ESSENTIALS
— OF —
BUSINESS LAW
AND THE LEGAL ENVIRONMENT
SIXTH EDITION

RICHARD A. MANN
Professor of Business Law,
The University of North Carolina at Chapel Hill
Member of the North Carolina Bar

BARRY S. ROBERTS
Professor of Business Law,
The University of North Carolina at Chapel Hill
Member of the North Carolina and Pennsylvania Bars

WEST
WEST EDUCATIONAL PUBLISHING COMPANY
An International Thomson Publishing Company

Publisher/Team Director: Jack W. Calhoun
Acquisitions Editor: Rob Dewey
Developmental Editor: Susanna Smart
Production Editors: Amy Hanson and Deanna Quinn
Production House: DPS Associates, Inc.
Cover Design: Tin Box Studio
Cover Illustration: Jane Starrett
Internal Design: Lesiak/Crampton Design
Sr. Marketing Manager: Scott D. Person

1 2 3 4 5 C5 1 0 9 8 7

Printed in the United States of America

ISBN 0-538-87876-2

Library of Congress Cataloging-in-Publication Data

Mann, Richard A.
   Essentials of business law and the legal environment / Richard A.
Mann, Barry S. Roberts. – 6th ed.
      p. cm.
   Includes index.
   ISBN 0-538-87876-2   (hard : alk. paper)
   1. Commercial law—United States.   I. Roberts, Barry S.
II. Title.
KF889.S55   1998
346.7307—DC21   97-21395
                                                             CIP

I⟨T⟩P®
International Thomson Publishing
West Educational Publishing is an ITP Company.
The ITP trademark is used under license.

Richard A. Mann received a B.S. in Mathematics from the University of North Carolina at Chapel Hill and a J.D. from Yale Law School. He is currently professor of Business Law at the Kenan-Flagler School of Business, University of North Carolina at Chapel Hill. Richard Mann is past president of the Southeastern Regional Business Law Association. He is a member of Who's Who in American Law, Outstanding Young Men of America, and the North Carolina Bar.

Professor Mann has written extensively on a number of legal topics including bankruptcy, sales, secured transactions, real property, insurance law, and bussiness associations. He has received the *American Business Law Journal's* award both for the best article and for the best comment and has, in addition, served as a reviewer and staff editor for the publication. He teaches in several executive education programs and is a founder, managing director, and instructor in the Carolina CPA Review. He is a co-author of *Smith and Robertson's Business Law, Tenth Edition,* as well as *Business Law and the Regulation of Business, Fifth Edition.*

Barry A. Roberts received a B.S. in Business Administration from Pennsylvania State University, a J.D. from the University of Pennsylvania, and an LL.M. from Harvard Law School. He served as a judicial clerk for the Pennsylvania Supreme Court prior to practicing law in Pittsburgh. Barry Roberts is currently professor of Business Law at the Kenan-Flagler School of Business, University of North Carolina at Chapel Hill. He is a member of Who's Who in American Law, Outstanding Young Men in America, and the North Carolina Bar.

Professor Roberts has written numerous articles on such topics as antitrust, products liability, constitutional law, banking law, employment law, and business associations. He has been a reviewer and staff editor for the *American Business Law Journal.* Professor Roberts is a founder, managing director, and instructor in the Carolina CPA Review. He is a co-author of *Smith and Robertson's Business Law, Tenth Edition,* as well as *Business Law and the Regulation of Business, Fifth Edition.*

CONTENTS IN BRIEF

CONTENTS

vii

P A R T   I X

Debtor and Creditor Relations 759

P A R T   X

Regulation of Business 827

MANAGERIAL INSIGHTS

CONSUMER INSIGHTS

THE LAW AND YOU

ETHICAL DILEMAS

The sixth edition of *Essentials of Business Law and the Legal Environment* continues the tradition of accuracy, comprehensiveness, and authoritativeness associated with its earlier editions. This text covers its subject material in a nontechnical but authoritative manner. It covers the material succinctly yet provides depth sufficient to ensure easy comprehension by today's students.

This text is designed for use in business law and legal environment courses generally offered in universities, colleges, and schools of business and commerce. By reason of the broad coverage and variety of the material, instructors may readily adapt this volume to specially designed courses in business law by assigning and emphasizing different combinations of the subject matter. All topics included in the CPA exam are covered by the text.

Emphasis has been placed upon the regulatory environment of business law: The first eight chapters introduce the legal environment of business, and Part Ten (Chapters 42 to 48) thoroughly addresses the area of government regulation of business.

To supplement the chapter on business ethics, we have added five new managerial case studies in business ethics. These case studies require the student to make the value trade-offs that confront business people in their professional lives. (We gratefully acknowledge the assistance of James Leis in writing the Mykon's Dilemma case.) Over half of the chapters also contain an "Ethical Dilemma," which presents a managerial situation involving ethical issues. A series of questions leads the student to explore the ethical dimensions of each situation. We wish to acknowledge and thank the following professors for their contribution in preparing the Ethical Dilemmas: Sandra K. Miller, Assistant Professor of Accounting and Taxation, *Widener University* and Gregory P. Cermignano, Associate Professor of Accounting, *Widener University*.

We have deemed it desirable to place primary emphasis on the text and to present the cases in summary fashion. Cases are briefed and integrated into the chapters. The facts are summarized in clear and understandable narrative using the names of the parties, and the legal issues and court decisions are explained carefully with a minimum of legal jargon. The opinions have been drastically shortened, the reductions affording more satisfactory material for purposes of instruction. Divided into four sections (FACTS, DECISION, OPINION, and INTERPRETATION), most cases are adequately covered in thirty lines or less.

From long classroom experience we are of the opinion that fundamental legal principles can be learned more effectively from text and case materials having at least a degree of human interest. Accordingly, we have included a large number of recent cases. Landmark cases, on the other hand, have not been neglected.

A number of chapters contain a feature, "The Law and You," consisting of excerpts from public service pamphlets published by state bar associations. These materials provide students with practical information about how the law affects them in their professional and personal lives. Topics include buying a car, tenants' and landlords' rights, applying for credit, what to do if involved in an automobile accident, what to do if arrested, and buying a home.

To improve readability throughout the text, all unnecessary "legalese" has been eliminated while necessary legal terms have been printed in boldface and clearly defined, explained, and illustrated. Definitions of essential terms and legal concepts also appear in the margins. The text is enriched by numerous illustrative hypothetical and case examples which help students relate material to real-life experiences.

Classroom-tested problems appear at the end of the chapters to test the student's understanding of major concepts. Each chapter contains several new, additional problems. We have used the problems and consider them excellent stimulants to classroom discussion. Students, in turn, have found the problems—many of which are taken from reported court decisions—helpful in enabling them to apply the basic rules of law to factual situations. Besides serving as a springboard for discussion, the problems readily suggest other and related problems to the inquiring, analytical mind. We also have included discussion questions at the end of all chapters to provide students another opportunity to assess their comprehension of the material.

We have incorporated approximately 160 classroom-tested figures, charts, and diagrams, about fifteen of which are new. The diagrams help the student conceptualize the many abstract concepts in the law; the charts not only summarize prior discussions but also indicate relationships between different legal rules. In addition, each chapter ends with a summary in the form of an annotated outline of the entire chapter, including key terms.

We have also added two new features—Insights (both managerial and consumer) and Internet Questions. The Managerial Insights provide both future and current managers legal information that will be helpful, and at times crucial, in the performance of their jobs. The Consumer Insights complement the Managerial Insights by exploring business regulations from a consumer's perspective. We wish to thank Linda Haac, Ginger Travis, and Beth Woods for their contribution to the Managerial and Consumer Insights.

The Internet Questions make the student explore the rich resources of the world wide web to obtain additional knowledge of the law. The internet is a large computer network that connects numerous information databases throughout the world. One caveat for students is that they should examine the reliability and currency of the information found; not all of it is current or accurate. Search engines are an excellent place to begin exploring the internet. Search engines include: yahoo (*http://www.yahoo.com,*) infoseek (*http://www.infoseek.com*), excite (*http://www. excite.com*), lycos (*http://www.lycos.com*) and webcrawler (*http://www. webcrawler.com*). There is also a search engine more specific to legal research: law crawler (*http://www.findlaw.com*).

Classroom use and study of this book should provide for the student the following benefits and skills:

1. Perception and appreciation of the scope, extent, and importance of the law
2. Basic knowledge of the fundamental concepts, principles, and rules of law that apply to business transactions

3. Knowledge of the function and operation of courts and governmental administrative agencies

4. Ability to recognize the potential legal problems that may arise in a doubtful or complicated situation, and the necessity of consulting a lawyer and obtaining competent professional legal advice

5. Development of analytical skills and reasoning power

We express our gratitude to the following professors for their helpful comments:

Bob Ek
Seminole Community College

James E. Holloway
East Carolina University

Tony Enerva
Lakeland Community College

John F. Mastriani
El Paso Community College

Karla Harbin Fox
University of Connecticut

L. K. O'Drudy, Jr.
University of Virginia

George Generas
University of Hartford

Michael J. O'Hara
University of Nebraska

Doug Gordon
Arapahoe Community College

Edward C. Wachter, Jr.
Point Park College

We also wish to thank the following professors for their assistance on the *fifth edition* of this text:

Michael Adighibe
Cheyney University

E. Sharon Hayenga
Minneapolis Community College

Terence Baird
Antelope Valley College

Trevor Howell
Belmont College

George S. Bohler
Embry-Riddle University

Mary Ellen Perri
SUNY-Farmingdale

Joyce Boland-DeVito
St. John's University

Todd B. Piller
SUNY-Cobleskill

Donald R. Brenner
American University

Pamela Poole Weber
Seminole Community College

Ed Dash
Pierce Junior College

Roger E. Reinsch
Emporia State University

David L. Davis
Tallahassee Community College

Owen T. Smith
Long Island University

Douglas C. Gordon
Arapahoe Community College

Dan Spielmann
University of Wisconsin—Green Bay

A. James Granito
Youngstown State University

Edward C. Wachter, Jr.
Point Park College

PREFACE

We also are grateful to those who provided us with comments regarding earlier editions of the book:

Michael E. Adighibe
Cheyney University

Jessica Allen
Suffolk Community College

Terence Baird
Antelope Valley College

Keith A. Beebe
SUNY-Cobleskill

Dawn Bennett-Alexander
University of Northern Florida

Janie Blankenship
DelMar College

Steven W. Bostian
Caston College

Norman E. Bradshaw
Alvin Community College

Donald R. Brenner
American University

Carroll Burrell
San Jacinto College

Jane Campbell
Jackson Community College

Vic Daniels
Tallahassee Community College

Joseph P. Davey
Hartnell College

Theodore M. Dinges
Longview Community College

Robert Ek
Seminole Community College

Allan M. Gerson
Palm Beach Community College

Douglas C. Gordon
Arapahoe Community College

Dan Huss
Miami University

Robert Inama
Ricks College

George Kepner
Hartwick College

Daniel A. Levin
University of Colorado/Boulder

David Ludwich
Belmont College

Bradley Lutz
Hillsborough Community College

Richard Lynn
Belmont College

Kyle McFatter
McNeese State University

James Miles
Anoka-Ramsey Community College

Dinah Payne
University of New Orleans

Mary Ellen Perri
SUNY-Farmingdale

Todd B. Piller
SUNY-Cobleskill

Richard W. Post
College of the Desert

M. Rose
Macomb County Community College

Herbert Rossman
Drexel University

Sylvia Samuels
Skyline College

Donald E. Sanders
Southwest Texas State University

Susan Schoeffler
Central Piedmont Community College

John E. H. Sherry
Cornell University

Michael D. Sommerville
St. Mary's College

Dan Spielmann
University of Wisconsin—Green Bay

Art Stelly
Baylor University

Robert J. Votta
Pierce Junior College

Larry Stephens
Gulf Coast College

Pamela Poole Weber
Seminole Community College

Stanley H. Stone
Valencia Community College—East Campus

Hugh Wilkoff
Cerritos College

We express our thanks and appreciation to Allison Rouse and Peggy Pickard for their help in the preparation of the manuscript. For their support we extend our thanks to Karlene Fogelin Knebel and Joanne Erwick Roberts. And we are grateful to Rob Dewey, Deanna Quinn, Amy Hanson, and Susanna Smart of West Educational Publishing Company for their invaluable assistance and cooperation in connection with the preparation of this text.

This text is dedicated also to our children Lilli-Marie Knebel Mann, Justin Erwick Roberts, and Matthew Charles Roberts.

Richard A. Mann

Barry S. Roberts

SUPPLEMENTAL MATERIALS

The **Study Guide,** prepared by Neely S. Inlow of Lynchburg College, provides for each chapter a brief statement of purpose, chapter checkpoints, chapter outline, key terms, and true/false, multiple choice, and short essay questions for students to test themselves. This edition of the study guide also includes CPA exam questions from previous CPA exams, designated as *CPA* at the beginning of each multiple choice CPA question. An additional feature is "TRY THE WEB," at the ends of selected chapters. One to three Internet exercises are designed to help students find legal information on the Internet.

The **Instructor's Manual** prepared by the text authors, with Beth D. Woods, contains for each chapter a chapter outline, list of chapter cases, and a list of transparency acetates, and is then outlined in lecture notes format, with teaching hints and discussion questions, cases, key terms and definitions, and answers to end-of-chapter questions and problems. Each part opener lists the chapters contained in the part, a list of ethics questions applicable to the part, and a list of suggested activities and research problems.

The **Test Bank**, prepared by Michelle Rehwinkel, Tallahassee Community College, includes true/false, multiple choice, short essay, and challenge questions, and end-of-part key terms and concepts matching questions suitable for quizzes.

Computerized Testing—WesTest provides the complete test bank on disk, allowing professors to generate a variety of tests using floppy diskettes for either IBM PCs and compatibles or for Apple II-family microcomputers. This is available to qualified adopters.

Transparency Acetates (full color) highlight text illustrations, with recommendations for their use included in the Instructor's Manual.

Library of Cases provides, on computer disk, the full text of all cases upon which many end-of-chapter problems have been based.

Instructor's Manual for *Drama of the Law* Video Series.

Multimedia Planning Guide.

Other available supplements:

Video library*

Legal REVIEW Software*

"You Be the Judge" Software*

Spanish Dictionary of Key Legal Terms

Interactive Software on Contracts and Sales*

Ten free hours of WESTLAW™*

CD-ROM Resources for Business Law and the Legal Environment of Business

*Available to qualified adopters. Please consult your local sales representative.

Introduction to Law and Ethics

CHAPTER 1

Introduction to Law

Law concerns the relations between individuals as such relations affect the social and economic order. It is both the product of civilization and the means by which civilization is maintained. As such, law reflects the social, economic, political, religious, and moral philosophy of society.

Law is an instrument of social control. Its function is to regulate, within certain limitations, human conduct and human relations. Accordingly, the laws of the United States affect the life of every U.S. citizen. At the same time, the laws of each state influence the life of each of its citizens and the lives of many noncitizens as well. The rights and duties of all individuals, as well as the safety and security of all people and their property, depend on the law.

The law is pervasive. It permits, forbids, and/or regulates practically every known human activity and affects all persons either directly or indirectly. Law is, in part, prohibitory: certain acts must not be committed. For example, one must not steal; one must not murder. Law is also partly mandatory: certain acts must be done or be done in a prescribed way. Thus, taxes must be paid; corporations must make and file certain reports with state authorities; traffic must keep to the right. Finally, law is permissive: certain acts may be done. For instance, one may or may not enter into a contract; one may or may not dispose of one's estate by will.

Because the areas of law are so highly interrelated, you will find it helpful to begin the study of the different areas of business law by first considering the nature, classification, and sources of law. This will enable you not only to understand better each specific area of law but also to understand its relationship to other areas of law.

NATURE OF LAW

The law has evolved slowly, and it will continue to change. It is not a pure science based on unchanging and universal truths. Rather, it results from a continuous striving to develop a workable set of rules that balance the individual and group rights of a society.

Definition of Law

Definition of law "a rule of civil conduct prescribed by the supreme power in a state, commanding what is right, and prohibiting what is wrong" (Blackstone)

Scholars and citizens in general often ask a fundamental but difficult question regarding law: What is it? Numerous philosophers and jurists (legal scholars) have attempted to define it. American jurists and Supreme Court Justices Oliver Wendell Holmes and Benjamin Cardozo defined law as predictions of the way in which a court will decide specific legal questions. The English jurist Blackstone, on the other hand, defined law as "a rule of civil conduct prescribed by the supreme power in a state, commanding what is right, and prohibiting what is wrong."

Because of its great complexity, many legal scholars have attempted to explain the law by outlining its essential characteristics. Roscoe Pound, a distinguished American jurist and former dean of the Harvard Law School, described law as having multiple meanings:

> First we may mean the legal order, that is, the régime of ordering human activities and relations through systematic application of the force of politically organized society, or through social pressure in such a society backed by such force. We use the term "law" in this sense when we speak of "respect for law" or for the "end of law."
>
> Second we may mean the aggregate of laws or legal precepts; the body of authoritative grounds of judicial and administrative action established in such a society. We may mean the body of received and established materials on which judicial and administrative determinations proceed. We use the term in this sense when we speak of "systems of law" or of "justice according to law."
>
> Third we may mean what Justice Cardozo has happily styled "the judicial process." We may mean the process of determining controversies, whether as it actually takes place, or as the public, the jurists, and the practitioners in the courts hold it ought to take place.

Functions of Law

At a general level the primary function of law is to maintain stability in the social, political, and economic system while simultaneously permitting change. The law accomplishes this basic function by performing a number of specific functions, among them dispute resolution, protection of property, and preservation of the state.

Disputes, which arise inevitably in any modern society, may involve criminal matters, such as theft, or noncriminal matters, such as an automobile accident. Because disputes threaten social stability, the law has established an elaborate and evolving set of rules to resolve them. In addition, the legal system has instituted societal remedies, usually administered by the courts, in place of private remedies such as revenge.

A second crucial function of law is to protect the private ownership of property and to assist in the making of voluntary agreements (called contracts) regarding exchanges of property and services. Accordingly, a significant portion of law, as well as this text, involves property and its disposition, including the law of property, contracts, sales, commercial paper, and business associations.

A third essential function of the law is preservation of the state. In our system, law ensures that changes in political structure and leadership are brought about by political action, such as elections, legislation, and referenda, rather than by revolution, sedition, and rebellion.

Law and Morals

Although moral concepts greatly influence the law, morals and law are not the same. You might think of them as two intersecting circles (see Figure 1–1). The more darkly shaded area common to both circles includes the vast body of ideas that are both moral and legal. For instance, "Thou shall not kill" and "Thou shall not steal" are both moral precepts and legal constraints.

On the other hand, that part of the legal circle which does not intersect the morality circle (the lightly shaded portion) includes many rules of law that are completely unrelated to morals, such as the rules stating that you must drive on

Functions of law to maintain stability in the social, political, and economic system through dispute resolution, protection of property, and the preservation of the state, while simultaneously permitting ordered change

Laws and morals are different but overlapping: law provides sanctions while morals do not

the right side of the road and that you must register before you can vote. Likewise, the part of the morality circle that does not intersect the legal circle includes moral precepts not enforced by legal sanctions, such as the idea that you should not silently stand by and watch a blind man walk off a cliff or that you should not foreclose a poor widow's mortgage.

Law and Justice

Law and justice are separate and distinct concepts; justice is the fair, equitable, and impartial treatment of competing interests with due regard for the common good

Law and justice represent separate and distinct concepts. Without law, however, there can be no justice. Although defining justice is at least as difficult as defining law, justice generally may be defined as the fair, equitable, and impartial treatment of the competing interests and desires of individuals and groups with due regard for the common good.

On the other hand, law is no guarantee of justice. Some of history's most monstrous acts have been committed pursuant to "law." For example, recall the actions of Nazi Germany during the 1930s and 1940s. Totalitarian societies often have shaped formal legal systems around the atrocities they have sanctioned.

CLASSIFICATION OF LAW

Because the subject is vast, classifying the law into categories is helpful. Though a number of categories is possible, the most useful ones are (1) substantive and procedural, (2) public and private, and (3) civil and criminal (see Figure 1–2).

Right legal capacity to require another person to perform or refrain from performing an act

Basic to understanding these classifications are the terms *right* and *duty*. A **right** is the capacity of a person, with the aid of the law, to require another person or persons to perform, or to refrain from performing, a certain act. Thus, if Alice sells and delivers goods to Bob for the agreed price of $500 payable at a certain date, Alice is capable, with the aid of the courts, of enforcing the payment by Bob of the

Duty legal obligation requiring a person to perform or refrain from performing an act

$500. A **duty** is the obligation the law imposes upon a person to perform, or to refrain from performing, a certain act. Duty and right are correlatives: no right can

FIGURE 1–1 Law and Morals

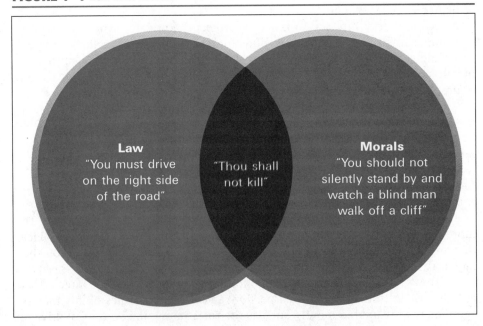

FIGURE 1–2 Classification of Law

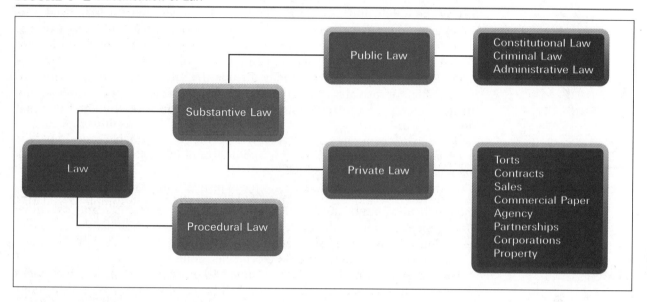

rest upon one person without a corresponding duty resting upon some other person, or in some cases upon all other persons.

Substantive and Procedural Law

Substantive law creates, defines, and regulates legal rights and duties. Thus, the rules of contract law that determine a binding contract are rules of substantive law. On the other hand, **procedural law** sets forth the rules for enforcing those rights that exist by reason of the substantive law. Thus, procedural law defines the method by which to obtain a remedy in court.

Substantive law *(sub'·stan·tive)* the basic law creating rights and duties

Procedural law the rules for enforcing substantive law

Public and Private Law

Public law is the branch of substantive law that deals with the government's rights and powers and its relationship to individuals or groups. Public law consists of constitutional, administrative, and criminal law. **Private law** is that part of substantive law governing individuals and legal entities (such as corporations) in their relationships with one another. Business law is primarily private law.

Public law the law dealing with the relationship between government and individuals

Private law the law involving relationships among individuals and legal entities

Civil and Criminal Law

The **civil law** defines duties the violation of which constitutes a wrong against the party injured by the violation. In contrast, the **criminal law** establishes duties the violation of which is a wrong against the whole community. Civil law is a part of private law, whereas criminal law is a part of public law. (The term *civil law* should be distinguished from the concept of a civil law *system*, which is discussed later in this chapter.) In a civil action the injured party **sues** to recover *compensation* for the damage and injury sustained as a result of the **defendant's** wrongful conduct. The party bringing a civil action (the **plaintiff**) has the burden of proof, which the plaintiff must sustain by a *preponderance* (greater weight) *of the evidence*. The purpose of the civil law is to compensate the injured party, not, as in the case of criminal law, to punish the wrongdoer. The principal forms of relief the civil law affords are a judgment for money damages and a decree ordering the defendant to perform a specified act or to desist from specified conduct.

Civil law the law dealing with the rights and duties of individuals among themselves

Criminal law the law that involves offenses against the entire community

Sue to begin a lawsuit in a court

Defendant the person against whom a legal action is brought

Plaintiff the person who initiates a civil suit

A crime is any act or omission prohibited by public law in the interest of protecting the public and made punishable by the government in a judicial proceeding brought **(prosecuted)** by it. The government must prove criminal guilt *beyond a reasonable doubt,* which is a significantly higher burden of proof than that required in a civil action. Crimes are prohibited and punished on the grounds of public policy, which may include the safeguarding of government, human life, or private property. Additional purposes of the criminal law include deterrence and rehabilitation. Figure 1–3 compares civil and criminal law.

SOURCES OF LAW

The sources of law in the U.S. legal system are the federal and state constitutions, federal treaties, interstate compacts, federal and state statutes and executive orders, the ordinances of countless local municipal governments, the rules and regulations of federal and state administrative agencies, and an ever-increasing volume of reported federal and state court decisions.

The *supreme law* of the land is the United States Constitution, which provides in turn that federal statutes and treaties shall be paramount to state constitutions and statutes. Federal legislation is of great significance as a source of law. Other federal actions having the force of law are executive orders by the president and rules and regulations set by federal administrative officials, agencies, and commissions. The federal courts also contribute considerably to the body of law in the United States.

The same pattern exists in every state. The paramount law of each state is contained in its written constitution. (Although a state constitution cannot deprive citizens of federal constitutional rights, it can guarantee rights beyond those provided in the United States Constitution.) Subordinate to the state constitution are the statutes enacted by the state's legislature and the case law developed by its judiciary. Likewise, rules and regulations of state administrative agencies have the force of law, as do executive orders issued by the governor. In addition, cities, towns, and villages have limited legislative powers to pass ordinances and resolutions within their respective municipal areas (see Figure 1–4).

FIGURE 1–3 Comparison of Civil and Criminal Law

	Civil Law	**Criminal Law**
Commencement of action	Aggrieved individual (plaintiff) sues	State or federal government prosecutes
Purpose	Compensation Deterrence	Punishment Deterrence Rehabilitation Preservation of peace
Burden of proof	Preponderance of the evidence	Beyond a reasonable doubt
Principal sanctions	Monetary damages Equitable remedies	Capital punishment Imprisonment Fines

Constitutional Law

A **constitution**—the fundamental law of a particular level of government—establishes the governmental structure and allocates power among governmental levels, thereby defining political relationships. One of the fundamental principles on which our government is founded is that of separation of powers. As incorporated into our Constitution this means that government consists of three distinct and independent branches—the federal judiciary, the Congress, and the executive branch.

A constitution also restricts the powers of government and specifies the rights and liberties of the people. For example, the Constitution of the United States not only specifically states what rights and authority are vested in the national government but also specifically enumerates certain rights and liberties of the people. Moreover, the Ninth Amendment to the U.S. Constitution makes it clear that this enumeration of rights does not in any way deny or limit other rights that the people retain.

All other law in the United States is subordinate to the federal Constitution. No law, federal or state, is valid if it violates the federal Constitution. Under the principle of **judicial review**, the Supreme Court of the United States determines the constitutionality of *all* laws.

Judicial Law

The U.S. legal system, a **common law system** like the system first developed in England, relies heavily on the judiciary as a source of law and on the adversary system for settling disputes. In an **adversary system** the parties, not the court, must initiate and conduct litigation. This approach is based on the belief that the truth is more likely to emerge from the investigation and presentation of evidence by two opposing parties, both motivated by self-interest, than from judicial investigation motivated only by official duty. In addition to the United States and England, the common law system is used in other English-speaking countries, including Canada and Australia.

In distinct contrast to the common law system are civil law systems, which are based on Roman law. **Civil law systems** depend on comprehensive legislative enactments (called codes) and an inquisitorial system of determining disputes. In the **inquisitorial system**, the judiciary initiates litigation, investigates pertinent facts, and conducts the presentation of evidence. The civil law system prevails in most of Europe, Scotland, the state of Louisiana, the province of Quebec, Latin America, and parts of Africa and Asia.

Common Law The courts in common law systems have developed a body of law that serves as precedent for determining later controversies. In this sense, common law, also called case law or judge-made law, is distinguished from other sources of law, such as legislation and administrative rulings.

In order to evolve in a stable and predictable manner, the common law has developed by application of *stare decisis*. Under the principle of **stare decisis** ("to stand by the decisions"), courts adhere to and rely on rules of law that they or superior courts relied on and applied in prior similar decisions. Judicial decisions thus have two uses: to determine with finality the case currently being decided and to indicate how the court will decide similar cases in the future. *Stare decisis* does not, however, preclude courts from correcting erroneous decisions or from choosing among conflicting precedents. Thus, the doctrine allows sufficient flexibility for the common law to change. The strength of the common law is its ability to adapt to change without losing its sense of direction.

Constitution fundamental law of a government establishing its powers and limitations

Judicial review authority of the courts to determine the constitutionality of legislative and executive acts

Common law system body of law originating in England and derived from judicial decisions

Adversary system *(ad'·ver·sa·ry)* system in which opposing parties initiate and present their case

Civil law system body of law derived from Roman law and based upon comprehensive legislative enactments

Inquisitorial system *(in·quis·i·to'·ri·al)* system in which the judiciary initiates, conducts, and decides cases

Stare decisis *(star'·e de·cis'·is)* principle that courts should apply rules decided in prior cases in deciding substantially similar cases

FIGURE 1–4 Hierarchy of Law

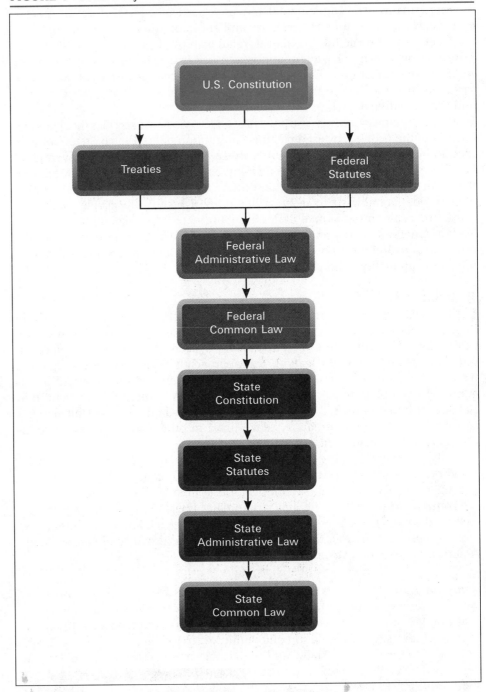

Equity As the common law developed in England, it became overly rigid and beset with technicalities. As a consequence, in many cases no remedies were provided because the judges insisted that a claim must fall within one of the recognized forms of action. Moreover, courts of common law could provide only limited remedies; the principal type of relief obtainable was a money judgment. Consequently, individuals who could not obtain adequate relief from monetary awards began to petition the king directly for justice. He, in turn, came to delegate these petitions to his chancellor.

Gradually, there evolved what was in effect a new and supplementary system of needed judicial relief for those who could not receive adequate remedies through the common law. This new system, called **equity**, was administered by a court of chancery presided over by the chancellor. The chancellor, deciding cases on "equity and good conscience," regularly provided relief where common law judges had refused to act or where the remedy at law was inadequate. Thus, there grew up, side by side, two systems of law administered by different tribunals, the common law courts and courts of equity.

> **Equity** body of law based upon principles distinct from common law and providing remedies not available at law

An important difference between common law and equity is that the chancellor could issue a **decree**, or order, compelling a defendant to do, or refrain from doing, a specified act. A defendant who did not comply with this order could be held in contempt of court and punished by fine or imprisonment. This power of compulsion available in a court of equity opened the door to many needed remedies not available in a court of common law.

> **Decree** decision of a court of equity

Courts of equity in some cases recognized rights that were enforceable at common law, but they provided more effective remedies. For example, in a court of equity, for breach of a land contract the buyer could obtain a decree of **specific performance** commanding the defendant seller to perform his part of the contract by transferring title to the land. Another powerful and effective remedy available only in the courts of equity was the **injunction**, a court order requiring a party to do or refrain from doing a specified act. Another remedy not available elsewhere was **reformation**, where, upon the ground of mutual mistake, an action could be brought to reform or change the language of a written agreement to conform to the actual intention of the contracting parties. An action for **rescission** of a contract, which allowed a party to invalidate a contract under certain circumstances, was another remedy.

> **Specific performance** decree ordering a party to perform a contractual duty
>
> **Injunction** a decree ordering a party to do or refrain from doing a specified act
>
> **Reformation** *(ref·or·ma'·tion)* equitable remedy rewriting a contract to conform with the original intent of the contracting parties
>
> **Rescission** *(re·scis'·sion)* an equitable remedy invalidating a contract

Although courts of equity provided remedies not available in courts of law, they granted such remedies only at their discretion, not as a matter of right. This discretion was exercised according to the general legal principles, or **maxims**, formulated by equity courts over the years.

> **Maxim** a general legal principle

In nearly every jurisdiction in the United States, courts of common law and equity have merged into a single court that administers both systems of law. Vestiges of the old division continue, however. For example, the right to a trial by jury applies only to actions at law, but not under federal law and in almost every state to suits filed in equity.

Restatements of Law The common law of the United States results from the independent decisions of the state and federal courts. The rapid increase in the number of decisions by these courts led to the establishment of the American Law Institute (ALI) in 1923. The ALI is composed of a distinguished group of lawyers, judges, and law teachers who set out to prepare "an orderly restatement of the general common law of the United States, including in that term not only the law developed solely by judicial decision, but also the law that has grown from the application by the courts of statutes that were generally enacted and were in force for many years."

Regarded as the authoritative statement of the common law of the United States, the Restatements cover many important areas of the common law, including torts, contracts, agency, property, and trusts. Although not law in themselves, they are highly persuasive, and courts frequently have used them to support

CONSUMER INSIGHT

Across the Globe: Four Major Legal Systems

Today, in an ever closer international world, nations and businesses find themselves dealing more and more with legal systems other than their own. As a result, they no longer can afford to ignore different types of legal reasoning.

Whereas national legal systems often differ in their particulars, they tend to fall into one of four major legal traditions, each of which represents a different approach to keeping the peace, maintaining stability, providing justice, and interpreting social reality. The four systems are

1. civil law,
2. common law,
3. socialist law, and
4. religious/customary law.

According to today's comparative legal scholars, civil law remains the oldest and most influential legal system operating in the modern Western world. The system derives from the Romano-Germanic tradition, which had its origins in the ancient Roman Empire. Sometime around 450 B.C., the Romans produced their first written legal code, known as the Twelve Tables of Rome. Later, as the Roman Empire spread from Greece to Gaul, the Romans carried with them their legal system, defined by administrative order, attention to detail, and official edict.

Once Rome crumpled under the invasion of Germanic tribes, however, this system of law might have been lost forever if the Byzantine Emperor Justinian I had not ordered the making of a written compilation in the sixth century. The Corpus Juris Civilis, or the Body of Civil Law, was completed around 534 A.D.

During the Renaissance, European scholars, such as those at the University of Bologna in Italy, eventually rediscovered the Justinian compilation when they turned to classical antiquity for intellectual models. So impressed were they with the Corpus

Juris Civilis that they lauded it as "written reason."

Hundreds of years later, when Europe began to produce stronger, more centralized governments, Roman law served as the foundation for national codes of law. In the seventeenth century, the Scandinavian countries developed the first such codes. Then, in 1804, under Napoleon Bonaparte, France enacted its Code Napoleon, which embodied the principles of the French Revolution and which came to represent the first modern civil law code. In 1896, Germany also enacted a civil code.

England, on the other hand, followed a course completely different from that of continental Europe. Even as part of the Roman Empire, England had managed to retain its local customs, which did not provide for a national, unified body of law. Not until William of Normandy invaded the island country in 1066 did Britain begin to develop a centralized legal system. That system would become known as the common law.

During the rule of William the Conqueror, English law grew out of the royal courts, where royal judges decided specific disputes of interest to the crown. Often, these disputes involved arguments over taxes, since William I was the first ruler of his time to impose a national tax on landed property. In fact, the Court of Exchequer, the first common law court, mainly decided tax disputes.

Unlike Europe's civil law, then, which developed as a law of principle and a systematic codification of justice, England's common law evolved as a law of procedure and precedent, used to solve practical problems. Judges, rather than university

scholars, created and furthered the system. Because of the nature of their courtrooms, they relied heavily on trial procedure, evidence, and case law, rather than code.

Today, England, Canada, Australia, New Zealand and the United States all use a form of common law. Continental Europe, Latin America, Japan, South Korea, and large areas of Africa employ a system of civil law.

In the twentieth century, still another legal system, socialism, has played an important role in such places as the former Soviet Union, the countries of Eastern Europe, the People's Republic of China, North Korea, and Cuba.

Socialism, largely the product of German and Russian thought of the late nineteenth and early twentieth centuries, is the youngest of the four major legal systems. Until 1917, Russia relied on a form of civil law; then, with the Bolshevik revolution, the country embraced a legal concept unlike anything the industrial world had seen before. Based on the philosophy of Karl Marx and Frederich Engels, socialism centered on a revolutionary idea: the turning of society's economic base away from capitalism would lead to a new social order, marked by collective ownership of the means of production and a proletarian equality. Law, then, could serve a revolutionary purpose, in that the state could use it not only to settle disputes or provide justice, but also to transform society.

Finally, religious law continues to be an important legal force in the world today, especially in Muslim countries. The Islamic religion, which calls on its believers to follow strict rules of conduct, is the national law in such places as Iran and Saudi Arabia. The law of Islam is known as Shari'a, which in Arabic translates as "jurisprudence." It is based primarily on the Koran, on sayings of the Prophet Muhammad, and on the writings of Islamic scholars.

their opinions. Because they provide a concise and clear statement of much of the common law, relevant portions of the Restatements are relied on frequently in this book.

Legislative Law

Since the end of the nineteenth century, legislation has become the primary source of new law and ordered social change in the United States. The annual volume of legislative law is enormous. Justice Felix Frankfurter's remarks to the New York City Bar in 1947 are even more appropriate today:

> . . . Inevitably the work of the Supreme Court reflects the great shift in the center of gravity of law-making. Broadly speaking, the number of cases disposed of by opinions has not changed from term to term. But even as late as 1875 more than 40 percent of the controversies before the Court were common-law litigation, fifty years later only 5 percent, while today cases not resting on statutes are reduced almost to zero. It is therefore accurate to say that courts have ceased to be the primary makers of law in the sense in which they "legislated" the common law. It is certainly true of the Supreme Court that almost every case has a statute at its heart or close to it.

This emphasis on legislative or statutory law has occurred because common law, which develops evolutionarily and haphazardly, is not well suited for making drastic or comprehensive changes. Moreover, while courts tend to be hesitant about overruling prior decisions, legislatures commonly repeal prior enactments. In addition, legislatures may choose the issues they wish to address, whereas courts may deal only with those issues presented by actual cases. As a result, legislatures are better equipped to make the dramatic, sweeping, and relatively rapid changes in the law that technological, social, and economic innovations compel.

While some business law topics, such as contracts, agency, property, and trusts, still are governed principally by the common law, most areas of commercial law, including partnerships, corporations, sales, commercial paper, secured transactions, insurance, securities regulation, antitrust, and bankruptcy have become largely statutory. Because most states enacted their own statutes dealing with these branches of commercial law, a great diversity developed among the states and hampered the conduct of commerce on a national scale. The increased need for greater uniformity brought about the formation of the National Conference of Commissioners on Uniform State Laws to prepare legislation that would reduce the conflicts among state laws.

The most successful example is the ***Uniform Commercial Code*** (UCC), which was prepared under the joint sponsorship and direction of the National Conference of Commissioners on Uniform State Laws and the American Law Institute. All fifty states (although Louisiana has adopted only Articles 1, 3, 4, 5, 7, and 8), the District of Columbia, and the Virgin Islands have adopted the Uniform Commercial Code.

Other uniform laws include the Uniform Partnership Act, the Uniform Limited Partnership Act, the Model Business Corporation Act, and the Uniform Probate Code.

Treaties A **treaty** is an agreement between or among independent nations. The United States Constitution authorizes the president to enter into treaties with the advice and consent of the Senate, "providing two thirds of the Senators present concur."

Treaties may be entered into only by the federal government, *not* by the states. A treaty signed by the president and approved by the Senate has the legal force

Treaty an agreement between or among independent nations

of a federal statute. Accordingly, a federal treaty may supersede a prior federal statute, while a federal statute may supersede a prior treaty. Like statutes, treaties are subordinate to the federal Constitution and subject to judicial review.

Executive Orders　In addition to his executive functions, the president of the United States also has authority to issue laws, which are called **executive orders**. This authority typically derives from specific delegation by federal legislation. An executive order may amend, revoke, or supersede a prior executive order. An example of an executive order is the one issued by President Johnson in 1965 prohibiting discrimination by federal contractors on the basis of race, color, sex, religion, or national origin in employment on any work the contractor performed during the period of the federal contract.

The governors of the states enjoy comparable authority to issue executive orders.

Administrative Law

Administrative law is the branch of public law that is created by administrative agencies in the form of rules, regulations, orders, and decisions to carry out the regulatory powers and duties of those agencies. It also deals with controversies arising among individuals and these public officials and agencies. Administrative functions and activities concern general matters of public health, safety, and welfare, including the establishment and maintenance of military forces, police, citizenship and naturalization, taxation, environmental protection, the regulation of transportation, interstate highways, waterways, television, radio, and trade and commerce.

Because of the increasing complexity of the nation's social, economic, and industrial life, the scope of administrative law has expanded enormously. In 1952 Justice Jackson stated that "the rise of administrative bodies has been the most significant legal trend of the last century, and perhaps more values today are affected by their decisions than by those of all the courts, review of administrative decisions apart." This is evidenced by the great increase in the number and activities of federal government boards, commissions, and other agencies. Certainly, agencies create more legal rules and decide more controversies than all the legislatures and courts combined.

LEGAL ANALYSIS

Decisions in state trial courts generally are not reported or published. The precedent a trial court sets is not sufficiently weighty to warrant permanent reporting. Except in New York and a few other states where selected opinions of trial courts are published, decisions in trial courts are simply filed in the office of the clerk of the court, where they are available for public inspection. Decisions of state courts of appeals are published in consecutively numbered volumes called "reports." In most states, court decisions are found in the official state reports of that state. In addition, state reports are published by West Publishing Company in a regional reporter called the National Reporter System, composed of the following: Atlantic (A. or A.2d); South Eastern (S.E. or S.E.2d); South Western (S.W. or S.W.2d); New York Supplement (N.Y.S. or N.Y.S.2d); North Western (N.W. or N.W.2d); North Eastern (N.E. or N.E.2d); Southern (So. or So.2d); and Pacific (P. or P.2d). A number of states no longer publish official reports and have designated a commercial reporter as the authoritative source of state case law.

Executive order legislation issued by the president or a governor

Administrative law is created by administrative agencies in the form of rules, regulations, orders, and decisions to carry out the regulatory powers and duties of those agencies

THE LAW AND YOU What You Should Know About Attorneys

What Is an Attorney?

An attorney is a person trained to assist people professionally with legal problems and to represent them before courts and government agencies.

Are Attorneys Necessary?

The law is an extremely complex network of statutes, regulations, and court decisions. Without law, our society would be chaotic and it would be unsafe for the individual to engage in most of the activities that we ordinarily take for granted.

It is impossible for anyone to know the meaning of all the law and to keep up with the changes which occur constantly unless he or she devotes full time to studying and working with the law. Therefore, it is essential to have attorneys who are skilled in this activity to advise others about their rights and handle legal matters for them.

Although it might be easier to understand a law or legal principle if all laws had a single source, laws come from many sources, and the laws arising from each source may have a different scope and effect. A lawyer must be familiar with all of them. In Ohio, the law which governs its citizens can be classified into four groups.

Constitutional law. The United States Constitution is the basic law of the nation, and the Ohio Constitution is the basic law of the State of Ohio. The two are similar in many respects, but where a conflict arises, the federal Constitution takes precedence.

Statutory law. Statutes are written laws adopted through legislation, and may come from several sources. Statutes affecting the entire state are enacted by the Ohio General Assembly. Federal statutes, enacted by Congress, also affect all of Ohio. Local laws, called ordinances, are enacted by city or village councils.

Administrative law. Many activities subject to statutes or ordinances are so technical or change so often or so fast that they cannot effectively be regulated by statutes or ordinances alone. In such cases, the government agency that administers these activities may be authorized to adopt written rules to supplement the statutes. These written rules are called administrative law.

Common law. Common law is a large body of principles, rules, and forms of proceedings that have no statutory or legislative law as their foundation, but have become interwoven with the written law through custom, use, and the reported decisions of judges in specific cases. Common law fills in the gaps and helps unify and clarify constitutional, statutory, and administrative law. It is, therefore, indispensable to an effective system of justice. Since it is based on generations of experience, it gives continuity and consistency to the law, while at the same time, it is responsible to changing needs.

What Are an Attorney's Qualifications?

To become an attorney in Ohio, a person must complete at least four years of college and an additional three years at an accredited law school. Courses taught at law school include contracts, real property, taxation, business organization, criminal law, domestic relations, and many other topics of the law.

After graduation from law school, the candidate for admission to the Bar must produce evidence from practicing lawyers of his or her good moral character and must successfully complete a comprehensive test administered by the Ohio Supreme Court, called the Bar Examination.

What Is Legal Advice?

When an attorney gives you "advice" it is a conclusion drawn from many years of training and study and perhaps many hours of searching through volumes of written material to be certain that it includes all the law affecting your problem. In preparing a contract, pleading, or other document for you, your attorney is bringing to that work the skill and knowledge of the legal profession.

After they are published, these opinions, or "cases," are referred to ("cited") by giving the name of the case; the volume, name, and page of the official state report, if any, in which it is published; the volume, name, and page of the particular set and series of the National Reporter System; and the volume, name, and page of any other selected case series. For instance, *Lefkowitz v. Great Minneapolis Surplus Store, Inc.,* 251 Minn. 188, 86 N.W.2d 689 (1957), indicates that the opinion in this case may be found in Volume 251 of the official Minnesota Reports at page 188 and in Volume 86 of the North Western Reporter, Second Series, at page 689, and that the opinion was delivered in 1957.

The decisions of courts in the federal system are found in a number of reports. Federal District Court opinions appear in the Federal Supplement (F.Supp.).

continued

When Should I Go to an Attorney?

The adage that "an ounce of prevention is worth a pound of cure" is just as applicable in law as it is in medicine. The best time to go to an attorney is before you are in legal difficulty. It is best to consult your attorney before you sign papers or take other action that might seriously alter your legal position.

You should consult your lawyer when—

- You are planning to enter into a verbal or written contract which has major financial consequences
- You are involved in an accident involving injury to persons or damage to property
- You are seeking to collect an account from another person, or someone is seeking to collect an account from you which you do not believe you owe or which you question
- You need an opinion about the title to real estate
- You want to plan your estate and make a will
- You are organizing or dissolving a business
- You are settling an estate
- You are involved in a family situation such as adoption, divorce, etc.
- Your rights as a consumer or employee are abused.

How Should I Go About Choosing an Attorney?

In choosing an attorney, you should follow the same steps as you would in choosing a doctor or dentist. If you do not know an attorney, ask your friends, neighbors, employer, or anyone in whom you have confidence, for a recommendation. In Ohio, there is a lawyer referral service in each metropolitan area, operated by the local bar association. The Ohio State Bar Association operates a statewide referral service for all areas of the state. Also, you may refer to the yellow pages of your local telephone directory.

Remember that when you have a legal problem, you should go to a lawyer. Beware of advice and "curbstone opinions" from persons who are not lawyers. To consult someone who is not an attorney about a legal problem is always risky and often costly. Generally, no two legal problems are alike.

What Is My Attorney's Duty to Me?

All attorneys take an oath, upon admission to practice, to uphold the constitutions and the law and to be faithful to their clients.

Just as your communications with your minister and physician are confidential, so are your private communications with your lawyer. Legal ethics rules prohibit your attorney from disclosing any information you give in the course of the attorney-client relationship without your permission—unless you say you intend to commit a crime. State law prevents forced disclosure of confidential communications between you and your attorney.

Your attorney's principal duty is to see that you are given the benefit of all your legal rights. An attorney is sworn to conduct cases in an orderly way that will assure that they may be decided upon their merits. Your attorney may not make any agreement or incur any obligations that might substantially prejudice your interests, without your prior approval.

What Is My Duty to My Attorney?

You should give your attorney **all** the facts concerning your case and make a full and fair disclosure of the entire situation. In order to serve you well, your lawyer must know not only the favorable facts but also those that may be unfavorable.

[The information contained in this feature is general. You should not apply it to a specific legal problem without first consulting an attorney.]

Reprinted by permission of the Ohio State Bar Association.

Decisions of the U.S. Court of Appeals are found in the Federal Reporter (Fed., F.2d, or F.3d), while the U.S. Supreme Court's opinions are published in the United States Supreme Court Reports (U.S.), Supreme Court Reporter (S.Ct.), and Lawyers Edition (L.Ed.).

In reading the title of a case, such as *"Jones v. Brown,"* the *"v."* or *"vs."* means versus or against. In the trial court, Jones is the ***plaintiff***, the person who filed the suit, and Brown is the ***defendant***, the person against whom the suit was brought. When the case is appealed, some, but not all, courts of appeals or appellate courts place the name of the party who appeals, or the **appellant**, first, so that *"Jones v. Brown"* in the trial court becomes, if Brown loses and hence becomes the appellant, *"Brown v. Jones"* in the appellate court. Therefore, it is not always possible to determine from the title itself who was the plaintiff and who was the defendant. You must carefully read the facts of each case and clearly

Appellant party who appeals

identify each party in your mind in order to understand the discussion by the appellate court. In a criminal case the caption in the trial court will first designate the prosecuting governmental unit and then will indicate the defendant, as in *"State v. Jones"* or *"Commonwealth v. Brown."*

The study of reported cases requires an understanding and application of legal analysis. Normally, the reported opinion in a case sets forth (a) the essential facts, the nature of the action, the parties, what happened to bring about the controversy, what happened in the lower court, and what pleadings are material to the issues; (b) the issues of law or fact; (c) the legal principles involved; (d) the application of these principles; and (e) the decision.

CHAPTER SUMMARY

Nature of Law	**Definition of Law** "a rule of civil conduct prescribed by the supreme power in a state, commanding what is right, and prohibiting what is wrong" (Blackstone) **Functions of Law** to maintain stability in the social, political, and economic system through dispute resolution, protection of property, and the preservation of the state, while simultaneously permitting ordered change **Law and Morals** are different but overlapping; law provides sanctions while morals do not **Law and Justice** are separate and distinct concepts; justice is the fair, equitable, and impartial treatment of competing interests with due regard for the common good

Classification of Law	**Substantive and Procedural** ■ *Substantive Law* law creating rights and duties ■ *Procedural Law* rules for enforcing substantive law **Public and Private** ■ *Public Law* law dealing with the relationship between government and individuals ■ *Private Law* law governing the relationships among individuals and legal entities **Civil and Criminal** ■ *Civil Law* law dealing with rights and duties the violation of which constitutes a wrong against an individual or other legal entity ■ *Criminal Law* law establishing duties which, if violated, constitute a wrong against the entire community

Sources of Law	**Constitutional Law** fundamental law of a government establishing its powers and limitations
	Judicial Law
	■ *Common Law* body of law developed by the courts that serves as precedent for determination of later controversies
	■ *Equity* body of law based upon principles distinct from common law and providing remedies not available at law
	Legislative Law statutes adopted by legislative bodies
	■ *Treaties* agreements between or among independent nations
	■ *Executive Orders* laws issued by the president or by the governor of a state
	Administrative Law is created by administrative agencies in the form of rules, regulations, orders, and decisions to carry out the regulatory powers and duties of those agencies

QUESTIONS

1. Identify and describe the basic functions of law.
2. Distinguish between law and justice.
3. Distinguish between law and morals.
4. Define and discuss substantive and procedural law.
5. Distinguish between public law and private law.
6. Distinguish between civil and criminal law.
7. Identify and describe the sources of law.
8. Distinguish between law and equity.
9. Explain the principle of *stare decisis*.
10. Identify and define five remedies available in equity.

Internet Question. For the federal government and for your state, find examples of the following sources of law: (a) constitutional law, (b) judicial law, (c) legislative law, and (d) administrative law. (If your state is not available, choose another state.)

Business Ethics

Business ethics is a subset of ethics: no special set of ethical principles applies only to the world of business. Immoral acts are immoral, whether or not a businessperson has committed them. In the last few years, countless business wrongs, such as insider trading, the Beech-Nut adulterated apple juice scandal, the Bhopal disaster, the Dalkon Shield tragedy, and the savings and loan industry collapse have been reported almost daily.

Ethics can be defined broadly as the study of what is right or good for human beings. It attempts to determine what people ought to do, or what goals they should pursue. **Business ethics,** as a branch of applied ethics, is the study and determination of what is right and good in business settings. Business ethics seeks to understand the moral issues that arise from business practices, institutions, and decision making and their relationship to generalized human values. Unlike legal analyses, analyses of ethics have no central authority, such as courts or legislatures, upon which to rely; nor do they follow clear-cut, universal standards. Nonetheless, despite these inherent limitations, it still may be possible to make meaningful ethical judgments. To improve ethical decision making, it is important to understand how others have approached the task.

Some examples of the many business ethics questions may help to clarify the definition of business ethics. In the employment relationship, countless ethical issues arise regarding the safety and compensation of workers, their civil rights (such as equal treatment, privacy, and freedom from sexual harassment), and the legitimacy of whistle blowing. In the relationship between business and its customers, ethical issues permeate marketing techniques, product safety, and consumer protection. The relationship between business and its owners bristles with ethical questions involving corporate governance, shareholder voting, and management's duties to the shareholders. The relationship among competing businesses involves numerous ethical matters, including fair competition and the effects of collusion. The interaction between business and society at large presents additional ethical dimensions: pollution of the physical environment, commitment to the community's economic and social infrastructure, and depletion of natural resources. Not only do all of these issues recur at the international level, but additional ones present themselves, such as bribery of foreign officials, exploitation of less-developed countries, and conflicts among differing cultures and value systems. (See "The Aftermath of Bhopal.")

In resolving the ethical issues raised by business conduct, it is helpful to utilize a seeing-knowing-doing model. First, the decision maker should *see* (identify) the ethical issues involved in the proposed conduct, including the ethical implications of the various available options. Second, the decision

Ethics study of what is right or good for human beings

Business ethics study of what is right and good in a business setting; includes the moral issues that arise from business practices, institutions, and decisions

maker should *know* (resolve) what to do by choosing the best option. Finally, the decision maker should *do* (implement) the chosen option by developing implementing strategies.

This chapter first surveys the most prominent ethical theories (the knowing part of the decision, on which the great majority of philosophers and ethicists have focused). The chapter then examines ethical standards in business and the ethical responsibilities of business. It concludes with five ethical business cases, which give the student the opportunity to apply the seeing-knowing-doing model. The student (1) identifies the ethical issues presented in these cases; (2) resolves these issues by using one of the ethical theories described in the chapter, some other ethical theory, or a combination of the theories; and (3) develops strategies for implementing the ethical resolution.

LAW VERSUS ETHICS

As discussed in Chapter 1, moral concepts strongly affect the law, but law and morality are not the same. Although it is tempting to say that "if it's legal, it's moral," such a proposition is generally too simplistic. For example, it would seem gravely immoral to stand by silently while a blind man walks off a cliff if one could prevent the fall by shouting a warning, even though one would not be legally obligated to do so. Similarly, moral questions arise concerning "legal" business practices, such as failing to fulfill a promise that is not legally binding; exporting products banned in the United States to third world countries where they are not prohibited; or slaughtering baby seals for fur coats. The mere fact that these practices are legal does not prevent them from being challenged on moral grounds.

Just as it is possible for legal acts to be immoral, it is equally possible for illegal acts to seem morally preferable to following the law. For example, it is the moral conviction of the great majority of people that those who sheltered Jews in violation of Nazi edicts during World War II and those who committed acts of civil disobedience in the 1950s and 1960s to challenge segregation laws in the United States were acting properly and that the laws themselves were immoral.

ETHICAL THEORIES

Philosophers have sought for centuries to develop dependable and universal methods for making ethical judgments. In earlier times, some thinkers analogized the discovery of ethical principles with the derivation of mathematical proofs. They asserted that people could discover fundamental ethical rules by applying careful reasoning *a priori*. (*A priori* reasoning is based on theory rather than experimentation and deductively draws conclusions from cause to effect and from generalizations to particular instances.) In more recent times, many philosophers have concluded that although careful reasoning and deep thought assist substantially in moral reasoning, experience reveals that the complexities of the world defeat most attempts to fashion precise, *a priori* guidelines. Nevertheless, a review of the most significant ethical theories is useful in the analysis of issues of business ethics.

Ethical Fundamentalism

Ethical fundamentalism individuals look to a central authority or set of rules to guide them in ethical decision making

Under **ethical fundamentalism**, or absolutism, individuals look to a central authority or set of rules to guide them in ethical decision making. Some look to the Bible; others look to the Koran or the writings of Karl Marx or to any

MANAGERIAL INSIGHT

The Aftermath of Bhopal

When corporations operate internationally, they confront ethical issues related to political, social, and cultural differences among countries. Take, for example, the case of Union Carbide.

In 1984, the multinational chemical company had interests in thirty-five countries and, at least in the United States, boasted one of the best safety records among major manufacturers of chemical products. That was before the tragedy at Bhopal, India.

Union Carbide owned nearly 51 percent of Union Carbide India Limited (UCIL), a publicly traded corporation in India that ranked at the time as the country's twenty-first largest company. At the urging of the Indian government, UCIL went into the pesticide business in the 1960s, a time when India was attempting to modernize its agricultural base and produce more food. Also, at the government's urging, UCIL located in India's Bhopal region, a densely populated but extremely impoverished area. In addition, the subsidiary installed a manually operated safety system at the Bhopal plant, rather than an automatic one. (The manual system provided more jobs, a goal of the Indian government.) By the early 1980s, the UCIL plant was losing money. Squeezed by a drop in the demand for pesticides, the plant was operating at only 40 percent of its capacity. It also had taken steps to cut costs. One was to manufacture the commonly used pesticide, Sevin, in bulk quantities, from start to finish, at the plant. This required UCIL not only to make large quantities of methyl isocyanate (MIC) but to store the highly dangerous, extremely volatile chemical on site. The company also cut its

workforce, which impaired plant maintenance.

Not long before midnight on Sunday, December 2, 1984, a Bhopal plant engineer, Suman Dey, noticed that the pressure and temperature gauges on tank E610, which held some forty-five tons of MIC, had climbed to the boiling point. The normally refrigerated tank held the chemical, deadly in its gaseous state, in a cool, liquid form. But now the tank had lost its refrigeration. Employees had reason to believe that the gauges did not work properly, yet they searched for a leak anyway. Then, shortly after midnight, Dey heard what sounded like an explosion in the tank. Within seconds, a toxic cloud of methyl isocyanate escaped. The silent, deadly fog enveloped the area close to the plant, then rolled down toward Bhopal's railroad station and its main city.

The UCIL plant had been built in what was, at the time, an open area, but by the time of the accident, a large, densely populated shanty town had grown up around it. Squatters had moved in as close as the plant's gate. In the early morning hours of December 3, many of these squatters died where they fell, their lungs seared by methyl isocyanate. Others were killed in the stampede to escape the deadly gas. As the cloud drifted over Bhopal, more victims fell in its wake. Of those who survived, many were permanently blinded or

otherwise disabled. In all, approximately 200,000 people were injured. Today, estimates of the death toll range from more than 2,000 victims to as many as 30,000 victims.

When Union Carbide's chairman, Warren M. Anderson, arrived in Bhopal shortly after the disaster, he was arrested and charged with homicide. In the United States, the company faced a takeover bid from GAF Corporation which it avoided only by selling off its consumer products division, maker of Prestone antifreeze, Eveready batteries, and Glad Bags.

In 1989, the Indian Supreme Court ordered Union Carbide, now only a shadow of its former self, to pay $470 million to compensate Bhopal victims. Criminal charges against the company and its officials, though, were dropped.

For a multinational corporation like Union Carbide, the lesson of Bhopal is simple: Be careful. Yet how careful should a company be? Should multinational corporations maintain in their overseas plants safety standards the same as those they maintain in their United States operations? Or should the governments of host countries determine required safety standards?

Whatever the answers, any corporation doing business in another country should consider the following: To operate successfully in a foreign land requires a deep understanding of the political, social, and cultural differences among countries. Often, such an enterprise also demands a keen sense of advanced technology's impact on underdeveloped nations.

number of living or deceased prophets. The essential characteristic of this approach is a reliance upon a central repository of wisdom. In some cases, such reliance is total. In others, followers of a religion or a spiritual leader may believe that all members of the group are obligated to assess moral dilemmas independently, according to each person's understanding of the dictates of the fundamental principles.

Ethical Relativism

Ethical relativism asserts that actions must be judged by what individuals subjectively feel is right or wrong for themselves

Ethical relativism is a doctrine asserting that actions must be judged by what individuals feel is right or wrong for themselves. It holds that when any two individuals or cultures differ regarding the morality of a particular issue or action, they are both correct because morality is relative. However, though ethical relativism promotes open-mindedness and tolerance, it has limitations. If each person's actions are always correct for that person, then his behavior is, by definition, moral and, therefore, exempt from criticism. Once a person concludes that criticizing or punishing behavior in some cases is appropriate, he abandons ethical relativism and faces the task of developing a broader ethical methodology.

Situational ethics a person's actions must be judged by first putting oneself in the actor's situation

Although bearing a surface resemblance to ethical relativism, situational ethics actually differs substantially. **Situational ethics** holds that developing precise guidelines for effectively navigating ethical dilemmas is difficult because real-life decision making is so complex. To judge the morality of someone's behavior, the person judging must actually put herself in the other person's shoes to understand what motivated the other to choose a particular course of action. Situational ethics, however, does not cede the ultimate judgment of the propriety of an action to the actor; rather, it insists that, prior to evaluation, a person's decision or act be viewed from the actor's perspective.

Utilitarianism

Utilitarianism (util'·i·tar·i·an·ism) moral actions are those that produce the greatest net pleasure compared to net pain

Utilitarianism is a doctrine that assesses good and evil in terms of the consequences of actions. Those actions that produce the greatest net pleasure compared to net pain are better in a moral sense than those that produce less net pleasure. As Jeremy Bentham, one of the most influential proponents of utilitarianism, proclaimed, a good or moral act is one that results in "the greatest happiness for the greatest number."

Act utilitarianism assesses each separate act according to whether it maximizes pleasure over pain

The two major forms of utilitarianism are act utilitarianism and rule utilitarianism. **Act utilitarianism** assesses each separate act according to whether it maximizes pleasure over pain. For example, if telling a lie in a particular situation produces more overall pleasure than pain, then an act utilitarian would support lying as the moral thing to do. Rule utilitarians, disturbed by the unpredictability of act utilitarianism and its potential for abuse, follow a different approach. **Rule utilitarianism** holds that general rules must be established and followed even though, in some instances, following rules may produce less overall pleasure than not following them. It applies utilitarian principles in developing rules; thus, it supports rules that on balance produce the greatest satisfaction. Determining whether telling a lie in a given instance would produce greater pleasure than telling the truth is less important to the rule utilitarian than deciding whether a general practice of lying would maximize society's pleasure. If lying would not maximize pleasure generally, then one should follow a rule of not lying even though on occasion telling a lie would produce greater pleasure than would telling the truth.

Rule utilitarianism supports rules that on balance produce the greatest good

Cost-benefit analysis quantify in monetary terms the benefits and costs of alternatives

Utilitarian notions underlie cost-benefit analysis, an analytical tool used by many business and government managers today. **Cost-benefit analysis** first quantifies in monetary terms and then compares the direct and indirect costs and benefits of program alternatives for meeting a specified objective. Cost-benefit analysis seeks the greatest economic efficiency, according to the underlying notion that given two potential acts, the act achieving the greatest output at the least cost promotes the greatest marginal happiness over the less efficient act, other things being equal.

The chief criticism of utilitarianism is that in some important instances it ignores justice. A number of situations would maximize the pleasure of the majority at great social cost to a minority. Another major criticism of utilitarianism is that measuring pleasure and pain in the fashion its supporters advocate is extremely difficult, if not impossible.

Deontology

Deontological theories (from the Greek word *deon,* meaning duty or obligation) address the practical problems of utilitarianism by holding that certain underlying principles are right or wrong irrespective of any pleasure or pain calculations. Believing that actions cannot be measured simply by their results but must be judged by means and motives as well, deontologists judge the morality of acts not so much by their consequences but by the motives that lead to them. A person not only must achieve just results but also must employ the proper means.

The best-known deontological theory was proffered by the eighteenth-century philosopher Immanuel Kant. Under Kant's *categorical imperative,* for an action to be moral it (1) must potentially be a universal law that could be applied consistently and (2) must respect the autonomy and rationality of all human beings and not treat them as an expedient. That is, one should not do anything that he or she would not have everyone do in a similar situation. For example, you should not lie to colleagues unless you support the right of all colleagues to lie to one another. Similarly, you should not cheat others unless you advocate everyone's right to cheat. We apply Kantian reasoning when we challenge someone's behavior by asking: What if everybody acted that way?

Under Kant's approach, it would be improper to assert a principle to which one claimed personal exception, such as insisting that it was acceptable for you to cheat but not for anyone else to do so. This principle could not be universalized since everyone would then insist on similar rules from which only they were exempt.

Kant's philosophy also rejects notions of the end justifying the means. To Kant, every person is an end in him- or herself. Each person deserves respect simply because of his or her humanity. Thus, any sacrifice of a person for the greater good of society would be unacceptable to Kant.

In many respects, Kant's categorical imperative is a variation of the Golden Rule; and, like the Golden Rule, the categorical imperative appeals to the individual's self-centeredness.

As does every theory, Kantian ethics has its critics. Just as deontologists criticize utilitarians for excessive pragmatism and flexible moral guidelines, utilitarians and others criticize deontologists for rigidity and excessive formalism. For example, if one inflexibly adopts as a rule to tell the truth, one ignores situations in which lying might well be justified. A person hiding a terrified wife from her angry, abusive husband would seem to be acting morally by falsely denying that the wife is at the person's house. Yet, a deontologist, feeling bound to tell the truth, might ignore the consequences of truthfulness, tell the husband where his wife is, and create the possibility of a terrible tragedy. Another criticism of deontological theories is that the proper course may be difficult to determine when values or assumptions conflict.

Social Ethics Theories

Social ethics theories assert that special obligations arise from the social nature of human beings. Such theories focus not only on each person's obligations to other

Deontology *(de'·on·tol·o·gy)* holds that actions must be judged by their motives and means as well as their results

Social ethical theories focus on a person's obligations to other members in society and also on the individual's rights and obligations

Social egalitarians
(e·gal'·i·tar·i·ans) believe that society should provide all members with equal amounts of goods and services irrespective of their relative contributions

Distributive justice stresses equality of opportunity rather than of results

members of society but also on the individual's rights and obligations within the society. For example, **social egalitarians** believe that society should provide each person with equal amounts of goods and services irrespective of the contribution each makes to increase society's wealth.

Two other ethics theories have received widespread attention in recent years. One is the theory of **distributive justice** proposed by Harvard philosopher John Rawls, which seeks to analyze the type of society that people in a "natural state" would establish if they could not determine in advance whether they would be talented, rich, healthy, or ambitious, relative to other members of society. According to distributive justice, the society contemplated through this "veil of ignorance" is the one that should be developed because it considers the needs and rights of all its members. Rawls did not argue that such a society would be strictly egalitarian. That would unfairly penalize those who turned out to be the most talented and ambitious. Instead, Rawls suggested that such a society would stress equality of opportunity, not of results. On the other hand, Rawls stressed that society would pay heed to the least advantaged to ensure that they did not suffer unduly and that they enjoyed society's benefits. To Rawls, society must be premised on justice. Everyone is entitled to his or her fair share in society, a fairness all must work to guarantee.

Libertarians *(lib'·er·tar·i·ans)* stress market outcomes as the basis for distributing society's rewards

In contrast to Rawls, another Harvard philosopher, Robert Nozick, stressed liberty, not justice, as the most important obligation that society owes its members. **Libertarians** stress market outcomes as the basis for distributing society's rewards. Only to the extent that one meets market demands does one deserve society's benefits. Libertarians oppose social interference in the lives of those who do not violate the rules of the marketplace, that is, in the lives of those who do not cheat others and who disclose honestly the nature of their transactions with others. The fact that some end up with fortunes while others accumulate little simply proves that some can play in the market effectively while others cannot. To libertarians, this is not unjust. What is unjust to them is any attempt by society to take wealth earned by citizens and distribute it to those who did not earn it.

These theories and others (e.g., Marxism) judge society in moral terms by its organization and by the way in which it distributes goods and services. They demonstrate the difficulty of ethical decision making in the context of a social organization: behavior that is consistently ethical from individual to individual may not necessarily produce a just society.

Other Theories

Intuitionism
(in'·tu·i·tion·ism) a rational person possesses inherent powers to assess the correctness of actions

Good person philosophy holds that individuals should seek out and emulate good role models

The preceding theories do not exhaust the possible approaches to evaluating ethical behavior; several other theories also deserve mention. **Intuitionism** holds that a rational person possesses inherent powers to assess the correctness of actions. Though an individual may refine and strengthen these powers, they are just as basic to humanity as our instincts for survival and self-defense. Just as some people are better artists or musicians, some people have more insight into ethical behavior than others. Consistent with intuitionism is the **good person philosophy**, which declares that if individuals wish to act morally, they should seek out and emulate those who always seem to know the right choice in any given situation and who always seem to do the right thing. One variation of these ethical approaches is the *"Television Test,"* which directs us to imagine that every ethical decision we make is being broadcast on nationwide television. An appropriate decision is one we would be comfortable broadcasting on national television for all to witness.

ETHICAL STANDARDS IN BUSINESS

In this section we will explore the application of the theories of ethical behavior to the world of business.

Choosing an Ethical System

In their efforts to resolve the moral dilemmas facing mankind, philosophers and other thinkers have struggled for years to refine the various systems previously discussed. All of the systems are limited, however, in terms of applicability and tend to produce unacceptable prescriptions for action in some circumstances. But to say that each system has limits is not to say it is useless. On the contrary, a number of these systems provide insight into ethical decision making and help us formulate issues and resolve moral dilemmas. Furthermore, concluding that moral standards are difficult to articulate and that moral boundaries are imprecise is not the same as concluding that moral standards are unnecessary or nonexistent.

Research by the noted psychologist Lawrence Kohlberg provides some insight into ethical decision making and lends credibility to the notion that moral growth, like physical growth, is part of the human condition. **Kohlberg** observed that people progress through sequential **stages of moral development** according to two major variables: age and reasoning. During the first level—the *preconventional level*—a child's conduct is a reaction to the fear of punishment and, later, to the pleasure of reward. Although people who operate at this level may behave in a moral manner, they do so without understanding why their behavior is moral. The rules are imposed upon them. During adolescence—Kohlberg's *conventional level*—people conform their behavior to meet the expectations of groups, such as family, peers, and eventually society. The motivation for conformity is loyalty, affection, and trust. Most adults operate at this level. According to Kohlberg, some reach the third level—the *postconventional level*—where they accept and conform to moral principles because they understand *why* the principles are right and binding. At this level, moral principles are voluntarily internalized, not externally imposed. Moreover, individuals at this stage develop their own universal ethical principles and may even question the laws and values that society and others have adopted (see Figure 2–1).

Kohlberg believed that not all people reach the third, or even the second, stage. He therefore argued that essential to the study of ethics was the exploration of ways to help people achieve the advanced stage of postconventional thought. Other psychologists assert that individuals do not pass sequentially from stage to stage but rather function in all three stages simultaneously.

Whatever the source of our ethical approach, we cannot avoid facing moral dilemmas that challenge us to recognize and to do the right thing. Moreover, for those who plan business careers, such dilemmas necessarily will have implications for many others—employees, shareholders, suppliers, customers, and society at large.

Corporations as Moral Agents

Because corporations are not persons but artificial entities created by the state, whether they can or should be held morally accountable is difficult to determine. Though, clearly, individuals within corporations can be held morally responsible, the corporate entity presents unique problems.

Kohlberg's stages of moral development see Figure 2–1

Corporations as moral agents because a corporation is a statutory entity, it is difficult to resolve whether it should be morally accountable

FIGURE 2–1 Kohlberg's Stages of Moral Development

Levels	Perspective	Justification
Preconventional (Childhood)	Self	Punishment/Reward
Conventional (Adolescence)	Group	Group Norms
Postconventional (Adulthood)	Universal	Moral Principles

Commentators are divided on the issue. Some insist that only people can engage in behavior that can be judged in moral terms. Opponents of this view concede that corporations are not persons in any literal sense but insist that the attributes of responsibility inherent in corporations are sufficient to justify judging corporate behavior from a moral perspective.

ETHICAL RESPONSIBILITIES OF BUSINESS

Many people assert that the only responsibility of business is to maximize profit and that this obligation overrides any ethical or social responsibility. Although our economic system of modified capitalism is based on the pursuit of self-interest, it also contains components to check this motivation of greed. Our system has always recognized the need for some form of regulation, whether it be by the "invisible hand" of competition, the self-regulation of business, or government regulation.

Regulation of Business

As explained and justified by Adam Smith in *The Wealth of Nations* (1776), the capitalistic system is composed of six "institutions": economic motivation, private productive property, free enterprise, free markets, competition, and limited government. As long as all these constituent institutions continue to exist and operate in balance, the factors of production—land, capital, and labor—combine to produce an efficient allocation of resources for individual consumers and for the economy as a whole. To achieve this outcome, however, Smith's model requires that a number of conditions be satisfied: "standardized products, numerous firms in markets, each firm with a small share and unable by its actions alone to exert significant influence over price, no barriers to entry, and output carried to the point where each seller's marginal cost equals the going market price." E. Singer, *Antitrust Economics and Legal Analysis*.

History has demonstrated that the actual operation of the economy has satisfied almost none of these assumptions. More specifically, the actual competitive process falls considerably short of the assumptions of the classic economic model of perfect competition:

> Competitive industries are never perfectly competitive in this sense. Many of the resources they employ cannot be shifted to other employments without substantial cost and delay. The allocation of those resources, as between industries or as to relative proportions within a single industry, is unlikely to have been made in a way that affords the best possible expenditure of economic effort. Information is incomplete, motivation confused, and decision therefore ill informed and often unwise. Variations in efficiency are not directly reflected in variations of profit. Success is derived in large part from competitive selling efforts, which in the aggregate may be wasteful, and from differentiation of products, which may be undertaken partly by methods designed to impair the opportunity of the buyer to compare quality and price. C. Edwards, *Maintaining Competition*.

In addition to capitalism's failure to allocate resources efficiently, it cannot be relied on to achieve all of the social and public policy objectives a pluralistic democracy requires. For example, the free enterprise model simply does not address equitable distribution of wealth, national defense, conservation of natural resources, full employment, stability in economic cycles, protection against economic dislocations, health and safety, social security, and other important social and economic goals. Increased **regulation of business** has occurred not only to preserve the competitive process in our economic system but also to achieve social goals extrinsic to the efficient allocation of resources, the "invisible hand" and self-regulation by business having failed to bring about these desired results. Such intervention attempts (1) to regulate both "legal" monopolies, such as those conferred by law through copyrights, patents, and trade symbols, and "natural" monopolies, such as utilities, transportation, and communications; (2) to preserve competition by correcting imperfections in the market system; (3) to protect specific groups, especially labor and agriculture, from marketplace failures; and (4) to promote other social goals. Successful government regulation involves a delicate balance between regulations that attempt to preserve competition and those that attempt to advance other social objectives. The latter should not undermine the basic competitive processes that provide an efficient allocation of economic resources.

Regulation of business government regulation is necessary because all the conditions for perfect competition have not been satisfied and free competition cannot by itself achieve other social goals

Corporate Governance

In addition to the broad demands of maintaining a competitive and fair marketplace, another factor demanding the ethical and social responsibility of business is the sheer size and power of individual corporations. The five thousand largest U.S. firms currently produce over half of the nation's gross national product.

In a classic study published in 1932, Adolf Berle and Gardner Means concluded that great amounts of economic power had been concentrated in a relatively few large corporations, that the ownership of these corporations had become widely dispersed, and that the shareholders had become far removed from active participation in management. Since their original study, these trends have continued steadily. Thus, vast amounts of wealth and power are controlled by a small number of corporations, which are in turn controlled by a small group of corporate officers.

These developments raise a large number of social, policy, and ethical issues about the governance of large, publicly owned corporations. Many observers insist that companies playing such an important economic role should have a responsibility to undertake projects that benefit society in ways that go beyond mere financial efficiency in producing goods and services. In some instances, the idea of corporate obligations come from industrialists themselves.

Corporate governance vast amounts of wealth and power have become concentrated in a small number of corporations, which are in turn controlled by a small group of people, and it is argued that they therefore have a responsibility to undertake projects to benefit society

Arguments against Social Responsibility

A number of arguments oppose business involvement in socially responsible activities: profitability, unfairness, accountability, and expertise.

Profitability As Milton Friedman and others have argued, businesses are artificial entities established to permit people to engage in profit-making, not social, activities. Without profits, they assert, there is little reason for a corporation to exist and no real way to measure the effectiveness of corporate activities. Businesses are not organized to engage in social activities; they are structured to produce goods and services for which they receive money. Their social obligation

Profitability the business of business is to engage in profit-making activity

is to return as much of this money as possible to their direct stakeholders. In a free market with significant competition, the selfish pursuits of corporations will lead to maximizing output, minimizing costs, and establishing fair prices. All other concerns distract companies and interfere with achieving these goals.

Unfairness Whenever companies stray from their designated role of profit-maker, they take unfair advantage of company employees and shareholders. For example, a company may support the arts or education or spend excess funds on health and safety; however, these funds rightfully belong to the shareholders or employees. The company's decision to disburse these funds to others who may well be less deserving than the shareholders and employees is unfair. Furthermore, consumers can express their desires through the marketplace, and shareholders and employees can decide privately if they wish to make charitable contributions. In most cases, senior management consults the board of directors about supporting social concerns but does not seek the approval of the company's major stakeholders, thereby effectively disenfranchising these shareholders from actions that reduce their benefits from the corporation.

Accountability Corporations, as previously noted, are private institutions that are subject to a lower standard of accountability than are public bodies. Accordingly, a company may decide to support a wide range of social causes and yet submit to little public scrutiny. But a substantial potential for abuse exists in such cases. For one thing, a company could provide funding for a variety of causes its employees or shareholders did not support. It also could provide money "with strings attached," thereby controlling the recipients' agendas for less than socially beneficial purposes. For example, a drug company that contributes to a consumer group might implicitly or explicitly condition its assistance on the group's agreement never to criticize the company or the drug industry.

This lack of accountability warrants particular concern because of the enormous power corporations wield in modern society. Many large companies, like General Motors or Exxon, generate and spend more money in a year than all but a handful of the world's countries. If these companies suddenly began to vigorously pursue their own social agendas, their influence might well rival, and perhaps undermine, that of their national government. In a country like the United States, founded on the principles of limited government and the balance of powers, too much corporate involvement in social affairs might well present substantial problems. Without clear guidelines and accountability, companies pursuing their private visions of socially responsible behavior might well distort the entire process of governance.

There is a clear alternative to corporations engaging in socially responsible action. If society wishes to increase the resources devoted to needy causes, it has the power to do so. Let the corporations seek profits without the burden of a social agenda, let the consumers vote in the marketplace for the products and services they desire, and let the government tax a portion of corporate profits for socially beneficial causes.

Expertise Even though a corporation has an expertise in producing and selling its product, it may not possess a talent for recognizing or managing socially useful activities. Corporations become successful in the market because they can identify and meet the needs of their customers. Nothing suggests that this talent spills over into nonbusiness arenas. In fact, critics of corporate participation in

Unfairness whenever corporations engage in social activities, they divert funds rightfully belonging to the shareholders or employees

Accountability a corporation is subject to less public accountability than are public institutions

Expertise although a corporation may have a high level of expertise in selling its goods and services, there is absolutely no guarantee that any promotion of social activities will be carried on with the same degree of competence

social activities worry that corporations will prove unable to distinguish the true needs of society from their own narrow self-interests.

Arguments in Favor of Social Responsibility

First, it should be recognized that even the critics of business acknowledge that the prime responsibility of business is to make a reasonable return on its investment by producing a quality product at a reasonable price. They do not suggest that business entities be charitable institutions. They do assert, however, that business has certain obligations beyond making a profit or not harming society. Such critics contend that business must help to resolve societal problems, and they offer a number of arguments in support of their position.

The Social Contract Society creates corporations and gives them a special social status, including the granting of limited liability, which insulates owners from liability for debts their organizations incur. Supporters of social roles for corporations assert that limited liability and other rights granted to companies carry a responsibility: Corporations, just like other members of society, must contribute to its betterment. Therefore, companies owe a moral debt to society to contribute to its overall well-being. Society needs a host of improvements, such as pollution control, safe products, a free marketplace, quality education, cures for illness, and freedom from crime. Corporations can help in each of these areas. Granted, deciding which social needs deserve corporate attention is difficult; however, this challenge does not lessen a company's obligation to choose a cause. Corporate America cannot ignore the multitude of pressing needs that remain, despite the efforts of government and private charities.

> **The social contract** since society allows for the creation of corporations and gives them special rights, including a grant of limited liability, corporations owe a responsibility to society

A derivative of the social contract theory is the **stakeholder model** for the societal role of the business corporation. Under the stakeholder model a corporation has fiduciary responsibilities—duty of utmost loyalty and good faith—to all of its stakeholders, not just its stockholders. Historically, the stockholder model for the role of business has been the norm. Under this theory, a corporation is viewed as private property owned by and for the benefit of its owners—the stockholders of the corporation. (For a full discussion of this legal model, see Chapter 37.) The stakeholder model, on the other hand, holds that corporations are responsible to society at large and more directly to all those constituencies on which they depend for their survival. Thus, it is argued that a corporation should be managed for the benefit of all of its stakeholders—stockholders, employees, customers, suppliers, and managers, as well as the local communities in which it operates. (See Figure 2–2; compare it with Figure 37–1.)

> **Stakeholder model** corporations have a fiduciary duty to all of their stakeholders, not just their stockholders

Less Government Regulation According to another argument in favor of corporate social responsibility, the more responsibly companies act, the less the government must regulate them. This idea, if accurate, would likely appeal to those corporations that typically view regulation with distaste, perceiving it as a crude and expensive way of achieving social goals. To them, regulation often imposes inappropriate, overly broad rules that hamper productivity and require extensive record-keeping procedures to document compliance. If companies can use more flexible, voluntary methods of meeting a social norm such as pollution control, then government will be less tempted to legislate norms.

> **Less government regulation** by taking a more proactive role in aiding with society's problems, corporations create a climate of trust and respect that has the effect of reducing government regulation

The argument can be taken further. Not only does anticipatory corporate action lessen the likelihood of government regulation, but social involvement by companies creates a climate of trust and respect that reduces the overall

FIGURE 2–2 The Stakeholder Model

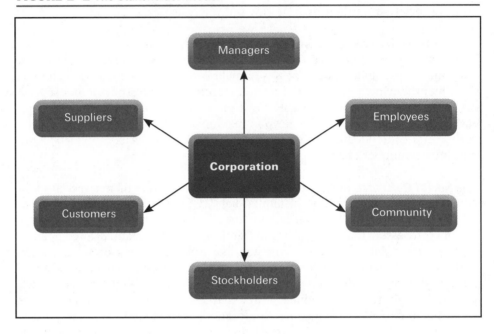

inclination of government to interfere in company business. For example, a government agency is much more likely to show some leniency toward a socially responsible company than toward one that ignores social plights.

Long-run profits corporate involvement in social causes creates goodwill, which simply makes good business sense

Long-Run Profits Perhaps the most persuasive argument in favor of corporate involvement in social causes is that such involvement actually makes good business sense. Consumers often support good corporate images and avoid bad ones. For example, consumers generally prefer to patronize stores with "easy return" policies. Even though such policies are not required by law, companies institute them because they create goodwill—an intangible though indispensable asset for ensuring repeat customers. In the long run, enhanced goodwill often rebounds to stronger profits. Moreover, corporate actions to improve the well-being of their communities make these communities more attractive to citizens and more profitable for business.

CHAPTER SUMMARY

Definitions	**Ethics** study of what is right or good for human beings **Business Ethics** study of what is right and good in a business setting

Ethical Theories	**Ethical Fundamentalism** individuals look to a central authority or set of rules to guide them in ethical decision making
	Ethical Relativism asserts that actions must be judged by what individuals subjectively feel is right or wrong for themselves
	Situational Ethics one must judge a person's actions by first putting oneself in the actor's situation
	Utilitarianism moral actions are those that produce the greatest net pleasure compared to net pain
	■ *Act Utilitarianism* assesses each separate act according to whether it maximizes pleasure over pain
	■ *Rule Utilitarianism* supports rules that on balance produce the greatest pleasure for society
	■ *Cost-Benefit Analysis* quantifies the benefits and costs of alternatives
	Deontology holds that actions must be judged by their motives and means as well as their results
	Social Ethics Theories focus on a person's obligations to other members in society and also on the individual's rights and obligations within society
	■ *Social Egalitarians* believe that society should provide all its members with equal amounts of goods and services irrespective of their relative contributions
	■ *Distributive Justice* stresses equality of opportunity rather than results
	■ *Libertarians* stress market outcomes as the basis for distributing society's rewards
	Other Theories
	■ *Intuitionism* a rational person possesses inherent power to assess the correctness of actions
	■ *Good Person* individuals should seek out and emulate good role models

Ethical Standards in Business	**Choosing an Ethical System** Kohlberg's stages of moral development is a widely accepted model (See Figure 2–1.)
	Corporations as Moral Agents because a corporation is a statutorily created entity, it is not clear whether it should be held morally responsible

Ethical Responsibilities of Business	**Regulation of Business** governmental regulation has been necessary because all the conditions for perfect competition have not been satisfied and free competition cannot by itself achieve other societal objectives
	Corporate Governance vast amounts of wealth and power have become concentrated in a small number of corporations, which are in turn controlled by a small group of corporate officers
	Arguments against Social Responsibility
	■ *Profitability* since corporations are artificial entities established for profit-making activities, their only social obligation should be to return as much money as possible to shareholders
	■ *Unfairness* whenever corporations engage in social activities, such as supporting the arts or education, they divert funds rightfully belonging to shareholders and/or employees to unrelated third parties

■ *Accountability* a corporation is subject to less public accountability than public bodies are

■ *Expertise* although a corporation may have a high level of expertise in selling its goods and services, there is absolutely no guarantee that any promotion of social activities will be carried on with the same degree of competence

Arguments in Favor of Social Responsibility

■ *The Social Contract* since society allows for the creation of corporations and gives them special rights, including a grant of limited liability, corporations owe a responsibility to our society

■ *Less Government Regulation* by taking a more proactive role in aiding with society's problems, corporations create a climate of trust and respect that has the effect of reducing government regulation

■ *Long-Run Profits* corporate involvement in social causes creates goodwill, which simply makes good business sense

QUESTIONS

1. Describe the differences between law and ethics.
2. List and contrast the various ethical theories.
3. Describe cost-benefit analysis and explain when it should be used and when it should be avoided.
4. Explain Kohlberg's stages of moral development.
5. Explain the ethical responsibilities of business.

Internet Question. Find and identify some web sites pertaining to business ethics that contain (a) political, social, or economic bias, (b) codes of conduct for companies, associations, or users, and (c) other significant material

PROBLEMS

1. You have an employee who has a chemical imbalance in the brain that causes her to be severely unstable. The medication that is available to deal with this schizophrenic condition is extremely powerful and decreases the taker's life span by one to two years for every year that the user takes it. You know that her doctors and family believe that it is in her best interest to take the medication. What course of action should you follow?

2. You have an employee from another country who is very shy. After a period of time, you notice that the quality of her performance is deteriorating rapidly. You find an appropriate time to speak with her and determine that she is extremely distraught. She informs you that her family has arranged a marriage for her and that she refuses to obey their contract. She further informs you that she is contemplating suicide. Two weeks later, after her poor performance continues, you determine that she is on the verge of a nervous breakdown; and once again she informs you that she is going to commit suicide. What should you do? Consider further that you can petition a court to have her involuntarily committed to a mental hospital. You know, however, that such a commitment would be considered an extreme insult by her family and that they might seek retribution. Does this alter your decision?

3. You receive a telephone call from a company you never do business with requesting a reference on one of your employees, Mary Sunshine. You believe Mary performs in a generally incompetent manner and would be delighted to see her take another job. You give her a glowing reference. Is this right? Explain.

4. You have just received a report suggesting that a chemical your company uses in its manufacturing process is very dangerous. You have not read the report, but you are generally aware of its contents. You believe that the chemical can be replaced fairly easily, but that if word gets out panic may set in among employees and community members. A reporter asks if you have seen the report, and you say no. Is your behavior right or wrong? Explain.

5. Joe Jones, your neighbor and friend, and you bought lottery tickets at the corner drugstore. While watching the lottery drawing on TV with you that night, Joe leaped from the couch, waved his lottery ticket, and shouted, "I've got the winning number!" Suddenly, he clutched his chest, keeled over, and died on the spot. You are the only living person who knows that Joe, not you, bought the winning ticket. If you substitute his ticket for yours, no one will know of the switch and you will be $10 million richer. Joe's only living relative is a rich aunt whom

he despised. Will you switch his ticket for yours? Explain.

6. Omega, Inc., a publicly held corporation, has assets of $100 million and annual earnings in the range of $13–$15 million. Omega owns three aluminum plants, which are profitable, and one plastics plant, which is losing $4 million a year. Because of its very high operating costs, the plastics plant shows no sign of ever becoming profitable, and there is no evidence that the plant and the underlying real estate will increase in value. Omega decides to sell the plastics plant. The only bidder for the plant is Gold, who intends to use the plant for a new purpose, to introduce automation, and to replace all existing employees. Would it be ethical for Omega to turn down Gold's bid and keep the plastics plant operating indefinitely, for the purpose of preserving the employees' jobs? Explain.

7. You are the sales manager of a two-year-old electronics firm. At times, the firm has seemed on the brink of failure, but recently has begun to be profitable. In large part, the profitability is due to the aggressive and talented sales force you have recruited. Two months ago, you hired Alice North, an honors graduate from the State University who decided that she was tired of the Research Department and wanted to try sales.

Almost immediately after you sent Alice out for training with Brad West, your best salesman, he began reporting to you an unexpected turn of events. According to Brad, "Alice is terrific: she's confident, smooth, and persistent. Unfortunately, a lot of our buyers are good old boys who just aren't comfortable around young, bright women. Just last week, Hiram Jones, one of our biggest customers, told me that he simply won't continue to do business with `young chicks' who think they invented the world. It's not that Alice is a know-it-all. She's not. It's just that these guys like to booze it up a bit, tell some off-color jokes, and then get down to business. Alice doesn't drink, and, although she never objects to the jokes, it's clear she thinks they're offensive." Brad felt that several potential deals had fallen through "because the mood just wasn't right with Alice there." Brad added, "I don't like a lot of these guys' styles myself, but I go along to make the sales. I just don't think Alice is going to make it."

When you call Alice in to discuss the situation, she concedes the accuracy of Brad's report, but indicates that she's not to blame and insists that she be kept on the job. You feel committed to equal opportunity, but don't want to jeopardize your company's ability to survive. What should you do?

The business ethics cases that follow are based on the kinds of situations that companies regularly face in conducting business. You should first read each case carefully and in its entirety before attempting to analyze it. Second, you should identify the most important ethical issues arising from the situation. Often it is helpful to prioritize these issues. Third, you should identify the viable options for addressing these issues and the ethical implications of the identified options. This might include examining the options from the perspectives of the various ethical theories as well as the affected stakeholders. Fourth, you should reach a definite resolution of the ethical issues by choosing what you think is the best option. You should have a well-articulated rationale for your resolution. Finally, develop a strategy for implementing your resolution.

Pharmakon Drug Company

BACKGROUND

William Wilson, senior vice president of research, development, and medical (R, D & M) at Pharmakon Drug Company received both his Ph.D. in biochemistry and his M.D. from the University of Oklahoma. Upon completion of his residency, Dr. Wilson joined the faculty at Harvard Medical School. He left Harvard after five years to join the research group at Merck & Co. Three years later, he went to Burroughs-Wellcome as director of R, D & M, and, after eight years, Dr. Wilson joined Pharmakon in his current position.

William Wilson has always been highly respected as a scientist, a manager, and an individual. He has also been an outstanding leader in the scientific community, particularly in the effort to attract more minorities into the field.

Pharmakon concentrates its research efforts in the areas of antivirals (with a focus on HIV), cardiovascular, respiratory, muscle relaxants, gastrointestinal, the central nervous system, and consumer health care (that is, nonprescription or over-the-counter medicines). Dr. Wilson is on the board of directors of Pharmakon and the company's executive committee. He reports directly to the chairman of the board and CEO, Mr. Jarred Swenstrum.

DECLINING GROWTH

During the previous eight years, Pharmakon experienced tremendous growth: 253 percent overall with yearly growth ranging from 12 percent to 25 percent. During this period, Pharmakon's R, D & M budget grew from $79 million to $403 million, and the number of employees rose from 1,192 to 3,273 (see Table 1).

During the previous two years, however, growth in revenue and earnings had slowed considerably. Moreover, in the current year, Pharmakon's revenues of $3.55 billion and earnings before taxes of $1.12 billion were up only 2 percent from the previous year. Furthermore, both revenues and earnings are projected to be flat or declining for the next five years.

The cessation of this period's tremendous growth and the likelihood of future decline have been brought about principally by two causes. First, a number of Pharmakon's most important patents have expired and competition from generics has begun, and could continue, to erode its products' market shares. Second, as new types of health-care delivery organizations evolve, pharmaceutical companies' revenues and earnings will in all likelihood be adversely affected.

PROBLEM AND PROPOSED SOLUTIONS

In response, the board of directors has decided that the company must emphasize two conflicting goals: increase the number of new drugs brought to market and cut back on the workforce in anticipation of rising labor and marketing costs and declining revenues. Accordingly, Dr. Wilson has been instructed to cut costs significantly and to reduce his workforce by 15 percent over the next six months.

Dr. Wilson called a meeting with his management team to discuss the workforce reduction. One of his managers, Leashia Harmon, argued that the layoffs should be made "so that recent gains in minority hiring are not wiped out." The percentage of minority employees had increased from 2.7 percent eight years ago to 8.3 percent in the previous year (see Table 1). The minority population in communities in which Pharmakon has major facilities has remained over the years at approximately 23 percent. About 20 percent of the R, D & M workforce have a Ph.D. in a physical science or in pharmacology, and another 3 percent have an M.D.

Dr. Harmon, a Ph.D. in pharmacology and head of clinical studies, is the only minority on Dr. Wilson's seven-member management team. Dr. Harmon argued that R, D & M has worked long and hard to increase minority employment and has been a leader in promoting Pharmakon's affirmative action plan (see Exhibit 1). Therefore, she asserted, all layoffs should reflect this commitment, even if it meant disproportionate layoffs of nonminorities.

TABLE 1 Pharmakon Employment

Attribute/ Years Ago	1	2	3	4	5	6	7	8
Total Employment	3,273	3,079	2,765	2,372	1,927	1,619	1,306	1,192
Minority Employment	272 (8.35)	238 (7.7%)	196 (7.15)	143 (6.0%)	109 (5.7%)	75 (4.6%)	53 (4.1%)	32 (2.7%)
Revenue ($ million)	3,481	3,087	2,702	2,184	1,750	1,479	1,214	986
Profit ($ million)	1,106	1,021	996	869	724	634	520	340
R, D & M Budget ($ million)	403	381	357	274	195	126	96	79

Dr. Anson Peake, another member of Dr. Wilson's management team and director of new products, argued that Pharmakon's R, D & M division has never discharged a worker except for cause and should adhere as closely as possible to that policy by terminating individuals solely based on merit. Dr. Rachel Waugh, director of product development, pointed out that the enormous growth in employment over the last seven years—almost a trebling of the workforce—had made the company's employee performance evaluation system less than reliable. Consequently, she contended that because laying off 15 percent of her group would be extremely difficult and subjective, she preferred to follow a system of seniority.

Dr. Wilson immediately recognized that any system of reducing the workforce would be difficult to implement. Moreover, he was concerned about fairness to employees and maintaining the best qualified group to carry out the area's mission. He was very troubled by a merit or seniority system if it could not maintain the minority gains. In fact, he had even thought about the possibility of using this difficult situation to increase the percentage of minorities to bring it more in line with the minority percentage of the communities in which Pharmakon had major facilities.

FIGURE 1 Pharmakon Affirmative Action Program

Pharmakon Drug Company
Equal Employment Opportunity
Affirmative Action Program

POLICY

It is the policy of Pharmakon Drug Co. to provide equal employment opportunities without regard to race, color, religion, sex, national origin, sexual preference, disability and veteran status. The Company will also take affirmative action to employ and advance individual applicants from all segments of our society. This policy relates to all phases of employment, including, but not limited to, recruiting, hiring, placement, promotion, demotion, layoff, recall, termination, compensation, and training. In communities where Pharmakon has facilities, it is our policy to be a leader in providing equal employment for all of its citizens.

RESPONSIBILITY FOR IMPLEMENTATION

The head of each division is ultimately responsible for initiating, administering, and controlling activities within all areas of responsibility necessary to ensure full implementation of this policy.

The managers of each location or area are responsible for the implementation of this policy.

All other members of management are responsible for conducting day-to-day activities in a manner to ensure compliance with this policy.

Mykon's Dilemma

Jack Spratt, the newly appointed CEO of Mykon Pharmaceuticals, Inc., sat at his desk and scratched his head for the thousandth time that night. His friends never tired of telling him that unless he stopped this habit he would remove what little hair he had left. Nevertheless, he had good reason to be perplexed—the decisions he made would determine the future of the company and, literally, the life or death of thousands of people.

As a young, ambitious scientist, Spratt had gained international fame and considerable fortune while rising quickly through the ranks of the scientists as Mykon. After receiving a degree from the Executive MBA program at the Kenan-Flagler Business School, University of North Carolina at Chapel Hill, he assumed, in rapid succession, a number of administrative positions at the company, culminating in his appointment as CEO. But no one had told him that finding cures for previously incurable diseases would be fraught with moral dilemmas. Although it was now 3:00 in the morning, Spratt remained at his desk, unable to stop thinking about his difficult choices. His preoccupation was made worse by the knowledge that pressure from governments and consumers would only increase each day he failed to reach a decision. This pressure had mounted relentlessly since the fateful day he had announced that Mykon had discovered the cure for AIDS. But the cure brought with it a curse: there was not enough to go around.

COMPANY BACKGROUND

Mykon, a major international research-based pharmaceutical group, engages in the research, development, manufacture, and marketing of human health-care products for sale in both the prescription and over-the-counter (OTC) markets. The company's principal prescription medicines include a range of products in the following areas: antiviral, neuromuscular blocking, cardiovascular, anti-inflammatory, immunosuppressive, systemic antibacterial, and central nervous system. Mykon also manufactures other products such as muscle relaxants, anti-depressants, anticonvulsants, and respiratory stimulants. In addition, the company markets drugs for the treatment of congestive heart failure and the prevention of organ rejection following transplant.

Mykon's OTC business primarily consists of cough and cold preparations and several topical antibiotics. The company seeks to expand its OTC business in various ways, including the reclassification of some of its prescription drugs to OTC status. Mykon's OTC sales represented 14 percent of the company's sales during last year.

Mykon has a long tradition of excellence in research and development (R & D). The company's expenditures on R & D for the last three financial years constituted 15 percent of its sales.

Mykon focuses its R & D on the following selected therapeutic areas, listed in descending order of expenditure amount: antivirals and other antibiotics, cardiovascular, central nervous system, anti-cancer, anti-inflammatory, respiratory, and neuromuscular.

Mykon sells its products internationally in over 120 countries and has a significant presence in two of the largest pharmaceutical markets—the United States and Europe—and a growing presence in Japan. It generated approximately 43 percent and 35 percent of the company's sales from the previous year in the United States and Europe, respectively. The company sells essentially the same range of products throughout the world.

PRODUCTION

Mykon carries out most of its production in Rotterdam in the Netherlands and in Research Triangle Park, North Carolina, in the United States. The latter is the company's world headquarters. The company's manufacturing processes typically consist of three stages: the manufacture of active chemicals, the incorporation of these chemicals into products designed for use by the consumer, and packaging. The firm has an ongoing program of capital expenditure to provide up-to-date production facilities and relies on advanced technology, automation, and computerization of its manufacturing capability to help maintain its competitive position.

Production facilities are also located in ten other countries to meet the needs of local markets and to overcome legal restrictions on the importation of finished products. These facilities principally engage in product formulation and packaging, although plants in certain countries manufacture active chemicals. Last year, Mykon had more than 17,000 employees, 27 percent of whom were in the United States. Approximately 21 percent of Mykon's employees were engaged in R & D, largely in the Netherlands and the United States. Although unions represent a number of the firm's employees, the firm has not experienced any significant labor disputes in recent years, and it considers its employee relations to be good.

RESEARCH AND DEVELOPMENT

In the pharmaceutical industry, R & D is both expensive and prolonged, entailing considerable uncertainty. The process of producing a commercial drug typically takes between eight and twelve years as it proceeds from discovery through development to regulatory approval and finally to the product launch. No assurance exists that new compounds will survive the development process or obtain the requisite regulatory approvals. In addition, research conducted by other pharmaceutical companies may lead at any time to the introduction of competing or improved treatments.

Last year Mykon incurred approximately 95 percent of its R & D expenditures in the Netherlands and the United States. Figure 2 sets out the firm's annual expenditure on R & D in dollars and as a percentage of sales for each of the last three financial years.

JACK SPRATT

Every society, every institution, every company, and most importantly, every individual should follow those precepts that society holds most dear. The pursuit of profits must be consistent with and subordinate to these ideals, the most important of which

FIGURE 2 Mykon R & D Expenditures

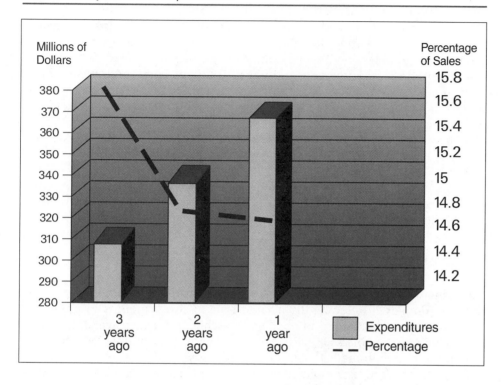

is the Golden Rule. To work for the betterment of humanity is the reason I became a scientist in the first place. As a child, Banting and Best were my heroes. I could think of no vocation that held greater promise to help mankind. Now that I am CEO I intend to have these beliefs included in our company's mission statement.

These sentiments, expressed by Jack Spratt in a newsmagazine interview, capture the intensity and drive that animate the man. None who knew him was surprised when he set out years ago—fueled by his prodigious energy, guided by his brilliant mind, and financed by Mykon—for the inner reaches of the Amazon Basin to find naturally occurring medicines. Spratt considered it to be his manifest destiny to discover the cure for some dread disease.

His search was not totally blind. Some years earlier, Frans Berger, a well-known but eccentric scientist, had written extensively about the variety of plant life and fungi that flourished in the jungles of the Bobonaza River region deep in the Amazon watershed. Although he spent twenty years there and discovered nothing of medical significance, the vast number and intriguing uniqueness of his specimens convinced Spratt that it was just a matter of time before a major breakthrough would occur.

Spratt also had some scientific evidence. While working in Mykon's laboratory to finance his graduate education in biology and genetics, Spratt and his supervisors had noticed that several fungi could not only restore damaged skin but when combined with synthetic polymers, had significant effects on internal cells. Several more years of scientific expeditions and investigations proved promising enough for Mykon to send Spratt and a twenty-person exploration team to the Amazon Basin for two years. Two years became five, and the enormous quantity of specimens sent back eventually took over an entire wing of the company's sizable laboratories in Research Triangle Park, North Carolina.

Upon Spratt's return, he headed up a group of Mykon scientists who examined the Amazonian fungi for pharmacological activity. After several years of promising beginnings and disappointing endings, they discovered that one fungus destroyed the recently identified virus, HIV. Years later, the company managed to produce enough of the drug (code named Sprattalin) derived from the fungus to inform the Food and Drug Administration (FDA) that it was testing what appeared to be a cure for HIV. It was the happiest moment of Jack Spratt's life. The years of determined effort, not to mention the $800 million Mykon had invested, would now more than fully be rewarded.

Spratt's joy was short-lived, though. Public awareness of the drug quickly spread and groups pressured the FDA to shorten or eliminate its normal approval process, which ordinarily takes more than seven years. People dying from the virus's effects demanded immediate access to the drug.

THE DRUG

Mirroring the insidiousness of HIV itself, the structure of Sprattalin is extraordinarily complex. Consequently, it takes four to seven months to produce a small quantity, only 25 percent of which is usable. It is expensive; each unit of Sprattalin costs Mykon $20,000 to produce. The projected dosage ranges from ten units for asymptomatic HIV-positive patients who have normal white blood cell counts to fifty units for patients with low white blood cell counts and a full-blown AIDS diagnosis. The drug appears to eliminate the virus from all patients regardless of their stage of the disease. However, it does not have any restorative effect on patients' compromised immune systems. Accordingly, it is expected that asymptomatic HIV-positive patients will revert to their normal life expectancies. It is not clear what the life expectancy will be of patients with full-blown AIDS, although it is almost certain that their life expectancy would be curtailed.

Supply of Sprattalin

The company has estimated that the first two years of production would yield enough Sprattalin to cure 20 percent of all asymptomatic HIV-positive patients. Alternatively, the supply would be sufficient to treat 14 percent of all patients with full-blown AIDS.

Interested parties have argued that the solution to production problems is clear: build larger facilities. However, even with production levels as low as they are, the bottleneck in supply occurs elsewhere. The fungus on which the whole process depends is incredibly rare, growing only in two small regions near Jatun Molino, Ecuador, along the Bobonaza River. At current harvesting rates, scientists predict that all known deposits will be depleted in three years, and many of them insist that production should be scaled back to allow the fungus to regenerate itself.

Presently there are no known methods of cultivating the fungus in the laboratory. Apparently, the delicate ecology that allows it to exist in only one region of the earth is somehow distressed enough by either transport or lab conditions to render it unable to grow and produce the drug's precursor. Scientists are feverishly trying to discover those factors that will support successful culture.

However, with limited quantities of the starting material and most of that pressured into production, the company has enjoyed no success in this endeavor. Because of Sprattalin's complexity, attempts to synthesize the drug have failed completely, mainly because, like aspirin, it is not known how the drug works; thus, Sprattalin's effectiveness remains shrouded in mystery.

Allocation of Sprattalin

In response to the insufficient supply, a number of powerful consumer groups have made public their suggestions regarding the allocation of Sprattalin. One proposition advanced would use medical records to establish a waiting list of possible recipients based on the length of time they have been in treatment for the virus. The argument is that those people who have waited the longest and are most in danger of dying should be the first to find relief.

Other groups propose an opposite approach, arguing that since supply is so drastically short, Mykon should make Sprattalin available only to asymptomatic HIV patients. They require the least concentrations of the drug to become well, thus extending the drug's supply. They also have the greatest likelihood of returning to full life expectancies. Under this proposal, people who have a full-blown AIDS diagnosis would be ineligible for treatment. Such patients have previously come to terms with their impending mortality, have less psychological adjustments to make, and represent, on a dosage basis, two to five healthier patients. In meting the drug out in this manner, proponents argue, the drug can more readily meet the highest public health objectives to eradicate the virus and prevent further transmission.

Others propose that only patients who contracted the virus without any fault of their own should have priority. This approach would first make Sprattalin available to children who were born with the virus, hemophiliacs and others who got the virus from blood transfusions, rape victims, and health-care workers.

One member of Sprattalin's executive committee has suggested a free market approach: the drug should go to the highest bidder.

Pricing of Sprattalin

In addition to supply problems, Mykon has also come under considerable criticism for its proposed pricing structure. Because of extraordinarily high development and production costs, the company has tentatively priced the drug at levels unattainable for most people afflicted with HIV. Perhaps never before in the history of medicine has the ability to pay been so starkly presented, since those that can pay, live, while those that cannot, die.

Even at these prices, though, demand far exceeds supply. Jack Spratt and the rest of the Mykon executives predict that the company could easily sell available supplies at twice the proposed price.

A growing number of Mykon executives disagree with the passive stance the company has taken in pricing the product. In their view, a 20 percent markup represents a meager return for the prolonged risk and high levels of spending that the company incurred to develop the drug. Moreover, it leaves little surplus for future investment. Furthermore, eight years is too long to amortize the R & D expenses since Sprattalin, though the first, is unlikely to be the last anti-HIV drug, now that Mykon has blazed a path. Other, more heavily capitalized, companies are racing to reverse engineer the drug, and the availability of competing drugs remains only a matter of time. Accordingly, the company cannot realistically count on an eight-year window of opportunity.

Foreign markets further exacerbate the pricing perplexity. Other countries, with less privatized health care, have already promised their citizens access to Sprattalin at any price. Some first world countries, for instance, are willing to pay up to $2 million per patient. They do not, however, wish to subsidize the drug for the United States. At the same time, some voices in the United States insist that supplies should go first to U.S. citizens.

On the other hand, countries with the most severe concentration of the HIV infection cannot afford to pay even Mykon's actual costs. Some regions in Africa and Asia have experienced rapid growth of the disease, reporting 50 percent to 80 percent of their population at some stage in the HIV cycle. Jack Spratt feels a very real moral obligation to help at least some of these people, whether they can pay or not.

MAKING THE DECISION

In the last few months, Jack Spratt had seen many aspects of the most important project in his life become not only public knowledge but also public domain. Because of the enormous social and political consequences of the discovery, it is unlikely that the government will allow Mykon to control the destiny of either Sprattalin or ultimately the company.

Addressing the public's concern over access to the drug while ensuring future prosperity of his company has become like walking a tightrope with strangers holding each end of the rope. He knew of no way to satisfy everyone. As Jack Spratt sat at his desk, sleep remained an eon away.

Oliver Winery, Inc.

BACKGROUND

Paul Oliver, Sr., immigrated to the United States in 1930 from Greece. After working for several wineries, he started Oliver Winery, Inc., which eventually found a market niche in nonvarietal jug wines. Through mass-marketing techniques, the company established a substantial presence in this segment of the market. Ten years ago, Paul, Jr., joined the firm after receiving a degree in enology (the study of wine making). He convinced his father of the desirability of entering a different segment of the wine market: premium varietals. In order to do this, the company needed a large infusion of capital to purchase appropriate vineyards. Reluctantly, Paul, Sr., agreed to take the company public. The initial public offering succeeded and 40 percent of the company's stock came into outsiders' hands. Also, for the first time, outsiders served on the board of directors. Although Paul, Jr., wanted to use a new name for the premium varietal to appeal to a more upscale market, his father insisted on using the name Oliver.

BOARD MEETING

The board of directors met, along with Janet Stabler, the director of Marketing of Oliver Winery, Inc. In attendance were:

Paul Oliver, Sr.,
  Chairman of the board and founder of the
  company
Paul Oliver, Jr., CEO,
  has an advanced degree in enology
Cyrus Abbott, CFO,
  has an MBA
Arlene Dale, comptroller,
  a CPA with a master's degree in Accounting
Raj Ray, COO,
  has a master's in Industrial Engineering

LaTasha Lane, VP Legal,
  has a J.D.
Elisabeth Constable, union representative to
  the board, has a GED
Rev. John W. Calvin, outside director,
  has a Doctor of Divinity degree
Carlos Menendez, outside director,
  has an MFA

Oliver, Sr.: The next item on the agenda is a proposal to develop a new line of wines. Janet Stabler will briefly present the proposal.

Stabler: Thank you. The proposal is to enter the fortified wine market. It's the only type of wine in which unit sales are increasing. We'll make the wines cheaply and package them in pint bottles with screw-on caps. Our chief competitors are Canandaigua with Richard's Wild Irish Rose, Gallo with Thunderbird and Night Train Express, and Mogen David with MD 20/20. We'll market the wine with little or no media advertising by strategically sampling the product to targeted consumers. That's it in a nutshell.

Oliver, Sr.: Any questions before we vote?

Menendez: Who'll buy this wine?

Calvin: From what I know about the consumers of your competitors, it appears to me that it's bought by homeless winos.

Stabler: Not entirely. For example, pensioners on a fixed income would find the price of the wine appealing. Thunderbird has been recently introduced into England and has become very popular with the yuppie crowd.

Calvin: Then why put it in pint bottles?

Stabler: For the convenience of consumers.

Menendez: Why would pensioners want a small bottle?

Calvin: Homeless people want it in pints so they can fit it in their hip pockets. They obviously don't have a wine cellar to lay away their favorite bottles of Mad Dog.

Stabler: The pint size also keeps the price as low as possible.

Calvin: Translation: the homeless don't have to panhandle as long before they can make a purchase. Also, why would you increase the alcoholic content to 18 percent and make it so sweet if it weren't for the wino market?

Stabler: Many people like sweet dessert wines and 18 percent is not that much more than other types of wines that have 12 percent alcohol.

Menendez: Is it legal?

Lane: Sure. We sell to the retailers. It may be against the law to sell to intoxicated persons, but that's the retailers' business. We cannot control what they do.

Calvin: Isn't this product intended for a perpetually intoxicated audience that many people consider to be ill? Wouldn't we be taking advantage of their illness by selling highly sugared alcohol that suppresses their appetite? I've spoken to drinkers who claim to live on a gallon of this type of product a day.

Oliver, Jr.: What will this do to our image? We're still trying to get our premium wines accepted.

Stabler: Of course we won't use the Oliver name on these wines. We will use another name.

Menendez: Is it okay to do that?

Stabler: Why not? Canandaigua, Gallo, and Mogen David all do the same thing. None of them put their corporate name on this low-end product.

Abbott: We're getting away from the crux of the matter. Profit margins would be at least 10 percent higher on this line than our others. Moreover, unit sales might increase over time. Our other lines are stagnant or decreasing. The public shareholders are grousing.

Dale: Not to mention that our stock options have become almost worthless. I'm only a few years from retirement. We need to increase the profitability of the company.

Ray: Operationally this proposal is a great fit. We can use the grapes we reject from the premium line. It will also insulate us from bad grape years since any grape will do for this wine. We can fill a lot of our unused capacity

Constable: And hire back some of the workers who were laid off!

Stabler: It's a marketing dream. Just give out some samples to "bell cows."

Menendez: What are bell cows?

Stabler: Opinion leaders who will induce other consumers to switch to our brand.

Calvin: You mean wino gurus?

Oliver, Sr.: Look, if we don't do it, others will. In fact, they already have.

Abbott: And they'll get richer and we'll get poorer.

Lane: Gallo pulled out of several of these skid row markets as did Canandaigua. Little good it did. The alcoholics just switched to malt liquor, vodka, or anything they could get their hands on.

Dale: I think our concern is misplaced. These people are the dregs of society. They contribute nothing.

Calvin: They're human beings who need help. We're profiting off their misfortune and misery.

Oliver, Sr.: We can take that up when we decide on what charities to support. Anyone opposed to the proposal?

Calvin: Is this a done deal? I believe we should contribute half of our profits from this product to support homeless shelters and other programs that benefit indigent and homeless people. If not, I must resign from this board.

Sources

Alix M. Freedman "Winos and Thunderbird Are a Subject Gallo Doesn't Like to Discuss," *The Wall Street Journal,* February 25, 1988, p.1.

Carrie Dolan "Gallo Conducts Test to Placate Critics of Its Cheap Wine," *The Wall Street Journal,* June 16, 1989, p. B3.

Frank J. Prial "Experiments by a Wine Maker Fails to Thwart Street Drunks," *New York Times,* February 11, 1990, p. A29.

JLM, Inc.

BACKGROUND

Sitting in her office, Ellen Fulbright, director of Human Resources for JLM, Inc., thought over the decisions confronting her. To help her decide, she mentally reviewed how they had arisen.

After receiving her MBA and JD degrees from a highly regarded university, she joined a prestigious New York law firm where she specialized in employment law. After seven years at the law firm, she was hired by one of the firm's clients as general counsel. When that company was acquired by JLM, she joined its legal staff and within a few years had been promoted to her current position.

Fulbright's rapid advancement resulted from her having made a positive impression on Rasheed Raven, JLM's CEO. Raven is a hard-driving, bottom-line–oriented pragmatist in his early forties. Raven, a graduate of Howard University, had begun his business career on Wall Street, which he astounded by his aggressive but successful takeover strategies. After acquiring fifteen unrelated manufacturing companies, he decided to try his hand at the turn-around business. He organized JLM as an umbrella for his acquired companies. Soon he earned the reputation as the best in the business by transforming JLM into the leader in the industry.

JLM is a highly successful turn-around company. Typically, JLM purchases companies that are in serious financial trouble and manages them until they become successful companies. At that time, JLM either retains them in its own portfolio of companies or sells them off to other enterprises.

REFERENCE LETTER POLICY

About a year after Fulbright had become director of human resources (HR), Raven called her into his office and showed her a newspaper article. It reported, in somewhat sensational fashion, that several defamation suits had resulted in multimillion dollar judgments against companies that had written negative letters of references about former employees. Raven told her that he was concerned about this and that he wanted her to develop an HR policy covering letters of reference.

In researching the issue, she discovered several articles in which the authors decried the recent spate of companies that had decided to stop writing letters of reference. According to their data, they believed that these companies had over-reacted to the actual risk posed by defamation suits. Based on these articles and her own inclination toward full disclosure, she proposed that the company continue to permit letters of reference but that all letters with negative comments must be reviewed by her.

Raven did not receive her proposal favorably and sought a second opinion from her old law firm. His analysis of the firm's advice was: "We get nothing but brownie points for writing reference letters, but we face the possibility of incurring the cost of a legal defense or, worse yet, a court judgment. This is a 'no-brainer.' We have no upside and all downside." Raven ordered that henceforth company employees would no longer write letters of reference but would simply verify dates of employment.

Although Fulbright was personally and professionally miffed by his decision, she drew up the policy statement as directed. Fulbright believed that since JLM frequently took over companies that needed immediate downsizing, this policy would be unfair and extremely detrimental to long-time employees of newly purchased companies.

TAKEOVER OF DIVERSIFIED MANUFACTURING, INC.

After a number of years of steady growth, Diversified Manufacturing began experiencing huge financial losses and its immediate survival was in serious doubt. After careful consideration, Raven decided that Diversified was an ideal takeover target in that its core businesses were extremely strong and presented great long-term economic viability.

Upon acquiring Diversified, JLM quickly decided that it had to rid Diversified of some of its poorly performing companies and that it had to reduce the size of Diversified's home office staff by 25 percent. Raven relentlessly orchestrated the reduction in force, but at Fulbright's urging he provided the discharged executives with above average severance packages, including excellent outplacement services.

THE PROBLEM

The reduction in force was disruptive and demoralizing in all the usual ways. But for Fulbright there was a further complication: the no reference letter policy. She was extremely troubled by its application to three discharged Diversified employees and to one discharged JLM employee.

The Salacious Sales Manager

Soon after taking over Diversified, Fulbright became all too aware of the story of Ken Byrd, Diversified's then national sales manager. Ken is an affable man of fifty who had been an unusually effective sales manager. Throughout his career, his sales figures had always doubled that of his peers. He achieved rapid advancement despite a fatal flaw: he is an inveterate and indiscreet womanizer. He could not control his hands, which slapped backs so well, nor his tongue, which persuaded so eloquently. He had two approaches to women. With a woman of equal or superior rank in the company, he would politely, but inexorably, attempt to sweep her off her feet. With these women, he would be extremely charming and attentive, taking great care to avoid being offensive or harassing. In contrast, with a woman of subordinate rank, he would physically harass her. Less openly, but much too often, he would come up behind a woman, reach around her, and grab her. He invariably found this amusing—his victims, however, did not.

Fulbright could not believe that such a manager had stayed employed at Diversified so long, let alone been continually promoted to positions of greater responsibility and power. As Fulbright investigated the situation, she discovered that numerous sexual harassment complaints had been filed with Diversified concerning Byrd's behavior. In order to protect Byrd, Diversified dealt with these complaints by providing money and undeserved promotions to the complainants to smooth over their anger. Thus, Diversified successfully kept the complaints in house and away from the courts and the Equal Employment Opportunity Commission.

After JLM's takeover of Diversified, Fulbright quickly discharged Byrd. Her satisfaction in getting rid of him was short-lived, however. His golden tongue and stellar sales record had landed him several job offers. Her dilemma was that she was uncomfortable about loosing this deviant on an unsuspecting new employer. But JLM's policy forbade her from writing any letters or answering questions from prospective employers.

The Fruitless Juice

Melissa Cuthbertson had been a vice president in procurement for Diversified's Birch-Wood division with direct responsibility over the ordering of supplies and raw materials. Birch-Wood manufactured a full line of baby food products, including fruit juices that were labeled "100% fruit juice." To cut costs, Stanley Aker, the division's president, had arranged for an unscrupulous supplier to provide high-fructose corn syrup labeled as juice concentrate. Because standard testing in the industry was unable to detect the substitution, the company did not get caught. Emboldened, Aker gradually increased the proportion of corn syrup until there were only trace amounts of fruit juice left in the "juice." A company employee discovered the practice and after the takeover brought the matter to Fulbright's attention through JLM's internal whistle-blowing channel, which Fulbright had established. She referred the matter to Raven, who called Aker and Cuthbertson in and confronted them with the accusation. They admitted it all, explaining that nutritionally the corn syrup was equivalent to the fruit juice. But at 60 percent of the cost of fruit juice, the corn syrup made a big difference to the bottom line. Raven told them that such conduct was not permitted and that they must properly dispose of the adulterated juice.

That night Aker and Cuthbertson had the juice moved from Birch-Wood's New York warehouse and shipped to its Puerto Rico warehouse. Over the course of the next few days, the "juice" was sold in Latin America as "apple juice." Aker reported to Raven that the juice had been properly disposed of and that Birch-Wood had sustained only a small loss during that quarter. When Raven discovered the truth, he immediately discharged Aker and Cuthbertson, telling them "that if he had anything to do with it, neither of them would ever work again." Fulbright was to meet soon with Raven to discuss what should be done about Aker and Cuthbertson.

The Compassionate CFO

Jackson Cobb, JLM's former chief financial officer, is a brilliant analyst. Through hard work he had earned an excellent education that honed his innate mathematical gifts. His natural curiosity led him to read widely and this enabled him to bring disparate facts and concepts to bear on his often novel analyses of financial matters. But he had no interest in implementing his insights, for his only enjoyment was the process of discovering connections. Fortune—or fate—had brought him together with Raven, who is twenty years younger than Cobb. Theirs was definitely a case of opposites attracting. Raven cared little about ideas; he cared primarily about money. Cobb cared little about money; he cared primarily about ideas. Raven took Cobb's insights and translated them into action with spectacular success. Their relationship brought new meaning to the concept of synergy. When Raven formed JLM, he brought Cobb on as chief financial officer and installed him in an adjoining office.

Their relationship continued to flourish, as did JLM's bottom line, until Cobb's wife became terminally ill. During the eighteen months she languished, Cobb spent as much time as he could taking care of her. After forty years of marriage, he was unwilling to leave her welfare to the "kindness of strangers." At his own expense, he installed a state-of-the-art communication center in his home. By virtue of computers, modems, video cameras, faxes, copiers, mobile telephones, and the like, he had available to him the same data and information as he had at his office. He could be reached by telephone at all times. But he was not in the office next to Raven; he was not present at Raven's daily breakfast meetings; he was not on the corporate jet en route to business meetings. After their many years of working together, Raven was enraged at the loss of immediate access to Cobb. He felt that Cobb had betrayed him and demanded that Cobb resume his old working hours. Cobb refused and Raven fired him. Because of his age, Cobb was experiencing difficulty in finding new employment, and Fulbright wanted to write a letter on his behalf.

Sword Technology, Inc.

BACKGROUND

Sitting in his office, Stephen Hag, CEO of Sword Technology, Inc., contemplated the problems that had been perplexing him for some time now. They began when he took his company international, and they kept coming. But today he was no more successful in devising a solution than he had been previously. Slowly, his thoughts drifted to those early days years ago when he and his sister Marian started the company.

The company's first product was an investment newsletter stressing technical analysis in securities investing. A few years later, he developed what became a "killer app": a computer program that defines an entirely new market and through customer loyalty substantially dominates that market. His software program enabled investors to track their investments in stocks, bonds, and futures. By combining powerful analytical tools with an accessible, graphical interface, it appealed to both professional and amateur investors. Moreover, it required users to download information from the company's database. With one of the most extensive databases and the cheapest downloading rates in the industry, the company soon controlled the U.S. market. Sword then went public through a highly successful IPO (an initial public offering of the company's common stock), and its stock is traded on the over-the-counter market. The company is required to file periodic reports with the Securities and Exchange Commission.

The company used cash from sales of software, on-line charges, and the IPO to try to enter the hardware side of the computer industry. It began manufacturing modems and other computer peripherals. A nagging problem, however, plagued the company's manufacturing efforts. Although Sword's modem could convert data more quickly and efficiently than most of its competitors, because of high labor costs it was unable to market its modem successfully. To reduce manufacturing costs, especially labor costs, the company decided to move its manufacturing facilities overseas. And that's when the trouble began.

Stephen's thoughts returned to the present. He reopened the folder labeled "Confidential: International Issues" and began perusing its contents.

TRANSFER PRICING

The first item he saw was an opinion letter from the company's tax attorney. It dealt with Excalibur Technology, the first overseas company Sword established. Excalibur, a wholly owned subsidiary of Sword, is incorporated in Tolemac, an emerging country with a rapidly growing economy. To encourage foreign investment, Tolemac taxes corporate profits at a significantly lower rate than the United States and other industrialized nations. Excalibur manufactures modems for Sword pursuant to a licensing agreement under which Excalibur pays Sword a royalty equal to a specified percentage of the modems' gross

CHAPTER 2 Business Ethics

sales. Excalibur sells all of its output at a fair market price to Sword, which then markets the modems in the United States. Stephen had been closely involved in structuring this arrangement and had insisted on keeping the royalty rate low in order to minimize taxable income for Sword. Stephen reread the opinion letter:

> Section 482 of the Internal Revenue Code authorizes the Internal Revenue Service to allocate gross income, deductions, credits, and other common allowances among two or more organizations, trades, or businesses under common ownership or control whenever it determines that this action is necessary "in order to prevent evasion of taxes or clearly to reflect the income of any such organizations, trades, or businesses." IRS Regulation 1.482-2(e) governing the sale or trade of intangibles between related persons mandates an appropriate allocation to reflect the price that an unrelated party under the same circumstances would have paid, which normally includes profit to the seller. The Regulations provide four methods for determining an arm's length price. In our opinion, under the only method applicable to the circumstances of Sword Technology, Inc., and Excalibur Technology, the royalty rate should be at least three times the current one. If the IRS were to reach the same conclusion, then the company would be liable for the taxes it underpaid because of the understatement of income. Moreover, the company would be liable for a penalty of either 20 percent or 40 percent of the tax deficiency, unless the company can show that it had reasonable cause and acted in good faith.

Stephen had spoken to the tax attorney at length and learned that the probability of an audit was about 10 percent and that many multinational companies play similar "games" with their transfer pricing. The attorney also told him that he believed that if the company were audited, there was at least a 90 percent probability that the IRS would agree with his conclusion and at least a 70 percent probability that it would impose a penalty. Because the dollar amount of the contingent tax liability was not an insignificant amount, Stephen had been concerned about it for the six weeks since he had received the letter.

CUSTOMS AND CUSTOMS

Soon after Excalibur had manufactured the first shipment of modems, a new problem arose: getting them out of Tolemac. It took far too long to clear customs, thus undermining their carefully planned just-in-time manufacturing schedules. Stephen hired a local export broker who distributed cash gifts to custom officials. Miraculously, the clearance time shortened and manufacturing schedules were maintained. The export broker billed the company for his services and the amount of the cash gifts. Although the broker assured Stephen that such gifts were entirely customary, Stephen was not entirely comfortable with the practice.

THE THORN IN HIS SIDE

Tolemac was not his only problem. Six months after commencing operations in Tolemac, Sword began serious negotiations to enter the Liarg market. Liarg is an undeveloped country with a large population and a larger national debt. Previously, Sword had encountered great difficulties in exporting products to Liarg. Stephen's sister, Marian, COO of Sword, took on the challenge of establishing a Liarg presence.

They decided that setting up a manufacturing facility in Liarg would achieve two objectives: greater access to the Liarg marketplace and lower-cost modems.

At first, the Liarg government insisted that Sword enter into a joint venture, with the government having a 51 percent interest. Sword was unwilling to invest in such an arrangement, countering with a proposal for a wholly owned subsidiary. Marian conducted extensive negotiations with the government, assisted by a Liarg consulting firm that specialized in lobbying governmental officials. As part of these negotiations, Sword made contributions to the reelection campaigns of key Liarg legislators who were opposed to wholly owned subsidiaries of foreign corporations. After the legislators' reelection, the negotiations quickly reached a successful conclusion. On closing the contract, Sword flew several Liarg officials and their wives to Lake Tahoe for a lavish, three-day celebration. All of these expenses were reported in the company's financial statements as payments for legal and consulting fees.

Marian then hired an international engineering firm to help design the manufacturing plant. Two weeks later, they submitted plans for the plant and its operations that fully complied with Liarg regulations regarding worker health and safety as well as environmental protection. But, as Marian had explained to Stephen, the plant's design fell far short of complying with U.S. requirements. Marian noted that under the proposed design the workers would face exposure to moderately high levels of toxic chemicals and hazardous materials. The design also would degrade the water supply of nearby towns. However, the design would generate very significant savings in capital and operational cost as compared to the design used in their U.S. facility. Marian assured Stephen that all quality control systems were in place so the modems produced in this plant would be indistinguishable from their U.S. counterparts. Stephen and Marian have had long discussions about what to do about the plant.

Stephen then took from the folder an article that had appeared in a number of U.S. newspapers.

Children and Chips

A twelve-year-old Liarg child recently spoke at an international conference in New York denouncing the exploitation of children in the Liarg computer chip industry. The child informed the outraged audience that he had worked in such a plant from age four to age ten. He asserted that he was just one of many children who were so employed. He described the deplorable working conditions: poor ventilation, long hours, inadequate food, and substandard housing. The pay was low. But, because their families could not afford to keep them at home, the children were hired out to the factory owners, who especially wanted young children because their small fingers made them adept at many assembly processes.

Stephen had read the article countless times, thinking about his own children. He knew that if they set up a plant in Liarg, they would have to buy chip components from Liarg suppliers. He also knew that there would be no way for Sword to insure that the chips had not been made with child labor.

He was also troubled by another labor issue. Marian told him that she had met considerable resistance from the Liarg executives they had hired when she suggested that women should be hired at the supervisory level. They maintained that it was not done and would make it impossible to hire and control a satisfactory workforce at the plant. Moreover, they insisted on hiring their relatives as supervisors. When Marian protested this nepotism, they assured her that it was customary and asserted that they could not trust anyone not related to them.

On top of all these concerns had come a letter from the company's outside legal counsel regarding payments made to foreign officials.

Memorandum of Law

The Foreign Corrupt Practices Act makes it unlawful for any domestic company or any of its officers, directors, employees, or agents or its stockholders acting on its behalf to offer or give anything of value directly or indirectly to any foreign official, political party, or political official for the purpose of

1. influencing any act or decision of that person or party in his or its official capacity,
2. inducing an act or omission in violation of his or its lawful duty, or
3. inducing such person or party to use its influence to affect a decision of a foreign government in order to assist the domestic concern in obtaining or retaining business.

An offer or promise to make a prohibited payment is a violation even if the offer is not accepted or the promise is not performed. The 1988 amendments explicitly excluded facilitating or expediting payments made to expedite or secure the performance of routine governmental actions by a foreign official, political party, or party official. Routine governmental action does not include any decision by a foreign official regarding the award of new business or the continuation of old business. The amendments also added an affirmative defense for payments that are lawful under the written laws or regulations of the foreign officials country. Violations are punishable by fines of up to $2 million for companies; individuals may be fined a maximum of $100,000 or imprisoned up to five years, or both. Fines imposed upon individuals may not be paid directly or indirectly by the domestic company on whose behalf they acted. In addition, the courts may impose civil penalties of up to $10,000.

The statute also imposes internal control requirements on all reporting companies. Such companies must

1. make and keep books, records, and accounts, which in reasonable detail, accurately and fairly reflect the transactions and dispositions of the assets of the company; and
2. devise and maintain a system of internal controls that assure that transactions are executed as authorized and recorded in conformity with generally accepted accounting principles, thereby establishing accountability with regard to assets and assuring that access to those assets is permitted only with management's authorization.

Any person who knowingly circumvents or knowingly fails to implement a system of internal accounting controls or knowingly falsifies any book, record, or account is subject to criminal liability.

The plant! Stephen wondered whether there ought to be a plant at all.

PART II

The Legal Environment of Business

CHAPTER 3

The Judicial System

As we discussed in Chapter 1, substantive law sets forth the rights and duties of individuals and other legal entities, whereas procedural law determines how these rights are asserted. Procedural law attempts to accomplish two competing objectives: (1) to be fair and impartial and (2) to operate efficiently. The judicial process in the United States represents a balance between these two objectives as well as a commitment to the adversary system.

In the first part of this chapter, we will describe the structure and function of the federal and state court systems. The second part deals with jurisdiction; the third part discusses civil dispute resolution, including the procedure in civil lawsuits.

THE COURT SYSTEM

Courts are impartial tribunals (seats of judgment) established by governmental bodies to settle disputes. A court may render a binding decision only when it has jurisdiction over the dispute and the parties to that dispute; that is, when it has a right to hear and make a judgment in a case. The United States has a dual court system: the federal government has its own independent system, as does each of the fifty states and the District of Columbia.

THE FEDERAL COURTS

Article III of the United States Constitution states that the judicial power of the United States shall be vested in one Supreme Court and such lower courts as Congress may establish. Congress has established a lower federal court system consisting of a number of special courts, district courts, and courts of appeals. Judges in the federal court system are appointed for life by the president, subject to confirmation by the Senate. The structure of the federal court system is illustrated in Figure 3–1.

District Courts

District courts trial courts of general jurisdiction that can hear and decide most legal controversies in the federal system

The **district courts** are general trial courts in the federal system. Most federal cases begin in the district court, and it is here that issues of fact are decided. The district court is generally presided over by *one* judge, although in certain cases three judges preside. In a few cases, an appeal from a judgment or decree of a district court is taken directly to the Supreme Court. In most cases, however, appeals go to the Circuit Court of Appeals of the appropriate circuit, the decision of which is final in most cases.

FIGURE 3–1 Federal Judicial System

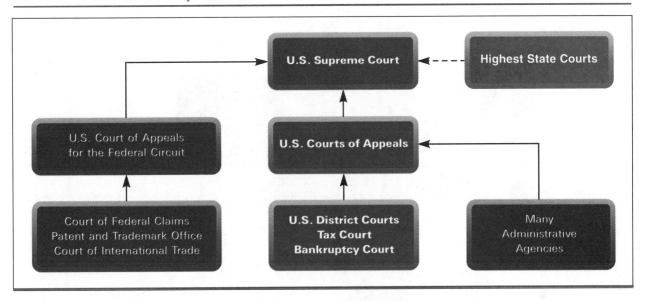

Congress has established judicial districts, each of which is located entirely in a particular state. All states have at least one district, while certain states contain more than one district. For instance, New York has four districts, Illinois has three, and Wisconsin has two, while a number of less populated states each make up a single district.

Courts of Appeals

Congress has established twelve judicial circuits (eleven numbered circuits plus the D.C. circuit), each having a court known as the Court of Appeals, which primarily hears appeals from the district courts located within its circuit (see Figure 3–2). In addition, these courts review decisions of many administrative agencies, the Tax Court, and the Bankruptcy Courts. Congress has also established the U.S. Court of Appeals for the Federal Circuit, which is discussed below in the section on "Special Courts." The United States Courts of Appeals generally hear cases in panels of *three* judges, although in some instances all judges of the circuit will sit *en banc* to decide a case.

The function of appellate courts is to examine the record of a case on appeal and to determine whether the trial court committed prejudicial error (error substantially affecting the appellant's rights and duties). If so, the appellate court will **reverse** or **modify** the judgment of the lower court and, if necessary, **remand** or send it back to the lower court for further proceeding. If there is no prejudicial error, the appellate court will **affirm** the decision of the lower court.

The Supreme Court

The nation's highest tribunal is the United States Supreme Court, which consists of nine justices (a Chief Justice and eight Associate Justices) who sit as a group in Washington, D.C. A quorum consists of any six justices. In certain types of cases, the United States Supreme Court has original jurisdiction (the right to hear a case first). The Court's principal function, nonetheless, is to review decisions of the Federal Courts of Appeals and, in some instances, those of the highest state

Courts of Appeals hear appeals from the district courts and review orders of certain administrative agencies

Reverse set aside the lower court's judgment

Modify change the lower court's judgment

Remand send the case back to the lower court

Affirm uphold the lower court's judgment

The Supreme Court nation's highest court whose principal function is to review decisions of the Federal Courts of Appeals and the highest state courts

FIGURE 3–2 Circuit Courts of the United States

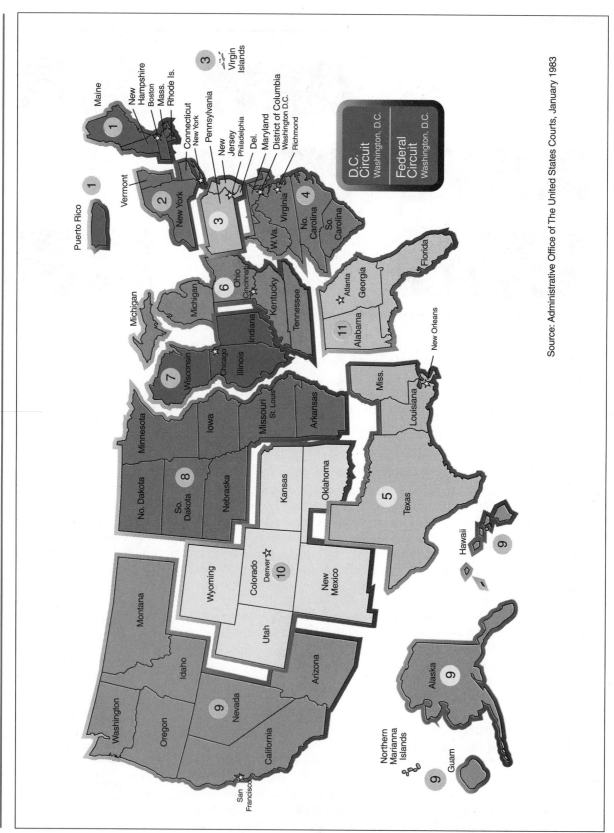

Source: Administrative Office of The United States Courts, January 1983

courts or other tribunals. Cases reach the Supreme Court under its appellate jurisdiction by one of two routes. Very few come by way of **appeal by right**. The Court must hear these cases if one of the parties requests the review. In 1988 Congress enacted legislation that almost completely eliminated the right to appeal to the U.S. Supreme Court.

The second way in which the Supreme Court may review a decision of a lower court is by the discretionary **writ of *certiorari***, which requires a lower court to produce the records of a case it has tried. Now almost all cases reaching the Supreme Court come to it by means of writs of *certiorari*. If four Justices vote to hear the case, the Court grants writs when there is a federal question of substantial importance or a conflict in the decisions of the U.S. Circuit Courts of Appeals. Only a small percentage of the petitions to the Supreme Court for review by *certiorari* are granted, however, as the Court uses the writ as a device to choose which cases it wishes to hear.

Special Courts

The **special courts** in the federal judicial system include the U.S. Court of Federal Claims, the U.S. Bankruptcy Courts, the U.S. Tax Court, and the U.S. Court of Appeals for the Federal Circuit. These courts have jurisdiction over particular areas. The U.S. Court of Federal Claims hears claims against the United States. The U.S. Bankruptcy Courts hear and decide certain matters under the Federal Bankruptcy Code, subject to review by the U.S. District Court. The U.S. Tax Court has jurisdiction over certain cases involving federal taxes. The U.S. Court of Appeals for the Federal Circuit reviews decisions of the Court of Federal Claims, the Patent and Trademark Office, patent cases decided by U.S. District Courts, the United States Court of International Trade, the Merit Systems Protection Board, and the U.S. Court of Veterans Appeals.

STATE COURTS

Each of the fifty states and the District of Columbia has its own independent court system. In most states, the voters elect judges for a stated term. The structure of state court systems varies from state to state. Figure 3–3 shows a typical system.

Inferior Trial Courts

At the bottom of the state court system are the **inferior trial courts**, which decide the least serious criminal and civil matters. Usually, inferior trial courts do not keep a complete written record of trial proceedings. Minor criminal cases such as traffic offenses are heard in inferior trial courts, which are referred to as municipal courts, justice of the peace courts, or traffic courts. These courts also conduct preliminary hearings in more serious criminal cases.

Small claims courts are inferior trial courts that hear civil cases involving a limited amount of money. Usually there is no jury, the procedure is informal, and neither side employs an attorney. An appeal from a small claims court is taken to the trial court of general jurisdiction, where a new trial (called a trial *de novo*), in which the small claims court's decision is given no weight, is begun.

Trial Courts

Each state has **trial courts** of general jurisdiction, which may be called county, district, superior, circuit, or common pleas courts. (In New York the trial court is

---

Appeal by right mandatory review by a higher court

Writ of certiorari *(sir'·sho·rare'·ee)* discretionary review by a higher court

Special courts have jurisdiction over cases in a particular area of federal law and include the U.S. Court of Federal Claims, the Tax Court, the U.S. Bankruptcy Courts, and the Court of Appeals for the Federal Circuit

Inferior trial courts hear minor cases such as traffic offenses and civil cases involving small amounts of money and conduct preliminary hearings in more serious criminal cases

Small claims courts inferior trial courts with jurisdiction over civil cases involving a limited dollar amount

Trial courts have general jurisdiction over civil and criminal cases

FIGURE 3–3 State Court System

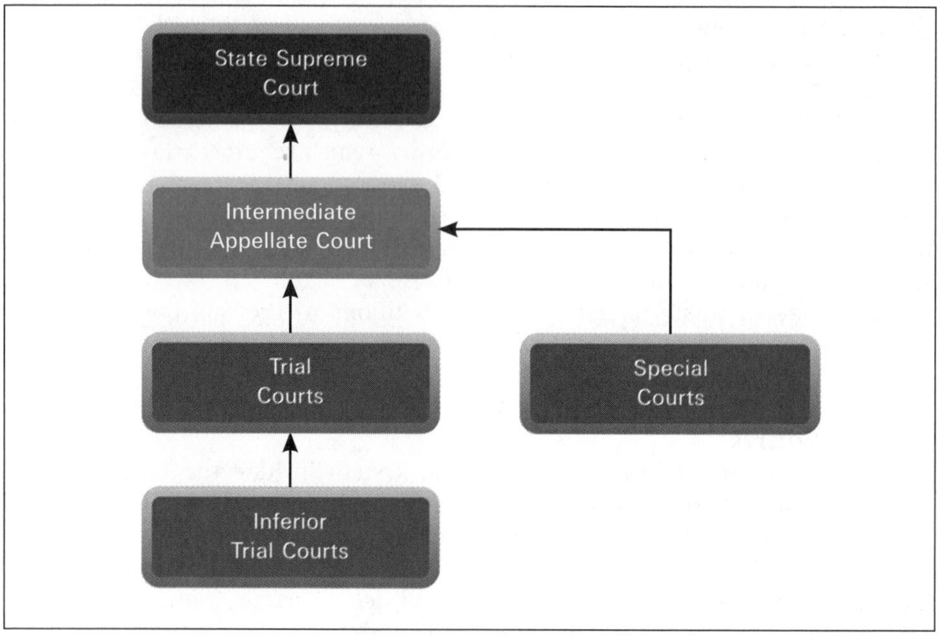

called the Supreme Court.) These courts do not have a dollar limitation on their jurisdiction in civil cases and hear all criminal cases other than minor offenses. Unlike the inferior trial courts, these trial courts of general jurisdiction maintain formal records of their proceedings as procedural safeguards.

Many states have special trial courts that have jurisdiction over particular areas. For example, many states have probate courts with jurisdiction over the administration of wills and estates and family courts with jurisdiction over divorce and child custody cases.

Special courts trial courts, such as probate courts and family courts, having jurisdiction over a particular area of state law

Appellate Courts

At the summit of the state court system is the state's court of last resort, a reviewing court generally called the supreme court of the state. Except for those cases in which review by the U.S. Supreme Court is available, the decision of the highest state tribunal is final. In addition, most states also have created intermediate **appellate courts** to handle the large volume of cases in which review is sought. Review by such a court is usually by right. Further review is in most cases at the highest court's discretion.

Appellate courts include one or two levels: the highest court's decisions are final except in those cases reviewed by the U.S. Supreme Court

JURISDICTION

Jurisdiction *(ju·ris·dic'·tion)* authority of a court to hear and decide a case

Jurisdiction means the power or authority of a court to hear and decide a given case. To resolve a lawsuit, a court must have two kinds of jurisdiction. The first is jurisdiction over the subject matter of the lawsuit. Where a court lacks jurisdiction over the subject matter of a case, no action it takes in the case will have legal effect.

The second kind of jurisdiction is over the parties to a lawsuit. This jurisdiction is required for the court to render an enforceable judgment that affects the parties' rights and duties. A court usually may obtain jurisdiction over the defendant in a lawsuit if the defendant lives and is present in the court's territory or the transaction giving rise to the case has a substantial connection to the court's territory. The court obtains jurisdiction over the plaintiff when the plaintiff voluntarily submits to the court's power by filing a complaint with the court. See Figure 3–6.

SUBJECT MATTER JURISDICTION

Subject matter jurisdiction refers to the authority of a particular court to judge a controversy of a particular kind. Federal courts have *limited* subject matter jurisdiction. State courts have jurisdiction over *all* matters that the Constitution or Congress neither denies them nor gives exclusively to the federal courts.

> **Subject matter jurisdiction** authority of a court to decide a particular kind of case

Federal Jurisdiction

The federal courts have, to the exclusion of the state courts, subject matter jurisdiction over some areas. Such jurisdiction is called **exclusive federal jurisdiction**. Federal jurisdiction is exclusive only if Congress so provides, either explicitly or implicitly. If Congress does not so provide and the area is one over which federal courts have subject matter jurisdiction, they share this jurisdiction with the state courts. Such jurisdiction is known as **concurrent federal jurisdiction**.

> **Exclusive federal jurisdiction** jurisdiction that permits only the federal courts to hear a case

> **Concurrent federal jurisdiction** authority of federal or state courts to hear the same case

Exclusive Federal Jurisdiction The federal courts have exclusive jurisdiction over federal criminal prosecutions; admiralty, bankruptcy, antitrust, patent, trademark and copyright cases; suits against the United States; and cases arising under certain federal statutes that expressly provide for exclusive federal jurisdiction.

Concurrent Federal Jurisdiction There are two types of concurrent federal jurisdiction: federal question jurisdiction and diversity jurisdiction. The first arises whenever there is a federal question over which the federal courts do not have exclusive jurisdiction. A **federal question** is any case arising under the Constitution, statutes, or treaties of the United States. There is no minimum dollar requirement in federal question cases.

> **Federal question** any case arising under the Constitution, statutes, or treaties of the United States

The second type of concurrent federal jurisdiction occurs in a civil suit where there is diversity of citizenship and the amount in controversy exceeds $75,000. As the following case explains, the jurisdictional requirement is satisfied if the claim for the amount is made in good faith, unless it is clear to a legal certainty that the claim does not meet or exceed the required amount. *Diversity of citizenship exists (1) when the plaintiffs are citizens of a state or states different from the state or states of which the defendants are citizens;* (2) when a foreign country brings an action against citizens of the United States; *or* (3) when the controversy is between citizens of the United States and citizens of a foreign country. The citizenship of an individual litigant (party in a lawsuit) is the state in which the individual resides or is domiciled, whereas that of a corporate litigant is both the state of incorporation and the state in which its principal place of business is located. For example, if the amount in controversy exceeds $75,000, then diversity of citizenship jurisdiction would be satisfied if Ada, a citizen of California, sues Bob, a citizen of Idaho. If, however, Carol, a citizen of Virginia, and Dianne, a citizen of North Carolina, sue Evan, a citizen of Georgia, and Farley, a citizen of North Carolina, there is *not* diversity of citizenship, because both Dianne, a plaintiff, and Farley, a defendant, are citizens of North Carolina.

When a federal district court hears a case solely under diversity of citizenship jurisdiction, no federal question is involved; and, accordingly, the federal courts must apply substantive state law. The conflict of law rules of the state in which the district court is located determine which state's substantive law is to be used in the case. (Conflict of laws is discussed later.) Federal courts apply federal procedural rules in diversity cases.

In any case involving concurrent jurisdiction, the plaintiff has the choice of bringing the action in either an appropriate federal court or state court. If the plaintiff brings the case in a state court, however, the defendant usually may have it removed (shifted) to a federal court for the district in which the state court is located.

DEUTSCH v. HEWES STREET REALTY CORP. U.S. Court of Appeals, Second Circuit, 1966, 359 F.2d 96

FACTS Mariana Deutsch worked as a knitwear mender and attended a school for beauticians. The sink in her apartment collapsed on her foot, fracturing her big toe and making it painful for her to stand. She claims that as a consequence of the injury she was compelled to abandon her plans to become a beautician because that job requires long periods of standing. She also asserts that she was unable to work at her current job for a month. She filed a tort claim against Hewes Street Realty for negligence in failing to maintain the sink properly. She brought the suit in federal district court, claiming damages of $25,000. Her medical expenses and actual loss of salary were less than $1,500; the rest of her alleged damages were for loss of future earnings as a beautician. Hewes Street moved to dismiss the suit on the basis that Deutsch's claim fell short of the jurisdictional requirement, which was then $10,000, and therefore the federal court lacked subject matter jurisdiction over her claim. The district court dismissed the suit, and Deutsch appealed.

DECISION District court's dismissal reversed.

OPINION The general rule for determining the $10,000 jurisdictional amount in controversy requirement is

that an amount alleged in good faith to exceed $10,000 will satisfy the requirement, unless it appears to a legal certainty that the claim is really for less than $10,000. The court may look beyond the face of the complaint, however, to determine the validity of the alleged amount. For example, the court may dismiss a suit for lack of jurisdiction: (1) if the damages claimed are not recoverable at all under applicable law, or (2) if the damages that are recoverable cannot as a matter of law exceed $10,000, or (3) if the amount of damages was inflated solely to gain access to the federal courts.

In this case, Deutsch's claim for unliquidated damages of $25,000 for her loss of future earnings as a beautician satisfies the jurisdictional requirement. Although it may seem unlikely that she could actually prove $25,000 in damages, it cannot be said with legal certainty that the damages do not exceed $10,000. Therefore, she should have an opportunity to have her claim decided on its merits in a federal court.

INTERPRETATION If it is not clear to a legal certainty that the damages claimed would not satisfy the jurisdictional amount requirement, the plaintiff is entitled to have her claim heard in a federal court.

Exclusive State Jurisdiction

The state courts have exclusive jurisdiction over all other matters. All matters not granted to the federal courts in the Constitution or by Congress are solely within the jurisdiction of the states. Accordingly, exclusive state jurisdiction would include cases involving diversity of citizenship where the amount in controversy is $75,000 or less. In addition, the state courts have exclusive jurisdiction over all cases to which the federal judicial power does not reach, including, but by no means limited to, property, torts, contract, agency, commercial transactions, and most crimes.

FIGURE 3–4 Federal and State Jurisdiction

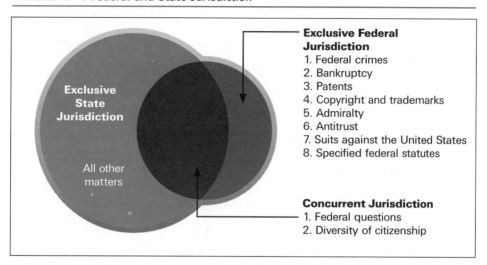

A court in one state may be a proper forum for a case even though some or all of the relevant events occurred in another state. For example, a California plaintiff may sue a Washington defendant in Washington over a car accident that occurred in Oregon. Because of Oregon's connections to the accident, Washington may choose, under its **conflict of laws** rules, to apply the substantive law of Oregon. Conflict of laws rules vary from state to state.

The jurisdiction of the federal and state courts is illustrated in Figure 3–4.

Stare Decisis in the Dual Court System

The doctrine of *stare decisis* presents certain problems when there are two parallel court systems. As a consequence, in the United States, *stare decisis* works approximately as follows (also illustrated in Figure 3–5):

FIGURE 3–5 *Stare Decisis* in the Dual Court System

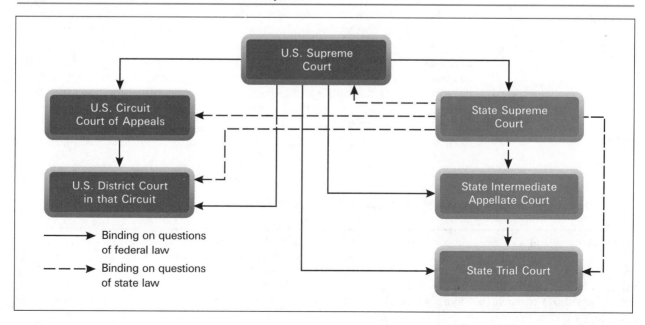

1. The United States Supreme Court has never held itself to be bound rigidly by its own decisions, and lower federal courts and state courts have followed that course with respect to their own decisions.
2. A decision of the U.S. Supreme Court on a federal question is binding on all other courts, federal or state.
3. On a federal question, although a decision of a federal court other than the Supreme Court may be persuasive in a state court, it is not binding.
4. A decision of a state court may be persuasive in the federal courts, but it is not binding except where federal jurisdiction is based on diversity of citizenship. In such a case, the federal courts must apply state law as determined by the highest state tribunal.
5. Decisions of the federal courts (other than the U.S. Supreme Court) are not binding on other federal courts of equal or inferior rank unless the latter owe obedience to the deciding court. For example, a decision of the Fifth Circuit Court of Appeals binds district courts in the fifth circuit but binds no other federal court.
6. A decision of a state court is binding on all courts inferior to it in its jurisdiction. Thus, the decision of the supreme court in a state binds all other courts in that state.
7. A decision of a state court is not binding on courts in another state except where the latter courts are required, under their conflict of laws rules, to apply the law of the first state as determined by the highest court in that state. For example, if a North Carolina court is required to apply Virginia law, it must follow decisions of the Virginia Supreme Court.

JURISDICTION OVER THE PARTIES

Jurisdiction over the parties power of a court to bind the parties to a suit

The second essential type of jurisdiction a court must have is the power to bind the parties involved in the dispute. This type of jurisdiction is called **jurisdiction over the parties**, and its requirements may be met in any of three ways: (1) *in personam* jurisdiction, (2) *in rem* jurisdiction, or (3) attachment jurisdiction. In addition, the exercise of jurisdiction must satisfy the constitutionally imposed requirements of reasonable notification and a reasonable opportunity to be heard. Moreover, the court's exercise of jurisdiction is valid under the due process clause of the U.S. Constitution only if the defendant has minimum contacts with the state sufficient to prevent the court's assertion of jurisdiction from offending "traditional notions of fair play and substantial justice." In order for a court constitutionally to assert jurisdiction over a defendant, the defendant must have engaged in either purposeful acts in the state or acts outside the state that are of such a nature that the defendant could reasonably foresee being sued in that state, as discussed in the next case.

WORLD-WIDE VOLKSWAGEN CORP. v. WOODSON Supreme Court of the United States, 1980, 444 U.S. 286, 100 S.Ct. 559, 62 L.Ed.2d 490

FACTS Harry and Kay Robinson purchased a new Audi automobile from Seaway Volkswagen, Inc. (Seaway) in Massena, New York. The Robinsons, who had resided in New York for years, left for a new home in Arizona. As they drove through Oklahoma, another car struck their Audi from behind, causing a fire that severely burned Kay and her two children.

The Robinsons brought a products-liability suit in the District Court in Oklahoma, claiming their injuries resulted from defective design of the Audi gas tank and

continued

fuel system. They joined as defendants the manufacturer (Audi), the regional distributor (World-Wide Volkswagen Corp.), and the retail distributor (Seaway).

World-Wide and Seaway entered special appearances, asserting that Oklahoma's exercise of jurisdiction over them offended limitations on state jurisdiction imposed by the due process clause of the Fourteenth Amendment. The Oklahoma Supreme Court upheld the assertion of state jurisdiction, and World-Wide and Seaway appealed.

DECISION Judgment of Oklahoma Supreme Court reversed.

OPINION The due process clause of the Fourteenth Amendment limits the power of a state court to render a valid personal judgment against a nonresident defendant. A judgment rendered in violation of due process is void in the rendering state and is not entitled to full faith and credit elsewhere. A state court may exercise personal jurisdiction over a nonresident defendant only so long as there exist "minimum contacts" between the defendant and the forum state. The defendant's contacts with the forum state must be such

that maintenance of the suit does not offend traditional notions of fair play and justice.

World-Wide is incorporated and has its place of business in New York. It distributes vehicles, parts, and accessories to retail dealers in New York, New Jersey, and Connecticut. Seaway, one of those retail dealers, is incorporated and has its place of business in New York. There is no evidence that either World-Wide or Seaway does any business in Oklahoma, ships or sells any products to or in that state, has an agent to receive process there, or purchases advertisements in any media calculated to reach Oklahoma. In fact, there is no showing that any automobile sold by World-Wide or Seaway has ever entered Oklahoma with the single exception of the Robinson's Audi. Thus, in this case, there is a total absence of those affiliating circumstances, or minimum contacts, that are a necessary predicate to any exercise of state court jurisdiction.

INTERPRETATION Sufficient minimal contacts between the defendant and the state must exist for a state to exercise jurisdiction.

In Personam Jurisdiction

***In personam* jurisdiction,** or personal jurisdiction, is the jurisdiction of a court over the parties to a lawsuit, in contrast to its jurisdiction over their property. A court obtains *in personam* jurisdiction over a person either (1) by serving process on the party within the state in which the court is located or (2) by reasonable notification to a party outside the state in those instances where a "long-arm statute" applies. To *serve process* means to deliver a summons, which is an order to respond to a complaint lodged against a party. (The terms *summons* and *complaint* are explained more fully later in this chapter.)

Personal jurisdiction may be obtained by personally serving process upon a person within a state if that person is domiciled in that state. The U.S. Supreme Court has held that a state may exercise personal jurisdiction over a nonresident defendant who is temporarily present if the defendant is personally served in that state. Personal jurisdiction may also arise from a party's consent. For example, parties to a contract may agree that any dispute concerning that contract will be subject to the jurisdiction of a specific court.

Most states have adopted ***long-arm statutes*** to expand their jurisdictional reach beyond those persons who may be personally served within the state. These statutes allow courts to obtain jurisdiction over nonresident defendants under the following conditions, as long as the exercise of jurisdiction does not offend traditional notions of fair play and substantial justice: if the defendant (1) has committed a tort (civil wrong) within the state, (2) owns property within the state and if that property is the subject matter of the lawsuit, (3) has entered into a contract within the state, or (4) has transacted business within the state and if that business is the subject matter of the lawsuit.

In personam **jurisdiction** *(per·sew'·num)* jurisdiction based on claims against a person, in contrast to jurisdiction over property

FIGURE 3–6 Jurisdiction

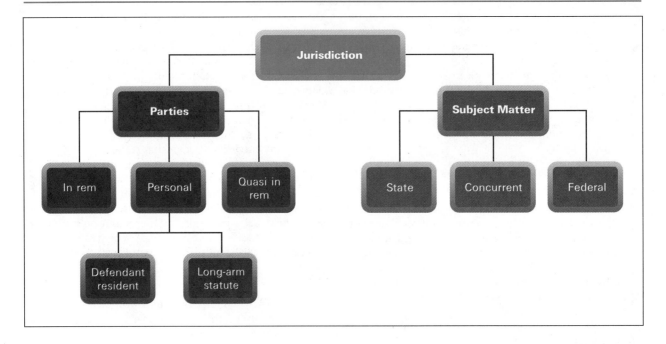

In Rem Jurisdiction

Courts in a state have the jurisdiction to adjudicate claims to property situated within the state if the plaintiff gives those persons who have an interest in the property reasonable notice and an opportunity to be heard. Such jurisdiction over property is called *in rem* **jurisdiction**. For example, if Carpenter and Miller are involved in a lawsuit over property located in Kansas, then an appropriate court in Kansas would have *in rem* jurisdiction to adjudicate claims over this property as long as both parties are given notice of the lawsuit and a reasonable opportunity to contest the claim.

In rem **jurisdiction**
jurisdiction based on claims against property

Attachment Jurisdiction

Attachment jurisdiction, or *quasi in rem* **jurisdiction**, like *in rem* jurisdiction, is jurisdiction over property rather than over a person. But attachment jurisdiction is invoked by seizing the defendant's property located within the state to obtain payment of a claim against the defendant that is *unrelated* to the property seized. For example, Allen, a resident of Ohio, has obtained a valid judgment in the amount of $20,000 against Bradley, a citizen of Kentucky. Allen can attach Bradley's automobile, which is located in Ohio, to satisfy his court judgment against Bradley.

Quasi in rem **jurisdiction**
(kwa´-zee) jurisdiction over property not based on claims against it

Venue

Venue, which often is confused with jurisdiction, concerns the geographical area in which a lawsuit *should* be brought. The purpose of venue is to regulate the distribution of cases within a specific court system and to identify a convenient forum. In the federal court system, venue determines the district or districts in a given state in which suit may be brought. State rules of venue typically require that a suit be initiated in a county where one of the defendants lives. In matters

Venue particular geographical place where a court with jurisdiction may hear a case involving real estate, most venue rules require that a suit be initiated in the county where the property is situated.

CIVIL DISPUTE RESOLUTION

As mentioned in Chapter 1, one of the primary functions of law is to provide for the peaceful resolution of disputes. Accordingly, our legal system has established an elaborate set of governmental mechanisms to settle disputes. The most prominent of these is judicial dispute resolution, called *litigation*. Judicial resolution of civil disputes is governed by the rules of civil procedure, which we will discuss in the first part of this section. Judicial resolution of criminal cases is governed by the rules of criminal procedure, which are covered in Chapter 6. Dispute resolution by administrative agencies, which is also very common, is discussed in Chapter 5.

As an alternative to governmental dispute resolution, several nongovernmental methods of dispute resolution, such as arbitration, have developed. We will discuss these in the second part of this section.

CIVIL PROCEDURE

A civil dispute that enters the judicial system must follow the rules of civil procedure. These rules are designed to resolve the dispute justly, promptly, and inexpensively.

To acquaint you with civil procedure, we will carry a hypothetical action through the trial court to the highest court of review in the state. Although there are technical differences in trial and appellate procedure among the states and the federal courts, the following illustration will give you a general understanding of the trial and appeal of cases. Assume that Pam Pederson, a pedestrian, is struck by an automobile driven by David Dryden while crossing a street in Chicago. Pederson suffers serious personal injuries, incurs heavy medical and hospital expenses, and is unable to work for several months. She desires that Dryden pay her for the loss and damages she sustained. After attempts at settlement fail, Pederson brings an action at law against Dryden. Thus, Pederson is the plaintiff and Dryden the defendant. Each is represented by a lawyer. Let us follow the progress of the case.

The Pleadings

The **pleadings** are a series of responsive, formal, written statements in which each side to a lawsuit states its claims and defenses. The purpose of pleadings is to give notice and to establish the issues of fact and law the parties dispute. An "issue of fact" is a dispute between the parties regarding the events that gave rise to the lawsuit. In contrast, an "issue of law" is a dispute between the parties as to what legal rules apply to these facts. Issues of fact are decided by the jury, or by the judge when there is no jury, whereas issues of law are decided by the judge.

Pleadings series of responsive, formal, written statements by each side to a lawsuit

Complaint and Summons A lawsuit begins when Pederson, the plaintiff, files with the clerk of the trial court a **complaint** against Dryden that contains (1) a statement of the claim and supporting facts showing that she is entitled to relief

Complaint initial pleading by the plaintiff stating his case and (2) a demand for that relief. Pederson's complaint alleges that while exercising due and reasonable care for her own safety, she was struck by Dryden's automobile, which was being driven negligently by Dryden, causing her personal injuries and damages of $50,000, for which Pederson requests judgment.

Once the plaintiff has filed a complaint, the clerk issues a **summons** to be served upon the defendant to notify him that a suit has been brought against him. If the defendant has contacts with the state sufficient to show that the state's assertion of jurisdiction over the defendant is constitutional, proper service of the summons establishes the court's jurisdiction over the person of the defendant. The county sheriff or a deputy sheriff serves a summons and a copy of the complaint on Dryden, the defendant, commanding him to file his appearance and answer with the clerk of the court within a specific time, usually thirty days from the date the summons was served.

Summons notice given to inform a person of a lawsuit against her

Responses to Complaint   At this point, Dryden has several options. If he fails to respond at all, a **default judgment** will be entered against him. He may make *pretrial motions* contesting the court's jurisdiction over him or asserting that the action is barred by the statute of limitations, which requires suits to be brought within a specified time. Dryden also may move, or request, that the complaint be made more definite and certain, or he may instead move that the complaint be dismissed for failure to state a claim on which relief may be granted. Such a motion is sometimes called a **demurrer**; it essentially asserts that even if all of Pederson's allegations were true, she still would not be entitled to the relief she seeks, and that therefore there is no need for a trial of the facts. The court rules on this motion as a matter of law. If it rules in favor of the defendant, the plaintiff may appeal the ruling.

Default judgment judgment against a defendant who fails to respond to a complaint

Demurrer *(de·mur'·rer)* motion to dismiss for failure to state a claim

If he does not make any pretrial motions, or if they are denied, Dryden will respond to the complaint by filing an **answer**, which may contain denials, admissions, affirmative defenses, and counterclaims. Dryden might answer the complaint by denying its allegations of negligence and stating that he was driving his car at a low speed and with reasonable care (a *denial*) when his car struck Pederson (an *admission*), who had dashed across the street in front of his car without looking in any direction to see whether cars or other vehicles were approaching; that, accordingly, Pederson's injuries were caused by her own negligence (an *affirmative defense*); and that, therefore, she should not be permitted to recover any damages. Dryden might further state that Pederson caused damage to his car and request a judgment for $2,000 (a *counterclaim*). These pleadings create an issue of fact regarding whether Dryden or Pederson, or both, failed to exercise due and reasonable care under the circumstances and were thus negligent and liable for their carelessness.

Answer defendant's pleading in response to the plaintiff's complaint

If the defendant counterclaims, the plaintiff must respond through a **reply**, which also may contain admissions, denials, or affirmative defenses.

Reply plaintiff's pleading in response to the defendant's answer

Pretrial Procedure

Judgment on the Pleadings   After the pleadings, either party may move for **judgment on the pleadings**, which requests the judge to rule as a matter of law whether the facts as alleged in the pleadings of the nonmoving party are sufficient to warrant granting the requested relief.

Judgment on the pleadings final binding determination on the merits made by the judge after the pleadings

Discovery In preparation for trial and even before completion of the pleadings stage, each party has the right to obtain relevant evidence, or information that may lead to evidence, from the other party. This procedure, known as **discovery,** includes (1) pretrial *depositions* consisting of sworn testimony, taken out of court, of the opposing party or other witnesses; (2) sworn answers by the opposing party to *written interrogatories,* or questions; (3) *production* of documents and physical objects in the possession of the opposing party; (4) *examination* by a physician of the opposing party, as needed; and (5) admissions of facts set forth in a *request for admissions* submitted to the opposing party. By using discovery properly, each party may become fully informed of relevant evidence and avoid surprise at trial. Another purpose of this procedure is to facilitate settlements by giving both parties as much relevant information as possible.

Discovery pretrial exchange of information between opposing parties to a lawsuit

Pretrial procedure process requiring the parties to disclose what evidence is available to prove the disputed facts; designed to encourage settlement of cases or to make the trial more efficient

Pretrial Conference Also furthering these objectives is the pretrial conference between the judge and the attorneys representing the parties. The basic purposes of the **pretrial conference** are (1) to simplify the issues in dispute by amending the pleadings, admitting or stipulating facts, and limiting the number of expert witnesses; and (2) to encourage settlement of the dispute without trial. If no settlement occurs, the judge will enter an order containing all of the amendments, stipulations, admissions, and other matters agreed to during the pretrial conference. The order supersedes the pleadings and controls the remainder of the trial.

Pretrial conference a conference between the judge and the attorneys to simplify the issues in dispute and to attempt to settle the dispute without trial

Summary Judgment The evidence disclosed by discovery may be so clear that a trial to determine the facts becomes unnecessary. If this is so, either party may move for a summary judgment, which requests the judge to rule that, because there are no issues of fact to be determined by trial, the party thus moving should prevail as a matter of law. A **summary judgment** is a final binding determination on the merits made by the judge before a trial. The following case involving the famous actress Shirley MacLaine explains the rules courts use to determine whether to grant summary judgment.

Summary judgment binding determination on the merits made by the judge before trial

---

PARKER v. TWENTIETH CENTURY-FOX FILM CORP. Supreme Court of California, 1970, 3 Cal.3d 176, 89 Cal.Rptr. 737, 474 P.2d 689

FACTS Shirley MacLaine Parker, a well-known actress, contracted with Twentieth Century-Fox Film Corporation in August 1965 to play the female lead in Fox's upcoming production of "Bloomer Girl," a motion picture musical that was to be filmed in California. Fox agreed to pay Parker $750,000 for fourteen weeks of her services. Fox decided to cancel its plans for "Bloomer Girl" before production had begun and, instead, offered Parker the female lead in another film, "Big Country, Big Man," a dramatic western to be filmed in Australia. The compensation offered was identical, but Parker's right to approve the director and screenplay would have been eliminated or altered by the "Big Country" proposal. She refused to accept and brought suit to recover the $750,000 for Fox's breach of the "Bloomer Girl" contract. Fox's sole defense in its answer was that it owed no money to Parker because she had deliberately failed to mitigate or reduce her damages by unreasonably refusing to accept the "Big Country" lead. Parker filed a motion for summary judgment. Fox, in opposition to the motion, claimed, in effect, only that the "Big Country" offer was not employment different from or inferior to that under the "Bloomer Girl" contract. The trial court granted Parker a summary judgment and Fox appealed.

DECISION Summary judgment affirmed.

OPINION The matter to be determined by a trial court on a motion for summary judgment is whether facts have been presented which give rise to a triable factual issue. The trial court may not pass upon the issue itself. Summary judgment is proper only if the affidavits or declarations in support of Parker, the moving party, would be sufficient to sustain a judgment in her favor

continued

and her opponent does not by affidavit show facts sufficient to present a triable issue of fact. The affidavits of the moving party are strictly construed, and doubts as to the propriety of summary judgment should be resolved against granting the motion. Such summary procedure is drastic and should be used with caution so that it does not become a substitute for the open trial method of determining facts.

Here, it is clear that the trial court correctly ruled that Parker's failure to accept Fox's tendered substitute employment could not be applied in mitigation of damages because the offer of the "Big Country" lead was of employment both different and inferior, and that no factual dispute was presented on that issue. Therefore, summary judgment in favor of Parker is granted for $750,000.

INTERPRETATION A court will grant summary judgment when there are no issues of fact to be determined by trial.

Trial

Trial determines the facts and the outcome of the case

In all federal civil cases at common law involving more than twenty dollars, the United States Constitution guarantees the right to a jury trial. In addition, nearly every state constitution provides a similar right. Under federal law and in almost all states, jury trials are *not* available in equity cases. Even in cases where a jury trial is available, the parties may waive (choose not to have) a trial by jury. When a trial is conducted without a jury, the judge serves as the fact finder and will make separate findings of fact and conclusions of law. When a trial is conducted *with* a jury, the judge determines issues of law and the jury determines questions of fact.

Voir dire *(vwar deer)* preliminary examination of potential jurors

Jury Selection Assuming a timely demand for a jury has been made, the trial begins with the selection of a jury. The jury selection process involves a ***voir dire***, an examination by the parties' attorneys (or in some courts by the judge) of the potential jurors. Each party has an unlimited number of ***challenges for cause***, which allow the party to prevent a prospective juror from serving if the juror is biased or cannot be fair and impartial. In addition, each party has a limited number of ***peremptory challenges*** for which no cause is required to disqualify a prospective juror. The Supreme Court has held that the U.S. Constitution prohibits discrimination in jury selection on the basis of race or gender.

EDMONSON v. LEESVILLE CONCRETE COMPANY, INC. Supreme Court of the United States, 1991, 500 U.S. 614, 111 S.Ct. 2077, 114 L.Ed.2d 660

FACTS Thaddeus Donald Edmonson, a construction worker, was injured in a job-site accident at Fort Polk, Louisiana. Edmonson sued Leesville Concrete Company for negligence in the U.S. District Court for the Western District of Louisiana, claiming that a Leesville employee permitted one of the company's trucks to roll backward and pin him against some construction equipment. Edmonson invoked his Seventh Amendment right to a trial by jury. During *voir dire*, Leesville used two of its three peremptory challenges authorized by statute to remove black persons from the prospective jury. When Edmonson, who is himself black, requested that the District Court require Leesville to articulate a race-neutral explanation for striking the two jurors, the District Court ruled that the precedent on which Edmonson's request relied applied only to criminal cases and allowed the strikes to stand.

A jury of eleven whites and one black brought in a verdict for Edmonson, assessing total damages at $90,000. It also attributed 80 percent of the fault to Edmonson's contributory negligence and awarded him only $18,000. On appeal, a divided *en banc* panel affirmed the judgment of the District Court, concluding that the use of peremptory challenges by private litigants did not constitute state action and, as a result, did not violate constitutional guarantees against racial discrimination. The U.S. Supreme Court granted *certiorari*.

DECISION Judgment for Edmonson.

OPINION Although the conduct of private parties lies beyond the Constitution's scope in most instances, governmental authority may dominate an activity to such an extent that its participants must be deemed to act with the authority of the government and, as a result,

continued

be subject to Constitutional constraints. In determining whether a particular course of action is governmental in character, it is relevant to examine (1) the extent to which the actor relies on governmental assistance and benefits, (2) whether the actor is performing a traditional governmental function, and (3) whether the injury caused is aggravated in a unique way by the incidents of governmental authority. The Court held that, based on these three principles, the exercise of peremptory challenges by the defendant in the district court was pursuant to a course of state action and therefore subject to Constitutional protection against discrimination on the basis of race.

Without significant participation of the government, the whole jury trial system, of which the peremptory challenge is a part, could not exist. In fact, peremptory challenges have no utility outside the jury system. Further, government statutes prescribe the qualifications for jury service, the procedures for jury selection, and lawful excuse from jury service. Trials are held in governmental buildings and presided over by judges who are state actors charged to use the utmost care to see that justice is done. And in all jurisdictions, a verdict will be incorporated in a judgment which is enforceable by the state. When private litigants participate in the judicial process—including the selection of jurors—they serve an important function within the government and act with its substantial assistance. Finally, the injury caused by discrimination in peremptory challenges is made more severe because it has occurred within the courthouse, where the law itself unfolds in an ongoing expression of Constitutional authority. To permit racial exclusion in this official forum offends the integrity of the court and compounds the racial insult inherent in judging a citizen by the color of his or her skin.

INTERPRETATION The U.S. Constitution imposes restrictions against racial discrimination in the jury selection process.

Conduct of Trial After the jury has been selected, both attorneys make an *opening statement* about the facts that they expect to prove in the trial. The plaintiff and plaintiff's witnesses then testify on *direct examination* by the plaintiff's attorney. Each is subject to *cross-examination* by the defendant's attorney. Pederson and her witnesses testify that the traffic light at the street intersection where she was struck was green for traffic in the direction in which she was crossing but changed to yellow when she was about one-third of the way across the street.

During the trial, the judge rules on the admission and exclusion of evidence. If the judge does not allow certain evidence to be introduced or certain testimony to be given, the attorney must make an *offer of proof* to preserve for review on appeal the question of its admissibility. The offer of proof is not regarded as evidence, and the offer, which consists of oral statements of counsel or witnesses showing for the record the evidence that the judge has ruled inadmissible, is not heard by the jury.

After cross-examination, followed by redirect examination of each of her witnesses, Pederson rests her case. At this time, Dryden may move for a directed verdict in his favor. A **directed verdict** is a final binding determination on the merits made by the judge after a trial has begun but before the jury renders a verdict. If the judge concludes that the evidence introduced by Pederson, which is assumed for the purposes of the motion to be true, would not be sufficient for the jury to find in favor of the plaintiff, then the judge will grant the directed verdict in favor of the defendant. In some states, the judge will deny the motion for a directed verdict if there is *any* evidence on which the jury might possibly render a verdict for the plaintiff.

If the judge denies the motion for a directed verdict, however, the defendant then has the opportunity to present evidence. Dryden and his witnesses testify that he was driving his car at a low speed when it struck Pederson and that Dryden at the time had the green light at the intersection. After the defendant has presented his evidence and both parties have rested (concluded), then either party may move for a directed verdict. By this motion the party contends that the

Conduct of trial consists of opening statements by attorneys, direct and cross-examination of witnesses, and closing arguments

Directed verdict final binding determination on the merits made by the judge after a trial has begun but before the jury renders a verdict

THE LAW AND YOU What You Should Know About Being a Witness

What Is a Witness?

Some day you may be called to court to relate facts you know—to be a **witness** in a lawsuit or trial. If so, don't refuse. Your testimony may be absolutely necessary for a just verdict in the case.

Our American system of justice requires trials to decide the rights of people, and trials require witnesses. If you do not testify voluntarily, the court can order you to appear by issuing a **subpoena** to you.

It is your duty as a citizen to give your testimony when it is needed. It may not always be convenient for you to leave your job or home and spend a day in court. But someday you may find the fate of your own case depending on the willingness of another person to come to court and tell what he or she knows.

What Is a Deposition?

In some cases, your testimony may be required before trial by one of the parties to the lawsuit. The taking and recording of such testimony prior to the actual trial is called **giving a deposition**. (The comments in this pamphlet apply to testimony as a witness whether in court or by deposition.)

What Are Rules of Evidence?

Rules of evidence control courtroom proceedings. Such rules are designed to eliminate testimony and other evidence that may not be trusted. For example, the "hearsay rule" is designed to prevent a witness from relating second-hand information, because the law generally does not regard that as a reliable method of proving the truth.

From time to time, the attorneys in a case may object to a particular question asked of you. If the judge overrules the objection, you may answer the question. If the judge sustains the objection, you will not be permitted to answer. When an objection is made to a question, wait for the judge's ruling before answering the question. During a deposition, which is taken without a judge being present, you will often be permitted to answer the question after an objection is made for the record by one of the attorneys.

If you feel that the answer to any particular question might tend to incriminate you (connect you with the commission of a crime), then you have a constitutional right to refuse to answer the question. If you are in doubt about the incriminating possibility of your answer, you have the right to consult with your own attorney.

How Are Witnesses Questioned?

One of the basic rules of the administration of justice, essential to learning the truth, is that both sides of a lawsuit must have a chance to question a witness.

This is called "examination" and "cross examination." The lawyer who calls you to testify will ask you questions designed to bring out the facts you know (direct examination.) After this is completed, the lawyer for the opposing side will be given an opportunity to ask you questions about the same information (cross examination). Often on deposition, and sometimes in court, the order of examination is reversed and the attorney calling you to testify will be permitted to cross-examine you first. The questions by both lawyers serve one purpose—to bring out the truth about the facts you know.

Don't be afraid of cross-examination. You may think the opposing lawyer is trying to pin you down to too much detail, but the opposition has the right to test your recollection to find out how your memory of the facts compares with the memories of others.

Keep in mind that it is natural for several persons to see and remember an event somewhat differently. Your memory may be clear on certain facts and dim on others. Your job as a witness is to testify from your own memory as accurately as possible.

Should I Discuss My Testimony in Advance?

If you are called as a witness in a case, the lawyer calling you may want to discuss the case with you beforehand. There is nothing improper in this. It is the lawyer's job to find out in advance what you know about the case. The attorney can explain courtroom procedures to you. Don't hesitate to ask about correct courtroom conduct. If you do not wish to discuss the case beforehand with the attorney, you are not obliged to do so.

Tips for Witnesses

• **Be truthful.** You are under oath when you testify in court or on deposition. Testifying falsely under oath can subject you to criminal penalties for perjury. Sometimes being truthful will require you to say "I don't know" or "I don't remember." Your truthfulness will help the judge or jury reach the right decision.

• **Never lose your temper!** A witness who gets angry is at the mercy of the cross-examiner. The witness appears to be prejudiced, and is less likely to be believed by judges and juries. Keep your temper. Your service as a witness will be more pleasant, and your testimony will be more valuable.

• **Be attentive.** You must be alert when you are in the witness chair so that you can hear, understand, and give an intelligent answer to every question. If the judge or jury gets the impression you are indifferent, they may not believe your story.

• **Think before you speak.** Hasty and thoughtless answers may be incorrect and may cause problems. This is particularly true when the opposing lawyer is cross-examining. The cross examiner may ask you leading questions—questions which suggest only one answer. Make sure

continued

you understand the question; then answer it as accurately as you can. If you do not know the answer or cannot remember, say so.

• **Speak clearly.** Nothing is more annoying to a court, jury, and lawyers than a witness who refuses to speak clearly enough to be heard. An inaudible voice not only detracts from the value of your testimony, but it also tends to make the court and jury think that you are not certain of what you are saying. Everyone in the courtroom is entitled to know what you have to say, and the court reporter who is recording the proceedings must be able to hear all your testimony.

• **If you don't understand a question, ask that it be explained.** Many times, a witness will not understand a question that has been asked, but will try to answer it anyway. This is confusing to the court, the jury, and the lawyers, and it extends the time a witness will be testifying because the lawyers must

go back and correct the misinformation.

• **Answer all questions directly!** Too often, a witness will be so anxious to tell the story that he or she will want to get it all told in answer to the first question. Listen to the question. If you can answer it with a "yes" or "no," do so.

• **Never volunteer information.** The information that you volunteer may have no bearing on the case and may delay the proceedings.

• **Stick to the facts.** Don't guess or speculate! The only thing you will be permitted to testify to is what you know personally. What you **know** is important; what you **think** is not.

• **Be helpful, not funny.** A trial is an important matter to the parties involved. Their money, property, or freedom may be risked by your testimony. Don't try to be a comedian.

• **Be fair.** Though you may be testifying for a friend whom you would like to see win, don't color your testimony

or try to overdo it. You will do the best service by making your testimony as objective as possible.

Why Is Being a Witness So Important?

Your obligation to serve as a witness is just as essential to the equal administration of justice as your duty to serve as a juror. When called, testify truthfully and fairly and leave with the satisfaction that you have performed a most important function in seeing that justice is accomplished. Just remember, you may have a lawsuit or trial of your own someday, and you will need witnesses who will testify for you in a fair and impartial way.

[The information contained in this pamphlet is general and should not be applied to specific legal problems without first consulting your own attorney.]

Reprinted by permission of the Ohio State Bar Association.

---

evidence is so clear that reasonable persons could not differ about the outcome of the case. If the judge grants the motion for a directed verdict, he takes the case away from the jury and enters a judgment for the party making the motion.

If these motions are denied, then Pederson's attorney makes a *closing argument* to the jury, reviewing the evidence and urging a verdict in favor of Pederson. Then Dryden's attorney makes a closing argument, summarizing the evidence and urging a verdict in favor of Dryden. Pederson's attorney is permitted to make a short argument in rebuttal.

Jury Instructions The attorneys have previously given written *jury instructions* on the applicable law to the trial judge, who gives to the jury those instructions that he approves and denies those that he considers incorrect. The judge also may give the jury instructions of his own. These instructions (called "charges" in some states) advise the jury of the particular rules of law that apply to the facts the jury determines from the evidence.

Jury instructions judge gives the jury the particular rules of law that apply to the case

Verdict The jury then retires to the jury room to deliberate and to reach its **verdict** in favor of one party or the other. If the jury finds the issues in favor of Dryden, its verdict is that he is not liable. If, however, it finds the issues for Pederson and against Dryden, its verdict will be that the defendant is liable and will specify the amount of the plaintiff's damages. In this case, the jury found that Pederson's damages were $35,000. On returning to the jury box, the foreperson either announces the verdict or hands it in written form to the clerk to give to

Verdict formal decision by the jury on questions submitted to it that is based on those facts the jury determines the evidence proves

the judge, who reads the verdict in open court. In some jurisdictions, a *special verdict*, by which the jury makes specific written findings on each factual issue, is used. The judge then applies the law to these findings and renders a judgment.

Motions Challenging Verdict The unsuccessful party may then file a written motion for a new trial or for judgment notwithstanding the verdict. A *motion for a new trial* may be granted if (1) the judge committed prejudicial error during the trial, (2) the verdict is against the weight of the evidence, (3) the damages are excessive, or (4) the trial was not fair. The judge has the discretion to grant a motion for a new trial (on ground 1, 3, or 4 above) even if the verdict is supported by substantial evidence. On the other hand, the motion for judgment notwithstanding the verdict (also called a judgment n.o.v.) must be denied if there is any substantial evidence supporting the verdict. This motion is similar to a motion for a directed verdict, only it is made after the jury's verdict. To grant the **motion for judgment notwithstanding the verdict**, the judge must decide that the evidence is so clear that reasonable people could not differ as to the outcome of the case. If these motions are denied, the judge enters *judgment on the verdict* for $35,000 in favor of the plaintiff.

Judgment notwithstanding the verdict a final binding determination on the merits made by the judge after and contrary to the jury's verdict

Appeal determines whether the trial court committed prejudicial error

Appeal

The purpose of an appeal is to determine whether the trial court committed prejudicial error. As a general rule, only errors of law are reviewed by an appellate court. Errors of law include the judge's decisions to admit or exclude evidence; the judge's instructions to the jury; and the judge's actions in denying or granting a motion for a demurrer, a summary judgment, a directed verdict, or a judgment notwithstanding the verdict. Errors of fact will be reversed only if they are so clearly erroneous that they are considered to be an error of law.

Let us assume that Dryden directs his attorney to appeal. The attorney files a notice of appeal with the clerk of the trial court within the prescribed time. Later, Dryden, as appellant, files in the reviewing court the record on appeal, which contains the pleadings, a transcript of the testimony, rulings by the judge on motions made by the parties, arguments of counsel, jury instructions, the verdict, posttrial motions, and the judgment from which the appeal is taken. In states having an intermediate court of appeals, such court will usually be the reviewing court. In states having no intermediate court of appeal, a party may appeal directly from the trial court to the state supreme court.

Dryden, as appellant, is required to prepare a condensation of the record, known as an abstract, or pertinent excerpts from the record, which he files with the reviewing court together with a brief and argument. His *brief* contains a statement of the facts, the issues, the rulings by the trial court that Dryden contends are erroneous and prejudicial, grounds for reversal of the judgment, a statement of the applicable law, and arguments on his behalf. Pederson, the appellee, files an answering brief and argument. Dryden may, but is not required to, file a reply brief. The case is now ready to be considered by the reviewing court.

The appellate court does not hear any evidence; rather, it decides the case on the record, abstracts, and briefs. After *oral argument* by the attorneys, if the court elects to hear one, the court takes the case under advisement, or begins deliberations. Then, having made a decision based on majority rule, the appellate court prepares a written opinion containing the reasons for its decision, the rules of law that apply, and its judgment. The judgment may affirm the judgment of the trial

CONSUMER INSIGHT

Downward Trends: The Verdict of Most States and the Judicial Conference Is . . . Smaller Juries Are More Efficient

While most states have settled the debate over the size of civil juries by deciding less is better, the issue remains contentious within the federal judiciary.

The United States Judicial Conference, in September, rejected a move to return to 12-member juries despite support for the proposal by its Committee on Rules of Practice and Procedure and an influential appellate judge.

The decision keeps federal courts in the mainstream on the issue. According to a 1993 survey by the National Center for State Courts, 39 states and the District of Columbia allowed in some way for civil juries of fewer than 12 members.

In some of those states a stipulation of the parties is required to reduce jury size; in some, smaller juries are permitted only in certain courts or for certain kinds of cases.

High Court Stimulates Change

Two U.S. Supreme Court decisions in the early 1970s held that 12-person juries are not constitutionally mandated. The rulings prompted many federal judges to drop the requirement in civil cases. In 1991, the Judicial Conference, which is the judiciary's policy-making body, amended Rule 48 of the Federal Rules of Civil Procedure to explicitly authorize the practice.

Chief Judge Gilbert S. Merritt, outgoing chair of the group's executive committee, says the debate was rekindled partly because of support for larger juries from Chief Justice Richard S. Arnold of the 8th U.S. Circuit Court of Appeals.

Arnold argued in a 1993 speech that juries were composed of 12 persons at the time of the adoption of the Seventh Amendment, which guarantees a right to a jury in civil trials. He also cited studies showing differences between 6- and 12-member juries.

"If the number 12 was settled on 500 years ago," he added, "and was used without interruption until 20 years ago, it carries with it a certain presumption of regularity, a certain entitlement of respect."

Arnold's speech was adapted for a 1993 law review article, "Trial by Jury: The Constitutional Right to a Jury of Twelve in Civil Trials," 22 *Hofstra L. Rev.* 1. Specifically, he and other proponents claim that 12-member juries would:

- Have a better chance of reflecting a diverse cross-section of the community, and be more likely to include people from different economic, racial, ethnic and religious backgrounds.
- Have a greater capacity for recalling all the facts and arguments presented at trial.
- Be less likely to be dominated by a single, aggressive juror.
- Pose only a small economic burden on the judiciary.

A report supporting the move said the cost would be roughly $10 million per year, but described the amount as "less than 13 percent of the funds allocated to pay for jurors' expenses and only one-third of 1 percent of the judiciary's overall $3 billion budget."

During the debate on the proposal, which lasted about 30 minutes, trial judges who worked with smaller juries had fairly strong views in favor of them, Merritt says. They contend the juries were more efficient, less expensive and took less time to empanel.

Meetings of the conference are closed to the public and neither the votes nor details of the debate are revealed.

Judges from the Southern District of New York are among those who support smaller juries. In February testimony before a conference subcommittee, U.S. District Judge John F. Keenan said the 8-person juries used there are diverse and cost-efficient.

"There is no data or reliable information to support the concept that 12-member juries achieve better results," he said.

The Next Jury Debate

Merritt says the conference will devote further study to a related issue: whether to relax the requirement that, absent consent of the parties, jury verdicts in federal civil trials must be unanimous. The 1993 National Center survey found that 34 states allow for less than unanimous verdicts, although two of them permit it only by stipulation of the parties.

In other action, the conference voted to send to Congress a request for an additional 21 permanent and 12 temporary district court judgeships. The last time new judgeships were created was in 1990.

By Henry J. Reske, *ABA Journal*, December 1996. Used with permission.

court, or, if the appellate court finds that reversible error was committed, the judgment may be reversed or modified or returned to the lower court (remanded) for a new trial. In some instances the appellate court will affirm the lower court's decision in part and will reverse it in part. The losing party may file a petition for rehearing, which is usually denied.

If the reviewing court is an intermediate appellate court, the party losing in that court may decide to seek a reversal of its judgment by filing within a prescribed time a notice of appeal, if the appeal is by right, or a petition for leave to appeal to the state supreme court, if the appeal is by discretion. This petition corresponds to a petition for a writ of *certiorari* in the United States Supreme Court. The party winning in the appellate court may file an answer to the petition for leave to appeal. If the petition is granted, or if the appeal is by right, the record is certified to the supreme court, where each party files a new brief and argument. The supreme court may hear oral argument or simply review the record; it then takes the case under advisement. If the supreme court concludes that the judgment of the appellate court is correct, it affirms. If it decides otherwise, it reverses the judgment of the appellate court and enters a reversal or an order of remand. The unsuccessful party may again file a petition for a rehearing, which is likely to be denied. Barring the remote possibility of an application for still further review by the United States Supreme Court, the case either has reached its termination or, on remand, is about to start its second journey through the courts, beginning, as it did originally, in the trial court.

Enforcement

Enforcement plaintiff with an unpaid judgment may resort to a writ of execution to have the sheriff seize property of the defendants and to garnishment to collect money owed to the defendant by a third party

If Dryden does not appeal, or if the reviewing court affirms the judgment if he does appeal, and Dryden does not pay the judgment, the task of enforcement will remain. Pederson must request the clerk to issue a ***writ of execution*** demanding payment of the judgment, which is served by the sheriff on the defendant. If the writ is returned "unsatisfied," that is, if Dryden still does not pay, Pederson may post bond or other security and order a levy on and sale of specific nonexempt property belonging to the defendant, which is then seized by the sheriff, advertised for sale, and sold at a public sale under the writ of execution. If the sale does not produce enough money to pay the judgment, Pederson's attorney may begin another proceeding in an attempt to locate money or other property belonging to Dryden. In an attempt to collect the judgment, Pederson's attorney may also proceed by ***garnishment*** against Dryden's employer to collect from his wages or against a bank in which he has an account.

The various stages in civil procedure are illustrated in Figure 3–7.

ALTERNATIVE DISPUTE RESOLUTION

Litigation is complex, time-consuming, and expensive. Furthermore, court adjudications involve long delays, lack special expertise in substantive areas, and provide only a limited range of remedies. Additionally, litigation is structured so that one party takes all with little opportunity for compromise and often causes animosity between the disputants. Consequently, in an attempt to overcome some of the disadvantages of litigation, several nonjudicial methods of dealing with disputes have developed. The most important of these alternatives to litigation is arbitration. Others include conciliation, mediation, and "mini-trials."

The various techniques differ in a number of ways, including (1) whether the process is voluntary, (2) whether the process is binding, (3) whether the disputants represent themselves or are represented by attorneys, (4) whether the decision is made by the disputants or by a third party, (5) whether the procedure utilized is formal or informal, and (6) whether the basis for the decision is law or some other criterion.

Which method of civil dispute resolution—litigation or one of the nongovernmental methods—is better for a particular dispute depends on several

FIGURE 3–7 Stages in Civil Procedure

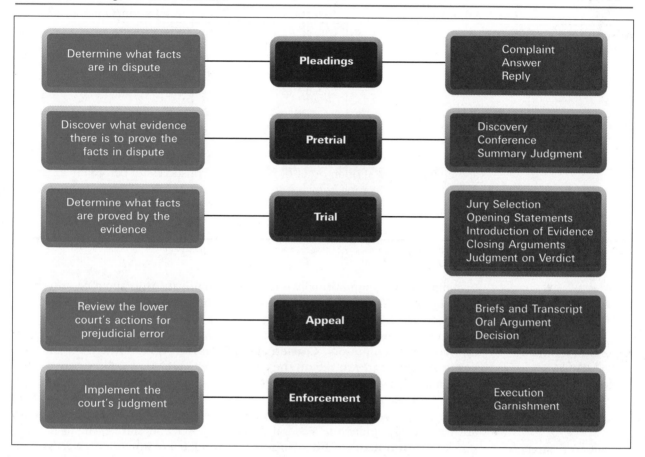

factors, including the financial circumstances of the disputants, the nature of the relationship (commercial or personal, ongoing or limited) between them, and the urgency of a quick resolution. Alternative dispute resolution methods are especially suitable when privacy, speed, preservation of continuing relations, and control over the process—including the flexibility to compromise—are important to the parties. Nevertheless, the disadvantages of using alternative dispute mechanisms may make court adjudication more appropriate. For example, with the exception of arbitration, only courts can compel participation and provide a binding resolution. In addition, only courts can establish precedents and create public duties. Furthermore, the courts provide greater due process protections and uniformity of outcome. Finally, the courts are independent of the parties and are publicly funded. See Figure 3–8.

Arbitration

In **arbitration**, the parties select a third person or persons (the arbitrator(s)) who render(s) a binding decision after hearing arguments and reviewing evidence. Because the presentation of the case is less formal and the rules of evidence are more relaxed, arbitration usually takes less time and costs less than litigation. Moreover, in many arbitration cases the parties are able to select an arbitrator with special expertise concerning the subject of the dispute. Thus, the quality of the arbitrator's decision may be higher than that available through the court system.

Arbitration nonjudicial proceeding where a neutral third party selected by disputants renders a binding decision

FIGURE 3–8 Comparison of Adjudication, Arbitration, and Mediation/Conciliation

	Court Adjudication	**Arbitration**	**Mediation/Conciliation**
Advantages	Binding Public norms Precedents Uniformity Publicly funded Compels participation	Binding Parties control process Privacy Special expertise Speedy resolution	Preserves relations Parties control process Privacy Flexible
Disadvantages	Expensive Time-consuming Long delays Limited remedies Lacks special expertise No compromise Disrupts relationships Publicity	No public norms No precedent No uniformity	Not binding Lacks finality No compelled participation No precedent No uniformity

Adapted from Table 4 of *Report of the Ad Hoc Panel on Dispute Resolution and Public Policy*, prepared by the National Institute for Dispute Resolution.

In addition, arbitration normally is conducted in private, thus avoiding unwanted publicity. Arbitration is commonly used in commercial and labor management disputes.

There are two basic types of arbitration—consensual, which is by far the most common, and compulsory. **Consensual arbitration** occurs whenever the parties to a dispute agree to submit the controversy to arbitration. They may do this in advance by agreeing in their contract that disputes arising out of their contract will be resolved by arbitration. Or they may do so after a dispute arises by then agreeing to submit the dispute to arbitration. In either instance, such agreements are enforceable under the Federal Arbitration Act and statutes in over forty states. In **compulsory arbitration**, which is relatively infrequent, a federal or state statute requires arbitration for specific types of disputes, such as those involving public employees like police officers or fire fighters.

The decision of the arbitrator, called an **award**, is binding on the parties. Nevertheless, it is subject to limited judicial review for such matters as illegality, fraud or other misconduct, lack of due process, or the arbitrator's having exceeded his or her powers. Historically, the courts were unfriendly to arbitration; however, the courts have dramatically changed their attitude and now favor arbitration.

Consensual arbitration
arbitration voluntarily entered into by the parties

Compulsory arbitration
arbitration required by statute for specific types of disputes

Award the decision of an arbitrator

ALLIED-BRUCE TERMINIX COMPANIES, INC. v. DOBSON Supreme Court of the United States, 1995, 513 U.S. 265, 115 S.Ct. 834, 130 L.Ed. 753

FACTS In August 1987, Steven Gwin bought a lifetime Termite Protection Plan for his home from the local office of Allied-Bruce, a franchise of Terminix International Company. The plan provided that Allied-Bruce would "protect" Gwin's house against termite infestation, reinspect periodically, provide additional treatment if necessary, and repair damage caused by new termite infestations. Terminix International guaranteed the fulfillment of these contractual provisions. The plan also provided that all disputes arising out of the contract would be settled exclusively by arbitration. In 1991, Gwin had Allied-Bruce reinspect the house in anticipa-

tion of selling it. Allied-Bruce gave the house a "clean bill of health." Gwin then sold the house and transferred the Termite Protection Plan to Dobson. Shortly thereafter, Dobson found the house to be infested with termites. Allied-Bruce attempted to treat and repair the house, using materials from out of state, but these efforts failed to satisfy Dobson. Dobson then sued Gwin, Allied-Bruce, and Terminix International in an Alabama state court. Allied-Bruce and Terminix International asked for a stay of these proceedings until arbitration could be carried out as stipulated in the contract. The trial court refused to grant the stay. The Alabama Supreme Court upheld

continued

that ruling, citing a state statute that makes predispute arbitration agreements unenforceable. The court found that the Federal Arbitration Act, which preempts conflicting state law, did not apply to this contract because its connection to interstate commerce was too slight. The U.S. Supreme Court agreed to hear this case.

DECISION Judgment reversed and remanded.

OPINION The Federal Arbitration Act § 2 provides that a "written provision in . . . a contract evidencing a transaction involving commerce to settle by arbitration a controversy thereafter arising out of such contract or transaction . . . shall be valid, irrevocable, and enforceable, save upon such grounds as exist at law or in equity for the revocation of any contract." The basic purpose of the Act is to overcome courts' refusals to enforce agreements to arbitrate; a policy arising from the ancient desire of courts to protect and extend their jurisdiction rather than to erode it. Congress based the act on the power to control interstate commerce, and it preempts state law if the transaction is within the scope of Congress's constitutional power to legislate these areas.

Furthermore, by using the word "involving," Congress intended the statute to exercise Congress's Commerce Clause powers to the full. Therefore, the statute covers transactions that are not strictly "within the flow of interstate commerce" but merely *affect* interstate commerce. In addition, the language "evidencing a transaction" allows the statute to apply where a transaction has *in fact* involved interstate commerce even though the parties did not contemplate interstate commerce when creating the contract. In this case, the parties do not contest that the transaction, in fact, involved interstate commerce. In addition to the multistate operations of Terminix and Allied-Bruce, the materials used by Allied-Bruce in its efforts to carry out the terms of the Termite Protection Plan came from outside Alabama. Therefore, the Federal Arbitration Act preempts Alabama's anti-arbitration statute and requires enforcement of the contract's arbitration provision.

INTERPRETATION Consensual arbitration agreements subject to the Federal Arbitration Act are enforceable, and the Act preempts conflicting state law.

Conciliation

Conciliation is a nonbinding, informal process in which a third party (the conciliator) selected by the disputing parties attempts to help them reach a mutually acceptable agreement. The duties of the conciliator include improving communications, explaining issues, scheduling meetings, discussing differences of opinion, and serving as an intermediary between the parties when they are unwilling to meet.

> **Conciliation** *(con·cil·i·a'·tion)* nonbinding process in which a third party acts as an intermediary between the disputing parties

Mediation

Mediation is a process in which a third party (the mediator) selected by the disputants helps them to resolve their disagreement. In addition to employing conciliation techniques to improve communications, the mediator, unlike the conciliator, proposes possible solutions for the parties to consider. Like the conciliator, the mediator does not have the power to render a binding decision.

Sometimes the techniques of arbitration and mediation are combined in a procedure called "med-arb." In **med-arb**, the neutral third party serves first as a mediator and, if all issues are not resolved through such mediation, then serves as an arbitrator authorized to render a binding decision on the remaining issues.

> **Mediation** *(me·di·a'·tion)* nonbinding process in which a third party acts as an intermediary between the disputing parties and proposes solutions for them to consider

> **Med-arb** binding process in which a third party serves first as a mediator and then as an arbitrator for those issues not resolved through mediation

Mini-Trial

A mini-trial typically occurs when both disputants are corporations. In a **mini-trial**, attorneys for the two corporations conduct limited discovery and then present evidence to a panel consisting of managers from each company, as well as to a neutral third party, who may be a retired judge or other attorney. After the lawyers complete their presentations, the managers try to negotiate a settlement without the attorneys. The managers may consult the third party on how a court might resolve the issues in dispute.

> **Mini-trial** nonbinding process in which attorneys for the disputing parties present evidence to managers of the disputing parties and a neutral third party, and then the managers attempt to negotiate a settlement in consultation with the third party

Summary Jury Trial

Summary jury trial mock trial followed by negotiations

A **summary jury trial** is a mock trial in which the parties present their case to a jury. Though not binding, the jury's verdict does influence the negotiations in which the parties must participate following the trial. If the parties do not reach a settlement, they may have a full trial *de novo*.

CHAPTER SUMMARY

The Court System

Federal Courts	
	District Courts trial courts of general jurisdiction that can hear and decide most legal controversies in the federal system
	Courts of Appeals hear appeals from the district courts and review orders of certain administrative agencies
	The Supreme Court nation's highest court whose principal function is to review decisions of the Federal Courts of Appeals and the highest state courts
	Special Courts have jurisdiction over cases in a particular area of federal law and include the U.S. Court of Federal Claims, the Tax Court, the U.S. Bankruptcy Courts, and the U.S. Court of Appeals for the Federal Circuit

State Courts	
	Inferior Trial Courts hear minor criminal cases such as traffic offenses and civil cases involving small amounts of money and conduct preliminary hearings in more serious criminal cases
	Trial Courts have general jurisdiction over civil and criminal cases
	Special Courts trial courts, such as probate courts and family courts, have jurisdiction over a particular area of state law
	Appellate Courts include one or two levels; the highest court's decisions are final except in those cases reviewed by the U.S. Supreme Court

Jurisdiction

Subject Matter Jurisdiction	
	Definition authority of a court to decide a particular kind of case
	Federal Jurisdiction
	■ *Exclusive Federal Jurisdiction* federal courts have sole jurisdiction over federal crimes, bankruptcy, antitrust, patent, trademark, copyright, and other special cases
	■ *Concurrent Federal Jurisdiction* authority of more than one court to hear the same case; state and federal courts have concurrent jurisdiction over (1) federal question cases (cases arising under the Constitution, statutes, or treaties of the United States) which do not involve exclusive federal jurisdiction and (2) diversity of citizenship cases involving more than $75,000
	State Jurisdiction state courts have exclusive jurisdiction over all matters to which the federal judicial power does not reach

Jurisdiction over the Parties	**Definition** the power of a court to bind the parties to a suit
	***In Personam* Jurisdiction** jurisdiction based upon claims against a person in contrast to jurisdiction over his or her property
	In Rem Jurisdiction jurisdiction based on claims against property
	Attachment Jurisdiction jurisdiction over a defendant's property to obtain payment of a claim not related to the property
	Venue geographical area in which a lawsuit should be brought

Civil Dispute Resolution

Civil Procedure	**The Pleadings** series of statements that give notice and establish the issues of fact and law presented and disputed
	■ *Complaint* initial pleading by the plaintiff stating his case
	■ *Summons* notice given to inform a person of a lawsuit against her
	■ *Answer* defendant's pleading in response to the plaintiff's complaint
	■ *Reply* plaintiff's pleading in response to the defendant's answer
	Pretrial Procedure process requiring the parties to disclose what evidence is available to prove the disputed facts; designed to encourage settlement of cases or to make the trial more efficient
	■ *Judgment on Pleadings* a final ruling in favor of one party by the judge based on the pleadings
	■ *Discovery* right of each party to obtain evidence from the other party
	■ *Pretrial Conference* a conference between the judge and the attorneys to simplify the issues in dispute and to attempt to settle the dispute without trial
	■ *Summary Judgment* final ruling by the judge in favor of one party based on the evidence disclosed by discovery
	Trial determines the facts and the outcome of the case
	■ *Jury Selection* each party has an unlimited number of challenges for cause and a limited number of peremptory challenges
	■ *Conduct of Trial* consists of opening statements by attorneys, direct and cross-examination of witnesses, and closing arguments
	■ *Jury Instructions* judge gives the jury the particular rules of law that apply to the case
	■ *Verdict* the jury's decision based on those facts the jury determines the evidence proves
	■ *Motions Challenging Verdict* include motions for a new trial and a motion for judgment notwithstanding the verdict
	Appeal determines whether the trial court committed prejudicial error
	Enforcement plaintiff with an unpaid judgment may resort to a writ of execution to have the sheriff seize property of the defendants and to garnishment to collect money owed to the defendant by a third party

Alternative Dispute Resolution	**Arbitration** a nonjudicial proceeding in which a neutral third party selected by the disputants renders a binding decision (award)
	Conciliation a nonbinding process in which a third party acts as an intermediary between the disputing parties
	Mediation a nonbinding process in which a third party acts as an intermediary between the disputing parties and proposes solutions for them to consider
	Mini-Trial a nonbinding process in which attorneys for the disputing parties (typically corporations) present evidence to managers of the disputing parties and a neutral third party, after which the managers attempt to negotiate a settlement in consultation with the third party
	Summary Jury Trial mock trial followed by negotiations

QUESTIONS

1. List and describe the courts in the federal court system and in a typical state court system.
2. Distinguish between appeal by right and by writ of *certiorari*.
3. Distinguish between subject matter jurisdiction and jurisdiction over the parties.
4. Distinguish between exclusive and concurrent federal jurisdiction. Identify the two types of federal concurrent jurisdiction.
5. Define and describe a typical long-arm statute.
6. List and distinguish among the three types of jurisdiction over the parties.
7. Describe the purpose of pleadings.
8. List and explain the various stages of a civil proceeding.
9. Compare and contrast the following: demurrer, judgment on the pleadings, summary judgment, directed verdict, and judgment notwithstanding the verdict.
10. Compare and contrast litigation, arbitration, conciliation, and mediation.

Internet Question. Find information about the structure and operations of (a) the federal court system and (2) your own state's court system. (If your state is not available, choose another state.)

PROBLEMS

1. On June 15 a newspaper columnist predicted that the coast of State X would be flooded on the following September 1. Relying on this pronouncement, Gullible quit his job and sold his property at a loss so as not to be financially ruined. When the flooding did not occur, Gullible sued the columnist in a State X court for damages. The court dismissed the case for failure to state a cause of action under applicable state law. On appeal, the State X Supreme Court upheld the lower court. Three months after this ruling, the State Y Supreme Court heard an appeal in which a lower court had ruled that a reader could sue a columnist for falsely predicting flooding.

    (a) Must the State Y Supreme Court follow the ruling of the State X Supreme Court as a matter of *stare decisis*?

    (b) Should the State Y lower court have followed the ruling of the State X Supreme Court until the State Y Supreme Court issued a ruling on the issue?

    (c) Once the State X Supreme Court issued its ruling, could the United States Supreme Court overrule the State X Supreme Court?

    (d) If the State Y Supreme Court and the State X Supreme Court rule in exactly opposite ways, must the United States Supreme Court resolve the conflict between the two courts?

2. State Senator Bowdler convinced the legislature of State Z to pass a law requiring all professors to submit their class notes and transparencies to a board of censors to be sure that no "lewd" materials were presented to students at state universities. Professor Rabelais would like to challenge this law as being violative of his First Amendment rights under the U.S. Constitution.

    (a) May Professor Rabelais challenge this law in the State Z courts?

    (b) May Professor Rabelais challenge this law in a federal district court?

3. While driving his car in Virginia, Carpe Diem, a resident of North Carolina, struck Butt, a resident of Alaska. As a result of the accident, Butt suffered over $60,000 in medical expenses. Butt would like to know if he personally serves the proper papers to Diem whether he can obtain jurisdiction against Diem for damages in the following courts:
   (a) Alaska state trial court
   (b) Federal Circuit Court of Appeals for the Ninth Circuit (includes Alaska)
   (c) Virginia state trial court
   (d) Virginia federal district court
   (e) Federal Circuit Court of Appeals for the Fourth Circuit (includes Virginia and North Carolina)
   (f) Virginia equity court
   (g) North Carolina state trial court.

4. Sam Simpleton, a resident of Kansas, and Nellie Naive, a resident of Missouri, each bought $85,000 in stock at local offices in their home states from Evil Stockbrokers, Inc. ("Evil"), a business incorporated in Delaware with its principal place of business in Kansas. Both Simpleton and Naive believe that they were cheated by Evil Stockbrokers and would like to sue Evil for fraud. Assuming that no federal question is at issue, assess the accuracy of the following statements:
   (a) Simpleton can sue Evil in a Kansas state trial court.
   (b) Simpleton can sue Evil in a federal district court in Kansas.
   (c) Naive can sue Evil in a Missouri state trial court.
   (d) Naive can sue Evil in a federal district court in Missouri.

5. The Supreme Court of State A ruled that, under the law of State A, pit bull owners must either keep their dogs fenced or pay damages to anyone bitten by the dogs. Assess the accuracy of the following statements:
   (a) It is likely that the United States Supreme Court would issue a writ of *certiorari* in the "pit bull" case.
   (b) If a case similar to the "pit bull" case were to come before the Supreme Court of State B in the future, the doctrine of *stare decisis* would leave the court no choice but to rule the same way as the "pit bull" case.

6. The Supreme Court of State G decided that the U.S. Constitution requires professors to warn students of their right to remain silent before questioning the students about cheating. This ruling directly conflicts with a decision of the Federal Court of Appeals for the circuit which includes State G.
   (a) Must the Federal Circuit Court of Appeals withdraw its ruling?
   (b) Must the Supreme Court of State G withdraw its ruling?

7. Thomas Clements brought an action to recover damages for breach of warranty against defendant, Signa Corporation. (A warranty is an obligation that the seller of goods assumes with respect to the quality of the goods sold.) Clements had purchased a motorboat from Barney's Sporting Goods, an Illinois corporation. The boat was manufactured by Signa Corporation, an Indiana corporation with its principal place of business in Decatur, Indiana. Signa has no office in Illinois and no agent authorized to do business on its behalf within Illinois. Clements saw Signa's boats on display at the Chicago Boat Show. In addition, literature on Signa's boats was distributed at the Chicago Boat Show. Several boating magazines, delivered to Clements in Illinois, contained advertisements for Signa's boats. Clements had also seen Signa's boats on display at Barney's Sporting Goods Store in Palatine, Illinois, where he eventually purchased the boat. A written warranty issued by Signa was delivered to Clements in Illinois. Although Signa was served with a summons, it failed to enter an appearance in this case. A default order was entered against Signa and subsequently a judgment of $6,220 was entered against Signa. Signa appealed. Decision?

8. Vette sued Aetna under a fire insurance policy. Aetna moved for summary judgment on the basis that the pleadings and discovered evidence showed a lack of an insurable interest in Vette. An "insurable interest" exists where the insured derives a monetary benefit or advantage from the preservation or continued existence of the property or would sustain an economic loss from its destruction. Aetna provided ample evidence to infer that Vette had no insurable interest in the contents of the burned building. Vette also provided sufficient evidence to put in dispute this factual issue. The trial court granted the motion for summary judgment. Vette appealed. Decision?

9. Mark Womer and Brian Perry were members of the U.S. Navy and were stationed in Newport, Rhode Island. On April 10, 1978, Womer allowed Perry to borrow his automobile so that Perry could visit his family in New Hampshire. Later that day, while operating Womer's vehicle, Perry was involved in an accident in Manchester, New Hampshire. As a result of the accident, Tzannetos Tavoularis was injured. Tavoularis brought this action against Womer in a New Hampshire superior court, contending that Womer was negligent in lending the automobile to Perry when he knew or should have known that Perry did not have a valid driver's license. Womer sought to dismiss the action on the ground that the New Hampshire courts lacked jurisdiction over him, citing the following facts: (1) he lived and worked in Georgia; (2) he had no relatives in New Hampshire; (3) he neither owned property nor possessed investments in New Hampshire; and (4) he had never conducted business in New Hampshire. Decision?

CHAPTER 4

Constitutional Law

You will recall from Chapter 1 that a constitution is the fundamental law of a particular level of government. It establishes the structure of government and defines the political relationships within it. It also places restrictions on the powers of government and guarantees the rights and liberties of the people.

The Constitution of the United States was adopted on September 17, 1787, by representatives of the thirteen newly created states. Its purpose is stated in the preamble:

> We the People of the United States, in Order to form a more perfect Union, establish Justice, insure domestic Tranquility, provide for the common defense, promote the general Welfare, and secure the Blessings of Liberty to ourselves and our Posterity, do ordain and establish this Constitution for the United States of America.

Although the framers of the U.S. Constitution stated precisely what rights and authority were vested in the new national government, they considered it unnecessary to list those liberties the people were to keep for themselves. Nonetheless, during the state conventions ratifying the document, people expressed fear that the federal government might abuse its powers. To calm these concerns, the first Congress approved ten amendments to the U.S. Constitution, now known as the Bill of Rights, which were adopted on December 15, 1791.

The Bill of Rights restricts the powers and authority of the federal government and establishes many of the civil and political rights enjoyed in the United States, including the right to due process of law and freedoms of speech, press, religion, assembly, and petition. Though the Bill of Rights does not apply directly to the states, the Supreme Court has held that the Fourteenth Amendment incorporates most of the principles of the Bill of Rights, thus making them applicable to the states.

This chapter concerns constitutional law as it applies to business and commerce. We will begin by surveying some of the basic principles of constitutional law, and will then examine the allocation of power between the federal and state governments with respect to the regulation of business. Finally, we will discuss the constitutional restrictions on the power of government to regulate business.

BASIC PRINCIPLES

Constitutional law in the United States involves several basic concepts. These fundamental principles, which apply both to the powers of and to the limitations on government, are (1) federalism, (2) federal supremacy and preemption, (3) judicial review, (4) separation of powers, and (5) state action.

Federalism

Federalism is the division of governing power between the federal government and the states. The U.S. Constitution enumerates the powers of the federal government and specifically reserves to the states or the people the powers not expressly delegated to the federal government. Accordingly, the federal government is a government of enumerated, or limited, powers; and a specified power must authorize each of its acts. The doctrine of enumerated powers is not, however, a significant limitation on the federal government because a number of these enumerated powers, in particular the power to regulate interstate and foreign commerce, have been broadly interpreted.

Furthermore, the Constitution grants Congress not only specified powers but also the power "[t]o make all Laws which shall be necessary and proper for carrying into Execution the foregoing Powers, and all other Powers vested by this Constitution in the Government of the United States, or in any Department or Officer thereof." U.S. CONST. art. I, § 8, cl. 18. In the Supreme Court's view, the "necessary and proper" clause enables Congress to legislate in areas not mentioned in the list of enumerated powers as long as such legislation reasonably relates to some enumerated power.

Federalism governing power is divided between the federal government and the states

Federal Supremacy and Preemption

Although under our federalist system the states retain significant powers, the **supremacy clause** of the U.S. Constitution provides that within its own sphere, federal law is supreme and that state law must, in case of conflict, yield. Accordingly, any state constitutional provision or law that conflicts with the U.S. Constitution or valid federal laws or treaties is unconstitutional and may not be given effect.

Under the supremacy clause, whenever Congress enacts legislation within its constitutional powers, the federal action **preempts** (overrides) any conflicting state legislation. (See *Perry v. Thomas* in Chapter 3) Even if a state regulation is not in conflict, it must still give way if Congress clearly has intended its action to preempt state legislation. This intent may be specifically stated in the legislation or inferred from the scope of the legislation, the need for uniformity, or the danger of conflict between coexisting federal and state regulation.

When Congress has *not* intended to displace all state legislation, then nonconflicting state legislation is permitted. The case of *Silkwood v. Kerr-McGee Corporation* illustrates this point. When Congress has not acted, the fact that it *has* the power to act does not prevent the states from acting. Until Congress exercises its power to preempt, state regulation is permitted.

Supremacy clause *(su·prem'·a·cy)* federal law takes precedence over conflicting state laws

Federal preemption *(pre·emp'·tion)* first right of the federal government to regulate matters within its powers to the possible exclusion of state regulation

---

SILKWOOD v. KERR-McGEE CORPORATION Supreme Court of the United States, 1984, 464 U.S. 238, 104 S.Ct. 615, 78 L.Ed.2d 443

FACTS Karen Silkwood was a laboratory analyst for Kerr-McGee Corporation at its Cimarron plant in Oklahoma. The plant made plutonium fuel pins for use as reactor fuel in nuclear power plants. Accordingly, the plant was subject to licensing and extensive federal regulation by the Nuclear Regulatory Commission (NRC), pursuant to the Atomic Energy Act, which preempts Oklahoma's regulation of the safety aspects of nuclear energy. During a three-day work period in 1974, Silkwood was contaminated by plutonium at the plant.

After high levels of contamination were detected on her when she arrived at work on the third day, Kerr-McGee ordered a decontamination squad to Silkwood's apartment, resulting in the unavoidable destruction of many of her personal belongings. Silkwood was sent to the Los Alamos Scientific Laboratory to determine the extent of the contamination in her body's vital organs. A week later she returned to work but died that night in an unrelated automobile accident. Her father, as administrator of her estate, filed a claim against Kerr-McGee

continued

under Oklahoma tort law for Karen's personal injuries and property damage resulting from her contamination. On the basis of the jury's verdict, the trial court awarded Silkwood $505,000 ($500,000 for personal injuries and $5,000 for property damage) plus punitive damages of $10,000,000. The appellate court held that because federal statutes regulate nuclear energy, punitive damages could not be awarded. Silkwood appealed.

DECISION Judgment of appellate court reversed.

OPINION The federal preemption of state regulation of the safety aspects of nuclear energy does not extend to a state-authorized award of punitive damages. Preemption concerning damages for radiation injuries should not be judged on the basis that the federal government has so completely occupied the field of safety that state remedies are foreclosed. Rather, preemption depends on whether there is an irreconcilable conflict between the state and federal standards or whether the imposition of a state standard in a damages suit would frustrate the objectives of the federal law.

Here, there is no conflict between the payment of a punitive damages award under Oklahoma state law and a federal fine imposed for an infraction of the NRC's standards. An examination of the statutory scheme and legislative history indicates that Congress did not intend to forbid the states from providing remedies for those suffering injuries from radiation in nuclear plants. Moreover, an award of punitive damages under state law does not hinder Congress's purpose of encouraging the development of atomic energy, nor do such damages frustrate the goal of precluding dual regulation of radiation hazards. On the contrary, Congress believed that the NRC should have exclusive regulatory authority over the safety aspects of nuclear development while at the same time plaintiffs like Silkwood should have the right under state law to recover for injuries caused by nuclear hazards.

INTERPRETATION When Congress has not intended to displace all state legislation, then nonconflicting state legislation is permitted.

Judicial Review

Judicial review power of the courts to determine the constitutionality of any legislative or executive act

Judicial review describes the process by which the courts examine governmental actions to determine whether they conform to the U.S. Constitution. If governmental action violates the U.S. Constitution, under judicial review the courts will invalidate that action. Judicial review extends to legislation, acts of the executive branch, and the decisions of inferior courts; such review scrutinizes actions of both the federal and state governments and applies to both the same standards of constitutionality. The U.S. Supreme Court is the final authority as to the constitutionality of any federal and state law.

Separation of Powers

Separation of powers allocation of powers among the legislative, executive, and judicial branches of government

Another basic principle on which our government is founded is that of **separation of powers.** Our Constitution vests power in three distinct and independent branches of government—the executive, legislative, and judicial branches. The purpose of the doctrine of separation of powers is to prevent any branch of government from gaining too much power. The doctrine also permits each branch to function without interference from any other branch. Basically, the legislative branch is granted the power to make the law, the executive branch to enforce the law, and the judicial branch to interpret the law. This separation of powers is not complete, however. For example, the executive branch has veto power over legislation enacted by Congress; the legislative branch must approve a great number of executive appointments; and the judicial branch may declare both legislation and executive actions unconstitutional. Nevertheless, our government generally operates under a three-branch scheme that provides for separation of powers and places checks and balances on the power of each branch. See Figure 4–1.

State Action

State action actions by governments as opposed to actions taken by private individuals

Most of the protections provided by the U.S. Constitution and its amendments apply only to governmental, or state, action. **State action** includes any actions

FIGURE 4–1 Separation of Powers: Checks and Balances

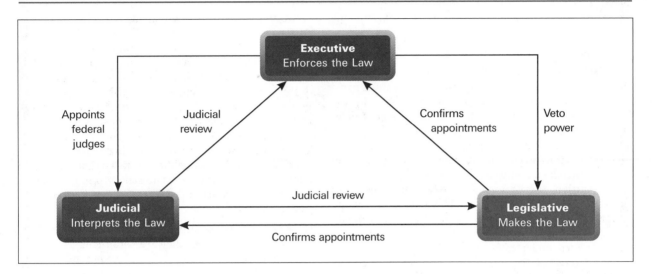

of the federal and state governments and their subdivisions, such as city or county governments and agencies. Only the Thirteenth Amendment, which abolishes slavery or involuntary servitude, applies to the actions of private individuals. The protections that guard against state action may, however, be extended by *statute* to apply to private activity.

Additionally, action taken by private citizens may constitute state action if the state exercises coercive power over the challenged private action or has encouraged the action significantly. For example, the Supreme Court found state action when the Supreme Court of Missouri ordered a lower court to enforce an agreement among white property owners that prohibited the transfer of their property to nonwhites. Moreover, if "private" individuals or entities engage in public functions, their actions may be considered state action subject to constitutional limitations. For example, the U.S. Supreme Court held that a company town was subject to the First Amendment because the state had allowed the company to exercise all of the public functions and activities usually conducted by a town government. Since that case, the Supreme Court has been less willing to find state action based upon the performance of public functions by private entities; the Court now limits such a finding to those functions "traditionally exclusively reserved to the state." The case *National Collegiate Athletic Ass'n v. Tarkanian* further illustrates this trend.

NATIONAL COLLEGIATE ATHLETIC ASS'N. v. TARKANIAN Supreme Court of the United States, 1988, 488 U.S. 179, 109 S.Ct. 454, 102 L.Ed.2d 469

FACTS When Jerry Tarkanian became head basketball coach at the University of Nevada at Las Vegas (UNLV) in 1973, he inherited a team with a 14—14 record. By 1977, the UNLV team had won 29 of 32 games and had made it to the "Final Four" of the National Collegiate Athletic Association (NCAA) tournament. Nevertheless, in 1977, UNLV informed Tarkanian that he was to be suspended from employment for at least two years. The suspension was motivated by a NCAA report detailing 38 violations of NCAA rules by UNLV personnel, including 10 involving Tarkanian.

Tarkanian brought suit in Nevada state court, alleging that both UNLV and the NCAA had deprived him of his Fourteenth Amendment due process rights. Ultimately, Tarkanian obtained injunctive relief and attorneys' fees against both UNLV and the NCAA,

continued

awards which were upheld by the Nevada Supreme Court. The NCAA appealed.

DECISION Judgment for the NCAA.

OPINION The NCAA's liability may be upheld only if its participation in the events that led to Tarkanian's suspension constituted "state action" prohibited by the Fourteenth Amendment and was performed "under color of" state law. Clearly UNLV's conduct was influenced by the NCAA. The question is, however, whether UNLV's actions in compliance with the NCAA rules and recommendations turned the NCAA's conduct into state action. UNLV, along with several hundred other member institutions, may have had some impact on the formulation of NCAA policy. By no stretch of the imagination, though, can this policy be said to have been formulated under color of Nevada law. Furthermore, UNLV retained the authority to withdraw from the

NCAA and establish its own standards. Thus, neither UNLV's decision to adopt the NCAA standards nor its minor role in their formulation is a sufficient reason for concluding that the NCAA was acting under color of Nevada law. It is true that a state may delegate authority to a private party and thereby make that party a state actor. However, UNLV delegated no power to the NCAA to take specific action against any UNLV employee. The NCAA did not, and indeed could not, directly discipline Tarkanian. Accordingly, the NCAA's participation in the events that led to Tarkanian's suspension did not constitute "state action" prohibited by the Fourteenth Amendment and was not performed "under color of" state law.

INTERPRETATION Conduct by private parties will constitute state action when they are performing a public function traditionally exclusively reserved to the state.

POWERS OF GOVERNMENT

The U.S. Constitution created a federal government of enumerated powers. Moreover, as the Tenth Amendment declares, "[t]he powers not delegated to the United States by the Constitution, nor prohibited by it to the States, are reserved to the States respectively, or to the people." Consequently, the legislation Congress enacts must be based on a specific power the Constitution grants to the federal government or be reasonably necessary for carrying out an enumerated power.

Some governmental powers may be exercised only by the federal government. These exclusive federal powers include the power to establish laws regarding bankruptcy, to establish post offices, to grant patents and copyrights, to coin currency, to wage war, and to enter into treaties. Conversely, both the federal government and the states may exercise concurrent governmental powers, which include taxation, spending, and police power (regulation of public health, safety, and welfare).

In this part of the chapter, we will examine the sources and extent of the powers of the federal government—as well as the power of the states—to regulate business and commerce.

Federal Commerce Power

The U.S. Constitution provides that Congress has the power to regulate commerce with other nations and among the states. This commerce clause has two important effects: (1) it provides a broad source of **commerce power** for the federal government to regulate the economy, and (2) it restricts state regulations that obstruct or unduly burden interstate commerce.

Commerce power
exclusive power granted by the U.S. Constitution to the federal government to regulate commerce with foreign countries and among the states

The U.S. Supreme Court interprets the commerce clause as granting virtually complete power to Congress to regulate the economy and business. A court may invalidate legislation enacted under the commerce clause only if it is clear: (1) that the activity the legislation regulates does not affect interstate commerce or (2) that there is no reasonable connection between the selected regulatory means and the stated ends. For example, activities conducted solely within one state, such as the practice of law or real estate brokerage agreements, are subject to federal antitrust laws under the power granted by the commerce clause if those activities (1) substantially affect interstate commerce or (2) are in the flow of commerce.

Because of the broad and permissive interpretation of the commerce power, Congress currently regulates a vast range of activities. Many of the activities discussed in this text are regulated by the federal government through its exercise of the commerce power; such activities include federal crimes, consumer warranties and credit transactions, electronic funds transfers, trademarks, unfair trade practices, other consumer transactions, residential real estate transactions, consumer and employee safety, labor relations, civil rights in employment, transactions in securities, and environmental protection.

State Regulation of Commerce

The commerce clause, as we have previously discussed, specifically grants to Congress the power to regulate commerce among the states. In addition to acting as a broad source of federal power, the clause also implicitly restricts the states' power to regulate activities if the result obstructs or unduly burdens interstate commerce.

Regulations The Supreme Court ultimately decides the extent to which state regulation may affect interstate commerce. In doing so, the Court weighs and balances several factors: (1) the necessity and importance of the state regulation, (2) the burden it imposes on interstate commerce, and (3) the extent to which it discriminates against interstate commerce in favor of local concerns. The application of these factors involves case-by-case analysis. In general, where a state statute regulates evenhandedly to accomplish a legitimate state interest and its effects on interstate commerce are only incidental, the Court will uphold the statute unless the burden imposed on interstate commerce is excessive compared to the local benefits. The Court will uphold a discriminatory regulation only if no other reasonable method of achieving a legitimate local interest exists. *Chemical Waste Management, Inc. v. Hunt* illustrates the application of this test.

State regulation of commerce the commerce clause of the Constitution restricts the states' power to regulate activities if the result obstructs interstate commerce

---

CHEMICAL WASTE MANAGEMENT, INC. v. HUNT Supreme Court of the United States, 1992, 504 U.S. 334, 112 S.Ct. 2009, 119 L.Ed. 2d 121

FACTS Alabama law imposes a fee of $97.50 per ton for hazardous wastes generated outside the state and disposed of at a commercial facility in Alabama. The fee for hazardous wastes generated within Alabama is $25.60 per ton. Chemical Waste Management, Inc., which operates a commercial hazardous waste land disposal facility in Emelle, Alabama, filed suit requesting a declaratory judgment that the Alabama law violated the commerce clause of the U.S. Constitution. Alabama argued that the additional fee of $72.00 served a legitimate local purpose related to its citizens' health and safety, given recent large increases in the hazardous waste received into the state and the possible adverse effects of such waste. The trial court found the additional fee to be in violation of the U.S.

Constitution, but the Alabama Supreme Court reversed that decision.

DECISION Decision of the Alabama Supreme Court reversed.

OPINION No state may attempt to isolate itself from a problem common to the several states by raising barriers to the free flow of interstate trade. Alabama's additional fee discriminates on its face against hazardous wastes generated in states other than Alabama. Generally, a state law that taxes a transaction more heavily when it crosses state lines than when it occurs entirely within the state is immediately struck down. Alabama, however, asserts a legitimate purpose behind the additional fees. We have held that a presumably

continued

legitimate goal sought to be achieved by the illegitimate means of isolating the state from the national economy amounts to economic protectionism and is barred by the commerce clause. In such a case, the burden is on the state to show that the discrimination is demonstrably justified by a valid factor unrelated to economic protectionism. A state meets that burden by demonstrating that there are no less discriminatory alternatives available to alleviate the concern or that there is an inherent danger associated with the out-of-state goods that is not present in the in-state goods.

In this case, the state's concern focuses on the volume of the waste entering the Emelle facility. Less discriminatory alternatives, however, are available to

lessen this concern, including a generally applicable per-ton additional fee on all hazardous waste disposed of within Alabama, a per-mile tax on all vehicles transporting hazardous waste on Alabama roads, or an evenhanded cap on the total tonnage disposed of at Emelle. Furthermore, the record establishes that the hazardous waste at issue is the same regardless of the point of origin and that, therefore, waste originating outside the state poses no unique threat.

INTERPRETATION The U.S. Constitution permits states to discriminate against interstate commerce only if there is no other reasonable method of achieving a legitimate local interest.

Taxation The commerce clause, in conjunction with the import-export clause, also limits the power of the state to tax. The import-export clause provides: "No State shall, without the Consent of the Congress, lay any Imposts or Duties on Imports or Exports." U.S. CONST. art. I, § 10, cl. 2. Together, the commerce clause and the import-export clause exempt from state taxation goods that have entered the stream of commerce, whether they are interstate or foreign and whether they are imports or exports. The purpose of this immunity is to protect goods in commerce from both discriminatory and cumulative state taxes. Once the goods enter the stream of interstate or foreign commerce, the power of the state to tax ceases and does not resume until the goods are delivered to the purchaser or the owner terminates the movement of the goods through commerce.

The due process clause of the Fourteenth Amendment also restricts the power of states to tax. Under the due process clause, for a state tax to be constitutional, a sufficient nexus must exist between the state and the person, thing, or activity to be taxed.

Federal Fiscal Powers

The federal government exerts a dominating influence over the national economy through its control of financial matters. Much of this impact results from the exercise of its regulatory powers under the commerce clause, as previously discussed. In addition, the government derives a substantial portion of its influence from powers that are independent of the commerce clause. These include (1) the power to tax, (2) the power to spend, (3) the power to borrow and coin money, and (4) the power of eminent domain.

Taxation The federal government's power to tax, although extremely broad, has three major limitations: (1) direct taxes must be apportioned among the states, (2) all custom duties and excise taxes must be uniform throughout the United States, and (3) no duties may be levied on exports from any state.

Besides raising revenues, taxes also have regulatory and socioeconomic effects. For example, import taxes and custom duties can protect domestic industry from foreign competition. Graduated or progressive tax rates and exemptions may further social policies seeking the redistribution of wealth. Tax credits encourage investment in favored enterprises to the disadvantage of unfavored businesses. A tax that does more than just raise revenue will be upheld "so long as the motive of Congress and the effect of its legislative action are to secure revenue for the benefit of the general government. . . ."

Spending Power The Constitution authorizes the federal government to pay debts and to spend for the common defense and general welfare of the United States. Like the power to tax, the spending power of Congress is extremely broad; this power will be upheld so long as it does not violate a specific constitutional limitation on federal power.

Furthermore, through its spending power, Congress may accomplish indirectly what it may not do directly. For example, the Supreme Court has held that Congress may condition a state's receipt of federal highway funds on that state's mandating twenty-one as the minimum drinking age, even though the Twenty-first Amendment grants the states significant powers with respect to alcohol consumption within their respective borders. As the Court noted, "Constitutional limitations on Congress when exercising its spending power are less exacting than those on its authority to regulate directly." Whether directly or indirectly, the power of the federal government to spend money represents an important regulatory force in the economy and significantly affects the general welfare of the United States.

Borrowing and Coining Money The U.S. Constitution also grants Congress the power to borrow money on the credit of the United States and to coin money. These two powers have enabled the federal government to establish a national banking system, the Federal Reserve System, and specialized federal lending programs such as the Federal Land Bank. Through these and other institutions and agencies, the federal government wields extensive control over national fiscal and monetary policies and exerts considerable influence over interest rates, the money supply, and foreign exchange rates.

Eminent Domain The government's power to take private property for public use, known as the power of **eminent domain,** is recognized, in the federal Constitution and in the constitutions of the states, as one of the inherent powers of government. At the same time, however, the power is carefully limited. The Fifth Amendment to the federal Constitution contains a "takings clause" that provides that private property shall not be taken for public use without just compensation. Although this amendment applies only to the federal government, the Supreme Court has held that the takings clause is incorporated through the Fourteenth Amendment and is therefore applicable to the states. Moreover, similar or identical provisions are found in the constitutions of the states.

Eminent domain the power of a government to take private property for public use upon payment of fair compensation

As the language of the takings clause indicates, the taking must be for a public use. Public use has been held to be synonymous with public purpose. Thus, private entities, such as railroads and housing authorities, may utilize the government's power of eminent domain so long as the entity's use of the property benefits the public. When the government or a private entity properly takes property under the power of eminent domain, the owners of the property must receive just compensation, which has been interpreted as the fair market value of the property. Eminent domain is discussed further in Chapter 53.

Figure 4–2 summarizes the powers granted to the federal government, the states, and the people.

FIGURE 4–2 Powers of Government

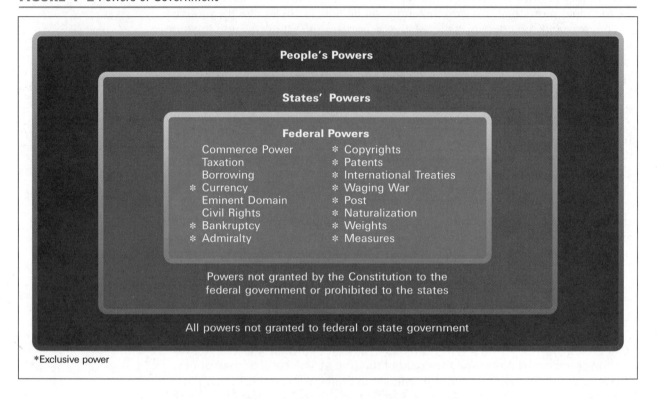

*Exclusive power

LIMITATIONS ON GOVERNMENT

As we have discussed, the U.S. Constitution grants certain specified powers to the federal government, while reserving other, unspecified powers to the states. The Constitution and its amendments, however, impose limits on the powers of both the federal government and the states. In this part of the chapter, we will discuss those limitations most applicable to business: (1) the contract clause, (2) the First Amendment, (3) due process, and (4) equal protection. The first of these—the contract clause—applies only to the actions of state governments, whereas the other three apply to both the federal government and the states.

None of these restrictions operates as an absolute limitation but instead triggers review or scrutiny by the courts to determine whether the governmental power exercised encroaches impermissibly upon the interest the Constitution protects. The U.S. Supreme Court has used different levels of scrutiny, depending on the interest affected and the nature of the governmental action. Although this differentiation among levels of scrutiny is most fully developed in the area of equal protection, it also occurs in other areas, including substantive due process and protection of free speech.

The least rigorous level of scrutiny is the **rational relationship test**, which requires that the regulation conceivably bear some rational relationship to a legitimate governmental interest that the regulation will attempt to further. The most exacting level of scrutiny is the **strict scrutiny test**, which requires that the regulation be necessary to promote a compelling governmental interest. Finally, under the **intermediate test**, the regulation must have a substantial

Rational relationship test requirement that regulation bear a rational relationship to a legitimate governmental interest

Strict scrutiny test requirement that regulation be necessary to promote a compelling governmental interest

Intermediate test requirement that regulation have a substantial relationship to an important governmental objective

relationship to an important governmental objective. These standards will be more fully explained below. Also see Figure 4–3.

Contract Clause

Article I, Section 10, of the Constitution provides: "No State shall . . . pass any . . . Law impairing the Obligation of Contracts. . . ." The Supreme Court has used the **contract clause** to restrict states from retroactively modifying public charters and private contracts. However, the Court, holding that the contract clause does *not* preclude the states from exercising eminent domain or their police powers, has ruled: "No legislature can bargain away the public health or the public morals." Although the contract clause does not apply to the federal government, due process limits the federal government's power to impair contracts.

Contract clause prohibition against the states' retroactively modifying public and private contracts

First Amendment

The First Amendment states:

> Congress shall make no law respecting an establishment of religion, or prohibiting the free exercise thereof; or abridging the freedom of speech, or of the press; or the right of the people peaceably to assemble, and to petition the Government for a redress of grievances.

The First Amendment's protection of **free speech** is not absolute. Some forms of speech, such as obscenity, receive no protection. Most forms of speech, however, are protected by the strict or exacting scrutiny standard, which requires the existence of a compelling and legitimate state interest to justify a restriction of speech. If such an interest exists, the legislature must use means that least restrict free speech. We will examine the application of the First Amendment's guarantee of free speech to (1) corporate political speech, (2) commercial speech, and (3) defamation.

Freedom of speech First Amendment protects most speech by utilizing a strict scrutiny standard

Corporate Political Speech Freedom of speech is indispensable to the discovery and spread of political truth; indeed, "the best test of truth is the power of the thought to get itself accepted in the competition of the market." To promote this competition of ideas, the First Amendment's guarantee of free speech applies not only to individuals but also to corporations. Accordingly, corporations may not be prohibited from speaking out on political issues. For example, the Supreme Court has held unconstitutional a Massachusetts criminal statute that prohibited banks and business corporations from making contributions and expenditures with regard to most referenda issues. The Court held that if speech is otherwise protected, the fact that the speaker is a corporation does not alter the speech's protected status.

Corporate political speech First Amendment protects a corporation's right to speak out on political issues

FIGURE 4–3 Limitations on Government

Term/Interest	Equal Protection	Substantive Due Process	Free Speech
Strict Scrutiny	Fundamental Rights Suspect Classifications	Fundamental Rights	Protected Noncommercial Speech
Intermediate	Gender Legitimacy		Commercial Speech
Rational Relationship	Economic Regulation	Economic Regulation	Nonprotected Speech

The Supreme Court retreated somewhat from this holding when it upheld a state statute prohibiting corporations, except media corporations, from using general treasury funds to make independent expenditures in elections for public office but permitting such expenditures from segregated funds used solely for political purposes. The Court held that the statute did not violate the First Amendment because the burden on corporations' exercise of political expression was justified by a compelling state interest in preventing corruption in the political arena: "the corrosive and distorting effects of immense aggregations of wealth that are accumulated with the help of the corporate form and that have little or no correlation to the public's support for the corporation's political ideas." The Court held that the statute was sufficiently narrowly tailored because it "is precisely targeted to eliminate the distortion caused by corporate spending while also allowing corporations to express their political views" by making expenditures through segregated funds.

Commercial speech
expression related to the economic interests of the speaker and his audience

Commercial Speech **Commercial speech** is expression related to the economic interests of the speaker and his audience, such as advertisements for a product or service. Since the mid-1970s, U.S. Supreme Court decisions have eliminated the doctrine that commercial speech is wholly outside the protection of the First Amendment. Rather, the Court has established the principle that speech proposing a commercial transaction is entitled to protection, which, although less than that accorded political speech, is still extensive. Protection is accorded commercial speech because of the interest such communication holds for the advertiser, consumer, and general public. Advertising and other similar messages convey important information for the proper and efficient distribution of resources in our free market system. At the same time, however, commercial speech is less valuable and less vulnerable than other varieties of speech and therefore does not merit complete First Amendment protection.

In cases determining the protection to be afforded commercial speech, a four-part analysis has developed. First, the court must determine whether the expression is protected by the First Amendment. For commercial speech to come within that provision, such speech, at the least, must concern lawful activity and not be misleading. Second, the court must determine whether the asserted governmental interest is substantial. If both inquiries yield positive answers, then, third, the court must determine whether the regulation directly advances the governmental interest asserted and, fourth, whether the regulation is not more extensive than is necessary to serve that interest. The Supreme Court recently held that governmental restrictions of commercial speech need not be absolutely the least severe so long as they are "narrowly tailored" to achieve the governmental objective.

Because the constitutional protection extended to commercial speech is based on the informational function of advertising, governments may regulate or suppress commercial messages that do not accurately inform the public about lawful activity. "The government may ban forms of communication more likely to deceive the public than to inform it, or commercial speech related to illegal activity." Therefore, governmental regulation of false and misleading advertising is permissible under the First Amendment.

RUBIN v. COORS BREWING COMPANY Supreme Court of the United States, 1995, 514 U.S. 476, 115 S.Ct. 1585, 131 L.Ed.2d 532

FACTS Coors Brewing Company brews beer. In 1987, in response to rumors that its beer was lower in alcohol content than that of other brands, Coors applied to the Bureau of Alcohol Tobacco and Firearms (BATF) for approval of proposed labels and advertisements that disclosed the alcohol content of its beer. Pursuant to a regulation promulgated under the Federal Alcohol Administration Act (FAAA) prohibiting statements of alcohol content in advertising or labeling unless required by state law, BATF rejected the application. Coors sued for a declaratory judgment that the regulation violated the First Amendment. The district court granted relief but the Court of Appeals reversed and remanded the case for the district court to determine whether the regulation directly advanced a substantial federal interest. The district court upheld the ban on advertising but invalidated the ban on labels. The government appealed the invalidation of the labeling ban and the Court of Appeals affirmed the district court.

DECISION Judgment affirmed.

OPINION Commercial speech has been held protected by the First Amendment subject to certain types of restrictions. Whether commercial speech will come within the protection of the First Amendment depends on several factors, which were set out in *Central Hudson Gas & Electric Corp. v. Public Serv. Comm'n of N.Y.* First, the statement must at least concern lawful activity and not be misleading. Second, the court must determine whether the governmental interest in regulating the speech is substantial. Finally, if the first two inquiries are answered affirmatively, the court must determine whether the regulation directly advances the governmental interest asserted and whether it is not more extensive than is necessary to serve that interest. Both parties agree that Coors seeks to disclose only truthful, verifiable, and nonmisleading factual information about the alcohol content of its beer. The government contends that it has a substantial interest in curbing "strength wars" between competing brewing companies. According to the government, the FAAA's restriction prevents a particular type of beer drinker—one who selects a beverage because of its high potency—from choosing beers solely for their alcohol content, which could lead to greater alcoholism and its attendant social costs. The

remaining *Central Hudson* factors consider the "fit" between the legislature's intended ends and the means chosen to accomplish those ends. The government's burden on this point is not satisfied by mere speculation and conjecture; rather, a governmental body seeking to sustain a restriction on commercial speech must demonstrate that the harms it recites are real and that its restriction will in fact alleviate the harms to a material degree. The BATF regulation in this case fails to advance the government's interest in preventing strength wars because of the overall irrationality of the government's regulatory scheme. First, while the laws governing labeling prohibit the disclosure of alcohol content unless required by state law, federal regulations apply a contrary policy to beer advertising. Restrictions on statements of alcohol content in beer advertising are prohibited only if the state affirmatively prohibits such advertising. Since only eighteen states have such prohibitions, brewing companies are free to advertise their beer's alcohol content in most states. Second, although this regulation bans the disclosure of alcohol content on beer labels, it allows the exact opposite in the case of wines and spirits. In fact, disclosures of alcohol content are required for wines with more than 14 percent alcohol. Furthermore, the regulation is not the least intrusive method that the government could have employed to achieve its goal. It could have directly limited alcohol content of beer, prohibited marketing efforts emphasizing high alcohol strength, or limited the labeling ban to malt liquors, which is the market segment allegedly threatened with a strength war. In sum, although the government may have a substantial interest in suppressing strength wars in the beer market, the FAAA's countervailing provisions prevent this regulation from furthering that purpose in a direct and material fashion. Moreover, there are less intrusive alternatives. Therefore, since the BATF regulation fails the *Central Hudson* test, it violates the First Amendment's protection of commercial speech.

INTERPRETATION Governmental regulation of nonmisleading commercial speech concerning lawful activity is permitted if the regulation directly advances a substantial governmental interest and the regulation is no more extensive than necessary.

Defamation **Defamation** is a civil wrong or tort that consists of disgracing or diminishing a person's reputation through the communication of a false statement. An example would be the publication of a statement that a person had committed a crime or had a loathsome disease. (Defamation is also discussed in Chapter 7.)

Defamation *(def·a·ma'·tion)* injury of a person's reputation by communication of false statements

ETHICAL DILEMMA Who Is Responsible for Commercial Speech?

FACTS Jane Stewart is an assistant manager of advertising for *Dazzling Magazine*, a fashion magazine aimed primarily at women between the ages of 25 and 35. Offering regular columns on health, beauty, fashion, and current events, the magazine has a small circulation and handles its advertising internally.

Having experienced declining sales in recent years, the magazine has downsized its operations by eliminating jobs and implementing cost-cutting measures. To prevent further declines in revenue, *Dazzling*'s marketing and editorial staffs are attempting to expand the magazine's appeal to include younger audiences between the ages of 16 and 24. Jane is in charge of making recommendations to the advertising manager with regard to new advertisements. The advertising manager, in turn, makes

the final recommendation to the head of the advertising department. Because of the magazine's overall decline in sales, the advertising unit has come under increased pressure to generate revenue from advertisements. Compensation of advertising unit employees is based in part on the earning of "bonus points" related to first-year revenues from new clients.

Jane has received advertisement offers from two cigarette companies and from one swimsuit manufacturer. Although the cigarette advertisements would generate twice as much revenue as the swimsuit advertisement, Jane is concerned that the cigarette advertisements would allure young women to smoke. She has recommended to her supervisor, Agnes Scott, that the cigarette advertisements be rejected. Scott adamantly

disagrees. She strongly recommends to the head of the advertising department that the cigarette advertisements be accepted.

Social, Policy, and Ethical Considerations

1. What should Jane do? What is best for (a) her company and (b) society? Should Jane raise her concerns to the department head?

2. Identify the competing social values at stake with regard to cigarette advertising. What role should the government play in regulating speech that promotes products such as tobacco and alcohol?

3. Should the age of *Dazzling*'s prospective audience influence the choice of advertisements? Explain.

Because defamation involves a communication, it receives the protection extended to speech by the First Amendment. Moreover, the Supreme Court has ruled that a public official who is defamed in regard to his conduct, fitness, or role as public official may *not* recover in a defamation action unless the statement was made with *actual malice*, which requires clear and convincing proof that the defendant had knowledge of the falsity of the communication or acted in reckless disregard of its truth or falsity. This restriction on the right to recover for defamation is based on "a profound national commitment to the principle that debate on public issues should be uninhibited, robust and wide-open, and that it may well include vehement, caustic, and sometimes unpleasantly sharp attacks on government and public officials." The communication may deal with the official's qualifications for and performance in office, which would likely include most aspects of character and public conduct. In addition, the Supreme Court has extended the same rule to public figures and candidates for public office. (The Court, however, has not precisely defined the term *public figure*.)

In a defamation suit brought by a private person (one who is neither a public official nor a public figure) against a member of the news media, the plaintiff must prove that the defendant published the defamatory and false comment with malice *or* negligence. In contrast, when a private person brings suit against a defendant who is *not* a member of the news media, it is currently unresolved whether the plaintiff must prove anything beyond the fact that a defamatory and false statement has been made.

Due Process

The Fifth and Fourteenth Amendments prohibit the federal and state governments, respectively, from depriving any person of life, liberty, or property without **due process** of law. Due process has two different aspects: *substantive* and *procedural*. As we discussed in Chapter 1, substantive law creates, defines, or regulates legal rights, whereas procedural law establishes the rules for enforcing those rights. Accordingly, **substantive due process** concerns the compatibility of a law or governmental action with fundamental constitutional rights such as free speech. In contrast, **procedural due process** involves the review of the decision-making process that enforces substantive laws and results in depriving a person of life, liberty, or property.

Substantive Due Process   Substantive due process, which involves a court's determination of whether a particular governmental action is compatible with individual liberties, addresses the constitutionality of a legal rule, not the fairness of the process by which the rule is applied. Legislation affecting economic and social interests satisfies substantive due process so long as the legislation is rationally related to legitimate governmental objectives. Where a rule affects individuals' fundamental rights under the Constitution, however, the Court will carefully scrutinize the legislation to determine if it is necessary to promote a compelling or overriding state interest.

Procedural Due Process   Procedural due process pertains to the governmental decision-making process that results in depriving a person of life, liberty, or property. As the Supreme Court has interpreted procedural due process, the government is required to provide an individual with a fair procedure if, but only if, the person faces deprivation of life, liberty, or property. When governmental action adversely affects an individual but does not deny life, liberty, or property, the government is not required to give the person any hearing at all.

For the purposes of procedural due process, **liberty** generally includes the ability of individuals to engage in freedom of action and choice regarding their personal lives. **Property** includes not only all forms of real and personal property but also certain benefits (entitlements) conferred by the government, such as social security payments and food stamps.

When applicable, procedural due process requires that a court utilize a fair and impartial procedure in resolving the factual and legal basis for a governmental action that results in a deprivation of life, liberty, or property.

Equal Protection

The Fourteenth Amendment provides that "nor shall any State . . . deny to any person within its jurisdiction the equal protection of the laws." Although this amendment applies only to the actions of state governments, the Supreme Court has interpreted the due process clause of the Fifth Amendment to subject federal actions to the same standards of review. The most important constitutional concept protecting individual rights, the guarantee of **equal protection** basically requires that similarly situated persons be treated similarly by governmental actions.

When governmental action involves classification of people, the equal protection guarantee comes into play. In determining whether governmental action satisfies the equal protection guarantee, the Supreme Court uses one of three standards of review, depending on the nature of the right involved. The three standards are (1) the rational relationship test, (2) the strict scrutiny test, and (3) the intermediate test.

Due process Fifth and Fourteenth Amendments prohibit the federal and state governments from depriving any person of life, liberty, or property without due process of law

Substantive due process requirement that governmental action be compatible with individual liberties

Procedural due process requirement that governmental action depriving a person of life, liberty, or property be done through a fair procedure

Liberty ability of individuals to engage in freedom of action and choice regarding their personal lives

Property includes real property, personal property, and certain benefits conferred by government

Equal protection requirement that similarly situated persons be treated similarly by government action

Rational relationship test a standard of review used to determine whether economic regulation satisfies the equal protection guarantee

Rational Relationship Test

The rational relationship test, which applies to economic regulation, simply requires that the classification *conceivably* bear some rational relationship to a legitimate governmental interest the classification seeks to further. Under this standard of review, the governmental action is permitted to attack part of the evil to which the action is addressed. Moreover, there is a strong presumption that the action is constitutional. Therefore, the courts will overturn the governmental action *only* if clear and convincing evidence shows that there is *no* reasonable basis justifying the action.

Strict scrutiny test exacting standard of review applicable to regulation affecting a fundamental right or involving a suspect classification

Strict Scrutiny Test

The strict scrutiny test is far more exacting than the rational relationship test. Under this test, the courts do not defer to the government; rather, they independently determine whether a classification of persons is constitutionally permissible. This determination requires that the classification be necessary to promote a compelling or overriding governmental interest.

The strict scrutiny test is applied when governmental action affects fundamental rights or involves suspect classifications. Fundamental rights include most of the provisions of the Bill of Rights and certain other rights, such as interstate travel, voting, and access to criminal justice. Suspect classifications include those made on the basis of race or national origin. A classic and important example of strict scrutiny applied to classifications based upon race is found in the 1954 school desegregation case of *Brown v. Board of Education of Topeka*, in which the Supreme Court ruled that segregated public school systems violated the equal protection guarantee. Subsequently, the Court has invalidated segregation in public beaches, municipal golf courses, buses, parks, public golf courses, and courtroom seating.

BROWN v. BOARD OF EDUCATION OF TOPEKA Supreme Court of the United States, 1954, 347 U.S. 483, 74 S.Ct. 686, 98 L.Ed. 873

FACTS These were consolidated cases from Kansas, South Carolina, Virginia, and Delaware, each with a different set of facts and local conditions but also presenting a common legal question. Black minors, through their legal representatives, sought court orders to obtain admission to the public schools in their community on a nonsegregated basis. They had been denied admission to schools attended by white children under laws requiring or permitting segregation according to race. The Supreme Court had previously upheld such laws under the "separate but equal" doctrine, which provided that there was equality of treatment of the races through substantially equal, though separate, facilities; and the lower courts had found that the white schools and the black schools involved had been or were being equalized with respect to buildings, curricula, qualifications and salaries of teachers, and other "tangible" factors. The black minors contended, however, that segregated public schools were not and could not be made "equal," and that hence they had been deprived of the equal protection of the laws guaranteed by the Fourteenth Amendment.

DECISION Judgment for plaintiffs.

OPINION Segregation of children in public schools solely on the basis of race generates a feeling of inferiority that diminishes their motivation to learn and affects "their hearts and minds in a way unlikely ever to be undone." Though the physical facilities and other "tangible" factors may be equal, segregation of the races with the sanction of law retards the educational and mental development of black children and deprives them of equal educational opportunities. Since separate educational facilities are inherently unequal, the "separate but equal" doctrine has no place in the field of public education. Therefore, segregation denies the black children the equal protection of the laws guaranteed by the Fourteenth Amendment.

INTERPRETATION When a governmentally imposed classification involves fundamental rights or suspect classifications, equal protection requires the classification to be necessary to promote a compelling or overriding governmental interest.

Another important example of strict scrutiny is the "one person, one vote" rule based upon the fundamental right to vote. Chief Justice Warren formulated the rule as follows:

> Legislators represent people, not trees or acres. . . . And, if a State should provide that the votes of citizens in one part of the State should be given two times, or five times, or ten times the weight of votes of citizens in another part of the State, it could hardly be contended that the right to vote of those residing in the disfavored areas had not been effectively diluted . . . [T]he Equal Protection Clause requires that the seats in both houses of a bicameral state legislature must be apportioned on a population basis.

Intermediate Test An intermediate test has been applied to governmental action based on gender and legitimacy. Under this test, the classification must have a substantial relationship to an important governmental objective. The intermediate standard eliminates the strong presumption of constitutionality to which the rational relationship test adheres. For example, the Court invalidated an Alabama law that allowed courts to grant alimony awards only from husbands to wives and not from wives to husbands. Similarly, where an Idaho statute gave preference to males over females in qualifying for selection as administrators of estates, the Court invalidated the statute because the preference did not bear a fair and substantial relationship to any legitimate legislative objective. On the other hand, not all legislation based upon gender is invalid. For example, the Court has upheld a California statutory rape law which imposed penalties only upon males, as well as the federal military selective service act, which exempted women from registering for the draft.

Intermediate test standard of review applicable to regulation based on gender and legitimacy

CHAPTER SUMMARY

Basic Principles	**Federalism** the division of governing power between the federal government and the states
	Federal Supremacy federal law takes precedence over conflicting state law
	Federal Preemption right of federal government to regulate matters within its power to the exclusion of regulation by the states
	Judicial Review examination of governmental actions to determine whether they conform to the U.S. Constitution
	Separation of Powers allocation of powers among executive, legislative, and judicial branches of government
	State Action actions of governments to which constitutional provisions apply

Powers of Government	**Federal Commerce Power** exclusive power of federal government to regulate commerce with other nations and among the states
	State Regulation of Commerce the commerce clause of the Constitution restricts the states' power to regulate activities if the result obstructs interstate commerce
	Federal Fiscal Powers
	■ *Taxation and Spending* the Constitution grants Congress broad powers to tax and spend; such powers are important to federal government regulation of the economy
	■ *Borrowing and Coining Money* enables the federal government to establish a national banking system and to control national fiscal and monetary policy
	■ *Eminent Domain* the government's power to take private property for public use with the payment of just compensation

Limitations on Government	**Contract Clause** restricts states from retroactively modifying contracts
	Freedom of Speech First Amendment protects most speech by utilizing a strict scrutiny standard
	■ *Corporate Political Speech* First Amendment protects a corporation's right to speak out on political issues
	■ *Commercial Speech* expression related to the economic interests of the speaker and its audience; such expression receives a lesser degree of protection
	■ *Defamation* a tort consisting of a false communication that injures a person's reputation; such a communication receives limited constitutional protection
	Due Process Fifth and Fourteenth Amendments prohibit the federal and state governments from depriving any person of life, liberty, or property without due process of law
	■ *Substantive Due Process* determination of whether a particular governmental action is compatible with individual liberties
	■ *Procedural Due Process* requires the governmental decision-making process to be fair and impartial if it deprives a person of life, liberty, or property
	Equal Protection requires that similarly situated persons be treated similarly by governmental actions
	■ *Rational Relationship Test* a standard of review used to determine whether economic regulation satisfies the equal protection guarantee
	■ *Strict Scrutiny Test* exacting standard of review applicable to regulation affecting a fundamental right or involving a suspect classification
	■ *Intermediate Test* standard of review applicable to regulation based on gender and legitimacy

QUESTIONS

1. List and distinguish the basic principles of constitutional law.
2. Explain the two effects of the commerce clause.
3. Distinguish the three levels of scrutiny used by the courts to determine the constitutionality of governmental action.
4. Explain the effect of the First Amendment upon (a) commercial speech and (b) defamation.

5. Explain the difference between substantive and procedural due process.

Internet Question. Find your state's constitution and compare its protection of individual rights with that of the U.S. Constitution. (If your state is not available, choose another state.)

PROBLEMS

1. In May, Patricia Allen left her automobile on the shoulder of a road in the city of Erewhon after the car stopped running. A member of the Erewhon city police department found the car later that day and placed on it a sticker stating that unless the car were moved, it would be towed. When after a week the car had not been removed, the police department authorized Baldwin Auto Wrecking Co. to tow it away and to store it on its property. Allen was told by a friend that her car was at Baldwin's. Allen asked Baldwin to allow her to take possession of her car, but Baldwin refused to relinquish the car until the $70 towing fee was paid. Allen could not afford to pay the fee, and the car remained at Baldwin's for six weeks. At that time, Baldwin requested the police department for a permit to dispose of the automobile. After the police department tried unsuccessfully to telephone Allen, the department issued the permit. In late July, Baldwin destroyed the automobile. Allen brings an action against the city and Baldwin for damages for loss of the vehicle, arguing that she was denied due process. Decision?

2. In 1967, large oil reserves were discovered in the Prudhoe Bay area of Alaska. As a result, state revenues increased from $124 million in 1969 to $3.7 billion in 1981. In 1980, the state legislature enacted a dividend program that would distribute annually a portion of these earnings to the state's adult residents. Under the plan, each citizen eighteen years of age or older receives one unit for each year of residency subsequent to 1959, the year Alaska became a state. The state advanced three purposes justifying the distinctions made by the dividend program: (a) creation of a financial incentive for individuals to establish and maintain residence in Alaska; (b) encouragement of prudent management of the earnings; and (c) apportionment of benefits in recognition of undefined "contributions of various kinds, both tangible and intangible, which residents have made during their years of residency." Crawford, a resident since 1978, brings suit challenging the dividend distribution plan as violative of the equal protection guarantee. Decision?

3. Maryland enacted a statute prohibiting any producer or refiner of petroleum products from operating retail service stations within the state. The statute also required that any producer or refiner discontinue operating its company-owned retail service stations. Approximately 3,800 retail service stations in Maryland sell over twenty different brands of gasoline. No petroleum products are produced or refined in Maryland, however, and only 5 percent of the total number of retailers are operated by a producer or refiner. Maryland enacted the statute because a survey conducted by the state comptroller indicated that gasoline stations operated by producers or refiners had received preferential treatment during periods of gasoline shortage. Seven major producers and refiners brought an action challenging the statute on the ground that it discriminated against interstate commerce in violation of the commerce clause of the U.S. Constitution. Decision?

4. The Federal Aviation Act of 1958 provides that "The United States of America is declared to possess and exercise complete and exclusive national sovereignty in the airspace of the United States." The city of Orion adopted an ordinance that makes it unlawful for jet aircraft to take off from its airport between 11 P.M. of one day and 7 A.M. of the next day. Jordan Airlines, Inc., is adversely affected by this ordinance and brings suit challenging it under the supremacy clause of the U.S. Constitution. Decision?

5. The Public Service Commission of State X issued a regulation completely banning all advertising that "promotes the use of electricity" by any electric utility company in State X. The commission issued the regulation in order to conserve energy. Central Electric Corporation of State X challenges the order in the state courts, arguing that the commission had restrained commercial speech in violation of the First Amendment. Decision?

6. E-Z-Rest Motel is a motel with 216 rooms located in the center of a large city in State Y. It is readily accessible from two interstate highways and three major state highways. The motel solicits patronage from outside State Y through various national advertising media, including magazines of national circulation. It accepts convention trade from outside State Y, and approximately 75 percent of its registered guests are from out of State Y. An action under the Federal Civil Rights Act of 1964 has been brought against E-Z-Rest Motel alleging that the motel discriminates on the basis of race and color. The motel contends that the statute cannot be applied to it because it is not engaged in interstate commerce. Decision?

7. State Z enacted a Private Pension Benefits Protection Act requiring private employers with 100 or more employees to pay a pension funding charge for terminating a pension plan or closing an office in State Z. Acme Steel Company closed its offices in State Z, whereupon the state assessed the company $185,000 under the vesting provisions of the act. Acme challenged the constitutionality of the act under the contract clause (Article I, Section 10) of the U.S. Constitution. Decision?

8. A state statute empowered public school principals to suspend students for up to ten days without any notice or hearing. A student who was suspended for ten days challenges the constitutionality of his suspension on the grounds that he was denied due process. Decision?

9. Iowa enacted a statute prohibiting the use of sixty-five-foot double trailer truck combinations. All of the other midwestern and western states permit such trucks to be used on their roads. Consolidated Freightways is adversely affected by this statute and brings suit against Iowa, alleging that the statute violates the commerce clause. Decision?

10. Metropolitan Edison Company is a privately owned and operated Pennsylvania corporation subject to extensive regulation by the Pennsylvania Public Utility Commission. Under a provision of its general tariff filed with the commission, Edison had the right to discontinue electric service to any customer on reasonable notice of nonpayment of bills. Catherine Jackson had been receiving electricity from Metropolitan Edison when her account was terminated in 1970 because of her delinquency in payments. Edison later opened a new account for her residence in the name of James Dodson, another occupant of Jackson's residence. In August 1971, Dodson moved away and no further payments were made to the account. Finally, in October 1971, Edison disconnected Jackson's service without any prior notice. Jackson brought suit claiming that her electric service could not be terminated without notice and a hearing. She further argued that such action, allowed by a provision of Edison's tariff filed with the commission, constituted "state action" depriving her of property in violation of the Fourteenth Amendment's guarantee of due process of law. Decision?

11. The McClungs own Ollie's Barbecue, a restaurant located a few blocks from the interstate highway in Birmingham, Alabama, with dining accommodations for whites only and a take-out service for blacks. In the year preceding the passage of the Civil Rights Act of 1964, the restaurant had purchased a substantial portion of the food it served from outside the state. The restaurant has refused to serve blacks since its original opening in 1927 and asserts that if it were required to serve blacks it would lose much of its business. The McClungs sought a declaratory judgment to render unconstitutional the application of the Civil Rights Act to their restaurant since their admitted racial discrimination did not restrict or significantly impede interstate commerce. Decision?

12. In the fall of 1971, Miss Horowitz was admitted as an advanced medical student at the University of Missouri-Kansas City. During the spring of 1972, several faculty members expressed dissatisfaction with Miss Horowitz's clinical performance, noting that it was below that of her peers, that she was erratic in attendance at her clinical sessions, and that she lacked a critical concern for personal hygiene. Upon the recommendation of the school's Council on Evaluation, she was advanced to her second and final year on a probationary basis. After subsequent unfavorable reviews during her second year and a negative evaluation of her performance by seven practicing physicians, the council recommended that Miss Horowitz be dismissed from the school for her failure to meet academic standards. The decision was approved by the dean and later affirmed by the provost after an appeal by Miss Horowitz. She brought suit against the school's Board of Curators, claiming that her dismissal violated her right to procedural due process under the Fourteenth Amendment and deprived her of "liberty" by substantially impairing her opportunities to continue her medical education or return to employment in a medically related field. The trial court found for the defendant, but the appellate court reversed. The Board of Curators appealed. Decision?

Administrative Law

Administrative law is the branch of public law that is created by administrative agencies in the form of rules, regulations, orders, and decisions, to carry out the regulatory powers and duties of those agencies. **Administrative agencies** are governmental entities—other than courts and legislatures—having authority to affect the rights of private parties through their operations. Administrative agencies, referred to by names such as commission, board, department, agency, administration, government corporation, bureau, or office, regulate a vast array of important matters involving national safety, welfare, and convenience. For instance, federal administrative agencies are charged with responsibility for national security, citizenship and naturalization, law enforcement, taxation, currency, elections, environmental protection, consumer protection, regulation of transportation, telecommunications, labor relations, trade, commerce, and securities markets, as well as providing health and social services.

Administrative agency
governmental entity (other than a court or legislature) having authority to affect the rights of private parties

Because of the increasing complexity of the social, economic, and industrial life of the nation, the scope of administrative law has expanded enormously. In 1952, Justice Jackson observed that "the rise of administrative bodies has been the most significant legal trend of the last century, and perhaps more values today are affected by their decisions than by those of all the courts, review of administrative decisions apart." This observation is even more true today, as evidenced by the great increase in the number and activities of federal government boards, commissions, and other agencies. Certainly, agencies create more legal rules and adjudicate more controversies than all the nation's legislatures and courts combined.

State agencies also play a significant role in the functioning of our society. Among the more important state boards and commissions are those that supervise and regulate banking, insurance, communications, transportation, public utilities, pollution control, and workers' compensation.

Much of the federal, state, and local law in this country is established by countless administrative agencies. These agencies, which many label the "fourth branch of government," possess tremendous power and have long been criticized as being "in reality miniature independent governments . . . [which are] a haphazard deposit of irresponsible agencies. . . ." 1937 Presidential Task Force Report.

Despite such criticism, these administrative entities clearly play a significant and necessary role in our society. Administrative agencies relieve legislatures from the impossible burden of fashioning legislation that deals with every detail of a specific problem. As a result, Congress can enact legislation, such as the Federal Trade Commission Act, which prohibits unfair and deceptive trade practices, without having to define such a phrase specifically or to anticipate all the particular problems that may arise. Instead, Congress may pass an *enabling statute* that creates an agency—in this example, the Federal Trade Commission—to which it can delegate the power to issue rules, regulations, and guidelines to carry out the statutory mandate. In addition, the establishment of separate, specialized bodies enables administrative agencies to be staffed by individuals with expertise in the field being regulated. Administrative agencies can thus develop the knowledge and devote the time necessary to provide continuous and flexible solutions to evolving regulatory problems.

In this chapter, we will discuss federal administrative agencies. Such agencies can be classified as either independent or executive. Executive agencies are those housed within the executive branch of government, while independent agencies are not. Many federal agencies are discussed in other parts of the text. More specifically, the Federal Trade Commission (FTC) and Department of Justice are discussed in Chapter 44; the FTC and the Consumer Product Safety Commission in Chapter 46; the Department of Labor, National Labor Relations Board (NLRB), and Equal Employment Opportunity Commission (EEOC) in Chapter 43; the Securities and Exchange Commission (SEC) in Chapters 42 and 45; and the Environmental Protection Agency (EPA) in Chapter 47.

OPERATION OF ADMINISTRATIVE AGENCIES

Administrative process
entire set of activities engaged in by administrative agencies while carrying out their rulemaking, enforcement, and adjudicative functions

Most administrative agencies perform three basic functions: (1) rulemaking, (2) law enforcement, and (3) adjudication of controversies. The term **administrative process** refers to the entire set of activities in which administrative agencies engage while carrying out these functions. Administrative agencies exercise powers that have been allocated by the Constitution to the three separate branches of government. More specifically, an agency exercises legislative power when it makes rules, executive power when it enforces its enabling statute and its rules, and judicial power when it adjudicates disputes. This concentration of power has raised questions regarding the propriety of having the same bodies that establish the rules also act as prosecutors and judges in determining whether those rules have been violated. To address this issue and to bring about certain additional procedural reforms, the Administrative Procedure Act (APA) was enacted in 1946.

Rulemaking

Rulemaking process by which an administrative agency promulgates rules of law

Rulemaking is the process by which an administrative agency enacts or promulgates rules of law. Under the APA, a **rule** is "the whole or a part of an agency statement of general or particular applicability and future effect designed to implement, interpret, or process law or policy." Once promulgated, rules are applicable to all parties. Moreover, the process of rulemaking notifies all parties that the impending rule is being considered and provides concerned individuals with an opportunity to be heard. Administrative agencies promulgate three types of rules: legislative rules, interpretative rules, and procedural rules.

Rule agency statement of general or particular applicability designed to implement, interpret, or process law or policy

Legislative Rules Legislative rules, often called regulations, are in effect "administrative statutes." **Legislative rules** are those issued by an agency having the ability, under a legislative delegation of power, to make rules having the force and effect of law. For example, the FTC has rulemaking power with which to elaborate upon its enabling statute's prohibition of unfair or deceptive acts or practices.

Legislative rules
substantive rules issued by an administrative agency under the authority delegated to it by the legislature

Legislative rules have the force of law if they are constitutional, within the power granted to the agency by the legislature, and issued according to proper procedure. To be constitutional, regulations must not violate any provisions of the U.S. Constitution, such as due process or equal protection. In addition, they may not involve an unconstitutional delegation of legislative power from the legislature to the agency. To be constitutionally permissible, the enabling statute granting power to an agency must establish reasonable standards to guide the agency in implementing the statute. This requirement has been met by statutory language such as "to prohibit unfair methods of competition," "fair and equitable," "public interest, convenience, and necessity," and other equally broad expressions. In any event, agencies may not exceed the actual authority granted by the enabling statute.

FCC v. MIDWEST VIDEO CORP. Supreme Court of the United States, 1979, 440 U.S. 689, 99 S.Ct. 1435, 59 L.Ed.2d 692

FACTS In May 1976, the Federal Communications Commission issued rules requiring cable television systems of a designated size (1) to develop a minimum 20-channel capacity by 1986, (2) to make available on a first-come, nondiscriminatory basis certain channels for access by third parties, and (3) to furnish equipment and facilities for such access. The purpose of these rules was to ensure public access to cable systems. Midwest Video Corporation claimed that the access rules exceeded the Commission's jurisdiction granted it by the Communications Act of 1934, because the rules infringe upon the cable systems' journalistic freedom by in effect treating the cable operators as "common carriers." A common carrier is one that "makes a public offering to provide [communication facilities] whereby all members of the public who choose to employ such facilities may communicate or transmit. . . ." The Commission contended that its expansive mandate under the Communications Act to supervise and regulate broadcasting encompassed the access rules since they were intended to promote these broad objectives.

DECISION Judgment for Midwest Video.

OPINION The Commission has the authority to issue rules to promote its long-established regulatory goals of increasing the number of outlets for local expression and diversifying programming. However, under the Communications Act of 1934 the Commission may not impose common carrier obligations on cable operators. This prohibition reflects a Congressional belief that the resulting intrusion upon the journalistic integrity of broadcasters would overshadow any benefits associated with increased public access. Since the access rules require cable operators to accept on a first-come, nondiscriminatory basis those members of the general public who wish to use the system, the operators become essentially common carriers and their editorial freedom to control the content of programming is lost. The authority to compel cable operators to provide this type of public access must come specifically from Congress. Thus, the FCC's access rules went beyond the boundaries of its jurisdiction granted by the Communications Act of 1934 and are, therefore, set aside.

INTERPRETATION To be valid, legislative rules must not exceed the actual authority granted to the agency by the enabling statute.

Legislative rules must be promulgated in accordance with the procedural requirements of the APA, although the enabling statute may impose more stringent requirements. Most legislative rules are issued in accordance with the *informal rulemaking* procedures of the APA, which require that the agency provide the following:

1. Prior notice of a proposed rule, usually by publication in the Federal Register
2. An opportunity for interested parties to participate in the rulemaking
3. Publication of a final draft containing a concise general statement of the rule's basis and purpose at least thirty days before its effective date

TENNESSEE GAS PIPELINE COMPANY v. FEDERAL ENERGY REGULATORY COMMISSION United States Court of Appeals, D.C. Circuit, 1992, 969 F.2d 1141

FACTS Pursuant to the Natural Gas Act of 1978, the Federal Energy Regulatory Commission's (FERC) regulations permit a natural gas pipeline company to replace existing facilities without prior authorization and provide automatic authorization for companies to construct facilities for the transportation of natural gas. On August 2, 1990, the FERC issued an interim rule requiring interstate natural gas pipelines to provide the FERC with thirty days' notice regarding any replacement of existing facilities and construction of new facilities. The FERC promulgated the interim rule without providing the notice and opportunity for comment required by the Administrative Procedure Act (APA). Tennessee Gas Pipeline Company filed a petition for review of the interim rule, claiming that FERC violated the APA.

DECISION Judgment for Tennessee Gas Pipeline Company.

OPINION The APA requires agencies to provide notice of a rule thirty days before it becomes effective and to give the public an opportunity to comment on it. An exception exists where the agency finds for good cause that notice and public comment are impracticable, unnecessary, or contrary to the public interest. The good cause exception, however, is to be narrowly construed, and an agency should limit its use of the exception to emergency situations. The FERC argues that the interim rule qualifies as a "good cause" exception because of (1) its interim nature and (2) the environmental damage that might result from a rush to

construct and replace pipeline to avoid the requirements of a final rule.

The interim status of a rule is a significant factor, and the less expansive the interim rule, the less the need for public comment. The rule in question is indeed interim, and the FERC has indicated that the notice requirements under the rule take only a few hours. Nevertheless, the limited nature of a rule cannot in itself justify a failure to follow notice and comment procedures; otherwise, the good cause exception would swallow the notice and comment rule.

The FERC's second justification for the interim rule rests on the regulator's prediction of the regulateds' reaction to its proposed rulemaking. At a minimum, an agency must indicate the basis for its prediction so that a reviewing court may be in a position to determine whether the agency acted reasonably. The FERC has provided little factual basis for its belief that pipeline operators will seek to avoid its future rule by rushing new construction and replacements and consequently damaging the environment. FERC has failed to demonstrate sufficient cause for setting aside the important APA safeguards of requiring an agency to have the benefit of informed comment before it issues regulations. Therefore, despite the minimal reach of the interim rule, the FERC has failed to provide a sufficient basis for invoking the good cause exception.

INTERPRETATION Unless there is good cause, an agency must provide notice of a proposed rule and give the public an opportunity to comment on it.

In some instances the enabling statute requires that certain rules be made only after the opportunity for an agency hearing. This formal rulemaking procedure is far more complex than the informal procedures and is governed by the same APA provisions that govern an adjudication, discussed below. In *formal rulemaking,* the agency must consider the record of the trial-like agency hearing and include a statement of "findings and conclusions, and the reasons or basis therefore, on all the material issues of fact, law, or discretion presented on the record" when making rules.

Some enabling statutes direct that the agency, in making rules, use certain procedures more formal than those in informal rulemaking but do not compel the full hearing that formal rulemaking requires. This intermediate procedure, known as *hybrid rulemaking,* results from combining the informal procedures of the APA with the additional procedures specified by the enabling statute. For example, an agency may be required to conduct a legislative-type hearing (formal) that permits no cross-examination (informal).

In 1990, Congress enacted the Negotiated Rulemaking Act to encourage the involvement of affected parties in the initial stages of the policy-making process prior to the publication of notice of a proposed rule. The Act authorizes agencies to use negotiated rulemaking but does not require it. If an agency decides to use negotiated rulemaking, the affected parties and the agency develop an agreement and offer it to the agency. If accepted, the agreement becomes a basis for the proposed regulation, which is then published for comment.

Interpretative Rules **Interpretative rules** are agency-issued statements that explain how the agency construes its governing statute. For instance, the Securities and Exchange Commission "renders administrative interpretations of the law and regulations thereunder to members of the public, prospective registrants and others, to help them decide legal questions about the application of the law and the regulations to particular situations and to aid them in complying with the law." *The Work of the SEC* (1980).

These interpretative rules, however, which are exempt from the APA's procedural requirements of notice and comment, are *not* automatically binding on the private parties the agency regulates or on the courts, although they are given substantial weight. As the Supreme Court has stated, "the weight of such [an interpretative rule] in a particular case will depend upon the thoroughness evident in its consideration, the validity of its reasoning, its consistency with earlier and later pronouncements, and all those factors which give it power to persuade. . . ."

Interpretative rules *(in·ter'·pre·ta·tive)* statements issued by an administrative agency indicating how it construes its governing statute

Procedural Rules **Procedural rules** are also exempt from the notice and comment requirements of the APA and are not law. These rules establish rules of conduct for practice before the agency, identify an agency's organization, and describe its method of operation. For example, the Securities and Exchange Commission's Rules of Practice deal with matters such as who may appear before the commission; business hours and notice of proceedings and hearings; settlements, agreements, and conferences; presentation of evidence and the taking of depositions and interrogatories; and review of hearings.

Procedural rules rules issued by an administrative agency establishing its organization, method of operation, and rules of conduct for practice before it

Enforcement

Agencies also investigate conduct to determine whether the enabling statute or the agency's legislative rules have been violated. In carrying out this executive function, the agencies traditionally have been accorded great discretion, subject to constitutional limitations, to compel the disclosure of information. These limitations require that (1) the investigation is authorized by law and undertaken for a legitimate purpose, (2) the information sought is relevant, (3) the demand for information is sufficiently specific and not unreasonably burdensome, and (4) the information sought is not privileged.

Enforcement process by which agencies determine whether their rules have been violated

For example, the following explains some of the investigative and enforcement functions of the Securities and Exchange Commission:

> Most of the Commission's investigations are conducted privately. Facts are developed to the fullest extent possible through informal inquiry, interviewing witnesses, examining brokerage records and other documents, reviewing and trading data, and similar means. The Commission is empowered to issue subpoenas requiring sworn testimony and the production of books, records, and other documents pertinent to the subject matter under investigation. In the event of refusal to respond to a subpoena, the Commission may apply to a Federal court for an order compelling obedience. *The Work of the SEC* (1986).

Adjudication

After concluding an investigation, the agency may use informal or formal methods to resolve the matter. Since the caseload of administrative agencies is vast, far greater than that of the judicial system, most matters are informally adjudicated. Informal procedures include advising, negotiating, and settling. In 1990, Congress enacted the Administrative Dispute Resolution Act to authorize and encourage federal agencies to use mediation, conciliation, arbitration, and other techniques for the prompt and informal resolution of disputes. The Act does not, however, require agencies to use alternative dispute resolution and the affected parties must consent to its use.

The formal procedure by which an agency resolves a matter (called *adjudication*) involves finding facts, applying legal rules to the facts, and formulating orders. An **order** "means the whole or a part of a final disposition, whether affirmative, negative, injunctive or declaratory in form, of an agency." In essence an administrative trial, adjudication is used when the enabling statute so requires.

The procedures employed by the various administrative agencies to adjudicate cases are nearly as varied as the agencies themselves. Nevertheless, the APA does establish certain mandatory standards for those federal agencies the act covers. For example, an agency must give notice of a hearing. The APA also requires that the agency give all interested parties the opportunity to submit and consider "facts, arguments, offers of settlement, or proposals of adjustment." In many cases this involves testimony and cross-examination of witnesses. If no settlement is reached, then a hearing must be held.

The hearing is presided over by an administrative law judge (ALJ) and is prosecuted by the agency. ALJs are appointed by the agency through a professional merit selection system and may be removed only for good cause. There are more than twice as many administrative law judges as there are federal judges. Juries are never used. Thus, the agency serves as both the prosecutor and decision maker. In order to reduce the potential for a conflict of interest, the APA provides for a separation of functions between those agency members engaged in investigation and prosecution and those involved in decision making.

Oral and documentary evidence may be introduced by either party, and all sanctions, rules, and orders must be based upon "consideration of the whole record or those parts cited by a party and supported by and in accordance with the reliable, probative, and substantial evidence." All decisions must include a statement of findings of fact and conclusions of law and the reasons or basis for them, as well as a statement of the appropriate rule, order, sanction, or relief.

If such are authorized by law and within its delegated jurisdiction, an agency may impose in its orders sanctions such as penalties; fines; the seizing of property; the assessment of damages, restitution, compensation, or fees; and the act of requiring, revoking, or suspending a license. In most instances, orders are final unless appealed; and failure to comply with an order subjects the party to a statutory penalty. If the order is appealed, the governing body of the agency may decide the case *de novo*. Thus, the agency may hear additional evidence and arguments in deciding whether to revise the findings and conclusions it made in the initial decision.

Although administrative adjudications mirror to a large extent the procedures of judicial trials, there are many differences between the two. "Agency hearings tend to produce evidence of general conditions as distinguished from facts relating solely to the respondent. Administrative agencies more consciously formulate policy by adjudicating (and rulemaking) than do courts. Consequently, administrative adjudications may require that the administrative

ETHICAL DILEMMA Should the Terminally Ill Be Asked to Await FDA Approval of Last-Chance Treatments?

FACTS Mrs. Barnett is a 63-year-old widow who has just been diagnosed with ovarian cancer. Because of the lack of adequate screening procedures for this type of cancer, Mrs. Barnett's cancer has long gone undetected and has progressed considerably.

Dr. Jason, Mrs. Barnett's doctor, will perform immediate surgery, but the surgery will not effectively cure the cancer. He has recommended that she undergo rigorous chemotherapy on a monthly basis for eighteen months following surgery. Thereafter, an exploratory operation can be conducted to assess the success of the treatment. The proposed chemotherapy, which involves the use of platinum, will cause severe side effects, including nausea, oral lesions, and complete hair loss.

Dr. Jason has informed Mrs. Barnett and her two daughters, June and Sarina, that although chemotherapy will defer their mother's immediate death, her chances of a recovery are slim. Dr. Jason stated that while, on average, one in three patients undergoing such treatment could expect to recover, he believed Mrs. Barnett's recovery was highly unlikely. A second opinion from a reputable cancer treatment center confirmed Dr. Jason's diagnosis and recommendations for treatment.

Sarina has heard of an experimental cancer drug being tested in Europe and Scandinavia. Thus far the results seem promising. Though the drug may be obtained in Norway, it is not yet legal in the United States. The Federal Drug Administration has just begun to review the drug, but it will be years before the drug could receive FDA approval.

Sarina is strongly opposed to the painful regimen of chemotherapy that has been proposed, particularly since the treatment seems futile. She wants to fly to Norway, obtain the experimental drug, and return with it to the United States. Mrs. Barnett is much too ill to travel. June, on the other hand, is opposed to any course of treatment that does not have the approval of the FDA. Mrs. Barnett, who is weak and confused, is looking to her daughters for guidance.

Social, Policy, and Ethical Considerations

1. If Mrs. Barnett were your mother, what recommendation would you make? Under the circumstances, is it unethical to use a drug that has not been approved by the Federal Drug Administration?
2. As a policy matter, how should the FDA handle drugs for life-threatening diseases?
3. Should individuals be allowed absolute freedom to take risks with drug therapy?
4. Should the FDA apply different drug approval standards with regard to children who suffer from life-threatening diseases?
5. As a policy matter, how should the government and nonprofit organizations allocate resources among research groups competing for funding? How should the government, through its administrative agencies, establish priorities for funding research on various illnesses?

law judge consider more consciously the impact of his decision upon the public interest as well as upon the particular respondent. . . . Even more important is the fact that an administrative hearing is tried to an *administrative law judge* and never to a *jury*. Since many of the rules governing the admission of proof in judicial trials are designed to protect the jury from unreliable and possibly confusing evidence, the rules need not be applied with the same vigor in proceedings solely before an administrative law judge. The administrative judge decides both the facts and the law to be applied." *McCormick on Evidence*, 3d ed., Section 350, p. 1005.

LIMITS ON ADMINISTRATIVE AGENCIES

An important and fundamental part of administrative law is the limits imposed by judicial review upon the activities of administrative agencies. On matters of policy, however, courts are not supposed to substitute their judgment for the agency's. Additional limitations arise from the legislature and the executive branch, which, unlike the judiciary, may address the wisdom and correctness of an agency's decision or action. See Figure 5–1. Moreover, legally required disclosure of agency actions provides further protection for the public.

FIGURE 5–1 Limits on Administrative Agencies

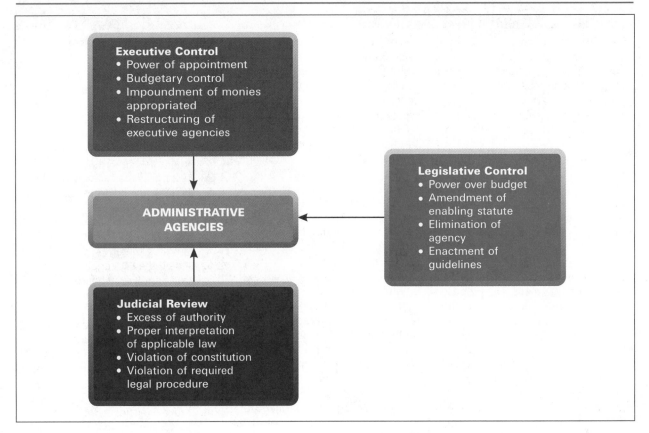

Judicial Review

Judicial review
acts as a control or check by
a court on a particular rule
or order of an administrative
agency

As discussed in Chapter 4, judicial review describes the process by which the courts examine governmental action. Judicial review, which is available unless a statute precludes such review or the agency action is committed to agency discretion by law, acts as a control or check on a particular rule or order of an administrative agency.

General Requirements Parties seeking to challenge agency action must have standing and must have exhausted their administrative remedies. Standing requires that the agency action injure the party in fact and that the party assert an interest that is in the "zone of interests to be protected or regulated by the statute in question." Judicial review is ordinarily available only for *final* agency action. Accordingly, if a party seeks review while an agency proceeding is in progress, a court will usually dismiss the action because the party has failed to exhaust his administrative remedies.

LUJAN v. DEFENDERS OF WILDLIFE Supreme Court of the United States, 1992, 504 U.S. 555,
112 S.Ct. 2130, 119 L.Ed.2d 351

FACTS This case involves a challenge to a rule promulgated by the Secretary of the Interior interpreting Section 7 of the Endangered Species Act of 1973 (ESA).

Section 7(a)(2) of the Act provides (in relevant part) that "[e]ach Federal agency shall, in consultation with and with the assistance of the Secretary (of the

continued

Interior), insure that any action authorized, funded, or carried out by such agency . . . is not likely to jeopardize the continued existence of any endangered species or threatened species or result in the destruction or adverse modification of habitat of such species which is determined by the Secretary, after consultation as appropriate with affected States, to be critical." In 1978, the Fish and Wildlife Service and the National Marine Fisheries Service, on behalf of the Secretary of the Interior and the Secretary of Commerce respectively, promulgated a joint regulation stating that the obligations imposed by section 7(a)(2) extend to actions taken in foreign nations. In 1983, the Interior Department proposed a revised joint regulation that would require consultation only for actions taken in the United States or on the high seas. Shortly thereafter, Defenders of Wildlife and other organizations filed this action against the Secretary of the Interior, seeking a declaratory judgment that the new regulation is in error as to the geographic scope of section 7(a)(2) and an injunction requiring the Secretary to promulgate a new regulation restoring the initial interpretation. The District Court granted the Secretary's motion to dismiss for lack of standing. The Court of Appeals for the Eighth Circuit reversed and remanded for judicial review of the regulation. On remand, the district court denied summary judgment on the standing issue based on the Eighth Circuit's earlier ruling and ordered the Secretary to publish a revised regulation.

DECISION Judgment reversed.

OPINION In addition to addressing concerns of judicial self-government, the doctrine of standing is an essential and unchanging part of the case-or-controversy requirement of Article III. Our cases have established that the irreducible constitutional minimum of standing contains three elements. First, the plaintiff must have suffered an "injury in fact"—an invasion of a legally protected interest that is (a) concrete and particularized, and (b) "actual or imminent," not conjectural or hypothetical. Second, there must be a causal connection between the injury and the conduct complained of—the injury has to be "fairly . . . trace[able] to the challenged action of the defendant, and not . . . th[e] result [of] the independent action of some third party not before the court." Third, it must be likely, as opposed to merely speculative, that the injury will be redressed by a favorable decision.

When the plaintiff is not himself the object of the government action or inaction he challenges, standing is not precluded, but it is ordinarily substantially more difficult to establish. The plaintiff must adduce facts showing that the third party affected has or will make choices that produce causation and permit redressability of the injury. Here, the plaintiffs rely on the affidavits of two of Defender's members that state that they have visited foreign regions of the world and observed the habitat of endangered species and that they intend to return and view the endangered animals directly at some later date. These affidavits allege that planned or existing government supported projects will adversely affect these habitats and therefore affect the affiants' future viewings of the endangered animals. Even if it is assumed that the governmental actions described will have the alleged effect, these affidavits contain no facts showing how damage to the species will produce "imminent" injury to the affiants. The affiants' profession of an "intent" to return to the places they had visited before—where they will presumably be deprived of the opportunity to observe animals of the endangered species—is simply not enough. Such "some day" intentions—without any description of concrete plans, or indeed even any specification of when the "some day" will be—do not support a finding of the "actual or imminent" injury that our cases require.

In addition to these affidavits, the respondents propose a series of novel standing theories. First, the "ecosystem nexus" theory proposes that any person who uses any part of a "contiguous ecosystem" adversely affected by a funded activity has standing even if the activity is located a great distance away. This approach is inconsistent with *National Wildlife Federation*, which held that a plaintiff claiming injury from environmental damage must use the area affected by the challenged activity and not an area roughly "in the vicinity" of it. Second, the "animal nexus" approach proposes that anyone who has an interest in studying or seeing the endangered animals anywhere on the globe has standing. Third, the "vocational nexus" approach proposes that anyone with a professional interest in such animals can sue. The latter two theories overlook that standing requires, at the summary judgment stage, a factual showing of perceptible harm. It goes beyond the limit and into pure speculation and fantasy to say that anyone who observes or works with an endangered species, anywhere in the world, is appreciably harmed by a single project affecting some portion of that species with which he has no more specific connection. Therefore, the plaintiffs lack standing to bring this action and the Court of Appeals erred in denying the summary judgment motion filed by the United States.

INTERPRETATION Parties seeking to challenge agency action must have standing, which requires that the agency action injure the party in fact and that the party assert an interest that is in the zone of interests to be protected or regulated by the statute in question.

In exercising judicial review, the court may decide either to compel agency action unlawfully withheld or to set aside impermissible agency action. In making its determination, the court must review the whole record and may set aside agency action only if the error is prejudicial.

Questions of Law When conducting a review, a court decides all relevant questions of law, interprets constitutional and statutory provisions, and determines the meaning or applicability of the terms of an agency action. This review of questions of law includes determining whether the agency has (1) exceeded its authority, (2) properly interpreted the applicable law, (3) violated any constitutional provision, or (4) acted contrary to the procedural requirements of the law.

Questions of Fact When reviewing factual determinations, the courts use one of three different standards. Where informal rulemaking or informal adjudication has occurred, the standard generally is the *arbitrary and capricious* test, which requires only that the agency had a rational basis for reaching its decision. See *Motor Vehicle Mfrs. Ass'n v. State Farm Mutual Automobile Ins. Co.* Where there has been a formal hearing, the substantial evidence test usually applies. It also applies to informal or hybrid rulemaking if the enabling statute so requires. The *substantial evidence* test requires the conclusions reached to be supported by "such relevant evidence as a reasonable mind might accept as adequate to support a conclusion." Finally, in rare instances the reviewing court may apply the *unwarranted by the facts* standard, which permits the court to try the facts *de novo*. This strict review is available only when the enabling statute so provides, when the agency has conducted an adjudication with inadequate fact-finding procedures, or when issues that were not before the agency are raised in a proceeding to enforce nonadjudicative agency action.

MOTOR VEHICLE MFRS. ASS'N. v. STATE FARM MUTUAL AUTOMOBILE INS. CO.

Supreme Court of the United States, 1983, 463 U.S. 29, 103 S.Ct. 2856, 77 L.Ed.2d 443

FACTS Congress enacted the National Traffic and Motor Vehicle Safety Act of 1966 (the Act) for the purpose of reducing the number of traffic accidents that result in death or personal injury. The Act directs the Secretary of Transportation to issue motor vehicle safety standards in order to improve the design and safety features of cars. The Secretary has delegated authority to promulgate safety standards to the National Highway Traffic Safety Administration (NHTSA). The Act also authorizes judicial review under the provisions of the Administrative Procedure Act (APA) of all orders establishing, amending, or revoking a federal motor vehicle safety standard issued by the NHTSA.

Pursuant to the Act, the NHTSA issued Motor Vehicle Safety Standard 208, which required all cars made after September 1982 to be equipped with passive restraints (either automatic seatbelts or airbags). The cost of implementing the standard was estimated to be around $1 billion. However, early in 1981, due to changes in economic circumstances and particularly due to complaints from the automotive industry,

the NHTSA rescinded Standard 208. The NHTSA had originally assumed that car manufacturers would install airbags in 60 percent of new cars and passive seatbelts in 40 percent. However, by 1981 it appeared that manufacturers were planning to install seatbelts in 99 percent of all new cars. Moreover, the majority of passive seatbelts could be easily and permanently detached by consumers. Therefore, the NHTSA felt that Standard 208 would not result in any significant safety benefits.

State Farm Mutual Automobile Insurance Company (State Farm) and the National Association of Independent Insurers (NAII) filed petitions in federal court for review of the NHTSA's rescission of Standard 208; the Court of Appeals consequently held that the agency's rescission was arbitrary and capricious. The NHTSA appealed.

DECISION Judgment for State Farm and NAII.

OPINION The Act indicates that motor vehicle safety standards are to be promulgated under the informal

continued

rulemaking procedure of the APA. The NHTSA's action in promulgating such standards therefore may be set aside if found to be "arbitrary, capricious, an abuse of discretion, or otherwise not in accordance with law." The scope of review under the arbitrary and capricious standard is narrow and a court is not to substitute its judgment for that of the agency. Nevertheless, the agency must demonstrate a rational connection between the facts found and the choice made.

The most obvious reason for finding the rescission arbitrary and capricious is that the NHTSA apparently gave no consideration whatever to modifying Standard 208 to require that airbag technology be utilized. Even if one accepts the NHTSA conclusion that detachable seatbelts will not attain anticipated safety benefits, this alone would not justify more than an amendment to Standard 208 to achieve the objectives of the Act. The logical response to the faults of the detachable seatbelts would be to require the installation of airbags. Clearly, an agency is not required to consider all policy alternatives in making decisions. However, the airbag is more than a policy alternative; it is an alternative technology already within the ambit of the existing standard.

INTERPRETATION Where informal rulemaking has occurred, the courts use the arbitrary and capricious standard that requires only that the agency had a rational basis for reaching its decision.

Legislative Control

The legislature may exercise control over administrative agencies in various ways. Through its budgetary power, it may greatly restrict or expand an agency's operations. Congress may amend an enabling statute to increase, modify, or decrease an agency's authority. Even more drastically, it may completely eliminate an agency. Or Congress may establish general guidelines to govern agency action, as it did by enacting the Administrative Procedure Act. Moreover, it may reverse or change an agency rule or decision by specific legislation. In addition, each house of Congress has oversight committees that review the operations of administrative agencies. Finally, the Senate has the power of confirmation over some high-level appointments to administrative agencies.

Control by Executive Branch

By virtue of his power to appoint and remove their chief administrators, the president has significant control over the administrative agencies housed within the executive branch. With respect to independent agencies, however, the president has less control because commissioners serve for a fixed term that is staggered with the president's term of office. Nevertheless, his power to appoint agency chairs and to fill vacancies confers considerable control, as does his power to remove commissioners for statutorily defined cause. The president's central role in the budgeting process of agencies also enables him to exert great control over agency policy and operations. Even more extreme is the president's power to impound monies appropriated to an agency by Congress. In addition, the president may radically alter, combine, or even abolish agencies of the executive branch unless either house of Congress disapproves such an act within a prescribed time.

Disclosure of Information

Requiring administrative agencies to disclose information about their actions makes them more accountable to the public. Accordingly, Congress has enacted disclosure statutes to enhance public and political oversight of agency activities. These statutes include the Freedom of Information Act and the Government in the Sunshine Act.

Freedom of Information Act First enacted in 1966, the Freedom of Information Act (FOIA) gives the public access to most records in the files of federal administrative agencies. Once a person has requested files, an agency must indicate within ten working days whether it intends to comply with the request and must within a reasonable time respond to the request. The agency may charge a fee for providing the records.

The FOIA permits agencies to deny access to nine categories of records: (1) records specifically authorized in the interest of national defense or foreign policy to be kept secret; (2) records that relate solely to the internal personnel rules and practices of an agency; (3) records specifically exempted by statute from disclosure; (4) trade secrets and commercial or financial information that is privileged or confidential; (5) inter- or intra-agency memorandums; (6) personnel and medical files, the disclosure of which would constitute a clearly unwarranted invasion of personal privacy; (7) investigatory records compiled for law enforcement purposes; (8) records that relate to the regulation or supervision of financial institutions; and (9) certain geological and geophysical information and data.

Government in the Sunshine Act The Government in the Sunshine Act requires meetings of many federal agencies to be open to the public. This act applies to multimember bodies whose members the president appoints with the advice and consent of the Senate, such as the Securities and Exchange Commission, the Federal Trade Commission, the Federal Communications Commission, the Consumer Product Safety Commission, and the Commodity Futures Trading Commission. The act does not cover executive agencies such as the Environmental Protection Agency, the Food and Drug Administration, and the National Highway Safety Administration.

Agencies generally may close meetings on the same grounds upon which they may refuse disclosure of records under the Freedom of Information Act. In addition, agencies such as the SEC and the Federal Reserve Board may close meetings in order to protect information the disclosure of which would lead to financial speculation or endanger the stability of financial institutions. The Sunshine Act also permits agencies to close meetings that concern agency participation in pending or anticipated litigation.

CHAPTER SUMMARY

Operation of Administrative Agencies	**Rulemaking** process by which an administrative agency promulgates rules of law
	  ■ *Legislative Rules* substantive rules issued by an administrative agency under the authority delegated to it by the legislature
	  ■ *Interpretative Rules* statements issued by an administrative agency indicating how it construes its governing statute
	  ■ *Procedural Rules* rules issued by an administrative agency establishing its organization, method of operation, and rules of conduct for practice before it
	Enforcement process by which agencies determine whether their rules have been violated
	Adjudication formal methods by which an agency resolves disputes

Limits on Administrative Agencies	**Judicial Review** acts as a control or check by a court on a particular rule or order of an administrative agency **Legislative Control** includes control over the agency's budget and enabling statute **Control by Executive Branch** includes the president's power to appoint members of the agency

QUESTIONS

1. List and explain the three basic functions of administrative agencies.
2. List and distinguish among the three types of rules promulgated by administrative agencies.
3. Explain the difference between formal and informal methods of adjudication.
4. List the questions of law determined by a court in conducting a review of a rule or order of an administrative agency.

5. List and explain the three standards of judicial review of factual determinations made by administrative agencies.

Internet Question. Find and explore several federal administrative agencies to learn about their (a) organization, (b) purpose, and (c) operations.

PROBLEMS

1. In 1942, Congress passed the Emergency Price Control Act in the interest of national defense and security. The stated purpose of the act was "to stabilize prices and to prevent speculative, unwarranted and abnormal increases in prices and rents. . . ." The act established the Office of Price Administration, which was authorized to establish maximum prices and rents that were to be "generally fair and equitable and [were to] effectuate the purposes of this Act." Stark was convicted for selling beef at prices in excess of those set by the agency. Stark appeals on the ground that the act unconstitutionally delegated to the agency the legislative power of Congress to control prices. Decision?

2. The Secretary of Commerce (Secretary) published notice in the *Federal Register* inviting comments regarding flammability standards for mattresses. Statistical data were compiled, consultant studies were conducted, and 75 groups submitted comments. The Secretary then determined that all mattresses, including crib mattresses, must pass a cigarette test, consisting of bringing a mattress in contact with a burning cigarette. Bunny Bear, Inc. now challenges the cigarette flammability test, asserting that the standard was not shown to be applicable to crib mattresses, since "infants and young children obviously do not smoke." The Secretary, according to Bunny Bear, has not satisfied the burden of proof justifying the inclusion of crib mattresses within this general safety standard. Decision?

3. National Airport in Washington, D.C., is one of the busiest and most crowded airports in the nation.

Accordingly, the Federal Aviation Administration (FAA) has restricted the number of commercial landing and takeoff slots at National to 40 per hour. Allocation of the slots among the air carriers serving National had been by voluntary agreement through an airline scheduling committee (ASC). When a new carrier, New York Air, requested 20 slots during peak hours, National's ASC was unable to agree on a slot allocation schedule. The FAA invited public comment as a means to solve the slot allocation dilemma. The FAA then issued Special Federal Aviation Regulation 43 (SFAR 43) based on public comments and a proposal made at the last National ASC meeting, thereby decreasing the number of slots held by current carriers and shifting some slots to less desirable times. SFAR 43 also granted 18 slots to New York Air. Northwest Airlines seeks judicial review of SFAR 43, claiming that it is arbitrary, capricious, and not a product of reasoned decision making, and that it capriciously favors the Washington-New York market as well as the carrier, New York Air. Decision?

4. Bachowski was defeated in a United Steelworkers of America union election. After exhausting his union remedies, Bachowski filed a complaint with Secretary of Labor Dunlop. Bachowski invoked the Labor-Management Reporting and Disclosure Act, which required Dunlop to investigate the complaint and determine whether to bring a court action to set aside the election. Dunlop decided such action was unwarranted. Bachowski then filed an action in District

Court to have Dunlop's decision declared arbitrary and capricious and to order Dunlop to file suit to set aside the election. The District Court dismissed the action, claiming a lack of authority to review Dunlop's discretionary decision. The Court of Appeals reversed and remanded, saying that Dunlop's decision, which was a final order by an administrative agency, was subject to judicial review under the Administrative Procedure Act. Dunlop maintains that judicial review is inappropriate in these circumstances and petitions to the U.S. Supreme Court. Decision?

5. The Federal Crop Insurance Corporation (FCIC) was created as a wholly government-owned corporation to insure wheat producers against unavoidable crop failure. As required by law, the FCIC published in the *Federal Register* conditions for crop insurance. Specifically, the FCIC published that spring wheat reseeded on winter wheat acreage was ineligible for coverage. When farmer Merrill applied for insurance on his wheat crop, he informed the local FCIC agent that 400 of his 460 acres of spring wheat were reseeded on the winter acreage. The agent advised Merrill that his entire crop was insurable. When drought destroyed Merrill's wheat, Merrill tried to collect the insurance, but the FCIC refused to pay, asserting that Merrill is bound by the notice provided by publication of the regulation in the *Federal Register*. Decision?

6. David Fenster, president and part owner of Utica Packing Company, was convicted of bribing a meat inspector. After an administrative hearing filed by the U.S. Department of Agriculture (USDA), the administrative law judge ordered withdrawal of inspection services from Utica. Upon judicial review of this decision, the court ordered Davis, the judicial officer for the USDA, to consider several mitigating circumstances. For example, there had been improper conduct by the inspectors, virulent anti-Semitic remarks by an inspector (Fenster is a Jewish survivor of the Holocaust), Fenster's serious health problems, and the fact that, despite the bribe, the Utica plant was clean. Davis ruled to reinstate inspection services to Utica. The USDA moved for reconsideration and replaced judicial officer Davis with Franke, who, unlike Davis, had no judicial background, could be fired at will, and who was assigned a legal adviser who worked with the prosecutors in the case. Fenster claims this violates his Fifth Amendment due process rights. The USDA responds that separation of investigative, prosecutorial, and adjudicative functions is relaxed in an administrative setting. Decision?

7. The Department of Energy (DOE) issued a subpoena requesting information regarding purchases, sales, exchanges, and other transactions in crude oil from Phoenix Petroleum Company (Phoenix). The aim of the DOE audit was to uncover violations of the Emergency Petroleum Allocation Act of 1973 (EPAA). The EPAA contained provisions for summary, or expedited, enforcement of DOE decisions. However, after the subpoena was issued but before Phoenix had responded, the EPAA expired. Furthermore, during this time, the President of the United States had ordered deregulation of DOE price and allocation controls. Utilizing the summary enforcement provisions of the now-defunct EPAA, the DOE sues to enforce the subpoena. Phoenix argues that since the EPAA has expired, the DOE lacks the authority either to issue the subpoena or to use the summary enforcement provisions. Decision?

CHAPTER 6

Criminal Law

As we discussed in Chapter 1, the civil law defines duties the violation of which constitutes a wrong against the injured party. The criminal law, on the other hand, establishes duties the violation of which is a societal wrong against the whole community. Civil law is a part of private law, whereas criminal law is a part of public law. In a civil action, the injured party sues to recover compensation for the damage and injury that he has sustained as a result of the defendant's wrongful conduct. The party bringing a civil action (the plaintiff) has the burden of proof, which he must sustain by a preponderance (greater weight) of the evidence. The purpose of the civil law is to compensate the aggrieved party.

Criminal law is designed to prevent harm to society by defining criminal conduct and establishing punishment for such conduct. In a criminal case, the defendant is prosecuted by the government, which must prove the defendant's guilt beyond a reasonable doubt, a significantly higher burden of proof than that required in a civil action. Moreover, under our legal system, guilt is never presumed. Indeed, the law presumes the innocence of the accused, and this presumption is unaffected by the defendant's failure to testify in her own defense. The government still has the burden of affirmatively proving the guilt of the accused beyond a reasonable doubt.

Of course, the same conduct may, and often does, constitute both a crime and a tort, which is a civil wrong. (We will discuss torts in Chapters 7 and 8.) But an act may be criminal without being tortious; by the same token, an act may be a tort but not a crime.

Because of the increasing use of criminal sanctions to enforce governmental regulation of business, criminal law is an essential part of business law. (See "Survey Finds that Crimes Cost $450 Billion a Year.") Moreover, businesses sustain considerable loss as victims of criminal actions. Accordingly, this chapter covers the general principles of criminal law and criminal procedure as well as specific crimes and defenses relevant to business.

NATURE OF CRIMES

A **crime** is any act or omission forbidden by public law in the interest of protecting society and made punishable by the government in a judicial proceeding brought by it. Punishment for criminal conduct includes fines, imprisonment, probation, and death. In addition, some states and the federal government have enacted victim indemnification statutes, which establish funds, financed by criminal fines, to provide indemnification in limited

Crime an act or omission in violation of a public law and punishable by the government

115

amounts to victims of criminal activity. Crimes are prohibited and punished on grounds of public policy, which may include the protection and safeguarding of government (as in treason), human life (as in murder), or private property (as in larceny). Additional purposes for criminal law include deterrence, rehabilitation, and retribution.

Historically, criminal law was primarily common law. Today, however, criminal law is almost exclusively statutory. All states have enacted comprehensive criminal law statutes (or codes) covering most, if not all, of the common law crimes. Moreover, these statutes have made the number of crimes defined in criminal law far greater than the number of crimes defined under common law. Some codes expressly limit crimes to those the code includes, thus abolishing common law crimes. Nonetheless, some states do not define all crimes statutorily; therefore, the courts must rely on common law definitions. Because there are no federal common law crimes, all federal crimes are statutory.

Within recent times the scope of the criminal law has increased greatly. The scope of traditional criminal behavior has been expanded by numerous regulations and laws, pertaining to nearly every phase of modern living, that contain criminal penalties. Typical examples in the field of business law are those laws concerning the licensing and conduct of a business, antitrust laws, and the laws governing the sales of securities.

Essential Elements

Actus reus *(act'·us ray'·us)*
wrongful or overt act

In general, a crime consists of two elements: (1) the wrongful or overt act (**actus reus**) and (2) the criminal or mental intent (**mens rea**). For example, to support a larceny conviction it is not enough to show that the defendant stole another's goods; it must also be established that he intended to steal the goods. Conversely, criminal intent without an overt act is not a crime. For instance, Ann decides to rob the neighborhood grocery store and then really "live it up." Without more, Ann has committed no crime.

Mens rea *(menz re·a)*
criminal intent or mental fault

Actus reus refers to all the nonmental elements of a crime, including the physical act that must be performed, the circumstances under which it must be performed, and the consequences of that act. The *actus reus* required for specific crimes will be discussed later in this chapter.

Mens rea, or mental fault, refers to the mental element of a crime. Most common law and some statutory crimes require subjective fault, whereas other crimes require objective fault; some statutory crimes require no fault at all. The American Law Institute's proposed Model Penal Code and most modern criminal statutes recognize three possible types of **subjective fault**: purposeful, knowing, and reckless. A person acts *purposely* or *intentionally* if his conscious object is to engage in the prohibited conduct or to cause the prohibited result. Thus, if Arthur, with the desire to kill Donna, shoots his rifle at Donna, who is seemingly out of gunshot range, and in fact does kill her, Arthur had the purpose or intent to kill Donna. If Benjamin, desiring to poison Paula, places a toxic chemical in the water cooler in Paula's office and unwittingly poisons Gail and Ram, Benjamin will be found to have purposefully killed Gail and Ram because Benjamin's intent to kill Paula is transferred to Gail and Ram, regardless of Benjamin's feelings toward Gail and Ram.

Subjective fault
purposeful, knowing, or reckless

A person acts *knowingly* if he is aware that his conduct is of a prohibited type or is practically certain to cause a prohibited result. A person acts *recklessly* if he consciously disregards a substantial and unjustifiable risk that his conduct is prohibited or that it will cause a prohibited result.

MANAGERIAL INSIGHT

Survey Finds that Crimes Cost $450 Billion a Year

Report Is Called Justification for Spending

Crime costs Americans at least $450 billion a year, according to the most comprehensive survey ever done on the price of violence.

The report, done for the Justice Department, is the first to try to measure the cost of child abuse and domestic violence along with crimes like murder, rape and robbery. It is also the first to estimate the mental health care costs and the reduced quality of life for victims of crime.

The report calculates out-of-pocket costs covering items like legal fees, lost work time and the cost of police work as well as intangibles, like the affection lost for a murder victim's family. The authors devised a formula for the intangibles.

The study excludes the cost of running the nation's prisons, jails and parole and probation systems, which would add $40 billion, bringing the total annual cost of crime to almost $500 billion, according to other Justice Department statistics. By comparison, the Defense Department's budget for 1995 is $252.6 billion.

"The estimate of $450 billion for crime is an amazing number which tells us just how heavy a burden that crime and the fear of crime place on our society," said Representative Charles E. Schumer of Brooklyn, the ranking Democratic member of the House Subcommittee on Crime.

"This report could change the debate" on crime, Mr. Schumer said, "because it shows that while most people think a $1 billion anti-crime program is a large number, it's really just a drop in the bucket."

The most important thing about the study, Mr. Schumer said, "is that it shows the cost of not doing anything" is much higher than any proposed anti-crime programs, like putting more police on the street, building more prisons or spending for violence prevention.

The report, "Victim Costs and Consequences: A New Look," was sponsored by the National Institute of Justice, the research arm of the Justice Department.

While the report has been praised by a number of academic specialists and law-enforcement authorities, others have raised questions about the methodology used in calculating the intangible costs like the value of a murder victim's life.

Representative Bill McCollum, Republican of Florida, the chairman of the House Subcommittee on Crime, agreed with Mr. Schumer, saying the report "demonstrates that the cost of building prisons and adding police are justified, in terms of the cost to our society." He said this was true even though many state governments were running out of money to build new prisons.

Mr. McCollum said the figures were worrisome "because they don't even take into account the new crime wave we expect over the next 10 years" as the number of teenagers increases by 20 percent. While homicide rates among adults have been falling over the past decade, they have more than doubled among youths under 18 years old.

The authors of the new report make no recommendations on the best mix of measures to control crime. But they point out that ignoring the intangible benefits of crime reduction "can lead to a misallocation of resources."

The average rape, for example, incurs "out-of-pocket costs" to the victim of $5,100, far less than the $20,000 annual cost of a prison cell, the authors said. But when the rape's effect on the victim's quality of life is calculated, the cost soars to $87,000, many times greater than the price of a prison cell, the study concludes.

Mark A. Cohen, one of the three authors and an associate professor at Vanderbilt University's Owen Graduate School of Management, said another study he had done found that longer prison sentences would be a cost-effective way to reduce rape, assault and automobile theft but not burglary and robbery. Building more prisons for burglars and robbers would cost more than the savings society would achieve from a reduction in the crimes, he said.

"We would like to do away with crime, but society cannot afford a zero crime rate," said Professor Cohen, an economist. It would require so many prisons, he said, "We would bankrupt ourselves and we'd also have a society we wouldn't like."

The other authors of the report are Ted R. Miller, associate director of the National Public Services Research Institute in Landover, Md., and Brian Wiersema, research coordinator for the Violence Research Group at the University of Maryland.

Some experts expressed skepticism about the $450 billion figure put forward in the report and had doubts about its methodology.

Alfred Blumstein, a professor at Carnegie Mellon University, said the report was "one more piece of shooting at a very-tough-to-get-at number." But he said the $450 billion-a-year estimate "is unreasonably high," giving too much weight to intangible factors like pain, suffering and reduction in the quality of life.

Professor Blumstein, a leading criminologist, and some other specialists expressed concern that the very high estimate made it easier to justify building expensive prisons and handing out longer sentences.

He also said it was very difficult to calculate the benefits of violence prevention programs. While the costs of crime are incurred now, he said, "we cannot see the benefits of prevention programs for 5 to 10

continued

years" or know how many crimes will be averted.

"The public and politicians demand immediate gratification, so there is considerable push for being tough with more mandatory sentences," Professor Blumstein said. "As a result, we have largely abandoned prevention and rehabilitation efforts for juveniles," he said, which has contributed to the rapid growth of violent crime among teenagers.

Among other findings in the report were these:

• Child abuse and domestic violence account for about one-third of the total annual costs of crime, a far higher figure than previous estimates. This does not include future costs that are likely to mount as children who have been physically or sexually abused perpetuate a cycle of violence by molesting their own offspring.

• Violent crime causes 3 percent of medical spending and 14 percent of injury-related medical spending. Crime also accounts for as much as 10 to 20 percent of mental health care expenditures.

• Intangible costs, like lost quality of life, are by far the largest cost component for crimes of violence, the authors claim, though they are also the most difficult to measure and therefore subject to the most debate. The study places the "lost quality of life" for a murder victim and his family at $1.9 million, while the average cost of police investigation into a murder is only $1,400.

The report calculated the out-of-pocket costs of crime at $105 billion annually, including medical bills, property losses, lost earnings and programs for victim assistance.

To measure the intangible costs of crime, including pain, suffering and lost quality of life, the authors adopted figures from jury awards to crime victims and other statistical studies of the value of life, in addition to including the cost of mental care.

In a separate study by Professor Cohen, now under preparation for the Justice Department, he found that preventing a "high risk" young person in a poor neighborhood from a troubled family from turning into a juvenile delinquent and adult criminal would save the country $1.5 million to $2 million.

By Fox Butterfield. *The New York Times*, p. A8. April 22, 1996. Used with permission.

JOHNSON v. FLORIDA Supreme Court of Florida, 1992, 597 So.2d 798.

FACTS Raymond Johnson snatched a purse that had been left in an unattended car at a gas station. The purse contained both money and a firearm. Johnson was convicted for the crimes of grand theft of property (cash and payroll check) and grand theft of a firearm. Johnson appealed, arguing that this conviction is a double jeopardy violation in that it constitutes multiple convictions for a single act.

DECISION Case remanded. Johnson cannot be separately convicted for grand theft of property and grand theft of a firearm.

OPINION The question presented is whether a defendant may be separately convicted and sentenced for grand theft of cash and grand theft of a firearm, the theft of which was accomplished by means of snatching a purse that contained both cash and a firearm

when the defendant did not know the nature of the purse's contents. When one commits a theft by taking the property of another, the degree of felony is defined by such factors as the value of the goods or whether a firearm is taken. However, these classifications do not constitute separate crimes. A separate crime occurs only when there are separate distinct acts of seizing the property of another. If Johnson had taken the purse and then picked up the gun separately, there could be two convictions for separate acts. However, in this case, there was *one intent* and one act of taking the handbag. Accordingly, there could be only one theft conviction.

INTERPRETATION An essential element of a crime is the mental intent (*mens rea*) to commit the crime.

Objective fault gross deviation from reasonable conduct

Objective fault involves a gross deviation from the standard of care that a reasonable person would observe under given circumstances. Criminal statutes refer to objective fault by terms such as *carelessness* or *negligence*. Such conduct occurs when a person *should* be aware of a substantial and unjustifiable risk that his conduct is prohibited or will cause a prohibited result. Examples of crimes requiring objective fault are involuntary manslaughter (negligently causing the death of another), carelessly driving an automobile, and, in some states, issuing a bad check.

Many regulatory statutes have totally dispensed with the mental element of a crime by imposing criminal liability without fault. Without regard to the care that a person exercises, criminal **liability without fault** makes it a crime for that person to do a specified act or to bring about a certain result. Statutory crimes imposing liability without fault include the sale of adulterated food, the sale of narcotics without a prescription, and the sale of alcoholic beverages to a minor. Most of these crimes involve regulatory statutes dealing with health and safety, and impose only fines for violations. See Figure 6–1.

Liability without fault crime to do a specific act or cause a certain result without regard to the care exercised

Classification

Historically, crimes have been classified *mala in se* (wrongs in themselves or morally wrong, such as murder) or *mala prohibita* (not morally wrong but declared wrongful by law, such as the failure to drive on the right side of the road). From the standpoint of the seriousness of the offense, crimes are also classified as a **felony**, or serious crime (any crime punishable by death or imprisonment in the penitentiary), or as a **misdemeanor**, a less serious crime (any crime punishable by a fine or imprisonment in a local jail).

Mala in se *(ma'·la in say)* wrongs in themselves or morally wrong

Mala prohibita *(ma'·la pro·hi'·bi·ta)* not morally wrong but declared wrongful by law

Felony serious crime

Misdemeanor less serious crime

Vicarious Liability

Vicarious liability is liability imposed upon one person for the acts of another. Employers are vicariously liable for the authorized criminal acts of their employees if the employer directed, participated in, or approved of the act. For example, if an employer directs its vice president of marketing to fix prices with its company's competitors, and the employee does so, both the employer and employee have criminally violated the Sherman Antitrust Act. On the other hand, employers ordinarily are not liable for the unauthorized criminal acts of their employees. As previously discussed, most crimes require mental fault; this element is not present, so far as criminal responsibility of the employer is concerned, where the employee's criminal act was not authorized.

Vicarious *(vi·car'·i·ous)* **liability** liability imposed on one for acts of another

Employers may, however, be subject to a criminal penalty for the unauthorized act of an adviser or manager acting in the scope of employment. Moreover, an employer may be criminally liable under a liability without fault statute for certain unauthorized acts of an employee, whether the employee is managerial or not. For example, many states have statutes that punish "every person who by himself or his employee or agent sells anything at short weight," or "whoever sells liquor to a minor and any sale by an employee shall be deemed the act of the employer as well."

FIGURE 6–1 Degrees of Mental Fault

Type	Fault Required	Examples
Subjective Fault	Purposeful Knowing Reckless	Larceny Embezzlement
Objective Fault	Negligent Careless	Careless driving Issuing bad check (some states)
Liability without Fault	None	Sale of alcohol to a minor Sale of adulterated food

Liability of a Corporation

Historically, corporations were not held criminally liable because, under the traditional view, a corporation could not possess the requisite criminal intent and, therefore, was incapable of committing a crime. The dramatic growth in size and importance of corporations changed this view. Under the modern approach, a corporation may be liable for violation of statutes imposing liability without fault. In addition, a corporation may be liable when the offense is perpetrated by a high corporate officer or the board of directors. The American Law Institute's Model Penal Code provides that a corporation may be convicted of a criminal offense for the conduct of its employees if

1. the legislative purpose of the statute defining the offense is to impose liability on corporations and the conduct is within the scope of the agent's office or employment;
2. the offense consists of an omission to discharge a specific, affirmative duty imposed upon corporations by law; or
3. the offense was authorized, requested, commanded, performed, or recklessly tolerated by the board of directors or by a high managerial agent of the corporation.

By necessity, punishment of a corporation for crimes is by fine rather than imprisonment. Nonetheless, those individuals bearing responsibility for the criminal act face either fines or imprisonment, or both. The Model Penal Code provides that the corporate agent having primary responsibility for the discharge of a duty imposed by law on the corporation is as accountable for the corporation's reckless omission to perform the required act as if the duty were imposed by law directly upon him.

On November 1, 1991, the Federal Organizational Corporate Sentencing Guidelines took effect. The overall purpose of the guidelines is to impose sanctions that will provide just punishment and adequate deterrence. To that end, the guidelines require corporations to formulate and implement compliance programs reasonably designed to prevent potential legal violations by the corporation and its employees.

The guidelines provide for a base corporate fine for each criminal offense, calculated by one of the following: (a) the amount listed in the guidelines' offense-level fine table (fines range from $5,000 to $72.5 million), (b) the pecuniary gain to the organization, or (c) the pecuniary loss as a result of the offense, to the extent that the loss was intentionally, knowingly, or recklessly caused. In addition, restitution is available to victims whenever possible. In the most extreme case, a corporation's charter can be revoked. For a corporation that has implemented an adequate compliance program, the fine can be reduced to as little as 5 percent of the scheduled amount. On the other hand, if a company does not have a proper program in place, the fine can be multiplied by up to four times.

An adequate compliance program should include the following:

1. a written code of conduct,
2. assignment of a senior corporate official to be responsible for the overall compliance program,
3. effective communication of the program to all employees and agents,
4. ongoing monitoring of the program,
5. proper delegation of program-related authority within the organization,
6. disciplinary measures appropriate to enforce the program, and
7. periodic reviews of the program.

WHITE-COLLAR CRIME

White-collar crime has been defined in various ways. The Justice Department defines it as nonviolent crime involving deceit, corruption, or breach of trust. It includes crimes committed by individuals—such as embezzlement and forgery—as well as crimes committed on behalf of a corporation—such as commercial bribery, product safety and health crimes, false advertising, and antitrust violations. Regardless of the definition, white-collar crime clearly costs society billions of dollars (estimates range from $40 billion to over $200 billion per year). Historically, prosecution of white-collar crime was deemphasized because such crime was not considered violent. Now, however, many contend that white-collar crime often inflicts violence but does so impersonally. For example, unsafe products cause injury and death to consumers, while unsafe working conditions cause injury and death to employees. Indeed, many contend that white-collar criminals should receive stiff prison sentences due to the magnitude of their crimes.

White-collar crime
nonviolent crime involving deceit, corruption, or breach of trust

Computer Crime

One special type of white-collar crime is computer crime. **Computer crime** involves the use of a computer to steal money or services, to remove personal or business information, and to tamper with information. Computer crimes fall into five general categories: (1) theft of computer hardware, software, or secrets; (2) unauthorized use of computer services; (3) theft of money by computer; (4) vandalism of computer hardware or software; and (5) theft of computer data.

Computer crime crime by, with, or at a computer

Detection of crimes involving computers is extremely difficult. In addition, computer crimes often are not reported because businesses do not want to give the impression that their security is lax. Nonetheless, losses due to computer crimes are estimated to be in the tens of billions of dollars. Moreover, given society's ever-increasing dependence upon computers, this type of crime will in all likelihood continue to increase.

Already, computer crimes have become commonplace. Examples abound: Software piracy (the unauthorized copying of copyrighted software) is now so widespread that an estimated two out of every three copies of software are illegally obtained. A computer consultant hired by Security Pacific Bank wrongfully transferred $10 million from the bank to his own Swiss bank account. Six employees stole TRW's credit rating data and offered to "repair" poor credit ratings for a fee. Disgruntled or discharged employees have used computer programs to destroy software.

As a consequence, enterprises are spending large sums of money to increase computer security. In addition, nearly all of the states have enacted computer crime laws. And though, despite numerous attempts, the federal government has not passed comprehensive legislation prohibiting computer crime, in 1984 Congress enacted specific legislation (the Counterfeit Access Device and Computer Fraud and Abuse Act) making unauthorized access to a computer a federal crime.

Racketeer Influenced and Corrupt Organizations Act (RICO)

The Racketeer Influenced and Corrupt Organizations Act (**RICO**) was enacted in 1970 with the stated purpose of terminating the infiltration by organized crime into legitimate business. The act subjects to severe civil and criminal penalties enterprises that engage in a pattern of racketeering, defined as the commission of two or more predicate acts within a period of ten years. A "predicate act" is any

RICO federal law intended to stop organized crime from infiltrating legitimate businesses

of several criminal offenses listed in RICO. Included are nine major categories of state crimes and twenty-six federal crimes, such as murder, kidnapping, arson, extortion, drug dealing, securities fraud, mail fraud, and bribery. The most controversial issue concerning RICO is its application to businesses that are not engaged in organized crime but that do meet the "pattern of racketeering" test under the act. Criminal conviction under the law may result in a prison term of up to twenty years plus a fine of up to $25,000 per violation. In addition, businesses forfeit any property obtained due to a RICO violation, and individuals harmed by RICO violations may invoke the statute's civil remedies, which include treble damage and attorney's fees.

H.J. INC. v. NORTHWESTERN BELL TELEPHONE COMPANY Supreme Court of the United States, 1989, 492 U.S. 229, 109, S.Ct. 2893

FACTS Northwestern Bell Telephone Company customers brought a class action suit against the telephone company, alleging that the company and some of its employees bribed members of the Minnesota Public Utilities Commission in order to get approval for unfair and unreasonable rate hikes. The plaintiffs argued that the bribes had continued for a six-year period from 1980 to 1986. They also alleged that the bribes included not only cash payments to commissioners but also negotiations with them concerning future employment, payment for parties and meals, and sporting event and airline tickets. The plaintiffs invoked the Racketeer Influenced and Corrupt Organizations Act and sought an injunction against the company and treble damages under the act's civil liability provisions. The U.S. District Court dismissed the case, saying that the plaintiffs had not shown multiple illegal schemes but rather just one single scheme. The plaintiffs appealed to the U.S. Court of Appeals, which affirmed the lower court's decision. The plaintiffs then appealed to the U.S. Supreme Court.

DECISION Opinion reversed and case remanded for further proceedings consistent with this opinion.

OPINION The Racketeer Influenced and Corrupt Organizations Act (RICO) imposes criminal and civil penalties on individuals who engage in prohibited activities (as defined by state and federal laws) that constitute a pattern of racketeering. As defined in the act, a "pattern" necessitates "at least two acts of racketeering activity" (although these two acts may not be sufficient in all cases) in a ten-year period. A plaintiff must show both the relationship between at least two

activities and the continuity, or its likelihood, of long-term criminal activity in order to demonstrate racketeering under RICO. Without proof of relationship or continuity, a plaintiff must show that the racketeering activity was undertaken to further multiple criminal schemes. Neither RICO's language nor its legislative history suggests that the act is limited solely to organized crime or corporations. Nor does the act require a defendant in a civil RICO case to have been convicted formerly of a criminal RICO offense. Moreover, the act does not necessarily require separate multiple illegal schemes in order to constitute a pattern of racketeering. The elements needed, instead, are related racketeering activities and a threat, or possible threat, of continued criminal activity. Racketeering that lasts for a week or a month does not satisfy the requirement of continuity, since Congress clearly intended the act to apply to long-term criminal activity. As such, the alleged acts of bribery in this case may be said at trial to relate to the common purpose of influencing the commissioners, thus demonstrating relationship. That the racketeering activities happened regularly over a six-year period may be sufficient to satisfy the need for continuity. Moreover, the alleged bribes may be demonstrated to be the normal way that Northwestern Bell Telephone Company conducts its ongoing business.

INTERPRETATION RICO imposes civil and criminal penalties on enterprises that engage in a pattern of racketeering, defined as the commission of two or more predicate acts within a period of ten years.

CRIMES AGAINST BUSINESS

Criminal offenses against property greatly affect businesses, amounting to losses worth hundreds of billions of dollars each year. In this section we will discuss the following crimes against property: (1) larceny, (2) embezzlement, (3) false pretenses, (4) robbery, (5) burglary, (6) extortion and bribery, (7) forgery, and (8) bad checks.

Larceny

The crime of **larceny** is the (1) trespassory (2) taking and (3) carrying away of (or exercising dominion or control over) (4) personal property (5) of another (6) with the intent to deprive the victim permanently of the goods. All six elements must be present for the crime to exist. Thus, if Carol takes Dan's 1968 automobile without Dan's permission, intending to use it for a joyride and to then return it to Dan, Carol has not committed larceny because she did not intend to deprive Dan permanently of the automobile. (Carol nevertheless has committed the offense of unauthorized use of an automobile, which is a crime in most states.) On the other hand, if Carol left Dan's 1968 car in a junkyard after the joyride, Carol most likely would be held to have committed a larceny because of the high risk that Dan would be permanently deprived of the car. The *Olivo* case, which follows, deals with the question of whether persons may be convicted of larceny for shoplifting if they are arrested before leaving the store.

> **Larceny** trespassory taking and carrying away of the goods of another with the intent to permanently deprive

---

PEOPLE v. OLIVO Court of Appeals of New York, 1981, 52 N.Y.2d 309, 438, N.Y.S.2d 242, 420, N.E.2d 40

FACTS Olivo was in the hardware area of a department store. A security guard saw him look around, take a set of wrenches, and conceal it in his clothing. Olivo looked around once more and proceeded toward an exit, passing several cash registers. The guard stopped him short of the exit. Olivo testified at trial that he was waiting in line at a cashier with the tools under his arm when he was seized by the guard. A jury found him guilty of larceny. Olivo then brought this appeal, maintaining that larceny is not legally established unless the defendant leaves a place of business without paying for merchandise in his possession.

DECISION Judgment affirmed.

OPINION A shoplifter need not leave the store to be guilty of larceny. The modern definition of larceny aims to protect individual property rights. If a shopper exercises dominion and control over merchandise wholly inconsistent with the continued rights of the owner, and the other elements of larceny are present, a larceny has occurred. A customer may exercise such dominion and control—and in a manner contrary to that of a prospective purchaser—without leaving the store. In this particular case, Olivo's suspicious survey of the area, concealment of the tools in his clothing, and movement toward an exit suggest an exercise of dominion and control inconsistent with the store's continued rights.

INTERPRETATION The crime of larceny is the trespassory taking and exercising control of personal property of another with intent to deprive the victim permanently of the goods.

Embezzlement

Embezzlement is the fraudulent conversion of another's property by one who was in lawful possession of it. A **conversion** is any act that seriously interferes with the owner's rights in the property; such acts may include exhausting the resources of the property, selling it, giving it away, or refusing to return it to its rightful owner. The key distinction between larceny and embezzlement, therefore, is whether the thief is in lawful possession of the property. While both situations concern misuse of the property of another, in embezzlement, the thief lawfully possesses the property; in larceny, she does not.

> **Embezzlement** taking the property of another in violation of a trust

False Pretenses

False pretenses is the crime of obtaining title to property of another by making materially false representations of an existing fact with knowledge of their falsity and with the intent to defraud. Larceny does not cover this situation

> **False pretenses** obtaining title to property of another by means of materially false representations of fact made with knowledge of their falsity and with the intent to defraud

because here the victim voluntarily transfers the property to the thief. For example, a con artist who goes door to door and collects money by saying he is selling stereo equipment, when he is not, is committing the crime of false pretenses.

Specialized crimes that are similar to false pretenses include mail fraud and securities fraud. *Mail fraud,* unlike the crime of false pretenses, does not require the victim to be actually defrauded; it simply requires the defendant to use the mails to carry out a scheme that attempts to defraud others. Securities fraud is discussed in Chapter 42.

Robbery

Robbery larceny from a person by force or threat of force

Robbery is a larceny with these additional elements: (1) the property is taken directly from the victim or in the immediate presence of the victim, and (2) the act is accomplished through either force or the threat of force. The defendant's force or threat of force need not be against the person from whom the property is taken. For example, a robber threatens Sam that unless Sam opens up his employer's safe, the robber will shoot Maria.

Many statutes distinguish between simple robbery and aggravated robbery. Robbery can be aggravated by any of several factors, including (1) robbery with a deadly weapon, (2) robbery where the robber has the intent to kill or would kill if faced with resistance, (3) robbery that involves serious bodily injury, or (4) robbery by two or more persons.

Burglary

Burglary breaking and entering the home of another at night with intent to commit a felony

At common law, **burglary** was defined as breaking and entering the dwelling of another at night with the intent to commit a felony. Modern statutes differ from the common law definition. Many of them simply require that there be (1) an entry (2) into a building (3) with the intent to commit a felony in the building. Nevertheless, the modern statutes vary so greatly it is nearly impossible to generalize.

Extortion and Bribery

Extortion making threats to obtain property

Although extortion and bribery are frequently confused, they are two distinct crimes. **Extortion**, or blackmail as it is sometimes called, is generally held to be the making of threats for the purpose of obtaining money or property. For example, Lindsey tells Jason that unless Jason pays her $10,000 she will tell Jason's customers that Jason was once arrested for disturbing the peace. Lindsey has committed the crime of extortion. In a few jurisdictions, however, the crime of extortion occurs only if the defendant actually causes the victim to relinquish money or property.

Bribery offering property to a public official to influence the official's decision

Bribery, on the other hand, is the offer of money or property to a public official to influence the official's decision. The crime of bribery is committed when the illegal offer is made, whether accepted or not. Thus, if Andrea offered Edward, the mayor of Allentown, a 20 percent interest in Andrea's planned real estate development if Edward would use his influence to have the development proposal approved, Andrea would be guilty of criminal bribery. In contrast, if Edward had threatened Andrea that unless he received a 20 percent interest in Andrea's development he would use his influence to prevent the approval of the development, Edward would be guilty of criminal extortion. Bribery of foreign officials is covered by the Foreign Corrupt Practices Act, discussed in Chapter 42.

Some jurisdictions have gone beyond the traditional bribery law to adopt statutes that make *commercial bribery* illegal. Commercial bribery is the use of bribery to acquire new business, obtain secret information or processes, or obtain kickbacks.

Forgery

Forgery is the intentional falsification or false making of a document with the intent to defraud. Accordingly, if William prepares a false certificate of title to a stolen automobile, he is guilty of forgery. Likewise, if an individual alters some receipts in order to increase her income tax deductions, she has committed the crime of forgery. The most common type of forgery is the signing of another's name to a financial document.

> **Forgery** intentional falsification of a document with intent to defraud

Bad Checks

All jurisdictions have enacted laws making it a crime to issue **bad checks**; that is, writing a check when there is not enough money in the account to cover the check. Most jurisdictions simply require that the check be issued; they do not require that the issuer receive anything in return for the check. Also, though most jurisdictions require that defendants issue a check with knowledge that they do not have enough money to cover the check, a few jurisdictions require only that there be insufficient funds.

> **Bad checks** checks issued with funds insufficient to cover them

---

STATE v. KELM Superior Court of New Jersey, 1996, 289 N.J.Super. 55, 672 A.2d 1261

FACTS On February 10, 1991, defendant Kelm secured a loan for $6,000 from Ms. Joan Williams. Kelm told Williams that the loan was to finance a real estate transaction. Five days later, Ms. Williams received a check drawn by Kelm in the amount of $6,000 from Kelm's attorney. Although the check was dated February 15, 1991, Kelm claims that she delivered the check to her attorney on February 10, 1991. The following week, Ms. Williams learned the check was uncollectible. Subsequently, Williams received assurances from Kelm but was unsuccessful in her efforts to obtain money from the drawee's bank. When Williams deposited the check, it was returned with a notation that it should not be presented again and that no account was on file. Bank records show that the account was closed on March 8, 1991, and that it had negative balances since February 10, 1991. Following a jury trial, Kelm was found guilty of issuing a bad check. Kelm appeals asserting that an intent to defraud is an element of the statutory offense of issuing a bad check and that the statutory provision exempts post-dated checks.

DECISION The jury verdict is affirmed.

OPINION The principal issue on appeal is whether an intent to defraud is an element of Section 2C:21-5 (issuing a bad check) of the New Jersey statutes. The statute provides:

> A person who issues or passes a check or similar sight order for the payment of money, knowing that it will not be honored by the drawee, commits an offense. . . . For the purposes of this section as well as in any prosecution for theft committed by means of a bad check, an issuer is presumed to know that the check or money order (other than a post-dated check or order) would not be paid, if:

***

> (b) Payment was refused by the drawee for lack of funds, upon presentation within 30 days after issue, and the issuer failed to make good within 10 days after receiving notice of that refusal. . . .

This statute, unlike its predecessor, does not contain the language "with intent to defraud." Kelm's reliance on cases interpreting the prior bad check statute is misplaced. An intent to defraud is not an element of the offense of issuing a bad check. Rather, the current statute requires mere knowledge at the time the check is issued or passed that it will not be honored by the drawee.

Addressing Kelm's second assertion, the statute's reference to postdated checks does not completely exempt such checks from its operation. That reference only exempts the drawer of a postdated check from the presumption of knowledge that the check will not be paid. In such cases, the State must prove such knowledge beyond a reasonable doubt.

The trial judge's charge to the jury correctly reflected the statutory requirement of knowledge. It

continued

also states that if the jury should find that the check was postdated, then the element of knowledge requires proof beyond a reasonable doubt. The jury was correctly instructed by this charge. Therefore, the jury's verdict is affirmed.

INTERPRETATION The New Jersey statute requires mere knowledge at the time the check is issued or passed that the check will not be honored by the drawee for the offense of issuing a bad check to exist.

DEFENSES TO CRIMES

Even though a defendant is found to have committed a criminal act, he will not be convicted if he has a valid defense. The defenses most relevant to white-collar crimes and crimes against business include defense of property, duress, mistake of fact, and entrapment. In some instances, a defense proves the absence of a required element of the crime; other defenses provide a justification or excuse that bars criminal liability.

Defense of Person or Property

Defense of person or property individuals may use reasonable force to protect themselves, other individuals, and their property

Individuals may use reasonable force to protect themselves, other individuals, and their property. This defense enables a person to commit, without any criminal liability, what would otherwise be considered the crime of assault, battery, manslaughter, or murder. Under the majority rule, deadly force is *never* reasonable to protect property because life is deemed more important than the protection of property. For this reason, individuals cannot use a deadly mechanical device, such as a spring gun, to protect their property. If, however, the defender's use of reasonable force in protecting his property is met with an attack upon his person, he then may use deadly force if the attack threatens him with death or serious bodily harm.

Duress

Duress coercion by threat of serious bodily injury

A person who is threatened with immediate, serious bodily harm to himself or another unless he engages in criminal activity has the valid defense of **duress** (sometimes referred to as compulsion or coercion) to criminal conduct other than murder. For example, Ann threatens to kill Ben if Ben does not assist her in committing larceny. Ben complies. Because of duress, he would not be guilty of the larceny.

Mistake of Fact

Mistake of fact honest and reasonable belief that conduct is not criminal is a defense

If a person reasonably believes the facts surrounding an act to be such that his conduct would not constitute a crime, then the law will treat the facts as he reasonably believes them to be. Accordingly, an honest and reasonable mistake of fact will justify the defendant's conduct. For example, if Ann gets into a car that she reasonably believes to be hers—the car is the same color, model, and year as hers, is parked in the same parking lot, and is started by her key—she will be relieved of criminal responsibility for taking Ben's automobile.

Entrapment

Entrapment the act of a government official in inducing another to commit a crime

The defense of **entrapment** arises when a law enforcement official induces a person to commit a crime when that person would not have done so without the persuasion of the police official. The rationale behind the rule, which applies only to government officials and agents, not to private individuals, is to prevent law enforcement officials from provoking crime and from engaging in improper conduct.

CRIMINAL PROCEDURE

Each of the states and the federal government have procedures for initiating and coordinating criminal prosecutions. In addition, the first ten amendments to the U.S. Constitution (called the Bill of Rights) guarantee many defenses and rights of an accused. The Fourth Amendment prohibits unreasonable searches and seizures to obtain incriminating evidence. The Fifth Amendment requires indictment by a grand jury for capital crimes, prevents double jeopardy, protects against self-incrimination, and prohibits deprivation of life or liberty without due process of law. The Sixth Amendment requires that an accused receive a speedy and public trial by an impartial jury and that he be informed of the nature of the accusation, be confronted with the witnesses who testify against him, be given the power to obtain witnesses in his favor, and have the right to competent counsel for his defense. The Eighth Amendment prohibits excessive bail, excessive fines, and cruel or unusual punishment. See Figure 6–2.

Most state constitutions have similar provisions to protect the rights of accused persons. In addition, the Fourteenth Amendment prohibits state governments from depriving any person of life, liberty, or property without due process of law. Moreover, the U.S. Supreme Court has held that most of the constitutional protections just discussed apply to the states through the operation of the Fourteenth Amendment.

Although various jurisdictions may differ in actual operational details, their criminal processes have a number of common objectives. The primary purpose of the process in any jurisdiction is the effective enforcement of the criminal law, but this purpose must be accomplished within the limitations imposed by other goals. These goals include advancing an adversary system of adjudication, requiring the government to bear the burden of proof, minimizing both erroneous convictions and the burdens of defense, respecting individual dignity, maintaining the appearance of fairness, and achieving equality in the administration of the process.

FIGURE 6–2 Constitutional Protection for the Criminal Defendant

Amendment	Protection Conferred
Fourth	Freedom from unreasonable search and seizure
Fifth	Right to due process Right to indictment by grand jury for capital crimes* Freedom from double jeopardy Freedom from self-incrimination
Sixth	Right to speedy, public trial by jury Right to be informed of accusations Right to confront witnesses Right to present witnesses Right to competent counsel
Eighth	Freedom from excessive bail Freedom from cruel and unusual punishment

*This right has *not* been applied to the states through the Fourteenth Amendment.

We will first discuss the steps in a criminal prosecution; we will then focus on the major constitutional protections for the accused in our system of criminal justice.

Steps in Criminal Prosecution

Steps in criminal prosecution generally include arrest, booking, formal notice of charges, preliminary hearing to determine probable cause, indictment or information, arraignment, and trial

Although the particulars of criminal procedure vary from state to state, the following provides a basic overview. After arrest, the accused is booked and appears before the magistrate, commissioner, or justice of the peace, where he is given formal notice of the charges and is advised of his rights, and where bail is set. Next, a **preliminary hearing** is held to determine whether there is probable cause to believe the defendant is the one who committed the crime. The defendant is usually entitled to be represented by counsel.

Preliminary hearing determines whether there is probable cause

If the magistrate concludes that there is probable cause, she will bind the case over to the next stage, which is either an indictment or information, depending upon the jurisdiction. The federal system and about one-third of the states require indictments for all felony prosecutions (unless waived by the defendant), while the other states permit, but do not mandate, indictments. A grand jury issues an **indictment** or true bill if it finds sufficient evidence to justify a trial on the charge brought. The grand jury, which traditionally consists of not less than sixteen and not more than twenty-three people, is not bound by the magistrate's decision at the preliminary hearing. Unlike the preliminary hearing, the grand jury does not hear evidence from the defendant; nor does the defendant appear before the grand jury. In contrast, an **information** is a formal accusation of a crime brought by a prosecuting officer, not a grand jury. Such a procedure is used in misdemeanor cases and in some felony cases in those states that do not require indictments. The indictment or information at times precedes the actual arrest.

Indictment grand jury charge that the defendant should stand trial

Information formal accusation of a crime brought by a prosecutor

At the **arraignment,** the defendant is brought before the trial court, where he is informed of the charge against him and where he enters his plea. The arraignment must be held promptly after the indictment or information has been filed. If his plea is "not guilty," the defendant must stand trial. He is entitled to a jury trial for all felonies and for misdemeanors punishable by more than six months' imprisonment. Most states also permit a defendant to request a jury trial for lesser misdemeanors. If the defendant chooses, however, he may have his guilt or innocence determined by the court sitting without a jury, which is called a "bench trial."

Arraignment (ar·raign'·ment) accused is informed of the charge against him and enters a plea

A criminal trial is similar to a civil trial, but there are some significant differences: (1) the defendant is presumed innocent, (2) the burden of proof on the prosecution is to prove criminal guilt **beyond a reasonable doubt** (proof that is entirely convincing, satisfied to a moral certainty), and (3) the defendant is not required to testify. The trial begins with the selection of the jury and the opening statements by the prosecutor and the attorney for the defense. The prosecution presents evidence first; then the defendant presents his. At the conclusion of the testimony, closing statements are made and the jury is instructed as to the applicable law and retires to arrive at a verdict. If the verdict is "not guilty," the matter ends there. The state has no right to appeal from an acquittal; and the accused, having been placed in "jeopardy," cannot be tried a second time for the same offense. If the verdict is "guilty," the judge will enter a judgment of conviction and set the case for sentencing. The defendant may make a motion for a new trial, asserting that prejudicial error occurred at his original trial, thus requiring a retrial of the case. He may appeal to a reviewing court, alleging error by the trial court and asking for either his discharge or a remandment of the case for a new trial.

Beyond a reasonable doubt proof that is entirely convincing; satisfied to a moral certainty

Fourth Amendment

The Fourth Amendment, which protects all individuals against unreasonable searches and seizures, is designed to guard the privacy and security of individuals against arbitrary invasions by government officials. Although the Fourth Amendment by its terms applies only to acts of the federal government, the Fourteenth Amendment makes it applicable to state government actions as well.

When a violation of the Fourth Amendment has occurred, the general rule prohibits the introduction of the illegally seized evidence at trial. The purpose of this **exclusionary rule** is to discourage illegal police conduct and to protect individual liberty, not to hinder the search for the truth. Nonetheless, in recent years the Supreme Court, as shown in *United States v. Leon*, has limited the exclusionary rule.

Fourth Amendment protects individuals against unreasonable searches and seizures

Exclusionary rule prohibition against the introduction of illegally seized evidence

---

UNITED STATES v. LEON Supreme Court of the United States, 1984, 468 U.S. 897, 104, S.Ct. 3405, 82 L.Ed.2d. 677

FACTS Officer Cyril Rombach of the Burbank Police Department, an experienced and well-trained narcotics officer, applied for a warrant to search several residences and automobiles for cocaine, methaqualone, and other narcotics. Rombach supported his application with information given to another police officer by a confidential informant of unproven reliability. He also based the warrant application on his own observations made during an extensive investigation—known drug offenders visiting the residences and leaving with small packages as well as a suspicious trip to Miami by two of the suspects. A state superior court judge issued a search warrant to Rombach based on this information. Rombach's searches netted large quantities of drugs and other evidence, which produced indictments of several suspects on charges of conspiracy to possess and distribute cocaine. The defendants moved to suppress the evidence on the grounds that the search warrant was defective in that Rombach had failed to establish the informant's credibility and that the information provided by the informant about the suspect's criminal activity was fatally stale. The district court declared that the search lacked probable cause, that the warrant was invalid, and that the obtained evidence must be excluded from the prosecution's case under the Fourth Amendment's exclusionary rule. The Court of Appeals for the Ninth Circuit affirmed.

DECISION Judgments of the district court and Court of Appeals reversed.

OPINION The Fourth Amendment contains no express provision mandating the exclusion of evidence obtained by an unlawful search and seizure. Consequently, an unlawful search and seizure will not automatically grant an individual a constitutional right to have the unlawfully obtained evidence excluded. When law enforcement officers act in good faith, pursuant to reasonable reliance upon a facially valid search warrant issued by a detached, neutral magistrate, the evidence obtained should not be excluded, even if the warrant is subsequently declared defective. To exclude such evidence would punish law enforcement officers, whose conduct is objectively reasonable, for a magistrate's error. It may also result in permitting some guilty defendants to go free or receive reduced sentences, simply because of a technical flaw in the application. These considerations weigh heavily in favor of recognizing a good faith exception to the exclusionary rule.

INTERPRETATION When a violation of the Fourth Amendment has occurred, the general rule prohibits the introduction of the illegally seized evidence at trial. Interpretation of the exclusionary rule, however, is frequently very difficult.

As indicated in *Leon,* to obtain a warrant to search a particular person, place, or thing, a law enforcement official must demonstrate to a magistrate that he has probable cause to believe that the search will reveal evidence of criminal activity. **Probable cause** means "[t]he task of the issuing magistrate is simply to make a practical, common-sense decision whether, given all the circumstances set forth . . . before him, . . . there is a fair probability that contraband or evidence of a crime will be found in a particular place." *Illinois v. Gates*, 462 U.S. 213 (1983).

Probable cause reasonable belief of the offense charged

THE LAW AND YOU Your Rights When Arrested

ARREST

1. When Are You Under Arrest?

Under Connecticut law, a police officer may make an arrest without a warrant under a variety of circumstances, most notably when the arresting officer has reasonable grounds to believe that an offense has been committed, or is in the process of being committed. As a consequence, the majority of arrests involving crimes that do not take place in the home are conducted without a warrant ever being issued.

Since most arrests take place without benefit of a warrant, it is important to know when an arrest has actually occurred in order to invoke the many important rights triggered by the act of arrest.

As a general rule, you are arrested whenever a law-enforcement officer takes you into custody or otherwise deprives you of your freedom of movement in any significant way. In fact, you may be under arrest even though no one has actually used the word "arrest" or any other comparable word. The fact that you have been deprived of your freedom of movement in some significant manner may amount legally to an arrest.

Under some circumstances a citizen has a limited power to conduct an arrest.

2. May a Law-Enforcement Officer Detain You Without Arresting You?

Based upon reasonable suspicion that you may be involved in criminal activity, a police officer may detain you and require you to identify yourself and explain your whereabouts at a particular time without arresting you. The officer may not, however, remove you from the immediate vicinity without making an arrest unless you voluntarily accompany the officer to some other location.

If the officer has reasonable grounds to believe you are armed or that you may be dangerous to him or her or others, the officer may conduct a limited pat-down of your outer garments for the purpose of detecting weapons. If this "frisk" results in the officer's reasonable belief that you are carrying a weapon, the officer may remove the suspicious object for the purpose of protecting him or herself. The officer must return to you any lawful object unless you are placed under arrest. Unless you are under arrest, the frisk or search is limited to suspected weapons.

The officer may ask you some questions in order to complete the field investigation. You have a constitutional right not to answer them, but it is nonetheless advisable to provide your name and address, as your failure to do so may suggest to the officer that criminal activity is afoot. Moreover, there is an infraction law requiring you to produce your license and registration to an officer when he or she stops a motor vehicle you are operating.

At the conclusion of this temporary detention, the officer must either arrest you or let you go. Ordinarily, such temporary detention should not exceed 20 minutes.

If you should enter a retail establishment where goods are placed on display for sale, the merchant or employees may detain you on the premises for a reasonable time for questioning if they have probable cause to believe that you have stolen or have attempted to steal goods for sale. Under such circumstances a police officer called to the scene may make an arrest for shoplifting even though the alleged offense was not committed in his or her presence.

3. What Are Your Rights After You Have Been Arrested?

An arrest triggers a number of constitutional protections which must be afforded by the arresting officer.

You have a right to know the crime or crimes with which you have been charged.

You have a right to know the identity of the policeman with whom you are dealing.

You have the right to communicate by telephone with your attorney, family, your friends, or a bondsman after you have been brought to the police station and booking procedures are completed.

You have the right to be represented by an attorney at all critical stages of your case, including police questioning. If you cannot afford an attorney, the court will appoint an attorney to represent you free of charge provided you qualify under existing guidelines as an insolvent person.

Remember, constitutional rights may be waived or given up voluntarily. Before you say or sign anything that might result in a waiver of a constitutional right, make sure you consult with an attorney.

4. What Rights Do You Have When Questioned by Police?

It is essential to understand that you are under absolutely no compulsion to cooperate with the police in any way should they begin questioning you about a crime for which you have been arrested, or any other crime.

You have an absolute right to remain silent. If you choose to speak, anything you say can be used against you in court. If you do decide to answer any questions, you may stop at any time and all questioning must cease.

You have a right to consult with your attorney before answering any questions.

You have the right to have your attorney present if you decide to answer any questions, and if you

---

continued

cannot afford an attorney, one will be provided for you or appointed for you by the court without cost to you, before any further questions may be asked.

5. What Should You Say?

The simple answer is that you should not say anything to anyone concerning any aspect of the offense with which you have been charged except, of course, to your attorney. You cannot legally be required or forced by a police officer or anyone else to talk, to answer questions, or sign any papers. If by threats, by persistent questions, or by other means of coercion, you are forced to give incriminating information, its use against you can be prevented in court.

Certain official parties, such as the bail commissioner, may, in the course of their duties, inquire as to certain aspects of your conduct in connection with the allegations being made. Politely refuse to respond until you have had a chance to talk to an attorney.

You may be required to provide certain nontestimonial evidence. In particular, you may be required to participate in a lineup, to prepare a sample of your penmanship, to speak phrases associated with the crime with which you are charged, to don certain wearing apparel, or to give a sample of your hair. You should ask to have your attorney present during any of these procedures. You have an absolute right to counsel if you are asked to participate in a lineup, after you have been formally charged by the prosecuting attorney.

You may also be required to be fingerprinted and photographed.

6. How Do You Arrange For a Lawyer?

If you do not know a lawyer in the area where you have been arrested and have no lawyer in your home town whom you would call, you may contact your county or city bar association for the name of an attorney on the lawyer referral list. Any attorney you contact will be happy to discuss fees with you and give you some idea of the cost involved. Normally, you have a right to a written fee agreement that outlines the basis of the fee and the scope of the matter to be handled by the attorney.

If you cannot afford a private lawyer, you should advise the judge of this fact at your first appearance or as soon after that as possible. The judge will ask you some questions to see if you are eligible for the services of an attorney at public expense. You will probably be asked to make a sworn statement as to your inability to afford a private attorney.

* * *

Record of Attest

If you are found not guilty of a charge for which you are arrested, or the charge is dismissed by the court, the law requires that all records of your arrest and prosecution be "erased" twenty (20) days after the dismissal. This does not mean the records are destroyed, but the clerk of the court and the police may not give information about your arrest to anyone. If the prosecutor "nolles" a charge for which you were arrested (that is, if he or she decides not to prosecute the case), all records of your arrest are also "erased," but not until 13 months after the nolle is entered.

This pamphlet, prepared by the Connecticut Bar Association, is based upon Connecticut law in effect at the time of its publication and is intended for general information purposes only. It is issued as a public service and is not a substitute for obtaining legal advice from a Connecticut attorney.

Reprinted by permission of the Connecticut Bar Association.

Even though the Fourth Amendment requires that a search and seizure generally be made after a valid search warrant has been obtained, in some instances a search warrant is not necessary. For example, it has been held that a warrant is not necessary where (1) there is hot pursuit of a fugitive, (2) the subject of the search voluntarily consents, (3) an emergency requires such action, (4) there has been a lawful arrest, (5) evidence of a crime is in plain view of the law enforcement officer, or (6) delay would present a significant obstacle to the investigation.

Fifth Amendment

The Fifth Amendment protects persons against self-incrimination, double jeopardy, and being charged with a capital or infamous crime except by grand jury indictment. The prohibitions against self-incrimination and double jeopardy also apply to the states through the due process clause of the Fourteenth Amendment; however, the grand jury clause does not.

The privilege against self-incrimination extends only to testimonial evidence, not to physical evidence. The Fifth Amendment "privilege protects an accused

Fifth Amendment
protects persons against self-incrimination, double jeopardy, and being charged with a capital crime except by grand jury indictment

only from being compelled to testify against himself, or otherwise provide the state with evidence of a testimonial or communicative nature." Therefore, a person can be forced to stand in an identification lineup, provide a handwriting sample, or take a blood test. Significantly, the Fifth Amendment does not protect the records of a business entity, such as a corporation or partnership; it applies only to papers of individuals. Moreover, the Fifth Amendment does not prohibit examination of an individual's business records as long as the individual is not compelled to testify against himself.

The Fifth Amendment and the Fourteenth Amendment also guarantee due process of law, which is basically the requirement of a fair trial. All persons are entitled to have the charges or complaints against them made publicly and in writing, whether in civil or criminal proceedings, and are to be given the opportunity to defend themselves against such charges. In criminal prosecutions, due process includes the right to counsel, to confront and cross-examine adverse witnesses, to testify in one's own behalf if desired, to produce witnesses and offer other evidence, and to be free from any and all prejudicial conduct and statements.

Sixth Amendment

Sixth Amendment
provides the accused with the right to a speedy and public trial, the opportunity to confront witnesses, process for obtaining witnesses, and the right to counsel

The Sixth Amendment provides that the federal government shall provide the accused with a speedy and public trial by an impartial jury, inform him of the nature and cause of the accusation, confront him with the witnesses against him, have compulsory process for obtaining witnesses in his favor, and allow him to obtain the assistance of counsel for his defense. The Fourteenth Amendment extends these guarantees to the states.

CHAPTER SUMMARY

Nature of Crimes	**Definition** any act or omission forbidden by public law
	Essential Elements
	■ *Actus Reus* wrongful or overt act
	■ *Mens Rea* criminal intent or mental fault
	Classification
	■ *Felony* a serious crime
	■ *Misdemeanor* a less serious crime
	Vicarious Liability liability imposed for acts of his or her employees if the employer directed, participated in, or approved of the acts
	Liability of a Corporation under certain circumstances a corporation may be convicted of crimes and punished by fines
	White-Collar Crime nonviolent crime involving deceit, corruption, or breach of trust
	Computer Crime use of a computer to commit a crime
	RICO federal law intended to stop organized crime from infiltrating legitimate businesses

Crimes Against Business	**Larceny** trespassory taking, and carrying away of personal property of another with the intent to deprive the victim permanently of the property **Embezzlement** taking of another's property by a person who was in lawful possession of the property **False Pretenses** obtaining title to property of another by means of representations one knows to be materially false, made with intent to defraud **Robbery** committing larceny with the use or threat of force **Burglary** under most modern statutes, an entry into a building with the intent to commit a felony **Extortion** the making of threats to obtain money or property **Bribery** offering money or property to a public official to influence the official's decision **Forgery** intentional falsification of a document in order to defraud **Bad Checks** knowingly issuing a check without funds sufficient to cover the check
Defenses to Crimes	**Defense of Person or Property** individuals may use reasonable force to protect themselves, other individuals, and their property **Duress** coercion by threat of serious bodily harm is a defense to criminal conduct other than murder **Mistake of Fact** honest and reasonable belief that conduct is not criminal is a defense **Entrapment** inducement by a law enforcement official to commit a crime is a defense
Criminal Procedure	**Steps in Criminal Prosecution** generally include arrest, booking, formal notice of charges, preliminary hearing to determine probable cause, indictment or information, arraignment, and trial **Fourth Amendment** protects individuals against unreasonable searches and seizures **Fifth Amendment** protects persons against self-incrimination, double jeopardy, and being charged with a capital crime except by grand jury indictment **Sixth Amendment** provides the accused with the right to a speedy and public trial, the opportunity to confront witnesses, process for obtaining witnesses, and the right to counsel

QUESTIONS

1. Discuss criminal intent and the various degrees of mental fault.
2. List and define the crimes against property.
3. Identify the significant features of white-collar crimes.
4. List and explain the constitutional amendments affecting criminal procedure.
5. Discuss the defenses of property, duress, mistake of fact, and entrapment.

Internet Question. Find and review (a) the Bureau of Justice's data for the burglary, theft, and motor vehicle theft rates for the last five years, and (b) information on computer crime and its trend.

PROBLEMS

1. Sam said to Carol, "Kim is going to sell me a good used car next Monday and then I'll deliver it to you in exchange for your microcomputer, but I'd like to have the computer now." Relying on this statement, Carol delivered the computer to Sam. Sam knew Kim had no car and would have none in the future, and he had no such arrangement with her. The appointed time of exchange passed, and Sam failed to deliver the car to Carol. Has a crime been committed? Discuss.

2. Sara, a lawyer, drew a deed for Robert by which Robert was to convey land to Rick. The deed was correct in every detail. Robert examined and verbally approved it but did not sign it. Sara erased Rick's name and substituted her own. Robert signed the deed with all required legal formalities without noticing the change. Was Sara guilty of forgery? Discuss.

3. Ann took Bonnie's watch before Bonnie was aware of the theft. Bonnie discovered her loss immediately and pursued Ann. Ann pointed a loaded pistol at Bonnie, who, in fear of being shot, allowed Ann to escape. Was Ann guilty of robbery? Of any other crime?

4. Jones and Wilson were on trial, separately, for larceny of a $1,000 bearer bond (payable to the holder of the bond, not a named individual) issued by Brown, Inc. The Commonwealth's evidence showed that the owner of the bond had dropped it accidentally in the street enclosed in an envelope bearing his name and address; that Jones found the envelope with the bond in it; that Jones could neither read nor write; that Jones presented the envelope and bond to Wilson, an educated man, and asked Wilson what he should do with it; that Wilson told Jones that the finder of lost property becomes the owner of it; that Wilson told Jones that the bond was worth $100 but that the money could only be collected at the issuer's home office; that Jones then handed the bond to Wilson, who redeemed it at the corporation's home office and received $1,000; that Wilson gave Jones $100 of the proceeds. What rulings?

5. Truck drivers for a hauling company, while loading a desk, found a $100 bill that had fallen out of the desk. They agreed to get it exchanged for small bills and divide the proceeds. En route to the bank, one of them changed his mind and refused to proceed with the scheme, whereupon the other pulled a knife and demanded the bill. A police officer intervened. It turned out that the bill was counterfeit money. What crimes have been committed?

6. Peter, an undercover police agent, was trying to locate a laboratory where it was believed that methamphetamine, or "speed"—a controlled substance—was being manufactured illegally. Peter went to Mary's home and said that he represented a large organization that was interested in obtaining methamphetamine. Peter offered to supply a necessary ingredient for the manufacture of the drug, which was very difficult to obtain, in return for one-half of the drug produced. Mary agreed and processed the chemical given to her by Peter in Peter's presence. Later Peter returned with a search warrant and arrested Mary. Mary was charged with various narcotics law violations. Mary asserted the defense of entrapment. Decision?

7. The police obtained a search warrant based on an affidavit that contained the following allegations: (a) Donald was seen crossing a state line on four occasions during a five-day period and going to a particular apartment; (b) telephone records disclosed that the apartment had two telephones; (c) Donald had a reputation as a bookmaker and as an associate of gamblers; and (d) the FBI was informed by a "confidential reliable informant" that Donald was conducting gambling operations. When a search was made based on the warrant, evidence was obtained that resulted in Donald's conviction of violating certain gambling laws. Donald challenged the constitutionality of the search warrant. Decision?

8. A national bank was robbed by a man with a small strip of tape on each side of his face. An indictment was returned against David. David was then arrested, and counsel was appointed to represent him. Two weeks later, without notice to David's lawyer, an FBI agent arranged to have the two bank employees observe a lineup, including David and five or six other prisoners. Each person in the lineup wore strips of tape, as had the robber, and each was directed to repeat the words "Put the money in the bag," as had the robber. Both of the bank employees identified David as the robber. At David's trial he was again identified by the two, in the courtroom, and the prior lineup identification was elicited on cross-examination by David's counsel. David's counsel moved the court either to grant a judgment of acquittal or alternatively to strike the courtroom identifications on the grounds that the lineup had violated David's Fifth Amendment privilege against self-incrimination and his Sixth Amendment right to counsel. Decision?

9. Waronek owned and operated a trucking rig, transporting goods for L.T.L. Perishables, Inc., of St. Paul, Minnesota. He accepted an offer to haul a trailer load of beef from Illini Beef Packers, Inc., in Joslin, Illinois, to Midtown Packing Company in New York City. After his truck was loaded with ninety-five forequarters and ninety-five hindquarters of beef in Joslin, Waronek drove north to his home in Watertown, Wisconsin, rather than east to New York. While in Watertown, he asked employees of the Royal Meat Company to

butcher and prepare four hindquarters of beef—two for himself and two for his friends. He also offered to sell ten hindquarters to one employee of the company at an alarmingly reduced rate. The suspicious employee contacted the authorities, who told him to proceed with the deal. When Waronek arrived in New York with his load short nineteen hindquarters, Waronek telephoned L.T.L. Perishables in St. Paul. He notified them "that he was short nineteen hindquarters, that he knew where the beef went, and that he would make good on it out of future settlements." L.T.L. told him to contact the New York police but he failed to do so. Shortly thereafter, he was arrested by the Federal Bureau of Investigation and indicted for the embezzlement of goods moving in interstate commerce. Decision?

10. Four separate cases involving similar fact situations were consolidated since they presented the same constitutional question. In each case, police officers, detectives, or prosecuting attorneys took a defendant into custody and interrogated him in a police station to obtain a confession. In none of these cases did the officials fully and effectively advise the defendant of his rights at the outset of the interrogation. The interrogations produced oral admissions of guilt from each defendant, as well as signed statements from three of them, which were used to convict them at their trials. The defendants appeal, arguing that the officials should have warned them of their constitutional rights and the consequences of waiving them before the questioning began. It was contended that to permit any statements obtained without such a warning violated their Fifth Amendment privilege against self-incrimination. Decision?

CHAPTER 7

Intentional Torts

Tort a civil wrong causing injury to persons, their property, or their economic interests

All forms of civil liability are either (1) voluntarily assumed, as by contract, or (2) involuntarily assumed, as imposed by law. Tort liability is of the second type. **Tort** law gives persons relief from civil wrongs or injuries to their persons, property, and economic interests. This law has three principal objectives: (1) to compensate persons who sustain harm or loss resulting from another's conduct, (2) to place the cost of that compensation only on those parties who should bear it, and (3) to prevent future harms and losses. Thus, the law of torts reallocates losses caused by human misconduct. In general, a tort is committed when (1) a duty owed by one person to another (2) is breached, (3) proximately causing (4) injury or damage to the owner of a legally protected interest.

Each person is legally responsible for the damages proximately caused by his tortious conduct. Moreover, as we will discuss in Chapter 30, businesses that conduct their business activities through employees are also liable for the torts their employees commit in the course of employment. The tort liability of employers makes the study of tort law essential to business managers.

Injuries may be inflicted intentionally, negligently, or without fault (strict liability). We will discuss intentional torts in this chapter and cover negligence and strict liability in Chapter 8.

The same conduct may, and often does, constitute both a crime and a tort. For example, let us assume that Johnson has committed an assault and battery against West. For the commission of this crime, the state may take appropriate action against Johnson. In addition, Johnson has violated West's right to be secure in his person, and so has committed a tort against West. Regardless of the criminal action brought by the state against Johnson, West may bring a civil tort action against Johnson for damages. But an act may be criminal without being tortious; by the same token, an act may be a tort but not a crime.

Punitive damages *(pu´·ni·tive)* damages awarded in excess of normal compensation to punish a defendant for a serious civil wrong

In a tort action, the injured party *sues* to recover *compensation* for the injury sustained as a result of the defendant's wrongful conduct. The purpose of tort law, unlike criminal law, is to compensate the injured party, not to punish the wrongdoer. In certain cases, however, courts may award exemplary or **punitive damages**, which are damages over and above the amount necessary to compensate the plaintiff. Where the defendant's tortious conduct has been intentional and outrageous, showing malice or a fraudulent or evil motive, most courts permit a jury to award punitive damages. The allowance of punitive damages is designed to punish and make an example of the defendant and thus deter others from similar conduct.

BMW OF NORTH AMERICA, INC. v. GORE United States Supreme Court, 1996, ____ U.S. ____ , 116 S.Ct. 1589, 134 L.Ed.2d 809

FACTS Gore purchased a BMW sports sedan from an authorized BMW dealer in Alabama for $40,750.88. The national distributor of BMW automobiles in America, BMW of North America (BMW), did not inform the dealer that the car had been repainted prior to delivery. BMW's policy at the time of sale was not to inform dealers of repairs costing less than 3 percent of the retail price of the car, a policy that was legal in many states. Gore noticed no flaws in the appearance of the automobile at the time of purchase. Nine months later, however, Gore took the car to a detailer who told him that the sedan appeared to have been repainted. Gore brought suit against BMW for actual and punitive damages, alleging that the failure to disclose the repainting of the car constituted suppression of a material fact. To support his claim for punitive damages, Gore introduced evidence that since 1983 BMW had without disclosure sold 983 refinished cars as new, including fourteen in Alabama. Using $4,000 per vehicle as actual damages, Gore argued that an appropriate punitive damage award would be $4 million for the approximately 1,000 vehicles sold for more than they were worth. The jury at trial awarded compensatory damages of $4,000 and punitive damages of $4,000,000. The trial judge denied BMW's posttrial motion to set aside the punitive damage award. On appeal, the Alabama Supreme Court held that the jury's calculation of the punitive award was improper because it considered BMW's conduct in other jurisdictions. The state high court reduced the punitive award to $2,000,000, which it considered "constitutionally reasonable," based on other punitive awards for comparable conduct in Alabama and other jurisdictions. The court expressly disclaimed any reliance on acts that had occurred in other jurisdictions.

DECISION Judgment reversed.

OPINION Principles of sovereignty and comity preclude a state from imposing economic sanctions on violators of its laws with the intent of changing the tortfeasors' lawful conduct in other states. Therefore, a state may not base a punitive award on out-of-state conduct.

To satisfy the Due Process Clause of the Fourteenth Amendment, a punitive damage award by a state court must not be "grossly excessive" in relation to the state's legitimate interests in punishment and deterrence. Based on BMW's conduct solely in Alabama, this punitive award is "grossly excessive." To ensure that a person has been given fair notice of possible punishment for his misconduct, three indices of excessiveness are applied to punitive damage awards: (1) the degree of reprehensibility of the conduct, (2) the ratio of punitive damages to compensatory damages, and (3) a comparison of the punitive award to the civil and criminal penalties that could be imposed for similar misconduct. The degree of reprehensibility of BMW's conduct is slight since the resulting harm was purely economic and the conduct created no risk to health or safety. The absence of such aggravating factors supports a finding that this punitive award was excessive. The disparity between the harm or potential harm and the punitive damages award here is extraordinarily large. Although no simple mathematical formula may be established as to what ratio is constitutionally reasonable, in this case the punitive award is a breathtaking five hundred times greater than the compensatory damages. Finally, the difference between the punitive award in this case and the civil penalties authorized or imposed in comparable cases is enormous. In Alabama, a violation of the Deceptive Trade Practices Act carries a maximum civil penalty of $2,000. The severest sanctions in other states are $5,000 to $10,000. None of these statutes would put a person on fair notice that such conduct would subject her to a multimillion dollar sanction. Also, there is no evidence that a more modest sanction would not have served the purpose of deterring future misconduct. In conclusion, each of the three indices stated above support a finding that this award was constitutionally excessive.

INTERPRETATION In most states a jury may award punitive damages if a defendant's tortious conduct is intentional and outrageous, but the amount of damages must not be grossly excessive.

Tort law is primarily common law, and, as we mentioned in Chapter 1, the Restatements, prepared by the American Law Institute, present many important areas of the common law, including torts. You will recall that although they are not law in themselves, the Restatements are highly persuasive in the courts.

Intent, as used in tort law, does not require a hostile or evil motive. Rather, it means that the actor desires to cause the consequences of his act *or* that he believes the consequences are substantially (almost) certain to result from it.

Intent desire to cause the consequences of an act or knowledge that the consequences are substantially certain to result from the act

(See Figure 7–1.) The following examples illustrate the definition of intent: (1) If Mark fires a gun in the middle of the Mojave Desert, he intends to fire the gun; but when the bullet hits Steven, who is in the desert without Mark's knowledge, Mark does not intend that result. (2) Mark throws a bomb into Steven's office in order to kill Steven. Mark knows that Carol is in Steven's office and that the bomb is substantially certain to injure Carol, although Mark has no desire to harm her. Mark is, nonetheless, liable to Carol for any injury caused Carol. Mark's intent to injure Steven is *transferred* to Carol.

Infants (persons who have not reached the age of majority) are held liable for their intentional torts. The infant's age and knowledge, however, are critical in determining whether the infant had sufficient intelligence to form the required intent. Incompetents, like infants, are generally held liable for their intentional torts.

Even though the defendant has intentionally invaded the interests of the plaintiff, the defendant will not be liable if such conduct was privileged. A defendant's conduct is **privileged** if it furthers an interest of such social importance that the law grants immunity from tort liability for damage to others. Examples of privilege include self-defense, defense of property, and defense of others. In addition, the plaintiff's consent to the defendant's conduct is a defense to intentional torts.

HARM TO THE PERSON

The law provides protection against harm to the person. Generally, intentional torts to the person entitle the injured party to recover damages for bodily harm, emotional distress, loss or impairment of earning capacity, reasonable medical expenses, and harm the tortious conduct caused to property or business.

FIGURE 7–1 Intent

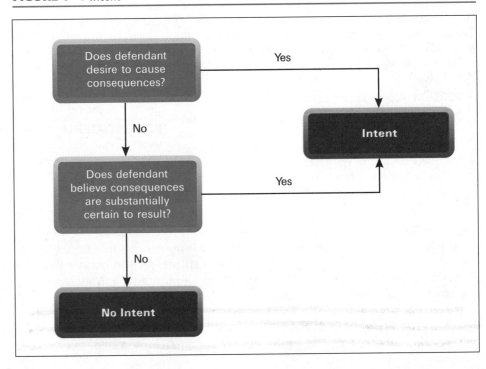

Battery

Battery is an intentional infliction of harmful or offensive bodily contact. It may consist of contact causing serious injury, such as a gunshot wound or a blow on the head with a club. Or it may involve contact causing little or no physical injury, such as knocking a hat off of a person's head or flicking a glove in another's face. Bodily contact is offensive if it would offend a reasonable person's sense of dignity. Such contact may be accomplished through the use of objects, such as Gustav's throwing a rock at Hester with the intention of hitting her. If the rock hits Hester or any other person, Gustav has committed a battery.

Battery intentional infliction of harmful or offensive bodily contact

Assault

Assault is intentional conduct by one person directed at another that places the other in apprehension of immediate bodily harm or offensive contact. It is usually committed immediately before a battery, but if the intended battery fails, the assault remains. Assault is essentially a mental rather than a physical intrusion. Accordingly, damages for it may include compensation for fright and humiliation. The person in danger of immediate bodily harm must have *knowledge* of the danger and be apprehensive of its imminent threat to his safety.

Assault intentional infliction of apprehension of immediate bodily harm or offensive contact

False Imprisonment

The tort of **false imprisonment** or **false arrest** is the act of intentionally confining a person against her will within fixed boundaries if the person is conscious of the confinement or harmed by it. Such restraint may be brought about by physical force, the threat of physical force, or by force directed against a person's property. Damages for false imprisonment may include compensation for loss of time, physical discomfort, inconvenience, physical illness, and mental suffering. As in *Peterson v. Sorlien,* merely obstructing a person's freedom of movement is not false imprisonment so long as a reasonable alternative exit is available.

False imprisonment intentional interference with a person's freedom of movement by unlawful confinement

Merchants occasionally encounter potential liability for false imprisonment when they seek to question a suspected shoplifter. If the merchant detains an innocent person, she may face a lawsuit for false imprisonment. However, most states have statutes protecting the merchant, provided she detains the suspect with probable cause, in a reasonable manner, and for not more than a reasonable time.

PETERSON v. SORLIEN Supreme Court of Minnesota, 1980, 299 N.W.2d 123

FACTS Susan Jungclaus Peterson was a twenty-one-year-old student at Moorhead State University who had lived most of her life on her family farm in Minnesota. Though Susan was a dean's list student during her first year, her academic performance declined after she became deeply involved in an international religious cult organization known locally as The Way of Minnesota, Inc. The cult demanded an enormous psychological and monetary commitment from Susan. Near the end of her junior year, her parents became alarmed by the changes in Susan's physical and mental well-being and concluded that she had been "reduced to a condition of psychological bondage by The Way." They sought help from Kathy Mills, a self-styled "deprogrammer" of minds brainwashed by cults.

On May 24, 1976, Norman Jungclaus, Susan's father, picked up Susan at Moorhead State. Instead of returning home, they went to the residence of Veronica Morgel, where Kathy Mills attempted to deprogram Susan. For the first few days of her stay, Susan was unwilling to discuss her involvement. She lay curled in a fetal position in her bedroom, plugging her ears and hysterically screaming and crying while her father pleaded with her to listen. By the third day, however, Susan's demeanor changed completely. She became friendly and vivacious and communicated with her father. Susan also went roller skating and played softball at a nearby park over the following weekend. She spent the next week in Columbus, Ohio, with a former cult member who had shared her experiences

continued

of the previous week. While in Columbus, she spoke daily by telephone with her fiancé, a member of The Way, who begged her to return to the cult. Susan expressed the desire to get her fiancé out of the organization, but a meeting between them could not be arranged outside the presence of other members of The Way. Her parents attempted to persuade Susan to sign an agreement releasing them from liability for their actions, but Susan refused. After nearly sixteen days of "deprogramming" Susan left the Morgel residence and returned to her fiancé and The Way. Upon the direction of The Way ministry, she brought this action against her parents for false imprisonment. Susan appealed from the trial court's judgment in favor of her parents.

DECISION Judgment for Mr. and Mrs. Jungclaus affirmed.

OPINION "If a person is aware of a reasonable means of escape that does not present a danger of bodily or material harm, a restriction is not total and complete and does not constitute unlawful imprisonment." Also, a person cannot recover damages for any period of detention to which she voluntarily consents. For the final thirteen days of the sixteen-day period Susan willingly remained in the company of her parents. She also had several reasonable and safe opportunities to escape while playing softball, roller skating, and traveling to and within Ohio. Given that the conditioning of the cult may have impaired her free will prior to her "deprogramming," it is reasonable to infer from her subsequent consent that she would have consented to the first three days' detention if she had had her full capacity. Furthermore, parents may place limitations on their adult child's mobility if they have a good-faith, reasonable belief that the child's judgmental capacity has been seriously affected by a cult and if she at some point assents to the limitations. Thus, Susan's assent during the thirteen-day period relieved her parents of liability for false imprisonment.

INTERPRETATION The key elements of false imprisonment are the plaintiff's being detained against his will and the plaintiff's knowing of no reasonable means of escape.

Infliction of Emotional Distress

Infliction of emotional distress extreme and outrageous conduct intentionally or recklessly causing severe emotional distress

Infliction of emotional distress occurs when a person by extreme and outrageous conduct intentionally or recklessly causes severe emotional distress to another, thereby imposing liability upon himself for such emotional distress as well as for any resulting bodily harm. As shown in *Agis v. Howard Johnson*, damages may be recovered for severe emotional distress even in the absence of any physical injury.

This cause of action does not protect a person from abusive language or rudeness but rather from atrocious, intolerable conduct beyond all bounds of decency. Examples of this tort include sexual harassment on the job and outrageous and prolonged bullying tactics employed by creditors or collection agencies attempting to collect a debt, or by insurance adjusters trying to force a settlement of an insurance claim.

AGIS v. HOWARD JOHNSON COMPANY Supreme Judicial Court of Massachusetts, 1976, 371 Mass. 140, 355 N.E.2d 315

FACTS Debra Agis was a waitress in a restaurant owned by the Howard Johnson Company. On May 23, 1975, Roger Dionne, manager of the restaurant, called a meeting of all waitresses at which he informed them that "there was some stealing going on." Dionne also stated that the identity of the party or parties responsible was not known and that he would begin firing all waitresses in alphabetical order until the guilty party or parties were detected. He then fired Debra Agis, who allegedly "became greatly upset, began to cry, sustained emotional distress, mental anguish, and loss of wages and earnings." Mrs. Agis brought this complaint against the Howard Johnson Company and Roger Dionne, alleging that the defendants acted recklessly and outrageously, intending to cause emotional distress and anguish. The defendants argued that damages for emotional distress are not recoverable unless physical injury occurs as a result of the distress. The judge dismissed the complaint, and Mrs. Agis appealed.

DECISION Judgment dismissing the complaint reversed.

continued

OPINION An individual "who, by extreme and outrageous conduct and without privilege, causes severe emotional distress to another is subject to liability for such emotional distress even though no bodily harm may result." Mrs. Agis successfully established the following four essential elements: (1) that the defendants intended to cause emotional distress or that they knew or should have known that emotional distress was likely to result from their conduct; (2) that the defendants'

conduct was "extreme and outrageous" and "beyond all possible bounds of decency"; (3) that the defendants' actions caused Mrs. Agis's distress; and (4) that Mrs. Agis's emotional distress was "severe" and such "that no reasonable man could be expected to endure it."

INTERPRETATION Physical injury is not required for a plaintiff to recover damages for severe emotional distress caused by extreme and outrageous conduct.

HARM TO THE RIGHT OF DIGNITY

The law also protects a person against intentional interference with, or harm to, his right of dignity. This protection covers a person's reputation, privacy, and right to freedom from unjustifiable litigation.

Defamation

As we discussed in Chapter 4, the tort of **defamation** is a false communication that injures a person's reputation by disgracing him and diminishing the respect in which he is held. An example would be the publication of a false statement that a person had committed a crime or had a loathsome disease.

Elements of Defamation The elements of a defamation action are (1) a false and defamatory statement concerning another, (2) an unprivileged publication (communication) to a third party, (3) in some cases, depending on the status of the defendant, some degree of fault on her part in knowing or failing to ascertain the falsity of the statement, and (4) in some cases, proof of special harm caused by the publication. The burden of proof is on the plaintiff to prove the falsity of the defamatory statement.

If the defamatory communication is handwritten, typewritten, printed, pictorial, or in any other medium with similar communicative power, such as a television or radio broadcast, it is designated as **libel**. If it is spoken or oral, it is designated as **slander**. In either case, it must be communicated to a person or persons other than the one who is defamed, a process referred to as its ***publication.*** Thus, if Maurice writes a defamatory letter about Pierre's character that he hands or mails to Pierre, this is not a publication because it is intended only for Pierre.

A significant new trend affecting business has been the bringing of defamation suits against former employers by discharged employees. It has been reported that such suits comprise approximately one-third of all defamation lawsuits. The following case demonstrates the consequences of failing to be careful in discharging an employee.

Defamation
(def·a·ma´·tion)
injury to a person's reputation by communication of false statements

Libel defamation communicated by writing, television, radio, or the like

Slander oral defamation

FRANK B. HALL & CO., INC. v. BUCK Court of Appeals of Texas, Fourteenth District, 1984, 678 S.W.2d 612

FACTS On June 1, 1976, Larry W. Buck, an established salesman in the insurance business, began working for Frank B. Hall & Co. In the course of the ensuing months, Buck brought several major accounts to Hall and produced substantial commission income for the

firm. In October 1976, Mendel Kaliff, then president of Frank B. Hall & Co. of Texas, informed Buck that his salary and benefits were being reduced because of his failure to generate sufficient income for the firm. On March 31, 1977, Kaliff and Lester Eckert, Hall's office

continued

manager, fired Buck. Buck was unable to procure subsequent employment with another insurance firm. He hired an investigator, Lloyd Barber, to discover the true reasons for his dismissal and for his inability to find other employment.

Barber contacted Kaliff, Eckert, and Virginia Hilley, a Hall employee, and told them he was an investigator and was seeking information about Buck's employment with the firm. Barber conducted tape-recorded interviews with the three in September and October of 1977. Kaliff accused Buck of being disruptive, untrustworthy, paranoid, hostile, untruthful, and of padding his expense account. Eckert referred to Buck as "a zero" and a "classical sociopath" who was ruthless, irrational, and disliked by other employees. Hilley stated that Buck could have been charged with theft for certain materials he brought with him from his former employer to Hall. Buck sued Hall for damages for defamation and was awarded over $1.9 million by a jury—$605,000 for actual damages and $1,300,000 for punitive damages. Hall then brought this appeal.

DECISION Judgment for Buck affirmed.

OPINION Any intentional or negligent communication of defamatory matter to a third person is a publication, unless the defamed individual authorized, invited, or procured the statement or statements and knew of their contents in advance. The Hall employees intentionally communicated disparaging remarks about Buck to Barber. While it may be true that Buck could assume the employees would express their opinion of him, he did not know they would defame him. Their accusations were not mere opinions but were untrue and derogatory statements of fact. Although the comments were directed at an individual acting at Buck's request, communication to an agent of the defamed individual qualifies as a publication unless the defamed individual or his agent invited the publication. In this case, neither Buck nor Barber induced the defamatory remarks.

INTERPRETATION The key elements of defamation are that the statements made are false, injure the plaintiff's reputation, and are published.

Privilege immunity from tort liability

Defenses to Defamation **Privilege** is an immunity from tort liability granted when the defendant's conduct furthers a societal interest of greater importance than the injury inflicted upon the plaintiff. Three kinds of privileges apply to defamation: absolute, conditional, and constitutional.

Absolute privilege, which protects the defendant regardless of his motive or intent, has been confined to those few situations where public policy clearly favors complete freedom of speech. Such privilege includes (1) statements made by participants regarding a judicial proceeding; (2) statements made by members of Congress on the floor of Congress; (3) statements made by certain executive branch officers while performing their governmental duties; and (4) statements regarding a third party made between spouses when they are alone.

Qualified or *conditional privilege* depends on proper use of the privilege. A person has a conditional privilege to publish defamatory matter to protect her own legitimate interests or, in some cases, the interests of another. Conditional privilege also extends to many communications in which the publisher and the recipient have a common interest, such as letters of reference. Conditional privilege, however, is forfeited by a publisher who acts in an excessive manner, without probable cause, or for an improper purpose.

The First Amendment to the U.S. Constitution guarantees freedom of speech and freedom of the press. The U.S. Supreme Court has applied these rights to the law of defamation by extending a form of *constitutional privilege* to comment about public officials or public figures so long as it is done without *malice*. For these purposes, "malice" is not ill will but clear and convincing proof of the publisher's knowledge of falsity or reckless disregard of the truth. Thus, under constitutional privilege, the public official or public figure must prove that the defendant published the defamatory and false comment with knowledge or in reckless disregard of the comment's falsity and its defamatory character.

MANAGERIAL INSIGHT

Employment References and Liability for Defamation

If you own or manage a business, you can expect employees to leave for a variety of reasons. When your present or former employees apply for work elsewhere, their potential new employers may well call you to verify their employment history and ask your opinion of them as employees. Should you give that information?

In the 1980s, many employers stopped giving meaningful references for former employees. Some employers would verify only employment dates and job titles of former employees. Others would give no information at all. The reason? Fear of liability for defamation and of incurring large legal expenses to defend a lawsuit.

Are those fears justified? Does the benefit of minimizing risk outweigh the cost of shutting down a legitimate and valuable information system?

Two researchers surveyed all published employee defamation cases in state and federal trial and appeals courts for 1965–69 and 1985–89, taking special note of cases involving employment references. They concluded that employers faced less risk in the 1980s. Although the number of lawsuits went up, plaintiffs won less often in the 1980s than in the 1960s, and damage awards decreased slightly. The researchers suggest that employers who stopped giving references may have overreacted to sensational newspaper accounts of large damage awards.

Points to consider:

- The law actually offers employers more protection since a key Supreme Court decision in 1974. Before that decision, an employer who published an employee-related statement that turned out to be untrue was strictly liable. Now the employer is liable for a false statement only if she was negligent in attempting to establish its truth.
- Employment references enjoy qualified privilege, unless the employer communicates the statements to people with no need to know their contents or publishes them out of spite.
- Employment references are valuable. Employers who expect to get useful information about job applicants should also be willing to give it.

You can reduce the risk of liability when giving employment references if you. . .

- Endeavor to ensure that all statements you publish about an employee are true. Your effort can be used as a defense against negligence.
- Make sure you publish statements only to people with a legitimate need to know, i.e., potential employers.
- Regulate the giving of references in your company. Make sure people who work for you understand who may give references and who may not. And make sure they know that no one is ever to publish statements maliciously.
- Ask your existing employees to give you written consent to provide references for them.

Source: Ramona L. Paetzold and Steven L. Wilborn, "Employer (Ir)rationality and the Demise of Employment References," *American Business Law Journal*, May 1992, 123–42.

In a defamation suit brought by a private person (one who is neither a public official nor a public figure) against a member of the news media, the plaintiff must prove that the defendant published the defamatory and false comment with malice *or* negligence. By comparison, in a suit brought by a private person against a defendant who is *not* a member of the news media, the question whether the plaintiff must prove anything beyond the fact that a defamatory statement has been made is currently unresolved.

Invasion of Privacy

The invasion of a person's right to privacy actually consists of four distinct torts: (1) appropriation of a person's name or likeness; (2) unreasonable intrusion on the seclusion of another; (3) unreasonable public disclosure of private facts; or (4) unreasonable publicity that places another in a false light in the public eye.

It is entirely possible and not uncommon for a person's right of privacy to be invaded in a manner entailing two or more of these related torts. For example, Bart forces his way into Cindy's hospital room, takes a photograph of Cindy, and publishes it to promote his cure for Cindy's illness along with false statements about Cindy that would be highly objectionable to a reasonable person. Cindy would be entitled to recover on any or all of the four torts comprising invasion of privacy.

Appropriation

(ap·pro·pri·a'·tion)
unauthorized use of another person's identity for one's own benefit

Appropriation **Appropriation** is the unauthorized use of another person's name or likeness for one's own benefit, as, for example, in promoting or advertising a product or service. The tort of appropriation, which seeks to protect the individual's right to the exclusive use of his identity, is also known as the "right of publicity." In the example above, Bart's use of Cindy's photograph to promote Bart's business constitutes the tort of appropriation. The following case involving Vanna White is also an example of appropriation.

WHITE v. SAMSUNG ELECTRONICS United States Court of Appeals, Ninth Circuit, 1992, 971 F.2d 1395

FACTS Plaintiff, Vanna White, is the hostess of *Wheel of Fortune,* one of the most popular game shows in television history. Samsung Electronics and David Deutsch Associates ran an advertisement for video cassette recorders that depicted a robot dressed in a wig, gown, and jewelry chosen to resemble White's hair and dress. The robot was posed in a stance, for which White is famous, next to a game board, which is instantly recognizable as the *Wheel of Fortune* game show set. The caption of the ad read: "Longest-running game show. 2012 A.D." Defendants referred to the ad as the "Vanna White" ad. White neither consented to the ads nor was she paid for them. White sued Samsung and Deutsch under the California common law right of publicity. The district court granted summary judgment against White on this claim.

DECISION Judgment reversed.

OPINION The law protects a person's exclusive right to exploit the value of her identity. To state a cause of action under the California common law right of publicity, a plaintiff must allege (1) the defendant's use of the plaintiff's identity; (2) the appropriation of the plaintiff's name or likeness to the defendant's advantage, commercially or otherwise; (3) lack of consent; and (4) resulting injury. In this case, the district court dismissed White's claim for failure to meet the second element. Although the robot ad did not make use of White's name or likeness, the common law right of publicity is not so confined. The "name or likeness" formulation originated not as an element of the right of publicity cause of action, but as a description of the types of cases in which the cause of action had been recognized. The case law has borne out that the right of publicity is not limited to the appropriation of name or likeness. The specific means of appropriation are relevant only for determining whether the defendant has

in fact appropriated the plaintiff's identity. It is not important how the defendant has appropriated the plaintiff's identity, but whether the defendant has done so.

To consider the means of appropriation as dispositive would not only weaken the right of publicity but would effectively eviscerate it. The identities of the most popular celebrities are not only the most attractive for advertisers but also the easiest to evoke without resorting to obvious means such as name, likeness, or voice. Consider a hypothetical advertisement that depicts a mechanical robot with male features, an African-American complexion, and a bald head. The robot is wearing black high-top Air Jordan basketball sneakers and a red basketball uniform with black trim, baggy shorts, and the number 23 (though not revealing "Bulls" or "Jordan" lettering). The ad depicts the robot dunking a basketball one-handed, stiff-armed, legs extended like open scissors, and tongue hanging out. Now envision that this ad is run on television during professional basketball games. Considered individually, the robot's physical attributes, its dress, and its stance tell us little. Taken together, they lead to the only conclusion that any sports viewer who has registered a discernible pulse in the past five years would reach: the ad depicts Michael Jordan.

Viewed together, the individual aspects of the ad in the present case leave little doubt about the celebrity the ad is meant to depict. Indeed, the defendants themselves referred to their ad as the "Vanna White" ad. Because White has alleged facts showing that Samsung and Deutsch had appropriated her identity, the district court erred by rejecting, on summary judgment, White's common law right of publicity claim.

INTERPRETATION The tort of appropriation protects a person's exclusive right to exploit the value of her identity.

Intrusion **Intrusion** is the unreasonable and highly offensive interference with the solitude or seclusion of another. Such unreasonable interference includes improper entry into another's dwelling, unauthorized eavesdropping on another's private conversations, and unauthorized examination of another's private papers and records. The intrusion must be offensive or objectionable to a reasonable person and must involve private matters. Thus, there is no liability if the defendant examines public records or observes the plaintiff in a public place. This form of invasion of privacy is committed once the intrusion occurs—publicity is not required.

> **Intrusion** unreasonable and highly offensive interference with the seclusion of another

Public Disclosure of Private Facts Under the tort of **public disclosure of private facts**, liability is imposed for *publicity* given to private information about another, if the matter made public would be highly offensive and objectionable to a reasonable person. Like intrusion, this tort applies only to private, not public, information about an individual; unlike intrusion, it requires publicity. Under the Restatement, the publicity required differs in degree from "publication" as used in the law of defamation. This tort requires that private facts be communicated to the public at large or that they become public knowledge, whereas publication of a defamatory statement need only be made to a single third party. Thus Kathy, a creditor of Gary, will not invade Gary's privacy by writing a letter to Gary's employer informing the employer of Gary's failure to pay the debt, but Kathy would be liable if she posted in the window of her store a statement that Gary will not pay a debt owed to her. Some courts, however, have allowed recovery where the disclosure was made to only one person. Also, unlike defamation, this tort applies to truthful private information if the matter published would be offensive and objectionable to a reasonable person of ordinary sensibilities.

> **Public disclosure of private facts** offensive publicity given to private information about another person

False Light The tort of **false light** imposes liability for highly offensive *publicity* placing another in a false light if the defendant *knew* that the matter publicized was false or acted in *reckless disregard* of the truth. For example, Edgar includes Jason's name and photograph in a public "rogues' gallery" of convicted criminals. Because Jason has never been convicted of any crime, Edgar is liable to Jason for placing him in a false light.

As with defamation, the matter must be untrue; unlike defamation, it must be "publicized," not merely "published." Although the matter must be objectionable to a reasonable person, it need not be defamatory. In many instances, the same facts will give rise to actions both for defamation and for false light.

> **False light** offensive publicity placing another in a false light

Defenses The defenses of *absolute, conditional,* and *constitutional* privilege apply to publication of any matter that is an invasion of privacy to the same extent that such defenses apply to defamation.

Misuse of Legal Procedure

Three torts comprise the **misuse of legal procedure:** malicious prosecution, wrongful civil proceedings, and abuse of process. Each protects an individual from being subjected to unjustifiable litigation. *Malicious prosecution* and *wrongful civil proceedings* impose liability for damages caused by improperly brought proceedings, including harm to reputation, credit, or standing; emotional distress; and the expenses incurred in defending against the wrongfully brought lawsuit. *Abuse of process* consists of using a legal proceeding (criminal or civil) to

> **Misuse of legal procedure** torts protecting an individual from unjustifiable litigation

accomplish a purpose for which the proceeding is not designed. This misuse of procedure applies even when there is probable cause or when the plaintiff or prosecution succeeds in the litigation.

HARM TO PROPERTY

The law also provides protection against invasions of a person's interests in property. Intentional harm to property includes the torts of (1) trespass to real property, (2) nuisance, (3) trespass to personal property, and (4) conversion.

Real Property

Real property is land and anything attached to it, such as buildings, trees, and minerals. The law protects the possessor's rights to the exclusive use and quiet enjoyment of the land. Accordingly, damages for harm to land include compensation for the resulting diminution in the value of the land, the loss of use of the land, and the discomfort caused to the possessor of the land.

Trespass A person is liable for **trespass to real property** if he intentionally (1) enters or remains on land in the possession of another, (2) causes a thing or a third person to so enter or remain, or (3) fails to remove from the land a thing that he is under a duty to remove. Liability exists even though no actual damage is done to the land.

It is no defense that the intruder acted under the mistaken belief of law or fact that he was not trespassing. If the intruder intended to be on the particular property, his reasonable belief that he owned the land or had permission to enter on it is irrelevant. However, an intruder is not liable if his presence on the land of another is not caused by his own actions. For example, if Shirley is thrown onto Roy's land by Jimmy, Shirley is not liable to Roy for trespass, although Jimmy is.

A trespass may be committed on, beneath, or above the surface of the land, although the law regards the upper air, above a prescribed minimum altitude for flight, as a public highway. No aerial trespass occurs unless the aircraft enters into the lower reaches of the airspace and substantially interferes with the landowner's use and enjoyment.

Nuisance A **nuisance** is a nontrespassory invasion of another's interest in the private use and enjoyment of land. In contrast to trespass, nuisance does not require interference with another's right to exclusive possession of land, but rather imposes liability for significant and unreasonable harm to another's use or enjoyment of land. Examples of nuisances include the emission of unpleasant odors, smoke, dust, or gas, as well as the pollution of a stream, pond, or underground water supply.

Personal Property

Personal property is any type of property other than an interest in land. The law protects a number of interests in the possession of personal property, including an interest in the property's physical condition and usability, an interest in the retention of possession, and an interest in the property's availability for future use.

Real property land and anything attached to it

Trespass to real property wrongful entry onto another's land

Nuisance nontrespassory invasion of another's interest in the private use and enjoyment of her land

Personal property any property other than an interest in land

Trespass **Trespass to personal property** consists of the intentional dispossession or unauthorized use of the personal property of another. Although the interference with the right to exclusive use and possession may be direct or indirect, liability is limited to instances in which the trespasser (1) dispossesses the other of the property; (2) substantially impairs the condition, quality, or value of the property; or (3) deprives the possessor of use of the property for a substantial time. For example, Albert parks his car in front of his house. Later, Ronald pushes Albert's car around the corner. Albert subsequently looks for his car but cannot find it for several hours. Ronald is liable to Albert for trespass.

Trespass to personal property intentional dispossession or unauthorized use of the personal property of another

Conversion **Conversion** is an intentional exercise of dominion or control over another's personal property that so seriously interferes with the other's right of control as justly to require the payment of full value for the property. Thus, all conversions are trespasses, but not all trespasses are conversions. Conversion may consist of the intentional destruction of the personal property or the use of the property in an unauthorized manner. For example, Barbara entrusts an automobile to Ken, a dealer, for sale. After he drives the car 8,000 miles on his own business, Ken is liable to Barbara for conversion. On the other hand, in the example in which Ronald pushed Albert's car around the corner, Ronald would *not* be liable to Albert for conversion.

Conversion intentional exercise of dominion or control over another's personal property

HARM TO ECONOMIC INTERESTS

Economic interests comprise a fourth set of interests the law protects against intentional interference. Economic or pecuniary interests include a person's existing and prospective contractual relations, a person's business reputation, a person's name and likeness (previously discussed under appropriation), and a person's freedom from deception. In this section, we will discuss business torts—those torts that protect a person's economic interests.

Interference with Contractual Relations
Interference with contractual relations involves interfering intentionally and improperly with the performance of a contract by inducing one of the parties not to perform it. (Contracts are discussed extensively in Part Three of this text.) The injured party may recover the economic loss resulting from the breach of the contract. The law imposes similar liability for intentional and improper interference with another's prospective contractual relation, such as a lease renewal or financing for construction.

Interference with contractual relations intentionally causing one of the parties to a contract not to perform the contract

In either case, the rule requires that a person act with the purpose or motive of interfering with another's contract or with the knowledge that such interference is substantially certain to occur as a natural consequence of her actions. The interference may be by prevention through the use of physical force or by threats. Frequently, the interference is accomplished by inducement, such as the offer of a better contract. For instance, Calvin may offer Becky, an employee of Fran under a contract that has two years left, a yearly salary of $5,000 per year more than the contractual arrangement between Becky and Fran. If Calvin is aware of the contract between Becky and Fran and of the fact that his offer to Becky will interfere with that contract, then Calvin is liable to Fran for intentional interference with contractual relations.

TEXACO, INC. v. PENNZOIL, CO. Court of Appeals of Texas, First District, 1987, 729 S.W.2d 768

FACTS Pennzoil negotiated with Gordon Getty and the J. Paul Getty Museum over the purchase by Pennzoil of all the Getty Oil stock held by each. Gordon Getty, who was also a director of Getty Oil, held about 40.2 percent of the outstanding shares of Getty Oil. The Museum held 11.8 percent. On January 2, a Memorandum of Agreement was drafted, setting forth the terms reached by Pennzoil, Gordon Getty, and the Museum. After increasing the offering price to $110 per share plus a $5 "stub" or bonus, the board of directors of Getty Oil voted on January 3 to accept the Pennzoil deal. Accordingly, on January 4 both Getty Oil and Pennzoil issued press releases, announcing an agreement in principle on the terms of the Memorandum of Agreement but at the higher price.

Having learned of the impending sale of Getty Oil stock to Pennzoil, Texaco hurriedly called several in-house meetings, and hired an investment banker as well, to determine a feasible price range for acquiring Getty Oil. On January 5, Texaco decided on $125 per share and authorized its officers to take any steps necessary to conclude a deal. Texaco met first with a lawyer for the Museum, then with Gordon Getty. Texaco stressed to Getty that if he hesitated in selling his shares, he might be "locked out" in a minority position. On January 6, the Getty Oil board of directors voted to withdraw from the Pennzoil deal and unanimously voted to accept the $125-per-share Texaco offer. Pennzoil sued and won an award of $7.53 billion in compensatory damages and $3 billion in punitive damages based on tortious interference with a contract. Texaco appealed.

DECISION Judgment of trial court affirmed.

OPINION New York law requires knowledge by a defendant of the existence of contractual rights as an element of the tort of inducing breach of that contract. Since there was no direct evidence of Texaco's knowledge of a contract, the question is whether there was legally and factually sufficient circumstantial evidence from which the knowledge could be inferred. Among the evidence were (1) Texaco's carefully mapped strategy to defeat Pennzoil's deal; (2) the notice of a contract in a January 5 *Wall Street Journal* article, although Texaco claimed that no one at Texaco had seen it; (3) the knowledge of an agreement that would arise from comparing the Memorandum of Agreement with the Getty press release; and (4) demands made by the Museum and Trust for full indemnity by Texaco against any claims by Pennzoil based on the Memorandum of Agreement. Clearly, the inference by the jury that Texaco had knowledge of contractual relations between Pennzoil and Gordon Getty and the Museum is supported by the evidence.

Another necessary element is a showing that the defendant took an active part in persuading a party to a contract to breach it. Merely entering into a contract with a party with the knowledge of that party's contractual obligations to someone else is not the same as inducing a breach. For tort liability to arise it is necessary that there be some act of interference or of persuading a party to breach, such as by offering better terms or other incentives. The evidence shows that Texaco knew it had only twenty-four hours to "stop the Pennzoil train." Furthermore, the evidence also shows that Texaco's strategy included pressure on Gordon Getty, as well as on key people at the Museum. This evidence contradicts the contention that Texaco passively accepted a deal proposed by the other parties.

INTERPRETATION The tort of interference with contractual relations protects a party to a contract from a third party who intentionally and improperly induces the other contracting party not to perform the contract.

Disparagement

Disparagement
(dis·par'·age·ment) publication of false statements resulting in harm to another's monetary interests

The tort of **disparagement** or injurious falsehood imposes liability upon one who publishes a false statement that results in harm to another's monetary interests if the publisher knows that the statement is false or acts in reckless disregard of its truth or falsity. This tort most commonly involves intentionally false statements that cast doubt on another's right of ownership in or on the quality of another's property or products. Thus Simon, while contemplating the purchase of a stock of merchandise that belongs to Marie, reads an advertisement in a newspaper in which Ernst falsely asserts he owns the merchandise. Ernst has disparaged Marie's property in the goods.

Absolute, conditional, and constitutional privilege apply to the same extent to the tort of disparagement as they do to defamation. In addition, a competitor has conditional privilege to compare her products favorably to those of a rival, even

ETHICAL DILEMMA What May One Do to Attract Clients from a Previous Employer?

FACTS Carl Adle and Louise Bart formed a law firm as partners, and Anne Lily, Marvin Thomas, and Tim Jones joined the newly formed firm of Adle & Bart as associates (non-partner employees). After about five years, Lily, Thomas, and Jones became disenchanted with the law firm and decided to form their own, to be called Lily, Thomas & Jones.

Lily and Thomas suggested to Jones that they contact approximately five hundred of Adle & Bart's current clients. Lily and Thomas had prepared a model letter to inform clients about the new law firm (Lily, Thomas & Jones) and to encourage them to leave Adle & Bart and to become clients of the new firm. The letter also indicated that Lily, Thomas & Jones would offer legal services far better than those of Adle & Bart: billing rates would be more reasonable, service more prompt, and legal representation more effective and successful. The reference to success was aimed, in part, at three large clients who recently lost lawsuits under Adle

& Bart representation. Although the losses had not resulted from malpractice or mishandling by Adle & Bart, Lily and Thomas knew that significant amounts of money had been at issue and that the clients were sensitive about the results of the lengthy litigation.

The letter included two postage-paid form letters for the prospective client to sign and mail. One form letter was addressed to Adle & Bart, informing them of the client's desire to discontinue the client-attorney relationship and requesting the firm to forward all files to Lily, Thomas & Jones. The other form letter, addressed to Lily, Thomas & Jones, requested representation.

Jones is reluctant about the proposed mailing. Lily and Thomas, in turn, argue that their new firm is not doing as well as they expected. They essentially give Jones an ultimatum: join in the letter or leave the firm. Jones, who has thoroughly alienated Adle & Bart, does not believe he has any immediate alternative job opportunities.

Social, Policy, and Ethical Considerations

1. Should Jones agree to the proposed mailing? Is it ethical for those forming the new firm to utilize a client list of their former employer when seeking clients?
2. What practical steps could Jones take to assist him in his decision?
3. What are the competing social interests at stake in this controversy?
4. How would your answers differ, if at all, if the firms were accounting firms rather than law firms?
5. In what manner, if at all, should the law protect existing businesses from competition? Under what circumstances might competition become unfair, and how should laws be tailored to deter unfair practices?
6. Should Jones be concerned about the comparisons the letter makes between the new firm and Adle & Bart?

though she does not believe that her products are superior. No privilege applies, however, if the comparison contains false assertions of specific unfavorable facts about the competitor's property.

The pecuniary loss an injured person may recover is that which directly and immediately results from impairment of the marketability of the property disparaged. Damages may also be recovered for expenses necessary to counteract the false publication, including litigation expenses, the cost of notifying customers, and the cost of publishing denials.

Fraudulent Misrepresentation

Fraudulent misrepresentation imposes liability for the monetary loss caused by a justifiable reliance on a misrepresentation of fact intentionally made for the purpose of inducing the relying party to act. For example, Smith misrepresents to Jones that a tract of land in Texas is located in an area where oil drilling has recently commenced. Smith makes this statement knowing it is not true. In reliance upon the statement, Jones purchases the land from Smith. Smith is liable to Jones for intentional or fraudulent misrepresentation. Although fraudulent misrepresentation is a tort action, it is closely connected with contractual negotiations; we will discuss its relationship to contracts in Chapter 11.

Fraudulent misrepresentation *(fraud'·u·lent)* false statement made with knowledge of its falsity and with intent to induce another to act

FIGURE 7–2 Intentional Torts

Interest Protected	Tort
Person	
Freedom from contact	Battery
Freedom from apprehension	Assault
Freedom of movement	False imprisonment
Freedom from distress	Infliction of emotional distress
Dignity	
Reputation	Defamation
Privacy	Appropriation
	Intrusion
	Public disclosure of private facts
	False light
Freedom from wrongful legal actions	Misuse of legal procedure
Property	
Real	Trespass
	Nuisance
Personal	Trespass
	Conversion
Economic	
Contracts	Interference with contractual rights
Goodwill	Disparagement
Freedom from deception	Fraudulent misrepresentation

CHAPTER SUMMARY

Harm to the Person	**Battery** intentional infliction of harmful or offensive bodily contact **Assault** intentional infliction of apprehension of immediate bodily harm or offensive contact **False Imprisonment** intentional confining of a person against her will **Infliction of Emotional Distress** extreme and outrageous conduct intentionally or recklessly causing severe emotional distress

Harm to the Right of Dignity	**Defamation** false communication that injures a person's reputation ■ *Libel* written or electronically transmitted defamation ■ *Slander* spoken defamation **Invasion of Privacy** ■ *Appropriation* unauthorized use of a person's identity ■ *Intrusion* unreasonable and offensive interference with the seclusion of another ■ *Public Disclosure of Private Facts* offensive publicity of private information ■ *False Light* offensive and false publicity about another **Misuse of Legal Procedure** torts of malicious prosecution, wrongful civil proceeding, and abuse of process that protect an individual from unjustifiable litigation

Harm to Property	**Real Property** land and anything attached to it ■ *Trespass* wrongfully entering on land of another ■ *Nuisance* a nontrespassory interference with another's use and enjoyment of land **Personal Property** any property other than land ■ *Trespass* an intentional taking or use of another's personal property ■ *Conversion* intentional exercise of control over another's personal property

Harm to Economic Interests	**Interference with Contractual Relations** intentionally causing one of the parties to a contract not to perform **Disparagement** publication of false statements about another's property or products **Fraudulent Misrepresentation** a false statement, made with knowledge of its falsity, intended to induce another to act

QUESTIONS

1. Identify and define the torts that protect against intentional interference with personal rights.
2. Explain the application of the various privileges to defamation suits and how they are affected by whether the plaintiff is a (a) public figure, (b) public official, or (c) private person.
3. Distinguish the four torts comprising invasion of privacy.
4. Identify and describe the torts that protect against harm to property.
5. Distinguish by example among interference with contractual relations, disparagement, and fraudulent misrepresentation.

Internet Question. Find information about punitive damages and review the proposed Model Punitive Damages Act.

PROBLEMS

1. The Penguin intentionally hits Batman with his umbrella. Batman, stunned by the blow, falls backwards, knocking Robin down. Robin's leg is broken in the fall, and he cries out, "Holy broken bat bones! My leg is broken." Who, if anyone, has liability to Robin? Why?
2. CEO was convinced by his employee, M. Ploy, that a coworker, A. Cused, had been stealing money from the company. At lunch that day in the company cafeteria, CEO discharged Cused from her employment, accused her of stealing from the company, searched through her purse over her objections, and finally forcibly escorted her to his office to await the arrival of the police, whom he had his secretary summon. Cused is indicted for embezzlement but subsequently is acquitted upon establishing her innocence. What rights, if any, does Cused have against CEO?
3. Ralph kisses Edith while she is asleep but does not waken or harm her. Edith sues Ralph for battery. Decision?
4. Claude, a creditor seeking to collect a debt, calls on Dianne and demands payment in a rude and insolent manner. When Dianne says that she cannot pay, Claude calls Dianne a deadbeat and says that he will never trust Dianne again. Is Claude liable to Dianne? If so, for what tort?
5. Lana, a ten-year-old child, is run over by a car negligently driven by Mitchell. Lana, at the time of the accident, was acting reasonably and without negligence. Clark, a newspaper reporter, photographs Lana while she is lying in the street in great pain. Two years later, Perry, the publisher of a newspaper, prints Clark's picture of Lana in his newspaper as a lead to an article concerning the negligence of children. The caption under the picture reads: "They ask to be killed." Lana, who has recovered from the accident, brings suit against Clark and Perry. What is the result?
6. In 1963, the *Saturday Evening Post* featured an article entitled "The Story of a College Football Fix," characterized in the subtitle as "A Shocking Report of How

Wally Butts and Bear Bryant Rigged a Game Last Fall." Butts was athletic director of the University of Georgia, and Bryant was head coach of the University of Alabama. The article was based on a claim by one George Burnett that he had accidentally overheard a long-distance telephone conversation between Butts and Bryant in the course of which Butts divulged information on plays Georgia would use in the upcoming game against Alabama. The writer assigned to the story by the *Post* was not a football expert, did not interview either Butts or Bryant, and did not personally see the notes Burnett had made of the telephone conversation. Butts admitted that he had a long-distance telephone conversation with Bryant but denied that any advance information on prospective football plays was given. Butts brought a libel suit against the *Post.* Decision?

7. A patient confined in a hospital, Joan has a rare disease that is of great interest to the public. Carol, a television reporter, requests Joan to consent to an interview. Joan refuses, but Carol, nonetheless, enters Joan's room over her objection and photographs her. Joan brings a suit against Carol. Decision?

8. Owner has a place on his land where he piles trash. The pile has been there for three months. John, a neighbor of Owner, without Owner's consent or knowledge, throws trash onto the trashpile. Owner learns that John has done this and sues him. What tort, if any, has John committed?

9. Chris leaves her car parked in front of a store. There are no signs that say Chris cannot park there. The store owner, however, needs the car moved to enable a delivery truck to unload. He releases the brake and pushes Chris's car three or four feet, doing no harm to the car. Chris returns and sees that her car has been moved and is very angry. She threatens to sue the store owner for trespass to her personal property. Can she recover?

10. Carr borrowed John's brand-new Ford for the purpose of going to the store. He told John he would be right back. Carr then decided, however, to go to the beach while he had the car. Can John recover from Carr the value of the automobile? If so, for what tort?

11. Marcia Samms, a respectable married woman, claimed that David Eccles had repeatedly and persistently called her at various hours, including late at night, from May to December, soliciting her to have illicit sexual relations with him. She also claimed that on one occasion Eccles came over to her residence to again solicit sex and indecently exposed himself to her. Mrs. Samms had never encouraged Eccles but had continuously repulsed his "insulting, indecent, and obscene" proposals. She brought suit against Eccles, claiming she suffered great anxiety and fear for her personal safety and severe emotional distress, demanding actual and punitive damages. Decision?

12. National Bond and Investment Company sent two of its employees to repossess Whithorn's car after he failed to complete the payments. The two repossessors located Whithorn while he was driving his car. They followed him and hailed him down in order to make the repossession. Whithorn refused to abandon his car and demanded evidence of their authority. The two repossessors became impatient and called a wrecker. They ordered the driver of the wrecker to hook Whithorn's car and move it down the street while Whithorn was still inside the vehicle. Whithorn started the car and tried to escape, but the wrecker lifted the car off the road and progressed seventy-five to one hundred feet until Whithorn managed to stall the wrecker. Whithorn sued National Bond for false imprisonment. Decision?

13. In March 1975, William Proxmire, a United States senator from Wisconsin, initiated the "Golden Fleece of the Month Award" to publicize what he believed to be wasteful government spending. The second of these awards was given to the federal agencies that had for seven years funded Dr. Hutchinson's research on stress levels in animals. The award was made in a speech Proxmire gave in the Senate; the text was also incorporated into an advance press release that was sent to 275 members of the national news media. Proxmire also referred to the research again in two subsequent newsletters sent to 100,000 constituents and during a television interview. Hutchinson then brought this action alleging defamation resulting in personal and economic injury. Decision?

14. Capune was attempting a trip from New York to Florida on an eighteen-foot-long paddleboard. The trip was being covered by various media to gain publicity for Capune and certain products he endorsed. Capune approached a pier by water. The pier was owned by Robbins, who had posted signs prohibiting surfing and swimming around the pier. Capune was unaware of these notices and attempted to continue his journey by passing under the pier. Robbins ran up yelling and threw two bottles at Capune. Capune was frightened and tried to maneuver his paddleboard to go around the pier. Robbins then threw a third bottle that hit Capune on the head. Capune had to be helped out of the water and taken to the hospital. He suffered a physical wound that required twenty-four sutures and, as a result, had to discontinue his trip. Capune brought suit in tort against Robbins. Is Robbins liable? If so, for which tort or torts?

15. Ralph Nader, who has been a critic of General Motors for several years, claims that when General Motors learned that Nader was about to publish a book entitled *Unsafe at Any Speed*, criticizing one of its automobiles, the company decided to conduct a campaign of intimidation against him. Specifically, Nader claims that GMC (1) conducted a series of interviews with Nader's

acquaintances, questioning them about his political, social, racial, and religious views; (2) kept him under surveillance in public places for an unreasonable length of time; (3) caused him to be accosted by women for the purpose of entrapping him into illicit relationships; (4) made threatening, harassing, and obnoxious telephone calls to him; (5) tapped his telephone and eavesdropped by means of mechanical and electronic equipment on his private conversations with others; and (6) conducted a "continuing" and harassing investigation of him. Nader brought suit against GMC for invasion of privacy. Which, if any, of the alleged actions would constitute invasion of privacy?

16. Bill Kinsey was charged with murdering his wife while working for the Peace Corps in Tanzania. After waiting six months in jail, he was acquitted at a trial that attracted wide publicity. Five years later, while a graduate student at Stanford University, Kinsey had a brief affair with Mary Macur. He abruptly ended the affair by telling Macur he would no longer be seeing her because another woman, Sally Allen, was coming from England to live with him. A few months later, Kinsey and Allen moved to Africa and were subsequently married. Soon after Bill ended their affair, Macur began a letter-writing campaign designed to expose Bill and his mistreatment of her. Macur sent several letters to both Bill and Sally Kinsey, their former spouses, their parents, their neighbors, their parents' neighbors, members of Bill's dissertation committee, other faculty, and the president of Stanford University. The letters contained statements accusing Bill of murdering his first wife, spending six months in jail for the crime, being a rapist, and other questionable behavior. The Kinseys brought an action for invasion of privacy, seeking damages and a permanent injunction. Decision?

17. Plaintiff, John W. Carson, was the host and star of *The Tonight Show,* a well-known television program broadcast by the National Broadcasting Company. Carson also appears as an entertainer in nightclubs and theaters around the country. From the time he began hosting *The Tonight Show* in 1962, he had been introduced on the show each night with the phrase "Here's Johnny." The phrase "Here's Johnny" is still generally associated with Carson by a substantial segment of the television viewing public. In 1967, Carson began authorizing use of this phrase by outside business ventures.

Defendant, Here's Johnny Portable Toilets, Inc., is a Michigan corporation engaged in the business of renting and selling "Here's Johnny" portable toilets. Defendant's founder was aware at the time he formed the corporation that "Here's Johnny" was the introductory slogan for Carson on *The Tonight Show.* He indicated that he coupled the phrase with a second one, "The World's Foremost Commodian," to make "a good play on a phrase." Carson brought suit for invasion of privacy. The trial court dismissed Carson's claim, and he appealed. Decision?

18. In 1981, Lemmie L. Ruffin, Jr., was an Alabama licensed agent for Pacific Mutual Life Insurance and for Union Fidelity Life Insurance Company. Union wrote group health insurance policies for municipalities, while Pacific did not. Plaintiffs Cleopatra Haslip, Cynthia Craig, Alma M. Calhoun, and Eddie Hargrove were employees of Roosevelt City, Alabama. Ruffin gave the city a single proposal for health and life insurance for its employees, which the city approved. Both companies provided the coverage, however: Union provided the health insurance and Pacific the life insurance. This packaging of coverage by two different and unrelated insurers was not unusual. Union would send its billings for health premiums to Ruffin at Pacific Mutual's office. The city clerk each month issued a check for those premiums and sent it to Ruffin. Ruffin, however, did not remit to Union the premium payments he received from the city; instead, he misappropriated most of them. Late in 1981, when Union did not receive payment from the city, it sent notices of lapsed health coverage to the plaintiffs, who did not know that their health policies had been canceled.

Plaintiff Haslip was hospitalized on January 23, 1982, and because the hospital could not confirm her health coverage, it required her to make a partial payment on her bill. Her physician, when he was not paid, placed her account with a collection agency, which obtained against Haslip a judgment that damaged her credit. Plaintiffs sued Pacific Mutual and Ruffin for fraud. The case was submitted to a jury, which was instructed that if it found liability for fraud, it could award punitive damages. The jury returned verdicts for the plaintiffs and awarded Haslip $1,040,000, of which at least $840,000 was punitive damages. The Supreme Court of Alabama affirmed the trial court's judgment. Pacific Mutual appealed. Decision?

CHAPTER 8

Negligence and Strict Liability

Whereas intentional torts deal with conduct that has a substantial certainty of causing harm, negligence involves conduct that creates an unreasonable risk of harm. The basis of liability for negligence is the failure to exercise reasonable care under the circumstances for the safety of another person or his property, which failure proximately causes injury to such person or damage to his property, or both. Thus, if the driver of an automobile intentionally runs down a person, she has committed the intentional tort of battery. If, on the other hand, the driver hits and injures a person while driving with no reasonable regard for the safety of others, she is negligent.

Strict liability is not based on the negligence or intent of the defendant but rather on the nature of the activity in which he is engaging. Under this doctrine, defendants who engage in certain activities, such as keeping animals or maintaining abnormally dangerous conditions, are held liable for injuries they cause, even if they have exercised the utmost care. The law imposes this liability in order to bring about a just reallocation of loss, given that the defendant engaged in the activity for his own benefit and probably is better prepared than the plaintiff is to manage the risk inherent in the activity through insurance or otherwise.

NEGLIGENCE

Negligence failure to exercise reasonable care under the circumstances

The Restatement defines **negligence** as "conduct that falls below the standard established by law for the protection of others against unreasonable risk of harm." The standard established by law is the conduct of a reasonable person acting prudently and with due care under the circumstances. The general rule is that a person is under a duty to all others at all times to exercise reasonable care for the safety of other persons and their property. This rule is subject to certain exceptions, however, which we will discuss below.

A person is not liable for injury caused to another by an unavoidable accident—an occurrence the person had not intended and could not have prevented by the exercise of reasonable care. Thus, no liability results from the loss of control of an automobile because the driver suddenly and unforeseeably suffers a heart attack, stroke, or fainting spell. If, however, the driver had warning of the imminent heart attack or other infirmity, it would be negligent for him to drive at all.

An action for negligence consists of three elements, each of which the plaintiff must prove:

1. **Breach of duty of care:** that a legal duty required the defendant to conform to the standard of conduct established for the protection of others *and* that the defendant failed to conform to that standard
2. **Proximate cause:** that the defendant's failure to conform to the required standard of conduct proximately caused the injury and harm the plaintiff sustained
3. **Injury:** that the injury and harm is of a type protected against the defendant's negligent conduct

BREACH OF DUTY OF CARE

Negligence consists of conduct that creates an unreasonable risk of harm. In determining whether a given risk of harm was unreasonable, the following factors are considered: (1) the probability that the harm would occur, (2) the gravity or seriousness of the resulting harm, (3) the social utility of the conduct creating the risk, and (4) the cost of taking precautions that would have reduced the risk. Thus, the standard of conduct, which is the basis for the law of negligence, is usually determined by a cost-benefit analysis.

Reasonable Person Standard

The duty of care imposed by law is measured by the degree of carefulness that a reasonable person would exercise in a given situation. The **reasonable person** is a fictitious individual who is always careful and prudent and never negligent. What the judge or jury determines a reasonable person would have done in light of the facts revealed by the evidence in a particular case sets the standard of conduct for that case. The reasonable person standard is thus *external* and *objective.*

> **Reasonable person standard** duty of care required to avoid being negligent; one who is careful, diligent, and prudent

Children The standard of conduct to which a child must conform to avoid being negligent is that of a reasonable person of like age, intelligence, and experience under like circumstances. The law applies a test that acknowledges these three factors, because children do not have the judgment, intelligence, knowledge, and experience of adults. Moreover, children as a general rule do not engage in activities entailing high risk to others, and their conduct normally does not involve a potential for harm as great as that of adult conduct. A child who engages in an adult activity, however, such as flying an airplane or driving a boat or car, is held in about half the states to the standard of care applicable to adults.

> **Children** must conform to conduct of a reasonable person of like age, intelligence, and experience

Physical Disability If a person is ill or otherwise physically disabled, the standard of conduct to which he or she must conform to avoid being negligent is that of a reasonable person having a like disability. Thus, a blind person must act as a reasonable person who is blind.

> **Physical disability** a disabled person's conduct must conform to that of a reasonable person under like disability

Mental Deficiency The law does not allow for the insanity, voluntary intoxication, or other mental deficiency (in terms, for example, of intelligence, judgment, memory, or emotional stability) of the defendant in a negligence case; rather, the defendant is held to the standard of conduct of a reasonable person who is *not* insane, intoxicated, or mentally deficient, even though the defendant is, in fact, incapable of conforming to the standard.

> **Mental deficiency** a mentally deficient person is held to the reasonable person standard of a reasonable person who is not mentally deficient

Superior skill or knowledge professionals must exercise the same care and skill normally possessed by members of their profession

Superior Skill or Knowledge Persons who are qualified and who practice a profession or trade that requires special skill and expertise are required to use the same care and skill that members of their profession or trade normally possess. This standard applies to such professionals as physicians, dentists, attorneys, pharmacists, architects, accountants, and engineers and to those who perform a skilled trade such as airline pilot, electrician, carpenter, and plumber. If a member of a profession or skilled trade possesses greater skill than that common to the profession or trade, she is required to exercise that greater degree of skill.

Emergency sudden, unexpected event calling for immediate action

Emergencies the reasonable person standard applies, but the emergency is considered part of the circumstances

Emergencies An **emergency** is a sudden and unexpected event that calls for immediate action and permits no time for deliberation. In determining whether a defendant's conduct was reasonable, the fact that he was at the time confronted with an emergency is taken into consideration. The standard is still that of a reasonable person under the circumstances—the emergency is simply part of the circumstances. If, however, the defendant's own negligent or tortious conduct created the emergency, he is liable for the consequences of this conduct even if he acted reasonably in the resulting emergency situation.

Violation of statute if the statute applies, the violation is negligence *per se*

Violation of Statute The reasonable person standard of conduct may be established by legislation. Some statutes do so by expressly imposing civil liability on violators. Where a statute does not expressly provide for civil liability, courts may adopt the requirements of the statute as the standard of conduct if the statute is intended to protect a class of persons that includes the plaintiff against the particular hazard and kind of harm that resulted.

Negligence *per se* *(per say')* conclusive on the issue of negligence (duty of care and breach)

If the statute is found to apply, the great majority of the courts hold that an unexcused violation is **negligence** *per se*; that is, the violation conclusively shows negligent conduct (breach of duty of care). In a minority of states, the violation is considered merely to be evidence of negligence. In either event, the plaintiff must also prove legal causation and injury.

For example, a statute enacted to protect employees from injuries requires that all factory elevators be equipped with specified safety devices. Arthur, an employee in Leonard's factory, and Marian, a business visitor to the factory, are injured when the elevator falls because the safety devices have not been installed. The court may adopt the statute as a standard of conduct as to Arthur, and hold Leonard negligent *per se* as to Arthur, but not as to Marian, because Arthur, not Marian, is within the class of persons the statute is intended to protect. Marian would have to establish that a reasonable person in the position of Leonard under the circumstances would have installed the safety device. (See Figure 8–1.)

On the other hand, compliance with a legislative enactment or administrative regulation does not prevent a finding of negligence if a reasonable person would have taken additional precautions. For instance, driving at the speed limit may not constitute due care when traffic or road conditions require a lower speed. Legislative or administrative rules normally establish *minimum* standards.

■ RYAN v. FRIESENHAHN Court of Appeals of Texas, 1995, 911 S.W.2d 113   ■

FACTS Todd Friesenhahn, son of Nancy and Frederick Friesenhahn, held an "open invitation" party at his parents' home that encouraged guests to "bring your own bottle." Sabrina Ryan attended the party, became intoxicated, and was involved in a fatal accident after she left the party. Sandra and Stephen Ryan, Sabrina's parents, sued the Friesenhahns for negligence, alleging that the Friesenhahns were aware of the underage drinking at

continued

the party and of Sabrina's condition when she left the party. The trial court granted summary judgment for the Friesenhahns.

DECISION Judgment reversed.

OPINION Accepting the Ryans' allegations as true, the Friesenhahns were aware that minors possessed and consumed alcohol on their property and specifically allowed Sabrina to become intoxicated. The Texas Alcoholic Beverage Code provides that a person commits an offense if, with criminal negligence, that person "makes available an alcoholic beverage to a minor." A violation of a statute constitutes negligence *per se* if the injured party is a member of the class protected by the statute. The Alcoholic Beverage Code was designed to protect the general public and minors in particular. Therefore, Sabrina was a member of the protected class, and we find that the Ryans have stated a cause of action against the Friesenhahns for violation of the Alcoholic Beverage Code.

In considering common-law negligence as a basis for social host liability, courts have relied on *Graff v. Board*, a prior Texas Supreme Court decision in which it was held that no third party liability should be imposed on social hosts who provide alcohol to adult guests. The Texas Supreme Court gave two reasons for its holding in *Graff:* first, the host cannot reasonably

know the extent of his guests' alcohol consumption level; second, the host cannot reasonably be expected to control his guests' conduct. However, this rationale does not apply where the guest is a minor. The adult social host need not estimate the extent of a minor's alcohol consumption, because serving minors *any* amount of alcohol is a criminal offense. Furthermore, the social host may control the minor, with whom there is a special relationship, in a manner analogous to that of parent-child.

While one adult has no general duty to control the behavior of another adult, one would hope that adults would exercise special diligence in supervising minors. When a party is for the purpose of engaging in the consumption of alcohol by minors, adults certainly have a greater duty of care. Moreover, in view of the legislature's determination that minors are not competent to understand the effects of alcohol, the court found sufficient legislative intent to support its holding that a duty exists between the adult social host and the minor guest. Accordingly, the court found that the Ryans' petition stated a common-law cause of action.

INTERPRETATION A violation of a statute constitutes negligence *per se* if the injured party is a member of the class protected by the statute.

Duty to Act

Except in special circumstances, no one is required to aid another in peril. For example, Adolf, an adult standing at the edge of a steep cliff, observes a baby carriage with a crying infant in it slowly heading toward the edge and certain doom. Adolf could easily prevent the baby's fall at no risk to his own safety. Nonetheless, Adolf does nothing, and the baby falls to its death. Adolf is under no legal duty to act and therefore incurs no liability for failing to do so. However, special relations that impose a duty on the defendant to aid or protect the other may exist between the parties. Thus, if Adolf were the baby's parent or babysitter, Adolf would be under a duty to act and would therefore be liable for not taking action.

A duty to act is also imposed on those whose conduct, whether tortious or innocent, has injured another and left him helpless and in danger of further harm. For example, Alice drives her car into Frank, rendering him unconscious. Alice leaves Frank lying in the middle of the road, where he is run over by a second car driven by Rebecca. Alice is liable to Frank for the additional injuries inflicted by Rebecca. Moreover, a person voluntarily coming to the assistance of another in need of aid incurs a duty to exercise care. In other words, the actor is liable if his failure to exercise reasonable care increases the risk of harm, causes harm, or leaves the other in a worse position. For example, Ann finds Ben drunk and stumbling along a dark sidewalk. Ann leads Ben halfway up a steep and unguarded stairway, where she then abandons him. Ben attempts to climb the stairs but trips and falls, suffering serious injury. Ann is liable to Ben for having left him in a worse position.

Duty to act except in special circumstances, no one is required to aid another in peril

FIGURE 8–1 Negligence and Negligence *Per Se*

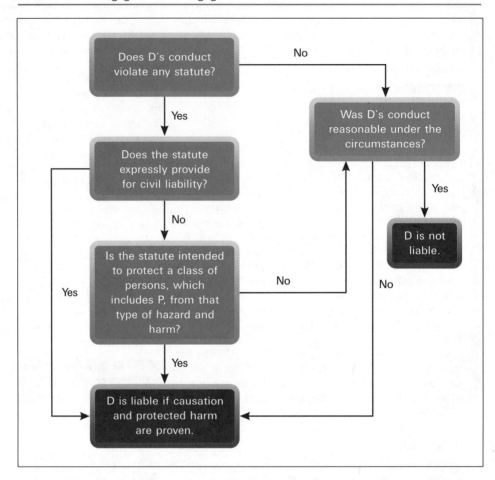

SOLDANO v. O'DANIELS California Court of Appeals, Fifth District, 1983, 141 Cal.App.3d 443, 190 Cal.Rptr. 310

FACTS On August 9, the plaintiff's father, Darrell Soldano, was shot and killed at the Happy Jack Saloon. The defendant owns and operates the Circle Inn, an eating establishment across the street from the Happy Jack Saloon. On the night of the shooting, a patron of the Happy Jack Saloon came into the Circle Inn and informed the Circle Inn bartender that a man had been threatened at Happy Jack's. The patron requested that the Circle Inn bartender either call the police or allow the patron to use the Circle Inn phone to call the police. The bartender refused either to make the call or to allow the Happy Jack patron to use the phone. The plaintiff alleges that the actions of the Circle Inn employee were a breach of the legal duty that the Circle Inn owed to the decedent. The defendant maintains that there was no legal obligation to take any action, and therefore there was no duty owed to the decedent. The trial court dismissed the case on the defendant's motion for summary judgment.

DECISION The appellate court reversed and remanded the case for trial.

OPINION Defendant points to the established rule that one who has not created a peril ordinarily does not have a duty to take affirmative action to assist an imperiled person. The courts have increased the instances in which affirmative duties are imposed, not by direct rejection of the common law rule but by expanding the list of special relationships that will justify departure from that rule. In this case, however, there was no special relationship between the defendant and the deceased. Nonetheless, the court determined to re-examine the common law rule of nonliability for nonfeasance in the special circumstances of this case. Imposing such a duty to third parties requires an examination and balancing of foreseeability of harm, certainty that the plaintiff would suffer injury, the connection between defendant's

continued

conduct and the injury, moral blame attached to defendant's conduct, the prevention of future harm, extent of the burden to the defendant, consequences to the community of imposing a duty to exercise care, and the availability, cost and prevalence of insurance for the particular risk involved. The court concluded, on these facts, that the Circle Inn's employee's conduct displayed a disregard for human life in that the burden on the defendant to respond was minimal. Balancing these factors, the court concluded that there was an affirmative duty on the defendant's part to respond and that his failure to respond resulted in a legal breach of duty of care. It bears emphasizing that the duty in this case does not require that one go to the aid of another. Rather, the use of a telephone, in the public portion of a business open to the public, during business hours, should not be refused for a legitimate emergency call.

INTERPRETATION Although a person may not have a duty to help another, in a case such as this, a person has a duty not to hinder others who are trying to help.

Duties of Possessors of Land

The right of possessors of land to use that land for their own benefit and enjoyment is limited by their duty to do so in a reasonable manner. By the use of their land, possessors of land cannot cause unreasonable risks of harm to others. Liability for breach of this obligation may arise from conduct in any of the three areas of torts discussed in this and the preceding chapter: intentional harm, negligence, or strict liability. Most of these cases fall within the classification of negligence.

In conducting activities on her land, the possessor of land is required to exercise reasonable care to protect others who are *not* on her property. For example, a property owner who constructs a factory on her premises must take reasonable care that it is not unreasonably dangerous to people off the site.

ETHICAL DILEMMA   What Are the Obligations of a Bartender to His Patrons?

FACTS John Campbell, age 22, was recently hired as a management trainee for the Stanton Hotel. The Stanton features a health club, swimming pool, ski slopes, and boating facilities. The management trainee program is an eighteen-month program during which the trainees rotate jobs to gain exposure to all phases of hotel operations. There is no formal orientation, and each trainee is randomly assigned to jobs.

John's first assignment was at the restaurant/bar working with Mr. Arnold, a bartender who was 50 years old and quite experienced. Mr. Arnold commented to John that John was lucky to be working the bar during the skiing season. Mr. Arnold explained that skiers frequently come in from the slopes to warm up. He told John that all tips are shared equally and that the more it snows and colder it gets, the better the bar business.

One day, John observed that Mr. Arnold was serving drinks to two young men who appeared to be about 22 or 23. John overheard the men planning to ski an hour or so more and then drive over to meet friends at a neighboring hotel. One of the men appeared self-contained and unaffected by the drinks. His friend, however, was gradually getting louder although he was not making a disturbance.

John noticed that Mr. Arnold had already served three rounds of bourbon to the men. When Mr. Arnold was preparing the fourth round, John said to him, "Don't you think they've had enough? They're going back on the slopes." Mr. Arnold replied, "Kid, you've got a lot to learn."

Social, Policy, and Ethical Considerations

1. What action, if any, should John take?
2. What are the potential risks to the two men who are drinking? Are public safety issues involved?
3. What management policies should the hotel institute with regard to its liquor policies and athletic operations?
4. Do the drinking companions bear an ethical responsibility for each other's drinking?
5. How should society balance the interests of freedom of business and individual conduct (i.e., drinking) with the competing interests of protecting public safety?

The duty of a possessor of land to persons who come on the land usually depends on whether those persons are trespassers, licensees, or invitees. A few states have abandoned these distinctions, however, and simply apply ordinary negligence principles of foreseeable risk and reasonable care.

Trespasser person who enters or remains on the land of another without permission or privilege to do so

Duty to trespassers not to injure intentionally

Duty to Trespassers A **trespasser** is a person who enters or remains on the land of another without permission or privilege to do so. The lawful possessor of the land is *not* liable to adult trespassers for his failure to maintain the land in a reasonably safe condition. Nonetheless, the lawful possessor is not free to inflict intentional injury on a trespasser. Moreover, some courts have held that upon discovery of the presence of trespassers on the land, the lawful possessor is required to exercise reasonable care for their safety.

Licensee *(li·cens·ee')* person privileged to enter or remain on land by virtue of the consent of the lawful possessor

Duty to licensees to warn of known dangerous conditions licensees are unlikely to discover for themselves

Duty to Licensees A **licensee** is a person who is privileged to enter or remain on land only by virtue of the lawful possessor's consent. Licensees include members of the possessor's household, *social guests,* and salespersons calling at private homes. A licensee will become a trespasser, however, if he enters a portion of the land to which he is not invited or remains on the land after his invitation has expired.

The possessor owes a higher duty of care to licensees than to trespassers. The possessor must warn the licensee of dangerous activities and conditions of which the possessor has knowledge and the licensee does not and is not likely to discover. If he is not warned, the licensee may recover if the activity or dangerous condition resulted from the possessor's failure to exercise reasonable care to protect him from the danger. To illustrate: Henry invites a friend, Anne, to his place in the country at eight o'clock on a winter evening. Henry knows that a bridge in his driveway is in a dangerous condition that is not noticeable in the dark. Henry does not inform Anne of this fact. The bridge gives way under Anne's car, causing serious harm to Anne. Henry is liable to Anne.

Some states have extended to licensees the same protection traditionally accorded invitees. A number of states have included social guests in the invitee category.

Invitee *(in·vi·tee')* person invited upon land as a member of the public or for a business purpose

Duty to invitees to exercise reasonable care to protect invitees against dangerous conditions the possessor should know of but invitees are unlikely to discover

Duty to Invitees An **invitee** is a person invited upon land as a member of the public or for a business purpose. A *public invitee* is a person who is invited to enter or remain on land as a member of the public for a purpose for which the land is held open to the public. Such invitees include those who utilize public parks, beaches, or swimming pools, as well as those who utilize governmental facilities, such as a post office or an office of the recorder of deeds, where business with the public is transacted openly. A *business visitor* is a person invited to enter or remain on premises for a purpose directly or indirectly concerning business dealings with the possessor of the land, such as one who enters a store or a worker who enters a residence to make repairs.

With respect to the condition of the premises, the possessor of land is under a duty to exercise reasonable care to protect invitees against dangerous conditions they are unlikely to discover. This liability extends not only to those conditions of which the possessor actually knows but also to those of which he *should* reasonably know. For example, David's store has a large glass front door that is well lighted and plainly visible. Maxine, a customer, mistakes the glass for an open doorway and walks into the glass, injuring herself. David is not liable to Maxine. If, on the other hand, the glass was difficult to see and a

FIGURE 8–2 Duties of Possessors of Land

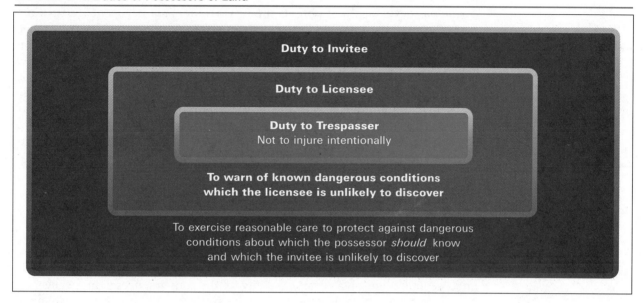

person foreseeably might have mistaken the glass for an open doorway, then David would be liable to Maxine if Maxine crashed into the glass while exercising reasonable care.

These three kinds of duties are illustrated in Figure 8–2.

YANIA v. BIGAN Supreme Court of Pennsylvania, 1959, 397 Pa. 316, 155 A.2d 343

FACTS Joseph Yania and Boyd Ross visited a coal strip-mining operation owned by John Bigan to discuss a business matter with Bigan. On Bigan's property there were several cuts and trenches he had dug to remove the coal underneath. While there, Bigan asked the two men to help him pump water from one of these cuts in the earth. This particular cut contained water eight to ten feet in depth with side walls or embankments sixteen to eighteen feet in height. The two men agreed, and the process began with Ross and Bigan entering the cut and standing at the point where the pump was located. Yania stood at the top of one of the cut's side walls. Apparently, Bigan taunted Yania into jumping into the water from the top of the side wall—a height of sixteen to eighteen feet. As a result, Yania drowned. His widow brought a negligence action against Bigan. She claims that Bigan was negligent "(1) by urging, enticing, taunting and inveigling Yania to jump into the water; (2) by failing to warn Yania of a dangerous condition on the land . . .; [and] (3) by failing to go to Yania's rescue after he jumped into the water." The trial court dismissed the action, and Yania's widow appealed.

DECISION Judgment for Bigan.

OPINION Taunting and enticement will constitute actionable negligence only if directed "at a child of tender years or a person mentally deficient." Therefore, Bigan's taunting of Yania, who was an adult in full possession of his mental faculties, is not negligence.

In addition, the owner of land ordinarily has, at the least, a duty to warn invitees of known or discoverable dangers the owner should realize involve an unreasonable risk of harm to them. This warning is required only if the owner has no reason to believe the invitee will discover the condition or realize the risk of harm. Here, however, the dangers of the water-filled trench were "obvious and apparent to Yania," who was also a coal strip-mine operator. Accordingly, Bigan is not negligent in failing to warn Yania of the obvious.

Finally, despite Bigan's tauntings, Yania jumped into the water of his own accord. Bigan was not legally responsible, in whole or in part, for placing Yania in his perilous and fatal position. Therefore, although he may have had a moral responsibility, Bigan did not have a legal responsibility to rescue Yania, who died of his own foolhardiness.

INTERPRETATION A possessor of land does not have a legal duty to warn business invitees of obvious dangers that invitees should be able to discover themselves.

Res Ipsa Loquitur

A rule has developed that permits the jury to infer *both* negligent conduct and causation from the mere occurrence of certain types of events. This rule, called *res ipsa loquitur*, meaning "the thing speaks for itself," applies when the event is of a kind that ordinarily would not occur in the absence of negligence and other possible causes are sufficiently eliminated by the evidence. For example, Camille rents a room in Leo's motel. During the night, a large piece of plaster falls from the ceiling and injures Camille. In the absence of other evidence, the jury may infer that the harm resulted from Leo's negligence in permitting the plaster to become defective. Leo is permitted, however, to introduce evidence to contradict the inference of negligence.

PROXIMATE CAUSE

Liability for the negligent conduct of a defendant requires not only that the conduct in fact caused injury to the plaintiff but also that it was the proximate cause of the injury. Most simply expressed, proximate cause consists of the judicially imposed limitations on a person's liability for the consequences of his negligence. As a matter of social policy, the courts have not permitted legal responsibility to follow all the consequences of a negligent act. Rather, they have limited responsibility—to a greater extent than with intentional torts—to those persons and results that are closely connected with the negligent conduct. Moreover, in strict liability cases the courts impose a narrower rule of proximate cause than they do in negligence cases.

Causation in Fact

To support a finding that the defendant's negligence was the proximate cause of the plaintiff's injury, it is first necessary to show that the defendant's conduct was the cause in fact (that is, the *actual cause*) of the injury. A widely applied test for causation in fact is the **but for rule**: A person's conduct is a cause of an event if the event would not have occurred *but for* the person's negligent conduct. Under this test, an act or omission to act is *not* a cause of an event if that event would have occurred regardless of the act or omission. For instance, Arnold fails to erect a barrier around an excavation. Doyle is driving a truck when its accelerator becomes stuck. Arnold's negligence is not a cause in fact of Doyle's death if the runaway truck would have crashed through the barrier even if it had been erected. Similarly, failure to install a proper fire escape to a hotel is not the cause in fact of the death of a person who is suffocated by the smoke while sleeping in bed.

The "but for" test, however, is not useful when two or more forces, each of which is sufficient to bring about the harm in question, are actively operating. For example, Wilson and Hart negligently set fires that combine to destroy Kennedy's property. Either fire would have destroyed the property. Under the "but for" test, either Wilson or Hart, or both, could argue that the fire caused by the other would have destroyed the property and that he, therefore, is not liable. The **substantial factor test** addresses this problem by stating that negligent conduct is a legal cause of harm to another if the conduct is a substantial factor in bringing about the harm. Under this test the conduct of both Wilson and Hart would be found to be a cause in fact of the destruction of Kennedy's property.

Res ipsa loquitur *(rez ip'·sa lock'·we·tur)* "the thing speaks for itself"; permits the jury to infer both negligent conduct and causation

But for rule conduct is a cause of an event if the event would not have occurred in the absence of the person's negligent conduct

Causation in fact the defendant's conduct was the actual cause of, or a substantial factor in causing, the injury

Limitations on Causation in Fact

As a matter of policy, the law imposes limitations on the causal connection between the defendant's negligence and the plaintiff's injury. Two of the principal factors that the courts consider in determining such limitations are (a) unforeseeable consequences and (b) superseding causes.

Unforeseeable Consequences Determining the liability of a negligent defendant for unforeseeable consequences has proved to be troublesome and controversial. The Restatement and a majority of the courts have adopted the following position: even if the defendant's negligent conduct is a cause in fact of harm to the plaintiff, the conduct is not a proximate cause *unless* the defendant could reasonably have anticipated injuring the plaintiff or a class of persons of which the plaintiff is a member. Proximate cause involves recognizing the risk of harm to the plaintiff individually or to a class of persons of which the plaintiff is a member.

For example, Steven, while negligently driving an automobile, collides with a car carrying dynamite. Steven is unaware of the contents of the other car and has no reason to know about them. The collision causes the dynamite to explode, shattering glass in a building a block away. The shattered glass injures Doria, who is inside the building. The explosion also injures Walter, who is walking on the sidewalk near the collision. Steven would be liable to Walter because Steven should have realized that his negligent driving might result in a collision that would endanger pedestrians nearby; and the fact that the actual harm resulted in an unforeseeable manner does not affect his liability. Doria, however, was beyond the zone of danger created by Steven's negligence, and Steven is therefore not liable to Doria. Steven's negligent driving is not deemed to be the "proximate cause" of Doria's injury because, looking back from the harm to Steven's negligence, it appears highly extraordinary that Steven's conduct should have brought about the harm to Doria. See Figure 8–3.

Unforeseeable consequences no liability if defendant could not reasonably have anticipated injuring the plaintiff or a class of persons to which the plaintiff belongs

FIGURE 8–3 Proximate Cause

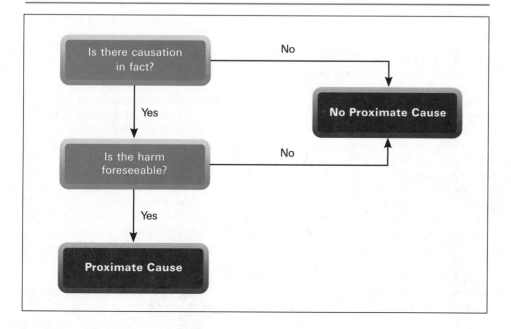

PALSGRAF v. LONG ISLAND RAILROAD CO. Court of Appeals of New York, 1928, 248 N.Y. 339, 162 N.E. 99

FACTS Palsgraf was on the railroad station platform buying a ticket when a train stopped at the station. As it began to depart, two men ran to catch it. After the first was safely aboard, the second jumped onto the moving car. When he started to fall, a guard on the train reached to grab him and another guard on the platform pushed the man from behind. They helped the man to regain his balance, but in the process they knocked a small package out of his arm. The package, which contained fireworks, fell onto the rails and exploded. The shock from the explosion knocked over a scale resting on the other end of the platform, and it landed on Mrs. Palsgraf. She then brought an action against the railroad to recover for the injuries she sustained. The railroad appealed from the trial and appellate courts' decisions in favor of Palsgraf.

DECISION Judgment for Palsgraf reversed.

OPINION Negligence is not actionable unless it involves the invasion of a legally protected interest or the violation of a right. In other words, in order for a given act to be held negligent, it must be shown that the charged party owed a duty to the complaining individual, the observance of which would have averted or avoided the injury.

Here, then, Palsgraf cannot recover because the railroad, although perhaps negligent as to the man carrying the package, was not negligent as to her. This was because the harm to her was not foreseeable. She cannot recover for injuries sustained merely because the railroad's agents were negligent as to the man they assisted.

INTERPRETATION Even if the defendant's negligent conduct in fact caused harm to the plaintiff, the defendant is not liable if the defendant could not have foreseen injuring the plaintiff or a class of persons to which the plaintiff belonged.

Superseding Cause An intervening cause is an event or act that occurs after the defendant's negligent conduct and with that negligence causes the plaintiff's harm. If the intervening cause is deemed a **superseding cause**, it relieves the defendant of liability for that harm.

Superseding cause
intervening event that occurs after the defendant's negligent conduct and relieves her of liability

For example, Adams negligently leaves in a public sidewalk an excavation without a fence or warning lights, into which Bogues falls at night. Darkness is an intervening, but not a superseding, cause of harm to Bogues because it is a normal consequence of the situation caused by Adams's negligence. Therefore, Adams is liable to Bogues. In contrast, if Adams negligently leaves an excavation in a public sidewalk into which Carson intentionally hurls Bogues, Adams is not liable to Bogues because Carson's conduct is a superseding cause that relieves Adams of liability.

PETITION OF KINSMAN TRANSIT CO. United States Court of Appeals, Second Circuit, 1964, 338 F.2d 708

FACTS The *MacGilvray Shiras* was a ship owned by the Kinsman Transit Company. During the winter months when Lake Erie was frozen, the ship and others moored at docks on the Buffalo River. As oftentimes happened, one night an ice jam disintegrated upstream, sending large chunks of ice downstream. Chunks of ice began to pile up against the *Shiras*, which at that time was without power and manned only by a shipman. The ship broke loose when a negligently constructed "deadman" to which one mooring cable was attached pulled out of the ground. The "deadman" was operated by Continental Grain Company. The ship began moving down the S-shaped river stern first and struck another ship, the *Tewksbury*. The *Tewksbury* also broke loose from its mooring, and the two ships floated down the river together. Although the crew manning the

Michigan Avenue Bridge downstream had been notified of the runaway ships, they failed to raise the bridge in time to avoid a collision because of a mixup in the shift changeover. As a result, both ships crashed into the bridge and were wedged against the bank of the river. The two vessels substantially dammed the flow of the river, causing ice and water to back up and flood installations as far as three miles upstream. The injured parties brought this action for damages against Kinsman, Continental, and the city of Buffalo. The trial court found the three defendants liable, and they appealed from that decree.

DECISION Decree of trial court affirmed as to liability.

OPINION A ship insecurely moored in a fast-flowing river is a known danger to the owners of all ships and

continued

structures down the river and to persons upon them. Kinsman and Continental, then, owed a duty of care to all within the foreseeable reach of the ships' destructive path. Similarly, the city is liable to those who foreseeably could have been injured by its negligent failure to raise the bridge in time to prevent the collision. Finally, although the exact type of harm that occurred was not foreseeable, this does not prevent liability. The damage resulted from the same physical forces whose existence required the exercise of greater care than was displayed and was of the same general type that was foreseeable. In short, the unforeseeability of the exact developments and of the extent of the loss will not limit liability where the persons injured and the general nature of the damage done were foreseeable.

INTERPRETATION The unforeseeability of the exact manner and extent of a loss will not limit liability where the persons injured and the general nature of the damage were foreseeable.

INJURY

The plaintiff must prove that the defendant's negligent conduct proximately caused harm to a legally protected interest. Certain interests receive little or no protection against such conduct, while others receive full protection. The courts determine the extent of protection for a particular interest as a matter of law on the basis of social policy and expediency. For example, negligent conduct that is the proximate cause of harmful contact with the person of another is actionable. Thus, if Bob negligently runs into Julie, a pedestrian, who is carefully crossing the street, Bob is liable for physical injuries Julie sustains as a result of the collision. On the other hand, if Bob's careless conduct causes only offensive contact with Julie's person, Bob is not liable.

The courts traditionally have been reluctant to allow recovery for negligently inflicted emotional distress. This view has gradually changed during this century, and the majority of courts now hold a person liable for negligently causing emotional distress if bodily harm—such as a heart attack—results from the distress. And though, in the great majority of states, a defendant is not liable for conduct resulting solely in emotional disturbance, a few courts have recently allowed recovery of damages for negligently inflicted emotional distress even in the absence of resultant physical harm.

Burden of proof plaintiff must prove that defendant's negligent conduct caused harm to a legally protected interest

Harm to legally protected interest courts determine which interests are protected from negligent interference

DEFENSES TO NEGLIGENCE

Although a plaintiff has established by a preponderance of the evidence all the required elements of a negligence action, he may nevertheless not recover damages if the defendant proves a valid defense. As a general rule, any defense to an intentional tort is also available in an action in negligence. In addition, there are defenses available in negligence cases that are not defenses to intentional torts. These are contributory negligence, comparative negligence, and assumption of risk. (See Figure 8–4.)

Contributory Negligence

Contributory negligence is defined as conduct on the part of the *plaintiff* that falls below the standard to which he should conform for his own protection and that is a legal cause of the plaintiff's harm. If negligence of the plaintiff together with negligence of the defendant proximately caused the injury and damage the plaintiff sustained, he cannot recover *any* damages from the defendant in those *few* states where contributory negligence is still recognized, no matter how slight the plaintiff's contributory negligence was.

Contributory negligence *(con·trib'·u·to·ry)* failure of a plaintiff to exercise reasonable care such that her failure legally causes the plaintiff's harm

FIGURE 8—4 Defenses to a Negligence Action

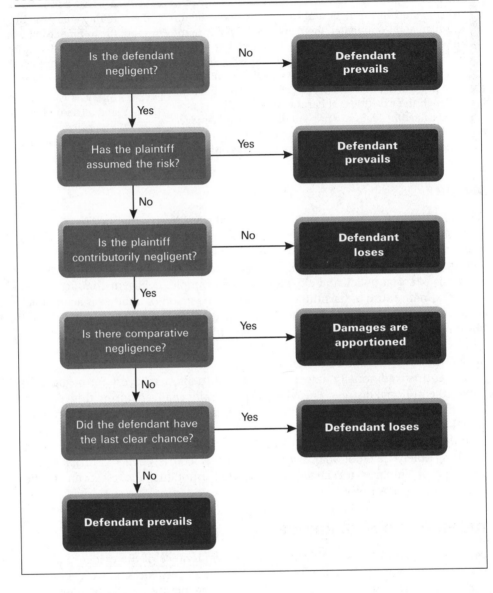

Notwithstanding the contributory negligence of the plaintiff, if the defendant had a **last clear chance** to avoid injury to the plaintiff but did not avail himself of such a chance, the contributory negligence of the plaintiff does not bar his recovery of damages.

Last clear chance final opportunity to avoid an injury

Comparative Negligence

The harshness of the contributory negligence doctrine has caused all but a few states to reject its all-or-nothing rule and to substitute the doctrine of **comparative negligence**. Under comparative negligence, damages are divided between the parties in proportion to the degree of fault or negligence found against them. For instance, Matthew negligently drives his automobile into Nancy, who is

Comparative negligence *(com·par'·a·tive)* doctrine dividing damages between the plaintiff and defendant where the negligence of each has caused the harm

crossing against the light. Nancy sustains damages in the amount of $10,000 and sues Matthew. If the trier of fact (the jury or judge, depending on the case) determines that Matthew's negligence contributed 70 percent to Nancy's injury and that Nancy's contributory negligence contributed 30 percent to her injury, then Nancy would recover $7,000.

Most states that have adopted the doctrine of comparative negligence have enacted statutes that do not permit any recovery to a plaintiff whose contributory negligence was equal to or greater than that of the defendant. Thus, in the example above, if the trier of fact determined that Matthew's negligence and Nancy's contributory negligence contributed 40 percent and 60 percent, respectively, to her injury, then Nancy would not recover anything from Matthew.

Assumption of Risk

A plaintiff who has *voluntarily* and *knowingly* assumed the risk of harm arising from the negligent or reckless conduct of the defendant cannot recover for such harm. Basically, **assumption of risk** is the plaintiff's express or implied consent to encounter a known danger. Thus, a spectator entering a baseball park may be regarded as consenting that the players may proceed with the game without taking precautions to protect him from being hit by the ball. The following case involves both contributory negligence and assumption of risk.

Assumption of risk
(as·sump'·tion) plaintiff's express or implied consent to encounter a known danger

A number of states have abolished or modified the defense of assumption of risk. Some have merged one or all of the types of assumption of risk into their comparative negligence or comparative fault systems.

FALGOUT v. WARDLAW Court of Appeal of Louisiana, Second Circuit, 1982, 423 So.2d 707

FACTS Carolyn Falgout accompanied William Wardlaw as a social guest to Wardlaw's brother's camp. After both parties had consumed intoxicating beverages, Falgout walked onto a pier that was then only partially completed. Wardlaw had requested that she not go on the pier. Falgout said, "Don't tell me what to do," and proceeded to walk on the pier. Wardlaw then asked her not to walk past the completed portion of the pier. She ignored his warnings and walked to the pier's end. When returning to the shore, Falgout got her shoe caught between the boards. She fell, hanging by her foot, with her head and arms in the water. Wardlaw rescued Falgout, who had seriously injured her knee and leg. She sued Wardlaw for negligence and subsequently appealed from the trial court's judgment for Wardlaw.

DECISION Judgment for defendant affirmed.

OPINION A plaintiff's conduct may constitute both assumption of risk and contributory negligence. To have assumption of risk, the plaintiff must have actual, *subjective* knowledge of the dangers involved. It is not enough that she is merely in a position to make

observations that would reveal the dangers. Only when she has actually made the observations and should then have reasonably known of the particular risk can she be held to have voluntarily assumed it. On the other hand, contributory negligence is determined by an *objective,* "reasonable person" standard. If the plaintiff's conduct falls below the standard, she is contributorily negligent. Both defenses relieve the defendant of liability because of the plaintiff's fault.

Here, Falgout actually observed the wide spacings in the pier when she walked to its end. Also, Wardlaw warned her not to go out on it. These two facts establish that Falgout both saw and understood the risks of walking on the pier and, yet, she voluntarily assumed them. Her conduct also constituted contributory negligence. Either defense relieves Wardlaw of liability to Falgout.

INTERPRETATION A plaintiff who has proven all of the elements of a negligence action nevertheless will be denied a full recovery if the plaintiff voluntarily and knowingly assumed the risk or negligently contributed to her injuries.

STRICT LIABILITY

Strict liability liability for nonintentional and nonnegligent conduct

In some instances a person may be held liable for injuries he has caused even though he has not acted intentionally or negligently. Such liability is called strict liability, absolute liability, or liability without fault. The courts have determined that certain types of otherwise socially desirable activities pose sufficiently high risks of harm regardless of how carefully they are conducted, and that therefore those who carry on these activities should bear the cost of any harm that such activities cause. The doctrine of strict liability is *not* based on any particular fault of the defendant, but rather on the nature of the activity in which he is engaging.

ACTIVITIES GIVING RISE TO STRICT LIABILITY

We will discuss in this section the following activities that give rise to strict liability: (1) performing abnormally dangerous activities, (2) keeping animals, and (3) selling defective, unreasonably dangerous products.

Abnormally Dangerous Activities

Abnormally dangerous activities involve a high degree of risk of serious harm and are not matters of common usage

The courts impose strict liability for harm resulting from extraordinary, unusual, abnormal, or exceptional activities, as determined in light of the place, time, and manner in which the activity was conducted. An **abnormally dangerous activity** is one that (1) necessarily involves a high degree of risk of serious harm to the persons and/or chattels of others, which risk cannot be eliminated by the exercise of reasonable care, *and* (2) is not a matter of common usage. Activities to which the rule has been applied include storing explosives or flammable liquids in large quantities; blasting or pile driving; crop dusting; drilling for or refining oil in populated areas; and emitting noxious gases or fumes into a settled community. On the other hand, courts have refused to apply the rule where the activity is a "natural" use of the land, such as drilling for oil in the oil fields of Texas or transmitting gas through a gas pipe or electricity through electric wiring.

KLEIN v. PYRODYNE CORPORATION Supreme Court of Washington, 1991, 117 Wash.2d 1, 810 P.2d 917

FACTS Pyrodyne Corporation contracted to display the fireworks at the Western Washington State Fairgrounds in Puyallup, Washington, on July 4, 1987. During the fireworks display, one of the five-inch mortars was knocked into a horizontal position. A shell inside ignited and discharged, flying five hundred feet parallel to the earth and exploding near the crowd of onlookers. Danny and Marion Klein were injured by the explosion. Mr. Klein suffered facial burns and serious injuries to his eyes. The parties provided conflicting explanations for the improper discharge, and because all the evidence had exploded, there was no means of proving the cause of the misfire. The Kleins brought suit against Pyrodyne under the theory of strict liability for participating in an abnormally dangerous activity.

DECISION Judgment for the Kleins.

OPINION Under the modern doctrine of strict liability for abnormally dangerous activities, a defendant will be liable when he damages another by a thing or activity unduly dangerous and inappropriate to the place where it is maintained, in light of the character of that place and its surroundings. The Restatement of Torts provides that any party carrying on an "abnormally dangerous activity" is strictly liable and lists six factors that courts are to consider in determining whether an activity is "abnormally dangerous." These factors are (a) the existence of a high degree of risk of some harm to the person, land, or chattels of others; (b) the likelihood that the harm resulting from the activity will be great; (c) the inability to eliminate the risk by the exercise of reasonable care; (d) the extent to which the activity is not a matter of common usage; (e) the inappropriateness of the activity to the place where it is

continued

carried on; and (f) the extent to which the activity's dangerous attributes outweigh its value to the community. Any one of these is not necessarily sufficient, and ordinarily a finding of strict liability will require several of them. The essential question is whether the risk the activity creates is so unusual as to justify the imposition of strict liability even though the activity is conducted with all reasonable care.

Factors (a), (b), and (c) are present in this case. Any time a person ignites aerial shells or rockets with the intention of sending them aloft in the presence of large crowds of people, a high risk of serious personal injury or property damage is created. That risk arises because of the possibility that a shell or rocket will malfunction or be misdirected. Furthermore, no matter how much care pyrotechnicians exercise, they cannot entirely eliminate the high risk inherent in setting off powerful explosives, such as fireworks, near crowds. Moreover, since relatively few persons conduct public fireworks displays, factor (d) is also present. Since the fairgrounds were an appropriate place for the fireworks and we as a society value fireworks on the Fourth of July more than we fear the risks, factors (e) and (f) are not present. Finding that four of the six conditions were present, the court holds that conducting public fireworks displays is an abnormally dangerous activity justifying strict liability.

INTERPRETATION The courts impose strict liability for harm resulting from an abnormally dangerous activity, as determined in light of the place, time, and manner in which the activity was conducted.

Keeping of Animals

Strict liability for harm caused by animals existed at common law and continues today with some modification. As a general rule, those who possess animals for their own purposes do so at their peril and must protect against harm those animals may cause to people and property.

Keeping of animals strict liability is imposed for wild animals and usually for trespassing domestic animals

Trespassing Animals Keepers of animals are generally held liable for any damage their animals cause by trespassing on the property of another. There are three exceptions to this rule: (1) keepers of cats and dogs are liable only for negligence; (2) keepers of animals are not strictly liable for animals straying from a highway on which they are being lawfully driven, although the owner may be liable for negligence if he fails to control them properly; and (3) in some western states, keepers of farm animals, typically cattle, are not strictly liable for harm caused by their trespassing animals that are allowed to graze freely.

Nontrespassing Animals Keepers of wild animals are strictly liable for harm caused by such animals, whether or not they are trespassing. *Wild animals* are defined as those that, in the particular region in which they are kept, are known to be likely to inflict serious damage and that cannot be considered safe, no matter how domesticated they are. Animals included in this category are bears, lions, elephants, monkeys, tigers, deer, and raccoons.

Domestic animals are those animals that are traditionally devoted to the service of mankind and that as a class are considered safe. Examples of domestic animals are dogs, cats, horses, cattle, and sheep. Keepers of domestic animals are liable if they knew, or should have known, of an animal's dangerous propensity. The animal's dangerous propensity must be the cause of the harm. For example, a keeper is not liable for a dog that bites a human merely because he knows that the dog has a propensity to fight with other dogs. On the other hand, a person whose 150-pound Old English sheepdog has a propensity to jump enthusiastically on visitors would be liable for any damage caused by the dog's playfulness.

THE LAW AND YOU What to Do in Case of an Auto Accident

1. *Stop!*

Failure to stop can result in serious criminal consequences.

2. *Render Aid*

If anyone is injured:

a. Render first aid if qualified.
b. Stop bleeding.
c. Call a doctor or an ambulance or both.
d. Do not move an injured person in any way that could possibly add to his or her injury.

3. *Protect the Scene from Further Damage*

You may be liable for damages to approaching drivers, unless they are properly warned.

If the highway is obstructed at night, illuminate the accident scene if possible.

4. *Call an Officer*

Policemen, Highway Patrolmen, Sheriffs and their deputies are trained accident investigators whose testimony may be invaluable in establishing your civil claim for damages.

5. *Gather Information/Write It Down*

Don't trust your memory. Don't guess—be specific.

a. Measure skid marks.
b. Step off distances.
c. Obtain names and addresses of witnesses.

Drivers are required by law to exhibit their driver's license to each other.

6. *Be Careful What You Say*

Even if you feel you might be at fault, it is best to make no admission. You may learn later that the other driver was equally at fault, or more so.

Emotional comments can be misconstrued by others, or may be misquoted.

At the scene of an accident, spectators are curious. It is best to remain silent.

Let your lawyer talk for you later—you get the **FACTS.**

7. *See Your Doctor*

Serious injuries do not always result in immediate pain or bloodshed. If there is the slightest chance you may be injured, see a doctor.

8. *Consult Your Lawyer Immediately*

The sooner your lawyer is brought into the matter, the better he or she can advise you and protect your rights. Your lawyer can obtain statements from the witnesses while their memories are fresh, and do many other things to insure that the true facts are preserved.

Get your lawyer's advice before giving any interviews or statements to investigators or adjusters.

9. *Report the Accident to the Department of Public Safety*

An accident report is required by law to be filed with the Dept. of Public Safety within 10 days from the date of the accident if there is an injury, death, or total damages exceeding $500.00. An official form is available from the Police, Sheriff's Dept., Highway Patrol, or Texas Dept. of Public Safety.

10. *Inform Your Insurance Company Promptly*

Failure to do so may void your policy. Effective January 1, 1982, vehicles operated on the streets and highways of Texas *must* be covered by liability insurance or other evidence of financial responsibility. The Dept. of Public Safety enforcement personnel will accept as evidence of insurance the insurance policy for the vehicle or an instrument issued by the insurance company confirming coverage of the vehicle. This instrument must contain at least:

a. A statement that the coverage meets the minimum prescribed by law;
b. The name of the insurance company;
c. The name of the insured;
d. The period of the policy; and
e. The policy number.

Evidence of insurance should be carried in the vehicle or with the driver of the vehicle. As a condition of driving, every owner and/or operator is required upon request to furnish such evidence to a law enforcement officer or to another person if involved in an accident.

Failure to show evidence of insurance or financial responsibility carries upon conviction certain statutory penalties including fine and suspension of license and registration privileges.

[The material in this feature was prepared as a public service and is intended for general information purposes only. The frequent changes in state law could affect this material, and such law also varies from state to state.]

Reprinted by permission from the State Bar of Texas.

Products Liability

A recent and important trend in the law is the imposition of a limited form of strict liability on manufacturers and merchants who sell goods in a *defective condition* unreasonably dangerous to the user or consumer. Such liability, imposed regardless of the seller's due care, applies to all merchant sellers. Nearly all states have adopted some version of strict products liability, a topic we will cover in Chapter 22.

DEFENSES TO STRICT LIABILITY

Because the strict liability of one who carries on an abnormally dangerous activity, keeps animals, or sells products is not based on his negligence, the ordinary **contributory negligence** of the plaintiff is *not* a defense to such liability. The law in imposing strict liability places the full responsibility for preventing harm on the defendant. Nevertheless, some states apply the doctrine of **comparative negligence** to some types of strict liability, in particular, to products liability.

Voluntary assumption of risk is a defense to an action based on strict liability. If the owner of an automobile knowingly and voluntarily parks the vehicle in a blasting zone, he may not recover for harm to his automobile. The assumption of risk, however, must be voluntary. Where blasting operations are established, for example, the possessor of nearby land is not required to move away and may recover for harm suffered.

> **Products liability** imposed upon manufacturers and merchants who sell goods in a defective condition unreasonably dangerous to the user or consumer

> **Contributory negligence** is *not* a defense to strict liability

> **Comparative negligence** most states apply this doctrine to products liability cases

> **Assumption of risk** is a defense to an action based upon strict liability

CHAPTER SUMMARY

Negligence

Breach of Duty of Care	**Definition of Negligence** conduct that falls below the standard established by law for the protection of others against unreasonable risk of harm
	Reasonable Person Standard degree of care that a reasonable person would exercise in a given situation
	■ *Children* must conform to conduct of a reasonable person of like age, intelligence, and experience
	■ *Physical Disability* a disabled person's conduct must conform to that of a reasonable person under like disability
	■ *Mental Deficiency* a mentally deficient person is held to the reasonable person standard of a reasonable person who is not mentally deficient
	■ *Superior Skill or Knowledge* professionals must exercise the same care and skill normally possessed by members of their profession
	■ *Emergencies* the reasonable person standard applies, but the emergency is considered part of the circumstances
	■ *Violation of Statute* if the statute applies, the violation is negligence *per se*
	Duty to Act except in special circumstances, no one is required to aid another in peril
	Duties of Possessors of Land
	■ *Duty to Trespassers* not to injure intentionally
	■ *Duty to Licensees* to warn of known dangerous conditions licensees are unlikely to discover for themselves
	■ *Duty to Invitees* to exercise reasonable care to protect invitees against dangerous conditions possessor should know of but invitees are unlikely to discover
	Res Ipsa Loquitur permits the jury to infer both negligent conduct and causation

Proximate Cause	**Causation in Fact** the defendant's conduct was the actual cause of, or a substantial factor in causing, the injury
	Limitations on Causation in Fact
	■ *Unforeseeable Consequences* no liability if defendant could not reasonably have anticipated injuring the plaintiff or a class of persons to which the plaintiff belongs
	■ *Superseding Cause* an intervening act that relieves the defendant of liability

| **Injury** | **Harm to Legally Protected Interest** courts determine which interests are protected from negligent interference |
| | **Burden of Proof** plaintiff must prove that defendant's negligent conduct caused harm to a legally protected interest |

Defenses to Negligence	**Contributory Negligence** failure of a plaintiff to exercise reasonable care for his own protection, which in a few states prevents the plaintiff from recovering anything
	Comparative Negligence damages are divided between the parties in proportion to their degree of negligence; applies in almost all states
	Assumption of Risk plaintiff's express or implied consent to encounter a known danger

Strict Liability

Activities Giving Rise to Strict Liability	**Definition of Strict Liability** liability for nonintentional and nonnegligent conduct
	Abnormally Dangerous Activities involve a high degree of risk of serious harm and are not matters of common usage
	Keeping of Animals strict liability is imposed for wild animals and usually for trespassing domestic animals
	Products Liability imposed upon manufacturers and merchants who sell goods in a defective condition unreasonably dangerous to the user or consumer

Defenses to Strict Liability	**Contributory Negligence** is *not* a defense to strict liability
	Comparative Negligence most states apply this doctrine to products liability cases
	Assumption of Risk is a defense to an action based upon strict liability

QUESTIONS

1. List and briefly describe the three required elements of an action for negligence.
2. Explain the duty of care that is imposed upon (a) adults, (b) children, (c) persons with a physical disability, (d) persons with a mental deficiency, (e) persons with superior knowledge, and (f) persons acting in an emergency.
3. Define trespassers, licensees, and invitees. Discuss the duties owed by possessors of land to each of these.
4. Identify the defenses that are available to a tort action in negligence and those that are available to a tort action in strict liability.
5. Identify and discuss those activities giving rise to a tort action in strict liability.

Internet Question. Find and review information about tort reform.

PROBLEMS

1. A statute that requires railroads to fence their tracks is construed as intended solely to prevent injuries to animals straying onto the right-of-way. B & A Railroad Company fails to fence its tracks. Two of Calvin's cows wander onto the track. Nellie is hit by a train. Elsie is poisoned by weeds growing beside the track. For which cows, if any, is B & A Railroad Company liable to Calvin? Why?

2. Martha invites John to come to lunch. Martha knows that her private road is dangerous to travel, having been guttered by recent rains. She doesn't warn John of the condition, reasonably believing that he will notice the gutters and exercise sufficient care. John's attention, while driving over, is diverted from the road by the screaming of his child, who has been stung by a bee. He fails to notice the condition of the road, hits a gutter, and skids into a tree. If John is not contributorily negligent, is Martha liable to John?

3. Nathan is run over by a car and left lying in the street. Sam, seeing Nathan's helpless state, places him in his car for the purpose of taking him to the hospital. Sam drives negligently into a ditch, causing additional injury to Nathan. Is Sam liable to Nathan?

4. Vance was served liquor while he was an intoxicated patron of the Clear Air Force Station Non-commissioned Officers' Club. He later injured himself as a result of his intoxication. An Alaska state statute makes it a crime to give or to sell liquor to intoxicated persons. Vance has brought an action seeking damages for the injuries he suffered. He argues that the United States was negligent *per se* by its employee's violation of the statute. Decision?

5. A statute requires all vessels traveling on the Great Lakes to provide lifeboats. One of Winston Steamship Company's boats is sent out of port without a lifeboat. Perry, a sailor, falls overboard in a storm so heavy that had there been a lifeboat it could not have been launched. Perry drowns. Is Winston liable to Perry's estate?

6. Lionel is negligently driving an automobile at excessive speed. Reginald's negligently driven car crosses the center line of the highway and scrapes the side of Lionel's car, damaging its fenders. As a result, Lionel loses control of his car, which goes into the ditch, wrecking the car and causing personal injuries to Lionel. What can Lionel recover?

7. **(a)** Ellen, the owner of a baseball park, is under a duty to the entering public to provide a reasonably sufficient number of screened seats to protect those who desire such protection against the risk of being hit by batted balls. Ellen fails to do so. Frank, a customer entering the park, is unable to find a screened seat and, although fully aware of the risk, sits in an unscreened seat. Frank is struck and injured by a batted ball. Is Ellen liable?

   (b) Gretchen, Frank's wife, has just arrived from Germany and is viewing baseball for the first time. Without asking any questions, she follows Frank to a seat. After the batted ball hits Frank, it caroms into Gretchen, injuring her. Is Ellen liable to Gretchen?

8. CC Railroad is negligent in failing to give warning of the approach of its train to a crossing and thereby endangers Larry, a blind man who is about to cross. Mildred, a bystander, in a reasonable effort to save Larry, rushes onto the track to push Larry out of danger. Although Mildred acts as carefully as possible, she is struck and injured by the train.
   (a) Can Mildred recover from Larry?
   (b) Can Mildred recover from CC Railroad?

9. An unidentified man was held up by two thugs in an alley in Manhattan. When the thieves departed with his possessions, the man quickly gave chase. He had almost caught one when the thief managed to force his way into an empty taxicab stopped at a traffic light. The cab was owned by the Peerless Transport Company. The thief pointed his gun at the driver's head and ordered him to drive on. The driver started

to follow the directions while closely pursued by a posse of good citizens, but then suddenly jammed on the brakes and jumped out of the car to safety. The thief also jumped out, but the car traveled on, injuring Mrs. Cordas and her two children. The Cordases then brought an action for damages, claiming that the cab driver was negligent in jumping to safety and leaving the moving vehicle uncontrolled. Decision?

10. Timothy keeps a pet chimpanzee that is thoroughly tamed and accustomed to playing with its owner's children. The chimpanzee escapes, despite every precaution to keep it on the owner's premises. It approaches a group of children. Wanda, the mother of one of the children, erroneously thinking the chimpanzee is about to attack the children, rushes to her child's assistance. In her hurry and excitement, she stumbles and falls, breaking her leg. Can Wanda recover from Timothy for her personal injuries?

11. Hawkins slipped and fell on a puddle of water just inside the automatic door to the H. E. Butt Grocery Company's store. The water had been tracked into the store by customers and blown through the door by a strong wind. The store manager was aware of the puddle and had mopped it up several times earlier in the day. Still, no signs had been placed to warn store patrons of the danger. Hawkins brought an action to recover damages for injuries sustained in the fall. Decision?

12. Escola, a waitress, was injured when a bottle of Coca-Cola exploded in her hand while she was putting it into the restaurant's cooler. The bottle came from a shipment that had remained under the counter for thirty-six hours after being delivered by the bottling company. The bottler had subjected the bottle to the method of testing for defects commonly used in the industry, and there is no evidence that Escola or anyone else did anything to damage the bottle between its delivery and the explosion. Escola brought an action against the bottler for damages. Since she is unable to show any specific acts of negligence on its part, she seeks to rely on the doctrine of *res ipsa loquitur*. Decision?

13. Hunn injured herself when she slipped and fell on a loose plank while walking down some steps that the hotel had repaired the day before. The night before, while entering the hotel, she had noticed that the steps were dangerous, and although she knew from her earlier stays at the hotel that another exit was available, she chose that morning to leave via the dangerous steps. The hotel was aware of the hazard, as one of three other guests who had fallen that night had reported his accident to the desk clerk then on duty. Still, there were no cautionary signs on the steps to warn of the danger, and they were not roped

off or otherwise excluded from use. Hunn brought an action against the hotel for injuries she sustained as a result of her fall. Decision?

14. Fredericks, a hotel owner, had a dog named Sport that he had trained as a watchdog. When Vincent Zarek, a guest at the hotel, leaned over to pet the dog, it bit him. Although Sport had never bitten anyone before, Fredericks was aware of the dog's violent tendencies and, therefore, did not allow it to roam around the hotel alone. Vincent brought an action for injuries sustained when the dog bit him. Decision?

15. Led Foot drives his car carelessly into another car. The second car contains dynamite, a fact which Led had no way of knowing. The collision causes an explosion that shatters a window of a building half a block away on another street. The flying glass inflicts serious cuts on Sally, who is working at a desk near the window. The explosion also harms Vic, who is walking on the sidewalk near the point of the collision. Toward whom is Led Foot negligent?

16. A foul ball struck Marie Uzdavines on the head while she was watching the Metropolitan Baseball Club (The Mets) play the Philadelphia Phillies at the Mets' home stadium in New York. The ball came through a hole in a screen designed to protect spectators sitting behind home plate. The screen contained several holes that had been repaired with baling wire, a lighter weight wire than that used in the original screen. Although the manager of the stadium makes no formal inspections of the screen, his employees do try to repair the holes as they find them. Weather conditions, rust deterioration, and baseballs hitting the screen are the chief causes of these holes. The owner of the stadium, the city of New York, leases the stadium to the Mets and replaces the entire screen every two years. Uzdavines sued the Mets for negligence under the doctrine of *res ipsa loquitur*. Decision?

17. Two-year-old David Allen was bitten by Joseph Whitehead's dog while he was playing on the porch at the Allen residence. Allen suffered facial cuts, a severed muscle in his left eye, a hole in his left ear, and scarring over his forehead. Through his father, David sued Whitehead, claiming that, as owner, Whitehead is responsible for his dog's actions. Whitehead admitted that (1) the dog was large, mean-looking, and frequently barked at neighbors; (2) the dog was allowed to roam wild; and (3) the dog frequently chased and barked at cars. He stated, however, that (1) the dog was friendly and often played with his and neighbors' children; (2) he had not received previous complaints about the dog; (3) the dog was neither aggressive nor threatening; and (4) the dog had never bitten anyone before this incident. Decision?

18. Larry VanEgdom, in an intoxicated state, bought alcoholic beverages from the Hudson Municipal Liquor Store in Hudson, South Dakota. Immediately following the purchase, VanEgdom, while driving a car, struck and killed Guy William Ludwig, who was stopped on his motorcycle at a stop sign. Lela Walz, as special administrator of Ludwig's estate, brought an action against the city of Judson, which operated the liquor store, for the wrongful death of Ludwig. Walz alleged that the store employee was negligent in selling intoxicating beverages to VanEgdom when he knew or could have observed that VanEgdom was drunk. The trial court dismissed the action, and Walz appealed. Decision?

PART III

Contracts

CHAPTER 9

Introduction to Contracts

Every business enterprise, whether large or small, must enter into contracts with its employees, its suppliers of goods and services, and its customers in order to conduct its business operations. Thus, contract law is an important subject for the business manager. Contract law is also basic to fields of law treated in other parts of this book, such as agency, partnerships, corporations, sales of personal property, commercial paper, and secured transactions.

Even the most common transaction may involve many contracts. For example, in a typical contract for the sale of land, the seller promises to transfer title, or right of ownership, to the land; and the buyer promises to pay an agreed-upon purchase price. In addition, the seller may promise to pay certain taxes; and the buyer may promise to assume a mortgage on the property or to pay the purchase price to a creditor of the seller. If the parties have lawyers, they very likely have contracts with these lawyers. If the seller deposits the proceeds of the sale in a bank, he enters into a contract with the bank. If the buyer rents the property, he enters into a contract with the tenant. When one of the parties leaves his car in a parking lot to attend to any of these matters, he assumes a contractual relationship with the owner of the lot. In short, nearly every business transaction is based on contract and the expectations the agreed-upon promises create. It is, therefore, essential that you know the legal requirements for making binding contracts.

DEVELOPMENT OF THE LAW OF CONTRACTS

Contract law, like the law as a whole, is not static. It has undergone—and is still undergoing—enormous changes. In the nineteenth century, almost total freedom in forming contracts was the rule. However, contract formation also involved many technicalities; and the courts imposed contract liability only when the parties complied strictly with the required formalities.

During the twentieth century, many of the formalities of contract formation have been relaxed. Today, contractual obligations are usually recognized whenever the parties clearly intend to be bound. In addition, an increasing number of promises are now enforced in certain circumstances, even though such promises do not comply strictly with the basic requirements of a contract. In brief, the twentieth century has left its mark on contract law by limiting the absolute freedom of contract and, at the same time, by relaxing the requirements of contract formation. Accordingly, we can say that now it is considerably easier both to get into a contract and to get out of one.

Common Law

Contracts are primarily governed by state common law. An orderly presentation of this law is found in the Restatements of the Law of Contracts, a valuable authoritative reference work extensively relied on and quoted in reported judicial opinions.

The Uniform Commercial Code

The sale of personal property is a large part of commercial activity. Article 2 of the **Uniform Commercial Code** (the Code, or UCC) governs such sales in all states except Louisiana. A **sale** is a contract involving the transfer of title to goods from seller to buyer for a price. The Code essentially defines **goods** as tangible personal property. **Personal property** is any property other than an interest in real property (land). For example, the purchase of a television set, an automobile, or a textbook is a sale of goods. All such transactions are governed by Article 2 of the Code, but where the Code has not specifically modified general contract law, the common law of contracts continues to apply. In other words, the law of sales is a specialized part of the general law of contracts, and the law of contracts governs unless specifically displaced by the Code. See *Pittsley v. Houser* in Chapter 19.

Uniform Commercial Code Article 2 of the UCC governs the sale of goods

Sale transfer of title from seller to buyer

Goods tangible personal property

Personal property property other than an interest in land

Types of Contracts Outside the Code

General contract law **(common law)** governs all contracts outside the scope of the Code. Such contracts play a significant role in commercial activities. For example, the Code does *not* apply to employment contracts, service contracts, insurance contracts, contracts involving **real property** (land and anything attached to it, including buildings), and contracts for the sale of intangibles such as patents and copyrights. These transactions continue to be governed by general contract law. Figure 9–1 summarizes the types of law governing contracts.

Common law most contracts are primarily governed by state common law including contracts involving employment, services, insurance, real property, patents, and copyrights

Real property land and anything attached to it

INSUL-MARK MIDWEST, INC. v. MODERN MATERIALS, INC. Supreme Court of Indiana, 1993, 612 N.E.2d 550

FACTS Insul-Mark is the marketing arm of Kor-It Sales, Inc. Kor-It manufactures roofing fasteners and Insul-Mark distributes them nationwide. In late 1985, Kor-It contracted with Modern Materials, Inc. to have large volumes of screws coated with a rust-proofing agent. The contract specified that the coated screws must pass a standard industry test and that Kor-It would pay according to the pound and length of the screws coated. Kor-It had received numerous complaints from customers that the coated screws were rusting, but Modern Materials unsuccessfully attempted to remedy the problem. Kor-It terminated its relationship with Modern Materials and brought suit for the deficient coating. Modern Materials counterclaimed for the labor and materials it had furnished to Kor-It. The trial court held that the contract (1) was for performance of a service, (2) not governed by the UCC, (3) governed by the common law of contracts, and (4) therefore barred by a two-year statute of limitations. Insul-Mark appealed to the Court of Appeals, which transferred the case to the Supreme Court of Indiana to resolve conflicting authority in the Court of Appeals.

DECISION The transaction is predominantly for the performance of a service and, therefore, is not governed by the sales article of the UCC.

OPINION Where a transaction is "mixed"—that is, it involves both goods and services—the sales article of the UCC will apply only where the "predominant thrust" of the transaction is a sale of goods with labor only incidentally involved. This court rejects the "bifurcation" approach, taken by some lower courts, whereby a mixed transaction is viewed as two transactions: one for the sale of goods governed by the UCC, and one for the performance of a service governed by the common law. The bifurcation approach is less sensitive to the parties' expectations than the predominant thrust approach and would not work where an agreement is not readily divisible.

Whether the predominant thrust of a transaction is the sale of goods or the performance of a service depends primarily on the language of the contract in light of the situation of the parties and the surrounding

continued

circumstances. Also relevant are the final product the purchaser bargained to receive and whether it may be described as a good or a service. Finally, the courts examine the costs involved for the goods and services, and whether the purchaser was charged only for a good or a price based on both goods and services.

The agreement between Kor-It and Modern Materials was predominantly for the performance of a service. The performance Kor-It contracted to obtain was the transformation of its screws from a noncoated form to a coated form with enhanced rust-resistance. Modern Materials' complex multistep application process was the crucial element completing this trans-

formation. The transfer of the coating material, a good, in the process was incidental to the larger service. This is evidenced by the fact that Kor-It did not involve itself in deciding which coating material Modern Materials would apply to the screws. Furthermore, the pricing method in this transaction reveals that its predominant thrust was the performance of a service: Kor-It was charged by the pound of screws coated rather than a price based on the gallons of coating used.

INTERPRETATION Where a contract provides for both goods and labor, the common law applies if the predominate thrust of the contract is the provision of labor.

DEFINITION OF CONTRACT

Contract binding agreement that the courts will enforce

Breach failure to properly perform a contractual obligation

Put simply, a **contract** is a binding agreement that the courts will enforce. The Restatement, Second, of Contracts, more precisely defines a contract as "a promise or a set of promises for the breach of which the law gives a remedy, or the performance of which the law in some way recognizes a duty." A *promise* manifests or demonstrates the intention to act or to refrain from acting in a specified manner.

Those promises that meet *all* of the essential requirements of a binding contract are contractual and will be enforced. All other promises are *not* contractual, and usually no legal remedy is available for a **breach** of, or a failure to properly perform, these promises. (The remedies provided for breach of contract, which include compensatory damages, equitable remedies, reliance damages, and restitution, are discussed in Chapter 18.) Thus, a promise may be contractual (and therefore binding) or noncontractual. In other words, all contracts are promises, but not all promises are contracts (see Figure 9–2).

FIGURE 9–1 Law Governing Contracts

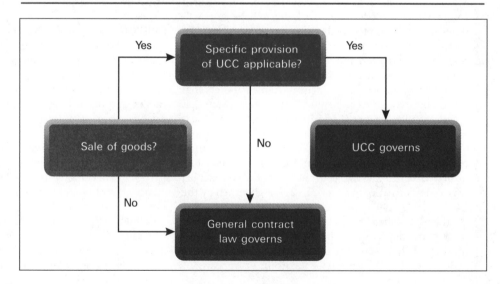

FIGURE 9–2 Contractual and Noncontractual Promises

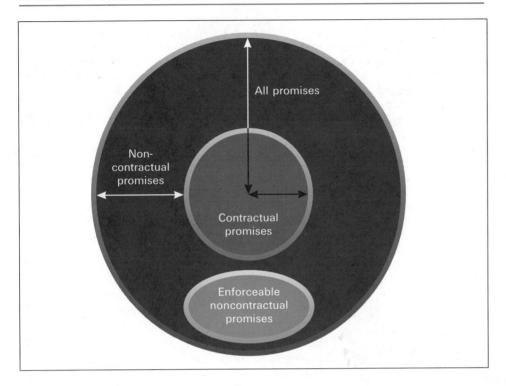

ESSENTIALS OF A CONTRACT

The four basic requirements of a contract are as follows:

1. **Mutual Assent.** The parties to a contract must manifest by words or conduct that they have agreed to enter into a contract. The usual method of showing mutual assent is by offer and acceptance.
2. **Consideration.** Each party to a contract must intentionally exchange a legal benefit or incur a legal detriment as an inducement to the other party to make a return exchange.
3. **Legality of Object.** The purpose of a contract must not be criminal, tortious, or otherwise against public policy.
4. **Capacity.** The parties to a contract must have contractual capacity. Certain persons, such as adjudicated incompetents, have no legal capacity to contract, while others, such as minors, incompetent persons, and intoxicated persons, have limited capacity to contract. All others have full contractual capacity.

In addition, though in a limited number of instances, a contract must be evidenced by a writing to be enforceable, in most cases an oral contract is binding and enforceable. Moreover, there must be an *absence* of invalidating conduct, such as duress, undue influence, misrepresentation, or mistake. (See Figure 9–3.) As the following two cases show, a promise meeting all of these requirements is contractual and legally binding. However, if any requirement is unmet, the promise is noncontractual. We will consider these essentials separately in succeeding chapters.

STEINBERG v. CHICAGO MEDICAL SCHOOL Illinois Court of Appeals, 1976, 41 Ill.App.3d 804, 354 N.E.2d 586

FACTS Robert Steinberg applied for admission to the Chicago Medical School as a first-year student and paid an application fee of $15. The school, a private educational institution, rejected his application. Steinberg brought an action against the school, claiming that it did not evaluate his and other applications according to the academic entrance criteria printed in the school's bulletin. Instead, he argues, the school based its decisions primarily on nonacademic considerations, such as family connections between the applicant and the school's faculty and members of its board of trustees and the ability of the applicant or his family to donate large sums of money to the school. Steinberg asserts that by evaluating his application according to these unpublished criteria, the school breached the contract it had created when it accepted his application fee. The trial court granted the defendant's motion to dismiss, and Steinberg appealed.

DECISION Trial court's dismissal reversed and case remanded.

OPINION A contract is a promise or set of promises for the breach of which the law gives a remedy. "A contract's essential requirements are: competent parties, valid subject matter, legal consideration, mutuality of obligation and mutuality of agreement." Generally, parties may contract in any situation where there is no legal prohibition. To be binding, however, the terms must be "reasonably certain and definite." The contract must also be supported by consideration. Defined in its most general terms, consideration is some benefit accruing to one party or some detriment undertaken by the other, such as the payment of or promise to pay money. In addition, the parties must mutually agree to the contract's essential terms and conditions to make the contract binding. Mutual consent is gathered from the language employed by the parties or manifested by their words or acts.

In this situation, the school's promise to evaluate the applications according to academic standards is stated in a "definitive manner" in its bulletin. Steinberg accepted this in good faith, and his $15 application fee served as valid consideration. When the school accepted this money, it bound itself to honor the obligations stated in its bulletin. Therefore, its failure to use the stated academic criteria in evaluating applications constituted a breach of its contractual obligation to Steinberg.

INTERPRETATION An agreement meeting all of the requirements of a contract is binding and legally enforceable.

PEARSALL v. ALEXANDER District of Columbia Court of Appeals, 1990, 572 A.2d 113

FACTS Harold Pearsall and Joe Alexander were friends for over twenty-five years. About twice a week they would get together after work and proceed to a liquor store, where they would purchase what the two liked to refer to as a "package"—a half-pint of vodka, orange juice, two cups, and two lottery tickets. Occasionally these lottery tickets would yield modest rewards of two or three dollars, which the pair would then "plow back" into the purchase of additional tickets. On December 16, 1992, Pearsall and Alexander visited the liquor store twice, buying their normal "package" on both occasions. For the first package, Pearsall went into the store alone, and when he returned to the car, he said to Alexander, in reference to the tickets, "Are you in on it?" Alexander said, "Yes." When Pearsall asked him for his half of the purchase price, though, Alexander replied that he had no money. When they went to Alexander's home, Alexander snatched the tickets from Pearsall's hand and "scratched" them, only to find that they were both worthless. Later that same evening, Alexander returned to the liquor store and bought a second "package." This time, Pearsall snatched the tickets from Alexander and said that he would "scratch" them. Instead, he gave one to Alexander, and each man scratched one of the tickets. Alexander's was a $20,000 winner. Alexander cashed the ticket and refused to give Pearsall anything. Pearsall brought suit against Alexander, claiming breach of an agreement to share the proceeds. The trial court dismissed Pearsall's complaint, and Pearsall appealed.

DECISION Judgment reversed and remanded with instructions to enter judgment in favor of Pearsall.

OPINION The record supports Pearsall's contention that an agreement to share the proceeds existed. The conduct of the two men on December 16, when the ticket was purchased, clearly demonstrates a meeting of the minds. After purchasing the first pair of tickets, Pearsall asked Alexander if he was "in on it." Not only did Alexander give his verbal assent, he also snatched both tickets from Pearsall and "scratched" them. It is clear that Alexander considered himself "in on" an agreement to share in the fortunes of the tickets. It is also clear that in giving over the tickets he purchased, Pearsall gave his assent to the agreement he had proposed

continued

earlier. This conduct took place within the context of a long-standing pattern of similar conduct, which included the parties' practice of "plowing back" small returns from tickets to purchase additional tickets. It is clear that by exchanging mutual promises to share in the proceeds, the parties entered into a valid, enforceable contract.

INTERPRETATION An agreement meeting all of the requirements of a contract is binding and legally enforceable.

FIGURE 9–3 Validity of Agreements

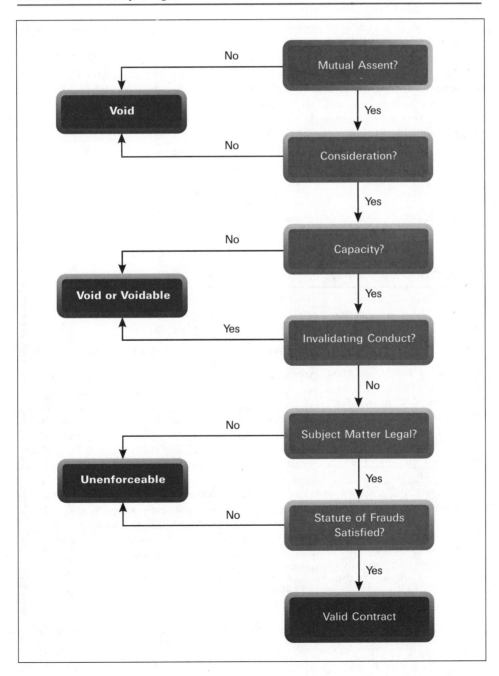

CLASSIFICATION OF CONTRACTS

Contracts can be classified according to various characteristics, such as method of formation, content, and legal effect. The standard classifications are (1) express or implied contracts; (2) bilateral or unilateral contracts; (3) valid, void/voidable, or unenforceable contracts; (4) executed or executory contracts; and (5) formal or informal contracts. These classifications are not mutually exclusive. For example, a contract may be express, bilateral, valid, executory, and informal.

Express and Implied Contracts

Parties to a contract may indicate their assent either in words or by conduct implying such willingness. For instance, a regular customer known to have an account at a drugstore might pick up an item at the drugstore, show it to the clerk, and walk out. This is a perfectly valid contract. The clerk knows from the customer's conduct that she is buying the item at the specified price and wants it charged to her account. Her actions speak as effectively as words. Such a contract, formed by conduct, is an implied or, more precisely, an **implied in fact contract**; in contrast, a contract in which the parties manifest assent in words is an **express contract**. Both are contracts, equally enforceable. The difference between them is merely the manner in which the parties manifest their assent.

Implied in fact contract
contract where agreement of the parties is inferred from their conduct

Express contract
agreement of parties that is stated in words either in writing or orally

---

RICHARDSON v. J. C. FLOOD CO. District Court of Appeals, 1963, 190 A.2d 259

FACTS Richardson hired J. C. Flood Company, a plumbing contractor, to correct a stoppage in the sewer line of her house. The plumbing company's "snake" device, used to clear the line leading to the main sewer, became caught in the underground line. To release it, the company excavated a portion of the sewer line in Richardson's backyard. In the process, the company discovered numerous leaks in a rusty, defective water pipe that ran parallel with the sewer line. To meet public regulations, the water pipe, of a type no longer approved for such service, had to be replaced either then or later, when the yard would have to be redug for such purpose. The plumbing company proceeded to repair the water pipe. Though Richardson inspected the company's work daily and did not express any objection to the extra work involved in replacing the water pipe, she refused to pay any part of the total bill after the company completed the entire operation. J. C. Flood Company then sued Richardson for the costs of labor and material it had furnished. Richardson argued that she only requested correction of a sewer obstruction and had

never agreed to the replacement of the water pipe. She appealed from a trial court judgment against her for costs of labor and materials.

DECISION Judgment for J. C. Flood Company affirmed.

OPINION Contracts are either expressed or implied—expressed when their terms are stated by the parties, implied when arising from a mutual agreement not set forth in words. An implied contract "may be presumed from the acts and conduct of the parties as a reasonable man would view them under all the circumstances." Here, Richardson made daily inspections yet failed to object to the replacement of the water pipe until after the work was completed. Although she did not expressly agree to this extra work, her acts and conduct indicate her consent to it. Therefore, she created an implied (in fact) contract obligating her to pay for the reasonable value of the company's services.

INTERPRETATION An implied in fact contract is formed by the conduct of the parties.

Bilateral and Unilateral Contracts

In the typical contractual transaction, each party makes at least one promise. For example, if Adelle says to Byron, "If you promise to mow my lawn, I will pay you ten dollars," and Byron agrees to mow Adelle's lawn, Adelle and Byron have made mutual promises, each agreeing to do something in exchange for the promise of the other. When a contract is formed by the exchange of promises, each party is under a duty to the other. This kind of contract is called a **bilateral contract**, because each party is both a **promisor** (a person making a promise) and a **promisee** (the person to whom a promise is made).

But suppose that only one of the parties makes a promise. Adelle says to Byron, "If you will mow my lawn, I will pay you ten dollars." A contract will be formed when Byron has finished mowing the lawn and not before. At that time, Adelle becomes contractually obligated to pay ten dollars to Byron. Adelle's offer was in exchange for Byron's act of mowing the lawn, not for his promise to mow it. Because Byron never made a promise to mow the lawn, he was under no duty to mow it. This is a **unilateral contract** because only *one* of the parties has made a promise.

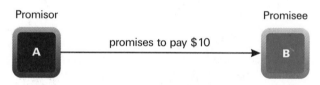

Thus, whereas a bilateral contract results from the exchange of a promise for a return promise, a unilateral contract results from the exchange of a promise either for performing an act or for refraining from doing an act. Where it is not clear whether a unilateral or bilateral contract has been formed, the courts presume that the parties intended a bilateral contract. Thus, if Adelle says to Byron, "If you will mow my lawn, I will pay you ten dollars," and Byron replies, "OK, I will mow your lawn," a bilateral contract is formed.

Valid, Void, Voidable, and Unenforceable Contracts

By definition a **valid contract** is one that meets all of the requirements of a binding contract. It is an enforceable promise or agreement.

A **void contract** is an agreement that does not meet all of the requirements of a binding contract. Thus, it is no contract at all; it is merely a promise or agreement that has no legal effect. An example of a void agreement is an agreement entered into by a person whom the courts have declared incompetent.

A voidable contract, on the other hand, though defective, is not wholly lacking in legal effect. A **voidable contract** *is* a contract; however, because of the manner in which the contract was formed or a lack of capacity of a party to it, the law permits one or more of the parties to avoid the legal duties the contract

Bilateral contract *(bi·lat'·er·al)* contract in which both parties exchange promises

Promisor person making a promise

Promisee person to whom a promise is made

Unilateral contract contract in which only one party makes a promise

Valid contract contract that meets all of the requirements of a binding contract

Void contract an agreement without legal effect

Voidable contract contract capable of being made void

MANAGERIAL INSIGHT

Can You Contract by Fax?

Roberta Maxwell is trying to buy a new home. She and her husband have made an offer on a two-story contemporary house in Chapel Hill, North Carolina. In fact, this dream home is the one for which Roberta and her husband have been searching for more than two years.

Now, after a few days of negotiation, the owner agrees to Roberta's price. There's only one glitch. The owner's wife, whose name is on the deed, has already moved to Ohio, and she will not be returning. The owner suggests that he fax the contract to his wife, who will sign it and zap it back. But will the contract be legal?

The answer is probably yes. Still, Roberta and her husband will need to be careful.

As fax machines proliferate, more and more business transactions, including contract negotiations, are being conducted long-distance. For the first time in history, parties can exchange written agreements within minutes, even if they are separated by an ocean or two, or one or more continents. With the invention of the fax, however, came a number of vexing legal questions, and so far, the courts have yet to address fully the issues raised. To protect yourself, consider the following when attempting to contract by fax:

- *Is the faxed document a copy of the original contract or the original contract itself?* To ensure that the fax serves as an original contract, have it signed. You may want to protect yourself even further by having any signature on the document notarized before the fax is sent. You also should state in the contract that both the faxed contract and the faxed signature are intended to serve as originals.

- *Is the fax a written contract or an oral contract?* Again, make certain that the fax document is signed if you want it to serve as a written contract. You should also include language in your faxed document that defines the document as a written contract. This is important because the statute of frauds requires certain contracts to be in writing and to be signed.

- *Will the printing on the faxed contract deteriorate over time?* If so, follow the fax up with an original hard copy sent by mail. To avoid any questions about the original nature of the faxed contract, add language to the contract that defines the hard copy as an original counterpart of the faxed contract.

- *Is the faxed contract a final agreement?* Because of the ease of transmission, faxed documents tend to fly back and forth between parties. To ensure that your faxed contract serves as the final agreement, state in the contract that it is the final and complete agreement of the parties. Also, be certain to date the faxed contract and to keep on file all faxed documents related to the negotiation.

- *Will the faxed contract stand up in court?* Most likely, if you have followed the steps outlined above. Section 2-206 of the Uniform Commercial Code allows for the acceptance of contracts by any reasonable manner and method under the circumstances. This part of the Code is meant to offer flexibility to contracting parties and to allow them to use new technologies. The Restatement of Contracts, Section 65, takes a similar approach.

- *Are there circumstances under which faxed contracts won't work?* Yes, there are times when you cannot contract by fax. For example, some states require that any land transfer be accompanied by a signed and sealed deed, which eliminates the use of a fax. In addition, a corporate seal is usually invalid if faxed. In the United States, different states have enacted different laws related to contracts, as have different countries. Therefore, always check appropriate legal requirements before you attempt to contract by fax.

creates. If the contract is voided, both of the parties are relieved of their legal duties under the agreement. For instance, through intentional misrepresentation of a material fact (*fraud*), Thomas induces Regina to enter into a contract. Regina may, upon discovery of the fraud, notify Thomas that by reason of the misrepresentation she will not perform her promise; and the law will support Regina. Although the contract induced by fraud is not void, it is voidable at the election of Regina, the defrauded party. Thomas, the fraudulent party, may make no such election. If Regina elects to avoid the contract, Thomas will be released from his promise under the agreement, although he may be liable for damages under tort law for fraud.

A contract that is neither void nor voidable may nonetheless be unenforceable. An **unenforceable contract** is one for the breach of which the law provides no remedy. For example, a contract may be unenforceable because of a failure to satisfy the requirements of the statute of frauds, which requires certain kinds of contracts to be evidenced by a writing to be enforceable. Also, the statute of limitations imposes restrictions on the time during which a party has the right to bring a lawsuit for breach of contract. After the statutory time period has passed, a contract is referred to as unenforceable, rather than void or voidable. See Figure 9–3.

Unenforceable contract
contract for the breach of which the law does not provide a remedy

Executed and Executory Contracts

A contract that has been fully carried out by all of the parties to it is an **executed contract**. Strictly speaking, an executed contract is no longer a contract, because all of the duties under it have been performed; but having a term for such a completed contract is useful. By comparison, the term **executory contract** applies to contracts that are still partially or entirely unperformed by one or more of the parties.

Executed contract
contract fully performed by all of the parties

Executory contract
(ex·ec´·u·to·ry) contract not fully performed

PROMISSORY ESTOPPEL

As a general rule, promises are not enforceable if they do not meet all the requirements of a contract. Nevertheless, in certain circumstances, the courts enforce noncontractual promises under the doctrine of **promissory estoppel** in order to avoid injustice. A noncontractual promise is enforceable when it is made under circumstances that should lead the promisor reasonably to expect that the promisee, in reliance on the promise, will be induced by it to take definite and substantial action or to forbear, and the promisee does take such action or does forbear. (See Figure 9–2). For example, Gordon promises Constance not to foreclose for a period of six months on a mortgage Gordon owns on Constance's land. Constance then expends $100,000 to construct a building on the land. His promise not to foreclose is binding on Gordon under the doctrine of promissory estoppel.

Promissory estoppel
(prom´·is·sory es·top´·pel) doctrine enforcing noncontractual promises where there has been justifiable reliance on the promise and justice requires enforcement

QUASI CONTRACTS

In addition to express and implied in fact contracts, there are *implied in law* or quasi contracts, which were not included in the previous classification of contracts for

FIGURE 9–4 Contracts, Promissory Estoppel, and Quasi Contracts

	Contract	Promissory Estoppel	Quasi Contract
Type of Promise	Contractual	Noncontractual	None Void Unenforceable Invalidated
Requirements	All of the essentials of a contract	Detrimental and justifiable reliance	Benefit conferred and knowingly accepted
Remedies	Equitable Compensatory Reliance Restitution	Promise enforced to the extent necessary to avoid injustice	Reasonable value of benefit conferred

the reason that a quasi (meaning "as if") contract is not a contract at all. The term "quasi contract" is used because the remedy granted for quasi contract is similar to one of the remedies available for breach of contract.

Quasi *(kwa·'zee)* **contract** obligation *not* based upon contract that is imposed by law to avoid injustice

A quasi contract is *not* a contract because it is based neither on an express nor on an implied promise. Rather, a **contract implied in law** or **quasi contract** is an obligation imposed by law to avoid injustice. For example, Willard by mistake delivers to Roy a plain, unaddressed envelope containing $100 intended for Lucia. Roy is under no contractual obligation to return it, but Willard is permitted to recover the $100 from Roy. The law imposes a quasi-contractual obligation on Roy in order to prevent his unjust enrichment at the expense of Willard. Such a recovery requires three essential elements: (1) a benefit conferred upon the defendant (Roy) by the plaintiff (Willard); (2) the defendant's (Roy's) appreciation or knowledge of the benefit; and (3) acceptance or retention of the benefit by the defendant (Roy) under circumstances making it inequitable for him to retain the benefit without compensating the plaintiff for its value.

Not infrequently, quasi contracts are used to provide a remedy when the parties enter into a void contract, an unenforceable contract, or a voidable contract that is avoided. In such a case, the law of quasi contracts will determine what recovery is permitted for any performance rendered by the parties under the invalid, unenforceable, or invalidated agreement.

WEICHERT CO. REALTORS v. RYAN Supreme Court of New Jersey, 1992, 128 N.J. 427, 608 A.2d 280

FACTS In March 1987, William Tackaberry, a real estate agent for Weichert Co. Realtors, informed Thomas Ryan, a local developer, that he knew of property Ryan might be interested in purchasing. Ryan indicated he was interested in knowing more about the property. Tackaberry disclosed the property's identity and the seller's proposed price. Tackaberry also stated that the purchaser would have to pay Weichert a ten percent commission. Tackaberry met with the property owner and gathered information concerning the property's current leases, income, expenses, and development plans. Tackaberry also collected tax and zoning documents relevant to the property. In a face-to-face meeting on April 4, Tackaberry gave Ryan the data he had gathered and presented Ryan with a letter calling for a ten percent finder's fee to be paid to Weichert by Ryan upon "successfully completing and closing of title." Tackaberry arranged a meeting, held three days later, where Ryan contracted with the owner to buy the land. Ryan refused, however, to pay the ten percent finder's fee to Weichert. The trial and appellate courts found that Ryan and Weichert had entered into a binding contract. Ryan appealed.

DECISION Judgment for Weichert modified and remanded to the trial court to determine the amount of plaintiff's recovery.

OPINION This case presents two issues: whether Ryan and Tackaberry entered into an enforceable agreement and, if not, whether Weichert is entitled to recover the reasonable value of Tackaberry's services on a theory of *quantum meruit*. The record is insufficient to support a finding that Tackaberry and Ryan mutually manifested assent to the essential terms of the contract. First, Ryan never expressly assented to the terms of Tackaberry's offer. Although Ryan expressed interest in learning more about the property, neither his expression of interest nor his agreement to meet with Tackaberry to learn more about the transaction was sufficient to establish the "unqualified acceptance" necessary to manifest express assent. Moreover, Ryan refused to agree to the ten percent figure during the April meeting and thereafter consistently rejected that term. Thus, the parties never formed an express contract.

In some circumstances, courts will allow recovery even though the parties' words and actions are insufficient to manifest an intention to agree to the proffered terms. Recovery based on a quasi contract, sometimes referred to as a contract implied in law, is wholly unlike recovery based on an express or implied in fact contract in that the law imposes it for the purpose of bringing about justice without reference to the parties' intentions. Applying that principle, courts have allowed quasi-contractual recovery for services rendered when a party confers a benefit with a reasonable expectation of payment. That type of quasi-contractual recovery, known as *quantum meruit*, entitles the performing party to recoup the reasonable value of the services he has rendered. In this case, Tackaberry furnished Ryan with information about the property with an expectation

continued

that Ryan would pay a brokerage fee, and Ryan himself admitted at trial that he had always intended to compensate Tackaberry for his services. To deny Tackaberry compensation for services rendered would unjustly enrich Ryan. The commission amount should be determined on the basis of proofs showing the reasonable value of Tackaberry's services, including evidence of customary brokers' fees for similar transactions.

INTERPRETATION The courts impose a quasi contractual obligation to pay the reasonable value of a benefit conferred in order to avoid unjust enrichment.

CHAPTER SUMMARY

Law of Contracts	**Definition of Contract** a binding agreement that the courts will enforce **Common Law** most contracts are primarily governed by state common law, including contracts involving employment, services, insurance, real property (land and anything attached to it), patents, and copyrights **Uniform Commercial Code** Article 2 of the UCC governs the sales of goods ■ *Sale* the transfer of title from seller to buyer ■ *Goods* tangible personal property (personal property is all property other than an interest in land)

Essentials of a Contract	**Mutual Assent** the parties to a contract must manifest by words or conduct that they have agreed to enter into a contract **Consideration** each party to a contract must intentionally exchange a legal benefit or incur a legal detriment as an inducement to the other party to make a return exchange **Legality of Object** the purpose of a contract must not be criminal, tortious, or otherwise against public policy **Capacity** the parties to a contract must have contractual capacity

Classification of Contracts	**Express and Implied Contracts** ■ *Express Contract* an agreement that is stated in words either orally or in writing ■ *Implied in Fact Contract* contract where the agreement of the parties is inferred from their conduct **Bilateral and Unilateral Contracts** ■ *Bilateral Contract* contract in which both parties exchange promises ■ *Unilateral Contract* contract in which only one party makes a promise **Valid, Void, Voidable, and Unenforceable Contracts** ■ *Valid Contract* one that meets all of the requirements of a binding contract ■ *Void Contract* no contract at all; without legal effect ■ *Voidable Contract* contract capable of being made void ■ *Unenforceable Contract* contract for the breach of which the law provides no remedy

Classification of Contracts	**Executed and Executory**
	▪ *Executed Contract* contract that has been fully performed by all of the parties
	▪ *Executory Contract* contract that has yet to be fully performed
	Promissory Estoppel doctrine enforcing noncontractual promises where there has been justifiable reliance on the promise and justice requires the enforcement of the promise
	Quasi Contract an obligation not based upon contract that is imposed by law to avoid injustice; also called an *implied in law* contract

QUESTIONS

1. Distinguish between contracts that are covered by the UCC and those covered by common law.
2. Define the terms *contract* and *breach*.
3. List the essential elements of a contract.
4. Distinguish between express and implied contracts.
5. Distinguish between unilateral and bilateral contracts.
6. Explain the differences among valid, void, voidable, and unenforceable contracts.
7. Distinguish between executed and executory contracts.
8. Explain the doctrine of promissory estoppel.
9. Identify the three elements of an enforceable quasi contract and explain how it differs from a contract.
10. What have been the most significant changes to contract law made during the twentieth century?

Internet Question. Find several samples of contracts.

PROBLEMS

1. Owen telephones an order to Hillary's store for certain goods which Hillary delivers to Owen. Nothing is said by either party about price or payment terms. What are the legal obligations of Owen and Hillary?
2. Minth is the owner of the Hiawatha Supper Club, which he leased during 1972 and 1973 to Piekarski. During the period of the lease, Piekarski contracted with Puttkammer for the resurfacing of the access and service areas of the supper club. The work, including labor and materials, had a reasonable value of $2,540, but Puttkammer was never paid because Piekarski went bankrupt. Puttkammer brought an action against Minth to recover the amount owed to him by Piekarski. Decision?
3. Jonathan writes to Willa, stating, "I'll pay you $150 if you reseed my lawn." Willa reseeds Jonathan's lawn as requested. Has a contract been formed? If so, what kind?
4. Calvin uses fraud to induce Maria to promise to pay money in return for goods he has delivered to her. Has a contract been formed? If so, what kind? What are the rights of Calvin and Maria?
5. Anna is about to buy a house on a hill. Prior to the purchase, she obtains a promise from Betty, the owner of the adjacent property, that Betty will not build any structure that would block Anna's view. In reliance on this promise Anna buys the house. Is Betty's promise binding? Why or why not?
6. Mary Dobos was admitted to Boca Raton Community Hospital in serious condition with an abdominal aneurysm. The hospital called upon Nursing Care Services, Inc., to provide around-the-clock nursing services for Mrs. Dobos. She received two weeks of in-hospital care, forty-eight hours of postrelease care, and two weeks of at-home care. The total bill was $3,723.90. Mrs. Dobos refused to pay, and Nursing Care Services, Inc., brought an action to recover. Mrs. Dobos maintained that she was not obligated to render payment in that she never signed a written contract, nor did she orally agree to be liable for the services. The necessity for the services, reasonableness of the fee, and competency of the nurses were undisputed. After Mrs. Dobos admitted that she or her daughter authorized the forty-eight hours of postrelease care, the trial court ordered compensation of $248 for that period. It did not allow payment of the balance, and Nursing Care Services, Inc., appealed. Decision?
7. St. Charles Drilling Co. contracted with Osterholt to install a well and water system that would produce a specified quantity of water. The water system failed to meet its warranted capacity, and Osterholt sued for breach of contract. Does the UCC apply to this contract?
8. On March 4, 1970, Helvey brought suit against REMC for breach of implied and express warranties. He alleged that REMC furnished electricity in excess of

135 volts to Helvey's home, damaging his 110-volt household appliances. This incident occurred on January 10, 1966. In defense, REMC pleads that the Uniform Commercial Code's Article 2 statute of limitations of four years has passed, thereby barring Helvey's suit. Helvey argues that providing electrical energy is not a transaction in goods under the UCC but rather a furnishing of services that would make applicable the general contract six-year statute of limitations. Decision?

9. In April 1980 Jack Duran, president of Colorado Carpet Installation, Inc., began negotiations with Fred and Zuma Palermo for the sale and installation of carpeting, carpet padding, tile, and vinyl floor covering in their home. Duran drew up a written proposal that referred to Colorado Carpet as "the seller" and to the Palermos as the "customer." The proposal listed the quantity, unit cost, and total price of each item to be installed. The total price of the job was $4,777.75. Although labor was expressly included in this figure, Duran estimated the total labor cost at $926. Mrs. Palermo orally accepted Duran's written proposal soon after he submitted it to her. After Colorado Carpet delivered the tile to the Palermo home, however, Mrs. Palermo had a disagreement with Colorado Carpet's tile man and arranged for another contractor to perform the job. Colorado Carpet brought an action against the Palermos for breach of contract. The trial court determined that the agreement between Colorado Carpet and the Palermos constituted a service contract for the performance of labor, not a contract for the sale of goods, and thus did not have to be in writing to be enforceable. The court of appeals reversed the decision, finding that the agreement was a contract for the sale of goods and was unenforceable under the "writing" requirement of the statute of frauds section of the Uniform Commercial Code. Decision?

10. On November 1, 1986, the Kansas City Post Office Employees Credit Union merged into the Kansas City Telephone Credit Union to form the Communications Credit Union (Credit Union). Systems Design and Management Information (SDMI) develops computer software programs for credit unions, using Burroughs (now Unisys) hardware. SDMI and Burroughs together offered to sell to Credit Union both a software package, called the Generic System, and Burroughs hardware. In November 1986, a demonstration of the software was held at SDMI's offices, and the Credit Union agreed to purchase the Generic System software. This agreement was oral. After Credit Union was converted to the SDMI Generic System, major problems with the system immediately became apparent.

SDMI filed suit against Credit Union to recover the outstanding contract price for the software. Credit Union counterclaimed for damages based upon breach of contract and negligent and fraudulent misrepresentation. The trial court entered judgment in favor of Credit Union on SDMI's claim and for SDMI on Credit Union's counterclaim. Both parties appealed. On its appeal, SDMI argued that the Uniform Commercial Code (UCC) should have governed this case because computer software is "goods" under the UCC. Decision?

CHAPTER 10

Mutual Assent

Although each of the requirements for forming a contract is essential to its existence, mutual assent is so basic that frequently a contract is referred to as an agreement between the parties. Enforcing the contract means enforcing the agreement; indeed, the agreement between the parties is the very core of the contract. As we discussed in Chapter 9, a contractual agreement always involves either a promise exchanged for a promise (*bilateral contract*) or a promise exchanged for a completed act or forbearance to act (*unilateral contract*), as shown by what the parties communicate to one another.

The way in which parties usually show mutual assent is by offer and acceptance. One party makes a proposal (offer) by words or conduct to the other party, who agrees by words or conduct to the proposal (acceptance).

A contract may be formed by conduct. Thus, though there may be no definite offer and acceptance, or definite acceptance of an offer, a contract exists if both parties' actions manifest a recognition by each of them of the existence of a contract. To form a contract, the agreement must be objectively manifested. The important thing is what the parties indicate to one another by spoken or written words or by conduct. Toward contracts, therefore, the law applies an *objective* standard and is concerned only with the assent, agreement, or intention of a party as it reasonably appears from his words or actions. The law of contracts is not concerned with what a party may have actually thought or the meaning that he intended to convey, insofar as his subjective understanding or intention differed from the meaning objectively manifested. For example, if Joanne seemingly offers to sell to Bruce her Chevrolet automobile but intended to offer and believes that she is offering her Ford automobile, and Bruce accepts the offer, reasonably believing it was for the Chevrolet, a contract has been formed for the sale of the Chevrolet. Subjectively, Joanne and Bruce are not in agreement as to the subject matter. Objectively, however, there is a manifestation of agreement; and this manifestation is binding.

The Code's treatment of mutual assent is covered in greater detail in Chapter 19.

OFFER

Offer a proposal indicating a willingness to enter into a contract

An **offer** is a definite undertaking or proposal made by one person to another indicating a willingness to enter into a contract. The person making the proposal is the **offeror**. The person to whom it is made is the **offeree**. When it is received, the offer confers on the offeree the power to create a contract by acceptance, which is an expression of the offeree's willingness to comply with the terms of the offer. Until the offeree exercises this power, the outstanding offer creates neither rights nor liabilities.

Offeror person making the offer

Offeree person to whom the offer is made

ESSENTIALS OF AN OFFER

An offer need not take any particular form to have legal effect. To be effective, however, it must (1) be communicated to the offeree; (2) manifest an intent to enter into a contract; and (3) be sufficiently definite and certain. If these essentials are present and the offer has not terminated, the offer gives the offeree the power to form a contract by accepting the offer.

Communication

To provide his part of the mutual assent required to form a contract, the offeree must know about the offer; he cannot agree to something about which he has no knowledge. Accordingly, the offeror must communicate the offer in an intended manner. For example, Oscar signs a letter containing an offer to Ellen and leaves it on top of the desk in his office. Later that day, Ellen, without prearrangement, goes to Oscar's office, discovers that he is away, notices the letter on his desk, reads it, and then writes on it an acceptance that she dates and signs. No contract is formed because the offer never became effective: Ellen became aware of the offer by chance, not by Oscar's intentional communication of it.

Not only must the offer be communicated to the offeree, but the communication must also be made or authorized by the offeror. If Jones tells Black that she plans to offer White $600 for a piano, and Black promptly informs White of Jones's intention, no offer has been made. There was no authorized communication of any offer by Jones to White. By the same token, if David should offer to sell to Lou his diamond ring, an acceptance of this offer by Tia would not be effective, as David made no offer to Tia.

An offer need not be stated or communicated by words. Conduct from which a reasonable person may infer a proposal in return for either an act or a promise amounts to an offer.

An offer may be made to the general public. No person can accept such an offer, however, until and unless he knows that the offer exists. For example, if a person, without knowing of an advertised reward for information leading to the return of a lost watch, gives information leading to the return of the watch, he is not entitled to the reward. His act was not an acceptance of the offer because he could not accept something of which he had no knowledge.

Communication offeree must have knowledge of the offer and the offer must be made by the offeror or her authorized agent to the offeree

Intent

To have legal effect, an offer must manifest an intent to enter into a contract. The intent of an offer is determined objectively from the manifestations of the parties. The meaning of either party's manifestation is based upon what a reasonable person in the other party's position would have believed.

Intent determined by an objective standard of what a reasonable offeree would have believed

CITY OF EVERETT v. ESTATE OF SUMSTAD Supreme Court of Washington 1981, 95 Wash.2d 853, 631, P.2d 366

FACTS On August 12, 1978, Mr. and Mrs. Mitchell, the owners of a small secondhand store, attended Alexander's Auction, where they bought a used safe for $50. The safe, part of the Sumstad estate, contained a locked inside compartment. This fact was known to both the auctioneer and the Mitchells. Soon after the auction, the Mitchells had the compartment opened by a locksmith, who discovered $32,207 inside. The Everett Police Department impounded the money. The city of Everett brought an action against the Sumstad estate and the Mitchells to determine the owner of the money. Both parties moved for summary judgment. The trial court entered summary judgment for the estate, and the court of appeals affirmed. The Mitchells appealed.

DECISION Case remanded to trial court for entry of summary judgment in favor of the Mitchells.

OPINION The subject matter transferred in a sale is determined by the outward manifestations of assent made by the parties entering into the contract. The intentions of the parties are revealed by a reasonable interpretation of their words and acts or by those words and acts "which ordinarily accompany and represent a known intent." Any unexpressed or subjective intention is irrelevant. In this case, the Mitchells understood that all auction sales were final, and the auctioneer reserved no rights of the estate to any contents of the safe. The reasonable conclusion is that the auctioneer objectively intended to sell both the safe and its contents and that the parties mutually assented to such a sale.

INTERPRETATION The intent of an offer is determined by an objective standard of what a reasonable offeree would have believed.

Occasionally, a person exercises her sense of humor by speaking or writing words that—taken literally and without regard to context or surrounding circumstances—could be construed as an offer. The promise is intended as a joke, however, and the promisee as a reasonable person should understand it to be such. Therefore, it is not an offer. Because the person to whom it is made realizes or should realize that it is not made in earnest, it should not create a reasonable expectation in his mind. No contractual intent exists on the part of the promisor, and the promisee is or reasonably ought to be aware of that fact. If, however, the intended jest is so seemingly earnest that the promisee as a reasonable person under all the circumstances believes that the joke is in fact an offer, and so believing accepts, the objective standard applies and the parties have entered into a contract. (See "Pepsi Premium Pickle.")

A promise made under obvious excitement or emotional strain is likewise not an offer. For example, Charlotte, after having her month-old Cadillac break down for the third time in two days, screams in disgust, "I will sell this car to anyone for $10.00!" Lisa hears Charlotte and hands her a ten-dollar bill. Under the circumstances, Charlotte's statement was not an offer if a reasonable person in Lisa's position would have recognized it merely as an excited, nonbinding utterance.

It is important to distinguish language that constitutes an offer from that which merely solicits or invites offers. Such proposals, although made in earnest, lack the intent to enter into a contract and are therefore not deemed offers. As a result, a purported acceptance does not bring about a contract but operates only as an offer. Proposals that invite offers include preliminary negotiations, advertisements, and auctions.

Preliminary Negotiations If a communication creates in the mind of a reasonable person in the position of the offeree an expectation that his acceptance will conclude a contract, then the communication is an offer. If it does not, then the communication is a preliminary negotiation. Initial communications between potential parties to a contract often take the form of preliminary negotiations, through which the parties either request or supply the terms of an offer that may or may not be made. A statement that may indicate a

MANAGERIAL INSIGHT

PEPSI PREMIUM PICKLE
Cola Maker Balks at Jet Payoff

One can only hope that John Leonard is never charged "an arm and a leg" for something he wishes to purchase.

When PepsiCo Inc. ran a television ad offering a Harrier military jet as a premium in its "Pepsi Stuff" campaign, the 21-year-old Leonard took it literally, even though most viewers recognized the soft drink maker's humorous use of exaggeration.

The ad, which first aired in late 1995, offered premiums such as sunglasses, clothes and beach towels in exchange for "Pepsi Points" obtained from packages of the soda. Text at the bottom of the ad offered the jet as a prize for 7 million points.

Leonard redeemed the minimum allowable 15 Pepsi Points and paid $700,008.50 to purchase the remaining points.

Leonard, a student at Shoreline Community College in Shoreline, Wash., raised the money from people he met on mountain-climbing expeditions.

Pepsi officials insisted in July that the Harrier jet "offer" was a joke. Leonard refused to retract his demand, and Pepsi sought declaratory judgment in federal court in New York to have his claim deemed frivolous.

Leonard countersued in Dade County, Fla., circuit court in August for breach of contract, fraud, deceptive and unfair trade practices, and misleading advertising. "I am simply trying to take Pepsi up on an offer it made to the public," he explains.

The whole dispute is moot, says Pentagon spokesman Kenneth Bacon, because military planes cannot be sold to civilians until they are discontinued, "demilitarized" and rendered flightless. "So even if the lad were able to ... get a plane from Pepsi, it would not be one he could fly," says Bacon.

By Brian Sullivan, Joseph Wharton, and Associated Press. Statistics compiled by John MacIntyre. *ABA Journal*, p.14. November 1996. Used with permission.

willingness to make an offer is not in itself an offer. For instance, if Brown writes to Young, "Will you buy my automobile for $3,000?" and Young replies, "Yes," there is no contract. Brown has not made an offer to sell her automobile to Young for $3,000. The offeror must manifest an intent to enter into a contract, not merely a willingness to enter into a negotiation.

Advertisements Merchants desire to sell their merchandise and thus are interested in informing potential customers about the goods, the terms of sale, and price. But if they make widespread promises to sell to each person on their mailing list, the number of acceptances and resulting contracts might conceivably exceed their ability to perform. Consequently, a merchant might refrain from making offers by merely announcing that he has goods for sale, describing the goods, and quoting prices. He is simply inviting his customers and, in the case of published advertisements, the public, to make offers to him to buy his goods. His advertisements, circulars, quotation sheets, and displays of merchandise are *not* offers because (1) they do not contain a promise, and (2) they leave unexpressed many terms that would be necessary to the making of a contract. Accordingly, his customers' responses are not acceptances because no offer to sell has been made.

Nonetheless, a seller is not free to advertise goods at one price and then raise the price once demand has been stimulated. Although, as far as contract law is concerned, the seller has made no offer, such conduct is prohibited by the Federal Trade Commission as well as by legislation in most states. Moreover, in some circumstances a public announcement or advertisement may constitute an offer if the advertisement or announcement contains a definite promise of something in exchange for something else and confers a power of acceptance on a specified person or class of persons. The typical offer of a reward is an example of a definite offer, as is the situation presented in the landmark *Lefkowitz* case, which follows.

LEFKOWITZ v. GREAT MINNEAPOLIS SURPLUS STORE, INC. Supreme Court of Minnesota 1957,
251 Minn. 188, 86 N.W.2d 689

FACTS On April 6, 1956, Great Minneapolis Surplus Store published an advertisement in a Minneapolis newspaper reporting that "Saturday, 9:00 a.m. sharp; 3 brand new fur coats worth up to $100; first come, first served, $1 each." Lefkowitz was the first to arrive at the store, but the store refused to sell him the fur coats because the "house rule" was that the offers were intended for women only and sales would not be made to men. The following week, Great Minneapolis published a similar advertisement for the sale of two mink scarves and a black lapin stole. Again Lefkowitz was the first to arrive at the store on Saturday morning, and once again the store refused to sell to him, this time because Lefkowitz knew of the house rule. This appeal was from a judgment awarding the plaintiff the sum of $138.50 as damages for breach of contract.

DECISION Judgment for Lefkowitz affirmed.

OPINION Whether a newspaper advertisement constitutes an offer, rather than a mere invitation to make an offer, depends upon the intention of the parties and the surrounding circumstances. If the facts show that some performance was promised in positive terms in return for something requested, then a newspaper advertisement addressed to the general public may lead to a binding obligation. Here the newspaper advertisements were clear, definite, and explicit, and left nothing open for negotiation. Lefkowitz was the first to arrive at the store and to offer to purchase the furs and, therefore, was entitled to performance on the part of the store.

INTERPRETATION Although advertisements generally do not constitute offers, under some circumstances they do.

Auction Sales The auctioneer at an auction sale does not make offers to sell the property being auctioned but invites offers to buy. The classic statement by the auctioneer is, "How much am I offered?" The persons attending the auction may make progressively higher bids for the property, and each bid or statement of a price or a figure is an offer to buy at that figure. If the bid is accepted, which customarily is indicated by the fall of the hammer in the auctioneer's hand, a contract results. A bidder is free to withdraw his bid at any time prior to its acceptance. The auctioneer is likewise free to withdraw the goods from sale *unless* the sale is advertised or announced to be without reserve.

Without reserve
auctioneer may not withdraw the goods from the auction

If the auction sale is advertised or announced in explicit terms to be **without reserve**, the auctioneer may not withdraw an article or lot put up for sale unless no bid is made within a reasonable time. Unless so advertised or announced, the sale is with reserve. A bidder at either type of sale may retract his bid at any time prior to its acceptance by the auctioneer; such retraction does not revive any previous bid.

Definiteness

Definiteness offer's terms must be clear enough to provide a court with a basis for giving an appropriate remedy

The terms of a contract, all of which are usually contained in the offer, must be clear enough to provide a court with a reasonable basis for determining the existence of a breach and for giving an appropriate remedy. It is a fundamental policy that contracts should be made by the parties and not by the courts; accordingly, remedies for a breach must in turn have their basis in the parties' contract.

Where the parties have intended to form a contract, the courts will attempt to find a basis for granting a remedy. Missing terms may be supplied by course of dealing, usage of trade, or by inference. Thus, uncertainty as to incidental matters seldom will be fatal so long as the parties intended to form a contract. Nevertheless, the more terms the parties leave open, the less likely it is that they have intended to form a contract. Moreover, given the great variety of contracts, stating the terms that are essential to all contracts is impossible. In most cases, however, material terms would include the subject matter, price, quantity, quality, terms of payment, and duration.

Open Terms With respect to agreements for the sale of goods, the Uniform Commercial Code provides standards by which the courts may determine omitted terms, provided the parties intended to enter into a binding contract. The Code provides missing terms in a number of instances, where, for example, the contract fails to specify the price, the time or place of delivery, or payment terms. The Restatement has adopted an approach similar to the Code's in supplying terms omitted from the parties' contract.

Under the Code, an offer for the purchase or sale of goods may leave open particulars of performance to be specified by one of the parties. Any such specification must be made in good faith and within limits set by commercial reasonableness. **Good faith** is defined as honesty in fact in the conduct or transaction concerned. **Commercial reasonableness** is a standard determined in terms of the business judgment of reasonable persons familiar with the practices customary in the type of transaction involved and in terms of the facts and circumstances of the case.

Good faith honesty in fact

Commercial reasonableness judgment of reasonable persons familiar with the business transaction

Output and Requirements Contracts An **output contract** is an agreement of a buyer to purchase a seller's entire output for a stated period. In comparison, a **requirements contract** is an agreement of a seller to supply a buyer with all his requirements for certain goods. Even though the exact quantity of goods is not specified and the seller may have some degree of control over his output and the buyer over his requirements, under the Code and the Restatement such agreements are enforceable by the application of an objective standard based on the good faith of both parties. Thus, a seller who operated a factory only eight hours a day before the agreement was made cannot operate the factory twenty-four hours a day and insist that the buyer take all of the output. Nor can the buyer expand his business abnormally and insist that the seller still supply all of his requirements.

Output contract an agreement of a buyer to purchase the entire output of a seller's factory

Requirements contract an agreement of a seller to supply a buyer with all his requirements for certain goods

DURATION OF OFFERS

An offer confers upon the offeree a power of acceptance, which continues until the offer terminates. The ways in which an offer may be terminated, other than by acceptance, are through (1) lapse of time; (2) revocation; (3) rejection; (4) counteroffer; (5) death or incompetency of the offeror or offeree; (6) destruction of the subject matter to which the offer relates; and (7) subsequent illegality of the type of contract the offer proposes.

Lapse of Time

The offeror may specify the time within which the offer is to be accepted, just as he may specify any other term or condition in the offer. Unless otherwise terminated, the offer remains open for the *specified* time period. Upon the expiration of that time, as demonstrated by *Newman v. Schiff*, the offer no longer exists and cannot be accepted. Any purported acceptance of an expired offer will serve only as a new offer.

If the offer does not state the time within which the offeree may accept, the offer will terminate after a *reasonable* time. Determining a "reasonable" time is a question of fact, depending on the nature of the contract proposed, the usages of business, and other circumstances of the case. For instance, an offer to sell a perishable good would be open for a far shorter period of time than an offer to sell undeveloped real estate.

Lapse of time offer remains open for the time period specified or, if no time is stated, for a reasonable period of time

NEWMAN v. SCHIFF United States Court of Appeals, Eighth Circuit, 1985, 778 F.2d 460

FACTS Irwin Schiff is a self-styled "tax rebel" who has made a career, and substantial profit, out of his tax protest activities. On February 7, 1983, Schiff appeared live on CBS News *Nightwatch*, a late-night program with a viewer participation format. During the broadcast Schiff repeated his assertion that nothing in the Internal Revenue Code stated that an individual was legally required to pay federal income tax. Schiff then challenged "[i]f anybody calls this show—I have the Code—and cites any section of this Code that says an individual is required to file a tax return, I will pay them $100,000." Call-in telephone numbers were periodically flashed on the screen. John Newman, an attorney, did not see Schiff's live appearance on Nightwatch. Newman did, however, see a two-minute videotaped segment, including Schiff's challenge, that was rebroadcast several hours later on the *CBS Morning News*. Newman researched the matter that same day, and on the following day, February 9, 1983, placed a call using directory assistance to *CBS Morning News* stating that the call was performance of the consideration requested by Mr. Schiff in exchange for his promise to pay $100,000. When Schiff refused to pay, Newman sued.

DECISION Judgment for Schiff.

OPINION Mutual assent is necessary for the formation of a contract. Courts will determine whether the parties expressed their assent to a contract by analyzing their agreement process in terms of offer and acceptance. An offer is the manifestation of willingness to enter into a bargain, so made as to justify another person in understanding that his assent to that bargain is invited and will conclude it. However, an offeror is the master of his offer, and it is clear that Schiff by his words "if anybody calls this show . . ." limited his offer in time to remain open only for the duration of the live Nightwatch broadcast. The *CBS Morning News* report on Schiff's offer did not serve to renew or extend the original offer. Newman's attempted acceptance was therefore untimely, and no contract was formed.

INTERPRETATION An offeror may limit the duration of an offer, either directly or by implied language.

Revocation

Revocation *(rev'·o·ca·tion)* cancellation of an offer by an offeror; generally an offer may be terminated at any time prior to its acceptance

The offeror generally may cancel or *revoke* an offer (**revocation**) at any time *prior* to its acceptance. If the offeror originally promises that the offer will be open for thirty days but wishes to terminate it after five days, he may do so merely by giving the offeree notice that he is withdrawing the offer. This notice may be given by any means of communication and effectively terminates the offer when *received* by the offeree. An offer made to the general public is revoked only by giving to the revocation publicity equivalent to that given the offer.

Notice of revocation may be communicated indirectly to the offeree through reliable information from a third person that the offeror has disposed of the property he has offered for sale or has otherwise placed himself in a position indicating an unwillingness or inability to perform the promise contained in the offer. For example, Aaron offers to sell his portable television set to Ted and tells Ted that he has ten days in which to accept. One week later, Ted observes the television set in Celia's house and is informed that Celia purchased it from Aaron. The next day, Ted sends to Aaron an acceptance of the offer. There is no contract because Aaron's offer was effectively revoked when Ted learned of Aaron's inability to sell the television set to Ted because he had sold it to Celia.

Certain limitations, however, restrict the offeror's power to revoke the offer at any time prior to its acceptance. These limitations apply to the following five situations.

Option contract providing that an offer will stay open for a specified period of time

Consideration the inducement to enter into a contract consisting of an act or promise that has legal value

Option Contracts

An **option** is a contract by which the offeror is bound to hold open an offer for a specified period of time. It must comply with all of the requirements of a contract, including the offeree's giving of **consideration** to the offeror. (Consideration, or the inducement to enter into a contract consisting of an act or promise that has legal value, is discussed in Chapter 12.) For example, if Ellen, in return for the payment of $500 to her by Barry, grants Barry an option, exercisable at any time within thirty days, to buy Blackacre at a price of $80,000, Ellen's offer is irrevocable. Ellen is legally bound to keep the offer open for thirty days, and any communication by Ellen to Barry giving notice of withdrawal of the offer is ineffective. Though Barry is not bound to accept the offer, the option contract entitles him to thirty days in which to accept.

FIRST DEVELOPMENT CORPORATION OF KENTUCKY v. MARTIN MARIETTA CORP.
United States Court of Appeals, Sixth Circuit, 1992, 959 F.2d 617

FACTS First Development Corporation of Kentucky (FDCK) sought to purchase a fifteen-acre parcel of riverfront property owned by Martin Marietta. On May 9, 1988, FDCK made an offer to purchase the property for $300,000, which it submitted to Coldwell Banker, Martin Marietta's real estate agent. This offer was accompanied by an earnest money deposit evidenced by a $1,000 check payable to Coldwell Banker. The deposit was fully refundable if transfer of title to FDCK was not completed for any reason except FDCK's failure to perform. After this offer expired without being accepted, FDCK asked Don Gilmour, Coldwell Banker's account agent, to seek a counteroffer. In a letter to Gilmour, dated September 7, 1988, Martin Marietta agreed to sell the property for $550,000. The counteroffer stated it was to remain open for thirty days. Gilmour informed Pollitt, president of FDCK, of the counteroffer by telephone on September 7 and sent a copy of the letter to Pollitt, which was received on September 12.

Within days of the expiration of FDCK's original offer, Bill Harvey, president of Harmony Landing, a development company, initiated direct negotiations with Martin Marietta to purchase the riverfront parcel. These negotiations resulted in a contract being executed on September 21 or 22. During a September 21 phone call, Gilmour advised Pollitt of Harmony Landing's interest in buying the property, but Pollitt remained noncommittal during the conversation. Later that day, Pollitt, along with his partner and engineer, visited the property and discussed various studies and arrived at a decision to accept the September 7, 1988, offer from Martin Marietta. However, Pollitt did not convey this acceptance to Gilmour. Rather, he consulted his attorneys regarding a contract to accept Martin Marietta's offer.

After consulting with his attorneys, Pollitt prepared an acceptance of Martin Marietta's offer but did not put it in the mail. The next morning, Pollitt placed the acceptance in his office suite's mail depository. However, after being informed by Gilmour that Martin Marietta had accepted Harmony Landing's option on the river property, Pollitt retrieved the acceptance and personally delivered it to Gilmour at 4:15 P.M. The acceptance was returned to Pollitt and he subsequently initiated this action for temporary and permanent injunction and specific performance. The district court ruled that the $1,000 check, payable to and in the possession of Coldwell Banker during the period of this controversy was, by operation of law, converted into consideration for a thirty-day irrevocable option in favor of FDCK to purchase the riverfront property in accordance with the terms of Martin Marietta's letter of September 7, 1988. Accordingly, the court granted a permanent injunction and ordered Martin Marietta to convey the parcel to FDCK.

DECISION Judgment reversed.

OPINION An option contract that is not supported by consideration can be withdrawn at any time before acceptance. The $1,000 deposit accompanying FDCK's initial offer was not consideration for an option contract. The documentation is explicitly clear that the parties, all of whom were sophisticated businesspeople experienced in brokering real estate, were negotiating for an unconditional sale rather than an option agreement. Further, a payment such as this deposit, which is simply an advance toward the purchase price if the sale is ultimately consummated, does not constitute consideration for an irrevocable option. It is clear that there was no monetary consideration to support the option contract here involved.

The next question is whether FDCK had, in fact and in law, accepted the Martin Marietta offer to sell its property before the offer was revoked or withdrawn. An offer must be accepted "before any intimation is received that the offer is withdrawn." An offer is revoked when the offeree learns of acts by the offeror that are inconsistent with the continuance of the offer or that imply that the offer has been revoked. It is clear from his conversations with Gilmour that Pollitt knew that the agreement between Martin Marietta and Harmony Landing was a contract to purchase the riverfront property and that the property was no longer available.

Under the "mailbox rule," an acceptance becomes effective when it is "put out of the offeree's possession." The rule, simply stated, is that "an offer may be

continued

accepted by mailing acceptance, properly stamped and addressed." The envelope containing FDCK's acceptance never left Pollitt's possession as evidenced by Pollitt's effortless retrieval of the documents from the office mail drop after he became aware of the contract in favor of Harmony Landing. At that point in time, the envelope had not even been stamp metered. He thereafter hand delivered the envelope to Gilmour at 4:15 P.M. This was approximately one hour and forty-five minutes after he knew the property was off the market. Accordingly, FDCK had not accepted Martin Marietta's offer to sell the riverfront property before it knew that the land was no longer available.

INTERPRETATION (1) An offeror generally can revoke an offer at any time prior to its acceptance. (2) For an option contract to exist, the offeree must give consideration.

Firm offer irrevocable offer by a merchant to sell or buy goods, made in a signed writing that gives assurance that it will not be rescinded for up to three months

Firm Offers under the Code The Code provides that a **merchant** is bound to keep an offer to buy or sell **goods** open for a stated period (or, if no time is stated, for a reasonable time) not exceeding three months if the merchant gives assurance in a **signed writing** that the offer will be held open. The Code, therefore, makes a merchant's **firm offer** (written promise not to revoke an offer for a stated period of time) enforceable even though no consideration is given the offeror for that promise (i.e., an option contract does not exist). A **merchant** is defined as a person (1) who is a dealer in a given type of goods, or (2) who by his occupation holds himself out as having knowledge or skill peculiar to the goods or practices involved, or (3) who employs an agent or broker whom he holds out as having such knowledge or skill.

Statutory irrevocability offer made irrevocable by statue

Statutory Irrevocability Certain offers, such as bids made to the state, municipality, or other governmental body for the construction of a building or some public work, are made irrevocable by statute. Another example is preincorporation stock subscription agreements, which are irrevocable for a period of six months under many state corporation statutes.

Irrevocable offer to unilateral contracts a unilateral offer may not be revoked for a reasonable time after performance is

Irrevocable Offers of Unilateral Contracts Where the offer contemplates a *unilateral* contract—that is, a promise for an act—injustice to the offeree may result if revocation is permitted after the offeree has started to perform the act requested in the offer and has substantially but not completely accomplished it. Such an offer is not accepted and no contract is formed until the offeree has completed the requested act. By simply starting performance, the offeree does not bind himself to complete performance; historically, he did not bind the offeror to keep the offer open, either. Thus, the offeror could revoke the offer at any time before the offeree's completion of performance. For example, Jordan offers Karlene $300 if Karlene will climb to the top of the flagpole in the center of campus. Karlene starts to climb, but when she is five feet from the top, Jordan yells to her, "I revoke."

The Restatement deals with this problem by providing that where the performance of the requested act necessarily requires the offeree to expend time and effort, the offeror is obligated not to revoke the offer for a reasonable time. This obligation, which arises when the offeree begins the invited performance, applies when the offeror's duty of performance is conditional on completion of the invited performance according to the terms of the offer. If, however, the offeror does not know of the offeree's performance and has no adequate means of learning of it within a reasonable time, the offeree must exercise reasonable diligence to notify the offeror.

Promissory Estoppel As discussed in the previous chapter, a noncontractual promise may be enforced when it is made under circumstances that should lead the promisor reasonably to expect that the promise will induce the promisee to take action in reliance on it. This doctrine has been used in some cases to prevent an offeror from revoking an offer prior to its acceptance.

Thus, Ramanan Plumbing Co. submits a written offer for plumbing work to be used by Resolute Building Co. as part of Resolute's bid as a general contractor. Ramanan knows that Resolute is relying on Ramanan's bid, and in fact Resolute submits Ramanan's name as the plumbing subcontractor in the bid. Ramanan's offer is irrevocable until Resolute has a reasonable opportunity to notify Ramanan that Resolute's bid has been accepted.

Rejection

An offeree is at liberty to accept or reject the offer as he sees fit. If he decides not to accept it, he is not required to reject it formally but may simply wait until the offer terminates by lapse of time. A **rejection** of an offer is a manifestation by the offeree of his unwillingness to accept. A communicated rejection terminates the power of acceptance. From the effective moment of rejection, which is the *receipt* of the rejection by the offeror, the offeree may no longer accept the offer. Rejection by the offeree may consist of express language or may be implied from language or conduct.

Counteroffer

A **counteroffer** is a counterproposal from the offeree to the offeror that indicates a willingness to contract but on terms or conditions different from those contained in the original offer. It is not an unequivocal acceptance of the original offer, and by indicating an unwillingness to agree to the terms of the offer, it generally operates as a rejection. It also operates as a new offer. (See *Zeller v. First National Bank & Trust*, on the following page). To illustrate further, assume that Worthy writes Joanne a letter stating that he will sell to Joanne a second-hand color television set for $300. Joanne replies that she will pay Worthy $250 for the set. This is a counteroffer that, on *receipt* by Worthy, terminates the original offer. Worthy may, if he wishes, accept the counteroffer and thereby create a contract for $250. If, on the other hand, Joanne in her reply states that she wishes to consider the $300 offer but is willing to pay $250 at once for the set, she is making a counteroffer that does *not* terminate Worthy's original offer. In the first instance, after making the $250 counteroffer, Joanne may not accept the $300 offer. In the second instance, she may do so, as the counteroffer was stated in such a manner as not to indicate an unwillingness to accept the original offer; and Joanne therefore did not terminate it. In addition, a mere inquiry about the possibility of obtaining different or new terms is not a counteroffer and does not terminate the original offer.

Another common type of counteroffer is the **conditional acceptance**, which claims to accept the offer but expressly makes the acceptance contingent on the offeror's assent to additional or different terms. Nonetheless, it is a counteroffer and generally terminates the original offer. The Code's treatment of acceptances containing terms that vary from the offer is discussed later in this chapter.

Promissory estoppel
noncontractual promise that binds the promisor because she should reasonably expect that the promise will induce the promisee (offeree) to take action in reliance on it

Rejection the refusal to accept an offer

Counteroffer
counterproposal to an offer; which generally terminates the original offer

Conditional acceptance
acceptance of an offer contingent upon the acceptance of an additional or different term, operates as a counteroffer

ZELLER v. FIRST NATIONAL BANK & TRUST Appellate Court of Illinois, First District, 1979,
79 Ill.App.3d 170, 34 Ill.Dec. 473, 398 N.E.2d 148

FACTS On December 23, 1977, Wyman, a lawyer representing First National Bank & Trust (defendant), wrote to Zeller (plaintiff) stating that he had been instructed to offer a building to Zeller for sale at a price of $240,000. Zeller had previously expressed an interest in purchasing the building for $240,000. The letter also set forth details concerning interest rates and loan fees.

After receiving the letter, Zeller instructed his attorney, Jamma, to send Wyman a written counteroffer of $230,000 with varying interest and loan arrangements. Jamma sent the written counteroffer, as instructed, on January 10. On the same day, Jamma telephoned Wyman and informed him of the counteroffer. Jamma then tried to telegraph acceptance of the original offer to Wyman. When Wyman refused to sell the property to him, Zeller brought this action to seek enforcement of the alleged contract. The trial court entered summary judgment against Zeller, and he appealed.

DECISION Summary judgment for defendant affirmed.

OPINION In order for an acceptance to create a binding contract, it must comply strictly with the terms of the offer. An acceptance requesting modification or containing terms that vary from those offered constitutes a rejection of the original offer and becomes a counteroffer that must be accepted by the original offeror before a valid, binding contract is formed. Here, in a telephone conversation on January 10, Jamma told Wyman of the $230,000 counteroffer, which operated as a rejection of the original offer and terminated Zeller's power of acceptance.

Finally, it matters not that the counteroffer was communicated orally in response to a written offer. If an offer requires a written acceptance, no other form will do. Here, however, no particular form of response was required; so the oral counteroffer was an effective rejection. As such, it is irrelevant that the written acceptance arrived prior to the written counteroffer since the oral counteroffer preceded them both.

INTERPRETATION A counteroffer generally operates as a rejection and terminates the original offer.

Death or Incompetency

Death or incompetency of either the offeror or the offeree terminates the offer

The death or incompetency of either the offeror or the offeree ordinarily terminates an offer. On his death or incompetency the offeror no longer has the legal capacity to enter into a contract; thus, all outstanding offers are terminated. Death or incompetency of the offeree also terminates the offer, because an ordinary offer is not assignable (transferable) and may be accepted only by the person to whom it was made. When the offeree dies or ceases to have legal capability to enter into a contract, no one else has the power to accept the offer. Therefore, the offer necessarily terminates.

The death or incompetency of the offeror or offeree, however, does *not* terminate an offer contained in an option.

Destruction of Subject Matter

Destruction of subject matter of an offer terminates the offer

Destruction of the specific subject matter of an offer terminates the offer. Suppose that Sarah, owning a Buick, offers to sell the car to Barbara and allows Barbara five days in which to accept. Three days later the car is destroyed by fire. On the following day, Barbara, without knowledge of the destruction of the car, notifies Sarah that she accepts Sarah's offer. There is no contract. The destruction of the car terminated Sarah's offer.

Subsequent Illegality

Subsequent illegality of the purpose or subject matter of the offer terminates the offer

One of the essential requirements of a contract, as we previously mentioned, is legality of purpose or subject matter. If performance of a valid contract is subsequently made illegal, the obligations of both parties under the contract are discharged. Illegality taking effect after the making of an offer but prior to acceptance has the same effect: The offer is legally terminated.

For an illustration of the duration of revocable offers, see Figure 10–1.

ACCEPTANCE OF OFFER

The acceptance of an offer is essential to the formation of a contract. Once an acceptance has been given, the contract is formed. **Acceptance** of an offer for a bilateral contract is some overt act by the offeree that manifests his assent to the terms of the offer, such as speaking or sending a letter, a telegram, or other explicit or implicit communication to the offeror. If the offer is for a unilateral contract, acceptance is the performance of the requested act with the intention of accepting. For example, if Joy publishes an offer of a reward to anyone who returns the diamond ring that she has lost (an offer to enter into a unilateral contract), and Bob, with knowledge of the offer, finds and returns the ring to Joy, Bob has accepted the offer.

> **Acceptance** manifestation of a willingness to enter into a contract on the terms of the offer

COMMUNICATION OF ACCEPTANCE

General Rule

Since acceptance is the manifestation of the offeree's assent to the offer, it must necessarily be communicated to the offeror. This is the rule as to all bilateral offers. In the case of unilateral offers, however, notice of acceptance to the offeror usually is not required. If, however, the offeree in a unilateral contract has reason to know that the offeror has no adequate means of learning of the offeree's performance with reasonable promptness and certainty, then the offeree must make reasonable efforts to notify the offeror of acceptance or lose the right to enforce the contract.

FIGURE 10–1 Duration of Revocable Offers

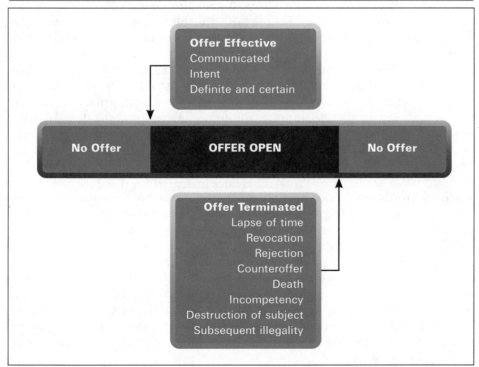

Silence as Acceptance

An offeree is generally under no legal duty to reply to an offer. Silence or inaction therefore does *not* indicate acceptance of the offer. By custom, usage, or course of dealing, however, the offeree's silence or inaction may operate as an acceptance. Thus, the silence or inaction of an offeree who fails to reply to an offer operates as an acceptance and causes a contract to be formed where by previous dealings the offeree has given the offeror reason to understand that the offeree will accept all offers unless the offeree sends notice to the contrary. Another example of silence operating as an acceptance occurs when the prospective member of a mail-order club agrees that his failure to return a notification card rejecting offered goods will constitute his acceptance of the club's offer to sell the goods.

Furthermore, if an offeror sends unordered or unsolicited merchandise to a person, stating that the goods may be purchased at a specified price and that the offer will be deemed to have been accepted unless the goods are returned within a stated period of time, the offer is one for an inverted unilateral contract (i.e., an act for a promise). This practice has led to abuse, however, prompting the federal government as well as most states to enact statutes that provide that in such cases the offeree-recipient of the goods may keep them as a gift and is under no obligation either to return them or to pay for them.

Effective Moment

Effective moment acceptance effective upon dispatch unless the offer specifically provides otherwise or the offeree uses an unauthorized means of communication, or the acceptance follows a prior rejection

As we discussed previously, an offer, a revocation, a rejection, and a counteroffer are effective when they are *received*. An acceptance, as shown in the following case, is generally effective upon **dispatch**. This is true unless the offer specifically provides otherwise, the offeree uses an unauthorized means of communication, or the acceptance follows a prior rejection.

Stipulated provisions in the offer the communication of acceptance must conform to the specification in the offer

Stipulated Provisions in the Offer If the offer specifically stipulates the means of communication to be used by the offeree, the acceptance must conform to that specification. Thus, if an offer states that acceptance must be made by registered mail, any purported acceptance not made by registered mail would be ineffective. Moreover, the rule that an acceptance is effective when dispatched or sent does not apply where the offer provides that the acceptance must be received by the offeror. If the offeror states that a reply must be received by a certain date or that he must hear from the offeree or uses other language indicating that the acceptance must be received by him, the effective moment of the acceptance is when the offeror receives it and not when the offeree sends or dispatches it.

Authorized Means Historically, an authorized means of communication was either the means the offeror expressly authorized in the offer or, if none was authorized, the means the offeror used in presenting the offer. If in reply to an offer by mail, the offeree places in the mail a letter of acceptance properly stamped and addressed to the offeror, a contract is formed at the time and place that the offeree mails the letter. This assumes, of course, that the offer was open at that time and had not been terminated by any of the methods previously discussed. The reason for this rule is that the offeror, by using the mail, impliedly authorized the offeree to use the same means of communication. It is immaterial if the letter of acceptance goes astray in the mails and is never received.

THE LAW AND YOU Marriage

Perhaps the most important decision one ever makes is the decision to marry. Certainly it greatly affects a person's personal happiness and future. But society at large also has an interest in marriage because marriage is the foundation of the family. To protect society's interest in the institution of marriage, therefore, each state has enacted laws designed to ensure both the legality and the stability of the marriage union.

Many couples view marriage as a serious religious or spiritual commitment. It is also a legal contract. Marriages are usually entered into on the basis of a couple's love, faith, and trust in each other, not on the basis of carefully drafted and negotiated documents. Nevertheless, marriage has many legal consequences that people who are about to marry should realize.

The purpose of this pamphlet is to help you understand North Carolina marriage laws and some of the legal matters that may affect the lives of any married couple.

Eligibility

North Carolina law establishes legal limitations concerning marriage that deal with age and blood relationships. In general, one must be at least 18 years of age to get married in this state. Minors 16–18 may marry with their parents' or guardians' consent. If a female 12–16 becomes pregnant, she and the child's father may legally marry if her parents or guardians consent. A physician's certificate is required to verify the pregnancy.

The law discourages marriage by persons who are in the same family. First cousins may marry, but persons who are closer kin than first cousins may not.

Common law marriage or marriage by consent is not recognized in North Carolina. Marriage between individuals of the same gender is not recognized as valid in North Carolina, regardless of where the marriage was obtained.

The License

You must obtain a marriage license before you may be legally married—whether in a civil or religious ceremony. A marriage license is secured from the register of deeds of the county where the marriage is to take place. No waiting period is required before the ceremony may take place. The license is good for sixty days after it is issued. Obtaining a license by misrepresentation may be punished by fine and/or imprisonment.

Premarital Agreements

Parties about to marry may enter into a contract before marriage with respect to a variety of matters so long as the contract meets the requirements of North Carolina law. Such a contract then becomes effective upon marriage of the parties. A Premarital Agreement cannot eliminate a child support obligation. If you are contemplating marriage and you have children or obligations from a prior marriage, have an expectation of significant gifts or inheritances from third parties, own property or wish to provide for disposition of assets and liabilities or exposure to future support obligations, it is wise to consult an attorney with an expertise in marital law before you marry. Keep in mind that these agreements can be complex in some circumstances, so they are best examined and drafted well in advance of the date of the marriage.

The Ceremony

Marriage ceremonies may be either religious or civil. A religious ceremony is performed by an ordained minister. A civil ceremony is conducted by a magistrate, the only civil officer authorized to perform marriages. There must be two witnesses at any marriage ceremony, whether it is civil or religious.

The Marriage Certificate

After a marriage ceremony, whoever performs the ceremony is required to give the couple a marriage certificate. This certificate includes the couple's names and addresses, the date of the marriage, the county that issued the marriage license, and the date of the license. The minister or magistrate must sign the license and return it to the register of deeds who issued the license; this is the official record of the ceremony.

Estate Planning and Inheritance

A new husband and wife automatically have new legal rights and responsibilities. Each spouse is now eligible to share in the estate of the other. As soon as children are born to the marriage or legally adopted, they also will become eligible to share in the estate of their parents. Stepchildren are not treated as children of the marriage unless adopted.

If you are contemplating marriage, you should consider writing a will. If a person dies without a will, state laws govern how that person's income and property will be distributed. Regardless of the amount of income or property involved, it is wise for each spouse to have a will to govern distribution of his or her estate and to take advantage of federal and state laws favorable to those who are married.

Name Change

A wife usually assumes her husband's last name. However, she is under no legal compulsion to do so, and she may retain her maiden name at the time of marriage with no formal legal proceedings. But if a wife who took her husband's name wants to resume her maiden name, she must petition the superior court in the county where she resides for the legal name change. A woman who is divorcing her husband may resume her maiden name by requesting this change in

continued

the divorce proceedings. If she wishes to take back her maiden name at some date before or after the divorce settlement, she must petition the court for the restoration of her name. She should contact the clerk for the necessary forms.

Sometimes a married couple may wish to assume a combined or hyphenated name that includes both of their names. The wife may assume this name at the time of marriage with no formal legal proceedings, but the husband must petition the court for a legal name change.

In any name change, it is important to keep all official records up to date. Any name change should be communicated to all government agencies that might be affected—such as the Social Security Administration, the Department of Motor Vehicles, and the Vital Statistics Office of the Department of Human Resources. Such private institutions as your bank, insurance company, employers, and others should also be notified of changes in your name and marital status.

Insurance

If you have life or health insurance and then marry, you should consider what changes should be made in your insurance program. All insurance companies that carry policies on you that may be affected by this change in status should be notified. Also, perhaps the beneficiaries of your life or health insurance policies need to be changed or expanded to include your spouse.

Income Tax Status

A married couple is entitled to file a joint federal income tax return if they were married at the end of the tax year. Filing a joint tax return can sometimes reduce taxes, but the financial advantage of the joint return varies with each couple's individual financial situation.

* * *

[The material in this feature was prepared as a public service by The Public Information Committee of the North Carolina Bar Association and is not intended to be a comprehensive statement of the law. North Carolina laws change frequently and could affect the information in this material.]

Reprinted by permission from "This Is the Law: Marriage in North Carolina," produced by the N.C. Bar Association, Public Information Committee. Copyright 1997.

The Restatement and the Code both now provide that where the language in the offer or the circumstances do not otherwise indicate, an offer to make a contract shall be construed as authorizing acceptance in any reasonable manner. Thus, an **authorized means** is usually any *reasonable* means of communication. These provisions are intended to allow flexibility of response and the ability to keep pace with new modes of communication.

Authorized means The Restatement and the Code provide that unless the offer provides otherwise, acceptance is authorized to be in any reasonable manner

Unauthorized Means When the method of communication used by the offeree is unauthorized, the traditional rule is that acceptance is effective when and if received by the offeror, provided that it is received within the time during which the authorized means would have arrived. The Restatement goes further by providing that if these conditions are met, then the effective time for the acceptance is the moment of dispatch.

Unauthorized means acceptance effective when received, provided that it is received within the time within which the authorized means would have arrived

Acceptance Following a Prior Rejection An acceptance sent after a prior rejection is not effective when sent by the offeree, but only when and if *received* by the offeror before he receives the rejection. Thus, when an acceptance follows a prior rejection, the *first communication* the offeror receives is the effective one. For example, Carlos in New York sends by airmail to Paula in San Francisco an offer that is expressly stated to be open for one week. On the fourth day, Paula sends to Carlos by airmail a letter of rejection, which is delivered on the morning of the sixth day. At noon on the fifth day, Paula dispatches a telegram of acceptance that Carlos receives before the close of business on that day. A contract was formed when Carlos received Paula's telegram of acceptance—it was the first communication he received.

Acceptance following a prior rejection first communication received by the offeror is effective

Defective Acceptances

A late or defective acceptance does not create a contract. After the offer has expired, it cannot be accepted. However, a late or defective acceptance does manifest a willingness on the part of the offeree to enter into a contract and therefore constitutes a new offer. In order to create a contract based on this offer, the original offeror must accept the new offer by manifesting his assent to it.

Defective acceptances does not create a contract but serves as a new offer

VARIANT ACCEPTANCES

A variant acceptance—one that contains terms different from or additional to those in the offer—receives distinctly different treatment under the common law and under the Code. See Figure 10–2.

Common Law

An acceptance must be *positive* and *unequivocal*. It may not change, add to, subtract from, or qualify in any way the provisions of the offer. In other words, it must be the **mirror image** of the offer. Any communication by the offeree that attempts to modify the offer is not an acceptance but a counteroffer, which does not create a contract.

Mirror image rule an acceptance cannot deviate from the terms of the offer

Code

The common law mirror image rule, by which the acceptance cannot vary or deviate from the terms of the offer, is modified by the Code. This modification is necessitated by the realities of modern business practices. A vast number of business transactions use standardized business forms. For example, a merchant buyer sends to a merchant seller on the buyer's order form a purchase order for one thousand dozen cotton shirts at $60 per dozen with delivery by October 1 at the buyer's place of business. On the reverse side of this standard form are twenty-five numbered paragraphs containing provisions generally favorable to the buyer. When the seller receives the buyer's order, he agrees to the buyer's quantity, price, and delivery terms and sends to the buyer on his acceptance form an unequivocal acceptance of the offer. However, on the back of his acceptance form, the seller has thirty-two numbered paragraphs generally favorable to himself and in significant conflict with the provisions on the buyer's form. Under the common law's *mirror image* rule, no contract would exist; for the seller has not accepted unequivocally all of the material terms of the buyer's offer. See Figure 10–3.

FIGURE 10–2 Offer and Acceptance

Communications by Offeror	Time Effective	Effect
Offer	Received by offeree	Creates power to form a contract
Revocation	Received by offeree	Terminates power
Communications by Offeror		
Rejection	Received by offeror	Terminates offer
Counteroffer	Received by offeror	Terminates offer
Acceptance	Sent by offeree	Forms a contract
Acceptance after prior rejection	Received by offeror	If received before rejections forms a contract

FIGURE 10–3 Mutual Assent

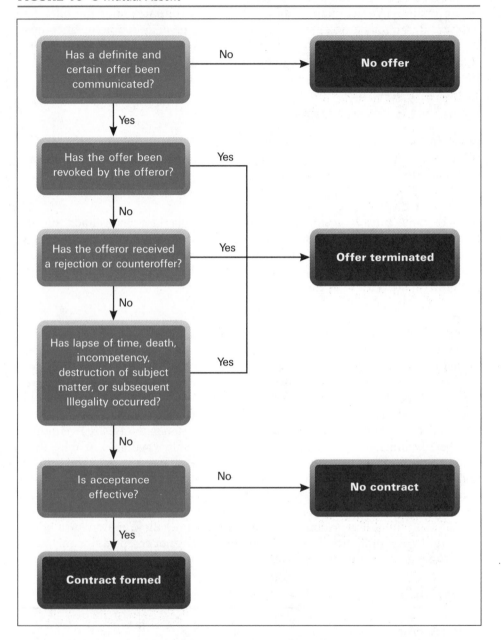

The Code attempts to alleviate this ***battle of the forms*** by focusing on the intent of the parties. If the offeree does not expressly make her acceptance conditional upon the offeror's assent to the additional or different terms, a contract is formed. The issue then becomes whether the offeree's different or additional terms become part of the contract. If both offeror and offeree are merchants, such *additional* terms may become part of the contract provided that they do not materially alter the agreement and are not objected to either in the offer itself or within a reasonable period of time. If either of the parties is not a merchant or if the additional terms materially alter the offer, then the additional terms are merely construed as proposals to the contract. *Different* terms proposed by the offeree will not become part of the contract unless accepted by the offeror. The courts are divided over what terms to include when the terms differ or conflict. Most courts hold that the offeror's terms govern; other courts hold that the terms cancel each other out and look to the Code to provide the missing terms. (See Figure 19–1 in Chapter 19.)

Let us apply the Code to the previous example involving the seller and the buyer: since both parties are merchants and the seller's acceptance was not conditional upon assent to the seller's additional or different terms, then either (1) the contract will be formed without the seller's different terms unless the buyer specifically accepts them; (2) the contract will be formed without the seller's additional terms (unless they are specifically accepted by the buyer) because the additional terms materially alter the offer; or (3) depending upon the jurisdiction, either (a) the buyer's conflicting terms will be included in the contract or (b) the Code will provide the missing terms, since the conflicting terms cancel each other out.

CHAPTER SUMMARY

Offer

Essentials of an Offer	**Definition** indication of willingness to enter into a contract **Communication** offeree must have knowledge of the offer and the offer must be made by the offeror or her authorized agent to the offeree **Intent** determined by an objective standard of what a reasonable offeree would have believed **Definiteness** offer's terms must be clear enough to provide a court with a basis for giving an appropriate remedy

Duration of Offers	**Lapse of Time** offer remains open for the time period specified or, if no time is stated, for a reasonable period of time **Revocation** generally, an offer may be terminated at any time before it is accepted, subject to the following exceptions ■ *Option Contracts* contract that binds offeror to keep an offer open for a specified time ■ *Firm Offer* a merchant's irrevocable offer to sell or buy goods in a signed writing that assures that the offer will not be terminated for up to three months ■ *Statutory Irrevocability* offer made irrevocable by statute ■ *Irrevocable Offer of Unilateral Contracts* a unilateral offer may not be revoked for a reasonable time after performance is begun ■ *Promissory Estoppel* noncontractual promise that binds the promisor because she should reasonably expect that the promise will induce the promisee (offeree) to take action in reliance on it ■ *Rejection* refusal to accept an offer terminates the power of acceptance ■ *Counteroffer* counterproposal to an offer that generally terminates the original offer ■ *Death or Incompetency* of either the offeror or the offeree terminates the offer ■ *Destruction of Subject Matter* of an offer terminates the offer ■ *Subsequent Illegality* of the purpose or subject matter of the offer terminates the offer

Acceptance

Requirements	**Definition** positive and unequivocal expression of a willingness to enter into a contract on the terms of the offer **Mirror Image Rule** except as modified by the Code, an acceptance cannot deviate from the terms of the offer

Communication of Acceptance	**General Rule** acceptance effective upon dispatch unless the offer specifically provides otherwise or the offeree uses an unauthorized means of communication **Stipulated Provisions in the Offer** the communication of acceptance must conform to the specifications in the offer **Authorized Means** *Restatement* and the Code provide that, unless the offer provides otherwise, acceptance is authorized to be in any reasonable manner **Unauthorized Means** acceptance effective when received, provided that it is received within the time within which the authorized means would have arrived **Acceptance Following a Prior Rejection** first communication received by the offeror is effective **Defective Acceptance** does not create a contract but serves as a new offer

QUESTIONS

1. Identify the three essentials of an offer and discuss briefly the requirements associated with each.
2. Identify and discuss briefly seven ways by which an offer may be terminated other than by acceptance.
3. Compare briefly the traditional and modern theories of definiteness of acceptance of an offer as shown by the common law "mirror image" rule and by the rule of the Uniform Commercial Code.
4. Discuss the five situations limiting an offeror's right to revoke her offer.
5. Explain the various rules that determine when an acceptance takes effect.

Internet Question. Compare the provisions governing offer and acceptance contained in the United Nations Convention on Contracts for the International Sale of Goods (Vienna, 1980) with those of the United States common law contracts.

PROBLEMS

1. Ames, seeking business for his lawn maintenance firm, posted the following notice in the meeting room of the Antlers, a local lodge: "To the members of the Antlers—Special this month. I will resod your lawn for four dollars per square foot using Fairway brand sod. This offer expires July 15."

   The notice also included Ames's name, address, and signature and specified that the acceptance was to be in writing.

   Bates, a member of the Antlers, and Cramer, the janitor, read the notice and were interested. Bates wrote a letter to Ames saying he would accept the offer if Ames would use Putting Green brand sod. Ames received this letter July 14 and wrote to Bates saying he would not use Putting Green sod. Bates received Ames's letter on July 16 and promptly wrote Ames that he would accept Fairway sod. Cramer wrote to Ames on July 10 saying he accepted Ames's offer.

   By July 15, Ames had found more profitable ventures and refused to resod either lawn at the specified price. Bates and Cramer brought an appropriate action against Ames for breach of contract. Decisions as to the respective claims of Bates and Cramer?

2. Justin owned four speedboats named Porpoise, Priscilla, Providence, and Prudence. On April 2, Justin made written offers to sell the four boats in the order named for $4,200 each to Charles, Diane, Edward, and Fran respectively, allowing ten days for acceptance. In which, if any, of the following four situations was a contract formed?

(a) Five days later, Charles received notice from Justin that he had contracted to sell Porpoise to Mark. The next day, April 8, Charles notified Justin that he accepted Justin's offer.

(b) On the third day, April 5, Diane mailed a rejection to Justin that reached Justin on the morning of the fifth day. At 10 a.m. on the fourth day, Diane sent an acceptance by telegram to Justin, who received it at noon the same day.

(c) Edward, on April 3, replied that he was interested in buying Providence but declared the price appeared slightly excessive and wondered if, perhaps, Justin would be willing to sell the boat for $3,900. Five days later, having received no reply from Justin, Edward accepted Justin's offer by letter, and enclosed a certified check for $4,200.

(d) Fran was accidently killed in an automobile accident on April 9. The following day, the executor of her estate mailed an acceptance of Justin's offer to Justin.

3. Alpha Rolling Mill Corporation (Alpha Corporation), by letter dated June 8, offered to sell Brooklyn Railroad Company (Brooklyn Company) 2,000 to 5,000 tons of fifty-pound iron rails on certain specified terms and added that, if the offer was accepted, Alpha Corporation would expect to be notified prior to June 20. Brooklyn Company, on June 16, by telegram, referring to Alpha Corporation's offer of June 8, directed Alpha Corporation to enter an order for 1,200 tons of fifty-pound iron rails on the terms specified. The same day, June 16, Brooklyn Company, by letter to Alpha Corporation, confirmed the telegram. On June 18, Alpha Corporation, by telegram, declined to fulfill the order. Brooklyn Company, on June 19, telegraphed Alpha Corporation: "Please enter an order for 2,000 tons of rails as per your letter of the eighth. Please forward written contract. Reply." In reply to Brooklyn Company's repeated inquiries concerning whether the order for 2,000 tons of rails had been entered, Alpha denied the existence of any contract between Brooklyn Company and itself. Thereafter, Brooklyn Company sued Alpha Corporation for breach of contract. Decision?

4. On April 8, Crystal received a telephone call from Akers, a truck dealer, who told Crystal that a new model truck in which Crystal was interested would arrive in one week. Although Akers initially wanted $10,500, the conversation ended after Akers agreed to sell and Crystal agreed to purchase the truck for $10,000, with a $1,000 down payment and the balance on delivery. The next day, Crystal sent Akers a check for $1,000, which Akers promptly cashed.

One week later, when Crystal called Akers and inquired about the truck, Akers informed Crystal he had several prospects looking at the truck and would not sell for less than $10,500. The following day Akers sent Crystal a properly executed check for $1,000 with the following notation thereon: "Return of down payment on sale of truck."

After notifying Akers that she will not cash the check, Crystal sues Akers for damages. Decision?

5. On November 15, Gloria, Inc., a manufacturer of crystalware, mailed to Benny Buyer a letter stating that Gloria would sell to Buyer one hundred crystal "A" goblets at $100 per goblet and that "the offer would remain open for fifteen (15) days." On November 18, Gloria, noticing the sudden rise in the price of crystal "A" goblets, decided to withdraw its offer to Buyer and so notified Buyer. Buyer chose to ignore Gloria's letter of revocation and gleefully watched as the price of crystal "A" goblets continued to skyrocket. On November 30, Buyer mailed to Gloria a letter accepting Gloria's offer to sell the goblets. The letter was received by Gloria on December 4. Buyer demands delivery of the goblets. What is the result?

6. On May 1, Melforth Realty Company offered to sell Greenacre to Dallas, Inc., for $1,000,000. The offer was made by telegraph and stated that the offer would expire on May 15. Dallas decided to purchase the property and sent a registered letter to Melforth on May 10 accepting the offer. As a result of unexplained delays in the postal service, the letter was not received by Melforth until May 22. Melforth wishes to sell Greenacre to another buyer who is offering $1,200,000 for the tract of land. Has a contract resulted between Melforth and Dallas?

7. Rowe advertised in newspapers of wide circulation and otherwise made known that she would pay $5,000 for a complete set, consisting of ten volumes, of certain rare books. Ford, not knowing of the offer, gave Rowe all but one of the set of rare books as a Christmas present. Ford later learned of the offer, obtained the one remaining book, tendered it to Rowe, and demanded the $5,000. Rowe refused to pay. Is Ford entitled to the $5,000?

8. Scott, manufacturer of a carbonated beverage, entered into a contract with Otis, owner of a baseball park, whereby Otis rented to Scott a large signboard on top of the center field wall. The contract provided that Otis should letter the sign as Scott desired and would change the lettering from time to time within forty-eight hours after receipt of written request from Scott. As directed by Scott, the signboard originally stated in large letters that Scott would pay $100 to any ballplayer hitting a home run over the sign.

In the first game of the season, Hume, the best hitter in the league, hit one home run over the sign. Scott immediately served written notice on Otis instructing Otis to replace the offer on the signboard with an offer to pay $50 to every pitcher who pitched a no-hit game in the park. A week after receipt of Scott's letter, Otis had not changed the wording on the sign; and on that day, Perry, a pitcher for a scheduled game, pitched a no-hit game and Todd, one of his teammates, hit a home run over Scott's sign.

Scott refuses to pay any of the three players. What are the rights of Scott, Hume, Perry, and Todd?

9. Barney accepted Clark's offer to sell to him a portion of Clark's coin collection. Clark forgot at the time of the offer and acceptance that her prized $20 gold piece was included in the portion that she offered to sell to Barney. Clark did not intend to include the gold piece in the sale. Barney, at the time of inspecting the offered portion of the collection, and prior to accepting the offer, saw the gold piece. Is Barney entitled to the $20 gold piece?

10. Small, admiring Jasper's watch, asked Jasper where and at what price he had purchased it. Jasper replied, "I bought it at West Watch Shop about two years ago for around $85, but I am not certain as to that." Small then said, "Those fellows at West are good people and always sell good watches. I'll buy that watch from you." Jasper replied, "It's a deal." The next morning, Small telephoned Jasper and said he had changed his mind and did not wish to buy the watch.

Jasper sued Small for breach of contract. In defense, Small has pleaded that he made no enforceable contract with Jasper because (a) the parties did not agree on the price to be paid for the watch, and (b) the parties did not agree on the place and time of delivery of the watch to Small. Are either, or both, of these defenses good?

11. Jeff says to Brenda, "I offer to sell you my IBM PC for $900." Brenda replies, "If you do not hear otherwise from me by Thursday, I have accepted your offer." Jeff agrees and does not hear from Brenda by Thursday. Does a contract exist between Jeff and Brenda? Explain.

12. On November 19, 1949, Hoover Motor Express Company sent to Clements Paper Company a written offer to purchase certain real estate. Sometime in December, Clements authorized Williams to accept. Williams, however, attempted to bargain with Hoover to obtain a better deal, specifically that Clements would retain easements on the property. In a telephone conversation on January 13, 1950, Williams first told Hoover of his plan to obtain the easements. Hoover replied, "Well, I don't know if we are ready. We have not decided, we might not want to go through with it." On January 20, Clements sent a written acceptance of Hoover's offer. Hoover refused to buy, claiming it had revoked its offer through the January 13 phone conversation. Clements then brought suit to compel the sale or obtain damages. Decision?

13. Walker leased a small lot to Keith for ten years at one hundred dollars a month, with a right for Keith to extend the lease for another ten-year term under the

same terms except as to rent. The renewal option provided:

> Rental will be fixed in such amount as shall actually be agreed upon by the lessors and the lessee with the monthly rental fixed on the comparative basis of rental values as of the date of the renewal with rental values at this time reflected by the comparative business conditions of the two periods.

Keith sought to exercise the renewal right and, when the parties were unable to agree on the rent, brought suit against Walker. Who prevails? Why?

14. The Brewers contracted to purchase Dower House from McAfee. Then, several weeks before the May 7 settlement date for the purchase of the house, the two parties began to negotiate for the sale of certain items of furniture in the house. On April 30, McAfee sent the Brewers a letter containing a list of the furnishings to be purchased at specific prices; a payment schedule including a $3,000 payment due on acceptance; and a clause reading: "If the above is satisfactory, please sign and return one copy with the first payment."

On June 3, the Brewers sent a letter to McAfee stating that enclosed was a $3,000 check; that the original contract had been misplaced and could another be furnished; that they planned to move into Dower House on June 12; and that they wished that the red desk be included in the contract. McAfee then sent a letter dated June 8 to the Brewers listing the items of furniture they had purchased.

The Brewers moved into Dower House in the middle of June. Soon after they moved in, they tried to contact McAfee at his office to tell him that there had been a misunderstanding relating to their purchase of the listed items. They then refused to pay him any more money, and he brought this action to recover the outstanding balance. Decision?

15. The Thoelkes were owners of real property located in Orange County, which the Morrisons agreed to purchase. The Morrisons signed a contract for the sale of that property and mailed it to the Thoelkes in Texas on November 26. The next day, the Thoelkes executed the contract and placed it in the mail addressed to the Morrisons' attorney in Florida. After the executed contract was mailed but before it was received in Florida, the Thoelkes called the Morrisons' attorney in Florida and attempted to repudiate the contract. Decision?

16. On December 20, 1952, Lucy and Zehmer met while having drinks in a restaurant. During the course of their conversation, Lucy apparently offered to buy Zehmer's 471.6-acre farm for $50,000 cash. Although Zehmer claims that he thought the offer was made in jest, he wrote the following on the back of a pad: "We hereby agree to sell to W. O. Lucy the Ferguson Farm complete for $50,000, title satisfactory to buyer."

Zehmer then signed the writing and induced his wife Ida to do the same. She claims, however, that she signed only after Zehmer assured her that it was only a joke. Finally, Zehmer claims that he was "high as a Georgia pine" at the time but admits that he was not too drunk to make a valid contract. Decision?

17. On July 31, Lee Calan Imports advertised a used Volvo station wagon for sale in the *Chicago Sun-Times*. As part of the information for the advertisement, Lee Calan Imports instructed the newspaper to print the price of the car as $1,795. However, due to a mistake made by the newspaper, without any fault on the part of Lee Calan Imports, the printed ad listed the price of the car as $1,095. After reading the ad and then examining the car, O'Brien told a Lee Calan Imports salesman that he wanted to purchase the car for the advertised price of $1,095. Calan Imports refuses to sell the car to O'Brien for $1,095. Is there a contract? If so, for what price?

18. On May 20, cattle rancher Oliver visited his neighbor Southworth, telling him, "I know you're interested in buying the land I'm selling." Southworth replied, "Yes, I do want to buy that land, especially since it adjoins my property." Although the two men did not discuss the price, Oliver told Southworth he would determine the value of the property and send that information to Southworth so that he would have "notice" of what Oliver "wanted for the land." On June 13, Southworth called Oliver to ask if he still planned to sell the land. Oliver answered, "Yes, and I should have the value of the land determined soon." On June 17, Oliver sent a letter to Southworth listing a price quotation of $324,000. Southworth then responded to Oliver by letter on June 21, stating that he accepted Oliver's offer. However, on June 24 Oliver wrote back to Southworth saying "There has never been a firm offer to sell, and there is no enforceable contract between us." Oliver maintains that a price quotation alone is not an offer. Southworth claims a valid contract has been made. Who wins? Discuss.

19. Cushing filed an application with the office of the Adjutant General of the State of New Hampshire for the use of the Portsmouth Armory to hold a dance on the evening of April 29, 1978. The application, made on behalf of the Portsmouth Area Clamshell Alliance, was received by the Adjutant General's office on or about March 30, 1978. On March 31 the Adjutant General mailed a signed contract after agreeing to rent the armory for the evening requested. The agreement required acceptance by the renter affixing his signature to the agreement and then returning the copy to the Adjutant General within five days after receipt. Cushing received the contract offer, signed it on behalf of the alliance, and mailed it on April 3. At 6:30 on the evening of April 4, Cushing received a telephone call from the Adjutant General revoking the rental offer. Cushing stated during the conversation that he had already signed and mailed the contract. The Adjutant General sent a written confirmation of the withdrawal on April 5. On April 6 the Adjutant General's office received by mail the signed contract dated April 3 and postmarked April 5. The trial court ruled that a binding contract existed and ordered the defendants to honor the contract. Decision?

CHAPTER 11

Conduct Invalidating Assent

In Chapter 10, we considered one of the essential requirements of a contract, namely, the objective manifestation of assent by each party to the other. In addition to requiring offer and acceptance, the law also requires that the agreement be voluntary and knowing. If either of these requirements is not met, then the agreement is voidable or void. This chapter deals with situations in which the consent manifested by one of the parties to the contract is not effective because it was not knowingly and voluntarily given. We consider five such situations in this chapter: duress, undue influence, fraud, nonfraudulent misrepresentation, and mistake.

DURESS

Duress *(du·ress′)* wrongful act or threat that overcomes the free will of a party

A person should not be held to an agreement he has not entered voluntarily. Accordingly, the law will not enforce any contract induced by **duress**, which in general is any wrongful act or threat that overcomes the free will of a party.

Physical Compulsion

Physical compulsion coercion involving physical force renders the agreement void

Duress is of two basic types. The first type, *physical duress*, occurs when one party compels another to manifest assent to a contract through actual physical force, such as pointing a gun at a person or taking a person's hand and compelling him to sign a written contract. This type of duress, while extremely rare, renders the agreement *void*.

Improper Threats

Improper threats improper threats or acts, including economic and social coercion, render the contract voidable

The second and more common type of duress involves the use of *improper threats* or acts, including economic and social coercion, to compel a person to enter into a contract. Though the threat may be explicit or may be inferred from words or conduct, in either case it must leave the victim with no reasonable alternative. This type of duress makes the contract *voidable* at the option of the coerced party. For example, if Ellen, a landlord, induces Vijay, an infirm, bedridden tenant, to enter into a new lease on the same apartment at a greatly increased rent by wrongfully threatening to terminate Vijay's lease and evict him, Vijay can escape or *avoid* the new lease by reason of the duress exerted on him. The following case illustrates how economic duress renders a contract voidable.

INTERNATIONAL UNDERWATER CONTRACTORS, INC. v. NEW ENGLAND TELEPHONE AND TELEGRAPH COMPANY
Appeals Court of Massachusetts, Suffolk, 1979, 8 Mass.App. 340, 393 N.E.2d 968

FACTS International Underwater Contractors, Inc. (IUC), entered into a written contract with New England Telephone and Telegraph Company (NET) to assemble and install certain conduits under the Mystic River for a lump sum price of $149,680. Delays caused by NET forced IUC's work to be performed in the winter months instead of during the summer as originally bid, and as a result, a major change had to be made in the system from that specified in the contract. NET repeatedly assured IUC that it would pay the cost if IUC would complete the work. The change cost IUC a total of $811,816.73; nevertheless, it signed a release settling the claim for a total sum of $575,000. IUC, which at the time was in financial trouble, now seeks to recover the balance due, arguing that the signed release is not binding because it was signed under economic duress. Summary judgment was entered in favor of NET.

DECISION Summary judgment reversed.

OPINION A release signed under economic pressure illegally or immorally applied is not binding. To prove that the release was signed under economic duress, IUC must show that: (1) one side involuntarily accepted the terms of the other; (2) the circumstances permitted no other alternative; and (3) the circumstances were the result of the coercive acts of the other party. Merely taking advantage of another's financial difficulty is not duress; rather, the party claiming duress must show that its financial difficulty was contributed to or caused by the one accused of coercion.

Here NET insisted on the change in the contract and repeatedly assured IUC that it would pay the substantial additional cost if IUC would complete the work. Furthermore, NET refused to make payments for almost a year, which in turn caused IUC's financial difficulties. Other factors also indicate the existence of economic duress, including the unequal bargaining power of the two parties and the disparity among IUC's actual costs ($811,816.73), the amount NET's engineers had recommended for settlement ($775,000), and the final amount offered on a take-it-or-leave-it basis with the release ($575,000).

INTERPRETATION Economic coercion that compels a person to enter into a contract renders the contract voidable.

The fact that the act or threat would not affect a person of average strength and intelligence is not important if it places fear in the person actually affected and induces her to act against her will. The test is *subjective*, and the question is this: Did the threat actually induce assent on the part of the person claiming to be the victim of duress?

Ordinarily, the acts or threats constituting duress are themselves crimes or torts. But this is not true in all cases. The acts need not be criminal or tortious in order to be *wrongful*; they merely need to be contrary to public policy or morally reprehensible. For example, if the threat involves a breach of a contractual duty of good faith and fair dealing, it is improper.

Moreover, it generally has been held that contracts induced by threats of criminal prosecution are voidable, regardless of whether the coerced party had committed an unlawful act. Similarly, threatening the criminal prosecution of a close relative is also duress. To be distinguished from such threats of prosecution are threats that resort to ordinary civil remedies to recover a debt due from another. It is not wrongful to threaten a civil suit against an individual to recover a debt. What is prohibited is threatening to bring a civil suit when bringing such a suit would be abuse of process.

JOHNSON v. INTERNATIONAL BUSINESS MACHINES CORPORATION
United States District Court, 1995, 891 F.Supp. 522

FACTS Ronald D. Johnson is a former employee of International Business Machines Corporation (IBM). In late 1993, as part of a downsizing effort, IBM discharged Johnson. In exchange for an enhanced severance package, Johnson signed a written release and covenant not to sue IBM. IBM's downsizing plan

continued

provided that surplus personnel were eligible to receive benefits, including outplacement assistance, career counseling, job retraining, and an enhanced separation allowance. These employees were eligible, at IBM's discretion, to receive a separation allowance of two weeks' pay. However, employees who signed a release could be eligible for an enhanced severance allowance equal to one week's pay for each six months of accumulated service with a maximum of twenty-six weeks' pay. Surplus employees could also apply for alternate, generally lower-paying, manufacturing positions. Johnson opted for the release and received the maximum twenty-six weeks' pay. He then alleged, among other claims, that IBM subjected him to economic duress when he signed the release and covenant-not-to-sue and he sought to rescind both.

DECISION Judgment for IBM.

OPINION Parties to a contract must freely and mutually consent to its terms. If consent to a contract is not freely given, the contract may be rescinded by the parties. In order to establish a claim for economic duress, the plaintiff must prove by a preponderance of evidence the following elements: (1) the defendant engaged in a sufficiently coercive wrongful act such that (2) a reasonably prudent person in the plaintiff's economic position would have no reasonable alternative but to succumb to the defendant's coercion;

(3) the defendant knew of the plaintiff's economic vulnerability; and (4) the defendant's coercive wrongful act actually caused or induced the plaintiff to enter into the contract. Johnson's case fails to meet any of these elements.

First, IBM did not commit a wrongful act by designating Johnson a surplus employee or by requiring that he choose between severance options. Although the wrongful act need not be criminal or tortious, being allowed a voluntary choice of perfectly legitimate alternatives is the antithesis of duress. Encouragement or incentives is a far cry from coercion or denial of choice.

Second, Johnson had reasonable alternatives to signing the release. In determining whether a reasonable alternative was available, courts employ an objective test dependent on the circumstances of each case. Johnson was not facing imminent bankruptcy or financial ruin. Regardless of what he may have subjectively believed, Johnson had reasonable alternatives available.

Third, IBM had no knowledge of Johnson's particular economic circumstances nor of any peculiar economic vulnerability he had. Finally, Johnson's decision was his own and was not caused by any unfair action on the part of IBM. Therefore, at the time he signed the release, Johnson was not subject to economic duress.

INTERPRETATION An act that is not wrongful or unfair does not constitute duress.

UNDUE INFLUENCE

Undue influence the unfair persuasion of a person by a party in a dominant position based on a relationship of trust and confidence

Undue influence is the unfair persuasion of a person by a party in a dominant position based on a *confidential relationship*. The law very carefully scrutinizes contracts between those in a relationship of trust and confidence that is likely to permit one party to take unfair advantage of the other. Examples are the relationships of guardian–ward, trustee–beneficiary, agent–principal, spouses, parent–child, attorney–client, physician–patient, and clergy–parishioner.

A transaction induced by undue influence on the part of the dominant party is **voidable**. The ultimate question in undue influence cases is whether the transaction was induced by dominating either or both the mind or emotions of a submissive party. The weakness or dependence of the person persuaded is a strong indicator of whether the persuasion may have been unfair. For example, Abigail, a person without business experience, has for years relied on Boris, who is experienced in business, for advice on business matters. Boris, without making any false representations of fact, induces Abigail to enter into a contract with Boris's confederate, Cassius, that is disadvantageous to Abigail, as both Boris and Cassius know. The transaction is voidable on the grounds of undue influence.

SCHANEMAN v. SCHANEMAN Supreme Court of Nebraska, 1980, 206 Neb. 113, 291 N.W.2d 412

FACTS Conrad Schaneman was a Russian immigrant who could neither read nor write the English language. In 1975, Conrad deeded (conveyed) a farm he owned to his eldest son, Laurence, for $23,500, which was the original purchase price of the property in 1945. The value of the farm in 1975 was between $145,000 and $160,000. At the time he executed the deed, Conrad was an eighty-two-year-old invalid, severely ill, and completely dependent on others for his personal needs. He weighed between 325 and 350 pounds, had difficulty breathing, could not walk more than fifteen feet, and needed a special jackhoist to get in and out of the bathtub. Conrad enjoyed a long-standing, confidential relationship with Laurence, who was his principal adviser and handled Conrad's business affairs. Laurence also obtained a power of attorney from Conrad and made himself a joint owner of Conrad's bank account and $20,000 certificate of deposit. Conrad brought this suit to cancel the deed, claiming it was the result of Laurence's undue influence. The district court found that the deed was executed as a result of undue influence, set aside the deed, and granted title to Conrad. Laurence appealed.

DECISION Judgment for Conrad Schaneman affirmed.

OPINION A confidential or fiduciary relationship exists between two persons if one has gained the confidence of the other and purports to act or advise with the other's interest in mind. In such a relationship, the court will scrutinize critically any transaction between the two parties, especially where age, infirmity, and instability are involved, to see that no injustice has occurred.

Here, the evidence shows that a confidential relationship existed between Conrad and Laurence and that due to age and physical infirmities, Conrad was, for all intents and purposes, an invalid at the time of the conveyance. It further supports a finding that Conrad's mental acuity was impaired at times and that he sometimes suffered from disorientation and lapse of memory. Conrad was subject to the influence of Laurence, who was acting in a confidential relationship; the opportunity to exercise undue influence existed; there was a disposition on the part of Laurence to exercise such undue influence; and the conveyance appeared to be the effect of such influence. Accordingly, the deed is canceled for undue influence.

INTERPRETATION Undue influence is the unfair persuasion of a person by a party in a dominant position based upon a confidential relationship.

FRAUD

Another factor affecting the validity of consent given by a contracting party is fraud, which prevents assent from being knowingly given. There are two distinct types of fraud: fraud in the execution and fraud in the inducement.

Fraud in the Execution

Fraud in the execution, which is extremely rare, consists of a misrepresentation that deceives the defrauded person as to the very nature of the contract. Such fraud occurs when a person does not know, or does not have reasonable opportunity to know, the character or essence of a proposed contract because the other party misrepresents its character or essential terms. Fraud in the execution renders the transaction *void*.

For example, Melody delivers a package to Ray, requests that Ray sign a receipt for it, holds out a simple printed form headed "Receipt," and indicates the line on which Ray is to sign. This line, which appears to Ray to be the bottom line of the receipt, is actually the signature line of a promissory note cleverly concealed underneath the receipt. Ray signs where directed without knowing that he is signing a note. This is fraud in the execution. The note is void and of no legal effect, for, although the signature is genuine and appears to manifest Ray's assent to the terms of the note, there is no actual assent. The nature of Melody's fraud precluded consent to the signing of the note because it prevented Ray from reasonably knowing what he was signing.

Fraud in the execution
misrepresentation that deceives the other party as to the nature of a document evidencing the contract

Fraud in the Inducement

Fraud in the inducement, generally referred to as fraud or deceit, is an intentional misrepresentation of material fact by one party to the other, who consents to enter into a contract in justifiable reliance on the misrepresentation. Fraud in the inducement renders the contract *voidable* by the defrauded party. For example, Alice, in offering to sell her dog to Bob, tells Bob that the dog won first prize in its class in the recent national dog show. In truth, the dog had not even been entered in the show. However, Alice's statement induces Bob to accept the offer and pay a high price for the dog. There is a contract, but it is voidable by Bob because Alice's fraud induced his assent.

The requisites for fraud in the inducement are

1. a false representation
2. of a fact
3. that is material and
4. made with knowledge of its falsity and the intention to deceive (scienter) and
5. which representation is justifiably relied on.

False Representation A basic element of fraud is a false representation or a **misrepresentation**, i.e., misleading conduct or an assertion not in accord with the facts, made through a positive statement. In contrast, **concealment** is an action intended or known to be likely to keep another from learning a fact he otherwise would have learned. Active concealment can form the basis for fraud, as, for example, when a seller puts heavy oil or grease in a car engine to conceal a knock. Truth may be suppressed by concealment as much as by misrepresentation. Expressly denying knowledge of a fact that a party knows to exist is a misrepresentation if it leads the other party to believe that the fact does not exist or cannot be discovered. Moreover, a statement of misleading half-truth is considered the equivalent of a false representation.

As a general rule, *silence* or nondisclosure alone does *not* amount to fraud when the parties deal at arm's length. An *arm's length transaction* is one in which the parties owe each other no special duties and each is acting in his or her self-interest. In most business or market transactions the parties deal at arm's length and generally have no obligation to tell the other party everything they know about the subject of the contract. Thus, it is not fraud when a buyer possesses advantageous information about the seller's property, information of which he knows the seller to be ignorant, and does not disclose such information to the seller. A buyer is under no duty to inform the seller of the greater value or other advantages of the property for sale. Assume, for example, that Sid owns a farm that, as a farm, is worth $10,000. Brenda, who knows that there is oil under Sid's farm, also knows that Sid is ignorant of this fact. Without disclosing this information to Sid, Brenda makes an offer to Sid to buy the farm for $10,000. Sid accepts the offer and a contract is duly made. Sid, on later learning the facts, can do nothing about the matter, either at law or in equity. As one case puts it, "a purchaser is not bound by our laws to make the man he buys from as wise as himself."

Although nondisclosure usually does not constitute a misrepresentation, in certain situations it does. One such situation arises when (1) a person fails to disclose a fact known to him; (2) he knows that the disclosure of that fact would

Fraud in the inducement misrepresentation regarding the subject matter of a contract that induces the other party to enter into the contract

Misrepresentation some positive statement or conduct that is not in accord with the facts

Concealment action taken to keep another from learning a fact

correct a mistake of the other party as to a basic assumption on which that party is making the contract; and (3) nondisclosure of the fact amounts to a failure to act in good faith and in accordance with reasonable standards of fair dealing. Accordingly, if the property at issue in the contract contains a substantial latent (hidden) defect, one that would not be discovered through an ordinary examination, the seller may be obliged to reveal it. Suppose, for example, that Judith owns a valuable horse, which Judith knows is suffering from a disease discoverable only by a competent veterinary surgeon. Judith offers to sell this horse to Curt, but does not inform Curt about the condition of her horse. Curt makes a reasonable examination of the horse and, finding it in apparently normal condition, purchases it from Judith. Curt, on later discovering the disease in question, can have the sale set aside. Judith's silence, under the circumstances, was a misrepresentation.

There are other situations in which the law imposes a duty of disclosure. For example, one may have a duty of disclosure because of prior representations innocently made before entering into the contract, which are later discovered to be untrue. Another instance in which silence may constitute fraud is a transaction involving a fiduciary. A **fiduciary** is a person in a confidential relationship who owes a duty of trust, loyalty, and confidence to another. For example, an agent owes a fiduciary duty to his principal, as does a trustee to the beneficiary of the trust and a partner to her copartners. A fiduciary may not deal at *arm's length*, as a party in most everyday business or market transactions may, but rather owes a duty to disclose fully all relevant facts when entering into a transaction with the other party to the relationship.

Fiduciary *(fi·du·ci·ar´·y)* person who owes a duty of trust, loyalty, and confidence to another

Fact The basic element of fraud is the misrepresentation of a material fact. A **fact** is an event that actually took place or a thing that actually exists. Suppose that Dale induces Mike to purchase shares in a company unknown to Mike at a price of $100 per share by representing that she had paid $150 per share for them during the preceding year, when in fact she had paid only $50. This representation of a past event is a misrepresentation of fact.

Fact an event that took place or a thing that exists

Actionable fraud rarely can be based upon what is merely a statement of opinion. A representation is one of **opinion** if it expresses only the uncertain belief of the representer as to the existence of a fact or his judgment as to quality, value, authenticity, or other matters of judgment.

Opinion belief in the existence of a fact or a judgment as to value

The line between fact and opinion is not an easy one to draw and in close cases presents an issue for the jury. The solution often will turn upon the superior knowledge of the person making the statement and the information available to the other party. Thus, if Dale said to Mike that the shares were "a good investment," she was merely stating her opinion; and normally Mike ought to regard it as no more than that. Other common examples of opinion are statements of value, such as "This is the best car for the money in town" or "This deluxe model will give you twice the wear of a cheaper model." Such exaggerations and commendations of articles offered for sale are to be expected from dealers, who are merely **puffing** their wares with "sales talk." If the representer is a professional advising a client, the courts are more likely to regard an untrue statement of opinion as actionable. Such a statement expresses the opinion of one holding himself out as having expert knowledge, and the tendency is to grant relief to those who have sustained loss by reasonable reliance on expert evaluation, as the next case shows.

Puffing sales talk that is considered general bragging or overstatement

VOKES v. ARTHUR MURRAY, INC Court of Appeal of Florida, 1968, 212 So.2d 906

FACTS Mrs. Audrey E. Vokes, a widow of fifty-one years and without family, purchased fourteen separate dance courses from J. P. Davenport's Arthur Murray, Inc., School of Dance. The fourteen courses totaled in the aggregate 2,302 hours of dancing lessons at a cost to Mrs. Vokes of $31,090.45. Mrs. Vokes was induced continually to reapply for new courses by representations made by Mr. Davenport that her dancing ability was improving, that she was responding to instruction, that she had excellent potential, and that they were developing her into an accomplished dancer. In fact, she had no dancing ability or aptitude and had trouble "hearing the musical beat." Mrs. Vokes brought action to have the contracts set aside. The plaintiff's complaint was dismissed for failure to state a cause of action, and she appealed.

DECISION Judgment reversed.

OPINION Ordinarily, for a misrepresentation to be actionable, it must be one of fact rather than of opinion.

Where, as here, however, a statement is made by a party having superior knowledge, that statement may be taken as one of fact, although it would be considered as one of opinion if the parties were dealing on equal terms. Here it could be said that Mr. Davenport had superior knowledge as to Mrs. Vokes's dancing potential and as to her degree of improvement and that he set forth those "facts" in a greatly exaggerated fashion to induce her to enter into new contracts. Even in contractual situations where a party to a transaction owes no duty to disclose facts within his knowledge or to answer inquiries as to those facts, if he undertakes to speak, he must disclose the whole truth.

INTERPRETATION Because of his superior knowledge, Davenport's statements regarding Mrs. Vokes dancing ability and potential may be taken as statements of fact.

Also to be distinguished from a representation of fact is a **prediction**. Predictions are similar to opinions, as no one can know with certainty what will happen in the future, and normally they are not regarded as factual statements. Likewise, promissory statements ordinarily do not constitute a basis of fraud, as a breach of promise does not necessarily indicate that the promise was fraudulently made. However, a promise that the promisor, at the time of making, had no intention of keeping is a misrepresentation of fact.

Historically, courts held that representations of **law** were not statements of fact but rather of opinion. The present trend is to recognize that a statement of law may have the effect of either a statement of fact or a statement of opinion. For example, a statement asserting that a particular statute has been enacted or repealed has the effect of a statement of fact. On the other hand, a statement as to the legal consequences of a particular set of facts is a statement of opinion.

Material of substantial importance; likely to induce a reasonable person to enter into the contract

Materiality In addition to the requirement that a misrepresentation be one of fact, it must also be material. A misrepresentation is **material** if (1) it would be likely to induce a reasonable person to manifest her assent or (2) the maker knows that it would be likely to induce the recipient to do so. Thus, in the sale of a racehorse, it may not be material whether the horse was ridden in its most recent race by a certain jockey, but its running time for the race probably would be. The Restatement of Contracts provides that a contract justifiably induced by a misrepresentation is voidable if the misrepresentation is *either* fraudulent *or* material. Therefore, a fraudulent misrepresentation does not have to be material to obtain rescission, but it must be material to recover damages.

The following case presents an unusual factual situation involving the duty to disclose a "material" fact. (See also "Harvard Withdraws Acceptance of Teen Convicted in Mom's Death.")

REED v. KING California Court of Appeals, 1983, 145 Cal.App.3d 261, 193 Cal.Rptr. 130

FACTS Dorris Reed bought a house from Robert King for $76,000. King and his real estate agent knew that a woman and her four children had been murdered in the house ten years earlier and allegedly knew that the event had materially affected the market value of the house. They said nothing about the murders to Reed, and King asked a neighbor not to inform her of them. After the sale, neighbors told Reed about the murders and informed her that the house was consequently worth only $65,000. Reed brought an action against King and the real estate agent, alleging fraud and seeking rescission and damages. The complaint was dismissed, and Reed appealed.

DECISION Judgment reversed.

OPINION The requisite elements of fraud are "(1) a *false representation* or concealment of a material fact (or, in some cases, an opinion) susceptible of knowledge, (2) made with *knowledge* of its falsity or without sufficient knowledge on the subject to warrant a representation, (3) with the *intent* to induce the person to whom it is made to act upon it; and such person must (4) act in *reliance* upon the representation (5) to his *damage*." The trial court determined that Reed failed to allege concealment of a material fact. Concealment, however, may include mere silence when a party has

a duty to disclose. This duty falls upon the seller of real property where he (1) knows of facts that have a material effect upon the value or desirability of the property and (2) knows that these facts are unknown to the buyer and inaccessible to the buyer through the exercise of ordinary diligence. The second of these conditions clearly applies. King knew that Reed was unaware of the murders, and Reed cannot reasonably be expected to anticipate and discover such an unlikely possibility. The issue therefore turns upon the question of materiality. Material nondisclosures in real property cases generally pertain to physical defects of the property or to legal impediments to its use. Murder, however, is a particularly disturbing event that may cause a buyer to be unable to live in a house where it has occurred and may thus deprive the buyer of the intended use of the property. Moreover, the content of the information not disclosed by the seller need not be the crucial factor. If Reed can prove that the murders significantly and measurably affected the market value of the premises, she should receive a favorable judgment on the issue of materiality and duty to disclose.

INTERPRETATION A representation is material if it is likely to influence or affect a reasonable person.

Knowledge of Falsity and Intention to Deceive To establish fraud, the misrepresentation must have been known by the one making it to be false and must be made with an intent to deceive. This element of fraud is known as **scienter**. Knowledge of falsity can consist of (a) actual knowledge, (b) lack of belief in the statement's truthfulness, or (c) reckless indifference as to its truthfulness.

Scienter *(sci·en´·ter)* guilty knowledge

Justifiable Reliance A person is not entitled to relief unless she has **justifiably relied** on the misrepresentation. If the complaining party's decision was in no way influenced by the misrepresentation, she must abide by the terms of the contract. She is not deceived if she does not rely on the misrepresentation. Justifiable reliance requires that the misrepresentation contribute substantially to the misled party's decision to enter into the contract. If the complaining party knew or it was obvious that the representation of the defendant was untrue, but she still entered into the contract, she has not justifiably relied on that representation. Moreover, where the misrepresentation is fraudulent, the party who relies on it is entitled to relief even though she does not investigate the statement or is contributorily negligent in relying on it. Not knowing or discovering the facts before making a contract does not make a person's reliance unjustified unless her reliance amounts to a failure to act in good faith and in accordance with reasonable standards of fair dealing. Thus, most courts will not allow a person who concocts a deliberate and elaborate scheme to defraud—one that the defrauded party should readily detect—to argue that the defrauded party did not justifiably rely upon the misrepresentation.

Justifiable reliance reasonably influenced by the misrepresentation

BOSTON—Gina Grant seemed to be the perfect candidate for Harvard University: an IQ of 150, honor society member, tennis team co-captain, tutor of underprivileged kids.

Now, Harvard has taken back its offer of early admission after learning that Grant bludgeoned her mother to death with a lead crystal candlestick five years ago.

"I deal with this tragedy every day on a personal level," Grant, 19, said in a statement. "It serves no good purpose for anyone else to dredge up the pain of my childhood. I'm especially distressed that my college career may now be in jeopardy."

The university would not comment on Grant's case, acknowledging only that an early admission offer had been rescinded. Spokesman Joe Wrinn said Friday that Harvard occasionally withdraws such offers because of a sudden drop in a student's academic performance or because a student lied on the application.

The Harvard application asks whether a student has ever been on probation. Grant had been on probation until she was 18 as a condition of pleading "no contest" to the September 1990 killing of her mother in Lexington, S.C.

The university did not release Grant's application. Grant's attorney, Margaret Burnham, said Grant was not obligated to disclose something that happened when she was a juvenile.

Burnham said in a statement that she hoped Harvard will reconsider its rejection. She did not mention possible legal action.

After the killing, Grant moved to Cambridge, Mass., to live with her aunt—the sister of her father, who died of cancer when she was 11—and uncle. When she was 16, she moved into her own apartment, supporting herself from a modest trust fund.

She began attending Cambridge Rindge and Latin High School in 1992. Officials there said she is a student in good standing.

Grant received her acceptance letter in January from Harvard. In the following weeks, someone anonymously provided Harvard officials with newspaper clippings about the killing.

Grant's mother, Dorothy Mayfield, 42, was hit at least 13 times. Mayfield, described in court as an alcoholic, died with a blood alcohol level of 0.30.

South Carolina prosecutor Donnie Myers said the killing was premeditated. Afterward, Grant and her football-player boyfriend, Jack Hook, tried to make the death look like suicide by sticking a carving knife into the side of her mother's neck. Hook pleaded "no contest" to being an accessory to murder after the fact.

A judge who placed Grant in juvenile detention for a few months granted her permission to move north and begin her life anew.

From *The Raleigh News & Observer,* April 8, 1995. Reprinted with permission of the Associated Press.

NONFRAUDULENT MISREPRESENTATION

Negligent misrepresentation made without due care

Innocent misrepresentation misrepresentation made without knowledge of its falsity but with due care

Nonfraudulent misrepresentation is a material, false statement that induces another to rely justifiably but is made *without* scienter. Such representation may occur in one of two ways. **Negligent misrepresentation** is a false representation that is made without due care in ascertaining its truthfulness; such representation renders an agreement voidable. **Innocent misrepresentation**, which also renders a contract voidable, is a false representation made without knowledge of its falsity but with due care. To obtain relief for nonfraudulent misrepresentation, all of the other elements of fraud must be present *and* the misrepresentation must be material. The remedies that may be available for nonfraudulent misrepresentation are rescission and damages (see Chapter 18).

MISTAKE

Mistake an understanding that is not in accord with existing fact

A **mistake** is a belief that is not in accord with the facts. Where the mistaken facts relate to the basis of the parties' agreement, the law permits the adversely affected party to avoid or reform the contract under certain circumstances. But because permitting avoidance for mistake undermines the objective approach to mutual assent, the law has experienced considerable difficulty in specifying those circumstances that justify permitting the subjective matter of mistake to invalidate an otherwise objectively satisfactory agreement. As a result, establishing clear rules to govern the effect of mistake has proven elusive.

The Restatement and modern cases treat mistakes of law in existence at the time of making the contract *no* differently than mistakes of fact. For example, Susan contracts to sell a parcel of land to James with the mutual understanding that James will build an apartment house on the land. Both Susan and James believe that such a building is lawful. Unknown to them, however, three days before they entered into their contract, the town in which the land was located had enacted an ordinance precluding such use of the land. In states that regard mistakes of law and fact in the same light, this mistake of law would be treated as a mistake of fact that would lead to the consequences discussed below.

Mutual Mistake

Mutual mistake occurs when *both* parties are mistaken as to the same set of facts. If the mistake relates to a basic assumption on which the contract is made and has a material effect on the agreed exchange, then it is *voidable* by the adversely affected party unless he bears the risk of the mistake.

Mutual mistake both parties have a common but erroneous belief forming the basis of a contract

Usually, market conditions and the financial situation of the parties are not considered basic assumptions. Thus, if Gail contracts to purchase Pete's automobile under the belief that she can sell it at a profit to Jesse, she is not excused from liability if she is mistaken in this belief. Nor can she rescind the agreement simply because she was mistaken as to her estimate of what the automobile was worth. These are the ordinary risks of business, and courts do not undertake to relieve against them. But suppose that the parties contract upon the assumption that the automobile is a 1992 Cadillac with fifteen thousand miles of use, when in fact the engine is that of a cheaper model and has been run in excess of fifty thousand miles. Here, a court likely would allow a rescission because of mutual mistake of a material fact. In a New Zealand case, the plaintiff purchased a "stud bull" at an auction. There were no express warranties as to "sex, condition, or otherwise." Actually, the bull was sterile. Rescission was allowed, the court observing that it was a "bull in name only."

WILKIN v. 1ST SOURCE BANK Court of Appeals of Indiana, 1990, 548 N.E.2d 170

FACTS At the time of her death in August 1984, Olga Mestrovic was the owner of a large number of works of art created by her late husband, Ivan Mestrovic, an internationally known sculptor and artist whose works were displayed throughout Europe and the United States. By the terms of Olga's will, all the works of art created by her husband were to be sold and the proceeds distributed to members of the Mestrovic family. Also included in the estate of Olga Mestrovic was certain real property which 1st Source Bank (the Bank), as personal representative of the estate of Olga Mestrovic, agreed to sell to Terrence and Antoinette Wilkin. The agreement of purchase and sale made no mention of any works of art, although it did provide for the sale of such personal property as a dishwasher, drapes, and French doors stored in the attic.

Immediately after closing on the real estate, the Wilkins complained to the Bank of the clutter left on the premises; the Bank gave the Wilkins an option of cleaning the house themselves and keeping any personal property they desired, to which the Wilkins agreed. At the time these arrangements were made, neither the Bank nor the Wilkins suspected that any works of art remained on the premises. During cleanup, however, the Wilkins found eight drawings and a sculpture created by Ivan Mestrovic to which the Wilkins claimed ownership based upon their agreement with the Bank that, if they cleaned the real property, they could keep such personal property as they desired.

DECISION Judgment for 1st Source Bank.

OPINION The parties in this case shared a common presupposition as to certain facts that proved false. The Bank and the Wilkins considered the real estate which Wilkins had purchased to be cluttered with items of personal property variously characterized as "junk," "stuff," or "trash." Neither party suspected

continued

that Mestrovic's works of art remained on the premises, and the discovery of those works of art by the Wilkins was unexpected. Where both parties share a common assumption about a vital fact, upon which they based their bargain, the transaction may be avoided if, because of the mistake, an exchange of values quite different from the exchange of values contemplated by the parties occurs. The gain to the Wilkins and the loss to the Bank were not contemplated when they made their agreement, and so a true meeting of the minds never occurred, allowing the Bank to avoid the agreement.

INTERPRETATION If both parties to a contract have a common but erroneous belief as to a basic assumption on which the contract is made, the contract is voidable.

Unilateral Mistake

Unilateral mistake
erroneous belief on the part of only one of the parties to a contract

Unilateral mistake occurs when only one of the parties is mistaken. Courts have been hesitant to grant relief for unilateral mistake, even though it relates to a basic assumption on which a party entered into the contract and has a material effect on the agreed exchange. Nevertheless, relief will be granted where the nonmistaken party knows, or reasonably should know, that such a mistake has been made (palpable unilateral mistake) or where the mistake was caused by the fault of the nonmistaken party. For example, suppose a building contractor makes a serious error in his computations and consequently submits a job bid that is one-half the amount it should be. If the other party knows that the contractor made such an error, or reasonably should have known it, she cannot, as a general rule, take advantage of the other's mistake by accepting the offer. In addition, many courts and the Restatement allow rescission where the effect of unilateral mistake makes enforcement of the contract unconscionable.

Assumption of Risk of Mistake

Assumption of risk of mistake a party may assume the risk of a mistake

A party who has undertaken to bear the risk of a mistake will not be able to avoid the contract, even though the mistake (which may be either mutual or unilateral) would have otherwise permitted the party to do so. This allocation of risk may occur by agreement of the parties. For instance, a ship at sea may be sold "lost or not lost." In such case the buyer is liable whether the ship was lost or not lost at the time the contract was made. There is no mistake; instead, there is a conscious allocation of risk.

The risk of mistake also may be allocated by conscious ignorance when the parties recognize that they have limited knowledge of the facts. For example, the Supreme Court of Wisconsin refused to set aside the sale of a stone for which the purchaser paid one dollar, but that was subsequently discovered to be an uncut diamond valued at $700. The parties did not know at the time of sale what the stone was and knew they did not know. Each consciously assumed the risk that the value might be more or less than the selling price.

Effect of Fault upon Mistake

Effect of fault upon mistake not a bar to avoidance unless the fault amounts to a failure to act in good faith

The Restatement provides that a mistaken party's fault in not knowing or discovering a fact before making a contract does not prevent him from avoiding the contract "unless his fault amounts to a failure to act in good faith and in accordance with reasonable standards of fair dealing." This rule does not, however, apply to a failure to read a contract. As a general proposition, a party is held to what she signs. Her signature authenticates the writing, and she cannot repudiate that which she has voluntarily approved. Generally, one who assents to a writing is presumed to know its contents and cannot escape being bound by its terms merely by contending that she did not read them; her assent is deemed to cover unknown as well as known terms.

FIGURE 11–1 Conduct Invalidating Assent

Conduct	Effect
Duress by physical force	Void
Duress by improper threats	Voidable
Undue influence	Voidable
Fraud in the execution	Void
Fraud in the inducement	Voidable
Nonfraudulent misrepresentation	Voidable
Mutual mistake of fact	Voidable

Mistake in Meaning of Terms

Somewhat related to mistakes of fact is the situation in which the parties misunderstand their manifestations of mutual assent. A famous case involving this problem is *Raffles v. Wichelhaus*, 2 Hurlstone & Coltman 906 (1864), popularly known as the *"Peerless"* case. A contract of purchase was made for 125 bales of cotton to arrive on the *Peerless* from Bombay. It happened, however, that there were two ships by the name of *"Peerless"* each sailing from Bombay, one in October and the other in December. The buyer had in mind the ship that sailed in October, while the seller reasonably believed the agreement referred to the *Peerless* sailing in December. Neither party was at fault, but both believed in good faith that a different ship was intended. The English court held that no contract existed.

The Restatement is in accord: There is no manifestation of mutual assent where the parties attach materially different meanings to their manifestations and neither party knows or has reason to know the meaning attached by the other. If blame can be ascribed to either party, however, that party will be held responsible. Thus, if the seller knew of the sailing from Bombay of two ships by the name of *Peerless*, then he would be at fault, and the contract would be for the ship sailing in October as the buyer expected. If neither party is to blame or both are to blame, there is no contract at all; that is, the agreement is void.

CHAPTER SUMMARY

Duress | **Definition** wrongful act or threat that overcomes the free will of a party
Physical Compulsion coercion involving physical force renders the agreement void
Improper Threats improper threats or acts, including economic and social coercion, render the contract voidable

Undue Influence | **Definition** taking unfair advantage of a person by reason of a dominant position based on a confidential relationship
Effect renders a contract voidable

Fraud	**Fraud in the Execution** a misrepresentation that deceives the other party as to the nature of a document evidencing the contract renders the agreement void
	Fraud in the Inducement renders the agreement voidable if the following elements are present:
	■ *False Representation* positive statement or conduct that misleads
	■ *Fact* an event that occurred or thing that exists
	■ *Materiality* of substantial importance
	■ *Knowledge of Falsity and Intention to Deceive* *(called scienter)* and includes (a) actual knowledge, (b) lack of belief in statement's truthfulness, or (c) reckless indifference to its truthfulness
	■ *Justifiable Reliance* a defrauded party is reasonably influenced by the misrepresentation

Nonfraudulent Misrepresentation	**Negligent Misrepresentation** misrepresentation made without due care in ascertaining its truthfulness; renders agreement voidable
	Innocent Misrepresentation misrepresentation made without knowledge of its falsity but with due care; renders contract voidable

Mistake	**Definition** an understanding that is not in accord with existing fact
	Mutual Mistake both parties have a common but erroneous belief forming the basis of the contract; renders the contract voidable by either party
	Unilateral Mistake courts are unlikely to grant relief unless the error is known or should be known by the nonmistaken party
	Assumption of Risk of Mistake a party may assume the risk of a mistake
	Effect of Fault upon Mistake not a bar to avoidance unless the fault amounts to a failure to act in good faith

QUESTIONS

1. Identify the types of duress and discuss the legal effect of each.
2. Identify the types of fraud and the elements that must be shown to establish the existence of each.
3. Discuss undue influence and identify some of the situations giving rise to a confidential relationship.
4. Identify and discuss the situations involving voidable mistakes.

5. Define the two types of nonfraudulent misrepresentation.

Internet Question. Find information for businesses and consumers about avoiding and detecting fraud and scams (including online, credit card, and telemarketing).

PROBLEMS

1. Anita and Barry were negotiating, and Anita's attorney prepared a long and carefully drawn contract that was given to Barry for examination. Five days later and prior to its execution, Barry's eyes became so infected that it was impossible for him to read. Ten days there-

after and during the continuance of the illness Anita called Barry and urged him to sign the contract, telling him that time was running out. Barry signed the contract despite the fact he was unable to read it. In a subsequent action by Anita, Barry claimed that the contract was not binding on him because it was impossible for him to read and he did not know what it contained prior to his signing it. Decision?

2. **(a)** William tells Carol that he paid $150,000 for his farm in 1985 and that he believes it is now worth twice that. Relying on these statements, Carol buys the farm from William for $225,000. William did pay $150,000 for the farm in 1985, but its value has increased only slightly, and it is presently not worth $300,000. On discovering this, Carol offers to reconvey the farm to William and sues for the return of her $225,000. Result?

   (b) Modify the facts in (a) by assuming that William had paid $100,000 for the property in 1985. What is the result?

3. On September 1, Adams in Portland, Oregon, wrote a letter to Brown in New York City offering to sell to Brown 1,000 tons of chromite at $48 per ton, to be shipped by *S.S. Malabar* sailing from Portland, Oregon, to New York City via the Panama Canal. Upon receiving the letter on September 5, Brown immediately mailed to Adams a letter stating that she accepted the offer. There were two ships by the name of *S.S. Malabar* sailing from Portland to New York City via the Panama Canal, one sailing in October and the other sailing in December. At the time of mailing her letter of acceptance, Brown knew of both sailings and further knew that Adams knew only of the December sailing. Is there a contract? If so, to which *S.S. Malabar* does it relate?

4. Adler owes Perreault, a police captain, $500. Adler threatens Perreault that unless Perreault gives him a discharge from the debt, Adler will disclose the fact that Perreault has on several occasions become highly intoxicated and has been seen in the company of certain disreputable persons. Perreault, induced by fear that such a disclosure would cost him his position or in any event lead to social disgrace, gives Adler a release, but subsequently sues to set it aside and recover on his claim. Decision?

5. Harris owned a farm that was worth about $600 an acre. By false representations of fact, Harris induced Pringle to buy the farm at $1,500 an acre. Shortly after taking possession of the farm, Pringle discovered oil under the land. Harris, on learning this, sues to have the sale set aside on the ground that it was voidable because of fraud. Decision?

6. On February 2, Phillips induced Mallor to purchase from her fifty shares of stock in the XYZ Corporation for $10,000, representing that the actual book value of each share was $200. A certificate for fifty shares was delivered to Mallor. On February 16, Mallor discovered that the February 2 book value was only $50 per share. Thereafter, Mallor sues Phillips. Decision?

7. Dorothy mistakenly accused Fred's son, Steven, of negligently burning down Dorothy's barn. Fred believed that his son was guilty of the wrong and that he, Fred, was personally liable for the damage, since Steven was only fifteen years old. Upon demand made by Dorothy, Fred paid Dorothy $2,500 for the damage to Dorothy's barn. After making this payment, Fred learned that his son had not caused the burning of Dorothy's barn and was in no way responsible for its burning. Fred then sued Dorothy to recover the $2,500 that he had paid her. Decision?

8. Jones, a farmer, found an odd-looking stone in his fields. He went to Smith, the town jeweler, and asked him what he thought it was. Smith said he did not know but thought it might be a ruby. Jones asked Smith what he would pay for it, and Smith said two hundred dollars, whereupon Jones sold it to Smith for $200. The stone turned out to be an uncut diamond worth $3,000. Jones brought an action against Smith to recover the stone. On trial, it was proved that Smith actually did not know the stone was a diamond when he bought it, but he thought it might be a ruby. Decision?

9. Decedent, Joan Jones, a bedridden, lonely woman, eighty-six years old, owned outright Greenacre, her ancestral estate. Biggers, her physician and friend, visited her weekly and was held in the highest regard by Joan. Joan was extremely fearful of pain and suffering and depended on Biggers to ease her anxiety and pain. Several months before her death, Joan deeded Greenacre to Biggers for $5,000. The fair market value of Greenacre at this time was $125,000. Joan was survived by two children and six grandchildren. Joan's children challenged the validity of the deed. Decision?

10. In February, Gardner, a schoolteacher with no experience in running a tavern, entered into a contract to purchase for $40,000 the Punjab Tavern from Meiling. The contract was contingent upon Gardner's obtaining a five-year lease for the tavern's premises and a liquor license from the state. Prior to the formation of the contract, Meiling had made no representations to Gardner concerning the gross income of the tavern. Approximately three months after the contract was signed, Gardner and Meiling met with an inspector from the Oregon Liquor Control Commission (OLCC) to discuss transfer of the liquor license. Meiling reported to the agent, in Gardner's presence, that the tavern's gross income figures for February, March, and April were $5,710, $4,918, and $5,009 respectively. The OLCC granted the required license, the transaction was closed, and Gardner took possession on June 10. After discovering that the tavern's income was very low and that the tavern had very few female patrons, Gardner contacted Meiling's bookkeeping service and learned that the actual gross income for those three months had been approximately $1,400 to $2,000. Gardner then sued for rescission of the contract. Decision?

11. Dorothy and John Huffschneider listed their house and lot for sale with C. B. Property. The asking price

was $165,000, and the owners told C. B. that the property contained 6.8 acres. Dean Olson, a salesman for C. B., advertised the property in local newspapers as consisting of six acres. James and Jean Holcomb signed a contract to purchase the property through Olson after first inspecting the property with Olson and being assured by Olson that the property was at least 6.6 acres. The Holcombs never asked for nor received a copy of the survey. In actuality, the lot was only 4.6 acres. The Holcombs now seek to rescind the contract. Decision?

12. Christine Boyd was designated as the beneficiary of a life insurance policy issued by Aetna Life Insurance Company on the life of Christine's husband, Jimmie Boyd. The policy insured against Jimmie's permanent total disability and also provided for a death benefit to be paid on Jimmie's death. Several years after the policy was issued, Jimmie and Christine separated. Jimmie began to travel extensively, and, therefore, Christine was unable to keep track of his whereabouts or his state of health. Jimmie, nevertheless continued to pay the premiums on the policy until Christine tried to cash in the policy to alleviate her financial distress. A loan had previously been made on the policy, however, leaving its cash surrender value, and thus the amount Christine received, at only $4.19. Shortly thereafter, Christine learned that Jimmie had been permanently and totally disabled before the surrender of the policy. Aetna also was unaware of Jimmie's condition, and Christine requested the surrendered policy be reinstated and that the disability payments be made. Jimmie died soon thereafter, and Christine then requested that Aetna pay the death benefit. Decision?

13. Beginning in 1971, Treasure Salvors and the state of Florida entered into a series of four annual contracts governing the salvage of the *Nuestra Senora de Atocha*. The *Atocha* is a Spanish galleon that sank in 1622, carrying a treasure now worth well over $250 million. Both parties had contracted under the impression that the seabed on which the *Atocha* lay was land owned by Florida. Treasure Salvors agreed to relinquish 25 percent of the items recovered in return for the right to salvage on state lands. In accordance with these contracts, Treasure Salvors delivered to Florida its share of the salvaged artifacts. In 1975 the United States Supreme Court held that the part of the continental shelf on which the *Atocha* was resting had *never* been owned by Florida. Treasure Salvors then brought suit to rescind the contracts and to recover the artifacts it had delivered to the state of Florida. The state appeals from a judgment in favor of Treasure Salvors. Decision?

14. Jane Francois married Victor H. Francois in 1984. At the time of the marriage, Victor was a fifty-year-old bachelor living with his elderly mother, and Jane was a thirty-year-old, twice-divorced mother of two. Victor had a

relatively secure financial portfolio; Jane, on the other hand, brought no money or property to the marriage.

The marriage deteriorated quickly over the next couple of years, with disputes centered on financial matters. During this period, Jane systematically gained a joint interest and took control of most of Victor's assets. Then, in September of 1987, Jane contracted Harold Monoson, an attorney, to draw up divorce papers. Victor was unaware of Jane's decision until he was taken to Monoson's office, where Monoson presented for Victor's signature a "Property Settlement and Separation Agreement." Monoson told Victor that he would need an attorney, but Jane vetoed Victor's choice. Monoson then asked another lawyer, Gregory Ball, to come into the office. Ball read the agreement and strenuously advised Victor not to sign it because it would commit him to financial suicide. The agreement transferred most of Victor's remaining assets to Jane. Victor, however, signed it because Jane and Monoson persuaded him that it was the only way that his marriage could be saved. In October of 1988, Jane informed Victor that she had sold most of his former property and that she was leaving him permanently. Victor brought this action to have the agreement set aside as a result of undue influence. Decision?

15. Iverson owned Iverson Motor Company, an enterprise engaged in the repair and sale of Oldsmobile, Rambler, and International Harvester Scout automobiles. Forty percent of the business's sales volume and net earnings came from the Oldsmobile franchise.

Whipp contracted to buy Iverson Motors, which Iverson said included the Oldsmobile franchise. After the sale, however, General Motors refused to transfer the franchise to Whipp. Whipp then returned the property to Iverson and brought this action seeking rescission of the contract. Decision?

16. On February 10, Mrs. Sunderhaus purchased a diamond ring from Perel & Lowenstein for $6,990. She was told by the company's salesman that the ring was worth its purchase price, and she also received at that time a written guarantee from the company attesting to the diamond's value, style, and trade-in value. When Mrs. Sunderhaus went to trade the ring for another, however, she was told by two jewelers that the ring was valued at $3,000 and $3,500, respectively. Mrs. Sunderhaus knew little about the value of diamonds and claims to have relied on the oral representation of the Perel & Lowenstein's salesman and the written representation as to the ring's value. She seeks rescission of the contract or damages in the amount of the sales price over the ring's value. Decision?

17. Division West Chinchilla Ranch advertised on television that a five-figure income could be earned by raising chinchillas with an investment of only $3.75 per animal per year and only thirty minutes of maintenance per

day. The minimum investment was $2,150 for one male and six female chinchillas. Division West represented to the plaintiffs that chinchilla ranching would be easy and that no experience was required to make ranching profitable. The plaintiffs, who had no experience raising chinchillas, each invested $2,150 or more to purchase Division's chinchillas and supplies. After three years without earning a profit, the plaintiffs sued Division West for fraud. Decision?

18. William Schmalz entered into an employment contract with Hardy Salt Company. The contract granted Schmalz six months' severance pay for involuntary termination but none for voluntary separation or termination for cause. Schmalz was asked to resign from his employment. He was informed that if he did not resign he would be fired for alleged misconduct. When Schmalz turned in his letter of resignation, he signed a release prohibiting him from suing his former employer as a consequence of his employment. Schmalz consulted an attorney before signing the release and upon signing it received $4,583.00 (one month's salary) in consideration. Schmalz now sues his former employer for the severance pay, claiming that he signed the release under duress. Decision?

19. Glen Haumont, who owned an equipment retail business in Broken Bow, Nebraska, owed the Security State Bank over $628,000 due to improper selling practices as well as business and inventory loans. Several times Glen tried to persuade his parents, Lee and Letha Haumont, to financially back his business debts; but each time they refused. Glen then told his parents that, according to his attorney and the bank, Glen could be prosecuted and sent to jail. Soon afterwards, David Schweitz, the president of the bank, drove out to the elder Haumonts' farm to convince them to sign as guarantors of Glen's debt. Both Schweitz and Glen stressed to the Haumonts that unless they agreed to guarantee his debt, Glen would go to jail. Letha asked that her attorney be allowed to read over the guaranty agreement, but Schweitz told her that he did not have time to wait and that she must decide right then whether Glen was to go to jail. As a result, the Haumonts signed the agreement, encumbering their previously debt-free family farm for over $628,000. At trial, the court set aside the guaranty agreement, holding that it was the result of duress. The bank appealed. Decision?

CHAPTER 12

Consideration

Consideration is the primary—but not the only—basis for the enforcement of promises in our legal system. **Consideration** is the inducement to make a promise enforceable. The doctrine of consideration ensures that promises are enforced only where the parties have exchanged something of value in the eye of the law. **Gratuitous** (gift) **promises**—those made without consideration—are not legally enforceable, except under certain circumstances, which are discussed later in the chapter.

Consideration, or that which is exchanged for a promise, is present only when the parties intend an exchange. The consideration exchanged for the promise may be an act, a forbearance to act, or a promise to do either of these. Thus, there are two basic elements to consideration: (1) legal sufficiency (something of value) and (2) bargained-for exchange. Both must be present to satisfy the requirement of consideration.

Consideration inducement to make a promise enforceable

Gratuitous promise *(gra·tu´·i·tous)* promise made without consideration

LEGAL SUFFICIENCY

To be **legally sufficient**, the consideration for the promise must be either a legal detriment to the promisee *or* a legal benefit to the promisor. In other words, the promisor must receive something of legal value or the promisee must give up something of legal value in return for the promise.

Legal detriment means (1) the doing of (or the undertaking to do) that which the promisee was under no prior legal obligation to do, *or* (2) the refraining from the doing of (or the undertaking to refrain from doing) that which he was previously under no legal obligation to refrain from doing. On the other hand, **legal benefit** means the obtaining by the promisor of that which he had no prior legal right to obtain. In most, if not all, cases where there is legal detriment to the promisee, there is also a legal benefit to the promisor. As the following case demonstrates, however, the presence of *either* is sufficient.

Legal sufficiency benefit to the promisor or detriment to the promisee

Legal detriment doing an act that one is not legally obligated to do or not doing an act that one has a legal right to do

Legal benefit obtaining something to which one had no legal right

---

COLLINS v. PARSONS COLLEGE Supreme Court of Iowa, 1973, 203 N.W..2d 594

FACTS Ben Collins was a full professor with tenure at Wisconsin State University in 1966. In March of 1966, Parsons College, in order to lure Dr. Collins from Wisconsin State, offered him a written contract promising him the rank of full professor with tenure and a salary of $25,000 for the 1966–67 academic year. The contract further provided that the College would increase his salary by $1,000 each year for the next five years. In return, Collins was to teach two trimesters of the academic year beginning in October 1966. In addition, the contract stipulated, by reference to the College's faculty bylaws, that tenured professors could only be dismissed for just cause and after written charges were filed with the Professional Problems Committee. The two parties signed the contract, and Collins resigned his position at Wisconsin State.

continued

In February of 1968, the College tendered a different contract to Collins to cover the following year. This contract reduced his salary to $15,000 with no provision for annual increments, but left his rank of full professor intact. It also required that Collins waive any and all rights or claims existing under any previous employment contracts with the College. Collins refused to sign this new contract and Parsons College soon notified him that he would not be employed the following year. The College did not give any grounds for his dismissal; nor did it file charges with the Professional Problems Committee. As a result, Collins was forced to take a teaching position at the University of North Dakota at a substantially reduced salary. He sued to recover the difference between the salary Parsons College promised him until 1971 and the amount he earned. The trial court ruled in favor of Parsons College, and Collins appealed.

DECISION Judgment reversed and remanded with directions.

OPINION The College's promise to employ Collins permanently (with tenure), at a specified salary with increments to 1971, must be supported by consideration from Collins to be enforceable. Collins did not promise to serve permanently or even until 1971 in exchange for the College's promise. Consideration, however, may consist of a detriment to the promisee (Collins), and benefit need not move to the promisor (the College). Parsons College promised Collins tenure, knowing that he would have to resign his permanent, tenured position at Wisconsin State. Therefore, Collins's surrender of his former position to accept the College's offer constituted binding consideration.

INTERPRETATION Collins provided consideration by resigning his permanent position at Wisconsin State (legal detriment to the promisee).

Adequacy

Legal sufficiency has nothing to do with **adequacy of consideration**. The items or actions that the parties agree to exchange do not need to have the same value. Rather, the law will regard the consideration as adequate if the parties have freely agreed to the exchange. The requirement of legally sufficient consideration is, therefore, *not* at all concerned with whether the bargain was good or bad or whether one party received disproportionately more or less than what he gave or promised in exchange. (Such facts, however, may be relevant to the availability of certain defenses—such as fraud, duress, or undue influence—or certain remedies—such as specific performance.) The requirement of legally sufficient consideration is simply (1) that the parties have agreed to an exchange and (2) that, with respect to each party, the subject matter exchanged, or promised in exchange, either imposed a legal detriment on the promisee or conferred a legal benefit on the promisor. If the purported consideration is clearly without value, however, such that the transaction is a sham, many courts would hold that consideration is lacking.

Adequacy of consideration not required where parties have freely agreed to the exchange

Unilateral Contracts

In a unilateral contract, a promise is exchanged for a completed act or a forbearance to act. Since only one promise exists, one party, the person making the promise, is the **promisor** and the other party, the person receiving the promise, is the **promisee**. For example, A promises to pay B $2,000 if B paints A's house. B paints A's house.

Promisor person making a promise

Promisee person receiving a promise

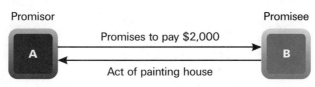

Promisor   Promisee

A → Promises to pay $2,000 → B
A ← Act of painting house ← B

A's promise is binding only if it is supported by consideration consisting of either a legal detriment to B, the promisee, or a legal benefit to A, the promisor. B's painting the house is a legal detriment to B, the promisee, because she was under no prior legal duty to paint A's house. Also, B's painting of A's house is a legal benefit to A, the promisor, because A had no prior legal right to have his house painted by B.

A unilateral contract may also consist of a promise exchanged for a forbearance. To illustrate, A negligently injures B, for which B may recover damages in a tort action. A promises B $5,000 if B forbears from bringing suit. B accepts by not suing.

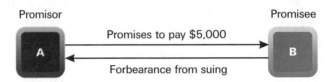

A's promise to pay B $5,000 is binding because it is supported by consideration; B, the promisee, has incurred a legal detriment by refraining from bringing suit, which he was under no prior legal obligation to refrain from doing. A, the promisor, has received a legal benefit because she had no prior legal right to B's forbearance from bringing suit.

Bilateral Contracts

In a bilateral contract there is an exchange of promises. Thus, each party is *both* a promisor and a promisee. For example, if A promises to purchase an automobile from B for $20,000 and B promises to sell the automobile to A for $20,000, the following relationship exists:

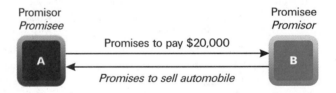

A as promisor: A's promise to pay B $20,000 is binding if that promise is supported by legal consideration, which may consist of either a legal detriment to B, the *promisee*, or a legal benefit to A, the *promisor*. B's promise to sell A the automobile is a legal detriment to B because he was under no prior legal duty to sell the automobile to A. Moreover, B's promise is also a legal benefit to A because A had no prior legal right to that automobile. Consequently, A's promise to pay $20,000 to B is supported by consideration and is enforceable.

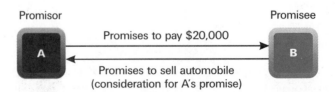

B as promisor: For **B's promise** to sell the automobile to A to be binding, it likewise must be supported by consideration, which may be either a legal detriment to A, the *promisee*, or a legal benefit to B, the *promisor*. A's promise to pay B $20,000 is a legal detriment to A because he was under no prior legal duty to pay $20,000 to B. At the same time, A's promise is also a legal benefit to B because B had no prior legal right to the $20,000. Thus, B's promise to sell the automobile **is** supported by consideration and is enforceable.

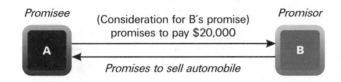

To summarize, for *A's promise* to B to be binding, it must be supported by legally sufficient consideration, which requires that the promise A receives from B in exchange either provides a legal benefit to *A* (*the promisor*) or constitutes a legal detriment to *B* (*the promisee*). B's return promise to A must also be supported by consideration. Thus, in a bilateral contract each promise is the consideration for the other, a relationship that has been referred to as **mutuality of obligation**. A general consequence of mutuality of obligation is that each promisor in a bilateral contract must be bound or neither is bound. See the Ethical Dilemma on the following page for a situation dealing with the disputed enforceability of a promise.

Illusory Promises

Words of promise that make the performance of the purported promisor entirely optional do not constitute a promise at all. Consequently, they cannot serve as consideration. In this section, we will distinguish such illusory promises from promises that do impose obligations of performance upon the promisor and thus can be legally sufficient consideration.

An **illusory promise** is a statement that is in the form of a promise but imposes no obligation upon the maker of the statement. An illusory promise is not consideration for a return promise. Thus, a statement committing the promisor to purchase such quantity of goods as he may "desire" or "want" or "wish to buy" is an illusory promise because its performance is entirely optional. For example, if Exxon offers to sell to Gasco as many barrels of oil as Gasco shall choose at $40 per barrel, there is no contract for lack of consideration. An offer containing such a promise, although accepted by the offeree, does not create a contract because the promise is illusory—Gasco's performance is entirely optional and no constraint is placed on its freedom. It is not bound to do anything, nor can Exxon reasonably expect it to do anything. Thus, Gasco, by its promise, suffers no legal detriment and confers no legal benefit.

Illusory promise
(il·lu´·so·ry) promise imposing no obligation on the promisor

Output and Requirements Contracts The agreement of a seller to sell her entire production to a particular purchaser is called an **output contract**. It gives the seller an assured market for her product. Conversely, a purchaser's agreement to purchase from a particular seller all the materials of a particular kind that the purchaser needs is called a **requirements contract**. It assures the buyer of a ready source of inventory or supplies. These contracts are *not* illusory. The buyer under a requirements contract does not promise to buy as much as she

Output contract
agreement to sell all of one's production

Requirements contract
agreement to buy all of one's needs from a particular seller

ETHICAL DILEMMA   Should a Spouse's Promise Be Legally Binding?

FACTS Joan Kantor is a social worker for the employees of Surf & Co., a towel manufacturer. Stan Koronetsky, a Surf employee, has confided the following problems to Kantor.

Koronetsky and his wife, Paula, have been married for ten years. Koronetsky states that three years ago his wife was unfaithful and Koronetsky began a divorce proceeding. When Paula Koronetsky promised to refrain from further infidelity and to attend marital counseling sessions, Koronetsky agreed to stop the divorce proceeding. However, although Stan dropped the divorce proceeding, his wife never attended counseling.

Koronetsky is also upset because he and his wife had agreed that she would attend medical school while he worked to support her. In exchange for his promise to put her through medical school, Paula promised that she would support him while he obtained his M.B.A. degree. But after Paula became a doctor, she refused to support him; consequently, Stan never got his master's degree.

Social, Policy, and Ethical Considerations

1. What should Joan Kantor do in this situation? What is the scope of her counseling responsibilities?
2. Should agreements between married parties be enforced in a court of law? If so, what types of agreements should be enforceable?
3. What are the individual interests at stake in this situation? Is it reasonable to assume that spouses make many private agreements, and that generally these agreements are made without the intention of their being legally binding?

---

desires to buy, but rather to buy as much as she *needs*. Similarly, under an output contract, the seller promises to sell to the buyer the seller's entire production, not merely as much as the seller desires.

Furthermore, the Code imposes a good faith limitation upon the quantity to be sold or purchased under an output or requirements contract. Thus, this type of contract involves such actual output or requirements as may occur in good faith, except that no quantity unreasonably disproportionate to any stated estimate or, in the absence of a stated estimate, to any normal prior output or requirements may be tendered or demanded. Therefore, after contracting to sell to Adler, Inc., its entire output, Benevito Company cannot increase its production from one eight-hour shift per day to three eight-hour shifts per day.

Exclusive dealing sole right to sell goods in a defined market

Exclusive Dealing Contracts An **exclusive dealing** agreement is a contract in which a manufacturer of goods grants to a distributor an exclusive right to sell its products in a designated market. Unless otherwise agreed, an implied obligation is imposed on the manufacturer to use its best efforts to supply the goods and on the distributor to use her best efforts to promote their sale. These implied obligations are sufficient consideration to bind both parties to the exclusive dealing contract.

Conditional promise obligations are contingent upon a stated event

Conditional Promises A **conditional promise** is a promise the performance of which depends upon the happening or nonhappening of an event not certain to occur (the condition). A conditional promise is sufficient consideration *unless* the promisor knows at the time of making the promise that the condition cannot occur.

Thus, if Joanne offers to pay Barry $8,000 for Barry's automobile, provided that Joanne receives such amount as an inheritance from the estate of her deceased uncle, and Barry accepts the offer, the duty of Joanne to pay $8,000 to Barry is *conditioned* on her receiving $8,000 from her deceased uncle's estate. The consideration moving from Barry to Joanne is the transfer of title to the automobile. The consideration moving from Joanne to Barry is the promise of $8,000 subject to the condition.

Preexisting Obligations

The law does not regard the performance of, or the promise to perform, a preexisting legal duty, public or private, as either a legal detriment or a legal benefit. A public duty does not arise out of a contract; rather, it is imposed on members of society by force of the common law or by statute. Illustrations, as found in the law of torts, include the duty not to commit assault, battery, false imprisonment, or defamation. The criminal law also imposes many public duties. Thus, if Norton promises to pay Holmes, the village ruffian, $100 not to injure him, Norton's promise is unenforceable because both tort and criminal law impose a preexisting public obligation on Holmes to refrain from such abuse.

Public officials, such as the mayor of a city, members of a city council, police, and firefighters, are under a preexisting obligation to perform their duties by virtue of their public office. See *Denney v. Reppert.*

The performance of, or the promise to perform, a ***preexisting contractual duty***, a duty the terms of which are neither doubtful nor the subject of honest dispute, is also legally insufficient consideration because the doing of what one is legally bound to do is neither a detriment to a promisee nor a benefit to the promisor. For example, if Anita employs Ben for one year at a salary of $1,000 per month, and at the end of six months promises Ben that in addition to the salary she will pay Ben $3,000 if Ben remains on the job for the remainder of the period originally agreed on, Anita's promise is not binding for lack of legally sufficient consideration. However, if Ben's duties were by agreement changed in nature or amount, Anita's promise would be binding because Ben's new duties are a legal detriment to Ben and a legal benefit to Anita.

The following case deals with both preexisting public and contractual obligations.

Preexisting public obligations public duties such as those imposed by tort or criminal law are neither a legal detriment nor a legal benefit

Preexisting contractual obligation performance of a preexisting contractual duty is not consideration

---

DENNEY v. REPPERT Court of Appeals of Kentucky, 1968, 432 S.W.2d 647

FACTS In June, three armed men entered and robbed the First State Bank of Eubank, Kentucky, of $30,000. Acting on information supplied by four employees of the bank, Denney, Buis, McCollum, and Snyder, three law enforcement officials apprehended the robbers. Two of the arresting officers, Godby and Simms, were state policemen, and the third, Reppert, was a deputy sheriff in a neighboring county. All seven claimed the reward for the apprehension and conviction of the bank robbers. The trial court held that only Reppert was entitled to the reward, and Denney appealed.

DECISION Judgment affirmed.

OPINION In general, when a reward is offered to the general public for the performance of some specified act, the reward may be claimed by the person who performs that act unless that person is an agent, employee, or public official acting within the scope of his employment or official duties. For this reason, the bank employees cannot recover. At the time of the robbery, they were under a duty to protect the bank's resources and to safeguard the institution furnishing them employment. Thus, in assisting the police officers in apprehending the bank robbers, the bank employees were merely doing their duty and, therefore, are not entitled to share in the reward.

Similarly, the state policemen, Godby and Simms, were exercising their duty as police officers in arresting the bank robbers and, thus, are not entitled to share in the reward. Reppert, on the other hand, was out of his jurisdiction at the time and, thus, was under no legal duty to arrest the bank robbers.

INTERPRETATION The law does not regard the performance of a preexisting duty as either a legal detriment or a legal benefit.

Modification of a Preexisting Contract A modification of a contract occurs when the parties to the contract mutually agree to change one or more of its terms. Under the common law, as shown in the following case, a modification of an existing contract must be supported by mutual consideration to be enforceable. In

Modification of a preexisting contract
under the common law a modification of a preexisting contract must be supported by mutual consideration; under the Code a contract can be modified without new consideration

other words, the modification must be supported by some new consideration beyond that which is already owing (thus, there must be a separate and distinct modification contract). For example, Diane and Fred agree that Diane shall put in a gravel driveway for Fred at a cost of $2,000. Subsequently, Fred agrees to pay an additional $3,000 if Diane will blacktop the driveway. Since Diane was not bound by the original contract to provide blacktop, she would incur a legal detriment in doing so and is therefore entitled to the additional $3,000. Similarly, consideration may consist of the promisee's refraining from exercising a legal right.

GROSS v. DIEHL SPECIALTIES INTERNATIONAL, INC. Missouri Court of Appeals, 1989, 776 S.W.2d 879

FACTS Dairy Specialties, Inc. was a company engaged in the business of formulating ingredients to produce nondairy products for use by customers allergic to cow's milk. Harry Schenberg, the owner of the company, hired the plaintiff, Gross, to help reformulate the product to withstand pasteurization. Gross successfully reformulated the product. On August 24, 1977, Gross and Dairy entered into a contract employing Gross for fifteen years as general manager of the company. Compensation was set at $14,400 annually plus cost-of-living increases. In addition, when 10 percent of Dairy's gross profits exceeded Gross's annual salary, he would receive additional compensation equal to the difference between his salary and 10 percent of the gross profits for such year. He also was to receive a royalty of 1 percent of the selling price for the use of his formulae. The royalty would increase to 2 percent after the term of the agreement. During the term of the agreement, Gross and Dairy would own the formulae equally; afterward, ownership would revert to Gross. Dairy had exclusive rights to use the formulae during the term and a nonexclusive right of use after the term.

In 1982, Schenberg sold Dairy to the Diehl family, and the company became Diehl Specialties International, Inc. Prior to the sale, Diehl insisted that unless a new contract between Gross and Dairy were executed, Diehl would reduce the amount to be paid for Dairy. Accordingly, on August 24, 1982, the parties executed a new contract. The new contract reduced the contract term to ten years, which provided the same expiration date as the original contract, and reinstated Gross's original base salary of $14,400, thereby eliminating accrued cost-of-living increases. It also provided that Diehl owned Gross's formulae exclusively both during and after the term of the contract. The new contract provided for no royalties to be paid after its termination. No other changes were made in the agreement. Gross received no compensation for executing the new contract, he was not a party to the sale of the company, and he received nothing tangible from the sale. After the sale, Gross was given additional duties but no additional compensation. Diehl Specialties terminated his

employment in October 1984, and Gross sued Diehl Specialties for breach of contract. The trial court held that the second contract was the operative one, and Gross appealed.

DECISION Trial court's decision that the second contract was operative reversed and case remanded for further proceedings.

OPINION A contract modification constitutes the making of a new contract, and such new contract must be supported by consideration. Where a contract has not been fully performed at the time of the new agreement, the substitution of a new provision which modifies the obligations on both sides is sufficient consideration for the new contract. While consideration may consist of either a detriment to the promisee or a benefit to the promisor, a promise to carry out an already existing contractual duty does not constitute consideration. Under the 1982 contract, Diehl Specialties assumed no detriment it did not already have. The term of the contract expired on the same date under both contracts, and Diehl Specialties assumed no greater obligations than it already had. Gross, on the other hand, received less than he had had under the original contract. In exchange for nothing, Diehl acquired exclusive ownership of the formulae during and after the agreement, eliminated the obligation to pay royalties after the agreement terminated, converted its right to non-exclusive use after termination into a right of exclusive use and control, and achieved a reduction in Gross's base salary.

Diehl asserts that consideration flowed to Gross because the purchase of Dairy might not have occurred without the agreement, and, consequently, the purchase of Dairy provided Gross with continued employment. There is no evidence to support this. Gross had continued employment under the 1977 contract. We have difficulty converting Schenberg's windfall benefit of receiving more from his sale because of the new contract into a benefit to Gross.

INTERPRETATION A modification of an existing contract must be supported by consideration to be enforceable.

The Code has modified the common law rule for contract modification by providing that the parties can effectively modify a contract for the sale of goods without new consideration, provided they both intend to modify the contract and act in good faith. Moreover, the Restatement has moved toward this position by providing that a modification of an executory contract is binding if it is fair and equitable in the light of surrounding facts that the parties had not anticipated when the contract was made. See Figure 12–1.

Substituted Contracts A **substituted contract** results when the parties to a contract mutually agree to rescind their original contract and enter into a new one. This situation actually involves three separate contracts: the original contract, the contract of rescission, and the substitute contract. Substituted contracts are perfectly valid, allowing the parties to effectively discharge the original contract and to impose obligations under the new one. The rescission is binding in that, as long as each party still had rights under the original contract, each has, by giving up those rights, provided consideration to the other.

> **Substituted contract**
> parties rescind their original contract and enter into a new one

Settlement of an Undisputed Debt An **undisputed debt** is an obligation that is not contested as to its existence or its amount. Under the common law, the payment of a lesser sum of money than is owed in consideration of a promise to discharge a fully matured, undisputed debt is legally insufficient to support

> **Undisputed debt**
> obligation whose existence and amount are not contested

FIGURE 12–1 Modification of a Preexisting Contract

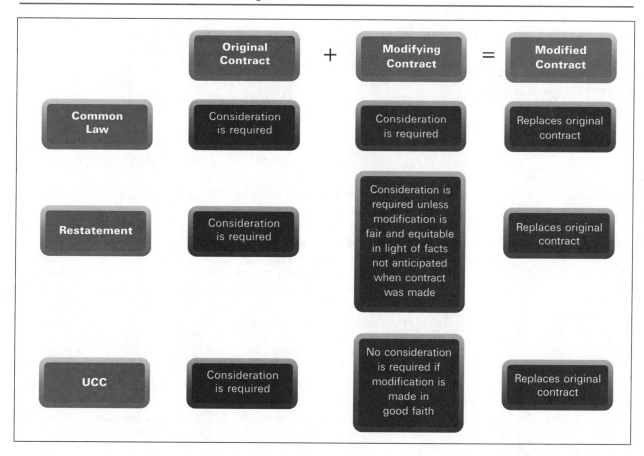

Settlement of an undisputed debt payment of a lesser sum of money to discharge an undisputed debt does not constitute legally sufficient consideration

the promise of discharge. To illustrate, assume that Barbara owes Arnold $100, and in consideration of Barbara's paying him $50, Arnold agrees to discharge the debt. In a subsequent suit by Arnold against Barbara to recover the remaining $50, at common law Arnold is entitled to a judgment for $50 on the ground that Arnold's promise of discharge is not binding because Barbara's payment of $50 was no legal detriment to the promisee, Barbara, as she was under a **preexisting legal obligation** to pay that much and more. Consequently, the consideration for Arnold's promise of discharge was legally insufficient, and Arnold is not bound by his promise. If, however, Arnold had accepted from Barbara any new or different consideration, such as the sum of $40 and a fountain pen worth $10 or less, or even the fountain pen with no payment of money, in full satisfaction of the $100 debt, the consideration moving from Barbara would be legally sufficient because Barbara was under no legal obligation to give a fountain pen to Arnold. In this example, consideration would also exist if Arnold had agreed to accept $50 *before* the debt became due, in full satisfaction of the debt. Barbara was under no legal obligation to pay any of the debt before its due date. Consequently, Barbara's early payment would constitute a legal detriment to Barbara as well as a legal benefit to Arnold. The common law is not concerned with the amount of the discount, because that is simply a question of adequacy. Likewise, Barbara's payment of a lesser amount on the due date at an agreed-upon different place of payment would be legally sufficient consideration. The Restatement, however, requires that the new consideration "differ[s] from what was required by the duty in a way which reflects more than a pretense of bargain."

Disputed debt obligation whose existence or amount is contested

Settlement of a disputed debt payment of a lesser sum of money to discharge a disputed debt is legally sufficient consideration

Settlement of a Disputed Debt A **disputed debt** is an obligation whose existence or amount is contested. A promise to settle a validly disputed claim in exchange for an agreed payment or other performance is supported by consideration. Where the dispute is based on contentions without merit or not made in good faith, the debtor's surrender of such contentions is not a legal detriment to the claimant. The Restatement adopts a different position by providing that the settlement of a claim that proves invalid is consideration if at the time of the settlement (1) the claimant honestly believed that the claim was valid *or* (2) the claim was in fact doubtful because of uncertainty as to the facts or the law.

For example, where a person has requested professional services from an accountant or a lawyer and no agreement has been made about the amount of the fee to be charged, the client has a legal obligation to pay the reasonable value of the services performed. Because no definite amount was agreed on, the client's obligation is uncertain. When the accountant or lawyer sends the client a bill for her services, even though the amount stated in the bill is her estimate of the reasonable value of the services, the debt does not become undisputed until and unless the client agrees to pay the amount of the bill. If the client honestly disputes the amount that is owing and offers in full settlement an amount less than the bill, acceptance of the lesser amount by the accountant or lawyer discharges the debt. Thus, if Andy sends to Bess, an accountant, a check for $120 in full payment of his debt to Bess for services rendered, which services Andy considered worthless but for which Bess billed Andy $600, Bess's acceptance (cashing) of the check releases Andy from any further liability. Andy has given up his right to dispute the billing further, and Bess has forfeited her right to further collection. Thus, there is mutuality of consideration.

MATHIS v. ST. ALEXIS HOSPITAL Court of Appeals of Ohio, 1994, 99 Ohio App.3d 159, 650 N.E.2d 141

FACTS Rodney and Donna Mathis (Mathis) filed a wrongful death action against St. Alexis Hospital and several physicians, arising out of the death of their mother, Mary Mathis. Several weeks before trial, an expert consulted by Mathis notified the trial court and Mathis's counsel that, in his opinion, Mary Mathis's death was not proximately caused by the negligence of the physicians. Shortly thereafter, Mathis voluntarily dismissed the wrongful death action. Mathis and St. Alexis entered into a covenant-not-to-sue in which Mathis agreed not to pursue any claims against St. Alexis or its employees in terms of the medical care of Mary Mathis. St. Alexis, in return, agreed not to seek sanctions, including attorney fees and costs incurred in defense of the previously dismissed wrongful death action. Subsequently, Mathis filed a second wrongful death action against St. Alexis Hospital, among others. Mathis asked the court to rescind the covenant-not-to-sue, arguing that since St. Alexis was not entitled to sanctions in connection with the first wrongful death action, there was no consideration for the covenant-not-to-sue. The trial court granted summary judgment for St. Alexis. Mathis appeals.

DECISION Judgment affirmed.

OPINION A promise to forbear pursuit of a legal claim can be sufficient consideration to support a contract when the promisor has a good faith belief in the validity of the claim. Mathis argues that any sanctions award should have been against Mathis's attorney. However, under the rules of civil procedure, an award of reasonable attorney's fees may be made against a party, his attorney, or both. Therefore, sanctions could have been awarded against Mathis.

Mathis also argues that St. Alexis had not shown that Mathis engaged in any frivolous conduct. However, the standard for evaluating the validity of a foregone claim is a subjective one. St. Alexis sufficiently asserted a good faith belief in the validity of its sanctions claims and asserted that its belief in the validity of its sanctions claim was based on Mathis's complete failure to produce any expert testimony on the issue of proximate cause. Since the only expert testimony presented on the issue indicated that St. Alexis's actions did not proximately cause Mary Mathis's death, St. Alexis's belief in the validity of its sanctions claim was reasonable. Thus, foregoing the claim would constitute sufficient consideration for the covenant-not-to-sue.

INTERPRETATION A promise to settle a validly disputed claim in exchange for an agreed payment or other performance is supported by consideration.

BARGAINED-FOR EXCHANGE

The central idea behind consideration is that the parties have intentionally entered into a **bargained-for exchange** with each other and have each given to the other something in a mutually agreed-upon exchange for his or her promise or performance. Thus, a promise to give someone a birthday present is without consideration, because the promisor received nothing in exchange for her promise of a present.

Bargained-for exchange mutually agreed-upon exchange

Past Consideration

Consideration, as previously defined, is the inducement for a promise or performance. The element of exchange is absent where a promise is given for an act already done. Therefore, unbargained-for past events are not consideration, despite their designation as **past consideration**. A promise made on account of something that the promisee has already done is not enforceable. For example, Diana installs Tom's complex new car stereo and speakers. Tom subsequently promises to reimburse Diana for her expenses, but his promise is not binding because there is no bargained-for exchange.

Past consideration unbargained-for past events

Third Parties

Consideration to support a promise may be given to a person other than the promisor if the promisor bargains for that exchange. For example, A promises to pay B $15 if B delivers a specified book to C.

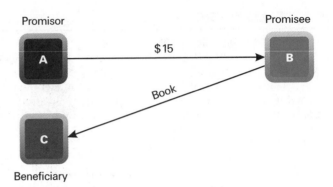

A's promise is binding because B incurred a legal detriment by delivering the book to C, as B was under no prior legal obligation to do so, and A had no prior legal right to have the book given to C. A and B have bargained for A to pay B $15 in return for B's delivering to C the book. A's promise to pay $15 is also consideration for B's promise to give C the book.

Conversely, consideration may be given by some person other than the promisee. For example, A promises to pay B $25 in return for D's promise to give A a radio. A's promise to pay $25 to B is consideration for D's promise to give A a radio and *vice versa*.

CONTRACTS WITHOUT CONSIDERATION

Certain transactions are enforceable even though they are not supported by consideration.

Promises to Perform Prior Unenforceable Obligations

In certain circumstances the courts will enforce new promises to perform an obligation that originally was not enforceable or that has become unenforceable by operation of law. These situations include promises to pay debts barred by the statute of limitations, debts discharged in bankruptcy, and voidable obligations. In addition, some courts will enforce promises to pay moral obligations.

Statute of limitation time period within which a lawsuit must be initiated

Promise to Pay Debt Barred by the Statute of Limitations Every state has a **statute of limitations** stating that legal actions to enforce a debt must be brought within a prescribed period of time after the rights to bring the action arose. Actions not begun within the specified period—such periods vary among the states and also with the nature of the legal action—will be dismissed.

Promise to pay debt barred by the statute of limitations a new promise by the debtor to pay the debt renews the running of the statute of limitations for a second statutory period

An exception to the past consideration rule extends to promises to pay all or part of a contractual or quasi-contractual debt barred by the statute of limitations. The new promise is binding according to its terms, without consideration, for a second statutory period. Any recovery under the new promise is limited to the terms contained in the new promise. Most states require that new promises falling under this rule, except those partially paid, must be in writing to be enforceable.

Promise to pay debt discharged in bankruptcy may be enforceable without consideration

Promise to Pay Debt Discharged in Bankruptcy A promise to pay a debt that has been discharged in bankruptcy is also enforceable without consideration. The Bankruptcy Code, however, imposes a number of requirements that must be met before such a promise may be enforced. These requirements are discussed in Chapter 39.

Voidable Promises Another promise that is enforceable without new consideration is a new promise to perform a voidable obligation that has not previously been avoided. The power of avoidance may be based on lack of capacity, fraud, misrepresentation, duress, undue influence, or mistake. For instance, a promise to perform an antecedent obligation made by a minor upon reaching the age of majority is enforceable without new consideration. To be enforceable, the promise itself must not be voidable. For example, if the new promise is made without knowledge of the original fraud or by a minor before reaching the age of majority, then the new promise is not enforceable.

Voidable promises a new promise to perform a voidable obligation that has not been previously avoided is enforceable

Moral Obligation Under the common law and in most states, a promise made in order to satisfy a preexisting moral obligation is made for past consideration and therefore is unenforceable for lack of consideration. Instances involving such moral obligations include promises to pay another for board and lodging the other previously furnished to one's needy relative and promises to pay debts owed by a relative.

Moral obligation a promise made to satisfy a preexisting moral obligation is generally unenforceable for lack of consideration

The Restatement and a minority of states recognize moral obligations as consideration. The Restatement provides that a promise made for "a benefit previously received by the promisor from the promisee is binding to the extent necessary to prevent injustice." For instance, under the Restatement, Tim's subsequent promise to Donna to reimburse her for expenses she incurred in rendering emergency services to Tim's son is binding even though it is not supported by new consideration.

Promissory Estoppel

As discussed in Chapter 10, in certain circumstances where there has been detrimental reliance, the courts enforce noncontractual promises under the doctrine of promissory estoppel. When applicable, the doctrine makes gratuitous promises enforceable to the extent necessary to avoid injustice. The doctrine applies when a promise that the promisor should reasonably expect to induce detrimental reliance does induce such action or forbearance.

Promissory estoppel doctrine that prohibits a party from denying his promise when the promisee takes action or forbearance to his detriment reasonably based upon the promise

Promissory estoppel does not mean that a promise given without consideration is binding simply because it is followed by a change of position on the part of the promisee. Such a change of position in justifiable reliance on the promise creates liability if injustice can be avoided only by the enforcement of the promise. For example, Ann promises Larry not to foreclose for a period of six months on a mortgage Ann owns on Larry's land. Larry then changes his position by spending $100,000 to construct a building on the land. Ann's promise not to foreclose is binding on her under the doctrine of promissory estoppel.

FEINBERG v. PFEIFFER CO. St. Louis Court of Appeals, Missouri, 1959, 322 S.W.2d 163

FACTS Anna Feinberg began working for the Pfeiffer Company in 1910 at age seventeen. By 1947, she had attained the position of bookkeeper, office manager, and assistant treasurer. In appreciation for her skill, dedication, and long years of service, the Pfeiffer board of directors resolved to increase Feinberg's monthly salary to $400 and to create for her a retirement plan. The plan allowed that Feinberg would be given the privilege of retiring from active duty at any time she chose and that she would receive retirement pay of $200 per month, although the Board expressed the hope that Feinberg would continue to serve the company for many years. Feinberg, however, chose to retire two years later, in 1949. The Pfeiffer Company paid Feinberg her retirement pay until 1956. The company thereafter discontinued payments, alleging that no contract had been made by the board of directors, since Feinberg had paid no consideration, and that the resolution was merely a promise to make a gift. Feinberg sued.

DECISION Judgment for Feinberg.

continued

OPINION The law is clear that past services performed do not constitute valid consideration for the formation of a contract. Here, promises made in appreciation of Feinberg's many years of work do not render those promises enforceable against the company. However, a promise that the promisor should reasonably expect to induce action or forbearance of a definite and substantial character on the part of the promisee and that does induce such action or forbearance is binding if injustice can be avoided only by enforcement of the promise. This doctrine is called promissory estoppel. Feinberg reasonably relied on the promise of $200 per-month retirement pay, and thereby abandoned her opportunity to continue in gainful employment. At the time payments were discontinued, Feinberg was sixty-three years old. Her chance of finding satisfactory employment, much less a position comparable to the one she gave up when she retired, is virtually nonexistent. Feinberg's reasonable and detrimental reliance upon the company's promise has created an enforceable contract.

INTERPRETATION A court may enforce noncontractual promises under the doctrine of promissory estoppel when failure to do so will result in injustice.

The most common application of the doctrine of promissory estoppel is to charitable subscriptions. Numerous churches, memorials, college buildings, stadiums, hospitals, and other structures used for religious, educational, or charitable purposes have been built with the assistance of contributions made through fulfillment of pledges or promises to contribute to particular worthwhile causes. Although the pledgor regards herself as making a gift for a charitable purpose and gift promises tend not to be enforceable, the courts have generally enforced charitable subscription promises. Although various reasons and theories have been advanced in support of liability, the one most commonly accepted is that the subscription has induced a change of position by the promisee (the church, school, or charitable organization) in reliance on the promise. The Restatement, moreover, has relaxed the reliance requirement for charitable subscriptions so that actual reliance need not be shown; the probability of reliance is sufficient.

Contracts Under Seal

Contracts under seal
where still recognized, the seal acts as a substitute for consideration

Under the common law, when a person desired to bind himself by bond, deed, or solemn promise, he executed his promise under seal. He did not have to sign the document; rather, his delivery of a document to which he had affixed his seal was sufficient. No consideration for his promise was necessary. In some states a promise under seal is still binding without consideration.

Nevertheless, most states have abolished by statute the distinction between contracts under seal and written unsealed contracts. In these states, the seal is no longer recognized as a substitute for consideration. The Code also has adopted this position, specifically eliminating the use of seals in contracts for the sale of goods.

Promises Made Enforceable by Statute

Some gratuitous promises that would otherwise be unenforceable have been made binding by statute. Most significant among these are (1) contract modifications, (2) renunciations, and (3) irrevocable offers.

Contract Modifications As mentioned previously, the Uniform Commercial Code has abandoned the common law rule requiring that a modification of an existing contract be supported by consideration in order to be valid. Instead, the Code provides that a contract for the sale of goods can be effectively modified without new consideration, provided the modification is made in good faith.

Renunciation Under the Code, any claim or right arising out of an alleged breach of contract can be discharged in whole or in part without consideration by a written waiver or renunciation signed and delivered by the aggrieved party.

Firm Offers Under the Code, a firm offer, a written offer signed by a merchant offeror to buy or sell goods, is not revocable for lack of consideration during the time within which it is stated to be open, not to exceed three months, or, if no time is stated, for a reasonable time. For a summary of consideration, see Figure 12–2.

FIGURE 12–2 Consideration

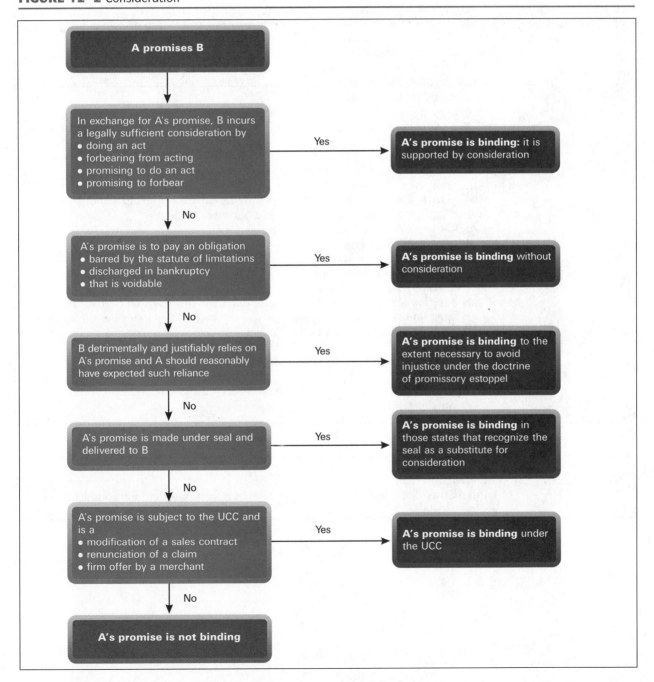

CHAPTER SUMMARY

Consideration	**Definition** the inducement to enter into a contract **Elements** legal sufficiency and bargained-for exchange

Legal Sufficiency of Consideration	**Definition** consists of either a benefit to the promisor or a detriment to the promisee ■ *Legal Benefit* obtaining something to which one had no prior legal right ■ *Legal Detriment* doing an act one is not legally obligated to do or not doing an act that one has a legal right to do **Adequacy of Consideration** not required where the parties have freely agreed to the exchange **Illusory Promise** promise that imposes no obligation on the promisor; the following promises are *not* illusory ■ *Output Contract* agreement to sell all of one's production to a single buyer ■ *Requirements Contract* agreement to buy all of one's needs from a single producer ■ *Exclusive Dealing Contract* grant to a franchisee or licensee by a manufacturer of the sole right to sell goods in a defined market ■ *Conditional Contract* one where the obligations are contingent upon the occurrence of a stated event **Preexisting Public Obligations** public duties such as those imposed by tort or criminal law are neither a legal detriment nor a legal benefit **Preexisting Contractual Obligation** performance of a preexisting contractual duty is not consideration ■ *Modification of a Preexisting Contract* under the common law a modification of a preexisting contract must be supported by mutual consideration; under the Code a contract can be modified without new consideration ■ *Substituted Contracts* the parties agree to rescind their original contract and to enter into a new one; rescission and new contract are supported by consideration ■ *Settlement of an Undisputed Debt* payment of a lesser sum of money to discharge an undisputed debt (one whose existence and amount are not contested) does not constitute legally sufficient consideration ■ *Settlement of a Disputed Debt* payment of a lesser sum of money to discharge a disputed debt (one whose existence or amount is contested) is legally sufficient consideration

Bargained-For Exchange	**Definition** a mutually agreed-upon exchange **Past Consideration** an act done before the contract is made is not consideration

Contracts without Consideration	**Promises to Perform Prior Unenforceable Obligations** ■ *Promise to Pay Debt Barred by the Statute of Limitations* a new promise by the debtor to pay the debt renews the running of the statute of limitations for a second statutory period ■ *Promise to Pay Debt Discharged in Bankruptcy* may be enforceable without consideration ■ *Voidable Promises* a new promise to perform a voidable obligation that has not been previously avoided is enforceable ■ *Moral Obligation* a promise made to satisfy a preexisting moral obligation is generally unenforceable for lack of consideration **Promissory Estoppel** doctrine that prohibits a party from denying his promise when the promisee takes action or forbearance to his detriment reasonably based upon the promise **Contracts under Seal** where still recognized, the seal acts as a substitute for consideration **Promises Made Enforceable by Statute** some gratuitous promises have been made enforceable by statute; the Code makes enforceable (1) contract modification, (2) renunciations, and (3) firm offers

QUESTIONS

1. Define consideration and what is meant by legal sufficiency.
2. Discuss illusory promises, output contracts, requirements contracts, exclusive dealing contracts, and conditional contracts.
3. Explain whether preexisting public and contractual obligations satisfy the legal requirement of consideration.
4. Explain the concept of bargained-for exchange. Is this element present with past consideration or third-party beneficiaries? Explain.
5. Identify and discuss those contracts that are enforceable even though they are not supported by consideration.

Internet Question. Find several sample contracts and determine what consideration is given by the parties.

PROBLEMS

1. In consideration of $800 paid to him by Joyce, Hill gave Joyce a written option to purchase his house for $80,000 on or before April 1. Prior to April 1, Hill verbally agreed to extend the option until July 1. On May 18, Hill, known to Joyce, sold the house to Gray, who was ignorant of the unrecorded option. Joyce brought suit against Hill. Decision?

2. (a) Ann owed $500 to Barry for services Barry rendered to Ann. The debt was due June 30, 1988. In March 1989, the debt was still unpaid. Barry was in urgent need of ready cash and told Ann that if she would pay $150 on the debt at once, Barry would release her from the balance. Ann paid $150 and stated to Barry that all claims had been paid in full. In August 1989, Barry demanded the unpaid balance and subsequently sued Ann for $350. Decision?

   (b) Modify the facts in (a) by assuming that Barry gave Ann a written receipt stating that all claims had been paid in full. Result?

   (c) Modify the facts in (a) by assuming that Ann owed Barry the $500 on Ann's purchase of a motorcycle from Barry. Result?

3. (a) Judy orally promises her daughter, Liza, that she will give her a tract of land for her home. Liza, as intended by Judy, gives up her homestead and takes possession of the land. Liza lives there for six months and starts construction of a home. Is Judy bound to convey the real estate?

   (b) Ralph, knowing that his son, Ed, desires to purchase a tract of land, promises to give him the $25,000 he needs for the purchase. Ed, relying on this promise, buys an option on the tract of land. Ralph now seeks to rescind his promise. Decision?

4. George owed Keith $800 on a personal loan. Neither the amount of the debt nor George's liability to pay the $800 was disputed. Keith had also rendered services as a carpenter to George without any agreement as to the price to be paid. When the work was completed, an honest and reasonable difference of opinion developed

between George and Keith with respect to the value of Keith's services. Upon receiving Keith's bill for the carpentry services for $600, George mailed in a properly stamped and addressed envelope his check for $800 to Keith. In an accompanying letter, George stated that the enclosed check was in full settlement of both claims. Keith endorsed and cashed the check. Thereafter, Keith unsuccessfully sought to collect from George an alleged unpaid balance of $600. Keith then sued George for $600. Decision?

5. The Snyder Mfg. Co., being a large user of coal, entered into separate contracts with several coal companies. In each contract, it was agreed that the coal company would supply coal during the year 1988 in such amounts as the manufacturing company might desire to order, at a price of $49 per ton. In February 1988, the Snyder Company ordered 1,000 tons of coal from Union Coal Company, one of the contracting parties. Union Coal Company delivered 500 tons of the order and then notified Snyder Company that no more deliveries would be made and that it denied any obligation under the contract. In an action by Union Coal to collect $49 per ton for the 500 tons of coal delivered, Snyder files a counterclaim, claiming damages of $1,500 for failure to deliver the additional 500 tons of the order and damages of $4,000 for breach of agreement to deliver coal during the balance of the year. Decision?

6. On February 5, Devon entered into a written agreement with Gordon whereby Gordon agreed to drill a well on Devon's property for the sum of $5,000 and to complete the well on or before April 15. Before entering into the contract, Gordon had made test borings and had satisfied himself as to the character of the subsurface. After two days of drilling, Gordon struck hard rock. On February 17, Gordon removed his equipment and advised Devon that the project had proved unprofitable and that he would not continue. On March 17, Devon went to Gordon and told Gordon that he would assume the risk of the enterprise and would pay Gordon $100 for each day required to drill the well, as compensation for labor, the use of Gordon's equipment, and Gordon's services in supervising the work, provided Gordon would furnish certain special equipment designed to cut through hard rock. Gordon said that the proposal was satisfactory. The work was continued by Gordon and completed in an additional fifty-eight days. Upon completion of the work, Devon failed to pay, and Gordon brought an action to recover $5,800. Devon answered that he had never become obligated to pay $100 a day and filed a counterclaim for damages in the amount of $500 for the month's delay based on an alleged breach of contract by Gordon. Decision?

7. Discuss and explain whether there is valid consideration for each of the following promises:

(a) A and B entered into a contract for the purchase and sale of goods. A subsequently promised to pay a higher price for the goods when B refused to deliver at the contract price.

(b) A promised in writing to pay a debt, which was due from B to C, on C's agreement to extend the time of payment for one year.

(c) A executed a promissory note to her son, B, solely in consideration of past services rendered to A by B, for which there had been no agreement or request to pay.

8. Alan purchased shoes from Barbara on open account. Barbara sent Alan a bill for $10,000. Alan wrote back that 200 pairs of the shoes were defective and offered to pay $6,000 and give Barbara his promissory note for $1,000. Barbara accepted the offer, and Alan sent his check for $6,000 and his note in accordance with the agreement. Barbara cashed the check, collected on the note, and one month later sued Alan for $3,000. Decision?

9. Nancy owed Sharon $1,500, but Sharon did not initiate a lawsuit to collect the debt within the time period prescribed by the statute of limitations. Nevertheless, Nancy promises Sharon that she will pay the barred debt. Thereafter, Nancy refuses to pay. Sharon brings suit to collect on this new promise. Decision?

10. Anthony lends money to Frank, who dies without having repaid the loan. Frank's widow, Carol, promises Anthony to repay the loan. Upon Carol's refusal to pay the loan, Anthony brings suit against Carol for payment. Decision?

11. The parties entered into an oral contract in June 1969, under which the plaintiff agreed to construct a building for the defendant on a time and materials basis, at a maximum cost of $56,146, plus sales tax and extras ordered by the defendant. When the building was 90 percent completed, the defendant told the plaintiff he was unhappy with the whole job as "the thing just wasn't being run right." The parties then, on October 17, signed a written agreement lowering the maximum cost to $52,000 plus sales tax. The plaintiff thereafter completed the building at a cost of $64,155. The maximum under the June oral agreement, plus extras and sales tax, totaled $61,040. The defendant contended that he was obligated to pay only the lower maximum fixed by the October 17 agreement. Decision?

12. Taylor assaulted his wife, who then took refuge in Ms. Harrington's house. The next day, Mr. Taylor entered the house and began another assault on his wife. Taylor's wife knocked him down and, while he was lying on the floor, attempted to cut his head open or decapitate him with an axe. Harrington intervened to stop the bloodshed, and was hit by the axe as it was descending. The axe fell upon her hand, mutilating it badly, but sparing Taylor his life. Afterwards, Taylor

orally promised to compensate Harrington for her injury. He paid a small sum but nothing more. Harrington sued to enforce Taylor's promise. Decision?

13. Jonnel Enterprises, Inc. contracted to construct a student dormitory at Clarion State College. On May 6, Jonnel entered into a written agreement with Graham and Long as electrical contractors to perform the electrical work and to supply materials for the dormitory. The contract price was $70,544.66. Graham and Long claim that they believed the May 6 agreement obligated them to perform the electrical work on only one wing of the building, but that three or four days after work was started, a second wing of the building was found to be in need of wiring. At that time, Graham and Long informed Jonnel that they would not wire both wings of the building under the present contract, so a new contract was orally agreed upon by the parties. Under the new contract, Graham and Long were obligated to wire both wings and were to be paid only $65,000, but they were relieved of the obligations to supply entrances and a heating system. Graham and Long resumed their work, and Jonnel made seven of the eight progress payments called for. When Jonnel did not pay the final payment, Graham and Long brought this action. Jonnel claims that the May 6 contract is controlling. Decision?

14. Baker entered into an oral agreement with Healey, the state distributor of Ballantine & Sons's liquor products, that Ballantine would supply Baker with its products on demand and that Baker would have the exclusive agency for Ballantine within a certain area of Connecticut. Shortly thereafter, the agreement was modified to give Baker the right to terminate at will. Eight months later, when Ballantine & Sons revoked its agency, Baker sued to enforce the oral agreement. Decision?

15. PLM, Inc. entered into an oral agreement with Quaintance Associates, an executive "headhunter" service, for the recruitment of qualified candidates to be employed by PLM. As agreed, PLM's obligation to pay Quaintance did not depend on PLM actually hiring a qualified candidate presented by Quaintance. After several months Quaintance sent a letter to PLM, admitting that it had so far failed to produce a suitable candidate, but included a bill for $9,806.61, covering fees and expenses. PLM responded that Quaintance's services were only worth $6,060.48, and that payment of the lesser amount was the only fair way to handle the dispute. Accordingly, PLM enclosed a check for $6,060.48, writing on the back of the check "IN FULL PAYMENT OF ANY CLAIMS QUAINTANCE HAS AGAINST PLM, INC." Quaintance cashed the check and then sued PLM for the remaining $3,746.13. Decision?

16. Red Owl Stores told the Hoffman family that upon the payment of approximately $18,000 a grocery store franchise would be built for them in a new location. On the advice of Red Owl, the Hoffmans bought a small grocery store in their hometown in order to get management experience. After the Hoffmans operated at a profit for three months, Red Owl advised them to sell the small grocery, assuring them that Red Owl would find them a larger store elsewhere. Although selling at that point would cost them much profit, the Hoffmans followed Red Owl's directions. Additionally, to raise the required money for the deal, the Hoffmans sold their bakery business in their hometown. The Hoffmans also sold their house and moved to a new home in the city where their new store was to be located. Red Owl then informed the Hoffmans that it would take $24,100, not $18,000, to complete the deal. The family scrambled to find the additional funds. However, when told by Red Owl that it would now cost them $34,000 to get their new franchise, the Hoffmans decided to sue instead. Decision?

17. The plaintiff, Brenner, entered into a contract with the defendant, Little Red School House, Ltd., which stated that in return for a nonrefundable tuition of $1,080 Brenner's son could attend the defendant's school for a year. When Brenner's ex-wife refused to enroll their son, the plaintiff sought and received a verbal promise of a refund. The defendant now refuses to refund the plaintiff's money for lack of consideration. Decision?

18. Tender Loving Care, Inc. (TLC), a corporation owned and operated by Virginia Bryant, eventually went out of business. The Secretary of State canceled its corporate charter, and a check drawn on TLC's account made out to the Department of Human Resources (DHR) to pay state unemployment taxes was returned for insufficient funds. Subsequently, Bryant filed individually for bankruptcy, listing the DHR as a creditor. This claim was not allowed, since Bryant was held not to be personally liable on the debts of TLC to the DHR. The DHR later called Bryant to its offices, where she was told that she needed to pay the debt owed to the DHR by TLC. Unable to contact her lawyer, Bryant eventually was persuaded to sign a personal guarantee to cover the debt. Later, when Bryant refused to pay, the DHR filed suit. Decision?

CHAPTER 13

Illegal Bargains

A legal objective is essential for a promise or agreement to be binding. When the formation or performance of an agreement is criminal, tortious, or otherwise contrary to public policy, the agreement is illegal and **unenforceable** (as opposed to being void). The law does *not* provide a remedy for the breach of an unenforceable agreement and thus "leaves the parties where it finds them." (It is preferable to use the term "illegal bargain" or "illegal agreement" rather than "illegal contract," because the word "contract," by definition, denotes a legal and enforceable agreement.) The illegal bargain is made unenforceable (1) to discourage such undesirable conduct in the future and (2) to avoid the inappropriate use of the judicial process in carrying out the socially undesirable bargain.

In this chapter, we will discuss (a) agreements in violation of a statute, (b) agreements contrary to public policy, and (c) the effect of illegality upon agreements.

VIOLATIONS OF STATUTES

Violations of statues the courts will not enforce agreements declared illegal by statute

The courts will not enforce an agreement declared illegal by statute. For example, "wagering or gambling contracts" are specifically declared unenforceable in most states. Likewise, an agreement induced by criminal conduct will not be enforced. For example, if Alice enters into an agreement with Brent Co. through the bribing of Brent Co.'s purchasing agent, the agreement would be unenforceable.

Licensing Statutes

License formal authorization to engage in certain practices

Every jurisdiction has laws requiring a **license** for those who engage in certain trades, professions, or businesses. Common examples are licensing statutes that apply to lawyers, doctors, dentists, accountants, brokers, plumbers, and contractors. Some licensing statutes mandate schooling and/or examination, while others require only financial responsibility and/or good moral character. Whether a person who has failed to comply with a licensing requirement may recover for services rendered depends on the terms or type of licensing statute.

The statute itself may expressly provide that an unlicensed person engaged in a business or profession for which a license is required shall not recover for services rendered. Where there is no express statutory provision, the courts commonly distinguish between regulatory statutes and those enacted merely to raise revenue through the issuance of licenses. If the statute is regulatory, a person cannot recover for professional services unless he has the required license, as long as the public policy behind the regulatory purpose clearly outweighs the person's interest in being paid for his services. Some courts balance the penalty suffered by the unlicensed party against the benefit received by the other party. In contrast, if the law is for revenue purposes only, agreements for unlicensed services are enforceable.

A **regulatory license** is a measure designed to protect the public from unqualified practitioners. Examples are licenses issued under statutes prescribing standards for those who seek to practice law or medicine or, as demonstrated by the case below, to engage in the construction business. A **revenue license**, on the other hand, does not seek to protect against incompetent or unqualified practitioners, but simply to raise money. An example is a statute requiring a license of plumbers but not establishing standards of competence for those who practice the trade. The courts regard this as a taxing measure lacking any expression of legislative intent to prevent unlicensed plumbers from enforcing their business contracts.

Regulatory license measure to protect the public from unqualified practitioners

Revenue license measure to raise money

HYDROTECH SYSTEMS, LTD. v. OASIS WATERPARK Supreme Court of California, 1991, 52 Cal.3d 988, 277 Cal.Rptr. 517, 803 P.2d 370

FACTS Oasis Waterpark, a California corporation, owns and operates a water-oriented amusement park in Palm Springs, California. Wessman Construction Company, Inc., the general contractor for construction of Oasis Waterpark, contracted with Hydrotech Systems, Ltd. to design and construct a 29,000-square-foot "surfing pool" for $850,000. Hydrotech, a New York corporation that manufactures and installs patented equipment designed to simulate ocean waves, claims that its product and its skills at installing the equipment are unique. Under the contract, Wessman was entitled to hold back a portion of the contract price until the satisfactory completion and operation of the pool, but it continued to withhold $110,000 long after the pool was completed and performing properly. Hydrotech brought this suit against Wessman and Oasis to recover the withheld portion of the contract price. As a defense, Wessman and Oasis asserted that section 7031 of the California Business and Professions Code prohibited Hydrotech's suit because Hydrotech was not licensed to do business in the state of California. Section 7031 states that "[n]o person engaged in the business or acting in the capacity of a contractor" may bring suit in a California court to recover "compensation for the performance of any act or contract for which a [California contractor's] license is required" without proving that he or she was a duly licensed contractor during the performance of the act or contract. Hydrotech argued that its claim was not prohibited by the statute because of exceptional circumstances. First, it claimed that it wanted only to supply the equipment and not to construct it, but that Wessman fraudulently induced it into entering a construction contract with promises that Wessman would arrange for a California contractor to work with Hydrotech on any activities that required a license. It also claimed that Wessman never intended to pay the full amount. As to these matters, Hydrotech claimed that section 7031 does not bar fraudulent inducement claims. Second, Hydrotech claimed that section 7031 does not bar claims by a nonresident who subcontracted to provide unique construction skills in an "isolated" transaction. The trial court dismissed the action against Oasis, and Hydrotech appealed. The Court of Appeal reinstated Hydrotech's fraud claim and affirmed the remainder of the trial court's decision.

DECISION Court of Appeal's decision in favor of Oasis affirmed; decision in favor of Hydrotech reversed.

OPINION The purpose of the California contractor's licensing law is to protect the public from incompetence and dishonesty with regard to those who provide building and construction services. The licensing requirements provide minimal assurance that all persons offering such services in California have the requisite skill and character, understand applicable local laws and codes, and know the rudiments of administering a contracting business. Section 7031 advances this purpose by withholding judicial aid from those who seek compensation for unlicensed contract work. The section applies despite the "exceptional circumstances" of this transaction. Because of the strength and clarity of this policy, it is well settled that section 7031 applies despite injustice to the unlicensed contractor. Hydrotech's reluctance to engage in the design and construction and Oasis's insistence that it do so are irrelevant. The deterrent purpose of section 7031 outweighs any harshness in a particular case. Furthermore, it is manifest that the concern for the public inherent in section 7031 is just as applicable to a project done by an out-of-state contractor who performs few jobs in California as it is to a project done by a California contractor who performs only one job in California. Moreover, subcontractors are also governed by the licensing law. Therefore, an unlicensed subcontractor may not recover from either the owner or the general contractor.

INTERPRETATION A regulatory license is a measure to protect the public from unqualified practitioners; the failure to comply with such a regulation prevents the noncomplying party from recovering for services rendered.

Gambling Statutes

Wager (gambling)
agreement that one party will win and the other lose depending upon the outcome of an event in which their only interest is the gain or loss

In a **wager**, the parties stipulate that one shall win and the other lose depending on the outcome of an event in which their only "interest" is the possibility of such gain or loss. All states have legislation on gambling or wagering, and U.S. courts generally refuse to recognize the enforceability of a gambling agreement. Thus, if Smith makes a bet with Brown on the outcome of a ball game, the agreement is unenforceable by either party. Some states, however, now permit certain kinds of regulated gambling. Wagering conducted by governmental agencies, principally state-operated lotteries, has come to constitute an increasingly important source of public revenues. (See "More Lottery Funds Headed for Education.")

Usury Statutes

Usury statute (u'·su·ry)
law establishing a maximum rate of interest

A **usury statute** is a law establishing a maximum rate of permissible interest for which a lender and borrower of money may contract. Although, historically, every state had a usury statute, the recent trend is to limit or relax such statutes. Maximum permitted rates vary greatly from state to state and among types of transactions. These statutes typically are general in their application, and certain types of transactions are exempted altogether. For example, many states impose no limit on the rate of interest that may be charged on loans to corporations. Furthermore, some states permit the parties to contract for any rate of interest on loans made to individual proprietorships or partnerships for the purpose of carrying on a business.

In addition to the exceptions affecting certain designated types of borrowers, a number of states have exempted specific lenders. For example, the majority of states have enacted installment loan laws, which permit eligible lenders a higher

CONSUMER INSIGHT

More Lottery Funds Headed for Education

A growing number of states that run lotteries are putting the proceeds into education or considering doing that, a *USA TODAY* survey shows.

It also found that states that already spend lottery dollars on education are talking about earmarking the money for specific programs.

Educators say such moves will appease voters who suspect that states use lottery money to replace, not supplement, education funding.

In Florida, for example, the share of state education funding averaged 60% before the lottery was introduced in 1988. By 1993, it had dipped to 51%.

President Clinton has made education a priority in his second term and applauded Georgia recently for its lottery-funded HOPE scholarship program.

It pays college tuition, fees and books to every state resident who maintains a B or better grade point average at state schools.

USA TODAY surveyed the 37 states and the District of Columbia that have lotteries and found at least 10 states are considering putting more money into education:

- Virginia is shifting lottery proceeds this year from its general fund to education for the first time; Texas is considering doing the same.
- Idaho, which now gives half its lottery proceeds to schools and half

to state buildings, may give 100% to schools.
- There's a push in Colorado to put some of the lottery money that goes to environmental programs into education.
- Ohio and Florida, which now put lottery money into a general education fund, are talking about earmarking the money for specific programs.

In fiscal year 1996, lottery sales totaled $33.6 billion nationwide. After prizes and operating expenses were paid, $11 billion went to various public programs.

Only 10 states gave all their lottery proceeds to education, a total of $5.7 billion.

By Haya El Nasser. *USA Today*, p.1. February 19, 1997. "Copyright 1997, USA TODAY. Reprinted with permission."

return on installment loans than would otherwise be permitted under the applicable general interest statute. These specific lender usury statutes, which have all but eliminated general usury statutes, vary greatly but generally encompass small consumer loans, retail installment sales acts, corporate loans, loans by small lenders, real estate mortgages, and numerous other transactions.

For a transaction to be usurious, courts usually require evidence of the following factors: (a) a loan (b) of money (c) that is repayable absolutely and in all events (d) for which an interest charge is exacted in excess of the interest rate allowed by law. Nevertheless, the law does permit certain expenses or charges in addition to the maximum legal interest, such as payments made by a borrower to the lender for expenses incurred or for services rendered in good faith in making a loan or in obtaining security for its repayment. Permissible expenses commonly incurred by a lender include the costs of examining title, investigating the borrower's credit rating, drawing necessary documents, and inspecting the property. If not excessive, such expenses are not considered in determining the rate of interest under the usury statutes. As shown in the following case, however, payments made to the lender from which he derives an advantage are considered if they exceed the reasonable value of services he actually rendered.

ABRAMOWITZ v. BARNETT BANKS OF WEST ORLANDO Florida Court of Appeals, 1981, 394 So.2d 1033

FACTS Abramowitz obtained a one-year mortgage loan from Barnett Bank for $400,000 at 9 percent interest with a 1 percent "point" or service fee. The maximum lawful rate of interest on such a loan is 10 percent. The bank deducted the $4,000 service fee from the loan proceeds, actually disbursing only $396,000 to Abramowitz. During the one-year term of his loan, Abramowitz was charged and he paid $36,347.78 in interest. He claims the loan was usurious since the $4,000 "service fee" plus the $36,347 interest charge exceeded the 10-percent limit on total interest. Abramowitz appealed from a judgment denying him any relief.

DECISION Judgment reversed and the case remanded for imposition of damages against the bank in favor of Abramowitz.

OPINION If the $4,000 was "interest," Abramowitz paid more than $40,000, or 10 percent in total interest

charges, on his $400,000 loan. If the loan was a "discount" loan, with interest paid in advance, then the rate should properly be gauged on the amount of principal actually disbursed to Abramowitz plus the legitimate expenses incurred by the bank. These expenses must be actual, reasonable expenses of making this particular loan and may not include the general overhead of the bank. The only reasonable, legitimate expense the bank suffered in making this loan amounted to $300. Thus, the lawful amount of interest on Abramowitz's loan is $39,630 (10 percent of $396,300—the actual principal disbursed plus the $300). But Abramowitz paid $36,347 plus the interest in advance of $3,700 ($4,000 less the $300 expense), which is greater than the lawful amount of $39,630.

INTERPRETATION Usury statutes establish a maximum rate of interest for which a lender may charge a borrower.

The legal effect of a usurious loan varies from state to state. In a few states, the lender forfeits both principal and interest. In some jurisdictions, the lender can recover the principal but forfeits all interest. In other states, only that portion of interest exceeding the permitted maximum is forfeited, whereas in still other states, the amount forfeited is a multiple (double or treble) of the interest charged. How the states deal with usurious interest already paid also varies. Some states do not allow the borrower to recover any of the usurious interest she has paid; others allow recovery of such interest or a multiple of it.

Sunday Statutes

In the absence of a statutory prohibition, the common law does not prohibit entering into contracts on Sunday. Some states, however, have legislation, referred to as **blue laws**, modifying this common law rule and prohibiting certain types of commercial activity on Sunday. Even in a state that prohibits contracts on Sunday, a court nonetheless will enforce a subsequent weekday ratification of a loan made on Sunday or a promise to pay for goods sold and delivered on Sunday. In addition, Blue Laws usually do not apply to activities of "necessity" and "charity."

VIOLATIONS OF PUBLIC POLICY

The reach of a statute may extend beyond its language. Sometimes the courts, by analogy, use a statute and the policy it embodies as a guide in determining a person's rights under a private contract. Conversely, the courts frequently must express the "public policy" of the state without significant help from statutory sources. This judicially declared public policy is very broad in scope, it often being said that agreements having "a tendency to be injurious to the public or the public good" are contrary to public policy. Contracts raising questions of public policy include agreements that (1) restrain trade, (2) excuse or exculpate a party from liability for his own negligence, (3) are unconscionable, (4) involve tortious conduct, or (5) tend to corrupt public officials or impair the legislative process.

Common Law Restraint of Trade

Restraint of trade agreement that eliminates or tends to eliminate competition

A **restraint of trade** is any contract or agreement that eliminates or tends to eliminate competition or otherwise obstructs trade or commerce. One type of restraint of trade is a **covenant not to compete**, which is an agreement to refrain from entering into a competing trade, profession, or business.

Covenant not to compete (*cov'·e·nant*) agreement to refrain from entering into a competing trade, profession, or business

Today, an agreement to refrain from a particular trade, profession, or business is enforceable if (1) the purpose of the restraint is to protect a property interest of the promisee, and (2) the restraint is no more extensive than is reasonably necessary to protect that interest. Restraints typically arise in two situations: (a) the sale of a business and (b) employment contracts.

Sale of a business the promise by the seller of a business not to compete in that particular business in a reasonable geographic area for a reasonable period of time is enforceable

Sale of a Business As part of an agreement to sell a business, the seller frequently promises not to compete in that particular type of business in a *defined area* for a stated period of *time* in order to protect the business's goodwill (an asset that the buyer has purchased). The courts will enforce such a covenant (promise) if the restraint is within reasonable limitations. The reasonableness of the restraint depends on the geographic area the restraint covers, the period for which it is to be effective, and the hardship it imposes on the promisor and the public.

For example, the promise of a person selling a service station business in Detroit not to enter the service station business in Michigan for the next twenty-five years is unreasonable as to both area and time. The business interest would not include the entire state, so the protection of the purchaser does not require that the seller be prevented from engaging in the service station business in all of Michigan or perhaps, for that matter, in the entire city of Detroit. Limiting the area to the neighborhood in which the station is located or to a radius of a few miles would probably be adequate protection. However, in the case of a citywide business, such as a laundry or cleaning establishment with neighborhood outlets, a covenant restraining competition anywhere in the city might well be reasonable.

The same type of inquiry must be made about time limitations. In the sale of a service station, a twenty-five-year ban on competition from the seller would be unreasonable, but a one-year ban probably would not. The courts consider each case on its own facts to determine what is reasonable under the particular circumstances.

Employment Contracts Salespeople, management personnel, and other employees are frequently required to sign employment contracts prohibiting them from competing with their employers during their employment and for some additional stated period after their termination. The same is also frequently true among corporations or partnerships involving professionals such as accountants, lawyers, investment brokers, stockbrokers, or doctors. Though the courts readily enforce a covenant not to compete during the period of employment, they subject the promise not to compete after termination of employment to a test of reasonableness stricter even than that applied to noncompetition promises included in a contract for the sale of a business.

Employment contracts an employment contract prohibiting an employee from competing with his employer for a reasonable period following termination is enforceable provided the restriction is necessary to protect legitimate interests of the employer

A court order enjoining (prohibiting) a former employee from competing in a described territory for a stated period of time is the usual way in which an employer seeks to enforce an employee's promise not to compete. However, before the courts will grant such injunctions, the employer must demonstrate that the restriction is *necessary* to protect his legitimate interests, such as trade secrets or customer lists. Because the injunction may have the practical effect of placing the employee out of work, the courts must carefully balance the public policy favoring the employer's right to protect his business interests against the public policy favoring full opportunity for individuals to gain employment. Some courts, rather than refusing to enforce an unreasonable restraint, will modify the restrictive covenant to make it reasonable under the circumstances.

Thus, one court has held unreasonable a contract covenant requiring a travel agency employee after termination of her employment to not engage in a like business in any capacity in either of two named towns or within a sixty-mile radius of those towns for two years. There was no indication that the employee had enough influence over customers to cause them to move their business to her new agency, nor was it shown that any trade secrets were involved.

INSULATION CORPORATION OF AMERICA v. BROBSTON Superior Court of Pennsylvania, 1995, 667 A.2d 729

FACTS Richard Brobston was hired by Insulation Corporation of America (ICA) in 1982. Initially, he was hired as a territory sales manager but was promoted to national account manager in 1986 and to general manager in 1990. In 1992, ICA was planning to acquire computer-assisted design (CAD) technology to upgrade its product line. Prior to acquiring this technology, ICA required that Brobston and certain other employees sign employment contracts that contained restrictive covenants or be terminated. These restrictive covenants provided that in the event of Brobston's termination for any reason, Brobston would not reveal any of ICA's trade secrets or sales information and would not enter into direct competition with ICA within three hundred miles of Allentown, Pennsylvania, for a period of two years from the date of termination. The purported consideration for Brobston's agreement was a $2,000 increase in his base salary and proprietary information concerning the CAD system, customers, and pricing. Brobston signed the proffered employment contract. In October 1992, Brobston became vice president of special products, which included responsibility for sales of the CAD system products as well as other products. Over the course of the next year, Brobston failed in several respects to properly perform his employment duties and on August 13, 1993, ICA terminated Brobston's employment. In December 1993, Brobston was hired by a competitor of ICA who was aware of

continued

ICA's restrictive covenants. ICA sought injunctive relief against Brobston and filed a petition to enforce the employment agreement by enjoining him from disclosing proprietary information about ICA and by restraining him from competing with ICA. The trial court issued a temporary restraining order and later granted a preliminary injunction that enjoined Brobston from disclosing ICA's trade secrets and from competing with ICA within three hundred miles of Allentown, Pennsylvania, for a period of two years from the date of Brobston's termination. Brobston appealed.

DECISION Preliminary injunction affirmed to the extent it enjoined Brobston from disclosing trade secrets and reversed to the extent that it restricted Brobston from competing with ICA.

OPINION In order for a noncompetition covenant to be valid, it must relate to a contract for employment, be supported by adequate consideration, and be reasonably limited in both time and territory. More specifically, where a restrictive covenant has been entered into between an employer and its employee, courts have permitted the enforcement of post-employment restraints only where they are ancillary to an employment relationship between the parties, the restrictions are reasonably necessary to protect the employer, and the restrictions are reasonably limited in duration and geographic extent. Brobston's agreement was ancillary since it was supported by new consideration in the form of the $2,000 annual raise and a change in employment status from at-will to a written year-to-year contract.

The more important issue in this case is whether the restrictions in Brobston's contract were reasonable. The

determination of reasonableness involves the weighing of competing interests—that of the employer's need for protection—against the hardship of the restriction upon the employee. Notably, there is a significant factual distinction between the hardship imposed by the enforcement of a restrictive covenant on an employee who voluntarily leaves his employer and that imposed upon an employee who is terminated for failing to do his job. In this case, Brobston was terminated for poor performance. Where an employer determines that an employee has failed to promote the employer's legitimate business interests, it clearly suggests an implicit decision on the part of the employer that its business interests are best promoted without the employee in its service. Such a determination by an employer diminishes the employer's need to protect itself and it is unreasonable as a matter of law to permit the employer to retain unfettered control over that which it has effectively deemed worthless to its business interests. Moreover, the nondisclosure agreement in this case renders the noncompetition agreement unnecessary. As the agreement states, its purpose was to protect the proprietary CAD technology. However, Brobston never actually received sufficient training to operate the CAD technology. He had access only to sales and profit margin information, the security of which is addressed adequately by the nondisclosure agreement. Therefore in this case, ICA's interests are sufficiently protected without enforcement of the noncompetition agreement.

INTERPRETATION In order for a covenant not to compete to be enforceable, it must relate to a contract for employment, be supported by adequate consideration, and be reasonably limited in time and territory.

Exculpatory Clauses

Exculpatory clause
(ex·cul'·pa·to·ry) a provision excusing one party from fault or liability, courts generally disapprove

Some contracts contain an **exculpatory clause** that excuses one party from liability for her own tortious conduct. While there is general agreement that exculpatory clauses relieving a person from tort liability for harm caused intentionally or recklessly are unenforceable as violating public policy, exculpatory clauses that excuse a party from liability for harm caused by negligent conduct undergo careful scrutiny by the courts, which often require that the clause be conspicuously placed in the contract and clearly written. Accordingly, an exculpatory clause on the reverse side of a parking lot claim check, which attempts to relieve the parking lot operator of liability for negligently damaging the customer's automobile, will generally be held unenforceable as against public policy.

Where one party's superior bargaining position has enabled him to impose an exculpatory clause upon the other party, the courts are inclined to nullify the provision. Such a situation, as shown in the case that follows, may arise in residential leases exempting a landlord from liability for his negligence. Moreover, an exculpatory clause may be unenforceable for unconscionability.

HENRIOULLE v. MARIN VENTURES, INC. Supreme Court of California, 1978, 20 Cal.3d 512,
573 P.2d 465, 143 Cal.Rptr. 247

FACTS Henrioulle, an unemployed widower with two children, received public assistance in the form of a rent subsidy. He entered into an apartment lease agreement with Marin Ventures that provided "INDEMNIFICA-TION: Owner shall not be liable for any damage or injury to the tenant, or any other person, or to any property, occurring on the premises, or any part thereof, and Tenant agrees to hold Owner harmless for any claims for damages no matter how caused." Henrioulle fractured his wrist when he tripped over a rock on a common stairway in the apartment building. At the time of the accident, the landlord had been having difficulty keeping the common areas of the apartment building clean. Henrioulle appealed from the trial court's orders granting Marin Ventures a judgment notwithstanding the jury's verdict and a new trial.

DECISION Orders of the trial court reversed and case remanded with directions to enter a judgment for Henrioulle on the verdict.

OPINION The criteria used to identify when an exculpatory clause is invalid as against public policy include whether (1) it concerns a business of a type generally thought suitable for public regulation; (2) the party seeking exculpation is engaged in performing a service of great importance to the public, which is often a matter of practical necessity for some members of the public; (3) the party seeking exculpation is in a superior bargaining position; (4) the exculpatory clause is part of a standard adhesion contract whose terms are stated on a "take-it-or-leave-it" basis. Here, the transaction, a residential rental agreement, meets these criteria, and, therefore, the exculpatory clause is invalid as contrary to public policy. Accordingly, Henrioulle is entitled to recover for his injuries.

INTERPRETATION An exculpatory clause is valid only if it is not contrary to public policy.

Unconscionable Contracts

The Uniform Commercial Code provides that a court may scrutinize every contract for the sale of goods to determine whether in its commercial setting, purpose, and effect the contract is **unconscionable**, or unfair. The court may refuse to enforce an unconscionable contract or any part of the contract it finds to be unconscionable. The Restatement has a similar provision.

Though neither the Code nor the Restatement defines the word *unconscionable*, the term is defined in the *New Webster's Dictionary* (Deluxe Encyclopedic Edition) as "contrary to the dictates of conscience; unscrupulous or unprincipled; exceeding that which is reasonable or customary; inordinate, unjustifiable."

The doctrine of unconscionability has been justified on the basis that it permits the courts to resolve issues of unfairness explicitly in terms of that unfairness without recourse to formalistic rules or legal fictions. In policing contracts for fairness, the courts have again demonstrated their willingness to limit freedom of contract in order to protect the less advantaged from overreaching by dominant contracting parties. The doctrine of unconscionability has evolved through its application by the courts to include both procedural and substantive unconscionability. **Procedural unconscionability** involves scrutiny for the presence of "bargaining naughtiness." In other words, was the negotiation process fair? Or were there procedural irregularities, such as burying important terms of the agreement in fine print or obscuring the true meaning of the contract with impenetrable legal jargon?

By comparison, in searching for **substantive unconscionability**, the courts examine the actual terms of a contract for oppressive or grossly unfair provisions such as exorbitant prices or unfair exclusions or limitations of contractual remedies. An all-too-common example of such a provision involves a buyer in pressing need who is in an unequal bargaining position with a seller who consequently obtains an exorbitant price for his product or service. In one case, a price of $749 ($920 if the purchaser wished to pay on credit over time) for a vacuum cleaner that cost the seller $140 was held unconscionable. In another case, the

Unconscionable
(un·con'·scion·a·ble) unfair or unduly harsh

Procedural unconscionability unfair or irregular bargaining

Substantive unconscionability oppressive or grossly unfair contractual terms

buyers, welfare recipients, purchased by a time payment contract a home freezer unit for $900 that, when time credit charges, credit life insurance, credit property insurance, and sales tax were added, cost $1,235. The purchase resulted from a visit to the buyers' home by a salesman representing Your Shop At Home Service, Inc.; the maximum retail value of the freezer unit at the time of purchase was $300. The court held the contract unconscionable and reformed it by reducing the price to the total payment ($620) the buyers had managed to make. Another landmark case follows.

Closely akin to the concept of unconscionability is the doctrine of contracts of adhesion. An *adhesion contract*, a standard-form contract prepared by one party, generally involves the preparer offering the other party the contract on a "take-it-or-leave-it" basis. Such contracts are not automatically unenforceable but are subject to greater scrutiny for procedural or substantive unconscionability. See Ethical Dilemma on the following page.

WILLIAMS v. WALKER-THOMAS FURNITURE CO. United States Court of Appeals, District of Columbia Circuit, 1965, 350 F.2d 445

FACTS Between 1957 and 1962, Williams purchased a number of household items on credit from Walker-Thomas Furniture Co., a retail furniture store. Walker-Thomas retained the right in its contracts to repossess an item if Williams defaulted on an installment payment. Each contract also provided that each installment payment by Williams would be credited *pro rata* to all outstanding accounts or bills owed to Walker-Thomas. As a result of this provision, an unpaid balance would remain on every item purchased until the entire balance due on all items, whenever purchased, was paid in full. Williams defaulted on a monthly installment payment in 1962, and Walker-Thomas sought to repossess all the items that Williams had purchased since 1957. Williams claimed that the contracts were unconscionable and therefore unenforceable. The trial court granted judgment for Walker-Thomas, and the District of Columbia Court of Appeals affirmed.

DECISION Judgment reversed and remanded to determine the possible unconscionability of the contracts.

OPINION In general, one who signs an agreement without knowledge of its terms is bound and is held to have assumed the risk that the bargain was one-sided. But if a party with little bargaining power and, therefore, no meaningful choice enters into a commercially unreasonable contract with little or no knowledge or understanding of its terms, one cannot say that the supposed acceptance was an objective manifestation of assent to all of the terms of the contract. In cases involving allegedly unconscionable terms, the court will examine the reasonableness or fairness of the term at the time that the contract was entered into to determine whether it should be enforced. Generally, the suspect term is evaluated in light of general commercial background and the particular reason for the term's inclusion. If the term is found to be so extreme as to be unconscionable, enforcement of that term should be denied. The contract provision as to prorating each payment on all purchases whenever made is unconscionable and therefore unenforceable.

INTERPRETATION The doctrine of unconscionability includes both procedural and substantive unconscionability.

Tortious Conduct

Tortious conduct an agreement that requires a person to commit a tort is unenforceable

An agreement that requires a person to commit a tort is an illegal agreement and thus is unenforceable. The courts will not permit contract law to violate the law of torts. Any agreement attempting to do so is considered contrary to public policy. For example, Ada and Bernard enter into an agreement under which Ada promises Bernard that in return for $5,000 she will disparage the product of Bernard's competitor, Cone, in order to provide Bernard with a competitive advantage. Ada's promise is to commit the tort of disparagement and is unenforceable as contrary to public policy.

ETHICAL DILEMMA Is It Fair to Reserve the Right to Withhold Test Scores?

FACTS Professor Cramer teaches business law at State University. She also serves as a pre-law adviser. Ed Brinter, a 21-year-old college senior, is one of her advisees. Last semester, Ed applied to five law schools. Since he was uncertain whether he wanted to attend law school or to pursue an M.B.A., Professor Cramer suggested that he also apply to three graduate business schools.

As required for admission, Ed took the GMAT and the LSAT, both administered by the Educational Testing Service (ETS). He obtained a good, but not outstanding, score on the GMAT and an excellent score on his LSAT. ETS, however, has refused to send either set of test scores to any of the schools to which Ed applied. According to an ETS testing specialist, Ed's correct and incorrect answers so closely correlated to those of another student that ETS is requiring both students to retake the LSAT before any test scores will be forwarded. ETS also refuses to forward Ed's GMAT scores.

The ETS maintains that Ed entered into a contract when he registered for the exams. The application form included a clause that states that ETS reserves the right to cancel any test score if there is adequate reason to question its validity.

Ed has come to Professor Cramer for advice. Professor Cramer has known Ed for two years and has never seen him do anything dishonest. Yet she has lingering doubts. She knows how desperately Ed wants to attend graduate school and is aware of the significant pressure he has been under from his family.

Social, Policy, and Ethical Considerations

1. Should Professor Cramer attempt to intervene on Ed's behalf? What actions should she take?
2. Is it fair for the Educational Testing Service to take the position that all applicants agree to specific terms and conditions by virtue of the application process?
3. What policy interests does ETS serve through such procedures? What competing issues do such procedures present?
4. What justification, if any, is there for withholding the second set of Ed's test scores?

Corrupting Public Officials

Agreements that may adversely affect the public interest through the corruption of public officials or the impairment of the legislative process are unenforceable. Examples include using improper means to influence legislation, to secure some official action, or to procure a government contract. Contracts to pay lobbyists for services to obtain or defeat official action by means of persuasive argument are to be distinguished from illegal influence-peddling agreements.

For example, a bargain by a candidate for public office to make a certain appointment following his election is illegal. In addition, an agreement to pay a public officer something extra for performing his official duty, such as promising a bonus to a police officer for strictly enforcing the traffic laws on her beat, is illegal. The same is true of an agreement in which a citizen promises to perform, or to refrain from performing, duties imposed on her by citizenship. Thus, a promise by Carl to pay $50 to Rachel if she will register and vote is opposed to public policy and illegal.

Corrupting public officials agreements that corrupt public officials are not enforceable

EFFECT OF ILLEGALITY

With few exceptions, illegal contracts are **_unenforceable_**. In most cases, neither party to an illegal agreement can sue the other for breach or recover for any performance rendered. It is often said that where parties are *in pari delicto* (in pa´·re de·lik´·tow)—in equal fault—a court will leave them where it finds them. The law will provide neither with any remedy. This strict rule of unenforceability is subject to certain exceptions, however, which is discussed on the following page.

Effect of illegality neither party may recover (unenforceable) under an illegal agreement where both parties are *in pari delicto* (in equal fault)

Party Withdrawing Before Performance

A party to an illegal agreement may, before performance, withdraw from the transaction and recover whatever she has contributed, if the party has not engaged in serious misconduct. A common example is recovery of money left with a stakeholder for a wager before it is paid over to the winner.

Party Protected by Statute

Sometimes an agreement is illegal because it violates a statute designed to protect persons from the effects of the prohibited agreement. For example, state and federal statutes prohibiting the sale of unregistered securities are designed primarily to protect investors. In such case, even though there is an unlawful agreement, the statutes usually expressly give the purchaser a right to withdraw from the sale and recover the money paid.

Party Not Equally at Fault

Where one of the parties is less at fault than the other, he may be allowed to recover payments made or property transferred. For example, this exception would apply where one party induces the other to enter into an illegal bargain through the exercise of fraud, duress, or undue influence.

Excusable Ignorance

An agreement that appears to be entirely permissible on its face may, nevertheless, be illegal by reason of facts and circumstances of which one of the parties is completely unaware. For example, a man and woman make mutual promises to marry, but unknown to the woman, the man is already married. This is an agreement to commit the crime of bigamy, and the marriage, if entered into, is void. In such case, the courts permit the party who is ignorant of the illegality to maintain a lawsuit against the other party for damages.

A party may also be excused for ignorance of legislation of a minor character. For instance, Jones and Old South Building Co. enter into a contract to build a factory that contains specifications in violation of the town's building ordinance. Jones did not know of the violation and had no reason to know. Old South's promise to build would not be rendered unenforceable on grounds of public policy, and Jones consequently would have a claim against Old South for damages for breach of contract.

Partial Illegality

A contract may be partly unlawful and partly lawful. The courts view such a contract in one of two ways. First, the partial illegality may be held to taint the entire contract with illegality, so that it is wholly unenforceable. Second, the court may determine it possible to separate the illegal from the legal part, in which case the illegal part only will be held unenforceable, while the legal part will be enforced. For example, if a contract contains an illegal covenant not to compete, the covenant will not be enforced, though the rest of the contract may be.

CHAPTER SUMMARY

Violations of Statutes	**General Rule** the courts will not enforce agreements declared illegal by statute **Licensing Statutes** require formal authorization to engage in certain trades, professions, or businesses ■ *Regulatory License* licensing statute that is intended to protect the public against unqualified persons; an unlicensed person may not recover for services he has performed ■ *Revenue License* licensing statute that seeks to raise money; an unlicensed person may recover for services he has performed **Gambling Statutes** prohibit wagers, which are agreements that one party will win and the other lose depending upon the outcome of an event in which their only interest is the gain or loss **Sunday Statutes** prohibition of certain types of commercial activity on Sunday (also called blue laws) **Usury Statutes** establish a maximum rate of interest
Violations of Public Policy	**Common Law Restraint of Trade** unreasonable restraints of trade are not enforceable ■ *Sale of a Business* the promise by the seller of a business not to compete in that particular business in a reasonable geographic area for a reasonable period of time is enforceable ■ *Employment Contracts* an employment contract prohibiting an employee from competing with his employer for a reasonable period following termination is enforceable provided the restriction is necessary to protect legitimate interests of the employer **Exculpatory Clauses** the courts generally disapprove of contractual provisions excusing a party from liability for his own tortious conduct **Unconscionable Contracts** unfair or unduly harsh agreements are not enforceable ■ *Procedural Unconscionability* unfair or irregular bargaining ■ *Substantive Unconscionability* oppressive or grossly unfair contractual terms **Tortuous Conduct** an agreement that requires a person to commit a tort is unenforceable **Corrupting Public Officials** agreements that corrupt public officials are not enforceable
Effect of Illegality	**Unenforceability** neither party may recover (unenforceable) under an illegal agreement where both parties are *in pari delicto* (in equal fault) **Exceptions** permit one party to recover payments ■ *Party Withdrawing Before Performance* ■ *Party Protected by Statute* ■ *Party Not Equally at Fault* ■ *Excusable Ignorance* ■ *Partial Illegality*

QUESTIONS

1. Define unenforceable. Why are illegal agreements unenforceable? What are the major exceptions to this rule?
2. Identify and distinguish between the two types of licensing statutes.
3. Distinguish between general and specific usury laws.
4. Describe when a covenant not to compete will be enforced and discuss the two situations in which these types of covenants most frequently arise.
5. Distinguish between procedural and substantive unconscionability.

Internet Question. Find and review information on lotteries, including which states have them and how the proceeds are used.

PROBLEMS

1. Johnson and Wilson were the principal shareholders in XYZ Corporation located in the city of Jonesville, Wisconsin. This corporation was engaged in the business of manufacturing paper novelties, which were sold over a wide area in the Midwest. The corporation was also in the business of binding books. Johnson purchased Wilson's shares in XYZ Corporation and, in consideration thereof, Wilson agreed that for a period of two years he would not (a) manufacture or sell in Wisconsin any paper novelties of any kind that would compete with those sold by XYZ Corporation, or (b) engage in the bookbinding business in the city of Jonesville. Discuss the validity and effect, if any, of this agreement.

2. Wilkins, a Texas resident licensed by that state as a certified public accountant, rendered service in his professional capacity in Louisiana to Coverton Cosmetics Company. He was not registered as a certified public accountant in Louisiana. His service under his contract with the cosmetics company was not the only occasion on which he had practiced his profession in that state. The company denied liability and refused to pay him, relying on a Louisiana statute declaring it unlawful for any person to perform or offer to perform services as a CPA for compensation until he has been registered by the designated agency of the state and holds an unrevoked registration card. The statute provides that a CPA certificate may be issued without examination to any applicant who holds a valid unrevoked certificate as a CPA under the laws of any other state. The statute provides further that rendering services of the kind performed by Wilkins, without registration, is a misdemeanor punishable by a fine or imprisonment in the county jail or by both fine and imprisonment. Wilkins brought action against Coverton, seeking to recover a fee in the amount of $1,500 as the reasonable value of his services. Decision?

3. Michael is interested in promoting the passage of a bill in the state legislature. He agrees with Christy, an attorney, to pay Christy for her services in writing the required bill, obtaining its introduction in the legislature, and making an argument for its passage before the legislative committee to which it will be referred. Christy renders these services. Subsequently, on Michael's refusal to pay Christy, Christy sues Michael for damages for breach of contract. Decision?

4. Anthony promises to pay McCarthy $10,000 if McCarthy reveals to the public that Washington is a communist. Washington is not a communist and never has been. McCarthy successfully persuades the media to report that Washington is a communist and now seeks to recover the $10,000 from Anthony, who refuses to pay. McCarthy initiates a lawsuit against Anthony. What result?

5. The Dear Corporation was engaged in the business of making and selling harvesting machines. It sold everything pertaining to its business to the HI Company, agreeing "not again to go into the manufacture of harvesting machines anywhere in the United States." The Dear Corporation, which had a national and international goodwill in its business, now begins the manufacture of such machines contrary to its agreement. Should the court stop it from doing so? Explain.

6. Charles Leigh, engaged in the industrial laundry business in Central City, employed Tim Close, previously employed in the home laundry business, as a route salesman. Leigh rents linens and industrial uniforms to commercial customers; the soiled linens and uniforms are picked up at regular intervals by the route drivers and replaced with clean ones. Every employee is assigned a list of customers whom he or she services. The contract of employment stated that in consideration of being employed, on termination of his employment, Close would not "directly or indirectly engage in the linen supply business or any competitive business within Central City, Illinois, for a period of one year from the date when his employment under this contract ceases." On May 10 of the following year, Close's employment was terminated by Leigh for valid reasons. Close then accepted employment with Ajax Linen Service, a direct competitor of Leigh in Central City. He began soliciting former customers he had called on for Leigh and obtained some of them as customers for Ajax. Leigh brings an action to enforce the provisions of the contract. Decision?

7. On July 5, 1988, Barbara and Kitty entered into a bet on the outcome of the 1988 presidential election. On January 28, 1989, Barbara, who bet on the winner, approached Kitty, seeking to collect the $3,000 Kitty had wagered. Kitty paid Barbara the wager but now seeks to recover the funds from Barbara. Result?

8. Carl, a salesman for Smith, comes to Benson's home and sells him a complete set of "gourmet cooking utensils" that are worth approximately $300. Benson, an eighty-year-old man who lives alone in a one-room efficiency apartment, signs a contract to buy the utensils for $1,450 plus a credit charge of $145 and to make payments in ten equal monthly installments. Three weeks after Carl leaves with the signed contract, Benson decides he cannot afford the cooking utensils and has no use for them. What can Benson do? Explain.

9. Consider the facts in problem 8 but assume that the price was $350. Assume, further, that Benson wishes to avoid the contract based on the allegation that Carl befriended and tricked him into the purchase. Decision?

10. Adrian rents a bicycle from Barbara. The bicycle rental contract Adrian signed provides that Barbara is not liable for any injury to the renter caused by any defect in the bicycle or the negligence of Barbara. Adrian is injured when she is involved in an accident due to Barbara's improper maintenance of the bicycle. Adrian sues Barbara for damages. Decision?

11. Merrill Lynch employed Post and Maney as account executives beginning on April 20, 1959, and May 15, 1961, respectively. Both men elected to be paid a salary and to participate in the firm's pension and profit-sharing plans rather than take a straight commission. Merrill Lynch terminated the employment of both Post and Maney on August 30, 1974. On September 4, 1974, both began working for Bache & Company, a competitor of Merrill Lynch. Merrill Lynch then informed them that all of their rights in the company-funded pension plan had been forfeited pursuant to a provision of the plan that permitted forfeiture in the event an employee directly or indirectly competed with the firm. Decision?

12. Tovar applied for the position of resident physician in Paxton Community Memorial Hospital. The hospital examined his background and licensing and assured him that he was qualified for the position. Relying upon the hospital's promise of permanent employment, Tovar resigned from his job and began work at the hospital. He was discharged two weeks later, however, because he did not hold a license to practice medicine in Illinois as required by state law. He had taken the examination but had never passed it. Tovar claims that the hospital promised him a position of permanent employment and that by discharging him it breached their employment contract. Decision?

13. Carolyn Murphy, a welfare recipient with four minor children, responded to an advertisement that offered the opportunity to purchase televisions without a deposit or credit history. She entered into a rent-to-own contract for a twenty-five-inch console color television set that required seventy-eight weekly payments of $16 (a total of $1,248, which was two and one-half times the retail value of the set). Under the contract, the renter could terminate the agreement by returning the television and forfeiting any payments already made. After Murphy had paid $436 on the television, she read a newspaper article criticizing the lease plan. She stopped payment and sued the television company. In response, the television company has attempted to take possession of the set. Decision?

14. Albert Bennett, an amateur cyclist, participated in a bicycle race conducted by the United States Cycling Federation. During the race, Bennett was hit by an automobile. He claims that employees of the Federation improperly allowed the car onto the course. The Federation claims that it cannot be held liable to Bennett because Bennett signed a release exculpating the Federation from responsibility for any personal injury resulting from his participation in the race. Decision?

15. In February of 1980, Brady, a general contractor, signed a written contract with the Fulghums to build for them a house in North Carolina. The contract price of the house was $106,850, and construction was to begin in March of 1980. Neither during the contract negotiations nor during the commencement of construction was Brady licensed as a general contractor as required by North Carolina law. In fact, Brady did not obtain his license until late October of 1980, at which time he had completed over two-thirds of the construction on the Fulghums' house. The Fulghums submitted to Brady total payments of $104,000 on the house. Brady sues for $2,850 on the original contract and $29,000 for additions and changes requested by the Fulghums during construction. Decision?

16. Robert McCart owned and operated an H & R Block tax preparation franchise. When Robert became a district manager for H & R Block, in accordance with company policy, he signed over his franchise to his wife June. June signed the new franchise agreement, which included a covenant not to compete for a two-year period within a 50-mile radius of the franchise territory should the H & R Block franchise be terminated, transferred, or otherwise disposed of. At all times Robert was aware of the terms of this agreement. Shortly after terminating her franchise agreement, June sent out letters to H & R Block customers, criticizing H & R Block's fees and informing that she and Robert would establish their own tax preparation services at the same address as the former franchise location. Each letter included a separate letter from Robert detailing the tax services to be offered by the McCarts' new business. H & R Block obtained an injunction against Robert, and Robert appealed. Decision?

CHAPTER 14

Contractual Capacity

A binding promise or agreement requires that the parties to the agreement have contractual capacity. Everyone is regarded as having such capacity unless the law, for public policy reasons, holds that the individual lacks such capacity. We will consider this essential ingredient of a contract by discussing those classes and conditions of persons who are legally limited in their capacity to contract: minors, incompetent persons, and intoxicated persons.

MINORS

Minor person under age of legal majority

A **minor**, also called an infant, is a person who has not attained the age of legal majority. At common law, a minor was an individual who had not reached the age of twenty-one years. Today the age of majority has been changed by statute in nearly all jurisdictions, usually to age eighteen. Almost without exception a minor's contract, whether executory or executed, is *voidable* at his or her option. Even an "emancipated" minor, one who, because of marriage or other reasons, is no longer subject to strict parental control, may nevertheless avoid contractual liability in most jurisdictions. Consequently, business people deal at their peril with minors and in situations of consequence generally require an adult to co-sign or guarantee the performance of the contract. Nevertheless, most states recognize special categories of contracts that cannot be avoided (such as student loans or contracts for medical care) or that have a lower age for capacity (such as bank accounts, marriage, and insurance contracts).

Liability on contracts minor's contracts are voidable at the minor's option

Liability on Contracts

A minor's contract is not entirely void and of no legal effect; rather, as we have said, it is voidable at the minor's option. The exercise of this power of avoidance, called a **disaffirmance**, releases the minor from any liability on the contract. On the other hand, after the minor comes of age, he may choose to adopt or ratify the contract, in which case he surrenders his power of avoidance and becomes bound by his **ratification**.

Disaffirmance *(dis´·af·fir·mance)* avoidance of the contract; may be done during minority and for a reasonable time after reaching majority

Disaffirmance As we stated earlier, a minor has the power to avoid liability. She or, in some jurisdictions, her guardian may exercise the power to disaffirm a contract through words or conduct showing an intention not to abide by it.

Ratification *(rat´·i·fi·ca·tion)* affirmation of the entire contract; may be done upon reaching majority

A minor may disaffirm a contract at any time before reaching the age of majority. Moreover, a minor generally may disaffirm a contract within a reasonable time after she comes of age as long as she has not already ratified the contract. A notable exception is that a minor cannot disaffirm a sale of land until after she reaches her majority.

In most states, determining a reasonable time depends upon circumstances such as the nature of the transaction, whether either party has caused the delay, and the extent to which either party has been injured by the delay. Some states, however, statutorily prescribe a time period, generally one year, in which the minor may disaffirm the contract.

Disaffirmance may be either *express* or *implied*. No particular form of language is essential, so long as it shows an intention not to be bound. This intention also may be manifested by acts or by conduct. For example, a minor agrees to sell property to Andy and then sells the property to Betty. The sale to Betty constitutes a disaffirmance of the contract with Andy.

A troublesome yet important problem in this area pertains to the minor's duty upon disaffirmance. The courts do not agree on this question. The majority hold that the minor must return any property she has received from the other party to the contract, provided she has it in her possession at the time of disaffirmance. Nothing more is required. If the minor disaffirms the purchase of an automobile and the vehicle has been wrecked, she need only return the wrecked vehicle. Other states require at least the payment of a reasonable amount for the use of the property or of the amount by which the property depreciated while in the hands of the minor. (See *Dodson v. Shrader*, below.) A few states, however, either by statute or court ruling, recognize a duty on the part of the minor to make *restitution*; that is, to return an equivalent of what has been received so that the seller will be in approximately the same position he would have occupied had the sale not occurred.

DODSON v. SHRADER Supreme Court of Tennessee, 1992, 824 S.W.2d 545

FACTS Joseph Eugene Dodson, age sixteen, purchased a used pickup truck from Burns and Mary Shrader. The Shraders owned and operated Shrader's Auto Sales in Columbia, Tennessee. Dodson paid $4,900 in cash for the truck. At the time of sale, the Shraders did not question Mr. Dodson's age, but thought he was eighteen or nineteen. Dodson made no misrepresentation concerning his age. Nine months after the date of purchase, the truck began to develop mechanical problems. A mechanic diagnosed the problem as a burnt valve, but could not be certain. Dodson, who could not afford the repairs, continued to drive the truck until one month later, when the engine "blew up." Dodson parked the vehicle in the front yard of his parents' home and contacted the Shraders to rescind the purchase of the truck and to request a full refund. The Shraders refused. Dodson filed an action, seeking to rescind the contract and to obtain a full refund of the money he had paid. Before the case was heard, the truck was hit by a hit-and-run driver. The trial judge granted the rescission and ordered the Shraders to reimburse the $4,900. The Court of Appeals affirmed.

DECISION Case remanded to determine the proper amount to be refunded.

OPINION The modern rule is that contracts of infants are voidable and subject to be affirmed by the minor either before or after he or she attains majority. Under this rule, rather than having the courts determine which contracts are beneficial and which are harmful, the infant is permitted to decide which contracts he wishes to invalidate. This rule is based upon the underlying purpose of protecting minors from their lack of judgment and "from squandering their wealth through improvident contracts with crafty adults who would take advantage of them in the marketplace." Now, however, two minority rules allow the adult who contracts with a minor to refund less than the full consideration in the event of rescission. The first rule, called the "Benefit Rule," holds that upon rescission, recovery of the full price is subject to a deduction for the minor's use of the merchandise. The other rule holds that the minor's recovery of the full purchase price is subject to a deduction for the minor's "use" of the consideration he or she received under the contract or for the "depreciation" or "deterioration" of the consideration while in his or her possession. We hold that where (1) the minor has not been overreached in any way, (2) there has been no undue influence, and (3) the contract is fair and reasonable, the minor may not recover the amount he or

continued

she actually paid without first allowing the seller reasonable compensation for the use and depreciation of, and willful or negligent damage to, the article purchased while it remained in the minor's hands. The rule does not apply, however, if the seller has perpetrated any fraud against, or has taken unfair advantage of, the minor. In this case, nine months after the date of purchase, Dodson continued to drive the truck after being informed of the probable nature of its problems. Whether or not this involved gross negligence or intentional conduct is a matter for determination at trial. In addition, the issue of liability for the damage to the truck after Dodson notified the Shraders is for the trial court to decide.

INTERPRETATION   Under the majority rule, a minor may disaffirm her contracts during minority and for a reasonable time thereafter; this case also presents two minority views.

Finally, can a minor disaffirm and recover property that he has sold to a buyer who in turn has sold it to a good-faith purchaser for value? Traditionally, the minor could avoid the contract and recover the property, even though the third person gave value for it and had no notice of the minority. Thus, in the case of the sale of real estate, a minor could take back a deed of conveyance even against a third-party good-faith purchaser of the land who did not know of the minority. The Uniform Commercial Code, however, has changed this principle in connection with sales of goods by providing that a person with voidable title (e.g., the person buying goods from a minor) has power to transfer valid title to a good-faith purchaser for value. For example, a minor sells his car to an individual who resells it to a used-car dealer, a good-faith purchaser for value. The used-car dealer would acquire legal title even though he bought the car from a seller who had only voidable title.

Ratification   A minor has the option of ratifying a contract after reaching the age of majority. Ratification makes the contract binding *ab initio* (from the beginning). That is, the result is the same as if the contract had been valid and binding from its inception. Ratification, once effected, is final and cannot be withdrawn; furthermore, it must be in total, validating the entire contract. The minor can ratify the contract only as a whole, both as to burdens and benefits. He cannot, for example, ratify so as to retain the consideration he received and escape payment or other performance on his part; nor can he retain part of the contract and disaffirm another part.

Note that a minor has *no* power to ratify a contract while he remains a minor. A ratification based on words or conduct occurring while the minor is still underage is no more effective than his original contractual promise. The ratification must take place after the individual has acquired contractual capacity by attaining his majority.

Ratification can occur in three ways: (1) through express language, (2) as implied from conduct, and (3) through failure to make a timely disaffirmance. Suppose that a minor makes a contract to buy property from an adult. The contract is voidable by the minor, and she can escape liability. But suppose that after reaching her majority she promises to go through with the purchase. She has *expressly* ratified the contract she entered when she was a minor. Her promise is binding, and the adult can recover for breach if the minor fails to carry out the terms of the contract.

Ratification also may be *implied* from a person's conduct. Suppose that the minor, after attaining her majority, uses the property involved in the contract, undertakes to sell it to someone else, or performs some other act showing an intention to affirm the contract. She may not thereafter disaffirm the contract but is bound by it. Perhaps the most common form of implied ratification occurs when a minor, after attaining her majority, continues to use the property that she purchased as a minor. This use is obviously inconsistent with the nonexistence of a contract. Whether the contract is performed or still partly executory, the continued use of the property amounts to a ratification and prevents a disaffirmance by the minor. Simply keeping the goods for an unreasonable time after attaining majority has also been construed as a ratification.

FLETCHER v. MARSHALL Appellate Court of Illinois, 1994, 260 Ill.App.3d 673, 198 Ill.Dec 494, 632 N.E.2d 1105

FACTS On April 29, 1991, the plaintiff, Kirsten Fletcher, and the defendant, John E. Marshall III, jointly signed a lease to rent an apartment for the term beginning on July 1, 1991, and ending on June 30, 1992, for a monthly rent of $525 per month. At the time the lease was signed, Marshall was not yet eighteen years of age. Marshall turned eighteen on May 30, 1991. Two weeks later, the couple moved into the apartment. About two months later, Marshall moved out to attend college, but Fletcher remained. She paid the rent herself for the remaining ten months of the lease and then sought contribution for Marshall's share of the rent plus court costs in the amount of $2,500. The trial court entered judgment in favor of Marshall because he was a minor at the time of contract formation.

DECISION Judgment reversed and remanded to determine damages the defendant owes the plaintiff.

OPINION A contract of a minor is not void, but is voidable at the election of the minor. After attaining majority, a minor may either disaffirm or ratify a contract that he entered into while he was still a minor. Also, once a contract is ratified by the minor, it cannot then be disaffirmed by subsequent conduct. Two weeks after becoming eighteen years of age, Marshall moved into the apartment and paid rent. He lived in the apartment for about one and a half months and never took any action to disaffirm the lease before moving out. Marshall's occupancy and payment of rent constitute unequivocal ratification of the lease. Because he had already ratified the lease, his later attempt to disaffirm it by moving out of the apartment and refusing to make further payments was of no effect. Accordingly, the trial court's judgment was against the manifest weight of the evidence. Marshall remained liable for the rent for the remainder of the lease term and is therefore liable to Fletcher for the rent payments she made on his behalf.

INTERPRETATION Ratification of a contract may be implicit from a person's conduct after the person attains his majority.

Liability for Necessaries

Contractual incapacity does not excuse a minor from an obligation to pay for **necessaries**, those things, such as food, shelter, medicine, and clothing, that suitably and reasonably supply his personal needs. Even here, however, the minor is not contractually liable for the agreed price but for the *reasonable* value of the items furnished. Recovery is based on quasi contract. Thus, if a clothier sells a minor a suit that the minor needs, the clothier can successfully sue the minor. The clothier's recovery, however, is limited to the reasonable value of the suit only, even if this amount is much less than the agreed-upon selling price. In addition, a minor is not liable for anything on the ground that the item is a necessary unless it has been actually furnished to him and used or consumed by him. In other words, a minor may disaffirm his executory contracts for necessaries and refuse to accept such clothing, lodging, or other items.

Defining "necessaries" is a difficult task. In general, the states regard as necessary those things that the minor needs to maintain himself in his particular station in life. Items necessary for subsistence and health, such as food, lodging, clothing, medicine, and medical services, are included. But other less essential

Necessaries items that reasonably supply a person's needs

Liability for necessaries a minor is liable for the reasonable value of necessary items

items, such as textbooks, school instruction, and legal advice, may be included as well. Further, some states enlarge the concept of necessaries to include articles of property and services that a minor needs to earn the money required to provide the necessities of life for himself and his dependents. Nevertheless, many states limit necessaries to items that are not provided to the minor. Thus, if a minor's guardian provides her with an adequate wardrobe, a blouse the minor purchased would *not* be considered a necessary.

The following is the leading case on the rights and obligations of minors for the purchase of "necessaries."

GASTONIA PERSONNEL CORP. v. ROGERS Supreme Court of North Carolina, 1970, 276 N.C. 279, 172 S.E.2d 19

FACTS Rogers was a nineteen-year-old (the age of majority then being twenty-one) high school graduate pursuing a civil engineering degree when he learned that his wife was expecting a child. As a result, he quit school and sought assistance from Gastonia Personnel Corporation in finding a job. Rogers signed a contract with the employment agency providing that he would pay the agency a service charge if it obtained suitable employment for him. The employment agency found him such a job, but Rogers refused to pay the service charge, asserting that he was a minor when he signed the contract. Gastonia sued to recover the agreed-upon service charge from Rogers. The trial court dismissed the plaintiff's claim and the Court of Appeals affirmed.

DECISION Judgment reversed and case remanded for a new trial in accordance with legal principles stated in the opinion.

OPINION In general, a contract with a minor is voidable by the minor unless the contract is for necessaries. The law is based on the idea that society has a moral obligation to protect the interests of minors from overreaching adults. In its effort to protect "older minors" from improvident or unfair contracts, however, the law should not deny them the opportunity and the right to obligate themselves for articles of property or services that are reasonably necessary to enable them to provide for the proper support of themselves and their dependents. Since the service provided by the employment agency in finding Rogers a suitable job qualifies as such a service, the contract is not voidable, and the agency can recover the reasonable service charge.

INTERPRETATION Contractual incapacity does not excuse a minor from an obligation to pay a reasonable value for a necessity.

Ordinarily, luxury items, such as cameras, tape recorders, stereo equipment, television sets, and motorboats, do not qualify as necessaries. The question concerning whether automobiles and trucks are necessaries has caused considerable controversy, but some courts have recognized that under certain circumstances an automobile may be a necessary where it is used by the minor for his business activities.

Liability for Misrepresentation of Age

Liability for misrepresentation of age prevailing view is that a minor may disaffirm the contract

The states do not agree whether a minor who fraudulently misrepresents her age when entering into a contract has the power to disaffirm. Suppose a contracting minor says that she is eighteen years of age (or twenty-one, if that is the year of attaining majority) and actually looks that old or even older. By the prevailing view in this country, despite her misrepresentation, the minor may nevertheless disaffirm the contract. Some states, however, prohibit disaffirmance if a minor misrepresented her age to an adult who, in good faith, reasonably relied on the misrepresentation. As shown in the following case, other states not following the majority rule either (a) require the minor to restore the other party to the position he occupied before making the contract or (b) allow the defrauded party to recover damages against the minor in tort.

KESER v. CHAGNON Supreme Court of Colorado, 1966, 159 Colo. 209, 410 P.2d 637

FACTS On June 11, 1964, Chagnon bought a 1959 Edsel from Keser for $995. Chagnon, who was then a twenty-year-old minor, obtained the contract by falsely advising Keser that he was over twenty-one years old, the age of majority. On September 25, 1964, two months and four days after his twenty-first birthday, Chagnon disaffirmed the contract and, ten days later, returned the Edsel to Keser. He then brought suit to recover the money he had paid for the automobile. Keser counterclaimed that he suffered damages as the direct result of Chagnon's false representation of his age. A trial was had to the court, sitting without a jury, all of which culminated in a judgment in favor of Chagnon against Keser in the sum of $655.78. This particular sum was arrived at by the trial court in the following manner: the trial court found that Chagnon initially purchased the Edsel for the sum of $995 and that he was entitled to the return of his $995; and then, by way of setoff, the trial court subtracted from the $995 the sum of $339.22, apparently representing the difference between the purchase price paid for the vehicle and the reasonable value of the Edsel on October 5, 1964, the date when the Edsel was returned to Keser.

DECISION Judgment affirmed except as to the calculation of damages for misrepresentation.

OPINION If a minor does not exercise his right to disaffirm a contract within a "reasonable time" after he reaches the age of majority, he loses that right. Here, however, Chagnon's disaffirmance just two months after reaching majority was within a reasonable time. Under the general rule, once he returned the car—the only consideration in his possession—he was entitled to recover the full $995. While a false representation of his age does not destroy a minor's right to disaffirm, it does permit the seller to deduct from the buyer's compensation any damages that the seller suffered due to the false representation. The measure of damages for the seller is the difference between the reasonable value of the property on the date of delivery and its reasonable value on the date of return. Since Chagnon obtained the contract by false representation of his age, he will not recover his full $995. Instead, his recovery is decreased by the amount of Keser's damages—the loss of the Edsel's reasonable value.

INTERPRETATION States vary on the rights of a minor and a defrauded party when a minor fraudulently misrepresents her age when entering into a contract.

Liability for Tort Connected with Contract

It is well settled that minors are generally liable for their torts. There is, however, a legal doctrine that if a tort and a contract are so "interwoven" that the court must enforce the contract to enforce the tort action, the minor is not liable in tort. Thus, if a minor rents an automobile from an adult, he enters into a contractual relationship obliging him to exercise reasonable care to protect the property from injury. By negligently damaging the automobile, he breaches that contractual undertaking. But his contractual immunity protects him from an action by the adult based on the contract. By the majority view, the adult cannot successfully sue the minor for damages on a tort theory. For, it is reasoned, a tort recovery would, in effect, be an enforcement of the contract and would defeat the protection that contract law gives the minor. Should the minor depart, however, from the terms of the agreement (by using a rental automobile for an unauthorized purpose, for example) and in so doing negligently cause damage to the automobile, most courts would hold that the tort is independent and that the adult can collect from the minor.

Liability for tort connected with contract if a tort and a contract are so intertwined that to enforce the tort the court must enforce the contract, the minor is not liable in tort

INCOMPETENT PERSONS

In this section, we will discuss the contract status of incompetent persons who are under court-appointed guardianship and those who are not adjudicated incompetents.

Guardianship
(guard´·i·an·ship) the relationship under which a person (the guardian) is appointed by a court to preserve and control the property of another (the ward)

Person under guardianship contracts made by a person placed under guardianship by court order are void

Person Under Guardianship

If a person is under **guardianship** by *court order*, her contracts are *void* and of no legal effect. A court appoints a *guardian*, generally under the terms of a statute, to control and preserve the property of a person (the *ward* or *adjudicated incompetent*) whose impaired capacity prevents her from managing her own property. (See The Law and You.) Nonetheless, a party dealing with an individual under guardianship may be able to recover the fair value of any necessaries provided to the incompetent. Moreover, the contracts of the ward may be ratified by her guardian during the period of guardianship or by the ward herself on termination of the guardianship.

THE LAW AND YOU What Is a Guardian and a Conservator?

Guardians and conservators are persons appointed by the Probate Court. The individual for whom they are appointed is called a ward.

A guardian is appointed for a ward when the Probate Court determines that one of the following circumstances exists:

1. The ward is a minor (less than 18 years old);
2. The ward is mentally ill, as evidenced by the opinion of a qualified physician;
3. The ward is mentally retarded, as evidenced by the opinion of a qualified physician;
4. The ward, because of excessive drinking, gambling and the like, wastes or lessens his estate, commonly called a "spendthrift."

In each of the foregoing situations, except in the case of minors, it must appear to the Probate Court that the ward is incapacitated to such a degree that he is unable to make informed decisions regarding his personal and financial affairs.

A conservator is appointed for a ward when the Probate Court determines that one of the following circumstances exists:

1. The ward suffers from mental weakness;
2. The ward is mentally retarded;
3. The ward suffers from physical incapacity;

4. The ward is unable to make or communicate informed decisions due to physical incapacity or illness.

In each of the foregoing situations, it must appear to the Probate Court that the ward is incapacitated to such a degree that he is unable to make informed decisions regarding his financial affairs.

What Are the Duties of a Guardian and a Conservator?

Guardians and conservators have many duties in common and are subject to supervision of the Probate Court. Some of these duties are set forth below. The list is not complete, but rather is a general indication of the scope of duties:

1. Pay the ward's debts;
2. Represent the ward in all lawsuits;
3. Control and manage the ward's property;
4. Invest the ward's funds;
5. Collect funds due the ward;
6. Support the ward and his family from the ward's funds;
7. Sell, lease or mortgage the ward's property, with the approval of the Probate Court.

A guardian, unlike a conservator, has custody of the person of his ward, Also, a guardian must consent

to such matters as medical treatment and where the ward will reside.

Who May Be a Guardian or a Conservator?

The law gives no preference to any particular class of persons or relatives. Any person who is proper and fit is eligible. The paramount consideration of the Probate Court is the welfare of the ward and the appropriateness of the appointment to meet the ward's needs.

Fees of a Guardian and Conservator

The reasonableness of fees is ultimately determined by the court. A court usually will take into account the size of the estate, the responsibilities placed upon the guardian or conservator and the amount of work involved. Corporate guardians and conservators, such as banks and trust companies, base their fees upon a percentage of income and principal each year. Banks publish fee schedules which are available to the public.

[This material was issued as a public service and does not constitute legal advice, which can only be given by an attorney. The contents of this feature pertain only to the laws of Massachusetts at the time of their publication.]

Reprinted with permission from the Massachusetts Bar Foundation, copyright September 1993.

Mental Illness or Defect

Because a contract is a consensual transaction, the parties to a valid contract must have a certain level of mental capacity. If a person lacks such capacity, or is **mentally incompetent**, the agreement is *voidable*.

Under the traditional cognitive ability test, a person is mentally incompetent if he is unable to comprehend the subject of the contract, its nature, and its probable consequences. Though he need not be proved permanently incompetent to avoid the contract, his mental defect must be something more than a weakness of intellect or a lack of average intelligence. In short, a person is competent unless he is unable to understand the nature and effect of his actions, in which case he may disaffirm the contract even if the other party did not know or had no reason to know of the incompetent's mental condition.

A second type of mental incompetence recognized by the Restatement and some states is a mental condition that impairs a person's ability to act in a reasonable manner. In other words, the person understands what he is doing but cannot control his behavior in order to act in a reasonable and rational way. If the contract he enters is entirely executory or grossly unfair, it is voidable. If, however, the contract is executed and fair and the competent party had no reason to suspect the incompetency of the other, the incompetent must restore the competent party to the *status quo* by returning the consideration he has received or its equivalent in money. If restoration to the *status quo* is impossible, avoidance will depend upon the equities of the situation.

Like minors and persons under guardianship, an incompetent person is liable on the principle of quasi contract for *necessaries* furnished him, the amount of recovery being the reasonable value of the goods or services. Moreover, an incompetent person may *ratify* or *disaffirm* his voidable contracts during a lucid period or when he becomes competent.

INTOXICATED PERSONS

A person may *avoid* any contract that he enters into if the other party has reason to know that the person, because of his intoxication, is unable to understand the nature and consequences of his actions or unable to act in a reasonable manner. Such contracts, as in the case that follows, are **voidable**, although they may be ratified when the intoxicated person regains his capacity. Slight intoxication will not destroy one's contractual capacity; on the other hand, to make a contract voidable, a person need not be so drunk that he is totally without reason or understanding.

The effect that the courts allow intoxication to have on contractual capacity is similar to the effect they allow contracts that are voidable because of incompetency, although the courts are even more strict with intoxication due to its voluntary nature. The courts, therefore, require that, to avoid a contract, the intoxicated person on regaining his capacity must act promptly to disaffirm and generally must offer to restore the consideration he has received. Individuals who are taking prescribed medication are treated the same as those who are incompetent under the cognitive ability test. As with incompetent persons, intoxicated persons are liable in quasi contract for necessaries furnished during their incapacity.

Mentally incompetent unable to understand the nature and effect of one's acts

Mental illness or defect a contract entered into by a mentally incompetent person is voidable

Intoxicated persons a contract entered into by an intoxicated person (one who cannot understand the nature and consequence of her actions) is voidable

FIRST STATE BANK OF SINAI v. HYLAND Supreme Court of South Dakota, 1987, 399 N.W.2d 894

FACTS Randy Hyland, unable to pay two promissory notes due September 19, 1981, negotiated with The First State Bank of Sinai (Bank) for an extension. The Bank agreed on the condition that Randy's father Mervin act as cosigner. Mervin, a good customer of the Bank, had executed and paid on time over sixty promissory notes within a seven-year period. Accordingly, the Bank drafted a new promissory note with an April 20, 1982, due date, which Randy took home for Mervin to sign. On April 20, 1982, the new note was unpaid. Randy, on May 5, 1982, brought the Bank a check signed by Mervin to cover the interest owed on the unpaid note and asked for another extension. The Bank agreed to a second extension, again on the condition that Mervin act as cosigner. Mervin, however, refused to sign the last note; and Randy subsequently declared bankruptcy. The Bank sued Mervin on December 19, 1982. Mervin responded that he was not liable since he had been incapacitated by liquor at the time he signed the note. He had been drinking heavily throughout this period, and in fact had been involuntarily committed to an alcoholism treatment hospital twice during the time of these events. In between commitments, however, Mervin had executed and paid his own promissory note with the Bank and had transacted business in connection with his farm. The trial court held that Mervin's contract as cosigner was void due to alcohol-related incapacity, and the Bank appealed.

DECISION Judgment for the Bank.

OPINION Mervin's obligation on the note was voidable, not void, due to his alcohol-related incapacity. Voidable contracts may be disaffirmed by the temporarily disabled party. Disaffirmance, however, must be prompt upon the recovery of the intoxicated person, or upon notice of the agreement if the once disabled person has forgotten it. A voidable contract may also be ratified by the party who contracted while disabled, resulting in a fully valid legal obligation. Ratification may be either express or implied by conduct. Furthermore, failure to disaffirm over a period of time may itself ripen into ratification, especially when voiding the contract will significantly prejudice the other party. Mervin had notice, both from Randy and the Bank, that the note he cosigned was overdue. Nevertheless, Mervin wrote a check paying the interest due. Such action amounts to ratification by conduct. Mervin also ratified the contract by waiting several months before attempting to disaffirm. The Bank has been significantly prejudiced by Mervin's delay since Randy has now been discharged through bankruptcy. Through his failure to disaffirm and subsequent ratification, the once voidable contract is now fully binding on Mervin.

INTERPRETATION An intoxicated party ratifies a contract by not disaffirming it when she is not intoxicated and learns of its existence and by making interest payments on it when she is not intoxicated.

Figure 14–1 summarizes the voidability of contracts made by persons with contractual incapacity.

FIGURE 14–1 Incapacity: Minors, Nonadjudicated Incompetents, and Intoxicated Persons

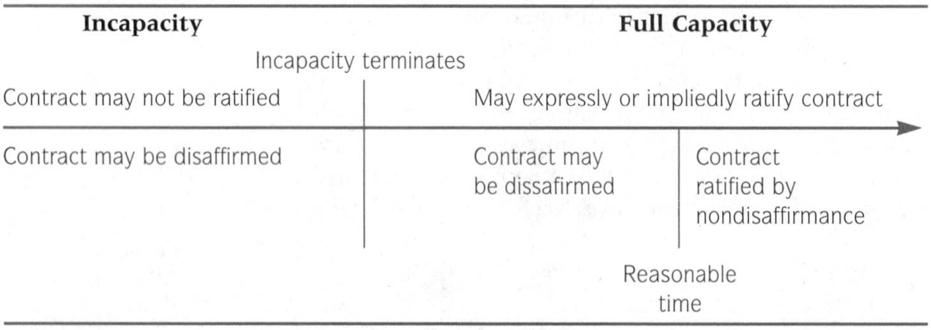

ETHICAL DILEMMA Should a Merchant Sell to One Who Lacks Capacity?

FACTS Alice Richards is a sales-clerk for an exclusive department store in Connecticut. She was working in the children's clothing department when an elderly woman, Carrie Johnson, entered the area and began to browse. Since part of her compensation is based on commissions and it had been a slow season, Richards was eager to help her. However, when Richards asked Johnson if she needed any help, Johnson replied, "No, I'm just looking for a new pocketbook." When Richards attempted to direct Johnson to the pocketbooks, Johnson did not appear to respond. Puzzled, Richards began to wonder whether the woman was mentally alert.

Johnson picked out infant's clothing and accessories worth approximately $250.00. At the cashier's counter she exclaimed how lovely everything was and explained that the jumpers and bath toys would go well with the other new clothes she had purchased for her son, who would soon be back from a cruise in the Bahamas.

Worried that the woman did not know what she was purchasing, Richards asked her manager for assistance. The manager said that the sale should be completed, as long as the store's credit policies were satisfied.

Social, Policy, and Ethical Considerations

1. What would you do?
2. What responsibility does a retail store have in stopping a sale where a reasonable person would assume that the customer lacks capacity? What business policies are appropriate?
3. What are the dangers in assuming a protective position? How can a retailer avoid discrimination and extend appropriate protection?
4. What alternatives does a family have when an elderly member begins to lose capacity?

CHAPTER SUMMARY

Minors	**Definition** person who is under the age of majority (usually 18 years)
	Liability on Contracts minor's contracts are voidable at the minor's option
	■ *Disaffirmance* avoidance of the contract; may be done during minority and for a reasonable time after reaching majority
	■ *Ratification* affirmation of the entire contract; may be done upon reaching majority
	Liability for Necessaries a minor is liable for the reasonable value of necessary items (those that reasonably supply a person's needs)
	Liability for Misrepresentation of Age prevailing view is that a minor may disaffirm the contract
	Liability for Tort Connected with Contract if a tort and a contract are so intertwined that to enforce the tort the court must enforce the contract, the minor is not liable in tort

Incompetent and Intoxicated Persons	**Person under Guardianship** contracts made by a person placed under guardianship by court order are void
	Mental Illness or Defect a contract entered into by a mentally incompetent person (one who is unable to understand the nature and consequences of his acts) is voidable
	Intoxicated Persons a contract entered into by an intoxicated person (one who cannot understand the nature and consequence of her actions) is voidable

QUESTIONS

1. How and when may a minor ratify a contract?
2. What is the liability of a minor who disaffirms a contract?
3. Define a necessary and explain how it affects the contracts of a minor.
4. Distinguish between the legal capacity of a person under guardianship and a mentally incompetent person who is not under guardianship.
5. What is the rule governing an intoxicated person's capacity to enter into a contract?

Internet Question. Find and review information on (a) laws governing the employment of minors, (b) gifts to minors, and (c) Uniform Guardianship and Protective Proceedings Act.

PROBLEMS

1. Mark, a minor, operates a one-man automobile repair shop. Rose, having heard of Mark's good work on other cars, takes her car to Mark's shop for a thorough engine overhaul. Mark, while overhauling Rose's engine, carelessly fits an unsuitable piston ring on one of the pistons, with the result that Rose's engine is seriously damaged. Mark offers to return the sum that Rose paid him for his work, but refuses to make good the damage. Rose sues Mark in tort for the damage to her engine. Decision?

2. (a) On March 20, Andy Small became seventeen years old, but he appeared to be at least eighteen (the age of majority). On April 1, he moved into a rooming house in Chicago and orally agreed to pay the landlady $300 a month for room and board, payable at the end of each month.

   (b) On April 4, he went to Honest Hal's Carfeteria and signed a contract to buy a used car on credit with a small down payment. He made no representation as to his age, but Honest Hal represented the car to be in top condition, which it subsequently turned out not to be.

   (c) On April 7, Andy sold and conveyed to Adam Smith a parcel of real estate that he owned.

   On April 30, Andy refused to pay his landlady for his room and board for the month of April; he returned the car to Honest Hal and demanded a refund of his down payment; and he demanded that Adam Smith reconvey the land, although the purchase price, which Andy received in cash, had been spent in riotous living. Decisions as to each claim?

3. Jones, a minor, owned a 1987 automobile. She traded it to Stone for a 1988 car. Jones went on a three-week trip and found that the 1988 car was not as good as the 1987 car. She asked Stone to return the 1987 car but was told that it had been sold to Tate, who did not know that the car had been obtained by Stone from a minor. Jones thereupon sued Tate for the return of the 1987 car. Decision?

4. On May 7, Roy, a minor, a resident of Smithton, purchased an automobile from Royal Motors, Inc., for $7,750 in cash. On the same day, he bought a motor scooter from Marks, also a minor, for $750 and paid him in full. On June 5, two days before attaining his majority, Roy disaffirmed the contracts and offered to return the car and the motor scooter to the respective sellers. Royal Motors and Marks each refused the offers. On June 16, Roy brought separate appropriate actions against Royal Motors and Marks to recover the purchase price of the car and the motor scooter. By agreement on July 30, Royal Motors accepted the automobile. Royal then filed a counterclaim against Roy for the reasonable rental value of the car between June 5 and July 30. The car was not damaged during this period. Royal knew that Roy lived twenty-five miles from his place of employment in Smithton and that he would probably use the car, as he did, for transportation. Decision as to (a) Roy's action against Royal Motors, Inc. and its counterclaim against Roy; (b) Roy's action against Marks?

5. On October 1, George Jones, who was then a minor, entered into a contract with Johnson Motor Company, a dealer in automobiles, to buy a car for $7,600. He paid $1,100 down and agreed to make monthly payments thereafter of $325 each. Although he made the first payment on November 1, he failed to make any more payments. Though Jones was seventeen years old at the time he made the contract, he represented to the company that he was twenty-one years old because he was afraid the company would not sell the car to him if it knew his real age. His appearance was that of a man of twenty-one years of age. On December 15, the company repossessed the car under the terms provided in the contract. At that time, the car had been damaged and was in need of repairs. On December 20, George Jones became of age and at once disaffirmed the contract and demanded the return of the $1,425 paid on the contract. When the company

refused to do so, Jones brought an action to recover the $1,425; and the company set up a counterclaim of $1,500 for expenses it incurred in repairing the car. Decision?

6. Rebecca entered into a written contract to sell certain real estate to Mary, a minor, for $80,000, payable $4,000 on the execution of the contract and $800 on the first day of each month thereafter until paid. Mary paid the $4,000 down payment and eight monthly installments before attaining her majority. Thereafter, Mary made two additional monthly payments and caused the contract to be recorded in the county where the real estate was located. Mary was then advised by her lawyer that the contract was voidable. After being so advised, Mary immediately tendered the contract to Rebecca, together with a deed reconveying all of Mary's interest in the property to Rebecca. Also, Mary demanded that Rebecca return the money paid under the contract. Rebecca refused the tender and declined to repay any portion of the money paid to her by Mary. Mary then brought an action to cancel the contract and recover the amount paid to Rebecca. Decision?

7. Anita sold and delivered an automobile to Marvin, a minor. Marvin, during his minority, returned the automobile to Anita, saying that he disaffirmed the sale. Anita accepted the automobile and said she would return the purchase price to Marvin the next day. Later in the day, Marvin changed his mind, took the automobile without Anita's knowledge, and sold it to Chris. Anita had not returned the purchase price when Marvin took the car. On what theory, if any, can Anita recover from Marvin? Explain.

8. Ira, who in 1987 had been found not guilty of a criminal offense because of insanity, was released from a hospital for the criminally insane during the summer of 1988 and since that time has been a reputable and well-respected citizen and businessman. On February 1, 1989, Ira and Shirley entered into a contract in which Ira would sell his farm to Shirley for $100,000. Ira now seeks to void the contract. Shirley insists that Ira is fully competent and has no right to avoid the contract. Who will prevail? Why?

9. Daniel, while under the influence of alcohol to the extent that he did not know the nature and consequences of his acts, agreed to sell his 1992 automobile to Belinda for $8,000. The next morning when Belinda went to Daniel's house with the $8,000 in cash, Daniel stated that he did not remember the transaction but that "a deal is a deal." One week after completing the sale, Daniel decides that he wishes to avoid the contract. What is the result?

10. Langstraat, age seventeen, owned a motorcycle that he insured against liability with Midwest Mutual Insurance Company. He signed a notice of rejection attached to the policy indicating that he did not desire to purchase uninsured motorists' coverage from the insurance company. Later he was involved in an accident with another motorcycle owned and operated by a party who was uninsured. Langstraat now seeks to recover from the insurance company, asserting that his rejection was not valid because he is a minor. Decision?

11. G.A.S. married his wife, S.I.S., on January 19, 1957. He began to have mental health problems in 1970; that year, he was hospitalized at the Delaware State Hospital for eight weeks. Similar illnesses occurred in 1972 and in the early part of 1974, with G.A.S. suffering from symptoms such as paranoia and loss of a sense of reality. In early 1975, G.A.S. was still committed to the Delaware State Hospital, attending a regular job during the day and returning to the hospital at night. During this time, he entered into a separation agreement prepared by his wife's attorney. G.A.S., however, never spoke with the attorney about the contents of the agreement; nor did he read it prior to signing. Moreover, G.A.S. was not independently represented by counsel when he executed this agreement. G.A.S. brings this action to disaffirm the separation agreement. Decision?

12. L. D. Robertson bought a pickup truck from King and Julian, who did business as the Julian Pontiac Company. At the time of purchase, Robertson was seventeen years old, living at home with his parents, and driving his father's truck around the county to different construction jobs. According to the sales contract, he traded in a passenger car for the truck and was given $723 credit toward the truck's $1,743 purchase price, agreeing to pay the remainder in monthly installments. After he paid the first month's installment, the truck caught fire and was rendered useless. The insurance agent, upon finding that Robertson was a minor, refused to deal with him. Consequently, Robertson sued to exercise his right as a minor to rescind the contract and to recover the purchase price he had already paid ($723 credit for the car traded in plus the one month's installment). The defendants argue that Robertson, even as a minor, cannot rescind the contract since it was for a necessary item. Decision?

13. A fifteen-year-old minor was employed by Midway Toyota, Inc., of Great Falls, Montana. On August 18, 1975, the minor, while engaged in lifting heavy objects, injured his lower back. In October 1975 he underwent surgery to remove a herniated disk. Midway Toyota paid him the appropriate amount of temporary total disability payments ($53.36 per week) from August 18, 1975, through November 15, 1976. In February 1977 a final settlement was reached for 150 weeks of permanent partial disability benefits totaling

$6,136.40. Tom Mazurek represented Midway Toyota in the negotiations leading up to the agreement and negotiated directly with the minor and his mother, Hermoine Parrent. The final settlement agreement was signed by the minor only. Mrs. Parrent was present at the time and did not object to the signing, but neither she nor anyone else of "legal guardian status" co-signed the agreement. The minor later sought to disaffirm the agreement and reopen his workers' compensation case. The workers' compensation court denied his petition, holding that Mrs. Parrent "participated fully in consideration of the offered final settlement and . . . ratified and approved it on behalf of her ward . . . to the same legal effect as if she had actually signed [it]. . . ." The minor appealed. Decision?

14. Rose, a minor, bought a new Buick Riviera from Sheehan Buick. Seven months later, while still a minor, he attempted to disaffirm the purchase. Sheehan Buick refused to accept the return of the car or to refund the purchase price. Rose, at the time of the purchase, gave all the appearance of being of legal age. The car had been used by him to carry on his school, business, and social activities. Decision?

15. Haydocy Pontiac sold Jennifer Lee an automobile for $1,552, of which $1,402 was financed with a note and security agreement. At the time of the sale, Lee, age twenty, represented to Haydocy that she was twenty-one years old, the age of majority, and capable of contracting. After receiving the car, Lee allowed John Roberts to take possession of it. Roberts took the car and has not returned. Lee has failed to make any further payments on the car. Haydocy has sued to recover on the note. Lee disaffirms the contract, claiming that she was too young to enter into a valid contract. Decision?

16. Carol White ordered a $225 pair of contact lenses through an optometrist. White, an emancipated minor, paid $100 by check and agreed to pay the remaining $125 at a later time. The doctor ordered the lenses, incurring a debt of $110. After the lenses were ordered, White called to cancel her order and stopped payment on the $100 check. The lenses could be used by no one but White. The doctor sued White for the value of the lenses. Decision?

17. Williamson, her mortgage in default, was threatened with foreclosure on her home. She decided to sell the house. The Matthewses learned of this and contacted her about the matter. Williamson claims that she offered to sell her equity for $17,000 and that the Matthewses agreed to pay off the mortgage. The Matthewses contend that the asking price was $1,700. On September 27, 1978, the parties signed a contract of sale, which stated the purchase price to be $1,800 ($100 increase to account for furniture in the house) plus the unpaid balance of the mortgage. The parties met again on October 10 to sign the deed. Later that day, Williamson, concerned that she had not received her full $17,000 consideration, contacted an attorney. On October 12, Williamson filed for injunctive relief, seeking to set aside the sale based upon inadequate consideration and mental weakness due to intoxication. Decision?

18. Halbman, a minor, purchased a 1968 Oldsmobile from Lemke for $1,250. Under the terms of the contract, Halbman would pay $1,000 down and the balance in $25 weekly installments. Upon making the down payment, Halbman received possession of the car, but Lemke retained the title until the balance was paid. After Halbman had made his first four payments, a connecting rod in the car's engine broke. Lemke denied responsibility but offered to help Halbman repair the engine if Halbman would provide the parts. Halbman, however, placed the car in a garage where the repairs cost $637.40. Halbman never paid the repair bill.

Hoping to avoid any liability for the vehicle, Lemke transferred title to Halbman even though Halbman never paid the balance owed. Halbman returned the title with a letter disaffirming the contract and demanded return of the money paid. Lemke refused. Since the repair bill remained unpaid, the garage removed the car's engine and transmission and towed the body to Halbman's father's house. Vandalism during the period of storage rendered the car unsalvageable. Several times Halbman requested Lemke to remove the car. Lemke refused. Halbman sued Lemke for the return of his consideration, and Lemke countersued for the amount still owed on the contract. Decision?

CHAPTER 15

Contracts in Writing

An *oral* contract, that is, one not in writing, is in every way as enforceable as a written contract *unless* otherwise provided by statute. Although most contracts do not need to be in writing to be enforceable, it is highly desirable that significant contracts be written. Written contracts avoid many problems that proving the terms of oral contracts inevitably involve. The process of setting down the contractual terms in a written document also tends to clarify the terms and bring to light problems the parties might not otherwise foresee. Moreover, the terms of a written contract do not change over time, whereas the parties' recollections of the terms might.

When the parties do reduce their agreement to a complete and final written expression, the law (under the parol evidence rule) honors this document by not allowing the parties to introduce any evidence in a lawsuit that would alter, modify, or vary the terms of the written contract. Nevertheless, the parties may differ as to the proper or intended meaning of language contained in the written agreement where such language is ambiguous or susceptible to different interpretations. To determine the proper meaning requires an interpretation, or construction, of the contract. The rules of construction permit the parties to introduce evidence to resolve ambiguity and to show the meaning of the language employed and the sense in which both parties used it.

In this chapter, we will examine (1) the types of contracts that must be in writing to be enforceable, (2) the parol evidence rule, and (3) the rules of contractual interpretation.

STATUTE OF FRAUDS

The **statute of frauds** requires that certain designated types of contracts be evidenced by a writing to be enforceable. Many more types of contracts are *not* subject to the statute of frauds than are subject to it. Most oral contracts, as previously indicated, are as enforceable and valid as written contracts. If, however, a given contract subject to the statute of frauds is said to be *within* the statute, to be enforceable it must comply with the requirements of the statute. All other types of contracts are said to be "not within" or "outside" the statute and need not comply with its requirements to be enforceable.

Statute of frauds specifies those contracts that must be evidenced by a writing to be enforceable

CONTRACTS WITHIN THE STATUTE OF FRAUDS

The following five kinds of contracts are within the statute of frauds as most states have adopted it. Compliance requires a writing signed by the party to be charged (the party against whom the contract is to be enforced).

1. Promises to answer for the duty of another
2. Promises of an executor or administrator to answer personally for a duty of the decedent whose funds he is administering
3. Agreements upon consideration of marriage
4. Agreements for the transfer of an interest in land
5. Agreements not to be performed within one year

A sixth type of contract within the original English statute of frauds applied to contracts for the sale of goods. The Uniform Commercial Code now governs the enforceability of contracts of this kind.

The various provisions of the statute of frauds apply independently. Accordingly, a contract for the sale of an interest in land may also be a contract in consideration of marriage, a contract not to be performed in one year, *and* a contract for the sale of goods.

In addition to those contracts specified in the original statute, most states require that other contracts be evidenced by a writing as well—for example, a contract to make a will, to authorize an agent to sell real estate, or to pay a commission to a real estate broker. Moreover, the UCC requires that contracts for the sale of securities, contracts creating certain types of security interests, and contracts for the sale of all other personal property for more than $5,000 be in writing.

Suretyship Provision

Suretyship provision
(sure´·ty·ship) promise to pay the debts of another

Surety person who promises to pay the debt of another

Principal debtor person whose debt is being supported

Collateral promise undertaking to be secondarily liable, that is, liable if the principal debtor does not perform

The **suretyship** provision applies to a contractual promise by a **surety** (*promisor*) to a **creditor** (*promisee*) to perform the duties or obligations of a third person (**principal debtor**) if the principal debtor does not perform. Thus, if a mother tells a merchant to extend $1,000 worth of credit to her son and says, "If he doesn't pay, I will," the promise is a suretyship and must be evidenced by a writing to be enforceable. The factual situation can be reduced to the simple idea that "If X doesn't pay, I will." The promise is said to be a **collateral promise**, in that the promisor is not primarily liable. The mother does not promise to pay in any event; her promise is to pay only if the one primarily obligated, the son, defaults.

Thus, a suretyship involves three parties and two contracts. The primary contract, between the principal debtor and the creditor, creates the indebtedness. The collateral contract is made by the third person (surety) directly with the creditor, whereby the surety promises to pay the debt to the creditor in case the principal debtor fails to do so. For a complete discussion of suretyship, see Chapter 40.

Original Promise If the promisor makes an **original promise** by undertaking to become primarily liable, then the statute of frauds does not apply. For example, a father tells a merchant to deliver certain items to his daughter and says, "I will pay $400 for them." The father is not promising to answer for the debt of another; rather, he is making the debt his own. It is to the father, and to the father alone, that the merchant extends credit; to the father alone, the creditor may look for payment. The statute of frauds does not apply, and the promise may be oral.

Original promise promise to become primarily liable

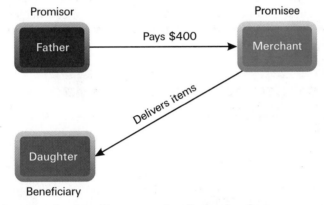

The following case further illustrates the distinction between suretyship and original promise.

SHANE QUADRI v. GOODYEAR SERVICE STORES Court of Appeals of Indiana, Third District, 1980, 412 N.E.2d 315

FACTS The defendant, Shane Quadri, contacted Don Hoffman, an employee of defendant Al J. Hoffman & Co., to procure car insurance. Later, Quadri's car was stolen on October 25 or 26, 1977. Quadri contacted Hoffman, who arranged with Budget Rent-a-Car, a plaintiff in this case, for a rental car for Quadri until his car was recovered. Hoffman authorized Budget Rent-a-Car to bill the Hoffman Agency. Later, when the stolen car was recovered, Hoffman telephoned the plaintiff, Goodyear, and arranged to have four new tires put on Quadri's car to replace those damaged during the theft. The plaintiffs (Budget and Goodyear) sued the defendants (Quadri and Hoffman) for payment of the car rental and tires. Judgment was entered in favor of Budget and Goodyear against defendant Hoffman but in favor of Quadri.

DECISION Judgment for Budget and Goodyear against Hoffman and judgment for Quadri affirmed.

OPINION Although the statute of frauds makes unenforceable oral contracts to pay the debts of a third person, it does not apply to original promises to pay for services rendered to a third person. Hoffman initiated the transactions with both Budget and Goodyear by telephone, indicating that Quadri was insured, and authorized the billing of the Hoffman Agency. By signing the rental agreement and tire invoice, Quadri merely obtained the benefits of the transactions authorized by Hoffman. Since credit was extended solely to the Hoffman Agency, the statute does not apply to Hoffman's oral promises. Thus, they are enforceable against Hoffman.

INTERPRETATION If the promisor makes an original promise to become primarily liable, then the statute of frauds does not apply.

Main Purpose Doctrine The courts have developed an exception to the suretyship provision called the "main purpose doctrine" or "leading object rule." Where the **main purpose** of the promisor is to obtain an economic benefit for herself that she did not previously have, then the promise comes within the exception and is *outside* the statute. The expected benefit to the surety "must be such as to justify the conclusion that his main purpose in making the promise is to advance his own interest." The fact that the surety received consideration for his promise or that he might receive a slight and indirect advantage is insufficient to bring the promise within the main purpose doctrine.

Main purpose object of promisor/surety is to provide an economic benefit for herself

Suppose that a supply company has refused to furnish materials on the credit of a building contractor. Faced with a possible slowdown in the construction of his building, the owner of the land promises the supplier that if the supplier will extend credit to the contractor, the owner will pay if the contractor does not. Here, the purpose of the promisor was to serve an economic interest of his own, even though the performance of the promise would discharge the duty of another. The intent to benefit the contractor was at most incidental, and courts will enforce oral promises of this type. Another application of the rule is provided in the following case.

STUART STUDIO, INC. v. NATIONAL SCHOOL OF HEAVY EQUIPMENT, INC. Court of Appeals of North Carolina, 1975, 25 N.C.App. 544, 214 S.E.2d 192

FACTS Stuart Studio, an art studio, prepared a new catalog for the National School of Heavy Equipment, a school run by Gilbert and Donald Shaw. When the artwork was virtually finished, Gilbert Shaw requested Stuart Studio to purchase and supervise the printing of 25,000 catalogs. Shaw told the art studio that payment of the printing costs would be made within ten days after billing and that if the "National School would not pay the full total that he would stand good for the entire bill." Shaw was chairman of the board of directors of the school, and he owned 100 percent of its voting stock and 49 percent of its nonvoting stock. The school became bankrupt, and Stuart Studio was unable to recover the sum from the school. Stuart Studio then brought this action against Shaw on the basis of his promise to pay the bill. The trial court granted Shaw's motion for a directed verdict, and Stuart Studio brought this appeal.

DECISION Judgment granting defendant's motion for directed verdict modified and remanded for trial on the issue of the liability of Shaw.

OPINION The statute of frauds requires promises to answer for the duties of another to be in writing to be enforceable. Where the promise is collateral and it appears that the promisor's main purpose in guaranteeing the obligation was to secure an advantage or economic benefit for himself, however, the promise is enforceable even though it was not in writing. The benefit accruing to a party merely by virtue of his position as a stockholder, officer, or director of a corporation alone is not such personal, immediate, and economic benefit as to invoke the main purpose rule. Rather, the court will examine the surety's position and ownership interest in the corporation to determine whether he has enough control of the corporation to benefit directly. Here, Gilbert Shaw exercised sufficient control over the National School to render his oral promise enforceable.

INTERPRETATION Where the main purpose of the promisor is to obtain an economic benefit for himself that he did not previously have, then the promise is outside the statute of frauds.

Promise Made to Debtor The suretyship provision has been interpreted *not* to include promises made to a *debtor*. For example, D owes a debt to C. S promises D to pay D's debt. Since the promise of S was made to the debtor (D), not the creditor, the promise is enforceable even if it is oral.

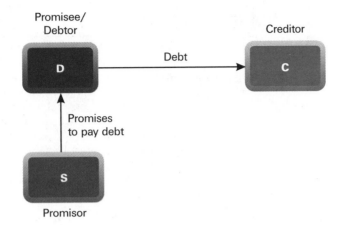

Executor-Administrator Provision

The executor-administrator provision applies to the promises of an executor of a decedent's will, or to those of the administrator of the estate if there is no will, to answer personally for a duty of the decedent. An **executor** or **administrator** is a person appointed by a court to carry out, subject to order of court, the administration of the estate of a deceased person. If the will of a decedent nominates a certain person as executor, the court usually appoints that person. (For a more detailed discussion of executors, administrators, and the differences between the two, see Chapter 54.) If an executor or administrator promises to answer personally for a duty of the decedent, the promise is unenforceable unless it is in writing. For example, Edgar, who is Donna's son and executor of Donna's will, recognizes that Donna's estate will not have enough funds to pay all of the decedent's debts. He orally promises Clark, one of Donna's creditors, that he will personally pay all of his mother's debts in full. Edgar's oral promise is not enforceable. This provision does not apply, however, to promises to pay debts of the deceased out of assets of the estate.

The executor-administrator provision is thus a specific application of the suretyship provision. Accordingly, the exceptions to the suretyship provision also apply to this provision.

Executor Administrator *(ex·ec'·u·tor)* person appointed to settle a decedent's estate

Executor-administrator provision applies to promises to answer personally for a duty of the decedent

Marriage Provision

The notable feature of the marriage provision is that it does *not* apply to mutual promises to marry. Rather, the provision applies only if a promise to marry is made in consideration for some promise other than a mutual promise to marry. Therefore, this provision covers Adams's promise to convey title to a certain farm to Barnes if Barnes accepts Adams's proposal of marriage. (See Consumer Insight: "I Will, I Do, I Don't, I Won't" on the following page.)

Marriage provision applies to promises in de in consideration of marriage but not to mutual promises to marry

Land Contract Provision

The land contract provision covers promises to transfer any **interest in land**, which includes any right, privilege, power, or immunity in real property. Thus, all promises to transfer, buy, or pay for an interest in land, including ownership interests, leases, mortgages, options, and easements, are within the provision.

The land contract provision does not include contracts to transfer an interest in personal property. It also does not cover short-term leases, which by statute in

Interest in land any right, privilege, power, or immunity in real property

Land contract provision applies to promises to transfer any right, privilege, power, or immunity in real property

CONSUMER INSIGHT

I Will, I Do, I Don't, I Won't: The Growing Popularity of Prenuptial Agreements

Once, only the rich and famous thought it necessary to draw up prenuptial agreements. Now, more and more middle-class couples are writing marriage contracts that include financial agreements before they exchange their wedding vows.

Prenuptial agreements came into vogue in the 1980s, after many states changed their divorce laws to allow for a more equitable distribution of property when a marriage dissolves. Some states, California being the notable example, even enacted community property laws that declared marital property to be jointly owned, no matter in whose name it was, unless the parties had signed a prenuptial agreement.

Today, with nearly half of all marriages ending in divorce, many people are entering their second marriage, or even their third, with some caution. Usually, they have assets that they want to protect. Often, they also have children from a previous marriage whom they want to look out for. Then, too, as people

in their twenties wait longer and longer before marrying, more women, and men as well, are walking down the aisle with considerable assets, from condominiums and houses to stocks and bonds.

Many couples are also realizing that marriage today has nearly as much to do with economics as it does with romance. In fact, along with sex and in-laws, money tops the list of topics that couples argue about the most.

As a result, prenuptial agreements are becoming more popular. They are also becoming more expensive. Today, a typical agreement may run in length to several written pages, spelling out in loads of fine print a financial blueprint for the marriage. It also may define a host of lifestyle issues, including arrangements for

child-rearing, rights of monetary support, and decisions about schooling and career relocations.

Generally, the courts have upheld most prenuptial contracts, as long as they have been written and are based on full disclosure of each party's finances. Legal and financial experts agree that those contemplating a prenuptial agreement should take into account the following points:

- Plan to act well in advance of the wedding, since it may take months to negotiate the contract.
- Make sure both of you hire your own attorney, to avoid a conflict of interest.
- Disclose honestly all of your assets and liabilities.
- Decide what property you will keep separate and what you will combine.
- Specify what will happen to assets accrued during the marriage.
- Put the agreement in writing and have it witnessed and notarized.

most states are those for one year or less; contracts to build a building on a piece of land; contracts to do work on the land; or contracts to insure a building.

An oral contract for the transfer of an interest in land may be enforced if the party seeking enforcement has so changed his position in reasonable reliance on the contract that a court can prevent injustice only by enforcing the contract. In applying this **part performance** exception, many states require the transferee to have paid a portion or all of the purchase price *and* either to have taken possession of the real estate or to have started to make valuable improvements on the land. Payment of part or all of the price is not sufficient in itself to make the contract enforceable under this exception. For example, Jane orally agrees to sell land to Jack for $30,000. With Jane's consent, Jack takes possession of the land, pays Jane $10,000, builds a house on the land, and occupies it. Several years later, Jane repudiates the contract. The courts will enforce the contract against Jane.

An oral promise by a purchaser is also enforceable if the seller fully performs by conveying the property to the purchaser.

One-year provision
applies to contracts that cannot be performed within one year

One-Year Provision

The statute of frauds requires that all contracts that *cannot* be fully performed within one year of the making of the contract be in writing.

The Possibility Test To determine whether a contract falls within the one-year provision, the courts ask whether it is *possible* for the performance of the contract to be completed within a year. Under the majority rule, the **possibility test** does not ask whether the agreement is likely to be performed within one year from the date it was formed; nor does it ask whether the parties think that performance will occur within the year. The enforceability of the contract depends *not* on probabilities or on actual subsequent events but on whether the terms of the contract make it possible for performance to occur within one year. For example, an oral contract between Alice and Bill for Alice to build a bridge, which should reasonably take three years, is generally enforceable if it is possible, although extremely unlikely and difficult, for Alice to perform the contract in one year. Similarly, if Alice agrees to employ Bill for life, this contract is also not within the statute of frauds. It is possible that Bill may die within the year, in which case the contract would be completely performed. The contract is therefore one that is *fully performable* within a year. Contracts of indefinite duration are likewise excluded from the provision. On the other hand, an oral contract to employ another person for thirteen months could not possibly be performed within a year and is therefore unenforceable.

> **Possibility test** is it possible for the agreement to be performed within one year?

PRICE v. MERCURY SUPPLY CO., INC. Court of Appeals of Tennessee, 1984, 682 S.W.2d 924

FACTS On July 5, 1970, Richard Price signed a written employment contract as a new salesman with the Mercury Supply Company. The contract was of indefinite duration and could be terminated by either party for any reason upon fifteen days' notice. Between 1970 and 1978, Price was promoted several times. In 1975, Price was made vice president of sales. In September of 1978, however, Price was told that his performance was not satisfactory and that if he did not improve he would be fired. In February of 1981, Price received notice of termination. Price claims that in 1975 he entered into a valid oral employment contract with Mercury Supply Company wherein he was made vice president of sales for life or until he should retire. The trial court ruled that the alleged oral contract was barred by the one-year provision of the statute of frauds.

DECISION Judgment for Mercury Sales because the enforceable oral contract was terminable at any time by either party.

OPINION The statute of frauds requires that all contracts that cannot *possibly* be completed within a year must be evidenced by a writing in order to be enforceable. Conversely, contracts that can possibly be performed within a year may still be enforced even if they are oral. The trial court in essence misapplied the law. The alleged oral contract of 1975 could be performed within one year because Price could have died or could have elected to retire within a year of making the alleged contract. The evidence, however, produced at trial showed that the alleged oral contract, if actually made, was still a terminable-at-will employment contract. Therefore, Mercury Supply Company could discharge Price at any time without breaching the valid oral contract.

INTERPRETATION If a contract is possible to perform fully within one year, it does not fall within the statute of frauds.

Computation of Time The year runs from the time the *agreement is made*, not from the time when the performance is to begin. For example, on January 1, 1997, A hires B to work for eleven months starting on May 1, 1997, under the terms of an oral contract. That contract will be fully performed on March 31, 1998, which is more than one year after January 1, 1997, the date the contract was made. Consequently, the contract is *within* the statute of frauds and unenforceable because it is oral.

> **Computation of time** the year runs from the time the agreement is made

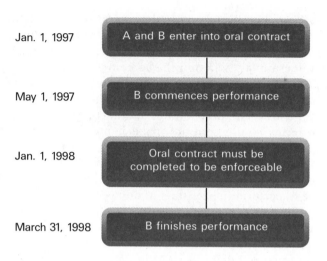

Similarly, a contract for a year's performance that is to begin three days after the date of the making of the contract is within the statute and, if oral, is unenforceable. If, however, the performance is to begin the day following the making or, under the terms of the agreement, *could* have begun the following day, it is not within the statute and need not be in writing.

Full Performance by One Party

Full performance by one party makes the promise of the other party enforceable under majority view

Where a contract has been fully performed by one party, most courts hold that the promise of the other party is enforceable even though by its terms its performance was not possible within one year. For example, Jane borrows $4,800 from Tom. Jane orally promises to pay Tom $4,800 in three annual installments of $1,600. Jane's promise is enforceable, despite the one-year provision, because Tom has fully performed by making the loan.

Sales of Goods

Sale of goods a contract for the sale of goods for the price of $500 or more must be evidenced by a writing to be enforceable

The English statute of frauds, which applied to contracts for the sale of goods, has been used as a prototype for the UCC, Article 2, statute of frauds provision. The UCC provides that a contract for the sale of goods for the price of ***$500 or more*** is not enforceable unless there is some writing sufficient to indicate that a contract for sale has been made between the parties. The Code defines goods as movable personal property.

Admission an admission in pleadings, testimony, or otherwise in court makes the contract enforceable for the quantity of goods admitted

Admission The Code permits an oral contract for the sale of goods to be enforced against a party who, in his pleading, testimony, or otherwise, admits in court that a contract was made; but the Code limits enforcement to the quantity of goods he admits. Moreover, some courts hold that, by performing over a period of time, for example, a party may implicitly admit the existence of a contract. Some courts now apply this exception to other statute of frauds provisions.

Specially manufactured goods an oral contract for specially manufactured goods is enforceable

Specially Manufactured Goods The Code permits enforcement of an oral contract for goods specially manufactured for a buyer, but only if evidence indicates that the goods were made for the buyer and the seller can show that he has made a *substantial beginning* of their manufacture before receiving any notice of repudiation. If the goods, although manufactured on special order, may be readily resold in the ordinary course of the seller's business, this exception does not apply.

Delivery or Payment and Acceptance Under the Code, delivery and acceptance of part of the goods, or payment and acceptance of part of the price, validates the contract but only for the goods that have been accepted or for which payment has been accepted. To illustrate, Liz orally agrees to buy 1,000 watches from David for $15,000. David delivers 300 watches to Liz, who receives and accepts the watches. The oral contract is enforceable to the extent of 300 watches ($4,500)—those received and accepted—but is unenforceable to the extent of 700 watches ($10,500).

A summary of the contracts within, and the exceptions to, the statute of frauds is provided in Figure 15–1.

Modification or Rescission of Contracts within the Statute of Frauds

Oral contracts modifying previously existing contracts are unenforceable if the resulting contract is within the statute of frauds. The reverse is also true: an oral modification of a prior contract is enforceable if the new contract is not within the statute of frauds.

Thus, examples of unenforceable oral contracts include an oral promise to guarantee the additional duties of another, an oral agreement to substitute different land for that described in the original contract, and an oral agreement to extend an employee's contract for six months to a total of two years. On the other hand, an oral agreement to modify an employee's contract from two years to six months at a higher salary is not within the statute of frauds and is enforceable.

Under the UCC, the decisive point is the contract price *after* modification. If the parties enter into an oral contract to sell for $450 a motorcycle to be delivered to the buyer and later, prior to delivery, orally agree that the seller shall

Delivery or payment and acceptance validates the contract only for the goods that have been accepted or for which payment has been accepted

Modification or Rescission of Contracts within the Statute of Frauds oral contracts modifying existing contracts are unenforceable if the resulting contract is within the statute of frauds

FIGURE 15–1 The Statute of Frauds

Contracts Within the Statute of Frauds	Exceptions
Suretyship—a promise to answer for the duty of another	• Main purpose rule • Original promise • Promise made to debtor
Executor-Administrator—a promise to answer personally for debt of decedent	• Main purpose rule • Original promise • Promise made to debtor
Agreements made upon consideration of marriage	• Mutual promises to marry
Agreements for the transfer of an interest in land	• Part performance plus detrimental reliance • Seller conveys property
Agreements not to be performed within one year	• Full performance by one party • Possibility of performance within one year
Sale of goods for $500 or more	• Admission • Specially manufactured goods • Delivery or payment and acceptance

paint the motorcycle and install new tires and that the buyer shall pay a price of $550, the modified contract is unenforceable. Conversely, if the parties have a written contract for the sale of 200 bushels of wheat at a price of $4 per bushel and later orally agree to decrease the quantity to 100 bushels at the same price per bushel, the agreement as modified is for a total price of $400 and thus is enforceable.

An oral rescission is effective and discharges all unperformed duties under the original contract. For example, Jones and Brown enter into a written contract of employment for a two-year term. Later they orally agree to rescind the contract. The oral agreement is effective, and the written contract is rescinded. Where land has been transferred, however, an agreement to rescind the transaction is a contract to retransfer the land and is within the statute of frauds.

COMPLIANCE WITH THE STATUTE OF FRAUDS

Even a contract within the statute of frauds will be enforced if it is contained in a *writing* or *memorandum* sufficient to satisfy the statute's requirements. As long as the writing meets those requirements, it need not be in any specific form, nor be an attempt by the parties to enter into a binding contract, nor represent their entire agreement.

General Contract Provisions

Compliance: General contract law the writing or writings must: specify the parties to the contract; specify the subject matter and essential terms; be signed by the party to be charged or by her agent

The English statute of frauds and most modern statutes of frauds require that the agreement be evidenced by a writing to be enforceable. The statute's purpose in requiring a writing is to ensure that the parties have actually entered into a contract. It is, therefore, not necessary that the writing be in existence when the parties initiate litigation; it is sufficient to show that the memorandum existed at one time. The note or memorandum, which may be formal or informal, must

1. specify the parties to the contract;
2. specify with reasonable certainty the subject matter and the essential terms of the unperformed promises; and
3. be signed by the party to be charged or by her agent.

The memorandum may be such that the parties themselves view it as having no legal significance whatever. For example, a personal letter between the parties, an interdepartmental communication, an advertisement, or the record books of a business may serve as a memorandum. The writing need not have been delivered to the party who seeks to take advantage of it, and it may even contain a repudiation of the oral agreement. For example, Sid and Gail enter into an oral agreement that Sid will sell Blackacre to Gail for $5,000. Sid subsequently receives a better offer and sends Gail a signed letter, which begins by reciting all the material terms of the oral agreement. The letter concludes: "Since my agreement to sell Blackacre to you for $5,000 was oral, I am not bound by my promise. I have since received a better offer and will accept that one." Sid's letter constitutes a sufficient memorandum for Gail to enforce Sid's promise to sell Blackacre. Because Gail did not sign the memorandum, however, the writing does not bind her. Thus, a contract may be enforceable against only one of the parties.

The "signature" may be initials or may even be typewritten or printed, as long as the party intended it to authenticate the writing. Furthermore, the signature need not be at the bottom of the page or at the customary place for a signature.

The memorandum may consist of *several* papers or documents, none of which would be sufficient by itself. The several memoranda, however, must together satisfy all of the requirements of a writing to comply with the statute of frauds and must clearly indicate that they relate to the same transaction. The latter requirement can be satisfied if (a) the writings are physically connected, (b) the writings refer to each other, or (c) an examination of the writings shows them to be in reference to each other.

ESTATE OF JACKSON v. DEVENYNS Supreme Court of Wyoming, 1995, 892 P.2d 786

FACTS On February 9, 1993, George Jackson and his neighbors, Karen and Steve Devenyn, drafted and signed a document that purports to convey a seventy-nine acre parcel of land owned by Jackson. By the terms of the agreement, Jackson wished to reserve a 1.3 acre portion of the parcel. Although the agreement contained a drawing and dimensions of the conveyance, it did not contain a specific description of the parcel. Jackson died on May 8, 1993, and his estate refused to honor the agreement. The Devenyns then filed a petition with the probate court to order a conveyance. Based on the parol evidence rule, the estate of Jackson objected to the admission of the witnesses' testimony that they could point out the specific area based on conversations with Jackson. However, the probate court heard the testimony and determined that, with the witnesses' testimony, a sufficient description of the parcel could be determined. Accordingly, it granted the petition. The estate appeals.

DECISION Judgment reversed.

OPINION A written memorandum purporting to convey real estate must sufficiently describe the property so as to comply with the requirements of the statute of frauds and permit specific performance. A valid contract to convey land must expressly contain a description of

the land, certain in itself or capable of being rendered certain by reference to an extrinsic source that the writing itself designates. It is expressly prohibited to supply the writing's essential provisions by inferences or presumptions deduced from oral testimony. This writing insufficiently describes the property it purports to convey, to reserve, and for which it grants an option to purchase. The writing's description of the property to be conveyed states: "George Jackson agrees to sell 79 acres . . . . " Such a description is insufficiently definite to identify the land without recourse to extrinsic evidence. When a writing only states the total acreage without any description of the location of the land involved, the statute of frauds' requirement that the subject matter be reasonably certain is not satisfied and the contract is void. The present description only provides the total acreage and does not provide any certainty that this particular tract was intended to be conveyed. Therefore, this agreement is too uncertain to be enforced.

INTERPRETATION A writing to comply with the general contract statute of frauds must (1) specify the parties to the contract, (2) specify with reasonable certainty the subject matter and the essential terms of the promises, and (3) be signed by the party to be charged or by her agent.

Sale of Goods

The statute of frauds provision under Article 2 (Sales) of the UCC is more liberal. For a sale of goods, the Code requires merely a writing (a) sufficient to indicate that a contract has been made between the parties; (b) signed by the party against whom enforcement is sought or by her authorized agent or broker; and (c) specifying the *quantity* of goods or securities to be sold. The writing is sufficient even if it omits or incorrectly states an agreed-upon term; however, if the quantity term is misstated, the contract can be enforced only to the extent of the quantity stated in the writing.

As with general contracts, several related documents may satisfy the writing requirement. Moreover, the "signature" may be by initials or even typewritten or printed, so long as the party intended to authenticate the writing.

In addition, between merchants, if one party, within a reasonable time after entering into the oral contract, sends a written confirmation of the contract for

Compliance: Sale of goods the writing or writings must (1) be sufficient to indicate that a contract has been made between the parties; (2) be signed by the party to be charged or his agent; and (3) specify the quantity of goods to be sold

a sale of goods to the other party and the written confirmation is sufficient against the sender, it is also sufficient against the recipient of the confirmation unless the recipient gives written notice of his objection within ten days after receiving the confirmation.

For example, Brown Co. and ANM Industries enter into an oral contract that provides that ANM will deliver 1,000 dozen shirts to Brown at $6 per shirt. Brown sends a letter to ANM acknowledging the agreement. The letter is signed by Brown's president, contains the quantity term but not the price, and is mailed to ANM's vice president for sales. Brown is bound by the contract once its authorized agent signs the letter, while ANM cannot raise the defense of the statute of frauds ten days after receiving the letter if it does not object within that time. Therefore, as further illustrated by the following case, merchants should examine written confirmations carefully and promptly to make certain that they are accurate.

THOMSON PRINTING MACHINERY CO. v. B. F. GOODRICH CO. United States Court of Appeals, Seventh Circuit, 1983, 714 F.2d 744

FACTS Thomson Printing Company is a buyer and seller of used machinery. On April 10, 1979, the president of the company, James Thomson, went to the surplus machinery department of B. F. Goodrich Company in Akron, Ohio, to examine some used equipment that was for sale. Thomson discussed the sale, including a price of $9,000, with Ingram Meyers, a Goodrich employee and agent. Four days later, on April 14, Thomson sent a purchase order to confirm the oral contract for purchase of the machinery and a partial payment of $1,000 to Goodrich in Akron. The purchase order contained Thomson Printing's name, address, and telephone number, as well as certain information about the purchase, but did not specifically mention Meyers or the surplus equipment department. Goodrich sent copies of the documents to a number of its divisions, but Meyers never learned of the confirmation until weeks later, by which time the equipment had been sold to another party. Thomson Printing brought suit against Goodrich for breach of contract. Goodrich claimed that no contract had existed and that at any rate the alleged oral contract could not be enforced because of the statute of frauds. The district court found the contract unenforceable, and Thomson Printing appealed.

DECISION District court's order granting judgment in favor of Goodrich reversed and the cause remanded for trial consistent with this opinion.

OPINION The merchants' confirmation exception to the statute of frauds provides that an oral contract between merchants may be enforced by the sender of a written confirmation of the agreement where the recipient of the confirmation has reason to know its contents and does not object to them in writing within ten days. Goodrich acknowledged receipt of the purchase order but claimed that it was not received by anyone who had reason to know its contents and that Thomson erred in not designating Meyers or the surplus equipment department on any of the materials it sent. The "merchants'" exception, however, does not expressly require that the confirmation be received by a particular individual. Moreover, even if such a requirement were in force, Section 1-201 of the Uniform Commercial Code states that notice received by an organization "is effective . . . from the time when it would have been brought to [the attention of the individual conducting that transaction] if the organization had executed due diligence." If Goodrich had exercised due diligence in this situation, the items would have come to Meyers's attention reasonably promptly. The purchase order should have immediately alerted the mailroom to the type of transaction involved and the intended destination of the documents. Alternatively, the mailroom could have placed a simple phone call to Thomson Printing.

INTERPRETATION Between merchants, if one party, within a reasonable time after entering into the oral contract, sends a written confirmation of the agreement for a sale of goods to the other party and the written confirmation is sufficient against the sender, it is also sufficient against the recipient of the confirmation unless the recipient give written notice of his objection within ten days after receiving the confirmation.

EFFECT OF NONCOMPLIANCE

Under both the statute of frauds and the Code, the basic legal effect is the same: a contracting party has a defense to an action by the other party for enforcement of an *unenforceable* oral contract—that is, an oral contract that falls within the statute and does not comply with its requirements. For example, if Kirkland, a painter, and Riggsbee, a homeowner, make an oral contract under which Riggsbee is to give Kirkland a certain tract of land in return for the painting of Riggsbee's house, the contract is unenforceable under the statute of frauds. It is a contract for the sale of an interest in land. Either party can repudiate and has a defense to an action by the other to enforce the contract.

Full Performance

After *all* the promises of an oral contract have been *performed* by all the parties, the statute of frauds no longer applies. Accordingly, neither party may ask the court to rescind the executed oral contract on the basis that it did not meet the statute's requirements. Thus, the statute applies to executory contracts only.

Full performance statute does not apply to executed contracts

Restitution

A party to a contract that is unenforceable because of the statute of frauds may have, nonetheless, acted in reliance upon the contract. In such a case the party may recover in restitution the benefits he conferred upon the other in relying upon the unenforceable contract. Thus, if Wilton makes an oral contract to furnish services to Rochelle that are not to be performed within a year and Rochelle discharges Wilton after three months, Wilton may recover as restitution the value of the services he rendered during the three months. Most courts require, however, that the party seeking restitution not be in default.

Restitution is available in quasi-contract for benefits conferred in reliance on the oral contract

Promissory Estoppel

A growing number of courts have used the doctrine of promissory estoppel to displace the requirement of a writing by enforcing oral contracts within the statute of frauds where the party seeking enforcement has reasonably and foreseeably relied upon a promise in such a way that the court can avoid injustice only by enforcing the promise. The remedy granted is limited, as justice requires, and depends upon such factors as the availability of other remedies; the foreseeability, reasonableness, and substantiality of the reliance; and the extent to which reliance corroborates evidence of the promise. The use of promissory estoppel, however, to avoid the writing requirement of the statute of frauds has gained little acceptance in cases involving the sale of goods.

Promissory estoppel oral contracts will be enforced where the party seeking enforcement has reasonably and justifiably relied upon the promise and the court can avoid injustice only by enforcement

PAROL EVIDENCE RULE

A contract reduced to writing and signed by the parties is frequently the result of many conversations, conferences, proposals, counterproposals, letters, and memoranda; and sometimes it is also the product of negotiations conducted, or partly conducted, by agents of the parties. At some stage in the negotiations, the parties or their agents may have reached tentative agreements that were superseded (or regarded as such by one of the parties) by subsequent negotiations. Offers may have been made and withdrawn, either expressly or by implication, or forgotten in the give-and-take of negotiations. Ultimately, though, the parties prepare and sign a final draft of the written contract, which may or may not include all of the points that they discussed and agreed upon in the course of the negotiations. By signing the agreement, despite its potential omissions, the parties have declared it to be their contract; and the terms as contained in it represent the contract they have made. As a rule of substantive law, neither party is later permitted to show that the contract they made is different from the terms and provisions that appear in the written agreement. This rule, which also applies to wills and deeds, is called the "parol evidence" rule.

THE RULE

Parol evidence rule
(pa·rol') excludes inconsistent prior and contemporaneous oral and written agreements not incorporated into the contract

Integrated contract
complete and exclusive agreement of the parties

When the parties express their contract in a writing that is intended to be the complete and final expression of their rights and duties, the **parol evidence rule** excludes *prior* oral or written negotiations or agreements of the parties or their *contemporaneous* oral agreements that *vary* or *change* an integrated written contract. The word *parol* literally means "speech" or "words." The term parol evidence refers to any evidence, whether oral or in writing, that is outside the written contract and not incorporated into it either directly or by reference.

The parol evidence rule applies only to an **integrated contract**, that is, one contained in a certain writing or writings to which the parties have assented as being the statement of the complete and exclusive agreement or contract between them. When there is such an integration of a contract, the courts will not permit parol evidence of any prior or contemporaneous agreement to vary, change, alter, or modify any of the terms or provisions of the written contract.

The reason for the rule is that the parties, by reducing their entire agreement to writing, are regarded as having intended the writing that they signed to include the whole of their agreement. The terms and provisions contained in the writing are there because the parties intended them to be in their contract. Conversely, the courts regard the parties as having omitted intentionally any provision not in the writing. The rule, by excluding evidence that would tend to change, alter, vary, or modify the terms of the written agreement, safeguards the contract as made by the parties. The rule, which applies to all integrated written contracts, deals with what terms are part of the contract. The rule differs from the statute of frauds, which governs what contracts must be evidenced by a writing to be enforceable. Does the parol evidence rule or the statute of frauds apply to the situation presented in the Ethical Dilemma later in this chapter?

LEITZ v. THORSON Court of Appeals of Oregon, 1992, 113 Or.App. 557, 833 P.2d 343

FACTS Plaintiffs leased commercial space from the defendant to open a florist shop. After the lease was executed, the plaintiffs learned that they could not place a freestanding sign along the highway to advertise their business because the Deschutes County Code allowed only one freestanding sign on the property, and the defendant already had one in place. The plaintiffs filed this action, alleging that defendant had breached the lease by failing to provide them with space in which they could erect a freestanding sign. Paragraph 16 of the lease provides as follows: "Tenant shall not erect or install any signs . . . visible from outside the leased premises with out [sic] the previous written consent of the Landlord." The trial court allowed the plaintiffs to introduce evidence that, before the lease was executed, the defendant told them that they could have a freestanding sign. The defendant objected to the testimony on the basis of the parol evidence rule and brought this appeal.

DECISION Affirmed; the evidence was properly admitted.

continued

OPINION The parol evidence rule is a rule of integration. It prohibits oral evidence of those aspects of the bargain that the parties intended to memorialize in their written agreement. If the parties did not intend the writing to represent their entire agreement, the agreement is only partially integrated, and prior consistent additional terms not evidenced by the writing may still form part of the entire agreement. An oral agreement is not integrated in a contemporaneous writing if it is not inconsistent with the written agreement and is such an agreement as the parties might naturally make as a separate agreement. We start with a presumption that the parties intend the writing to be a complete integration. The integration clause in this lease indicates that the lease was intended to be a complete agreement, but it is not conclusive. The defendant testified that he told plaintiffs that they could have a sign and that he did not require them to obtain his written consent, despite the words in paragraph 16 of the lease. There was evidence to support the trial court's holding that the parties did not intend the written lease to reflect their entire agreement, thereby overcoming the presumption of integration. The next question is whether a separate oral agreement to allow a freestanding sign was inconsistent with the written lease. No provision of the lease prohibits a freestanding sign; thus, the disputed parol evidence was not inconsistent with the written agreement. The evidence is therefore admissible.

INTERPRETATION The parol evidence rule only applies to an integrated contract; i.e., one where the parties intend the writing to represent their complete agreement.

SITUATIONS TO WHICH THE RULE DOES NOT APPLY

The parol evidence rule, in spite of its name, is not an exclusionary rule of evidence; nor is it a rule of construction or interpretation. Rather, it is a rule of substantive law that defines the limits of a contract. Bearing this in mind, as well as the reason underlying the rule, you will readily understand that the rule does ***not*** apply to any of the following situations (also see Figure 15-2):

1. A contract that is *partly written* and partly oral; that is, a contract in which the parties do not intend the writing to be their entire agreement. See *Leitz v. Thorson*, above
2. A clerical or *typographical error* that obviously does not represent the agreement of the parties. Where, for example, a written contract for the services of a skilled mining engineer provides that his rate of compensation is to be $2 per day, a court of equity would permit reformation (correction) of the contract to correct the mistake if both parties intended the rate to be $200 per day.
3. The lack of *contractual capacity* of one of the parties through, for instance, minority, intoxication, or mental incompetency. Such evidence would not tend to vary, change, or alter any of the terms of the written agreement but rather would show that the written agreement was voidable or void.
4. A *defense* of fraud, misrepresentation, duress, undue influence, mistake, illegality, lack of consideration, or other invalidating cause. Evidence establishing any of these defenses would not purport to vary, change, or alter any of the terms of the written agreement but rather would show such agreement to be voidable, void, or unenforceable.
5. A *condition precedent* to which the parties agreed orally at the time of the execution of the written agreement and to which the entire agreement was made subject. Such evidence does not tend to vary, alter, or change any of the terms of the agreement; rather, it shows whether the entire unchanged written agreement ever became effective.
6. A *subsequent mutual rescission* or *modification* of the written contract. Parol evidence of a later agreement does not tend to show that the integrated writing did not represent the contract between the parties at the time the writing was made.

7. *Parol evidence*. Such evidence is admissible to explain *ambiguous* terms in the contract. To enforce a contract, it is necessary to understand its intended meaning. Nevertheless, such interpretation is not to alter, change, or vary the terms of the contract.

FIGURE 15–2 Parol Evidence Rule

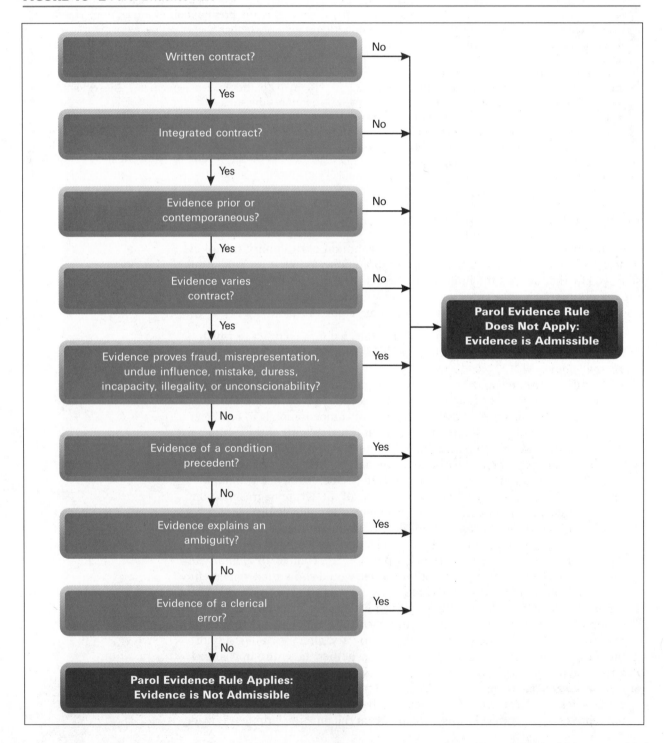

8. A *separate contract*. The rule does not prevent a party from proving the existence of a separate, distinct contract between the same parties.

SUPPLEMENTAL EVIDENCE

Although a written agreement cannot be contradicted by evidence of a prior agreement or of a contemporaneous agreement, under the Restatement and the Code a written contract may be explained or supplemented by (1) course of dealing between the parties; (2) usage of trade; (3) course of performance; or (4) evidence of consistent additional terms, unless the writing was intended by the parties to be a complete and exclusive statement of their agreement.

A **course of dealing** is a sequence of previous conduct between the parties that a court may fairly regard as having established a common basis of understanding for interpreting their expressions and other conduct.

Course of dealing previous conduct between the parties

A **usage of trade** is a practice or method of dealing regularly observed and followed in a place, vocation, or trade.

Usage of trade practice engaged in by the trade or industry

Course of performance refers to the manner in which and the extent to which the respective parties to a contract have accepted without objection successive tenders of performance by the other party.

Course of performance conduct between the parties concerning performance of the particular contract

The Restatement and the Code permit *supplemental consistent evidence* to be introduced into a court proceeding. Such evidence, however, is admissible only if it does not contradict a term or terms of the original agreement and would probably not have been included in the original contract.

ETHICAL DILEMMA   What's (Wrong) in a Contract?

FACTS Rick Davidson was an All-American point guard on Donaldson University's varsity basketball team. He was a four-year starter and, through the cooperation of several accommodating professors, was able to graduate on time—with one small catch: he really couldn't read or write. But his classroom experiences helped convince him that he could handle any situation, and when he was drafted in the first round by an NBA team, he decided to act as his own agent.

During the negotiations, John Stock, general manager for the team, made Rick an offer of $2,400,000 to play for the team for three years. After seeing that other first-round draft choices were receiving closer to $3,000,000 for the same three years, Rick made it known to Stock that the team's offer

was unacceptable. Stock told Rick that because of the salary cap (each NBA team has a limit on the total amount of salaries it can pay its players), he would be willing to raise the offer to $2,800,000 but that the extra $400,000 could not be written into the contract. This would be an oral agreement that would avoid disclosing the salary cap violation to the league. After considering the offer, Rick signed the contract for $2,400,000 for three years' service, and he and Stock shook hands on the deal for the additional $400,000 for the same three years. The contract stated that it was the complete and final agreement between the parties.

After Rick's first year, it was obvious to the team that Rick was not worth the money, and Stock decided not to pay him the first year's portion

of the extra $400,000. Stock claimed that since this agreement was not in writing, it was not enforceable.

Social, Policy, and Ethical Considerations

1. What would you do?
2. Is the team legally obligated to pay the additional $400,000? Is it ethically obligated to do so?
3. What policy interests are served by the team's decision not to pay Rick the extra money? Would the fact that NBA policy makes it impossible for a player to leave a team and play for another NBA team change your answer?
4. What responsibility does the university bear in this situation?
5. What is the nature of Rick's responsibility with respect to the above facts? What should he do?

INTERPRETATION OF CONTRACTS

Interpretation
construction or meaning
given the contract

Although parol evidence may not change the written words or language in which the parties embodied their agreement or contract, the ascertainment (determination) of the meaning to be given to the written language is outside the scope of the parol evidence rule. Though the written words embody the terms of the contract, these words are but symbols; and, if their meaning is ambiguous, the courts may clarify this meaning by applying rules of interpretation or construction and by using extrinsic (external) evidence where necessary.

The Restatement defines **interpretation** as the ascertainment of the meaning of a promise or agreement or of a term of the promise or agreement. Where the language in a contract is unambiguous, a court will not accept extrinsic evidence tending to show a meaning different from that which the words clearly convey. To perform its function of interpreting and construing written contracts and documents, the court adopts rules of interpretation to apply a legal standard to the words contained in the agreement. These are among the rules that aid interpretation:

1. Words and other conduct are interpreted in the light of all the circumstances, and if the principal purpose of the parties is ascertainable, it is given great weight.
2. A writing is interpreted as a whole, and all writings that are part of the same transaction are interpreted together.
3. Unless the parties manifest a different intention, language that has a commonly accepted meaning is interpreted in accordance with that meaning.
4. Unless a different intention is manifested, technical terms and words of art are given their technical meanings.
5. Wherever reasonable, the parties' manifestations of intention regarding a promise or agreement are interpreted as consistent with each other and with any relevant course of performance, course of dealing, or usage of trade.
6. An interpretation that gives a reasonable, lawful, and effective meaning to all the terms is preferred over an interpretation that leaves a part unreasonable, unlawful, or of no effect.
7. Specific and exact terms are given greater weight than general language.
8. Separately negotiated or added terms are given greater weight than standardized terms or other terms not separately negotiated.
9. Express terms, course of performance, course of dealing, and usage of trade are weighted in that order.
10. Where a term or promise has several possible meanings, it will be interpreted against the party who supplied the contract or the term.
11. Where written provisions are inconsistent with typed or printed provisions, the written provision is given preference. Likewise, typed provisions are given preference to printed provisions.
12. If the amount payable is set forth in both figures and words and the amounts differ, the words control the figures.

We may observe that, through the application of the parol evidence rule (where properly applicable) and the above rules of interpretation and construction, the law not only enforces a contract but, in so doing, exercises great care both that the contract being enforced is the one the parties made and that the sense and meaning of the parties' intentions are carefully ascertained and given effect.

CHAPTER SUMMARY

Statute of Frauds

Contracts within the Statute of Frauds	**Rule** contracts within the statute of frauds must be evidenced by a writing to be enforceable **Suretyship Provision** applies to promises to pay the debt of another ■ *Promise Must Be Collateral* promisor must be secondarily, not primarily, liable ■ *Main Purpose Doctrine* if primary object is to provide an economic benefit to the surety, then the promise is not within the statute **Executor-Administrator Provision** applies to promises to answer personally for a duty of the decedent **Marriage Provision** applies to promises in consideration of marriage but not to mutual promises to marry **Land Contract Provision** applies to promises to transfer any right, privilege, power, or immunity in real property **One-Year Provision** applies to contracts that cannot be performed within one year ■ *The Possibility Test* the criterion is whether it is possible, not likely, for the agreement to be performed within one year ■ *Computation of Time* the year runs from the time the agreement is made ■ *Full Performance by One Party* makes the promise of the other party enforceable under majority view **Sale of Goods** a contract for the sale of goods for the price of $500 or more must be evidenced by a writing to be enforceable ■ *Admission* an admission in pleadings, testimony, or otherwise in court makes the contract enforceable for the quantity of goods admitted ■ *Specially Manufactured Goods* an oral contract for specially manufactured goods is enforceable ■ *Delivery or Payment and Acceptance* validates the contract only for the goods that have been accepted or for which payment has been accepted **Modification or Rescission of Contracts within the Statute of Frauds** oral contracts modifying existing contracts are unenforceable if the resulting contract is within the statute of frauds
Methods of Compliance	**General Contract Law** the writing or writings must: ■ specify the parties to the contract ■ specify the subject matter and essential terms ■ be signed by the party to be charged or by her agent **Sale of Goods** provides a general method of compliance for all parties and an additional one for merchants ■ *Writing or Writings Must:* (1) be sufficient to indicate that a contract has been made between the parties, (2) be signed by the party against whom enforcement is sought or by her authorized agent, and (3) specify the quantity of goods to be sold ■ *Written Confirmation* between merchants, a written confirmation that is sufficient against the sender is also sufficient against the recipient unless the recipient gives written notice of his objection within ten days

Effect Of Noncompliance	**Oral Contract within Statute of Frauds** is unenforceable **Full Performance** statute does not apply to executed contracts **Restitution** is available in quasi-contract for benefits conferred in reliance on the oral contract **Promissory Estoppel** oral contracts will be enforced where the party seeking enforcement has reasonably and justifiably relied upon the promise and the court can avoid injustice only by enforcement

Parol Evidence Rule and Interpretation of Contracts

Parol Evidence Rule	**Statement of Rule** when parties express a contract in a writing that they intend to be the final expression of their rights and duties, evidence of their prior oral or written negotiations or agreements of their contemporaneous oral agreements that vary or change the written contract are not admissible **Situations to Which the Rule Does Not Apply** ■ a contract that is not an integrated document ■ correction of a typographical error ■ showing that a contract was void or voidable ■ showing whether a condition has in fact occurred ■ showing a subsequent mutual rescission or modification of the contract **Supplemental Evidence** may be admitted ■ *Course of Dealing* previous conduct between the parties ■ *Usage of Trade* practice engaged in by the trade or industry ■ *Course of Performance* conduct between the parties concerning performance of the particular contract ■ *Supplemental Consistent Evidence*

Interpretation of Contracts	**Definition** the ascertainment of the meaning of a promise or agreement or a term of the promise or agreement **Rules of Interpretation** include ■ all the circumstances are considered and the principal purpose of the parties is given great weight ■ a writing is interpreted as a whole ■ commonly accepted meanings are used unless the parties manifest a different intention ■ wherever possible, the intentions of the parties are interpreted as consistent with each other and with course of performance, course of dealing, or usage of trade ■ technical terms are given their technical meaning ■ specific terms are given greater weight than general language ■ separately negotiated terms are given greater weight than standardized terms or those not separately negotiated ■ the order for interpretation is express terms, course of performance, course of dealing, and usage of trade ■ where a term has several possible meanings, the term will be interpreted against the party who supplied the contract or term ■ written provisions are given preference over typed or printed provisions and typed provisions are given preference over printed provisions ■ if an amount is set forth in both words and figures and they differ, words control the figures

QUESTIONS

1. Identify and discuss the five types of contracts covered by the general contract statute of frauds and the contracts covered by the UCC statute of frauds provision.
2. Describe the writing that is required to satisfy the general contract and UCC statute of frauds provisions.
3. Identify and discuss the other methods of complying with the UCC statute of frauds provision.
4. Explain the parol evidence rule and identify the situations to which the rule does not apply.
5. Discuss the rules that aid in the interpretation of a contract.

Internet Question. Determine whether the United Nations Convention on Contracts for the International Sale of Goods (Vienna, 1980) contains a writing requirement.

PROBLEMS

1. Rafferty was the principal shareholder in Continental Corporation, and, as a result, he received the lion's share of Continental Corporation's dividends. Continental Corporation was anxious to close an important deal for iron ore products to use in its business. A written contract was on the desk of Stage Corporation for the sale of the iron ore to Continental Corporation. Stage Corporation, however, was cautious about signing the contract; and it did not sign until Rafferty called Stage Corporation on the telephone and stated that if Continental Corporation did not pay for the ore, he would pay. Business reverses struck Continental Corporation, and it failed. Stage Corporation sued Rafferty. What defense, if any, has Rafferty? Decision?

2. Green was the owner of a large department store. On Wednesday, January 26, he talked to Smith and said, "I will hire you to act as sales manager in my store for one year at a salary of $18,000. You are to begin work next Monday." Smith accepted and started work on Monday, January 31. At the end of three months, Green discharged Smith. On May 15, Smith brought an action against Green to recover the unpaid portion of the $18,000 salary. Decision?

3. Rowe was admitted to the hospital suffering from a critical illness. He was given emergency treatment and later underwent surgery. On at least four occasions, Rowe's two sons discussed with the hospital the payment for services to be rendered by the hospital. The first of these four conversations took place the day after Rowe was admitted. The sons informed the treating physician that their father had no financial means but that they themselves would pay for such services. During the other conversations, the sons authorized whatever treatment their father needed, assuring the hospital that they would pay for the services. After Rowe's discharge, Dr. Peterson brought this action against the sons to recover the unpaid bill for the services rendered to their father. Decision?

4. Ames, Bell, Cain, and Dole each orally ordered color television sets from Marvel Electronics Company, which accepted the orders. Ames's set was to be specially designed and encased in an ebony cabinet. Bell, Cain, and Dole ordered standard sets described as "Alpha Omega Theatre." The price of Ames's set was $1,800, and the sets ordered by Bell, Cain, and Dole were $700 each. Bell paid the company $75 to apply on his purchase; Ames, Cain, and Dole paid nothing. The next day, Marvel sent Ames, Bell, Cain, and Dole written confirmations captioned "Purchase Memorandum," numbered 12345, 12346, 12347, and 12348 respectively, containing the essential terms of the oral agreements. Each memorandum was sent in duplicate with the request that one copy be signed and returned to the company. None of the four purchasers returned a signed copy. Ames promptly sent the company a repudiation of the oral contract, which it received before beginning manufacture of the set for Ames or making commitments to carry out the contract. Cain sent the company a letter reading in part, "Referring to your Contract No. 12347, please be advised I have canceled this contract. Yours truly, (Signed) Cain." The four television sets were duly tendered by Marvel to Ames, Bell, Cain, and Dole, all of whom refused to accept delivery. Marvel brings four separate actions against Ames, Bell, Cain, and Dole for breach of contract. Decide each claim.

5. Moriarity and Holmes enter into an oral contract by which Moriarity promises to sell and Holmes promises to buy Blackacre for $10,000. Moriarity repudiates the contract by writing a letter to Holmes in which she states accurately the terms of the bargain, but adds "our agreement was oral. It, therefore, is not binding upon me, and I shall not carry it out." Thereafter, Holmes sues Moriarity for specific performance of the contract. Moriarity interposes the defense of the statute of frauds, arguing that the contract is within the statute and hence unenforceable. Decision?

6. On March 1, Lucas called Craig on the telephone and offered to pay him $90,000 for a house and lot that Craig owned. Craig accepted the offer immediately on the telephone. Later in the same day, Lucas told

Annabelle that if she would marry him, he would convey to her the property then owned by Craig that was the subject of the earlier agreement. On March 2 Lucas called Penelope and offered her $16,000 if she would work for him for the year commencing March 15, and she agreed. Lucas and Annabelle were married on June 25. By this time, Craig had refused to convey the house to Lucas. Thereafter, Lucas renounced his promise to convey the property to Annabelle. Penelope, who had been working for Lucas, was discharged without cause on July 5; Annabelle left Lucas and instituted divorce proceedings in July.

What rights, if any, have (a) Lucas against Craig for his failure to convey the property; (b) Annabelle against Lucas for failure to convey the house to her; (c) Penelope against Lucas for discharging her before the end of the agreed term of employment?

7. Blair orally promises Clay to sell him five crops of potatoes to be grown on Blackacre, a farm in Idaho; and Clay promises to pay a stated price for them on delivery. Is the contract enforceable?

8. Rachel leased an apartment to Bertha for the term May 1, 1993, to April 30, 1994, at $500 a month, "payable in advance on the first day of each and every month of said term." At the time the lease was signed, Bertha told Rachel that she received her salary on the tenth of the month, and that she would be unable to pay the rent before that date each month. Rachel replied that would be satisfactory. On June 2, Bertha not having paid the June rent, Rachel sued Bertha for the rent. At the trial, Bertha offered to prove the oral agreement as to the date of payment each month. Decision?

9. Ann bought a car from the Used Car Agency (Used) under a written contract. She purchased the car in reliance on Used's agent's oral representations that it had never been in a wreck and could be driven at least 2,000 miles without adding oil. Thereafter, Ann discovered that the car had, in fact, been previously wrecked and rebuilt, that it used excessive quantities of oil, and that Used's agent was aware of these facts when the car was sold. Ann brought an action to rescind the contract and recover the purchase price. Used objected to the introduction of oral testimony concerning representations of its agent, contending that the written contract alone governed the rights of the parties. Decision on the objection?

10. In a contract drawn up by Goldberg Company, it agreed to sell and Edwards Contracting Company agreed to buy wood shingles at $650. After the shingles were delivered and used, Goldberg Company billed Edwards Company at $650 per bunch of 900 shingles. Edwards Company refused to pay because it thought the contract meant $650 per thousand shingles. Goldberg Company brought action to recover on the basis of $650 per bunch. The evidence showed that there was no applicable custom or usage in the trade and that each party held its belief in good faith. Decision?

11. Amos orally agrees to hire Elizabeth for an eight-month trial period. Elizabeth performs the job magnificently, and after several weeks Amos orally offers Elizabeth a six-month extension at a salary increase of 20 percent. Elizabeth accepts the offer. At the end of the eight-month trial period, Amos discharges Elizabeth, who brings suit against Amos for breach of contract. Is Amos liable? Why?

12. Halsey, a widower, was living without family or housekeeper in his house in Howell, New York. Burns and his wife claim that Halsey invited them to give up their house and business in Andover, New York, to live in his house and care for him. In return, they allege, he promised them the house and its furniture upon his death. Acting upon this proposal, the Burnses left Andover, moved into Halsey's house, and cared for him until he died five months later. No deed, will, or memorandum exists to authenticate Halsey's promise. McCormick, the administrator of the estate, claims the oral promise is unenforceable under the statute of frauds. Decision?

13. Ethel Greenberg acquired the ownership of the Carlyle Hotel on Miami Beach but had little experience in the hotel business. She asked Miller to participate in and counsel her operation of the hotel, which he did. He claims that, because his efforts produced a substantial profit, Ethel made an oral agreement for the continuation of his services. Miller alleges that in return for his services, Ethel promised to marry him and to share the net income resulting from the operation of the hotel. Miller maintains that he rendered his services to Ethel in reliance upon her promises and that the couple planned to wed in the fall of 1955. Ethel, due to physical illness, decided not to marry. Miller sued for damages for Ethel's breach of agreement. Decision?

14. Dean was hired on February 12, 1962, as a sales manager of the Co-op Dairy for a minimum period of one year with the dairy agreeing to pay his moving expenses. By February 26, 1962, Dean had signed a lease, moved his family from Oklahoma to Arizona, and reported for work. After he worked for a few days, he was fired. Dean then brought this action against the dairy for his salary for the year, less what he was paid. The dairy argues that enforcement of the oral contract is barred by the statute of frauds because the contract was not to be performed within one year. Decision?

15. Yokel, a grower of soybeans, had sold soybeans to Campbell Grain and Seed Company and other grain companies in the past. Campbell entered into an oral contract with Yokel to purchase soybeans from him. Promptly after entering into the oral contract,

Campbell signed and mailed to Yokel a written confirmation of the oral agreement. Yokel received the written confirmation but did not sign it or object to its content. Campbell now brings this action against Yokel for breach of contract upon Yokel's failure to deliver the soybeans. The trial court ruled in favor of the defendant, Yokel, on the ground that the defendant is not a "merchant" within the meaning of the Code. Decision?

16. Presti claims that he reached an oral agreement with Wilson by telephone in October 1970 to buy a horse for $60,000. Presti asserts that he sent Wilson a bill of sale and a postdated check, which Wilson retained. Presti also claims that Wilson told him that he wished not to consummate the transaction until January 1, 1971, for tax reasons. The check was neither deposited nor negotiated. Wilson denies that he ever agreed to sell the horse or that he received the check and bill of sale from Presti. Presti's claim is supported by a copy of his check stub and by the affidavit of his executive assistant, who says that he monitored the telephone call and prepared and mailed both the bill of sale and the check. Wilson argues that the statute of frauds governs this transaction and that since there was no writing, the contract claim is barred. Decision?

17. Louie E. Brown worked for the Phelps Dodge Corporation under an oral contract for approximately twenty-three years. In 1967, he was suspended from work for unauthorized possession of company property. In 1968, Phelps Dodge fired Brown after discovering that he was using company property without permission and building a trailer on company time. Brown sued Phelps Dodge for benefits under an unemployment benefit plan. According to the plan, "in order to be eligible for unemployment benefits, a laid-off employee must: (1) Have completed 2 or more years of continuous service with the company, and (2) Have been laid off from work because the company had determined that work was not available for him." The trial court held that the wording of the second condition was ambiguous and should be construed against Phelps Dodge, the party who chose the wording. A reading of the entire contract, however, indicates that the plan was not intended to apply to someone who was fired for cause. Decision?

18. Katz offered to purchase land from Joiner, and, after negotiating the terms, Joiner accepted. On October 13, over the telephone, both parties agreed to extend the time period for completing and mailing the written contract until October 20. Although the original paperwork deadline in the offer was October 14, Katz stated he had inserted that provision "for my purpose only." All other provisions of the contract remained unchanged. Accordingly, Joiner completed the contract and mailed it on October 20. Immediately after, however, Joiner sent Katz a telegram stating that "I have signed and returned contract, but have changed my mind. Do not wish to sell property." Joiner now claims an oral modification of a contract within the statute of frauds is unenforceable. Katz counters that the modification is not material, and therefore does not affect the underlying contract. Decision?

19. When Mr. McClam died, he left the family farm, heavily mortgaged, to his wife and children. In order to save the farm from foreclosure, Mrs. McClam planned to use insurance proceeds and her savings to pay off the debts. She was unwilling to do so, however, unless she had full ownership of the property. Mrs. McClam wrote her daughter, stating that the daughter should deed over her interest in the family farm to her mother. Mrs. McClam promised that upon her death all the children would inherit the farm from their mother equally. The letter further explained that if foreclosure occurred, each child would receive very little, but if they complied with their mother's plan, each would eventually receive a valuable property interest upon her death. Finally, the letter stated that all the other children had agreed to this plan. The daughter also agreed. Years later, Mrs. McClam tried to convey the farm to her son Donald. The daughter challenged, arguing that the mother was contractually bound to convey the land equally to all children. Donald says this was an oral agreement to sell land, and is unenforceable. The daughter says the letter satisfies the statute of frauds, making the contract enforceable. Who gets the farm? Explain.

20. Butler Brothers Building Company sublet all of the work in a highway construction contract to Ganley Brothers, Inc. Soon thereafter, Ganley brought this action against Butler for fraud in the inducement of the contract. The contract, however, provided: "The contractor [Ganley] has examined the said contracts . . ., knows all the requirements, and is not relying upon any statement made by the company in respect thereto." Decision?

21. Alice solicited an offer from Robett Manufacturing Company to manufacture certain clothing that Alice intended to supply to the government. Alice contends that in a telephone conversation Robett made an oral offer that she immediately accepted. She then received the following letter from Robett, which, she claims, confirmed their agreement:

Confirming our telephone conversation, we are pleased to offer the 3,500 shirts at $4.00 each and the trousers at $3.80 each with delivery approximately ninety days after receipt of order. We will try to cut this to sixty days if at all possible.

This, of course, is quoted f.o.b. Atlanta and the order will not be subject to cancellation, domestic pack only.

Thanking you for the opportunity to offer these garments, we are

Very truly yours,
ROBETT MANUFACTURING CO., INC.

Alice sued to enforce this agreement. Decision?

22. Enrique Gittes was a financial consultant for NCC, an English holding company that invested capital in other businesses in return for a stake in those businesses. One of NCC's investments was a substantial holding in Simplicity Pattern Company. Gittes's consulting contract was subsequently transferred to Simplicity, and Gittes was elected to the Simplicity board of directors.

When NCC fell into serious financial straits, it became imperative that it sell its interest in Simplicity. Accordingly, a buyer was found. The buyer insisted that before closing the deal all current Simplicity directors, including Gittes, must resign. Gittes, however, refused to resign. Edward Cook, the largest shareholder of NCC and the one with the most to lose if the Simplicity sale was not completed, orally offered Gittes a five-year, $50,000-per-year consulting contract with Cook International if Gittes would resign from the Simplicity board.

Gittes and Cook never executed a formal contract. However, Cook International did issue two writings, a prospectus and a memo, that mentioned the employment of Gittes for five years at $50,000 per year. Neither writing described the nature of Gittes's job or any of his duties. In fact, Gittes was given no responsibilities, and was never paid. Gittes sued to enforce the employment contract. Cook International contended that the statute of frauds made the oral contract unenforceable. Decision?

CHAPTER 16

Third Parties to Contracts

In prior chapters, we considered situations that essentially involved only two parties. In this chapter, we deal with the rights and duties of third parties, namely, persons who are not parties to the contract but who have a right to or an obligation for its performance. These rights and duties arise either by (1) an assignment of the rights of a party to the contract, (2) a delegation of the duties of a party to the contract, or (3) the express terms of a contract entered into for the benefit of a third person. In an assignment or delegation, the third party's rights or duties arise *after* the original contract is made, whereas in the third situation the third-party beneficiary's rights arise at the time the contract is formed. We will consider these three situations in that order.

ASSIGNMENT OF RIGHTS

Every contract creates both rights and duties. A person who owes a duty under a contract is an **obligor**, while a person to whom a contractual duty is owed is an **obligee**. For instance, Ann promises to sell to Bart an automobile for which Bart promises to pay $10,000 by monthly installments over the next three years. Ann's right under the contract is to receive payment from Bart, whereas Ann's duty is to deliver the automobile. Bart's right is to receive the automobile; his duty is to pay for it.

Obligor party owing a duty under original contract

Obligee (*ob·li·gee'*) party to whom a contractual duty of performance is owed

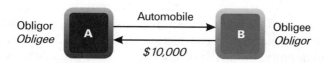

An **assignment of rights** is the voluntary transfer to a third party of the rights arising from the contract. In the above example, if Ann were to transfer her right under the contract (the installment payments due from Bart) to Clark for $8,500 in cash, this would constitute a valid assignment of rights. In this case, Ann would be the **assignor**, Clark would be the **assignee**, and Bart would be the *obligor*.

Assignment of rights voluntary transfer to a third party of the rights arising from a contract

Assignor (*as·sign·or'*) party making an assignment

Assignee (*as·sign·ee'*) party to whom contractual rights are assigned

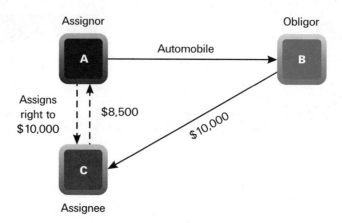

An effective assignment terminates the assignor's right to receive performance by the obligor. After an assignment, *only* the assignee has a right to the obligor's performance.

On the other hand, if Ann and Doris agree that Doris should deliver the automobile to Bart, this would constitute a delegation, not an assignment, of duties between Ann and Doris. A **delegation of duties** is a transfer to a third party of a contractual obligation. In this instance, Ann would be the **delegator**, Doris would be the **delegatee**, and Bart would be the *obligee*.

Requirements of an Assignment

The Restatement defines an assignment of a right as a manifestation of the assignor's intention to transfer the right so that the assignor's right to the performance of the obligor is extinguished either in whole or in part and the assignee acquires a right to such performance. No special form or particular words are necessary to create an assignment. Any words that fairly indicate an intention to make the assignee the owner of the right are sufficient.

Unless otherwise provided by statute, an assignment may be oral. The UCC imposes a writing requirement on all assignments beyond $5,000. In addition, Article 9 requires certain assignments to be in writing.

Consideration is *not* required for an effective assignment. Consequently, gratuitous assignments are valid and enforceable. By giving value, or consideration, for the assignment, the assignee indicates his assent to the assignment as part of the bargained-for exchange. On the other hand, when the assignment is gratuitous, the assignee's assent is not always required. Any assignee who has not assented to an assignment may, however, disclaim the assignment within a reasonable time after learning of its existence and terms.

Revocability of Assignments When the assignee gives consideration in exchange for an assignment, a contract exists between the assignor and the assignee. Consequently, the assignor may not revoke the assignment without the assignee's assent. In contrast, a gratuitous assignment is revocable by the assignor and is terminated by the assignor's death, incapacity, or subsequent assignment of the right, *unless* the assignor has made an effective delivery of the assignment to the assignee, as in the case of *Speelman v. Pascal*. Such delivery can be accomplished by transferring a deed or other document evidencing the right, such as a stock certificate or savings passbook. Delivery may also consist of physically delivering a signed, written assignment of the contract right. A gratuitous assignment is also made irrevocable if, before the

---

Delegation of duty *(del·e·ga´·tion)* transfer to a third party of a contractual obligation

Delegator *(del´·e·ga·tor)* party delegating his duty to a third party

Delegatee *(del·e·ga·tee´)* third party to whom the delegator's duty is delegated

Revocability of assignment when the assignee gives consideration, the assignor may not revoke the assignment without the assignee's consent

attempted revocation, the donee-assignee receives payment of the claim from the obligor, obtains a judgment against the obligor, or obtains a new contract with the obligor.

SPEELMAN v. PASCAL Court of Appeals of New York, 1961, 10 N.Y.2d 313, 222 N.Y.S.2d 324, 178 N.E.2d 723

FACTS In 1952, the estate of George Bernard Shaw granted to Gabriel Pascal Enterprises, Limited, the exclusive rights to produce a musical play and a motion picture based on Shaw's play *Pygmalion*. The agreement contained a provision terminating the license if Gabriel Pascal Enterprises did not arrange for well-known composers, such as Lerner and Loewe, to write the musical and produce it within a specified period of time. George Pascal, owner of 98 percent of Gabriel Pascal Enterprises' stock, attempted to meet these requirements but died in July 1954 before negotiations had been completed. In February 1954, however, while the license had two years yet to run, Pascal had sent a letter to Kingman, his executive secretary, granting to her certain percentages of his share of the profits from the expected stage and screen productions of *Pygmalion*. Subsequently, Pascal's estate arranged for the writing and production of the highly successful *My Fair Lady*, based on Shaw's *Pygmalion*.

Kingman then sued to enforce Pascal's gift assignment of the future royalties. The trial court entered judgment for Kingman.

DECISION Judgment for Kingman affirmed.

OPINION Assignments of rights to sums that are expected to become due to the assignor are enforceable. To make a gift of such an assignment, the donor need only demonstrate a present intent to transfer irrevocably his right to the donee. Although at the time of the delivery of the letter there was no musical play or motion picture in existence, Pascal's letter was intended to transfer irrevocably by assignment a percentage of the royalties from the future productions to Kingman. Therefore, the assignment is enforceable as a valid gift.

INTERPRETATION A gratuitous assignment becomes irrevocable upon the assignor's making an effective delivery of the assignment to the assignee.

Partial Assignments A **partial assignment** is a transfer of a portion of the contractual rights to one or more assignees, as in the case above. The obligor, however, may require all the parties entitled to the promised performance to litigate the matter in one action, thus ensuring that all parties are present and avoiding the undue hardship of multiple lawsuits. For example, Jack owes Richard $2,500. Richard assigns $1,000 to Mildred. Neither Richard nor Mildred can maintain an action against Jack if Jack objects, unless the other is joined in the proceeding against Jack.

Partial assignment
transfer of a portion of contractual rights to one or more assignees

Rights That Are Assignable
As a general rule, most contract rights, including rights under an option contract, are assignable. The most common contractual right that may be assigned is the right to the payment of money. A contract right to other property, such as land or goods, is likewise assignable.

Rights That Are Not Assignable
In order to protect the obligor or the public interest, some contract rights are not assignable. These nonassignable contract rights include those that (1) materially increase the duty, risk, or burden upon the obligor; (2) transfer highly personal contract rights; (3) are expressly prohibited by the contract; or (4) are prohibited by law.

Assignments That Materially Increase the Duty, Risk, or Burden An assignment is ineffective if performance by the obligor to the assignee would differ materially from the obligor's performance to the assignor; that is, if the assignment would significantly change the nature or extent of the obligor's duty. Thus, an automobile liability insurance policy issued to Alex is not assignable by Alex to Betty. The risk assumed by the insurance company was liability for Alex's negligent operation of the automobile. Liability for Betty's operation of the same automobile would be a risk entirely different than the one the insurance company had assumed. Similarly, Candice would not be allowed to assign to Eunice, the owner of a twenty-five room mansion, Candice's contractual right to have David paint her small, two-bedroom house. Clearly, such an assignment would materially increase David's duty of performance. By comparison, the right to receive monthly payments under a contract may be assigned; for mailing the check to the assignee costs no more than mailing it to the assignor.

Assignments of Personal Rights When the rights under a contract are highly personal, in that they are limited to the person of the *obligee*, such rights are not assignable. An extreme example of such a contract is an agreement of two persons to marry one another. The prospective groom obviously may not transfer the prospective bride's promise to marry to some third party. A more typical example of contract involving personal rights would be a contract between a teacher and a school. The teacher could not assign her right to a faculty position to another teacher. Similarly, a student who is awarded a scholarship cannot assign his right to some other person. The next case involves another example.

REISER v. DAYTON COUNTRY CLUB COMPANY United States Court of Appeals, 1992, 972 F.2d 689

FACTS The Dayton Country Club Company (the Club) offers many social activities to its members. However, the privilege to play golf at the Club is reserved to a special membership category for which additional fees are charged. The Club chooses golfing memberships from a waiting list of members according to detailed rules, regulations, and procedures. Magness and Redman were golfing members of the Club. Upon their filing for bankruptcy, their trustee sought to assign by sale their rights under these memberships to (1) other members on the waiting list, (2) other members not on the waiting list, or (3) the general public, provided the purchaser first acquired membership in the Club. The bankruptcy court found that the Club's rules governing golf membership were essentially anti-assignment provisions and therefore the estate could not assign rights contained in the membership agreement. On appeal to the district court, the bankruptcy court's ruling was affirmed. The district court added that this case was not a lease but rather a "non-commercial dispute over the possession of a valuable membership in a recreational and social club."

DECISION Judgment affirmed.

OPINION The Court of Appeals found that the memberships of Magness and Redman were personal contracts that are not assignable. A personal contract is one in which "the personality of one of the parties is material." The determination of whether a contract is personal is a question of intent as shown by the language used in the contract and the nature of the contract. In this case, "[t]he contracts creating the complex relationships among the parties and others are not in any way commercial. They create personal relationships among individuals who play golf, who are waiting to play golf, who eat together, swim and play together." Therefore, the parties intended these contracts to be personal and thus they are nonassignable.

INTERPRETATION When rights under a contract are personal, they may not be assigned.

Express Prohibition against Assignment Though contract terms prohibiting assignment of rights under the contract are strictly construed, most courts interpret a general prohibition against assignments as a mere promise not to assign. As a consequence, the general prohibition, if violated, gives the obligor a right to damages for breach of the terms forbidding assignment but does *not* render the assignment ineffective.

The Restatement and Article 2 of the Code provide that, unless circumstances indicate the contrary, a contract term prohibiting assignment of the *contract* bars only the delegation to the assignee (delegatee) of the assignor's (delegator's) *duty* of performance, not the assignment of *rights*. Thus, Norman and Lucy contract for the sale of land by Lucy to Norman for $30,000 and provide in their contract that Norman may not assign the contract. Norman pays Lucy $30,000, thereby fulfilling his duty of performance under the contract. Norman then assigns his rights to George, who consequently is entitled to receive the land from Lucy (the obligor) despite the contractual prohibition of assignment.

Article 2 of the Code provides that a right to damages for breach of the whole contract or a right arising out of the assignor's due performance of his entire obligation can be assigned despite a contractual provision to the contrary. Article 9 of the Code makes ineffective any term in a contract prohibiting the assignment of any right to payment for goods sold or leased or for services rendered.

ALDANA v. COLONIAL PALMS PLAZA, INC. District Court of Appeal of Florida, Third District, 1991, 591 So.2d 953

FACTS Colonial Palms Plaza, Inc. (Landlord) entered into a lease agreement with Abby's Cakes On Dixie, Inc. (Tenant). The lease included a provision in which Landlord agreed to pay Tenant a construction allowance of up to $11,250 after Tenant completed certain improvements. Prior to completion of the improvements, Tenant assigned its right to receive the first $8,000 of the construction allowance to Robert Aldana in return for a loan of $8,000 to finance the construction. Aldana sent notice of the assignment to Landlord. When Tenant completed the improvements, Landlord ignored the assignment and paid Tenant the construction allowance. Aldana sued Landlord for the money due pursuant to the assignment. Landlord relied on an anti-assignment clause in the lease to argue that the assignment was void. That clause states in part: "TENANT agrees not to assign, mortgage, pledge, or encumber this Lease, in whole or in part, to sublet in whole or any part of the DEMISED PREMISES . . . without first obtaining the prior, specific written consent of the LANDLORD at LANDLORD'S sole discretion. . . . Any such assignment . . . without such consent shall be void." The trial court granted Landlord summary judgment.

DECISION Summary judgment reversed and case remanded.

OPINION Aldana argued that under ordinary contract principles the lease provision does not prevent the assignment of the right to receive contractual payments. The appellate court agreed. Tenant did not assign the lease but instead assigned a right to receive the construction allowance. The law in this area is summarized in the Restatement of Contracts as follows: "Unless the circumstances indicate the contrary, a contract term prohibiting assignment of `the contract' bars only the delegation to an assignee of the performance by the assignor of a duty or condition." As a rule of construction, a prohibition against assignment of a contract (in this case, the lease) will prevent assignment of contractual duties but does not prevent assignment of the right to receive payments due—unless circumstances indicate otherwise. Having received notice of the assignment, Landlord was bound by the assignment.

INTERPRETATION Unless circumstances indicate the contrary, a contract term prohibiting assignment of the contract bars only delegation of the assignor's contractual duties.

Assignments Prohibited by Law Various federal and state statutes, as well as public policy, prohibit or regulate the assignment of certain types of contract rights. For instance, assignments of future wages are subject to such statutes, some of which prohibit these assignments altogether, whereas others require the assignments to be in writing and subject them to certain restrictions. Moreover, an assignment that violates public policy will be unenforceable even in the absence of a prohibiting statute.

Rights of the Assignee

Rights of assignee assignee stands in the shoes of the assignor

Obtains Rights of Assignor   The general rule is that an assignee **stands in the shoes** of the assignor. She acquires the rights of the assignor but *no* new or additional rights, and she takes with the assigned rights all of the defenses, defects, and infirmities to which they would be subject in an action against the obligor by the assignor. Thus, in an action brought by the assignee against the obligor, the obligor may plead fraud, duress, undue influence, failure of consideration, breach of contract, or any other defense arising out of the original contract against the assignor. The obligor may also assert rights of **setoff** or counterclaim arising out of entirely separate matters that he may have against the assignor, as long as they arose before he had notice of the assignment.

Setoff   claim by obligor against assignor arising out of an entirely separate transaction

The Code permits the buyer under a contract of sale to agree as part of the contract that he will not assert against an assignee any claim or defense that the buyer may have against the seller if the assignee takes the assignment for value and in good faith. Such a provision in an agreement renders the seller's rights more marketable. The Federal Trade Commission, however, has invalidated such waiver of defense provisions in consumer credit transactions. This rule is discussed more fully in Chapter 26.

Notice   The obligor need not receive notice for an assignment to be valid. Giving notice of assignment is advisable, however, because an assignee will lose his rights against the obligor if the obligor, without notice of the assignment, pays the assignor. Compelling an obligor to pay a claim a second time, when she was unaware that a new party was entitled to payment, would be unfair. For example, Donald owes Gary $1,000 due on September 1. Gary assigns the debt to Paula on August 1, but neither Gary nor Paula informs Donald. On September 1, Donald pays Gary. Donald is fully discharged from his obligation, whereas Gary is liable for $1,000 to Paula. On the other hand, if Paula had given notice of the assignment to Donald before September 1 and Donald had paid Gary nevertheless, Paula would then have the right to recover the $1,000 from either Donald or Gary. Furthermore, notice cuts off any defenses based on subsequent agreements between the obligor and assignor and, as already indicated, subsequent setoffs and counterclaims of the obligor that may arise out of entirely separate matters.

Implied Warranties of Assignor

Implied warranty obligation imposed by law upon the transferor of property or contract rights

An **implied warranty** is an obligation imposed by law upon the transferor of property or contract rights. In the absence of an express intention to the contrary, an assignor who receives value makes the following implied warranties to the assignee with respect to the assigned right:

1. that he will do nothing to defeat or impair the assignment;
2. that the assigned right actually exists and is subject to no limitations or defenses other than those stated or apparent at the time of the assignment;
3. that any writing that evidences the right and that is delivered to the assignee or exhibited to him as an inducement to accept the assignment is genuine and what it purports to be; and

4. that the assignor has no knowledge of any fact that would impair the value of the assignment.

Thus, Eric has a right against Julia and assigns it for value to Gwen. Later, Eric gives Julia a release. Gwen may recover damages from Eric for breach of the first implied warranty.

Express Warranties of Assignor

An **express warranty** is an explicitly made contractual promise regarding the property or contract rights transferred. The assignor is further bound by any specific express warranties he makes to the assignee about the right assigned. Unless he explicitly states as much, however, the assignor does *not* guarantee that the obligor will pay the assigned debt or otherwise perform.

Express warranty
explicitly made contractual promise regarding the property or contract rights transferred

Successive Assignments of the Same Right

The owner of a right could conceivably make successive assignments of the same claim to different persons. Although this action is morally and legally inappropriate, it raises the question of what rights successive assignees have. Assume, for example, that B owes A $1,000. On June 1, A for value assigns the debt to C. Thereafter, on June 15, A assigns it to D, who in good faith gives value and has no knowledge of the prior assignment by A to C. If the assignment is subject to Article 9, then the article's priority rules will control, as discussed in Chapter 39. Otherwise, the priority is determined by the common law. The majority rule in the United States is that the *first assignee in point of time* (C) prevails over later assignees. By way of contrast, in England and in a minority of the states, the first assignee to notify the obligor prevails.

Successive assignments
the majority rule is that the first assignee in point of time prevails over later assignees; minority rule is that the first assignee to notify the obligor prevails

The Restatement adopts a third view: a prior assignee is entitled to the assigned right and its proceeds to the exclusion of a subsequent assignee, *except* where the prior assignment is revocable or voidable by the assignor or the subsequent assignee in good faith and without knowledge of the prior assignment gives value and obtains one of the following: (1) payment or satisfaction of the obligor's duty, (2) a judgment against the obligor, (3) a new contract with the obligor, or (4) possession of a writing of a type customarily accepted as a symbol or evidence of the right assigned.

DELEGATION OF DUTIES

As we indicated earlier, contractual *duties* are *not* assignable, but their performance generally may be *delegated* to a third person. A delegation of duties is a transfer of a contractual obligation to a third party. For example, A promises to sell B a new automobile, for which B promises to pay $10,000 by monthly installments over the next three years. If A and D agree that D should deliver the automobile to B, this would not constitute an assignment but would be a delegation of duties between A and D. In this instance, A would be the *delegator*, D would be the *delegatee*, and B would be the *obligee*. A delegation of duty does *not* extinguish the delegator's obligation to perform because A remains liable to B. When the delegatee accepts, or **assumes**, the delegated duty, *both* the delegator and delegatee are liable for performance of the contractual duty to the obligee.

Delegation of duties
transfer to a third party of a contractual obligation

Assumes delegatee agrees to perform the contractual obligation of the delegator

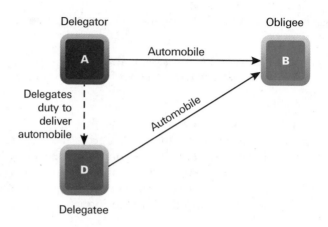

Delegator   Obligee

A   Automobile → B

Delegates duty to deliver automobile

Automobile

D

Delegatee

Delegable Duties

Though contractual duties generally are delegable, a delegation will not be permitted if

1. the nature of the duties are personal in that the obligee has a substantial interest in having the delegator perform the contract;
2. the performance is expressly made nondelegable; or
3. the delegation is prohibited by statute or public policy.

The courts will examine a delegation more closely than an assignment because a delegation compels the nondelegating party to the contract (the obligee) to receive performance from a party with whom she has not dealt.

For example, a school teacher may not delegate her performance to another teacher, even if the substitute is equally competent; for this contract is personal in nature. On the other hand, under a contract in which performance by a party involves no special skill and in which no personal trust or confidence is involved, the party may delegate performance of his duty. For example, the duty to pay money, to deliver fungible goods such as corn, or to mow a lawn is usually delegable. The next case deals with this type of delegation.

MACKE COMPANY v. PIZZA OF GAITHERSBURG, INC. Court of Appeals of Maryland, 1970,
259 Md. 479, 270 A.2d 645

FACTS In 1966, Pizza of Gaithersburg and The Pizza Shops contracted with Virginia Coffee Service to have vending machines installed in each of their pizza establishments. One year later, the Macke Company purchased Virginia's assets, and the vending machine contracts were assigned to Macke. When The Pizza Shops attempted to terminate their contracts for vending services, Macke brought suit for damages for breach of contract. The Pizza Shops argued that they had dealt with Macke before but had chosen Virginia because they preferred the way it conducted its business. They contended that since there was a material difference between the performance of Virginia and that of Macke, they were justified in refusing to recognize Virginia's delegation of its duties to Macke. Macke appealed from a judgment for the defendants.

DECISION Judgment reversed.

OPINION A contractual duty may be delegated and the promisee cannot rescind the contract if the quality of the performance remains materially the same. Here, the original contract was for the installation, maintenance, and stocking of a vending machine. It involved either a license granted to Virginia by The Pizza Shops or a lease of a portion of their premises. It did not involve a contract for personal services. Since the quality of performance remained substantially the same under Macke, Virginia's delegation of its duties was entirely permissible and enforceable.

INTERPRETATION Contractual duties, unless otherwise stated, are delegable if the quality of performance remains materially the same.

Duties of the Parties

Even when permitted, a **delegation** of a duty to a third person leaves the delegator bound to perform. If the delegator desires to be discharged of the duty, she may enter into an agreement by which she obtains the consent of the obligee to substitute a third person (the delegatee) in her place. This is a **novation**, whereby the delegator is discharged and the third party becomes directly bound on his promise to the obligee.

Though a delegation authorizes a third party to perform a duty for the delegator, the delegatee becomes liable for performance only if he assents to perform the delegated duties. Thus, if Frank owes a duty to Grace, and Frank delegates that duty to Henry, Henry is not obligated to either Frank or Grace to perform the duty unless Henry agrees to do so. If, however, Henry promises either Frank (the delegator) or Grace (the obligee) that he will perform Frank's duty, Henry is said to have *assumed the delegated duty* and becomes liable for nonperformance to both Frank and Grace. Accordingly, when there is both a delegation of duties *and* an assumption of the delegated duties, *both* the delegator and the delegatee are liable to the obligee for proper performance of the original contractual duty.

The question of whether a party has assumed contractual duties frequently arises in the following ambiguous situation: Marty and Carol agree to an assignment of Marty's *contract* with Bob. The Restatement and the Code clearly resolve this ambiguity by providing that unless the language or circumstances indicate the contrary, an assignment of "the contract" or of "all my rights under the contract" or an assignment in similar general terms is an assignment of rights *and* a delegation of performance of the duties of the assignor, and its acceptance by the assignee constitutes a promise by her to perform those duties. For example, Cooper Oil Company has a contract to deliver oil to Halsey. Cooper makes a written assignment to Lowell Oil Company "of all Cooper's rights under the contract." Lowell is under a duty to Halsey to deliver the oil called for by the contract, and Cooper is liable to Halsey if Lowell does not perform. You should also recall that the Restatement and the Code provide that a clause prohibiting an assignment of "the contract" is to be construed as barring only the delegation to the assignee (delegatee) of the assignor's (delegator's) performance, unless the circumstances indicate the contrary.

THIRD-PARTY BENEFICIARY CONTRACTS

A contract in which a party (the *promisor*) promises to render a certain performance not to the other party (the *promisee*) but to a third person (the beneficiary) is called a **third-party beneficiary contract**. The third person is merely a beneficiary of the contract, not a party to it. The law divides such contracts into two types: (1) intended beneficiary contracts and (2) incidental beneficiary contracts. An **intended beneficiary** is intended by the two parties to the contract (the promisor and promisee) to receive a benefit from the performance of their agreement. Accordingly, the courts generally enforce intended beneficiary third-party contracts. For example, Abbot promises Baldwin to deliver an automobile to Carson if Baldwin promises to pay $10,000. Carson is the intended beneficiary.

Delegation delegator is still bound to perform original obligation

Novation contract, to which the obligee is a party, substituting a new promisor for an existing promisor, who is consequently no longer liable on the original contract and is not liable as a delegator

Third-party beneficiary contract contract in which one party promises to render a performance to a third person

Intended beneficiary third party intended by the two contracting parties to receive a benefit from their contract

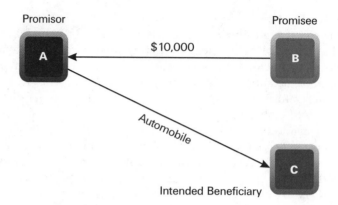

Incidental beneficiary
third party whom the two parties to a contract have no intention of benefiting by their contract

In an **incidental beneficiary** contract the third party is not intended to receive a benefit under the contract. Accordingly, courts do not enforce the third party's right to the benefits of the contract. For example, Abbot promises to purchase and deliver to Baldwin an automobile for $10,000. In all probability Abbot would acquire the automobile from Davis. Davis would be an incidental beneficiary.

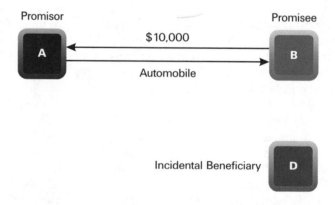

Intended Beneficiary
There are two types of intended beneficiaries: (1) donee beneficiaries and (2) creditor beneficiaries.

Donee beneficiary
a third party intended to receive a benefit from the contract as a gift

Donee Beneficiary A third party is an intended *donee* beneficiary if the promisee's purpose in bargaining for and obtaining the contract with the promisor was to make a gift to the beneficiary. The ordinary life insurance policy illustrates this type of intended beneficiary third-party contract. The insured (the promisee) makes a contract with an insurance company (the promisor), which promises, in consideration of premiums paid to it by the insured, to pay upon the death of the insured a stated sum of money to the named beneficiary (generally a relative or close friend), who is an intended donee beneficiary.

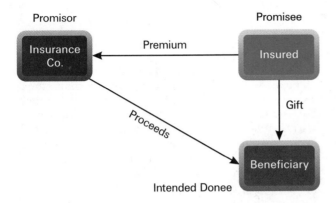

Creditor Beneficiary A third person is an intended *creditor* beneficiary if the promisee intends the performance of the promise to satisfy a legal duty owed to the beneficiary, who is a creditor of the promisee. The contract involves consideration moving from the promisee to the promisor in exchange for the promisor's engaging to pay a debt or to discharge an obligation the promisee owes to the third person.

Creditor beneficiary a third person intended to receive a benefit from the agreement to satisfy a legal duty owed to him

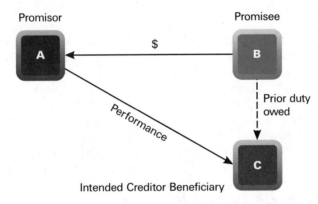

To illustrate: in the contract for the sale by Wesley of his business to Susan, she promises Wesley that she will pay all of his outstanding business debts, as listed in the contract. Wesley's creditors are intended creditor beneficiaries.

Rights of Intended Beneficiary Though an intended *creditor* beneficiary may sue either or both parties, an intended *donee* beneficiary may enforce the contract against the promisor only. He cannot maintain an action against the promisee, since the promisee was under no legal obligation to him.

In turn, in an action by the intended beneficiary of a third-party contract to enforce the promise, the promisor may assert any defense that would be available to him if the action had been brought by the promisee. The rights of the third party are based on the promisor's contract with the promisee. Thus, the promisor may assert against the intended beneficiary the absence of mutual assent or consideration, lack of capacity, fraud, mistake, and the like.

Rights of intended beneficiaries an intended donee beneficiary may enforce the contract against the promisor; an intended creditor beneficiary may enforce the contract against either or both the promisor and the promisee

BROWN v. NATIONAL SUPERMARKETS, INC. Missouri Court of Appeals, Eastern District, Division Three, 1984, 679 S.W.2d 307

FACTS Pauline Brown was shot and seriously injured by an unknown assailant in the parking lot of National Supermarkets. Pauline and George Brown brought a negligence action against National, Sentry Security Agency, and T. G. Watkins, a security guard and Sentry employee. The Browns maintained that the defendants have a legal duty to protect National's customers both in the store and in the parking lot and that this duty was breached. The defendants denied this allegation and were granted summary judgment by the trial court. The Browns appealed.

DECISION Trial court decision for summary judgment reversed and case remanded for action consistent with this opinion.

OPINION The Browns argue that National and Sentry entered into a contract whereby Sentry was to provide protection against criminal activities for National and its patrons. The National store manager stated that he understood the contract to include the area both inside and outside the store. On the other hand, Watkins, the security guard, claimed that he was never told to patrol the parking lot. Depending upon the terms of the contract and the surrounding circumstances, National and Sentry may or may not have assumed a duty to the Browns. If the contract was formed for the primary benefit of such third parties as the Browns, then the Browns are third-party beneficiaries to the agreement. In such a situation, the Browns, as third-party beneficiaries, may sue in tort or contract for any contract breach by Sentry or its employees. Since questions of fact remain in this case, summary judgment was inappropriate.

INTERPRETATION Third-party intended beneficiaries may maintain an action based on the underlying contract.

Vesting of rights if the beneficiary's rights vest, the promisor and promisee may not thereafter vary or discharge these vested rights

Vesting of Rights A contract for the benefit of an intended beneficiary confers upon that beneficiary rights that the beneficiary may enforce. Until these rights vest (take effect), however, the promisor and promisee may, by later agreement, vary or completely discharge them. There is considerable variation among the states as to when vesting occurs. Some states hold that vesting takes place immediately upon the making of the contract. In other states, vesting occurs when the third party learns of the contract and assents to it. In another group of states, vesting requires the third party to change his position in reliance upon the promise made for his benefit. The Restatement has adopted the following position: If the contract between the promisor and promisee provides that its terms may not be varied without the consent of the beneficiary, such a provision will be upheld. If there is no such provision, the parties to the contract may rescind or vary the contract unless the intended beneficiary (1) has brought an action on the promise, (2) has changed her position in reliance on it, or (3) has assented to the promise at the request of the promisor or promisee.

On the other hand, the promisor and promisee may provide that the benefits will *never* vest. For example, Mildred purchases an insurance policy on her own life, naming her husband as beneficiary. The policy, as such policies commonly do, reserves to Mildred the right to change her beneficiary or even to cancel the policy entirely.

Incidental beneficiary third party whom the two parties to the contract have no intention of benefitting by their contract and who acquires no rights under the contract

Incidental Beneficiary

An incidental third-party beneficiary is a person to whom the parties to a contract did not intend a benefit but who nevertheless would derive some benefit by its performance. For instance, a contract to raze an old, unsightly building and to replace it with a costly modern house would benefit the owner of the adjoining property by increasing his property's value. He would have no rights under the contract, however, as the benefit to him would be unintended and incidental.

A third person who may benefit incidentally by the performance of a contract to which he is not a party has no rights under the contract, since neither the promisee nor the promisor intended that the third person benefit. Assume that for a stated consideration Charles promises Madeline that he will purchase and deliver to Madeline a new Sony television of the latest model. Madeline performs. Charles does not. Reiner, the local exclusive Sony dealer, has no rights under the contract, although performance by Charles would produce a sale from which Reiner would derive a benefit; for Reiner is only an incidental beneficiary.

CHAPTER SUMMARY

Assignment of Rights	**Definition of Assignment** voluntary transfer to a third party of the rights arising from a contract so that the assignor's right to performance is extinguished
	■ *Assignor* party making an assignment
	■ *Assignee* party to whom contract rights are assigned
	■ *Obligor* party owing a duty to the assignor under the original contract
	■ *Obligee* party to whom a duty of performance is owed under a contract
	Requirements of an Assignment include intent but not consideration
	■ *Revocability of Assignment* when the assignee gives consideration, the assignor may not revoke the assignment without the assignee's consent
	■ *Partial Assignment* transfer of a portion of contractual rights to one or more assignees
	Assignability most contract rights are assignable *except*:
	■ Assignments that materially increase the duty, risk, or burden upon the obligor
	■ Assignments of personal rights
	■ Assignments expressly forbidden by the contract
	■ Assignments prohibited by law
	Rights of Assignee assignee stands in the shoes of the assignor
	■ *Defenses of obligor* may be asserted against the assignee
	■ *Notice* is not required but is advisable
	Implied Warranties obligation imposed by law upon the assignor of a contract right
	Express Warranty explicitly made contractual promise regarding contract rights transferred
	Successive Assignments the majority rule is that the first assignee in point of time prevails over later assignees; minority rule is that the first assignee to notify the obligor prevails

| **Delegation of Duties** | **Definition of Delegation** transfer to a third party of a contractual obligation
■ *Delegator* party delegating his duty to a third party
■ *Delegatee* third party to whom the delegator's duty is delegated
■ *Obligee* party to whom a duty of performance is owed by the delegator and delegatee
Delegability most contract duties may be delegated *except*:
■ Duties that are personal
■ Duties that are expressly nondelegable
■ Duties whose delegation is prohibited by statute or public policy
Duties of Parties
■ *Delegation* delegator is still bound to perform original obligation
■ *Novation* contract, to which the obligee is a party, substituting a new promisor for an existing promisor, who is consequently no longer liable on the original contract and is not liable as a delegator |
| **Third-Party Beneficiary Contracts** | **Definition** a third-party beneficiary contract is one in which one party promises to render a performance to a third person (the beneficiary)
Intended Beneficiaries third parties intended by the two contracting parties to receive a benefit from their contract
■ *Donee Beneficiary* a third party intended to receive a benefit from the contract as a gift
■ *Creditor Beneficiary* a third person intended to receive a benefit from the agreement to satisfy a legal duty owed to him
■ *Rights of Intended Beneficiaries* an intended donee beneficiary may enforce the contract against the promisor; an intended creditor beneficiary may enforce the contract against either or both the promisor and the promisee
■ *Vesting of Rights* if the beneficiary's rights vest, the promisor and promisee may not thereafter vary or discharge these vested rights
Incidental Beneficiary third party whom the two parties to the contract have no intention of benefitting by their contract and who acquires no rights under the contract |

QUESTIONS

1. Distinguish between an assignment of rights and a delegation of duties.
2. Identify (a) the requirements of an assignment of contract rights and (b) those rights that are *not* assignable.
3. Identify those situations in which a delegation of duties is not permitted.

4. Distinguish between an intended beneficiary and an incidental beneficiary.
5. When do the rights of an intended beneficiary vest?

Internet Question. Find a sample of one of the following: (a) an assignment of a contract, (b) a delegation of a contractual duty, or (c) a third-party beneficiary contract.

PROBLEMS

1. On December 1, Euphonia, a famous singer, contracted with Boito to sing at Boito's theater on December 31 for a fee of $25,000 to be paid immediately after the performance.
   (a) Euphonia, for value received, assigns this fee to Carter.
   (b) Euphonia, for value received, assigns this contract to sing to Dumont, an equally famous singer.
   (c) Boito sells his theater to Edmund and assigns his contract with Euphonia to Edmund.
   State the effect of each of these assignments.

2. The Smooth Paving Company entered into a paving contract with the city of Chicago. The contract contained the clause "contractor shall be liable for all damages to buildings resulting from the work performed." In the process of construction, one of the bulldozers of the Smooth Paving Company struck and broke a gas main, causing an explosion and a fire that destroyed the house of John Puff. Puff brought an appropriate action against the Smooth Paving Company to recover damages for the loss of his house. Decision?

3. Anne, who was unemployed, registered with the Speedy Employment Agency. A contract was then made under which Anne, in consideration of such position as the agency would obtain for her, agreed to pay the agency one-half of her first month's salary. The contract also contained an assignment by Anne to the agency of one-half of her first month's salary. Two weeks later, the agency obtained a permanent position for Anne with the Bostwick Co. at a monthly salary of $900. The agency also notified Bostwick Co. of the assignment by Anne. At the end of the first month, Bostwick Co. paid Anne her salary in full. Anne then quit and disappeared. The agency now sues Bostwick Co. for $450 under the assignment. Decision?

4. Georgia purchased an option on Blackacre from Pamela for $1,000. The option contract contained a provision by which Georgia promised not to assign the option contract without Pamela's permission. Georgia, without Pamela's permission, assigned the contract to Michael. Michael now seeks to exercise the option, and Pamela refuses to sell Blackacre to him. Decision?

5. Julia contracts to sell to Hayden, an ice cream manufacturer, the amount of ice Hayden may need in his business for the ensuing three years to the extent of not more than 250 tons a week at a stated price per ton. Hayden makes a corresponding promise to Julia to buy such an amount of ice. Hayden sells his ice cream plant to Reed and assigns to Reed all Hayden's rights under the contract with Julia. On learning of the sale, Julia refuses to furnish ice to Reed. Reed sues Julia for damages. Decision?

6. Brown enters into a written contract with Ideal Insurance Company under which, in consideration of Brown's payment of her premiums, the insurance company promises to pay XYZ College the face amount of the policy, $100,000, on Brown's death. Brown pays the premiums until her death. Thereafter, XYZ College makes demand for the $100,000, which the insurance company refuses to pay on the ground that XYZ College was not a party to the contract. Decision?

7. Grant and Debbie enter into a contract binding Grant personally to do some delicate cabinetwork. Grant assigns his rights and delegates performance of his duties to Clarence.
   (a) On being informed of this, Debbie agrees with Clarence, in consideration of Clarence's promise to do the work, that Debbie will accept Clarence's work, if properly done, instead of the performance promised by Grant. Later, without cause, Debbie refuses to allow Clarence to proceed with the work, though Clarence is ready to do so, and makes demand on Grant that Grant perform. Grant refuses. Can Clarence recover damages from Debbie? Can Debbie recover from Grant?
   (b) Debbie refuses to permit Clarence to do the work, employs another carpenter, and brings an action against Grant, claiming as damages the difference between the contract price and the cost to employ the other carpenter. Decision?

8. Rebecca owes Lewis $2,500 due on November 1. On August 15, Lewis assigns this right for value received to Julia, who gives notice on September 10 of the assignment to Rebecca. On August 25, Lewis assigns the same right to Wayne, who in good faith gives value and has no prior knowledge of the assignment by Lewis to Julia. Wayne gives Rebecca notice of the assignment on August 30. What are the rights and obligations of Rebecca, Lewis, Julia, and Wayne?

9. Lisa hired Jay in the spring, as she had for many years, to set out in beds the flowers Lisa had grown in her greenhouses during the winter. The work was to be done in Lisa's absence for $300. Jay became ill the day after Lisa departed and requested his friend, Curtis, to set out the flowers, promising to pay Curtis $250 when Jay received his payment. Curtis agreed. On completion of the planting, an agent of Lisa's, who had authority to dispense the money, paid Jay, and Jay paid Curtis. Within two days, it became obvious that the planting was a disaster. Because he did not operate Lisa's automatic watering system properly, everything set out by Curtis had died of water rot.
   May Lisa recover damages from Curtis? May Lisa recover damages from Jay, and, if so, does Jay have an action against Curtis?

10. Caleb, operator of a window-washing business, dictated a letter to his secretary addressed to Apartments, Inc., stating, "I will wash the windows of your apartment buildings at $4.10 per window to be paid on completion of the work." The secretary typed the letter, signed Caleb's name, and mailed it to Apartments, Inc. Apartments, Inc., replied, "Accept your offer."

   Caleb wrote back, "I will wash them during the week starting July 10 and direct you to pay the money you will owe me to my son, Bernie. I am giving it to him as a wedding present." Caleb sent a signed copy of the letter to Bernie.

   Caleb washed the windows during the time stated and demanded payment to him of $8,200 (2,000 windows at $4.10 each), informing Apartments, Inc., that he had changed his mind about having the money paid to Bernie.

   What are the rights of the parties?

11. On April 1, 1980, members of Local 100, Transport Workers Union of America (TWU), began an eleven-day mass transit strike that paralyzed the life and commerce of the city of New York. Jackson, Lewis, Schnitzler & Krupman, a Manhattan law firm, brought a class action suit against the TWU for the direct and foreseeable damages it suffered as a result of the union's illegal strike. The law firm sought to recover as a third-party beneficiary of the collective bargaining agreement between the union and New York City. The agreement contains a no-strike clause and states that the TWU agreed to cooperate with the city to provide a safe, efficient, and dependable mass transit system. The law firm argues that its members are a part of the general public that depends on the mass transit system to go to and from work. Therefore, they are in the class of persons for whose benefit the union has promised to provide dependable transportation service. Decision?

12. Northwest Airlines leased space in the terminal building at the Portland Airport from the Port of Portland. Crosetti entered into a contract with the Port to furnish janitorial services for the building, which required Crosetti to keep the floor clean, to indemnify the Port against loss due to claims or lawsuits based upon Crosetti's failure to perform, and to provide public liability insurance for the Port and Crosetti. A patron of the building who was injured by a fall caused by a foreign substance on the floor at Northwest's ticket counter brought suit for damages against Northwest, the Port, and Crosetti. Upon settlement of this suit, Northwest sued Crosetti to recover the amount of its contribution to the settlement and other expenses on the grounds that Northwest was a third-party beneficiary of Crosetti's contract with the Port to keep the floors clean and, therefore, within the protection of Crosetti's indemnification agreement. Decision?

13. Tompkins-Beckwith, as the contractor on a construction project, entered into a subcontract with a division of Air Metal Industries. Air Metal procured American Fire and Casualty Company to be surety on certain bonds in connection with contracts it was performing for Tompkins-Beckwith and others. As security for these bonds, on January 3, 1962, Air Metal executed an assignment to American Fire of all accounts receivable under the Tompkins-Beckwith subcontract. On November 26, 1962, Boulevard National Bank lent money to Air Metal. To secure the loans, Air Metal purported to assign to the bank certain accounts receivable it had under its subcontract with Tompkins-Beckwith.

   In June 1963, Air Metal defaulted on various contracts bonded by American Fire. On July 1, 1963, American Fire served formal notice on Tompkins-Beckwith of Air Metal's assignment. Tompkins-Beckwith acknowledged the assignment and agreed to pay. In August 1963, Boulevard National Bank notified Tompkins-Beckwith of its assignment. Tompkins-Beckwith refused to recognize the bank's claim and, instead, paid all remaining funds that had accrued to Air Metal to American Fire. The bank then sued to enforce its claim under Air Metal's assignment. Decision?

14. The International Association of Machinists (the union) was the bargaining agent for the employees of Powder Power Tool Corporation. On August 24, 1953, the union and the corporation executed a collective bargaining agreement providing for retroactively increased wage rates for the corporation's employees effective as of April 1, 1953. Three employees who were working for Powder before and for several months after April 1, 1953, but who were not employed by the corporation when the agreement was executed on August 24, 1953, were paid to the time their employment terminated at the old wage scale. The three employees assigned their claims to Springer, who brought this action against the corporation for the extra wages. Decision?

15. In March 1962, Adrian Saylor sold government bonds owned exclusively by him and with $6,450 of the proceeds opened a savings account in a bank in the name of "Mr. or Mrs. Adrian M. Saylor." In June 1963 Saylor deposited the additional sum of $2,132 of his own money in the account. There were no other deposits and no withdrawals prior to the death of Saylor in May 1964. Is the balance of the account on Saylor's death payable wholly to Adrian Saylor's estate, wholly to his widow, or half to each?

16. Linda King was found liable to Charlotte Clement as the result of an automobile accident. King, who was insolvent at the time, declared bankruptcy and directed her attorney, Prestwich, to list Clement as an unsecured creditor. The attorney failed to carry out

this duty, and consequently King sued him for legal malpractice. When Clement pursued her judgment against King, she received a written assignment of King's legal malpractice claim against Prestwich. Clement has attempted to bring the claim, but Prestwich alleges that a claim for legal malpractice is not assignable. Decision?

17. Rensselaer Water Company contracted with the city of Rensselaer to provide water to the city for use in homes, public buildings, industry, and fire hydrants. During the term of the contract a building caught fire. The fire spread to a nearby warehouse and destroyed it and its contents. The water company knew of the fire but failed to supply adequate water pressure at the fire hydrant to extinguish the fire. The warehouse owner sued the water company for failure to fulfill its contract with the city. Decision?

18. McDonald's granted to Copeland a franchise in Omaha, Nebraska. In a separate letter, it also granted him a right of first refusal for future franchises to be developed in the Omaha-Council Bluffs area. Copeland then sold all rights in his six McDonald's franchises to Schupack. When McDonald's offered a new franchise in the Omaha area to someone other than Schupack, he attempted to exercise the right of first refusal. McDonald's would not recognize the right in Schupack, claiming that it was personal to Copeland and, therefore, nonassignable without its consent.

Schupack brought an action for specific performance, requiring McDonald's to accord him the right of first refusal. Decision?

19. While under contract to play professional basketball for the Philadelphia 76ers, Billy Cunningham negotiated a three-year contract with the Carolina Cougars, another professional basketball team. The contract with the Cougars was to begin at the expiration of the contract with the 76ers. In addition to a signing bonus of $125,000, Cunningham was to receive under the new contract a salary of $100,000 for the first year, $110,000 for the second, and $120,000 for the third. The contract also stated that Cunningham "had special, exceptional and unique knowledge, skill and ability as a basketball player" and that Cunningham therefore agreed the Cougars could enjoin him from playing basketball for any other team for the term of the contract. In addition, the contract contained a clause prohibiting its assignment to another club without Cunningham's consent. In 1971, the ownership of the Cougars changed, and Cunningham's contract was assigned to Munchak Corporation, the new owners, without his consent. When Cunningham refused to play for the Cougars, Munchak Corporation sought to enjoin his playing for any other team. Cunningham asserts that his contract was not assignable. The trial court denied injunctive relief and Munchak appealed. Decision?

CHAPTER 17

Performance, Breach, and Discharge

The subject of discharge of contracts concerns the termination of contractual duties. In earlier chapters we have seen how parties may become contractually bound by their promises. It is also important to know how a person may become unbound from a contract. For although contractual promises are made for a purpose, and the parties reasonably expect this purpose to be fulfilled by performance, performance of a contractual duty is only one method of discharge.

Whatever causes a binding promise to cease to be binding is a discharge of the contract. In general, there are four kinds of discharge: (1) performance by the parties, (2) material breach by one or both of the parties, (3) agreement of the parties, and (4) operation of law. Moreover, many contractual promises are not absolute promises to perform but rather are conditional—that is, they depend on the happening or nonhappening of a specific event. After we discuss the subject of conditions, we will cover the four kinds of discharge.

CONDITIONS

Condition an uncertain event whose happening or nonhappening affects the duty of performance

A **condition** is an event whose happening or nonhappening affects a duty of performance under a contract. Some conditions must be satisfied before any duty to perform arises; others terminate the duty to perform; still others either limit or modify the duty to perform. A condition is inserted in a contract to protect and benefit the promisor. The more conditions to which a promise is subject, the less content the promise has. For example, a promise to pay $8,000 provided that such sum is realized from the sale of an automobile, provided the automobile is sold within sixty days, and provided that the automobile, which has been stolen, can be found, is clearly different from, and worth considerably less than, an unconditional promise by the same promisor to pay $8,000.

A fundamental difference exists between the breach or nonperformance of a contractual promise and the failure or nonhappening of a condition. A breach of contract subjects the promisor to liability. It may or may not, depending on its materiality, excuse the nonbreaching party's nonperformance of his duty under the contract. The happening or nonhappening of a condition, on the other hand, either prevents a party from acquiring a right or deprives him of a right, but subjects neither party to any liability.

Conditions may be classified by *how* they are imposed: express conditions, implied-in-fact conditions, or implied-in-law conditions (also called constructive conditions). They also may be classified by *when* they affect a duty of performance: conditions concurrent, conditions precedent, or conditions subsequent. These two ways of classifying conditions are not mutually exclusive; for example, a condition may be constructive and concurrent, or express and precedent.

Express Conditions

An **express condition** is explicitly set forth in language. No particular form of words is necessary to create an express condition, as long as the event to which the performance of the promise is made subject is clearly expressed. An express condition is usually preceded by words such as "provided that," "on condition that," "if," "while," "after," "upon," or "as soon as."

The basic rule applied to express conditions is that they must be fully and literally performed before the conditional duty to perform arises. However, where application of the full and literal performance test would result in a forfeiture, the courts usually apply to the completed portion of the condition a *substantial satisfaction* test, as discussed in this chapter under substantial performance.

Satisfaction of a Contracting Party The parties to a contract may agree that performance by one of them shall be to the **satisfaction** of the other, who will not be obligated to perform unless he is satisfied. This is an express condition to the duty to perform. Assume that tailor Ken contracts to make a suit of clothes to Dick's satisfaction, and that Dick promises to pay Ken $350 for the suit if he is satisfied with it when completed. Ken completes the suit using materials ordered by Dick. The suit fits Dick beautifully, but Dick tells Ken that he is not satisfied with it and refuses to accept or pay for it. Ken is not entitled to recover $350 or any amount from Dick because the express condition did not happen. This is so if Dick's dissatisfaction is honest and in good faith, even if it is unreasonable. Where satisfaction relates to a matter of personal taste, opinion, or judgment, the law applies the **subjective satisfaction** standard; and the condition has not occurred if the promisor is in good faith dissatisfied.

If the contract does not clearly indicate that satisfaction is subjective, or if the performance contracted for relates to mechanical fitness or utility, the law assumes an **objective satisfaction** standard. For example, the objective standard of satisfaction would apply to the sale of a building or standard goods. In such cases, the question would not be whether the promisor was actually satisfied with the performance by the other party but whether, as a reasonable person, he ought to be satisfied.

Satisfaction of a Third Party A contract may condition the performance of a party upon the approval of a third party. For example, building contracts commonly provide that before the owner is required to pay, the builder shall furnish the architect's certificate stating that the building has been constructed according to the plans and specifications upon which the builder and the owner agreed. For even though the price is being paid for the building, not for the certificate, the owner must have both the building and the certificate before she will be obliged to pay. The duty of payment was made expressly conditional on the presentation of the certificate.

Implied-in-Fact Conditions

Implied-in-fact conditions are similar to express conditions in that they must fully and literally occur and in that they are understood by the parties to be part of the agreement. They differ in that they are not stated in express language; rather, they are necessarily inferred from the terms of the contract, the nature of the transaction, or the conduct of the parties. Thus, if Edna, for $750, contracts to paint Sy's house any color Sy desires, it is necessarily implied in fact that Sy will inform Edna of the desired color before Edna begins to paint. The notification of

---

Express condition performance is explicitly made contingent on the happening or nonhappening of a stated event

Satisfaction express condition making performance contingent upon one party's approval of the other's performance

Subjective satisfaction approval based upon a party's honestly held opinion

Objective satisfaction approval based upon whether a reasonable person would be satisfied

Implied-in-fact condition contingency understood but not expressed by the parties

choice of color is an implied-in-fact condition, an operative event that must occur before Edna is subject to the duty of painting the house.

Implied-in-Law Conditions

Implied-in-law condition
contingency that arises from operation of law

An **implied-in-law condition**, or a *constructive condition*, is imposed by law in order to accomplish a just and fair result. It differs from an express condition and an implied-in-fact condition in two ways: (1) it is not contained in the language of the contract or necessarily inferred from the contract, and (2) it need only be substantially performed. For example, Fernando contracts to sell a certain tract of land to Marie for $18,000, but the contract is silent as to the time of delivery of the deed and payment of the price. According to the law, the contract implies that payment and delivery of the deed are not independent of each other. The courts will treat the promises as mutually dependent and will therefore hold that a delivery or tender of the deed by Fernando to Marie is a condition to the duty of Marie to pay the price. Conversely, payment or tender of $18,000 by Marie to Fernando is a condition to the duty of Fernando to deliver the deed to Marie.

Concurrent Conditions

Concurrent conditions
performance by the parties is to occur simultaneously

Concurrent conditions occur when the mutual duties of performance are to take place simultaneously. As we indicated in the section above, in the absence of agreement to the contrary, the law assumes that the respective performances under a contract are concurrent conditions. See *K & G Construction Co. v. Harris* later in this chapter for an illustration of mutually dependent, concurrent conditions.

Condition Precedent

Condition precedent an event that must occur or not occur before performance is due

A **condition precedent** is an event that must occur before performance is due under a contract. In other words, the immediate duty of one party to perform is subject to the condition that some event must first occur. For instance, Steve is to deliver shoes to Nancy on June 1, and Nancy is to pay for the shoes on July 15. Steve's delivery of the shoes is a condition precedent to Nancy's performance. Similarly, if Rachel promises to buy Justin's land for $50,000, provided Rachel can obtain financing in the amount of $40,000 at 10 percent or less for thirty years within sixty days of signing the contract, Rachel's obtaining the specified financing is a condition precedent to her duty. If the condition is satisfied, Rachel is bound to perform; if it is not met, she is not bound to perform. Rachel, however, is under an implied-in-law duty to use her best efforts to obtain financing under these terms.

Condition Subsequent

Condition subsequent an event that terminates a duty of performance

A **condition subsequent** is an event that terminates an existing duty. For example, where goods are sold under terms of "sale or return," the buyer has the right to return the goods to the seller within a stated period but is under an immediate duty to pay the price unless the parties have agreed on credit. The duty to pay the price is terminated by a return of the goods, which operates as a condition subsequent. Conditions subsequent occur very infrequently in contract law, while conditions precedent are quite common.

Discharge termination of a contractual duty

DISCHARGE BY PERFORMANCE

Performance fulfillment of a contractual obligation

Discharge is the termination of a contractual duty. **Performance** is the fulfillment of a contractual obligation. Discharge by performance is undoubtedly the most frequent method of discharging a contractual duty. If a promisor exactly performs his duty under the contract, he is no longer subject to that duty.

Tender is an offer by one party—who is ready, willing, and able to perform— to the other party to perform his obligation according to the terms of the contract. Under a bilateral contract, the refusal or rejection of a tender, or offer of performance, by one party may be treated as a repudiation, excusing or discharging the tendering party from further duty of performance under the contract. A tender of payment of a debt past due, however, does not discharge the debt if the creditor refuses to accept the tender; instead, further accumulation of interest on the debt will stop.

> **Tender** offer of performance

DISCHARGE BY BREACH

A **breach** of a contract is a wrongful failure to perform its terms. Breach of contract always gives rise to a cause of action for damages by the aggrieved (injured) party. It may, however, have a more important effect: an uncured (uncorrected) *material* breach by one party operates as an excuse for nonperformance by the other party and discharges the aggrieved party from any further duty under the contract. If, on the other hand, the breach is not material, the aggrieved party is not discharged from the contract, although she may recover money damages. Under the Code's perfect tender rule, which applies *only* to sales transactions, *any* deviation discharges the aggrieved party.

> **Breach** wrongful failure to perform the terms of a contract; gives rise to a right of damages by the injured party

Material Breach
An unjustified failure to perform *substantially* the obligations promised in a contract is a **material breach**. The key is whether the aggrieved party obtained substantially what he bargained for, despite the breach, or whether the breach significantly impaired his rights under the contract. A material breach discharges the aggrieved party from his duty of performance. For instance, Joe orders a specially made, tailored suit from Peggy to be made of wool; but Peggy makes the suit of cotton instead. Peggy has materially breached the contract. Consequently, Joe is discharged from his duty to pay for the suit; and he may also recover money damages from Peggy for her breach.

> **Material breach** nonperformance that significantly impairs the aggrieved party's rights under the contract; discharges the injured party from any further duty under the contract

Although there are no clear-cut rules as to what constitutes a material breach, several basic principles apply. First, partial performance is a material breach of a contract if it omits some essential part of the contract. Second, the courts will consider a breach material if it is quantitatively or qualitatively serious. Third, an *intentional* breach of contract is generally held to be material. Fourth, a failure to perform a promise promptly is a material breach if time is of the essence; that is, if the parties have clearly indicated that a failure to perform by a stated time is material; otherwise, the aggrieved party may recover damages only for loss caused by the delay. Fifth, the parties to a contract may, within limits, specify what breaches are to be considered material.

K & G CONSTRUCTION CO. v. HARRIS Court of Appeals of Maryland, 1960, 223 Md. 305, 164 A.2d 451

FACTS K & G Construction Co. was the owner of and the general contractor for a housing subdivision project. Harris contracted with the company to do excavating and earth-moving work on the project. Certain provisions of the contract stated that (1) K & G was to make monthly progress payments to Harris; (2) no such payments were to be made until Harris obtained liability insurance; and (3) all of Harris's work on the project must be performed in a workmanlike manner. On August 9, a bulldozer operator, working for Harris,

continued

drove too close to one of K & G's houses, causing the collapse of a wall and other damage. When Harris and his insurance carrier denied liability and refused to pay for the damage, K & G refused to make the August monthly progress payment. Harris, nonetheless, continued to work on the project until mid-September, when the excavator ceased its operations due to K & G's refusal to make the progress payment. K & G had another excavator finish the job at an added cost of $450. It then sued Harris for the bulldozer damage, alleging negligence, and also for the $450 damages for breach of contract. Harris claims that K & G defaulted first, having no legal right to refuse the August progress payment. The trial court entered judgment for Harris, and K & G appealed.

DECISION Judgment for Harris reversed and judgment entered in favor of K & G Construction Co. for $450.

OPINION Contractual obligations are either independent of each other or mutually dependent. They are independent if the parties intend that performance by each of them is in no way conditioned upon performance by the other. Failure of one party to perform its independent promise does not excuse the other's nonperformance. On the other hand, promises are concurrent conditions and mutually dependent if the parties intend performance by one to be conditioned upon performance by the other. A material breach of a mutually dependent promise by one party excuses the other's performance of his contractual obligations. The modern rule is that there is a presumption that mutual promises are concurrent and dependent, and are to be so regarded, whenever possible.

Here, the bulldozer operator's negligent damage to the house was a material breach of Harris's promise to perform in a workmanlike manner. Under a reasonable interpretation of the circumstances and the contract, the progress payment was conditioned upon Harris's nonnegligent, workmanlike performance. Hence, the promises are concurrent and mutually dependent. K & G then had a right to refuse making the progress payment without canceling the contract, based upon Harris's negligence.

INTERPRETATION A material breach of a mutually dependent duty discharges the nonbreaching party's duty to perform.

Prevention of performance one party's substantial interference with or prevention of performance by the other constitutes a material breach that discharges the other party to the contract

Prevention of Performance One party's substantial interference with, or prevention of, performance by the other generally constitutes a material breach that discharges the other party to the contract. For instance, Dale prevents an architect from giving Lucy a certificate that is a condition to Dale's liability to pay Lucy a certain sum of money. Dale may not then use Lucy's failure to produce a certificate as an excuse for nonpayment. Likewise, if Maude has contracted to grow a certain crop for Harold, and Harold plows the field and destroys the seedlings Maude has planted, his interference with Maude's performance discharges Maude from her duty under the contract. It does not, however, discharge Harold from his duty under the contract.

Perfect tender rule standard under the UCC that performance must comply strictly with contractual duties and that any deviation discharges the injured party

Perfect Tender Rule The Code greatly alters the common law doctrine of material breach by adopting what is known as the perfect tender rule. The **perfect tender rule**, which we will discuss more fully in Chapter 20, essentially provides that *any* deviation from the promised performance in a sales contract under the Code constitutes a material breach of the contract and discharges the aggrieved party from his duty of performance.

Substantial performance performance that is incomplete but does not defeat the purpose of the contract; does not discharge the injured party but entitles him to damages

Substantial Performance

Substantial performance is performance that, though incomplete, does not defeat the purpose of the contract. If a party substantially, but not completely, performs her obligations under a contract, the common law generally will allow her to obtain the other party's performance, less any damages the partial performance caused. If no harm has been caused, the breaching party will obtain the other party's full contractual performance. Thus, in the specially ordered suit illustration, if Peggy, the tailor, used the correct fabric but improperly used black buttons instead of blue, she would be permitted to collect from Joe the contract price of the suit less the damage, if any, caused to Joe by the substitution of the wrongly colored buttons. The doctrine of substantial performance assumes particular importance in the construction industry in cases where a structure is built on the aggrieved party's land. Consider the following: Adam builds a $300,000 house for Betty but deviates from the specifications, causing Betty $10,000 in damages. If the courts considered this a material breach, Betty would not have to pay for the house that is now on her land, a result that would clearly constitute an unjust forfeiture on Adam's part. Therefore, because Adam's performance has been substantial, the courts would probably not deem the breach material; and he would be able to collect $290,000 from Betty.

MOUNTAIN RESTAURANT CORPORATION v. PARKCENTER MALL ASSOCIATES
Court of Appeals of Idaho, 1992, 122 Idaho 261, 833 P.2d 119

FACTS Mountain Restaurant Corporation (Mountain) leased commercial space in the ParkCenter Mall to operate a restaurant called Zac's Grill. The lease specified that the shopping center should always have as a part of it, or upon premises immediately next to it, a minimum of 500 parking spaces at all times. While developing the mall, ParkCenter entered into two agreements that restricted the amount of parking at their mall to fewer than 500 spaces. Neither agreement was shown to Mountain before it signed the lease.

Zac's Grill was to be a fast-food restaurant where tables were anticipated to "turn over" twice during lunch. Zac's operated successfully until parking close to the restaurant became restricted. Two other restaurants opened and began competing for parking spaces, and the parking lot would become full between 12:00 and 12:30 P.M. Parking, however, was always available at other areas of the mall. Business declined for Zac's, which fell behind on the rent due to ParkCenter until finally the restaurant closed. Mountain filed for rescission of the lease, and ParkCenter counterclaimed for the rent owed. The trial court found that ParkCenter had not materially breached its contract and that, therefore, Mountain was not entitled to rescission of the lease.

DECISION Trial court decision affirmed.

OPINION A material breach of contract is a breach so substantial and fundamental that it defeats the object of the parties in entering into the contract. It affects the substantive rights of the parties, and, in the face of such a breach, a court may order a rescission of the contract. Rescission is not warranted, however, where the breach is incidental and subordinate to the main purpose of the contract. Thus, there is no material breach where substantial performance has been rendered. Substantial performance is performance that, despite deviation or omission, provides the important and essential benefits of the contract to the promisee. Whether a breach of contract is material is a question of fact.

The evidence in this case supports the finding that there was no material breach of contract. There was a breach of contract by ParkCenter: It had expressly agreed to provide 500 parking spaces "immediately contiguous [to the mall] or adjacent thereto," but during normal business hours on weekdays it provided only 387 spaces. This deviation was not material, however, because the evidence showed that parking was always available on the mall property. Although Mountain may have believed that having parking available right next to its location was extremely important to its business, the lease did not so provide. Thus, the fact that spaces in close proximity to the restaurant were generally not available during the lunch hour does not provide support for the claim that there was a material breach of the lease because the lease simply did not provide that parking in that area would be reserved for Mountain's customers.

INTERPRETATION Incomplete performance that does not defeat the purpose of the contract does not discharge the injured party but entitles him to damages.

CONSUMER INSIGHT

AOL Offers Refunds to Angry Customers

America Online agreed Wednesday to give disgruntled users of its overburdened network up to $39.90 or a free month of service.

The Dulles, Va.-based company, the world's largest online service, will offer refunds for December and January when many customers had trouble logging on.

"You can't offer something to a subscriber and then not be able to deliver," said Illinois Attorney General James Ryan, who led the efforts of 36 state attorneys general to hold AOL accountable.

AOL's stock rose $2 to 37¼ as investors cheered the move. But analysts are unsure of the settlement's cost.

The agreement calls for AOL to offer full refunds to customers nationwide who used the service less than two hours in either December or January. Those who used it for 2–8 hours are entitled to a 50% refund; 8–15 hours, a 25% refund. Or users can opt for one month of free service.

"We're hitting the issues head on," says Steve Case, AOL's chief executive.

AOL's recent problems began when it offered customers unlimited usage for $19.95 a month late last year. The new plan led to major traffic jams.

AOL also agreed to reduce its advertising in February to help hold its customer base at about 8 million. Also, AOL will:

- Mention in ads and inform new users that its network might not always be accessible.
- Hire 600 more customer service representatives.
- Make it easier to cancel subscriptions.

AOL customers must file for a refund with their state attorney general or AOL Member Refunds, P.O. Box 511, Ogden, Utah 84402-0511.

Anticipatory Repudiation

Anticipatory repudiation *(an·tic'·i·pa·to·ry)* an inability or refusal to perform, before performance is due, that is treated as a breach, allowing the nonrepudiating party to bring suit immediately

A breach of contract, as previously discussed, is a failure to perform the terms of a contract. While it is logically and physically impossible to fail to perform a duty before the date on which that performance is due, a party may announce before the due date that she will not perform, or she may commit an act that makes her unable to perform. Either act is a repudiation of the contract, which notifies the other party that a breach is imminent. Such repudiation before the date fixed by the contract for performance is called an **anticipatory repudiation**. The courts, as shown in the leading case that follows, view it as a breach that discharges the nonrepudiating party's duty to perform and permits her to bring suit immediately. Nonetheless, the nonbreaching party *may* wait until the time the performance is due, to see if the repudiator will retract his repudiation and perform his contractual duties. If the repudiator does perform, then there is a discharge by performance; if he does not perform, there is a material breach.

HOCHSTER v. DE LA TOUR Queen's Bench of England, 1853, 2 Ellis and Blackburn Reports 678

FACTS On April 12, 1852, Hochster contracted with De La Tour to serve as a guide for De La Tour on his three-month trip to Europe, beginning on June 1 at an agreed-upon salary. On May 11, De La Tour notified Hochster that he would not need Hochster's services. He also refused to pay Hochster any compensation. Hochster brought this action to recover damages for breach of contract.

DECISION Judgment for Hochster.

OPINION Hochster may treat the repudiation by De La Tour as a breach of contract and immediately bring suit. Otherwise, Hochster would have to remain ready to perform and to refrain from accepting other employment in order to tender his services on June 1. It is far more rational, upon repudiation of the contract by one of the parties, to allow the other party to consider his performance under the contract as excused and seek other employment while retaining his right to sue for damages.

INTERPRETATION An anticipatory breach discharges the injured party and entitles her to bring suit immediately.

Material Alteration of Written Contract

An unauthorized alteration or change of *any* of the material terms or provisions of a written contract or document is a discharge of the *entire* contract. An alteration is material if it would vary any party's legal relations with the maker of the alteration or would adversely affect that party's legal relations with a third person. To constitute a discharge, the alteration must be material and fraudulent and must be the act of either a party to the contract or someone acting on his behalf. An unauthorized change in the terms of a written contract by a person who is not a party to the contract does not discharge the contract.

> **Material alteration** a material and fraudulent alteration of a written contract by a party to the contract discharges the entire contract

DISCHARGE BY AGREEMENT OF THE PARTIES

By agreement, the parties to a contract may discharge each other from performance under the contract. They may do this by rescission, substituted contract, accord and satisfaction, or novation.

Mutual Rescission

A **rescission** is an agreement between the parties to terminate their respective duties under the contract. It is, literally, a contract to end a contract; and it must contain all of the essentials of a contract. In rescinding an executory, bilateral contract, each party furnishes consideration in giving up his rights under the contract in exchange for the other party's doing the same. If one party has already fully performed, however, a mutual rescission is not binding at common law because of lack of consideration.

> **Mutual rescission** agreement of the parties to terminate their contractual duties

Substituted Contracts

A **substituted contract** is a new contract accepted by both parties in satisfaction of the parties' duties under the original contract. A substituted contract immediately discharges the original contract and imposes new obligations under its own terms.

> **Substituted contract** a new contract accepted in satisfaction of the parties' duties under the original contract

Accord and Satisfaction

An **accord** is a contract by which an obligee promises to accept a stated performance in *satisfaction* of the obligor's *existing* contractual duty. The performance of the accord, called a **satisfaction**, discharges the original duty. Thus, if Dan owes Sara $500, and the parties agree that Dan will paint Sara's house in satisfaction of the debt, the agreement is an executory accord. When Dan performs the accord by painting Sara's house, he will by satisfaction discharge the $500 debt.

> **Accord and satisfaction** substituted duty (accord) and the discharge of the prior contractual obligation by performance of the new duty (satisfaction)

ENGLAND v. HORBACH Court of Appeals of Utah, 1995, 905 P.2d 301

FACTS In late 1989 or early 1990, the plaintiff, Lan England, agreed to sell 258,363 shares of stock to the defendant, Eugene Horbach, for $2.75 per share, resulting in a total price of $710,498.25. Although the purchase money was to be paid in the first quarter of 1990, the defendant made periodic payments on the stock at least through September 1990. The parties met in May of 1991 to finalize the transaction. At this time, the plaintiff believed that the defendant owed at least $25,000 of the original purchase price. The defendant did not dispute that amount. The parties then reached a second agreement whereby the defendant agreed to pay to the plaintiff an additional $25,000 and to hold in trust 2 percent of the stock for the plaintiff. In return, the plaintiff agreed to transfer the stock and to forego his right to sue the defendant for breach of the original agreement.

In December 1992, the plaintiff made a demand for the 2 percent stock, but the defendant refused, contending that the 2 percent agreement was meant only

continued

to secure his payment of the additional $25,000. The plaintiff sued for breach of the 2 percent agreement. Prior to trial, the defendant discovered additional business records that the defendant claimed documented he had, before entering into the second agreement, actually overpaid the plaintiff for the purchase of the stock. The trial court dismissed the plaintiff's complaint, ruling that the plaintiff could not enforce the second agreement as an accord and satisfaction because it was not supported by consideration and because it was based upon a mutual mistake that the defendant owed additional money on the original agreement.

DECISION Judgment reversed.

OPINION An accord and satisfaction arises when the parties to a contract mutually agree that a performance different than that required by the original contract will be made in substitution of the performance originally agreed upon and that the substituted agreement calling for a different performance will discharge the obligation created under the original agreement. The elements of an accord and satisfaction include: (1) a bona fide dispute or uncertainty over an unliquidated amount; (2) a payment tendered in full settlement of the entire dispute; and (3) an acceptance of the payment. In addition, for an accord and satisfaction to have any legal effect, the elements of a contract, including consideration, must be present. It is clear that consideration for an accord may consist of a compromise of a bona fide dispute or uncertainty as to the amount actually owing. Moreover, it is not necessary for the dispute to be well-founded so long as it is in good faith. Thus, if the parties, in good faith, believe there is a disputed or uncertain claim, mere

settlement of the amount due and acceptance of that amount constitutes the consideration necessary to support the contract. At the meeting in May, 1991, the parties both believed that there was a dispute as to the amount that had been paid. Although unfounded, the plaintiff asserted in good faith that he believed additional money was still owing. The defendant accepted this representation without dispute and accepted the plaintiff's settlement proposal. Therefore, the settlement agreement is supported by consideration.

The trial court also erred in determining that the accord and satisfaction was unenforceable because of a mutual mistake of fact. A mutual mistake occurs when both parties, at the time of contracting, share a misconception about a basic assumption or vital fact upon which they based their bargain. It is true that, when the settlement agreement was made, neither party was aware that the defendant had already paid the original purchase agreement in full. However, this mistake did not go to the terms of the parties' accord; rather, it merely demonstrates their accord was indeed a compromise of a bona fide dispute that was not necessarily well-founded, but was made in good faith. The accord and satisfaction accurately reflects the intent of the parties at the time it was entered. Therefore, as there was no mistake regarding a basic assumption underlying the accord and satisfaction, it is enforceable.

INTERPRETATION An accord (a duty substituted for the original contractual duty) and satisfaction (performance of the substituted duty) discharges the original contractual duty.

Novation

Novation *(no·va´·tion)* substituted contract involving a new third-party promisor or promisee

A **novation** is a substituted contract that involves an agreement among *three* parties to substitute a new promisee for the existing promisee or to replace the existing promisor with a new one. A novation discharges the old obligation by creating a new contract in which there is either a new promisee or a new promisor. Thus, if B owes A $500, and A, B, and C agree that C will pay the debt and B will be discharged, the novation is the substitution of the new promisor C for B. Alternatively, if the three parties agree that B will pay $500 to C instead of to A, the novation is the substitution of a new promisee (C for A). In each instance, the debt B owes A is discharged.

DISCHARGE BY OPERATION OF LAW

In this chapter, we have considered various ways by which contractual duties may be discharged. In all of these cases, the discharge resulted from the action of one or both of the parties to the contract. In this section, we will examine discharge brought about by the operation of law.

Impossibility

If a particular contracting party is unable to perform because of financial inability or lack of competence, for instance, this **subjective impossibility** does not excuse the promisor from liability for breach of contract, as the next case shows. Historically, the common law excused a party from contractual duties only for **objective impossibility**; that is, for situations where no one could render performance. Thus, the death or illness of a person who has contracted to render personal services is a discharge of his contractual duty. Furthermore, the contract is discharged if, for example, a jockey contracts to ride a certain horse in the Kentucky Derby and the horse dies prior to the derby; for it is objectively impossible for this or any other jockey to perform the contract. Also, if Ken contracts to lease to Karlene a certain ballroom for a party on a scheduled future date, destruction of the ballroom by fire without Ken's fault before the scheduled event discharges the contract. Destruction of the subject matter or of the agreed-upon means of performance of a contract, without the fault of the promisor, is excusable impossibility.

Subjective impossibility the promisor—but not all promisors—cannot perform; does not discharge the promisor

Objective impossibility no promisor is able to perform; generally discharges the promisor

---

CHRISTY v. PILKINTON Supreme Court of Arkansas, 1954, 224 Ark. 407, 273 S.W.2d 533

FACTS The Christys entered into a written contract to purchase an apartment house from Pilkinton for $30,000. Pilkinton tendered a deed to the property and demanded payment of the unpaid balance of $29,000 due on the purchase price. As a result of a decline in Christy's used car business, the Christys did not possess and could not borrow the unpaid balance and, thus, asserted that it was impossible for them to perform their contract. This suit was brought by Pilkinton to enforce the sale of the apartment house.

DECISION Judgment for Pilkinton.

OPINION There is an important distinction between objective impossibility, which amounts to saying, "the thing cannot be done," and subjective impossibility—"I cannot do it." The latter, which is well illustrated by a promisor's financial inability to pay, does not discharge the contractual duty.

INTERPRETATION Subjective impossibility (the promisor, but not all promisors, cannot perform) does not discharge the promisor's contractual duty.

Subsequent Illegality If the performance of a contract that was legal when formed becomes illegal or impractical because of a subsequently enacted law, the duty of performance is discharged. For example, Linda contracts to sell and deliver to Carlos ten cases of a certain whiskey each month for one year. A subsequent prohibition law makes the manufacture, transportation, or sale of intoxicating liquor unlawful. The contractual duties that Linda has yet to perform are discharged.

Subsequent illegality if performance becomes illegal or impractical as a result of a change in the law, the duty of performance is discharged

Frustration of Purpose Where, after a contract is made, a party's principal purpose is substantially frustrated without his fault by the occurrence of an event whose nonoccurrence was a basic assumption on which the contract was made, his remaining duties to render performance are discharged, unless the party has assumed the risk. This rule developed from the so-called "coronation cases." When, on the death of his mother, Queen Victoria, Edward VII became King of England, impressive coronation ceremonies were planned, including a

Frustration of purpose
principal purpose of a
contract cannot be fulfilled
because of a subsequent
event

procession along a designated route through London. Owners and lessees of buildings along the route made contracts to permit the use of rooms on the day scheduled for the procession. The king became ill, however, and the procession did not take place. Consequently the rooms were not used. Numerous suits were filed, some by landowners seeking to hold the would-be viewers liable on their promises, and some by the would-be viewers seeking to recover money they had paid in advance for the rooms. Though the principle involved was novel, from these cases evolved the **frustration of purpose** doctrine, under which a contract is discharged if supervening circumstances make impossible the fulfillment of the purpose that both parties had in mind, unless one of the parties has contractually assumed that risk.

Commercial impracticability
(im·prac·ti·ca·bil'·i·ty) where
performance can only be
accomplished under
unforeseen and unjust
hardship, the contract is
discharged under the Code
and the Restatement

Commercial Impracticability The Restatement and Code have relaxed the traditional test of objective impossibility by providing that performance need not be actually or literally impossible; rather, **commercial impracticability**, or unforeseen and unjust hardship, will excuse nonperformance. This does not mean mere hardship or an unexpectedly excessive cost of performance. A party will be discharged from performing her duty only when her performance is made impracticable by a supervening event not caused by her own fault. Moreover, the nonoccurrence of the subsequent event must have been a "basic assumption" made by both parties when entering into the contract, neither party having assumed the risk that the event would occur.

NORTHERN CORP. v. CHUGACH ELECTRICAL ASSOCIATION Supreme Court of Alaska, 1974, 518 P.2d 76

FACTS Northern Corporation (Northern) entered into a contract with Chugach Electrical Association (Chugach) in August 1966 to repair and upgrade the upstream face of Cooper Lake Dam in Alaska. The contract required Northern to obtain rock from a quarry site at the opposite end of the lake and to transport the rock to the dam during the winter across the ice on the lake. In December 1966, Northern cleared a road on the ice to permit deeper freezing, but thereafter water overflowed on the ice, preventing use of the road. Northern complained of the unsafe conditions of the lake ice, but Chugach insisted on performance. In March 1967, one of Northern's loaded trucks broke through the ice and sank. Northern continued to encounter difficulties and ceased operations with the approval of Chugach. However, on January 8, 1968, Chugach notified Northern that it would be in default unless all rock was hauled by April 1. After two more trucks broke through the ice, causing the deaths of the drivers, Northern ceased operations and notified Chugach that it would make no more attempts to haul across the lake. Northern advised Chugach that it considered the contract terminated for

impossibility of performance and commenced suit to recover the cost incurred in attempting to complete the contract. The trial court found for Northern.

DECISION Judgment for Northern affirmed.

OPINION Northern's contract to perform was discharged by impossibility of performance. The particular method of performance specified in the contract presupposed the existence of ice frozen to sufficient depth to permit hauling of rock across the lake. This expectation by both parties was never fulfilled. A party is discharged from its contractual obligation, even if it is technically possible to perform, if the cost of performance would be so greatly disproportionate to that reasonably contemplated by the parties that performance would be commercially impracticable. In addition, a serious risk to life or health will excuse nonperformance.

INTERPRETATION Commercial impracticability (unforeseen and unjust hardship) will excuse performance.

Bankruptcy

Bankruptcy is a discharge of a contractual duty by operation of law available to a debtor who, by compliance with the requirements of the Bankruptcy Code, obtains an order of discharge by the bankruptcy court. It applies only to obligations that the Bankruptcy Code provides are dischargeable in bankruptcy. (We will treat the subject of bankruptcy in Chapter 41.)

Bankruptcy discharge available to a debtor who obtains an order of discharge by the bankruptcy court

Statute of Limitations

At common law a plaintiff was not subject to any time limitation within which to bring an action. Now, however, all states have statutes providing such a limitation. The majority of courts hold that the running of the period of the statute of limitations does not operate to discharge the obligation, but only to bar the creditor's right to bring an action.

For a summary of discharge of contracts, see Figure 17–1.

Statute of limitations after the statute of limitations has run, the debt is not discharged, but the creditor cannot maintain an action against the debtor

FIGURE 17–1 Discharge of Contracts

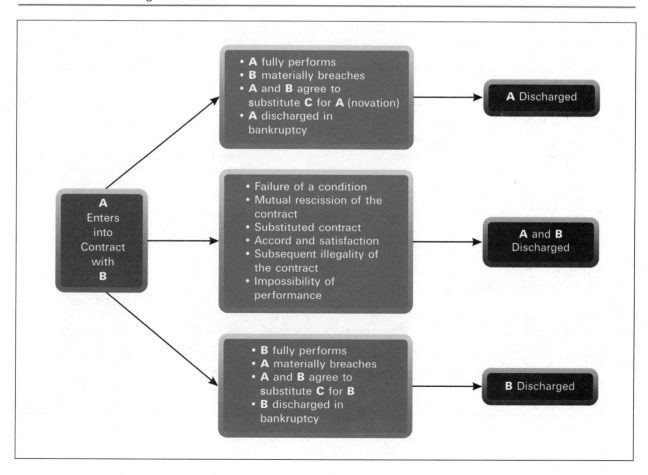

CHAPTER SUMMARY

Conditions	**Definition of a Condition** an event whose happening or nonhappening affects a duty of performance
	Express Condition contingency explicitly set forth in language
	  ■ *Satisfaction* express condition making performance contingent upon one party's approval of the other's performance
	  ■ *Subjective Satisfaction* approval based upon a party's honestly held opinion
	  ■ *Objective Satisfaction* approval based upon whether a reasonable person would be satisfied
	Implied-in-Fact Condition contingency understood by the parties to be part of the agreement, though not expressed
	Implied-in-Law Condition contingency not contained in the language of the contract but imposed by law; also called a constructive condition
	Concurrent Conditions conditions that are to take place at the same time
	Condition Precedent an event which must or must not occur before performance is due
	Condition Subsequent an event that terminates a duty of performance

Discharge by Performance	**Discharge** termination of a contractual duty **Performance** fulfillment of a contractual obligation resulting in a discharge

Discharge by Breach	**Definition of Breach** a wrongful failure to perform the terms of a contract that gives rise to a right to damages by the injured party
	Material Breach nonperformance that significantly impairs the injured party's rights under the contract and discharges the injured party from any further duty under the contract
	  ■ *Prevention of Performance* one party's substantial interference with or prevention of performance by the other constitutes a material breach and discharges the other party to the contract
	  ■ *Perfect Tender Rule* standard under the UCC that a seller's performance under a sales contract must strictly comply with contractual duties and that any deviation discharges the injured party
	Substantial Performance performance that is incomplete but that does not defeat the purpose of the contract; does not discharge the injured party but entitles him to damages
	Anticipatory Repudiation an inability or refusal to perform, before performance is due, that is treated as a breach, allowing the nonrepudiating party to bring suit immediately
	Material Alteration a material and fraudulent alteration of a written contract by a party to the contract discharges the entire contract

Discharge by Agreement of the Parties	**Mutual Rescission** an agreement between the parties to terminate their respective duties under the contract **Substituted Contract** a new contract accepted by both parties in satisfaction of the parties' duties under the original contract **Accord and Satisfaction** substituted duty under a contract (accord) and the discharge of the prior contractual obligation by performance of the new duty (satisfaction) **Novation** a substituted contract involving a new third-party promisor or promisee

Discharge by Operation of Law	**Impossibility** performance of contract cannot be done ■ *Subjective Impossibility* the promisor—but not all promisors—cannot perform; does not discharge the promisor ■ *Objective Impossibility* no promisor is able to perform; generally discharges the promisor ■ *Subsequent Illegality* if performance becomes illegal or impractical as a result of a change in the law, the duty of performance is discharged ■ *Frustration of Purpose* principal purpose of a contract cannot be fulfilled because of a subsequent event ■ *Commercial Impracticability* where performance can only be accomplished under unforeseen and unjust hardship, the contract is discharged under the Code and the Restatement **Bankruptcy** discharge available to a debtor who obtains an order of discharge by the bankruptcy court **Statute of Limitations** after the statute of limitations has run, the debt is not discharged, but the creditor cannot maintain an action against the debtor

QUESTIONS

1. Identify and distinguish among the six types of conditions.
2. Distinguish between full performance and tender of performance.
3. Explain the difference between material breach and substantial performance. Explain how the UCC perfect tender rule differs from these rules.
4. Distinguish among a mutual rescission, substituted contract, accord and satisfaction, and novation.
5. Identify and discuss the ways discharge may be brought about by operation of law.

Internet Question. Compare the provisions governing performance and breach of contract contained in the Principles of European Contract Law with the provisions of the U.S. common law.

PROBLEMS

1. A-1 Roofing Co. entered into a written contract with Jaffe to put a new roof on the latter's residence for $1,800, using a specified type of roofing, and to complete the job without unreasonable delay. A-1 undertook the work within a week thereafter, and when all the roofing material was at the site and the labor 50 percent completed, the premises were totally destroyed by fire caused by lightning. A-1 submitted a bill to Jaffe for $1,200 for materials furnished and labor performed up to the time of the destruction of the premises. Jaffe refused to pay the bill, and A-1 sued Jaffe. Decision?

2. By contract dated January 5, Rebecca agreed to sell to Nancy, and Nancy agreed to buy from Rebecca, a certain parcel of land then zoned commercial. The specific intent of Nancy, which was known to Rebecca, was to erect a storage plant on the land; and the contract stated that the agreement was conditioned on Nancy's ability to construct such a plant on the land. The closing date for the transaction was set for April 1. On February 15, the city council rezoned the land from commercial to residential, which precluded the erection of the storage plant. As the closing date drew near, Nancy made it known to Rebecca that she did not intend to go through with the purchase because the land could no longer be used as intended. On April 1, Rebecca tendered the deed to Nancy, who refused to pay Rebecca the agreed purchase price. Rebecca brought an action against Nancy for breach of contract. Decision?

3. The Perfection Produce Company entered into a written contract with Hiram Hodges for the purchase of 200 tons of potatoes to be grown on Hodges's farm in Maine at a stipulated price per ton. Though the land would ordinarily produce 1,000 tons and although the planting and cultivation were properly done, Hodges was able to deliver only 100 tons because an unprecedented drought caused a partial crop failure. Hodges sued the produce company to recover an unpaid balance of the agreed price for 100 tons of potatoes. The produce company, by an appropriate counterclaim against Hodges, sought damages for his failure to deliver the additional 100 tons. Decision?

4. On November 23, Sally agreed to sell to Bart her Pontiac automobile for $7,000, delivery and payment to be made on December 1. On November 26, Bart informed Sally that he wished to rescind the contract and would pay Sally $350 if Sally agreed. Sally agreed and took the $350 in cash. On December 1, Bart tendered to Sally $6,650 and demanded that Sally deliver the automobile. Sally refused, and Bart initiated a lawsuit. Decision?

5. Webster, Inc., dealt in automobile accessories at wholesale. Although it manufactured a few items in its own factory, among them windshield wipers, Webster purchased most of its supplies from a large number of other manufacturers. In January, Webster entered into a written contract to sell Hunter 2,000 windshield wipers for $1,900, delivery to be made June 1. In April, Webster's factory burned to the ground and Webster failed to make delivery on June 1. Hunter, forced to buy windshield wipers elsewhere at a higher price, brought an action against Webster for breach of contract. Decision?

6. Erwick Construction Company contracted to build a house for Charles. The specifications called for the use of Karlene Pipe for all plumbing. Erwick, nevertheless, got a better price on Boynton Pipe and substituted the equally good Boynton Pipe for Karlene Pipe. Charles's inspection revealed the change, and Charles now refuses to make the final payment. The contract price was for $200,000, and the final payment is $20,000. Erwick now brings suit seeking the $20,000. Decision?

7. Green owed White $3,500, which was due and payable on June 1. White owed Brown $3,500, which was due and payable on August 1. On May 25, White received a letter signed by Green stating, "If you will cancel my debt to you, in the amount of $3,500, I will pay, on the due date, the debt you owe Brown, in the amount of $3,500." On May 28, Green received a letter signed by White stating, "I received your letter and agree to the proposals recited therein. You may consider your debt to me canceled as of the date of this letter." On June 1, White, needing money to pay his income taxes, made a demand upon Green to pay him the $3,500 due on that date. Is Green obligated to pay the money demanded by White?

8. By written contract, Ames agreed to build a house on Bowen's lot for $45,000, commencing within ninety days of the date of the contract. Prior to the date for beginning construction, Ames informed Bowen that he was repudiating the contract and would not perform. Bowen refused to accept the repudiation and demanded fulfillment of the contract. Eighty days after the date of the contract, Bowen entered into a new contract with Curd for $42,000. The next day, without knowledge or notice of Bowen's contract with Curd, Ames began construction. Bowen ordered Ames from the premises and refused to allow him to continue. Ames sued Bowen for damages. Decision?

9. Judy agreed in writing to work for Northern Enterprises, Inc., for three years as superintendent of Northern's manufacturing establishment and to devote herself entirely to the business, giving it her full time, attention, and skill, for which she was to receive $24,000 per annum in monthly installments of $2,000. Judy worked and was paid for the first twelve months, when, through no fault of her own or Northern's, she was arrested and imprisoned for one month. It became imperative for Northern to employ another, and it treated the contract with Judy as breached and abandoned, refusing to permit Judy to resume work on her release from jail. What rights, if any, does Judy have under the contract?

10. The Park Plaza Hotel awarded its valet and laundry concession to Larson for a three-year term. The contract contained the following provision: "It is distinctly understood and agreed that the services to be rendered by Larson shall meet with the approval of the Park Plaza Hotel, which shall be the sole judge of the sufficiency and propriety of the services." After seven months, the hotel gave a month's notice to discontinue

services based on the failure of the services to meet its approval. Larson brought an action against the hotel, alleging that its dissatisfaction was unreasonable. The hotel defended on the ground that subjective or personal satisfaction may be the sole justification for termination of the contract. Decision?

11. Schlosser entered into an agreement to purchase a cooperative apartment from Flynn Company. The written agreement contained the following provision: "This entire agreement is conditioned on Purchaser's being approved for occupancy by the board of directors of the Cooperative. In the event approval of the Purchaser shall be denied, this agreement shall thereafter be of no further force or effect." When Schlosser unilaterally revoked her "offer," Flynn sued for breach of contract. Schlosser claims the approval provision was a condition precedent to the existence of a binding contract and, thus, she was free to revoke. Decision?

12. Jacobs, owner of a farm, entered into a contract with Earl Walker in which Walker agreed to paint the buildings on the farm. Walker purchased the paint from Jones. Before the work was completed, however, Jacobs ordered Walker to stop because she was dissatisfied with the results. Both Jones and Walker made offers to complete the job, but Jacobs declined to permit Walker to fulfill his contract. Jones and Walker brought an action against Jacobs for breach of contract. Decision?

13. Barta entered into a written contract to buy the K&K Pharmacy, located in a local shopping center. Included in the contract was a provision stating that "this Agreement shall be contingent upon Buyer's ability to obtain a new lease from Landlord for the premises presently occupied by Seller. In the event Buyer is unable to obtain a lease satisfactory to Buyer, this Agreement shall be null and void." Barta planned to sell "high-traffic" grocery items, such as bread, milk, and coffee, in order to attract customers to his drugstore. A grocery store in the shopping center, however, already held the exclusive right to sell grocery items. Barta, therefore, could not obtain a leasing agreement meeting his approval. When Barta refused to close the sale, K&K Pharmacy sued him for breach of contract. Decision?

14. Victor Packing Co. (Victor) contracted to supply Sun Maid Raisin Growers 1,800 tons of raisins from the current year's crop. After delivering 1,190 tons of raisins by August, Victor refused to supply any more. Although Victor had until the end of the crop season to ship the remaining 610 tons of raisins, Sun Maid treated Victor's repeated refusals to ship any more raisins as a repudiation of the contract. In order to prevent breaching its own contracts, Sun Maid went into the marketplace to "cover" and bought the raisins needed. Unfortunately, between the time Victor refused delivery and Sun Maid entered the market, disastrous rains had caused the price of raisins to skyrocket. May Sun Maid recover from Victor the difference between the contract price and the market price before the end of the current crop year?

15. On August 20, 1981, Hildebrand entered into a written contract with the city of Douglasville whereby he was to serve as community development project engineer for three years at a monthly fee of $1,583.33. This salary figure could be changed without affecting the other terms of the contract. One of the provisions for termination of the contract was written notice by either party to the other at any time at least ninety days prior to the intended date of termination. The contract listed a number of services and duties Hildebrand was to perform for the city, among which were (1) keeping the community development director (Hildebrand's supervisor) informed at all times of his whereabouts and how he could be contacted and (2) attending meetings at which his presence was requested. On September 20, 1983, by which time Hildebrand's fee had risen to $1,915.83 per month, the city fired Hildebrand effective immediately, citing "certain material breaches . . . of the . . . agreement." Hildebrand sued the mayor and city for breach of his employment contract, seeking damages in the amount of $5,747.49 because of the city's failure to give him ninety days' notice prior to termination. The city contended that Hildebrand repeatedly violated the terms and conditions of the contract. The city specifically charged that he did not attend the necessary meetings although requested to do so and seldom if ever kept his supervisor informed of his whereabouts and how he could be contacted. The trial court granted summary judgment to Hildebrand, and the city appealed. Decision?

16. Walker & Co. contracted to provide a sign for Harrison to place above his dry cleaning business. According to the contract, Harrison would lease the sign from Walker, making monthly payments for thirty-six months. In return, Walker agreed to maintain and service the sign at its own expense. Walker installed the sign in July 1953, and Harrison made the first rental payment. Shortly thereafter, someone hit the sign with a tomato. Harrison also claims he discovered rust on its chrome and little spiderwebs in its corners. Harrison repeatedly called Walker for the maintenance work promised under the contract, but Walker did not respond. Harrison then telegraphed Walker that, due to Walker's failure to perform the maintenance services, he held Walker in material breach of the contract. Decision?

17. In May 1976, Watts was awarded a construction contract, based on its low bid, by the Cullman County

Commission. The contract provided that it would not become effective until approved by the state director of the Farmers Home Administration. In September, construction still had not been authorized and Watts wrote to the County Commission requesting a 5-percent price increase to reflect seasonal and inflationary price increases. The County Commission countered with an offer of 3.5 percent. Watts then wrote the commission, insisting on a 5-percent increase and stating that if this was not agreeable, it was withdrawing its original bid. The commission obtained another company to perform the project, and on October 14, 1976, informed Watts that it had accepted the withdrawal of the bid. Watts sued for breach of contract. The trial court granted the county's motion for summary judgment. Decision?

Remedies

When one party to a contract breaches the contract by failing to perform his contractual duties, the law provides a remedy for the injured party. While the primary objective of contract remedies is to compensate the injured party for the loss resulting from the breach, it is impossible for any remedy to equal the promised performance. The relief a court can give an injured party is what it regards as an *equivalent* of the promised performance.

In this chapter, we will examine the most common remedies available for breach of contract: (1) monetary damages, (2) the equitable remedies of specific performance and injunction, and (3) restitution. Sales of goods are governed by Article 2 of the Uniform Commercial Code, which provides specialized remedies that we will discuss in Chapter 23. Contract remedies are available to protect one or more of the following interests of the injured parties:

1. their *expectation interest*, which is their interest in having the benefit of their bargain by being put in a position as good as the one they would have been in had the contract been performed;
2. their *reliance interest*, which is their interest in being reimbursed for loss caused by reliance on the contract by being put in a position as good as the one they would have been in had the contract not been made; or
3. their *restitution interest*, which is their interest in having restored to them any benefit that they had conferred on the other party.

The expectation interest is protected by the contract remedies of compensatory damages, specific performance, and injunction. The reliance interest is protected by the contractual remedy of reliance damages, while the contractual remedy of restitution protects the restitution interest.

MONETARY DAMAGES

A judgment awarding monetary damages is the most frequently granted judicial remedy for breach of contract. Monetary damages, however, will be awarded only for losses that are foreseeable, established with reasonable certainty, and not avoidable. The equitable remedies discussed in this chapter are discretionary and are available only if monetary damages are inadequate.

Compensatory Damages

The right to recover compensatory damages for breach of contract is always available to the injured party. The purpose in allowing **compensatory damages** is to place the injured party in a position as good as the one he would have been

Compensatory damages *(com·pen'·sa·to·ry)* contract damages placing the injured party in as good a position as if the other party had performed; equals loss of value minus loss avoided by injured party plus incidental damages plus consequential damages

in had the other party performed under the contract. These damages are intended to protect the injured party's **expectation interest**, which is the value he expected to derive from the contract. Thus, the amount of compensatory damages is the loss of value to the injured party caused by the other party's failure to perform or by the other's deficient performance *minus* the loss or cost avoided by the injured party *plus* incidental damages *plus* consequential damages.

Loss of value value of promised performance minus value of actual performance

Loss of Value In general, **loss of value** is the *difference between the value of the promised performance* of the breaching party *and the value of the actual performance* rendered by the breaching party. If no performance is rendered at all, the loss of value is the value of the promised performance. If defective or partial performance is rendered, the loss of value is the difference between the value that the full performance would have had and the value of the performance actually rendered. Thus, where there has been a breach of warranty, the injured party may recover the difference between the value the goods would have had, had they been as warranted, and the value of the goods in the condition in which the buyer actually received them. To illustrate, Jacob sells an automobile to Juliet, expressly warranting that it will get forty-five miles per gallon; but the automobile gets only twenty miles per gallon. The automobile would have been worth $8,000 if as warranted, but it is worth only $6,000 as delivered. Juliet would recover $2,000 in damages for loss of value.

Expenses saved loss or costs the injured party avoids by not having to perform

Expenses Saved The recovery by the injured party is reduced, however, by any cost or loss she has avoided by not having to perform. For example, Clinton agrees to build a hotel for Debra for $1,250,000 by September 1. Clinton breaches by not completing construction until October 1. As a consequence, Debra loses revenues for one month in the amount of $10,000 but saves operating expenses of $6,000. Therefore, she may recover damages for $4,000. Similarly, in a contract in which the injured party has not fully performed, the injured party's recovery is reduced by the value to the injured party of the performance the injured party promised but did not render. For example, Victor agrees to convey land to Joan in return for Joan's promise to work for Victor for two years. Joan repudiates the contract before Victor has conveyed the land to Joan. Victor's recovery for loss from Joan is reduced by the value to Victor of the land.

Incidental damages damages arising directly out of a breach of contract

Incidental Damages **Incidental damages** are damages that arise directly out of the breach, such as costs incurred to acquire the nondelivered performance from some other source. For example, Agnes employs Benton for nine months for $20,000 to supervise construction of a factory. She then fires Benton without cause after three weeks. Benton, who spends $350 in reasonable fees attempting to find comparable employment, may recover $350 in incidental damages in addition to any other actual loss he has suffered.

Consequential damages damages not arising directly out of a breach but as a foreseeable result of the breach

Consequential Damages **Consequential damages** are damages not arising directly out of a breach but arising as a foreseeable result of the breach. Consequential damages include lost profits and injury to person or property. Thus, if Tracy leases to Sean a defective machine that causes $4,000 in property damage and $12,000 in personal injuries, Sean may recover, in addition to damages for loss of value and incidental damages, $16,000 as consequential damages.

Reliance Damages

Instead of seeking compensatory damages, the injured party may seek reimbursement for foreseeable loss caused by her reliance on the contract. The purpose of **reliance damages** is to place the injured party in a position as good as the one she would have been in had the contract *not been made*. Reliance damages include expenses incurred in preparing to perform, in actually performing, or in forgoing opportunities to enter into other contracts. An injured party may prefer damages for reliance to compensatory damages when she is unable to establish her lost profits with reasonable certainty or when the contract is itself unprofitable. For example, Donald agrees to sell his retail store to Gary, who spends $50,000 in acquiring inventory and fixtures. Donald then repudiates the contract, and Gary sells the inventory and fixtures for $35,000. Because neither party can establish with reasonable certainty what profit Gary would have made, Gary may recover from Donald as damages the loss of $15,000 he sustained on the sale of the inventory and fixtures plus any other costs he incurred in entering into the contract.

Reliance damages contract damages placing the injured party in as good a position as he would have been in had the contract not been made

Nominal Damages

An action to recover damages for breach of contract may be maintained even though the plaintiff has not sustained or cannot prove any injury or loss resulting from the breach. In such case he will be permitted to recover **nominal damages**—a small sum fixed without regard to the amount of loss. Such a judgment may also include an award of court costs.

Nominal damages a small sum awarded where a contract has been breached but the loss is negligible or unproved

Damages for Misrepresentation

The basic remedy for misrepresentation is rescission (avoidance) of the contract. When appropriate, restitution will also be required. At common law, an alternative remedy to rescission is a suit for damages. The Code liberalizes the common law by not restricting a defrauded party to an election of remedies. That is, the injured party may both rescind the contract by restoring the other party to the status quo and recover damages or obtain any other remedy available under the Code. In most states, the measure of damages for misrepresentation depends upon whether the misrepresentation was fraudulent or nonfraudulent.

Fraud A party who has been induced by fraud to enter into a contract may recover general damages in a tort action. A minority of states allows the injured party to recover, under the "**out-of-pocket**" rule, general damages equal to the difference between the value of what she has received and the value of what she has given for it. The great majority of states, however, permits the intentionally defrauded party to recover, under the "**benefit-of-the-bargain**" rule, general damages that are equal to the difference between the value of what she has received and the value of the fraudulent party's performance as represented. The Restatement of Torts provides the fraudulently injured party with the option of either out-of-pocket or benefit-of-the-bargain damages. To illustrate, Emily intentionally misrepresents the capabilities of a printing press and thereby induces Melissa to purchase the machine for $20,000. Though the value of the press as delivered is $14,000, the machine would be worth $24,000 if it performed as represented. Under the out-of-pocket rule, Melissa would recover $6,000, whereas under the benefit-of-the-bargain rule, she would recover $10,000. In addition to a recovery of general damages under one of the measures

Out-of-pocket damages difference between the value received and the value given

Benefit-of-the-bargain damages difference between the value received and the value of the fraudulent party's performance as represented

just discussed, consequential damages may be recovered to the extent they are proved with reasonable certainty and to the extent they do not duplicate general damages. Moreover, where the fraud is gross, oppressive, or aggravated, punitive damages are permitted.

Nonfraudulent Misrepresentation Where the misrepresentation is negligent, the deceived party may recover general damages, under the out-of-pocket measure, and consequential damages. Furthermore, some states permit the recovery of general damages under the benefit-of-the-bargain measure. Where the misrepresentation is neither fraudulent nor negligent, however, the Restatement of Torts limits damages to the out-of-pocket measure.

Punitive Damages

Punitive damages are monetary damages in addition to compensatory damages awarded to a plaintiff in certain situations involving willful, wanton, or malicious conduct. Their purpose is to punish the defendant and thus discourage him and others from similar wrongful conduct. The purpose of allowing contract damages, on the other hand, is to compensate the plaintiff for the loss he sustained because of the defendant's breach of contract. Accordingly, the Restatement provides that punitive damages are *not* recoverable for a breach of contract unless the conduct constituting the breach is also a tort for which the plaintiff may recover punitive damages.

> **Punitive damages** are generally *not* recoverable for breach of contract

Liquidated Damages

A contract may contain a **liquidated damages** provision by which the parties agree in advance to the damages to be paid in event of a breach. Such a provision will be enforced if it amounts to a reasonable forecast of the loss that may or does result from the breach. If, however, the sum agreed on as liquidated damages bears no reasonable relationship to the amount of probable loss, it is unenforceable as a penalty. (A penalty is a contractual provision designed to deter a party from breaching her contract and to punish her if she does breach it.) Such equivalence is required because the objective of contract remedies is compensatory, not punitive. By examining the substance of the provision, the nature of the contract, and the extent of probable harm that a breach may reasonably be expected to cause the promisee, the courts will determine whether the agreed amount is proper as liquidated damages or unenforceable as a penalty. If a liquidated damages provision is not enforceable, the injured party nevertheless is entitled to the ordinary remedies for breach of contract.

> **Liquidated damages** reasonable damages agreed to in advance by the parties to a contract

WATSON v. INGRAM Supreme Court of Washington, 1994, 124 Wash.2d 845, 881 P.2d 247

FACTS Watson agreed to buy Ingram's house for $355,000. The contract required Ingram to perform certain repairs at his expense. The contract also provided that Watson deposit $15,000 as earnest money and that "[i]n the event of default by the Buyer, earnest money shall be forfeited to Seller as liquidated damages, unless Seller elects to seek actual damages or specific performance." The contract also stipulated that the "Buyer represents that Buyer has sufficient funds available to close this sale in accordance with this agreement, and is not relying on any contingent source of funds unless otherwise set forth in this agreement." In fact, Watson did not have sufficient funds available but planned to assume Ingram's mortgage on the house. When this arrangement did not materialize, Watson sought to modify the terms of sale so as to defer payment in exchange for giving Ingram a lien on certain real estate owned by Watson. Ingram rejected this modification and stated that he intended to strictly enforce the original terms. Watson secured

continued

other, contingent financing but Ingram refused to grant Watson an extension, and the sale to Watson was not completed, Finally, nine months after the Watson sale was to occur, Ingram sold the house to a third party for $355,000. Ingram and Watson each sought to recover Watson's $15,000 earnest money, which was being held in escrow. The trial court found that the earnest money "was clearly intended by both parties to be nonrefundable" if Watson defaulted and determined that $15,000 was a reasonable forecast by Ingram and Watson of damages that would be incurred by Ingram if Watson failed to complete the purchase. The court entered judgment in favor of Ingram for the amount of the earnest money plus interest and attorney's fees pursuant to the parties' agreement. The Court of Appeals affirmed. Watson appealed.

DECISION   Judgment affirmed.

OPINION   This case presents a single issue for review: whether the parties' contract provision requiring Watson to forfeit a $15,000 nonrefundable earnest money deposit is enforceable as liquidated damages. To determine the enforceability of liquidated damages clauses, courts apply a two-part test from the Restatement of Contracts. Liquidated damages clauses are upheld if the amount fixed is a reasonable forecast of just compensation for the harm that it caused by the breach and the harm is such that it is incapable or very difficult of ascertainment.

The reasonableness of the forecast is judged at the time the contract was entered (prospectively) rather than at the time of trial (retrospectively). The prospective approach concentrates on whether the liquidated sum represents a reasonable prediction of the harm to the seller if the buyer breaches the agreement and ignores actual damages, except as evidence of the reasonableness of the estimate of potential damage. The court concluded that the prospective approach better fulfills the underlying purposes of liquidated damages clauses and gives greater weight to the parties' expectations. Liquidated damages permit parties to allocate business and litigation risks and resolve disputes efficiently. Even if the estimates of damages are not exact, parties can allocate and quantify those risks and can negotiate adjustments to the contract price in light of the allocated risks. Watson argues that the prospective approach treats buyers unfairly because it permits a seller to retain earnest money even when the seller suffers no actual damage, thus violating the principle that contract damages should be compensatory only. The retrospective approach fails to give proper weight to the parties negotiations by focusing on the actual damage that occurs in determining the reasonableness of the

parties' forecast. The parties themselves know best what motivations and considerations influenced their bargaining, and while the result of the bargain may be unfortunate for one party, it is not the role of the court to relieve parties from the consequences of their own improvidence.

Having adopted the date of contract formation as the proper time frame for evaluating the Restatement test, the second requirement loses independent significance. The central inquiry is whether the specified liquidated damages were reasonable at the time of contract formation. The greater the prospective difficulty of estimating possible damages, the greater the range of reasonableness used in assessing a liquidated damages provision. In sum, so long as the agreed-upon earnest money agreement, viewed prospectively, is a reasonable prediction of potential damage suffered by the seller, the agreement should be enforced without regard to the actual damages incurred or the difficulty of proving them.

Under the prospective test, the liquidated damages provision in the Watson-Ingram agreement is valid and enforceable. First, evaluating the agreement at the time of contract formation, the liquidated sum was a reasonable forecast of just compensation for the harm that would be suffered by Ingram in the event of breach by Watson. The $15,000 earnest money deposit represented several variables, including the value of the improvements Ingram was required to make, fluctuations in the real estate market, and lost value of the use of the net sale proceeds prior to the eventual sale of the property. Each of these variables represents a potential loss to Ingram in the event of breach by Watson. Additionally, Ingram was seeking a quick sale in anticipation of his moving to California, and the liquidated sum may have reflected a personal cost to Ingram. Under these circumstances, the sum of $15,000 is a reasonable forecast of Ingram's damages in the event of breach by Watson.

The court likewise found that Ingram's potential damages were difficult to ascertain at the time of contracting: the parties could not know what delays might ensue, what might occur in the real estate market, or how a failed sale might affect Ingram's plans. Real estate purchase-and-sale agreements are precisely the type of contracts that are amenable to liquidated damages provisions. Therefore, the liquidated damages provision is valid and enforceable.

INTERPRETATION   A liquidated damages provision is enforceable if it is a reasonable forecast of the loss that may or does result from the breach.

Limitations on Damages

In order to accomplish the basic purposes of contract remedies, the limitations of foreseeability, certainty, and mitigation have been imposed upon monetary damages. These limitations are intended to ensure that damages can be taken into account at the time of contracting, that they are compensatory and not speculative, and that they do not include loss that could have been avoided by reasonable efforts.

Foreseeability of Damages Contracting parties are generally expected to consider foreseeable risks at the time they enter into the contract. Therefore, compensatory or reliance damages are recoverable only for loss that the party in breach had reason to foresee as a *probable* result of a breach when the contract was made. The breaching party is not liable for loss that was not foreseeable at the time of entering into the contract. The test of **foreseeable damages** is *objective*, based on what the breaching party had reason to foresee. Loss may be deemed foreseeable as a probable result of a breach because it followed from the breach (a) in the ordinary course of events or (b) as a result of special circumstances, beyond the ordinary course of events, about which the party in breach had reason to know.

A leading case on the subject of foreseeability of damages is *Hadley v. Baxendale*, decided in England in 1854.

Foreseeable damages loss that the party in breach had reason to anticipate when the contract was made

---

HADLEY v. BAXENDALE Court of Exchequer, 1854, 9 Ex. 341, 156 Eng.Rep. 145

FACTS The plaintiffs operated a flour mill at Gloucester. They had to stop operating the mill because of a broken crankshaft attached to the steam engine that furnished power to the mill. It was necessary to send the broken shaft to a foundry in Greenwich so that a new shaft could be made. The plaintiffs delivered the broken shaft to the defendants, who were common carriers, for immediate transportation from Gloucester to Greenwich but did not inform the defendants that the mill had ceased operating because of the broken crankshaft. The defendants received the shaft, collected the freight charges in advance, and promised the plaintiffs to deliver the shaft for repairs the following day. The defendants did not make prompt delivery as promised. As a result, the plaintiffs could not operate the mill for several days, thus losing profits that they otherwise would have received. The defendants contended that the loss of profits was too remote, and therefore unforeseeable, to be recoverable. In awarding damages to the plaintiffs, the jury was permitted to consider the loss of these profits.

DECISION Judgment for defendants.

OPINION The appellate court reversed the decision and ordered a new trial on the ground that the special circumstances that caused the loss of profits, namely, the continued stoppage of the mill while awaiting the return of the new crankshaft, had never been communicated by the plaintiffs to the defendants. A common carrier would not reasonably foresee that the plaintiff's mill would be shut down as a result of delay in transporting the broken crankshaft. Damages for "breach of contract should be such as may fairly and reasonably be considered either arising naturally, i.e., according to the usual course of things, from such breach . . . or such as may reasonably be supposed to have been in the contemplation of both parties at the time they made the contract, as the probable result of the breach of it."

INTERPRETATION Damages are recoverable only for those damages that were foreseeable at the time of entering into the contract.

On the other hand, if the defendants in *Hadley v. Baxendale* had been informed that the shaft was necessary for the operation of the mill, or otherwise had reason to know this fact, they would be liable for the plaintiffs' loss of profit during that period of the shutdown caused by their delay. Under these circumstances, the loss would be the "foreseeable" and "natural" result of the breach.

Should a plaintiff's expected profit be extraordinarily large, the general rule is that the breaching party will be liable for such special loss only if he had reason to know of it. In any event, the plaintiff may recover for any ordinary loss resulting from the breach. Thus, if Madeline breaches a contract with Jane, causing Jane, due to special circumstances, $10,000 in damages where ordinarily such a breach would only result in $6,000 in damages, Madeline would be liable to Jane for $6,000, not $10,000, provided that Madeline was unaware of the special circumstances causing Jane the unusually large loss.

Certainty of Damages Damages are not recoverable for loss beyond an amount that the injured party can establish with reasonable certainty. If the injured party cannot prove a particular element of her loss with reasonable certainty, she nevertheless will be entitled to recover the portion of her loss that she can prove with reasonable certainty. The certainty requirement creates the greatest challenge for plaintiffs seeking the recovery of consequential damages for lost profits on related transactions. Similar difficulty arises in proving lost profits caused by breach of a contract to produce a sporting event or to publish a new book, for example.

Certainty of damages damages are not recoverable beyond an amount that can be established with reasonable certainty

Mitigation of Damages Under the doctrine of **mitigation of damages**, the injured party may not recover damages for loss that he could have avoided with reasonable effort and without undue risk, burden, or humiliation. Thus, if Earl is under a contract to manufacture goods for Karl and Karl repudiates the contract after Earl has begun performance, Earl will not be allowed to recover for losses he sustains by continuing to manufacture the goods, if to do so would increase the amount of damages. The amount of loss that could reasonably have been avoided is deducted from the amount that would otherwise be recoverable as damages. On the other hand, if the goods were almost completed when Karl repudiated the contract, completing the goods might reduce the damages, because the finished goods may be resalable whereas the unfinished goods may not.

Similarly, if Harvey contracts to work for Olivia for one year for a weekly salary and after two months is wrongfully discharged by Olivia, Harvey must use reasonable efforts to mitigate his damages by seeking other employment. If, after such effort, he cannot obtain other employment of the same general character, he is entitled to recover full pay for the contract period during which he is unemployed. He is not obliged to accept a radically different type of employment or to accept work at a distant place. For example, a person employed as a schoolteacher or accountant who is wrongfully discharged is not obliged to accept employment as a chauffeur or truck driver. The next case involving Shirley MacLaine turns on whether acting in a western is employment equivalent to singing and dancing in a musical.

Mitigation of damages *(mit·i·ga'·tion)* the injured party may not recover damages for loss he could have avoided by reasonable effort

---

PARKER v. TWENTIETH CENTURY FOX FILM CORP. Supreme Court of California, 1970, 3 Cal.3d 176, 89 Cal.Rptr. 737, 474 P.2d 689

FACTS Shirley MacLaine Parker, a well-known actress, contracted with Twentieth Century-Fox Film Corporation (Fox) in August 1965 to play the female lead in Fox's upcoming production of *Bloomer Girl*, a motion picture musical that was to be filmed in California. The contract provided that Fox would pay Parker a minimum "guaranteed compensation" of $750,000 for fourteen weeks of Parker's services, beginning May 23, 1966. By letter dated April 4, 1966, Fox notified Parker of its intention not to produce the film and, instead, offered to employ Parker in the female lead of another film entitled *Big Country, Big Man*, a dramatic

continued

western to be filmed in Australia. The compensation offered and most of the other provisions in the substitute contract were identical to the *Bloomer Girl* provisions, except that Parker's right to approve the director and screenplay would have been eliminated or reduced under the *Big Country* contract. Parker refused to accept and brought suit against Fox to recover $750,000 for breach of the *Bloomer Girl* contract. Fox contended that it owed no money to Parker because she had deliberately failed to mitigate or reduce her damages by unreasonably refusing to accept the *Big Country* lead. The trial court granted Parker a summary judgment. [The court's opinion with respect to the rules for determining whether to grant summary judgment appears in Chapter 3.]

DECISION   Judgment for Parker affirmed.

OPINION   A wrongfully discharged employee generally has a duty to mitigate her damages either by attempting to find or by actually finding substitute employment. The measure of recovery is typically the amount of salary promised under the original contract minus the amount the employer proves the employee

has earned, or with reasonable effort might have earned, from other, "substantially similar" employment. The employee's rejection of or failure to seek other employment of a different or inferior kind cannot be used to mitigate damages.

Bloomer Girl was to be a musical revue calling upon Parker's talents as a dancer as well as an actress and was to be filmed in Los Angeles. On the other hand, *Big Country, Big Man* was a straight acting, "western type" motion picture taking place in an opal mine in Australia. In addition, Parker would have had her right to approve the director and screenplay eliminated or impaired by the *Big Country* contract. Such disparities between the two projects render the substitute *Big Country* lead of a kind different and inferior to the *Bloomer Girl* role. Therefore, Parker need not accept or seek such inferior employment and could reject Fox's substitute offer with no reduction in her award for failure to mitigate.

INTERPRETATION   An injured party's damages may not be reduced by mitigation for her failure to accept or seek other employment of a different or inferior kind.

REMEDIES IN EQUITY

At times, damages will not adequately compensate an injured party. In these cases, equitable relief in the form of specific performance or an injunction may be available to protect the injured party's interest. Such remedies are not a matter of right but rest in the discretion of the court. Consequently, they will not be granted where there is an adequate remedy at law; where it is impossible to enforce them, as where the seller has already transferred the subject matter of the contract to an innocent third person; where the terms of the contract are unfair; where the consideration is grossly inadequate; where the contract is tainted with fraud, duress, undue influence, mistake, or unfair practices; or where the relief would cause the defendant unreasonable hardship. See *Tamarind Lithography Workshop v. Sanders* on page 341.

On the other hand, a court may grant specific performance or an injunction despite a provision for liquidated damages. Moreover, a court will grant specific performance or an injunction even though a term of the contract prohibits equitable relief, if denying such relief would cause the injured party unreasonable hardship.

Reformation
(ref·or·ma´·tion) equitable remedy correcting a written contract to conform with the original intent of the contracting parties

Another equitable remedy is **reformation**, a process whereby the court "rewrites" or "corrects" a written contract to make it conform to the true agreement of the parties. The purpose of reformation is *not* to make a new contract for the parties but rather to express adequately the contract they have made for themselves. The remedy of reformation is granted when the parties agree on a contract but write it in a way that inaccurately reflects their actual agreement. For example, Acme Insurance Co. and Bell agree that for good consideration Acme will issue an annuity paying $500 per month. Because of a clerical error, the annuity policy is issued for $50 per month. A court of equity, upon satisfactory proof of the mistake, will reform the policy to provide for the correct amount—$500 per month.

Specific Performance

Specific performance is the equitable remedy that compels the defaulting party to perform her contractual obligations. As with all equitable remedies, it is available only when there is no adequate remedy at law. Ordinarily, for instance, in a case in which a seller breaches her contract for the sale of personal property, the buyer has a sufficient remedy at law. Where, however, the ***personal property*** contracted for is rare or *unique*, this remedy is inadequate. Examples of such property would include a famous painting or statue, an original manuscript or a rare edition of a book, a patent, a copyright, shares of stock in a closely held corporation, or an heirloom. Articles of this kind cannot be purchased elsewhere. Accordingly, on breach by the seller of her contract for the sale of any such article, money damages will not adequately compensate the buyer. Consequently, the buyer may avail herself of the equitable remedy of specific performance.

While courts of equity will grant specific performance in connection with contracts for the sale of personal property only in exceptional circumstances, they will always grant it in case of breach of contract for the sale of ***real property***. The reason for this is that every parcel of land is regarded as unique. Consequently, if the seller refuses to convey title to the real estate contracted for, the buyer may seek the aid of a court of equity to compel the seller to convey the title. Most courts of equity will likewise compel the buyer in a real estate contract to perform at the suit of the seller.

Courts of equity will not grant specific performance of contracts for personal services. In the first place, there is the practical difficulty, if not impossibility, of enforcing such a decree. In the second place, it is against the policy of the courts to force one person to work for or to serve another against his will, even though he has contracted to do so. Such enforcement would closely resemble involuntary servitude. For example, if Carmen, an accomplished concert pianist, agrees to appear at a certain time and place to play a specified program for Rudolf, a court would not issue a decree of specific performance upon her refusal to appear.

> **Specific performance**
> court decree ordering breaching party to render promised performance

---

TAMARIND LITHOGRAPHY WORKSHOP, INC. v. SANDERS Court of Appeal of California,
Second District, 1983, 143 Cal.App.3d 571, 193 Cal.Rptr. 409

FACTS In 1969, Sanders agreed in writing to write, direct, and produce a motion picture on the subject of lithography for the Tamarind Lithography Workshop. After the completion of this film, *Four Stones for Kanemitsu*, litigation arose concerning the parties' rights and obligations under their 1969 agreement. Tamarind and Sanders resolved this dispute by a written settlement agreement, whereby Tamarind promised to provide Sanders a screen credit stating: "A Film by Terry Sanders." Tamarind did not comply with this agreement and failed to include a screen credit for Sanders in the prints it subsequently distributed. In the ensuing litigation, Sanders sought damages for Tamarind's breach of the settlement agreement and specific performance to compel Tamarind's compliance with its obligation to provide a screen credit. The trial court denied Sanders's

request for specific performance, and he brought his case to the Court of Appeal.

DECISION Decision for Sanders granting specific performance.

OPINION To obtain specific performance, Sanders must show (1) the inadequacy of his legal remedy; (2) an underlying contract that is both reasonable and supported by adequate consideration; (3) the existence of mutuality of remedies; (4) contractual terms that are sufficiently definite; and (5) a substantial similarity of the requested performance to that promised in the contract. Sanders's legal remedy is inadequate here because, first, an accurate assessment of damages for lost public acclaim is far too difficult and requires too much speculation; and, second, any future showings of

continued

the film might be deemed a further breach creating "the danger of an untold number of lawsuits." The remedy of specific performance avoids these difficulties and provides Sanders with the contracted-for public acclaim. Since the other requisites for granting specific performance have been met, Sanders is entitled to a writ of specific performance requiring Tamarind to add a screen credit to the film.

INTERPRETATION Specific performance is an appropriate remedy when there is no adequate remedy at law.

Injunctions

Injunction court order prohibiting a party from doing a specific act

The **injunction**, as used as a contract remedy, is a formal court order enjoining (commanding) a person to refrain from doing a specific act or to cease engaging in specific conduct. A court of equity, at its discretion, may grant an injunction against breach of a contractual duty where damages for a breach would be inadequate. For example, Clint enters into a written contract to give Janice the right of first refusal on a tract of land owned by Clint. Clint, however, subsequently offers the land to Blake without first offering it to Janice. A court of equity may properly enjoin Clint from selling the land to Blake. Similarly, valid covenants not to compete may be enforced by an injunction.

An employee's promise of *exclusive* personal services may be enforced by an injunction against serving another employer as long as the probable result will not deprive the employee of other reasonable means of making a living. Suppose, for example, that Allan makes a contract with Marlene, a famous singer, under which Marlene agrees to sing at Allan's theater on certain dates for an agreed fee. Before the date of the first performance, Marlene makes a contract with Craig to sing for Craig at his theater on the same dates. Although, as we have already discussed, Allan cannot obtain specific performance of his contract by Marlene, a court of equity will, on suit by Allan against Marlene, issue an injunction against her ordering her not to sing for Craig. This is the situation in the case of *Madison Square Garden Corp., Ill. v. Carnera*. Also, see the Managerial Insight on the following page for another example of an injunction.

Where the services contracted for are *not* unusual or extraordinary in character, the injured party cannot obtain injunctive relief. His only remedy is an action at law for damages.

MADISON SQUARE GARDEN CORP., ILL. v. CARNERA Circuit Court of Appeals, Second Circuit, 1931, 52 F.2d 47

FACTS Carnera (defendant) agreed with Madison Square Garden (plaintiff) to render services as a boxer in his next contest with the winner of the Schmeling-Stribling contest for the heavyweight championship title. The contract also provided that prior to the match Carnera would not engage in any major boxing contest without the permission of Madison Square Garden. Without obtaining such permission, Carnera contracted to engage in a major boxing contest with Sharkey. Madison Square Garden brought suit requesting an injunction against Carnera's performing his contract to box Sharkey. The trial court granted a preliminary injunction.

DECISION Order for Madison Square Garden affirmed.

OPINION The affidavits in support of the request for a preliminary injunction adequately show that Carnera's services are unique and extraordinary. While specific performance will not be ordered to compel Carnera to render personal services, the court will specifically enforce a negative covenant by injunctive order where damages are not readily ascertainable.

INTERPRETATION Where damages are not adequate, an injunction may be used to enforce an agreement to perform exclusive services that are unusual and extraordinary.

MANAGERIAL INSIGHT

Parcells: Pats Exit Blocked

NEW YORK—If Bill Parcells wants to coach another team, he must get permission from the New England Patriots, NFL Commissioner Paul Tagliabue ruled Wednesday.

Parcells and his lawyers argued that he could resign, pay New England one year's salary ($1.3 million) and coach another NFL team.

But Tagliabue determined that Parcells' stance would render the 1996 amendment "meaningless and of no effect" and would be "contrary to common sense, as well as to Massachusetts law."

Tagliabue's finding severely limits Parcells, 55, if he does not wish to continue with the AFC champions next season in what would conclude the original five-year contract.

It is virtually certain owner Robert Kraft would demand compensation if Parcells left. The division rival New York Jets, who have yet to interview a candidate for their coaching vacancy, are thought to have interest in the two-time Super Bowl winner.

"It does not mean he can go in some other capacity to another team," NFL spokesman Greg Aiello said. "He can't be a GM for another team in 1997. The contract gives the Patriots exclusive option on (Parcells') NFL services in 1997."

Parcells could elect to pursue broadcasting or other opportunities outside the NFL. Neither Parcells nor his agent, Robert Fraley, could be reached for comment.

The Patriots issued a statement welcoming the decision and saying, "Bill Parcells has been an important part of the success of this organization. It is now time for the Patriots to move ahead and build on the success of the 1996-97 season."

Parcells and Kraft had requested Tagliabue's intervention.

When Kraft was asked where the two sides are headed, he replied, "I don't know."

By Tom Pedulla. *USA TODAY*, p.1C. January 30, 1997. "Copyright 1997, USA TODAY. Reprinted with permission."

RESTITUTION

One of the remedies that may be available to a party to a contract is restitution. **Restitution** is the act of returning to the aggrieved party the consideration, or its value, that he gave to the other party. The purpose of restitution is to restore the injured party to the position he was in before the contract was made. Therefore, the party seeking restitution must return what he has received from the other party.

Restitution is available in several contractual situations: (1) for a party injured by breach, as an alternative remedy; (2) for a party in default; (3) for a party who may not enforce a contract because of the statute of frauds; and (4) for a party wishing to rescind (avoid) a voidable contract.

Restitution restoration of the injured party to the position he was in before the contract was made

Party Injured by Breach

A party is entitled to restitution if the other party totally breaches the contract by nonperformance or repudiation. For example, Benedict agrees to sell land to Beatrice for $60,000. After Beatrice makes a partial payment of $15,000, Benedict wrongfully refuses to transfer title. As an alternative to damages or specific performance, Beatrice may recover the $15,000 in restitution.

Party injured by breach a party is entitled to restitution if the other party totally breaches the contract by nonperformance or repudiation

Party in Default

Where a party, after having partly performed, commits a breach by nonperformance or repudiation that discharges the other party's duty to perform, the party in default is entitled to restitution for any benefit she has conferred in excess of the loss she has caused by her breach. For example, Nathan agrees to sell land to Milly for $60,000, and Milly makes a partial payment of $15,000. Milly then repudiates the contract. Nathan sells the land to Murray in good faith for $55,000. Milly may recover from Nathan in restitution the part payment of the

Party in default the party in default is entitled to restitution for any benefit conferred in excess of the loss caused by the breach

$15,000 *less* the $5,000 damages Nathan sustained because of Milly's breach, which equals $10,000.

Statute of Frauds

Statute of frauds where a contract is unenforceable because of the statute of frauds, a party may recover the benefits conferred on the other party in reliance on the contract

A party to a contract that is unenforceable because of the statute of frauds may, nonetheless, have acted in reliance on the contract. In such a case, that party may recover in restitution the benefits he conferred on the other in relying on the unenforceable contract. In most states the party seeking restitution must not be in default. Thus, if Wilton makes an oral contract to furnish services to Rochelle that are not to be performed within a year, and Rochelle discharges Wilton after three months, Wilton may recover as restitution the value of the services rendered during the three months.

Voidable Contracts

Voidable contracts a party who has avoided a contract is entitled to restitution for any benefit conferred on the other party

A party who has rescinded or avoided a contract for lack of capacity, duress, undue influence, fraud, misrepresentation, or mistake is entitled to restitution for any benefit he has conferred on the other. For example, Samuel fraudulently induces Edith to sell land for $60,000. Samuel pays the purchase price, and Edith conveys the land. She then discovers the fraud. Edith may disaffirm the contract and recover the land as restitution. Generally, the party seeking restitution must return any benefit that he has received under the agreement; however, as we found in our discussion of contractual capacity (Chapter 14), this is not always the case.

Figure 18–1 summarizes the remedies for breach of contract.

FIGURE 18–1 Contract Remedies

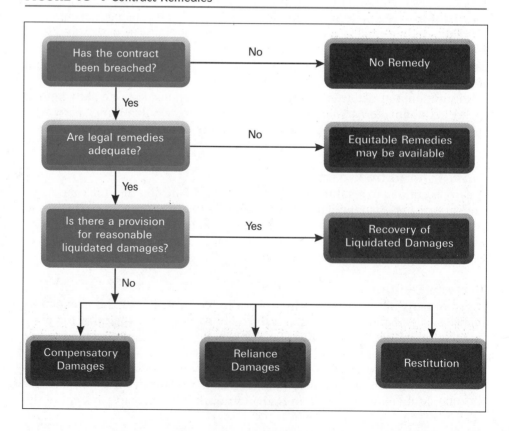

LIMITATIONS ON REMEDIES

Election of Remedies

If a party injured by a breach of contract has more than one remedy available to him, his manifestation of a choice of one remedy, such as bringing suit, does not prevent him from seeking another unless the remedies are inconsistent and the other party materially changes his position in reliance on the manifestation. For example, a party who seeks specific performance, an injunction, or restitution may be entitled to incidental damages, such as those brought about by delay in performance. Damages for total breach, however, are inconsistent with the remedies of specific performance, injunction, and restitution. Likewise, the remedy of specific performance or an injunction is inconsistent with that of restitution.

> **Election of remedies** if remedies are not inconsistent, a party injured by a breach of contract may seek more than one remedy

With respect to contracts for the sale of goods, the Code rejects any doctrine of election of remedies. Thus, the remedies it provides, which are essentially cumulative, include all of the remedies available for breach. Under the Code, whether one remedy prevents the use of another depends upon the facts of the individual case.

HEAD & SEEMAN, INC. v. GREGG Court of Appeals of Wisconsin, 1981, 104 Wis.2d 156, 311 N.W.2d 667

FACTS Bettye Gregg offered to purchase a house from Head & Seeman, Inc. (seller). Though she represented in writing that she had between $15,000 and $20,000 in equity in another home that she would pay to the seller after she sold the other home, she knew that she did not have such equity. In reliance upon these intentionally fraudulent representations, the seller accepted Gregg's offer and the parties entered into a land contract. After taking occupancy, Gregg failed to make any of the contract payments. The seller's investigations then revealed the fraud. Head & Seeman then brought suit seeking rescission of the contract, return of the real estate, and restitution. Restitution was sought for the rental value for the five months of lost use of the property and the seller's out-of-pocket expenses made in reliance upon the bargain. Gregg contends that under the election of remedies doctrine the seller cannot both rescind the contract and recover damages for its breach. The trial court denied recovery for rental value and out-of-pocket expenses.

DECISION Order reversed.

OPINION The election of remedies doctrine bars a plaintiff from maintaining inconsistent theories or forms of relief. Its purpose is to prevent a double recovery for the same wrong. Under the doctrine, a defrauded party must choose either (1) to rescind or (2) to affirm the contract and seek damages. This rule applies where the defrauded party is seeking benefit-of-the bargain damages. It does not, however, prevent a defrauded party from rescinding and recovering "restorative" damages that put the defrauded party back in the position he held prior to the making of the contract. Rescission and restitutionary (restorative) damages are consistent remedies and are not subject to the election of remedies doctrine.

Here, the restoration of the rental value and out-of-pocket expenses works consistently with rescission of the contract to restore Head & Seeman to its pre-contract position. There is no possibility of the corporation obtaining an inconsistent or double recovery. Therefore, the election of remedies does not apply.

INTERPRETATION The purpose of the doctrine of election of remedies is to prevent double recovery for the same loss, not to bar an injured party from seeking more than one remedy so long as those remedies are consistent.

Loss of Power of Avoidance

A party with a power of avoidance for lack of capacity, duress, undue influence, fraud, misrepresentation, or mistake may lose that power if (1) she affirms the contract, (2) she delays unreasonably in exercising the power of disaffirmance, or (3) the rights of third parties intervene.

> **Loss of power of avoidance** a party with the power to avoid a contract may lose that power by (1) affirming the contract, (2) delaying unreasonably in exercising the power of avoidance, or (3) being subordinated to the intervening rights of third parties

Affirmance A party who has the power to avoid a contract for lack of capacity, duress, undue influence, fraud in the inducement, nonfraudulent misrepresentation, or mistake will lose that power by affirming the contract. Affirmance occurs where the party, with full knowledge of the facts, either declares his intention to proceed with the contract or takes some other action from which such intention may reasonably be inferred. Thus, suppose that Pam was induced to purchase a ring from Sally through Sally's fraudulent misrepresentation. If, after learning the truth, Pam undertakes to sell the ring to Janet or does something else that is consistent only with her ownership of the ring, she may no longer rescind the transaction with Sally. In the case of incapacity, duress, or undue influence, affirmance is effective only after the circumstances that made the contract voidable cease to exist. Where there has been fraudulent misrepresentation, the defrauded party may affirm only after he knows of the misrepresentation; if the misrepresentation is nonfraudulent or a mistake is involved, affirmance may occur only after the defrauded party knows or should know of the misrepresentation or mistake.

Delay The power of avoidance may be lost if the party who has the power to do so does not rescind within a reasonable time after the circumstances that made the contract voidable have ceased to exist. Determining a reasonable time depends on all the circumstances, including the extent to which the delay enables the party with the power of avoidance to speculate at the other party's risk. To illustrate, a defrauded purchaser of stock cannot wait unduly to see if the market price or value of the stock appreciates sufficiently to justify retaining the stock.

Rights of Third Parties The intervening rights of third parties further limit the power of avoidance and the accompanying right to restitution. If A transfers property to B in a transaction that is voidable by A, and B sells the property to C (a good faith purchaser for value) before A exercises her power of avoidance, A will lose the right to recover the property.

Thus, if a third party (C), who is a good faith purchaser for value, acquires an interest in the subject matter of the contract before A has elected to rescind, no rescission is permitted. Because the transaction is voidable, B acquires a voidable title to the property. Upon a sale of the property by him to C, who is a purchaser in good faith and for value, C obtains good title and is allowed to retain the property. Since both A and C are innocent, the law will not disturb the title held by C, the good faith purchaser. In this case, as in all cases where rescission is not available, A's only recourse is against B.

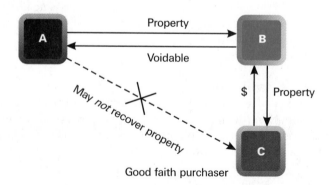

The one notable exception to this rule is the situation involving a sale, *other than a sale of goods,* by a minor who subsequently wishes to avoid the transaction, in which the property has been retransferred to a good faith purchaser. Under this special rule, a good faith purchaser is deprived of the protection generally provided such third parties. Therefore, the third party in a transaction not involving goods is no more protected from the minor's disaffirmance than is the person dealing directly with the minor.

CHAPTER SUMMARY

Monetary Damages	**Compensatory Damages** contract damages placing the injured party in a position as good as the one he would have held had the other party performed; equals loss of value minus loss avoided by injured party plus incidental damages plus consequential damages
	◾ *Loss of Value* value of promised performance minus value of actual performance
	◾ *Expenses Saved* loss or costs the injured party avoids by not having to perform
	◾ *Incidental Damages* damages arising directly out of a breach of contract
	◾ *Consequential Damages* damages not arising directly out of a breach but arising as a foreseeable result of the breach
	Reliance Damages contract damages placing the injured party in as good a position as she would have been in had the contract not been made
	Nominal Damages a small sum awarded where a contract has been breached but the loss is negligible or unproved
	Damages for Misrepresentation
	◾ *Benefit-of-the-Bargain Damages* difference between the value of the fraudulent party's performance as represented and the value the defrauded party received
	◾ *Out-of-Pocket Damages* difference between the value given and the value received
	Punitive Damages are generally *not* recoverable for breach of contract
	Liquidated Damages reasonable damages agreed to in advance by the parties to a contract
	Limitations on Damages
	◾ *Foreseeability of Damages* potential loss that the party now in default had reason to know of when the contract was made
	◾ *Certainty of Damages* damages are not recoverable beyond an amount that can be established with reasonable certainty
	◾ *Mitigation of Damages* injured party may not recover damages for loss he could have avoided by reasonable effort

Remedies in Equity	**Availability** only where there is no adequate remedy at law
	Types
	◾ *Specific Performance* court decree ordering breaching party to render promised performance
	◾ *Injunction* court order prohibiting a party from doing a specific act
	◾ *Reformation* court order correcting a written contract to conform with the intent of the contracting parties

Restitution	**Definition of Restitution** restoration of the injured party to the position she was in before the contract was made **Availability** ■ *Party Injured by Breach* if the other party totally breaches the contract by nonperformance or repudiation ■ *Party in Default* for any benefit conferred in excess of the loss caused by the breach ■ *Statute of Frauds* where a contract is unenforceable because of the statute of frauds, a party may recover the benefits conferred on the other party in reliance on the contract ■ *Voidable Contracts* a party who has avoided a contract is entitled to restitution for any benefit conferred on the other party
Limitations on Remedies	**Election of Remedies** if remedies are not inconsistent, a party injured by a breach of contract may seek more than one remedy **Loss of Power of Avoidance** a party with the power to avoid a contract may lose that power by ■ Affirming the contract ■ Delaying unreasonably in exercising the power of avoidance ■ Being subordinated to the intervening rights of third parties

QUESTIONS

1. Explain how compensatory damages are computed.
2. Explain how reliance damages are computed.
3. Define (a) nominal damages, (b) incidental damages, (c) consequential damages, (d) foreseeability of damages, (e) punitive damages, (f) liquidated damages, and (g) mitigation of damages.
4. Define the various types of equitable relief and discuss when the courts will grant such relief.
5. Identify and discuss the situations in which restitution is available as a contractual remedy.

Internet Question. Compare the provisions governing remedies for breach of contract contained in the Principles of European Contract Law with the provisions of the U.S. common law.

PROBLEMS

1. Edward contracted to buy 1,000 barrels of sugar from Marcia. Marcia failed to deliver, and because Edward could not buy any sugar in the market, he was forced to shut down his candy factory. (a) What damages is Edward entitled to recover? (b) Would it make any difference if Marcia had been told by Edward that he wanted the sugar to make candies for the Christmas trade and that he had accepted contracts for delivery by certain dates?

2. Daniel agreed to erect an apartment building for Steven for $750,000, and that Daniel would suffer a deduction of $1,000 per day for every day of delay. Daniel was twenty days late in finishing the job, losing ten days because of a strike and ten days because the material suppliers were late in furnishing him with materials. Daniel claims that he is entitled to payment in full (a) because the agreement as to $1,000 a day is a penalty and (b) because Steven has not shown that he has sustained any damage. Discuss each contention and decide.

3. Sharon contracted with Jane, a shirtmaker, for 1,000 shirts for men. Jane manufactured and delivered 500 shirts, for which Sharon paid. At the same time, Sharon notified Jane that she could not use or dispose of the other 500 shirts and directed Jane not to manufacture any more under the contract. Nevertheless, Jane made up the other 500 shirts and tendered them to Sharon. Sharon refused to accept the shirts. Jane then sued for the purchase price. Decision?

4. Stuart contracts to act in a comedy for Charlotte and to comply with all theater regulations for four seasons. Charlotte promises to pay Stuart $800 for each performance and to allow Stuart one benefit performance each season. It is expressly agreed that "Stuart shall not be employed in any other production for the period of the contract." Stuart and Charlotte, during the first year of the contract, have a terrible quarrel. Thereafter, Stuart signs a contract to perform in Elaine's production and ceases performing for Charlotte. Charlotte seeks (a) to prevent Stuart from performing for Elaine and (b) to require Stuart to perform his contract with Charlotte. What result?

5. Louis leased a building to Pam for five years at a rental of $1,000 per month, commencing July 1, 1993. Pam was to deposit $10,000 as security for performance of all her promises in the lease, which was to be retained by Louis in case of any breach on Pam's part, otherwise to be applied in payment of rent for the last ten months of the term of the lease. Pam defaulted in the payment of rent for the months of May and June 1997. After proper notice to Pam of the termination of the lease for nonpayment of rent, Louis sued Pam for possession of the building and recovered a judgment for possession. Thereafter, Pam sued Louis to recover the $10,000, less the amount of rent due Louis for May and June 1997. Decision?

6. (a) Mary and Anne enter into a written agreement under which Mary agrees to sell and Anne agrees to buy for $10 per share 100 shares of the 300 shares outstanding of the capital stock of the Infinitesimal Steel Corporation, whose shares are not listed on any exchange and are closely held. Mary refuses to deliver when tendered the $1,000, and Anne sues in equity for specific performance, tendering the $1,000. Decision?

    (b) Modifying (a) above, assume that the subject matter of the agreement is stock of the United States Steel Corporation, which is traded on the New York Stock Exchange. Decision?

    (c) Modifying (a) above, assume that the subject matter of the agreement is undeveloped farmland of little commercial value. Decision?

7. On March 1, Joseph sold to Sandra fifty acres of land in Oregon that Joseph at the time represented to be fine black loam, high, dry, and free of stumps. Sandra paid Joseph the agreed price of $40,000 and took from Joseph a deed to the land. Sandra subsequently discovered that the land was low, swampy, and not entirely free of stumps. Sandra, nevertheless, undertook to convert the greater part of the land into cranberry bogs. After one year of cranberry culture, Sandra became entirely dissatisfied, tendered the land back to Joseph, and demanded from Joseph the return of the $40,000. On Joseph's refusal to repay the money, Sandra brought an action at law against him to recover the $40,000. What judgment?

8. James contracts to make repairs to Betty's building in return for Betty's promise to pay $12,000 on completion of the repairs. After partially completing the repairs, James is unable to continue. Betty hires another builder, who completes the repairs for $5,000. The building's value to Betty has increased by $10,000 as a result of the repairs by James, but Betty has lost $500 in rents because of the delay caused by James's breach. James sues Betty. How much, if any, may James recover in restitution from Betty?

9. Linda induced Sally to enter into a purchase of a stereo amplifier by intentionally misrepresenting the power output to be sixty watts at rated distortion, when in fact it delivered only twenty watts. Sally paid $450 for the amplifier. Amplifiers producing twenty watts generally sell for $200, whereas amplifiers producing sixty watts generally sell for $550. Sally decides to keep the amp and sue for damages. How much may Sally recover in damages from Linda?

10. Virginia induced Charles to sell Charles's boat to Virginia by misrepresentation of material fact on which Charles reasonably relied. Virginia promptly sold the boat to Donald, who paid fair value for it and knew nothing concerning the transaction between Virginia and Charles. Upon discovering the misrepresentation, Charles seeks to recover the boat. What are Charles's rights against Virginia and Donald?

11. Felch was employed as a member of the faculty of Findlay College on a continuing basis. He was dismissed by action of the president and board of trustees, who did not comply with a contractual provision for dismissal that requires a hearing. Felch requested the court to enjoin Findlay College to continue Felch as a member of the faculty and to pay him the salary agreed upon. Decision?

12. Copenhaver, the owner of a laundry business, contracted with Berryman, the owner of a large apartment complex, to allow Copenhaver to own and operate the laundry facilities within the apartment complex. Berryman terminated the five-year contract with Copenhaver with forty-seven months remaining. Within six months, Copenhaver placed the equipment into use in other locations. He then filed suit, claiming that he was entitled to conduct the laundry operations for an additional forty-seven months and that, through such operations, he would have earned a profit of $13,886.58, after deducting Berryman's share of the gross receipts and other operating expenses. Decision?

13. Billy Williams Builders and Developers (Williams) entered into a contract with Hillerich under which Williams agreed to sell to Hillerich a certain lot and to construct on it a house according to submitted plans

and specifications. The house built by Williams was defectively constructed. Hillerich brought suit for specific performance of the contract and for damages resulting from the defective construction and delay in performance. Williams argued that Hillerich was not entitled to have both specific performance and damages for breach of the contract because the remedies were inconsistent and Hillerich had to elect one or the other. Decision?

14. Developers under a plan approved by the city of Rye had constructed six luxury cooperative apartment buildings and were to construct six more. In order to obtain certificates of occupancy for the six completed buildings, the developers were required to post a bond with the city to insure completion of the remaining buildings. The developers posted a $100,000 bond upon which the defendant, Public Service Mutual Insurance Company, as guarantor or surety, agreed to pay $200 for each day after April 1, 1971, that the remaining buildings were not completed. After the April deadline, more than 500 days passed without completion of the buildings. The city sued the developers and the insurance company to recover $100,000 on the bond. Decision?

15. Kerr Steamship Company sent a telegram to the Philippines through the Radio Corporation of America. The telegram, which contained instructions for loading cargo on one of Kerr's ships, was mislaid and never delivered. Consequently, the ship was improperly loaded and the cargo was lost. Kerr sued the Radio Corporation for the $6,675.29 in profits the company lost on the cargo because of the Radio Corporation's failure to deliver the telegram. Decision?

16. El Dorado Tire Company fired Bill Ballard, a sales executive. Ballard had a five-year contract with El Dorado but was fired after only two years of employ-

ment. Ballard sued El Dorado for breach of contract. El Dorado claims that any damages due to breach of the contract should be mitigated because of Ballard's failure to seek other employment after he was fired. Decision?

17. California and Hawaiian Sugar Company (C and H) is an agricultural cooperative in the business of growing sugarcane in Hawaii and transporting the raw sugar to its refinery in California for processing. Because of the seasonal nature of the sugarcane crop, availability of ships to transport the raw sugar immediately after harvest is imperative. In 1979, C and H lost the services of the shipping company it previously used. To fill the void, C and H decided to build its own ship, a Macababoo, which had two components, a tug and a barge. C and H contracted with Halter Marine to build the tug and with Sun Ship to build the barge. In finalizing the contract for construction of the barge, both C and H and Sun Ship were represented by senior management and by legal counsel. The resulting contract called for a liquidated damages payment of $17,000 per day that delivery of the completed barge was delayed. Delivery of both the barge and the tug were significantly delayed. Sun Ship paid the $17,000 per day liquidated damages amount and then sued to recover it, claiming that without the liquidated damages provision, C and H's legal remedy for money damages would have been significantly less than that paid by Sun Ship pursuant to the liquidated damages provision. The trial court found in favor of C and H, upholding the validity of the liquidated damages provision. Sun Ship appealed, claiming that the liquidated damages provision was invalid as a penalty since Halter Marine was also significantly late in delivery of the tug, without which the barge was useless to C and H. Decision?

PART IV

Sales

CHAPTER 19

Introduction to Sales

Sales are the most common and important of all commercial transactions. In an exchange economy such as ours, sales are the essential means by which the various units of production exchange their outputs, thereby providing the opportunity for specialization and enhanced productivity. An advanced, complex, industrialized economy with highly coordinated manufacturing and distribution systems requires a reliable mechanism for assuring that *future* exchanges can be entered into today and fulfilled later. Because practically everyone in our economy is a purchaser of both durable and consumable goods, the manufacture and distribution of goods involve numerous sales transactions. The critical role of the law of sales is to establish a framework in which these present and future exchanges may take place in a predictable, certain, and orderly fashion with a minimum of transaction costs.

Leases of personal property, also of great economic significance, exceed $100 billion annually. Leases range from a consumer's renting an automobile or a lawnmower to a Fortune 500 corporation's leasing heavy industrial machinery.

In this chapter, we will discuss the nature and formation of sales contracts and the fundamental principles of leases.

NATURE OF SALES CONTRACTS

The law of sales, which governs contracts involving the sale of goods, is a specialized branch of both the law of contracts (discussed in Chapters 9–18) and the law of personal property (discussed in Chapter 48). This section will cover the definition of a sales contract and the fundamental principles of Article 2 of the Code.

DEFINITIONS

Sale transfer of title to goods from seller to buyer for a price

Goods movable personal property

The Code defines a **sale** as the transfer of title to goods from seller to buyer for a price. The price can be money, other goods, real estate, or services. **Goods** are essentially defined as movable, tangible, personal property. For example, the sale of a bicycle, stereo set, or this textbook is considered a sale of goods. "Goods" also include the unborn young of animals, growing crops, and, if removed by the seller, timber, minerals, or a building attached to real property.

Sales transactions are governed by Article 2 of the Uniform Commercial Code, which has been adopted in all states—except Louisiana—plus the District of Columbia and the Virgin Islands. Where the Code has not modified general contract law, such law continues to apply. In other words, the law of sales is a specialized part of the general law of contracts, and the law of contracts continues to govern unless specifically displaced by the Code.

General contract law also continues to govern all contracts outside the scope of the Code. Transactions not within the scope of Article 2 include employment contracts, service contracts, insurance contracts, contracts involving real property, and contracts for the sale of intangibles such as stocks, bonds, patents, and copyrights. For an illustration of the law governing contracts, see Figure 9–1. In determining whether a contract containing both a sale of goods and a service is a UCC contract or general contract, the majority of states follows the predominant purpose test. This test, as in *Pittsley v. Houser*, below, and in *Insul-Mark Midwest, Inc. v. Modern Materials, Inc.* in Chapter 9, holds that if the predominant purpose of the whole transaction is a sale of goods, then Article 2 applies to the entire transaction. If, on the other hand, the predominant purpose is the nongood or service portion, then Article 2 does not apply at all. A few states apply Article 2 only to the goods part of a transaction and general contract law to the nongoods or service part of the transaction.

PITTSLEY v. HOUSER Idaho Court of Appeals, 1994, 875 P.2d 232

FACTS Jane Pittsley contracted with Donald Houser, who was doing business as Hilton Contract Co. (Hilton), to install carpet in her home. The total contract price was $4,402. From this sum, Hilton paid the installers $700 to put the carpet in Pittsley's home. Following installation, Pittsley complained to Hilton that the installation was defective in several respects. Hilton attempted to fix the installation but was unable to satisfy Pittsley. Eventually, Pittsley refused any further efforts to fix the carpet. She sued for rescission of the contract and return of the $3,500 she had previously paid on the contract plus incidental damages. Hilton counterclaimed for the balance due on the contract. The magistrate determined that the breach was not so material as to justify rescission of the contract and awarded Pittsley $250 in repair costs plus $150 in expenses. The magistrate also awarded Hilton the balance of $902 remaining on the contract. Pittsley appealed to the district court, which reversed and remanded the case to the magistrate for additional findings of fact and to apply the UCC to the transaction. Hilton appeals this ruling, asserting that application of the UCC is inappropriate since the only defects alleged were in the installation of the carpet, not in the carpet itself.

DECISION The judgment of the magistrate is vacated and the case remanded.

OPINION The subject transaction is a hybrid transaction, involving both the sale of goods (carpet) and services (installation). There are two lines of authority addressing the question of whether such transactions are governed by the UCC or by common law. The majority position utilizes the "predominant factor" test. This test essentially involves consideration of the contract in its entirety, applying the UCC to the entire contract or not at all. In considering the applicability of the UCC to a hybrid transaction, a court must determine whether its predominant factor, its thrust, its purpose, is the rendition of service, with goods incidentally involved, or is a transaction of sale, with labor incidentally involved. The second line of authority, which Hilton urged, allows the contract to be severed into different parts, applying the UCC to the goods involved in the contract, but not to the nongoods involved. Thus an action focusing on defects or problems with the goods themselves would be covered by the UCC, while a suit based on the service or other nongoods provided would not be covered by the UCC.

The predominant factor test is the more prudent rule. Severing contracts into various parts, attempting to label each as goods or nongoods and applying different law to each separate part clearly contravenes the UCC's declared purpose to simplify, clarify, and modernize the law governing commercial transactions. In addition, severing contracts would present difficult problems of proof in segregating assets and determining damages.

Under the predominant factor test, the UCC is applicable to the subject transaction in the present case. It appears that Pittsley entered into this contract for the purpose of obtaining carpet of a certain quality and color. The contract called for "165 yds Masterpiece No. 2122—Installed" and there was a separate charge for the removal of the old carpet. However, the installation service does not appear to have been a factor in inducing

continued

Pittsley to choose Hilton as the carpet supplier. Pittsley specified neither who would provide the service or the nature of the work. Since the sale of carpet was the predominant factor in this transaction, the UCC applies to the entire transaction.

INTERPRETATION If the predominant purpose of the whole transaction is a sale of goods, then Article 2 applies to the whole transaction; if the predominant purpose is the nongood or service component, then Article 2 does not apply.

FUNDAMENTAL PRINCIPLES OF ARTICLE 2

Purpose of Article 2 to modernize, clarify, simplify, and make uniform the law of sales

The purpose of Article 2 is to modernize, clarify, simplify, and make uniform the law of sales. Furthermore, the article is to be interpreted according to these principles and not according to some abstraction such as the passage of title. The Code "is drawn to provide flexibility so that, since it is intended to be a semi-permanent piece of legislation, it will provide its own machinery for expansion of commercial practices. It is intended to make it possible for the law embodied in this Act to be developed by the courts in the light of unforeseen and new circumstances and practices. However, the proper construction of the Act requires that its interpretation and application be limited to its reason." (*General Provisions* in Comment to Section 1-102). This open-ended drafting includes the following fundamental concepts.

Good Faith

Good faith the Code requires all sales contracts to be performed in good faith, which means honesty in fact in the conduct or transaction concerned; in the case of a merchant, it also includes the observance of reasonable commercial standards

All parties who enter into a contract or duty within the scope of the Code must perform their obligations in good faith. The Code defines **good faith** as "honesty in fact in the conduct or transaction concerned." For a merchant, good faith also requires the observance of reasonable commercial standards of fair dealing in the trade. For instance, if the parties agree that the seller is to set the price term, the seller must establish the price in good faith.

Unconscionability

Unconscionability a court may refuse to enforce an unconscionable contract or any part of a contract found to be unconscionable

The courts may scrutinize every contract of sale to determine whether in its commercial setting, purpose, and effect it is unconscionable. The reviewing court may refuse to enforce a contract (or any part of it) found to be unconscionable or may limit its application to prevent an unconscionable result. The Code does not define *unconscionable*; however, the term is defined in the *New Webster's Dictionary* (Deluxe Encyclopedic Edition) as "contrary to the dictates of conscience; unscrupulous or unprincipled; exceeding that which is reasonable or customary; inordinate, unjustifiable."

The Code denies or limits enforcement of an unconscionable contract for the sale of goods to promote fairness and decency and to correct harshness or oppression in contracts resulting from the unequal bargaining positions of the parties.

The doctrine of unconscionability permits the courts to resolve issues of unfairness explicitly on that basis without recourse to formalistic rules or legal fictions. In policing contracts for fairness, the courts have demonstrated their willingness to limit freedom of contract in order to protect the less advantaged from the overreaching of dominant contracting parties.

Procedural unconscionability unreasonable bargaining process

The doctrine of unconscionability has evolved through its application by the courts to include both procedural and substantive unconscionability. **Procedural unconscionability** involves scrutiny for the presence of "bargaining naughtiness." In other words, was the negotiation process fair? Or were there procedural irregularities such as burying important terms of the agreement in fine print or obscuring the true meaning of the contract with impenetrable legal jargon?

In the search for **substantive unconscionability**, the court examines the actual terms of the contract, seeking oppressive or grossly unfair provisions such as an exorbitant price or an unfair exclusion or limitation of contractual remedies. An all-too-common example involves a necessitous buyer in an unequal bargaining position with a seller who consequently has obtained an exorbitant price for his product or service.

The following case illustrates the application of the doctrine of unconscionability, as does *Williams v. Walker-Thomas Furniture Co.* in Chapter 13.

> **Substantive unconscionability** grossly unfair contractual terms

CONSTRUCTION ASSOCIATES, INC. v. FARGO WATER EQUIPMENT CO.
North Dakota Supreme Court, 1989, 446 N.W.2d 237

FACTS Construction Associates (CA) was the successful bidder to construct a water supply line for the city of Breckenridge, Minnesota. CA purchased a large amount of polyvinyl chloride pipe manufactured by the Johns-Manville Sales Corporation (J-M) in order to construct the pipeline. CA, however, did not have any direct contact with J-M; instead, it purchased the pipe through a supply company (Fargo Water Equipment). J-M shipped the pipe directly to the work site, and included with each shipment an installation guide written for those who actually directed the installation of the pipe. On page three of the installation guide, J-M expressly warranted the pipe to be free from defects in workmanship and materials. In addition, J-M set forth a limitation of liability clause, which stated there would be no liability except for breach of the express warranty, and that J-M would be responsible only for resupplying a like quantity of nondefective pipe. J-M stated that it would not be liable for any incidental, consequential, or other damages.

Eventually the Breckenridge pipeline developed over seventy leaks. The only way these leaks could be repaired was to remove the defective joints and replace them with stainless steel sleeves. After incurring over $140,000 in repairing the pipeline, CA sued J-M and Fargo. CA won a jury award of over $140,000 in damages from J-M. J-M appealed, claiming that the limitation of liability clause should be enforced.

DECISION Judgment for CA affirmed.

OPINION The Uniform Commercial Code expressly allows a party to a contract to limit or exclude conse-quential damages, unless the limitation or exclusion is unconscionable. The UCC, however, also states that "if the court as a matter of law finds the contract or any clause of the contract to have been unconscionable at the time it was made the court may refuse to enforce the contract, or it may enforce the remainder of the contract without the unconscionable clause, or it may limit the application of any unconscionable clause as to avoid any unconscionable result."

Courts will determine whether the unconscionability in question is procedural or substantive in nature. Procedural unconscionability includes unfair surprise, oppression, and inequality of bargaining power, while harshness or one-sidedness of contractual provisions are types of substantive unconscionability. From a procedural viewpoint, the limitation of liability clause was never negotiated, and in fact was only seen by lower-level CA employees at the work site. In addition, even though this is a commercial setting, there is significant inequality of bargaining power between the local contractor CA and the international conglomerate J-M. Substantively, all J-M is required to do under the limitation of liability clause is resupply more pipe. Since the only way to repair the installed pipe is with stainless steel sleeves, this remedy is virtually worthless. Given both the procedural and substantive unconscionability in this instance, the decision of the trial court is affirmed.

INTERPRETATION A court can override a term of a contract if it finds that term to be unconscionable or the result of an unconscionable negotiation process.

Expansion of Commercial Practices
An underlying policy of the Code is "to permit the continued expansion of commercial practices through custom, usage and agreement of the parties." In

ETHICAL DILEMMA What Constitutes Unconscionability in a Business?

FACTS Frank's Maintenance and Repair, Inc., orally placed with C. A. Roberts Co. an order for steel tubing to use in manufacturing front fork tubes for motorcycles. Front fork tubes bear the bulk of a motorcycle's weight, so Frank's had to use high-quality steel.

Soon, Frank's received from Roberts Co. an acknowledgment of the order. This acknowledgment included the conditions of sale, which limited consequential damages, as well as a description of restricted remedies that were available upon the contract's breach. The sale conditions required that the buyer make any claim for defective equipment promptly upon receipt of the goods. These conditions were printed on the back of the acknowledgment. On the front, a legend that read "conditions of sale on reverse side" had been stamped over in such a way that the words at first appeared to read "No conditions of sale on reverse side."

Roberts delivered the steel to Frank's in December 1975. The steel had no visible defects. When Frank's began using the material in its manufacturing process in the summer of 1976, however, the company discovered that the steel was hopelessly pitted and cracked. Frank's Maintenance and Repair informed Roberts Co. of the defects, revoked its acceptance of the steel, and sued for breach of the warranty of merchantability.

Social, Policy, and Ethical Considerations

1. Did Frank's Maintenance and Repair have a reasonable opportunity to understand the terms of its contract with C. A. Roberts Co.? Given the contract that Frank's received, was the company able to make a meaningful choice with regard to the terms of the agreement? Why or why not?

2. Who bears the responsibility in a situation such as this, where both parties are businesspersons and thus should know enough to read all contracts carefully and thoroughly?

3. With or without the stamp, did Roberts act unconscionably in drawing up its contract? Moreover, should Roberts have the right to restrict a buyer's remedies if its steel may have a latent defect?

particular, the Code emphasizes the course of dealing and the usage of trade in interpreting agreements.

A **course of dealing** is a sequence of previous conduct between the parties that may fairly be regarded as establishing a common basis of understanding for interpreting their expressions and agreement.

A **usage of trade** is a practice or method of dealing regularly observed and followed in a place, vocation, or trade. To illustrate: Connie contracts to sell Ward 1,000 feet of San Domingo mahogany. By usage of dealers in mahogany, known to Connie and Ward, good figured mahogany of a certain density is known as San Domingo mahogany, though it does not come from San Domingo. Unless otherwise agreed, the usage is part of the contract.

Sales by and between Merchants

The Code establishes some separate rules that apply to transactions between merchants or to transactions involving a merchant as a party. A **merchant** is defined as a person (1) who is a dealer in a particular type of goods, or (2) who by his occupation holds himself out as having knowledge or skill peculiar to certain goods or practices, or (3) who employs an agent or broker whom he holds out as having such knowledge or skill. These rules exact higher standards of conduct from merchants because of their knowledge of trade and commerce and because merchants as a class generally set these standards for themselves. The more significant of these merchant provisions are good faith, confirmation of oral contracts, firm offers, "battle of the forms," warranty of title, warranty of merchantability, sales on approval, retention of possession of goods by seller, entrusting of goods, risk of loss, and duties after rightful rejection.

Course of dealing
sequence of previous conduct between parties establishing a basis for interpreting their agreement

Usage of trade
practice or method of dealing regularly observed and followed in a place, vocation, or trade

Merchant dealer in goods or person who by his occupation holds himself out as having knowledge or skill peculiar to the goods

Liberal Administration of Remedies

The Code provides that its remedies shall be liberally administered in order to place the aggrieved party in a position as good as the one she would have held, had the defaulting party fully performed. The Code does make it clear, however, that remedies are limited to compensation and may not include consequential or punitive damages, unless specifically provided by the Code. According to its provisions, for cases in which the Code itself does not expressly provide a remedy for a right or obligation, the courts should provide an appropriate remedy. Remedies are discussed in Chapter 23.

Freedom of Contract

Most of the Code's provisions are not mandatory but permit the parties by agreement to vary or displace them altogether. However, the obligations of good faith, diligence, reasonableness, and care may not be disclaimed by agreement, though the parties may by agreement determine the standards by which to measure the performance of these obligations, as long as the standards are not obviously unreasonable.

Freedom of contract most provisions of the Code may be varied by agreement

Validation and Preservation of Sales Contracts

One of the requirements of commercial law is the establishment of rules that determine when an agreement is valid. The Code approaches this requirement by reducing formal requisites to the bare minimum and by attempting to preserve agreements whenever the parties manifest an intent to enter into a contract.

Validation and preservation of sales contract the Code reduces formal requisites to the bare minimum and attempts to preserve agreements whenever the parties manifest an intention to enter into a contract

FUNDAMENTALS OF ARTICLE 2A—LEASES

Despite the frequent and widespread use of personal property leases, the law governing these transactions had been patched together from the common law of personal property, real estate leasing law, and the Uniform Commercial Code (Articles 2 and 9). Except for several provisions, the UCC did not directly apply to leases. Though some courts, nevertheless, have held that a lease is a transaction in goods and therefore within the scope of the UCC, other courts have refused to apply the Code to leases because actual title to the goods never passes. Still other courts have applied the Code by analogy to leases. In any event, no unified or uniform statutory law governed leases of personal property for most of the twentieth century.

To fill this void, the drafters of the Code approved "Article 2A—Leases" in 1987 and subsequently amended the Article in 1990. An analogue of Article 2, the new Article adopts many of the rules contained in Article 2. Article 2A is an attempt to codify in one statute all the rules governing the leasing of personal property. Two states have enacted the 1987 version of Article 2A while over forty other states and the District of Columbia have adopted the 1990 version.

Definition of a Lease

Within Article 2A, a **lease** of goods is defined as a "transfer of the right to possession and use of goods for a term in return for consideration, but . . . retention or creation of a security interest is not a lease." If a transaction is within this definition of a lease, it is governed by Article 2A; but if the transaction is a security interest disguised as a lease, it is governed by Article 9.

Lease transfer of the right to possession and use of goods for a term in return for consideration

Warranties

Article 2A carries over the warranty provisions of Article 2 with relatively minor revision to reflect differences in style, leasing terminology, or leasing practices. Article 2 and Article 2A diverge somewhat, however, in their treatment of the warranties of title and infringement as well as in their provisions for the exclusion and modification of warranties.

Default and Remedies

The approach to default and remedies within Article 2A is a synthesis of the treatments found in Article 2 and Article 9. Provisions are made both for the lessor's remedies upon the lessee's default and for the lessee's remedies upon the lessor's default. This is a substantial departure from Article 9, which provides remedies only for the secured party. As is true elsewhere in Article 2A, the sections on default and remedies emphasize the freedom of the parties to contract among themselves. The lease agreement may include rights and remedies for default in addition to, or in substitution for, those provided in Article 2A.

Consumer Leases

Article 2A affords special treatment for consumer leases. The definition of a consumer lease requires that (1) the transaction meet the definition of a lease under Article 2A; (2) the lessor be regularly engaged in the business of leasing *or* selling goods; (3) the lessee be an individual, not an organization; (4) the lessee take the lease interest primarily for a personal, family, or household purpose; and (5) the total payments under the lease do not exceed an amount to be specified by each state. Although consumer protection for lease transactions is primarily left to other state and federal law, Article 2A does contain several provisions that apply to consumer leases and that may *not* be varied by agreement of the parties. In terms of *all* leases, the Article provides that a court faced with an unconscionable contract or clause may refuse to enforce either the entire contract or just the unconscionable clause; or the court may limit the application of the unconscionable clause to avoid an unconscionable result.

Finance Leases

A finance lease is a special type of lease transaction generally involving three parties instead of two. Whereas in the typical lease situation the lessor also supplies the goods, in a finance lease arrangement the lessor and the supplier are separate parties. The lessor's primary function in a finance lease is to provide financing to the lessee for a lease of goods provided by the supplier. For example, under a finance lease arrangement, a manufacturer supplies goods pursuant to the lessee's instructions or specifications. The party functioning as the lessor will then either purchase those goods from the supplier or act as the prime lessee to lease them from the supplier. In turn, the lessor leases or subleases the goods to the lessee. Because the finance lessor functions merely as a source of credit, he typically will have no special expertise as to the goods. Due to the finance lessor's usually limited role, Article 2A imposes fewer obligations upon him.

FORMATION OF A SALES CONTRACT

As we have stated previously, the Code's basic approach to validation is to recognize contracts whenever the parties manifest such an intent. This is so whether or not the parties can identify the precise moment at which they formed the contract.

MANIFESTATION OF MUTUAL ASSENT

In order for a contract to exist there must be an objective manifestation of mutual assent: an offer and an acceptance. In this section, we will examine the UCC rules that affect offers and acceptances.

Definiteness of an Offer

At common law, the terms of a contract were required to be definite and complete. The Code has rejected the strict approach of the common law by recognizing an agreement as valid, despite missing terms, if there is any reasonably certain basis for granting a remedy. Accordingly, the Code provides that even though a contract may omit one or more terms, the contract need not fail for indefiniteness. The Code provides standards by which the courts may ascertain and supply omitted essential terms, provided the parties intended to enter into a binding agreement. Nevertheless, the more terms the parties leave open, the less likely their intent to enter into a binding contract.

> **Definiteness of an offer**
> the Code provides that a contract does not fail for indefiniteness even though one or more terms may have been omitted; the Code provides standards by which missing essential terms may be supplied

Open Price The parties may enter into a contract for the sale of goods even though they have reached no agreement on the price. In such a case, the price is a reasonable price at the time for delivery. A contract has an open price term if the agreement (1) says nothing as to price; (2) provides that the parties shall agree later as to the price and they fail to so agree; or (3) fixes the price in terms of some agreed market or other standard, as set by a third person or agency, and the price is not so set.

Open Quantity: Output and Requirements Contracts As we discussed in Chapters 10 and 12, an output contract is the agreement of a buyer to purchase the entire output of a seller for a stated period, whereas a requirements contract is an agreement of a seller to supply a buyer with all her requirements for certain goods. Even though the exact quantity of goods is not specified and even though the seller may have some control over his output and the buyer over her requirements, such agreements are enforceable through the application of an objective standard based on the good faith of both parties. Moreover, the parties may not produce or request quantities disproportionate to any stated estimate of need or production or to prior output or requirements.

EMPIRE GAS CORP. v. AMERICAN BAKERIES CO. United States Court of Appeals, 7th Circuit, 1988, 5 UCC Rep.Serv.2d 545

FACTS Due to high gasoline prices, American Bakeries Company (ABC) considered converting its fleet of over 3,000 vehicles to a much less expensive propane fuel system. After negotiations with Empire Gas Corporation (Empire), ABC signed a contract for approximately three thousand converter units, "more or less depending upon requirements of Buyer," as well as agreeing to buy all propane to be used for four years from Empire. Without

continued

giving any reasons, however, ABC never ordered any converter units or propane from Empire, having apparently decided not to convert its vehicles. Empire brought suit against ABC and won a jury award of $3,254,963, representing lost profits on 2,242 converter units and the propane that would have been consumed during the contract period. ABC appealed.

DECISION Judgment for Empire affirmed.

OPINION The UCC, which governs requirements contracts, provides that "a term which measures the quantity by the output of the seller or the requirements of the buyer means such actual output or requirements as may occur in *good faith*, except that *no quantity unreasonably disproportionate to any stated estimate. . .* may be tendered or demanded." The Court held that the "unreasonably disproportionate" proviso should not be read literally when a buyer is demanding less, rather than more, of a stated estimate. The Court, however,

held that a requirements contract was not, from a buyer's standpoint, in essence an option to purchase up to or slightly beyond a stated estimate on terms specified in the contract. For purposes of a requirements contract, the buyer's "requirements" must be more than purely subjective needs. The good faith requirement, moreover, would preclude the buyer from merely having second thoughts about the terms of the contract and desiring to get out of it. The Court concluded that American Bakeries had acted in bad faith in deciding for undisclosed reasons not to convert its fleet to propane, thereby reducing its requirements to zero.

INTERPRETATION Even though the exact quantity of goods under a requirements contract is not specified, such requirements are enforceable through the application of an objective standard based on good faith of both parties.

Irrevocable Offer

An offeror generally may withdraw an offer at any time prior to its acceptance. To be effective, the notice revoking the offer must reach the offeree before he has accepted.

Option contract to hold open an offer

An **option** is a contract by which the offeror is bound to hold open an offer for a specified time. It must comply with all of the requirements of a contract, including consideration. Option contracts apply to all types of contracts, including sales of goods.

Firm offer signed writing by merchant to hold open an offer for the scale or purchase of goods

The Code has made certain offers—called **firm offers**—irrevocable without the offeree giving any consideration for the promise to keep the offer open. The Code provides that a merchant is bound to keep an offer open for a maximum of three months if the merchant gives assurance in a signed writing that it will be held open. The Code, therefore, makes a merchant's written promise not to revoke an offer for a stated period of time enforceable even though no consideration is given the merchant-offeror for that promise.

Variant Acceptances

Variant acceptances the inclusion of different or additional terms in an acceptance is addressed by focusing on the intent of the parties

The common law *mirror image* rule, by which the acceptance cannot vary or deviate from the terms of the offer, has been modified by the Code. This modification has been necessitated by the realities of modern business practices, notably by the fact that a vast number of businesses use standardized business forms. For example, a buyer sends to the seller on the buyer's order form a purchase order for 1,000 dozen cotton shirts at $60 per dozen with delivery by October 1 at the buyer's place of business. On the reverse side of this standard form are twenty-five numbered paragraphs containing provisions generally favorable to the buyer. When the seller receives the buyer's order and agrees to the buyer's quantity, price, and delivery terms, he sends to the buyer an unequivocal acceptance of the offer on his acceptance form. On the back of his acceptance form, however, the seller has thirty-two numbered paragraphs generally favorable to himself and in significant conflict with the provisions in the buyer's form. Under the

common law's "mirror image" rule, no contract would exist, for the seller has not accepted unequivocally all of the material terms of the buyer's offer.

The Code attempts to reconcile this **battle of the forms** by focusing on the intent of the parties. If the offeree expressly makes his acceptance conditional upon assent to the additional or different terms, no contract is formed. If, however, the offeree does not expressly require such a condition, a contract is formed. The issue then becomes whether the offeree's different or additional terms become part of the contract. If both offeror and offeree are merchants, **additional** terms (terms the offeree proposed for the contract for the first time) will become part of the contract if they do not materially alter the agreement and are not objected to either in the offer itself or within a reasonable time. If either of the parties is not a merchant, or if the terms materially alter the offer, the additional terms are merely construed as proposals for addition to the contract. **Different** terms (terms that contradict or conflict with terms of the offer) proposed by the offeree also will generally not become part of the contract unless specifically accepted by the offeror.

The courts are divided over what terms are included when the terms conflict. The majority of courts hold that the terms cancel each other out and look to the Code to provide the missing terms; other courts hold that the offeror's terms govern. Some states follow a third alternative and apply the additional terms test to different terms. See Figure 19–1.

Applying Section 2-207 to the example above: since both parties are merchants and the seller did not condition his acceptance upon the buyer's assent to the additional or different terms, then (1) the contract will be formed without the *seller's different terms* unless the buyer specifically accepts them; (2) the contract will be formed without the *seller's additional terms* unless (a) the buyer specifically accepts or (b) the additional terms do not materially alter the offer and the buyer does not object to them; and (3) depending upon the jurisdiction, either (a) the *conflicting terms* cancel each other out and the Code provides the missing terms, (b) the *buyer's conflicting terms* are included in the contract, or (c) the additional terms test is applied.

Finally, subsection 3 of 2-207 deals with those situations in which the writings do not form a contract but the conduct of the parties recognizes the existence of one. For instance, Ernest makes an offer to Gwen, who replies with a conditional acceptance. Although no contract has been formed, Gwen ships the ordered goods and Ernest accepts the goods. Subsection 3 provides that in this instance the contract consists of the written terms to which both parties agreed together with supplementary provisions of the Code.

McJUNKIN CORPORATION v. MECHANICALS, INC. United States Court of Appeals, Sixth Circuit, 1989, 888 F.2d 481

FACTS Emery Industries (Emery) contracted with Mechanicals, Inc. (Mechanicals), to install a pipe system to carry chemicals and fatty acids under high pressure and temperature. The system required stainless steel "stub ends" (used to connect pipe segments), which Mechanicals ordered from McJunkin Corporation (McJunkin). McJunkin in turn ordered the stub ends from the Alaskan Copper Companies, Inc. (Alaskan). McJunkin's purchase order required the seller to certify the goods and to relieve the buyer of liabilities which might arise from defective goods.

After shipment of the goods to McJunkin, Alaskan sent written acknowledgment of the order, containing terms and conditions of sale different from those in McJunkin's purchase order. The acknowledgment provided a disclaimer of warranty and a requirement for inspection of the goods within ten days of receipt. The acknowledgment also contained a requirement that the buyer accept all of the seller's terms.

The stub ends were delivered to Mechanicals in several shipments over a five-month period. Each shipment included a document reciting terms the

FIGURE 19–1 Battle of the Forms

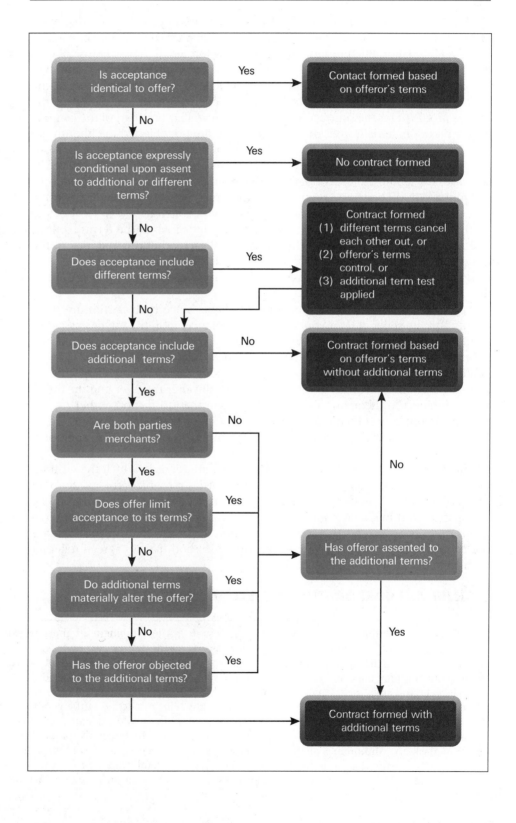

continued

same as those on Alaskan's initial acknowledgment. Apparently, McJunkin never objected to any of the terms contained in any of Alaskan's documents.

After the stub ends were installed, they were found to be defective. Mechanicals had to remove and replace them, causing Emery to close its plant for several days. McJunkin filed a complaint alleging that Mechanicals had failed to pay $26,141.88 owed on account for the stub ends McJunkin supplied. Mechanicals filed an answer and counterclaim against McJunkin, alleging $93,586.13 in damages resulting from the replacement and repair of the defective stub ends. McJunkin filed a third-party complaint against Alaskan, alleging that Alaskan was liable for any damages Mechanicals incurred as a result of the defective stub ends. The district court entered a $68,000 judgment for Mechanicals against McJunkin ($87,000 in damages minus $19,000 owed McJunkin on its account). The court granted Alaskan a judgment against McJunkin based on Alaskan's liability limitation provision. McJunkin appealed the judgment in favor of Alaskan.

DECISION Judgment for Alaskan vacated and remanded.

OPINION This conflict requires a court to declare a victor in a classic Uniform Commercial Code "battle of the forms." We must determine whether, under the facts here, a liability limitation contained in the acknowledgment form of Alaskan Copper Companies precludes McJunkin Corporation from recovering damages from Alaskan.

The problem underlying any "battle of the forms" is that the parties have failed to incorporate into one formal, signed writing the explicit terms of their contract. Instead, each has been content to rely upon standard terms included in its own purchase orders or acknowledgments, even though these terms often conflict with those in the other party's documents. Usually, these standard terms mean little, for a contract is designed for fulfillment and rarely anticipates its breach. Generally, if the parties are equal in bargaining power, the Code gives them the right to agree upon contractual terms that might otherwise violate the Code, including liability limitations.

Nevertheless, under the facts of this case, Alaskan's liability limitation is inoperative. Although Alaskan and McJunkin had a contract, the contract existed by virtue of the parties' conduct, not by virtue of the exchange of forms. The contract thus incorporated only the terms in both parties' standardized forms; the liability limitation was not a term in McJunkin's purchase order, so it did not bind McJunkin.

INTERPRETATION Subsection 3 of Section 2-207 deals with those situations in which the writings do not form a contract but the conduct of the parties recognizes the existence of one: the contract consists of the written terms to which both parties agreed, together with supplementary provisions of the UCC.

Manner of Acceptance

As is true of contracts under common law, the offeror may specify the manner in which the offer must be accepted. If the offeror does not so specify and the circumstances do not otherwise clearly indicate, an offer to make a sales contract invites acceptance, effective upon dispatch, in any manner and in any medium reasonable in the circumstances. The Code therefore allows flexibility of response and the ability to keep pace with new modes of communication.

An offer to buy goods for prompt or current shipment may be accepted either by a prompt promise to ship or by prompt shipment. Acceptance by performance requires notice within a reasonable time, or the offer may be treated as lapsed.

Manner of acceptance an acceptance can be made in any reasonable manner and is effective upon dispatch

CONSIDERATION

In several respects, the Code has relaxed the common law requirements regarding consideration. For example, the Code provides that a contract for the sale of goods can be modified without new consideration, provided the modification is made in good faith. In addition, any claim of right arising out of an alleged breach of contract can be discharged in whole or in part without consideration by a written waiver or renunciation signed and delivered by the aggrieved party. As previously noted, a firm offer is not revocable for lack of consideration.

Contractual modifications the Code provides that a contract for the sale of goods may be modified without new consideration if the modification is made in good faith

FORM OF THE CONTRACT

Statute of Frauds

Statute of frauds sale of
goods costing $500 or more
must be evidenced by a
signed writing to be
enforceable

The original statute of frauds, which applied to contracts for the sale of goods, has been used as a prototype for the Article 2 statute of frauds provision. The Code provides that a contract for the sale of goods costing ***$500 or more*** is not enforceable unless there is some writing sufficient to evidence the existence of a contract between the parties.

Modification of Contracts An agreement modifying a contract must be in writing if the resulting contract is within the statute of frauds. Conversely, if a contract that was previously within the statute of frauds is modified so as to no longer fall within it, the modification is enforceable even if it is oral. Thus, if the parties enter into an oral contract to sell for $450 a dining room table, to be delivered to the buyer, and later, prior to delivery, *orally* agree that the seller shall stain the table and that the buyer shall pay a price of $550, the modified contract is unenforceable. In contrast, if the parties have a written contract for the sale of 150 bushels of wheat at a price of $4.50 per bushel and, later, orally agree to decrease the quantity to 100 bushels at the same price per bushel, the agreement, as modified, is enforceable.

Written compliance the
Code requires some writing
or writings sufficient to
indicate that a contract has
been made between the
parties, signed by the party
against whom enforcement is
sought or by her authorized
agent or broker, and
including a term specifying
the quantity of goods

Written Compliance The statute of frauds compliance provisions under the Code are more liberal than the rules under general contract law. The Code requires merely some writing (1) sufficient to indicate that a contract has been made between the parties, (2) signed by the party against whom enforcement is sought or by her authorized agent or broker, and (3) including a term specifying the quantity of goods to be exchanged. Whereas general contract law requires that the writing include all essential terms, under the Code a writing may be sufficient even if it omits or incorrectly states an agreed-upon term. This is consistent with other provisions of the Code that permit contracts to be enforced even though material terms are omitted. Nevertheless, the contract is enforceable only to the extent of the quantity of goods stated. Given proof that a contract was intended and that a signed writing describes the goods, the quantity of goods, and the names of the parties, the court, under the Code, can supply omitted terms such as price and particulars of performance. Moreover, several related documents together may satisfy the writing requirement.

Between merchants, a written confirmation, if sufficient against the sender, is also sufficient against the recipient unless the recipient gives written notice of her objection within ten days after receiving the confirmation.

Exceptions A contract that does not satisfy the writing requirement but is otherwise valid is enforceable in the following instances.

The Code permits an oral contract for the sale of goods to be enforced against a party who in his pleading, testimony, or otherwise in court ***admits*** that a contract was made; but the Code limits enforcement to the quantity of goods he admits. This provision recognizes that the policy behind the statute of frauds does not apply when the party seeking to avoid the oral contract admits under oath the existence of the contract.

The Code also permits enforcement of an oral contract for goods *specially manufactured* for the buyer. Nevertheless, if the goods are readily marketable in the ordinary course of the seller's business, even though they were manufactured on special order, the contract is not enforceable unless it is in writing.

Under the Code, delivery and acceptance of part of the goods or payment and acceptance of part of the price validates the contract, but only for the goods that have been *delivered and accepted* or for which *payment* has been *accepted*. To illustrate, Debra orally agrees to buy 1,000 watches from Brian for $15,000. Brian delivers 300 watches to Debra, who receives and accepts them. The oral contract is enforceable to the extent of 300 watches ($4,500)—those received and accepted—but is unenforceable to the extent of 700 watches ($10,500).

Parol Evidence

Contractual terms that are set forth in a writing intended by the parties as a final expression of their agreement may not be contradicted by evidence of any prior agreement or of a contemporaneous oral agreement, but, under the Code, the terms may be explained or supplemented by (a) course of dealing, usage of trade, or course of performance, and (b) evidence of consistent additional terms, unless the writing was intended as the complete and exclusive statement of the terms of the agreement.

Parol evidence contractual terms that are set forth in a writing intended by the parties as a final expression of their agreement may not be contradicted by evidence of any prior agreement or of a contemporaneous oral agreement, but such terms may be explained or supplemented by course of dealing, usage of trade, course of performance, or consistent additional evidence

Seal

The Code makes seals inoperative with respect to contracts for the sale of goods or an offer to buy or sell goods.

For a comparison of general contract law and the law governing the sale of goods, see Figure 19–2.

FIGURE 19–2 Contract Law Compared with Law of Sales

	Contract	**Law of Sales**
Definiteness	Contract must include all material terms.	Open terms permitted if parties intend to make a contract.
Counteroffers	Acceptance must be a mirror image of offer. Counteroffer and conditional acceptance are rejections.	Battle of Forms, see Figure 19–1.
Modification of Contract	Consideration is required.	Consideration is not required.
Irrevocable Offers	Options.	Options. Firm offers up to three months' duration binding without consideration.
Statute of Frauds	Writing must include all material terms.	Writing must include quantity term. Specially manufactured goods. Confirmation by merchants. Delivery or payment and acceptance. Admissions.

THE LAW AND YOU Buying a Car

Buying a Car

The purchase of a new or used car will probably be one of your biggest expenditures outside of purchasing a home. How can you be sure you will get what you are paying for?

The ISBA [Illinois State Bar Association] suggests you consider a number of things before you make this investment.

Before You Buy

Begin by deciding what things you need your car to do and what cars are available. Consider what size car you need, what type of car you want, and how much you can afford to spend. Publications like *Consumer Reports* offer reviews and repair records for most domestic and foreign vehicles. Your insurance company may have safety information and records. A little work before you buy can prevent disappointment later.

If you are interested in a particular car, ask your salesperson for a written proposal. This should give you a figure with all charges and credits, such as trade-in, dealer preparation fees, taxes, and other charges. You can then compare this proposal with other dealerships' proposals.

Do not make your final decision on the spur of the moment. Reputable dealerships will not try to force you into an immediate sale because they are confident that their proposal is comparable to that of their competitors. Except for scarce vehicles and year-end models, new car dealers can probably obtain a similar car to sell to you in the near future should the car you are interested in be sold.

Borrowing Money

If you are not going to purchase a car for cash, call your lending institution for their finance rate before you go shopping for a car. You can then compare their rate with the financing made available through the dealership. You may also want to consider leasing as an alternative to an outright loan. Lease payments are generally less than loan payments, but you need to remember that you will not own the car when the lease ends.

Review all documents carefully before you sign them. They should set out everything you have agreed to, including price, interest rates, length of payments and total cost of the vehicle including all charges.

Make sure that you understand all of the other terms of the financing agreement, especially what happens if you are late or miss a payment.

Checking Over a Used Car

When you buy a used car, you should let an independent mechanic check the car. The mechanic can estimate mileage based on tire and brake wear, and the general condition of the car. In many cases he can advise you of potential problems and the cost of repairing those problems if they are not covered under any warranty.

Prior to buying a used car, you may wish to learn the names of the previous owners to check with them about problems they've had with the vehicle. You may determine this by obtaining a copy of the vehicle identification number for the vehicle and inquiring with the Secretary of State, Dept. of Motor Vehicles to obtain a history of ownership.

State and federal law require accurate odometer (mileage meter) readings. These laws require the seller to record on the title the odometer reading at the time of transfer, the date of the transfer and the seller's name and address. An odometer which shows fewer miles than that recorded on the transfer statement or a transfer statement that indicates that the true mileage is unknown, should raise a red flag to the buyer and the consumer should take extra care in examining this car.

After You Buy

A new vehicle is covered by a manufacturer's warranty. You should make sure the dealer explains to you the terms of the warranty, its length, and what is not covered. Most manufacturers have a customer service network that works with customers who are not satisfied with their new car. Many manufacturers also have an independent arbitration system in place to deal with customer problems. These channels for customer relief will be set out in the new car warranty.

A buyer of a new car may also seek relief under state or federal statutes. In Illinois, a buyer may be able to obtain a replacement vehicle or a refund of part or all of the purchase price if: a) the car has a defect which substantially impairs the value, the safety or the use of the car; b) the defect occurs within 12 months or 12,000 miles (whichever occurs first after delivery); and c) the seller is unable to correct the defect after a reasonable time. Reasonable time generally means after four (4) or more repair attempts for the same problem or if the car is out of service for thirty (30) days or more. The buyer must give the seller a reasonable opportunity to repair the vehicle prior to taking advantage of these statutes.

Purchasing a used car is another matter. Used cars may be sold "as is" or with a limited warranty. If you purchase a car "as is" you are obtaining no warranty and in most cases the dealer is not obligated to stand by any oral representations he may have made prior to the purchase. If you are buying a car "as is" and the

continued

dealer has made certain representations about the car or has promised to repair certain problems with the car, get these promises in **writing**. Make the dealer set out what he is willing to do on the bill of sale. If the vehicle has a limited warranty, make sure the dealer puts in writing what the warranty is, what it covers, and how long it lasts. Obtaining representations or promises in writing will eliminate problems later on.

If the car you buy does not work as promised, or if the seller will not make repairs as promised, you have several options. One option would be to sue under the Illinois Consumer Fraud and Deceptive Business Practices Act. If successful,

you might be able to force a dealer to repair the problem, and also to pay your attorneys' fees. If the misrepresentations are serious, the Court could find that the dealer must buy back the vehicle. Another alternative would be to file a complaint with the Attorney General's office. The Attorney General's Office may be able to contact the dealer and resolve the complaint to the satisfaction of all parties. If the Attorney General's Office receives a number of complaints about a dealership, it may initiate further action on behalf of the complaining consumers under the Illinois Consumer Fraud and Deceptive Business Practices Act.

If you notice problems with either a new or used vehicle, keep written records of all of your complaints as problems occur. Keep copies of all of your repair orders and receipts even if a warranty covers the repair cost. Complete and accurate records will greatly increase your chances of achieving the results you want should it be necessary to go to arbitration or to file suit.

Reprinted with permission from the Illinois State Bar Association. Copyright, Illinois State Bar Association, 1990. This pamphlet is prepared and published by the Illinois State Bar Association as a public service. Its purpose is to inform citizens of their legal rights and obligations. Consult your lawyer if you have questions about application of the law in a particular case.

CHAPTER SUMMARY

Nature of Sales Contracts

Definitions	**Sale** transfer of title to goods from seller to buyer for a price **Goods** movable personal property **Governing Law** ■ *Sales Transactions* governed by Article 2 of the Code, except where general contract law has not been specifically modified by the Code, general contract law continues to apply ■ *Transactions outside the Code* include employment contracts, service contracts, insurance contracts, contracts involving real property, and contracts for the sale of intangibles
Fundamental Principles of Article 2	**Purpose** to modernize, clarify, simplify, and make uniform the law of sales **Good Faith** the Code requires all sales contracts to be performed in good faith, which means honesty in fact in the conduct or transaction concerned; in the case of a merchant, it also includes the observance of reasonable commercial standards **Unconscionability** a court may refuse to enforce an unconscionable contract or any part of a contract found to be unconscionable ■ *Procedural Unconscionability* unfairness of the bargaining process ■ *Substantive Unconscionability* oppressive or grossly unfair contractual provisions

Expansion of Commercial Practices
- *Course of Dealing* a sequence of previous conduct between the parties establishing a common basis for interpreting their agreement
- *Usage of Trade* a practice or method of dealing regularly observed and followed in a place, vocation, or trade

Sales by and Between Merchants the Code establishes separate rules that apply to transactions between merchants or involving a merchant (a dealer in goods or a person who by his occupation holds himself out as having knowledge or skill peculiar to the goods or practices involved, or who employs an agent or broker whom he holds out as having such knowledge or skill)

Liberal Administration of Remedies

Freedom of Contract most provisions of the Code may be varied by agreement

Validation and Preservation of Sales Contract the Code reduces formal requisites to the bare minimum and attempts to preserve agreements whenever the parties manifest an intention to enter into a contract

---

Fundamentals of Article 2A—Leases

Definition a transfer of right to possession and use of goods in return for consideration

Warranties applies Article 2 warranty provisions with relatively minor revision

Default and Remedies article provides both for lessor's remedies upon the lessee's default and for lessee's remedies upon the lessor's default

Consumer Leases Article 2A affords special protection for consumer leases

Finance Leases special type of lease transaction generally involving three parties instead of two

---

Formation of a Sales Contract

Manifestation of Mutual Assent

Definiteness of an Offer the Code provides that a contract does not fail for indefiniteness even though one or more terms may have been omitted; the Code provides standards by which missing essential terms may be supplied

Irrevocable offers
- *Option* a contract to hold open an offer
- *Firm Offer* a signed writing by a merchant to hold open an offer for the purchase or sale of goods for a maximum of three months

Variant Acceptances the inclusion of different or additional terms in an acceptance is addressed by focusing on the intent of the parties

Manner of Acceptance an acceptance can be made in any reasonable manner and is effective upon dispatch

---

Consideration

Contractual Modifications the Code provides that a contract for the sale of goods may be modified without new consideration if the modification is made in good faith

Firm Offers are not revocable for lack of consideration

Form of the Contract	**Statute of Frauds** sale of goods costing $500 or more must be evidenced by a signed writing to be enforceable ■ ***Written Compliance*** the Code requires some writing or writings sufficient to indicate that a contract has been made between the parties, signed by the party against whom enforcement is sought or by her authorized agent or broker, and including a term specifying the quantity of goods ■ ***Alternative Methods of Compliance*** written confirmation between merchants, admission, specially manufactured goods, and delivery or payment and acceptance **Parol Evidence** contractual terms that are set forth in a writing intended by the parties as a final expression of their agreement may not be contradicted by evidence of any prior agreement or of a contemporaneous oral agreement, but such terms may be explained or supplemented by course of dealing, usage of trade, course of performance, or consistent additional evidence

QUESTIONS

1. Distinguish a sale from a lease of personal property.
2. Identify and discuss the fundamental principles of Article 2.
3. Discuss how Article 2 has changed the need for an offer to include all material terms.
4. Distinguish between the common law's mirror image rule and the Code's provisions for dealing with variant acceptances.
5. Discuss (a) the Code's approach to the requirement that certain contracts must be in writing and (b) the alternative methods of compliance.

Internet Question. Compare the provisions governing the formation of sales contracts under the United Nations Convention on Contracts for the International Sale of Goods (Vienna, 1980) with the provisions of Article 2 of the Uniform Commercial Code.

PROBLEMS

1. Dickison orders 1,000 widgets at $5 per widget from International Widget to be delivered within sixty days. After the contract is consummated and signed, Dickison orally requests that International deliver the widgets within thirty days rather than sixty days. International agrees. Is the contractual modification binding?

2. In question 1, what effect, if any, would the following telegram have?

   International Widget:

   In accordance with our agreement of this date you will deliver the 1,000 previously ordered widgets within thirty days. Thank you for your cooperation in this matter.

   (signed) Dickison

3. Hicks, a San Francisco company, orders from U.S. Electronics, a New York company, 10,000 electronic units. Hicks's order form provides that any dispute would be resolved by an arbitration panel located in San Francisco. U.S. Electronics executes and delivers to Hicks its acknowledgment form accepting the order and containing the following provision: "All disputes will be resolved by the state courts of New York." A dispute arises concerning the workmanship of the parts, and Hicks wishes the case to be arbitrated in San Francisco. What result?

4. Explain how the result in problem 3 might change if the U.S. Electronics form contained the following provisions:
   (a) "The seller's acceptance of the purchase order to which this acknowledgment responds is expressly made conditional on the buyer's assent to any or different terms contained in this acknowledgment."
   (b) "The seller's acceptance of the purchase order is subject to the terms and conditions on the face and reverse side hereof, which the buyer accepts by accepting the goods described herein."

(c) "The seller's terms govern this agreement—this acknowledgment merely constitutes a counter-offer."

5. Reinfort executed a written contract with Bylinski to purchase an assorted collection of shoes for $3,000. A week before the agreed shipment date, Bylinski called Reinfort and said, "We cannot deliver at $3,000; unless you agree to pay $4,000, we will cancel the order." After considerable discussion, Reinfort agreed to pay $4,000 if Bylinski would ship as agreed in the contract. After the shoes had been delivered and accepted by Reinfort, Reinfort refused to pay $4,000 and insisted on paying only $3,000. Decision?

6. On November 23, Blackburn, a dress manufacturer, mailed to Conroy a written and signed offer to sell 1,000 sundresses at $50 per dress. The offer stated that it would "remain open for ten days" and that it could "not be withdrawn prior to that date."

Two days later, Blackburn, noting a sudden increase in the price of sundresses, changed his mind. Blackburn therefore sent Conroy a letter revoking the offer. The letter was sent on November 25 and received by Conroy on November 28.

Conroy chose to disregard the letter of November 25; instead, she happily continued to watch the price of sundresses rise. On December 1, Conroy sent a letter accepting the original offer. The letter, however, was not received by Blackburn until December 9, due to a delay in the mails.

Conroy has demanded delivery of the goods according to the terms of the offer of November 23, but Blackburn has refused. Decision?

7. Henry and Wilma, an elderly immigrant couple, agreed to purchase from Harris a refrigerator with a fair market value of $450 for twenty-five monthly installments of $60 per month. Henry and Wilma now wish to void the contract, asserting that they did not realize the exorbitant price they were paying. Result?

8. Courts Distributors needed 200 compact refrigerators on a rush basis. It contacted Eastinghouse Corporation, a manufacturer of refrigerators. Eastinghouse said it would take some time to quote a price on an order of that size. Courts replied, "Send the refrigerators immediately and bill us later." The refrigerators were delivered three days later, and the invoice arrived ten days after that. The invoice price was $140,000. Courts believes that the wholesale market price of the refrigerators is only $120,000. Discuss.

9. While adjusting a television antenna beside his mobile home and underneath a high-voltage electric transmission wire, Prince received an electric shock resulting in personal injury. He claims the high-voltage electric current jumped from the transmission wire to the antenna. The wire, which carried some 7,200 volts of electricity, did not serve his mobile home but ran directly above it. Prince sued the Navarro County Electric Co-Op, the owner and operator of the wire, for breach of implied warranty of merchantability under the Uniform Commercial Code. He contends that the Code's implied warranty of merchantability extends to the container of a product—in this instance the wiring—and that the escape of the current shows that the wiring was unfit for its purpose of transporting electricity. The electric company argues that the electricity passing through the transmission wire was not being sold to Prince and that, therefore, there was no sale of goods to Prince. Decision?

10. HMT, already in the business of marketing agricultural products, decided to try its hand at marketing potatoes for processing. Nine months before the potato harvest, HMT contracted to supply Bell Brand with 100,000 sacks of potatoes. At harvest time, Bell Brand would only accept 60,000 sacks. HMT sues for breach of contract. Bell Brand argues that custom and usage in marketing processing potatoes allows buyers to give *estimates* in contracts, not fixed quantities, since the contracts are established so far in advance. HMT responds that the quantity term in the contract was definite and unambiguous. Can custom and trade usage be used to interpret an unambiguous contract? Discuss.

11. Schreiner, a cotton farmer, agreed over the telephone to sell 150 bales of cotton to Loeb & Co. Schreiner had sold cotton to Loeb & Co. for the past five years. Written confirmation of the date, parties, price, and conditions was mailed to Schreiner, who did not respond to the confirmation in any way. Four months later, when the price of cotton had doubled, Loeb & Co. sought to enforce the contract. Is the contract enforceable?

12. American Sand & Gravel Inc. agreed to sell sand to Clark at a special discount if 20,000–25,000 tons were ordered. The discount price was 45¢ per ton, compared to the normal price of 55¢ per ton. Two years later, Clark orders, and receives, 1,600 tons of sand from American Sand & Gravel. Clark refuses to pay more than 45¢ per ton. American Sand & Gravel sues for the remaining 10¢ per ton. Decision?

13. In September 1973, Auburn Plastics (defendant) submitted price quotations to CBS (plaintiff) for the manufacture of eight cavity molds to be used in making parts for CBS's toys. Each quotation specified that the offer would not be binding unless accepted within fifteen days. Furthermore, CBS would be subject to an additional 30-percent charge for engineering services upon delivery of the molds. In December 1973 and January 1974, CBS sent detailed purchase orders to Auburn Plastics for cavity molds. The purchase order forms stated that CBS reserved the right to

remove the molds from Auburn Plastics without an additional or "withdrawal" charge. Auburn Plastics acknowledged the purchase order and stated that the sale would be subject to all conditions contained in the price quotation. CBS paid Auburn for the molds, and Auburn began to fabricate toy parts from the molds for CBS. Later, Auburn announced a price increase, and CBS demanded delivery of the molds. Auburn refused to deliver the molds unless CBS paid the additional charge for engineering services. CBS claimed that the contract did not provide for a withdrawal charge. Decision?

14. Terminal Grain Corporation brought an action against Glen Freeman, a farmer, to recover damages for breach of an oral contract to deliver grain. According to the company, Freeman orally agreed to two sales of wheat to Terminal Grain of 4,000 bushels each at $1.65 a bushel and $1.71 a bushel, respectively. Dwayne Maher, merchandising manager of Terminal Grain, sent two written confirmations of the agreements to Freeman. Freeman never made any written objections to the confirmations. After the first transaction had occurred, the price of wheat rose to between $2.25 and $2.30 per bushel, and Freeman refused to deliver the remaining 4,000 bushels at the agreed-upon price. Freeman denies entering into any agreement to sell the second 4,000 bushels of wheat to Terminal Grain but admits that he received the two written confirmations sent by Maher. Decision?

15. The defendant, Gray Communications, desired to build a television tower. After a number of negotiation sessions conducted by telephone between the defendant and the plaintiff, Kline Iron, the parties allegedly reached an oral agreement under which the plaintiff would build a tower for the defendant for a total price of $1,485,368. A few days later, the plaintiff sent a written document, referred to as a proposal, for execution by the defendant. The proposal indicated that it had been prepared for immediate acceptance by the defendant and that prior to formal acceptance by the defendant it could be modified or withdrawn without notice. A few days later, without having executed the proposal, the defendant advised the plaintiff that a competitor had provided a lower bid for construction of the tower. The defendant requested that the plaintiff explain its higher bid price, which the plaintiff failed to do. The defendant then advised the plaintiff by letter that it would not be retained to construct the tower. The plaintiff then commenced suit, alleging breach of an oral contract, and asserting that the oral agreement was enforceable because the common law of contracts, not the UCC, governed the transaction and that under the common law a writing is not necessary to cover this type of transaction. Even if the transaction was subject to the UCC, the plaintiff alternatively argued, the contract was within the UCC "merchant's exception." Decision?

CHAPTER 20

Performance

Performance fulfillment of a contractual obligation

Performance is the process of discharging contractual obligations by carrying out those obligations according to a contract's terms. The basic obligation of the seller in a contract for the sale of goods is to transfer and deliver goods that conform to the terms of the contract. The basic obligation of the buyer is to accept and pay for conforming goods in accordance with the contract. A contract of sale also requires that each party not impair the other party's expectation of having the contract performed.

The obligations of the parties are determined by their contractual agreement. Thus, the contract of sale may expressly state, for example, whether the seller must deliver the goods before receiving payment of the price or whether the buyer must pay the price before receiving the goods. If the contract does not sufficiently cover the particulars of performance, these terms will be supplied by the Code, common law, course of dealings, usage of trade, and course of performance. In all events, both parties to the sales contract must perform their contractual obligations in good faith.

In this chapter, we will examine the performance obligations of the seller and the buyer as well as the contractual obligations that apply to both of them.

PERFORMANCE BY THE SELLER

Unless the parties have agreed otherwise, tender (offer) of performance by one party is a condition to performance by the other party. Tender of conforming goods by the seller entitles him to acceptance of them by the buyer and to payment of the contractually agreed-upon price. Nonetheless, the terms of the contract may establish other rights for the parties. For example, if the seller has agreed to sell goods on sixty or ninety days' credit, he is required to perform his part of the contract by delivering the goods before the buyer performs.

Tender of delivery seller makes available to buyer goods conforming to the contract and so notifies the buyer

Tender of delivery requires that the seller put and hold goods that conform to the contract at the buyer's disposition and that he give the buyer reasonable notification to enable her to take delivery. Tender must also be made at a reasonable time and be kept open for a reasonable period. For example, Jim agrees to sell Joan a stereo system composed of a CD player, a receiver, a tape deck, and two speakers. Each component is specified by manufacturer and model number, and delivery is to be at Jim's store. Jim obtains the ordered equipment in accordance with the contractual specifications and notifies Joan that she may pick up the system at her convenience. Jim has now tendered and thus has performed his obligations under the sales contract: he holds goods that conform to the contract, he has placed them at the buyer's disposition, and he has notified the buyer of their readiness.

Time and Manner of Tender

Tender must be at a *reasonable* time, and the goods tendered must be kept available for the period reasonably necessary to enable the buyer to take possession of them. If the contract terms set no definite time for delivery, the seller is allowed a reasonable time after entering into the contract within which to tender the goods to the buyer. Likewise, the buyer has a reasonable time within which to accept delivery. What length of time is reasonable depends on the facts and circumstances of each case.

A contract may not be performed piecemeal or in installments unless the parties specifically so agree. Otherwise, all of the goods called for by a contract must be tendered in a single delivery; and payment is due at the time of such tender.

> **Time of tender** tender must be made at a reasonable time and kept open for a reasonable period of time

Place of Tender

If the contract does not specify the place for delivery of the goods, the place for delivery is the *seller's place of business* or, if he has no place of business, his residence. If the contract is for the sale of identified goods that the parties know at the time of making the contract are not located either at the seller's place of business or at his residence, the *location* of the goods is then the place for delivery.

The parties frequently agree expressly on the place of tender, typically by using one of the various *delivery terms*. These terms specify whether the contract is a shipment or destination contract and determine where the seller must tender delivery of the goods.

> **Place of tender** if none is specified, place for delivery is the seller's place of business or, if he has no such place, his residence

Shipment Contracts

The delivery terms *F.O.B. place of shipment, F.A.S. seller's port, C.I.F.,* and *C. & F.* are all shipment contracts. Under a **shipment contract**, the seller is required or authorized to send the goods to the buyer, but the contract does not obligate her to deliver them at a particular destination. In these cases, the seller's tender of performance occurs at the point of shipment, provided the seller meets certain specified conditions designed to protect the interests of the absent buyer.

The initials **F.O.B.** and **F.A.S.** mean "free on board" and "free alongside," respectively. Under the Code, these are delivery terms, even though they are used only in connection with a stated price. A contract providing that the sale is *F.O.B. place of shipment* or *F.A.S. port of shipment* is a shipment contract. Under a **C.I.F.** ("cost, insurance, and freight") contract, in consideration for an agreed unit price for the goods, the seller pays all costs of transportation, insurance, and freight to the destination. Under a **C. & F.** contract, he will pay "cost and freight."

A seller under a shipment contract is required to (1) deliver the goods to a carrier; (2) make a contract for their transportation that is reasonable according to the nature of the goods and other circumstances; (3) obtain and promptly deliver or tender to the buyer any document necessary to enable the buyer to obtain possession of the goods from the carrier; and (4) promptly notify the buyer of the shipment.

> **Shipment contract** seller is required to tender delivery of the goods to a carrier for delivery to buyer

> **F.O.B.** free on board
>
> **F.A.S.** free alongside
>
> **C.I.F.** cost, insurance, and freight: a shipment contract
>
> **C. & F.** cost and freight: a shipment contract

Destination Contracts

The delivery terms *F.O.B. city of buyer, ex-ship,* and *no arrival, no sale* are destination contracts. Since a **destination contract** requires the seller to *tender* delivery of conforming goods at a *specified*

> **Destination contract** seller is required to tender delivery of the goods at a named destination

destination, the seller must place the goods at the buyer's disposition and give the buyer reasonable notice to enable him to take delivery. In addition, if the destination contract involves documents of title, the seller must tender the necessary documents.

Where the contract provides that the sale is *F.O.B. place of destination,* the seller must at his own expense and risk transport the goods to that place and there tender delivery of them to the buyer. For example, if the buyer is in Boston and the seller is in Chicago, a contract providing F.O.B. Boston is a destination contract under which the seller must tender the goods at the designated place in Boston at his own expense and risk. A contract that provides for delivery **ex-ship**, or "from the ship," is also a destination contract, requiring the seller to unload the goods from the carrier at a named destination. Finally, if the contract contains the terms "**no arrival, no sale**," the title and risk of loss do not pass to the buyer until the seller makes a tender of the goods after they arrive at their destination.

> **Ex-ship** "from the ship": a destination contract
>
> **No arrival, no sale** a destination contract, but if goods do not arrive, seller is excused from liability unless it is due to the seller's fault
>
> **Goods held by bailee** seller must either tender to the buyer a document of title or obtain an acknowledgment from the bailee

Goods Held by Bailee   Where goods are in the possession of a bailee and are to be delivered without being moved, in most instances the seller may either tender to the buyer a document of title or obtain an acknowledgment by the bailee of the buyer's right to possess the goods. This acknowledgment permits the buyer to obtain the goods directly from the bailee.

For a summary of performance by the seller, see Figure 20–1.

Perfect Tender Rule

> **Perfect tender rule** seller's tender of performance must conform exactly to the contract, subject to
> (1) agreement of parties
> (2) cure by seller, and
> (3) installment contracts

The Code's **perfect tender rule** imposes on the seller the obligation to conform her tender of goods *exactly* to the terms of the contract. If either the tender of delivery or the goods fail in any respect to conform to the contract, the buyer may (1) reject the whole lot, (2) accept the whole lot, or (3) accept any commercial unit or units and reject the rest. A *commercial unit* means such a unit of goods that by commercial usage is a single unit and that, if divided, would be materially impaired in character or value.

Thus, a buyer may rightfully reject the delivery of 110 dozen shirts under an agreement calling for delivery of 100 dozen shirts. The size or extent of the breach does *not* affect the right to reject. The following case further illustrates the perfect tender rule.

MOULTON CAVITY & MOLD INC. v. LYN-FLEX IND. Supreme Court of Maine, 1979, 396 A.2d 1024

FACTS Moulton Cavity & Mold Inc. agreed to manufacture twenty-six innersole molds to be purchased by Lyn-Flex. Moulton delivered the twenty-six molds to Lyn-Flex after Lyn-Flex allegedly approved the sample molds. However, Lyn-Flex rejected the molds, claiming that they did not satisfy the specifications exactly, and denied that it had ever approved the sample molds. Moulton then sued, contending that Lyn-Flex wrongfully rejected the molds. Lyn-Flex, arguing that the Code's perfect tender rule permitted its rejection of the imperfect molds, regardless of Moulton's substantial performance, appealed from a judgment entered by the trial court in favor of Moulton.

DECISION Judgment for Moulton reversed and a new trial ordered.

OPINION Under the Code's perfect tender provision, "if the goods or the tender of delivery fail in any respect to conform to the contract, the buyer may reject the whole." Therefore, Moulton's substantial performance does not obligate Lyn-Flex to accept the molds. If they failed to meet the contract's specifications in any respect, Lyn-Flex was entitled to reject them without liability.

INTERPRETATION If the seller does not perform his contractual obligations exactly, the buyer may rightfully reject the seller's performance.

FIGURE 20–1 Tender of Performance by Seller

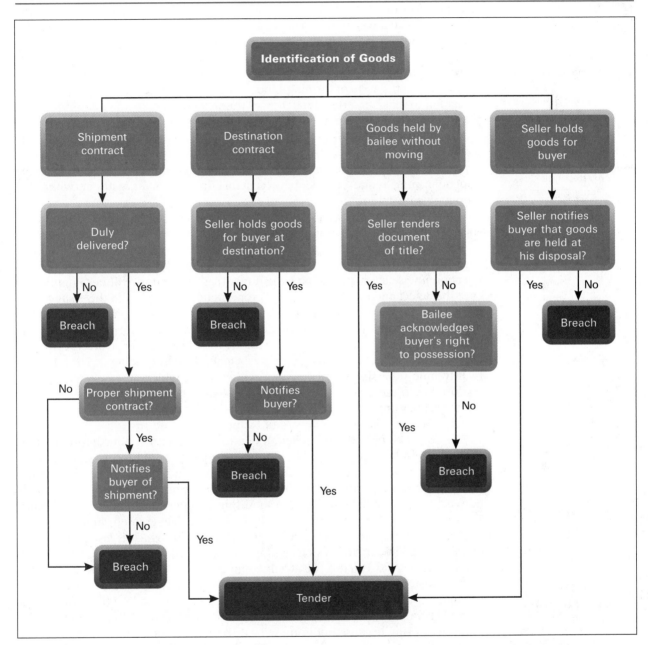

Three basic conditions qualify the buyer's right to reject the goods upon the seller's failure to comply with the perfect tender rule: (1) agreement between the parties limiting the buyer's right to reject nonconforming goods, (2) cure by the seller, and (3) the existence of an installment contract. In addition, the perfect tender rule does not apply to a seller's breach of her obligation under a shipment contract to make a proper contract for transportation or to give proper notice of the shipment. A failure to perform either of these obligations is a ground for rejection only if material loss or delay results.

Agreement Between the Parties The parties may contractually agree to limit the operation of the perfect tender rule. For example, they may agree that the seller shall have the right to repair or replace any defective parts or goods. We will discuss these contractual limitations in Chapter 23.

Cure by the Seller The Code recognizes two situations in which a seller may *cure*, or correct, a nonconforming tender of goods. This relaxation of the seller's obligation to make a perfect tender gives the seller an opportunity either to make a second delivery or to make a substitute tender. The first opportunity for cure occurs when the time for performance under the contract has not expired. The second opportunity for cure is available after the time for performance has expired but only if the seller had reasonable grounds to believe that the nonconforming tender would be acceptable to the buyer with or without a monetary adjustment.

Where the buyer refuses to accept a tender of goods that do not conform to the contract, the seller, by acting promptly and within the time allowed for performance, may make a proper tender or delivery of conforming goods and thereby cure his defective tender or performance. Upon notice of the buyer's rightful rejection, the seller must first give the buyer reasonable notice of her intention to cure the defect and must then make a proper tender according to the *original* contract. This rule gives the seller the full contractual period in which to perform but does not cause any harm to the buyer, who receives full performance within the time agreed to in the contract. For example, Neal is to deliver to Jessica twenty-five blue shirts and fifty white shirts by October 15. On October 1, Neal delivers twenty-nine blue shirts and forty-six white shirts, which Jessica rejects as not conforming to the contract. Jessica notifies Neal of her rejection and the reasons for it. Neal has until October 15 to cure the defect by making a perfect tender, provided he seasonably notifies Jessica of his intention to do so.

The Code also provides the seller an opportunity to cure a nonconforming tender that the seller had reasonable grounds to believe would be acceptable to the buyer with or without a money allowance. If, on the buyer's notice of rejection, the seller seasonably notifies the buyer of his intention to cure, the seller is permitted a reasonable time in which to substitute a conforming tender. For example, Tim orders from Noel a model 110X television to be delivered on January 20. The 110X is unavailable, but Noel can obtain a model 110, which is last year's model of the same television and which lists for 5 percent less than the 110X. On January 20, Noel delivers to Tim the 110 at a discount price of 10 percent less than the contract price for the 110X. Tim rejects the substituted television set. Noel, who promptly notifies Tim that she will obtain and deliver a model 110X, will have a reasonable time beyond the January 20 deadline in which to deliver the 110X television set to Tim, because under these facts she had reasonable grounds to believe the model 110 would be acceptable with the money allowance in Tim's favor.

Installment Contracts Unless the parties have otherwise agreed, the buyer does not have to pay any part of the price of the goods until the seller has delivered or tendered to her the entire quantity specified in the contract. An **installment contract** represents an instance in which the parties have otherwise agreed. It expressly provides for delivery of the goods in separate lots or installments and usually provides for payment of the price in installments. If the contract is silent about payment, the Code provides that the seller may demand the price, if it can be apportioned, for each lot.

Agreement between the parties the parties may contractually limit the operation of the perfect tender rule

Cure by the seller when the time for performance under the contract has not expired or when the seller has shipped nonconforming goods in the belief that the nonconforming tender would be acceptable, a seller may cure or correct his nonconforming tender

Installment contracts when the contract calls for the goods to be delivered in separate lots, the buyer may reject a nonconforming installment if it substantially impairs the value of that installment and cannot be cured; but if nonconformity or default of one or more of the installments substantially impairs the value of the whole contract, the buyer can treat the breach as a breach of the whole contract

Although the buyer may reject any nonconforming installment if the non-conformity *substantially* impairs the value of *that installment* and cannot be cured, the buyer cannot reject the installment if the installment substantially impairs the value of the installment but not the value of the entire contract if the seller gives adequate assurance of the installment's cure. However, whenever the nonconformity or default of one or more of the installments substantially impairs the value of the *whole contract*, the buyer can treat the breach as a breach of the whole contract.

PERFORMANCE BY THE BUYER

A buyer is obliged to accept conforming goods and to pay for them according to the contract terms. Payment or tender of payment by the buyer, unless otherwise agreed, is a condition of the seller's duty to tender and to complete any delivery. The buyer is not obliged to accept a tender or delivery of goods that do not conform to the contract. Upon determining that the tender or delivery is nonconforming, the buyer has three choices. He may (1) reject all of the goods, (2) accept all of the goods, or (3) accept any commercial unit or units of the goods and reject the rest. The buyer must pay the contract rate for the commercial units he accepts.

Inspection

Unless the parties agree otherwise, the buyer has a right to inspect the goods before payment or acceptance. This **inspection** enables her to determine whether the goods tendered or delivered conform to the contract. If the contract requires payment before acceptance (where, for example, the contract provides for shipment C.O.D., collect on delivery), payment must be made prior to inspection; however, such payment is not an acceptance of the goods and impairs neither the buyer's right to inspect nor any of her remedies.

Inspection unless otherwise agreed, the buyer has a reasonable time in which to inspect the goods before payment or acceptance to determine whether they conform

The buyer, allowed a reasonable time to inspect the goods, may lose the right to reject or revoke acceptance of nonconforming goods by failing to inspect them within such time. Nevertheless, although the buyer must bear the expenses of inspection, she may recover them from the seller if the goods do not conform and are rightfully rejected.

Rejection

Rejection is a manifestation by the buyer of her unwillingness to become owner of the goods. It must be made within a reasonable time after the goods have been tendered or delivered and is not effective unless the buyer reasonably notifies the seller.

Rejection buyer's manifestation of unwillingness to become the owner of the goods; must be made within a reasonable time after the goods have been tendered or delivered and gives the buyer the right to
(1) reject the goods
(2) accept all of the goods, or
(3) accept any commercial unit(s) and reject the rest

Rejection of the goods may be rightful or wrongful, depending on whether the goods tendered or delivered conform to the contract. The buyer's rejection of nonconforming goods or tender is rightful under the perfect tender rule.

If the buyer refuses a tender of goods or rejects it as nonconforming without disclosing to the seller the nature of the defect, she may not assert such defect as an excuse for not accepting the goods or as a breach of contract by the seller if the defect is curable.

After the buyer has rejected the goods, the Code allows her to exercise no ownership of them. If the buyer possesses the rejected goods but has no security interest in them, she is obliged to hold them with reasonable care for a time sufficient to permit the seller to remove them. The buyer who is not a merchant is under no further obligation with regard to goods rightfully rejected.

However, a merchant buyer of goods who has rightfully rejected them is obligated to follow reasonable instructions from the seller regarding disposal of the goods in her possession or control when the seller has no agent or business at the place of rejection. If the merchant buyer receives no instructions from the seller within a reasonable time after giving notice of the rejection, and if the rejected goods are perishable or threaten to decline in value speedily, she is obligated to make reasonable efforts to sell them for the seller's account. Otherwise, she may (1) store the goods for the seller's account, (2) reship them to the seller, or (3) resell them for the seller's account. Such action is not an acceptance of the goods. When the buyer sells the rejected goods, she is entitled to reimbursement for the reasonable expenses of caring for and selling them and to a reasonable selling commission not to exceed 10 percent of the gross proceeds.

FURLONG v. ALPHA CHI OMEGA SORORITY Bowling Green County Municipal Court, 1993, 73 Ohio Misc.2d 26, 657 N.E.2d 866

FACTS Alpha Chi Omega (AXO) entered into an oral contract with Furlong to buy 168 "custom designed" sweaters for the Midnight Masquerade III. The purchase price of $3,612 was to be paid as follows: $2,000 down payment when the contract was made and $1,612 upon delivery. During phone conversations with Furlong, Emily, the AXO social chairperson, described the design to be imprinted on the sweater. She also specified the colors to be used in the lettering (hunter green on top of maroon outlined in navy blue) and the color of the mask design (hunter green). Furlong promised to have a third party imprint the sweaters as specified. Furlong later sent to Emily a sweater with maroon letters to show her the color. He then sent her a fax illustrating the sweater design with arrows indicating where each of the three colors was to appear. On the day before delivery was due, Argento, Furlong's supplier, requested design changes, which Furlong approved without the consent of AXO. These changes included deleting the navy blue outline, reducing the number of colors from three to two, changing the maroon lettering to red, and changing the color of the masks from hunter green to red. Upon delivery, AXO gave a check to Furlong's agent for the balance of the purchase price. Later that day, Emily inspected the sweaters and screamed her dismay at the design changes. AXO immediately stopped payment on the check. Amy, the president of AXO, phoned Furlong, stating that the sweaters were not what AXO had ordered. She gave the specifics as to why the sweaters were not as ordered and offered to return them. Furlong refused but offered to reduce the unit price of the sweaters if AXO agreed to accept them. AXO refused this offer. Furlong then filed suit against AXO for the unpaid portion of the sweaters' purchase price ($1,612) and AXO counterclaimed for return of the down payment ($2,000).

DECISION Judgment for AXO. The court ordered

Furlong to pay $2,000 plus interest and costs and AXO to return the sweaters upon such payment.

OPINION As this is a sale of goods, the provisions of the Uniform Commercial Code apply. The design specifications were part of the basis of the bargain and as such became an express warranty under U.C.C. §2-313. This warranty was created in three ways that are consistent and, therefore, cumulative (U.C.C. §2-317). First, Furlong's promise during the phone call to have the sweaters printed as specified was sufficient to have created an express warranty under U.C.C. §2-313(1)(a). Second, the sweater with maroon lettering that Furlong sent was sufficient to create an express warranty as a sample under subsection (1)(c). Third, Furlong's fax to Emily was sufficient to create an express warranty as a description under subsection (1)(b). By delivering nonconforming goods, Furlong breached the express warranty to meet the bargained-for specifications and, therefore, breached the contract. Since AXO seasonably notified the seller of the nonconformity by phone "within a reasonable time" (on the same day as delivery), its rejection of the goods was rightful under U.C.C. §2-602(1). Under U.C.C. §2-601(a), AXO was within its rights to reject the whole lot of sweaters: "if the goods . . . fail[ed] in any respect to conform to the contract, . . . " Here, the goods materially failed to conform in many respects. Since AXO never accepted the goods, the duty to pay the purchase price never arose (U.C.C. §2-607(1)). Therefore, AXO did not breach the contract. Moreover, although the law allowed AXO to accept Furlong's offer of compromise (U.C.C. §2-601(b)), it did not require AXO to do so. Finally, because Furlong breached the contract, AXO may cancel the contract and recover the partial payment of the contract price.

INTERPRETATION If the goods fail in any respect to conform to the contract, the buyer may reject the whole lot.

Acceptance

Acceptance of goods means a willingness by the buyer to become the owner of the goods tendered or delivered to her by the seller. Acceptance of the goods, which precludes any later rejection of them, includes overt acts or conduct that manifest such willingness. Such acts or conduct may include express words, the presumed intention of the buyer through her failure to act, or conduct of the buyer inconsistent with the seller's ownership of the goods. More specifically, acceptance occurs when the buyer, after a reasonable opportunity to inspect the goods (1) signifies to the seller that the goods conform to the contract, (2) signifies to the seller that she will take the goods or retain them in spite of their nonconformity to the contract, or (3) fails to make an effective rejection of the goods.

Acceptance of any part of a commercial unit is acceptance of the entire unit. The buyer must pay at the contract rate for any goods she accepts but may recover damages for any nonconformity of the goods, provided the buyer reasonably notifies the seller of any breach. For example, Nancy agrees to deliver to Paul 500 light bulbs, 100 watts each, for $300 and 1,000 light bulbs, 60 watts each, for $500. Nancy delivers on time, but the shipment contains only 400 of the 100-watt bulbs and 750 of the 60-watt bulbs. If Paul accepts the shipment, he must pay Nancy $240 for the 100-watt bulbs accepted and $375 for the 60-watt bulbs accepted, less the amount of damages Nancy's nonconforming delivery caused him.

> **Acceptance** buyer's express or implied manifestation of a willingness to become owner of the goods

Revocation of Acceptance

A buyer might accept defective goods either because it is difficult to discover the defect by inspection or because the buyer reasonably assumes that the seller will correct the defect. In either instance, the buyer may revoke his acceptance of the goods if the uncorrected defect substantially impairs the value of the goods to him. **Revocation of acceptance** gives the buyer the same rights and duties with respect to the goods as he would have acquired by rejecting them.

More specifically, the buyer may revoke his acceptance of goods that do not conform to the contract if the nonconformity *substantially* impairs the value of the goods to him, provided that his acceptance was (1) premised on the reasonable assumption that the seller would cure the nonconformity, and it was not seasonably cured or (2) made without discovery of the nonconformity, and such acceptance was reasonably induced by the difficulty of discovery before acceptance or by the seller's assurances. Determining substantial impairment of the value to the buyer of nonconforming goods is a *subjective* test, rather than an objective one.

Revocation of acceptance is not effective until notification is given to the seller. This, as stated in the case above, must be done within a reasonable time after the buyer discovers or should have discovered the grounds for revocation and before the goods have undergone any substantial change not caused by their own defects.

The following case deals with the question of whether a party forfeits the right to revoke an acceptance by the continuing use of a good.

> **Revocation of acceptance** rescission of buyer's acceptance of the goods if nonconformity of the goods substantially impairs their value, provided that the acceptance was (1) premised on the assumption that the nonconformity would be cured by the seller and it was not, or (2) the nonconformity was an undiscovered hidden defect

---

IN RE STEM Alabama Supreme Court, 1990, 571 So.2d 1112

FACTS On February 26, 1987, William Stem purchased a used BMW from Gary Braden for $6,600. Stem's primary purpose for buying the car was to use it to transport his child. Braden indicated to Stem that the car had not been wrecked and that it was in good condition. Stem thought the car had been driven only 70,000 miles. Less than a week after the purchase, Stem discovered a disconnected plug that, when plugged in, caused the oil warning light to turn on. When Stem then took his car to a mechanic, the mechanic discovered that the front end was that of a 1979 BMW and the rear end was that of a 1975 BMW. Further investigation

continued

revealed that the front half had been driven 170,000 miles. On March 10, 1987, Stem sent a letter informing Braden that he refused the automobile and that he intended to rescind the sale. Braden refused. Stem filed an action against Braden, seeking to rescind the sale, and the trial court awarded Stem the purchase price of the car, plus interest. The Court of Appeals reversed, holding that Stem had accepted the automobile by driving it for seven months and nearly 9,000 miles after sending the letter to Braden.

DECISION Decision of the Court of Appeals reversed and the case remanded.

OPINION Even if Stem had accepted the automobile, rescission may still have been available to him. The proper analysis is whether Stem revoked his acceptance of the sale under the UCC. Revocation of acceptance is available when the nonconformity is such as will in fact cause a substantial impairment of value to the buyer, even though the seller had no advance knowledge as to the buyer's particular circumstances.

The record of this case shows that the trial court could have found that the automobile's nonconformities substantially impaired its value to Stem. The court could also have found that Stem's acceptance was reasonably induced by Braden's assurances, that Stem revoked his acceptance within a reasonable time, and that he met the notice requirements of the UCC.

When Stem revoked his acceptance, he had the same rights and duties with regard to the automobile that he would have had, had he rejected it. After rejection, however, any exercise of ownership by the buyer with respect to any commercial unit is wrongful as against the seller. Consequently, although Stem revoked his acceptance, his continued use of the automobile was wrongful as against Braden, and the Court of Appeals accordingly held that the use constituted "acceptance." Nevertheless, the courts of many other states have held that in some circumstances continued use after revocation, although "wrongful," does not constitute acceptance. This reasoning is based on the fact that often it may be a financial burden for a party to do without an automobile until litigation is complete. These courts held, however, that such "wrongful" use by the buyer entitles the seller to prove the reasonable value of the use and to set off that amount from what the seller owes the buyer. In this case, it would have been a great burden on Stem to find another way to transport his child. Therefore, his use did not constitute an acceptance, but Braden may deduct the value of Stem's use from what he owes Stem.

INTERPRETATION After rightfully revoking acceptance, the buyer may continue to use the goods if such use is reasonable, but this use may entitle the seller to a setoff in the amount of the value of the buyer's use.

Obligation of Payment

Obligation of payment in the absence of an agreement, payment is due at the time and place the buyer is to receive the goods

The terms of the contract may expressly state the time and place at which the buyer is obligated to pay for the goods. If so, these terms are controlling. Thus, if the buyer has agreed to pay either the seller or a carrier for the goods in advance of delivery, his duty to pay is not conditional on performance or a tender of performance by the seller. Further, where the sale is on credit, the buyer is not obligated to pay for the goods when he receives them. The credit provision in the contract will control the time of payment.

In the absence of agreement, payment is due at the time and place the buyer is to receive the goods, even though the place of shipment is the place of delivery. This rule is understandable in view of the right of the buyer, in the absence of agreement to the contrary, to inspect the goods before being obliged to pay for them. Tender of payment is sufficient when made by any means or in any manner current, such as a check, in the ordinary course of business, unless the seller demands cash and allows the buyer a reasonable time within which to obtain it.

For a summary of performance by the buyer, see Figure 20–2.

OBLIGATIONS OF BOTH PARTIES

Contracts for the sale of goods necessarily involve risks concerning future events that may or may not occur. Though in some instances the parties explicitly allocate

FIGURE 20–2 Performance by the Buyer

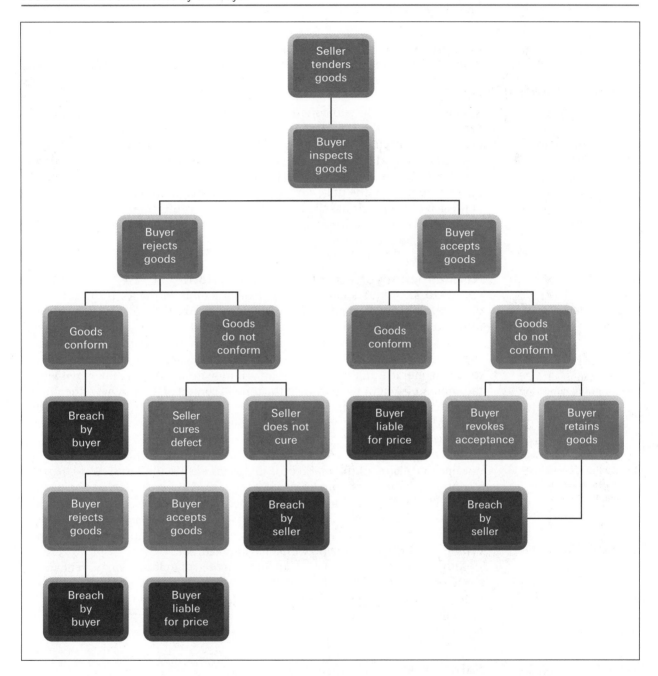

these risks, in most instances they do not. The Code contains three sections that allocate these risks when the parties fail to do so. Each provision, when applicable, relieves the parties from the obligation of full performance under the sales contract. (Also see Ethical Dilemma.)

Related to the subject of whether the Code will excuse performance is the question of whether both parties will be able and willing to perform. In such instances, the Code allows the insecure party to seek reasonable assurance of the potentially defaulting party's willingness and ability to perform. In addition, if one of the parties clearly indicates an unwillingness or inability to perform, the Code protects the other party.

Casualty to Identified Goods

If goods are destroyed before an offer to sell or to buy them is accepted, the offer is terminated by general contract law. But what if the goods are destroyed after the sales contract is formed? The rules for the passage of risk of loss, as discussed in Chapter 21, apply with one exception: if the contract is for goods that are **identified** when the contract was made and these goods are totally lost or damaged, without fault of either party, before the risk of loss passes to the buyer, the contract is avoided. This means that each party is excused from his obligation to perform under the contract: the seller is no longer obligated to deliver, and the buyer need not pay the price. In the case of a partial destruction or deterioration of the goods, the buyer has the option to avoid the contract or to accept the goods with due allowance or deduction from the contract price sufficient to account for the deterioration or deficiency in quantity.

Nonhappening of Presupposed Condition

Central to the Code's approach to impossibility of performance is the concept of **commercial impracticability**. Under this concept, the Code will excuse performance that, even though not actually or literally impossible, is commercially impracticable. This, however, requires more than mere hardship or increased cost of performance. In order for a party to be discharged, performance must be rendered impracticable as a result of an unforeseen supervening event not within the contemplation of the parties at the time of contracting. Moreover, the nonoccurrence of the event must have been a "basic assumption" that both parties made when entering into the contract. See *Northern Corp. v. Chugach Electrical Association* in Chapter 17.

Increased production cost alone does not excuse performance by the seller, nor does a collapse of the market for the goods excuse the buyer. But a party to a contract for the sale of programs for a scheduled Super Bowl that is called off, for the sale of tin horns for export that become subject to embargo, or for the production of goods at a designated factory that becomes damaged or destroyed by fire would be excused from performance: in each case, an unforeseen supervening event has rendered performance impracticable.

Although the nonhappening of presupposed conditions may relieve the seller of her contractual duty, if the contingency affects only a part of the seller's capacity to perform, she must, to the extent of her remaining capacity, allocate delivery and production in a fair and reasonable manner among her customers.

Substituted Performance

The Code provides that where neither party is at fault and the agreed-upon manner of delivering the goods becomes commercially impracticable—because of the failure of loading or unloading facilities, or the unavailability of an agreed-upon type of carrier, for example—a substituted manner of performance, if commercially reasonable, must be tendered and accepted. Where a practical alternative or substitute exists, the Code excuses neither seller nor buyer on the ground that delivery in the express manner provided in the contract is impossible.

ETHICAL DILEMMA Should a Buyer Refuse to Perform a Contract Because a Legal Product May Be Unsafe?

FACTS Carson and Olson are partners in a landscape and gardening business that operates out of three major locations and employs approximately 30 people. The business provides general lawn care predominately for residential homes; its services include grass cutting, fertilizing, and trimming of shrubbery. Carson and Olson also provide landscape design services.

One year ago, Carson and Olson entered into a two-year contract with Chem-Care, which manufactures chemical-based fertilizers effective in weed control. Because the contract was for a long term and because Carson and Olson have been excellent Chem-Care customers for the past fifteen years, they obtained an extremely favorable price of $40,000 for a two-year supply of Chem-Care fertilizers.

Now, however, due to publicity concerning health problems associated with certain chemical lawn treatments, the majority of Carson's and Olson's customers have decided that they no longer want chemical lawn treatments. Concerned by the health hazards associated with chemical fertilizers, the customers insist upon natural fertilizers.

Chem-Care fertilizers have been approved by the government and do not violate any standards currently in place. Nevertheless, a congressional committee has begun studying approximately 100 chemical treatments, including the fertilizers used by Chem-Care. The study will take at least a year to complete.

Carson wants to cancel the contract with Chem-Care. But Olson feels a sense of loyalty to Chem-Care and wants to honor the contract by trying to find new customers who would be willing to use the Chem-Care products.

Social, Policy, and Ethical Considerations

1. Should Carson and Olson attempt to invalidate the contract? Compare the social value of enforcing promises made with the good faith intention of being legally bound against the value of protecting the public from health or environmental threats.

2. Is it premature to characterize Chem-Care products as a threat to health or the environment?

3. Should the law excuse the performance of contracts that involve products which are under investigation for posing health or environmental problems?

4. As a practical matter, what should Carson and Olson do? Given the question as to the safety of Chem-Care products, does Olson's suggestion of getting new customers for Chem-Care products make sense from an ethical or a business standpoint?

Right to Adequate Assurance of Performance

A contract of sale also requires that each party not impair the other party's expectation of having the contract performed. Therefore, when reasonable grounds for insecurity arise regarding either party's performance, the other party may demand written assurance and suspend his own performance until he receives that assurance. The failure to provide adequate assurance of performance within a reasonable time, not exceeding thirty days, constitutes a repudiation of the contract.

Right to adequate assurance of performance when reasonable grounds for insecurity arise regarding either party's performance, the other party may demand written assurance and suspend his own performance until he receives that assurance

Right to Cooperation

Where one party's cooperation is necessary to the agreed performance but is not timely forthcoming, the other party is excused with regard to any resulting delay in her own performance. The nonbreaching party either may proceed to perform in any reasonable manner or, if the time for her performance has occurred, may treat the other's failure to cooperate as a breach. In either event, the nonbreaching party has access to any other remedies the Code may provide, as discussed in Chapter 23.

Right to cooperation where one party's required cooperation is untimely, the other party is excused from any resulting delay in her performance

Anticipatory Repudiation

While a repudiation in itself is a clear indication by either party to a contract that he is unwilling or unable to perform his obligations under the contract, an **anticipatory repudiation** is a repudiation made *before* the time to perform occurs. It may occur by express communication or by the repudiating party's taking an

Anticipatory repudiation if either party clearly indicates an unwillingness or inability to perform before the performance is due, the other party may await performance for a reasonable time or resort to any remedy for breach

action that makes performance impossible, such as selling unique goods to a third party. It also may result from the failure of a party to give timely assurance of performance after a justifiable demand. If an anticipatory repudiation substantially impairs the value of the contract, the aggrieved party may (1) await performance for a commercially reasonable time or (2) resort to any remedy for breach. In either case, he may suspend his own performance. The repudiating party may retract his anticipatory repudiation and thereby reinstate the contract unless the aggrieved party has canceled the contract, has materially changed his position, or has otherwise indicated that she considers the anticipatory repudiation final.

NEPTUNE RESEARCH & DEVELOPMENT, INC. v. TEKNICS INDUSTRIAL SYSTEMS, INC.
New Jersey Superior Court, Appellate Division, 1989, 235 N.J. Super. 522, 563 A.2d 465

FACTS Neptune Research & Development, Inc. (the buyer), which manufactured solar-operated valves used in scientific instruments, saw advertised in a trade journal a hole-drilling machine with a very high degree of accuracy, which was manufactured and sold by Teknics Industrial Systems, Inc. (the seller). As the machine's specifications met the buyer's needs, the buyer contacted the seller in late March and ordered one of the machines to be delivered in mid-June. There was no "time-of-the-essence" clause in the contract.

Although the buyer made several calls to the seller throughout the month of June, the seller never delivered the machine and never gave the buyer any reasons for the nondelivery. By late August, the buyer desperately needed the machine. The buyer went to the seller's place of business to examine the machine and discovered that the still unbuilt machine had been redesigned, omitting a particular feature that the buyer had wanted. Nonetheless, the buyer agreed to take the machine, and the seller promised that it would be ready on September 5. The seller also agreed to call the buyer on September 3 in order to give the buyer two days to arrange for transportation of the machine.

The seller failed to telephone the buyer on September 3 as agreed. On September 4, the buyer called the seller to find out the status of the machine, and was told by the seller that "under no circumstances" could the seller have the machine ready by September 5. At this point, the buyer notified the seller that the order was canceled. One hour later, the seller called the buyer, retracted its earlier statement, and indicated that the machine would be ready by the

agreed September 5 date. The buyer sued for the return of its $3,000 deposit.

DECISION Judgment for the buyer affirmed.

OPINION The UCC's right to cure provisions apply only where a seller has made actual delivery of goods, and therefore are not applicable here. Moreover, time was not of the essence in the original contract, so the seller's failure to deliver on the mid-June original delivery date was not an anticipatory breach entitling the buyer to cancel the contract. The seller, however, had repudiated the contract when it stated on September 4 that under no circumstances could the agreed-upon delivery date be met. This repudiation impaired the value of the contract to the buyer. A contract need not expressly state that time is of the essence in order for timely delivery to be deemed essential. Here the seller delayed delivery for an inordinate amount of time.

Nonetheless, under some circumstances, a party may retract a repudiation. The Code states that "until the repudiating party's next performance is due he can retract his repudiation unless the aggrieved party has since the repudiation cancelled or materially changed his position or otherwise indicated that he considers the repudiation final." Here, the buyer communicated its cancellation of the contract to the seller before the attempted retraction. Therefore, the cancellation by the buyer is effective.

INTERPRETATION A buyer's cancellation of a contract based on the seller's anticipatory repudiation is effective if the cancellation precedes the seller's attempt to retract her repudiation.

CHAPTER SUMMARY

Performance by the Seller	**Tender of Delivery** the seller makes available to the buyer goods conforming to the contract and so notifies the buyer ■ Buyer is obligated to accept conforming goods ■ Seller is entitled to receive payment of the contract price **Time of Tender** tender must be made at a reasonable time and kept open for a reasonable period of time **Place of Tender** if none is specified, place for delivery is the seller's place of business or, if he has no such place, his residence ■ *Shipment Contracts* seller is required to tender delivery of the goods to a carrier for delivery to buyer; shipment terms include the following: F.O.B. place of shipment, F.A.S. port of shipment, C.I.F., C. & F. ■ *Destination Contracts* seller is required to tender delivery of the goods at a named destination; destination terms include the following: F.O.B. place of destination; ex-ship; no arrival, no sale ■ *Goods Held by Bailee* seller must either tender to the buyer a document of title or obtain an acknowledgment from the bailee **Perfect Tender Rule** the seller's tender of performance must conform exactly to the contract, subject to the following qualifications: ■ *Agreement Between the Parties* the parties may contractually limit the operation of the perfect tender rule ■ *Cure by the Seller* when the time for performance under the contract has not expired or when the seller has shipped nonconforming goods in the belief that the nonconforming tender would be acceptable, a seller may cure or correct his nonconforming tender ■ *Installment Contracts* when the contract calls for the goods to be delivered in separate lots, the buyer may reject a nonconforming installment if it substantially impairs the value of that installment and cannot be cured; but if nonconformity or default of one or more of the installments substantially impairs the value of the whole contract, the buyer can treat the breach as a breach of the whole contract

Performance by the Buyer	**Inspection** unless otherwise agreed, the buyer has a reasonable time in which to inspect the goods before payment or acceptance to determine whether they conform **Rejection** buyer's manifestation of unwillingness to become the owner of the goods; must be made within a reasonable time after the goods have been tendered or delivered and gives the buyer the right to (1) reject all of the goods, (2) accept all of the goods, or (3) accept any commercial unit(s) and reject the rest **Acceptance** buyer's express or implied manifestation of a willingness to become the owner of the goods **Revocation of Acceptance** rescission of buyer's acceptance of the goods if nonconformity of the goods substantially impairs their value, provided that the acceptance was (1) premised on the assumption that the nonconformity would be cured by the seller and it was not, or (2) the nonconformity was an undiscovered hidden defect **Obligation of Payment** in the absence of an agreement, payment is due at the time and place the buyer is to receive the goods

Obligations of Both Parties	**Casualty to Identified Goods** if the contract is for goods that were identified when the contract was made and those goods are totally lost or damaged without fault of either party and before the risk of loss has passed to the buyer, the contract is avoided **Nonhappening of Presupposed Condition** the seller is excused from the duty of performance on the nonoccurrence of presupposed conditions that were a basic assumption of the contract, unless the seller has expressly assumed the risk **Substituted Performance** where neither party is at fault and the agreed manner of delivery of goods becomes commercially impracticable, a substituted manner of performance must be tendered and accepted **Right to Adequate Assurance of Performance** when reasonable grounds for insecurity arise regarding either party's performance, the other party may demand written assurance and suspend his own performance until he receives that assurance **Right to Cooperation** if one party's required cooperation is untimely, the other party is excused from any resulting delay in her own performance **Anticipatory Repudiation** if either party clearly indicates an unwillingness or inability to perform before the performance is due, the other party may await performance for a reasonable time or resort to any remedy for breach

QUESTIONS

1. Explain the requirements of tender of delivery with respect to time, manner, and place of delivery.
2. Explain the perfect tender rule and the three limitations upon it.
3. Explain when the buyer has the right to reject the goods and what obligations the buyer has upon rejection.
4. Discuss the buyer's right to revoke acceptance.
5. Identify and discuss the excuses for nonperformance.

Internet Question. Compare the performance obligations of the seller and buyer under the United Nations Convention on Contracts for the International Sale of Goods (Vienna, 1980) with their obligations under Article 2 of the Uniform Commercial Code.

PROBLEMS

1. Tammie contracted with Kristine to manufacture, sell, and deliver to Kristine and put in running order a certain machine. After Tammie set up the machine and put it in running order, Kristine found it unsatisfactory and notified Tammie that she rejected the machine. She continued to use it for three months but continually complained of its defective condition. At the end of the three months, she notified Tammie to come and get it. Has Kristine lost her right (a) to reject the machine? (b) to revoke acceptance of the machine?

2. Smith, having contracted to sell to Beyer thirty tons of described fertilizer, shipped to Beyer by carrier thirty tons of fertilizer that he stated conformed to the contract. Nothing was stated in the contract as to time of payment, but Smith demanded payment as a condition of handing over the fertilizer to Beyer. Beyer refused to pay unless he were given the opportunity to inspect the fertilizer. Smith sued Beyer for breach of contract. Decision?

3. Benny and Sheree entered into a contract for the sale of one hundred barrels of flour. No mention was made of any place of delivery. Thereafter, Sheree demanded that Benny deliver the flour at her place of business, and Benny demanded that Sheree come and take the flour from his place of business. Neither party acceded to the demand of the other. Has either one a right of action against the other?

4. Johnson, a manufacturer of air-conditioning units, made a written contract with Maxwell to sell to Maxwell forty units at a price of $200 each and to deliver them at a certain apartment building owned by Maxwell for installation by Maxwell. On the arrival of Johnson's truck for delivery at the apartment building, Maxwell examined the units on the truck, counted only thirty units, and asked the driver if that was the total delivery. The driver replied that it was as far as he knew. Maxwell told the driver that she would not accept delivery of the units. The next day, Johnson telephoned

Maxwell and inquired why delivery was refused. Maxwell stated that the units on the truck were not what she ordered, that she ordered forty units, that only thirty were tendered, and that she was going to buy air-conditioning units elsewhere. In an action by Johnson against Maxwell for breach of contract, Maxwell defends on the ground that the tender of thirty units was improper, as the contract called for delivery of forty units. Is this a valid defense?

5. Edwin sells a sofa to Jack for $800. Edwin and Jack both know that the sofa is in Edwin's warehouse, located approximately ten miles from Jack's home. The contract does not specify the place of delivery, and Jack insists that the place of delivery is either his house or Edwin's store. Is Jack correct?

6. On November 4, Kim contracted to sell to Lynn 500 sacks of flour at $4 each to be shipped in November to Lynn. On November 27, Kim shipped the flour. By December 5, when the car arrived, containing only 450 sacks, the market price of flour had fallen. The usual time required for shipment was five to twelve days. Lynn refused to accept delivery or to pay. Kim shipped 50 more sacks of flour, which arrived December 10. Lynn refused delivery. Kim resold the flour for $3 per sack. What are Kim's rights against Lynn?

7. Farley and Trudy entered into a written contract whereby Farley agreed to sell and Trudy agreed to buy 6,000 bushels of wheat at $3.75 per bushel, deliverable at the rate of 1,000 bushels a month commencing June 1, the price for each installment being payable ten days after delivery thereof. Though Farley delivered and received payment for the June installment, he defaulted by failing to deliver the July and August installments. By August 15, the market price of wheat had increased to $4 per bushel. Trudy thereupon entered into a contract with Albert to purchase 5,000 bushels of wheat at $4 per bushel deliverable over the ensuing four months. In late September, the market price of wheat started to decline and by December 1 was $3.25 per bushel. Trudy brings an action against Farley for breach of contract. Decision?

8. Bain ordered from Marcum a carload of lumber, which he intended to use in the construction of small boats for the U.S. Navy, pursuant to contract. The order specified that the lumber was to be free from knots, wormholes, and defects. The lumber was shipped, and immediately on receipt Bain looked into the door of the fully loaded car, ascertained that there was a full carload of lumber, and acknowledged to Marcum that the carload had been received. On the same day, Bain moved the car to his private siding and sent to Marcum full payment in accordance with the terms of the order.

A day later, the car was moved to the work area and unloaded in the presence of the navy inspector, who refused to allow three-fourths of it to be used because of excessive knots and wormholes in the lumber. Bain then informed Marcum that he was rejecting the order and requested refund of the payment and directions on disposition of the lumber. Marcum replied that since Bain had accepted the order and unloaded it, he was not entitled to return of the purchase price. Bain thereupon brought an action against Marcum to recover the purchase price. Decision?

9. The plaintiff, a seller of milk, had for ten years bid on contracts to supply milk to the defendant school district, and had supplied milk to other school districts in the area. On June 15, 1987, the plaintiff contracted to supply the defendant's requirements of milk for the school year 1987–88, at a price of $.0759 per half-pint. The price of raw milk delivered from the farm had for years been controlled by the U.S. Department of Agriculture. On June 15, 1987, the department's administrator for the New York-New Jersey area had mandated a price for raw milk of $8.03 per hundred-weight. By December 1987, the mandated price had been raised to $9.31 per hundredweight, an increase of nearly 20 percent. If required to complete deliveries at the contract price, the plaintiff would lose $7,350.55 on its contract with the defendant and would face similar losses on contracts with two other school districts. The plaintiff sued for a judgment that its performance had become impracticable through unforeseen events, particularly unanticipated grain crop failures and the huge amounts of grain sold to Russia in mid-1987. Decision?

10. In April of 1957, F. W. Lang Company (Lang) purchased an ice cream freezer and refrigeration compressor unit from Fleet for $2,160. Although the parties agreed to a written installment contract providing for an $850 down payment and eighteen installment payments, Lang made only one $200 payment upon receipt of the goods. One year later, Lang moved to a new location and took the equipment along without notifying Fleet. Then, in May or June of 1959, Lang disconnected the compressor from the freezer and used it to operate an air conditioner. Lang continued to use the compressor for that purpose until the sheriff seized the equipment and returned it to Fleet pursuant to a court order. Fleet then sold the equipment for $500 in what both parties conceded was a fair sale. Lang then brought an action charging that the equipment was defective and unusable for its intended purpose and sought to recover the down payment and expenses incurred in repairing the equipment. Fleet counterclaimed for the balance due under the installment contract less the proceeds from the sale. Decision?

11. Deborah McCullough bought a new car from Bill Swad Chrysler-Plymouth, Inc. The car was protected by both a limited warranty and an extended warranty.

McCullough immediately encountered problems with the automobile's brakes, transmission, and air-conditioning and discovered a number of cosmetic defects as well. She returned the car to Swad for repairs, but Swad did not fix the brakes properly or perform any of the cosmetic work. Moreover, new problems appeared with respect to the car's steering mechanism. McCullough returned the car twice more for repairs, but on each occasion, old problems persisted and new ones emerged. After the engine abruptly shut off on a short trip away from home and the brakes again failed on a more extensive excursion, McCullough presented Swad with a list of thirty-two of the car's defects and demanded their correction. When Swad failed to remedy more than a few of the problems, McCullough wrote a letter to Swad calling for rescission of the purchase agreement and a refund of the purchase price and offering to return the car upon receipt of shipping instructions from Swad. Swad did not respond to the letter, and McCullough brought an action against Swad. She continued to operate the vehicle until the time of trial, some seventeen and one-half months (and 23,000 miles) later. Decision?

12. On March 17, 1976, Peckham bought a new car from Larsen Chevrolet for $6,400.85. During the first one and one-half months after the purchase, Peckham discovered that the car's hood was dented, its gas tank contained no baffles, its emergency brake was inoperable, the car did not have a jack or a spare tire, and neither the clock nor the speedometer worked. Larsen claimed that Peckham knew of the defects at the time of the purchase. Peckham, on the other hand, claimed that despite his repeated efforts the defects were not repaired until June 11, 1976. Then, on July 15, the car's dashboard caught fire, leaving the car's interior damaged and the car itself inoperable. Peckham then returned to Larsen Chevrolet and told Larsen that Larsen had to repair the car at his own expense or that he, Peckham, would either rescind the contract or demand a new automobile. Peckham also claimed that at the end of their conversation he notified Larsen Chevrolet that he was electing to rescind the contract and demanded the return of the purchase price. Larsen denied having received that oral notification. On October 12, 1976, Peckham sent a written notice of rescission to Larsen. Decision?

13. Joc Oil bought a cargo of fuel oil for resale. The certificate from the foreign refinery stated the sulphur content of the oil was 0.5 percent. Joc Oil entered into a written contract with Con Ed for the sale of this oil. The contract specified a sulphur content of 0.5 percent. Joc Oil knew, however, that Con Ed was authorized to buy and burn oil of up to 1 percent sulphur content and that Con Ed often bought and mixed oils of varying contents to stay within this limit. The oil under contract was delivered to Con Ed, but independent testing revealed a sulphur content of 0.92 percent. Con Ed promptly rejected the nonconforming shipment. Joc Oil immediately offered to substitute a conforming shipment of oil, although the time for performance had expired after the first shipment of oil. Con Ed refused to accept the substituted shipment. Joc Oil sues Con Ed for breach of contract. Judgment?

14. The plaintiff, a West German wine producer and exporter, contracted to ship 620 cases of wine to the defendant distributor in North Carolina. The contract was silent as to the shipment destination. During the next several months, the defendant called repeatedly to find out the status of the shipment. Later, without notifying the defendant, the plaintiff delivered the wine to a shipping line in Rotterdam, destined for Wilmington, N.C. The ship and the wine were lost at sea en route to Wilmington. When the defendant refused to pay on the contract, the plaintiff sued. Decision?

15. Can-Key Industries, Inc., manufactured a turkey-hatching unit, which it sold to Industrial Leasing Corporation (ILC), which leased it to Rose-A-Linda Turkey Farms. ILC conditioned its obligation to pay on Rose-A-Linda's acceptance of the equipment. Rose-A-Linda indicated its dissatisfaction with the equipment, and ILC refused to perform its obligations under the contract. Can-Key then brought suit against ILC for breach of contract. It argued that Rose-A-Linda accepted the equipment, since it used it for fifteen months between March 1976 and May 1977. ILC contended that the equipment was unacceptable and asked that it be removed. It claimed that Can-Key refused and failed to instruct Rose-A-Linda to refrain from using the equipment. Therefore, ILC argued, Rose-A-Linda effectively rejected the turkey-hatching unit, relieving ILC of its contractual obligations. Decision?

16. Frederick Manufacturing Corp. ordered 500 dozen units of Import Traders' rubber pads for $2,580. The order indicated that the pads should be "as soft as possible." Import Traders delivered the rubber pads to Frederick Manufacturing on November 19, 1981. Frederick failed to inspect the goods upon delivery, even though the parties recognized that there might be a problem with the softness. Frederick finally complained about the nonconformity of the pads in April 1982, when Import Traders requested the contract price for the goods. Traders then sued Frederick to recover the contract price. Decision?

Transfer of Title and Risk of Loss

Historically, the principle of title governed nearly every aspect of the rights and duties of the buyer and seller arising out of a sales contract. In an attempt to add greater precision and certainty to sales contracts, the Code has abandoned the common law's reliance on title. Instead, the Code approaches each legal issue arising out of a sales contract on its own merits and provides separate and specific rules to control various transactional situations. In this chapter, we will cover the Code's approach to the transfer of title and other property rights, the passage of risk of loss, and the transfer of goods sold in bulk.

TRANSFER OF TITLE

As previously stated, a sale of goods is defined as the transfer of title from the seller to the buyer for a consideration known as the price. Transfer of title is, therefore, fundamental to a sale of goods. Title, however, cannot pass under a contract for sale until existing goods have been identified as those to which the contract refers. Future goods (goods that are not both existing and identified) cannot constitute a present sale.

If the buyer rejects the goods, whether justifiably or not, title revests to the seller.

Identification

Identification is the designation of specific goods as goods to which the contract of sale refers. Identification may be made by either the seller or the buyer and may be made at any time and in any manner agreed upon by the parties. To illustrate, suppose Barringer contracts to purchase a particular Buick automobile from Stevenson's car lot. Identification occurs as soon as the parties enter the contract. If, however, Barringer agreed to purchase a television set from Stevenson, who has his storeroom filled with such televisions, identification will not occur until either Barringer or Stevenson selects a particular television to fulfill the contract.

If the goods are **fungible** (the equivalent of any other unit), identification of a share of undivided goods occurs when the contract is entered into. Thus, if Barringer agreed to purchase 1,000 gallons of gasoline from Stevenson, who owns a 5,000 gallon tank of gasoline, identification occurs as soon as the contract is formed.

Security Interest   The Code defines a **security interest** as an interest in personal property or fixtures that ensures payment or performance of an

Identification designation of specific goods as goods to which the contract of sale refers

Fungible *(fun'·gi·ble)* the equivalent of any other unit

Security interest interest in personal property or fixtures that ensures payment or performance of an obligation

obligation. Any reservation by the seller of a title to goods *delivered* to the buyer is limited in effect to a reservation of a security interest. Security interests in goods are governed by Article 9 of the Code (discussed in Chapter 39).

Insurable Interest In order for a contract or policy of insurance to be valid, the insured must have an **insurable interest** in the subject matter. At common law, only a person with title or a **lien** (a legal claim of a creditor on property) could insure his interest in specific goods. The Code extends an insurable interest to a buyer's interest in goods that have been identified as goods to which the contract refers. This ***special property interest*** of the buyer, which arises upon identification, enables her to purchase insurance protection on goods that she does not presently own but that she will own upon delivery by the seller. The seller also has an insurable interest in the goods, as long as he has title to them or any security interest in them.

Passage of Title

Title passes when the parties *intend* it to pass, provided the goods are in existence and have been identified. Where the parties have no explicit agreement as to transfer of title, the Code provides rules that determine when title passes to the buyer.

Physical Movement of the Goods When delivery is to be made by moving the goods, title passes at the time and place the seller completes his performance with reference to delivery of the goods. When and where delivery occurs depends upon whether the contract is a shipment contract or a destination contract.

A **shipment contract** requires or authorizes the seller to send the goods to the buyer but does not require the seller to deliver them to a particular destination. Under a shipment contract, title passes to the buyer at the time and place the seller delivers the goods to the carrier for shipment to the buyer.

A **destination contract** requires the seller to deliver the goods to a particular destination. Under a destination contract, title passes to the buyer on tender of the goods at that destination. **Tender**, as discussed in Chapter 20, requires that the seller, at a reasonable time, (1) put and hold conforming goods at the buyer's disposition, (2) give notice to the buyer that the goods are available, and (3) keep the goods available for a reasonable period of time.

Insurable interest interest in property that may be insured against loss

Lien a nonconsensual claim against property

Passage of title title passes when the parties intend it to pass; when the parties do not specifically agree, the Code provides rules to determine when title passes

Physical movement of the goods when delivery is to be made by moving the goods, title passes at the time and place where the seller completes his performance with reference to delivery

Shipment contract seller is required to deliver the goods to a carrier for delivery to buyer

Destination contract seller is required to tender delivery of the goods at a particular destination

Tender seller offers conforming goods to buyer and gives buyer notice that the goods are available

---

PITTSBURGH INDUSTRIAL FURNACE COMPANY v. UNIVERSAL CONSOLIDATED COMPANIES, INC. United States District Court, W.D. Pennsylvania, 1991, 789 F.Supp. 184

FACTS During 1988, Universal Consolidated Companies, Inc. (Universal) entered into negotiations with the China Metallurgical Import and Export Corporation (CMIEC), Tianjin branch, People's Republic of China, to provide seven lines of new and used equipment for a cold-rolling steel mill. The project required that Universal provide twelve anneal furnaces. Pittsburgh Industrial Furnace Company (Pifcom) contracted with Universal in January 1989 to provide the necessary engineering, equipment, and materials for construction of these furnaces. The contract provided for Pifcom to receive $955,000 in four installments. Universal paid $295,000, with the balance of $660,000 due upon shipment. The contract called for

Pifcom to ship the materials and equipment "FOB Points of Shipment." Pifcom performed its part of the contract and shipped most of the equipment to EMPE, Inc., Universal's engineering consultant. In September 1989, CMIEC terminated its contract with Universal, and in October 1989, Universal informed Pifcom that CMIEC had ended the contract and requested Pifcom to suspend its performance. At this time, the balance of the goods not already received had already been shipped. Pifcom did not take any steps to stop delivery or to reclaim any of the remaining equipment until December 8, 1989, when Pifcom instructed EMPE to stop any delivery to Universal. Trustcorp Financing Services, Inc. (TFSI) had

continued

provided financing for the Universal/CMIEC project. After CMIEC canceled, TFSI declared its loan in default and repossessed the materials at EMPE, in which, it asserted, Universal had granted it a security interest. Pifcom sued for title of the equipment it had delivered to EMPE, claiming that Pifcom had not intended for title to the goods to pass until it was paid. Pifcom argued that it had an understanding with EMPE that EMPE would act as a bailee in storing the goods for Pifcom.

DECISION Judgment for TFSI.

OPINION The Uniform Commercial Code provides that under an "FOB place of shipment contract," the seller must bear the risk and expense of putting the goods in the possession of an independent carrier at the seller's location. Once the goods are delivered to the carrier, the seller has given up possession of the goods and title passes to the buyer, because the seller's performance with regard to the physical delivery of the goods is completed. Pifcom's claim that it entered into an oral agreement that modified the original terms of the contract is unsupported.

INTERPRETATION Under a shipment contract, title passes to the buyer at the time and place the seller delivers the goods to the carrier.

No Movement of the Goods   When delivery is to be made without moving the goods, unless otherwise agreed, title passes (a) on delivery of a document of title, where the contract calls for delivery of such document (documents of title are documents that evidence a right to receive specified goods; they are discussed more fully in Chapter 50); or (b) at the time and place of contracting, if the goods at that time have been identified by either the seller or the buyer as the goods to which the contract refers and no documents are to be delivered. Where the goods are not identified at the time of contracting, title passes when the goods are identified.

Power to Transfer Title

It is important to understand under what circumstances a seller has the right or **power to transfer title** to a buyer. If the seller is the rightful owner of goods or is authorized to sell the goods for the rightful owner, the seller has the *right* to transfer title. But when a seller possesses goods that he neither owns nor has authority to sell, the sale is not rightful. In some situations, however, unauthorized sellers may have the *power* to transfer good title to certain buyers. This section pertains to such sales by a person in possession of goods that he neither owns nor has authority to sell.

The rule of property law protecting existing ownership of goods is the starting point for any discussion of a sale of goods by a nonowner. One of the law's most basic tenets, expressly stated in the Code, is that a purchaser of goods obtains such title as his transferor had or had power to transfer. Likewise, the purchaser of a limited interest in goods acquires rights only to the extent of the interest that he purchased. By the same token, no one can transfer what he does not have. A purported sale by a thief or finder or ordinary bailee of goods does not transfer title to the purchaser.

The principal reason underlying the policy of the law in protecting existing ownership of goods is that a person should not be required to retain possession at all times of all the goods that he owns in order to maintain his ownership of them. One valuable incident of the ownership of goods is the freedom of the owner to make a bailment of his goods as he pleases; the mere possession of goods by a bailee does not authorize the bailee to sell them.

Another legal policy conflicts, however, with the policy protecting existing ownership of goods; this latter protection, the protection of the good faith purchaser, is based on the importance in trade and commerce of ensuring the security

Power to transfer title   the purchaser of goods obtains such title as his transferor either has or had the power to transfer; however' to encourage and make secure good faith acquisitions of goods, it is necessary to protect certain third parties under certain circumstances

of good faith transactions in goods. To encourage and make secure good faith acquisitions of goods, *bona fide* (good faith) purchasers for value must be protected under certain circumstances. A **good faith purchaser** is defined as one who acts honestly, gives value, and takes the goods without notice or knowledge of any defect in the title of his transferor.

Void and Voidable Title to Goods   A **void title** is no title. A person claiming ownership of goods by an agreement that is void obtains no title to the goods. Thus, a thief or a finder of goods or a person who acquires goods from someone under physical duress or under guardianship has no title to them and can transfer none.

A **voidable title** is one acquired under circumstances that permit the former owner to rescind the transfer and revest herself with title, as in the case of mistake, common duress, undue influence, fraud in the inducement, misrepresentation, mistake, or sale by a person without contractual capacity (other than an individual under guardianship). In these situations, the buyer has acquired legal title to the goods, which may be divested by action of the seller. If, however, the buyer were to resell the goods to a good faith purchaser for value, before the seller has rescinded the transfer of title, the right of rescission in the seller is cut off, and the good faith purchaser acquires good title. The Code defines **good faith** as "honesty in fact in the conduct or transaction concerned" and value to include a consideration sufficient to support a simple contract.

The distinction between a void and voidable title is, therefore, extremely important in determining the rights of good faith purchasers of goods. The good faith purchaser always believes that she is buying the goods from the owner or from one with authority to sell. Otherwise, she would not be acting in good faith. In each situation, the party selling the goods appears to be the owner, whether his title is valid, void, or voidable. Given a case involving two innocent persons—the true owner who has done nothing wrong and the good faith purchaser who has done nothing wrong—the law will not disturb the legal title but will rule in favor of the one who has it. Thus, where A transfers possession of goods to B under such circumstances that B acquires no title or a void title, and B thereafter sells the goods to C, a good faith purchaser for value, B has nothing to transfer to C except possession. In a lawsuit between A and C involving the right to the goods, A will win because she has the legal title. (See Figure 21–1.) C's only recourse is against B for breach of warranty of title, which we will discuss in

Good faith purchaser buyer who acts honestly, gives value, and takes the goods without notice or knowledge of any defect in the title of her transferor

Void title no title can be transferred

Voidable title the good faith purchaser acquires good title

Good faith honesty in fact in the conduct or transaction concerned

FIGURE 21–1 Void Title

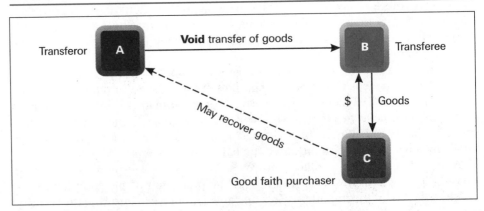

Chapter 22. If, however, B acquired a voidable title from A and resold the goods to C, in a suit between A and C over the goods, C would win. In this case, B had title, though voidable, which she transferred to the good faith purchaser. The title thus acquired by C will be protected. The voidable title in B is title until it has been avoided, and, after transfer to a good faith purchaser, it may not be avoided. (See Figure 21–2.) A's only recourse is against B for restitution or damages.

ROBINSON v. DURHAM Alabama Court of Civil Appeals, 1988, 537 So.2d 966

FACTS Mike Durham bought a used 1968 Chevrolet Camaro from Ronald and Wyman Robinson, owners of Friendly Discount Auto Sales. Unknown to either Durham or the Robinsons, the car had been stolen. In fact, when he first bought the car, Wyman Robinson had obtained tag receipts from what turned out to be the car thief, and had subsequently registered the car in his name. Durham had received all prior documentation upon purchase of the car. However, the FBI seized the car from Durham and returned it to the original owner. Durham sued the Robinsons, alleging, among other things, breach of the warranty of title. The jury awarded Durham $5,200, the amount he had paid for the car. The Robinsons appealed.

DECISION Judgment for Durham.

OPINION The Robinsons assert that since they were good faith purchasers for value when they bought the car for their business, they had good title and therefore passed good title to Durham. Alternatively, the Robinsons maintain that they had at least a voidable title, and thus could pass good title to Durham, who was himself a good faith purchaser for value. Both arguments are without merit. It is clear that a thief gets only void title, and without more, cannot pass *any* title to a subsequent purchaser, not even to a good faith purchaser for value. Since the Robinsons obtained no title from the thief, they could not pass good title to Durham. This clearly constitutes a breach of warranty of title between the Robinsons and Durham.

INTERPRETATION A void title is no title.

The Code has enlarged the common law voidable title doctrine by providing that a good faith purchaser for value obtains valid title from one possessing voidable title even if that person obtained voidable title by (1) fraud as to her identity; (2) exchange for a subsequently dishonored check; (3) an agreement that the transaction was to be a cash sale, and the sales price has not been paid; or (4) criminal fraud punishable as larceny.

In addition, the Code has expanded the rights of good faith purchasers with respect to sales by *minors*. While the common law permitted a minor seller of goods to disaffirm the sale and to recover the goods from a third person who had purchased them in good faith from the party who had acquired the goods from the minor, the Code changed this rule by no longer permitting a minor seller to prevail over a good faith purchaser for value.

FIGURE 21–2 Voidable Title

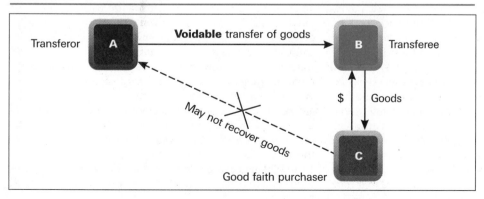

Entrusting of goods to a merchant buyers in the ordinary course of business acquire good title when buying from merchants

Buyer in ordinary course of business person who buys from a person in the business of selling goods of that kind, in good faith, and without knowledge that the sale to him is in violation of anyone's ownership rights

Entrusting transfer of possession of goods

Entrusting of Goods to a Merchant Frequently, an owner of goods entrusts (transfers possession of) goods to a bailee for resale, repair, or some other use. In some instances, the bailee violates this entrusting by selling the goods to a third party without the owner's permission or by keeping the proceeds of such a sale. Although the "true" owner has a right of recourse against the bailee for the value of the goods, what right, if any, should the true owner of the goods have against the third party? Once again the law must balance the right of ownership against the rights of market transactions.

The Code protects buyers of goods in the ordinary course of business from merchants who deal in goods of that kind, where the owner has entrusted possession of the goods to the merchant. The Code defines a **buyer in the ordinary course of business** as a person who in good faith and without knowledge that the sale to him is in violation of the ownership rights or security interest of another buys the goods in the ordinary course of business from a person, other than a pawnbroker, in the business of selling goods of that kind. Because the merchant who deals in goods of that kind is cloaked with the appearance of ownership or apparent authority to sell, the Code seeks to protect the innocent third-party purchaser. Any such **entrusting** of possession bestows on the merchant the power to transfer all rights of the entruster to a buyer in the ordinary course of business. For example, A brings his stereo for repair to B, who also sells both new and used stereo equipment. C purchases A 's stereo from B in good faith and in the ordinary course of business. The Code protects the rights of C and defeats the rights of A, whose only recourse is against B.

The Code, however, does not go so far as to protect the buyer in the ordinary course of business from a merchant to whom the goods have been entrusted by a thief, a finder, or a completely unauthorized person. It merely grants the buyer in the ordinary course of business the rights of the entruster.

Where a buyer of goods to whom title has passed leaves the seller in possession of the goods, the buyer has "entrusted the goods" to the seller. If that seller is a merchant and resells and delivers the goods to another buyer in the ordinary course of business, this second buyer acquires good title to the goods. Thus, Dennis sells certain goods to Sylvia, who pays the price but allows possession to remain with Dennis. Dennis thereafter sells the same goods to Karen, a buyer in the ordinary course of business. Karen takes delivery of the goods. Sylvia does not have any rights against Karen or to the goods. Sylvia 's only remedy is against Dennis.

HEINRICH v. TITUS-WILL SALES, INC. Court of Appeals of Washington, 1994, 73 Wash.App. 147, 868 P.2d 169.

FACTS In 1989, Michael Heinrich retained James Wilson to purchase a new Ford pickup truck for him. Wilson had held himself out as a dealer/broker, but unbeknownst to Heinrich, Wilson had lost his vehicle dealer license. Wilson negotiated with Titus-Will Ford Sales, Inc. (Titus-Will) to purchase the truck for Heinrich. Titus-Will had dealt with Wilson as a dealer before, but also did not know that he had lost his dealer license. All payments for the truck went through Wilson, and the purchase order indicated that the truck was being sold to Wilson as a dealer for resale. Wilson agreed to deliver the truck to Heinrich at Titus-Will on Saturday, October 21, 1989. Wilson delivered to a clerk at Titus-Will a postdated check for the balance of the purchase price, which the clerk accepted, and in return delivered to Wilson a packet containing the keys to the truck, the owner's manual, an odometer disclosure statement, and the warranty card. The odometer statement showed that Wilson was the transferor and Titus-Will did not fill out the warranty card since the sale appeared to be dealer to dealer. Wilson's check, however, did not clear and Titus-Wilson demanded the return of the truck. On November 6, Wilson picked up the truck from Heinrich, telling him he would have Titus-Will make certain repairs under the warranty, and returned the truck to Titus-Will. On November 9, 1989,

continued

Wilson admitted to Heinrich that he did not have funds to cover his check and that Titus-Will would not release the truck without payment. Heinrich then asked Titus-Will for the truck but was refused. Heinrich sued Titus-Will and Wilson, seeking return of the truck and damages for his loss of use. By pretrial arrangement, Heinrich regained possession of, but not clear title to the truck. Heinrich also obtained a default order against Wilson. After a bench trial, the court awarded Heinrich title to the truck and $3,050 in damages for loss of its use. Titus-Will appeals.

DECISION Judgment affirmed.

OPINION Titus-Will argues that the trial court erroneously applied the entrustment doctrine of UCC. To prevail under this provision, Heinrich must show (1) Titus-Will "entrusted" the truck to Wilson and, thus, empowered Wilson subsequently to transfer all rights of Titus-Will in the truck to Heinrich; (2) Wilson was a merchant dealing in automobiles; and (3) Heinrich bought the truck from Wilson as a "buyer in the ordinary course of business."

Titus-Will did entrust the truck to Wilson, who was a merchant dealing in automobiles. The UCC does not require proper state licensing for merchant status. Wilson held himself out as a dealer in automobiles and appeared to be a dealer in automobiles.

There is also substantial evidence that Heinrich was a "buyer in the ordinary course of business." A buyer in the ordinary course of business is

a person who in good faith and without knowledge that the sale to him is in violation of the ownership rights or security interest of a third party in the goods buys in ordinary course from a person in the business of selling goods of that kind.

Good faith is "honesty in fact in the conduct or transaction concerned." There was no showing that Heinrich acted other than in good faith. He gave substantial value for the truck, more than Wilson agreed to pay Titus-Will. Nor did Heinrich know or have a basis to believe that Wilson's sale of the truck to him violated Titus-Will's ownership or security interest rights. Therefore, Wilson's illegal fraudulent activity does not taint Heinrich's status as a buyer.

Titus-Will not only entrusted Wilson with the truck but also with the signed odometer disclosure statement, the owner's manual, the warranty card, and the keys. By doing so, Titus-Will enabled Wilson to complete the sales transaction. In addition, the entrustment allowed Wilson to continue to deceive Heinrich from the date of delivery to the date when Wilson finally admitted the truth. Under these circumstances, application of the entrustment doctrine furthers the policy of protecting the buyer who relies on the merchant's apparent legal ability to sell goods in the merchant's possession.

INTERPRETATION A buyer in the ordinary course of business acquires good title when buying from a merchant seller who was entrusted with possession of the goods.

RISK OF LOSS

Risk of loss, as the term is used in the law of sales, addresses the allocation of loss between seller and buyer where the goods have been damaged, destroyed, or lost *without the fault* of either the seller or the buyer. If the loss is placed on the buyer, he is under a duty to pay the price for the goods even though they were damaged or he never received them. If placed on the seller, she has no right to recover the purchase price from the buyer, although she does have a right to the return of the damaged goods.

In determining who has the risk of loss, the Code provides definite rules for specific situations—a sharp departure from the common law concept, which essentially determined risk of loss according to who had ownership of the goods and which depended on whether title had been transferred. The Code's transactional approach is necessarily detailed and for this reason is probably more understandable and meaningful than the common law's reliance on the abstract concept of title. The Code has adopted rules for determining the risk of loss in the absence of breach separate from those that apply where a breach of the sales contract has occurred.

Risk of loss allocation of loss between seller and buyer where the goods have been damaged, destroyed, or lost

Risk of Loss Where There Is a Breach

Where one party breaches the contract, the Code places the risk of loss on that party, even though this allocation differs from the passage of risk of loss in the absence of a breach. Nevertheless, where the nonbreaching party is in control of the goods, the Code places the risk of loss on him to the extent of his insurance coverage.

Breach by the seller if the seller ships to the buyer goods that do not conform to the contract, the risk of loss remains on the seller until the buyer has accepted the goods or until the seller has remedied the defect

Breach by the Seller   If the seller ships to the buyer goods that do not conform to the contract, the risk of loss remains on the seller until the buyer has accepted the goods or until the seller has remedied the defect.

Where the buyer has accepted nonconforming goods but thereafter by timely notice to the seller rightfully revokes his acceptance (discussed in Chapter 20), he may treat the risk of loss as resting from the beginning on the seller, to the extent of any deficiency in the buyer's effective insurance coverage. For example, Stuart delivers to Bernard nonconforming goods, which Bernard accepts. Subsequently, Bernard discovers a hidden defect in the goods and rightfully revokes his prior acceptance. If the goods are destroyed through no fault of either party, and Bernard has insured the goods for 60 percent of their fair market value of $10,000, then the insurance company will cover $6,000 of the loss and Stuart will cover the remainder, or $4,000. Had the buyer's insurance coverage been $10,000, Stuart would not bear any of the loss.

Breach by the buyer the seller may treat the risk of loss as resting on the buyer for a commercially reasonable time to the extent of any deficiency in the seller's effective insurance coverage

Breach by the Buyer   Where conforming goods have been identified to a contract that the buyer repudiates or breaches before risk of loss has passed to him, the seller may treat the risk of loss as resting on the buyer "for a commercially reasonable time" to the extent of any deficiency in the seller's effective insurance coverage. For example, Susan agrees to sell 40,000 pounds of plastic resin to Bella, F.O.B. Bella 's factory, delivery by March 1. On February 1, Bella wrongfully repudiates the contract by telephoning Susan and telling her that she does not want the resin. Susan immediately seeks another buyer, but before she is able to locate one, and within a commercially reasonable time, the resin is destroyed by a fire through no fault of Susan's. The fair market value of the resin is $35,000. Because Susan's insurance covers only $15,000 of the loss, Bella is liable for $20,000.

Risk of Loss in Absence of a Breach

Where there is no breach, the parties may allocate the risk of loss by agreement. Where there is no breach and the parties have not otherwise agreed, the Code places the risk of loss, for the most part, on the party who is more likely to have greater control over the goods, is more likely to insure the goods, or is better able to prevent the loss of the goods.

Agreement of the parties the parties may by agreement allocate the risk of loss

Agreement of the Parties   The parties, by agreement, not only may shift the allocation of risk of loss but also may divide the risk between them. Such agreement is controlling. Thus, for example, the parties may agree that a seller shall retain the risk of loss even though the buyer is in possession of the goods or has title to them. Furthermore, the agreement may provide that the buyer bears 60 percent of the risk and that the seller bears 40 percent.

Trial Sales   Some sales are made with the understanding that the buyer can return the goods even though they conform to the contract. These trial sales permit the buyer to try the goods for a period of time in order to determine if she wishes either to keep them or to try to resell them. The Code recognizes two types of trial sales—a sale on approval and a sale or return—and provides a test for distinguishing between them: unless otherwise agreed, if the goods are delivered primarily for the buyer's use, the transaction is a sale on approval; if they are delivered primarily for resale by the buyer, it is a sale or return.

In a **sale on approval**, possession of, but not title to, the goods is transferred to the buyer for a stated period of time or, if no time is stated, for a reasonable time, during which period the buyer may use the goods to determine whether she wishes to accept them. Both title and risk of loss remain with the *seller* until the buyer "approves," or accepts, the goods. Until acceptance by the buyer, the sale is a bailment with an option to purchase.

Although use of the goods consistent with the purpose of approval by the buyer is not acceptance, the buyer's failure to notify the seller within a reasonable time of her election to return the goods *is* an acceptance. The buyer also may manifest approval by exercising any dominion or control over the goods inconsistent with the seller's ownership. On approval, title and risk of loss pass to the buyer, who then becomes liable to the seller for the purchase price of the goods. If, however, the buyer then decides to return the goods and so notifies the seller, the return is at the seller's risk and expense.

In a **sale or return**, the goods are sold and delivered to the buyer with an option to return them to the seller. The risk of loss is on the *buyer*, who also has title until she revests it in the seller by returning the goods. The return of the goods is at the buyer's risk and expense.

A **consignment** is a delivery of possession of personal property to an agent for sale by the agent. Under the Code, a sale on consignment is regarded as a sale or return. Therefore, the creditors of the consignee (the agent who receives the merchandise for sale) prevail over the consignor and may obtain possession of the consigned goods, provided the consignee maintains a place of business where he deals in goods of the kind involved under a name other than the name of the consignor. Nevertheless, the consignor will prevail if she (a) complies with applicable state law requiring a consignor's interest to be evidenced by a sign, (b) establishes that the consignee is generally known by his creditors to be substantially engaged in selling the goods of others, or (c) complies with the filing provisions of Article 9 (Secured Transactions).

Contracts Involving Carriers   Sales contracts frequently contain terms indicating the agreement of the parties as to delivery by a carrier. These terms identify the contract as a shipment contract or as a destination contract and, by implication, indicate the time at which the risk of loss passes. If the contract does not require the seller to deliver the goods to a particular destination but merely to the common carrier (a ***shipment contract***), risk of loss passes to the buyer when the seller delivers the goods to the carrier. If the seller is required to deliver them to a particular destination (a ***destination contract***), risk of loss passes to the buyer at destination when the goods are tendered to the buyer.

The following case deals with the question of when the risk of loss passes between parties whose sales contract contains no specific provision or any delivery term. The case demonstrates that if the contract is not clearly a destination contract or a shipment contract, the law assumes that it is a shipment contract.

Sale on approval transfer of possession without title to the buyer for trial period; risk of loss remains with the seller until approved or accepted by the buyer

Sale or return sale where buyer has option to return goods to the seller; risk of loss is on the buyer until goods are returned

Consignment delivery of possession of personal property to an agent for sale

Contracts involving carriers in shipment contracts, the seller bears the risk of loss and expense until the goods are delivered to the carrier for shipment; in destination contracts, the seller bears the risk of loss and expense until tender of the goods at a particular destination

PESTANA v. KARINOL District Court of Appeals of Florida, Third District, 1979, 367 So.2d 1096

FACTS Nahim Amar B. contracted with Karinol for the purchase of electronic watches. The contract contained no explicit provisions specifying who would bear the risk of loss while the watches were in the carrier's possession. Nor were there any F.O.B., F.A.S., or C. & F. terms in the contract. It did, however, contain a notation specifying Chetumal, Mexico, as the destination. Karinol delivered the watches to its agent for delivery to Amar. Karinol's carrier obtained insurance for the two cartons of watches, naming Karinol as the insured. The goods were then shipped by air to Belize, where they were to be shipped by truck to Chetumal. Upon their arrival in Belize, Amar paid Pestana, the executor of Amar's estate, the balance due on the contract. But when customs officials and an agent of Amar opened the cartons in Belize for customs clearance, they found the packages were empty.

Pestana contended that the "send to Chetumal, Mexico," notation made the contract a destination contract. Therefore, he argued, Karinol should bear the loss of the watches since its carrier had not yet tendered delivery of them in Chetumal. Pestana appealed from a verdict in favor of Karinol.

DECISION Judgment for Karinol affirmed.

OPINION In a destination contract, the seller bears the risk of loss of the goods until tender of delivery to the buyer. On the other hand, in a shipment contract, risk of loss passes to the buyer when the seller delivers the goods to the carrier. The parties must explicitly agree to a destination contract; otherwise, it is considered a shipment contract.

Here, there were no specific provisions in the contract allocating the risk of loss of the goods while in transit and no delivery terms, such as F.O.B. Chetumal. The "send to" term, common to all contracts requiring the delivery of goods, by itself is not enough to convert a shipment contract into a destination contract. The contract, therefore, was a shipment contract with Amar bearing the risk of loss after Karinol delivered the watches to its carrier. Thus, Amar may not recover the purchase price of the watches from Karinol.

INTERPRETATION Unless specifically designated as a destination contract, a sales contract that involves shipment by a carrier is a shipment contract.

Goods in Possession of Bailee In some sales, the goods, at the time the contract is made, are held by a bailee and are to be delivered without being moved. For instance, a seller may contract with a buyer to sell grain that is located in a grain elevator and that the buyer intends to leave in the same elevator. In such situations, the time at which the risk of loss passes to the buyer depends on the document of title involved—or, as the case may be, on whether the transaction involves such a document at all: (1) If a negotiable document of title (discussed in Chapter 50) is involved, the risk of loss passes when the buyer *receives* the document. (2) If a nonnegotiable document of title is involved, the risk passes when the document is *tendered* to the buyer. (3) If no documents of title are employed, it passes either (a) when the seller *tenders* to the buyer written directions to the bailee to deliver the goods to the buyer or (b) when the bailee acknowledges the buyer's right to possession of the goods.

In situations 2 and 3a, if the buyer seasonably objects, the risk of loss remains upon the seller until the buyer has had a reasonable time to present the document or direction to the bailee.

All other sales for merchant seller, risk of loss passes to buyer on the buyer's receipt of goods; for nonmerchant seller, risk of loss passes to buyer upon tender of goods

All Other Sales If the buyer possesses the goods when the contract is formed, risk of loss passes to the buyer at that time.

All other sales not involving breach are covered by the Code's catchall provision, which applies to those instances in which the buyer picks up the goods at the seller's place of business or those in which the seller delivers the goods using her own transportation. In these cases, risk of loss depends on whether the seller is a merchant. If the seller is a *merchant*, risk of loss passes to the buyer on the buyer's *receipt* of the goods. If the seller is *not a merchant*, it passes on *tender* of the goods from the seller to the buyer. The policy behind this rule is that so long as the merchant seller is making delivery at her place of business or with her own vehicle, she continues to control the goods and can be expected to insure them. The buyer, on the other hand, has no control over the goods and is not likely to have insurance on them.

Suppose Ted goes to Jack's furniture store, selects a particular set of dining room furniture, and pays Jack the agreed price of $800 on Jack's agreement to stain the set a darker color and to deliver it. Jack stains the furniture and notifies Ted that he will deliver it the next day. That night, the furniture is accidentally destroyed by fire. Ted can recover the $800 payment from Jack. The risk of loss is on the seller, Jack, because he is a merchant and the goods were not received by Ted but were only tendered to him.

On the other hand, suppose Debra, an accountant, having moved to a different city, contracts to sell her household furniture to Dwight for $3,000 by a written agreement signed by Dwight. Though she notifies Dwight that the furniture is available for Dwight to pick up, he delays picking it up for several days; in the interim, the furniture is stolen from Debra's residence through no fault of Debra's. Debra may recover the $3,000 purchase price from Dwight. The risk of loss is on the buyer, Dwight, because, since the seller, Debra, is not a merchant, tender is sufficient to transfer the risk of loss.

MARTIN v. MELLAND'S INC. Supreme Court of North Dakota, 1979, 283 N.W.2d 76

FACTS Martin entered into a written agreement with Melland's, Inc., a farm implement dealer, to purchase a truck and attached haystack mover. According to the contract, Martin was to trade in his old truck and haystack mover unit; to mail or bring the certificate of title to the old unit to Melland's within a week; and to retain the use and possession of the old unit until Melland's had the new one ready. The contract contained no provision allocating the risk of loss of the trade-in unit. After Martin mailed the certificate to Melland's, but while he still had possession of the trade-in unit itself, the unit was destroyed by fire. Martin then sued to compel Melland's to bear the loss of the trade-in, claiming that title had passed to Melland's before the destruction of the old unit. The district court dismissed the cause of action, and Martin appealed.

DECISION Judgment for Melland's Inc. affirmed.

OPINION Under the Code, the passage of title is irrelevant to the determination of who bears the risk of loss. The risk of loss is determined by specific provisions of the Code. The provision applicable here states: "The risk of loss passes to the buyer on his receipt of the goods if the seller is a merchant; otherwise the risk passes to the buyer on tender of delivery." Because Martin was the original owner of the trade-in unit, he is considered the seller of it. Moreover, Martin, by his own admission, is not a merchant seller. Thus, the risk of loss would shift to Melland's only after Martin had tendered delivery of the unit. Since both parties agreed that Martin would keep the old unit until the new one was ready, tender of delivery had not been made when the unit was destroyed. Consequently, Martin must bear the loss.

INTERPRETATION In a sale involving a nonmerchant seller, the risk of loss stays with the seller until the goods are tendered to the buyer.

See Figure 21–3 for an illustration of risk of loss in the absence of breach. See also Ethical Dilemma.

BULK SALES

A sale of goods in bulk occurs when a merchant sells all or a major portion of his inventory at once. Creditors have an obvious interest in such a bulk disposal of merchandise made not in the ordinary course of business, for a debtor may secretly liquidate all or a major part of his tangible assets by a bulk sale and conceal or divert the proceeds of the sale without paying his creditors. The central purpose of bulk sales law is to deter two common forms of commercial fraud. These occur (a) when the merchant, owing debts, sells out his stock in trade to

FIGURE 21–3 Passage of Risk of Loss in Absence of Breach

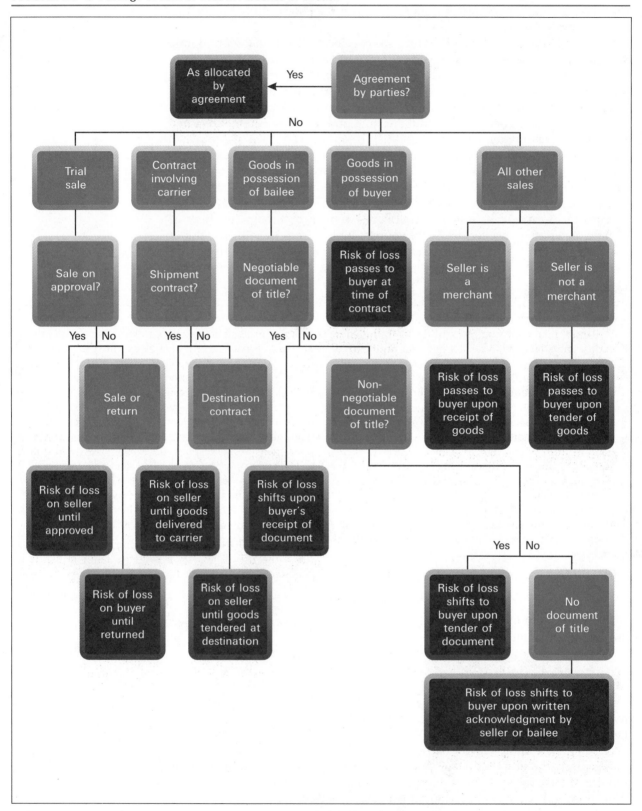

a friend for a low price, pays his creditors less than he owes them, and hopes to come back into the business "through the back door" sometime in the future; and (b) when the merchant, owing debts, sells out his stock in trade to anyone for any price, pockets the proceeds, and disappears without paying his creditors.

Article 6 of the Code, which applies to such sales, defines a **bulk transfer** as "any transfer in bulk and not in the ordinary course of the transferor's business of a major part of the materials, supplies, merchandise, or other inventory." The transfer of a substantial part of equipment is a bulk transfer only if made in connection with a bulk transfer of inventory. Those subject to Article 6 of the Code are merchants whose principal business is the sale of merchandise from stock, including those who manufacture what they sell.

The Code provides that a bulk transfer of assets is ineffective against any creditor of the transferor, unless the transfer meets certain Article 6 requirements designed to give the creditor notice of the bulk transfer. Should the transferor fail to comply with these requirements, the goods in the possession of the transferee continue to be subject to the claims of the transferor's unpaid creditors.

In 1988, the National Conference of Commissioners on Uniform State Laws and the American Law Institute jointly issued a recommendation stating "that changes in the business and legal contexts in which sales are conducted have made regulation of bulk sales unnecessary." They therefore recommended the

Requirements of Article 6 transfer is ineffective against any creditor of the transferor, unless certain requirements are met

Bulk transfer transfer of a major part of the transferor's inventory made not in the ordinary course of his business

ETHICAL DILEMMA Who Should Bear the Loss?

FACTS Stratton Corporation, a regional pharmaceutical company located in Smithville, has embarked on a policy that encourages its employees to become computer literate. Accordingly, it has made a deal with BMI, a computer manufacturer, to have computers available for purchase by Stratton's employees at considerable savings from the standard retail price. The computers, which Stratton purchases in bulk, are delivered to the home office in Smithville.

The state in which Smithville is located imposes a 7 percent sales tax on any sale that takes place in the state. For state tax purposes, the place of sale is the point of delivery. To help reduce the costs to its employees, Stratton has arranged for its personnel to pick up their purchased computers at its Somerton office, located about 25 miles from Smithville in a neighboring state that does not impose a sales tax.

Arthur Johnson, a Stratton employee, took advantage of the offer and purchased a computer through Stratton on December 1, 1992. The computer arrived in Smithville on December 18, 1992, and was immediately placed on a Stratton pickup truck for transfer to Somerton. Johnson, however, wanting the computer home by Christmas, suggested that he put the unit in his car and deliver it to Somerton himself, where he would immediately pick it up. Stratton, seeing a chance to save time and money, agreed to the suggestion.

On December 19, 1992, in a heavy snowfall, Johnson left Smithville with the computer bound for Somerton. Even as he turned onto the highway, the snowfall became a whiteout. Hearing on his car radio that blizzard conditions had already made the roads into Somerton impassable, Johnson brought the computer to his home, planning to hold it there until he could deliver it to Somerton. On the night of December 21, 1992, when snow still blocked the Somerton roads, the Johnson home and many of its furnishings were destroyed by fire. Unfortunately, Johnson had no fire insurance at the time. The computer was among the items that were destroyed. Stratton refused to accept the loss on the computer and demanded that Johnson pay for it in full. Johnson refuses.

Social, Policy, and Ethical Considerations

1. From a legal standpoint, who must bear the risk of loss for the computer? From an ethical standpoint, who should bear the loss?

2. What social responsibility did Stratton violate in setting up the computer delivery scheme? Did it have a legitimate reason for implementing the plan?

3. Do cost savings ever give a business the right to violate a social or ethical responsibility?

4. Are there any similarities between Stratton's actions in this case and a company's decision to close one of its plants?

repeal of Article 6 or, for those states that felt the need to continue the regulation of bulk sales, the adoption of a revised Article 6 designed to afford better protection to creditors while minimizing the obstacles to good faith transactions. Over half of the states have repealed Article 6; only a few states have adopted Revised Article 6.

CHAPTER SUMMARY

Transfer of Title	**Identification** designation of specific goods as goods to which the contract of sale refers
	■ *Security Interest* an interest in personal property or fixtures that ensures payment or performance of an obligation
	■ *Insurable Interest* buyer obtains an insurable interest and specific remedies in the goods by the identification of existing foods as goods to which the contract of sale refers
	Passage of Title title passes when the parties intend it to pass; when the parties do not specifically agree, the Code provides rules to determine when title passes
	■ *Physical Movement of the Goods* when delivery is to be made by moving the goods, title passes at the time and place where the seller completes his performance with reference to delivery
	■ *No Movement of the Goods*
	Power to Transfer Title the purchaser of goods obtains such title as his transferor either has or had the power to transfer; however, to encourage and make secure good faith acquisitions of goods, it is necessary to protect certain third parties under certain circumstances
	■ *Void Title* no title can be transferred
	■ *Voidable Title* the good faith purchaser acquires good title
	■ *Entrusting of Goods to a Merchant* buyers in the ordinary course of business acquire good title when buying from merchants

Risk of Loss	**Definition** allocation of loss between seller and buyer where the goods have been damaged, destroyed, or lost without the fault of either party
	Risk of Loss Where There is a Breach
	■ *Breach by the Seller* if the seller ships to the buyer goods that do not conform to the contract, the risk of loss remains on the seller until the buyer has accepted the goods or until the seller has remedied the defect
	■ *Breach by the Buyer* the seller may treat the risk of loss as resting on the buyer for a commercially reasonable time to the extent of any deficiency in the seller's effective insurance coverage
	Risk of Loss in Absence of a Breach
	■ *Agreement of the Parties* the parties may by agreement allocate the risk of loss
	■ *Trial Sales* unless otherwise agreed, if the goods are delivered primarily for the buyer's use, the transaction is a sale on approval (risk of loss remains with the seller until "approval" or acceptance of the goods by the buyer); if they are delivered primarily for resale by the buyer, it is a sale or return (the risk of loss is is on the buyer until she returns the goods)

- ■ *Contracts Involving Carriers* in shipment contracts, the seller bears the risk of loss and expense until the goods are delivered to the carrier for shipment; in destination contracts, the seller bears the risk of loss and expense until tender of the goods at a particular destination
- ■ *All Other Sales* for merchant seller, risk of loss passes to buyer on the buyer's receipt of the goods; for nonmerchant seller, risk of loss passes to buyer upon tender of goods

Bulk Sales

Definition a transfer, not in the ordinary course of the transferor's business, of a major part of inventory

Requirements of Article 6 transfer is ineffective against any creditor of the transferor, unless certain requirements are met

QUESTIONS

1. Explain the relative importance of title under the common law and Article 2.
2. Distinguish between a shipment contract and a destination contract. When does title and risk of loss pass under each?
3. When does the seller have a right or power to transfer title? When is the transfer void or voidable? By whom? Against whom?
4. Discuss the rules covering (a) risk of loss in the absence of a breach and (b) risk of loss when there is a breach.
5. Discuss bulk transfers. How do such transfers concern creditors? How does the Code attempt to regulate bulk transfers?

Internet Question. Compare the provisions governing risk of loss contained in the United Nations Convention on Contracts for the International Sale of Goods (Vienna, 1980) with those of Article 2 of the Uniform Commercial Code.

PROBLEMS

1. Stein, a mechanic, and Beal, a life insurance agent, entered into a written contract for the sale of Stein's tractor to Beal for $2,800 cash. It was agreed that Stein would tune the motor on the tractor. Stein fulfilled this obligation and on the night of July 1 telephoned Beal that the tractor was ready to be picked up on Beal's making payment. Beal responded, "I'll be there in the morning with the money." On the next morning, however, Beal was approached by an insurance prospect and decided to get the tractor at a later date. On the night of July 2, the tractor was destroyed by fire of unknown origin. Neither Stein nor Beal had any fire insurance. Who must bear the loss?

2. Regan received a letter from Chase, the material portion of which stated, "Chase hereby places an order with you for fifty cases of Red Top Tomatoes. Ship them C.O.D." As soon as he received the letter, Regan shipped the tomatoes to Chase. While en route, the railroad car carrying the tomatoes was wrecked. When Chase refused to pay for the tomatoes, Regan started an action to recover the purchase price. Chase defended on the ground that because the shipment was C.O.D., neither title to the tomatoes nor risk of loss passed until their delivery to Chase. Decision?

3. On May 10, the Adair Company, acting through Brown, entered into a contract with Clark for the installation of a milking machine at Clark's farm. Following the enumeration of the articles to be furnished, together with the price of each article, the written contract provided: "This machinery is subject to thirty days' free trial and is to be installed about June 1." Within thirty days after installation, all the purchased machinery, except for a double utility unit, was destroyed by fire through no fault of Clark's. The Adair Company sued Clark to recover the value of the articles destroyed. Decision?

4. Brown contracted to buy sixty cases of Lovely Brand canned corn from Smith, a Toledo seller, at a contract price of $600. Based on the contract, Smith selected and set aside sixty cases of Lovely Brand canned corn

and tagged them "For Brown." The contract required Smith to ship the corn to Brown via T Railroad, F.O.B. Toledo. Before Smith delivered the corn to the railroad, the sixty cases were stolen from Smith's warehouse.

(a) Who is liable for the loss of the sixty cases of corn, Brown or Smith?

(b) Suppose Smith had delivered the corn to the railroad in Toledo. After the corn was loaded on a freight car but before the train left the yard, the car was broken open and its contents, including the corn, were stolen. Who is liable for the loss, Brown or Smith?

(c) Would your answer in question (b) be the same if this contract were F.O.B. Brown's warehouse, and all other facts remained the same?

5. Farber owned a quantity of corn that was stored in a corncrib located on Farber's farm. On March 12, Farber wrote a letter to Barber stating that he would sell to Barber all of the corn in this crib, which he estimated at between 900 and 1,000 bushels, for $3.60 per bushel. Barber received this letter on March 13, and on the same day immediately wrote and mailed a letter to Farber stating that he would buy the corn. The corncrib and contents were accidentally destroyed by a fire that broke out about 3:00 a.m. on March 14. What are the rights of the parties? What difference, if any, in result would there be if Farber were a merchant?

6. Franco, a New York dealer, purchased twenty-five barrels of specially graded and packed apples from a producer at Hood River, Oregon. He afterward resold the apples to Harris under a contract that specified an agreed price on delivery at Harris's place of business in New York. The apples were shipped to Franco from Oregon but, through no fault of either Franco or Harris, were totally destroyed before reaching New York. Does any liability rest on Franco?

7. Smith was approached by a man who introduced himself as Brown of Brown & Co. Smith, who did not know Brown, asked Dun & Bradstreet for a credit report on Brown. He thereupon sold Brown some expensive gems and billed Brown & Co. "Brown" turned out to be a clever jewel thief, who later sold the gems to Brown & Co. for valuable consideration. Brown & Co. was unaware of "Brown's" transaction with Smith. Smith sued Brown & Co. for either the return of the gems or the price as billed to Brown & Co. Decision?

8. Charlotte, the owner of a new Cadillac automobile, agreed to loan the car to Ellen for the month of February while she (Charlotte) went to Florida for a winter vacation. It was understood that Ellen, who was a small-town Cadillac dealer, would merely place Charlotte's car in her showroom for exhibition and sales promotion purposes. While Charlotte was away, Ellen sold the car to Bob. When Charlotte returned from Florida, she sued to recover the car from Bob. Decision?

9. Steven offered to sell his used automobile to Benito for $2,600 cash. Benito agreed to buy the car, gave Steven a check for $2,600, and drove away in the car. The next day, Benito sold the car for $3,000 to Jose, a good faith purchaser. The bank returned Benito's $2,600 check to Steven because of insufficient funds in Benito's account. Steven brings an action against Jose to recover the automobile. What is the judgment?

10. Justin told Jennifer he wished to buy Jennifer's automobile. He drove the car for about ten minutes, returned to Jennifer, stated he wanted to take the automobile to show it to his wife, and then left with the automobile and never returned. Justin sold the automobile in another state to Thomas and gave him a bill of sale. Jennifer sued Thomas to recover the automobile. Decision?

11. On February 7, Pillsbury purchased 8,000 bushels of wheat from Landis. The wheat was being stored at the Greensville Grain Company. Pillsbury also intended to store the wheat with Greensville. On February 10, the wheat was destroyed. Landis demands payment for the wheat from Pillsbury. Who prevails? Who has title? Who has the risk of loss? Explain.

12. Johnson, who owns a hardware store, was indebted to Hutchinson, one of his suppliers. Johnson sold his business to Lockhart, one of Johnson's previous competitors. Lockhart combined the inventory from Johnson's store with his own and moved the combined inventory to a new, larger store. Hutchinson claims that Lockhart must pay Johnson's debt because the sale of the business had been made without complying with the requirements of the bulk sales law. Decision?

13. A seller had manufactured 40,000 pounds of plastic resin pellets specially for a buyer, who agreed to accept them at the rate of 1,000 pounds per day upon his issuance of shipping instructions. Despite numerous requests by the seller, the buyer issued no such instructions. On August 18, the seller, after warehousing the goods for forty days, demanded by letter that the buyer issue instructions. The buyer agreed to issue them beginning August 20, but never did. On September 22, a fire destroyed the seller's plant containing the goods, which were not covered by insurance. Who bears the risk of loss? Why?

14. McCoy, an Oklahoma cattle dealer, orally agreed with Chandler, a Texas cattle broker, to ship cattle to a New Mexico feedlot for delivery to Chandler. The agreement was for six lots of cattle valued at $119,000. After McCoy delivered the cattle, he presented invoices to Chandler that described the cattle and set forth the sales price. McCoy then demanded payment, which Chandler refused. Unknown to McCoy, Chandler had obtained a loan from First National Bank and had pledged the subject cattle as collateral. The bank had no knowledge of any interest that

McCoy may have had in the cattle. McCoy sued to recover the cattle. The bank counterclaimed that it had a perfected security interest in the cattle that was superior to any interest of McCoy's. The trial court ruled in favor of the bank, and McCoy appeals. Decision?

15. Porter, the owner of a collection of artworks, had a number of art transactions with Harold Von Maker, who used, among other names, that of Peter Wertz. Porter permitted Von Maker to temporarily have a painting by Maurice Utrillo, *Chateau de Lion-sur-Mer*, to hang in his home until he decided whether to purchase it. A few months later, Porter sought the return of the Utrillo painting but was unable to reach Von Maker. Porter subsequently discovered that he was not dealing with the "real" Peter Wertz but with Harold Von Maker, a man with an extensive criminal record, including a conviction for defrauding the Chase Manhattan Bank. When Porter finally reached him, Von Maker claimed the Utrillo was on consignment with a client. Von Maker then agreed in writing either to return the painting to Porter within ninety days or to make compensation for it. At the time he entered this agreement, Von Maker had already sold the painting. He had used the real Peter Wertz, a delicatessen employee and acquaintance, to effect the sale of the Utrillo to Feigen for $20,000. Feigen, an art dealer, then sold the painting to Brenner, and it is now somewhere in Venezuela. Porter brought suit against Feigen and the others involved to recover possession of either the Utrillo or its value. Decision?

16. Home Indemnity, an insurance company, paid one of its insureds after the theft of his car. The car reappeared in another state and was sold to Michael Schrier for $4,300 by a used car dealer. The dealer promised to give Mr. Schrier a certificate of title. One month later, the car was seized by the police on behalf of Home Indemnity. Mr. Schrier sued for the return of the car and won. Home Indemnity seeks reversal of that decision and possession of the car. Decision?

17. Fred Lane, who sells boats, motors, and trailers, sold a boat, motor, and trailer to John Willis in exchange for a check for $6,285.00. The check was not honored when Lane attempted to use the funds. Willis subsequently left the boat, motor, and trailer with John Garrett, who sold the items to Jimmy Honeycutt for $2,500.00. Honeycutt was surprised at how inexpensive the boat was, considering its quality. He did not know where Garrett got the boat, but he had dealt with Garrett before and described him as a "sly businessman." Garrett did not sell boats; normally, he sold fishing tackle and provisions. Honeycutt also received a forged certificate for the boat, on which he had observed Garrett forge the purported owner's signature. Lane sues Honeycutt for return of the boat, motor, and trailer. Decision?

18. Mike Moses purchased a mobile home, including installation, from Gary Newman. Newman delivered the home to Moses's lot. Upon inspection of the home, Moses's fiancée found a broken window and water pipe. Moses also had not received keys to the front door. Before Newman corrected these problems, a windstorm destroyed the home. Moses sued Newman for loss of the home. Decision?

19. United Road Machinery Company, a dealer in heavy road equipment (including truck scales supplied by Thurman Scale Company), received a telephone call on July 21 from James Durham, an officer of Consolidated Coal Company, seeking to acquire truck scales for his coal mining operation. United and Consolidated entered into a twenty-four-month lease-purchase agreement. United then notified Thurman that Consolidated would take possession of the scales directly. United paid for the scales and Consolidated took possession of them, but the latter never signed and returned the contract papers forwarded to it by United. Consolidated also never made any of the rental payments ($608/month) due under the lease. On September 20, Consolidated, through its officer Durham, sold the scales to Kentucky Mobile Homes for $8,500. Kentucky's president, Ethard Jasper, checked the county records prior to the purchase and found no lien or encumbrance on the title; likewise, he denied knowledge of the dispute between Consolidated and United. On September 22, Kentucky sold the scales to Clyde Jasper, individually, for $8,500. His search also failed to disclose any lien on the title to the scales, and he denied knowledge of the dispute between Consolidated and United. United brought suit to recover the scales from Jasper. Decision?

20. Harrison, a men's clothing retailer located in Westport, Connecticut, ordered merchandise from Ninth Street East, Ltd., a Los Angeles–based clothing manufacturer. Ninth Street delivered the merchandise to Denver-Chicago Trucking Company (Denver) in Los Angeles and then sent four invoices to Harrison that bore the notation "F.O.B. Los Angeles." Denver subsequently transferred the merchandise to a connecting carrier, Old Colony Transportation Company, for final delivery to Harrison's Westport store. When Old Colony tried to deliver the merchandise, Harrison's wife asked the truck driver to deliver the boxes inside the store; but the driver refused. The dispute remained unresolved, and the truck departed with Old Colony still in possession of the goods. By letter, Harrison then notified Ninth Street of the nondelivery; but Ninth Street was unable to locate the shipment. Ninth Street then sought to recover the contract purchase price from Harrison. Harrison refused, contending that risk of loss remained with Ninth Street because of its refusal to deliver the merchandise to Harrison's place of business. Decision?

CHAPTER 22

Products Liability: Warranties and Strict Liability

In this chapter, we will consider the liability of manufacturers and sellers of goods to buyers, users, consumers, and bystanders for damages caused by defective products. The rapidly expanding development of case law has established product liability as a distinct field of law that combines and enforces rules and principles of contracts, sales, negligence, strict liability, and statutory law.

One reason for the expansion of such liability has been the modern method of distributing goods. Today, retailers serve principally as a conduit of goods that are prepackaged in sealed containers and that are widely advertised by the manufacturer or distributor. This has hastened the extension of product liability coverage to include manufacturers and other parties within the chain of distribution. The extension of product liability to manufacturers, however, has not noticeably lessened the liability of a seller to his immediate purchaser. Rather, it has broadened the base of liability through the development and application of new principles of law.

Currently, the entire area of product liability has attracted a great deal of public attention. The cost of maintaining product liability insurance has skyrocketed, causing great concern in the business community. In response to the clamor over this insurance crisis, over forty states have revised their tort law to make successful product liability lawsuits more difficult to bring.

The liability of manufacturers and sellers of goods for a defective product, or for its failure to perform adequately, may be based on one or more of the following: (1) negligence, (2) misrepresentation, (3) violation of statutory duty, (4) warranty, and (5) strict liability in tort. We covered the first three of these causes of actions in Chapters 8 and 11. In this chapter, we will explore the last two.

WARRANTIES

Warranty obligation of the seller concerning title, quality, characteristics, or condition of goods

A **warranty** creates a duty on the part of the seller to assure that the goods he sells will conform to certain qualities, characteristics, or conditions. A seller, however, is not required to warrant the goods; and, in general, he may, by appropriate words, disclaim (exclude) or modify a particular warranty or even all warranties.

In bringing a warranty action, the buyer must prove that (1) a warranty existed, (2) the warranty has been breached, (3) the breach of the warranty proximately caused the loss suffered, and (4) notice of the breach of warranty was given to the seller. The seller has the burden of proving defenses based on the buyer's conduct. If the seller breaches his warranty, the buyer may reject or revoke acceptance of the goods. Moreover, whether the goods have been accepted or rejected, the buyer may recover a judgment against the seller for damages. Harm for which damages are recoverable include personal injury, damage to property, and economic loss. Economic loss most commonly involves damages for loss of bargain and consequential damages for lost profits. (Damages for breach of warranty are discussed in detail in the next chapter.) In this section, we will examine the various types of warranties, as well as the obstacles to a cause of action for breach of warranty.

TYPES OF WARRANTIES

A warranty may arise out of the mere existence of a sale (a warranty of title), out of any affirmation of fact or promise made by the seller to the buyer (an express warranty), or out of the circumstances under which the sale is made (an implied warranty). In a contract for the sale of goods, it is possible to have both express and implied warranties, as well as a warranty of title. All warranties are construed as consistent with each other and cumulative, unless such construction is unreasonable.

Warranty of Title

Under the Code's **warranty of title**, the seller implicitly warrants (1) that the title conveyed is good and its transfer rightful and (2) that the goods are subject to no security interest or other lien (a claim on property by another for payment of debt) of which the buyer did not know at the time of contracting.

Warranty of title obligation to convey the right of ownership without any lien

Let us assume that Steven acquires goods from Nancy in a transaction that is void and then sells the goods to Rachel. Nancy brings an action against Rachel and recovers the goods. Steven has breached the warranty of title because he did not have good title to the goods and, therefore, his transfer of the goods to Rachel was not rightful. Accordingly, Steven is liable to Rachel for damages.

The Code does not label the warranty of title an implied warranty, even though it arises out of the sale and not out of any particular words or conduct. Instead, the Code has a separate disclaimer provision for warranty of title; thus, the Code's general disclaimer provision for implied warranties does not apply.

Express Warranties

An **express warranty** is an explicit undertaking by the seller with respect to the quality, description, condition, or performability of the goods. The undertaking may consist of an affirmation of fact or a promise that relates to the goods, a description of the goods, or a sample or model of the goods. In each of these instances, in order for an express warranty to be created, the undertaking must become or be made part of the basis of the bargain. It is not necessary, however, that the seller have a specific intention to make a warranty or use formal words such as "warrant" or "guarantee." Moreover, it is not necessary that, in order to be liable for breach of express warranty, a seller know of the falsity of a statement she makes; the seller may be acting in good faith. For example, if John mistakenly asserts to Sam that a rope will easily support 300 pounds and Sam is injured

Express warranty affirmation of fact or promise about the goods, which may consist of a description or a sample, and which becomes part of the basis of the bargain

when the rope breaks while supporting only 200 pounds, John is liable for breach of an express warranty.

Creation A seller can create an express warranty either orally or in writing. One way in which the seller may create such a warranty is by an ***affirmation of fact*** or a ***promise*** that relates to the goods. For example, a statement made by a seller that an automobile will get 42 miles to the gallon of gasoline or that a camera has automatic focus is an express warranty.

The Code further provides that an affirmation of the ***value*** of the goods or a statement purporting merely to be the seller's ***opinion*** or recommendation of the goods does not create a warranty. Such statements are not factual and do not deceive the ordinary buyer, who accepts them merely as opinions or as puffery (sales talk). A statement of value, however, may be an express warranty where the seller states the price at which the goods were purchased from a former owner, or where she gives market figures relating to sales of similar goods. These are affirmations of facts. They are statements of events, not mere opinions; and the seller is liable for breach of warranty if they are untrue. Also, although a statement of opinion by the seller is not ordinarily a warranty, the seller who is an expert and who gives her opinion as such may be liable for breach of warranty.

A seller also can create an express warranty by the use of a ***description*** of the goods that becomes a part of the basis of the bargain. Under such a warranty, the seller expressly warrants that the goods shall conform to the description. Examples include statements regarding a particular brand or type of goods, technical specifications, and blueprints.

The use of a ***sample*** or model is another means of creating an express warranty. Where a sample or model is a part of the basis of the bargain, the seller expressly warrants that the entire lot of goods sold shall conform to the sample or model. A sample is a good that is actually drawn from the bulk of goods that is the subject matter of the sale. By comparison, a model is offered for inspection when the subject matter is not at hand; it is not drawn from the bulk.

Basis of Bargain The Code does not require that the affirmations, promises, descriptions, samples, or models the seller makes or uses be relied on by the buyer but only that they constitute a part of the **basis of the bargain**. In other words, if they are part of the buyer's assumption underlying the sale, reliance by the buyer is presumed. Some courts merely require that the buyer know of the affirmation or promise for it to be presumed to be part of the basis of the bargain, while others require some showing of reliance. See the case that follows.

> **Basis of the bargain** part of the buyer's assumption underlying the sale

---

CIPOLLONE v. LIGGETT GROUP, INC. United States Court of Appeals, Third Circuit, 1990, 893 F.2d 541, aff'd in part and rev'd in part, 505 U.S. 504, 112 S.Ct. 2608, 120 L.Ed.2d 407 (1992)

FACTS Between 1942 and her death in 1984, Rose Cipollone smoked between one and two packs of cigarettes a day. Upon her death in 1984 from lung cancer, Rose's husband, Antonio Cipollone, filed suit against Liggett Group, Inc., Lorillard, Inc., and Philip Morris, Inc., three of the leading firms in the tobacco industry, for the wrongful death of his wife. Many theories of liability and defenses were asserted in this decidedly complex and protracted litigation.

One theory of liability claimed by Mr. Cipollone was breach of express warranty. It is uncontested that all three manufacturers ran multimedia ad campaigns that contained affirmations, promises, or innuendos that smoking cigarettes was safe. For example, ads for Chesterfield cigarettes boasted that a medical specialist could find no adverse health effects in subjects after six months of smoking. Chesterfields were also advertised as being manufactured with "electronic miracle" technology that

continued

made them "better and safer for you." Another ad stated that Chesterfield ingredients were tested and approved by scientists from leading universities. Another brand, L&M, publicly touted the "miracle tip" filter, claiming it was "just what the doctor ordered."

At trial, the defendant tobacco companies were not permitted to try and prove that Mrs. Cipollone disbelieved or placed no reliance on the advertisements and their safety assurances. The jury returned a verdict for $400,000 on the breach of express warranty claim. The defendant tobacco companies appealed.

DECISION Demand for a new trial on the issue of breach of express warranty. The court also ruled that the Federal Cigarette Labeling Act preempted claims arising from smoking after January 1, 1966, based upon the adequacy of warnings.

OPINION The central concern in a breach of express warranty case is the nature of the reliance interest required by the UCC. According to this section, any affirmation or promise, any description, or any sample or model must be made part of the basis of the bargain in order to create an express warranty. On one hand, the tobacco companies contend that Mr. Cipollone must prove that Mrs. Cipollone actually relied on the advertisements and was induced to buy the cigarettes because of the advertisements. On the other extreme, the trial court seemed to feel that any affirmations made in any advertisements became a basis of the bargain between Mrs. Cipollone and the tobacco companies, regardless of whether Mrs. Cipollone actually knew of the ad. The court noted that the district court's interpretation of this requirement would be met even if Mrs. Cipollone had not read or heard the advertisements. Rather, the court noted that a plaintiff satisfies the "basis of the bargain" requirement establishing breach of express warranty by proving that he or she read, heard, saw, or knew of ads containing affirmation of fact or promise. Once the buyer has become aware of such affirmations or promises, those statements are presumed to be part of the basis of the bargain unless the seller, by clear affirmative proof, shows that the buyer knew that the affirmation or promise was untrue.

INTERPRETATION Merely knowing of an express warranty may be sufficient to claim that the warranty is part of the basis of the bargain.

[Author's note: This case was appealed on the issue of federal preemption of common law claims arising after January 1, 1966, and was reversed in part and affirmed in part by the U.S. Supreme Court.]

Like statements in advertisements or catalogs, statements or promises made by the seller to the buyer prior to the sale may be express warranties, since they may form a part of the basis of the bargain. In addition, under the Code, statements or promises made by the seller subsequent to the making of the contract of sale may become express warranties even though no new consideration is given.

Implied Warranties

An implied warranty, unlike an express warranty, is not found in the language of the sales contract or in a specific affirmation or promise by the seller. Instead, it exists by operation of law. An **implied warranty** arises out of the circumstances under which the parties enter into their contract and depends on factors such as the type of contract or sale entered into, the seller's merchant or non-merchant status, the conduct of the parties, and the applicability of other statutes.

Merchantability Under the Code, a *merchant seller* makes an implied warranty of the merchantability of goods that are of the kind in which he deals. The implied warranty of **merchantability** provides that the goods are reasonably fit for the *ordinary* purposes for which they are manufactured and sold, and also that they are of fair, average quality.

Fitness for Particular Purpose Unlike the warranty of merchantability, the implied warranty of fitness for a particular purpose applies to *any* seller, whether he is a merchant or not. The implied warranty of **fitness for a particular purpose** arises if at the time of contracting the seller had reason to know the buyer's

Implied warranty contractual obligation arising out of certain circumstances of the sale

Merchantability warranty by a merchant seller that the goods are fit for their ordinary purpose

Fitness for a particular purpose warranty that goods are fit for a stated purpose, provided the seller selects the product knowing the buyer's intended use and that the buyer is relying on the seller's judgment

particular purpose and to know that the buyer was relying on the seller's skill and judgment to select suitable goods.

The implied warranty of fitness for a particular purpose does not require any specific statement by the seller. Rather, it requires only that the seller know that the buyer, in selecting a product for her specific purpose, is relying on the seller's expertise. The buyer need not specifically inform the seller of her particular purpose; it is sufficient if the seller has reason to know it. On the other hand, the implied warranty of fitness for a particular purpose would not arise in a situation where the buyer insists on a particular product and the seller simply conveys it to her.

In contrast to the implied warranty of merchantability, the implied warranty of fitness for a particular purpose pertains to a specific purpose for, rather than the ordinary purpose of, the goods. A particular purpose may be a specific use or may relate to a special situation in which the buyer intends to use the goods. Thus, if the seller has reason to know that the buyer is purchasing a pair of shoes for mountain climbing and that the buyer is relying on the seller's judgment to furnish suitable shoes for this purpose, a sale of shoes suitable only for ordinary walking purposes would be a breach of this implied warranty. Likewise, if a buyer indicates to a seller that she needs a stamping machine to stamp 10,000 packages in an eight-hour period and that she relies upon the seller to select an appropriate machine, the seller, by selecting a machine, impliedly warrants that the machine selected will stamp 10,000 packages in an eight-hour period.

Frequently, as in the case that follows, a seller's conduct may involve both the implied warranty of merchantability *and* the implied warranty of fitness for a particular purpose.

IN RE L. B. TRUCKING, INC. United States Bankruptcy Court, 1994, 163 BR 709, 23 UCC Rep. Serv.2d 1093

FACTS Dudley B. Durham, Jr., and his wife, Barbara Durham, owned and operated a trucking company, L. B. Trucking, Inc., and a farm, Double-D Farms, Inc. In April, 1983, Dudley Durham met with Richard Thomas of Southern States Cooperative—which is in the business of supplying various agricultural supplies to farmers—about arranging for the application of herbicides to the Durhams' fields.

At a subsequent meeting in early May, Durham met with Thomas to complete credit arrangements and to arrange the application of herbicides. Durham told Thomas, "Richard, you know I'm trying to pay, get straightened around and get all my stuff straightened around. I want it done the cheapest way, the best way it can be done." Thomas responded, "Will do." Thomas then outlined with some specificity the chemicals he proposed to use on the Durhams' fields. The plan included the use of a water-based carrier that was recommended by local experts, rather than a more expensive nitrogen solution. Durham had no experience or expertise on herbicidal chemicals and relied on Thomas's briefing on the various herbicide mixtures in choosing which ones to apply.

When the herbicides were actually to be applied, Southern States herbicide applicator, Gilbert McClements, received from Mr. Thomas instructions concerning which chemicals to apply and would mix the chemicals each day prior to spraying. Apparently, though, Mr. McClements used a nitrogen solution to prepare the herbicides and did not make extensive pre-spraying inspections of the grass and weeds in the fields to be sprayed. When Durham noticed a significant number of weeds and grasses had survived the herbicidal treatment, he promptly notified Southern States. Southern States attempted to remedy the problem, but the harvest was dismal and far below the county average.

In 1983, the Durhams and both their businesses filed for bankruptcy. Southern States brought a claim against the consolidated bankruptcy estate to collect payment for the herbicides as well as application and other services provided. The trustee of the estate asserted counterclaims against Southern States for negligence and breach of warranties in the application of herbicides that caused severe damage to the Durhams' 1983 crop.

DECISION Judgment for the trustee.

continued

OPINION The warranty provisions of the UCC are applicable in this case since the predominant purpose of the contract was the sale of herbicides and the service of their application was merely incidental to that sale. Furthermore, the facts of the case lead to the conclusion that Southern States breached both express and implied warranties in its sale of herbicides to the Durhams.

Thomas created at least two express warranties by his statements to Durham. First, he warranted that water would be the carrier used to distribute the herbicides. Second, Thomas made statements about the effectiveness of the herbicides in removing weeds and grass. These statements became a part of the basis of the bargain. They were not puffing or mere "seller's talk" but rather specific statements about the product. Moreover, Durham, because of his limited knowledge, relied on these statements in deciding to purchase from Southern States. The first express warranty was breached by the use of the nitrogen solution, notwithstanding Southern States argument that the use of nitrogen solution was common trade usage in 1983. The standard for evaluating whether conduct is a breach of warranty is the affirmation of fact or promise made by the seller, not common trade usage. The second express warranty was breached since the herbicide failed to kill weeds effectively. Expert testimony established that these breaches were a proximate cause of the damage to the 1983 crop.

In addition to express warranties, Southern States also breached implied warranties created by the UCC. Under the implied warranty of merchantability, a merchant warrants that goods are merchantable at the time of sale. There is no doubt that Southern States is a merchant as defined under the UCC, because it "deals in goods of the kind." To be merchantable, goods must pass without objection in the trade and be fit for the ordinary purposes for which they were intended. Herbicides are intended to be used as chemical agents that will kill weeds without damaging the primary crops. The herbicides in this case failed to control 85 percent of the weeds. Instead, the weeds flourished and the crops died. Therefore, the herbicides were not merchantable as they were unfit for the ordinary purpose for which they were intended to be used.

Southern States also breached the implied warranty that the herbicides were fit for a particular purpose. Under this warranty, if a seller "has reason to know of a particular purpose for which the goods are required and that the buyer is relying on the seller's skill or judgment to select or furnish suitable goods, the seller warrants that the goods sold shall be fit for such purpose." UCC § 2-315. Durham relied on Thomas's skill and judgment in selecting suitable herbicides to conduct no-till farming on his farms. However, the herbicides did not effectively do their job. As a result, the herbicides' failure to do their intended task coupled with Durham's reliance on Southern States' judgment and skill in formulating, mixing, and applying the herbicidal chemicals breached the implied warranty of fitness for a particular purpose.

INTERPRETATION In a contract for a sale of goods, it is possible to breach multiple warranties.

OBSTACLES TO WARRANTY ACTIONS

A number of technical obstacles, which vary considerably from jurisdiction to jurisdiction, limit the effectiveness of warranty as a basis for recovery. These include disclaimers of warranties, limitations or modifications of warranties, privity, notice of breach, and the conduct of the plaintiff.

Disclaimer of Warranties

To be effective, a **disclaimer** (negation of warranty) must be positive, explicit, unequivocal, and conspicuous. The Code calls for a reasonable construction of words or conduct to disclaim or limit warranties.

Express Exclusions In general, a seller cannot provide an **express warranty** and then disclaim it. A seller can, however, avoid making an express warranty by carefully refraining from making any promise or affirmation of fact relating to the goods, by refraining from making a description of the goods, or by refraining from using a sample or model in a sale. Oral warranties made before the execution of a written agreement containing an express disclaimer are subject to the parol evidence rule, however. Thus, as discussed in Chapter 15, if the parties intend the written contract to be the final and *complete* statement of the

Disclaimer negation of a warranty

Express warranty not usually possible to disclaim

agreement between them, parol evidence of a warranty that *contradicts* the terms of the written contract is inadmissible.

A **warranty of title** may be excluded only by specific language or by certain circumstances, including a judicial sale or sales by sheriffs, executors, or foreclosing lienors. In the latter cases, the seller is clearly offering to sell only such right or title as he or a third person might have in the goods, because it is apparent that the goods are not the property of the person selling them.

To exclude or to modify an **implied warranty of merchantability**, the language of disclaimer or modification must mention *merchantability* and, in the case of a writing, must be *conspicuous*.

To exclude or to modify an **implied warranty of fitness** for the particular purpose of the buyer, the disclaimer must be in *writing* and *conspicuous*.

All implied warranties, unless the circumstances indicate otherwise, are excluded by expressions like "*as is*" or "with all faults" or by other language plainly calling the buyer's attention to the exclusion of warranties. Most courts require the "as is" clause to be conspicuous. Implied warranties may also be excluded by course of dealing, course of performance, or usage of trade.

The courts will invalidate disclaimers they consider unconscionable. The Code, as discussed in Chapter 19, permits a court to limit the application of any contract or contractual provision that it finds unconscionable.

Buyer's Examination or Refusal to Examine If the buyer inspects the goods before entering into the contract, **implied warranties** do not apply to defects that are apparent on examination. Moreover, there is no implied warranty on defects that an examination ought to have revealed, not only where the buyer has examined the goods as fully as she desired, but also where the buyer has *refused* to examine the goods.

Warranty of title may be excluded or modified by specific language or by certain circumstances

Implied warranty of merchantability the disclaimer must mention "merchantability" and in the case of writing, must be conspicuous

Implied warranty of fitness for a particular purpose the disclaimer must be in writing and conspicuous

Other disclaimers of implied warranties the implied warranties may also be disclaimed (1) by expressions like "as is," "with all faults," or other similar language; (2) by course of dealing, course of performance, or usage of trade; or (3) as to defects an examination ought to have revealed where the buyer has examined the goods or where the buyer has refused to examine the goods

---

TRANS-AIRE INTERNATIONAL, INC. v. NORTHERN ADHESIVE CO., INC. United States Court of Appeals, Seventh Circuit 1989, 882 F.2d 1254

FACTS Trans-Aire International, Inc. (TAI) converts ordinary automotive vans into recreational vehicles. TAI had been installing carpet and ceiling fabrics in the converted vans with an adhesive made by the 3M Company. Unfortunately, during the hot summer months the 3M adhesive would often fail to hold the carpet and fabrics in place.

TAI contacted Northern Adhesive Company (Northern), seeking a "suitable" product to replace the 3M adhesive. Northern sent samples of several adhesives, commenting that hopefully one or more "might be applicable." Northern also informed TAI that one of the samples, Adhesive 7448, was a "match" for the 3M adhesive. After testing all the samples under cool plant conditions, TAI's chief engineer determined that Adhesive 7448 was better than the 3M adhesive. When TAI's president asked if the new adhesive should be tested under summerlike conditions, the chief engineer responded that it was unnecessary to do so. The president then asked if Adhesive 7448 came with any warranties. A Northern representative stated that there were no warranties, except that the orders shipped would be identical to the sample.

After converting over 500 vans using Adhesive 7448, TAI became aware that high summer temperatures were causing the new adhesive to fail. TAI sued Northern, claiming breach of an implied warranty of fitness for a particular purpose and breach of an implied warranty of merchantability, as well as breach of express warranty. The trial court ruled for Northern, and TAI appealed.

DECISION Judgment for Northern.

OPINION The UCC provides that "when the buyer before entering into a contract has examined the goods or the sample or model as fully as he desired or has refused to examine the goods there is no implied warranty with regard to defects which an examination ought in the circumstances to have revealed to him." The facts clearly show that TAI refused to do any further testing of Adhesive 7448 to determine the effect of summerlike heat upon the adhesive. Had it done so, TAI would have discovered that Adhesive 7448 fared

continued

no better than the 3M adhesive it had been using. Moreover, Northern did not breach an implied warranty of fitness for a particular purpose, since TAI did not rely on Northern's skill or judgment in selecting Adhesive 7448. Northern, furthermore, did not breach any express warranties, for Northern made no affirmations or promises when it supplied TAI with samples. At most, Northern claimed that Adhesive 7448 was a "match" for the 3M adhesive, which in fact turned out to be true.

INTERPRETATION If the buyer inspects the goods before entering into the contract, implied warranties do not apply to defects that are apparent.

Federal Legislation Relating to Warranties of Consumer Goods To protect purchasers of **consumer goods** (defined as "tangible personal property normally used for personal, family or household purposes"), Congress enacted the *Magnuson-Moss Warranty Act*. The purpose of the act is to prevent deception and to make sure that consumer purchasers are adequately informed about warranties.

The Federal Trade Commission administers and enforces the act. The commission's guidelines for the type of consumer product warranty information a seller must supply are aimed at providing the consumer with clear and useful information. More significantly, the act provides that a seller who makes a written warranty *cannot* disclaim *any* implied warranty. For a complete discussion of the act, see Chapter 46.

For a summary of the types of warranties and the ways in which they can be disclaimed, see Figure 22–1.

Federal legislation relating to warranties of consumer goods the Magnuson-Moss Warranty Act protects purchasers of consumer goods by providing that warranty information be clear and useful and that a seller who makes a written warranty cannot disclaim any implied warranty

Consumer goods goods normally used for personal, family, or household purposes

FIGURE 22–1 Warranties

Type of Warranty	How Created	What Is Warranted	How Disclaimed
Title	• Seller contracts to sell goods	• Good title • Rightful transfer • Not subject to lien	• Specific language • Circumstances giving reason to know that seller does not claim title
Express	• Affirmation of fact • Promise • Description • Sample or model	• Conform to affirmation • Conform to promise • Conform to sample, model or description	• Usually not possible
Merchantability	Merchant sells goods	• Fit for ordinary purposes • Adequately contained, packaged, and labeled	• Must mention "merchantability" • If in writing, must be conspicuous • As-is sale • Buyer examination • Course of dealing, course of performance, usage of trade
Fitness for a particular purpose	Seller knows buyer is relying upon seller to select goods suitable for buyer's particular purpose	Fit for particular purpose	• No specific words necessary • In writing and conspicuous • As-is sale • Buyer examination • Course of dealing, course of performance, usage of trade

Limitation or Modification of Warranties

Limitation or modification of warranties permitted as long as it is not unconscionable

The Code permits a seller to **limit** or **modify** the buyer's remedies for breach of warranty. One important exception to this right is the prohibition against a seller's "unconscionable" limitations or exclusions of consequential damages. Specifically, the "[l]imitation of consequential damages for injury to the person in the case of consumer goods is prima facie unconscionable. . . ." In some cases, a seller may seek to impose time limits within which the warranty is effective. Except where such clauses result in unconscionability, the Code permits them; it does not, however, permit any attempt to shorten the time period for filing an action for personal injury to less than one year.

Privity of Contract

Privity contractual relationship

Because of the close association between warranties and contracts, a principle of law in the nineteenth century established that a plaintiff could not recover for breach of warranty unless he was in a contractual relationship with the defendant. This relationship is known as **privity** of contract.

Under this rule, a warranty by seller Ingrid to buyer Sylvester, who resells the goods to purchaser Lyle under a similar warranty, gives Lyle no rights against Ingrid. There is no privity of contract between Ingrid and Lyle. In the event of breach of warranty, Lyle may recover only from his seller, Sylvester, who in turn may recover from Ingrid.

Horizontal privity determines who benefits from a warranty and therefore may bring a cause of action

Horizontal privity determines who benefits from a warranty and who may therefore sue for its breach. Horizontal privity pertains to noncontracting parties who are injured by the defective goods; this group would include users, consumers, and bystanders who are not the contracting purchaser.

The Code relaxes the requirement of horizontal privity of contract by permitting recovery on a seller's warranty, at a minimum, to members of the buyer's family or household or to a guest in his home. The Code provides three alternative sections from which the states may select. Alternative A, the least comprehensive and most widely adopted alternative, provides that a seller's warranty, whether express or implied, extends to any natural person who is in the family or household of the buyer or who is a guest in his home, if it is reasonable to expect that such person may use, consume, or be affected by the goods, and who is injured in person by breach of the warranty. Alternative B extends Alternative A to "any natural person who may reasonably be expected to use, consume or be affected by the goods." Alternative C further expands the coverage of the section to any person, not just natural persons, and to property damage as well as personal injury. (A natural person would not include artificial entities such as corporations, for example.) A seller, however, may not exclude or limit the operation of this section for injury to a person.

Nonetheless, the Code was not intended to establish outer boundaries for third-party recovery for injuries caused by defective goods. Rather, it sets a minimum standard that the states may expand through case law. Most states have judicially accepted the Code's invitation to relax the requirements of horizontal privity and, for all practical purposes, have *eliminated* horizontal privity in warranty cases.

Vertical privity determines who is liable for breach or warranty

Vertical privity, in determining who is liable for breach of warranty, pertains to remote sellers within the chain of distribution, such as manufacturers and wholesalers, with whom the consumer purchaser has not entered into a contract. Although the Code adopts a neutral position regarding vertical privity, the courts in most states have *eliminated* the requirement of vertical privity in warranty actions.

Notice of Breach of Warranty

When a buyer has accepted a tender of goods that are not as warranted by the seller, she is required to notify the seller of any breach of warranty, express or implied, as well as any other breach, within a reasonable time after she has discovered or should have discovered it. If the buyer fails to notify the seller of any breach within a reasonable time, she is barred from any remedy against the seller. In determining whether notice was provided in a reasonable period of time, commercial standards apply to a merchant buyer while different standards apply to a retail consumer, so as not to deprive a good faith consumer of her remedy.

Notice of breach if the buyer fails to notify the seller of any breach within a reasonable time, she is barred from any remedy against the seller

Plaintiff's Conduct

Because of the development of warranty liability in the law of sales and contracts, **contributory negligence** of the buyer is *no* defense to an action against the seller for breach of warranty. Comparative negligence statutes do apply, however, to warranty actions in some states. (Comparative negligence is discussed later in this chapter.)

Contributory negligence is not a defense

If the buyer discovers a defect in the goods that may cause injury and nevertheless proceeds to make use of them, he will not be permitted to recover damages from the seller for loss or injuries caused by such use. This is not contributory negligence but **voluntary assumption** of a known risk.

Voluntary assumption of risk is a defense

STRICT LIABILITY IN TORT

The most recent and far-reaching development in the field of product liability is that of strict liability in tort. All but a very few states have now accepted the concept, which is embodied in **Section 402A** of the Restatement, Second, of Torts.

Section 402A imposes strict liability in tort

Section 402A imposes **strict liability in tort** on merchant sellers both for personal injuries and for property damage that result from selling a product in a *defective condition, unreasonably dangerous* to the user or consumer. Section 402A applies even though "the seller has exercised all possible care in the preparation and sale of his product." Thus, negligence is not the basis of liability in strict liability cases. The essential distinction between the two doctrines is that actions in strict liability do not require the plaintiff to prove that the injury-producing defect resulted from any specific act of negligence of the seller. Strict liability actions focus on the *product*, not on the *conduct* of the manufacturer. Courts in strict liability cases are interested in the fact that a product defect arose—not in *how* it arose. Thus, even an "innocent" manufacturer—one who has not been negligent—may be liable if his product turns out to contain a defect that injures a consumer. Although liability for personal injuries caused by a defective condition that makes goods unreasonably dangerous is usually associated with sales of such goods, this type of liability also exists with respect to *leases* and *bailments* of defective goods.

Strict liability in tort merchant seller is liable for selling a product in a defective condition, unreasonably dangerous to the user or consumer

REQUIREMENTS OF STRICT LIABILITY IN TORT

Section 402A imposes strict liability in tort if (1) the defendant was engaged in the business of selling a product such as the defective one; (2) the defendant sold the product in a defective condition; (3) the defective condition made the product unreasonably dangerous to the user or consumer or to his property;

(4) the defect in the product existed when it left the defendant's hands; (5) the plaintiff sustained physical harm or property damage by using or consuming the product; and (6) the defective condition was the proximate cause of the injury or damage.

This liability is imposed by law as a matter of public policy and does not depend on contract, either express or implied. Nor does it require reliance by the injured user or consumer on any statements made by the manufacturer or seller. It is not limited to persons in a buyer-seller relationship; thus, neither vertical nor horizontal privity is required. No notice of the defect is required to have been given by the injured user or consumer. The liability, furthermore, generally is not subject to disclaimer, exclusion, or modification by contractual agreement. Rather, it is solely in tort and arises out of the common law. It is not governed by the provisions of the Uniform Commercial Code. The majority of courts considering the question, however, have held that Section 402A imposes liability only for injury to person and damage to property, not for commercial loss (such as loss of bargain or profits), which is recoverable in an action for breach of warranty.

Merchant Sellers

Section 402A imposes liability only upon a person who is in the *business* of selling the product involved. It does not apply to an occasional seller, such as a person who trades in his used car or who sells his lawn mower to a neighbor. In this respect, the section is similar to the implied warranty of merchantability, which applies only to sales by a merchant of goods that are of the type in which he deals. A growing number of jurisdictions recognize the applicability of strict liability in tort even to merchant-sellers of *used* goods.

Defective Condition

In an action to recover damages under the rule of strict liability in tort, though the plaintiff must prove a defective condition in the product, she is not required to prove how or why or in what manner the product became defective. The plaintiff must, however, show that at the time she was injured, the condition of the product was not substantially changed from the condition in which the manufacturer or seller sold it. In general, defects may arise through faulty manufacturing, through faulty product design, or through inadequate warnings, labeling, packaging, or instructions.

Manufacturing defect not produced according to specifications

Manufacturing Defect A **manufacturing defect** occurs when the product is not properly made; that is, it fails to meet its own manufacturing specifications. For instance, suppose a chair is manufactured with legs designed to be attached by four screws and glue. If the chair was produced without the appropriate screws, this would constitute a manufacturing defect.

Design defect plans or specifications inadequate to ensure the product's safety

Design Defect A product contains a **design defect** when, despite its being produced as specified, the product is dangerous or hazardous because its design is inadequate. Design defects can result from a number of causes, including poor engineering, poor choice of materials, and poor packaging. An example of a design defect that received great notoriety was the fuel tank assembly of the Ford Pinto. A number of courts found the car to be inadequately designed because the fuel tank had been placed too close to its rear axle, causing the tank to rupture when the car was hit from behind.

Section 402A provides no guidance in determining which injury-producing designs should give rise to strict liability and which should not. Consequently, the courts have adopted widely varying approaches in applying 402A to defective design cases. Nevertheless, virtually none of the courts has upheld a judgment in a strict liability case in which the defendant demonstrated that the "**state of the art**" was such that the manufacturer (1) neither knew nor could have known of a product hazard, or (2) if he knew of the product hazard, could have designed a safer product given existing technology. Thus, almost all courts evaluate the design of a product on the basis of the dangers that the manufacturer could have known at the time he produced the product.

> **State of the art**
> the state of technology current at the time the product is made

---

HECKMAN v. FEDERAL PRESS CO. United States Court of Appeals, Third Circuit, 1978, 587 F.2d 612

FACTS Heckman, an employee of Clark Equipment Company, severely injured his left hand when he caught it in a power press that he was operating at work. The press was manufactured by Federal Press Company and sold to Clark in 1970. It could be operated either by hand controls that required the use of both hands away from the point of operation or by an optional foot pedal. When the foot pedal was used without a guard, nothing remained to keep the operator's hands from the point of operation. Federal Press did not provide safety appliances unless the customer requested them, but when it delivered the press to Clark with the optional pedal, it suggested that Clark install a guard. The press had a similar warning embossed on it. Clark did, in fact, purchase a guard for $100, but it was not mounted on the machine at the time of the injury; nor was it believed to be an effective safety device.

Heckman argued that one type of guard, if installed, would have made the press safe in 95 percent of its customary uses. Federal, in turn, argued that the furnishing of guards was not customary in the industry; that the machine's many uses made it impracticable to design and install any one guard as standard equipment; that Clark's failure to obey Federal's warning was a superseding cause of the injury; and that state regulations placed responsibility for the safe operation of presses on employers and employees. The jury awarded Heckman $750,000, and Federal appealed.

DECISION The judgment as to Federal's liability is affirmed, but a new trial is granted due to reversible error in the award of damages.

OPINION A failure to provide proper safety devices constituted a design defect that subjected Federal to liability. The question whether Federal's guardless press created an unreasonable risk of harm to the user was a question for the jury to decide after considering such factors as (1) the feasibility of incorporating safety features during manufacture; (2) the likelihood that users would not secure adequate protective devices; (3) whether the machine was of standard make or custom built; (4) the relative expertise of the manufacturer and the customer with regard to the product; (5) the extent of risk to the user; and (6) the seriousness of the injury that could be anticipated.

INTERPRETATION If a manufacturer knows of a potential risk of injury arising from a defective design and can easily change the design to reduce this risk but does not do so, he is liable for injuries caused by the design defect.

Failure to Warn A seller is under a duty to provide adequate warning of a product's possible danger, to provide appropriate directions for its safe use, and to package the product safely. Warnings do not, however, always protect sellers from liability. A seller who could have designed or manufactured a product in a safe yet cost-effective manner, but who instead chooses to produce the product cheaply and to provide a warning of the product's hazards, cannot escape liability simply by the warning. Warnings usually will avoid liability only if no cost-effective designs or manufacturing processes are available to reduce a risk of injury.

The duty to give a warning arises from a foreseeable danger of physical harm that could result from the normal or probable use of the product and from the likelihood that, unless warned, the user or consumer would not ordinarily be aware of such danger or hazard.

> **Failure to warn** failure to provide adequate warning of possible danger or to provide appropriate directions for use of a product

ROHRBAUGH v. OWENS CORNING FIBERGLASS CORP. United States Court of Appeals, Tenth Circuit, 1992, 965 F.2d 844

FACTS For sixteen years, the late Mrs. Dorothy Mae Palmer was married to Mr. Schultz, an insulator who worked with asbestos products. Mrs. Palmer was not exposed to asbestos dust in a factory setting; rather, she was exposed when Mr. Schultz brought his work clothes home to be washed. Mrs. Palmer died of mesothelioma in 1986. This product liability suit was brought by Mrs. Palmer's daughters, Suzan Rohrbaugh, Barbara Ann Clay, and Debra Mae Ambler, to recover for the alleged wrongful death of their mother. The daughters claim that Mrs. Palmer's mesothelioma was the result of exposure to asbestos-containing products manufactured by Owens-Corning. The daughters claim that the asbestos products were defective and unreasonably dangerous and that Owens-Corning was negligent in failing to warn of the dangers associated with their products. The trial jury found in favor of Mrs. Palmer's daughters and awarded them damages in the amount of $450,000. Owens-Corning asserted that instructions given to the jury indicated that the manufacturer was obligated to warn Mrs. Palmer of the dangers of their products and appealed on the basis of incorrect instructions given to the jury.

DECISION Judgment of the district court vacated and remanded for further proceedings.

OPINION Under Oklahoma law, a manufacturer may have a duty to warn consumers of potential hazards that occur from the use of its products. A failure to warn may result in a product's being found to be defective and unreasonably dangerous. This duty to warn, however, extends only to the ordinary consumer and user of the product (defined as "one who would be foreseeably expected to purchase the product"). According to these facts, Owens-Corning did not have the obligation to warn Mrs. Palmer because she was not the ordinary consumer of the asbestos-containing products.

Additionally, at the time the asbestos products in question were sold, Owens-Corning had no knowledge of their dangers. In fact, the prevailing scientific opinion of the time was that the type of asbestos involved in this case did NOT cause mesothelioma. The Oklahoma Supreme Court had earlier ruled that "the manufacturer of a product has a duty to warn the consumer of potential dangers which may occur from the use of the product when it is known or should be known that the hazards exist."

INTERPRETATION A manufacturer can be held responsible only for failure to warn the consumers it expects to use its products with regard only to dangers it knows or should know about.

Unreasonably Dangerous

Unreasonably dangerous
danger beyond that which the ordinary consumer contemplates

Section 402A liability applies only if the defective product is unreasonably dangerous to the user or consumer. An **unreasonably dangerous** product is one that contains a danger beyond that which would be contemplated by the ordinary consumer who purchases it with common knowledge of its characteristics. Thus, Comment i to Section 402A describes the difference between reasonable and unreasonable dangers: "good whiskey is not unreasonably dangerous merely because it will make some people drunk, and is especially dangerous to alcoholics; but bad whiskey, containing a dangerous amount of fusel oil, is unreasonably dangerous. Good tobacco is not unreasonably dangerous merely because the effects of smoking may be harmful; but tobacco containing something like marijuana may be unreasonably dangerous. Good butter is not unreasonably dangerous merely because, if such be the case, it deposits cholesterol in the arteries and leads to heart attacks; but bad butter, contaminated with poisonous fish oil, is unreasonably dangerous." Most courts have left the question of reasonable consumer expectations to the jury.

OBSTACLES TO RECOVERY

Few of the obstacles to recovery in warranty cases present serious problems to plaintiffs in strict liability actions brought pursuant to Section 402A because this section was drafted largely to avoid such obstacles.

Disclaimers and Notice

Comment m to Section 402A provides that the basis of strict liability rests solely in tort and therefore is not subject to contractual defenses. The comment specifically states that strict product liability is not governed by the Code, that it is not affected by contractual limitations or disclaimers, and that it is not subject to any requirement that notice be given to the seller by the injured party within a reasonable time. Nevertheless, most courts have *allowed* clear and specific disclaimers of Section 402A liability in *commercial* transactions between merchants of relatively equal economic power.

Privity

With respect to horizontal privity, the strict liability in tort of manufacturers and other sellers extends not only to buyers, users, and consumers, but also to injured bystanders.

In terms of vertical privity, strict liability in tort imposes liability on any seller who is engaged in the business of selling the product, including a wholesaler or distributor as well as the manufacturer and retailer. The rule of strict liability in tort also applies to the manufacturer of a defective component that is used in a larger product if the manufacturer of the finished product has made no essential change in the component.

Plaintiff's Conduct

Many product liability defenses relate to the conduct of the plaintiff. The claim common to all of them is that the plaintiff's improper conduct so contributed to the plaintiff's injury that it would be unfair to blame the product or its seller.

Contributory Negligence **Contributory negligence** is conduct on the part of the plaintiff (1) that falls below the standard to which he should conform for his own protection and (2) that is the legal cause of the plaintiff's harm. Because strict liability is designed to assess liability without fault, Section 402A rejects contributory negligence as a defense. Thus, a seller cannot defend a strict liability lawsuit on the basis of a plaintiff's negligent failure to discover a defect or to guard against its possibility. But, as discussed below, contributory negligence in the form of an assumption of the risk can bar recovery under Section 402A.

Contributory negligence not a defense in the majority of states

Comparative Negligence Under **comparative negligence**, the court apportions damages between the parties in proportion to the degree of fault or negligence it finds against them. Despite Section 402A's bar of contributory negligence in strict liability cases, most courts apply comparative negligence to strict liability cases. (Some courts use the term comparative responsibility rather than comparative negligence.) There are two basic types of comparative negligence or comparative responsibility. One is pure comparative responsibility, which simply reduces the plaintiff's recovery in proportion to her fault, whatever that may be. Thus, the recovery of a plaintiff found to be 80 percent at fault in causing an accident in which she suffered a $100,000 loss would be limited to 20 percent of her damages, or $20,000. Under the other type of negligence, modified comparative responsibility, the plaintiff recovers according to the general principles of comparative responsibility *unless* she is more than 50 percent responsible for her injuries, in which case she recovers nothing. The majority of comparative negligence states follows the modified comparative responsibility approach.

Comparative negligence most states have applied the rule of comparative negligence to strict liability in tort

ETHICAL DILEMMA When Should a Company Order a Product Recall?

FACTS Walter Jones was feeding his five-month-old daughter Millie plums from a jar of Winkler baby food when she suddenly began to choke on a piece of aluminum foil that had come from the jar. Walter rushed her to the hospital, where more foil was found in her stomach. Although the amount of aluminum found was not in itself deadly, Millie was nauseous for several hours, and her parents had trouble getting her to eat for many days thereafter.

Walter sued Winkler. A number of similar incidents involving Winkler products had occurred at about the same time. Although the incidents covered a wide geographic area, their total number was not great, and the FDA decided not to require a recall of the baby food. Winkler faced two choices: (1) to do nothing and settle the cases as they arose, or (2) to recall all jars of the same lot to protect other children from the possibility of ingesting foreign substances.

Social, Policy, and Ethical Considerations

1. What are the social and ethical issues Winkler must consider in choosing its course of action? Should the fact that none of the incidents had been fatal affect the company's decision? What should Winkler do?
2. Would the first option be good for business? Who eventually bears the cost of the lawsuits or recalls? Who should bear the cost?
3. What actions should be taken by the baby's parents? Do they have any social responsibility in this case to seek publicity sufficient to warn others?

Voluntary Assumption of the Risk Assumption of risk is a defense in an action based on strict liability in tort. Basically, *assumption of the risk* is the plaintiff's express or implied consent to encounter a known danger. Thus, a person who drives an automobile after realizing that the brakes are not working and an employee who attempts to remove a foreign object from a high-speed roller press without shutting off the power have assumed the risk of their own injuries.

Voluntary assumption of the risk is a defense

To establish such a defense, the defendant must show that (1) the plaintiff actually knew and appreciated the particular risk or danger the defect created; (2) the plaintiff voluntarily encountered the risk while realizing the danger; and (3) the plaintiff's decision to encounter the known risk was unreasonable.

Misuse or Abuse of the Product Closely connected to voluntary assumption of the risk is the valid defense of misuse or abuse of the product by the injured party. *Misuse* or *abuse* occurs when the injured party knows, or should know, that he is using the product in a manner the seller did not contemplate. The major difference between misuse or abuse and assumption of the risk is that the former includes actions that the injured party does not know to be dangerous, whereas the latter does not include such conduct. Instances of such misuse or abuse include standing on a rocking chair to change a light bulb or using a lawn mower to trim hedges. The courts, however, have significantly limited this defense by requiring that the misuse or abuse not be foreseeable by the seller. If a use is foreseeable, then the seller must take measures to guard against it.

Misuse or abuse of the product is a defense

Subsequent Alteration

Subsequent alteration liability exists only if the product reaches the user or consumer without substantial change in the condition in which it is sold

Section 402A provides that liability exists only if the product reaches "the user or consumer without substantial change in the condition in which it is sold." Accordingly, most, but not all, courts would not hold a manufacturer liable for a faulty carburetor if a car dealer had removed the part and made significant changes in it before reinstalling it in an automobile.

Statute of Repose

A number of lawsuits have been brought against manufacturers many years after a product was first sold. In response, many states have adopted statutes of repose. These enactments limit the period—typically between six and twelve years—for which a manufacturer is liable for injury caused by a defective product. After the statutory time period has elapsed, a manufacturer ceases to be liable for such harm.

Statue of repose limits the time period for which a manufacturer is liable for injury caused by its product

Figure 22–2 compares strict liability in tort with the implied warranty of merchantability. Also see Ethical Dilemma: "When Should a Company Order a Product Recall?" and the Managerial Insight ("A. H. Robins: What Went Wrong?")

FIGURE 22–2 Products Liability

	Merchantability*	**Strict Liability in Tort**
Condition of Goods Creating Liability	Not fit for ordinary purposes	Defective condition, unreasonably dangerous
Type of Transaction Covered	Sales; some courts apply to leases and bailments of goods	Sales, leases, and bailments of goods
Disclaimer	Must mention "merchantability" If in writing, must be conspicuous Must not be unconscionable Subject to Magnuson-Moss Act	Not possible in consumer transactions; may be permitted in commercial transactions
Notice to Seller	Required within reasonable time	Not required
Causation	Required	Required
Who May Sue	In some states, buyer and the buyer's family or guests in home; in other states, any person who may be expected to use, consume, or be affected by goods	Any user or consumer of product; also, in most states, any bystander
Compensable Harms	Personal injury, property damage, economic loss	Personal injury, property damage
Who May Be Sued	Seller who is a merchant with respect to the goods sold	Seller who is engaged in business of selling such a product

*The warranty of fitness for a particular purpose differs from the warranty of merchantability in the following respects: (1) the condition that triggers liability is the failure of the goods to perform according to the particular purpose described in the warranty, and (2) a disclaimer need not mention "fitness for a particular purpose."

MANAGERIAL INSIGHT

A. H. Robins: What Went Wrong?

Until the 1970s, A. H. Robins of Richmond, Virginia, operated as a relatively small, essentially family-run company with a fairly wholesome image. Nearly a decade later, however, the company's name rang sourly in the public ear.

For years, the pharmaceutical firm had been headed by E. Claiborne Robins, Sr., its chairman, and his son, E. Claiborne Robins, Jr., its chief executive officer. Both men were well respected in Richmond, and the elder Robins was known as a generous man who donated millions to educational and other concerns. Initially, A. H. Robins made such popular products as Robitussin cough medicine, Chap Stick lip balm, and Sergeant's flea and tick collars. Then the company decided to get into the birth control business, and there its troubles began.

With the sexual revolution of the Sixties and the advent of the birth-control pill, corporate America sensed profits to be made from any new form of birth control. Potentially large profits. But the trick was to find a safe, easy-to-use, acceptable product.

At the prestigious Johns Hopkins Hospital in Baltimore in the late 1960s, Dr. Hugh J. Davis, director of the hospital's birth-control clinic, was testing a new intrauterine device, known as the Dalkon Shield. The plastic, nickel-sized, crab-like instrument was inserted into a woman's uterus as a way to prevent pregnancy. No one knew why or how IUDs worked.

In February 1970, Davis reported in the American Journal of Obstetrics and Gynecology that the pregnancy rate for his Dalkon Shield was 1.1 percent, a rate similar to or lower than that of the birth-control pill. He did not disclose, however, that he was part owner of the small Dalkon Corporation that made the new IUD.

A few months later, A. H. Robins took notice of the Dalkon Shield at a physician's conference in Pennsylvania. By June of that year, the firm had acquired the rights to the device and had hired Davis on as a consultant. Yet within two weeks of the Dalkon Shield's purchase, A. H. Robins began to hear of problems. One of its own officials cited potential difficulties with the device's tail, which, unlike the tails of other IUDs, consisted of hundreds of tiny filaments enclosed in a nylon shield that was open at one end. The tail's exposed threads could potentially attract bacteria and thus cause infection.

Still, A. H. Robins rushed the Dalkon Shield into production. The company made a few design changes but conducted no more research on the device. Nor did the Food and Drug Administration require the company to get approval for the device before introducing it, since the Dalkon Shield was classified as a medical device, not a drug.

Within six months of buying the Dalkon Shield, A. H. Robins launched a major marketing campaign. Thousands of reprints of Davis's study that included his 1.1-percent pregnancy rate were distributed across the country. Less than a year later, the Dalkon Shield had captured 60 percent of the IUD market in the United States.

Sales mounted, and the money rolled in. By February 1971, however, the company had received two reports of women developing pelvic inflammatory disease, a painful infection that can lead to sterility. Soon, more adverse evidence surfaced. New reports suggested that

the pregnancy rate for the Dalkon Shield ran as high as 4.3 percent. Another study suggested that as many as 1 in 14 Dalkon Shield wearers suffered from infections. But that wasn't the only danger. While some Dalkon Shield wearers were hospitalized for infection, others were admitted for perforated uteruses or, if they happened to be pregnant, for ectopic pregnancies, for septic (or infected) abortions, or for premature labor and delivery. Some became sterile. Some died. By 1973, A. H. Robins had evidence that six women wearing the Dalkon Shield had died from septic abortions. Yet it did little.

Nor did the Food and Drug Administration (FDA) respond quickly. Not until June of 1973 did the FDA write A. H. Robins to tell the company that it should stop selling the Dalkon Shield because of safety questions. Two days later, A. H. Robins voluntarily withdrew the device from the U. S. market. Yet the company waited nearly another year before banning international sales of the Dalkon Shield.

By early 1974, A. H. Robins faced another threat: lawsuits from injured women. The company, however, fought back fiercely, often playing hardball with women who pressed their claims, questioning them vociferously about their sex lives and suggesting that their own behavior led to any problems that they might be having. Until 1979, the company was able to settle many cases out of court for an average of $11,000 each.

But then things began to unravel for A. H. Robins. In 1979, a Denver jury decided against the company, awarding an injured woman more than $6.8 million, most of it in punitive damages.

By 1984, the company had paid out $314 million in some 8,300 lawsuits. It still faced 3,800 additional lawsuits, and women were filing new

continued

suits every day. Pressure was beginning to mount. Then, in February of that year, Judge Miles Lord of the U.S. District Court in Minneapolis, exasperated by the number of Dalkon Shield lawsuits that he had presided over, made national news when he summoned three top A. H. Robins executives, including CEO E. Claiborne Robins, Jr., to his courtroom and lashed out at the officers, condemning them for their hardheartedness and begging them to take action to protect the women who still wore the Dalkon Shield.

Obviously, the company had to do something. So, by October, A. H. Robins launched a major advertising campaign to tell women that it would pay for the removal of their Dalkon Shields. But it did not issue a recall.

Then it asked the U.S. District Court in Richmond, Virginia, to set one national trial as part of a class action suit to determine if punitive damages should be awarded to claimants and, if so, how much. The company also moved to establish a reserve fund of $615 million to pay for pending and future claims. The fund was the biggest ever to be set aside to settle liability claims for a medical device. Unfortunately, the company underestimated the Dalkon Shield's costs.

By August 1985, A. H. Robins was in deep trouble. The company and its insurer, Aetna Life and Casualty Co., had lost $530 million in 9,500 lawsuits, and they were facing 5,200 more cases. Meanwhile, 400 new cases were being filed each month. Plus, the company had been forced to stare down a shareholders' lawsuit, which it settled for $6.9 million. With nowhere else to go, A. H. Robins filed for bankruptcy.

The end had come. But how could things have gone so terribly wrong? How could a company such as A. H. Robins have miscalculated so badly?

Despite evidence of the Dalkon Shield's risks, the company, according to its critics, did not act quickly or responsibly to warn physicians and women of the danger. In fact, A. H. Robins, these critics say, attempted to slide over the problem. Moreover, to date the company has never issued a recall of the Dalkon Shield and has always said publicly that the device was neither defective nor unreasonably dangerous.

CHAPTER SUMMARY

Warranties

Types of Warranties	**Definition of Warranty** an obligation of the seller to the buyer concerning title, quality, characteristics, or condition of goods
	Warranty of Title the obligation of a seller to convey the right of ownership without any lien
	Express Warranty an affirmation of fact or promise about the goods or a description, including a sample, of the goods, which becomes part of the basis of the bargain
	Implied Warranty a contractual obligation, arising out of certain circumstances of the sale, imposed by operation of law and not found in the language of the sales contract
	■ *Merchantability* warranty by a merchant seller that the goods are reasonably fit for the ordinary purpose for which they are manufactured or sold and that they are of fair, average quality
	■ *Fitness for Particular Purpose* warranty by any seller that goods are reasonably fit for a particular purpose if, at the time of contracting, the seller had reason to know the buyer's particular purpose and that the buyer was relying on the seller's skill and judgment to furnish suitable goods

| **Obstacles to Warranty Action** | **Disclaimer of Warranties** a negation of a warranty
■ *Express Warranty* not usually possible to disclaim
■ *Warranty of Title* may be excluded or modified by specific language or by certain circumstances, including judicial sale or a sale by a sheriff, executor, or foreclosing lienor
■ *Implied Warranty of Merchantability* the disclaimer must mention "merchantability" and, in the case of a writing, must be conspicuous
■ *Implied Warranty of Fitness for a Particular Purpose* the disclaimer must be in writing and conspicuous
■ *Other Disclaimers of Implied Warranties* the implied warranties of merchantability and fitness for a particular purpose may also be disclaimed (1) by expressions like "as is," "with all faults," or other similar language; (2) by course of dealing, course of performance, or usage of trade; or (3) as to defects an examination ought to have revealed where the buyer has examined the goods or where the buyer has refused to examine the goods
■ *Federal Legislation Relating to Warranties of Consumer Goods* the Magnuson-Moss Warranty Act protects purchasers of consumer goods by providing that warranty information be clear and useful and that a seller who makes a written warranty cannot disclaim any implied warranty
Limitation or Modification of Warranties permitted as long as it is not unconscionable
Privity of Contract a contractual relationship between parties that was necessary at common law to maintain a lawsuit
■ *Horizontal Privity* doctrine determining who benefits from a warranty and who therefore may bring a cause of action; the Code provides three alternatives
■ *Vertical Privity* doctrine determining who in the chain of distribution is liable for a breach of warranty; the Code has not adopted a position on this
Notice of Breach if the buyer fails to notify the seller of any breach within a reasonable time, she is barred from any remedy against the seller
Plaintiff's Conduct
■ *Contributory Negligence* is not a defense
■ *Voluntary Assumption of the Risk* is a defense |

Strict Liability in Tort

| **Nature** | **General Rule** imposes tort liability on merchant sellers for both personal injuries and property damage for selling a product in a defective condition unreasonably dangerous to the user or consumer
Defective Condition
■ *Manufacturing Defect* by failing to meet its own manufacturing specifications, the product is not properly made
■ *Design Defect* the product, though made as designed, is dangerous because the design is inadequate
■ *Failure to Warn* failure to provide adequate warning of possible danger or to provide appropriate directions for use of a product
Unreasonably Dangerous contains a danger beyond that which would be contemplated by the ordinary consumer |

Obstacles to Recovery

Contractual Defenses defenses such as privity, disclaimers, and notice generally do not apply to tort liability

Plaintiffs Conduct
- *Contributory Negligence* not a defense in the majority of states
- *Comparative Negligence* most states have applied the rule of comparative negligence to strict liability in tort
- *Voluntary Assumption of the Risk* is a defense
- *Misuse or Abuse of the Product* is a defense

Subsequent Alteration liability exists only if the product reaches the user or consumer without substantial change in the condition in which it is sold

Statute of Repose limits the time period for which a manufacturer is liable for injury caused by its product

QUESTIONS

1. Identify and describe the types of warranties.
2. Discuss the various defenses that may be successfully raised to a warranty action.
3. Describe the elements of an action based upon strict liability in tort.
4. Discuss the obstacles to an action based upon strict liability in tort.
5. Compare strict liability in tort with the implied warranty of merchantability.

Internet Question. Find and review information about product liability reform.

PROBLEMS

1. At the start of the social season, Aunt Lavinia purchased a hula skirt in Sadie's dress shop. The salesperson told her, "This superior garment will do things for a person." Aunt Lavinia's houseguest, her niece, Florabelle, asked and obtained her aunt's permission to wear the skirt to a masquerade ball. In the midst of the festivity, where there was much dancing, drinking, and smoking, the long skirt brushed against a glimmering cigarette butt. Unknown to Aunt Lavinia and Florabelle, its wearer, the garment was made of a fine unwoven fiber that is highly flammable. It burst into flames, and Florabelle suffered severe burns. Aunt Lavinia notified Sadie of the accident and of Florabelle's intention to recover from Sadie. Florabelle seeks to recover damages in an action against Sadie, the proprietor of the dress shop, and Exotic Clothes, Inc., the manufacturer from which Sadie purchased the skirt. Decision?

2. The Talent Company, manufacturer of a widely advertised and expensive perfume, sold a quantity of this product to Young, a retail druggist. Dorothy and Bird visited the store of Young, and Dorothy, desiring to make a gift to Bird, purchased a bottle of this perfume from Young, asking for it by its trade name. Young wrapped up the bottle and handed it directly to Bird. The perfume contained a foreign chemical that upon the first use of the perfume by Bird severely burned her face and caused a permanent facial disfigurement. What are the rights of Bird, if any, against Dorothy, Young, and the Talent Company?

3. John Doe purchased a bottle of "Bleach-All," a well-known brand, from Roe's combination service station and grocery store. When John used the "Bleach-All," his clothes severely deteriorated due to an error in mixing the chemicals during the detergent's manufacture. John brings an action against Roe to recover damages. Decision?

4. A route salesperson for Ideal Milk Company delivered a half-gallon glass jug of milk to Allen's home. The next day, when Allen grasped the milk container by its neck to take it out of his refrigerator, it shattered in his hand and caused serious injury. Allen paid Ideal on a monthly basis for the regular delivery of milk. Ideal's milk bottles each contained the legend "Property of Ideal—to be returned," and the route salesman would pick up the empty bottles when he delivered milk.

Allen brought an action against Ideal Milk Company. Decision?

5. While Butler and his wife, Wanda, were browsing through Sloan's used car lot, Butler told Sloan that he was looking for a safe but cheap family car. Sloan said, "That old Cadillac hearse ain't hurt at all, and I'll sell it to you for $2,950." Butler said, "I'll have to take your word for it because I don't know a thing about cars." Butler asked Sloan whether he would guarantee the car, and Sloan replied, "I don't guarantee used cars." Then Sloan added, "But I have checked that Caddy over, and it will run another 10,000 miles without needing any repairs." Butler replied, "It has to because I won't have an extra dime for any repairs." Butler made a down payment of $400 and signed a printed form contract, furnished by Sloan, that contained a provision: "Seller does not warrant the condition or performance of any used automobile."

As Butler drove the car out of Sloan's lot, the left rear wheel fell off and Butler lost control of the vehicle. It veered over an embankment, causing serious injuries to Wanda. What is Sloan's liability to Butler and Wanda?

6. John purchased for cash a Revenge automobile manufactured by Japanese Motors, Ltd., from an authorized franchised dealer in the United States. The dealer told John that the car had a "twenty-four month 24,000-mile warranty." Two days after John accepted delivery of the car, he received an eighty-page manual in fine print that stated, among other things, on page 72:

The warranties herein are expressly in lieu of any other express or implied warranty, including any implied warranty of merchantability or fitness, and of any other obligation on the part of the company or the selling dealer.

Japanese Motors, Ltd., and the selling dealer warrant to the owner each part of this vehicle to be free under use and service from defects in material and workmanship for a period of twenty-four months from the date of original retail delivery of first use or until it has been driven for 24,000 miles, whichever first occurs.

Within nine months after the purchase, John was forced to return the car for repairs to the dealer on thirty different occasions; and the car has been in the dealer's custody for over seventy days during these nine months. The dealer has been forced to make major repairs to the engine, transmission, and steering assembly. The car is now in the custody of the dealer for further major repairs, and John has demanded that it keep the car and refund his entire purchase price. The dealer has refused on the ground that it has not breached its contract and is willing to continue repairing the car during the remainder of the "twenty-four–twenty-four" period. What are the rights and liabilities of the dealer and John?

7. Fred Lyon of New York, while on vacation in California, rented a new model Home Run automobile from Hart's Drive-A-Car. The car was manufactured by the Ange Motor Company and was purchased by Hart's from Jammer, Inc., an automobile importer. Lyon was driving the car on a street in San Jose when, due to a defect in the steering mechanism, it suddenly became impossible to steer. The speed of the car at the time was thirty miles per hour, but before Lyon could bring it to a stop, the car jumped a low curb and struck Peter Wolf, who was standing on the sidewalk, breaking both of his legs and causing other injuries. Wolf sues Hart's Drive-A-Car, the Ange Motor Company, Jammer, and Lyon. Decisions?

8. The plaintiff brings this cause of action against a manufacturer for the loss of his leg below the hip. The leg was lost when caught in the gears of a screw auger machine sold and installed by the defendant. Shortly before the accident, the plaintiff's co-employees had removed a covering panel from the machine by use of sledgehammers and crowbars in order to do repair work. When finished with their repairs, they replaced the panel with a single piece of cardboard instead of restoring the equipment to its original condition. The plaintiff stepped on the cardboard in the course of his work and fell, catching his leg in the moving parts. Decision?

9. The plaintiff, while driving a pickup manufactured by the defendant, was struck in the rear by another motor vehicle. Upon impact, the plaintiff's head was jarred backward against the rear window of the cab, causing the plaintiff serious injury. The pickup was not equipped with a headrest, and none was required at the time. Should the plaintiff prevail on a cause of action based upon strict liability in tort? Why? Why not?

10. The plaintiff, while dining at the defendant's restaurant, ordered a chicken pot pie. While she was eating, she swallowed a sliver of chicken bone, which became lodged in her throat, causing her serious injury. The plaintiff brings a cause of action. Should she prevail? Why?

11. Salem Supply Co. sells new and used gardening equipment. Ben Buyer purchased a slightly used riding lawn mower for $1,500. The price was considerably less than that of comparable used mowers. The sale was clearly indicated to be "as is." Two weeks after Ben purchased the mower, the police arrived at his house with Owen Owner, the true owner of the lawn mower, which was stolen from his yard, and reclaimed the mower. What recourse, if any, does Ben have?

12. Seigel, a seventy-three-year-old man, was injured at one of Giant Food's retail food stores when a bottle of Coca-Cola exploded as he was placing a six-pack of Coke into his shopping cart. The explosion caused him to lose his balance and fall, with injuries resulting. Seigel brought suit against Giant Food for damages allegedly

caused by Giant's breach of its implied warranty of merchantability. The trial court granted judgment in favor of Giant, and Seigel brought this appeal. Decision?

13. Guarino and two others (plaintiffs) died of gas asphyxiation and five others were injured when they entered a sewer tunnel without masks to answer the cries for help of their crew leader, Rooney. Rooney had left the sewer shaft and entered the tunnel to fix a water leakage problem. Having corrected the problem, Rooney was returning to the shaft when he apparently was overcome by gas because of a defect in his oxygen mask, which was manufactured by Mine Safety Appliance Company (defendant). The plaintiffs brought this action against the defendant for breach of warranty, and the defendant raised the defense of the plaintiffs' voluntary assumption of the risk. Decision?

14. Green Seed Company packaged, labeled, and marketed a quality tomato seed known as "Green's Pink Shipper" for commercial sale. Brown Seed Store, a retailer, purchased the seed from Green Seed and then sold it to Guy Jones, an individual engaged in the business of growing tomato seedlings for sale to commercial tomato growers. Williams purchased the seedlings from Jones and then transplanted and raised them in accordance with accepted farming methods. The plants, however, produced not the promised "Pink Shipper" tomatoes but rather an inferior variety that spoiled in the field. Williams then brought an action against Green Seed for $900, claiming that his crop damage had been caused by Green Seed's breach of an express warranty. Green Seed argued in defense that its warranty did not extend to remote purchasers and that the company did not receive notice of the claimed breach of warranty. Decision?

15. Shell Oil Company leased to Flying Tiger Line a gasoline tank truck with a movable ladder for refueling certain types of aircraft. Under the terms of the lease, Flying Tiger was to maintain the equipment in safe operating order, but Shell was obligated to make most of the repairs at Flying Tiger's request. Four years after the lease was entered, Shell, at Flying Tiger's request, replaced the original ladder with a new one built by an undisclosed manufacturer. Both Flying Tiger and Shell inspected the new ladder. Two years later, however, Price, an aircraft mechanic employed by Flying Tiger, was seriously injured when the ladder's legs split while he was climbing onto an airplane wing. Decision?

16. Mobley purchased from Century Dodge a car described in the contract as new. The contract also contained a disclaimer of all warranties, express or implied. Subsequently, Mobley discovered that the car had, in fact, been involved in an accident. He then sued Century Dodge to recover damages, claiming the dealer had breached its express warranty that the car was new. Century Dodge argues that it had adequately disclaimed all warranties. Decision?

17. On August 22, 1975, O'Neil purchased a used diesel tractor-trailer combination from International Harvester. O'Neil claimed that International Harvester's salesman had told him that the truck had recently been overhauled and that it would be suitable for hauling logs in the mountains. The written installment contract signed by the parties provided that the truck was sold "AS IS WITHOUT WARRANTY OF ANY CHARACTER express or implied." O'Neil admitted that he had read the disclaimer clause but claimed that he understood it to mean that the tractor-trailer would be in the condition that International Harvester's salesman had promised.

O'Neil paid the $1,700 down payment, but he failed to make any of the monthly payments. He claimed that he refused to pay because his employee had many problems with the truck when he took it to the mountains. Delays resulting from those problems, O'Neil argued, had caused him to lose his permit to cut firewood and, therefore, the accompanying business. An International Harvester representative agreed to pay for one-half of the cost of certain repairs, but the several attempts made to fix the truck were unsuccessful. O'Neil then tried to return the truck and to rescind the sale, but International Harvester refused to cooperate. Decision?

18. Mrs. Embs went into Stamper's Cash Market to buy soft drinks for her children. She had removed five bottles from an upright soft drink cooler, placed them in a carton, and turned to move away from the display when a bottle of Seven-Up in a carton at her feet exploded, cutting her leg. Apparently, several other bottles had exploded that same week. Stamper's Cash Market received its entire stock of Seven-Up from Arnold Lee Vice, the area distributor. Vice in turn received his entire stock of Seven-Up from Pepsi-Cola Bottling Co. Decision?

19. Catania wished to paint the exterior of his house. He went to Brown, a local paint store owner, and asked him to recommend a paint for the job. Catania told Brown that the exterior walls were stucco and in a chalky, powdery condition. Brown suggested Pierce's shingle and shake paint. Brown then instructed Catania how to mix the paint and how to use a wire brush to prepare the surface. Five months later, the paint began to peel, flake, and blister. Catania brings an action against Brown. Decision?

20. Robinson, a truck driver for a moving company, decided to buy a used truck from the company. Branch, the owner, told Robinson that the truck was being repaired and that Robinson should wait and inspect the truck before signing the contract. Robinson, who had driven the truck before, felt that inspection was unnecessary. Again, Branch suggested Robinson wait to inspect the truck, and again Robinson declined. Branch then told Robinson he was

buying the truck "as is." Robinson then signed the contract. After the truck broke down four times, Robinson sued. Decision?

21. Perfect Products manufactures balloons, which are then bought and resold by wholesale novelty distributors. Mego Corp. manufactures a doll called "Bubble Yum Baby." A balloon is inserted in the doll's mouth with a mouthpiece, and the doll's arm is pumped to inflate the balloon, simulating the blowing of a bubble. Mego Corp. used Perfect Products balloons in the dolls, bought through independent distributors. The plaintiff's infant daughter died after swallowing a balloon removed from the doll. The plaintiff sues Perfect Products and others on a theory of strict liability. Decision?

22. Patient was injured when the footrest of an adjustable X-ray table collapsed, causing Patient to fall to the floor. G.E. manufactured the X-ray table and the footrest. At trial, evidence was introduced that G.E. had manufactured for several years another footrest model complete with safety latches. However, there was no evidence that the footrest involved was manufactured defectively. The action is based on a theory of strict liability. Who wins? Why?

23. Vlases, a coal miner who had always raised small flocks of chickens, spent two years building a new two-story chicken coop large enough to house 4,000 chickens. After its completion, he purchased 2,200 one-day-old chicks from Montgomery Ward for the purpose of producing eggs for sale. He had selected them from Ward's catalog, which stated that these chicks, hybrid Leghorns, were noted for their excellent egg production. Vlases had equipped the coop with brand-new machinery and had taken further hygiene precautions for the chicks' health. Almost one month later, Vlases noticed that their feathers were beginning to fall off. A veterinarian's examination revealed signs of drug intoxication and hemorrhagic disease in a few of the chicks. Eight months later, it was determined that the chicks were suffering from visceral and ocular leukosis, or bird cancer, which reduced their egg-bearing capacity to zero. Avian leukosis may be transmitted either genetically or by unsanitary conditions. Subsequently, the disease infected the entire flock. Vlases then brought suit against Montgomery Ward for its breach of the implied warranties of merchantability and of fitness for a particular purpose. Ward claimed that there was no way to detect the disease in the one-day-old chicks, nor was there medication available to prevent this disease from occurring. Montgomery Ward brought this appeal from a judgment in favor of Vlases. Decision?

Remedies

A contract for the sale of goods may be completely performed at one time or may be performed in stages, according to the parties' agreement. At any stage, one of the parties may repudiate the contract, may become insolvent, or may breach the contract by failing to perform her obligations under it. In a sales contract, breach may consist of the seller's delivering defective goods, too few goods, the wrong goods, or no goods. The buyer may breach by not accepting conforming goods or by failing to pay for conforming goods that she has accepted. Breach may occur when the goods are in the possession of the seller, in the possession of a bailee of the buyer, in transit to the buyer, or in the possession of the buyer.

Remedies, therefore, need to address not only the type of breach of contract but also the situation with respect to the goods. Consequently, the Code provides separate and distinct remedies for the seller and for the buyer, each specifically keyed to the type of breach and the situation of the goods.

In all events, the purpose of the Code is to put the aggrieved party in a position as good as the one she would have been in, had the other party fully performed. To accomplish this purpose, the Code has provided that the courts should liberally administer its remedies. Moreover, damages do not have to be "calculable with mathematical precision"; they simply must be proved with "whatever definiteness and accuracy the facts permit, but no more." The purpose of remedies under the Code is compensation; therefore, punitive damages are generally not available.

Finally, the Code has rejected the doctrine of election of remedies. Essentially, the Code provides that remedies for breach are cumulative. Whether one remedy bars another depends entirely on the facts of the individual case.

REMEDIES OF THE SELLER

A **buyer's default** in performing any of his contractual obligations deprives the seller of the rights for which he bargained. Such default may consist of any of the following acts: wrongfully rejecting the goods, wrongfully revoking acceptance of the goods, failing to make a payment due on or before delivery, or repudiating (indicating an intention not to perform) the contract in whole or in part. The Code catalogs the seller's remedies for each of these defaults. These remedies allow the seller to (1) withhold delivery of the goods, (2) stop delivery of the goods by a carrier or other bailee, (3) identify to the contract conforming goods not already identified, (4) resell the goods and recover damages, (5) recover damages for nonacceptance of the goods or repudiation of the contract, (6) recover the price, (7) recover incidental damages, (8) cancel the contract, and (9) reclaim the goods on the buyer's insolvency.

Buyer's default the seller's remedies are triggered by the buyer's actions in wrongfully rejecting or revoking acceptance of the goods, in failing to make payment due on or before delivery, or in repudiating the contract

It is useful to note that the first three and the ninth remedies indexed above are *goods-oriented*—that is, they relate to the seller's exercising control over the goods. The fourth through seventh remedies are *money-oriented* because they provide the seller with the opportunity to recover monetary damages. The eighth remedy is *obligation-oriented* because it allows the seller to avoid his obligation under the contract.

Moreover, if the seller delivers goods on credit and the buyer fails to pay the price when due, the seller's sole remedy, unless the buyer is insolvent, is to sue for the unpaid price. If, however, the buyer received the goods on credit while insolvent, the seller may be able to reclaim the goods. The Code defines insolvency to include both its equity meaning and its bankruptcy meaning. The **equity** meaning of **insolvency** is the inability to pay debts in the ordinary course of business or as they become due. The **bankruptcy** meaning of **insolvency** is that total liabilities exceed the total value of all assets.

As noted, the Code's remedies are cumulative. Thus, by way of example, an aggrieved seller may (1) identify goods to the contract, *and* (2) withhold delivery, *and* (3) resell or recover damages for nonacceptance or recover the price, *and* (4) recover incidental damages, *and* (5) cancel the contract.

To Withhold Delivery of the Goods

A seller may withhold delivery of goods to a buyer who has wrongfully rejected or revoked acceptance of the goods, who has failed to make a payment due on or before delivery, or who has repudiated the contract. This right is essentially that of a seller to withhold or discontinue performance of her side of the contract because of the buyer's breach.

Where the contract calls for installments, any breach of an installment that impairs the value of the *whole* contract will permit the seller to withhold the entire undelivered balance of the goods. In addition, on discovery of the buyer's insolvency, the seller may refuse to deliver the goods except for cash, including payment for all goods previously delivered under the contract.

To Stop Delivery of the Goods

An extension of the right to withhold delivery is the right of an aggrieved seller to **stop the delivery** of goods in transit to the buyer or in the possession of a bailee. A seller who discovers that the buyer is insolvent may stop any delivery. If the buyer is not insolvent but repudiates or otherwise breaches the contract, the seller may stop carload, truckload, planeload, or larger shipments. To stop delivery, the seller must notify the carrier or other bailee soon enough for the bailee to prevent delivery of the goods. After this notification, the carrier or bailee must hold and deliver the goods according to the directions of the seller, who is liable to the carrier or bailee for any charges or damages incurred. If a negotiable document of title has been issued for the goods, the bailee need not obey a notification until surrender of the document.

To Identify Goods to the Contract

On a breach of the contract by the buyer, the seller may proceed to identify to the contract conforming goods in her possession or control that were not so identified at the time she learned of the breach. This enables the seller to exercise the remedy of resale of goods (discussed below). Furthermore, the seller may resell any unfinished goods that have been demonstrably intended to fulfill the particular contract. The seller may either complete the manufacture of unfinished

---

Insolvency *(in·sol'·ven·cy)* **(equity)** inability to pay debts in ordinary course of business or as they become due

Insolvency (bankruptcy) total liabilities exceed total value of assets

To stop delivery if the buyer is insolvent, the seller may stop any delivery; if the buyer repudiates or otherwise breaches, the seller may stop carload, truckload, planeload, or larger shipments

goods and identify them to the contract or cease their manufacture and resell the unfinished goods for scrap or salvage value. In so deciding, the seller must exercise reasonable commercial judgment to minimize her loss.

To Resell the Goods and Recover Damages

Under the same circumstances that permit the seller to withhold delivery of goods to the buyer (i.e., wrongful rejection or revocation, repudiation, or failure to make timely payment), the seller may **resell the goods** concerned or the undelivered balance of the goods. If the resale is made in good faith and in a commercially reasonable manner, the seller may recover from the buyer the *difference between the contract price and the resale price, plus* any incidental damages (discussed below), *less* expenses saved because of the buyer's breach. For example, Floyd agrees to sell goods to Beverly for a contract price of $8,000 due on delivery. Beverly repudiates the contract and refuses to pay Floyd anything. Floyd resells the goods in strict compliance with the Code for $6,000, incurring incidental damages for sales commissions of $500 but saving $200 in transportation costs. Floyd would recover from Beverly the difference between the contract price ($8,000) and the resale price ($6,000), plus incidental damages ($500), minus expenses saved ($200), which equals $2,300.

The resale may be a public or private sale, and the goods may be sold as a unit or in parcels. Where the resale is a private sale, the seller must give the buyer reasonable notice of his intention to resell. Where the resale is at a public sale (such as an auction), it must be made at a usual place or market for public sale if one is reasonably available. The seller must give the buyer reasonable notice of the time and place of the resale, unless the goods are perishable or threaten to decline in value speedily. In addition, the seller may be a purchaser of the goods at the public sale. In choosing between a public and private sale, the seller must observe relevant trade practices and usages and take into account the character of the goods.

The seller is not accountable to the buyer for any profit made on any resale of the goods. Moreover, a good faith purchaser at a resale takes the goods free of any rights of the original buyer, even if the seller has failed to comply with one or more of the requirements of the Code in making the resale.

Failure to act in good faith and in a commercially reasonable manner deprives the seller of this remedy and relegates him to the remedy of recovering damages for nonacceptance or repudiation (discussed next).

To Recover Damages for Nonacceptance or Repudiation

In the event of the buyer's wrongful rejection or revocation, repudiation, or failure to make timely payment, the seller may recover damages from the buyer equal to the **market price differential,** or the *difference between the unpaid contract price and the market price* at the time and place of tender of the goods, *plus* incidental damages, *less* expenses saved because of the buyer's breach. This remedy is an alternative to the remedy of reselling the goods.

For example, Joyce in Seattle agrees to sell goods to Maynard in Chicago for $20,000 F.O.B. Chicago, delivery on June 15. Maynard wrongfully rejects the goods. The market price would be ascertained as of June 15 in Chicago because F.O.B. Chicago is a destination contract in which the place of tender would be Chicago. The market price of the goods on June 15 in Chicago is $15,000. Joyce, who incurred $1,000 in incidental expenses while saving $500 in expenses, would recover from Maynard the difference between the contract price

To resell the goods the seller may resell the goods concerned or the undelivered balance of the goods and recover the difference between the contract price and the resale price, together with any incidental damages, less expenses saved

Market price differential the seller may recover damages from the buyer measured by the difference between the unpaid contract price and the market price at the time and place of tender of the goods, plus incidental damages, less expenses saved

($20,000) and the market price ($15,000), plus incidental damages ($1,000), minus expenses saved ($500), which equals $5,500.

Lost profit if the market price differential will not place the seller in as good a position as performance would have, the seller may recover the lost profit, including reasonable overhead, plus incidental damages, less expenses saved

If the difference between the contract price and the market price will not place the seller in as good a position as performance would have, then the measure of damages is the **profit**, including reasonable overhead, that the seller would have realized from full performance by the buyer, plus any incidental damages, less expenses the seller saved because of the buyer's breach. For example, Green, an automobile dealer, enters into a contract to sell a large, fuel-inefficient luxury car to Holland for $32,000. The price of gasoline increases 20 percent, and Holland repudiates. The market value of the car is still $32,000, but because Green cannot sell as many cars as he can obtain, Green's sales volume has decreased by one as a result of Holland's breach. Therefore, Green would be permitted to recover the profits he lost on the sale to Holland (computed as the contract price, minus what the car costs Green, plus an allocation of overhead), plus any incidental damages. The following case further explains the computation of lost profits.

UNIQUE DESIGNS, INC v. PITTARD MACHINERY CO. Court of Appeals of Georgia, 1991, 200 Ga.App. 647, 409 S.E.2d 241

FACTS Unique Designs, Inc. contacted Pittard Machinery Co. to ask for assistance in disposing of a lathe that Unique had purchased from a competing dealer. During the conversation, Unique indicated that it would purchase a new lathe from Pittard. Pittard arranged for an international broker of machinery to sell the old lathe, but Pittard received no commission for this service as Pittard expected Unique to purchase a new lathe from Pittard. Thereafter, the parties negotiated a price of $104,000 or $104,850 for a new lathe. However, the next day, Unique canceled its order for the new lathe. Apparently, Unique had been negotiating all along with one of Pittard's competitors and had used the deal with Pittard as leverage in obtaining a reduced price for a lathe. Pittard resold the lathe that was the subject matter of the repudiated contract to one of its regular customers for $110,000. Pittard then brought suit against Unique for breach of its agreement to purchase a lathe. The trial court granted summary judgment on the issue of liability, ruling that the oral contract was valid because of Unique's admissions during pleadings, and that Pittard was a high-volume dealer entitled to recover its lost profits pursuant to UCC §2-708(2). The jury awarded general damages of $18,000 and the court entered final judgment in that amount. Unique appeals, contending that the trial court erred in adopting the "lost volume dealer" rule in this case and that the calculation of damages was incorrect.

DECISION Judgment affirmed.

OPINION Under UCC §2-708(2), if damages measured by the market price/contract price differential are inadequate to put the seller in as good a position as performance would have done, then the measure of damages is the profit that the seller would have made from full performance by the buyer. Therefore, when the seller is a "lost volume dealer," he is entitled to recover lost profits and incidental damages from a repudiating buyer, even though the seller has resold the goods to another buyer at the same prices as the original buyer had contracted to pay, for the reason that if the original buyer had not repudiated, the seller would have been able to make two sales and thus obtain two profits.

In order for a seller to establish that he is a "lost volume dealer," he must prove that, even though he later resold the repudiated contract goods, the sale to the third party would have been made regardless of the buyer's breach so that the seller would have realized two profits from two sales. Thus, the key inquiry is whether the seller could have provided the product to both the buyer and the resale buyer. In this case, the record reveals that Pittard carries a large inventory of lathes; that the lathe purchased by Unique was a stock item not specially ordered, made, or adapted to any specifications; and that the sale to the resale buyer would have occurred even if Unique had not repudiated its contract. Thus, Pittard has clearly established itself as a lost volume dealer.

Unique further argues that under UCC §2-708(2) Pittard should be required to give Unique due credit for the proceeds of the resale of the lathe. Such a strict construction of §2-708(2) would undermine its intended effect to put the lost volume seller in as good a position as if there had been performance. In essence, the original sale and the second sale are independent events, becoming related only after breach, as the original sale goods are applied to the second sale. Therefore, Unique's contention is without merit.

INTERPRETATION An aggrieved seller who can resell the goods to another buyer may recover lost expected profits if the contract breach decreases the seller's sales volume.

To Recover the Price

The Code permits the seller to **recover the price** plus incidental damages in three situations: (1) where the buyer has accepted the goods; (2) where conforming goods have been lost or damaged after the risk of loss has passed to the buyer; and (3) where the goods have been identified to the contract and there is no ready market available for their resale at a reasonable price. For example, Kelly, in accordance with her agreement with Sally, prints ten thousand letterheads and envelopes with Sally's name and address on them. Sally wrongfully rejects the stationery, and Kelly is unable to resell it at a reasonable price. Kelly is entitled to recover the price plus incidental damages from Sally.

A seller who sues for the price must hold for the buyer any goods that have been identified to the contract and are still in her control. If resale becomes possible, the seller may resell the goods at any time before the collection of the judgment, and the net proceeds of such resale must be credited to the buyer. Payment of the judgment entitles the buyer to any goods not resold.

> **To recover the price** the seller may recover the price: (1) where the buyer has accepted the goods, (2) where the goods have been lost or damaged after the risk of loss has passed to the buyer, or (3) where the goods have been identified to the contract and there is no ready market available for their resale

To Recover Incidental Damages

In addition to recovering damages for the difference between the contract price and the resale price, recovering damages for nonacceptance or repudiation, or recovering the price, the seller also may recover in the same action her incidental damages in order to recoup expenses she reasonably incurred as a result of the buyer's breach. The Code defines a **seller's incidental damages** to include any commercially reasonable charges, expenses, or commissions incurred in stopping delivery; in the transportation, care, and custody of goods after the buyer's breach; in connection with return or resale of the goods; or otherwise resulting from the breach.

> **Seller's incidental damages** commercially reasonable charges, expenses, or commissions directly resulting from breach

To Cancel the Contract

Where the buyer wrongfully rejects or revokes acceptance of the goods, fails to make a payment due on or before delivery, or repudiates the contract in whole or in part, the seller may cancel the part of the contract that concerns the goods directly affected. If the breach is of an installment contract and it substantially impairs the whole contract, the seller may cancel the entire contract.

The Code defines **cancellation** as one party's putting an end to the contract because of a breach by the other. The obligation of the canceling party for any future performance under the contract is discharged, although he retains any remedy for breach of the whole contract or for any unperformed balance. Thus, if the seller has the right to cancel, he may recover damages for breach without having to tender any further performance.

> **Cancellation** one party's putting an end to a contract because of a breach by the other

To Reclaim the Goods upon the Buyer's Insolvency

In addition to the right of an unpaid seller to withhold and stop delivery of the goods, he may reclaim them from an insolvent buyer by demand made to the buyer within ten days after the buyer has received the goods. However, if the buyer has committed fraud by misrepresenting her solvency to the seller in writing within three months prior to delivery of the goods, the ten-day limitation does not apply.

The seller's right to **reclaim the goods** is subject to the rights of a buyer in the ordinary course of business or to the rights of any other good faith purchaser. In addition, a seller who successfully reclaims goods from an insolvent buyer is excluded from all other remedies with respect to those goods. (See Figure 23–1.)

> **To reclaim the goods** an unpaid seller may reclaim goods from an insolvent buyer under certain circumstances

FIGURE 23–1 Remedies of the Seller

Buyer's Breach	Obligation-Oriented	Goods-Oriented	Money-Oriented
Buyer wrongfully rejects goods	Cancel	• Withhold delivery of goods • Stop delivery of goods in transit • Identify conforming goods to the contract	• Resell and recover damages • Recover difference between unpaid contract and market prices *or* lost profits • Recover price
Buyer wrongfully revokes acceptance	Cancel	• Withhold delivery of goods • Stop delivery of goods in transit • Identify conforming goods to the contract	• Resell and recover damages • Recover difference between unpaid contract and market prices *or* lost profits • Recover price
Buyer fails to make payment	Cancel	• Withhold delivery of goods • Stop delivery of goods in transit • Identify conforming goods to the contract • Reclaim goods upon buyer's insolvency	• Resell and recover damages • Recover difference between unpaid contract and market prices *or* lost profits • Recover price
Buyer repudiates	Cancel	• Withhold delivery of goods • Stop delivery of goods in transit • Identify conforming goods to the contract	• Resell and recover damages • Recover difference between unpaid contract and market prices *or* lost profits • Recover price

REMEDIES OF THE BUYER

Seller's default the buyer's remedies arise where the seller fails to make delivery or repudiates the contract, or where the buyer rightfully rejects or justifiably revokes acceptance of goods tendered or delivered

Basically, a **seller** may **default** in one of three different ways: she may repudiate; she may fail to deliver the goods without repudiation; or she may deliver or tender goods that do not conform to the contract. The Code provides remedies for each of these breaches. Some remedies are available for all three types of breaches, whereas others are not. Moreover, the availability of some remedies depends on the buyer's actions. For example, if the seller tenders nonconforming goods, the buyer may reject or accept them. If the buyer rejects them, he can choose from a number of remedies. On the other hand, if the buyer accepts the nonconforming goods and does not justifiably revoke his acceptance, he limits himself to recovering damages.

Where the seller fails to make delivery or repudiates, or where the buyer rightfully rejects or justifiably revokes acceptance, the buyer may, with respect to any goods involved, or with respect to the whole if the breach goes to the whole contract, (1) cancel *and* (2) recover payments made. In addition, the buyer may (3) "cover" and obtain damages, *or* (4) recover damages for nondelivery. Where the seller fails to deliver or repudiates, the buyer, where appropriate, may also (5) recover identified goods if the seller is insolvent, *or* (6) "replevy" the goods, *or* (7) obtain specific performance. Moreover, on rightful rejection or justifiable revocation of acceptance, the buyer (8) has a security interest in the goods. Where the buyer has accepted goods and notified the seller of their nonconformity, the buyer may (9) recover damages for breach of warranty. Finally, in addition to the remedies listed above, the buyer may, where appropriate, (10) recover incidental damages and (11) recover consequential damages.

We might observe that the first remedy cataloged above is *obligation-oriented*; the second through fourth and ninth through eleventh are *money-oriented*; and the fifth through eighth are *goods-oriented*.

The buyer may deduct from the price due any damages resulting from any breach of contract by the seller. The buyer must, however, give notice to the seller of her intention to withhold such damages from payment of the price due.

To Cancel the Contract

Where the seller fails to make delivery or repudiates the contract, or where the buyer rightfully rejects or justifiably revokes acceptance of goods tendered or delivered to him, the buyer may cancel the contract with respect to any goods involved; and, if the breach by the seller concerns the whole contract, the buyer may cancel the entire contract. The buyer, who must give the seller notice of his cancellation, is excused from further performance or tender on his part.

To Recover Payments Made

The buyer, on the seller's breach, may also recover as much of the price as he has paid. For example, Jonas and Sheila enter into a contract for a sale of goods for a contract price of $3,000, and Sheila, the buyer, has made a down payment of $600. Jonas delivers nonconforming goods to Sheila, who rightfully rejects them. Sheila may cancel the contract and recover the $600 plus whatever other damages she can prove.

To Cover

On the seller's breach, the buyer may protect herself by obtaining cover. **Cover** means that the buyer may in good faith and without unreasonable delay proceed to purchase needed goods or make a contract to purchase such goods in substitution for those due under the contract from the seller.

On making a reasonable contract of cover, the buyer may recover from the seller the *difference between the cost of cover and the contract price*, *plus* any incidental and consequential damages (discussed below), *less* expenses saved because of the seller's breach. For example, Phillip, whose factory is in Oakland, agrees to sell goods to Edith, in Atlanta, for $22,000 F.O.B. Oakland. Phillip fails to deliver, and Edith covers by purchasing substitute goods for $25,000, incurring $700 in sales commissions. Edith suffers no other damages as a consequence of Phillip's breach. Shipping costs from Oakland to Atlanta for the goods are $1,300. Edith would recover the difference between the cost of cover ($25,000) and the contract price ($22,000), plus incidental damages ($700 in sales commissions), plus consequential damages ($0 in this example), minus expenses saved (the $1,300 in shipping costs that Edith need not pay under the contract of cover), which equals $2,400.

The buyer is not required to obtain cover, and his failure to do so does not bar him from any other remedy the Code provides. The buyer may not, however, recover consequential damages that he could have prevented by cover.

To cover the buyer may obtain cover by proceeding in good faith and without unreasonable delay to purchase substitute goods; the buyer may recover the difference between the cost of cover and the contract price, plus any incidental and consequential damages, less expenses saved

BIGELOW-SANFORD, INC v. GUNNY CORP. United States Court of Appeals, Fifth Circuit, 1981, 649 F.2d 1060

FACTS The plaintiff, Bigelow-Sanford, Inc., contracted with the defendant, Gunny Corp., for the purchase of 100,000 linear yards of jute at $.64 per yard. Gunny delivered 22,228 linear yards in January 1979. The February and March deliveries required under the contract were not made, and 8 rolls (each roll containing 66.7 linear yards) were delivered in April. With 72,265 linear yards undelivered, Gunny told Bigelow-Sanford that no more would be delivered. In mid-March, Bigelow-Sanford turned to the jute spot market to replace the balance of the order at a price of $1.21 per linear yard. Since several other companies had also defaulted on their jute contracts with Bigelow-Sanford, the plaintiff purchased a total of 164,503 linear yards

continued

on the spot market. The plaintiff sued the defendant to recover losses sustained as a result of the breach of contract. Gunny appealed from a judgment in favor of Bigelow-Sanford.

DECISION Judgment for Bigelow-Sanford affirmed.

OPINION The Code permits a buyer to "cover" his damages due to the seller's breach by purchasing goods in substitution for those due from the seller. The buyer, however, must make the substitute purchases in good faith and without unreasonable delay. If he does so, the buyer may recover as damages the difference between the cost of cover and the contract price plus any incidental damages, but less expenses saved in consequence of the seller's breach.

Here, Gunny breached when it notified Bigelow-Sanford in February that no more jute would be delivered. Bigelow-Sanford made its first spot market purchases to cover by mid-March. Thus, Bigelow-Sanford covered without undue delay. Since its purchases were also reasonable and made in good faith, Bigelow-Sanford is entitled to damages. Bigelow did not specifically allocate the spot market replacements to the individual sellers' accounts. Therefore, it is reasonable to determine the cost of cover by multiplying the average cost of the spot market purchases times the amount of jute Gunny had failed to deliver.

INTERPRETATION If the buyer makes substitute purchases in good faith and without unreasonable delay, he may recover as damages the difference between the cost of cover and the contract price plus any incidental damages, but minus any expenses he saved because of the seller's breach.

To Recover Damages for Nondelivery or Repudiation

To recover damages for nondelivery or repudiation the buyer may recover the difference between the market price at the time the buyer learned of the breach and the contract price, plus any incidental and consequential damages but less expenses saved

If the seller repudiates the contract or fails to deliver the goods, or if the buyer rightfully rejects or justifiably revokes acceptance of the goods, the buyer is entitled to recover damages from the seller equal to the ***difference between the market price*** at the time the buyer learned of the breach ***and the contract price***, together *with* incidental and consequential damages, *less* expenses saved because of the seller's breach. This remedy is a complete alternative to the remedy of cover and is available only to the extent the buyer has not covered. As previously indicated, the buyer who elects this remedy may not recover consequential damages that she could have avoided by cover.

The market price is to be determined as of the place for tender or, in the event that the buyer has rightfully rejected the goods or has justifiably revoked his acceptance of them, as of the place of arrival. For example, Janet, in Boston, agrees to sell goods to Laura, in Denver, for $7,000 C.O.D., with delivery by November 15. Janet fails to deliver. As a consequence, Laura suffers incidental damages of $1,500 and consequential damages of $1,000. In the case of nondelivery or repudiation, market price is determined as of the place of tender. Since C.O.D. is a shipment contract, the place of tender would be the seller's city. Therefore, the market price must be the market price in Boston, the seller's city, on November 15, when Laura learned of the breach. At this time and place, the market price is $8,000. Laura would recover the difference between the market price ($8,000) and the contract price ($7,000), plus incidental damages ($1,500), plus consequential damages ($1,000), less expenses saved ($0 in this example), which equals $3,500.

In the example above, if Janet had instead delivered nonconforming goods that Laura rejected, the market price would be determined at Denver, Laura's place of business; if Janet had repudiated the contract on November 1, instead of November 15, then the market price would be determined as of November 1.

To Recover Identified Goods on the Seller's Insolvency

To recover identified goods on the seller's insolvency for which the buyer has paid all or part of the price

Where existing goods are identified to the contract of sale, the buyer acquires a ***special property interest*** in the goods. This interest exists even if the goods are nonconforming and the buyer therefore has the right to return or reject them. Either the buyer or the seller may identify the goods to the contract.

The Code gives the buyer a right, which does not exist at common law, to recover from an insolvent seller the goods in which the buyer has a special property interest and for which he has paid part or all of the price. This right exists where the seller, who is in possession or control of the goods, becomes insolvent within ten days after receiving the first installment of the price. To exercise it, the buyer must tender to the seller any unpaid portion of the price. If the special property interest exists by reason of an identification made by the buyer, he may recover the goods only if they conform to the contract for sale.

To Sue for Replevin

Replevin is an action at law to recover from a defendant's possession specific goods that are being unlawfully withheld from the plaintiff. Where the seller has repudiated or breached the contract, the buyer may maintain against the seller an action for replevin for goods that have been identified to the contract if (1) the buyer after a reasonable effort is unable to obtain cover for such goods or (2) the goods have been shipped under reservation of a security interest in the seller and satisfaction of this security interest has been made or tendered.

To Sue for Specific Performance

Specific performance is an equitable remedy compelling the party in breach to perform the contract according to its terms. At common law, specific performance is available only if legal remedies are inadequate. For example, where the contract is for the purchase of a unique item, such as a work of art, a famous racehorse, or an heirloom, money damages may not be an adequate remedy. In such a case, a court of equity has the discretion to order the seller specifically to deliver to the buyer, on payment of the price, the goods described in the contract.

The Code not only has continued the availability of specific performance but also has sought to promote a more liberal attitude toward its use. Accordingly, it does not expressly require that the remedy at law be inadequate. Instead, the Code states that "specific performance may be decreed where the goods are unique or in other proper circumstances."

To Enforce a Security Interest in the Goods

A buyer who has rightfully rejected or justifiably revoked acceptance of goods that remain in her possession or control has a security interest in these goods for any payments she has made on their price and for any expenses she reasonably has incurred in their inspection, receipt, transportation, care, and custody. The buyer may hold such goods and resell them in the same manner as an aggrieved seller may resell goods. In the event of resale, the buyer is accountable to the seller for any amount of the net proceeds of the resale that exceeds the amount of her security interest.

To Recover Damages for Breach in Regard to Accepted Goods

Where the buyer has accepted nonconforming goods and has timely notified the seller of the breach of contract, the buyer is entitled to recover from the seller the damages resulting in the ordinary course of events from the seller's breach as determined in any reasonable manner. Nonconformity includes breaches of warranty as well as any failure of the seller to perform according to her obligations under the contract. Thus, even if a seller cures a nonconforming tender, the

---

To sue for replevin *(re·plev'·in)* the buyer may recover goods identified to the contract if (1) the buyer is unable to obtain cover or (2) the goods have been shipped under reservation of a security interest in the seller

Specific performance equitable remedy compelling the party in breach to perform the contract according to its terms where the goods are unique or in other proper circumstances

To enforce a security interest a buyer who has rightfully rejected or justifiably revoked acceptance of goods that remain in her possession has a security interest in these goods for any payments that she has made on their price and for any expenses she has reasonably incurred

To recover damages for breach in regard to accepted goods the buyer may recover damages resulting in the ordinary course of events from the seller's breach; in the case of breach of warranty, such recovery is the difference between the value the goods would have had if they had been as warranted and the value of the nonconforming goods that have been accepted

buyer may recover under this section for any injury he suffered because the original tender was nonconforming.

In the event of breach of warranty, the measure of damages is the **difference** at the time and place of acceptance **between the value of the goods that have been accepted and the value** that the goods would have had if they had been **as warranted**, unless special circumstances show proximate damages of a different amount. Where appropriate, incidental and consequential damages may also be recovered. The contract price of the goods does not figure in this computation because the buyer is entitled to the benefit of his bargain, which is to receive goods that are as warranted. For example, Eleanor agrees to sell goods to Timothy for $1,000. While the value of the goods accepted by Timothy is $800, if they had been as warranted, their value would have been $1,200. Timothy's damages for breach of warranty are $400, which he may deduct from any unpaid balance due on the purchase price, on notice to Eleanor of his intention to do so.

VOLKSWAGEN OF AMERICA, INC v. DILLARD Alabama Supreme Court, 1991, 570 So.2d 1301

FACTS In July 1988, Dillard purchased a new 1987 Volkswagen Scirocco for $16,449.56. During his first year and a half of ownership, Dillard brought the car in for repair twenty-one times. Dillard experienced a "hesitation, stalling, jerking problem" and a grinding noise with his car. There was no pattern to these problems, and because the car "cut off" and "stopped" unexpectedly when he pulled out in front of oncoming traffic, he had to allow for the possibility that the car would not accelerate. On occasion, the car would overheat and die, forcing Dillard to push it out of the street and wait until the engine reached normal operating temperatures. The car also had a problem that caused smoke to come out of the exhaust; several times this prevented Dillard from seeing the cars behind him. Sometimes the smoke would fill the inside of the car. Dillard sued Volkswagen, alleging breach of warranty and claiming damages for loss of the value of the car. Dillard also claimed damages for mental anguish, arguing that the car's stalling, cutting off, and losing power in the face of oncoming traffic had caused him anxiety, embarrassment, and anger. The trial court instructed the jury that it could compensate for mental anguish for breach of contract "where a contractual duty is so related with matters of mental concern or apprehensiveness or with the feelings of the parties to whom the duty is owed that a breach of that duty will necessarily or reasonably result in mental anguish or suffering and such matters were reasonably within the contemplation of the parties when the warranty became effective." The jury returned a verdict for Dillard for breach of express warranty, assessing damages of $7,000 for loss of value and $8,000 for mental anguish. Volkswagen appealed, arguing that damages for mental anguish were not recoverable in a breach of warranty action for the sale of an automobile.

DECISION Decision of the trial court affirmed.

OPINION The general rule in Alabama is that a plaintiff may not recover for mental anguish under a breach of contract because the damages are too remote and are not within the contemplation of the parties and because a breach of contract is not, as such, a natural cause of mental anguish. Yet the Alabama courts have recognized an exception to this rule by permitting damages for mental anguish where the contractual duty or obligation is so coupled with matters of mental concern or with the feelings of the party to whom the duty is owed that a breach of that duty necessarily or reasonably will result in the party's mental anguish or suffering. Because Alabama's version of the UCC permits damages for injury to the person in a breach of warranty case to include those damages ordinarily allowable in such actions at law, the appellate court interpreted the Alabama UCC as not restricting damages for breach of warranty for injury to the person solely to physical injury. Therefore, the appellate court was correct in concluding that the trial court had properly instructed the jury and that the jury could have found damages for mental anguish as the result of a breach of warranty.

INTERPRETATION A buyer may recover consequential damages for breach of warranty, and under Alabama's version of the Code these damages may include mental anguish if the seller's failure to perform his duty was closely related to such anguish.

To Recover Incidental Damages

In addition to remedies such as covering, recovering damages for nondelivery or repudiation, or recovering damages for breach in regard to accepted goods, including breach of warranty, the buyer may recover incidental damages. A **buyer's incidental damages** provide reimbursement for the buyer who incurs reasonable expenses in handling rightfully rejected goods or in effecting cover. The buyer's incidental damages resulting from the seller's breach include expenses reasonably incurred in inspection, receipt, transportation, and care and custody of goods rightfully rejected; any commercially reasonable charges, expenses, or commissions in connection with obtaining cover; and any other reasonable expense connected to the delay or other breach. For example, the buyer of a racehorse who justifiably revokes acceptance because the horse does not conform to the contract will be allowed to recover as incidental damages the cost of caring for the horse from the date the horse was delivered until the buyer returns it to the seller.

> **Buyer's incidental damages** reimbursement for reasonable expenses incurred in handling rightfully rejected goods or in effecting cover

To Recover Consequential Damages

In many cases, the remedies discussed above will not fully compensate the aggrieved buyer for her losses. For example, nonconforming goods that are accepted may in some way damage or destroy the buyer's warehouse and its contents, or undelivered goods may have been the subject of a lucrative contract of resale, the profits from which are now lost. The Code responds to this problem by providing the buyer with the opportunity to recover **consequential damages** resulting from the seller's breach, including (1) any loss resulting from the buyer's requirements and needs of which the seller at the time of contracting had reason to know and which the buyer could not reasonably prevent by cover or otherwise and (2) injury to person or property proximately resulting from any breach of warranty.

> **Consequential damages** damages resulting from buyer's requirements of which seller had reason to know at the time of contracting, as well as injury to person or property proximately resulting from breach of warranty

With respect to the first type of consequential damages, *particular* needs of the buyer usually must be made known to the seller, whereas *general* needs usually need not be. In the case of a buyer who is in the business of reselling goods, resale is one requirement of which the seller has reason to know. For example, Supreme Machine Co., a manufacturer, contracts to sell Allied Sales, Inc., a dealer in used machinery, a used machine that Allied plans to resell. After Supreme repudiates and Allied is unable to obtain a similar machine elsewhere, Allied's damages include the net profit that it would have made on resale of the machine. A buyer may not, however, recover consequential damages he could have prevented by cover. For instance, Supreme Machine Co. contracts to sell Capitol Manufacturing Co. a used machine for $10,000 to be delivered at Capitol's factory by June 1. Supreme repudiates the contract on May 1. By reasonable efforts, Capitol could buy a similar machine from United Machinery Inc. for $11,000 in time for a June 1 delivery. Capitol fails to do so, losing a $5,000 profit that it would have made from the resale of the machine. Though it can recover $1,000 from Supreme, Capitol's damages do *not* include the loss of the $5,000 profit.

An example of the second type of consequential damage would be as follows: Federal Machine Co. sells a machine to Southern Manufacturing Co., warranting its suitability for Southern's purpose. However, the machine is not suitable for Southern's purpose and causes $10,000 in damage to Southern's property and $15,000 in personal injuries. Southern can recover the $25,000 in consequential damages in addition to any other loss suffered. (See Figure 23–2.)

FIGURE 23–2 Remedies of the Buyer

Seller's Breach	Obligation-Oriented	Goods-Oriented	Money-Oriented
Buyer rightfully reject goods	Cancel	Have a security interest	• Recover payments made • Cover and recover damages • Recover damages for nondelivery
Buyer justifiably revokes acceptance	Cancel	Have a security interest	• Recover payments made • Cover and recover damages • Recover damages for nondelivery
Seller fails to deliver	Cancel	• Recover identified goods if seller is insolvent • Replevy goods • Obtain specific performance	• Recover payments made • Cover and recover damages • Recover damages for nondelivery
Seller repudiates	Cancel	• Recover identified goods if seller is insolvent • Replevy goods • Obtain specific performance	• Recover payments made • Cover and recover damages • Recover damages for nondelivery
Buyer accepts nonconforming goods			• Recover damages for breach of warranty

CONTRACTUAL PROVISIONS AFFECTING REMEDIES

Within specified limits, the Code permits the parties to a sales contract to modify, exclude, or limit by agreement the remedies or damages that will be available for breach of that contract. Two basic types of contractual provisions affect remedies: (1) liquidation or limitation of damages and (2) modification or limitation of remedy.

Liquidation or Limitation of Damages

Liquidation or limitation of damages the parties may specify the amount or measure of damages that may be recovered in the event of a breach if the amount is reasonable

The parties may provide for liquidated damages in their contract by specifying the amount or measure of damages that either party may recover in the event of a breach by the other. The amount of such damages must be reasonable in light of the anticipated or actual loss resulting from a breach, the difficulties of proof of loss, and the inconvenience or lack of feasibility of otherwise obtaining an adequate remedy. A contract provision that fixes unreasonably large liquidated damages is void as a penalty. By comparison, an unreasonably small amount might be stricken on the grounds of unconscionability.

To illustrate, Sterling Cabinetry Company contracts to build and install shelves and cabinets for an office building being constructed by Baron Construction Company. The contract price is $120,000, and the contract provides that Sterling would be liable for $100 per day for every day's delay beyond the completion date specified in the contract. The stipulated sum of $100 per day is reasonable and commensurate with the anticipated loss. Therefore, it is enforceable as liquidated damages. If, instead, the sum stipulated had been $5,000 per day, it would be unreasonably large and would, therefore, be void as a penalty.

CONSUMER INSIGHT

Warranty of Title: Who Pays Attorney's Fees When a Dispute Arises?

When Mr. De La Hoya walked into Slim's Gun Shop in California, he wanted only to purchase a gun. Unfortunately, he got more than he bargained for.

Because Slim's Gun Shop advertised itself as a licensed dealer, Mr. De La Hoya figured he had nothing to worry about. So he picked out a handgun and paid his money.

The particular gun that Mr. De La Hoya chose, however, had been purchased earlier from a third party. The owner of Slim's Gun Shop believed all to be fine with the gun. After all, he had filed the necessary federal and state reports, both when he purchased the gun and also when he sold it to Mr. De La Hoya.

A short time later, Mr. De La Hoya went target shooting with his new handgun. But after his practice session began, a police officer walked up and asked Mr. De La Hoya about the weapon. Upon tracing the gun's serial number, the officer found out that the weapon had been reported stolen. Mr. De La Hoya was promptly arrested.

To escape criminal charges, Mr. De La Hoya was forced to hire a lawyer. Once his name was cleared, he sued the owner of Slim's Gun Shop, intent on receiving damages for a breach of warranty of title. In the end, the trial court awarded Mr. De La Hoya $949, which included $140 for the confiscated handgun and $800 for his attorney's fees. Slim's Gun Shop appealed.

The dispute came down to whether the gun shop should pay Mr. De La Hoya's attorney's fees. In cases involving a breach of contract, the law allows only damages that both contracting parties can anticipate at the time they make their agreement. Slim's Gun Shop argued that no one could have foreseen that Mr. De La Hoya would be arrested for possession of a stolen gun. No one had even known that the gun was stolen.

The California Court of Appeal, however, found for Mr. De La Hoya. The court reasoned that the owner of Slim's Gun Shop could have anticipated that if Mr. De La Hoya were questioned about the handgun and the gun happened to be stolen, Mr. De La Hoya might find himself in deep trouble.

Under a breach of warranty of title, Mr. De La Hoya also had a strong case, the court wrote. In so opining, the court pointed to California's Uniform Commercial Code, Section 3312, which reads: "The detriment caused by the breach of warranty of the title of personal property sold is deemed to be the value thereof to the buyer, when he is deprived of its possession, together with any costs which he has become liable to pay in an action brought for the property by the true owner."

Thus, although Mr. De La Hoya faced arrest for possessing stolen property, he did not have to pay for his release. That fell to Slim's Gun Shop, which had violated Mr. De La Hoya's warranty of title, even if it had done so unwittingly.

Modification or Limitation of Remedy by Agreement

The contract between the seller and buyer may expressly provide for remedies in addition to or instead of those provided in the Code and may limit or change the measure of damages recoverable in the event of breach. For instance, the contract may validly limit the buyer's remedy to a return of the goods and a refund of the price, or to the replacement of nonconforming goods or parts.

A contractual remedy is optional, however, unless the parties expressly agree that it is to be exclusive of other remedies, in which event it becomes the sole remedy. Moreover, where circumstances cause an exclusive or limited remedy to fail in its essential purpose, the parties may resort to the remedies provided by the Code.

The contract may expressly limit or exclude consequential damages unless such limitation or exclusion would be unconscionable. Limitation of consequential damages for personal injuries resulting from breach of warranty in the sale of consumer goods is *prima facie* unconscionable, whereas limitation of such damages for commercial loss is not. For example, Ace Motors, Inc., sells a pickup truck to Brenda, a consumer. The contract of sale excludes liability for all consequential damages. The next day, the truck explodes, causing serious personal injury to Brenda. Brenda would recover for her personal injuries unless Ace could prove that the exclusion of consequential damages was *not* unconscionable.

Modification or limitation of remedy by agreement the contract between the parties may expressly provide for remedies in addition to those in the Code, or it may limit or change the measure of damages recoverable for breach

MARTIN v. SHEFFER Court of Appeals of North Carolina, 1991, 102 N.C.App. 802, 403 S.E.2d 555

FACTS Daniel Martin and John Duke contracted with J & S Distributors, Inc. to purchase a KIS Magnum Speed printer for $17,000. The parties agreed that Martin and Duke would send one half of the money as a deposit and would pay the balance upon delivery. When the machine arrived five days late, Martin and Duke refused to accept it, stating that they had purchased a substitute machine elsewhere. Martin and Duke requested the return of their deposit, but J & S refused. Martin and Duke sued Jeff Sheffer and J & S for breach of contract, fraud, breach of good faith, and unfair and deceptive trade practices. The defendants counterclaimed for full performance of the contract pursuant to a clause in the contract that provides:

> In the event of nonpayment of the balance of the purchase price reflected herein on due date and in the manner recorded or on such extended date which may be caused by late delivery on the part of [the seller], the Customer shall be liable for: (1) immediate payment of the full balance recorded herein; and (2) payment of interest at the rate of 12% per annum calculated on the balance due, when due, together with any attorney's fees, collection charges and other necessary expenses incurred by [the seller].

The trial court granted summary judgment to the defendants on both the claim against them and their counterclaim and ordered specific performance of the contract. Plaintiffs appeal.

DECISION Judgment affirmed.

OPINION Martin and Duke argue that seller's damages are controlled by UCC §2-708 and are limited to lost profits. However, §1-102 clearly allows parties to vary the provisions of the Code by agreement, except that the obligations of good faith, diligence, reasonableness and care prescribed by the Code may not be disclaimed.

Also, §2-719(1)(a) provides that a contract for the sale of goods "may provide for remedies in addition to or in substitution for those provided in this article and may limit or alter the measure of damages recoverable under this article, . . ." A contractual provision expanding the seller's damages upon breach of the buyer will therefore be upheld where the contractual provision is reasonable and in good faith. Martin and Duke do not argue that they were fraudulently induced into signing the contract, that the clause authorizing specific enforcement is ambiguous or a mistake, or that the seller breached the contract by failing to deliver at the time promised.

Martin and Duke argue that the contract provision is an "unconscionable and oppressive" liquidated damages clause. However, a contract clause authorizing specific performance is different from a liquidated damages provision. Even if this were not the case, enforcement of the price the plaintiff freely agreed to pay for the machine cannot be considered unreasonable or a penalty. Furthermore, to find unconscionability, there must be an absence of meaningful choice on the part of one of the parties together with contract terms that are unreasonably favorable to the other. As a merchant, Martin and Duke are presumed to be familiar with the terms and practices of contracts for the purchase of the tools of their trade. It is rare that a limitation of remedy will be held unconscionable in a commercial setting, since the relationship between parties is usually not so one-sided as to force an unconscionable limitation on a party.

The contractual clause authorizing specific performance does not undermine the essential purpose of the contract. Therefore, the clause is enforceable.

INTERPRETATION A sales contract may provide for remedies in addition to or instead of those provided by the Code.

WILSON TRADING CORP v. DAVID FERGUSON, LIMITED Court of Appeals of New York, 1968, 23 N.Y. 2d 398, 297 N.Y.S.2d 108, 244 N.E.2d 685

FACTS Wilson Trading Corp. agreed to sell David Ferguson a specified quantity of yarn for use in making sweaters. The written contract provided that notice of defects, to be effective, had to be received by Wilson before knitting or within ten days of receipt of the yarn. When the knitted sweaters were washed, the color of the yarn "shaded" (i.e., variations in color from piece to piece appeared). David Ferguson immediately notified Wilson of the problem and refused to pay for the yarn, claiming that the defect made the sweaters unmarketable. Wilson brought suit against Ferguson. The trial court granted Wilson summary

judgment for the contract price and the appellate court affirmed.

DECISION Order of appellate court reversed and Wilson's motion for summary judgment denied.

OPINION Ordinarily, a buyer who accepts goods has a reasonable time after he discovers or should have discovered a breach to notify the seller of the breach. At the same time, however, parties can within limits modify or exclude warranties and fashion their own remedies for the breach of those warranties. Nevertheless, if the remedies available are unconscionably limited, the

continued

limiting terms are subject to replacement by the general remedial provisions of the UCC. Since the notice provision in effect precluded buyers from giving notice of latent defects, the provision failed in its essential purpose and left David Ferguson without a remedy. To that extent, the contract provision was displaced by the rule that Ferguson had a reasonable time to notify Wilson of the defect.

INTERPRETATION Where circumstances cause an exclusive or limited remedy to fail in its essential purpose, the aggrieved party may resort to the remedies provided by the Code.

CHAPTER SUMMARY

Remedies of the Seller	**Buyer's Default** the seller's remedies are triggered by the buyer's action in wrongfully rejecting or revoking acceptance of the goods, in failing to make payment due on or before delivery, or in repudiating the contract
	To Withhold Delivery
	To Stop Delivery if the buyer is insolvent (one who is unable to pay his debts as they become due or one whose total liabilities exceed his total assets), the seller may stop any delivery; if the buyer repudiates or otherwise breaches, the seller may stop carload, truckload, planeload, or larger shipments.
	To Identify Goods
	To Resell the Goods the seller may resell the goods concerned or the undelivered balance of the goods and recover the difference between the contract price and the resale price, together with any incidental damages, less expenses saved
	◼ *Type of Resale* may be public or private
	◼ *Manner of Resale* must be made in good faith and in a commercially reasonable manner
	To Recover Damages for Nonacceptance or Repudiation
	◼ *Market Price Differential* the seller may recover damages from the buyer measured by the difference between the unpaid contract price and the market price at the time and place of tender of the goods, plus incidental damages, less expenses saved
	◼ *Lost Profit* in the alternative, the seller may recover the lost profit, including reasonable overhead, plus incidental damages, less expenses saved
	To Recover the Price the seller may recover the price:
	◼ where the buyer has accepted the goods
	◼ where the goods have been lost or damaged after the risk of loss has passed to the buyer
	◼ where the goods have been identified to the contract and there is no ready market available for their resale
	To Recover Incidental Damages incidental damages include any commercially reasonable charges, expenses, or commissions directly resulting from the breach
	To Cancel the Contract
	To Reclaim the Goods upon the Buyer's Insolvency an unpaid seller may reclaim goods from an insolvent buyer under certain circumstances

Remedies of the Buyer	**Seller's Default** the buyer's remedies arise where the seller fails to make delivery or repudiates the contract, or where the buyer rightfully rejects or justifiably revokes acceptance of goods tendered or delivered
	To Cancel the Contract
	To Recover Payments Made
	To Cover the buyer may obtain cover by proceeding in good faith and without unreasonable delay to purchase substitute goods; the buyer may recover the difference between the cost of cover and the contract price, plus any incidental and consequential damages, less expenses saved
	To Recover Damages for Nondelivery or Repudiation the buyer may recover the difference between the market price at the time the buyer learned of the breach and the contract price, plus any incidental and consequential damages, but less expenses saved
	To Recover Identified Goods on the Seller's Insolvency for which he has paid all or part of the price
	To Sue for Replevin the buyer may recover goods identified to the contract if (1) the buyer is unable to obtain cover or (2) the goods have been shipped under reservation of a security interest in the seller
	To Sue for Specific Performance the buyer may obtain specific performance where the goods are unique or in other proper circumstances
	To Enforce a Security Interest a buyer who has rightfully rejected or justifiably revoked acceptance of goods that remain in her possession has a security interest in these goods for any payments that she has made on their price and for any expenses she has reasonably incurred
	To Recover Damages for Breach in Regard to Accepted Goods the buyer may recover damages resulting in the ordinary course of events from the seller's breach; in the case of breach of warranty, such recovery is the difference between the value the goods would have had if they had been as warranted and the value of the nonconforming goods that have been accepted
	To Recover Incidental Damages the buyer may recover incidental damages, which include any commercially reasonable expenses connected with the delay or other breach
	To Recover Consequential Damages the buyer may recover consequential damages resulting from the seller's breach, including (1) any loss resulting from the buyer's requirements and needs of which the seller at the time of contracting had reason to know and which the buyer could not reasonably prevent by cover or otherwise, and (2) injury to person or property proximately resulting from any breach of warranty

Contractual Provisions Affecting Remedies	**Liquidation or Limitation of Damages** the parties may specify the amount or measure of damages that may be recovered in the event of a breach if the amount is reasonable
	Modification or Limitation of Remedy by Agreement the contract between the parties may expressly provide for remedies in addition to those in the Code, or it may limit or change the measure of damages recoverable for breach

QUESTIONS

1. Identify and discuss the goods-oriented remedies of the seller and the buyer.
2. Identify and discuss the obligation-oriented remedies of the seller and the buyer.
3. Identify and discuss the money-oriented damages of the seller and the buyer.
4. Identify and discuss the "specific performance" remedies of the seller and the buyer.
5. Describe the basic types of contractual provisions affecting remedies and the limitations the Code imposes upon these provisions.

Internet Question. Compare the remedies of the seller and buyer under the United Nations Convention on Contracts for the International Sale of Goods (Vienna, 1980), with their remedies under Article 2 of the Uniform Commercial Code.

PROBLEMS

1. Mae contracted to sell 1,000 bushels of wheat to Lloyd at $4 per bushel. Just before Mae was to deliver the wheat, Lloyd notified her that he would not receive or accept the wheat. Mae sold the wheat for $3.60 per bushel, the market price, and later sued Lloyd for the difference of $400. Lloyd claims he was not notified by Mae of the resale and hence is not liable. Decision?

2. On December 15, Judy wrote a letter to David stating that she would sell to David all of the mine-run coal that David might need to buy during the next calendar year for use at David's factory, delivered at the factory at a price of $40 per ton. David immediately replied by letter to Judy stating that he accepted the offer, that he would purchase all of his mine-run coal from Judy, and that he would need 200 tons of coal during the first week in January. During the months of January, February, and March, Judy delivered to David a total of 700 tons of coal, for which David made payment to Judy at the rate of $40 per ton. On April 10, David ordered 200 tons of mine-run coal from Judy, who replied to David on April 11 that she could not supply David with any more coal except at a price of $48 per ton delivered. David thereafter purchased elsewhere at the market price, namely $48 per ton, all of his factory's requirements of mine-run coal for the remainder of the year, amounting to a total of 2,000 tons of coal. David now brings an action against Judy to recover damages at the rate of $8 per ton for the coal thus purchased, amounting to $16,000. Decision?

3. On January 10, Betty, of Emanon, Missouri, visited the showrooms of the Forte Piano Company in St. Louis and selected a piano. A sales memorandum of the transaction signed both by Betty and by the salesman of the Forte Piano Company read as follows: "Sold to Betty one new Andover piano, factory number 46832, price $3,300, to be shipped to the buyer at Emanon, Missouri, freight prepaid, before February 1. Prior to shipment, seller will stain the case a darker color in accordance with buyer's directions and will make the tone more brilliant." On January 15, Betty repudiated the contract by letter to the Forte Piano Company. The company subsequently stained the case, made the tone more brilliant, and offered to ship the piano to Betty on January 26. Betty persisted in her refusal to accept the piano. In an action by the Forte Piano Company against Betty to recover the contract price, what would be the judgment?

4. Sims contracted in writing to sell Blake 100 electric motors at a price of $100 each, freight prepaid to Blake's warehouse. By the contract of sale, Sims expressly warranted that each motor would develop twenty-five brake horsepower. The contract provided that the motors would be delivered in lots of twenty-five per week beginning January 2 and that Blake should pay for each lot of twenty-five motors as delivered, but that Blake was to have right of inspection on delivery. Immediately on delivery of the first lot of twenty-five motors on January 2, Blake forwarded Sims a check for $2,500, but on testing each of the twenty-five motors, Blake determined that none of them would develop more than fifteen brake horsepower. State all of the remedies available to Blake.

5. Henry and Mary entered into a written contract whereby Henry agreed to sell and Mary agreed to buy a certain automobile for $3,500. Henry drove the car to Mary's residence and properly parked it on the street in front of Mary's house, where he tendered it to Mary and requested payment of the price. Mary refused to take the car or pay the price. Henry informed Mary that he would hold her to the contract; but before Henry had time to enter the car and drive it away, a fire truck, answering a fire alarm and traveling at a high speed, crashed into the car and demolished it. Henry brings an action against Mary to recover the price of the car. Who is entitled to judgment? Would there be any difference in result if Henry were a dealer in automobiles?

6. Jane sells and delivers to Gerald on June 1 certain goods and receives from Gerald at the time of delivery

Gerald's check in the amount of $900 for the goods. The following day, Gerald is petitioned into bankruptcy; and Gerald's bank dishonors the check. On June 5, Jane serves notice on Gerald and the trustee in bankruptcy that she reclaims the goods. The trustee is in possession of the goods and refuses to deliver them to Jane. What are the rights of the parties?

7. The ABC Company, located in Chicago, contracted to sell a carload of television sets to Dodd in St. Louis, Missouri, on sixty days' credit. ABC Company shipped the carload to Dodd. On arrival of the car at St. Louis, Dodd paid the freight charges and reshipped the car to Hines of Little Rock, Arkansas, to whom he had previously contracted to sell the television sets. While the car was in transit to Little Rock, Dodd went bankrupt. ABC Company was informed of this at once and immediately telegraphed XYZ Railroad Company to withhold delivery of the television sets. What should the XYZ Railroad Company do?

8. Robert in Chicago entered into a contract to sell certain machines to Terry in New York. The machines were to be manufactured by Robert and shipped F.O.B. Chicago not later than March 25. On March 24, when Robert was about to ship the machines, he received a telegram from Terry wrongfully repudiating the contract. The machines cannot readily be resold for a reasonable price because they are a special kind used only in Terry's manufacturing processes. Robert sues Terry to recover the agreed price of the machines. What are the rights of the parties?

9. Calvin purchased a log home construction kit, manufactured by Boone Homes, Inc., from an authorized Boone dealer. The sales contract stated that Boone would repair or replace defective materials and that this was the exclusive remedy available against Boone. The dealer assembled the house, which was defective in a number of respects. The knotholes in the logs caused the walls and ceiling to leak. A support beam was too small and therefore cracked, causing the floor to crack also. These defects could not be completely cured by repair. Calvin sues Boone for breach of warranty to recover damages for the loss in value. Decision?

10. Margaret contracted to buy a 1973 Rolls-Royce Corniche from Paragon Motors, Inc. Only 100 Corniches are built each year. She paid a $3,000 deposit on the car but Paragon sold the car to Gluck. What remedy, if any, does Margaret have against Paragon?

11. Technical Textile agreed by written contract to manufacture and sell 20,000 pounds of yarn to Jagger Brothers at a price of $2.15 per pound. After Technical had manufactured, delivered, and been paid for 3,723 pounds of yarn, Jagger Brothers by letter informed Technical that it was repudiating the contract and that it would refuse any further yarn deliveries. On August 12,

the date of the letter, the market price of yarn was $1.90 per pound. Technical was awarded $4,069.25 in damages by the trial court, an amount equal to 16,277 times the difference between the contract price ($2.15) and the market price ($1.90) of the yarn on the repudiation date. Jagger Brothers appealed, contending that the proper measure of damages was the difference between the contract price and the cost of manufacture and that, because no evidence was offered as to the cost of manufacture, Technical was entitled only to nominal damages. Decision?

12. Sherman Burrus, a job printer, purchased a printing press from the Itek Corporation for a price of $7,006.08. Before making the purchase, Burrus was assured by an Itek salesman, Mr. Nessel, that the press was appropriate for the type of printing Burrus was doing. Burrus encountered problems in operating the press almost continuously from the time he received it. Burrus, his employees, and Itek representatives spent many hours in an unsuccessful attempt to get the press to operate properly. Burrus requested that the press be replaced, but Itek refused. Burrus then brought an action against Itek for (1) damages for breach of the implied warranty of merchantability and (2) consequential damages for losses resulting from the press's defective operation. The trial court awarded damages of $10,435 to Burrus, and Itek appealed. Decision?

13. A farmer made a contract in April to sell a grain dealer 40,000 bushels of corn to be delivered in October. On June 3, the farmer unequivocally informed the grain dealer that he was not going to plant any corn, that he would not fulfill the contract, and that if the buyer had commitments to resell the corn he should make other arrangements. The grain dealer waited in vain until October for performance of the repudiated contract. Then he bought corn at a greatly increased price on the market in order to fulfill commitments to his purchasers. The grain dealer sued for damages. Decision?

14. Through information provided by S-2 Yachts, Inc., the plaintiff, Barr, located a yacht to his liking at the Crow's Nest marina and yacht sales company. When Barr asked the price, he was told that, although the yacht normally sold for $102,000, Crow's Nest was willing to sell this particular one for only $80,000 in order to make room for a new model from the manufacturer, S-2 Yachts, Inc. Barr was assured that the yacht in question came with full manufacturer's warranties. Barr asked if the yacht was new and if anything was wrong with it. Crow's Nest told him that nothing was wrong with the yacht and that there were only 20 hours of use on the engines.

Once the yacht had been delivered and Barr had taken it for a test run, he noticed several problems associated with saltwater damage, such as rusted screws, a rusted stove, and faulty electrical wiring. Barr was assured that Crow's Nest would pay for these repairs.

However, as was later discovered, the yacht was in such a damaged condition that Barr experienced great personal hazard the two times that he used the boat. Examination by a marine expert revealed clearly that the boat had been sunk in salt water prior to Barr's purchase. The engines were severely damaged, and there was significant structural and equipment damage as well. According to the expert, not only was the yacht not new, it was worth at most only a half of the new value of $102,000. Barr sued both S-2 Yachts and Crow's Nest for breach of warranties. Decision?

15. Lee Oldsmobile sells Rolls-Royce automobiles. Mrs. Kaiden sent Lee a $5,000 deposit on a $29,500 1973 Rolls-Royce. Although Lee informed Mrs. Kaiden that the car would be delivered in November, the order form did not indicate the delivery date and contained a disclaimer for delay or failure to deliver due to circumstances beyond the dealer's control. On November 21, Mrs. Kaiden purchased another car from another dealer and canceled her car from Lee. When Lee attempted to deliver a Rolls-Royce to Mrs. Kaiden on November 29, Mrs. Kaiden refused to accept delivery. Lee later sold the car for $26,495.00. Mrs. Kaiden sued Lee for her $5,000 deposit plus interest. Lee counterclaims, based on the terms of the contract, for liquidated damages of $5,000 (the amount of the deposit) as a result of Mrs. Kaiden's breach of contract. Decision?

16. Servebest contracted to sell Emessee 200,000 pounds of 50-percent lean beef trimmings for $105,000. Upon a substantial fall in the market price, Emessee refused to pay the contract price and informed Servebest that the contract was canceled. Servebest sues Emessee for breach of contract including (a) damages for the difference between the contract price and the resale price of the trimmings and (b) incidental damages. Decision?

17. Mrs. French was the highest bidder on eight antique guns at an auction held by Sotheby & Company. When Sotheby's billed Mrs. French $24,886.27 for the guns, she refused to pay. Sotheby's sued Mrs. French for the price of the guns. Decision?

18. Teledyne Industries, Inc., entered into a contract with Teradyne, Inc., to purchase a T-347A transistor test system for the list and fair market price of $98,400 less a discount of $984. After they system was packed for shipment, Teledyne canceled the order, offering to purchase a Field Effects Transistor System for $65,000. Teradyne refused the offer and sold the T-347A to another purchaser pursuant to an order that was on hand prior to the cancellation. Teradyne then sued Teledyne for breach of contract. Judgment was entered in favor of Teradyne for lost profits, and Teledyne appealed. Decision?

PART V

Negotiable Instruments

CHAPTER 24

Form and Content

In July 1990, the American Law Institute and the National Conference of Commissioners on Uniform Laws approved a Revised Article 3 to the UCC. Named "Negotiable Instruments," the new Article, now adopted by nearly all of the states, maintains the basic scope and content of prior Article 3 (Commercial Paper). This part of the text will discuss Revised Article 3, but will also point out the major changes from prior Article 3. Revised Article 3 is presented in Appendix C.

Negotiable instruments
include drafts, checks, promissory notes, and certificates of deposit

Negotiable instruments, also referred to simply as **instruments**, include checks, drafts, promissory notes, and certificates of deposit. These instruments are crucial to the sale of goods and services as well as to the financing of most businesses. The use of negotiable instruments has increased to such an extent that payments made with these instruments, with checks in particular, are now many times greater than payments made with cash. In fact, currency now is used primarily for smaller transactions. Accordingly, the vital importance of negotiable instruments as a method of payment cannot be overstated.

Modern business could not be conducted without the use of negotiable instruments. A tremendous number of transactions involve the writing of one or more checks. Drafts, of which checks are a specialized form, provide an important monetary and credit function in the business world, both inside and outside the banking system. Promissory notes serve an essential business purpose, not only in areas of high finance, but also at the level of the consumer and small businessperson as well. In recent years, individuals have increasingly used certificates of deposit instead of savings accounts.

NEGOTIABILITY

Negotiability
(ne·go·ti·a·bil'·i·ty) invests instruments with a high degree of marketability and commercial utility by conferring upon certain good faith transferees immunity from most defenses to the instrument

Negotiability is a legal concept that makes written instruments freely transferable and therefore a readily accepted form of payment in substitution for money.

Development of Law of Negotiable Instruments

The starting point for an understanding of negotiable instruments is recognizing that four or five centuries ago in England a contract right to the payment of money was not assignable because a contractual promise ran to the promisee. The fact that performance could be rendered only to him constituted a hardship for the owner of the right because it prevented him from selling or disposing of it. Eventually, however, the law permitted recovery upon an assignment by the assignee against the obligor.

An innocent assignee bringing an action against the obligor was subject to all defenses available to the obligor. Such an action would result in the same outcome whether it was brought by the assignee or assignor. Thus, a contract right became assignable but not very marketable because merchants had little interest in buying into a possible lawsuit. This remains the law of *assignments: the assignee stands in the shoes of his assignor.* For a discussion of assignments, see Chapter 16.

With the flourishing of trade and commerce, it became essential to develop a more effective means of exchanging contractual rights for money. For example, a merchant who sold goods for cash might use the cash to buy more goods for resale. If he were to make a sale on credit in exchange for a promise to pay money, why should he not be permitted to sell that promise to someone else for cash with which to carry on his business? One difficulty was that the buyer of the goods gave the seller only a promise to pay money to him. The seller was the only person to whom performance or payment was promised. If, however, the seller obtained from the buyer a promise in writing to pay money to anyone in possession (a *bearer*) of the writing (the *paper* or *instrument*) or to anyone the seller (or *payee* in this case) designated, then the duty of performance would run directly to the holder (the bearer of the paper or to the person to whom the payee ordered payment to be made). This is one of the essential distinctions between negotiable and nonnegotiable instruments. Although a negotiable instrument has other formal requirements, this particular one eliminates the limitations of a promise to pay money only to a named promisee.

Moreover, if the promise to pay were not subject to all of the defenses available against the assignor, a transferee would not only be more willing to acquire the promise but also would pay more for it. Accordingly, the law of negotiable instruments developed the concept of the **holder in due course,** whereby certain good faith transferees who gave value acquired the right to be paid, free of most of the defenses to which an assignee would be subject. By reason of this doctrine, a transferee of a negotiable instrument could acquire *greater* rights than his transferor, whereas an assignee would acquire *only* the rights of his assignor. With these basic innovations, negotiable instruments enabled merchants to sell their contractual rights more readily and thereby keep their capital working.

Assignment Compared with Negotiation

Negotiability invests negotiable instruments with a high degree of marketability and commercial utility. It allows negotiable instruments to be freely transferable and enforceable by a person with the rights of a holder in due course against any person obligated on the instrument, subject only to a limited number of defenses. To illustrate, assume that George sells and delivers goods to Elaine for $50,000 on sixty days' credit and that, a few days later, George assigns this account to Marsha. Unless Elaine is duly notified of this assignment, she may safely pay the $50,000 to George on the due date without incurring any liability to Marsha, the assignee. Assume next that the goods were defective and that Elaine, accordingly, has a defense against George to the extent of $20,000. Assume also that Marsha duly notified Elaine of the assignment. The result is that Marsha can recover only $30,000, not $50,000, from Elaine because Elaine's defense against George is equally available against George's assignee, Marsha. In other words, an assignee of contractual rights merely "steps into the shoes" of her assignor and, hence, acquires only the same rights as her assignor—and no more.

Assume, instead, that upon the sale by George to Elaine, Elaine executes and delivers her negotiable note to George for $50,000, payable to George's order in sixty days, and that, a short time later, George duly negotiates (transfers) the note to Marsha. In the first place, Marsha is not required to notify Elaine that she has acquired the note from George, since one who issues a negotiable instrument is held to know that the instrument may be negotiated and is generally obligated to pay the holder of the instrument, whoever that may be. In the second place, Elaine's defense is not available against Marsha if Marsha acquired the note in good faith and for value and had no knowledge of Elaine's defense against George and took it without reason to question its authenticity. Marsha, therefore, is entitled to hold Elaine for the full face amount of the note at maturity, namely, $50,000. In other words, Marsha, by the negotiation of the negotiable note to her, acquired rights greater than those George had, since, by keeping the note, George could have recovered only $30,000 on it because Elaine successfully could have asserted her defense in the amount of $20,000 against him.

To have the full benefit of negotiability, negotiable instruments not only must meet the requirements of negotiability but also must be acquired by a holder in due course. This chapter discusses the formal requirements instruments must satisfy to be negotiable. Chapter 25 deals with the manner in which a negotiable instrument must be negotiated to preserve its advantages. Chapter 26 covers the requisites and rights of a holder in due course. Finally, Chapter 27 examines the liability of all the parties to a negotiable instrument.

TYPES OF NEGOTIABLE INSTRUMENTS

There are four types of negotiable instruments: drafts, checks, notes, and certificates of deposit. The first two contain *orders* or directions to pay money; the last two involve *promises* to pay money.

Drafts

Drafts a draft involves three parties: the drawer orders the drawee to pay a fixed amount of money to a payee

Drawer issuer of an order to pay (draft or check)

Drawee party ordered to pay a draft or a check

Payee person to receive payment on any instrument

A **draft** involves three parties, each in a distinct capacity. One party, the **drawer**, *orders* a second party, the **drawee**, to pay a fixed amount of money to a third party, the **payee** (see Figure 24–1). The drawee is ordinarily a person or entity who either is in possession of money belonging to the drawer or owes money to him. A sample draft is reproduced in Figure 24–2. The same party may appear in more than one capacity; for instance, the drawer may also be the payee.

Drafts may be either "time" or "sight." A *time draft* is one payable at a specified future date, whereas a *sight draft* is payable on demand (that is, immediately upon presentation to the drawee).

FIGURE 24–1 Order to Pay: Draft or Check

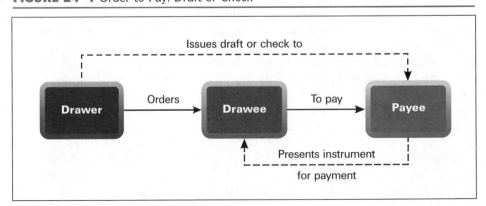

FIGURE 24–2 Draft

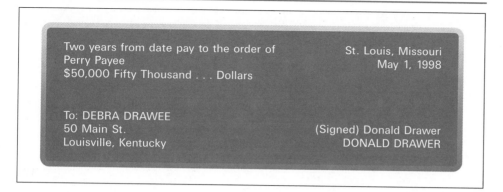

Two years from date pay to the order of
Perry Payee

$50,000 Fifty Thousand . . . Dollars

St. Louis, Missouri
May 1, 1998

To: DEBRA DRAWEE
50 Main St.
Louisville, Kentucky

(Signed) Donald Drawer
DONALD DRAWER

Checks

A **check** is a specialized form of draft, namely, an order to pay money drawn on a *bank* and payable on *demand* (that is, upon the payee's request for payment). Once again, there are parties involved in three distinct capacities: the *drawer*, who orders the *drawee*, a bank, to pay the payee on **demand** (see Figure 24–3). Checks are by far the most widely used form of negotiable instruments. Each year over ten billion checks are written in the United States for a total of over five trillion dollars.

A *cashier's check* is a check drawn by a bank upon itself to the order of a named payee.

Checks a specialized form of draft that is drawn on a bank and payable on demand; the drawer orders the drawee (bank) to pay the payee on demand

Demand request for payment made by the holder of an instrument

Notes

A **promissory note** is an instrument involving two parties in two capacities. One party, the **maker**, promises to pay a second party, the payee, a stated sum of money, either on demand or at a stated future date (see Figure 24–4). The note may range from a simple "I promise to pay $X to the order of Y" form to more complex legal instruments such as installment notes, collateral notes, mortgage notes, and judgment notes. Figure 24–5 is a note payable at a definite time—six months from the date of April 7, 1998—and hence is referred to as a *time note*. A note payable upon the request or demand of the payee or holder is a *demand note*.

Promissory note a written promise by a maker (issuer) to pay a payee

Maker issuer of a promissory note or certificate of deposit

FIGURE 24–3 Check

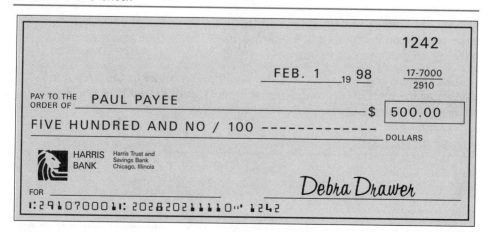

1242

FEB. 1 19 98   17-7000
                2910

PAY TO THE ORDER OF PAUL PAYEE $ 500.00

FIVE HUNDRED AND NO / 100 ------------- DOLLARS

HARRIS BANK   Harris Trust and Savings Bank
              Chicago, Illinois

FOR   Debra Drawer

⑈291070001⑈ 20282021111 0⑈ 1242

FIGURE 24–4 Promise to Pay: Promissory Note or Certificate of Deposit

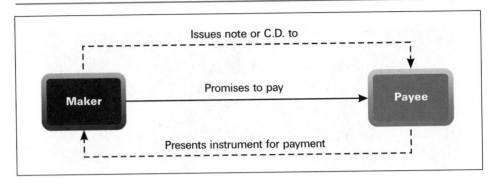

Certificates of Deposit

Certificate of deposit a specialized form of note that is given by a bank or thrift association

A certificate of deposit, or CD, as it is frequently called, is a specialized form of *promise* to pay money given by a *bank*. A **certificate of deposit** is a written acknowledgment by a bank of the receipt of money that it promises to repay. The issuing party, the *maker*, which is always a bank, promises to pay a second party, the payee, who is named in the CD (see Figure 24–6).

FORMAL REQUIREMENTS OF NEGOTIABLE INSTRUMENTS

Formal requirements negotiability is wholly a matter of form, and all the requirements for negotiability must be met within the "four corners" of the instrument

To perform its function in the business community effectively, negotiable instruments must be able to pass freely from person to person. The fact that *negotiability* is wholly a matter of form makes such freedom possible. The instrument must contain within its "four corners" all the information required to determine whether it is negotiable. No reference to any other source is permitted. For this reason, a negotiable instrument is called a "courier without luggage." In addition, indorsements *cannot* create or destroy negotiability.

In order to be negotiable, the *instrument* must

1. be in writing,
2. be signed,
3. contain a promise or order to pay,
4. be unconditional,
5. be for a fixed amount,
6. be for money,
7. contain no other undertaking or instruction,
8. be payable on demand or at a definite time, and
9. be payable to order or to bearer.

If these requirements are not met, the undertaking is not negotiable (nor is it a negotiable instrument or simply an instrument), and the rights of the parties are governed by the law of contract (assignment).

FIGURE 24–5 Note

| $10,000 | Albany, N.Y. | April 7, 1998 |

Six months from date I promise to pay to the order of Pat Payee ten thousand dollars.

(signed) Matthew Maker

FIGURE 24–6 Certificate of Deposit

NEGOTIABLE CERTIFICATE OF DEPOSIT

The Mountain Bank
No. 13900   Mountain, N.Y.   June 1, 1998

THIS CERTIFIES THAT THERE HAS BEEN DEPOSITED
with the undersigned the sum of $200,000.00

Two hundred thousand . . . . .Dollars

Payable to the order of Pablo Payee on December 1, 2000,
with interest only to maturity at the rate of Seven percent (7%)
per annum upon surrender of this certificate properly indorsed.

The Mountain Bank

By (Signature) Malcolm Maker, Vice President

Authorized Signature

Writing

The requirement that the instrument be in **writing** is broadly construed. Printing, typewriting, handwriting, or any other tangible expression is sufficient to satisfy the requirement. Most negotiable instruments, of course, are written on paper, but this is not required. In one instance, a check was reportedly written on a coconut.

Writing any reduction to tangible form is sufficient

Signed

A note or certificate of deposit must be signed by the maker; a draft or check must be signed by the drawer. As in the case of a writing, extreme latitude is granted in determining what constitutes a **signature**, which is any symbol a party executes or adopts with the *intent* to validate a writing. Moreover, it may consist of any word or mark used in place of a written signature, such as initials, an X, or a thumbprint. It may be a trade name or an assumed name. Even the location of the signature on the document is unimportant. Normally, a maker or drawer signs in the lower right-hand corner of the instrument, but this is not required. Negotiable instruments are frequently signed by an agent for her principal. For a discussion of the appropriate way in which an agent should sign a negotiable instrument, see Chapter 27.

Signature any symbol executed or adopted by a party with the intention to validate a writing

Promise or Order to Pay

A negotiable instrument must contain either a promise to pay money, in the case of a note or certificate of deposit, or an order to pay, in the case of a draft or check.

Promise to Pay A **promise to pay** is an undertaking and must be more than the mere acknowledgment or recognition of an existing obligation or debt. The so-called due bill or IOU is not a promise but merely an acknowledgment of indebtedness. Accordingly, an instrument reciting "due Adam Brown $100" or "IOU, Adam Brown, $100" is not negotiable because it does not contain a promise to pay.

Promise to pay an undertaking to pay, which must be more than a mere acknowledgment or recognition of an existing debt

Order to Pay An **order to pay** is an instruction to pay. It must be more than an authorization or request and must identify with reasonable certainty the person to be paid. The usual way to express an order is by use of the word *pay*:

Order to pay instruction to pay

"*Pay* to the order of John Jones" or "*Pay* bearer." The addition of words of courtesy, such as *please pay* or *kindly pay*, will not destroy the negotiability. Nonetheless, caution should be exercised in employing words that modify the prototypically correct "*pay.*" For example, the use of the words "I wish you would pay" has been held to destroy the negotiability of an instrument and to render its transfer a contractual assignment.

Unconditional

The requirement that the promise or order be unconditional is to prevent the inclusion of any term that could reduce the promisor's obligation to pay. Conditions limiting a promise would diminish the payment and credit functions of negotiable instruments by necessitating costly and time-consuming investigations to determine the degree of risk such conditions imposed. Moreover, if the holder (transferee) had to take an instrument subject to certain conditions, her risk factor would be substantial, and this would lead to limited transferability. Substitutes for money must be capable of rapid circulation at a minimum risk.

Unconditional an absolute promise to pay that is not subject to any contingencies

A promise or order to pay is **unconditional** if it is absolute and not subject to any contingencies or qualifications. Thus, an instrument would not be negotiable if it stated that "ABC Corp. promises to pay $100,000 to the order of Johnson provided the helicopter sold meets all contractual specifications." On the other hand, suppose that upon delivering an instrument that provided, "ABC Corp. promises to pay $100,000 to the order of Johnson," Meeker, the president of ABC, stated that the money would be paid only if the helicopter met all contractual specifications. The instrument would be negotiable because negotiability is determined solely by examining the instrument itself and is not affected by matters beyond the instrument's face.

A promise or order is unconditional unless it states: (a) that there is an express condition to payment, (b) that the promise or order is subject to or governed by another writing, or (c) that rights or obligations concerning the order or promise are stated in another writing. A mere reference to another writing, however, does not make the promise or order conditional.

An instrument is not made conditional by the fact that it is subject to implied or constructive conditions; the condition must be expressed to destroy negotiability. Implications of law or fact are not to be considered in deciding whether an instrument is negotiable. Thus, a statement in an instrument that it is given for an executory promise does *not* imply that the instrument is conditioned upon performance of that promise.

Reference to another agreement does not destroy negotiability unless the recital makes the instrument subject to or governed by the terms of another agreement

Reference to Other Agreements   The restriction against **reference to another agreement** is to enable any person to determine the right to payment provided by the instrument without having to look beyond its four corners. If such right is made subject to the terms of another agreement, the instrument is nonnegotiable.

A distinction is to be made between a mere recital of the *existence* of a separate agreement (this does not destroy negotiability) and a recital that makes the instrument *subject* to the terms of another agreement (this does destroy negotiability).

A statement in a note such as

> This note is given in partial payment for a color TV set to be delivered two weeks from date in accordance with a contract of this date between the payee and the maker.

does not impair negotiability. It merely describes the consideration and the transaction giving rise to the note. It does not place any restriction or condition on the maker's obligation to pay. The promise is not made subject to any other agreement. The following is an example of added words that *would* impair negotiability:

> This note is subject to all terms of said contract.

Such words make the promise to pay conditional upon the adequate performance of the television set in accordance with the terms of the contract and thus render the instrument nonnegotiable.

HOLLY HILL ACRES, LIMITED v. CHARTER BANK OF GAINESVILLE District Court of Appeals of Florida, Second District, 1975, 314 So.2d 209

FACTS Holly Hill Acres, Ltd., executed and delivered a promissory note and a purchase money mortgage to Rogers and Blythe. The note provided that it was secured by a mortgage on certain real estate and that the terms of that mortgage "are by this reference made a part hereof." Rogers and Blythe then assigned the note to Charter Bank, and the bank sought to foreclose on the note and mortgage. Holly Hill Acres refused to pay, claiming that it was defrauded by Rogers and Blythe. Holly Hill appealed from a summary judgment in favor of the plaintiff, Charter Bank.

DECISION Summary judgment reversed and case remanded for further proceedings.

OPINION A note that states that it is subject to or governed by any other agreement does not contain an unconditional promise to pay and, therefore, is not a negotiable instrument. Here, the note executed by Holly Hill Acres provided that it was secured by a mortgage on real estate. This is a common commercial practice, and such a reference does not in itself destroy the negotiability of the note. In addition, however, the note states that the terms of the mortgage are by reference made a part of the note. This condition on the promise to pay renders the note nonnegotiable because it depends on terms not appearing on the face of the instrument. And since the note, therefore, is nonnegotiable, Charter Bank, as the assignee of a mortgage securing a nonnegotiable note, must take subject to all defenses available against Rogers and Blythe.

INTERPRETATION A reference in a negotiable instrument to the existence of a separate agreement (e.g., secured by a mortgage) does not destroy its negotiability; but a reference that is subject to another agreement does destroy its negotiability.

The Particular Fund Doctrine Revised Article 3 eliminates the **particular fund doctrine** by providing that a promise or order is *not* made conditional because payment is to be made only out of a particular fund.

Under prior Article 3, an order or promise to pay only out of a particular fund was conditional and destroyed negotiability because payment depended upon the existence and sufficiency of the particular fund. On the other hand, a promise or order to pay that merely indicated a particular fund out of which reimbursement was to be made or a particular account to be debited with the amount did not impair negotiability since the promise or order relied on the drawer's or maker's general credit and since charging a particular account was merely a bookkeeping entry to be followed after payment.

Particular fund doctrine an order or promise to pay only out of a particular fund is no longer conditional and does not destroy negotiability

Fixed Amount

The purpose of the requirement of a **fixed amount** in money is to enable the person entitled to enforce the instrument to determine from the instrument itself the amount that he is entitled to receive.

The requirement that payment be of a "fixed amount" must be considered from the point of view of the person entitled to enforce the instrument, not the maker or drawer. (Prior Article 3 used the term "sum certain," which means fundamentally the same as "fixed amount.") The holder must be assured of a

Fixed amount the holder must be assured of a determinable minimum principal payment, although provisions in the instrument may increase the amount of recovery under certain circumstances

determinable minimum payment, although provisions of the instrument may increase the recovery under certain circumstances. Revised Article 3, however, applies the fixed amount requirement only to the *principal*. Thus, the fixed amount portion does not apply to interest or to the charges, such as collection fees or attorney's fees.

Moreover, negotiability of an instrument is not affected by the inclusion or omission of a stated rate of interest. If the instrument does not state a rate of interest, it is payable without interest. If the instrument states that it is payable "with interest" but does not specify a rate, the judgment rate of interest applies.

Most significantly, Revised Article 3 provides that "Interest may be stated in an instrument as a fixed or variable amount of money or it may be expressed as a fixed or variable rate or rates." Moreover, determination of the rate of interest "may require reference to information not contained in the instrument." Variable rate mortgages, therefore, may be negotiable; this result is consistent with the rule that the fixed amount requirement applies only to the principal.

Under prior Article 3, both principal and interest had to be determined from the face of the instrument. Thus, courts held that variable interest rate provisions destroyed negotiability because the interest rate was tied to a published index external to the instrument.

A sum payable is a fixed amount even though it is payable in installments or payable with a fixed discount, if paid before maturity, or with a fixed addition, if paid after maturity. This is because it is always possible to use the instrument itself to compute the amount due at any given time.

Money

Money legal tender authorized or adopted by a sovereign government as part of its currency

The term **money** means a medium of exchange authorized or adopted by a sovereign government as part of its currency. Consequently, even though local custom may make gold or diamonds a medium of exchange, an instrument payable in such commodities would be nonnegotiable because of the lack of governmental sanction of such media as legal tender. On the other hand, an instrument paying a fixed amount in French francs, German marks, Italian lira, Japanese yen, or other foreign currency is negotiable.

No Other Undertaking or Instruction

No other undertaking or instruction a promise or order to do an act in addition to the payment of money destroys negotiability

A negotiable instrument must contain a promise or order to pay money, but it may not "state any other undertaking or instruction by the person promising or ordering payment to do any act in addition to the payment of money." Accordingly, an instrument containing an order or promise to do an act in addition to or in lieu of the payment of money is not negotiable. For example, a promise to pay $100 "and a ton of coal" would be nonnegotiable.

The Code sets out a list of terms and provisions that may be included in instruments without adversely affecting negotiability. Among these are (1) an undertaking or power to give, maintain, or protect collateral in order to secure payment, (2) an authorization or power to confess judgment (written authority by the debtor to allow the holder to enter judgment against the debtor in favor of the holder) on the instrument, (3) an authorization or power to sell or dispose of collateral upon default, and (4) a waiver of the benefit of any law intended for the advantage or protection of the obligor. It is important to note that the Code does not render any of these terms legal or effective; it merely provides that their inclusion will not affect negotiability.

Payable on Demand or at a Definite Time

A negotiable instrument must "be payable on demand or at a definite time." This requirement, like the other formal requirements of negotiability, is designed to promote certainty in determining the present value of a negotiable instrument.

Demand "Payable upon demand" means that the money owed under the instrument must be paid upon the holder's request. **Demand paper** always has been considered sufficiently certain as to time of payment to satisfy the requirements of negotiability because it is the person entitled to enforce the instrument who makes the demand and who thus sets the time for payment. Any instrument in which no time for payment is stated—a check, for example— is payable on demand. An instrument also qualifies as being payable on demand if it is payable at sight or on presentment.

Demand paper payable on request

NATIONSBANK OF VIRGINIA, N.A. v. BARNES Virginia Circuit Court, 1994, 24 UCC.Rep. Serv.2d 782

FACTS In 1991, Ad Barnes and Elaine Barnes (Barnes) executed a promissory note for $200,000 to Sovran Bank, N.A. (Sovran). The note was executed on a standard form and a box marked payable "on demand" was checked. There was no set time for repayment, only a provision requiring monthly payments of interest. NationsBank of Virginia, N.A. (NationsBank) became the successor by merger to Sovran and is now the holder of this note. By a letter dated February 17, 1993, NationsBank made a demand for payment on the note. Barnes did not make payment and NationsBank brought this action to recover payment. NationsBank filed a motion for partial summary judgment on the issue of liability. Barnes argued that NationsBank must make a showing of good faith before it may demand payment on the note.

DECISION Summary judgment granted for NationsBank.

OPINION Under any contract providing for accelerated payment at will, the UCC provides that the option is to be exercised only in the good faith belief that the prospect of payment or performance is impaired. However, the Code also indicates that this rule is not applicable to a demand note. Barnes argued that the note in this case was not a demand note and therefore NationsBank must show good faith before it can recover. To support this argument, Barnes argued that the detailed enumeration of events constituting default is inconsistent with a demand note.

UCC Revised § 3-108(a) states that a note is payable "on demand" if it says it is payable on demand or states no time for payment. In this case, the box marked payable "on demand" was checked and no payment date was stated. The note is unambiguous and it is clearly a demand note. Therefore, no showing of good faith is required before NationsBank may demand payment. Since NationsBank has demanded payment, Barnes is liable on the note.

INTERPRETATION An instrument payable on demand must be paid upon the holder's request.

Definite Time Instruments payable at a definite time are called **time paper**. A promise or order is payable at a definite time if it is payable:

Time paper payable at definite time

1. at a fixed date or dates,
2. at a definite period of time after sight or acceptance, or
3. at a time readily ascertainable at the time the promise or order is issued.

An instrument is payable at a definite time if it is payable "on or before" a stated date. The person entitled to enforce the instrument is thus assured that she will have her money by the maturity date at the latest, although she may receive it sooner. This right of anticipation enables the obligor, at his option, to pay before the stated maturity date (*prepayment*) and thereby stop the further accrual of interest or, if interest rates have gone down, to refinance at a lower rate of interest. Nevertheless, it constitutes sufficient certainty so as not to impair negotiability.

Frequently, instruments are made payable at a fixed period after a stated date. For example, the instrument may be made payable "thirty days after date." This means it is payable thirty days after the date of issuance, which is recited on the instrument. Such an instrument is payable at a definite time, for its exact maturity date can be determined by simple math.

An undated instrument payable "thirty days after date" is not payable at a definite time, since the date of payment cannot be determined from its face. It is therefore nonnegotiable until it is completed.

An instrument, which by its terms is otherwise payable only upon an act or event whose time of occurrence is uncertain, is *not* payable at a definite time. An example would be a note providing for payment to the order "when X dies." However, as previously stated, a time that is readily ascertainable at the time the promise or order is issued is a definite time. This changes prior Article 3 and seemingly would permit a note reading "payable on the day of the next presidential election." As long as the scheduled event is certain to happen, Revised Article 3 appears to be satisfied.

The clause "at a fixed period after sight" is frequently used in drafts. Because a fixed period after sight means a fixed period after acceptance, a simple mathematical calculation makes the maturity date certain; and the instrument is, therefore, negotiable.

An instrument payable at a fixed time subject to *acceleration* by the holder also satisfies the requirement of being payable at a definite time. Indeed, such an instrument would seem to have a more certain maturity date than a demand instrument because it at least states a definite maturity date. In addition, the acceleration may be contingent upon the happening of some act or event.

Finally, a provision in an instrument granting the *holder* an option to extend the maturity of the instrument for a definite *or* indefinite period does not impair its negotiability. Nor does a provision permitting the *obligor* of an instrument to extend the maturity date to a further *definite* time. For example, a provision in a note, payable one year from date, that the maker may extend the maturity date six months does not impair negotiability. If the obligor is given an option to extend the maturity of the instrument for an *indefinite* period, however, his promise is illusory; and there is no certainty regarding time of payment. Such an instrument is nonnegotiable. If the obligor's right to extend is limited to a definite time, the extension clause is no more indefinite than an acceleration clause with a time limitation.

In addition, extension may be made automatic upon or after a specified act or event, provided a definite time limit is stated. An example of such an extension clause is, "I promise to pay to the order of John Doe the sum of $2,000 on December 1, 1997, but it is agreed that if the crop of sections 25 and 26 of Twp. 145 is below eight bushels per acre for the 1997 season, this note shall be extended for one year."

At a Definite Time and On Demand If the instrument, payable at a fixed date, *also* provides that it is payable on demand made before the fixed date, it is still a negotiable instrument. Revised Article 3 provides that the instrument is payable on demand until the fixed date and, if demand is not made prior to the specified date, becomes payable at a definite time on the fixed date.

Payable to Order or to Bearer

A negotiable instrument must contain words indicating that the maker or drawer intends that it may pass into the hands of someone other than the payee. While the "magic" words of negotiability typically are **payable to order or to bearer,** other clearly equivalent words also may fulfill this requirement. The use of synonyms, however, only invites trouble. Moreover, as noted above, indorsements cannot create or destroy negotiability, which must be determined from the "face" of the instrument. Words of negotiability must be present when the instrument is issued or first comes into possession of a holder.

Revised Article 3 provides that a ***check*** that meets all requirements of being a negotiable instrument except that it is not payable to bearer or order is nevertheless a negotiable instrument. This rule does *not* apply to instruments other than checks and does not exist under prior Article 3.

Payable to order or to bearer a negotiable instrument must contain words indicating that the maker or drawer intends that it pass into the hands of someone other than the payee

Payable to Order An instrument is **payable to order** if it is payable (a) to the order of an identified person or (b) to an identified person or order. If an instrument is payable to bearer, it cannot be payable to order; an instrument that is ambiguous as to this point is payable to bearer. Prior Article 3 provided that use of the word "assigns" met the requirement of words of negotiability; Revised Article 3, however, does not so provide.

Payable to order payable to the "order of" a named person or anyone designated by that person

Moreover, in every instance the person to whose order the instrument is payable must be designated with reasonable certainty. Within this limitation a broad range of payees is possible, including an individual, two or more payees, an office, an estate, a trust or fund, a partnership or unincorporated association, and a corporation.

This requirement should not be confused with the requirement that the instrument contain an order or promise to pay. An order to pay is an instruction to a third party to pay the instrument as drawn. The word "order" in terms of an "order instrument," on the other hand, pertains to the transferability of the instrument rather than to instructions directing a specific party to pay.

A writing, other than a *check*, that names a specified person without indicating that it is payable to order—for example, "Pay to Justin Matthew"—is not payable to order or to bearer. Such a writing is not a negotiable instrument and is not covered by Article 3. On the other hand, a check that meets all of the requirements of a negotiable instrument, except that it does not provide the words of negotiability, is still a negotiable instrument and falls within the purview of Article 3. Thus, a check "payable to Justin Matthew" is a negotiable check.

COOPERATIVE CENTRALE RAIFFEISEN-BOERENLEENBANK B.A. v. BAILEY United States District Court, Central District of California, 1989, 710 F. Supp. 737

FACTS William Bailey, M.D., executed a promissory note to California Dreamstreet, a joint venture that solicited investments in cattle breeding operations. California Dreamstreet subsequently sold the note to Cooperative Centrale Raiffeisen-Boerenleenbank B.A. (Bank).

The wording on the promissory note was unusual. In pertinent part it read: "DR. WILLIAM BAILEY . . . hereby promises to pay to the order to CALIFORNIA DREAMSTREET . . . the sum of Three Hundred Twenty-Nine Thousand Eight Hundred ($329,800) Dollars."

Dr. Bailey contended that the atypical wording "pay to the order to" rendered the note nonnegotiable, and refused to pay the Bank. The Bank, asserting that the note was negotiable, sued for payment.

DECISION Judgment for the Bank.

OPINION Whether an instrument is negotiable is a question of law to be determined solely from the face of the instrument, without reference to the intent of the parties. According to the UCC, in order to be negotiable an instrument must "be payable to order or bearer." The UCC further defines "payable to order" as follows: "An instrument is payable to order when by its terms it is payable to the order . . . of any person therein specified with reasonable certainty, or to him or his order, or when it is conspicuously designated on its face as 'exchange' or the like and names a payee."

continued

It is well established that a promissory note is non-negotiable if it states only "payable to (payee)" rather than "payable to the order of (payee)." Dr. Bailey argues that the promissory note in question falls somewhere in between and therefore should be deemed nonnegotiable. One of the basic concepts underlying the requirements of UCC Article 3 is to promote the negotiability of instruments by establishing certainty. While the wording of this particular note is unclear, it can plausibly be construed only to mean "pay to the order of." No other interpretation is realistic.

INTERPRETATION An instrument is payable to order if it is payable to the order of an identified entity.

Payable to Bearer The UCC states that an instrument fulfills the requirements of being **payable to bearer** if it (1) states it is payable to bearer or the order of bearer, (2) does not state a payee, or (3) states it is payable to "cash" or to the order of "cash." An instrument made payable both to order and to bearer, that is, "pay to the order of Mildred Courts or bearer," is payable to bearer.

Payable to bearer payable to the holder of the instrument; includes instruments payable (1) to bearer or the order of bearer, (2) does not specify a payee, or (3) to "cash" or to order of "cash"

An instrument that does not state a payee is payable to bearer. Thus, if a drawer leaves blank the "pay to order of" line of a check or the maker of a notes writes "pay to _____," the instrument is a negotiable bearer instrument.

Terms and Omissions and Their Effect on Negotiability
The negotiability of an instrument may be questioned because of an omission of certain provisions or because of ambiguity. Problems may also arise in connection with the interpretation of an instrument, whether or not negotiability is called into question. Accordingly, the Code contains rules of construction that apply to every instrument.

Dating of the Instrument The negotiability of an instrument is not affected by the fact that it is antedated or postdated. If the instrument is undated, its date is the date of its issuance. If it is unissued, its date is the date it first comes into the possession of a holder.

Incomplete Instruments Occasionally, a party will sign a paper that clearly is intended to become an instrument but that, either by intention or through oversight, is incomplete because of the omission of a necessary element such as a promise or order, a designated payee, an amount payable, or a time for payment. The Code provides that such an instrument is not negotiable until completed.

If, for example, an undated instrument is delivered on November 1, 1997, payable "thirty days after date," the payee has implied authority to fill in "November 1, 1997." Until he does so, however, the instrument is not negotiable because it is not payable at a definite time. If the payee completes the instrument by inserting an erroneous date, the rules as to material alteration, covered in Chapter 27, apply.

Ambiguous Instruments Rather than commit the parties to the use of parol evidence to establish the interpretation of an instrument, Article 3 establishes rules to resolve common ambiguities. This promotes negotiability by providing added certainty to the holder.

Where it is doubtful whether the instrument is a draft or note, the holder may treat it as either and present it for payment to the drawee or the person signing it. For example, an instrument reading

> To X: On demand, I promise to pay $500 to the order of Y.
>
>   Signed, Z

may be presented for payment to X as a draft or to Z as a note.

An instrument naming no drawee but stating

> On demand, pay $500 to the order of Y.
>
>   Signed, Z

although in the form of a draft, may be treated as a note and presented to Z for payment.

If a printed form of note or draft is used and the party signing it inserts handwritten or typewritten language that is inconsistent with the printed words, the handwritten words control the typewritten and the printed words, and the typewritten words control the printed.

If the amount payable is set forth on the face of the instrument in both figures and words and the amounts differ, the words control the figures. It is presumed that the maker or drawer would be more careful with words. If the words are ambiguous, however, then the figures control.

CHAPTER SUMMARY

Negotiability	**Rule** invests instruments with a high degree of marketability and commercial utility by conferring upon certain good faith transferees immunity from most defenses to the instrument **Formal Requirements** negotiability is wholly a matter of form, and all the requirements for negotiability must be met within the "four corners" of the instrument

Types of Negotiable Instruments	**Orders to Pay**
	  ■ *Drafts* a draft involves three parties: the drawer orders the drawee to pay a fixed amount of money to the payee
	  ■ *Checks* a specialized form of draft that is drawn on a bank and payable on demand; the drawer orders the drawee (bank) to pay the payee on demand (upon the request of the holder)
	Promises to Pay
	  ■ *Notes* a written promise by a maker (issuer) to pay a payee
	  ■ *Certificates of Deposit* a specialized form of note that is given by a bank or thrift association

Formal Requirements of Negotiable Instruments	**Writing** any reduction to tangible form is sufficient
	Signature any symbol executed or adopted by a party with the intention to validate a writing
	Promise or Order to Pay
	   ■ *Promise to Pay* an undertaking to pay, which must be more than a mere acknowledgment or recognition of, an existing debt
	   ■ *Order to Pay* instruction to pay
	Unconditional an absolute promise to pay that is not subject to any contingencies
	   ■ *Reference to Other Agreements* does not destroy negotiability unless the recital makes the instrument subject to or governed by the terms of another agreement
	   ■ *The Particular Fund Doctrine* an order or promise to pay only out of a particular fund is no longer conditional and does not destroy negotiability
	Fixed Amount the holder must be assured of a determinable minimum principal payment, although provisions in the instrument may increase the amount of recovery under certain circumstances
	Money legal tender authorized or adopted by a sovereign government as part of its currency
	No Other Promise or Order a promise or order to do an act in addition to the payment of money destroys negotiability
	Payable on Demand or at a Definite Time an instrument is demand paper if it must be paid upon request: an instrument is time paper if it is payable at a definite time
	Payable to Order or to Bearer a negotiable instrument must contain words indicating that the maker or drawer intends that it pass into the hands of someone other than the payee
	   ■ *Payable to Order* payable to the "order of" (or other words that mean the same) a named person or anyone designated by that person
	   ■ *Payable to Bearer* payable to the holder of the instrument; includes instruments payable (1) to bearer or the order of bearer, (2) does not specify a payee, or (3) to "cash" or to order of "cash"

QUESTIONS

1. Discuss the concept and importance of negotiability.
2. Identify and discuss the types of negotiable instruments involving an order to pay.
3. Identify and discuss the types of negotiable instruments involving a promise to pay.
4. List and discuss the formal requirements that an instrument must meet in order to be negotiable.

5. Discuss the effect on the negotiability of an instrument of (1) the instrument's being undated, antedated, or postdated, (2) its lack of completion, and (3) ambiguity.

Internet Question. Find which version of UCC Article 3 your state has adopted. (If your state is not available, choose another state.)

PROBLEMS

1. State whether the following provisions impair or preclude negotiability, the instrument in each instance being otherwise in proper form. Answer each statement with either the word "Negotiable" or "Nonnegotiable" and explain why.

   (a) A note for $2,000 payable in twenty monthly installments of $100 each that provides the

following: "In case of death of maker, all payments not due at date of death are canceled."

   (b) A note stating, "This note is secured by a mortgage of even date herewith on personal property located at 351 Maple Street, Smithton, Illinois."

   (c) A certificate of deposit reciting, "June 6, 1997, John Jones has deposited in the Citizens Bank of

Emanon, Illinois, Two Thousand Dollars, to the credit of himself, payable upon the return of this instrument properly indorsed, with interest at the rate of 6 percent per annum from date of issue upon ninety days' written notice. (Signed) Jill Crystal, President, Citizens Bank of Emanon."

(d) An instrument reciting, "IOU, Mark Noble, $1,000.00."

(e) A note stating, "In accordance with our contract of December 13, 1997, I promise to pay to the order of Sam Stone $100 on March 13, 1998."

(f) A draft drawn by Brown on the Acme Publishing Company for $500, payable to the order of the Sixth National Bank of Erehwon, directing the bank to "Charge this draft to my royalty account."

(g) A note executed by Pierre Janvier, a resident of Chicago, for $2,000, payable in Swiss francs.

(h) An undated note for $1,000 payable "six months after date."

(i) A note for $500 payable to the order of Ray Rodes six months after the death of Albert Olds.

(j) A note of $500 payable to the assigns of Levi Lee.

(k) A check made payable "to Ketisha Johnson."

2. State whether the following provisions in a note impair or preclude negotiability, the instrument in each instance being otherwise in proper form. Answer each statement with either the word "Negotiable" or "Nonnegotiable" and explain why.

(a) A note signed by Henry Brown in the trade name of the Quality Store.

(b) A note for $450, payable to the order of TV Products Company, "If, but only if, the color television set for which this note is given proves entirely satisfactory to me."

(c) A note executed by Adams, Burton, and Cady Company, a partnership, for $1,000, payable to the order of Davis, payable only out of the assets of the partnership.

(d) A note promising to pay $500 to the order of Leigh and to deliver ten tons of coal to Leigh.

(e) A note for $10,000 executed by Eaton payable to the order of the First National Bank of Emanon, in which Eaton promises to give additional collateral if the bank deems itself insecure and demands additional security.

(f) A note reading, "I promise to pay to the order of Richard Roe $2,000 on January 31, 1998, but it is agreed that if the crop of Blackacre falls below ten bushels per acre for the 1997 season, this note shall be extended indefinitely."

(g) A note payable to the order of Ray Rogers fifty years from date but providing that payment shall be accelerated by the death of Silas Hughes to a point of time four months after his death.

(h) A note for $4,000 calling for payments of installments of $250 each and stating, "In the event any installment hereof is not paid when due, this note shall immediately become due at the holder's option."

(i) An instrument dated September 17, 1998, in the handwriting of John Henry Brown, which reads in full: "Sixty days after date, I, John Henry Brown, promise to pay to the order of William Jones $500."

(j) A note reciting, "I promise to pay Ray Reed $100 on December 24, 1997."

3. On March 10, Tolliver Tolles, also known as Thomas Towle, delivered to Alonzo Craig and Abigail Craig the following instrument, written by him in pencil:

> For value received, I, Thomas Towle, promise to pay to the order of Alonzo Craig or Abigail Craig One Thousand Seventy-Five ($1,000.75) Dollars six months after my mother, Alma Tolles, dies with interest at the rate of 9 percent from date to maturity and after maturity at the rate of 9¾ percent. I hereby waive the benefit of all laws exempting real or personal property from levy or sale.

Is this instrument negotiable? Explain.

4. Henry Hughes, who operates a department store, executed the following instrument:

> $2,600   Chicago, March 5, 1998
> On July 1, 1998, I promise to pay Daniel Dalziel, or order, the sum of Twenty-Six Hundred Dollars for the privilege of one framed advertising sign, size 24 x 36 inches, at one end of each of two hundred sixty motor coaches of the New Omnibus Company for a term of three months from May 15, 1998.
>   Henry Hughes.

Is this instrument negotiable? Explain.

5. Pablo agreed to lend Marco $500. Thereupon Marco made and delivered his note for $500 payable to Pablo or order "ten days after my marriage." Shortly thereafter Marco was married. Is the instrument negotiable? Explain.

6. For the balance due on the purchase of a tractor, Henry Brown executed and delivered to Jane Jones his promissory note containing the following language:

> January 1, 1998, I promise to pay to the order of Jane Jones the sum of $7,000 to be paid only out of my checking account at the XYZ National Bank of Pinckard, Illinois, in two installments of $3,500 each, payable on May 1, 1998, and on July 1, 1998, provided that if I fail to pay the first installment on the due date, the entire sum shall become immediately due. (Signed) Henry Brown.

Is the note negotiable? Explain.

7. Sam Sharpe executed and delivered to Don Dole the following instrument:

> Knoxville, Tennessee
> May 29, 1995
>
> Thirty days after date I promise to pay Don Dole or order Five Thousand Dollars. The holder of this instrument shall have the election to require the assignment and delivery to him of my 100 shares of Brookside Iron Works Corporation stock in lieu of the payment of Five Thousand Dollars in money.
>
> (Signed) Sam Sharpe.

Is this instrument negotiable? Explain.

8. Is the following instrument negotiable?

> March 1, 1997
>
> One month from date, I, James Jimson, hereby promise to pay Edmund Edwards: Six thousand, Seven hundred Fifty ($6,750.00) dollars, plus 8¾% interest. Payment for cutting machines to be delivered on March 15, 1997.
>
> James Jimson

9. Broadway Management Corporation obtained a judgment against Briggs. The note on which the judgment was based reads in part: "Ninety Days after date, I, we, or either of us, promise to pay to the order of Three Thousand Four Hundred Ninety Eight and 45/100——Dollars." (The underlined words and symbols were typed in; the remainder was printed.) There are no blanks on the face of the instrument, any unused space having been filled in with hyphens. The note contains clauses permitting acceleration in the event the holder deems itself insecure and authorizes judgment "if this note is not paid at any stated or accelerated maturity." Briggs appeals, claiming that the note is not negotiable order paper. Decision?

10. Sandra and Thomas McGuire entered into a purchase-and-sale agreement for "Becca's Boutique" with Pascal and Rebecca Tursi. The agreement provided that the McGuires would buy the store for $75,000, with a down payment of $10,000 and the balance of $65,000 to be paid at closing on October 5, 1979. The settlement clause stated that the sale was contingent upon the McGuires obtaining a Small Business Administration loan of $65,000. On September 4, 1979, Mrs. McGuire signed a promissory note in which the McGuires promised to pay to the order of the Tursis and the Green Mountain Inn the sum of $65,000. The note specified that interest payments of $541.66 would become due and payable on the fifth days of October,

November, and December 1979. The entire balance of the note, with interest, would become due and payable at the option of the holder if any installment of interest was not paid according to that schedule.

The Tursis had for several months been negotiating with Parker Perry for the purchase of the Green Mountain Inn in Stowe, Vermont. On September 7, 1979, the Tursis delivered to Perry a $65,000 promissory note payable to the order of Green Mountain Inn, Inc. This note was secured by transfer to the Green Mountain Inn of the McGuires' note to the Tursis. Subsequently, Mrs. McGuire learned that her Small Business Administration loan had been disapproved. On December 5, 1979, the Tursis defaulted on their promissory note to the Green Mountain Inn. On June 11, 1980, PP, Inc., formerly Green Mountain Inn, Inc., brought an action against the McGuires to recover on the note held as security for the Tursis' promissory note. Decision?

11. On September 2, 1976, Levine executed a mortgage bond under which she promised to pay the Mykoffs a preexisting obligation of $54,000. On October 14, 1979, the Mykoffs transferred the mortgage to Bankers Trust Co., indorsing the instrument with the words "Pay to the Order of Bankers Trust Company Without Recourse." The Lincoln First Bank, N.A., brought this action asserting that the Mykoffs' mortgage is a nonnegotiable instrument because it is not payable to order or bearer; thus it is subject to Lincoln's defense that the mortgage was not supported by consideration since an antecedent debt is not consideration. Decision?

12. Horne executed a $100,000 note in favor of R. C. Clark. On the back of the instrument was a restriction stating that the note could not be transferred, pledged, or otherwise assigned without Horne's written consent. As part of the same transaction between Horne and Clark, Horne gave Clark a separate letter authorizing Clark to pledge the note as collateral for a loan of $50,000 that Clark intended to secure from First State Bank. Clark did secure the loan and pledged the note, which was accompanied by Horne's letter authorizing Clark to use the note as collateral. First State contacted Horne and verified the agreement between Horne and Clark as to using the note as collateral. Clark defaulted on the loan. When First Bank later attempted to collect on the note, Horne refused to pay arguing that the note was not negotiable since it could not be transferred without obtaining Horne's written consent. This suit was instituted. Decision?

CHAPTER 25

Transfer

The primary advantage of negotiable instruments is their ease of transferability. Nonetheless, although both negotiable instruments and nonnegotiable undertakings are transferable by assignment, only negotiable instruments can result in the transferee becoming a holder. This distinction is highly significant. If the transferee of a negotiable instrument is entitled to payment by the terms of the instrument, he is a holder of the instrument. Only holders may be holders in due course and thus may be entitled to greater rights in the instrument than the transferor may have possessed. These rights, discussed in the next chapter, are the reason why negotiable instruments move freely in the marketplace. This chapter discusses the methods by which negotiable instruments may be transferred.

NEGOTIATION

A **holder** is broadly defined in Section 1–201(20) as "a person who is in possession of . . . an instrument . . . drawn, issued, or indorsed to him or his order or to bearer or in blank." **Negotiation** is the transfer of possession, whether voluntary or involuntary, by a person other than the issuer of a negotiable instrument in such a manner that the transferee becomes a holder. An instrument is transferred when a person other than its issuer delivers it for the purpose of giving the recipient the right to enforce the instrument. Accordingly, to qualify as a holder a person must have possession of an instrument that runs to him. Thus, there are two ways in which a person can be a holder: (1) the instrument has been issued to that person, or (2) the instrument has been transferred to that person by negotiation.

The transfer of a nonnegotiable promise or order operates as an assignment, as does the transfer of a negotiable instrument by a means that does not render the transferee a holder. As discussed in Chapter 16, an **assignment** is the voluntary transfer to a third party of the rights arising from a contract.

Whether a transfer is by *assignment* or by *negotiation*, the transferee acquires the rights his transferor had. The transfer need not be for value: if the instrument is transferred as a gift, the donee acquires all the rights of the donor. If the transferor was a holder in due course, the transferee acquires the rights of a holder in due course, which rights he in turn may transfer. This rule, sometimes referred to as the **shelter rule**, existed at common law and still exists under the UCC. The shelter rule is discussed more fully in Chapter 26.

The requirements for negotiation depend upon whether the instrument is bearer paper or order paper.

Holder possessor of an instrument with all necessary indorsements

Negotiation transfer such that transferee becomes a holder

Assignment voluntary transfer to a party of the rights arising from a contract

Shelter rule transferee gets rights of transferor

Negotiation of Bearer Paper

If an instrument is payable to bearer, it may be negotiated by transfer of possession alone. Because bearer paper (an instrument payable to bearer) runs to whoever is in possession of it, a finder or a thief of bearer paper would be a holder even though he did not receive possession by voluntary transfer. For example, P loses an instrument payable to bearer that I had issued to her. F finds it and sells and delivers it to B, who thus receives it by negotiation and is a holder. F also qualified as a holder because he was in possession of bearer paper. As a holder, F had the power to negotiate the instrument, and B, the transferee, may be a holder in due course if he meets the Code's requirements for such a holder (discussed in Chapter 26). See Figure 25–1 for an illustration of this example. Since a bearer instrument is transferred by mere *possession*, it is comparable to cash.

Negotiation of Order Paper

If the instrument is order paper, (an instrument payable to order), both (a) transfer of its *possession* and (b) its *indorsement* (signature) by the appropriate parties are necessary for the transferee to become a holder. Figure 25–2 compares the negotiation of bearer and order paper.

Any transfer for *value* of an instrument not payable to bearer gives the transferee the specifically enforceable right to have the unqualified indorsement of the transferor, unless the parties agree otherwise. The parties may agree that the transfer is to be an assignment rather than a negotiation, in which case no indorsement is required. Absent such agreement, the courts presume that negotiation was intended where value is given. Where a transfer is not for value, the transaction is normally noncommercial; thus, the courts do not presume the intent to negotiate.

Until the necessary indorsement has been supplied, the transferee has nothing more than the contract rights of an assignee. Negotiation takes effect only when a proper indorsement is made, at which time the transferee becomes a holder of the instrument.

If a customer deposits a check or other instrument for collection without properly indorsing the item, the depository bank becomes a holder when it accepts the item for deposit if the depositor is a holder. It no longer needs to supply the customer's indorsement.

FIGURE 25–1 Bearer Paper

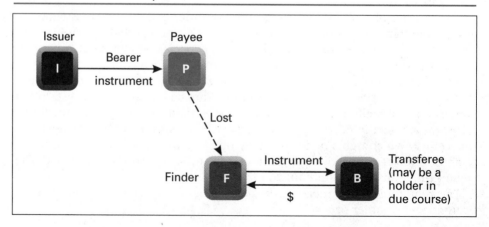

FIGURE 25–2 Negotiation of Bearer and Order Paper

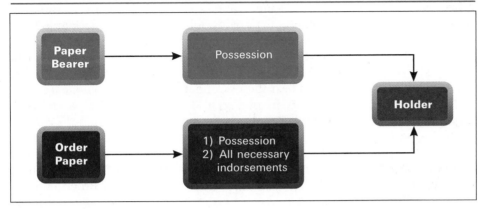

The Impostor Rule Negotiation of an order instrument requires a valid indorsement by the person to whose order the instrument is payable. The impostor rule governing unauthorized signatures is an *exception* to this general rule. Usually, the impostor rule comes into play in situations involving a confidence man who impersonates a respected citizen and who deceives a third party into delivering a negotiable instrument to the impostor in the name of the respected citizen. For instance, John Doe, falsely representing himself as Richard Roe, a prominent citizen, induces Ray Davis to loan him $10,000. Davis draws a check payable to the order of Richard Roe and delivers it to Doe, who then forges Roe's name to the check and presents it to the drawee for payment. The drawee pays it. Subsequently, Davis, the drawer, denies the drawee's right of reimbursement upon the ground that the drawee did not pay in accordance with his order: Davis ordered payment to Roe or to Roe's order. Roe did not order payment to anyone; therefore, the drawee would not acquire a right of reimbursement against Davis. The general rule governing unauthorized signatures supports this argument in favor of the drawer.

Nevertheless, the indorsement of the impostor (Doe) or of any other person in the name of the named payee is *effective* as the indorsement of the payee if the impostor has induced the maker or drawer (Davis) to issue the instrument to him or his confederate using the name of the payee (Roe). It is as if the named payee had indorsed the instrument. The reason for this rule is that the drawer or maker is to blame for failing to detect the impersonation by the impostor. Thus, in the above example, the drawee would be able to debit the drawer's account. Moreover, Revised Article 3 expands the impostor rule by extending its coverage to include an impostor who is impersonating an agent. Thus, if an impostor impersonates Jones and induces the drawer to draw a check to the order of Jones, the impostor can negotiate the check. Moreover, under the Revision, if an impostor impersonates Jones, the president of Jones Corporation, and the check is to the order of Jones Corporation, the impostor can negotiate the check.

If the person paying the instrument fails to exercise ordinary care, the issuer may recover from the payor to the extent the payor's negligence contributed to the loss. If the issuer is also negligent, comparative negligence would apply.

The Fictitious Payee Rule The rule just discussed also applies when a person who does not intend the payee to have an interest in the instrument signs as or on behalf of a maker or drawer. In such a situation, any person's indorsement in

The impostor rule an indorsement of an impostor or of any other person in the name of the named payee is effective if the impostor has induced the maker or drawer to issue the instrument to him using the name of the payee

The fictitious payee rule an indorsement by any person in the name of the named payee is effective if an agent of the maker or drawer has supplied her with the name of the payee for fraudulent purposes

the name of the named payee is *effective* if the person identified as the payee is a fictitious person. For instance, Palmer gives Albrecht, her employee, authority to write checks in order to pay Palmer's debts. Albrecht writes a check for $2,000 to Foushee, a fictitious payee, which Albrecht takes and indorses in Foushee's name to Albrecht. Albrecht cashes the check at Palmer's bank, which can debit Palmer's account because Albrecht's signature in Foushee's name is effective against Palmer. Palmer should bear the risk of her unscrupulous employees.

In a similar situation also involving a disloyal employee, a drawer's employee falsely tells the drawer that money is owed to Leon, and the drawer writes a check payable to the order of Leon and hands it to the agent for delivery to him. The agent forges Leon's name to the check and obtains payment from the drawee bank. The drawer then denies the bank's claim to reimbursement upon the ground that the bank did not comply with her order; that the drawer had ordered payment to Leon or order; that the drawee did not make payment either to Leon or as ordered by him, inasmuch as the forgery of Leon's signature is wholly inoperative; and that the drawee paid in accordance with the scheme of the faithless agent and not in compliance with the drawer's order. Under the Code, an employer has liability on the instrument when one of its employees, who is entrusted with responsibility with respect to such an instrument, makes a fraudulent indorsement if: (1) the instrument is payable to the employer and the employee forges the indorsement of the employer or (2) the instrument is issued by the employer and the employee forges the indorsement of the person identified as the payee. The example above falls under the second part of the rule just stated. Accordingly, the employee's indorsement is effective as that of the unintended payee, and the drawee bank will be able to debit the drawer's (employer's) account. See "Details of $1 Million Embezzlement Case Emerge" in the Managerial Insight.

This rule also applies to a situation (number 1 of the paragraph above) not involving a fictitious payee: a fraudulent indorsement made by an employee entrusted with responsibility with respect to an instrument payable to the employer. For example, an employee, whose job involves posting amounts of checks payable to her employer, steals some of the checks and forges her employer's indorsement. The indorsement is effective as the employer's indorsement because the employee's duties included processing checks for bookkeeping purposes.

This section provides, however, that the employer may recover from the drawee bank to the extent the loss resulted from the bank's failure to exercise ordinary care. If the employer is also negligent, a rule of comparative negligence applies.

SHEARSON LEHMAN BROTHERS, INC. v. WASATCH BANK United States District Court,
D. Utah, C.D., 1992, 788 F. Supp. 1184

FACTS Stanley A. Erb became a vice president of the Shearson Lehman Brothers, Inc. branch office in Provo, Utah, in 1987. That year, Erb was contacted by McKay Matthews, the controller for the Orem, Utah, based WordPerfect Corporation and its sister corporation, Utah Softcopy. At Matthews's request, Erb established and managed three separate investment accounts at Shearson. The accounts were for the benefit of the WordPerfect and Utah Softcopy corporations, and one account was for the WordPerfect principals, Allen Ashton, Bruce Bastian, and Willard Peterson. In March 1987, Erb personally accepted from Matthews a check drawn by Utah Softcopy for $460,150.23 and payable to the order of "ABP Investments." At that time, there was no ABP investment account at Shearson, although the WordPerfect principals maintained accounts elsewhere

continued

in that name. Erb accepted the check, but rather than deposit it in one of the three authorized accounts, Erb opened a new account at Shearson in the name of "ABP Investments," apparently by forging the signature of Bruce Bastian on the new account documents. Over the next eleven months, Erb induced Shearson to draft thirty-seven checks on the ABP Investment account, payable to ABP Investments, by submitting falsified payment requests to Shearson's cashier. The checks were mailed to an Orem post office box unknown to WordPerfect and its principals. Erb would obtain the checks and indorse them in the name of ABP Investments. He took the checks to Wasatch Bank for deposit into his personal account. Wasatch accepted the deposits and later allowed Erb to withdraw $504,295.30, the entire amount, from the account. Shearson discovered Erb's activities after Erb had left Shearson in 1989. Shearson settled with WordPerfect and its principals and was assigned all their legal rights.

Shearson brought suit against Wasatch. Wasatch moved for summary judgment, claiming under the "fictitious payee" rule that it was not liable.

DECISION Summary judgment for Wasatch.

OPINION As a general rule, forged indorsements are ineffective to pass title or authorize a drawee to pay, and when a collecting bank makes payment over a forged indorsement, it is generally liable for the amount paid. Under this rule, Wasatch clearly would be liable. Wasatch argues that it should be allowed to avoid such liability under an exception to the rule, known as the "fictitious payee" rule. For this defense to apply, an employee or agent of the drawer must "supply" the name of the payee and intend that the payee have no interest in the instrument. The payee named does not need to be fictitious, and the term "supply" can mean merely that the employee has initiated a normal business procedure to produce a check for an unauthorized transaction. The policy underlying the fictitious payee rule is to place the risk of loss of forgery on the party in the best position to avoid or insure against such loss. Erb, an employee of the drawer of the checks, supplied the name of the payee and intended that the named payee have no interest in the checks. Under these facts, the "fictitious payee" defense applies, and the drawer, Shearson, bears the loss.

INTERPRETATION An indorsement by any person in the name of the named payee is effective if an agent of the drawer supplied the name of the payee and intended the payee to have no interest in the instrument.

Negotiations Subject to Rescission

A negotiation conforming to the requirements discussed above is effective to transfer the instrument even if it is

1. made by an infant, a corporation exceeding its powers, or a person without capacity; or
2. obtained by fraud, duress, or mistake; or
3. made in breach of a duty or as part of an illegal transaction.

Thus, a negotiation is valid even though the transaction in which it occurs is voidable or even void. In all of these instances, the transferor loses all rights in the instrument until he regains possession of it. His right to do so, determined by state law, is valid against the immediate transferee and all subsequent holders, but not against a subsequent holder in due course or a person paying the instrument in good faith and without notice.

Negotiations subject to rescission negotiation is valid even though a transaction is void or voidable

INDORSEMENTS

An **indorsement** is "a signature, other than that of a signer as maker, drawer, or acceptor, that alone or accompanied by other words is made on an instrument for the purpose of (i) negotiating the instrument, (ii) restricting payment of the instrument, or (iii) incurring the indorser's liability on the instrument, but regardless of the intent of the signer, a signature and its accompanying words is

Indorsement signature (on the instrument) of a payee, drawee, accommodation party, or holder

MANAGERIAL INSIGHT

Details of $1 Million Embezzlement Case Emerge

RALEIGH—A glimpse into how an obscure accountant allegedly embezzled more than $1 million from Carolina Power & Light Co. is emerging as prosecutors prepare to seek an indictment against him.

Authorities now say they think Tony Creech stole $1.08 million since 1987 by tricking the utility into issuing checks to vendors that didn't exist or to which he owed money.

So far investigators have tracked down only $28,000, a house in Cary and three high-priced cars to show for Creech's alleged eight-year spree. But police and utility auditors are still looking.

"It's an incredibly complex investigation," CP&L spokesman Rick White said. "It's not going to be over as soon as I thought it would be. It's an extensive, methodical process. They're pulling one string at a time."

Creech, 46, remains in the Wake County Jail, where he has been held since his arrest June 15, and has not entered a plea. His bail has been raised to a $500,000 secured bond, and his assets have been frozen.

Six charges of obtaining property by false pretenses have been added to 15 counts of embezzlement against Creech.

Wake County Assistant District Attorney Susan Spurlin will ask a county grand jury July 10 to indict Creech on those charges, which account for $1,083,174.38 in CP&L money.

Creech, a mid-level accountant in the utility's downtown Raleigh office, was arrested after CP&L auditors and security officers began checking irregularities in the books several weeks ago. Just how they think Creech stole the money has remained a mystery until now.

In part, that's because they still don't know the size of the alleged swindle and are making sure it doesn't happen again.

"That's why we're still reluctant to say a whole lot," CP&L's White said. "They haven't had a chance to talk with everybody they have to talk to yet. They hope to finally do that this week."

But prosecutor Spurlin has disclosed in court some of the case against Creech, who was one of about 140 employees in the accounting department.

She said Creech embezzled the money two ways, using his position to submit bogus check requests for payments to vendors.

In one scheme, Creech set up an account at Wachovia Bank for a phony company, she said. When CP&L paid the non-existent firm, Creech simply transferred the money into his personal Wachovia account, she said.

That's how he funneled about $500,000 into a single fake firm, called G&C Associates, Spurlin said.

In the other, more complicated, method, Spurlin said, Creech had CP&L issue checks to real people who were also vendors, and he used that money to pay his own debts to them.

Investigators are trying to determine whether any of the companies knew those checks were not a legitimate way for Creech to pay them.

Spurlin said that anyone who took CP&L's checks to pay Creech's debts, knowing that he wasn't entitled to that money, could be prosecuted as a co-conspirator.

Creech allegedly funneled money through eight vendor accounts, using real and phony firms. Spurlin would not identify the vendors.

White said CP&L regularly pays 3,000 to 4,000 vendors, covering an array of services: janitors, security, temporary workers, supplies and equipment and vehicles, for example.

Most of the money Creech is accused of embezzling was taken during a two-month stretch more than a year ago, although the thefts began in 1987, according to the charges.

One warrant that suggests Creech embezzled nearly a quarter million dollars on one day in 1987 is misleading. Police and utility officials now say that amount was taken over several months that year.

CP&L is bonded for such losses, so rate-payers won't bear the cost.

"We feel very much like a victim," White said.

Meanwhile, investigators discovered that last week Creech's mother had withdrawn $53,000 from his personal checking account, using the power of attorney he granted her.

Investigators found $28,000 of that money, and it was seized and is being held by the court pending a review. The rest hasn't been accounted for.

Creech's mother, Ellen Smith Mitchell of Goldsboro, declined to discuss her son's case Tuesday. Spurlin said she didn't break the law by withdrawing the money.

After her son was arrested, Mitchell posted a $50,000 cash bond for his release. Creech was awaiting final arrangements to surrender his passport, but the judge raised the bail Thursday.

If Creech comes up with the $500,000 bond, he will have to submit to an alcohol abuse assessment and seek any treatment that is recommended, according to the court's conditions.

Cary police have arrested Creech twice in the past 14 months on charges of driving while intoxicated in his 1990 Corvette.

Creech claimed he was indigent after CP&L fired him in early June and applied for a court-appointed attorney, saying he had only $12,000 in the bank. His request was denied, and he has hired Raleigh attorney Philip Redwine. —*By Craig Jarvis.*

Reprinted with permission of *The News & Observer of Raleigh*, North Carolina.

an indorsement unless the accompanying words, terms of the instrument, place of the signature, or other circumstances unambiguously indicate that the signature was made for a purpose other than indorsement."

An indorsement may be complex or simple. It may be dated and may indicate where it is made, but neither date nor place is required to be shown. The simplest type is merely the signature of the indorser. Since the indorser undertakes certain obligations, as explained later, an indorsement consisting of merely a signature may be said to be the shortest contract known to the law. A forged or otherwise unauthorized signature necessary to negotiation is inoperative and thus breaks the chain of title to the instrument.

The type of indorsement used in first negotiating an instrument affects its subsequent negotiation. Every indorsement is (1) either blank or special, (2) either restrictive or nonrestrictive, and (3) either qualified or unqualified. These categories are not mutually exclusive. Indeed, each indorsement may be placed within three of these six categories because all indorsements disclose three things: (1) the method to be employed in making subsequent negotiations (this depends upon whether the indorsement is blank or special); (2) the kind of interest that is being transferred (this depends upon whether the indorsement is restrictive or nonrestrictive); and (3) the liability of the indorser (this depends upon whether the indorsement is qualified or unqualified). For instance, an indorser who merely signs her name on the back of an instrument is making a blank, nonrestrictive, unqualified indorsement. See Figure 25–3 on page 477 for further illustrations.

Revised Article 3 identifies an additional type of indorsement—an anomalous indorsement. An anomalous indorsement is "an indorsement made by a person that is not the holder of the instrument." The only effect of an anomalous indorsement is to make the signer liable on the instrument as an indorser. Such an indorsement does not affect the manner in which the instrument may be negotiated.

The effectiveness of an indorsement as well as the rights of the transferee and transferor depend upon whether the indorsement meets certain formal requirements. This section will cover the different kinds of indorsements and the formal requirements of each.

Blank Indorsements

A **blank indorsement,** which specifies no indorsee, may consist solely of the signature of the indorser or her authorized agent. Such an indorsement converts order paper into bearer paper and leaves bearer paper as bearer paper. Thus, an instrument indorsed in blank may be negotiated by delivery alone without further indorsement. Hence, the holder should treat it with the same care as cash. See *Palmer & Ray Dental Supply of Abilene, Inc. v. First National Bank* on page 475.

Blank indorsement one specifying no indorsee and making the instrument bearer paper

Special Indorsements

A **special indorsement** specifically identifies the person to whom or to whose order the instrument is to be payable. Thus, if Peter, the payee of a note, indorses it "Pay to the order of Andrea," or even "Pay Andrea," the indorsement is special because it names the transferee. Words of negotiability—"pay to order or bearer"— are *not* required in an indorsement. Thus, an indorsement reading "Pay Edward" is interpreted as meaning "Pay to the order of Edward." Any further negotiation of the instrument would require Edward's indorsement.

Special indorsement one identifying an indorsee to be paid and making the instrument order paper

Moreover, a holder of an instrument with a blank indorsement may protect himself by converting the blank indorsement to a special indorsement by writing over the signature of the indorser words identifying the person to whom the instrument is payable. For example, on the back of a negotiable instrument appears the blank indorsement "Sally Seller." Harry Holder, who receives the instrument from Seller, may convert this bearer instrument into order paper by inserting above Seller's signature "Pay Harry Holder" or other similar words.

CASAREZ v. GARCIA Court of Appeals of New Mexico, 1983, 99 N.M. 508, 660 P.2d 598

FACTS Arthur and Lucy Casarez contracted with Blas Garcia, who purported to be a representative of the Albuquerque Fence Company, for the construction of a new home. Blas introduced the Casarezes to Cecil Garcia, who agreed to make a loan to them to be used as a down payment on the project. Cecil then obtained a loan from Rio Grande Valley Bank in the form of a $25,000 cashier's check payable to himself, which he indorsed over to Lucy Casarez. Lucy indorsed the check with the words "Pay to the order of Albuquerque Fence Company, Lucy N. Casarez" and delivered it to Blas Garcia. Claiming he was following Cecil's instructions, Blas indorsed the check with the words "Alb. Fence Co." and gave the check to Cecil. Cecil signed his own name under "Alb. Fence Co." and presented the check to the bank in exchange for $25,000. The Casarezes soon learned that Blas and Cecil Garcia had never been in any way affiliated with or employed by the Albuquerque Fence Company. Lucy brought suit against the bank, claiming that the unauthorized signatures of Blas and Cecil Garcia invalidated the special indorsement to Albuquerque Fence Company and that therefore the bank negligently cashed the check, rendering the bank liable to Lucy for the amount of the check. The court granted the bank's motion for directed verdict, and Casarez appealed.

DECISION Judgment granting bank's motion for directed verdict reversed.

OPINION A special indorsement specifies to whom or to whose order it makes the instrument payable. If an instrument is specially indorsed to an organization, only one authorized by the organization may indorse it. Here, Lucy specially indorsed the check to the Albuquerque Fence Company. Blas indorsed it without proper authority from the company, rendering Lucy's special indorsement ineffective to pass title to Cecil and preventing its further negotiation. Cecil, having knowledge of Lucy's special indorsement and Blas's lack of authority, could gain no more authority to indorse than Blas could. Thus, Lucy remained the owner of the check. The bank, therefore, is liable to Lucy, the owner of the cashier's check, since it negligently failed to check the validity of the indorsements.

INTERPRETATION To negotiate an instrument that has been specially indorsed requires the signature of the named indorsee.

Restrictive Indorsements

Restrictive indorsement one attempting to limit the rights of the indorsee

As the term implies, a **restrictive indorsement** attempts to restrict the rights of the indorsee in some fashion. It limits the purpose for which the proceeds of the instrument can be applied. The Code discusses four types of indorsements as restrictive: conditional indorsements, indorsements prohibiting further transfer, indorsements for deposit or collection, and indorsements in trust. Only the last two are effective. An **unrestrictive indorsement**, in contrast, does not attempt to restrict the rights of the indorsee.

Unrestrictive indorsement one that does not attempt to restrict the rights of the indorsee

Indorsements for deposit or collection effectively limit further negotiation to those consistent with the indorsement

Indorsements for Deposit or Collection The most frequently used form of restrictive indorsement is that designed to place the instrument in the banking system for deposit or collection. Indorsements of this type, collectively referred to as "collection indorsements," include "for collection," "for deposit," and "pay any bank." Such an indorsement *effectively limits* further negotiation to those consistent with its limitation and binds (1) all nonbanking persons, (2) a depository bank that purchases the instrument or takes it for collection, and

(3) a payor bank that is also the depository bank or that takes the instrument for immediate payment over the counter from a person other than a collecting bank. Thus, a collection indorsement binds all parties except an intermediary bank (discussed in Chapter 28) or a payor bank that is not also the depository bank. Compare the following two cases.

PALMER & RAY DENTAL SUPPLY OF ABILENE, INC. v. FIRST NATIONAL BANK Court of Civil Appeals of Texas, 1972, 477 S.W.2d 954

FACTS Mrs. Wilson was employed as the office manager of Palmer & Ray Dental Supply of Abilene, Inc. Soon after an auditor discovered a discrepancy in the company's inventory, Mrs. Wilson confessed to cashing thirty-five checks that she was supposed to deposit on behalf of the company. Palmer & Ray Dental Supply used a rubber stamp to indorse checks. The stamp listed the company's name and address but did not read "for deposit only." Mrs. Wilson was authorized by the company's president, James Ray, to indorse checks with this stamp. All checks were cashed at First National Bank. Palmer & Ray Dental Supply claimed that First National converted the company's funds by giving Mrs. Wilson cash instead of depositing the checks into the company's bank account. Summary judgment was granted in favor of First National, and Palmer & Ray appealed.

DECISION Judgment for First National Bank affirmed.

OPINION A blank indorsement is one that specifies no particular indorsee and that may consist of a mere signature. A restrictive indorsement, on the other hand, includes one that uses the words "for deposit." The rubber stamp used by Mrs. Wilson to indorse the checks on the company's behalf was a blank indorsement, as it stated only the company's name and address. Moreover, Mrs. Wilson indorsed the checks under the actual implied or apparent authority granted by Mr. Ray, the company president. Accordingly, when First National Bank delivered cash to Mrs. Wilson instead of depositing the proceeds from the checks into the company's account, the bank acted in conformity with the indorsement.

INTERPRETATION A blank indorsement may be negotiated by delivery alone and does not restrict proceeds of the instrument to the depositor's account.

STATE OF QATAR v. FIRST AMERICAN BANK OF VIRGINIA United States District Court, E.D. Va., 1995, 885 F.Supp. 849, 27 U.C.C. Rep. Serv.2d 168

FACTS From 1986 to 1992, Bassam Salous defrauded his employer, the state of Qatar, by drawing checks on Qatar's account to pay false or duplicate invoices that he himself had created. He then deposited the checks into his personal account at First American Bank of Virginia (First American). At the time they were deposited, the checks bore the forged indorsement of the named payee, followed by the stamped restriction "for deposit only." Qatar has sued First American for conversion.

DECISION Judgment for Qatar.

OPINION The UCC makes clear that the phrase "for deposit only" is a restrictive indorsement. Although the meaning of the term is not defined, the clear purpose of the restriction is to avoid the hazards of indorsing a check in blank. A stolen check that is indorsed in blank is essentially cash, and can be freely negotiated by the bearer. To protect against the vulnerability, the payee can add the restriction "for deposit only" to the indorsement, and the depository bank is required to handle the check in a manner consistent with that restriction.

First American contends that its action of depositing the funds into Salous's account was consistent with the restriction "for deposit only." However, the payee's intent in adding such a restriction plainly is to direct that the funds be deposited into her own account, not simply that the funds be deposited into any account. Without such a construction, the phrase is without commercial utility. It is virtually impossible to imagine a scenario in which a payee cares only that a check be deposited and is indifferent as to the particular account to which the funds are to be credited.

By depositing the checks made payable to others and restrictively indorsed "for deposit only," into Bassam Salous's account, First American violated the restrictive indorsements on those checks. Therefore, First American is liable to Qatar for conversion in the amount of the total face values of the checks.

INTERPRETATION A "for deposit only" restrictive indorsement effectively limits the depository bank to handle the instrument in a manner consistent with the restriction.

Indorsements in trust
effectively require the
indorsee to pay or apply all
funds in accordance with the
indorsement

Indorsements in Trust Another common kind of restrictive indorsement is that in which the indorser creates a trust for the benefit of himself or others. If an instrument is indorsed "Pay Thelma in trust for Barbara," "Pay Thelma for Barbara," "Pay Thelma for account of Barbara," or "Pay Thelma as agent for Barbara," Thelma is a fiduciary, subject to liability for any breach of her obligation to Barbara. Trustees commonly and legitimately sell trust assets, and, consequently, a trustee has power to negotiate an instrument. The first taker under an indorsement to her in trust (Thelma in the above examples) is under a duty to pay or apply, in a manner consistent with the indorsement, all the funds she receives. Thelma's immediate transferee may safely pay Thelma for the instrument if he does not have *notice* of any breach of fiduciary duty. Subsequent indorsements or transferees are not bound by such indorsement *unless* they *know* that the trustee negotiated the instrument for her own benefit or otherwise in breach of her fiduciary duty.

**Indorsements with
ineffective restrictions**
include conditional
indorsements and
indorsements attempting to
prohibit further negotiation

Indorsements with Ineffective Restrictions A conditional indorsement is one by which the indorser makes the rights of the indorsee subject to the happening or nonhappening of a specified event. Suppose Marcin makes a note payable to Parker's order. Parker indorses it "Pay Rodriguez, but only if the good ship Jolly Jack arrives in Chicago harbor by November 15, 1997." If Marcin had used this language in the instrument itself, it would be nonnegotiable because her promise to pay must be unconditional to satisfy the formal requisites of negotiability. Revised Article 3 makes such indorsements ineffective by providing that an indorsement stating a condition to the right of a holder to receive payment does not affect the right of the indorsee to enforce the instrument.

An indorsement may by its express terms attempt to prohibit further transfer by stating "Pay [name] only" or language to similar effect. Such an indorsement, or any other purporting to prohibit further transfer, is designed to restrict the rights of the indorsee. To remove any doubt as to the effect of such a provision, the Code provides that *no* indorsement limiting payment to a particular person or otherwise prohibiting further transfer is effective. As a result, an indorsement that purports to *prohibit* further transfer of the instrument is given the same effect as an unrestricted indorsement.

Qualified and Unqualified Indorsements

Unqualified indorsement
one that imposes liability on
the indorser

Unqualified indorsers promise that they will pay the instrument according to its terms at the time of their indorsement to the holder or to any subsequent indorser who paid it. In short, an unqualified indorser guarantees payment of the instrument if certain conditions are met.

An indorser may disclaim her liability on the contract of indorsement, but only if the indorsement so declares and the disclaimer is written on the instrument. The customary manner of disclaiming an indorser's liability is to add the words *"without recourse,"* either before or after her signature. A "without recourse" indorsement, called a **qualified** indorsement, does not, however, eliminate all of an indorser's liability. As discussed in Chapter 27, a qualified indorsement disclaims contract liability but does not entirely remove the warranty liability of the indorser. A qualified indorsement and delivery is a negotiation and transfers legal title to the indorsee, but the indorser does *not* guarantee payment of the instrument. Furthermore, a qualified indorsement does not

Qualified indorsement
without recourse, one that
limits the indorser's liability

destroy negotiability or prevent further negotiation of the instrument. For example, assume that an attorney receives a check payable to her order in payment of a client's claim. She may indorse the check to the client without recourse, thereby disclaiming liability as a guarantor of payment of the check. The qualified indorsement plus delivery would transfer title to the client.

Formal Requirements of Indorsements

Place of Indorsement An indorsement must be written on the instrument or on a paper, called an **allonge**, affixed to the instrument. An allonge may be used even if the instrument contains sufficient space for the indorsement.

Allonge piece of paper affixed to the instrument

Customarily, indorsements are made on the back or reverse side of the instrument, starting at the top and continuing down. Under Federal Reserve Board guidelines, indorsements of checks must be in ink of an appropriate color, such as blue or black, and must be made within 1½ inches of the trailing (left) edge of the back of the check. The remaining space is reserved for bank indorsements. (See Figure 25–4.) Nevertheless, failure to comply with the guidelines does not destroy negotiability, and there are no penalties for violating the standard.

Occasionally, however, a signature may appear on an instrument in such a way that it is impossible to tell with certainty the nature of the liability the signer intended to undertake. In such an event, the Code specifies that the signer is to be treated as an indorser. In keeping with the rule that a transferee must be able to determine her rights from the face of the instrument, the person who signed in an ambiguous capacity may not introduce parol evidence to establish that she intended to be something other than an indorser.

Incorrect or Misspelled Indorsements If an instrument is payable to a payee or indorsee under a misspelled name or a name different from that of the holder, the holder may require the indorsement in the name stated or in the holder's correct name or both. Nevertheless, the person paying or taking the instrument for value may require the indorser to sign both names.

FIGURE 25–3 Indorsements

Indorsement	Type of Indorsement	Interest Transferred	Liability of Indorser
1. "John Doe"	Blank	Nonrestrictive	Unqualified
2. "Pay to Richard Roe, John Doe"	Special	Nonrestrictive	Unqualified
3. "Without recourse, John Doe"	Blank	Nonrestrictive	Qualified
4. "Pay to Richard Roe in trust for John Roe, without recourse, John Doe"	Special	Restrictive	Qualified
5. "For collection only, without recourse, John Doe"	Blank	Restrictive	Qualified
6. "Pay to XYZ Corp., on the condition that it delivers goods ordered this date, John Doe"	Special	Restrictive	Unqualified

FIGURE 25–4 Placement of Indorsement

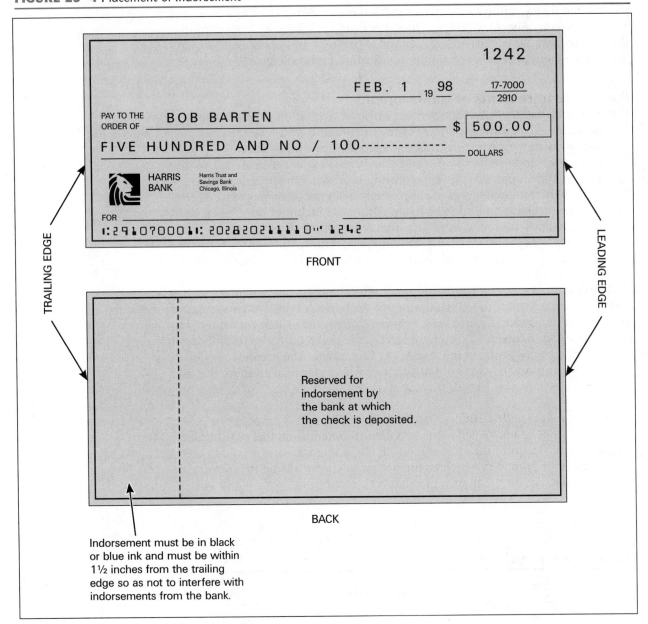

FRONT

BACK

TRAILING EDGE

LEADING EDGE

Reserved for
indorsement by
the bank at which
the check is deposited.

Indorsement must be in black
or blue ink and must be within
1½ inches from the trailing
edge so as not to interfere with
indorsements from the bank.

CHAPTER SUMMARY

Negotiation	**Holder** possessor of an instrument with all necessary indorsements

Holder possessor of an instrument with all necessary indorsements
Shelter Rule transferee gets rights of transferor
Negotiation of Bearer Paper transferred by mere possession
Negotiation of Order Paper transferred by possession and indorsement by all appropriate parties
- *The Impostor Rule* an indorsement of an impostor or of any other person in the name of the named payee is effective if the impostor has induced the maker or drawer to issue the instrument to him using the name of the payee
- *The Fictitious Payee Rule* an indorsement by any person in the name of the named payee is effective if an agent of the maker or drawer has supplied her with the name of the payee for fraudulent purposes

Negotiations Subject to Rescission negotiation is valid even though a transaction is void or voidable

Indorsement

Definition signature (on the instrument) of a payee, drawee, accommodation party, or holder
Blank Indorsement one specifying no indorsee and making the instrument bearer paper
Special Indorsement one identifying an indorsee to be paid and making the instrument order paper
Unrestrictive Indorsement one that does not attempt to restrict the rights of the indorsee
Restrictive Indorsement one attempting to limit the rights of the indorsee
- *Indorsements for Deposit or Collection* effectively limit further negotiation to those consistent with the indorsement
- *Indorsements in Trust* effectively require the indorsee to pay or apply all funds in accordance with the indorsement
- *Indorsements with Ineffective Restrictions* include conditional indorsements and indorsements attempting to prohibit further negotiation

Unqualified Indorsement one that imposes liability on the indorser
Qualified Indorsement without recourse, one that limits the indorser's liability
Formal Requirements of Negotiation
- *Place of Indorsement*
- *Incorrect or Misspelled Indorsement*

QUESTIONS

1. Distinguish among (1) transfer, (2) negotiation, and (3) assignment.

2. What is necessary to become a holder of an instrument?

3. Distinguish between a blank indorsement and a special one.

4. Distinguish between a qualified and an unqualified indorsement.

5. Discuss the various types of effective and ineffective restrictive indorsements.

Internet Question. Compare the provisions governing transfer and negotiation contained in the United Nations Convention on International Bills of Exchange and International Promissory Notes with those of Article 3 of the Uniform Commercial Code.

PROBLEMS

1. Roy Rand executed and delivered the following note to Sue Sims: "Chicago, Illinois, June 1, 1996; I promise to pay to Sue Sims or bearer, on or before July 1, 1996, the sum of $7,000. This note is given in consideration of Sims's transferring to the undersigned title to her 1991 Buick automobile. (signed) Roy Rand." Rand and Sims agreed that delivery of the car be deferred to July 1, 1996. On June 15, Sims sold and delivered the note, without indorsement, to Karl Kaye for $6,200. What rights, if any, has Kaye acquired?

2. Lavinia Lane received a check from Wilmore Enterprises, Inc., drawn on the Citizens Bank of Erehwon, in the sum of $10,000. Mrs. Lane indorsed the check "Mrs. Lavinia Lane for deposit only, Account of Lavinia Lane," placed it in a "Bank by Mail" envelope addressed to the First National Bank of Emanon, where she maintained a checking account, and placed the envelope over a tier of mailboxes in her apartment building along with other letters to be picked up by the postman the next day.

   Flora Fain stole the check, went to the Bank of Omaha, where Mrs. Lane was unknown, represented herself to be Lavinia Lane, and cashed the check. Has Bank of Omaha taken the check by negotiation? Why or why not?

3. What types of indorsements are the following:
   (a) "Pay to Monseen without recourse."
   (b) "Pay to Allinore for collection."
   (c) "I hereby assign all my rights, title, and interest in this note to Fullilove in full."
   (d) "Pay to the Southern Trust Company."
   (e) "Pay to the order of the Farmers Bank of Nicholasville for deposit only."

   Indicate whether the indorsement is (1) blank or special, (2) restrictive or nonrestrictive, and (3) qualified or unqualified.

4. Explain whether each of the following transactions results in a valid negotiation:
   (a) Arnold gives a negotiable check payable to bearer to Betsy without indorsing it.
   (b) Golden indorses a negotiable, promissory note payable to the order of Golden, "Pay to Chambers and Rambis, (signed) Golden."
   (c) Porter lost a negotiable check payable to his order. Kersey found it and indorsed the back of the check as follows: "Pay to Drexler, (signed) Kersey."
   (d) Thomas indorsed a negotiable promissory note payable to the order of Thomas, "(signed) Thomas," and delivered it to Sally. Sally then wrote above Thomas's signature, "Pay to Sally."

5. Alpha issues a negotiable check to Beta payable to the order of Beta in payment of an obligation Alpha owed Beta. Beta delivers the check to Gamma without indorsing it in exchange for 100 shares of General Motors stock owned by Gamma. How has Beta transferred the check? What rights, if any, does Gamma have against Beta?

6. Margarita executed and delivered to Poncho a negotiable promissory note payable to the order of Poncho as payment for 100 bushels of wheat Poncho had sold to Margarita. Poncho indorsed the note "Pay to Randy only, (signed) Poncho" and sold it to Randy. Randy then sold the note to Stephanie after indorsing it "Pay to Stephanie, (signed) Randy." What rights, if any, does Stephanie acquire in the instrument?

7. Simon Sharpe executed and delivered to Ben Bates a negotiable promissory note payable to the order of Ben Bates for $500. Bates indorsed the note, "Pay to Carl Cady upon his satisfactorily repairing the roof of my house, (signed) Ben Bates," and delivered it to Cady as a down payment on the contract price of the roofing job. Cady then indorsed the note and sold it to Timothy Tate for $450. What rights, if any, does Tate acquire in the promissory note?

8. Debbie Dean issued a check to Betty Brown payable to the order of Cathy Cain and Betty Brown. Betty indorsed the check, "Payable to Elizabeth East, (signed) Betty Brown." What rights, if any, does Elizabeth acquire in the check?

9. Triplett attempted to arrange a $2,850,000 loan through Meyer Rabin and his Consumer's Investment Company (CIC). CIC issued a commitment letter conditioned on the payment of a $14,250 commitment fee and the personal guarantee of C. D. Wyche. Triplett sought an additional loan from E. S. Tubin to cover the commitment fee. Tubin agreed to provide the $14,250 if the money would be "safe" pending the closing of the $2,850,000 loan and if he would receive $4,500 for the use of his money. Triplett agreed, and Tubin purchased a $14,250 cashier's check payable to Melvin Rueckhaus, his attorney. Rueckhaus typed the following indorsement on the back of the check: "PAY TO THE ORDER—CONSUMERS INVESTMENT CO. and CHARLES D. WYCHE, SR . . . "

   Rabin presented the check to Fair Park National Bank for immediate credit to CIC's account. Not knowing that Wyche's signature had been forged by Rabin, the bank complied, and Rabin subsequently depleted CIC's account. The loan was never closed, and the $14,250 was never returned to Tubin. Tubin then brought this suit against Fair Park National Bank. Decision?

10. The drawer, Commercial Credit Corporation (Corporation), issued two checks payable to Rauch Motor Company. Rauch indorsed the checks in blank,

deposited them to its account in University National Bank, and received a corresponding amount of money. The Bank stamped "pay any bank" on the checks and initiated collection. However, the checks were dishonored and returned to the Bank with the notation "payment stopped." Rauch, through subsequent deposits, repaid the bank. Later, to compromise a lawsuit, the Bank executed a special two-page indorsement of the two checks to Lamson. Lamson then sued the Corporation for the face value of the checks, plus interest. The Corporation contends that Lamson was not a holder of the checks because the indorsement was not in conformity with the UCC in that it was stapled to the checks. Decision?

11. Edmund Jezemski, estranged and living apart from his wife, Paula, was administrator and sole heir-at-law of his deceased mother's estate, one asset of which was real estate in Philadelphia. Without Edmund's knowledge or consent, and with the assistance of John M. McAllister, an attorney, and Anthony DiBenedetto, a real estate broker, Paula arranged for a mortgage on the property through Philadelphia Title Insurance Company. Shortly before settlement, Paula represented to McAllister and DiBenedetto that her husband would be unable to attend the closing on the mortgage. She appeared at McAllister's office in advance of the closing accompanied by a man whom she introduced to McAllister and DiBenedetto as her husband. She and this man, in the presence of McAllister and DiBenedetto, executed a deed conveying the property from the estate to her husband and herself as tenants by the entireties and also executed the mortgage. McAllister and DiBenedetto were witnesses. Thereafter, McAllister, DiBenedetto, and Paula met at the office of the Title Company on the closing date, produced the signed deed and mortgage, and Paula obtained from Title Company its check for the mortgage loan proceeds of $15,640.82, payable to the order of Edmund Jezemski and Paula Jezemski individually and to Edmund as administrator.

Paula cashed the check, bearing the purported indorsements of all the payees, at Penns Grove National Bank and Trust Company. Edmund received none of the proceeds, either individually or as administrator. His purported indorsements were forgeries. In the collection process, the check was presented to and paid by the drawee bank, Fidelity-Philadelphia Trust Company, and charged against the drawer Title Company's account. Upon discovery of the existence of the mortgage, Edmund brought an action that resulted in the setting aside of the deed and mortgage and the repayment of the amount advanced by the mortgagee. Title Company thereupon sued the drawee bank (Fidelity) to recover the amount of the check, $15,640.82. Decision?

12. Cole was supervisor of the shipping department of Machine Mfg. Inc. In February, Cole found herself in need of funds and, at the end of that month, submitted to Ames, the treasurer of the corporation, a payroll listing that showed as an employee, among others, "Ben Day," to whom was allegedly owed $800 for services rendered during February. Actually, there was no employee named Day. Relying upon the word of Cole, Ames drew and delivered to her a series of corporate payroll checks, drawn upon the corporate account in the Capital Bank, one of which was made payable to the order of "Ben Day" for $800. Cole took the check, indorsed on its back "Ben Day," cashed it at the Capital Bank, and pocketed the proceeds. She repeated the same procedure at the end of March, April, and May. In mid-June, Machine Mfg. Inc. learned of Cole's fraudulent conduct, fired her, and brought an appropriate action against Capital Bank, seeking a judgment for $3,200. Decision?

13. While assistant treasurer of Travco Corporation, Frank Mitchell caused two checks, each payable to a fictitious company, to be drawn on Travco's account with Brown City Savings Bank. In each case, Mitchell indorsed the check in his own name and then cashed it at Citizens Federal Savings & Loan Association of Port Huron. Both checks were cleared through normal banking channels and charged against Travco's account with Brown City. Travco subsequently discovered the embezzlement, and after its demand for reimbursement was denied, it brought this suit against Citizens. Decision?

CHAPTER 26

Holder in Due Course

The unique and most significant aspect of negotiability is the concept of the holder in due course. While a mere holder acquires a negotiable instrument subject to all claims and defenses to it, a holder in due course, *except* in *consumer* credit transactions, takes the instrument free of all claims of other parties and free of all defenses to the instrument except for a very limited number. The law has conferred this preferred position upon the holder in due course in order to encourage the free transferability of negotiable instruments by minimizing the risks assumed by an innocent purchaser of the instrument. The transferee of a negotiable instrument wants payment for it; he does not want to be subject to any dispute between the obligor and the obligee (generally the original payee). This chapter discusses the requirements of becoming a holder in due course and the benefits conferred upon a holder in due course.

REQUIREMENTS OF A HOLDER IN DUE COURSE

To acquire the preferential rights of a holder in due course, a person either must meet the requirements of the Code or must "inherit" these rights under the shelter rule (discussed later in this chapter). To satisfy the requirements of the Code, a transferee must

1. be a holder of a negotiable instrument;
2. take it for value;
3. take it in good faith; and
4. take it without notice
   (a) that it is overdue or has been dishonored, or
   (b) that the instrument contains an unauthorized signature or an alteration, or
   (c) that any person has any defense against or claim to it; and
5. take it without reason to question its authenticity due to apparent evidence of forgery, alteration, incompleteness, or other irregularity.

Figure 26–1 illustrates the various requirements of becoming a holder in due course and the consequence of meeting or not meeting these requirements.

Holder

Holder a person who has both possession of an instrument and all indorsements necessary to it

In order to become a **holder** in due course, the transferee must first be a holder. A holder, as discussed in Chapter 25, is a person who is in possession of a negotiable instrument that is "payable to bearer or, in the case of an instrument payable to an identified person, if the identified person is in possession." In other words, a holder is a person who has both possession of an instrument and all indorsements necessary to it. Whether the holder is the owner of the instrument

FIGURE 26–1 Rights of Transferees

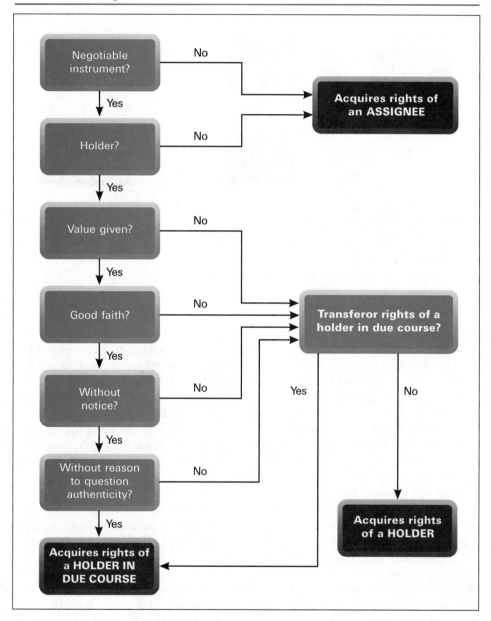

or not, he may transfer it, negotiate it, enforce payment of it (subject to valid claims and defenses), or, with certain exceptions, discharge it.

The following factual situation, illustrated in Figure 26–2, defines the significance of being a holder. Poe indorsed her paycheck in blank and cashed it at a hardware store where she was a well-known customer. Shortly thereafter, a burglar stole the check from the hardware store. The owner of the hardware store immediately notified Poe's employer, who gave the drawee bank a stop payment order (an order not to pay the instrument). The burglar indorsed the check in a false name and transferred it to a grocer who took it in good faith and for value. The check was dishonored (not paid) when presented to the drawee bank. The

FIGURE 26-2 Stolen Bearer Paper

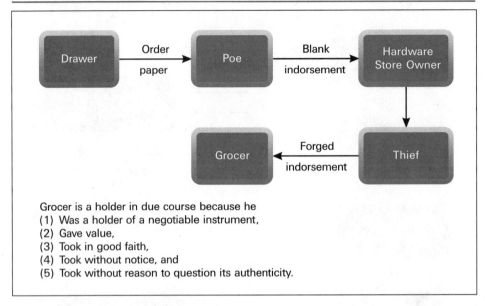

Grocer is a holder in due course because he
(1) Was a holder of a negotiable instrument,
(2) Gave value,
(3) Took in good faith,
(4) Took without notice, and
(5) Took without reason to question its authenticity.

paycheck became bearer paper when Poe indorsed it in blank. It retained this character in the hands of the owner of the hardware store, in the hands of the burglar, and in the hands of the grocer, who became a holder in due course even though he had received it from a thief who had indorsed it with a false name. Because an indorsement is not necessary to the negotiation of bearer paper, the fact that the indorsement was forged was immaterial. The thief was a "holder" of the check and may negotiate an instrument "whether or not he is the owner." Accordingly, one who, like the grocer, takes from a holder for value, in good faith, without notice, and without reason to question its authenticity, becomes a holder in due course. Furthermore, in the absence of a real defense, discussed later in this chapter, the grocer will be entitled to payment from the drawer.

This rule does not apply to a stolen order instrument. In the above example, assume that the thief had stolen the paycheck from Poe prior to indorsement. The thief then forged Poe's signature and transferred the check to the grocer, who again took it in good faith, for value, without notice, and without reason to question its authenticity. Negotiation of an order instrument requires a valid indorsement by the person to whose order the instrument is payable, in this case Poe. A forged indorsement is not valid. Consequently, the grocer has not taken the instrument with all necessary indorsements, and, therefore, he could not be a holder or a holder in due course. The grocer's only recourse would be to collect the amount of the check from the thief. Figure 26–3 illustrates this example.

In addition, certain other persons are entitled to enforce an instrument even though the person is not the owner of the instrument or is in wrongful possession of the instrument. These other persons entitled to enforce an instrument include a nonholder in possession of the instrument who has the rights of a holder, and a person not in possession of the instrument who is entitled to enforce the instrument pursuant to special situations, such as where the instrument has been lost, destroyed, or stolen or where the instrument has been paid or accepted by mistake and the payor or acceptor has recovered the money or revoked acceptance.

TURMAN v. WARD'S HOME IMPROVEMENT, INC. Virginia Circuit Court, 1995, 26 U.C.C. Rep. Serv.2d 175

FACTS On February 23, 1993, Turman executed a deed of trust note for $107,500 payable to Ward's Home Improvement, Inc. (Ward's). The note was in consideration of a contract for Ward's to build a house on Turman's property. On the same day, Ward's executed an assignment of the note to Robert Pomerantz for which Pomerantz paid Ward's $95,000. Although the document uses the word "assignment," no notation or indorsement was made on the note itself. Subsequently, Ward's failed to complete the house, and to do so would require the expenditure of an additional $42,000. The commissioner in this case found that Pomerantz was a holder in due course and awarded payment to Pomerantz. Turman appealed.

DECISION Judgment reversed and remanded.

OPINION Pomerantz is not a holder in due course. "[I]f an instrument is payable to an identified person, negotiation requires its indorsement by the holder."

An assignment is not an indorsement, and, consequently, the transaction between Ward and Pomerantz was not a negotiation and Pomerantz is not a holder.

An assignment vests in the transferee any rights of the transferor to enforce the contract. The rights of the transferee are derivative of the transferor's. Therefore, the assignee of a negotiable instrument is subject to defenses that the maker could assert against the assignor. One such defense is failure of consideration. If an instrument is issued for a promise, the issuer has a defense to the extent performance of the promise is due and the promise has not been performed. Since Pomerantz is not a holder in due course, he is subject to this defense as if it were being asserted against Ward.

INTERPRETATION A holder is a person who has both possession of an instrument and all indorsements necessary to it.

Value

The law requires a holder in due course to give value. An obvious case of the failure to do so is where the holder makes a gift of the instrument to a third person.

The concept of value in the law of negotiable instruments is not the same as that of consideration under the law of contracts. **Value**, for purposes of negotiable instruments, is defined as (1) the actual *performing* of the agreed promise (executory promises are excluded since they have not been performed); (2) the acquiring of a security interest or other lien in the instrument other than a judicial lien; (3) the taking of the instrument in payment of or as security for an antecedent debt; (4) the giving of a negotiable instrument; and (5) the giving of an irrevocable obligation to a third party.

Executory Promise An executory promise, though clearly valid consideration to support a contract, is *not* the giving of value to support holder in due course status because such a promise has yet to be performed. A purchaser of a note or

Value differs from contractual consideration and consists of (1) the timely performance of legal consideration (which excludes executory promises); (2) the acquisition of a security interest in or a lien on the instrument; (3) taking the instrument in payment of or as security for an antecedent debt; (4) the giving of a negotiable instrument; or (5) the giving of an irrevocable commitment to a third party

FIGURE 26–3 Stolen Order Paper

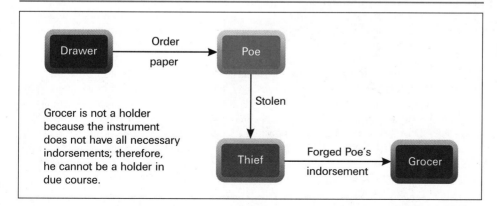

Grocer is not a holder because the instrument does not have all necessary indorsements; therefore, he cannot be a holder in due course.

draft who has not yet given value may rescind the transaction if she learns of a defense to the instrument. A person who has given value, however, cannot do this; to recover value, she needs the protection accorded a holder in due course.

For example, Mike executes and delivers a $1,000 note payable to the order of Pat, who negotiates it to Henry, who promises to pay Pat for it a month later. During the month, Henry learns that Mike has a defense against Pat. Henry can rescind the agreement with Pat and return or tender the note back to her. Because this makes him whole, Henry has no need to cut off Mike's defense. Assume, on the other hand, that Henry has paid Pat for the note before he learns of Mike's defense. Because he may be unable to recover his money from Pat, Henry needs holder in due course protection, which permits him to recover on the instrument from Mike.

A holder therefore takes an instrument for value to the extent that the agreed promise of performance has been performed provided the performance was given prior to the holder's learning of any defense or claim to the instrument. Assume that in the previous example Henry had agreed to pay Pat $900 for the note. If Henry had paid Pat $600, he could be a holder in due course to the extent of $666.67 ($600/900 \times 1000), and if a defense were available, it would be valid against him only to the extent of the balance. When Henry paid the $300 balance to Pat, he would become a holder in due course as to the full $1,000 face value of the note, provided payment was made prior to Henry's discovery of Mike's defense. If he made the $300 payment after discovering the defense or

ETHICAL DILEMMA What Responsibility Does a Holder Have in Negotiating Commercial Paper?

FACTS Marcus Moore and David Arnold are subcontractors specializing in the installation of electrical wiring for commercial office space. They have incorporated their business as Moore & Arnold, Inc. Over the last two years, their business has been extremely slow. Recently, they obtained an offer to install wiring for a general contractor, Barnes & Sons, which was in charge of renovating an office to be occupied by three major tenants. The job was substantial and would pay $35,000.

Marcus and David disagreed on whether to accept the job. Marcus was concerned with the business reputation of Barnes & Sons. For years, the business had been reputably operated by Tom Barnes, the original owner, but when his son, John, assumed control of operations, problems began. The partnership was recently sued for negligence in connection with a major construction project in a mall. It is well known that John is a gambler, and the business has gained the reputation of being slow to pay creditors.

Marcus and David finally decided to accept the job. Upon their completing the work, John Barnes handed Marcus a negotiable promissory note drawn by John Major, one of three different names Barnes & Sons has been trading under during the last year. The note was payable to Moore & Arnold, Inc., one month from date.

Marcus is instinctively nervous about accepting the note. He is aware of the cash flow problems and the litigation pending against Barnes & Sons and has become increasingly suspicious because of the different trade names the contractor uses. David, who is more trusting, wants to accept the note and negotiate it to Wire Ways, Inc., one of their major suppliers of electrical wiring. Marcus

wants to demand cash and, if Barnes refuses, to refer the account to a collection agency.

Social, Policy, and Ethical Considerations

1. Would it be ethical for Marcus and David to accept the note and negotiate it to Wire Ways, Inc.? Why?
2. What ethical responsibilities does one have to review the business reputations of prospective clients or customers and to refuse to do business with disreputable persons?
3. What risks did Moore & Arnold, Inc., assume in accepting the business? Was the risk limited to the failure to obtain payment?
4. Could Marcus and David have structured the business transaction in any way to insulate Moore & Arnold, Inc., from the risks it assumed?

claim, Henry would be a holder in due course only to the extent of $666.67. A holder in due course, to give value, need pay only the amount he agreed to pay, not the face amount of the instrument.

The Code provides an exception to the executory promise rule in two situations: (1) the giving of a negotiable instrument and (2) the making of an irrevocable obligation to a third party.

KORZENIK v. SUPREME RADIO, INC. Supreme Judicial Court of Massachusetts, 1964, 347 Mass. 309, 197 N.E.2d 702

FACTS Supreme Radio, Inc., issued to Southern New England Distributing Corporation (Southern) two notes worth $1,900. The two notes and others, all of a total face value of about $15,000, were transferred to Korzenik, an attorney, by his client Southern "as a retainer for services to be performed" by Korzenik. Although Korzenik was unaware of the fact, Southern had obtained the notes by fraud. Southern retained Korzenik on October 25 in connection with certain antitrust litigation, and the notes were transferred on October 31. The value of the services Korzenik performed during that time is unclear. Korzenik brought this action against Supreme Radio to recover $1,900 on the notes.

DECISION Judgment for Supreme Radio affirmed.

OPINION In order to qualify as a holder in due course, a holder of an instrument must take for value. A holder takes an instrument for value (a) to the extent that the agreed consideration has been performed or that he acquires a security interest in or a lien on the instrument otherwise than by legal process; or (b) when he takes the instrument in payment of or as security for an antecedent claim against any person whether or not the claim is due; or (c) when he gives a negotiable instrument for it or makes an irrevocable commitment to a third person. Value is divorced from consideration and, except as is provided in (c), an executory promise to give value is not value. Here, Korzenik has failed to show the extent to which the agreed consideration has been performed and, hence, the value that has been given.

INTERPRETATION A holder takes an instrument for value to the extent that the agreed consideration has been *given*, provided the consideration was given prior to the holder's learning of any defense or claim to the instrument.

Security Interest Where an instrument is given as security for an obligation, the lender is regarded as having given value to the extent of his security interest. Sections 3–302(e) and 3–303(a). For example, Pedro is the holder of a $1,000 note payable to his order, executed by Monica, and due in twelve months. Pedro uses the note as security for a $700 loan made to him by Larry. Larry has advanced $700; therefore, he has met the requirement of value to the extent of $700.

Likewise, a *bank* gives value when a depositor is allowed to withdraw funds against a deposited item. The provisional or temporary crediting of a depositor's account (discussed in Chapter 28) is not sufficient. If a number of checks have been deposited, and some but not all of the funds have been withdrawn, the Code traces the deposit by following the "FIFO" or "first-in, first-out" method of accounting.

Antecedent Debt Under general contract law, an antecedent debt (a preexisting obligation) is not consideration. Under the Code, however, a holder gives value when she takes an instrument in payment of or as security for an antecedent debt. Thus, Martha makes and delivers a note for $1,000 to the order of Penny, who indorses the instrument and delivers it to Howard in payment of an outstanding debt of $970 that she owes him. Howard has given value.

Antecedent debt
preexisting obligation

Good Faith

Good faith honesty in fact
and the observance of
reasonable commercial
standards of fair dealing

Revised Article 3 defines **good faith** as "honesty in fact and the observance of reasonable commercial standards of fair dealing." Thus, Revised Article 3 adopts a definition of good faith that has both a subjective and objective component. The subjective component ("honesty in fact") measures good faith by what the purchaser knows or believes. The objective component ("the observance of reasonable commercial standards of fair dealing") is comparable to the definition of good faith applicable to *merchants* under Article 2 in that it includes the requirement of the observance of reasonable commercial standards of fairness. Buying an instrument at a discounted price does not demonstrate lack of good faith.

Lack of Notice

To become a holder in due course, a holder must also take the instrument without notice that it is (1) overdue, (2) dishonored, (3) forged or altered, or (4) subject to any claim or defense. Notice of any of these matters should alert the purchaser that she may be buying a lawsuit and that, consequently, she may not be accorded the favored position of a holder in due course. The Code defines *notice* as follows: "A person has 'notice' of a fact when (a) he has actual knowledge of it; or (b) he has received a notice or notification of it; or (c) from all the facts and circumstances known to him at the time in question, he has reason to know that it exists." Whereas the first two clauses of this definition impose a wholly subjective standard, the last clause provides a partially objective one: the presence of suspicious circumstances does not adversely affect the purchaser, unless he has reason to recognize them as suspicious. Since the applicable standard is "actual notice," "notice received," or "reason to know," constructive notice through public filing or recording is not of itself sufficient notice to prevent a person from being a holder in due course.

To be effective, notice must be received at a time and in a manner that the recipient will have a reasonable opportunity to act on it.

**Notice an instrument is
overdue** time paper is
overdue after its stated date;
demand paper is overdue
after demand has been
made or after it has been
outstanding for an
unreasonable period of time

Notice an Instrument Is Overdue   To be a holder in due course, the purchaser must take the instrument without notice that it is overdue. This requirement is based on the idea that overdue paper conveys a suspicion that something is wrong. *Time paper* is due on its stated due date if the stated date is a business day or, if not, on the next business day. It "becomes overdue on the day after the due date." Thus, if an instrument is payable on July 1, a purchaser cannot become a holder in due course by buying it on July 2, provided that July 1 was a business day. In addition, in the case of an installment note or of several notes issued as part of the same transaction with successive specified maturity dates, the purchaser has notice that an instrument is overdue if he has reason to know that any part of the principal amount is overdue or that there is an uncured default in payment of another instrument of the same series.

Demand paper is overdue for purposes of preventing a purchaser from becoming a holder in due course if the purchaser has notice that she is taking the instrument on a day after demand has been made or after it has been outstanding for an unreasonably long time. The Code provides that for checks a reasonable time is ninety days after its date. For all other demand instruments the reasonable period of time varies depending upon the facts of the particular case. Thus, the particular situation, business custom, and other relevant factors must be considered in determining whether an instrument is overdue: no hard-and-fast rules are possible.

Acceleration clauses have caused problems. If an instrument's maturity date has been accelerated, the instrument becomes overdue on the day after the accelerated due date even though the holder may be unaware that it is past due.

Notice an Instrument Has Been Dishonored

Dishonor is the refusal to pay or accept an instrument when it becomes due. If a transferee has notice that an instrument has been dishonored, he cannot become a holder in due course. For example, a person who takes a check stamped "NSF" (not sufficient funds) or "no account" has notice of dishonor and will not be a holder in due course.

Notice of a Claim or Defense

A purchaser of an instrument cannot become a holder in due course if he purchases it with notice of "any claim to the instrument described in Section 3–306" or "a defense or claim in recoupment described in Section 3–305(a)." A **defense** protects a person from liability on an instrument, whereas a **claim** to an instrument asserts ownership to it.

Claims covered by Section 3–306 "include not only claims to ownership but also any other claim of a property or possessory right. It includes the claim to a lien or the claim of a person in rightful possession of an instrument who was wrongfully deprived of possession." Claims to instruments may be made against thieves, finders, or possessors with void or voidable title. In many instances, both a defense and claim will be involved. For example, Donna is fraudulently induced to issue a check to Pablo. Donna has a claim to ownership of the instrument as well as a defense to Pablo's demand for payment.

Section 3–305(a), which is more fully discussed later in this chapter, provides that personal defenses are valid against a holder, while real defenses are effective against both holders and holders in due course. In addition, a person without the rights of a holder in due course is subject to an obligor's claim in recoupment "against the original payee of the instrument if the claim arose from the transaction that gave rise to the instrument." For example, Buyer gives Seller a negotiable note in exchange for Seller's promise to deliver certain goods. Seller delivers nonconforming goods that Buyer elects to accept. Buyer has a cause of action under Article 2 for breach of warranty under the contract, which a "claim may be asserted against Seller as a counterclaim or as a claim in recoupment to reduce the amount owing on the note. It is not relevant whether Seller knew or had notice that Buyer had the warranty claim."

Buying an instrument at a discount or for a price less than face value does not mean that the buyer had notice of any defense or claim against the instrument. Nonetheless, a court may construe an unusually large discount as notice of a claim or defense.

Without Reason to Question Its Authenticity

Under prior Article 3, a purchaser had notice of a claim or defense if the instrument was so incomplete, contained such visible evidence of forgery or alteration, or was otherwise so irregular as to call into question its validity. Courts differed greatly as to how irregular an instrument had to be for a holder to have notice. Revised Article 3 provides that a party may become a holder in due course only if the instrument issued or negotiated to the holder "does not bear such apparent evidence of forgery or alteration or is not otherwise so irregular or incomplete as to call into question its authenticity." According to the comments to this section, the term "authenticity" clarifies the idea that the irregularity or incompleteness must indicate that the instrument may not be what it purports to be.

The Revision takes the position that persons who purchase such instruments do so at their own peril and should not be protected against defenses of the obligor or claims of prior owners. In addition, the Revision takes the position that it makes no difference if the holder does not have notice of such irregularity or incompleteness, it depends only upon whether the instrument's defect is apparent and whether the taker should have reason to know of the problem.

ST. PAUL FIRE AND MARINE INSURANCE CO. v. STATE BANK OF SALEM Court of Appeals of Indiana, First District, 1980, 412 N.E.2d 103

FACTS Stephens delivered 184 bushels of corn to Aubrey, for which he was to receive $478.23. Aubrey issued a check with $478.23 typewritten in numbers, and on the line customarily used to express the amount in words appeared "$100478 and 23 cts" imprinted in red with a check-writing machine. Before Stephens cashed the check, someone crudely typed "100" in front of the typewritten $478.23. When Stephens presented this check to the State Bank of Salem, Anderson, the manager, questioned Stephens. Anderson knew that Stephens had just declared bankruptcy and was not accustomed to making such large deposits. Stephens told Anderson he had bought and sold a large quantity of corn at a great profit. Anderson accepted the explanation, applied the monies to nine promissory notes, an installment payment, and accrued interest owed by Stephens. Stephens also received $2,000 in cash, with the balance deposited in his checking account.

Later that day, Anderson reexamined the check and discovered the suspicious appearance of the typewriting. He then contacted Aubrey, who said a check in that amount was suspicious, whereupon Anderson froze the transaction. When Aubrey stopped payment on the check, the bank sustained a $28,193.91 loss because Stephens could not be located. The bank then sued Aubrey for the loss. As defenses, Aubrey claimed that (1) the bank did not take the check for value and that (2) the typed "100" put the bank on notice of Aubrey's defense. Thus, Aubrey contended that the bank was not a holder in due course and could not collect on the check from Aubrey. The trial court ruled in favor of the bank, and Aubrey appealed.

DECISION Judgment for State Bank of Salem affirmed.

OPINION Under the UCC, value is given for an instrument when the instrument is taken in payment for an antecedent debt. Moreover, when credit is drawn upon, value is given to that extent. Value is also given to the extent that the funds represented by the check are applied to an overdrawn account. Here, the bank's application of funds, made available by the Aubrey check to Stephen's indebtedness, and the surrender of the notes constituted taking the instrument for value.

Furthermore, the bank took the check without notice of Aubrey's defense. In case of ambiguity, typewritten terms control printed terms and words control figures. The court determined that the impressions made by the check imprinter were not "printed" terms but should be considered "words," since they were on the line typically used for expressing the amount in words, not figures. Moreover, Aubrey did not prove that Anderson violated customary banking standards by not comparing the two amounts. Consequently, Anderson's reliance upon the amount expressed by the check imprinter was reasonable. In addition, the typed figure "100" was not such visible evidence of an alteration of the check as to put the bank on notice of Aubrey's defense.

Finally, the circumstances surrounding such a transaction may be so irregular as to put a reasonably prudent banker on notice of a defense or claim. Anderson's knowledge of Stephen's questionable general financial position, by itself, however, is insufficient to defeat the bank's holder in due course status. Thus, the bank can enforce the check against Aubrey to the extent it gave value for it.

INTERPRETATION Under Revised Article 3, the key question would have been should the bank have reason to know of the irregularity.

HOLDER IN DUE COURSE STATUS

A holder who meets the requirements discussed in the previous section obtains the preferred position of holder in due course status. This section discusses whether a payee may become a holder in due course. It also addresses the rights of a transferee from a holder in due course under the shelter rule. Finally, it identifies those special circumstances that prevent a transferee from acquiring holder in due course status.

A Payee May Be a Holder in Due Course

A payee may be a holder in due course. This does not mean that a payee automatically is a holder in due course but that he *may* be one if he satisfies the requirements for such status. For example, if a seller delivers goods to a buyer and accepts a current check in payment, the seller will be a holder in due course if he acted in good faith and had no notice of defenses or claims and no reason to question its authenticity. Nevertheless, the holder in due course doctrine is irrelevant when the issuer and payee are the only parties to the instrument. In such a situation, the seller/payee takes the instrument subject to all claims and defenses; the doctrine of the preferred position of a holder in due course "applies only to cases in which more than two parties are involved. Its essence is that the holder in due course does not have to suffer the consequences of a defense of the obligor on the instrument that arose from an occurrence with a third party."

In some situations, the payee is not an immediate party to the transaction and therefore will not be subject to any claims and most defenses if he meets the requirements of a holder in due course. In such a situation, the transaction involves three parties, and the defense involves the parties other than the payee. For example, after purchasing goods from Punky, Robin fraudulently obtains a check from Clem payable to the order of Punky and forwards it to Punky. Punky takes it for value and without any knowledge that Robin had defrauded Clem into issuing the check. In such a case, the payee, Punky, is a holder in due course and takes the instrument free and clear of Clem's defense of fraud in the inducement. See also *John Deere Co. v. Boelus State Bank* on page 497.

A payee may be a holder in due course the payee's rights as a holder in due course are limited to defenses of persons with whom he has not dealt

The Shelter Rule

Through operation of the **shelter rule**, the transferee of an instrument acquires the *same* rights in the instrument as the transferor had. Therefore, even a holder who does not comply fully with the requirements for being a holder in due course nevertheless acquires all the rights of a holder in due course if some previous holder of the instrument had been a holder in due course. For example, Prosser induces Mundheim, by fraud in the inducement, to make a note payable to her order and then negotiates it to Henn, a holder in due course. After the note is overdue, Henn gives it to Corbin, who has notice of the fraud. Corbin is not a holder in due course, since he has taken the instrument when overdue, did not pay value, and has notice of Mundheim's defense. Nonetheless, through the operation of the shelter rule, Corbin acquires Henn's rights as a holder in due course, and Mundheim cannot successfully assert his defense against Corbin. The purpose of the shelter provision is not to benefit the transferee but to assure the holder in due course of a free market for the negotiable instrument he acquires.

The shelter rule, however, provides that a transferee who has himself been a party to any fraud or illegality affecting the instrument cannot subsequently acquire the rights of a holder in due course. For example, Parker induces Miles, by fraud in the inducement, to make an instrument payable to the order of Parker, who subsequently negotiates the instrument to Henson, a holder in due course. If Parker later reacquires it from Henson, Parker will not succeed to Henson's rights as a holder in due course and will remain subject to the defense of fraud.

Shelter rule the transferee of an instrument acquires the same rights that the transferor had in the instrument

THE PREFERRED POSITION OF A HOLDER IN DUE COURSE

In a *nonconsumer transaction*, a holder in due course takes the instrument (1) free from all *claims* on the part of any person and (2) free from all *defenses* of any party with whom he has not dealt, except for a limited number of defenses that are available against anyone, including a holder in due course. Such defenses are referred to as **real defenses**, as opposed to defenses which may not be asserted against a holder in due course, which are referred to as **personal**, or **contractual**, **defenses**.

Real defenses real defenses are available against all holders, including holders in due course

Personal (contractual) defenses all other defenses that might be asserted in the case of any action for breach of contract

Real Defenses

The real defenses available against *all* holders, including holders in due course, are

1. Infancy, to the extent that it is a defense to a simple contract
2. Any other incapacity, duress, or illegality of the transaction that renders the obligation void
3. Fraud in the execution
4. Discharge in insolvency proceedings
5. Any other discharge of which the holder has notice when he takes the instrument
6. Unauthorized signature and
7. Fraudulent alteration

Infancy All states have a firmly entrenched public policy of protecting minors from persons who might take advantage of them through contractual dealings. The Code does not state when minority is available as a defense or the conditions under which it may be asserted. Rather, it provides that minority (infancy) is a defense available against a holder in due course to the extent that it is a defense to a contract under the laws of the state involved. See Chapter 14.

Void Obligations Where the obligation on an instrument originates in such a way that it is *void* or null under the law of the state involved, the Code authorizes the use of this defense against a holder in due course. This follows from the idea that where the party was never obligated, it is unreasonable to permit an event over which she has no control—negotiation to a holder in due course—to convert a nullity into a valid claim against her.

Incapacity, duress, and the illegality of a transaction are defenses that may render the obligation of a party either voidable or void, depending upon the law of the state involved as applied to the facts of a given transaction. To the extent the obligation is rendered void (because of duress by physical force, because the party is a person under guardianship, or, in some cases, because the contract is illegal), the defense may be asserted against a holder in due course. To the extent it is voidable, which is generally the case, the defense (other than minority, as discussed previously) is not effective against a holder in due course.

FEDERAL DEPOSIT INSURANCE CORPORATION v. MEYER United States District Court, District of Columbia, 1991, 755 F. Supp. 10

FACTS Certain partners of the Finley Kumble law firm signed promissory notes that secured loans made to the law firm by the National Bank of Washington (NBW). When Finley Kumble subsequently declared bankruptcy and defaulted on the loans, NBW filed suit to collect on the notes. Then NBW itself became insolvent, and the Federal Deposit Insurance Corporation (FDIC) was appointed as receiver. The FDIC moved for summary judgment against each defendant on the grounds that the Federal Deposit Insurance Act (FDIA) of 1950 places the FDIC in the position of a holder in due course and thus bars all personal defenses against FDIC

continued

claims as a matter of law. Twenty of the Finley partners opposed the motion, claiming that they signed the notes under the threat that their wages and standing in the firm would decrease if they refused to sign. Such a threat constituted economic duress, which, they contended, is not a personal defense but a real one. They argued that the FDIA does not bar real defenses.

DECISION Summary judgment granted in favor of FDIC.

OPINION The FDIA bars only personal defenses, not real defenses. A real defense renders an instrument entirely void, leaving no interest that could be "diminished or defeated." The question is whether the Finley partners' defense is real or personal. If the Finley partners' defense of economic duress were a real defense, then their promissory notes were void from the beginning and the FDIC had no interest from the start. On the other hand, if their defense were a personal defense, then the FDIC received voidable title to the notes from the NBW, and the defense would be cut off.

The Finley partners argued that duress of any type is a real defense under the UCC. The UCC, however, does not make such a blanket classification. Rather, it suggests that only those types of duress that are so severe as to render an obligation a nullity are real defenses. The Official Comment declares that local law determines what type of duress is severe enough to render the obligation a nullity. The Restatement of Contracts states that duress by threat, rather than by physical compulsion, renders a contract voidable rather than void. Thus, there are two forms of duress. In one, a person physically compels a party to engage, with apparent assent, in conduct in which the party has no real intention of engaging. Conduct thus compelled is not effective to create a contract, i.e., the "agreement" is void. In the other type of duress, an improper threat that induces an assent creates a contract that is voidable by the victim.

Economic duress does not reach the level of physical compulsion capable of rendering a transaction entirely void. NBW held voidable title when the FDIC took over as receiver. Thus, the Finley partners' personal defense of economic duress is not valid against the FDIC.

INTERPRETATION Where the obligation of an instrument is void, the Code authorizes the use of this real defense against a holder in due course.

Fraud in the Execution Fraud in the execution of the instrument renders the instrument void and therefore is a defense valid against a holder in due course. The Code describes this type of fraud as misrepresentation that induced the party to sign the instrument with neither knowledge nor reasonable opportunity to learn of its character or its essential terms. For example, Francis is asked to sign a receipt and does so without realizing or having the opportunity of learning that her signature is going on a promissory note cleverly concealed under the receipt. Because her signature has been obtained by fraud in the execution, Francis would have a valid defense against a holder in due course.

Discharge in Insolvency Proceedings If a party's obligation on an instrument is discharged in a proceeding for bankruptcy or for any other insolvency, he has a valid defense in any action brought against him on the instrument, including one brought by a holder in due course. Thus, a debtor, whose obligation on a negotiable instrument is discharged in an insolvency proceeding, is relieved of payment, even to a holder in due course.

Discharge of Which the Holder Has Notice Any holder, including a holder in due course, takes the instrument subject to *any* discharge of which she has notice at the time of taking. If only some, but not all, of the parties to the instrument have been discharged, the purchaser can still become a holder in due course. The discharged parties, however, have a real defense against a holder in due course who has notice of their discharge. For example, Harris, who is in possession of a negotiable instrument, strikes out the indorsement of Jones. The instrument is subsequently negotiated to Stephen, a holder in due course, against whom Jones has a real defense.

Unauthorized Signature A person's signature on an instrument is unauthorized when it is made without express, implied, or apparent authority. Because he has not made a contract, a person whose signature is unauthorized or forged cannot be held liable on the instrument in the absence of estoppel or ratification, even if the instrument is negotiated to a holder in due course. Similarly, if Joan's signature were forged on the back of an instrument, Joan could not be held as an indorser, since she was not made a contract. Thus, any unauthorized signature is totally invalid as that of the person whose name is signed unless she ratifies it or is precluded from denying it; the unauthorized signature operates only as the signature of the unauthorized signer.

Fraudulent Alteration An alteration is (1) an unauthorized change that modifies the obligation of any party to the instrument or (2) an unauthorized addition or change to an incomplete instrument concerning the obligation of a party.

An alteration that is fraudulently made discharges a party whose obligation is affected by the alteration except where that party assents or is precluded by his own negligence from raising the defense. All other alterations do not discharge any party, and the instrument may be enforced according to its original terms. Thus, if an instrument has been nonfraudulently altered, it may be enforced, but only to the extent of its original tenor (that is, according to its initially written terms). See Figure 26–4.

A discharge under the Code for fraudulent alteration, however, is not effective against a holder in due course who took the instrument without notice of the alteration. Such a subsequent holder in due course may always enforce the instrument according to its original terms and, in the case of an incomplete instrument, may enforce it as completed. The following examples demonstrate the operation of these rules (Figure 26–5 illustrates these examples).

1. M executes and delivers a note to P for $2,000, which P subsequently indorses and transfers to A for $1,900. A intentionally and skillfully changes the figure on the note to $20,000 and then negotiates it to B, who takes it, in good faith, without notice of any wrongdoing and without reason to question its authenticity, for $19,000. B is a holder in due course and, therefore, can collect the original amount of the note ($2,000) from M or P and the full amount ($20,000) from A, less any amount paid by the other parties.

2. Assume the facts in (1), except that B is not a holder in due course. M and P are both discharged by A's fraudulent alteration. B's only recourse is against A for the full amount ($20,000).

3. M issues his blank check to P, who is to complete it when the exact amount is determined. Though the correct amount is set at $2,000, P fraudulently fills in $4,000 and then negotiates the check to T. If T is a holder in due course, she can collect the amount as completed ($4,000) from either M or P. If T is not a holder in due course, however, she has no recourse against M but may recover the full amount ($4,000) from P.

4. Assume the facts in (3), except that P filled in the $4,000 amount in good faith. No party is discharged from liability on the instrument because the alteration was not fraudulent. If T is not a holder in due course, M is liable for the correct amount ($2,000). If T is a holder in due course, T is entitled to receive $4,000 from M because she can enforce an incomplete instrument as completed. Whether or not T is a holder in due course, T may recover $4,000 from P.

FIGURE 26–4 Effects of Alterations

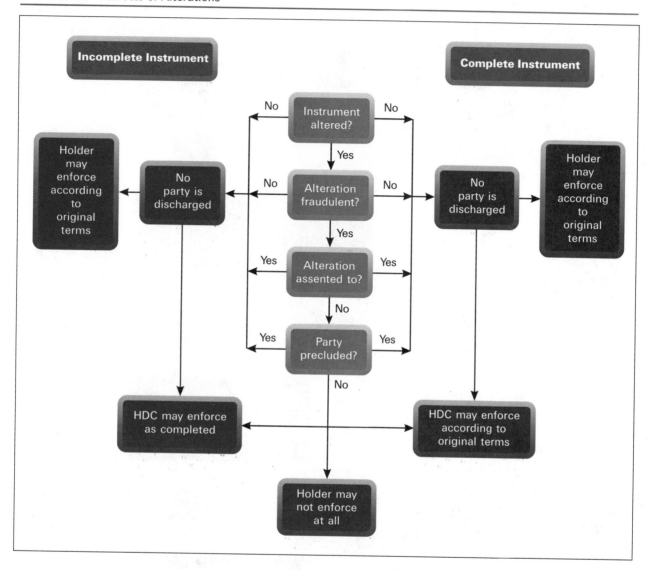

Personal Defenses

Defenses to an instrument may arise in many ways, either when the instrument is issued or later. In general, the numerous defenses to liability on a negotiable instrument, which are similar to those that may be raised in an action for breach of contract, are available against any holder of the instrument unless she has the rights of a holder in due course. Among the personal defenses are (1) lack of consideration; (2) failure of consideration; (3) breach of contract; (4) fraud in the inducement; (5) illegality that does not render the transaction void; (6) duress, undue influence, mistake, misrepresentation, or incapacity that does not render the transaction void; (7) setoff or counterclaim; (8) discharge of which the holder in due course does not have notice; (9) nondelivery of an instrument, whether complete or incomplete; (10) unauthorized completion of an incomplete instrument; (11) payment without obtaining surrender of the instrument; (12) theft of a bearer instrument or of an instrument payable to

FIGURE 26–5 Material Alteration

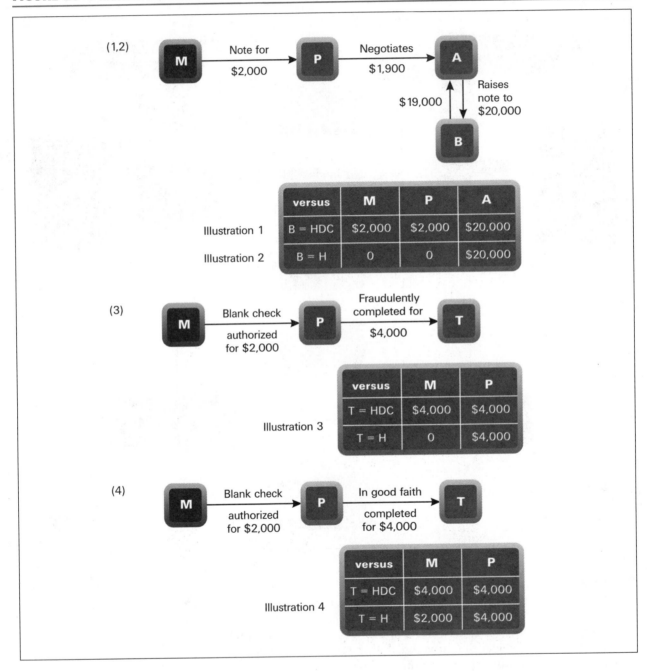

him; and (13) lack of authority of a corporate officer, agent, or partner as to the particular instrument, where such officer, agent, or partner had general authority to issue negotiable paper for his principal or firm.

These situations are the most common examples, but others exist. Indeed, the Code does not attempt to detail defenses that may be cut off. It is content to state that a holder in due course takes the instrument free and clear of all claims and defenses, except those listed as real defenses. See Figure 26–6.

JOHN DEERE CO. v. BOELUS STATE BANK Supreme Court of Nebraska, 1989, 233 Neb. 818, 448 N.W.2d 163

FACTS Walter Duester purchased a John Deere combine from St. Paul Equipment. John Deere Co. was the lender and secured party under the agreement. The combine was pledged as collateral. Duester defaulted on his debt, and the manager of St. Paul, Hansen, was instructed to repossess the combine. Hansen went to Duester's farm to accomplish this. Duester told him that he had received some payments for custom combining and would immediately purchase a cashier's check to pay the John Deere debt. Hansen followed Duester to the defendant, Boelus State Bank. Hansen remained outside, and Duester returned in a few minutes with a cashier's check in the amount of the balance of his indebtedness payable to John Deere. The check had been signed by an authorized bank employee. When John Deere, however, presented the check to the bank for payment shortly thereafter, the bank refused to pay, claiming that Duester acquired the cashier's check by theft. The trial court found for John Deere.

DECISION Judgment for John Deere affirmed.

OPINION Theft of an instrument constitutes a personal defense. The UCC provides that a holder in due course takes an instrument free of the personal defense of theft of the instrument. The court concluded that John Deere was indeed a holder in due course since it had given value in the form of taking an instrument in payment of an antecedent debt and that it had acted in good faith and without notice that any claim or defense was applicable to the instrument. Although the bank subsequently informed John Deere of the theft, the court stated that subsequent knowledge of a defense or claim does not impair holder in due course status.

In addition, the payee of a negotiable instrument may be a holder in due course provided he meets the requirements. In obtaining the check drawn on the defendant bank, John Deere did not deal with the bank, and took the instrument for value, in good faith, and without notice.

INTERPRETATION A holder in due course takes an instrument free of personal defenses.

LIMITATIONS UPON HOLDER IN DUE COURSE RIGHTS

The preferential position enjoyed by a holder in due course has been severely limited by a Federal Trade Commission rule restricting the rights of a holder in

FIGURE 26–6 Availability of Defenses Against Holders and Holders in Due Course

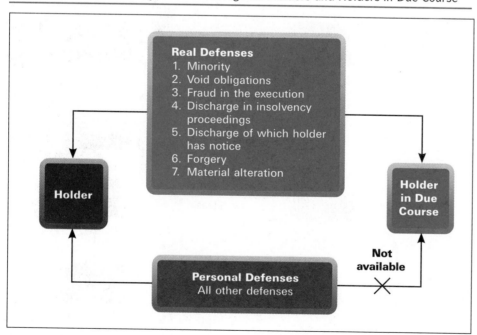

Limitations on rights of holder in due course the preferential position of a holder in due course has been severely limited by a Federal Trade Commission rule that applies to consumer credit contracts; under which, a transferee of consumer credit contracts cannot take as a holder in due course

due course of an instrument concerning a debt arising out of a *consumer credit contract*, which includes negotiable instruments. The rule, entitled "Preservation of Consumers' Claims and Defenses," applies to sellers and lessors of consumer goods, which are goods for personal, household, or family use. It also applies to lenders who advance money to finance a consumer's purchase of consumer goods or services. The rule is intended to prevent consumer purchase transactions from being financed in such a manner that the purchaser is legally obligated to make full payment of the price to a third party, even though the dealer from whom she bought the goods committed fraud or the goods were defective. Such obligations arise when a purchaser executes and delivers to a seller a negotiable instrument that the seller negotiates to a holder in due course. The buyer's defense that the goods were defective or that the seller committed fraud, although valid against the seller, is not valid against the holder in due course. See Figure 26–7.

In order to correct this situation, the Federal Trade Commission rule preserves claims and defenses of consumer buyers and borrowers against holders in due

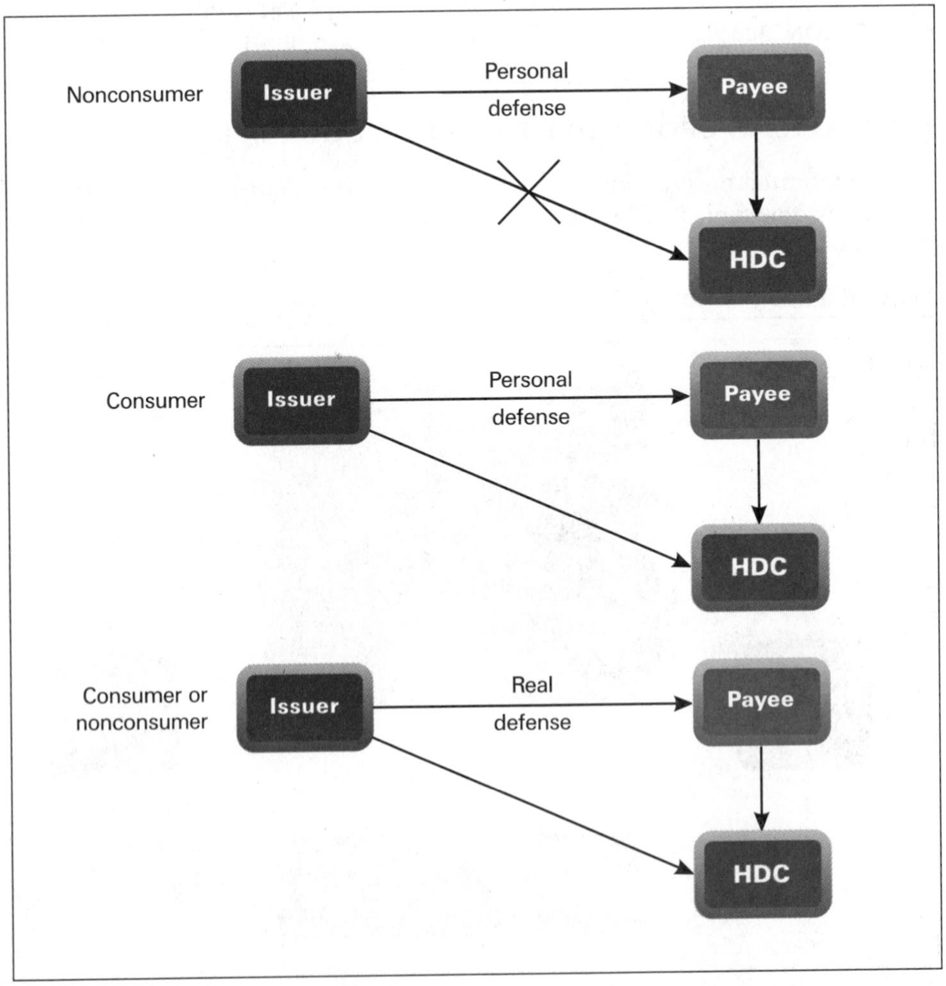

FIGURE 26–7 Rights of Holder in Due Course Under FTC Rule

course. The rule states that no seller or creditor can take or receive a consumer credit contract unless the contract contains this conspicuous provision:

> NOTICE: ANY HOLDER OF THIS CONSUMER CREDIT CONTRACT IS SUBJECT TO ALL CLAIMS AND DEFENSES WHICH THE DEBTOR COULD ASSERT AGAINST THE SELLER OF THE GOODS OR SERVICES OBTAINED PURSUANT HERETO OR WITH THE PROCEEDS HEREOF. RECOVERY HEREUNDER BY THE DEBTOR SHALL NOT EXCEED AMOUNTS PAID BY THE DEBTOR HEREUNDER.

The purpose of this notice is to inform any holder in due course of a paper or negotiable instrument that he takes the instrument subject to all claims and defenses that the buyer could assert against the seller. The effect of the rule is to place the holder in due course in the position of an assignee.

CHAPTER SUMMARY

Requirements of Holder in Due Course	**Holder** a person who has both possession of an instrument and all indorsements necessary to it **Value** differs from contractual consideration and consists of any of the following: ■ the timely performance of legal consideration (which (excludes executory promises); ■ the acquisition of a security interest in or a lien on the instrument; ■ taking the instrument in payment of or as security for an antecedent debt; ■ the giving of a negotiable instrument; or ■ the giving of an irrevocable commitment to a third party **Good Faith** honesty in fact and the observance of reasonable commercial standards of fair dealing **Lack of Notice** ■ *Notice an Instrument Is Overdue* time paper is overdue after its stated date; demand paper is overdue after demand has been made or after it has been outstanding for an unreasonable period of time ■ *Notice an Instrument Has Been Dishonored* dishonor is the refusal to pay or accept an instrument when it becomes due ■ *Notice of Claim or Defense* a defense protects a person from liability while a claim is an assertion of ownership **Without Reason to Question Its Authenticity** instrument cannot bear such apparent evidence of forgery or alteration or otherwise be so irregular or incomplete as to call into question its authenticity
Holder in Due Course Status	**A Payee May Be a Holder in Due Course** the payee's rights as a holder in due course are limited to defenses of persons with whom he has not dealt **The Shelter Rule** the transferee of an instrument acquires the same rights that the transferor had in the instrument

The Preferred Position of a Holder in Due Course	**Real Defenses** real defenses are available against all holders, including holders in due course; such defenses are as follows: ■ *Infancy* ■ *Void Obligations* ■ *Fraud in the Execution* ■ *Discharge in Insolvency Proceedings* ■ *Discharge of which the Holder Has Notice* ■ *Unauthorized Signature* ■ *Fraudulent Alteration* **Personal (Contractual) Defenses** all other defenses that might be asserted in the case of any action for breach of contract **Limitations on Rights of Holder in Due Course** the preferential position of a holder in due course his been severely limited by a Federal Trade Commission rule that applies to consumer credit contracts; under which, a transferee of consumer credit contracts cannot take as a holder in due course

QUESTIONS

1. Discuss the requirements for becoming a holder in due course.
2. Discuss (a) the shelter rule and (b) the rights of a payee.
3. Define, identify, and discuss the real defenses.
4. Define and discuss personal defenses.
5. Discuss the limitations the Federal Trade Commission imposes upon the rights of a holder in due course.

Internet Question. Compare the provisions governing holders and protected holders contained in the United Nations Convention on International Bills of Exchange and International Promissory Notes with those governing holders and holders in due course under Article 3 of the Uniform Commercial Code.

PROBLEMS

1. Marcus issues a negotiable promissory note payable to the order of Parish for the amount of $3,000. Parish raises the amount to $13,000 and negotiates it to Hilda for $12,000.
   (a) If Hilda is a holder in due course, how much can she recover from Marcus? How much from Parish? If Marcus's negligence substantially contributed to the making of the alteration, how much can Hilda recover from Marcus and Parish, respectively?
   (b) If Hilda is not a holder in due course, how much can she recover from Marcus? How much from Parish? If Marcus's negligence substantially contributed to the making of the alteration, how much can Hilda recover from Marcus and Parish, respectively?

2. On December 2, 1997, Miles executed and delivered to Proctor a negotiable promissory note for $1,000, payable to Proctor or order, due March 2, 1998, with interest at 14 percent from maturity, in partial payment of a printing press. On January 3, 1998, Proctor, in need of ready cash, indorsed and sold the note to Hughes for $800. Hughes paid $600 in cash to Proctor on January 3 and agreed to pay the balance of $200 one week later, namely, on January 10. On January 6, Hughes learned that Miles claimed a breach of warranty by Proctor and, for this reason, intended to refuse to pay the note when it matured. On January 10, Hughes paid Proctor $200, in conformity with their agreement of January 3. Following Miles's refusal to pay the note on March 2, 1998, Hughes sues Miles for $1,000. Decision?

3. Thornton fraudulently represented to Daye that he would obtain for her a new car to be used in Daye's business for $7,800 from Pennek Motor Company. Daye thereupon executed her personal check for $7,800 payable to the order of Pennek Motor Company and delivered the check to Thornton, who immediately delivered it to the motor company in payment of his own prior indebtedness. The motor company had no knowledge of the representations made by Thornton to Daye. Pennek Motor Company now brings an action on the check against Daye, who defends on the ground of failure of consideration. Decision?

4. Adams, who reads with difficulty, arranged to borrow $200 from Bell. Bell prepared a note, which Adams read laboriously. As Adams was about to sign it, Bell diverted Adams's attention and substituted the following paper, which was identical to the note Adams had read except that the amounts were different:

> On June 1, 1997, I promise to pay Ben Bell or order Two Thousand Dollars with interest from date at 16 percent. This note is secured by certificate No. 13 for 100 shares of stock of Brookside Mills, Inc.

Adams did not detect the substitution, signed as maker, handed the note and stock certificate to Bell, and received from Bell $200. Bell indorsed and sold the paper to Fore, a holder in due course, who paid him $1,800. Fore presented the note at maturity to Adams, who refused to pay. What are Fore's rights, if any, against Adams?

5. On January 2, 1997, Martin, seventeen years of age, as a result of Dealer's fraudulent misrepresentation, bought a used motorboat to use in his fishing business for $2,000 from Dealer, signed an installment contract for $1,500, and gave Dealer the following instrument as down payment:

> Dated:_____1997
>
> I promise to pay to the order of Dealer, six months after date, the sum of $500 without interest. This is given as a down payment on an installment contract for a motorboat.
>
> (signed) Martin

Dealer, on July 1, sold his business to Henry and included this note in the transaction. Dealer indorsed the note in blank and handed it to Henry, who left the note in his office safe. On July 10, Sharpie, an employee of Henry, without authority, stole the note and sold it to Bert for $300, indorsing the note "Sharpie." At the time, in Bert's presence, Sharpie filled in the date on the note as February 2, 1997. Bert demanded payment from Martin, who refused to pay. What are Bert's rights against Martin?

6. McLaughlin borrowed $1,000 from Adler, who, apprehensive about McLaughlin's ability to pay, demanded security. McLaughlin indorsed and delivered to Adler a negotiable promissory note executed by Topping for $1,200 payable to McLaughlin's order in twelve equal monthly installments. The note did not contain an acceleration clause, but it recited that the consideration for the note was McLaughlin's promise to paint and shingle Topping's barn. At the time McLaughlin transferred the note to Adler, the first installment was overdue and unpaid. Adler was unaware that the installment had not been paid. Topping did not pay any of the installments on the note. When the last installment became due, Adler presented the note to Topping for payment. Topping refused upon the ground that McLaughlin had not painted or reshingled her barn.

What are Adler's rights, if any, against Topping on the note?

7. McEnolly purchased a refrigerator for his home from Perrault Appliance Store for $700. McEnolly paid $200 in cash and signed an installment contract for $500, which in its entirety stated:

> January 15, 1997
>
> I promise to pay to the order of Perrault Appliance Store the sum of $500 in ten equal monthly installments.
>
> (signed) McEnolly

Perrault negotiated the installment contract to Hughes, who took the instrument for value, in good faith, without notice of any claim or defense of any party, and without question of the instrument's authenticity. After McEnolly had paid two installments, the refrigerator ceased operating, and McEnolly wishes to recover his down payment and first two monthly payments and to discontinue further payments. What outcome?

8. Adams, by fraudulent representations, induced Barton to purchase 100 shares of the capital stock of the Evermore Oil Company. The shares were worthless. Barton executed and delivered to Adams a negotiable promissory note for $5,000, dated May 5, in full payment for the shares, due six months after date. On May 20, Adams indorsed and sold the note to Cooper for $4,800. On October 21, Barton, having learned that Cooper now held the note, notified Cooper of the fraud and stated he would not pay the note. On December 1, Cooper negotiated the note to Davis who, while not a party, had full knowledge of the fraud perpetrated on Barton. Upon refusal of Barton to pay the note, Davis sues Barton for $5,000. Decision?

9. Donna gives Peter a check for $5,000 in return for a personal computer. The check is dated December 2. Peter transfers the check for value to Howard on December 14, and Howard deposits it in his bank on December 20. In the meantime, Donna has discovered that the personal computer is not what was promised and has stopped payment on the check. If Peter and Howard disappear, may the bank recover from Donna notwithstanding her defense of failure of consideration? What will be the bank's cause of action?

10. Eldon's Super Fresh Stores, Inc., is a corporation engaged in the retail grocery business. William Drexler was the attorney for and the corporate secretary of Eldon's and was also the personal attorney of Eldon Prinzing, the corporation's president and sole shareholder. From January 1989 through January 1990, Drexler maintained an active stock trading account in his name with Merrill Lynch. Eldon's had no such

account. On August 12, 1989, Drexler purchased 100 shares of Clark Oil & Refining Company stock through his Merrill Lynch stockbroker. He paid for the stock with a check drawn by Eldon's, made payable to Merrill Lynch and signed by Prinzing. On August 15, 1989, Merrill Lynch accepted the check as payment for Drexler's stock purchase. There was no communication between Eldon's and Merrill Lynch until November 1990, fifteen months after the issuance of the check. At that time, Eldon's asked Merrill Lynch about the whereabouts of the stock certificate and asserted a claim to its ownership. It then brought this action, claiming that it gave the check to Drexler to be delivered to Merrill Lynch for Eldon's benefit. Decision?

11. Consolidated Business Forms leased a Phillips business computer from Benchmark. Benchmark subsequently transferred the lease and promissory note to Exchange International Leasing Corporation. Consolidated stopped making rental payments when the computer malfunctioned, and Exchange International brought this suit to recover the payments due on the promissory note. Consolidated defends on the grounds that Benchmark prevented its agent, Mr. Spohn, from examining the contents of the agreement between the two companies and further represented that the computer would be removed with a complete refund if it failed to operate properly. Decision?

12. In 1973, Litton decided to purchase photocopiers to use in its offices. Angelo Buquicchio, a Royal (a division of Litton) salesman, recommended that Litton lease the machines from Regent. Regent was a company totally independent of Litton and had agreed to give Buquicchio "service fees" or, more appropriately, bribes. Regent borrowed money from Bankers Trust to finance purchases and transferred the Litton leases as security. A clause in the leases permitted transfer and provided that the transferee's rights would be independent of any claims or offsets of Litton as against Regent. Litton defaulted on the obligations, and the primary question was whether Regent's bribery of Royal's employee rendered Litton's obligations a nullity and a defense against the banks as holders in due course. Decision?

CHAPTER 27

Liability of Parties

The preceding chapters discussed the requirements of negotiability, the transfer of negotiable instruments, and the preferred position of a holder in due course. When parties issue negotiable instruments, they do so with the expectation that they, either directly or indirectly, will satisfy their obligation under the instrument. Likewise, when a person accepts, indorses, or transfers an instrument, he incurs liability for the instrument under certain circumstances. This chapter examines the liability of parties arising out of negotiable instruments and the ways in which liability may be terminated.

Two types of potential liability are associated with negotiable instruments: contractual liability and warranty liability. The law imposes **contractual liability** on those who *sign*, or have representative agent sign, a negotiable instrument. Because some parties to a negotiable instrument never sign it, they never assume contractual liability.

Contractual liability obligation on a negotiable instrument based upon signing the instrument

Warranty liability, on the other hand, is not based on signature; thus, it may be imposed on both signers and nonsigners. **Warranty liability** applies (1) to persons who transfer an instrument and (2) to persons who obtain payment or acceptance of an instrument.

Warranty liability applies to persons who transfer an instrument or receive payment for or acceptance of it

CONTRACTUAL LIABILITY

All parties whose signatures appear on a negotiable instrument incur certain contractual obligations, unless they disclaim liability. The *maker* of a promissory note and the *acceptor* of a draft assume primary, or unconditional, liability, subject to valid claims and defenses, to pay according to the terms of the instrument at the time they sign it or as completed according to the rules for incomplete instruments, discussed in Chapter 26. **Primary liability** means that a party is legally obligated to pay without the holder's having to resort first to another party. *Indorsers* of all instruments incur secondary, or conditional, liability if the instrument is not paid. **Secondary liability** means that a party is legally obligated to pay only after another party, who is expected to pay, fails to do so. The liability of drawers of drafts and checks is also conditional because it is generally contingent upon the drawee's dishonor of the instrument. A *drawee* has *no* liability on the instrument until he *accepts* it.

Primary liability absolute obligation to pay a negotiable instrument

Secondary liability obligation to pay a negotiable instrument is subject to conditions precedent

An **accommodation party** signs the instrument to lend her credit to another party to the instrument and is a direct beneficiary of the value received. The liability of an accommodation party, who generally signs as a co-maker, or anomalous indorser, is determined by the capacity in which she signs. If she

Accommodation party signs an instrument to lend her credit to the instrument; her liability is determined by the capacity in which she signs

signs as a maker, she incurs primary liability; if she signs as an anomalous indorser, she incurs secondary liability.

SIGNATURE

Signature a signature may be made by the individual herself or by her authorized agent

The word **signature**, as discussed in Chapter 24, is broadly defined to include any name, word, or mark, whether handwritten, typed, printed, or in any other form, made with the intention of authenticating an instrument. The signature may be made by the individual herself or on behalf by the individual's authorized agent.

Authorized Signatures

Authorized signatures an agent who executes a negotiable instrument on behalf of his principal is not liable if the instrument is executed properly and as authorized

Authorized agents often execute negotiable instruments on behalf of their principals. The agent is not liable if she is authorized to execute the instrument and does so properly (e.g., "Prince, principal, by Adams, agent"). If these two conditions are met, then only the principal is liable on the instrument. (For a comprehensive discussion of the principal-agent relationship, see Chapters 29 and 30.)

Occasionally, however, the agent, although fully authorized, uses an inappropriate form of signature that may mislead holders or prospective holders as to the identity of the obligor. Although incorrect signatures by agents assume many forms, they can be conveniently sorted into three groups.

The first type occurs when an agent signs only his own name to an instrument, neither indicating that he is signing in a representative capacity nor stating the name of the principal. For example, Adams, the agent of Prince, makes a note on behalf of Prince but signs it "Adams." The signature does not indicate that Adams has signed in a representative capacity or that he has made the instrument on behalf of Prince. In this situation, only the agent is liable on the instrument; Prince is not liable because his name does not appear on the instrument. Prince may be liable to Adams or a third party, however, on the basis of contract or agency law.

The second type of incorrect form occurs when an authorized agent indicates that he is signing in a representative capacity but does not disclose the name of his principal. For example, Adams, executing an instrument on behalf of Prince, merely signs it "Adams, agent." In this situation, Prince is liable if the payee is an immediate party to the instrument and knows that Adams represents Prince. But as to any subsequent party, and as to the payee if he does not know that Adams represents Prince, Prince is not liable on the instrument; Adams alone is liable. As with the first situation, Prince may be liable to Adams, or to a third party, based on contract or agency law.

The third type of inappropriate signature occurs when an agent reveals both her name and her principal's name, but does not indicate that she has signed in a representative capacity. For example, Adams, signing an instrument on behalf of Prince, signs it "Adams and Prince." Because a subsequent holder might reasonably believe that Adams and Prince were co-makers, both are fully liable. But if the party who dealt with Adams knew or should have known that Adams was acting on behalf of Prince without intending to incur personal liability, Adams may prove this fact by parol evidence and avoid liability to this immediate party.

Under Revised Article 3, if a representative (an agent) signs his name as the drawer of a *check* without indicating his representative status and the check is payable from an account of the represented person (the principal) who is identified on the check, the representative is not liable on the check if he is an authorized agent. Some courts reached this result under prior Article 3.

COHEN v. DISNER California Court of Appeal, 1995, 36 Cal. App.4th 855, 42 Cal. Rptr. 2d 782, 27 UCC Rep. Serv. 2d 540

FACTS Attorney Eliot Disner tendered a check for $100,100 to Sidney and Lynne Cohen. In drawing the check, Disner was serving as an intermediary for his clients, Irvin and Dorothea Kipnes, who owed the money to the Cohens as part of a settlement agreement. The Kipneses had given Disner checks totaling $100,100, which he had deposited into his professional corporation's client trust account. After confirming with the Kipneses' bank that their account held sufficient funds, Disner wrote and delivered a trust account check for $100,100 to the Cohens' attorney, with this note: "Please find $100,100 in settlement (partial) of Cohen v. Kipnes, et al[.] Per our agreement, delivery to you constitutes timely delivery to your clients." Also typed on the check was a notation identifying the underlying lawsuit.

Without Disner's knowledge, the Kipneses stopped payment on their checks, leaving insufficient funds in the trust account to cover the check to the Cohens. The trust account check therefore was not paid due to insufficient funds; the Kipneses declared bankruptcy; and the Cohens served Disner and his professional corporation (jointly, Disner) with demand for payment. The Cohens sought the amount written on the check plus a $500 statutory penalty. The trial court entered summary judgment for Disner, reasoning he is not liable on the check because he was a mere conduit or agent for transferring money from the Kipneses to the Cohens. The Cohens appeal from the judgment.

DECISION Judgment affirmed.

OPINION The drawer of a check that is rejected for insufficient funds is not liable for payment if there is no enforceable obligation to pay. However, the Cohens contend that California Civil Code § 1719 rejects the "representative capacity" defense, and imposes strict liability against the drawer of a check drawn on an account lacking sufficient funds.

If § 1719 imposed strict liability, it would conflict with the pre-existing law of negotiable instruments. However, as worded, § 1719 may readily be harmonized with the UCC to impose liability only when there is an enforceable obligation to pay the check. By acknowledging that there must be an enforceable obligation to pay, § 1719 echoes the UCC, which precludes recovery where the payee has no "right to enforce the obligation of a party to pay an instrument." If the drawer has no enforceable obligation to pay a dishonored check, there is no amount "owing upon that check" under the plain language of § 1719. Had the legislature intended § 1719 to be a strict liability statute, it would have imposed liability for "the amount written upon that check" rather than "the amount owing upon that check."

Under the "representative capacity" defense, a representative, signing the representative's name, is only liable on the instrument to a holder in due course without notice of his representative capacity if the form of the signature does not show unambiguously that the signature is made in a representative capacity and the represented party is not identified on the instrument. However, where the holder has notice of the drawer's representative status, it is not required that the representative indicate his representative capacity in the signature even if the check is payable from the account of the representative. Disner is not liable on the check because he has no enforceable obligation to pay and it was drawn by him in a representative capacity.

INTERPRETATION Where a holder has notice that the drawer's signature is in the capacity of an agent, the drawer is not personally liable on the instrument.

Unauthorized Signatures

Unauthorized signatures include both forgeries and signatures made by an agent without authority. Though generally not binding on the person whose name appears on the instrument, the unauthorized signature is binding upon the unauthorized signer, whether her own name appears on the instrument or not, to any person who in good faith pays or gives value for the instrument. Section 3–403(a). Thus, if Adams, without authority, signed Prince's name to an instrument, Adams, not Prince, would be liable on the instrument. The rule, therefore, is an exception to the principle that only those whose names appear on a negotiable instrument can be liable on it.

> **Unauthorized signatures** include forgeries and signatures made by an agent without proper power; are generally not binding on the person whose name appears on the instrument but are binding on the unauthorized signer

Ratification of Unauthorized Signature An unauthorized signature may be *ratified* by the person whose name appears on the instrument. Although the ratification may relieve the actual signer from liability on the instrument, it does not itself affect any rights the person ratifying the signature may have against the actual signer.

Negligence Contributing to Unauthorized Signature Any person who by his *negligence* substantially contributes to the making of an unauthorized signature may *not* assert the lack of authority as a defense against a holder in due course or a person who in good faith pays the instrument or takes it for value or for collection. Nevertheless, if the person asserting the preclusion also fails to exercise reasonable care, Revised Article 3 adopts a comparative negligence standard.

LIABILITY OF PRIMARY PARTIES

There is a primary party on every note: the *maker*. The maker's commitment is unconditional. No one, however, is unconditionally liable on a draft or check as issued. A *drawee* is *not* liable on the instrument unless he accepts it. If, however, the drawee accepts the draft, after which he is known as the *acceptor*, he becomes primarily liable on the instrument. **Acceptance** or, in the case of a check, certification is the drawee's signed promise to pay a draft as presented. Presentment (that is, a demand for payment) is not a condition to the holder's right to recover from parties with primary liability.

Acceptance a drawee's signed commitment to honor the instrument

Makers

The **maker** of a note is obligated to pay the instrument according to its terms at the time of issuance or, if the instrument is incomplete, according to its terms when completed, as discussed in Chapter 26. The obligation of the maker is owed to a person entitled to enforce the instrument or to an indorser who paid the instrument.

Maker guarantees that he will pay the note according to its original terms

Primary liability also applies to issuers of cashier's checks and to issuers of drafts drawn on the drawer (that is, where the issuer is both the drawee and the drawer).

Acceptors

A drawee has no liability on the instrument until she accepts it, at which time she becomes an **acceptor** and, like the maker, primarily liable. The acceptor becomes liable on the draft according to its terms at the time of acceptance or as completed according to the rules for incomplete instruments as discussed in Chapter 26. Nevertheless, if the acceptor does not state the amount accepted and the amount of the draft is later raised, a subsequent holder in due course can enforce the instrument against the acceptor according to the terms at the time the holder in due course took possession. Thus, an acceptor should always indicate on the instrument the amount that it is accepting. The acceptor owes the obligation to pay a person entitled to enforce the instrument or to the drawer or an indorser who paid the draft under drawer's or indorser's liability.

Acceptor a drawee has no liability on the instrument until she accepts it; she then becomes primarily liable

An acceptance must be written on the draft. Having met this requirement, it may take many forms. It may be printed on the face of the draft, ready for the drawee's signature. It may consist of a rubber stamp, with the signature of the drawee added. It may be the drawee's signature, preceded by a word or phrase such as "Accepted," "Certified," or "Good." It may consist of nothing more than the drawee's signature. Normally, but by no means necessarily, an acceptance is written vertically across the face of the draft. It must not, however, contain any words indicating an intent to refuse to honor the draft. Furthermore, no writing separate from the draft and no oral statement or conduct of the drawee will convert the drawee into an acceptor.

Checks, when accepted, are said to be certified. **Certification** is a special type of acceptance consisting of the drawee bank's promise to pay the check when subsequently presented for payment.

Certification acceptance of a check by a bank

The drawee bank has no obligation to certify a check, and its refusal to certify does not constitute dishonor of the instrument. If the drawee refuses to accept or pay the instrument, he may be liable to the drawer for breach of contract.

LIABILITY OF SECONDARY PARTIES

Parties with secondary (conditional) liability do not unconditionally promise to pay the instrument; rather, they engage to pay the instrument if the party expected to pay does not do so. The drawer is liable if the drawee dishonors the instrument. Indorsers (including the payee if he indorses) of an instrument are also conditionally liable; their liability is subject to the conditions of dishonor and notice of dishonor. If an instrument is *not* paid by the party expected to pay and the conditions precedent to the liability of a secondary party are satisfied, a secondary party is liable unless he has disclaimed his liability or he possesses a valid defense to the instrument.

Indorsers and drawers if the instrument is not paid by a primary party and if the conditions precedent to the liability of secondary parties are satisfied, indorsers and drawers are secondarily (conditionally) liable unless they have disclaimed their liability or have a valid defense to the instrument

Drawers

A drawer of a draft orders the drawee to pay the instrument and does not expect to pay the draft personally. The drawer is obligated to pay the draft only if the drawee fails to pay the instrument. The drawer of an *unaccepted draft* is obligated to pay the instrument upon its dishonor according to its terms at the time it was issued or, in the case of an incomplete instrument, according to the rules discussed in Chapter 26. Under Revised Article 3, the drawer's liability is contingent only upon dishonor and does not require notice of dishonor. The drawer's obligation on an unaccepted draft is owed to a person entitled to enforce the instrument or to an indorser who paid the instrument under indorser's liability.

If the draft has been accepted and the acceptor is not a bank, the obligation of the drawer to pay the instrument is then contingent upon both dishonor of the instrument and notice of dishonor; the drawer's liability in this instance is equivalent to that of an indorser.

DAVIS v. WATSON BROTHERS PLUMBING, INC. Court of Civil Appeals of Texas, Dallas, 1981, 615 S.W.2d 844

FACTS Arnett Lee presented a $152.38 check for cashing to the plaintiff, liquor store operator Troy Davis. After Davis gave Lee the cash, Lee requested a bottle of scotch and a six-pack of beer. As Davis turned to fill the order, a thief stole $110.00 of the $152.38. Lee immediately contacted the defendant—drawer of the check, Watson Brothers Plumbing, Inc.—and notified them of the loss. The defendant then issued another check for $152.38 and stopped payment on the first check held by Davis. Davis brought this action against the defendant for the full face amount of the check.

DECISION Judgment for Davis for $152.38.

OPINION Davis was the holder of the check, and Watson Brothers Plumbing failed to raise any valid defense to enforcement of the check against it. Any party "who is in possession of . . . an instrument . . . indorsed to him . . . in blank" is a holder. Since Lee indorsed the check in blank to Davis, Davis is a holder. The holder of a draft is entitled to receive its full amount from the drawer upon dishonor of the check, unless the drawer has a valid defense to the holder's enforcement

continued

of the check against it. Watson Brothers Plumbing, the drawer of the check, argues that it may raise the defense of insufficiency or failure of consideration in the transaction between Davis and Lee. But the transfer of the check by Lee to Davis has no effect upon Watson Brothers Plumbing's obligation to pay the check according to its tenor. "Consideration" is concerned with Lee's transaction with Watson Brothers Plumbing, not with whether Davis gave anything in consideration for the check to Lee. Since Watson Brothers Plumbing has no defense to enforcement of the check against Lee, it has no defense against Davis, regardless of whether Davis gave full consideration for the check.

INTERPRETATION The drawer's liability is contingent upon dishonor of the instrument.

Indorsers

An indorser promises that upon dishonor of the instrument *and* notice of dishonor she will pay the instrument according to the terms of the instrument at the time it was indorsed or, if an incomplete instrument when indorsed, according to its terms when completed, as discussed in Chapter 26. Once again, this obligation is owed to a person entitled to enforce the instrument or to a subsequent indorser who paid the instrument under indorser's liability.

Effect of Acceptance

Effect of acceptance when a draft is accepted by a bank, the drawer and all prior indorsers are discharged from contractual liability

Where a *draft* is accepted by a *bank*, the drawer and all prior indorsers are discharged. The liability of indorsers subsequent to certification is not affected. When the bank accepts a draft, it should withhold from the drawer's account funds sufficient to pay the instrument. Since the bank is primarily liable on its acceptance and has the funds whereas the drawer does not, the discharge is reasonable.

Disclaimer of Liability by Secondary Parties

Disclaimer by secondary parties a drawer (except of a check) or indorser may disclaim liability by a qualified drawing or indorsing ("without recourse")

Both drawers and indorsers *may* disclaim their normal conditional liability by drawing or indorsing an instrument *"without recourse."* However, drawers of *checks* may not disclaim contractual liability. The use of the qualifying words *without recourse* is understood to place purchasers on notice that they may not rely on the credit of the person using this language. A person drawing or indorsing an instrument in this manner does not incur the normal contractual liability of a drawer or indorser to pay the instrument, but he may nonetheless be liable for breach of warranty.

Conditions Precedent to Liability

A *condition precedent* is an event or events that must occur before liability arises. The condition precedent to the liability of the drawer of an *unaccepted* draft is dishonor. Condition precedent to the liability of any indorser or the drawer of an *accepted* draft by a nonbank are dishonor and notice of dishonor. If the conditions to secondary liability are not met, a party's conditional obligation on the instrument is discharged, unless the conditions are excused.

Dishonor generally involves the refusal to pay an instrument when it is presented

Presentment demand for payment or acceptance of an instrument

Dishonor Dishonor generally involves the refusal to pay an instrument when it is presented. **Presentment** is a demand made by or on behalf of a person entitled to enforce the instrument for (1) *payment* by the drawee or other party obligated to pay the instrument or (2) *acceptance* by the drawee of a draft. The return of any instrument for lack of necessary indorsements or for failure of the presentment to comply with the terms of the instrument, however, is not a dishonor.

What constitutes dishonor varies depending upon the type of instrument and whether presentment is required.

1. Note—A *demand note* is dishonored if the maker does not pay it on the day of presentment. If the note is payable at a *definite time and* (1) the terms of the note require presentment or (2) the note is payable at or through a bank, the note is dishonored if it is not paid on the date it is presented or its due date, whichever is later. All *other time notes* need not be presented and are dishonored if they are not paid on their due dates. Nevertheless, since makers are primarily liable on their notes, their liability is not affected by failure of proper presentment.

2. Drafts—An *unaccepted draft* (other than a check, discussed below) that is payable on *demand* is dishonored if presentment is made and it is not paid on the date presented. A *time draft* presented for *payment* is due on the due date or presentment date, whichever is later. A *time draft* presented for *acceptance* prior to its due date is dishonored if it is not accepted on the day presented. Refusal to *accept* a *demand instrument* is not a dishonor, although acceptance may be requested. Of course, if an instrument is payable at a certain time period after acceptance or sight, a refusal to accept the draft on the day presented is a dishonor.

   An *accepted demand draft* is dishonored if the acceptor (who is primarily liable on the instrument) does not pay it on the day presented for payment. An *accepted time draft* is dishonored if it is not paid on the due date for payment or on the presentment date, whichever is later.

   Drawers, with the exception of drafts accepted by a bank, are not discharged from liability by a delay in presentment. Once an instrument has been properly presented and dishonored, a drawer becomes liable to pay the instrument. As previously indicated, drawers and prior indorsers are discharged from liability when a draft is accepted by a bank.

3. Checks—If a *check* is presented for payment directly to the payor/drawee bank for immediate payment, a refusal to pay the check on the day presented constitutes dishonor. In the more common situation of a check being presented through the normal collection process, a check is dishonored if the payor bank makes timely return of the check, sends timely notice of dishonor or nonpayment, or becomes accountable for the amount of the check (until that payment has been made, the check is dishonored. As more fully explained in Chapter 28, under Article 4 a bank in most instances has a midnight deadline (before midnight of the next banking day) in which to decide whether to honor or dishonor an instrument. Thus, depending on the number of banks involved in the collection process, the time for dishonor can greatly vary.

   Delay in presentment discharges an *indorser* only if the instrument is a check and it is not presented for payment or given to a depositary bank for collection within thirty days after the day the indorsement was made. The same rule does not apply, however, to a drawer. If a person entitled to enforce a check fails to present a check within thirty days after its date, the drawer will be discharged only if the delay deprives the drawer of funds because of the suspension of payments by the drawee bank such as would result from a bank failure. This discharge is quite unlikely because of federal bank insurance but would be available where an account is not fully insured because it exceeds $100,000 or because the account doesn't qualify for deposit insurance.

Notice of Dishonor The obligation of an indorser of any instrument and of a drawer of a draft accepted by a nonbank is not enforceable unless the indorser or drawer is given notice of dishonor or the notice is otherwise excused. Thus, lack of proper notice discharges the liability of an indorser; for this purpose a drawer of a draft accepted by a party other than a bank is treated as an indorser. Notice of dishonor is *not* required to retain the liability of drawers of unaccepted drafts. In addition, as previously mentioned, a drawer is discharged when a draft is accepted by a *bank*. In short, a drawer's liability is *usually* not contingent upon receiving notice of dishonor whereas an indorser's liability is.

Notice of dishonor is normally given by the holder or by an indorser who has himself received notice. For example, Michael makes a note payable to the order of Phyllis; Phyllis indorses it to Arthur; Arthur indorses it to Bambi; and Bambi indorses it to Henry, the last holder. Henry presents it to Michael within a reasonable time, but Michael refuses to pay. Henry may give notice of dishonor to all secondary parties: Phyllis, Arthur, and Bambi. If he is satisfied that Bambi will pay him or if he does not know how to contact Phyllis or Arthur, he may notify only Bambi, who then must see to it that Arthur or Phyllis is notified, or she will have no recourse. Bambi may notify either or both. If she notifies Arthur only, Arthur will have to see to it that Phyllis is notified, or Arthur will have no recourse. When properly given, notice benefits all parties who have rights on the instrument against the party notified. Thus, Henry's notification to Phyllis operates as notice to Phyllis by both Arthur and Bambi. Likewise, if Henry notifies only Bambi and Bambi notifies Arthur and Phyllis, then Henry has the benefit of Bambi's notification of Arthur and Phyllis. Nonetheless, it would be advisable for Henry to give notice to all prior parties because Bambi may be insolvent and thus may not bother to notify Arthur or Phyllis.

If, in the above example, Henry were to notify Phyllis alone, Arthur and Bambi would be discharged. Because she has no claim against Arthur or Bambi, who indorsed after she did, Phyllis would have no ground for complaint. It cannot matter to Phyllis that she is compelled to pay Henry rather than Arthur. Therefore, subsequent parties are permitted to skip intermediate indorsers if they want to discharge them and are willing to look solely to prior indorsers for recourse.

Any necessary notice must be given by a *bank* before midnight on the *next* banking day following the banking day on which it receives notice of dishonor. Any *nonbank* with respect to an instrument taken for collection must give notice within thirty days following the day on which it received notice. In all other situations, notice of dishonor must be within thirty days following the day on which dishonor occurred. For instance, Donna draws a check on Youngstown Bank payable to the order of Pablo; Pablo indorses it to Andrea; Andrea deposits it to her account in Second Chicago National Bank; Second Chicago National Bank properly presents it to Youngstown Bank, the drawee; and Youngstown dishonors it because the drawer, Donna, has insufficient funds on deposit to cover it. Youngstown has until midnight of the following day to notify Second Chicago National, Andrea or Pablo, of the dishonor. Second Chicago National then has until midnight on the day after receipt of notice of dishonor to notify Andrea, or Pablo. That is, if Second Chicago National received the notice of dishonor on Monday, it would have until midnight on Tuesday to notify Andrea or Pablo. If it failed to notify Andrea, it could not charge the item back to her. Andrea, in turn, has thirty days after receipt of notice of dishonor to notify Pablo. Donna, a drawer of an unaccepted draft, is not discharged from liability for failure to receive notice of dishonor.

Frequently, notice of dishonor is given by returning the unpaid instrument with an attached stamp, ticket, or memorandum stating that the item was not paid and requesting that the recipient make good on it. But since the purpose of notice is to give knowledge of dishonor and to inform the secondary party that he may be held liable on the instrument, any kind of notice that informs the recipient of his potential liability is sufficient. No formal requisites are imposed—notice may be given by any commercially reasonable means, including oral, written, or electronic communication. An oral notice, while sufficient, is inadvisable because it may be difficult to prove. Notice of dishonor must reasonably identify the instrument.

Presentment and Notice of Dishonor Excused The Code excuses *presentment* for payment or acceptance if (1) the person entitled to enforce the instrument cannot with reasonable diligence present the instrument; (2) the maker or acceptor of the instrument has repudiated the obligation to pay, is dead, or is in insolvency proceedings; (3) the terms of the instrument do not require presentment in order to hold the indorsers or drawer liable; (4) the drawer or indorser has waived the right of presentment; or (5) the drawer instructed the drawee not to pay or accept the draft; or (6) the drawee was not obligated to the drawer to pay the draft.

Notice of dishonor is excused if the terms of the instrument do not require notice in order to hold the party liable or if notice has been waived by the party whose obligation is being enforced. Moreover, a waiver of presentment is also a waiver of notice of dishonor. Finally, delay in giving notice of dishonor is excused if the delay is caused by circumstances beyond the control of the person giving notice and that person exercised reasonable diligence in giving notice after the cause of the delay ceased to exist. See Figure 27–1.

Liability of Conversion

Conversion is a *tort* by which a person becomes liable in damages because of his wrongful control over the personal property of another. The law applicable to conversion of personal property applies to instruments. An instrument is so converted if the instrument "is taken by transfer, other than by negotiation, from a person *not* entitled to enforce the instrument or a bank makes or obtains payment

Liability for conversion conversion occurs (1) when a drawee refuses to return a draft that was presented for acceptance, (2) when any person refuses to return an instrument after he dishonors it, or (3) when an instrument is paid on a forged indorsement

FIGURE 27–1 Contractual Liability

Party	Instrument	Liability	Conditions
Maker	Note	Unconditional	None
Acceptor	Draft	Unconditional	None
Drawer	Unaccepted-draft	Conditional	Dishonor
	Draft accepted by a nonbank	Conditional	Dishonor and notice
	Cashier's check	Unconditional	None
	Draft drawn on drawer	Unconditional	None
	Draft accepted by a bank	None	
	Draft (not check) drawn without recourse	None	
Indorser	Note or draft	Conditional	Dishonor and notice
	Draft subsequently accepted by a bank	None	
	Note or draft indorsed without recourse	None	
Drawee	Draft	None	

with respect to the instrument for a person *not* entitled to enforce the instrument or receive payment." Section 3–420(a) (emphasis added). Examples of conversion thus would include a drawee bank that pays an instrument containing a forged indorsement or a bank that pays an instrument containing only one of two required indorsements.

TERMINATION OF LIABILITY

Eventually, every commercial transaction must end, terminating the potential liabilities of the parties to the instrument. The Code specifies the various methods by and extent to which the liability of *any* party, primary or secondary, is discharged. It also specifies when the liability of *all* parties is discharged. No discharge of a party is effective against a subsequent holder in due course, however, unless she has notice of the discharge when she takes the instrument. In addition, discharge of liability is not always final; liability under certain circumstances (e.,g., coming into possession of a subsequent holder in due course) can be revived.

Payment
The most obvious and common way for a party to discharge liability on an instrument is to pay a party entitled to enforce the instrument. An instrument is paid to the extent that payment is made by or for a person obligated to pay the instrument and to a person entitled to enforce the instrument. Subject to three exceptions, such payment results in a discharge even though it is made with knowledge of another person's claim to the instrument, unless such other person either supplies adequate indemnity or obtains an injunction in a proceeding to which the holder is made a party.

The person making payment should, of course, take possession of the instrument or have it canceled—marked "paid" or "canceled"—so that it cannot pass to a subsequent holder in due course against whom his discharge would be ineffective.

Tender of Payment
Any party liable on an instrument who makes proper tender of full payment to a person entitled to enforce the instrument when or after payment is due is discharged from liability for interest after the due date. If her tender is refused, she is not discharged from liability for the face amount of the instrument or for any interest accrued until the time of tender. Moreover, if an instrument requires presentment and the obligor is ready and able to pay the instrument when it is due at the place of payment specified in the instrument, such readiness is the equivalent of tender.

Occasionally a person entitled to enforce an instrument will refuse a tender of payment for reasons known only to himself. It may be that he believes his rights exceed the amount of the tender or that he desires to enforce payment against another party. In any event, his refusal of the tender wholly discharges to the extent of the amount of tender every party who has a right of recourse against the party making tender.

Cancellation and Renunciation
The Code provides that a person entitled to enforce an instrument may discharge the liability of any party to an instrument by an intentional voluntary act, such as by canceling the instrument or the signature of the party or parties to be discharged, by mutilating or destroying the instrument, by obliterating a signature,

or by adding words indicating a discharge. A party entitled to enforce an instrument may also renounce his rights by a writing, signed and delivered, promising not to sue or otherwise renouncing rights against the party. Like other discharges, however, a written renunciation is of no effect against a subsequent holder in due course who takes without knowledge of the renunciation.

Cancellation or renunciation is effective even without consideration.

LIABILITY BASED ON WARRANTY

Article 3 imposes two types of implied warranties: (a) transferor's warranties and (b) presenter's warranties. Although these warranties are effective whether the transferor or presenter signs the instrument or not, the extension of the transferor's warranty to subsequent holders does depend on whether one or the other has indorsed the instrument. Like other warranties, these may be disclaimed by agreement between immediate parties. In the case of an indorser, his disclaimer of transfer warranties and presentment warranties must appear in the indorsement itself and be effective, except with respect to checks. Such disclaimers must be specific, such as "without warranty." The use of "without recourse" will only disclaim contract liability, not warranty liability.

WARRANTIES ON TRANSFER

Any person who transfers an instrument, whether by negotiation or assignment, and receives *consideration* makes certain **transferor's warranties**. Any consideration sufficient to support a contract will support transfer warranties. If transfer is by delivery alone, warranties on transfer run only to the immediate transferee. If the transfer is made by indorsement, whether qualified or unqualified, the transfer warranty runs to "any subsequent transferee." Transfer means that the delivery of possession is voluntary. The warranties of the transferor are as follows.

> **Transferor's warranties**
> any person who transfers an instrument and receives consideration makes certain transferor's warranties
>
> **Beneficiary** if the transfer is by delivery, the warranties run only to the immediate transferee; if the transfer is by indorsement, the warranties run to any subsequent holder who takes the instrument in good faith

Entitlement to Enforce

The first warranty that the Code imposes on a transferor is that the transferor is a person entitled to enforce the instrument. This warranty "is in effect a warranty that there are no unauthorized or missing indorsements that prevent the transferor from making the transferee a person entitled to enforce the instrument." The following example illustrates this rule. Mitchell makes a note payable to the order of Penelope. A thief steals the note from Penelope, forges Penelope's indorsement, and sells the instrument to Aaron. Aaron is not entitled to enforce the instrument because the break in the indorsement chain prevents him from being a holder. If Aaron transfers the instrument to Judith for consideration, Judith can hold Aaron liable for breach of warranty. The warranty action is important to Judith because it enables her to hold Aaron liable, even if Aaron indorsed the note "without recourse."

Authentic and Authorized Signatures

The second warranty imposed by the Code is that *all* signatures are authentic and authorized. In the example presented above, this warranty would also be breached. If, however, the signature of a maker, drawer, drawee, acceptor, or indorser not in the chain of title is unauthorized, there is a breach of this warranty but no breach of the warranty of entitlement to enforce.

No Alteration

The third warranty is the warranty against alteration. Suppose that Maureen makes a note payable to the order of the payee in the amount of $100. The payee, without authority, alters the note so that it appears to be drawn for $1,000 and negotiates the instrument to Lois, who buys it without knowledge of the alteration. Lois, indorsing "without recourse," negotiates the instrument to Kyle for consideration. Kyle presents the instrument to Maureen, who refuses to pay more than $100 on it. Kyle can collect the difference from Lois, for although her qualified indorsement saves Lois from liability to Kyle on the indorsement contract, she is liable to him for breach of warranty. If Lois had not qualified her indorsement, Kyle would be able to recover against her on the basis of either warranty or the indorsement contract.

No Defenses

The fourth transferor's warranty imposed by the Code is that the instrument is not subject to a defense or claim in recoupment of any party. A claim in recoupment, as discussed in Chapter 26, is a counterclaim that arose from the transaction that gave rise to the instrument. Suppose that Madeline, a minor and a resident of a state where minors' contracts for nonnecessaries are voidable, makes a note payable to bearer in payment of a motorcycle. Pierce, the first holder, negotiates it to Iola by mere delivery. Iola indorses it and negotiates it to Justin, who unqualifiedly indorses it to Hector. All negotiations are made for consideration. Because of Madeline's minority (a real defense), Hector cannot recover upon the instrument against Iola. Hector therefore recovers against Justin or Iola on either the breach of warranty that no valid defenses exist to the instrument or the indorsement contract. Justin, if he is forced to pay Hector, can in turn recover against Iola on either a breach of warranty or the indorsement contract. Justin, however, cannot recover against Pierce. Pierce is not liable to Justin as an indorser because he did not indorse the instrument. Although Pierce, as a transferor, warrants that there are no defenses good against him, this warranty extends only to his immediate transferee, Iola. Therefore, Justin cannot hold Pierce liable. Iola, however, can recover from Pierce on either warranty or contract.

No Knowledge of Insolvency

Any person who transfers a negotiable instrument warrants that he has no knowledge of any insolvency proceedings instituted with respect to the maker, acceptor, or drawer of an unaccepted instrument. Insolvency proceedings include bankruptcy and "any assignment for the benefit of creditors or other proceedings intended to liquidate or rehabilitate the estate of the person involved." Thus, if Marcia makes a note payable to bearer, and the first holder, Taylor, negotiates it for consideration without indorsement to Ursula, who then negotiates it for consideration by qualified indorsement to Valerie, both Taylor and Ursula warrant that they do not know that Marcia is in bankruptcy. Valerie could not hold Taylor liable for breach of warranty, however, because Taylor's warranty runs only in favor of her immediate transferee, Ursula, since Taylor transferred the instrument without indorsement. If Valerie could hold Ursula liable on her warranty, Ursula could thereupon hold Taylor, her immediate transferor, liable. Figure 27–2 summarizes liabilities on transfer.

FIGURE 27–2 Liability on Transfer

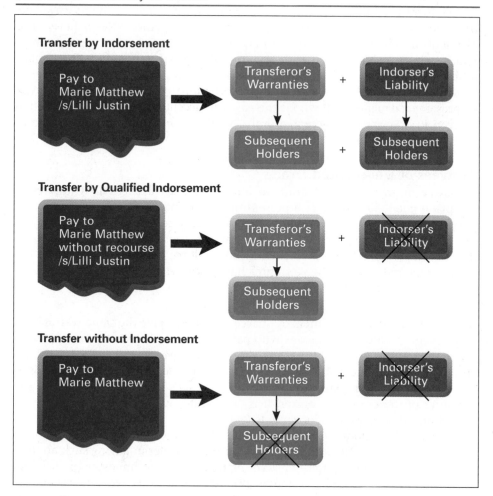

WARRANTIES ON PRESENTMENT

Any party who pays or accepts an instrument must do so in strict compliance with the orders that instrument contains. For example, the payment or acceptance must be made to a person entitled to receive payment or acceptance, the amount paid or accepted must be the correct amount, and the instrument must be genuine and unaltered. If the payment or acceptance is incorrect, the payor or acceptor potentially will incur a loss. In the case of a note, a maker who pays the wrong person will not be discharged from his obligation to pay the correct person. If the maker pays too much, the excess comes out of his pocket. If a drawee pays the wrong person, he generally cannot charge the drawer's account; if he pays too much, he generally cannot charge the drawer's account for the excess. Indorsers who pay an instrument may make similar incorrect payments.

After paying or accepting an instrument to the wrong person, for the wrong amount, or in some other incorrect way, does the person who incorrectly paid or accepted have any recourse against the person who received the payment or acceptance? The Code addresses this critical question by providing that "if an instrument has been paid or accepted by mistake . . . the person paying or accepting may, to the extent permitted by the law governing mistake and restitution, (i) recover the payment from the person to whom or for whose benefit payment was made or (ii) in the case of acceptance, may revoke the acceptance." Nevertheless, this payment or acceptance is *final* and may not be asserted against a person who took the instrument in good faith and for value or who in good faith changed position in reliance on the payment or acceptance, unless there has been a breach of the implied **warranties on presentment**. What warranties are given by presenters depend upon who is the payor or acceptor. The greatest protection is given to drawees of unaccepted drafts, while all other payors receive significantly less protection.

Warranties on presentment all people who obtain payment or acceptance of an instrument as well as all prior transferors give the presenter's warranties

Beneficiary the presenter's warranties run to any person who in good faith pays or accepts an instrument

Drawees of Unaccepted Drafts

A drawee of an unaccepted draft (including uncertified checks), who pays or accepts in good faith, receives a presentment warranty from the person obtaining payment or acceptance and from all prior transferors of the draft. These parties warrant to the drawee making payment or accepting the draft in good faith that: (1) the warrantor is a person entitled to enforce the draft, (2) the draft has not been altered, and (3) the warrantor has no knowledge that the drawer's signature is unauthorized.

Entitled to Enforce Presenters of unaccepted checks give the same warranty of entitlement to enforce to persons who pay or accept as is granted to transferees under the transferor's warranty. Thus, the presenter warrants that she is a person entitled to enforce the instrument. As explained above, this warranty extends to the genuineness and completeness of the indorser's signatures but not to the signature of the drawer or maker. It is "in effect a warranty that there are no unauthorized or missing indorsements."

For example, if Donnese draws a check to Peter or order, and Peter's indorsement is forged, the bank does not follow Donnese's order in paying such an item and therefore cannot charge her account (except in the impostor or fictitious payee situations discussed in Chapter 25). The bank, however, can recover for breach of the presenter's warranty of entitlement to enforce the instrument from the person who obtained payment of the check from the bank. Although it should know the signatures of its own customers, the bank should not be expected to know the signatures of payees or other indorsers of checks; the bank, therefore, should not have to bear this loss.

TRAVELERS INDEMNITY CO. v. STEDMAN U.S. District Court, Eastern District of Pennsylvania, 1995, 895 F.Supp. 742, 27 UCC Rep. Serv. 2d 1347

FACTS In November 1988, the plaintiff, Travelers Indemnity Co., issued a comprehensive crime insurance policy to the American Lung Association (ALA), insuring the ALA against financial losses due to employee fraud or dishonesty. Shortly thereafter, in October of 1989, the ALA hired the defendant, Nancy Stedman, as the Director of Bureau Affairs. In this capacity, Stedman embezzled $129,624.23 of ALA funds by writing seventeen checks against the ALA's account with Merrill, Lynch, Pierce, Fenner & Smith (Merrill Lynch). Stedman deposited six of these checks into her personal checking account with the other defendant, Main Line Federal Savings Bank (Main Line). The checks were subsequently presented to and honored by Merrill Lynch. These checks bore two forged drawer's signatures and at least one forged indorsement. To recover its losses in paying the ALA's insurance claim, Travelers sued Stedman, Main Line, and Merrill Lynch. Merrill Lynch subsequently advanced a claim for indemnity and for breach of presentment warranties against Main Line. Main Line seeks judgment on the pleadings or partial summary judgment on Merrill Lynch's claims.

continued

DECISION Judgment for Main Line.

OPINION Liability or loss allocation, under the UCC, for honoring negotiable instruments containing forged or unauthorized signatures is governed by whether the forgery at issue is that of a drawer's signature or of the indorsement of a payee or holder. Generally, a drawee bank is strictly liable to its customer, the drawer, for payment over either a forged drawer's signature or a forged indorsement. Moreover, when a drawee bank honors an instrument bearing a forged drawer's signature, that payment is final in favor of a holder in due course or one who has in good faith changed his position in reliance on the payment. As a result, where the only forgery is of the signature of the drawer and not of the indorsement, the negligence of a holder in taking the forged instrument will not allow a drawee bank to shift liability to a prior collecting or depositary bank, unless such negligence amounts to a lack of good faith, or unless the payee bank returns the instrument or sends notice of dishonor within the limited time provided. However, where the only forged signature is an indorsement, the drawee normally may pass liability back through the collection chain to the depositary or collecting bank, or to the forger herself if she is available, by a claim for breach of presentment warranties.

Regrettably, the drafters of the UCC failed to address the allocation of liability for honoring instruments containing both a forged drawer's signature and a forged indorsement, the so called "double forgeries." However, based on a thorough examination of the rationales behind the allocation of liability in "single forgery" cases, the Court of Appeals for the Fifth and Sixth Circuits concluded that double forgeries should be treated as though only containing forged drawer's signatures. The Courts observed that in a double forgery case no valid check had been drawn, and therefore no payee could validly claim a loss as a result of the forged indorsement. The loss incurred would be the result of the drawee bank paying the check over the forged drawer's signature. Therefore, under the UCC, checks containing both a forged drawer's signature and a forged indorsement should be treated, for loss allocation purposes, as though bearing only a forged drawer's signature. As a result, the negligence of a holder in taking a double forgery will not allow a drawee bank, such as Merrill Lynch, to shift liability to a prior collecting or depositary bank, such as Main Line, unless such negligence amounts to a lack of good faith, or unless the drawee bank returns the instrument or sends notice of dishonor within the limited time provided by the UCC.

Thus, because it is uncontested that all of the checks at issue bear forged drawer's signatures, liability for honoring these checks is assessed under the loss allocation rules relevant to checks bearing only forged drawer's signatures. Therefore, Merrill Lynch is precluded by the operation of law from asserting a claim for breach of presentment warranties under the loss allocation scheme of the UCC.

INTERPRETATION The presentment warranties extend to the genuineness of the indorser's signatures but not to the signature of the drawer.

No Alteration Presenters also give a warranty of no alteration. For example, if Dolores makes a check payable to Porter's order in the amount of $30, and the amount is fraudulently raised to $30,000, the drawee bank cannot charge to the drawer's account the $30,000 it pays out on the check. The drawee bank can charge the drawer's account only $30, because that is all the drawer ordered it to pay. Nonetheless, because the presenter's warranty of no alteration has been breached, the drawee bank can collect the difference from all warrantors.

Genuineness of Drawer's Signature Presenters lastly warrant that they have no knowledge that the signature of the drawer is unauthorized. Thus, unless the presenter has knowledge that the drawer's signature is unauthorized, the drawee bears the risk that the drawer's signature is unauthorized.

Figure 27–3 summarizes liabilities based on warranty.

All Other Payors

In all instances other than a drawee of an unaccepted draft or uncertified check, the only presentment warranty that is given is that the warrantor is a person

FIGURE 27–3 Liability Based on Warranty

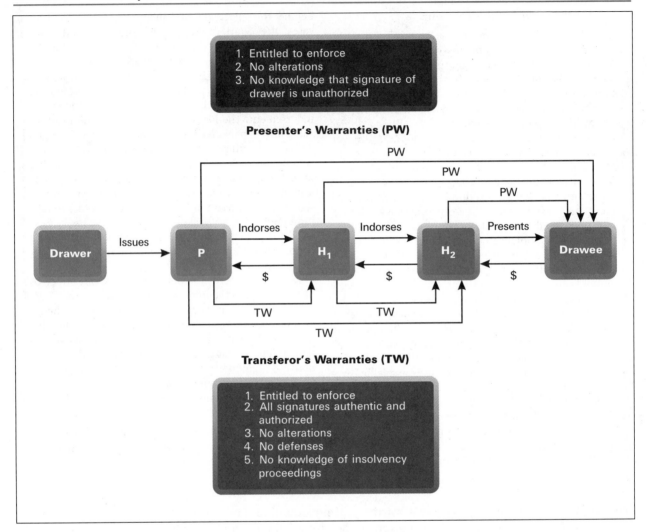

entitled to enforce the instrument or is authorized to obtain payment on behalf of the person entitled to enforce the instrument. This warranty is given by the person obtaining payment and prior transferors and applies to the presentment of notes and accepted drafts for the benefit of any party obliged to pay the instrument, including an indorser. It also applies to presentment of dishonored drafts if made to the drawer or an indorser.

The warranties of no alteration and authenticity of the drawer's signature are not given to all other payors. These warranties are not necessary for makers and drawers since they should know their own signatures and the terms of their instruments. Similarly, indorsers have already warranted the authenticity of signatures and that the instrument was not altered. Finally, acceptors should know the terms of the instrument when they accepted it; moreover, they did receive the full presentment warranties when they as drawees accepted the draft upon presentment.

ETHICAL DILEMMA Who Gets to Pass the Buck on a Forged Indorsement?

FACTS Tom West goes to Libertyville Currency Exchange to cash a check for $3,525. The check belongs to West's friend, John Reston, who accompanies him. The check is a certified check drawn on NationsBank and made payable to the order of "Piscitello Enterprises, Inc." and indorsed on the reverse side by "Joe Piscitello."

Since West often transacts business at the currency exchange, the clerk, Rita Bosworth, recognizes him as soon as he walks in. West indorses the check and hands it to Bosworth, who dispenses the cash. West immediately turns to Reston, giving him some money.

Later, Libertyville Currency Exchange deposits the check with First National Bank, which eventually files a claim against the currency exchange because the indorsement "Joe Piscitello" has been forged. The currency exchange pays the claim, then brings an action against West.

During the trial, Bosworth testifies that she saw Reston hand some money back to West when the two men turned away from her. West vehemently denies this. He says that he received no money in exchange for helping Reston.

Libertyville Currency Exchange claims that West breached his warranty of good title under the transferor's warranty by obtaining payment for a check on which the payee's indorsement was forged. West, on the other hand, argues that he signed the check to lend his name to another party and that he is thus an accommodation party. He maintains that he is not liable to Libertyville Currency Exchange because NationsBank did not give him timely notice that the signature on the check was forged and also because the Currency Exchange paid the check, thus releasing him from liability as an accommodation indorser.

Social, Policy, and Ethical Considerations

1. How could the bank have prevented this problem? Is a clerk responsible for knowing exactly who is cashing a check and who gave value for it? What steps, if any, could Rita Bosworth have taken to verify the check's indorsements?

2. Did Tom West have a responsibility to ensure that his friend's check was legitimate? Should he have inquired about the indorsement?

3. What issues relating to the transfer of a negotiable instrument are involved here? What liability does the bank face? What liability does Tom West face? What warranties apply to each party?

CHAPTER SUMMARY

Contractual Liability

General Principles	**Liability on the Instrument** no person has contractual liability on an instrument unless her signature appears on it
	Signature a signature may be made by the individual herself or by her authorized agent
	■ *Authorized Signatures* an agent who executes a negotiable instrument on behalf of his principal is not liable if the instrument is executed properly and as authorized
	■ *Unauthorized Signatures* include forgeries and signatures made by an agent without proper power; are generally not binding on the person whose name appears on the instrument but are binding on the unauthorized signer

Liability of Primary Parties	**Primary Liability** absolute obligation to pay a negotiable instrument
	Makers the maker guarantees that he will pay the note according to its original terms
	Acceptors a drawee has no liability on the instrument until she accepts it; she then becomes primarily liable
	  ■ *Acceptance* a drawee's signed engagement to honor the instrument
	  ■ *Certification* acceptance of a check by a bank

Liability of Secondary Parties	**Secondary (Conditional) Liability** obligation to pay a negotiable instrument that is subject to conditions precedent
	Indorsers and Drawers if the instrument is not paid by a primary party and if the conditions precedent to the liability of secondary parties are satisfied indorsers and drawers are secondarily (conditionally) liable unless they have disclaimed their liability or have a valid defense to the instrument
	Effect of Acceptance when a draft is accepted by a bank, the drawer and all prior indorsers are discharged from contractual liability
	Disclaimer by Secondary Parties a drawer (except of a check) or indorser may disclaim liability by a qualified drawing or indorsing ("without recourse")
	Conditions Precedent to Liability
	  ■ *Drawer* liability is generally only contingent upon dishonor and does not require notice
	  ■ *Indorser* liability is contingent upon dishonor and notice of dishonor

Liability for Conversion	**Tort Liability** conversion occurs (1) when a drawee refuses to return a draft that was presented for acceptance, (2) when any person refuses to return an instrument after he dishonors it, or (3) when an instrument is paid on a forged indorsement

Termination of Liability	**Effect of Discharge** potential liability of parties to the instrument is terminated
	Discharge
	  ■ *Performance*
	  ■ *Tender of Payment* for interest, costs, and attorney's fees
	  ■ *Cancellation*
	  ■ *Renunciation*

Liability Based on Warranty

Warranties on Transfer	**Parties** ■ *Warrantor* any person who transfers an instrument and receives consideration makes certain transferor's warranties ■ *Beneficiary* if the transfer is by delivery, the warranties run only to the immediate transferee; if the transfer is by indorsement, the warranties run to any subsequent holder who takes the instrument in good faith **Warranties** ■ *Entitled to Enforce* ■ *All Signatures Are Authentic and Authorized* ■ *No Alteration* ■ *No Defenses* ■ *No Knowledge of Insolvency*

Warranties on Presentment	**Parties** ■ *Warrantor* all people who obtain payment or acceptance of an instrument as well as all prior transferors give the presenter's warranties ■ *Beneficiary* the presenter's warranties run to any person who in good faith pays or accepts an instrument **Warranties** ■ *Entitled to Enforce* ■ *No Alteration* ■ *Genuineness of Drawer's Signature*

QUESTIONS

1. Discuss contractual liability, warranty liability, and liability for conversion.
2. Discuss the liability of makers, acceptors, drawees, drawers, indorsers, and accommodation parties.
3. Discuss the conditions precedent to the liability of secondary parties.
4. Compare the warranties on transfer with the warranties on presentment.
5. Discuss the methods by which liability on an instrument may be terminated.

Internet Question. Compare the provisions governing liability and discharge contained in the United Nations Convention on International Bills of Exchange and International Promissory Notes with those of Article 3 of the Uniform Commercial Code.

PROBLEMS

1. $800.00   Smalltown, Illinois
                                                November 15, 1997

The undersigned promises to pay to the order of John Doe, Nine Hundred Dollars with interest from date of note. Payment to be made in five monthly installments of One Hundred Eighty Dollars, plus accrued interest beginning on December 1, 1997. In the event of default in the payment of any installment or interest on installment date, the holder of this instrument may declare the entire obligation due and owing and proceed forthwith to collect the balance due on this instrument.

                                                (signed) Acton, agent

On December 18, no payment having been made on the note, Doe indorsed and delivered the instrument to Todd to secure a preexisting debt in the amount of $800.

On January 18, 1998, Todd brought an action against Acton and Phi Corporation, Acton's principal, to collect the full amount of the instrument with interest. Acton defended on the basis that he signed the instrument in a representative capacity and that Doe had failed to deliver the consideration for which the instrument had been issued. Phi Corporation defended on the basis that it did not sign the instrument and that its name does not appear on the instrument.

For what amount, if any, are Acton and Phi Corporation liable?

2. While employed as a night watchman at the place of business of A. B. Cate Trucking Company, Fred Fain observed that the office safe had been left unlocked. It contained fifty payroll checks, which were ready for distribution to employees two days later. The checks had all been signed by the sole proprietor, Cate. Fain removed five of these checks and two blank checks that were also in the safe. Fain forged the indorsements of the payees on the five payroll checks and cashed them at local supermarkets. He then filled out one of the blank checks, making himself payee, and forged Cate's signature as drawer. After cashing that check at a supermarket, Fain departed by airplane to Jamaica. The six checks were promptly presented for payment to the drawee bank, the Bank of Emanon, which paid each one. Shortly thereafter, Cate learned about the missing payroll checks and forgeries and demanded that the Bank of Emanon credit his account with the amount of the six checks.

Must the Bank comply with Cate's demand? What are the Bank's rights, if any, against the supermarkets? You may assume that the supermarkets cashed all of the checks in good faith.

3. A negotiable promissory note executed and delivered by B to C passed in due course to and was indorsed in blank by C, D, E, and F. G, the present holder, strikes out D's indorsement. What is the liability of D on her indorsement?

4. On June 15, 1992, Joanne, for consideration, executed a negotiable promissory note for $10,000, payable to Robert on or before June 15, 1997. Joanne subsequently suffered financial reverses. In January of 1997, Robert on two occasions told Joanne that he knew she was having a difficult time, that he, Robert, did not need the money, and that the debt should be considered completely canceled with no other act or payment being required. These conversations were witnessed by three persons, including Larry. On March 15, 1997, Robert changed his mind and indorsed the note for value to Larry. The note was not paid by June 15, 1997, and Larry sued Joanne for the amount of the note. Joanne defended upon the ground that Robert had canceled the debt and renounced all rights against Joanne and that Larry had notice of this fact. Decision?

5. Tate and Fitch were longtime friends. Tate was a man of considerable means; Fitch had encountered finan-

cial difficulties. In order to bolster his failing business, Fitch desired to borrow $6,000 from Farmers Bank of Erehwon. To accomplish this, he persuaded Tate to aid him in the making of a promissory note by which it would appear that Tate had the responsibility of maker, but with Fitch's agreeing to pay the instrument when due. Accordingly, they executed the following instrument:

> December 1, 1997
> Thirty days after date and for value received, I promise to pay to the order of Frank Fitch the sum of $6,000.
>
> /s/ Timothy Tate

On the back of the note, Fitch indorsed, "Pay to the order of Farmers Bank of Erehwon /s/ Frank Fitch" and delivered it to the bank in exchange for $6,000.

When the note was not paid at maturity, the bank, without first demanding payment by Fitch, brought an action on the note against Tate. (a) Decision? (b) If Tate voluntarily pays the note to the bank, may he then recover on the note against Fitch, who appears as an indorser?

6. Alpha orally appointed Omega as his agent to find and purchase for him a 1930 Dodge automobile in good condition, and Omega located such a car. Its owner, Roe, agreed to sell and deliver the car on January 10, 1998, for $9,000. To evidence the purchase price, Omega mailed to Roe the following instrument:

> December 1, 1997
> $9,000.00
>
> We promise to pay to the order of bearer Nine Thousand Dollars with interest from date of this instrument on or before January 10, 1998. This note is given in consideration of John Roe's transferring title to and possession of his 1930 Dodge automobile.
>
> (Signed) Omega, agent

Smith stole the note from Roe's mailbox, indorsed Roe's name on the note, and promptly discounted it with Sunset Bank for $8,700. Not having received the note, Roe sold the car to a third party. On January 10, 1998, the bank, having discovered all the facts, demanded payment of the note from Alpha and Omega. Both refused payment.

What are Sunset Bank's rights with regard to Omega? Its rights with regard to Roe and Smith?

7. In payment of the purchase price of a used motorboat that had been fraudulently misrepresented, Young signed and delivered to Armstrong his negotiable note in the amount of $2,000 due October 1, with Selby as an accommodation co-maker. Young intended to use the boat for his fishing business. Armstrong indorsed the note in blank preparatory to discounting it. Tillman

stole the note from Armstrong and delivered it to McGowan on July 1 in payment of a past-due debt in the amount of $600 that he owed to McGowan, with McGowan making up the difference by giving Tillman his check for $800 and an oral promise to pay Tillman an additional $600 on October 1.

When McGowan demanded payment of the note on December 1, both Young and Selby refused to pay the note because the note had not been presented for payment on its due date and because Armstrong had fraudulently misrepresented the motorboat for which the note had been executed.

What are McGowan's rights, if any, against Young, Selby, Tillman, and Armstrong, respectively?

8. On July 1, Anderson sold D'Aveni, a jeweler, a necklace containing imitation gems, which Anderson fraudulently represented to be diamonds. In payment for the necklace, D'Aveni executed and delivered to Anderson her promissory note for $25,000 dated July 1 and payable on December 1 to Anderson's order with interest at 12 percent per annum.

The note was thereafter successively indorsed in blank and delivered by Anderson to Bylinski, by Bylinski to Conrad, and by Conrad to Shearson, who became a holder in due course on August 10. On November 1, D'Aveni discovered Anderson's fraud and immediately notified Anderson, Bylinski, Conrad, and Shearson that she would not pay the note when it became due. Bylinski, a friend of Shearson, requested that Shearson release him from liability on the note, and Shearson, as a favor to Bylinski and for no other consideration, struck out Bylinski's indorsement.

On November 15, Shearson, who was solvent and had no creditors, indorsed the note to the order of Frederick, his father, and delivered it to Frederick as a gift. At the same time, Shearson told Frederick of D'Aveni's statement that D'Aveni would not pay the note when it became due. Frederick presented the note to D'Aveni for payment on December 1, but D'Aveni refused to pay. Thereafter, Frederick gave due notice of dishonor to Anderson, Bylinski, and Conrad.

What are Frederick's rights, if any, against Anderson, Bylinski, Conrad, and D'Aveni on the note?

9. Saul sold goods to Bruce, warranting that the goods were of a specified quality. The goods were not of the quality warranted, however, and Saul knew this at the time of the sale. Bruce drew and delivered a check payable to Saul and drawn on Third National Bank in the amount of the purchase price. Bruce subsequently discovered the goods were faulty and stopped payment on the check. Saul brings a suit against Bruce. Decision?

10. R & A Concrete Contractors, Inc., executed a promissory note that identifies both R & A Concrete and Grover Roberts as its makers. On the reverse side of the note, the following appears: "X John Ament Sec. & Treas." National Bank of Georgia, the payee, now sues both R & A Concrete and Ament on the note. Decision?

11. On August 10, 1964, Theta Electronic Laboratories, Inc. executed a promissory note to George and Marguerite Thomson. Three other individuals, Gerald Exten, Emil O'Neil, and James Hane, and their wives also indorsed the note. The note was then transferred to Hane by the Thomsons on November 26, 1965. Although a default occurred at this time, it was not until April 1967, eighteen months later, that Hane gave notice of the dishonor and made a demand for payment on the Extens as indorsers. Hane appeals from a judgment in favor of the Extens. Decision?

CHAPTER 28

Bank Deposits, Collections, and Funds Transfers

In today's society, most goods and services are bought and sold without a physical transfer of "money." Credit cards, charge accounts, and various deferred payment plans have made cash sales increasingly rare. But even credit sales must ultimately be settled—when they are, payment is usually made by check rather than with cash. If the parties to a sales transaction happen to have accounts at the same bank, a transfer of credit is easily accomplished. In the vast majority of cases, however, the parties do business at different banks. Then the buyer's check must journey from the seller-payee's bank (the depositary bank), where the check is deposited by the seller for credit to his account, to the buyer-drawer's bank (the payor bank) for payment. In this collection process, the check frequently passes through one or more other banks (intermediary banks), each of which must accurately record its passing, before it may be collected. Our banking system has developed a network to handle the collection of checks and other instruments.

In recent years, the amount of payment made by electronic funds transfers has increased at an astounding rate. The dollar volume of commercial payments made by wire transfer far exceeds the dollar amount made by checks or credit cards. In addition, electronic fund transfers have become exceedingly popular with consumers. Consumer electronic funds transfers are covered by the Federal Electronic Fund Transfer Act; nonconsumer (wholesale) electronic transfers are covered by Article 4A of the Uniform Commercial Code.

This chapter will cover both the bank deposit–collection system and electronic funds transfers.

BANK DEPOSITS AND COLLECTIONS

Article 4 of the UCC, entitled "Bank Deposits and Collections," provides the principal rules governing the bank collection process. Since items in the bank collection process are essentially those covered by Article 3, "Commercial Paper," and to a lesser extent by Article 8, "Investment Securities," these Articles often apply to a bank collection problem. In addition, Articles 3 and 4 are supplemented and, at times, preempted by Federal law: the Expedited Funds Availability Act and its implementing Federal Reserve Regulation (Regulation CC). This section will cover the collection of an item through the banking system and the relationship between the payor bank and its customer.

COLLECTION OF ITEMS

When a person deposits a check in his bank (the **depositary bank**), the bank credits his account by the amount of the check. This initial crediting is **provisional**. Normally, a bank does not permit a customer to draw funds against a provisional credit; by permitting its customer to thus draw, the bank will have given *value* and, provided it meets the other requirements, will be a holder in due course. Under the customer's contract with his bank, the bank is obligated to make a reasonable effort to obtain payment of all checks deposited for collection. When the amount of the check has been collected from the payor bank (the drawee), the credit becomes a **final credit**.

The Competitive Equality Banking Act of 1987 has expedited the availability of funds by establishing maximum time periods for which a bank may hold (and thereby deny a customer access to the funds represented by) various types of instruments. Under the Act, (1) cash deposits, wire transfers, government checks, the first $100 of a day's check deposits, cashier's checks, and checks deposited in one branch of a depositary institution and drawn on the same or another branch of the same institution must clear by the next business day; (2) local checks must clear within one intervening business day; and (3) nonlocal checks must clear in no more than four intervening business days.

If the payor bank (the drawee bank) does not pay the check for some reason, such as a stop payment order or insufficient funds in the drawer's account, the depositary bank reverses the provisional credit to the account, debits his account for that amount, and returns the check to him with a statement of the reason for nonpayment. If, in the meantime, the customer has been permitted to draw against the provisional credit, the bank may recover the payment from him.

In some cases, the bank involved is both the depositary bank and the payor bank. In most cases, however, the depositary and payor banks are different, in which event the bank collection aspects of Article 4 come into play. Where the depositary and payor banks differ, it is necessary for the item to pass from one to the other, either directly through a clearinghouse or through one or more **intermediary banks** (banks, other than the depositary or payor bank, that are involved in the collection process, such as one of the twelve Federal Reserve Banks), as illustrated in Figure 28–1. A **clearinghouse** is an association, composed of banks or other payors, whose members settle accounts with each other on a daily basis. Each member of the clearinghouse forwards all deposited checks drawn on other members and receives from the clearinghouse all checks drawn on it. Balances are adjusted and settled each day.

Collecting Banks

A **collecting bank** is any bank, other than the payor bank, handling an item for payment. In the usual situation, where the depositary and payor banks are different, the depositary bank gives a provisional credit to its customer, transfers the item to the next bank in the chain, and receives a provisional credit or "settlement" from it; the process repeats until the item reaches the payor bank, which gives a provisional settlement to its transferor. When the item is paid, all the provisional settlements given by the respective banks in the chain become final, and the particular transaction has been completed. Because this procedure simplifies bookkeeping by necessitating only one entry if the item is paid, no adjustment is necessary on the books of any of the banks involved.

Depositary bank the bank in which the payee or holder deposits the check for credit

Provisional credit tentative credit for the deposit of an instrument until final credit is given

Final credit payment of the instrument by the payor bank; if the payor bank (drawee) does not pay the check, the depositary bank reverses the provisional credit

Intermediary bank a bank, other than the depositary or payor bank, involved in the collection process

Clearinghouse an association of banks for the purpose of settling accounts on a daily basis

Collecting bank any bank (other than the payor bank) handling the item for payment

FIGURE 28–1 Bank Collections

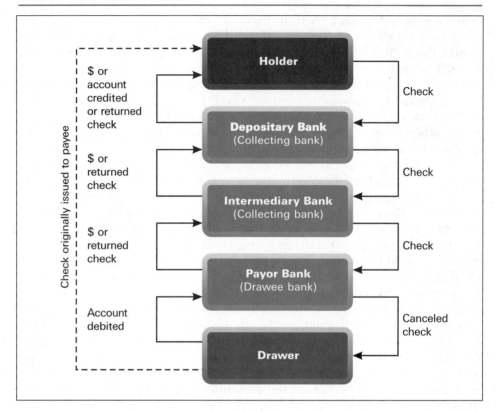

If, however, the payor bank does not pay the check, it returns the item, and each intermediary or collecting bank reverses the provisional settlement or credit it previously gave to its forwarding bank. Ultimately, the depositary bank will charge (remove the provisional credit from) the account of the customer who deposited the item. The customer must then seek recovery from the indorsers or the drawer.

Agent collecting bank is an agent or subagent of the owner of the check until the settlement becomes final

A collecting bank is an **agent** or subagent of the owner of the item until the settlement becomes final. Unless otherwise provided, any credit given for the item initially is provisional. Once settled, the agency relationship changes to one of *debtor-creditor*. The effect of this agency rule is that the risk of loss remains with the owner and that any chargebacks go to her, not to the collecting bank.

All collecting banks have certain responsibilities and duties in collecting checks and other items. These will now be discussed.

Duty of care a collecting bank must exercise ordinary care in handling an item

Duty of Care A collecting bank must exercise ordinary care in handling an item transferred to it for collection. The steps it takes in presenting an item or sending it for presentment are of particular importance. It must act within a reasonable time after receipt of the item and must choose a reasonable method of forwarding the item for presentment. It also is responsible for using care in routing and in selecting intermediary banks or other agents.

Duty to act timely a collecting bank acts timely if it takes proper action before its midnight deadline

Duty to Act Timely Closely related to the collecting bank's duty of care is its duty to act in a timely manner. A collecting bank acts timely in any event if it takes proper action, such as forwarding or presenting an item before the "midnight deadline" following its receipt of the item, notice, or payment. If the bank adheres to this standard, the timeliness of its action cannot be challenged; should it, however, take a reasonably longer time, the bank bears the burden of proof in establishing timeliness. The **midnight deadline** is the midnight of the banking day following the banking day on which the bank received the item or notice. Thus, if a bank receives a check on Monday, it must take proper action by midnight on the next banking day, or Tuesday. A banking day means the part of a day on which a bank is open to the public for carrying on substantially all of its banking functions.

The midnight deadline presents a problem because it takes time to process an item through a bank—whether it be the depositary, intermediary, or payor bank. If a day's transactions are to be completed without overtime work, the bank must either close early or fix an earlier cutoff time for the day's work. Accordingly, the Code provides that for the purpose of allowing time to process items, prove balances, and make the bookkeeping entries necessary to determine its position for the day, a bank may fix an afternoon hour of 2:00 P.M. or later as a cutoff point for handling money and items and for making entries on its books. Items received after the cutoff hour fixed as the close of the banking day are considered to have been received at the opening of the next banking day, and the time for taking action and for determining the bank's midnight deadline begins to run from that point.

Recognizing that everyone involved will be greatly inconvenienced if an item is not paid, the Code provides that unless otherwise instructed, a collecting bank in a good faith effort to secure payment may, in the case of a specific item drawn on a payor other than a bank, waive, modify, or extend the time limits, but not in excess of two additional banking days. This extension may be made without the approval of the parties involved and without discharging drawers or indorsers. This section does not apply to checks and other drafts drawn on a bank. The Code also authorizes delay when communications or computer facilities are interrupted as a result of blizzard, flood, hurricane, or other disaster; the suspension of payments by another bank; war; emergency conditions; failure of equipment; or other circumstances beyond the bank's control. Nevertheless, such delay will be excused only if the bank exercises such diligence as the circumstances require.

Indorsements   An item restrictively indorsed with words such as "pay any bank" is locked into the bank collection system, and only a bank may acquire the rights of a holder. When forwarding an item for collection, a bank normally indorses the item "pay any bank," irrespective of the type of indorsement, if any, that the item carried at the time of receipt. This serves to protect the collecting bank by making it impossible for the item to stray from regular collection channels.

If the item had no indorsement when the depositary bank received it, the bank nonetheless becomes a holder of the item at the time it takes possession of the item for collection if the customer was a holder at the time of delivery to the bank and, if the bank satisfies the other requirements of a holder in due course, it will become a holder in due course in its own right. In return, the bank warrants to the collecting banks, the payor, and the drawer that it has paid the amount of the item to the customer or deposited that amount to the customer's account. This rule speeds up the collection process by eliminating the necessity of returning checks for indorsement when the depositary bank knows they came from its customers.

Warranties customers and collecting banks give warranties on transfer, presentment, and encoding

Warranties Customers and collecting banks give substantially the same warranties as those given by parties under Article 3 upon presentment and transfer, which were discussed in Chapter 27. In addition, under Article 4, customers and collecting banks may give encoding warranties. Each customer or collecting bank who transfers an item and receives a settlement or other consideration warrants to his transferee and any subsequent collecting bank that (1) he is a person entitled to enforce the item; (2) *all* signatures are authentic and authorized; (3) the item has not been altered; (4) he is not subject to any defense or claim in recoupment; and (5) he has no knowledge of any insolvency proceeding involving the maker or acceptor or the drawer of an unaccepted draft. Moreover, each customer or collecting bank who obtains payment or acceptance from a drawee on a draft as well as each prior transferor warrants to the drawee who pays or accepts the draft in good faith that (1) she is a person entitled to enforce the draft; (2) the item has not been altered; and (3) she has no knowledge that the signature of the drawer is unauthorized.

Processing of checks is now done by Magnetic Ink Character Recognition (MICR). When a check is deposited, the depositary bank magnetically encodes the check with the amount of the check (all checks are pre-encoded with the drawer's account number and the designation of the drawee bank), after which the processing occurs automatically, without further human involvement. Despite its efficiency, the magnetic encoding of checks has created several problems. The first is the problem a bank encounters when paying a postdated instrument prior to its date. The Revision changes prior law by providing that the drawee may debit the drawer's account, unless the drawer timely informs the drawee that the check is postdated. A second difficulty arises when a depositing bank or its customer who encodes her own checks miscodes a check. Revised Article 4 provides that such an encoder warrants to any subsequent collecting bank and to the payor that information on a check is properly encoded. If the encoding is done by the customer, the depositary bank also makes the warranty.

GREAT LAKES HIGHER EDUCATION CORP. v. AUSTIN BANK OF CHICAGO United States District Court, Northern District of Illinois, E.D., 1993, 837 F. Supp. 892

FACTS Between October 1990, and January, 1992, Great Lakes Higher Education Corp. (Great Lakes), a not-for-profit student loan servicer, issued 224 student loan checks totaling $273,152.88. The checks were drawn against Great Lakes's account at First Wisconsin National Bank of Milwaukee (First Wisconsin). Each of the 224 checks were presented to Austin Bank of Chicago (Austin Bank) without indorsement of the named payee. Austin Bank accepted each check for purposes of collection and without delay forwarded each check to First Wisconsin for that purpose. First Wisconsin paid Austin Bank the face amount of each check even though the indorsement signature of the payee was not on any of the checks. In February, 1992, First Wisconsin, claiming breach of warranty due to the absence of proper indorsements, requested that Austin Bank refund these payments. Austin Bank did not respond to this request. Subsequently, First Wisconsin and Great Lakes filed suit, claiming, among other things, negligence in the presentment of certain checks and breach of warranty to a third party.

DECISION Negligence claims and breach of warranty to a third party are dismissed with prejudice.

OPINION [Author's Note: This case applies Revised Articles 3 and 4.] The plaintiffs have claimed negligence in the presentment of checks as a theory of recovery. Presentment under the UCC means "a demand made by or on behalf of a person entitled to enforce an instrument. . . ." Under the Code, a collecting bank such as Austin Bank is required to use ordinary care in the presentment of checks or the sending of checks for presentment. Comments to this section of the Code further indicate that where the collecting bank is itself presenting the check for payment, it must use ordinary care with respect to the time and manner of the presentment. However, where the collecting bank is merely sending the check for presentment, it must exercise ordinary care

continued

in the routing of the check and the selection of intermediary banks. In this case, Austin Bank was merely sending the checks for presentment. Therefore, since Austin Bank used ordinary care with respect to routing and choosing intermediaries, it is not liable.

Great Lakes also alleges that it is the third-party beneficiary of a transfer warranty owed by Austin Bank to First Wisconsin. The Code provides, in relevant part, "a customer or collecting bank . . . warrants to the transferee and to any subsequent collecting bank that . . . all signatures on the item are authentic and authorized."

However, the majority of courts and the comments to the Code do not allow a drawer to maintain an action as a third-party beneficiary. Therefore, Great Lakes's claim that it is entitled to relief as a third-party beneficiary of Austin Bank's warranty to First Wisconsin is dismissed.

INTERPRETATION A collecting bank must use ordinary care in handling an item for collection and it does not owe a transfer warranty to a drawer of the instrument.

THE FIRST NATIONAL BANK OF BOSTON v. FIDELITY BANK, N. A. United States District Court,
E.D. Pennsylvania, 1989, 724 F.Supp. 1168, aff'd, 908 F.2d. 962 (3rd Cir. 1990)

FACTS On September 22, 1986, New York City Shoes (NYCS) issued a check in the amount of $100,000 to the Maxwell Shoe Company (Maxwell). The check was drawn on one of NYCS's accounts at Pennsylvania Fidelity Bank. Maxwell deposited the check in its account at the First National Bank of Boston (Boston), which credited Maxwell's account with the face amount of the check and then processed the check through the Federal Reserve system. Checks presently are processed by Magnetic Ink Character Recognition (MICR). Under this procedure, each bank check is preprinted with magnetic characters along the lower left-hand edge. These characters designate the bank upon which the check is drawn and the account number of the drawer. When a check is presented to another bank (the depositary bank), that bank adds additional magnetic encoding, at the lower right-hand side of the check, specifying the amount of the check. From there, the check goes through the bank clearing system to the bank on which the check is drawn (the payor bank) and is charged against the drawer's account without further human intervention.

In this case, Boston properly encoded NYCS's check, but NYCS's account contained insufficient funds; consequently, Fidelity returned the check to Boston. Boston did not charge Maxwell's account because of the check's uncollectibility, but instead re-presented the check to Fidelity. To the bottom of the check, Boston attached a "tape skirt," on which it re-encoded the check so that it could be processed through the Federal Reserve system. Boston's encoder made an error, however, and encoded the amount of the check as $10,000, rather than $100,000. The computers that processed the check did not detect the error. When the check arrived at Fidelity on October 3, 1986, it was charged against NYCS's account in the amount of $10,000. Boston, which became aware of the error only after

that sum was forwarded to it, then made demand on Fidelity for $90,000. Fidelity replied that it was unable to honor the request because NYCS's account was insufficient to cover it.

Boston filed suit against Fidelity for the $90,000, arguing that Fidelity was liable under the "final payment" rule of the UCC, which provides that "[a]n item is finally paid by a payor bank when the bank . . . has completed the process of posting the item to the indicated account of the drawer, maker or other person to be charged therewith. . . . Upon a final payment . . . the payor bank shall be accountable for the amount of the item."

Boston argued that Fidelity did post the check against NYCS's account on October 3, 1986, and therefore, under the Code, was accountable to Boston for the amount of the check. Boston further argued that it was irrelevant that the check was encoded in the wrong amount, since it was undisputed that Fidelity "completed the process of posting the item to the indicated account of the drawer" on October 3, 1986. Fidelity countered that for purposes of the Code, the "amount of the item" for which the payor bank must account should be the encoded amount of the check, rather than its actual face amount.

DECISION Judgment for Fidelity.

OPINION We reject Fidelity's argument that under the final payment rule, the "amount of the item" is the encoded amount, rather than the face amount, of the check. If the encoded amount were greater than the face amount of the check, the error would produce a windfall for the collecting bank and would unjustifiably increase the potential liability of the payor bank, the drawer, or both. Rather, the "amount of the item" under the final payment rule is the face amount of the check or the encoded amount, whichever is less. This basically means

continued

that as between the encoding bank and all other banks in the collecting process, including the payor bank, the encoder is estopped from claiming more than the encoded amount of the check. Therefore, Fidelity is not liable to Boston under the Code's final payment rule.

INTERPRETATION   Revised Article 4 provides that an encoder warrants that information on a check is properly encoded.

Final Payment   The provisional settlements made in the collection chain are all directed toward final payment of the item by the payor bank. From this turnaround point in the collection process, the proceeds of the item begin their return flow, and provisional settlements become final. For example, a customer of the California Country State Bank may deposit a check drawn on the State of Maine Country National Bank. The check may then take a course such as follows: from the California Country State Bank to a correspondent bank in San Francisco, to the Federal Reserve Bank of San Francisco, to the Federal Reserve Bank of Boston, to the payor bank. Provisional settlements are made at each step. When the payor finally pays the item, the proceeds begin to flow back over the same course.

The critical question, then, is the point at which the payor has *paid* the item, since this not only commences the payment process but also affects questions of priority between the payment of an item and actions such as the filing of a stop payment order against it. Under the Code, **final payment** occurs when the payor bank first does any of the following: (1) pays an item in cash; (2) settles an item and does not have the right to revoke the settlement through statute, clearinghouse rule, or agreement; or (3) makes a provisional settlement and does not revoke it within the time and in the manner permitted by statute, clearinghouse rule, or agreement.

Payor Banks

The **payor** or drawee **bank**, under its contract of deposit with the drawer, agrees to pay to the payee or his order a check issued by the drawer, provided that the order is not countermanded, and that there are sufficient funds in the drawer's account.

The tremendous increase in volume of bank collections has necessitated deferred posting procedures, whereby items are sorted and proved on the day of receipt but are not posted to customers' accounts or returned until the next banking day. The UCC not only approves such procedures but establishes specific standards to govern their application to the actions of payor banks.

When a payor bank that is not also a depositary bank receives a demand item other than for immediate payment over the counter, it must either return the item or give its transferor a provisional settlement before midnight of the banking day on which the item is received. Otherwise, the bank becomes liable to its transferor for the amount of the item, unless it has a valid defense, such as breach of a presentment warranty.

If the payor bank gives the provisional settlement as required, it has until the midnight deadline to return the item or, if the item is held for protest or is otherwise unavailable for return, to send written notice of dishonor or nonpayment. After doing this, the bank is entitled to revoke the settlement and recover any payment it has made. Should it fail to return the item or send notice before its

Final payment occurs when the payor bank does any of the following, whichever happens first: (1) pays an item in cash; (2) settles and does not have the right to revoke the settlement; or (3) makes a provisional settlement and does not properly revoke it

Payor bank under its contract with the drawer, the payor or drawee bank agrees to pay to the payee or his order checks that are issued by the drawer, provided the order is not countermanded by a stop payment order and provided there are sufficient funds in the drawer's account

midnight deadline, the payor bank will be accountable for the amount of the item unless it has a valid defense for its inaction.

There are innumerable reasons why a bank may dishonor an item and return it or send notice. The following situations are the most common: the drawer or maker may have no account or may have funds insufficient to cover the item; a signature on the item may be forged; or the drawer or maker may have stopped payment of the item.

RELATIONSHIP BETWEEN PAYOR BANK AND ITS CUSTOMER

The relationship between a payor bank and its checking account customer is primarily the product of their contractual arrangement. Although the parties have relatively broad latitude in establishing the terms of their agreement and in altering the provisions of the Code, a bank may not validly (1) disclaim responsibility for its lack of good faith, (2) disclaim responsibility for its failure to exercise ordinary care, or (3) limit its damages for a breach comprising such lack or failure. The parties may by agreement, however, determine the standards by which the bank's responsibility is to be measured, if these standards are not clearly unreasonable.

Contractual relationship the relationship between a payor bank and its checking account customer is primarily the product of their contractual arrangement

Payment of an Item

A payor owes a duty to its customer, the drawer, to pay checks properly drawn by him on an account having funds sufficient to cover the items. A check or draft, however, is not an assignment of the drawer's funds that are in the drawee's possession. Moreover, as discussed in Chapter 27, the drawee is not liable on a check until it accepts the item. Therefore, the *holder* of a check has no right to require the drawee bank to pay it, whether the drawer's account contains sufficient funds or not. But if a payor bank improperly refuses payment when presented with an item, it will incur a liability to the *customer* from whose account the item should have been paid. If the customer has adequate funds on deposit, and there is no other valid basis for the refusal to pay, the bank is liable to its customer for damages proximately caused by the *wrongful dishonor*. Liability is limited to actual damages proved and may include damages for arrest, prosecution, or other consequential damages.

Payment of an item when a payor receives an item for which the funds in the account are insufficient, the bank may either dishonor the item and return it or pay the item and charge the customer's account even though an overdraft is created

When a payor bank receives an item properly payable from a customer's account but the funds in the account are insufficient to pay it, the bank may (1) dishonor the item and return it or (2) pay the item and charge its customer's account, even though the actions create an overdraft. The item authorizes or directs the bank to make the payment and hence carries with it an enforceable implied promise to reimburse the bank. Further, the customer may be liable to pay the bank a service charge for its handling of the overdraft or to pay interest on the amount of the overdraft. A customer, however, is not liable for an overdraft if the customer did not sign the item or benefit from the proceeds of the item.

A payor bank is under no obligation to its customer to pay an uncertified check that is over six months old. This rule reflects the usual banking practice of consulting a depositor before paying a *stale* item (one over six months old) on her account. The bank is not required to dishonor such an item, however; and if the bank makes payment in good faith, it may charge the amount of the item to its customer's account.

Stop Payment Orders

A check drawn on a bank is an order to pay a sum of money and an authorization to charge the amount to the drawer's account. The customer, or any person authorized to draw on the account, may countermand this order, however, by means of a **stop payment order**. If the order does not come too late, the bank is bound by it. If the bank inadvertently pays a check over a valid stop order, it is *prima facie* liable to the customer, but only to the extent of the customer's loss resulting from the payment. The burden of establishing the fact and amount of loss is on the customer.

To be effective, a stop payment order must be received in time to provide the bank a reasonable opportunity to act on it. An oral stop order is binding on the bank for only fourteen calendar days. If the customer confirms an oral stop order in writing within the fourteen-day period, the order is effective for six months and may be renewed in writing for additional six-month periods.

The fact that a drawer has filed a stop payment order does not automatically relieve her of liability. If the bank honors the stop payment order and returns the check, the holder may bring an action against the drawer. If the holder qualifies as a holder in due course, personal defenses that the drawer might have to such an action would be of no avail.

Stop payment order an oral stop payment order (a command for a drawer to a drawee not to pay an instrument) is binding for fourteen calendar days; a written order is effective for six months and may be renewed in writing

---

SINISCALCHI v. VALLEY BANK OF NEW YORK District Court, Nassau County, Second District, 1974, 79 Misc.2d 64, 359 N.Y.S.2d 173

FACTS On Tuesday, June 11, Siniscalchi issued a $200 check on the drawee, Valley Bank. On Saturday morning, June 15, the check was cashed. This transaction, as well as others taking place on that Saturday morning, was not recorded or processed through the bank's bookkeeping system until Monday, June 17. On that date, Siniscalchi arrived at the bank at 9:00 A.M. and asked to place a stop payment order on the check. A bank employee checked the bank records, which at that time indicated the instrument had not cleared the bank. At 9:45 A.M., she gave him a printed notice confirming his request to stop payment. Siniscalchi sought to recover the $200 paid on the check.

DECISION Judgment for Valley Bank granted.

OPINION A customer has a right to stop payment on a check, but the stop payment order must be received at such time and in such manner as to afford the bank a reasonable opportunity to act on the stop payment. Here, the check was cashed before the stop payment order was issued, and, hence, the stop payment order did not effectively bind Valley Bank.

INTERPRETATION To be effective, a stop payment order must be received in time to provide the bank a reasonable opportunity to act on it.

Bank's Right to Subrogation on Improper Payment

If a payor bank pays an item over a stop payment order, after an account has been closed, or otherwise in violation of its contract with the drawer or maker, the payor bank is subrogated to (obtains) the rights of (1) any holder in due course on the item against the drawer or maker; (2) the payee or any other holder against the drawer or maker; and (3) the drawer or maker against the payee or any other holder. For instance, over the drawer's stop payment order, a bank pays a check presented to the bank by a holder in due course. The drawer's defense is that the check was obtained by fraud in the inducement. The drawee bank is subrogated to the rights of the holder in due course, who would not be subject to the drawer's personal defense, and thus can debit the drawer's account. The same would be true if the presenter were the payee, against whom the drawer did not have a valid defense.

Bank's right to subrogation on improper payment if a payor bank pays an item over a stop payment order or otherwise in violation of its contract, the payor bank is subrogated to (obtains) the rights of (1) any holder in due course on the item against the drawer or maker; (2) the payee or any other holder against the drawer or maker; and (3) the drawer or maker against the payee or any other holder

Disclosure Requirements

In 1992, Congress enacted the Truth in Savings Act, which requires all depositary institutions (including commercial banks, savings and loan associations, savings banks, and credit unions) to disclose in great detail to consumers the terms and conditions of their deposit accounts. The stated purpose of the Act is to allow consumers to make informed decisions regarding deposit accounts by mandating standardized disclosure of rates of interest and fees in order to facilitate meaningful comparison of different deposit products.

More specifically, the Act provides that the disclosures must be made in a clear and conspicuous writing and must be given to the consumer when an account is opened or service is provided. These disclosures must include the following: (1) the annual percentage yield (APY) and the percentage rate; (2) how variable rates are calculated and when the rates may be changed; (3) balance information (including how the balance is calculated); (4) when and how interest is calculated and credited; (5) the amount of fees that may be charged and how they are calculated; and (6) any limitation on the number or amount of withdrawals or deposits. In addition, the Act requires the depositary institution to disclose the following information with periodic statements it sends to its customers: (1) the APY earned; (2) any fees debited during the covered period; (3) the dollar amount of the interest earned during the covered period; and (4) the dates of the covered period.

Customer's Death or Incompetence

The general rule is that death or incompetence revokes all agency agreements. Furthermore, adjudication of incompetency by a court is regarded as notice to the world of that fact. Actual notice is not required. The Code modifies these stringent rules in several ways with respect to bank deposits and collections.

First, if either a payor or collecting bank does not know that a customer has been adjudicated incompetent, the existence of such incompetence at the time an item is issued or its collection undertaken does not impair either bank's authority to accept, pay, or collect the item or to account for proceeds of its collection. The bank may pay the item without incurring any liability.

Second, neither death nor adjudication of incompetence of a customer revokes a payor or collecting bank's authority to accept, pay, or collect an item until the bank knows of the condition and has a reasonable opportunity to act on this knowledge.

Finally, even though a bank knows of the death of its customer, it may for ten days after the date of his death pay or certify checks drawn by the customer unless a person claiming an interest in the account, such as an heir, executor, or administrator, orders the bank to stop making such payments.

Customer's Duties

The Code imposes certain affirmative duties on bank customers and fixes time limits within which they must assert their rights. The duties arise and the time starts to run from the point at which the bank either sends or makes available to its customer a statement of account showing payment of items against the account. The statement of account will suffice provided it describes by item the number of the item, the amount, and the date of payment. The customer must exercise reasonable promptness in examining the bank statement or the items to discover whether any payment was unauthorized due to an *unauthorized signature* on or any *alteration* of an item. Since he is not presumed to know the

Customer's duties the customer must examine bank statements and items carefully and promptly to discover any unauthorized signatures or alterations

signatures of payees or indorsers, this duty of prompt and careful examination applies only to alterations and the customer's own signature, both of which he should be able to detect immediately. If he discovers an unauthorized signature or an alteration, he must notify the bank promptly. A failure to fulfill these duties of prompt examination and notice precludes the customer from asserting against the bank his unauthorized signature or any alteration if the bank establishes that it suffered a loss by reason of such failure.

Furthermore, the customer will lose his rights in a potentially more serious situation. Occasionally, a forger, possibly an employee who has access to his employer's checkbook, carries out a series of transactions involving the account of the same individual. He may forge one or more checks each month until he is finally detected. The bank, noticing nothing suspicious, might pay one or more of the customer's checks bearing the false signatures before the customer detects the forgery, months or even years later. The Code deals with these situations by stating that once the statement and items become available to him, the customer must examine them within a reasonable period, which in no event may exceed thirty calendar days and which may, under certain circumstances, be less and notify the bank. Any instruments containing alterations or unauthorized signatures by the same wrongdoer that the bank pays during that period will be the bank's responsibility, but any paid thereafter but before the customer notifies the bank may not be asserted against it. This rule is based on the concept that the loss involved is directly traceable to the customer's negligence and that, as a result, he should stand the loss.

These rules depend, however, on the bank's exercising ordinary care in paying the items involved. If it does not and that failure by the bank substantially contributed to the loss, the loss will be allocated between the bank and the customer based on their comparative negligence. But whether the bank exercised due care or not, the customer must in all events report any alteration or his unauthorized signature within one year from the time the statement or items are made available to him or be barred from asserting them against the bank. Any *unauthorized indorsement* must be asserted within three years under the Article's general Statute of Limitations provisions.

Consistent with modern automated methods for processing checks, Articles 3 and 4 provide that "ordinary care" does not require a bank to examine every check if the failure to do so does not vary unreasonably from general banking usage.

TALLY v. AMERICAN SECURITY BANK United States District Court, District of Columbia, 1982, 35 UCC Rep.Serv. 215

FACTS Tally held a savings account with American Security Bank. On seven occasions, Tally's personal secretary, who received his bank statements and had custody of his passbook, forged Tally's name on withdrawal slips that she then presented to the bank. The secretary obtained $52,825 in this manner. She confessed this to Tally after avoiding detection for several years. Tally brought an action against American Security Bank to recover the funds. The bank moved for partial summary judgment.

DECISION Partial summary judgment for American Security Bank granted.

OPINION The UCC imposes a duty upon a bank customer to inspect promptly statements and items either sent to the customer or reasonably made available to him. A customer must report any unauthorized signature on an item within one year from the time the item is made available. Tally first notified the bank of the irregularities some three years after his secretary's last withdrawal. Tally claims, however, that the one-year time limit only holds when the periodic account statement is accompanied by the items supporting it. In this case, the savings withdrawal slips were retained on file by the bank. They were, however,

continued

effectively made available to Tally when the statement was sent. Tally should have reviewed the statement and reported any problems to the bank. Since he did not do so within the specified one-year time period, he cannot recover for the allegedly forged withdrawal orders paid by the bank.

INTERPRETATION The customer must report any alteration or his unauthorized signature within one year from the statement or items that are made available to him; otherwise, he would be prohibited from asserting them against the bank.

ELECTRONIC FUND TRANSFER

As previously mentioned, the use of negotiable instruments for payment has transformed the United States into a virtually cashless society. The advent and technological advances of computers makes it likely that in the foreseeable future **electronic fund transfer** systems (EFTS) will bring about a society that is virtually checkless as well. Financial institutions seek to substitute EFTS for checks for two principal reasons. The first is to eliminate the ever-increasing paperwork involved in processing the billions of checks issued annually. The second is to eliminate the "float" that a drawer of a check currently enjoys by maintaining the use of his funds during the processing period between the time at which he issues the check and final payment.

An electronic fund transfer (EFT) has been defined as "any transfer of funds, other than a transaction originated by check, draft, or similar paper instrument, which is initiated through an electronic terminal, telephonic instrument, or computer or magnetic tape so as to order, instruct or authorize a financial institution to debit or credit an account." For example, with an EFT, William in New York would be able to pay a debt he owes to Yvette in Illinois by entering into his computer an order to his bank to pay Yvette. The drawee bank would then instantly debit William's account and transfer the credit to Yvette's bank, where Yvette's account would immediately be credited in that amount. The entire transaction would be completed in minutes.

Although EFTs are still in their formative stages, their use has generated considerable confusion concerning the legal rights of customers and financial institutions. Congress provided a partial solution to these legal issues in 1978 by enacting the Electronic Fund Transfer Act (EFTA), discussed later. But significant and numerous legal problems remain. In an attempt to resolve some of these questions, the Permanent Editorial Board of the Uniform Commercial Code has promulgated Article 4A—Fund Transfer.

Electronic fund transfer any transfer of funds, other than a transaction originated by check, draft, or similar paper instrument, which is initiated through an electronic terminal, telephonic instrument, or computer or magnetic tape so as to order, instruct, or authorize a financial institution to debit or credit an account

TYPES OF ELECTRONIC FUNDS TRANSFERS

Although a number of new EFTs are likely to appear in the coming years, five main types of EFTs are currently in use: (1) automated teller machines, (2) point-of-sale systems, (3) direct deposit and withdrawal of funds, (4) pay-by-phone systems, and (5) wholesale wire transfers.

Automated Teller Machines

Now available throughout the country, automated teller machines (ATMs), permit customers to conduct various transactions with their bank through the use

ETHICAL DILEMMA   Can Embezzlement Ever Be a Loan?

FACTS Susan Jennings was the head cashier for Pears, a highly respected discount store located in the heart of Chicago. Her job included distributing funds to each cashier, periodically collecting any large amounts from them, making a collection at the end of each shift, and depositing the previous day's receipts each morning. When a cashier brought money to Susan, the cashier would count the money and Susan would check it. At the end of each day, Susan would make out a deposit slip for the amount of cash and checks received, giving a copy of the slip to the accounting department for proper book entry. She would indorse each check with a company stamp marked "For Deposit Only."

On December 1, 1992, Alvin Troop, a new cashier, finished his shift and brought his money tray to Susan. While counting his receipts, he had noticed a check for $120 that had been made out without a payee. Alvin brought the check to Susan's attention. Matching his receipts to the cash register tape, Susan found that Alvin was exactly $120 over. Susan told him not to worry and said that she would fill in the store's name when she made the next deposit and would reconcile the receipts to the tape.

On December 2, 1992, Susan deposited the previous day's receipts in Pear's account in the First Sandy Hill Bank of Chicago, but decided to borrow $120 for her Christmas shopping. Short of cash and wanting to take advantage of a special sale, she intended to make up the difference on December 5, 1992, which was a pay day. She filled her name in on the blank check, which also was drawn on the First Sandy Hill Bank, and the bank cashed it. Three days later, she replaced the money. No one knew what she had done until the customer who had written the check received his bank statement and demanded that the bank credit his account for the amount of the check that showed Susan as the payee.

Social, Policy, and Ethical Considerations

1. Were Susan's actions unethical or illegal? Explain. Would Susan's using the money for essential items, such as food or medicine, change your answer?
2. What should Susan have done?
3. What responsibility does the First Sandy Hill Bank have to its customers? In general, are banking procedures and standards established for the benefit of the bank or for that of the public?
4. If the bank teller had any idea that Susan had done something wrong, does the fact that he may have followed banking rules relieve him of any ethical responsibility?

of electronic terminals. After activating an ATM with a plastic identification card and a personal identification number, or PIN, a customer can deposit and withdraw funds from her account, transfer funds between accounts, obtain cash advances, and make payments on loan accounts. (See Consumer Insight, "Thwarting ATM Fraud.")

Point-of-Sale Systems

Computerized point-of-sale (POS) systems permit consumers to transfer funds from their bank accounts to a merchant automatically. The POS machines, located within the merchant's store and activated by the consumer's identification card and code, instantaneously debit the consumer's account and credit the merchant's account.

Direct Deposits and Withdrawals

Another type of EFT involves deposits, authorized in advance by a customer, that are made directly to his account through an electronic terminal. Examples include direct payroll deposits, deposits of Social Security payments, and deposits of pension payments. Conversely, automatic withdrawals are preauthorized electronic funds transfers from the customer's account for regular payments to some party other than the financial institution at which the funds are deposited. Automatic withdrawals to pay insurance premiums, utility bills, or automobile loan payments are common examples of this type of EFT.

CONSUMER INSIGHT

Thwarting ATM Fraud

What is the easiest way to rob a bank these days? Head for your local ATM, or automatic teller machine. With nearly 90,000 machines open virtually round the clock nationwide, ATMs offer thieves a wide new frontier.

Thieves get sophisticated

These days, you still may find yourself held up by some robber who pulls a gun and demands your ATM withdrawal, but other thieves have gotten much more sophisticated. Often, ATM robbers will use binoculars or video cameras to record your finger movements as you enter your personal identification number at an ATM. Then they'll match your PIN with your account number on the ATM receipt that you perhaps carelessly threw away. If they encounter a problem, they'll even call you at home, posing as bank officials seeking to verify your PIN. You should know, however, that banks never do this sort of thing.

To reduce street crime around ATMs, banks have begun installing the machines in well-lighted public places such as 24-hour grocery stores and shopping malls. They have also teamed up with city officials in such places as Chicago and Los Angeles to install bank machines in police stations.

Malls become targets

Such measures, however, haven't stopped more cunning ATM robbers. One group, for example, carried out the most sophisticated heist so far in Manchester, Connecticut, in April and May 1993. That spring, operators approached mall officials at the Buckland Hills Mall about installing an ATM. Before a contract could be signed, the thieves rolled in a temporary-looking machine, which they left in the mall for two weeks, during which time shoppers who slipped in their cards and entered their PINs

received an apologetic message saying that the machine was out of service. Often, a "repairman" stood by, ostensibly waiting to fix the machine. Even to mall employees, the ATM looked legitimate. Yet the machine, which rested on wheels, could have been carted away at any moment. Finally, two men dressed in uniforms, came on Mother's Day and did just that. Then, using the stolen PIN and account numbers that the machine had recorded, the robbers made fake cash cards, traveled to midtown Manhattan, and went on a banking spree that netted them $50,000 in one day.

Banks held liable

Fraud like this is costing banks plenty. According to the American Bankers Association, banks lost $18 million to ATM fraud in 1991, the latest year for which figures are available.

One problem that banks face is that thieves like those in Connecticut can now buy used ATMs for as little as $6,000. Another is that customers often carelessly toss their ATM cards, PINs, or account receipts around. Many times, in fact, customers fall victim to friends or relatives who "borrow" their cards to make withdrawals.

Moreover, under the Electronic Funds Transfer Act, customers can limit their liability for unauthorized withdrawals. If, as a customer, you lose your card or it is stolen, you have two days to notify the bank from the time that you discover the problem. By acting quickly, you reduce your liability to no more than $50; if you wait four days, however, your liability shoots up to $500.

If you discover an unauthorized withdrawal on your monthly statement, you have sixty days from the postmark on the statement's envelope to report the problem. Again, your liability will be limited to $50. If you become the victim of a criminal who makes a fake ATM card for your account, you face no liability. Whatever the circumstance, the burden of proof rests with the bank. If your bank refuses to reimburse you in a timely manner, you can sue.

Precautions to consider

Today, ATMs account for more than seven billion transactions each year in the United States, and that number is growing. Increasingly, banks are using ATMs to sell everything from American Express traveler's checks to home equity loans. The list keeps expanding. And if you travel, some ATMs in foreign countries will even allow you to link up with your local bank, withdraw money from your account, and receive it in the local coin. To thwart would-be robbers, then, you may want to remember these important safety tips:

- Keep your ATM card and your PIN in separate places.
- Better yet, memorize your PIN, and never give it out to anyone.
- If you must keep a record of your PIN, put it in your safe deposit box at your bank.
- Never write your PIN on your ATM card or keep your PIN in your wallet.
- Avoid using the first part of your social security number, your driver's license number, your telephone number, or your birthday for your PIN.
- Don't leave your ATM card lying around the house for someone else to pick up.

continued

- Keep all your ATM withdrawal receipts, rather than tossing them away.
- Take someone with you to the cash machine and watch out for people who are loitering nearby.
- Head for ATMs in well-lighted, protected locations, such as grocery stores or malls.
- Never let a stranger into an ATM

area with you, and get in and out quickly.
- Try to use ATMs during the day and have your card ready before you approach the machine.

- Conceal your finger movements from view as you enter your PIN.
- Opt for drive-through ATMs and keep your car windows and doors locked, except for the driver's side.
- Put your money away as soon as you get it and count it later.
- Finally, regularly compare your monthly statements with your ATM receipts.

Pay-by-Phone Systems

Recently, some financial institutions have instituted a service that permits customers to pay bills by telephoning the bank's computer system and directing a transfer of funds to a designated third party. This service also permits customers to transfer funds between accounts.

Wholesale Electronic Funds Transfers

Wholesale electronic funds transfers, commonly called wholesale wire transfers, involve the movement of funds between financial institutions, between financial institutions and businesses, and between businesses. More than one *trillion* dollars is transferred this way each business day over the two major transfer systems—the Federal Reserve wire transfer network system (Fedwire) and the New York Clearing House Interbank Payment System (CHIPS). In addition, a number of private wholesale wire systems exist among the large banks. Limited aspects of wholesale wire transfers are governed by uniform rules promulgated by the Federal Reserve, CHIPS, and the National Automated Clearing House Association.

CONSUMER FUNDS TRANSFERS

Electronic Fund Transfer Act provides a basic framework establishing the rights, liabilities, and responsibilities of participants in consumer electronic fund transfers

In 1978, Congress determined that the use of electronic systems to transfer funds provided the potential for substantial benefits to consumers. Existing consumer protection legislation failed to account for the unique characteristics of such systems, however, leaving the rights and obligations of consumers and financial institutions undefined. Accordingly, Congress enacted Title IX of the Consumer Protection Act, called the **Electronic Fund Transfer Act** (EFTA), to "provide a basic framework establishing the rights, liabilities, and responsibilities of participants in electronic fund transfers" with primary emphasis on "the provision of individual consumer rights." Because the EFTA deals exclusively with the protection of *consumers*, it does not govern electronic transfers between financial institutions, between financial institutions and businesses, and between businesses. The act is similar in many respects to the Fair Credit Billing Act (see Chapter 46, which applies to credit card transactions. The Electronic Fund Transfer Act is administered by the Board of Governors of the Federal Reserve System, which is mandated to prescribe regulations to carry out the purposes of the act. Pursuant to this congressional mandate, the Federal Reserve has issued Regulation E.

Disclosure

The EFTA is primarily a disclosure statute and as such requires that the terms and conditions of electronic funds transfers involving a consumer's account be disclosed in readily understandable language at the time the consumer contracts for such services. Included among the required disclosures are the consumer's liability for unauthorized transfers, the kinds of EFTs allowed, the charges for transfers or for the right to make transfers, the consumer's right to stop payment of preauthorized EFTs, the consumer's right to receive documentation of EFTs, rules concerning disclosure of information to third parties, procedures for correcting account errors, and the financial institution's liability to the consumer under the Act.

Documentation and Periodic Statements

The Act requires the financial institution to provide the consumer with written documentation of each transfer made from an electronic terminal at the time of transfer—a receipt. The receipt must clearly state the amount involved, the date, the type of transfer, the identity of the account(s) involved, the identity of any third party involved, and the location of the terminal involved.

In addition, the financial institution must provide each consumer with a periodic statement for each account of the consumer that may be accessed by means of an EFT. The statement must describe the amount, date, and location for each transfer; the fee, if any, to be charged for the transaction; and an address and phone number for questions and information.

Preauthorized Transfers

A preauthorized transfer *from* a consumer's account must be authorized in advance by the consumer in *writing*, and a copy of the authorization must be provided to the consumer when the transfer is made. Up to three business days before the scheduled date of the transfer, a consumer may stop payment of a preauthorized EFT by notifying the financial institution orally or in writing, though the financial institution may require the consumer to provide written confirmation of an oral notification within fourteen days.

Error Resolution

The consumer has sixty days after the financial institution sends a periodic statement in which to notify the institution of any errors appearing on that statement. The financial institution is required to investigate alleged errors and report its findings within ten business days. If the financial institution needs more than ten days to investigate, it may take up to forty-five days, provided it recredits the consumer's account for the amount alleged to be in error. If it determines that an error did occur, it must properly correct the error. Failure to investigate in good faith makes the financial institution liable to the consumer for treble damages (that is, three times the amount of provable damages).

Consumer Liability

A consumer's liability for an unauthorized electronic fund transfer is limited to a maximum of $50 if the consumer notifies the financial institution within *two days* after he *learns* of the loss or theft. If the consumer does not report the loss or theft within two days, he is liable for losses up to $500. If the consumer fails to report the unauthorized use within *sixty days* of transmittal of a periodic statement, he is liable for losses resulting from *any* unauthorized EFT that appeared on the statement if the financial institution can show that the loss would not have occurred had the consumer reported the loss within sixty days.

Liability of Financial Institution

Financial institution responsibility liable to a consumer for all damage proximately caused by its failure to properly handle an EFT transaction

A financial institution is liable to a consumer for all damages proximately caused by its failure to make an EFT in accordance with the terms and conditions of an account, in the correct amount, or in a timely manner when properly instructed to do so by the consumer. There are, however, exceptions to such liability. The financial institution will not be liable if

1. the consumer's account has insufficient funds through no fault of the financial institution,
2. the funds are subject to legal process,
3. the transfer would exceed an established credit limit,
4. an electronic terminal has insufficient cash, or
5. circumstances beyond the financial institution's control prevent the transfer.

The financial institution is also liable for failure to stop payment of a preauthorized transfer from a consumer's account when instructed to do so in accordance with the terms and conditions of the account.

WHOLESALE FUNDS TRANSFERS

Wholesale funds transfers the movement of funds through the banking system; excludes all transactions governed by the Electronic Fund Transfer Act

Article 4A, Funds Transfers, is designed to provide a statutory framework for a payment system that is not covered by existing Articles of the Uniform Commercial Code or by the Electronic Fund Transfer Act. The typical wholesale wire transfer involves sophisticated parties who desire great speed in transferring large sums of money. Article 4A has been universally adopted by the states and territories.

Article 4A provides that the parties to a funds transfer generally may by agreement vary their rights and obligations. Moreover, funds-transfer system rules governing banks that use the system may be effective even if such rules conflict with Article 4A. Rights and obligations under Article 4A can also be changed by Federal Reserve regulations and operating circulars of Federal Reserve Banks.

Scope of Article

Article 4A, which covers wholesale funds transfers, defines a funds transfer as a "series of transactions, beginning with the originator's payment order, made for the purpose of making payment to the beneficiary of the order. The term includes any payment order issued by the originator's bank or an intermediary bank intended to carry out the originator's payment order. A funds transfer is completed by acceptance by the beneficiary's bank of a payment order for the benefit of the beneficiary of the originator's payment order." The Article, therefore, covers the transfers of credit that move from an originator to a beneficiary through the banking system. If any step in the process is governed by the Electronic Fund Transfer Act, however, the entire transaction is excluded from the Article's coverage.

The following examples illustrate the coverage of the Article

1. Johnson Co. instructs its bank, First National Bank (FNB), to pay $2 million to West Co., also a customer of FNB. FNB executes the payment order by crediting West's account with $2 million and notifying West that the credit has been made and is available.
2. Assume the same facts as those in the first example, except that West's bank is Central Bank (CB). FNB will execute the payment order of Johnson Co. by issuing to CB its own payment order instructing CB to credit the account of West.
3. Assume the facts presented in the second example with the added fact that FNB does not have a correspondent relationship with CB. In this instance, FNB will have to issue its payment order to Northern Bank (NB), a bank that does have a correspondent relationship with CB, and NB will then issue its payment order to CB.

Payment Order   A **payment order** is a sender's instruction to a receiving bank to pay, or to cause another bank to pay, a fixed or determinable amount of money to a beneficiary. The instruction may be communicated orally, electronically, or in writing. To be a payment order, the instruction must

> **Payment order** an instruction of a sender to a receiving bank to pay, or to cause another bank to pay, a fixed amount of money to a beneficiary

1. contain no condition to payment other than the time of payment;
2. be sent to a receiving bank that is to be reimbursed either by debiting an account of the sender or by otherwise receiving payment from the sender; and
3. be transmitted by the sender directly to the receiving bank or indirectly through an agent, a funds-transfer system, or a communication system.

The payment order is issued when sent and, if more than one payment is to be made, each payment represents a separate payment order. In the examples above, there is one payment order in the first example (from Johnson Co.), two in the second example (from Johnson Co. and from First National Bank), and three in the third example (from Johnson Co., from First National Bank, and from Northern Bank).

> **Originator** sender of the first payment order
>
> **Sender** party who gives an instruction to the receiving bank

Parties   The **originator** is either the sender of the payment order or, in a series of payment orders, the sender of the first payment order. A **sender** is the party who gives an instruction to the **receiving bank**, or the bank to which the sender's instruction is addressed. The receiving bank may be the originator's bank, an intermediary bank, or the beneficiary's bank. The **originator's bank** is either the bank that receives the original payment order or the originator if the originator is a bank. The **beneficiary's bank**, the last bank in the chain of a funds transfer, is the bank instructed in the payment order to credit the beneficiary's account. The **beneficiary** is the person to be paid by the beneficiary bank. An **intermediary bank** is any receiving bank, other than the originator's bank or the beneficiary's bank, that receives the payment order. Thus, in the above examples,

> **Receiving bank** bank that receives the sender's instructions
>
> **Originator's bank** either the bank that receives the original payment order or the originator if a bank
>
> **Beneficiary's bank** bank identified in a payment order to credit the beneficiary's account
>
> **Beneficiary** person to be paid by the beneficiary bank
>
> **Intermediary bank** any receiving bank other than an originator's or beneficiary's bank

1. Johnson Co. is the *originator* in all three examples;
2. Johnson Co. is a *sender* in all three examples, FNB is a sender in examples 2 and 3, and NB is a sender in example 3;
3. FNB is the *receiving bank* of Johnson Co.'s payment order in all three examples; in example 2, CB is the receiving bank of FNB's payment order; and, in

example 3, CB is the receiving bank of NB's payment order and NB is the receiving bank of FNB's payment order;

4. FNB is the *originator's bank* in all three examples;
5. FNB is the *beneficiary's bank* in example 1; CB is the beneficiary's bank in examples 2 and 3;
6. West is the *beneficiary* in all three examples;
7. NB is an *intermediary bank* in example 3.

See Figure 28–2 for a summary of the parties in these three examples. In some instances, the originator and the beneficiary may be the same party. For example, a corporation may wish to transfer funds from one account to another account that is in the same or a different bank.

Excluded Transactions As previously mentioned, if any part of a funds transfer is governed by the Electronic Fund Transfer Act, then the transfer is excluded from Article 4A coverage. In addition, Article 4A covers only credit transactions; it therefore excludes debit transactions. If the person making the payment gives the instruction, the transfer is a credit transfer. If, however, the person receiving the payment gives the instruction, the transfer is a debit transfer. For example, a seller of goods obtains authority from the purchaser to debit the purchaser's account after the seller ships the goods. Article 4A does not cover this transaction because the instructions to make payment issue from the beneficiary (the seller), not from the party whose account is to be debited (the purchaser). See Figure 28–3.

Acceptance

Rights and obligations arise as a result of a receiving bank's acceptance of a payment order. The effect of acceptance depends upon whether the payment order was issued to the beneficiary's bank or to a receiving bank other than the beneficiary's bank.

If a receiving bank is not the beneficiary's bank, the receiving bank does not subject itself to any liability until it accepts the instrument. Acceptance by a receiving bank other than the beneficiary's bank occurs when the receiving bank

Acceptance rights and obligations that arise as a result of a receiving bank's acceptance of a payment order

FIGURE 28–2 Parties to a Funds Transfer

	Example 1	Example 2	Example 3
Originator	Johnson Co.	Johnson Co.	Johnson Co.
Sender(s)	Johnson Co.	Johnson Co. FNB	Johnson Co. FNB NB
Receiving Bank(s)	FNB	FNB CB	FNB CB NB
Orginator's Bank	FNB	FNB	FNB
Beneficiary's Bank	FNB	CB	CB
Beneficiary	West	West	West
Intermediary Bank	—	—	NB

FIGURE 28–3 Credit Transaction

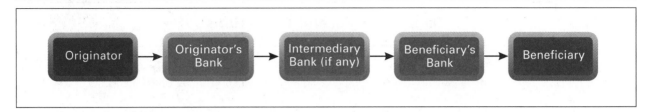

executes the sender's order. Such execution occurs when the receiving bank "issues a payment order intended to carry out" the sender's payment order. When the receiving bank executes the sender's payment order, the bank is entitled to payment from the sender and can debit the sender's account.

The beneficiary's bank may accept an order in any of three ways, and acceptance occurs at the earliest of these events: (1) when the bank (a) pays the beneficiary or (b) notifies the beneficiary that the bank has received the order or has credited the beneficiary's account with the funds; (2) when the bank receives payment of the sender's order; or (3) the opening of the next funds-transfer business day of the bank after the payment date of the order if the order was not rejected and funds are available for payment.

If a beneficiary's bank accepts a payment order, the bank is obliged to pay the beneficiary the amount of the order. The bank's acceptance of the payment order does not, however, create any obligation to either the sender or the originator.

Erroneous Execution of Payment Orders

If a receiving bank mistakenly executes a payment order for an amount greater than the amount authorized, the bank is entitled to payment only in the amount of the sender's correct order. To the extent allowed by the law governing mistake and restitution, the receiving bank may then recover from the beneficiary of the erroneous order the amount in excess of the authorized amount. If the wrong beneficiary is paid, however, the bank that issued the erroneous payment order is entitled to payment neither from its sender nor from prior senders and has the burden of recovering the payment from the improper beneficiary.

Unauthorized Payment Orders

If a bank wishing to prevent unauthorized transactions establishes commercially reasonable security measures, to which a customer agrees, and the bank properly follows the process it has established, the customer must pay an order even if it was unauthorized. The customer, however, can avoid liability by showing that the unauthorized order was *not* caused directly or indirectly by (1) a person with access to confidential security information who was acting for the customer or (2) a person who obtained such information from a source controlled by the customer.

CHAPTER SUMMARY

Bank Deposits and Collections

Collection of Items	**Depositary Bank** the bank in which the payee or holder deposits a check for credit **Provisional Credit** tentative credit for the deposit of an instrument until final credit is given **Final Credit** payment of the instrument by the payor bank; if the payor bank (drawee) does not pay the check, the depositary bank reverses the provisional credit **Intermediary Bank** a bank, other than the depositary or payor bank, involved in the collection process **Collecting Bank** any bank (other than the payor bank) handling the item for payment ■ *Agency* a collecting bank is an agent or subagent of the owner of the check until the settlement becomes final ■ *Duty of Care* a collecting bank must exercise ordinary care in handling an item ■ *Duty to Act Timely* a collecting bank acts timely if it takes proper action before its midnight deadline (midnight of the next banking day) ■ *Indorsements* if an item is restrictively indorsed "for deposit only," only a bank may be a holder ■ *Warranties* customers and collecting banks give warranties on transfer, presentment, and encoding ■ *Final Payment* occurs when the payor bank does any of the following, whichever happens first: (1) pays an item in cash; (2) settles and does not have the right to revoke the settlement; or (3) makes a provisional settlement and does not properly revoke it **Payor Bank** under its contract with the drawer, the payor or drawee bank agrees to pay to the payee or his order checks that are issued by the drawer, provided the order is not countermanded by a stop payment order and provided there are sufficient funds in the drawer's account
Relationship between Payor Bank and Its Customers	**Contractual Relationship** the relationship between a payor bank and its checking account customer is primarily the product of their contractual arrangement **Payment of an Item** when a payor receives an item for which the funds in the account are insufficient, the bank may either dishonor the item and return it or pay the item and charge the customer's account even though an overdraft is created **Stop Payment Orders** an oral stop payment order (a command from a drawer to a drawee not to pay an instrument) is binding, for fourteen calendar days; a written order is effective for six months and may be renewed in writing **Bank's Right to Subrogation on Improper Payment** if a payor bank pays an item over a stop payment order or otherwise in violation of its contract, the payor bank is subrogated to (obtains) the rights of (1) any holder in due course on the item against the drawer or maker; (2) the payee or any holder against the drawer or maker and (3) the drawer or maker against the payee or any other holder **Customer's Duties** the customer must examine bank statements and items carefully and promptly to discover any unauthorized signatures or alterations

Electronic Funds Transfers

Nature and Types of Electronic Funds Transfers	**Definition** any transfer of funds, other than a transaction originated by check, draft, or similar paper instrument, which is initiated through an electronic terminal, telephonic instrument, or computer or magnetic tape so as to order, instruct, or authorize a financial institution to debit or credit an account **Purpose** to eliminate the paperwork involved in processing checks and the "float" available to a drawer of a check **Types of Electronic Funds Transfers** ■ *Automated Teller Machines* ■ *Point-of-Sale Systems* ■ *Direct Deposits and Withdrawals* ■ *Pay-by-Phone Systems* ■ *Wholesale Electronic Funds Transfers*

Consumer Funds Transfers	**Electronic Fund Transfer Act** provides a basic framework establishing the rights, liabilities, and responsibilities of participants in consumer electronic fund transfers **Financial Institution Responsibility** liable to a consumer for all damage proximately caused by its failure to properly handle an EFT transaction

Article 4A–Funds Transfers	**Scope** ■ *Wholesale Funds Transfers* the movement of funds through the banking system; excludes all transactions governed by the Electronic Fund Transfer Act ■ *Payment Order* an instruction of a sender to a receiving bank to pay, or to cause another bank to pay, a fixed amount of money to a beneficiary ■ *Parties* include originator, sender, receiving bank, originator's bank, beneficiary's bank, beneficiary, and intermediary banks **Acceptance** rights and obligations that arise as a result of a receiving bank's acceptance of a payment order

QUESTIONS

1. Distinguish among depositary, payor, intermediary, and collecting banks.
2. Discuss the duties of collecting banks.
3. Discuss the obligations between a customer and a drawee bank.
4. Define a consumer electronic fund transfer and outline the major provisions of the Electronic Fund Transfer Act.

5. Define a wholesale funds transfer and identify the parties to such a transfer.

Internet Question. Find and review information about (a) electronic banking, (b) the Federal Reserve System, and (c) the Federal Deposit Insurance Company.

PROBLEMS

1. On December 9, Jane Jones writes a check for $500 payable to Ralph Rodgers in payment for goods to be received later in the month. Before the close of business on the ninth, Jane notifies the bank by telephone to stop payment on the check. On Monday, December 19, Ralph gives the check to Bill Briggs for value and without notice. On the twentieth, Bill deposits the check in his account at Bank A. On the twenty-first, Bank A sends the check to its correspondent, Bank B. On the twenty-second, Bank B presents the check through the clearinghouse to Bank C. On the twenty-third, Bank C presents the check to Bank P, the payor bank. On Wednesday, December 28, the payor bank makes payment of the check final. Jane Jones sues the payor bank. Decision?

2. Howard Harrison, a longtime customer of Western Bank, operates a small department store, Harrison's Store. Since his store has few experienced employees, Harrison frequently travels throughout the United States on buying trips, although he also runs the financial operations of the business. On one of his buying trips, Harrison purchased a gross of sport shirts from Well-Made Shirt Company and paid for the transaction with a check on his store account with Western Bank in the amount of $1,000. Adams, an employee of Well-Made who deposits its checks in Security Bank, sloppily raised the amount of the check to $10,000 and indorsed the check, "Pay to the order of Adams from Pension Plan Benefits, Well-Made Shirt Company by Adams." He cashed the check and cannot be found. Western Bank processed the check, paid it, and sent it to Harrison's Store with the monthly statement. After briefly examining the statement, Harrison left on another buying trip for three weeks.
   (a) Assuming the bank acted in good faith and the alteration is not discovered and reported to the bank until an audit conducted thirteen months after the statement was received by Harrison's Store, who must bear the loss on the raised check?
   (b) Assume that Harrison, who was unable to examine his statement promptly because of his buying trips, left instructions with the bank to carefully examine and to notify him of any item over $5,000 to be charged to his account; assume further that the bank nevertheless paid the item in his absence. Who bears the loss if the alteration is discovered one month after the statement was received by Harrison's Store? If the alteration is discovered thirteen months later?

3. Tom Jones owed Bank of Cleveland $10,000 on a note due November 17, with 1 percent interest due the bank for each day delinquent in payment. Jones issued a $10,000 check to Bank of Cleveland and deposited it

in the night vault the evening of November 17. Several days later, he received a letter saying he owed one day's interest on the payment because of a one-day delinquency in payment. Jones refused because he said he had put the payment in the vault on November 17. Decision?

4. Assume that Davis draws a check on Dallas Bank, payable to the order of Perkins; that Perkins indorses it to Cooper; that Cooper deposits it to her account in Houston Bank; that Houston Bank presents it to Dallas Bank, the drawee; and that Dallas Bank dishonors it because of insufficient funds. Houston Bank receives notification of the dishonor on Monday but, because of an interruption of communication facilities, fails to notify Cooper until Wednesday. What result?

5. Jones, a food wholesaler whose company has an account with City Bank in New York City, is traveling in California on business. He finds a particularly attractive offer and decides to buy a carload of oranges for delivery in New York. He gives Saltin, the seller, his company's check for $25,000 to pay for the purchase. Saltin deposits the check, with others he received that day, with his bank, the Carrboro Bank. Carrboro Bank sends the check to Downs Bank in Los Angeles, which in turn deposits it with the Los Angeles Federal Reserve Bank (L.A. Fed). The L.A. Fed sends the check, with others, to the New York Federal Reserve Bank (N.Y. Fed), which forwards the check to City Bank, Jones's bank, for collection.
   (a) Is City Bank a depository bank? A collecting bank? A payor bank?
   (b) Is Carrboro a depository bank? A collecting bank?
   (c) Is the N.Y. Fed. an intermediary bank?
   (d) Is Downs Bank a collecting bank?
   Explain.

6. On April 1, Moore gave Pipkin a check properly drawn by Moore on Zebra Bank for $500 in payment of a painting to be framed and delivered the next day. Pipkin immediately indorsed the check and gave it to Yeager Bank as payment in full of his indebtedness to the bank on a note he previously had signed. Yeager Bank canceled the note and returned it to Pipkin.

   On April 2, upon learning that the painting had been destroyed in a fire at Pipkin's studio, Moore promptly went to Zebra Bank, signed a printed form of stop payment order, and gave it to the cashier. Zebra Bank refused payment on the check upon proper presentment by Yeager Bank.
   (a) What are the rights of Yeager Bank against Zebra Bank?
   (b) What are the rights of Yeager Bank against Moore?

(c) Assuming that Zebra Bank inadvertently paid the amount of the check to Yeager Bank and debited Moore's account, what are the rights of Moore against Zebra Bank?

7. As payment in advance for services to be performed, Acton signed and delivered the following instrument:

> December 1, 1997
>
> LAST NATIONAL BANK
> MONEYVILLE, STATE X
>
> Pay to the order of Olaf Owen $1,500.00 _____Fifteen Hundred Dollars_____ For services to be performed by Olaf Owen starting on December 6, 1997.
>
> (signed) Arthur Acton

Owen requested and received Last National Bank's certification of the check even though Acton had only $900 on deposit. Owen indorsed the check in blank and delivered it to Dan Doty in payment of a preexisting debt.

When Owen failed to appear for work, Acton issued a written stop payment order ordering the bank not to pay the check. Doty presented the check to Last National Bank for payment. The bank refused payment.

What are the bank's rights and liabilities relating to the transactions described?

8. Jones drew a check for $1,000 on The First Bank and mailed it to the payee, Thrift, Inc. Caldwell stole the check from Thrift, Inc., chemically erased the name of the payee, and inserted the name of Henderson as payee. Caldwell also increased the amount of the check to $10,000 and, by using the name of Henderson, negotiated the check to Willis. Willis then took the check to The First Bank, obtained its certification on the check, and negotiated the check to Griffin, who deposited the check in The Second National Bank for collection. The Second National forwarded the check to the Detroit Trust Company for collection from The First Bank, which honored the check. Griffin exhausted her account in the Second National Bank, and the account was closed. Shortly thereafter, The First Bank learned that it had paid an altered check.

What are the rights of each of the parties?

9. On July 21, Boehmer, a customer of Birmingham Trust, secured a loan from that bank for the principal sum of $5,500 in order to purchase a boat allegedly being built for him by A. C. Manufacturing Company, Inc. After Boehmer signed a promissory note, Birmingham Trust issued a cashier's check to Boehmer and A. C. Manufacturing Company as payees. The check was given to Boehmer, who then forged A. C. Manufacturing Company's indorsement and deposited the check in his own account at Central Bank. Central Bank credited Boehmer's account and then placed the legend "P.I.G.," meaning "Prior Indorsements Guaranteed," on the check. The check was presented to and paid by Birmingham Trust on July 22. When the loan became delinquent in March of the following year, Birmingham Trust contacted A. C. Manufacturing Company to learn the location of the boat. They were informed that it had never been purchased, and they soon after learned that Boehmer had died on January 24 of that year. On May 1, Birmingham Trust sought reimbursement from Central Bank under the latter's warranty of prior indorsements. Decision?

10. Jason, who has extremely poor vision, went to an ATM to withdraw $200 on February 1. Joshua saw that Jason was having great difficulty reading the computer screen and offered to help. Joshua obtained Jason's personal identification number and secretly exchanged one of his old credit cards for Jason's ATM card. Between February 1 and February 15, Joshua withdrew $1,600 from Jason's account. On February 15, Jason discovered that his ATM card was missing and immediately notified his bank. The bank closed Jason's ATM account on February 16, by which time Joshua had withdrawn another $150. What is Jason's liability, if any, for the unauthorized use of his account?

11. Advanced Alloys, Inc., issued a check in the amount of $2,500 to Sergeant Steel Corporation. The check was presented for payment fourteen months later to the Chase Manhattan Bank, which made payment on the check and charged Advanced Alloy's account. Advanced Alloys now seeks to recover the payment made on the check. Decision?

12. Laboratory Management deposited into its account at Pulaski Bank a check issued by Fairway Farms in the amount of $150,000. The date of deposit was February 5, 1985. Pulaski, the depositary bank, initiated the collection process immediately by forwarding the check to Worthen Bank on the sixth. Worthen sent the check on for collection to M Bank Dallas, and M Bank Dallas, still on February 6, delivered the check to M. Bank Fort Worth. That same day, M Bank Fort Worth delivered the check to the Fort Worth Clearinghouse. Since TAB/West Side, the drawee/payor bank, was not a clearinghouse member, it had to rely on TAB/Fort Worth for further transmittal of the check. TASI, a processing center used by both TAB/Fort Worth and TAB/West Side, received the check on the sixth and processed it as a reject item because of insufficient funds. On the seventh, TAB/West Side determined to return the check unpaid. TASI gave M Bank Dallas telephone notice of the return on February 7, but physically misrouted the check. Because of this, M Bank Dallas did not physically receive the check until February 19. However, M Bank notified Worthen telephonically on the fifteenth of the dishonor and return

of the check. Worthen received the check on the twenty-first and notified Pulaski by telephone on the twenty-second. Pulaski actually received the check from Worthen on the twenty-third. On February 22 and 23, Lab Management's checking account with Pulaski was $46,000. Pulaski did not freeze the account because it considered the return to be too late. The Lab Management account was finally frozen on April 30, 1985, when it had a balance of $1,400. Pulaski brings this suit against TAB/Fort Worth, TAB/Dallas, and TASI, alleging their notice of dishonor was not timely relayed to Pulaski. The trial court found in favor of Pulaski, but awarded a nominal amount of damages. Pulaski appeals, claiming that the liability of the collecting and payor banks was absolute. Decision?

13. On November 22, 1971, a $25,000 check drawn on the First National Bank of Nevada was deposited with Lincoln First Bank-Central. Lincoln forwarded the check to Nevada via Hartford National Bank and Trust Company and Wells Fargo Bank. Nevada received the check on Friday, December 10, and discovered that it was drawn on insufficient funds. That same day, Nevada informed Wells Fargo by telephone that the check had been dishonored. On Monday, December 13, Nevada mailed the check to Wells Fargo, which received it on Friday, December 17. Upon receiving the check, Wells Fargo promptly wired notice of the dishonor to Hartford and mailed the check to Hartford. Hartford received the check on December 21 and mailed it to Lincoln, which received it on December 27. Lincoln refused to accept the check, claiming that the notice of dishonor had arrived too late. Wells Fargo, which eventually ended up with the check and the $25,000 loss, brought an action to reverse the $25,000 credit it had given to Hartford in the course of handling the check. Decision?

PART | VI

Agency

CHAPTER 29

Relationship of Principal and Agent

By using agents, one person (the principal) may enter into any number of business transactions as though he had carried them out personally, thus multiplying and expanding his business activities. The law of agency, like the law of contracts, is basic to almost every other branch of business law.

Practically every type of contract or business transaction can be created or conducted through an agent. Therefore, the place and importance of agency in the practical conduct and operation of business cannot be overemphasized, particularly in the case of partnerships and corporations. Partnership is founded on the agency of the partners. Each partner is an agent of the partnership and as such has the authority to represent and bind the partnership in all usual transactions pertaining to the partnership's business. Corporations, in turn, must function through the agency of their officers and employees. Thus, practically and legally, agency is an integral part of partnerships and corporations. In addition, sole proprietors also may employ agents in the operations of their businesses. Business, therefore, is very largely conducted by representatives or agents, not by the owners themselves.

Although some overlap occurs, the law of agency divides broadly into two main parts: the internal and the external. An agent functions as an agent by dealing with third persons, thereby establishing legal relations between her principal and those third persons. These relations are the external part of agency law, which we will discuss in the next chapter. In this chapter, we will consider the nature and function of agency, as well as other topics concerning the internal part of the law of agency.

Agency is primarily governed by state common law. An orderly presentation of this law is found in the Restatement of the Law of Agency. Regarded as a valuable authoritative reference work, the Restatement is extensively cited and quoted in reported judicial opinions.

NATURE OF AGENCY

Agency is a relationship between two persons, the **principal** and the **agent**, through which the agent is authorized to act for and on behalf of the principal. An agent is, therefore, one who represents another, the principal, in business dealings with a third person; and the operation of agency therefore involves three persons: the principal, the agent, and a third person. In dealings with a third person, the agent acts for and in the name and place of the principal, who,

Agency relationship authorizing one party (agent) to act for and on behalf of the other party (principal)

Principal person who authorizes another to act on her behalf

Agent person authorized to act on another's behalf

along with the third person, is a party to the transaction, which is usually contractual. The result of the agent's functioning is exactly the same as if the principal had dealt directly with the third person. However, if the existence and identity of the principal are disclosed, the agent acts not as a party but simply as an intermediary.

Within the scope of the authority granted to her by her principal, the agent may negotiate the terms of contracts with others and bind her principal to such contracts. Moreover, the negligence of an agent who is an employee in conducting the business of her principal exposes the principal to tort liability for injury and loss suffered by third persons.

HANSON v. KYNAST Supreme Court of Ohio, 1986, 24 Ohio St.3d 171, 494 N.E.2d 1091

FACTS On May 1, 1982, Brian Hanson sustained a paralyzing injury while playing in a lacrosse match between Ohio State University and Ashland University. Hanson had interceded in a fight between one of his teammates and an Ashland player, William Kynast. Hanson grabbed Kynast in a bear hug, but Kynast threw Hanson off his back. Hanson's head struck the ground, resulting in serious injuries. An ambulance was summoned, and after several delays Hanson was transported to a local hospital where he underwent surgery. Doctors determined that Hanson had suffered a compression fracture of his sixth spinal vertebra. Hanson, now an incomplete quadriplegic, subsequently filed suit against William Kynast and Ashland University, maintaining that because Kynast was acting as the agent of Ashland, the university was therefore liable for Kynast's alleged wrongful acts under the doctrine of *respondeat superior*.

DECISION Judgment for Ashland.

OPINION The relationship of principal and agent exists only when one party exercises the right of control over the actions of another and those actions are directed toward the attainment of an objective that the former seeks. Here, however, Kynast's relationship with Ashland is typical of that of most students attending a university. A university such as Ashland offers classroom instruction in a great variety of subjects, as well as optional participation in events such as school clubs

and sports. These offerings are designed to expand and enrich the overall educational experience. The student pays a fee and agrees to abide by the university's rules. In exchange, the university provides the student with a worthwhile education. This relationship does not constitute a principal-agent relationship. The student is a buyer of education rather than an agent.

While the degree of control necessary to establish agency has not been clearly defined, it is evident that there is no agency relationship between Kynast and Ashland. A student who attends a university of his choice, receives no scholarship or compensation, voluntarily becomes a member of the university's lacrosse team for which games no attendance fee is charged, who purchases his own equipment and who receives instruction from a coach while preparing and playing such games but is not otherwise controlled by the coach, and who participates in the game as a part of his total educational experience while attending school is not the agent of the university at the time he is playing the game of lacrosse. Ashland is therefore not liable to Hanson under the doctrine of *respondeat superior*.

INTERPRETATION The relationship of principal and agent exists only when one party exercises the right of control over the actions of another and those actions are directed toward the attainment of an objective that the former seeks.

Scope of Agency Purposes

As a general rule, a person may do through an agent whatever business activity he may accomplish personally. Conversely, whatever he cannot legally do himself, he cannot authorize another to do for him. In addition, a person may not appoint an agent to perform acts that are so personal that their performance may not be delegated to another, as in the case of a contract for personal services.

> **Scope of agency purposes** whatever business activity a person may accomplish personally he generally may do through an agent

Other Legal Relations

Two other legal relationships overlap with agency: employer-employee and principal-independent contractor. In the **employment relationship**, the employer has the right to *control* the physical conduct of the employee. In contrast, a person

> **Employment relationship** one in which the employer has the right to control the physical conduct of the employee

Independent contractor
person who contracts with another to do a particular job and is *not* subject to the other's control

who engages an **independent contractor** to do a specific job does *not* have the right to control the conduct and activities of the independent contractor in the performance of his contract. The latter simply contracts to do a job and is free to choose the method and manner in which to perform it. For example, a full-time chauffeur is an employee, whereas a taxicab driver hired to carry a person to the airport is an independent contractor engaged by the passenger.

Although all employees are agents, not all agents are employees. Agents who are not employees are independent contractors. For instance, an attorney retained to handle a particular transaction would be an independent contractor-agent for that particular transaction. Finally, not all independent contractors are agents. For example, the taxicab driver in the example above is not an agent. Likewise, if Pam hires Bill to build a stone wall around her property, Bill is an independent contractor who is not an agent.

The distinction between employee and independent contractor has a number of important legal consequences. For example, as we will discuss in the next chapter, a principal is liable for the torts an employee commits within the scope of her employment but ordinarily is not liable for torts committed by an independent contractor. The following two cases further explain the differences between an employee and an independent contractor.

JAEGER v. WESTERN RIVERS FLY FISHER United States District Court, 1994, 855 F.Supp. 1217

FACTS Western operates under license of the U.S. Forest Service as an "outfitter," a corporation in the business of arranging fishing expeditions on the Green River. The defendant, Michael D. Petragallo, is licensed by the Forest Service as a guide to conduct fishing expeditions but cannot do so by himself, as the Forest Service only licenses outfitters to float patrons down the Green River. Western and several other licensed outfitters contact Petragallo to guide clients on fishing trips. Because the Forest Service licenses only outfitters to sponsor fishing expeditions, every guide must display on the boat and vehicle he uses the insignia of the outfitter sponsoring the particular trip. Petragallo may agree or refuse to take individuals Western refers to him, and Western does not restrict him from guiding expeditions for other outfitters. Western pays Petragallo a certain sum per fishing trip and does not make any deductions from his compensation. The Internal Revenue Service has determined that, for tax purposes, Western is properly treating guides it hires as independent contractors. Petragallo's responsibilities include transporting patrons to the Green River, using his own boat for fishing trips, providing food and overnight needs for patrons, assisting patrons in fly fishing, and transporting them from the river to their vehicles.

Robert McMaster contacted Western and arranged for a fishing trip for himself and two others. The plaintiff, Jaeger, was a member of McMaster's fishing party. McMaster paid Western, which set the price for the trip, planned the itinerary for the McMaster party, rented fishing rods to them, and arranged for Petragallo to be their guide. When Petragallo met the McMaster party, he answered affirmatively when the plaintiff asked him if he worked for Western. Petragallo provided his own vehicle and boat and supplied the food, equipment, and gasoline for the trip. Both the vehicle and the boat had signs bearing Western's identification and logo. While driving the McMaster party back to town at the conclusion of the fishing trip, Petragallo lost control of his vehicle, injuring the plaintiff. The plaintiff brought suit against Western, Petragallo, and others. Western moved for summary judgment, arguing that, because Petragallo is an independent contractor and was never its employee, it is not liable, as a matter of law, for Petragallo's acts in causing the plaintiff's injuries.

DECISION Motion for summary judgment denied.

OPINION The plaintiff argues that Petragallo was Western's employee, and, thus, Western is liable for Petragallo's actions under the doctrine of *respondeat superior*. Western contends Petragallo is an independent contractor for whose conduct Western is not liable. In general, an employee is one who is hired and paid a salary, a wage, or at a fixed rate, to perform the employer's work as directed by the employer and who is subject to a comparatively high degree of control by the employer in performing those duties. In contrast, an independent contractor is one who is engaged to do some particular project or piece of work, usually for a set total sum, who may do the job in his own way, subject to only minimal restrictions or controls and is responsible only for its satisfactory completion. Factors

continued

a court may consider in determining the nature of the relationship include (1) whatever agreements exist concerning the right of direction and control over the employee, whether express or implied; (2) the right to hire and fire; (3) the method of payment—whether in wages or fees, as compared to payment for a complete job or project; and (4) the furnishing of the equipment. None of these factors separately is controlling.

The facts of this case, relative to whether Petragallo is Western's employee or an independent contractor, do not point only to a single conclusion. On the one hand, the facts suggest Petragallo may be an independent contractor. Western engages Petragallo to guide particular fishing trips, for a set sum, allowing him to conduct the trips in his own discretion. Petragallo may even choose to refuse to guide patrons Western has referred to him. Western's actions appear to involve setting up the parameters of a fishing trip and place "only minimal restrictions or controls" upon Petragallo. Moreover, although Petragallo must operate under Western's license, as required by the Forest Service, Western does not control the manner in which Petragallo conducts fishing trips. Apparently, once Western sets up a fishing trip and engages Petragallo as a guide, it relies upon and expects Petragallo to use his own discretion in doing everything else to ensure patrons have an enjoyable experience, including using his own expertise, vehicle, boat, and equipment. Finally, because Forest Service

licensing regulations prohibit an individual river guide from conducting tours unless sponsored by an outfitter, it may be argued that, if Petragallo is subject to any control, it is by the Forest Service, not Western.

On the other hand, the facts may indicate Petragallo is an employee. It is actually a judgment call as to how much control Western has over Petragallo through its advertising and arranging of fishing expeditions. Although Petragallo may refuse to guide patrons, Western apparently contacts Petragallo only after Western has planned the fishing trip, without involving him, and may provide him with a set itinerary. Also, Forest Service licensing regulations place Western in a position of having the ultimate right to control Petragallo's work as, without solicitations from Western and other outfitters, Petragallo would be prohibited completely from conducting fishing expeditions.

In applying the above factors and standards, the court concludes that determining the nature of Petragallo's relationship with Western is a factual issue inappropriate for summary judgment.

INTERPRETATION Factors relevant to determining whether an employment relationship exists include (1) the principal's right to control the agent, (2) the right to hire and fire, and (3) the method of payment, and (4) the furnishing of equipment.

WILSON v. ST. LOUIS AREA COUNCIL, BOY SCOUTS OF AMERICA Missouri Court of Appeals, Eastern District, Division Two, 1992, 845 S.W.2d 568

FACTS Tony Wilson was a member of Troop 392 of the Boy Scouts of America (BSA) and of the St. Louis Area Council (Council). On September 23, 1988, Tony went on a trip with the troop to Fort Leonard Wood, Missouri. Five adult volunteer leaders accompanied the troop. The troop stayed in a building that had thirty-foot-long aluminum pipes stacked next to it. At 10:00 P.M., Tony and other scouts were outside the building, and the leaders were inside. Tony and two others picked up a pipe and raised it so that it touched a 7200-volt power line. All three were electrocuted, and Tony died. His parents brought suit against the Council for Tony's wrongful death, claiming that the volunteer leaders were agents or servants of the Council and that the Council was vicariously liable for their negligence. The Council disclaimed liability for the following reason: The BSA chartered local councils in certain areas, and the councils in turn granted charters to local sponsors such as schools, churches, or civic organizations. The councils did not administer the scouting program for the sponsor, did not select volunteers, did not prescribe training for

volunteers, and did not direct or control troop activities. Furthermore, troops were not required to obtain the local council's permission to participate in activities. The trial court granted summary judgment for the Council.

DECISION Judgment of the trial court affirmed.

OPINION Under the doctrine of *respondeat superior*, an employer is liable for those negligent acts or omissions of his employee that the employee commits within the scope of his employment. Liability based on *respondeat superior* requires some evidence that a master-servant relationship existed between the parties. The test to determine if *respondeat superior* applies to a tort is whether the person sought to be charged as the "master" had the right or power to control and direct the physical conduct of the other in the performance of the act. If there was no right to control, there is no liability, because those who render services but retain control over their own movements are not servants. A party's liability under the doctrine of *respondeat superior* therefore depends on the facts

continued

and circumstances in evidence in each particular case, and no single test is conclusive of the issue.

Central to determining liability in the volunteer situation is the charitable organization's control over, or its right to control, the volunteer's activities. In this case, the structure of the BSA established the autonomy of the troop and its leaders over troop activities. With regard to the troop's trip to Fort Leonard Wood, the Council did not grant permission for, direct, or have knowledge of the troop's participation. There was no evidence that the Council either controlled or had the right to control the leaders' activities. Thus, the leaders were not the Council's servants or agents while participating in the program at the fort. Therefore, there was no vicarious liability on the part of the Council.

INTERPRETATION The principal's right to control the conduct of the agent is the most significant factor in determining whether an employment relationship exists.

In addition, under numerous federal and state statutes, the obligations of a principal apply only to agents who are employees. Examples of these statutes are the Social Security Act, the National Labor Relations Act, and workers' compensation acts. We will discuss these and other statutory enactments affecting the employment relationship in Chapter 43. See the following Managerial Insight.

MANAGERIAL INSIGHT

Ruling Against Microsoft Is Boon to Independent Contract Workers

In a decision that could make it harder for companies to treat workers as independent contractors, a federal appeals court has ordered the Microsoft Corp. to pay employee benefits to hundreds of workers who, the court found, were regular employees and not independent contractors, as Microsoft insisted.

The 9th U.S. Circuit Court of Appeals in San Francisco looked to rulings of the Internal Revenue Service and payroll records to conclude that the workers were not contractors, but regular employees, and thus entitled to participate in Microsoft's 401(k) plan and buy its shares at discount just like other employees.

The court said that the workers, who held jobs like software tester and proofreader, deserved these benefits even though Microsoft specifically told them when they were hired that they would not take part in the 401(k) plan or stock purchase plan.

Many labor lawyers predict that the opinion, which was issued last week, will have far-reaching implications for companies across the nation because independent contractors represent almost 7 percent of the work force and are being used with increasing frequency, especially in high-tech industries. These lawyers said the opinion showed that some courts were increasingly looking askance at companies that rely on independent contractors to avoid paying benefits.

"This opinion is precedent-setting because companies, by treating workers as contractors, have been trying to reduce what they spend on benefits and to avoid having to follow new laws, like the disability act and the family medical leave act," said Jay Krupin, a Washington-based lawyer who specializes in employment matters.

In the first sentence of a 2-to-1 decision, Judge Stephen Reinhardt showed his displeasure with the trend among corporations to use independent contractors. "Large corporations have increasingly adopted the practice of hiring temporary employees or independent contractors as a means of avoiding payment of employee benefits and thereby increasing their profits," he wrote.

Mark Murray, a Microsoft spokesman, said the company would appeal the decision in the hope that the full panel of judges on the 9th Circuit would rehear the case. He said the number of employees involved in the case was in "the high hundreds," although Stephen Strong, a lawyer for the plaintiffs, insisted that more than 1,000 workers were involved.

"We do not believe this is the final word on this case," Murray said. "We believe that we have treated all or our workers fairly."

The appeals court sent the case back to a district court to determine how many workers should get the benefits and how much that should be. Murray said it was difficult to determine how much Microsoft would owe, if it lost the appeal, because the workers have to invest money of their own in the 401(k) plan and stock discount plan to enjoy their benefits.

"Court Decides Microsoft Owes Some Benefits to Freelancers" by Steven Greenhouse, 10/12/96, *The New York Times*.

CREATION OF AGENCY

The relationship of principal and agent is consensual and not necessarily contractual; therefore, it may exist without consideration. An agency created without consideration is a **gratuitous agency**. The power of a gratuitous agent to affect the principal's relations with third persons is the same as that of a paid agent, and his liabilities to and rights against third persons are the same as well. Nonetheless, agency by contract, the most usual method of creating the relationship, must satisfy all of the requirements of a contract.

Gratuitous agency (*gra·tu'·i·tous*) an agency created without consideration

Formalities

As a general rule, a contract of agency requires no particular formality; and usually the contract either may be oral or may be inferred from the conduct of the principal. In some cases, however, the contract must be in writing. For example, the appointment of an agent for a period of more than a year comes within the one-year clause of the statute of frauds and thus must be in writing. In some states, the authority of an agent to sell land must be set down in a writing signed by the principal.

A **power of attorney** is a formal appointment of an agent who is known as an attorney in fact. Under a power of attorney, a principal may, for example, appoint an agent not only to execute a contract for the sale of the principal's real estate but also to execute the deed conveying title to the real estate to the third party.

Formalities no particular formality is usually required in a contract of agency, although appointments of agents for a period of more than one year must be in writing

Power of attorney written, formal appointment of an agent

Capacity

The capacity to be a principal, and thus to act through an agent, depends on the **capacity of** the **principal** to do the act herself. For example, contracts entered into by a minor or an incompetent not under a guardianship are voidable. Consequently, the appointment of an agent by a minor or an incompetent not under a guardianship and any resulting contracts are voidable, regardless of the agent's contractual capacity.

On the other hand, because the act of the agent is considered the act of the principal, the incapacity of an agent to bind himself by contract does *not* disqualify him from making a contract that is binding on his principal. Thus, any person has the capacity to be an agent. Although the contract of agency may be voidable, an authorized contract between the principal and the third person who dealt with the agent is valid. Nonetheless, some mental capacity is necessary in an agent; therefore, very young minors and mental incompetents may not have the capacity to act as agents in certain situations.

Capacity of principal if the principal is a minor or an incompetent not under a guardianship, his appointment of another to act as an agent is voidable

Capacity of agent any person may act as an agent since the act of the agent is considered the act of the principal

DUTIES OF AGENT TO PRINCIPAL

Because the principal-agent relationship is ordinarily created by contract, the duties of the agent to the principal are determined primarily by the provisions of the contract. In addition to these contractual duties, the agent is subject to various other duties imposed by law, unless the parties agree otherwise. Normally, a principal bases the selection of an agent on the agent's ability, skill, and integrity. Moreover, the principal not only authorizes and empowers the agent to bind him on contracts with third persons, but often places the agent in possession of his money and other property. As a result, the agent is in a position to injure the principal, either through negligence or dishonesty.

Accordingly, an agent, as a fiduciary (a person in a position of trust and confidence), owes her principal the duties of obedience, diligence, and loyalty; the duty to inform; and the duty to provide an accounting. Moreover, an agent is liable for any loss she causes to the principal through her breach of these duties.

A gratuitous agent is subject to the same duty of loyalty that is imposed upon a paid agent and is equally liable to the principal for the harm he causes by his careless performance. Although the lack of consideration usually places a gratuitous agent under no duty to perform for the principal, such an agent may be liable to the principal for failing to perform a promise on which the principal has relied.

Duty of Obedience

Duty of obedience an agent must act in the principal's affairs only as authorized by the principal and must obey all reasonable instructions and directions

The **duty of obedience** requires the agent to act in the principal's affairs only as authorized by the principal and to obey all reasonable instructions and directions of the principal. An agent is not, however, under a duty to follow orders to perform illegal or unethical acts, such as misrepresenting the quality of his principal's goods or those of a competitor. The agent may be subject to liability to her principal for breach of the duty of obedience (1) if she entered into an unauthorized contract for which her principal is now liable; (2) if she has improperly delegated her authority; or (3) if she has committed a tort for which the principal is now liable. Thus, an agent who sells on credit in violation of his principal's explicit instructions has breached the duty of obedience and is liable to the principal for any amounts the purchaser does not pay. Moreover, an agent who breaches her duty of obedience loses her right to compensation.

Duty of Diligence

Duty of diligence an agent must act with reasonable care and skill in performing the work for which he is employed

A paid agent must act with reasonable care and skill in performing the work for which he is employed. He must also exercise any special skill that he may have. An agent who does not exercise the required care and skill is liable to his principal for any resulting loss. For example, Peg appoints Alvin as her agent to sell goods in markets where the highest price can be obtained. Although he could have obtained a higher price in a nearby market by carefully obtaining information, Alvin sells goods in a glutted market and obtains a low price. Consequently, he is liable to Peg for breach of the duty of diligence.

Duty to Inform

Duty to inform an agent must use reasonable efforts to give the principal information relevant to the affairs entrusted to her

An agent must use reasonable efforts to provide the principal with information that is relevant to the affairs entrusted to her and that, as the agent knows or should know, the principal would desire to have. The rule of agency providing that notice to an agent is notice to her principal makes this duty essential. Examples of information that an agent is under a duty to communicate may include the following: a customer of the principal has become insolvent; a debtor of the principal has become insolvent; a partner of a firm with which the principal has previously dealt, and with which the principal or agent is about to deal, has withdrawn from the firm; or property that the principal has authorized the agent to sell at a specified price can be sold at a higher price.

Duty to Account

Duty to account an agent must maintain and provide the principal with a true and complete account of money or other property that the agent has received or expended on behalf of the principal

The agent is under a duty to maintain and to provide to the principal a true and complete account of money or other property that the agent has received or expended on the principal's behalf. An agent must also keep the principal's property separate from his own.

Fiduciary Duty

A **fiduciary duty**, arising out of a relationship of trust and confidence, is one of *utmost loyalty and good faith*. A duty imposed by law, it is owed by an agent to his principal and by an employee to his employer. It is also owed by a trustee to a beneficiary of a trust, by an officer or director of a corporation to the corporation and its shareholders, and by a lawyer to his clients. But fiduciary duties are not limited to these situations: such duties exist wherever the law authorizes one person in a relationship to place trust and confidence in another.

An agent who violates his fiduciary duty is liable to his principal for breach of contract, in tort for losses caused, and in restitution for profits he made or property he received in breach of the fiduciary duty. Moreover, he loses the right to compensation. The principal may avoid a transaction in which the agent breached his fiduciary duty, even though the principal suffered no loss. A breach of fiduciary duty may also constitute just cause for discharge of the agent.

Although the fiduciary duty is not limited to the following situations, they occur most frequently.

Conflicts of Interest   An agent must act solely in the interest of his principal, not in his own interest or in the interest of another. In addition, an agent may not represent his principal in any transaction in which the agent has a personal interest. Nor may the agent act on behalf of adverse parties to a transaction without both principals' approval to the dual agency. An agent may take a position that conflicts with the interest of his principal *only* if the principal, with full knowledge of all of the facts, consents. For example, A, an agent of P who desires to purchase land, agrees with C, who represents B, a seller of land, that A and C will endeavor to effect a transaction between their principals and will pool their commissions. A and C have committed a breach of fiduciary duty to P and B.

The courts closely scrutinize transactions between an agent and her principal. The agent may not deal at arm's length with her principal. The agent thus owes her principal a duty of full disclosure regarding all relevant facts that affect the transaction. Moreover, the transaction must be fair. Thus, Penny employs Albert to purchase for her a site suitable for a shopping center. Albert owns such a site and sells it to Penny at the fair market value, but does not disclose to Penny that he had owned the land. Penny may rescind the transaction. The agent's loyalty must be undivided, and he must devote his actions exclusively to the representation and promotion of his principal's interests.

Duty Not to Compete   An agent cannot compete with his current principal or act on behalf of a competitor. After the agency terminates, however, unless otherwise agreed, the agent may compete with his former principal. The courts will enforce by injunction a contractual agreement by the agent not to compete after termination (see Chapter 13) if the restriction is reasonable as to time and place and necessary to protect the principal's legitimate interest.

Confidential Information   An agent may not use or disclose confidential information obtained in the course of the agency for her own benefit or

Fiduciary *(fi·du'·cia·ry)* **duty** duty of utmost loyalty and good faith owed by agent to principal

contrary to the interest of her principal. Confidential information is information that, if disclosed, would harm the principal's business or that has value because it is not generally known. Confidential information includes unique business methods, trade secrets, business plans, and customer lists. An agent may, however, reveal confidential information that the principal is committing, or is about to commit, a crime.

Once the agency terminates, unless otherwise agreed, the agent may not use or disclose to third persons confidential information. The agent may, however, use the skills, knowledge, and general information she acquired during the agency relationship.

Duty to Account for Financial Benefits Unless otherwise agreed, an agent must account to the principal for any financial benefit she receives as a direct result of transactions she conducts on behalf of the principal. Such benefits would include bribes, kickbacks, and gifts. Moreover, an agent may not make a secret profit from any transaction subject to the agency. All such profits belong to the principal, to whom the agent must account. Thus, if an agent, authorized to sell certain property of her principal for $1,000, sells it for $1,500, she may not secretly pocket the additional $500.

DETROIT LIONS, INC. v. ARGOVITZ United States District Court, Eastern District of Michigan, 1984, 580 F.Supp. 542

FACTS Jerry Argovitz was employed as an agent of Billy Sims, a professional football player. Early in 1983, Argovitz informed Sims that he was awaiting the approval of his application for a United States Football League franchise in Houston. Sims was unaware, however, of Argovitz's extensive ownership interest in the new Houston Gamblers organization. Meanwhile, during the spring of 1983, Argovitz continued contract negotiations on behalf of Sims with the Detroit Lions of the National Football League. By June 22, Argovitz and the Lions were very close to an agreement, although Argovitz represented to Sims that the negotiations were not proceeding well. Argovitz then sought an offer for Sims's services from the Gamblers. The Gamblers offered Sims a $3.5 million five-year deal. Argovitz told Sims that he thought the Lions would match this figure; however, he did not seek a final offer from the Lions and then present the terms of both packages to Sims. Sims, convinced that the Lions were not negotiating in good faith, signed with the Gamblers on July 1, 1983. On December 16, 1983, Sims signed a second contract with the Lions. The Lions and Sims brought an action against Argovitz, seeking to invalidate Sims's contract with the Gamblers on the ground that Argovitz breached his fiduciary duty when negotiating the contract with the Gamblers.

DECISION Judgment for the Lions and Sims rescinding the Gamblers' contract with Sims.

OPINION Argovitz, as Sims's agent, owed Sims the fiduciary duties of loyalty, good faith, and fair and honest dealing. The duty of loyalty requires that an agent not represent his principal in a transaction in which the agent has a personal stake that conflicts with the principal's interest. Therefore, an agent may not deal on his principal's behalf with a third party in which the agent has an interest. An agent who does so is presumed to have acted fraudulently and must show that the principal freely consented to the transaction with full knowledge of every material fact known to the agent that might affect the principal. In this case, Argovitz had an ownership interest in the Gamblers and thus had a personal interest, contrary to Sims's interest, in signing Sims with the team. Fraud on Argovitz's part is therefore presumed, and Sims may rescind the contract with the Gamblers unless Argovitz can demonstrate that Sims was aware of all material facts that might have influenced his decision. Argovitz failed to show either that he informed Sims of the material facts or that these facts would have had no impact upon Sims's decision to sign the contract with the Gamblers. Indeed, Argovitz did not solicit a final contract offer from the Lions because he knew that the Lions would match the Gamblers' offer and that Sims would be lost to the Gamblers, a team that Argovitz owned.

INTERPRETATION In agent's fiduciary duty precludes the agent from acting in his own interest or in the interests of another if such action would conflict with his principal's interests.

DUTIES OF PRINCIPAL TO AGENT

Although, in terms of the rights and duties arising out of the agency relationship, the duties of the agent receive more emphasis than those of the principal, an agent nonetheless has certain rights against the principal, both under the contract and by the operation of law. Connected to these rights are certain duties, based in contract and tort law, that the principal owes to the agent. For a summary of the primary duties in the principal-agent relationship, see Figure 29–1.

Contractual Duties

The contractual duties owed by a principal to an agent are the duties of compensation, reimbursement, and indemnification; each may be excluded or modified by agreement between the principal and agent. Although a gratuitous agent is not owed a duty of compensation, she is entitled to reimbursement and indemnification.

Depending on the particular case, the principal must furnish either the agent's means of employment or the opportunity for work. For example, a principal who employs an agent to sell his goods must supply the agent with conforming goods. It is also the duty of the principal not to terminate the agency wrongfully.

Compensation A principal has a duty to compensate her agent unless the agent has agreed to serve gratuitously. If the agreement does not specify a definite compensation, a principal is under a duty to pay the reasonable value of authorized services the agent has performed. An agent loses the right to compensation by (1) breaching the duty of obedience, (2) breaching the duty of loyalty, or (3) willfully and deliberately breaching the agency contract. Furthermore, an agent whose compensation is dependent upon her accomplishing a specific result is entitled to the agreed compensation only if she achieves the result in the time specified or in a reasonable time, if no time is

Compensation a principal must compensate the agent as specified in the contract, or for the reasonable value of the services provided, if no amount is specified

FIGURE 29–1 Duties of Principal and Agent

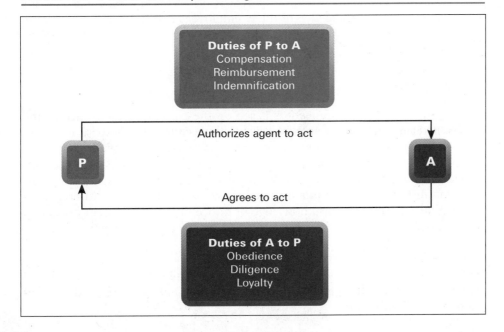

stated. A common example is a listing agreement between a seller and a real estate broker providing for a commission to the broker if he finds a buyer ready, willing, and able to buy the property on the terms specified in the agreement.

Reimbursement duty owed by principal to pay agent for authorized payments made on principal's behalf

Reimbursement A principal is under a duty to reimburse his agent for authorized payments the agent makes on the principal's behalf and for authorized expenses the agent incurs. For example, an agent who reasonably and properly pays a fire insurance premium for the protection of her principal's property is entitled to reimbursement for the payment.

Indemnification *(in·dem·ni·fi·ca'·tion)* duty owed by principal to pay for losses agent incurred while acting as directed by principal

Indemnification The principal is under a duty to indemnify the agent for losses the agent incurred or suffered while acting as directed by the principal in a transaction that is not illegal or not known by the agent to be wrongful. To indemnify is to make good or pay a loss. Suppose that Perry, the principal, has in his possession goods belonging to Margot. Perry directs Alma, his agent, to sell these goods. Alma, believing Perry to be the owner, sells the goods to Turner. Margot then sues Alma for the conversion of her goods and recovers a judgment, which Alma pays to Margot. Alma is entitled to payment from Perry for her loss, including the amount she reasonably expended in defense of the lawsuit brought by Margot.

Tort Duties

Tort duties include the duty to provide an employee with reasonably safe conditions of employment and to warn the employee of any unreasonable risk involved in the employment

A principal owes to any agent the same duties under tort law that the principal owes to all parties. Moreover, a principal is under a duty to disclose to an agent those risks of which the principal knows or should know, if the principal should realize that the agent is unaware of such risks in the agency. For instance, in directing his agent to collect rent from a tenant who is known to have assaulted rent collectors, a principal has a duty to warn the agent of this risk.

Where the agent is an employee, the principal owes the agent additional duties. Among these is the duty to provide the employee with reasonably safe conditions of employment and to warn the employee of any unreasonable risk involved in the employment. An employer is also liable to his employees for injury caused by the negligence of other employees and of other agents doing work for him. We will discuss the tort duties owed by an employer to an employee more fully in Chapter 43.

TERMINATION OF AGENCY

Because the authority of an agent is based on the consent of the principal, the agency is terminated when such consent is withdrawn or otherwise ceases to exist. On termination of the agency, the agent's actual authority ends, and she is not entitled to compensation for services subsequently rendered, although her fiduciary duties may continue. As discussed in Chapter 30, in some situations apparent authority also terminates, whereas in others apparent authority continues until a third party has knowledge or notice of the termination of agency. Termination may take place by the acts of the parties or by operation of law.

Acts of the Parties

Termination by the acts of the parties may occur by the provisions of the original agreement, by the subsequent acts of both principal and agent, or by the subsequent act of either one.

Lapse of Time Authority conferred upon an agent for a specified time terminates when that period expires. If no time is specified, authority terminates at the end of a reasonable period. For example, Palmer authorizes Avery to sell a tract of land for him. After ten years pass without communication between Palmer and Avery, Avery purports to sell the tract. But his authorization has terminated due to lapse of time.

Fulfillment of Purpose The authority of an agent to perform a specific act or to accomplish a particular result terminates when the agent performs the act or accomplishes the result. Thus, if Porter authorizes Alford to sell or lease Porter's land, Alford's authority terminates when he leases the land to Taft; and he may not thereafter sell or lease the land without new authorization.

Mutual Agreement of the Parties The agency relationship is created by agreement and may be terminated at any time by mutual agreement of the principal and the agent.

Revocation of Authority A principal may revoke an agent's authority at any time. But if such revocation constitutes a breach of contract by the principal, as in the next case, the agent may recover damages from the principal. Nonetheless, where the agent has seriously breached the agency contract, has willfully disobeyed, or has violated the fiduciary duty, the principal is not liable for revocation. In addition, if the agency is gratuitous, the principal ordinarily may revoke it without liability to the agent.

HILGENDORF v. HAGUE Supreme Court of Iowa, 1980, 293 N.W.2d 272

FACTS Harvey Hilgendorf was a licensed real estate broker acting as the agent of the Hagues in the sale of eighty acres of farmland. The Hagues, however, terminated Hilgendorf's agency before the expiration of the listing contract when they encountered financial difficulties and decided to liquidate their entire holdings of land at one time. Hilgendorf brought this action for breach of the listing contract. The Hagues, who maintained that Hilgendorf's duty of loyalty required him to give up the listing contract, appealed from the trial court's judgment in favor of Hilgendorf.

DECISION Judgment for Hilgendorf affirmed.

OPINION Since agency is a consensual relationship, a principal has the power to terminate an agency that is not coupled with an interest even though the term of the agency has not yet expired. But without a legal reason for doing so, the principal does not have the right to terminate an unexpired agency contract and may subject himself to liability for doing so. Although an agent's duty of loyalty does require him to place the principal's interests first in dealing with third parties, in the contract of agency itself between the agent and the principal, each is acting in his own behalf. The Hagues' financial difficulties did not give them the legal right to terminate the agency relationship, and Hilgendorf was under no duty to relinquish his role as their agent simply because the principal encountered financial problems. Therefore, Hilgendorf may recover damages for breach of the listing contract.

INTERPRETATION A principal may revoke an agent's authority at any time, but if such revocation constitutes a breach of contract, the agent may recover damages from the principal.

Renunciation by the Agent The agent also has the power to end the agency by notice to the principal that she renounces the authority given her by the principal. If the agency is gratuitous, the agent ordinarily may renounce it without liability to the principal. However, if the parties have contracted for the agency to continue for a specified time, an unjustified renunciation prior to the expiration of that time is a breach of contract.

Operation of Law

By the operation of law, the occurrence of certain events will automatically terminate an agency relationship. These events either make it impossible for the agent to perform or unlikely that the principal would want the agent to act. As a matter of law, the occurrence of any of the following events ordinarily terminates agency.

Bankruptcy Bankruptcy is a federal court proceeding to afford relief to financially troubled debtors. The filing of a petition in bankruptcy, which initiates the proceedings, usually terminates all the debtor's existing agency relationships. Bankruptcy is discussed in Chapter 41.

Death The death of the principal terminates the authority of the agent. For example, Polk employs Allison to sell Polk's line of goods under a contract that specifies Allison's commission and the one-year period for which the employment is to continue. Unbeknownst to Allison, Polk dies; Allison no longer has authority to sell Polk's goods. Similarly, the authority a principal gives to an agent is strictly personal; the agent's death terminates the agency.

Incapacity Incapacity of the principal that occurs after the formation of the agency terminates the agent's authority. Likewise, the subsequent incapacity of an agent to perform the acts authorized by the principal terminates the agent's authority. Almost all of the states have statutes providing for a durable power of attorney. If made in compliance with one of these statutes, an appointment of an agent survives the incapacity of the *principal*.

Change in Circumstances The authority of an agent is terminated by notice or knowledge of a change in the value of the subject matter or of a change in business conditions from which the agent should reasonably infer that the principal would not wish the agent to exercise the authority given him. For example, Patricia authorizes Aaron to sell her eighty acres of farmland for $800 per acre. Subsequently, oil is discovered on nearby land, and Patricia's land greatly increases in value. Because Aaron knows of this, whereas Patricia does not, Aaron's authority to sell the land is terminated.

Loss or Destruction of the Subject Matter Where a specific subject matter to which an agent's authority relates becomes lost or is destroyed, such authority is thereby terminated. This corresponds to the rule stating that loss or destruction of the subject matter of an offer terminates the offer. For example, Pauline authorizes Abraham to make a contract for the sale of Pauline's residence. The next week, the residence burns completely, as Abraham is aware. Abraham's authority is terminated.

Disloyalty of Agent If an agent, without the knowledge of her principal, acquires interests adverse to those of the principal or otherwise breaches her duty of loyalty to the principal, her authority to act on behalf of the principal is terminated. Thus, Parker employs Agnes, a realtor, to sell Parker's land. Unknown to Parker, Agnes has been authorized by Trent to purchase this land from Parker. Agnes is not authorized to sell the land to Trent.

Change in Law A change in the law that takes effect after the employment of the agent may make the performance of an authorized act illegal or criminal. Such a change terminates the authority of the agent. Thus, Paul directs his agent, Allan, to ship young elm trees from State X to State Y. In order to control elm disease, State X establishes a quarantine on the shipment of elm trees to any other state, and any such shipment is punishable by fine. Allan's authority to ship the elm trees is terminated.

Outbreak of War Where the outbreak of war places the principal and agent in the position of alien enemies, the authority of the agent is terminated because its exercise is illegal.

Irrevocable Agencies

In the foregoing discussion of the various ways in which the authority of an agent may be terminated, the agency relationship was assumed to be the ordinary one in which the agent has no security interest in the power conferred on him by the principal. Where the **agency** is **coupled with an interest** of the agent in the subject matter, as, for example, where the agent has advanced funds on behalf of the principal and his power to act is given as security for the loan, the principal may *not* revoke the authority of the agent. In addition, neither the incapacity nor the bankruptcy of the principal will terminate the authority or power of the agent in such a situation. Not even the death of the principal will terminate the agency, unless the duty for which the security was given terminates with her death.

Agency coupled with an interest irrevocable agency where agent has a security interest in the subject matter of the agency

---

ETHICAL DILEMMA Is Medicaid Designed to Protect Inheritances?

FACTS Mrs. Singer is a seventy-eight year-old widow. Although she remains somewhat active and lives in her own apartment, her physical and mental abilities are declining. She fell recently and needs assistance with bathing and some routine chores.

Mrs. Singer has two children, a son, Steven, who lives within fifteen minutes of her home, and a daughter, Kate, who lives a great distance away. While Mrs. Singer sees Kate only once a year, she remains in close contact with Steven, who does her grocery shopping, takes her to the doctor, and provides transportation, thereby enabling Mrs. Singer to maintain some social life.

Steven has become increasingly concerned about his mother's declining condition and is unsure how much longer she can remain in her apartment. Steven has consulted his lawyer, who suggested that Mrs.

Singer give Steven a durable power of attorney authorizing Steven to manage most of her financial affairs. It would also give Steven the power to transfer Mrs. Singer's assets to himself so that Mrs. Singer will qualify for Medicaid, should she need to enter a nursing home. Steven's lawyer explained that in order to qualify for Medicaid, Mrs. Singer must meet asset and income limits that are quite low.

Mrs. Singer has substantial assets. She has a portfolio of investments in stocks, bonds, and certificates of deposit worth over $700,000. The durable power of attorney would enable Steven to strip Mrs. Singer of her assets within the time frame necessary to allow the declining Mrs. Singer to qualify for Medicaid.

Mrs. Singer has agreed to execute the power. But Kate objects to the plan. She does not get along with

Steven, does not trust his judgment, and is concerned that he will not properly share his mother's assets.

Social, Policy, and Ethical Considerations

1. Is it ethical for Steven to execute the power of attorney in an effort to enable his mother to qualify for Medicaid?

2. Should Medicaid be available only to those with low income and few assets? Could a national health care plan provide a solution?

3. What role, if any, should private insurance play in providing a safety net against the catastrophic costs of nursing home care?

4. What questions of family ethics does a plan such as Steven's raise?

CHAPTER SUMMARY

Nature of Agency

Definition of Agency relationship authorizing one party (the agent) to act for and on behalf of the other party (the principal)

Scope of Agency Purposes whatever business activity a person may accomplish personally he generally may do through an agent

Other Legal Relations
- *Employment Relationship* one in which the employer has the right to control the physical conduct of the employee
- *Independent Contractor* a person who contracts with another to do a particular job and who is not subject to the control of the other

Creation of Agency

Formalities though agency is a consensual relationship that may be formed by contract or agreement between the principal and agent, agency may exist without consideration
- *Requirements* no particular formality is usually required in a contract of agency, although appointments of agents for a period of more than one year must be in writing
- *Power of Attorney* written, formal appointment of an agent

Capacity
- *Principal* if the principal is a minor or an incompetent not under a guardianship, his appointment of another to act as an agent is voidable
- *Agent* any person may act as an agent since the act of the agent is considered the act of the principal

Duties of Agent to Principal

Duty of Obedience an agent must act in the principal's affairs only as authorized by the principal and must obey all reasonable instructions and directions

Duty of Diligence an agent must act with reasonable care and skill in performing the work for which he is employed

Duty to Inform an agent must use reasonable efforts to give the principal information relevant to the affairs entrusted to her

Duty to Account an agent must maintain and provide the principal with a true and complete account of money or other property that the agent has received or expended on behalf of the principal

Fiduciary Duty an agent owes a duty of utmost loyalty and good faith to the principal
- *Conflicts of Interest*
- *Duty Not to Compete*
- *Confidential Information*
- *Duty to Account for Financial Benefits*

Duties of Principal to Agent	**Contractual Duties** ■ *Compensation* a principal must compensate the agent as specified in the contract, or for the reasonable value of the services provided, if no amount is specified ■ *Reimbursement* the principal must pay back to the agent authorized payments the agent has made on the principal's behalf ■ *Indemnification* the principal must pay the agent for losses the agent incurred while acting, as directed by the principal **Tort Duties** include the duty to provide an employee with reasonably safe conditions of employment and to warn the employee of any unreasonable risk involved in the employment

Termination of Agency	**Acts of the Parties** ■ *Lapse of Time* ■ *Fulfillment of Purpose* ■ *Mutual Agreement of the Parties* ■ *Revocation of Authority* ■ *Renunciation by the Agent* **Operation of Law** ■ *Bankruptcy* the bankruptcy of the principal usually terminates all of the principal's agency relationships; if the credit of the agent is important to the agency relationship, the relationship will be terminated by the bankruptcy of the agent ■ *Death* of either the principal or the agent ■ *Incapacity* of either the principal or the agent ■ *Change in Circumstances* ■ *Loss or Destruction of the Subject Matter* ■ *Disloyalty of Agent* ■ *Change in Law* ■ *Outbreak of War* **Irrevocable Agencies** an agency coupled with an interest is irrevocable and occurs where the agent has a security interest in the subject matter of the agency

QUESTIONS

1. Distinguish among the following relationships: (a) agency, (b) employment, and (c) independent contractor.
2. Discuss the requirements for creating an agency relationship.
3. Discuss the duties owed by an agent to her principal.
4. Discuss the duties owed by a principal to his agent.

5. Identify the ways in which an agency relationship may be terminated.

Internet Question. Compare the formation and termination of an agency relationship under the Convention on Agency in the International Sale of Goods (Geneva, 17 February 1983) with formation and termination under the U.S. common law.

PROBLEMS

1. Parker, the owner of certain unimproved real estate in Chicago, employed Adams, a real estate agent, to sell the property for a price of $25,000 or more and agreed to pay Adams a commission of 6 percent for making a sale. Adams negotiated with Turner, who was interested in the property and willing to pay as much as $28,000 for it. Adams made an agreement with Turner that if Adams could obtain Parker's signature to a contract to sell the property to Turner for $25,000, Turner would pay Adams a bonus of $1,000. Adams prepared and Parker and Turner signed a contract for the sale of the property to Turner for $25,000. Turner refuses to pay Adams the $1,000 as promised. Parker refuses to pay Adams the 6 percent commission. In an action by Adams against Parker and Turner, what is the judgment?

2. Perry employed Alice to sell a parcel of real estate at a fixed price without knowledge that David had previously employed Alice to purchase the same property for him. Perry gave Alice no discretion as to price or terms, and Alice entered into a contract of sale with David on the exact terms authorized by Perry. After accepting a partial payment, Perry discovered that Alice was employed by David and brought an action to rescind. David resisted on the ground that Perry had suffered no damage because Alice had been given no discretion and the sale was made on the exact basis authorized by Perry. Decision?

3. Packer owned and operated a fruit cannery in Southton, Illinois. He stored a substantial amount of finished canned goods in a warehouse in East St. Louis, Illinois, owned and operated by Alden, in order to have goods readily available for the St. Louis market. On March 1, he had 10,000 cans of peaches and 5,000 cans of apples in storage with Alden. On the day named, he borrowed $5,000 from Alden, giving Alden his promissory note for this amount due June 1, together with a letter authorizing Alden, in the event the note was not paid at maturity, to sell any or all of his goods in storage, pay the indebtedness, and account to him for any surplus. Packer died on June 2 without having paid the note. On June 8, Alden told Taylor, a wholesale food distributor, that he had for sale, as agent of the owner, 10,000 cans of peaches and 5,000 cans of apples. Taylor said he would take the peaches and would decide later about the apples. A contract for the sale of 10,000 cans of peaches for $6,000 was thereupon signed "Alden, agent for Packer, seller; Taylor, buyer." Both Alden and Taylor knew of the death of Packer. Delivery of the peaches and payment were made on June 10. On June 11, Alden and Taylor signed a similar contract covering the 5,000 cans of apples, delivery and payment to be made June 30. On June 23, Packer's executor, having learned of these contracts, wrote Alden and Taylor stating that Alden had no authority to make the contracts, demand-

ing that Taylor return the peaches, and directing Alden not to deliver the apples. Discuss the correctness of the contentions of Packer's executor.

4. Green, a licensed real estate broker in Illinois, and Jones, also an Illinois resident, while both in New York, signed a contract whereby Green agreed to endeavor to find a buyer for certain Illinois real estate owned by Jones, who agreed to pay Green a commission of $10,000 in the event of a sale. Green found a buyer, a resident of New York, to whom the land was sold. Thereafter, Jones refused to pay the commission, and Green commenced an action in Illinois to recover it. Jones defended on the sole ground that the brokerage contract was unenforceable because Green was not a licensed real estate broker in New York. Relevant provisions of the applicable New York statute forbid any person from holding himself out or acting temporarily as a real estate broker or salesman without first procuring a license. A violation is declared to be a misdemeanor, and the commission of a single prohibited act is a violation for which the statute provides a penalty. For whom should judgment be rendered?

5. Palmer made a valid contract with Ames under which Ames was to sell Palmer's goods on commission from January 1 to June 30. Ames made satisfactory sales up to May 15 and was about to close an unusually large order when Palmer suddenly and without notice revoked Ames's authority to sell. Can Ames continue to sell Palmer's goods during the unexpired term of her contract?

6. Piedmont Electric Co. gave a list of delinquent accounts to Alexander, an employee, with instructions to discontinue electric service to delinquent customers. Among those listed was Todd Hatchery, which was then in the process of hatching chickens in a large, electrically heated incubator. Todd Hatchery told Alexander that it did not consider its account delinquent, but Alexander nevertheless cut the wires leading to the hatchery. Subsequently, Todd Hatchery recovered a judgment of $5,000 in an action brought against Alexander for the loss resulting from the interruption of the incubation process. Alexander has paid the judgment and brings a cause of action against Piedmont Electric Co. Decision?

7. In October 1992, Black, the owner of the Grand Opera House, and Harvey entered into a written agreement to lease the opera house to Harvey for five years at a rental of $30,000 a year. Harvey engaged Day as manager of the theater at a salary of $175 per week plus 10 percent of the profits. One of Day's duties was to determine the amounts of money taken in each night and, after deducting expenses, to divide the profits between Harvey and the manager of the particular attraction playing at the theater. In September 1997, Day went to

Black and offered to rent the opera house from Black at a rental of $37,500 per year, whereupon Black entered into a lease with Day for five years at this figure. When Harvey learned of and objected to this transaction, Day offered to assign the lease to him for $60,000 per year. Harvey refused and brought an appropriate action seeking to have Day declared a trustee of the opera house lease on behalf of Harvey. Decision?

8. Timothy retains Cynthia, an attorney, to bring a lawsuit upon a valid claim against Vincent. Recently enacted legislation has shortened the statute of limitations for this type of legal action. Cynthia fails to make herself aware of this new statute. Consequently, she files the complaint after the statute of limitations has run. As a result, the lawsuit is dismissed. What rights, if any, does Timothy have against Cynthia?

9. Wilson engages Ruth to sell Wilson's antique walnut chest to Harold for $2,500. The next day, Ruth learns that Sandy is willing to pay $3,000 for Wilson's chest. Ruth nevertheless sells the chest to Harold. Wilson then discovers these facts. What are Wilson's rights, if any, against Ruth?

10. Morris is a salesman for Acme, Inc., a manufacturer of household appliances. Morris receives a commission on all sales made and no further compensation. He drives his own automobile, pays his own expenses, and calls on whom he pleases. While driving to make a call on a potential customer, Morris negligently collides with Hudson. Hudson sues Acme and Morris. Who should be held liable?

11. Sierra Pacific Industries purchased various areas of timber and six other pieces of real property, including a ten-acre parcel on which five duplexes and two single-family units were located. Sierra Pacific requested the assistance of Joseph Carter, a licensed real estate broker, in selling the nontimberland properties. It commissioned him to sell the property for an asking price of $85,000, of which Sierra Pacific would receive $80,000 and Carter would receive $5,000 as a commission. Unable to find a prospective buyer, Carter finally sold the property to his daughter and son-in-law for $85,000 and retained the $5,000 commission without informing Sierra Pacific of his relationship to the buyers. After learning of these facts, Sierra Pacific brought this action for fraud against Carter. Decision?

12. Murphy, while a guest at a motel operated by the Betsy-Len Motor Hotel Corporation, sustained injuries from a fall allegedly caused by negligence in maintaining the premises. At that time, Betsy-Len was under a license agreement with Holiday Inns, Inc. The license contained provisions permitting Holiday Inns to regulate the architectural style of the buildings as well as the type and style of the furnishings and equipment. The contract, however, did not grant Holiday Inns the power to control the day-to-day operations of Betsy-Len's motel, to fix customer rates, or to demand a share of the profits.

Betsy-Len could hire and fire its employees, determine wages and working conditions, supervise the employee work routine, and discipline its employees. In return, Betsy-Len used the trade name, "Holiday Inns," and paid a fee for use of the license and Holiday Inns' national advertising. Murphy sued Holiday Inns, claiming Betsy-Len was its agent. Decision?

13. Hunter Farms contracted with Petrolia Grain & Feed Company, a Canadian company, to purchase a large supply of the farm herbicide Sencor from Petrolia for resale. Petrolia learned from the U.S. Customs Service that the import duty for the Sencor would be 5 percent but that the final rate could only be determined upon an inspection of the Sencor at the time of importation. Petrolia forwarded this information to Hunter. Meanwhile, Hunter employed F. W. Myers & Company, an import broker, to assist in moving the herbicide through customs. When customs later determined that certain chemicals in the herbicide, not listed on its label, would increase the customs duty from $30,000 to $128,000, Myers paid the additional amount under protest and turned to Hunter for indemnification. Hunter refused to pay Myers, claiming that Myers breached its duty of care as an import broker in failing to inform Hunter that the 5 percent duty rate was subject to increase. Myers brought an action against Hunter, arguing that it was not employed to give advice to Hunter on matters of importation. Decision?

14. Tube Art was involved in moving a reader board sign to a new location. Tube Art's service manager and another employee went to the proposed site and took photographs and measurements. Later, a Tube Art employee laid out the exact size and location for the excavation by marking a four-by-four square on the asphalt surface with yellow paint. The dimensions of the hole, including it's depth of six feet, were indicated with spray paint inside the square. After the layout was painted on the asphalt, Tube Art engaged a backhoe operator, Richard F. Redford, to dig the hole. Redford began digging in the early evening hours at the location designated by Tube Art. At approximately 9:30 P.M., the bucket of Redford's backhoe struck a small natural gas pipeline. After examining the pipe and finding no indication of a break or leak, he concluded that the line was not in use and left the site. Shortly before 2:00 a.m. on the following day, an explosion and fire occurred in the building serviced by that gas pipeline. As a result, two people in the building were killed, and most of its contents were destroyed.

Massey and his associates, as tenants of the building, brought an action against Tube Art and Richard Redford for the total destruction of drawings, plan, sketches, prototype machine components, castings, and other work products. The trial court entered judgment on a jury verdict awarding $143,000 in damages to Massey. Tube Art appealed. Decision?

CHAPTER 30

Relationship with Third Parties

The purpose of an agency relationship is to allow the principal to extend his business activities by authorizing agents to enter into contracts with third persons on his behalf. Accordingly, it is important that the law balance the competing interests of principals and third persons. The principal wants to be liable *only* for those contracts he actually authorizes the agent to make for him. The third party, on the other hand, wishes the principal bound on *all* contracts that the agent negotiates on the principal's behalf. As we will discuss in this chapter, the law has adopted an intermediate outcome: the principal and the third party are bound to those contracts the principal *actually* authorizes *plus* those the principal has *apparently* authorized.

While pursuing her principal's business, an agent may tortiously injure third parties, who then may seek to hold the principal personally liable. Under what circumstances should the principal be held liable? Similar questions arise concerning a principal's criminal liability for an agent's violation of the criminal law. The law of agency has established rules to determine when the principal is liable for the torts and crimes his agents commit. We will discuss these rules in this chapter.

Finally, what liability to the third party should the agent incur and what rights should she acquire against the third party? Usually, the agent has no liability for, or rights under, contracts made on behalf of a principal. As we will discuss in this chapter, however, in some situations the agent has contractually created obligations or rights or both.

RELATIONSHIP OF PRINCIPAL AND THIRD PERSONS

In this section, we will first consider the contract liability of the principal; then we will examine the principal's potential tort liability.

CONTRACT LIABILITY OF THE PRINCIPAL

Power ability of an agent to change the legal status of his principal

The **power** of an agent is his ability to change the legal status of his principal. An agent who has either actual *or* apparent authority has the power to bind his principal. Thus, whenever an agent, acting within his authority, makes a contract for his principal, he creates new rights or liabilities for his principal and thus changes his principal's legal status. This power of an agent to act for his principal in business transactions is the basis of agency.

A principal's contract liability also depends upon whether she is disclosed, partially disclosed, or undisclosed. The principal is a **disclosed principal** if at the time of a transaction conducted by an agent, the other party has notice that the agent is acting for a principal and also has notice of the principal's identity. The principal is a **partially disclosed principal** if at the time of the transaction conducted by the agent, the other party has notice that the agent is or may be acting for a principal but has no notice of the principal's identity. The principal is an **undisclosed principal** if the other party has no notice that the agent is acting for a principal.

Disclosed principal one whose existence and identity are known

Partially disclosed principal one whose existence is known but whose identity is not known

Undisclosed principal one whose existence and identity are not known

Types of Authority

Authority is of two basic types: actual and apparent. **Actual authority** exists when the principal gives actual consent to the agent. Such authority may be either express or implied. In either case, it is binding and gives the agent both the

Actual authority power conferred upon the agent by actual consent given by the principal

---

MANAGERIAL INSIGHT

Undisclosed Principal Working Through Agents Assembles Home for Famous Mouse, Duck, and Friends

One of the most ambitious, successful land purchases ever made by agents for an undisclosed principal took place in Orange County, Florida, in 1964 and 1965. In just eighteen months, buyers working for a mysterious developer assembled a piece of land twice the size of Manhattan. Rumors regarding the developer's identity were rampant as agents bought up cattle ranches and road frontage, scrub woods and swampland. When the agents were finished, they had acquired about 27,400 acres at an average reported price per acre of $185, for a total expenditure of somewhat more than $5 million.

The mystery ended in 1965.

Walt Disney Productions announced its intention to build Disney World, an amusement park and resort, on 2,500 acres within the large tract. Disney World would be modeled on Disneyland Park, which had opened in 1955 in Anaheim, California. But Disney World would dwarf the 289 acres at Disneyland.

Disney's announcement set off the biggest wave of land speculation Florida had seen in fifty years. David Nusbickel, an Orlando real estate broker, worked with Disney's

attorneys to help buy land. Several years after Disney's announcement of its purchase had set off a buying frenzy, Nusbickel said of the land speculators, "These guys, who obviously know their business, don't even blink when you quote them a price of $75,000 to $150,000 for an acre of property that maybe went for $3,000 a few years back." *Business Week* estimated that between 1965 and 1971 more than $200 million in property changed hands—confirming the wisdom of Disney's secret buying.

Walt Disney World, as the project became known, opened on October 1, 1971. While still under construction, it was called by *Newsweek* the world's largest nongovernmental construction project. Despite occupying 2,500 acres of land, however, phase one of Walt Disney World took up slightly less than one-tenth of the total parcel Disney had assembled. Why had Disney directed its agents to buy so much land?

In Anaheim, hotels and restaurants had sprung up on the perimeter of Disneyland. The value of room and food revenues, which far exceeded the park's revenues, went to the owners and operators of the hotels and restaurants, not to Disney. And having developed without a plan, the hotels, restaurants, and stores gave the impression of clutter. Walt Disney's response: "It is necessary to control the environment. We learned this at Disneyland." Accordingly, Walt and his brother, Roy, decided to take their plan for Walt Disney World one step further. Not only would the company put restaurants, hotels, and golf courses inside the park, it would also buy enough land to develop housing—thus, the huge land purchase.

Said Roy Disney, who ran the financial side of the company, "I think we will make a lot more on the land than we ever will on the park. The development of this 20,000 acres can give us a future. And we will keep that future right in our own company."

Sources: *Newsweek*, 29 November 1965, 82, and 19 April 1971, 103–4; *Time*, 18 October 1971, 52–53; and *Business Week*, 11 September 1971, 80.

power and the right to create or to affect the principal's legal relations with third persons. Where the principal is undisclosed, an agent acting with actual authority in making a contract will contractually bind the principal and the third party unless the terms of the contract exclude the principal from being a party or unless her existence is fraudulently concealed from the third party.

Apparent authority power conferred upon the agent by acts or conduct of the principal that reasonably lead a third party to believe that the agent has such power

Apparent authority is based on acts or conduct of the principal that lead a third person to believe that the agent has actual authority, on which belief the third person *justifiably* relies. This manifestation, which confers upon the agent the power to create a legal relationship between the principal and a third party, may consist of words or actions of the principal as well as other facts and circumstances that induce the third person reasonably to rely on the existence of an agency relationship.

Express authority actual authority derived from written or spoken words of the principal

Actual Express Authority The **express authority** of an agent, found in the spoken or written words the principal communicates to the agent, is actual authority stated in language directing or instructing the agent to do something specific. Thus, if Lee, orally or in writing, requests his agent, Anita, to sell his automobile for $6,500, Anita's authority to sell the car for this sum is actual and express.

Implied authority actual authority inferred from words or conduct manifested to the agent by the principal

Actual Implied Authority **Implied authority** is not found in express or explicit words of the principal but is inferred from words or conduct that the principal manifests to the agent, who has implied authority to do what she reasonably infers the principal desires her to do, in light of the principal's manifestations to her and all other facts she knows or should know. Implied authority may arise from customs and usages of the principal's business. In addition, the authority granted to an agent to accomplish a particular purpose necessarily includes the authority to employ the means reasonably required to accomplish it. For example, Helen authorizes Clyde to manage her eighty-two-unit apartment complex but says nothing about expenses. In order to manage the building, Clyde must employ a janitor, purchase fuel for heating, and arrange for ordinary maintenance. Even though Helen has not expressly granted him the authority to incur such expenses, Clyde may, because such expenses are necessary to proper management, infer the authority to incur them from the express authority to manage the building.

Unless otherwise agreed, the authority to make a contract is inferred from the authority to conduct a transaction, if the making of such a contract is incidental to the transaction, usually accompanies such a transaction, or is reasonably necessary to accomplish it. Thus, Paragon, Inc., appoints Astor as the general manager of Paragon's manufacturing business. Astor's authority is interpreted as including the authority to make contracts for the employment of necessary employees. On the other hand, suppose Paige employs Arthur, a real estate broker, to find a purchaser for her residence at a stated price. Arthur has no authority to contract for its sale.

Unless otherwise agreed, general authority to manage or operate a business for a principal confers on an agent the implied authority (1) to buy and sell property for the principal; (2) to make contracts that are incidental or reasonably necessary to such business; (3) to acquire equipment and supplies; (4) to make repairs; (5) to employ, supervise, and discharge employees; (6) to receive payments due the principal and to pay debts due from the principal; and (7) to direct the ordinary operations of the business.

Apparent Authority Apparent authority is power arising from the conduct or words of a disclosed or partially disclosed principal that, when manifested to third persons, reasonably induce them to rely upon the assumption that actual authority exists. Apparent authority confers upon the agent, or supposed agent, the power to bind the disclosed or partially disclosed principal in contracts with third persons and prevents the principal from denying the existence of actual authority. Thus, when authority is apparent but not actual, the disclosed or partially disclosed principal is nonetheless bound by the act of the agent. By exceeding his actual authority, however, the agent violates his duty of obedience and is liable to the principal for any loss the principal suffers as a result of the agent's acting beyond his actual authority. See Figures 30–1 and 30–2.

For example, Peter writes a letter to Alice authorizing her to sell his automobile and sends a copy of the letter to Thomas, a prospective purchaser. On the following day, Peter writes a letter to Alice revoking the authority to sell the car but does not send a copy of the second letter to Thomas, who is not

FIGURE 30–1 Contract Liability of Disclosed Principal

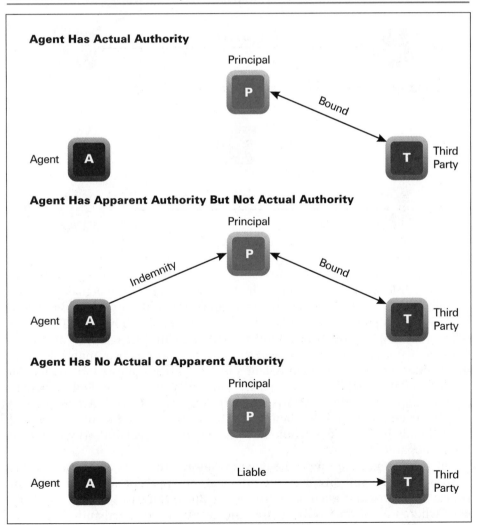

FIGURE 30–2 Contract Liability of Partially Disclosed Principal

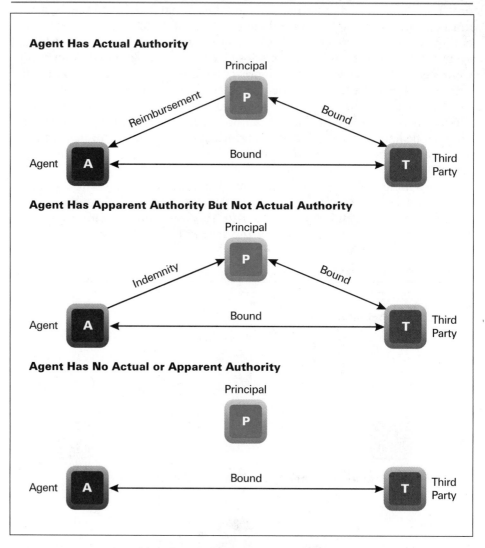

otherwise informed of the revocation. Although Alice has no actual authority to sell the car, she continues to have apparent authority with respect to Thomas. Or suppose that Arlene, in the presence of Polly, tells Thad that Arlene is Polly's agent to buy lumber. Although this statement is not true, Polly does not deny it, as she easily could. Thad, in reliance upon the statement, ships lumber to Polly on Arlene's order. Polly is obligated to pay for the lumber because Arlene had apparent authority to act on Polly's behalf. Arlene's apparent authority exists only with respect to Thad. If Arlene were to give David an order for a shipment of lumber to Polly, David would not be able to hold Polly liable. Arlene would have had neither actual authority nor, as to David, apparent authority.

Since apparent authority is the power resulting from acts that appear to the third party to be authorized by the principal, no apparent authority can exist where the principal is *undisclosed*. See Figure 30–3. Nor can apparent authority exist where the third party *knows* that the agent has no actual authority.

FIGURE 30–3 Contract Liability of Undisclosed Principal

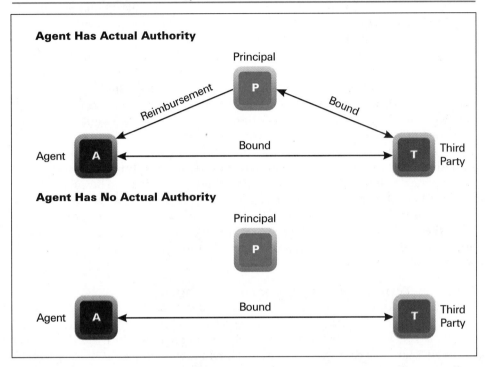

SCHOENBERGER v. CHICAGO TRANSIT AUTHORITY Appellate Court of Illinois, First District, First Division, 1980, 84 Ill.App.3d 1132, 39 Ill.Dec. 941, 405 N.E.2d 1076

FACTS Schoenberger applied for and interviewed concerning a position with the Chicago Transit Authority (C.T.A.). He met several times with Frank ZuChristian, who was in charge of recruiting for the C.T.A. Data Center. At the third of these meetings, ZuChristian informed Schoenberger that he wanted to employ him at a salary of $19,800 and that he was making a recommendation to that effect. When the formal offer was made by the placement department, however, the salary was stated at $19,300. Schoenberger did not accept the offer immediately but instead called ZuChristian for an explanation of the salary difference. After making inquiries, ZuChristian informed Schoenberger that a clerical error had been made and that it would take some time to correct. He urged Schoenberger to accept the job at $19,300 and said that he would see that the $500 was made up to him at one of the salary reviews in the following year. When the increase was not given, Schoenberger resigned and filed this suit to recover damages. The trial court ruled in favor of C.T.A., and Schoenberger appealed.

DECISION Judgment for Chicago Transit Authority affirmed.

OPINION ZuChristian had neither the actual nor the apparent authority to bind the C.T.A. for the additional $500. The actual authority of an agent may come only from the principal and must be founded on the words or acts of the principal, not on the acts or words of the agent. Apparent authority, in contrast, is such authority as the principal knowingly permits the agent to assume or holds out his agent as possessing. It is such authority as a reasonable, prudent person, exercising diligence and discretion, in view of the principal's conduct, would naturally suppose the agent to possess.

Here, two of ZuChristian's superiors testified that he had no actual authority to make an offer of a specific salary to Schoenberger or to make any promise of additional compensation. Moreover, ZuChristian did not have the apparent authority to do either. The mere fact that he was allowed to interview prospective employees does not establish that the C.T.A. held him out as possessing the authority to hire or to set salaries. Furthermore, Schoenberger was told that the formal offer would be made by the placement department.

INTERPRETATION In order for an agent to bind a principal, she must have either actual authority or apparent authority, either of which must come from the conduct or words of the principal.

Delegation of Authority

Because the appointment of an agent reflects the principal's confidence in the agent's personal skill, integrity, and other qualifications, the agent ordinarily has no power to delegate her authority to a subagent.

In certain situations, however, it is clear that the principal intended to permit the agent to delegate her granted authority. Such an intention may be gathered from the express authorization of the principal, the character of the business, the usages of trade, or the prior conduct of the parties. For example, if a check is deposited in a bank for collection at a distant place, the bank is impliedly authorized to employ another bank at the place of payment.

If an agent is authorized to appoint or select other persons, called **subagents**, to perform or to assist in the performance of the agent's duties, the acts of the subagent are as binding on the principal as those of the agent. The subagent, an agent of both the principal and the agent, owes a fiduciary duty to both.

If no authority exists to delegate the agent's authority, but the agent does so nevertheless, the acts of the subagent do not impose on the principal any obligations or liability to third persons. Likewise, the principal acquires no rights against such third persons.

Effect of Termination of Agency on Authority

When an agency terminates, the agent's *actual authority* ceases. When the termination is by the death or incapacity of the principal or agent, the agent's *apparent authority* also expires. Notice of such termination to third persons is *not* required. Thus, in a case where Thomas, a tenant of the principal, Perry, paid rent to Perry's agent, Augustus, in ignorance of Perry's death, and Augustus failed to account for the payment, Thomas is liable to Perry's estate for payment of the amount of the rent. The same holds where the performance of an authorized transaction becomes impossible, such as where the subject matter of the transaction is destroyed or the transaction is made illegal. The bankruptcy of the principal terminates without notice the power of an agent to affect the principal's property which has passed to the bankruptcy trustee.

In other cases, apparent authority continues until the third party has actual knowledge or receives actual notice, if the third party is one (1) with whom the agent had previously dealt on credit, (2) to whom the agent has been specially accredited, or (3) with whom the agent has begun to deal, as the principal should know. **Actual notice** requires a communication to the third party, either oral or written. All other third parties as to whom there was apparent authority must have actual knowledge or be given **constructive notice**, through publication, for example, in a newspaper of general circulation in the area where the agency is regularly carried on. See Figure 30–4.

To illustrate: Alfred is the general agent of Pace, who carries on business in Chicago. Carol knows of the agency, but has never dealt with Alfred. Daphne sells goods on credit to Alfred, as the agent of Pace. Pace revokes Alfred's authority and publishes a statement to that effect in a newspaper of general circulation published in Chicago. Carol does not see the statement and deals with Alfred in reliance upon the former agency. Daphne, who also does not see the statement and who has no knowledge of the revocation, sells more goods to Alfred, as the agent of Pace. Pace has given sufficient notice of revocation as to Carol, and, therefore, Alfred's apparent authority has terminated with respect to Carol. On the other hand, Pace has not given sufficient notice of revocation as to Daphne, and Pace is bound to Daphne by the contract of sale Alfred made on Pace's behalf.

FIGURE 30–4 Termination of Apparent Authority

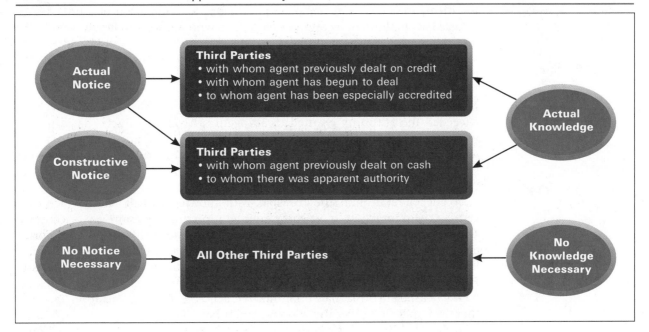

ZUKAITIS v. AETNA CASUALTY AND SURETY CO. Supreme Court of Nebraska, 1975, 195 Neb. 59, 236 N.W.2d 819

FACTS Raymond Zukaitis was a physician practicing medicine in Douglas County, Nebraska. Aetna issued a policy of professional liability insurance to Zukaitis through its agent, the Ed Larsen Insurance Agency. The policy covered the period from August 31, 1969, through August of the following year. On August 7, 1971, Dr. Zukaitis received a written notification of a claim for malpractice that had occurred on September 27, 1969. Dr. Zukaitis notified the Ed Larsen Insurance Agency immediately and forwarded the written claim to them. The claim was then mistakenly referred to St. Paul Fire and Marine Insurance Company, the company that currently insured Dr. Zukaitis. Apparently without notice to Dr. Zukaitis, the agency contract between Larsen and Aetna had been canceled on August 1, 1970, and St. Paul had replaced Aetna as the insurance carrier. However, when St. Paul discovered it was not the carrier on the date of the alleged wrongdoing, it notified Aetna and withdrew from Dr. Zukaitis's defense. Aetna also refused to represent Dr. Zukaitis, contending that it was relieved of its obligation to Dr. Zukaitis because he had not notified Aetna immediately of the claim. Dr. Zukaitis then secured his own attorney to defend against the malpractice claim and brought this action against Aetna to recover attorney's fees and other expenses incurred in the defense. The trial court found for Aetna, and Dr. Zukaitis appealed.

DECISION Judgment for Aetna reversed and remanded.

OPINION Aetna is responsible for the defense of Dr. Zukaitis. The notice given by Dr. Zukaitis to Larsen, the agent of Aetna, constitutes notice to Aetna and obligates it to carry out the terms of its insurance contract with Dr. Zukaitis. A revocation of the agent's authority does not become effective between the principal and third persons until they receive notice of the termination. More specifically, when an insurer terminates the agency contract, it has a duty to notify third persons, such as the insureds with whom the agent dealt, and inform them of such termination. If it does not do so and such third persons or insureds deal with the agent without notice or knowledge of the termination and in reliance on the apparently continuing authority of the agent, the insurer is bound by the acts of the former agent. Therefore, the notice given by Zukaitis to Larsen, the agent of Aetna, obligates Aetna to carry out the terms of its insurance contract with Dr. Zukaitis and to provide for his defense against the malpractice claim.

INTERPRETATION A revocation of an agent's authority does not bind third parties until they receive notice of the revocation.

Ratification

Ratification affirmation by one person of a prior unauthorized act that another has done as her agent or as her purported agent

Ratification is the confirmation or affirmance by one person of a prior unauthorized act performed by another who is, or who purports to be, his agent. The ratification of such act or contract binds the principal and the third party as if the agent or purported agent had been authorized initially. Once made, a valid ratification is irrevocable.

Requirements of Ratification Ratification may relate to acts that have exceeded the authority granted to an agent, as well as to acts that a person without any authority performs on behalf of an alleged principal. For the act to be ratified, however, the actor must have indicated to the third person that he was acting on a principal's behalf. There can be no ratification by an undisclosed principal.

To effect a ratification, the principal, with knowledge of all material facts concerning the transaction, must show an intent to ratify the entire act or contract. The principal does not need to communicate this intent either to the purported agent or to the third person. It may be manifested by express language or implied from conduct of the principal. Thus, if Amanda, without authority, contracts in Penelope's name for the purchase of goods from Tate on credit, and Penelope, having learned of Amanda's unauthorized act, accepts the goods from Tate, she thereby impliedly ratifies the contract and is bound on it.

To be effective, ratification must occur before the third person gives notice of his withdrawal to the principal or agent. If the affirmance of a transaction occurs when the situation has so materially changed that it would be inequitable to subject the third party to liability, the third party may elect to avoid liability. For example, Alex has no authority, but, purporting to act for Penny, he contracts to sell Penny's house to Taylor. The next day, the house burns down. Penny then affirms. Taylor is not bound. Moreover, the power to ratify would be terminated by the third party's death or loss of capacity and by the lapse of a reasonable time.

Finally, for ratification to be effective, the purported principal must have been in existence when the act was done. For example, a promoter of a corporation not yet in existence may enter into contracts on behalf of the corporation. However, in the majority of states, these acts cannot be *ratified* by the corporation because it did not exist when the contracts were made. In contrast, a contract that is voidable because of the principal's incapacity may be ratified by the principal after the incapacity is removed. Thus, after she reaches majority, a principal may ratify an unauthorized contract made on her behalf while she was a minor.

Effect of Ratification Ratification is equivalent to prior authority, which means that the effect of ratification is substantially the same as if the purported agent had been duly authorized when he performed the act. The respective rights, duties, and remedies of the principal and the third party are the same as if the agent had originally possessed due authority. Both the principal and the agent are in a position the same as the one they would have been in, had the principal authorized the act originally. The agent is entitled to her due compensation. Moreover, she is freed from liability to the principal for acting as his agent without authority or for exceeding her authority, as the case may be. Between the agent and the third party, the agent is released from any liability she may have to the third party by reason of her having induced the third party to enter into the contract without the principal's authority.

ETHICAL DILEMMA When Should an Agent's Power to Bind His Principal Terminate?

FACTS Tim Banks was an employee of Golden Harvest Florists International (GHFI). GHFI operated a wholesale florist business on the East Coast and also maintained a small chain of retail shops in the Washington, D.C.-Baltimore area. Tim, whose responsibilities included buying large quantities of fresh cut flowers from various greenhouses along the East Coast, had established an excellent rapport with all of his suppliers and was well respected throughout the entire industry.

Because of his good reputation, Tim was shocked to discover on April 1, 1993 that he had been released by GHFI. This notice came after five years of faithful service to the company. Though the company would not tell Tim why he had been fired, Tim learned that GHFI felt threatened by his reputation and was worried that he was becoming better known and more important than the company itself.

GHFI did not, moreover, notify any of Tim's suppliers of his release until January 1, 1994. The company was worried that notice might undermine the suppliers' confidence in the company and could possibly cause prices to rise. Meanwhile, deciding to begin his own business, Tim continued to purchase flowers from the same greenhouses. He was able to pay his supply bills from April through November of 1993, but, when his funds were low in December, he charged the flowers to GHFI. GHFI refused to pay, and the greenhouses have filed suit against Tim and GHFI.

Social, Policy, and Ethical Considerations

1. Who is legally responsible for the bills? Who is ethically responsible?
2. What is the social policy behind the requirement of notice prior to termination of a principal-agent relationship?
3. Does Tim have a responsibility to the greenhouses to notify them of the source of his funds, as long as the bill is paid?

Fundamental Rules of Contractual Liability

The following rules summarize the contractual relations between the principal and the third party:

1. A disclosed principal and the third party are contractually bound if the agent acts within her *actual* or *apparent* authority in making the contract. See Figure 30–1.
2. A partially disclosed principal and the third party are contractually bound if the agent acts within her *actual* or *apparent* authority in making the contract. See Figure 30–2.
3. An undisclosed principal and the third party are contractually bound if the agent acts within her *actual* authority in making the contract unless (a) the terms of the contract exclude the principal, or (b) his existence is fraudulently concealed. See Figure 30–3.
4. No principal is contractually bound to a third party if the agent acts *without* any authority, unless a disclosed or partially disclosed principal ratifies the contract.

See Figure 30–5.

FIGURE 30–5 Types of Agency and Authority

Authority	Disclosed	Partially Disclosed	Undisclosed
Actual	Yes	Yes	Yes
Apparent	Yes	Yes	No
Neither	Yes	Yes	Yes
Ratification	Yes	Maybe*	No

* If principal is one intended or identified.

TORT LIABILITY OF THE PRINCIPAL

In addition to being contractually liable to third persons, a principal may be liable in tort to third persons because of the acts of her agent. Tort liability may arise directly or indirectly (vicariously) from authorized or unauthorized acts of an agent. Also, a principal is liable for the unauthorized torts an agent commits in connection with a transaction that the purported principal, with full knowledge of the tort, subsequently ratifies. Cases involving unauthorized but ratified torts are extremely rare. Of course, in all of these situations the wrongdoing agent is personally liable to the injured person because the agent committed the tort. See Figure 30–6.

Direct Liability of Principal

Direct liability of principal a principal is liable for his own tortious conduct involving the use of agents

A principal is liable for his *own* tortious conduct involving the use of agents. Such liability may arise in two primary ways. First, a principal is directly liable in damages for harm resulting from his directing an agent to commit a tort. Second, the principal is directly liable if he fails to exercise care in employing competent agents.

FIGURE 30–6 Tort Liability

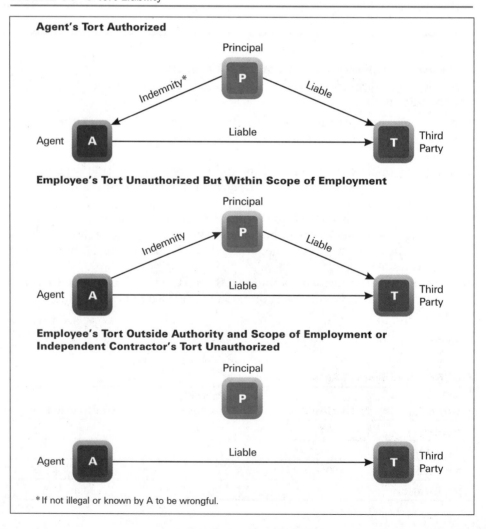

Authorized Acts of Agent A principal who authorizes his agent to commit a tortious act concerning the property or person of another is liable for the injury or loss that person sustains. The authorized act is that of the principal. Thus, if Phillip directs his agent, Anthony, to enter on Clark's land and cut timber, which neither Phillip nor Anthony has any right to do, the cutting of the timber is a trespass, and Phillip is liable to Clark. Or suppose Phillip instructs his agent, Anthony, to make certain representations as to Phillip's property that Anthony is authorized to sell. Phillip knows these representations are false, but Anthony does not. Such representations by Anthony to Dryden, who buys the property in reliance on them, constitute a deceit for which Phillip is liable to Dryden.

Authorized acts of agent a principal is liable for torts she authorizes another to commit

Unauthorized Acts of Agent A principal who conducts activities through an employee or other agent is liable for harm resulting from the principal's negligence or recklessness in hiring, instructing, supervising, or controlling the employee or other agent.

The liability of a principal under this provision—called negligent hiring—arises when the principal does not exercise proper care in selecting an agent for the job to be done. For example, if Patricia lends to her employee, Art, a company car with which to run a business errand, knowing that Art is incapable of driving the vehicle, Patricia would be liable for her own negligence to anyone injured by Art's unsafe driving. The negligent hiring doctrine has also been used to impose liability on a principal for intentional torts committed by an agent against customers of the principal or members of the public, where the principal either knew or should have known that the agent was violent or aggressive.

Unauthorized acts of agent a principal is liable for failing to exercise care in employing agents whose unauthorized acts cause harm

CONNES v. MOLALLA TRANSPORT SYSTEM, INC. Supreme Court of Colorado, 1992, 831 P.2d 1316

FACTS Terry Taylor was an employee of Molalla Transport. In hiring Taylor, Molalla followed its standard hiring procedure, which includes a personal interview with each applicant and requires the applicant to fill out an extensive job application form and to produce a current driver's license and a certificate from a medical examiner. Molalla also contacts prior employers and other references about the applicant's qualifications and conducts an investigation of the applicant's driving record in the state where the applicant obtained the driver's license. Although applicants are asked whether they have been convicted of a crime, Molalla does not conduct an independent investigation to determine whether or not an applicant has ever been convicted. Approximately three months after Taylor began working for Molalla, he was assigned to transport freight from Kansas to Oregon. While traveling through Colorado, Taylor left the highway and drove by a hotel where Grace Connes was working as a night clerk. Observing that Connes was alone in the lobby, Taylor pulled his truck into the parking lot and entered the lobby. Once inside, Taylor sexually assaulted Connes at knifepoint. Although Taylor denied any prior criminal convictions on his application and during his interview, police and court records obtained since these events show that Taylor had been convicted of three felonies in Colorado and had been issued three citations for lewd conduct and another citation for simple assault in Seattle, Washington.

Connes sued Molalla on the theory of negligent hiring, claiming that Molalla knew or should have known that Taylor would come into contact with members of the public, that Molalla had a duty to hire and retain high-quality employees so as not to endanger members of the public, and that Molalla had breached its duty by failing to investigate fully and adequately Taylor's criminal background. The district court granted Molalla's motion for summary judgment. The Court of Appeals upheld the lower court's ruling, holding that Molalla had no legal duty to investigate the nonvehicular criminal record of its driver prior to hiring him as an employee. Connes appealed.

DECISION Judgment affirmed.

OPINION The tort of negligent hiring is based on the principle that a person conducting an activity through employees is subject to liability for harm resulting from negligent conduct "in the employment of improper persons or instrumentalities in work involving risk of harm to others." Restatement (Second) of Agency § 213(b). In recognizing the tort of negligent hiring, we emphasize that an employer is not an insurer for violent acts

continued

committed by an employee against a third person. On the contrary, liability is predicated on the employer's hiring of a person under circumstances antecedently giving the employer reason to believe that the person, by reason of some attribute of character or prior conduct, would create an undue risk of harm to others in carrying out his or her employment responsibilities.

The scope of the employer's duty in exercising reasonable care in a hiring decision will depend largely on the anticipated degree of contact that the employee will have with other persons in performing his or her employment duties. Where the employment calls for minimum contact between the employee and other persons, there may be no reason for an employer to conduct an investigation of the applicant's background beyond obtaining past employment information. However, where the employee will come into frequent contact with members of the public, or close contact with particular individuals with whom the employer has a special relationship, the employer's duty necessarily will be greater and may require an independent investigation of the applicant's background.

In the present case, Molalla had no reason to foresee that its hiring of Taylor under the circumstances of this case would create a risk that Taylor would sexually assault or otherwise endanger a member of the public by engaging in violent conduct. Far from requiring frequent conduct with members of the public or close contact with persons having a special relationship with the employer, Taylor's duties were restricted to the hauling of freight and involved only incidental contact with third persons having no special relationship to either Molalla or Taylor. Furthermore, nothing in the hiring process gave Molalla reason to foresee that Taylor would pose an unreasonable risk of harm to members of the public. Therefore, we hold that Molalla had no legal duty to conduct an independent investigation into Taylor's nonvehicular criminal background in order to protect a member of the public, such as Connes, from a sexual assault committed by Taylor in the course of making a long-haul trip.

INTERPRETATION   An employer's liability for negligent hiring is based on the employer's hiring a person under circumstances antecedently giving the employer reason to believe that the person would create an undue risk of harm to others in carrying out his employment duties.

Vicarious Liability of Principal for Unauthorized Acts of Agent

Vicarious liability
(vi·car'·i·ous) indirect legal responsibility for the act of another

The **vicarious liability** of a principal for unauthorized torts by an agent depends primarily on whether the agent is an employee or not. An employee is an agent whose physical conduct in the performance of services for the principal-employer is controlled by the principal or subject to the principal's right to control. By comparison, an agent whose physical conduct is not controlled by, or subject to the control of, the principal is not an employee but an independent contractor. The general rule is that a principal is *not* liable for physical harm caused by the tortious conduct of an agent who is an independent contractor if the principal did not intend or authorize the result or the manner of performance. Conversely, a principal is liable for an unauthorized tort committed by an employee in the course of his employment.

On the other hand, the liability of a principal whose agent makes an unauthorized yet tortious *misrepresentation* does not depend upon whether the agent is an employee. Rather, the principal is liable for loss caused to another who relies upon a tortious representation made by an agent (whether an employee or an independent contractor) if the representation is *apparently* authorized. For example, Pillsbury engages Adams as an agent to sell some land. While negotiating with Trent, Adams states that a stream running through the property has not overflowed its banks during the past ten years. Adams knows that this is untrue. In reliance upon this false statement, Trent purchases the land. Pillsbury is liable to Trent for fraudulent misrepresentation.

Respondeat Superior   An employer may be liable for an unauthorized tort committed by his employee, even one that is in flagrant disobedience of his instructions, if the employee committed the tort in the course of her employment.

This form of employer liability without fault is based on the doctrine of **respondeat superior**, or "let the superior respond." The rationale behind this doctrine is that a person who conducts his business activities through the use of employees should be liable for their tortious conduct in carrying out those activities. It does not matter how carefully the employer selected the employee if, in fact, the latter tortiously injures a third person while engaged in the employer's business. Under the Restatement, even an undisclosed principal employer is liable for the torts his employee commits within the scope of employment.

Respondeat superior an employer is liable for unauthorized torts committed by an employee in the course of his employment

The liability of the principal under *respondeat superior* is vicarious or derivative and depends on proof of wrongdoing by the employee *in the course of his employment*. Frequently, both principal and employee are defendants in the same suit. If the employee is not held liable, the principal is not liable either, because the employer's liability is based upon the employee's tortious conduct. A principal who is held liable for her employee's tort has a right of **indemnification** against the employee, which is the right to be reimbursed for the amount that she was required to pay as a result of the employee's wrongful act. Frequently, however, an employee is not able to reimburse his employer, and the principal must bear the brunt of the liability.

The wrongful act of the employee must be connected with his employment and within its scope if the principal is to be held liable for resulting injuries or damage to third persons. For example, Hal, delivering gasoline for Martha, lights his pipe and negligently throws the blazing match into a pool of gasoline that has dripped on the ground during the delivery. The gasoline ignites, burning Arnold's filling station. Martha is subject to liability for the resulting harm because the negligence of the employee who delivered the gasoline relates directly to the manner in which he handled the goods in his custody. But if a chauffeur, while driving his employer's car on an errand for his employer, suddenly decides to shoot his pistol at pedestrians on the sidewalk, the employer would not be liable to the pedestrians. This willful and intentional misconduct is not related to the performance of the services for which the chauffeur was employed.

The same rule applies to an employee's tortious conduct that is unrelated to his employment. If Page employs Edward to deliver merchandise to Page's customers in a given city, and while driving a delivery truck to or from a place of delivery Edward negligently causes the truck to hit and injure Fred, Page is liable to Fred for injuries sustained. But if, after making the scheduled deliveries, Edward drives the truck to a neighboring city to visit a friend and while so doing negligently causes the truck to hit and injure Debra, Page is not liable. In the latter case, Edward is said to be on a "frolic of his own." By using the truck to accomplish his own purposes, not those of his employer, he has deviated from the purpose of his employment.

CLOVER v. SNOWBIRD SKI RESORT Supreme Court of Utah, 1991, 808 P.2d 1037

FACTS Chris Zulliger was a chef at the Plaza Restaurant in the Snowbird Ski Resort in Utah. The restaurant is located at the base of a mountain. As a chef for the Plaza, Zulliger was instructed by his supervisor and the restaurant manager to make periodic trips to inspect the Mid-Gad Restaurant, which was located halfway up the mountain. Because skiing helped its employees to get to work, Snowbird preferred that its employees know how to ski and gave them ski passes as part of their compensation. Prior to beginning work at the Plaza on December 5, 1985, Zulliger went skiing. The restaurant manager asked Zulliger to stop at the Mid-Gad before

continued

beginning work that day, and Zulliger stopped at the Mid-Gad during his first run and inspected the kitchen. He then skied four runs before heading down the mountain to begin work. On the last run, Zulliger decided to take a route often taken by Snowbird employees. About midway down, Zulliger decided to jump off a crest on the side of an intermediate run. Because of the drop, a skier above the crest cannot see if there are skiers below, and Zulliger ran into Margaret Clover, who was below the crest. The jump was well known to Snowbird; the resort's ski patrol often instructed people not to jump, and there was a sign instructing skiers to take it slow at that point. Clover sued Zulliger and, under the doctrine of *respondeat superior*, Snowbird, claiming that Zulliger had been acting within the scope of his employment. Zulliger settled prior to trial. The trial court granted summary judgment for Snowbird, ruling as a matter of law that Zulliger was not acting within the scope of his employment. Clover appealed.

DECISION Decision of the trial court reversed and remanded for further proceedings.

OPINION Under the doctrine of *respondent superior*, employers are held vicariously liable for the torts their employees commit while acting within the scope of their employment. In deciding this issue, three criteria apply: (1) the employee's conduct must be of the kind the employee is hired to do and not a personal endeavor; (2) the employee's conduct must occur substantially within the hours and ordinary physical boundaries of the employment; and (3) the employee's conduct must be motivated at least in part by the purpose of serving the employer's interest.

Relating those factors to this case, if Zulliger had returned to the Plaza Restaurant immediately after inspecting the Mid-Gad, his actions clearly would have been within the scope of his employment. First, Zulliger's actions could be considered to have been of a kind that he was employed to perform. Evidence showed that it was part of Zulliger's job to monitor the operations at the Mid-Gad and that he was directed to monitor the operations on the day of the accident. Evidence showed also that Snowbird intended Zulliger to use the ski lifts and the ski runs on his trips to the Mid-Gad. Second, Zulliger's actions clearly occurred within the hours and normal spatial boundaries of his employment. Zulliger was expected to monitor the operations at the Mid-Gad during the time the lifts were operating and when he was not working at the Plaza. The trip was also on Snowbird's premises. Lastly,

it is clear that Zulliger's actions could be considered to have been motivated, at least in part, by the purpose of serving his employer's interest.

The difficulty in determining Snowbird's liability, if any, arises from the fact that Zulliger did not return to the Plaza immediately after he inspected the Mid-Gad. Rather, he made four runs and went to the top of the mountain before returning to the Plaza. Under the dual purpose doctrine, if an employee's actions are motivated by the dual purpose of benefiting the employer and of serving some personal interest, the actions will fall within the scope of employment. However, if the purpose for acting is primarily personal, the incidental business duty will not make the conduct fall within the scope of employment. Where a trip is involved, a useful test is to see if the trip is one that would have required the employer to send another employee over the same route or to perform the same function if the first employee had not made the trip. In this case, if Zulliger had not inspected Mid-Gad, it would have been necessary for Snowbird to send another employee to make the inspection. Furthermore, the second employee most likely would have used the ski lifts and ski runs in traveling to and from the restaurant. Therefore, ample evidence shows a predominant business purpose for Zulliger's trip to the Mid-Gad.

Since the evidence demonstrates a primarily employment-related purpose for Zulliger's actions, this case should be analyzed as an instance where an employee has taken a personal detour in the process of carrying out his duties. If the detour is such a substantial deviation from the employee's duties that it constitutes a complete abandonment of employment, then the employee was acting outside the scope of his employment as a matter of law. However, if reasonable minds could differ regarding whether the detour constituted an abandonment or not, it is a question for the jury.

In this case, reasonable minds could have differed. It is possible for a jury to believe that Zulliger resumed his employment after a detour. If that is in fact what he did, his actions would have been conduct of the kind for which he was hired and would have been motivated, at least in part, by employment-related purposes.

INTERPRETATION Under *respondeat superior*, an employer may be liable for torts committed by an employee who, after conducting personal business, has resumed his employment-related duties.

RUBIN v. YELLOW CAB COMPANY Appellate Court of Illinois, First District, Fifth Division, 1987, 154 Ill. App.3d 336, 107 Ill.Dec. 450, 507 N.E.2d 114

FACTS Rubin, the plaintiff, was driving on one of the city's streets when he inadvertently obstructed the path of a taxicab, causing the cab to come into contact with his vehicle. Angered by the plaintiff's sudden blocking of his traffic lane, the defendant taxi driver exited his cab, approached Rubin, and struck him about the head and shoulders with a metal pipe. Rubin filed suit against the cab driver to recover for bodily injuries resulting from the altercation. He also sued the Yellow Cab Company (Yellow Cab), asserting that the company was vicariously liable under the doctrine of *respondeat superior*. The trial court ruled in favor of Yellow Cab, and the plaintiff appealed.

DECISION Judgment for Yellow Cab affirmed.

OPINION It is well established that an employer may be held vicariously liable under the doctrine of *respondeat superior* for the negligent, willful, malicious, or criminal acts of its employees where such acts are committed in the course of employment and in furtherance of the business of the employer. However, when the acts complained of are committed solely for the benefit of the employee, the employer will not be held liable to an injured third party. The plaintiff contends that the driver's acts were committed within the course and scope of his employment, and were designed to further the business purposes of Yellow Cab. The plaintiff asserts that the driver's acts (1) fulfilled his obligation to investigate and report accidents damaging company property, (2) were performed pursuant to his obligation to protect property owned by Yellow Cab, and (3) were meant to prevent the plaintiff and others from delaying his progress to obtain fares.

The court flatly rejected the plaintiff's argument. The driver's act of hitting the plaintiff has no relation whatsoever to the business of driving a cab. The nature of some jobs, such as a bouncer or bartender, makes the use of force during the course of employment highly probable. The assault on the plaintiff in this case, however, amounted to a deviation from the conduct generally associated with the enterprise of cab driving. The driver was not acting to further the business purposes of Yellow Cab. Accordingly, Yellow Cab is not vicariously liable for the battery of the plaintiff by the driver.

INTERPRETATION Under *respondeat superior,* an employer's liability for torts extends only to torts committed within the scope of employment.

Torts of Independent Contractor An **independent contractor** is not the employee of the person for whom he is performing work or rendering services. Hence, the doctrine of *respondeat superior* generally does not apply to torts committed by an independent contractor. For example, Parnell authorizes Bob, his broker, to sell land for him. Parnell, Teresa, and Bob meet in Teresa's office; and Bob arranges the sale to Teresa. While Bob is preparing a deed for Parnell to sign, he negligently knocks over an inkstand and ruins a valuable rug belonging to Teresa. Bob, but *not* Parnell, is liable to Teresa.

Independent contractor a principal is usually not liable for the unauthorized torts of an independent contractor

However, under some circumstances, a principal will be liable for torts committed by an independent contractor. Certain duties imposed by law are nondelegable, and a person may not escape the consequences of their nonperformance by having entrusted them to an independent contractor. For example, a landowner who permits an independent contractor to maintain a dangerous condition on his premises, such as an excavation, neither surrounded by a guardrail nor lit at night, that adjoins a public sidewalk, is liable to a member of the public who is injured by falling into the excavation.

Moreover, the principal may be directly liable if he should know that there is an undue risk that the independent contractor will be negligent and harm others. Thus, Melanie, who knows that Gordon is an alcoholic, employs Gordon as an independent contractor to repair her roof. Gordon attempts the repairs while heavily intoxicated and drops a fifty-pound bundle of shingles upon Eric, a pedestrian walking by on the public sidewalk. Both Gordon and Melanie are liable to Eric.

A principal is also liable for an independent contractor's conduct in carrying on an ultrahazardous activity. Finally, a principal is liable if an independent contractor negligently conducts an inherently dangerous activity, such as excavating a public road, demolishing a building, or spraying crops.

CRIMINAL LIABILITY OF THE PRINCIPAL

Authorized acts the principal is liable if he directed, participated in, or approved the criminal acts of his agents

A principal is liable for the **authorized** criminal **acts** of his agents only if the principal directed, participated in, or approved of the acts. For example, if an agent, at his principal's direction or with his principal's knowledge, fixes prices with the principal's competitors, both the agent and the principal have criminally violated the antitrust laws. Otherwise, a principal ordinarily is not liable for the unauthorized criminal acts of his agents. One of the elements of a crime is mental fault, and this element is absent, so far as the principal's criminal responsibility is concerned, where the principal did not authorize the agent's act.

Unauthorized acts the principal may be liable either for a criminal act of managerial person or under liability without fault statutes

An employer may, nevertheless, be subject to a criminal penalty for the unauthorized act of an advisory or managerial employee acting in the scope of her employment. Moreover, an employer may be criminally liable under liability without fault statutes for certain **unauthorized acts** of an employee, whether the employee is managerial or not. These statutes are usually regulatory and do not require mental fault. For example, many states have statutes that punish "every person who by himself or his employee or agent sells anything at short weight," or "whoever sells liquor to a minor and any sale by an employee shall be deemed the act of the employer as well." Another example is a statute prohibiting the sale of unwholesome or adulterated food. See Chapter 6 for a more detailed discussion of this topic.

RELATIONSHIP OF AGENT AND THIRD PERSONS

The function of an agent is to assist in the conduct of the principal's business by carrying out his orders. Generally, the agent acquires no rights against third parties and likewise incurs no liabilities to them. There are, however, several exceptions to this proposition. In certain instances, an agent may become personally liable to the third party for contracts she made on behalf of her principal. Occasionally, the agent also may acquire rights against the third party. In addition, an agent who commits a tort is personally liable to the injured third party. In this section, we will cover these circumstances involving the personal liability of an agent, as well as those in which an agent may acquire rights against third persons.

CONTRACT LIABILITY OF AGENT

The agent normally is not a party to the contract he makes with a third person on behalf of a disclosed principal. An agent who exceeds his actual and apparent authority may, however, be personally liable to the third party. In addition, an agent acting for a disclosed principal may become liable if he expressly assumes liability on the contract. When an agent enters into a contract on behalf of a partially disclosed principal or an undisclosed principal, the agent becomes personally liable to the third party on the contract. Furthermore, an agent who knowingly enters into a contract on behalf of a nonexistent or incompetent principal is personally liable to the third party on that contract.

Disclosed Principal

When transacting business with an agent who is acting for an identified principal, a third person is on notice that the agent is not personally undertaking to perform the contract, but is simply negotiating on behalf of her principal. The resulting contract, if within the agent's actual authority, is between the third person and the principal. The agent ordinarily incurs no liability on the contract to either party. (See Figure 30–1.) This is also true of unauthorized contracts that are subsequently ratified by the principal. However, if the agent has apparent authority but no actual authority, the agent has no liability to the third party but is liable to the principal for any loss the agent has caused by exceeding his actual authority.

Unauthorized Contracts If an agent exceeds his actual *and* apparent authority, the principal is not bound. The fact that the principal is not bound does not, however, make the agent a party to the contract. The agent's liability, if any, arises from express or implied representations about his authority that he makes to the third party. For example, an agent may ***expressly warrant*** that he has authority by stating that he has authority and that he will be personally liable to the third party if he does not in fact have the authority to bind his principal.

Moreover, a person who undertakes to make a contract on behalf of another gives an ***implied warranty*** that he is in fact authorized to make the contract on behalf of the party whom he purports to represent. If the agent does not have authority to bind the principal, the agent is liable to the third party for damages unless the principal ratifies the contract or unless the third party knew that the agent was unauthorized. No implied warranty exists, however, if the contract expressly provides that the agent shall not be responsible for any lack of authority or if the agent, acting in good faith, discloses to the third person all of the facts upon which his authority rests. For example, agent Larson has received an ambiguous letter of instruction from his principal, Dan. Larson shows it to Carol, stating that it represents all of the authority that he has to act, and both Larson and Carol rely upon its sufficiency. In this case, Larson has made to Carol no implied or express warranty of his authority.

If a purported agent ***misrepresents*** to a third person that he has authority to make a contract on behalf of a principal whom he has no power to bind, he is liable in a tort action to the third person for the loss she sustained in reliance upon the misrepresentation. However, if the third party knows that the representation is false, the agent is not liable.

Agent Assumes Liability By making the contract in her own name, by co-making the contract with the principal, or by guaranteeing that the principal will perform the contract between the third party and the principal, an agent may agree to become liable on a contract between the principal and the third party. In all of these situations, the agent's liability is separate unless the parties agree otherwise. Therefore, the third party may sue the agent separately without joining the principal and may obtain a judgment against either the principal or the agent or both. If the principal satisfies the judgment, the agent is discharged. If the agent pays the judgment, he usually will have a right of reimbursement from the principal. This right is based upon the principles of suretyship, discussed in Chapter 40.

Partially Disclosed Principal

An agent, as we discussed previously, acts for a partially disclosed principal if the third party has notice that the agent is acting for a principal but has no notice of

Disclosed principal the agent is not normally a party to the contract she makes with a third person if she is authorized or if the principal ratifies an unauthorized contract

Unauthorized contracts if an agent exceeds her actual and apparent authority, the principal is not bound but the agent may be liable for breach of warranty or for misrepresentation

Agent assumes liability an agent may agree to become liable on a contract between the principal and the third party

the principal's identity. Thus, though the third person is aware that the agent is acting on behalf of another, he does not know the principal's name or identity. Using a partially disclosed principal may be helpful where, for example, the third party might inflate the price of property he is selling if he knew the identity of the principal. Partial disclosure may also occur inadvertently, when the agent fails through neglect to inform the third party of the principal's identity.

Partially disclosed principal an agent who acts for a partially disclosed principal is a party to the contract with the third party unless otherwise agreed

Unless otherwise agreed, an agent making a contract for a **partially disclosed principal** is a party to the contract. For example, Ashley writes to Terrence offering to sell a rare painting on behalf of its owner, who wishes to remain unknown. Terrence accepts. Ashley is a party to the contract.

Whether the particular transaction is authorized or not, an agent for a partially disclosed principal is liable on the contract to the third party. (See Figure 30–2.) If the agent is actually authorized to make the contract, both the agent and the partially disclosed principal are liable. In any event, the agent is separately liable, and the third party may sue her individually, without joining the principal, and the agent or the principal may obtain a judgment against either or both. If the principal satisfies the judgment, the agent is discharged. If the agent pays the judgment, he has the right to be reimbursed by the principal.

VAN D. COSTAS, INC. v. ROSENBERG   District Court of Appeal of Florida, Second District, 1983, 432 So.2d 656

FACTS Van D. Costas, Inc. (Costas) entered into a contract to remodel the entrance of the Magic Moment Restaurant owned by Seascape Restaurants, Inc. Rosenberg, part owner and president of Seascape, signed the contract on a line under which was typed "Jeff Rosenberg, The Magic Moment." When a dispute arose over the performance and payment of the contract, Costas brought suit against Rosenberg for breach of contract. Rosenberg contended that he had no personal liability for the contract and that only Seascape, the owner of the restaurant, was liable. Costas claimed that Rosenberg signed for an undisclosed principal and, therefore, was individually liable. The trial court held that Rosenberg was not liable on the contract. Costas appealed.

DECISION Reversed (Rosenberg individually liable).

OPINION To avoid personal liability, an agent must disclose both that he is acting as an agent and the identity of his principal. If the contracting party knows the identity of the principal for whom the agent is acting, the principal is considered disclosed. It is not the contracting party's duty, however, to seek out the identity of the principal.

Here, nothing indicates that Costas had ever heard of Seascape at the time the contract was signed. Moreover, use of a trade name (here, Magic Moment) is not sufficient disclosure of the identity of the principal. Rosenberg knew that Seascape was the owner, and he could have avoided personal liability by properly disclosing the identity of his principal. Since he did not, Rosenberg is personally liable.

INTERPRETATION To avoid personal liability on a contract, an agent must disclose both that she is acting as an agent and the identity of her principal.

Undisclosed Principal

An agent acts for an undisclosed principal when she appears to be acting on her own behalf and the third person with whom she is dealing has no knowledge that she is acting as an agent. The principal has instructed the agent to conceal not only the principal's identity but also the agency relationship. Such concealment can also occur if the agent simply neglects to disclose the existence and identity of her principal. Thus, the third person is dealing with the agent as though the agent were a principal.

Undisclosed principal an agent who acts for an undisclosed principal is personally liable on the contract to the third party

The agent is personally liable upon a contract she enters into with a third person on behalf of an **undisclosed principal**, unless the third person, after discovering the existence and identity of the principal, elects to hold the principal to the contract. (See Figure 30–3.) The reason for the agent's liability is that the third person has relied upon the agent individually and has accepted the agent's personal undertaking to perform the contract. Obviously, where the principal is undisclosed, the third person does not know of the interest of anyone in the contract other than that of himself and the agent.

After learning the identity of the undisclosed principal, the third person may hold either the principal or the agent to performance of the contract, but not both; and his choice, once made, binds him irrevocably. However, to avoid the risk that evidence at trial may fail to establish the agency relationship, the third person may bring suit against both the principal and agent. In most states, this act of bringing suit and proceeding to trial against both is not an election, but, before the entry of any judgment, the third person is compelled to make an election because he is not entitled to a judgment against both. A judgment against the agent by a third party who knows the identity of the previously undisclosed principal discharges the principal's liability to the third party but leaves her liable to the agent, who would have the right to be reimbursed by the principal. If the third party obtains a judgment against the agent before learning the identity of the principal, the principal is not discharged. Finally, the agent is discharged from liability if the third party obtains a judgment against the principal.

Nonexistent or Incompetent Principal

A person who purports to act as agent for a principal whom both the agent and the third party know to be nonexistent or wholly incompetent is personally liable on a contract entered into with a third person on behalf of such a principal. An agent who makes a contract for a disclosed principal whose contracts are voidable for lack of contractual capacity is *not* liable to the third party, with two exceptions: (1) if the agent warrants or represents that the principal has capacity or (2) if the agent has reason to know both of the principal's lack of capacity and of the third party's ignorance of that incapacity.

TORT LIABILITY OF AGENT

An agent is personally liable for his tortious acts that injure third persons, whether such acts are authorized by the principal or not and whether the principal may also be liable or not. For example, an agent is personally liable if he converts the goods of a third person to his principal's use. An agent is also liable for making representations that he knows to be fraudulent to a third person who in reliance sustains a loss.

RIGHTS OF AGENT AGAINST THIRD PERSON

Though an agent for an **undisclosed principal** or a **partially disclosed principal** may maintain in her own name an action against a third person for breach of contract, an agent who makes a contract with a third person on behalf of a **disclosed principal** usually has no right of action against the third person for breach of contract; for the agent is not a party to the contract. An agent for a disclosed principal may sue on the contract, however, if it provides that the agent is a party to the contract.

Nonexistent or incompetent principal a person who purports to act as agent for a principal whom both the agent and the third party know to be nonexistent or wholly incompetent is personally liable on a contract entered into with a third person on behalf of such a principal

Tort liability of agent the agent is liable to the third party for his own torts

Undisclosed principal the agent may enforce the contract against the third party

Partially disclosed principal the agent may enforce the contract against the third party

Disclosed principal the agent usually has no rights against the third party

CHAPTER SUMMARY

Principal and Third Persons

Contract Liability of Principal

Types of Principals
- *Disclosed Principal* principal whose existence and identity are known
- *Partially Disclosed Principal* principal whose existence is known but whose identity is not known
- *Undisclosed Principal* principal whose existence and identity are not known

Authority power of an agent to change the legal status of the principal
- *Actual Authority* power conferred upon the agent by actual consent given by the principal
- *Actual Express Authority* actual authority derived from written or spoken words of the principal
- *Actual Implied Authority* actual authority inferred from words or conduct manifested to the agent by the principal
- *Apparent Authority* power conferred upon the agent by acts or conduct of the principal that reasonably lead a third party to believe that the agent has such power

Delegation of Authority is usually not permitted unless expressly or impliedly authorized by the principal; if the agent is authorized to appoint other subagents, the acts of these subagents are as binding on the principal as those of the agent

Effect of Termination of Agency on Authority ends actual authority
- *Termination by Operation of Law* apparent authority also ends without notice to third parties
- *Termination by Act of Parties* apparent authority ends when third parties have actual knowledge or when appropriate notice is given to third parties; actual notice must be given to third parties with whom the agent had previously dealt on credit, has been specially accredited, or has begun to deal; all other third parties as to whom there was apparent authority need only be given constructive notice

Ratification affirmation by one person of a prior unauthorized act that another has done as her agent or as her purported agent

Fundamental Rules of Contractual Liability
- *Disclosed Principal* is contractually bound with the third party if the agent acts within her actual or apparent authority in making the contract
- *Partially Disclosed Principal* is contractually bound with the third party if the agent acts within her actual or apparent authority in making the contract
- *Undisclosed Principal* is contractually bound with the third party if the agent acts within her actual authority in making the contract

Tort Liability of Principal

Direct Liability of Principal a principal is liable for his own tortious conduct involving the use of agents
- *Authorized Acts of Agent* a principal is liable for torts she authorizes another to commit
- *Unauthorized Acts of Agent* a principal is liable for failing to exercise care in employing agents whose unauthorized acts cause harm

Vicarious Liability of Principal for Unauthorized Acts of Agent
- *Respondeat Superior* an employer is liable for unauthorized torts committed by an employee in the course of his employment
- *Independent Contractor* a principal is usually not liable for the unauthorized torts of an independent contractor

Criminal Liability of Principal

Authorized Acts the principal is liable if he directed, participated in, or approved the acts of his agents

Unauthorized Acts the principal may be liable either for a criminal act of a managerial person or under liability without fault statutes

Agents and Third Persons

Contract Liability of Agent

Disclosed Principals the agent is not normally a party to the contract she makes with a third person if she is authorized or if the principal ratifies an unauthorized contract
- *Unauthorized Contracts* if an agent exceeds her actual and apparent authority, the principal is not bound but the agent may be liable for breach of warranty or for misrepresentation
- *Agent Assumes Liability* an agent may agree to become liable on a contract between the principal and the third party

Partially Disclosed Principal an agent who acts for a partially disclosed principal is a party to the contract with the third party unless otherwise agreed

Undisclosed Principal an agent who acts for an undisclosed principal is personally liable on the contract to the third party

Nonexistent or Incompetent Principal a person who purports to act as agent for a principal whom both the agent and the third party know to be nonexistent or wholly incompetent is personally liable on a contract entered into with a third person on behalf of such a principal

Tort Liability of Agent

Authorized Acts the agent is liable to the third party for his own torts

Unauthorized Acts the agent is liable to the third party for his own torts

Rights of Agent

Disclosed Principal the agent usually has no rights against the third party

Partially Disclosed Principal the agent may enforce the contract against the third party

Undisclosed Principal the agent may enforce the contract against the third party

QUESTIONS

1. Distinguish among actual express authority, actual implied authority, and apparent authority.
2. Discuss the contractual liability of the principal, agent, and third party when the principal is (a) disclosed, (b) partially disclosed, and (c) undisclosed.
3. Distinguish between actual and constructive notice.
4. Discuss the doctrine of ratification.
5. Discuss the tort liability of a principal for the (a) authorized acts of agents, (b) unauthorized acts of employees, and (c) unauthorized acts of independent contractors.

Internet Question. Compare the rules determining the authority of agents and the liability of principals for acts of agents under the Convention on Agency in the International Sale of Goods (Geneva, 17 February 1983) with the rules under the U.S. common law.

PROBLEMS

1. Alice was Peter's traveling salesperson and was also authorized to collect accounts. Before the agreed termination of the agency, Peter wrongfully discharged Alice. Alice then called on Tom, an old customer, and collected an account from Tom. She also called on Laura, a new prospect, as Peter's agent, secured a large order, collected the price of the order, sent the order to Peter, and disappeared with the collections. Peter delivered the goods to Laura per the order.
   (a) Peter sues Tom for his account. Decision?
   (b) Peter sues Laura for the agreed price of the goods. Decision?

2. Paula instructed Alvin, her agent, to purchase a quantity of hides. Alvin ordered the hides from Ted in his own (Alvin's) name and delivered the hides to Paula. Ted, learning later that Paula was the principal, sends the bill to Paula, who refuses to pay Ted. Ted sues Paula and Alvin. Decision?

3. Stan sold goods to Bill in good faith, believing him to be a principal. Bill in fact was acting as agent for Nancy and within the scope of his authority. The goods were charged to Bill, and, on his refusal to pay, Stan sued Bill for the purchase price. While this action was pending, Stan learned of Bill's relationship with Nancy. Nevertheless, thirty days after learning of that relationship, Stan obtained judgment against Bill and had an execution issued that was never satisfied. Three months after the judgment was made, Stan sued Nancy for the purchase price of the goods. Decision?

4. Green Grocery Company employed Jones as its manager and gave her authority to purchase supplies and goods for resale. Jones had conducted business for several years with Brown Distributing Company, although her purchases had been limited to groceries. Jones contacted Brown Distributing Company and had it deliver a color television set to her house. She told Brown Company that the set was to be used in promotional advertising to increase Green Grocery Company's business. The advertising did not develop, and Jones disappeared from the area, taking the television set with her. Brown Company sued Green Grocery Company for the purchase price of the set. Decision?

5. Stone was the agent authorized to sell stock of the Turner Company at $10 per share and was authorized in case of sale to fill in the blanks in the certificates with the name of the purchaser, the number of shares, and the date of sale. He sold 100 shares to Barrie, and without the knowledge or consent of the company and without reporting to the company, he indorsed the back of the certificate as follows:

   It is hereby agreed that Turner Company shall, at the end of three years after the date, repurchase the stock at $11 per share on thirty days' notice. Turner Company, by Stone.

   After three years, demand was made on Turner Company to repurchase. The company refused the demand and repudiated the agreement on the ground that the agent had no authority to make the agreement for repurchase. Barrie sued Turner Company. Decision?

6. Helper, a delivery boy for Gunn, delivered two heavy packages of groceries to Reed's porch. As instructed by Gunn, Helper rang the bell to let Reed know the groceries had arrived. Mrs. Reed came to the door and asked Helper if he would deliver the groceries into the kitchen because the bags were heavy. Helper did so, and on leaving he observed Mrs. Reed having difficulty in moving a cabinet in the dining room. He undertook to assist her, but being more interested in watching Mrs. Reed than in noting the course of the cabinet, he failed to observe a small, valuable antique table, which he smashed into with the cabinet and totally destroyed. Does Reed have a cause of action against Gunn for the value of the destroyed antique?

7. Driver picked up Friend to accompany him on an out-of-town delivery for his employer, Speedy Service. A "No Riders" sign was prominently displayed on the

windshield of the truck, and Driver violated specific instructions of his employer by permitting an unauthorized person to ride in the vehicle. While discussing a planned fishing trip with Friend, Driver ran a red light and collided with an automobile driven by Motorist. Both Friend and Motorist were injured. Is Speedy Service liable to either Friend or Motorist for the injuries they sustained?

8. Cook's Department Store advertises that it maintains a barber shop in its store and that the shop is managed by Hunter, a Cook's employee. Actually, Hunter is not an employee of the store but merely rents space in the store. While shaving Jordan in the barber shop, Hunter negligently puts a deep gash, requiring ten stitches, into one of Jordan's ears. Jordan sues Cook's Department Store for damages. Decision?

9. The following contract was executed on August 22:

> Ray agrees to sell and Shaw, the representative of Todd and acting on his behalf, agrees to buy 10,000 pounds of 0.32 x $1^5/_8$ stainless steel strip type 410.
>
> (signed) Ray
> (signed) Shaw

On August 26 Ray informs Shaw and Todd that the contract was in reality signed by him as agent for Upson. What are the rights of Ray, Shaw, Todd, and Upson in the event of a breach of the contract?

10. Harris, owner of certain land known as Red Bank, mailed a letter to Byron, a real estate broker in City X, stating, "I have been thinking of selling Red Bank. I have never met you, but a friend has advised me that you are an industrious and honest real estate broker. I therefore employ you to find a purchaser for Red Bank at a price of $35,000." Ten days after receiving the letter, Byron mailed the following reply to Harris: "Acting pursuant to your recent letter requesting me to find a purchaser for Red Bank, this is to advise that I have sold the property to Sims for $35,000. I enclose your copy of the contract of sale signed by Sims. Your name was signed to the contract by me as your agent." Is Harris obligated to convey Red Bank to Sims?

11. While crossing a public highway in the city, Joel was struck by a horse-drawn cart driven by Morison's agent. The agent was traveling between Burton Crescent Mews and Finchley on his employer's business and was not supposed to go into the city at all.

Apparently, the agent was on a detour to visit a friend when the accident occurred. Joel brought this action against Morison for the injuries he sustained as a result of the agent's negligence. Morison argues that he is not liable for his agent's negligence because the agent had strayed from his assigned path. Decision?

12. Serges is the owner of a retail meat marketing business. His managing agent borrowed $3,500 from David, on Serges's behalf, for use in Serges's business. Serges paid $200 on the alleged loan and on several other occasions told David that the full balance owed would eventually be paid. He then disclaimed liability on the debt, asserting that he had not authorized his agent to enter into the loan agreement. David brought this action to collect on the loan. Decision?

13. In 1978, Sherwood negligently ran into the rear of Austen's car, which was stopped at a stoplight. As a result, Austen received bodily injuries and her car was damaged. Sherwood, arts editor for the *Mississippi Press Register*, was en route from a concert he had covered for the newspaper. When the accident occurred, he was on his way to spend the night at a friend's house. Austen sued Sherwood and—under the doctrine of *respondeat superior*—Sherwood's employer, the *Mississippi Press Register*. Decision?

14. Aretta J. Parkinson owned a 200-acre farm. Prior to her death on December 23, 1976, Parkinson deeded a one-eighth undivided interest in the farm to each of her eight children as tenants in common. On January 15, 1977, one of the daughters, Roma Funk, approached Barbara Bradshaw about selling the Parkinson farm. They orally agreed to a selling price of $33,000. After this meeting, Funk contacted Bryant Hansen, a real estate broker, to assist her in completing the transaction. Hansen prepared an earnest money agreement that was signed by the Bradshaws but by none of the Parkinson children. Hansen also prepared warranty deeds, which were signed by three of the children. Several of the children subsequently refused to convey their interests in the farm to the Bradshaws. The Bradshaws brought an action against the defendants, seeking specific performance of the oral contract of sale. The trial court ruled for the Bradshaws, finding that the defendants ratified the oral contract by their knowledge of and failure to repudiate it. The defendants appealed. Decision?

PART | VII

Unincorporated Business Associations

CHAPTER 31

Formation of General Partnerships

A business enterprise may be operated or conducted by a sole proprietor, a joint venture, a general partnership, a limited partnership, a limited liability company, a corporation, or by some other form of business organization. The owner or owners of the enterprise determine the form of business unit they wish to use. Various factors, not the least of which are federal and state income tax laws, affect the decision to use one medium rather than another. Other factors include ease of formation, capital requirements, flexibility of management and control, extent of external liability, and the duties imposed by law on management. For a concise comparison of general partnerships, limited partnerships, limited liability companies, and corporations, see Figure 35–2 in Chapter 35.

Although corporations today outnumber unincorporated business associations (general partnerships, joint ventures, limited partnerships, and limited liability companies) by about two to one and generate greater revenues by over twenty to one, unincorporated business associations are common in a number of areas. General partnerships, for example, are utilized frequently in finance, insurance, accounting, real estate, wholesale and retail trade, law, and other services. Joint ventures have enjoyed popularity among major corporations planning to engage in cooperative research; in the exploitation of land and mineral rights; in the development, promotion, and sale of patents, trade names, and copyrights; and in manufacturing operations in foreign countries. Limited partnerships have been widely used for enterprises such as real estate investment and development, motion picture and theater productions, oil and gas ventures, and equipment leasing. In the last few years, the states have authorized the formation of limited liability companies. This form of business organization will probably be attractive to a number of businesses, including real estate ventures, high-technology enterprises, transactions involving foreign investors, professional organizations, corporate joint ventures, start-up businesses, and venture capital projects.

See The Law and You on the next page.

In Chapters 31 through 33, we will examine general partnerships, commonly called partnerships; in Chapter 34, we will discuss limited partnerships, limited liability companies, and other types of unincorporated business associations. Part Eight covers corporations.

NATURE OF PARTNERSHIP

Partnerships are extremely important in that they allow individuals with different expertise, backgrounds, resources, and interests to combine their various skills to form a more competitive enterprise. In 1914, the National Conference

THE LAW AND YOU Buying a Franchise

Franchising Facts

While the information contained in this pamphlet is believed to be accurate, it is general in nature. It is not a legal opinion of The Florida Bar but rather a summary of certain legal matters and should not be relied on as legal advice.

This pamphlet is designed to give basic information to those thinking of expanding their business through franchising (a prospective franchisor) and to those thinking of buying a franchise (a prospective franchisee). We hope it steers you in the right direction.

A myriad of products and services in our state are sold by concerns doing business under what is called product or business format franchising. Today, nearly 40 percent of all retail sales are made from franchise outlets. These include not only fast food operations, but also the sale of automobile products, accounting services, independent post offices, advertising services, employment services, home furnishings, lawn and garden supplies, hotels and motels, pet care, hair salons, printing and copy centers, real estate sales, travel, weight control, dry cleaning and more. U.S. Department of Commerce statistics estimate that a new franchise outlet opens in the nation about every 17 minutes.

What is Franchising?

Franchising is a method of doing business, of selling goods or services where one party (a franchisor) allows another (a franchisee) to use its trademark and its business system in exchange for a fee. The term "franchise" can refer to the relationship between the franchisor and the franchisee, or is sometimes used to refer to the business itself which the franchisee buys.

The legal definition of a franchise under federal law is a written contract (regardless of what it's called) where three elements exist:

1. the use of another's trademark, trade name, etc;
2. the payment of $500 or more during the first six months of operations (excluding wholesale purchases of inventory); and
3. significant assistance and/or significant control of the operations.

If these three elements exist, it's a franchise under federal law.

Franchising comes in various forms. One is the franchise of an entire retail business operation, such as a fast food restaurant or real estate sales office (a "business format" franchise). Another is a product distribution system, where a franchisee distributes the franchisor's products, such as automobiles, gasoline, or soft drinks under the manufacturer's name (a "product" franchise).

The appeal of franchising is that it is supposed to provide a pretested formula for success. It provides a mechanism for rapid growth of the franchisor's outlets of distribution and, at the same time, increases the likelihood of success of the small business person, the franchisee. Franchisors should provide a business system, managerial training and assistance on an ongoing basis, and the franchisee must comply with the controls and procedures established by the franchisor.

The U.S. Department of Commerce reports that less than 5 percent of franchised business outlets have been discontinued each year since 1985. Other statistics provided by the U.S. Small Business Administration show that 38 percent of all business start-ups are discontinued in the first year. After five years, 90 percent of franchises are still in business, while only 23 percent of independent operations are still in existence after five years.

Who Regulates Franchising in Florida?

Franchisors must comply with Federal Trade Commission regulations regarding disclosure (the "FTC Franchise Rule"). Under the FTC Franchise Rule, every franchisor must prepare an extensive document with information about the company that must be given to a franchisee (an "Offering Circular"). This Offering Circular contains information about the business, including fees, investment required, bankruptcies and litigation history of the company, the term of the franchise or how long it will last, financial statements of the company, and earnings claims (if any are made—and usually they aren't). A current Offering Circular must be given to a prospective franchisee at least 10 business days before any agreement is executed or the franchisee pays any money to the franchisor.

Florida is one of the majority of states that does not specifically regulate franchising. There is no state registration or disclosure law as such. However, certain Florida statutes govern some aspects of the franchise relationship, such as misrepresentations by franchisors, deceptive and unfair trade practices, state registration of trademarks, antitrust violations, and regulation of so-called "business opportunities" which are not usually, but in some instances also can be franchises.

Where You Can Find More Information

The U.S. Department of Commerce and the International Franchise Association or "IFA" 1-800-543-1038 or (202) 628-8000 have publications listing franchise companies and other pamphlets to aid you if you are thinking about franchising or considering a franchise purchase. Other sources include American Association of Franchises and Dealers, (619) 235-2556 and

continued

American Franchisee Association, (312) 431-0545.

What to Ask Before Buying a Franchise

The IFA recommends you investigate the following:

- the type of experience required in the franchised business—Do you have the right background for this business? Find out what you need to know;
- the operational characteristics of the business;
- the hours and personal commitment necessary to run the business;
- who the franchisor is, what its track record has been, and the business experience of the officers and directors;
- how other franchisees in the same system are doing—Contact as many of the current franchisees as you can as well as ones who have left in the past year and talk to them;
- how much it's going to cost to get into the franchise;
- how much you're going to pay for the continuing right to operate the business;
- if there are any products or services you must buy from the franchisor and how and by whom they are supplied;
- Does the franchisor own the trademark? Is it federally registered? Will the franchisor indemnify you for trademark infringement?
- the terms and conditions under which the franchise relationship can be terminated, and how many have been terminated during the past few years; and
- the financial condition of the franchisor and its system.

Are All Claims Made Truthful?

While penalties may be imposed on franchisors for inaccuracies and misrepresentations contained in the Offering Circular, you must act to protect yourself. One of the best ways to do this is to make sure you talk to the other franchisees who have already purchased franchises from the franchisor. Find out if they are "satisfied customers."

You should also have a lawyer experienced in franchise law and your accountant assist you in reviewing the Offering Circular. By obtaining the Offering Circular of several companies in which you are interested, you'll be better able to "comparison shop."

How to Protect Yourself

Due largely to its success, franchising, as with other business methods, has attracted its share of unqualified promoters. Many government agencies and local Better Business Bureaus attempt to check on companies or individuals selling franchises, but your best protection rests with you and your professional advisors. You must thoroughly investigate the specific franchisor, its reputation, its business record and its industry. The best way to do this is with the assistance of a qualified franchise lawyer who understands the complex nature of franchising, especially the antitrust laws, the trademark laws, and the FTC Franchise Rule. You should also have a competent accountant examine your purchase before you buy.

[The material in this feature was prepared as a public service and is intended for general information purposes only. The frequent changes in state law could affect this material, and such law also varies from state to state.]

of Commissioners on Uniform State Laws promulgated the Uniform Partnership Act (UPA). Since then it has been adopted in all states (except Louisiana), as well as by the District of Columbia, the Virgin Islands, and Guam. Although the UPA (reprinted in Appendix C) is fairly comprehensive, it does not cover all legal issues concerning partnerships. Accordingly, the UPA provides that any situation for which it does not provide shall be governed by the rules of law and equity.

In August 1986, the UPA Revision Subcommittee of the Committee on Partnerships and Unincorporated Business Organizations of the American Bar Association's Section of Corporation, Banking and Business Law and the National Conference of Commissioners on Uniform State Laws undertook a complete revision of the Uniform Partnership Act. The revision was approved in August 1992, and was amended in 1993 and 1994. Only eight states have adopted the revised act. In this chapter, therefore, we will discuss the original 1914 UPA.

Definition of Partnership

The UPA's definition of a **partnership** is "an association of two or more persons to carry on as co-owners a business for profit." The UPA broadly defines "person" to include "individuals, partnerships, corporations, and other associations." A business is defined by the UPA to include every trade, occupation, or profession.

Partnership an association of two or more persons to carry on as co-owners a business for profit

Entity Theory

A **legal entity** is an organization having a legal existence separate from that of its members. It therefore is a unit able to possess legal rights and to be subject to legal duties. A legal entity may acquire, own, and dispose of property. It may enter into contracts, commit wrongs, sue, and be sued. Each business corporation is a legal entity having a distinct legal existence separate from that of its shareholders.

Legal entity an organization having a legal existence separate from that of its members

A partnership was regarded by the common law as a **legal aggregate,** a group of individuals having no legal existence apart from that of its members. The UPA, however, has partially rejected the common law view of partnerships. Accordingly, it treats partnerships as legal entities for some purposes and as legal aggregates for others.

Legal aggregate *(ag'·gre·gate)* a group of individuals *not* having a legal existence separate from that of its members

Partnership as a Legal Entity The UPA recognizes a partnership as an entity legally distinct from its members in several ways: (1) the assets of the firm are treated as those of the business and are considered separate and distinct from the individual assets of the members; (2) title to real estate may be acquired by a partnership in the partnership name; (3) a partner is accountable as a fiduciary to the partnership; (4) every partner is considered an agent of the partnership; and (5) under the doctrine of marshaling of assets—which applies in insolvency cases administered by a state court of equity—partnership creditors have a prior right to partnership assets, while creditors of the individual members have a prior right to the separate assets of their individual debtors.

Partnership as a Legal Aggregate Because a partnership is considered an aggregate for some purposes, it can neither sue nor be sued in the firm name unless a statute specifically allows such an action. Similarly, the debts of the partnership are ultimately the debts of the individual partners, and any one partner may be held liable for the partnership's entire indebtedness. Thus, if Meg and Mike enter into a partnership that becomes insolvent, as does Meg, Mike is fully liable for the partnership's debts.

In addition, a partnership generally lacks continuity of existence: whenever any partner ceases to be associated with the partnership, it is dissolved. Likewise, though a partner may assign her interest in the partnership, the assignee does not become a partner without the consent of all the partners.

Finally, the Internal Revenue Code treats a partnership as an aggregate. A partnership is not required to pay federal income tax but must file an information return stating the name of each partner and the amount of income each derives from the partnership. It is the responsibility of each partner to include his share of partnership income in his individual tax return and to pay the tax on his share. Partnership income is taxed to the individual partners regardless of whether the income is distributed.

PATE v. MARTIN Court of Appeals of Arkansas, Division I, 1985, 13 Ark.App. 182, 681, S.W.2d 410

FACTS Troy Martin notified the Arkansas Workers' Compensation Commission (Commission) that he had been injured within the scope of his employment with P & P Fabrication. After a hearing, the Commission awarded Martin all medical costs and accrued benefits, to be paid by P & P Fabrication. Reference was made neither to whether P & P Fabrication was a corporation or partnership nor to the identity of any copartners. It is undisputed, however, that Jimmie Pate and Jimmie Pate, Jr., were equal partners and owners of P & P Fabrication. In fact, both Pate and Pate, Jr., appeared before the Commission to defend against Martin's claim. When P & P Fabrication failed to pay, Martin obtained a writ of garnishment against Pate. Pate responded that since the Commission award did not name him specifically and individually, he was not liable for payment. The trial court ruled that because Pate had notice, had appeared and defended before the Commission, and was co-owner and copartner in P & P Fabrication, the court was entitled to find that Pate was liable even though the Commission had not named him. Pate appealed.

DECISION Judgment for Pate.

OPINION At common law, a partnership was not recognized as a legal entity separate and apart from the individuals owning it and had no capacity to sue or be sued. Martin argues that under the Uniform Partnership Act (UPA), a partnership may now be sued under the firm name, and liability will thereby be imposed upon the partners. The UPA, however, defines a partnership as "an association of two or more persons to carry on as co-owners a business for profit." Furthermore, the Arkansas legislature did not accept an alternative definition that a partnership was a "legal person" in its own right; nor did the legislature adopt provisions for the liability of individual partners sued in the partnership name. Rather, the UPA adopts the common law aggregate approach, with modifications consistent with the entity approach for certain specific circumstances, such as the acquisition and transfer of property and marshaling of assets. Since the award of the Commission was against P & P Fabrication only, with no mention of any individual partners, the award may not be enforced against a partner.

INTERPRETATION The UPA treats a partnership as a legal entity for some purposes and a legal aggregate for other purposes.

Types of Partners

Partners can be classified as either general or limited. In addition, a partner may be silent, secret, or dormant.

General partner member of either a general or limited partnership with unlimited liability for its debts, full management powers, and a right to share in the profits

A **general partner** is a partner of either a general or limited partnership whose liability for partnership indebtedness is unlimited, who has full management powers, and who shares in the profits. Most partnerships consist of only general partners and are referred to as "general partnerships" or just "partnerships."

Limited partner member of a limited partnership with liability for its debts only to the extent of her capital contribution

A special or **limited partner** is one who, as a member of a limited partnership, is liable for firm indebtedness only to the extent of the capital he has contributed or has agreed to contribute. Limited partnerships, discussed in Chapter 34, are formed by compliance with a number of statutory requirements.

A *silent partner* is a partner who has no voice and elects to take no part in the partnership business.

A *secret partner* is a partner whose membership in the firm is not disclosed to the public.

A *dormant partner* is a partner who is both a silent and a secret partner.

FORMATION OF A PARTNERSHIP

The formation of a partnership is relatively simple and may be done consciously or unconsciously. A partnership may result from an oral or written agreement between the parties, from an informal arrangement, or from the conduct of the parties. Persons become partners by associating themselves in a business as co-owners. Consequently, if two or more individuals share the control and profits of a business, the law may deem them partners without regard to how they themselves might characterize their relationship.

Articles of Partnership

To achieve a more clear, definite, and complete understanding between the partners, it is preferable, although not usually required, that partners put their agreement in writing. A written agreement creating a partnership is referred to as a partnership agreement or **articles of partnership.** Unless the agreement provides otherwise, the partners may amend it only by unanimous consent. Any partnership agreement should include (1) the firm name and the identity of the partners; (2) the nature and scope of the partnership business; (3) the duration of the partnership; (4) the capital contributions of each partner; (5) the division of profits and sharing of losses; (6) the management duties of each partner; (7) a provision for salaries, if desired; (8) restrictions, if any, on the authority of particular partners to bind the firm; (9) the right, if desired, of a partner to withdraw from the firm, and the terms, conditions, and notice such withdrawal would require; and (10) a provision for the continuation of the business by the remaining partners, if desired, in the event of the death of a partner or other dissolution, and a statement of the method or formula for appraising and paying the interest of the deceased or former partner. Figure 31–1 shows a sample partnership agreement.

> **Articles of partnership** it is preferable, although not usually required, that the partners enter into a written partnership agreement (articles of partnership)

Because the statute of frauds does not apply specifically to a contract for the formation of a partnership, usually no writing is required to create the relationship. However, a contract to form a partnership to continue for a period longer than one year is *within* the statute and requires a writing in order to be enforceable. Moreover, a contract for the transfer of an interest in real estate to or by a partnership is governed by the statute of frauds and requires a writing to be enforceable.

Tests of Partnership Existence

Partnerships can be formed without the slightest formality. Consequently, it is important that the law establish a test for determining whether a partnership has been formed. As we mentioned earlier, the UPA provides the basic definition of a partnership: an association of two or more persons to carry on as co-owners a business for profit. Thus, this definition contains three components, all of which must be present for a partnership to exist: (1) an association of two or more persons (2) conducting, for profit, a business (3) that they co-own.

> **Tests of partnership existence** the formation of a partnership requires all of the following: (1) association, (2) business for profit, and (3) co-ownership

Association A partnership must consist of two or more persons who have agreed to become partners. Any natural person having full *capacity* may enter into a partnership. To the extent that a minor has capacity to act as a principal or agent, she may become a partner, although she has the right both to disaffirm the partnership agreement at any time before reaching majority and to avoid personal liability to partnership creditors.

The position of a nonadjudicated incompetent is basically the same as that of a minor, except that his incompetency may afford his copartners a ground for seeking dissolution by court decree. Since all contracts of an adjudicated incompetent are void, not voidable, a partnership agreement entered into by such an individual is void.

A corporation is defined as a "person" by the UPA and is, therefore, legally capable of entering into a partnership in those states whose incorporation

FIGURE 31–1 Sample Partnership Agreement

THIS PARTNERSHIP AGREEMENT is entered into this _____ day of _____ , 19 ___ , between the following persons whose names and addresses are set forth below:

The above partners hereby agree that upon the commencement date of this partnership they shall be deemed to have become partners in business. The purposes, terms and conditions of this partnership are as follows:

1. NAME—The firm name of the partnership shall be

2. PRINCIPAL PLACE OF BUSINESS—The principal place of the partnership shall be

3. PURPOSE—The business of the partnership is set forth below and includes any other business related thereto.

4. TERM—The partnership shall commence on _____ , 19 ___ , and shall continue for an indefinite time.

5. CAPITAL CONTRIBUTION: DISTRIBUTION OF PROFITS AND LOSSES

Name of Partner	Capital Contribution		Percentage Distribution of Profit and Loss
	Specific Contribution	Agreed Upon Cash Valuation of Contribution	

A division of profits and losses shall be made at such time as may be agreed upon by the partners and at the close of each fiscal year. The profits and losses of the partnership shall be divided between the partners according to the above Schedule of "Distribution of Profits and Losses."

6. CONTROL—The partners shall have the exclusive control over the business of the partnership and each partner shall have equal rights in the management and conduct of the partnership business. Any differences arising as to the ordinary matters connected with the partnership business shall be decided by a numerical majority of the partners. Any act beyond the scope of this partnership agreement or any contract which may subject this partnership to liability in excess of _____ DOLLARS shall be subject to the prior written consent of all the partners.

7. DISSOLUTION—In the event of retirement, expulsion, bankruptcy, death, or insanity of a general partner, the remaining partners have the right to continue the business of the partnership under the same name by themselves, or in conjunction with any other persons they select.

IN WITNESS WHEREOF, the parties hereto have signed this partnership agreement on the day and year first written above.

_____
                 PARTNER

_____
                 PARTNER

_____
                 PARTNER

Source: "West's Book of Legal Forms," by Robert D. McNutt, Copyright © 1981 by West Publishing Co. Reprinted with permission.

statutes authorize a corporation to do so. Furthermore, a partnership may be a member of other partnerships.

Business for Profit   The UPA provides that co-ownership does not in itself establish a partnership, even though the co-owners share the profits they derive from use of the property. For a partnership to exist, there must be a business in addition to co-ownership of property. Moreover, to be a partnership, the business carried on by the association of two or more persons must be "for profit." This requirement therefore excludes social clubs, fraternal orders, civic societies, and charitable organizations from being partnerships. Such organizations that do not incorporate are considered to be unincorporated nonprofit associations and are governed by state common law and statutes. These laws, however, do not address the issues facing nonprofit associations in a systematic or integrated fashion. Consequently, in 1996, the National Conference of Commissioners on Uniform State Laws promulgated a Uniform Unincorporated Nonprofit Association Act to reform the common law concerning unincorporated nonprofit associations in a limited number of major issues, including ownership of property, authority to sue and be sued, and the contract and tort liability of officers and members of the association.

Nor does a partnership result when persons are associated for mutual financial gain on a temporary or limited basis involving a single transaction or a relatively few isolated transactions: the parties are not engaged in the continuous series of commercial activities necessary to constitute a business. Co-ownership of the means or instrumentality of accomplishing a particular business transaction or a limited series of transactions may result in a **joint venture**, but not in a general partnership. (We will discuss joint ventures in Chapter 34.)

For example, Emmett and Beth have joint ownership of shares of the capital stock of a corporation, have a joint bank account, and have inherited or purchased real estate as joint tenants or tenants in common. They share the dividends paid on the stock, the interest on the bank account, and the net proceeds from the sale or lease of the real estate. But Emmett and Beth are not partners. Although they are co-owners and share profits, they are not engaged in carrying on a business; hence, no partnership exists. On the other hand, if Emmett and Beth continuously bought and sold real estate over a period of time and carried on a business of trading in real estate, a partnership relation would exist between them, regardless of whether they considered themselves partners or not.

Co-ownership   Although co-ownership of *property* used in a business is a condition neither necessary nor sufficient for the existence of a partnership, the co-ownership of a *business* is essential. In determining the element of business co-ownership, the two most important factors are the sharing of profits and the right to manage and control the business.

That a person receives a share of the ***profits*** from a business is *prima facie* evidence that he is a partner in the business. The UPA provides, however, that a partnership relation shall not be inferred to exist where such profits are received in payment (1) of a debt; (2) of wages of an employee or rent to a landlord; (3) of an annuity to a representative of a deceased partner; (4) of interest on a loan, though the amount of payment may vary with the profits of the business; or (5) as consideration for the sale of the goodwill of a business

Joint venture an association of two or more persons to carry on a particular business enterprise for profit

or other property. It is possible, nonetheless, to establish that such a person is a partner by proof of other facts and circumstances, such as the sharing of control.

The sharing of *gross returns*, in contrast to profits, does *not* of itself establish a partnership. This is so whether or not the persons sharing the gross returns have a joint or common interest in any property from which the returns are derived. Thus, two brokers who share commissions are not necessarily partners, or even presumed to be. Similarly, an author who receives royalties (a share of gross receipts from the sales of a book) is not a partner with her publisher.

An agreement to share in or contribute to the *losses* of a business, however, affords strong evidence of an ownership interest. For a partnership to exist, few jurisdictions insist on an express loss-sharing agreement; but all consider such an agreement compelling proof of a partnership's existence.

By itself, evidence as to participation in the *management* or *control* of a business is not conclusive proof of a partnership relation, but it is persuasive. The right to participate in control is considered by the courts in conjunction with other factors, particularly with profit sharing.

Figure 31–2 illustrates the tests for determining whether a partnership exists, as does the following case.

CHAIKEN v. EMPLOYMENT SECURITY COMMISSION Superior Court of Delaware, 1971, 274 A.2d 707

FACTS Chaiken entered into separate but nearly identical agreements with Strazella and Spitzer to operate a barber shop. Under the terms of the "partnership" agreements, Chaiken would provide barber chairs, supplies, and licenses, while the other two would provide tools of the trade. The agreements also stated that gross returns from the partnership were to be divided on a percentage basis among the three men and that Chaiken would decide all matters of partnership policy. Finally, the agreements stated hours of work and holidays for Strazella and Spitzer and required Chaiken to hold and distribute all receipts. The Delaware Employment Security Commission (Commission), however, determined that Strazella and Spitzer were not partners of Chaiken but rather were his employees. The Commission then brought this action to assess unemployment compensation contributions against Chaiken for the two barbers. Chaiken contended that they were not employees but partners pursuant to written partnership agreements. As their partner, rather than their employer, Chaiken would not be liable for unemployment compensation contributions.

DECISION Judgment for the Commission.

OPINION A partnership is an association of two or more persons to carry on as co-owners a business for profit. The mere existence of a writing labeled "partnership agreement" and the characterization of its signatories as "partners" does not conclusively establish the existence of a partnership. Rather, the intention of the parties, as explained by the wording of the agreement, is controlling.

Here, several aspects of the agreements between Chaiken and the two barbers, when considered as a whole, negate the finding of a partnership arrangement. First, Chaiken reserved the exclusive right to determine partnership policy. Second, distribution of assets upon dissolution of a partnership is to occur only after all partnership liabilities have been satisfied. Here, however, there was no such condition placed on postdissolution distributions to Strazella and Spitzer. Third, the agreements set forth holidays and hours of work for the two barbers, subjects not commonly found in partnership agreements. Finally, and of most importance, the agreements provided for a division of gross returns, not of net profits. The intent to divide profits is an indispensable requisite of a partnership. All of these factors taken together negate a finding of partnership intent here. Rather, Strazella and Spitzer are employees of Chaiken, who must pay unemployment compensation contributions on their behalf.

INTERPRETATION Two important tests for the existence of a partnership are (1) the sharing of profits (not gross receipts) by the partners and (2) participation by the partners in control of the business.

FIGURE 31–2 Tests for Existence of a Partnership

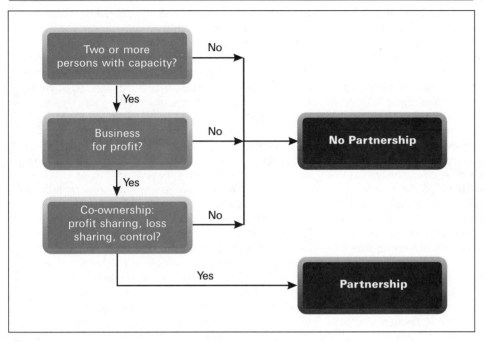

Partnership Capital and Property

The total money and property the partners contribute and dedicate to use in the enterprise is the **partnership capital**. Though a partnership is not required to have a minimum amount of capitalization before starting business, a partner may withdraw no part of his capital contribution without the consent of all the partners, except when the partnership is dissolved.

Whereas partnership capital is a fixed amount that may change only through an amendment to the articles of partnership, **partnership property**, or the sum of all of the partnership assets, may vary in amount. All property originally brought into the partnership or subsequently acquired by it is partnership property. Given no contrary intention, property acquired with partnership funds is partnership property.

Title to real estate that is properly a partnership asset (purchased with partnership funds or specifically made a capital contribution, for example) may stand in the name of the partnership, an individual partner, or a third party. The UPA alters the common law by permitting title to real estate to be conveyed to a partnership in the partnership name; title so acquired may be subsequently conveyed only in the partnership name.

A question may arise concerning whether property that a partner owned before the partnership formed and that was used in the partnership business is a capital contribution and thus an asset of the partnership. Where there is no express agreement, an intention to consider property as partnership property may be inferred from any of the following facts: (1) the property was improved with partnership funds; (2) the property was carried on the books of the partnership as an asset; (3) taxes, liens, or expenses, such as insurance or repairs, were paid by the partnership; (4) income or proceeds of the property were treated as partnership funds; or (5) the partners admit or declare the property to be partnership property.

Partnership capital total money and property contributed by the partners for permanent use by the partnership

Partnership property sum of all of the partnership's assets, including all property brought into the partnership or subsequently acquired by it

STANDRING v. STANDRING   Colorado Court of Appeals, 1990, 794 P.2d 1089

FACTS Frank Standring, the defendant, and Stephen Standring, the plaintiff, are father and son. Frank owned two parcels of property: a house on West Myrtle Street and a shop on South College Avenue where he ran Mountain Armory, a shop dealing in firearms and other sporting goods. In 1972, Frank constructed a new building for the shop, securing a loan using both properties as collateral. In 1975, Frank formed a partnership concerning Mountain Armory with Stephen and a third party, Dennis Combs. Subsequently, Combs withdrew from the partnership, and Frank raised Stephen's partnership interest to 49 percent. The partnership income included money from the rental of the Myrtle Street house, and Stephen testified that his duties included maintenance of both the shop and the house. Both parcels were consistently listed as assets in partnership tax returns. Although title to both parcels remained in Frank Standring's name, Stephen testified that he understood them to belong to the partnership. In 1986, Frank and Stephen had a dispute and Frank told Stephen he never wanted to see him again. Stephen subsequently brought this action to dissolve the partnership. The court granted the dissolution and declared the shop a partnership asset that was to be sold with the proceeds divided 51 percent to Frank and 49 percent to Stephen. Stephen appeals the court's ruling that the house was not a partnership asset.

DECISION Judgment affirmed.

OPINION Partners have the right to contribute any property they wish to the partnership. Whether the property has been contributed to a partnership depends on whether the parties agreed to do so. Thus, the determination whether real property purchased by and held in the name of a single partner is a private or partnership asset depends on the intent of the parties. Some of the factors reflecting the parties' intent to contribute individually held property to a partnership include the language of any partnership agreement; the use of the property in the partnership business; the listing of the property as an asset and of its mortgage as a liability in the partnership books and tax returns; the construction or improvements using partnership money; payment of taxes and insurance premiums on the property out of partnership funds; a party's declaration of intent, such as by letter or will, accompanying his act of entering the partnership; and, generally, the conduct of the parties with respect to the property. In this case, the trial court considered several of the above factors in determining which of the parcels were partnership property and, in the absence of competent evidence to the contrary, its ruling is binding on appeal. Here, the trial court's ruling is supported by the record. Although both parcels were listed on tax returns and income from both was "run through" the partnership, only the College Street property was used in the business of the partnership. Also, there is conflicting evidence concerning whether Stephen spent time or partnership money maintaining the Myrtle Street property. Finally, notes written by the attorney who simultaneously formulated the partnership and Frank's will indicate that Frank intended to devise the Myrtle Street house through his will. This evidence supports an inference that Frank intended to retain the house as a personal asset. Therefore, the trial court's ruling is binding on appeal.

INTERPRETATION Whether property is partnership property depends upon the intent of the parties as indicated by factors such as their express agreement; the use of the property in the partnership business; the listing of the property as an asset on the partnership's books; the improvement of the property with partnership assets; and the payment by the partnership of taxes, insurance, and other expenses of property ownership.

Rights in Specific Partnership Property

A partner's ownership interest in any specific item of partnership property is that of a **tenant in partnership.** This type of ownership, which exists only in a partnership, has the following principal characteristics:

Tenancy in partnership
type of joint ownership that determines partners' rights in specific partnership property

1. Each partner has a right equal to those of his copartners to possess partnership property for partnership purposes, but he has no right to possess it for any other purpose without his copartners' consent.
2. A partner may not make an individual assignment of his right in specific partnership property.
3. A partner's interest in specific partnership property is not subject to attachment or execution by his individual creditors. It is subject to attachment or execution only on a claim against the partnership.

4. Upon the death of a partner, his right in specific partnership property vests in the surviving partner or partners. Upon the death of the last surviving partner, his right in the property vests in his legal representative.

Partner's Interest in the Partnership

In addition to owning as a tenant in partnership every specific item of partnership property, each partner has an **interest in the partnership**, defined as his share of the profits and surplus. This interest is expressly stated to be personal property.

Interest in partnership partner's share in the partnership's profits and surplus

Assignability A partner may sell or assign his interest in the partnership. The new owner, however, does *not* become a partner, does not succeed to the partner's rights to participate in the management, and does not have access to the information available to a member of the firm as a matter of right. He is merely entitled to receive the share of profits and rights on liquidation to which the assigning partner would otherwise have been entitled. An assignment does not dissolve the partnership, and the assigning partner remains a partner, with all of a partner's other rights and duties.

Assignability a partner may sell or assign his interest in the partnership; the new owner becomes entitled to the assigning partner's share of profits and surplus but does not become a partner

Creditors' Rights A partner's interest is subject to the claims of that partner's creditors, who may obtain a **charging order** (a type of judicial lien) against the partner's interest. A creditor who has charged the interest of a partner with a judgment debt may apply for the appointment of, and the court may then appoint, a receiver, who will receive and hold for the benefit of the creditor the share of profits that ordinarily would be paid to the partner. Neither the judgment creditor nor the receiver becomes a partner, and neither is entitled to participate in the partnership's management or to have access to information. In addition, neither the charging order nor its sale upon foreclosure causes a dissolution.

Creditor's rights a partner's interest is subject to the claims of creditors, who may obtain a charging order against the partner's interest

Charging order judicial lien against a partner's interest in the partnership

Figure 31–3 compares a partner's rights in specific partnership property with his interest in the partnership, as does the next case.

BOHONUS v. AMERCO Supreme Court of Arizona, 1979, 124 Ariz. 88, 602 P.2d 469

FACTS Amerco secured a personal judgment against Bohonus. The company sought to enforce that judgment by requesting a judicial sale of the assets and property of a partnership of which Bohonus was a member and in which he had an interest.

DECISION Judgment for the partnership.

OPINION The property rights of a partner include his rights in specific partnership property, his interest in the partnership, and his right to participate in management. But only the partner's interest in the partnership—his share of the profits and surplus—can be charged and sold to satisfy the individual debt of that partner. In contrast, his right in specific partnership property is not subject to attachment or execution except on a claim against the partnership. Accordingly, a court cannot order the sale of partnership assets to satisfy the individual debt of Bohonus.

INTERPRETATION A partner's interest is subject to the claims of his creditors, but a partner's rights in specific partnership property is not.

FIGURE 31–3 Partnership Property Compared with Partner's Interest

	Partnership Property	**Partner's Interest**
Definition	Tenant in partnership	Share of profits and surplus
Possession	For partnership purposes, not individual purposes	Intangible, personal property right
Assignability	NO: unless all other partners assign their rights in the property	YES: but the assignee does not become a partner
Attachment	YES: but only for a claim against the partnership	YES: by a charging order
Inheritance	NO: goes to surviving partner(s)	YES: passes to the personal representative

CHAPTER SUMMARY

Nature	**Definition of Partnership** an association of two or more persons to carry on as co-owners of a business for profit **Entity Theory** 　■ *Legal Entity* an organization having a legal existence separate from that of its members; UPA considers a partnership a legal entity for some purposes 　■ *Legal Aggregate* a group of individuals not having a legal existence separate from that of its members; the UPA considers a partnership a legal aggregate for some purposes **Types of Partners** 　■ *General Partner* member of either a general or limited partnership with unlimited liability for its debts, full management powers, and a right to share profits 　■ *Limited Partner* member of a limited partnership with liability for its debts only to the extent of her capital contribution 　■ *Silent Partner* partner who takes no part in the partnership business 　■ *Secret Partner* partner whose membership in the partnership is not disclosed to the public 　■ *Dormant Partner* partner who is both a silent and a secret partner

Formation	**Articles of Partnership** it is preferable, although not usually required, that the partners enter into a written partnership agreement (articles of partnership) **Tests of Existence** the formation of a partnership requires all of the following: 　■ *Association* two or more persons with legal capacity who agree to become partners 　■ *Business for Profit* 　■ *Co-ownership* includes sharing of profits, losses, and control of the business **Partnership Capital** total money and property contributed by the partners for permanent use by the partnership **Partnership Property** sum of all of the partnership's assets, including all property brought into the partnership or subsequently acquired by it **Tenancy in Partnership** type of joint ownership that determines partners' rights in specific partnership property

> **Interest in Partnership** partner's share in the partnership's profits and surplus
> - *Assignability* a partner may sell or assign his interest in the partnership; the new owner becomes entitled to the assigning partner's share of profits and surplus but does not become a partner
> - *Creditor's Rights* a partner's interest is subject to the claims of creditors, who may obtain a charging order (judicial lien) against the partner's interest

QUESTIONS

1. Distinguish between a legal entity and a legal aggregate. Identify those purposes for which a partnership is treated as a legal entity and those purposes for which it is treated as a legal aggregate.
2. List the main provisions that should be included in a partnership agreement.
3. Discuss the tests for the existence of a partnership.
4. Distinguish between partnership capital and partnership property.
5. Distinguish between a partner's rights in specific partnership property and a partner's interest in the partnership.

Internet Question. Find and review information about the selection of a form of business organization.

PROBLEMS

1. Lynn and Jack jointly own shares of stock of a corporation, have a joint bank account, and have purchased and own as tenants in common a piece of real estate. They share equally the dividends paid on the stock, the interest on the bank account, and the rent from the real estate. Without Lynn's knowledge, Jack makes a trip to inspect the real estate and on his way runs over Samuel. Samuel sues Lynn and Jack for his personal injuries, joining Lynn as defendant on the theory that Lynn was Jack's partner. Is Lynn liable?

2. Smith, Jones, and Brown were creditors of White, who operated a grain elevator known as White's Elevator. White was heavily in debt and was about to fail when the three creditors mentioned agreed to take title to his elevator property and pay all the debts. It was also agreed that White should continue as manager of the business at a salary of $1,500 per month and that all profits of the business were to be paid to Smith, Jones, and Brown. It was further agreed that they could dispense with White's services at any time, and that he was also at liberty to quit when he pleased. White accepted the proposition and continued to operate the business as before, buying and selling grain, incurring obligations, and borrowing money at the bank in his own name for the business. He did, however, tell the banker of the transaction with Smith, Jones, and Brown; and other former creditors of the business knew of it. It worked successfully and for several years paid substantial profits, enough so that Smith, Jones, and Brown had received back nearly all that they had originally advanced. Were Smith, Jones, and Brown partners? Explain.

3. James and Suzanne engaged in the grocery business as partners. In one year they earned considerable money, and at the end of the year, they invested a part of the profits in oil land, taking title to the land in their names as tenants in common. The investment was fortunate, for oil was discovered near the land; and its value increased many times. Who owns the land? Why?

4. Sheila owned an old roadside building that she believed could be easily converted into an antique shop. She talked to her friend Barbara, an antique fancier, and they executed the following written agreement:
   (a) Sheila would supply the building, all utilities, and $10,000 capital for purchasing antiques.
   (b) Barbara would supply $3,000 for purchasing antiques, Sheila to repay her when the business terminated.
   (c) Barbara would manage the shop, make all purchases, and receive a salary of $100 per week plus 5 percent of the gross receipts.
   (d) Fifty percent of the net profits would go into the purchase of new stock. The balance of the net profits would go to Sheila.
   (e) The business would operate under the name Roadside Antiques.

   Business went poorly, and after one year, Sheila and Barbara owed a debt of $4,000 to Old Fashioned, Inc., the principal supplier of antiques purchased by

Barbara in the name of Roadside Antiques. Old Fashioned sues Roadside Antiques, and Sheila and Barbara as partners. Decision?

5. Clark owned a vacant lot. Bird was engaged in building houses. Clark and Bird entered into an oral agreement by which Bird was to erect a house on the lot. When the house and lot were sold, Bird was to have his money first. Clark was then to have the agreed value of the lot, and the profits were to be equally divided. Did a partnership exist?

6. Grant, Arthur, and David formed a partnership for the purpose of betting on boxing matches. Grant and Arthur would become friendly with various boxers and offer them bribes to lose certain bouts. David would then place large bets, using money contributed by all three, and would collect the winnings. After David had accumulated a large sum of money, Grant and Arthur demanded their share, but David refused to make any split. Grant and Arthur then brought suit in a court of equity to compel David to account for the profits of the partnership. What decision?

7. Virginia, Georgia, Caroline, and Louise, residents of state X, were partners doing business under the trade name of Morning Glory Nursery. Virginia owned a one-third interest, and Georgia, Caroline, and Louise owned two-ninths each. The partners acquired three tracts of land in state X for the purpose of the partnership. Two of the tracts were acquired in the names of the four partners, "trading and doing business as Morning Glory Nursery." The third tract was acquired in the names of the individuals, the trade name not appearing in the deed. This third tract was acquired by the partnership out of partnership funds and for partnership purposes. Who owns each of the three tracts? Why?

8. Teresa, Peter, and Walker were partners under a written agreement made in January that the partnership should continue for ten years. During the same year, Walker, being indebted to Rebecca, sold and conveyed his interest in the partnership to Rebecca. Teresa and Peter paid Rebecca $5,000 as Walker's share of the profits for that year but refused Rebecca permission to inspect the books or to come into the managing office of the partnership. Rebecca brings an action setting forth the above facts and asks for an account of partnership transactions and an order to inspect the books and to participate in the management of the partnership business.

   (a) Does Walker's action dissolve the partnership?

   (b) To what is Rebecca entitled with respect to (1) partnership profits, (2) inspection of partnership books, (3) an account of partnership transactions, and (4) participation in the partnership management?

9. Horn's Crane Service furnished supplies and services under a written contract to a partnership engaged in operating a quarry and rock-crushing business. Horn brought this action against Prior and Cook, the individual members of the partnership, to recover a personal judgment against them for the partnership's liability under that contract. Horn has not sued the partnership itself, nor does he claim that the partnership property is insufficient to satisfy its debts. Decision?

10. Richard DeLong and Ken Birch formed Birch-DeLong Construction Company in 1972 as a partnership. They initially agreed that all disbursements would be only on mutual agreement. Later, though, DeLong agreed to allow Birch to disburse funds solely on Birch's signature. Around 1980, DeLong realized that Birch was using partnership funds for personal expenses. Birch admitted this. After the partnership filed for bankruptcy in 1981, DeLong reported the disbursement problems to the state. In 1982, three counts of first degree theft and one count of second degree theft were filed against Birch. The trial court held as a matter of law that a partner could not be charged with embezzling partnership funds because the partner would not be exercising unauthorized control over the property of another. The state appealed. Decision?

11. Smithtown General Hospital was operated as a forty-two-member general partnership. The hospital was criminally indicted for (1) allowing an unauthorized individual to take part in a surgical procedure on an uninformed, nonconsenting patient and (2) falsifying records in an effort to conceal the offense. The partnership moved to dismiss the indictment, claiming that it was not an entity distinct from the aggregate of the forty-two individual partners and thus could not be indicted without a showing of culpable intent on the part of each partner. Decision?

12. Cutler worked as a bartender for Bowen until they orally agreed that Bowen would have the authority and responsibility for the entire active management and operation of the tavern business known as the Havana Club. Each was to receive $100 per week plus half of the net profits. The business continued under this arrangement for four years until the building was taken over by the Salt Lake City Redevelopment Agency. The agency paid $10,000 to Bowen as compensation for disruption. The business, however, was terminated after Bowen and Cutler failed to find a new, suitable location. Cutler, alleging a partnership with Bowen, then brought this action against him to recover one-half of the $10,000. Bowen contends that he is entitled to the entire $10,000 because he was the sole owner of the business and that Cutler was merely his employee. Cutler argues that although Bowen owned the physical assets of the business, she, as a partner in the business, is entitled to one-half of the compensation that was paid for the business's goodwill and going-concern value. Decision?

13. In 1966, Gauldin and Corn entered into a partnership for the purpose of raising cattle and hogs. The two men were to share equally all costs, labor, losses, and profits. The business was started on land owned initially by Corn's parents but later acquired by Corn and his wife. No rent was ever requested or paid for use of the land. Partnership funds were used to bulldoze and clear the land, to repair and build fences, and to seed and fertilize the land. In 1970, at a cost of $2,487.50, a machine shed was built on the land. In 1975, a Cargill unit was built on the land at a cost of $8,000. When the partnership dissolved in 1976, Gauldin paid Corn $7,500 for the "removable" assets; however, the two had no agreement regarding the distribution of the barn and the Cargill unit. Gauldin sues Corn, claiming he is entitled to one-half of the value of the two buildings. Decision?

14. In 1976, Peter D. Norman and John C. Norman inherited a one-third undivided interest in commercial property in Greenville, Alabama. The other interests were owned by Ellis Oil Company and by the estate of Charlie Haigler, Sr. The three families operated a business on the property until the early 1980s. Then they rented the property to an unrelated business and designated the Normans to act as rental agents on the property to collect and disburse the rental income. The Normans established a bank account under the name of "Norman Properties," into which they deposited monthly rental checks and other income from the property. The Normans paid out of this account the pro rata shares of the rental income to the Haigler estate and to Ellis Oil Co., but they allowed their shares to accumulate in the account. On January 21, 1981, the Normans purchased a piece of commercial property in Greenville, the title to which was taken in the names of Peter D. Norman and John C. Norman, as tenants in common. In purchasing the property, the Normans drew checks on the "Norman Properties" account. On December 9, 1986, Robert Dwayne Bozeman and Elizabeth Bozeman sued Norman Properties, alleging fraud and breach of the warranty of habitability with regard to a new house the Normans had built. On August 26, 1988, the trial court entered a judgment against Norman Properties for $50,000, which the Bozemans filed. On July 31, 1989, the Normans sold the Greenville commercial property to Earnest Dean, who assumed the existing mortgages. On February 15, 1991, the Bozemans filed this action, seeking to have the trial court declare that the Greenville property sold to Dean was partnership property, and therefore was subject to sale to satisfy the judgment. The Normans argued that the Greenville property was individually owned by them. The trial court granted summary judgment for the Bozemans, and the Normans appealed. Decision?

CHAPTER 32

Operation of General Partnerships

The operation and management of a partnership involve interactions among the partners as well as their interactions with third persons. In this chapter, we will consider both of these relationships. The first part of the chapter will focus on the rights and duties of the partners among themselves, which are determined by the partnership agreement, the common law, and the Uniform Partnership Act. The second part of the chapter will focus on the relations of partners to third persons who deal with the partnership, which are governed by the laws of agency, contracts, and torts, as well as by the UPA.

RELATIONSHIPS AMONG PARTNERS

When parties enter into a partnership, the law imposes certain obligations on them and also gives them specific rights. So long as the rights of third parties are not affected and standards of fairness are maintained, the parties may, by agreement, vary these rights and obligations.

DUTIES AMONG PARTNERS

The principal legal duties imposed upon the relationship of partners among themselves are (1) the fiduciary duty (the duty of loyalty), (2) the duty of obedience, and (3) the duty of care. In addition, each partner has a duty to inform his copartners and a duty to account to the partnership. (These additional duties will be discussed later, in a section covering the rights of partners.) All of these duties correspond precisely with those duties owed by an agent to his principal and reflect the fact that much of the law of partnership is the law of agency.

Fiduciary Duty

A fiduciary relationship, based on high standards of trust and confidence, exists among the members of a partnership. Each partner owes a duty of utmost good faith, fairness, and loyalty to his partners. Only on such a basis can so intimate a business relationship function.

Fiduciary duty duty of utmost loyalty, fairness, and good faith owed by partners to each other and to the partnership

The **fiduciary duty** requires that a partner not make a profit other than his agreed compensation, not compete with the partnership, and not otherwise profit from the relationship at the expense of the partnership. The UPA states that every partner must account to the partnership for any benefit he receives and hold as trustee for it any profits he makes without the consent of the other partners from any transaction connected with the formation, conduct, or liquidation of the partnership or from any use he makes of its property. He may not prefer

610

himself over the firm, nor may he even deal at arm's length with his partners. His duty is one of undivided and continuous loyalty to them.

The extent of this fiduciary duty, which binds all fiduciaries and not just partners, has been most eloquently expressed by the often-quoted words of Judge (later Justice) Cardozo:

> Joint adventurers, like copartners, owe to one another, while the enterprise continues, the duty of the *finest loyalty*. Many forms of conduct permissible in a workaday world for those acting at arm's length, are forbidden to those bound by fiduciary ties. A trustee is held to something stricter than the morals of the market place. *Not honesty alone, but the punctilio of an honor the most sensitive, is then the standard of behavior.* As to this there has developed a tradition that is unbending and inveterate. Uncompromising rigidity has been the attitude of courts of equity when petitioned to undermine the rule of undivided loyalty by the "disintegrating erosion" of particular exceptions. Only thus has the level of conduct for fiduciaries been kept at a level higher than that trodden by the crowd. It will not consciously be lowered by any judgment of this court. [Emphasis added.]

Within the demands of the fiduciary duty, a partner cannot acquire for herself a partnership asset or opportunity without the consent of all the partners. The duty also applies to the purchase of a partner's interest from another partner. Each partner owes the highest duty of honesty and fair dealing to the other partners, including the obligation to disclose fully and accurately all material facts.

The next case illustrates how rigorously the courts enforce the fiduciary duty.

CLEMENT v. CLEMENT Supreme Court of Pennsylvania, 1970, 436 Pa. 466, 260 A.2d, 728

FACTS Charles and L. W. Clement were brothers who had formed a partnership lasting forty years. In 1964, Charles discovered that his brother, who was the brighter of the two and who kept the partnership's books, had made several substantial personal investments with funds improperly withdrawn from the partnership. He then brought an action in equity seeking dissolution of the partnership, appointment of a receiver, and an accounting. The chancellor of the court of equity issued a decree in favor of Charles, but the court *en banc* reversed his decision. Charles appealed.

DECISION Order of the court *en banc* reversed and case remanded.

OPINION There is a fiduciary relationship between partners such that a person does not have to deal with his partner as though he were the opposite party in an arm's length transaction. Where a partner commingles partnership funds with his own and generally deals loosely with partnership assets, he has the burden of proving that he did not breach his fiduciary duty. Here, L.W. dealt loosely with partnership funds. At various times he made substantial investments in his own name, but he was unable to explain where he got the funds to make those investments. The burden is on L. W. to show the source of the funds that have gone into his investments. L.W. has not satisfied that burden, and, therefore, Charles is entitled to recover even though he cannot trace the money invested by his brother dollar for dollar from the diverted partnership funds.

INTERPRETATION Partners are held to a fiduciary duty in their dealings with each other, which includes the obligation to disclose accurately to their partners all material facts.

Duty of Obedience

A partner owes his partners a duty to act in obedience to the partnership agreement and to any business decisions properly made by the partnership. A partner who violates this duty is individually liable to his partners for any resulting loss. For example, a partner who, in violation of a specific agreement not to extend credit, advances money from partnership funds and sells goods on credit to an insolvent party is personally liable to his partners for the unpaid debt.

Duty of obedience duty to act in accordance with the partnership agreement and any business decisions properly made by the partners

Duty of Care

Duty of care duty owed by partners to manage the partnership affairs without culpable negligence

Culpable negligence greater than ordinary negligence but less than gross negligence

A partner must manage partnership affairs without culpable negligence. **Culpable negligence** is something more than ordinary negligence, yet short of gross negligence. Thus, a partner who makes honest errors of judgment or who fails to use ordinary skill in transacting partnership business does not breach her duty of care, so long as she is not culpably negligent. Assume, for example, that a partner assigned to keep the partnership books uses an overly complicated bookkeeping system and, consequently, makes numerous mistakes. Since these errors result simply from poor judgment rather than fraud and are not intended to and do not operate to the personal advantage of the negligent bookkeeping partner, she is *not* liable to her copartners for any resulting loss.

RIGHTS AMONG PARTNERS

The law provides partners with certain rights, which include (1) their rights in specific partnership property as tenants in partnership; (2) their interest in the partnership; (3) their right to share in distributions; (4) their right to participate in management; (5) their right to choose associates; and (6) their right of enforcement. We discussed the first two of these rights in Chapter 31. The four remaining rights among partners will be discussed in this section.

Right to Share in Distributions

Distribution transfer of partnership property from the partnership to a partner

A **distribution** is a transfer of partnership property from the partnership to a partner. Distributions include a division of profits, a return of capital contributions, a repayment of a loan or advance made by a partner to the partnership, and a payment made to compensate a partner for services rendered to the partnership.

Profits each partner is entitled to an equal share of the profits unless otherwise agreed

Right to Share in Profits Because a partnership is an association to carry on a business for profit, each partner is entitled, unless otherwise agreed, to a share of the **profits**. Conversely, unless otherwise agreed, each partner must contribute toward any losses the partnership sustains. If the partners do not have an agreement about dividing the profits, they share the profits *equally*, regardless of the ratio of their financial contributions or their degree of participation in the management. Moreover, they bear losses in a proportion the *same* as that in which they share profits, unless the partnership agreement provides otherwise—which it validly may do.

For example, Alice, Betty, and Carol form a partnership, with Alice contributing $10,000; Betty, $20,000; and Carol, $30,000. They could agree that Alice would receive 20 percent of the profits and assume 30 percent of the losses; that Betty would receive 30 percent of the profits and assume 50 percent of the losses; and that Carol would receive 50 percent of the profits and assume 20 percent of the losses. However, if their agreement is silent as to the sharing of profits and losses, each would have an equal one-third share of both profits and losses.

Capital after all partnership creditors have been paid, each partner is entitled to be repaid his capital contribution when the firm is terminated

Right to Return of Capital After all partnership creditors have been paid, each partner is entitled to repayment of his **capital** contribution when the firm is terminated. Unless otherwise agreed, a partner is not entitled to interest on his capital contribution. However, if the return of his capital contribution is delayed, he is entitled to interest at the legal rate from the date when the contribution should have been repaid.

FELTON INVESTMENT GROUP v. TAURMAN   Supreme Court of Montana, 1986, 722 P.2d 1135

FACTS Wayne Taurman and Derrold Paige, employees of Felton Construction Company, were members of Felton Investment Group (FIG), a partnership of employee contributors to a retirement fund. The partnership agreement included a provision "that if a member ceases employment or is discharged for misconduct, his interest shall be returned in an amount equal to contributions paid into the fund plus 4% simple interest." In December 1978, Paige decided that his investment in FIG was in jeopardy and stopped contributing to the fund; however, he remained an employee of Felton. About a year later, Paige received a check from FIG, reflecting his contributions to the fund plus interest, in satisfaction of his claim in the partnership. He refused to indorse and cash the check. Taurman continued to invest in FIG until July 1980. At that time, he and Paige were both terminated by Felton for refusing to accept nonunion work. Taurman was then offered by FIG an amount equal to his contribution plus interest in satisfaction of his claim in the partnership, but he too refused to indorse and cash the check. FIG filed a complaint requesting that Taurman and Paige be ordered to accept the amounts offered in satisfaction of their claims in the partnership. Taurman and Paige filed a complaint seeking the judicial dissolution of FIG, a formal accounting of the partnership, and *pro rata* shares in the partnership's assets. FIG appealed from a trial court judgment for Taurman and Paige.

DECISION Judgment for Taurman and Paige affirmed.

OPINION The partnership agreement addressed the voluntary termination of a partner's employment with Felton as well as his discharge for misconduct. The agreement did not cover the effect of a partner's involuntary termination from Felton in the absence of misconduct. Taurman and Paige were both long-time employees of Felton whose discharge was solely determined by their refusal to break with their union. Since no misconduct was present, their rights were not set forth in the partnership agreement. Therefore, the provisions of the Uniform Partnership Act are controlling. The relevant section states that "[e]ach partner shall be repaid his contributions . . . and share equally in the profits and surplus remaining after all liabilities . . . are satisfied . . ." Taurman and Paige are entitled to receive their *pro rata* shares of the fair market value of the assets of FIG as of the date their employment with Felton terminated.

INTERPRETATION Upon withdrawal, a partner is entitled to the return of his capital contribution and to receive his share of the profits and surplus.

Right to Return of Advances If a partner makes an **advance** (loan) over and above his agreed capital contribution, he is entitled to repayment of the advance plus interest on it. His claim as a creditor of the firm, though subordinate to the claims of creditors who are not partners, is superior to the partners' rights to return of capital. In addition, a partner who has incurred personal liabilities in the ordinary and proper conduct of the firm's business or who has made payments on behalf of the partnership is entitled to indemnification or repayment on footing equal to that afforded the repayment of advances made by partners.

Advance if a partner makes an advance (loan) to the firm, he is entitled to repayment of the advance plus interest; but his repayment is subordinate to that of nonpartner creditors

Right to Compensation The UPA provides that, unless otherwise agreed, *no* partner is entitled to remuneration (payment) for acting in the partnership business. Even a partner who works more than any of the others to conduct the business is entitled to no salary but only to his share of the profits. A partner may, however, by agreement among all of the partners, receive a salary or a disproportionate percentage of the profits. Moreover, a surviving partner is entitled to reasonable compensation for his services in winding up the partnership affairs.

Compensation unless otherwise agreed, no partner is entitled to payment for acting in the partnership business

Right to Participate in Management
Each of the partners, unless otherwise agreed, has an *equal* voice in the **management** of the business. The majority generally governs the actions and decisions of the partnership, with the principal exception that *all* the partners must

Management each partner has an equal voice in management unless otherwise agreed

consent to any actions that are contrary to the partnership agreement. In their partnership agreement, the partners may provide for unequal voting rights. Large partnerships often concentrate most or all management authority in a committee of a few partners or even in just one partner. Classes of partners with different management rights may also be created. This is a common practice in accounting and law firms, which may have two classes (junior and senior partners) or three classes (junior, senior, and managing partners).

Right to Choose Associates

Choice of associates under the doctrine of *delectus personae*, no person can become a member of a partnership without the consent of all of the partners

No partner may be forced to accept as a partner any person the choice of whom she does not approve. This is partly because of the fiduciary relationship between the partners and partly because each partner has a right to participate in the management of the business, to handle the partnership assets for partnership purposes, and to act as an agent of the partnership. It is possible that an ill-chosen partner, by negligence, poor judgment, or dishonesty, may bring financial loss or ruin to a partnership. Because of the close relationships they involve, partnerships must necessarily be founded on mutual trust and confidence. All this finds expression in the term ***delectus personae*** (literally, "choice of the person"), which indicates the right one has to select her partners. This principle is embodied in the UPA, which provides: "No person can become a member of a partnership without the consent of ***all*** the partners" (emphasis added). It is because of *delectus personae* that a purchaser of a partner's interest does not become a partner and is not entitled to participate in the management. The partnership agreement, however, may provide for admission of a new partner by a less-than-unanimous vote.

Delectus personae (de·lek'·tus per·so'·nee) partner's right to choose who may become a member of the partnership

Enforcement Rights

As we have discussed, the partnership relationship creates a number of duties and rights among partners. Accordingly, partnership law provides partners with the means to enforce these rights and duties.

Information each partner may demand full information about all partnership matters, and each partner has a duty to supply other partners with full and accurate information

Right to Information and Inspection of the Books Each partner may demand to have full **information** about all partnership matters, and, in turn, each partner has a duty to supply other partners with full and accurate information about all things that affect the partnership. Unless the partners agree otherwise, the books of the partnership are to be kept at the principal place of business at all times; and each partner has a right to have access to, to inspect, and to copy any of them. This right may also be exercised by a duly authorized agent on behalf of a partner.

Formal account complete review of all financial transactions of a partnership

Right to an Account A **formal account** is a complete review of all financial transactions of the partnership, including financial statements. The UPA grants to each partner the right to an account whenever (1) his copartners wrongfully exclude him from the partnership business or possession of its property, (2) the partnership agreement so provides, (3) a partner makes a profit in violation of his fiduciary duty, or (4) other circumstances render it just and reasonable.

Accounting equitable proceeding for a complete settlement of all partnership affairs

If a partner does not receive a requested account or is dissatisfied with it, she may bring an enforcement action called an **accounting**, which is an equitable proceeding for a comprehensive and effective settlement of all partnership affairs.

ETHICAL DILEMMA When Is an Opportunity a Partnership Opportunity?

FACTS Ted Johnson is a real estate manager and investor. Nearly twenty years ago, Ted embarked on a partnership with Karla Jones to improve and operate an office building in New Haven, Connecticut. The building and land are owned by James Jason. James gave Ted and Karla a twenty-year lease. At the end of twenty years, the lease would terminate and the property would revert to James. Pursuant to their partnership agreement, Ted and Karla each provided 50 percent of the capital for improvements of the office space and received 50 percent of allocable net profits.

Ted has successfully managed the building and during the past twenty years has accumulated some additional capital. Six months before the twenty-year lease was scheduled to expire, he and James had dinner together. Indicating how pleased he had been with Ted's management skills, James offered to lease the property for another twenty-year term and mentioned the idea of knocking down the present structure and building a small mall. In light of the recent building of luxury condominiums and exclusive restaurants in the neighborhood, the development of a mall appears to be a sound idea.

Though he no longer needs Karla's capital for the project, Ted suspects that Karla would be interested in participating in the mall development. However, it was not clear whether James made the offer to renew the lease solely to Ted or to the partnership. Since Karla had not been invited to dinner and her name had never been mentioned, Ted believes that the offer was made solely to him.

Social, Policy, and Ethical Considerations

1. Does Ted have an ethical responsibility to inform Karla of the opportunity to renew the lease?
2. Does it matter that the renewal offer for the long-term lease was initially raised in a dinner conversation between Ted and James?
3. Should Ted be free to sever relations with Karla with regard to the property? Consider that Ted has managed the property and no longer needs Karla's capital. What competing social values does his dilemma involve?

RELATIONSHIP BETWEEN PARTNERS AND THIRD PARTIES

In the course of doing business, partners may also acquire rights over and incur duties to third parties. For example, under the law of agency, a principal is liable on contracts made on his behalf by his duly authorized agents and is liable in tort for the wrongful acts his employees commit in the course of their employment. A large part of the law of partnership is the law of agency, and most problems arising between partners and third persons require the application of principles of agency law.

CONTRACTS OF PARTNERSHIP

The act of every partner binds the partnership on transactions *within* the scope of the partnership business unless the partner does not have actual or apparent authority to so act. If the partnership is bound, each general partner has *unlimited* **personal liability** for that partnership obligation. The UPA provides that partners are jointly liable on all debts and contract obligations of the partnership. Under **joint liability**, a creditor must bring suit against all of the partners as a group. Consequently, any suit against a partner must name all the partners as defendants.

Personal liability if the partnership is contractually bound, each partner has joint, unlimited personal liability

Joint liability liability where a creditor must sue all of the partners as a group

Authority to Bind Partnership

A partner may bind the partnership by her act if (a) she has actual authority, express or implied, to perform the act or (b) she has apparent authority to perform the act. If the act is not apparently within the scope of the partnership

Authority to bind partnership a partner who has actual authority (express or implied) or apparent authority may bind the partnership

business, the partnership is bound only where the partner has actual authority. In such a case, the third person dealing with the partner assumes the risk of the existence of such actual authority. Where there is no actual or apparent authority, the partnership is bound only if it ratifies the act. (Ratification was discussed in Chapter 30.) See Figure 32–1.

Actual express authority
authority set forth in the partnership agreement, in additional agreements among the partners, or in decisions made by a majority of the partners regarding the ordinary business of the partnership

Actual Express Authority The **actual express authority** of partners may be written or oral; it may be specifically set forth in the partnership agreement or in an additional agreement between the partners. In addition, it may arise from decisions made by a majority of the partners regarding ordinary matters connected with the partnership business.

The UPA provides that the following acts do *not* bind the partnership unless authorized by *all* of the partners: (1) assignment of partnership property for the benefit of its creditors; (2) disposal of the goodwill of the business; (3) any act that would make it impossible to carry on the ordinary business of the partnership; (4) confession of a judgment (a written agreement by a debtor authorizing a

FIGURE 32–1 Contract Liability

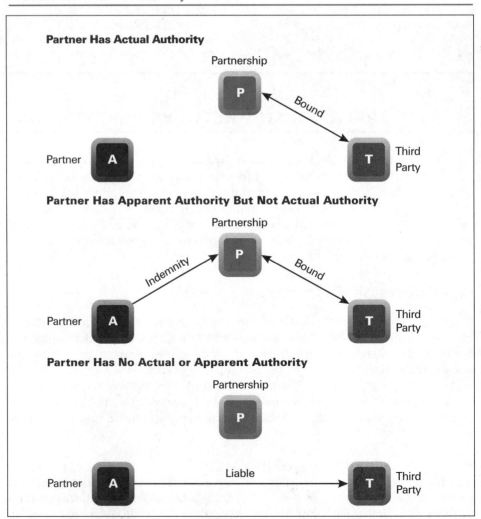

creditor to obtain a court judgment in the event the debtor defaults); or (5) submission of a partnership claim or liability to arbitration.

In addition, a partner who does not have actual authority from all of her partners may not bind the partnership by any act that does not apparently relate to the usual conduct of the partnership business. Such acts would include the following, which under ordinary circumstances would be clearly outside the scope of the partnership: (1) execution of contracts of guaranty or suretyship in the firm name, (2) sale of partnership property not held for sale in the usual course of business, and (3) payment of individual debts out of partnership assets.

Actual Implied Authority   **Actual implied authority** is authority neither expressly granted nor expressly denied but reasonably deduced from the nature of the partnership, the terms of the partnership agreement, or the relations of the partners. For example, a partner has implied authority to hire and fire employees whose services are necessary to carry on the partnership business. In addition, a partner has implied authority to purchase property necessary for the business, to receive performance of obligations due the partnership, and to bring legal actions to enforce claims of the partnership.

> **Actual implied authority**
> authority that is reasonably deduced from the nature of the partnership, the terms of the partnership agreement, or the relations of the partners

Apparent Authority   **Apparent authority** (which may or may not be actual) is authority that a third person, in view of the circumstances, the conduct of the parties, and a lack of notice or knowledge to the contrary, may reasonably consider to exist. For example, a partner has apparent authority to indorse checks and notes, to make representations and warranties in selling goods, and to enter into contracts for advertising. However, a third person may not rely on apparent authority in any situation where he is put on notice or already knows that the partner does not have actual authority.

> **Apparent authority**
> authority that a third person may reasonably assume to exist in light of the conduct of the partners, so long as that third person has no knowledge or notice of the lack of actual authority

FIRST NATIONAL BANK AND TRUST COMPANY OF WILLISTON v. SCHERR Supreme Court of North Dakota, 1991, 467 N.W.2d 427

FACTS Scherr and Scherr is a partnership formed by Pius Scherr and Albinus Scherr in 1981 for the purpose of constructing and investing in buildings. In September 1981, Scherr and Scherr opened a checking account with First National Bank and Trust Company of Williston (Bank). The signature card for the account, signed by each of the partners, allowed either of the two partners to bind the partnership concerning "checks, endorsements, notes, . . . mortgages or any other instruments for the deposit or withdrawal of funds, for borrowing money and pledging or mortgaging assets of the partnership as security for the payment thereof and for the transaction of any other business with it." In December 1981, the partnership delivered to the Bank, at its request, a copy of a partnership agreement signed by both Pius and Albinus. This agreement provided: "[w]ithout the written consent of the other partner, neither partner shall on behalf of the partnership borrow or lend money, or make, deliver or accept any commercial paper, or execute any mortgage, security agreement, bond or lease, or purchase or contract to purchase, or sell or contract to sell any property for or of the partnership."

Beginning in November 1981, and continuing into 1984, Scherr and Scherr borrowed large sums from the Bank to acquire property and to construct various buildings. One venture was the construction of a building leased to a Famous Recipe Chicken fast-food franchisee. This project began with a mortgage, signed by both Pius and Albinus, to the Bank on April 29, 1983, for a construction advance of $100,000. Subsequent notes drawing on this short-term loan were signed solely by Pius, but these were later converted into a long-term note for $100,000 and a long-term mortgage, both signed by Pius and Albinus. A final short-term partnership note for $65,000 was signed solely by Pius. Scherr and Scherr defaulted on their obligations concerning the Famous Recipe Chicken project. The Bank foreclosed on the $100,000 mortgage and sued the partnership to collect the $65,000 note. The trial court granted summary judgment for the Bank against Pius, Albinus, and the partnership for the $65,000 balance due on the note. On

continued

appeal, the Supreme Court of North Dakota affirmed the judgment against Pius and reversed the judgment against Albinus and the partnership. It remanded for trial on the effect of the restriction in the partnership agreement on the liability of Albinus and the partnership to the Bank. On remand, the trial court determined that Albinus and the partnership were not liable on the note and entered judgment dismissing the Bank's claim against them. The Bank appealed.

DECISION Judgment affirmed.

OPINION The Bank argues that the signature card authorization was a controlling agreement between the Bank and the partnership because Albinus thereby consented to Pius's lone signature on the $65,000 note. The Bank further argues that the agreement between the partners did not alter the direct authorization given to the bank, even though the bank knew about it. The Uniform Partnership Act regulates the authority of partners to act for the partnership. Section 9(1) of the UPA states that a partner as an agent of the partnership normally binds the partnership by executing any instrument that carries on the business of the partnership in the usual way. This is so unless the partner has no authority to act and the person with whom he is dealing has knowledge of the fact that he has no such authority. This qualification is repeated in Section 9(4): "No act of a partner in contravention of a restriction on

authority shall bind the partnership to persons having knowledge of the restriction." Standing alone, the partnership agreement would compel judgment for Albinus and the partnership.

In this case, Pius had initial authority to act individually for the partnership in borrowing money from the Bank through the signature card authorization. Afterward, the partnership agreement restricted that authority. Under the Restatement (Second) of Agency § 136(2)(a), the continuing authority of an agent to accept credit from a third person on behalf of a principal may be terminated by the principal giving notice of the revocation of the agent's authority to the third person. The question in this case is whether delivery of the written partnership agreement to the Bank was effective notice that Pius's individual authorization had been restricted. The trial court determined as a matter of fact that effective notice of the restriction had been given. Under agency principles and the Uniform Partnership Act, the trial court's factual determinations that Pius acted in contravention of a restriction on his authority as a partner, known to the Bank, controls this case.

INTERPRETATION A third person may not rely on apparent authority in any situation where he is put on notice or already knows that the partner does not have actual authority.

Partnership by Estoppel

Partnership by estoppel imposes partnership duties and liabilities on a nonpartner who either has represented himself or has consented to be represented as a partner. It extends to a third person to whom such a representation is made and who justifiably relies on the representation.

For example, Marks and Saunders are partners doing business as Marks and Company. Marks introduces Patterson to Taylor, describing Patterson as a member of the partnership. Believing that Patterson is a member of the partnership and relying on Patterson's good credit standing, Taylor sells goods on credit to Marks and Company. In an action by Taylor against Marks, Saunders, and Patterson as partners to recover the price of the goods, Patterson is liable even though he is not a partner in Marks and Company. Taylor had justifiably relied on the representation that Patterson was a partner, to which representation Patterson, by his silence, consented. However, if Taylor had known at the time of the sale that Patterson was not a partner, his reliance on the representation would not have been justified; and Patterson would not be liable.

TORTS OF PARTNERSHIP

The UPA provides that a partnership is liable for the loss or injury any partner causes by any wrongful act or omission while acting within the ordinary course of the partnership business or with the authority of his copartners. If the partnership is liable, each partner has ***unlimited personal liability*** for the partnership obligation. The liability of partners for a tort or breach of trust committed by any partner or by an employee of the firm in the course of partnership business is **joint and several**, which means that all of the partners may be sued jointly in one action or that separate actions (leading to separate judgments) may be maintained against each of them. Judgments obtained are enforceable, however, only against property of the defendant or defendants named in the suit; and payment of any one of the judgments satisfies all of them.

This liability is comparable to the vicarious liability that the doctrine of ***respondeat superior*** imposes on a principal for the torts of an employee. The partner committing the tort is directly liable to the third party and must also ***indemnify*** the partnership for any damages it pays to the third party (see Figure 32–2). Tort liability of the partnership may include not only the negligence of the partners but also trespass, fraud, defamation, and breach of fiduciary duty, so long as the tort is committed in the course of partnership business. Moreover, though the fact that a tort is intentional does not necessarily remove it from the course of business, such intent is a factor to be considered.

> **Joint and several liability** the partners are jointly and severally liable for a tort or breach of trust committed by any partner or by an employee of the firm in the course of partnership business; under such liability, the creditors may sue the partners jointly as a group or separately as individuals
>
> ***Respondeat superior*** the partnership is liable for loss or injury caused by any wrongful act or omission of any partner while acting within the ordinary course of the business or with the authority of his copartners

---

HUSTED v. McCLOUD Supreme Court of Indiana, 1983, 450 N.E.2d 491

FACTS Herman McCloud retained the firm of Husted and Husted, a partnership consisting of Selwyn and Edgar Husted, to act as attorneys for his mother's estate. After the estate was closed, an additional estate tax liability of $18,006.73 was assessed by the IRS. Edgar falsely represented to McCloud that the precise amount of this liability was unknown and then induced McCloud to issue a check for $18,800 to a fictitious Husted and Husted trust account. Edgar indicated that he would pay the tax liability out of this sum and keep the remainder as his fee. Instead, he converted all of McCloud's funds to his own use, convincing local bank officials to issue a check from another estate for the McCloud estate tax liability. When Edgar's illegal conduct was subsequently discovered, the IRS canceled the satisfaction of the McCloud estate tax liability and reassessed the additional tax due with additional interest, which McCloud then paid. Edgar Husted was sentenced to prison, and McCloud brought an action against the partnership of Husted and Husted, seeking compensatory and punitive damages. The trial court awarded compensatory and punitive damages against Edgar Husted and the partnership. The Court of Appeals affirmed the decision.

DECISION Punitive damages awarded against Edgar Husted and the partnership set aside.

OPINION The Uniform Partnership Act of Indiana imposes liability upon a partnership for the wrongful act of any partner acting in the ordinary course of the partnership's business. A partnership is also liable where one partner, acting with apparent authority, misapplies the property of a third party or where any partner misapplies such property after it is received by the partnership in the course of its business. The partnership in this case claims that Edgar's acts were not within the ordinary course of business and that the partnership never had possession of the McCloud funds. Edgar, in requesting the money from McCloud, was, however, acting well within the ordinary course of a law partnership's business and was acting with apparent authority. Furthermore, the partnership was in possession of the McCloud funds, since Edgar converted the money to his own use only after receiving it in the ordinary course of the partnership's business. The partnership, however, is liable only for compensatory damages, since Edgar's tort itself was well removed from the ordinary course of the partnership's business. Moreover, punitive damages are intended to punish the wrongdoer, and Selwyn Husted, Edgar's partner, was innocent of any misconduct in the matter.

INTERPRETATION A partnership is liable in *compensatory* damages for the injury or loss caused by the wrongful act of any partner in the course of the partnership business

FIGURE 32–2 Tort Liability

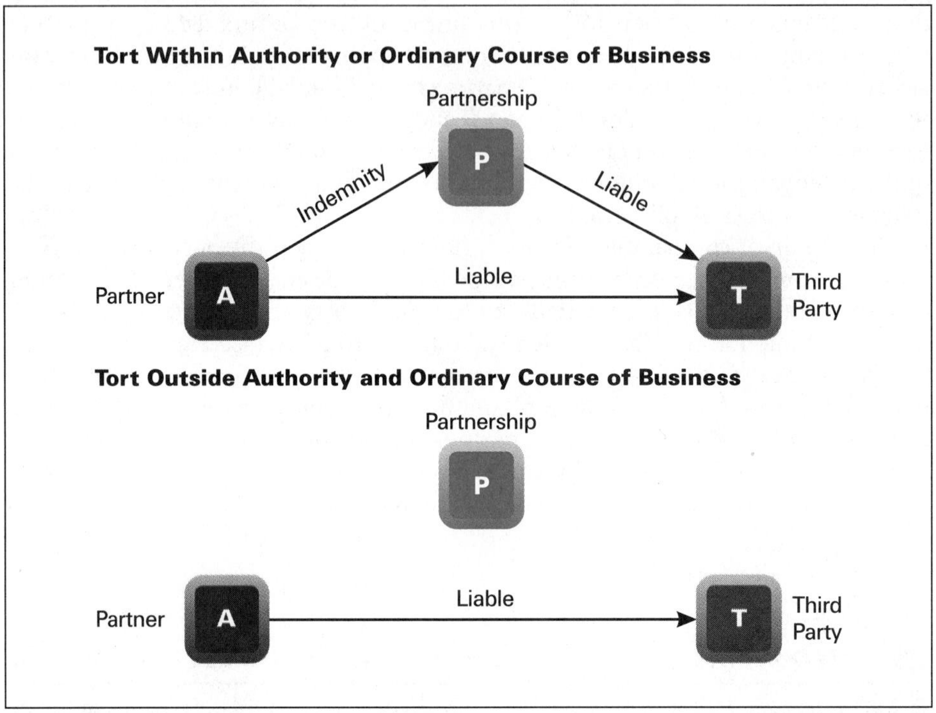

Tort Within Authority or Ordinary Course of Business

Tort Outside Authority and Ordinary Course of Business

ADMISSIONS OF AND NOTICE TO A PARTNER

Admission an admission by one partner within the scope of his authority may be used as evidence against the partnership

An **admission** or representation by any partner regarding partnership affairs within the scope of his authority may be used as evidence against the partnership. One person's admission that a partnership exists does not prove its existence. But once competent evidence establishes such an existence, one partner's admission may be used against the entire partnership, provided the partner is acting within the scope of the partnership business.

Notice a partnership is bound by notice to and knowledge of a partner

A partnership is bound (1) by **notice** to any partner of any matter relating to partnership affairs; (2) by the knowledge of a partner acting in a particular matter, if he acquired such knowledge while he was a partner; and (3) by the knowledge of any other partner who reasonably could and should have communicated it to the acting partner.

Demand a demand on one partner is a demand on the partnership

A **demand** on one partner as a representative of the firm is a demand on the partnership.

LIABILITY OF INCOMING PARTNER

Antecedent debts the liability of an incoming partner for antecedent debts of the partnership is limited to his capital contribution

A person admitted as a partner into an existing partnership is as liable for the **antecedent debts** (partnership obligations that arose before his admission) as he would have been, had he been a partner when such obligations were incurred, although this liability may be satisfied *only* out of partnership property. This means that an incoming partner's liability for the preexisting debts and obligations of a firm is limited to his capital contribution. This restriction does not apply, of course, to **subsequent debts** (obligations arising after his admission into the partnership), for which obligations his liability is *unlimited*. For example,

Subsequent debts the liability of an incoming partner for subsequent debts of the partnership is unlimited

Nash is admitted to Higgins, Cooke and White Co., a partnership. Nash's capital contribution is $7,500, which she paid in cash upon her admission to the partnership. A year later, when liabilities of the firm exceed its assets by $40,000, the partnership is dissolved. Porter had lent the firm $15,000 eight months before Nash was admitted; Skinner lent the firm $20,000 two months after Nash was admitted. Nash has no liability to Porter *except* to the extent of her capital contribution, but she is *personally* liable to Skinner.

CHAPTER SUMMARY

Relationship Among Partners

Duties Among Partners	**Fiduciary Duty** duty of utmost loyalty, fairness, and good faith owed by partners to each other and to the partnership **Duty of Obedience** duty to act in accordance with the partnership agreement and any business decisions properly made by the partners **Duty of Care** duty owed by partners to manage the partnership affairs without culpable negligence, which is greater than ordinary negligence but less than gross negligence
Rights Among Partners	**Tenancy in Partnership** **Interest in Partnership** **Distributions** transfer of partnership property from the partnership to a partner ■ *Profits* each partner is entitled to an equal share of the profits unless otherwise agreed ■ *Capital* after all partnership creditors have been paid, each partner is entitled to be repaid his capital contribution when the firm is terminated ■ *Advances* if a partner makes an advance (loan) to the firm, he is entitled to repayment of the advance plus interest; but his repayment is subordinate to that of nonpartner creditors ■ *Compensation* unless otherwise agreed, no partner is entitled to payment for acting in the partnership business **Management** each partner has an equal voice in management unless otherwise agreed **Choice of Associates** under the doctrine of *delectus personae*, no person can become a member of a partnership without the consent of all of the partners **Enforcement Rights** ■ *Information* each partner may demand full information about all partnership matters, and each partner has a duty to supply other partners with full and accurate information ■ *Formal Account* complete review of all financial transactions of a partnership ■ *Accounting* equitable proceeding for a complete settlement of all partnership affairs

Relationship Between Partners and Third Parties

Contracts	**Authority to Bind Partnership** a partner who has actual authority (express or implied) or apparent authority may bind the partnership

- *Actual Express Authority* authority set forth in the partnership agreement, in additional agreements among the partners, or in decisions made by a majority of the partners regarding the ordinary business of the partnership
- *Actual Implied Authority* authority that is reasonably deduced from the nature of the partnership, the terms of the partnership agreement, or the relations of the partners
- *Apparent Authority* authority that a third person may reasonably assume to exist in light of the conduct of the partners, so long as that third person has no knowledge or notice of the lack of actual authority

Partners' Liability
- *Personal Liability* if the partnership is contractually bound, each partner has joint, unlimited personal liability
- *Joint Liability* a creditor must sue all of the partners as a group

Partnership by Estoppel imposes partnership duties and liabilities on a nonpartner who has either represented himself or consented to be represented as a partner

Torts	*Respondeat Superior* the partnership is liable for loss or injury caused by any wrongful act or omission of any partner while acting within the ordinary course of the business or with the authority of his copartners

Joint and Several Liability the partners are jointly and severally liable for a tort or breach of trust committed by any partner or by an employee of the firm in the course of partnership business; under such liability, the creditors may sue the partners jointly as a group or separately as individuals

Other Powers	**Admissions** an admission by one partner within the scope of his authority may be used as evidence against the partnership

Notice a partnership is bound by notice to and knowledge of a partner

Demand a demand on one partner is a demand on the partnership

Liability of Incoming Partner	**Antecedent Debts** the liability of an incoming partner for antecedent debts of the partnership is limited to his capital contribution

Subsequent Debts the liability of an incoming partner for subsequent debts of the partnership is unlimited

QUESTIONS

1. Discuss the three principal duties owed by a partner to her copartners.
2. Identify and discuss the principal rights of partners (four are discussed in this chapter and two in the previous chapter).
3. Discuss the contract liability of a partnership and the partners.
4. Discuss the tort liability of a partnership and the partners.
5. Distinguish between the liability of an incoming partner for debts arising before his admission and those arising after his admission.

PROBLEMS

1. Albert, Betty, and Carol own and operate the Roy Lumber Company. Each contributed one-third of the capital, and they share equally in the profits and losses. Their partnership agreement states that all purchases over $500 must be authorized in advance by two partners and that only Albert is authorized to draw checks. Unknown to Albert or Carol, Betty purchases on the firm's account a $2,500 diamond bracelet and a $5,000 forklift and orders $2,000 worth of logs, all from Doug, who operates a jewelry store and is engaged in various activities connected with the lumber business. Before Betty made these purchases, Albert told Doug that Betty is not the log buyer. Albert refuses to pay Doug for Betty's purchases. Doug calls at the mill to collect, and Albert again refuses to pay him. Doug calls Albert an unprintable name, and Albert then punches Doug in the nose, knocking him cold. While Doug is lying unconscious on the ground, an employee of Roy Lumber Company negligently drops a log on Doug's leg, breaking three bones. The firm and the three partners are completely solvent. What are the rights of Doug?

2. Paula, Fred, and Stephanie agree that Paula and Fred will form and conduct a partnership business and that Stephanie will become a partner in two years. Stephanie agrees to lend the firm $5,000 and take 10 percent of the profits in lieu of interest. Without Stephanie's knowledge, Paula and Fred tell Harold that Stephanie is a partner, and Harold, relying on Stephanie's sound financial status, gives the firm credit. Later, the firm becomes insolvent, and Harold seeks to hold Stephanie liable as a partner. Should Harold succeed?

3. Anita and Duncan had been partners for many years in a mercantile business. Their relationship deteriorated to the point where Anita threatened to bring an action for an accounting and dissolution of the firm. Duncan then offered to buy Anita's interest in the partnership for $25,000. Anita refused the offer and told Duncan that she would take no less than $36,000.

A short time later, James approached Duncan and informed him he had inside information that a proposed street change would greatly benefit the business and that he, James, would buy the entire business for $100,000 or buy a one-half interest for $50,000. Duncan made a final offer of $35,000 to Anita for her interest. Anita accepted this offer, and the transaction was completed. Duncan then sold the one-half interest to James for $50,000. Several months later, Anita learned for the first time of the transaction between Duncan and James. What rights, if any, does Anita have against Duncan?

4. Anthony and Karen were partners doing business as the Petite Garment Company. Leroy owned a dye plant that did much of the processing for the company. Anthony and Karen decided to offer Leroy an interest in their company, in consideration for which Leroy would contribute his dye plant to the partnership. Leroy accepted the offer and was duly admitted as a partner. At the time he was admitted as a partner, Leroy did not know that the partnership was on the verge of insolvency. About three months after Leroy was admitted to the partnership, a textile firm obtained a judgment against the partnership in the amount of $50,000. This debt represented an unpaid balance that had existed before Leroy was admitted as a partner. The textile firm brought an action to subject the partnership property, including the dye plant, to the satisfaction of its judgment. The complaint also requested that, in the event the judgment was unsatisfied by sale of the partnership property, Leroy's home be sold and the proceeds applied to the balance of the judgment. Anthony and Karen own nothing but their interest in the partnership property. What should be the result with regard to (a) the dye plant and (b) Leroy's home?

5. Jones and Ray formed a partnership on January 1, known as JR Construction Co., to engage in the construction business, each partner owning a one-half interest. On February 10, while conducting partnership

business, Jones negligently injured Ware, who brought an action against Jones, Ray, and JR Construction Co. and obtained judgment for $25,000 against them on March 1. On April 15, Muir joined the partnership by contributing $10,000 cash, and by agreement each partner was entitled to a one-third interest. In July, the partners agreed to purchase new construction equipment for the partnership, and Muir was authorized to obtain a loan from XYZ Bank in the partnership name for $20,000 to finance the purchase. On July 10, Muir signed a $20,000 note on behalf of the partnership, and the equipment was purchased. In November, the partnership was in financial difficulty, its total assets amounting to $5,000. The note was in default, with a balance of $15,000 owing to XYZ Bank. Muir has substantial resources, while Jones and Ray each individually have assets of $2,000. What is the extent of Muir's personal liability and the personal liability of Jones and Ray as to (a) the judgment obtained by Ware and (b) the debt owing to XYZ Bank?

6. Apex Company is a general partnership organized under the UPA. It consists of Dianne, Greg, Knox, and Laura, whose capital contributions were as follows: Dianne = $5,000, Greg = $7,500, Knox = $10,000, and Laura = $5,000. The partnership agreement provided that the partnership would continue for a three-year period and that no withdrawals of capital were to be made without the consent of all the partners. The agreement also provided that all advances would be entitled to interest at 10 percent per year. Six months after the partnership was formed, Dianne made an advance to the partnership of $10,000. At the end of the first year, net profits were realized in the amount of $11,000 before any moneys had been distributed to the partners. How should the $11,000 be allocated to Dianne, Greg, Knox, and Laura? Explain.

7. Adams, a consulting engineer, entered into a partnership with three others for the practice of their profession. The only written partnership agreement is a brief document specifying that Adams is entitled to 55 percent of the profits and the others to 15 percent each. The venture is a total failure. Creditors are pressing for payment, and some have filed suit. The partners are in fundamental disagreement as to their future course of action. How many of the partners must agree to achieve each of the following objectives?
   (a) To add Jones, also an engineer, as a partner, where Jones would be willing to contribute a substantial amount of new capital.
   (b) To sell a vacant lot held in the partnership name, which had been acquired as the site of a future office for the partnership.
   (c) To move the offices of the partnership to less expensive quarters.
   (d) To demand a formal accounting.
   (e) To dissolve the partnership.

   (f) To agree to submit certain disputed claims to arbitration, which Adams believes will prove less expensive than litigation.
   (g) To sell all of the partnership's personal property, where Adams has what he believes to be a good offer for the property from a newly formed engineering firm.
   (h) To alter the respective interests of the parties in the profits and losses by decreasing Adams's share to 40 percent and increasing the others' shares accordingly.
   (i) To assign all the assets to a bank in trust for the benefit of creditors, hoping to work out satisfactory arrangements without formal bankruptcy.

8. Charles and Jack orally agreed to become partners in a small tool and die business. Charles, who had experience in tool and die work, was to operate the business. Jack was to take no active part but was to contribute the entire $50,000 capitalization. Charles worked ten hours a day at the plant, for which he was paid nothing. However, despite Charles's best efforts, the business failed. The $50,000 capital was depleted, and the partnership owed $50,000 in debts. Before the business failed, Jack became personally insolvent; consequently, the creditors of the partnership collected the entire $50,000 indebtedness from Charles, who was forced to sell his home and farm to satisfy the debt. Jack later regained his financial responsibility, and Charles brought an appropriate action against Jack for (a) one-half of the $50,000 he had paid to partnership creditors and (b) one-half of $18,000, the reasonable value of Charles's services during the operation of the partnership. Decision?

9. Glenn refuses an invitation to become a partner of Dorothy and Cynthia in the retail grocery business. Nevertheless, Dorothy inserts an advertisement in the local newspaper representing Glenn as their partner. Glenn takes no steps to deny the existence of a partnership between them. Ron, who extended credit to the firm, seeks to hold Glenn liable as a partner. Decision?

10. Hanover leased a portion of his farm to Brown and Black, doing business as the Colorite Hatchery. Brown went on the premises to remove certain chicken sheds that he and Black had placed there for hatchery purposes. Hanover thought Brown intended to remove certain other sheds that were Hanover's property, and an altercation occurred between them. Brown willfully struck Hanover and knocked him down. Then Brown ran to the Colorite truck, which he had previously loaded with chicken coops, and drove back to the hatchery. On the way, he picked up George, who was hitchhiking to the city to look for a job. Brown was in a hurry and was driving at seventy miles per hour down the highway. At an open intersection with another highway, Brown ran a stop sign and struck

another vehicle. The collision caused severe injuries to George. Brown and Black's partnership was dissolved directly after these incidents, and Brown was insolvent. Hanover and George each bring separate actions against Black as copartner for the alleged tort committed by Brown against each. What would be the judgments as to each?

11. Phillips and Harris are partners in a used car business. Under their oral partnership, each has an equal voice in the conduct and management of the business. Because of the irregular business hours the two keep, it was further agreed that they could use any partnership vehicle as desired. This includes use for transportation to and from work, even though the vehicles are for sale at all times. While driving a partnership vehicle home from the used car lot, Harris hit a car driven by Cook, who brought this action against Harris and Phillips individually and as copartners for his injuries. Decision?

12. Stroud and Freeman are general partners in Stroud's Food Center, a grocery store. Nothing in the articles of partnership restricts the power or authority of either partner to act in respect to the ordinary and legitimate business of the Food Center. In October, however, Stroud informed National Biscuit that he would not be personally responsible for any more bread sold to the partnership. Then, in February of the following year, at the request of Freeman, National Biscuit sold and delivered more bread to the Food Center. When payment was refused, National Biscuit brought this action against Stroud and the partnership to recover the value of the bread delivered to the Food Center. Decision?

13. Hodge and Voeller, the managing partner of the Pay-Out Drive-In Theatre, signed a contract for the sale of a small parcel of land belonging to the partnership. Except for the last twenty feet, which was necessary for the theatre's driveway, the parcel was not used in theatre operations. The agreement stated that it was between Hodge and the partnership, with Voeller signing for the partnership. Voeller claims that he told Hodge before signing that a plat plan would have to be approved by the other partners before the sale. Hodge denies this and sues for specific performance, claiming that Voeller had actual and apparent authority to bind the partnership. The partners argue that Voeller had no such authority and that Hodge knew this. Decision?

14. L.G. and S.L. Patel, husband and wife, owned and operated the City Center Motel in Dureka. On April 16, 1986, Rajeshkumar, the son of L.G. and S.L. formed a partnership with his parents and became owner of 35 percent of the City Center Motel. The partnership agreement required that Rajeshkumar approve any sale of the motel. Record title to the motel was not changed, however, to reflect his interest. On April 21, L.G. and S.L. listed their motel for sale with a real estate broker. On May 2, P.V. and Kirit Patel made an offer on the motel, which L.G. and S.L. accepted. Neither the broker nor the purchasers know of the son's interest in the motel. When L.G. and S.L. notified Rajeshkumar of their plans, to their surprise, he refused to sell his 35 percent of the motel. On May 4, L.G. and S.L. notified P.V. and Kirit that they wished to withdrawal their acceptance. They offered to pay $10,000 in damages and to give the purchasers a right of first refusal for five years.

Rather than accept the offer, on May 29, P.V. and Kirit filed an action for specific performance and incidental damages. L.G., S.L., and Rajeshkumar responded that the contract could not be lawfully enforced. After trial, the court found that but for Rajeshkumar's undisclosed partnership interest, P.V. and Kirit would be entitled to specific performance of the contract. Nevertheless, the trial court found that the sale, which would make it impossible to continue the partnership business, was barred unless all partners agreed to it. Accordingly, the court held the contract unenforceable and denied specific performance. It also denied damages for the alleged "run-down" condition of the motel and for loss of profits. However, because L.G. and S.L. had lured P.V. and Kirit into spending money to perfect the sale, the court ruled that P.V. and Kirit were entitled to compensation for those expenses—down payments, commission, escrow fees, title insurance fees, loan fees, and any other costs—thus restoring them to the position they had occupied before the unenforceable contract was executed. Decision?

CHAPTER 33

Dissolution of General Partnerships

Three stages lead to the extinguishment of a partnership: (1) dissolution, (2) winding up or liquidation, and (3) termination. Dissolution occurs when the partners cease to carry on the business together. Upon dissolution, the partnership is not terminated but continues until the winding up of its affairs is complete. During winding up, unfinished business is completed, receivables are collected, payments are made to creditors, and the remaining assets are distributed to the partners. Termination occurs when the process is finished.

DISSOLUTION

Dissolution *(dis·so·lu'·tion)* change in the relation of partners caused by any partner's ceasing to be associated with the carrying on of the business

The Uniform Partnership Act defines **dissolution** as the change in the relation of the partners caused by any partner's ceasing to be associated in the carrying on, as distinguished from the winding up, of the business. In this section, we will discuss the causes and effects of dissolution.

Causes of Dissolution

Dissolution may be brought about by (1) an act of the partners, (2) operation of law, or (3) court order. A number of events that were considered causes of dissolution under the common law are no longer considered so under the UPA. For example, the assignment of a partner's interest, a creditor's charging order (judicial lien) on a partner's interest, and an accounting do *not* cause a dissolution.

Dissolution by act of the partners a partner always has the power to dissolve a partnership, but the partnership agreement determines whether he has the right to do so

Dissolution by Act of the Partners A partnership is a personal relationship, and a partner always has the *power* to dissolve it by his actions; but whether he has the *right* to do so is determined by the partnership agreement. A partner who has withdrawn from the partnership in violation of the partnership agreement is liable to the remaining partners for damages resulting from a *wrongful dissolution*.

A partnership is *rightfully dissolved*—that is, dissolved without violation of the partnership agreement—by the act of the partners (1) when all the partners who have not assigned their interests or permitted their interests to be charged expressly agree to dissolve the partnership; (2) when the time period provided in the agreement has ended or the purpose for which the partnership was formed has been accomplished; (3) when a partner withdraws from a **partnership at will**, that is, a partnership with no definite term or specific undertaking; or (4) when a partner is expelled in accordance with a power to expel conferred by the partnership agreement.

Partnership at will one with no definite term or specific undertaking

RODGERS v. RAB INVESTMENTS, LTD. Court of Appeals of Texas, 1991, 816 S.W.2d 543

FACTS Stephen B. Rodgers, Newell Boughton, and RAB Investments, Ltd., a general partnership, formed Viola Courts Partnership (Viola) to renovate the Viola Courts apartment complex. The partnership agreement required unanimous consent for dissolution of the partnership and transfers of partnership interests. RAB invested $150,000 and received a 50 percent interest in the partnership. Rodgers and Boughton each received 25 percent for originating the deal. Viola initially obtained a $500,000 loan. Because of cost overruns and delays, Viola borrowed an additional $150,000. RAB formed a limited partnership, Viola Investors, Ltd., and RAB transferred its interest in Viola to the Viola Investors. Rodgers and Boughton demanded that RAB contribute more capital, but RAB refused. On April 11, 1985, Rodgers and Boughton expelled RAB from Viola. Rodgers and Boughton sued RAB, alleging that RAB breached the partnership agreement by failing to contribute more capital. RAB counterclaimed, arguing that a dissolution of the partnership occurred by operation of law when Rodgers and Boughton purportedly expelled RAB. RAB requested that it be paid the value of its interest in the partnership.

The trial court determined that the expulsion of RAB caused a dissolution of the partnership as a matter of law, and the jury awarded RAB $613,400 as the value of its interest in the partnership as of April 11, 1985. Rodgers and Boughton were denied relief. Although the jury found that RAB had breached the partnership agreement by transferring its partnership interest in Viola to Viola Investors, Rodgers and Boughton did not ask the jury for damages resulting from this breach, and no damages were given them. Rodgers and Boughton appealed, arguing that the expulsion of RAB did not dissolve the partnership.

DECISION Judgment of the trial court that Rodgers and Boughton caused a dissolution is affirmed.

OPINION Every partner has the inherent power to dissolve a partnership, even if the dissolution violates the partnership agreement. A partner always has the power, although perhaps not the legal right, to dissolve the partnership. No partner has to continue in a partnership against his will. An ouster of a partner is a sufficient expression of will to dissolve the partnership, though the partnership continues to exist, at least for the purposes of winding up. Only on termination of the partnership does the relationship end. The outgoing partner may claim the value of his interest at dissolution and either interest on that value from the date of dissolution or profits attributable to the use of his right in the partnership property from the date of dissolution. The outgoing partner's right to profits ends when he receives the value of his interest.

The partnership agreement in this case prohibits dissolution except by a unanimous vote of the partners. The agreement also provides that a partner may be expelled by the unanimous vote of the other partners for conduct that tends to affect prejudicially the carrying on of partnership affairs. The letter notifying RAB of its expulsion stated that RAB's refusal to make contributions was conduct that prejudicially affected the carrying on of partnership affairs. This letter clearly expressed the will of Rodgers and Boughton to dissolve the partnership. Therefore, the trial court was correct in determining that Rodgers and Boughton caused a dissolution as a matter of law when they expelled RAB and that RAB should be awarded the value of its interest in Viola as of the date of RAB's expulsion.

INTERPRETATION Every partner has the power—although not always the right—to dissolve a partnership, and the expulsion of a partner causes the dissolution of a partnership.

Dissolution by Operation of Law A partnership is dissolved by operation of law upon (1) the death of a partner, (2) the bankruptcy of a partner or of the partnership, or (3) the subsequent illegality of the partnership, which includes any event that makes it unlawful for the partnership business to be carried on or for the members to carry on the business in partnership form. For example, a partnership of lawyers would be dissolved if one of its members were disbarred from the practice of law.

Dissolution by Court Order After application by or for a partner, a court will order a dissolution if it finds that (1) a partner has been adjudicated mentally incompetent or suffers some other incapacity that prevents him from functioning as a partner; (2) a partner is guilty of conduct prejudicial to the business, has willfully or persistently breached the partnership agreement, or

Dissolution by operation of law a partnership is dissolved by operation of law upon (1) the death of a partner, (2) the bankruptcy of a partner or of the partnership, or (3) the subsequent illegality of the partnership

Dissolution by court order a court will order dissolution of a partnership under certain conditions

has conducted himself so that it is impracticable to carry on business; (3) the business can be carried on only at a loss; or (4) other circumstances render a dissolution equitable.

An assignee of a partner's interest or a partner's personal creditor who has obtained a charging order against the partner's interest is entitled to a dissolution by court decree. If the partnership is not at will, however, the partnership will not be dissolved until after the specified term or particular undertaking is complete.

Effects of Dissolution

Effects of dissolution
upon dissolution a partnership is not terminated but continues until the winding up is completed

On dissolution, the partnership is *not* terminated but continues until the winding up of its affairs is complete. Moreover, dissolution does *not* discharge the **existing liability** of any partner, though it *does* restrict the authority of partners to act for the partnership.

Existing liability
dissolution does not in itself discharge the existing liability of any partner

On dissolution, the actual **authority** of a partner to act for the partnership terminates, except so far as may be necessary to wind up partnership affairs. Actual authority to wind up includes the authority to complete existing contracts, to collect debts owed the partnership, to sell partnership assets, and to pay partnership obligations.

Authority a partner's actual authority to act for the partnership terminates, except so far as may be necessary to wind up partnership affairs; apparent authority continues unless notice of the dissolution is given to a third party

Although actual authority terminates on dissolution, *apparent authority* still binds the partnership for acts within the scope of the partnership business unless the third party is given notice of the dissolution. A third party who had extended credit to the partnership before dissolution may hold the partnership liable for any transaction that would have bound the partnership had dissolution not occurred, unless the third party has knowledge or actual notice of the dissolution. **Actual notice** requires a verbal statement to the third party or actual delivery of a written statement. On the other hand, a third party who knew of or had dealt with the partnership, but who had not extended credit to it before its dissolution, cannot hold the partnership liable if he has knowledge, actual notice, or constructive notice of dissolution. **Constructive notice** consists of advertising a dissolution notice in a newspaper of general circulation in the places at which the partnership business was regularly conducted. *No* notice need be given to third parties who had no knowledge of the partnership before its dissolution.

Actual notice knowledge actually and expressly communicated

Constructive notice
knowledge imputed by law

WINDING UP

Winding up completing unfinished business, collecting debts, and distributing assets to creditors and partners; also called liquidation

Whenever a dissolved partnership is not to be continued, the partnership must be liquidated. The process of *liquidation,* called **winding up**, involves completing unfinished business, collecting debts, taking inventory, reducing assets to cash, auditing the partnership books, paying creditors, and distributing the remaining assets to the partners. During this period, the fiduciary duties of the partners continue in effect.

▌ **HOOPER v. YODER** Supreme Court of Colorado, 1987, 737 P.2d 852

FACTS Hooper and Yoder entered into an oral partnership agreement in the fall of 1976 to manufacture and market frozen yogurt bars. In the spring of 1977, just as the yogurt bars were being produced and made ready for market, the partners decided to incorporate their business as Beautiful Daydreams, Inc. Yoder and Hooper were the only members of the board of directors and held all the corporate offices. However, the two decided to defer issuing stock in the corporation in exchange for the partnership assets. Subsequently, Market West

continued

Brokers agreed to loan money to Beautiful Daydreams, Inc., provided that Market West employee Brian Bradley was made a member of the board of directors. Bradley and Hooper later called a meeting of the board of directors of Beautiful Daydreams without informing Yoder, at which time a resolution was passed to issue ninety-five shares of stock to Hooper and five to Market West in partial cancellation of indebtedness. No stock was to be issued to Yoder, and he was later removed as a director of Beautiful Daydreams and fired as an employee of the company.

After discovering all the actions taken without his knowledge or consent, including the fact that Hooper had drawn over $141,500 in salary despite an agreement not to draw salaries until the company was more financially stable, Yoder filed suit against Hooper. The trial court held, and the court of appeals affirmed, that (1) a partnership was formed between Hooper and Yoder, (2) the parties agreed to continue their partnership in corporate form, (3) any stock issued would go in equal amounts to Hooper and Yoder, and (4) Hooper breached the agreement and his fiduciary duty to Yoder. Hooper was found to hold one-half of the $141,500 salary and one-half the ninety-five shares in constructive trust for Yoder. Hooper appealed.

DECISION Judgment for Yoder affirmed.

OPINION As a general rule, when partners organize a corporation to operate the business of the partnership and transfer the assets to the corporation, the partnership is dissolved. Such actions usually reflect the express will of the parties that the partnership be dissolved. Here, based on the record, the partnership between Hooper and Yoder was dissolved upon incorporation of Beautiful Daydreams, Inc.

The dissolution of a partnership, however, does not automatically terminate the existence of the partnership. Rather, the partnership continues until the winding up of partnership affairs is completed. The winding up of a partnership includes the transfer of the partnership assets to the corporation in exchange for corporate stock. Since no stock was issued upon the incorporation of Beautiful Daydreams, Inc., the partnership continued to exist.

The fiduciary duty that one partner owes to another also continues to exist throughout the winding up of partnership business. Each partner has the right to demand and expect a full, fair, open, and honest disclosure of everything affecting the partnership. Hooper's actions in issuing shares to himself and drawing a salary without Yoder's approval or knowledge, in direct violation of the partnership agreement to share equally, is the antithesis of the fair dealing required between partners.

INTERPRETATION Fiduciary duties remain in effect during the winding up of a dissolved partnership.

The Right to Wind Up

On dissolution, any partner, except one who has wrongfully dissolved the partnership or who has been rightfully expelled according to the terms of the partnership agreement, has the right to insist on the winding up of the partnership, unless the partnership agreement provides otherwise. Unless otherwise agreed, all nonbankrupt partners who have not wrongfully dissolved the partnership have the right to wind up the partnership affairs. A court, on the petition of a partner, his legal representative, or his assignee, may appoint a receiver for all of the partnership's property and assets. The receiver has authority to wind up the business under the court's direction. The appointment of a receiver is discretionary, based upon a showing of cause.

Right to wind up on dissolution, any partner has the right to insist on the winding up of the partnership unless the partnership agreement provides otherwise; however, a partner who has wrongfully dissolved the partnership or who has been properly expelled cannot force the liquidation of the partnership

Distribution of Assets

After all the partnership assets have been collected and reduced to cash, they are distributed to the creditors and partners. The UPA sets forth the rules for settling accounts between the parties after dissolution. It states that the liabilities of a partnership are to be paid out of partnership assets in the following order:

1. Amounts owing to nonpartner creditors
2. Amounts owing to partners other than for capital and profits

Distribution of assets the liabilities of a partnership are to be paid out of partnership assets in the following order: (1) amounts owing to nonpartner creditors, (2) amounts owing to partners other than for capital and profits, (3) amounts owing to partners for capital contributions, and (4) amounts owing to partners for profits

3. Amounts owing to partners for capital contributions
4. Amounts owing to partners for profits

The partners may, by agreement among themselves, change the internal priorities of distribution (numbers 2, 3, and 4) but not the preferred position of third parties (number 1). The UPA defines partnership assets to include all partnership property as well as the contributions necessary for the payment of all partnership liabilities, which consist of numbers 1, 2, and 3. In addition, the UPA provides that, in the absence of any contrary agreement, each partner shall share equally in the profits and surplus remaining after all liabilities (numbers 1, 2, and 3) are satisfied and must contribute, according to his share in the profits, toward the losses, capital or otherwise, that the partnership sustained. Thus, the proportion in which the partners bear losses, capital or otherwise, depends not on their relative capital contributions but on their agreement. If no specific agreement exists, the partners bear losses in the same proportion in which they share profits.

If the partnership is insolvent, the partners individually must contribute their respective share of the losses in order to pay the creditors. Furthermore, if one or more of the partners is insolvent or bankrupt or is out of the jurisdiction and refuses to contribute, the other partners must contribute the additional amount necessary to pay the firm's liabilities in the relative proportions in which they share profits. Any partner who has paid an amount in excess of his proper share of the losses has a right of contribution against the partners who have not paid their share.

The following examples illustrate these rules.

Solvent Partnership Assume that A, B, and C formed ABC Company, a partnership, with A contributing $6,000 capital, B contributing $4,000 capital, and C contributing services but no capital. A also loaned the partnership $3,000, which has not been repaid. There is no agreement as to the proportions in which profits and losses are to be shared. After a few years of operation, the partnership is liquidated. At this time, the assets of ABC Company are $54,000, and its liabilities to creditors are $26,000. The partnership is thus solvent and has enjoyed a profit of $15,000, calculated by subtracting the total liabilities ($39,000) from the total assets ($54,000). The total liabilities consist of the amount owed to creditors ($26,000), the amount owed to partners other than for capital and profits ($3,000 owed to A for his loan), and the capital contributions of the partners ($10,000: $6,000 from A and $4,000 from B). Because A, B, and C have not explicitly agreed on a profit-sharing ratio, they share the profits equally, in this case receiving $5,000 ($15,000 ÷ 3) each. After the creditors have been paid in full, A will receive $14,000 ($3,000 for repayment of the loan, $6,000 for capital, and $5,000 for share of profits); B will receive $9,000 ($4,000 for capital and $5,000 for share of profits); and C will receive $5,000 (for share of profits).

Insolvent Partnership Assume the same partnership had experienced financial adversity. It still owes its creditors $26,000, but its total assets only amount to $12,000. In this case, the partnership has sustained an aggregate loss of $27,000, which is calculated by subtracting the total liabilities ($39,000, calculated as in the example above) from the total assets ($12,000). If the agreement makes no other arrangement, the losses are shared as the profits are, which in this case is equally. Accordingly, each partner's share of the loss will be $9,000 ($27,000 ÷ 3). After the creditors are paid ($26,000), A will receive nothing ($3,000 owed for the loan plus $6,000 for capital *minus* $9,000 for his share of losses); B must make an additional *contribution* of $5,000 to make good his share of the loss ($4,000 owed for capital *minus* $9,000 for his share of losses); and C must contribute $9,000 (his share of losses).

	Loans	+	Capital Contribution	–	Share of Loss	=	Share of Assets or (Additional Contributions Owed)
A	$3,000		$ 6,000		–$ 9,000		$ 0
B	0		$ 4,000		–$ 9,000		$ (5,000)
C	0		0		–$ 9,000		$ (9,000)
Total	$3,000		$10,000		–$27,000		$(14,000)

Contribution of Partner on Insolvency In the insolvent partnership example above, if A were individually insolvent, the results would not change, because A was not required to contribute any additional moneys. If A and B were solvent and C were individually insolvent, C would be unable to pay any of his share of the loss. A and B would then have to contribute equally, because that is the relative proportion in which they share profits, in order to make good the amount of C's share. C's share of the loss is $9,000; therefore, A and B would each have to contribute an additional $4,500. This would mean that, in total, A would have to contribute $4,500 and B $9,500 in order to satisfy the unpaid claims of partnership creditors. On the other hand, if A and C were individually insolvent and B were solvent, B would be required to pay the entire balance of $14,000 due to partnership creditors, representing his unpaid share of the loss plus a contribution of the full amount of C's unpaid share of the loss.

LANGNESS v. "O" STREET CARPET SHOP, INC. Supreme Court of Nebraska, 1984, 217 Neb. 569, 353 N.W.2d 709

FACTS Herbert Friedman, Strelsa Langness, and "O" Street Carpet Shop ("O" Street), through its president, Gerald Neva, formed a partnership known as NFL Associates. "O" Street contributed a $56,000 purchase agreement on property valued at $65,000, for a $9,000 net contribution. During the life of the partnership, "O" Street contributed an additional $4,005 in capital. Friedman contributed his legal services, although no value was ever assigned to this contribution. Langness contributed $14,000 in cash, $8,000 of which went to "O" Street and $6,000 of which was used to fund partnership operations. By agreement, the profits or losses were to be split as follows: 45 percent to "O" Street, 45 percent to Langness, and 10 percent to Friedman. Also, Langness was to receive payments of $116.66 per month from the partnership. Neva personally guaranteed the payments should the partnership funds prove insufficient. Langness received an amount equal to 54 payments over the life of the partnership.

Eventually the partnership was dissolved, its property sold, and, after paying the creditors, $48,824.41 in assets remained. Neva and Friedman calculated the final distribution as follows: Langness was to receive $16,792.01, "O" Street would get $26,808.58, and Friedman would receive $5,223.82. Langness disagreed with this division of assets and brought suit for an accounting. The trial court determined that Langness was owed an additional $7,290.42. Friedman appealed.

DECISION Judgment for Langness affirmed as modified.

OPINION "O" Street initially contributed property worth $9,000. However, $8,000 of Langness's cash contribution went to "O" Street, thereby reducing "O" Street's net contribution to $1,000. "O" Street made further contributions totaling $4,005. Thus, "O" Street's total capital contribution was $5,005. Friedman contributed no money or property. It is the general rule that a partner who contributes only services is not deemed to have made a capital contribution to the partnership such as to require capital repayment upon dissolution, unless the parties have agreed to the contrary. There was no such agreement here. Langness contributed $14,000 in cash to the partnership, but the $116-per-month payments to Langness were properly treated as capital withdrawals reducing her initial

continued

capital contribution to $7,699.70 as of the date of final distribution.

Of the $48,824.41 in assets to be distributed, $7,699.70 is to be paid to Langness for her capital contribution, and $5,005 goes to "O" Street as repayment of capital. The $36,119.71 remaining is to be divided as agreed on a 45-45-10 basis. Langness and "O" Street will each receive $16,253.87 of the profits and Friedman will receive $3,611.97. Therefore, Langness is owed a total of $23,953.57 (capital repayment of $7,699.70 plus share of profits of $16,253.87). Since Langness has only received $16,792.01, her former partners are liable to her for $7,161.56.

INTERPRETATION   The assets of a dissolved partnership are distributed in the following order: (1) debts owed to nonpartners, (2) debts owed to partners, (3) capital contributions owed to partners, and (4) profits owed to partners.

Marshaling of Assets

The doctrine of marshaling of assets applies *only* when the assets of a partnership and of its members are administered by a court of equity. **Marshaling of assets** means segregating and considering separately the assets and liabilities of the partnership and the respective assets and liabilities of the individual partners. **Partnership creditors** are entitled to be satisfied first out of partnership assets and may recover any deficiency out of the individually owned assets of the partners; this latter right is subordinate, however, to the rights of **nonpartnership creditors** to those assets. Conversely, the nonpartnership creditors have first claim to the individually owned assets of their respective debtors; their claims to partnership assets are subordinate to claims of partnership creditors.

Finally, the assets of an insolvent partner are distributed in the following order: (1) debts and liabilities owing to nonpartnership creditors, (2) debts and liabilities owing to partnership creditors, and (3) contributions owing to other partners who have paid more than their respective shares of the firm's liabilities to partnership creditors.

This rule, however, is *no longer* followed if the partnership is a debtor under the Bankruptcy Code. In a proceeding under the **federal bankruptcy** law, a trustee is appointed to administer the estate of the debtor. If the partnership property is insufficient to pay all the claims against the partnership, the statute directs the trustee to first seek recovery of the deficiency from the general partners who are not bankrupt. The trustee may then seek recovery against the estates of bankrupt partners on the same basis as other creditors of the bankrupt partner. This provision, although contrary to the UPA's doctrine of marshaling of assets, governs whenever partnership assets are being administered by a bankruptcy court.

CONTINUATION AFTER DISSOLUTION

Dissolution leads to one of two outcomes: either the partnership is liquidated or the remaining partners continue the partnership. Liquidation sacrifices the value of a going concern; continuation of the partnership after dissolution avoids this loss. Nonetheless, the UPA gives each partner the right to have the partnership liquidated, except in a limited number of instances where the remaining partners have the right to continue the partnership.

Right to Continue Partnership

After dissolution, the remaining partners have the right to continue the partnership when (1) the partnership has been dissolved in violation of the partnership

---

Marshaling of assets only applies when a state court of equity administers the assets of a partnership and of its members; the process of segregating and considering separately the assets and liabilities of the partnership and the respective assets and liabilities of the individual partners

Partnership creditors are entitled to be first satisfied out of partnership assets

Nonpartnership creditors have first claim to the individually owned assets of their respective debtor-partners

Federal bankruptcy marshaling of assets is not followed if the partnership is a debtor

Right to continue partnership the remaining partners have the right to continue the partnership in the following situations: (1) wrongful dissolution, (2) expulsion, or (3) agreement of the partners

agreement, (2) a partner has been expelled in accordance with the partnership agreement, or (3) all the partners agree to continue the business. Nevertheless, the noncontinuing partner, or his legal representative, has a right to an account of his interest against the person or partnership continuing the business as of the date of dissolution, unless otherwise agreed. Moreover, when a partner dies or retires and the business is continued by the surviving partners, the retired partner or the legal representative of the deceased partner is entitled to be paid the value of his interest as of the date of the dissolution as an ordinary creditor of the partnership. In addition, he is entitled to receive interest on this amount or, at his option, in lieu of interest, the profits of the business attributable to the use of his right in the property of the dissolved partnership. His rights are subordinate, however, to those of creditors of the dissolved partnership.

Continuation After Wrongful Dissolution   A partner who wrongfully withdraws cannot force the liquidation of the firm. The aggrieved partners have the option of either liquidating the firm and recovering damages for the breach of the partnership agreement or continuing the partnership by buying out the withdrawing partner, who is entitled to realize his interest in the partnership less the amount of the damages that the other partners have sustained because of his breach. The withdrawing partner's interest is computed without considering the goodwill of the business. In addition, the remaining partners may use the capital contributions of the wrongdoing partner for the unexpired period of the partnership agreement. They must, however, indemnify the former partner against all present and future partnership liabilities.

Continuation after wrongful dissolution the aggrieved partners can continue the firm by paying the withdrawing partner the value of his interest less the amount of damages they sustained as a result of the breach

Continuation After Expulsion   A partner expelled according to the partnership agreement cannot force the liquidation of the partnership. He is entitled only (1) to be discharged from all partnership liabilities either by payment or by a novation with the creditors and (2) to receive in cash the net amount due him from the partnership.

Continuation after expulsion the expelled partner is entitled to be discharged from partnership liabilities and to receive cash in the net amount due him from the partnership

Continuation Agreement of the Partners   By far the best and most reliable way of preserving a partnership business after dissolution is through a continuation agreement. Such agreements are frequently used to ensure continuity in the event of a partner's death or retirement. A continuation agreement permits the remaining partners to keep the partnership property, to carry on its business, and to specify a settlement with the outgoing partners.

Figure 33–1 summarizes the causes and consequences of dissolution.

Continuation agreement of the partners permits the remaining partners to keep partnership property and to carry on its business; provides a specified settlement to the departing partner

Rights of Creditors

The continuation of a partnership after dissolution creates a new partnership, even though a majority of the old partnership's members may be present in the new organization. The creditors of the old partnership may pursue their claims against the new partnership and also may proceed to hold all of the members of the dissolved partnership personally liable. If a withdrawing partner has made arrangements with those who continue the business, whereby they assume and pay all debts and obligations of the firm, the partner is still liable to creditors whose claims arose prior to the dissolution. However, a withdrawing partner who is compelled to pay such debts has a right of indemnity against her former partners, who had agreed to pay the debts but failed to do so.

Rights of creditors the creditors of the old partnership have claims against the continuing (new) partnership and may also proceed against all the members of the dissolved partnership

FIGURE 33–1 Causes and Effects of Dissolution

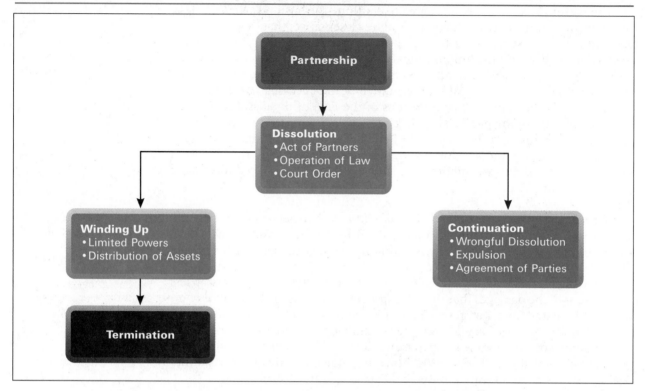

Figure 33–2 illustrates the liability of incoming and retiring partners.

A retiring partner may be discharged from his existing liabilities by entering into a ***novation*** with the continuing partners and the creditors. A creditor must agree to a novation, although his consent may be inferred from his course of dealing with the partnership after dissolution. Whether such dealings with a continuing partnership constitute an implied novation is a factual question of intent.

A withdrawing partner may protect herself against liability on contracts the firm enters into after her withdrawal by giving notice that she is no longer a member of the firm. Otherwise, she will be liable for debts thus incurred to creditors who had no notice or knowledge of the partner's withdrawal. Actual notice must be given to persons who had extended credit to the partnership prior to its dissolution, whereas constructive notice by newspaper publication will suffice for those who knew of the partnership but who had not extended credit to it before its dissolution.

Figure 33–2 illustrates the liability of incoming and retiring partners.

FIGURE 33–2 Liability of Incoming and Retiring Partners

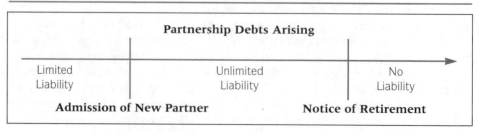

VICTORIA AIR CONDITIONING, INC. v. SOUTHWEST TEXAS MECHANICAL INSULATION CO. Court of Appeals of Texas, 1993, 850 S.W.2d 720

FACTS In August, 1988, Victoria Air Conditioning, Inc. (VAC) entered into a subcontract for insulation services with Southwest Texas Mechanical Insulation Company (SWT), a partnership comprised of Charlie Jupe and Tommy Nabors. In February, 1989, Jupe and Nabors dissolved the partnership, but VAC did not receive notice of the dissolution at that time. Sometime later, insulation was removed from Nabors's premises to Jupe's possession and Jupe continued the insulation project with VAC. From then on, Nabors had no more involvement with SWT. One month later, Nabors informed VAC's project manager, Von Behrenfeld, that Nabors was no longer associated with SWT, had formed his own insulation company, and was interested in bidding on new jobs. Subsequently, SWT failed to perform the subcontract and Jupe could not be found. VAC brought suit for breach of contract against SWT, Jupe, and Nabors. Nabors claims that several letters and change orders introduced by both parties show that VAC knew of the dissolution and impliedly agreed to discharge Nabors from liability. These documents indicated that VAC had dealt with Jupe, and had not dealt with Nabors, after the dissolution. The jury found that VAC, Jupe, and Nabors had agreed to discharge Nabors from liability on the subcontract. VAC appealed, denying that the course of dealings between VAC and Jupe was the type from which an agreement to discharge Nabors could be inferred.

DECISION Judgment affirmed.

OPINION The general rule is that the dissolution of a partnership does not of itself discharge any existing liabilities of a partner. UPA § 36(1). However, an exception to the general rule exists when the retired partner, the person continuing the partnership's business, and the partnership creditor agree that the retired partner will be discharged from liability. Furthermore, such an agreement may be inferred from the course of dealing between the creditor having knowledge of the dissolution and the person continuing the partnership's business. UPA § 36(2).

We must determine whether the evidence is factually sufficient to support the jury's finding that there was an agreement between VAC, Jupe, and Nabors to discharge Nabors from liability. First, the evidence supports the jury's finding that VAC knew of the dissolution of the SWT partnership. Behrenfeld testified that as of February 1989 he knew that Nabors was "no longer involved in the company." Also, the letters and change orders subsequent to dissolution support the contention that VAC was aware of SWT's change of address. Finally, following a meeting between Heilker, the president of VAC, and Jupe, the salutation in the letters changed from "Gentlemen" to "Dear Charlie" or "Dear Mr. Jupe." Second, the course of dealing between Jupe and VAC after the dissolution supports the jury's finding that there was an implied agreement between the parties to discharge Nabors from liability. VAC never objected to Nabors's absence from the project and never requested that Nabors remain liable. This is true even though VAC and Jupe engaged in considerable negotiations from the time of dissolution until the breach of contract. Also, the record reflects that VAC failed to contact Nabors regarding the default until suit was filed in this matter, even though Nabors was available at all times and his whereabouts were known. After the breach, all demands were addressed to Jupe. We therefore hold that sufficient evidence of a course of dealing exists in the record from which the jury could have inferred that an agreement existed between VAC, Jupe, and Nabors to discharge Nabors from liability.

INTERPRETATION Although the dissolution of a partnership does not of itself discharge any existing liability of a partner, a novation among a retiring partner, the continuing partners, and a creditor will discharge the retiring partner's obligations to that creditor. Moreover, a novation may be inferred from a creditor's course of dealing with the partnership after dissolution if the creditor has knowledge of the dissolution.

ETHICAL DILEMMA   What Duty of Disclosure Is Owed to Incoming Partners?

FACTS James Edwards was just appointed managing partner of the northeastern division of Banks & Borre, a prestigious national CPA firm operating as a partnership. The position is an excellent one, and James is the youngest partner ever to have served as a regional managing partner. However, although Banks & Borre is a well-established firm, it recently has been subject to several sizable lawsuits that allege the firm's misconduct in services it provided to several banks and certain tax shelters.

Robert Smith, the national manager, has given James clear guidelines on management strategy for the northeastern division. Smith has emphasized the importance of expanding the client base in light of the pending lawsuits. A principal strategy is to expand through acquisition of smaller firms. Because of his position as manager of the northeastern division, James receives both a salary and a percentage of new client revenues.

Jones, Jones, & Frank is a medium-sized CPA firm which provides auditing, tax, and management advisory services to a variety of clients. Brothers Ken Jones and Richard Jones began the practice twenty-five years ago. Donald Frank began as an employee but was brought into the partnership in its fifth year.

Jones, Jones, & Frank has been considering the possibility of merging its practice with that of a larger firm. Ken and Richard are in their late fifties and no longer want managerial responsibilities. Nevertheless, they wish to remain active in the practice.

James Edwards initiated discussions with Jones, Jones, & Frank regarding the possibility of a merger. James indicated that he could arrange attractive compensation packages for the partners of the smaller firm. Ken, Richard, and Donald have inquired about the lawsuits pending against Borre. Not having been involved in the services that gave rise to the lawsuits, James does not know most of the details. He does know, however, that concern about the litigation could destroy all prospects for the merger. James reassures Ken, Richard, and Donald that he does not know much about the lawsuits but is under the impression that they are not significant.

Social, Policy, and Ethical Considerations

1. Should James make a point of acquainting himself with the details of the litigation? Were his preliminary statements about the lawsuits justifiable?

2. Is it ethical for Banks & Borre to recruit new partners and to institute a policy which encourages mergers, given the pending litigation?

3. If a merger takes place, could Ken, Richard, and Donald be held liable for any judgments arising from the litigation?

4. How might a CPA firm insulate its partners from personal liability?

5. What actions should Jones, Jones, & Frank take to investigate Banks & Borre before proceeding with the merger?

CHAPTER SUMMARY

Dissolution	**Definition of Dissolution** the change in the relation of partners caused by any partner's ceasing to be associated with the carrying on of the business **Causes of Dissolution** ▪ *Dissolution by Act of the Partners* a partner always has the power to dissolve a partnership, but the partnership agreement determines whether he has the right to do so ▪ *Dissolution by Operation of Law* a partnership is dissolved by operation of law upon (1) the death of a partner, (2) the bankruptcy of a partner or of the partnership, or (3) the subsequent illegality of the partnership ▪ *Dissolution by Court Order* a court will order dissolution of a partnership under certain conditions

Effects of Dissolution upon dissolution a partnership is not terminated but continues until the winding up is completed
- ■ *Authority* a partner's actual authority to act for the partnership terminates, except so far as may be necessary to wind up partnership affairs; apparent authority continues unless notice of the dissolution is given to a third party
- ■ *Existing Liability* dissolution does not in itself discharge the existing liability of any partner

Winding Up

Definition of Winding Up completing unfinished business, collecting debts, and distributing assets to creditors and partners; also called liquidation

Right to Wind Up on dissolution, any partner has the right to insist on the winding up of the partnership unless the partnership agreement provides otherwise; however, a partner who has wrongfully dissolved the partnership or who has been properly expelled cannot force the liquidation of the partnership

Distribution of Assets the liabilities of a partnership are to be paid out of partnership assets in the following order: (1) amounts owing to nonpartner creditors, (2) amounts owing to partners other than for capital and profits, (3) amounts owing to partners for capital contributions, and (4) amounts owing to partners for profits

Marshaling of Assets only applies when a state court of equity administers the assets of a partnership and of its members; the process of segregating and considering separately the assets and liabilities of the partnership and the respective assets and liabilities of the individual partners
- ■ *Partnership Creditors* are entitled to be first satisfied out of partnership assets
- ■ *Nonpartnership Creditors* have first claim to the individually owned assets of their respective debtor-partners
- ■ *Federal Bankruptcy* marshaling of assets is not followed if the partnership is a debtor

Continuation After Dissolution

Right to Continue Partnership the remaining partners have the right to continue the partnership in the following situations:
- ■ *Continuation After Wrongful Dissolution* the aggrieved partners can continue the firm by paying the withdrawing partner the value of his interest less the amount of damages they sustained as a result of the breach
- ■ *Continuation After Expulsion* the expelled partner is entitled to be discharged from partnership liabilities and to receive cash in the net amount due him from the partnership
- ■ *Continuation Agreement of the Partners* permits the remaining partners to keep partnership property and to carry on its business; provides a specified settlement to the departing partner

Rights of Creditors the creditors of the old partnership have claims against the continuing (new) partnership and may also proceed against all the members of the dissolved partnership

QUESTIONS

1. Identify the causes of dissolution of a partnership.
2. Explain the effect of dissolution upon the authority and liability of the partners.
3. Explain the order in which the assets of a partnership are distributed to creditors and partners.
4. Distinguish between the relative rights of partnership creditors and partners' creditors under the UPA and the Bankruptcy Code.
5. Identify and discuss the conditions under which partners have the right to continue the partnership after dissolution.

PROBLEMS

1. Simmons, Hoffman, and Murray were partners doing business under the firm name of Simmons & Co. The firm borrowed money from a bank and gave the bank the firm's note for the loan. In addition, each partner guaranteed the note individually. The firm became insolvent, and a receiver was appointed. The bank claims that it has a right to file its claim as a firm debt and also that it has a right to participate in the distribution of the assets of the individual partners before partnership creditors receive any payment from such assets.
    (a) Explain the principle involved in this case.
    (b) Is the bank correct?
2. Lauren, Matthew, and Susan form a partnership, Lauren contributing $10,000, Matthew $5,000, and Susan her time and skill. Nothing is said as to the division of profits. The firm becomes insolvent, and after payment of all firm debts owed to third parties, $6,000 is left. Lauren claims that she is entitled to the entire $6,000. Matthew contends that the distribution should be $4,000 to Lauren and $2,000 to Matthew. Susan claims the $6,000 should be divided equally among the partners. Who is correct? Explain.
3. Martin, Mark, and Marvin formed a retail clothing partnership named M Clothiers and conducted a business for many years, buying most of their clothing from Hill, a wholesaler. On January 15, Marvin retired from the business, but Martin and Mark decided to continue it. As part of the retirement agreement, Martin and Mark agreed in writing with Marvin that Marvin would not be responsible for any of the partnership debts, either past or future. A news item concerning Marvin's retirement appeared in the local newspaper on January 15.

    Before January 15, Hill was a creditor of M Clothiers to the extent of $10,000; and on January 30, he extended additional credit of $5,000. Hill was not advised and did not in fact know of Marvin's retirement and the change of the partnership. On January 30, Ray, a competitor of Hill, extended credit for the first time to M Clothiers in the amount of $3,000.

    On February 1, Martin and Mark departed for parts unknown and left no partnership assets with which to pay the described debts. What is Marvin's liability, if any, (a) to Hill and (b) to Ray?
4. Ben, Dan, and Lilli were partners sharing profits in proportions of one-fourth, one-third, and five-twelfths, respectively. Their business failed, and the firm was dissolved. At the time of dissolution, no financial adjustments between the partners were necessary with reference to their respective capital contributions, but the firm's liabilities to creditors exceeded its assets by $24,000. Without contributing any amount toward the payment of the liabilities, Dan moved to a destination unknown. Ben and Lilli are financially responsible. How much must each contribute?
5. Indicate which of the following statements are true and which are false:
    (a) Creditors having claims based on torts committed by partners in the course of business of the partnership are preferred over creditors with claims based on contracts.
    (b) Partners who wish to continue the business have a prior right to purchase the assets.
    (c) In the absence of a contract providing otherwise, the distribution to partners of accrued profits should be in equal parts, regardless of the fact that the partners had contributed to the firm unequally.
    (d) Advances in the nature of loans made by the various partners to the partnership share in the firm assets on the same basis as debts due other creditors.
    (e) Between the partners, the assets of the partnership must be applied to pay the claims of partners with respect to capital ahead of the claims of partners with respect to profits.
    (f) Debts owing to partners (other than for capital and profits) rank ahead of debts owing to partners with respect to capital and profits.
6. Ames, Bell, and Cole were equal partners in the ABC Construction Company. They had no formal or written partnership agreement. Cole died on June 30,

and his widow, Cora Cole, qualified as executor of his will. Ames and Bell continued the business of the partnership until December 31, when they sold all of the assets of the partnership. After paying all partnership debts, they distributed the balance equally among themselves and Mrs. Cole as executor.

Subsequently, Mrs. Cole learned that Ames and Bell had made and withdrawn a net profit of $20,000 during the period from July 1 to December 31. The profit was made through new contracts using the partnership name and assets. Ames and Bell had concealed from Mrs. Cole such contracts and profit, and she learned about them from other sources. Immediately after acquiring this information, Mrs. Cole demanded one-third of the profit of $20,000 from Ames and Bell. They rejected her demand. What are the rights and remedies, if any, of Cora Cole as executor?

7. David and Barbara were partners in Miami. Steven, a traveling salesman for Karen, called on them and on January 14 received from them an order for merchandise. Steven forwarded the order to Karen in New York on January 15; David and Barbara dissolved their partnership by agreement between them on January 18. On January 19, Karen, without knowledge of the dissolution, acknowledged receipt of the order, accepted it, and shipped the goods the next day. Barbara received them on January 23. On January 25, notice of the dissolution of David and Barbara's partnership was duly published. Karen sues David and Barbara for the purchase price of the merchandise sold. Decision?

8. The articles of partnership of the firm of Wilson and Company provide:

> William Smith to contribute $50,000; to receive interest thereon at 13 percent per annum and to devote such time as he may be able to give; to receive 30 percent of the profits.
> John Jones to contribute $50,000; to receive interest on same at 13 percent per annum; to give all of his time to the business and to receive 30 percent of the profits.
> Henry Wilson to contribute all of his time to the business and to receive 20 percent of the profits.
> James Brown to contribute all of his time to the business and to receive 20 percent of the profits.

There is no provision for sharing losses. After six years of operations, the firm has assets of $400,000 and liabilities to creditors of $420,000. Upon dissolution and winding up, what are the rights and liabilities of the respective parties?

9. Harold Fuller, Mary Warner, and Tom Clardy were copartners in a cattle-raising operation. Fuller and Clardy were both killed as the result of a common disaster. Mary Warner took charge of the partnership business and spent considerable time and effort in winding it up. In a suit brought for an accounting, Mary Warner made a claim for a reasonable allowance for services rendered in winding up the affairs of the partnership. The partnership agreement contained no payment provision for such services. What decision?

10. Adam, Stanley, and Rosalind formed a partnership in state X to distribute beer and wine. Their agreement provided that the partnership would continue until December 31, 2003. Which of the following events would cause the partnership to dissolve? If so, when would the partnership be dissolved?
    (a) Rosalind assigns her interest in the partnership to Mary on April 1, 1999.
    (b) Stanley dies on June 1, 2003.
    (c) Adam withdraws from the partnership on September 15, 2002.
    (d) A creditor of Stanley obtains a charging order against Stanley's interest on October 9, 2000.
    (e) In 2001, the legislature of state X enacts a statute making the sale or distribution of alcoholic beverages illegal.
    (f) Stanley has a formal accounting of partnership affairs on September 19, 2000.

11. Stark, Henning & Co., a partnership formed by Stark and Henning for the purpose of acting as sales representatives for various firms in upstate New York, contracted with Utica Screw Product, Inc., on June 19, 1975, to act as its sales representative for most of New York State. On October 22, 1976, Stark sent a letter to Henning terminating the partnership. A copy of this letter was also sent to the president of Utica. When Utica refused to pay commissions owed to the partnership for orders the partnership had obtained for Utica between February 10, 1976, and October 20, 1976, Stark brought this action on behalf of the partnership to recover the commissions due. Utica contended that Stark had no standing to sue because he had not received authority from his partner, Henning, to institute this action. Decision?

12. In 1946, Donald Petersen joined his father, William Petersen, in a chicken hatchery business William had previously operated as a sole proprietorship. When the partnership was formed, William contributed the assets of the proprietorship, which included cash, equipment, and inventory having a total value of $41,000. Donald contributed nothing. From 1946 until his death in 1964, Donald took over the operation of the hatchery. This suit was brought on behalf of Donald's estate when William refused to distribute any of the partnership assets to the estate. William contended that the total value of the partnership property at the time of Donald's death was $18,572.

He claimed the full amount on the theory that he was entitled to the return of his capital investment of $41,000 before Donald's estate could recover anything. Decision?

13. Davis and Shipman founded a partnership in 1954 under the name of Shipman & Davis Lumber Company. On September 20, 1955, the partnership was dissolved by written agreement. Notice of the dissolution was published in a newspaper of general circulation in Merced County, where the business was conducted. No actual notice of dissolution was given to firms that had previously extended credit to the partnership. By the dissolution agreement, Shipman, who was to continue the business, was to pay all of the partnership's debts. He continued the business as a sole proprietorship for a short time until he formed a successor corporation, Shipman Lumber Servaes Co. After the partnership's dissolution, two firms that had previously done business with the partnership extended credit to Shipman for certain repair work and merchandise. The partnership also had a balance due to Valley Typewriter Company for the prior purchase of a calculator. In 1956, two checks were drawn by Shipman Lumber Servaes Co. and accepted by Valley Typewriter as partial payment on this debt. Credit Bureaus of Merced County, as assignee of these three accounts, sued the partnership as well as Shipman and Davis individually. Davis argued that the dissolution of the partnership relieved him of personal liability for the accounts. The trial court entered judgment in favor of the Credit Bureaus for all three accounts. Decision?

CHAPTER 34

Limited Partnerships and Limited Liability Companies

In this chapter, we will consider other types of unincorporated business associations: limited partnerships, limited liability companies, joint ventures, limited liability partnerships, limited liability limited partnerships, and business trusts. These organizations have developed to meet special business and investment needs. Each has characteristics that make it appropriate for certain purposes.

LIMITED PARTNERSHIPS

The limited partnership has proved to be an attractive vehicle for a variety of investments because of its tax advantages and the limited liability it confers upon the limited partners. Unlike general partnerships, limited partnerships are statutory creations. Before 1976, the governing statute in all states except Louisiana was the Uniform Limited Partnership Act (ULPA), which was promulgated in 1916. In 1976, the National Conference of Commissioners on Uniform State Laws promulgated the Revised Uniform Limited Partnership Act (RULPA). In 1985, the National Conference revised the RULPA; the resulting 1985 Act is substantially similar to the 1976 RULPA and does not alter its underlying philosophy or thrust. All but two states have adopted either the 1976 Act or the 1985 Act. More than twice as many states have adopted the 1985 version as have adopted the 1976 version.

In this chapter, we will discuss the 1985 RULPA. The ULPA, the 1976 RULPA, and the 1985 RULPA are supplemented by the Uniform Partnership Act, which applies to limited partnerships in any case for which the Limited Partnership Act does not provide. For a concise comparison of general and limited partnerships, see Figure 35–2 in the next chapter.

In addition, limited partnership interests are almost always considered to be securities, and their sale is therefore subject to state and federal regulation, as we will discuss in Chapter 42.

Definition

A **limited partnership** is a partnership, formed by two or more persons under the laws of a state, that has one or more general partners and one or more limited partners. A *person* includes a natural person, a partnership, a limited partnership, a trust, an estate, an association, or a corporation. Such a partnership differs from a general partnership in several respects, three of which are fundamental:

Limited partnership a partnership, formed in compliance with a state statute, composed of one or more general partners and one or more limited partners

1. A statute providing for the formation of limited partnerships must be in effect.
2. The limited partnership must substantially comply with the requirements of that statute.
3. The *liability* of a *limited* partner for partnership debts or obligations is **limited** to the extent of the capital he has contributed or has agreed to contribute.

Formation

Formation a limited partnership can only be formed by substantial compliance with a state limited partnership statute

Although the **formation** of a *general* partnership requires no special procedures, the formation of a *limited* partnership requires substantial compliance with the limited partnership statute. Failure to comply may result in the limited partners *not* obtaining limited liability.

Filing of certificate two or more persons must file a signed certificate of limited partnership

Filing of Certificate The RULPA provides that two or more persons desiring to form a limited partnership shall file in the office of the secretary of state of the state in which the limited partnership has its principal office a signed certificate of limited partnership. The certificate must include the following information: (1) the name of the limited partnership; (2) the address of its office and the name and address of the agent for service of process; (3) the name and the business address of each general partner; (4) the latest date upon which the limited partnership is to dissolve; and (5) any other matters the general partners decide to include in the certificate.

The certificate of limited partnership must be amended if a new general partner is admitted, a partner withdraws, or a general partner becomes aware that any statement in the certificate was or has become false. In addition, the certificate may be amended at any time for any other purpose the general partners deem proper. As discussed later, false statements in a certificate or amendment that cause loss to third parties who rely on the statements may result in liability for the general partners.

Name inclusion of a limited partner's surname in the partnership name in most instances will result in the loss of the limited partner's limited liability

Name Including the surname of a limited partner in the partnership name is prohibited unless it is also the surname of a general partner or unless the business had been carried on under that name before the admission of that limited partner. A limited partner who knowingly permits his name to be used in violation of this provision is liable to any creditor who did not know that he was a limited partner. The RULPA also prohibits a partnership name that is the same as, or deceptively similar to, that of any corporation or other limited partnership. Finally, the name of the limited partnership must contain, unabbreviated, the words "limited partnership."

Contribution may be cash, property, services, or a promise to contribute cash, property, or services

Contributions The contribution of a partner may be cash, property, services rendered, a promissory note, or an obligation to contribute cash or property or to perform services. A promise by a limited partner to contribute to the limited partnership is not enforceable unless it is in a signed writing. Should a partner fail to make a required capital contribution described in a signed writing, the limited partnership may hold her liable to contribute the cash value of the stated contribution.

Defective formation if no certificate is filed or if the one filed does not substantially meet the statutory requirements, the formation is defective and the limited liability of the limited partners is jeopardized

Defective Formation A limited partnership is formed when a certificate of limited partnership that substantially complies with the statutory requirements is filed. Therefore, if no certificate is filed or if the certificate filed does not substantially meet the statutory requirements, the formation is defective. In either case, the limited liability of limited partners is jeopardized. The RULPA provides that a person who has contributed to the capital of a business (an "equity participant"), believing erroneously and in good faith that he has become a limited partner in a limited partnership, is not liable as a general partner, provided that on ascertaining the mistake he either (1) withdraws from the business and renounces *future* profits or (2) files a certificate or an amendment curing the defect. However, the equity participant will be liable to any third party who transacted business with the enterprise before the withdrawal or amendment and who in good faith believed that the equity participant was a general partner at the time of the transaction.

The 1985 Act does not require that the limited partners be named in the certificate. This greatly reduces the risk that an inadvertent omission of such information will expose a limited partner to liability.

IN RE WESTOVER HILLS LTD. United States Bankruptcy Court, District of Wyoming, 1985, 46 B.R. 300

FACTS Dale Fullerton was chairman of the board of Envirosearch and the sole stockholder in Westover Hills Management. James Anderson was president of AGFC. Fullerton and Anderson agreed to form a limited partnership to purchase certain property from WYORCO, a joint venture of which Fullerton was a member. The parties intended to form a limited partnership with Westover Hills Management as the sole general partner and AGFC and Envirosearch as limited partners. The certificate filed with the Wyoming secretary of state, however, listed all three companies as both general and limited partners of Westover Hills Ltd. Anderson and Fullerton later became aware of this error and filed an amended certificate of limited partnership, which correctly named Envirosearch and AGFC as limited partners only. When Westover Hills Ltd. became bankrupt, the court sought to determine whether the enterprise was a general or limited partnership for the purposes of determining eligibility for relief under the Bankruptcy Code.

DECISION Westover Hills Ltd. held to be a limited partnership for purposes of bankruptcy.

OPINION Under the Uniform Limited Partnership Act, if the parties intend to form a limited partnership, failure to comply with the requirements regarding the certificate of partnership results only in the nonformation of the limited partnership, not in the formation of a general partnership. The parties in this case clearly intended to form a limited partnership. The Revised Uniform Limited Partnership Act of 1976 provides that an intended limited partner who subsequently discovers that the limited partnership has been defectively formed may remedy the situation either by causing an appropriate certificate of amendment to be filed or by withdrawing from the enterprise and renouncing future profits. AGFC complied with the first alternative, thereby ensuring that it did not lose its limited partner status. Therefore, Westover Hills Ltd. is a limited partnership for the purposes of bankruptcy.

INTERPRETATION A limited partnership exists only after a certificate is filed in compliance with the limited partnership statute.

Foreign Limited Partnerships A limited partnership is considered "foreign" in any state other than the one in which it was formed. The laws of the state in which a foreign limited partnership is organized govern its organization, its internal affairs, and the liability of its limited partners. In addition, the RULPA requires all foreign limited partnerships to register with the secretary of state before transacting any business in a state. Any foreign limited partnership transacting business without so registering may not bring enforcement actions in the state's courts until it registers, although it may defend itself in the state's courts.

Foreign limited partnerships a limited partnership is considered "foreign" in any state other than that in which it was formed

Rights
Because limited partnerships are organized pursuant to statute, the rights of the parties are usually set forth in the articles of limited partnership and in the

Rights a general partner has all the rights and powers of a partner in a general partnership

limited partnership agreement. Unless otherwise agreed or provided in the act, a general partner of a limited partnership has all the rights and powers of a partner in a partnership without limited partners. A general partner may also be a limited partner and thereby may also share in profits, losses, and distributions as a limited partner.

Control the general partners have almost exclusive control and management of the limited partnership; a limited partner who participates in the control of the limited partnership may lose limited liability

Control   The general partners of a limited partnership have almost exclusive control and management of the limited partnership. A limited partner, on the other hand, cannot share in this management or control; if he does, he may forfeit his limited liability. Under the 1976 Act, a limited partner whose participation in control *is* substantially the same as the exercise of the powers of a general partner assumes the liability of a general partner to *all* third parties who transact business with the partnership. However, a limited partner whose participation in control of the business is *not* substantially the same as the exercise of the powers of a general partner is liable as a general partner for the obligations of the limited partnership *only* to those persons who transact business with the limited partnership with *actual knowledge* of the limited partner's participation in control.

The 1985 Act has eliminated the broader liability of a limited partner whose participation is substantially the same as that of a general partner. Under the 1985 Act, a limited partner who participates in the control of the business is liable only to those persons who transact business with the limited partnership reasonably believing, based upon the limited partner's conduct, that the limited partner is a general partner.

Moreover, both versions of the RULPA provide a "safe harbor" by enumerating certain activities, any or all of which a limited partner may perform without being deemed to have participated in control of the business. They include (1) being a contractor for, or an agent or employee of, the limited partnership or a general partner; (2) consulting with and advising a general partner with respect to the business of the limited partnership; (3) acting as surety for the limited partnership; (4) approving or disapproving an amendment to the partnership agreement; and (5) voting on various fundamental changes in the limited partnership.

ALZADO v. BLINDER, ROBINSON & CO., INC.   Supreme Court of Colorado, 1988, 752 P.2d 544

FACTS In 1979, Lyle Alzado and two business associates formed Combat Promotions, Inc., to promote an eight-round exhibition boxing match in Denver, Colorado, between Alzado and Muhammad Ali. Ali agreed to participate on the condition that prior to the match he would receive an irrevocable letter of credit guaranteeing payment of $250,000. Combat Promotions persuaded Blinder, Robinson & Company, Inc. (B-R) to put up the $250,000 letter of credit. B-R, however, insisted on several conditions. First, B-R required the formation of a limited partnership, Combat Associates, with B-R as limited partner and Combat Promotions as general partner. Second, B-R required that the partnership agreement provide that the letter of credit be paid off as a partnership expense. Finally, B-R required Alzado's personal secured guarantee to reimburse B-R for any losses it might suffer. In a separate transaction Alzado

signed an agreement with Combat Associates stating that he would be paid $100,000 for the match, but subordinating that right to payment for expenses of the promotion.

B-R used its office as a ticket outlet, gave two parties to promote the exhibition match, and gave several promotional TV interviews. Nonetheless, few tickets were sold and the exhibition boxing match was a financial disaster. After Ali collected on the letter of credit as he was entitled to do, Combat Associates could pay B-R only $65,000, and paid nothing to Alzado or other creditors. B-R then sued Alzado for $185,000 in damages. Alzado counterclaimed, alleging that B-R should be deemed a general partner of Combat Associates and therefore liable to Alzado for $100,000. The jury awarded Alzado $92,500. B-R appealed, and the Colorado Court of Appeals

continued

reversed. Alzado then appealed to the Colorado Supreme Court.

DECISION Judgment of the Court of Appeals for Blinder, Robinson & Co., Inc., reversing the trial court's award to Alzado, affirmed.

OPINION A limited partner may become liable to partnership creditors as a general partner if the limited partner assumes control of partnership business. The RULPA, however, allows a limited partner to participate in a number of activities without losing limited liability. Any determination of whether a limited partner's conduct amounts to control over the partnership business requires analysis of several factors, including the purpose of the partnership, the administrative activities undertaken, the manner in which the partnership actually functioned, and the nature and frequency of the limited partner's activities.

B-R made no investment, accounting, or other financial decisions for the partnership, nor did B-R foster the appearance of being in control of the partnership. The evidence establishes at most that B-R engaged in a few promotional activities. It does not establish that B-R took part in management or control of the business affairs of Combat Associates. Rather, B-R at all times remained a limited partner.

INTERPRETATION The RULPA permits limited partners to carry on certain specified activities without losing their limited liability.

Voting Rights The partnership agreement may grant to all or a specified group of general or limited partners the right to vote on any matter. If, however, the agreement grants limited partners voting powers beyond the act's safe harbor provisions, a court *may* hold that the limited partners have participated in control of the business. The RULPA does not require that limited partners have the right to vote on matters as a class separate from the general partners, although the partnership agreement may provide such a right.

Choice of Associates After the formation of a limited partnership, the admission of additional limited partners requires the written consent of all partners, unless the partnership agreement provides otherwise. Regarding additional general partners, the written partnership agreement determines the procedure for authorizing their admission. The written consent of all partners is required only if the partnership agreement fails to deal with this issue.

Choice of associates no person may be added as a general partner or a limited partner without the consent of all partners

Withdrawal A general partner may **withdraw** from a limited partnership at any time by giving written notice to the other partners. If the withdrawal violates the partnership agreement, the limited partnership may recover damages from the withdrawing general partner. A limited partner may withdraw as provided in the limited partnership certificate or, under the 1985 Act, the written partnership agreement. If the certificate (or written partnership agreement, under the 1985 Act) does not specify when a limited partner may withdraw, she may do so upon giving at least six months' prior written notice to each general partner. Upon withdrawal, a withdrawing partner is entitled to receive any distribution to which she is entitled under the partnership agreement, subject to the amount restrictions discussed below. The partner is also entitled to receive the fair value of her interest in the limited partnership as of the date of withdrawal, based upon her right to share in distributions from the limited partnership, if the partnership agreement does not provide otherwise.

Withdrawal a general partner may withdraw from a limited partnership at any time by giving written notice to the other partners; a limited partner may withdraw as provided in the limited partnership certificate

Assignment of Partnership Interest A partnership interest is a partner's share of the profits and losses of a limited partnership and the right to receive distributions of partnership assets. A partnership interest is personal property. Unless the partnership agreement provides otherwise, a partner may assign his

Assignment of partnership interest unless otherwise provided in the partnership agreement, a partner may assign his partnership interest; an assignee may become a limited partner if all other partners consent

partnership interest. An assignment does not dissolve the limited partnership. The assignee does not become a partner and may not exercise any rights of a partner: the assignment entitles the assignee only to receive, to the extent of the assignment, the assigning partner's share of distributions. However, an assignee of a partnership interest, including an assignee of a general partner, may become a *limited* partner if all the other partners consent or if the assigning partner, having such power provided to her in the certificate (or in the partnership agreement, under the 1985 Act), grants the assignee this right. Except as otherwise provided in the partnership agreement, a partner ceases to be a partner upon assignment of all his partnership interest.

A creditor of a partner may obtain a charging order against a partner's interest in the partnership. To the extent of the charging order, the creditor has the rights of an assignee of the partnership interest.

Profit and loss sharing
profits and losses are allocated among the partners as provided in the partnership agreement; if the partnership agreement has no such provision, then profits and losses are allocated on the basis of the contributions each partner actually made

Profit and Loss Sharing The profits and losses are allocated among the partners as provided in the partnership agreement. If the partnership agreement makes no such provision in writing, the profits and losses are allocated on the basis of the value of the contributions each partner has actually made. Nonetheless, limited partners are usually not liable for losses beyond their capital contribution. The 1985 Act requires the agreement for sharing profits and losses to be in writing.

Distributions the partners share distributions of cash or other assets of a limited partnership as provided in the partnership agreement

Distributions The partners share **distributions** of cash or other assets of the limited partnership as provided in writing in the partnership agreement. The RULPA allows partners to share in distributions in a proportion different than that in which they share profits. If the partnership agreement does not allocate distributions in writing, they are made on the basis of the contributions each partner actually made. A partner who becomes entitled to a distribution has the status of a creditor with respect to that distribution. A partner may not receive a distribution from a limited partnership unless its post-distribution assets would be sufficient to pay all of its liabilities other than liabilities to partners on account of their partnership interests.

Loans both general and limited partners may be secured or unsecured creditors of the partnership

Loans Both general and limited partners may be secured or unsecured creditors of the partnership with rights the same as those of a person who is not a partner, subject to applicable state and federal bankruptcy and fraudulent conveyance statutes.

Information each partner has the right to inspect and copy the partnership records

Information The partnership must continuously maintain within the state an office at which basic organizational and financial records are kept. Each partner has the right to inspect and copy any of the partnership records.

Derivative actions a limited partner may sue on behalf of a limited partnership if the general partners refuse to bring the

Derivative Actions A limited partner has the right to bring an action on behalf of a limited partnership to recover a judgment in its favor if the general partners having authority to bring the action have refused to do so.

Duties and Liabilities
The duties and liabilities of general partners in a limited partnership are quite different from those of a limited partner. A general partner is subject to all the duties and restrictions of a partner in a partnership without limited partners, whereas a limited partner is subject to few, if any, duties and enjoys limited liability.

Duties A *general partner* of a limited partnership has a ***fiduciary*** relationship to her general and limited partners. This fiduciary duty of the general partner is extremely important to the limited partners because of their circumscribed roles in the control and management of the business enterprise. Conversely, it remains unclear whether a limited partner owes a fiduciary duty to his general partners or to the limited partnership itself. The very limited judicial authority on this question seems to indicate that he does not.

The RULPA does not distinguish between the duty of care owed by a general partner to a general partnership and that owed by a general partner to a limited partnership. Thus, a general partner owes her partners a duty not to be culpably negligent, as such negligence was discussed in Chapter 32. As in the next case, however, some courts have imposed upon general partners a higher duty of care toward *limited partners*. On the other hand, a limited partner owes no duty of care to a limited partnership as long as she remains a limited partner.

> **Duties** general partners owe a duty of care and loyalty (fiduciary duty) to the general partners, the limited partners, and the limited partnership; limited partners do not

---

WYLER v. FEUER
California Court of Appeal, Second District, Division 2, 1978, 85 Cal.App.3d 392, 149 Cal.Rptr. 626

FACTS Feuer and Martin, associated as Feuer and Martin Productions, Inc. (FMPI), had been successful producers of Broadway musical comedies. Their first motion picture, *Cabaret*, received eight Academy Awards in 1973. In 1972, FMPI bought the motion picture and television rights to Simone Berteaut's best-selling book about her life with her half-sister Edith Piaf. To finance a movie based on this novel, FMPI sought a substantial private investment from Wyler. In July 1973, Wyler signed a final limited partnership agreement with FMPI. The agreement stated that Wyler would provide, interest free, 100 percent financing for the proposed $1.6 million project in return for a certain portion of the profits, not to exceed 50 percent. In addition, FMPI would obtain $850,000 in production financing by September 30, 1973. The contract specifically provided that FMPI's failure to raise this amount by September 30, 1973, "shall not be deemed a breach of this agreement" and that Wyler's sole remedy would be a reduction in the producer's fee.

A year after its release in 1974, the motion picture proved less than an overwhelming success—costing $1.5 million and taking in total receipts of only $478,000. From the receipts, Wyler received $313,500 for his investment. FMPI had failed to obtain an amount even close to the required $850,000 for production financing. Wyler then sued Feuer, Martin, and FMPI for mismanagement of the limited partnership business and to recover his $1.5 million as damages. The trial court found in favor of Feuer, Martin, and FMPI.

DECISION Judgment for Feuer, Martin, and FMPI affirmed.

OPINION In a limited partnership, the limited partner restricts his liability to the amount of his capital investment. In return, the limited partner surrenders the right to manage and control the partnership business. The general partner owes to the limited partner a duty of reasonable care in his management of the business. But the general partner may not be held liable to the limited partner for mistakes made or losses incurred in the good faith exercise of reasonable business judgment.

Here, Wyler proved only that the motion picture did not make money, was not sought after by distributors, and did not live up to its producer's expectations. He failed to show that Feuer and Martin's decisions and efforts breached the standards of good faith and reasonableness. Therefore, he cannot recover damages from Feuer and Martin for an investment that simply turned sour.

INTERPRETATION A general partner is not liable for business losses if he or she conducts the business prudently and in good faith.

Liabilities One of the most appealing features of a limited partnership is the limited personal liability it offers to limited partners. **Limited liability** means that a limited partner who has paid her contribution has no further liability to the limited partnership or its creditors. Thus, if a limited partner buys a 25 percent share of a limited partnership for $50,000 and does not forfeit her limited liability, her liability is limited to the $50,000 she contributed, even if the

> **Limited liability** limited partners have liability for partnership debts or obligations only to the extent of the capital that the limited partner contributed or agreed to contribute

partnership suffers losses of $500,000. See Figure 34–1 for a comparison of general and limited partners.

This protection is subject to three conditions discussed earlier: (1) that the partnership has substantially complied in good faith with the requirement that a certificate of limited partnership be filed; (2) that the surname of the limited partner does not appear in the partnership name; and (3) that the limited partner does not take part in control of the business. In addition, if the certificate contains a false statement, anyone who suffers loss by reliance on that statement may hold liable any party to the certificate who knew the statement to be false when the certificate was executed. As long as the limited partner abides by these conditions, his liability for any and all obligations of the partnership is limited to his capital contribution. See Figure 34–2 for a summary of the liability of limited partners.

Liability of general partners the general partners have unlimited liability

At the same time, the general partners of a limited partnership have unlimited external liability. Also, any general partner who knew or *should have known* that the limited partnership certificate contained a false statement is liable to anyone who suffers loss by reliance on that false statement. Moreover, a general partner who knows or should know that a statement has *become* false, but who does not amend the certificate within a reasonable time, is liable as well.

Any partner to whom any part of her contribution has been returned *without* violation of the partnership agreement or of the limited partnership act is liable for one year to the limited partnership, to the extent necessary to pay creditors who extended credit during the period the partnership held the contribution. In contrast, any partner to whom any part of her contribution was returned *in violation* of the partnership agreement or the limited partnership act is liable to the limited partnership for six years for the amount of the contribution wrongfully returned.

Dissolution

Causes the limited partners have neither the right nor the power to dissolve the partnership, except by decree of the court. The following events trigger a dissolution: (1) the expiration of the time period; (2) the withdrawal of a general partner, unless all partners agree to continue the business; or (3) a decree of judicial dissolution

As with a general partnership, extinguishing a limited partnership involves three steps: (1) dissolution, (2) winding up or liquidation, and (3) termination. The causes of dissolution and the priorities in distributing the assets, however, differ somewhat from those in a general partnership.

Causes In a limited partnership, the limited partners have *no* right or power to dissolve the partnership, except by court decree. The death or bankruptcy of a

FIGURE 34–1 Comparison of General and Limited Partners

	General Partner	**Limited Partner**
Control	Has all the rights and powers of a partner in a partnership without limited partners	Has no right to take part in management or control
Liability	Unlimited	Limited, unless partner takes part in control or partner's name is used
Agency	Is an agent of the partnership	Is not an agent of the partnership
Fiduciary Duty	Yes	No
Duty of Care	Yes	No

FIGURE 34-2 Liability of Limited Partners

Activity	Consequences
Defective formation	Unlimited liability to third parties who transacted business before withdrawal or amendment and in good faith believed the "equity participant" was a general partner
Participation in control is substantially the same as powers of a general partner	1976 Act: Unlimited liability to all third parties who transact business with the partnership
	1985 Act: Unlimited liability to third parties who transacted business with reasonable belief, based on the limited partner's conduct, that the limited partner was a general partner
Participation in control is *not* substantially the same as powers of a general partner	1976 Act: Unlimited liability to those persons who transact business with actual knowledge of the limited partner's participation in control
	1985 Act: Same as 1985 Act, where participation in control is substantially the same as powers of a general partner
Name used with permission	Unlimited liability to third parties who did not have actual knowledge that she was a limited partner

limited partner does *not* dissolve the partnership. The RULPA specifies the events that will trigger a dissolution, after which the partnership affairs must be liquidated: (1) the expiration of the time period specified in the certificate; (2) the happening of events specified in writing in the partnership agreement; (3) the unanimous written consent of all the partners; (4) the withdrawal of a general partner, unless either (a) the written provisions of the partnership agreement permit the remaining general partners to continue the business or (b) all partners agree in writing to continue the business; or (5) a decree of judicial dissolution, which may be granted whenever it is not reasonably practicable to carry on the business in conformity with the partnership agreement. A general partner's withdrawal includes his retirement, the assignment of all his general partnership interest, removal, bankruptcy, death, and adjudication of incompetency. A certificate of cancellation must be filed when the limited partnership dissolves and winding up commences.

Winding Up Unless otherwise provided in the partnership agreement, the general partners who have not wrongfully dissolved the limited partnership may wind up its affairs. The limited partners may wind up the limited partnership if the general partners all have wrongfully dissolved the partnership. But, by showing cause, any partner, his legal representative, or his assignee may obtain a winding up by the court.

Distribution of Assets The priorities in distributing the assets of a limited partnership are as follows:

1. to creditors, including partners who are creditors except with respect to liabilities for distributions;

Winding up unless otherwise provided in the partnership agreement, the general partners who have not wrongfully dissolved the partnership may wind up its affairs

Distribution of assets the priorities for distribution are as follows: (1) creditors, including partners who are creditors; (2) partners and ex-partners in satisfaction of liabilities for unpaid distributions; (3) partners for the return of contributions, except as otherwise agreed; and (4) partners for their partnership interests in the proportions in which they share in distributions, except as otherwise agreed

2. to partners and ex-partners in satisfaction of liabilities for unpaid distributions;

3. to partners for the return of their contributions, except as otherwise agreed; and

4. to partners for their partnership interests in the proportions in which they share in distributions, except as otherwise agreed.

General and limited partners rank equally unless the partnership agreement provides otherwise.

LIMITED LIABILITY COMPANIES

A limited liability company (LLC) is another form of unincorporated business association. Prior to 1990, only two states had statutes permitting LLCs. Now all states have enacted LLC statutes. Until 1995, there was no uniform statute on which states might base their LLC legislation, and as of July 1997, only four states had adopted the uniform statute. Therefore, the enabling legislation varies from state to state. Nevertheless, the LLC statutes generally share certain characteristics.

A **limited liability company** is a noncorporate business organization that provides limited liability to *all* of its owners (members), permits all of its members to participate in management of the business, and, if properly structured, is taxed as a partnership. Thus, the LLC provides many of the advantages of a general partnership plus limited liability for all its members. Its benefits outweigh those of a limited partnership in that all members of an LLC not only enjoy limited liability but also may participate in management and control of the business. Ownership interests in a limited liability company *may* be considered to be securities, especially interests in those LLCs operated by managers. If a particular LLC interest is considered a security, its sale would be subject to state and federal regulation, as discussed in Chapter 42. See Figure 35–1.

Formation

The **formation** of a limited liability company requires substantial compliance with a state's limited liability company statute. About two-thirds of the statutes require an LLC to have at least two members. Once formed, an LLC is a separate legal entity that is distinct from its members, who are normally not liable for its debts and obligations. An LLC can contract in its own name and is generally empowered to carry on any lawful business purpose, although some statutes restrict the permissible activities of LLCs.

Filing The LLC statutes generally require the central filing of *articles of organization* in a designated state office. The states vary regarding the information they require the articles to include. Some LLC statutes limit LLCs to a duration of thirty years or less, while other statutes require the articles to specify the latest date on which the LLC is to dissolve.

Name LLC statutes generally require the name of the LLC to include the words "limited liability company" or the abbreviation "LLC." Some states also permit the use of the name "limited company" and the abbreviation "LC."

Contribution The contribution of a member to a limited liability company may be cash, property, services rendered, a promissory note, or other obligation to

---

Limited liability company a noncorporate business organization that provides limited liability to *all* of its owners (members), permits all of its members to participate in management of the business, and, if properly structured, is taxed as a partnership

Formation the formation of a limited liability company requires substantial compliance with a state's limited liability company statute

Filing the LLC statutes generally require the central filing of articles of organization in a designated state office

Name LLC statutes generally require the name of the LLC to include the words "limited liability company" or the abbreviation "LLC"

Contribution the contribution of a member to a limited liability company may be cash, property, services rendered, a promissory note, or other obligation to contribute cash, property, or to perform services

contribute cash, property, or to perform services. Members are liable to the LLC for failing to make an agreed contribution.

Operating Agreement The members of an LLC adopt an **operating agreement**, which is the basic contract governing the affairs of a limited liability company and stating the various rights and duties of the members. Some states require the entire operating agreement to be in writing, while other states permit unwritten operating agreements to govern at least some of the relations among the members.

Foreign Limited Liability Companies A limited liability company is considered "foreign" in any state other than that in which it was formed. LLC statutes typically provide that the laws of the state in which a foreign LLC is organized govern its organization, its internal affairs, and the liability of its members and managers. Foreign limited liability companies must register with the secretary of state before transacting any business in a state. Any foreign limited liability company transacting business without so registering may not bring enforcement actions in the state's courts until it registers, although it may defend itself in the state's courts.

Rights of Members
A member has no property interest in property owned by the LLC. On the other hand, a member does have an interest in the LLC, which is personal property. A member's interest in the LLC includes two components:

1. The *financial interest,* which is the right to distributions, and
2. the *management interest,* which consists of all other rights granted to a member by the LLC operating agreement and the LLC statute. The management interest typically includes the right to manage, vote, obtain information, and bring enforcement actions.

Profit and Loss Sharing The LLC's operating agreement determines how the partners allocate the profits and losses. If the LLC's operating agreement makes no such provision, the profits and losses are typically allocated on the basis of the value of the members' contributions.

Distributions The members share distributions of cash or other assets of a limited liability company as provided in the operating agreement. If the LLC's operating agreement does not allocate distributions, they are typically made on the basis of the contributions each member made.

Withdrawal Most statutes permit a member to withdraw and demand payment of her interest upon giving the notice specified in the statute or the LLC's operating agreement. Some of the statutes permit the operating agreement to deny members the right to withdraw from the LLC.

Management Most LLC statutes provide that, in the absence of a contrary agreement, each member has equal rights in the management of the LLC. All LLC statutes permit LLCs to be managed by one or more managers who may, but need not, be members. In a member-managed LLC, the members have actual and apparent authority to bind the LLC. In a manager-managed LLC, the

---

Operating agreement is the basic contract governing the affairs of a limited liability company and stating the various rights and duties of the members

Foreign limited liability companies a limited liability company is considered "foreign" in any state other than that in which it was formed

Rights of members a member's interest in the LLC includes the financial interest (the right to distributions) and the management interest (which consists of all other rights granted to a member by the LLC operating agreement and the LLC statute)

Profit and loss sharing the LLC's operating agreement determines how the partners allocate the profits and losses; if the LLC's operating agreement makes no such provision, the profits and losses are typically allocated on the basis of the value of the members' contributions

Distributions the members share distributions of cash or other assets of a limited liability company as provided in the operating agreement; if the LLC's operating agreement does not allocate distributions, they are typically made on the basis of the contributions each member made

Withdrawal a member may withdraw and demand payment of her interest upon giving the notice specified in the statute or the LLC's operating agreement

Management in the absence of a contrary agreement, each member has equal rights in the management of the LLC; but LLCs may be managed by one or more managers who may be members

managers have this authority, while the members have *no* actual or apparent authority to bind the manager-managed LLC.

Voting A number of the LLC statutes specify the voting rights of members, subject to a contrary provision in an LLC's operating agreement. Typically, members have the right to vote on proposals to (1) adopt or amend the operating agreement, (2) admit any person as a member, (3) sell all or substantially all of the LLC's assets prior to dissolution, and (4) merge the LLC with another LLC.

Derivative Actions A member has the right to bring an action on behalf of a limited liability company to recover a judgment in its favor if the managers or members with authority to bring the action have refused to do so.

Assignment of LLC Interest Unless otherwise provided in the LLC's operating agreement, a member may assign his financial interest in the LLC. An assignment does not dissolve the LLC. The assignee does not become a member and may not exercise any rights of a member. The assignment only entitles the assignee to receive, to the extent of the assignment, the assigning member's share of distributions. However, an assignee of a financial interest in an LLC may acquire the other rights by being admitted as a member of the company by all the remaining members. A judgment creditor of a member may obtain a charging order against the member's financial interest in the LLC.

Duties

As with general partnerships and limited partnerships, the duties of care and loyalty also apply to LLCs. In a number of states, the LLC statute expressly imposes these duties. In other states, the common law imposes these duties. Who has these duties in a limited liability company depends upon whether the LLC is a manager-managed LLC or a member-managed LLC.

Manager-managed LLCs Most LLC statutes impose upon the managers of an LLC a duty of care. In some states, this is a duty to refrain from grossly negligent, reckless, or intentional conduct; in other states, it is a duty to act as a prudent person would in similar circumstances. Managers also have a fiduciary duty, although the statutes vary in how they specify that duty. Usually, members of manager-managed LLCs have no duties to the LLC or its members by reason of being a member.

Member-managed LLCs Members of member-managed LLCs have the same duties of care and loyalty that managers have in manager-managed LLCs.

Liabilities

One of the most appealing features of a limited liability company is the limited personal liability it offers to *all* its members and managers. Statutes typically provide that no member or manager of a limited liability company shall be obligated personally for any debt, obligation, or liability of the limited liability company solely by reason of being a member or acting as a manager of the limited liability company.

As mentioned earlier, a member who fails to make an agreed contribution is liable to the limited liability company for the deficiency. Moreover, under the great majority of statutes, any member who receives a return of her contribution

Voting LLC statutes often specify the voting rights of members, subject to a contrary provision in an LLC's operating agreement

Derivative actions a member has the right to bring an action on behalf of a limited liability company to recover a judgment in its favor if the managers or members with authority to bring the action have refused to do so

Assignment of LLC interest unless otherwise provided in the LLC's operating agreement, a member may assign his *financial interest* in the LLC; an assignee of a financial interest in an LLC may acquire the other rights by being admitted as a member of the company by all the remaining members

Manager-managed LLCs the managers of a manager-managed LLC have a duty of care and loyalty; usually, members of manager-managed LLCs have no duties to the LLC or its members by reason of being a member

Member-managed LLCs members of member-managed LLCs have the same duties of care and loyalty that managers have in manager-managed LLCs

Liabilities no member or manager of a limited liability company is obligated personally for any debt, obligation, or liability of the limited liability company solely by reason of being a member or acting as a manager of the limited liability company in violation of the LLC's operating agreement or the limited liability company act is liable to the limited liability company for the amount of the contribution wrongfully returned. Under a few of the statutes, even members who receive a return of their capital contribution *without* violating the LLC agreement or the limited liability company act remain liable to the limited liability company for a specified time to the extent necessary to pay creditors.

Dissolution

Limited liability company statutes generally provide that an LLC will automatically dissolve upon

1. the dissociation of a member,
2. the expiring of the LLC's agreed duration or the happening of any of the events specified in the articles,
3. the unanimous written consent of all the members, or
4. a decree of judicial dissolution.

Dissociation **Dissociation** means that a member has ceased to be associated with the company and includes voluntary withdrawal, death, incompetence, expulsion, or bankruptcy. Most statutes permit the nondissociating members by unanimous consent to continue the LLC after a member dissociates. Some allow continuation by majority vote.

Distribution of Assets Most statutes provide default rules for distributing the assets of a limited liability company as follows:

1. to creditors, including members and managers who are creditors, except with respect to liabilities for distributions;
2. to members and former members in satisfaction of liabilities for unpaid distributions, except as otherwise agreed;
3. to members for the return of their contributions, except as otherwise agreed; and
4. to members for their limited liability company interests in the proportions in which members share in distributions, except as otherwise agreed.

Dissolution an LLC will automatically dissolve upon (1) the dissociation of a member, (2) the expiration of the LLC's agreed duration or the happening of any of the events specified in the articles, (3) the unanimous written consent of all the members, or (4) a decree of judicial dissolution

Dissociation means that a member has ceased to be associated with the company and includes voluntary withdrawal, death, incompetence, expulsion, or bankruptcy

Distribution of assets the default rules for distributing the assets of a limited liability company are (1) to creditors, including members and managers who are creditors; (2) to members and former members in satisfaction of liabilities for unpaid distributions; (3) to members for the return of their contributions, except as otherwise agreed; and (4) to members for their limited liability company interests in the proportions in which members share in distributions, except as otherwise agreed

---

IN THE MATTER OF DAUGHERTY CONSTRUCTION, INC. United States Bankruptcy Court, 1995, 188 B.R. 607

FACTS Daugherty Construction, Inc. (DCI), a debtor under Chapter 11 of the Federal Bankruptcy Act, is a member of a number of Nebraska limited liability companies (LLCs), including Folsom Ridge Apartments, L.L.C. (Folsom) and Lakeview Park Apartments, L.L.C. (Lakeview), which were formed to develop two apartment complexes in Lincoln, Nebraska. DCI's membership capital contribution to each LLC was to provide general contractor services for construction of the apartment buildings. Lakeview and Folsom are LLCs organized pursuant to Nebraska's Limited Liability Companies Act. The articles of organization and operating agreements of the two LLCs incorporate Section 21-2621 of the Nebraska statute, which states that the bankruptcy of a member constitutes an act of dissolu-

tion, unless two-thirds of the remaining members vote to continue the LLC.

The nondebtor members of Lakeview and Folsom treated DCI's bankruptcy filing as an event of dissolution and voted to continue the respective LLCs and to terminate DCI as general contractor on the respective LLC construction projects. In addition, the nondebtor members voted to remove Rick Daugherty (the president and sole shareholder of DCI) as general manager of each LLC.

The court must determine the validity of Nebraska's statutory provisions that dissolve a limited liability company upon the filing of a bankruptcy petition by one of its members. No cases are reported in any jurisdiction that deal with such a provision in a limited liability company act.

continued

DECISION Nebraska's LLC statutory provision dissolving a limited liability company upon a member's filing a bankruptcy petition is not enforceable in a Chapter 11 bankruptcy case.

OPINION The Nebraska Limited Liability Companies Act was adopted in Nebraska in 1993 as part of a growing national trend. Such a company is a hybrid business entity comprised of attributes from both corporations and partnerships. The primary purpose of an LLC is to provide the best aspects of both entities: the conduit taxation of a partnership with the limited liability of a corporation. To preserve conduit taxation attributes, limited liability company acts contain provisions calculated to diminish the corporate attributes of an LLC enough for the LLC to qualify under Treasury Regulations for taxation as a partnership.

One attribute of corporate existence sought to be avoided or diminished is continuity of LLC life. In order to establish an entity without continuity of life, the Nebraska statute provides that the death, insanity, bankruptcy, retirement, resignation, or expulsion of any member will cause a dissolution of the organization.

Termination of an LLC upon bankruptcy of a member may also be in response to other concerns. Like a partnership, members of the LLC have voluntarily associated in a business enterprise, and the relationship among members may be personal in character. Indeed, there are very strict limitations upon the transfer of a member's interest in the two LLCs involved in this case. These problems and concerns are addressed in LLC statutes by provisions that dissolve the LLC upon bankruptcy and provide that if the nonbankrupt members of the LLC vote to continue the business of the LLC, the interest of the bankrupt member is terminated.

Congress, however, has also dealt with this problem in the context of bankruptcy cases in a manner inconsistent with the Nebraska LLC statute. Under the Supremacy Clause of the United States Constitution, federal law must prevail. Accordingly, the Nebraska Limited Liability Companies Act provisions dissolving an LLC upon a member's filing a Chapter 11 bankruptcy case are not enforceable because they are in conflict with specific provisions of the Bankruptcy Code. First, the debtor's interest in the LLCs constitutes property of the bankruptcy estate, and state law purporting to terminate that interest is unenforceable under Section 541(c). Second, under Section 363, the debtor has the right to use, sell, or lease all property of the estate, including the debtor's membership interest in the LLC, despite state law purporting to terminate the debtor's interest. Third, the LLC articles of organization and the operating agreement among the LLC members constitute, on the facts of this case, executory contracts that the debtor may attempt to assume under Section 365, despite provisions of these contracts that purport to terminate the debtor's interest upon the commencement of a bankruptcy case. Therefore, despite the Nebraska Limited Liability Companies Act, the membership of DCI in Folsom and Lakeview did not terminate upon the commencement of this Chapter 11 bankruptcy case, the LLCs continued to exist, and the LLC articles and agreements constitute an executory contract under the Bankruptcy Code.

INTERPRETATION A state LLC statutory provision dissolving an LLC upon a member's filing a bankruptcy petition may not be enforceable in a federal bankruptcy proceeding.

OTHER UNINCORPORATED BUSINESS ASSOCIATIONS

Joint Ventures

Joint venture association of two or more persons to engage in a particular business transaction for a profit

A **joint venture** or joint adventure is a business association composed of persons who combine their property, money, efforts, skill, and knowledge for the purpose of carrying out a particular business enterprise for profit. Thus, a joint venture usually contemplates a single transaction, or a related series of transactions. Usually, although not necessarily, it is of short duration and therefore differs from a partnership, which is formed to carry on a business over a considerable or indefinite period of time. Each joint venturer has authority to act and bind the other venturers within the actual or apparent scope of the business. An example of a joint venture is a securities underwriting syndicate or a syndicate formed to acquire a certain tract of land for subdivision and resale. Other common examples include joint research conducted by corporations, exploitation of mineral rights, and manufacturing operations in foreign countries. Except for a few differences, a joint venture is generally governed by the law of partnerships.

HIRSCHFELD PRESS, INC. v. WESTON GROUP, INC. Court of Appeals of Colorado, Div. I, 1991, 824 P.2d. 44

FACTS Page Gallery Productions, Inc. (PGP) had a nonassignable license with the National Football League (NFL) to print football posters. PGP, on the advice of a marketing consultant, entered into negotiations with Weston Group, Inc. to market its posters. PGP and Weston exchanged several written proposals and finally agreed on a contract, but PGP declined to sign the agreement because it was dissatisfied with Weston's marketing efforts as of that date.

PGP previously had contracted to have Hirschfeld Press print posters in connection with a pizza chain promotion but did not mention this promotion during the negotiations with Weston. Hirschfeld subsequently agreed to print NFL posters for PGP. PGP and Hirschfeld did not enter into a separate contract for the new NFL poster agreement, nor did Hirschfeld establish a new account receivable for the NFL project. During the course of negotiations with Weston, PGP experienced financial problems and was unable to pay Hirschfeld. PGP requested and obtained a loan from Weston, for which PGP signed a promissory note to Weston. PGP made payments of $49,000 to Hirschfeld, either from the proceeds of poster sales or from the funds it had borrowed from Weston, without specifying to Hirschfeld how the payments should be allocated. Hirschfeld allocated the payments to the printing of bills for the pizza chain promotion, then filed suit against PGP for the payment of bills for the NFL posters. Neither Weston nor Hirschfeld was aware of the other's dealings with PGP. However, after filing suit against PGP and learning of Weston's involvement with PGP, Hirschfeld amended its pleadings and asserted a claim against Weston.

The trial court found that PGP and Weston orally agreed that Weston would promote and market football posters, that Weston would receive 50 percent of the profits, and that the parties' share of any losses would be deducted from any future profits. The court also found that the parties intended to enter into a joint venture and that all elements of a joint venture were present in their dealings. Weston appeals, asserting that the judgment should be reversed as a matter of law because there is not enough evidence of a joint venture.

DECISION Decision of the trial court affirmed.

OPINION A joint venture is a partnership formed for a limited purpose, and it is unnecessary to execute a written agreement in order to form the venture. The evidence must only establish an express or implied agreement for (1) a joint interest in the property; (2) an agreement to share in the profits and losses of the venture; and (3) actions and conduct showing the parties' cooperation in the project. In this case, the parties' failure to sign their contract was not based on a failure to reach an agreement on the venture terms. Therefore, the failure to sign does not prevent the conclusion that a joint venture existed.

Weston contends that the evidence is insufficient to show that the parties had a joint interest in the property since the nonassignable NFL license was solely in PGP's name and PGP owned the posters and transparencies. A joint interest arises when the parties agree to commit their property, money, credit, labor, and skills to the venture. There is no requirement that they convey title to all property interests to the joint venture. Rather, the joint interest contemplated is that of making a profit from shared property interests or contract rights. The evidence here confirms that the parties by their actions and conduct joined efforts to produce and market the NFL posters. The parties communicated with each other on a regular basis, jointly decided on which posters to print and how many, and agreed on an accounting system to track revenue and costs associated with the poster project; and PGP undertook production of the posters while Weston initiated marketing efforts.

The acts of one joint venturer are binding upon other joint venturers if those acts pertain to matters within the scope of the joint venture and the joint venturer had authority to act. Here, the printing of posters was an integral part of the venture, and the parties had contemplated the expenses of that printing. Since the printing expenses were within the scope of the agreement, PGP had authority to bind the joint venture even though Hirschfeld had no knowledge of the venture.

INTERPRETATION A joint venture is a business association composed of persons who combine their property, money, efforts, skill, and knowledge for the purpose of carrying out a particular venture for profit. Each joint venturer has authority to act and bind the other venturers within the scope of the business.

Limited Liability Partnerships

Beginning in 1991, about forty states have enacted statutes enabling the formation of limited liability partnerships (LLPs). There is no uniform LLP statute, so the enabling statutes vary from state to state. A registered **limited liability partnership** is a general partnership that, by making the statutorily required filing,

> **Limited liability partnership** is a general partnership that, by making the statutorily required filing, limits the liability of its partners for some or all of the partnership's obligations

limits the liability of its partners for some or all of the partnership's obligations. To become an LLP, a general partnership must file with the secretary of state an application containing specified information. Most of the statutes require only a majority of the partners to authorize registration as an LLP; others require unanimous approval. Some statutes require renewal of registrations annually; other statutes require periodic reports; and a few require no renewal. Some statutes require a new filing after any change in membership of the partnership, but a few of the statutes do not.

Designation the name of the LLP must include the words "limited liability partnership" or "registered limited liability partnership," or the abbreviation "LLP"

Designation All statutes require LLPs to designate themselves as such. Most statutes require the name of the LLP to include the words "limited liability partnership" or "registered limited liability partnership," or the abbreviation "LLP." Most statutes provide that the laws of the jurisdiction under which a foreign LLP is registered shall govern its organization, internal affairs, and the liability and authority of its partners. Many, but not all, of the statutes require a foreign LLP to register or obtain a certificate of authenticity.

Liability limitation some statutes limit liability only for *negligent* acts; others limit liability to any partnership tort or contract obligation that arose from negligence, malpractice, wrongful acts, or misconduct committed by any partner, employee, or agent of the partnership; while some provide limited liability for *all* debts and obligations of the partnership

Liability Limitation LLP statutes have taken three different approaches to limiting the liability of partners for the partnership's obligations. The earliest statutes limited liability only for *negligent* acts; they retain unlimited liability for *all* other obligations. The next generation of statutes extended limited liability to any partnership tort or contract obligation that arose from negligence, malpractice, wrongful acts, or misconduct committed by any partner, employee, or agent of the partnership. Unlimited liability remained for ordinary contract obligations, such as those owed to suppliers, lenders, and landlords. Some of the more recent statutes have provided limited liability for *all* debts and obligations of the partnership.

The statutes, however, generally provide that the limitation on liability will *not* affect the liability of (1) a partner who committed the wrongful act giving rise to the liability and (2) a partner who supervised the partner, employee, or agent of the partnership who committed the wrongful act. The statutes also provide that the limitations on liability will apply only to claims that arise while the partnership was a registered limited liability partnership. Accordingly, partners would have unlimited liability for obligations that either arose before registration or after registration lapses.

Although limited liability company statutes provide greater protection against liability than most LLP statutes, the LLP form has attracted some businesses, especially professional firms. One advantage of the LLP is that an existing general partnership may become an LLP without forming a new organization or negotiating a new operating agreement.

Limited Liability Limited Partnerships

Limited liability limited partnership is a limited partnership in which the liability of the general partners has been limited to the same extent as in an LLP

A **limited liability limited partnership** (LLLP) is a limited partnership in which the liability of the general partners has been limited to the same extent as in an LLP. A few states have statutes expressly providing for LLLPs. In other states, by operation of the provision in the RULPA that a general partner in a limited partnership has the liabilities of a general partner in a general partnership, the LLP statute may provide limited liability to general partners in a limited partnership that registers as an LLLP under the LLP statute. Where authorized, the general partners in an LLLP will obtain the same degree of liability limitation that general partners can achieve in LLPs. Where available, a limited partnership may register as an LLLP without having to form a new organization, as would be the case in converting to an LLC.

Business Trusts

A trust is a transfer of the legal title to certain specific property to one person for the use and benefit of another. An express trust that results from a contract is an agreement commonly known as a declaration of trust. It customarily designates the property, the duration of the trust, the exact functions and duties of the trustees concerning the management of the property, the persons to whom the income of the trust is to be paid and the share to be received by each, the method of winding up the trust, and the person or persons entitled to share in the trust property on termination. See Chapter 54 for a discussion of trusts.

Like an ordinary trust between natural persons, a business trust may be created by a voluntary agreement without state authorization or consent. A **business trust** has three distinguishing characteristics: (1) the trust estate is devoted to the conduct of a business; (2) by the terms of the agreement, each beneficiary is entitled to a certificate evidencing his ownership of a beneficial interest in the trust that he is free to sell or otherwise transfer; and (3) the trustees have the exclusive right to manage and control the business. If the third condition is not met, the trust may fail; for the beneficiaries, by participating in control, would become personally liable as partners for the obligations of the business.

Business trust a trust (managed by a trustee for the benefit of a beneficiary) established to conduct a business for a profit

The trustees are personally liable for the debts of the business unless the trustee obtains the agreement of the other contracting party to look solely to the assets of the trust. The personal liability of the trustees for their own torts or the torts of their agents and servants employed in the operation of the business stands on a different footing. While this liability cannot be avoided, the risk involved may be reduced substantially or eliminated altogether by insurance. In most jurisdictions, the beneficiaries of a business trust have no liability for obligations of the trust.

CHAPTER SUMMARY

Limited Partnership	**Definition of a Limited Partnership** a partnership formed by two or more persons under the laws of a state and having one or more general partners and one or more limited partners
	Formation a limited partnership can only be formed by substantial compliance with a state limited partnership statute
	■ *Filing of Certificate* two or more persons must file a signed certificate of limited partnership
	■ *Name* inclusion of a limited partner's surname in the partnership name in most instances will result in the loss of the limited partner's limited liability
	■ *Contributions* may be cash, property, services, or a promise to contribute cash, property, or services
	■ *Defective Formation* if no certificate is filed or if the one filed does not substantially meet the statutory requirements, the formation is defective and the limited liability of the limited partners is jeopardized
	■ *Foreign Limited Partnerships* a limited partnership is considered "foreign" in any state other than that in which it was formed
	Rights a general partner in a limited partnership has all the rights and powers of a partner in a general partnership

- **Control** the general partners have almost exclusive control and management of the limited partnership; a limited partner who participates in the control of the limited partnership may lose limited liability
- **Choice of Associates** no person may be added as a general partner or a limited partner without the consent of all partners
- **Withdrawal** a general partner may withdraw from a limited partnership at any time by giving written notice to the other partners; a limited partner may withdraw as provided in the limited partnership certificate
- **Assignment of Partnership Interest** unless otherwise provided in the partnership agreement, a partner may assign his partnership interest; an assignee may become a limited partner if all other partners consent
- **Profit and Loss Sharing** profits and losses are allocated among the partners as provided in the partnership agreement; if the partnership agreement has no such provision, then profits and losses are allocated on the basis of the contributions each partner actually made
- **Distributions** the partners share distributions of cash or other assets of a limited partnership as provided in the partnership agreement
- **Loans** both general and limited partners may be secured or unsecured creditors of the partnership
- **Information** each partner has the right to inspect and copy the partnership records
- **Derivative Actions** a limited partner may sue on behalf of a limited partnership if the general partners refuse to bring the action

Duties and Liabilities
- **Duties** general partners owe a duty of care and loyalty (fiduciary duty) to the general partners, the limited partners, and the limited partnership; limited partners do not
- **Liabilities** the general partners have unlimited liability; the limited partners have limited liability (liability for partnership obligations only to the extent of the capital that the limited partner contributed or agreed to contribute)

Dissolution
- **Causes** the limited partners have neither the right nor the power to dissolve the partnership, except by decree of the court. The following events trigger a dissolution: (1) the expiration of the time period; (2) the withdrawal of a general partner, unless all partners agree to continue the business; or (3) a decree of judicial dissolution
- **Winding Up** unless otherwise provided in the partnership agreement, the general partners who have not wrongfully dissolved the partnership may wind up its affairs
- **Distribution of Assets** the priorities for distribution are as follows: (1) creditors, including partners who are creditors; (2) partners and ex-partners in satisfaction of liabilities for unpaid distributions; (3) partners for the return of contributions, except as otherwise agreed; and (4) partners for their partnership interests in the proportions in which they share in distributions, except as otherwise agreed

---

Limited Liability Company

Definition a limited liability company is a noncorporate business organization that provides limited liability to *all* of its owners (members), permits all of its members to participate in management of the business, and, if properly structured, is taxed as a partnership

Formation the formation of a limited liability company requires substantial compliance with a state's limited liability company statute

- ■ *Filing* the LLC statutes generally require the central filing of articles of organization in a designated state office
- ■ *Name* LLC statutes generally require the name of the LLC to include the words "limited liability company" or the abbreviation "LLC"
- ■ *Contribution* the contribution of a member to a limited liability company may be cash, property, services rendered, a promissory note, or other obligation to contribute cash, property, or to perform services
- ■ *Operating Agreement* is the basic contract governing the affairs of a limited liability company and stating the various rights and duties of the members
- ■ *Foreign Limited Liability Companies* a limited liability company is considered "foreign" in any state other than that in which it was formed

Rights of Members a member's interest in the LLC includes the financial interest (the right to distributions) and the management interest (which consists of all other rights granted to a member by the LLC operating agreement and the LLC statute)

- ■ *Profit and Loss Sharing* the LLC's operating agreement determines how the partners allocate the profits and losses; if the LLC's operating agreement makes no such provision, the profits and losses are typically allocated on the basis of the value of the members' contributions
- ■ *Distributions* the members share distributions of cash or other assets of a limited liability company as provided in the operating agreement; if the LLC's operating agreement does not allocate distributions, they are typically made on the basis of the contributions each member made
- ■ *Withdrawal* a member may withdraw and demand payment of her interest upon giving the notice specified in the statute or the LLC's operating agreement
- ■ *Management* in the absence of a contrary agreement, each member has equal rights in the management of the LLC; but LLCs may be managed by one or more managers who may be members
- ■ *Voting* LLC statutes often specify the voting rights of members, subject to a contrary provision in an LLC's operating agreement
- ■ *Derivative Actions* a member has the right to bring an action on behalf of a limited liability company to recover a judgment in its favor if the managers or members with authority to bring the action have refused to do so
- ■ *Assignment of LLC Interest* unless otherwise provided in the LLC's operating agreement, a member may assign his *financial interest* in the LLC; an assignee of a financial interest in an LLC may acquire the other rights by being admitted as a member of the company by all the remaining members

Duties

- ■ *Manager-managed LLCs* the managers of manager-managed LLCs have a duty of care and loyalty; usually, members of a manager-managed LLC have no duties to the LLC or its members by reason of being a member
- ■ *Member-managed LLCs* members of member-managed LLCs have the same duties of care and loyalty that managers have in manager-managed LLCs

Liabilities no member or manager of a limited liability company is obligated personally for any debt, obligation, or liability of the limited liability company solely by reason of being a member or acting as a manager of the limited liability company

Dissolution an LLC will automatically dissolve upon (1) the dissociation of a member, (2) the expiration of the LLC's agreed duration or the happening of any of the events specified in the articles, (3) the unanimous written consent of all the members, or (4) a decree of judicial dissolution

- ■ *Dissociation* means that a member has ceased to be associated with the company and includes voluntary withdrawal, death, incompetence, expulsion, or bankruptcy
- ■ *Distribution of Assets* the default rules for distributing the assets of a limited liability company are (1) to creditors, including members and managers who are creditors, except with respect to liabilities for distributions; (2) to members and

former members in satisfaction of liabilities for unpaid distributions, except as otherwise agreed; (3) to members for the return of their contributions, except as otherwise agreed; and (4) to members for their limited liability company interests in the proportions in which members share in distributions, except as otherwise agreed

Other Unincorporated Business Associations

Joint Venture association of two or more persons to engage in a particular business transaction for a profit

Limited Liability Partnership is a general partnership that, by making the statutorily required filing, limits the liability of its partners for some or all of the partnership's obligations
- *Designation* the name of the LLP must include the words "limited liability partnership" or "registered limited liability partnership," or the abbreviation "LLP"
- *Liability Limitation* some statutes limit liability only for *negligent* acts; others limit liability to any partnership tort or contract obligation that arose from negligence, malpractice, wrongful acts, or misconduct committed by any partner, employee, or agent of the partnership; while some provide limited liability for *all* debts and obligations of the partnership

Limited Liability Limited Partnership is a limited partnership in which the liability of the general partners has been limited to the same extent as in an LLP

Business Trust a trust (managed by a trustee for the benefit of a beneficiary) established to conduct a business for a profit

QUESTIONS

1. Distinguish between a general partnership and a limited partnership.
2. Identify those activities in which a limited partner may engage without forfeiting limited liability.
3. Explain the order in which the assets of a limited partnership are distributed to creditors, limited partners, and general partners.
4. Distinguish between a limited partnership and a limited liability company.
5. Discuss the basic characteristics of joint ventures, limited liability partnerships, and business trusts.

Internet Question. Find and review information about (a) limited partnerships, (b) limited liability partnerships, and (c) real estate investment trusts.

PROBLEMS

1. John Palmer and Henry Morrison formed the partnership of Palmer & Morrison for the management of the Huntington Hotel. The partnership agreement provided that Palmer would contribute $40,000 and be a general partner and that Morrison would contribute $30,000 and be a limited partner. Palmer was to manage the dining and cocktail rooms, and Morrison was to manage the rest of the hotel. Nanette, a popular French singer, who knew nothing of the partnership affairs, appeared for four weeks in the Blue Room at the hotel and was not paid her fee of $8,000. Subsequently, Palmer and Morrison had a difference of opinion, and Palmer bought Morrison's interest in the partnership for $20,000. Palmer later went into bankruptcy. Nanette sued Morrison for $8,000. For how much, if anything, is Morrison liable?

2. A limited partnership was formed consisting of Webster as the general partner and Stevens and Stewart as the limited partners. The limited partnership was

organized in strict compliance with the limited partnership statute. Stevens was employed by the partnership as a purchasing agent. Stewart personally guaranteed a loan made to the partnership. Both Stevens and Stewart consulted with Webster about partnership business, voted on a change in the nature of the partnership business, and disapproved an amendment to the partnership agreement proposed by Webster. The partnership experienced serious financial difficulties, and its creditors seek to hold Webster, Stevens, and Stewart personally liable for the debts of the partnership. Decision?

3. Fox, Dodge, and Gilbey agreed to become limited partners in Palatine Ventures, a limited partnership. The certificate of limited partnership stated that each would contribute $20,000. Fox's contribution consisted entirely of cash; Dodge contributed $12,000 in cash and gave the partnership her promissory note for $8,000; and Gilbey's contribution was his promise to perform 500 hours of legal services for the partnership. What liability, if any, do Fox, Dodge, and Gilbey have to the partnership by way of capital contribution?

4. Madison and Tilson agree to form a limited partnership with Madison as general partner and Tilson as the limited partner, each to contribute $12,500 as capital. No papers are ever filed, and after ten months the enterprise fails with liabilities exceeding assets by $30,000. Creditors of the partnership seek to hold Madison and Tilson personally liable for the $30,000. Decision?

5. Kraft is a limited partner of Johnson Enterprises, a limited partnership. As provided in the limited partnership agreement, Kraft decided to leave the partnership and demanded that her capital contribution of $20,000 be returned. At this time, the partnership assets were $150,000 and liabilities to all creditors totaled $140,000. The partnership returned to Kraft her capital contribution of $20,000. What liability, if any, does Kraft have to the creditors of Johnson Enterprises?

6. Gordon is the only limited partner in a limited partnership whose general partners are Daniels and McKenna. Gordon contributed $10,000 for his limited partnership interest and loaned the partnership $7,500. Daniels and McKenna each contributed $5,000 by way of capital. After a year, the partnership is dissolved, at which time it owes $12,500 to its only creditor, Dickel, and has assets of $30,000. How should these assets be distributed?

7. Discuss whether a limited partner does or does not have the following rights or powers: (a) to assign his interest in the limited partnership, (b) to receive repayment of loans made to the partnership on a *pro rata* basis with general creditors, (c) to manage the affairs of the limited partnership, (d) to receive his share of the profits before the general partners receive their share of the profits, and (e) to dissolve the partnership if he withdraws from the partnership.

8. Dr. Vidricksen contributed $25,000 to become a limited partner in a Chevrolet car agency business with Thom, the general partner. Articles of limited partnership were drawn up, but no effort was made to comply with the state's statutory requirement of recording the certificate of limited partnership. In March 1961, Vidricksen learned that, because of the failure to file, he might not have formed a limited partnership. At this time, the business developed financial difficulties and went into bankruptcy on September 11, 1961. Eight days later, Vidricksen filed a renunciation of the business's profits. The trustee in bankruptcy now seeks to have Dr. Vidricksen adjudged a general partner for bankruptcy purposes. Decision?

9. Weil organized Diversified Properties as a limited partnership with varying degrees of ownership in several apartment complexes and other real estate located in Maryland. The parties signed a formal written agreement in July 1967, and the partnership was properly registered in the District of Columbia. Weil was the only general partner and managed the partnership's affairs until May 1, 1968. At that time, the partnership encountered cash flow problems; and, to help matters, Weil gave up both his office and his salary. At a partnership meeting held the following week, two third parties, Rubenstein and Tempchin, were selected by the limited partners to manage the partnership properties on a commission basis in accordance with a proposal that Weil had advanced earlier. Weil began working for another real estate company as a vice president, but he remained a general partner of Diversified Properties. Creditors of the partnership, therefore, turned to him with demands for payment of the partnership debts that had not been met. Weil claims that after he surrendered his office and his salary, he remained as the general partner but that his directions were ignored. He also claims that the limited partners at various times gave direct orders to Rubenstein and Tempchin as to how to manage the partnership's affairs. Accordingly, he brings this action seeking to have the limited partners declared general partners. Decision?

10. On September 23, 1971, Campbell, while driving a farm vehicle owned by Lytton, struck an automobile owned and operated by Willie Wilson. When the accident occurred, Lytton had been employing Campbell as a farmhand. Prior to the accident, Lytton, a tomato farmer, had entered into an arrangement with Florida Tomato Packers, Inc., a corporation engaged in the business of packing, selling,

wholesaling, and distributing tomatoes. According to this agreement, Lytton planted and raised the tomatoes and transported them to Florida Tomato Packers' warehouse. Florida Tomato Packers paid all of Lytton's farming bills, including land and equipment rentals, equipment repair, gasoline and oil, seeds and fertilizer, and all labor. The corporation also packed, crated, shipped, and sold the crop after it arrived at the packing house. Lytton and the corporation divided equally any profits from the sale of the tomatoes. The Wilsons sued Florida Tomato Packers for the damages caused by the accident with Campbell. Decision?

PART VIII

Corporations

CHAPTER 35

Nature and Formation

A corporation is an entity created by law that exists separately and distinctly from the individuals whose contributions of initiative, property, and control enable it to function. The corporation is the dominant form of business organization in the United States, accounting for 90 percent of the gross revenues of all business entities (see Figure 35–1). Over three million domestic corporations are currently doing business in the United States, with annual revenues and assets in the trillions of dollars. Approximately thirty million Americans own shares of stock, while more than one hundred million additional people own stock indirectly through institutional investors such as banks, insurance companies, pension funds, and investment companies. Corporations have achieved this dominance because their attributes of limited liability, free transferability of shares, and continuity have attracted great numbers of widespread investors. Moreover, the centralized management of corporations has facilitated the development of large organizations that employ great quantities of invested capital, thereby taking advantage of economies of scale.

Use of the corporation as an instrument of commercial enterprise has made possible the vast concentrations of wealth and capital that have largely transformed this country's economy from an agrarian to an industrial one. Due to its size, power, and impact, the business corporation is a key institution not only in the American economy but also in the world power structure.

In 1946, a committee of the American Bar Association, after careful study and research, submitted a draft of a Model Business Corporation Act (MBCA). The Model Act has been amended frequently since then. Its provisions do not become law until a state enacts them, but the influence of the act has been widespread: a majority of the states have adopted it in whole or in part.

In 1984, the Revised Model Business Corporation Act (RMBCA) was promulgated. The Revised Act, as amended, will be used throughout the chapters on corporations in this text and will be referred to as the Revised Act or the RMBCA. Appendix D contains selected provisions of the RMBCA, as amended.

NATURE OF CORPORATIONS

Creature of the state a corporation may be formed only by substantial compliance with a state incorporation statute

A corporation is a **creature of the state**: it may be formed only by substantial compliance with a state incorporation statute. To understand corporations, it is helpful to examine the various types of corporations and their common attributes. We will discuss both of these topics in this section.

FIGURE 35–1 Business Entities

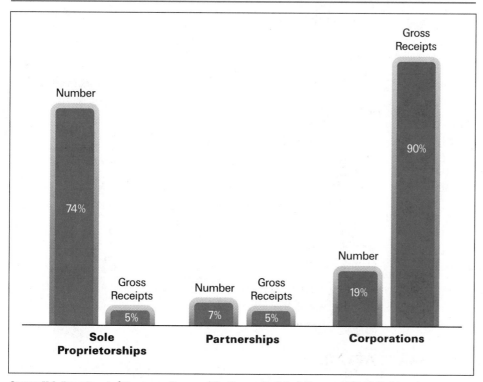

Source: U.S. Department of Commerce, Bureau of the Census, Statistical Abstract of the United States (Washington, D.C.: U.S. Government Printing Office, 1996).

MANAGERIAL INSIGHT

Why Delaware?

If you owned a business and wanted to operate it as a corporation, in what state would you incorporate? Wouldn't you choose your home state?

Then why are the following companies incorporated in Delaware, even though their headquarters are elsewhere?

- McDonald's (Oak Brook, Illinois)
- Wal-Mart (Bentonville, Arkansas)
- Microsoft (Redmond, Washington)
- Ford (Dearborn, Michigan)

Since World War I, Delaware has been the favorite state of incorporation, and many Fortune 500 companies are its citizens. (Many actually reincorporated there.) This situation did not come about by accident. Corporations are chartered by the states, not by the federal government,

and laws of incorporation vary significantly from state to state. New Jersey, for example, was the favorite domicile of large corporations early in the 20th century, but later fell behind Delaware, partly because it failed to update its corporation laws often enough.

Delaware purposely has made itself attractive to corporations, and the reason is money. Franchise taxes paid by Delaware corporations are a very significant source of income for that small state. The preamble to the 1963 revision of the Delaware General Corporation Law plainly acknowledges this fact:

. . . the favorable climate which the State of Delaware has traditionally provided for corporations has been a leading source of revenue for the State;

. . . the General Assembly of the State of Delaware declares it to be the public policy of the State to maintain a favorable business climate and to encourage corporations to make Delaware their domicile. . . .

Delaware has long offered an incorporation law that favors management. And over the years Delaware's General Assembly has revised and amended the Delaware General Corporation Law to keep it attractive to corporate managements. (Remember that laws of incorporation also should protect the rights of shareholders and creditors.) In addition, the Delaware law is

continued

considered to be both clear and up to date.

Delaware's courts, which have been characterized as "a judiciary of corporate specialists," are another significant attraction. Delaware judges have created a large body of case law that is "well-settled law with unique predictability" and that allows corporations to be flexible in their operations.

Specifically, a few of the advantages of Delaware incorporation are as follows:

- incorporating is quick and easy;
- fees and taxes are moderate;
- the only specification the state sets for purposes of incorporation is that they be lawful;
- there is no minimum capital requirement, and shares may be issued for cash, property, or services;
- provisions allow a single incorporator and a single director;
- directors have no residence requirements, and directors' and shareholders' meetings expressly may be held outside of Delaware;
- directors and officers are indemnified more liberally than in other states;
- the charter may limit or eliminate the personal liability of directors to the corporation or its shareholders;
- there are restrictions on shareholders' derivative actions;
- voting trusts are authorized; and
- there are broad provisions for mergers and consolidations.

Today, other states share many of Delaware's favorable provisions, but none has had so many for so long. And Delaware's great body of legal precedents has helped to give the state a head start that is hard to overcome.

Sources: William L. Cary and Melvin Aron Eisenberg: *Case and Materials on Corporations*, 7th ed., 1988, 125–132; Alfred F. Conard, Robert L. Knauss, and Stanley Siegel, *Enterprise Organization*, 1987, 527; Harry G. Henn and John R. Alexander, *Laws of Corporations*, 1983, 186–201; and Detlev F. Vagts, *Basic Corporation Law*, 1989, 77.

CORPORATE ATTRIBUTES

These are the principal attributes of a corporation: (1) it is a legal entity; (2) it provides limited liability to its shareholders; (3) its shares of stock are freely transferable; (4) its existence may be perpetual; (5) its management is centralized; and it is considered, for some purposes, (6) a person and (7) a citizen.

Legal Entity

Legal entity a corporation is an entity apart from its shareholders, with entirely distinct rights and liabilities

A corporation is a **legal entity** separate from its shareholders, with rights and liabilities entirely distinct from theirs. It may sue or be sued by, as well as contract with, any other party, including any one of its shareholders. A transfer of stock in the corporation from one individual to another has no effect on the legal existence of the corporation. Title to corporate property belongs not to the shareholders but to the corporation. Even where a single individual owns all of the stock of the corporation, the shareholder and the corporation have distinct existences.

Limited Liability

Limited liability a shareholder's liability is limited to the amount invested in the business enterprise

A corporation is a legal entity and is therefore liable out of its own assets for its debts. Generally, the shareholders have **limited liability** for the corporation's debts—their liability does not extend beyond the amount of their investment—although later in this chapter we will discuss certain circumstances under which a shareholder may be personally liable.

Free Transferability of Corporate Shares

Free transferability unless otherwise specified in the charter, corporate shares are freely transferable

In the absence of contractual restrictions, shares in a corporation may be freely transferred by sale, gift, or pledge. The ability to transfer shares is a valuable right and may enhance their market value. Transfers of shares of stock (discussed in Chapter 36) are governed by Article 8 of the Uniform Commercial Code, Investment Securities.

Perpetual Existence

A corporation has **perpetual existence** unless otherwise stated in its articles of incorporation. Consequently, the death, withdrawal, or addition of a shareholder, director, or officer does not terminate its existence.

Centralized Management

The shareholders of a corporation elect a board of directors that manages the business affairs of the corporation. The board must then appoint officers to run the day-to-day operations of the business. Because neither the directors nor the officers (collectively referred to as "management") need be shareholders, it is entirely possible, and in large corporations quite typical, for the ownership of the corporation to be separate from its management. We will discuss the management structure of corporations in Chapter 37.

As a Person

Whether a corporation is a "person" within the meaning of a constitution or statute is a matter of construction based on the intent of the lawmakers in using the word. For example, a corporation is considered a person within the provisions in the Fifth and Fourteenth Amendments to the U.S. Constitution that no "person" shall be "deprived of life, liberty, or property, without due process of law" and in the Fourteenth Amendment provision that no state shall "deny to any person within its jurisdiction the equal protection of the laws." A corporation also enjoys the right of a person to be secure against unreasonable searches and seizures, as provided for in the Fourth Amendment. On the other hand, a corporation is not considered to be a person within the Fifth Amendment clause that protects a "person" against self-incrimination.

As a Citizen

A corporation is considered a citizen for some purposes but not for others. For instance, a corporation is not a citizen as the term is used in the Fourteenth Amendment, which provides, "No state shall make or enforce any law which shall abridge the privileges or immunities of citizens of the United States."

A corporation is, however, regarded as a citizen of the state of its incorporation and of the state in which it has its principal office for the purpose of determining whether diversity of citizenship exists between the parties to a lawsuit, so as to provide a basis for federal court jurisdiction.

Corporations differ from partnerships because of these and other attributes. Figure 35–2 further outlines the differences and similarities of general partnerships, limited partnerships, corporations, and limited liability companies.

CLASSIFICATION OF CORPORATIONS

Corporations may be classified as public or private, profit or nonprofit, domestic or foreign, publicly held or closely held, and professional. As you will see, these classifications are not mutually exclusive. For example, a corporation may be a closely held, professional, private, profit, domestic corporation.

Public or Private

A **public corporation** is one that is created to administer a unit of local civil government, such as a county, city, town, village, school district, or park district,

FIGURE 35–2 General Partnership, Limited Partnership, Corporation, and Limited Liability Company

	General Partnership	Limited Partnership	Public Corporation	Close Corporation	Limited Liability Company
Transferability	Financial interest may be assigned; membership requires consent of all partners	Financial interest may be assigned, and assignee may become limited partner if all partners consent	Freely transferable	Freely transferable unless shareholders agree otherwise	Financial interest may be assigned; membership requires consent of all members
Liability	Partners have unlimited liability	General partners have unlimited liability; limited partners have limited liability	Shareholders have limited liability	Shareholders have limited liability	All members have limited liability
Control	By all partners	By general partners, not limited partners	By board of directors elected by shareholders	By board of directors elected by shareholders	By all members
Continuity	Dissolved by death, bankruptcy, or withdrawal of partner	Dissolved by death, bankruptcy, or withdrawal of general partner	Unaffected by death, bankruptcy, or withdrawal of shareholder	Unaffected by death, bankruptcy, or withdrawal of shareholder	Dissolved by death, bankruptcy, or withdrawal of member
Taxation	Only partners taxed	Only partners taxed	Corporation and shareholders taxed	Corporation taxed unless Subchapter S applies; shareholders taxed	Only members taxed

Private corporation one founded by and composed of private persons for private purposes and having no governmental duties

Profit corporation one founded for the purpose of operating a business for profit

Nonprofit corporation one whose profits must be used exclusively for the charitable, educational, or scientific purpose for which it was formed

Domestic corporation corporation created under the laws of a given state

Foreign corporation corporation created under the laws of any other state, government, or country; it must obtain a certificate of authority from each state in which it does intrastate business

or one created by the United States to conduct public business, such as the Tennessee Valley Authority or the Federal Deposit Insurance Corporation. A public corporation is usually created by specific legislation, which determines the corporation's purpose and powers. Many public corporations are also referred to as municipal corporations.

A **private corporation** is founded by and composed of private persons for private purposes and has no governmental duties. A private corporation may be for profit or nonprofit.

Profit or Nonprofit

A **profit corporation** is one founded for the purpose of operating a business for profit from which payments are made to the corporation's shareholders in the form of dividends.

Although a **nonprofit** (or not-for-profit) **corporation** may make a profit, the profit may not be distributed to its members, directors, or officers but must be used exclusively for the charitable, educational, or scientific purpose for which the corporation was organized. Most states have special incorporation statutes governing nonprofit corporations, most of which are patterned after the Model Nonprofit Corporation Act first published in 1952 and most recently revised in 1987.

Domestic or Foreign

A corporation is a **domestic corporation** in the state in which it is incorporated. It is a **foreign corporation** in every other state or jurisdiction. A corporation may not do business, except for acts in interstate commerce, in a state other than the state of its incorporation without the permission and authorization of the other state. Every state, however, provides for the issuance of certificates of authority, which allow foreign corporations to do business within its borders, and for the taxation of such foreign businesses. Obtaining a certificate (or "qualifying") usually involves filing certain information with the secretary of state, paying prescribed fees, and designating a resident agent. Conduct typically requiring a certificate of authority includes maintaining an office to conduct local intrastate business, selling personal property not in interstate commerce, entering into contracts relating to local business or sales, and owning or using real estate for general corporate purposes. A single agreement or isolated transaction within a state does not constitute doing business.

A foreign corporation that transacts business without having first qualified may be subject to a number of penalties. Most statutes provide that an unlicensed foreign corporation doing business in the state shall not be entitled to maintain a suit in a state court until it has obtained a certificate of authority. However, the failure to obtain a certificate of authority to transact business in the state does not impair the validity of a contract entered into by the corporation and does not prevent it from defending any action or proceeding brought against it in the state. In addition, many states impose fines on corporations that do not obtain certificates, and a few states also impose fines on the corporation's officers and directors, as well as holding them personally liable on contracts made within the state.

TILLER CONSTRUCTION CORP. v. NADLER Court of Appeals of Maryland, 1994, 334 Md. 1, 637 A.2d 1183

FACTS Ronald Nadler was a resident of Maryland and the chief executive officer of Glenmar Cinestate, Inc., a Maryland corporation, as well as its principal, if not only, stockholder. Glenmar leased certain space in the Westridge Square Shopping Center, located in Frederick, Maryland, and in Cranberry Mall, located in Westminster, Maryland. Tiller Construction Corporation and Nadler entered into two contracts for the construction of movie theaters at these locations, one calling for Tiller to do "the work" for Nadler at Westridge for $637,000, and the other for Tiller to do "the work" for Nadler at Cranberry for $688,800. Ronald Nadler requested that Tiller send all bills to Glenmar, the lessee at both shopping malls, but agreed to be personally liable to Tiller for the payment of both contracts.

At the time of the suit, there was a net balance due for the Cranberry project in the amount of $229,799.46, and on the Westridge project for the sum of $264,273.85, which Nadler refused to pay, even though he had approved all work and the work had been performed in a timely, good, and workmanlike manner. Tiller Construction Corporation sued Ronald Nadler and Glenmar Cinestate, Inc., for breach of contract in the amounts due under the Cranberry and Westridge contracts.

Nadler submitted a motion to dismiss based on § 7–301 of the Maryland's business corporation statute.

This section prohibits foreign corporations that conduct intrastate business in Maryland but fail to register or qualify under Maryland law from maintaining a suit in Maryland courts. Nadler asserted that Tiller was a New York Corporation that has never qualified to transact business in the state of Maryland. Tiller conceded that the corporation had not qualified to do business in Maryland but argued that Tiller was not required to qualify because its activities did not constitute, in the contemplation of the statute, doing business in the state since Tiller just had occasional business in Maryland. Nadler countered by asserting that the two separate contracts to build movie theaters, each "in excess of one-half million dollars," involved the employment of a substantial number of subcontractors (most of whom were Maryland subcontractors), the maintaining of a supervisor on each job, and the opening of Maryland bank accounts. The trial court granted Nadler's motion to dismiss.

DECISION Judgment affirmed.

OPINION In *Snavely, Inc. v. Wheeler*, the Court of Special Appeals made a thorough analysis of the principles that have been applied to determine when a foreign corporation is doing intrastate business in Maryland. The court concluded that a foreign corporation is doing business within a state when it transacts some substantial part of its ordinary business in that

continued

state. Where, however, the corporation does not engage in significant business activity in Maryland, § 7–301 has been interpreted to permit a corporation to maintain an action in the courts of this state even though it has neither registered nor qualified.

Whether the acts engaged in by a foreign corporation are sufficient to constitute "doing business" must be determined from the facts of each case, with particular emphasis on the nature and extent of the business and activities occurring in the state. Among the factors to be considered are: (1) whether the foreign corporation pays state taxes; (2) whether it maintains property, an office, telephone listings, employees, agents, inventory, research and development facilities, advertising and bank accounts in the state; (3) whether it makes contracts in the state; and (4) whether its management functions in the state are pervasive.

The trial court looked at the facts of this case in the light of these *Snavely* factors. The court found that all inventory was bought and paid for locally and that Tiller had paid sales tax in Maryland. The court also found that, although there was no formal office in the state, Tiller leased a motel room for a considerable period of time, posted a sign at the job site, and maintained telephones listed in information. In addition, Tiller engaged in fairly pervasive management functions, and the value of the projects comprised a substantial part of Tiller's revenues during the period. From this the court properly determined that Tiller was doing business in Maryland by assessing its activities pursuant to the factors noted in our appellate opinions and concluding that Tiller had indeed transacted some substantial part of its ordinary business in Maryland.

INTERPRETATION A foreign corporation must obtain a certificate of authority in every state in which it conducts intrastate business.

Publicly Held or Closely Held

Publicly held corporation
corporation whose shares are owned by a large number of people and are widely traded

A **publicly held corporation** is one whose shares are owned by a large number of people and are widely traded. There is no accepted minimum number of shareholders, but any corporation required to register under the Federal Securities and Exchange Act of 1934 is considered to be publicly held. In addition, corporations that have issued securities subject to a registered public distribution under the Federal Securities Act of 1933 are also usually considered publicly held. (The federal securities laws are discussed in Chapter 42.)

Closely held corporation
corporation that is owned by few shareholders and whose shares are not actively traded

A **closely held corporation** is one whose outstanding shares of stock are held by a small number of persons, frequently relatives or friends. In most closely held corporations, the shareholders are active in the management and control of the business. Accordingly, the shareholders, concerned about the identities of their fellow shareholders, frequently restrict the transfer of shares in order to prevent "outsiders" from obtaining the stock. Although a vast majority of corporations in the United States are closely held, they account for only a small fraction of corporate revenues and assets.

In most states, closely held corporations are subject to the general incorporation statute that governs all corporations. The Revised Act includes a number of liberalizing provisions for closely held corporations. In addition, some states have enacted special legislation to accommodate the needs of closely held corporations, and a Statutory Close Corporation Supplement to the Model and Revised Acts (the Supplement) has been promulgated.

The Supplement applies only to an eligible corporation (one having fewer than fifty shareholders) that elects statutory close corporation status. A corporation may voluntarily terminate statutory close corporation status. We will discuss other provisions of the Supplement in this and other chapters. See the Managerial Insight.

Subchapter S Corporation

Subchapter S corporation
eligible corporation electing to be taxed as a partnership under the Internal Revenue Code

Subchapter S of the Internal Revenue Code permits a **corporation** meeting specified requirements to elect to be taxed essentially as though it were a partnership.

Under subchapter S, a corporation's income is taxed only once at the individual shareholder level.

MANAGERIAL INSIGHT

Re-Defining Close Corporations

Courts, Legislatures Move to Protect Minority Shareholders

The ineffectiveness of traditional corporate law principles in protecting minority shareholders in closely-held, or "close," corporations has resulted in increased judicial and legislative intervention to prohibit attempts by majority shareholders to squeeze out minority shareholders.

Increasingly, courts and legislatures are recognizing that the inherent relationship among shareholders of a close corporation unmistakably resembles a partnership, and, consequently, they are applying partnership principles to settle shareholder disputes.

Generally, a close corporation has a relatively small number of shareholders. The corporation's shares are not traded publicly and are rarely bought and sold. In many cases, the shareholders of the corporation are also its directors, officers and employees.

The active participation of all or substantially all shareholders in the management of the close corporation has been viewed as evidence of the shareholders' intent to establish a partnership relationship. Therefore, close corporations are sometimes referred to as "chartered partnerships" or "incorporated partnerships."

Because of the unusual and intimate relationship between shareholders and the actual operations of the close corporation, many courts have recognized that control of this entity is peculiarly susceptible to misuse or abuse by majority shareholders, including failure to declare dividends, unfair distribution of business profits to majority shareholders in the form of salaries or bonuses, and discharge of minority shareholders as corporate employees.

To avoid such misuse or abuse, courts have held shareholders of a close corporation to owe each other the same heightened fiduciary duty that exists between partners, a duty of utmost good faith and loyalty. *Crosby v. Bean*, 47 Ohio St. 3d 105 (1989); *Hagshenas v. Gaylord*, 557 N.E.2d 316 (Ill.App. 1990); *Donahue v. Rodd Electrotype Co.*, 328 N.E.2d 505 (Mass. 1975).

Many states have adopted laws to codify the partnership features that apply to close corporations. *See* Arizona Rev. Stat. Ann., Sec. 10-205; New York Bus. Corp. Law, Sec. 620. Other states have adopted statutes that specifically permit the use of close corporations to take advantage of the limited liability, tax benefits and perpetual existence features of a corporation while permitting the parties to set forth the terms of their business relationship in an agreement similar to those describing partnerships. *See* Ohio Revised Code Sec. 1701.591(F); Delaware Code Annotated, Title 8, Sec. 354.

Limiting Rights to Control

The treatment of close corporations as "incorporated partnerships" has resulted in other developments. For example, while majority shareholders frequently assume that their actions are justifiable if they have a legitimate business purpose, since they have the right to control the corporation, their heightened partner-like fiduciary duty in close corporations actually limits their rights to control.

In addition, some courts have determined that majority shareholders should not be permitted to exercise powers arbitrarily or without regard to the legitimate expectations of minority shareholders.

Accordingly, the principle of good faith and fair dealing among shareholders of a close corporation may override traditional corporate principles of majority control. Principles of fiduciary duty are even being applied to close corporations in the absence of any formal agreement among shareholders. *Hagshenas, supra; Blackwell v. Nixon*, 1991 Del. Ch. Lexis 150 (Del. Ch. 1991).

Generally, a shareholder seeking to recover for breach of fiduciary duty by a director or controlling shareholder must bring a derivative action on behalf of the corporation against the director or shareholder. Recently, however, courts have recognized that, where a majority shareholder in a close corporation breaches his or her heightened fiduciary duty to a minority shareholder who is individually harmed, the minority shareholder may bring a direct, rather than derivative, action against the majority shareholder.

Courts are increasingly willing to allow minority shareholders to sue majority shareholders directly because any derivative recoveries would remain under the control of the majority shareholders. In addition, instead of applying traditional remedies, such as judicial dissolution of the corporation, to resolve shareholder disputes, courts may order a close corporation to purchase the shares of a minority shareholder at fair value. At least two states have enacted statutes that contain such buy-out provisions. *See* Minnesota Statutes

continued

Ann., Sec. 302A.751(2); New Jersey Statutes, Sec. 14A: 12-7(c)(8).

The unusual relationship among shareholders in a close corporation has resulted in the development of governing principles that should be considered in the formation of such a business entity.

It is important that a close corporation agreement be used to clarify the relationship of the shareholders. The use of outside or disinterested directors also may serve to avoid disputes between majority and minority shareholders and the manipulative use of corporate control by majority shareholders to unfairly deprive minority shareholders of the advantages and opportunities to which they are entitled.

Source: Ivery D. Foreman, *ABA Journal*, March 1992. Reprinted with permission from the March 1992 issue of the *ABA Journal*, published by the American Bar Association.

Professional Corporations

Professional corporation
corporate form under which duly licensed individuals may practice their professions

All of the states have **professional** association or **corporation** statutes that permit duly licensed professionals to practice in the corporate form. Some statutes apply to all professions licensed to practice within the state, whereas others apply only to specified professions. There is a Model Professional Corporation Supplement to the MBCA.

FORMATION OF A CORPORATION

The formation of a corporation under a general incorporation statute requires action by various groups, individuals, and state officials.

ORGANIZING THE CORPORATION

The procedure to organize a corporation begins with the promotion of the proposed corporation by its organizers, also known as promoters, who procure offers by interested persons, known as subscribers, to buy stock in the corporation, once created, and who also prepare the necessary incorporation papers. The incorporators then execute the articles of incorporation and file them with the secretary of state, who issues the charter or certificate of incorporation. Finally, an organizational meeting is held.

Promoters

Promoter person who takes the preliminary steps to organize a corporation

A **promoter** is a person who takes the preliminary steps to organize a corporation. The promoter arranges for the capital and financing of the corporation; assembles the necessary assets, equipment, licenses, personnel, leases, and services; and attends to the actual legal formation of the corporation. On incorporation, the promoter's organizational task is finished.

Promoters' contracts
promoters remain liable on preincorporation contracts made in the name of the corporation unless the contract provides otherwise or unless a novation is effected

Promoters' Contracts In addition to procuring subscriptions and preparing the incorporation papers, promoters often enter into contracts in anticipation of the creation of the corporation. The contracts may be ordinary agreements necessary for the eventual operation of the business, such as leases, purchase orders, employment contracts, sales contracts, or franchises. If the promoter executes these contracts in her own name and there is no further action, the promoter is liable on such contracts; the corporation, when created, is not liable. Moreover, a preincorporation contract made by a promoter in the name of the corporation and on its behalf does not bind the corporation. Before its formation, a corporation has no capacity to enter into contracts or to employ agents or representatives. After its formation, it is not liable at common law on any prior contract, even one made in its name, unless it adopts the contract expressly, impliedly, or by knowingly accepting benefits under it.

A promoter who enters into a preincorporation contract in the name of the corporation usually remains liable on that contract even if the corporation adopts it. This liability results from the rule of agency law stating that a principal, in order to be able to ratify a contract, must be in existence when the contract is made. A promoter will be relieved of liability, however, if the contract itself provides that adoption shall terminate the promoter's liability or if the promoter, the third party, and the corporation enter into a novation substituting the corporation for the promoter.

Figure 35–3 summarizes the liability of the promoter and the corporation for preincorporation contracts.

COOPERS & LYBRAND v. FOX Colorado Court of Appeals, Division IV, 1988, 758 P.2d 683

FACTS Fox met with a representative of Coopers & Lybrand (C&L), a national accounting firm, to obtain accounting services. Fox informed C&L that he was acting on behalf of a corporation he was in the process of forming, to be called "G. Fox and Partners, Inc." C&L accepted the engagement with the knowledge that the corporation was not yet in existence. C&L completed the assignment and billed Fox for a reasonable fee of $10,827. When neither Fox nor G. Fox and Partners, Inc., paid, C&L sued Fox for breach of express and implied contracts based on a theory of promoter liability. Fox insisted that he was acting as an agent for the future corporation. The trial court ruled for Fox after determining that there was no agreement that would obligate Fox individually to pay the fee. C&L appealed.

DECISION Judgment for Coopers & Lybrand.

OPINION We reject Fox's argument that he was acting solely as an agent for the yet unformed corporation. A person may not act as an agent of a nonexistent principal. Rather, Fox is squarely within the definition of a promoter. As a general rule, promoters are personally liable for the contracts they make on behalf of a corporation to be formed. A well-recognized exception is that if the contracting party knows the corporation is not in existence but nevertheless agrees to look solely to the corporation, the promoter incurs no liability. In the absence of an express agreement, an agreement may be implied by circumstances making it reasonably certain that the parties intended to look only to the corporation. Here, the trial court found that there was no agreement, either express or implied, regarding Fox's liability. Thus, in the absence of any agreement releasing him from liability, Fox is personally liable.

INTERPRETATION A promoter is personally liable for the contracts he makes on behalf of a future corporation unless there is an agreement releasing him from liability.

Promoters' Fiduciary Duty The promoters of a corporation have a fiduciary relationship among themselves as well as with the corporation, its subscribers, and its initial shareholders. This duty requires good faith, fair dealing, and full disclosure to an independent board of directors. If an independent board has not been elected, full disclosure must be made to all shareholders. Accordingly, the promoters are under a duty to account for any secret profit they realize. Failure to disclose may also violate federal or state securities laws.

Promoters' fiduciary duty promoters owe a fiduciary duty among themselves and to the corporation, its subscribers, and its initial shareholders

Subscribers

A *preincorporation subscription* is an offer to purchase capital stock in a corporation yet to be formed. The offeror is called a **subscriber**. Courts traditionally have viewed subscriptions in one of two ways. The majority regards a subscription as a continuing offer to purchase stock from a nonexisting entity incapable of accepting the offer until it exists. Under this view, a subscription

Subscriber person who agrees to purchase initial stock in a corporation

FIGURE 35–3 Promoters' Preincorporation Contracts

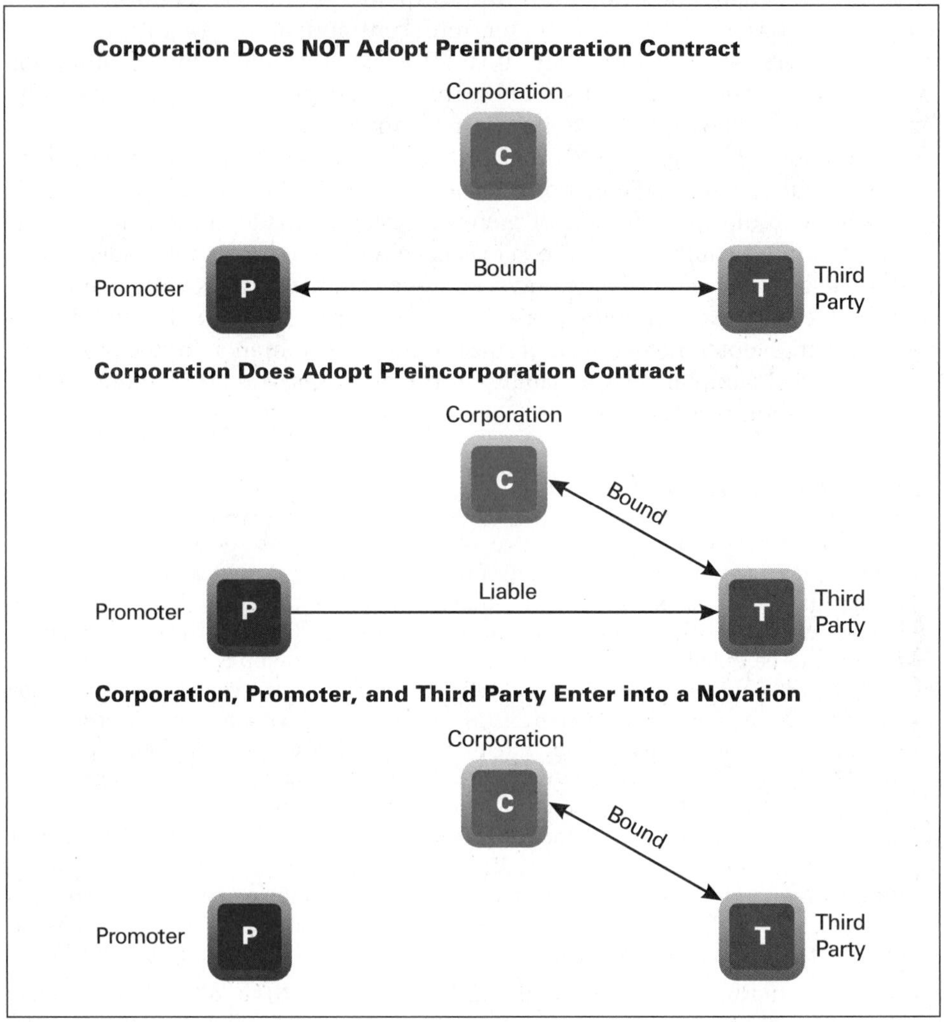

Corporation Does NOT Adopt Preincorporation Contract

Corporation

Promoter   P ⟵ Bound ⟶ T Third Party

Corporation Does Adopt Preincorporation Contract

Corporation

C ⟷ Bound ⟶ T

Promoter   P ⟶ Liable ⟶ T Third Party

Corporation, Promoter, and Third Party Enter into a Novation

Corporation

C ⟷ Bound ⟶ T

Promoter   P   T Third Party

may be revoked at any time prior to its acceptance. By comparison, a minority of jurisdictions treat a subscription as a contract among the various subscribers, making the subscription irrevocable except with all of the subscribers' consent. Modern incorporation statutes have adopted an intermediate position. For example, the Revised Act provides that a preincorporation subscription is irrevocable for six months, unless the subscription agreement provides a different period or all of the subscribers consent to the revocation. If the corporation accepts the subscription during the period of irrevocability, the subscription becomes a contract binding on both the subscriber and the corporation.

FORMALITIES OF INCORPORATION

Although the procedure involved in organizing a corporation varies somewhat from state to state, typically the incorporators execute and deliver articles of incorporation to the secretary of state or to another designated official. The Revised Act provides that after incorporation, the board of directors named in the articles of incorporation shall hold an organizational meeting for the purpose of adopting bylaws, appointing officers, and carrying on any other business brought before the meeting. After completion of these organizational details, the corporation's business and affairs are managed by its board of directors and by its officers.

Selection of Name

Most general incorporation laws require that the name contain a word or words that clearly designate the organization as a corporation, such as "corporation," "company," "incorporated," "limited," "Corp.," "Co.," "Inc.," or "Ltd." A corporate name must be distinguishable from the name of any domestic corporation or any foreign corporation authorized to do business within the state.

Selection of name the name must clearly designate the entity as a corporation

Incorporators

The **incorporators** are the persons who sign the articles of incorporation filed in the state of incorporation with the secretary of state. Although they perform a necessary function, their services as incorporators are perfunctory and short-lived, ending with the organizational meeting following incorporation. Furthermore, modern statutes have greatly relaxed the qualifications of incorporators and have also reduced the number required. The Revised Act, for example, provides that only one person need act as the incorporator, though more may do so. Under the Revised Act, "person" includes individuals and entities; "entities," in turn, include domestic and foreign corporations, not-for-profit corporations, profit and not-for-profit unincorporated associations, business trusts, estates, partnerships, and trusts.

Incorporators the persons who sign the articles of incorporation

Articles of Incorporation

The **articles of incorporation** or charter is generally a rather simple document that under the Revised Act *must* include the name of the corporation, the number of authorized shares, the street address of the registered office and the name of the registered agent, and the name and address of each incorporator. The Revised Act also permits the charter to include optional information such as the identities of the corporation's initial directors; corporate purposes; management of internal affairs; powers of the corporation; par value of shares; and any provision required or permitted to be set forth in the bylaws.

In order to form a corporation, the charter, once drawn up, must be executed and filed with the secretary of state. The charter then becomes the basic governing document of the corporation, so long as its provisions are consistent with state and federal law. Figure 35–4 shows a sample charter.

Articles of incorporation the charter or basic organizational document of a corporation

Organizational Meeting

As previously mentioned, the Revised Act requires that an **organizational meeting** be held to adopt the new corporation's bylaws, appoint officers, and carry on any other business brought before it. If the articles do not name the corporation's initial directors, the incorporators hold the organizational meeting to elect directors; and either the incorporators or the directors then complete the organization of the corporation.

Organizational meeting the first meeting, held to adopt the bylaws and appoint officers

Bylaws

The **bylaws** are the rules and regulations that govern the internal management of a corporation. Because bylaws are necessary to the organization of the

Bylaws rules and regulations governing a corporation's internal management

corporation, their adoption is one of the first items of business at the organizational meeting held promptly after incorporation. The bylaws may contain any provision for managing the business and regulating the affairs of the corporation that is not inconsistent with law or the articles of incorporation. Under the Revised Act, the shareholders may amend or repeal the bylaws, which, in contrast to the certificate of incorporation embodying the articles of incorporation, do not have to be publicly filed. In addition, the board of directors also may amend or repeal the bylaws, unless the articles of incorporation or other sections of the RMBCA reserve that power exclusively to the shareholders in whole or in part.

FIGURE 35–4 Sample Articles of Incorporation

Articles of Incorporation of [Corporate Name]

The undersigned, acting as incorporator(s) of a corporation under the _____ Business Corporation Act, adopt(s) the following Articles of Incorporation for such corporation:

First: The name of the corporation is _____

_____

Second: The period of its duration is _____

_____

Third: The purpose or purposes for which the corporation is organized are:_____

_____

Fourth: The aggregate number of shares which the corporation shall have authority to issue is _____

_____

Fifth: Provisions granting preemptive rights are: _____

Sixth: Provisions for the regulation of the internal affairs of the corporation are: _____

Seventh: The address of the initial registered office of the corporation is _____
and the name of its initial registered agent at such address is _____

Eighth: The number of directors constituting the initial board of directors of the corporation is _____, and the names and addresses of the persons who are to serve as directors until the first annual meeting of shareholders or until their successors are elected and shall qualify are:

Name	**Address**
_____	_____
_____	_____
_____	_____

Ninth: The name and address of each incorporator is:

Name	**Address**
_____	_____
_____	_____
_____	_____

Dated _____, 19_____.   _____

_____

_____

Incorporator(s)

Source: Reprinted with permission from Henn & Alexander, *Corporations*, 3rd ed. Copyright © 1983 by West Publishing Company.

The Statutory Close Corporation Supplement permits close corporations to avoid adopting bylaws by including, either in a shareholder agreement or in the articles of incorporation, all the information necessary to corporate bylaws.

RECOGNITION OR DISREGARD OF CORPORATENESS

Business associates choose to incorporate to obtain one or more of the corporate attributes, primarily limited liability and perpetual existence. Because a corporation is a creature of the state, such attributes are recognized when the enterprise complies with the state's requirements for incorporation. Although the formal procedures are relatively simple, errors or omissions sometimes occur. In some cases the mistakes may be trivial, such as incorrectly stating an incorporator's address in the charter; in other instances the error may be more significant, such as a complete failure to file the articles of incorporation. The consequences of procedural noncompliance depend on the seriousness of the error. Conversely, even when a corporation has been formed in strict compliance with the incorporation statute, a court may disregard the corporateness of the enterprise if justice requires.

DEFECTIVE INCORPORATION

Although modern corporation statutes have greatly simplified incorporation procedures, defective incorporations do occur. The possible consequences of a defective incorporation include the following: (1) the state brings an action against the association for involuntary dissolution; (2) the associates are held personally liable to a third party; (3) the association asserts that it is not liable on an obligation; or (4) a third party asserts that it is not liable to the association. Corporate statutes addressing this issue have taken an approach considerably different from that of the common law.

Common Law Approach
Under the common law, a defectively formed corporation was, under certain circumstances, accorded corporate attributes. The courts developed a set of doctrines granting corporateness to *de jure* (of right) corporations, *de facto* (of fact) corporations, and corporations by estoppel, but denying corporateness to corporations that were too defectively formed.

Corporation de Jure A **corporation** *de jure* is one that has been formed in substantial compliance with the incorporation statute and the required organizational procedure. Once a *de jure* corporation is formed, its existence may not be challenged by anyone, even the state in a direct proceeding for this purpose.

Corporation de Facto Although it fails to comply in some way with the incorporation statute and, hence, is not *de jure*, a **corporation** *de facto* is nevertheless recognized for most purposes as a corporation. A failure to form a *de jure* corporation may result in the formation of a *de facto* corporation if the following requirements are met: (1) the existence of a general corporation statute, (2) a bona fide attempt to comply with that law in organizing a corporation under the statute, and (3) the actual exercise of corporate power by conducting business in the belief that a corporation has been formed. The

Corporation *de jure*
(dee jur'·ee) one that has been formed in substantial compliance with the incorporation statute and having all corporate attributes

Corporation *de facto* *(di fak'·to)* one not formed in compliance with the statute but recognized for most purposes as a corporation

existence of a *de facto* corporation can be challenged only by the state in an action of *quo warranto* ("by what right").

Corporation by estoppel prevents a person from raising the question of a corporation's existence

Corporation by Estoppel   The doctrine of **corporation by estoppel** is distinct from that of corporation *de facto*. Estoppel does not create a corporation. It operates only to prevent a person or persons under the facts and circumstances of a particular case from questioning a corporation's existence or its capacity to act or to own property. Corporation by estoppel requires a holding out by a purported corporation or its associates and reliance by a third party. In addition, application of the doctrine depends on equitable considerations. A person who has dealt with a defectively organized corporation may be precluded or estopped from denying its corporate existence if the necessary elements of holding out and reliance are present. The doctrine can be applied not only to third parties but also to the purported corporation and to the associates who held themselves out as a corporation.

Defective corporation the associates are denied the benefits of incorporation

Defective Corporation   If the associates who purported to form a corporation fail to comply with the requirements of the incorporation statute to such an extent that neither a *de jure* nor a *de facto* corporation is formed and the circumstances do not justify applying the corporation by estoppel doctrine, the courts generally deny the associates the benefits of incorporation. Some or all of the associates are then held unlimitedly liable for the obligations of the business.

Statutory Approach

While the common law approach to defective incorporation is cumbersome in both theory and application, under the Revised Act **(RMBCA)**, the *filing* of the articles of incorporation by the secretary of state is conclusive proof that the incorporators have satisfied all conditions precedent to incorporation, except in a proceeding brought by the state. The Revised Act imposes liability only on persons who, in purporting to act as or on behalf of a corporation, *knew that there was no incorporation.*

RMBCA liability is imposed only on persons who act on behalf of a defectively formed corporation knowing that there was no incorporation

MBCA unlimited personal liability is imposed on all persons who act on behalf of a defectively formed corporation

The Model Act **(MBCA)** and many states provide that a "certificate of incorporation shall be conclusive evidence that all conditions precedent required to be performed by the incorporators have been complied with and that the corporation has been incorporated under this Act, except as against this state." With respect to the attribute of limited liability, the Model Act provides that all persons who assume to act as a corporation without authority to do so shall have joint and several unlimited liability for all debts and liabilities incurred or arising as a result of their so acting.

Consider two illustrations: First, Smith had been shown executed articles of incorporation some months before he invested in the corporation and became an officer and director. He was also told by the corporation's attorney that the articles had been filed; however, because of confusion in the attorney's office, they had not in fact been filed. Under the Revised Act and many court decisions, Smith would not be held liable for the obligations of the defective corporation. Second, knowing that no corporation has been formed because no attempt has been made to file articles of incorporation, Jones represents that a corporation exists and enters into a contract in the corporate name. Jones would be held liable for the obligations of the defective corporation under the Model Act, the Revised Act, and most court decisions involving similar situations.

Figure 35–5 illustrates the approach to defective incorporation taken by the Model Act and the Revised Act.

FIGURE 35–5 Recognition of Corporate Attributes: Statutory Approach

	Nonrecognition of Corporateness	Recognition of Corporateness
RMBCA Approach	**No Filing of Articles of Incorporation** No corporate attributes Joint and several liability for those who act knowing that there was no incorporation	**Filing of Articles of Incorporation** Corporate attributes Limited liability Insulation from collateral suits
MBCA Approach	**No Certificate Issued** No corporate attributes Joint and several liability for all who assume to act as a corporation	**Certificate Issued** Corporate attributes Limited liability Insulation from collateral suits

HARRIS v. LOONEY Court of Appeals of Arkansas, 1993, 43 Ark.App. 127, 862 S.W.2d 282

FACTS On February 1, 1988, Robert L. Harris sold his business and its assets to J & R Construction. Joe Alexander, one of three J & R incorporators, signed the contract on behalf of J & R Construction with Harris. On the same day, the incorporators (Joe Alexander, Avanell Looney, and Rita Alexander) signed the articles of incorporation for J & R Construction, but they were not filed with the secretary of state's office until February 3, 1988. In 1991, J & R Construction defaulted on its contract and promissory note, and Harris sued the three incorporators of J & R Construction for the corporation's debt of $49,696.21. Joe Alexander and Avanell Looney stated that they were both present at the signing. Harris testified, however, that only he, his wife, and Joe Alexander were present when the contract was signed and that he does not remember Avanell Looney being present. Kathryn Harris testified that Alexander and Looney were not present when the contract was signed. The trial court held that Joe Alexander was personally liable for the debt because he was the contracting party who dealt on behalf of the corporation. The court refused to hold Avanell Looney or Rita Alexander liable because neither of them had acted for or on behalf of the corporation. Harris appealed.

DECISION Judgment affirmed.

OPINION Revised Model Business Corporation Act § 2.04 states, "All persons purporting to act as or on behalf of a corporation, knowing there was no incorporation under this Act, are jointly and severally liable for all liabilities created while so acting." The comment to this section explains that it seems appropriate to impose liability only on persons who act as or on behalf of corporations knowing that no corporation exists. Thus this provision protects persons who "erroneously but in good faith believe" that a corporation existed. In adopting the Revised Act, the Arkansas General Assembly adopted a heightened standard for imposing personal liability for transactions entered into before incorporation. In order to find liability under § 2.04, the persons sought to be charged must have acted as or on behalf of the corporation and must have known there was no incorporation under this Act.

The trial court found the evidence to show that Avanell Looney and Rita Alexander had not acted as or on behalf of the corporation. The evidence showed that the contract to purchase Harris's business and the promissory note were signed only by Joe Alexander on behalf of the corporation. There was conflicting evidence as to who else was present at the signing of the contract. Since the trial court's finding is not clearly erroneous or clearly against the preponderance of the evidence, we find no error in the court's refusal to award Harris a judgment against Rita Alexander or Avanell Looney.

INTERPRETATION The Revised Act imposes liability on all persons who purport to act as or on behalf of a corporation if they knew there was no incorporation.

PIERCING THE CORPORATE VEIL

If substantial compliance with the incorporation statute results in a *de jure* or *de facto* corporation, the general rule is that the courts will recognize corporateness and its attendant attributes—including limited liability. Nonetheless, the courts will disregard the corporate entity when it is used to defeat public convenience, commit a wrongdoing, protect fraud, or circumvent the law. Reaching behind a corporate shield to prevent individuals from insulating themselves against personal accountability and the consequences of their wrongdoing is known as **piercing the corporate veil**. Where they deem it necessary, courts will pierce the corporate veil to remedy wrongdoing. They have done so most frequently with closely held corporations and with parent-subsidiary relationships.

Piercing the corporate veil
the courts will disregard the corporate entity when it is used to defeat public convenience, commit a wrongdoing, protect fraud, or circumvent the law

Closely Held Corporations

The joint and active management by all the shareholders of closely held corporations frequently results in a tendency to forgo corporate formalities, such as holding meetings of the board and shareholders, while the small size of close corporations often renders certain creditors unable to fully satisfy their claims against the corporation. Such frustrated creditors will likely ask the court to disregard the organization's corporateness and to impose personal liability for the corporate obligations on the shareholders. Courts have responded by piercing the corporate veil where the shareholders (1) have not conducted the business on a corporate basis, (2) have not provided an adequate financial basis for the business, or (3) have used the corporation to defraud. Conducting the business on a corporate basis involves separately maintaining the corporation's and the shareholders' funds, maintaining separate financial records, holding regular directors' meetings, and generally observing corporate formalities. Adequate capitalization requires that the shareholders invest capital sufficient to meet the reasonably anticipated requirements of the enterprise.

KINNEY SHOE CORP. v. POLAN United States Court of Appeals, Fourth Circuit, 1991, 939 F.2d 209

FACTS In 1984, Lincoln M. Polan (Polan) formed two corporations, Industrial Realty Company (Industrial) and Polan Industries, Inc. Polan was the owner of both corporations. Although certificates of incorporation were issued, no organizational meetings were held and no officers were elected for either corporation. Polan and Kinney Shoe Corp. negotiated a sublease to Industrial of a building in which Kinney had a leasehold interest. The term of the sublease from Kinney to Industrial commenced in December 1984. On April 15, 1985, Industrial subleased part of the building to Polan Industries for fifty percent of the rental amount due Kinney. Polan signed both subleases on behalf of the respective companies. Other than the sublease with Kinney, Industrial had no assets, no income, and no bank account. It issued no stock, and its only income was from its sublease to Polan Industries. The first rental payment to Kinney was made out of Polan's personal funds, and no further payments were made by Polan or by Polan Industries, Inc., either to Industrial or to Kinney. Kinney filed suit against Industrial for unpaid rent and obtained a judgment in the amount of $166,400. Kinney then filed this action against Polan individually to collect the amount owed by Industrial. The district court ruled that Polan was not individually liable on the lease between Kinney and Industrial, and Kinney appealed.

DECISION Judgment in favor of Polan reversed.

OPINION A corporation is an entity separate and distinct from its officers and stockholders, and the individual stockholders are not responsible for the debts of the corporation. This is, however, a legal fiction, and the courts can disregard it when it is used with the wrong intent and in such a way that it could produce injustice. Piercing the corporate veil is an equitable remedy; the burden of proof rests with the party seeking such relief. The courts have devised a two-pronged test to determine if the corporate veil should be pierced: First, is the unity of interest and ownership such that the separate personalities of the corporation and the individual shareholders no longer exist? Second, would an equitable result occur if the acts in question were treated as those of the corporation alone? When deciding these questions, a court considers many factors, including whether there is adequate capitalization and a regard for corporate formalities. Grossly inadequate capitalization and disregard for corporate formalities that together cause unfairness are sufficient to justify piercing the corporate veil.

In this case, it is undisputed that Industrial was not adequately capitalized. It had *no* capital. Also, Polan did not observe any corporate formalities outside of obtaining the certificate. He bought no stock, made no capital contribution, kept no minutes, and elected no officers

continued

for Industrial. In addition, Polan attempted to protect his assets by placing them in Polan Industries, Inc. and interposing Industrial between Polan Industries, Inc. and Kinney so as to prevent Kinney from going against the corporation with assets. Polan, who gave no explanation or justification for the existence of Industrial as the intermediary between Polan Industries, Inc. and Kinney, was obviously trying to limit his liability and the liability of Polan Industries, Inc. by setting up a paper curtain constructed of nothing more than Industrial's certificate of incorporation. These facts present the classic scenario for an action to pierce the corporate veil so as to reach the responsible party and produce an equitable result.

INTERPRETATION As piercing the corporate veil is an equitable remedy, the courts decide each case based on its facts. Courts will impose personal liability on the shareholders when doing so is fair and just, given the circumstances.

The Statutory Close Corporation Supplement validates a number of arrangements that allow the shareholders to relax traditional corporate formalities. The Supplement is intended to prevent the shareholders in a statutory close corporation from being held individually liable for the debts and torts of the business merely because the corporation does not follow the traditional corporate model. While courts may still pierce the corporate veil of a statutory close corporation if the same circumstances would justify imposing personal liability on the shareholders of a general business corporation, the Supplement simply prevents a court from piercing the corporate veil just because the corporation is a statutory close corporation.

Parent-Subsidiary

A corporation wishing to risk only a portion of its assets in a particular enterprise may choose to form a subsidiary corporation. A **subsidiary corporation** is one in which another corporation, the **parent corporation**, owns at least a majority of the shares and over which the parent corporation therefore has control. Courts will pierce the corporate veil and hold the parent liable for the debts of its subsidiary if (1) both corporations are not adequately capitalized, *or* (2) the formalities of separate corporate procedures are not observed, *or* (3) each corporation is not held out to the public as a separate enterprise, *or* (4) the funds of the two corporations are commingled, *or* (5) the parent corporation completely dominates the subsidiary only to advance the parent's own interests. So long as a parent-subsidiary duo avoids these pitfalls, the courts generally will recognize the subsidiary as a separate entity, even if the parent owns all the subsidiary's stock and the two corporations share directors and officers.

Subsidiary corporation *(sub·sid'·iary)* corporation controlled by another corporation

Parent corporation corporation that controls another corporation

BERGER v. COLUMBIA BROADCASTING SYSTEM, INC. United States Court of Appeals, Fifth Circuit, 1972, 453 F.2d 991

FACTS Berger was planning to produce a fashion show in Las Vegas. In April 1965, Berger entered into a written licensing agreement with CBS Films, Inc., a wholly owned subsidiary of CBS, for presentation of the show. In 1966, Stewart Cowley decided to produce a fashion show similar to Berger's and entered into a contract with CBS. CBS broadcasted Cowley's show, but not Berger's; and Berger brought this action against CBS to recover damages for breach of his contract with CBS Films. Berger claimed that CBS was liable because CBS Films was its instrumentality or *alter ego*, and that the court should disregard the parent-subsidiary form. In support of this claim, Berger showed that CBS Films' directors were employees of CBS, that CBS's organizational chart included CBS Films, and that all lines of employee authority from CBS Films passed through CBS employees to the CBS chairman of the board. CBS, in turn, argued that Berger had failed to justify piercing the corporate veil and disregarding the corporate identity of CBS Films

continued

in order to hold CBS liable. The trial court found for Berger.

DECISION Judgment of the trial court reversed.

OPINION Generally, a corporation is a creature of the law, endowed with a personality separate and distinct from that of its owners. A principal reason that legal recognition is given to the separate corporate personality is to allow stockholders an opportunity to limit their personal liability. Therefore, in order to justify the application of the instrumentality rule holding the parent liable for the acts of its subsidiary, Berger must have shown (1) that the parent controlled and completely

dominated the subsidiary; (2) that the parent used such control to commit fraud or wrong; and (3) that the control and breach of duty is the proximate cause of the injury complained of. Here, the evidence does not sustain any finding that CBS completely dominated the finances, policy, and business practices of CBS Films. Therefore, the instrumentality rule is inapplicable, and the parent, CBS, cannot be held liable for any breach of contract by its subsidiary, CBS Films.

INTERPRETATION A parent will be held liable for the debts of a subsidiary if the parent has dominated the finances, policy, and business practices of the subsidiary.

CORPORATE POWERS

Because a corporation derives its existence and all of its powers from its state of incorporation, it possesses only those powers that the state has conferred on it. Corporate powers include those expressly set forth in the statute and articles of incorporation and those reasonably implied from these documents.

SOURCES OF CORPORATE POWERS

Statutory Powers

Statutory powers typically include perpetual existence, right to hold property in the corporate name, and all powers necessary or convenient to effect the corporation's purposes

Typical of the general powers granted by incorporation statutes are those provided by the Revised Act, which include the following: (1) to have perpetual succession; (2) to sue and be sued in the corporate name; (3) to acquire and dispose of property, including shares or other interests in, or obligations of, any other entity; (4) to make contracts, borrow money, and secure any corporate obligations; (5) to lend money; (6) to be a promoter, partner, member, associate, or manager of any partnership, joint venture, trust, or other entity; (7) to conduct business within or without the state of incorporation; (8) to establish pension plans, profit sharing plans, share option plans, and other employee benefit plans; and (9) to make charitable donations. The Revised Act also grants to all corporations the same powers individuals have to do all things necessary or convenient to carry out their business and affairs.

Express Charter Powers

Express charter powers those stated in the articles of incorporation

The objects or purposes for which a corporation is formed are stated in its articles of incorporation, which outline in general language the type of business activities in which the corporation proposes to engage. The express powers must relate to a legitimate business activity or industry within the purview of the general statute.

Implied Powers

Implied powers those necessary or convenient to and consistent with the express powers

A corporation may take any action necessary or convenient to and consistent with the execution of its express powers and the operation of the business that it was formed to conduct. This power exists by implication: it depends not on express language in the charter or statute but on reasonable inference as to the proper scope and content of such language, considering the facts and circumstances of the particular case.

ULTRA VIRES ACTS

Because a corporation has authority to act only within its express and implied powers, any corporate action or contract that exceeds these powers is **ultra vires**. The doctrine of *ultra vires* is less significant today because modern statutes permit incorporation for any lawful purpose and most articles of incorporation do not limit corporate powers. As a consequence, far fewer acts are *ultra vires*.

Ultra vires acts *(ul'·tra vi'·reez)* any action or contract that goes beyond a corporation's express and implied powers

Effect of *Ultra Vires* Acts

Traditionally, *ultra vires* contracts were unenforceable as null and void. Under the modern approach, courts allow the *ultra vires* defense where the contract is wholly executory on both sides. A corporation having received full performance from the other party to the contract is not permitted to escape liability by a plea of *ultra vires*. Conversely, the other party may not use the defense of *ultra vires* against a corporation suing for breach of a contract that has been fully performed on its side. Almost all statutes, including the Revised Act, have abolished the defense of *ultra vires* in an action by or against a corporation. These statutes do not, however, validate illegal corporate actions.

Effect of *ultra vires* acts under RMBCA, *ultra vires* acts and conveyances are not invalid

Remedies for *Ultra Vires* Acts

Although *ultra vires* under modern statutes may no longer be used as a shield against liability, corporate activities that are *ultra vires* may be redressed in any of three ways, as provided by the Revised Act:

Remedies for *ultra vires* acts the RMBCA provides three possible remedies

1. in a proceeding by a shareholder against the corporation to enjoin the act, if equitable and if all affected persons are parties to the proceeding, the court may award damages for loss suffered by the corporation or another party because of the enjoining of the unauthorized act;
2. in a proceeding by the corporation, or a shareholder derivatively, against the incumbent or former directors or officers for exceeding their authority; or
3. in a proceeding by the attorney general of the state of incorporation to dissolve the corporation or to enjoin it from the transaction of unauthorized business.

LIABILITY FOR TORTS AND CRIMES

A corporation is liable for the **torts** its agents commit in the course of their employment. The doctrine of *ultra vires*, even in those jurisdictions where it is permitted as a defense, does not apply to wrongdoing by the corporation. Rather, the doctrine of *respondeat superior* imposes full liability on a corporation for such agent and employee torts. For example, Robert, a truck driver employed by the Webster Corporation, while on a business errand, negligently runs over Pamela, a pedestrian. Both Robert and the Webster Corporation are liable to Pamela in her action to recover damages for the injuries she sustained. A corporation may also be found liable for fraud, false imprisonment, malicious prosecution, libel, and other torts; but some states hold the corporation liable for *punitive* damages only if it authorized or ratified the agent's act.

Torts under the doctrine of *respondeat superior*, a corporation is liable for torts committed by its employees within the course of their employment

Historically, corporations were not held criminally liable because, under the traditional view, a corporation could not possess the criminal intent requisite for committing a **crime**. The dramatic growth in size and importance of corporations has changed this view. Under the modern approach, a corporation may be liable

Crimes a corporation may be criminally liable for violations of statutes imposing liability without fault or for an offense perpetrated by a high corporate officer or its board of directors for violating statutes imposing liability without fault. In addition, a corporation may be liable for an offense perpetrated by a high corporate officer or by its board of directors. Punishment of a corporation for crimes is necessarily by fine, not imprisonment.

CHAPTER SUMMARY

Nature of Corporations

Corporate Attributes	**Creature of the State** a corporation may be formed only by substantial compliance with a state incorporation statute **Legal Entity** a corporation is an entity apart from its shareholders, with entirely distinct rights and liabilities **Limited Liability** a shareholder's liability is limited to the amount invested in the business enterprise **Free Transferability of Corporate Shares** unless otherwise specified in the charter **Perpetual Existence** unless the charter provides otherwise **Centralized Management** shareholders of a corporation elect the board of directors to manage its business affairs; the board appoints officers to run the day-to-day operations of the business **As a Person** a corporation is considered a person for some but not all purposes **As a Citizen** a corporation is considered a citizen for some but not all purposes

Classification of Corporations	**Public or Private** ■ *Public Corporation* one created to administer a unit of local civil government or one created by the United States to conduct public business ■ *Private Corporation* one founded by and composed of private persons for private purposes; has no governmental duties **Profit or Nonprofit** ■ *Profit Corporation* one founded to operate a business for profit ■ *Nonprofit Corporation* one whose profits must be used exclusively for charitable, educational, or scientific purposes **Domestic or Foreign** ■ *Domestic Corporation* one created under the laws of a given state ■ *Foreign Corporation* one created under the laws of any other state or jurisdiction; it must obtain a certificate of authority from each state in which it does intrastate business **Publicly Held or Closely Held** ■ *Publicly Held* corporation whose shares are owned by a large number of people and are widely traded ■ *Closely Held* corporation that is owned by few shareholders and whose shares are not actively traded **Subchapter S Corporation** eligible corporation electing to be taxed as a partnership under the Internal Revenue Code **Professional Corporations** corporate form under which duly licensed individuals may practice their professions

Formation of a Corporation

Organizing the Corporation

Promoter person who takes the preliminary steps to organize a corporation
- *Promoters' Contracts* promoters remain liable on preincorporation contracts made in the name of the corporation unless the contract provides otherwise or unless a novation is effected
- *Promoters' Fiduciary Duty* promoters owe a fiduciary duty among themselves and to the corporation, its subscribers, and its initial shareholders

Subscribers persons who agree to purchase the initial stock in a corporation

---

Formalities of Incorporation

Selection of Name the name must clearly designate the entity as a corporation
Incorporators the persons who sign the articles of incorporation
Articles of Incorporation the charter or basic organizational document of a corporation
Organizational Meeting the first meeting, held to adopt the bylaws and appoint officers
Bylaws rules governing a corporation's internal management

Recognition or Disregard of Corporateness

Defective Incorporation

Common Law Approach
- *Corporation de Jure* one formed in substantial compliance with the incorporation statute and having all corporate attributes
- *Corporation de Facto* one not formed in compliance with the statute but recognized for most purposes as a corporation
- *Corporation by Estoppel* prevents a person from raising the question of a corporation's existence
- *Defective Corporation* the associates are denied the benefits of incorporation

Statutory Approach the filing of the articles of incorporation is generally conclusive proof of proper incorporation
- *RMBCA* liability is imposed only on persons who act on behalf of a defectively formed corporation knowing that there was no incorporation
- *MBCA* unlimited personal liability is imposed on all persons who act on behalf of a defectively formed corporation

---

Piercing the Corporate Veil

General Rule the courts will disregard the corporate entity when it is used to defeat public convenience, commit a wrongdoing, protect fraud, or circumvent the law
Application most frequently applied to
- *Closely Held Corporations*
- *Parent-Subsidiary Corporations*

Corporate Powers

Sources of Corporate Powers	**Statutory Powers** typically include perpetual existence, right to hold property in the corporate name, and all powers necessary or convenient to effect the corporation's purposes
	Express Charter Powers those stated in the articles of incorporation
	Implied Powers those necessary or convenient to and consistent with the express powers

Ultra Vires Acts	**Definition of *Ultra Vires* Acts** any action or contract that goes beyond a corporation's express and implied powers
	Effect of *Ultra Vires* Acts under RMBCA, *ultra vires* acts and conveyances are not invalid
	Remedies for *Ultra Vires* Acts the RMBCA provides three possible remedies

Liability for Torts and Crimes	**Torts** under the doctrine of *respondeat superior*, a corporation is liable for torts committed by its employees within the course of their employment
	Crime a corporation may be criminally liable for violations of statutes imposing liability without fault or for an offense perpetrated by a high corporate officer or its board of directors

QUESTIONS

1. Identify the principal attributes of a corporation and explain how these distinguish it from a partnership, a limited partnership, and a limited liability company.
2. Discuss (a) the liability of promoters on preincorporation contracts and (b) the nature of their fiduciary duty.
3. Distinguish between the common law and statutory approaches to defective formation of a corporation.
4. Explain how the doctrine of piercing the corporate veil applies to (a) closely held corporations and (b) parent-subsidiary corporations.
5. Distinguish between the common law and statutory approaches to the effect of *ultra vires* acts.

Internet Question. Find samples of (a) articles of incorporation and (b) corporate bylaws.

PROBLEMS

1. After part of the shares of a proposed corporation had been successfully subscribed, one of the promoters hired a carpenter to repair a building that was intended to be conveyed to the proposed corporation. The promoters subsequently secured subscriptions to the balance of the shares and completed the organization, but the corporation, finding the building to be unsuitable for its purposes, declined to use the building or to pay the carpenter. The carpenter brought suit against the corporation for the amount that the promoter agreed would be paid to him. Decision?

2. C. A. Nimocks was a promoter engaged in organizing the Times Printing Company. On September 12, on behalf of the proposed corporation, he made a contract with McArthur for her services as comptroller for a one-year period beginning October 1. The Times Printing Company was incorporated October 16, and on that date McArthur commenced her duties as comptroller. Neither the board of directors nor any officer took formal action on her employment, but all the shareholders, directors, and officers knew of the contract made by Nimocks. On December 1, McArthur

was discharged without cause. Has she a cause of action against the Times Printing Company?

3. Todd and Elaine obtained an option on a building that was used for manufacturing pianos. They acted as the promoters for a corporation and turned the building over to the new corporation for $500,000 worth of stock. In truth, their option on the building called for a purchase price of only $300,000. The other shareholders desire to have $200,000 of the common stock canceled. Can they succeed in this action?

4. Wayne signed a subscription agreement for ten shares of stock, having a value of $100 per share, of the proposed ABC Company. Two weeks later, the company was incorporated. A certificate was duly tendered to Wayne, but he refused to accept it. He was notified of all shareholders' meetings, but he never attended. A dividend check was sent to him, but he returned it. ABC Company brings a legal action against Wayne to recover $1,000. He defends on the ground that his subscription agreement was an unaccepted offer, that he had done nothing to ratify it, and that he was therefore not liable on it. Decision?

5. Julian, Cornelia, and Sheila petitioned for a corporate charter for the purpose of conducting a retail shoe business. They complied with all the statutory provisions except having their charter recorded. This was simply an oversight on their part, and they felt that they had fully complied with the law. They operated the business for three years, after which time it became insolvent. The creditors desire to hold the members personally and individually liable. May they do so?

6. Arthur, Barbara, Carl, and Debra decided to form a corporation for bottling and selling apple cider. Arthur, Barbara, and Carl were to operate the business, while Debra was to supply the necessary capital but was to have no voice in the management. They went to Jane, a lawyer, who agreed to organize a corporation for them under the name A-B-C Inc., and paid her funds sufficient to accomplish the incorporation. Jane promised that the corporation would definitely be formed by May 3. On April 27, Arthur telephoned Jane to inquire how the incorporation was progressing, and Jane said she had drafted the articles of incorporation and would send them to the secretary of state that very day. She assured Arthur that incorporation would occur before May 3.

Relying on Jane's assurance, Arthur, with the approval of Barbara and Carl, on May 4 entered into a written contract with Grower for his entire apple crop. The contract was executed by Arthur on behalf of "A-B-C Inc." Grower delivered the apples as agreed. Unknown to Arthur, Barbara, Carl, Debra, or Grower, the articles of incorporation were never filed, through Jane's negligence. The business subsequently failed.

What are Grower's rights, if any, against Arthur, Barbara, Carl, and Debra as individuals?

7. The Pyro Corporation has outstanding 20,000 shares of common stock, of which 19,000 are owned by Peter B. Arson; 500 shares are owned by Elizabeth Arson, his wife; and 500 shares are owned by Joseph Q. Arson, his brother. These three individuals are the officers and directors of the corporation. The Pyro Corporation obtained a $250,000 fire insurance policy to cover a certain building it owned. Thereafter, Peter B. Arson set fire to the building, and it was totally destroyed. The corporation now brings an action against the fire insurance company to recover on the $250,000 fire insurance policy. What judgment?

8. A corporation is formed for the purpose of manufacturing, buying, selling, and dealing in drugs, chemicals, and similar products. The corporation, under authority of its board of directors, contracted to purchase the land and building it occupied as a factory and store. Collins, a shareholder, sues in equity to restrain the corporation from completing the contract, claiming that as the certificate of incorporation contained no provision authorizing the corporation to purchase real estate, the contract was *ultra vires*. Decision?

9. Amalgamated Corporation, organized under the laws of State S, sends traveling salespersons into State M to solicit orders, which are accepted only at the home office of Amalgamated Corporation in State S. Riley, a resident of State M, places an order that is accepted by Amalgamated Corporation in State S. The Corporation Act of State M provides that "no foreign corporation transacting business in this state without a certificate of authority shall be permitted to maintain an action in any court of this state until such corporation shall have obtained a certificate of authority." Riley fails to pay for the goods, and when Amalgamated Corporation sues Riley in a court of State M, Riley defends on the ground that Amalgamated Corporation does not possess a certificate of authority from State M. Result?

10. Dr. North, a surgeon practicing in Georgia, engaged an Arizona professional corporation consisting of twenty lawyers to represent him in a dispute with a Georgia hospital. West, a member of the law firm, flew to Atlanta and hired local counsel with Dr. North's approval. West represented Dr. North in two hearings before the hospital and in one court proceeding, as well as negotiating a compromise between Dr. North and the hospital. The total bill for the law firm's travel costs and professional services was $21,000, but Dr. North refused to pay $6,000 of it. The law firm brought an action against Dr. North for the balance owed. Dr. North argued that the action should be dismissed because the law firm failed to register as a foreign corporation in accordance with the Georgia Corporation Statute. Decision?

11. An Arkansas statute provides that if any foreign corporation authorized to do business in the state should remove to the federal court any suit brought against it

by an Arkansas citizen or initiate any suit in the federal court against a local citizen, without the consent of the other party, Arkansas's secretary of state should revoke all authority of the corporation to do business in the state. The Burke Construction Company, a Missouri corporation authorized to do business in Arkansas, has brought a suit in federal court and has also removed to the federal court a state suit brought against it. Burke now seeks to enjoin the secretary of state from revoking its authority to do business in Arkansas, contending that the Arkansas statute is unconstitutional. Decision?

12. Little Switzerland was incorporated on January 28, 1968. On February 18, Ellison and Oxley were made directors of the company after they purchased some stock. Then, on September 25, Ellison and Oxley signed stock subscription agreements to purchase 5,000 shares each. Under the agreement, they both issued a note that indicated that they would pay for the stock "at their discretion." In March 1970, the board of directors passed a resolution canceling the stock subscription agreements of Ellison and Oxley. The creditors of Little Switzerland brought suit against Ellison and Oxley to recover the money owed under the subscription agreements. Decision?

13. Oahe Enterprises was formed by the efforts of Emmick, who acted as a promoter and contributed shares of Colonial Manors, Inc. (CM) stock in exchange for stock in Oahe. The CM stock had been valued by CM's directors for internal stock option purposes at $19 per share. However, one month prior to Emmick's incorporation of Oahe Enterprises, CM's board reduced the stock value to $9.50 per share. Although Emmick knew of this reduction before the meeting to form Oahe Enterprises, he did not disclose this information to the Morrises, the other shareholders of the new corporation. Oahe Enterprises then brought this action to recover the shortfall. Decision?

14. In April 1961, Cranson was asked to invest in a new business corporation that was about to be created. He agreed to purchase stock and to become an officer and director. After his attorney advised him that the corporation had been formed under the laws of Maryland, Cranson paid for and received a stock certificate evidencing his ownership of shares. The business of the new venture was conducted as if it were a corporation. Cranson was elected president, and he conducted all of his corporate actions, including those with IBM, as an officer of the corporation. At no time did he assume any personal obligation or pledge his individual credit to IBM. As a result of an oversight of the attorney, of which Cranson was unaware, the certificate of incorporation, which had been signed and acknowledged prior to May 1, 1961, was not filed until November 24, 1961. Between May 1 and November 8, the "corporation" purchased eight typewriters from IBM. After the corporation made only partial payment, IBM brought suit against Cranson seeking to hold him personally liable for the $4,333.40 balance due. Decision?

15. On September 14, 1971, Healthwin-Midtown Convalescent Hospital, Inc. (Healthwin), was incorporated in California for the purpose of operating a health care facility. From that date until November 30, 1974, it participated as a provider of services under the federal Medicare Act and received periodic payments from the United States Department of Health, Education and Welfare. Undisputed audits revealed that a series of overpayments had been made to Healthwin in the total amount of $30,481.00. The United States brought an action to recover this sum from the defendants, Healthwin and Israel Zide. Zide was a member of the board of directors of the Healthwin corporation, the administrator of its health care facility, its president, and owner of 50 percent of its stock. Only Zide could sign the corporation's checks without prior approval of another corporate officer. In addition, Zide had a 50 percent interest in a partnership that owned both the realty in which Healthwin's health care facility was located and the furnishings used at that facility. The corporation was initially undercapitalized, and its liabilities continued to exceed its assets substantially. Zide exercised control over Healthwin, causing its finances to become inextricably intertwined both with his personal finances and with his other business holdings. The United States contends that the corporate veil should be pierced and that Zide should be held personally liable for the Medicare overpayments made to Healthwin. Decision?

16. MPL Leasing Corporation is a California corporation that provides financing plans to dealers of Saxon Business Products. MPL invited Jay Johnson, a Saxon dealer in Alabama, to attend a sales seminar in Atlanta. MPL and Johnson entered into an agreement under which Johnson was to lease Saxon copiers with an option to buy. MPL shipped the equipment into Alabama and filed a financing statement with the secretary of state. When Johnson became delinquent with his payments to MPL, MPL brought an action against Johnson in an Alabama court. Johnson moved to dismiss the action, claiming that MPL was not qualified to conduct business in Alabama and was thus barred from enforcing its contract with Johnson in an Alabama court. The trial court entered judgment in favor of MPL. Decision?

CHAPTER 36

Financial Structure

Capital is necessary for any business to function. Two of the principal sources for corporate financing involve debt and equity investment securities. While equity securities represent an ownership interest in the corporation and include both common and preferred stock, corporations finance most of their continued operations through debt securities. Debt securities, which include notes and bonds, do not represent an ownership interest in the corporation; rather, they create a debtor-creditor relationship between the corporation and the bondholder. The third principal way in which a corporation may meet its financial needs is through retained earnings.

All states have statutes regulating the issuance and sale of corporate shares and other securities. Popularly known as **Blue Sky Laws**, these statutes typically contain provisions prohibiting fraud in the sale of securities. In addition, a number of states require the registration of securities, and some states also regulate brokers, dealers, and others who engage in the securities business.

Blue Sky Laws state laws regulating the issuance and sale of securities

In 1933, Congress passed the first federal statute for the regulation of securities offered for sale and sold through the use of the mails or otherwise in interstate commerce. The statute requires a corporation to disclose certain information about a proposed security in a registration statement and in its *prospectus* (an offer a corporation makes to interest people in buying securities). Although the SEC does not examine the merits of the proposed security and although registration does not guarantee the accuracy of the facts presented in the registration statement or prospectus, the law does prohibit false and misleading statements under penalty of fine or imprisonment or both.

Under certain conditions, a corporation may receive an exemption from the requirement of registration under the Blue Sky Laws of most states and the Securities Act of 1933. If no exemption is available, a corporation offering for sale or selling its shares of stock or other securities, as well as any person selling such securities, is subject to court injunction, possible criminal prosecution, and civil liability in damages to the persons to whom securities are sold in violation of the regulatory statute. A discussion of federal regulation of securities appears in Chapter 42.

In this chapter, we will discuss debt and equity securities as well as the payment of dividends and other distributions to shareholders. We will also examine the manner in which debt and equity investment securities are transferred.

DEBT SECURITIES

Debt security source of capital creating no ownership interest and involving the corporation's promise to repay funds lent to it

Bond a debt security

Corporations frequently find it advantageous to use debt as a source of funds. **Debt securities** (also called **bonds**) generally involve the corporation's promise to repay the principal amount of a loan at a stated time and to pay interest, usually at a fixed rate, while the debt is outstanding. In addition to bonds, a corporation may finance its operations through other forms of debt, such as credit extended by its suppliers and short-term commercial paper. Some states, but not the Revised Act, permit articles of incorporation to confer voting rights on debt security holders; a few states allow other shareholder rights to be conferred on bondholders.

AUTHORITY TO ISSUE DEBT SECURITIES

Authority to issue debt securities each corporation has the power to issue debt securities as determined by the board of directors

The Revised Act provides that every corporation has the power to borrow money and to issue its notes, bonds, and other obligations. The board of directors may issue bonds without the authorization or consent of the shareholders.

TYPES OF DEBT SECURITIES

Indenture (in·den'·ture) debt agreement specifying loan terms

Depending on their characteristics, debt securities can be classified into various types, each offering numerous variants and combinations. A corporation typically issues debt securities under an **indenture** or debt agreement, which specifies in great detail the terms of the loan.

METROPOLITAN LIFE INSURANCE COMPANY v. RJR NABISCO, INC. United States District Court, S.D. New York, 1989, 716 F.Supp. 1504

FACTS On October 20, 1988, F. Ross Johnson, then the CEO of RJR Nabisco (RJR), proposed a $17 billion leveraged buyout (LBO) of RJR's shareholders at $75 dollars per share. (An LBO occurs when a group of investors, usually including the company's management, buy the company with little equity and significant new debt. The debt typically is financed through mortgages or high-risk/high-yield bonds, known as "junk bonds." A portion of this debt normally is secured by the company's assets. After the transaction is complete, some of these assets usually are sold to reduce the debt.) Within a few days, the investment group led by Johnson, the Kohlberg Kravis Roberts & Co. (KKR) investment firm, and others began a bidding war. On December 1, 1988, an RJR committee recommended that RJR accept KKR's proposal of a $24 billion LBO at $109 per share. Metropolitan Life Insurance Co. (MetLife), a life insurance company with $88 billion in assets and $49 billion in debt securities holdings, owned $340,542,000 in principal amount of RJR Nabisco bonds purchased between July 1975 and July 1988. These bonds bore interest rates from 8 to 10.25 percent. Jefferson-Pilot Life Insurance Co., with $3 billion in assets, of which $1.5 billion was in debt securities, owned $9.34 million in principal of RJR bonds purchased between June 1978 and June 1988.

MetLife and Jefferson-Pilot (plaintiffs) argued that RJR had an implied duty of good faith and fair dealing not to incur the debt involved in the LBO. They asserted that RJR consistently had reassured its bondholders that it had a "mandate" from its board of directors to maintain RJR's preferred credit rating. The plaintiffs alleged that RJR's actions drastically impaired the value of their bond holdings, in effect misappropriated the value of those bonds to finance the LBO, and distributed the windfall to the company's shareholders. They declared that these actions constituted a breach of the implied duty and betrayed the fundamental basis of their bargain with RJR. The plaintiffs alleged that they unfairly suffered a multimillion dollar loss in the value of their bonds and that, therefore, RJR should redeem their bonds.

RJR defended the LBO by pointing to express provisions in the bond indentures that permitted mergers and the assumption of additional debt. These provisions, RJR pointed out, were known to the market and to the plaintiffs, who were sophisticated investors who freely bought the bonds and who were equally free to sell them at any time. RJR argued that no legal grounds supported the existence of an implied duty and that any attempt to enforce such a duty would constitute an impermissible invasion of the free and open operation of the marketplace.

continued

DECISION Judgment for RJR.

OPINION Although the numbers in this case are large and the financing is unprecedented, the legal principles governing the bonds are familiar: detailed bond indentures, which are in turn governed by New York contract law. The holders of public bonds often enter the market after the indentures have been negotiated and memorialized. Thus, those indentures are often not the product of face-to-face negotiations between the ultimate holders and the issuing company. Underwriters ordinarily negotiate the terms of the indentures with the issuers while keeping the buyers in mind. Moreover, the indentures in this case were not secret agreements imposed upon unwitting participants in the bond market. Indeed, sophisticated investors like the plaintiffs are well aware of indenture terms and presumably review them carefully before lending hundreds of millions of dollars to any company. Furthermore, the prospectus for the indentures contained this statement: "The Indenture contains no restrictions on the creation of unsecured short-term debt by [RJR]."

Under certain circumstances, courts will consider extrinsic evidence to evaluate the scope of an implied duty of good faith. In contracts like bond indentures, however, an implied duty derives its substance directly from the language of the indenture and cannot give the holders of debentures any rights inconsistent with those set out in the indenture. The appropriate analysis, then, is to examine the indentures to determine the fruits of the agreement and to decide whether those "fruits" have been spoiled. The court holds that the "fruits" of these indentures do not include an implied duty that would prevent the incurrence of new debt to facilitate the LBO. The plaintiffs do not invoke an implied duty of good faith to protect a legitimate, mutually contemplated benefit of the indentures. Rather, they seek to create an additional benefit for which they did not bargain and which, if granted, would interfere with and destabilize the market.

INTERPRETATION Bond indentures are highly detailed contracts specifying the terms of the underlying loan. The courts will not imply any duties that are inconsistent with the terms of such a contract.

Unsecured Bonds

Unsecured bonds, usually called **debentures**, have only the obligation of the corporation behind them. Debenture holders are thus unsecured creditors and rank equally with other general creditors. To protect the unsecured bondholders, indentures frequently impose limitations on the corporation's borrowing, its payment of dividends, and its redemption and reacquisition of its own shares. An indenture may also require a corporation to maintain specified minimum reserves.

> **Unsecured bonds** called **debentures**, have only the obligation of the corporation behind them

Secured Bonds

A secured creditor is one whose claim is not only enforceable against the general assets of the corporation but is also a lien on specific property. Thus, **secured** or mortgage **bonds** provide the security of specific corporate property in addition to the general obligation of the corporation. After resorting to the specified security, the holder of secured bonds becomes a general creditor for any unsatisfied amount of the debt.

> **Secured bonds** are claims against a corporation's general assets and also a lien on specific property

Income Bonds

Traditionally, debt securities bear a fixed interest rate that is payable without regard to the financial condition of the corporation. **Income bonds**, on the other hand, condition the payment of interest to some extent on corporate earnings. **Participating bonds** call for a stated percentage of return regardless of earnings, with additional payments dependent on earnings.

> **Income bonds** bonds that condition payment of interest on corporate earnings

> **Participating bonds** bonds that call for a stated percentage of return regardless of earnings, with additional payments dependent upon earnings

Convertible Bonds

Usually at the option of the holder, **convertible bonds** may be exchanged, in a specified ratio, for other securities of the corporation. For example, a convertible bond may provide that the bondholder shall have the right for a specified time to exchange each bond for twenty shares of common stock.

> **Convertible bonds** bonds that may be exchanged for other securities of the corporation

Callable Bonds

Callable bonds bonds that are subject to redemption (reacquisition) by the corporation

Callable bonds are bonds subject to a redemption provision that permits the corporation to redeem or call (pay off) all or part of the issue before maturity at a specified redemption price.

CONSUMER INSIGHT

Bond Ratings: What Do They Tell Us? Who Makes Them?

"Triple-A," "investment grade," and "junk" are familiar terms to those who invest in bonds. All three terms refer to a central concern of investors: what is the probability that the issuer of bonds will repay the principal at maturity and make scheduled interest payments on time? Put another way, what is the risk of default?

A high rating is supposed to reflect a high probability of repayment. The greater this probability, the less risk to the investor. Conversely, lower rated bonds are judged to be riskier. Generally, safer bonds have a lower yield, riskier bonds a higher yield. Investors taking greater risks demand a higher return.

Independent rating agencies analyze the companies and municipalities that issue bonds and assign ratings to reflect the creditworthiness of the issuer. The best-known agencies in the United States are Standard and Poor's and Moody's Investor Service. Standard and Poor's bond ratings, from highest to lowest, are AAA, AA, A; BBB, BB, B; CCC, CC, C; and D (in payment default). Moody's ratings are comparable: Aaa, Aa, A; Baa, Ba, B; and Caa, Ca, C. Moody's does not give a D.

"Investment grade" refers to the top four ratings, denoting bonds that are relatively safe investments for individuals and institutions. In contrast, "junk bonds" (generally anything rated below the top four ratings) are low-rated, risky, and high-yielding. Junk bonds were a favorite financing vehicle for leveraged buyouts during

the 1980s. The bonds attracted buyers hungry for yield and not very concerned about safety. However, they put a huge debt burden on the issuing companies—some of which went into highly publicized bankruptcies.

The relationship of risk to return in the bond markets can be checked in the financial pages of a newspaper such as *The Wall Street Journal*. For example, on October 6, 1993, bonds of American Home Products (an AAA-rated company), with a maturity date in the year 2023, were priced to yield 6.569 percent. On the same day, bonds of USX (a BB+-rated company), with a maturity date in 2013, were priced to yield 8.619 percent.

The quality of a particular bond can change over time as business conditions change for the issuer. For this reason, bond ratings have a subjective component. Analysts look not only at an issuing company's financial statements but also at trends in the industry—and adjust their ratings accordingly. For example, a recent *New York Times* article described the efforts of big bank holding companies such as Chase Manhattan Corp., Citicorp, and Chemical Banking Corp. to raise their ratings. Formerly rated as high as AAA in the 1970s, these banks had seen their ratings decline to BBB by the early 1990s through a succession of woes: new competition from Wall Street and from banks

abroad, then losses on loans to Latin American countries, followed by bad real estate loans in the United States. Structural changes in the banking industry have made high ratings much harder to obtain. The *Times* quoted a Moody's official: "Most institutions think, 'If we get our financial ratios back to where they were when we were double-A, we will be double-A again.' That is not going to happen. The bar is getting higher."

Raising its rating can save a company money when it issues new bonds: with a higher rating the company pays a lower interest rate, resulting in savings that can directly affect the bottom line. For example, one of the big banks in the *Times* story, with a stated goal of raising its rating from triple-B in 1993 to double-A in 1994, figured that the upgrade could increase its annual earnings by at least $150 million.

If a rating tells us how risky a bond is, then what, if anything, does it not tell us?

Bond ratings relate to bond issuers, not investors. Thus, the ratings do not say whether a particular bond is an appropriate investment for a particular buyer. And ratings do not forecast the movement of interest rates, movement that causes bond prices to rise or fall.

In other words, bond ratings are only a tool for investors, not a substitute for good judgment.

Sources: "Big Banks' Goal: Higher Ratings," *The New York Times*, 8 June 1993, C1; "Bond Market Data Bank 10/6/93," *The Wall Street Journal*, 7 October 1993, C21; *Moody's Bond Record*, 3; and *Understanding Wall Street*, 3d ed., 131.

EQUITY SECURITIES

An **equity security** is a source of capital creating an ownership interest in the corporation. The holders of equity securities, as owners of the corporation, occupy a position financially riskier than that of creditors; and changes in the corporation's fortunes and general economic conditions have a greater effect on shareholders than on any other class of investor.

Equity security source of capital creating an ownership interest in the corporation

Though a proportionate proprietary interest in a corporate enterprise can be described in terms of the **shares** a person owns, shares do not in any way vest their owner with title to any of the corporation's property. However, shares do confer on their owner a threefold interest in the corporation: (1) the right to participate in control, (2) the right to participate in the earnings of the corporation, and (3) the right to participate in the residual assets of the corporation on dissolution. The shareholder's interest is usually represented by a certificate of ownership and is recorded by the corporation.

Shares proportionate ownership interest in a corporation

ISSUANCE OF SHARES

The state of incorporation regulates the issuance of shares by determining the type of shares that may be issued, the kinds and amount of consideration for which shares may be issued, and the rights of shareholders to purchase a proportionate part of additionally issued shares. Moreover, the federal government and each state in which the shares are issued or sold regulate the issuance and sale of shares.

Authority to Issue

The initial amount of shares to be issued is determined by the promoters or incorporators and is generally governed by practical business considerations and financial needs. A corporation is limited, however, to selling only the amount of shares that has been authorized in its articles of incorporation. Unauthorized shares of stock that are purportedly issued by a corporation are void. The rights of parties entitled to these overissued shares are governed by Article 8 of the Uniform Commercial Code, which provides that the corporation must either obtain an identical security, if one is reasonably available, for the person entitled to the security or pay that person the price he (or the last purchaser for value) paid for it, with interest.

Authority to issue only those shares authorized in the articles of incorporation may be issued

Once the amount of shares that the corporation is authorized to issue has been established and specified in the charter, it cannot be increased or decreased without amendment to the charter. Consequently, articles of incorporation commonly specify more shares than are to be issued immediately.

Preemptive Rights

A shareholder's proportionate interest in a corporation can be changed by either a nonproportionate issuance of additional shares or a nonproportionate reacquisition of outstanding shares. Management is subject to fiduciary duties in both types of transactions. Moreover, when a corporation issues additional shares, a shareholder may have the **preemptive right** to purchase a proportionate part of the new issue. Preemptive rights are used far more frequently in closely held corporations than in publicly traded corporations, possibly because, without such rights, a shareholder may be unable to prevent a dilution of his ownership interest in the corporation. For example, Leonard owns 200 shares of stock of the Fordham

Preemptive right (pre·emp'·tive) shareholder's right to purchase a *pro rata* share of new stock offerings

Company, which has a total of 1,000 shares outstanding. The company decides to increase its capital stock by issuing 1,000 additional shares of stock. If Leonard has preemptive rights, he and every other shareholder will be offered one share of the newly issued stock for every share they own. If he accepts the offer and buys the stock, he will have 400 shares out of a total of 2,000 outstanding, and his relative interest in the corporation will be unchanged. Without preemptive rights, however, he would have only 200 out of the 2,000 shares outstanding; instead of owning 20 percent of the stock, he would own 10 percent.

At common law, shareholders have preemptive rights to the issuance of additionally authorized shares. Such rights do not apply, however, to the reissue of previously issued shares, shares issued for noncash consideration, or shares issued in connection with a merger or consolidation. The jurisdictions are divided over whether preemptive rights apply to the issuance of unissued shares that were originally authorized.

Modern statutes expressly authorize articles of incorporation to deny or limit preemptive rights. In some states, preemptive rights exist unless denied by the charter; in others, they do not exist unless the charter so provides. The Revised Act adopts the latter approach: shareholders have no preemptive rights unless the charter provides for them. If the charter simply states that the corporation elects to have preemptive rights, the shareholders have a preemptive right to acquire proportional amounts of the corporation's unissued shares but have no such right with respect to (1) shares issued as compensation to directors, officers, and employees; (2) shares issued within six months of incorporation; and (3) shares issued for consideration other than money. In addition, holders of nonvoting preferred stock have no preemptive rights with respect to *any* class of shares; and holders of voting common shares have no preemptive rights with respect to preferred stock unless the preferred stock is convertible into common stock. The articles of incorporation may expressly provide that any one or all of these limitations do not apply.

Amount of Consideration for Shares

Amount of consideration for shares shares are deemed fully paid and nonassessable when a corporation receives the consideration for which the board of directors authorized the issuance of the shares, which in the case of par value stock must be at least par

The board of directors usually determines the price for which the corporation will issue shares, although the charter may reserve this power to the shareholders. Shares are deemed fully paid and nonassessable when the corporation receives the consideration for which the board of directors authorized their issuance. The amount of consideration depends on the kind of shares being issued.

Par Value Stock Par value shares may be issued for any amount, not less than par, set by the board of directors or shareholders. The par value of stock must be stated in the articles of incorporation. The consideration received constitutes *stated capital* to the extent of the par value of the shares; any consideration in excess of par value constitutes *capital surplus*.

The Revised Act, the 1980 amendments to the MBCA, and about twenty states have eliminated the concepts of par value, stated capital, and capital surplus. Under these acts, *all* shares may be issued for such consideration as authorized by the board of directors or, if the charter so provides, the shareholders. A corporation *may*, however, elect to issue shares with par value.

No Par Value Stock Shares without par value may be issued for any amount set by the board of directors or shareholders. Under incorporation statutes recognizing par value, stated capital, and capital surplus, the entire consideration a corporation receives for such stock constitutes *stated capital* unless the board of directors allocates a portion of the consideration to capital surplus. The directors are free to allocate any or all of the consideration received, unless the no par stock has a liquidation preference. In that event, only the consideration in excess of the amount of liquidation preference may be allocated to capital surplus. No par shares provide the directors with great latitude in establishing capital surplus, which can, in some jurisdictions, provide greater flexibility in terms of subsequent distributions to shareholders.

Treasury Stock **Treasury stock** is shares that a corporation buys back after it has issued them. Treasury shares are *issued but not outstanding*, in contrast to shares owned by shareholders, which are deemed issued *and* outstanding. A corporation may sell treasury shares for any amount the board of directors determines, even if the shares have a par value that is more than the sale price. Treasury shares do not provide voting rights or preemptive rights. In addition, no dividend is paid on treasury stock.

Treasury stock shares reacquired by a corporation

The Revised Act carries forward the 1980 amendments to the MBCA, which eliminated the concept of treasury shares. Under the Revised Act, all shares reacquired by a corporation are authorized but unissued shares, unless the articles of incorporation prohibit reissue, in which event the authorized shares are reduced by the number of shares reacquired.

Figure 36–1 illustrates the categorization of authorized shares.

FIGURE 36–1 Issuance of Shares

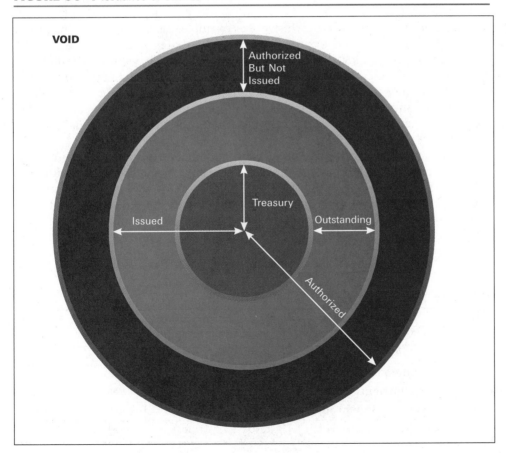

Payment for shares may be cash, property, and services actually rendered, as determined by the board of directors; under the Revised Act, promises to contribute cash, property, or services are also permitted

Payment for Shares

Payment for shares involves two major issues. First, what type of consideration may the corporation validly accept in payment for shares? Second, who shall determine the value to be placed upon the consideration the corporation receives in payment for shares?

Type of Consideration The definition of consideration for the issuance of capital stock is somewhat more limited than the definition of consideration under contract law. In about thirty states, cash, property, and services actually rendered to the corporation are generally acceptable as valid consideration, whereas promissory notes and promises regarding the performance of future services are not. Some states permit shares to be issued for preincorporation services; other states do not.

The Revised Act greatly liberalized these rules by specifically validating for the issuance of shares consideration consisting of any tangible or intangible property or *benefit* to the corporation, including cash, services performed, *contracts for future services*, and *promissory notes*. Figure 36–2 compares the types of valid capital contributions.

Valuation of Consideration Determining the value to be placed on the consideration that stock purchasers will exchange for shares is the responsibility of the directors. The majority of jurisdictions holds that this valuation is a matter of opinion and that, in the absence of fraud in the transaction, the judgment of the board of directors as to the value of the consideration the corporation receives for shares shall be conclusive. For example, assume that the directors of Elite Corporation authorize the issuance of 2,000 shares of common stock for $5 per share to Kramer for property the directors purportedly value at $10,000. The valuation, however, is fraudulent; and the property is actually worth only $5,000. Kramer is liable to Elite Corporation and its creditors for $5,000. If, on the other hand, the directors had made the valuation without fraud and in good faith, Kramer would not be liable, even though the property is actually worth less than $10,000.

Under the Revised Act, the directors simply determine whether the consideration received (or to be received) for shares is *adequate*.Their determination is "conclusive insofar as the adequacy of consideration for the issuance of shares relates to whether the shares are validly issued, fully paid, and nonassessable." Under the Revised Act, the articles of incorporation may reserve to the shareholders the powers granted to the board regarding the issuance of shares.

FIGURE 36–2 Valid Capital Contributions

Kind	ULPA	RULPA	MBCA	RMBCA
Cash	Yes	Yes	Yes	Yes
Property	Yes	Yes	Yes	Yes
Services rendered	No	Yes	Yes	Yes
Promise to contribute cash	No	Yes	No	Yes
Promise to contribute property	No	Yes	No	Yes
Promise to perform services	No	Yes	No	Yes

Liability for Shares

A purchaser of shares has no liability to the corporation or its creditors with respect to shares except to pay the corporation either the consideration for which the shares were authorized to be issued or the consideration specified in the preincorporation stock subscription. When the corporation receives that consideration, the shares are fully paid and nonassessable. A transferee who acquires shares in good faith and without knowledge or notice that the full consideration had not been paid is *not* personally liable to the corporation or its creditors for the unpaid portion of the consideration.

CLASSES OF SHARES

Corporations are generally authorized by statute to issue different classes of stock, which may vary with respect to their rights to dividends, their voting rights, and their right to share in the assets of the corporation on liquidation. The usual stock classifications are common and preferred shares. Although the Revised Act has eliminated the terms "preferred" and "common," it permits the issuance of shares with different preferences, limitations, and relative rights. The Revised Act, however, explicitly requires a corporation's charter to authorize "(1) one or more classes of shares that together have unlimited voting rights, and (2) one or more classes of shares (which may be the same class or classes as those with voting rights) that together are entitled to receive the net assets of the corporation upon dissolution." In most states, however, even nonvoting shares may vote on certain mergers, share exchanges, and other fundamental changes that affect that class of shares as a class. See Chapter 38.

Common Stock

Common stock does not have any special contract rights or preferences. Frequently the only class of stock outstanding, it generally represents the greatest proportion of the corporation's capital structure and bears the greatest risk of loss, should the enterprise fail.

> **Common stock** stock not having any special contract rights

Preferred Stock

Stock generally is considered **preferred stock** if it has contractual rights superior to those of common stock with regard to dividends, assets on liquidation, or both. Other special rights or privileges generally do not remove stock from the common stock classification. The articles of incorporation must provide for the contractual rights and preferences of an issue of preferred stock.

> **Preferred stock** stock having contractual rights superior to those of common stock

Dividend Preferences Though the holders of an issue of preferred stock with a **dividend preference** will receive full dividends before any dividend may be paid to holders of common stock, no dividend is payable on any class of stock, common or preferred, unless the board of directors has declared such dividend.

> **Dividend preference** must receive full dividends before any dividend may be paid on common stock

Preferred stock may provide that dividends are cumulative, noncumulative, or cumulative to the extent earned. For *cumulative* dividends, if the board does not declare regular dividends on the preferred stock, such omitted dividends cumulate, and no dividend may be declared on the common stock until all dividend arrearages on the preferred stock are declared and paid. If *noncumulative*, regular dividends do not cumulate on the board's failure to declare them, and all rights to a dividend for the period omitted are gone forever. Accordingly, noncumulative stock has priority over common stock only in the fiscal period during which a dividend on common stock is declared. Unless the charter expressly makes the dividends on preferred stock noncumulative, the courts generally hold them to be cumulative. *Cumulative-to-the-extent-earned* shares cumulate unpaid dividends only to the extent funds were legally available to pay such dividends during that fiscal period.

Preferred stock also may be *participating*, although generally it is not. The nature and extent of such participation on a specified basis with the common stock must be stated in the articles of incorporation. For example, a class of participating preferred stock could be entitled to share at the same rate with the common stock in any additional distribution of earnings for a given year *after* provision has been made for payment of the prior preferred dividend and for payment of dividends on the common stock at a rate equal to the fixed rate of the preferred.

Liquidation Preferences After a corporation has been dissolved, its assets liquidated, and the claims of its creditors satisfied, the remaining assets are distributed *pro rata* among the shareholders according to their priority as provided in the articles of incorporation. If a class of stock with a dividend preference does not expressly provide for a preference of any kind on dissolution and liquidation, its holders share *pro rata* with the common shareholders.

Liquidation preference
priority over common stock in corporate assets upon liquidation

When the articles provide a **liquidation preference**, preferred stock has priority over common to the extent the articles state. In addition, if specified, preferred shares may participate beyond the liquidation preference in a stated ratio with other classes of shares. Such shares are said to be participating preferred with reference to liquidation. Preferred shares not so specified do not participate beyond the liquidation preference.

Stock Rights

Stock options contractual rights to purchase stock from a corporation

A corporation may issue stock rights or **stock options** entitling their holders to purchase from the corporation shares of a specified class or classes. A *stock warrant* is a type of stock option that typically has a longer term and is freely transferable. The board of directors determines the terms upon which stock rights, options, or warrants are issued; their form and content; and the consideration for which the shares are to be issued. One use of stock options and warrants is in incentive compensation plans for directors, officers, and employees. Another is to assist a corporation in raising capital by making one class of securities more attractive by including in it the right to purchase shares in another class.

Figure 36–3 compares debt and equity securities.

DIVIDENDS AND OTHER DISTRIBUTIONS

The board of directors, in its discretion, determines the time and amount in which to declare distributions and dividends. The corporation's working capital requirements, shareholder expectations, tax consequences, and other factors influence the board in forming distribution policy.

TYPES OF DIVIDENDS AND OTHER DISTRIBUTIONS

Distribution transfer of property from a corporation to any of its shareholders

The Revised Act defines a **distribution** as "a direct or indirect transfer of money or other property (except its own shares) or incurrence of indebtedness by a

FIGURE 36–3 Debt and Equity Securities

	Debt	Equity	
		Common	**Preferred**
Ownership Interest	No	Yes	Yes
Obligation to Repay Principal	Yes	No	No
Fixed Maturity	Yes	No	No
Obligation to Pay Income	Yes	No	No
Preference on Income	Yes	No	Yes
Preference on Liquidation	Yes	No	Yes
Voting Rights	Some states	Yes, unless denied	Yes, unless denied
Redeemable	Yes	In some states	Yes
Convertible	Yes	In some states	Yes

corporation to or for the benefit of its shareholders in respect of any of its shares. A distribution may be in the form of a declaration or payment of a dividend; a purchase, redemption, or other acquisition of shares; a distribution of indebtedness; or otherwise." A stock or share dividend is a ratable distribution of additional shares of the corporation's capital stock to its shareholders. In a stock split, the corporation simply breaks each of the issued and outstanding shares into a greater number of shares, each representing a proportionately smaller interest in the corporation. Neither a stock dividend nor a stock split is a distribution.

Cash Dividends

The most customary type of dividend is a cash dividend, declared and paid at regular intervals from legally available funds. These dividends may vary in amount, depending on the policy of the board of directors and the earnings of the enterprise.

Property Dividends

Although dividends are almost always paid in cash, shareholders occasionally have received a **property dividend**, a distribution of earnings in the form of property. On one occasion, a distillery declared and paid a dividend in bonded whiskey.

Property dividend distribution in form of property

Liquidating Dividends

Although dividends ordinarily are identified with the distribution of profits, a distribution of capital assets to shareholders is referred to as a **liquidating dividend** in some jurisdictions. Incorporation statutes usually require that the shareholder be informed when a distribution is a liquidating dividend.

Liquidating dividend a distribution of capital assets to shareholders

Redemption of Shares

Redemption is the corporation's repurchase of its own shares, usually at its own option. Though the Model Act and the statutes of many states permit preferred shares to be redeemed, they do not allow the redemption of common stock; in contrast, the Revised Act does not prohibit redeemable common stock. The power of redemption must be expressly provided for in the articles of incorporation.

Redemption of shares a corporation's exercise of the right to repurchase its own shares

Acquisition of Shares

A corporation may acquire its own shares. Such shares, unless canceled, are referred to as treasury shares. Under the Revised Act, such shares are considered

Acquisition of shares a corporation's repurchase of its own shares

authorized but unissued. As with redemption, the acquisition of shares constitutes a distribution to shareholders and has an effect similar to a dividend.

LEGAL RESTRICTIONS ON DIVIDENDS AND OTHER DISTRIBUTIONS

Legal restrictions on distributions distributions may be paid only if the cash flow and applicable balance sheet tests are satisfied

A number of **legal restrictions** limit the amount of **distributions** the board of directors may declare. All states have statutes restricting the funds that are legally available for dividends and other distributions of corporate assets. In many instances, contractual restrictions imposed by lenders provide even more stringent limitations on the declaration of dividends and distributions.

Cash flow test a corporation must not be or become insolvent

States restrict the payment of dividends and other distributions in order to protect creditors. All states impose a "**cash flow test**," the *equity insolvency test*, which prohibits the payment of any dividend or other distribution when the corporation either is insolvent or would become so through the payment of the dividend or distribution. **Insolvent** indicates the inability of a corporation to pay its debts as they become due in the usual course of business. In addition, each state imposes further restrictions on what funds are legally available to pay dividends and other distributions. These additional "**balance sheet**" restrictions are based upon the corporation's assets, whereas the equity insolvency test is based upon the corporation's cash flow.

Insolvent (equity) unable to pay debts as they become due in the usual course of business

Balance sheet test varies among the states and includes the earned surplus test (available in all states), the surplus test, and the net assets test (used by the Model and Revised Acts)

Definitions

The legal, asset-based restrictions on the payment of dividends or other distributions involve the concepts of earned surplus, surplus, net assets, stated capital, and capital surplus (see Figure 36–4).

FIGURE 36–4 Key Concepts in Legal Restrictions Upon Distributions

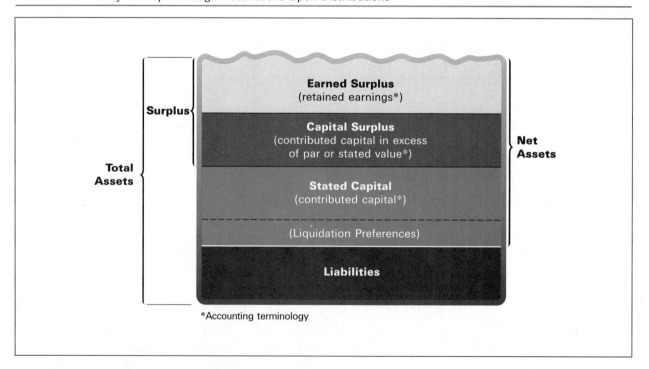

*Accounting terminology

Earned surplus consists of the corporation's undistributed net profits, income, gains, and losses, computed from its date of incorporation.

Surplus is the amount by which the net assets of a corporation exceed its stated capital.

Net assets equal the amount by which the total assets of a corporation exceed its total debts.

Stated capital is the sum of the consideration the corporation has received for its issued stock (except that part of the consideration properly allocated to capital surplus), including any amount transferred to stated capital when stock dividends are declared. In the case of par value shares, the amount of stated capital is the total par value of all the issued shares. In the case of no par stock, it is the consideration the corporation has received for all the no par shares it has issued, except that amount allocated in a manner permitted by law, to an account designated as capital surplus or paid-in surplus.

Capital surplus means the entire surplus of a corporation other than its earned surplus. It may result from an allocation of part of the consideration received for no par shares, from any consideration in excess of par value received for par shares, or from a higher reappraisal of certain corporate assets.

Earned surplus undistributed net profits, income, gains, and losses

Surplus excess of net assets over stated capital

Net assets total assets minus total debts

Stated capital consideration, other than that allocated to capital surplus, received for issued stock

Capital surplus surplus other than earned surplus

Legal Restrictions on Cash Dividends

Earned Surplus Test Unreserved and unrestricted earned surplus is available for dividends in all jurisdictions. Many states permit dividends to be paid *only* from earned surplus; corporations in these jurisdictions may not pay dividends out of capital surplus or stated capital. In addition, dividends may not be paid if the corporation is or would be rendered insolvent in the equity sense by the payment. The MBCA used this test until 1980.

Surplus Test A number of less-restrictive states permit dividends to be paid out of any surplus—earned or capital. Some of these states express a surplus test by prohibiting dividends that impair stated capital. Moreover, dividends may not be paid if the corporation is or would be rendered insolvent in the equity sense by the payment.

Net Assets Test The MBCA, as amended in 1980, and the Revised Act have adopted a net asset test that permits a corporation to pay dividends unless its total assets after such payment would be less than the sum of its total liabilities and the maximum amount that then would be payable for all outstanding shares having preferential rights in liquidation.

Legal Restrictions on Liquidating Distributions

Even those states that do not permit cash dividends to be paid from capital surplus usually will permit distributions, or dividends, in partial liquidation from that source. Prior to 1980, the Model Act had such a provision. A distribution paid out of such surplus returns to the shareholders part of their investment.

No such distribution may be made, however, when the corporation is insolvent or would become insolvent by the distribution. Distributions from capital surplus are also restricted to protect the liquidation preference and cumulative dividend arrearages of preferred shareholders. Unless provided for in the articles of incorporation, a liquidating dividend must be authorized not only by the board

Legal restrictions on liquidating distributions states usually permit distribution in partial liquidation from capital surplus unless the company is insolvent

of directors but also by the affirmative vote of the holders of a majority of the outstanding shares of stock of each class.

Because the Revised Act does not distinguish between cash and liquidating dividends, it therefore imposes the same limitations upon both.

Legal Restrictions on Redemption and Acquisition of Shares

Legal restrictions on redemption of shares in most states, a corporation may not redeem shares when insolvent or when such redemption would render it insolvent

Legal restrictions on acquisition of shares restrictions similar to those on cash dividends usually apply

To protect creditors and holders of other classes of shares, most states have statutory restrictions on redemption. A corporation may not redeem or purchase its redeemable shares when insolvent or when such redemption or purchase would render it insolvent or would reduce its net assets below the aggregate amount payable on shares having prior or equal rights to the corporation's assets upon involuntary dissolution.

A corporation may purchase its own shares only out of earned surplus or, if the articles of incorporation permit or if the shareholders approve, out of capital surplus. As with redemption, the corporation may make no purchase of shares when it is insolvent or when such purchase would make it insolvent.

The Revised Act permits a corporation to purchase, redeem, or otherwise acquire its own shares unless (1) the corporation's total assets after the distribution would be less than the sum of its total liabilities and the maximum amount that then would be payable for all outstanding shares having preferential rights in liquidation or (2) the corporation would be unable to pay its debts as they become due in the usual course of its business.

Additional restrictions may apply to a corporation's acquisition of its own shares. In close corporations, for example, courts may scrutinize acquisitions for compliance with the good faith and fair dealing requirements of the fiduciary duty. See *Donahue v. Rodd Electrotype Co., Inc.* in Chapter 37.

NEIMARK v. MEL KRAMER SALES, INC. Court of Appeals of Wisconsin, 1981, 102 Wis.2d 282, 306 N.W.2d 278

FACTS Mel Kramer was the founder and majority shareholder of Mel Kramer Sales, Inc. (MKS), a closely held Wisconsin corporation. Shortly before Kramer's death, MKS and all of its shareholders (Kramer, Delores Kramer, Jack Neimark, and Jerome Sadowsky) entered into a stock redemption agreement. The agreement required MKS to buy, and a deceased stockholder's estate to sell, all shares of MKS for a specified price. Under the agreement Mel Kramer's majority block of shares was to be redeemed for a net price of $358,000, to be paid in installments of $100,000 at the closing of his estate, and the balance in five consecutive annual installments. The agreement also provided that if MKS did not have sufficient surplus or retained earnings to redeem shares, the parties would contribute the necessary capital to enable MKS to lawfully redeem the shares.

After Mel Kramer died, his widow, Delores, was reluctant to have her husband's shares redeemed, since a third party had recently offered to buy MKS for an amount that would make those shares worth more than the redemption price. Jack Neimark, who was vice president, stockholder, and director of MKS, sued derivatively to compel specific performance of the stockholder redemption agreement. Delores Kramer contended that redemption of her husband's shares would be illegal, since it would render MKS insolvent. The trial court ordered specific performance of the stock redemption agreement.

DECISION Judgment vacated and remanded.

OPINION The Wisconsin statute requires that a stock redemption be paid for out of earned surplus (surplus cutoff test) and prohibits a stock redemption if the corporation would thereby be rendered insolvent (insolvency test). According to the surplus cutoff test, a corporation must have unrestricted earned surplus equal to the cost of the shares to be redeemed. As for the insolvency test, insolvent in the equity sense means an inability of the debtor to pay his debts as they mature.

The use of installment payments, however, makes the application of the surplus cutoff and insolvency tests more complicated. This court agrees with the reasoning of a majority of American courts that the insolvency test should be applied both at the time of repurchase *and* when each installment payment is made. Furthermore, the amount of each payment, and

continued

not the total purchase price, should be the figure used to determine solvency.

The surplus cutoff test is to be handled differently from the insolvency test. This court is persuaded that the surplus cutoff determination should be made only once, at the time of redemption. It is apparent from financial statements that MKS lacks sufficient surplus or retained earnings to satisfy the surplus cutoff test. However, all four stockholders signed the agreement providing that if MKS lacked sufficient surplus to redeem shares according to the redemption agreement,

the stockholders would contribute the necessary capital to enable MKS lawfully to redeem the shares. Therefore, this case is sent back to the trial court to make the necessary findings with regard to providing sufficient earned surplus and assuring solvency as a condition to specific performance.

INTERPRETATION When a corporation redeems its own stock by installment payments, the earned surplus test is applied only at the time of the redemption, whereas the insolvency test is applied both at redemption and when each installment payment is made.

DECLARATION AND PAYMENT OF DISTRIBUTIONS

The board of directors of a corporation declares dividends and other distributions, and this power may not be delegated. If the charter clearly and expressly provides for mandatory dividends, however, the board must comply with the provision. Nonetheless, such provisions are extremely infrequent, and shareholders cannot assume this power in any other way, although it is in their power to elect a new board. Moreover, the board cannot discriminate in its declaration of dividends among shareholders of the same class.

Shareholders' Right to Compel a Dividend

If the directors fail to declare a dividend, a shareholder may bring a suit in equity against them and the corporation to seek a mandatory injunction requiring the directors to declare a dividend. However, courts of equity are reluctant to order an injunction of this kind; for such a judgment involves substituting the court's business judgment for that of the directors elected by the shareholders. With respect to the directors' discretion regarding the declaration of dividends, a preferred shareholder having prior rights with respect to dividends is in the same position as the holder of common shares.

Shareholders' right to compel a dividend the declaration of distributions is within the discretion of the board of directors and only rarely will a court substitute its business judgment for that of the board's

DODGE v. FORD MOTOR CO. Supreme Court of Michigan, 1919, 204 Mich. 459, 170 N.W. 668

FACTS Ford Motor Company had made large profits for several years. Henry Ford, Ford's president and the dominant figure on its board of directors, declared that although it had paid special dividends in the past, Ford would not, as a matter of policy, pay any special dividends in the future but instead would reinvest the profits in the proposed expansion of the company. At the conclusion of Ford's most prosperous year, John and Horace Dodge, minority shareholders in Ford, brought this action against Ford's directors to compel the declaration of dividends and to enjoin the expansion of the business. The Dodges complained that the reinvestment of the profits was not in the best interests of Ford and its shareholders and that it was an arbitrary action of the directors. The trial court entered a decree requiring the directors to declare and pay a dividend of $19,275,385.96.

DECISION That part of the decree fixing and determining the specific amount to be distributed to stockholders affirmed; decree reversed in other respects.

OPINION In general, it is not a violation of a corporation's charter to accumulate profits for reinvestment in the company. As the managers of a corporation, the directors are impliedly invested with discretionary power as to the time and manner of distributing the company's profits. But while the court is reluctant to substitute its judgment for that of the directors, their refusal to declare and pay special dividends in light of the large surplus was not an exercise of discretion but an arbitrary refusal to do what the circumstances required to be done.

INTERPRETATION The right of shareholders to receive a share of the corporation's profits may not be arbitrarily withheld by the directors.

Effect of Declaration

Effect of declaration once properly declared, a cash dividend is considered a debt the corporation owes to the shareholders

Once lawfully and properly declared, a cash dividend is considered a debt the corporation owes to the shareholders. It follows from this debtor-creditor relationship that, once declared, a declaration of a cash dividend cannot be rescinded without the shareholders' consent; a stock dividend, however, may be revoked unless actually distributed.

LIABILITY FOR IMPROPER DIVIDENDS AND DISTRIBUTIONS

The Revised Act imposes personal liability on the directors of a corporation who vote for or assent to the declaration of a dividend or other distribution of corporate assets contrary to the incorporation statute or the articles of incorporation. Directors generally are liable either to the corporation or to the corporation's creditors. The Revised Act expressly provides that the directors who vote for or assent to an illegal dividend or distribution are liable to the corporation. The damages equal the amount of the dividend or distribution in excess of the amount that the corporation lawfully may have paid.

Directors' liability the directors who assent to an improper dividend are liable for the unlawful amount of the dividend

A director is not liable if she acted in good faith, with due care, and in a manner she reasonably believed to be in the best interests of the corporation. (This standard of conduct is discussed in the next chapter.) In discharging this duty, a director is entitled to rely in good faith on financial statements presented by the corporation's officers, public accountants, or finance committee. Such statements must be prepared on the basis of "accounting practices and principles that are reasonable in the circumstances or on a fair valuation or other method that is reasonable in the circumstances." According to the Comments to the Revised Act, generally accepted accounting principles are *always* reasonable in the circumstances; other accounting principles *may* be acceptable under a general standard of reasonableness.

Shareholders' liability a shareholder must return illegal dividends if he knew of the illegality, if the dividend resulted from his fraud, or if the corporation is insolvent

A shareholder's obligation to repay an illegally declared dividend depends on a variety of factors, which may include the faith, good or bad, in which the shareholder accepted the dividend, his knowledge of the facts, the solvency or insolvency of the corporation, and, in some instances, special statutory provisions. The existence of statutory liability on the part of directors does not relieve shareholders from the duty to make repayment.

A shareholder who receives illegal dividends with knowledge of their unlawful character is under a duty to refund them to the corporation. Where the corporation is insolvent, the shareholder may not retain even a dividend received in good faith. However, where an unsuspecting shareholder receives an illegal dividend from a solvent corporation, the majority rule is that the corporation cannot compel a refund.

Figure 36–5 compares the liability of directors and shareholders for improper distributions.

TRANSFER OF INVESTMENT SECURITIES

Any investor has the right to transfer her securities by sale, gift, or pledge, just as she has the inherent right to transfer any other properties she may own. The right to transfer is a valuable one, and easy transferability adds to the value and marketability of securities. The availability of a ready market for any security affords liquidity and makes the security both attractive to investors and useful as collateral.

The Uniform Commercial Code, Article 8, Investment Securities, contains the statutory rules applicable to transfers of securities; these rules are similar to those

FIGURE 36–5 Liability for Improper Distributions

	Corporation Solvent	Corporation Insolvent
Nonbreaching Director	No	No
Breaching Director	Yes	Yes
Knowing Shareholder	Yes	Yes
Innocent Shareholder	No	Yes

in Article 3, which concerns negotiable instruments. Article 8 applies not only to shares but also to bonds, debentures, voting trust certificates, certificates of beneficial interest in business trusts, and any other "interest in property of or an enterprise of the issuer or an obligation of the issuer" that is of a "class or series" and "issued or dealt in as a medium for investment." In 1994, a revision of Article 8 was promulgated, and some states have already adopted the revision. This chapter discusses the pre-1994 version of Article 8.

Several aspects of the transfer of securities are also regulated by federal securities laws, which we will discuss in Chapter 42.

OWNERSHIP OF SECURITIES

Record Ownership

A security is intangible personal property and exists independently of a certificate. Article 8 permits the issuance and transfer of **certificated securities** and **uncertificated securities**. The transfer of uncertificated securities is registered on books maintained for that purpose by or on behalf of the issuer.

Certificated security
security represented by a certificate

The Revised Act permits the board of directors to authorize the issue of some or all of any or all of a corporation's classes of shares without certificates. The rights and obligations of holders of uncertificated shares and holders of certificated shares of the same class and series are identical.

Uncertificated security
security not represented by a certificate

Duty of Issuer to Register Transfer of Certificated Security

The issuing corporation is under a duty to register the transfer of its certificated securities and to issue new certificates to a new owner if certain conditions are met. The owner or purchaser is entitled to registration in order to vote and to receive dividends, notices, periodic reports of the corporation, and the actual certificate, because the only way to sell, pledge, or dispose of certificated securities is by transferring the certificate itself.

Lost, Destroyed, or Stolen Certificated Securities

If a certificated security has been lost, destroyed, or stolen, the owner is entitled to a new certificate to replace the missing one, provided she (1) requests it before the issuer has notice that the "missing" certificate has been acquired by a *bona fide* purchaser, (2) files a sufficient indemnity bond with the issuer, and (3) satisfies other reasonable requirements of the issuer, such as furnishing a sworn statement of the facts connected with the loss.

TRANSFER OF SECURITIES

Restrictions on Transfer

In the absence of a specific agreement, shares of stock are freely transferable. Although free transferability of shares is usually considered an advantage of the corporate form, in some situations the shareholders may prefer to restrict the transfer of shares. In closely held corporations, for example, stock transfer restrictions are used to control who may become shareholders. They are also used to maintain statutory close corporation status by restricting the number of persons who may become shareholders. In publicly held corporations, restrictions on the transfer of shares are used to preserve exemptions under state and federal securities laws. (These are discussed in Chapter 42.)

Most incorporation statutes have no provisions governing share transfer restrictions. The common law validates such restrictions if they are adopted for a lawful purpose and do not unreasonably restrain or prohibit transferability. In addition, the UCC provides that an otherwise valid share transfer restriction is ineffective against a person without actual knowledge of it unless the restriction is conspicuously noted on the share certificate or, for an uncertificated security, in the initial transaction statement.

Restrictions on transfer must be reasonable and conspicuously noted on stock certificate

The Revised Act and the statutes of several states permit the articles of incorporation, bylaws, or a shareholder agreement to impose **transfer restrictions** but require that the restriction be noted conspicuously on the certificate or that, for uncertificated securities, it be contained in the information statement. The Revised Act authorizes restrictions for any reasonable purpose.

DEAN WITTER REYNOLDS, INC. v. SELECTRONICS, INC. Supreme Court, Appellate Division, 1993, 188 A.D.2d 117, 594 N.Y.S.2d 174

FACTS Selectronics, Inc. transferred five shares of Selectronics stock to Stephen R. Nagel, a director and officer of the company. In reliance upon the "private placement" exemption authorized under section 4(2) of the Securities Act of 1933, Selectronics did not register the transfer with the Securities Exchange Commission. Selectronics failed to place any markings on the certificates to alert subsequent transferees that the securities were unregistered and had been distributed in a private placement. Although Nagel later exchanged the certificates for the five common stock securities in question here, Selectronics again chose not to file a registration statement or record restrictive legends on the shares. The stock, which was pledged by Nagel as security for a loan from the defendant, F.I.G. Corporation, ultimately came into possession of Banque Internationale a Luxembourg (Suisse) S.A. (BIL), which deposited the shares with Dean Witter with instructions to sell the stock. Dean Witter proceeded to sell the stock and remitted the proceeds to BIL. However, when Selectronics's transfer agent, Mellon Bank, sent the shares for re-registration, the securities clearinghouse refused the certificates and returned them to Dean Witter with, for the first time, restrictive legends shown on their face. When BIL refused to return to Dean Witter the funds it had previously forwarded, Dean Witter commenced this action against BIL and Selectronics.

In granting Dean Witter's motion for partial summary judgment, the trial court determined that the defendants were liable under UCC § 8–204 for neglecting to indicate on the face of the stock certificates any restrictions on transfer and remanded the matter for an immediate assessment of damages. Following reargument, the trial judge modified her decision to allow discovery as to whether Dean Witter lacked actual knowledge of the restrictions as required by UCC § 8–204. On appeal, the defendants urged that the complaint should have been dismissed because UCC § 8–204 does not create a cause of action for failure to legend stock certificates, and, in any event, this provision applies only to restrictions imposed by the issuer and not by law. The defendants contend that the restriction on transfer due to private placement is imposed by the Securities Act of 1933 and not by any action of Selectronics.

DECISION Judgment affirmed.

OPINION Section 8–204 of the Uniform Commercial Code states that "[a] restriction on transfer of a security imposed by the issuer even though otherwise lawful is ineffective against any person without actual knowledge of it unless (a) the security is certificated and the restriction is noted conspicuously thereon." The sixth comment accompanying this provision observes that it "deals only with restrictions imposed by the issuer and restrictions imposed by statute are not affected." Nevertheless, contrary to the defendants' contention, the restrictions involved here were established by the issuer and not by any statute. The

continued

relevant federal legislation certainly does not require the imposition of restrictions but merely authorizes issuers and transferors to register their securities or, alternatively, qualify for statutory exemptions. Thus, while a party desiring to invoke a specified exemption may be compelled to place restrictions on transfer, it is not the securities law that imposes the restrictions. Rather, it is the issuer, by electing to rely upon an exemption instead of registering the securities in question, that makes the operative choice. Thus, Selectronics could have chosen to file a registration statement for Nagel's shares, in which case the stock would be freely tradeable. Instead, it opted to exempt the securities from registration by making use of the private placement exemption. Thus, UCC § 8–204 does create liability for damages upon an issuer and/or transfer agent who fails to include restrictions on the face of securities. Accordingly, the trial court's decision was in all respects proper.

INTERPRETATION An otherwise valid share transfer restriction is ineffective against a person without actual knowledge of it unless the restriction is conspicuously noted on the share certificate.

Statute of Frauds

A contract for the sale of securities is not enforceable unless one of the following conditions is satisfied: (1) a writing indicating that a contract has been made for the sale of a stated quantity of described securities at a defined or stated price is signed by the party against whom enforcement is sought; (2) performance occurs, as evidenced by acceptance of delivery or acceptance of payment, but only to the extent of such delivery or payment; (3) the receiver fails to object in writing within ten days to a written confirmation binding on the sender; or (4) the party against whom enforcement is sought admits in pleading, testimony, or otherwise in court that a contract was made.

> **Statute of frauds** a contract for the sale of securities must be in writing or must otherwise satisfy the statute of frauds

Manner of Transfer

Under the Code, certificated securities are transferred either by delivery of the certificate alone, if it is in bearer form or indorsed in blank, or, if it is in registered form, which is more usual, by delivery of the certificate either (1) with the indorsement of "an appropriate person" on it or (2) accompanied by a separate document of assignment and transfer signed by "an appropriate person." The term "appropriate person" includes the person specified in the certificate or entitled to it by special indorsement, his successors in interest, or the authorized agent of a person so specified or so entitled. A transfer of uncertificated securities occurs when the transfer is registered.

> **Manner of transfer** made by delivery of the certificate if it is in bearer form or indorsed in blank, or, if in registered form, with either an indorsement or a separate assignment, each signed by an appropriate person

The delivery of an unindorsed certificate by the owner with the intention of transferring title to the securities represented thereby gives the intended transferee as against the transferor complete rights in the certificate and in the certificated securities, including the right to compel indorsement. He becomes a *bona fide* purchaser of the certificated securities, however, only when the indorsement is supplied.

Bona Fide Purchasers

A "*bona fide* purchaser" is a purchaser for value in good faith and without notice of any adverse claim who takes delivery of a certificated security either in bearer form or in registered form issued to her, indorsed to her, or in blank. The negotiation and transfer of a security to a *bona fide* purchaser passes title to her free of all adverse claims not conspicuously noted on the certificate. Such claims would include contentions that a transfer was or would be wrongful or that a particular adverse person is the owner of or has an interest in the security. Thus, the *bona fide* purchaser from a thief, finder, or other unauthorized person is protected.

Transfer Warranties

Transfer warranties by transferring securities represented by a certificate, a person gives certain warranties

A person transferring certificated securities to a purchaser for value warrants that (1) the transfer is effective and rightful; (2) the security is genuine and has not been materially altered; and (3) he knows of no fact that might impair the validity of the security.

A person who presents a certificated security for registration of transfer or for payment or exchange warrants to the issuer that he is entitled to the registration, payment, or exchange; but a purchaser for value and without notice of adverse claims who receives a new, reissued, or registered certificated security on registration of transfer warrants only that he has no knowledge of any unauthorized signature in a necessary indorsement.

Forged or Unauthorized Indorsement

Forged or unauthorized indorsement the owner of securities represented by a certificate is not deprived of his title by a transfer of the certificate bearing a forged or unauthorized indorsement

The owner of certificated securities is not deprived of his title by a transfer of the certificate bearing a **forged or unauthorized indorsement**. However, the purchaser of a security bearing such an indorsement who resells and transfers it to a *bona fide* purchaser breaches the warranty that the transfer is effective and rightful and consequently is liable to the purchaser for the value of the securities at the time of sale. Neither party is owner of the securities, as title cannot be transferred through a forged or unauthorized indorsement.

CHAPTER SUMMARY

Debt Securities

Authority to Issue Debt Securities	**Definitions** ■ *Debt Security* source of capital creating no ownership interest and involving the corporation's promise to repay funds lent to it ■ *Bond* a debt security **Rule** each corporation has the power to issue debt securities as determined by the board of directors
Types of Debt Securities	**Unsecured Bonds** called debentures, have only the obligation of the corporation behind them **Secured Bonds** are claims against a corporation's general assets and also a lien on specific property **Income Bonds** condition to some extent the payment of interest on corporate earnings **Participating Bonds** call for a stated percentage of return regardless of earnings, with additional payments dependent upon earnings **Convertible Bonds** may be exchanged for other securities **Callable Bond** bonds subject to redemption

Equity Securities

Issuance of Shares	**Definitions** ■ *Equity Security* source of capital creating an ownership interest in the corporation ■ *Share* a proportionate ownership interest in a corporation ■ *Treasury Stock* shares reacquired by a corporation **Authority to Issue** only those shares authorized in the articles of incorporation may be issued **Preemptive Rights** right to purchase a *pro rata* share of new stock offerings **Amount of Consideration for Shares** shares are deemed fully paid and nonassessable when a corporation receives the consideration for which the board of directors authorized the issuance of the shares, which in the case of par value stock must be at least par **Payment for Newly Issued Shares** may be cash, property, and services actually rendered, as determined by the board of directors; under the Revised Act, promises to contribute cash, property, or services are also permitted

Classes of Shares	**Common Stock** stock not having any special contract rights **Preferred Stock** stock having contractual rights superior to those of common stock ■ *Dividend Preferences* must receive full dividends before any dividend may be paid on common stock ■ *Liquidation Preferences* priority over common stock in corporate assets upon liquidation **Stock Rights** contractual right to purchase stock from a corporation

Dividends and Other Distributions

Types of Dividends and Other Distributions	**Distributions** transfers of property by a corporation to any of its shareholders in respect to its shares; become debts of the corporation, if and when declared by the board **Cash Dividends** the most common type of distribution **Property Dividends** distribution in form of property **Stock Dividends** a ratable distribution of additional shares of stock **Stock Splits** each of the outstanding shares is broken into a greater number of shares **Liquidating Dividends** a distribution of capital assets to shareholders **Redemption of Shares** a corporation's exercise of the right to repurchase its own shares **Acquisition of Shares** a corporation's repurchase of its own shares

Legal Restrictions on Dividends and Other Distributions	**Legal Restrictions on Cash Dividends** dividends may be paid only if the cash flow and applicable balance sheet tests are satisfied ■ *Cash Flow Test* a corporation must not be or become insolvent (unable to pay its debts as they become due in the usual course of business) ■ *Balance Sheet Test* varies among the states and includes the earned surplus test (available in all states), the surplus test, and the net assets test (used by the Model and Revised Acts)

Legal Restrictions on Liquidating Distributions states usually permit distribution in partial liquidation from capital surplus unless the company is insolvent

Legal Restrictions on Redemptions of Shares in most states, a corporation may not redeem shares when insolvent or when such redemption would render it insolvent

Legal Restrictions on Acquisition of Shares restrictions similar to those on cash dividends usually apply

Declaration and Payment of Distributions

Shareholders' Right to Compel a Dividend the declaration of dividends is within the discretion of the board of directors and only rarely will a court substitute its business judgment for that of the board

Effect of Declaration once properly declared, a cash dividend is considered a debt the corporation owes to the shareholders

Liability for Improper Dividends and Distributions

Directors the directors who assent to an improper dividend are liable for the unlawful amount of the dividend

Shareholders a shareholder must return illegal dividends if he knew of the illegality, if the dividend resulted from his fraud, or if the corporation is insolvent

Transfer of Securities

Restrictions on Transfer must be reasonable and conspicuously noted on stock certificate

Statute of Frauds a contract for the sale of securities must be in writing or must otherwise satisfy the statute of frauds

Manner of Transfer made by delivery of the certificate if it is in bearer form or indorsed in blank, or, if in registered form, with either an indorsement or a separate assignment, each signed by an appropriate person

Transfer Warranties by transferring securities represented by a certificate, a person gives certain warranties

Forged or Unauthorized Indorsement the owner of securities represented by a certificate is not deprived of his title by a transfer of the certificate bearing a forged or unauthorized indorsement

QUESTIONS

1. Distinguish between equity and debt securities.
2. Identify and describe the principal kinds of equity and debt securities.
3. Explain what type and amount of consideration a corporation may validly receive for the shares it issues.
4. Explain the legal restrictions imposed upon dividends and other distributions.
5. Identify the warranties a person transferring investment securities makes to a purchaser for value.

Internet Question. Using the Security and Exchange Commission's EDGAR database, find the Annual Report (Form 10-K) and, if necessary, the proxy statement (DEF 14A) of three companies of interest and determine with respect to their common stock: (a) on which exchanges it is listed, (b) earnings for the most recent quarter, (c) annual dividends, and (d) the high and low price for the stock over the previous 52 week period.

1. Frank McAnarney and Joseph Lemon entered into an agreement to promote a corporation to engage in the manufacture of farm implements. Before the corporation was organized, McAnarney and Lemon solicited subscriptions to the stock of the corporation and presented a written agreement for the subscribers to sign. The agreement provided that the subscribers would pay $100 per share for stock in the corporation in consideration of McAnarney's and Lemon's agreement to organize the corporation and to advance the preincorporation expenses. Thomas Jordan signed the agreement, making application for 100 shares of stock. After the filing of the articles of incorporation with the secretary of state, but before the charter to the corporation was issued, Jordan died. The administrator of Jordan's estate notified McAnarney and Lemon that the estate would not honor Jordan's subscription.

   After the formation of the corporation, Franklin Adams signed a subscription agreement making application for 100 shares of stock. Before the corporation accepted the subscription, Adams informed the corporation that he was canceling it.

   (a) The corporation brings an appropriate action against Jordan's estate to enforce Jordan's stock subscription. Decision?

   (b) The corporation brings an appropriate action to enforce Adams's stock subscription. Decision?

2. The XYZ Corporation was duly organized on July 10. Its certificate of incorporation provides for a total authorized capital of $100,000, consisting of 1,000 shares of common stock with a par value of $100 per share. The corporation issues for cash a total of fifty certificates, numbered one to fifty inclusive, representing various amounts of shares in the names of various individuals. The shares were all paid for in advance, so the certificates are all dated and mailed on the same day. The fifty certificates of stock represent a total of 1,050 shares. Certificate 49 for thirty shares was issued to Jane Smith. Certificate 50 for twenty-five shares was issued to William Jones. Is there any question concerning the validity of any of the stock thus issued? What are the rights of Smith and Jones?

3. Doris subscribed for 200 shares of 12 percent cumulative, participating, redeemable, convertible, preferred shares of the Ritz Hotel Company with a par value of $100 per share. The subscription agreement provided that she was to receive a bonus of one share of common stock of $100 par value for each share of preferred stock. Doris fully paid her subscription agreement of $20,000 and received the 200 shares of preferred and the bonus stock of 200 shares of the par value common. The Ritz Hotel company later becomes insolvent. Ronald, the receiver of the corporation, brings suit for $20,000, the par value of the common stock. What judgment?

4. The Hyperion Company has an authorized capital stock of 1,000 shares with a par value of $100 per share, of which 900 shares, all fully paid, are outstanding. Having an ample surplus, the Hyperion Company purchases from its shareholders 100 shares at par. Subsequently, the Hyperion Company, needing additional working capital, issues the 200 shares in question to Alexander at $80 per share. Two years later, the Hyperion Company is forced into bankruptcy. The trustee in bankruptcy now sues Alexander for $4,000. Decision?

5. For five years, Henry and James had been engaged as partners in building houses. They owned the equipment necessary to conduct the business and had an excellent reputation. In March, Joyce, who previously had been in the same kind of business, proposed that Henry, James, and Joyce form a corporation for the purpose of constructing medium-priced houses. They engaged attorney Portia, who did all the work required and caused the business to be incorporated under the name of Libra Corp.

   The certificate of incorporation authorized one hundred shares of $100 par value stock. At the organizational meeting of the incorporators, Henry, James, and Joyce were elected directors, and Libra Corp. issued a total of sixty-five shares of its stock. Henry and James each received twenty shares in consideration for transferring to Libra Corp. the equipment and goodwill of their partnership, which had a combined value of over $4000. Joyce received twenty shares as an inducement to work for Libra Corp. in the future, and Portia received five shares as compensation for the legal services she rendered in forming Libra Corp.

   Later that year, Libra Corp. had a number of financial setbacks and in December ceased operations. What rights, if any, does Libra Corp. have against Henry, James, Joyce, and Portia in connection with the original issuance of its shares?

6. Paul Bunyan is the owner of noncumulative 8 percent preferred stock in the Broadview Corporation, which had no earnings or profits in 1995. In 1996, the corporation had large profits and a surplus from which it might properly have declared dividends. However, the directors refused to do so, using the surplus instead to purchase goods necessary for the corporation's expanding business. The corporation earned a small profit in 1997. The directors at the end of 1997 declared a 10 percent dividend on the common stock and an 8 percent dividend on the preferred stock without paying preferred dividends for 1996.

   (a) Is Bunyan entitled to dividends for 1995? For 1996?

   (b) Is Bunyan entitled to a dividend of 10 percent rather than 8 percent in 1997?

7. Alpha Corporation has outstanding 400 shares of $100 par value common stock, which has been issued and sold at $105 per share for a total of $42,000. Alpha is incorporated in State X, which has adopted the earned surplus test for all distributions. At a time when the assets of the corporation amount to $65,000 and the liabilities to creditors total $10,000, the directors learn that Rachel, who holds 100 of the 400 shares of stock, is planning to sell her shares on the open market for $10,500. Believing that this will not be in the best interest of the corporation, the directors enter into an agreement with Rachel to buy the shares for $10,500. About six months later, when the assets of the corporation have decreased to $50,000 and its liabilities, not including its liability to Rachel, have increased to $20,000, the directors use $10,000 to pay a dividend to all of the shareholders. The corporation later becomes insolvent.

   (a) Does Rachel have any liability to the corporation or its creditors in connection with the corporation's reacquisition of the 100 shares?

   (b) Was the payment of the $10,000 dividend proper?

8. Almega Corporation, organized under the laws of State S, has outstanding 20,000 shares of $100 par value nonvoting preferred stock calling for noncumulative dividends of $5 per year; 10,000 shares of voting preferred stock of par $50 value, calling for cumulative dividends of $2.50 per year; and 10,000 shares of no par common stock. State S has adopted the earned surplus test for all distributions. As of the end of 1992, the corporation had no earned surplus. In 1993, the corporation had net earnings of $170,000; in 1994, $135,000; in 1995, $60,000; in 1996, $210,000; and in 1997, $120,000. The board of directors passed over all dividends during the four years from 1993 to 1996, since the company needed working capital for expansion purposes. In 1997, however, the directors declared a dividend of $5 per share on the noncumulative preferred shares, a dividend of $12.50 per share on the cumulative preferred shares, and a dividend of $30 per share on the common stock. The board submitted its declaration to the voting shareholders, and they ratified it. Before the dividends were paid, Payne, the record holder of 500 shares of the noncumulative preferred stock, brought an appropriate action to restrain any payment to the cumulative preferred or common shareholders until the company paid a full dividend for the period from 1993 to 1997. Decision?

9. Sayre learned that Adams, Boone, and Chase were planning to form a corporation for the purpose of manufacturing and marketing a line of novelties to wholesale outlets. Sayre had patented a self-locking gas tank cap but lacked the financial backing to market it profitably. He negotiated with Adams, Boone, and Chase, who agreed to purchase the patent rights for $5,000 in cash and 200 shares of $100 par value preferred stock in a corporation to be formed.

   The corporation was formed and Sayre's stock issued to him, but the corporation has refused to make the cash payment. It has also refused to declare dividends, although the business has been very profitable because of Sayre's patent and has a substantial earned surplus with a large cash balance on hand. It is selling the remainder of the originally authorized issue of preferred shares, ignoring Sayre's demand to purchase a proportionate number of these shares. What are Sayre's rights, if any?

10. A bylaw of Betma Corporation provides that no shareholder can sell his shares unless he first offers them for sale to the corporation or its directors. The bylaw also states that this restriction shall bind all present or future owners or holders and shall be printed or stamped on each stock certificate. Betma Corporation did not comply with this latter provision. Shaw, having knowledge of the bylaw restriction, nevertheless purchased twenty shares of the corporation's stock from Rice, without having Rice first offer them for sale to the corporation or its directors. When Betma Corporation refused to effectuate a transfer of the shares to her, Shaw sued to compel a transfer and the issuance of a new certificate to her. Decision?

11. Wood, the receiver of Stanton Oil Company, sued Stanton's shareholders to recover dividends paid to them for three years, claiming that at the time these dividends were declared, Stanton was in fact insolvent. Wood did not allege that the present creditors were also creditors when the dividends were paid. Decision?

12. Olympic National Agencies was organized with an authorized capitalization of preferred stock and common stock. The articles of incorporation provided for a 7 percent annual dividend for the preferred stock. The articles further stated that the preferred stock would be given priority interests in the corporation's assets up to the par value of the stock. In 1965, the shareholders voted to dissolve Olympic. Because Olympic's assets greatly exceeded its liabilities, the liquidating trustee petitioned the court for instructions on the respective rights of the shareholders in the assets of the corporation upon dissolution. Decision?

13. International Distributing Export Company (IDE) was organized as a corporation on September 7, 1948, under the laws of New York and commenced business on November 1, 1948. IDE formerly had been in existence as an individual proprietorship. On October 31, 1948, the newly organized corporation had liabilities of $64,084. Its only assets, in the sum of $33,042, were those of the former sole proprietorship. The corporation, however, set up an asset on its balance sheet in the amount of $32,000 for goodwill. As a result of this entry, IDE had a surplus at the end of each of its fiscal years from 1949 until 1954. Cano, a shareholder, received $7,144 in dividends from IDE during the period from 1950 to 1955. Fried, the trustee in bankruptcy of IDE, brought an action against Cano to recover the amount of these dividends, alleging that they had been paid when IDE was insolvent or when its capital was impaired. Decision?

CHAPTER 37

Management Structure

The corporate management structure, as required by state incorporation statutes, is pyramidal. At the base of the pyramid are the *shareholders*, who are the residual owners of the corporation. Basic to their role in controlling the corporation is the right to elect representatives to manage the ordinary business matters of the corporation and the right to approve all extraordinary matters.

The *board of directors*, as the shareholders' elected representatives, are delegated the power to manage the business of the corporation. Directors exercise dominion and control over the corporation, hold positions of trust and confidence, and determine questions of operating policy. Because they are not expected to devote their full time to the corporation's affairs, directors have broad authority to delegate power to agents and to *officers*, who hold their offices at the will of the board. These officers, in turn, hire and fire all necessary operating personnel and run the day-to-day affairs of the corporation. The pyramid structure of corporate management under the statutory model is illustrated in Figure 37–1.

CORPORATE GOVERNANCE

The statutory model of corporate management, although required by most states, accurately describes the actual governance of only a few corporations. The great majority of corporations are closely held: they have a small number of stockholders and no ready market for their shares, and most of the shareholders actively participate in the management of the business. Typically, the shareholders of a closely held corporation are also its directors and officers. Figure 37–2 depicts the actual management structure of a typical closely held corporation.

Although the statutory model and the actual governance of closely held corporations diverge, in most states closely held corporations must adhere to the general corporate statutory model. One of the greatest burdens conventional general business corporation statutes impose on closely held corporations is a set of rigid corporate formalities. Although these formalities may be necessary and desirable in publicly held corporations having separate management and ownership, in a closely held corporation, where the owners are usually the managers, many of these formalities are unnecessary and meaningless. Consequently, shareholders in closely held corporations tend to disregard the formalities, sometimes forfeiting their limited liability as a result. In response to this problem, the 1969 amendments to the MBCA, which were carried over to the Revised Act, included several liberalizing provisions for closely held corporations. Moreover, some states have enacted special legislation to accommodate the needs of closely held corporations, and, as noted in Chapter 35, a Statutory Close Corporation Supplement (the Supplement) to the Model and Revised Acts has been promulgated.

The Supplement has relaxed most of the nonessential corporate formalities. It permits operation without a board of directors, authorizes broad use of shareholder agreements (including their use in place of bylaws), makes annual meetings optional, and authorizes one person to execute documents in more than one capacity. Most importantly, it prevents courts from denying limited liability simply because the corporation is a statutory close corporation. The general incorporation statute applies to closely held corporations except to the extent that it is inconsistent with the Supplement.

In sharp contrast is the large, publicly held corporation with a vast market for its shares. These shares typically are widely dispersed, and very few are owned by management. Approximately one-half are held by institutional investors (such as insurance companies, pension funds, mutual funds, and trusts), which manage funds for individual investors; the remaining shares are owned directly by individual investors. Whereas the great majority of institutional investors exercise their right to vote their shares, most individual investors do not. Nonetheless, virtually all shareholders who vote for the directors do so through the use of a **proxy**—an authorization by a shareholder to an agent (usually the chief executive officer of the corporation) to vote his shares. The majority of shareholders who return their proxies vote as management advises. As a result, incumbent management prevails in nearly all elections and actually determines its own membership. Figure 37–3 illustrates the actual management structure of a typical large, publicly held corporation.

Proxy authorization by a shareholder to have another vote his shares

Thus, the 500 to 1,000 large, publicly held corporations—which own the great bulk of the industrial wealth of the United States—are controlled by a small group of corporate officers. This great concentration of the control over wealth, and the power that results from it, raises social, policy, and ethical issues concerning the governance of these corporations and the accountability of their management. The actions (or inactions) of these powerful corporations greatly affect the national economy, employment policies, the health and safety of the workplace and the environment, the quality of products, and the effects of overseas operations. Accordingly, the accountability of management is a critical issue.

Nevertheless, the structure and governance of corporations must adhere to incorporation statute requirements. Therefore, in this chapter we will discuss the rights, duties, and liabilities of shareholders, directors, and officers under these statutes.

ROLE OF SHAREHOLDERS

The role of the shareholders in managing the corporation is generally restricted to the election of directors, the approval of certain extraordinary matters, the approval of corporate transactions that are void or voidable unless ratified, and the right to bring suits to enforce these rights.

VOTING RIGHTS OF SHAREHOLDERS

The shareholder's right to vote is fundamental to the concept of the corporation and its management structure. In most states today, a shareholder is entitled to one vote for each share of stock that she owns, unless the articles of incorporation provide otherwise; the articles may provide for more or less than one vote

FIGURE 37–1 Management Structure of Corporations: The Statutory Model

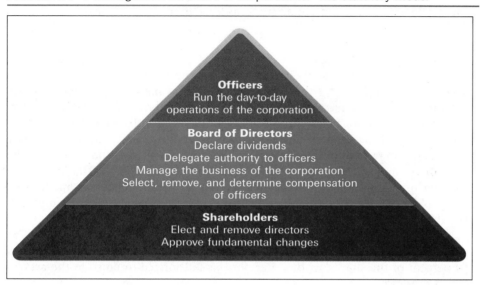

Officers
Run the day-to-day
operations of the corporation

Board of Directors
Declare dividends
Delegate authority to officers
Manage the business of the corporation
Select, remove, and determine compensation
of officers

Shareholders
Elect and remove directors
Approve fundamental changes

FIGURE 37–2 Management Structure of Typical Closely Held Corporations

Shareholders = Directors = Officers

FIGURE 37–3 Management Structure of Typical Publicly Held Corporation

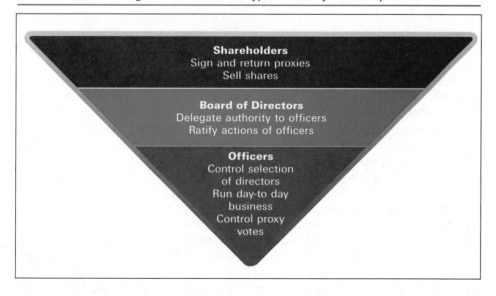

Shareholders
Sign and return proxies
Sell shares

Board of Directors
Delegate authority to officers
Ratify actions of officers

Officers
Control selection
of directors
Run day-to day
business
Control proxy
votes

for any share. In addition, incorporation statutes generally permit the issuance of one or more classes of nonvoting stock, as long as at least one class of shares has voting rights.

Shareholder Meetings

Shareholder meetings shareholders may exercise their voting rights at both annual and special shareholder meetings

Shareholders may exercise their voting rights at both annual and special **shareholder meetings**. Under the Revised Act, *annual meetings* are required and must be held at a time fixed by the corporation's bylaws. If the annual shareholder meeting is not held within the earlier of six months after the end of the corporation's fiscal year or fifteen months after its last annual meeting, any shareholder may petition and obtain a court order requiring that a meeting be held. By comparison, the Close Corporation Supplement provides that no annual meeting of shareholders need be held unless a written request is made by a shareholder at least thirty days in advance of the date specified for the meeting. The date may be established in the articles of incorporation, in the bylaws, or in a shareholder agreement.

Special meetings may be called by the board of directors, by holders of at least 10 percent of the shares, or by other persons authorized to do so in the articles of incorporation.

Written notice stating the date, time, and place of the meeting and, in the case of a special meeting, the purposes for which it is called must be given in advance. Notice, however, may be waived in writing by any shareholder entitled to notice.

A number of states permit shareholders to conduct business without a meeting if all the shareholders consent in writing to the action taken. Some states have further relaxed the formalities of shareholder action by permitting shareholders to act without a meeting with the written consent of only the number of shares required to act on the matter.

Quorum and Voting

Quorum *(kwor'·im)* minimum number necessary to be present at a meeting in order to transact business

A **quorum** of shares must be presented at the meeting, either in person or by proxy. Unissued shares and treasury stock may not be voted or counted in determining whether a quorum exists. Decisions made at the meeting will have no effect if a quorum is not present. Once a quorum is present at a meeting, it is deemed present for the rest of the meeting, even if shareholders withdraw in an effort to break it. Unless the articles of incorporation otherwise provide, a majority of shares entitled to vote constitutes a quorum. In most states and under the Model Act, a quorum may not consist of less than one-third of the shares entitled to vote; the Revised Act and some states do not contain a statutory minimum for a quorum. Because state statutes do not impose an upper limit upon a quorum, it may be set higher than a majority and may even require *all* the outstanding shares.

Most states require shareholder actions to be approved by a majority of the shares represented at the meeting and entitled to vote. The Revised Act and some states, however, provide a different rule: if a quorum exists, a shareholder action (other than the election of directors) is approved if the votes cast for the action exceed the votes cast against it. Moreover, virtually all states permit the articles of incorporation to increase the percentage of shares required to take any action that is subject to shareholder approval. A provision that increases the voting requirements is commonly called a "supermajority provision." Close corporations frequently have used supermajority shareholder voting requirements to protect minority shareholders from oppression by the majority. Recently, some publicly held corporations have used them to defend against hostile takeover bids as well.

Election of Directors

The shareholders elect directors each year at the annual shareholders' meeting. Most states provide that where a corporation's board consists of nine or more directors, the charter or bylaws may provide for a *classification* of directors, that is, a division into two or three classes to be as nearly equal in number as possible and to serve for staggered terms. If the directors are divided into two classes, the members of each class are elected once a year in alternate years for a two-year term; if divided into three classes, they are elected for three-year terms. This permits one-half of the board to be elected every two years or one-third to be elected every three years, thus providing continuity in the board's membership. Moreover, given two or more classes of shares and the authorization for such an action in the articles of incorporation, each class may elect a specified number of directors.

Election of directors the shareholders elect the board at the annual meeting of the corporation

Straight Voting Normally, each shareholder has one vote for each share owned, and directors are elected by a *plurality* of the votes, though the charter may increase the percentage of shares required for the election of directors.

Straight voting directors are elected by a plurality of votes

Cumulative Voting In certain states shareholders electing directors have the right of cumulative voting. In most states, and under the Revised Act, cumulative voting is permissive, not mandatory. **Cumulative voting** entitles shareholders to multiply the number of votes they are entitled to cast by the number of directors for whom they are entitled to vote and to cast the product for a single candidate or distribute the product among two or more candidates. Cumulative voting permits a minority shareholder, or a group of minority shareholders acting together, to obtain minority representation on the board if they own a certain minimum number of shares. In the absence of cumulative voting, the holder or holders of 51 percent of the voting shares can elect all of the members of the board.

Cumulative voting entitles shareholders to multiply the number of votes they are entitled to cast by the number of directors for whom they are entitled to vote and to cast the product for a single candidate or to distribute the product among two or more candidates

The formula for determining how many shares a minority shareholder with cumulative voting rights must own, or have proxies to vote, in order to secure representation on the board is as follows:

$$X = \frac{ac}{b+1} + 1$$

where

a = number of shares voting
b = number of directors to be elected
c = number of directors desired to be elected
X = number of shares necessary to elect the number of directors desired to be elected.

For example, Gray Corporation has two shareholders, Stephanie with sixty-four shares and Thomas with thirty-six shares. The board of directors of Gray Corporation consists of three directors. Under "straight" or noncumulative voting, Stephanie could cast sixty-four votes for each of her three candidates, and Thomas could cast thirty-six votes for his three candidates. As a result, all three of Stephanie's candidates would be elected. On the other hand, if cumulative voting were in force, Thomas could elect one director:

$$X = \frac{ac}{b+1} + 1$$

$$X = \frac{100\,(1)}{3+1} + 1 = 26 \text{ shares}.$$

Since Thomas has the right to vote more than twenty-six shares, he would be able to elect one director. Stephanie, of course, with her sixty-four shares, could elect the remaining two directors.

Removal of Directors

Removal of directors the shareholders may by majority vote remove directors with or without cause, subject to cumulative voting rights

By a majority vote, shareholders may remove any director or the entire board of directors, with or without cause, in a meeting called for that purpose. In the case of a corporation having cumulative voting, however, removal of a director requires sufficient votes to prevent his election. We will discuss the removal of directors more fully later in this chapter.

Approval of Fundamental Changes

Approval of fundamental changes shareholder approval is required for charter amendments, most acquisitions, and dissolution

The board of directors manages the ordinary business affairs of the corporation. Extraordinary matters involving fundamental changes in the corporation require shareholder approval; such matters include amendments to the articles of incorporation, a sale or lease of all or substantially all of the corporate assets not in the regular course of business, most mergers, consolidations, compulsory share exchanges, and dissolution. We will discuss fundamental changes in Chapter 38.

Concentrations of Voting Power

Certain devices enable groups of shareholders to combine their voting power for purposes such as obtaining or maintaining control or maximizing the impact of cumulative voting. The most important methods of concentrating voting power are proxies, voting trusts, and shareholder agreements. See Figure 37–4.

Proxies A shareholder may vote either in person or by written proxy. As we mentioned earlier, a proxy is a shareholder's authorization to an agent to vote his shares at a particular meeting or on a particular question. Generally, proxies must be in writing to be effective; and statutes typically limit the duration of proxies to no more than eleven months, unless the proxy specifically provides otherwise. Since a proxy is the appointment of an agent, it is revocable, as all agencies are, unless conspicuously stated to be irrevocable *and* coupled with an interest, such as shares held as collateral. The solicitation of proxies by publicly held corporations is also regulated by the Securities Exchange Act of 1934, as we will discuss in Chapter 42.

FIGURE 37–4 Concentrations of Voting Power

	Proxy	**Voting Trust**	**Shareholder Agreement**
Definition	Authorization of an agent to vote shares	Conferral of voting rights on trustee	Agreement among shareholders on voting of shares
Formalities	Signed writing delivered to corporation	Signed writing delivered to corporation	Signed writing
Duration	Eleven months, unless otherwise agreed	Ten years; may be extended	No limit
Revocability	Yes, unless coupled with an interest	No	Only by unanimous agreement
Prevalence	Publicly held	Publicly and closely held	Closely held

Voting Trusts Voting trusts, which are devices designed to concentrate corporate control in one or more persons, have been used in both publicly held and closely held corporations. A **voting trust** is a device by which one or more shareholders separate the voting rights of their shares from the ownership of them. Under a voting trust, one or more shareholders confer on a trustee the right to vote or otherwise act for them by signing an agreement setting out the provisions of the trust and transferring their shares to the trustee. In most states, voting trusts are permitted by statute but are usually limited in duration to ten years.

Voting trust transfer of corporate shares' voting rights to a trustee

Shareholder Voting Agreements In most jurisdictions, shareholders may agree in writing to vote in a specified manner for the election or removal of directors or on any matter subject to shareholder approval. Unlike voting trusts, **shareholder voting agreements** are not limited in duration. Shareholder agreements are used frequently in closely held corporations, especially in conjunction with restrictions on the transfer of shares, in order to provide each shareholder with greater control and *delectus personae* (the right to choose those who will become shareholders).

Shareholder voting agreement used to provide shareholders with greater control over the election and removal of directors and other matters

---

GALLER v. GALLER Supreme Court of Illinois, 1964, 32 Ill.2d 16, 203 N.E.2d 577

FACTS In 1927, two brothers, Benjamin and Isadore Galler, incorporated the Galler Drug Co., a wholesale drug business that they had operated as equal partners since 1919. The company continued to grow, and in 1955 the two brothers and their wives, Emma and Rose Galler, entered into a written shareholder agreement to leave the corporation in equal control of each family after the death of either brother. Specifically, the agreement provided that the corporation should continue to provide income for the support and maintenance of their immediate families and that the parties should vote for directors so as to give the estate and heirs of a deceased shareholder the same representation as before.

Benjamin died in 1957, and shortly thereafter his widow, Emma, requested that Isadore, the surviving brother, comply with the terms of the agreement. When he refused and proposed that certain changes be made in the agreement, Emma brought this action seeking specific performance of the agreement. Isadore and his wife, Rose, defended on the ground that the shareholder agreement was against public policy and the state's corporation law. The trial court entered a decree of specific performance in favor of Emma. On appeal, the decree was reversed.

DECISION Judgment of appellate court reversed.

OPINION A close corporation is one in which the stock is held in a few hands and is rarely traded. In contrast to a shareholder in a public corporation, who may easily trade his shares on the open market when he disagrees with its management over corporate policy, the shareholder of a closely held corporation often has no ready market in which to sell his shares should he wish to do so. Moreover, the shareholder in a closely held corporation often has most of his capital invested in the corporation and, therefore, views himself not only as a mere investor but also as a participant in the management of the business. Without a shareholder agreement subject to specific performance by the courts, the minority shareholder might find himself at the mercy of the controlling majority shareholder. In short, the detailed shareholder agreement is the only sound means by which the minority shareholder can protect himself. Therefore, since the agreement was reasonable in its scope and purpose of providing continuing support for the Galler brothers' families, it should be enforced.

INTERPRETATION Written shareholder agreements are an important means of enabling minority shareholders in a close corporation to maintain *delectus personae* and control as well as otherwise protecting their interest in the corporation.

ENFORCEMENT RIGHTS OF SHAREHOLDERS

To protect a shareholder's interests in the corporation, the law provides shareholders with certain enforcement rights. These include the right to obtain information, the right to sue the corporation directly or to sue on the corporation's behalf, and the right to dissent.

Right to Inspect Books and Records

Right to inspect books and records shareholder has the right if the demand is made in good faith and for a proper purpose

Most states have enacted statutory provisions granting shareholders the **right to inspect**, for a *proper purpose*, **books and records** in person or through an agent and to copy parts of them. The Revised Act provides that *every* shareholder is entitled to examine specified corporate records upon prior written request if the demand is made in good faith, for a proper purpose, and during regular business hours at the corporation's principal office. Many states, however, limit this right to shareholders who own a minimum number of shares or to those who have been shareholders for a minimum period of time. For example, the Model Act requires that a shareholder either must own 5 percent of the outstanding shares or must have owned his shares for at least six months (though a court may order an inspection even when neither condition is met).

A ***proper purpose*** for inspection is one that is reasonably relevant to that shareholder's interest in the corporation. Proper purposes include determining the financial condition of the corporation, the value of shares, the existence of mismanagement, or the names of other shareholders in order to communicate with them about corporate affairs. The right of inspection is subject to abuse and will be denied a shareholder who is seeking information for an improper purpose. Examples of improper purposes include obtaining information for use by a competing company or obtaining a list of shareholders in order to offer it for sale.

COMPAQ COMPUTER CORP. v. HORTON Supreme Court of Delaware, 1993, 631 A.2d 1

FACTS Charles E. Horton has beneficially owned 112 shares of common stock in Compaq Computer Corporation (Compaq) continuously since December 6, 1990. On July 22, 1991, Horton and seventy-eight other parties sued Compaq, fifteen of its advisors, and certain management personnel, alleging that Compaq and its codefendants violated the Texas Security Act and the Texas Deceptive Trade Practices Consumer Protection Act as well as committing fraud and breaching their fiduciary duty. All these claims arise from the contention that Compaq misled the public regarding the true value of its stock at a time when members of management were selling their own shares.

On September 22, 1992, Horton delivered a letter demanding to inspect Compaq's stock ledger and related information for the period from October 1, 1990, to June 30, 1991. The demand letter stated that the purpose of the request was to enable Horton to communicate with other Compaq shareholders to inform them of the pending shareholders' suit and to ascertain whether any of them would desire to become associated with that suit or bring similar actions against Compaq and assume a *pro rata* share of the litigation expenses. On September 30, 1992, Compaq refused the demand, stating that the purpose described in the letter was not a "proper purpose" under Section 220(b) of the General Corporation Law of the state of Delaware.

Horton brought suit and the trial court concluded that the plaintiff's desire to contact other stockholders and solicit their involvement in the litigation was a purpose reasonably related to his interest as a stockholder. Accordingly, the trial court ordered Compaq to permit Horton to inspect and copy the stockholder lists and related stockholder information requested in his demand letter. Compaq appealed.

DECISION Judgment affirmed.

OPINION In Delaware, a shareholder's common law right to inspect the corporation's stock ledger is codified in section 220(b), which provides in pertinent part:

> Any stockholder . . . shall, upon written demand under oath stating the purpose thereof, have the right during the usual hours for business to inspect *for any proper purpose* the corporation's stock ledger. . . . A proper purpose shall mean a purpose reasonably related to such person's interest as a stockholder.

Under this section, when a stockholder complies with the section's requirements as to form and manner of making a demand, then the corporation bears the burden of proving that the demand is for an improper purpose. If there is any doubt, it must be resolved in favor of the stockholder's statutory right to inspect.

Essentially, Horton alleges that it is in the interests of Compaq's shareholders to know that acts of mismanagement and fraud are continuing and cannot

continued

be overlooked. Thus, it is assumed that the resultant filing of a large number of individual damage claims might well discourage further acts of misconduct by the defendants. In this specific context, the antidotal effect of the Texas litigation may indeed serve a purpose reasonably related to Horton's current interest as a Compaq stockholder.

We recognize that even though a purpose may be reasonably related to one's interest as a stockholder, it cannot be adverse to the corporation's interests. In this respect it becomes clear that a stockholder's right to inspect and copy a stockholder list is not absolute. Rather, it is a qualified right depending on the facts presented. Horton's ultimate objective, to solicit additional parties to the Texas litigation, may impose substantial expenses upon the company. Therefore, Compaq argues that such a purpose is per se improper as being adverse to the interests of the corporation. Yet, insofar as law and policy require corporations and their agents to answer for the breaches of their duties to shareholders, Compaq has no legitimate interest in avoiding the payment of compensatory damages that it, its management, or its advisors may owe to those who own the enterprise. Thus, common sense and public policy dictate that a proper purpose may be stated in these circumstances, notwithstanding the lack of a direct benefit flowing to the corporation.

This conclusion does not suggest that Compaq's burden of showing an improper purpose is impossible to bear. Previous cases provide valuable examples of the degree to which a stated purpose is so indefinite, doubtful, uncertain, or vexatious as to warrant denial of the right of inspection. On the whole, a fair reading of these cases leads to the conclusion that where the person making the demand is acting in bad faith or for reasons wholly unrelated to his or her role as a stockholder, access to the ledger will be denied. That simply is not the case here. Horton seeks in good faith to solicit the support of other similarly situated Compaq stockholders, not only to seek monetary redress for their individual economic injuries, but also to prevent further acts of fraud or mismanagement from disrupting the fair market value of Compaq's stock.

The court found, therefore, that Compaq's arguments fail to meet its burden to show that Horton acts from an improper purpose. First, Compaq's contention that Horton's demand is not connected to his status as a stockholder is unsubstantiated. Horton's demand is connected to his stockholder status because he seeks to bring an end to injuries sustained that directly and adversely affect his stock ownership. Second, Compaq's complaint that Horton seeks a historical stock list is inconsequential as many cases recognize a stockholder's right to investigate past acts of mismanagement. Furthermore, Section 220 expressly grants the right to inspect not only a corporation's list of present stockholders but also its stock ledger. Third, Compaq's accusation that Horton seeks inspection only for his personal gain is immaterial. So long as Horton establishes a single proper purpose related to his role as a stockholder, all other purposes are irrelevant. Finally, Compaq's contention that Horton's purpose is contrary to the best interests of the corporation and its current stockholders is both speculative and specious. Any harm that may accrue to the corporation as a result of releasing the list is too remote and uncertain to warrant denial of the stockholder's statutory right to inspection. If anything, the corporation and its stockholders, as well as public policy, will best be served by exposure of the fraud, if that is the case, and restoration of the stock to a value set by a properly informed market.

INTERPRETATION Upon demand, a stockholder has the right to inspect for a proper purpose the corporation's books and records. A proper purpose means a purpose reasonably related to that shareholder's interest in the corporation.

Shareholder Suits

The ultimate recourse of a shareholder, short of selling his shares, is to bring suit against or on behalf of the corporation. Shareholder suits are essentially of two kinds: direct suits and derivative suits.

Direct Suits A shareholder may bring a **direct suit** to enforce a claim that she has *against* the corporation, based on her ownership of shares. Any recovery in a direct suit goes to the shareholder plaintiff. Examples of direct suits include shareholder actions to compel payment of dividends properly declared, to enforce the right to inspect corporate records, to enforce the right to vote, to protect preemptive rights, and to compel dissolution. A **class suit** is a direct suit

Direct suit suit brought by a shareholder against the corporation based on his ownership of shares

Class suit direct suit in which one or more shareholders purport to act as a representative of a class of shareholders to recover for injuries to the entire class

in which one or more shareholders purport to act as a representative for a class of shareholders in order to recover for injuries to the entire class. Such a suit is a direct suit because the representative claims that all similarly situated shareholders were injured by an act that did not injure the corporation.

Derivative suit suit brought by a shareholders on behalf of the corporation to enforce a right belonging to it

Derivative Suits A **derivative suit** is a cause of action brought by one or more shareholders on *behalf* of the corporation to enforce a right belonging to it. Shareholders may bring such an action when the board of directors refuses to so act on the corporation's behalf. Recovery usually goes to the corporation's treasury, so that all shareholders can benefit proportionately. Examples of derivative suits are actions to recover damages from management for an *ultra vires* act, to recover damages for a managerial breach of duty, and to recover improper dividends. In such situations, the board of directors may well be hesitant to bring suit against the corporation's officers or directors. Consequently, a shareholder derivative suit is the only recourse.

In most states, a shareholder must have owned his shares at the time the transaction complained of occurred in order to bring a derivative suit. In addition, the shareholder must first make demand on the board of directors to enforce the corporate right.

Figure 37–5 compares direct and derivative suits.

RICHARDSON v. ARIZONA FUELS CORP. Supreme Court of Utah, 1980, 614 P.2d 636

FACTS Donald J. Richardson, Grove L. Cook, and Wayne Weaver were stockholders of Major Oil. They brought an action, individually and on behalf of all other stockholders of Major, against certain directors and other officers of the corporation. In all, the complaint stated twelve causes of action. The first eight causes alleged some misappropriation of Major's assets by the defendants and sought to require the defendants to return the assets to Major. Three of the remaining four causes alleged breaches of fiduciary duty implicit in those fraudulent acts and sought compensatory or punitive damages for the injury that resulted. The final cause sought the appointment of a receiver. Richardson, Cook, and Weaver moved for an order certifying the suit as a class action. The motion was granted by the district court, and the defendants appealed.

DECISION Judgment certifying the suit as a class action reversed and remanded.

OPINION The critical distinction in this case is that between a derivative action and a class action. Derivative actions seek to enforce rights belonging to the corporation, and may be initiated by a stockholder only after the corporation has failed to do so. The shareholder has no right, title, or interest in the claim itself and recovers nothing. Class actions seek to enforce the individual rights of the representative of the class and all other class members. In a class action

against a corporation, the injury sued upon is an injury to the individual plaintiff shareholders, and the recovery belongs directly to the shareholders. In this case, the first eight causes of action concern injury to the corporation only, which the plaintiff stockholders can assert only derivatively on behalf of the corporation. The ninth, tenth, and eleventh causes of action, which allege breaches of the defendants' fiduciary duty to the corporation and its stockholders, are also based upon claims for relief that belong to the corporation only and not to the individual stockholders. Generally, the directors and other officers of a corporation owe a fiduciary duty to the corporation and to the stockholders collectively, but breach of this duty results in a corporate claim only. The ninth cause of action also accused the defendants of mismanaging the business affairs of Major Oil. Again, however, corporate mismanagement gives rise to a cause of action in the corporation and not with the stockholders individually, even though the mismanagement may injure the stockholders by reducing the value of the corporation's shares.

INTERPRETATION A class action is a direct suit *against* the corporation and seeks recovery for the shareholders as individuals. A derivative suit is brought by shareholders *on behalf* of the corporation and seeks recovery for the corporation so that all shareholders benefit proportionately.

FIGURE 37–5 Shareholder Suits

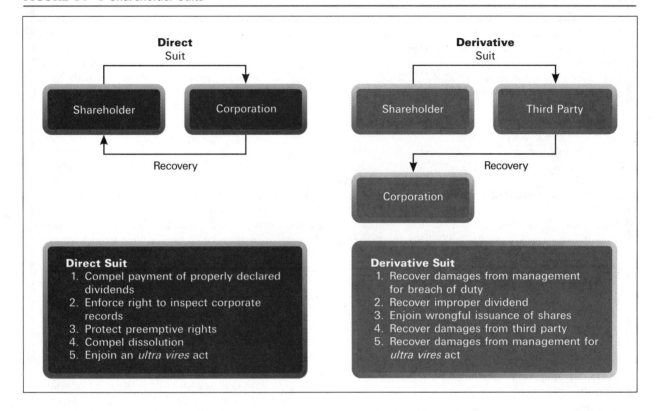

Shareholder's Right to Dissent

A shareholder has the right to dissent from certain corporate actions that require shareholder approval. These actions include most mergers, consolidations, compulsory share exchanges, and a sale or exchange of all or substantially all the assets of the corporation not in the usual and regular course of business. We will discuss the shareholder's right to dissent in Chapter 38.

Shareholder's right to dissent a shareholder has the right to dissent from certain corporate actions that require shareholder approval

ROLE OF DIRECTORS AND OFFICERS

Management of a corporation is vested by statute in its board of directors, which determines general corporate policy and appoints officers to execute that policy and to administer the day-to-day operations of the corporation. Both the directors and officers of the corporation owe certain duties to the corporate entity as well as to the corporation's shareholders and are liable for breaching these duties.

In the following sections we will discuss the roles of corporate directors and officers. In some instances, controlling shareholders (those who own a number of shares sufficient to allow them effective control over the corporation) are held to the same duties as directors and officers, which we will discuss later in this chapter. Moreover, in close corporations, some courts impose upon *all* the shareholders a fiduciary duty similar to that imposed upon partners.

DONAHUE v. RODD ELECTROTYPE CO., INC.   Massachusetts Supreme Court, 1975, 367 Mass. 578, 328 N.E.2d 505

FACTS Euphemia Donahue was a minority stockholder in the Rodd Electrotype Company of New England, Inc. Rodd Electrotype was, by definition, a close corporation. Members of the Rodd and Donahue families were the sole owners of the corporate stock, and no ready market for the shares existed. Moreover, the Rodds effectively controlled the corporation through their control of the chief management positions and their ownership of the majority of the stock. When Harry Rodd, a director, officer, and controlling stockholder of Rodd Electrotype, retired from the business, Rodd Electrotype purchased his shares in the corporation for $36,000. Donahue, who was not offered an equal opportunity to sell her shares to the corporation, brought an action against Rodd Electrotype, Harry Rodd, and the present directors of the corporation, claiming that the defendants breached their fiduciary duty to her in causing the corporation to purchase the shares of Harry Rodd. She sought rescission of the purchase and repayment by Harry Rodd to Rodd Electrotype of the purchase price of the shares plus interest. The trial court dismissed the case, and the appellate court affirmed.

DECISION Judgment reversed and relief granted to the plaintiff.

OPINION By definition, the close corporation strongly resembles a partnership. Moreover, just as in a partnership, all stockholders in a close corporation must have trust and confidence in one another. Specifically, the minority shareholders must rely upon the loyalty and abilities of the majority and especially of those stockholders who hold office. For instance, the majority stockholders in a corporation, through their control of the board of directors, are in a position to employ certain "freeze-out" techniques that may oppress or disadvantage the minority shareholders. The minority is unable to challenge the policies of the directors "unless a plain abuse of discretion is made to appear," and, by definition lacking fifty percent of the shares, the minority cannot cause the dissolution of the corporation. In a close corporation, a minority shareholder's recourse is further limited by the fact that no ready market for the shares is available. Therefore, the standard of duty owed by the stockholders in a close corporation is more rigorous than the general good faith and inherent fairness standard of conduct to which directors and stockholders of all corporations must adhere. Stockholders in a close corporation owe one another substantially the same fiduciary duty that partners owe to one another, where the standard of duty owed by partners is the "utmost good faith and loyalty." As a result, when a close corporation purchases the shares of a controlling stockholder, the corporation must offer each stockholder an equal chance to sell a proportional number of his shares at the same price. Without such an opportunity, the purchase of shares from a member of the controlling group (1) provides an exclusive market for shares from which minority shareholders are shut out and (2) functions as a preferential distribution of the corporation's assets. This advantage is inconsistent with the strict fiduciary duty imposed upon the stockholders of close corporations. In this case, the Rodd family is a single controlling group, and the purchase of Harry Rodd's shares is a violation of the fiduciary duty owed by the controlling shareholders, the Rodds, to Donahue, a minority shareholder.

INTERPRETATION Recognizing the strong resemblance of a close corporation to a partnership, some courts impose upon all shareholders in a close corporation substantially the same fiduciary duty that partners owe each other.

FUNCTION OF THE BOARD OF DIRECTORS

Although the shareholders elect them to manage the corporation, the directors are neither trustees nor agents of the shareholders or the corporation. They are, however, fiduciaries who must perform their duties in good faith, in the best interests of the corporation, and with due care.

The Revised Act states that "[a]ll corporate powers shall be exercised by or under the authority of, and the business and affairs of the corporation managed under the direction of, its board of directors, subject to any limitation set forth in the articles of incorporation." In some corporations, the board members are all actively involved in the management of the business. In these cases, the corporate powers are exercised *by* the board of directors. On the other hand, in publicly held corporations, a majority of board members often are not actively involved in management. Here, the corporate powers are exercised *under* the authority of the board, which formulates major management policy but does not involve itself in day-to-day management.

In publicly held corporations, the directors who are also officers or employees of the corporation are ***inside directors***, while the directors who are not officers or employees are ***outside directors***. Outside directors who have no business contacts with the corporation are ***unaffiliated directors***; outside directors having business contacts—such as investment bankers, lawyers, or suppliers—are ***affiliated directors***. Under the Revised Act, a corporation having fifty or fewer shareholders may dispense with or limit the authority of a board of directors by designating in its articles of incorporation those who will perform some or all of the duties of a board.

The board determines corporate policy in a number of areas, including (1) selecting and removing officers, (2) determining the corporation's capital structure, (3) initiating fundamental changes, (4) declaring dividends, and (5) setting management compensation.

Selection and Removal of Officers

In most states, the board of directors is responsible for choosing the corporation's officers and may remove any officer at any time. Officers are corporate agents who are delegated their responsibilities by the board of directors.

Capital Structure

The board of directors determines the capital structure and financial policy of the corporation. For example, the board of directors has the power (1) to fix the selling price of newly issued shares, unless the articles of incorporation reserve to the shareholders the power to do so; (2) to determine the value of the consideration the corporation will receive in payment for the shares it issues; (3) to borrow money, issue notes, bonds, and other obligations, and secure any of the corporation's obligations; and (4) to sell, lease, or exchange assets of the corporation in the *usual* and *regular* course of business.

Fundamental Changes

The board of directors has the power to amend or repeal the bylaws, unless the articles of incorporation reserve this power exclusively to the shareholders. In addition, the board initiates certain actions that require shareholder approval. For instance, the board initiates proceedings to amend the articles of incorporation; to effect a merger, consolidation, compulsory share exchange, or the sale or lease of all or substantially all of the assets of the corporation *other* than in the usual and regular course of business; and to dissolve the corporation.

Fundamental changes the directors have the power to make, amend, or repeal the bylaws, unless this power is exclusively reserved to the shareholders

Dividends

The board of directors declares the amount and type of **dividends**, subject to restrictions in the state incorporation statute, the articles of incorporation, and corporate loan and preferred stock agreements. The board also may purchase, redeem, or otherwise acquire shares of the corporation's equity securities.

Dividends directors declare the amount and type of dividends

Management Compensation

The board of directors usually determines the compensation of officers. In addition, a number of states allow the board to fix the compensation of its members.

CONSUMER INSIGHT

Those !!$%&?! CEO Salaries

The screed against greed in the executive suite is hardly new—it's an American populist tradition. The latest variation on the theme is the attack on corporate chieftains whose salaries, often pegged to rising stock prices, are surging when average workers' wages aren't keeping pace with under-3 percent inflation.

Last year was a case in point, according to Graef Crystal, an executive-compensation expert who surveyed 1995 data from 76 of the 150 largest companies. Pay and bonus packages for leading chief executives jumped by some 15 percent, a heady rise over the 11 percent rate of recent years. Demagoguery aside, from an investor standpoint, the present system often lavishes rewards on executives who deliver results that are no better than average.

The poster boy in the current debate is AT&T Chairman Robert Allen, whose total pay package for 1995 included $5.2 million in base pay and $11 million in stock options. Early this year, he announced that 40,000 jobs would be eliminated as part of a massive restructuring that would break AT&T into three new companies. The real issue is not the layoffs, however, but the degree to which Allen's long-term record justifies extra rewards or bonuses of any kind. Since he moved to the top spot in 1988, AT&T's stock has appreciated by 12 percent a year, no better and no worse than the performance of the Standard & Poor's 500-stock index. And let's not forget the ill-conceived purchase in 1991 of computer maker NCR that subsequently resulted in a multibillion-dollar write-off. Allen presided over that fiasco.

Benchmarks Wanted

There's nothing wrong with giving executives incentives to increase shareholder value. The challenge is to relate them to consistent and sustainable results and not simply to make them a free ride on a rising stock market.

A proper "pay for performance" program, says Crystal, should start with a low base salary. Michael Eisner, the chairman of Disney, for example, has been making $750,000 a year in base pay since 1984. At Bear Stearns, Chairman Ace Greenberg gets $200,000. Any bonus "should be really sensitive to company performance and not just be one that soars in good times and merely floats in bad times," adds Crystal. In his view, stock options should be handed out only after a company's results exceed a threshold figure. "Just getting the stock price up by 5 percent means nothing to shareholders, who could earn the same in a bond," Crystal argues.

To prevent rewarding executives for mediocre results, a few corporations have initiated compensation programs in which share prices must rise by a pre-determined number before bonuses for top managers kick in. The most notable company to adopt such a value-added approach is Transamerica, the big West Coast insurer. Stock options for senior executives aren't triggered until net income rises by at least 10 percent.

The debate pitting Wall Street (downsizing is good and pushes up share prices) against Main Street (layoffs hurt real people) is phony. A look at companies that have created the top stockholder returns over the past decade—such as Coca-Cola, Amgen and Applied Materials—indicates that the engine for these gains has been growth, not cost-cutting layoffs.

While Wall Street may respond initially to restructuring announcements from companies by boosting their share prices, these gains could be short-lived. "With all the downsizing and restructuring that's going on and the increasing emphasis on improving profitability, what's lacking often is an emphasis on future growth," declares James Knight, a managing partner with Strategic Compensation Associates, which advises blue-chip firms on payout policies and helped devise the Transamerica plan.

With corporate annual reports filling mailboxes, investors should look for sharp statements of strategy and believable action plans as signs that management truly wants to build shareholder value. "Too much talk about earnings per share," says Knight, "shows a worrisome short-term focus."

By Jack Egan. Copyright, April 8, 1996, *U.S. News & World Report*.

ELECTION AND TENURE OF DIRECTORS

The incorporation statute, the articles of incorporation, and the bylaws determine the qualifications necessary to those who would be directors of the corporation. They also determine election procedures for and the number, tenure, and compensation of directors.

Election, Number, and Tenure of Directors

The initial board of directors generally is named in the articles of incorporation and serves until the first meeting of the shareholders at which directors are elected. Thereafter, directors are elected at annual meetings of the shareholders and hold office for one year unless their terms are staggered. However, if the shares represented at a meeting in person or by proxy are insufficient to constitute a quorum or if the shareholders are deadlocked and unable to elect a new board, the incumbent directors continue in office as "holdover" directors until their successors are duly elected and qualified. Though state statutes traditionally required each corporation to have three or more directors, the modern trend is to permit the board to consist of one or more members. Moreover, the number of directors may be increased or decreased, within statutory limits, by amendment to the bylaws or charter.

Vacancies and Removal of Directors

The Revised Act provides that a vacancy in the board may be filled either by the shareholders or by the affirmative vote of a majority of the remaining directors, even if they should constitute less than a quorum of the board. The term of a director elected to fill a vacancy expires at the next shareholders' meeting at which directors are elected.

Some states have no statutory provision for the removal of directors, although a common law rule permits removal for cause by action of the shareholders. The Revised Act and an increasing number of other statutes permit the shareholders to remove one or more directors or the entire board, with or without cause, at a special meeting called for that purpose, subject to cumulative voting rights, if applicable. However, the Revised Act also permits the articles of incorporation to provide that directors may be removed only for cause.

Compensation of Directors

Traditionally, directors did not receive salaries for their directorial services, although they commonly received a fee or honorarium for their attendance at meetings. The Revised Act and a number of incorporation statutes now specifically authorize the board of directors to fix the compensation of directors, unless a contrary provision exists in the articles of incorporation or bylaws.

EXERCISE OF DIRECTORS' FUNCTIONS

Though they are powerless to bind the corporation when acting individually, directors do have this power when acting as a board. The board may act only through a meeting of the directors or through written consent signed by all of the directors, if such consent without a directors' meeting is authorized by the incorporation statute and is not contrary to the charter or bylaws.

Meetings are either held at a regular time and place fixed in the bylaws or called at special times. Notice of meetings must be given as prescribed in the bylaws. A director's attendance at any meeting is a waiver of such notice, unless the director attends only to object to the holding of the meeting or to the transaction of business at it and does not vote for or assent to action taken at the meeting. Waiver of notice also may be given in a signed writing. Most modern statutes provide that meetings of the board may be held either in or outside of the state of incorporation.

Exercise of directors' functions directors have the power to bind the corporation only when acting as a board

Quorum and Voting

A majority of the board members constitutes a quorum (the minimum number of members that must be present at a meeting in order to transact business). Although most states do not permit a quorum to be set at less than a majority, the Revised Act *allows* the articles of incorporation or the bylaws to authorize a quorum consisting of as few as one-third of a board's members. In contrast, however, the articles of incorporation or bylaws may require a number *greater* than a simple majority. If a quorum is present at any meeting, the act of a majority of the directors in attendance is the act of the board, unless the articles of incorporation or bylaws require the act of a greater number.

Closely held corporations sometimes use supermajority or unanimous quorum requirements. In addition, they may require a supermajority or unanimous vote of the board for some or all matters.

By requiring a quorum to be present when "a vote is taken," the Revised Act makes it clear that the board may act only when a quorum is present. This rule is in contrast to the rule governing shareholder meetings: recall that, once a quorum of shareholders is obtained, it *cannot* be broken by the withdrawal of shareholders. In any event, directors may not vote by proxy, although most states permit directors to participate in meetings through teleconference.

A director present at a board meeting at which action on any corporate matter is taken is deemed to have assented to such action unless, in addition to dissenting from it, he (1) has his dissent entered in the minutes of the meeting, (2) files his written dissent to such action with the presiding officer before the meeting adjourns, or (3) delivers his written dissent to the corporation immediately after adjournment.

Action Taken without a Meeting

Action taken without a meeting permitted if a consent in writing is signed by all of the directors

The Revised Act and most states provide that unless the articles of incorporation or bylaws provide otherwise, any action the statute requires or permits to be taken at a meeting of the board may be taken without a meeting if consent in writing is signed by all of the directors.

Delegation of Board Powers

Delegation of board powers committees may be appointed to perform some but not all of the board's functions

Unless otherwise provided by the articles of incorporation or the bylaws, the board of directors may, by majority vote of the *full* board, appoint one or more committees, all of whose members must be directors. Many state statutes permit committees only if the charter or bylaws expressly authorize their formation. Committees may exercise all the authority of the board, except with regard to certain matters specified in the incorporation statute, such as declaring dividends and other distributions, filling vacancies on the board or on any of its committees, amending the bylaws, recommending fundamental changes to the shareholders, approving a merger or charter amendment not requiring shareholder approval, and authorizing the sale or reacquisition of stock. Delegating authority to a committee does not relieve any board member of his duties to the corporation. Commonly used committees include executive committees, audit committees (to recommend and oversee independent public accountants), compensation committees, finance committees, nominating committees, and investment committees.

Directors' Inspection Rights

Directors' inspection rights directors have the right to inspect corporate books and records

So that they can perform their duties competently and fully, directors have the right to inspect corporate books and records. This right is considerably broader than a shareholder's right to inspect.

OFFICERS

The board of directors appoints the officers of a corporation to hold the offices provided for in the bylaws, which set forth the respective duties of each officer. Statutes generally require as a minimum that the officers consist of a president; one or more vice presidents, as prescribed by the bylaws; a secretary; and a treasurer. With the exception that the same person may not hold the office of president and secretary at the same time, a person may hold more than one office.

The Revised Act permits every corporation to designate whatever officers it wants. Although the act specifies no particular number of officers, one of them must be delegated responsibility to prepare the minutes of directors' and shareholders' meetings and to authenticate corporate records. The Revised Act permits the same individual to hold *all* of the offices of a corporation.

Selection and Removal of Officers

Most state statutes provide that officers be appointed by the board of directors and that they serve at the pleasure of the board. Accordingly, the board may remove officers with or without cause. Of course, if the officer has an employment contract that is valid for a specified time period, removing the officer without cause before the contract expires would constitute a breach of the employment contract. The board also determines the compensation of officers.

Role of Officers

The officers are, like the directors, fiduciaries to the corporation. On the other hand, unlike the directors, they are agents of the corporation. The roles of officers are set forth in the corporate bylaws.

Authority of Officers

The Revised Act provides that each officer has the authority provided in the bylaws or prescribed by the board of directors, to the extent that such prescribed authority is consistent with the bylaws. Like that of other agents, the authority of an officer to bind the corporation may be (1) actual express, (2) actual implied, or (3) apparent.

Actual Express Authority **Actual express authority** results from the corporation's manifesting to the officer its assent that the officer should act on the corporation's behalf. Actual express authority arises from the incorporation statute, the articles of incorporation, the bylaws, and resolutions of the board of directors. The last provide the principal source of actual express authority.

> **Actual express authority** arises from the incorporation statute, the charter, the bylaws, and resolutions of the directors

Actual Implied Authority Officers, as agents of the corporation, have **actual implied authority** to do what is reasonably necessary to perform their actual, delegated authority. In addition, a common question is whether officers possess implied authority merely by virtue of their positions. The courts have been cautious in granting such implied or inherent authority. However, any act requiring board approval, such as issuing stock, is clearly beyond the implied authority of any officer.

> **Actual implied authority** authority to do what is reasonably necessary to perform actual authority

Apparent Authority **Apparent authority** arises from acts of the corporation that lead third parties to believe reasonably and in good faith that an officer has the required authority. Apparent authority might arise when a third party relies

> **Apparent authority** acts of the principal that lead a third party to believe reasonably and in good faith that an officer has the required authority

on the fact that an officer has exercised the same authority in the past with the consent of the board of directors.

Ratification A corporation may ratify the unauthorized acts of its officers. Equivalent to the corporation's having granted the officer prior authority, **ratification** relates back to the original transaction and may be either express or implied from the corporation's acceptance of the contract's benefits with full knowledge of the facts.

DUTIES OF DIRECTORS AND OFFICERS

Generally, directors and officers owe the duties of obedience, diligence, and loyalty to the corporation. These duties are for the most part judicially imposed. By imposing liability upon directors and officers for specific acts, state and federal statutes supplement the common law, which nonetheless remains the most significant source of duties.

A corporation may not recover damages from its directors and officers for losses resulting from their poor business judgments or honest mistakes of judgment. Directors and officers are not duty-bound to ensure business success. They are required only to be obedient, reasonably diligent, and completely loyal.

Duty of Obedience

Directors and officers must act within their respective authority. For any loss the corporation suffers because of their unauthorized acts, they are held absolutely liable in some jurisdictions; in others, they are held liable only if they exceeded their authority intentionally or negligently.

Duty of Diligence

In discharging their duties, directors and officers must exercise ordinary care and prudence. Some states interpret this standard to mean that directors and officers must exercise "the same degree of care and prudence that [those] promoted by self-interest generally exercise in their own affairs." Most states, as well as the Revised Act, hold that the test requires a director or officer to discharge corporate duties (1) in good faith; (2) with the care an ordinarily prudent person in a like position would exercise under similar circumstances; and (3) in a manner the director or officer reasonably believes to be in the best interests of the corporation. A director or officer whose performance of her duties complies with these requirements is not liable for any action she takes as a director or officer or for any failure to act.

So long as the directors and officers act in good faith and with due care, the courts will not substitute their judgment for that of the board or officer—the so-called business judgment rule. Directors and officers will nevertheless be held liable for bad faith or negligent conduct. Moreover, they may be liable for failing to act. In one instance, a bank director, who in the five-and-one-half years that he had been on the board had never attended a board meeting or examined the institution's books and records, was held liable for losses resulting from the unsupervised acts of the president and cashier, who had made various improper loans and had permitted large overdrafts.

Reliance on Others Directors and officers are permitted to entrust important work to others, and if they have selected employees with care, they are not personally liable for the negligent acts or willful wrongs of those selected.

Ratification a corporation may ratify the unauthorized acts of its officers

Duty of obedience must act within respective authority

Duty of diligence must exercise ordinary care and prudence

However, a reasonable amount of supervision is required; and an officer or director who knew or should have known or suspected that an employee was incurring losses through carelessness, theft, or embezzlement will be held liable for such losses.

Directors also may rely on information provided them by officers or employees of the corporation, committees of the board of directors, or legal counsel or public accountants. An officer is also entitled to rely upon this information, but this right may, in many circumstances, be more limited than a director's because of the officer's greater familiarity with the affairs of the corporation.

Business Judgment Rule Directors and officers are continuously called on to make decisions that require balancing benefits and risks to the corporation. Although hindsight may reveal that some of these decisions were not the best, the **business judgment rule** precludes imposing liability on the directors or officers for honest mistakes of judgment. To later benefit from the business judgment rule, a director or officer must make an informed decision without any conflict of interests, have a rational basis for making it, and reasonably believe it is in the corporation's best interests. Moreover, where this standard of conduct has not been met, the director's action (or inaction) must be shown to be the proximate cause of damage to the corporation.

Hasty or ill-advised action also can render directors liable. In a recent case, the Supreme Court of Delaware held directors liable for approving the terms of a cash-out merger. The court found that the directors did not adequately inform themselves of the company's intrinsic value and were grossly negligent in approving the terms of the merger upon two hours' consideration and without prior notice.

> **Business judgment rule**
> precludes imposing liability on directors and officers for honest mistakes in judgment if they act with due care, in good faith, and in a manner reasonably believed to be in the best interests of the corporation

FRANCIS v. UNITED JERSEY BANK Supreme Court of New Jersey, 1981, 87 N.J. 15, 432 A.2d 814

FACTS Pritchard & Baird was a reinsurance broker. A reinsurance broker arranges contracts between insurance companies so that companies that have sold large policies may sell participations in these policies to other companies in order to share the risks. Pritchard & Baird was controlled for many years by Charles Pritchard, who died in December 1973. Prior to his death, he brought his two sons, Charles, Jr. and William, into the business. The pair assumed an increasingly dominant role in the affairs of the business during the elder Charles's later years. Starting in 1970, Charles, Jr. and William began to withdraw from the corporate account ever-increasing sums that were designated as "loans" on the balance sheet. These "loans," however, represented a significant misappropriation of funds belonging to the corporation's clients. By late 1975, Charles, Jr. and William had plunged the corporation into hopeless bankruptcy. A total of $12,333,514.47 in "loans" had accumulated by October of that year. Mrs. Lillian Pritchard, the widow of the elder Charles, was a member of the corporation's board of directors until her resignation on December 3, 1975, the day before the corporation filed for bankruptcy. Francis, as trustee in the bankruptcy proceeding, brought suit against United Jersey Bank, the administrator of the estate of Charles, Sr. He also charged that Lillian Pritchard, as a director of the corporation, was personally liable for the misappropriated funds on the basis of negligence in discharging her duties as director. The trial court found Lillian Pritchard liable, and the appellate court affirmed.

DECISION Judgment for Francis affirmed.

OPINION All corporate directors, as fiduciaries of the corporation and its stockholders, are responsible for managing the business and affairs of the corporation. They must exercise their duties in good faith and with the diligence, care, and skill of an ordinarily prudent individual. At the very least, a director should have some basic understanding of the corporation's business and activities. A director should also keep abreast of the financial status of the enterprise by regularly reviewing its financial statements. This review may result in a duty to investigate any suspicious matters. Depending upon the outcome of such an investigation, a director may have a duty to object to any improprieties, to

continued

resign if the objection goes unheeded, and even to seek the advice of counsel.

Here, Mrs. Pritchard should have known that Pritchard & Baird was in the reinsurance business as a broker and that it annually handled millions of dollars belonging to, or owing to, ceding companies and reinsurers. Charged with that knowledge, a director in Mrs. Pritchard's position had, at the bare minimum, an obligation to ask for and read the annual financial statements of the corporation. She would then have had the obligation to react appropriately to what a reading of the statements would have revealed. Mrs. Pritchard never knew what Charles, Jr. and William were doing because she never made the slightest effort to discharge any of her responsibilities as a director of

Pritchard & Baird. Nonetheless, her negligence would not result in liability unless it were a proximate cause of the corporation's losses. Mrs. Pritchard had the power and the duty to prevent the losses. Her objection to the "loans" might well have deterred her sons, and even if it had not, her consultation with an attorney and the threat of a lawsuit would certainly have averted the losses. Therefore, since Mrs. Pritchard breached her duty as a director of Pritchard & Baird, she is liable for the misappropriations.

INTERPRETATION   In exercising their duties, all corporate directors must act in good faith, in the corporation's best interests, and with the diligence, care, and skill of an ordinarily prudent individual.

Duty of Loyalty

Duty of loyalty requires undeviating loyalty to the corporation

The officers and directors of a corporation owe a duty of loyalty (a *fiduciary duty*) to the corporation and to its shareholders. The essence of a fiduciary duty is the subordination of self-interest to the interest of the person or persons to whom the duty is owing. It requires officers and directors to be constantly loyal to the corporation, which they both serve and control.

An officer or director is required to disclose fully to the corporation any financial interest he may have in any contract or transaction to which the corporation is a party. (This is a corollary to the rule that forbids fiduciaries from making secret profits.) His business conduct must be insulated from self-interest, and he may not advance his personal interest at the corporation's expense. Moreover, an officer or director may not represent conflicting interests; her duty is one of strict allegiance to the corporation.

The remedy for breach of fiduciary duty is a suit in equity by the corporation, or more often a derivative suit instituted by a shareholder, to require the fiduciary to pay to the corporation the profits she obtained through the breach. It need not be shown that the corporation could otherwise have made the profits that the fiduciary realized. The object of the rule is to discourage breaches of duty by taking from the fiduciary all of the profits she has made. Though the enforcement of the rule may result in a windfall to the corporation, this is incidental to the rule's deterrent objective. Whenever a director or officer breaches his fiduciary duty, he forfeits his right to compensation during the period he engaged in the breach.

Conflict of Interests   A contract or other transaction between an officer or a director and the corporation inherently involves a conflict of interest. Contracts between officers and the corporation are covered under the law of agency. (See Chapter 29.) Early on, the common law viewed all director-corporation transactions as automatically void or voidable but eventually recognized that this rule was unreasonable because it would prevent directors from entering into contracts beneficial to the corporation. Now, therefore, if such a contract is honest and fair, the courts will uphold it. In the case of contracts between corporations having an interlocking directorate (corporations whose boards of directors share one or more members), the courts subject the contracts to scrutiny and will set them aside unless the transaction is shown to have been entirely fair and entered in good faith.

The Revised Act and most states address these related problems by providing that such transactions are neither void nor voidable if, after full disclosure, they are approved by either the board of disinterested directors or the shareholders or if they are fair and reasonable to the corporation.

Loans to Directors The Model Act and some states permit a corporation to lend money to its directors only with its shareholders' authorization for each loan. The statutes in most states permit such loans either on a general or limited basis. The Revised Act initially permitted such loans if each particular loan was approved (1) by a majority of disinterested shareholders or (2) by the board of directors after determining that the loan would benefit the corporation; however, the 1988 amendments to the Revised Act deleted this section, subjecting loans to directors to the procedure that applies to directors' conflicting-interest transactions.

Corporate Opportunity Directors and officers may not usurp any corporate opportunity that in all fairness should belong to the corporation. A corporate opportunity is one in which the corporation has a right, property interest, or expectancy; whether such an opportunity exists depends on the facts and circumstances of each case. A corporate opportunity must be promptly offered to the corporation, which, in turn, should promptly accept or reject it. Rejection may be based on one or more of several factors, such as the corporation's lack of interest in the opportunity, its financial inability to acquire the opportunity, legal restrictions on its ability to accept the opportunity, or a third party's unwillingness to deal with the corporation.

┃ KLINICKI v. LUNDGREN Supreme Court of Oregon, 1985, 298 Or. 662, 695 P.2d 906

FACTS Klinicki and Lundgren, both furloughed Pan Am pilots stationed in West Germany, decided to start their own charter airline company. They therefore formed Berlinair, Inc., a closely held Oregon corporation. Lundgren was president and a director in charge of developing the business. Klinicki was vice president and a director in charge of operations and maintenance. Klinicki, Lundgren, and Lelco, Inc. (Lundgren's family business) each owned one-third of the stock. Klinicki and Lundgren, as representatives of Berlinair, met with BFR, a consortium of Berlin travel agents, to negotiate a lucrative air transportation contract. When Lundgren learned of the likelihood of actually obtaining the BFR contract, he formed his own solely owned company, Air Berlin Charter Company (ABC); and, though he continued to negotiate for the BFR contract, he did so on behalf of ABC, not Berlinair. Eventually BFR awarded the contract to ABC. Klinicki commenced a derivative action on behalf of Berlinair and a suit against Lundgren individually for usurping a corporate opportunity of Berlinair. The trial court found that ABC, acting through Lundgren, had indeed usurped such an opportunity. Additionally, the trial court determined that Lundgren had breached the fiduciary duties of good faith, fair dealing, and full disclosure he owed to Klinicki and to Berlinair. The Court of Appeals affirmed the trial court opinion. ABC through Lundgren appealed, claiming that Berlinair was not financially able to undertake the BFR contract and that, therefore, no usurpation of corporate opportunity could occur.

DECISION Judgment for Klinicki affirmed.

OPINION There is no dispute that the corporate opportunity doctrine precludes corporate fiduciaries from diverting to themselves business opportunities in which the corporation has an expectation, property interest, or right, and which in fairness should otherwise belong to the corporation. The doctrine follows from a corporate fiduciary's duty of undivided loyalty to the corporation. A director or senior executive may take advantage of a corporate opportunity *only after full disclosure* and only if the opportunity is rejected by a majority of the disinterested directors or, if there are no disinterested directors, by a majority of the disinterested shareholders. If, after full disclosure, the disinterested directors or shareholders unreasonably fail

continued

to reject the offer, the interested director or principal senior executive may proceed to take the opportunity if he can prove the taking was otherwise "fair" to the corporation. Lundgren, as director and principal executive officer, owed a fiduciary duty to Berlinair and to Klinicki, a minority shareholder. Lundgren's failure to disclose fully the BFR opportunity to Berlinair and his

appropriation of the opportunity for ABC were clearly an illegal taking of a corporate opportunity.

INTERPRETATION Corporate directors and officers may not usurp any opportunity in which the corporation has a right, property interest, or expectancy that in all fairness should belong to the corporation.

Transactions in Shares The issuance of shares at favorable prices to management by excluding other shareholders normally will constitute a violation of the fiduciary duty. So might the issuance of shares to a director at a fair price if the purpose of the issuance is to perpetuate corporate control rather than to raise capital or to serve some other corporate interest. Officers and directors have access to inside advance information, unavailable to the public, that may affect the future market value of the corporation's shares. Federal statutes have attempted to deal with this trading advantage by prohibiting officers and directors from purchasing or selling shares of their corporation's stock without adequately disclosing all material facts in their possession that may affect the stock's actual or potential value. We will discuss these matters more fully in Chapter 42.

Although state law has inconsistently imposed liability on officers and directors for secret, profitable use of inside information, the trend is toward holding them liable for breach of fiduciary duty to shareholders from whom they purchase stock without disclosing facts that give the stock added potential value. They are also held liable to the corporation for profits they realize on a sale of the stock when undisclosed conditions of the corporation make a substantial decline in value practically inevitable.

Duty Not to Compete As fiduciaries, directors and officers owe to the corporation the duty of undivided loyalty, which means that they may not compete with the corporation. A director or officer who breaches his fiduciary duty by competing with the corporation is liable for damages caused to the corporation. Although directors and officers may engage in their own business interests, courts will closely scrutinize any interest that competes with the corporation's business. Moreover, an officer or director may not use corporate personnel, facilities, or funds for her own benefit or disclose trade secrets of the corporation to others.

Indemnification of Directors and Officers

Indemnification a corporation may indemnify a director or officer for liability incurred if he acted in good faith and was not adjudged negligent or liable for misconduct

Directors and officers incur personal liability for breaching any of the duties they owe to the corporation and its shareholders. Under many modern incorporation statutes, a corporation may indemnify a director or officer for liability incurred if he acted in good faith and in a manner he reasonably believed to be in the best interests of the corporation, so long as he has not been judged negligent or liable for misconduct. The Revised Act provides for *mandatory* indemnification of directors and officers for reasonable expenses they incur in the wholly successful defense of any proceeding brought against them because they are or were directors or officers. These provisions, however, may be limited by the articles of incorporation. In addition, a corporation may purchase insurance

ETHICAL DILEMMA   Whom Does a Director Represent?   What Are a Director's Duties?

FACTS Maulington's, a large, publicly held food processing company, is run by an old, dictatorial CEO, who is also chairman of the board—a board packed with inside directors and retired chief executive officers of other businesses. Industry analysts regard Maulington's as stodgy and unimaginative in its use of capital. Yet its profits are dependable, it pays a decent dividend, and its stock is widely held by conservative investors. In the city where the company has its headquarters, it is regarded as a good corporate citizen. Many community organizations depend on its charitable contributions.

Upon the unexpected death of a director, the remaining directors nominate a forty-year-old doctor and children's health advocate, Peter Maxwell-Deane, who has wide community connections but little business experience. The directors reason that the board could use some youth, at least for appearances. Dr. Maxwell-Deane is duly elected to the board. He knows the visibility will help his career. He also hopes to influence the company to donate to his favorite children's health projects.

After his election, Dr. Maxwell-Deane is approached by Carola Campbell, a woman he knows from his charitable work and who, in fact, he once dated for several months. Campbell is the granddaughter of the company's founder, owns one percent of the company's shares, and is feuding with the current CEO. She says that the CEO has held Maulington's back, thereby hurting its share price, and that she thinks he should have retired long ago. She tells Maxwell-Deane that the board's compensation committee has improperly given stock options to the current CEO and other inside directors. Campbell, who has no friends on the board, appeals to Maxwell-Deane for help. Specifically, she asks him to sound out other outside directors to see if they also find the stock option deals fishy. Finally, she tells him that she is thinking about requesting a list of shareholders from the board so that she can communicate directly with other shareholders about the management of the corporation. She wonders whether, if she has any trouble obtaining the list, Maxwell-Deane will help her.

Social, Policy, and Ethical Considerations

1. Does Dr. Maxwell-Deane, as a director, represent Carola Campbell? Should he quietly sound out the other directors, as she asks? What risks would he run by doing so?

2. Does Maxwell-Deane have a duty to disclose to the board his previous relationship with Campbell? What details, if any, of his conversation with her should he report to the board?

3. What duty does Maxwell-Deane have to follow up on Campbell's allegation that stock options were improperly awarded to the CEO and other inside directors?

4. What should Maxwell-Deane do?

to indemnify officers and directors for liability arising out of their corporate activities, including liabilities against which the corporation is not empowered to indemnify directly.

Liability Limitation Statutes

At least forty states have recently enacted legislation limiting the liability of directors. Most of these states, including Delaware, have authorized corporations—with shareholder approval—to limit or eliminate the liability of directors for some breaches of duty. A few states permit shareholders to limit the liability of officers. The Delaware statute provides that the articles of incorporation may contain a provision eliminating or limiting the personal liability of a director to the corporation or its stockholders for monetary damages for breach of directorial duty, provided that such provision does not eliminate or limit the liability of a director (1) for any breach of the director's duty of loyalty to the corporation or its stockholders, (2) for acts or omissions lacking good faith or involving intentional misconduct or a knowing violation of law, (3) for liability for unlawful dividend payments or redemptions, or (4) for any transaction from which the director derived an improper personal benefit.

A handful of states have directly eliminated personal liability for money damages, subject to certain exceptions. For example, under the Indiana statute, a

Liability limitation statutes many states now authorize corporations—with shareholder approval—to limit or eliminate the liability of directors for some breaches of duty

director is liable only if she has breached or failed to perform her duties in compliance with the statutory standard of care and the breach or failure to perform constitutes willful misconduct or recklessness. A third approach, taken by some states, limits the amount of money damages that may be assessed against a director or officer.

The Revised Act authorizes the articles of incorporation to include a provision eliminating or limiting—with certain exceptions—the liability of a director to the corporation or its shareholders for any action he takes, or fails to take, as a director. The exceptions, for which his liability would not be affected, are (1) the amount of any financial benefit the director receives to which he is not entitled, such as a bribe, kickback, or profits from a usurped corporate opportunity; (2) an intentional infliction of harm on the corporation or the shareholders; (3) liability under Section 8.33 for unlawful distributions; and (4) an intentional violation of the criminal law.

CHAPTER SUMMARY

Role of Shareholders

Voting Rights of Shareholders	**Management Structure of Corporations** see Figures 37–1, 2, and 3 for illustrations of the statutory model of corporate governance, the structure of the typical closely held corporation, and the structure of the typical publicly held corporation **Shareholder Meetings** shareholders may exercise their voting rights at both annual and special shareholder meetings **Quorum** minimum number necessary to be present at a meeting in order to transact business **Election of Directors** the shareholders elect the board at the annual meeting of the corporation ■ *Straight Voting* directors are elected by a plurality of votes ■ *Cumulative Voting* entitles shareholders to multiply the number of votes they are entitled to cast by the number of directors for whom they are entitled to vote and to cast the product for a single candidate or to distribute the product among two or more candidates **Removal of Directors** the shareholders may by majority vote remove directors with or without cause, subject to cumulative voting rights **Approval of Fundamental Changes** shareholder approval is required for charter amendments, most acquisitions, and dissolution **Concentrations of Voting Power** ■ *Proxy* authorization to vote another's shares at a shareholder meeting ■ *Voting Trust* transfer of corporate shares' voting rights to a trustee ■ *Shareholder Voting Agreement* used to provide shareholders with greater control over the election and removal of directors and other matters

| Enforcement Rights of Shareholders | **Right to Inspect Books and Records** if the demand is made in good faith and for a proper purpose
Shareholder Suits
■ *Direct Suits* brought by a shareholder or a class of shareholders against the corporation based upon the ownership of shares
■ *Derivative Suits* brought by a shareholder on behalf of the corporation to enforce a right belonging to the corporation
Shareholder's Right to Dissent a shareholder has the right to dissent from certain corporate actions that require shareholder approval |

Role of Directors and Officers

| Function of the Board of Directors | **Selection and Removal of Officers**
Capital Structure
Fundamental Changes the directors have the power to make, amend, or repeal the bylaws, unless this power is exclusively reserved to the shareholders
Dividends directors declare the amount and type of dividends
Management Compensation
Vacancies in the Board may be filled by the vote of a majority of the remaining directors |

| Exercise of Directors' Functions | **Meeting** directors have the power to bind the corporation only when acting as a board
Action Taken Without a Meeting permitted if a consent in writing is signed by all of the directors
Delegation of Board Powers committees may be appointed to perform some but not all of the board's functions
Directors' Inspection Rights directors have the right to inspect corporate books and records |

| Officers | **Role of Officers** officers are agents of the corporation
Authority of Officers
■ *Actual Express Authority* arises from the incorporation statute, the charter, the bylaws, and resolutions of the directors
■ *Actual Implied Authority* authority to do what is reasonably necessary to perform actual authority
■ *Apparent Authority* acts of the principal that lead a third party to believe reasonably and in good faith that an officer has the required authority
■ *Ratification* a corporation may ratify the unauthorized acts of its officers |

Duties of Directors and Officers	**Duty of Obedience** must act within respective authority
	Duty of Diligence must exercise ordinary care and prudence
	Duty of Loyalty requires undeviating loyalty to the corporation
	Business Judgment Rule precludes imposing liability on directors and officers for honest mistakes in judgment if they act with due care, in good faith, and in a manner reasonably believed to be in the best interests of the corporation
	Indemnification a corporation may indemnify a director or officer for liability incurred if he acted in good faith and was not adjudged negligent or liable for misconduct
	Liability Limitation Statutes many states now authorize corporations—with shareholder approval—to limit or eliminate the liability of directors for some breaches of duty

QUESTIONS

1. Compare the actual governance of closely held corporations, the actual governance of publicly held corporations, and the statutory model of corporate governance.
2. Distinguish between (a) straight and cumulative voting, (b) proxies and voting trusts, and (c) direct suits and derivative suits.
3. Identify the areas of corporate policy determined by the board of directors.
4. Discuss the business judgment rule.
5. Identify and discuss the most important situations that involve management's duties of loyalty, obedience, and diligence.

Internet Question. Using the Security and Exchange Commission's EDGAR database, find the Annual Report (Form 10-K) and, if necessary, the proxy statement (DEF 14A) of three companies of interest and determine (a) the number of inside and outside directors, (b) what committees the board of directors has established, (c) the compensation for the three highest paid officers (including the value of stock options), and (d) whether any person owns more than five percent of the outstanding shares of common stock.

PROBLEMS

1. Brown, the president and director of a corporation engaged in owning and operating a chain of motels, was advised, on what seemed to be good authority, that a superhighway was to be constructed through the town of X, which would be a most desirable location for a motel. Brown presented these facts to the board of directors of the motel corporation and recommended that the corporation build a motel in the town of X at the location described. The board of directors agreed, and the new motel was constructed. However, the superhighway plans were changed after the motel was constructed, and the highway was never built. Later, a packinghouse was built on property adjoining the motel, and as a result the corporation sustained a considerable loss. The shareholders brought an appropriate action against Brown, charging that his proposal had caused the corporation a substantial loss. Decision?
2. A, B, C, D, and E constituted the board of directors of the X Corporation. While D and E were out of

town, A, B, and C held a special meeting of the board. Just as the meeting began, C became ill. He then gave a proxy to A and went home. A resolution was then adopted directing and authorizing the X Corporation's purchase of an adjoining piece of land owned by S as a site for an additional factory building. A and B voted for the resolution, and A, as C's proxy, cast C's vote in favor of the resolution. The X Corporation then made a contract with S for the purchase of the land. After the return of D and E, another special meeting of the board was held with all five directors present. A resolution was then unanimously adopted to cancel the contract with S. So notified, S now sues X Corporation for damages for breach of contract. Decision?
3. Bernard Koch was president of United Corporation, a closely held corporation. Koch, James Trent, and Henry Phillips made up the three-person board of directors. At a meeting of the board, Trent was elected president, replacing Koch. At the same meeting, Trent

attempted to have the salary of the president increased. He was unable to obtain board approval of the increase because although Phillips voted for the increase, Koch voted against it. Trent was disqualified from voting by the charter. As a result, the directors, by a two-to-one vote, amended the bylaws to provide for the appointment of an executive committee composed of three reputable business persons to pass upon and fix all matters of salary for employees of the corporation. Subsequently, the executive committee, consisting of Jane Jones, James Black, and William Johnson, increased the salary of the president. Koch brought an appropriate action against the corporation, Trent, and Phillips to enjoin them from paying compensation to the president above that fixed by the board of directors. What decision?

4. Zenith Steel Company operates a prosperous business. In January, its president, Roe, who is also a director, was voted a $100,000 bonus by the board of directors for valuable services he provided to the company during the previous year. Roe received an annual salary of $85,000 from the company. Black, a minority shareholder in Zenith Steel Company, brings an appropriate action to enjoin the payment by the company of the $100,000 bonus. Decision?

5. (a) Smith, a director of the Sample Corporation, sells a piece of vacant land to the Sample Corporation for $50,000. The land cost him $20,000.

 (b) Jones, a shareholder of the Sample Corporation, sells a used truck to the Sample Corporation for $8,400, although the truck is worth $6,000.

 Raphael, a minority shareholder of the Sample Corporation, claims that these sales are void and should be annulled. Is he correct? Why?

6. The X Corporation manufactures machine tools. Its two principal competitors are Y Corporation and Z Corporation. The five directors of X Corporation are Black, White, Brown, Green, and Crimson. At a duly called meeting of the board of directors of X Corporation in January, all five directors were present. A contract for the purchase of $1 million worth of steel from the D Company, of which Black, White, and Brown are directors, was discussed and approved by a unanimous vote. There was a lengthy discussion about entering into negotiations for the purchase of Q Corporation, which allegedly was about to be sold for around $15 million. By a three-to-two vote, it was decided not to open such negotiations.

 Three months later, Green purchased Q Corporation for $15 million. Shortly thereafter, a new board of directors for X Corporation took office. X Corporation now brings actions to rescind its contract with D Company and to compel Green to assign to X Corporation his contract for the purchase of Q Corporation. Decisions as to each action?

7. Gore had been the owner of one percent of the outstanding shares of the Webster Company, a corporation since its organization ten years ago. Ratliff, the president of the company, was the owner of 70 percent of the outstanding shares. Ratliff used the shareholders' list to submit to the shareholders an offer of $50 per share for their stock. Gore, on receiving the offer, called Ratliff and told him that the offer was inadequate and advised that she was willing to offer $60 per share and for that purpose demanded a shareholders' list. Ratliff knew that Gore was willing and able to supply the funds necessary to purchase the stock, but he nevertheless refused to supply the list to Gore. Further, he did not offer to transmit Gore's offer to the shareholders of record. Gore then brought an action to compel the corporation to make the shareholders' list available to her. Decision?

8. Mitchell, Nelson, Olsen, and Parker, experts in manufacturing baubles, each owned fifteen out of one hundred authorized shares of Baubles, Inc., a corporation of State X that does not permit cumulative voting. On July 7, 1987, the corporation sold forty shares to Quentin, an investor, for $1,500,000, which it used to purchase a factory building. On July 8, 1987, Mitchell, Nelson, Olsen, and Parker contracted as follows:

> All parties will act jointly in exercising voting rights as shareholders. In the event of a failure to agree, the question shall be submitted to George Yost, whose decision shall be binding upon all parties.

 Until a meeting of shareholders on April 17, 1992, when a dispute arose, all parties to the contract had voted consistently and regularly for Nelson, Olsen, and Parker as directors. At that meeting, Yost considered the dispute and decided and directed that Mitchell, Nelson, Olsen, and Parker vote their shares for the latter three as directors. Nelson, Olsen, and Parker so voted. Mitchell and Quentin voted for themselves and Olsen as directors.

 (a) Is the contract of July 8, 1987, valid, and, if so, what is its effect?

 (b) Who were elected directors of Baubles, Inc. at the meeting of its shareholders on April 17, 1992?

9. Acme Corporation's articles of incorporation require cumulative voting for the election of its directors. The board of directors of Acme Corporation consists of nine directors, each elected annually.

 (a) Peter owns 25 percent of the outstanding shares of Acme Corporation. How many directors can he elect with his votes?

 (b) If Acme Corporation were to classify its board into three classes, each consisting of three directors elected every three years, how many directors would Peter be able to elect?

10. Neese, trustee in bankruptcy for First Trust Company, brings a suit against the directors of the company for losses the company sustained as a result of the directors' failure to use due care and diligence in the discharge of their duties. The specific acts of negligence alleged are (1) failure to give as much time and attention to the affairs of the company as its business interests required; (2) abdication of their control of the corporation by turning the entire management of the corporation over to its president, Brown; (3) failure to keep informed as to the affairs, condition, and management of the corporation; (4) taking no action to direct or control the corporation's affairs; (5) permitting large, open, unsecured loans to affiliated but financially unsound companies that were owned and controlled by Brown; (6) failure to examine financial reports that would have shown illegal diversions and waste of the corporation's funds; and (7) failure to supervise properly the corporation's officers and directors. Decision?

11. Minority shareholders of Midwest Technical Institute Development Corporation, a closed-end investment company owning assets consisting principally of securities of companies in technological fields, brought a shareholder derivative suit against officers and directors of Midwest, seeking to recover on Midwest's behalf the profits the officers and directors realized through dealings in stock held in Midwest's portfolio in breach of their fiduciary duty. Approximately three years after commencement of the action, a new corporation, Midtex, was organized to acquire Midwest's assets. The shareholders now seek to add Midtex as a party defendant to their suit. Decision?

12. Litton, an officer and the dominant shareholder of Dixie Splint Coal Company, transferred the company's remaining assets to himself when the company came to the verge of bankruptcy. The transfer allegedly was in satisfaction of an accrued salary claim that Litton had not enforced until the company came into financial difficulty. The trustee in bankruptcy seeks to have Litton's claim disallowed. Decision?

13. Riffe, while serving as an officer of Wilshire Oil Company, received a secret commission for work he did on behalf of a competing corporation. Wilshire Oil brings this action against Riffe to recover these secret profits and, in addition, to recover the compensation Wilshire Oil paid to Riffe during the period that he acted on behalf of the competitor. Decision?

14. Muller, a shareholder of SCM, brought an action against SCM over his unsuccessful negotiations to purchase some of SCM's assets overseas. He then formed a shareholder committee to challenge the position of SCM's management in that suit. In order to conduct a proxy battle for management control at the next election of directors, the committee sought to obtain the list of shareholders who would be eligible to vote. At the time, however, no member of the committee had owned stock in SCM for the six-month period required to gain access to such information. Then Lopez, a former SCM executive and a shareholder for over one year, joined the committee and demanded to be allowed to inspect the minutes of SCM shareholder proceedings and to gain access to the current shareholder list. His stated reason for making the demand was to solicit proxies in support of the committee's nominees for positions as directors. Lopez brought this action after SCM rejected his demand. Decision?

Fundamental Changes

Certain extraordinary changes affect a corporation so fundamentally that they fall outside the authority of the board of directors and require shareholder approval. Such fundamental changes include charter amendments, mergers, consolidations, compulsory share exchanges, dissolution, and the sale or lease of all or substantially all of the corporation's assets (other than those in the regular course of business), all of which alter the corporation's basic structure. Although each of these actions is authorized by state incorporation statutes that impose specific procedural requirements, they are also subject to equitable limitations imposed by the courts.

Since shareholder approval for fundamental changes usually does not need to be unanimous, such changes frequently will be approved despite opposition by minority shareholders. Shareholder approval means a majority (or some other specified fraction) of *all* votes *entitled* to be cast, rather than a majority (or other fraction) of votes represented at a shareholders' meeting at which a quorum is present. In some instances, minority shareholders have the right to dissent and to recover the fair value of their shares if they follow the prescribed procedure for doing so. This right is called the appraisal remedy. We will discuss the legal aspects of fundamental changes in this chapter.

CHARTER AMENDMENTS

Shareholders do not have a vested property right resulting from any provision in the articles of incorporation. Accordingly, the corporate charter may be amended by following proper procedures. The amended articles of incorporation, however, may contain only those provisions that might lawfully be contained in the articles of incorporation at the time of the amendment.

Authority to amend statutes permit charters to be amended

Approval by Directors and Shareholders

Under modern statutes, the typical **procedure** for amending the articles of incorporation requires the board of directors to adopt a resolution setting forth the proposed amendment, which must then be approved by a majority vote of the shareholders entitled to vote, although some older statutes require a two-thirds shareholder vote. After the shareholders approve the amendment, the corporation executes articles of amendment and delivers them to the secretary of state for filing. The amendment does not affect the existing rights of nonshareholders.

Under the Revised Act, *dissenting shareholders* receive the appraisal remedy *only* if an amendment materially and adversely affects their rights by (1) altering or abolishing a preferential right of the shares; (2) creating, altering, or abolishing a

Procedure the board of directors adopts a resolution, which must be approved by a majority vote of the shareholders

right involving the redemption of the shares; (3) altering or abolishing a pre-emptive right of the holder of such shares; (4) excluding or limiting a shareholder's right to vote on any matter or to cumulate his votes; or (5) reducing to a fraction of a share the number of shares a shareholder owns, if the fractional share is to be acquired for cash.

Under the Revised Act, the shareholder approval required for an amendment depends upon the nature of the amendment. An amendment that would give rise to dissenters' rights must be approved by a majority of all votes *entitled* to be cast on the amendment, unless the act or the charter requires a greater vote. All other amendments must be approved by a majority of all votes *cast* on the amendment, unless the act or the charter requires a greater vote.

Approval by Directors

The Revised Act permits the board of directors to adopt certain amendments without shareholder action, unless the articles of incorporation provide otherwise. These amendments include (1) extending the duration of a corporation that was incorporated when limited duration was required by law, (2) changing each issued and unissued authorized share of an outstanding class into a greater number of whole shares if the corporation has only one class of shares, and (3) making minor name changes.

COMBINATIONS

Acquiring all or substantially all of the assets of another corporation or corporations may be both desirable and profitable for a corporation. To accomplish this, the corporation may (1) purchase or lease other corporations' assets, (2) purchase a controlling stock interest in other corporations, (3) merge with other corporations, or (4) consolidate with other corporations. Any method of combination that involves issuing shares, proxy solicitations, or tender offers may be subject to federal securities regulation, as we will discuss in Chapter 42. Moreover, when a combination may have a detrimental effect on competition, federal antitrust laws, as discussed in Chapter 44, may apply.

Purchase or Lease of All or Substantially All of the Assets

Purchase or lease of all or substantially all of the assets results in no change in the legal personality of either corporation

When one corporation purchases or leases all or substantially all of the assets of another corporation, the legal personality of neither corporation changes. The purchaser or lessee corporation simply acquires ownership or control of additional physical assets. The selling or lessor corporation, in exchange for its physical properties, receives cash, other property, or a stipulated rental. Each corporation continues its separate existence, having altered only the form or extent of its assets.

Generally, a corporation that purchases the assets of another corporation does not assume the other's liabilities unless (1) the purchaser expressly or impliedly agrees to assume the seller's liabilities; (2) the transaction amounts to a consolidation or merger of the two corporations; (3) the purchaser is a mere continuation of the seller; or (4) the sale is for the fraudulent purpose of avoiding the seller's liabilities. Some courts, as the next case illustrates, recognize a fifth exception (called the "product line" exception), which imposes strict tort liability upon the purchaser for defects in products manufactured and distributed by the seller corporation when the purchaser corporation continues the product line.

RAY v. ALAD CORP. Supreme Court of California, 1977, 19 Cal.3d 22, 136 Cal.Rptr. 574, 560 P.2d 3

FACTS On March 24, 1969, Ray fell from a defective ladder while working for his employer. Ray brought suit in strict tort liability against the Alad Corporation (Alad II), which neither manufactured nor sold the ladder to Ray's employer. Prior to the accident, Alad II succeeded to the business of the ladder's manufacturer, the now-dissolved "Alad Corporation" (Alad I), through a purchase of Alad I's assets for an adequate cash consideration. Alad II acquired Alad I's plant, equipment, inventory, trade name, and goodwill and continued to manufacture the same line of ladders under the "Alad" name, using the same equipment, designs, and personnel. In addition, Alad II solicited through the same sales representatives with no outward indication of any change in the ownership of the business. The parties had no agreement, however, concerning Alad II's assumption of Alad I's tort liabilities. Ray appealed from a judgment for Alad II.

DECISION Judgment reversed.

OPINION Generally, a purchaser does not assume a seller's liabilities unless (1) there is an express or implied agreement of such assumption; (2) the transaction is a consolidation or merger; (3) the purchasing corporation is a mere continuation of the seller; or (4) the transfer of assets to the purchaser is for the fraudulent purpose of escaping liability for the seller's debts. Here, there was no express or implied agreement of an assumption of tort liability, nor were the assets transferred for a fraudulent purpose. Also, the second and third exceptions were not met, because the purchase of Alad I's assets did not amount to a consolidation or merger.

Since the general rule did not render Alad II liable, the court looked to the policy considerations underlying strict tort liability—the protection of otherwise defenseless victims of manufacturing defects and the spreading throughout society of the costs of compensating them. Justification for imposing strict liability upon Alad II rests upon (1) the virtual destruction of Ray's remedies against Alad I due to the purchase; (2) Alad II's ability to assume Alad I's risk-spreading role; and (3) the fairness of requiring Alad II to assume the responsibility for the defective product since it continued to enjoy Alad I's goodwill. The presence of these three factors renders Alad II strictly liable.

INTERPRETATION If a purchaser of all of a corporation's assets continues the seller's product line, some courts impose upon the purchaser strict tort liability for defects in products previously manufactured by the seller corporation.

Regular Course of Business If the sale or lease of all or substantially all of its assets is in the selling or lessor corporation's usual and regular course of business, approval by its board of directors is required but shareholder authorization is not. In addition, a mortgage or pledge of any or all of a corporation's property and assets—whether in the usual or regular course of business or *not*—also requires only the approval of the board of directors. The Revised Act considers a transfer of any or all of a corporation's assets to a wholly owned subsidiary to be a sale in the regular course of business.

Regular course of business approval by the selling corporation's board of directors is required, but shareholder authorization is not

Other Than in Regular Course of Business Shareholder approval is necessary only for a sale or lease of all or substantially all of a corporation's assets that is *not* in the usual and regular course of business. The selling corporation, by liquidating its assets, or the lessor corporation, by placing its physical assets beyond its control, has significantly changed its position and perhaps its ability to carry on the type of business contemplated by its charter. For this reason, such a sale or lease must be approved not only by action of the directors but also by the affirmative vote of the holders of a majority of the corporation's shares entitled to be cast at a shareholders' meeting called for this purpose. In most states, *dissenting shareholders* of the selling corporation are given an appraisal remedy.

Other than in regular course of business approval by the board of directors and shareholders of the selling corporation is required

Purchase of Shares

An alternative to the purchase of another corporation's assets is the purchase of its stock. When one corporation acquires all of or a controlling interest in the stock of another corporation, the legal existence of neither corporation changes.

Purchase of shares a transaction by which one corporation acquires all of or a controlling interest in the stock of another corporation; no change occurs in the legal existence of either corporation and no formal shareholder approval of either corporation is required

The acquiring corporation acts through its board of directors, while the corporation that becomes a subsidiary does not act at all, because the decision to sell stock is made by the individual shareholders, not by the corporation itself. The capital structure of the subsidiary remains unchanged, and that of the parent is usually not altered unless financing the acquisition requires a change in capital. Because formal approval is required of neither corporation's shareholders, there is *no* appraisal remedy (see Figure 38–1).

Sale of Control   When one or a few shareholders own a controlling interest, she or they may privately negotiate a sale of such interest, though the courts require that these transactions be made with due care. The controlling shareholders must make a reasonable investigation so as not to transfer control to purchasers who wrongfully plan to steal or "loot" the corporation's assets or to act against its best interests. In addition, purchasers frequently are willing to pay a premium for a block of shares that conveys control. Although historically some courts have required that this so-called "control premium" inure to the benefit of the corporation, today virtually all courts permit the controlling shareholders to retain the full amount of the control premium.

Tender offer general invitation to all of the shareholders of a target company to tender their shares for sale at a specified price

Tender Offer   When one or a few shareholders do not hold a controlling interest, the acquisition of a corporation through the purchase of shares may take the form of a tender offer. A **tender offer** is a general invitation to all shareholders of a target company to tender their shares for sale at a specified price. The offer may be for all of the target company's shares or for just a controlling interest. Tender offers for publicly held companies, which are subject to federal securities regulation, will be discussed in Chapter 42.

Compulsory Share Exchange

Compulsory share exchange a transaction by which a corporation becomes the owner of all of the outstanding shares of one or more classes of stock of another corporation by an exchange that is compulsory on all owners of the acquired shares; the board of directors of each corporation and the shareholders of the corporation whose shares are being acquired must approve

The Revised Act and some states provide different procedures where a corporation acquires shares through a **compulsory share exchange**, a transaction by which the corporation becomes the owner of *all* the outstanding shares of one or more classes of another corporation by an exchange that is *compulsory* on *all* owners of the acquired shares. The corporation may acquire the shares with its or any other corporation's shares, obligations, or other securities, or with cash or other property. For example, if A Corporation acquires all of B Corporation's outstanding shares through a compulsory exchange, B becomes a wholly owned subsidiary of A. A compulsory share exchange does not affect the separate existence of the corporate parties to the transaction. Although their results are similar to those of mergers, as discussed below, compulsory share exchanges are used

FIGURE 38–1 Purchase of Shares

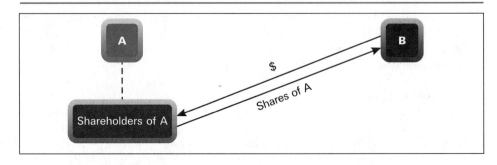

instead of mergers when it is desirable that the acquired corporation remain in existence, as, for example, in the formation of holding company systems for insurance companies and banks.

A compulsory share exchange requires approval from the board of directors of each corporation and from the shareholders of the corporation whose shares are being acquired. Each class of shares included in the exchange must vote separately. The transaction need *not* be approved by the shareholders of the corporation acquiring the shares. After the shareholders adopt and approve the compulsory share exchange plan, it is binding on all who hold shares of the class to be acquired. Dissenting shareholders of the corporation whose shares are acquired are given an appraisal remedy.

Merger

A **merger** of two or more corporations is the combination of all of their assets. One of the corporations, known as the ***surviving corporation***, receives title to all the assets. The other party or parties to the merger, known as the ***merged corporation*** or corporations, is merged into the surviving corporation and ceases to exist as a separate entity. Thus, if A Corporation and B Corporation combine into the A Corporation, A is the surviving corporation and B the merged corporation. The shareholders of the merged corporation may receive stock or other securities issued by the surviving corporation or other consideration, as provided in the merger agreement. Moreover, the surviving corporation assumes all debts and other liabilities of the merged corporation.

A merger requires the approval of each corporation's board of directors, as well as the affirmative vote of each corporation's holders of a majority of the shares entitled to vote. Dissenting shareholders of each corporation have an appraisal remedy. In a **short-form merger**, however, a corporation that owns at least *90 percent* of the outstanding shares of each class of a subsidiary may merge the subsidiary into itself *without* approval by the shareholders of either corporation. The parent's 90 percent ownership precludes the need to seek direct approval either from the shareholders or from the subsidiary's board of directors. All that is required is a resolution by the board of directors of the parent corporation.

Whereas the dissenting shareholders of the subsidiary have the right to obtain payment from the parent for their shares, the shareholders of the parent do not have this appraisal remedy, because the transaction has not materially changed their rights. Instead of indirectly owning 90 percent of the subsidiary's assets, the parent now directly owns 100 percent of the same assets.

Merger combination of the assets of two or more corporations into one of the corporations

Effect the surviving corporation receives title to all of the assets of the merged corporation and assumes all of its liabilities; the merged corporation ceases to exist

Procedure requires approval by the board of directors and shareholders of each corporation

Short-form merger a corporation that owns at least 90 percent of the outstanding shares of a subsidiary may merge the subsidiary into itself without approval by the shareholders of either corporation

---

SHELL PETROLEUM v. SMITH Supreme Court of Delaware, 1992, 606 A.2d 112

FACTS In early 1984, Royal Dutch Petroleum Company (Royal Dutch), through various subsidiaries, controlled approximately 70 percent of the outstanding common shares of Shell Oil Co. (Shell). On January 24, 1984, Royal Dutch announced its intention to merge Shell into SPNV Holdings, Inc. (SPNV), which is now Shell Petroleum, Inc., by offering the minority shareholders $55 per share. Shell's board of directors, however, rejected the offer as inadequate. Royal Dutch then withdrew the merger proposal and initiated a tender offer at $58 per share. As a result of the tender offer, SPNV's ownership interest increased to 94.6 percent of Shell's outstanding stock. SPNV then initiated a short-form merger. Under the terms of the merger, Shell's minority stockholders were to receive $58 per share. However, if before July 1, 1985, a shareholder waived his right to seek an appraisal, he would receive an extra $2 per share. In conjunction with the short-form merger, SPNV distributed several documents to the minority, including a document entitled "Certain Information About Shell" (CIAS).

continued

The CIAS included a table of discounted future net cash flows (DCF) for Shell's oil and gas reserves. However, due to a computer programming error, the DCF failed to account for the cash flows from approximately 295 million barrel equivalents of U.S. proved oil and gas reserves. Shell's failure to include the reserves in its calculations resulted in an understatement of its discounted future net cash flows of approximately $993 million to $1.1 billion or $3.00 to $3.45 per share. Moreover, as a result of the error, Shell stated in the CIAS that there had been a slight decline in the value of its oil and gas reserves from 1984 to 1985. When properly calculated, the value of the reserves had actually increased over that time period.

Shell's minority shareholders sued in the Court of Chancery, asserting that the error in the DCF along with other alleged disclosure violations constituted a breach of SPNV's fiduciary "duty of candor." After trial, the Court of Chancery held that the error in the DCF was both material and misleading. Moreover, the trial court concluded that SPNV, by virtue of its substantial role in preparing and distributing the disclosure materials, was liable to the minority shareholders for the error. The court then awarded the shareholder class $2 per share. SPNV appealed, arguing that the court's decision was incorrect because (1) the error was insignificant when viewed in context, (2) the error was not significant enough to affect a shareholder's decision whether to seek an appraisal, and (3) the error was not material because the DCF was only an estimate.

DECISION Judgment affirmed.

OPINION The question whether the disclosures to Shell's minority shareholders were adequate is a mixed one of law and fact, requiring an assessment of the inferences a reasonable shareholder would draw and the significance of those inferences to the individual shareholder.

SPNV's duty with respect to disclosure is clear. As the majority shareholder, SPNV bears the burden of showing complete disclosure of all material facts relevant to a minority shareholder's decision whether to accept the short-form merger consideration or to seek an appraisal. Thus, the question is one of materiality. A fact is considered material if there is a substantial likelihood that the disclosure of the omitted fact would have been viewed by the reasonable investor as having significantly altered the "total mix" of information made available. While it need not be shown that an omission or distortion would have made an investor change his overall view of a proposed transaction, it must be shown that the fact in question would have been relevant to him.

The Court of Chancery concluded that the understatement of Shell's oil and gas reserves by 294.6 million barrel equivalents, with a value of approximately $993 million to $1.1 billion or $3.00 to $3.45 per share would have been viewed by a reasonable investor as significantly altering the total mix of information available. It is clear from the Vice Chancellor's decision that he applied the proper legal standards and carefully considered the evidence presented.

SPNV contends that the billion-dollar error was insignificant because it resulted in only a 5.5 percent understatement in the total discounted cash flows reported. However, the significance of the error is clearly demonstrated by the fact that a Shell executive vice president stated in *The Wall Street Journal* that a 220 million barrel discovery in the Gulf of Mexico was considered a major find. Thus, it is difficult to accept SPNV's argument that the failure to report cash flows from 295 million barrels was insignificant, when the discovery of 220 million barrels was considered important enough to merit coverage on the first page of *The Wall Street Journal*.

SPNV also argues that a $3-per-share error was not significant enough to make a reasonable stockholder change his decision and seek an appraisal. However, the question is not whether the information would have changed the stockholder's decision to accept the merger consideration, but whether the fact in question would have been relevant to him. We cannot agree that a billion-dollar understatement of the value of Shell's reserves would have been anything but highly relevant and material to a reasonable stockholder.

Finally, SPNV contends that the DCF is only an estimate of future cash flows and, therefore, it would be unreasonable for a shareholder to conclude that Shell's oil and gas reserves were worth the amount presented in the DCF. In fact, according to SPNV, a reasonable shareholder should anticipate a certain margin of error simply due to the uncertainties inherent in the estimate process. Although the DCF presents an estimate of future cash flows, a shareholder could reasonably conclude that the DCF was accurately prepared based on all available information. Moreover, a reasonable shareholder could conclude that the 1985 DCF was prepared in a manner consistent with the 1984 DCF. Thus, a comparison of the 1984 and 1985 DCFs should present an accurate indication of whether the value of Shell's reserves was increasing or decreasing. Such was not the case. A comparison of the 1984 and 1985 DCFs inevitably leads to the erroneous conclusion, as stated in the CIAS, that the value of Shell's reserves had declined. Most importantly, the misleading statement that the

continued

value of the reserves had declined was not based on the inherent inaccuracies of the estimate process, but on an error made by Shell. The fact that the error was included in a schedule that contained estimates does not diminish its materiality.

INTERPRETATION In seeking shareholders' waivers of their appraisal remedy in a short-form merger, management owes the shareholders a fiduciary duty of accurate disclosure of all material facts.

Consolidation

A **consolidation** of two or more corporations is a combination of all of their assets, the title to which is taken by a newly created corporation known as the *consolidated corporation*. Each constituent corporation ceases to exist, and all of its debts and liabilities are assumed by the new corporation. The shareholders of each constituent corporation receive stock or other securities, not necessarily of the same class, issued to them by the new corporation, or other consideration provided in the plan of consolidation. A consolidation requires the approval of each corporation's board of directors, as well as the affirmative vote of each corporation's holders of a majority of the shares entitled to vote. Dissenting shareholders have an appraisal remedy. The Revised Act, however, has deleted all references to consolidations, since in modern corporate practice ensuring the survival of one corporation is almost always advantageous.

Consolidation combination of two or more corporations into a new corporation

Effect each constituent corporation ceases to exist; the new corporation assumes all of their debts and liabilities

Procedure requires approval of the board of directors and shareholders of each corporation

Going Private Transactions

Corporate combinations are sometimes used to take a publicly held corporation private in order to eliminate minority interests, to reduce the burdens of certain provisions of the federal securities laws, or both. One method of going private is for the corporation or its majority shareholder to acquire the corporation's shares through purchases on the open market or through a tender offer for the shares. Other methods include a cash-out combination (a merger or a sale of assets) with a corporation controlled by the majority shareholder. If the majority shareholder is a corporation, it may arrange a cash-out combination with itself or, if it owns enough shares, may use a short-form merger. In recent years, a new type of going private transaction—a management buyout—has become much more frequent. In this section, we will examine cash-out combinations and management buyouts.

Going private transactions a combination that makes a publicly held corporation a private one; includes cash-out combinations and management buyouts

Cash-out Combinations Cash-out combinations are used to eliminate minority shareholders by forcing them to accept cash or property for their shares. A cash-out combination often follows the acquisition, by a person, group, or company, of a large interest in a target company (T) through a tender offer. The tender offeror (TO) then seeks to eliminate all other shareholders, thereby achieving complete control of T. To do so, TO might form a new corporation (Corporation N) and take 100 percent of its stock. TO then arranges a cash-out merger of T into N, with all the shareholders of T, other than TO, to receive cash for their shares. Since TO owns all the stock of N and a controlling interest in T, the shareholders of both companies will approve the merger. Alternatively, TO could purchase for cash or notes the assets of T, leaving the minority shareholders with only an interest in the proceeds of the sale. The use of cash-out combinations has raised questions concerning both their purpose and their fairness to minority shareholders. Some states require that cash-out combinations have a valid business purpose and that they be fair to all concerned. Fairness, in this context, includes both fair dealing (which involves the procedural aspects of the transaction) and fair price (which involves the financial considerations of the merger). Other states require only that the transaction be fair.

ALPERT v. 28 WILLIAMS ST. CORP. New York Court of Appeals, 1984, 63 N.Y.2d 557, 483 N.Y.S.2d 667, 473 N.E.2d 19

FACTS 79 Realty Corporation owned a valuable seventeen-story office building in Manhattan. The plaintiffs in this action held 26 percent of the outstanding shares of 79 Realty Corporation. The defendants formed a limited partnership, Madison 28 Associates, to buy the building. This limited partnership created 28 Williams Street Corporation to act as the nominal purchaser. The defendants planned to achieve the purchase by means of a "two-step" merger in which Madison Associates would buy control of the majority shares of Realty Corporation and then merge Realty Corporation with Williams Street, "freezing out" the minority shareholders of Realty Corporation through a cash buyout. All shareholders of Realty Corporation were sent a statement of intent explaining the details of the proposed merger. Soon after the merger was approved, and in accordance with the merger plan, Realty Corporation, the surviving corporation, was dissolved, and title to the building passed to Madison Associates. The plaintiffs brought an action for equitable relief in the form of rescission of the merger. The trial court found for 28 Williams Street Corporation, and the appellate court affirmed.

DECISION Judgment for 28 Williams Street Corporation affirmed.

OPINION The directors and majority shareholders of a corporation have a fiduciary duty to treat all shareholders fairly and equally. The concept of fairness has two main components: fair dealing toward the minority shareholders and fair price. In a case such as this, fair dealing may include efforts to simulate arm's length negotiations, the procedural fairness of the transaction, and complete and candid disclosure of all the material facts of the proposed merger. A fair price need not equal the exact "fair value" of the shares but should reflect such factors as net asset value, book value, earnings, market value, and investment value. In this case, the majority shareholders' exclusion of the minority interests through the two-step merger was, viewed as a whole, fair to the minority shareholders. The minority shareholders, however, clearly were not treated equally with other shareholders, for they had no choice but to surrender their shares in the corporation for cash. Nonetheless, in a freeze-out merger, such variant treatment of the minority shareholders is permissible where it relates to the advancement of some independent corporate purpose. Here, at least one business purpose, obtaining additional capital for building repairs, justified the exclusion of the plaintiffs' interests. The evidence indicates that such capital would not have been available through the merger without eliminating the plaintiffs' interests in the corporation. Therefore, since the merger dealt with the minority shareholders fairly, advanced an independent corporate purpose, and was untainted by fraud or illegality, no breaches of fiduciary duty occurred and the merger may be upheld.

INTERPRETATION In a cash-out merger, the directors and majority shareholders have a fiduciary duty to treat all shareholders fairly, the merger must have an independent business purpose, and the transaction must be conducted without fraud and illegality.

Management Buyout A management buyout is a transaction by which existing management increases its ownership of a corporation while eliminating the entity's public shareholders. The typical procedure is as follows. The management of an existing company (Corporation A) forms a new corporation (Corporation B), in which the management owns some of the stock and institutional investors own the rest. Corporation B issues bonds to institutional investors to raise cash, with which it purchases the assets or stock of Corporation A. The assets of Corporation A are used as security for the bonds issued by Corporation B. (Because of the extensive use of borrowed funds, a management buyout is commonly called a **leveraged buyout** (LBO).) The result of this transaction is twofold: the public shareholders of Corporation A no longer have any proprietary interest in the assets of Corporation A, and management's equity interest in Corporation B is greater than its interest was in Corporation A.

A critical issue is a management buyout's fairness to the shareholders of Corporation A. The transaction inherently presents a potential conflict of interest for those in management, who owe a fiduciary duty to represent the interests of the shareholders of Corporation A. As substantial shareholders of Corporation B, however, those in management have a personal and probably adverse financial interest in the transaction.

Dissenting Shareholders

The shareholder's right to dissent, a statutory right to obtain payment for shares, is accorded to shareholders who object to certain fundamental changes in the corporation.

> **Dissenting shareholder** one who opposes a fundamental change and has the right to receive the fair value of her shares

Transactions Giving Rise to Dissenters' Rights Most states grant dissenters' rights to (1) dissenting shareholders of a corporation *selling* or *leasing* all or substantially all of its property or assets not in the usual or regular course of business; (2) dissenting shareholders of each corporation that is a party to a *merger*, except in short-form mergers, where only the dissenting shareholders of the subsidiary have dissenters' rights; and (3) dissenting shareholders of each corporation that is a party to a *consolidation*. In addition to the first and second fundamental changes, the Revised Act also provides a right to dissent to (1) any plan of compulsory share exchange in which the corporation will be the one acquired; (2) any amendment to the articles of incorporation that materially and adversely affects the dissenter's rights with respect to shares; and (3) any other corporate action taken pursuant to a shareholder vote with respect to which the articles of incorporation, the bylaws, or a resolution of the board of directors provides that shareholders shall have a right to dissent and obtain payment for their shares.

A number of states, however, have a stock market exception to the appraisal remedy. Under these statutes, the right to dissent does not exist if an established market, such as the New York Stock Exchange, exists for the shares. The Revised Act does not contain this exception.

Procedure The corporation must notify the shareholders of the existence of dissenters' rights before taking the vote on the corporate action. A shareholder who dissents and strictly complies with the provisions of the statute is entitled to receive the fair value of his shares. However, unless he makes written demand within the prescribed time period, he is not entitled to payment for his shares.

> **Appraisal remedy** the right of a dissenter to receive the fair value of his shares (the value of shares immediately before the corporate action to which the dissenter objects takes place, excluding any appreciation or depreciation in anticipation of such corporate action unless such exclusion would be inequitable)

Appraisal Remedy A dissenting shareholder who complies with all applicable requirements is entitled to an **appraisal remedy**, which is the corporation's payment of the fair value of the shares, plus accrued interest. The *fair value* is that value immediately preceding the corporate action to which the dissenter objects, excluding any appreciation or depreciation that occurs in anticipation of such corporate action, unless such exclusion would be inequitable. The next case explains how fair value is determined.

IN RE VALUATION OF COMMON STOCK OF MCLOON OIL CO. Supreme Judicial Court of Maine, 1989, 565 A.2d 997

FACTS McLoon, Morse Bros., and T-M Oil Companies were closely held companies entirely owned by members of the Pescosolido family, under the leadership of Carl Pescosolido, Sr. His sons, Carl Jr. and Richard, each held shares in McLoon, Morse Bros., and T-M. Together, their shares constituted 50 percent of the McLoon and Morse Bros. common stock and 14.3 percent of the T-M common stock. In December 1975, Carl Sr. proposed to merge all of the family-held companies into Lido Inc., over which he would exercise

continued

sole voting control. Carl Jr. and Richard (the dissenters) objected to the proposed merger. On December 6, 1976, the parties executed a merger agreement in which the dissenters expressly preserved their statutory appraisal rights. On December 15, 1976, the dissenters individually wrote to each of the three Maine companies and requested payment for their shares. Lido responded by offering each dissenter $128,685.55 for his combined interests in all three companies. Both dissenters rejected that offer.

On April 1, 1977, the dissenters filed a suit for valuation of their stock in all three companies. Ten years later, on May 22, 1987, the court appointed a referee to determine all the issues in the case, including the stock value. The referee held eight days of hearings. The dissenters offered two expert appraisal witnesses, who testified to the value of the real estate owned by the three companies and the companies' net asset value. One of Lido's expert witnesses countered by presenting a discounted cash analysis for T-M and McLoon and a net asset valuation for Morse Bros. The other expert for Lido testified about hypothetical returns on investments in comparable business properties. In his report, the referee weighed the discounted cash analysis and the net asset analysis for T-M and McLoon—seventy-five percent and twenty-five percent, respectively—and accepted fully the net asset valuation of Morse Bros. The referee held that the fair value of each dissenter's stock was his proportionate share of the full value of each company, as determined from the expert testimony. Lido objected to the report, contending that the referee should discount the full value of each company because of the minority status and lack of marketability of the dissenters' stock. The court accepted the referee's report in full, ordering Lido to pay each dissenter $334,925 with 8 percent simple interest from December 6, 1976. Lido appealed.

DECISION Judgment affirmed.

OPINION For statutory appraisal purposes, a stock's fair value can be determined by weighing three factors—the stock's market price, the company's net asset value, and the company's investment value—with the weight to be accorded each factor depending on its reliability as an indicator of fair value. Although the reliability of each factor will vary with each case, the court should still consider all three elements of fair value. In this case, the referee did so.

Lido contends that the referee's finding of fair value was inaccurate since it did not consider any minority or nonmarketability discount. The appellate court rejected this argument. The appraisal remedy for dissenting shareholders evolved as it became clear that unanimous consent was inconsistent with the growth and development of large business enterprises. Under the appraisal statute, the shareholder who disapproves of a proposed merger or other major corporate change gives up his right to veto the change in exchange for the right to be bought out—not at market value, but at "fair value." Although courts use the discount method in valuing stock for tax, probate, and other purposes where the market value is essential, the discount method has no place in the dissenter shareholder situation. The purpose of applying discount variables is to determine the investment value or fair market value of a minority interest in the context of a hypothetical sale between a willing seller and buyer. The involuntary change of ownership caused by a merger, however, requires as a matter of fairness that a dissenting shareholder be compensated for the loss of his proportionate interest in the business. The valuation focus under the appraisal statute is not the stock as a commodity, but rather the stock as a proportionate part of the enterprise as a whole. The question is simply: What is the best price a single buyer could reasonably be expected to pay for the firm as an entity? After answering that question, the court simply prorates the value among the shares, as was done in this case.

INTERPRETATION In determining the fair value of shares in a close corporation for the appraisal remedy, the court should prorate among the shares the highest price a single buyer would reasonably pay for the whole enterprise.

A shareholder who has a right to obtain payment for her shares does not have the right to attack the validity of the corporate action that gives rise to the right to obtain payment or to have the action set aside or rescinded, except when the corporate action is unlawful or fraudulent with regard to the complaining shareholders or to the corporation. Where the corporate action is not unlawful or fraudulent, many states make the appraisal remedy exclusive, and the shareholder may not challenge the action. Some states make the appraisal remedy exclusive in all cases; others, in contrast, make it nonexclusive in all cases.

DISSOLUTION

Although a corporation may have perpetual existence, its life may be terminated in a number of ways. Incorporation statutes usually provide for both voluntary and involuntary dissolution. Dissolution itself does not terminate the corporation's existence but does require that the corporation *wind up* its affairs and *liquidate* its assets.

Voluntary Dissolution

A board of directors may effect a **voluntary dissolution** by a resolution approved by the affirmative vote of the holders of a majority of the corporation's shares entitled to vote at a shareholders' meeting duly called for this purpose. Though shareholders who object to dissolution usually have no right to dissent and recover the fair value of their shares, the Revised Act grants dissenters' rights in connection with a sale or exchange of all or substantially all of a corporation's assets not made in the usual or regular course of business, *including* a sale in dissolution. However, the act *excludes* such rights in sales by court order and in sales for cash on terms requiring that all or substantially all of the net proceeds be distributed to the shareholders within one year.

The Statutory Close Corporation Supplement gives shareholders who elect such a right in the articles of incorporation the power to dissolve the corporation. Unless the charter specifies otherwise, an amendment to include, modify, or delete a power to dissolve must be approved by *all* of the shareholders. The power to dissolve may be conferred upon any shareholder or holders of a specified number or percentage of shares of any class and may be exercised at will or upon the occurrence of a specified event or contingency.

See Figure 38–2 for a comparison of the types of fundamental changes.

> **Voluntary dissolution** may be brought about by a resolution of the board of directors that is approved by the shareholders

Involuntary Dissolution

A corporation may be involuntarily dissolved by administrative dissolution or by judicial dissolution.

Administrative Dissolution The secretary of state may commence an administrative proceeding to dissolve a corporation if (1) the corporation does not pay within sixty days after they are due any franchise taxes or penalties; (2) the corporation does not deliver its annual report to the secretary of state within sixty days after it is due; (3) the corporation is without a registered agent or registered office in the state for sixty days or more; (4) the corporation does not notify the secretary of state within sixty days that it has changed its registered agent or registered office, that its registered agent has resigned, or that it has discontinued its registered office; or (5) the corporation's period of duration stated in its articles of incorporation expires.

Judicial Dissolution Judicial dissolution may be brought by the state, a shareholder, or a creditor. A court may dissolve a corporation in a proceeding brought by the attorney general if it is proved that the corporation obtained its charter through fraud or has continued to exceed or abuse the authority conferred upon it by law.

A court may dissolve a corporation in a proceeding brought by a shareholder if it is established that (1) the directors are deadlocked in the management of the corporate affairs, the shareholders are unable to break the deadlock, and

> **Involuntary dissolution** may occur by administrative or judicial action taken (1) by the attorney general, (2) by shareholders under certain circumstances, and (3) by a creditor on a showing that the corporation has become unable to pay its debts and obligations as they mature in the regular course of its business

FIGURE 38–2 Fundamental Changes

Change	Board of Director Resolution Required	Shareholder Approval Required	Shareholders' Appraisal Remedy Available
A amends its articles of incorporation	A: Yes	A: Yes	A: No, unless amendment materially and adversely affects rights of shares
B sells its assets in usual and regular course of business to A	B: Yes	B: No	B: No
B sells its assets not in usual and regular course of business to A	B: Yes	B: Yes	B: Yes
A voluntarily purchases shares of B	A: Yes B: No	A: No B: No, individual shareholders decide	A: No B: No
A acquires shares of B through a compulsory exchange	A: Yes B: Yes	A: No B: Yes	A: No B: Yes
A and B merge	A: Yes B: Yes	A: Yes B: Yes	A: Yes B: Yes
A merges its 90 percent subsidiary B into A	A: Yes B: No	A: No B: No	A: No B: Yes
A and B consolidate	A: Yes B: Yes	A: Yes B: Yes	A: Yes B: Yes
A voluntarily dissolves	A: Yes	A: Yes	A: No (usually)

the corporation is threatened with or is suffering irreparable injury; (2) the acts of the directors or those in control of the corporation are illegal, oppressive, or fraudulent; (3) the corporate assets are being misapplied or wasted; or (4) the shareholders are deadlocked and have failed to elect directors for at least two consecutive annual meetings.

A creditor may bring a court action to dissolve a corporation on showing that the corporation has become unable to pay its debts and obligations as they mature in the regular course of its business and that either (1) the creditor has reduced his claim to a judgment and an execution issued on it has been returned unsatisfied; or (2) the corporation has admitted in writing that the claim of the creditor is due and owing.

MATTER OF KEMP & BEATLEY, INC. Court of Appeals of New York, 1984, 64 N.Y.2d 63, 484 N.Y.S.2d 799, 473 N.E.2d 1173

FACTS Kemp & Beatley was a company incorporated under the laws of New York. Eight shareholders held the corporation's outstanding 1,500 shares of stock. Petitioners Dissin and Gardstein together owned 20.33 percent of the stock, and each had been longtime employees of the corporation. Kemp & Beatley had a long-standing practice of awarding compensation bonuses based upon stock ownership..However, when the policy was changed in 1979 to compensation based on service to the corporation, and not on stock ownership, Dissin resigned. Gardstein was terminated in 1980. They commenced suit in 1981, seeking involuntary dissolution of the corporation and alleging that the corporation's board of directors had acted in a "fraudulent and oppressive" manner toward them, rendering their stock virtually worthless. According to the petitioners, their "reasonable expectations" regarding this business venture had been frustrated by the directors'

continued

actions. The trial court referred the matter for a hearing before a referee, who concluded that the corporation should be dissolved or, in the alternative, be required to purchase the petitioners' stock. The trial court confirmed the referee's recommendation, and the Appellate Division affirmed. Kemp & Beatley appealed, maintaining that the corporation statute, which allows for involuntary dissolution when the directors or those in control of the corporation have been guilty of oppressive actions toward the complaining shareholders, was improperly applied in this case.

DECISION Judgment for petitioners Dissin and Gardstein affirmed as modified.

OPINION Oppressive action within the meaning of the statute exists when the conduct of the majority serves substantially to defeat the objectively reasonable expectations of minority shareholders. Shareholders in a closely held corporation such as Kemp & Beatley often are involved in the day-to-day operations of the business as officers or employees, and usually look to their salaries, bonuses, and retirement benefits rather than to dividends for a return on their investment. Here, petitioners reasonably expected that their ownership in the corporation would entitle them to certain benefits.

Kemp & Beatley had a tradition of awarding *de facto* dividends to shareholders in the form of compensation bonuses based on stock ownership. Shortly before the petitioners' complaint was initiated, this policy was changed. The fact finder did not err in finding that the change in policy was, in effect, an attempt to exclude the petitioners from gaining a return on their investment in the company.

Once the petitioners had shown that the directors' conduct was oppressive, the corporation had the burden of demonstrating the existence of an adequate alternative remedy short of dissolution or buyout. The stock of closely held corporations is not readily salable. Thus, unless the corporation buys the petitioners' shares, the petitioners will be stuck with what is to them worthless stock. Therefore, the trial court did not abuse its discretion by ordering the dissolution of Kemp & Beatley, subject to the opportunity to buy out the petitioners' shares.

INTERPRETATION A court may dissolve a corporation in a proceeding brought by a shareholder if it is established that the acts of the directors are oppressive—that is, they serve substantially to defeat the objectively reasonable expectations of the minority shareholders.

Liquidation

As we mentioned earlier, dissolution requires that the corporation devote itself to winding up its affairs and liquidating its assets. After dissolution, the corporation must cease carrying on its business except as is necessary to wind up. When a corporation is dissolved, its assets are liquidated and used first to pay the expenses of **liquidation** and its creditors according to their respective contract or lien rights. Any remainder is proportionately distributed to shareholders according to their respective contract rights; stock with a liquidation preference has priority over common stock. Voluntary liquidation is carried out by the board of directors, who serve as trustees; involuntary liquidation may be conducted by a court-appointed receiver.

Liquidation when a corporation is dissolved, its assets are liquidated and used first to pay its liquidation expenses and its creditors according to their respective contract or lien rights; any remainder is proportionately distributed to shareholders according to their respective contract rights

Protection of Creditors

The statutory provisions governing dissolution and liquidation usually prescribe procedures to safeguard the interests of the corporation's creditors. Such procedures typically include the required mailing of notice to known creditors, a general publication of notice, and the preservation of claims against the corporation.

ETHICAL DILEMMA What Rights Do Minority Shareholders Have?

FACTS Frank, James, and Thomas were fraternity brothers who graduated from college in the same year. Shortly after graduation they began a private security company incorporated as Secure, Inc. The company specialized in providing systems and personnel keyed to improving retail loss prevention efforts. The company also offered electronic theft detection systems for both homes and businesses.

When the company was formed, Frank put up the majority of the capital and became a 60 percent shareholder. James and Thomas had gone through college on scholarships and had little capital to invest. They received minority interests of 20 percent each.

The business became successful. Frank was excellent at customer and personnel relations, accounting, and routine business management. James and Thomas, however, were the real brains behind the business. They developed innovative techniques and systems that were highly attractive to customers. Their innovations attracted attention in the business community, and the company was the focus of a feature article in a major newspaper.

Safety First, Inc. has made an offer that would merge Secure, Inc. into Safety First, Inc. Frank wants to accept the merger proposal, but James and Thomas are adamantly opposed. They believe that in the long run they will make considerably more money if they operate the business independently for at least five to ten more years before considering selling out. The initial intention of Secure, Inc. was to enable the three shareholders to operate an independent business. James and Thomas do not want their technology and systems sold to another company.

Social, Policy, and Ethical Considerations

1. What moral or fiduciary obligation does Frank have to James and Thomas? What obligations do James and Thomas have to Frank?
2. To what extent should initial expectations as to business goals and operations continue to bind business associates morally? To what extent should associates spell out their expectations in advance?
3. What types of legal remedies, if any, are necessary where business associates no longer agree on fundamental business plans? To what extent should the law intervene in private management disputes among members of closely held businesses?
4. If Frank pays James and Thomas the fair value of their shares and proceeds with a merger, will this provide sufficient compensation to James and Thomas? Who owns the technological advances?

CHAPTER SUMMARY

Charter Amendments	**Authority to Amend** statutes permit charters to be amended **Procedure** the board of directors adopts a resolution, which must be approved by a majority vote of the shareholders

Combinations	**Purchase or Lease of All or Substantially All of the Assets** results in no change in the legal personality of either corporation ■ *Regular Course of Business* approval by the selling corporation's board of directors is required, but shareholder authorization is not ■ *Other Than in Regular Course of Business* approval by the board of directors and shareholders of the selling corporation is required **Purchase of Shares** a transaction by which one corporation acquires all of, or a controlling interest in, the stock of another corporation; no change occurs in the legal existence of either corporation and no formal shareholder approval of either corporation is required

Compulsory Share Exchange a transaction by which a corporation becomes the owner of all of the outstanding shares of one or more classes of stock of another corporation by an exchange that is compulsory on all owners of the acquired shares; the board of directors of each corporation and the shareholders of the corporation whose shares are being acquired must approve

Merger the combination of the assets of two or more corporations into one of the corporations

- *Procedure* requires approval by the board of directors and shareholders of each corporation
- *Short-Form Merger* a corporation that own at least 90 percent of the outstanding shares of a subsidiary may merge the subsidiary into itself without approval by the shareholders of either corporation
- *Effect* the surviving corporation receives title to all of the assets of the merged corporation and assumes all of its liabilities; the merged corporation ceases to exist

Consolidation the combination of two or more corporations into a new corporation

- *Procedure* requires approval of the board of directors and shareholders of each corporation
- *Effect* each constituent corporation ceases to exist; the new corporation assumes all of their debts and liabilities

Going Private Transactions a combination that makes a publicly held corporation a private one; includes cash-out combinations and management buyouts

Dissenting Shareholder one who opposes a fundamental change and has the right to receive the fair value of her shares

- *Availability* dissenters' rights arise in (1) mergers, (2) consolidations, (3) sales or leases of all or substantially all of the assets of a corporation not in the regular course of business, (4) compulsory share exchanges, and (5) amendments that materially and adversely affect the rights of shares
- *Appraisal Remedy* the right of a dissenter to receive the fair value of his shares (the value of shares immediately before the corporate action to which the dissenter objects takes place, excluding any appreciation or depreciation in anticipation of such corporate action unless such exclusion would be inequitable)

Dissolution

Voluntary Dissolution may be brought about by a resolution of the board of directors that is approved by the shareholders

Involuntary Dissolution may occur by administrative or judicial action taken (1) by the attorney general, (2) by shareholders under certain circumstances, and (3) by a creditor on a showing that the corporation has become unable to pay its debts and obligations as they mature in the regular course of its business

Liquidation when a corporation is dissolved, its assets are liquidated and used first to pay its liquidation expenses and its creditors according to their respective contract or lien rights; any remainder is proportionately distributed to shareholders according to their respective contract rights

QUESTIONS

1. Which charter amendments (a) do not require shareholder approval and (b) give dissenting shareholders an appraisal remedy?
2. Which combinations (a) do not require shareholder approval and (b) give dissenting shareholders an appraisal remedy?
3. Distinguish between a tender offer and a compulsory share exchange.
4. Compare and contrast a cash-out combination and a management buyout.
5. Identify the ways by which voluntary and involuntary dissolution may occur.

Internet Question. Find your state's incorporation statute and determine what kinds of fundamental changes it recognizes. (If your state is not available, choose another state.)

PROBLEMS

1. The stock in Hotel Management, Inc., a hotel management corporation, was divided equally between two families. For several years the two families had been unable to agree on or cooperate in the management of the corporation. As a result, no meeting of shareholders or directors had been held for five years. There had been no withdrawal of profits for five years, and last year the hotel operated at a loss. Although the corporation was not insolvent, such a state was imminent because the business was poorly managed and its properties were in need of repair. As a result, the owners of half the stock brought an action in equity for dissolution of the corporation. What decision?

2. **(a)** When may a corporation sell, lease, exchange, mortgage, or pledge all or substantially all of its assets in the usual and regular course of its business?

   (b) When may a corporation sell, lease, exchange, mortgage, or pledge all or substantially all of its assets other than in the usual and regular course of its business?

   (c) What are the rights of a shareholder who dissents from a proposed sale or exchange of all or substantially all of the assets of a corporation other than in the usual and regular course of its business?

3. The Cutler Company was duly merged into the Stone Company. Yetta, a shareholder of the former Cutler Company, having paid only one-half of her subscription, is now sued by the Stone Company for the balance of the subscription. Yetta, who took no part in the merger proceedings, denies liability on the ground that, inasmuch as the Cutler Company no longer exists, all her rights and obligations in connection with the Cutler Company have been terminated. Decision?

4. Smith, while in the course of his employment with the Bee Corporation, negligently ran the company's truck into Williams, injuring him very severely. Subsequently, the Bee Corporation and the Sea Corporation consolidated, forming the SeaBee Corporation. Williams filed suit against the SeaBee Corporation for damages, and the SeaBee Corporation argued the defense that the injuries Williams sustained were not caused by any of SeaBee's employees, that SeaBee was not even in existence at the time of the injury, and that the SeaBee Corporation was therefore not liable. What decision?

5. The Johnson Company, a corporation organized under the laws of State X, after proper authorization by the shareholders, sold its entire assets to the Samson Company, also a State X corporation. Ellen, an unpaid creditor of the Johnson Company, sues the Samson Company on her claim. Decision?

6. Zenith Steel Company operates a prosperous business. The board of directors voted to spend $20 million of the company's surplus funds to purchase a majority of the stock of two other companies—the Green Insurance Company and the Blue Trust Company. The Green Insurance Company is a thriving business whose stock is an excellent investment at the price at which it will be sold to Zenith Steel Company. The principal reasons for Zenith's purchase of the Green Insurance stock are to invest surplus funds and to diversify its business. The Blue Trust Company owns a controlling interest in Zenith Steel Company. The main purpose for Zenith's purchase of the Blue Trust Company stock is to enable the present management and directors of Zenith Steel Company to continue their management of the company. Jones, a minority shareholder in Zenith Steel Company, brings an appropriate action to enjoin the purchase by Zenith Steel Company of the stock of either the Green Insurance Company or of the Blue Trust Company. Decision?

7. Mildred, Deborah, and Bob each own one-third of the stock of Nova Corporation. On Friday, Mildred received an offer to merge Nova into Buyer Corporation. Mildred, who agreed to call a shareholders' meeting to discuss the offer on the following Tuesday, telephoned Deborah and Bob and informed them of the offer and the scheduled meeting.

Deborah agreed to attend. Bob was unable to attend because he was leaving on a trip on Saturday and asked if the three of them could meet Friday night to discuss the offer. Mildred and Deborah agreed. The three shareholders met informally Friday night and agreed to accept the offer only if they received preferred stock of Buyer Corporation for their shares. Bob then left on his trip. On Tuesday, at the time and place appointed by Mildred, Mildred and Deborah convened the shareholders' meeting. After discussion, they concluded that the preferred stock payment limitation was unwise and passed a formal resolution to accept Buyer Corporation's offer without any such condition. Bob files suit to enjoin Mildred, Deborah, and the Nova Corporation from implementing this resolution. Decision?

8. Tretter alleged that his exposure over the years to asbestos products manufactured by Philip Carey Manufacturing Corporation caused him to contract asbestosis. Tretter brought an action against Rapid American Corporation, which was the surviving corporation of a merger between Philip Carey and Rapid American. Rapid American denied liability, claiming that immediately after the merger it had transferred its asbestos operations to a newly formed subsidiary corporation. Decision?

9. Wilcox, chief executive officer and chairman of the board of directors, owned 60 percent of the shares of Sterling Corporation. When the market price of Sterling's shares was $22 per share, Wilcox sold all of his shares in Sterling to Conrad for $29 per share. The minority shareholders of Sterling brought suit against Wilcox to demand a portion of the amount Wilcox received in excess of the market price. Decision?

10. All Steel Pipe and Tube is a closely held corporation engaged in the business of selling steel pipes and tubes. Leo and Scott Callier are its two equal shareholders. Scott is Leo's uncle. Leo is one of the company's two directors and is president of the corporation. Scott is the general manager. Scott's father and Leo's grandfather, Felix, is the other director. Over the years, Scott and Leo have had differences of opinion about various aspects of the operation of the business. However, despite the deterioration of their relationship, the company has flourished. When negotiations aimed at the redemption of Scott's shares by Leo began, the parties could not reach an agreement. The discussion then turned to voluntary dissolution and liquidation of the corporation, but still no agreement could be reached. Finally, Leo fired Scott and began to wind down All Steel's business and to form a new corporation, Callier Steel Pipe and Tube. Leo then brought this action seeking a dissolution and liquidation of All Steel. Decision?

11. The shareholders of Endicott Johnson who had dissented from a proposed merger of Endicott with McDonough Corporation brought a proceeding to fix the fair value of their stock. At issue was the proper weight to be given the market price of the stock in fixing its fair value. The shareholders argued that the market value should not be considered because of McDonough's control of Endicott's stock and the stock's subsequent delisting from the New York Stock Exchange. Decision?

PART | IX

Debtor and Creditor Relations

CHAPTER 39

Secured Transactions in Personal Property

Today our economy literally runs on borrowed funds. An absence of loans would severely restrict the goods and services that units of production could provide and would greatly limit consumers in the quantities they could afford to purchase.

A lender typically incurs two basic collection risks. The first is that the borrower is unwilling to repay the loan even though he is *able* to do so. The second and more significant collection risk is that the borrower may prove to be *unable* to repay the loan. In addition to the remedies dealing with the first of these risks, which we will discuss in Chapter 41, the law has developed several devices to maximize the likelihood of repayment. The most important of these are consensual security interests. A consensual security interest (also known as a secured transaction) is a borrower's agreement granting a lender the right to reach specified property of the borrower to pay off the debt if the borrower fails to do so.

A secured transaction therefore includes two elements: (1) a debt or obligation to pay money and (2) an interest of the creditor in specific property of the debtor that secures performance of the obligation. An obligation or debt can also exist without security. In fact, a vast amount of indebtedness is unsecured, the debtor's integrity, reputation, and net worth being deemed adequate by the creditor. In many situations, however, businesses or other individuals cannot obtain credit without giving adequate security. In other cases, the borrower can obtain an unsecured loan, but giving security results in a lower interest rate.

Financing transactions involving security in personal property are governed by *Article 9* of the Uniform Commercial Code, Secured Transactions. This article provides a simple and unified structure within which the tremendous variety of current secured financing transactions can take place with less cost and with greater certainty. Moreover, the article's flexibility and simplified formalities allow new forms of secured financing to fit comfortably under its provisions. In this chapter, we will also discuss secured transactions in personal property. We will also discuss secured transactions involving real property, which Article 9 does not cover, in Chapter 53.

ESSENTIALS OF SECURED TRANSACTIONS

Secured transaction an agreement by which one party obtains a security interest in the personal property of another to secure the payment of a debt

Secured transactions in personal property are governed by Article 9 if the debtor *consents* to provide a security interest in such property to secure the payment of a debt. Article 9 does *not* apply to security interests without consent that arise by operation of law, such as mechanics' or landlords' liens. A common type of consensual secured transaction covered by Article 9 occurs when a person who wants to buy goods does not have either the cash or a sufficient credit standing to obtain the goods on open credit, and the seller obtains a security interest in the goods to secure payment of all or part of the price. Alternatively, the buyer may borrow the purchase price from a third party and pay the seller in cash. The third-party lender may then take a security interest in the goods to secure repayment of the loan.

Every consensual secured transaction involves a debtor, a secured party, collateral, a security agreement, and a security interest. As defined in the Code, a **debtor** is a person who owes payment or performance of an obligation. A **secured party** is the creditor-lender, seller, or other person who possesses the security interest in the collateral. **Collateral** is the property subject to the security interest. A **security agreement** is an agreement that creates or provides for a **security interest**, which in its broadest sense is an interest in personal property or fixtures that secures payment or performance of an obligation. A seller of goods who retains a security interest in them by a security agreement has a **purchase money security interest** (PMSI). Similarly, a third-party lender who advances funds to enable the debtor to purchase goods has a purchase money security interest if she has a security agreement and the debtor in fact uses the funds to purchase the goods.

Thus, a security interest is created when an automobile dealer sells and delivers a car to an individual (the *debtor*) under a retail installment contract (a *security agreement*) through which the dealer (the *secured party*) obtains a *security interest* (a *purchase money security interest*) in the car (the *collateral*) until the price is paid. A security interest in property cannot exist apart from the debt it secures, and discharging the debt in any way terminates the security interest in the property. Figure 39–1 illustrates the fundamental rights of the debtor and the secured party in a secured transaction.

CLASSIFICATION OF COLLATERAL

Although most of the provisions of Article 9 apply to all kinds of personal property, some provisions state special rules that apply only to particular kinds of collateral. Under the Code, collateral is classified according to its nature and its use. The classifications according to nature are (a) goods, (b) indispensable paper, and (c) intangibles.

Goods
Goods, or tangible personal property that can be moved when the security interest in it becomes enforceable, are subdivided into (1) consumer goods, (2) farm

Debtor person who owes payment or performance of an obligation

Secured party creditor who possesses a security interest in collateral

Collateral property subject to a security interest

Security agreement agreement that grants a security interest

Security interest right in personal property to ensure payment of an obligation

Purchase money security interest security interest in goods purchased; interest is retained either by the seller of the goods or by a lender who advances the purchase price

Goods movable, tangible personal property

FIGURE 39–1 Fundamental Rights of Debtor and Secured Party

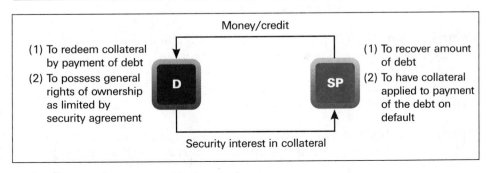

Money/credit

(1) To redeem collateral by payment of debt
(2) To possess general rights of ownership as limited by security agreement

D

SP

(1) To recover amount of debt
(2) To have collateral applied to payment of the debt on default

Security interest in collateral

products, (3) inventory, and (4) equipment. Goods that become affixed to real estate are called fixtures. Depending on its use or purpose, the same item of goods may fall into different classifications. For example, a refrigerator purchased by a physician to store medicines in his office is classified as equipment, but the same refrigerator would be classified as consumer goods if the physician had purchased it for home use. In the hands of a refrigerator retailer or manufacturer, the refrigerator would be classified as inventory.

Consumer Goods Goods used or bought for use primarily for personal, family, or household purposes are **consumer goods**.

Farm Products The Code defines **farm products** as "crops or livestock or supplies used or produced in farming operations or if they are products of crops or livestock in their unmanufactured states." Thus, farm products would include wheat growing on the farmer's land; the farmer's pigs, cows, and hens; and the hens' eggs.

Inventory **Inventory** includes goods held for sale or lease and the raw materials, work in process, or materials used or consumed in a business. Thus, a retailer's or wholesaler's merchandise, as well as a manufacturer's materials, is inventory.

Equipment Goods used or purchased for use primarily in business (including farming or a profession) are classified as **equipment**, provided they are not included in the definition of inventory, farm products, or consumer goods. This category is broad enough to include a lawyer's library, a physician's office furniture, or machinery in a factory.

Fixtures Goods that have become so related to particular *real property* that an interest in them arises under real estate law are called **fixtures**. Thus, state law other than the Code determines whether and when goods become fixtures. In general terms, fixtures are goods so firmly attached to real estate that they are considered part of the real estate. Examples are furnaces, central air-conditioning units, and plumbing fixtures. (See Chapter 49 for a further discussion of fixtures.) A security interest under Article 9 may be created in fixtures, and under certain circumstances a perfected security interest in fixtures will have priority over a conflicting security interest or mortgage in the real property to which the goods are attached.

Indispensable Paper

Three kinds of collateral involve rights evidenced by **indispensable paper**: (1) chattel paper, (2) instruments, and (3) documents.

Chattel Paper **Chattel paper** is a writing or writings that evidence both a monetary obligation and a security interest in or a lease of specific goods. Frequently, a secured party may borrow against or sell the security agreement of his debtor along with his interest in the collateral. In this type of transaction, the secured party's collateral is chattel paper.

Instruments **Instruments** include negotiable instruments, stocks, bonds, and other investment securities. An instrument is any writing that evidences

---

Consumer goods goods bought or used primarily for personal, family, or household purposes

Farm products crops, livestock, or supplies used or produced in farming

Inventory goods held for sale or lease or consumed in a business

Equipment goods used primarily in business

Fixtures goods that are so firmly attached to real property that they are considered part of the real estate

Indispensable paper chattel paper, instruments, and documents

Chattel paper writings that evidence both a debt and a security interest

Instruments negotiable instruments, stocks, bonds, and other investment securities

a right to payment of money, that is transferable by delivery with any necessary indorsement or assignment, and that is not of itself a security agreement or lease.

Documents The term **document** includes documents of title, such as bills of lading and warehouse receipts, that may be either negotiable or nonnegotiable. A document of title is negotiable if by its terms the goods it covers are deliverable to bearer or to the order of a named person. Any other document is nonnegotiable.

Document documents of title

Intangibles

The Code also recognizes two kinds of collateral that are neither goods nor indispensable paper, namely, accounts and general intangibles. These types of **intangible** collateral are not evidenced by any indispensable paper, such as a stock certificate or a negotiable bill of lading.

Intangibles accounts and general intangibles

Accounts The term **account** or *account receivable* refers to the right, not evidenced by an instrument or chattel paper, to payment for goods sold or leased or for services rendered, whether such right has been earned by performance or not. The definition of account includes contract rights.

Account right to payment for goods sold or services rendered

General Intangibles The term **general intangibles** applies to any personal property other than goods, accounts, chattel paper, documents, instruments, and money. Except for those interests it specifically excludes, this is a catchall category for interests not otherwise covered, leaving room for the use of new kinds of collateral for financing purposes. General intangibles include goodwill, literary rights, and interests in patents, trademarks, and copyrights to the extent they are not regulated by federal statute.

General intangibles catchall category of collateral not otherwise covered

ATTACHMENT

Attachment is the Code's term to describe the creation of a security interest that is *enforceable* against the debtor. Attachment is also a prerequisite to a security interest's enforceability against parties other than the debtor, though in some instances attachment is sufficient in itself.

Until a security interest "attaches," it is ineffective against the debtor. The security interest created by a security agreement attaches to the described collateral once the following events have occurred: (1) the secured party has given value; (2) the debtor has acquired rights in the collateral; and (3) a security agreement has been formed.

Attachment security interest that is enforceable against the debtor

Value

The term **value** is broadly defined and includes consideration under contract law, a binding commitment to extend credit, and an antecedent debt. For example, Buyer purchases goods from Seller on credit. When Buyer fails to make timely payment, Seller and Buyer enter into a security agreement that grants Seller a security interest in the goods. By entering the agreement, Seller has given value, even though he does not provide any new consideration but instead relies on an antecedent debt—the original transfer of goods to Buyer. Moreover, Seller is not limited to acquiring a security interest in the goods he sold to Buyer but may also obtain a security interest in other personal property of Buyer.

Value includes contract consideration, a binding commitment to extend credit, and an antecedent debt

Debtor's Rights in Collateral

Rights in collateral
personal property the
debtor owns, possesses, or
is in the process of acquiring

As a general rule, the debtor is deemed to have **rights in collateral** that he owns or possesses as well as in those items that he is in the process of acquiring from the seller. For example, if Julia borrows money from Nick and grants him a security interest in corporate stock that she owns, then Julia had rights in the collateral before entering into the secured transaction. If Susan sells goods to Peter on credit and he provides Susan with a security interest in the goods, Peter will acquire rights in the collateral on identification of the goods to the contract.

Security Agreement

Security agreement
agreement between debtor
and creditor creating a
security interest that (1)
must be in writing, unless
the secured party has
possession of the collateral;
(2) must be signed by the
debtor; and (3) must contain
a reasonable description of
the collateral

A security interest cannot attach unless an agreement between the debtor and creditor grants, creates, or provides the creditor a security interest in the debtor's collateral. With the exception of pledges, the agreement must (1) be *in writing*, (2) be *signed* by the *debtor*, and (3) contain a *reasonable description* of the collateral. In addition, if the collateral is crops growing or to be grown or timber to be cut, the agreement must contain a reasonable description of the land on which the collateral is or will be located. Figure 39–2 provides a sample security agreement.

Pledge delivery of collateral
to creditor as security for
payment of a debt

Under the Code, the security agreement does not have to be in writing when the collateral is pledged or in the possession of the secured party pursuant to an agreement. A **pledge** is the delivery of personal property to a creditor as security for the payment of a debt. A pledge requires that the secured party (the pledgee) and the debtor agree to the pledge of the collateral and that the collateral be delivered to the pledgee.

The following case illustrates how a security interest attaches when an agreement grants, creates, or provides a creditor a security interest in a debtor's collateral.

NEW WEST FRUIT CORPORATION v. COASTAL BERRY CORPORATION California Court of Appeal, Sixth District, 1991, 1 Cal.App.4th 92, 1 Cal.Rptr. 2d 664

FACTS New West Fruit Corporation (New West) and Coastal Berry Corporation are both brokers of fresh strawberries. In the second half of 1984, New West's predecessor, Monc's Consolidated Produce, Inc., loaned money and strawberry plants to a group of strawberry growers known as Cooperativa La Paz (La Paz). In September 1984, Monc's and La Paz signed a "Sales and Marketing Agreement" to allow Monc's the exclusive right to market the strawberries grown by La Paz during the 1984–85 season. The agreement did not mention the advances of money or plants, but did give Monc's a security interest in all crops and proceeds on specified property in the 1984–85 season. The financing statement was properly signed and filed. Monc's closed down in January 1985, and its assets were assigned to New West. In April, New West learned that La Paz had agreed to market its 1985 crop through Coastal Berry. New West immediately arranged a meeting to advise the Coastal Berry officers of its contract with the growers. New West requested that Central Berry either pay New West the amounts owed by the growers or allow New West to market the berries to recover the money. Coastal Berry did not respond.

After Coastal Berry began marketing the berries, New West sent letters demanding payment of the proceeds. In August 1985, New West filed suit against Coastal Berry, La Paz, the individual growers, and a berry freezing company that had accepted some of the berries. All the defendants except Coastal Berry settled with New West before trial. An outstanding claim of over $14,000 remained.

At trial, New West asserted that its security interest was valid and that it had duly notified Coastal Berry both through the financing statement on file and through the letters it had sent to Coastal Berry directly. Coastal Berry claimed that the security agreement was not effective because it did not specifically identify the debt (money and plants) being secured.

DECISION Judgment for New West.

OPINION A security agreement in some form is necessary to create a valid security interest. Although the writing does not need to be formally designated "Security Agreement," it must contain language that grants rights in the collateral. A nonpossessory security interest becomes enforceable when (1) the debtor has

continued

signed an agreement containing a description of the collateral (including a description of the land in the case of crops), (2) value has been given, and (3) the debtor has rights in the collateral.

In this case, the Sales and Marketing Agreement, though poorly written, was sufficient to create a security agreement because it did grant to New West rights in the collateral (the crops). The agreement described the crops and the land and was signed by a represen-

tative from La Paz, New West (Monc's) had given value, and La Paz had rights in the crops.

Additionally, Coastal Berry was given sufficient notice of the debt and should have retained funds from the sales to cover it.

INTERPRETATION A security interest must (1) be in writing, unless the secured party has possession of the collateral; (2) be signed by the debtor; and (3) contain a reasonable description of the collateral.

FIGURE 39–2 Sample Security Agreement

SECURITY AGREEMENT

August 22, 1997

Daniel Debtor of 113 Hillsborough Street, City of Raleigh, County of Wake, State of North Carolina, hereinafter called the "Debtor," does hereby grant to S.P. & Assoc., Inc., of Raleigh, North Carolina, hereinafter called "S.P.," its successors and assigns, a security interest in the following described property, hereinafter called the "Collateral," to-wit:

One (1) Deluxe Personal Computer
Serial number VDL16794321
Manufacturer: Apex Mechanical Equipment Co.
Model 420A

to secure the payment of Debtor's note or notes of even date herewith in the aggregate principal or aggregate face amount of Seven Thousand Five Hundred Dollars ($7,500.00), together with interest and any renewal or extension thereof, in whole or in part, and any and all other debts, obligations, and liabilities of any kind of Debtor to S.P., however created, arising, or evidenced, whether direct or indirect, joint or several, whether as maker, indorser, surety, guarantor or otherwise, whether now or hereafter existing, whether due or not due, and however acquired by S.P. (all hereinafter called the "Obligations").

DEBTOR WARRANTS AND AGREES THAT:

1. Except for the security interest hereby granted, the Debtor will use the proceeds of advances made hereunder, which proceeds may be paid by the S.P. directly to the seller of the Collateral, to become the owner of marketable title to the Collateral free from any prior lien, security interest or encumbrance, and the Debtor will defend the Collateral against all claims and demands of all persons at any time claiming an interest therein.
2. The Collateral is and will be used primarily for personal, family, or household purposes, and the Debtor's residence is that shown at the beginning of this Agreement.
3. The Collateral will be kept at the Debtor's address shown at the beginning of this Agreement.
4. There are no financing statements covering any of the Collateral on file in any public office, and the Debtor has not executed in favor of other secured parties financing statements that could be placed on file prior to any of S.P.'s financing statements.

5. **DEBTOR AGREES THAT:**

   A. He will pay to S.P. all amounts due on the note or notes mentioned above and the other Obligations secured hereby as and when same shall be due and payable, whether by maturity, acceleration, or otherwise, and will pay to S.P. reasonable attorney's fees incurred by S.P. in collection of said Obligations or enforcement of this Security Agreement.
   B. He will maintain all mechanical equipment and machinery hereby covered in sound and efficient operating condition, including the procurement and installation of such new parts, attachments, and replacements as may be necessary or desirable to maintain said Collateral in proper operating condition.
   C. He will maintain such insurance upon all of the Collateral as S.P. may require, payable to Debtor and S.P. as their interest may appear, in an amount not less than the actual value of the Collateral.

FIGURE 39–2 *continued*

D. He will pay all insurance premiums and taxes, licenses, or other charges assessed against the Collateral or required to be paid in connection with the use and ownership of the Collateral. If Debtor shall fail to pay such insurance premiums, taxes, licenses, or other charges when they are due, S.P. at its opinion, may pay the cost thereof, and the amounts so paid and advanced shall be added to the indebtedness secured hereby and shall bear interest at the maximum rate permitted by Law.

E. He will not (a) permit any liens or security interest to attach to any of the Collateral; (b) permit any of the Collateral to be levied upon under any legal process; (c) sell or dispose of any of the Collateral without prior written consent of S.P.; (d) permit anything to be done that may impair the value of the Collateral or the security intended to be afforded by this Agreement.

F. He will immediately notify S.P. in writing of any change of the Debtor's place of residence, place or places of business, or the location of the Collateral.

G. He will not remove the Collateral from the State of North Carolina without prior written consent by S.P.

6. IT IS FURTHER AGREED THAT THE DEBTOR SHALL BE IN DEFAULT UNDER THIS AGREEMENT:

A. If the Debtor uses any of the Collateral in violation of any statute or ordinance or the Debtor is found to have a record or reputation for violating the laws of the United States or any State relating to liquor or narcotics; or

B. If the Debtor shall fail to perform any covenant or Agreement made by him herein; or

C. If the Debtor shall fail to make due and punctual payment of any of the Obligations secured hereby when and as any part or all of such Obligation becomes due and payable; or

D. If any warranty, representation, or statement made or furnished to S.P. by or on behalf of the Debtor in connection with this Agreement proves to have been false in any material respect when made or furnished; or

E. If the Collateral suffers material damage or destruction; or

F. If any bankruptcy or insolvency proceedings are commenced by or against the Debtor or any guarantor or surety for the Debtor; or

G. If the Debtor dies, becomes incompetent, is dissolved, or the Debtor's existence otherwise terminates.

Upon the happening of any of the above events of default or in the event that S.P., in good faith, deems itself insecure, S.P. may at its option, declare all Obligations secured hereby due and payable immediately and have, in addition to other rights and remedies, the rights and remedies of a secured party upon default under the North Carolina Uniform Commercial Code.

The waiver of any particular default of the Debtor hereunder shall not be a waiver of any other or subsequent default of the Debtor.

Any requirement of the North Carolina Uniform Commercial Code of reasonable notification of time and place of public sale, or the time on or after which private sale may be held, may be met by sending written notice by registered or certified mail to the above address of the Debtor at least five (5) days prior to public sale or the date after which private sale may be made.

The Debtor shall be and remain liable for any deficiency remaining after applying the proceeds of disposition of the Collateral first to the reasonable expenses of re-taking, holding, preparing for sale, selling, and the like, including the reasonable attorney's fees, incurred by S.P. in connection therewith, and then to satisfaction of the Obligations secured hereby.

This Agreement and all rights, remedies, and duties hereunder, including matters of construction, shall be governed by the laws of North Carolina.

This Agreement shall apply to, inure to the benefit of, and be binding upon the heirs, administrators, executors, and assigns of S.P. and the Debtor. This is the entire agreement of the parties, and no amendment, alteration, deletion, or addition hereto shall be effective and binding unless it is in writing and signed by the parties.

Debtor acknowledges that this Agreement is and shall be effective upon execution by the Debtor and delivery hereof to S.P., and it shall not be necessary for S.P. to execute or otherwise signify its acceptance hereof.

Signed and delivered on the day first above written.

_____ (SEAL)

Daniel Debtor
S.P. & Assoc., Inc.
(Secured Party)
By: _____

Consumer Goods Federal regulation prohibits a credit seller or lender from obtaining a consumer's grant of a security interest in household goods. However, this rule does *not* apply to purchase money security interests or to nonpossessory security interests (pledges). Household goods are defined to include clothing, furniture, appliances, kitchenware, personal effects, one radio, and one television; the definition specifically excludes works of art, other electronic entertainment equipment, antiques, and jewelry.

Consumer goods Federal regulation prohibits a credit seller or lender from obtaining a consumer's grant of a nonpossessory security interest in household goods

After-Acquired Property A security agreement may provide a secured party with a security interest in **after-acquired property**, property that the debtor currently neither owns nor has rights to but may acquire at some time. For example, after-acquired property clauses in a security agreement may include all present and subsequently acquired inventory, accounts, or equipment of the debtor. Article 9 therefore accepts the concept of a "continuing general lien" or a *floating lien*; nevertheless, it limits the operation of an after-acquired property clause against *consumers*. A security interest cannot be claimed in consumer goods, except accessions, that are acquired more than ten days after the secured party gives value. An *accession* is property installed in or affixed to other property. For example, a new engine placed in an old automobile is an accession.

After-acquired property property the debtor may acquire at some time after the security interest attaches

Proceeds **Proceeds** include whatever is received from the sale, exchange, collection, or other disposition of the collateral. These proceeds may be in the form of money, checks, deposit accounts, promissory notes, or other types of personal property. Unless otherwise agreed, a security agreement gives the secured party rights to proceeds.

Proceeds consideration received for the sale, exchange, or other disposition of the collateral

Future Advances The obligations a security agreement covers may include **future advances**. Frequently, a debtor will obtain a line of credit from a creditor for advances to be made at some later time. For instance, a manufacturer may provide a retailer with a $60,000 line of credit, of which the retailer initially uses only $20,000. The security agreement between the manufacturer and the retailer grants the manufacturer a security interest in the retailer's inventory to secure not only the initial $20,000 advance but also any future advances against the $60,000 line of credit.

Future advances a security agreement may include future advances

PERFECTION

To be effective against third parties (including other creditors of the debtor, the debtor's trustee in bankruptcy, and transferees of the debtor), the security interest must be perfected. **Perfection** of a security interest occurs when it has attached *and* when all the applicable steps required for perfection have been taken. If these steps precede attachment, the security interest is perfected at the time it attaches. Once a security interest becomes perfected, as the official comments to the Code provide, it "may still be or become subordinate to other interests but in general after perfection the secured party is protected against creditors and transferees of the debtor and in particular against any representative of [the] creditor in insolvency proceedings instituted by or against the debtor."

Perfection enforceability of a security interest against third parties; attachment plus any steps necessary for perfection

Depending upon the type of collateral, a security interest may be perfected (1) by the secured party's filing a financing statement in the designated public office; (2) by the secured party's taking or retaining possession of the collateral; (3) automatically, on the attachment of the security interest; or (4) temporarily, for

FIGURE 39–3 Requirements for Enforceability of Security Interests

I. Attachment	II. Perfection

A. Agreement
   1. in writing (unless SP has possession),
   2. providing a security interest,
   3. in described collateral,
   4. signed by debtor,
 B. Value given by secured party, and
 C. Debtor has rights in collateral
	A. Files a financing statement, or
	 B. SP takes possession, or
	 C. Automatically, or
	 D. Temporarily.

a period specified by the Code. Figure 39–3 lists the requirements for enforceability of security interests.

Filing a Financing Statement

Filing a financing statement is the general method of perfecting a security interest under Article 9. Filing may be used to perfect a security interest in any kind of collateral, with the *exception* of instruments. The form of the **financing statement**, filed to give public notice of the security interest, may vary from state to state. The financing statement must contain the names and addresses of the secured party and the debtor, a reasonable description of the type or items of collateral, and the signature of the debtor. Figure 39–4 shows a sample financing statement.

Financing statement document filed by the secured party to provide notice of the security interest; may be used for all collateral except instruments

---

NATIONAL CASH REGISTER CO. v. FIRESTONE & CO. Supreme Judicial Court of Massachusetts, 1963, 346 Mass. 255, 191 N.E.2d 471

FACTS National Cash Register Company (NCR), a manufacturer of cash registers, entered into a sales contract for a cash register with Edmund Carroll. On November 18, 1960, Firestone and Company made a loan to Carroll, who conveyed certain property to Firestone as collateral under a security agreement. The property outlined in the security agreement included "[a]ll contents of luncheonette including equipment such as * * * [twenty-five different listed items,] * * * together with all property and articles now, and which may hereafter be, used * * * with, [or] added * * * to * * * any of the foregoing described property." A similarly detailed description of the property conveyed as collateral appeared in Firestone's financing statement, but the financing statement made no mention of property to be acquired thereafter, and neither document made a specific reference to a cash register. NCR delivered the cash register to Carroll in Canton between November 19 and November 25 and filed a financing statement with the town clerk of Canton on December 20 and with the secretary of state on December 21. Carroll subsequently defaulted both on the contract with NCR and on the security agreement with Firestone. Firestone took possession of the cash register and sold it at auction. NCR brought an action against Firestone for conversion of the cash register. The trial court and the appellate court ruled in favor of NCR, and Firestone appealed.

DECISION Judgment reversed and new judgment issued in favor of Firestone.

OPINION NCR could have protected itself completely by perfecting its interest in the cash register before or within ten days of delivery to Carroll. Since it did not do so, the issue is whether Firestone's security interest includes the after-acquired cash register. The language of the security agreement appears to cover all the contents of the luncheonette, not just the listed items, and is therefore broad enough to include the cash register. The only potential problem for Firestone is that its financing statement did not mention property to be acquired subsequently. The UCC, however, has adopted the "notice filing" system in which only a simple notice describing the collateral must be filed by the secured party either before the security interest attaches or thereafter. This system is designed to "give subsequent potential creditors and other interested persons information and procedures adequate to enable the ascertainment of the fact they need to know." The Firestone financing statement met this requirement. The words "All contents of luncheonette . . ." were enough to put NCR on notice to determine what those contents were.

INTERPRETATION A perfected security interest is enforceable and effective against claims by third parties.

FIGURE 39–4 Sample Financing Statement

UNIFORM COMMERCIAL CODE—FINANCING STATEMENT
APPROVED FOR USE IN NORTH CAROLINA AND THE FOLLOWING STATES

Alabama	Delaware	Maine	New Jersey	Tennessee
Alaska	Hawaii	Maryland	New Mexico	Virginia
Arkansas	Idaho	Massachusetts	North Dakota	West Virginia
Arizona	Indiana	Mississippi	Ohio	Wyoming
Colorado	Kansas	Montana	Oklahoma	District of Columbia
Connecticut	Kentucky	New Hampshire	South Carolina	

UCC-1

This FINANCING STATEMENT is presented to a Filing Officer for filing pursuant to the Uniform Commercial Code.

No. of Additional Sheets Presented:

(1) Debtor(s) (Last Name First) and Address(es):

(2) Secured Party(ies) Name(s) and Address(es):

(3) (a) ❑ Collateral is or includes fixtures.
   (b) ❑ Timber, Minerals or Accounts Subject to UCC–9–103 (5) are covered.
   (c) ❑ Crops are growing or to be grown on Real Property Described in Section (5). If either block 3(a) or block 3(b) applies, describe real estate, including record owner(s), in section (5).

(4) Assignee(s) of Secured Party, Address(es):

For Filing Officer

---

(5) This Financing Statement covers the following types [or items] of property.

❑ Products of the Collateral are also covered.

---

(6) Signatures: Debtor(s)

Secured Party(ies) [or Assignees]

(By) _____

Standard Form Approved by N.C. Sec. of State and other states shown above.

(1) Filing Officer Copy—Numerical

(By) _____

Signature of Secured Party Permitted in Lieu of Debtor's Signature:
(1) Collateral is subject to Security Interest in Another Jurisdiction and ❑
   ❑ Collateral Is Brought into This State
   ❑ Debtor's Location Changed to This State
(2) For Other Situations See: UCC–9–402 (2)

UCC-1

Duration of Filing A financing statement on which is stated no maturity date is effective for *five years* from the date of filing. If the secured party files a **continuation statement** within six months prior to expiration, the effectiveness of the filing will be extended for another five years.

In most states, security interests in ***motor vehicles*** must be perfected by a notation on the certificate of title, rather than by the filing of a financing statement. A **certificate of title** is an official representation of ownership. Nevertheless, in most states, certificate of title laws do not apply to motor vehicles that are held as inventory for sale by a dealer.

Certificate of title official representation of ownership

Place of Filing The Code provides three alternative provisions regarding the proper place at which to file a financing statement. The alternatives differ as to which types of collateral are to be filed **locally** (in the county) or **centrally** (with the secretary of state or with another designated state official).

The first alternative, which only a few states have adopted, provides that where the collateral is fixtures, timber to be cut, or minerals to be extracted, the financing statement should be filed locally in the office where a mortgage on real estate would be filed or recorded. All other filings should be made centrally with the secretary of state or with another designated state official.

The second, and most widely adopted, alternative stipulates local filing for fixtures, farm products, consumer goods, timber, minerals, and farming equipment. All other filings are to be made in the office of the secretary of state or another designated state official.

The third alternative is the same as the second except that where central filing is required, the secured party must *also* file locally if the debtor has a place of business in only one county or if the debtor has no place of business in the state but resides in the state.

Improper Filing If a secured party fails to file the financing statement in the proper location or fails to file it in all the required locations, the filing is *ineffective*, subject to two exceptions. First, a filing made in good faith is effective for any collateral for which the filing complies with the requirements of Article 9. This exception applies when a filing that covers several different kinds of collateral is proper for some but not all of them. Second, a filing made in good faith is also effective for collateral covered by the financing statement against any person who has knowledge of the contents of that financing statement. This exception has been limited by the 1972 amendments to the article, which give a lien creditor priority over an unperfected security interest without regard to whether the lien creditor knew of the unperfected security interest.

Possession

While possession by the secured party perfects a security interest in goods, instruments, negotiable documents, or chattel paper, possession does *not* perfect a security interest in accounts and general intangibles. With the limited exception of the twenty-one-day temporary period of perfection discussed later in this chapter, **possession** is the *only* way to perfect a security interest in instruments. In addition, the usual and advisable method of perfecting a security interest in both negotiable documents and chattel paper is by possession. Although both types of collateral may be perfected by filing, reliance on filing is not advisable.

A pledge or possessory security interest is the delivery of personal property to a creditor, or to a third party acting as an agent or bailee for the creditor, as security for the payment of a debt. Perhaps the most common pledge is that of a borrower who pledges corporate stock by delivering the certificates to a bank in order to secure a loan.

One kind of pledge is the **field warehouse**. This common arrangement for financing inventory allows the debtor access to the pledged goods and simultaneously gives the secured party control over the pledged property. In this arrangement, a professional warehouseman generally establishes a warehouse on the debtor's premises—usually by enclosing a portion of the premises and posting appropriate signs—to store the debtor's unsold inventory. Nonnegotiable receipts for the goods are then typically issued by the warehouseman

Possession by the secured party (a pledge); may be used for goods, instruments, documents, or chattel paper

Field warehouse secured party takes possession of the goods, but the debtor has access to them

to the secured party, who then may authorize the warehouseman to release a portion of the goods to the debtor as the goods are sold, at a specified quantity per week, or at any rate on which the parties agree. Thus, the secured party legally possesses the goods but allows the debtor easy access to the inventory.

Automatic Perfection

In some situations, a security interest is automatically perfected on attachment. The most important situation to which **automatic perfection** applies is a purchase money security interest in consumer goods. In addition, a partial or isolated assignment of accounts that transfers a less-than-significant part of the assignor's outstanding accounts is also automatically perfected.

Automatic perfection perfection upon attachment

A purchase money security interest in consumer goods, with the exception of motor vehicles, is perfected automatically on attachment without the necessity of filing a financing statement. For example, Don purchases a refrigerator from Carol on credit for his own personal, family, or household use. Don takes possession of the refrigerator and then grants Carol a security interest in the refrigerator according to a written security agreement. On Don's granting Carol the security interest in the refrigerator, Carol's security interest attaches and is automatically perfected. The same is also true if Don purchased the refrigerator for cash but borrowed the money from Laura, to whom he granted a security interest in the refrigerator pursuant to a written security agreement. Laura's security interest attached and was automatically perfected when Laura received the security agreement from Don. But, because an automatically perfected PMSI in consumer goods does not protect the secured party as fully as a filed PMSI does, secured parties frequently file a financing statement, rather than simply rely on automatic perfection.

KIMBRELL'S OF SANFORD, INC. v. KPS, INC. Court of Appeals of North Carolina, 1994, 113 N.C.App. 830, 440 S.E.2d 329.

FACTS The defendant, Burns, purchased a VCR at Kimbrell's of Sanford. At the time of sale, Burns signed a purchase money security agreement with Kimbrell's. However, Kimbrell's did not file a financing statement to perfect its purchase money security interest. Burns immediately pawned the VCR to KPS, Inc. After Burns defaulted on the security agreement, Kimbrell's filed suit in small claims court to recover the VCR. The magistrate entered judgment denying recovery. On appeal to the district court, the judgment was affirmed. Kimbrell's appeals.

DECISION Judgment reversed.

OPINION At the time the defendant purchased the VCR from Kimbrell's, he granted Kimbrell's a purchase money security interest in the VCR. Since a VCR is a consumer good, Kimbrell's did not have to file a financing statement in order to perfect its purchase money security interest in the VCR—it automatically perfected. Therefore, when Burns defaulted on the purchase money security agreement, Kimbrell's became entitled to recover possession of the VCR.

INTERPRETATION A purchase money security interest in consumer goods, with the exception of motor vehicles, is perfected automatically on attachment.

Temporary Perfection

Security interests in certain collateral are automatically perfected but only for a temporary period, depending on the type of collateral. After that period expires, the security interest becomes unperfected unless it is perfected by other means. A security interest in *negotiable documents* or *instruments* is automatically perfected, without filing or taking possession, for **twenty-one days** from the time it

Temporary perfection a security interest in certain collateral is automatically perfected for a limited time, depending upon the collateral

attaches, to the extent that it arises for new value given under a written security agreement. The secured party, however, runs the risk of loss or impairment of his security interest during the twenty-one-day period; for although his interest is temporarily perfected, a holder in due course of a negotiable instrument or a holder to whom a document has been duly negotiated will take priority over his security interest.

The Code further provides that a security interest remains perfected for *twenty-one days* where a secured party, who already has a perfected security interest in an instrument, negotiable document, or goods in possession of a bailee (provided the secured party has not issued a negotiable document for the goods), under certain circumstances delivers the instrument to the debtor, releases the document to her, or makes the goods available to her. Moreover, a security interest in proceeds is automatically perfected for *ten days* after receipt of the proceeds, if the security interest in the original collateral was perfected.

Figure 39–5 lists the methods of perfecting security interests available for different types of collateral.

PRIORITIES AMONG COMPETING INTERESTS

Priority precedence in order of right to collateral

As we noted previously, a security interest must be perfected to be effective against other creditors of the debtor, the debtor's trustee in bankruptcy, and transferees of the debtor. Nonetheless, perfection of a security interest does *not* provide the secured party with a **priority** over *all* third parties with an interest in the collateral. On the other hand, even an unperfected but attached security interest has priority over a limited number of third parties and is enforceable against the debtor. Article 9 establishes a complex set of rules that determines the relative priorities among these parties.

Figure 39–6 on page 779 summarizes these priorities among selected parties who have competing interests in collateral.

FIGURE 39–5 Methods of Perfecting Security Interests

Collateral	Applicable Method of Perfection			
	Filing	**Possession**	**Automatic**	**Temporary**
Goods				
Consumer	•	•	PMSI	
Equipment	•	•		
Farm products	•	•		
Inventory	•	•		
Fixtures	•	•		
Indispensable Paper				
Chattel Paper	•	•		
Instrument		•		21 days
Document	•	•		21 days
Intangibles				
Account	•		Isolated Assignment	
General intangibles	•			

Against Unsecured Creditors

Once a security interest *attaches*, it has priority over claims of other creditors who do not have a security interest or a lien. This priority does not depend upon perfection. If a security interest does not attach, the creditor is merely an unsecured or general creditor of the debtor.

Against Other Secured Creditors

The rights of a secured creditor against other secured creditors depend upon the security interests perfected, when they are perfected, and the type of collateral. Notwithstanding the rules of priority, it is possible for a secured party entitled to priority to subordinate her interest to that of another secured creditor. This may be done by agreement between the secured parties, and nothing need be filed.

Perfected versus Unperfected A creditor with a *perfected* security interest has greater rights in the collateral than a creditor with an unperfected security interest, whether the unperfected security interest has attached or not.

Perfected versus Perfected Two parties each having a *perfected* security interest rank according to priority in *time of filing or perfection*. Priority dates from the time a filing covering the collateral is first made or the time the security interest is first perfected, whichever is earlier, provided that in no subsequent period there is neither filing nor perfection. This rule favors filing because it can occur prior to attachment and thus can grant priority from a time that may precede perfection.

For example, Darwin Store and Surety Bank enter into a loan agreement under the terms of which Surety agrees to lend $5,000 on the security of Darwin's existing store equipment. A financing statement is filed, but no funds are advanced. One week later, Darwin enters into a loan agreement with Reserve Bank, and Reserve Bank agrees to lend $5,000 on the security of the same store equipment. The funds are advanced, and a financing statement is filed. One week later, Surety Bank advances the agreed sum of $5,000. Darwin Store defaults on both loans. Between Surety Bank and Reserve Bank, Surety has priority. When both security interests are perfected by filing, the order of filing determines priority. Reserve Bank should have checked the financing statements on file. Had it done so, it would have discovered that Surety Bank claimed a security interest in the equipment. Once Surety's financing statement was on file, with no prior secured party of record, Surety was not required to check the files prior to advancing funds to Darwin Store in accordance with its loan commitment.

Where there is a *purchase money security interest* in the collateral, the rules depend on whether the collateral is noninventory or inventory:

1. A purchase money security interest in *noninventory* collateral takes priority over a conflicting security interest if the purchase money security interest is perfected at the time the debtor receives possession of the collateral *or* within *ten days* of receipt. Section 9-312(4). Thus the secured party has a ten-day grace period in which to perfect. Almost all of the states have extended the grace period to twenty days, although a few have extended the period to some other number of days (15, 21, or 30 days).

For example, Dawkins Manufacturing Co. enters into a loan agreement with Larkin Bank which loans money to Dawkins on the security of Dawkins's existing and future equipment and files a financial statement stating that the collateral is "all equipment presently owned and subsequently acquired" by Dawkins.

At a later date, Dawkins buys new equipment from Parker Supply Co., paying 25 percent of the purchase price, with Parker retaining a security interest in the equipment to secure the remaining balance. If Parker files a financing statement within the time provided under the statutory grace period of Dawkins's obtaining possession of the equipment, Parker's purchase money security interest in the new equipment purchased from Parker has priority over Larkin's interest. If, however, Parker files one day beyond the statutory grace period, Parker's interest is subordinate to Larkin's.

MATTER OF ULTRA PRECISION INDUSTRIES, INC. United States Court of Appeals, Ninth Circuit, 1974, 503 F.2d 414

FACTS National Acceptance Company loaned Ultra Precision Industries $692,000, and to secure repayment of the loan Ultra executed a chattel mortgage security agreement on National's behalf on March 7, 1967. National perfected the security interest by timely filing a financing statement. Although the security interest covered specifically described equipment of Ultra, both the security agreement and the financing statement contained an after-acquired property clause that did not refer to any specific equipment.

Later in 1967 and in 1968, Ultra placed three separate orders for machines from Wolf Machinery Company. In each case it was agreed that after the machines had been shipped to Ultra and installed, Ultra would be given an opportunity to test them in operation for a reasonable period. If the machines passed inspection, Wolf would then provide financing that was satisfactory to Ultra. In all three cases, financing was arranged with Community Bank (Bank) and accepted, and a security interest was given in the machines. Furthermore, in each case a security agreement was entered into, and a financing statement was then filed by the secured parties within ten days. Ultra became bankrupt on October 7, 1969. National claimed that its security interest in the after-acquired machines should take priority over those of Wolf and Bank because their interests were not perfected by timely filed financing statements. The district court affirmed the referee's ruling in favor of Wolf and Bank. National appealed.

DECISION Judgment for Wolf and Bank affirmed.

OPINION Wolf and Bank provided funds for Ultra to purchase the machines and, therefore, had an interest classified as a purchase money security interest in equipment. National, on the other hand, had an ordinary secured interest in the equipment that it had properly perfected. Between these two conflicting interests, the purchase money security interest in the equipment would have priority if it was perfected at the time that the debtor, Ultra, received possession of the collateral or within ten days thereafter. Here, Wolf and Bank filed financing statements long after the debtor received physical delivery of the machines but within ten days of when Ultra completed testing and secured financing and thereby incurred the obligation to purchase the machines. Only when Ultra executed and delivered the security agreements on the machines did it become a debtor. Therefore, since the financing statements were filed within ten days of that date, Wolf and Bank had properly perfected purchase money security interests in the machines that take priority over National's claims.

INTERPRETATION A financing statement filed within the statutory grace period under a PMSI in equipment takes priority over an earlier perfected security interest.

See also *National Cash Register Co. v. Firestone & Co.*, earlier in this chapter.

2. A purchase money security interest in **inventory** has priority over conflicting security interests if the following requirements are met. The purchase money security holder must perfect his interest in the inventory at the time the debtor receives the inventory. Also, he must notify, in writing, all holders of conflicting security interests who have filed financing statements covering inventory of the same type as his acquisition, to inform them of his purchase money security interest, and must give a description of the secured inventory.

For example, Dodel Store and San Diego Bank enter into a loan agreement in which San Diego agrees to finance Dodel's entire inventory of stoves, refrigerators, and other kitchen appliances. A financing statement is filed, and San Diego advances funds to Dodel. Subsequently, Dodel enters into an agreement in which Regina Stove Co. will supply Dodel with stoves, retaining a purchase money security interest in this inventory. Regina will have priority on the inventory it supplies to Dodel, provided that a financing statement is filed by the time Dodel receives possession of the stoves and that Regina notifies San Diego that it is going to engage in this purchase money financing of the described stoves. If Regina fails to give the required notice or to file a timely financing statement, San Diego will have priority over Regina on the stoves it supplies to Dodel. As we have mentioned, the Code adopts a priority system for notice filing; and secured parties who fail to check the financing statements on file proceed at their peril.

Unperfected versus Unperfected If neither security interest is perfected, the first to attach has priority. If neither attaches, both creditors are general, unsecured creditors.

Against Buyers

A security interest continues even in collateral that is sold, unless the secured party authorizes the sale. The security interest also continues in any identifiable proceeds from the sale. In some instances, however, buyers of collateral sold without the secured party's authorization take it free of the security interest. Some of these purchasers take the collateral free of even a perfected security interest; others take it free of only an unperfected security interest.

Buyers in the Ordinary Course of Business A **buyer in the ordinary course of business** takes collateral free of any security interest created by *her* seller, even if the security interest is perfected and the buyer knows of its existence. This rule does not, however, apply to a person buying farm products from a person engaged in farming operations. A buyer in the ordinary course of business is a person who, without knowledge that a sale will violate a security interest of a third party, buys in good faith from a person in the business of selling goods of that kind. Thus, this rule applies primarily to purchasers of inventory. For example, a consumer who purchases a sofa from a furniture dealer and the dealer who purchases the sofa from another dealer are both buyers in the ordinary course of business. On the other hand, a person who purchases a sofa from a dentist who used the sofa in a waiting room or from an individual who used the sofa at home is not a buyer in the ordinary course of business.

To illustrate further: a person who in the ordinary course of business buys an automobile from an automobile dealership will take free and clear of a security interest created by the dealer from whom the buyer purchases the car. However, that same buyer in the ordinary course of business will *not* take clear of a security interest created by any person who owned the automobile prior to the dealer.

Buyer in the ordinary course of business a person who buys from a merchant in good faith, without knowledge that the sale violates a security interest

---

EXCHANGE BANK OF OSCEOLA v. JARRETT Supreme Court of Montana, 1979, 588 P.2d 1006

FACTS On September 8, 1976, Daniel Holland purchased for his own use a tractor-scraper through the Exchange Bank of Osceola located in Kissimmee, Florida. The bank retained a security interest in the tractor for the full $13,000 purchase price and then perfected that security interest in Florida.

On February 1, 1977, Holland sold the tractor, without the Exchange Bank's permission, to C. B. and O. Equipment Company, a Council Bluffs, Iowa, farm implements merchant. The tractor arrived in Iowa on February 7, 1977, and on February 21, 1977, Jarrett, a Montana contractor, purchased it and transported it to

continued

Montana. Exchange Bank then properly filed a financing statement in both Iowa and Montana. When Holland subsequently defaulted on his obligation to Exchange Bank, the bank brought this action to foreclose on its security interest in the tractor. Exchange Bank appealed from a judgment granting the defendant's motion to dismiss for failure to state a cause of action.

DECISION Judgment reversed and remanded.

OPINION Exchange Bank perfected its security interest in the tractor when it filed the financing statement in Florida. Generally, a security interest continues in the collateral despite the debtor's sale or exchange of the collateral unless the secured party authorized the transfer in the security agreement or otherwise. Therefore, since Holland sold the tractor without Exchange Bank's permission, the purchaser, C. B. and O. Equipment Company, took the tractor subject to Exchange Bank's security interest.

Jarrett, moreover, did not take the tractor free of Exchange Bank's security interest. Although Jarrett was a buyer in the ordinary course of business because he purchased in good faith, without knowledge that the sale to him was in violation of Exchange Bank's security interest, from a person in the business of selling tractors, a buyer in the ordinary course only takes free of security interests created by *his* seller. Here, Exchange Bank created the security interest, which remained perfected, while C. B. and O. Equipment Company sold the tractor to Jarrett. Accordingly, Jarrett did not take free of Exchange Bank's security interest in the tractor, and the bank is entitled to foreclose because of Holland's default.

INTERPRETATION A buyer in the ordinary course of business takes collateral free of any security interest created by his seller.

Buyers of Farm Products Buyers in the ordinary course of business of farm products, although not protected by Article 9, are protected by the Federal Food Security Act. This act defines a buyer in the ordinary course of business more broadly than does the Code as "a person who, in the ordinary course of business, buys farm products from a person engaged in farming operations who is in the business of selling farm products." The act provides that such a buyer shall take free of most security interests created by the seller, even if the security interest is perfected and the buyer knows of its existence. However, three exceptions in the act make the security interest effective against the buyer. Two of the exceptions depend upon the state's enactment of a central filing system, as specified in the act; the third applies if the creditor, in a form specified by the act, gives the buyer written notice of the creditor's interest within one year before the sale.

Buyers of Consumer Goods In the case of consumer goods, a buyer who buys without knowledge of a security interest, for value, and for personal, family, or household use takes the goods free of any purchase money security interest automatically perfected, but not free of a security interest perfected by filing. For example, Ann purchases on credit a refrigerator from Steve for use in her home and grants Steve a security interest in the refrigerator. Steve does not file a financing statement but has a perfected security interest by attachment (automatic perfection). Ann subsequently sells the refrigerator to her neighbor, Nick, for use in Nick's home. Nick does not have knowledge of Steve's security interest and therefore takes the refrigerator free of the interest. If Steve had filed a financing statement, however, Steve's security interest would continue in the collateral even in Nick's hands.

Other Buyers An unperfected security interest is subordinate to the following rights: (1) in the case of goods, instruments, documents, and chattel paper, of a purchaser who gives value for the collateral and who takes it without knowledge of the existing security interest, before the interest is perfected; and (2) in the case

of accounts and general intangibles of a purchaser who takes the collateral for value, without knowledge of the security interest, and before perfection. If either of these purchasers has knowledge of the unperfected security interest, he takes the collateral subject to the interest.

A purchaser who gives new value and takes possession of chattel paper or an instrument in the ordinary course of his business has priority over a perfected security interest in the chattel paper or instrument if he acts without knowledge that the specific paper or instrument is subject to a security interest. A holder in due course of a negotiable instrument, a holder to whom a negotiable document of title has been duly negotiated, and a *bona fide* purchaser of an investment security take priority over an earlier security interest, even if it is perfected. Filing under Article 9 does *not* constitute notice of the security interest to such holders or purchasers.

Against Lien Creditors

A **lien creditor** is a creditor who has acquired a lien in the property by judicial decree; this includes an assignee for the benefit of creditors and a receiver in equity, as well as a trustee in bankruptcy. (A **trustee in bankruptcy** is a representative of an estate in bankruptcy who is responsible for collecting, liquidating, and distributing the debtor's assets.) Whereas a *perfected* security interest has priority over the liens of creditors who acquire those liens after perfection, an *unperfected* security interest is subordinate to the rights of one who becomes a lien creditor before the security interest is perfected. However, a secured party who files with respect to a *purchase money security interest* within ten days after the debtor receives possession of the collateral takes priority over the rights of a lien creditor that arise between the time the security interest attaches and the time of filing. Approximately half of the states have expanded the grace period from ten days to twenty days.

Lien creditor a creditor who has acquired a lien on property by attachment

Trustee in bankruptcy representative of an estate in bankruptcy who is responsible for collecting, liquidating, and distributing the debtor's assets

Against Trustee in Bankruptcy

The Bankruptcy Code empowers a trustee in bankruptcy to invalidate secured claims in certain instances. It also imposes some limitations on the rights of secured parties. In this section, we will examine the power of a trustee in bankruptcy (a) to take priority over an unperfected security interest and (b) to avoid preferential transfers.

Priority over Unperfected Security Interest A trustee in bankruptcy may invalidate any security interest that is voidable by a creditor who obtained a judicial lien on the date the bankruptcy petition was filed. Under the UCC and the Bankruptcy Code, the trustee, as a hypothetical *lien creditor*, has priority over a creditor whose security interest was not perfected when the bankruptcy petition was filed. A creditor with a purchase money security interest who files within the statutory grace period after the debtor receives the collateral will defeat the trustee, even if the debtor files the petition before the creditor perfects and after the creation of the security interest. For example, David borrowed $5,000 from Cynthia on September 1 and gave her a security interest in the equipment he purchased with the borrowed funds. On October 3, before Cynthia perfected her security interest, David filed for bankruptcy. The trustee in bankruptcy can invalidate Cynthia's security interest because it was unperfected when the bankruptcy petition was filed. If, however, David had filed for bankruptcy on September 8 and Cynthia had perfected the security within the statutorily provided grace period, Cynthia would prevail.

Avoidance of Preferential Transfers The Bankruptcy Code provides that a trustee in bankruptcy may invalidate any transfer of property—including the granting of a security interest—from the debtor, provided that the transfer (1) was to or for the benefit of a creditor; (2) was made on account of an antecedent debt; (3) was made at a time the debtor was insolvent; (4) was made on or within ninety days before the filing of the bankruptcy petition or, if made to an insider, was made within one year before the date of the filing; and (5) enabled the transferee to receive more than he would have received in bankruptcy. (An insider includes a relative or general partner of a debtor, as well as a partnership in which the debtor is a general partner or a corporation of which the debtor is a director, officer, or person in control.) In determining whether the debtor is insolvent, the act establishes a rebuttable presumption of insolvency for the ninety days prior to the filing of the bankruptcy petition. To avoid a transfer to an insider that occurred more than ninety days before bankruptcy, the trustee must prove that the debtor was insolvent when the transfer was made. If a security interest is invalidated as a preferential transfer, the creditor still may make a claim for the unpaid debt, though the claim will be unsecured.

To better understand this rule, consider the following. On May 1, Debra bought and received merchandise from Stuart and gave him a security interest in the goods for the unpaid price of $20,000. On May 20, Stuart filed a financing statement. On August 1, Debra filed a petition for bankruptcy. The trustee in bankruptcy may avoid the perfected security interest as a preferential transfer because (1) the transfer of the perfected security interest on June 5 was to benefit a creditor (Stuart); (2) the transfer was on account of an antecedent debt (the $20,000 Debra owed from the sale of the merchandise); (3) the debtor was insolvent at the time (the act presumes the debtor's insolvency for the ninety days preceding the date the bankruptcy petition was filed—August 1); (4) the transfer was made within ninety days of bankruptcy (June 5 is less than ninety days before August 1); and (5) the transfer enabled the creditor to receive more than he would have received in bankruptcy (Stuart would have a secured claim, on which he would recover more than he would on an unsecured claim).

DEFAULT

After default, the security agreement and the applicable provisions of the Code govern the rights and remedies of the parties. In general, the secured party may ask for a judgment or foreclosure or otherwise enforce the security interest by available judicial procedure. Unless he has waived his rights in the collateral after default, the debtor has a right of **redemption** (to free the collateral of the security interest by paying off the loan) at any time before the secured party has disposed of the collateral, has entered into a contract to dispose of it, or has discharged the obligation by retaining the collateral. The rights and remedies of the creditor are cumulative.

Redemption freeing the collateral of the security interest by paying off the loan

Repossession

Unless the parties have agreed otherwise, the secured party may take possession of the collateral on default without judicial process if she can do so without a breach of the peace. The Code leaves the term "breach of the peace" for the courts to define. Courts usually do not permit a creditor to repossess if the debtor has orally protested the repossession.

Repossession of collateral the secured party may take possession of the collateral on default without judicial process if it can be done without a breach of the peace

FIGURE 39–6 Priorities

vs	Unsecured creditor	Creditor with unperfected security interest	Creditor with perfected security interest	Creditor with perfected purchase money security interest
Unsecured creditor	=	↑	↑	↑
Creditor with unperfected security interest	←	first to attach	↑	↑
Creditor with perfected security interest—noninventory	←	←	first to file or perfect	↑ if PMSI perfected within grace period
Creditor with perfected security interest—inventory	←	←	first to file or perfect	↑ if PMSI gives notice and perfects by time debtor gets possession
Buyer in ordinary course of business	←	←	← if created by immediate seller	←
Consumer buyer of consumer goods	←	←	↑	← if not filed
Lien creditor (including trustee in bankruptcy)	←	←	first in time	first in time but PMSI has grace period
Trustee in bankruptcy—voidable preferences	←	←	↑ if secured party perfects within grace period	↑ if PMSI perfects within grace period

After default, instead of repossessing the collateral, the secured party may render it unusable and leave it on the debtor's premises until disposing of it.

Sale of Collateral

The secured party may sell, lease, or otherwise dispose of any collateral either in the condition in which it exists at the time of default or following any commercially reasonable preparation or processing. The debtor is entitled to any surplus and is liable for any deficiency, except in the case of a sale of accounts or chattel paper, where he is entitled or liable only if the security agreement so provides.

A purchaser for value of the collateral obtains all of the debtor's rights in the collateral and also discharges the security interest under which the sale occurred as well as all subordinate security interests and liens.

The collateral may be disposed of at *public* or *private* sale, so long as all aspects of its disposition, including the method, time, place, and terms, are "commercially reasonable." The fact that the secured party could have received a better price "is not of itself sufficient to establish that the sale was not made in a commercially reasonable manner." Unless the collateral is perishable or threatens to decline speedily in value or is of a type customarily sold in a recognized market, the secured party must give, to the debtor and, except in the case of consumer goods, to other secured parties who have filed, or who are known by the secured party to have security interests in the collateral, reasonable *notice* of a public sale, or of the time after which a private disposition will be made.

Sale of collateral the secured party may sell, lease, or otherwise dispose of any collateral

THE LAW AND YOU Ohio's Credit Laws

Signing a credit purchase slip or other sales contract can have major legal consequences, creating rights and liabilities for you as well as others. Treat your signature with the importance it deserves. Do not use it carelessly. If you are ever in doubt about signing a document, see an attorney before you sign it.

What Documents Are Needed for Installment Purchases?

Most of us have bought merchandise on the "time payment" or "installment plan." Buying on the installment plan is the most common method of credit buying. When you buy an item such as a television set or car on the installment plan, you must sign certain papers before you can take the item. Some of these papers can be lengthy and hard to read. These papers may be one or a combination of legal documents: a retail installment sales contract, a security agreement, a conditional sales contract, and/or a promissory note. A combination of these instruments may be found in the same paper. Sometimes you may be required to sign in more than one place.

What Does a Retail Sales Contract Involve?

In Ohio, all retail installment sales contracts or agreements for the purchase of consumer goods must be in writing. The seller is **required** to give the buyer a copy of this document either when it is signed or when the goods are delivered. There is usually a statement in the contract whereby the buyer acknowledges receipt of a copy of it when it is signed. The receipt in the body of the contract which the buyer has signed is proof that the buyer has received a copy of the contract.

Certain details must appear in the written contract, including the **price, down payment, cost of insurance** (if any), **finance charges, balance due** under the contract and details of **payments.**

By law, a retail seller is allowed to collect certain finance charges. Many retail installment sales contracts provide for an additional charge or penalty against the buyer who is late in making a payment. There are restrictions about when this charge may be made and its amount. If charges are in excess of those allowed by law, the contract may be unenforceable against the buyer. If you believe you are being overcharged, it would be wise to contact an attorney.

What Is a Security Agreement?

You may have heard the term "chattel mortgage," "conditional sale," or "security agreement." No matter what they are called, these documents are designed to create for the seller or lender a security interest in the goods that you are purchasing or are putting up as collateral for your loan.

This security interest is designed to secure payment of your debt. The seller or lender, by obtaining such an interest, will have important rights, including the right to repossess the goods should you fall behind in your payments. The creation of this interest will normally not interfere with your keeping and using the goods unless or until they are repossessed.

What Is a Promissory Note?

A promissory note is a written promise to pay a sum of money to another person or a company. This note may be sold to a finance company, a bank, or an individual. The buyer of the note will generally acquire the same security interest in what you purchased as the original seller had before the note was sold. There are provisions which let you claim, in an action against you for non-payment of the note, legal defenses based upon the seller's breach of warranty, fraud and breach of contract. In a consumer transaction, these legal defenses are as good against the buyer of the note as against the original creditor.

A promissory note usually provides that when you fail to pay an installment within a certain period after it is due, the entire balance may become immediately due and payable. This is called an **acceleration provision**.

What If I Can't Make the Payments?

Should you default in making your payments, the seller or lender has the right to repossess the goods which serve as collateral for the debt. After the seller has taken the goods back, they may be sold after notification to you and you may find yourself liable for the difference between the price for which they are sold and the amount you still owe. The law gives you certain rights to redeem the collateral before the seller or lender disposes of it.

On the other hand, the seller or lender may, after notifying you, choose to keep the goods to satisfy your obligation. If the goods are "consumer goods" (that is, they are used or bought for use primarily for personal, family, or household purposes), and you have paid at least 60 percent of the purchase price, the seller or lender may not keep the goods but must sell them.

In any case, when goods you have purchased are repossessed, it would be wise to see your attorney. He or she can tell you what rights you have with respect to the goods or the payments you have made.

If you fail to pay an installment, the seller or owner of the promissory note may, instead of repossessing the article you purchased, take a judgment against you for the balance owed.

What About Insurance?

A common misunderstanding on auto insurance should be avoided when you sign to buy a car on time. When autos are sold on an installment plan, the seller or financing agency insists on your insuring the auto to protect the unpaid balance. This is NOT liability insurance and it does not insure you against claims by others in case of accident or injury. For your own protection, you should have liability and property damage insurance. "Credit life insurance" may—or may not—be included in

continued

the transaction. If you want this type of insurance, investigate it thoroughly. **Check Before You Sign** **Read** every paper you are asked to sign, including the fine print. **Don't sign** any paper that has **blank spaces** on it. Every space should be filled in.	**Compare** the total charge—cost of item plus credit charges, etc.—with the cash price. **Don't rely on sales talk**. Oral promises usually are not enforceable unless included in the contract. Don't sign if you can't understand the words. **Ask questions!** **Take your time**. Don't be in a hurry. If in doubt, consult your attorney,	who can do more good **before** you sign than **after**. [The information contained in this feature is general and should not be applied to specific legal problems without first consulting an attorney.] Reprinted with permission from the Ohio State Bar Association.

The secured party may buy at a public sale and at a private sale if the collateral is customarily sold in a recognized market or is the subject of widely distributed standard price quotations. See Ethical Dilemma below.

Retention of Collateral

The secured party may, after default and repossession, send written notice to the debtor and, except in the case of consumer goods, to other secured parties that he proposes to retain the collateral in complete satisfaction of the obligation; and he may retain the collateral if he receives no objection within twenty-one days. If there is an objection, however, the secured party must dispose of the collateral as provided in the Code. In the case of *consumer* goods, if the debtor has paid *60 percent* of the obligation and has not, after default, signed a statement renouncing her rights, the secured party who has taken possession of the collateral must dispose of it by sale within ninety days after repossession or the debtor may recover, in conversion or under the Code, not less than the credit service charge, plus 10 percent of the principal amount of the debt or the time price differential, plus 10 percent of the cash price.

Retention of collateral the secured party, unless the debtor objects, may (with the exception of the compulsory disposition of some consumer goods) retain the collateral in satisfaction of the obligation

ETHICAL DILEMMA What Price Is "Reasonable" in Terms of Repossession?

FACTS On credit, Jill Carr purchased a $1,000 television set at the Ryko Appliance Store. The store's credit policy required Jill to give Ryko a security interest in the television set to secure her payment of the purchase price. Though she did not clearly comprehend the repossession procedures, Jill basically understood the terms; and she signed the credit slip and the security agreement on the reverse side.

Set at $40 per month, Jill's payments to Ryko were to extend for three years. Jill made the first six payments without a problem, but then, beset with large medical bills, she defaulted on the seventh payment. Her payments up to that point had reduced her principal balance by

$180. Ryko exercised its option to repossess the set.

Ryko's standard operating procedure was to offer repossessed sets at a special sale, to take the best price offered, and to make arrangements for the defaulting customer to pay any deficiency between the resale price and the balance due on the original selling price. But Marge Glass, the store manager, saw Jill's set and realized that it was just the type her husband wanted. She also knew that if she paid even a minimal price for the set, Ryko would eventually get the rest of the money from Jill. Thus, Marge paid Ryko $100 for the set; and the store proceeded to make arrangements to collect the balance from Jill. Marge stated that $100 was the high-

est price anyone would have offered for the set and that her actions were, therefore, commercially reasonable.

Social, Policy, and Ethical Considerations

1. Is a store responsible for ensuring a customer's understanding of the nature and consequences of a sales transaction? Why? Why not?
2. Did Marge and Ryko act ethically or legally? Explain. In what ways would Jill's full understanding of the repossession process change your answer?
3. What ethical or social implications does Article 9 of the Uniform Commercial Code have in this situation?

CHAPTER SUMMARY

Essentials of Secured Transactions

Definition of Secured Transaction an agreement by which one party obtains a security interest in the personal property of another to secure the payment of a debt
- ■ *Debtor* person who owes payment or performance of an obligation
- ■ *Secured Party* creditor who possesses a security interest in collateral
- ■ *Collateral* property subject to a security interest
- ■ *Security Agreement* agreement that grants a security interest
- ■ *Security Interest* right in personal property to ensure payment of an obligation
- ■ *Purchase Money Security Interest* security interest in goods purchased; interest is retained either by the seller of the goods or by a lender who advances the purchase price
- ■ *Financing Statement* document filed to provide notice of a security interest

Fundamental Rights of Debtor
- ■ to redeem collateral by payment of the debt
- ■ to possess general rights of ownership

Fundamental Rights of Secured Party
- ■ to recover amount of debt
- ■ to have collateral applied to payment of debt upon default

Classification of Collateral

Goods movable, tangible personal property
- ■ *Consumer Goods* goods bought or used primarily for personal, family, or household purposes
- ■ *Farm Products* crops, livestock, or supplies used or produced in farming
- ■ *Inventory* goods held for sale or lease and raw materials used in business
- ■ *Equipment* goods used primarily in business
- ■ *Fixtures* goods that are so firmly attached to real property that they are considered part of the real estate

Indispensable Paper
- ■ *Chattel Paper* writing that evidences both a debt and a security interest
- ■ *Instruments* negotiable instruments and investment securities
- ■ *Documents* documents of title

Intangibles
- ■ *Account* right to payment for goods sold or leased or for services rendered
- ■ *General Intangibles* catchall category of collateral not otherwise covered

Attachment

Definition security interest that is enforceable against the debtor
Value consideration under contract law, a binding commitment to extend credit, or an antecedent debt
Debtor's Rights in Collateral personal property the debtor owns, possesses, or is in the process of acquiring
Security Agreement agreement between debtor and creditor creating a security interest that (1) must be in writing, unless the secured party has possession of the collateral; (2) must be signed by the debtor; and (3) must contain a reasonable description of the collateral

- ■ *Consumer Goods* Federal regulation prohibits a credit seller or lender from obtaining a consumer's grant of a nonpossessory security interest in household goods.
- ■ *After-Acquired Property Clause* property the debtor may acquire in the future and may be covered by a security agreement
- ■ *Proceeds* consideration received for the sale, exchange, or other disposition of the collateral; the secured party, unless the security agreement states otherwise, has rights to the proceeds
- ■ *Future Advances* a security agreement may include future advances

Perfection

Definition attachment plus any steps required for perfection
Effect enforceable against third parties
Methods of Perfecting
- ■ *Filing a Financing Statement* may be used for all collateral except instruments
- ■ *Possession* by the secured party (a pledge); may be used for goods, instruments, documents, or chattel paper
- ■ *Automatic Perfection* perfection upon attachment; applies to a purchase money security interest in consumer goods
- ■ *Temporary Perfection* a security interest in certain collateral is automatically perfected for a limited time, depending upon the collateral

Priorities among Secured Parties

See Figure 39–6 for a summary of the priority rules

Default

Repossession of Collateral the secured party may take possession of the collateral on default without judicial process if it can be done without a breach of the peace
Sale of Collateral the secured party may sell, lease, or otherwise dispose of any collateral
Retention of Collateral the secured party, unless the debtor objects, may (with the exception of the compulsory disposition of some consumer goods) retain the collateral in satisfaction of the obligation

QUESTIONS

1. Name and define the various kinds of collateral.
2. Define attachment, its purpose, and its requirements.
3. Define perfection and the various methods of perfecting.
4. Discuss the priorities among the various parties who may have competing interests in collateral.

5. Discuss the rights and remedies of the parties to a security agreement after default by the debtor.

Internet Question. Find which alternative of Section 9-401 for place of filing your state has adopted. (If your state is not available, choose another state.)

PROBLEMS

1. Victor sells to Bonnie a refrigerator under a conditional sales contract for $600 payable in monthly installments of $30 for twenty months. The refrigerator is installed in the kitchen of Bonnie's apartment. No financing statement is filed. Assume that after Bonnie has made the first three monthly payments:
   (a) Bonnie moves from her apartment and sells the refrigerator in place to the new occupant for $350 cash. What are the rights of Victor?
   (b) Bonnie is adjudicated bankrupt, and her trustee in bankruptcy claims the refrigerator. What are the rights of the parties?

2. On January 2, Burt asked Logan to loan him money "against my diamond ring." Logan agreed to do so. To guard against intervening liens, Logan received permission to record his interest; and Burt and Logan signed a security agreement giving Logan an interest in the ring. Burt also signed a financing statement, which Logan properly filed on January 3. On January 4, Burt borrowed money from Tillo, pledging his ring to secure the debt. Tillo took possession of the ring and paid Burt the money on the same day. The next day, January 5, Logan loaned Burt the money under the assumption that Burt still had the ring. Who has priority, Logan or Tillo? Explain.

3. Joanna takes a security interest in the equipment in Jason Store and files a financing statement claiming "equipment and all after-acquired equipment." Berkeley later sells Jason Store a cash register on conditional sale and (a) files nine days after Jason receives the register or (b) files fifteen days after Jason receives the register. If Jason fails to pay both Joanna and Berkeley and they foreclose their security interests, who has priority on the cash register?

4. Finley Motor Company sells an automobile to Sara and retains a security interest in it. The automobile is insured, and Finley is named beneficiary. The automobile is totally destroyed in an accident, and three days later Sara files a petition in bankruptcy. Who is entitled to the insurance proceeds, Finley or Sara's trustee in bankruptcy?

5. On September 5, Wanda, a widow who occasionally teaches piano and organ in her home, purchased an electric organ from Murphy's music store for $4,800, trading in her old organ for $1,200 and promising in writing to pay the balance at $120 per month and granting to Murphy a security interest in the property in terms consistent with and incorporating provisions of the UCC. A financing statement covering the transaction was also properly filled out and signed, and Murphy properly filed it. After Wanda did not make the December or January payments, Murphy went to her home to collect the payments or to take the organ. Finding no one home and the door unlocked, he went in and took the organ. Two hours later, Tia, a third party and the present occupant of the house, who had purchased the organ for her own use, stormed into Murphy's store to demand the return of the organ. She exhibited a bill of sale from Wanda to her, dated December 15, that listed the organ and other furnishings in the house.
   (a) What are the rights of Murphy, Tia, and Wanda?
   (b) Would your answer change if Murphy had not filed a financing statement? Why?
   (c) Would your answer change if the organ had been used principally to give lessons? Explain.

6. On May 1, Lincoln lends Donaldson $20,000, receives from Donaldson his promissory note for this amount due in two years, and takes a security interest in the machinery and equipment in Donaldson's factory. A proper financing statement is filed with respect to the security agreement. On August 1, on Lincoln's request, Donaldson executes an addendum to the security agreement covering after-acquired machinery and equipment in Donaldson's factory. A second financing statement is filed covering the addendum. In September, Donaldson acquires $5,000 worth of new equipment from Thompson, which Donaldson installs in his factory. In December, Carter, a judgment creditor of Donaldson, causes an attachment to issue against the new equipment. What are the rights of Lincoln, Donaldson, Carter, and Thompson? What can the parties do to best protect themselves?

7. Anita bought a television set from Bertrum for her personal use. Bertrum, who was out of conditional sales contracts, showed Anita a form he had executed with Clarkson, another consumer. Anita and Bertrum orally agreed to the terms of the form. Anita subsequently defaults on payment, and Bertrum seeks to repossess the television. Decision? Would the result differ if Bertrum had filed a financing statement?

8. Aaron bought a television set for his own use from Penny. Aaron properly signed a security agreement and paid Penny $25 down as their agreement required. Penny did not file a financing statement, and subsequently Aaron sells the television to Nathaniel, his neighbor, for $300 for Nathaniel to use in his hotel lobby.
   (a) When Aaron fails to make the January and February payments, may Penny repossess the television from Nathaniel?
   (b) What if, instead of Aaron's selling the television set to Nathaniel, a judgment creditor levied (sought possession) on the television? Who would prevail?
   (c) What if Nathaniel intended to use the television set in his home? Who would prevail?

9. Standridge purchased a 1965 Chevrolet automobile from Billy Deavers, an agent of Walker Motor

Company. According to the sales contract, the balance due after the trade-in allowance was $282.50, to be paid in twelve weekly installments. Standridge claims that he was unable to make the second payment and that Billy Deavers orally agreed that he could make two payments the next week. The day after the double payment was due, Standridge still had not paid. That day, Ronnie Deavers, Billy's brother, went to Standridge's place of employment to repossess the car. Rather than consenting to the repossession, Standridge drove the car to the Walker Motor Company's place of business and tendered the overdue payments. The Deaverses refused to accept the late payment and instead demanded the entire unpaid balance. Standridge could not pay it. The Deaverses then blocked Standridge's car with another car and told him he could just "walk his _____ home." Standridge brought suit, seeking damages for the Deaverses' wrongful repossession of his car. The Deaverses deny that they granted Standridge permission to make a double payment; that Standridge tendered the double payment; and that they rejected it. They claim that he made no payment and that, therefore, they were entitled to repossess the car. Decision?

10. Jones bought a used car from the A–Herts Car Rental System, which regularly sold its used equipment at the end of its fiscal year. First National Bank of Roxboro had previously obtained a perfected security interest in the car, based upon its financing of A–Herts's automobiles. Upon A–Herts's failure to pay, First National sought to repossess the car from Jones. Decision?

11. On May 1, Charlie purchased on credit a refrigerator for his own use from XYZ for $600 and gave XYZ a security interest in the refrigerator. On May 5, Charlie borrowed $500 from the Friendly Finance Company and gave Friendly a security interest in the refrigerator. Friendly properly perfected its security interest by filing. On May 15, one of Charlie's creditors obtained a judgment lien against Charlie and properly recorded the lien. On May 20, after Charlie had failed to make his payment on the refrigerator, XYZ properly filed a financing statement. On May 30, Charlie sold the refrigerator at a yard sale to one of his neighbors for $200. All are claiming priority to the refrigerator. Who will prevail? Why?

12. Plant Reclamation Company sold equipment to Amex-Protein Development Corporation on an open account. Later, Plant Reclamation substituted a promissory note for the open account indebtedness and caused to be signed and filed a financing statement that provided notice of the parties' intention to create a security interest in the property sold as collateral for

the note. The note stated that it was secured by a security interest in the property "as per invoices." Amex-Protein subsequently declared bankruptcy, and the validity of Plant Reclamation's security interest in the property is now in issue. The trustee asserts that the promissory note does not constitute a valid security agreement and questions the adequacy of the collateral description contained in that instrument. Decision?

13. Eggeman and his wife gave Western National Bank a $41,000 promissory note securing the debt by a mortgage on two adjoining tracts of land. Sometime later, Eggeman gave the bank an additional $8,625 note, which was secured by "inventory and accounts receivable" described more fully in the security agreement. When Eggeman defaulted on both notes, Western National filed a complaint against Eggeman requesting the sale of the mortgaged land in satisfaction of the balance due on the first note and the sale of the collateral in satisfaction of the balance due on the second note. The judgment authorizing the foreclosure sale provided, with respect to the second note, "that the collateral listed in the security agreement be sold under and pursuant to the judgment of this Court." The inventory and accounts receivable were not listed or itemized in the judgment or at the sale. When the sale was held, both tracts of land, the inventory, and the accounts receivable were offered only as a whole and in one group. They were purchased by James T. Frost for $67,500. Eggeman moved to vacate the sale, claiming that the remedy taken by Western National with reference to the second note was not pursuant to law. Western National countered that the sale was proper as a judicial sale. Decision?

14. Joseph Modafferi, CPA, borrowed $10,000 from Peg-Leg Productions, Inc. The debt was evidenced by a written promissory note that was silent as to any collateral securing payment. Shortly after making the loan, Peg-Leg Productions filed a UCC-1 financing statement at the appropriate filing office, which stated that the debt was secured by office equipment, furniture, and all accounts payable. Modafferi, however, had signed only the financing statement and the promissory note. He had not signed any document referred to as or constituting a security agreement. On Modafferi's subsequent bankruptcy, Peg-Leg Productions filed a proof of claim with the trustee, claiming the status of a perfected secured creditor. The trustee responded that Peg-Leg was not a perfected secured creditor since it did not have a signed security agreement and that the company therefore must be grouped with unsecured creditors in the bankruptcy proceeding. Decision?

CHAPTER 40

Suretyship

In many business transactions involving the extension of credit, the creditor will require that someone in addition to the debtor promise to fulfill the obligation. This promisor generally is known as a **surety**. In a contract involving a minor, a surety commonly will act as a party with full contractual capacity who can be held responsible for the obligations arising from the contract. Sureties are often used in *addition* to security to further reduce the risks involved in the extension of credit and are used *instead* of security interests when security is unavailable or when the use of a secured transaction is too expensive or inconvenient. Employers frequently use sureties to protect against losses caused by employees' embezzlement, while property owners use sureties to bond the performance of contracts for the construction of commercial buildings. Similarly, statutes commonly require that contracts for work to be done for governmental entities have the added protection of a surety. Premiums for compensated sureties exceed $1 billion annually in the United States.

NATURE AND FORMATION

A surety promises to answer for the payment of a debt or the performance of a duty owed to one person (called the ***creditor***) by another (the ***principal debtor***) on the principal debtor's *failure* to make payment or otherwise to perform the obligation. Thus, the suretyship relationship involves three parties—the principal debtor, the creditor, and the surety—and three contractual obligations, as illustrated by Figure 40–1. Two or more persons bound for the same debt of a principal debtor are **cosureties**.

The creditor's rights against the principal debtor are determined by the contract between them. The creditor also may take action on any collateral that the creditor or the surety holds to secure the principal debtor's performance. In addition, the creditor may proceed against the surety if the principal debtor defaults. If the surety is an **absolute surety**, the creditor may hold the surety liable as soon as the principal debtor defaults. The creditor need *not* proceed first against the principal debtor. In contrast, a surety who is a **conditional guarantor of collection** is liable only when the creditor exhausts his legal remedies against the principal debtor. Thus, a conditional guarantor of collection is liable if the creditor first obtains, but is unable to collect, a judgment against the principal debtor.

A surety who is required to pay the creditor is entitled to be exonerated (relieved of liability) and reimbursed by the principal debtor. In addition, the surety is subrogated to (assumes) the rights of the creditor and has a right to contribution from cosureties (see Figure 40–1). The rights of sureties will be discussed more fully later in this chapter.

Surety *(shur'·i·tee)* one who promises to pay the debt of another if the other party fails to perform

Cosureties each of two or more sureties bound for the same debt of a principal debtor

Absolute surety surety liable to a creditor immediately upon the default of the principal debtor

Conditional guarantor of collection surety liable to creditor only after creditor exhausts his legal remedies against the principal debtor

FIGURE 40–1 Suretyship Relationship

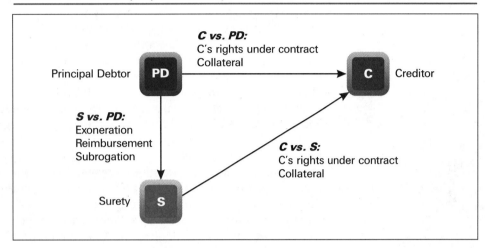

Although in theory a distinction exists between a surety and a guarantor, the two terms are almost synonymous in common usage. Strictly speaking, a surety is bound with the principal debtor as a primary obligor, usually, although not necessarily, on the same instrument, whereas the guarantor is separately or collaterally bound to pay if the principal debtor does not. For convenience, and because the rights and duties of a surety and a guarantor are almost indistinguishable, the term "surety" will be used to include both of these terms.

UNITED STATES v. TILLERAAS United States Court of Appeals, Sixth Circuit, 1983, 709 F.2d 1088

FACTS Elizabeth Tilleraas received three student loans totaling $3,500 under the Federal Insured Student Loan Program (FISLP) of the Higher Education Act of 1965. These loans were secured by three promissory notes executed in favor of Dakota National Bank & Trust Co., Fargo, North Dakota. Under the terms of these student loans, periodic payments were required beginning twelve months after Tilleraas ceased to carry at least one-half of a full-time academic workload at an eligible institution. Her student status terminated on January 28, 1971, and the first installment payment thus became due January 28, 1972. She never made any payment on any of her loans. Under the provisions of the FISLP, the United States assured the lender bank repayment in event of any failure to pay by the borrower.

The first payment due on the loans was in "default" on July 27, 1972, 180 days after the failure to make the first installment payment. On December 17, 1973, Dakota National Bank & Trust sent notice of its election under the provisions of the loan to accelerate the maturity of the note. The bank demanded payment in full by December 27, 1973. It then filed FISLP insurance claims against the United States on May 6, 1974, and assigned the three Tilleraas notes to the United States on May 10, 1974. The government, in turn, paid the

bank's claim in full on July 5, 1974. On June 4, 1980, the government filed suit against Tilleraas. The district court found for the United States.

DECISION Judgment for the United States affirmed.

OPINION A surety is responsible for the payment of the debt of another should the principal debtor fail to repay the creditor. The purpose of the arrangement is to induce the creditor to extend a loan where he might otherwise be unwilling to do so. The benefit thus received by the debtor places the debtor under an implied legal obligation to reimburse the surety for any payment made by the surety to the creditor. In this case, Tilleraas was able to borrow money from Dakota National with no collateral and upon favorable terms. The United States insured repayment to Dakota National in the event of default by Tilleraas. Therefore, a surety-principal/debtor-lender relationship was created. When Tilleraas in fact defaulted and the United States, the surety-guarantor, paid Dakota National's claim, it obtained the right to sue Tilleraas on the underlying loan.

INTERPRETATION A surety who is required to pay the creditor is entitled to reimbursement by the principal debtor.

Types of Sureties

A suretyship arrangement is frequently used by creditors seeking to reduce the risk of default by their debtors. For example, Philco Developers, a closely held corporation, applies to Caldwell Bank, a lending institution, for a loan. After scrutinizing Philco's assets and financial prospects, the lender refuses to extend credit unless Simpson, Philco's sole shareholder, promises to repay the loan if Philco does not. Simpson agrees, and Caldwell Bank makes the loan. Simpson's undertaking is that of a surety. Similarly, Philco Developers wishes to purchase goods on credit from Bird Enterprises, the seller, who agrees to extend credit only if Philco Developers obtains an acceptable surety. Simpson agrees to pay Bird Enterprises for the goods if Philco Developers does not. Simpson is a surety. In each of these examples, the surety's promise gives the creditor recourse for payment against two persons—the principal debtor and the surety—instead of one, thereby reducing the creditor's risk of loss.

Another common suretyship relation arises when an owner of property subject to a mortgage sells the property to a purchaser who **assumes the mortgage**. Though, by assuming the obligation, the purchaser becomes the principal debtor and therefore personally obligated to pay the seller's debt to the lender, the seller nevertheless remains liable to the lender and is a surety on the obligation the purchaser has assumed (see Figure 40–2). However, a purchaser who does *not* assume the mortgage but simply takes the property subject to the mortgage is *not* personally liable for the mortgage; nor is he a surety for the mortgage obligation. In this case, the purchaser's potential loss is limited to the value of the property; for, although the mortgagee creditor may foreclose against the property, she may not hold the purchaser personally liable for the debt.

In addition to the more general kinds of sureties, there are numerous specialized kinds of suretyship, the most important of which are (1) fidelity, (2) performance, (3) official, and (4) judicial. A surety undertakes a **fidelity bond** to protect an employer against employee dishonesty. **Performance bonds** guarantee the performance of the terms and conditions of a contract. These bonds are used frequently in the construction industry to protect an owner from losses that may result from a contractor's failure to perform a building contract. **Official bonds** arise from statutes requiring public officers to furnish bonds for the faithful performance of their duties. Such bonds obligate a surety for all losses an officer causes through negligence or through nonperformance of her

FIGURE 40–2 Assumption of Mortgage

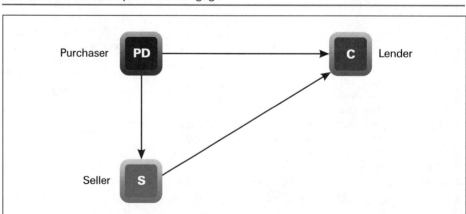

duties. *Judicial bonds*, provided on behalf of a party to a judicial proceeding, cover losses caused by delay or by the deprivation of the use of property resulting from the institution of the action. In criminal proceedings, the purpose of a judicial bond, called a *bail bond*, is to assure the appearance of the defendant in court.

Formation

The suretyship relationship is contractual and must satisfy all the usual elements of a contract. No particular words are required to constitute a contract of suretyship or guaranty.

As we discussed in Chapter 15, under the *statute of frauds* the contractual promise of a surety to the creditor must be in writing to be enforceable. This requirement, which applies only to collateral promises, is subject to the exception known as the *main purpose doctrine*. Under this doctrine, if the leading object, or main purpose, of the promisor (surety) is to obtain an economic benefit that he did not previously enjoy, the promise is *not* within the statute of frauds.

The promise of a surety is *not* binding without **consideration**. Because the surety generally makes her promise to induce the creditor to confer a benefit on the principal debtor, the consideration that supports the principal debtor's promise usually supports the surety's promise as well. Thus, if Constance lends money to Philip on Sally's promise to act as a surety, Constance's extension of credit is the consideration to support not only Philip's promise to repay the loan but also Sally's suretyship undertaking. However, a surety's promise made *after* the principal debtor's receipt of the creditor's consideration must be supported by new consideration. Accordingly, if Constance has already sold goods on credit to Philip, a subsequent guaranty by Sally will not be binding unless new consideration is given.

Formation the promise of the surety must satisfy all the elements of a contract and must also be in writing

RIGHTS OF SURETY

A surety whose principal debtor defaults has certain rights against the principal debtor, third parties, and cosureties. These rights include (1) exoneration, (2) reimbursement, (3) subrogation, and (4) contribution. As discussed above, a surety or absolute guarantor has *no* right to compel the creditor to collect from the principal debtor or to take action on collateral provided by the principal debtor. Nor is the creditor required to give the surety notice of the principal debtor's default, unless the contract of suretyship provides otherwise. A conditional guarantor of collection, on the other hand, has no liability until the creditor exhausts his legal remedies of collection against the principal debtor.

Exoneration

The ordinary expectation in a suretyship relation is that the principal debtor will perform the obligation and the surety will not be required to perform. Therefore, the surety has the right to require that her principal debtor pay the creditor when the obligation is due. This right of the surety against the principal debtor, called the right of **exoneration**, is enforceable at equity. If the principal debtor fails to pay the creditor when the debt is due, the surety may obtain a decree ordering the principal debtor to pay the creditor. However, this remedy in no way affects the creditor's right to proceed against the surety.

Exoneration *(ex·on·er·a´·tion)* the right of a surety to be relieved of his obligation to the creditor by having the principal debtor perform the obligation

A surety also has a right of exoneration against his cosureties. When the principal debtor's obligation becomes due, each surety owes every other cosurety the duty to pay her proportionate share of the principal debtor's obligation to the creditor. Accordingly, a surety may bring an action in equity to obtain an order requiring his cosureties to pay their share of the debt.

Reimbursement

Reimbursement the right of a surety who has paid the creditor to be repaid by the principal debtor

When, on the default of the principal debtor, a surety pays the creditor, the surety has the right of **reimbursement** (repayment) against the principal debtor. This right arises, however, only when the surety actually has made payment, and then applies only to the extent of the payment. Thus, a surety who advantageously negotiates a defaulted obligation and settles it at a compromise figure less than the original sum may recover from the principal debtor only the sum the surety actually paid, not the sum before negotiation.

Subrogation

Subrogation *(sub·ro·ga´·tion)* the right of a surety who has paid the creditor to assume all the rights the creditor has against or through the principal debtor

On payment of the principal debtor's *entire* obligation, the surety "steps into the shoes" of the creditor. Called **subrogation**, this confers on the surety all the rights the creditor has against or through the principal debtor. These include the creditor's rights

1. against the principal debtor, including the creditor's priorities in a bankruptcy proceeding;
2. in security of the principal debtor;
3. against third parties such as co-makers, who also are obligated on the principal debtor's obligation; and
4. against cosureties.

Contribution

Contribution the right of a surety to payment from each cosurety of his proportionate share of the amount paid to the creditor

Up to the amount of each surety's undertaking, cosureties are *jointly and severally* liable for the principal debtor's default. The creditor may proceed against any or all of the cosureties and collect from any of them the amount that that surety has agreed to guarantee, up to and including the entire amount of the principal debtor's obligation.

A surety who pays her principal debtor's obligation may require her cosureties to pay to her their proportionate shares of the obligation she paid. This right of **contribution** arises when a surety has paid more than her proportionate share of a debt, even though the cosureties originally were unaware of each other or were bound on separate instruments. They need only be sureties for the same principal debtor and the same obligation. The contractual agreement among the cosureties determines the right and extent of contribution for each. If no such agreement exists, sureties obligated for equal amounts share equally; where they are obligated for varying amounts, the proportion of the debt that each surety must contribute is determined by proration according to each surety's undertaking. For example, if X, Y, and Z are cosureties for PD to C in the amounts of $5,000, $10,000, and $15,000 respectively, which totals $30,000, then X's share of the total is one-sixth ($5,000/$30,000), Y's share is one-third ($10,000/$30,000), and Z's share is one-half ($15,000/$30,000).

FIRST AMERICAN BANK OF NEW YORK v. FALLOVA SHREDDER CO., INC. Supreme Court, Albany County, 1992, 155 Misc.2d 143, 587 N.Y.S.2d 119

FACTS Between November 10, 1986, and January 28, 1987, the First American Bank (Bank) loaned a total of $120,000 to the Fallova Shredder Co. The debt was guaranteed by Louis F. Fallova, Jr., Wayne Emerick, Everett Strong, Jr., and Edward J. Raymond, the shareholders of the company. On December 10, 1987, Fallova, Strong, and Raymond sold their shares to Emerick and Warren Hunt. Strong prospectively revoked his personal guaranty, which revocation the Bank accepted. The corporation thereafter defaulted on its loans, and the Bank sued the corporation, Emerick, and Strong. As to Strong, the Bank sought to recover only the debts owed prior to December 10, 1987. In that suit, Strong was held responsible for $121,000. Strong then commenced a third-party action against Raymond, Fallova, and Hunt. Strong made a motion seeking a pro rata share of $121,000 from Fallova, arguing that at common law a guarantor could obtain contribution from a co-guarantor for the amount the guarantor paid over his proportionate share. Fallova asserted that under the language of the guaranty, the Bank could release any one of the co-guarantors without the consent of the others. He argued that the Bank released him from the guaranty when it chose not to sue him and that he therefore also was released from any liability to his co-guarantors.

DECISION Judgment for Strong.

OPINION Where one joint obligor pays more than his proportionate share of the common liability, he is entitled to contribution from the other joint obligors. Also, where a creditor releases one co-guarantor without the consent of the others, all of the guarantors are released. Most lending institutions, such as the Bank in this case, alter this common law rule by contracting that the release of one co-guarantor does not release the others. Such a contract brings to bear two legal principles. First, if a creditor releases one of the co-sureties and recovers judgment on the debt against the remaining sureties, the released surety remains liable for contribution to the paying sureties. Second, where the creditor releases one of two sureties with the consent of the other, the released surety's obligation ends, and if the consenting surety pays the debt, he has no right of contribution from the surety who was released.

Fallova contends that when Strong signed the standard form required by the Bank containing the language allowing the principal and co-guarantors to be released, Strong brought himself within the second principle. Strong argues that his contract with the Bank was not intended to release his entitlement to contribution from his co-guarantors and that he therefore comes within the first principle. Policy considerations lead the court to accept Strong's position. The language of the contract with the lending institution is designed to protect the lending institution. It was not inserted to keep co-guarantors from contributing simply because the Bank chose not to sue them. Thus, the four guarantors of the corporate debt are each one-quarter responsible for the money the corporation owed to the Bank prior to December 10, 1987. Strong is entitled to recover from Fallova the sum of money that he paid beyond his one-quarter responsibility up to Fallova's one-quarter share.

INTERPRETATION A surety who pays more than his proportionate share is entitled to contribution from his cosureties.

DEFENSES OF SURETY AND PRINCIPAL DEBTOR

The obligations the principal debtor and the surety owe to the creditor arise out of contracts. Accordingly, the usual contractual defenses apply, such as those that result from (1) the nonexistence of the principal debtor's obligation, (2) a discharge of the principal debtor's obligation, (3) a modification of the principal debtor's contract, or (4) a variation of the surety's risk. Some of these defenses are available only to the principal debtor, some only to the surety, and others to both parties (see Figure 40–3).

Personal Defenses of Principal Debtor

The defenses available *only* to a principal debtor are known as the **personal defenses of the principal debtor**. For example, *incapacity* due to infancy or mental incompetency may serve as a defense for the principal debtor, but *not* for the surety. If, however, the principal debtor disaffirms the contract *and* returns

Personal defenses of principal debtor defenses available only to the principal debtor, including her incapacity, discharge in bankruptcy, and setoff

FIGURE 40–3 Defenses of Surety and Principal Debtor

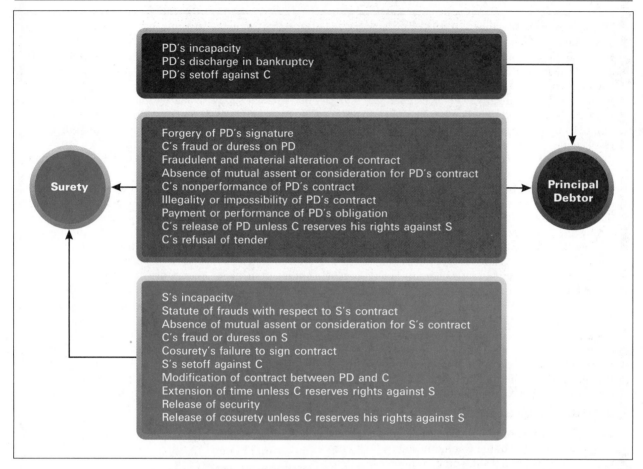

the consideration he received from the creditor, the surety is discharged from his liability. A discharge of the principal debtor's obligation in **bankruptcy**, by comparison, does not discharge the surety's liability to the creditor on that obligation. In addition, the surety may not use as a **setoff** any claim that the principal debtor has against the creditor.

Personal Defenses of Surety

Personal defenses of surety defenses available only to the surety, including her own incapacity, the statute of frauds, contract defenses to her suretyship undertaking, setoff, modification of the contract between the creditor and the principal debtor, and the creditor's release of security or cosurety

Those defenses that only the surety may assert are called **personal defenses of the surety**. The surety may use, as a defense, his own *incapacity*, noncompliance with the *statute of frauds*, or the absence of mutual assent or consideration to support his obligation. *Fraud* or *duress* practiced by the creditor on the surety is also a defense. Although, as a general rule, the creditor's nondisclosure of material facts to the surety is not fraud, there are two important exceptions. If a prospective surety requests information, the creditor must disclose it; and the concealment of material facts will constitute fraud. Second, a creditor who knows, or who should know, that a surety is being deceived is under a duty to disclose this information; and nondisclosure is considered fraud upon the surety. Fraud on the part of the principal debtor may *not* be asserted against the creditor, if the creditor is unaware of such fraud. Similarly, duress exerted by the principal debtor on the surety is not a defense against the creditor.

A surety is not liable if an intended cosurety, as named in the contract instrument, does not sign. A surety may *set off* his claims against a solvent creditor. Against an insolvent creditor, the surety may use his claim only if the principal debtor is also insolvent.

If a principal debtor and a creditor enter into a binding *modification* of their contract, a surety who does not assent to such modification may be discharged. The courts vary in their approach to modifications made without the surety's assent. An uncompensated surety (an *accommodation surety*) is more likely to be discharged for any material modification, even one that does not prejudice his rights. In contrast, when contemplating the discharge of a compensated surety, a number of courts require the alteration to be both material and prejudicial to the surety's interests.

Modifications possibly leading to a surety's discharge include valid and binding extensions of the time of payment *unless* the creditor expressly reserves his rights against the surety. An extension of time with reservation is construed only as an agreement by the creditor not to sue the principal debtor for the period of the extension. Accordingly, the surety's rights of exoneration, reimbursement, and subrogation are *not* postponed. Thus, the surety's risk is not changed and he is not discharged.

If the creditor releases or impairs the value of the security, the surety is discharged to the extent of the value of the security released or impaired. Similarly, if the creditor releases a cosurety, the other cosureties are discharged to the extent of the released surety's contributive share. If the creditor reserves his rights against the remaining cosureties, however, the release is considered a promise not to sue. As a result, the remaining cosureties are not discharged.

FIRST NATIONAL BANK OF ANTHONY v. DUNNING Court of Appeals of Kansas, 1993,
18 Kan.App.2d 518, 855 P.2d 493

FACTS In 1987, Floyd Dunning, Jr. was indebted to the First National Bank of Anthony (Bank) and his business was struggling. To help him stay in business, the Bank agreed to restructure Floyd's debt and loan him an additional $65,000. His total debt of $451,000 was to be paid off in ten installments that were to be made over twenty years. As part of the agreement, the Bank required Floyd to provide additional collateral. To satisfy this requirement, Floyd had his mother, Minnie Dunning, execute a mortgage to a quarter section of land that they jointly owned—Minnie $^{11}/_{12}$ and Floyd $^{1}/_{12}$.

Floyd's first payment was due in August 1988, but he failed to pay it. In January 1989, the Bank extended the due date for the first payment to April 1989. In September 1989, the Bank extended the due date for the second payment due in August 1989 to October 31, 1989. Minnie was never informed of either of these changes. When Floyd failed to make the second payment, the bank accelerated the note, sold Floyd's collateral, and foreclosed on the mortgage. The trial court discharged Minnie as surety because the time to make the two payments had been extended.

DECISION Judgment reversed and remanded.

OPINION A gratuitous surety is a "favorite of the law." In keeping with this rule, the obligation underlying a surety agreement cannot be modified without the surety's assent. A modification that materially alters the surety's obligation will discharge the surety. Accordingly, it has been held that a surety is discharged when the time to pay a debt is extended. However, in this case the time to pay the debt was not extended, but rather the time to make installment payments was extended. Whether these facts indicate a material modification is an issue of first impression.

The "material change" doctrine as set out in Restatement of Security § 128 provides that: "Where, without the surety's consent, the principal and the creditor modify their contract otherwise than by extension of time of payment the surety, other than a compensated surety, is discharged unless the modification is

continued

of a sort that can only be beneficial to the surety." A material change has also been defined as a change that a careful and prudent person would regard as substantially increasing the risk of loss.

Minnie was a gratuitous surety because she was not compensated for her obligation to pay. However, the extensions of installment due dates were not material modifications of the agreement to which she consented. The time for repayment of the entire debt was not extended or reduced and the interest rate was not changed except in accordance with the agreement. The only change was to give Floyd a measure of flexibility in repaying his debt. If this had not been done, the Bank could have foreclosed sooner. Therefore, it is difficult to see how these modifications could have in any way prejudiced Minnie. Since there was no material modification of the surety agreement, Minnie should not have been released as a surety.

INTERPRETATION An uncompensated surety is discharged from her obligation if the principal debtor and the creditor enter into a binding modification of their contract and that modification is material.

Defenses of Both Surety and Principal Debtor

Defenses of both surety and principal debtor
include contract defenses to the contract between the creditor and the principal debtor

A number of defenses are available to both the surety and the principal debtor. If the principal debtor's signature on an instrument is *forged* or if the creditor has exerted *fraud* or *duress* on the principal debtor, neither the principal debtor nor the surety is liable. Likewise, if the creditor has fraudulently and *materially altered* the contract instrument, both the principal debtor and the surety are discharged.

The absence of mutual assent or consideration to support the principal debtor's obligation is a defense for both the principal debtor and the surety. In addition, both may assert as defenses the *illegality* and the *impossibility* of performance of the principal debtor's contract.

Payment or *performance* of the principal debtor's obligation discharges both the principal debtor and the surety. If the principal debtor owes several debts to the creditor and makes a payment to the creditor without specifying the debt to which the payment should apply, the creditor is free to apply it to any one of them. For example, Pam owes Charles two debts, one for $5,000 and another for $10,000. Susan is a surety on the $10,000 debt. Pam sends Charles a payment in the amount of $3,500. If Pam directs Charles to apply the payment to the $10,000 debt, Charles must do so. Otherwise, Charles may, if he pleases, apply the payment to the $5,000 debt.

If the creditor *releases* the principal debtor, the surety is also discharged unless the surety consents to the release. If the creditor reserves his rights against the surety, however, the surety is *not* discharged. Such a release with reservation is construed as a promise not to sue, which leaves the surety's rights against the principal debtor unimpaired. Therefore, the surety is not discharged.

The creditor's refusal to accept *tender* of payment or performance by either the principal debtor or the surety completely discharges the surety. However, the creditor's refusal to accept a tender of payment by the principal debtor does *not* discharge the principal debtor. Rather, such refusal stops further accrual of interest on the debt and deprives the creditor of court costs on a subsequent suit by him to recover the amount due.

CHAPTER SUMMARY

Nature and Formation	**Definition of Surety** a person who promises to answer for the payment of a debt or the performance of a duty owed to the creditor by the principal debtor, upon the principal debtor's failure to perform ■ *Principal Debtor* the party primarily liable on the obligation ■ *Cosurety* each of two or more sureties who are liable for the same debt of the principal debtor ■ *Absolute Surety* surety liable to a creditor immediately upon the default of a principal debtor ■ *Conditional Guarantor of Collection* surety liable to a creditor only after the creditor has exhausted the legal remedies against the principal debtor **Types of Sureties** ■ *Party Assuming a Mortgage* ■ *Fidelity Bonds* ■ *Performance Bonds* ■ *Official Bonds* ■ *Judicial Bonds* **Formation** the promise of the surety must satisfy all the elements of a contract and must also be in writing
Rights of Surety	**Exoneration** the right of a surety to be relieved of his obligation to the creditor by having the principal debtor perform the obligation **Reimbursement** the right of a surety who has paid the creditor to be repaid by the principal debtor **Subrogation** the right of a surety who has paid the creditor to assume all the rights the creditor has against or through the principal debtor **Contribution** the right of a surety to payment from each cosurety of his proportionate share of the amount paid to the creditor
Defenses of Surety and Principal Debtor	**Personal Defenses of Principal Debtor** defenses available only to the principal debtor, including her incapacity, discharge in bankruptcy, and setoff **Personal Defenses of Surety** defenses available only to the surety, including her own incapacity, the statute of frauds, contract defenses to her suretyship undertaking, setoff, modification of the contract between the creditor and the principal debtor, and the creditor's release of security or a cosurety **Defenses of Both Surety and Principal Debtor** include contract defenses to the contract between the creditor and the principal debtor

QUESTIONS

1. Identify five types of sureties.
2. Explain the requirements for the formation of a suretyship relationship.
3. Explain the rights of a creditor against a surety.
4. Explain the rights of a surety, including those of a cosurety.
5. Identify (a) the personal defenses of the principal debtor, (b) the personal defenses of the surety, and (c) the defenses of both the surety and the principal debtor.

Internet Question. Find and examine (a) some surety and fidelity companies, and (b) the federal Small Business Administration's surety bond guarantee program.

PROBLEMS

1. Allen, Barker, and Cooper are cosureties on a $750,000 loan by Durham National Bank to Kingston Manufacturing Co., Inc. The maximum liability of the sureties is as follows: Allen, $750,000; Barker, $300,000; and Cooper, $150,000. If Kingston defaults on the entire $750,000 loan, what are the liabilities of Allen, Barker, and Cooper?

2. Peter Diamond owed Carter $500,000 secured by a first mortgage on Diamond's plant and land. Stephens was a surety on this obligation in the amount of $250,000. After Diamond defaulted on the debt, Carter demanded and received payment of $250,000 from Stephens. Carter then foreclosed upon the mortgage and sold the property for $375,000. What rights, if any, does Stephens have in the proceeds from the sale of the property?

3. Adams sold his house to Baldwin for $80,000, with Baldwin expressly assuming a mortgage held by Evans on the property in the amount of $60,000. The property has a fair market value of $140,000. Six months later, Baldwin defaulted in his payments to Evans on the mortgage.
   (a) What are Evans's rights, if any, against Baldwin?
   (b) What are Evans's rights, if any, against Adams?
   (c) What are Adams's rights, if any, against Baldwin?

4. Paula Daniels purchased an automobile from Carey on credit. At the time of the sale, Scott agreed to be a surety for Paula, who is sixteen years old. The automobile's odometer stated 52,000 miles, but Carey had turned it back from 72,000 miles. Paula refuses to make any payments due on the car. Carey proceeds against Paula and Scott. What defenses, if any, are available to (a) Paula and (b) Scott?

5. Stafford Surety Co. agreed to act as the conditional guarantor of collection on a debt owed by Preston Decker to Cole. Stafford was paid a premium by Preston to serve as surety. Preston defaults on the

obligation. What are Cole's rights against Stafford Surety Co.?

6. Campbell loaned Perry Dixon $7,000, which was secured by a possessory security interest in stock owned by Perry. The stock had a market value of $4,000. In addition, Campbell insisted that Perry obtain a surety. For a premium, Sutton Surety Co. agreed to act as a surety for the full amount of the loan. Prior to the due date of the loan, Perry convinced Campbell to return the stock because its value had increased and he wished to sell it in order to realize the gain. Campbell released the stock and Perry subsequently defaulted. Campbell proceeds against Sutton. Decision?

7. Pamela Darden owed Clark $5,000 on an unsecured loan. On May 1, Pamela approached Clark for an additional loan of $3,000. Clark agreed to make the loan only if Pamela could obtain a surety. On May 5, Simpson agreed to be a surety on the $3,000 loan, which was granted that day. Both loans were due on October 1. On June 15, Pamela sent $1,000 to Clark but did not provide any instructions.
   (a) What are Clark's rights?
   (b) What are Simpson's rights?

8. Patrick Dillon applied for a $10,000 loan from Carlton Savings & Loan. Carlton required him to obtain a surety. Patrick approached Sinclair Surety Co., which insisted that Patrick provide it with a financial statement. Patrick did so, but the statement was materially false. In reliance upon the financial statement and in return for a premium, Sinclair agreed to act as surety. Upon Sinclair's commitment to act as surety, Carlton loaned Patrick the $10,000. After one payment of $400, Patrick defaulted. Patrick then filed a voluntary petition in bankruptcy. Carlton proceeds against Sinclair. Decision?

9. On June 1, Smith contracted with Martin, d/b/a Martin Publishing Company, to distribute Martin's

newspapers and to account for the proceeds. As part of the contract, Smith agreed to furnish Martin a bond in the amount of $10,000 guaranteeing the payment of the proceeds. At the time the contract was executed and the credit extended the bond was not furnished and no mention was made as to the prospective sureties. On July 1, Smith signed the bond with Black and Blue signing as sureties. The bond recited the awarding of the contract for distribution of the newspapers as consideration for the bond.

On December 1, there was due from Smith to Martin the sum of $3,600 under the distributor's contract. Demand for payment was made, but Smith failed to make payment. As a result, Martin brought an appropriate action against Black and Blue to recover the $3,600. What decision?

10. Diggitt Construction Company was the low bidder on a well-digging job for the Village of Drytown. On April 15, Diggitt signed a contract with Drytown for the job at a price of $40,000. At the same time, pursuant to the notice of bidding, Diggitt prevailed upon Ace Surety Company to execute a performance bond indemnifying Drytown on the contract. On May 1, after having put in three days on the job, the president of Diggitt refigured his bid and realized that if his company were to complete the job it would lose $10,000. Accordingly, Diggitt notified Drytown that it was canceling the contract, effective immediately. What are the rights and duties of Ace Surety Company?

11. On March 10, 1972, L.R.Z.H. Corporation made and delivered to Langeveld its promissory note in the sum of $57,500. The indebtedness evidenced by the note was secured by a mortgage in the same amount on real property owned by the corporation. By an instrument of guaranty set forth at the bottom of the note, Higgins guaranteed performance of all obligations of the corporation under the note. The note became due on February 15, 1973, and was not paid. At this time, Higgins discovered that Langeveld had never recorded the mortgage securing the note. Langeveld then recorded the mortgage on March 1, 1973. In the year intervening between the execution of the mortgage and its recordation, another mortgage and two liens in substantial amounts had been filed. Langeveld brought suit against Higgins on the guaranty. Higgins argues that the creditor, Langeveld, owed a duty to him as surety for the debt to protect the security and to allow nothing to impair its value. Since Langeveld failed to fulfill this duty, Higgins argues, he, Higgins, should be released from all liability on his guaranty. Decision?

12. Throckmorton and Collins were the sole stockholders (as well as the officers and directors) in Central Ceilings, Inc. (Central). On March 26, 1973, Central borrowed $10,000 from the Wilmington Trust Company (the bank); a demand note was therefore executed by the corporate officers. On the back of the note, Throckmorton, Collins, and their wives unconditionally guaranteed payment of the note. In August 1973, Collins left the employ of Central and ceased to be actively involved in management. By mid-1975, Central had become insolvent. Central made no payments on the note after 1973, and the bank became concerned about Central's ability to repay. On May 30, 1975, Throckmorton and his wife took out a $15,402 loan, using $9,668.73 to satisfy the 1973 note. In return, the bank assigned its rights to Throckmorton. Throckmorton then sued both Collins and his wife, each for one-quarter of the $9,668.73 plus interest and attorney's fees. The Collinses claim that Throckmorton's wife paid half of the total, or $4,834.36. Of the half that he paid, Throckmorton was only personally liable for half, $2,417.18, or one-quarter of the total. Therefore, they assert, he can recover only $2,417.18 total from the Collinses—the excess of the amount he personally paid—not $2,417.18 from each. Decision?

13. The Army-Navy '83 Foundation was formed to facilitate preparations for the 1983 Army-Navy football game. The Foundation and Army and Navy Athletic Associations contracted to play the 1983 game at the Rose Bowl in Pasadena, California, as opposed to the traditional site in Philadelphia. Under the contract, the Foundation was entitled to revenues generated both from ticket sales and from TV broadcast rights. The Foundation was obligated to pay each Academy $875,000 ($550,000 from TV revenues and $325,000 from ticket sales and concession proceeds). The cost of transporting cadets, midshipmen, and support personnel would be funded by the Foundation, which was also required to compensate each Academy up to $100,000 for additional costs incurred in conjunction with moving the site. The contract further required the Foundation to obtain two bonds. The first bond would secure the Foundation's $650,000 obligation for ticket sales and concession proceeds. The second bond would guarantee the Foundation's obligation to pay up to $200,000 in additional expenses. The Foundation obtained both bonds from Reliance Insurance Company (Reliance) by assuring Reliance that the Foundation was entitled to the TV revenues from the game and promising to assign those revenues to Reliance up to the face amount of the bonds.

Thereafter, the Foundation and the Academies modified the contract three times. The second modification provided for the direct payment of the TV revenues to Army as the host school, rather than to the Foundation. As a result of this modification, the Foundation was entitled to only $350,000 of the TV revenues obligation under the original contract. The third modification required the Academies, instead of the Foundation, to pay for transportation because the airlines would only accept money in advance. The Foundation, however, would remain ultimately liable for the cost of transportation. Furthermore, the Foundation waived its rights to ticket and TV revenues in excess of $1,100,000 (i.e., $350,000, which was its only remaining revenue after the second modification.) Reliance was never informed of the modifications to the contract between the Foundation and the Academies.

When the Foundation failed to pay the Academies for additional expenses, they filed an action to recover on the second bond issued by Reliance. Reliance argued that the modifications of the bonded contract exonerated Reliance from payment on the bond. The district court held for Reliance, and the Academies appealed. Decision?

Bankruptcy

A debt is an obligation to pay money owed by a debtor to a creditor. Debts are created daily by countless purchasers of goods at the consumer level; by retailers of goods in buying merchandise from a manufacturer, wholesaler, or distributor; by borrowers of funds from various lending institutions; and through the issuance and sale of debentures, corporate mortgage bonds, and other types of debt securities. Multitudes of business transactions are entered into daily on a credit basis. Commercial activity would be greatly restricted if credit were not readily obtainable or if needed funds were unavailable for lending.

Fortunately, most debts are paid when due, thus justifying the extension of credit and encouraging its continuation. Though defaults may create credit and collection problems, normally the total amount in default represents a very small percentage of the total amount of outstanding indebtedness. Nevertheless, both individuals and corporations encounter financial crises and business misfortune. An accumulation of debts that exceeds total assets may confront an individual as well as a business. Or these debtors might have assets in excess of total indebtedness but in such noncash form that they are unable to pay their debts as they mature. For both businesses and individuals, relief from pressing debt and from the threat of impending lawsuits by creditors is frequently necessary for economic survival.

The conflict between creditor rights and debtor relief has engendered various solutions, such as compromises requiring installment payments to creditors over a period of time during which they agree to withhold legal action. Other voluntary methods include compositions and assignments of assets by a debtor to a trustee or assignee for the benefit of creditors. In addition, creditors sometimes file equity receiverships or insolvency proceedings in a state court, according to statute. Nonetheless, the most adaptable and frequently used method of debtor relief—one that also affords protection to creditors—is a proceeding in a federal court under federal bankruptcy law.

FEDERAL BANKRUPTCY LAW

Bankruptcy legislation serves a dual purpose: (1) to bring about a quick, *equitable distribution* of the debtor's property among her creditors and (2) to *discharge* the debtor from her debts, enabling her to rehabilitate herself and to start afresh. Other purposes are to provide uniform treatment of similarly situated creditors, to preserve existing business relations, and to stabilize commercial usages.

The U.S. Bankruptcy Code consists of eight odd-numbered chapters and one even-numbered chapter. Chapters 7, 9, 11, 12, and 13 provide five different types of proceedings; Chapters 1, 3, and 5 apply to those five proceedings. *Straight*, or ordinary, *bankruptcy* (Chapter 7) provides for the liquidation and termination of the debtor's business, whereas the other proceedings provide for the *reorganization* and adjustment of the debtor's debts and the continuance of the debtor's business. In reorganization cases the creditors usually look to the debtor's future earnings, whereas in liquidation cases the creditors look to the debtor's property at the commencement of the bankruptcy proceeding.

Chapter 7 applies to *all* debtors, with the exception of railroads, insurance companies, banks, savings and loan associations, homestead associations, licensed small business investment companies, and credit unions. Moreover, Chapter 7 has special provisions for liquidating the estates of stockbrokers and commodity brokers. Railroads and any person who may be a debtor under Chapter 7 (except a stockbroker or a commodity broker) may be debtors under Chapter 11. Chapter 9 applies only to municipalities that are generally authorized to be debtors under that chapter, that are insolvent, and that desire to effect plans to adjust their debts. Chapter 12 applies to individuals, or individuals and their spouses, engaged in farming if 50 percent of their gross income is from farming, their aggregate debts do not exceed $1.5 million, and at least 80 percent of their debts arise from farming operations. Corporations or partnerships may also qualify for Chapter 12. Chapter 13 applies to individuals with regular income who owe liquidated unsecured debts of less than $250,000 and secured debts of less than $750,000. (See Figure 41–1.)

The 1994 amendments to the Bankruptcy Act require that every three years, beginning in 1998, the U.S. Judicial Conference adjust for inflation the

FIGURE 41–1 Bankruptcy Filings

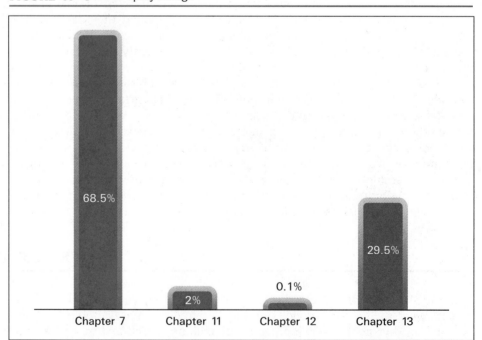

Source: U.S. Department of Commerce, Bureau of the Census, *Statistical Abstract of the United States* (Washington, D.C.: U.S. Government Printing Office, 1996).

dollar amounts of the following provisions: eligibility for Chapter 13, requirements for filing involuntary cases, priorities, exemptions, and exceptions to discharge.

The Bankruptcy Code grants to U.S. District Courts original and exclusive jurisdiction over all bankruptcy cases and original, but not exclusive, jurisdiction over civil proceedings arising under bankruptcy cases. The district court must, however, abstain from related matters that, except for their relationship to bankruptcy, could not have been brought in a federal court. The district court in which a bankruptcy case is commenced has exclusive jurisdiction over all of the debtor's property. In addition, within each federal district court is established a bankruptcy court staffed by bankruptcy judges. Bankruptcy courts are authorized to hear certain matters specified by the Bankruptcy Code and to enter appropriate orders and judgments subject to review by the district court or, where established, by a panel of three bankruptcy judges. The federal circuit court of appeals has jurisdiction over appeals from the district court or panel. In all other matters, unless the parties agree otherwise, only the district court may issue a final order or judgment based upon proposed findings of fact and conclusions of law submitted to the court by the bankruptcy judge.

CASE ADMINISTRATION—CHAPTER 3

Chapter 3 of the Bankruptcy Code contains provisions dealing with the commencement of a case in bankruptcy, the meetings of creditors, the officers who administer the case, and the officers' administrative powers.

Commencement of the Case

The filing of a voluntary or involuntary petition begins the jurisdiction of the bankruptcy court and the operation of the bankruptcy laws.

Voluntary Petitions More than 99 percent of all bankruptcy petitions are filed voluntarily. Any person eligible to be a debtor under a given bankruptcy proceeding may file a **voluntary petition** under that chapter, and need *not* be insolvent to do so. The commencement of a voluntary case constitutes an automatic *order for relief*. The petition must include a list of all creditors (secured and unsecured), a list of all property the debtor owns, a list of property that the debtor claims is exempt, and a statement of the debtor's affairs.

Involuntary Petitions An **involuntary petition** in bankruptcy may be filed only under Chapter 7 (liquidation) or Chapter 11 (reorganization). It may be filed (1) by three or more creditors who have unsecured claims that total $10,000 or more, or (2) if the debtor has fewer than twelve creditors, by one or more creditors whose total unsecured claims equal $10,000 or more. An involuntary petition may not be filed against a farmer or against a banking, insurance, or nonprofit corporation.

If the debtor does not contest the involuntary petition, the court will enter an order for relief against the debtor. However, if the debtor opposes the petition, the court may enter an order of relief only (1) if the debtor is generally not paying his debts as they become due or (2) if, within 120 days before the filing of the petition, a custodian or receiver took possession of substantially all of the debtor's property to enforce a lien against that property.

Commencement of the case the filing of a voluntary or involuntary petition begins jurisdiction of the bankruptcy court

Voluntary petitions available to any debtor even if solvent

Involuntary petitions may be filed only under Chapter 7 or 11 if the debtor is generally not paying his debts as they become due

Automatic Stays

The filing of a voluntary or involuntary petition operates as a stay against (that is, it prevents) attempts by creditors to begin or continue to recover claims against the debtor, to enforce judgments against the debtor, or to create or enforce liens against property of the debtor. This stay applies to both secured and unsecured creditors, although a secured creditor may petition the court to terminate the stay as to her security on showing that she lacks adequate protection in the secured property. An automatic stay ends when the bankruptcy case is closed or dismissed or when the debtor receives a discharge.

Trustees

A **trustee** is the representative of an estate and has the capacity to sue and be sued. In proceedings under Chapter 7, trustees are selected by a vote of the creditors. The 1994 amendments allow the creditors to elect a trustee in a Chapter 11 proceeding if the court orders the appointment of a trustee for cause. In Chapters 12 and 13 the trustee is appointed. Responsible, under Chapter 7, for collecting, liquidating, and distributing the debtor's estate, the trustee has, among others, the following duties and powers: (1) using, selling, or leasing property of the estate; (2) depositing or investing money of the estate; (3) employing attorneys, accountants, appraisers, or auctioneers; and (4) assuming or rejecting any executory contract or unexpired lease of the debtor. Trustees under Chapters 11, 12, and 13 perform some but not all of the duties of a Chapter 7 trustee.

Meetings of Creditors

Within a reasonable time after relief is ordered, a **meeting of creditors** must be held. Though the court may not attend this meeting, the debtor must appear and submit to an examination of his financial situation by the creditors and the trustee. In a proceeding under Chapter 7, qualified creditors at this meeting elect a permanent trustee.

CREDITORS, THE DEBTOR, AND THE ESTATE—CHAPTER 5

Creditors

The Bankruptcy Code defines a **creditor** as any entity having a claim against the debtor that arose at the time of or before the order for relief. A **claim** is a right to payment.

Proofs of Claim Creditors who wish to participate in the distribution of the debtor's estate may file a proof of claim. If a creditor does not do so in a timely manner, the debtor or trustee may file a proof of such claim. By doing this the debtor may prevent a claim from becoming nondischargeable. Filed claims are allowed unless a party, who has an interest, objects. If an objection is made, the court determines, after a hearing, the amount and validity of the claim. The court will not allow any claim that (1) is unenforceable against the debtor or her property, (2) is for unmatured interest, (3) may be offset against a debt owing the debtor, or (4) is for insider or attorney services in excess of the reasonable value of such services. An **insider** includes a relative or general partner of a debtor, as well as a partnership in which the debtor is a general partner or a corporation of which the debtor is a director, officer, or person in control.

Secured Claims An allowed claim of a creditor who has a lien on property of the estate is a **secured claim** to the extent of the value of the creditor's interest in the property. The creditor's claim is unsecured to the extent of the difference between the value of his secured interest and the allowed amount of his claim. Thus, if Alice has an allowed claim of $5,000 against the estate of debtor Bart and has a security interest in property of the estate that is valued at $3,000, Alice has a secured claim in the amount of $3,000 and an unsecured claim for $2,000.

Priority of Claims   After secured claims have been satisfied, the remaining assets are distributed among creditors with unsecured claims. Certain classes of unsecured claims, however, have a **priority**, which means that they must be paid in full before any distribution is made to claims of lesser rank. Each claimant within a priority class shares *pro rata* if the assets are insufficient to satisfy all claims in that class. The claims having a priority and the order of their priority are as follows:

Priority the right of certain claims to be paid before claims of lesser rank

1. *Expenses of administration* of the debtor's estate, including the filing fees paid by creditors in involuntary cases, the expenses of creditors in recovering concealed assets for the benefit of the bankrupt's estate, the trustee's necessary expenses, and reasonable compensation to receivers, trustees, and their attorneys, as allowed by the court;
2. Unsecured claims in an involuntary case arising in the ordinary course of the debtor's business after the commencement of the case but before the earlier of either the appointment of the trustee or the entering of the order for relief (such claimants are referred to as *"gap" creditors*);
3. Allowed, unsecured claims up to $4,000 for *wages, salaries, or commissions* earned within ninety days before the filing of the petition or before the date on which the debtor's business ceases, whichever comes first;
4. Allowed, unsecured claims for contributions to *employee benefit plans* arising from services rendered within 180 days before the filing of the petition or the cessation of the debtor's business, whichever occurs first, but limited to $4,000 multiplied by the number of employees covered by the plan, less the aggregate amount paid to such employees under number 3 above;
5. Allowed, unsecured claims up to $4,000 for *grain* or *fish producers* against a storage facility;
6. Allowed, unsecured claims up to $1,800 for *consumer deposits*; that is, moneys deposited in connection with the purchase, lease, or rental of property or the purchase of services for personal, family, or household use;
7. *Alimony* and *support* of a child or spouse;
8. Specified income, property, employment, or excise *taxes owed to governmental units*.

After creditors with secured claims and creditors with claims having a priority have been satisfied, creditors with allowed, unsecured claims share proportionately in any remaining assets.

Subordination of Claims   A subordination agreement is enforceable under the Bankruptcy Code to the same extent that it is enforceable under nonbankruptcy law. In addition to statutory and contract priorities, the bankruptcy court itself can, at its discretion in proper cases, apply equitable priorities. The court accomplishes this through the doctrine of subordination of claims, whereby, assuming two claims of equal statutory priority, the court declares that one claim must be paid in full before the other claim can be paid anything. Bankruptcy courts apply subordination where allowing a claim in full, such as the inflated salary claims of officers in a closely held corporation, would be unfair and inequitable to other creditors. In such cases, the court does not disallow the claim but merely orders that it be paid after all other claims are paid in full. For example, the court may subordinate the claim of a parent corporation against its bankrupt subsidiary to the claims of the subsidiary's other creditors if the parent has so mismanaged the subsidiary to the detriment of its innocent creditors that this unconscionable conduct precludes the parent from seeking the court's aid.

Debtors

As previously indicated, the purpose of the Bankruptcy Code is to bring about an equitable distribution of the debtor's assets and to provide him a discharge. Accordingly, the Code explicitly subjects the debtor to specified duties, while exempting some of his property and discharging most of his debts.

Debtor's duties the debtor must file specified information, cooperate with the trustee, and surrender all property of the estate

Debtor's Duties Under the Bankruptcy Code, the debtor must file a list of creditors, a schedule of assets and liabilities, and a statement of her financial affairs. In any case in which a trustee is serving, the debtor must cooperate with the trustee and surrender to the trustee all property of the estate and all records relating to such property.

Debtor's Exemptions The Bankruptcy Code exempts specified property of an individual debtor from bankruptcy proceedings, including the following: (1) up to $15,000 in equity in property used as a residence or burial plot; (2) up to $2,400 in equity in one motor vehicle; (3) up to $400 for any particular item of household furnishings, household goods, wearing apparel, appliances, books, animals, crops, or musical instruments that are primarily for personal, family, or household use; (4) up to $1,000 in jewelry; (5) any property up to $800 plus any unused amount of the first exemption; (6) up to $1,500 in implements, professional books, or tools of the debtor's trade; (7) unmatured life insurance contracts owned by the debtor, other than a credit life insurance contract; (8) professionally prescribed health aids; (9) social security, veteran's, and disability benefits; (10) unemployment compensation; (11) alimony and support payments, including child support; (12) payments from pension, profit-sharing, and annuity plans; and (13) payments from an award under a crime victim's reparation law, a wrongful death award, and up to $15,000, not including compensation for pain and suffering or for actual pecuniary loss, from a personal injury award. In addition, the debtor may avoid judicial liens on any exempt property and nonpossessory, nonpurchase money security interests on household goods, tools of the trade, and professionally prescribed health aids.

The debtor has the option of using either the exemptions provided by the Bankruptcy Code or those available under state law. Nevertheless, a state may, by specific legislative action, limit its citizens to the exemptions provided by state law. More than two-thirds of the states have enacted such legislation.

Discharge relief from liability for all debts except those the Bankruptcy Code specifies as not dischargeable

Discharge **Discharge** relieves the debtor from liability for all his dischargeable debts. A discharge of a debt voids any judgment obtained at any time concerning that debt and operates as an injunction against the commencement or continuation of any action to recover it.

No private employer may terminate the employment of, or discriminate with respect to employment against, an individual who is or has been a debtor under the Bankruptcy Code solely because such debtor (1) is or has been such a debtor; (2) has been insolvent before the commencement of a case or during the case; or (3) has not paid a debt that is dischargeable in a case under the Bankruptcy Code.

An agreement between a debtor and a creditor permitting the creditor to enforce a discharged debt is enforceable to the extent state law permits but only if (1) the agreement was made before the discharge was granted; (2) the debtor does not rescind the agreement within thirty days after it becomes enforceable; (3) the court informs a debtor who is an individual that he is not required to enter into such an agreement and explains the legal effect of the agreement; and (4) with regard to a consumer debt, the court has confirmed that the agreement does not impose an undue hardship on the debtor and is in the debtor's best interest.

The Bankruptcy Code provides that certain debts of an individual are **not dischargeable** in bankruptcy. This provision applies to individuals receiving discharges under Chapters 7, 11, 12, and, as discussed later in this chapter, the "hardship discharge" provision of Chapter 13. The nondischargeable debts are

1. Certain taxes and customs duties
2. Legal liabilities resulting from obtaining money or property by false pretenses or false representations
3. Legal liability for willful and malicious injuries to the person or property of another
4. Alimony and support of a spouse or a child
5. Debts not scheduled, unless the creditor knew of the bankruptcy
6. Debts the debtor created by fraud or embezzlement while acting in a fiduciary capacity
7. Student loans that first became due less than seven years before the filing of the petition, unless the debt would impose undue hardship
8. Debts that were or could have been listed in a previous bankruptcy in which the debtor waived or was denied a discharge
9. Consumer debts for luxury goods or services in excess of $1,000 per creditor if incurred by an individual debtor on or within sixty days before the order for relief
10. Cash advances aggregating more than $1,000 obtained by an individual debtor under an open-ended credit plan within sixty days before the order for relief
11. Liability for a court judgment based upon the debtor's operation of a motor vehicle while legally intoxicated
12. Fines, penalties, or forfeitures owed to a governmental entity.

In Chapter 13 cases, usually the only debts *not* discharged are the above numbered debts: four, seven, eleven, and twelve.

The following illustrates the operation of discharge. Donaldson files a petition in bankruptcy. Donaldson owes Anders $1,500, Boynton $2,500, and Conroy $3,000. Assume that Anders's claim is not dischargeable in bankruptcy, while Boynton's and Conroy's are. Anders receives $180 from the liquidation of Donaldson's bankruptcy estate, Boynton receives $300, and Conroy receives $360. If Donaldson receives a bankruptcy discharge, Boynton and Conroy will be precluded from pursuing Donaldson for the remainder of their claims ($2,200 and $2,640 respectively). Anders, on the other hand, because his debt is not dischargeable, may pursue Donaldson for the remaining $1,320, subject to the applicable statute of limitations. If Donaldson does *not* receive a discharge, Anders, Boynton, and Conroy may all pursue Donaldson for the unpaid portions of their claims.

The Estate

Estate all legal and
equitable interests of a
debtor in nonexempt
property

The commencement of a bankruptcy case creates an **estate** consisting of all legal and equitable interests of the debtor in nonexempt property at that time. The estate also includes property that the debtor acquires, within 180 days after the filing of the petition, by inheritance, by a property settlement, by divorce decree, or as a beneficiary of a life insurance policy. In addition, the estate includes proceeds, rents, and profits from property of the estate and any interest in property that the estate acquires after the case commences. Finally, the estate includes property that the trustee recovers under her powers (1) as a lien creditor, (2) to avoid voidable preferences, (3) to avoid fraudulent transfers, and (4) to avoid statutory liens. While the estate does *not* include earnings from services an individual debtor performs after the case commences, it *does* include, in a Chapter 12 or 13 case, wages the debtor earns and property she acquires *after* the case commences.

Trustee as lien creditor
trustee gains the rights and
powers of a creditor with a
judicial lien

Judicial lien property
interest obtained by court
action to secure payment of
a debt

Trustee as Lien Creditor When the case commences, the trustee gains the rights and powers of any creditor with a judicial lien against the debtor that is returned unsatisfied, whether such a creditor exists or not. Obtained by a judgment, a levy, or some other legal or equitable process, a **judicial lien** is a charge or interest in property to secure payment of a debt or performance of an obligation. The trustee is made an ideal creditor possessing every right and power conferred by the law of the state on its most favored creditor who has acquired a lien by legal or equitable proceedings. Because the trustee assumes the rights and powers of a purely hypothetical lien creditor, she need not locate an actual existing lien creditor.

Thus, under the Uniform Commercial Code and the Bankruptcy Code, the trustee, as a hypothetical lien creditor, has priority over a creditor with a security interest that was not perfected when the bankruptcy petition was filed. A creditor with a purchase money security interest who files within the grace period allowed under state law, which in most states is twenty days after the debtor receives the collateral, however, will defeat the trustee, even if the petition is gap-filed before the creditor perfects and after the security interest is created. For example, Donald borrows $5,000 from Cathy on September 1 and gives her a security interest in the equipment he purchases with the borrowed funds. On October 3, before Cathy perfects her security interest, Donald files for bankruptcy. The trustee in bankruptcy can invalidate Cathy's security interest because it was unperfected when the bankruptcy petition was filed. Cathy would be able to assert a claim as an unsecured creditor. If, however, Donald had filed for bankruptcy on September 18 and Cathy had perfected the security interest on September 19, Cathy would prevail because she perfected her purchase money security interest within twenty days after Donald received the equipment.

Voidable preferences
Bankruptcy Code invalidates
certain preferential transfers
made before the date of
bankruptcy from the debtor
to favored creditors

Voidable Preferences The Bankruptcy Code invalidates certain preferential transfers from the debtor to favored creditors before the date of bankruptcy. A creditor who has received a transfer invalidated as preferential may still make a claim for the unpaid debt, but the property he received under the preferential transfer becomes a part of the debtor's estate to be shared by all creditors. The trustee may recover any *transfer* of the debtor's property (1) to or for the benefit of a creditor; (2) for or on account of an antecedent debt the debtor owed before the transfer was made; (3) made while the debtor was insolvent; (4) made on or within ninety days before the date of the filing of the petition; or, if the creditor was an "insider" (as defined earlier), within one year of the date of the filing of the petition; *and* (5) that enables such creditor to receive more than he would have received under Chapter 7.

A transfer is any means, direct or indirect, voluntary or involuntary, of disposing of property or an interest in property, including the retention of title as a security interest. The Bankruptcy Code presumes that the debtor has been insolvent on and during the ninety days immediately preceding the date of the filing of the petition. **Insolvency** is a financial condition such that the sum of one's debts exceeds the sum of all one's property at fair valuation.

For example, on March 3, David borrows $15,000 from Carla, promising to repay the loan on April 3. David repays Carla on April 3. Then, on June 1, David files a petition in bankruptcy. His assets are sufficient to pay general creditors only $.40 on the dollar. David's repayment of the loan is a voidable preference, which the trustee may recover from Carla. The transfer (repayment) on April 3 (1) was to a creditor (Carla); (2) was on account of an antecedent debt (the $15,000 loan made on March 3); (3) was made while the debtor was insolvent (the debtor is presumed insolvent for the ninety days preceding the filing of the bankruptcy petition—June 1); (4) was made within ninety days of bankruptcy (April 3 is less than ninety days before June 1); and (5) enabled the creditor to receive more than she would have received under Chapter 7 (Carla received $15,000; she would have received .40 × $15,000 = $6,000 in bankruptcy). After returning the property to the trustee, Carla would have an unsecured claim of $15,000 against David's estate in bankruptcy, for which she would receive $6,000.

Consider another example. On May 1, Debra buys and receives merchandise from Stuart and gives him a security interest in the goods for the unpaid price of $20,000. On May 25, Stuart files a financing statement. On August 1, Debra files a petition for bankruptcy. The trustee in bankruptcy may avoid the perfected security interest as a preferential transfer. The transfer of the perfected security interest on May 25 (1) was to benefit a creditor (Stuart); (2) the transfer was on account of an antecedent debt (the $20,000 owed from the sale of the merchandise); (3) the debtor was insolvent at the time (the debtor's insolvency is presumed for the ninety days preceding the filing of the bankruptcy petition—August 1); (4) the transfer was made within ninety days of bankruptcy (May 25 is less than ninety days before August 1); and (5) the transfer enabled the creditor to receive more than he would have received in bankruptcy (on his secured claim, Stuart would recover more than he would on an unsecured claim).

Nevertheless, not all transfers made within ninety days of bankruptcy are voidable. The Bankruptcy Code makes exceptions for certain pre-bankruptcy transfers, including

1. **Exchanges for new value.** If, for example, within ninety days before the petition is filed, the debtor purchases an automobile for $9,000, this transfer of property (i.e., the $9,000) is *not* voidable because it was not made for an antecedent debt but rather as a substantially contemporaneous exchange for new value.

2. **Enabling security interests.** If the creditor gives the debtor new value that the debtor uses to acquire property in which he grants the creditor a security interest, the security interest is not voidable if the creditor perfects

Insolvency financial condition where debts exceed fair value of assets

it within twenty days after the debtor receives possession of the property. For example, if within ninety days of the filing of the petition, the debtor purchases a refrigerator on credit and grants the seller or lender a security interest in the refrigerator, the transfer of that interest is not voidable if the secured party perfects *within twenty days* after the debtor receives possession of the property.

3. **Payments in ordinary course.** The trustee may *not* avoid a transfer (1) in payment of a debt incurred in the ordinary course of business or financial affairs of the debtor and the transferee, (2) made in the ordinary course of business or financial affairs of the debtor and transferee, and (3) made according to ordinary business terms.

4. **Consumer debts.** This exception, added in 1984, provides that if the debtor is an individual whose debts are primarily consumer debts, the trustee may not avoid any transfer of property valued at less than $600.

5. **Alimony and support**. This exception, added in 1994, provides that the trustee may not avoid any transfer that is a *bona fide* payment of a debt for alimony, maintenance, or support made to a spouse, former spouse, or a child of the debtor.

UNION BANK v. WOLAS Supreme Court of the United States, 1991, 502 U.S. 151, 112 S.Ct. 527, 116 L.Ed.2d 514

FACTS On December 17, 1986, ZZZZ Best Co., Inc. (the debtor) borrowed seven million dollars from Union Bank (the bank). On July 8, 1987, the debtor filed a voluntary petition for bankruptcy under Chapter 7. During the preceding ninety days, the debtor had made interest payments of $100,000 to the bank on the loan. Wolas, appointed trustee of the debtor's estate, filed a complaint against the bank to recover those payments as a voidable preference.

The bankruptcy court held that the payments were not voidable because they came within the ordinary course of business exception. This exception provides that the trustee may not avoid a transfer that was (a) in payment of a debt incurred by the debtor in the ordinary course of business or financial affairs of the debtor and the transferee; (b) made in the ordinary course of business or financial affairs of the debtor and the transferee; and (c) made according to ordinary business terms. The bankruptcy court found that the loans had been made in the ordinary course of business or financial affairs of both the debtor and the bank and that the interest had been paid according to ordinary business terms. The district court affirmed. Wolas appealed, arguing that the exception applied only to short-term debt, not to long-term debt. The Court of Appeals reversed, and the bank appealed.

DECISION Decision of the Court of Appeals reversed and decision of the bankruptcy court reinstated.

OPINION The Bankruptcy Code authorizes bankruptcy trustees to avoid any transfer of the debtor's interest in property if five conditions are satisfied: (1) the transfer benefits a creditor; (2) is on account of an antecedent debt; (3) is made while the debtor is insolvent; (4) is made within the ninety days before the filing of the petition for bankruptcy; and (5) enables the creditor to receive a larger share of the estate than he or she would have received if the transfer had not been made. All five conditions are present in this case. However, the Bankruptcy Code provides an exception for payments made in the ordinary course of business. This exception does not distinguish between long-term debt and short-term debt. Rather, it focuses on whether the debt was incurred, and payment made, in the "ordinary course of business of the debtor and transferee." Thus, there is no textual support for a contention that the exception's coverage is limited to short-term debt.

INTERPRETATION The exception to voidable preferences for payments made in the ordinary course of business applies to both long-term and short-term debt.

Fraudulent transfers
trustee may avoid fraudulent transfers made on or within one year before the date of bankruptcy

Fraudulent Transfers The trustee may avoid **fraudulent transfers** made on or within one year before the date of the filing of the petition. One type of fraudulent transfer consists of the debtor's transferring property with the actual intent to hinder, delay, or defraud any of her creditors. Another consists of the debtor's transferring property for less than a reasonably equivalent consideration when she is insolvent or when the transfer would make her so. For example, Carol, who is in debt, transfers title to her house to Wallace, her father, without any payment by Wallace to Carol and with the understanding that when the house is no longer in danger of seizure by creditors, Wallace will reconvey it to Carol. Carol's transfer of the house is a fraudulent transfer.

Statutory Liens A **statutory lien** arises solely by force of a statute and does *not* include a security interest or judicial lien. The trustee may avoid a statutory lien on property of the debtor if the lien (1) first becomes effective when the debtor becomes insolvent, (2) is not perfected or enforceable against a *bona fide* purchaser on the date the petition was filed, *or* (3) is for rent.

Statutory lien interest in property to secure payment of a debt that arises solely by statute

LIQUIDATION—CHAPTER 7

To accomplish its dual goals of distributing the debtor's property fairly and providing the debtor with a fresh start, the Bankruptcy Code has established two approaches: liquidation and adjustment of debts. Chapter 7 uses liquidation, whereas Chapters 11, 12, and 13, discussed later, use the adjustment of debts. Liquidation involves terminating the business of the debtor, distributing his nonexempt assets, and, usually, discharging all his dischargeable debts.

Purpose of Chapter 7 to distribute equitably the debtor's nonexempt assets and usually to discharge all dischargeable debts of the debtor

Proceedings

Proceedings under Chapter 7 apply to all debtors except railroads, insurance companies, banks, savings and loan associations, homestead associations, and credit unions. A petition commencing a case under Chapter 7 may be either voluntary or involuntary. After the order for relief, an interim trustee is appointed, who serves until the creditors select a permanent trustee. If the creditors do not elect a trustee, the interim trustee becomes the permanent trustee. Under Chapter 7, the trustee collects and reduces to money the property of the estate; accounts for all property received; investigates the financial affairs of the debtor; examines and, if appropriate, challenges proofs of claims; opposes, if advisable, the discharge of the debtor; and makes a final report of the administration of the estate.

The creditors also may elect a committee of not fewer than three and not more than eleven unsecured creditors to consult with the trustee, to make recommendations to him, and to submit questions to the court.

Dismissal

The court on its own motion, after notice and a hearing, may dismiss a case filed by an individual debtor whose debts are primarily consumer debts if the court finds that granting relief would substantially abuse the provisions of Chapter 7.

Distribution of the Estate

After the trustee has collected all the assets of the debtor's estate, she distributes them to the creditors (and, if any assets remain, to the debtor) in the following order:

1. Secured creditors, on their security interests;
2. Creditors entitled to a priority, in the order provided;

Distribution of the estate in the following order: (1) secured creditors, (2) creditors entitled to a priority, (3) unsecured creditors, and (4) the debtor

3. Unsecured creditors who filed their claims on time (or tardily, if they did not have notice or actual knowledge of the bankruptcy);
4. Unsecured creditors who filed their claims late;
5. Claims for fines and multiple, exemplary, or punitive damages;
6. Interest at the legal rate from the date of the filing of the petition, to all of the above claimants; and
7. Whatever property remains, to the debtor.

Claims of the same rank are paid proportionately. For example: Donley has filed a petition for a Chapter 7 proceeding. The total value of Donley's estate *after* paying the expenses of administration is $25,000. Evans, who is owed $15,000, has a security interest in property valued at $10,000. Fishel has an unsecured claim of $6,000, which is entitled to a priority of $2,000. The United States has a claim for income taxes of $4,000. Green has an unsecured claim of $9,000 that was filed on time. Hiller has an unsecured claim of $12,000 that was filed on time. Jerdee has a claim of $8,000 that was filed late. The distribution would be as follows: (1) Evans receives $11,500; (2) Fishel receives $3,200; (3) the United States receives $4,000; (4) Green receives $2,700; (5) Hiller receives $3,600; and (6) Jerdee receives $0.

Let us analyze this distribution: Evans receives $10,000 as a secured creditor and has an unsecured claim of $5,000. Fishel receives $2,000 on the portion of his claim entitled to a priority and has an unsecured claim of $4,000. The United States has a priority of $4,000. After paying $10,000 to Evans, $2,000 to Fishel, and $4,000 to the United States, there remains $9,000 ($25,000 − $10,000 −$2,000 − $4,000) to be distributed *pro rata* to unsecured creditors who filed on time. Their claims total $30,000 (Evans = $5,000, Fishel = $4,000, Green = $9,000, and Hiller = $12,000). Therefore, each will receive $9,000/$30,000, or $.30 on the dollar. Accordingly, Evans receives an additional $1,500, Fishel receives an additional $1,200, Green receives $2,700, and Hiller receives $3,600. Because the assets were insufficient to pay all unsecured claimants who filed on time, Jerdee, who filed tardily, receives nothing. However, if Jerdee's claim were filed late because Donley had failed to schedule the claim, Donley's debt to Jerdee would not be discharged unless Jerdee knew or had notice of the bankruptcy.

Figure 41–2 summarizes the collection and distribution of the debtor's estate.

Discharge

Discharge granted by the court unless the debtor has committed an offense under the Bankruptcy Code or has received a discharge within six years

A **discharge** under Chapter 7 relieves the debtor of all debts that arose before the date of the order for relief, except for those debts that are not dischargeable. After distribution of the estate, the court will grant the debtor a discharge unless the debtor (1) is not an individual (partnerships and corporations may *not* receive a discharge under Chapter 7); (2) has destroyed, falsified, concealed, or failed to keep records and books of account; (3) has knowingly and fraudulently made a false oath or account, presented or used a false claim, or given or received bribes; (4) has transferred, removed, destroyed, or concealed any of his property with intent to hinder, delay, or defraud his creditors within twelve months before the filing of the bankruptcy petition; (5) has within six years before the bankruptcy been granted a discharge under Chapter 7 or 11; (6) has refused to obey any lawful order of the court or to answer any question approved by the court; (7) has failed to explain satisfactorily any losses of assets or any deficiency of assets to meet his liabilities; or (8) has executed a written waiver of discharge approved by the court. A debtor also will be denied a discharge under Chapter 7 if she

FIGURE 41–2 Collection and Distribution of the Debtor's Estate

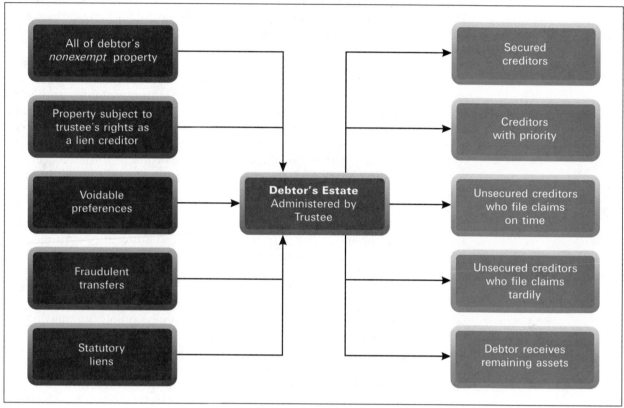

received a discharge under Chapter 12 or 13 within the past six years, unless payments under that chapter's plan totaled at least (1) 100 percent of the allowed unsecured claims or (2) 70 percent of such claims and the plan was the debtor's best effort.

On request of the trustee or a creditor and after notice and a hearing, the court may revoke within one year a discharge the debtor obtained through fraud.

REORGANIZATION—CHAPTER 11

Reorganization is the process of correcting or eliminating the factors that caused the distress of a business enterprise and thereby preserving both the enterprise and its value as a going concern. Chapter 11 of the Bankruptcy Code governs reorganization of eligible debtors—including partnerships, corporations, and individuals—and permits the restructuring of their finances. The main objective of a reorganization proceeding is to develop and carry out a fair, equitable, and feasible plan of reorganization. After a plan has been prepared and filed, a hearing held before the court determines whether or not it will be confirmed.

Purpose of Chapter 11 to preserve a distressed entity and its value as a going concern

Proceedings

Any person who may be a debtor under Chapter 7 (except a stockbroker or a commodity broker) and railroads may be debtors under Chapter 11. Petitions may be voluntary or involuntary. See *In Re Johns-Manville Corp.* on page 814.

The 1994 amendments permit small businesses to elect to be subject to streamlined procedures designed to expedite the administration of Chapter 11. The amendments define "small business" to include persons engaged in commercial or business activities whose aggregate, noncontingent, liquidated debts do not exceed $2 million.

As soon as possible after the order for relief, a committee of unsecured creditors (usually those who hold the seven largest unsecured claims against the debtor) is appointed. In addition, the court may order the appointment of additional committees of creditors or of equity security holders, if necessary, to assure adequate representation. The committee may, with the court's approval, employ attorneys, accountants, and other agents to represent or perform services for the committee. The committee should consult with the debtor or trustee concerning the administration of the case and may investigate the debtor's affairs and participate in formulating a reorganization plan.

The debtor will remain in possession and management of the property of the estate unless the court orders the appointment of a trustee, who may then operate the debtor's business. The court will order the appointment of a trustee only for cause (including fraud, dishonesty, incompetence, or gross mismanagement of the debtor's affairs) or if the appointment is in the interests of creditors or equity security holders. The 1994 amendments allow the creditors to elect the trustee.

The duties of a trustee in a case under Chapter 11 include the following: (1) to be accountable for all property received; (2) to examine proofs of claims; (3) to furnish information to all parties with an interest; (4) to provide the court and taxing authorities with financial reports of the debtor's business operations; (5) to make a final report and account of the administration of the estate; (6) to investigate the debtor's financial condition and to determine whether continuing the debtor's business is desirable; and (7) to file a plan or to file a report on why there will be no plan, or to recommend either dismissal of the case or its conversion to Chapter 7.

At any time before confirming a plan, the court may terminate the trustee's appointment and restore the debtor to possession and management of the estate property and the operation of the debtor's business. When a trustee has not been appointed, the debtor in possession performs many of the functions and duties of a trustee, with the principal exception of (self-) investigation.

The Bankruptcy Amendments Act of 1984 added a new provision dealing with the rejection of union-drafted collective bargaining agreements. It provides that subsequent to filing and prior to seeking such rejection, the trustee or debtor-in-possession must propose the necessary labor contract modifications that will enable the debtor to reorganize and that will also provide for the fair and equitable treatment of all parties concerned. The provision also requires that good faith meetings to reach a mutually satisfactory agreement be held between management and the union. It authorizes the court to approve rejection of the collective bargaining agreement only if the court finds that the proposal for rejection was made in accordance with these conditions, that the union refused the proposal without good cause, and that the balance of equities clearly favors rejection.

Plan of Reorganization

The debtor may file a plan at any time and has the exclusive right to file a plan during the 120 days after the order for relief, unless a trustee has been appointed. Then other parties in interest, including the trustee, if one has been appointed, or a creditors' committee, may file a plan.

A plan of reorganization must divide creditors' claims and shareholders' interests into classes, specify how each class will be treated, deal with claims within each class equally, and provide adequate means for implementing the plan. After a plan has been filed, the plan and a written disclosure statement approved by the court as containing adequate information must be transmitted to each holder of a claim before seeking acceptance or rejection of the plan. Adequate information is that which would enable a hypothetical reasonable investor to make an informed judgment about the plan.

Acceptance of Plan

Each class of claims and interests has the opportunity to accept or reject the proposed plan. To be accepted by a *class of claims*, a plan must be accepted by creditors that hold at least two-thirds in amount and more than one-half in number of the allowed claims of such class. Acceptance of a plan by a *class of interests*, such as shareholders, requires acceptance by holders of at least two-thirds in amount of the allowed interests of such class.

A class that is not impaired under a plan is deemed to have accepted the plan. Basically, a class is not impaired if the plan leaves unaltered the legal, equitable, and contractual rights to which the holder of such claim or interest is entitled. However, a class that will receive no distribution under a plan is automatically deemed *not* to have accepted the plan.

Acceptance of plan requires a specified proportion of creditors to approve the plan

Confirmation of Plan

The court must confirm a plan before it is binding on any parties, and a court will confirm only a plan that meets all the requirements of the Bankruptcy Code. The most important of these requirements are the following:

1. The plan must have been proposed in *good faith*.
2. The court must find that confirmation of the plan is *feasible* and not likely to be followed by the debtor's liquidation or by its need for further financial reorganization.
3. Certain classes of creditors must have their allowed claims paid in full in *cash* immediately or, in some instances, on a deferred basis.
4. The plan must be *accepted* by at least *one* class of claims, and with respect to *each* class, each holder must either accept the plan *or* receive not less than the amount he would have received under Chapter 7. In addition, each class must accept the plan or be unimpaired by it. Nonetheless, under certain circumstances, the court may confirm a plan that is not accepted by all impaired classes by determining that the plan does not discriminate unfairly and that it is fair and equitable. Under these circumstances, a class of claims or interests may, despite its objections, be subjected to the provisions of a plan.

Confirmation of plan requires (1) good faith, (2) feasibility, (3) cash payments to certain creditors, and usually (4) acceptance by creditors

Effect of Reorganization

After its confirmation, the plan governs the debtor's performance obligations. The plan binds the debtor and any creditor, equity security holder, or general partner of the debtor. After the entry of a final decree closing the proceedings, the debtor is discharged from all of its debts and liabilities that arose before the date the plan was confirmed, except as otherwise provided in the plan, the order of confirmation, or the Bankruptcy Code. The confirmation of a plan does not discharge an *individual* debtor from debts that are not dischargeable.

Effect of reorganization binds the debtor and creditors and discharges the debtor

IN RE JOHNS-MANVILLE CORPORATION United States Bankruptcy Court, Southern District of New York, 1984, 36 B.R. 727

FACTS Johns-Manville Corporation and its affiliated companies (Manville) were highly successful industrial enterprises among the nation's "Fortune 500." As of August 26, 1982, Manville had some 16,000 asbestos-related health suits pending against it because of its longtime use of products containing this deadly substance. The number of lawsuits was expected to multiply over the next two or three decades as individuals who had been exposed to asbestos began to develop asbestos-related diseases. Moreover, the insurance industry had generally disclaimed any liability to Manville on policies written for this purpose. Therefore, as a result of this mammoth economic burden, Manville filed for protection under Chapter 11 of the Bankruptcy Code on August 26, 1982. Four separate motions to dismiss Manville's petition were lodged before the court.

DECISION Motions to dismiss the Manville petition denied.

OPINION The Bankruptcy Code enables a financially beleaguered debtor to resort to the bankruptcy process before its economic situation is beyond repair. This possibility is consistent with the key aim of Chapter 11 of the Code: to avoid the liquidation of the enterprise.

Reorganization is more efficient than liquidation because valuable productive assets as well as jobs are preserved. Liquidation of Manville would result not only in the sale of valuable assets for scrap and the loss of jobs but also in the denial of just compensation of some present asbestos victims and all future claimants. Manville is a real business, with real debt and real creditors, in desperate need of economic reorganization. As of the filing date, the settlement demand for the pending health lawsuits approached $1 billion. Manville is projected to be liable to various school authorities for $500 million to $1.4 billion in asbestos-related property damage claims. Other debts of Manville run into the hundreds of millions of dollars. Manville's cash and liquid assets are insufficient to meet these obligations, and its insurance carriers are unwilling to contribute to the payment of the debt. Thus, the economic reality of Manville's dangerous financial situation, due to crushing real debt, requires that its petition for bankruptcy be sustained.

INTERPRETATION The main objective of a Chapter 11 proceeding is to effect a reorganization of the debtor so as to preserve the enterprise and its value as a going concern.

ADJUSTMENT OF DEBTS OF A FAMILY FARMER— CHAPTER 12

Purpose of Chapter 12 to permit a family farmer to file a repayment plan that will discharge him from most debts

Proceedings available to a farmer who receives at least 50 percent of his income from farming and who meets certain debt limitations

In 1986, Congress amended the Bankruptcy Act by adding Chapter 12, which provides for the adjustment of the debts of a family farmer with regular annual income. Family farmers are defined as individuals, or individuals and their spouses, who are engaged in farming and who receive 50 percent of their gross income from farming. Their aggregate debts may not exceed $1.5 million, and at least 80 percent of those debts must arise from the farming operation. A corporation or partnership may also qualify as a family farmer if, in addition to meeting the requirements just mentioned, one family holds 50 percent of the stock or equity, and more than 80 percent of the assets of the corporation or partnership are related to the farming operation.

Chapter 12 has a "sunset" provision: it will expire in 1998 unless Congress reenacts it. Its purpose is to provide a proceeding for family farmers who do not qualify for Chapter 13 and who find Chapter 11 proceedings overly burdensome. The provisions of Chapter 12 are based on and are substantially the same as those of Chapter 13.

ADJUSTMENT OF DEBTS OF INDIVIDUALS—CHAPTER 13

Purpose of Chapter 13 to permit an individual debtor to file a repayment plan that will discharge her from most debts

Chapter 13 of the Bankruptcy Code permits an individual debtor to file a repayment plan that, if confirmed by the court, will discharge him from almost all of his debts when he completes his payments under the plan.

ETHICAL DILEMMA For a Company Contemplating Bankruptcy, When Is Disclosure the Best Policy?

FACTS Doris Williams is a senior executive for Foundation Insurance Corporation, a publicly held insurance company that issues a broad range of policies. Early in January, Williams was appointed to serve on a management team composed of herself and four other executive officers. The team reviews and finalizes recommendations for establishing loss reserves, recommendations regarding dividend payments to shareholders, and proposals for press releases.

For the past few years, Foundation has experienced increasingly alarming financial difficulties. Ten years ago, in order to compete with alternative investments, the company developed many innovative life insurance products to provide both traditional insurance and an attractive savings vehicle for the insured. However, to meet the high interest payments on these new insurance products, management invested in risky real estate ventures that promised—but often failed to deliver—high returns. Foundation's property and casualty lines also experienced increased losses due to poor actuarial decisions and an unexpected rise in workers' compensation claims.

Toward the end of the first quarter, during the management team's review of dividend payments, Williams recommended slashing dividend payments, bolstering loss reserves, and publicly disclosing the company's growing financial problems. The four other committee members disagreed. They feared that the public would panic and that the effect on the market would be disastrous. They wanted more time to attempt to turn the business around. Williams went along with the committee for the first and second quarters. By the third quarter, however, the committee could no longer avoid recommending an unprecedented reduction in dividends and a dramatic increase in reserves. By the end of the year, the company, having become insolvent, filed for bankruptcy protection. The current management team now wishes to reorganize the company.

Social, Political, and Ethical Considerations

1. Was it ethical for Williams to acquiesce with regard to the first and second quarters? Consider the interests of the consumer/policyholder, the company, the shareholders, and the members of the committee. Was there merit to the committee's request for more time to remedy the company's problems?
2. Should bankrupt insurers be treated differently than other bankrupt corporations? What role, if any, should government play in insuring insurance companies?
3. Should the old management team be allowed to retain control of Foundation? Why? Why not?

Proceedings

Chapter 13 provides a procedure for the adjustment of debts of an *individual* with regular income who owes liquidated, unsecured debts of less than $250,000 and secured debts of less than $750,000. Sole proprietorships that meet these debt limitations are also eligible; partnerships and corporations are not. A case under Chapter 13 may be initiated *only* by a voluntary petition, and a trustee is appointed in every Chapter 13 case. Property of the estate in Chapter 13 includes wages the debtor earned and property she acquired after the Chapter 13 filing.

The Plan

The debtor files the plan and may modify it at any time before confirmation. The plan must meet three requirements:

1. It must require the debtor to submit all or any portion of her future earnings or income, as is necessary for the execution of the plan, to the trustee's supervision and control.
2. It must provide for full payment on a deferred basis of all claims entitled to a priority unless a holder of a claim agrees to a different treatment of such claim.
3. If the plan classifies claims, it must provide the same treatment for each claim in the same class.

In addition, the plan *may* modify the rights of unsecured creditors and the rights of secured creditors, except those secured only by a security interest in the debtor's principal residence. The plan may *not* provide for payments over a period longer than three years, unless the court approves, for cause, a longer period not to exceed five years.

Confirmation

Confirmation of plan requires (1) good faith, (2) that the value of property distributed to creditors not be less than the amount that would be paid them under Chapter 7, (3) that secured creditors accept the plan, and (4) that the debtor be able to make all payments and comply with the plan

To be confirmed by the court, the plan must meet certain requirements. First, the plan must comply with applicable law and be proposed in good faith. Second, the value of the property to be distributed to unsecured creditors must not be less than the amount they would receive under Chapter 7. Third, either the secured creditors must accept the plan, the plan must provide that the debtor will surrender the collateral to the secured creditors, *or* the plan must permit the secured creditors to retain their security interests and the value of the property to be distributed to them is not less than the allowed amount of their claim. Fourth, the debtor must be able to make all payments and comply with the plan. Fifth, if the trustee or the holder of an unsecured claim objects to the plan's confirmation, then the plan must either provide for payment in full of that claim or provide that all of the debtor's disposable income for three years be applied to payments under the plan. For purposes of this provision, *disposable income* means income received by the debtor that is not reasonably necessary for the maintenance or support of the debtor or a dependent of the debtor or, if the debtor is engaged in business, for the payment of expenditures necessary for continuing, preserving, and operating the business.

Effect of Confirmation

The provisions of a confirmed plan bind the debtor and all of her creditors. The confirmation of a plan vests in the debtor all property of the estate free and clear of any creditor's claim or interest for which the plan provides, except as otherwise provided in the plan or in the order confirming the plan. A plan may be modified after confirmation at the request of the debtor, the trustee, or a holder of an unsecured claim.

Discharge

After a debtor completes all payments under the plan, the court will grant him a discharge of all debts for which the plan provides, except the nondischargeable debts for alimony, maintenance, support, most student loans, liability for driving while intoxicated, governmental fines, and certain long-term obligations on which payments extend beyond the term of the plan. This discharge is considerably more extensive than that granted under Chapter 7. Moreover, though a debtor who receives a discharge under Chapter 7 cannot obtain another discharge under that chapter for six years, a debtor discharged under Chapter 13 is not subject to that limitation if payments under the plan totaled at least (1) 100 percent of unsecured claims or (2) 70 percent of such claims *and* the plan was the debtor's best effort.

Even if the debtor fails to make all payments, the court may, after a hearing, grant a "hardship discharge" if the debtor's failure is due to circumstances for which the debtor is not justly accountable, the value of property actually distributed is not less than what the creditors would have received under Chapter 7, and modification of the plan is not practicable. This discharge is subject, however, to the same exceptions for nondischargeable debts as a discharge under Chapter 7.

Figure 41–3 compares proceedings under Chapters 7, 11, 12, and 13.

IN RE CHRISTOPHE United States Bankruptcy Court, 1993, 151 B.R. 475

FACTS Yolanda Christophe filed her Chapter 13 petition on April 19, 1992. Her scheduled debts consist of $11,100 of secured debt, $9,300 owed on an unsecured student loan, and $6,960 of other unsecured debt. Christophe asserts that the student loan is nondischargeable under § 523(a)(8), and that assertion has not been questioned. However, none of the details of this loan were presented as evidence before the court. Christophe's proposed amended Chapter 13 plan calls for fifty-six monthly payments of $440 a month. The questioned provision in that plan is the division of the unsecured creditors into two classes. The general unsecured creditors would receive 32 percent and the separately classified student loan creditor would receive 100 percent.

DECISION Confirmation of the debtor's Chapter 13 plan is denied.

OPINION A bankruptcy judge may not confirm a Chapter 13 plan that is not presented in good faith or unfairly discriminates in violation of § 1322(b)(1), because such a plan would not fulfill the requirement of § 1325(a)(1) that it comply with the provisions of Chapter 13. Section 1322(b)(1) provides that a debtor may designate classes of unsecured claims but may not discriminate unfairly against any class of claims. However, if an individual is liable on consumer debts, the plan may treat claims for these debts differently than other unsecured claims.

The student loan claimant is an unsecured, nonpriority creditor. Christophe has proposed to place that creditor in a separate class and proposes to treat it differently from all other unsecured, nonpriority creditors. Therefore, it must be determined whether this disparate treatment constitutes unfair discrimination under § 1322(b)(1) or bad faith under § 1322(b)(3).

The statute provides no standards for determining when a plan discriminates "unfairly." However, courts have recognized four issues relevant to determining whether discrimination is unfair: (1) whether the discrimination has a reasonable basis; (2) whether the debtor can carry out a plan without the discrimination; (3) whether the plan is proposed in good faith; and (4) whether the degree of discrimination is directly related to the basis or rationale for the discrimination.

Discrimination is considered to be reasonable and therefore fair when it is related to the debtor's objective interest in completing the plan and obtaining a fresh start or maintaining a decent quality of life. The special rights of student loan creditors may in some circumstances form a reasonable basis for allowing a debtor to treat such creditors favorably. A creditor holding a nondischargeable student loan may sue to enforce a debtor's obligation in state court, and obtain a judgment against that debtor. Such action would often cause such a debtor to default on the Chapter 13 plan, and might thereby cause the Chapter 13 case to be dismissed or converted to a Chapter 7 liquidation case. Thus, a debtor's objective interest in fulfilling a Chapter 13 plan may be advanced by allowing the full payment of what is actually due under the student loan agreement.

However, finding a reasonable basis for discrimination does not end the analysis of whether unfair discrimination is present. The court must consider whether the basis for the discrimination directly supports the nature and degree of disparate treatment proposed in the plan. This question expresses a concern that debtors should not engage in any discrimination beyond what is necessary to accomplish the reasonable goal behind the discriminatory treatment. If a Chapter 13 debtor has an obligation to pay the student loan lender $100 a month for the next ten years, then nondischargeability of that obligation merely means that the debtor will continue to owe that $100 every month for the remaining term of the student loan. Furthermore, if an arrearage exists on the date that the Chapter 13 petition is filed, the Chapter 13 plan can reasonably and fairly provide for the regular monthly payments plus additional funds to cure the arrearage. Thus, debtors may provide for the preferential treatment of student loan creditors by providing in their plans for the funding of all monthly payments as they become due, plus the curing of arrearages.

Christophe has not shown that her plan does not exceed the necessity for discrimination. The missing details that would be particularly relevant to the analysis below are the following: (1) what payments were due under the loan agreement; (2) when is the last payment due under the loan agreement; (3) do any arrearages exist; (4) have the payments been accelerated pursuant to the loan agreement before the bankruptcy petition was filed; and (5) would the proposed 100 percent payout accelerate payments under the loan agreement. If the student loan creditor is not entitled to 100 percent repayment of its loan before the scheduled completion of the Chapter 13 plan, then a plan that pays 100 percent of that student loan during that period would accelerate payment of the student loan debt. That would be unfair to the other unsecured creditors, because the debtor would be forcing them to bear the cost of early payment of the student loan without a corresponding justification. Because Christophe has failed to prove that her Chapter 13 plan does not discriminate unfairly and is presented in good faith, it must be denied.

INTERPRETATION A bankruptcy judge may not confirm a Chapter 13 plan if it is not presented in good faith or if it unfairly discriminates.

FIGURE 41–3 Comparison of Bankruptcy Proceedings

	Chapter 7	**Chapter 11**	**Chapter 12**	**Chapter 13**
Objective	Liquidation	Reorganization	Adjustment	Adjustment
Eligible Debtors	Most debtors	Most debtors, including railroads	Family farmer who meets certain debt limitations	Individual with regular income who meets certain debt limitations
Type of Petition	Voluntary or involuntary	Voluntary or involuntary	Voluntary	Voluntary
Trustee	Usually selected by creditors; otherwise appointed	Only if court orders appointment for cause; creditors then may select trustee	Appointed	Appointed

CREDITORS' RIGHTS AND DEBTOR'S RELIEF OUTSIDE OF BANKRUPTCY

The rights and remedies of debtors and creditors outside of bankruptcy are governed mainly by state law. Because of the expense and notoriety associated with bankruptcy, resolving claims outside of a bankruptcy proceeding is often in the best interests of both debtor and creditor. Accordingly, bankruptcy is usually considered a last resort.

Outside of bankruptcy, the rights and remedies of creditors are varied. In the first part of this section, we will examine the basic right of *all* creditors to pursue their overdue claims to judgment and to satisfy that judgment out of property belonging to the debtor. (Other rights and remedies are discussed elsewhere in this book.) The second part of this section will describe the various forms of non-bankruptcy compromises that provide relief to debtors who have become overextended and who are unable to pay all of their creditors.

CREDITORS' RIGHTS

When a debtor fails to pay a debt, the creditor may file suit to collect it. The goal is to obtain a judgment against the debtor and to collect on that judgment.

Prejudgment Remedies

Because litigation takes time, a creditor attempting to collect on a claim through the judicial process will almost always experience delay in obtaining judgment. To prevent the debtor from meanwhile disposing of his assets, the creditor may use, when available, certain prejudgment remedies. The most important of these is **attachment**, the process of seizing property, through a judicial order, and bringing the property into the court's custody to secure satisfaction of the judgment ultimately to be entered in the action. Most states limit attachment to specified grounds and provide the debtor an opportunity for a hearing before a judge prior to the issuance of a writ of execution. In addition, the plaintiff generally

Attachment seizure of property to bring it under the custody of the court

must post a bond to compensate the defendant for loss should the plaintiff not prevail in the cause of action.

Similar in purpose is the remedy of prejudgment **garnishment**, which is a statutory proceeding directed at a third person who owes a debt to the debtor or who has property belonging to the debtor. Garnishment is most commonly used against the debtor's employer and the bank in which the debtor has a savings or checking account. Garnished property remains in the hands of the third party pending the outcome of the suit.

Garnishment proceeding by a creditor against a third person who owes money to the debtor

Postjudgment Remedies

If the debtor still has not paid the claim, the creditor may proceed to trial and try to obtain a court judgment against the debtor. Although necessary, obtaining a judgment is, nevertheless, only the first step. If the debtor does not voluntarily pay the judgment, the creditor will have to take additional steps to collect on it. These steps are called "postjudgment remedies."

First, the judgment creditor will have the court clerk issue a **writ of execution** demanding payment of the judgment, which is served by the sheriff upon the defendant debtor. Upon return of the writ "unsatisfied," the judgment creditor may post bond or other security and order a levy on and sale of specified nonexempt property belonging to the defendant debtor, which is then seized by the sheriff, advertised for sale, and sold at public sale under the writ of execution.

Writ of execution order served by a sheriff upon the debtor, demanding payment of a court judgment against the debtor

The writ of execution is limited to nonexempt property of the debtor. All states restrict creditors from recourse to certain property, the type and amount of which varies greatly from state to state.

If the proceeds of the sale do not produce funds sufficient to pay the judgment, the creditor may institute a *supplementary proceeding* in an attempt to locate money or other property belonging to the defendant. She may also proceed by *garnishment* against the debtor's employer or against a bank in which the debtor has an account.

DEBTOR'S RELIEF

The rights of creditors and the debtor's need for relief involve inherent conflicts arising from the following: (1) the right of diligent creditors to pursue their claims to judgment and to satisfy their judgments by sale of property of the debtor; (2) the right of unsecured creditors who have refrained from suing the debtor; and (3) the social policy of giving relief to a debtor who has contracted debts beyond his ability to pay and who therefore may carry a lifetime burden. Various forms of nonbankruptcy compromises have been developed to resolve these conflicts.

Compositions

A common law or nonstatutory **composition** is an ordinary contract or agreement between the debtor and her creditors under which the creditors receive a proportional part of their claims and the debtor is discharged from the balance of the claims. As a contract, it requires contractual formalities. For example, debtor D, owing debts of $5,000 to A, $2,000 to B, and $1,000 to C, offers to settle these claims by paying a total of $4,000 to A, B, and C. If A, B, and C accept the offer, a composition results, with A receiving $2,500, B $1,000, and C $500. The consideration for the promise of A to forgive the balance of his claim consists of the promises of B and C to forgive the balance of their claims. By avoiding a conflict among themselves to obtain the debtor's limited assets, all the creditors benefit.

Composition agreement between debtor and two or more of her creditors that each will take a portion of his claim as full payment

THE LAW AND YOU Bankruptcy for Individuals

Is There More than One Kind of Bankruptcy for Individuals?

Yes, the two main types of bankruptcy cases for individuals are Chapter 7 liquidation cases and Chapter 13 debt adjustments. Individuals are also eligible to file Chapter 11 reorganizations, but because of the complexity and expense of Chapter 11, it is normally used only by persons in business or those with excessive debts. Individuals engaged in farming also may be eligible for relief under Chapter 12.

What Happens When I File a Chapter 7 Case?

You turn over all of your non-exempt property to a person known as a "trustee in bankruptcy" who sells it and distributes the proceeds to your creditors under certain priorities prescribed in the bankruptcy laws. In exchange, unless you have committed certain wrongful or fraudulent acts prior to or during the bankruptcy or there are other unusual circumstances, you will receive a discharge (or cancellation) of all of your "dischargeable" debts.

In addition, once you file a bankruptcy case your creditors, generally, are prohibited, without having first obtained approval of the bankruptcy judge, from taking any further steps to collect any money you may owe them.

What Property May I Keep If I File a Chapter 7?

As of January 1, 1991, Illinois law permits you to retain as "exempt" up to $7,500 of equity in your residence and up to $1,200 in value in your car. In addition, you may keep up to $2,000 in personal property such as cash and furniture and all your necessary clothing, books and family pictures. You may also keep up to $750 in any implements, professional books or tools of the trade as well as all professionally prescribed health aids for you or your family. Additional exemptions are available and the amounts of these exemptions may change from time to time. However, to avail yourself of these "exemptions" you must properly request them in your bankruptcy case. These exemptions are available to each individual, so if both you and your spouse file a bankruptcy case each of you would be entitled to these exemptions.

Which of My Debts Are Not Discharged in a Chapter 7?

A discharge in Chapter 7 will not affect some of your debts such as alimony, child support, certain taxes, fines, certain debts arising from educational loans, and debts you fail to disclose properly to the bankruptcy court. At the request of a creditor, the bankruptcy judge may also exclude from your discharge debts resulting from loans you received by giving a lender a false financial statement as well as debts arising from fraud, embezzlement, drunken driving, larceny or certain other willful or malicious acts.

What Happens When I File a Chapter 13 Case?

Normally, in Chapter 13, you keep all or most of your property and propose a plan to repay all or some of your debts over time. During the period the "plan" is in effect, which can be as long as five years, you make regular payments (typically once a month) to a Chapter 13 Trustee, who, in turn, distributes the money to your creditors. Under certain circumstances, the bankruptcy court may approve a "plan" permitting you to keep all of your property even though you repay less than the full amount of your debts. Certain debts not dischargeable in Chapter 7, such as those based on fraud, may be discharged if you successfully complete your Chapter 13 plan. In order to be eligible to file a Chapter 13 case, you must have regular income and owe less than $100,000 [now $250,000] in unsecured debts and $350,000 [now $750,000] in secured debts.

How Will a Chapter 7 or Chapter 13 Case Affect My Future Credit and My Job?

Different people have different experiences obtaining credit after they file a bankruptcy case. Some find it more difficult. Others find it easier because they have relieved themselves of their prior debts or because their creditors know they cannot file another bankruptcy case for a period of time. Some people may discover that obtaining future credit is easier if they file a Chapter 13 and repay some of their debts than if they file a Chapter 7 and make no effort to repay. The bankruptcy laws prohibit your employer from discharging or discriminating against you solely because you have filed a bankruptcy case.

If I Own a Home, Will I Lose It If I File a Chapter 7 or Chapter 13 Case?

The answer depends on many factors. Many homeowners who file bankruptcy do not lose their homes. You should consult with an experienced bankruptcy attorney to obtain an answer.

Does My Spouse Have to File a Bankruptcy Too?

No, but you may discover that your spouse also owes many of your debts and that it would be beneficial for your spouse also to file a bankruptcy.

Do I Need a Lawyer to Represent Me If I File a Bankruptcy Case?

You have the absolute right to file your own bankruptcy case and represent yourself at all court hearings. However, in any bankruptcy case, you must complete and file with the bankruptcy court several detailed forms concerning your property,

debts and financial condition. Many people find it easier to complete these forms with the assistance of experienced bankruptcy counsel. In addition, you may discover, especially if you own significant property or if your creditors object to your discharge, that your case will develop complications requiring the advice and assistance of a lawyer.

[The material in this feature was originally prepared and published by the Illinois State Bar Association as a public service. Its purpose is to inform citizens of their legal rights and obligations. Consult your lawyer if you have questions about application of the law in a particular case.]

We should note, however, that the debtor in a composition is discharged from liability only on the claims of those creditors who voluntarily consent to the composition. If, in the illustration above, C had refused to accept the offer of composition and had refused to take the $500, he could attempt to collect his full $1,000 claim. Likewise, if D owed additional debts to X, Y, and Z, these creditors would not be bound by the agreement between D and A, B, and C. Another disadvantage of the composition is the fact that any creditor can attach the debtor's assets during the bargaining period that usually precedes the execution of the composition agreement. For instance, once D had advised A, B, and C that he was offering to compose the claims, any one of the creditors could seize D's property.

Assignments for Benefit of Creditors

A common law or nonstatutory **assignment for the benefit of creditors**, or a general assignment, as it is sometimes called, is a debtor's voluntary transfer of some or all of her property to a trustee, who applies the property to the payment of all the debtor's debts. For instance, debtor D transfers title to her property to trustee T, who converts the property into money and pays it to all of the creditors on a *pro rata* basis.

The advantage of the assignment over the composition is that it prevents the debtor's assets from being attached or executed and halts diligent creditors in their race to attach. On the other hand, though the common law assignment does not require the creditors' consent, the trustee's payment of part of the claims does not discharge the debtor from the balance of them. Thus, in the previous example, even after T pays A $2,500, B $1,000, and C $500 (and makes appropriate payments to all other creditors), A, B, and C and the other creditors may still attempt to collect the balance of their claims.

> **Assignment for benefit of creditors** voluntary transfer by the debtor of some or all of his property to a trustee, who applies the property to the payment of all the debtor's debts

Statutory Assignments

Because assignments benefit creditors by protecting the debtor's assets from attachment, many statutory enactments have endeavored to combine the idea of the assignment with a corresponding benefit that would discharge the debtor from the balance of his debts. However, since the United States Constitution prohibits a state from impairing a contractual obligation between private citizens, it is impossible for a state to force all creditors to discharge a debtor on a *pro rata* distribution of assets, although, as previously discussed, the federal government *does* have such power and exercises it in the Bankruptcy Code. Accordingly, the states generally have enacted assignment statutes permitting the debtor to obtain *voluntary* releases

> **Statutory assignment** provides a voluntary release of balance of claims from creditors who accept partial payments made by the trustee for the debtor

of the balance of claims from creditors who accept partial payments, thus combining the advantages of common law compositions and assignments.

Equity Receiverships

Equity receivership receiver is a disinterested person appointed by the court to collect and preserve the debtor's assets and income and to dispose of them at the direction of the court

One of the oldest remedies in equity is the court's appointment of a receiver, a disinterested person who collects and preserves the debtor's assets and income and disposes of them at the court's direction. The court may instruct the receiver (1) to liquidate the assets by public or private sale; (2) to operate the business as a going concern temporarily; or (3) to conserve the assets until final disposition of the matter before the court.

A receiver will be appointed on the petition (1) of a secured creditor seeking foreclosure of his security; (2) of a judgment creditor who has exhausted legal remedies to satisfy the judgment; or (3) of a shareholder of a corporate debtor whose assets will likely be dissipated by fraud or mismanagement. The receiver is always appointed at the discretion of the court. Insolvency, in the equity sense of the debtor's inability to pay her debts as they mature, is one of the factors the court considers in appointing a receiver.

CHAPTER SUMMARY

Federal Bankruptcy Law

Case Administration—Chapter 3	**Commencement of the Case** the filing of a voluntary or involuntary petition begins jurisdiction of the bankruptcy court ■ *Voluntary Petitions* available to any debtor even if solvent ■ *Involuntary Petitions* may be filed only under Chapter 7 or 11 if the debtor is generally not paying his debts as they become due **Automatic Stay** prevents attempts by creditors to recover claims against the debtor **Trustee** responsible for collecting, liquidating, and distributing the debtor's estate **Meeting of Creditors** debtor must appear and submit to an examination of her financial situation
Creditors, the Debtor, and the Estate—Chapter 5	**Creditor** any entity that has a claim against the debtor ■ *Claim* a right to payment ■ *Secured Claim* claim with a lien on property of the debtor ■ *Unsecured Claim* portion of a claim that exceeds the value of any property securing that claim ■ *Priority of Claim* the right of certain claims to be paid before claims of lesser rank **Debtors** ■ *Debtor's Duties* the debtor must file specified information, cooperate with the trustee, and surrender all property of the estate ■ *Debtor's Exemptions* determined by state or federal law, depending upon the state ■ *Discharge* relief from liability for all debts except those the Bankruptcy Code specifies as not dischargeable

The Estate all legal and equitable interests of a debtor in nonexempt property
- *Trustee as Lien Creditor* trustee gains the rights and powers of a creditor with a judicial lien (an interest in property, obtained by court action, to secure payment of a debt)
- *Voidable Preferences* Bankruptcy Code invalidates certain preferential transfers made before the date of bankruptcy from the debtor to favored creditors
- *Fraudulent Transfers* trustee may avoid fraudulent transfers made on or within one year before the date of bankruptcy
- *Statutory Liens* trustee may avoid statutory liens that first become effective on insolvency, are not perfected at commencement of the case, or are for rent

Liquidation— Chapter 7

Purpose to distribute equitably the debtor's nonexempt assets and usually to discharge all dischargeable debts of the debtor
Proceedings apply to most debtors
Distribution of the Estate in the following order: (1) secured creditors, (2) creditors entitled to a priority, (3) unsecured creditors, and (4) the debtor
Discharge granted by the court unless the debtor has committed an offense under the Bankruptcy Code or has received a discharge within six years

Reorganization— Chapter 11

Purpose to preserve a distressed entity and its value as a going concern
Proceedings debtor usually remains in possession of the property of the estate
Acceptance of Plan requires a specified proportion of creditors to approve the plan
Confirmation of Plan requires (1) good faith, (2) feasibility, (3) cash payments to certain creditors, and usually (4) acceptance by creditors
Effect of Reorganization binds the debtor and creditors and discharges the debtor

Adjustment of Debts of a Family Farmer— Chapter 12

Purpose to permit a family farmer to file a repayment plan that will discharge him from most debts
Proceedings available to a farmer who receives at least 50 percent of his income from farming and who meets certain debt limitations
Confirmation of Plan same as a Chapter 13 proceeding
Discharge after a debtor completes all payments under the plan

Adjustment of Debts of Individuals— Chapter 13

Purpose to permit an individual debtor to file a repayment plan that will discharge her from most debts
Confirmation of Plan requires (1) good faith, (2) that the value of property distributed to creditors not be less than the amount that would be paid them under Chapter 7, (3) that secured creditors accept the plan, and (4) that the debtor be able to make all payments and comply with the plan
Discharge after a debtor completes all payments under the plan

Creditors' Rights and Debtor's Relief Outside of Bankruptcy

Creditors' Rights	**Prejudgment Remedies** includes attachment and garnishment **Postjudgment Remedies** include writ of execution and garnishment

Debtor's Relief	**Compositions** agreement between debtor and two or more of her creditors that each will take a portion of his claim as full payment **Assignment for Benefit of Creditors** voluntary transfer by the debtor of some or all of his property to a trustee, who applies the property to the payment of all the debtor's debts **Statutory Assignment** provides a voluntary release of balance of claims from creditors who accept partial payments made by the trustee for the debtor **Equity Receivership** receiver is a disinterested person appointed by the court to collect and preserve the debtor's assets and income and to dispose of them at the direction of the court

QUESTIONS

1. List (a) the priorities of creditors' claims, (b) the debtor's exemptions, and (c) the debts that are not dischargeable in bankruptcy.
2. Discuss the rights of a trustee (a) as a lien creditor, (b) to avoid preferential transfers, (c) to avoid fraudulent transfers, and (d) to avoid statutory liens.
3. State the order in which the debtor's estate is distributed under Chapter 7.
4. Compare the adjustment of debt proceedings under Chapters 11, 12, and 13.

5. Identify and define the nonbankruptcy compromises between debtors and creditors.
Internet Question Using the American Bankruptcy Institute's site, find (a) the total number of bankruptcy filings, (b) the number of nonbusiness filings according to chapter of the Bankruptcy Code, and (c) the number of business filings.

PROBLEMS

1. (a) Benson goes into bankruptcy. His estate has no assets. Are Benson's taxes discharged by the proceedings? Why or why not?
   (b) Benson obtains property from Anderson on credit by representing that he is solvent when in fact he knows he is insolvent. Is Benson's debt to Anderson discharged by Benson's discharge in bankruptcy?
2. Bradley goes into bankruptcy owing $5,000 as wages to his four employees. There is enough in his estate to pay all costs of administration and enough to pay his employees, but nothing will be left for general creditors. Do the employees take all the estate? If so, under what conditions? If the general creditors received nothing at all, would these debts be discharged?

3. Jessica sold goods to Stacy for $2,500 and retained a security interest in them. Three months later, Stacy filed a petition in bankruptcy under Chapter 7. At this time, Stacy still owed Jessica $2,000 for the purchase price of the goods, whose value was $1,500.
   (a) May the trustee invalidate Jessica's security interest? If so, under what provision?
   (b) If the security interest is invalidated, what is Jessica's status in the bankruptcy proceeding?
   (c) If the security interest is *not* invalidated, what is Jessica's status in the bankruptcy proceeding?
4. A debtor went through bankruptcy and received his discharge. Which of the following debts were completely discharged, and which remain as future debts against him?

(a) A claim of $900 for wages earned within three months immediately prior to bankruptcy.

(b) A judgment of $3,000 against the debtor for breach of contract.

(c) Sales taxes of $1,800.

(d) $1,000 in past alimony and support money owed to his divorced wife for herself and their child.

(e) A judgment of $4,000 for injuries received because of the debtor's negligent operation of an automobile.

5. Rosinoff and his wife, who were business partners, entered bankruptcy. A creditor, Baldwin, objected to their discharge in bankruptcy on the grounds that

(a) the partners had obtained credit from Baldwin on the basis of a false financial statement;

(b) the partners had failed to keep books of account and records from which their financial condition could be determined; and

(c) Rosinoff had falsely sworn that he had taken $70 from the partnership account when he had actually taken $700.

Were the debtors entitled to a discharge?

6. X Corporation is a debtor in a reorganization proceeding under Chapter 11 of the Bankruptcy Code. By fair and proper valuation, its assets are worth $100,000. The indebtedness of the corporation is $105,000, and it has outstanding preferred stock of par value of $20,000 and common stock of par value of $75,000. The plan of reorganization submitted by the trustees would eliminate the common shareholders and give bonds of the face amount of $5,000 to the creditors and common stock in the ratio of 84 percent to the creditors and 16 percent to the preferred shareholders. Should this plan be confirmed?

7. Alex is a wage earner with a regular income. He has unsecured debts of $42,000 and secured debts owing to Betty, Connie, David, and Eunice totaling $120,000. Eunice's debt is secured only by a mortgage on Alex's house. Alex files a petition under Chapter 13 and a plan providing payment as follows: (a) 60 percent of all taxes owed, (b) 35 percent of all unsecured debts, and (c) $100,000 in total to Betty, Connie, David, and Eunice. Should the court confirm the plan? If not, how must the plan be modified or what other conditions must be satisfied?

8. John Bunker has assets of $130,000 and liabilities of $185,000 owed to nine creditors. Nonetheless, his cash flow is positive and he is making payment on all of his obligations as they become due. I. M. Flintheart, who is owed $22,000 by Bunker, files an involuntary petition in bankruptcy against Bunker. Bunker contests the petition. Decision?

9. Karen has filed a petition for a Chapter 7 proceeding. The total value of Karen's estate is $35,000. Ben, who is owed $18,000, has a security interest in property valued at $12,000. Lauren has an unsecured claim of $9,000, which is entitled to a priority of $2,000. The United States has a claim for income taxes of $7,000. Steve has an unsecured claim of $10,000 that was filed on time. Sarah has an unsecured claim of $17,000 that was filed on time. Wally has a claim of $14,000 that he filed late, even though Wally was aware of the bankruptcy proceedings. What should each of the creditors receive in a distribution under Chapter 7?

10. Landmark at Plaza Park, Ltd., filed a plan of reorganization under Chapter 11 of the Bankruptcy Code. Landmark is a limited partnership whose only substantial asset is a 200-unit garden apartment complex. City Federal holds the first mortgage on the property in the face amount of $2,250,000. The mortgage bears an interest rate of 9.5 percent and is due and payable on October 1, 1986.

Landmark has proposed a plan of reorganization under which the property now in possession of City Federal would be returned. Landmark will then deliver a nonrecourse note, payable in three years, in the face amount of $2,705,820.31 to City Federal in substitution of all of the partnership's existing liabilities. On the sixteenth month through the thirty-sixth month after the effective date of the plan, Landmark will make monthly interest payments at a rate of 12.5 percent computed on a property value of $2,260,000. Finally, the note will be secured by the existing mortgage. Landmark's theory is that the note will be paid off at the end of thirty-six months by a combination of refinancing and accumulation of cash from the project. The key is Landmark's proposal to obtain a new first mortgage in three years in the face amount of $2,400,000.

City Federal is a first mortgagee without recourse that has been collecting rents pursuant to a rent assignment agreement since the default on the mortgage in December of 1979, eleven months ago. City Federal is impaired by the plan, has rejected the plan, and seeks to complete its foreclosure action. Decision?

11. Freelin Conn filed a voluntary petition under Chapter 7 of the Bankruptcy Code on September 30, 1980. Conn listed BancOhio National Bank as having a claim incurred in October of 1979 in the amount of $4,000 secured by a 1978 Oldsmobile Omega. The car is listed as having a market value of $3,500. During the period from June 30, 1980, to September 30, 1980, Conn made three payments totaling $439.17 to BancOhio. The net payoff balance on the installment loan was $4,015.91 on September 30, the date on which the bankruptcy petition was filed. The trustee in bankruptcy now seeks to set aside those three payments as voidable preferences. Decision?

12. On March 6, 1985, the debtor negotiated a loan with Interfirst Bank of Dallas (the Bank) and signed a

promissory note for the purchase of a BMW from Howard Thornton Ford for his daughter. The daughter picked up the car on March 8, 1985, but the Bank did not perfect the purchase money security interest until March 19, 1985, which was within the twenty-day limit for perfecting a purchase money security interest under Texas law. On May 23, 1985, the debtor filed a bankruptcy petition, and on August 25, 1985, the Bank repossessed the daughter's BMW. The bankruptcy trustee sought recovery of the BMW as an asset of the estate, arguing that the transfer of the collateral (the BMW) to the Bank was a voidable preference under the Bankruptcy Code because the Bank's security interest in the car was not perfected within the ten-day grace period then required by the Bankruptcy Code. The bankruptcy court held for the trustee, and the district court affirmed. The Bank appealed. Decision?

PART X

Regulation of Business

827

CHAPTER 42

Securities Regulation

The primary purpose of federal securities regulation is to prevent fraudulent practices in the sale of securities and thereby to foster public confidence in the securities market. Federal securities law consists principally of two statutes: the Securities Act of 1933, which focuses on the issuance of securities, and the Securities Exchange Act of 1934, which deals mainly with trading in issued securities. These "secondary" transactions greatly exceed in number and dollar value the original offerings by issuers.

Both statutes are administered by the Securities and Exchange Commission (SEC), an independent, quasi-judicial agency consisting of five commissioners. The SEC has the power to seek civil injunctions in a federal district court against violation of the statutes, to recommend that the Justice Department bring criminal prosecutions, and to issue orders censuring, suspending, or expelling broker-dealers, investment advisers, and investment companies. The Securities Enforcement Remedies and Penny Stock Reform Act of 1990 granted the SEC the power to issue cease-and-desist orders and to impose administrative, civil penalties up to $550,000. Congress enacted the Private Securities Litigation Reform Act of 1995 (Reform Act) to amend both the 1933 Act and the 1934 Act. One of its provisions grants authority to the SEC to bring civil actions for specified violations of the 1934 Act against aiders and abettors (those who knowingly provide substantial assistance to a person who violates the statute).

The 1933 Act has two basic objectives: (1) to provide investors with material information concerning securities offered for sale to the public and (2) to prohibit misrepresentation, deceit, and other fraudulent acts and practices in the sale of securities generally, whether they are required to be registered or not.

The 1934 Act extends protection to investors trading in securities that are already issued and outstanding. The 1934 Act also imposes disclosure requirements on publicly held corporations and regulates tender offers and proxy solicitations.

Effective October 6, 1995, the SEC provided interpretative guidance for the use of electronic media for the delivery of information required by the federal securities laws. The SEC defined electronic media to include audiotapes, videotapes, facsimiles, CD-ROM, electronic mail, bulletin boards, Internet Web sites, and computer networks. Basically, electronic delivery must provide notice, access, and evidence of delivery comparable to that provided by paper delivery.

In addition to the federal laws regulating the sale of securities, each state has its own laws regulating such sales within its borders. Commonly called Blue Sky laws, these statutes all have provisions prohibiting fraud in the sale of securities. In addition, most states require the registration of securities and also regulate brokers and dealers.

Any person who sells securities must comply with the federal securities laws as well as with the securities laws of each state in which he intends to offer his securities. However, in 1996 Congress enacted the National Securities Markets Improvements Act, which preempted state regulation of the offerings of certain securities. Because state securities laws vary greatly, we will discuss only the 1933 Act and the 1934 Act in this chapter.

THE SECURITIES ACT OF 1933

The 1933 Act, also called the "Truth in Securities Act," requires that a registration statement be filed with the SEC and that it become effective before any securities may be offered for sale to the public, unless either the transaction in which the securities are offered or the securities themselves are exempt from registration. The purpose of registration is to disclose financial and other information about the issuer and those who control it, so that potential investors may consider the merits of the securities. The 1933 Act also requires that potential investors be furnished with a *prospectus* (a document offering the securities for sale to interested buyers) containing the important data set forth in the registration statement. The 1933 act prohibits fraud in *all* sales of securities involving interstate commerce or the mails, even if the securities are exempt from the 1933 Act's registration and disclosure requirements. Civil and criminal liability may be imposed for violations of the 1933 Act.

The National Securities Markets Improvements Act of 1996 broadly authorized the SEC to issue regulations or rules exempting any person, security, or transaction from any of the provisions of the 1933 Act or the SEC's rules promulgated under that act. This authorization extends so far as such exemption is necessary or appropriate in the public interest and is consistent with the protection of investors.

DEFINITION OF A SECURITY

The 1933 Act defines the term **security** to include any note, stock, bond, debenture, evidence of indebtedness, preorganization certificate or subscription, investment contract, voting-trust certificate, fractional undivided interest in oil, gas, or other mineral rights, or, in general, any interest or instrument commonly known as a security. This definition broadly includes the many types of instruments that fall within the ordinary concept of a security. Furthermore, the courts generally have interpreted the statutory definition to include nontraditional forms of investments. The Supreme Court, more specifically, employs a two-tier analysis to identify securities. Under this analysis, the Court will presumptively treat as a security a financial instrument designated as a note, stock, bond, or other instrument specifically named in the act.

On the other hand, if a financial transaction lacks the traditional characteristics of an instrument specifically named in the act, the Court has used a three-part test, derived from *Securities and Exchange Commission v. W.J. Howey Co.*, to determine whether that financial transaction constitutes an investment contract and thus a security. Under the *Howey* test, a financial instrument or transaction constitutes an **investment contract** if it involves (1) an investment in a common venture (2) premised on a reasonable expectation of profit (3) to be derived from the entrepreneurial or managerial efforts of others. In certain circumstances, investments

Security includes any note, stock, bond, preorganization subscription, and investment contract

Investment contract any investment of money or property made in expectation of receiving a financial return solely from the efforts of others in limited partnership interests, citrus groves, whiskey warehouse receipts, real estate condominiums, cattle, franchises, and pyramid schemes have been held to be securities under this test.

REVES v. ERNST & YOUNG Supreme Court of the United States, 1990, 494 U.S. 56, 110 S.Ct. 945, 108 L.Ed.2d 47

FACTS In order to raise money to support its business, the Farmer's Cooperative of Arkansas and Oklahoma (the Co-Op) sold promissory notes payable on demand by the holder. The notes were uncollateralized and uninsured, but they paid a variable interest rate, adjusted monthly. In offering the notes to members and nonmembers as part of an "Investment Program," the Co-Op advertised the notes in newsletters by stating, "YOUR CO-OP has more than $11,000,000 in assets to stand behind your investments. The investment is not Federal [sic] insured but is . . . Safe . . . Secure and available when you need it." In 1984, the Co-Op filed for bankruptcy. At that time, 1,600 people held notes worth a total of $10 million. A class of holders (plaintiffs) filed suit against Arthur Young & Co. (Young), the firm that audited the Co-Op's financial statements (and the predecessor to Ernst & Young). The plaintiffs alleged that Young intentionally failed to follow generally accepted accounting principles in its audit and that it did so in an effort to inflate the Co-Op's assets and net worth. Specifically, the plaintiffs claimed that Young overvalued the Co-Op's gasohol plant, a major asset, and that if Young had treated the plant properly in its audit, they would not have purchased the demand notes. On these grounds, the plaintiffs argued that Young had violated the antifraud provisions of the Securities Exchange Act of 1934.

The plaintiffs won at trial and were awarded $6.1 million. On appeal, Young argued that the demand notes were not securities under the 1934 Act. The Court of Appeals reversed, and the plaintiffs appealed.

DECISION Judgment of the Court of Appeals reversed and remanded.

OPINION Congress's purpose for enacting securities laws was to eliminate serious abuses in a largely unregulated securities market. To this end, Congress determined that the best way to protect investors was to define the term "security" in sufficiently broad and general terms. We have consistently held that the definition of a security under both the 1993 and 1934 Acts is broad enough to encompass virtually any instrument that might be sold as an investment. Congress did not, however, intend to provide a broad federal remedy for all fraud, and left the SEC and the federal courts to decide which financial transactions the acts cover. We must, then, analyze the economic realities of a transaction to determine if the federal securities acts apply.

Since the acts define "security" to include "any note," every note is presumed to be a security; but this presumption may be rebutted under the following standards: First, we must examine the motivations that prompted the seller and buyer to enter into the transaction. If the seller's purpose were to raise money for the general use of a business enterprise or to finance substantial investments and the buyer were interested in the expected profit from the note, then the instrument would likely be a "security." If, on the other hand, the note were exchanged to facilitate the purchase and sale of a minor asset or consumer good, to correct for the seller's cash-flow problems, or to advance some other commercial purpose, the note would likely not be a "security." Second, we must examine the "plan of distribution" of the instrument to see if such plan represents an investment in which there is "common trading for speculation or investment." Third, we must examine the reasonable expectations of the investing public. Finally, we must consider whether any factor, such as the presence of another regulatory scheme that reduces the risk of the instrument, renders the application of the securities acts unnecessary.

Under this four-part test, the notes in this case are "securities." The Co-Op sold the notes in an effort to raise capital for its business operations, and the purchasers bought the notes in order to earn a profit in the form of interest. Although the notes were not sold on an exchange, the "plan of distribution" covered a broad segment of the public, and that is sufficient to establish "common trading." The advertisements characterized the notes as an "investment," and nothing would have led a reasonable person to question that characterization. Furthermore, there are no risk-reducing factors to suggest that these uncollateralized and uninsured instruments are not securities. Unlike certificates of deposit, which are insured by the Federal Deposit Insurance Corporation and regulated by federal banking laws, and unlike pension plans, which are regulated by federal law, the notes in this case would escape federal regulation entirely if the securities acts were held not to apply.

INTERPRETATION In determining whether a financial transaction is a security, the courts examine the economic realities of the transaction.

REGISTRATION OF SECURITIES

The 1933 Act prohibits the offer or sale of any security through the use of the mails or any means of interstate commerce unless a registration statement for that security is in effect or the issuer secures an exemption from registration. The purpose of registration is to adequately and accurately disclose financial and other information on which investors may judge the merits of securities. However, registration does not insure investors against loss—the SEC does *not* judge the financial merits of any security. Moreover, the SEC does *not* guarantee the accuracy of the information presented in the registration statement.

Registration of securities disclosure of accurate material information required in all public offerings of nonexempt securities unless offering is an exempt transaction

Disclosure Requirements

In general, registration calls for disclosure of information such as (1) a description of the registrant's properties and business, (2) a description of the significant provisions of the security to be offered for sale and its relationship to the registrant's other capital securities, (3) information about the management of the registrant, and (4) financial statements certified by independent public accountants. In 1992, the SEC imposed new disclosure requirements regarding compensation paid to senior executives and directors. The registration statement must be signed by the issuer, its chief executive officer, its chief financial officer, its chief accounting officer, and a majority of its board of directors.

A registration statement and prospectus become public immediately on filing with the SEC. The effective date of a registration statement is the twentieth day after filing, although the commission, at its discretion, may advance the effective date or require an amendment to the filing, which will begin a new twenty-day period.

Before the filing of the registration statement, it is unlawful to sell, offer to sell, or offer to buy the securities; after the filing, the issuer still may not lawfully sell the securities until the effective date. Nevertheless, before filing, the issuer may give notice that it proposes to make a public offer. Furthermore, after the filing but before the statement's effective date, the issuer may *offer* the securities (1) orally; (2) by certain summaries of the information in the registration statement, as permitted by SEC rules; (3) by a "tombstone advertisement" that identifies the security, its price, and by whom orders will be executed; or (4) by a preliminary prospectus, called a "red herring," which may contain substantially the same information as a final prospectus but which must have a legend in red ink stating that the registration statement has not become effective. After the effective date, the issuer may make sales, provided the purchaser has received a final prospectus. See Figure 42–1.

Integrated Disclosure

The disclosure system under the 1933 Act developed independently of that required by the 1934 Act, which we will discuss later in this chapter. As a result, issuers subject to both statutes were compelled to provide duplicative or overlapping disclosure. Then, in 1982, the SEC, in an effort to reduce or eliminate unnecessary duplication of corporate reporting, adopted an integrated system that provides for three levels of disclosure, depending on the issuer's reporting history and market following. All issuers may use the detailed form described previously. Corporations that have reported continuously under the 1934 Act for at least three years are permitted to disclose less detailed information in the 1933 Act registration statement and to incorporate some information by reference to

FIGURE 42-1 Permissible Sales Activities

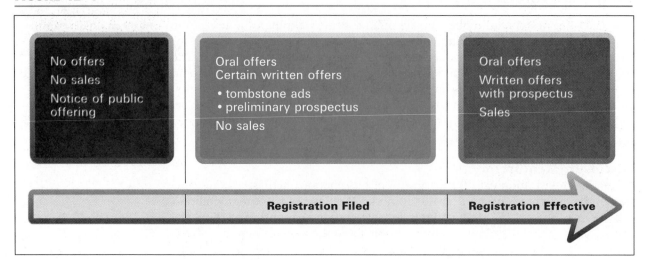

reports filed under the 1934 Act. Those corporations that have filed continuously under the 1934 Act for at least one year and that have a minimum market value of publicly held voting stock of $75 million are permitted to disclose even less detail in the 1933 Act registration and to incorporate even more information by reference to 1934 Act reports.

In 1992, the SEC issued new rules establishing an integrated registration and reporting system for small business issuers. These rules are intended to facilitate access to the public financial markets for start-up and developing companies and to reduce costs for small business issuers wishing to have their securities traded in public markets. The rules define a small business issuer as a noninvestment company whose annual revenues total less than $25 million and whose voting stock has a market value of less than $25 million.

Shelf Registrations

Shelf registrations permit certain qualified issuers to register securities that are to be offered and sold "off the shelf" on a delayed or continuous basis in the future. The information in the original registration must be kept accurate and current and the issuer must reasonably expect that the securities will be sold within two years of the effective date of the registration. Only companies eligible to use the shortest form of registration qualify for shelf registrations.

EXEMPT SECURITIES

Exempt security security not subject to registration requirements of the 1933 Act

The 1933 Act exempts a number of specific securities (called **exempt securities**) from its registration requirements. Because these exemptions apply to the securities themselves, they also may be resold without registration.

Short-Term Commercial Paper

The act exempts any note, draft, or bankers' acceptance (a draft accepted by a bank), issued for working capital, that has a maturity of not more than nine months when issued. This exemption is not available, however, if the proceeds are to be used for permanent purposes, such as the acquisition of a plant, or if the paper is of a type not ordinarily purchased by the general public.

Other Exempt Securities

The 1933 Act also exempts the following kinds of securities from registration: (1) securities issued or guaranteed by domestic governmental organizations, such as municipal bonds; (2) securities of domestic banks and savings and loan associations; (3) securities of nonprofit charitable organizations; (4) certain securities issued by federally regulated common carriers; and (5) insurance policies and annuity contracts issued by state-regulated insurance companies. In addition, the Bankruptcy Code exempts securities issued by a debtor under a reorganization plan in exchange for a claim or interest in the debtor.

EXEMPT TRANSACTIONS FOR ISSUERS

In addition to exempting specific types of securities, the 1933 Act also exempts *issuers* from the registration requirements for certain kinds of transactions. These **exempt transactions** include (1) private placements (Rule 506), (2) limited offers not exceeding $5 million (Rule 505), (3) limited offers not exceeding $1 million (Rule 504), and (4) limited offers solely to accredited investors (Section 4(6)). Except for Rule 504, these registration exemptions apply only to the transaction in which the securities are issued; therefore, any resale must be made by registration, unless the resale qualifies as an exempt transaction.

Exempt transaction issuance of securities not subject to the registration requirements of the 1933 Act

In addition, the 1933 Act identifies a number of securities exemptions that are in effect transaction exemptions. These include intrastate issues, exchanges between an issuer and its security holders, and reorganization securities issued and exchanged with court or other governmental approval. These exemptions apply only to the original issuance, and resales may be made only by registration, unless the resale qualifies as an exempt transaction.

Another transaction exemption is Regulation A, which permits an issuer to sell a limited amount of securities in an unregistered public offering, if certain conditions are met. Unlike other transaction exemptions, Regulation A places no restrictions upon the resale of securities issued pursuant to it.

Figure 42–2 illustrates registration and exemptions from registration under the 1933 Act.

Limited Offers

The 1933 Act exempts, or authorizes the SEC to exempt, transactions that do not require the protection of registration because they either involve a small amount of money or are made in a limited manner. Promulgated in 1982 to simplify and clarify the transaction exemptions relating to small issues and small issuers, *Regulation D* contains three separate exemptions (Rules 504, 505, and 506), each involving limited offers. Section 4(6), also aimed at small issues, is a companion section to the exemptions under Regulation D.

Securities sold pursuant to these exemptions (with the exception of those sold pursuant to Rule 504) are considered **restricted securities** and may be resold only by registration or in another transaction exempt from registration. An issuer who uses these exemptions must take reasonable care to prevent nonexempt, unregistered resales of restricted securities. Reasonable care includes, but is not limited to, the following: (a) making a reasonable inquiry to determine if the purchaser is acquiring the securities for herself or for other persons; (b) providing written disclosure, prior to the sale to each purchaser, that the securities have not been registered and therefore cannot be resold unless they are registered or unless an exemption from registration is available; and (c) placing a legend on

Restricted securities securities issued under an exempt transaction and subject to resale restrictions

FIGURE 42–2 Registration and Exemptions Under the 1933 Act

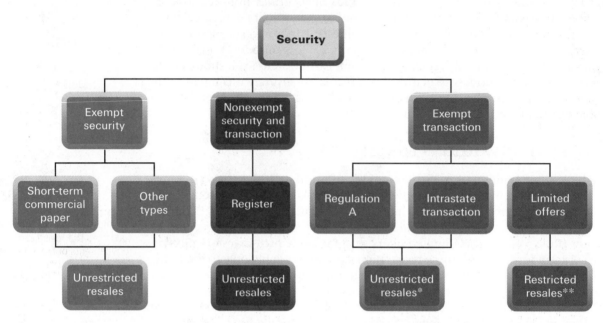

* Under intrastate exemption, resales to nonresidents may only be made nine months after the last sale in the initial issuance.
** Except under Rule 504.

the securities certificate stating that the securities have not been registered and that they are restricted securities.

Private Placements The most important transaction exemption for issuers is the so-called private placement provision of the act, which exempts "transactions by an issuer not involving any public offering." SEC **Rule 506** establishes a nonexclusive safe harbor for limited offers and sales without regard to the dollar amount of the offering. Satisfying the rule assures the exemption, but there is no presumption that the exemption is unavailable for transactions that do not comply with the rule.

Securities sold under this exemption are restricted securities and may be resold only by registration or in a transaction exempt from registration. General advertising or solicitation is not permitted. The issue may be purchased by an unlimited number of "accredited investors" and by no more than thirty-five other purchasers. **Accredited investors** include banks, insurance companies, investment companies, executive officers or directors of the issuer, savings and loan associations, registered broker-dealers, certain employee benefit plans with total assets in excess of $5 million, any person whose net worth exceeds $1 million, and any person whose income exceeded $200,000 in each of the two preceding years and who reasonably expects an income in excess of $200,000 in the current year. If the sale involves any nonaccredited investors, the issuer must, before the sale, give such purchasers specified material information about the issuer, its business, and the securities being offered. If all the purchasers are accredited investors, such disclosure is not mandatory. The issuer must reasonably believe that each purchaser who is not an accredited investor has sufficient knowledge and experience in financial and business matters to evaluate the merits and risks of the investment or has the services of a representative who possesses such knowledge and experience. The issuer must notify the SEC of sales made under the exemption and must take precautions against nonexempt, unregistered resales.

Limited Offers Not Exceeding $5 Million SEC **Rule 505** exempts from registration those offerings by noninvestment company issuers that do not exceed $5 million over twelve months. Securities sold under this exemption are restricted securities and may be resold only by registration or in a transaction exempt from registration. General advertising or general solicitation is not permitted. The issue may be purchased by an unlimited number of accredited investors and by no more than thirty-five other purchasers. If the sale involves any nonaccredited investors, the issuer must, before the sale, give them specified material information about the issuer, its business, and the securities being offered; otherwise, such disclosure is not required. Unlike the issuer under Rule 506, however, the issuer under Rule 505 is *not* required to believe reasonably that each nonaccredited investor, either alone or with his representative, has sufficient knowledge and experience in financial matters to be capable of evaluating the investment's merits and risks. As under Rule 506, the issuer must take precautions against nonexempt, unregistered resales and must notify the SEC of sales made under the exemption.

Limited Offers Not Exceeding $1 Million As amended in 1992, SEC **Rule 504** provides private, noninvestment company issuers with an unconditional exemption from registration for small issues not exceeding $1 million within twelve months. (Issuers required to report under the 1934 Act and investment companies may not use Rule 504.) The issuer is to notify the SEC of sales under the rule, which permits sales to an unlimited number of investors and does not require the issuer to furnish any information to them. The exemption does not forbid general solicitations, and acquired shares are freely transferable.

Limited Offers Solely to Accredited Investors In 1980, Congress added **Section 4(6)**, which provides an exemption for offers and sales, not in excess of $5 million, made by an issuer *solely* to accredited investors. General advertising or public solicitation is not permitted. As with Rules 505 and 506, an unlimited number of accredited investors may purchase the issue; however, Section 4(6) allows *no* unaccredited investors to purchase. No information is required to be furnished to the purchasers. Securities sold under this exemption are restricted securities and may be resold only by registration or in a transaction exempt from registration. The issuer must notify the SEC of sales made under the exemption and must take precautions against nonexempt, unregistered resales.

Regulation A

As amended in 1992, Regulation A permits an issuer to offer up to $5 million of securities in any twelve-month period without registering them, provided that the issuer files an offering statement with the SEC's regional office prior to the sale of the securities. An offering circular must also be provided to offerees and purchasers. The issuer may make offers upon filing the offering statement but may make sales only after the SEC has qualified it. (Issuers required to report under the 1934 Act and investment companies may not use Regulation A.)

Regulation A filings are less detailed and time-consuming than full registration statements, and the required financial statements are simpler and need not be audited unless the issuer is a reporting company under the 1934 Act. Issuers now may use an optional, simplified question-and-answer disclosure document.

Regulation A sets no restrictions regarding the number or qualifications of investors who may purchase securities under its provisions. Furthermore, securities sold under Regulation A may be resold freely after they are issued.

Intrastate Issues

The 1933 Act also exempts from registration any security that is a part of an issue offered and sold *only* to persons who live in a single state where the issuer of such security is resident and doing business. This exemption is intended to apply to local issues representing local financing carried out by local persons through local investments. The exemption does not apply if *any* offeree, who need not become a purchaser, is not a resident of the state in which the issuer is resident.

Rule 147, promulgated by the SEC, provides a nonexclusive safe harbor for securing the intrastate exemption. While satisfying the rule assures the exemption, the exemption is not presumed to be unavailable for transactions that do not comply with the rule. Rule 147 requires that (1) the issuer be incorporated or organized in the state in which the issuance occurs; (2) the issuer be doing business principally in that state, meaning that the issuer must derive 80 percent of its gross revenues from that state, 80 percent of its assets must be located in that state, and it must use 80 percent of the net proceeds from the issue in that state; (3) all of the *offerees* and purchasers be residents of that state; (4) no resales to nonresidents be made during the period of sale and for nine months after the last sale; and (5) the issuer take precautions against interstate distributions. Such precautions include (a) placing on the security certificate a legend stating that the securities have not been registered and that resales can be made only to residents of the state and (b) obtaining a written statement of residence from each purchaser.

Figure 42–3 summarizes transactions that are exempt for issuers.

EXEMPT TRANSACTIONS FOR NON-ISSUERS

Exempt transactions for non-issuers resales by persons other than the issuer that are exempted from the registration requirements of the 1933 Act

Affiliate person who controls, is controlled by, or is under common control with the issuer

Control the direct or indirect possession of the power to direct the management and policies of a person through ownership of securities, by contract, or otherwise

The 1933 Act requires registration for any sale by *any* person (including non-issuers) of any nonexempt security, unless a statutory exemption can be found for the transaction. The act, however, provides a transaction exemption for any person other than an issuer, underwriter, or dealer. In addition, the act exempts most transactions by dealers and brokers. These three provisions exempt from the registration requirements of the 1933 Act most secondary transactions; that is, the numerous resales that occur on an exchange or in the over-the-counter market. Nevertheless, these exemptions do not extend to some situations involving resales by non-issuers, in particular to (1) resales of restricted securities acquired under Regulation D (Rules 506, 505, or 504) or Section 4(6) and (2) sales of restricted *or* nonrestricted securities by affiliates. Such sales must be made pursuant to registration, Rule 144, or Regulation A, subject to the limited exception provided some issuances under Rule 504. An **affiliate** is a person who controls, is controlled by, or is under common control with the issuer. **Control** is the direct or indirect possession of the power to direct the management and policies of a person through ownership of securities, by contract, or otherwise.

FIGURE 42–3 Exempt Transactions for Issuers Under the 1933 Act

Exemption	Price Limitation	Information Required	Limitations on Purchasers	Resales
Regulation A	$5 million	offering circular	none	unrestricted
Intrastate Rule 147	none	none	intrastate only	only to residents before 9 months
Rule 506	none	material information to unaccredited purchasers	unlimited accredited; 35 unaccredited	restricted
Rule 505	$5 million	material information to unaccredited purchasers	unlimited accredited; 35 unaccredited	restricted
Rule 504	$1 million	none	none	unrestricted
Section 4(6)	$5 million	none	only accredited	restricted

Rule 144

Rule 144 of the SEC sets forth conditions that, if met by an affiliate or by any person selling restricted securities, exempt her from registering such securities. The rule requires that there be adequate current public information about the issuer, that the person selling under the rule have owned the securities for at least two years, that she sell them only in limited amounts in unsolicited brokers' transactions, and that notice of the sale be provided to the SEC. A person who is *not* an affiliate of the issuer when the restricted securities are sold and who has owned the securities for at least three years, however, may sell them in unlimited amounts and is not subject to *any* of the other requirements of Rule 144. Sales by an affiliate are subject to Rule 144 whether the securities are restricted or nonrestricted; however, compliance with the two-year holding period is not required when an affiliate sells *nonrestricted* securities.

Regulation A

Regulation A, in addition to providing issuers an exemption from registration for securities up to $5 million, also provides an exemption for non-issuers. The regulation places a $1.5 million limit on the total amount of securities sold by all non-issuers in any twelve-month period. Use of this exemption requires compliance with all of the conditions Regulation A imposes upon issuers, as discussed previously.

LIABILITY

To implement its objectives of providing full disclosure and preventing fraud in the sale of securities, the 1933 Act imposes a number of sanctions for noncompliance with its requirements. These sanctions include administrative remedies by the SEC, civil liability to injured investors, and criminal penalties. In addition, the court may award attorneys' fees against any party who brings suit or asserts a defense without merit.

The Reform Act provides "forward-looking" statements (predictions) a "safe harbor" from civil liability under the 1933 Act that is based on an untrue statement of material fact or an omission of a material fact necessary to make the statement not misleading. The safe harbor applies only to issuers required to report under the 1934 Act. The safe harbor eliminates civil liability if a forward looking statement is (1) immaterial, *or* (2) made without actual knowledge that it was false or misleading, *or* (3) identified as a forward-looking statement and is accompanied by meaningful cautionary statements identifying important factors that could cause actual results to differ materially from those predicted. "Forward-looking" statements include projections of revenues, income, earnings per share, capital expenditures, dividends, or capital structure; management's plans and objectives for future operations; and statements of future economic performance. The safe harbor provision, however, does not cover statements made in connection with an initial public offering, a tender offer, a going private transaction, or offerings by a partnership or a limited liability company.

Unregistered Sales

Unregistered sales absolute civil liability is imposed as there are no defenses

Section 12(1) of the act imposes express civil liability for the sale of an unregistered security that is required to be registered, the sale of a registered security without delivery of a prospectus, the sale of a security by use of an outdated prospectus, or the offer of a sale before the filing of the registration statement. Liability is strict or absolute, as there are no defenses. The person who purchases a security sold in violation of this provision has the right to tender it back to the seller and recover the purchase price. If the purchaser no longer owns the security, he may recover monetary damages from the seller.

False Registration Statements

False registration statements liability is imposed on the issuer, all persons who signed the statement, every director or partner, experts who prepared or certified any part of the statement, and all underwriters; defendants other than issuer may assert the defense of due diligence

When securities have been sold subject to a registration statement, Section 11 of the act imposes express liability on those who have included any untrue statement of a material fact in the registration statement or who have omitted any material fact from it. **Material** matters are those to which a reasonable investor would be substantially likely to attach importance in determining whether to purchase the security registered. Usually, proof of reliance upon the misstatement or omission is not required. The section imposes liability on (1) the issuer; (2) all persons who signed the registration statement, including the principal executive officer, principal financial officer, and principal accounting officer; (3) every person who was a director or partner; (4) every accountant, engineer, appraiser, or expert who prepared or certified any part of the registration statement; and (5) all underwriters. These persons are jointly and severally liable for the amount paid for the security, less either its value at the time of suit or the price for which it was sold, to any person who acquires the security without knowledge of the untruth or omission.

Material matters to which a reasonable investor would attach importance in deciding whether to purchase a security

Due diligence defense defense to liability for false registration statements available to defendants who had a reasonable (nonnegligent) belief that there were no untrue statements and no material omissions

An expert is liable only for misstatements or omissions in the portion of the registration that she prepared or certified. Moreover, any defendant, other than the issuer (who has strict liability), may assert the defense of due diligence. The **due diligence defense** generally requires the defendant to show that he had reasonable grounds to believe and did believe that there were no untrue statements or material omissions. In some instances, due diligence requires a reasonable investigation to determine grounds for belief. The standard of reasonableness for such investigation and such grounds is that required of a prudent person in the management of his or her own property.

ESCOTT v. BARCHRIS CONST. CORP. United States District Court, Southern District of New York, 1968, 283 F.Supp. 643

FACTS BarChris Construction Corporation sold shares of common stock to the public in December 1959. By early 1961, BarChris needed additional working capital and sold debentures to meet this need. A registration statement was filed with the SEC in March 1961, with amendments filed in May. By the time BarChris received the net proceeds of this sale, it was experiencing financial difficulties. Eventually BarChris filed for bankruptcy. Escott, a purchaser of the debentures, brought suit under the Securities Act of 1933 against BarChris, the underwriters, the company's auditors (Peat, Marwick, Mitchell & Co.), and the persons who signed the registration, alleging that the registration statement contained materially false statements and material omissions. The defendants denied the falsity of the statements and their materiality. Furthermore, all of the defendants, except BarChris, claimed that they individually had exercised due diligence in connection with the statement so as to be free from liability under the statute.

DECISION Judgment for Escott granted.

OPINION The registration statement contained a number of false statements and omissions, many of which were material. Although the 1933 Act does provide a "due diligence" defense to all defendants other

than the issuer, BarChris, none of them sustained the burden of proving this defense. A nonexpert (the defendants other than the auditor) is not liable for material misstatements or omissions in a registration statement not based on an expert's authority if the nonexpert made a reasonable investigation from which he had reasonable grounds to believe the statements were true. A nonexpert is not liable for material misstatements or omissions made on the authority of an expert if the nonexpert had reasonable grounds to believe and did believe they were true. The due diligence defense for an expert, such as the auditors, requires reasonable grounds to believe that there were no material misstatements or omissions based upon a reasonable investigation. The standard of reasonableness is that of a prudent person in the management of his or her own property.

INTERPRETATION The 1933 Act imposes liability for material misstatements and omissions in a registration statement on the issuer, the directors, certain officers, experts, and the underwriters. These parties, except the issuer, may avoid liability by proving that they exercised due diligence in executing their duties with respect to the registration process.

Antifraud Provisions

The 1933 Act also contains two antifraud provisions: Section 12(2) and Section 17(a). In addition, Rule 10b-5 of the *1934 Act* applies to the issuance or sale of all securities, even those exempted by the 1933 Act. Rule 10b-5 is discussed later in this chapter.

Section 12(2) imposes express liability on any person who offers or sells a security by means of a prospectus or oral communication that contains an untrue statement of material fact or omits a material fact. This liability extends only to the immediate purchaser, provided she did not know of the untruth or omission. The seller may avoid liability by proving that he did not know, and in the exercise of reasonable care could not have known, of the untrue statement or omission. The seller is liable to the purchaser for the amount paid on tender of the security. If the purchaser no longer owns the security, she may recover damages from the seller.

Section 17(a) makes it unlawful for any person in the offer or sale of any securities, whether registered or not, to do any of the following when using any means of transportation or communication in interstate commerce or the mails: (1) employ any device, scheme, or artifice to defraud; (2) obtain money or property by means of any untrue statement of a material fact or any statement that omits a material fact, without which the information is misleading; or (3) engage in any transaction, practice, or course of business that operates or would operate as a fraud or deceit upon the purchaser. There is some doubt whether the courts may imply a private right of action for persons injured by violations of this section. The Supreme Court has reserved this question and the lower courts are

Section 12(2) liability is imposed upon the seller to the immediate purchaser, provided the purchaser did not know of the untruth or omission; the seller is not liable if he did not know, and in the exercise of reasonable care could not have known, of the untrue statement or omission

divided on the issue. The SEC may, however, bring enforcement actions under Section 17(a).

Criminal Sanctions

Criminal sanctions
willful violations are subject to a fine of not more than $10,000 and/or imprisonment of not more than five years

The 1933 Act imposes **criminal sanctions** on any person who willfully violates any of the provisions of the act or the rules and regulations promulgated by the SEC pursuant to the act. Conviction may carry a fine of not more than $10,000 or imprisonment of not more than five years, or both.

The registration and liability provisions of the 1933 Act are summarized in Figure 42–4.

THE SECURITIES EXCHANGE ACT OF 1934

The Securities Exchange Act of 1934 deals mainly with the secondary distribution (resale) of securities. The 1934 Act's definition of a security is substantially the same as that of the 1933 Act. The act seeks to ensure fair and orderly securities markets by establishing rules for market operations and by prohibiting fraudulent and manipulative practices. It protects holders of *all* securities listed on national exchanges, as well as holders of *equity* securities of companies traded

FIGURE 42–4 Registration and Liability Provisions of the 1933 Act

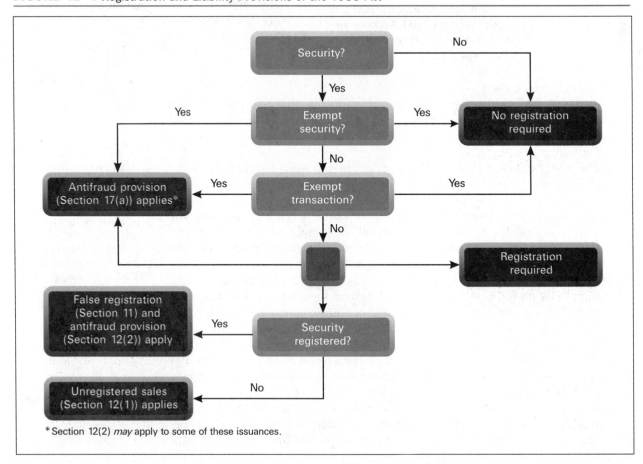

*Section 12(2) *may* apply to some of these issuances.

over the counter, whose corporate assets exceed $5 million and whose equity securities include a class with 500 or more shareholders. Companies must register such securities and are also subject to the 1934 Act's periodic reporting requirements, short-swing profits provision, tender offer provisions, and proxy solicitation provisions, as well as the internal control and record-keeping requirements of the Foreign Corrupt Practices Act. In addition, issuers of securities, whether registered under the 1934 Act or not, must comply with the antifraud and antibribery provisions of the act. (See Figure 42–5.)

The National Securities Markets Improvements Act of 1996 broadly authorized the SEC to issue regulations, rules, or orders exempting any person, security, or transaction from any of the provisions of the 1934 Act or the SEC's rules promulgated under that act. This authorization extends so far as such exemption is necessary or appropriate in the public interest and is consistent with the protection of investors. This exemptive authority does not, however, extend to the regulation of government securities broker-dealers.

DISCLOSURE

The 1934 Act imposes significant disclosure requirements upon reporting companies. These include the filing of securities registrations, periodic reports, disclosure statements for proxy solicitations, and disclosure statements for tender offers, as well as compliance with the accounting requirements imposed by the Foreign Corrupt Practices Act. As part of its integrated registration and reporting system for small business issuers, in 1992 the SEC developed a new series of forms for qualifying issuers to use for registration and periodic reporting under the 1934 Act. Also in 1992, the SEC required disclosure of the compensation paid to senior executives and directors in registration statements, periodic reports, and proxy statements.

FIGURE 42–5 Applicability of the 1934 Act

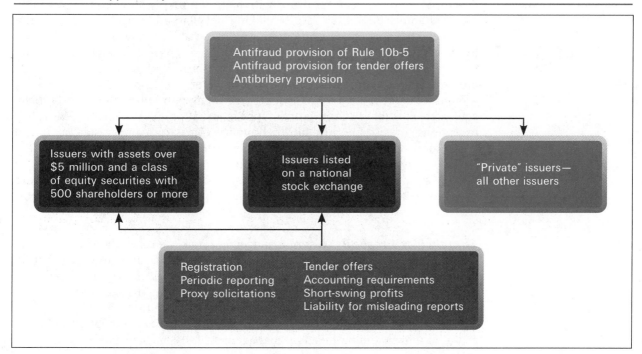

Registration Requirements for Securities

The 1934 Act requires all regulated publicly held companies to register with the SEC. These one-time registrations apply to an entire class of securities. Thus, they differ from registrations under the Securities Act of 1933, which relate only to the securities involved in a specific offering. Registration requires disclosure of information such as the organization, financial structure, and nature of the business; the terms, positions, rights, and privileges of the different classes of outstanding securities; the names of the directors, officers, and underwriters and of each security holder owning more than 10 percent of any class of nonexempt equity security; bonus and profit-sharing arrangements; and balance sheets and profit-and-loss statements for the three preceding fiscal years.

Periodic Reporting Requirements

Following registration, an issuer must file specified annual and periodic reports to update the information contained in the original registration. The act also requires that each director, officer, and any person who owns more than 10 percent of a registered equity security file reports with the SEC for any month in which changes in his ownership of such equity securities have occurred.

Proxy Solicitations

Proxy writing signed by a shareholder authorizing a named person to vote his stock at a specified meeting

A **proxy** is a writing signed by a shareholder authorizing a named person to vote his shares of stock at a specified shareholders' meeting. To ensure that shareholders have adequate information upon which to vote, the 1934 Act regulates the proxy solicitation process. The act makes it unlawful for any person to solicit any proxy concerning any registered security "in contravention of such rules and regulations as the Commission may prescribe." **Solicitation** includes any request for a proxy, any request not to execute a proxy, or any request to revoke a proxy.

Proxy statements proxy disclosure statements are required when proxies are solicited or an issuer submits a matter to a shareholder vote

Proxy Statements The 1934 Act prohibits solicitation of a proxy unless each person solicited has been furnished with a written **proxy statement** containing specified information. An issuer making solicitations must furnish security holders with a *proxy statement* describing all material facts concerning the matters being submitted to their vote, together with a *proxy form* on which the security holders can indicate their approval or disapproval of each proposal to be presented. Even a company that does not solicit proxies from its shareholders but submits a matter to their vote must provide them with information substantially equivalent to that which would appear in a proxy statement. With few exceptions, the issuer must file preliminary copies of a proxy statement and proxy form with the SEC at least ten days prior to the first date on which the forms are to be sent. In addition, in an election of directors, solicitations of proxies by a person other than the issuer are subject to similar disclosure requirements. The *issuer* in such an election also must include an annual report with the proxy statement.

Shareholder Proposals Where management makes a solicitation, any security holder entitled to vote has the opportunity to communicate with other security holders. On written request, the corporation must mail the communication at the security holder's expense or, at its option, promptly furnish to that security holder a current list of security holders.

If an eligible security holder entitled to vote submits a timely proposal for action at a forthcoming meeting, management must include the proposal in its proxy statement along with a brief statement explaining the shareholder's reasons for making the proposal. Management may omit a proposal if, among other things, (1) under state law it is not a proper subject for shareholder action, (2) it would require the company to violate any law, (3) it is beyond the issuer's power to accomplish, or (4) it relates to the conduct of the issuer's ordinary business operations.

Tender Offers

A **tender offer** is a general invitation to a company's shareholders to purchase their shares at a specified price for a specified time. In 1968, Congress enacted the Williams Act, which amended the 1934 Act to extend reporting and disclosure requirements to tender offers and other block acquisitions. The purpose of the Williams Act is to provide public shareholders with full disclosure by both the bidder and the target company, so that the shareholders may make an informed decision.

> **Tender offer** general invitation to all shareholders to purchase their shares at a specified price for a specified time

Disclosure Requirements The 1934 Act imposes **disclosure requirements** in three situations: (1) when a person or group acquires more than 5 percent of a class of voting securities registered under the 1934 Act, (2) when a person makes a tender offer for more than 5 percent of a class of registered equity securities, or (3) when the issuer makes an offer to repurchase its own registered shares. Although different rules govern each situation, the disclosure required is substantially the same. The acquiring entity must file with the SEC a statement containing (1) the acquisitor's background; (2) the source of the funds it will use to acquire the securities; (3) the purpose of the acquisition, including any plans to liquidate the company or to make major changes in the corporate structure; (4) the number of shares the acquisitor owns; and (5) any relevant contracts, arrangements, or understandings. This disclosure is also required of anyone soliciting shareholders to accept or reject a tender offer. A copy of the statement must be furnished to each offeree and sent to the issuer.

> **Disclosure requirements** a statement disclosing specified information must be filed with the SEC and furnished to each offeree

The target company has ten days in which to respond to the bidder's tender offer by (1) recommending acceptance or rejection, (2) expressing no opinion and remaining neutral, or (3) stating that it is unable to take a position. The target company's response must include the reasons for the position it takes.

Figure 42–6 summarizes the disclosure requirements under the 1934 Act.

Required Practices A tender offer either by a third party or by the issuer is subject to the following rules: The tender offer must be kept open for at least twenty business days and for at least ten days after any change in terms. Shareholders who tender their shares may withdraw them at any time during the offering period. The tender offer must be open to all holders of the class of shares subject to the offer. All shares tendered must be purchased for the same price; thus, if an offering price is increased, both those who have tendered and those who have yet to tender will receive the benefit of the increase. A tender offeror who offers to purchase less than all of the outstanding securities of the target must accept, on a *pro rata* basis, securities tendered during the offer. During the tender offer, the bidder may buy shares of the target only through that tender offer.

Defensive Tactics When confronted by an uninvited takeover bid—or by a potential, uninvited bid—management of the target company may decide either to oppose the bid or to seek to prevent it. The defensive tactics management

FIGURE 42–6 Disclosure Under the 1934 Act

	Initial Registration	Periodic Reporting	Insider Reporting	Proxy Statement	Tender Offer
Registrant	Issuer if regulated, publicly held company	Issuer if regulated publicly held company	Statutory insiders (directors, officers, and principal stockholders)	Issuer and other persons soliciting proxies	5 percent stockholder, tender offeror, or issuer
Information	Nature of business Financial structure Directors and executive officers Financial statements	Annual, quarterly, or current report updating information in initial registration	Initial statement of beneficial ownership of equity securities Changes in beneficial ownership	Details of solicitation Legal terms of proxy Annual report (if directors to be elected)	Identity and background Terms of transaction Source of funds Intentions
Filing Date	Within 120 days after becoming a reporting company	Annual: within 90 days after year's end Quarterly: within 45 days after quarter's end Current: within 15 days after any material change	Within 10 days of (1) becoming a statutory insider or (2) the end of a month in which a change in owner-ship takes place	10 days before final proxy statement is distributed	5 percent stockholder: within 10 days after acquir-ing more than 5 per-cent of a class of registered securities Tender offeror: before tender offer is made Issuer: before offer to repurchase
Purpose of Disclosure	Adequate and accurate disclosure of material facts regarding securities listed on a national exchange or traded publicly over the counter	Update informa-tion contained in initial registration	Prevent unfair use of information that may have been obtained by a statutory insider	Full disclosure of material information Facilitation of shareholder proposals	Adequate and accurate disclosure of material facts Opportunity to reach uncoerced decision

employs to prevent or defend against undesired tender offers have developed (and are still evolving) into a highly ingenious, and metaphorically named, set of maneuvers, some of which require considerable planning—and some of which are of questionable legality.

State Regulation More than two-thirds of the states have enacted statutes regulating tender offers. Although they vary greatly, most of these statutes tend to protect the target company from an unwanted tender offer. Some empower the state to review the merits of the offer or the adequacy of disclosure. Many impose waiting periods before the tender offer becomes effective. The state statutes generally require disclosures more detailed than those the Williams Act requires, and many of them exempt tender offers supported by the target company's management. A number of states have adopted fair price statutes, which require the acquisitor to pay to all shareholders the highest price paid to any shareholder. Some states have enacted business combination statutes prohibiting transactions with an acquisitor for a specified period after a change in control, unless disinterested shareholders approve.

Foreign Corrupt Practices Act

In 1977, Congress enacted the Foreign Corrupt Practices Act (FCPA) as an amendment to the 1934 Act. Amended in 1988, the act imposes internal control requirements on companies with securities registered under the 1934 Act and prohibits all domestic concerns from bribing foreign governmental or political officials (an activity we will discuss later in this chapter). The accounting requirements of the FCPA reflect the ideas that accurate record keeping is essential to managerial responsibility and that investors should be able to rely on the financial reports they receive. Accordingly, the accounting requirements were enacted (1) to assure that an issuer's books accurately reflect financial transactions, (2) to protect the integrity of independent audits of financial statements, and (3) to promote the reliability of financial information required by the 1934 Act.

Foreign Corrupt Practices Act imposes internal control requirements on companies with securities registered under the 1934 Act

LIABILITY

To implement its objectives, the 1934 Act imposes sanctions for noncompliance with its disclosure and antifraud requirements. These sanctions include civil liability to injured investors and issuers, civil penalties, and criminal penalties.

The Reform Act contains several provisions that affect civil liability under the 1934 Act. First, the Reform Act imposes on a plaintiff in any private action under the 1934 Act the burden of proving that the defendant's alleged violation of the 1934 Act caused the loss for which the plaintiff seeks to recover damages. Second, the Reform Act imposes a limit on the amount of damages a plaintiff can recover in any private action under the 1934 Act based on a material misstatement or omission in which she seeks to establish damages by reference to the market price of a security. The plaintiff may not recover damage in excess of the difference between the purchase or sale price she paid or received for the security and the mean trading price of that security during the ninety-day period beginning on the date when the information correcting the misstatement or omission is disseminated to the market. Third, the Reform Act provides a "safe harbor" from civil liability under the 1934 Act based on an untrue statement of material fact or an omission of a material fact necessary to make the statement not misleading. The safe harbor applies to issuers required to report under the 1934 Act and who make "forward-looking" statements (predictions) if the statements meet specified requirements. The requirements of the safe harbor and the transactions to which it does not apply were discussed earlier in this chapter.

Misleading Statements in Reports

Section 18 imposes express civil liability upon any person who makes or causes to be made any false or misleading statement with respect to any material fact in any application, report, document, or registration filed with the SEC under the 1934 Act. Any person who purchased or sold a security in reliance upon such a false or misleading statement without knowing that it was false or misleading may recover under this section. A person is not liable, however, if she proves that she acted in good faith and had no knowledge that such statement was false or misleading. The court may award attorneys' fees against either the plaintiff or the defendant.

Misleading statements in reports Section 18 imposes civil liability for any false or misleading statement made in a registration or report filed with the SEC

Short-Swing Profits

Section 16(b) of the 1934 Act imposes express liability upon insiders—directors, officers, and any person owning more than 10 percent of the stock of a corporation listed on a national stock exchange or registered with the SEC—for all profits resulting from their "short-swing" trading in such stock. If any insider sells such stock within six months from the date of its purchase or purchases such stock within six months from the date of a sale of the stock, the corporation is entitled to recover any and all profit the insider realizes from these transactions. The "profit" recoverable is calculated by matching the highest sale price against the lowest purchase price within the relevant six-month period. Losses cannot be offset against profits. Suit to recover such profit may be brought by the issuer or by the owner of any security of the issuer in the name and on behalf of the issuer if the issuer fails or refuses to bring such suit within sixty days of the owner's request.

Antifraud Provision

Section 10(b) of the 1934 Act and SEC **Rule 10b–5** make it unlawful for any person using the mails or facilities of interstate commerce in connection with the purchase or sale of any security (1) to employ any device, scheme, or artifice to defraud; (2) to make any untrue statement of a material fact; (3) to omit to state a material fact without which the information is misleading; or (4) to engage in any act, practice, or course of business that operates or would operate as a fraud or deceit upon any person.

Rule 10b–5 applies to any purchase or sale of *any* security, whether it is registered under the 1934 Act or not, whether it is publicly traded or closely held, whether it is listed on an exchange or sold over the counter, or whether it is part of an initial issuance or a secondary distribution. There are *no* exemptions. The implied liability under Rule 10b–5 applies to purchaser as well as seller misconduct and allows both defrauded sellers and buyers to recover.

Requisites of Rule 10b–5 Recovery of damages under Rule 10b–5 requires proof of (1) a misstatement or omission (2) that is material, (3) made with *scienter*, and (4) relied upon (5) in connection with the purchase or sale of a security. This rule differs from common law fraud in that Rule 10b–5 imposes an affirmative duty of disclosure. A misstatement or omission is *material* if there is a substantial likelihood that a reasonable investor would consider it important in deciding whether to purchase or sell the security. Examples of material facts include substantial changes in dividends or earnings, significant misstatements of asset value, and the fact that the issuer is about to become a target of a tender offer. In an action for damages under Rule 10b–5, it must be shown that the violation was committed with **scienter**, or intentional misconduct. Negligence is not sufficient. Although the Supreme Court has not yet decided whether reckless conduct is sufficient to satisfy the requirement of *scienter*, a great majority of circuit and district courts have held recklessness to be sufficient.

Remedies for Rule 10b–5 violations include rescission, damages, and injunctions. The courts, however, are divided over the measure of damages to impose.

BASIC INC. v. LEVINSON United States Supreme Court, 1988, 458 U.S. 224, 108 S.Ct. 978, 99 L.Ed.2d 194

FACTS Prior to December 20, 1978, Basic Inc. was a publicly traded company engaged in the business of manufacturing chemical refractories for the steel industry. Beginning in September 1976, Combustion Engineering, Inc. and Basic began discussions concerning the possibility of a merger of the two companies. Nevertheless, during 1977 and 1978, Basic made three public statements denying that it was engaged in

continued

merger negotiations. On December 18, 1978, Basic asked the New York Stock Exchange to suspend trading in its shares and issued a statement saying that it had been "approached" by another company concerning a merger. On December 20, Basic publicly announced its approval of Combustion's offer for all its outstanding shares. The plaintiffs were former owners of Basic stock who sold their shares after Basic publicly denied that it was engaged in merger negotiations. The plaintiffs brought a class action suit against Basic and its directors, alleging that they had released false or misleading information in violation of Section 10(b) of the 1934 Act and in violation of Rule 10b–5. The plaintiffs claimed that they were injured by selling their shares at prices that were artificially depressed as a consequence of Basic's misleading public statements. The Court of Appeals held that the plaintiffs had carried their burden of proof. The defendants appealed, claiming that the plaintiffs had not proven that they had, in fact, relied upon the misleading statements in selling their stock.

DECISION   Judgment for former shareholders.

OPINION   The lower court was correct in applying a presumption of reliance supported in part by the "fraud-on-the-market" theory, instead of requiring each plaintiff to show individual direct reliance on Basic's statements. A presumption of reliance upon public information is warranted in an impersonal, efficient market. It would be extremely burdensome to require plaintiffs to prove that they personally knew about the misleading or false information and actually relied upon it. A presumption of reliance also is consistent with the legislative policy embodied in the 1934 Act. Congress expressly relied upon the fact that securities markets are affected by information and that a free and open market relies upon the theory that the market price reflects a just price. Further, a presumption of reliance is supported by empirical evidence and common sense. Studies have confirmed the fact that market price generally reflects all publicly available information, and reasonable people would not take the risk of trading in a market in which such integrity of market price did not exist.

The defendants may rebut this presumption of reliance by showing either that their misrepresentations did not affect the respondents' decision to trade at the fair market price or that the price at which the plaintiffs sold their shares was unaffected by the misrepresentations. For example, the defendants could rebut this presumption by proving that the plaintiffs believed that Basic's statements concerning the merger were false and their shares were undervalued as a consequence but that they sold their shares anyway.

INTERPRETATION   The reliance requirement of Rule 10b–5 may be satisfied by the "fraud-on-the-market" presumption of reliance instead of requiring each plaintiff to prove individual direct reliance on the defendant's statements.

Insider Trading   Rule 10b–5 applies to sales or purchases of securities made by an "insider" who possesses material information that is not available to the general public. An insider who fails to disclose such information before trading on it will be liable under Rule 10b–5 unless he waits for the information to become public. **Insiders**, for the purpose of Rule 10b–5, include directors, officers, employees, and agents of the security issuer, as well as those with whom the issuer has entrusted information solely for corporate purposes, such as underwriters, accountants, lawyers, and consultants. In some instances, the rule also precludes persons who receive material, nonpublic information from insiders—tippees—from trading on that information. A tippee is under a duty not to trade on inside information from an insider who has breached his fiduciary duty to the shareholders by disclosing the information to the tippee, who knows or should know that such a breach has occurred. (See Figure 42–7.)

Although both Section 16(b) and Rule 10b–5 address the problem of insider trading and both may apply to the same transaction, they differ in several respects. First, Section 16(b) applies only to transactions involving registered equity securities; Rule 10b–5 applies to all securities. Second, the definition of *insider* under Rule 10b–5 extends beyond directors, officers, and owners of more than 10 percent of a company's stock, whereas the definition under Section 16(b) does not. Third, Section 16(b) does *not* require that the insider possess material,

Insider trading "insiders" are liable under Rule 10b–5 for failing to disclose material, nonpublic information before trading on the information

Insiders directors, officers, employees, and agents of the issuer, as well as those with whom the issuer has entrusted information solely for corporate purposes

FIGURE 42–7 Parties Forbidden to Trade on Inside Information

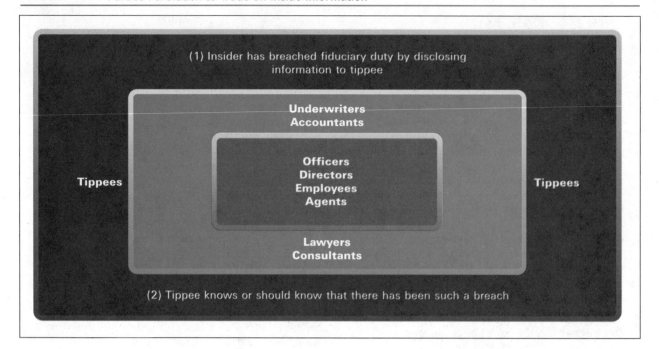

nonpublic information; liability is strict. Rule 10b–5 applies to insider trading only where such information is not disclosed. Fourth, Section 16(b) applies only to transactions occurring within six months of each other; Rule 10b–5 has no such limitation. Fifth, under Rule 10b–5, injured investors may recover damages on their own behalf; under Section 16(b), although shareholders may bring suit, any recovery is on behalf of the corporation.

Express Insider Trading Liability

Express insider trading liability is imposed on any person who sells or buys a security while in possession of inside information

Section 20A imposes express civil liability upon any person who violates the act by purchasing or selling a security while in possession of material, nonpublic information. Any person who contemporaneously sold or purchased securities of the same class as those improperly traded may bring a private action against the trader to recover damages for the violation. The total amount of damages may not exceed the profit gained or loss avoided by the violation, diminished by any amount the violator disgorges to the SEC pursuant to a court order. The action must be brought within five years after the date of the last transaction that is the subject of the violation. Tippers are jointly and severally liable with tippees who commit a violation by trading on the inside information.

Civil Penalties for Insider Trading

Civil penalties for inside trading may be imposed on inside traders in an amount up to three times the gains they made or losses they avoided

In addition to the remedies discussed above, the SEC is authorized to bring an action in a U.S. district court to have a civil penalty imposed upon any person who purchases or sells a security while in possession of material, nonpublic information. Liability also extends to any person who by communicating material, nonpublic information aids and abets another person in such a violation. Liability may also be imposed on any person who directly or indirectly

ETHICAL DILEMMA What Information May a Corporate Employee Disclose?

FACTS Sam Thompson is the director of tax research in the tax department of Anna Louise, Inc., a publicly traded clothing manufacturer. Formed by James and Anna Louise around the turn of the century, the corporation has been managed ever since by family members, who still own a controlling interest.

While studying certain tax matters in connection with a highly sensitive marketing project, Sam learned that an international company has offered to purchase a controlling interest in Anna Louise. Later, while he was having lunch with Mike, his good friend and stockbroker, Mike began pressuring Sam for information about the

offer. Mike is ambitious and is attempting to build a solid client base. He is a diligent worker, performs extensive research to support recommendations to clients, and socializes a great deal with the business community. Mike told Sam that he could tell something special was going on at Sam's office. Sam had been working overtime and for the past two weeks had been unable to meet Mike as usual on Friday evening for drinks after work.

Social, Policy, and Ethical Considerations

1. What are Sam's ethical responsibilities to his employer with

regard to information he obtains at work? How should he respond to Mike's requests for information?

2. If Sam took Mike into his confidence, what ethical responsibilities would Mike have to Sam to keep the information to himself?

3. Does Mike have any duties of loyalty to Sam's employer?

4. As a practical matter, to what extent must one keep in confidence information obtained in one's employment? Is it "safe," for example, to discuss matters with one's closest friends or one's spouse?

controlled a person who ultimately committed a violation if the controlling person knew or recklessly disregarded the likelihood that the controlled person would commit a violation and consequently failed to take appropriate steps to prevent the transgression. The violating transaction must be on or through the facilities of a national securities exchange or from or through a broker or dealer. Purchases that are part of a public offering by an issuer of securities are not subject to this provision.

The civil penalty for a person who trades on inside information is determined by the court in light of the facts and circumstances but may not exceed three times the profit gained or loss avoided as a result of the unlawful purchase or sale. The maximum amount that may be imposed upon a controlling person is the greater of $1.1 million or three times the profit gained or loss avoided as a result of the controlled person's violation. If that violation consists of tipping inside information, the court measures the controller's liability by the profit gained or loss avoided by the person to whom the controlled person directed the tip. For the purpose of this provision, "profit gained" or "loss avoided" is "the difference between the purchase or sale price of the security and the value of that security as measured by the trading price of the security a reasonable period after public dissemination of the nonpublic information."

Civil penalties for insider trading are payable into the United States Treasury. The SEC is authorized to award bounties of up to 10 percent of a recovered penalty to informants who provided information leading to the imposition of the penalty. An action to recover a penalty must be brought within five years after the date of the purchase or sale.

Misleading Proxy Statements

Any person who distributes a materially false or **misleading proxy statement** may be liable to a shareholder who relies upon the statement in purchasing or selling a security and consequently suffers a loss. In this context, a misstatement or omission is material if there is a substantial likelihood that a reasonable

Misleading proxy statement any person who distributes a false or misleading proxy statement is liable to injured investors

Insider Trading: Oughta Be a Law

Say you are planning a hostile takeover with your lawyer, your investment banker, and your trusted friend the newspaper columnist. After you leave the room, each confidant makes a hushed telephone call to buy stock in the target company.

Until recently, this grade B Hollywood stuff was criminal securities fraud, a.k.a. "insider trading." Depending on how the Supreme Court rules on a coming case—the U.S. government will file its brief tomorrow—it could be business as usual.

The case involves James O'Hagan, a Minneapolis lawyer who illegally used money from two client accounts—one of them was the Mayo Clinic. Allegedly needing money to repay his clients, Mr. O'Hagan loaded up on stock and short-term options in Pillsbury, then the target of a planned takeover by Grand Metropolitan, a client of Mr. O'Hagan's firm. When Grand Met tendered for Pillsbury, Mr. O'Hagan made $4.3 million overnight.

Mr. O'Hagan was convicted of "theft by temporary control" (he eventually repaid his clients) and did time in state prison. He also was convicted in federal court for trading on Grand Met's then-secret takeover plans. But his federal conviction was overturned by a broad-brush ruling from the U.S. Court of Appeals for the Eighth Circuit, in St. Louis. If the Supreme Court goes along, it soon will be open season for trading on many kinds of misappropriated—even stolen—nonpublic information.

Put in terms that even a lawyer could understand, it would be all right to trade on secret dope that you weren't supposed to trade on—that is, to cheat. And the basic premise of the little guy investor—that prices are set by market participants with roughly equivalent access to information—would go out the window.

It would still be illegal to use inside tips to trade on your own—or on your own client's—stock. But a huge moral inconsistency would linger over markets. Consider the case where two lawyers—one for the target, one for the bidder—learn of a pending acquisition. If they each buy stock in the target, the first goes to Sing Sing, the second to, well, how does Waikiki beach strike you? When similar behavior is treated differently, it suggests a problem.

But it's far from clear whether the problem lies in the courts or in the vagueness of the law. When Congress created the Securities and Exchange Commission in 1934, it deliberately avoided trying to spell out specific securities crimes. Instead, it broadly allowed the SEC to write rules proscribing "any manipulative or deceptive device" in connection with trading. (Wall Street wanted it that way; in the 1930s, as distinct from now, faith in rule by expert agencies was high.)

In the 1980s, prosecutors developed the "misappropriation" theory: If you wrongly get hold of and trade on inside dope, you are "deceiving" the person from whom the information was taken and breaking the law. Various courts, including the important Second Circuit in Manhattan, approved the theory, but the Supreme Court never has. (In one prior decision, involving a former reporter for *The Wall Street Journal* who tipped a broker in advance of stories, the high court split 4-4, leaving the lower-court ruling standing.)

In the O'Hagan case, the appeals court threw out the misappropriation theory, reckoning, in effect, that since a lawyer for a bidder doesn't owe a fiduciary duty to the target, there is no "deception" involved in buying the target's stock. Moreover, it threw out a conviction based on a narrower SEC rule prohibiting inside trading in advance of tender offers, on the grounds that the SEC had overreached. Finally, it knocked out the prosecutors usual fail-safe conviction on mail fraud.

Some big-name law professors are filing a friend-of-the-court brief urging the Supreme Court to reinstate the convictions—and affirm the misappropriation theory. If the government loses, "it would leave a gaping hole," says Jack Coffee, a Columbia law school professor in the group. "You would expect a lot more inside trading if you're not facing 10 years in prison."

The sure next step: The SEC would dust off a proposal for a bill explicitly banning insider trading. And that wouldn't be bad. The SEC refrained from pushing for legislation in the past because it was winning in the courts, didn't seem to need one, and feared that once Congress took up the idea, there was no telling where it would go. But there was always a little leap to get from the statute to the broader purpose of prosecutors—which is preventing inside trading that tarnishes market fairness. As Richard Walker, SEC general counsel says, "We want to protect confidence in markets."

Mr. Coffee hopes the Supreme Court will draw a "bright line" against inside trading. It's possible, but I think a weak line or murky line is just as possible. Securities lawyers such as Harvey Pitt, while granting that Mr. O'Hagan hardly elicits sympathy, say the government could well lose.

This argues for legislation. The details will be controversial (Wall Street will lobby to protect its current unfair practice of hinting to big investors before earnings announcements). But a statute could and should get writ. If behavior that has been widely and rightly condemned for more than a decade remains only borderline illegal, there oughta be a law against it.

[The U.S. Supreme Court upheld the misappropriation theory and the SEC rule.]

shareholder would consider it important in deciding how to vote. A number of courts have held that negligence is sufficient for an action under the proxy rule's antifraud provisions. In addition, when the proxy disclosure or filing requirement has been violated, a court may, if appropriate, enjoin a shareholder meeting or any action taken at that meeting. Other remedies are rescission, damages, and attorneys' fees.

Fraudulent Tender Offers

Section 14(e) makes it unlawful for any person to make any untrue statement of material fact, to omit to state any material fact, or to engage in any fraudulent, deceptive, or manipulative practices in connection with any tender offer. This provision applies even if the target company is not subject to the 1934 Act's reporting requirements.

Some courts have implied civil liability for violations of Section 14(e). Because of the small number of cases, however, the requirements for such an action are not entirely clear. A target company may seek an injunction, and a shareholder of the target may be able to recover damages or obtain rescission. The courts are likely to require *scienter*.

> **Fraudulent tender offers**
> Section 14(e) imposes civil liability for false and material statements or omissions or fraudulent, deceptive, or manipulative practices in connection with any tender offer

---

SCHREIBER v. BURLINGTON NORTHERN, INC. Supreme Court of the United States, 1985, 472 U.S. 1, 105 S.Ct. 2458, 86 L.Ed.2d 1

FACTS On December 21, 1982, Burlington Northern, Inc. made a hostile tender offer for El Paso Gas Co., proposing to purchase 25.1 million El Paso shares at $24 per share. The shareholders of El Paso fully subscribed the offer by the December 30, 1982, deadline. Burlington refused to accept those tendered shares and instead announced the terms of a new and friendly takeover agreement on January 10, 1983. Under this agreement, Burlington withdrew the December tender offer and substituted a new tender offer for 21 million shares at $24 per share. Over 40 million shares were tendered in response to this offer. Thus, the new offer disadvantaged those shareholders who had tendered during the first offer, for those who retendered were subject to substantial proration and hence received a diminished payment. Barbara Schreiber, one of the disadvantaged shareholders, brought an action against Burlington, El Paso, and members of El Paso's board, claiming that Burlington's rescission of the first tender offer and substitution of the new one was a "manipulative" distortion of the market for El Paso stock, which is prohibited by Section 14(e) of the Securities Exchange Act. The District Court dismissed the suit for failure to state a claim, and the Court of Appeals affirmed.

DECISION Judgment of the Court of Appeals affirmed.

OPINION Section 14(e) of the Securities Exchange Act forbids "fraudulent, deceptive or manipulative

acts or practices . . . in connection with any tender offer." Shreiber interprets the prohibition of "manipulative acts or practices" to include fully disclosed acts that nonetheless "artificially" affect the price of the takeover target's stock. This interpretation conflicts with the usual meaning of the term "manipulative." In a prior decision, the word "manipulative" was held to refer to "intentional or willful conduct designed to deceive or defraud investors by controlling or artificially affecting the price of securities." Thus, the term "manipulative" requires some sort of misrepresentation or nondisclosure. Moreover, Section 14(e) was added to the Securities Exchange Act simply to make sure that public shareholders have sufficient information with which to respond to a cash tender offer for their stock. The section does not attempt to address the substantive fairness of tender offers. It only imposes upon a tender offeror an obligation to disclose fully all material information, and Burlington complied with this requirement. Since Burlington's cancellation of the first tender offer was not accompanied by any misrepresentation, nondisclosure, or deception, no violation of Section 14(e) of the Securities Exchange Act occurred.

INTERPRETATION Shareholders have a right to full and accurate disclosure of information from those making tender offers to them.

Antibribery Provision of FCPA

The Foreign Corrupt Practices Act makes it unlawful for *any* domestic concern or any of its officers, directors, employees, or agents to offer or give anything of value directly or indirectly to any foreign official, political party, or political official for the purpose of (1) influencing any act or decision of that person or party in his or its official capacity, (2) inducing an act or omission in violation of his or its lawful duty, or (3) inducing such person or party to use his or its influence to affect a decision of a foreign government in order to assist the domestic concern in obtaining or retaining business. An offer or promise to make a prohibited payment is a violation even if the offer is not accepted or the promise is not performed. The 1988 amendments to the act explicitly excluded routine governmental action not involving the official's discretion, such as obtaining permits or processing applications. They also added an affirmative defense for payments that are lawful under the written laws or regulations of the foreign officials' country.

Violations can result in fines of up to $2 million for companies; individuals may be fined a maximum of $100,000 or be imprisoned for up to five years, or both. Fines imposed upon individuals may not be paid directly or indirectly by the domestic concern on whose behalf they acted. In addition, civil penalties up to $11,000 may be imposed.

Criminal Sanctions

Criminal sanctions
individuals who willfully violate the 1934 Act are subject to a fine of not more than $1 million and/or imprisonment of not more than ten years

Section 32 of the 1934 Act imposes **criminal sanctions** on any person who willfully violates any provision of the act (except the antibribery provision) or the rules and regulations promulgated by the SEC pursuant to the act. For individuals, conviction may carry a fine of not more than $1 million or imprisonment of not more than ten years, or both, with one exception: a person who proves she had no knowledge of the rule or regulation is not subject to *imprisonment*. If the person, however, is not a natural person (for example, a corporation), a fine not exceeding $2.5 million may be imposed.

Figure 42–8 summarizes the civil liability provisions under the 1933 and 1934 Acts.

FIGURE 42–8 Civil Liability Under the 1933 and 1934 Acts

Provision	Conduct	Plaintiffs	Defendants	Standard of Culpability	Reliance Required	Type of Liability	Remedies
Section 12(1) 1933 Act	Unregistered sale or sale without prospectus	Purchasers from a violator	Sellers in violation	Strict liability	No	Express	Rescission Damages Attorneys' fees
Section 11 1933 Act	Registration statement containing material misstatement or omission	Purchasers of registered security	Issuer Directors Signers Underwriters Experts	Strict liability for issuer Negligence for others	No	Express	Damages Attorneys' fees
Section 12(2) 1933 Act	Material misstatement or omission	Purchasers from a violator	Sellers in violation	Negligence	No	Express	Rescission Damages Attorneys' fees
Section 18 1934 Act	False or misleading statements in a document filed with SEC	Purchasers or sellers	Persons making filing in violation	Knowledge or bad faith	Yes	Express	Damages Attorneys' fees
Section 16(b) 1934 Act	Short-swing profit by insider	Issuer Shareholder of issuer	Directors Officers 10 percent shareholders	Strict liability	No	Express	Damages
Rule 10b-5 1934 Act	Deception Material misstatement or omission	Purchasers or sellers	Purchasers or sellers in violation	Scienter	Yes	Implied	Rescission Damages Injunction
Section 20A 1934 Act	Insider trading	Contemporane-ous purchasers or sellers	Inside traders	Scienter	No	Express	Damages
Section 14(a) 1934 Act	Materially false or misleading proxy solicitation	Shareholders	Persons making proxy solicitation in violation	Negligence (probably)	Probably	Implied	Rescission Damages Injunction Attorneys' fees
Section 14(e) 1934 Act	Tender offer with deception, or manipulation, or material misstatement or omission	Target company Shareholders of target	Persons making tender offer in violation	Scienter (probably)	Probably	Implied	Rescission Damages Injunction

CHAPTER SUMMARY

Securities Act of 1933

Definition of a Security	**Security** includes any note, stock, bond, preorganization subscription, and investment contract **Investment Contract** any investment of money or property made in expectation of receiving a financial return solely from the efforts of others
Registration of Securities	**Disclosure Requirements** disclosure of accurate material information required in all public offerings of nonexempt securities unless offering is an exempt transaction **Integrated Disclosure and Shelf Registrations** permitted for certain qualified issuers
Exempt Securities	**Definition** securities not subject to the registration requirements of the 1933 Act **Types** exempt securities include short-term commercial paper, municipal bonds, and certain insurance policies and annuity contracts
Exempt Transactions for Issuers	**Definition** issuance of securities not subject to the registration requirements of the 1933 Act **Types** exempt transactions include limited offers under Regulation D and Section 4(6), Regulation A, and intrastate issues
Exempt Transactions for Non-Issuers	**Definition** resales by persons other than the issuer that are exempted from the registration requirements of the 1933 Act **Types** exempt transactions include Rule 144 and Regulation A
Liability	**Unregistered Sales** absolute civil liability is imposed as there are no defenses **False Registration Statements** Section 11 imposes liability on the issuer, all persons who signed the statement, every director or partner, experts who prepared or certified any part of the statement, and all underwriters; defendants other than issuer may assert the defense of due diligence **Antifraud Provisions** Section 12(2) imposes liability upon the seller to the immediate purchaser, provided the purchaser did not know of the untruth or omission; but the seller is not liable if he did not know, and in the exercise of reasonable care could not have known, of the untrue statement or omission. Section 17(a) broadly prohibits fraud in the sale of securities **Criminal Sanctions** willful violations are subject to a fine of not more than $10,000 and/or imprisonment of not more than five years

Securities Exchange Act of 1934

Disclosure

Registration and Periodic Reporting Requirements apply to all regulated publicly held companies and include one-time registration as well as annual, quarterly, and monthly reports

Proxy Solicitations
- *Definition of a Proxy* a signed writing by a shareholder authorizing a named person to vote her stock at a specified meeting of shareholders
- *Proxy Statements* proxy disclosure statements are required when proxies are solicited or an issuer submits a matter to a shareholder vote

Tender Offers
- *Definition of a Tender Offer* a general invitation to shareholders to purchase their shares at a specified price for a specified time
- *Disclosure Requirements* a statement disclosing specified information must be filed with the SEC and furnished to each offeree

Foreign Corrupt Practices Act imposes internal control requirements on companies with securities registered under the 1934 Act

Liability

Misleading Statements in Reports Section 18 imposes civil liability for any false or misleading statement made in a registration or report filed with the SEC

Short-Swing Profits Section 16(b) imposes liability on certain insiders (directors, officers, and shareholders owning more than 10 percent of the stock of a corporation) for all profits made on sales and purchases within six months of each other, with any recovery going to the issuer

Antifraud Provision Rule 10b–5 makes it unlawful to (1) employ any device, scheme, or artifice to defraud; (2) make any untrue statement of a material fact; (3) omit to state a material fact; or (4) engage in any act that operates as a fraud
- *Requisites of Rule 10b–5* recovery requires (1) a misstatement or omission, (2) materiality, (3) scienter (intentional and knowing conduct), (4) reliance, and (5) connection with the purchase or sale of a security
- *Insider Trading* "insiders" are liable under Rule 10b–5 for failing to disclose material, nonpublic information before trading on the information

Express Insider Trading Liability is imposed on any person who sells or buys a security while in possession of inside information

Civil Penalties for Inside Trading may be imposed on inside traders in an amount up to three times the gains they made or losses they avoided

Misleading Proxy Statement any person who distributes a false or misleading proxy statement is liable to injured investors

Fraudulent Tender Offers Section 14(e) imposes civil liability for false and material statements or omissions or fraudulent, deceptive, or manipulative practices in connection with any tender offer

Antibribery Provision of FCPA prohibited bribery can result in fines and imprisonment

Criminal Sanctions individuals who willfully violate the 1934 Act are subject to a fine of not more than $1 million and/or imprisonment of not more than ten years

QUESTIONS

1. Distinguish between exempt securities and exempt transactions under the 1933 Act. List four examples of each.
2. Discuss the potential civil liabilities under the 1933 Act.
3. Distinguish between publicly held companies under the 1934 Act and those that are not publicly held. Which provisions of the 1934 Act apply only to publicly held companies and which apply to all companies?

4. Discuss the requirements and applications of Rule 10b–5.
5. Discuss (a) tender offers and (b) proxy solicitations.

Internet Question. Find the Securities and Exchange Commission Web site and learn about the agency's (a) structure, (b) functions, and (c) current activities.

PROBLEMS

1. Acme Realty, a real estate development company, is a limited partnership organized in Georgia. It is planning to develop a 200-acre parcel of land for a regional shopping center and needs to raise $1,250,000. As part of its financing, Acme plans to offer $1,250,000 worth of limited partnership interests to about 100 prospective investors in the southeastern United States. It anticipates that about forty to fifty private investors will purchase the limited partnership interests.
   (a) Must Acme register this offering? Why or why not?
   (b) If Acme must register but fails to do so, what are the legal consequences?
2. Bigelow Corporation has total assets of $850,000, sales of $1,350,000, one class of common stock with 375 shareholders and a class of preferred stock with 250 shareholders, both of which are traded over the counter. Which provisions of the Securities Exchange Act of 1934 apply to Bigelow Corporation?
3. Capricorn, Inc. is planning to "go public" by offering its common stock, which previously had been owned by only three shareholders. The company intends to limit the number of purchasers to twenty-five persons resident in the state of its incorporation. All of Capricorn's business and all of its assets are located in its state of incorporation. Based on these facts, what exemptions from registration, if any, are available to Capricorn, and what conditions would each of these available exemptions impose on the terms of the offer?
4. The boards of directors of DuMont Corp. and Epsot, Inc. agreed to enter into a friendly merger, with DuMont Corp. to be the surviving entity. The stock of both corporations was listed on a national stock exchange. In connection with the merger, both corporations distributed to their shareholders proxy statements seeking approval of the proposed merger. The shareholders of both corporations voted to approve the merger. About three weeks after the merger was consummated, the price of DuMont stock fell from $25 to

$13 as a result of the discovery that Epsot had entered into several unprofitable long-term contracts two months before the merger had been proposed. The contracts will result in substantial losses from Epsot's operations for at least the next four years. The existence and effect of these contracts, although known to both corporations at the time of the proposed merger, were not disclosed in the proxy statements of either corporation. Shareholders of DuMont bring suit against DuMont under the 1934 Act. Decision?
5. Farthing is a director and vice president of Garp, Inc., whose common stock is listed on the New York Stock Exchange. Farthing engaged in the following transactions in the same calendar year: on January 2, Farthing sold 500 shares at $30 per share; on January 15, she purchased 300 shares at $30 per share; on February 1, she purchased 200 shares at $45 per share; on March 1, she purchased 300 shares at $60 per share; on March 15, she sold 200 shares at $55 per share; and on April 1, she sold 100 shares at $40 per share. Howell brings suit on behalf of Garp, alleging that Farthing has violated the Securities Act of 1934. Farthing defends on the ground that she lost money on the transactions in question. Decision?
6. Intercontinental Widgets, Inc. had applied for a patent for a new state-of-the-art widget that, if patented, would significantly increase the value of Intercontinental's shares. On September 1, the Patent Office notified Jackson, the attorney for Intercontinental, that the patent application had been approved. After informing Kingsley, the company's president, of the good news, Jackson called his broker and purchased 1,000 shares of Intercontinental at $18 per share. He also told his partner, Lucas, who immediately proceeded to purchase 500 shares at $19 per share. Lucas then called his brother-in-law, Mammon, and told him the news. On September 3, Mammon bought 4,000 shares at $21 per share. On September 4, Kingsley issued a press release that accurately reported that a

patent had been granted to Intercontinental. On the next day, Intercontinental's stock soared to $38 per share. A class action suit is brought against Jackson, Lucas, Mammon, and Intercontinental for violations of Rule 10b–5. Who, if anyone, is liable?

7. Nova, Inc. sought to sell a new issue of common stock. It registered the issue with the SEC but included false information in both the registration statement and the prospectus. The issue was underwritten by Omega & Sons and was sold in its entirety by Periwinkle, Rameses, and Sheffield, Inc., a securities broker-dealer. Telford purchased 500 shares at $6 per share. Three months later, the falsity of the information contained in the prospectus was made public, and the price of the shares fell to $1 per share. The following week, Telford brought suit against Nova, Inc.; Omega & Sons; and Periwinkle, Rameses, and Sheffield, Inc. under the Securities Act of 1933.

   (a) Who, if anyone, is liable under the 1933 Act?

   (b) What defenses, if any, are available to the various defendants?

8. Tanaka, a director and officer of Deep Hole Oil Company, approached Romani for the purpose of buying 200 shares of Deep Hole Company stock owned by Romani. During the period of negotiations, Tanaka concealed his identity and did not disclose the fact that earlier in the day he had received a report of two rich oil strikes on the oil company's property. Romani sold his 200 shares to Tanaka for $10 per share. Taking into consideration the new strikes, the fair value of the stock was approximately $20 per share. Romani sues Tanaka to recover damages. Decision?

9. Venable Corporation has 750,000 shares of common stock outstanding, which are owned by 640 shareholders. The assets of Venable Corporation are valued at over $5 million. In March, Underhill began purchasing shares of Venable's common stock in the open market. By April, he had acquired 40,000 shares at prices ranging from $12 to $14. Upon discovering Underhill's activities in late April, the directors of Venable had the corporation purchase the 40,000 shares from Underhill for $18 per share. Which provisions of the 1934 Act, if any, have been violated?

10. In 1973, Dirks was an officer of a New York broker-dealer firm who specialized in providing investment analysis of insurance company securities to institutional investors. On March 6, Dirks received information from Ronald Secrist, a former officer of Equity Funding of America. Secrist alleged that the assets of Equity Funding, a diversified corporation primarily engaged in selling life insurance and mutual funds, were vastly overstated as the result of fraudulent corporate practices. Dirks decided to investigate the allegations. He visited Equity Funding's headquarters in Los Angeles and interviewed several officers and employees of the corporation. The senior management denied any wrongdoing, but certain corporation employees corroborated the charges of fraud. Neither Dirks nor his firm owned or traded any Equity Funding stock, but throughout his investigation he openly discussed the information he had obtained with a number of clients and investors. Some of these persons sold their holdings of Equity Funding securities, including five investment advisers who liquidated holdings of more than $16 million.

While Dirks was in Los Angeles, he was in touch regularly with William Blundell, *The Wall Street Journal*'s Los Angeles bureau chief. Dirks urged Blundell to write a story on the fraud allegations. Blundell did not believe, however, that such a massive fraud could go undetected and declined to write the story. He feared that publishing such damaging hearsay might be libelous.

During the two-week period in which Dirks pursued his investigation and spread word of Secrist's charges, the price of Equity Funding stock fell from $26 per share to less than $15 per share. This led the New York Stock Exchange to halt trading on March 27. Shortly thereafter, California insurance authorities impounded Equity Funding's records and uncovered evidence of the fraud. Only then did the Securities and Exchange Commission (SEC) file a complaint against Equity Funding.

The SEC began an investigation into Dirks's role in the exposure of the fraud. After a hearing by an administrative law judge, the SEC found that Dirks had aided and abetted violations of Section 10(b) of the Securities Exchange Act of 1934 and SEC Rule 10b–5 by repeating the allegations of fraud to members of the investment community who later sold their Equity Funding stock. Recognizing, however, that Dirks "played an important role in bringing Equity Funding's massive fraud to light," the SEC only censured him. Dirks appealed. Decision?

11. Texas Gulf Sulphur Company (TGS) was a corporation engaged in exploring for and mining certain minerals. A particular tract of Canadian land looked very promising as a source of desired minerals, and Texas Gulf drilled a test hole on November 8, 1963. Because the core sample of the hole contained minerals of amazing quality, Texas Gulf began to acquire surrounding tracts of land. Stevens, the president of Texas Gulf, instructed all on-site personnel to keep the find a secret. Because subsequent test drillings were performed, the amount of activity surrounding the drilling had resulted in rumors as to the size and quality of the find. To counteract these rumors, Stevens authorized a press release denying the validity of the rumors and describing them as excessively optimistic. The release was issued on April 12, 1964, though

drilling continued through April 15. In the meantime, several officers, directors, and employees had purchased or accepted options to purchase additional Texas Gulf stock on the basis of the information concerning the drilling. They also recommended similar purchases to outsiders without divulging the inside information to the public. At 10:00 a.m. on April 16, an accurate report on the find was finally released to the American financial press. The SEC brought this action against Texas Gulf Sulphur and several of its officers, directors, and employees to enjoin conduct alleged to violate Section 10(b) of the Securities Act of 1934 and to compel rescission by the individual defendants of securities transactions assertedly conducted in violation of Rule 10b–5. Decision?

12. W. J. Howey Co. and Howey-in-the-Hills Service, Inc. were Florida corporations under direct common control and management. The Howey Company owned large tracts of citrus acreage in Florida. The service company cultivated, harvested, and marketed the crops. For several years, Howey Company offered one-half of its planted acreage to the public to help it "finance additional development." Each prospective customer was offered both a land sales contract and a service contract with Howey-in-the-Hills after being told that it was not feasible to invest in the grove without a service arrangement. Upon payment of the purchase price, the land was conveyed by warranty deed. The service company was given full discretion over cultivating and marketing the crop. The purchaser had no right of entry to market the crop. The service company also was accountable only for an allocation of the net profits after the companies pooled the produce. The purchasers were predominantly nonresident businesspersons attracted by the expectation of substantial profits. Contending that this arrangement was an investment contract within the coverage of the Securities Act of 1933, the Securities and Exchange Commission brought this action against the two companies to restrain them from using the mails and instrumentalities of interstate commerce in the offer and sale of unregistered and nonexempt securities. Decision?

CHAPTER 43

Employment Law

Though the common law originally governed the relationship between employer and employee in terms of tort and contract duties (rules that are a part of the law of agency, as discussed in Chapter 29—Relationship of Principal and Agent), this common law has been supplemented—and in some instances replaced—by statutory enactments, principally at the federal level. In fact, government regulation now affects the balance and working relationship between employers and employees in three principal areas. First, the general framework in which management and labor negotiate the terms of employment is regulated by federal statutes designed to promote both labor-management harmony and the welfare of society at large. Second, federal law has been enacted to prohibit employment discrimination based upon race, sex, religion, age, handicap, or national origin. Finally, Congress, in response to the changing nature of American industry and the tremendous number of industrial accidents, has intervened by mandating that employers provide their employees with a safe and healthy work environment. Moreover, all of the states have adopted workers' compensation acts to provide compensation to employees injured during the course of employment.

In this chapter, we will focus upon these three categories of government regulation of the employment relationship: (1) labor law, (2) employment discrimination law, and (3) employee protection.

LABOR LAW

Traditionally, **labor law** opposed concerted activities by workers (such as strikes, picketing, and refusals to deal) to obtain higher wages and better working conditions. At various times, such activities were found to constitute criminal conspiracy, tortious conduct, and violation of antitrust law. Eventually, public pressure in response to the adverse treatment accorded labor forced Congress to intervene.

Norris-LaGuardia Act

Congress enacted the **Norris-LaGuardia Act** in 1932 in response to growing criticism of the use of injunctions in peaceful labor disputes. The act withdrew from the federal courts the power to issue injunctions in nonviolent **labor disputes**, broadly defined to include any controversy concerning terms or conditions of employment or union representation, regardless of whether the parties stood in an employer-employee relationship or not. More significantly, the act declared it to be United States policy that labor was to have full freedom to form unions, without employer interference. Accordingly, the act prohibited

Labor law provides the general framework in which management and labor negotiate terms of employment

Norris-LaGuardia Act established as United States policy the full freedom of labor to form labor unions without employer interference and withdrew from the federal courts the power to issue injunctions in nonviolent labor disputes

Labor dispute any controversy concerning terms or conditions of employment or union representation

the so-called "yellow dog" contracts through which employers coerced their employees into promising that they would not join a union.

National Labor Relations Act

National Labor Relations Act (1) declares it a federally protected right of employees to unionize and to bargain collectively; (2) identifies five unfair labor practices by an employer; and (3) created the NLRB to administer these rights

Unfair labor practice conduct in which an employer or union is prohibited from engaging

Unfair employer practice conduct in which an employer is prohibited from engaging

Enacted in 1935, the **National Labor Relations Act** (NLRA), or the *Wagner Act*, marked the federal government's effort to support collective bargaining and unionization. The act provides that "the right to self-organization, to form, join or assist labor organizations, to bargain collectively through representatives of their own choosing, and to engage in concerted activities for the purpose of collective bargaining or other mutual aid or protection" is, for workers, a federally protected right. Thus, the act gave employees the right to union representation when negotiating employment terms with their employers.

Moreover, the act sought to enforce the collective bargaining right by prohibiting certain employer and union activities deemed to be **unfair labor practices**. For example, the act identifies the following activities as **unfair employer practices**: (1) to interfere with employees' rights to unionize and bargain collectively; (2) to dominate the union; (3) to discriminate against union members; (4) to discriminate against an employee who has filed charges or testified under the NLRA; and (5) to refuse to bargain in good faith with duly established employee representatives.

LECHMERE, INC v. NATIONAL LABOR RELATIONS BOARD Supreme Court of the United States, 1992, 502 U.S. 527 112 S.Ct. 841, 117 L.Ed.2d 79

FACTS Local 919 of the United Food and Commercial Workers Union, AFL-CIO, began to organize the 200 employees at a Lechmere, Inc. retail store in Connecticut. Nonemployee union organizers entered Lechmere's parking lot and began placing handbills on car windshields in an area used mostly by employees. Lechmere's manager immediately confronted the organizers and informed them that handbill distribution of any kind was prohibited. The union organizers tried to distribute these handbills on several subsequent occasions; each time they were asked to leave, and the handbills were removed. The organizers then relocated to a public grassy strip beside Lechmere's parking lot and tried to pass out handbills to drivers entering and leaving the parking lot. The organizers continued this for one month; after that, they distributed handbills intermittently for another six months. They also recorded license plate numbers and, through the Division of Motor Vehicles, secured the names and addresses of forty-one employees, to whom they mailed letters and placed telephone calls. Their efforts resulted in one signed union authorization card.

The union filed an unfair labor practice charge against Lechmere with the National Labor Relations Board (NLRB), alleging that Lechmere had violated the National Labor Relations Act (NLRA) by barring the organizers from its property. The administrative law judge recommended that Lechmere be ordered to cease and desist from barring the organizers from the parking lot and to put up conspicuous signs proclaiming specifically that the union would not be barred from the property or prohibited from distributing union material. The NLRB affirmed, and the Court of Appeals enforced the NLRB's order. Lechmere appealed.

DECISION Decision of the Court of Appeals reversed and enforcement of the order of the NLRB denied.

OPINION Section 7 of the NLRA provides that "[e]mployees shall have the right to self-organization, to form, join, or assist labor organizations." Section 8(a)(1) of the act makes it an unfair labor practice for an employer "to interfere with, restrain, or coerce employees in the exercise of rights guaranteed in [Section 7]." Thus, the NLRA confers rights only on employees, not on unions. Employees' right to self-organization, depends, however, on their ability to learn the advantages of self-organization from others; consequently, Section 7 may restrict an employer's right to exclude nonemployee union organizers from his property.

The rights guaranteed under Section 7 in all access cases must be examined according to three factors: (1) the degree of impairment of the Section 7 right if access should be denied, balanced against (2) the degree of impairment of the private property right if access should be granted, and (3) the availability of reasonably effective alternative means. Essentially, a balance should exist between the employee's rights and

continued

the employer's property rights. However, so long as nonemployee union organizers have reasonable access to employees outside an employer's property, a court need not work to balance those rights further. In this case, the union's ability to make contact through the mail and by telephone suggests that the employees were accessible outside Lechmere's property. Although the union had little success through these contacts, the access, not the success, is the critical issue. Therefore, the NLRB erred in concluding that Lechmere had committed an unfair labor practice by barring nonemployee union organizers from its property.

INTERPRETATION The NLRA prohibits certain types of conduct as unfair employer practices. The action in this case did not constitute such action.

The act also established the ***National Labor Relations Board*** (NLRB) to monitor and administer these employee rights. The NLRB is empowered to order employers to remedy their unfair labor practices and to supervise elections by secret ballot so that employees can freely select a representative organization.

Labor-Management Relations Act

Following the passage of the National Labor Relations Act, the country underwent a tremendous increase in union membership and labor unrest. In response to this trend, Congress passed the **Labor-Management Relations Act** (the *LMRA*, or *Taft-Hartley Act*) in 1947. The act prohibits certain **unfair union practices** and separates the NLRB's prosecutorial and adjudicative functions. More specifically, the act amended the NLRA by declaring the following seven union activities to be ***unfair labor practices***: (1) coercing an employee to join a union, (2) causing an employer to discharge or discriminate against a nonunion employee, (3) refusing to bargain in good faith, (4) levying excessive or discriminatory dues or fees, (5) causing an employer to pay for work not performed ("featherbedding"), (6) picketing an employer to require it to recognize an uncertified union, and (7) engaging in secondary activities. A secondary activity is a boycott, strike, or picketing of an employer with whom a union has no labor dispute in order to persuade the employer to cease doing business with the company that is the target of the labor dispute. For example, assume that a union is engaged in a labor dispute with Anderson Company. To coerce Anderson into resolving the dispute in the union's favor, the union organizes a strike against Brooking Company, with which the union has no labor dispute. The union agrees to cease striking Brooking Company if Brooking agrees to cease doing business with Anderson. The strike against Brooking is a secondary activity prohibited as an unfair labor practice. See Figure 43–1 for a summary of union and employer unfair labor practices.

In addition to prohibiting unfair union practices, the act also fosters employer free speech by declaring that unions or employees wishing to identify an employer labor practice as unfair cannot use as proof any employer statement of opinion or argument that contains no threat of reprisal.

The LMRA also prohibits the closed shop but permits union shops, unless a state right-to-work law prohibits the latter. A **closed shop** contract requires the employer to hire only union members. A **union shop** contract permits the employer to hire nonunion members but requires the employee to become a union member within a specified time after gaining employment and to remain a member in good standing as a condition of employment. A **right-to-work law** is a state statute that prohibits union shop contracts. However, most states permit the existence of union shops.

Labor-Management Relations Act the act (1) prohibits unfair union practices, (2) prohibits closed shops, and (3) allows union shops

Unfair union practice conduct in which a union is prohibited from engaging

Closed shop employer can hire only union members

Union shop employer can hire nonunion members, but the employee must join the union

Right-to-work law state statute that prohibits union shop contracts

FIGURE 43–1 Unfair Labor Practices

Unfair Employer Practices	Unfair Union Practices
• Interfering with right to unionize • Refusing to bargain in good faith • Discriminating against union members • Dominating the union • Discriminating against an employee	• Coercing an employee to join the union • Refusing to bargain in good faith • Causing an employer to discriminate against a nonunion employee • Featherbedding • Picketing an employer to require recognition of an uncertified union • Engaging in secondary activity • Levying excessive or discriminatory dues

Finally, the act reinstates the availability of civil injunctions in labor disputes if requested of the NLRB in order to prevent an unfair labor practice. The act also empowers the president of the United States to obtain an injunction for an eighty-day cooling-off period for a strike that is likely to endanger the national health or safety.

Labor-Management Reporting and Disclosure Act

Labor-Management Reporting and Disclosure Act aimed at eliminating corruption in labor unions

The **Labor-Management Reporting and Disclosure Act**, also known as the *Landrum-Griffin Act*, is aimed at eliminating corruption in labor unions. The act, which was passed in 1959, attempts to eradicate corruption through an elaborate reporting system and a union "bill of rights" designed to make unions more democratic. The latter provides union members with the right to nominate candidates for union offices, to vote in elections, to attend membership meetings, to participate in union business, to express themselves freely at union meetings and conventions, and to be accorded a full and fair hearing before the union takes any disciplinary action against them.

EMPLOYMENT DISCRIMINATION LAW

A number of federal statutes prohibit discrimination in employment on the basis of race, sex, religion, national origin, age, and handicap. The cornerstone of federal employment discrimination law is Title VII of the 1964 Civil Rights Act, but other statutes and regulations are significant as well, including two recently enacted discrimination laws: the *Civil Rights Act of 1991* and the *Americans with Disabilities Act of 1990*. In addition, most states have enacted similar laws prohibiting discrimination based on race, sex, religion, national origin, and handicap.

Equal Pay Act

Equal Pay Act prohibits an employer from discriminating between employees on the basis of gender by paying unequal wages for the same work

The **Equal Pay Act** prohibits an employer from discriminating between employees on the basis of *gender* by paying unequal wages for the same work. The act forbids an employer from paying wages at a rate less than the rate at which he pays wages to employees of the opposite sex for equal work at the same establishment. Most courts define *equal work* to mean "substantially equal" rather than identical. The burden of proof is on the claimant to make a *prima facie* showing that the employer pays unequal wages for work requiring equal skill, effort, and responsibility under similar working conditions. Once the employee has demonstrated that the employer pays unequal wages for *equal* work to members of the opposite sex, the burden shifts to the employer to prove that the pay differential is based on (1) a seniority system, (2) a merit system, (3) a system that measures earnings by quantity or quality of production, or (4) any factor except gender.

Remedies include awarding back pay, awarding liquidated damages (an additional amount equal to back pay), and enjoining the employer from further unlawful conduct. Though the Department of Labor is the federal agency designated by the statute to interpret and enforce the act, in 1979 these functions were transferred to the Equal Employment Opportunity Commission.

Civil Rights Act of 1964

Title VII of the **Civil Rights Act of 1964** *prohibits* **employment discrimination** on the basis of race, color, gender, religion, or national origin in hiring, firing, compensating, promoting, training, and other employment-related processes. The act applies to employers engaged in an industry affecting commerce and having fifteen or more employees.

When Congress passed the *Pregnancy Discrimination Act of 1978*, it extended the benefits of Title VII to pregnant women. Under the act, an employer cannot refuse to hire a pregnant woman, fire her, or force her to take maternity leave unless the employer can establish a *bona fide* occupational qualification defense (discussed later in this section). The act, which protects the job reinstatement rights of women returning from maternity leave, requires employers to treat pregnancy as they would a temporary disability.

The enforcement agency for Title VII is the **Equal Employment Opportunity Commission (EEOC)**. The EEOC is empowered (1) to file legal actions in its own name or to intervene in actions filed by third parties; (2) to attempt to resolve alleged violations through informal means prior to bringing suit; (3) to investigate all charges of discrimination; and (4) to issue guidelines and regulations concerning enforcement policy.

Proving Discrimination Each of the following constitutes discriminatory conduct prohibited by the act:

1. **Disparate Treatment.** Such treatment occurs when an employer uses a prohibited criterion in making an employment decision. The Supreme Court has held that the plaintiff will have shown a *prima facie* case of discrimination if she (a) is within a protected class, (b) had applied for an open position, (c) was qualified for the position, (d) was denied the job, and (e) the employer continued to try to fill the position from a pool of applicants with the complainant's qualifications. Once the plaintiff establishes a *prima facie* case, the burden shifts to the defendant to "articulate legitimate and nondiscriminatory reasons for the plaintiff's rejection." If the defendant so rebuts, the plaintiff then has the opportunity to demonstrate that the employer's stated reason was merely a pretext.

2. **Present Effects of Past Discrimination.** Such effects result when an employer engages in conduct that on its face is "neutral"—that is, nondiscriminatory—but that actually perpetuates past discriminatory practices. For example, it has been held illegal for a union that previously had limited its membership to whites to adopt a requirement that new members be related to or recommended by existing members.

3. **Disparate Impact.** This occurs when an employer adopts "neutral" rules that adversely affect a protected class and that are not justified as being necessary to the business. See *Griggs v. Duke Power Co.* Despite the employee's

Civil Rights Act of 1964 prohibits employment discrimination on the basis of race, color, gender, religion, or national origin

Employment discrimination hiring, firing, compensating, promoting, or training of employees based on race, color, gender, religion, or national origin

Equal Employment Opportunity Commission (EEOC) enforcement agency for the Civil Rights Act of 1964

Discrimination prohibited by the act; includes (1) using proscribed criteria to produce disparate treatment, (2) engaging in nondiscriminatory conduct that perpetuates past discrimination, and (3) adopting neutral rules that have a disparate impact

proof of disparate impact, the employer may prevail if it can demonstrate that the challenged practice is "job related for the position in question and consistent with business necessity." Nevertheless, under the Civil Rights Act of 1991, even if the employer can demonstrate the business necessity of the questioned practice, the complainant will still prevail if she shows that a nondiscriminatory alternative practice exists.

GRIGGS v. DUKE POWER CO. Supreme Court of the United States, 1971, 401 U.S. 424, 91 S.Ct. 849, 28 L.Ed.2d 158

FACTS During the years prior to the passage of the Civil Rights Act of 1964, Duke Power openly discriminated against African-Americans by allowing them to work only in the labor department of the plant's five departments. The highest paying job in the labor department paid less than the lowest paying jobs in the other four "operating" departments, in which only whites were employed. In 1955, the company began requiring a high school education for initial assignment to any department except labor. However, when Duke Power stopped restricting African-Americans to the labor department in 1965, it made completion of high school a prerequisite to transfer from labor to any other department. White employees hired before the high school education requirement was adopted continued to perform satisfactorily and to achieve promotions in the "operating" departments.

In 1965, the company also began requiring new employees in the departments other than labor to register satisfactory scores on two professionally prepared aptitude tests, in addition to having a high school education. In September 1965, Duke Power began to permit current employees to qualify for transfer to another department from labor by passing the two tests, neither of which was directed or intended to measure the ability to learn to perform a particular job or category of jobs. Griggs brought suit against Duke Power, claiming that the high school education and testing requirements were discriminatory and therefore prohibited by the Civil Rights Act of 1964. The district court held that Title VII was prospective only and that Duke's earlier policy of racial discrimination was thus beyond the reach of the act. The Court of Appeals rejected the district court's holding that residual discrimination from previous employment practices was beyond the scope of the act, but it held the district court was correct in its conclusion that there was no showing of a racial purpose or invidious intent in the promulgation of the new hiring requirements. The Court of Appeals, therefore, held that the act did not prohibit the use of such standards.

DECISION Judgment of the Court of Appeals in favor of Duke Power reversed.

OPINION The objective of the Civil Rights Act of 1964 is to achieve equality of employment opportunities and remove barriers that have operated to favor white employees over other employees. The act proscribes not only overt discrimination but also practices, procedures, and tests that are fair in form, but discriminatory in operation. The standard is business necessity. If an employment practice operates to exclude African-Americans and is not related to job performance, the practice is prohibited.

Here, employees who had not completed high school or taken the tests nonetheless continued to perform satisfactorily and made progress in those departments that used these criteria. Neither high school completion nor the general intelligence test was shown to bear a demonstrable relationship to successful job performance. Rather, these requirements served a covert discriminatory function and are, therefore, prohibited by the Civil Rights Act of 1964.

INTERPRETATION "Neutral" tests or job requirements that do not relate to job performance and discriminate based on race violate the Civil Rights Act of 1964.

Defenses The act provides three basic defenses: (1) a *bona fide* seniority or merit system; (2) a professionally developed ability test; and (3) a *bona fide* occupational qualification (BFOQ). The BFOQ defense does not apply to discrimination based on race. A fourth defense, business necessity, is available in a disparate impact case.

Remedies Remedies for violation of the act include enjoining the employer from engaging in the unlawful behavior, taking appropriate affirmative action, and reinstating employees to their rightful place (which may include promotion) and awarding them back pay from a date not more than two years prior to the filing of the charge with the EEOC. First promulgated by executive order, as discussed below, **affirmative action** generally means the active recruitment of minority applicants, although courts also have used the remedy to impose numerical hiring ratios (quotas) and hiring goals based on race and gender. In 1985, the EEOC defined affirmative action in employment as "actions appropriate to overcome the effects of past or present practices, policies, or other barriers to equal employment opportunity."

Affirmative action active recruitment of a designated group of applicants

Prior to 1991, only victims of *racial* discrimination could recover compensatory and punitive damages from the courts. Today, however, under the Civil Rights Act of 1991, *all* victims of *intentional discrimination* based on race, gender, religion, national origin, or disability can recover compensatory and punitive damages, except in cases involving disparate impact. In cases not involving race, the act limits the amount of recoverable damages according to the number of persons the defendant employs. Companies with 15 to 100 employees are required to pay no more than $50,000; companies with 101 to 200 employees, no more than $100,000; those with 201 to 500 employees, no more than $200,000; and those with 501 or more employees, no more than $300,000. Either party may demand a jury trial. Victims of racial discrimination are still entitled to recover unlimited compensatory and punitive damages.

Reverse Discrimination A major controversy has arisen over the use of reverse discrimination in achieving affirmative action. In this context, **reverse discrimination** refers to affirmative action that directs an employer to remedy the underrepresentation of a given race or gender in a traditionally segregated job by considering an individual's race or gender when hiring or promoting. An example would be an employer who discriminates against white males in order to increase the proportion of females or racial minority members in a company's work force.

Reverse discrimination employment decisions taking into account race or gender in order to remedy past discrimination

Due to the absence of state action, challenges to affirmative action plans adopted by private employers—those that are not governmental units at the local, state, or federal level—are tested under Title VII of the Civil Rights Act of 1964, not under the Equal Protection Clause of the U.S. Constitution. In 1987, the United States Supreme Court, under a Title VII cause of action, upheld an employer's right to promote a female employee rather than a white male employee who had scored higher on a qualifying examination.

When a state or local government adopts an affirmative action plan that is challenged as constituting illegal reverse discrimination, the plan is subject to strict scrutiny under the *Equal Protection Clause* of the Fourteenth Amendment. Under the strict scrutiny test, the subject classification must (1) be justified by a compelling governmental interest and (2) be the least intrusive means available. (For a fuller discussion of the Equal Protection Clause and the standards of review, see Chapter 4.)

With regard to racial discrimination, the U.S. Supreme Court has held that the federal government has "unique remedial powers" far exceeding those of state and local governments and that federal programs enacted to address such discrimination "are subject to a different [and less burdensome] standard than such classifications prescribed by state and local governments." Thus, the Court has upheld Federal Communication Commission programs giving preference to minorities applying for licenses to operate television and radio stations.

Sexual Harassment In 1980, the EEOC issued a definition of sexual harassment:

Sexual harassment is an illegal form of sexual discrimination that includes unwelcome sexual advances, requests for sexual favors, and other verbal or physical conduct of a sexual nature

Unwelcome sexual advances, requests for sexual favors, and other verbal or physical conduct of a sexual nature constitute sexual harassment when

1. submission to such conduct is made either explicitly or implicitly a term or condition of an individual's employment,
2. submission to or rejection of such conduct by an individual is used as the basis for employment decisions affecting such individual, or
3. such conduct has the purpose or effect of reasonably interfering with an individual's work performance or creating an intimidating, hostile or offensive working environment.

The courts, including the Supreme Court, have held that sexual harassment may constitute illegal sexual discrimination in violation of Title VII. Moreover, an employer will be held liable for sexual harassment committed by one of its employees if it does not take immediate action when it knows or should have known of the harassment. When the employee engaging in sexual harassment is an agent of the employer or holds a supervisory position over the victim, the employer may be liable without knowledge or reason to know. (See the following *The Law and You*.)

MERITOR SAVINGS BANK, FSB v. VINSON Supreme Court of the United States, 1986, 477 U.S. 57, 106 S.Ct. 2399, 91 L.Ed.2d 49

FACTS Mechelle Vinson was an employee of Meritor Savings Bank for approximately four years. Beginning as a teller-trainee, she ultimately advanced to the position of assistant branch manager. Her promotions were based solely upon merit. Sidney Taylor, a vice president of the bank and manager of the branch office in which Vinson worked, was Vinson's supervisor throughout her employment with the bank. After the bank fired Vinson for her abusive use of sick leave, Vinson brought an action against Taylor and the bank, alleging that during her employment she had "constantly been subjected to sexual harassment" by Taylor in violation of Title VII of the Civil Rights Act of 1964. At trial, Vinson stated that Taylor repeatedly demanded sexual favors from her, fondled her in front of other employees, and forcibly raped her on a number of occasions. Taylor and the bank categorically denied Vinson's allegations. The district court denied relief to Vinson, finding that any sexual relationship between Vinson and Taylor "was a voluntary one having nothing to do with her continued employment . . . or her advancement or promotions at that institution." Notwithstanding this conclusion, the district court went on to determine that "the bank was without notice [of Taylor's alleged conduct] and cannot be held liable for the alleged actions of Taylor." The Court of Appeals reversed.

DECISION Judgment of the Court of Appeals in reversing the district court affirmed and case remanded for proceedings consistent with this opinion.

OPINION Title VII of the Civil Rights Act of 1964 prohibits sexual discrimination in the workplace "against any individual with respect to his compensation, terms, conditions, or privileges of employment." The Court of Appeals correctly held that sexual harassment that creates a hostile or offensive working environment, even if it does not condition employment benefits upon sexual favors, is a violation. The language of Title VII and the guidelines issued by the Equal Employment Opportunity Commission in 1980 both support this conclusion. Moreover, the district court's finding that any sexual relationship between Vinson and Taylor "was a voluntary one" is no defense to the charge of sexual harassment under Title VII. Vinson's willingness is immaterial if Taylor's alleged advances were unwelcome or if Taylor made Vinson's compliance with the advances a condition of her continued employment. The Court of Appeals was wrong, however, in holding that employers who neither know nor reasonably could know of alleged employee misconduct are nonetheless strictly liable for a hostile working environment created by a supervisor's sexual advances. While lack of notice to an employer may not necessarily protect the employer from liability, Congress, by defining "employee" to include any "agent" of an employer, apparently intended to put limits on the acts of employees for which employers are to be held liable under Title VII.

INTERPRETATION Title VII of the Civil Rights Act of 1964 prohibits sexual harassment that creates a hostile work environment.

THE LAW AND YOU Sexual Harassment in the Workplace

"The American Psychological Association estimates that 71 percent of working women will be subjected to sexual harassment during their careers."

Sexual Harassment Is Illegal and Should Not Be Tolerated by Employers or Employees

Harassment on the basis of sex is a violation of state and federal law. Sexual harassment is defined as any form of unwelcome physical conduct of a sexual nature.

What Is Sexual Harassment?

The most extreme form of sexual harassment occurs when an employee loses a job, benefit or other privilege of employment, or is fired or loses a benefit or opportunity because the employee has rejected sexual demands.

However, a determination of sexual harassment does not depend on whether the victim was threatened with the loss of a job or other benefit. Conduct which unreasonably interferes with an individual's work performance or which creates an intimidating, hostile or offensive work environment is also prohibited by law.

Finally, retaliation by an employer against one who resists sexual harassment or who reports acts of sexual harassment involving co-workers is also illegal.

Examples of conduct which may be prohibited by law include but are not limited to, the following:

- Unwanted sexual advances, flirtations or propositions.
- Demands for sexual favors in exchange for favorable treatment or continued employment.
- Unwanted sexually oriented jokes or remarks.
- Verbal abuse of a sexual nature.
- Graphic verbal commentary about an individual's body, sexual prowess or sexual deficiency.
- A display in the workplace of sexually suggestive objects, pictures, posters or reading materials.
- A coerced sexual act or assault.
- Physical contact of a sexual nature such as pinching, grabbing, patting or brushing unnecessarily against another person's body.
- Leering, whistling or gestures of a sexual nature.

An Employer Can Prevent Sexual Harassment from Occurring in the Workplace

Prevention is the best tool for the elimination of sexual harassment. An employer should take all steps necessary to prevent sexual harassment from occurring, such as affirmatively raising the subject, expressing strong disapproval, developing appropriate sanctions, informing employees of their right to raise the issue of harassment, and developing methods to sensitize all concerned. Suggested strategies for preventing sexual harassment include the following:

1. Develop a written sexual harassment policy statement. This policy statement should begin by stating that sexual harassment is illegal and will not be tolerated. The policy statement may further include the employees' right to work in an environment free from harassment and from retaliation for reporting harassment, the fact that sexual harassment is a violation of state and federal law, identification of specific behaviors that constitute sexual harassment, and an outline of consequences for engaging in harassing behavior.
2. Communicate the policy by posting it in the workplace and including the policy in employee handbooks or policy manuals.
3. Develop procedures that will be followed upon filing a claim of sexual harassment and identify the person(s) to whom the employee should report the harassment.
4. Charge employees with the responsibility to report harassment or discriminatory practices.

A Victim of Harassment Can Seek Relief

There are a number of options available for seeking relief from sexual harassment. An employee may wish to resolve the complaint informally through use of the employer's established procedures. However, if no complaint procedures have been estab- lished in the workplace and the employee feels unable to report the harassment to supervisory personnel, the employee may seek relief in an external forum such as the United States Equal Employment Opportunity Commission, the Florida Commission on Human Relations or the judicial system.

United States Equal Employment Opportunity Commission
1-800-669-4000

[This pamphlet is provided as a public service by the Florida Bar Public Information and Bar Services Department, and the Florida Commission on the Status of Women with the understanding that it does not purport to give legal advice. The general information within is not intended as a substitute for the specific and personalized services of a competent lawyer or other professional.]

Reprinted with permission of the Florida Bar Association.

Comparable Worth Industrial statistics on salaries indicate that women earn approximately two-thirds as much as men do. Because the Equal Pay Act only requires equal pay for equal work, it does not apply to different jobs even if they are comparable. Thus, that statute provides no remedy for women who have been systematically undervalued and underpaid in "traditional" occupations, such as secretary, teacher, or nurse. As a result, women have sought redress under Title VII by arguing that the failure to pay comparable worth is discrimination on the basis of gender. The concept of **comparable worth** provides that employers should measure the relative values of different jobs through a job evaluation rating system that is free of any potential gender bias. Theoretically, the consistent application of objective criteria (including factors such as skill, effort, working conditions, responsibility, and mental demands) across job categories will ensure fair payment for all employees. For example, if evaluation under such a system found the jobs of truck driver and nurse to be at the same level, workers in both jobs would receive the same pay.

> **Comparable worth** equal pay for jobs of equal value to the employer

In a 1981 case, the Supreme Court held that a claim of discriminatory undercompensation based on sex could be brought under Title VII, even where female plaintiffs were performing jobs different than those of their male counterparts. As the Court noted, however, the case involved a situation in which the defendant intentionally discriminated in wages; and the defendant, not the courts, had compared the jobs in terms of value. The Court also held that the four defenses available under the Equal Pay Act would apply to a Title VII claim. Since this decision, the concept of comparable worth has met with limited success in the courts. Nonetheless, more than a dozen states have adopted legislation requiring public and private employers to pay equally for comparable work.

Executive Order

> **Executive Order** prohibits discrimination by federal contractors on the basis of race, color, gender, religion, or national origin on any work the contractors perform during the period of the federal contract

In 1965, President Johnson issued an **Executive Order** that prohibits discrimination by federal contractors on the basis of race, color, gender, religion, or national origin in employment on *any work* the contractor performs during the period of the federal contract. Federal contractors are also required to take affirmative action in recruiting. The Secretary of Labor, *Office of Federal Contract Compliance Programs* (OFCCP), administers enforcement of the program.

The program applies to all contractors and all of their subcontractors in excess of $10,000 who enter into a federal contract to be performed in the United States. Compliance with the affirmative action requirement differs for construction and nonconstruction contractors. All *nonconstruction* contractors with fifty or more employees or with contracts for more than $50,000 must have a written affirmative action plan in order to be in compliance. The plan must include a work force analysis; planned corrective action, if necessary, with specific goals and timetables; and procedures for auditing and reporting. The director of the OFCCP periodically issues goals and timetables for each segment of the *construction* industry in each region of the country. As a condition precedent to bidding on a federal contract, a contractor must agree to make a good faith effort to achieve current published goals.

Age Discrimination in Employment Act of 1967

> **Age Discrimination in Employment Act (ADEA)** prohibits discrimination on the basis of age in hiring, firing, or compensating

The **Age Discrimination in Employment Act (ADEA)** prohibits discrimination on the basis of age in employment areas that include hiring, firing, and compensating. The act applies to private employers having twenty or more employees and to all governmental units, regardless of size. The act also prohibits mandatory retirement for most employees, no matter what their age, unless the retirement is justified by a suitable defense.

The major statutory defenses include (1) a *bona fide* occupational qualification, (2) a *bona fide* seniority system, and (3) any other reasonable action. Remedies include back pay, injunctive relief, affirmative action, and liquidated damages equal to the amount of the award for "willful" violations.

Handicap Discrimination

The ***Rehabilitation Act of 1973*** attempts to assist the handicapped in obtaining rehabilitation training, access to public facilities, and employment. The act requires federal contractors and federal agencies to take affirmative action to hire qualified handicapped persons. It also prohibits discrimination on the basis of handicap in federal programs and programs receiving federal financial assistance.

A *handicapped person* is defined as an individual who (1) has a physical or mental impairment that substantially affects one or more of her major life activities, (2) has a history of major life activity impairment, *or* (3) is regarded as having such an impairment. Major life activities include functions such as caring for oneself, seeing, speaking, or walking. Alcohol and drug abuses are not considered handicapping conditions for the purposes of this statute.

The ***Americans with Disabilities Act (ADA) of 1990*** forbids an employer from discriminating against any person with a handicap with regard to "hiring or discharge . . ., employee compensation, advancement, job training and other terms, conditions and privileges of employment." In addition, businesses must make special accommodations, such as installing wheelchair-accessible bathrooms, for handicapped workers and customers unless the cost is unduly burdensome. An employer may use qualification standards, tests, or selection criteria that screen out disabled workers if these measures are job related and consistent with business necessity *and* if no reasonable accommodation is possible. The ADA took effect on July 26, 1992, for employers with twenty-five or more employees and on July 26, 1994, for employers with fifteen or more employees. Remedies for violation of the ADA are those generally allowed under Title VII and include injunctive relief, reinstatement, back pay, and, for intentional discrimination, compensatory and punitive damages (capped according to company size by the Civil Rights Act of 1991).

In addition, the ***Vietnam Veterans Readjustment Act of 1974*** requires firms having $10,000 or more in federal contracts to engage in affirmative action for disabled veterans and Vietnam-era veterans.

See Figure 43–2 for an overview of the federal statutes prohibiting employment discrimination.

Handicap discrimination several federal acts, including the Americans with Disabilities Act, provide assistance to the handicapped in obtaining rehabilitation training, access to public facilities, and employment

EMPLOYEE PROTECTION

Employees are accorded a number of job-related protections. These include a limited right not to be unfairly dismissed, a right to a safe and healthy workplace, compensation for injuries sustained in the workplace, and some financial security upon retirement or loss of employment. This section discusses (1) employee termination at will, (2) occupational safety and health, (3) employee privacy, (4) workers' compensation, (5) Social Security and unemployment insurance, (6) the Fair Labor Standards Act, (7) employee notice of termination or layoff, and (8) family and health leave.

FIGURE 43–2 Federal Employment Discrimination Laws

	Protected Characteristics	Prohibited Conduct	Defenses	Remedies
Equal Pay Act	Sex	Wages	Seniority Merit Quality or quantity measures Any factor other than sex	Back pay Injunction Liquidated damages Attorneys' fees
Title VII of Civil Rights Act	Race Color Sex Religion National origin	Terms, conditions, or privileges of employment	Seniority Ability test BFOQ (except for race) Business necessity (disparate impact only)	Back pay Injunction Reinstatement Compensatory and punitive damages for intentional discrimination • unlimited for race • limited for all others Attorneys' fees
Age Discrimination in Employment Act	Age	Terms, conditions, or privileges of employment	Seniority BFOQ Any other reasonable act	Back pay Injunction Reinstatement Liquidated damages for willful violation Attorneys' fees
Americans with Disabilities Act	Disability	Terms, conditions, or privileges of employment	Undue hardship Job-related criteria and business necessity Risk to public health and safety	Back pay Injunction Reinstatement Compensatory and punitive damages for intentional discrimination (limited) Attorneys' fees

Employee Termination at Will

Employee termination at will under the common law, a contract of employment for other than a definite term is terminable at will by either party

Under the common law, a contract of employment for other than a definite term is terminable at will by either party. Accordingly, under the common law, employers may "dismiss their employees at will for good cause, for no cause or even for cause morally wrong, without being thereby guilty of legal wrong." In recent years, however, a growing number of judicial exceptions to the rule, based on implied contract, tort, and public policy, have developed. A number of federal and state statutes enacted in the last fifty years also limit the rule, which may in addition be restricted by contractual agreement between employer and employee. In particular, most collective bargaining agreements negotiated through union representatives contain a provision prohibiting dismissal "without cause."

Statutory limitations have been enacted by the federal government and some states

Statutory Limitations Federal legislation has been passed that limits the employer's right to discharge. These statutes fall into three categories: (1) those protecting certain employees from discriminatory discharge, (2) those protecting certain employees in their exercise of statutory rights, and (3) those protecting certain employees from discharge without cause.

At the state level, statutes protect workers from discriminatory discharge for filing workers' compensation claims. Also, many state statutes parallel federal legislation. Some states have adopted statutes similar to the NLRA, and many states prohibit discrimination in employment on the basis of factors such as race, creed, nationality, gender, or age. In addition, some states have statutes prohibiting discharge or other punitive actions taken for the purpose of influencing voting or, in some states, political activity.

Judicial Limitations **Judicial limitations** on the employment-at-will doctrine have been based on contract law, tort law, and public policy. Cases founded in contract theory have relied on arguments maintaining, among other things, (1) that the dismissal was improper because the employee had detrimentally relied on the employer's promise of work for a reasonable time; (2) that the employment was not at will because of implied-in-fact promises of employment for a specific duration, which meant that the employer could not terminate the employee without just cause; (3) that the employment contract implied or expressly provided that the employee would not be dismissed so long as he satisfactorily performed his work; (4) that the employer had assured the employee that he would not be dismissed except for cause; or (5) that, upon entering into the employment contract, the employee gave consideration over and above the performance of services to support a promise of job security.

> **Judicial limitations** based on contract law, tort law, or public policy

Courts have also created exceptions to the employment-at-will doctrine by imposing tort obligations on employers, most particularly with respect to the torts of intentional infliction of emotional distress and of interference with employment relations.

The most frequent basis for finding a discharge to be wrongful is that the discharge violates statutory or other established public policy. In general, these cases involve dismissal for (1) refusing to violate a statute, (2) exercising a statutory right, (3) performing a statutory obligation, or (4) reporting an alleged violation of a statute that is of public interest.

HUNGER v. GRAND CENTRAL SANITATION Superior Court of Pennsylvania, 1996, 670 A.2d 173

FACTS Mark Hunger was the safety director at Grand Central Sanitation (Grand Central). On September 7, 1991, Hunger "became aware" that hazardous materials consisting of blasting caps were being deposited into garbage containers at Shu-Deb, Inc. (Shu-Deb). Grand Central collected garbage from these containers and dumped it at a dump site. Hunger knew that Grand Central was not licensed to dispose of hazardous materials and believed that it would violate state and/or federal law if the company transported or disposed of hazardous materials. Hunger also became concerned about the safety of company employees from the danger of transporting blasting caps. On September 9, 1991, Hunger informed Grand Central's owner and vice president, Gary Perin, of the information he received about the blasting caps. On September 12, 1991, Hunger, accompanied by Pennsylvania state police and

agents of the Federal Bureau of Alcohol, Tobacco, and Firearms, went to search the contents of Shu-Deb's containers. However, the garbage had already been collected, so Hunger and the police located the garbage truck that had collected the garbage and searched it. No hazardous materials were found in the truck. On October 4, 1991, Hunger was terminated because of the incident. Hunger sued for wrongful discharge. The trial court granted summary judgment to Grand Central and Hunger appealed.

DECISION Judgment affirmed.

OPINION As a general rule, no common law cause of action exists against an employer for termination of an at-will employment relationship. In a limited number of circumstances, an exception is made where the discharge of an at-will employee violates public policy.

continued

To state a public policy exception to the at-will employment doctrine, the employee must point to a clear public policy articulated in the constitution, in legislation, in administrative regulation, or in judicial decision. Hunger is correct in noting that it is illegal for unlicensed parties to transport hazardous materials. However, his actions in this case were premature. He provides no specifics about how he "became aware" of the blasting caps. Furthermore, no blasting caps were found and Grand Central did not violate the law. If Hunger had observed a deliberate or knowing violation of law by Grand Central, then his case might warrant a public policy exception to the at-will employment doctrine. However, since Hunger did not witness such illegal activity, Grand Central was within its rights to terminate his employment.

INTERPRETATION Wrongful discharge only exists when an employer's termination of an employee violates public policy as evidenced in the constitution, in legislation, in administrative regulation, or in judicial decision.

Occupational Safety and Health Act

Occupational Safety and Health Act enacted to assure workers of a safe and healthful work environment

In 1970, Congress enacted the **Occupational Safety and Health Act** to assure, as far as possible, a safe and healthful working environment for every worker. The act established the *Occupational Safety and Health Administration (OSHA)* to develop standards, conduct inspections, monitor compliance, and institute enforcement actions against those who are not in compliance.

Upon each employer who is engaged in a business affecting interstate commerce, the act imposes a general duty to provide a work environment that is "free from recognized hazards that are causing or likely to cause death or serious physical harm to his employees." In addition to this general duty, the employer must comply with specific OSHA-promulgated safety rules. The act also requires employees to comply with all OSHA rules and regulations. Finally, the act prohibits any employer from discharging or discriminating against an employee who exercises her rights under the act.

Enforcing the act generally involves OSHA inspections and citations of employers, as appropriate, for (1) breach of the general duty obligation, (2) breach of specific safety and health standards, or (3) failure to keep records, make reports, or post notices required by the act.

When a violation is discovered, the offending employer receives a written citation, a proposed penalty, and a date by which the employer must remedy the breach. Citations may be contested; in such cases, the Occupational Safety and Health Review Commission assigns administrative law judges to hold hearings. The commission, at its discretion, may grant review of an administrative law judge's decision; review is not a matter of right. If no such review occurs, the judge's decision becomes the commission's final order thirty days after receipt, and the aggrieved party may then appeal the order to the appropriate United States Circuit Court of Appeals.

Penalties for violations are both civil and criminal. In cases involving civil penalties, serious violations require that a penalty be proposed; in contrast, for nonserious violations, penalties are discretionary and rarely proposed. The act further empowers the Secretary of Labor to obtain temporary restraining orders in situations where regular OSHA procedures are insufficient to halt imminently hazardous or deadly business operations.

One stated purpose of the act is to encourage state participation in regulating safety and health. The act therefore permits a state to regulate the safety and health of the work environment within its borders, provided that OSHA approves the plan. The act sets minimum acceptable standards for the states to impose, but does not require that a state plan be identical to the OSHA guidelines. More than half of the states regulate health and safety in the workplace through state-promulgated plans.

Employee Privacy

Over the last decade, employee privacy has become a major issue. The fundamental right to privacy is a product of common law protection, discussed in Chapter 7. Thus, the tort of invasion of privacy safeguards employees from unwanted searches, electronic monitoring and other forms of surveillance, and disclosure of confidential records. The tort actually consists of four different torts: (1) unreasonable intrusion into the seclusion of another; (2) unreasonable public disclosure of private facts; (3) unreasonable publicity that places another in a false light; and (4) appropriation of a person's name or likeness. In addition, the federal government and some states have legislatively supplemented the common law in certain areas.

Drug and Alcohol Testing Although no federal legislation deals comprehensively with **drug and alcohol tests**, legislation in a number of states either prohibits such tests altogether or prescribes certain scientific and procedural standards for conducting them. In the absence of a state statute, *private* sector employees have little or no protection from such tests. The NLRB has held, however, that drug and alcohol testing in a union setting is a mandatory subject of collective bargaining.

Drug and alcohol testing some states either prohibit such tests or prescribe certain scientific and procedural safeguards

In 1989, the U.S. Supreme Court ruled that the employer of a *public* sector employee whose position involved public health or safety or national security could subject the employee to a drug or alcohol test without either first obtaining a search warrant or having reasonable grounds to believe the individual had engaged in any wrongdoing. Based on Supreme Court and lower court decisions, it appears that a government employer may use (1) random or universal testing where the public health or safety or national security is involved and (2) selective drug testing where there is sufficient cause to believe an employee has a drug problem.

Lie Detector Tests The *Federal Employee Polygraph Protection Act of 1988* prohibits private employers from requiring employees or prospective employees to undergo a **lie detector test**, inquiring about the results of such a test, or using the results of such a test or the refusal to be thus tested as grounds for an adverse employment decision. The act exempts government employers and, in certain situations, Energy Department contractors or persons providing consulting services for federal intelligence agencies. In addition, security firms and manufacturers of controlled substances may use a polygraph to test prospective employees. Moreover, an employer, as part of an ongoing investigation of economic loss or injury to its business, may utilize a polygraph test. Nevertheless, the use of the test must meet the following requirements: (1) it must be designed to investigate a specific incident or activity, not to document a chronic problem; (2) the employee to be tested must have had access to the property that is the subject of the investigation; and (3) the employer must have reason to suspect the particular employee.

Lie detector tests federal statute prohibits private employers from requiring employees or prospective employees to take such tests

Employees and prospective employees tested under any of these exemptions cannot be terminated, disciplined, or denied employment solely as a result of the test. The act further provides that those subjected to a polygraph test (1) cannot be asked intrusive or degrading questions regarding topics such as their religious beliefs, opinions as to racial matters, political views, or sexual preferences or behaviors; (2) must be given the right to review all questions before the test and to terminate the test at any time; and (3) must receive a complete copy of the test results.

Workers' Compensation

Workers' compensation
compensation awarded to an injured employee whose injury arose out of and in the course of his employment

In order to provide speedier and more certain relief to injured employees, all states have adopted statutes providing for **workers' compensation**. (Several states, however, exempt specified employers from workers' compensation statutes.) These statutes create commissions or boards that determine whether an injured employee is entitled to receive compensation and, if so, how much. The basis of recovery under workers' compensation is strict liability: the employee does not have to prove that the employer was negligent. The common law defenses of contributory negligence, voluntary assumption of risk, and the fellow servant rule (which covers injury caused by the negligence of a fellow employee) are *not* available to employers in workers' compensation proceedings. Such defenses are *abolished*. The *only* requirement is that the employee be injured and that the injury arise out of and in the course of his employment. The amounts recoverable are fixed by statute for each type of injury and are lower than the amounts a court or jury would probably award in an action at common law. The courts, therefore, do not have jurisdiction over such cases, except to review decisions of the board or

---

ETHICAL DILEMMA What (Unwritten) Right Does an Employee Have to a Job?

FACTS Gary Johnson was a six-year employee of Simon Corporation, a manufacturer of small appliances. Gary worked part of the time on the production line, where he manufactured fruit juicers, and the rest of the time as a quality control inspector.

Two years ago, the line foreman, James Sullivan, Gary's good and long-standing friend, observed that Gary was intoxicated on the job. James warned his friend privately against drinking on the job. Two months later, James again noticed that Gary was intoxicated; again he warned Gary that such conduct could not be tolerated. Because of the recession, James was worried about causing his friend to lose his job and therefore remained silent. Finally, after another month passed and James again noticed that Gary was intoxicated, he reported the problem to his supervisor.

The company's employee handbook explained that alcohol and drugs were prohibited on the job and that all employees identified as drug or alcohol dependent were to attend an alcohol and drug dependence program. After talking to James, the supervisor informed Gary that he must attend the company's program. Gary refused to cooperate and was fired.

Simon Corporation had regularly rehired employees who had been fired for intoxication but who had subsequently overcome their addiction. Although the rehiring practice was not spelled out in the handbook, the corporation had consistently followed the unwritten policy for ten years. However, though Gary eventually overcame his addiction, the corporation refused to rehire him. Gary is now suing the company to rehire him, alleging that his original employment contract implied that he would be rehired if he demonstrated that he had overcome an addiction.

Social, Policy, and Ethical Considerations

1. Should James have waited so long before reporting the problem to his supervisor? Explain.
2. Does the nature of the product and the role of the employee affect the ethical considerations in such a decision? Assume, for example, that the juicer Gary produced would be potentially harmful if defective and consider, as well, his role in quality control.
3. How should a company handle alcohol and drug abuse among its employees?
4. Compare the goal of supporting recovering addicts with the need to ensure that the best employees are selected to perform a job.
5. How, if at all, should the state or federal government be involved in this type of situation?

commission; even then, the courts may only determine whether such decisions are in accordance with the statute. If a third party, however, causes the injury, the employee may bring a tort action against that third party.

Early workers' compensation laws did not provide coverage for occupational disease, and most courts held that occupational injury did not include disease. Today, virtually all states provide general compensation coverage for occupational diseases, although the coverage varies greatly from state to state.

Social Security and Unemployment Insurance

Social Security was enacted in 1935 in an attempt to provide limited retirement and death benefits to certain employees. Since then, the benefits have greatly increased; and the federal Social Security system, which has expanded to cover almost all employees, now contains four major benefit programs: (1) Old-Age and Survivors Insurance (OASI) (providing retirement and survivor benefits), (2) Disability Insurance (DI), (3) Hospitalization Insurance (Medicare), and (4) Supplemental Security Income (SSI).

> **Social Security** measures by which the government provides economic assistance to disabled or retired employees and their dependents

The system is financed by contributions (taxes) paid by employers, employees, and self-employed individuals. Employees and employers pay matching contributions. It is the employer's responsibility to withhold the employee's contribution and to forward the full amount of the tax to the Internal Revenue Service. Employee-made contributions are not tax deductible by the employee, whereas those made by the employer are. Self-employed persons are also required to report their taxable income and to pay the Social Security tax.

The federal *unemployment insurance* system was initially created by Title IX of the Social Security Act of 1935. Subsequently, Title IX was supplemented by the Federal Unemployment Tax Act and by numerous other federal statutes. This complex system depends upon the cooperation of state and federal programs. Federal law provides the general guidelines, standards, and requirements, while the states administer the program through their own employment laws. The system is funded by employer taxes: federal taxes generally pay the program's administrative costs, and state contributions pay for the actual benefits.

The purpose of the Federal Unemployment Tax Act is to provide **unemployment compensation** to workers who have lost their jobs, usually through no fault of their own, and cannot find other employment. Payments, generally made weekly, are based on a particular state's formula.

> **Unemployment compensation** compensation awarded to workers who have lost their jobs and cannot find other employment

Fair Labor Standards Act

The **Fair Labor Standards Act** (**FLSA**) regulates the employment of child labor outside of agriculture. The act prohibits the employment of anyone under fourteen years of age in nonfarm work, except for newspaper deliverers and child actors. Fourteen- and fifteen-year-olds may work for a limited number of hours outside of school hours, under specific conditions, in certain *nonhazardous* occupations. Sixteen- and seventeen-year-olds may work in any *nonhazardous* job, while persons eighteen years old or older may work in *any* job, whether it is hazardous or not. The Secretary of Labor determines which occupations are considered hazardous.

> **Fair Labor Standards Act** (**FLSA**) regulates the employment of child labor outside of agriculture

In addition, the FLSA imposes wage and hour requirements upon covered employers. The act provides for a minimum hourly wage and overtime pay of time-and-a-half for hours worked in excess of forty hours per week. However, the FLSA exempts certain workers from both its minimum wage and overtime provisions; those excluded include professionals, managers, and outside salespersons.

THE LAW AND YOU   Workers' Compensation

Who Is Covered by Workers' Compensation?

Workers' compensation applies to all employees with the exception of casual workers performing services not related to an employer's business or persons employed in a limited function. Domestic service workers are also excluded unless the employer has purchased workers' compensation insurance coverage. Corporate officers may elect to not be covered.

What Injuries Are Covered?

All injuries that arise in the course of employment and are related to that work are covered regardless of the worker's previous physical condition. Categorized occupational diseases are also covered as well as aggravations of prior pulmonary difficulties resulting from an employee's continued exposure at the work place.

The law applies to all injuries occurring in Pennsylvania as well as occupational diseases resulting from exposure while working within the state. For claims arising from coal workers' pneumoconiosis, silicosis and asbestosis, the Act requires an aggregate employment of at least two years in Pennsylvania during the 10 years prior to disability under certain circumstances.

An employee's negligence will not preclude him/her from receiving compensation for the injury. However, compensation will not be paid for injury or death which was intentionally self-inflicted or the result of an employee's violation of the law. In general, injuries caused by a third person are covered as long as they occur in the course of employment.

Is an Employer Required to Pay Workers' Compensation?

Yes. It is required by law that all employers provide payment of workers' compensation except in cases where employees are not specifically covered. An employee cannot contract away his rights to compensation.

When Will I Receive Compensation?

Generally, compensation is paid beginning with the eighth day of the disability. Compensation will not be paid for the first seven days unless your disability lasts longer than 14 days. The first payment of compensation must begin no later than the 21st day after your employer knew of your injury. If you have not received compensation within that time, you should call the Bureau of Workers' Compensation.

If you do receive a Notice of Compensation Payable, a Temporary Notice of Compensation Payable, or are asked to enter into an Agreement for Compensation, make sure that the description of the injury or disease and all of the statements in the Notice or Agreement are correct. Any corrections should be made through the Bureau of Workers' Compensation.

How Long Will the Benefits Continue?

Full disability payments will continue as long as the employee is totally disabled. Partial disability may be paid if an injury does not result in complete loss of earnings, but it is generally paid for a period not exceeding 500 weeks.

However, for injuries that occur on or after June 24, 1996, total disability benefits may not extend beyond two years. In most cases that do not involve serious injuries, the worker is less than 50 percent impaired according to AMA Guidelines and the employer may obtain an impairment rating exam. If the claimant, after an impairment exam, is found to be less than 50 percent impaired under the AMA Guidelines, benefits will be limited to partial disability. Unless it is established that the claimant has earning power, partial disability is paid at the total disability rate for 500 weeks.

Partial disability may also be paid if a claimant returns to work but does not receive earnings equal to the pre-injury wages. The period of payment cannot exceed 500 weeks, which is a little more than 9½ years.

If I Receive Compensation, Can I Still Sue My Employer?

No. Because the law makes the employer responsible for a worker's injuries regardless of the employee's carelessness, the law also provides that employees do not have the right to recover from the employer in any legal action other than workers' compensation. However, if the employer fails to provide for workers' compensation payments as required by law, the employee can sue for damages. If your work injury is caused by a third party, that party is subject to a civil suit.

How Should I Proceed If I Am Injured On The Job?

If you are injured on the job or suspect that you have an occupational disease, you should:

- Report the injury or suspicion of disease immediately to your employer, his/her representative or the person in charge of your job. If you are unable to do so because of the injury, your union representative or another person may notify the employer for you.
- Report the injury to your union representative or call the Bureau of Workers' Compensation at 1-800-482-2383.
- Get medical treatment. If you need medical attention, ask for it immediately. Make sure that you report to your physician the time that the injury occurred at work and that you take note of related dates and keep copies of all medical bills. You may go to the

continued

physician of your choice unless a list of at least six health care providers has been posted by the employer for workers' compensation purposes. In this case, you must seek treatment from one of these six providers during the first 90 days after your injury. After that time you may go to the provider of your choice, but the provider must file periodic reports to your employer outlining your progress.

- Act quickly. The law requires that you give notice to your employer of an injury within 21 days of the injury and no later than 120 days after the injury. This means that, if you report the injury to your employer within 21 days, you will receive compensation dating from the day of the injury. If you do not report the injury to your employer until after 21 days but within the 120 day limit, you will only receive compensation dating from the day that you reported the injury to your employer. In

addition, you must bring your claim within three years of the date of injury. Failing to meet these time requirements may result in a denial of your claim.

Your employer is required to issue a Notice of Workers' Compensation Denial within 21 days if compensation is not to be paid or, alternatively, a Temporary Notice of Compensation Payable may be used by your employer for not more than six weeks of compensation. If you are denied compensation, you should file a claim petition with the Bureau of Workers' Compensation in Harrisburg or at the nearest district workers' compensation office.

What Shouldn't I Do?

- Do not sign any incomplete papers.
- Do not sign any papers or statements unless you completely understand them.
- Do not sign any written statements about your injury or

exposure to disease unless you have a witness, union representative, or your attorney present and you fully agree with the written statements. Always get a copy of any statements you sign.

- Do not sign any Supplemental Agreements unless they correctly represent the current status of your disability. It may also help to have the Supplemental Agreement reviewed by a lawyer.
- Do not sign a Final Receipt of compensation unless you are fully recovered from your injury.

[The material in this feature has been issued to inform and not to advise. It is based on Pennsylvania law. The statements are general, and individual facts in a given case may alter their application or involve other laws not referred to here.]

Worker Adjustment and Retraining Notification Act

The **Worker Adjustment and Retraining Notification Act (WARN)** requires an employer to provide sixty days' advance notice of a plant closing or mass layoff. A "plant closing" is defined as the permanent or temporary shutting down of a single site or units within a site if the shutdown results in fifty or more employees losing employment during any thirty-day period. A "mass layoff" is defined as a loss of employment during a thirty-day period either for 500 employees or for at least one-third of the employees at a given site, if that one-third equals or exceeds fifty employees. WARN requires that notification be given to specified state and local officials as well as to the affected employees or their union representatives. The act, which reduces the notification period with regard to failing companies and emergency situations, applies to employers with a total of 100 or more employees who in the aggregate work at least 2,000 hours per week, not including overtime.

> **Worker Adjustment and Retraining Notification Act (WARN)** federal statute that requires an employer to provide sixty days' advance notice of a plant closing or mass layoff

Family and Medical Leave Act of 1993

The **Family and Medical Leave Act of 1993** requires employers with fifty or more employees and governments at the federal, state, and local levels to grant employees up to twelve weeks of leave during any twelve-month period for the birth of a child; adopting or gaining foster care of a child; or the care of a spouse, child, or parent who suffers from a serious health condition. The act defines a

> **Family and Medical Leave Act of 1993** requires some employers to grant employees leave for serious health conditions or certain other events

"serious health condition" as an "illness, injury, impairment or physical or mental condition" that involves inpatient medical care at a hospital, hospice, or residential care facility or continuing medical treatment by a health-care provider. Employees are eligible for such leave if they have been employed by their present employer for at least twelve months and have worked at least 1,250 hours for their employer during the twelve months preceding the leave request. The requested leave may be paid, unpaid, or a combination of both.

CHAPTER SUMMARY

Labor Law	**Purpose** to provide the general framework in which management and labor negotiate terms of employment
	Norris-LaGuardia Act established as United States policy the full freedom of labor to form labor unions without employer interference and withdrew from the federal courts the power to issue injunctions in nonviolent labor disputes (any controversy concerning terms or conditions of employment or union representation)
	National Labor Relations Act
	■ *Right to Unionize* declares it a federally protected right of employees to unionize and to bargain collectively
	■ *Prohibits Unfair Employer Practices* the act identifies five unfair labor practices by an employer
	■ *National Labor Relations Board (NLRB)* created to administer these rights
	Labor-Management Relations Act
	■ *Prohibits Unfair Union Practices* the act identifies seven unfair labor practices by a union
	■ *Prohibits Closed Shops* agreement that mandates that an employer can hire only union members
	■ *Allows Union Shops* an employer can hire nonunion members, but the employee must join the union
	Labor-Management Reporting and Disclosure Act aimed at eliminating corruption in labor unions

Employment Discrimination Law	**Equal Pay Act** prohibits an employer from discriminating between employees on the basis of gender by paying unequal wages for the same work
	Civil Rights Act of 1964 prohibits employment discrimination on the basis of race, color, gender, religion, or national origin
	■ *Equal Employment Opportunity Commission (EEOC)* enforcement agency for the act
	■ *Affirmative Action* the active recruitment of a designated group of applicants
	■ *Discrimination* prohibited by the act; includes (1) using proscribed criteria to produce disparate treatment, (2) engaging in nondiscriminatory conduct that perpetuates past discrimination, and (3) adopting neutral rules that have a disparate impact

■ *Reverse Discrimination* affirmative action that directs an employer to consider an individual's race or gender when hiring or promoting for the purpose of remedying underrepresentation of that race or gender in traditionally segregated jobs

■ *Sexual Harassment* is an illegal form of sexual discrimination that includes unwelcome sexual advances, requests for sexual favors, and other verbal or physical conduct of a sexual nature

■ *Comparable Worth* equal pay for jobs that are of equal value to the employer

Executive Order prohibits discrimination by federal contractors on the basis of race, color, gender, religion, or national origin on any work the contractors perform during the period of the federal contract

Age Discrimination in Employment Act prohibits discrimination on the basis of age in hiring, firing, or compensating

Handicap Discrimination several federal acts, including the Americans with Disabilities Act, provide assistance to the handicapped in obtaining rehabilitation training, access to public facilities, and employment

---

Employee Protection

Employee Termination at Will under the common law, a contract of employment for other than a definite term is terminable at will by either party

■ *Statutory Limitations* have been enacted by the federal government and some states

■ *Judicial Limitations* based on contract law, tort law, or public policy

■ *Limitations Imposed by Union Contract*

Occupational Safety and Health Act enacted to assure workers of a safe and healthful work environment

Employee Privacy

■ *Drug and Alcohol Testing* some states either prohibit such tests or prescribe certain scientific and procedural safeguards

■ *Lie Detector Tests* federal statute prohibits private employers from requiring employees or prospective employees to take such tests

Workers' Compensation compensation awarded to an employee who is injured in the course of his or her employment

Social Security measures by which the government provides economic assistance to disabled or retired employees and their dependents

Unemployment Compensation compensation awarded to workers who have lost their jobs and cannot find other employment

Fair Labor Standards Act regulates the employment of child labor outside of agriculture

Worker Adjustment and Retraining Notification Act federal statute that requires an employer to provide sixty days' advance notice of a plant closing or mass layoff

Family and Medical Leave Act of 1993 requires some employers to grant employees leave for serious health conditions or certain other events

---

QUESTIONS

1. List and briefly discuss the major labor law statutes.
2. Distinguish between the prohibited unfair labor practices that apply to employers and those that apply to unions.

3. Discuss the defenses available to an employer under (1) the Equal Pay Act and (b) the Civil Rights Act of 1964.

4. Discuss (a) the various types of conduct prohibited as employment discrimination, (b) reverse discrimination, (c) sexual harassment, and (d) comparable worth.

5. Discuss the traditional common law, the statutory, and the recent judicial approaches to the termination-at-will doctrine.

Internet Question. Find the Occupational Safety and Health Administration's home page and (a) explore "what's new," (b) determine what OSHA is doing about workplace violence, (c) examine the Occupational Injury and Illness Incidence Rates, and (d) review the latest News Releases.

PROBLEMS

1. Gooddecade manufactures and sells automobile parts throughout the eastern part of the United States. Among its full-time employees are 220 fourteen- and fifteen-year-olds. These teenagers are employed throughout the company and are paid at an hourly wage rate of $3 per hour. Discuss the legality of this arrangement.

2. Janet, a twenty-year-old woman, applied for a position driving a truck for Federal Trucking, Inc. Janet, who is 5'4" tall and weighs 135 lbs, was denied the job because the company requires that all employees be at least 5'6" tall and weigh at least 150 lbs. Federal justifies this requirement on the basis that its drivers are frequently forced to move heavy loads in making pickups and deliveries. Janet brings a cause of action. Decision?

3. N.I.S. promoted John, a forty-two-year-old employee, to a foreman's position while passing over James, a fifty-eight-year-old employee. N.I.S. told James he was too old for the job and that it preferred a younger man. James brings a cause of action. Decision?

4. Anthony was employed as a forklift operator for Blackburn Construction Company. While on the job, Anthony operated the forklift in a manner that was careless and in direct violation of Blackburn's procedural manual, and as a result, caused himself severe injury. Blackburn denies liability based on Anthony's (a) gross negligence, (b) disobedience of the procedural manual, and (c) written waiver of liability. Anthony now brings a cause of action. Decision?

5. Hazelwood School District is located in Sleepy Hollow Township. It is being sued by several teachers who applied for teaching positions with the school but were rejected. The plaintiffs, who are all African-Americans, produce the following evidence:

   (a) 1.8 percent of the Hazelwood School District's teachers are African-Americans, whereas 15.4 percent of the teachers in Sleepy Hollow Township are African-Americans; and

   (b) the hiring decisions by Hazelwood School District are based solely on subjective criteria.

   Decision?

6. T. W. E., a large manufacturer, prohibited its employees from distributing union leaflets to other employees while on the company's property. Richard, an employee of T. W. E., disregarded the prohibition and passed out the leaflets before his work shift began. T. W. E. discharged Richard for his actions. Has T. W. E. committed an unfair labor practice?

7. Erwick was dismissed from her job at the C & T Steel Company because she was "an unsatisfactory employee." At the time, Erwick was active in an effort to organize a union at C & T. Is the dismissal valid?

8. Johnson, president of the First National Bank of A, believes that it is appropriate to employ only female tellers. Hence, First National refuses to employ Ken Baker as a teller but does offer him a maintenance position at the same salary. Baker brings a cause of action against First National Bank. Decision?

9. Section 103 of the Federal Public Works Employment Act of 1977 establishes the MBE (Minority Business Enterprise) program and requires that, absent a waiver by the secretary of commerce, 10 percent of all federal grants given by the Economic Development Administration be used to purchase services or supplies from businesses owned and controlled by U.S. citizens belonging to one of six minority groups: African-American, Spanish-speaking, Oriental, Native American, Eskimo, and Aleut. White owners of businesses contend the act constitutes illegal reverse discrimination. Discuss.

10. Worth H. Percivil, a mechanical engineer, was employed by General Motors for twenty-six years until he was discharged. At the time his employment was terminated, Percivil was head of GM's Mechanical Development Department. Percivil sued GM for wrongful discharge. He contends that he was discharged as a result of a conspiracy among his fellow executives to force him out of his employment because of his age, because he had legitimately complained about certain deceptive practices of GM, because he had refused to give the government false information although urged to do so by his superiors, and because he had, on the contrary, undertaken to correct certain alleged misrepresentations made to the government. General Motors claims that Percivil's employment was terminable at the will of GM for any reason and with or without cause, provided that the discharge was not prohibited by statute. Decision?

11. On May 26, 1950, the trial examiner issued his Intermediate Report finding that the respondent

(Sailors' Union) had not engaged in unfair union practices under Section 8(b) in their dispute with Samsoc. With respect to the unfair labor practices, the complaint alleged that the respondent induced and encouraged employees of Moore Dry Dock Company to engage in a strike or concerted refusal in the course of their employment to perform services for Moore in connection with the conversion into a bulk gypsum carrier of the S. S. *Phopho*, a vessel owned by Samsoc, the object being to force Moore to cease doing business with Samsoc and thus force Samsoc to resolve its dispute with the respondent. The General Counsel and Moore appealed. Decision?

12. In 1974, the United Steelworkers of America and Kaiser Aluminum entered into a master collective bargaining agreement covering terms and conditions of employment at fifteen Kaiser plants. The agreement contained an affirmative action plan designed to eliminate conspicuous racial imbalances in Kaiser's then almost exclusively white craftwork forces. African-American craft-hiring goals were set for each Kaiser plant equal to the percentage of African-Americans in the respective local labor forces. To meet these goals, on-the-job training programs were established to teach unskilled production workers—African-Americans and whites—the skills necessary to become craftworkers. The plan reserved for African-American employees 50 percent of the openings in these newly created in-plant training programs.

Pursuant to the national agreement, Kaiser altered its craft-hiring practice in its Gramercy, Louisiana, plant by establishing a program to train its production workers to fill craft openings. Selection of craft trainees was made on the basis of seniority. At least 50 percent of the new trainees were to be African-American until the percentage of African-American skilled craftworkers in the Gramercy plant approximated the percentage of African-Americans in the local labor force. During this affirmative action plan's first year of operation, thirteen craft trainees (seven African-American, six white) were selected from Gramercy's production work force. The most senior African-American selected had less seniority than several white production workers who were denied admission to the program. Weber, one of these white employees, brought suit claiming that the affirmative action plan discriminated against white employees and therefore violated the Civil Rights Act of 1964. Decision?

13. At Whirlpool's manufacturing plant in Ohio, overhead conveyors transported household appliance components throughout the plant. A wire mesh screen was positioned below the conveyors in order to catch falling components and debris. Maintenance employees frequently had to stand on the screens to clean them. In 1973, Whirlpool began installing heavier wire

because several employees had fallen partly through the old screens and one had fallen completely through to the plant floor. At this time, the company warned workers to walk only on the frames beneath the wire but not on the wire itself. Before the heavier wire had been completely installed, a worker fell to his death through the old screen. A short time after this incident, Deemer and Cornwell, two plant employees, met with the plant safety director to discuss the mesh, to voice their concerns, and to obtain the name, address, and telephone number of the local Occupational Safety and Health Administration (OSHA) representative. The next day, the two employees refused to clean a portion of the old screen. They were then ordered to punch out for the remainder of the shift without pay and also received written reprimands, which were placed in their employment files. Secretary of Labor Marshall brought suit, claiming that Whirlpool's actions against Deemer and Cornwell constituted discrimination in violation of the Occupational Safety and Health Act. Decision?

14. The defendant, Berger Transfer and Storage, operated a national moving and transfer business employing approximately forty persons. In May and June of 1979, Local 705 of the International Brotherhood of Teamsters spoke with a number of Berger employees, obtaining twenty-eight cards signed in support of the union. The management of Berger, unwilling to work with the union, attempted to prevent it from representing Berger employees. The company first assigned all work to those with high seniority, in effect temporarily laying off low-seniority employees. The management then threatened to lay off permanently those with low seniority and threatened all employees with a total closedown of the plant. The management interrogated several employees about their union involvement and attempted to extract information about other employees' activities. When the union presented the company with the signed cards and recognition agreement, Berger refused to acknowledge the union's existence or its right to bargain on behalf of the employees. The union then called a strike, with employees picketing the Berger warehouse. During the picketing, the company threatened to terminate the picketers if they did not return to work. Later, one manager on two occasions recklessly drove a truck through the picket line, striking employees. Finally, the company contacted several of the employees and offered them the "grievance procedures and job security" the union would provide. The employees refused the offer. On June 15, the strike ended, with most of the picketers returning to work. Local 705 filed a complaint with the National Labor Relations Board, alleging that Berger had committed unfair labor practices in violation of the National Labor Relations Act. Decision?

15. The appellant—City of Richmond, Virginia (the City)—adopted a Minority Business Utilization Plan requiring prime contractors awarded city construction contracts to subcontract at least 30 percent of the dollar amount of each contract to one or more Minority Business Enterprises (MBEs). The plan defined an MBE to include a business from anywhere in the country that is at least 51 percent owned and controlled by African-American, Spanish-speaking, Oriental, Native American, Eskimo, or Aleut citizens. Although the plan declared that it was "remedial" in nature, it was adopted after a public hearing at which no direct evidence was presented that the City had discriminated on the basis of race in letting contracts or that its prime contractors had discriminated against minority subcontractors. The evidence introduced in support of the plan included a statistical study indicating that, although the City's population was 50 percent African-American, less than 1 percent of its prime construction contracts had been awarded to minority businesses in recent years. Additional evidence showed that a variety of local contractors' trade associations had virtually no MBE members. The appellee, J. A. Croson Co., the sole bidder on a city contract, was denied a waiver and lost its contract because of the plan. The appellee brought suit, alleging that the plan was unconstitutional under the Fourteenth Amendment's Equal Protection Clause. Decision?

16. Burdine, a woman, was hired by the Texas Department of Community Affairs as a clerk in the Public Service Careers Division (PSC). The PSC provides training and employment opportunities for unskilled workers. At the time she was hired, Burdine already had several years' experience in employment training. She was soon promoted, and later, when her supervisor resigned, she performed additional duties that usually had been assigned to the supervisor. Burdine applied for the position of supervisor, but the position remained unfilled for six months, until a male employee from another division was brought in to fill it. Burdine alleges discrimination violating Title VII of the 1964 Civil Rights Act. The defendant Texas Department of Community Affairs responds that nondiscriminatory evaluation criteria were used to choose the new supervisor. In order to comply with Title VII, must the Texas Department of Community Affairs hire Burdine as supervisor if she and the male candidate are equally qualified? Explain.

17. Ms. Wise was fired from her job at the Mead Corporation after she was involved in a fight with a coworker. On four other unrelated occasions, fights occurred between male coworkers. Only one of the males was fired, but this was after his second fight, in which he seriously injured another employee. There is no dispute that Ms. Wise was qualified and performed her duties adequately. Ms. Wise successfully establishes a *prima facie* case of discrimination. However, the defendant, Mead Corporation, meets its burden to "articulate legitimate and nondiscriminatory reasons" for firing Ms. Wise. Can she prevail? Explain.

18. John Novosel was employed by Nationwide Insurance Company from December 1966 until November 1981. Novosel had been a model employee and, at the time of discharge, was a district claims manager and a candidate for the position of division claims manager. In October 1981, Nationwide circulated a memorandum requesting the participation of all employees in an effort to lobby the Pennsylvania state legislature for the passage of a certain bill before the body. Novosel, who had privately indicated his disagreement with Nationwide's political views, refused to lend his support to the lobby, and his employment with Nationwide was terminated. Novosel brought two separate claims against Nationwide, arguing, first, that his discharge for refusing to lobby the state legislature on behalf of Nationwide constituted the tort of wrongful discharge in that it was arbitrary, malicious, and contrary to public policy. Novosel also contended that Nationwide breached an implied contract guaranteeing continued employment so long as his job performance was satisfactory. The district court dismissed both claims, and Novosel appealed. Decision?

CHAPTER 44

Antitrust

The economic community is best served in normal times by free competition in trade and industry. It is in the public interest that quality, price, and service in an open, competitive market for goods and services be determining factors in the business rivalry for the customer's dollar. Rather than compete, however, businesses would prefer to eliminate their competition and, consequently, to enjoy a position from which they could dictate both the price of their goods and the quantity they produce. While eliminating competition by producing a better product is the proper goal of a business, some businesses effect this elimination through illegitimate means, such as fixing prices and allocating exclusive territories to certain competitors within an industry. The law of antitrust prohibits such activities and attempts to assure free and fair competition in the marketplace.

The common law has traditionally favored competition and has held that agreements and contracts in restraint of trade are illegal and unenforceable. In addition, though several states enacted antitrust statutes during the 1800s, the latter half of the nineteenth century revealed concentrations of economic power in the form of "trusts" and "combinations" that were too powerful and widespread to be curbed effectively by state action. In 1890, this awesome and uncontrollable growth of power prompted Congress to enact the Sherman Antitrust Act, the first federal statute in this field. Since then, Congress has enacted other antitrust statutes, including the Clayton Act, the Robinson-Patman Act, and the Federal Trade Commission Act. These statutes prohibit anticompetitive practices and seek to prevent unreasonable concentrations of economic power that stifle or weaken competition.

SHERMAN ANTITRUST ACT

Section 1 of the Sherman Act prohibits contracts, combinations, and conspiracies that restrain trade, while Section 2 outlaws both monopolies and attempts to monopolize. Failure to comply with either section is a criminal violation and subjects the offender to fine or imprisonment or both. As amended by the 1990 Antitrust Amendments, the act subjects individual offenders to imprisonment of up to three years and fines up to $350,000, while corporate offenders are subject to fines of up to $10,000,000 per violation. Moreover, the act empowers the federal district courts to issue injunctions restraining violations; and anyone injured by a violation is entitled to recover in a civil action **treble damages** (that is, three times the amount of the actual loss sustained). The United States Department of Justice and the Federal Trade Commission have the duty to institute appropriate enforcement proceedings other than treble damages actions.

Treble damages three times actual loss

In 1992, the Justice Department expanded its enforcement policy regarding the Sherman Act to cover conduct by foreign companies that harms U.S. exports. Under the new policy, the department examines conduct to determine whether it would violate the law if it occurred within borders of the United States. The department has indicated that it will focus primarily on boycotts and cartels that injure the export of U.S. products and services.

Restraint of Trade

Restraint of trade
Section 1 prohibits contracts, combinations, and conspiracies that restrain trade

Section 1 of the Sherman Act provides that "[e]very contract, combination in the form of trust or otherwise, or conspiracy, in restraint of trade or commerce among the several states, or with foreign nations is hereby declared to be illegal." Because the section's language is so broad, identifying the elements that constitute a violation has been largely a product of judicial interpretation.

Standards As noted above, Section 1 prohibits every contract, combination, or conspiracy in restraint of trade. Taken literally, this prohibition would invalidate every unperformed contract. To avoid such an unrealistic application, the courts have interpreted this section to invalidate only *unreasonable* restraints of trade. This standard is known as the **rule of reason** test, a flexible standard under which the courts, in determining whether a challenged practice unreasonably restricts competition, consider a variety of factors, including the makeup of the relevant industry, the defendants' positions within that industry, the ability of the defendants' competitors to respond to the challenged practice, and the defendants' purpose in adopting the restraint. After reviewing the various factors, a court determines whether the challenged restraint unreasonably restricts competition.

Rule of reason standard that balances the restraint's anticompetitive effects against its procompetitive effects

By requiring the courts to balance the *anticompetitive* effects of every questioned restraint against its *procompetitive* effects, this standard placed a substantial burden upon the judicial system. The Supreme Court addressed this problem by declaring certain categories of restraints to be unreasonable by their very nature, that is, **illegal** *per se*. Characterizing a type of restraint as *per se* illegal significantly affects the prosecution of an antitrust suit. In such a case, the plaintiff need only show that the type of restraint occurred; she need not prove that the restraint limited competition. The defendants, in turn, may not defend on the basis that the restraint is reasonable. Furthermore, the court is not required to conduct extensive, and often difficult, economic analysis.

Illegal *per se* conclusively presumed unreasonable and therefore illegal

BCB ANESTHESIA CARE, LTD. v. PASSAVANT MEMORIAL AREA HOSPITAL ASSOCIATION United States Court of Appeals, Seventh Circuit, 1994, 36 F.3d 664

FACTS Certified registered nurse anesthetists (CRNAs) compete with physician-anesthesiologists (MDAs) to provide anesthesia services. BCB Anesthesia Care, Ltd. (BCB) is comprised of three CRNAs who, prior to July 29, 1991, were employed by Passavant Memorial Area Hospital Association (Passavant). Prior to July 29, 1991, Dr. Peter Roodhouse, a physician-anesthesiologist working as an independent contractor, provided anesthesia services at the hospital. On July 29, 1991, BCB entered into an agreement with Passavant to provide anesthesia services to Passavant's patients, billing patients directly.

During the last five months of 1991, BCB and other staff physicians performed all but three anesthesia procedures at the hospital. However, BCB alleges that Dr. Roodhouse billed patients and third-party payers for services he did not perform, causing patients to complain about double billing and interfering with BCB's ability to collect payments. Dr. Roodhouse also derided BCB's billing practices to local physicians, causing them to believe that BCB billings were either too high or unethical. Beginning in April 1992, Dr. Roodhouse scheduled anesthesia services at the hospital so as to perform the majority of those services during that

continued

month. On May 20, 1992, Passavant terminated its contract with BCB. Subsequently, Passavant entered into an agreement with Dr. Roodhouse and raised the price it charged patients for anesthesia from $11 to $17 per unit.

BCB alleges that all of this constitutes a conspiracy in restraint of trade to limit their practice, to initiate a tying agreement between Passavant and Dr. Roodhouse, to boycott the plaintiffs, and to fix prices illegally. The district court dismissed the complaint on the grounds that BCB had not alleged a sufficient nexus with interstate commerce to invoke Sherman Act jurisdiction.

DECISION Judgment affirmed on different grounds.

OPINION The proper inquiry to determine if a restraint of trade is governed by the Sherman Act is to ask whether or not activities allegedly infected by the restraint had a more than insubstantial effect on interstate commerce. The facts of this case indicate that BCB's complaint should not have been dismissed on jurisdictional grounds. First, BCB alleges that Passavant derives substantial revenue from interstate insurance and federal Medicare and Medicaid payments, and that it purchased substantial quantities of medical supplies coming from other states. BCB further alleges that Passavant treats out-of-state patients and states that BCB's billing is performed by an out-of-state agency. BCB also alleges that Passavant's change to MDA services resulted in a higher cost for Federal and third-party payers as well as out-of-state patients. Therefore, BCB has alleged a more than insubstantial effect on interstate commerce.

Although the complaint should not have been dismissed on jurisdictional grounds, the plaintiffs have not stated a claim under Section 1 of the Sherman Act. Under the Sherman Act, only unreasonable restraints of trade are illegal. Where certain conduct has both procompetitive and anticompetitive effects, courts apply a rule of reason test. This analysis raises questions of market definition and market power. This case involves one hospital's decisions about staff privileges and staffing patterns. There is nothing obviously anticompetitive about a hospital choosing one staffing pattern over another or in restricting the staffing to some rather than many. A hospital has an unquestioned right to exercise some control over the identity and number to whom it accords staff privileges. Here, there is little reason to infer that there is an impact on competition within the relevant market defined by BCB, and no reason to infer such an impact with the broader relevant market that must be considered. How one hospital staffs its needs is so unlikely to be within the ambit of Section 1 of the Sherman Act that it does not justify a detailed examination of purpose and effect unless the plaintiffs give far better reasons for that examination than they have here.

INTERPRETATION Under Section 1 of the Sherman Act, only unreasonable restraints of trade are illegal.

Horizontal and Vertical Restraints A trade restraint may be classified as either horizontal or vertical. A **horizontal restraint** involves collaboration among competitors at the same level in the chain of distribution. For example, an agreement among manufacturers, among wholesalers, or among retailers would be horizontal.

> **Horizontal restraints** agreements among competitors

On the other hand, an agreement among parties who are not in direct competition at the same distribution level is a **vertical restraint**. Thus, an agreement between a manufacturer and a wholesaler is vertical. Although the distinction between horizontal and vertical restraints can become blurred, it often determines whether a restraint is illegal *per se* or should be judged by the rule of reason test. For instance, horizontal market allocations are illegal *per se*, whereas vertical market allocations are subject to the rule of reason test.

> **Vertical restraints** agreements among parties at different levels in the chain of distribution

Concerted Action Section 1 does not prohibit **unilateral** conduct; rather, it forbids **concerted** action. Thus, one person or business by itself cannot violate the section. As the United States Supreme Court held in *Monsanto Co. v. Spray-Rite Service Corporation*, an organization has the "right to deal, or refuse to deal, with whomever it likes, as long as it does so independently." For example, if a manufacturer announces its resale prices in advance and refuses to deal with those who disagree with the pricing, there is no violation of Section 1 because the manufacturer has acted alone. On the other hand, if a manufacturer and its retailers together agree that the manufacturer will sell only to those retailers who agree to sell at a specified price, a violation of Section 1 may exist.

For purposes of the concerted action requirement, the courts view a firm and its employees as one entity. In 1984, the Supreme Court expanded this class to include a corporation and its wholly owned subsidiaries; thus, the Sherman Act is not violated when a parent and its wholly owned subsidiary agree to a restraint in trade.

Conscious parallelism
(con'·scious pa'·ral·lel·ism)
similar patterns of conduct among competitors

The concerted action requirement may be established by an express agreement. Not surprisingly, however, express agreements often are nonexistent, leaving the court to infer an inter-party agreement from circumstantial evidence. Nonetheless, similar patterns of conduct among competitors, called **conscious parallelism**, are not sufficient in themselves to imply a conspiracy in violation of Section 1. Actual conspiracy requires an *additional* factor—such as complex actions that would benefit each competitor only if all of them acted—or indications of a traditional conspiracy—such as identical sealed bids from each competitor.

Joint ventures (discussed in Chapter 34) are a form of business association organized to carry out a particular business enterprise. Competitors frequently will join their resources in order to share costs and to eliminate wasteful redundancy. The validity under antitrust law of a joint venture generally depends on the competitors' primary purpose in forming it. A joint venture that was not formed to fix prices or divide markets will be judged under the rule of reason.

However, because uncertainty about the legality of joint ventures seemed to discourage their use for joint research and development, Congress passed the National Cooperative Research Act in order to facilitate such applications. The act provides that the courts must judge joint ventures in the research and development of new technology under the rule of reason test and that treble damages do *not* apply to ventures formed in violation of Section 1 if those forming the venture have notified the Justice Department and the FTC of their intent to form the joint venture.

Price fixing an agreement with the purpose or effect of inhibiting price competition; both horizontal and vertical agreements are *per se* illegal

Price Fixing **Price fixing** is an agreement with the purpose or effect of inhibiting price competition; such agreements may, among other things, raise, depress, fix, peg, or stabilize prices. Price fixing is the primary and most serious example of a *per se* violation under the Sherman Act. All ***horizontal*** price-fixing agreements are illegal *per se*. This prohibition covers any agreement by which sellers establish *maximum* prices at which certain commodities or services are to be offered for sale, as well as those by which they set *minimum* prices. The law also prohibits sellers' agreements to change the prices of certain commodities or services simultaneously or to not advertise their prices. (See generally, "MIT Fights Charge of Price Fixing in the Ivy League.")

The U.S. Supreme Court has condemned not only agreements among horizontal competitors that directly fix prices but also agreements that affect price indirectly. For example, in finding an agreement among beer wholesalers to eliminate interest-free short-term credit on sales to beer retailers to be illegal *per se*, the Court viewed the credit terms "as an inseparable part of price" and concluded that the agreement to eliminate interest-free short-term credit was equivalent to an agreement to eliminate discounts and, thus, was an agreement to fix prices.

CONSUMER INSIGHT

MIT Fights Charge of Price-Fixing in the Ivy League

When the U.S. Justice Department went after the Massachusetts Institute of Technology and eight other Ivy League schools back in 1991 for price fixing related to student aid, MIT held its ground. The school, argued its lawyers, had not violated any antitrust laws. And it intended to fight back.

Since 1958, MIT had been part of the Overlap group, a collection of nearly two dozen officials from elite colleges in the Northeast who met regularly to discuss prospective students who needed financial aid. The group had a common interest: Many students applied to more than one college in the group (hence the name Overlap). No college, however, wanted to get in a bidding war with another school over a particular student, so the officials compared notes. They talked about aid amounts, tuition increases, and a student's mix of loans, grants, and work-study money. They then offered students the same financial aid packages, no matter which schools accepted them.

After the Justice Department cried foul, the eight Ivy League schools—Brown, Columbia, Cornell, Dart-mouth, Harvard, the University of Pennsylvania, Princeton, and Yale—signed a consent decree, agreeing to stop the practice. But MIT refused to go along. Instead the school argued that as a nonprofit institution it was not involved in any kind of commerce. The student-aid packages, the school said, had nothing to do with pricing. The aid was a gift, and MIT was dispensing charity.

Judge Louis C. Bechtle of the U.S. District Court in Philadelphia disagreed. In his 1992 ruling, he scoffed at MIT's reasoning, writing, "The court can conceive of few aspects of higher education that are more commercial than the price charged students." MIT appealed.

In September 1993, the U.S. Court of Appeals in Philadelphia reversed the lower court's decision. Saying that MIT had violated no antitrust laws, the court returned the case to the district court, adding that the earlier decision had overlooked two of the case's most important aspects: the mitigating circumstances involved and the social welfare justifications for the Overlap group's meetings.

The overriding issue in the case comes down to this: Which financial aid practices help students the most? The U.S. Justice Department has argued that real competition among schools would lead to better deals for individual students, who could more easily negotiate for larger aid packages. MIT takes another view. It argues that the Overlap group originally benefited more students, especially poorer and minority students, by basing its financial aid decisions purely on need and thus spreading limited funds more evenly.

Today, prestigious colleges face increasing pressure related to financial aid, especially as they try to diversify their student bodies. Many schools say they struggle to admit students without concern for their ability to pay, a practice known as need-blind admissions. At Ivy League schools once involved in the Overlap group, in fact, one-third to one-half of the current student body receives some kind of financial aid.

Adding a legal sting to the situation are angry students who claim that they have been victims of price collusion. Under federal law, such victims can sue for damages three times higher than any overcharge. In a weird twist, one MIT graduate, David Hoicka, countersued the school in January 1993 for price fixing after MIT sued him for nonpayment of his student loan. Hoicka, now an attorney, claimed that the school owed him reparations for overcharges, in part because MIT, as part of the Overlap group, had limited his ability to negotiate a better aid package, thus increasing his debt burden.

Congress may soon come to the rescue. Already, legislators have passed new guidelines that allow colleges to exchange general information about their financial aid programs, as long as the schools do not talk about individual students. The decision of the U.S. Court of Appeals only increased the heat. Now colleges will most likely redouble their efforts to remove financial aid from the antitrust arena.

Similarly, it is illegal *per se* for a seller to fix the price at which its purchasers must resell its product. This **vertical** form of price fixing—usually called retail price maintenance—is considered a *per se* violation of Section 1.

Despite its early and consistent condemnation of resale price maintenance agreements, the Supreme Court has found no Section 1 violation when a manufacturer who announces in advance that it will not sell to dealers who cut prices then terminates its dealers who have cut prices. Not surprisingly, courts sometimes have difficulty distinguishing between an illegal resale price maintenance agreement and a manufacturer's legal refusal to deal with a retailer who refuses to charge the manufacturer's dictated minimum price.

Market Allocations Direct price fixing is not the only way to control prices. Another method is through **market allocation**, whereby competitors agree not to compete with each other in specific markets, which may be defined by geographic area, customer type, or product class. All *horizontal* agreements to divide markets have been declared illegal *per se* because they grant to the firm remaining in the market a monopolistic control over price. Thus, if RAC and Sonny, both manufacturers of color televisions, agree that RAC shall have the exclusive right to sell color televisions in Illinois and Iowa and that Sonny shall have the exclusive right in Minnesota and Wisconsin, RAC and Sonny have committed a *per se* violation of Section 1 of the Sherman Act. Likewise, if RAC and Sonny agree that RAC shall have the exclusive right to sell color televisions to Sears and that Sonny shall sell exclusively to JCPenney or that RAC shall have exclusive rights to manufacture twenty-inch color televisions and that Sonny shall manufacture thirteen-inch sets, they are also in *per se* violation of Section 1 of the Sherman Antitrust Act.

No longer illegal *per se* vertical territorial and customer restrictions are now judged by the rule of reason. This change in approach results from the Supreme Court's decision in *Continental T.V., Inc. v. GTE Sylvania, Inc.*, which mandated the lower federal courts to balance the positive effect of vertical market restrictions on interbrand competition against the negative effects on intrabrand competition. Consequently, in some situations, vertical territorial restrictions will be found legitimate if, on balance, they do not inhibit competition in the relevant market.

Market allocation division of markets by customer type, geography, or products; horizontal agreements are *per se* illegal, while vertical agreements are judged by the rule of reason standard

---

CONTINENTAL T.V., INC. v. GTE SYLVANIA, INC. United States Supreme Court, 1977, 433 U.S. 36, 97 S.Ct. 2549, 53 L.Ed.2d 568

FACTS As part of a corporate plan to stimulate sagging color television sales, GTE Sylvania began to phase out its wholesale distributors and to sell its television sets directly to a smaller and more select group of franchised retailers. To this end, Sylvania limited the number of franchises granted for any given area and required each franchisee to sell Sylvania products only from the location or locations at which he was franchised. A franchise did not constitute an exclusive territory, and Sylvania retained sole discretion to increase the number of retailers in an area in light of the success or failure of existing retailers. The strategy apparently was successful, as Sylvania's national market share increased from less than 2 percent to 5 percent.

In the course of carrying out its plan, Sylvania franchised Young Brothers as a television retailer at a San Francisco location one mile from that of Continental T.V., Inc., one of Sylvania's most successful franchisees. A course of feuding began between Sylvania and Continental that reached a head when Sylvania refused Continental's request for permission to open a store in Sacramento. Continental opened the Sacramento store

anyway and began shipping merchandise there from its San Jose warehouse. Shortly thereafter, Sylvania terminated Continental's franchise.

Continental brought this action against Sylvania, claiming that the franchise location restriction is *per se* violative of the Sherman Act. The jury found for Continental and assessed damages at $591,505, which were trebled. On appeal, the Court of Appeals for the Ninth Circuit, sitting *en banc*, reversed the judgment.

DECISION Judgment of the Court of Appeals for Sylvania affirmed.

OPINION In an earlier decision, the Court erroneously held that territorial and customer restrictions on sales by wholesalers in the purchasing and selling of Schwinn bicycles were *per se* illegal. *Per se* rules of illegality are appropriate, however, only when they relate to conduct that is manifestly anticompetitive. Vertical market allocation restrictions in franchise agreements are not manifestly anticompetitive and, therefore, should be judged under the prevailing standard of analysis, the "rule of reason."

continued

Under the rule of reason analysis, the court must weigh all of the circumstances of the case in deciding whether a restrictive practice should be prohibited as imposing an unreasonable restraint on competition. The market impact of vertical restrictions is complex because of their potential for simultaneously reducing intrabrand competition and stimulating interbrand competition. On one hand, location restrictions and other vertical restraints reduce intrabrand competition by limiting the number of sellers of a particular product competing for the business of a given group of buyers. On the other hand, these vertical restrictions promote interbrand competition by allowing the manufacturer to achieve certain efficiencies in the distribution of his products. Overall, the franchise location clause imposed by Sylvania does not impose an unreasonable restraint on trade and, therefore, does not violate the Sherman Act.

INTERPRETATION Vertical market allocations are to be judged under a rule of reason standard.

In 1985, the United States Department of Justice issued a "market structure screen," under which the department will challenge no restraints by a firm having a less than 10 percent share of the relevant market or a "Vertical Restraint Index" (a measure of relative market share) indicating that neither collusion nor exclusion is possible. We will discuss the concept of relevant market later, in the section on monopolization.

Boycotts As we noted earlier, Section 1 of the Sherman Act applies not to unilateral action but only to agreements or combinations. Accordingly, a seller's refusal to deal with any particular buyer does not violate the act; and a manufacturer can thus refuse to sell to a retailer who persists in selling below the manufacturer's suggested retail price. On the other hand, when two or more firms agree not to deal with a third party, their agreement represents a ***concerted refusal to deal***, or a group **boycott**, which may violate Section 1 of the Sherman Act. Such a boycott may be clearly anticompetitive, eliminating competition or reducing market entry.

Boycott agreement among parties not to deal with a third party; *per se* illegal

Some group boycotts are illegal *per se* while others are subject to the rule of reason. Group boycotts designed to eliminate a competitor or to force that competitor to meet a group standard are illegal *per se* if the group has market power. On the other hand, cooperative arrangements "designed to increase economic efficiency and render markets more, rather than less, competitive" are subject to the rule of reason. Finally, most courts hold that the *per se* rule of illegality for concerted refusals to deal extends only to horizontal boycotts, not to vertical refusals to deal. Most courts have interpreted *Sylvania* to hold that a rule of reason test should govern all nonprice vertical restraints, including concerted refusals to deal.

Tying Arrangements A **tying arrangement** occurs when the seller of a product, service, or intangible (the "tying" product) conditions its sale on the buyer's purchasing a second product, service, or intangible (the "tied" product) from the seller. For example, imagine that Xerox, a major manufacturer of photocopying equipment, required all purchasers of its photocopiers also to purchase from Xerox all of the paper they would use with the copiers. Xerox would thereby tie the sale of its photocopier—the *tying* product—to the sale of paper—the *tied* product.

Tying arrangement conditioning a sale of a desired product (tying product) on the buyer's purchasing a second product (tied product); *per se* illegal if the seller has considerable power in the tying product or affects a more than insubstantial amount of interstate commerce in the tied product

Because tying arrangements limit buyers' freedom of choice and may exclude competitors, the law closely scrutinizes such agreements. A tying arrangement exists when a seller exploits its economic power in one market to expand its empire into another market. When the seller has considerable economic power in the tying product and affects a more than insubstantial amount of interstate commerce in the tied product, the tying arrangement will be *per se* illegal. Economic power may be demonstrated by showing that (1) the seller occupied a dominant position in the tying market; (2) the seller's product enjoys an advantage not shared by its competitors in the tying market; or (3) a substantial number of customers have accepted the tying arrangement, and the only explanation for their willingness to comply is the seller's economic power in the tying market. If the seller lacks economic power, the tying arrangement is judged by the rule of reason test.

EASTMAN KODAK CO. v. IMAGE TECHNICAL SERVICES, INC. United States Supreme Court, 1992, 504 U.S. 451, 112 S.Ct. 2072, 119 L.Ed.2d 265

FACTS Eastman Kodak Co. manufactures and sells photocopiers and micrographic equipment. Kodak also services the equipment and sells replacement parts. Image Technical Services, Inc. is a group of independent service organizations (ISOs) that in the early 1980s began servicing Kodak equipment. Kodak subsequently established policies of selling parts only to buyers of the Kodak equipment who used Kodak service or who repaired their own machines. As part of the same policy, Kodak sought to limit ISO access to other sources of Kodak parts (such as those manufactured by original equipment manufacturers—OEMs). Kodak made an agreement with the OEMs not to sell parts to ISOs and pressured individual equipment owners and independent parts distributors not to sell Kodak parts. Kodak succeeded in its intention to restrict ISOs from servicing Kodak machines. Some ISOs were forced out of business; others lost significant revenue. Customers were forced to switch to Kodak service, even if they preferred ISO service.

In 1987, the ISOs filed an action alleging that Kodak had unlawfully tied the sale of service to the sale of parts, in violation of Section 1 of the Sherman Act, and had unlawfully monopolized and attempted to monopolize the sale of service for Kodak machines, in violation of Section 2 of the Sherman Act. Kodak filed for summary judgment.

DECISION Summary judgment denied.

OPINION In order to defeat Kodak's motion for summary judgment, the ISOs must demonstrate, first, that service and parts are two distinct products and therefore able to be tied and, second, that Kodak had indeed tied the two products. Evidence presented showed that historically, service and parts have been sold separately and, therefore, that they are separate products. The question remains whether Kodak possessed significant economic power in the tying market. The ISOs claim that because some parts are

available only from Kodak, Kodak has excluded service competition, boosted service prices, and forced unwilling consumption of Kodak service. This evidence alone is sufficient to entitle respondents to a trial on their market power claim. Kodak counters, however, that because it does not possess market power in the equipment market, it cannot possess market power in the parts sales and service market. Its logic is that if it were to boost prices in the parts sales and service markets, it would lose sales in the equipment market—its main sales area—because customers would buy equipment with more attractive service costs. This, however, must be determined by the economic realities of the marketplace, not by Kodak's theoretical disclaimers.

Regarding the second part of the allegations—that Kodak has monopolized or attempted to monopolize the service and parts market—it is clear that Kodak has succeeded in controlling almost 100 percent of the market of Kodak parts. The question remains as to whether controlling one brand of parts constitutes a market. Kodak claims that one brand cannot define a market, but the respondents claim that because the parts are not interchangeable with other brands, Kodak parts are, from the consumer's perspective, the entire relevant product market.

In the end, of course, it may be decided that Kodak's parts, service, and equipment are one unified market or that the equipment market competition does discipline the aftermarkets of service and parts so that all three are competitively priced. Nonetheless, in this case, when we weigh the risk of deterring procompetitive behavior by proceeding to trial against the risk that illegal behavior will go unpunished, the balance tips against summary judgment.

INTERPRETATION One who possesses sufficient economic power in one market will not be permitted to gain unfair advantage in a different or tied market.

Figure 44–1 summarizes how these trade restraints are judged under Section 1. See also Ethical Dilemma on page 892.

Monopolies

Economic analysis indicates that a monopolist will use its power to limit production and increase prices. Therefore, a monopolistic market will produce fewer goods than a competitive market would, and will sell these goods at higher prices. Addressing the problem of monopolization, Section 2 of the Sherman Act prohibits monopolies and any attempts or conspiracies to monopolize. Thus, Section 2 prohibits both agreements among businesses and, unlike Section 1, unilateral conduct by one firm.

> **Monopolies** Section 2 prohibits monopolization, attempts to monopolize, and conspiracies to monopolize

Monopolization Although the language of Section 2 ostensibly prohibits *all* monopolies, the courts have required that a firm not only must possess market power but must also have attained the monopoly power unfairly or abused that power, once attained. By itself, the possession of monopoly power is not considered a violation of Section 2 because a firm may have obtained such power through its skills in developing, marketing, and selling products—that is, through the very competitive conduct that the antitrust laws are designed to promote.

> **Monopolization** requires market power (ability to control or exclude others from the marketplace) plus either the unfair attainment of the power or the abuse of such power

Since it is extremely rare to find an unregulated industry with only one firm, determining the presence of monopoly power involves defining the degree of market dominance that constitutes such power. **Monopoly power** is the ability to control price or to exclude competitors from the marketplace. In grappling with this question of power, the courts have developed a number of criteria; but the most common test is market share. A market share greater than 75 percent generally indicates monopoly power, while a share less than 50 percent does not. A share between 50 and 75 percent is, in itself, inconclusive.

> **Monopoly power** ability to control price or exclude others from the marketplace

Market share is a firm's fractional share of the total relevant product and geographic markets, but defining these relevant markets is often a difficult and subjective project for the courts. The relevant *product market*, as demonstrated in the following case, includes products that are substitutable for the firm's product on the basis of price, quality, and adaptability for other purposes. For example, although brick and wood siding are both used on building exteriors, it is unlikely they would be considered part of the same product market. On the other hand, Coca-Cola and Seven-Up are both soft drinks and would be considered part of the same product market.

FIGURE 44–1 Restraints of Trade Under Sherman Act

Type of Restraint	Standard	
	Per Se **Illegal**	**Rule of Reason**
Price fixing	Horizontal Vertical	
Market allocations	Horizontal	Vertical
Group boycotts or refusals to deal	Horizontal Vertical (minority)	Vertical (majority)
Tying arrangements	If seller has economic power in tying product and affects a substantial amount of interstate commerce in the tied product	If seller lacks economic power in tying product

UNITED STATES v. E. I. DU PONT DE NEMOURS & CO.   United States Supreme Court, 1956, 351 U.S. 377, 76 S.Ct. 994, 100 L.Ed. 1264

FACTS   In 1923, du Pont was granted the exclusive right to make and sell cellophane in North America. In 1927, the company introduced a moistureproof brand of cellophane that was ideal for various wrapping needs. Although more expensive than most competing wrapping, it offered a desired combination of transparency, strength, and cost. Except for its permeability to gases, however, cellophane had no qualities that a number of competing materials did not possess as well. Cellophane sales increased dramatically, and by 1950, du Pont produced almost 75 percent of the cellophane sold in the United States. Nevertheless, sales of the material constituted less than 20 percent of the sales of "flexible packaging materials."

The United States brought this action, contending that by so dominating cellophane production, du Pont had monopolized a part of trade or commerce in violation of the Sherman Act. Du Pont argued that it had not monopolized because it did not have the power to control the price of cellophane or to exclude competitors from the market for flexible wrapping materials. The government took a direct appeal from a ruling in favor of du Pont.

DECISION   Judgment for du Pont affirmed.

OPINION   The first step in determining whether du Pont has monopolized is to determine whether the company has monopoly power in the relevant market. Monopoly power is the power to control prices or to exclude competition in the relevant market. The relevant market consists of commodities reasonably interchangeable by consumers for the same purposes. Control of the relevant market, in turn, depends on the availability and interchangeability of competing products. A measure of this interchangeability is the cross-elasticity of demand between cellophane and the other wrappings—that is, the responsiveness of the sales of cellophane to changes in the price of other wrapping materials. Here, the evidence shows that sales of the other materials were highly sensitive to changes in the price of cellophane, thus indicating that the products compete in the same market. In other words, the interchangeability of cellophane with other wrapping materials suffices to define the relevant market for purposes of determining whether du Pont has monopolized the market for all flexible wrapping materials. Although it accounted for over 17 percent of the sales in that larger market, du Pont cannot be said, by that proportion of sales, to have the power to control prices or exclude competition.

INTERPRETATION   The relevant product includes products that are substituted for the firm's product on the basis of price, quality, and adaptability.

ETHICAL DILEMMA   When Is an Agreement Anticompetitive?

FACTS   Robert Crane has been hired as a manager of Sandra Renee, Inc., a prosperous fashion design manufacturer. A maker of women's dresses, Sandra Renee specializes in formal gowns. An important and growing segment of its business consists of renting gowns to retail chains. Because high prices often deter consumers from purchasing formalwear, the design industry as a whole has been benefiting from formal gown rentals. Under its rental arrangement, Sandra Renee receives a percentage from each rental. The rental also provides increased exposure and advertising for Sandra Renee.

Robert was sent to a meeting of the Association of Fashion Design Manufacturers. At the meeting, representatives from throughout the industry discussed the advantages of rentals; and two members raised the question of what action should be taken if a retailer sold one of the gowns. After a brief debate, the members agreed that gowns should no longer be provided to such retailers. The representatives also discussed the different pricing mechanisms their respective firms used in dealing with renting retailers. They generally agreed that a flat dollar fee plus a significant percentage of the rental fee was the best pricing scheme.

Robert grew concerned that this discussion was inappropriate. But because he was new to the association, he was uncertain what to do. He considered voicing his objection, leaving the meeting, or staying but remaining silent.

Social, Policy, and Ethical Considerations

1. Was Robert's sense of discomfort with the discussion justified? Explain.
2. What action should Robert have taken?
3. Whose interests were at stake at this meeting? How might such a meeting affect the public, Sandra Renee, and the company's competitors?
4. To what extent should employees be informed about the ethical and legal obligations of trade associations before attending meetings such as this?
5. What actions are open to an employee who disagrees with a company position that violates the law?

The relevant *geographic market* is the territory in which the firm sells its products or services. This may be at the local, regional, or national level. For instance, the relevant geographic market for the manufacture and sale of aluminum might be national, whereas that of a taxi company would be local. The scope of a geographic market depends on factors such as transportation costs, the type of product or service, and the location of competitors and customers.

If sufficient monopoly power has been proved, the law must then show that the firm has engaged in **unfair conduct**. However, the courts have yet to agree on what constitutes such conduct. One judicial approach is to place upon a firm possessing monopoly power the burden of proving that it acquired such power passively or that the power was "thrust" upon it. An alternative view is that monopoly power, combined with conduct designed to exclude competitors, violates Section 1. A third approach requires monopoly power plus some type of predatory practice, such as pricing below marginal costs. For example, one case that adopted the third approach held that a firm does not violate Section 2 of the Sherman Act if it attained its market share (1) through research, technical innovation, or a superior product or (2) through ordinary marketing methods available to all. In a decision that appears to combine these approaches, the Supreme Court has held that "[i]f a firm has been attempting to exclude rivals on some basis other than efficiency, it is fair to characterize its behavior as predatory."

To date, however, the United States Supreme Court has yet to identify the exact conduct, beyond the mere possession of monopoly power, that violates Section 2. To do so, the Court must resolve the complex and conflicting market and business policies this most basic question of monopolies involves.

Attempts to Monopolize Section 2 also prohibits **attempts to monopolize**. As with monopolization, the courts have had difficulty developing a standard that distinguishes undesirable conduct likely to engender a monopoly from healthy, competitive conduct. The standard test applied by the courts requires proof of a specific intent to monopolize plus a dangerous probability of success; however, among other things, this test neither defines an "intent" nor offers a standard of power by which to measure "success." Recent cases suggest that the greater the measure of market power a firm acquires, the less flagrant must its conduct be to constitute an attempt. These cases, however, do not specify any threshold level of market power.

Attempt to monopolize specific intent to monopolize, plus a dangerous probability of success

Conspiracies to Monopolize Section 2 also condemns conspiracies to monopolize. Few cases involve this offense alone, as any conspiracy to monopolize would also constitute, in violation of Section 1, a combination in restraint of trade.

CLAYTON ACT

In 1914, Congress strengthened the Sherman Act by adopting the Clayton Act, which was expressly designed "to supplement existing laws against unlawful restraints and monopolies." The Clayton Act provides only for civil actions, not for criminal penalties. Private parties may bring civil actions in federal court for *treble* damages and attorneys' fees. In addition, the Justice Department and the Federal Trade Commission are authorized to bring civil actions, including proceedings in equity, to prevent and restrict violations of the act.

The major provisions of the Clayton Act deal with price discrimination, tying contracts, exclusive dealing, and mergers. Section 2, which deals with price discrimination, was amended and rewritten by the Robinson-Patman Act, which we will discuss below. The Clayton Act exempts labor, agricultural, and horticultural organizations from all antitrust laws.

Tying Contracts and Exclusive Dealing

Tying arrangement
prohibited if it tends to create a monopoly or may substantially lessen competition

Section 3 of the Clayton Act prohibits **tying arrangements** and exclusive dealing, selling, or leasing arrangements that prevent purchasers from dealing with the seller's competitors where such arrangements *may* substantially lessen competition or *tend* to create a monopoly. This section is intended to stifle fledgling anticompetitive practices before they grow into violations of Section 1 or 2 of the Sherman Act. Unlike the Sherman Act, however, Section 3 applies only to practices involving commodities, not to those that involve services, intangibles, or land.

Tying arrangements, which we discussed earlier, have been labeled by the Supreme Court as serving "hardly any purpose beyond the suppression of competition." While the Court at one time indicated that the standards applied under the Sherman Act differed from those applied under the Clayton Act, recent lower court cases suggest that the same rules now govern both types of actions.

Exclusive dealing
arrangement by which a party has sole right to a market; prohibited if it tends to create a monopoly or may substantially lessen competition

Exclusive dealing arrangements are agreements by which the seller or lessor of a product conditions the agreement upon the buyer's or lessee's promise not to deal in a competitor's goods. For example, a manufacturer of razors might require retailers wishing to sell its line of shaving equipment to agree not to carry competing merchandise. Such conduct, although treated more leniently than tying arrangements, violates Section 3 if it tends to create a monopoly or may substantially lessen competition. The courts treat exclusive dealing arrangements more leniently because such arrangements may bolster competition to the extent that they benefit buyers, and thus, indirectly, the ultimate consumers, by assuring supplies, deterring price increases, and enabling long-term planning on the basis of known costs.

Mergers

Merger prohibited if it tends to create a monopoly or may substantially lessen competition

Horizontal merger
acquisition by one company of a competing company

Vertical merger acquisition by one company of one of its suppliers or customers

Conglomerate merger an acquisition by one company of another that is not a competitor, customer, or supplier

In the United States, corporate mergers have helped to reshape both corporate structure and our economic system. **Mergers** are horizontal, vertical, or conglomerate, depending on the relationship between the acquirer and the company acquired. A **horizontal merger** involves a company's acquisition of all or part of the stock or assets of a competing company. For example, if IBM were to acquire Apple, this would be a horizontal merger. A **vertical merger** is a company's acquisition of one of its customers or suppliers. A vertical merger is a *forward* merger if the acquiring company purchases a *customer*, such as the purchase of Revco Discount Drug Stores by Procter & Gamble. A vertical merger is a *backward* merger if the acquiring company purchases a supplier; for example, IBM's purchase of a microchip manufacturer. The third type of merger, the **conglomerate merge**r, is a catchall category that covers all acquisitions not involving a competitor, customer, or supplier.

Section 7 of the Clayton Act prohibits a corporation from merging or acquiring another corporation's stock or assets where such an action would substantially lessen competition or would tend to create a monopoly. Currently, the law regarding horizontal, vertical, and conglomerate mergers is, particularly with respect to the last two, in a state of flux.

The principal objective of the antitrust law governing mergers is to maintain competition. Accordingly, the courts scrutinize the legality of horizontal mergers most carefully. Factors that affect this review include the market share of each of the merging firms, the degree of industry concentration, the number of firms in the industry, entry barriers, market trends, the vigor and strength of other competitors in the industry, the character and history of the merging firms, market demand, and the extent of industry price competition. The leading Supreme Court cases on horizontal mergers date from the 1960s and early 1970s. Since then, lower federal courts, the Department of Justice, and the FTC have emphasized antitrust's goal of promoting economic efficiency. Accordingly, while the Supreme Court cases remain the law of the land, recent lower court decisions reflect a greater willingness to tolerate industry concentrations. Nevertheless, the government continues to prosecute, and the courts continue to condemn, horizontal mergers that are likely to harm consumers.

HOSPITAL CORP. OF AMERICA v. FTC U.S. Court of Appeals, Seventh Circuit, 1986, 807 F.2d 1381

FACTS Hospital Corporation of America (HCA), the largest proprietary hospital chain in the United States, originally owned one hospital in the Chattanooga, Tennessee, area. Between 1981 and 1982, at a cost of $700 million, HCA acquired two hospital corporations, which also owned or managed hospitals in the Chattanooga area. After this acquisition, HCA owned or managed 5 out of the 11 hospitals in the area. This acquisition also raised HCA's market share in the Chattanooga area from 14 percent to 26 percent. This made HCA the second largest provider of hospital services in a highly concentrated market where the four largest firms now had a collective market share of 91 percent, compared to a pre-acquisition share of 79 percent. After investigation, the Federal Trade Commission (FTC) ruled that the acquisitions by HCA violated § 7 of the Clayton Act. HCA appealed.

DECISION Judgment for the FTC affirmed.

OPINION Section 7 of the Clayton Act prohibits a merger or acquisition by a corporation that may lessen competition substantially or tend to create a monopoly.

The application of § 7 necessarily requires a prediction of the merger's impact, both present and future, on competition. The United States Supreme Court has repeatedly said that the economic concept of competition, rather than any desire to preserve rivals as such, is the lodestar that shall guide the application of the antitrust laws, including §7 of the Clayton Act. In applying § 7, the FTC is required to judge whether the challenged acquisition is likely to hurt consumers by making it easier for the firms in the market to collude, expressly or tacitly, and thereby force prices above the competitive level. § 7 does not require proof that a merger or other acquisition has created higher prices in the affected market. All that is necessary is that the merger create an appreciable danger of such consequences in the future. The challenged acquisition gave four firms control over an entire market, and as a result they would have little to fear if they raised prices above the competitive level.

INTERPRETATION A merger is illegal if it tends to create a monopoly or would substantially lessen competition.

Though far less likely to challenge vertical mergers, the Justice Department and the FTC will attack vertical mergers that are likely to raise entry barriers in the industry or to bar other firms in the acquiring firm's industry from competitively significant customers or suppliers. While the Supreme Court has not decided a vertical merger case since 1972, recent decisions indicate that at least some lower courts have been willing to condemn only those vertical mergers that clearly show anticompetitive effects.

Finally, conglomerate mergers have been challenged only (1) where one of the merging firms would be highly likely to enter the other firm's market or (2) where the merged company would be disproportionately large, compared with the largest competitors in its industry.

ROBINSON-PATMAN ACT

Originally, Section 2 of the Clayton Act only prohibited sellers from differentially pricing their products in order to injure local or regional competitors. In 1936, in an attempt to limit the power of large purchasers, Congress amended Section 2 of the Clayton Act by adopting the Robinson-Patman Act, which further prohibits **price discrimination** in interstate commerce concerning commodities of like grade and quality. More specifically, the act prohibits buyers from inducing and sellers from granting discrimination in prices. In order to constitute a violation, the price discrimination must substantially lessen competition or tend to create a monopoly.

Price discrimination the act prohibits buyers from inducing or sellers from giving different prices to buyers of commodities of similar grade and quality

Under this act, a seller of goods may not grant discounts to buyers, including allowances for advertisements, counter displays, and samples, unless the seller offers the same discounts to all other purchasers on proportionately equal terms. The act also prohibits other types of discounts, rebates, and allowances and makes it unlawful to sell goods at unreasonably low prices for the purpose of destroying competition or eliminating a competitor. The act also makes it unlawful for a person knowingly to "induce or receive" an illegal discrimination in price, thus imposing liability on the buyer as well as the seller. Violation of the Robinson-Patman Act, with limited exceptions, is civil, not criminal, in nature. Price differentials may be justified by proof of either a cost savings to the seller or a good faith price reduction to meet a competitor's lawful price.

Primary-Line Injury

In enacting Section 2 of the Clayton Act in 1914, Congress was concerned with sellers who sought to harm or eliminate their competitors through price discrimination. Injuries accruing to a seller's competitors are called **"primary-line" injuries**. Because the act forbids price discrimination only where such discrimination may substantially lessen competition or may tend to create a monopoly, the plaintiff in a Robinson-Patman primary-line injury case must either show that the defendant, with the intention of harming competition, has engaged in predatory pricing or present a detailed market analysis that demonstrates how the defendant's price discrimination actually harmed competition. To prove predatory intent, a plaintiff may rely either on direct evidence of such intent or, more commonly, on inferences drawn from the defendant's conduct, such as below-cost or unprofitable pricing for a significant period of time. A predatory pricing scheme may also be challenged under the Sherman Act.

Primary-line injury injury to a seller's competitors

Secondary- and Tertiary-Line Injury

In amending Section 2 of the Clayton Act through the adoption of the Robinson-Patman Act, Congress was concerned primarily with small buyers, who were harmed by the discounts that sellers granted to large buyers. Injuries that accrue to some buyers because of the lower prices granted to others are called "secondary-line" injuries. To prove the required harm to competition, a plaintiff in a **secondary-line injury** case must either show substantial and sustained intra-market price differentials or offer a detailed market analysis that demonstrates actual harm to competition. Because courts have been willing in secondary-line injury cases to infer harm to competition from a sustained and substantial price differential, proving a secondary-line injury is generally easier than proving a primary-line injury.

Secondary-line injury injury to competitors of the buyers

Tertiary-line injury occurs when the recipient of a favored price passes the benefits of the lower price on to the next level of distribution. Purchasers from other secondary-line sellers are injured in that they do not receive the benefits of the lower price; these purchasers may recover damages from the original discriminating seller.

Tertiary-line injury
(ter'·ti·a·ri) injury to purchasers from other secondary-line sellers

Cost Justification

If a seller can show that it costs less to sell a product to a particular buyer, the seller may lawfully pass along the cost savings. Section 2(a) provides that the Clayton Act does not "prevent differentials which make only due allowance for differences in the cost of manufacture, sale, or delivery resulting from the differing methods or quantities in which . . . commodities are . . . sold or delivered." For example, if retailer A orders goods from Seller X by the carload, whereas retailer B orders in small quantities, Seller X, who delivers F.O.B. buyer's warehouse, may pass along the transportation savings to buyer A. Nonetheless, although it is possible to pass along transportation savings, passing along alleged savings in manufacturing or distribution is extremely difficult because calculating and proving such savings is a complex task. Therefore, sellers rarely rely upon the defense of cost justification.

Meeting Competition

A seller may lower its price in a good faith attempt to meet competition. To illustrate:

1. Manufacturer X sells its motor oil to retail outlets for 65 cents per can. Manufacturer Y approaches A, one of Manufacturer X's customers, and offers to sell a comparable type of motor oil for 60 cents per can. Manufacturer X will be permitted to lower its price to A to 60 cents per can and need not lower its price to its other retail customers—B, C, and D. However, Manufacturer X may *not* lower its price to A to 55 cents unless it also offers this price to B, C, and D.
2. Manufacturer X will not be permitted to lower its price to A without also lowering its price to B, C, and D, in order to allow A to meet the lower price A's competitor, N, charges when selling Manufacturer Y's oil. The "meeting competition" defense is available only to meet the competition of the seller: the defense does not extend to a competitor's price to a specific, individual *purchaser* (see Figure 44–2).

A seller may beat its competitor's price, however, if it does not know the competitor's price, cannot reasonably determine the competitor's price, and acts reasonably in setting its own price.

FEDERAL TRADE COMMISSION ACT

In 1914, through the enactment of the **Federal Trade Commission Act**, Congress created the Federal Trade Commission (FTC), charged with preventing unfair methods of competition and unfair or deceptive acts or practices in commerce. To this end, the five-member commission is empowered to conduct appropriate investigations and hearings and to issue against violators cease and desist orders that are enforceable in the federal courts. The Supreme Court has commented on the breadth of the commission's power:

Federal Trade Commission Act
to prevent unfair methods of competition and unfair or deceptive practices, actions may be brought by the FTC, not by private individuals

FIGURE 44–2 Meeting Competition Defense

Illustration One

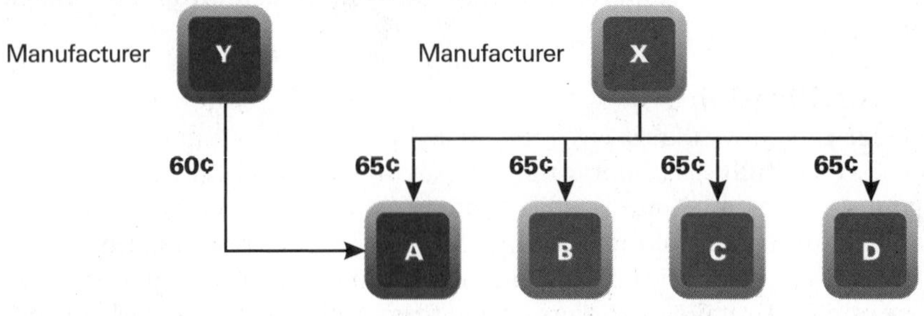

Manufacturer Y   Manufacturer X

60¢   65¢   65¢   65¢   65¢

A   B   C   D

Result: Manufacturer **X** may lower its price to A to 60¢ without lowering its price to B, C, and D.

Illustration Two

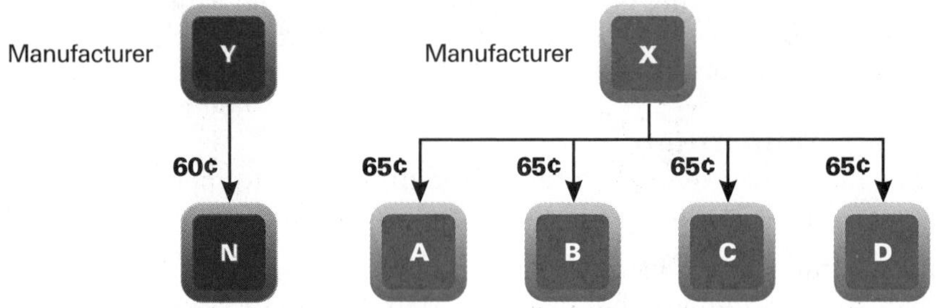

Manufacturer Y   Manufacturer X

60¢   65¢   65¢   65¢   65¢

N   A   B   C   D

Result: Manufacturer **X** may *not* lower its price to A to 60¢ without lowering its price to B, C, and D.

The "unfair methods of competition," which are condemned by . . . the Act, are not confined to those that were illegal at common law or that were condemned by the Sherman Act. . . . It is also clear that the Federal Trade Commission Act was designed to supplement and bolster the Sherman Act and the Clayton Act . . . *to stop in their incipiency acts and practices which, when full blown, would violate those Acts.* (Emphasis added.)

Complaints may be instituted by the FTC, which, after a hearing, "has wide latitude for judgment and the courts will not interfere except where the remedy selected has no reasonable relation to the unlawful practices found to exist." Although the FTC most frequently enters a cease and desist order having the effect of an injunction, it may order other relief, such as affirmative disclosure, corrective advertising, and the granting of patent licenses on a reasonable royalty basis. Appeals may be taken from orders of the FTC to the United States Courts of Appeals, which have exclusive jurisdiction to enforce, set aside, or modify FTC orders.

In performing its duties, the FTC investigates not only possible violations of the antitrust laws but also unfair methods of competition. For a more detailed discussion of the FTC and its powers, see Chapter 46.

CHAPTER SUMMARY

Sherman Antitrust Act	**Restraint of Trade** Section 1 prohibits contracts, combinations, and conspiracies that restrain trade

Restraint of Trade Section 1 prohibits contracts, combinations, and conspiracies that restrain trade
- ■ *Rule of Reason* standard that balances the anticompetitive effects against the procompetitive effects of the restraint
- ■ *Per Se Violations* conclusively presumed unreasonable and therefore illegal
- ■ *Horizontal Restraints* agreements among competitors
- ■ *Vertical Restraints* agreements among parties at different levels in the chain of distribution

Application of Section 1
- ■ *Price Fixing* an agreement with the purpose or effect of inhibiting price competition; both horizontal and vertical agreements are *per se* illegal
- ■ *Market Allocation* division of markets by customer type, geography, or products; horizontal agreements are *per se* illegal, while vertical agreements are judged by the rule of reason standard
- ■ *Boycott* agreement among competitors not to deal with a supplier or customer; *per se* illegal
- ■ *Tying Arrangement* conditioning a sale of a desired product (tying product) on the buyer's purchasing a second product (tied product); *per se* illegal if the seller has considerable power in the tying product or affects a more than insubstantial amount of interstate commerce in the tied product

Monopolies Section 2 prohibits monopolization, attempts to monopolize, and conspiracies to monopolize
- ■ *Monopolization* requires market power (ability to control or exclude others from the marketplace) plus either the unfair attainment of the power or the abuse of such power
- ■ *Attempt to Monopolize* specific intent to monopolize, plus a dangerous probability of success
- ■ *Conspiracies to Monopolize*

Sanctions
- ■ *Treble Damages* three times actual loss
- ■ *Criminal Penalties*

Clayton Act

Tying Arrangement prohibited if it tends to create a monopoly or may substantially lessen competition

Exclusive Dealing arrangement by which a party has sole right to a market; prohibited if it tends to create a monopoly or may substantially lessen competition

Merger prohibited if it tends to create a monopoly or may substantially lessen competition
- ■ *Horizontal Merger* one company's acquisition of a competing company
- ■ *Vertical Merger* a company's acquisition of one of its suppliers or customers
- ■ *Conglomerate Merger* the acquisition of a company that is not a competitor, customer, or supplier

Sanctions treble damages

Robinson-Patman Act	**Price Discrimination** the act prohibits buyers from inducing or sellers from giving different prices to buyers of commodities of similar grade and quality **Injury** plaintiff may prove injury to competitors of the seller (primary-line injury), to competitors of other buyers (secondary-line injury), or to purchasers from other secondary-line sellers (tertiary-line injury) **Defenses** (1) cost justification, (2) meeting competition, and (3) functional discounts **Sanctions** civil (treble damages); criminal in limited situations

Federal Trade Commission Act	**Purpose** to prevent unfair methods of competition and unfair or deceptive practices **Sanctions** actions may be brought by the FTC, not by private individuals

QUESTIONS

1. Discuss horizontal restraints of trade.
2. Discuss vertical restraints of trade.
3. Discuss monopolization.
4. Discuss the Clayton Act and its rules governing (a) tying contracts, (b) exclusive dealing, (c) vertical mergers, (d) horizontal mergers, and (e) conglomerate mergers.

5. Discuss the Robinson-Patman Act and the various defenses to it.

Internet Question. At the home pages for the Federal Trade Commission and the Department of Justice, explore the business and consumer issues these two agencies are currently examining.

PROBLEMS

1. Discuss the validity and effect of each of the following situations:
   (a) A, B, and C, manufacturers of radios, orally agree that due to the disastrous, cutthroat competition in the market, they will establish a reasonable price to charge their purchasers.
   (b) A, B, C, and D, newspaper publishers, agree not to charge their customers more than thirty cents per newspaper.
   (c) A, a distiller of liquor, and B, A's retail distributor, agree that B should charge a price of $5 per bottle.
2. Discuss the validity of the following:
   (a) A territorial allocation agreement between two manufacturers of the same type of products, whereby neither will sell its products in the area allocated to the other.
   (b) An agreement between manufacturer and distributor not to sell a dealer a particular product or parts necessary for the product's repair.
3. Universal Video sells $40 million worth of video recording equipment in the United States. The total sales of such equipment in the United States is $100 million. One-half of Universal's sales are to Giant Retailer, a company that possesses 50 percent of the

retail market. Giant is presently seeking (1) to obtain an exclusive dealing arrangement with Universal or (2) to acquire Universal. Advise Giant as to the validity of its alternatives.

4. Z sells cameras to A, B, C, and D for $60 per camera. Y, one of Z's competitors, sells a comparable camera to A for $58.50. Z, in response to this competitive pressure from Y, lowers its price to A to $58.50. B, C, and D insist that Z lower its price to them to $58.50, but Z refuses. B, C, and D sue Z for unlawful price discrimination. Decision? Would your answer differ if Z reduced its price to A to $58?

5. Discount is a discount appliance chain store that continually sells goods at a price below manufacturers' suggested retail prices. A, B, and C, the three largest manufacturers of appliances, agree that unless Discount ceases its discount pricing, they will no longer sell to Discount. Discount refuses, and A, B, and C refuse to sell to Discount. Discount sues A, B, and C. Decision?

6. Taylor Company produces 77 percent of the coal used in the United States. Coal provides 25 percent of the energy used in the United States. In a suit brought by the United States against Taylor for violation of the antitrust laws, what is the result?

7. Whirlpool Corporation manufactured vacuum cleaners under both its own name and under the Kenmore name. Oreck exclusively distributed the vacuum cleaners sold under the Whirlpool name. Sears, Roebuck & Co. exclusively distributed the Kenmore vacuum cleaners. Oreck alleged that its exclusive distributorship agreement with Whirlpool was not renewed because an unlawful conspiracy existed between Whirlpool and Sears. Oreck further contended that a *per se* rule was applicable because the agreement was (a) price fixing or (b) a group boycott, or both. Decision?

8. Indian Coffee of Pittsburgh, Pennsylvania, marketed vacuum-packed coffee under the Breakfast Cheer brand name in the Pittsburgh and Cleveland, Ohio, areas. Later in 1971, Folger Coffee, a leading coffee seller, began selling coffee in Pittsburgh. In order to make inroads into the new territory, Folger sold its coffee at greatly reduced prices. At first, Indian Coffee met Folger's prices but could not continue operating at such a reduced price and was forced out of the market. Indian Coffee brings an antitrust action. Decision?

9. Justin Manufacturing Company sells high-fashion clothing under the prestigious "Justin" label. The company has a firm policy that it will not deal with any company that sells below its suggested retail price. Justin is informed by one of its customers, XYZ, that its competitor, Duplex, is selling the "Justin" line at a great discount. Justin now demands that Duplex comply with the agreement not to sell the "Justin" line below the suggested retail price. Discuss the implications of this situation.

10. Jay Corporation, the largest manufacturer of bicycles in the United States with 40 percent of the market, has recently entered into an agreement with Retail Bike, the largest retailer of bicycles in the United States with 37 percent of the market, under which Jay will furnish its bicycles only to Retail, and Retail will sell only Jay's bicycles. The government is now questioning this agreement. Discuss.

11. Von's Grocery, a large retail grocery chain in Los Angeles, sought to acquire Shopping Bag Food Stores, a direct competitor. At the time of the proposed merger, Von's sales ranked third in the Los Angeles area and Shopping Bag's ranked sixth. Both chains were increasing their number of stores. The merger would have created the second largest grocery chain in Los Angeles, with total sales in excess of $170 million. Prior to the proposed merger, the number of owners operating single stores declined from 5,365 in 1950 to 3,590 by 1963. During this same period, the number of chains with two or more stores rose from 96 to 150. The United States brought suit against Von's to prevent the merger, claiming that the proposed merger violated Section 7 of the Clayton Act in that it could result in the substantial lessening of competition or could tend to create a monopoly. Decision?

12. Boise Cascade Corporation is a wholesaler and retailer of office products. The Federal Trade Commission issued a complaint charging that Boise had violated the Robinson-Patman Act by receiving a wholesaler's discount from certain suppliers on products that Boise resold at retail, in competition with other retailers that could not obtain wholesale discounts. Decision?

13. Zenith, an American manufacturer of television sets, and National Union Electric Corporation (NUE), the successor company to an American television-manufacturing firm that had since withdrawn from the market, sued twenty-one Japanese-controlled corporations that manufactured or sold consumer electronic products (CEP), claiming that these petitioners/defendants, over a twenty-year period, had legally conspired to drive American firms from the American CEP market by engaging in a scheme to fix and maintain artificially high prices for television sets sold by the petitioners in Japan, while simultaneously maintaining low prices for sets exported to and sold in the United States. The respondents claimed that such activity was concerted action in violation of Section 1 of the Sherman Act. The District Court held for the petitioners, finding that the bulk of the evidence on which the respondents relied was inadmissible, that the admissible evidence did not raise a genuine issue of material fact as to the existence of the alleged conspiracy, and that any inference of conspiracy was unreasonable. The Court of Appeals reversed, holding that the District Court erred in granting summary judgment in that there was both direct and circumstantial admissible evidence of a conspiracy. Decision?

14. Great Atlantic and Pacific Tea Company desired to achieve cost savings by switching to the sale of "private label" milk. A&P asked Borden company, its longtime supplier of "brand label" milk, to submit a bid to supply certain A&P private label dairy products. A&P was not satisfied with Borden's bid, however; so it solicited other offers. Bowman Dairy, a competitor of Borden's, submitted a lower bid. At this point, A&P contacted Borden and asked it to rebid on the private label contract. A&P included a warning that Borden would have to lower its original bid substantially in order to undercut Bowman's bid. Borden offered a bid that doubled A&P's potential annual cost savings. A&P accepted Borden's bid. The Federal Trade Commission then brought this action, charging that A&P had violated the Robinson-Patman Act by knowingly inducing or receiving illegal price discrimination from Borden. Decision?

15. Clorox is the nation's leading manufacturer of household liquid bleach (accounting for 49 percent—$40,000,000—of sales annually) and is the only brand

sold nationally. Clorox and its next largest competitor, Purex, hold 65 percent of national sales; and the top four bleach manufacturers control 80 percent of sales. Since all bleach is chemically identical, Clorox spends over $5,000,000 each year in advertising to attract and keep customers.

Procter & Gamble is the dominant national manufacturer of household cleaning products, with yearly sales of $1.1 billion. As with bleach, advertising is vital in the household cleaning products industry. Procter & Gamble annually spends over $127,000,000 in advertising and promotions. Procter & Gamble decided to diversify into the bleach business, since its household cleaning products and bleach are both low-cost, high-turnover consumer goods, are dependent on mass advertising, and are sold to the same customers at the same stores by the same merchandising methods. Procter & Gamble decided to merge with Clorox, rather than start its own bleach division, in order to secure the dominant position in the bleach market immediately. Should the FTC take action against this merger, and, if so, what decision?

16. In 1981, the NCAA adopted a plan for televising college football games in order to reduce the adverse effect of TV coverage on spectator attendance. The plan limited the total number of televised intercollegiate football games and also limited the number of games any one school could televise. No member of the NCAA was permitted to sell any television rights except in accordance with the plan. As part of the plan, the NCAA had agreements with the American Broadcasting Company (ABC) and the Columbia Broadcasting System (CBS) to pay to each school at least a specified minimum price for televising football games. Several member universities now join to bring suit against the NCAA, claiming the new plan is a horizontal price fixing agreement and output limitation and as such is illegal *per se*. The NCAA counters that the existence of the product, college football, depends upon member compliance with restrictions and regulations. According to the NCAA, its restrictions, including the TV plan, have a procompetitive effect. Is the TV plan valid? Explain.

17. The National Society of Professional Engineers (Society) had an ethics rule that prohibited member engineers from disclosing or discussing price/fee information with customers until after the customer had hired a particular engineer. This rule against competitive bidding was designed to maintain high standards in the field of engineering. The Society felt that competitive pressure to offer engineering services at the lowest possible price would encourage engineers to design and specify inefficient, unsafe, and unnecessarily expensive structures and construction methods. According to the Society, awarding engineering contracts to the lowest bidder, regardless of quality, would be dangerous to the public health, safety, and welfare. The Society emphasizes that the rule is not an agreement to fix prices. Rather, it claims the rule was drafted by experienced, highly trained professional engineers to prevent public harm and is therefore reasonable. The government contends that the rule unreasonably restrains trade and thus violates § 1 of the Sherman Act. Decision?

18. In the early 1930s, intense price competition characterized both the retail and the wholesale oil markets. At times, prices in the wholesale market fell below the manufacturer's cost. One cause of the volatile situation was the supply of "distress gasoline" placed on the market by seventeen independent refiners. These independent refiners had no retail sales outlets and little storage capacity, so they were forced to sell their product at "distress prices." In spite of their unprofitable operations, they could not afford to shut down; for, if they did so, they would be apt to lose both their oil connections in the field and their regular customers.

In an attempt to remedy this problem, the major oil companies entered into an informal agreement whereby each selected as its "dancing partner" one or more independent refiners having distress gasoline. The major oil company would then assume responsibility for purchasing the independent's distress supply at the "fair going market price." As a result, the market price of oil rose in 1935 and 1936, and the spot market became stable. The United States then brought this criminal action against the major companies, charging them with horizontal price fixing in violation of the Sherman Act. Decision?

CHAPTER 45

Accountants' Legal Liability

An accountant is subject to potential civil liability arising from the professional services he provides to his clients and third parties. This legal liability is imposed by both the common law at the state level and by federal securities laws. In addition, an accountant may violate federal and state criminal law through the performance of his professional activities. In this chapter, we will discuss accountants' legal liability under both state and federal law.

COMMON LAW

An accountant's legal responsibility under state law may be based on (1) contract law, (2) tort law, or (3) criminal law. In addition, the common law gives accountants certain rights and privileges; in particular, the ownership of their working papers and, in some states, a limited accountant-client privilege.

Contract Liability

The employment contract between an accountant and her client is subject to the general principles of contract law. All of the requirements of a common law contract must be present for the contract to be binding, including offer and acceptance, capacity, consideration, legality, and a writing if, as is often the case, the agreement falls within the one-year provision of the statute of frauds.

On entering into a binding contract (frequently referred to as an **engagement**), the accountant is bound to perform all the duties she *explicitly* agrees to provide under the contract. For example, if an accountant agrees to complete her audit of a client by October 15 so that the client may release its annual report on time, the accountant is under a contractual obligation to do so. Likewise, an accountant who contractually promises to conduct an audit to detect possible embezzlement is under a contractual obligation to provide for her client an expanded audit *beyond* Generally Accepted Auditing Standards (GAAS).

By entering into a contract, an accountant also *implicitly* agrees to perform the contract in a competent and professional manner. By agreeing to render professional services, an accountant is held to those standards that are generally accepted by the accounting profession, such as GAAS and Generally Accepted Accounting Principles (GAAP). Although accountants need not insure the absolute accuracy of their work, they must exercise the care of a reasonably skilled professional.

An accountant who breaches his contract will incur liability not only to his client but also to certain third-party beneficiaries. As you will recall from Chapter 16, a **third-party beneficiary** is a noncontracting party whom the contracting parties *intend* to receive the *primary* benefit under the contract. For example, Otis Manufacturing Co. hires Adler, an accountant, to prepare a financial statement for

Contract liability the employment contract between an accountant and her client is subject to the general principles of contract law

Engagement binding contract for an accountant's services

Explicit duties the accountant is bound to perform all the duties she expressly agrees to provide

Implicit duties the accountant impliedly agrees to perform the contract in a competent and professional manner

Third-party beneficiary noncontracting party whom the contracting parties intend to receive a primary benefit; contract liability extends to the client/contracting party and to third-party beneficiaries

Otis to use in obtaining a loan from Chemical Bank. Chemical Bank is a third-party beneficiary of the contract between Otis and Adler. Another example of a potential third party is an investor considering the purchase of part or all of a particular company. For a more detailed discussion of third-party beneficiaries, see Chapter 16.

Breach of contract general contract law principles apply

Following general contract principles, an accountant who *materially breaches* his contract will be entitled to no compensation. Thus, if an accountant does not perform an audit on time when time is of the essence, or completes only 60 percent of the audit, she has committed a material breach. On the other hand, an accountant who *substantially performs* his contractual duties is generally entitled to be compensated for the contractually agreed-upon fee, less any damages or loss his nonmaterial breach has caused the client. (See Chapter 18.)

Tort Liability

Tort a private or civil wrong or injury other than a breach of contract

In performing his professional services, an accountant may incur **tort** liability to his client or third parties for negligence or fraud. A tort, as we discussed in Chapter 7, is a private or civil wrong or injury, other than a breach of contract, for which the courts will provide a remedy in the form of an action for damages.

Negligence an accountant is liable for failing to exercise the degree of care a reasonably competent accountant would exercise under the circumstances; most courts have extended an accountant's liability for negligence beyond the client and third-party beneficiaries to foreseen third parties

Negligence An accountant is **negligent** if she does not exercise the degree of care a reasonably competent accountant would exercise under the circumstances. For example, Arthur, an accountant, is engaged to audit the books of Zebra Corporation. During the audit, Olivia, an officer of Zebra Corporation, notifies Arthur that she suspects that Terrance, the company's treasurer, is engaged in a scheme to embezzle from the corporation. Previously informed that Olivia and Terrance are on bad terms, Arthur does not pursue the matter. Terrance is, in fact, engaged in a commonly used embezzlement scheme. Arthur is negligent for failing to conduct a reasonable investigation of the alleged defalcation. Nonetheless, as we mentioned earlier, an accountant is *not* liable for honest inaccuracies or errors of judgment, so long as she exercises reasonable care in performing her duties. Moreover, an accountant need *not guarantee* the accuracy of her reports, provided she acts in a reasonably competent and professional manner.

Most courts do not permit an accountant to raise the defense of the plaintiff's contributory (or comparative) negligence. Nevertheless, a few courts do permit such a defense despite the fact that they recognize "that professional malpractice actions pose peculiar problems and that the comparison of fault between a layperson and a professional should be approached with caution."

Privity contractual relationship

Historically, an accountant's liability for negligence extended only to the client and to third-party beneficiaries. Under this view, **privity** of contract was a requirement for a cause of action based on negligence. This approach was established by the landmark case of *Ultramares Corp. v. Touche*.

Foreseen users those who the accountant knew would use the work or those who use the work for a purpose of which the accountant knew

In recent years, a majority of the states have adopted a **foreseen users** or **foreseen class of users** test. This approach, which also has been adopted by the Restatement of Torts, expands the class of protected individuals to include those the accountant knew would use the work product *or* those who use the accountant's work for a purpose for which the accountant knew the work would be used. For instance, Denise, an accountant, knows that her client will use a work product to try to obtain a bank loan from Nationsbank. Even if the client uses the audited financial statements to obtain a loan from a different bank, Denise would be liable to that second bank for any negligent misrepresentations in the financial statements. This class of protected individuals does not, however, include potential investors and the general public.

BILY v. ARTHUR YOUNG & CO. Supreme Court of California, En Banc, 1992, 3 Cal.4th 370, 11 Cal.Rptr.2d 51, 834 P.2d 745

FACTS Osborne Computer Corporation manufactured the first portable personal computer for the mass market. Shipments began in 1981, and by fall 1982, sales of the company's sole product, the Osborne I, had reached $10 million per month. In late 1982, the company began planning for an early 1983 initial public offering of its stock. In order to obtain the financing it needed to meet its capital requirements until the offering, the company issued warrants to investors, in exchange for direct loans or letters of credit, to secure bank loans to the company. The warrants entitled their holders to purchase blocks of the company's stock at favorable prices that were expected to yield a sizable profit when the public offering took place. The company retained Arthur Young & Company, which issued unqualified or "clean" audit opinions on the company's 1981 and 1982 financial statements. Each opinion appeared on Arthur Young's letterhead and stated that (1) Arthur Young had examined the accompanying financial statements in accordance with the accounting profession's Generally Accepted Auditing Standards (GAAS); (2) the statements had been prepared in accordance with Generally Accepted Accounting Principles (GAAP); and (3) the statements "presented fairly" the company's financial position. The 1981 financial statement showed a net operating loss of approximately $1 million on sales of $6 million. The 1982 financial statement revealed a modest net operating profit of $69,000 on sales of more than $68 million. As the warrant transaction closed on April 8, 1983, the company's financial performance began to falter, and the company later filed for bankruptcy. Investors who had purchased Osborne stock and warrants (plaintiffs) brought suit against Arthur Young, claiming that they had made their investments in reliance on Arthur Young's unqualified audit. The plaintiffs presented evidence that Arthur Young's audit was not performed in accordance with GAAS and that, as a result, Osborne's financial statements had overstated the company's profits by $3 million. The plaintiffs also presented evidence that Arthur Young had discovered material weaknesses in the company's accounting controls but had failed to report these weaknesses to management.

The court instructed the jury on fraud, negligent misrepresentation, and professional negligence. With respect to third parties, the negligence instructions stated that "[a]n accountant owes a further duty of care to those third parties who reasonably and foreseeably rely on an audited financial statement prepared by the accountant. A failure to fulfill any such duty is negligence." The jury found Arthur Young liable only for professional negligence and awarded the plaintiffs $4.3 million. The Court of Appeals affirmed.

DECISION Judgment reversed and remanded.

OPINION Negligence is conduct that falls below the standard established by law for the protection of others. Viewing this case, the court declines to permit all merely foreseeable third-party users of audit reports to sue the auditor on a theory of professional negligence. The main reason is that, given the "watchdog" role of the auditor, the complexity of the professional opinions rendered in audit reports, and the difficult and potentially tenuous relationships between audit reports and economic losses from investment and credit decisions, the auditor exposed to negligence claims from all foreseeable third parties would face potential liability far out of proportion to its fault. Thus, an auditor owes no general duty of care, regarding the conduct of an audit, to persons other than the client. Therefore, the verdict and judgment in the plaintiff's favor based on negligence is reversed.

Nevertheless, an auditor may be held liable to reasonably foreseeable third persons for intentional fraud in the preparation and dissemination of an audit report. Moreover, as provided by the Restatement of Torts, an auditor may be held liable for negligent misrepresentations in an audit report to those persons who act in reliance upon those misrepresentations in a transaction which the auditor intended to influence. Negligent misrepresentation is a separate and distinct tort and a species of the tort of deceit. Where the defendant makes false statements, honestly believing that they are true but having no reasonable ground for such belief, he may be liable for negligent misrepresentation. Under certain circumstances, expressions of professional opinion are treated as representations of fact. When a statement is not a casual expression of belief but a deliberate affirmation of the matters stated, it may be regarded as a positive assertion of fact. Moreover, when a party possesses or holds itself out as possessing superior knowledge or special information or expertise regarding the subject matter and a plaintiff is so situated that it may reasonably rely on such supposed knowledge, information, or expertise, the defendant's representation may be treated as one of material fact. There is no dispute that Arthur Young's statements in audit opinions fall within these principles. However, the jury rejected the plaintiff's claims based on intentional fraud and negligent misrepresentation.

INTERPRETATION This case adopts the Restatement position for negligent misrepresentation and the privity standard for other types of negligence.

Some courts have extended liability to benefit an even broader group: reasonably foreseeable plaintiffs who are neither known to the accountant nor members of a class of intended recipients. A few states have adopted this test, which requires only that the accountant reasonably foresee that such an individual might use the financial statements. The rationale behind the foreseeability standard of the law of negligence is that a tort-feasor should be fully liable for all the reasonably foreseeable consequences of her conduct. See Figure 45–1 for the various tests applied to accountants' liability to third parties for negligent misrepresentation.

Fraud an accountant who commits a fraudulent act is liable for both compensatory and punitive damages to any person who he should have reasonably foreseen would be injured; a fraudulent act is a false representation of fact that is material, is made with knowledge of its falsity and with the intention to deceive, and is justifiably relied on

Fraud An accountant who commits a fraudulent act is liable to any person the accountant *should have* reasonably foreseen would be injured through justifiable reliance on the misrepresentation. The required elements of **fraud**, which were more fully discussed in Chapter 11, are (1) a false representation (2) of fact (3) that is material and (4) made with knowledge of its falsity and with the intention to deceive, (5) is justifiably relied on, and (6) causes injury to the plaintiff. An accountant who commits fraud may be held liable for *both* compensatory and punitive damages.

In recent years, accountants also have been subject to a number of civil lawsuits based on the Racketeering Influenced and Corrupt Organizations Act (RICO). For a discussion of this act, see Chapter 6.

Criminal liability state law imposes criminal liability on accountants for willfully certifying false documents, altering or tampering with accounting records, using false financial reports, giving false testimony, and committing forgery

Criminal Liability

An accountant's potential **criminal liability** in rendering professional services is based primarily on the federal law of securities regulation and taxation. Nonetheless, an accountant would violate state criminal law by knowingly and

FIGURE 45–1 Accountants' Liability to Third Parties for Negligent Misrepresentation

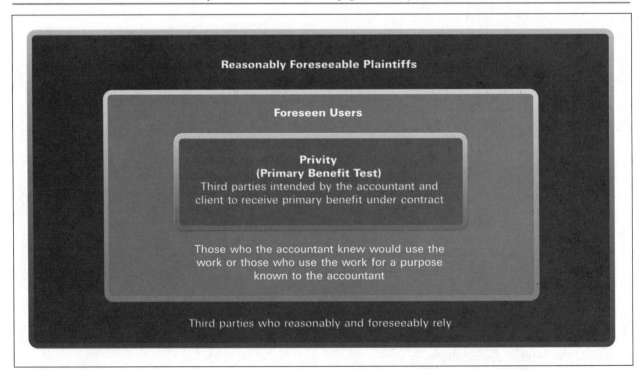

willfully certifying false documents, altering or tampering with accounting records, using false financial reports, giving false testimony under oath, or committing forgery.

Criminal sanctions may be imposed under the Internal Revenue Code for knowingly preparing false or fraudulent tax returns or documents used in connection with a tax return. Such liability also extends to willfully assisting or advising a client or others to prepare a false return. Penalties for tax fraud may be a fine not to exceed $100,000 ($500,000 for a corporation) or three years' imprisonment, or both.

Client Information

In providing services for his client, an accountant necessarily obtains information concerning the client's business affairs. Two legal issues arise concerning this client information: (1) who owns the working papers the accountant generates and (2) whether the information is privileged.

Working Papers Audit **working papers** include an auditor's records of the procedures she followed, the tests she performed, the information she obtained, and the conclusions she reached in connection with an audit. All relevant information that pertains to the examination should be included in the working papers. Because an accountant is held to be the owner of his working papers, he need not surrender them to his client. Nevertheless, the accountant may not disclose the contents of these papers unless (1) the client consents or (2) a court orders the disclosure.

> **Working papers** an accountant is considered the owner of his working papers but may not disclose their contents unless the client agrees or a court orders the disclosure

Accountant-Client Privilege The issue of confidentiality as it concerns accountant-client communication is important, for if such information is considered to be privileged, it may not be admitted into evidence over the objection of the person possessing the privilege. The question of a possible **accountant-client privilege** frequently arises in tax disputes, criminal prosecution, and civil litigation.

Neither the common law nor federal law recognizes such a privilege. Nevertheless, some states have adopted statutes granting some form of accountant-client privilege. Most of these statutes grant the privilege to the client, although a few extend the prerogative to the accountant. Regardless of whether the privilege exists or not, it is generally considered to be professionally unethical for an accountant to disclose confidential communications from a client unless the disclosure is in accordance with (1) American Institute of Certified Public Accountants (AICPA) or GAAS requirements, (2) a court order, or (3) the client's request.

> **Accountant-client privilege** not recognized by the common law or federal law, although some states have adopted statutes granting some form of privilege

---

UNITED STATES v. ARTHUR YOUNG & COMPANY Supreme Court of the United States, 1984, 465 U.S. 805, 104 S.Ct. 1495, 79 L.Ed.2d 826

FACTS Arthur Young & Co., a firm of certified public accountants, was the independent auditor for Amerada Hess Corporation. During its review of Amerada's financial statements as required by federal securities laws, Young confirmed Amerada's statement of its contingent tax liabilities and prepared tax accrual work papers. These work papers, which pertained to Young's evaluation of Amerada's reserves for contingent tax liabilities, included discussions of questionable positions Amerada might have taken on its tax returns. The Internal Revenue Service initiated a criminal investigation of Amerada's tax returns when, during a routine audit, it discovered questionable payments made by Amerada from a "special disbursement account." The

continued

IRS summoned Young to make available all its information relating to Amerada, including the tax accrual work papers. Amerada instructed Young not to obey the summons. The IRS then brought an action against Young to enforce the administrative summons. Though the district court declined to recognize an accountant-client privilege that would protect the work papers from disclosure, the Court of Appeals, holding that some form of work-product immunity should shield the work papers, affirmed in part and reversed in part.

DECISION The judgment of the Court of Appeals affirmed in part and reversed in part, and the case remanded.

OPINION The system of federal taxation demands forthright disclosure of all material information to the taxing authorities. Hence, the IRS has been given extensive information-gathering authority by Congress. This authority should be curtailed only by congressional action.

The argument comparing a work-product immunity for accountants' tax accrual work papers to the attorney work-product doctrine is based upon a misunderstanding of the differing roles of the private attorney and the independent certified public accountant. The attorney is his client's loyal and confidential adviser and advocate. The CPA, in certifying a corporation's financial statements, is a "public watchdog" who "assumes a public responsibility transcending any employment relationship with the client" and "owes ultimate allegiance to the corporation's creditors and stockholders, as well as to the investing public."

Moreover, in contrast with the view of the court of appeals, allowing the IRS access to tax accrual work papers poses no danger to the integrity of the securities markets. The court of appeals expressed the fear that, if tax accrual work papers were available to the IRS, a business might be tempted to withhold certain relevant and material information from its auditor. Such an action, however, could result in the auditor issuing a qualified opinion as to the accuracy of the financial statements, a possibility that responsible corporate management would be unwilling to risk.

INTERPRETATION Neither the common law nor Federal law recognizes an accountant-client privilege.

FEDERAL SECURITIES LAW

Accountants may be both civilly and criminally liable under provisions of the 1933 and 1934 Acts. This liability is more extensive and has fewer limitations than liability under the common law.

1933 Act

Civil liability Section 11 imposes express civil liability upon accountants if the financial statements they prepare or certify for a registration statement contain any untrue statement or omit any material fact, unless the accountant proves his due diligence defense, which requires that the accountant had, after reasonable investigation, reasonable grounds to believe and did believe that the financial statements were true, complete, and accurate

Criminal liability a willful violator of Section 11 is subject to fines of not more than $10,000 and/or imprisonment of not more than five years

Accountants are subject to express **civil liability** under Section 11 of the 1933 Act if the financial statements they prepare or certify for inclusion in a registration statement contain any untrue statement or omit any material fact. This liability extends to anyone who acquires the security without knowledge of the untruth or omission. Not only does such liability require no proof of privity between the accountant and the purchasers, but proof of reliance on the financial statements also is not usually required under Section 11. An accountant will not be liable, however, if he can prove "due diligence." The defense of **due diligence** requires that the accountant had, after reasonable investigation, reasonable grounds to believe and did believe, at the *time* the registration statement became *effective*, that the financial statements were true, complete, and accurate. The standard of reasonableness is that required of a prudent person in the management of his or her own property. Thus, Section 11 imposes liability on accountants for **negligence** in the conduct of an audit or in the presentation of information in the financial statements.

Moreover, an accountant who *willfully* violates this section may be held **criminally** liable for a fine of not more than $10,000 or imprisonment of not more than five years, or both.

1934 Act

Civil Liability **Section 18** of the 1934 Act imposes express *civil* liability on an accountant who makes or causes to be made any false or misleading statement about any material fact in any application, report, document, or registration filed with the SEC under the 1934 Act. Liability extends to any person who purchased or sold a security in reliance on that statement without knowing that it was false or misleading. An accountant is not liable, however, if she proves that she acted in good faith and had no knowledge that such statement was false or misleading. Thus, an accountant is not liable for false or misleading statements that result from negligence.

Accountants may also be held *civilly* liable for violations of **Rule 10b–5**. Rule 10b–5, as discussed in Chapter 42, is extremely broad in that it applies to *both* oral and written misstatements or omissions of material fact and to *all* securities. An accountant may be liable for a violation of the rule to those who rely on the misstatement or omission of material fact when purchasing or selling a security. However, liability is imposed only if the accountant acted with **scienter**, or intentional or knowing conduct. Therefore, accountants are not liable under Rule 10b–5 for mere negligence, although most courts have held that reckless disregard of the truth is sufficient. See Figure 45–2.

> **Section 18** imposes express civil liability on an accountant who knowingly makes any false or misleading statement about any material fact in any report, document, or registration filed with the SEC

> **Rule 10b–5** an accountant is civilly liable under this rule if he acts with scienter in making oral or written misstatements or omissions of material fact in connection with the purchase or sale of a security

> **Scienter** intentional or knowing conduct

ERNST & ERNST v. HOCHFELDER Supreme Court of the United States, 1976, 425 U.S. 185, 96 S.Ct 1375, 47 L.Ed.2d 668

FACTS The defendant, Ernst & Ernst, was an accounting firm. From 1946 through 1967, it was retained by First Securities Company of Chicago, a small brokerage firm and member of the Midwest Stock Exchange and the National Association of Securities Dealers, to perform periodic audits of the firm's books and records. In connection with these audits, Ernst & Ernst prepared for filing with the Securities and Exchange Commission the annual reports required of First Securities under the 1934 Act. It also prepared First Securities's responses to the financial questionnaires of the Midwest Stock Exchange.

Hochfelder and others (plaintiffs) were customers of First Securities who invested in a fraudulent securities scheme perpetrated by Leston B. Nay, president of the firm and owner of 92 percent of its stock. This fraud came to light in 1968 when Nay committed suicide, leaving a note that described First Securities as bankrupt and the escrow accounts as "spurious." Plaintiffs subsequently filed this action for damages against Ernst & Ernst under § 10(b) of the 1934 Act. The complaint charged that Nay's escrow scheme violated § 10(b) and Commission Rule 10b–5 and that Ernst & Ernst had "aided and abetted" Nay's violations by its "failure" to conduct proper audits of First Securities. The plaintiffs' cause of action rested on a theory of negligent nonfeasance—that, by failing to use "appropriate auditing procedures" in its audits of First Securities, Ernst & Ernst had thereby failed to discover internal practices of the firm said to prevent an effective audit. The District Court dismissed the action, but the Court of Appeals reversed and remanded.

DECISION Judgment of the Court of Appeals reversed.

OPINION Section 10(b) of the 1934 Act and SEC Rule 10b–5 apply only to intentional conduct, not negligence. The legislative intent of the act was to promote ethical standards of honesty and fair dealing by requiring regular accounting reports from corporations listed on national securities exchanges. In addition, Section 10 speaks specifically in terms of manipulation and deception and of implementing devices and contrivances. This is the commonly understood terminology of intentional wrongdoing. Based on this language and legislative history, the Supreme Court refused to expand the statute's scope to include negligent conduct. Because Ernst & Ernst's misconduct was merely negligent, not intentional, it is not liable to Hochfelder and the other shareholders.

INTERPRETATION Accountants are not liable under Rule 10b–5 for mere negligence.

FIGURE 45–2 Accountants' Liability under Federal Securities Law

	Section 11 (1933 Act)	Section 18 (1934 Act)	Rule 10b-5 (1934 Act)
Conduct	Registration statement containing material misstatement or omission	False or misleading statements in a document filed with SEC	Deception or material misstatement or opinion
Fault	Negligence	Knowledge or bad faith	Scienter
Plaintiff's knowledge is a defense	Yes	Yes	Yes
Reliance required	No	Yes	Yes
Privity required	No	No	No

Criminal liability a willful violator of either Section 18 or Rule 10b–5 is subject to fines of not more than $1 million and/or imprisonment of not more than ten years

Criminal Liability Those who willfully violate Section 18 or Rule 10b–5 also may be held *criminally* **liable**. For an accountant, conviction may carry a fine of not more than $1 million or imprisonment for not more than ten years, or both, while an accounting firm may be fined up to $2.5 million

ETHICAL DILEMMA Between Ethics, Advancement, and Friendship, Where Lies an Accountant's Responsibility to Disclose Possible Fraud?

FACTS John Rizzo, who recently graduated from college, was hired as a staff accountant for Alexander & Louis, a medium-sized CPA firm. John is now on the audit staff, where he will remain for two years. In his third year, he will divide his time between the tax and management advisory services departments. The reporting arrangements at Alexander & Louis are traditional: staff accountants report to senior accountants, and senior accountants report to managers, who in turn report to the particular partner in charge of the account.

Although John received three offers from excellent firms, he selected Alexander & Louis because one of his best friends, Wayne Mart, was a senior accountant at the firm and strongly recommended that John join the firm.

John's latest assignment was to audit Exit, Inc., a mail-order corporation that specializes in women's apparel. Wayne was the senior accountant on the job. John was auditing the sales account by review-ing a statistically selected sample of 60 sales transactions. He was tracing these sales by comparing sales invoices to shipping documents and ultimately to cash receipts or to receipts documented through autho-rized credit card companies. John noticed three transactions whose documentation contained discrepan-cies. He grew concerned that these sales were fictitious and brought the problem to Wayne's attention. In reply, Wayne stressed that the time spent on the audit was subject to a strict budget. "Drop it, John," he said. "Discrepancies like these are not a big issue."

Wayne's manager, Joan Keller, had repeatedly warned Wayne not to exceed the budget on the audit. During the last three audits under Wayne's supervision, total staff time had exceeded budget by 20 to 35 percent. Joan emphasized that such excesses thwarted Wayne's pros-pects for promotion and could ulti-mately threaten his job. As a result, Wayne grew very nervous. When an audit approached its budgetary lim-its, he would cut corners wherever possible and would intentionally fail to report all of the hours he actually worked on the job.

Social, Policy, and Ethical Considerations

1. What action, if any, should John take with respect to the sales transactions? What are his com-peting loyalties?

2. Under what circumstances, if any, should an employee leave a job because he disagrees with the way in which management conducts business? Discuss.

3. What role should an auditor play in the detection of fraud or other illegal acts?

4. What are the conflicting con-cerns of Alexander & Louis with regard to the pricing and man-agement of audits? Given these conflicts in the private sector, what industries should be sub-ject to government audit and regulation?

Audit Requirements The Private Securities Litigation Reform Act of 1995 (Reform Act) imposed a significant set of obligations upon independent public accountants who audit financial statements required by the 1934 Act. The Reform Act authorizes the SEC to adopt rules that modify or supplement the practices or procedures followed by auditors in the conduct of an audit. Moreover, the act requires auditors to establish procedures capable of detecting material illegal acts, identifying material-related party transactions, and evaluating whether there is a substantial doubt about the issuer's ability to continue as a going concern during the next fiscal year.

If the auditor becomes aware of information indicating an illegal act, it must determine whether an illegal act occurred and the illegal act's possible effect on the issuer's financial statements. Then the auditor must inform the issuer's management about any illegal activity and assure itself that the audit committee of the board of directors is adequately informed. If the auditor concludes that (1) the illegal act has a material effect on the issuer's financial statement, (2) neither senior management nor the board has taken timely and appropriate remedial action, *and* (3) the failure to take remedial action is reasonably expected to warrant departure from a standard auditor report or warrant resignation from the auditor's engagement, then the auditor promptly must report its conclusions to the issuer's board.

Within one day of receiving such report, the issuer must notify the SEC and furnish the auditor with a copy of that notice. If the auditor does not receive such notice, then the auditor must either resign or furnish the SEC with its report to the board. If the auditor resigns, it must furnish the SEC with a copy of its report.

The Reform Act provides that an auditor shall not be held liable in a private action for any finding, conclusion, or statement expressed in the report the act requires the auditor to make to the SEC. The SEC can impose civil penalties against an auditor who willfully violates the Reform Act by failing to resign or to furnish a report to the SEC.

Audit requirements auditors must establish procedures capable of detecting material illegal acts, identifying material-related party transactions, and evaluating whether there is a substantial doubt about the issuer's ability to continue as a going concern during the next fiscal year

CHAPTER SUMMARY

Common Law	**Contract Liability** the employment contract between an accountant and her client is subject to the general principles of contract law
	■ *Explicit Duties* the accountant is bound to perform all the duties she expressly agrees to provide
	■ *Implicit Duties* the accountant impliedly agrees to perform the contract in a competent and professional manner
	■ *Beneficiaries* contract liability extends to the client/contracting party and to third-party beneficiaries (noncontracting parties intended by the contracting parties to receive the primary benefit under the contract)
	■ *Breach of Contract* general contract law principles apply
	Tort Liability a tort is a private or civil wrong or injury other than a breach of contract
	■ *Negligence* an accountant is liable for failing to exercise the degree of care a reasonably competent accountant would exercise under the circumstances; most courts have extended an accountant's liability for negligence beyond the client and third-party beneficiaries to foreseen third parties

- **Fraud** an accountant who commits a fraudulent act is liable for both compensatory and punitive damages to any person who he should have reasonably foreseen would be injured; a fraudulent act is a false representation of fact that is material, is made with knowledge of its falsity and with the intention to deceive, and is justifiably relied on

Criminal Liability state law imposes criminal liability on accountants for willfully certifying false documents, altering or tampering with accounting records, using false financial reports, giving false testimony, and committing forgery

Client Information

- **Working Papers** an accountant is considered the owner of his working papers but may not disclose their contents unless the client agrees or a court orders the disclosure
- **Accountant-Client Privilege** not recognized by the common law or federal law, although some states have adopted statutes granting some form of privilege

---

Federal Securities Law

1933 Act

- **Civil Liability** Section 11 imposes express civil liability upon accountants if the financial statements they prepare or certify for a registration statement contain any untrue statement or omit any material fact, unless the accountant proves his due diligence defense, which requires that the accountant had, after reasonable investigation, reasonable grounds to believe and did believe that the financial statements were true, complete, and accurate
- **Criminal Liability** a willful violator of Section 11 is subject to fines of not more than $10,000 and/or imprisonment of not more than five years

1934 Act

- **Section 18** imposes express civil liability on an accountant who knowingly makes any false or misleading statement about any material fact in any report, document, or registration filed with the SEC
- **Rule 10b–5** an accountant is civilly liable under this rule if he acts with *scienter* in making oral or written misstatements or omissions of material fact in connection with the purchase or sale of a security
- **Criminal Liability** a willful violator of either Section 18 or Rule 10b–5 is subject to fines of not more than $1 million and/or imprisonment of not more than ten years

Audit Requirements auditors must establish procedures capable of detecting material illegal acts, identifying material-related party transactions, and evaluating whether there is a substantial doubt about the issuer's ability to continue as a going concern during the next fiscal year

---

QUESTIONS

1. Explain the contract liability of an accountant to her client.
2. For what and to whom does an accountant have tort liability?
3. Explain who owns the working papers an accountant generates and whether client information is privileged.
4. Discuss the potential civil and criminal liability of an accountant under the 1933 Act.
5. Discuss the potential civil and criminal liability of an accountant under the 1934 Act.

Internet Question. Find information about the structure and mission of the Financial Accounting Standards Board and examine its recent announcements and documents.

PROBLEMS

1. Baldwin Corporation made a public offering of $25,000,000 of convertible debentures and registered the offering with the SEC. The registration statement contained financial statements certified by Adams and Allen, CPAs. The financial statements overstated Baldwin's net income and assets by 20 percent, while understating the company's liability by 15 percent. Because Adams and Allen did not carefully follow GAAS, it failed to detect these inaccuracies, the discovery of which has caused the bond prices to drop from their original selling price of $1,000 per bond to $720. Conrad, who purchased $10,000 of the debentures, has brought suit against Adams and Allen. Decision?

2. Ingram is a CPA employed by Jordan, Keller and Lane, CPAs, to audit Martin Enterprises, Inc., a fast-growing service firm that went public two years ago. The financial statements that Ingram audited were included in a proxy statement proposing a merger with several other firms. The proxy statement was filed with the SEC and included several inaccuracies. First, approximately $1 million, or more than 20 percent, of the previous year's "net sales originally reported" had proven nonexistent by the time the proxy statement was filed and had been written off on Martin's own books. This was not disclosed in the proxy statement, in violation of Accounting Board Opinion Number 9. Second, Martin's net sales for the current year were stated as $11,300,000, when in truth they were less than $10,500,000. Third, Martin's net profits for the current year were reported as $700,000, when in fact the firm had no earnings at all.
   (a) What civil liability, if any, does Ingram have?
   (b) What criminal liability, if any, does Ingram have?

3. Girard & Company, CPAs, audited the financial statements included in the annual report submitted by PMG Enterprises, Inc. to the SEC. The audit failed to detect numerous false and misleading statements contained in the financial statements.
   (a) Investors who subsequently purchased PMG stock have brought suit against Girard under Section 18 of the 1934 Act. What defenses, if any, are available to Girard?
   (b) The SEC has initiated criminal proceedings under the 1934 Act against Girard. What must be proven for Girard to be held criminally liable?

4. Dryden, a certified public accountant, audited the books of Elixir, Inc., and certified incorrect financial statements in a form that was filed with the SEC. Shortly thereafter, Elixir, Inc. went bankrupt. Investigation into the bankruptcy disclosed that through an intricate and clever embezzlement scheme, Kraft, the president of Elixir, had siphoned off substantial sums of money that now support Kraft in a luxurious lifestyle in South America. Investors who purchased shares of Elixir have brought suit against Dryden under Rule 10b–5. At trial, Dryden produces evidence that demonstrates that his failure to discover the embezzlement resulted merely from negligence on his part and that he had no knowledge of the fraudulent conduct. Decision?

5. Johnson Enterprises, Inc. contracted with the accounting firm of P, A & E to perform an audit of Johnson. The accounting firm performed its duty in a nonnegligent, competent manner but failed to discover a novel embezzlement scheme perpetrated by Johnson's treasurer. Shortly thereafter, Johnson's treasurer disappeared with $75,000 of the company's money. Johnson now refuses to pay P, A & E its $20,000 audit fee and is seeking to recover $75,000 from P, A & E.
   (a) What are the rights and liabilities of P, A & E and Johnson? Explain.
   (b) Would your answer to (a) differ if the scheme was a common embezzlement scheme that GAAS should have disclosed? Explain.

6. The accounting firm of T, W & S was engaged to perform an audit of Progate Manufacturing Company. During the course of its investigation, T, W & S discovered that the company had overvalued its inventory by carrying the inventory on the books at the previous year's prices, which were significantly higher than current prices. When T, W & S approached Progate's president, Lehman, about the improper valuation of inventory, Lehman became enraged and told T, W & S that unless the firm accepted the valuation, Progate would sue T, W & S. Although T, W & S knew that Progate's suit was frivolous and unfounded, it wished to avoid the negative publicity that would arise from any suit brought against it. Therefore, on the assumption that the overvaluation would not harm anybody, T, W & S accepted Progate's inflated valuation of inventory. Progate subsequently went bankrupt, and T, W & S is now being sued by (1) First National Bank, a bank that relied upon T, W & S's statement to loan money to Progate, and (2) Thomas, an investor who purchased 20 percent of Progate's stock after receiving T, W & S's statement. What are the rights and liabilities of First National Bank, Thomas, and T, W & S?

7. J, B & J, CPAs, has audited the Highcredit Corporation for the past five years. Recently, the SEC has commenced an investigation of Highcredit for possible violations of federal securities law. The SEC has subpoenaed all of J, B & J's working papers pertinent to the audit of Highcredit. Highcredit insists that J, B & J not turn over the documents to the SEC. What action should J, B & J take? Why?

8. On February 1, the Gazette Corporation hired Susan Sharp to conduct an audit of its books and to prepare

financial statements for the corporation's annual meeting on July 1. Sharp made every reasonable attempt to comply with the deadline but could not finish the report on time due to delays in receiving needed information from Gazette. Gazette now refuses to pay Sharp for her audit and is threatening to bring a cause of action against Sharp. What course of action should Sharp pursue? Why?

9. John P. Butler Accountancy Corporation agreed to audit the financial statements of Westside Mortgage, Inc., a mortgage company that arranged financing for real property, for the year ending December 31, 1978. On March 22, 1979, after completing the audit, Butler issued unqualified audited financial statements listing Westside's corporate net worth as $175,036. The primary asset on the balance sheet was a $100,000 note receivable that had, in reality, been rendered worthless in August 1977 when the trust deed on real property securing the note was wiped out by a prior foreclosure of a superior deed of trust. The note constituted 57 percent of Westside's net worth and was thus material to an accurate representation of Westside's financial position. In October 1979, International Mortgage Company (IMC) approached Westside for the purpose of buying and selling loans on the secondary market. IMC signed an agreement with Westside in December after reviewing Westside's audited financial statements. In June 1980, Westside issued a $475,293 promissory note to IMC, on which it ultimately defaulted. IMC brought an action against Westside, its owners, principals, and Butler. IMC alleged negligence and negligent misrepresentation against Butler in auditing and issuing without qualification the defective financial statements on which IMC relied in deciding to do business with Westside. Butler moved for summary judgment, claiming that it owed no duty of care to IMC, a third party who was not specifically known to Butler as an intended recipient of the audited financial statements. The trial court granted Butler's motion, and IMC appealed. Decision?

CHAPTER 46

Consumer Protection

Consumer transactions have increased enormously since World War II, and today they amount to hundreds of billions of dollars. Although the definition varies, a consumer transaction generally involves goods, credit, services, or land acquired for personal, household, or family purposes. Historically, consumers were subject to the rule of *caveat emptor*—let the buyer beware. The law, however, has largely abandoned this principle and now offers greater protection to consumers. Most of this protection takes the form of statutory enactments at both the state and federal levels, and a wide variety of governmental agencies are charged with enforcing these statutes. This enforcement varies enormously. In some cases, only government agencies may exercise enforcement rights, through the imposition of criminal penalties, civil penalties, injunctions, and cease and desist orders. In other cases, in addition to government's enforcement rights, consumers may privately seek the rescission of contracts and damages for harm resulting from violations of consumer protection laws. Finally, under certain consumer protection statutes such as state "lemon laws," consumers alone may exercise enforcement rights. In this chapter, we will examine state and federal consumer protection agencies and consumer protection statutes.

STATE AND FEDERAL CONSUMER PROTECTION AGENCIES

Through the enactment of laws and regulations, legislatures and administrative bodies at the federal, state, and local levels all actively seek to shield consumers from an enormous range of harm. The most common abuses involving consumer transactions occur in the extension of credit, deceptive trade practices, unsafe products, and unfair pricing.

State and Local Consumer Protection Agencies

The many consumer protection agencies at the state and local levels typically deal with fraudulent and deceptive trade practices and fraudulent sales practices, such as false statements about a product's value or quality. In most jurisdictions, consumer protection agencies also help to resolve consumer complaints about defective goods or poor service.

Most state attorneys general facilitate consumer protection by enforcing laws against consumer fraud through judicially imposed injunctions and restitution. In recent years, as the federal government's role in consumer protection has diminished in response to the deregulatory movement, the states have correspondingly expanded their role. The National Association of

Attorneys General (NAAG) has been active in coordinating lawsuits among the states. Under NAAG's guidance, several states will often simultaneously file lawsuits against a company that has been engaging in fraudulent acts involving more than one state.

In some instances, however, states have not coordinated their efforts and have, instead, acted inconsistently with respect to consumer protection, especially in health and safety matters. This lack of coordination can present serious problems to companies that sell large numbers of products in interstate commerce.

The Federal Trade Commission

At the federal level, the most significant consumer protection agency is the **Federal Trade Commission** (FTC). Established in 1914, the FTC has two major functions: (1) under its mandate to prevent "unfair methods of competition in commerce," it is responsible for roughly half of the antitrust enforcement at the federal level (the FTC's role in antitrust enforcement was discussed in Chapter 44); and (2) under its mandate to prevent "unfair and deceptive" trade practices, it is responsible for stopping fraudulent sales techniques.

In addressing unfair and deceptive trade practices, the five-member commission (no more than three of whose members may be from the same political party) has the power to issue substantive "trade regulation rules" and to conduct appropriate investigations and hearings. Among the rules it has issued so far are those regulating used car sales, franchising and business opportunity ventures, funeral home services, and the issuance of consumer credit, as well as those requiring a "cooling-off" period for door-to-door sales (discussed later in this chapter).

In many instances, the agency, in considering a deceptive trade practice, may seek a cease and desist order rather than issue a substantive trade rule. A **cease and desist order** directs a party to stop a certain practice or face punishment such as a fine. In a typical situation, the FTC staff discovers a potentially deceptive practice, investigates the matter, files (if appropriate) a complaint against the alleged offender (usually referred to as the respondent), and after a hearing in front of an administrative law judge (ALJ) to determine whether a violation of the law has occurred, obtains a cease and desist order if the ALJ finds that one is necessary. The respondent may appeal to the FTC commissioners to reverse or modify the order. Appeals from orders issued by the commissioners go to the United States Courts of Appeals, which have exclusive jurisdiction to enforce, set aside, or modify orders of the commission.

Standards Though the FTC act does not define the words *unfair* or *deceptive*, the commission has issued three policy statements addressing the meaning of **unfairness** and has provided that an injury is unfair if it is substantial, not outweighed by any benefits to consumers or competition, and is one that consumers themselves could not reasonably have avoided. The standard, therefore, applies a cost-benefit analysis to the issue of unfairness.

The second policy statement deals with the meaning of **deception**—the basis of most FTC consumer protection actions—by providing that the commission will find deception in a misrepresentation, omission, or practice that is likely to mislead a consumer acting reasonably in the circumstances, to the consumer's detriment. The following case illustrates this standard for deception.

Federal Trade Commission prevents unfair methods of competition and unfair or deceptive acts or practices

Cease and desist order orders a party to stop a certain practice

Unfairness requires injury to be (1) substantial, (2) not outweighed by any countervailing benefit, and (3) unavoidable by reasonable consumer action

Deception misrepresentation, omission, or practice that is likely to mislead the consumer acting reasonably in the circumstances

IN RE CLIFFDALE ASSOCIATES, INC. Federal Trade Commission, 1984, 46 Antitrust & Trade Reg. Rep. 703

FACTS The FTC brought this action, claiming that Cliffdale Associates engaged in unfair and deceptive trade practices by advertising its "new air bleed" engine attachment, known as the Ball-Matic Gas Save Valve, as an "amazing automobile discovery" and as "the most significant breakthrough in the last ten years." The device was designed to allow more air to enter an automobile's engine and thus increase the automobile's efficiency and gas mileage. The Administrative Law Judge (ALJ) ruled in favor of the FTC and ordered Cliffdale to cease and desist from engaging in these unfair and deceptive trade practices.

DECISION Judgment for FTC.

OPINION Unfair and deceptive trade practices violate the Federal Trade Commission Act. An act or practice is deceptive if (1) there is a representation, omission, or practice that is (2) material and (3) likely to mislead consumers acting reasonably under the circumstances. Using these criteria, Cliffdale made several deceptive claims regarding the Ball-Matic. First, Cliffdale's advertisements characterizing the Ball-Matic as an "amazing automobile discovery" and a "significant automotive breakthrough" made the express claim that the Ball-Matic was an important and unique new invention. In reality, the Ball-Matic is similar to other simple air-bleed devices that have been sold over the years and are considered to be of little value by the automobile industry. The claim that the Ball-Matic was a new invention was false, material, and deceptive. Second, Cliffdale stated that the Ball-Matic would yield up to a 20 percent increase in fuel economy and implied that competent scientific tests backed this claim. But the highest savings established by any of the tests results introduced as evidence by Cliffdale was 11 percent. Thus, the performance claims made for the Ball-Matic were also deceptive. Finally, Cliffdale printed testimonials of Ball-Matic users that implicitly made performance claims akin to the false and deceptive express claims in the advertisements. Moreover, a number of the testimonials, while implicitly claiming to be unrestrained and impartial, came from business associates of Ball-Matic marketers. Cliffdale's failure to disclose this relationship was material and deceptive in that consumers were likely to rely on the endorsements of other users.

INTERPRETATION A misrepresentation or material omission that is likely to mislead a consumer to the consumer's detriment is grounds for a claim of deception.

Deception may occur either through false representation or material omission. Examples of deceptive practices have included advertising that a certain product would save consumers 25 percent on their automotive motor oil, when the product simply replaced a quart of oil in the engine (which normally contains four quarts of oil) and was, in fact, more expensive than the oil it replaced; placing marbles in a bowl of vegetable soup in order to displace the vegetables from the bottom of the bowl and therefore make the soup look thicker; and claiming that one drug provided greater pain relief than another named drug, when evidence actually was insufficient to prove the claim to the medical community.

Deception can also occur through a failure to *disclose* important product information if such disclosure is necessary to correct a false and material expectation created in the consumer's mind by the product or by the circumstances of sale. For example, the FTC has insisted that the failure to disclose a product's country of origin constitutes a deceptive omission, based on the agency's view that consumers assume the United States to be the country of origin of a product that bears no other country's name.

The third policy statement issued by the commission involves **ad substantiation**. This policy requires that advertisers have a reasonable basis for their claims at the time they make such claims. Moreover, in determining the reasonableness of a claim, the commission places great weight upon the cost and benefits of substantiation.

Ad substantiation requires advertisers to have a reasonable basis for their claims

Remedies

In addition to the remedies discussed above, the FTC has employed three other remedies: (1) affirmative disclosure, (2) corrective advertising, and (3) multiple

Affirmative disclosure
requirement that an
advertiser include in its
advertisements information
that will render the ads
nondeceptive

Corrective advertising
disclosure in an advertisement that previous ads were
deceptive

product orders. **Affirmative disclosure**, a remedy frequently employed by the FTC, requires an offender to include in its advertisements certain information that will prevent the ads from being considered deceptive.

Corrective advertising goes beyond affirmative disclosure by requiring an advertiser who has made a deceptive claim to disclose in future advertisements that such prior claims were in fact untrue. The theory behind this requirement is that a previous deception's effects will continue until expressly corrected. The following case provides an example of this remedy.

WARNER-LAMBERT CO. v. FTC United States Court of Appeals, District of Columbia Circuit, 1977, 562 F.2d 749

FACTS The FTC ordered Warner-Lambert to cease and desist from advertising that its product, Listerine antiseptic mouthwash, prevents, cures, or alleviates the common cold and sore throats. The order further required Warner-Lambert to disclose in future advertisements that "[c]ontrary to prior advertising, Listerine will not help prevent colds or sore throats or lessen their severity." Warner-Lambert contended that even if its past advertising claims were false, the corrective advertising portion of the order exceeded the FTC's statutory power. The FTC claimed that corrective advertising was necessary in light of Warner-Lambert's 100 years of false claims and the resulting persistence of erroneous consumer beliefs.

DECISION Order of the FTC affirmed as modified by this opinion.

OPINION Congress intended for the FTC to have broad remedial powers in order to protect the public from deceptive trade practices. Corrective advertising represents an appropriate remedy in this case because of Warner-Lambert's long history of deceptive advertising, the success of the advertising campaign in creating a false image in the public's mind, and the fact that this false perception would continue if not corrected.

INTERPRETATION Corrective advertisements may be required to remedy the effects of previous deceptive advertisements.

Multiple product order
requires advertiser to cease
and desist from deceptive
statements on all products it
sells

Multiple product orders require a deceptive advertiser to cease and desist from any future deception not only in regard to the product in question but also in regard to all products sold by the company. This remedy is particularly useful in dealing with companies that have repeatedly violated the law.

The Consumer Product Safety Commission

**Consumer Product Safety
Act** federal statute enacted
to (1) protect public against
unsafe products; (2) assist
consumers in evaluating
products; (3) develop
uniform safety standards;
and (4) promote safety
research

The **Consumer Product Safety Act** (CPSA) established an independent federal regulatory agency, the Consumer Product Safety Commission (CPSC). The purposes of the CPSA are (1) to protect the public against unreasonable risks of injury associated with consumer products, (2) to assist consumers in evaluating the comparative safety of consumer products, (3) to develop uniform safety standards for consumer products and to minimize conflicting state and local regulations, and (4) to promote research and investigation into the causes and prevention of product-related deaths, illnesses, and injuries.

Consisting of five commissioners, no more than three of whom can be from the same political party, the CPSC has authority to set safety standards for consumer products; to ban unsafe products; to issue administrative recall orders to compel repair, replacement, or refunds for products found to present substantial hazards; and to seek court orders requiring the recall of "imminently hazardous" products. In addition, Congress requires businesses under CPSC jurisdiction to notify the agency of any information indicating that their products contain defects that "could create" substantial product hazards. By triggering investigations that may lead to product recalls, these reports play a major role in the agency's regulatory activities.

The CPSC also enforces four statutes previously enforced by other agencies. These acts, commonly referred to as the "transferred acts," are the Federal Hazardous Substances Act, the Flammable Fabrics Act, the Poison Prevention Packaging Act, and the Refrigerator Safety Act. Whenever the CPSC can regulate a product under one of these specific acts, rather than under the more general CPSA, the agency is directed to do so unless it specifically finds that regulation under the CPSA is in the public interest. Thus, a large number of CPSC regulations, such as those for toys, children's flammable sleepwear, and hazard warnings on household chemical products, arise under the transferred acts rather than under the CPSA.

When first established, the CPSC promulgated a number of **mandatory safety standards**; manufacturers either must follow these rules, which regulate product design, packaging, and warning labels, or face legal sanctions. To save time and money, the agency began to rely on industry to establish **voluntary safety standards**—rules for which noncompliance does not violate the law—reserving mandatory standards for those instances in which voluntary standards proved inadequate. In 1981, Congress enacted legislation requiring the CPSC to rely on voluntary standards "whenever compliance with such voluntary standards would eliminate or adequately reduce the risk of injury addressed and there is substantial compliance with such voluntary standards." Although the 1981 amendments do not bar the CPSC from writing mandatory standards, the CPSC has promulgated few such standards since the law was amended.

Other Federal Consumer Protection Agencies

Among the many other federal agencies that play a major consumer protection role are the **National Highway Traffic Safety Administration (NHTSA)** and the **Food and Drug Administration (FDA)**.

Established in 1966 to reduce the number of deaths and injuries resulting from highway crashes, NHTSA has the authority to set motor vehicle safety standards that promote crash prevention and crashworthiness. Manufacturers are required to report possible safety defects, and the agency may seek a recall if it determines that a particular automobile model presents a sufficiently great hazard. NHTSA is also authorized to provide grants-in-aid for state highway safety programs and to conduct research on improving highway safety. See *Motor Vehicle Mfrs. Ass'n v. State Farm Mutual Automobile Ins. Co.* in Chapter 5.

The Food and Drug Administration is the oldest federal consumer protection agency, dating back to 1906. The FDA enforces the Food, Drug and Cosmetic Act, enacted in 1938, which authorizes the agency to regulate "adulterated and misbranded" products. The agency uses two basic enforcement methods: it sets standards for products or requires their premarket approval. The products most often subject to premarket approval are drugs. Since 1976, the agency also has had the authority to subject medical devices such as pacemakers and intrauterine devices to premarket approval; it recently has been requiring a large and increasing number of such devices to undergo this approval process.

Although the FTC, CPSC, NHTSA, and FDA are perhaps the best known federal consumer protection agencies, numerous others play important roles. For example, the United States Postal Service brings many cases every year to close down mail fraud operations; the Interstate Commerce Commission (ICC) enforces rules to prevent unfair business practices by interstate moving companies; and the Securities and Exchange Commission (SEC), as we discussed in

Chapter 42, protects consumers against fraud in the sale of securities. In addition, many other agencies assist consumers with specific types of problems that fall within an agency's scope.

CONSUMER PURCHASES

Whenever a consumer purchases a product or obtains a service, certain rights and obligations arise. (The extent to which these rights and obligations apply to all contracts was discussed more fully in Chapters 9 through 18; the extent to which they apply to a sale of goods under the Uniform Commercial Code was discussed in Chapters 19 through 23.) Although a number of consumer protection laws have been enacted in recent years, they still leave much of a consumer's rights and duties to state contract law. In particular, Article 2 of the Uniform Commercial Code provides the basic rules governing when a contract for the sale of goods is formed, what constitutes a breach of contract, and what rights an innocent party has against a party who commits a breach. Though many consumer protection laws add rights the UCC does not contain, they still use its tenets as building blocks. For example, many states have passed so-called "lemon laws" to provide additional contract cancellation rights to dissatisfied automobile purchasers.

Federal Warranty Protection

Warranty creates a duty on the seller's part to assure that the goods or services she sells will conform to certain qualities, characteristics, or conditions. A seller is not required, however, to warrant what she sells; and in general she may, by appropriate words, disclaim (exclude) or modify a particular warranty or all warranties. Because a seller's power to disclaim or modify is so flexible, consumer protection laws have been enacted to ensure that consumers understand the warranty protection provided them.

In 1974, to protect buyers and to prevent deception in selling, Congress enacted the *Magnuson-Moss Warranty Act*, which requires sellers of consumer products to provide adequate information about warranties. The FTC administers and enforces the act, which provides for (1) disclosure in clear and understandable language of the warranty that is to be offered, (2) a description of the warranty as either "full" or "limited," (3) a prohibition against disclaiming implied warranties if a written warranty is given, and (4) an optional informal settlement mechanism.

The act applies to consumer products with *written warranties*. A **consumer product** is any item of tangible personal property that is *normally* used for family, household, or personal use and that is distributed in commerce. The act does *not* protect commercial purchasers, partly because they are considered sufficiently knowledgeable, in terms of contracting, to protect themselves. Also, they are able to employ their own attorneys to protect themselves and, in the marketplace, can spread the cost of their injuries.

Presale Disclosures The act contains **presale disclosure** provisions calculated to prevent confusion and deception and to enable purchasers to make educated product comparisons. A person making a warranty must, to the extent required by the rules of the Federal Trade Commission, fully and conspicuously disclose in simple and readily understood language the terms and conditions of such warranty. Separate rules apply to mail order, catalog, and door-to-door sales.

Warranty creates a duty on the seller's part to assure certain features of goods or services

Federal warranty protection applies to sellers of consumer goods who give written warranties

Consumer product tangible personal property normally used for family, household, or personal purposes

Presale disclosure requires terms of warranty to be simple and readily understood and to be made available before the sale

Labeling Requirements The act further divides written warranties into two categories—limited and full—either of which, for any product costing more than $10, must be designated on the written warranty itself. The purpose of this provision is to enable the consumer to make an initial comparison of the legal rights under certain warranties. Under a **warranty** designated as **full**, the warrantor must agree to repair the product, without charge, to conform with the warranty; no limitation may be placed on the duration of any implied warranty; the consumer must be given the option of a refund or replacement if repair is unsuccessful; and consequential damages may be excluded only if the warranty conspicuously indicates their exclusion. A limited warranty is any warranty not designated as full.

Limitations on Disclaimers Most significantly, the act provides that a *written* warranty, whether full or limited, may ***not** disclaim any implied* warranty. Specifically, a full warranty may not disclaim, modify, or limit any implied warranty; and a limited warranty may not disclaim or modify any implied warranty but may limit its duration to that of the written warranty, provided that the limitation is reasonable, conscionable, and conspicuously displayed. Some states, however, do not allow limitations in the duration of implied warranties.

For example, GE sells consumer goods to Barry for $150 and provides a written warranty regarding the quality of the goods. GE must designate the warranty as full or limited, depending on the warranty's characteristics, and may not disclaim or modify any implied warranty. On the other hand, had GE not provided Barry with a written warranty, the Magnuson-Moss Act would not apply; and GE could disclaim any and all implied warranties (see Figure 46–1).

State "Lemon Laws"

A number of state legislatures have enacted **lemon laws** that attempt to provide new car purchasers with rights that are similar to full warranties under the Magnuson-Moss Warranty Act. (Some states have broadened their laws to cover

Labeling requirement requires warrantor to inform consumers of their legal rights under a warranty (full or limited)

Full warranty one under which warrantor will repair the product and, if unsuccessful, will replace or refund

Disclaimer limitation prohibits a written warranty from disclaiming any implied warranty

State "lemon laws" state laws that attempt to provide new car purchasers with rights similar to full warranties under Magnuson-Moss

FIGURE 46–1 Magnuson-Moss Act

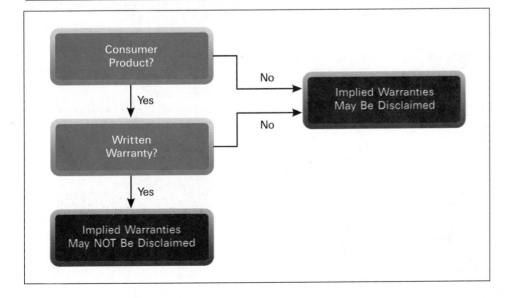

used cars; some also cover motorcycles.) There are many different lemon laws, but most define a *lemon* as a car that continues to have a defect that substantially impairs its use, value, or safety, even after the manufacturer has made reasonable attempts to correct the problem. If a consumer can prove that her car is a lemon, most lemon laws require the manufacturer either to replace the car or to refund its retail price, less an allowance for the consumer's use of the car. In addition, most lemon laws provide that the consumer may recover attorneys' fees and expenses if the case goes to litigation.

Consumer Right of Rescission

Rescission right to cancel

In most cases, a consumer is legally obligated once he has signed a contract. Many states, however, have statutes allowing a consumer a brief period—generally two or three days—during which he may **rescind** an otherwise binding credit obligation if the sale was solicited in his home. Moreover, the Federal Trade Commission has also set forth a trade regulation that applies to door-to-door sales, leases, or rentals of goods and services for $25 or more, whether the sale is for cash or on credit. The regulation permits a consumer to rescind a contract within *three days* of signing.

Consumer right of rescission in certain instances a consumer is granted a brief period of time during which she may rescind (cancel) an otherwise binding obligation

The right of **rescission** also exists under the *Federal Consumer Credit Protection Act* (discussed more fully in the next section), which allows a consumer three days during which he may withdraw from any credit obligation secured by a mortgage on his home, unless the extension of credit was made to acquire the dwelling. After the consumer rescinds, the creditor has twenty days to return any money or property he has received from the consumer.

The *Interstate Land Sales Full Disclosure Act* requires a developer of unimproved land to file a detailed statement of record containing specified information about specified subdivisions with the Department of Housing and Urban Development before offering the lots for sale or lease. The developer must provide a property report (a condensed version of the statement of record) to each prospective purchaser or lessee. The act provides that a purchaser or lessee may revoke any contract or agreement for sale or lease at her option within seven days of signing the contract, and that the contract must clearly provide this right. A purchaser or lessee who does not receive a property report before signing a contract may revoke the contract within two years from the date of signing.

For a summary of consumer rescission rights, see Figure 46–2.

FIGURE 46–2 Consumer Rescission Rights

Law	Rescission Period	Door-to-Door Solicitation Required?	Credit or Cash
State "cooling-off" laws	Varies	Yes	Varies
FTC trade regulation	Within 3 days of signing the contract	Yes	Both
Consumer Credit Protection Act (CCPA)	Within 3 days of signing the contract	No	Credit only
Interstate Land Sales Full Disclosure Act	Within 7 days of signing the contract	No	Both

CONSUMER CREDIT TRANSACTIONS

In the absence of special regulation, consumer credit transactions are governed by the laws that regulate commercial transactions generally. A **consumer credit transaction** is customarily defined as any credit transaction involving goods, services, or land acquired for personal, household, or family purposes. The following examples illustrate consumer credit transactions: Atkins borrows $600 from a bank to pay a dentist bill or to take a vacation; Bevins buys a refrigerator for her home from a department store and agrees to pay the purchase price in twelve equal monthly installments; Carpenter has an oil company credit card with which he purchases gasoline and tires for his family car.

Regulation of consumer credit has increased considerably because of the dramatic expansion of consumer credit and the numerous abuses in credit transactions, including misleading credit disclosures, unfair marketing practices, and oppressive collection methods. In 1968, in response to concerns about consumer credit, Congress passed the *Federal Consumer Credit Protection Act (FCCPA)*, which requires creditors to disclose finance charges (including interest and other charges) and credit extension charges, and sets limits on garnishment proceedings. Since 1968, Congress has added titles to this law. Also in 1968, the National Conference of Commissioners on Uniform State Laws (the group that drafted the Uniform Commercial Code) promulgated the *Uniform Consumer Credit Code (UCCC)*, which consolidated into one recommended law the regulation of all consumer credit transactions—loans and purchases on credit. Though only a few states have adopted the UCCC, its impact on the development of consumer credit has extended well beyond their borders.

Access to the Market

The *Equal Credit Opportunity Act*, enacted by Congress in 1974 and revised several times since then, prohibits all businesses that regularly extend credit from discriminating against any credit applicant on the basis of gender, marital status, race, color, religion, national origin, or age. Under the act, a creditor must notify an applicant, within thirty days of receiving an application, of the action the creditor has taken and must give specific reasons for denying credit. Although several federal agencies administer and enforce the act, the FTC has overall enforcement authority. A credit applicant aggrieved by a violation of the act may recover actual and punitive damages, plus attorneys' fees.

Disclosure Requirements

Title One of the FCCPA, also known as the **Truth-in-Lending Act**, has superseded state disclosure requirements relating to credit terms for both consumer loans and credit sales under $25,000. The act does not cover credit transactions for business, commercial, or agricultural purposes. Creditors in every state not specifically exempted by the Federal Reserve Board must comply with federal disclosure standards.

Before a consumer formally incurs a contractual obligation for credit, both state and federal statutes require the creditor to present to the consumer a written statement containing certain information about contract terms. Generally, the required disclosure concerns the cost of credit, that is, interest or sales finance charges. An important requirement in the Truth-in-Lending Act is that sales finance and interest rates must be quoted in terms of an **APR** *(annual percentage rate)* and must be calculated on a uniform basis. Congress required disclosure of

Consumer credit transaction any credit transaction involving goods, services, or land for personal, household, or family purposes

Access to the market discrimination in extending credit on the basis of gender, marital status, race, color, religion, national origin, or age is prohibited

Truth-in-Lending Act requires creditor to provide certain information about contract terms, including APR (annual percentage rate), to the consumer before he formally incurs the obligation

APR annual percentage rate

this information to encourage consumers to compare credit terms, to increase competition among financial institutions, and to facilitate economic stability. Enforcement and interpretation of the Truth-in-Lending Act was assigned to the Federal Reserve Board, which issued **Regulation Z** to carry out this responsibility.

The **Fair Credit and Charge Card Disclosure Act of 1988** adds to the Truth-in-Lending Act a new section requiring all credit and charge card applications and solicitations to include extensive disclosures whose requirements depend upon the type of card involved and whether the application or solicitation is by mail, telephone, or other means.

Credit Accounts In addition to the cost of the credit, under the Truth-in-Lending Act a creditor must inform consumers who open revolving or open-ended credit accounts about how the finance charge is computed and when it is charged, what other charges may be imposed, and whether the creditor retains or acquires a security interest. An **open-ended credit** account permits the debtor to enter into a series of credit transactions that he may pay off either in installments or in a lump sum. Examples of this type of credit include most department store credit cards, most gasoline credit cards, VISA cards, and MasterCards.

Open-ended credit
account permitting debtor to enter into a series of credit transactions

Close-ended credit, in contrast, is credit extended for a specified time, during which the debtor generally makes periodic payments in an amount and at a time agreed upon in advance. Examples of this type of credit include most automobile financing agreements, most real estate mortgages, and numerous other major purchases. For nonrevolving or closed-ended credit accounts, the creditor must provide the consumer with information about the total amount financed; the cash price; the number, amount, and due date of installments; delinquency charges; and a description of the security, if any.

Close-ended credit
credit extended to debtor for a specified time

ARMs In 1987, the Federal Reserve Board amended Regulation Z to deal with variable or adjustable rate mortgages (ARMs). The *ARM disclosure rules* apply to any loan that is (1) a closed-ended consumer transaction, (2) secured by the consumer's principal residence, (3) longer than one year in duration, and (4) subject to interest rate variation. This coverage excludes open-ended lines of credit secured by the consumer's principal dwelling. The disclosures must be made when a creditor furnishes an application to a prospective borrower or before the creditor receives payment of a nonrefundable fee, whichever occurs first. The ARM disclosure rules require that the creditor provide the consumer with a consumer handbook on ARMs and a loan program disclosure statement covering the terms of each ARM that the creditor offers.

Home Equity Loans In recent years a popular method of consumer borrowing has been the home equity loan. In order to regulate the disclosures and advertising of these loans, in 1988 Congress enacted the **Home Equity Loan Consumer Protection Act (HELCPA)**. HELCPA amends the Truth-in-Lending Act to require that lenders provide a disclosure statement and consumer pamphlet at (or, in some limited instances, within three days of) the time they provide an application to a prospective consumer borrower. HELCPA applies to all open-ended credit plans for consumer loans that are secured by the consumer's principal dwelling. Unlike other Truth-in-Lending statutes, HELCPA defines a principal dwelling to include second or vacation homes. The disclosure statement must include a statement that (1) a default on the loan may result in the consumer's loss of the dwelling; (2) some conditions must be met, such as a time by which the consumer must submit an application in order to obtain the specific terms; and (3) the creditor, under certain circumstances, may terminate the plan and accelerate the outstanding balance, prohibit further extension of credit, reduce the plan's credit limit, or impose fees upon the termination of the account. In addition, if the plan contains a fixed interest rate, the creditor must disclose each APR imposed. If the plan involves an ARM, it must include how the rate is computed, the manner in which rates will be changed, the initial rate and how it was determined, the maximum rate change that may occur in any one year, the maximum rate that can be charged under the plan, the earliest time at which the maximum interest can be reached, and an itemization of all fees the plan imposes. Regulation Z provides the consumer with the right to rescind such a plan until midnight of the third day following the opening of the plan, until delivery of a notice of the right to rescind, or until delivery of all material disclosures, whichever comes last.

Billing Errors   In 1975, the ***Fair Credit Billing Act*** went into effect to relieve some of the problems and abuses associated with credit card billing errors. The act establishes procedures for the consumer to follow in making complaints about specified billing errors and requires the creditor to explain or correct such errors. Until it responds to the complaint, the creditor may not take any action to collect the disputed amount, restrict the use of an open-ended credit account because the disputed amount is unpaid, or report the disputed amount as delinquent.

In 1974, Congress enacted the ***Real Estate Settlement Procedures Act (RESPA)*** to provide consumer home purchasers with greater and more timely information on the nature and costs of the settlement process and to protect them from unnecessarily high settlement charges. The act, which applies to all federally related mortgage loans, requires advance disclosure to home buyers and sellers of all settlement costs, including attorneys' fees, credit reports, title insurance, and, if relevant, an initial escrow account statement. Nearly all first mortgage loans fall within the scope of the act. RESPA, which is administered and enforced by the Secretary of Housing and Urban Development, prohibits kickbacks and referral fees and limits the amount home buyers must place in escrow accounts to insure payment of real estate taxes and insurance. In 1990, the National Affordable Housing Act amended RESPA to require an annual analysis of escrow accounts.

Contract Terms

Consumer credit is marketed on a mass basis. Frequently, contract documents are printed forms containing blank spaces to accommodate the contractual details the creditor will normally negotiate at the time she extends credit. Standardization and uniformity of contract terms facilitate the transfer of the creditor's rights (in most situations, those of a seller) to a third party, usually a bank or finance company.

Almost all states impose statutory ceilings on the amount that creditors may charge for the extension of consumer credit. Statutes regulating rates also specify what other charges may be made. Most statutes require a creditor to permit the debtor to pay her obligation in full at any time before the maturity date of the final installment. If the interest charge for the loan period was computed in advance and added to the principal of the loan, a debtor who prepays in full is entitled to a refund of the unearned interest already paid.

Contract terms statutory and judicial limitations have been imposed on consumer obligations

In the past, certain purchases involving consumer goods were financed in such a way that a consumer was legally obligated to make full payment of the price to a third party, even though the dealer from whom she bought the goods had committed fraud or the goods were defective. This occurred when the purchaser executed and delivered to the seller a negotiable instrument (a promissory note, draft, or check), and the seller negotiated it to a holder in due course, who purchased the note for value, in good faith, and without notice that it was overdue or that it had any defenses or claims attached to it. Though valid against the seller, the buyer's defenses—that the goods were defective or that the seller had committed fraud—were not valid against a holder in due course of the note. To preserve the claims and defenses of consumer buyers and borrowers and to make such claims and defenses available against holders in due course, the FTC adopted a rule that limits the rights of a holder in due course of an instrument evidencing a debt that arises out of a *consumer credit contract*. The rule, which we discussed in Chapter 26, applies to sellers and lessors of goods.

A similar rule applies to credit card issuers under the ***Fair Credit Billing Act***. The act preserves a consumer's defense against the issuer (provided the consumer has made a good faith attempt to resolve the dispute with the seller), but only if (1) the seller is controlled by the card issuer or is under common control with the issuer, (2) the issuer has included the seller's promotional literature in the monthly billing statements sent to the card holder, or (3) the sale involves more than $50 and the consumer's billing address is in the same state as, or within one hundred miles of, the seller's place of business.

Consumer Credit Card Fraud

Credit Card Fraud Act prohibits certain fraudulent practices and limits a card holder's liability for unauthorized use of a credit card to $50

In 1984, Congress enacted the ***Credit Card Fraud Act***, which closed many loopholes in prior law. The act prohibits the following practices: (1) possessing unauthorized cards, (2) counterfeiting or altering credit cards, (3) using account numbers alone, and (4) using cards obtained from a third party with his consent, even if the third party conspires to report the cards as stolen. It also imposes stiffer, criminal penalties for violation.

The FCCPA protects the *credit card holder* from loss by limiting to $50 the card holder's liability for another's unauthorized use of the holder's card. However, the card issuer may collect up to that amount for unauthorized use only if (1) the holder has accepted the card; (2) the issuer has furnished adequate notice of potential liability to the card holder; (3) the issuer has provided the card holder with a statement describing the means by which the holder may notify the card issuer of the loss or theft of the credit card; (4) the unauthorized use occurs before the card holder has notified the card issuer of the loss or theft; and (5) the card issuer has provided a method by which the person using the card can be identified as the person authorized to use the card.

Fair Reportage

Fair credit reporting consumer credit reports are prohibited from containing inaccurate or obsolete information

Because creditors usually grant consumers credit only after investigating their creditworthiness, it is essential that the information on which creditors base such decisions is accurate and current. To this end, in 1970 Congress enacted the ***Fair Credit Reporting Act***, which applies to consumer reports used to secure employment, insurance, and credit. The act prohibits the inclusion of inaccurate or specified obsolete information in consumer reports and requires consumer reporting agencies to give consumers written advance notice before making an investigative report. The consumer may request information regarding the nature and substance of all information in the consumer reporting agency's files, the source of the information, and the names of all who received the consumer reports furnished for employment purposes within the preceding two years and for other purposes within the preceding six months.

If the consumer does not agree that the information in the file is accurate and complete, and so notifies the agency, the agency must then reinvestigate the matter within a reasonable time, unless the complaint is frivolous or irrelevant. If reinvestigation proves that the information is inaccurate, it must promptly be deleted. If the dispute remains unresolved after reinvestigation, the consumer may submit to the agency a brief statement setting forth the nature of the dispute, and this statement must be incorporated into the report.

HENSON v. CSC CREDIT SERVICES   United States Court of Appeals, Seventh Circuit, 1994, 29 F.3d 280

FACTS   In 1990, Greg Henson sold his 1980 Chevrolet Camaro Z-28 to his brother, Jeff Henson. To purchase the car, Jeff secured a loan with Cosco Federal Credit Union (Cosco). Soon thereafter, the car was stolen and Jeff stopped making payments on his loan from Cosco. At the time, Cosco was unsure if Greg retained an interest in the car so Cosco sued both Jeff and Greg for possession of the car. The trial court rendered a default judgment against Jeff and ruled that Greg had no longer any interest in the car. The court further entered a deficiency judgment against Jeff in the amount of $4,076. However, the clerk erroneously noted in the judgment docket that the money judgment had been rendered against Greg as well as against Jeff. However, the official record of judgments and orders correctly reflected that only Jeff was affected by the money judgment. Two credit agencies, CSC Credit Services (CSC) and Trans Union Corporation (Trans Union), relied on the state court judgment docket and indicated in Greg's credit report that he owed the money judgment. Greg and his wife, Mary Henson, allege that they then "contacted Trans [Union] twice, in writing, to correct this horrible injustice." When Trans Union did not respond, the Hensons brought this action alleging violations of the Federal Credit Reporting Act (FCRA). The district court, noting that to state a claim under FCRA a consumer must allege that a credit reporting agency prepared a credit report containing inaccurate information, granted the defendants' motions to dismiss.

DECISION   Judgment affirmed in part and reversed in part and remanded.

OPINION   Under FCRA, a consumer reporting agency is required to follow "reasonable procedures to assure maximum possible accuracy" of the information contained in a consumer's credit report. A credit reporting agency is not liable under the FCRA if it followed "reasonable procedures to assure maximum possible accuracy," but nonetheless reported inaccurate information in the consumer's credit report.

First, the information reported by CSC and Trans Union was inaccurate. Contrary to CSC and Trans Union's contention that the judgment docket conclusively shows that a money judgment was entered against Greg Henson, it is the physical placing of the judgment into the "Record of Judgments and Orders" that constitutes the official entry of judgment. The official record conclusively establishes that no money judgment was rendered against Greg.

Although the information they reported was inaccurate, CSC and Trans Union are not liable under the FCRA if they followed "reasonable procedures to assure maximum possible accuracy" of the information reported. It may be said that the judgment docket is a presumptively reliable source and therefore it is reasonable to rely on it as an initial source of information. Thus, as a matter of law, a credit reporting agency is not liable under the FCRA for reporting inaccurate information obtained from a court's judgment docket, absent prior notice from the consumer that the information may be inaccurate.

Finally, the Hensons' allegation that they contacted Trans Union in an attempt to remedy the situation implicates Trans Union's duty to reinvestigate. A credit reporting agency that has been notified of potentially inaccurate information in a consumer's credit report is in a very different position than one who has no such notice. A credit reporting agency may initially rely on public court documents, because to require more may be unduly burdensome in the normal case. However, such exclusive reliance may not be justified once the credit reporting agency receives notice that the consumer disputes information contained in his credit report. The reasonableness of the defendant's conduct must be resolved by the trial court on remand.

INTERPRETATION   The FCRA prohibits the reporting of inaccurate or specified obsolete information.

Creditors' Remedies

A primary concern of creditors involves their rights should a debtor default or become late in payment. When the credit charge is precomputed, the creditor may impose a delinquency charge for late payments, subject to statutory limits for such charges. If, instead of being delinquent, the consumer defaults, the creditor may declare the entire balance of the debt immediately due and payable and may sue on the debt. The other courses of action that are open to the creditor depend on his security. Security provisions in consumer credit contracts may require a cosigner, an assignment of wages, a security interest in the goods sold, a security interest in other real or personal property of the debtor, and a confession of judgment clause (i.e., a clause by the defendant giving the plaintiff power to enter judgment against the defendant).

Wage assignments and garnishment most states limit the amount that may be deducted from an individual's wages through either assignment or garnishment

Wage Assignments and Garnishment Wage assignments are prohibited by some states. In most states and under the FCCPA, a limitation is imposed on the amount that may be deducted from an individual's wages during any pay period. In addition, the FCCPA prohibits an employer from discharging an employee solely because of a creditor's exercise of an assignment of wages in connection with any one debt.

Even where wage assignments are prohibited, the creditor may still reach a consumer's wages through garnishment. But garnishment is available only in a court proceeding to enforce the collection of a judgment. The FCCPA and state statutes contain exemption provisions that limit the amount of wages subject to garnishment.

Security interest seller may retain a security interest in goods sold or other collateral of the buyer, although some restrictions are imposed

Security Interest In the case of credit sales, the seller may retain a **security interest** in the goods sold. Many states impose restrictions on other security the creditor may obtain. Where the debt is secured by property as collateral, the creditor, on default by the debtor, may take possession of the property and, subject to the provisions of the Uniform Commercial Code, either retain it in full satisfaction of the debt or sell it and, if the proceeds are less than the outstanding debt, sue the debtor for the balance and obtain a deficiency judgment. The UCC provides that where a buyer of goods has paid 60 percent of the purchase price or 60 percent of a loan secured by consumer goods, the secured creditor may not retain the property in full satisfaction but must sell the goods and pay to the buyer that part of the sale proceeds in excess of the balance due. (We discussed secured transactions in Chapter 39.)

In addition, federal regulation prohibits a credit seller or lender from obtaining a consumer's grant of a nonpossessory security interest in household goods. Household goods include clothing, furniture, appliances, kitchenware, personal effects, one radio, and one television; such goods specifically exclude works of art, other electronic entertainment equipment, antiques, and jewelry. This rule, which does not apply to purchase money security interests or to pledges, prevents a lender or seller from obtaining a nonpurchase money security interest covering the consumer's household goods.

Debt collection practices abusive, deceptive, and unfair practices by debt collectors in collecting consumer debts are prohibited by the Fair Debt Collection Practices Act

Debt Collection Practices In 1977, Congress enacted the *Fair Debt Collection Practices Act* to prevent debt collection agencies from employing abusive, deceptive, and unfair practices in the collection of consumer debts. The act, which is enforced by the Federal Trade Commission, does not apply to creditors

ETHICAL DILEMMA Should Some Be Protected from High-Pressure Sales?

FACTS Glen Thomas, a recent college graduate, was hired as a rental agent by New Vistas Condominiums, Inc., of Old Saybrook, Connecticut. Initially responsible for handling rentals on two apartment buildings, Glen was also assigned to an aggressive sales program for new time-share condominiums to be developed in Florida.

Under the new sales program, Glen was to be trained as a marketing specialist. His boss, Sabrina Cassey, explained that the marketing plan would target those between the ages of sixty and eighty. The condominiums would feature an attractive communal social program that would include swimming exercises, Friday night bingo games, and monthly movies. Also available, for additional fees, would be special services, such as food delivery, shopping, and domestic help.

In the following months, in marketing the new condominiums, New Vistas makes particular efforts to interest those who have recently lost their spouses. The company has devised a system for following obituaries and has purchased lists that direct its marketing personnel to recent widows and widowers at certain income levels.

For the new condominiums, Sabrina's marketing team has concocted a presentation she terms "lethal." The program begins with a direct mailing. Thereafter, individuals are invited to a party and are promised free prizes. A movie is shown that features elderly people socializing around a pool, playing cards, and having intimate candlelight dinners. Wine and dessert are served afterward. Then, once the terms of the condominium purchase have been explained, New Vistas salespeople distribute contracts and pressure the attendees to sign the contracts before the distribution of gifts. At the meetings, Sabrina's job is to explain the condominiums; Glen's role is to get the contracts signed.

On the first night of the sales promotion, Glen meets Irving Sherman, who happens to be the father of a girl Glen dated in high school. Irving tells Glen that his wife has recently died, succumbing to a three-year battle with cancer. Glen knows that Irving has been through quite an ordeal, since Irving himself had suffered from colon cancer several years earlier. When it comes time to press for signatures on the contracts, Glen becomes very uncomfortable and wants to leave.

Social, Policy, and Ethical Considerations

1. What should Glen do? Why? What alternative sales methods are available?

2. Is there anything ethically wrong with gearing sales to a special segment of the population? Should certain segments of the population be protected from high-powered sales programs?

3. Can the public ever be overprotected with regard to sales promotions? To what extent, if any, should individuals be limited in the nonfraudulent marketing of their products?

themselves. Rather, the act provides that any debt collector who communicates with a person other than the consumer for the purpose of acquiring information about the consumer's location may not state that the consumer owes any debt. Moreover, the act prohibits a number of abusive collection practices, including (1) communication with the consumer at unusual or inconvenient hours; (2) communication with the consumer if she is represented by an attorney; (3) harassing, oppressive, or abusive conduct, such as obscene language or threats of violence; (4) false, deceptive, or misleading representations or means of collection; and (5) unfair or unconscionable means to collect any debt.

The act requires a debt collector, within five days of the initial communication with a consumer, to provide the consumer with a written notice that includes (1) the amount of the debt; (2) the name of the current creditor; and (3) a statement informing the consumer that she can request verification of the alleged debt. The consumer may recover damages from the collection agency for violations of the act.

MILLER v. PAYCO-GENERAL AMERICAN CREDITS, INC. United States Court of Appeals, Fourth Circuit, 1991, 943 F.2d 482

FACTS Lenvil Miller owed $2,501.61 to the Star Bank of Cincinnati. Star Bank referred collection of Miller's account to Payco-General American Credits, Inc. (Payco), a debt collection agency. Payco sent Miller a collection form. Across the top of the form was the caption, "DEMAND FOR PAYMENT," in large, red, boldface type. The middle of the page stated "THIS IS A DEMAND FOR IMMEDIATE FULL PAYMENT OF YOUR DEBT," also in large, red, boldface type. That statement was followed in bold by "YOUR SERIOUSLY PAST DUE ACCOUNT HAS BEEN GIVEN TO US FOR IMMEDIATE ACTION. YOU HAVE HAD AMPLE TIME TO PAY YOUR DEBT, BUT YOU HAVE NOT. IF THERE IS A VALID REASON, PHONE US AT [. . .] TODAY. IF NOT, PAY US—NOW." The word "NOW" covered the bottom third of the form. At the very bottom in the smallest type to appear on the form was the statement, "NOTICE: SEE REVERSE SIDE FOR IMPORTANT INFORMATION." The notice was printed in white against a red background. On the reverse side were four paragraphs in gray ink. The last three paragraphs contained the validation notice required by the Fair Debt Collection Practices Act (FDCPA) to inform the consumer how to obtain verification of the debt.

Miller sued Payco on the ground that the validation notice did not comply with the FDCPA. Miller argued that despite the fact that the validation notice contained all the necessary information, it violated the FDCPA because it contradicted other parts of the collection letter, was overshadowed by the demands for payment, and was not effectively conveyed to the consumer. The District Court granted summary judgment for Payco, concluding that Payco had complied with the FDCPA by including all the FDCPA-mandated information on the back of the form. Miller appealed.

DECISION Judgment of the District Court reversed and remanded.

OPINION The FDCPA requires a debt collector to send a consumer, either in its initial communication or within five days of the initial communication, a written notice containing (1) the debt amount; (2) the name of the current creditor; (3) a statement that if the consumer disputes the debt in writing within thirty days, the collector will send verification of the debt to the consumer; (4) a statement that if the consumer does not dispute the debt within thirty days, the collector will assume the debt to be valid; and (5) a statement that the collector will provide the name of the original creditor, upon the consumer's written request within thirty days. If the consumer, in writing, disputes the debt or requests the name of the original creditor, the collector must halt all collection efforts until it mails the debt verification or the creditor's name to the consumer.

The FDCPA was enacted to eliminate abusive debt collection practices. Congress included the debt validation provision in order to guarantee that consumers would receive adequate notice of their legal rights. Thus, a debt collector does not comply with FDCPA merely by including the required debt validation notice in a collection form. Rather, the collector must convey the notice effectively to the debtor. Furthermore, in order to be effective, the notice must not be overshadowed or contradicted by other messages or notices appearing in the initial communication.

The form Miller received from Payco prevents the effective conveying of notice by contradicting and overshadowing the validation notice. The large-print statements "IMMEDIATE FULL PAYMENT," "PHONE US TODAY," and "NOW" flatly contradict the information contained on the back of the form, which provides the consumer with thirty days in which to decide to request validation. Plus, if a consumer followed the commands to telephone, he could lose his rights for validation under the FDCPA, since the act requires that a consumer submit debt disputes in writing. If Miller had called to dispute the debt, Payco would have been under no statutory obligation to send the debt validation or to cease collection efforts.

INTERPRETATION In order to protect a consumer's right to verify a debt, a collection agency letter must contain a validation notice that other messages in the letter neither overshadow nor contradict.

THE LAW AND YOU Applying for Credit

Credit is used often in many forms. You use credit when you borrow money, buy a car or furniture with installment payments, or use a credit card. Federal laws says all consumers should get an equal chance to receive credit. Not everyone who applies for credit will get credit. The Equal Credit Opportunity Act states that it is illegal for creditors to discriminate against applicants on the basis of their sex, race, marital status, national origin, religion, age or because they get public assistance income.

A *creditor* is any bank, finance company, store, credit card company, car dealer or other business entity to which you owe money. Creditors look at your income, expenses, debts and credit history before deciding whether to give you credit. Any creditor who regularly extends credit, must follow the federal law.

Your Application Rights

You have the right to know whether your application was accepted or rejected within 30 days of filing.

You also have the right to know why your application was rejected. For example: Your income is to low or you have not worked at your job long enough. If you do not understand the reason, ask for a specific explanation you can understand.

Co-Signers

In some situations, a co-signer is required for receiving credit. A *co-signer* is someone who is equally responsible for the amount of the debt. If your credit is good enough, the creditor cannot require you to use a co-signer. If you are married and must use a co-signer, it does not necessarily have to be your spouse.

Credit Terms

You have the right to learn why you were offered less favorable terms (higher finance charges or less money) than what you wanted.

Accounts

You have the right to know why your account was closed, unless you are behind in your payments.

You have the right to keep your own account after you change your name, marital status, after you retire or reach a certain age.

Women have the right to their own credit history if the account was opened after June 1, 1977. If your account was opened before that time, it may only be in your husband's name. Ask the creditor to put your name on the account too.

On the application, a creditor may not discriminate against you because of your sex, marital status, age, religion, race, national origin, or because you receive public assistance income. That means that the creditor cannot make it hard for you to apply for credit, refuse to take your application, or refuse to give you credit for any of those reasons.

A Creditor May Not

- Ask whether you are divorced or widowed;
- Ask whether you are married or applying for a separate, unsecured account;
- Ask about your spouse unless you are applying together;
- Ask about your plans for having children;
- Ask if you are receiving alimony or child support unless you will rely on it for your credit; or
- Ask you about the race of the people who live in the neighborhood where you want to buy or improve your home.

A creditor can ask if you are *paying* alimony or child support.

In deciding whether to give you credit, a creditor may not consider your age unless you are under 18 or over 62. A creditor may not consider whether you have a telephone listed in your name. However, a creditor can ask whether there is a phone in your home.

Income

If you have a regular public assistance income, the creditor must count it the same as any other income. A creditor cannot count your income less because of your sex or marital status. A creditor cannot count income less or ignore income that is received from part-time work or from retirement programs. A creditor cannot refuse to count alimony or child support if you can prove that this income has been received regularly.

Discrimination—What to Do?

If you think you have been discriminated against, complain to the creditor in writing and tell the creditor that you know about the Equal Credit Opportunity Act. The creditor may change its decision or correct an error.

Contact the U.S. Attorney General's Office at the Federal Department of Justice to see if the creditor has violated Federal laws.

Contact your local Legal Services Office to see if a case can be brought in state or federal court against the creditor. Look for the telephone number in the phone book.

Shopping for Credit

Credit can be provided in different ways depending on whether you are buying a house, using a charge account or credit card, or buying an item with installment payments. Open-end and close-end credit are two ways credit can be given.

Open-end credit is credit given on a charge account or an overdraft checking account. Open-end credit usually involves several purchases, paid for on a monthly billing cycle. A finance charge can be added if the monthly bill is not paid on time.

This brochure will not tell you about open-end credit or buying a

continued

house on credit. We will look at close-end credit, which is borrowing money for a fixed amount and number of payments.

Confused About Where to Get the Cheapest Loan?

ASK for TRUTH IN LENDING information from the creditor. The federal Truth in Lending Law requires creditors that regularly extend credit (banks, finance companies, car dealers, retail stores) to tell you what it will cost you to borrow money.

The creditor must tell you

- The APR (annual percentage rate) or the cost of the yearly interest rate
- The FINANCE CHARGE (the dollar amount the credit will cost you)
- The AMOUNT FINANCED (the amount of credit provided to you or on your behalf)
- The TOTAL OF ALL PAYMENTS (the amount you will have to pay after you have made all the payments as scheduled)
- The NUMBER OF PAYMENTS
- The AMOUNT OF EACH PAYMENT and
- WHEN payments are DUE

Compare the APR and the finance charge of each creditor to find the best credit terms. You want the lowest APR and the smallest finance charge.

Credit insurance is usually not required in order to get credit. Before signing for credit life, credit disability, or credit life and disability insurance, decide whether you really need insurance. Consider whether or not anyone else who uses the item purchased on credit can afford to make payments if you cannot pay because of death or disability. Also consider the cost of credit insurance in comparison to the cost of other insurance. Although you can save money by not buying credit insurance, you may wish to compare the cost of the insurance with the risk of default and loss of item if you become disabled or die.

Credit Bureaus—What's in Your Credit File?

Credit bureaus, also called Consumer Reporting Agencies, keep files on individuals who borrow money or use credit cards. Most individuals have a file called a "consumer report" with their local credit bureau. A federal law called the Fair Credit Reporting Act gives you rights when dealing with your local credit bureau.

You have the right to review this file and make sure the information is correct and complete.

Check your credit report. The Consumer Report is a file which has information about how you pay your bills, or whether you have filed for bankruptcy.

You can call your local Credit Reporting Agency or Credit Bureau by looking for the telephone number in the yellow pages. If you have lived in more than one city, try to contact the Credit Bureau of each city that you lived in.

You have the right to know what the Credit Bureau report says. The Credit Bureau does not have to give you a copy of the report but many do. The Credit Bureau will not give you information about your credit over the phone. You must write or go in person to the Credit Bureau. You can also ask for the name of anyone who has received a report about you in the past six months (or if the report was about a job application you can get the names of those who received a report during the past two years).

It is important to check your credit report to make sure it is accurate and complete. If you are denied a loan, check with the Credit Bureau that was listed in the denial. There is no charge if you ask the Credit Bureau within 30 days after receiving the denial credit notice. There may be a small fee if you check with the Credit Bureau when you have not received a denial notice within the last 30 days.

What If the Report Is Wrong? — Correcting the Credit Report

There are "credit fix-up" agencies which can help you obtain a copy of your credit report as well as update or correct your credit report. The fees charged for this service commonly range from $100–$500. The services offered by a "credit fix-up" agency are actions you can take yourself without any expense.

If you see that information is missing or wrong:

1. Send a letter to the Credit Bureau explaining why the report is wrong and keep a copy for yourself. The Credit Bureau can send you a copy of the correction as well as send a copy of the correction to anyone who received your report in the last six months (or within the last two years if it is a job report).

2. If the Credit Bureau will not change its report, you can request that the Credit Bureau include your version of what the report presents. The Credit Bureau, at your request will send your version to anyone who received a copy of the old report. You must write your version of what happened in 25 words or less and ask the Bureau to send it to anyone who received the old report.

Bad Credit Reports—How Long Will It Hurt You?

Bad credit information cannot be reported after *seven* years as a general rule. However, a bankruptcy can be reported for *10* years.

[The material in this feature was prepared as a public service and is intended for general information purposes only. The frequent changes in state law could affect this material, and such law also varies from state to state.]

The material in this feature is reprinted by permission from The Florida Bar Information and Bar Services Department as a public service of The Florida Bar.

CHAPTER SUMMARY

Federal Trade Commission	**Purpose** to prevent unfair methods of competition and unfair or deceptive acts or practices **Standards** ■ *Unfairness* requires injury to be (1) substantial, (2) not outweighed by any countervailing benefit, and (3) unavoidable by reasonable consumer action ■ *Deception* misrepresentation, omission, or practice that is likely to mislead the consumer acting reasonably in the circumstances ■ *Ad Substantiation* requires advertisers to have a reasonable basis for their claims **Remedies** ■ *Cease and Desist Order* command to stop doing the act in question ■ *Affirmative Disclosure* requires an advertiser to include certain information in its ad so that the ad is not deceptive ■ *Corrective Advertising* requires an advertiser to disclose that previous ads were deceptive ■ *Multiple Product Order* requires an advertiser to cease and desist from deceptive statements regarding all products it sells

Consumer Health and Safety	**Consumer Product Safety Act** federal statute enacted to ■ *Protect Public Against Unsafe Products* ■ *Assist Consumers in Evaluating Products* ■ *Develop Uniform Safety Standards* ■ *Promote Safety Research* **Other Federal Consumer Protection Agencies**

Consumer Purchases	**Federal Warranty Protection** applies to sellers of consumer goods who give written warranties ■ *Presale Disclosure* requires terms of warranty to be simple and readily understood and to be made available before the sale ■ *Labeling Requirement* requires warrantor to inform consumers of their legal rights under a warranty (full or limited) ■ *Disclaimer Limitation* prohibits a written warranty from disclaiming any implied warranty **State "Lemon Laws"** state laws that attempt to provide new car purchasers with rights similar to full warranties under Magnuson-Moss **Consumer Right of Rescission** in certain instances a consumer is granted a brief period of time during which she may rescind (cancel) an otherwise binding obligation

Consumer Credit Transactions	**Definition** any credit transaction involving goods, services, or land for personal, household, or family purposes
	Access to the Market discrimination in extending credit on the basis of gender, marital status, race, color, religion, national origin, or age is prohibited
	Truth-in-Lending Act requires creditor to provide certain information about contract terms, including APR (annual percentage rate), to the consumer before he formally incurs the obligation
	Contract Terms statutory and judicial limitations have been imposed on consumer obligations
	Credit Card Fraud Act prohibits certain fraudulent practices and limits a card holder's liability for unauthorized use of a credit card to $50
	Fair Credit Reporting consumer credit reports are prohibited from containing inaccurate or obsolete information
	Creditors' Remedies
	■ *Wage Assignments and Garnishment* most states limit the amount that may be deducted from an individual's wages through either assignment or garnishment
	■ *Security Interest* seller may retain a security interest in goods sold or other collateral of the buyer, although some restrictions are imposed
	■ *Debt Collection Practices* abusive, deceptive, and unfair practices by debt collectors in collecting consumer debts are prohibited by the Fair Debt Collection Practices Act

QUESTIONS

1. Discuss the role of the FTC and the major enforcement sanctions that it may use.
2. Discuss the role and workings of the CPSC.
3. Discuss the principal provisions of the Magnuson-Moss Act and distinguish between a full and a limited warranty.
4. Discuss what information a creditor must provide a consumer before the consumer incurs the obligation. Distinguish between open-ended and closed-ended credit.

5. Outline the major remedies that are available to a creditor.

Internet Question. Learn about the consumer protection activities of (a) the Federal Trade Commission, (b) the Consumer Product Safety Commission, (c) the National Highway Safety Administration, (d) the Food and Drug Administration, and (e) the Federal Reserve.

PROBLEMS

1. The FTC brings a deceptive trade practice action against Beneficial Finance Company based on Beneficial's use of its "instant tax refund" slogan. The FTC argues that Beneficial's advertising a tax refund loan or instant tax refund is deceptive in that the loan is not in any way connected with a tax refund but is merely Beneficial's everyday loan based on the applicant's creditworthiness. Decision?
2. Brenda borrows $1,000 from Lincoln for one year, agreeing to pay Lincoln $200 in interest on the loan

and to repay the loan in twelve monthly installments of $100. The contract that Lincoln provides and Brenda signs specifies that the APR is 20 percent. Brenda now contends that the contract violates the FCCPA. Decision?
3. A consumer entered into an agreement with Rent-It Corporation for the rental of a television set at a charge of $17 per week. The agreement also provides that if the renter chooses to rent the set for seventy-eight consecutive weeks, title will be transferred. The

consumer now contends that the agreement is really a sales agreement, not a lease, and therefore is a credit sale subject to the Truth-in-Lending Act. Decision?

4. Central Adjustment Bureau allegedly threatened Consumer with a lawsuit, service at his office, and attachment and sale of his property in order to collect a debt, although it did not intend to carry out the threat and did not have the authority to commence litigation. On some notices sent to Consumer, Central failed to disclose that it was attempting to collect a debt. In addition, Consumer contends that Central sent notices demanding payment that were purportedly from attorneys but were written, signed, and sent by Central. Decision?

5. The Giant Development Company undertakes a massive real estate venture to sell 9,000 one-acre unimproved lots in Utah. The company advertises the project nationally. Arrington, a resident of New York, learns of the opportunity and requests information about the project. The company provides Arrington with a small advertising brochure that contains no information about the developer and the land. The brochure consists of vague descriptions of the joys of home ownership and nothing else. Arrington purchases a lot. Two weeks after entering into the agreement, Arrington wishes to rescind the contract. Will Arrington prevail?

6. Jane Jones, a married woman, applies for a credit card from Exxon but is refused credit. Jane is bewildered as to why she was turned down. What are her legal rights in this situation?

7. On a beautiful Saturday in October, Francie decides to take the twenty-mile ride from her home in New Jersey into New York City in order to do some shopping. Francie finds that Brown's Retail Sales, Inc. has a terrific sale on television sets and decides to surprise her husband with a new color TV. She purchases the set from Brown's on her American Express credit card for $450. When the set is delivered, Francie discovers that it does not work. Brown's refuses to repair or replace it or to credit Francie's charge account. Francie therefore refuses to pay American Express for the television. American Express brings a suit against Francie. Decision?

8. Frank finds Thomas's wallet, which contains many credit cards and Thomas's identification. By using Thomas's identification and Visa card, Frank goes on a shopping spree and runs up $5,000 in charges. Thomas does not discover that he has lost his wallet until the following day, when he promptly notifies his Visa bank. How much can Visa collect from Thomas?

9. Robert applies to Northern National Bank for a loan. Before granting the loan, Northern requests that Callis Credit Agency provide it with a credit report on Robert. Callis reports that three years previously, Robert had embezzled money from his employer. Based on this report, Northern rejects Robert's loan application.

(a) Robert demands to know why the loan was rejected, but Northern refuses to divulge the information, arguing that it is privileged. Is Robert entitled to the information?

(b) Assume that Robert obtains the information and alleges that it is inaccurate. What recourse does Robert have?

10. Colgate-Palmolive Co. produced a television advertisement that dramatically demonstrated the effectiveness of its Rapid Shave shaving cream. The ad purported to show the shaving cream being used to shave sandpaper. But because actual sandpaper appeared on television to be regular colored paper, Colgate substituted a sheet of Plexiglas with sand sprinkled on it. The FTC brought an action against Colgate, claiming that Colgate's ad was deceptive. Colgate defended on the ground that the consumer was merely being shown a representation of the actual test. Decision?

11. In 1982, several manufacturers introduced into the American market a product known as all-terrain vehicles (ATVs). ATVs are motorized bikes that sit on three or four low-pressure balloon tires and are meant to be driven off paved roads. Almost immediately, the Consumer Product Safety Commission began receiving reports of deaths and serious injuries. As the number of injuries and deaths increased, the CPSC began investigating ATV hazards. According to CPSC staff, children under the age of sixteen accounted for roughly half the deaths and injuries associated with this product. What type of rule, if any, may the CPSC issue for ATVs?

12. In the early 1970s, Sears formulated a plan to increase sales of its top-of-the-line Lady Kenmore brand dishwasher. Sear's plan sought to change the Lady Kenmore's image without reengineering or making any mechanical improvements in the dishwasher itself. To accomplish this, Sears undertook a four-year, $8 million advertising campaign that claimed that the Lady Kenmore completely eliminated the need to prerinse and prescrape dishes. As a result of this campaign, sales rose by more than 300 percent. The "no scraping, no pre-rinsing" claim was not true, however; and Sears had no reasonable basis for asserting the claim. In addition, the owner's manual that customers received after they purchased the dishwasher contradicted the claim.

After a thorough investigation, the Federal Trade Commission, in 1977, filed a complaint against Sears, alleging that the advertisements were false and misleading. The final FTC order required Sears to stop making the no scraping, no pre-rinsing claim. The order also prevented Sears from (1) making any "performance claims" for "major home appliances" without first possessing a reasonable basis consisting of substantiating tests or other evidence; (2) misrepresenting any test, survey, or demonstration regarding "major home appliances"; and (3) making any advertising statements not consistent with statements in postpurchase materials supplied to purchasers of "major home appliances." Sears contends the order is too broad, since it covers appliances other than dishwashers, and includes "performance claims" as well. Decision?

13. Onondaga Bureau of Medical Economics (OBME), a collection agency for physicians, sent the plaintiff, Seabrook, a letter demanding payment for a $198.00 physicians' bill. In addition to demanding payment, the letter stated that the bureau's client could commence against Seabrook a legal action that could result in a garnishment of his wages. Seabrook sued OBME, alleging that the letter violated the Fair Debt Collection Practices Act in that it did not give him required notice and threatened legal action against him. Decision?

14. William Thompson was denied credit based on an inaccurate credit report compiled by the San Antonio Retail Merchant's Association. The Association confused Thompson's credit history with that of another William Thompson and failed to use social security numbers to distinguish the two men. The second Mr. Thompson had a poor credit history. Thompson made numerous attempts to have the Association correct its mistake, but the error was never corrected. Thompson sued the Association for violation of the Fair Credit Reporting Act. Decision?

15. Thompson Medical Company manufactures and sells Aspercreme, a topical analgesic. Aspercreme is a pain reliever that contains no aspirin. Thompson's advertisements strongly suggest that Aspercreme is related to aspirin, however, by claiming that it provides "the strong relief of aspirin right where you hurt." The Federal Trade Commission brought a complaint against Thompson for false and misleading advertising of Aspercreme. Decision?

16. Mary Smith bought a car from Doug Chapman under an installment sales contract. Smith carried the insurance on the car, as required by the contract. Shortly after Smith purchased the car, it was wrecked in an accident. Smith's insurance company paid Chapman the installments still owed on the car, as well as Smith's equity in the car. Smith requested a new car from Chapman under an installment plan the same as the one under which she had purchased the first car. Chapman refused, claiming that the contract for the first car allowed him to retain the equity amount as security interest and that Smith understood this as a term of the contract. The provision relating to the security interest appeared on the back of the contract, although the Truth-in-Lending Act required it to be on the front side. The front side had a notice referring to provisions on the back side. Smith sued Chapman for violation of the Truth-in-Lending Act. Decision?

CHAPTER 47

Environmental Law

As technology has advanced and people have become more urbanized, their effect on the environment has increased. Our air has become dirtier; our waters have become more polluted. While individuals and environmental groups have brought private actions against some polluters, the common law has proved unable to control environmental damage. Because of this inadequacy, the federal and state governments have enacted a variety of statutes designed to promote environmental concerns and prevent environmental harm. Although in recent years certain developed countries, such as the United States, have made significant progress in controlling pollutants, such is not the case worldwide. Moreover, even as we have enjoyed some success in controlling some pollutants, a new generation of environmental problems has arisen. In this chapter, we will discuss both common law causes of action for environmental damage and federal regulation of the environment.

COMMON LAW ACTIONS FOR ENVIRONMENTAL DAMAGE

Private tort actions may be used to recover for harm to the environment. For example, if Alice's land is polluted by the mill next door, Alice may sue the mill in tort for the damage to her land. In suing to recover for environmental damage, plaintiffs generally have relied on the theories of nuisance, trespass, and strict liability.

NUISANCE

The term "nuisance" encompasses two distinct types of wrong: private nuisance and public nuisance. A private nuisance involves an interference with a person's use and enjoyment of his or her land, while a public nuisance is an act that interferes with a public right.

Private Nuisance

To establish a **private nuisance**, a plaintiff must show that the defendant has substantially and unreasonably interfered with the use and enjoyment of the plaintiff's land. In an action for damages, the plaintiff need not prove that the defendant's conduct was unreasonable, only that the interference was unreasonable. Thus, assuming all other requirements are met, the question in a private nuisance suit for damages is whether the defendant should pay for the harm it caused the plaintiff, even if the defendant's action was not unreasonable. For example, in one case, an electric utility using a coal-burning electric generator that employed the latest scientific methods for reducing emissions was held liable

Private nuisance
substantial and unreasonable interference with use and enjoyment of a person's land

for the harm it caused its neighbor's alfalfa crops, even though the utility was performing the socially useful function of creating electric power.

While a plaintiff need not prove the defendant's conduct is unreasonable to recover in a private nuisance action for damages, such reasonableness is an issue when the plaintiff sues for an injunction. In determining whether an injunction against a nuisance is appropriate, a court will "balance the equities" by considering a number of factors, including the gravity of the harm to the plaintiff, the social value of the defendant's activity that is causing the harm, the feasibility and costs of avoiding the harm, and the public interest, if any.

The need to balance the equities has meant that courts often deny injunctions when the defendant is engaged in a socially useful activity. Additionally, injunctions are frequently denied because the defendant successfully raises an equitable defense. Consequently, private nuisance actions have been of limited value in controlling environmental damage.

Public Nuisance

Public nuisance
interference with health, safety, or comfort of the public

To be treated as a **public nuisance**, an activity must somehow interfere with the health, safety, or comfort of the public. For example, the actions of an industrial plant in polluting a stream will be treated as a private nuisance if such actions inconvenience only the owners of land downstream but will be treated as a public nuisance if they kill the stream's marine life. Generally, only a public representative, such as the attorney general, may sue to stop a public nuisance. If, however, the nuisance inflicts upon an individual some unique harm that the general populace does not suffer, that individual may also sue to halt the nuisance. Out of concern about the economic impact of closing an industrial operation, public representatives frequently are unwilling to sue to abate a public nuisance. Consequently, because these representatives often will not, and private parties may not, sue, relatively few public nuisance actions have been brought against polluters.

TRESPASS TO LAND

Trespass to land
interference with the right of exclusive possession of the property

To establish **trespass to land**, a plaintiff must show an invasion that interferes with the plaintiff's right of exclusive possession of the property and that is the direct result of an action by the defendant. For example, entering or throwing trash on someone else's land without permission constitutes a trespass. Trespass differs from private nuisance in that trespass requires an interference with the plaintiff's possession of the land. Thus, sending smoke or gas onto another's property may constitute a private nuisance but does not constitute a trespass.

Trespass often is difficult to establish in actions for environmental damage, either because the plaintiff is not in possession of the property or because the injury does not stem from an invasion of the property. Trespass actions have thus been of limited benefit in halting environmental damage. For a more complete discussion of trespass, see Chapter 8.

STRICT LIABILITY FOR ABNORMALLY DANGEROUS ACTIVITIES

Strict liability liability without fault

While they generally base tort liability on fault, the courts may hold **strictly liable**, that is, liable without fault, a person engaged in an abnormally dangerous activity. To establish such strict liability, a plaintiff must show that the defendant is carrying on an unduly dangerous activity in an inappropriate location and that the plaintiff has suffered damage because of this activity. For example, a person who operates an oil refinery in a densely populated area may be held strictly liable for any damage the refinery causes. The requirement that the activity engaged in be (1) ultrahazardous and (2) inappropriate for its locale has limited the number of strict liability actions brought against polluters.

PROBLEMS COMMON TO PRIVATE CAUSES OF ACTION

In addition to the shortcomings of each tort theory discussed above, using a private cause of action to control environmental damage presents its own problems. The costs associated with private litigation (including the payment of one's own legal fees) are high, and while overall the environmental damage may be considerable, the extent of any particular injury may not warrant pursuing a private lawsuit. Furthermore, tort actions generally do not provide relief for aesthetic, as opposed to physical, injury. Additionally, in many tort actions a significant issue of causation arises. For example, if a landowner lives near several plants, each of which emits pollution and none of which, by itself, would cause the amount of damage the landowner's property has suffered, the landowner may have difficulty recovering from any of the plant owners. Finally, even if a private plaintiff is successful, his recovery may be limited to monetary damages, leaving the defendant free to continue to pollute.

FEDERAL REGULATION OF THE ENVIRONMENT

Because private causes of action have proved inadequate to recompense and prevent environmental damage, the federal, state, and some local governments have enacted statutes designed to protect the environment. In this chapter, we will consider some of the more important federal environmental laws. In addition, the Environmental Protection Agency (EPA) has encouraged companies to conduct voluntary environmental audits. One of the key issues surrounding such self-audits is whether these audits are discoverable by state or federal prosecutors.

THE NATIONAL ENVIRONMENTAL POLICY ACT

In 1969, Congress enacted the **National Environmental Policy Act (NEPA)** to establish environmental protection as a goal of federal policy. The NEPA's declaration of national environmental policy states:

> The Congress, recognizing the profound impact of man's activity on the interrelations of all components of the natural environment, particularly the profound influences of population growth, high-density urbanization, industrial expansion, resource exploitation, and new and expanding technological advances, and recognizing further the critical importance of restoring and maintaining environmental quality to the overall welfare and development of man, declares that it is the continuing policy of the Federal Government, in cooperation with State and local governments . . . to use all practicable means and measures . . . in a manner calculated to foster and promote the general welfare, to create and maintain conditions under which man and nature can exist in productive harmony, and fulfill the social, economic and other requirements of present and future generations of Americans.

National Environmental Policy Act (NEPA) establishes environmental protection as a goal of federal policy

The NEPA has two major substantive sections, one creating the Council on Environmental Quality (CEQ) and the other requiring that each federal agency, when recommending or reporting on proposals for legislation or other major federal action, prepare an **environmental impact statement (EIS)** if the legislation or federal action will have a significant environmental effect.

The Council on Environmental Quality

The **Council on Environmental Quality (CEQ)**, a three-member advisory group, is not a separate administrative agency but rather is part of the Executive Office of the President; as such, it makes recommendations to the president on environmental matters and prepares annual reports on the condition of the environment. Although not expressly authorized to do so by statute, the CEQ, acting under a series of executive orders, has issued regulations regarding the content and preparation of environmental impact statements. The federal courts generally have deferred to these regulations.

Environmental Impact Statements

Unlike most federal environmental statutes, the NEPA does not focus on a particular type of environmental damage or harmful substance but instead expresses the federal government's continuing concern with protection of the environment. The NEPA's promotion of environmental considerations is effected through the EIS requirement.

Procedure for Preparing an EIS When proposing legislation or considering a major federal action, the CEQ regulations require that a federal agency initially make an "environmental assessment," which is a short analysis of the need for an EIS. If the agency decides that no EIS is required, it must make this decision available to the public. If, on the other hand, the agency concludes that an EIS is required, the agency must engage in "scoping," which consists of consulting other relevant federal agencies and the public to determine the significant issues the EIS will address and the statement's appropriate scope. After scoping, the agency prepares a draft EIS, for which there is a comment period. After the comment period ends and revisions, if necessary, are made, a final EIS is published.

Scope of EIS Requirement The EIS requirement of the NEPA applies to a broad range of projects:

> [T]here is "Federal action" within the meaning of the statute not only when an agency proposes to build a facility itself, but also whenever an agency makes a decision which permits action by other parties which will affect the quality of the environment. NEPA's impact statement procedure has been held to apply where a federal agency approves a lease of land to private parties, grants licenses and permits to private parties, or approves and funds state highway projects. In each of these instances the federal agency took action affecting the environment in the sense that the agency made a decision which permitted some other party—private or governmental—to take action affecting the environment.

The NEPA's EIS requirement applies not only to a broad range of projects but also to a broad range of environmental effects. The NEPA has been held to apply not only to the natural environment but also to the urban environment.

The Act [NEPA] must be construed to include protection of the quality of life for city residents. Noise, traffic, overburdened mass transportation systems, crime, congestion and even availability of drugs all affect the urban "environment" and are surely results of the "profound influences of . . . high-density urbanization [and] industrial expansion."

While effects on health, including psychological health, are considered environmental effects under the NEPA, the Supreme Court has held that an effect is environmental only if it has a reasonably close causal relation to an impact on the physical environment. Accordingly, the Nuclear Regulatory Commission was not required to prepare an EIS before permitting one of the Three Mile Island reactors to resume operation, even though such resumption would cause residents of nearby areas to suffer psychological stress.

Content of an EIS The NEPA requires that an EIS describe in detail the environmental impact of a proposed action, any adverse environmental effects that could not be avoided if the proposal were implemented, alternatives to the proposed action, the relationship between local short-term uses of the environment and the maintenance and enhancement of long-term productivity, and any irreversible and irretrievable commitments of resources the proposed action would involve if it were implemented. Impact statements provide a basis for evaluating the benefits of a proposed project in light of its environmental risks and for comparing its environmental risks with those of alternatives.

Content the EIS must contain, among other items, a detailed statement of the environmental impact of the proposed action, any adverse environmental effects that cannot be avoided, and alternative proposals

The Supreme Court has held that a federal agency is required to consider only all *reasonable* alternatives in its EIS. Thus, when reviewing the licensing of a nuclear power plant, the Court held that the Atomic Energy Commission (the predecessor to the Nuclear Regulatory Commission) was not required to consider energy conservation as an alternative, because at the time the license was granted energy conservation was not a widely discussed issue and the plaintiffs, during the administrative procedure leading to the granting of the license, had not adequately raised the issue of energy conservation. When analyzing alternatives, a federal agency is required to consider only the reasonable impacts of such alternatives.

Nature of EIS Requirement Whether the NEPA was solely procedural or whether it had a substantive component was initially unclear. The Supreme Court resolved the issue by holding that the NEPA's requirements are primarily procedural and that the NEPA does not require that the relevant federal agency attempt to mitigate the adverse effects of a proposed federal action.

ROBERTSON v. METHOW VALLEY CITIZENS COUNCIL Supreme Court of the United States, 1989, 109 S.Ct. 1835

FACTS When considering an application for a special use permit to develop and operate a ski resort at Sandy Butte, a mountain in Washington that is part of a national forest, the Forest Service prepared an EIS. The EIS recommended the issuance of a special use permit for what was to be a sixteen-lift ski area, and the regional forester issued the permit as recommended. Four organizations sued, claiming that the EIS was inadequate. The lower court held that the EIS was ade-

quate, but the Court of Appeals reversed, concluding that the NEPA required that actions be taken to mitigate the adverse effects of a major federal action and that the EIS contain a detailed mitigation plan.

DECISION Decision of the Court of Appeals reversed and remanded.

OPINION The NEPA ensures governmental commitment to protecting environmental quality by establishing

continued

important "action-forcing" procedures. Pursuant to these procedures, a federal agency must prepare an EIS that forces the agency to take a "hard look" at the environmental consequences of proposed actions. It is implicit that through such procedures the NEPA requires that EIS discuss which adverse effects are avoidable. The NEPA, however, only mandates certain procedures, not particular results. An agency that adequately identifies and evaluates the adverse environmental effects of a proposed action in its EIS is not constrained by the NEPA from deciding that other values outweigh the environmental costs. Thus, the NEPA requires neither that action be taken to mitigate the adverse effects of federal actions nor that an EIS include specific measures to mitigate the adverse impacts of the proposed action. The NEPA only prohibits uninformed—rather than unwise—agency action and is procedural, not substantive, in nature.

INTERPRETATION The NEPA requires careful evaluation of a proposed federal action, but does not require that any actions be taken to reduce harmful impact.

THE CLEAN AIR ACT

Clean Air Act created to control and reduce air pollution

Initially, the federal government's role in controlling air pollution was quite limited. The states had primary responsibility for air pollution control, and the federal government merely supervised their efforts and offered technical and financial assistance. When state efforts proved inadequate to alleviate the problem, Congress enacted the **Clean Air Act** Amendments of 1970, greatly expanding the federal role in antipollution efforts. Major revisions to the Clean Air Act were enacted in 1977 and 1990. The act establishes two regulatory schemes, one for existing sources and one for new stationary sources. The states retain primary responsibility for regulating existing stationary sources and motor vehicles then in use (that is, in use when the act, or its subsequently enacted amendments, took effect), while the federal government regulates new sources, new vehicles, and hazardous air pollutants.

Under the act, the Environmental Protection Agency (EPA) may impose civil penalties of up to $25,000 per day of violation. Criminal penalties, which depend on the type of violation, vary greatly providing for a maximum fine of $1 million per violation and/or fifteen years' imprisonment for a knowing violation that endangers a person. For repeat convictions, the act doubles the maximum punishments.

Existing Stationary Sources and Motor Vehicles Then in Use

Because the states had not managed adequately to control air pollution, the 1970 amendments provided that, with respect to existing stationary sources and motor vehicles then in use, the federal government would set national air quality standards that the states would be primarily responsible for achieving.

National ambient air quality standards (NAAQS) allowable limits for air pollutants that endanger the public health and welfare

National Ambient Air Quality Standards Under the act, the EPA administrator is required to establish **national ambient air quality standards (NAAQS)** for air pollutants that endanger the public health and welfare. The EPA administrator must establish "primary" standards to protect the public health, allowing for an adequate safety margin, and "secondary" standards to protect elements relating to the public welfare, such as animals, crops, and structures. The NAAQS for a particular pollutant specifies the concentration of that pollutant that will be allowed in the outside air over designated periods of time.

The EPA administrator established quality standards for seven major classes of pollutants—carbon monoxide, particulates, sulfur dioxide, nitrogen dioxide, hydrocarbons, ozone, and lead, although the hydrocarbon NAAQS was subsequently withdrawn as no longer being necessary. Recognizing that many areas would not meet the 1977 NAAQS deadline, Congress, in the 1977 amendments to the act, extended the deadline to December 1982 and further provided that states demonstrating the impossibility of meeting the 1982 deadline "despite the implementation of all reasonably available measures" could obtain an extension until December 1987. In 1987, Congress extended the deadline for another eight months. The August 1988 deadline expired without extension, but the EPA has not vigorously enforced it.

The 1990 amendments sought to hasten attainment of the standards and provided that the EPA must establish new standards for major pollutants every five years. The amendments also imposed tighter standards with regard to ozone pollution, due to the lack of progress in this area.

State Implementation Plans Once the EPA promulgates a new NAAQS, each state must submit to the agency a **state implementation plan (SIP)** detailing how the state will implement and maintain the NAAQS within the state. If the state adopted the SIP after public hearings and the SIP meets certain statutory conditions, the EPA is required to approve it. Foremost among the statutory conditions is the requirement that under the SIP the state will attain primary standards as soon as practicable but in any case within three years after the EPA approves the SIP. If the EPA determines that under an SIP a state will not attain an NAAQS within the designated time and the state fails to make the necessary amendments, the EPA is authorized to make amendments that will be binding on the state.

State implementation plan (SIP) plan detailing with how a state will implement and maintain an NAAQS within its borders

Under the 1990 amendments, the EPA also must decide whether an SIP is complete. If it is not, the EPA may treat the plan as a nullity in whole or in part. If it is complete, the EPA must approve or disapprove the plan within a year. Once the EPA approves a SIP, the plan is regarded as both state and federal law, enforceable by either its state of implementation or the federal government.

Prevention of Significant Deterioration Areas Prior to the 1977 amendments, an issue arose as to whether air that was cleaner than required by an applicable NAAQS would be allowed to deteriorate to the NAAQS level. This issue was significant because much of the United States, particularly land in the Southwest, had air whose quality was higher than that required by applicable standards. Responding to this issue, Congress, in the 1977 amendments, established a policy to prevent the quality of such air from deteriorating. To effectuate this policy, Congress established rules for areas whose air quality was higher than the applicable NAAQS required it to be or for which information was insufficient to determine the air quality (so-called **prevention of significant deterioration (PSD) areas**). Because the rules classified an area on a pollutant-by-pollutant basis, a particular area might be a PSD area with respect to one pollutant and an area that had not met the applicable NAAQS with respect to another pollutant.

Prevention of significant deterioration areas rules for areas where air quality is higher than required

In PSD areas, only limited increases in air pollution are allowed. Before a major stationary source in a PSD area may be constructed or modified, the owner or operator of the source must receive a permit from the applicable state regulator.

In order to receive a permit, the owner/operator must demonstrate that the source will not increase pollution beyond permitted levels and must show that the source will utilize the best control technology available.

Nonattainment Areas The 1977 and 1990 amendments also established special rules for areas that did not meet applicable NAAQSs, so-called **nonattainment areas**. Before a major stationary source may be constructed or modified in a nonattainment area, the owner/operator of the source must receive a permit from the applicable state regulator. In order to receive a permit, the owner/operator must show that the source will comply with the lowest achievable emission rate, which is the more stringent of either the most stringent emission limitation contained in any SIP or the most stringent emission limitation actually achieved. Additionally, total emissions from existing stationary sources and the proposed new or modified source together must be less than the total emissions allowed from existing sources at the time the permit is sought. Thus, to obtain a permit in a nonattainment area, an owner/operator must in some way reduce total emissions from all sources (existing and new/modified). Under the 1990 amendments, the reduction required varies with the severity of the area's nonattainment problem. One way to reduce total emissions from all sources is to pay the owner/operator of another source to reduce its emissions by either installing more advanced emission control technology or closing its source. Alternatively, an owner/operator may reduce its own total emissions by altering the mix of emission controls at its plant. Under the EPA's "**bubble concept**," an entire plant is viewed as one source; consequently, the permit process applies only if total emissions from the plant increase. If, instead, the EPA treated each unit at a plant as a separate source, the owner/operator would be required to obtain a permit whenever it made a change to one unit. The bubble concept thus enables an owner/operator to bypass the permit process in some instances. Though environmental groups challenged the concept on this basis, in 1984 the Supreme Court upheld the bubble concept, finding the regulation to be a reasonable exercise of the EPA's discretion.

Nonattainment areas areas that do not meet NAAQSs

Bubble concept views an entire plant as one source of pollution

New Source Standards
The scheme of federal NAAQSs and state SIPs applies to existing stationary sources and to motor vehicles then in use. In contrast, the Clean Air Act authorizes the federal government to establish national emission standards for new stationary sources, hazardous air pollutants, and new vehicles.

New Stationary Sources The act requires the EPA administrator to establish performance standards for stationary sources that are constructed or modified after the publication of applicable regulations. The standard of performance must "reflect the degree of emission limitation and percentage reduction achievable through application of the best technological system of continuous emission reduction which . . . has been adequately demonstrated." As the following case indicates, the standard governing new sources is more stringent than the standard governing existing sources; accordingly, it is, from industry's perspective, better to be considered an existing source than a new or modified one.

New stationary sources owner/operator must employ the best technological system of continuous emission reduction that has been adequately demonstrated

NATIONAL-SOUTHWIRE ALUMINUM CO. v. EPA United States Court of Appeals, Sixth Circuit, 1988, 838 F.2d 835

FACTS National-Southwire Aluminum Company (NSA) owns and operates a plant that emits fluoride. In 1982, when its wet scrubbers were turned off as part of its regular maintenance program, NSA discovered no appreciable change in ambient fluoride levels. Because of the expense of operating the scrubbers and its belief that using the scrubbers did not significantly affect ambient fluoride levels, NSA desired to turn the scrubbers off permanently. Accordingly, NSA sought a determination from the EPA that turning off the scrubbers would not constitute a modification requiring the application of new source performance standards to the plant. Turning off the scrubbers would result in an increase of over 1,100 tons per year of fluoride emissions with no decrease in the emission of any other pollutant. This increase was nearly 400 times the level the EPA had established as inconsequential. The EPA determined that turning off the scrubbers would constitute a "new source" modification. Accordingly, NSA was required either to leave the scrubbers on or to install new pollutant control equipment. NSA appealed.

DECISION Determination of the EPA affirmed.

OPINION The Clean Air Act defines "modification" as any physical change or change in operation of a "stationary source" that increases the emission of air pollutants. Under NSA's argument, a "modification" depends on the amount of pollutant the pollution-generating equipment creates, without regard to the amount of pollution actually emitted into the atmosphere. The trial court disagreed. It is clear from EPA regulations that "modification" includes any change in operation that increases the emission of any air pollutant. The proposal to turn off the wet scrubbers does not suggest the addition or use of any device whose primary function is the reduction of air pollutants. Rather, the proposal involves the removal or replacement of a system, and in such a case, the EPA can determine that such a change is a modification if it results in less environmentally beneficial operations. Here, it is clear that turning off the scrubbers is less environmentally beneficial, since it would increase the emission of fluorides without decreasing the emission of other pollutants.

INTERPRETATION A plant modification that will increase emissions of pollutants requires the EPA administrator to apply new source performance standards.

New Vehicles The Clean Air Act requires the EPA administrator to establish emission standards for **new** motor **vehicles** and new motor vehicle engines. The 1970 amendments mandated a 90 percent reduction, from 1970 levels, in hydrocarbons and carbon monoxide by 1975 and a 90 percent reduction, from 1971 levels, in nitrogen oxide emissions by 1976. Both Congress and the EPA administrator have extended these deadlines several times. The 1990 amendments significantly tightened emission standards by mandating that hydrocarbon and nitrogen oxide emissions be cut by 30 and 60 percent, respectively, below prior standards by 1998. In addition, the amendments mandate a further 50 percent reduction in emission standards by the year 2003, unless the EPA determines that these more stringent standards are either unnecessary or infeasible.

New vehicles extensive emission standards are established

The 1990 amendments also require the use of reformulated automotive fuels to reduce ozone and carbon monoxide pollution. The reformulated gasoline must contain more oxygen and less in terms of volatile organic compounds.

Hazardous Air Pollutants The act authorizes the EPA administrator to establish national emission standards for **hazardous** or toxic **air pollutants**, defined as "air pollutant[s] . . . caus[ing], or contribut[ing] to, air pollution which may reasonably be anticipated to result in an increase in mortality or an increase in serious irreversible, or incapacitating reversible, illness." The standard must be set at a level that "provides an ample margin of safety to protect the public health."

Hazardous air pollutants to protect the public health, the EPA administrator must establish for hazardous air pollutants standards that provide ample safety margins

The 1990 amendments list 189 hazardous chemicals that the EPA must regulate. For each chemical, the EPA is to set standards for "major" and "area" (nonmajor) sources requiring the installation of maximum achievable control technology. The final deadline for regulating all 189 chemicals is the year 2000.

Acid rain standards are
established to protect
against acid rain
(precipitation that contains
high levels of sulfuric or nitric
acid)

Acid Rain The 1990 amendments attempt to halt environmental destruction caused by **acid rain**—precipitation that contains high levels of sulfuric or nitric acid. Because sulfur dioxide (which forms sulfuric acid in the atmosphere and comes back as acid rain) is primarily released into the atmosphere by electric utilities, the 1990 amendments regulate such utilities by allotting them emission allowances with regard to the amount of sulfur dioxide they may release into the atmosphere, based upon past emissions and fuel consumption. The amendments establish an allowance schedule that will significantly reduce emissions of sulfur dioxide and nitrous oxides by the year 2000. The amendments also permit each utility to bank or sell its emission allowances.

THE CLEAN WATER ACT

Clean Water Act created
to protect against water
pollution

As with air pollution control, the primary responsibility for controlling water pollution fell initially to the states. When their efforts proved inadequate, Congress fundamentally revised the nation's water pollution laws in its 1972 amendments to the Federal Water Pollution Control Act (subsequently renamed the **Clean Water Act**). Substantially amended again in 1977, 1981, and 1987, the act attempts comprehensively to restore and maintain the chemical, physical, and biological integrity of the nation's waters.

The EPA may impose civil penalties of up to $25,000 per day for each violation. Maximum criminal penalties for knowing violations are $50,000 per day of violation and/or three years' imprisonment. For repeat convictions, the maximum punishments are doubled.

Like the Clean Air Act, the Clean Water Act establishes different schemes for existing sources and new sources. Additionally, the act provides different programs for point and nonpoint sources of pollution. A **point source** is "any discernible, confined and discrete conveyance . . . from which pollutants are or may be discharged." A **nonpoint source**, in contrast, is a land use that causes pollution, such as a pesticide runoff from farming operations.

Point source any
discernible, confined, and
discrete conveyance from
which pollutants are or may
be discharged

Nonpoint source land use
that causes pollution

The scope of the act is extremely broad, applying not only to all navigable waters in the United States but also to tributaries of navigable waters, interstate waters and their tributaries, the use of nonnavigable intrastate waters (if their misuse could affect interstate commerce), and freshwater wetlands.

Point Sources

The act mandates that the EPA administrator establish effluent limitations for categories of existing point sources. An **effluent limitation** is a technology-based standard that limits the amount of a pollutant that a point source may discharge into a body of water. The act effectuates such limitations through the *National Pollutant Discharge Elimination System (NPDES)*, a permit system.

Effluent limitation
technology-based standard
that limits the amount of
pollutant that a point source
may discharge

Effluent Limitations Under the 1972 amendments, effluent limitations for existing point sources, other than publicly owned treatment works, required application of the best practicable control technology currently available (**BPT**) by 1977 and application of the best available technology economically achievable (**BAT**) by 1983. According to the EPA, BPT is "the average of the best existing performance by well-operated plants within each industrial category or subcategory," while BAT is "the very best control and treatment measures that have been or are capable of being achieved." Somewhat different standards apply to publicly owned treatment works.

BPT best practicable
control technology currently
available

BAT best available
technology economically
achievable

The National Pollutant Discharge Elimination System The National Pollutant Discharge Elimination System (NPDES), the permit system through which effluent limitations are to be achieved, requires that any person responsible for the discharge from a point source of a pollutant into U.S. waters must obtain a discharge permit from the EPA, the Army Corps of Engineers, or, in some circumstances, the relevant state. An NPDES permit incorporates the applicable effluent limitations and establishes a schedule for compliance. The holder of an NPDES permit is required to notify the appropriate authority if the holder will not meet its obligations under the permit. A discharge not in compliance with a permit is unlawful. With limited exceptions, new permits for existing facilities cannot be less stringent than current permits.

ARKANSAS v. OKLAHOMA Supreme Court of the United States, 1992, 112 S.Ct. 1046

FACTS The Clean Water Act provides for two water quality measures: effluent limitations, which are promulgated by the Environmental Protection Agency (EPA), and water quality standards, which are promulgated by the states. In order to discharge effluents into a navigable body of water, a point source must obtain a National Pollutant Discharge Elimination System (NPDES) permit from a relevant state or the EPA. The city of Fayetteville, Arkansas, received an EPA-issued NPDES permit for the discharge of sewage into a stream that ultimately reaches the Illinois River, twenty-two miles upstream from the Oklahoma border. The EPA permit limited the effluent discharge to comply with Oklahoma water quality standards, but the EPA stated that those standards would be violated only if the discharge would cause an actual, detectable violation of Oklahoma standards. Oklahoma appealed the permit, arguing that the permit violated Oklahoma water quality standards, which allow no degradation of water quality. The Court of Appeals denied the permit, holding that the act does not allow a permit where a proposed source would discharge effluent that would contribute to conditions currently constituting a violation of water quality

standards and that the Illinois River was already degraded.

DECISION Decision of the Court of Appeals reversed.

OPINION Affected states cannot block an EPA-issued permit, but instead must seek to have the EPA administrator disapprove the permit on the grounds that the discharge will have an undue impact on the interstate waterway. In issuing the permit at issue, the EPA required that the discharge not violate Oklahoma's water quality standards. This is a reasonable exercise of the EPA's broad discretionary power under the Clean Water Act to establish conditions for issuing NPDES permits. Thus, the Court of Appeals incorrectly held that the Clean Water Act provides that no discharge of an effluent can enter a waterway already in violation of existing water quality standards. Instead, the act vests in the EPA and the states broad authority to develop long-range, area-wide programs to alleviate and eliminate existing pollution.

INTERPRETATION The EPA has broad discretionary power in administering the Clean Water Act.

The 1977 Amendments Recognizing that the application deadlines it had set in the 1972 amendments would not be met, Congress extended and modified the deadlines in 1977. The 1977 amendments to the Clean Water Act divided pollutants into three categories—toxic, conventional, and nonconventional (any pollutants that are neither toxic nor conventional)—and established different deadlines and standards for each category. For toxic pollutants, the 1983 BAT deadline was extended to 1984; for nonconventional pollutants, this standard was to be achieved by 1984 or within three years after the effluent limitation was established, whichever was later. For conventional pollutants, a new standard, best conventional pollution control technology (**BCT**), was to be achieved by 1984. These deadlines were subsequently extended to 1989.

BCT best conventional pollution control technology

Nonpoint Source Pollution

Controlling nonpoint source pollution—such as agricultural and urban runoff—is inherently more difficult than controlling point source pollution.

> There is no effective way as yet, other than land use control, by which you can intercept that runoff and control it in a way that you do a point source. We have not yet developed technology to deal with that kind of a problem. We need to find ways to deal with it, because a great quantity of pollutants [are] discharged by runoff, not only from agriculture but from construction sites, from streets, from parking lots, and so on, and we have to be concerned with developing controls for them.

Although Congress tried to address the problem of nonpoint source pollution in the 1972 amendments, little effective control of nonsource pollution occurred before 1987. The 1987 amendments require states to identify state waters that will not meet the act's requirements without the management of nonpoint sources of pollution and to institute "best management practices" to control such sources. The EPA must approve each state's management plan.

New Source Performance Standards

The act requires the EPA administrator to establish federal performance standards for new sources. A performance standard should "reflect the greatest degree of effluent reduction . . . achievable through application of the best available demonstrated control technology." The preferred standard for new sources is one "permitting no discharge of pollutants." Violation of a standard by an owner/operator of a new source is unlawful.

HAZARDOUS SUBSTANCES

Technological advances have enabled human beings to produce numerous artificial substances, some of which have proven extremely hazardous to health. As the potential and actual harm from these latter substances became clear, Congress responded by enacting various substances-related statutes. In this section, we will consider some of the most important federal statutes governing hazardous substances: the Federal Insecticide, Fungicide and Rodenticide Act (FIFRA); the Toxic Substances Control Act (TSCA); the Resource Conservation and Recovery Act (RCRA); the Comprehensive Environmental Response, Compensation and Liability Act (CERCLA, or the Superfund); and the Superfund Amendments and Reauthorization Act of 1986 (SARA).

The Federal Insecticide, Fungicide and Rodenticide Act

FIFRA the Federal Insecticide, Fungicide and Rodenticide Act regulates the sale and distribution of pesticides

The federal government began regulating pesticides in 1910 and greatly expanded its control over such substances in 1947 with the passage of the Federal Insecticide, Fungicide and Rodenticide Act. Concern about pesticides increased dramatically after the publication in 1962 of *Silent Spring*, by Rachel Carson, and Congress has amended the FIFRA several times in the last thirty years.

The FIFRA requires that a pesticide be registered with the EPA before any person in any state may distribute it. Such registration is legal only if the pesticide's composition warrants the claims its manufacturer proposes for it, the pesticide will perform its intended function without "unreasonable adverse effects on the environment," the pesticide generally will not cause unreasonably adverse environmental effects when used in accordance with widespread and commonly recognized practice, and the pesticide complies with FIFRA labeling requirements.

ETHICAL DILEMMA Distant Concerns

FACTS In February 1990, an American chemical manufacturer gave the Environmental Protection Agency test results suggesting that one of the company's chemicals causes tumors and reproductive problems in laboratory mice. The chemical, known at R-11 (scientific name—2,3,4,5-Bis (2 butylene) tetrahydro-2 furaldehyde), repelled biting flies and was sold by its manufacturer to other companies that made and marketed insecticides for human use. Such insecticides included familiar national brands sold in drugstores and other retail outlets to families, anglers, boaters, hikers, and campers.

The U.S. makers of name-brand insecticides immediately stopped adding R-11 to their products, and they notified retailers to take products containing it off their shelves. (The maker of R-11 had already stopped shipping it to the insecticide manufacturers.) In early April 1990, the Canadian government banned the use of R-11 in Canada. In late April, the EPA issued a public warning to U.S. consumers not to use products containing the chemical. By the end of April, the EPA had not yet banned the chemical but was expected to do so any day. After the ban, retail stores would have just sixty days to get rid of any products containing R-11.

J. Randolph Ewing, an American entrepreneur with trading partners in the Caribbean and South America, had contracted with a small manufacturer of insecticides for a shipment of mosquito and biting-fly repellent containing R-11. Ewing planned to sell the insecticide, through his trading partners, under a variety of his own labels. He took delivery in the United States April 1 and shipped about half of the insecticides out at once. He heard about the EPA waring in late April. Anticipating a ban, Ewing thought about what to do next. He had several thousand dollars invested in the insecticides. Should he ship the rest of the insecticides overseas immediately and not mention the EPA warning to his foreign trading partners? Should he tell his trading partners about the warning and offer to take the product back? Should he be concerned at all?

Social, Policy, and Ethical Considerations

1. What should Ewing do?
2. Would your advice to Ewing be any different if R-11 were already banned in the United States?
3. If a chemical is banned in the United States but not in certain foreign nations, should the U.S. government prohibit the manufacturer from making the chemical here and exporting it to countries where it's not banned? What about a U.S. company that manufactures a banned chemical offshore, for example, in joint venture with a foreign partner?
4. In answering question 3, would you take a chemical-by-chemical approach? Or would you stand for or against an export ban based on the principle that what's not safe enough for Americans is not safe enough for others?
5. What, if any, would be the justifications for a double standard of safety for Americans and the rest of the world's citizens?

The FIFRA defines "unreasonable adverse effects on the environment" as any unreasonable risk to humans or the environment, taking into account the economic, social, and environmental costs and benefits of the use of any pesticide. Thus, unlike many environmental statutes, the FIFRA expressly requires the EPA to consider the costs of the action it takes under the statute.

If a pesticide is registered and subsequent data reveals additional hazards, the EPA may cancel the registration after an administrative hearing. The 1988 amendments placed upon industry the cost of disposing of canceled pesticides. Cancellation proceedings typically take years, both because of the numerous stages of the administrative process and because of the required use of a scientific advisory committee. While the cancellation process is in progress, the pesticide may be manufactured and sold. If additional hazard is imminent, however, the product's registration may be suspended until the cancellation proceeding is completed. Once its registration has been suspended, the pesticide may not be manufactured or distributed.

Until recently, the FIFRA did not adequately address the problem of old pesticides that had been registered under earlier and less strict standards. Concerned that these pesticides did not meet current standards, Congress in 1988 amended the FIFRA to require the re-registration of pesticides registered before 1984. U.S. exports are not subject to most of the act's requirements, though an exported pesticide not registered under the FIFRA must bear a label stating "Not Registered for Use in the United States of America."

The EPA may impose civil penalties of up to $5,000 for each offense. Maximum criminal penalties for knowing violations are a $50,000 fine and/or one year imprisonment.

The Toxic Substances Control Act

TSCA the Toxic Substances Control Act provides a comprehensive scheme for regulation of toxic substances

Congress passed the Toxic Substances Control Act (TSCA) in 1976 in an effort to provide a comprehensive scheme for regulating toxic substances. The TSCA contains provisions on the manufacture of new chemicals, the testing of suspect chemicals, the regulation of chemicals that present an unreasonable risk of injury to health and the environment, and the inventorying of all chemicals.

Under the act, a manufacturer must notify the EPA before it manufactures a new chemical or makes a significant new use of an existing chemical. If the EPA administrator concludes that the information submitted is insufficient to permit a reasoned evaluation of the health and environmental effects of the chemical and the chemical may present an unreasonable risk of injury to health or the environment, the administrator may limit or prohibit the chemical's manufacture or distribution.

The act authorizes the EPA to require the testing of any substance, whether existing or new, if (1) the manufacture or distribution of the substance may present an unreasonable risk of injury to health or the environment, (2) the data on the effects of the substance on health and the environment is insufficient, and (3) testing is necessary to develop such data. In *Chemical Manufacturers Association v. EPA*, the court considers the meaning of "unreasonable risk."

CHEMICAL MANUFACTURERS ASSOCIATION v. EPA United States Court of Appeals, District of Columbia Circuit, 1988, 859 F.2d 977 United States Court of Appeals, Fifth Circuit, 1990, 899 F.2d 344

FACTS Chemical Manufacturers Association (CMA) and four companies that manufacture chemicals challenged a test rule promulgated by the Environmental Protection Agency under the TSCA. The plaintiffs asserted that the EPA must find that the existence of an unreasonable risk of injury to health is more probable than not before it may issue a test rule under the act. In response, the EPA claimed that it may issue a test rule under the TSCA if the agency determines that there is a substantial probability of an unreasonable risk of injury to health. The test rule required toxicological testing to determine the health effects of the chemical, 2-ethylhexanoic acid, and imposed on exporters of this chemical a duty to file certain notices with the EPA.

DECISION The EPA's interpretation of the TSCA upheld.

OPINION The act establishes a two-tier structure: the EPA must find that a chemical substance "presents or will present an unreasonable risk of injury to health or the environment" in order to regulate that substance.

In contrast, the EPA has the authority to require testing if the substance "*may* present an unreasonable risk to health or the environment." The question here is whether the "unreasonable risk" must be more probable than not, as CMA contends, or must only be a probability that is more than merely theoretical or speculative, as the EPA contends. The court concluded that an "unreasonable risk" need not be established to a more-probable-than-not degree. If the EPA were required to find that a substance *presents* an unreasonable risk, then the EPA could regulate the substance and there would be no role for required testing. While Congress did not intend to authorize the EPA to issue test rules on the basis of mere hunches, the EPA's reading of the TSCA is a reasonable accommodation of the congressional policies regarding the gathering of information about suspect chemicals.

INTERPRETATION The definition of "unreasonable risk" under the TSCA is more permissive for the sake of testing a substance than for regulating it.

Because of the many substances that might be subject to testing under the statutory standard, the TSCA mandates that the EPA establish a priority list for testing that contains no more than fifty substances at any time. This list is established by a committee whose members come from eight specified agencies.

Once the EPA determines, either through its testing program or through the premanufacturing notice process, that a substance "presents or will present an unreasonable risk of injury to health or the environment," the agency may restrict or prohibit use of the substance.

If the EPA administrator believes that a substance presents an imminent hazard, he is authorized to bring an action in federal district court for seizure of the substance or other appropriate relief. The statute defines an "imminently hazardous chemical substance or mixture" as one that presents an unreasonable risk of serious or widespread injury to health or the environment.

The TSCA requires the EPA to compile and keep current a list of each chemical substance manufactured or processed in the United States. The EPA's initial inventory of existing chemicals, completed in 1980, listed approximately 55,000 substances. A chemical not listed on the inventory is subject to premanufacture review, even if it was in fact previously manufactured. While not explicitly required to do so by the TSCA, the EPA reviews the substances on the inventory to determine their safety.

The EPA may impose civil penalties of up to $20,000 per day for a violation of the TSCA. Maximum criminal penalties for knowing violations are $25,000 fines for each day of violation and/or one year imprisonment.

The Resource Conservation and Recovery Act

In 1976, Congress enacted the Resource Conservation and Recovery Act (RCRA) to provide a comprehensive scheme for the treatment of solid waste, particularly hazardous waste. The statute provides that the states are primarily responsible for nonhazardous waste, while the EPA regulates all phases of hazardous waste—generation, transportation, and disposal. Under the act, the federal government must establish criteria for identifying hazardous waste, taking into account factors that include toxicity, persistence, degradability, flammability, and corrosiveness.

RCRA the Resource Conservation and Recovery Act provides a comprehensive scheme for treatment of solid waste, particularly hazardous waste

The act prescribes for generators (entities that produce hazardous waste) standards concerning record keeping, labeling, the use of appropriate containers, and reporting. The statute requires the EPA to establish a *manifest system* to be used by generators. A manifest is a form on which the generator must specify the quantity, composition, origin, routing, and destination of hazardous waste. On the manifest the generator also must certify that the volume and toxicity of the waste have been reduced to the greatest degree economically practicable and that the method of treatment, storage, and disposal minimizes the threat to health and the environment.

Transporters must maintain records and properly label the waste they transport. Furthermore, they must comply with manifests and may transport hazardous waste only to facilities that have an RCRA hazardous waste facility permit.

Owners/operators of hazardous waste treatment, storage, and disposal sites must maintain records and comply with generator manifests. Facilities for hazardous waste treatment, storage, and disposal must obtain an RCRA hazardous waste facility permit. To obtain a permit, a facility must comply with relevant EPA standards. Failure to comply may subject the owner/operator to civil or criminal penalties.

The act authorizes the EPA administrator to sue in federal court for an injunction if the administrator has evidence that "the past or present handling, storage, treatment, transportation or disposal of any solid waste or hazardous waste may present an imminent and substantial endangerment to health or the environment." Moreover, the EPA may impose civil penalties of up to $25,000 per day of violation. Maximum criminal penalties for knowing violations are $50,000 for each day of violation and/or five years' imprisonment. Where a knowing violation endangers a person, the maximum criminal penalty is a $1 million fine and/or fifteen years' imprisonment.

The Superfund

Superfund the Comprehensive Environmental Response, Compensation and Liability Act (CERCLA) establishes (1) a National Contingency Plan for responding to releases of hazardous substances and (2) a trust fund to pay for removal and cleanup of hazardous waste

While the RCRA regulates current and future generation, transportation, and disposal of hazardous waste, the act provides only limited authority for the cleanup of abandoned or inactive hazardous waste sites. To fill this gap, Congress in 1980 enacted the Comprehensive Environmental Response, Compensation and Liability Act (CERCLA, or the Superfund). By 1986, the EPA, working under the act, had spent $1.6 billion and had begun the cleanup of only eight sites. This record and other problems with the initial legislation prompted Congress to amend the CERCLA by enacting the Superfund Amendments and Reauthorization Act of 1986 (SARA).

CERCLA requires the federal government to establish a National Contingency Plan (NCP) prescribing procedures and standards for responding to hazardous substance releases. The NCP specifies criteria for determining the priority of sites to be cleaned. The plan also identifies, on at least an annual basis, the sites that most require immediate cleanup.

Under the act, the federal government has authority to take either removal or remedial actions in response to a release or threatened release of hazardous substances, as long as such removal or remedial actions are consistent with the NCP. Removal typically is an immediate response to control a specific release of a hazardous substance. Remedial actions, on the other hand, consist of efforts to prevent or reduce the release of hazardous substances; such actions are intended to be long-term solutions. The president may impose a civil penalty of up to $25,000 per day of violation; for repeat violations, the penalty may reach up to $75,000 per day of violation.

States and private parties also may engage in response actions, although such actions must meet certain conditions in order for the responder to recover its costs from either the governmental trust fund or the parties responsible under CERCLA for the release or threatened release of hazardous substances.

CERCLA establishes a trust fund to pay for hazardous waste removal and other remedial actions. The trust fund is financed in part by a surtax on businesses with annual incomes over $2 million, a tax on petroleum, and a tax on chemical feedstocks. An additional part of the trust fund comes from money recovered from persons responsible for the release of hazardous substances. These parties include the owners and operators of a hazardous waste disposal facility from which there has been a release, as well as any generator of hazardous wastes that were disposed of at that facility.

Because CERCLA initially imposed liability on all owners of contaminated property, some parties were held liable even though they had acquired the land either involuntarily or without knowledge of the hazardous wastes stored there.

For example, after foreclosing on a mortgage of $335,000 and taking title to a piece of property, a bank was held liable for Superfund costs of more than $555,000. Responding to the inequity of such situations, Congress in SARA established a new defense to CERCLA liability for "innocent landowners." To qualify as an innocent landowner, one "must have undertaken, at the time of acquisition, all appropriate inquiry into the previous ownership and uses of the property consistent with good commercial or customary practice in an effort to minimize liability."

Figure 47–1 summarizes the major federal environmental statutes.

FIGURE 47–1 Major Federal Environmental Statutes

Act	Major Purpose	Maximum Civil Penalty	Maximum Criminal Penalty
National Environmental Policy Act (NEPA)	• Establish environmental protection as a major national goal • Mandate environmental impact statements prepared prior to federal action having a significant environmental effect	None	None
Clean Air Act	• Control and reduce air pollution • Establish National Ambient Air Quality Standards	$25,000 per day of violation	$1,000,000 fine per violation and/or 15 years' imprisonment*
Clean Water Act	• Protect against water pollution • Establish effluent limitations	$25,000 per day of violation	$50,000 per day of violation and/or 3 years' imprisonment*
Federal Insecticide, Fungicide and Rodenticide Act (FIFRA)	• Regulate the sale and distribution of pesticides • Prevent pesticides having an unreasonably adverse effect on the environment	$5,000 per offense	$50,000 fine and/or 1 year imprisonment
Toxic Substances Control Act (TSCA)	• Regulate toxic substances • Prevent unreasonable risk of injury to health and the environment from toxic substances	$20,000 per day of violation	$25,000 fine per day of violation and/or 1 year imprisonment
Resource Conservation and Recovery Act (RCRA)	• Regulate the disposal of solid waste • Establish standards to protect human health and the environment from hazardous wastes	$25,000 per day of violation	$1,000,000 fine and/or 15 years' imprisonment
Comprehensive Environmental Response, Compensation and Liability Act (CERCLA, or the Superfund) and Superfund Amendments and Reauthorization Act (SARA)	• Establish a national contingency plan for responding to releases of hazardous substances • Establish a trust fund to pay for removal of hazardous waste and other remedial actions	$25,000 per day of violation; $75,000 for repeat violations	None

*Doubled for repeat convictions.

INTERNATIONAL PROTECTION OF THE OZONE LAYER

Montreal Protocol treaty by which countries agreed to cut production of chlorofluorocarbons (CFCs) by 50 percent

U.S. Executive Order to eliminate CFCs and halon in the United States

In 1987, the United States and twenty-three other countries entered into the Montreal Protocol on Substances that Deplete the Ozone Layer, a treaty designed to prevent pollution that harms the ozone layer. The treaty requires all signatories to reduce their production and consumption of all chemicals, in particular chlorofluorocarbons (CFCs, more commonly called freon), that deplete the ozone layer. Although having excessive ozone in the air we breathe can be hazardous, the ozone layer in the stratosphere helps to protect the earth from harmful ultraviolet radiation. By 1985, scientists believed that the release of CFCs into the atmosphere had caused a hole to develop in the ozone layer over Antarctica.

Most of the countries signing the Montreal Protocol agreed to cut their production of CFCs by 50 percent by 1998. By 1990, however, mounting evidence underscored the serious harm being done to the ozone layer. Consequently, a new treaty was signed in London, England, requiring that CFCs and halon (a fire fighting chemical) be eliminated by the year 2000. In 1992, President Bush issued an executive order mandating the elimination of CFCs and halon in the United States by the year 1995. Due to the difficulty in finding substitutes for CFCs, this deadline was extended to 1996 by order of President Clinton.

THE LAW AND YOU Environmental Concerns for Home Buyers and Sellers

General

The purchase or sale of a home or residential lot is a significant event involving a variety of practical, legal and financial considerations. As a buyer, environmental concerns are an important part of the transaction because they affect your health and the value of the home or lot you are purchasing, and may have other legal and financial consequences.

A seller may require you to buy the home or lot "as is" and you therefore want to be alert to environmental problems and have appropriate inspections done before legally obligating yourself to purchase the home or lot. Your lender may also have requirements you have to fulfill with respect to environmental concerns.

As a seller, if you are aware of environmental problems with the home or lot you are selling, you may have an obligation to disclose those problems to a potential buyer. You may be asked by the buyer to reduce the price of the home or lot, clean up the environmental problem, or agree in the contract between you

and the buyer to be responsible for the problem.

The buyer or the seller may be required by federal, state or local environmental laws and regulations to clean up certain environmental hazards. Title insurance and other types of insurance typically do not cover environmental problems, and obtaining insurance to cover those problems can be very expensive. You may have an action against the person or company who caused the environmental problem, but they may not be able to pay.

This pamphlet has been prepared to inform you of some of the common environmental concerns confronting buyers and sellers of homes or residential lots in North Carolina today, and some of their legal, financial and health consequences.

If you suspect that the home or residential lot you are buying or selling has these or other environmental problems, it is important that you consult the appropriate legal or environmental professionals to assist you in determining how best to identify

and deal with those problems. It is also important that you be sure that your contract of sale adequately addresses these concerns. You do not want to wait until your closing to deal with environmental issues.

Environmental problems may be found both in the home itself and in the land on which the home is situated or, if undeveloped, a residential lot.

Lead Hazards

There are two primary sources of residential lead poisoning; lead-based paint and lead in drinking water from lead pipes and solder in home plumbing. In 1971, the federal government passed laws limiting the amount of lead in residential paint, but many older houses—especially those built before 1950—will likely have lead-based paint. (Effective Oct. 28, 1994, a seller of a home built prior to 1978 must disclose to any potential purchaser the possibility of lead paint hazards in that home. The purchaser has 10 days to conduct a risk assessment or inspection of the

continued

house. An attorney can advise you about the obligations of the seller and the rights of the potential purchaser.)

Lead pipes and solder were used as recently as the late 1980s, when their use was banned. Lead poisoning is a serious illness caused by swallowing or breathing too much lead. Lead is most dangerous to children under six years old and pregnant women (who can pass lead through the bloodstream to the unborn baby). Low level poisoning can slow a child's development and cause learning and behavioral problems; high level poisoning can damage the brain, kidneys, and nervous system, or even cause death.

What can I do if I suspect that the home contains lead hazards? Lead-based paint can be replaced or covered by a variety of methods. However, *be very careful* in how you deal with lead-based paint. The removal of lead paint produces paint chips, dust, smoke and fumes, which themselves contain lead and can be hazardous. Be sure you know the proper procedures to follow before replacing or covering lead-based paint yourself or hiring someone to do it.

Have your home inspected for lead pipes or soldering. If your inspector finds lead pipes or soldering, have the water tested. If the home contains lead hazards, state regulations may require the owner to develop a plan to remove the hazard. An environmental consultant can help develop and implement the plan (which will vary in simplicity and cost depending on the nature and extent of the lead hazard).

Asbestos

Asbestos is a fibrous mineral which because of its fire-retardant and insulative properties has been used in a variety of building materials, including: asbestos cement siding, roofing materials, vinyl floor tiles and

linoleum and adhesives used to install them, joint compound used in sheetrock walls and ceilings, acoustic ceiling tiles and sprayed on decorative ceilings, and various types of insulation used on hot water pipes, small boilers and heating, ventilation, and air conditioning systems.

Asbestos is dangerous if its fibers are released into the air. This usually happens when asbestos material becomes damaged or "friable" (meaning it can be crumbled or reduced to powder by hand pressure), or when asbestos material is disturbed by remodeling or renovations. People who breathe asbestos fibers for a prolonged period may develop asbestosis (a serious lung disease), lung cancer, mesothelioma (a cancer of the lining of the lung or abdominal cavity), or other lung and respiratory problems. These diseases usually develop 20 years or more after lengthy exposure to asbestos fibers.

What should I do if I suspect that the home contains asbestos? You cannot tell simply by looking whether a material contains asbestos (unless it is labeled). If you suspect that the home may contain asbestos, you can have it inspected and have samples analyzed by a qualified professional. If the asbestos material is in good shape and will not be disturbed, removal is not required and the United States Environmental Protection Agency (EPA) recommends doing nothing. If it is damaged or will be disturbed by renovations, you should consider having it removed or repaired by a qualified asbestos abatement company licensed in North Carolina. Homeowners should *not* handle asbestos materials or perform repairs or removal on their own.

Radon Gas

Radon is a radioactive gas produced by decaying uranium found in rock and soil. Radon gas is invisible and odorless. It permeates the atmos-

phere and buildings, and can contaminate well water. Studies have shown that significant exposure to elevated levels of radon may cause cancer.

What can I do if I suspect that the home contains radon gas? The EPA recommends testing all areas of a home below the third floor for radon gas. Testing is inexpensive and easy. When buying an existing home, ask for documentation of past radon tests. If none have been performed, the purchase contract may be drafted to require that a short-term test be performed prior to closing. When building a new home, state or local law may require that radon-resistant construction features be used. Investigate to ensure that such features are built into the home. High radon levels in most homes can be reduced to safe levels through a variety of methods, typically costing between $500 to $2,500. Having the results of a recent radon test will make your home more attractive to prospective purchasers.

Indoor Air Pollution

Indoor air pollution is caused by gases and particles released in the air. There are many potential sources, including asbestos and radon gas discussed above. Other sources include vapors from urea formaldehyde foam insulation, pesticides, combustible appliances such as unvented gas stoves, leaking chimneys and furnaces and wood stoves, and new or wet carpets that can emit chemicals.

Inadequate ventilation and high humidity and temperature levels can increase the concentration of some pollutants. The health hazards caused by indoor air pollutants vary depending upon the amount of the pollutant, how hazardous it is and the age and health of the individual exposed. Generally, immediate health effects from indoor air pollution may include irritation of the

continued

eyes, nose and throat, headaches, dizziness and fatigue. Long term effects from greater exposure may include respiratory diseases, cancer and kidney or liver damage.

What should I do if I suspect that the home contains sources of indoor air pollution? Look for sources of indoor air pollution in the home and for signs of problems with ventilation or air flow, including smelly air, dirty central heating and air cooling equipment, damaged flues and chimneys, and moisture, mold or water damage. If there are signs of poor air flow or specific potential sources of air pollution, you may need to consult with a professional who has experience in solving indoor air quality problems in homes.

Stump Holes

A stump hole, also regulated as a "Land Clearing and Inert Debris (LCID) Landfill," is a disposal site for stumps, limbs, and construction debris left from clearing land and building houses. An unapproved or unrecorded LCID Landfill is of environmental concern because methane gas that may form during the decay of organic matter in it may contaminate the water supply and also may migrate under the home, creating a risk of an explosion.

Environmental authorities may require a "cleanup" of an LCID Landfill releasing methane gas, which can be extremely expensive, sometimes impossible and could severely decrease the value of a home. Depending on the circumstances, the seller or buyer may be required to pay for the cleanup.

What can I do if I suspect that a stump hole is located on the property? In general, the process of decay, settling and formation of methane gas occurs within 5–10 years of the creation of an LCID Landfill, and therefore buyers of homes more than 10 years old may be less concerned about an LCID

Landfill. A potential purchaser of a home less than 10 years old should ask the owner, builder, or developer, and also be alert for cracking or shifting in the foundation, ground depressions and corrosion of electrical receptacles that are caused by methane gas. State regulations enacted in the early 1980s require that all LCID Landfills be recorded. Thus, a title search *may* reveal whether an LCID Landfill is located on a particular piece of property.

Underground Storage Tanks

An underground storage tank (UST) is a tank located all or partially under ground that is designed to hold gasoline, heating oil or other petroleum products or chemical solutions. The primary danger of a UST on the property is that it may leak, causing soil and/or groundwater contamination. This poses not only a health risk, particularly if the home's water source is a private well, but also a risk of liability for cleanup of the leaked substance.

If you buy or own property on which a leaking UST is located, you may have to pay for cleanup even if you did not install the UST, do not use it and did not cause the leak. Removal of a UST and cleanup of leaked substances can be expensive and banks may refuse to lend money for property that is contaminated by such a release.

What can I do if I suspect that an underground storage tank is located on the property? Ask the sellers or prior owners of the property whether there is a UST on the property, or whether they know of any prior use of the property by a home or business that may have installed a UST. If there is a UST on the property, you may want to consider testing soil in the area of the UST to determine if there is contamination. Also, the contract for sale and deed can specifically provide that ownership of the UST is not conveyed to the buyer if the seller agrees.

Hazardous Substances

Hazardous substances are materials that pose a threat to human health or the environment. Typical hazardous substances are toxic, corrosive, ignitable, explosive or chemically reactive. Many manufacturing businesses such as dry cleaners, auto mechanics shops and print shops use hazardous substances.

If hazardous substances have not been disposed of properly, they can be a serious health risk from contamination of the soil and water supply. In addition, the buyer, the seller or both may be held responsible for the costs of cleaning up the hazardous substances, even if neither the buyer nor the seller was responsible for the substances.

What can I do if I suspect that hazardous substances are located on the property? Investigate the history of use of the property, particularly if it is in a commercial or industrial area. One way to do this is by asking adjoining landowners. A history of industrial uses on or near the property is cause for concern. It may be advisable for you to have the property analyzed by an environmental consulting firm.

Be on the lookout for telltale signs of potential contamination, such as pipes sticking out of the ground, dying vegetation, oily puddles of water, discolored dirt or corroded barrels. . . . If you make "appropriate inquiry" into the previous owners and uses of the property, you *may* have a defense to liability for cleanup costs if hazardous waste contamination is later found on the property and you did not know or have reason to know it was there.

Water Quality and Supply

Water quality and supply concerns the safety and quantity of the drinking water used in the home. Your drinking water may be supplied by a well on the property, by a community source or by the

continued

municipality. Problems with the quantity and quality of your water can range from low pressure to poor yield and from bad smell or taste to contamination.

Contamination can come from sources such as lead pipes and soldering, methane gas from stump holes, oil from leaking underground storage tanks and septic tanks located too close to the water source. Contamination is more likely to be a problem where the water source is a private well.

What can I do if I suspect that there are problems with water quality and supply? If you are buying a home, be sure to taste and smell the water. If the water source is a private well, it is your responsibility. Local environmental or health officials may test private well water for bacteria, but probably will not test for chemicals. You may want to have further tests performed. If you are considering using a home water treatment system, contact the Better Business Bureau or the Consumer Protection Division of the North Carolina Attorney General's Office to be sure you are dealing with a reputable merchant.

Wetlands

Wetlands are marshes, swamps, and bogs that are inundated with surface or groundwater to the extent that there is a "prevalence of vegetation typically adapted for life in saturated soil conditions." They exist in all areas of the state, not just on the coast. Wetlands may not even seem "wet" on the ground surface, or they may be wet only at certain times of the year. Federal law restricts the destruction or disturbing of wetlands. Proper permits must be obtained if wetlands will be affected by construction activity. If wetlands are filled illegally, the developer or landowner may be forced to restore them to their original condition. You may have an action against whomever illegally filled the wetlands to recover the costs you may incur, which may include losing your home. However, those parties may not be able to pay.

What can I do if I suspect wetlands are located on the property? You should request a copy of the surveys and permits from the developer or former landowner to ensure that any wetlands were filled properly and legally. You might want to obtain your own survey illustrating wetland areas that still exist or have been filled. Also, local planning or zoning officials may have information about designated wetlands.

Conclusion

It is important for you to understand the environment of the community in which you live or will live. In addition to the concerns discussed in this pamphlet, you should be aware, for example, of rivers and flooding, noise from traffic or airports, rural or farm odors and suburban or industrial sources of pollution such as a paper mill or wastewater treatment plant. Understanding and addressing environmental concerns will make buying or selling your home a safer, more satisfying experience.

[Published as a Public Service by the Environmental Issues Committee Young Lawyers Division of the North Carolina Bar Association. This pamphlet is not intended to be a comprehensive statement of law. If you have specific questions, consult an attorney.]

Reprinted by permission of the North Carolina Bar Association.

CHAPTER SUMMARY

Common Law Actions for Environmental Damage

Nuisance	**Private Nuisance** substantial and unreasonable interference with the use and enjoyment of a person's land **Public Nuisance** interference with the health, safety, or comfort of the public

Other Common Law Actions	**Trespass** an invasion of land that interferes with the right of exclusive possession of the property **Strict Liability for Abnormally Dangerous Activities** liability without fault for an individual who engages in an unduly dangerous activity in an inappropriate location

Federal Regulation of the Environment

National Environmental Policy Act (NEPA)	**Purpose** to establish environmental protection as a goal of federal policy **Council on Environmental Quality** three-member advisory group in the Executive Office of the President that makes recommendations to the president on environmental matters **Environmental Impact Statement** a detailed statement concerning the environmental impact of a proposed federal action ■ *Scope* NEPA applies to a broad range of activities, including direct action by a federal agency as well as any action by a federal agency that permits action by other parties that will affect the quality of the environment ■ *Content* the EIS must contain, among other items, a detailed statement of the environmental impact of the proposed action, any adverse environmental effects that cannot be avoided, and alternative proposals

Clean Air Act	**Purpose** to control and reduce air pollution **Existing Sources** ■ *National Ambient Air Quality Standards (NAAQSs)* the EPA administrator must establish NAAQSs for air pollutants that endanger the public health and welfare ■ *State Implementation Plan* each state must submit a plan for each NAAQS detailing how the state will implement and maintain the standard **New Sources** ■ *New Stationary Sources* owner/operator must employ the best technological system of continuous emission reduction that has been adequately demonstrated ■ *New Vehicles* extensive emission standards are established ■ *Hazardous Air Pollutants* to protect the public health, the EPA administrator must establish for hazardous air pollutants standards that provide ample safety margins ■ *Acid Rain* standards are established to protect against acid rain (precipitation that contains high levels of sulfuric or nitric acid)

Clean Water Act	**Purpose** protect against water pollution **Point Sources** act establishes National Pollutant Discharge Elimination System (NPDES), a permit system, to control the amount of pollutants that may be discharged by a point source into U.S. waters **Nonpoint Sources** act requires the states to use the best management practices to control water runoff from agricultural and urban areas

Hazardous Substances	**FIFRA** the Federal Insecticide, Fungicide and Rodenticide Act regulates the sale and distribution of pesticides
	TSCA the Toxic Substances Control Act provides a comprehensive scheme for regulation of toxic substances
	RCRA the Resource Conservation and Recovery Act provides a comprehensive scheme for treatment of solid waste, particularly hazardous waste
	Superfund the Comprehensive Environmental Response, Compensation and Liability Act (CERCLA) establishes (1) a National Contingency Plan for responding to releases of hazardous substances and (2) a trust fund to pay for removal and cleanup of hazardous waste

| International Protection of the Ozone Layer | **Montreal Protocol** treaty by which countries agreed to cut production of chlorofluorocarbons (CFCs) by 50 percent |
| | **U.S. Executive Order** to eliminate CFCs and halon in the United States by 1996 |

QUESTIONS

1. Discuss the common law actions for environmental damage and the difficulties involved in prevailing in such actions.
2. Discuss the major substantive provisions of the National Environmental Policy Act.
3. Discuss the regulatory schemes of the Clean Air Act.
4. Discuss the regulation of both point and nonpoint sources of pollution by the Clean Water Act.
5. Discuss (a) the Federal Insecticide, Fungicide and Rodenticide Act; (b) the Toxic Substances Control Act;

(c) the Resource Conservation and Recovery Act; and (d) the Superfund.

Internet Question. Find information about the United States Environmental Protection Agency, then choose a state and determine if it has a state environmental protection agency and, if so, what are its responsibilities.

PROBLEMS

1. Atlantic Cement operated a large cement plant. Neighboring landowners sued for damages and an injunction, claiming that their properties were injured by the dirt, smoke, and vibrations coming from the plant. The lower court found that the plant constituted a nuisance and granted temporary damages but refused to grant an injunction because the benefits of operating the plant outweighed the harm to the plaintiffs' properties. The landowners appealed. Decision?
2. Seindenberg and Hutchinson (the site owners) leased a four-acre tract of land (the Bluff Road site) to a chemical manufacturing corporation (COCC). While the lease initially was for the sole purpose of allowing COCC to store raw materials and finished products in a warehouse on the land, COCC later expanded its business to

include the brokering and recycling of chemical waste generated by third parties. COCC's owners subsequently formed a new corporation, South Carolina Recycling and Disposal, Inc. (SCRDI) for the purpose of taking over COCC's waste-handling business. The site owners accepted rent from SCRDI. The waste stored at Bluff Road contained many chemical substances that federal law defines as hazardous. In 1980, the EPA concluded that the site was a major fire hazard. The federal government contracted with a third party to perform a partial cleanup of the site. South Carolina completed the cleanup. The federal government and South Carolina sued SCRDI, COCC, the site owners, and three third-party generators as responsible parties under RCRA and CERCLA. Decision?

3. The state of Y submits a plan under the Clean Air Act to attain national ambient air quality standards. Can the EPA administrator deny approval of the state plan because it is (a) less stringent or (b) more stringent than the agency believes is feasible? Explain.

4. Kennecott Copper Corp. brings this challenge to an EPA order that rejected a portion of the state of Nevada's implementation plan dealing with the control of stationary sources of sulfur dioxide (SO_2). All of the SO_2 emissions come from a single source—the Kennecott copper smelter at McGill. The EPA based its decision on the belief that the Clean Air Act NAAQS must be met by continuous emission limitations to the maximum extent possible and that the act permits the intermittent use of emission controls only when continuous controls are not economically feasible. Kennecott contends that the EPA must approve any state implementation plan that will attain and maintain an NAAQS within the statutory time period. Decision?

5. The EPA administrator issued an order suspending the registration of the pesticides heptachlor and chlordane under the FIFRA. Velsicol Chemical Corp., the sole manufacturer of these pesticides, brings this action, contending that the evidence does not support the administrator's contention that the continued use of these chemicals poses an imminent hazard to human health. Velsicol and the U.S. Department of Agriculture (USDA) contend (1) that the EPA's laboratory tests on mice and rats do not "conclusively" show that either chemical is carcinogenic; (2) that mice are too prone to tumors to be reliable test subjects; and (3) that human exposure to these chemicals is insufficient to create a risk. Nonetheless, human epidemiology studies on both chemicals provide no basis for concluding that either pesticide is safe. The administrator based part of his claim on residues of these chemicals found in soil, air, and the aquatic ecosystem over long periods of time and on the presence of these chemicals in the human diet and human tissue. Decision?

6. The U.S. Department of the Interior filed an environmental impact statement with regard to its proposal to lease approximately eighty tracts of submerged land, primarily located off the coast of Louisiana, for oil and gas exploration. Adjacent to the proposed area is the greatest estuarine coastal marsh in the United States. This marsh provides rich nutrients for the Gulf of Mexico, the most productive fishing region of the country. The EIS focused primarily on oil pollution and its negative environmental effect. Three conservation groups contend that the EIS is insufficient in that it does not properly discuss alternatives. The government contends that (a) it need only provide a detailed statement of the alternatives, not a discussion of their environmental impact, and (b) the only alternatives the NEPA requires it to discuss are those that can be adopted and implemented by the agency issuing the impact statement. Decision?

CHAPTER 48

International Business Law

Today every aspect of business, including business law, requires some understanding of international business practices. Since World War II, the global economy has become increasingly interconnected. Many U.S. corporations now have investments or manufacturing facilities in other countries; simultaneously, the number of foreign corporations with business operations in the United States has increased dramatically. Furthermore, whether a domestic corporation exports goods or not, it competes with imports from many other countries. For example, U.S. firms face competition from Japanese electronics and automobiles, French wines and fashions, German machinery, and Taiwanese textiles. In order to compete effectively, U.S. firms need to be aware of international business practices and developments.

Laws vary greatly from country to country: what one nation requires by law, another may forbid. To complicate matters, there is no single authority in international law that can compel countries to act. When the laws of two or more nations conflict, or when one party has violated an agreement and the other party wishes to enforce it or to recover damages, establishing who will adjudicate the matter, which laws will be applied, what remedies will be available, or where the matter should be decided often is very confusing. Nonetheless, given the growing impact of the global economy, a basic understanding of international business law is essential.

THE INTERNATIONAL ENVIRONMENT

International law deals with the conduct and relations between nation-states and international organizations, as well as some of their relations with persons. Unlike domestic law, international law generally cannot be enforced. Consequently, international courts do not have compulsory jurisdiction, though they do have authority to resolve an international dispute if the parties to the dispute *accept* the court's jurisdiction over the matter. Furthermore, a sovereign nation that has adopted an international law will enforce that law to the same extent as all of its domestic laws. In this section, we will examine some of the sources and institutions of international law.

International law deals with the conduct and relations of nation-states and international organizations

International Court of Justice
The United Nations, which is probably the most famous international organization, has a judiciary branch called the **International Court of Justice** (ICJ). The ICJ consists of fifteen judges, no two of whom may be from the same sovereign state, elected for nine-year terms by a majority of both the U.N. General

International Court of Justice judicial branch of the United Nations having voluntary jurisdiction over nations

Assembly and the U.N. Security Council. The usefulness of the ICJ is limited, however, because only nations (not private individuals or corporations) may be parties to an action before the court. Furthermore, the ICJ has contentious jurisdiction only over nation-parties who agree both to allow the ICJ to decide the case and to be bound by its decision. Moreover, because the ICJ cannot enforce its rulings, countries displeased with an ICJ decision may simply ignore it. Consequently, few nations submit their disputes to the ICJ.

The ICJ also has advisory jurisdiction if requested by a U.N. organ or specialized U.N. agency. Neither sovereign states nor individuals may request an advisory opinion. These opinions are nonbinding, and the U.N. agency requesting the opinion usually votes to decide whether to follow it.

Regional Trade Communities

Regional trade communities international organizations, conferences, and treaties focusing on business and trade regulations; the EU (the European Union) is the most prominent of these

Of much greater significance are international organizations, conferences, and treaties that focus on business and trade regulation. **Regional trade communities**, such as the European Union (EU), promote common trade policies among member nations. Other important regional trade communities include the Central American Common Market (CACM), the Caribbean Common Market (CARICOM), the Association of Southeast Asian Nations (ASEAN), the Andean Economic Community (ANDEAN), and the Economic Community of West African States (ECOWAS).

European Union (EU) The European Community (EC), the predecessor to the European Union, was formed in 1967 through a merger between the European Economic Community (better known as the Common Market), the European Coal and Steel Community, and the European Atomic Energy Community (Euratom). The EC worked to remove trade barriers between its member nations and to unify their economic policies. The EC had the power to make rules that bound member nations and that preempted its members' domestic laws.

In 1993 the Treaty on European Union (popularly called the Maastricht Treaty) took effect. It changed the name of the EC to the European Union (EU) and stated the Union's objectives to include (1) promoting economic and social progress by creating an area without internal borders and by establishing an economic and monetary union; (2) asserting its identity on the international scene by implementing a common foreign and security policy; (3) strengthening the protection of the rights and interests of citizens of its member states; and (4) developing close cooperation on justice and home affairs. The EU currently has fifteen full members: Austria, Belgium, Denmark, Finland, France, Germany, Greece, Ireland, Italy, Luxembourg, the Netherlands, Portugal, Spain, Sweden, and the United Kingdom. These countries have a combined population of over 350 million people and a combined annual gross product of about $7 trillion.

NAFTA The North American Free Trade Agreement, which took effect in 1994, established a free trade area among the United States, Canada, and Mexico. Its objectives are to (1) eliminate trade barriers to the movement of goods and services across the borders, (2) promote conditions of fair competition in the free trade area, (3) increase investment opportunities in the area, and (4) provide adequate and effective enforcement of intellectual property rights. Over fifteen years, the treaty will gradually eliminate all tariffs between the three countries.

International Treaties

A **treaty** is an agreement between or among independent nations. As we discussed in Chapter 1, the U.S. Constitution authorizes the president to enter into treaties with the advice and consent of the Senate "providing two-thirds of the Senators present concur." The U.S. Constitution provides that all valid treaties are "the law of the land," having the legal force of a federal statute.

Nations have entered into bilateral and multilateral treaties in order to facilitate and regulate trade and to protect their national interests. In addition, treaties have been used to serve as constitutions of international organizations, to establish general international law, to transfer territory, to settle disputes, to secure human rights, and to protect investments. The Treaty Section of the Office of Legal Affairs within the United Nations Secretariat is responsible for registering and publishing treaties and agreements among member nations. Since its inception in 1946, the U.N. Secretariat has registered and published over 30,000 treaties that expressly or indirectly concern international business.

Probably the most important multilateral trade treaty is the General Agreement on Tariffs and Trade (GATT). The basic purpose of GATT (now called the World Trade Organization) is to facilitate the flow of trade by establishing agreements on potential trade barriers such as import quotas, customs, export regulations, antidumping restrictions (the prohibition against selling goods for less than their fair market value), subsidies, and import fees. Such agreements arise under GATT's *most favored nation provision*, which states that all signatories must treat each other as favorably as they treat any other country. Thus, any privilege, immunity, or favor given to one country must be given to all. Nevertheless, nations may give preferential treatment to developing nations and also may enter into free trade areas with one or more other nations. A free trade area permits countries to discriminate in favor of their free trade partners, provided that the agreement covers substantially all trade among the partners. A second important principle adopted by GATT is that the protection offered domestic industries should take the form of customs tariffs, rather than other, more trade-inhibiting measures.

The most recent set of accords, adopted in 1994, included agreements on such matters as agricultural products, textiles and clothing, technical barriers to trade, trade-related investment measures, customs valuation, subsidies and countervailing measures, trade in services, antidumping measures, and protection of intellectual property rights. It also created the Dispute Settlement Body and increased the scope of GATT's dispute resolution process.

JURISDICTION OVER ACTIONS OF FOREIGN GOVERNMENTS

In this section, we will focus on a sovereign nation's power—and the factors limiting that nation's power—to exercise jurisdiction over a foreign nation or to take over property owned by foreign citizens. More specifically, we will examine state immunities (the principle of sovereign immunity and the act of state doctrine) and the power of a state to take foreign investment property.

Sovereign Immunity

One of the oldest concepts in international law is that each nation has absolute and total authority over the events occurring within its territory. It has also been long recognized, however, that in order to maintain international relations and trade, a host country must refrain from imposing its laws on a foreign sovereign

Treaty agreement between or among independent nations

International treaties agreements between or among independent nations, such as the General Agreement on Tariffs and Trade (GATT), now called the World Trade Organization

Sovereign immunity
(sov'·er·eign) foreign country's freedom from a host country's laws

nation present within its borders. This absolute immunity from the courts of a host country is known as **sovereign immunity**. Originally, all acts of a foreign sovereign nation within a host country were considered immune from the host country's laws. In modern times, however, international law distinguishes between a foreign nation's public acts and its commercial ones. Only public acts, such as those concerning diplomatic activity, internal administration, or armed forces, will be granted sovereign immunity. By engaging in trade or commercial activities, a foreign nation subjects itself to the jurisdiction of its host country's courts with respect to any disputes that arise out of those commercial activities.

In 1976, Congress enacted the Foreign Sovereign Immunities Act in order to establish exactly the circumstances under which the United States would extend immunity to foreign nations. The act specifically provides that a foreign state shall be immune from *neither* federal nor state court jurisdiction if the suit is based upon (1) a commercial activity conducted in the United States by the foreign state, (2) an act that the foreign state performed in the United States in connection with a commercial activity it conducted elsewhere, or (3) a commercial activity performed outside the United States that nonetheless directly affects the United States. Examples of commercial activities include a contract by a foreign government to buy provisions or equipment for its armed forces; a foreign government's contract to construct or repair a government building; and a foreign government's sale of a service or a product or its leasing of property, borrowing of money, or investing in a security of a U.S. corporation. Examples of public (noncommercial) activities to which sovereign immunity would extend include nationalizing a corporation, determining limitations upon the use of the foreign state's natural resources, and the granting of licenses to export a natural resource.

SAUDI ARABIA v. NELSON Supreme Court of the United States, 1993, 507 U.S. 349, 113 S.Ct. 1471, 123 L.Ed.2d 47

FACTS The Kingdom of Saudi Arabia owns and operates King Faisal Specialist Hospital in Riyadh (Hospital). The Hospital Corporation of America, Ltd. (HCA), an independent corporation existing under the laws of the Cayman Islands, recruits Americans for employment at the Hospital under an agreement signed with Saudi Arabia in 1973. HCA placed an advertisement in a periodical seeking applicants for a monitoring systems engineer position at the Hospital. Scott Nelson saw the ad in September 1983 while he was in the United States. After interviewing for the position in Saudi Arabia, Nelson returned to the United States, where he signed an employment contract with the Hospital, satisfied personnel processing requirements, and attended an orientation session that HCA conducted for Hospital employees. In December 1983, Nelson went to Saudi Arabia and began work at the Hospital. In March 1984, he discovered safety defects in the Hospital's oxygen and nitrous oxide lines that posed fire hazards. Nelson repeatedly advised Hospital officials of the safety defects and reported the defects to a Saudi government commission. On September 27, 1984, the Saudi government arrested him. Agents transported Nelson to a jail cell, where they shackled, tortured, and beat him and kept him for four

days without food. Government agents forced him to sign a statement written in Arabic, which language Nelson did not know. Two days later, government agents transferred Nelson to the Al Sijan Prison to await trial. Nelson was confined in an overcrowded cell infested with rats, where he had to fight other prisoners for food and from which he was taken only once a week for fresh air and exercise. Only after the personal request of a U.S. senator did the Saudi government release Nelson, thirty-nine days after his arrest. Seven days later, the Saudi government allowed him to leave the country.

In 1988, Nelson filed suit against Saudi Arabia in the United States District Court for the Southern District of Florida, seeking damages for personal injury. The District Court dismissed the case for lack of subject-matter jurisdiction under the Foreign Sovereign Immunities Act of 1976. The Court of Appeals reversed, holding that under the act, a foreign state is not immune from the jurisdiction of United States courts in any case involving an action based upon a commercial activity carried on in the United States by the foreign state. It concluded that Nelson's recruitment and hiring were commercial activities of Saudi Arabia and the Hospital carried on in the United States.

continued

DECISION Decision of the Court of Appeals reversed.

OPINION The Foreign Sovereign Immunities Act provides the sole basis for obtaining jurisdiction over a foreign state in the courts of this country. Under the act, a foreign state is presumptively immune from the jurisdiction of United States courts. The act, however, provides an exception for commercial activities carried on by a foreign state and having substantial contact with the United States. The statute provides that such a commercial activity may be either a regular course of commercial conduct or a particular commercial transaction or act. The commercial character of the conduct or act is determined by reference to its "nature," rather than its "purpose." A state engages in commercial activity where it exercises only those powers that also can be exercised by private citizens. Thus, a foreign state engages in commercial activity only where it acts in the manner of a private player within the market. Whether a state acts in the manner of a private party is a question of behavior, not motivation. The question is not whether the foreign government is motivated by profit or by the desire to fulfill uniquely sovereign objectives. Rather, the issue is whether the particular actions that the foreign state performs are of the type by which a private party engages in trade or commerce.

In this case, Saudi Arabia recruited and signed an employment contract with Nelson in the United States. While these activities led to the conduct that eventually injured Nelson, they are not the basis for the suit. Nelson has not alleged breach of contract, but personal injuries caused by Saudi Arabia's intentional wrongs. Nevertheless, such intentional conduct cannot qualify as commercial activity under the act. The conduct boils down to the Saudi government's abuse of the power of its police, and however monstrous such abuse undoubtedly may be, a foreign state's exercise of the powers of its police and penal officers has long been understood to be sovereign in nature. The exercise of such powers is not the sort of action by which private parties can engage in commerce. Such acts as legislation, or the expulsion of an alien, or a denial of justice cannot be performed by an individual acting in his own name. They can be performed only by the state acting as such.

INTERPRETATION Only lawsuits based on the commercial activities of a foreign state are subject to the jurisdiction of the state or federal courts in the United States.

Act of State Doctrine

The **act of state doctrine** provides that a nation's judicial branch should not question the validity of the actions a foreign government takes within that foreign sovereign's own borders. In 1897, the U.S. Supreme Court described the act of state doctrine in terms that remain valid today: "Every sovereign State is bound to respect the independence of every other sovereign State, and the courts of one country will not sit in judgment on the acts of the government of another done within its own territory."

> **Act of state doctrine** rule that a court should not question the validity of actions a foreign government takes in its own country

---

UNITED STATES v. BELMONT United States Supreme Court, 1937, 301 U.S. 324, 57 S.Ct. 758, 81 L.Ed. 1134

FACTS Prior to 1918, a Russian corporation had deposited sums of money with August Belmont, a private banker doing business in New York City. In 1918, the Soviet government nationalized the corporation and appropriated all of the corporation's property and assets, including the deposit account with Belmont. The deposit became the property of the Soviet government until 1933, when it was released and assigned to the U.S. government as part of an international compact between the United States and the Soviet Union. The purpose of this arrangement was to bring about a final settlement of the claims and counterclaims between the two countries. The United States brought an action to recover the deposit from Belmont. The district court held against the United States because the act of nationalization by the Soviets was a confiscation prohibited by the Fifth Amendment to the U.S. Constitution and was also a violation of New York public policy. The Court of Appeals affirmed, and the United States appealed.

DECISION Judgment reversed.

OPINION Governmental power over external affairs is vested exclusively in the national government, not the several states. Accordingly, the laws of New York cannot prevail against the international compact involved in this case. Principles of international comity forbid the courts of one country to examine the validity of the acts of a foreign government done within its own territory. "What another country has done in the way of taking over property of its nationals, and especially of its

continued

corporations, is not a matter for judicial consideration." Our Constitution, laws, and policies have no extraterritorial operation, except with respect to U.S. citizens. No U.S. interests were involved here, since August Belmont was merely a custodian for the deposit account.

INTERPRETATION Under the act of state doctrine, the United States has no jurisdiction over the internal actions of a sovereign nation.

In the United States, there are several possible exceptions to the act of state doctrine. Some courts hold (1) that a sovereign may waive its right to raise the act of state defense and (2) that the doctrine may be inapplicable to commercial activities of a foreign sovereign. In addition, by federal statute, courts will not apply the act of state doctrine to a claim to specific property located in the United States when such a claim is based on the assertion that a foreign state confiscated the property in violation of international law, unless the president of the United States determines that the doctrine should be applied to that particular case.

Taking of Foreign Investment Property

Investing in foreign states involves the risk that the host nation's government may take the investment property. An **expropriation** or nationalization occurs when a government seizes foreign-owned property or assets for a public purpose and pays the owner just compensation for what is taken. In contrast, **confiscation** occurs when a government offers no payment (or a highly inadequate payment) in exchange for seized property, or seizes it for a nonpublic purpose. Confiscations violate generally observed principles of international law, whereas expropriations do not. In either case, few remedies are available to injured parties. One precaution that U.S. firms can take is to obtain insurance from a private insurer or from the Overseas Private Investment Corporation (OPIC), an agency of the U.S. government.

Expropriation
(ex·pro·pri·a´·tion)
governmental taking, with payment, of foreign-owned property for a public purpose

Confiscation governmental taking of foreign-owned property without payment

TRANSACTING BUSINESS ABROAD

Transacting business abroad may involve activities such as selling goods, information, or services; investing capital; or arranging for the movement of labor. Because these transactions may affect the national security, economy, foreign policy, and interests of both the exporting and importing countries, nations have imposed measures to restrict or encourage such transactions. In this section, we will examine the legal controls imposed upon the flow of trade, labor, and capital across national borders.

Flow of Trade

Flow of trade controlled by trade barriers on imports and exports

Advances in modern technology, communication, transportation, and production methods have swelled the flow of goods across national boundaries. The governments within each country thereby face a dilemma. On the one hand, they wish to protect and stimulate domestic industry. On the other hand, they want to provide their citizens with the best quality goods at the lowest possible prices and to encourage exports from their own countries.

Tariff duty or tax imposed on goods moving into or out of a country

Governments have used a variety of trade barriers to protect domestic businesses. A frequently applied device is the **tariff**, which is a duty or tax imposed on goods moving into or out of a country. Tariffs raise the price of imported

goods, prompting some consumers to purchase less expensive, domestically produced items. Governments can also use *nontariff barriers* to give local industries
a competitive advantage. Examples of nontariff barriers include unilateral or
bilateral import quotas, import bans, overly restrictive safety or manufacturing
standards, complicated and time-consuming customs procedures, and subsidies
to local industry.

Governments also control the flow of goods out of their countries by imposing quotas, tariffs, or total prohibitions. *Export controls* or restrictions usually
result from important policy considerations, such as national defense, foreign
policy, or the protection of scarce national resources. For example, the United
States passed the Export Administration Act of 1979, which, as amended in 1985
and 1988, restricts the flow of technologically advanced goods and data from the
United States to other countries. Nonetheless, in order to assist domestic businesses, countries generally encourage exports through the use of *export incentives* and *export subsidies*.

Flow of Labor

The **flow of labor** across national borders generates policy questions concerning
the employment needs of local workers. Each country has its own immigration
policies and regulations. Almost all countries require that foreigners obtain valid
passports before entering their borders; citizens, in turn, often must have passports in order to leave or reenter the country. In addition, a country may issue
foreign citizens visas that permit them to enter the country for identified purposes or for specific periods of time. For example, the U.S. Immigration and
Naturalization Service issues various types of visas to persons who are temporarily visiting the United States for pleasure or business, to persons who enter the
United States to perform services that the unemployed in this country cannot
perform, and to persons who are transferred to the United States by their
employers.

> **Flow of labor** controlled through passport, visa, and immigration regulations

Flow of Capital

Multinational businesses frequently need to transfer funds to, and receive
money from, operations in other countries. Because there is no international
currency, nations have sought to ease the **flow of capital** among themselves.
In 1945, the International Monetary Fund (IMF) was established to facilitate the
expansion and balanced growth of international trade, to assist in the elimination of foreign exchange restrictions that hamper such growth, and to shorten
the duration and ease the disequilibrium in the international balance of payments between the members of the fund. Currently, more than 140 countries
are members of the IMF.

Nations also have cooperated in forming international and regional banks to
facilitate the flow of capital and trade. Such banks include the International Bank
for Reconstruction and Development (part of the World Bank), the African
Development Bank, the Asian Development Bank, the European Investment
Bank, and the Inter-American Development Bank.

> **Flow of capital**
> International Monetary Fund facilitates the expansion and balanced growth of international trade, assists in eliminating foreign exchange restrictions, and smooths the international balance of payments

International Contracts

The legal issues inherent in domestic commercial contracts also arise in **international contracts**. Moreover, additional issues, such as differences in language,
customs, legal systems, and currency, are peculiar to international contracts.
Such a contract should specify its official language and include definitions for all

> **International contracts**
> involve additional issues beyond those in domestic contracts, such as differences in language, legal systems, and currency

ETHICAL DILEMMA Who May Seek Economic Shelter Under U.S. Trade Law?

FACTS Stanlon, Inc., a U.S. manufacturer of educational computer software for children, has grown into a major employer in New England. Over the past eight years, Stanlon has developed programs on reading readiness and basic phonics aimed at preschool children. This innovative software, which recognizes the cultural diversity in America, sells for an average price of $150.00. Stanlon sells its products primarily through several subsidiary companies that retail children's educational toys. The retailers accept cash, checks, and major credit cards. They have no arrangements for installment sales. Over the past eight years, Stanlon, Inc., has enjoyed an excellent sales record.

Two years ago, Soeki, Ltd., a Japanese corporation, entered the market. Soeki sells substantially similar products for $75.00 per software package. In addition, the retail stores through which Soeki sells offer liberal credit terms, including installment sales. Soeki's stores are located in neighborhoods of various social and economic classes, and several are located near stores operated by Stanlon, whose retailers are located primarily in affluent neighborhoods.

Since Soeki entered the market, Stanlon's sales have plummeted. Now, having begun to lay off substantial numbers of workers, Stanlon has instituted a lawsuit against Soeki, Ltd., alleging that Soeki is selling its software at unprofitable prices in order to drive Stanlon from the market.

Social, Policy, and Ethical Considerations

1. Should a foreign corporation be free to sell goods at the lowest price possible? What is the social policy behind laws that prohibit foreign companies from selling below cost? What cost should be considered fair?

2. Is it in U.S. consumers' interest to encourage all competition from foreign enterprises?

3. How would your answers change if a foreign drug company were selling a medically valuable drug at a price significantly below that charged by its U.S. competitors?

---

the significant legal terms used in it. In addition, it should specify the acceptable currency (or currencies) and payment method. The contract should include a choice of law clause designating what law will govern any breach or dispute regarding the contract, and a choice of forum clause designating whether the parties will resolve disputes through one nation's court system or through third-party arbitration. Finally, the contract should include a *force majeure* (unavoidable superior force) clause apportioning the parties' liabilities and responsibilities in the event of an unforeseeable occurrence, such as a typhoon, tornado, flood, earthquake, war, or nuclear disaster.

CISG United Nations Convention on Contracts for the International Sales of Goods governs all contracts for international sales of goods between parties located in different nations that have ratified the CISG

CISG The United Nations Convention on Contracts for the International Sales of Goods (**CISG**), which has been ratified by the United States and more than forty other countries, governs all contracts for the international sales of goods between parties located in different nations that have ratified the CISG. Since treaties are federal law, the CISG supersedes the Uniform Commercial Code in any situation to which either could apply. The CISG includes provisions dealing with interpretation, trade usage, contract formation, obligations and remedies of sellers and buyers, and risk of loss. Parties to an international sales contract may, however, expressly exclude CISG governance from their contract. The CISG specifically excludes sales of (1) goods bought for personal, family, or household use; (2) ships or aircraft; and (3) electricity. In addition, it does not apply to contracts in which the primary obligation of the party furnishing the goods consists of supplying labor or services.

Letters of Credit International trade involves a number of risks not usually encountered in domestic trade, most notably governmental controls over the export or import of goods and currency. The most effective means of managing these risks—as well as the ordinary trade risks of nonperformance by seller and buyer—is the irrevocable documentary letter of credit. A **letter of credit** is a promise by a buyer's bank to pay the seller, provided certain conditions are met. The letter of credit transaction involves three or four different parties and three underlying contracts. To illustrate: a U.S. business wishes to sell computers to a Belgian company. The U.S. and Belgian firms enter into a sales agreement that includes details such as the number of computers, the features they will have, and the date they will be shipped. The buyer then enters into a second contract with a local bank, called an *issuer*, committing the bank to pay the agreed price upon receiving specified documents. These documents normally include a bill of lading (proving that the seller has delivered the goods for shipment), a commercial invoice listing the purchase terms, proof of insurance, and a customs certificate indicating that customs officials have cleared the goods for export. The buyer's bank's commitment to pay is the irrevocable letter of credit. Typically, a *correspondent* or *paying bank* located in the seller's country makes payment to the seller. Here, the Belgian issuing bank arranges to pay the U.S. correspondent bank the agreed sum of money in exchange for the documents. The issuer then sends the U.S. computer firm the letter of credit. When the U.S. firm obtains all the necessary documents, it presents them to the U.S. correspondent bank, which verifies the documents, pays the computer company in U.S. dollars, and sends the documents to the Belgian issuing bank. Upon receiving the required documents, the issuing bank pays the correspondent bank and then presents the documents to the buyer. In our example, the Belgian buyer pays the issuing bank in Belgian francs for the letter of credit when the buyer receives the specified documents from the bank.

Letter of credit bank's promise to pay the seller, provided certain conditions are met; used to manage the payment risks in international trade

Antitrust Laws

Section 1 of the Sherman Act provides that U.S. **antitrust laws** shall have a broad, extraterritorial reach. As we discussed in Chapter 44, contracts, combinations, or conspiracies that restrain trade with foreign nations, as well as among the domestic states, are deemed illegal. Therefore, agreements among competitors to increase the cost of imports, as well as arrangements to exclude imports from U.S. domestic markets in exchange for agreements not to compete in other countries, clearly violate U.S. antitrust laws. The antitrust provisions are also designed to protect U.S. exports when privately imposed restrictions seek to exclude U.S. competitors from foreign markets. Amendments to the Sherman Act and the Federal Trade Commission Act limit their application to unfair methods of competition that have a direct, substantial, and reasonably foreseeable effect on U.S. domestic commerce, U.S. import commerce, or U.S. export commerce.

Antitrust laws of the U.S. apply to unfair methods of competition that have a direct, substantial, and reasonably foreseeable effect on the domestic, import, or export commerce of the United States

Securities Regulation

The securities markets have become increasingly internationalized, thereby raising questions regarding which country's law governs a particular transaction in securities. (U.S. federal securities laws are discussed in Chapter 42.) Foreign issuers who issue securities in the United States must register them under the 1933 Act unless an exemption is available. Foreign issuers whose securities are sold in the secondary market in the United States must register under the 1934 Act unless the issuer is exempt. Some nonexempt foreign issuers may avoid registration under the 1934 Act by providing the SEC with copies of all information material to investors that they have made public in their home country. The

Securities regulation foreign issuers who issue securities, or whose securities are sold in the secondary market, in the United States must register them unless an exemption is available; the antifraud provisions apply where there is either *conduct* or *effects* in the United States relating to a violation of the federal securities laws

antifraud provisions of the U.S. securities laws apply to securities sold by the use of any means or instrumentality of interstate commerce. In determining the extraterritorial application of these provisions, the courts have generally found jurisdiction where there is either *conduct* or *effects* in the United States relating to a violation of the federal securities laws.

ITOBA LIMITED v. LEP GROUP PLC United States Court of Appeals, Second Circuit, 1995, 54 F.3d 118

FACTS The corporate defendant in this case, Lep Group PLC (Lep), is a London-based holding company with some fifty subsidiaries in thirty countries. Lep's "ordinary shares," the British equivalent of common stock, are registered in the United Kingdom, obligating the company to comply with United Kingdom securities laws. In 1988, to create a United States market for its ordinary shares, Lep deposited 12,842,850 of its approximately 136 million shares in an American depository, which in turn issued an American Depository Receipt (ADR) for each five ordinary shares of Lep deposited. Because these ADRs trade in the form of American Depository Shares (ADSs) on the National Association of Securities Dealers Automated Quotation System (NASDAQ), Lep is subject to the reporting and disclosure requirements of United States securities law.

Itoba Limited is a wholly owned subsidiary of A.D.T. Limited (ADT). ADT is a transnational holding company based in Bermuda. Its shares are listed on the New York Stock Exchange and approximately 50 percent of its shareholders of record reside in the United States. ADT also is the corporate parent of A.D.T. Securities Systems, Inc., a Delaware-based firm and one of America's largest suppliers of security and protection services.

In mulling over expansion plans for A.D.T. Securities Systems, ADT considered the possible acquisition of one of A.D.T. Securities Systems's largest competitors in the American security market, National Guardian. ADT already owned a small interest in that corporation through shares it held of Lep, the parent company of National Guardian. Because ownership of Lep would lead to control of National Guardian, ADT considered increasing its Lep holdings.

At the same time, Canadian Pacific was pondering a sizable investment in Lep, so Canadian Pacific and ADT agreed to explore a joint purchase of Lep. Canadian Pacific hired S.G. Warburg, a London investment bank, to evaluate Lep's business operations. ADT also performed an in-house valuation of Lep. In December 1989, S.G. Warburg issued an extensive report assessing Lep's prospects. The analysis in this report was based on Lep's U.K. annual reports; the Form 20-F that Lep filed with the United States Securities and Exchange Commission for the year ended December 31, 1988; Lep's shareholder register; and broker reports. Shortly after the Warburg report was issued,

Canadian Pacific abandoned the proposed joint venture. ADT's interest, on the other hand, did not diminish. ADT continued its examination of Lep, relying heavily on the Warburg report. To supplement its research, ADT obtained from Canadian Pacific a copy of Lep's Form 20-F for 1988.

Based on its own analyses and a review of the Warburg report, ADT decided to acquire Lep by making anonymous purchases on the market through Itoba. By November 1990, Itoba had acquired over 37 million Lep ordinary shares for approximately $114 million, paid for by ADT. Before ADT could complete its planned acquisition, however, Lep disclosed a series of business reversals that decimated its share value; Lep's stock price plummeted 97 percent and the value of Itoba's holdings in Lep declined by nearly $111 million. Lep wrote off approximately $522 million from its books for the fiscal year ended December 31, 1991.

Itoba sued Lep and its officers in a U.S. District Court, asserting violations of the Securities Exchange Act of 1934 (the Act). According to Itoba, Lep failed to disclose material matters in statements filed with the SEC. Specifically, Itoba alleged that Lep made high-risk investments and engaged in speculative business ventures without informing the investing public. Itoba claimed that had these matters been properly disclosed, it would not have purchased Lep's stock at artificially inflated prices. The defendants moved to dismiss Itoba's claims for lack of subject matter jurisdiction, and the district court granted the motion. Itoba appealed.

DECISION Judgment reversed and remanded for trial.

OPINION It is well recognized that the Securities Exchange Act is silent as to its extraterritorial application. Two jurisdictional tests have emerged under this Court's decisions: the "conduct test" and the "effects test." There is no requirement that these two tests be applied separately and distinctly from each other. Indeed, a combination of the two often gives a better picture of whether there is sufficient United States involvement to justify the exercise of jurisdiction by an American court.

Under the conduct test, a federal court has subject matter jurisdiction if (1) the defendant's activities in the United States were more than "merely preparatory" to a securities fraud conducted elsewhere, and (2) these

continued

activities or culpable failures to act within the United States "directly caused" the claimed losses. Inherent in the conduct test is the principle that Congress does not want "the United States to be used as a base for manufacturing fraudulent security devices for export, even when these are peddled only to foreigners."

The conduct test requires Itoba to prove that Lep's United States-based activities directly caused Itoba's financial losses. The lower court's finding that ADT and Itoba did not read and rely on the SEC filing in making their purchase decision must be rejected in view of the clearly established fact that the executives of Itoba and ADT based their investment decision on the Warburg report. The analyses and conclusions in this report were predicated on information found in the Form 20-F that Lep filed with the SEC. Moreover, the ADT executive responsible for assessing investment prospects used his own copy of the 1988 Form 20-F to formulate his purchase recommendations. The acquisition plan that Itoba's directors approved was formulated and funded by ADT, which in turn relied on its financial officer's analysis of the Warburg report and Lep's SEC filing. The contents of Lep's 1988 Form 20-F were thus a "substantial" and "significant contributing cause" to Itoba's purchase decision.

The lower court's second reason for denying jurisdiction—that the SEC filings were made in connection with Lep's ADSs and ADRs, not its ordinary shares—is also without merit. The ADRs were simply a grouping into one security of five ordinary shares. Inevitably, there was a direct linkage between the prices of the ADRs representing five ordinary shares and the prices of the single ordinary shares themselves. If the ordinary share price fell on the London Exchange, the market price of an ADR would decrease in similar manner, and vice versa. Moreover, the making of the allegedly false and misleading filings with the SEC was not "merely preparatory to the fraud." A material fact that is undisclosed in an SEC filing remains undisclosed absent public enlightenment. Lep's uncorrected nondisclosure played as much a role in Itoba's purchases as the price listings on the London Exchange and NASDAQ. In view of the deleterious effect this continued nondisclosure had on the thousands of ADT shareholders in the United States, it cannot be described correctly as incidental or preparatory.

This argument, of course, combines pertinent principles of both the conduct and effects tests, the latter one being based on fraud that takes place abroad, which impacts on stock registered and listed on an American national securities exchange and is detrimental to the interests of American investors. Here, we have fraud occurring on an American exchange and persisting abroad that has impacted detrimentally upon thousands of United States shareholders in the defrauded company, amounting to more than $100 million lost in the shareholders' corporate equity. In short, we hold that a sufficient combination of ingredients of the conduct and effects tests is present in this case to justify the exercise of jurisdiction by the district court.

INTERPRETATION The U.S. securities laws apply extraterritorially where there is either conduct or effects in the United States relating to a violation of the federal securities laws.

Protection of Intellectual Property

The U.S. laws protecting intellectual property (discussed in Chapter 50) do not apply to transactions in other countries. Generally, the owner of an intellectual property right must comply with each country's requirements to obtain from that country whatever protection is available. The requirements vary substantially from country to country, as does the degree of protection. The United States belongs to multinational treaties that try to coordinate the application of member nations' intellectual property laws. These treaties include the Paris Convention for the Protection of Industrial Property, the Patent Cooperation Treaty, the Berne Convention for the Protection of Literary and Artistic Works, and the Trade-Related Aspects of Intellectual Property Rights portion of the World Trade Organization Agreement.

Protection of intellectual property the owner of an intellectual property right must comply with each country's requirements to obtain from that country whatever protection is available

Foreign Corrupt Practices Act

In 1977, Congress enacted the **Foreign Corrupt Practices Act (FCPA)** prohibiting all domestic concerns from bribing foreign governmental or political officials. The FCPA makes it unlawful for *any* domestic concern or any of its

Foreign Corrupt Practices Act prohibits all U.S. companies from bribing foreign governmental or political officials officers, directors, employees, or agents to offer or give anything of value directly or indirectly to any foreign official, political party, or political official for the purpose of (1) influencing any act or decision of that person or party in his or its official capacity, (2) inducing an act or omission in violation of his or its lawful duty, or (3) inducing such person or party to use his or its influence to affect a decision of a foreign government in order to assist the domestic concern in obtaining or retaining business. An offer or promise to make a prohibited payment is a violation even if the offer is not accepted or the promise is not performed. The 1988 amendments to the FCPA explicitly excluded routine governmental actions not involving the discretion of the official, such as obtaining permits or processing applications. They also added an affirmative defense for payments that are lawful under the written laws or regulations of foreign official's country.

Violations can result in fines of up to $2 million for companies; individuals may be fined a maximum of $100,000 or imprisoned up to five years, or both. Fines imposed upon individuals may not be paid directly or indirectly by the domestic concern on whose behalf they acted. In addition, the courts may impose civil penalties of up to $11,000.

MANAGERIAL INSIGHT

Tradition in India vs. a Patent in the U.S.

NEW DELHI, Sept. 14 — For more than 50 years, Dr. Vaidya Satya Pal has sat in his apothecary's shop in the teeming heart of this capital, dispensing the 2,000 ancient Indian remedies that cram the cupboards around him. Often, his treatment of choice is a derivative of the neem tree, a hardwood that is as common in India as a pine is in New England.

So when Dr. Pal heard that W.R. Grace & Company had an American patent granted in 1992 for a pesticide based on neem, and that the patent was under challenge from an international coalition that regarded it as a piracy of India's knowledge of the neem tree and its properties, he rose irritably from his table and pushed out among the throng gathered in the dimly lit pharmacy.

"It is ridiculous, just ridiculous," the 75-year-old physician said. "People in India have been using the neem tree since the beginning of time, since we learned to make fire. For anybody to say he has a patent on the neem tree, well, it only shows, anybody who has the muscle power and the money power, he will snatch whatever he can."

Similar opinions were common in India today as a legal petition challenging Grace's patent was presented to the United States Patent and Trademark Office in Washington. The Foundation on Economic Trends, the group that is heading the challenge, said the petition was backed by the signatures of more than 100,000 Indians, as well as by more than 225 agricultural, scientific and trade groups in 45 countries.

To its backers, the bid to strip Grace of the patent on Neemix, a nontoxic pesticide gaining popularity among American farmers for use on food crops, marks a watershed in the international battle over rights to intellectual property. With today's legal challenge, these groups say, developing nations have begun a counteroffensive against rich countries that have accused poorer nations of rampant intellectual piracy because of underground industries that make counterfeit copies of computer software and movie videos.

"What many Americans have not realized is that the anger, frustration and resentment in the developing countries against what they regard as piracy of their heritage is every bit as intense as the outrage that has been drummed up by the United States over the violation of our intellectual copyrights in the developing world," said Jeremy Rifkin, president of the Foundation on Economic Trends. "What we began today is the other side of the equation."

continued

In documents supporting the petition, the foundation, which is based in Washington, and its allies portrayed the battle over the neem patent as a symbol of a looming confrontation over what they call "legalized bio-piracy," which they regard as a multibillion-dollar issue involving the world's forests, fields and oceans.

One organization backing the challenge, the Rural Advancement Foundation International, listed more than 40 companies and organizations, most of them American, that have extensive "bio-prospecting" programs in developing nations. Among them: Merck & Company, which is searching the tropical forests of Costa Rica for fungi and plants that could be used in developing anti-coagulants and other drugs, and the National Cancer Institute, a Government-financed body that has a program to collect organisms that could be helpful in developing cancer-fighting treatments.

Beyond the challenge to the neem patent, organizations like Mr. Rifkin's would like to see international legal standards adopted to guarantee poorer nations a greater share of profits earned from the exploitation of biological resources.

But the first step sought is a halt to what these groups say is an attempt, through the patenting process in the United States and other rich countries, to get a legal hammerlock on resources that they view as belonging to mankind at large.

"The real battle is whether the genetic resources of the planet will be maintained as a shared commons or whether this common inheritance will be commercially enclosed and become the intellectual property of a few big corporations," Mr. Rifkin said. "We're talking here of something that is critical to future generations."

The battle over Grace's patent for Neemix is likely to hinge on judgments about the scientific work needed to bring it to market. In their legal challenge, Mr. Rifkin and his allies argue that the patent should be voided under a legal concept known as "prior art," meaning that a product cannot be patented if the technology is substantially the same as that in existing products. In the case of Neemix, the petitioners say, Grace is using a process little different from the one farmers in India have used for at least 2,500 years to protect their crops: grinding up the seeds of the neem tree, immersing them in water and spraying the resulting emulsion on their crops.

While the most widespread use of neem in India is as a crop spray, it has also been used for thousands of years to treat conditions as varied as ulcers, eczema, acne and prickly heat; twigs are even chewed by people too poor to buy toothpaste.

Chuck Suits, a spokesman for Grace, said by telephone from the company's headquarters in Boca Raton, Fla., that the company's research had resulted in a crucial breakthrough that extended the shelf life of the active neem ingredient, azadirachtin, from a few days to at least two years.

Mr. Suits said he had no figures on the amount spent developing the pesticide, which is made in the United States from a concentrate produced for Grace in the southern Indian city of Bangalore by the P.J. Margo Company, an Indian company in which Grace has a minority holding. While Neemix makes up only a small fraction of Grace's $5 billion in annual sales, critics of the company contend that its sales of Neemix could eventually be far greater than the company has stated.

By John F. Burns, From The New York Times, September 15, 1995. Page C4.

FORMS OF MULTINATIONAL ENTERPRISES

The term **multinational enterprise** (or MNE) refers to any business that engages in transactions involving the movement of goods, information, money, people, or services across national borders. Such an enterprise may conduct its business in any of several forms: through direct sales, foreign agents, distributorships, licensing, joint ventures, and wholly owned subsidiaries. A number of considerations determine which form of business organization would be best to use in conducting international transactions. These factors include financing, tax consequences, legal restrictions imposed by the host country, and the degree to which the multinational enterprise wishes to control the business.

Multinational enterprise business that engages in transactions involving the movement of goods, information, money, people, or services across national borders

Forms of MNE the choice of form depends upon a number of factors, including financing considerations, tax consequences, and degree of control

Direct Export Sales

Direct export sales seller contracts directly with the buyer in the other country

Under a **direct export sale**, the seller contracts directly with the buyer in the other country. This is the simplest and least involved multinational enterprise.

Foreign Agents

Foreign agents a local agent in the host country is used to provide limited involvement for an MNE

An agency relationship often is used by multinational enterprises seeking limited involvement in an international market. The principal firm will appoint a local agent, who may be empowered to enter into contracts in the agent's country on the principal's behalf or who may be authorized only to solicit and take orders. The agent generally does not take title to the merchandise.

Distributorships

Distributorship MNE sells to a foreign distributor who takes title to the merchandise

A commonly used form of multinational enterprise is the **distributorship**, in which a producer of goods appoints a foreign distributor. Unlike an agent, a distributor takes title to the merchandise it receives; in other words, the distributor, not the producer, bears many of the risks connected with commercial sales. The distributorship format, however, is especially susceptible to antitrust violations. Therefore, both the producer and the distributor must take special care to ensure that the arrangement does not violate the antitrust laws of their respective governments.

Licensing

Licensing MNE sells a foreign company the right to use technology or information

A multinational enterprise wishing to exploit an intellectual property right, such as a patent, trademark, trade secret, or an unpatented but innovative production technology, may choose to sell a foreign company the right to use such property, rather than enter the foreign market itself. The sale of such rights, called **licensing**, is one of the major means by which technology and information are transferred among nations. Normally, the foreign firm will pay royalties in exchange for the information, technology, or patent. Franchising is a form of licensing in which the owner of intellectual property grants permission to a foreign business under carefully specified conditions.

Joint Ventures

Joint ventures two independent businesses from different countries share profits, liabilities, and duties

In a **joint venture**, two or more independent businesses from different countries agree to coordinate their efforts to achieve a common result. The sharing of profits and liabilities, as well as the delegation of responsibilities, is fixed by contract. One advantage of the joint venture is that each company can be responsible for that which it does best. In order to promote local ownership of investments, several developing nations and regional groups have enacted legislation that prohibits foreign businesses from owning more than 49 percent of any business enterprise in those countries. In addition, each country may require that its citizens comprise the majority of an enterprise's management.

Wholly Owned Subsidiaries

Wholly owned subsidiary enables an MNE to retain control and authority over all phases of operation

By far, **wholly owned subsidiaries** require the most active participation by a parent firm. Nevertheless, creating a foreign wholly owned subsidiary corporation can offer a firm numerous advantages, most significantly the ability to retain authority and control over all phases of operation. This is especially attractive to businesses wishing to safeguard their technology.

BULOVA WATCH COMPANY, INC. v. K. HATTORI & CO. United States District Court, Eastern District of New York, 1981, 508 F.Supp. 1322

FACTS The plaintiff, Bulova Watch Company, was a New York corporation with its principal place of business in Flushing, New York. As both a manufacturer and seller of watches, Bulova claimed to have the largest direct sales marketing system in the watch business. The defendant, K. Hattori & Company (Hattori), incorporated under the laws of Japan with its principal office in Tokyo, was the parent company of the wholly owned subsidiary Seiko Corporation of America (SCA), a New York corporation. SCA, in turn, owned all the stock of three "sub-subsidiaries"—namely, Seiko Time Corp., Pulsar Time, and SPD Precision Inc.—all of which were incorporated under New York law. While the United States was Hattori's largest market, accounting for over one-half billion dollars in sales, Hattori distributed its products in over one hundred countries, using wholly owned subsidiaries in ten of those countries. For the remaining countries, Hattori employed independent distributors who conducted their own marketing and advertising activities and maintained their own repair centers. Desiring to expand the markets of its U.S.-based wholly owned subsidiaries, Hattori masterminded certain advertising campaigns and began recruiting and hiring several high-level direct sales marketing personnel from the Bulova company. Bulova filed this action against Hattori, alleging unfair competition, disparagement, and conspiracy to raid the plaintiff's marketing personnel. The defendant moved to dismiss the case for lack of jurisdiction, claiming that the Japanese parent company, Hattori, was an entity distinct and separate from its American subsidiaries and therefore lacked sufficient control over the subsidiaries to satisfy jurisdictional requirements.

DECISION Motion to dismiss denied.

OPINION Recognizing that the means by which a multinational corporation exercises control over its widely dispersed components may vary, the court emphasized that the degree and nature of control may depend upon such factors as the nationality of the corporate parent, the type and range of products being sold, and the age and stage of corporate evolution attained by those connected to the parent corporation. The choice among the various modes of entering a market (such as licensing arrangement, joint venture, minority-, majority-, or wholly owned subsidiary) has very significant implications for the control exercised by the parent. A wholly owned, marketing-based subsidiary is used where retaining unambiguous control of foreign operations is critical to the firm's strategy. Furthermore, enterprises with narrow product lines, such as Hattori with its exclusive manufacture of timepieces, tend to organize their operations on a highly integrated basis, linking production and marketing into tight strategic patterns. Again, the use of the wholly owned subsidiary form here reflects the desire for unambiguous control over sales and marketing to ensure uniform quality and promotion of the product sold. Finally, although Hattori's various subsidiaries may likely evolve into more autonomous units—characteristic of the later stages of multinational enterprise development—Hattori is currently a highly effective export manufacturer, more akin to the hub at the center of a wheel, with its various foreign subsidiaries and distributors as spokes. Accordingly, Hattori enjoys sufficient control over the activities of its wholly owned U.S. subsidiaries to support jurisdiction of U.S. courts in the action filed by the Bulova Watch Company.

INTERPRETATION Wholly owned subsidiaries are established by a parent company seeking to retain unambiguous control over the subsidiary's operation. Such control over a U.S. subsidiary may be sufficient to support jurisdiction by the U.S. courts over the parent.

CHAPTER SUMMARY

The International Environment	**International Law** includes law that deals with the conduct and relations of nation-states and international organizations as well as some of their relations with persons; such law is enforceable by the courts of a nation that has adopted the international law as domestic law **International Court of Justice** judicial branch of the United Nations having voluntary jurisdiction over nations **Regional Trade Communities** international organizations, conferences, and treaties focusing on business and trade regulations; the EU (the European Union) is the most prominent of these **International Treaties** agreements between or among independent nations, such as the General Agreement on Tariffs and Trade (GATT), now called the World Trade Organization

Jurisdiction Over Actions of Foreign Governments	**Sovereign Immunity** foreign country's freedom from a host country's laws **Act of State Doctrine** rule that a court should not question the validity of actions taken by a foreign government in its own country **Taking of Foreign Investment Property** ■ *Expropriation* governmental taking of foreign-owned property for a public purpose and with payment of just compensation ■ *Confiscation* governmental taking of foreign-owned property without payment (or for a highly inadequate payment) or for a nonpublic purpose

Transacting Business Abroad	**Flow of Trade** controlled by trade barriers on imports and exports ■ *Tariff* duty or tax imposed on goods moving into or out of a country ■ *Nontariff Barriers* includes quotas, bans, safety standards, and subsidies **Flow of Labor** controlled through passport, visa, and immigration regulations **Flow of Capital** International Monetary Fund facilitates the expansion and balanced growth of international trade, assists in eliminating foreign exchange restrictions, and smooths the international balance of payments **International Contracts** involve additional issues beyond those in domestic contracts, such as differences in language, legal systems, and currency ■ *CISG* United Nations Convention on Contracts for the International Sales of Goods governs all contracts for international sales of goods between parties located in different nations that have ratified the CISG ■ *Letter of Credit* bank's promise to pay the seller, provided certain conditions are met; used to manage the payment risks in international trade **Antitrust Laws** of the U.S. apply to unfair methods of competition that have a direct, substantial, and reasonably foreseeable effect on the domestic, import, or export commerce of the United States **Securities Regulation** foreign issuers who issue securities, or whose securities are sold in the secondary market in the United States, must register them unless an exemption is available; the antifraud provisions apply where there is either *conduct* or *effects* in the United States relating to a violation of the federal securities laws

	Protection of Intellectual Property the owner of an intellectual property right must comply with each country's requirements to obtain from that country whatever protection is available **Foreign Corrupt Practices Act** prohibits all U.S. companies from bribing foreign governmental or political officials
Forms of Multinational Enterprises	**Definition of Multinational Enterprise (MNE)** any business that engages in transactions involving the movement of goods, information, money, people, or services across national borders **Forms of MNE** the choice of form depends upon a number of factors including financing considerations, tax consequences, and degree of control ■ *Direct Export Sales* seller contracts directly with the buyer in the other country ■ *Foreign Agents* a local agent in the host country is used to provide limited involvement for an MNE ■ *Distributorship* MNE sells to a foreign distributor who takes title to the merchandise ■ *Licensing* MNE sells a foreign company the right to use technology or information ■ *Joint Ventures* two independent businesses from different countries share profits, liabilities, and duties ■ *Wholly Owned Subsidiary* enables an MNE to retain control and authority over all phases of operation

QUESTIONS

1. Discuss the purpose and major provisions of GATT (WTO).
2. Discuss and compare the doctrines of sovereign immunity and act of state.
3. Contrast expropriation and confiscation.
4. Briefly discuss the legal controls imposed on the flow of trade, labor, and capital across national borders.

5. List and briefly describe the various forms in which a multinational enterprise may conduct its business in a foreign country.

Internet Question. Find information about (a) the United Nations, (b) the International Court of Justice, (c) GATT (WTO), (d) NAFTA, and (e) the European Union.

PROBLEMS

1. Three banks that are wholly owned by the Republic of Costa Rica had issued promissory notes, payable in U.S. dollars in New York City. The notes are now in default due solely to actions of the Costa Rican government, which had suspended all payments of external debt because of escalating economic problems. Efforts by Costa Rica to curb foreign debt payment difficulties conflicted with U.S. policy for debt resolution procedures as conducted under the auspices of the International Monetary Fund. A syndicate of U.S. banks brought suit to recover on the promissory notes. The three Costa Rican banks assert the act of state doctrine as a defense. Decision?

2. Six U.S. manufacturers of broad-spectrum antibiotics derived a large percentage of their sales from overseas markets, including India, Iran, the Philippines, Spain, South Korea, West Germany, Colombia, and Kuwait. The manufacturers agreed to a common plan of marketing, whereby territories were divided and prices for products were set. The plan members also agreed not to grant foreign producers licenses to the manufacturing technology of any of their "big money" drugs. The above foreign countries bring suit for treble damages for violation of the U.S. antitrust laws. Decision?

3. After reading attractive brochures advertising a package tour of the Dominican Republic, a U.S. family decided to

purchase tickets for the family vacation plan. The tour was a product of four different business entities, two domestic (U.S.) and two foreign. Sheraton Hotels & Inns, World Corporation, was to provide food and lodging; Dominicana Airlines, wholly owned by the government of the Dominican Republic, which routinely flew into Miami International Airport and sold tickets within the United States, was to provide round-trip air transportation and "tourist cards" necessary for entry into the Dominican Republic; and two U.S. firms organized and sold the tour. Problems for the family began when their Dominicana flight landed in the Dominican Republic, and immigration officials denied them entry. Forced to leave, the family was shuttled first to Puerto Rico and then to Haiti, where they had to secure their own passage back to the United States at additional expense. The family brings suit against all four different business entities. Decision?

4. A privately owned business in a developing country determines that current computer technology could solve many of the problems faced by its country's private and public sectors. This business, however, lacks the capital resources necessary for research and development to acquire such computer technology, even if trained personnel were available. Furthermore, despite a sense of patriotism, the business concludes that its national government could not efficiently or effectively handle such a development project. What business forms are available to this business for acquiring sophisticated computer technology? What are the advantages and problems inherent in the various options?

5. King Faisal II of Iraq was killed on July 14, 1958, in the midst of a revolution in that country which led to the establishment of a republic subsequently recognized by the U.S. government. On July 19, 1958, the new republic issued a decree that all property of the former ruling dynasty, regardless of location, should be confiscated. Subsequently, the Republic of Iraq brought suit in the United States to obtain possession of money and stocks deposited in the deceased king's U.S. bank account in New York City. Decision?

6. A business entity incorporated under the laws of one of the EU member nations contracts with the government of a developing nation to form a joint venture for the mining and refining of a scarce raw material used by several developed nations in the manufacture of highly sensitive weapons systems. The contract calls for the EU-based corporation to invest money and technology that will be used to build permanent refinery plants that will eventually revert to the developing nation. The developing nation also reserves the right to set quotas on sales of this scarce resource and to choose the destination of exports. Due to political conflicts, the developing nation refuses to allow any exports of the scarce material to the United States. This causes a sharp price increase in exports to the United States by other suppliers. The United States asserts antitrust violations against the EU-based corporation for the effects produced within the United States. Decision?

7. A Panamanian corporation lends money to a Turkish enterprise, which issues a promissory note. The loan contract specifies that payment on the interest and principal shall be made to the Chemical Bank of New York City, where both parties maintain accounts. The loan contract contains no choice of law designation, but the Panamanian and Turkish companies have referred to the Chemical Bank in New York as their "legal address." As a result of a contractual performance dispute, the Turkish company suspends payments on the loan. The Panamanian corporation then brings suit in the United States to recover the balance of the payments due. What possible options for choice of law apply?

8. New England Petroleum Corporation (NEPCO), a New York corporation, was in the business of selling fuel oil in the United States. PETCO, a refinery incorporated in the Bahamas, was a wholly owned subsidiary of NEPCO. In 1968, PETCO entered into a long-term contract to purchase crude oil from Chevron Oil Trading (COT), which held 50 percent of an oil concession in Libya. In 1973, Libya nationalized COT and several other foreign-owned oil concessions, thereby forcing COT to terminate its contract with PETCO. In order to secure needed oil supplies, PETCO entered into a new contract with National Oil Corporation (NOC), which was wholly owned by the Libyan government. This contract was at a substantially higher price than the original contract with COT. The following month, Libya declared an oil embargo on exports to the United States, the Netherlands, and the Bahamas. Accordingly, NOC canceled its contracts with PETCO. After oil prices rose dramatically, NOC accepted bids for new contracts to replace the ones inactivated by the embargo. NEPCO brought suit against the Libyan government and NOC, alleging breach of contract. The district court dismissed the case for lack of jurisdiction, and the plaintiff appealed. Decision?

9. Nigeria, experiencing an economic boom due to exports of high-grade oil, embarked on an infrastructure development plan. Accordingly, Nigeria entered into at least 109 contracts with 68 suppliers for the purchase of cement at a price of almost $1 billion. Among the contracting suppliers were four American corporations, including Texas Trading & Milling Corporation. Nigeria misjudged the cement market (having anticipated only a 20 percent fulfillment rate) and was forced to repudiate most of the contracts. Texas Trading & Milling Corporation and three other American companies brought suit, alleging anticipatory breach of contract. Nigeria claimed immunity under the Foreign Sovereign Immunities Act of 1976. In three of the cases, the district court held jurisdiction to be present and proceeded to trial. In one of the cases, the district court dismissed for lack of jurisdiction. Decision?

PART XI

Property

979

CHAPTER 49

Introduction to Property and Property Insurance

In our democratic and free enterprise society, the importance of the concept of property is second only to that of the idea of liberty. Although many of our rules of property stem directly from English law, in the United States property occupies a unique status because of the protection expressly granted it by the United States Constitution and by most state constitutions as well. The Fifth Amendment to the federal Constitution provides that "No person shall be . . . deprived of life, liberty, or property, without due process of law; nor shall private property be taken for public use, without just compensation." The Fourteenth Amendment contains a similar requirement: "No State shall . . . deprive any person of life, liberty, or property, without due process of law." Under the police power, however, this protection afforded to property owners is subject to regulation for the public good. In the first part of this chapter, we will provide a general introduction to the law governing real and personal property. The second part of this chapter deals specifically with personal property; the last part covers property insurance.

INTRODUCTION TO PROPERTY AND PERSONAL PROPERTY

Property interest that is legally protected

Property is a legally protected interest or group of interests. It is valuable only because our law provides that certain consequences follow from the ownership of it. The right to use property, to sell it, and to control to whom it shall pass on the death of the owner are all included within the term property. Thus, a person who speaks of "owning property" may have one of two separate ideas in mind: (1) the *physical thing* itself, as when a homeowner says, "I just bought a piece of property in Oakland," meaning complete ownership of a physically identifiable parcel of land, or (2) a *right* or *interest* in a physical object (for example, with respect to land, a tenant under a lease has a property interest in the leased land, although he does not own the land).

KINDS OF PROPERTY

Property may be classified as (1) tangible or intangible and (2) real or personal (see Figure 49–1), but these classifications are not mutually exclusive.

Tangible property physical objects

Intangible property protected interest in a nonphysical thing

Tangible and Intangible

A forty-acre farm, a chair, and a household pet are tangible property. Each of these *physical* objects embodies the group of rights or interests known as "title" to or "ownership" of **tangible property**. **Intangible property**, in contrast, does *not* exist in a physical form. For example, a stock certificate, a promissory note,

FIGURE 49–1 Kinds of Property

	Personal	Real
Tangible	Goods	Land
		Buildings
		Fixtures
Intangible	Commercial paper	Leases
	Stock certificates	Easements
	Contract rights	Mortgages
	Copyrights	
	Patents	

and a deed granting Jones a right-of-way over Smith's land are intangible property. Each represents certain rights that defy reduction to physical possession but have a legal reality in that the courts will protect them.

The same item may be the object of both tangible and intangible property rights. Suppose Ann purchases a book published by Brown & Sons. On the first page is the statement "Copyright 1995 by Brown & Sons." Ann owns the volume she has purchased. She has the right to exclusive physical possession and use of that particular copy. It is a tangible piece of property of which she is the owner. Brown & Sons, however, has the exclusive right to publish copies of the book, a right granted the publisher by the copyright laws. The courts will protect this intangible property of Brown & Sons, as well as Ann's right to her particular volume.

Real and Personal

The most significant practical distinction between types of property is the classification into real and personal property. To define this distinction simply, land and all interests in it are **real property** (also called realty), and every other thing or interest identified as property is **personal property** (also called *chattel*). This easy description encompasses most property, with the exception of certain physical objects that are personal property under most circumstances but that may, because of their attachment to land or their use in connection with land, become a form of real property called fixtures.

Fixtures

As we noted above, a **fixture** is an article or piece of personal property that has been attached in such a manner to land or a building that an interest in the object arises under *real* property law. For example, building materials are clearly personal property; but when worked into a building as its construction progresses, such materials become real property, since buildings are a part of the land they occupy. Thus, clay in its natural state is, of course, real property; when made into bricks, it becomes personal property; and if the bricks are then built into the wall of a house, the "clay" once again becomes real property.

Although doing so may be difficult, determining whether various items are personal property or real property may be the only way to settle certain conflicting ownership claims. Unless otherwise provided by agreement, personal property remains the property of the person who placed it on the real estate. On the other hand, property that has been affixed so as to become a fixture (an actual part of the real estate) becomes the property of the real estate owner.

In determining whether personal property has become a fixture, the intention of the parties, as expressed in their agreement, will control the settlement

Real property land and interests in land

Personal property all property that is not real property

Fixture personal property so firmly attached to real property that an interest in it arises under real property law

of conflicting claims. In the absence of an agreement, the following factors are relevant in determining whether any particular item is a fixture:

1. the physical relationship of the item to the land or building;
2. the intention of the person who attached the item to the land or building;
3. the purpose the item serves in relation to the land or building and in relation to the person who brought it there; and
4. the interest of that person in the land or building at the time of the item's attachment.

Although physical attachment is significant, a more important test is whether the item can be removed without causing material injury to the land or building on the land. If it *cannot* be so removed, the item is generally held to have become part of the realty.

By comparison, the test of purpose or use applies only if the item (1) is affixed to the realty in some way but (2) can be removed without material injury to the realty. (See *Sears, Roebuck & Co. v. Seven Palms Motor Inn, Inc.*) In such a situation, if the use or purpose of the item is peculiar to a particular owner or occupant of the premises, the courts will tend to let him remove the item when he leaves. Accordingly, in the law of landlord and tenant, the tenant may remove **trade fixtures** (that is, items used in connection with a trade), provided that she can accomplish this without material injury to the realty. On the other hand, doors may be removed without injury to the structure; yet, because they are necessary to the ordinary use of the building and are not peculiar to the use of the occupant, they are considered to be fixtures and thus part of the real property.

SEARS ROEBUCK & CO. v. SEVEN PALMS MOTOR INN, INC. Supreme Court of Missouri, 1975, 530 S.W.2d 695

FACTS Sears had sold to and installed in Seven Palms Motor Inn a number of furnishings, including drapes and bedspreads, in connection with the construction of a motel on land Seven Palms owned. Sears did not receive payment in full for the materials and labor and brought suit to recover $8,357.49, with interest, and to establish a mechanic's lien on the motel and land for the unpaid portion of the furnishings. Seven Palms asserted that neither the drapes nor bedspreads were fixtures and that, thus, Sears could not obtain a mechanic's lien on them. Nevertheless, the trial court decided that Sears was entitled to recover $8,357.49, with interest, and that it did have a mechanic's lien. The Court of Appeals affirmed the money judgment but reversed the mechanic's lien, holding that the bedspreads were not lienable items and that their inclusion would void the entire lien.

DECISION Judgment for Sears, affirming the money judgment and granting a mechanic's lien for the draperies but not the bedspreads.

OPINION The characterization of an otherwise personal item as a fixture depends on (1) the item's annexation to the realty, (2) adaption of the item to the use to which the realty is devoted, and (3) the annexor's intent that the object become a permanent accession to the realty. Here, the draperies were hung from traverse rods that were attached to the walls. The purpose of hanging the drapes was to grant the motel's guest the control of light in his room or his privacy. The traverse rod, itself, did not accomplish this purpose. Rather, the rod and drapes, as a unit, were adapted to the proper use of the motel rooms. They were placed in the rooms with the intent that they would form a part of the special purpose for which the building was designed. Thus, the draperies are as much fixtures as the rods.

On the other hand, the bedspreads were not physically attached to the realty in any way. They cannot be "constructively annexed" merely because they match the drapes. The bedspreads were not essential to the use of a fixture (e.g., the drapes). In addition, it was not shown that they could not readily be used independently elsewhere. The bedspreads, therefore, are not fixtures.

INTERPRETATION A fixture is personal property so firmly attached to real property that an interest in it arises under real property law.

TRANSFER OF TITLE TO PERSONAL PROPERTY

The transfer of title to real property typically is a formal affair. In contrast, title to personal property may be acquired and transferred with relative ease and little formality. Such facility with regard to the transfer of personal property is essential within a society whose trade and industry are based principally upon transactions in personal property. In a free economy, stocks, bonds, merchandise, and intellectual property must be sold with minimal delay. It is only natural that the law will reflect these needs.

Accordingly, the law concerning personal property has been largely codified. The Uniform Commercial Code includes the law of sales of goods (Article 2), as well as the law governing the transfer and negotiation of commercial paper (Article 3) and of investment securities (Article 8). Nonetheless, the Code does not cover a number of issues (addressed in the remainder of this chapter) involving the ownership and transfer of title to personal property. In addition, personal property may be, and often is, acquired by producing the item, rather than by selling or transferring it.

By Sale

By definition, a **sale** of *tangible* personal property (goods) is a transfer of title to specified existing goods for a consideration known as the price. Title passes when the parties intend it to pass, and transfer of possession is not required for a transfer of title. For a discussion of transfer of title, see Chapter 21.

Sale transfer of property for consideration

Sales of *intangible* personal property also involve the transfer of title. Many of these sales also are governed by UCC provisions, while some, such as sales of copyrights and patents, are governed by specialized federal legislation.

By Gift

A **gift** is a transfer of property from one person to another without consideration. This lack of consideration is the basic distinction between a gift and a sale. Because a gift involves no consideration or compensation, it must be completed by delivery of the gift to be effective. A gratuitous promise to make a gift is not binding. In addition, there must be intent on the part of the maker (the **donor**) of the gift to make a present transfer, and there must be acceptance by the recipient (the **donee**) of the gift.

Gift transfer of property without consideration

Donor maker of a gift

Donee recipient of a gift

Delivery Delivery is essential to a valid gift. The term *delivery* has a very special meaning that includes, but is not limited to, the manual transfer of the item to the donee. A donor may effect an irrevocable delivery by, for example, turning an item over to a third person with instructions to give it to the donee. Frequently, an item, because of its size, location, or intangibility, is incapable of immediate manual delivery. In such cases, an irrevocable gift may be effected through the delivery of something that symbolizes dominion over the item. This is referred to as **constructive delivery**. For example, if Joanne declares that she gives an antique desk and all its contents to Barry and hands Barry the key to the desk, in many states a valid gift has been made.

Delivery includes both manual transfer of the item and constructive delivery

Constructive delivery delivery of something that symbolizes control over the item

---

ESTATE OF ROSS v. ROSS Supreme Court of Utah, 1981, 626 P.2d 489

FACTS David E. Ross, his two brothers, and their families operated and owned the entire stock of five businesses. Ross had three children: Rod, David II, and Betsy. David II and Betsy were not involved in the operation of the companies, but Rod began working for one of the firms, Equitable Life and Casualty Insurance

continued

Company, in 1972. Between 1974 and 1978, the elder Ross informed a number of persons of his desire to reward Rod for his work with Equitable Life by giving him stock in addition to the stock he would inherit. He subsequently executed several stock transfers to Rod, representing shares in various family businesses, which were reflected by appropriate entries on the corporate books. Certificates were issued in Rod's name and placed in an envelope identified with the name Rod Ross, but they were kept with the other family stock certificates in an office safe to which Rod did not have access. In all, one-fourth of the stock holdings of David E. Ross were transferred to Rod in this manner. This fact is consistent with the elder Ross's expressed intention that Rod should ultimately receive a total of one-half of the stock upon his father's death. David E. died in April 1978. His will divided the estate equally among the three children and made no reference to prior gifts of stock to Rod. David II and Betsy brought an action contesting the validity of the stock transfers. The district court held that the *inter vivos* gifts of the stock were valid, and David II and Betsy appealed.

DECISION Judgment for Rod Ross affirmed.

OPINION A donee must prove the existence of a gift by "clear and convincing" evidence. The three essential elements are a clear intention on the part of the donor to pass immediate ownership, an irrevocable delivery, and acceptance. David II and Betsy contend that the element of irrevocable delivery was not adequately established. They claim that their father should have physically conveyed the stock certificates to Rod and that the transfer of ownership on the corporate books did not effect a delivery. But "transferring the shares . . . upon the books of the company . . . stands in the place of a delivery" and "[t]he best evidence of [the donee's] ownership is the transfer on the books of the company." Other opinions support this position. David II and Betsy cite the Utah Uniform Commercial Code requirement that a donor must make actual manual delivery of stock certificates to his donee to effect a valid gift. Courts have generally concluded, however, that rigid application of this provision to stock gifts is inappropriate. Rather, the transfer of ownership on the corporate records, plus evidence of donative intent, may constitute a sufficient constructive delivery.

In this case, manual delivery of the certificates to Rod was not essential to a valid gift. The elder Ross clearly intended that Rod be made the owner of the stock. The change in ownership was recorded on the books, and new certificates were issued in Rod's name. While Rod's father may have maintained physical custody of the certificates, he did not exercise control or possessory rights over any of that stock.

INTERPRETATION The delivery necessary for an effective gift may be accomplished constructively.

Intent The law also provides clearly that the donor must intend to make a present gift of the property. Thus, if Jack leaves a packet of stocks and bonds with Joan, her acquiring good title to them depends on whether Jack intended to make a gift of them or simply intended to place them in Joan's hands for safekeeping. A voluntary, uncompensated delivery made with the intent to give the recipient title constitutes a gift when the donee accepts the delivery. If these conditions are met, the donor has no further claim to the property.

Gifts, therefore, cannot be conditional. There is, however, one major exception to this rule: an engagement gift given in anticipation of marriage. If the marriage does not take place, the donor usually can recover the gift unless the donor broke the engagement without justification. But the courts will not apply the exception when a marriage is called off due to the death of one of the engaged parties.

Acceptance The final requirement of a valid gift is acceptance by the donee. In most instances, of course, the donee will accept the gift gratefully. Accordingly, the law usually presumes that the donee has accepted. But certain circumstances may render acceptance objectionable, such as when a gift would impose a burden upon the donee. In such cases, the law will not require the recipient to accept an unwanted gift. For example, a donee may prudently reject a gift of an elephant or a wrecked car in need of extensive repairs.

Classification Gifts may be either *inter vivos* or *causa mortis*. An *inter vivos* gift is a gift made by a donor during her lifetime. A gift *causa mortis* is a gift made by a donor in contemplation of her imminent death. A gift *causa mortis* is a conditional gift, contingent upon (1) the donor's death as she anticipated, (2) the donor's not revoking the gift prior to her death, and (3) the donee's surviving the donor.

By Will or Descent

Title to personal property frequently is acquired by inheritance from a person who dies, either with or without a will. We will discuss this method of acquiring title in Chapter 54.

By Accession

Many of the practical problems surrounding the right to title to personal property stem from its principal characteristic—movability. The phrase "title by accession" denotes one general solution to the movability problem. **Accession**, in its strict sense, means the right of the owner of property to any increase in it, whether natural or man-made. For example, the owner of a cow acquires title by accession to any calves born to that cow.

Accession right of the owner of property to any increase in it

By Confusion

The basic problem of confusion is somewhat similar to problems involving title by accession. **Confusion** arises when identical goods belonging to different people become so *commingled* (mixed) that the owners cannot identify their own property. For example, Hereford cattle belonging to Benton become mixed with Hereford cattle belonging to Armstrong, and neither can specifically identify his herd as a result; or grain owned by Courts is combined inseparably with similar grain owned by Reichel. Confusion may result from accident, mistake, willful act, or agreement of the parties. If the goods can be apportioned, each owner who can prove his proportion of the whole is entitled to receive his share. If, however, the confusion results from the willful and wrongful act of one of the parties, he will lose his entire interest if he cannot prove his share. Frequently, problems arise not because the owners cannot prove their original interests but because there is not enough left to distribute a full share to each. In such cases, if the confusion was due to mistake, accident, or agreement, each owner will bear the loss in proportion to his share. If the confusion resulted from an intentional and unauthorized act, the wrongdoer will first bear any loss.

Confusion intermixing of goods belonging to two or more owners such that none of them can identify his property except as part of a mass of like goods

By Possession

Sometimes a person may acquire title to movable personal property by taking possession of it. If the property has been intentionally **abandoned** (intentionally disposed of), a *finder* is entitled to the property. Moreover, under the general rule, a finder is entitled to **lost** (unintentionally left) **property** against everyone except the true *owner*. Suppose Zenner, the owner of an apartment complex, leases a kitchenette apartment to Terrell. One night, Waters, Terrell's mother-in-law, is invited to sleep in the convertible bed in the living room. In the course of preparing the bed, Waters finds an emerald ring caught on the springs under the mattress. She turns the ring over to the police, but diligent inquiry fails to ascertain the true owner. As the finder, Waters will be entitled to the ring.

Possession a person may acquire title by taking possession of property

Abandoned property intentionally disposed of by the owner; the finder is entitled to the property

Lost property unintentionally left by the owner; the finder is generally entitled to the property

A different rule applies when the lost property is in the ground. Here, the owner of the land has a claim superior to that of the finder. For example, Josephs employs Kasarda to excavate a lateral sewer. Kasarda uncovers ancient Native American artifacts. Josephs, not Kasarda, has the superior claim.

A further exception to the rule gives the finder first claim against all but the true owner. If property is intentionally placed somewhere by the owner, who then unintentionally leaves it, it becomes **mislaid property**. Most courts hold that if property has been mislaid, not lost, then the owner of the premises, not the finder, has first claim if the true owner is not discovered. This doctrine is frequently invoked in cases involving items found in restaurants or on trains, buses, or airplanes.

Mislaid property intentionally placed by the owner but unintentionally left; the owner of the premises is generally entitled to the property

Many states, including Illinois, as shown in the following case, now have statutes that provide a means of vesting title to lost property in the finder where a prescribed search for the owner proves fruitless. Under these statutes, a finder generally may assert the right to possession against any party other than the true owner.

PASET v. OLD ORCHARD BANK AND TRUST CO. Appellate Court of Illinois, First District, 1978, 62 Ill.App.3d 534, 19 Dec. 389, 378 N.E.2d 1264

FACTS While in the examination booth in the safety deposit vault of Old Orchard Bank, Brenice Paset found $6,235 in currency in the seat of a chair that was partially under the table. She notified the bank officials and turned the money over to them. They told her that they would try to locate the owner but that, if they failed to locate the owner within one year, she, Brenice, could have the money. The bank then sent a notice to all of its safety deposit box customers asking if they had lost some property. Though it received no response within a year, the bank still refused to turn over the money, contending that it had to hold the money for the true owner. Brenice then brought this action to establish herself as the owner of the money by her compliance with the requirements of the applicable state statute. The bank argued that the money was mislaid and that therefore the statute was not applicable. The trial court adopted the bank's argument, and the plaintiff appealed.

DECISION Judgment reversed and remanded with directions to enter judgment for the finder, Brenice Paset.

OPINION Traditionally, found property could be classified as either mislaid, lost, or abandoned. Mislaid property is property that is intentionally put in a certain place and then later forgotten; at common law, a finder acquires rights to mislaid property. In contrast, property is deemed lost when it is unintentionally separated from the dominion of its owner; the finder of lost property is entitled to possession against everyone except the true owner. Finally, abandoned property is that which the owner, intending to relinquish all claim to the property, leaves free to be appropriated by any other person.

Here, the money was not mislaid as the bank claims, because if it was intentionally placed on the chair by someone who forgot where he left it, the bank's notice to the safety deposit box subscribers should have alerted the owner. Rather, the money was lost, and thus the statute is applicable. Since Brenice complied with the requirements of the statute and no claim to the money was made within the one-year period, she is entitled to recover it from the bank.

INTERPRETATION Property is considered lost when it is unintentionally left. The finder of lost property is entitled to possession against everyone except the true owner.

PROPERTY INSURANCE

Insurance covers a vast range of contracts, each of which distributes *risk* among a large number of members (the ***insureds***) through an insurance company (the ***insurer***). **Insurance** is a contractual undertaking by the insurer to pay a sum of money or give something of value to the insured or a beneficiary upon the happening of a contingency or fortuitous event that is beyond the control of the contracting parties.

Insurance contractual arrangement that distributes risk of loss among a large number of people

Insurance coverage of one form or another affects every commercial activity. Through insurance, a business can safeguard its tangible assets against almost any form of damage or destruction, whether resulting from natural causes or from the accidental or improper actions of people. Insurance may also protect a business from tort liability, including assertions involving strict liability, negligence, or the intentional acts of its representatives. A business may procure credit insurance to guard against losses from poor credit risks and fidelity bonds to secure it against losses incurred through employee defalcations. If a business hires a famous pianist, it may insure the latter's hands; if it decides to present an outdoor concert, it may insure against the possibility of rain. A business may purchase life insurance on its key executives to reimburse it for financial losses arising from their deaths, or it may purchase such life insurance payable to the families of executives as part of their compensation. An additional, increasingly important use of insurance is to carry out pension commitments arising from agreements with employees. Nonetheless, the remaining sections of this chapter will focus on the insurance of property.

The McCarran-Ferguson Act, enacted by Congress in 1945, left insurance regulation to the states. Statutes in each state regulate domestic insurance companies and establish standards for foreign (out-of-state) insurance companies wishing to do business within the state. Most state legislation relates to the incorporation, licensing, supervision, and liquidation of insurers and to the licensing and supervision of agents and brokers.

Because the insurance relationship arises from a contract of insurance between the insurer and the insured, the law of insurance is a branch of contract law. For this reason, the doctrines of offer and acceptance, consideration, and other rules applicable to contracts in general are equally applicable to insurance contracts. Beyond that, however, insurance law, like the law of sales, bailments, negotiable instruments, or other specialized types of contracts, contains numerous modifications of fundamental contract law, which we will examine in the following sections.

FIRE AND PROPERTY INSURANCE

Fire and property insurance protects the owner (or another person with an insurable interest, such as a secured creditor or mortgagee) of real or personal property against loss resulting from damage to or destruction of the property by fire and certain related perils. Most fire insurance policies also cover damage caused by lightning, explosion, earthquake, water, wind, rain, collision, and riot.

> **Fire (property) insurance** provides protection against loss due to fire or other related perils

Fire insurance policies are standardized in the United States, either by statute or by order of the state insurance departments, but their coverage is frequently enlarged through an "endorsement" or "rider" to include other perils or to benefit the insured in ways the provisions in the standard form do not. These policies normally are written for periods of one or three years.

For a general discussion of insurance fraud, see Consumer Insight.

Types of Fire

Fire insurance policies usually are held to cover damage from "hostile" fires, but they do not cover losses caused by "friendly" fires. A **friendly fire** is one contained in its intended location (for instance, a fire in a fireplace, furnace, or stove). A **hostile fire** is any other fire—all fires outside their intended or usual locales. Thus, a friendly fire becomes hostile if it escapes from its usual confines.

> **Friendly fire** fire contained where it is intended to be
>
> **Hostile fire** any fire outside its intended or usual place

CONSUMER INSIGHT

Insurance Fraud, Supposedly the Victimless Crime—Who Pays? Who Cares?

Here's a little quiz. Which of the following do you think are examples of insurance fraud? Who, if anyone, should be punished?

- A show horse, insured for several hundred thousand dollars, turns out to be a loser on the show-jumping circuit. The horse costs a lot to feed and train, and its selling price would be far less than the amount for which it's currently insured. The owner hires a hit man to electrocute the horse, a death that resembles death from colic. The owner collects the insurance and pays the hit man.

- A bus rear-ends another vehicle in heavy city traffic. Several people standing on the sidewalk see the accident and jump onto the bus. They then claim to have been injured in the accident and get cooperative doctors to diagnose accident-related injuries.

- Several apartment managers, having the power to pick contractors to repair fire- and accident-related damage to their buildings, charge their chosen contractors 10 percent kickbacks for being awarded repair jobs. The contractors, in turn, jack up their charges to cover the cost of the kickbacks.

- An insurance company calculates the pay of an independent insurance adjuster as a percentage of each claim she evaluates. The adjuster persuades policyholders to inflate their claims so that she—and they—can collect more money. She also bribes employees of the insurance company to approve the claims.

- Auto owners in states X and Y insure their cars in nearby state Z, which has lower auto insurance rates. The cars, of course, are kept at the owners' residences in states X and Y and are driven almost exclusively in those states.

- A beachside restaurant goes up in flames one night at the end of

summer. No one can prove arson, but the owner has been floundering in cash flow problems.

Now consider one more scenario:

Your apartment is broken into, and the thief takes your leather jacket, camera, two bikes, sound system, and about 200 tapes and CDs. You have renter's insurance. You're relieved that you can replace the clothes and music, but the bikes make you stop and think. You're a bike nut. You know your two bikes won't get you more than $750 from the insurance company, but with $1,800 you could buy the racing bike of your dreams. What do you tell the insurance company on your claim form?

Insurance fraud is a huge problem in the United States (and a growing problem in Europe). Fraudulent claims may total as much as $100 billion a year in the United States. Part of the problem is that people use a double standard to judge insurance fraud. We think it's outrageous when a ring of crooks sets small fires in shops (after bribing the owners), makes inflated claims, bribes insurance brokers and adjusters as part of the scheme, and pockets millions. But, ironically, many of us can't see the harm in padding our own claims just a little when we lose property by theft or fire. After all, some faraway, faceless company is the one who pays.

Wrong. We all pay. Ten cents of every dollar spent to purchase property and casualty insurance goes toward covering the cost of fraud. According to one U.S. insurer, fraud is second only to tax evasion in the list of largest economic crimes. Or, as

expressed slightly differently by a British insurance investigator, "Insurance fraud is second only to tax fraud as a socially acceptable crime."

Insurers in the United States have stepped up their fight against claims made for staged accidents, padded body shop repair bills, faked bodily injury reports, cars falsely reported stolen, and actual auto theft. Insurers are pressing the battle on two fronts: public opinion and criminal investigation. Of the two, insurance companies believe that public opinion will make the bigger difference—*if* attitudes really can be changed. In an interesting comparison, one insurer notes that drunk driving, considered a trivial offense just a decade ago, is now the target of laws that are increasingly tough *and* increasingly apt to be enforced, as a result of the public campaign waged by Mothers Against Drunk Drivers and similar grassroots groups.

Behavioral tip-offs—a person's eagerness for a quick settlement, use of a post office box or hotel as an address, or insistence on pursuing a claim in person rather than by mail or over the phone—lead insurers to investigate claims for fraud. They likewise become suspicious when a surprisingly large number of people submit medical bills from the same doctor or clinic.

However, insurance companies would very much like to win the hearts and minds of the public in fighting insurance fraud—first, so that ordinary law-abiding citizens resist the temptation to cheat (one poll reports that 23 percent of Americans think it's OK to pad a claim) and, second, to encourage the honest majority to report those who do cheat. For example, one insurer advises its policyholders to do the following to fight fraud:

- If you're in an accident, report it to the police. If you witness an accident, report it. Your report

continued

can help to determine whether or not a claim is legitimate.

- When you've been in an accident, call your insurer immediately. Obtain a police report and get the other driver's name, address, and license number and his car's registration number. Write down what happened while your memory is fresh.
- Call the police and your insurance company if someone tells you about a doctor or lawyer who will help you to falsify or inflate a claim. Do the same if a body shop says it can inflate its estimate for you.

- Pay attention when you're car shopping: don't buy a car that you suspect may be stolen. You should look at the vehicle identification number to see whether it appears to have been changed. Other red flags: a new paint job, remade keys, and a lack of title or registration.

- Make yourself heard with your state legislators. Ask them to support antifraud legislation and regulations.
- If you suspect fraud, report it. One organization you can call is the National Insurance Crime Bureau. Its toll-free hotline is 1-800-835-6422.

Sources: *The New York Times*, 14 March 1994, B3; 23 September 1993, B4; and 5 September 1993, A1; "Taking Fraud Seriously," *Amica Annual Report 1992*, 6–9; and *The Wall Street Journal*, 28 December 1993, B1; 18 January 1993; and 1 April 1992.

A standard insurance policy therefore will not cover heat or soot damage to a fireplace resulting from its continual use or damage done to personal property accidentally thrown into a stove. Damages caused by smoke, soot, water, and heat from a hostile fire are covered by the standard fire insurance policy, whereas such damages caused by a friendly fire generally are not. Moreover, most policies do not cover recovery for business interruption, unless they contain endorsements specifically covering such loss.

Co-insurance Clauses

An arrangement common in property insurance, **co-insurance** is a means of sharing the risk between insurer and insured. For example, under the typical 80 percent co-insurance clause, the insured may recover the full amount of loss, not to exceed the face amount of the policy, provided the policy is for an amount not less than 80 percent of the property's insurable value. If the policy is for less than 80 percent, the insured recovers that proportion of the loss that the amount of the policy bears, up to 80 percent of the insurable value. The formula for recovery is as follows:

Co-insurance insurance in which a person insures property for less than its full or stated value and agrees to share the risk of loss

$$\text{Recovery} = \frac{\text{Face Value of Policy}}{\text{Fair Market Value of Property} \times \text{Co-insurance \%}} \times \text{Loss}$$

Thus, if the co-insurance percentage is 80 percent, the value of the property is $100,000, and the policy is for $80,000 or more, the insured is fully protected against loss not to exceed the policy amount. If the policy amount is less than 80 percent of the property value, however, the insured receives only the proportion of the loss amount as determined in the formula above. Thus, in the above example, if the fire policy was for $60,000 and the property was 50 percent destroyed, the loss would be $50,000, of which the insurer would pay $37,500, which is $60,000/($100,000 × 80%) of $50,000. On a total loss, the recovery could not, of course, exceed the face amount of the policy. Some states do not favor co-insurance clauses and strictly construe the applicable statute against their validity. In addition, property insurance is not held to be co-insurance unless the policy specifically so provides.

Other Insurance Clauses

Other insurance clauses if multiple insurers are involved, liability is distributed *pro rata*

Recovery under property insurance policies typically is also limited by **other insurance clauses**, which generally require that liability be distributed *pro rata* among the various insurers. For example, Alexander insures his $120,000 building with Hamilton Insurance Co. for $60,000 and Jefferson Insurance Co. for $90,000. Alexander's building is partially destroyed by fire, causing Alexander $20,000 in damages. Alexander will collect two-fifths ($60,000/$150,000) of his damages from Hamilton ($8,000) and three-fifths ($90,000/$150,000) from Jefferson ($12,000). See *Alberici v. Safeguard Mutual Insurance Company* on page 991.

Types of Policies

Valued policy covers full value of policy as agreed upon by the parties at the time the policy is issued

Open policy covers fair market value of property calculated immediately prior to the loss

Property insurance may be either a **valued policy** or an open policy. A valued policy is one providing for the full value of the property, upon which value the insured and the insurer specifically agree at the time the policy is issued. Should total loss occur, the insurer must pay this amount, not the actual or fair market value of the property. By comparison, no agreement in an **open policy** specifies the property's value; instead, the insurer pays the fair market value of the property calculated immediately prior to its loss. Thus, if Latrisha insures her building for $650,000 and at the time of its loss the property is valued at $600,000, under an open policy Latrisha would recover $600,000, while under a valued policy she would recover $650,000. If she insured the building for $700,000, and it was valued at that amount just prior to being blown apart by a tornado, under both types of policies Latrisha would recover $700,000. Insurance of property under a marine policy (insurance covering marine vessels and cargo) is generally considered to be valued, whereas non-marine property insurance is presumed to be unvalued or open.

NATURE OF INSURANCE CONTRACTS

Nature of insurance contracts basic principles of contract law apply

The basic principles of *contract* law apply to insurance policies. Furthermore, because insurance companies engage in a large volume of business over wide areas, they tend to standardize their policies. In some states, standardization is required by statute. This usually means that the insured must accept a given policy or do without the desired insurance.

Offer and Acceptance

No matter how many stories tell of insurance agents aggressively soliciting would-be insureds to take out policies, the applicant usually makes the offer, and the contract is created when the insurance company accepts that offer. The company may condition its acceptance—upon payment of the premium, for instance. It also may write a policy that differs from the application, thereby making a counteroffer that the applicant may or may not choose to accept.

Binder making an agreement legally binding until the completion of the formal contract

In fire and casualty insurance, agents often have authority to make the insurance effective immediately, when needed, by means of a **binder**. Should a loss occur before the company actually issues a policy, the binder will be effective on the same terms and conditions the policy would have had if it had been issued.

In general, insurance contracts have not been held to be subject to the statute of frauds; thus, courts have held oral contracts for insurance to be enforceable. As a practical matter, however, oral contracts for insurance are very infrequent.

Insurable Interest

The concept of insurable interest has been developed over many years, primarily to eliminate gambling and to lessen the moral hazard. If a person could obtain an enforceable fire insurance policy on property that he did not own or in which he had no interest, he would be in a position to profit unfairly by the destruction of such property. An **insurable interest** is a relationship a person has with respect to certain property such that the happening of a possible, specific, damage-causing contingency would result in direct loss or injury to her. The purpose of insurance is protection against the risk of loss that would result from such a happening, not the realization of gain or profit.

Whether sole or concurrent, ownership obviously creates an insurable interest in property. Moreover, a right deriving from a contract concerning the property also gives rise to an insurable interest. For instance, shareholders in a closely held corporation have been held to have an insurable interest in the corporation's property to the extent of their interest. Likewise, lessees of property have insurable interests, as do holders of security interests, such as mortgagees or sellers with a purchase money security interest. The insurable interest must exist at the time the property *loss* occurs, although some courts speak in terms of having the insurable interest at the time of insuring *and* at the time of loss. Property insurance policies are freely assignable after, but not before, a loss occurs.

Insurable interest a financial interest in property that justifies insuring such property

ALBERICI v. SAFEGUARD MUTUAL INSURANCE COMPANY Superior Court of Pennsylvania, 1995, 444 Pa.Super. 351, 664 A.2d 110

FACTS In May 1977, Joseph Alberici entered an agreement to purchase a theater for $210,000. The named purchaser was "Joseph Alberici or his nominee" and the down payment of $21,000 was paid from a joint savings account owned by Alberici and his wife, Theresa. Joseph then purchased six fire insurance policies. Four of the policies named both Joseph and Theresa as insured parties, but the other two named only Joseph. Prior to closing, the property was seriously damaged by fire. The Albericis closed on the property by mortgaging other real estate that they jointly owned. Subsequently, Joseph came under suspicion for arson and was convicted of mail fraud for filing insurance claims related to the fire. When the insurers refused to pay the Alberici's claim, the couple sued. Because of Joseph's mail fraud conviction, the trial court granted summary judgment to the insurers. On appeal, the Superior Court held that if Theresa could show an insurable interest, she could recover under the policies. On remand, the trial court found that Theresa did have an insurable interest and could recover. In accordance with the insurance contracts, the court prorated Theresa's recovery by apportioning liability among all six insurers and allowed her to recover under the policies in which she was named as an insured. The insurers and Theresa both appeal.

DECISION Judgment affirmed.

OPINION On appeal, the four insurers challenge whether Theresa Alberici had an insurable interest in the theater property. Any person who derives benefit or advantage from the continued existence of property or who will suffer pecuniary loss from its destruction has an insurable interest in the property. Furthermore, a purchaser's insurable interest is in the entire property, not merely the extent to which he or she has made payments toward the purchase price. In this case, although the agreement of sale did not specifically identify Theresa as a purchaser, it did designate "Joseph Alberici or his nominee." Also, both Joseph and Theresa had approached the purchase as if they were purchasing the property jointly. They went together to inspect the property and the monies for the purchase came from liquidation of assets held jointly by Joseph and Theresa. Since Theresa was a purchaser, she had an insurable interest in the property amounting to the entire value of the property.

The second issue on appeal was whether the court correctly apportioned liability among the carriers who insured the interest of Joseph and Theresa Alberici. By state law, all policies for fire insurance include a

continued

proration clause that allows the liability of one insurer to be measured by the proportion that its policy bears to the total insurance on the property. In order for proration to apply, there must be two or more policies covering the same risk, the same subject matter, and the same interest. Theresa Alberici contends that the trial court erred by apportioning liability among all six insurers. She argues that the policies issued to Joseph Alberici individually did not apply to the same interest as those in which they are named as co-insureds. Two or more policies cover the same interest where there is a potential for the insured to experience a double recovery. The trial court found that the insurable interest that

Theresa acquired was that of purchaser. Joseph Alberici's interest was also that of purchaser. If both Joseph and Theresa were paid the full purchase price, there clearly would be a double recovery. There could not be full recovery for both. Under these circumstances, it seems clear that all policies insured a single interest, that of the purchaser. Therefore, the trial court's apportionment was correct.

INTERPRETATION The plaintiff had an insurable interest in the property, but under the other insurance clause the liability must be distributed *pro rata* among the insurers.

Premiums

Premiums amount to be paid for an insurance policy

Premiums are the consideration paid for an insurance policy. Property insurance policies are written only for periods lasting a few years at most. Long, continued liability on this type of policy is the exception rather than the rule. The rates that may be charged for fire and various kinds of casualty insurance are regulated by state law. The regulatory authorities are under a duty to require that the companies' rates be reasonable, not unfairly discriminatory, and neither excessively high nor inordinately low.

Defenses of the Insurer

In addition to the ordinary defenses to a contract, the insurer may assert the closely related defenses of misrepresentation, breach of warranty, and concealment.

Misrepresentation A representation is a statement made by or on behalf of an applicant for insurance to induce an insurer to enter into a contract. The representation is not a part of the insurance contract, but if the application containing the representation is incorporated by reference into the contract, the representation becomes a warranty. For a **misrepresentation** to have legal consequences, it must be material, the insurer must have relied on it as an inducement to enter into the contract, and it must either have been substantially false when the insured made it or have become so, to the insured's knowledge, before the contract was created. The principal remedy of the insurer on discovery of the material misrepresentation is rescission of the contract. To rescind the contract, the insurer must tender to the insured all premiums that have been paid, unless the misrepresentation was fraudulent. To be effective, rescission must be made as soon as possible after discovery of the misrepresentation.

Misrepresentation false representation of a material fact made by the insured that is justifiably relied upon by the insurer

Breach of warranty the failure of a required condition; generally an insurer may avoid liability for a breach of warranty only if the breach is material

Breach of Warranty Warranties are of great importance in insurance contracts because they operate as conditions that *must* exist before the contract is effective or before the insurer's promise to pay is enforceable. Failure of the condition to exist or to occur relieves the insurer from any obligation to perform its promise. Broadly speaking, a condition is simply an event whose happening or failure to happen either precedes the existence of a legal relationship or terminates one previously existing. Conditions are either precedent or subsequent. For example, payment of the premium is a condition precedent to the enforcement of the insurer's promise, as is the happening of the insured event. A condition subsequent is an operative event the happening of which terminates an existing, matured legal obligation. A provision in a policy to the effect that the insured shall not be liable unless suit is brought within twelve months from the date on which the loss occurs is an example of a condition subsequent.

To be a warranty, the provision must be expressly included in the insurance contract or clearly incorporated by reference. Usually, the policy statements that the insurer considers to be express warranties are characterized by words such as *warrant, on condition that, provided that,* or words of similar import. Other statements important to the risk assumed, such as the address of a building in a case where personal property at a particular location is insured against fire, are sometimes held to be informal warranties.

Generally, it is becoming more difficult for an insurer to avoid liability on a policy when an insured breaches a warranty. For example, a number of states now require a breach to be material before the insurer may avoid liability.

Concealment **Concealment** is the failure of an applicant for insurance to disclose material facts that the insurer does not know. The nondisclosure normally must be fraudulent as well as material to invalidate the policy; the applicant must have had reason to believe the fact was material; and its disclosure must have affected the insurer's acceptance of the risk.

Waiver and Estoppel

In certain instances, an insurer who normally would be entitled to deny liability under a policy because of a misrepresentation, breach of condition, or concealment is "estopped" from taking advantage of the defense or else is said to have "waived" the right to rely on it because of other facts.

The terms "waiver" and "estoppel" are used interchangeably, although by definition they are not synonymous. As generally defined, **waiver** is the intentional relinquishment of a known right; and **estoppel** means that a person is prevented by his own conduct from asserting a position inconsistent with such conduct, on which another person has justifiably relied.

Because a corporation such as an insurance company can act only through agents, situations involving waiver invariably are based on an agent's conduct. The higher the agent's position in the company's organization, the more likely his conduct is to bind the company, since an agent acting within the scope of his authority binds his principal. Insureds have the right to rely on representations made by the insurer's employees, and where such representations reasonably induce or cause the insured to change her position or prevent her from causing a condition to occur, the insurer may not assert as a defense the condition's failure to occur, whether the term applied to her situation be waiver or estoppel. Companies have tried with little success to limit the authority of local selling agents to bind the company through waiver or estoppel.

Termination

Most insurance contracts are performed according to their terms, and due *performance* terminates the insurer's obligation. Normally, the insurer pays the principal sum due and the contract is thereby performed and discharged.

Cancellation by mutual consent is another way of terminating an insurance contract. Cancellation by the insurer alone means that the insurer remains liable, according to the terms of the policy, until such time as the cancellation is effective. To cancel a policy, the insurer must tender the unearned portion of the premium to the insured.

Concealment fraudulent failure of an applicant for insurance to disclose material facts that the insurer does not know; allows the insurer to rescind the contract

Waiver an insurer intentionally relinquishes the right to deny liability

Estoppel an insurer is prevented by its own conduct from asserting a defense

Termination an insurance contract may be terminated by due performance or cancellation

CHAPTER SUMMARY

Introduction to Property and Personal Property

Kinds of Property	**Definition** interest, or group of interests, that is legally protected
	Tangible Property physical objects
	Intangible Property property that does not exist in a physical form
	Real Property land and interests in land
	Personal Property all property that is not real property
	Fixture personal property so firmly attached to real property that an interest in it arises under real property law

Transfer of Title to Personal Property	**Sale** transfer of property for consideration (price)
	Gift transfer of property without consideration
	■ *Delivery* includes both manual transfer of the item and constructive delivery (delivery of something that symbolizes control over the item)
	■ *Intent*
	■ *Acceptance*
	■ *Classification*
	Will right to property acquired upon death of the owner
	Accession right of a property owner to any increase in such property
	Confusion intermixing of goods belonging to two or more owners such that they can identify their individual property only as part of a mass of like goods
	■ If due to mistake, accident, or agreement, loss shared proportionately
	■ If caused by an intentional or unauthorized act, wrongdoer bears loss
	Possession a person may acquire title by taking possession of property
	■ *Abandoned Property* intentionally disposed of by the owner; the finder is entitled to the property
	■ *Lost Property* unintentionally left by the owner; the finder is generally entitled to the property
	■ *Mislaid Property* intentionally placed by the owner but unintentionally left; the owner of the premises is generally entitled to the property

Property Insurance

Fire and Property Insurance	**General Definition of Insurance** contractual arrangement that distributes risk of loss among a large number of members (the insureds) through an insurance company (the insurer)
	Coverage of fire and property insurance provides protection against loss due to fire or related perils
	Types of Fire
	■ *Friendly Fire* fire contained in its intended location
	■ *Hostile Fire* any fire outside its intended or usual location
	Co-insurance insurance in which a person insures property for less than its full or stated value and agrees to share the risk of loss

Other Insurance Clauses if multiple insurers are involved, liability is distributed *pro rata*

Types of Policies
- *Valued Policy* covers full value of property as agreed upon by the parties at the time the policy is issued
- *Open Policy* covers fair market value of property as calculated immediately prior to the loss

Nature of Insurance Contracts

General Contract Law basic principles of contract law apply

Insurable Interest a financial interest or close ownership interest in someone's property that justifies insuring the property and exists at the time the property loss occurs

Premiums amount to be paid for an insurance policy

Defenses of the Insurer
- *Misrepresentation* false representation of a material fact made by the insured that is justifiably relied upon by the insurer; enables the insurer to rescind the contract within a specified time
- *Breach of Warranty* the failure of a required condition; generally an insurer may avoid liability for a breach of warranty only if the breach is material
- *Concealment* fraudulent failure of an applicant for insurance to disclose material facts that the insurer does not know; allows the insurer to rescind the contract
- *Waiver* an insurer intentionally relinquishes the right to deny liability
- *Estoppel* an insurer is prevented by its own conduct from asserting a defense

Termination an insurance contract may be terminated by due performance or cancellation

QUESTIONS

1. Distinguish between (a) tangible and intangible property and (b) real and personal property.
2. Define and give three examples of a fixture.
3. Identify and discuss the three elements of a valid gift.
4. With respect to property insurance contracts, explain (a) the co-insurance clause and (b) an insurable interest.
5. Compare the defenses of misrepresentation, concealment, breach of warranty, and estoppel.

Internet Question. Find information about (a) business insurance, (b) homeowner's insurance, and (c) the ten largest home insurers and their market shares.

PROBLEMS

1. In January, Roger Burke loaned his favorite nephew, Jimmy White, his valuable Picasso painting. Knowing that Jimmy would celebrate his twenty-first birthday on May 15, Burke sent a letter to Jimmy on April 14 stating:

Dear Jimmy,

Tomorrow I leave on my annual trip to Europe, and I want to make you a fitting birthday gift, which I do by sending you my enclosed promissory note. Also I want you to keep the Picasso that I loaned you last January, and you may now consider it yours. Happy birthday!

Affectionately,
/s/ Uncle Roger

The negotiable promissory note for $5,000 sent with the letter was signed by Roger Burke, payable to Jimmy White or bearer, and dated May 15. On May 21,

Burke was killed in an automobile accident while motoring in France.

First Bank was appointed administrator of Burke's estate. Jimmy presented the note to the administrator and demanded payment, which was refused. Jimmy brought an action against First Bank as administrator, seeking recovery on the note. The administrator in turn brought an action against Jimmy, seeking the return of the Picasso.

(a) What decision in the action on the note?

(b) What decision in the action to recover the painting?

2. Several years ago, Pierce purchased a tract of land on which stood an old, vacant house. Recently, Pierce employed Fried, a carpenter, to repair and remodel the house. While Fried was tearing out a partition to enlarge one of the rooms, he found a metal box hidden in the wall. After breaking open the box and discovering that it contained $2,000 in gold and silver coins and old-style bills, Fried took the box and its contents to Pierce and told her where he had found it. When Fried handed the box and the money over to Pierce, he said, "If you do not find the owner, I claim the money." Pierce placed the money in an envelope and deposited it in her safe deposit box, where it presently remains. No one has ever claimed the money, but Pierce refuses to give it to Fried.

Fried brings an action against Pierce to recover the money. Decision?

3. Gable, the owner of a lumber company, was cutting trees over the boundary line between his property and property owned by Lane. Although he realized he had crossed onto Lane's property, Gable continued to cut trees of the same kind as those he had cut on his own land. While on Lane's property, he found a diamond ring on the ground, which he took home. All of the timber Gable cut that day was commingled.

What are Lane's rights, if any, (a) in the timber and (b) in the ring?

4. Decide each of the following problems.

(a) A chimney sweep found a jewel and took it to a goldsmith, whose apprentice removed the stone and refused to return it. The chimney sweep sues the goldsmith.

(b) One of several boys walking along a railroad track found an old stocking. All started playing with it until it burst in the hands of its discoverer, revealing several hundred dollars. The original discoverer claims all of the money; the other boys claim it should be divided equally.

(c) A traveling salesman leaving a store notices a parcel of bank notes on the floor. He picks them up and gives them to the owner of the store to keep for the true owner. After three years, they have not been reclaimed, and the salesman sues the storekeeper.

(d) Frank is hired to clean the swimming pool at the country club. He finds a diamond ring on the bottom of the pool. The true owner cannot be found. The country club sues Frank for possession of the ring.

(e) A customer found a pocketbook lying on a barber's table. He gave it to the barber to hold for the true owner, who failed to appear. The customer sues the barber.

5. Jones had 50 crates of oranges equally divided between grades A, B, and C, grade A being the highest quality and C being the lowest. Smith had 1,000 crates of oranges, about 90 percent of which were grade A, but some of which were grades B and C, the exact percentage of each being unknown. Smith willfully mixed Jones's crates with his own so that it was impossible to identify any particular crate. Jones seized the whole lot. Smith demanded 900 crates of grade A and 50 crates each of grades B and C. Jones refused to give them up unless Smith could identify particular crates. This Smith could not do. Smith brought an action against Jones to recover what he demanded or its value. Judgment for whom, and why?

6. Barnes, the owner and operator of Blackacre, decided to cease farming operations and liquidate his holdings. Barnes sold fifty head of yearling Merino sheep to Billing and then sold Blackacre to Clifton. He executed and delivered to Billing a bill of sale for the sheep and was paid for them. It was understood that Billing would send a truck for the sheep within a few days. At the same time, Barnes executed a warranty deed conveying Blackacre to Clifton. Clifton took possession of the farm and brought along one hundred head of his yearling Merino sheep and turned them into the pasture, not knowing the sheep Barnes sold Billing were still in the pasture. After the sheep were mixed, it was impossible to identify the fifty head belonging to Billing. After proper demand, Billings sued Clifton to recover the fifty head of sheep. Decision?

7. Susan permitted Kevin to take her very old grandfather clock on the basis of Kevin's representations that he was skilled at repairing such clocks and restoring them to their original condition and could do the job for $60. The clock had been badly damaged for years. Kevin immediately sold the clock to Fixit Shop for $30. Fixit Shop was in the business of repairing a large variety of items and also sold used articles. Three months later, Susan was in the Fixit Shop and clearly identified a grandfather clock Fixit Shop had for sale as the one she had given Kevin to repair. Fixit Shop had replaced more than half of the moving parts by having exact duplicates custom-made; the clock's exterior had been restored by a skilled cabinetmaker; and the clock's face had been replaced by a duplicate. All materials belonged to Fixit Shop, and the work

was accomplished by its employees. Fixit Shop asserts it bought the clock in the normal course of business from Kevin, who represented that it belonged to him. The fair market value of the clock in its damaged condition was $30, and the value of repairs made is $220.

Susan sued Fixit Shop for return of the clock. Fixit Shop defended that it now had title to the clock and, in the alternative, that Susan must pay the value of the repairs if she is entitled to regain possession. Decision?

8. Hyer rented a vacant lot from Bateman for a filling station under an oral agreement and placed on it a lightly constructed building bolted to a concrete slab and storage tanks laid on the ground in a shallow excavation. Later, Hyer prepared a lease providing that he might remove the equipment at the termination of the lease. This lease was not executed, having been rejected by Bateman because of a renewal clause it contained; but several years later another lease was prepared, which both Hyer and Bateman did sign. This lease did not mention removal of the equipment. At the termination of this lease, Hyer removed the equipment, and Bateman brought an action to recover possession of the equipment. What judgment?

9. Elvers sold a parcel of real estate, describing it by its legal description and making no mention of any improvements or fixtures on it. The land had upon it a residence, a barn, a rail fence, a stack of hay, some growing corn, and a windmill. The residence had a mirror built into the west wall of the living room and a heating system consisting of a furnace, steam pipes, and coils. In the house were chairs, beds, tables, and other furniture. On the house was a lightning rod. In the basement were screens for the windows. Which of these things passed by the deed and which did not?

10. John Swan rented a safety deposit box at the Tenth Citizens Bank of Emanon, State of X. On December 17, 1993, Swan went to the bank with stock certificates to place in the safety deposit box. After he was admitted to the vault and had placed the stock certificates in the box, Swan found lying on the floor of the vault a $5,000 negotiable bearer bond issued by the State of Wisconsin with coupons attached, due June 30, 1999. Swan picked up the bond and, observing that it did not carry the name of the owner, left the vault and went to the office of the president of the bank. He told the president what had occurred and delivered the bond to the president only after obtaining his promise that, should the owner not call for the bond or become known to the bank by June 30, 1994, the bank would redeliver the bond to Swan. On July 1, 1994, Swan learned that the owner of the bond had not called for it; nor was his identity known to the bank. Swan then asked that the bond be returned to him. The bank

refused, stating that it would continue to hold the bond until the owner claimed it. Swan brings an action against the bank to recover possession of the bond. Decision?

11. Lile, an insurance broker who handled all insurance for Tempo Co., purchased a fire policy from Insurance Company insuring Tempo Co.'s factory against fire in the amount of $150,000. Before the policy was delivered to Tempo and while it was still in Lile's hands, Tempo advised Lile to cancel the policy. Prior to cancellation, however, Tempo suffered a loss. Tempo now makes a claim against Insurance Company on the policy. The premium had been billed to Lile but was unpaid at the time of loss. In an action by Tempo Co. against Insurance Company, what judgment?

12. On July 15, Adler purchased in Chicago a Buick sedan, intending to drive it that day to St. Louis, Missouri. He telephoned a friend, Maruchek, who was in the insurance business, and told him that he wanted liability insurance on the automobile, limited in amount to $50,000 for injuries to one person and to $100,000 for any one accident. Maruchek took the order and told Adler over the telephone that he was covered and that his policy would be written by the Young Insurance Company. Later that same day and before Maruchek had informed the Young Insurance Company of Adler's application, Adler negligently operated the automobile and seriously injured Brown, who brings suit against Adler. Is Adler covered by liability insurance?

13. Graham owns a building having a fair market value of $120,000. She takes out a fire insurance policy from the Bentley Insurance Company for $72,000; the policy contains an 80 percent co-insurance clause. The building is damaged by fire to the extent of $48,000. How much insurance is Graham entitled to collect?

14. Scarola purchased an automobile for value and without knowledge that it was stolen. After he insured the car with Insurance Company of North America (INA), the car was stolen once again. When INA refused to reimburse Scarola for the loss, contending that he did not have an insurable interest in the car, Scarola brought an action. Decision?

15. In 1976, Butler purchased a 1967 Austin-Healy for $3,500. He received an Arizona certificate of title and was unaware that the vehicle had been stolen previously. Two years later, Tucson police seized the automobile and returned it to its lawful owner. Butler was insured against loss of the vehicle by Farmers Insurance Company of Arizona. When Farmers Insurance denied his claim for benefits, Butler brought suit. Farmers Insurance based its refusal to reimburse Butler upon lack of insurable interest. Both parties moved for summary judgment. Decision?

Intellectual Property

Intellectual property is an economically significant type of intangible personal property that includes trade secrets, trade symbols, copyrights, and patents. These interests are protected from **infringement**, or unauthorized use, by others. Such protection is essential to the conduct of business. For example, a company would be far less willing to invest considerable resources in research and development if resulting discoveries, inventions, and processes were not protected by patents and by regulations safeguarding trade secrets. Similarly, a company would not be secure in devoting time and money to marketing its products and services without laws to defend its trade symbols and trade names. Moreover, without copyright protection, the publishing, entertainment, and computer software industries would be vulnerable to piracy, both by competitors and by the general public. In this chapter, we will discuss the law protecting (1) trade secrets; (2) trade symbols, including trademarks, service marks, certification marks, collective marks, and trade names; (3) copyrights; and (4) patents.

TRADE SECRETS

Every business has secret information. Such information may include customer lists or contracts with suppliers and customers; it may also consist of secret formulas, processes, and production methods that are vital to the successful operation of the business. A business may disclose a trade secret in confidence to an employee with the understanding that the employee will not, in turn, reveal the information. To the extent the owner of the information obtains a patent on it, it is no longer a trade secret but is protected by patent law. Some businesses, however, choose not to obtain a patent because it provides protection for only a limited time, whereas state trade secret law protects a trade secret as long as it is kept secret.

Definition

Basically, a **trade secret** is commercially valuable information that is guarded from disclosure and is not general knowledge. The Uniform Trade Secrets Act defines a trade secret as

> information, including a formula, pattern, compilation, program, device, method, technique, or process that:
> (i) derives independent economic value, actual or potential, from not being generally known to, and not being readily ascertainable by proper means by, other persons who can obtain economic value from its disclosure or use, and

(ii) is the subject of efforts that are reasonable under the circumstances to maintain its secrecy.

A famous example of a trade secret is the formula for Coca-Cola.

Misappropriation

Misappropriation of a trade secret is the wrongful use of a trade secret. Basically, trade secrets are misappropriated in two ways: (1) an employee wrongfully uses or discloses such secrets; or (2) a competitor wrongfully obtains them.

Misappropriation wrongful use

An employee is under a duty of loyalty to his employer, which, among other things, charges the employee not to disclose trade secrets to competitors. It is wrongful, in turn, for a competitor to obtain vital secret trade information from an employee through bribery or other means. Besides breaching the duty of loyalty, the faithless employee who divulges secret trade information also commits a tort. In the absence of a contract restriction, an employee is under no duty upon termination of her employment to refrain from working for a competitor of, or competing with, a former employer; but she may not use trade secrets or disclose them to third persons. The employee is entitled, however, to use the skill, knowledge, and general information she acquired during the previous employment relationship.

Another improper method of acquiring trade secrets is industrial espionage conducted through methods such as electronic surveillance or spying. Improper means of acquiring another person's trade secrets also include theft, bribery, fraud, unauthorized interception of communications, and inducement or knowing participation in a breach of confidence. In the broadest sense, discovering another's trade secrets by any means other than independent research or personal inspection of the finished product is improper unless the other party voluntarily discloses the secret or fails to take reasonable precautions to protect its secrecy.

Remedies

Remedies for misappropriation of trade secrets are damages and, where appropriate, injunctive relief. Damages are awarded in the amount of either the pecuniary loss to the plaintiff caused by the misappropriation or the pecuniary gain to the defendant, whichever is greater. A court will grant an injunction to prevent a continuing or threatened misappropriation of a trade secret for as long as is necessary to protect the plaintiff from any harm attributable to the misappropriation and to deprive the defendant of any economic advantage attributable to the misappropriation.

B.C. ZIEGLER AND COMPANY v. EHREN Court of Appeals of Wisconsin, 1987, 141 Wis.2d 19, 414 N.W.2d 48

FACTS B. C. Ziegler and Company (Ziegler) was a securities company located in West Bend. It had established an internal procedure by which its customer lists were treated confidentially. This procedure included burning or shredding any paper to be disposed of that contained a customer name or information. Nonetheless, in late 1985, Ziegler delivered a number of boxes of unshredded scrap paper to Lynn's Waste Paper Company for disposal. One of Lynn's employees, Ehren, who had been in the securities business and had worked for two of Ziegler's competitors, noticed the information contained in the delivery from Ziegler and purchased six boxes of the Ziegler wastepaper for $16.75 from Lynn's. Shortly thereafter, Ehren and his daughter sorted through the information and ultimately obtained 11,600 envelopes of information on Ziegler's customers, including names, account summaries, and other information. Ehren sold this information to Thorson, a broker in competition with Ziegler. Thorson then sent a mailing to the

continued

Ziegler customers to solicit security sales for his firm and obtained an abnormally high response rate as a result. Ziegler, with the help of the West Bend Police Department, traced the dissemination of this information to Ehren and obtained a judgment from the trial court permanently enjoining Ehren from using or disclosing the information regarding Ziegler's clients. Ehren appealed that holding, claiming that such information was not a trade secret belonging to Ziegler.

DECISION Judgment of trial court affirmed.

OPINION The court stated that in determining whether a trade secret exists under the common law, factors to be considered include (1) the extent to which the information is known outside of the business of the party asserting trade secret status; (2) the extent to which it is known by employees and others involved in the business; (3) the extent to which measures taken guard the secrecy of the information; (4) the value the information represents to the party seeking to protect it and to that party's competitors; (5) the amount of effort or money expended by the party developing the information; and (6) the ease or difficulty with which others could properly acquire or duplicate such information. Each factor should indicate that trade secrets exist if the information is to be afforded protection. Applying these factors, the court concluded that Ziegler's customer information qualified for trade secret status. As to Ehren's argument that trade secret status does not survive an accidental or negligent disclosure, the court stated that trade secret status would be unimpaired even presuming negligent disclosure by Ziegler. Public policy would be harmed and it would be inequitable to allow Ehren to take advantage of Ziegler's confidential information, even though Ehren committed no wrongdoing in acquiring the information in the first place.

INTERPRETATION Discovery of another's trade secret by any means other than independent research or one's own inspection of the finished product is improper unless the other party voluntarily discloses the secret.

Criminal Penalties

In 1996 Congress enacted the Economic Espionage Act of 1996 prohibiting the theft of trade secrets and providing criminal penalties for violations. (The statute does not provide any civil remedies.) The statute defines trade secrets to mean "all forms and types of financial, business, scientific, technical, economic, or engineering information, including patterns, plans, compilations, program devices, formulas, designs, prototypes, methods, techniques, processes, procedures, programs, or codes, whether tangible or intangible, and whether or how stored, compiled, or memorialized physically, electronically, graphically, photographically, or in writing if (a) the owner thereof has taken reasonable measures to keep such information secret; and (b) the information derives independent economic value, actual or potential, from not being generally known to, and not being readily ascertainable through proper means by the public."

The act broadly defines theft to include all types of conversion of trade secrets including:

1. stealing, obtaining by fraud, or concealing such information;
2. without authorization copying, duplicating, sketching, drawing, photographing, downloading, uploading, photocopying, or mailing such information;
3. purchasing or possessing a trade secret with knowledge that it has been stolen.

The act punishes thefts of trade secrets, as well as attempts and conspiracies to steal secrets, with fines of up to $500,000, imprisonment for up to 10 years, or both. Organizations that violate the act are subject to fines of up to $5 million. The act imposes more severe penalties on thefts of trade secrets for the benefit of any foreign government, any entity that is controlled by a foreign government, or any agent of a foreign government. The act also authorizes the court to order a violator to forfeit to the United States (1) any property constituting, or derived from, the proceeds of violations, and (2) any property used, or intended to be used, to commit or facilitate a violation.

TRADE SYMBOLS

One of the earliest forms of unfair competition was the fraudulent marketing of one person's goods as those of another. Still common today, this unlawful practice is sometimes referred to as "passing off" or "palming off." Basically, "cashing in" fraudulently on the goodwill, good name, and reputation of a competitor and his products deceives the public and deprives honest businesses of trade. The Federal Trademark Act (the Lanham Act) prohibits businesses from using a false designation of origin in connection with any goods or services. This act also prohibits a business from falsely describing or representing its own goods and services. In 1988, Congress amended the act to prohibit the misrepresentation of *another* person's goods, services, or commercial activities.

The Lanham Act also established federal registration of trade symbols and protection against misuse or infringement by injunctive relief and a right of action for damages against the infringer. An infringement involves passing off one's goods or services as those of the owner of the mark in a manner that deceives the public and constitutes unfair competition.

Types of Trade Symbols

The Lanham Act recognizes four types of trade symbols or **marks**. A **trademark** is a *distinctive* mark, word, letter, number, design, picture, or combination in any arrangement that a person adopts or uses to identify the goods he manufactures or sells, as well as to distinguish them from those manufactured or sold by others. Examples of trademarks include Kodak, Xerox, and the rainbow apple logo on Apple computers. A trademark can also consist of goods' "trade dress," which is the appearance or image of goods as presented to prospective purchasers. Trade dress would include the distinctive but nonfunctional design of packaging labels, containers, and the product itself or its features. Examples include the Campbell Soup label and the shape of the Coca-Cola bottle.

Similar in function to the trademark, which identifies tangible goods and products, is a **service mark**, used to identify and distinguish the services of one person from those of others. For example, the titles, character names, and other distinctive elements of radio and television shows may be registered as service marks. Service marks may also consist of trade dress such as the decor or shape of buildings in which services are provided. Examples include the Fotomart kiosk and Howard Johnson's orange roof.

A **certification mark** is used on or in connection with goods or services to certify their regional or other origin, composition, mode of manufacture, quality, accuracy, or other characteristics, or that the work or labor in the goods or services was performed by members of a union or other organization. The marks "Good Housekeeping Seal of Approval" and "Underwriter's Laboratory" are examples of certification marks. The owner of the certification mark does *not* produce or provide the goods or services with which the mark is used.

A **collective mark** is a distinctive mark or symbol used to indicate either that the producer or provider belongs to a trade union, trade association, fraternal society, or other organization, or that the goods or services are produced by members of a collective group. Like the owner of a certification mark, the owner of a collective mark is not the producer or provider but rather is the

Mark trade symbol

Trademark distinctive symbol, work, or design on a good that is used to identify the manufacturer

Service mark distinctive symbol, work, or design that is used to identify the services of a provider

Certification mark distinctive symbol, word, or design used with goods or services to certify specific characteristics

Collective mark distinctive symbol used to indicate membership in an organization

group of which the producer or provider is a member. An example of a collective mark is the union mark that indicates a product's manufacture by a unionized company.

Registration

To be protected by the Lanham Act, a mark must be distinctive enough to identify clearly the origin of goods or services; it may not be immoral, deceptive, or scandalous. A trade symbol may satisfy the distinctiveness requirement in either of two ways. First, it may be *inherently distinctive* if prospective purchasers are likely to associate it with the product or service it designates because of the nature of the designation and the context in which it is used. Fanciful or arbitrary marks satisfy the distinctiveness requirement. In contrast, a descriptive or geographic designation is *not* inherently distinctive. Such a designation is one that is likely to be perceived by prospective purchasers as merely descriptive of the nature, qualities, or other characteristics of the goods or service with which it is used. Thus, the word *Plow* cannot be a trademark for plows, although it may be a trademark for shoes.

Descriptive or geographic designations may, however, satisfy the distinctiveness requirement through the second method: acquiring distinctiveness through a "secondary meaning." A designation acquires a *secondary meaning* when a substantial number of prospective purchasers associate the designation with the product or service it identifies.

A *generic designation* is one that is understood by prospective purchasers to denominate the general category, type, or class of goods or services with which it is used. A user *cannot* acquire rights in a generic designation as a trade symbol. Moreover, a trade symbol will lose its eligibility for protection if prospective purchasers *come to* perceive a trade symbol primarily as a generic description for the category, type, or class of goods or services with which it is used. Under the Lanham Act, the test for when this has occurred is "the primary significance of the registered mark to the relevant public rather than purchaser motivation." Examples of marks that have lost protection because they became generic include "aspirin," "thermos," "escalator," and "cellophane." To guard against losing the distinctiveness of their trade symbols, some manufacturers advertise the proper use of their marks; examples include Teflon, Kleenex, and Xerox.

To obtain federal protection, which has a ten-year term with unlimited ten-year renewals, the mark must be registered with the Patent and Trademark Office. The registrant must either (1) have actually used the mark in commerce or (2) demonstrate a *bona fide* intent to use the mark in commerce and actually use it within six months.

Registration provides numerous advantages. It gives nationwide constructive notice of the mark to all later users. It permits the registrant to use the federal courts to enforce the mark and constitutes *prima facie* evidence of the registrant's exclusive right to use the mark. This right becomes incontestable, subject to certain specified limitations, after five years. Finally, registration provides the registrant with Customs Bureau protection against imports that threaten to infringe upon the mark.

To retain trademark protection, the owner of a mark must not abandon it by failing to make *bona fide* use of it in the ordinary course of trade. Abandonment occurs when an owner does not use a mark and no longer intends to use it. Three years of nonuse raises a presumption of abandonment, which the owner may rebut by proving her intent to resume use.

MILLER BREWING COMPANY v. G. HEILEMAN BREWING COMPANY, INC. United States
Court of Appeals, Seventh Circuit, 1977, 561 F.2d 75

FACTS In 1967, a Chicago brewer, Meister Brau, Inc., began making and selling a reduced-calorie, reduced-carbohydrate beer under the name "LITE." Late in 1968, that company filed applications to register "LITE" as a trademark in the United States Patent Office, which ultimately approved three registrations of labels containing the name "LITE" for "beer with no available carbohydrates." In 1972, Meister Brau sold its interest in the "LITE" trademarks and the accompanying goodwill to Miller Brewing Company. Miller decided to expand its marketing of beer under the brand "LITE." It developed a modified recipe, which resulted in a beer lower in calories than Miller's regular beer but not without available carbohydrates. The label was revised, and one of the registrations was amended to show "LITE" printed rather than in script. In addition, Miller undertook an extensive advertising campaign. From 1973 through 1976, Miller expanded its annual sales of "LITE" from 50,000 barrels to 4,000,000 barrels and increased its annual advertising expenditures from $500,000 to more than $12,000,000.

Beginning in early 1975, a number of other brewers, including G. Heileman Brewing Company, introduced reduced-calorie beers labeled or described as "light." In response, Miller began filing trademark infringement actions against competitors to enjoin the use of the word "light." The District Court enjoined Heileman from continuing to sell, advertise, and distribute beer anywhere in the United States under a brand name incorporating the word "Light," and Heileman appealed.

DECISION Preliminary injunction reversed.

OPINION Registering a mark creates *prima facie* evidence of the registrant's exclusive right to use the registered mark in commerce on the goods or services specified in the registration, subject to any conditions or limitation the registration may state. Miller relies on registrations that specify the term "LITE" for "beer with no available carbohydrates" as the goods on which the registered mark is to be used. Therefore, the registrations are not *prima facie* evidence for Miller's exclusive

right to use the word "LITE" on a beer with available carbohydrates. Accordingly, Miller's claim must be evaluated under the common law of trademarks without the benefit of registration.

A generic or common descriptive term is one that is commonly used to name or describe a kind of goods. It cannot become a trademark under any circumstance. Changing the spelling of a term to a phonetic equivalent will not remove this barrier. For example, if "light" is a generic term, then "LITE" is as well. A type of term that is similar to a generic term is the merely descriptive term, which specifically describes a characteristic or an ingredient of an article. Under certain circumstances, such as extensive use, the term can acquire a secondary meaning. In that case, the merely descriptive term can become distinctive of the applicant's goods and thus a valid trademark.

Miller argues that "light" is a merely descriptive term that has acquired a secondary meaning through Miller's promotions. The court disagrees. The fact that "light" is an adjective does not prevent it from being a generic or common descriptive word. Otherwise, a competitor could not describe his goods as what they are. Indeed, "light" is a generic or common descriptive term when used with beer, and the beer industry has used the word "light" widely for many years to describe a beer's color, flavor, body, or alcoholic content. The use of that word by Heileman and other brewers long antedated either Miller's or Meister Brau's use of "LITE." State statutes even use "light beer" as a generic or common descriptive term.

In conclusion, since the word "light," including its phonetic equivalent "lite," is a generic or common descriptive term as applied to beer, Miller could not appropriate it exclusively as a trademark. This is true despite whatever promotional effort Miller may have expended to exploit the term.

INTERPRETATION A generic or common descriptive word—one that is commonly used as the name or description of a kind of good—cannot become a trademark.

Infringement
Infringement of a mark occurs when a person without authorization uses an identical or substantially indistinguishable mark that is likely to cause confusion, to cause mistake, or to deceive. The intention to confuse purchasers is not required, nor is proof of actual confusion, although likelihood of confusion may be inferred from either. Infringement occurs if an appreciable number of ordinarily prudent purchasers are *likely* to be misled or confused as to the source of the goods or services. In deciding whether infringement has occurred, the courts

Infringement occurs when a person without authorization uses a substantially indistinguishable mark that is likely to cause confusion, mistake, or deception

consider various factors, including the strength of the mark, the intent of the unauthorized user, the degree of similarity between the two marks, the relation between the two products or services the marks identify, and the marketing channels through which the goods or services are purchased.

Remedies

Remedies the Lanham Act provides the following remedies for infringement: injunctive relief, profits, damages, destruction of infringing articles, costs, and, in exceptional cases, attorneys' fees

The Lanham Act provides several **remedies** for infringement: (1) injunctive relief, (2) an accounting for profits, (3) damages, (4) destruction of infringing articles, (5) attorneys' fees in exceptional cases, and (6) costs. In assessing profits, the plaintiff has only to prove the gross sales made by the defendant; the defendant, in contrast, must prove any costs to be deducted in determining profits. If the court finds that the amount of recovery based on profits is either inadequate or excessive, the court may, in its discretion, award an amount it determines to be just. In assessing damages, the court *may* award up to three times the actual damages, according to the circumstances of the case. When an infringement is knowing and intentional, the court *shall* award attorneys' fees plus the greater of treble profits or treble damages, unless there are extenuating circumstances.

Where a defendant has intentionally and knowingly used a *counterfeit* mark, the court may impose criminal sanctions; and goods bearing the counterfeit mark may be destroyed. A *counterfeit mark* means a spurious mark that is identical with, or substantially indistinguishable from, a registered mark. Criminal sanctions include a fine of up to $250,000 or imprisonment of up to five years, or both. For a repeat offense, the limits are $1 million and fifteen years, respectively. For an offender who is not an individual (a corporation, for example), the fine may be up to $1 million for a first offense and up to $5 million for a repeat offense.

TRADE NAMES

Trade name any name used to identify a business, vocation, or occupation; may not be registered under the Lanham Act, but infringement is prohibited and damages and injunctions are available if infringement occurs

A **trade name** is any name used to identify a business, vocation, or occupation. Descriptive and generic words, and personal and generic names, although not proper trademarks, may become protected as trade names upon acquiring a special significance in the trade. A name acquires such significance, frequently referred to as a "secondary meaning," through its continuing and extended use in connection with specific goods or services, whereby the name's acquired meaning eclipses its primary meaning in the minds of many purchasers or users. Although they may *not* be federally registered under the Lanham Act, trade names are protected, and a person who palms off her goods or services under the trade name of another is liable in damages and also may be enjoined from doing so.

COPYRIGHTS

Copyright exclusive right, usually for the author's life plus fifty years, to original works of authorship

Copyright is a form of protection provided by the Federal Copyright Act to authors of original works, which include literary, musical, and dramatic works; pantomimes; choreographic works; pictorial, graphic, and sculptural works; motion picture and other audiovisual works; sound recordings; and architectural works. This listing is illustrative, not exhaustive, as the act extends **copyright** protection to "original works of authorship in any tangible medium of expression, now known or later developed." Moreover, in 1980, the Copyright Act was amended to extend copyright protection to computer programs. On

MANAGERIAL INSIGHT

Licensed Trademarks Beset by Pirates, Counterfeiters, and Copycats

Before the information age with its high-speed global communications and internationally recognized corporate symbols, trademark law existed as a sleepy corner of intellectual property law. Today, however, things have changed.

Now, companies are much more ready to go to court to protect their registered trademarks. In fact, they often have too much to lose to do otherwise.

These days, a registered trademark can provide a company with an essential marketing tool: worldwide name recognition. In addition, a well-known trademark encourages brand loyalty, as well as offering an implicit guarantee of consistent product quality.

But a trademark can also present problems for a company. There is always the danger that an aggressive competitor will infringe upon the trademark, dilute its distinctive nature by improper use, or, worse still, transform it into a generic label, which spells legal death for a trademark in the United States.

How difficult is it, then, to fend off trademark assaults? Ask Rollerblade, Inc. The Minneapolis-based company was the first to market in-line skates, a product that since has captured the sports world. With its success, however, the company found itself struggling to maintain its hold on its trademark. Rollerblade, despite public misuse of the word, is a federally registered trademark and not, as the company notes, the specific name of a sport or the general name of a skate. Neither "rollerblading" nor "rollerblades" is an appropriate use of the term. Today, Rollerblade, Inc., must battle daily with the media, the public and its competitors to keep its trademark from becoming a generic label.

As global competition intensifies, companies such as Rollerblade are also finding that they must protect their trademarks overseas. Rollerblade, for instance, markets its in-line

skates in Europe, Australia, and Japan, among other places. Currently, though, neither Rollerblade nor any other company can turn to a single international law that would give it worldwide rights to a trademark, patent, or copyright. Rather, companies must work within each individual country to protect their rights.

Increasingly, companies are reaping substantial profits from their trademarks, which is why they have turned to the courts for protection. Numerous companies, for example, are profiting from the hot new area of trademark licensing, which is especially lucrative when it comes to athletic sportswear. At the same time, companies are facing new challenges. They are being threatened as never before by cheap knockoffs and flagrant piracy. They are also being called on to deal with the popular culture's assimilation of corporate symbols.

Like everyone else, companies want to protect their good names. As a result, more and more of them are seeking trademark protection, sometimes with mixed results. A few noteworthy examples:

• Walt Disney, Inc., as well as many other companies, breathed a sigh of relief when Poland gave in to international pressure in 1994 and passed a strengthened copyright law that would subject violators to heavy fines and imprisonment. American companies had been losing millions of dollars under Poland's lax policing of copyright piracy and trademark infringement, which had led to the marketing of such items as fake Mickey Mouse dolls and contraband *Jurassic Park* videos.

• Several companies, notably Warner-Lambert and American Home Products, have dragged the Perrigo corporation to court for its knockoff versions of over-the-counter drugstore items. Warner-Lambert is the manufacturer of Cool Mint Listerine mouthwash, so it didn't much like it when Perrigo took to describing its own mouthwash as "Blue Mint" antiseptic mouth rinse. Nor did American Home Products, which makes Advil, fancy Perrigo bottling up its own ibuprofen tablets in Advil-style packaging. To American Home Products' dismay, though, it lost its case.

• The Cousteau Society took offense when Clover-Stornetta Farms decked out a cow in diving gear and plastered her picture on a billboard to advertise its dairy. Clo the Cow, the dairy's advertising symbol, had turned up previously as Christopher Cowlumbus, with nary a complaint. But Jacques Cowsteau got a chillier reception. The real-life Cousteau and his environmental society filed a $1.2 million trademark infringement lawsuit, which was settled out of court.

• French champagne makers protested when Yves Saint Laurent decided to name his new perfume Champagne. In France, a product with such an appellation must come from the region of Champagne. Otherwise, the name represents a violation of French trademark law. Although French vintners won in court and Saint Laurent was forced to rename his perfume after himself, he did retain the perfume's specially crafted bottle, shaped like a champagne cork. He also will be allowed to market the perfume in the United States as Champagne, since the American and French legal systems don't follow the same rules.

March 1, 1989, the United States joined the Berne Convention, an international treaty protecting copyrighted works.

In no case does the copyright protection for an original work of authorship protect also any idea, procedure, process, system, method of operation, concept, principle, or discovery, regardless of the form in which it is described, explained, illustrated, or embodied in such work. Copyright protection extends only to an *original expression* of an idea. For example, the idea of interfamily feuding cannot be copyrighted; but a particular expression of that idea in the form of a novel, drama, movie, or opera may be thus protected.

Procedure

Procedure registration is not required but provides additional remedies for infringement

Copyright applications are filed with the Register of Copyrights in Washington, D.C. While registration of the copyright is not required, since copyright protection begins as soon as the work is fixed in a tangible medium, registration is advisable nonetheless, being a condition of the remedies of statutory damages and attorneys' fees for copyright infringement. When a work is published, it is advisable, though no longer required, to place a copyright notice on all publicly distributed copies, so as to notify users about the copyright claim. If proper notice appears on the published copies to which a defendant in a copyright infringement case had access, the defendant will be unable to mitigate actual or statutory damages by asserting a defense of innocent infringement.

Rights

Rights copyright protection provides the exclusive right to (1) reproduce the copyrighted work, (2) prepare derivative works based on the work, (3) distribute copies of the work, and (4) perform or display the work publicly

In most instances, copyright protection lasts the duration of the author's life plus an additional fifty years. The Copyright Act gives the copyright owner the exclusive **right**, and the right to authorize others, to reproduce the copyrighted work, prepare derivative works based upon the copyrighted work, distribute copies or recordings of the copyrighted work, perform the work publicly, and display the work publicly.

These broad rights are subject, however, to several limitations, the most important of which are "compulsory licenses" and "fair use." *Compulsory licenses* permit certain limited uses of copyrighted material upon the payment of specified royalties and compliance with statutory conditions. The Copyright Act provides that the *fair use* of a copyrighted work for purposes such as criticism, comment, news reporting, teaching (including multiple copies for classroom use), scholarship, or research is *not* an infringement of copyright. In determining whether the use made of a work in any particular case is fair, the courts consider the following factors: (1) the purpose and character of the use, including whether such use is of a commercial nature or is for nonprofit educational purposes; (2) the nature of the copyrighted work; (3) the amount and substantiality of the portion used in relation to the copyrighted work as a whole; and (4) the effect of the use upon the potential market for or value of the copyrighted work.

CAMPBELL v. ACUFF-ROSE MUSIC, INC. Supreme Court of the United States, 1994, 510 U.S. 569, 114 S.Ct. 1164, 127 L.E.2d 500

FACTS In 1964, Roy Orbison and William Dees wrote a rock ballad entitled "Oh, Pretty Woman." Acuff-Rose Music, Inc. (Acuff-Rose) acquired the rights to this song and registered it for copyright protection. In 1989, Luther R. Campbell, a member of the popular rap music band, 2 Live Crew, wrote a song entitled "Pretty Woman" that was intended, "through comical lyrics, to satirize the original work." Campbell's version copied a readily recognizable portion of "Oh, Pretty Woman," including the characteristic opening bass riff and the first line of lyrics.

On July 5, 1989, 2 Live Crew's manager sent a letter to Acuff-Rose stating that 2 Live Crew had written a

continued

parody of "Oh, Pretty Woman" and that they were willing to pay for the use they wished to make of it and to credit ownership and authorship to Orbison, Dees, and Acuff-Rose. This letter was accompanied by a recording of the song and the lyrics. Acuff-Rose refused to grant permission, stating that they could not "permit the use of a parody of 'Oh, Pretty Woman.'" Nonetheless, 2 Live Crew released recordings in an album entitled *As Clean As They Wanna Be*, which contained the song "Pretty Woman." The album cover identifies the author of "Pretty Woman" as Orbison and Dees and its publisher as Acuff-Rose.

Acuff-Rose sued 2 Live Crew and its record company, Luke Skywalker Records, for copyright infringement. The district court granted summary judgment to 2 Live Crew, reasoning that the parody was a fair use of the original version. The Court of Appeals reversed.

DECISION Judgment of the Court of Appeals is reversed and remanded.

OPINION From the infancy of copyright protection, some opportunity for fair use of copyrighted materials has been thought necessary to fulfill copyright's very purpose, "[t]o promote the Progress of Science and useful Arts." U.S. Const., Art. I, § 8. Accordingly, the judicial doctrine of fair use developed. The Copyright Act of 1976 § 107 restates the judicial doctrine of fair use. The fair use doctrine permits and requires courts to avoid rigid application of the copyright statute when, on occasion, it would stifle the very creativity that that law is designed to foster.

The first factor in a fair use inquiry is to what extent the use of copyrighted material is "transformative"; that is, to what extent it adds something new, with a further purpose or different character, altering the original with new expression, meaning, or message. The threshold question when fair use is raised in defense of parody is whether a parodic character may be reasonably perceived. Although one might not assign a high rank to the parodic element here, 2 Live Crew's version reasonably could be perceived as commenting on the original or criticizing it to some degree. The new version's juxtaposition of romantic musings with degrading taunts, a bawdy demand for sex, and a sigh of relief from paternal responsibility could be seen as a rejection of the original version's sentiment, which ignores the ugliness of street life and the debasement that it signifies. Although 2 Live Crew's use of the original did have a commercial element, that does not raise a presumption of unfair use. The statute makes clear that the commercial purpose of the use is merely a separate factor that weighs to varying degrees against a finding of fair use. For example, use of copyrighted material to advertise a product will weigh more heavily against a

finding of fair use than the sale of a parody for its own sake, let alone one performed a single time by students in school.

The second factor, the nature of the copyrighted work, embodies the notion that some works are closer to the core of intended copyright protection than others and that fair use is more difficult to establish when the former works are copied. However, this factor is of little value in parody cases where the copied work is almost invariably a publicly known, expressive work, which is at the core of copyright's protective purposes.

The third factor asks whether the amount and substantiality of the material that was copied, in relation to the copyrighted work as a whole, was reasonable in light of the purpose for which it was copied. The purpose in this case was to parody the original. Parody's humor, or in any event its comment, necessarily springs from recognizable allusion to its object through distorted imitation. While in quoting the opening bass riff and lyrics, 2 Live Crew could be said to have taken the heart of the original; it is the heart of the song that most readily conjures up the song for parody. Therefore, the Court of Appeals erred in determining that 2 Live Crew's use was unreasonable as a matter of law, because the portion taken was the original's heart.

The fourth factor in the fair use analysis examines the effect of the use upon the potential market for or value of the copyrighted work. In this analysis, the extent to which the new work "supersedes" the old work in the market will weigh against a finding of fair use. The Court of Appeals presumed that because 2 Live Crew made commercial use of the original, it harmed the market for "Oh, Pretty Woman." However, where the new work is transformative, as it is in this case, market substitution is far from certain. A parody, like a scathing theater review, may legitimately seek to garrote the original, destroying it commercially as well as artistically. Therefore courts must distinguish between uses that usurp the original and those that criticize it.

The Court of Appeals erred in making evidentiary presumptions in addressing both the first and fourth factors of the § 107 fair use analysis of 2 Live Crew's parodic use of "Oh, Pretty Woman." No such presumptions are available. It was also error to hold that 2 Live Crew copied excessively from the original, considering the parodic use made of the copied material. Therefore, the judgment of the Court of Appeals is reversed.

INTERPRETATION Fair use of a copyrighted work is not infringement.

Ownership

The author of a creative work owns the entire copyright. Although the actual creator of a work is usually the author, in two situations under the doctrine of *works for hire*, she is not considered the author. First, if an employee prepares a work within the scope of her employment, her employer is considered the author of the work. Second, if a work is specially ordered or commissioned for certain purposes specified in the copyright statute *and* the parties expressly agree in writing that the work shall be considered a work for hire, the person commissioning the work is deemed to be the author.

The ownership of a copyright may be transferred in whole or in part by conveyance, will, or intestate succession. However, a transfer of copyright ownership, other than by operation of law, is not valid unless a note or memorandum chronicles the transfer in writing and is signed by the owner of the rights conveyed or by the owner's duly authorized agent. An author may terminate any transfer of copyright ownership, other than that of a work for hire, during the five-year period beginning thirty-five years after the transfer was granted.

Ownership of a copyright, or of any of the exclusive rights under a copyright, is distinct from the ownership of any material object that embodies the work. The transfer of ownership of any material object, including the copy or recording in which the work was first fixed, does not in itself convey any rights in the copyrighted work the object embodies; nor, in the absence of an agreement, does the transfer of copyright ownership or of any exclusive rights under a copyright convey property rights in any material object. Thus, the purchase of this textbook neither affects the publisher's copyright nor authorizes the purchaser to make and sell copies of the book, though the purchaser may rent, lend, or resell it. Were this a recorded text, however, the purchaser's latter rights would be somewhat more limited: in 1990, amendments to the Copyright Act prohibited the rental, lease, or commercial lending of sound recordings and computer programs unless authorized by the copyright owner.

Infringement and Remedies

Infringement occurs whenever somebody exercises, without authorization, the rights exclusively reserved for the copyright owner. Infringement need *not* be intentional. To prove infringement, the plaintiff must simply establish that he owns the copyright and that the defendant violated one or more of the plaintiff's exclusive rights under the copyright. Proof of infringement usually consists of showing that the allegedly infringing work is substantially similar to the copyrighted work and that the alleged infringer had access to the copyrighted work.

In order for the owner to sue for infringement, the copyright must be registered with the Copyright Office, unless the work is a Berne Convention work whose country of origin is not the United States. For an infringement occurring *after* registration, the following **remedies** are available: (1) injunction; (2) impoundment and possible destruction of infringing articles; (3) actual damages plus profits made by the infringer that are additional to those damages, *or* statutory damages of at least $500 but no more than $20,000 (though the ceiling may reach $100,000 if the infringement is willful), according to what the court determines to be just; (4) costs and, in the court's discretion, reasonable attorneys' fees to the prevailing party; or (5) criminal penalties of a fine of up to $10,000 or up to one year's imprisonment for willful infringement for purposes of commercial advantage or private gain. The Piracy and Counterfeiting Amendments Act of 1982

ETHICAL DILEMMA Who Holds the Copyright on Lecture Notes?

FACTS Tom Rigsby considers himself a young, aspiring entrepreneur. At twenty-three, he has already established a highly successful small business, Take Note, which provides students at the University of the Midwest with detailed class notes for approximately seventy-five university courses, covering subjects that range from business law to modern literature. For each of his note sets, Rigsby charges $35.

He also offers, for $25, an exam package that includes summary notes as well as exam questions that professors have used in the past, which many fraternities on campus already keep on file exclusively for their members.

To make a profit, Rigsby has concentrated on the university's more popular courses, which often pack up to 500 students into a single lecture hall. At present, he is grossing about $400,000 a year.

Most students who have used Rigsby's notes consider them to be of exceptionally high quality. Many believe that the notes have made the difference between an "A" and a "B" in their courses.

Rigsby received his degree from the University of the Midwest, where he graduated summa cum laude.

Until recently, when he expanded his business, he based his Take Note packages either on notes he had taken while a regular student or on notes from classes he audited after he graduated. Now, he has hired two additional notetakers, both 4.0 students at the university. He pays them each a small salary plus royalties of 12 percent on every sale of their notes that he makes.

To the dismay of many professors at the university, though, Rigsby has never sought their permission to distribute notes of their classes. He doesn't see why he should. In fact, he believes that any question of copyright here should be answered in favor of the notetaker, not the professor. He acknowledges that in other states, businesses such as his pay royalties to professors, but he thinks such expenditures unnecessary.

Now, on behalf of the University of the Midwest and its professors, lawyers for the university have sued Rigsby for copyright infringement. He, in turn, has filed a countersuit, charging disparagement. Rigsby was planning to expand his business to three other midwestern states, but now he says the university has disrupted his business with false accusations.

Social, Policy, and Ethical Considerations

1. Who does hold the copyright in this case? Did Rigsby act ethically in not seeking the professors' permission? Should he be required to share a part of his profits as royalties with the professors whose classes are covered by his Take Note packages?

2. Are the students acting ethically in buying Rigsby's Take Note packages? Does using one of Rigsby's exam packages constitute cheating? Does employing someone else's notes or old exam questions to study for an exam differ from using someone else's notes or outline to write a term paper?

3. Is the University of the Midwest acting responsibly in scheduling such large classes? What responsibility does it have to protect students from an impersonal or inadequate education? Is the university acting responsibly toward its professors? How should the university protect a professor's intellectual work?

imposes harsher punishments for large-scale piracy: a $250,000 fine and five years' imprisonment for those who pirate 1,000 recordings or 65 films within 180 days.

PATENTS

Through a **patent**, the federal government grants an inventor a monopolistic right to make, use, or sell an invention to the absolute exclusion of others for the period of the patent. The patent owner may also profit by licensing others to use the patent on a royalty basis. However, the patent may not be renewed: upon expiration, the invention enters the "public domain," and anyone may then use it.

Patent exclusive right to an invention

Patentability
The Patent Act specifies those inventions that may be patented as *utility patents*: any new and useful process, machine, manufacture, or composition of matter or

any new and useful improvement thereof. Thus, naturally occurring substances are not patentable, as the invention must be made or modified by humans. For example, the discovery of a bacterium with useful properties is *not* patentable, whereas the manufacture of a genetically engineered bacterium is. By the same token, laws of nature, principles, bookkeeping systems, fundamental truths, calculation methods, and ideas are not patentable. Accordingly, Einstein could not have patented his law that $E = mc^2$; nor could Newton have patented the law of gravity. Similarly, isolated computer programs are not patentable, although, as we mentioned above, they may be copyrighted.

To be patentable as a utility patent, the process, machine, manufacture, or composition of matter must meet three criteria: (1) novelty, (2) utility, and (3) nonobviousness.

In addition to utility patents, the Patent Act provides for plant patents and design patents. A ***plant patent*** protects a new and distinctive variety of asexually producing plant. Plant patents require (1) novelty, (2) distinctiveness, and (3) nonobviousness. A ***design patent*** protects a new, original, ornamental design for an article of manufacture. Design patents require (1) novelty, (2) ornamentality, and (3)nonobviousness.

Utility and plant patents have a term that begins on the date of the patent's grant and ends twenty years from the date of *application*. Design patents have a term of fourteen years from the date of grant.

Procedure

Procedure patents are issued upon application to and after examination by the U.S. Patent and Trademark Office

The United States Patent and Trademark Office issues a patent upon the basis of a patent application containing a *specification*, which describes how the invention works, and *claims*, which describe the features that make the invention patentable. The applicant must be the inventor. Before granting a patent, the Patent Office carefully and thoroughly examines the prior art and determines whether the submitted invention has novelty (does not conflict with a prior pending application or a previously issued patent) and utility, and is nonobvious. A patent application is confidential, and the Patent Office will not divulge its contents. This confidentiality ends, however, upon the granting of the patent.

An applicant whose application is rejected may apply for reexamination. If the application is again rejected, the applicant may appeal to the Patent and Trademark Office's Board of Appeals, and from there to the federal courts.

FIGURE 50–1 Intellectual Property

	Trade Secrets	**Trade Symbols**	**Copyright**	**Patents**
What Is Protected	Information	Mark	Work of authorship	Invention
Rights Protected	Use or sell	Use or sell	Reproduce, prepare derivative works, distribute, perform, or display	Make, use, or sell
Duration	Until disclosed	Until abandoned	Usually author's life plus 50 years	For utility and plant patents, 20 years from application; 14 years for design patents
Federally Protected	No	Yes	Yes	Yes
Requirements for Protection	Valuable secret	Distinctive	Original and fixed	Novel, useful, and nonobvious

Infringement

Anyone who, without permission, makes, uses, or sells a patented invention is a *direct infringer*, whereas a person who actively encourages another to make, use, offer to sell, or sell a patented invention without permission is an *indirect infringer*. A *contributory infringer* is one who knowingly sells, or offers to sell, a part or component of a patented invention, unless the component is a staple or commodity or is suitable for a substantial noninfringing use. Though good faith and ignorance *are* defenses to contributory infringement, they are *not* defenses to direct infringement.

Infringement occurs when anyone without permission makes, uses, or sells a patented invention

Remedies

The **remedies** for infringement under the Patent Act are (1) injunctive relief; (2) damages adequate to compensate the plaintiff but "in no event less than a reasonable royalty for the use made of the invention by the infringer"; (3) treble damages, when appropriate; (4) attorneys' fees in exceptional cases, such as those that involve knowing infringement; and (5) costs.

Remedies for infringement of a patent are (1) injunctive relief; (2) damages; (3) treble damages, where appropriate; (4) attorneys' fees; and (5) costs

CHAPTER SUMMARY

Trade Secrets	**Definition of Trade Secret** commercially valuable, secret information **Protection** owner of a trade secret may obtain damages or injunctive relief when the secret is misappropriated (wrongfully used) by an employee or a competitor **Criminal Penalties** federal law imposes penalties for the theft of trade secrets
Trade Symbols	**Types of Trade Symbols** ■ *Trademark* distinctive symbol, word, or design on a good that is used to identify the manufacturer ■ *Service Mark* distinctive symbol, word, or design that is used to identify a provider's services ■ *Certification Mark* distinctive symbol, word, or design used with goods or services to certify specific characteristics ■ *Collective Mark* distinctive symbol used to indicate membership in an organization **Registration** to be registered and thus protected by the Lanham Act, a mark must be distinctive and not immoral, deceptive, or scandalous **Infringement** occurs when a person without authorization uses a substantially indistinguishable mark that is likely to cause confusion, mistake, or deception **Remedies** the Lanham Act provides the following remedies for infringement: injunctive relief, profits, damages, destruction of infringing articles, costs, and, in exceptional cases, attorneys' fees

Trade Names	**Definition of Trade Name** any name used to identify a business, vocation, or occupation
	Protection may not be registered under the Lanham Act, but infringement is prohibited
	Remedies damages and injunctions are available if infringement occurs

Copyrights	**Definition of Copyright** exclusive right, usually for the author's life plus fifty years, to original works of authorship
	Procedure registration is not required but provides additional remedies for infringement
	Rights copyright protection provides the exclusive right to (1) reproduce the copyrighted work, (2) prepare derivative works based on the work, (3) distribute copies of the work, and (4) perform or display the work publicly
	Ownership the author of the copyrighted work is usually the owner of the copyright, which may be transferred in whole or in part
	Infringement occurs when someone exercises the copyright owner's rights without authorization
	Remedies if infringement occurs after registration, the following remedies are available: (1) injunction, (2) impoundment and possible destruction of infringing articles, (3) actual damages plus profits or statutory damages, (4) costs, and (5) criminal penalties

Patents	**Definition of Patent** the exclusive right to an invention for twenty years from the date of application for utility and plant patents; fourteen years from grant for design patents
	Patentability to be patentable, the invention must be (1) novel, (2) useful, and (3) not obvious
	Procedure patents are issued upon application to and after examination by the U.S. Patent and Trademark Office
	Infringement occurs when anyone without permission makes, uses, or sells a patented invention
	Remedies for infringement of a patent are (1) injunctive relief; (2) damages; (3) treble damages, where appropriate; (4) attorneys' fees; and (5) costs

QUESTIONS

1. Explain what trade secrets protect and how they may be infringed.
2. Distinguish among the various types of trade symbols.
3. Explain the extent to which trade names are protected.
4. Explain what copyrights protect and the remedies for infringement.
5. Explain what patents protect and the remedies for infringement.

Internet Question. Find information about the organization and procedures of (a) the United States Copyright Office, and (b) the United States Patent and Trademark Office.

PROBLEMS

1. Keller, a professor of legal studies at Rhodes University, is a diligent instructor. Late one night, while reading a newly published, copyrighted treatise of 1,800 pages written by Gilbert, he came across a three-page section discussing the subject matter he intended to cover in class the next day. Keller considered the treatment to be illuminating and therefore photocopied the three pages and distributed the copies to his class. One of Keller's students is a second cousin of Gilbert, the author of the treatise; and she showed Gilbert the copies. Instead of being flattered, Gilbert sued Keller for copyright infringement. Decision?

2. Jennings conceived a secret process for the continuous freeze-drying of foodstuffs and related products and constructed a small pilot plant that practiced the process. However, Jennings lacked the financing necessary to develop the commercial potential of the process and, in hopes of obtaining a contract for its development and the payment of royalties, disclosed it in confidence to Merrick, a coffee manufacturer, who signed an agreement not to disclose it to anyone else. At the same time, Jennings signed an agreement not to disclose the process to any other person as long as Jennings and Merrick were considering a contract for its development. Upon Jennings's disclosure of the process, Merrick became extremely interested and offered to pay Jennings the sum of $1,750,000 if, upon further development, the process proved to be commercially feasible. While negotiations between Jennings and Merrick were in progress, Nelson, a competitor of Merrick, learned of the process and requested a disclosure from Jennings, who informed Nelson that the process could not be disclosed to anyone unless negotiations with Merrick were broken off. Nelson offered to pay Jennings $2,500,000 for the process, provided it met certain defined objective performance criteria. A contract was prepared and executed between Jennings and Nelson on this basis, without any prior disclosure of the process to Nelson. Upon the making of this contract, Jennings rejected Merrick's offer. The process was thereupon disclosed to Nelson, and demonstration runs of the pilot plant in the presence of Nelson representatives were conducted under varying conditions. After three weeks of experimental demonstrations, compiling data, and analyzing results, Nelson informed Jennings that the process did not meet the performance criteria in the contract and that for this reason Nelson was rejecting the process. Two years later, Nelson placed on the market freeze-dried coffee that resembled in color, appearance, and texture the product of Jennings's pilot plant. What are the rights of the parties?

3. Stella, a chemist, was employed by Johnson, a manufacturer, to work on a secret process for Johnson's product under an exclusive three-year contract. Dabney, a salesman, was employed by Johnson on a week-to-week basis. Stella and Dabney resigned their employment with Johnson and accepted employment in their respective capacities with Washington, a rival manufacturer. Dabney began soliciting patronage from Johnson's former customers, whose names he had memorized. What are the rights of the parties in (a) a suit by Johnson to enjoin Stella from working for Washington, and (b) a suit by Johnson to enjoin Dabney from soliciting Johnson's customers?

4. Conrad and Darby were competitors in the business of dehairing raw cashmere, the fleece of certain Asiatic goats. Dehairing is the process of separating the commercially valuable soft down from the matted mass of raw fleece, which contains long coarse guard hairs and other impurities. Machinery for this process is not readily available on the open market. Each company in the business designed and built its own machinery and kept the nature of its process secret. Conrad contracted with Lawton, owner of a small machine shop, to build and install new improved dehairing machinery of increased efficiency for which Conrad furnished designs, drawings, and instructions. Lawton, who knew that the machinery design was confidential, agreed that he would manufacture the machinery exclusively for Conrad and that he would not reproduce the machinery or any of its essential parts for anyone else. Darby purchased from Lawton a copy of the dehairing machinery that Conrad had specially designed. What are Conrad's rights against (a) Darby and (b) Lawton?

5. Sally, having filed locally an affidavit required under the assumed name statute, has been operating and advertising her exclusive toy store for twenty years in Centerville, Illinois. Her advertising has consisted of large signs on her premises reading "The Toy Mart." Bob, after operating a store in Chicago under the name of "The Chicago Toy Mart," relocated in Centerville, Illinois, and erected a large sign reading "TOY MART" with the word "Centerville" written underneath in substantially smaller letters. Thereafter, Sally's sales declined, and many of Sally's customers patronized Bob's store, thinking it to be a branch of Sally's business. What are the rights of the parties?

6. Ryan Corporation manufactures and sells a variety of household cleaning products in interstate commerce. On national television, Ryan falsely advertises that its laundry liquid is biodegradable. Has Ryan violated the Lanham Act?

7. Gibbons, Inc. and Marvin Corporation are manufacturers who sell a variety of household cleaning products in interstate commerce. On national television Gibbons states that its laundry liquid is biodegradable and that Marvin's is not. In fact, both products are biodegradable. Has Gibbons violated the Lanham Act?

8. George McCoy of Florida has been manufacturing and distributing a cheesecake for over five years, labeling his product with a picture of a cheesecake, which serves as a background for a Florida bathing beauty and under which is written the slogan "McCoy All Spice Florida Cheese Cake." George McCoy has not registered his trademark. Subsequently, Leo McCoy of California begins manufacturing a similar product on the West Coast using a label similar in appearance to that of George McCoy, containing a picture of a Hollywood star and the words "McCoy's All Spice Cheese Cake." Leo McCoy begins marketing his products in the eastern United States, using labels with the word "Florida" added, as in George McCoy's label. Leo McCoy has registered his product under the Federal Trademark Act. To what relief, if any, is George McCoy entitled?

9. Sony Corporation manufactured and sold home video recorders, specifically Betamax videotape recorders (VTRs). Universal City Studios, Inc. (Universal) owned the copyrights on some programs aired on commercially sponsored television. Individual Betamax owners frequently used the device to record some of Universal's copyrighted television programs for their own noncommercial use. Universal brought suit, claiming that the sale of the Betamax VTRs to the general public violated its rights under the Copyright Act. It sought no relief against any Betamax consumer. Instead, Universal sued Sony for contributory infringement of its copyrights, seeking money damages, an equitable accounting of profits, and an injunction against the manufacture and sale of Betamax VTRs. Decision?

10. The Coca-Cola Company manufactures a carbonated beverage, Coke, made from coca leaves and cola nuts. The Koke Company of America introduced into the beverage market a similar product named Koke. The Coca-Cola Company brought a trademark infringement action against Koke. Coke claimed unfair competition within the beverage business due to Koke's imitation of the Coca-Cola product and Koke's attempt to reap the benefit of consumer identification with the Coke name. Decision?

11. Vuitton, a French corporation, manufactures high-quality handbags, luggage, and accessories. Crown Handbags, a New York corporation, manufactures and distributes ladies' handbags. Vuitton handbags are sold exclusively in expensive department stores, and distribution is strictly controlled to maintain a certain retail selling price. The Vuitton bags bear a registered trademark and a distinctive design. Crown's handbags appear identical to the Vuitton bags but are of inferior quality. Vuitton sues Crown for manufacturing counterfeit handbags and selling them at a discount. Decision?

12. T.G.I. Friday's, a New York corporation and registered service mark, entered into an exclusive licensing agreement with Tiffany & Co. that allowed Tiffany to open a Friday's restaurant in Jackson, Mississippi. International Restaurant Group, operated by the owners of Tiffany, applied for a license to open a Friday's in Baton Rouge, Louisiana, but was refused. In Baton Rouge, International then opened a restaurant, called E.L. Saturday's, or Ever Lovin' Saturday's, which had the same type of menu and decor as Friday's. Friday's sues International for trademark infringement. Decision?

13. As part of its business, Kinko's Graphics Corporation (Kinko's) copied excerpts from books, compiled them in "packets," and sold the packets to college students. Kinko's did this without permission from the owners of the copyrights to the books and without paying copyright fees or royalties. Kinko's has over 200 stores nationwide and reported $15 million in assets and $3 million in profits for 1989. Basic Books, Harper & Row, John Wiley & Sons, and others (plaintiffs) sued Kinko's for violation of the Copyright Act of 1976. The plaintiffs owned copyrights to the works copied and sold by Kinko's and derived substantial income from royalties. They argued that Kinko's had infringed on their copyrights by copying excerpts from their books and selling the copies to college students for profit. Kinko's admitted that it had copied excerpts without permission and had sold them in packets to students, but it contended that its actions constituted a fair use of the works in question under the Copyright Act. Decision?

Bailments and Documents of Title

A **bailment** is the relationship created when one person (the bailor) transfers the possession of personal property by delivery, without transfer of title, to another (the bailee) for the accomplishment of a certain purpose, after which the bailee is to return the property to the bailor or dispose of it according to the bailor's directions. One of the most common occurrences in everyday life, bailments are of great commercial importance. Bailments include the transportation, storage, repair, and rental of goods, which together involve billions of dollars in transactions each year. The following are common examples of bailments: keeping a car in a public garage; leaving a car, a watch, or any other article to be repaired; renting a car or truck; checking a hat or coat at a theater or restaurant; leaving clothes to be laundered; delivering jewelry, stocks, bonds, or other valuables to secure the payment of a debt; storing goods in a warehouse; and shipping goods by public or private transportation.

Documents of title are commonly used in bailment transactions. The most frequently used documents of title are the warehouse receipts issued by warehousers and the bills of lading issued by carriers.

Bailment the temporary transfer of personal property by one party to another

BAILMENTS

A bailment is the temporary transfer of possession, without title, of personal property by one party (the **bailor**) to another (the **bailee**). The benefit of a bailment may, by its terms, accrue solely to the bailor, solely to the bailee, or to both parties. A bailment may be with or without compensation. On these bases, bailments are classified as follows:

Bailor transferor of the bailed property

Bailee recipient of the bailed property

1. *Bailments for the bailor's sole benefit* include the gratuitous custody of personal property and the gratuitous services that involve custody of personal property, such as repairs or transportation. For example, if Sherry stores, repairs, or transports Tim's goods without compensation, this is a bailment for the sole benefit of the bailor, Tim.
2. *Bailments for the bailee's sole benefit* are usually limited to the gratuitous loan of personal property for use by the bailee, as where Tim, without compensation, lends his car, lawn mower, or book to Sherry for her use.
3. *Bailments for the mutual benefit of both parties* include ordinary commercial bailments, such as the delivery of goods to a repairman, jewels to a pawnbroker, or an automobile to a parking lot attendant.

Essential elements
(1) delivery of possession;
(2) personal property;
(3) possession, but not ownership, for a determinable time; and
(4) restoration of possession to the bailor

Essential Elements of a Bailment

The basic elements of a bailment are (1) the delivery of possession from a bailor to a bailee; (2) the delivery of personal property, not real property; (3) possession without ownership by the bailee for a determinable period; and (4) an absolute duty on the bailee to return the property to the bailor or to dispose of it according to the bailor's directions.

In most cases, two simple elements determine the existence of a bailment: (1) a separation of ownership and possession of the property (possession without ownership) and (2) a duty on the party in possession to redeliver the identical property to the owner or to dispose of it according to the owner's directions.

LITTLE, BROWN AND COMPANY v. AMERICAN PAPER RECYCLING CORP. United States

District Court, District of Massachusetts, 1993, 824 F.Supp. 11

FACTS Little, Brown and Company (Little, Brown), a publisher of books, entered into an agreement with American Paper Recycling Corp. (APR) whereby APR was to recycle books for Little, Brown. After the books were destroyed, APR was to pay Little, Brown ten dollars per usable ton and also, upon request, to provide Little, Brown with a certificate of destruction with respect to any shipment of books. In late October and early November 1990, APR picked up four shipments of books from Little, Brown. However, rather than destroying the books, APR sold the books to Advantage Paper Stock, Inc. (Advantage). Advantage's agreement with APR was to purchase "books for cutting" at $30 per ton. Advantage also did not destroy the books but sold them to another recycling company for $40 per ton. Following a series of transfers, some of the books ended up in the possession of book retailers. Little, Brown is suing APR for breach of a bailment contract.

DECISION Judgment for Little, Brown.

OPINION The parties in this case disagree about whether this is a contract for services with the parties in a bailor/bailee relationship or whether it is a contract for the sale of goods. The facts indicate that this contract contemplates a service and a bailment rather than an outright sale of goods. By definition a bailment is

the delivery of personal property by one person to another in trust for a specific purpose, with a contract, express or implied, that the trust shall be faithfully executed, and the property returned or duly accounted for when the special purpose is accomplished, or kept until the bailor reclaims it.

The undisputed evidence shows that APR paid Little, Brown not for the value of the books as books but rather for the usable weight of paper after the bindings and covers had been removed from the books. The parties also agree that the books had been consigned to APR by Little, Brown. Moreover, the amount to be paid by APR under the contract could not be established until the books had been destroyed. Lastly, APR was contractually obligated to certify, upon request, that the service of destroying the books had been performed. Under these circumstances, this contract must be interpreted as contemplating the destruction of books accompanied by a bailment lasting until the books were destroyed.

APR breached this contract for services in two ways. First, APR did not fully perform the service it agreed to perform. Although APR could delegate its duty to destroy the books, it could not delegate its duty to certify that the books had been destroyed. Since some of the books were not destroyed, APR could not possibly fulfill its obligation to certify their destruction. Second, APR sold the books while legal title was still in Little, Brown. A bailment does not contemplate any change of ownership rights. The bailor retains legal title and the bailee merely has the right to possession. By selling the books while they were still books, APR violated the bailor/bailee relationship and breached its contract with Little, Brown.

INTERPRETATION Under a bailment, the bailee must faithfully execute the purpose of the bailment.

Delivery of Possession Possession by a bailee involves (1) the bailee's power to control the personal property and (2) either the bailee's intention to control the property or her awareness that the rightful possessor has given up physical control of it. Thus, for example, when a restaurant customer hangs his hat or coat on a hook furnished for that purpose, the hat or coat is within an area under the restaurant owner's physical control. But the restaurant owner is not a bailee of the hat or coat unless he clearly signifies an intention to exercise control over the hat or coat. On the other hand, when a clerk in a store helps a customer to remove his coat in order to try on a new one, the owner of the store usually is held to have become a bailee of the old coat through the clerk, her employee. Here, the clerk has signified an intention to control the coat by taking it from the customer, and a bailment results.

Personal Property The bailment relationship can exist only with respect to personal property. The delivery of possession of real property by the owner to another is covered by real property law. Bailed property need not be tangible. Intangible property, such as promissory notes, corporate bonds, shares of stock, documents of title, and life insurance policies that are evidenced by written instruments and are thus capable of delivery, may be and frequently are the subject matter of bailments.

Possession for a Determinable Time To establish a bailment relationship, the person receiving possession must be under a duty to return the personal property and must not obtain title to it. If the identical property transferred is to be returned, even in an altered form, the transaction is a bailment; however, if other property of equal value or the money value of the original property may be returned, a transfer of title has occurred, and the transaction is a sale.

Restoration of Possession to the Bailor The bailee is legally obligated to restore the property to the bailor's possession when the bailment period ends. Normally, the bailee is required to return the identical goods bailed, although their condition may be changed because of the work that the bailee was required to perform on them. An exception to this rule concerns **fungible goods**, such as grain, which, for all practical purposes, consist of particles that are the equivalent of every other particle and which are expected to be mingled with other like goods during a bailment. Given such goods, a bailee obviously cannot be required to return the identical goods bailed. His obligation is simply to return goods of the same quality and quantity.

> **Fungible goods** equivalent goods, each unit being the equivalent of every other unit

A bailee has a duty to return the property to the right person. Her mistake in delivering property to the wrong person does not excuse her, even when the bailor's negligence induces the mistake. A bailee who, through mistake or intention, *misdelivers* the property to a third person who has no right to its possession is guilty of conversion and is liable to the bailor.

Rights and Duties of Bailor and Bailee

The bailment relationship creates rights and duties on the part of the bailor and the bailee. The bailee is under a duty to exercise due care for the safety of the property and to return it to the right person; conversely, the bailee has the exclusive right to possess the property for the term of the bailment. In addition, depending on the nature of the transaction, a bailee may have the right to limit his liability, as well as to receive compensation and reimbursement of expenses. The bailor, in turn, has certain duties with respect to the condition of the bailed goods.

Bailee's Duty to Exercise Due Care The bailee must exercise due care not to permit injury to or destruction of the property by the bailee or by third parties. The degree of care depends on the nature of the bailment relationship and the character of the property. In the context of a **commercial bailment**, from

> **Commercial bailment** parties derive a mutual benefit

Bailee's duty to exercise due care the bailee must exercise reasonable care to protect the safety of the property and to return it to the proper person

which the parties derive a mutual benefit, the law requires the bailee to exercise the care that a reasonably prudent person would exercise under the same circumstances. Where the bailment benefits the bailee alone (Tim's borrowing Michael's truck without payment would be an example), the law requires more-than-reasonable care of the bailee. On the other hand, where the bailee accepts the property for the bailor's sole benefit, the law requires a lesser degree of care (see Figure 51–1). Nevertheless, the amount of care required to satisfy any of the standards will vary with the character of the property.

When the property is lost, damaged, or destroyed while in the bailee's possession, it is often impossible for the bailor to obtain enough information to show that the loss or damage was due to the bailee's failure to exercise required care. The law aids the bailor in this respect by *presuming* that the bailee was at fault. The bailor is merely required to show that certain property was delivered by way of bailment and that the bailee either has failed to return it or has returned it in a damaged condition. The burden is then on the bailee to prove that he exercised the degree of care required of him.

Bailee's absolute liability occurs when (1) the parties so agree; (2) the custom of the industry requires the bailee to insure the property against the risk in question, but he fails to do so; or (3) the bailee uses the bailed property in an unauthorized manner

Bailee's Absolute Liability to Return Property As we discussed earlier, the bailee is free from liability if she exercised the degree of care required of her under the particular bailment while the property was within her control. This general rule has certain important exceptions that impose an absolute duty on the bailee to return the property undamaged to the proper person.

Where the bailee has an obligation by express *agreement* with the bailor or by *custom* to insure the property against certain risks but fails to do so, and the property is destroyed or damaged through such risks, she is liable for the damage or nondelivery, even if she has exercised due care.

Where the bailee uses the bailed property in a manner *not* authorized by the bailor or by the character of the bailment, and during the course of such use the property is damaged or destroyed, without fault on the bailee's part, the bailee is nonetheless absolutely liable for the damage or destruction. The wrongful use by the bailee automatically terminates her lawful possession: she becomes a trespasser as to the property and, as such, is absolutely liable for whatever harm befalls it.

Bailee's right to limit liability certain bailees are not permitted to limit their liability for breach of their duties, except as provided by statute

Bailee's Right to Limit Liability Certain bailees—namely common carriers, public warehousers, and innkeepers—may limit their liability for breach of their duties to the bailor only as provided by statute. Other bailees, however, may vary their duties and liabilities by contract with the bailor. Where liability may be limited by contract, the law requires that any such limitation be properly brought to the bailor's attention before he bails the property. This is especially true in the case of "professional bailees," such as repair garages, who make it their business

FIGURE 51–1 Duties in a Bailment

Type of Bailment	Bailee's Duty of Care	Bailor's Duty
For sole benefit of bailor	Slight care	To warn of defects of which she knew or should have known
For sole benefit of bailee	Utmost care	To warn of known defects
For mutual benefit	Ordinary care	To warn of defects of which she knew or should have known

to act as bailees and who deal with the public on a uniform, rather than on an individual, basis. Thus, a variation or limitation in writing, contained, for example, in a claim check or stub given to the bailor or posted on the walls of the bailee's place of business, ordinarily will *not* bind the bailor unless the bailee (a) draws the bailor's attention to the writing, (b) informs the bailor that it contains a limitation or variation of liability, and (c) the limitation is not the result of unequal bargaining power. Some states do not permit professional bailees (who commonly include warehousers, garagers, and parking lot owners) to disclaim liability for their own negligence.

AMERICAN NURSERY PRODUCTS, INC. v. INDIAN WELLS ORCHARDS Supreme Court of
Washington, 1990, 115 Wash.2d 217, 707 P.2d 477

FACTS In the fall of 1983, Indian Wells Orchards decided to acquire apple trees for development of an orchard. After contacting several nurseries, Indian Wells entered into a contract with American Nursery Products, Inc., doing business as Mount Arbor Nurseries (Mt. Arbor). Under the terms of the agreement, Mt. Arbor was to grow 200,000 grafted apple trees and 500,000 budded apple trees for Indian Wells. Indian Wells was to provide the 700,000 trees for growing, and Mt. Arbor was to provide up to 65,000 understocks for grafting and budding as necessary to compensate for mortality during the nursery phase. The parties agreed they were entering into a service agreement, and they provided no warranties beyond the conditions and services in the contract. They did agree that Indian Wells could reject any tree that did not have a caliper size greater than five-sixteenths of an inch. Once the trees were accepted, the contract placed the risk of loss upon Indian Wells. Moreover, the contract provided that Mt. Arbor would not be subject to or liable for incidental or consequential damages. Pursuant to the contract, Indian Wells delivered the rootstocks and the budding and grafting wood to Mt. Arbor. Mt. Arbor dipped the rootstocks in Ridomil 2E, which is an erratic fungicide, and many of the rootstocks died. Consequently, Mt. Arbor delivered only 108,158 of the 200,000 grafted trees and 372,360 of the 500,000 budded trees. Of those trees, Indian Wells rejected 32,750. Of those trees that were accepted, 89,983 later died. Indian Wells did not pay. Mt. Arbor brought suit against Indian Wells to recover the amount due on the contract. Indian Wells counterclaimed, alleging negligence and breach of contract.

The trial court, sitting without a jury, found that the dipping of the rootstocks in Ridomil had caused over $2.3 million in direct and consequential damages and constituted negligence *per se* and a breach of contract. The court reduced the damages by the $383,528 due under the contract and awarded $2,081,854 to Indian Wells. Though Mt. Arbor argued that the exclusionary clause in the contract prevented liability on its part for

negligence, the trial court held that the agreement excluding incidental and consequential damages was unconscionable, unenforceable, and against public policy. Mt. Arbor appealed.

DECISION Award of damages for breach of contract affirmed; award of incidental and consequential damages reversed.

OPINION The general rule is that a party to a contract can limit liability for damages resulting from negligence. However, specific exceptions render limitations on liability void as against public policy. One such exception prohibits professional bailees from limiting their liability for negligence. Here, the trial court held the exclusionary clause invalid on public policy grounds because bailees for mutual benefit are not permitted to disclaim or limit liability for negligence. The court did not, however, distinguish between professional bailees and bailees for mutual benefit. The law treats professional bailees differently than other bailees because the equality of bargaining power of the two parties to the professional bailment contract is largely theoretical. The bailor needs the bailee's services, is usually in no position to take his trade elsewhere, and, consequently, is compelled to agree to the terms the bailee stipulates.

The distinction between bailments for mutual benefit and professional bailments is somewhat blurred. While professional bailments are necessarily bailments for mutual benefit, not all bailments for mutual benefit are professional bailments. Bailments for mutual benefit, which include all nongratuitous bailments, arise when both parties to the contract benefit from the bailment. The benefit to the bailee need not be in the form of cash. Instead, the benefit may derive from a bailment that is incidental to the performance of services for which the bailee is to receive compensation or to the conduct of business from which the bailee hopes to derive profit. Such a benefit may also accrue where the bailor's desire to promote a sale motivates the bailment. Thus, bailments arising from service transactions are

continued

bailments for mutual benefit, and the bailees involved are not professional bailees. Therefore, they may validly contract to limit their liability for negligence.

Mt. Arbor was to receive compensation for the service it performed upon the bailed goods. Mt. Arbor and Indian Wells had equal bargaining strength, and Indian Wells was free to choose another commercial nursery for the needed service. Mt. Arbor was not a professional bailee; rather, the bailment was incidental to the performance of the service. Thus, no rule prohibits Mt. Arbor, as a bailee for mutual benefit, from contractually limiting its liability for negligence.

INTERPRETATION Professional bailees, in some states, are not permitted to disclaim liability for their own negligence.

Bailee's right to compensation entitled to reasonable compensation for work or services performed on the bailed goods

Bailee's Right to Compensation A bailee who by express or implied agreement undertakes to perform work on or render services in connection with the bailed goods is entitled to reasonable compensation for those services or that work. In most cases, the agreement between bailor and bailee fixes the amount of compensation and provides how it shall be paid. In the absence of a contrary agreement, the compensation is payable when the bailee completes the work or performs the services. If, after such completion or performance but before the redelivery of the goods to the bailor, the goods are lost or damaged through no fault of the bailee, the bailee is still entitled to compensation for his work and services.

Most bailees who are entitled to compensation for work and services performed in connection with bailed goods acquire a possessory lien on the goods to secure the payment of such compensation. In most jurisdictions, the bailee has a statutory right to obtain a judicial foreclosure of his lien and a sale of the goods. Many statutes also provide that the bailee does not lose his lien on redelivery of the goods to the bailor, as was the case at common law. Instead, the lien will continue for a specified period after redelivery, if the bailee timely records with the proper authorities an instrument claiming such a lien.

Bailor's duties in bailment for sole benefit of bailee, the bailor warrants that she is unaware of any defects; in all other bailments, the bailor has a duty to warn of all known defects and all defects she should discover upon a reasonable inspection

Bailor's Duties In a bailment for the sole benefit of the bailee, the bailor warrants that she is unaware of any defects in the bailed property. In all other instances, the bailor has a duty to warn the bailee of all defects she knows of or should have discovered upon a reasonable inspection of the bailed property. (See Figure 51–1). A number of courts have extended strict liability in tort and the implied warranties under Article 2 of the UCC to leases and bailments. Proposed Article 2A imposes implied warranties on the lease of goods.

Special Types of Bailments

Although the general principles that apply to all bailees govern pledgees, warehousers, and safe deposit companies, certain special features about the transactions in which they respectively engage subject them to extraordinary duties of care and liability. Innkeepers and common carriers may also be said to be *extraordinary* bailees, whereas all other bailees are *ordinary* bailees. This distinction is based on the character and extent of the liability of these two classes of bailees for the loss of or injury to bailed goods. As we have seen, an **ordinary**

Ordinary bailee one who must exercise due care

Extraordinary bailee one who is absolutely liable for the safety of the bailed property without regard to the cause of any loss

bailee is liable for only the loss or injury that results from his failure to exercise ordinary or reasonable care. The liability of the **extraordinary bailee**, on the other hand, is, in general, *absolute*. Just as an insurer, in general, becomes automatically liable to the insured on the happening of the hazard insured against, regardless of the cause, the extraordinary bailee becomes liable to the bailor for any loss or injury to the goods, regardless of the cause and without regard to the question of his care or negligence. Thus, he insures the safety of the goods.

Pledges A **pledge** is a bailment for security in which the owner gives possession of her personal property to another (the secured party) to secure a debt or the performance of some obligation. The secured party does not have title to the property involved but merely a possessory interest. Pledges of most types of personal property for security purposes are governed by Article 9 of the Uniform Commercial Code, which we discussed in Chapter 39. In most respects, the secured party's duties and liabilities are the same as those of a bailee for compensation.

Pledge security interest by possession

Warehousing A **warehouser** is a bailee who, for compensation, receives goods to be stored in a warehouse. Under the common law, his duties and liabilities were identical to those of the ordinary bailee for compensation. Today, because a strong public interest affects their activities, warehousers are subject to extensive state and federal regulation. Warehousers must also be distinguished from ordinary bailees in that the receipts they issue for storage have acquired a special status in commerce. Regarded as documents of title, these receipts are governed by Article 7 of the Uniform Commercial Code. (We will discuss documents of title later in this chapter.)

Warehouser storer of goods for compensation; warehouser must exercise reasonable care to protect the safety of the stored goods and to deliver them to the proper person

---

ETHICAL DILEMMA Who Is Responsible for the Operation of Rental Property?

FACTS Bobby Jones, a schoolteacher from a suburb of Atlanta, rents a fourteen-foot aluminum boat for the three-day Memorial Day weekend from Riverside Canoe and Boat Rentals on the Chattahoochee River. The manager of boat rentals gives Jones general instructions concerning the use of the craft and provides him with a booklet entitled "Boating Safety Rules." The manager also follows the routine procedure of examining the fuel line of the boat and starting the motor to ensure its serviceability.

On Memorial Day, while Jones is operating the boat on the Chattahoochee River, the motor stalls, forcing Jones to row the boat back to shore. Later that same day, Jones takes six minor children out in the boat to give them a ride on the river. Jones has been drinking beer nonstop since 8 A.M., and at the time of the afternoon boat ride his blood alcohol level is 0.22 percent. Jones recklessly moves into the swift current and heads toward a concrete dam and spillway. When he finally tries to reverse course, the motor stalls again, the boat is swept over the dam, and all of the children drown. Improbably, Jones lives.

Social, Policy, and Ethical Considerations

1. Could the boat rental company (and manager) have done more to prevent the accident that resulted in the children's deaths? Should the manager have done more?
2. Much rental property, including boats, cars, and power tools such as mowers and saws, is either potentially or inherently dangerous. What is the responsibility of the owner of such equipment to the renter of it? What, if anything, is the responsibility of

the renter to the owner? Should the owner be held strictly liable for the renter's accidents with the property, regardless of fault? Why or why not? Who do you think was at fault in this accident?
3. Jones's neighbors, the Corcorans and Duvals, are the parents of four of the drowned children. Together, in their anger, they consult a lawyer to explore the idea of suing either Jones or Riverside Canoe and Boat Rentals, or both. What cause might their lawyer try to make against Jones? Against Riverside Canoe and Boat Rentals? Do you think they should sue? Why or why not?
4. Are some items of equipment so dangerous the state legislatures should pass laws forbidding their rental? If so, what items?

Safe Deposit Boxes A majority of states hold that a person who rents a safe deposit box from a bank enters into a bailment relationship. As this constitutes a bailment for the parties' mutual benefit, the bailee bank owes the customer the duty to act with ordinary due care and is liable only if negligent.

Carriers of Goods In the broadest sense, anyone who transports goods from one place to another, either gratuitously or for compensation, is a **carrier**. Carriers are classified primarily as common carriers and private carriers. A **common carrier** offers its services and facilities to the public on terms and under circumstances indicating that the offering is made to all persons. Stated somewhat differently, the criteria that define common carriers are as follows: (1) the carriage must be part of its business; (2) the carriage must be for remuneration; and (3) the carrier must represent to the general public that it is willing to serve the public in the transportation of property. Common carriers of goods include railroad, steamship, aircraft, public trucking, and pipeline companies. In contrast, a **private** or **contract carrier** is one who carries the goods of another on isolated occasions or who serves a limited number of customers under individual contracts without offering the same or similar contracts to the public at large.

The person who delivers goods to a carrier for shipment is known as the **consignor** or shipper. The person to whom the carrier is to deliver the goods is known as the **consignee**. The instrument containing the terms of the contract of transportation, which the carrier issues to the shipper, is called a *bill of lading* (discussed later in this chapter).

A common carrier is under a duty to serve the public to the limits of its capacity and, within those limits, to accept for carriage goods of the kind that it normally transports. A private carrier, by comparison, has no duty to accept goods for carriage, except where it agrees by contract to do so. Whether common or private, the carrier is under an absolute duty to deliver the goods to the person to whom the shipper has consigned them.

A private carrier, in the absence of special contract terms, is liable as a bailee for the goods it undertakes to carry. The liability of a common carrier, on the other hand, approaches that of an insurer of the safety of the goods, except where loss or damage is caused by an act of God, an act of a public enemy, the acts or fault of the shipper, the inherent nature of or a defect in the goods, or an act of public authority. The carrier, however, is permitted, through its contract with the shipper, to limit its liability, provided the carrier gives the shipper notice of this limitation and the opportunity to declare a higher value for the goods.

Innkeepers At common law, **innkeepers** (today better known as hotel and motel owners or operators) are held to the same *strict or absolute liability* for their guests' belongings as are common carriers for the goods they carry. This rule of strict liability applies only to those who furnish lodging to the public for compensation as a regular business and extends only to the belongings of lodgers who are guests. Today, in almost all jurisdictions, case law and statute have substantially modified the innkeeper's strict liability under common law.

DOCUMENTS OF TITLE

A **document of title** is a warehouse receipt, bill of lading, or other document evidencing a right to receive, hold, and dispose of the document *and* the goods it

Carrier transporter of goods

Common carrier carrier that offers its services to the general public; is an extraordinary bailee

Private carrier carrier that limits its services and does not offer them to the general public; is an ordinary bailee

Consignor shipper of goods

Consignee person to whom the goods are to be shipped

Innkeeper hotel or motel operator; is an extraordinary bailee except as limited by statute or case law

Document of title instrument evidencing ownership of the document and the goods it covers

covers. To be a document of title, a document must be issued by or addressed to a bailee and must cover goods in the bailee's possession that are either identified or are fungible portions of an identified mass.

Briefly, a document of title symbolizes ownership of the goods it describes. Because of the document's legal characteristics, its ownership is equivalent to the ownership or control of the goods it represents, without the necessity of actual or physical possession of the goods. Likewise, its transfer transfers the ownership or control of the goods without necessitating the physical transfer of the goods themselves. For these reasons, documents of title are a convenient means of handling the billions of dollars' worth of goods that are transported by carriers or are stored with warehousers. Documents of title also facilitate the transfer of title to goods and the creation of a security interest in goods. Article 7 of the UCC governs documents of title.

Types of Documents of Title

Warehouse Receipts A **warehouse receipt** is a receipt issued by a person engaged in the business of *storing* goods for hire. A warehouser is liable for damages for loss or injury to the goods caused by his failure to exercise such care in regard to them as a reasonably careful person would exercise under the circumstances. The warehouser must deliver the goods to the person entitled to receive them under the terms of the warehouse receipt. Though a warehouser *may* limit his liability through a provision in the warehouse receipt fixing a specific maximum liability per article or item or unit of weight, this limitation, as shown in the case below, does not apply when a warehouser converts goods to his own use.

> **Warehouse receipt** receipt issued by a person storing goods

To enforce the payment of her charges and necessary expenses in connection with keeping and handling the goods, a warehouser has a lien on the goods that enables her to sell them at public or private sale after notice and to apply the net proceeds of the sale to the amount of her charges. The Code, moreover, provides the warehouser a definite procedure for enforcing her lien against the goods stored and in her possession.

I.C.C. METALS, INC. v. MUNICIPAL WAREHOUSE CO. Court of Appeals of New York, 1980, 50 N.Y.2d 657, 431 N.Y.S.2d 372, 409 N.E.2d 849

FACTS In the fall of 1974, I.C.C. Metals, Inc. delivered three lots of indium, an industrial metal, to Municipal Warehouse Company for safekeeping. The indium had an aggregate weight of 845 pounds and was worth $100,000. The warehouse supplied I.C.C. with receipts for each lot. Printed on the back of these receipts were the terms and conditions of the bailment, including an exculpatory clause limiting the liability of the warehouse to a maximum of $50. For two years, the warehouse billed I.C.C. for storage of the indium, and I.C.C. paid each invoice. In 1976, I.C.C. requested the return of the indium. For the first time, the warehouse told I.C.C. it was unable to locate any of the indium. I.C.C. brought an action in conversion to recover the full value of the indium. The warehouse defended on the ground that the metal had been stolen through no fault of its own and that its liability was limited to $50 in accordance with the terms of the warehouse receipts. The trial court granted summary judgment to I.C.C. for the full value of the stored property, and the appellate court affirmed.

DECISION Judgment for I.C.C. affirmed.

OPINION Absent an agreement to the contrary, a warehouse is not an insurer of goods. Thus, it may not be held liable for any injury to or loss of property not due to its own fault. As a bailee, however, a warehouse must exercise reasonable care to prevent loss or damage to the bailed property. It is also required to refrain from converting the goods left in its care. If a warehouse loses bailed property due to its own negligence, it will be liable for the full value of the goods, unless the

continued

parties have agreed to limit the warehouse's liability. A warehouse can, under certain conditions, limit its liability for its negligence. Nevertheless, if the warehouse converts the goods, liability cannot be limited. When a warehouse converts public property, it loses the protections afforded by its storage agreement.

Here, I.C.C. proved that it delivered the indium to Municipal and that it made a proper demand for its return, which Municipal failed to honor. Municipal's unsupported claim that the metal was stolen does not sufficiently explain the loss. The court then determined that under these circumstances, I.C.C.'s action in conversion could stand. Thus, the contractual limitation on Municipal's liability is ineffective.

INTERPRETATION A warehouser, as a bailee, must exercise ordinary care to prevent loss or damage to the bailed property.

Bill of lading document issued to the shipper by the carrier (1) as a receipt for the goods, (2) as evidence of their carriage contract, and (3) as a document of title

Bills of Lading A **bill of lading** is a document issued by a carrier on receipt of goods for *transportation*. It serves a threefold function: (1) as a receipt for the goods, (2) as evidence of the contract of carriage, and (3) as a document of title. A bill of lading is negotiable if, by its terms, the goods are deliverable to bearer or to the order of a named person. Any other document is nonnegotiable.

Under the Code, bills of lading may be issued not only by common carriers but also by contract carriers, freight forwarders, or any person engaged in the business of transporting or forwarding goods.

The carrier must deliver the goods to the person entitled to receive them under the terms of the bill of lading. Common carriers are extraordinary bailees under the law and are subject to greater liability than are ordinary bailees, such as warehousers.

The Code allows a carrier to limit its liability by contract in all cases where its rates depend on the value of the goods and the carrier allows the shipper an opportunity to declare a higher value. The limitation does not apply, however, when the carrier converts goods to its own use.

CALVIN KLEIN, LTD. v. TRYLON TRUCKING CORP. U.S. Court of Appeals, Second Circuit, 1989, 892 F.2d 191

FACTS Calvin Klein, Ltd. (Calvin Klein), a New York clothing company, had used the services of Trylon Trucking Corporation (Trylon) for over three years, involving hundreds of shipments, prior to the lost shipment at issue. After completing each carriage, Trylon would forward to Calvin Klein an invoice that contained a limitation of liability provision. The provision stated, "In consideration of the rate charged, the shipper agrees that the carrier shall not be liable for more than $50.00 on any shipment accepted for delivery to one consignee unless a greater value is declared, in writing, upon receipt at time of shipment and charge for such greater value paid, or agreed to be paid, by shipper."

On April 2, Trylon dispatched its driver Jamahl Jefferson to the J.F.K. International Airport to pick up 2,833 blouses sent from Hong Kong to Calvin Klein. The driver disappeared, stealing both the truck and the blouses. Calvin Klein sued Trylon for the full value of the blouses. The trial court ruled for Calvin Klein, holding that the limitation of liability provision did not extend to

the shipment at issue, due to lack of assent and consideration. While Trylon concedes that it was grossly negligent in the hiring and supervision of its driver, Trylon argues that such negligence is irrelevant here, and that the liability limitation provision should be enforced.

DECISION Judgment for Trylon.

OPINION According to the UCC, a shipper and a common carrier may contract to limit the carrier's liability in cases of loss to an amount agreed to by the parties, so long as the language of limitation is clear, the shipper is aware of the terms of the limitation, and the shipper can change the terms by indicating the true value of the goods being shipped. Such a limitation agreement usually is valid and enforceable, despite carrier negligence. The shipper can calculate the specific amount of its potential damages in advance, declare the value of the shipment based on that calculation, and pay a commensurately higher rate for carriage of the goods. In effect, the shipper can thus buy additional insurance from the common carrier.

continued

Here, Calvin Klein and Trylon were business entities with an ongoing commercial relationship spanning over three years and numerous transactions. In this commercial setting the clear limitation agreement between Calvin Klein and Trylon will be enforced. This is not a case where the shipper was dealing with the carrier for the first time, or under new or changed terms. Calvin Klein was aware of the terms and was free to adjust the limitation upon a written declaration of the value of a given shipment, but failed to do so with the shipment at issue. The terms of the unmodified liability limitation provision must be enforced despite Trylon's admitted gross negligence. Therefore, Trylon must pay Calvin Klein $50.00 for the lost shipment.

INTERPRETATION A carrier may limit its liability, even if the harm is caused by the carrier's negligence.

On goods in its possession that are covered by a bill of lading, the carrier has a lien for the charges and expenses necessary for its preservation of such goods. Against a purchaser for value of a negotiable bill of lading, this lien is limited to charges stated in the bill or in the applicable published tariff or, if no charges are so stated, to a reasonable charge.

The carrier may enforce its lien by public or private sale of the goods after notice to all persons known by the carrier to claim an interest in them. The sale must be on terms that are "commercially reasonable," and the carrier must conduct it in a "commercially reasonable manner."

A purchaser in good faith of goods sold to enforce the lien takes free of any rights of persons against whom the lien was valid, even if the enforcement of the lien does not comply with Code requirements. This rule applies both to carrier's and to warehouser's liens.

Negotiability of Documents of Title

The concept of negotiability has long been established in law. It is important not only in connection with documents of title but also in connection with commercial paper and investment securities, topics treated in other chapters of this book.

The Code provides that a warehouse receipt, bill of lading, or other document of title is negotiable if, by its terms, the goods are to be delivered to bearer or to the order of a named person or where, in overseas trade, the document runs to a named person or assigns. *Any* other document is nonnegotiable.

A nonnegotiable document, such as a straight bill of lading or a warehouse receipt under which the goods are deliverable only to a person named in the bill and not to the order of any person or to bearer, may be transferred by assignment but may not be negotiated. Only a negotiable document or instrument may be negotiated.

> **Negotiability** a document of title is negotiable if, by its terms, the goods are to be delivered to bearer or to the order of a named person

Due Negotiation

The Code sets forth the manner in which a negotiable document of title may be negotiated and the requirements of due negotiation. An order form negotiable document of title running to the order of a named person is negotiated by her indorsement and delivery. After such indorsement in blank or to bearer, the document may be negotiated by delivery alone. A special indorsement, by which the document is indorsed over to a specified person, requires the indorsement of the special indorsee as well as delivery to accomplish a further negotiation.

Due negotiation, a term peculiar to Article 7, requires not only that the purchaser of the negotiable document take it in good faith, without notice of any

> **Due negotiation** transfer of a negotiable document in the regular course of business to a holder who takes in good faith, without notice of any defense or claim, and for value

adverse claim or defense, and pay value, but also that she take it in the regular course of business or financing, not in settlement or payment of a money obligation. Thus, a transfer for value of a negotiable document of title to a nonbanker or to a person not in business, such as a college professor or student, would not be a due negotiation.

Due negotiation creates new rights in the holder of the document. The transferee does not stand in the shoes of his transferor; in other words, the defects and defenses available against the transferor are not available against the new holder. Newly created by the negotiation, his rights are free of such defects and defenses. This enables bankers and business persons to extend credit on documents of title without concern about possible adverse claims or the rights of third parties.

The rights of a holder of a negotiable document of title to whom it has been duly negotiated include (1) title to the document; (2) title to the goods; (3) all rights accruing under the law of agency or estoppel, including rights to goods delivered to the bailee after the document was issued; and (4) the issuer's direct obligation to hold or deliver the goods according to the document's terms.

Warranties

Warranties a person who negotiates or transfers a document of title for value, other than a collecting bank or other intermediary, incurs certain warranty obligations unless otherwise agreed

A person, other than a collecting bank or other intermediary, who either negotiates or transfers a document of title for value incurs certain warranty obligations, unless otherwise agreed. Such transferor warrants to her immediate purchaser (1) that the document is genuine, (2) that she had no knowledge of any fact that would impair its validity or worth, and (3) that her negotiation or transfer is rightful and fully effective with respect to the title to the document and the goods it represents.

Ineffective Documents of Title

Ineffective documents in order for a person to obtain title to goods by negotiation of a document, the goods must have been delivered to the issuer of the document by their owner or by one to whom the owner has entrusted actual or apparent authority

In order for a person to obtain title to goods through the negotiation of a document to him, the goods must have been delivered to the document's issuer by their owner or by either one to whom the owner has delivered the goods or one whom the owner has entrusted with actual or apparent authority to ship, store, or sell them. A warehouser or carrier, however, may deliver goods according to the terms of the document that it has issued or otherwise dispose of the goods as provided in the Code without incurring liability, even if the document did not represent title to the goods. The warehouser or carrier need only have acted in good faith and complied with reasonable commercial standards in both the receipt and delivery or other disposition of the goods. Such a bailee has no liability even though the person from whom the bailee received the goods had no authority to obtain the issuance of the document or to dispose of the goods, and the person to whom it delivered the goods had no authority to receive them.

Thus, a carrier or warehouser who receives goods from a thief or finder and later delivers them to a person to whom the thief or finder ordered them to be delivered is not liable to the true owner of the goods. Even a sale of the goods by the carrier or warehouser to enforce a lien for transportation or storage charges and expenses would not subject it to liability.

CHAPTER SUMMARY

Bailments	**Definition** the temporary transfer of personal property by one party (the bailor) to another (the bailee) **Classification of Bailments** ■ *For the Bailor's Sole Benefit* ■ *For the Bailee's Sole Benefit* ■ *For Mutual Benefit* includes ordinary commercial bailments **Essential Elements** ■ *Delivery of Possession* ■ *Personal Property* ■ *Possession, But not Ownership, for a Determinable Time* ■ *Restoration of Possession to the Bailor* **Rights and Duties** ■ *Bailee's Duty to Exercise Due Care* the bailee must exercise reasonable care to protect the safety of the property and to return it to the proper person ■ *Bailee's Absolute Liability* occurs when (1) the parties so agree; (2) the custom of the industry requires the bailee to insure the property against the risk in question, but he fails to do so; or (3) the bailee uses the bailed property in an unauthorized manner ■ *Bailee's Right to Limit Liability* certain bailees are not permitted to limit their liability for breach of their duties, except as provided by statute ■ *Bailee's Right to Compensation* entitled to reasonable compensation for work or services performed on the bailed goods ■ *Bailor's Duties* in bailment for sole benefit of bailee, the bailor warrants that she is unaware of any defects; in all other bailments, the bailor has a duty to warn of all known defects and all defects she should discover upon a reasonable inspection **Special Types** ■ *Pledge* security interest by possession ■ *Warehouser* storer of goods for compensation; warehouser must exercise reasonable care to protect the safety of the stored goods and to deliver them to the proper person ■ *Carrier of Goods* transporter of goods; a common carrier is an extraordinary bailee, while a private carrier is an ordinary bailee ■ *Innkeeper* hotel or motel operator; is an extraordinary bailee except as limited by statute or case law
Documents of Title	**Definition** an instrument evidencing ownership of the document and the goods it covers **Types** ■ *Warehouse Receipt* receipt issued by person storing goods ■ *Bill of Lading* document issued to the shipper by the carrier (1) as a receipt for the goods, (2) as evidence of their carriage contract, and (3) as a document of title **Negotiability** a document of title is negotiable if, by its terms, the goods are to be delivered to bearer or to the order of a named person **Due Negotiation** transfer of a negotiable document in the regular course of business to a holder, who takes in good faith, for value, and without notice of any defense or claim **Warranties** a person who negotiates or transfers a document of title for value, other than a collecting bank or other intermediary, incurs certain warranty obligations unless otherwise agreed **Ineffective Documents** in order for a person to obtain title to goods by negotiation of a document, the goods must have been delivered to the issuer of the document by their owner or by one to whom the owner has entrusted actual or apparent authority

QUESTIONS

1. Discuss the essential elements of a bailment.
2. Discuss the rights and duties of the bailor and bailee.
3. Discuss the duties of (a) a warehouser, (b) a common carrier, and (c) an innkeeper.
4. Define a document of title. Identify and discuss the various types of documents of title.
5. Discuss the negotiability of documents of title and the rights acquired by due negotiation.

Internet Question. Renting an automobile and shipping a package by express transportation are both examples of a bailment. Find and compare the rates and contract provisions of (a) three automobile rental companies, and (b) two express package transportation companies.

PROBLEMS

1. Phil was the owner of a herd of twenty highly bred dairy cows. He was a prosperous farmer, but his health was very poor. On the advice of his doctor, Phil decided to winter in Arizona. Before he left, he made an agreement with Freya under which Freya was to keep the cows on Freya's farm through the winter, pay Phil the sum of $800, and return to Phil the twenty cows at the close of the winter. For reasons that Freya thought made good farming sense, Freya sold six of the cows and replaced them with six other cows. After winter was over, Phil returned from Arizona. When he saw that Freya had replaced six of his cows, he sued Freya for the conversion of the original six cows. Decision?

2. Hines stored her furniture, including a grand piano, in Arnett's warehouse. Needing more space, Arnett stored Hines's piano in Butler's warehouse next door. As a result of a fire, which occurred without any fault of Arnett or Butler, both warehouses and their contents were destroyed. Hines sues Arnett for the value of her piano and furniture. Decision?

3. Curtis rented a safe deposit box from Reliable Safe Deposit Company, in which he deposited valuable securities and $4,000 in cash. Later, after opening the box and discovering $1,000 missing, Curtis brought an action against Reliable. At the trial, the company showed that its customary procedure was as follows: that there were two keys for each box furnished to each renter; that if a key was lost, the lock was changed; that new keys were provided for each lock each time a box was rented; that there were two clerks in charge of the vault; and that one of the clerks was always present to open the box. Reliable Safe Deposit Company also proved that two keys were given to Curtis at the time he rented his box; that his box could not be opened without the use of one of the keys in his possession; and that the company had issued no other keys to Curtis's box. Decision?

4. A, B, and C each stored 5,000 bushels of yellow corn in the same bin in X's warehouse. X wrongfully sold 10,000 bushels of this corn to Y. A contends that inasmuch as his 5,000 bushels of corn were placed in the bin first, the remaining 5,000 bushels belong to him. What are the rights of the parties?

5. (a) On April 1, Mary Rich, at the solicitation of Super Fur Company, delivered a $3,000 mink coat to the company at its place of business for storage in its vaults until November 1. On the same day, she paid the company its customary charge of $20 for such storage. After Mary left the store, the general manager of the company, on finding that its storage vaults were already filled to capacity, delivered Mary's coat to Swift Trucking Company for shipment to Fur Storage Company. En route, the truck in which Mary's coat was being transported was badly damaged by fire caused by the driver's negligence, and Mary's coat was totally destroyed. Is Super Fur Company liable to Mary for the value of her coat? Why?

   (b) Would your answer be the same if Mary's coat had been safely delivered to Fur Storage Company and had been stolen from the company's storage vaults without negligence on its part? Why?

6. Rich, a club member, left his golf clubs with Bogan, the pro at the Happy Hours Country Club, to be refinished at Bogan's pro shop. The refinisher employed by Bogan suddenly left town, taking Rich's clubs with him. The refinisher had previously been above suspicion, although Bogan had never checked on the man's character references. A valuable sand wedge that Bogan had borrowed from another member, Smith, for his own use in an important tournament was also stolen by the refinisher, as well as several pairs of golf shoes that Bogan had checked for members without charge as an accommodation. The club members concerned each made claims against Bogan for their losses. Can (a) Rich, (b) Smith, and (c) the other members compel Bogan to make good their respective losses?

7. Donna drove an automobile into Terry's garage and requested him to make repairs for which the charge would be $125. Donna, however, never returned to get the automobile. Two months later, Carla saw the automobile in Terry's garage and claimed it as her own, asserting that it had been stolen from her. Terry told Carla that she could have the automobile if she paid for the repairs and storage. One week later, Molly appeared and proved that the automobile was hers, that it had been stolen from her, and that neither Donna nor Carla had any rights in it. Molly brings an action against Terry for conversion of the automobile. Decision?

8. On June 1, Cain delivered his 1984 automobile to Barr, the operator of a repair shop, for necessary repairs. Barr put the car in his lot on Main Street. The lot, which is fenced on all sides except along Main Street, holds one hundred cars and is unguarded at night, although the police make periodic checks. The lot is well lighted. The cars do not have the keys in them when left out overnight. At some time during the night of June 4, the hood, starter, alternator, and gearshift were stolen from Cain's car. The car remained on the lot, and during the evening of June 5, the transmission was stolen from the car. The cost to replace the parts stolen in the first theft was $600 and in the second theft $500. Cain sued Barr to recover $1,100. Decision?

9. Seton, in Phoenix, according to a contract with Rider in New York, ships to Rider goods conforming to the contract and takes from the carrier a shipper's order bill of lading that Seton indorses in blank and forwards by mail to Clemson, his agent in New York, with instructions to deliver the bill of lading to Rider on receipt of payment of the price for the goods. Forest, a thief, steals the bill of lading from Clemson and transfers it for value to Pace, a *bona fide* purchaser. Before the goods arrive in New York, Rider is petitioned into bankruptcy. What are the rights of the parties?

10. Rutger, a Philadelphia merchant, purchased merchandise from Walsh in Chicago. The contract of sale provided that the merchandise was sold F.O.B. Chicago, payment to be made sixty days after delivery. Walsh delivered the goods to the railroad carrier in Chicago, took an order bill of lading in the name of Rutger, and forwarded it to Rutger. Before the goods arrived in Philadelphia, Walsh learned that Rutger had become insolvent and exercised a right of stoppage in transit by proper notice to the railroad company. Thereafter, and before the shipment reached Philadelphia, Rutger indorsed and delivered the bill of lading to Lee, an innocent purchaser for value. Lee claimed the goods by reason of holding the bill of lading. To whom should the goods be awarded?

11. Mrs. Laval was a patient of Dr. Leopold, a practicing psychiatrist. Dr. Leopold shared an office with two associates practicing in the same field. No receptionist or other employee attended the office. Mrs. Laval placed her coat in the clothes closet in the office reception room. Later, when she returned to retrieve the coat to leave, she found it missing. Mrs. Laval then brought this action to recover $1,725, the value of her coat. Decision? Explain.

12. Robert L. Moore, a United States Army sergeant stationed at Fort Benning, Georgia, rented a fourteen-foot aluminum boat from the Fort Benning Morale Support Activities Division, Outdoor Rentals. The manager of the rentals section gave Moore general instructions concerning the use of the craft and provided Moore with a copy of the Fort Benning Boating Safety Rules. He also followed the routine procedure of examining the fuel line of the boat and starting the motor to insure its serviceability. Three days later, while Moore was operating the boat on the Chattahoochee River, the motor stalled, forcing Moore to row the boat back to shore. Later that same day, Moore took six minor children out in the boat to give them a ride on the river. At the time, Moore's blood alcohol level was 0.29 percent, a level that would have made it extremely difficult to operate a boat with any type of proficiency. Moore recklessly moved into the swift current and headed toward a concrete dam and spillway. When he finally reversed course, the motor stalled again, the boat was swept over the dam, and the children were drowned. Juanita Craine and Nancy Brown, parents of four of the drowned children, brought an action against the United States, claiming that the government breached its duty to warn Moore and that the government is liable as the owner of a vessel that was negligently operated. Decision?

13. Mr. Sewall left his car in a parking lot owned by Fitz-Inn Auto Parks, Inc. The lot was approximately 100 by 200 feet in size and had a chain link fence along the rear boundary to separate the lot from a facility of the Massachusetts Bay Transportation Authority. Although the normal entrance and exit were located at the front of the lot, it was also possible to leave by way of small side streets on either side of the lot. Upon entering the lot, the driver would pay the attendant on duty a fee of twenty-five cents to park. The attendant's duties were limited to collecting money from patrons and directing them to parking spaces. Ordinarily, the attendant remained on duty until 11:00 a.m., after which time the lot was left unattended. Furthermore, a patron could remove his car from the lot at any time without interference by any employee of the parking lot.

On the morning of April 15, 1970, Sewall entered the lot, paid the twenty-five cent fee, parked his car in a space designated by the attendant, locked it, and took the keys with him. This was a routine he had followed for several years. When he returned to the unattended lot that evening, however, he found that his car was gone, apparently having been stolen by an unidentified third person. He then brought this action against Fitz-Inn, the owner of the lot, to recover the value of the car. Decision?

14. Mrs. Mieske delivered thirty-two fifty-foot reels of developed movie film to the Bartell Drug Company to be spliced together into four reels for viewing convenience. She placed the films, which contained irreplaceable pictures of her family's activities over a period of years, into the order in which they were to be spliced and then delivered them to the manager of Bartell. The manager placed a film processing packet on the bag of films and gave Mrs. Mieske a receipt that stated "We assume no responsibility beyond retail cost of film unless otherwise agreed to in writing." Although the disclaimer was not discussed, Mrs. Mieske's parting words to the store manager were "Don't lose these. They are my life."

Bartell sent the film to its processing agent, GAF Corporation, which intended to send them to another processing lab for splicing. While at the GAF laboratory, however, the film was accidently placed in the garbage dumpster and was never recovered. Upon learning of the loss of their film, the Mieskes brought this action to recover damages from Bartell and GAF. The defendants argued that their liability was limited to the cost of the unexposed film. A jury verdict was entered for the Mieskes for $7,500, and the defendants appealed. Decision?

Interests in Real Property

Interests in real property may be divided into possessory and nonpossessory interests. Possessory interests in real property, called estates, are classified, according to the quantity, nature, and extent of the rights they involve, into two major categories: freehold estates (those existing for an indefinite time or for the life of a person) and estates less than freehold (those that exist for a predetermined time), called leasehold estates. Both freehold estates and leasehold estates are regarded as possessory interests in property. In addition, there are several nonpossessory interests in property, including easements, *profits à prendre*, and licenses. The ownership of interests in property may be held by one individual or concurrently by two or more persons, each of whom is entitled to an undivided interest in the entire property. We will consider all of these topics in this chapter.

FREEHOLD ESTATES

As we mentioned above, a **freehold estate** is a right of ownership of real property for an indefinite time (fee estate) or for the life of a person (life estate). Of all the estates in real property, the most valuable are usually those present estates that combine the enjoyment of immediate possession with ownership at least for life. These estates are either some form of fee estates or estates for life. In addition, either type of estate may be created without immediate right to possession; such an estate is known as a future interest.

Freehold estate ownership of real property for an indefinite time or for the life of a person

Fee Estates

Fee estates include the right to immediate possession for an indefinite time and the right to transfer the interest by deed or will. Fee estates include both fee simple and qualified fee estates.

Fee estate right to immediate possession for an indefinite period of time

Fee Simple Estate **Fee simple** means that the property is owned absolutely and can be sold or passed on at will. The absolute rights to transfer ownership and to transmit such ownership through inheritance are basic characteristics of a fee simple estate. Fee simple is the largest estate in land; all other estates are derived from it.

Fee simple absolute ownership

A fee simple is created by any words that indicate an intent to convey absolute ownership. "To B in fee simple" will accomplish the purpose, as will "to B forever." The general presumption is that a conveyance is intended to convey full and absolute title in the absence of a clear intent to the contrary. A practical consequence of a fee simple title is not only that it may be transferred voluntarily, but also that it may be levied on and sold at the insistence of judgment creditors of the fee simple holder (the owner).

Qualified fee ownership subject to its being taken away upon the happening of an event

Qualified or Base Fee Estate It is possible to convey or will property to a person to enjoy absolutely, *subject* to its being taken away at a later date should a certain event occur. The estate thus created is known as a **qualified fee**, base fee, conditional fee, or fee simple defeasible. For example, Abe may provide in his will that his widow is to have his house and lot in "fee simple forever so long as she does not remarry." If his widow dies without remarrying, the property is transferred to her heirs as if she had owned it absolutely. However, if she remarries or sells the land to Ben and then remarries, the widow and Ben would respectively lose their title to the land; and it would revert to Abe's heirs.

The holder of a qualified fee interest may transfer the property by deed or will, and the property will pass by intestate succession. All transferees, however, take the property subject to the initial condition imposed upon the interest.

Life Estates

Life estates are divided into two major classes: (1) conventional life estates, or those created by voluntary act, and (2) those established by law, the most significant example of which is a wife's dower right in her husband's property.

Life estate ownership right for the life of a designated person

Remainder ownership estate that takes effect when the prior estate terminates

Conventional Life Estates A **life estate** is an ownership right in property for the life of a designated individual, while a **remainder** is the ownership estate that takes effect when the prior life estate terminates. For example, a grant or a devise (grant by will) "to Alex for life" creates in Alex an estate that terminates on his death. Such a provision may stand alone, in which case the property will revert to the grantor and his heirs; or, as is more likely, the provision will be followed by a subsequent grant to another party, such as "to Alex for life and then to Mario and his heirs." Alex is the *life tenant*, and Mario generally is described as the *remainderman*. Alex's life, however, need not be the measure of his life estate, as where an estate is granted "to Alex for the life of Bob." On Bob's death, Alex's interest terminates; if Alex dies before Bob, Alex's interest passes to his heirs or as he directs in his will for the remainder of Bob's life.

No particular words are necessary to create a life estate, as long as the words chosen clearly reflect the grantor's intent. Life estates arise most frequently in connection with the creation of trusts, which we will discuss in Chapter 54.

Waste any act or omission that permanently injures the realty or unreasonably changes its value

Generally, a life tenant may make reasonable use of the property as long as he does not commit "waste." Any act or omission that permanently injures the realty or unreasonably changes its characteristics or value constitutes **waste**. For example, the failure to repair a building, the unreasonable cutting of timber, or the neglect of an adequate conservation policy may subject the life tenant to an action by the remainderman to recover damages for waste.

A conveyance by the life tenant passes only her interest. The life tenant and the remainderman may, however, join in a conveyance to pass the entire fee to the property, or the life tenant may terminate her interest by conveying it to the remainderman.

Dower widow's estate in the real property of her husband

Life Estates Established by Law Under common law, **dower** is a life estate a widow has in one-third of all the real property her husband owned during their marriage. Arising by operation of law, it exists regardless of the intent or wishes of the parties.

Curtesy widower's estate in the real property of his wife

At common law, a surviving *husband* had a life estate, known as **curtesy**, in the real property of his wife, an estate similar to, though not identical with, a widow's dower. Unlike dower, curtesy did not exist unless a child had been born of the marriage.

Almost all of the states have substantially modified or entirely abolished the estates of dower and curtesy; in their place, some states by statute allow the surviving spouse a share in the estate of the deceased spouse.

Future Interests

Not all interests in property carry the right to immediate possession, even though the right and title to the interest are absolute. Thus, where property is conveyed or devised by will "to A during his life and then to B and her heirs," B has a definite, existing *interest* in the property, but she is not entitled to immediate *possession*. This right and similar rights, generically referred to as future interests, are of two principal types: reversions and remainders.

Reversions   If Anderson conveys property "to Benson for life" and makes no disposition of the remainder of the estate, Anderson holds the **reversion**—the grantor's right to the property on the death of the life tenant. Thus, Anderson would regain ownership to the property when Benson dies. However, because Anderson has only to await the termination of his grantee's estate before he regains ownership, a reversion in Anderson is also created if he conveys property "to Caldwell for ten years." Reversions may be transferred by deed or will and pass by intestate succession.

Reversion grantor's right to property upon termination of another estate

A conditional reversionary interest, a **possibility of reverter** exists where property may return to the grantor or his successor in interest because an event on which a fee simple estate was to terminate has occurred. This potential reversion is present in the grant of a base or qualified fee, previously discussed in this chapter. Thus, Karlene has a possibility of reverter if she dedicates property to a public use "so long as it is used as a park." If, in one hundred years, the city ceases to use the property for a park, Karlene's heirs will be entitled to the property. A possibility of a reverter may pass by will or intestate succession. In some states, it may be transferred by deed.

Possibility of reverter conditional reversionary interest

Remainders   A remainder, as we discussed earlier, is an estate in property that, like a reversion, will take effect in possession, if at all, on the termination of a prior estate created by the *same instrument*. Unlike a reversion, a remainder is held by a person other than the grantor or his successors. A grant from Gwen "to Lew for his life and then to Robert and his heirs" creates a remainder in Robert. On the termination of the life estate, Robert will be entitled to possession as remainderman, taking his title not from Lew but from the original grantor, Gwen.

A **vested remainder** is one in which the only contingency to possession by the remainderman is the termination of all preceding estates created by the transferor. When Richard has a remainder in fee, subject only to a life estate in Laura, the only obstacle to the right of immediate possession by Robert or his heirs is Laura's life. Laura's death is sufficient and necessary to place Robert in possession. The law considers this unconditional or vested remainder as a fixed, *present* interest to be enjoyed in the future.

Vested remainder unconditional remainder that is a fixed, present interest to be enjoyed in the future

By comparison, a **contingent remainder** is one in which the right to possession is dependent or conditional on the happening of some event *in addition* to the termination of the preceding estates. The contingent remainder may be conditioned on the existence of someone yet to be born or on the happening of an event that may never occur. A provision in a will "to David for life and then to his children, but if he has no children then to Julie" creates contingent

Contingent remainder remainder interest conditional upon the happening of an event in addition to the termination of the preceding estate

remainders both as to the children and as to Julie. Transferable by deed in most states, a contingent remainder is also inheritable, unless limited to termination prior to the death of the remainderman. For a comparison of the different free-hold estates see Figure 52–1.

LEASEHOLD ESTATES

Landlord owner of land who grants a leasehold interest to another

Tenant possessor of the leasehold interest

Leasehold estate right to possess real property

A lease is both a contract and a grant of an estate in land. It is a contract by which the owner of the land, the **landlord**, grants to another, the **tenant**, an exclusive right to use and possess the land for a definite or ascertainable period or term. The possessory term thus granted is an estate in land called a **leasehold estate**. The landlord retains an interest, or a *reversion*, in the property. A leasehold estate has two principal characteristics: it continues for a definite or ascertainable term and carries with it the tenant's obligation to pay rent to the landlord. Thus, if Linda, the owner of a house and lot, rents both to Ted for a year, Linda, of course, still holds title to the property; but she has sold to Ted the right to occupy it. Ted's right to occupy the property is superior to that of Linda, and as long as Ted occu-pies the property according to the terms of the lease contract, he has, as a prac-tical matter, exclusive possession against all the world as though he were the actual owner.

Creation and Duration

Because leaseholds are created by contract, the usual requirements for contract formation therefore apply. In most jurisdictions, leases for a term longer than a statutorily specified period, generally fixed at either one or three years, must be in writing. A few states require that all leases be in writing.

Definite term lease that automatically expires at end of the term

Definite Term A lease for a **definite term** automatically expires at the end of the term. Such a lease is frequently termed an *estate for years*, even though the duration may be one year or less. No notice to terminate is required.

Periodic tenancy lease with a definite term that is to be continued

Periodic Tenancy A **periodic tenancy** is a lease of indefinite duration that continues for successive periods unless terminated by notice to the other party.

FIGURE 52–1 Freehold Estates

Interest	Complementary Estate	Duration	Transfer by Deed	Transfer by Will or Intestacy
Fee Simple	None	Perpetual	Yes	Yes
Qualified Fee	Possibility of reverter	Until contingency occurs	Yes	Yes
Life Estate	Reversion or remainder	Life of indicated person	Yes	No, unless measuring life is not life tenant's
Reversion	Life estate	Perpetual	Yes	Yes
Possibility of Reverter	Qualified fee	Perpetual if contingency occurs	In some states	Yes
Vested Remainder	Life estate	Perpetual	Yes	Yes
Contingent Remainder	Life estate	Perpetual if contingency occurs	In most states	Yes, unless it is limited such that it terminates before the death of the remainderman

For example, a lease "to Ted from month to month" or "from year to year" creates a periodic tenancy. Periodic tenancies arise frequently by implication. For example, Laura leases to Ted without stating any term in the lease. This creates a tenancy at will. If Ted pays rent to Laura at the beginning of each month and Laura accepts such payments, most courts would hold that the tenancy at will has been transformed into a tenancy from month to month.

Either party may terminate a periodic tenancy at the expiration of any one period, but only on adequate notice to the other party. If the lease contains no specific agreement, the common law requires six months' notice in tenancies from year to year. However, in most jurisdictions, this period has been shortened by statute to periods ranging between thirty and ninety days in duration. In periodic tenancies involving periods of less than one year, the notice required at common law is one full period in advance; but, again, this may be subject to statutory regulation.

Tenancy at Will A lease containing a provision that either party may terminate at any time creates a **tenancy at will**. A lease that does not specify a duration also creates a tenancy at will. At common law, such tenancies were terminable without any prior notice, but many jurisdictions now have statutes requiring a period of notice before termination, usually thirty days.

Tenancy at will lease that is terminable at any time

Tenancy at Sufferance A **tenancy at sufferance** arises upon a tenant's failure to vacate the premises when the lease expires. Under the common law, the landlord may elect either to dispossess such tenant or to hold her for another term. Until the landlord makes this election, a tenancy at sufferance exists.

Tenancy at sufferance possession of real property without a valid lease

Transfer of Interests
Both the tenant's possessory interest in the leasehold and the landlord's reversionary interest in the property may be freely transferred in the absence of contractual or statutory prohibition. This general rule is subject to one major exception: the tenancy at will. Any attempt by either party to transfer her interest is usually considered an expression of the intent to terminate the tenancy.

Transfers by Landlord After conveying the leasehold interest, a landlord is left with a reversionary interest in the property plus the right to rent and other benefits acquired under the lease. The landlord may transfer either or both of these interests. The party to whom the reversion is transferred takes the property subject to the tenant's leasehold interest, if the transferee has actual or constructive notice of the lease. For example, Linda leases Whiteacre to Tina for five years, and Tina records the lease with the register of deeds. Linda then sells Whiteacre to Arthur. Tina's lease is still valid and enforceable against Arthur, whose right to possession of Whiteacre begins only after the lease expires.

Transfers by Tenant A tenant may dispose of his interest either by (1) assignment or (2) sublease, and in the absence of a lease provision to the contrary the tenant may do both. As a result, most standard leases expressly require the landlord's consent to an assignment or subletting of the premises. However, under the majority view, a covenant against assignment of a lease does not prohibit the tenant from subleasing the premises; conversely, a prohibition against subleasing does not restrict the right to assign the lease.

Assignment transfer of all a tenant's interest in the leasehold

A tenant who transfers *all* interest in a leasehold (consequently forfeiting her reversionary rights) has made an **assignment**. The tenant's agreement to pay rent and certain other contractual **covenants** (express promises) pass to and obligate the assignee of the lease as long as the assignee remains in possession of the leasehold estate. Although the assignee is thus bound to pay rent, the original tenant is *not* relieved of her contractual obligation to do so. If the assignee fails to pay the stipulated rent, the original tenant will have to pay, though she will have a right to be reimbursed by the assignee. Thus, after an assignment of a tenant's interest, *both* the original tenant and the assignee are liable to the landlord for failure to pay rent.

Covenants express promises

Sublease transfer of less than all of the tenant's interest in the leasehold

A **sublease** differs from an assignment in that the tenant transfers *less* than all her rights in the lease and thereby retains a reversion in the leasehold. For example, T is a tenant under a lease from L that is to terminate on December 31, 1994. If T leases the premises to SL for a shorter period than that covered by her own lease, say, until November 30, 1994, T, in transferring less than her whole interest in the lease, has subleased the premises.

The legal effects of a sublease are entirely different from those of an assignment. In a sublease, the sublessee, SL in the example above, has no obligation to T's landlord, L. SL's obligations run solely to T, the original tenant; and T is not relieved of any of her obligations under the lease. Thus, L has no right of action against T's sublessee, SL, under any covenants contained in the original lease between him and T, because that lease has not been assigned to SL. T, of course, remains liable to L for the rent and for all other covenants in the original lease.

Tenant's Obligations

Tenant's obligations the tenant has an obligation to pay a specified rent at specified times or, if none is specified, to pay a reasonable amount at the end of the term

Although the leasehold estate carries with it only an implied obligation on the part of the tenant to pay reasonable rent, the lease contract almost always contains an express promise or covenant by the tenant to pay rent in specified amounts at specified times. In the absence of a covenant specifying the rent amount and payment times, the rent will be a *reasonable* amount *payable only at the end of the term*.

Most leases provide that if the tenant breaches any of the covenants in the lease, the landlord may declare the lease at an end and regain possession of the premises. The tenant's express undertaking to pay rent thus becomes one of the covenants on which this provision can operate. If a lease contains no such provision, at common law, the tenant's failure to pay rent when due gives the landlord only the right to recover a judgment for the amount of such rent; it does *not* give him the right to oust the tenant from the premises. In most jurisdictions, however, statutory changes to the common law rule allow the landlord to dispossess the tenant for nonpayment of rent, even if the lease does not provide the landlord with such a right.

Unless the lease specifically provides otherwise, a tenant is under *no* duty to make any repairs to the leased premises. He is not obliged to repair or restore substantial or extraordinary damage occurring without his fault, nor to repair damage caused by ordinary wear and tear. However, the tenant is obliged to use the premises so that no substantial injury is caused them. The law imposes this duty; it need not be expressly stated in the lease. For example, a tenant who overloads an electrical connection and consequently shorts out a wiring system is liable to the landlord.

Destruction of the Premises Where the tenant leases land together with a building, and the building is destroyed by fire or some other chance event, the common law does not relieve him of his obligation to pay rent or permit him to terminate the lease. Most states, however, have statutorily modified the rule to exclude tenants who occupy only a portion of a building and who have no interest in the building as a whole, such as apartment tenants. Most leases contain clauses covering the accidental destruction of the premises.

Destruction of the premises under the common law, if the premises are destroyed, the tenant is not relieved of his obligation to pay rent and cannot terminate the lease

Eviction When the tenant breaches a covenant in her lease, such as the covenant to pay rent, and the landlord **evicts** or removes her from the premises according to a specific lease provision or under a statute authorizing him to do so, the lease is terminated. Because breaching the covenant to pay rent does not injure the premises and because the landlord's action in evicting the tenant terminates the lease, the evicted tenant normally is not liable to the landlord for any future rent installments. Most long-term leases, however, contain a *survival clause* providing that the tenant's eviction for nonpayment of rent will not relieve her of liability for damages equal to the difference between the rent specified in the lease and the rent the landlord is able to obtain when reletting the premises.

Eviction if the tenant breaches one of the covenants of her lease, the landlord may terminate the lease and evict (remove) her from the premises

Unlike authorized eviction, the landlord's wrongful eviction of the tenant terminates the tenant's obligations under the lease. Moreover, as discussed later, the landlord is liable for breach of the tenant's right of quiet enjoyment.

Abandonment If the tenant wrongfully abandons the premises before the lease term expires and the landlord reenters the premises or relets them to another, a majority of the courts hold that the tenant's obligation to pay rent terminates after such reentry. ("Reenter" in this case means to occupy the premises.) The landlord who desires to hold the tenant to his obligation to pay rent must either leave the premises vacant or have another "survival clause" in the lease that covers this situation.

Abandonment if tenant abandons property and the landlord reenters or relets it, tenant's obligation to pay rent terminates

Landlord's Obligations

Under the Fair Housing Act, a landlord cannot discriminate against a tenant with regard to race, color, gender, religion, national origin, or familial status (except under the housing for older persons exception). Nevertheless, unless the lease contains specific provisions, the landlord, under the common law, has few obligations to her tenant. Under the majority rule, at the beginning of the lease, the landlord has only to give the tenant actual possession. In a minority of states, she has only to give the right to possession. Thus, in these states, if the previous tenant refuses to move out when his lease terminates, the landlord must bring dispossession proceedings to oust him; but she is not responsible to the new tenant for the resulting delay, which, further, does not relieve the new tenant of the obligation to pay rent from the starting date of the lease.

Quiet Enjoyment The landlord may not interfere with the tenant's right to physical possession, use, and enjoyment of the premises. Rather, the landlord is bound to provide the tenant with quiet and peaceful enjoyment, a duty known as the landlord's covenant of **quiet enjoyment**. The landlord breaches this covenant, which arises by implication, whenever he wrongfully evicts the tenant. The law also regards the landlord as having breached this covenant if the tenant is evicted by someone having better title to the property than the

Quiet enjoyment tenant's right to physical possession of the premises free of interference by the landlord

landlord. The landlord is not responsible, however, for the wrongful acts of third parties unless they are done with his assent and under his direction.

Eviction need not be actual. Under the doctrine of **constructive eviction**, a failure by the landlord in any of her obligations under the lease that causes a substantial and lasting injury to the tenant's beneficial enjoyment of the premises is regarded as being, in effect, an eviction of the tenant. Under such circumstances, the courts permit the tenant to abandon the premises and terminate the lease. However, in order to claim that a constructive eviction occurred, the tenant must abandon possession within a reasonable time.

Constructive eviction
failure by the landlord in any obligation under the lease that causes a substantial and lasting injury to the tenant's enjoyment of the premises

---

HOME RENTALS CORP. v. CURTIS Appellate Court of Illinois, Fifth District, 1992, 236 Ill.App.3d 994, 176 Ill. Dec. 913

FACTS In February 1989, Home Rentals agreed to rent a single-family residence to Chris Curtis, Ed Domaracki, Mike Fraser, and Carson Flugstad (tenants), all of whom were students at Southern Illinois University. The terms of the written lease stated that the lease was to commence on August 17, 1989, and to expire on August 13, 1990. The tenants were to receive the premises in "good order and repair," rent was to be $740 per month, and a $500 deposit was required. The tenants initially paid $1,980 to cover the deposit and advance rent for the last two months of the lease. Although the house was fine when the tenants signed the lease in February, when they arrived on August 15, it was not. The electricity had not yet been turned on. Roaches had overrun the rooms, and the kitchen was so filthy and so infested by bugs that food could not be stored there. The carpet smelled, and one could see outside through holes in the wall. The bathrooms were unsanitary, no toilets worked, one of the bathtubs did not drain, and an open sewage drain emptied bathroom wastewater onto the basement floor. The tenants notified Home Rentals on the sixteenth that the place was uninhabitable because of the filth and roaches. Home Rentals responded that the tenants should just clean the place up and that it would reimburse them. Accordingly, the tenants attempted to clean the house, but the roach problem continued even after professional extermination, and Home Rentals did nothing about the plumbing. The tenants were never able to stay in the house. On August 21, the tenants finally sought housing elsewhere. They advised Home Rentals that they would not be living in the house, returned the keys, and reported the condition of the house to the city of Carbondale's Code Enforcement Division. The city notified Home Rentals on August 25, 1989, that it had found numerous city code violations and warned the corporation that the house would be posted "occupancy prohibited" unless all violations were corrected within seventy-two hours. By August 28, 1989, eleven days after the tenants' lease was to have commenced, Home Rentals had finally remedied all the violations. The city withdrew its threat, but Home Rentals did not rent the house to anyone else. Instead, it sued the tenants for breach of the lease and claimed $6,900 for all twelve months under the lease, less the deposit. The tenants denied the allegations and raised as affirmative defenses breach of the implied warranty of habitability and constructive eviction. Based on the latter theory, they asserted a counterclaim seeking the return of the $500 deposit and the $1,480 they had paid in advance rent. The trial court found for the tenants in the amount of $1,980, and Home Rentals appealed.

DECISION Judgment for the tenants affirmed.

OPINION A constructive eviction occurs where a landlord has done something grave and permanent with the intention of depriving the tenant of enjoyment of the premises. Constructive eviction does not require a finding that the landlord had the express intention to compel a tenant to leave the leased premises or to deprive him of their beneficial enjoyment. The landlord need only have committed acts or omissions that have rendered the leased premises useless to the tenant or that have deprived the tenant of the possession and enjoyment of the premises, in whole or part, making it necessary for the tenant to move.

In this case, the house did not simply fail to meet the tenants' expectations. It is scarcely unreasonable, for $740 a month, to expect flushing toilets, sewage-free basements, and kitchens not overrun by roaches. Basically, Home Rentals provided a house that was clearly unfit for people to occupy. It is true that a tenant may not abandon premises under the theory of constructive eviction without first affording the landlord a reasonable opportunity to correct the defects in the property. However, such an opportunity existed here. Considering the magnitude of the problem, four days was opportunity enough for Home Rentals to act.

INTERPRETATION If a landlord's failure to meet any of his obligations under a lease causes a substantial and lasting injury to the tenant's beneficial enjoyment of the premises, that failure, in effect, is a constructive and wrongful eviction of the tenant.

Fitness for Use Since the lease's primary value to the tenant is land, the landlord, under the common law, is under *no* obligation to provide or maintain the premises in a livable condition or to make them fit for any purpose, unless the lease specifically so provides. Most courts, however, have abandoned this rule in residential leases, instead imposing an **implied warranty of habitability** that requires leased premises to be habitable, that is, fit for ordinary residential purposes. These courts also have held that the covenant to pay rent is conditioned on the landlord's performance of this warranty. Courts reaching these results have emphasized that the tenant's interest is in a place to live, not merely in land.

> **Implied warranty of habitability** warranty that the leased premises are fit for ordinary residential purposes

A number of states have statutes requiring landlords to keep residential premises fit for occupation. Zoning ordinances, health and safety regulations, and building and housing codes also may impose certain duties on the landlord.

JAVINS v. FIRST NATIONAL REALTY CORP. United States Court of Appeals, District of Columbia Circuit, 1970, 428 F.2d 1071

FACTS By separate leases, Javins and a few others rented an apartment at the Clifton Terrace apartment complex. When they defaulted on their rent payments, the landlord, First National Realty, brought an action to evict them. The tenants admitted to the default but defended on the ground that the landlord had failed to maintain the premises in compliance with the Washington, D.C., Housing Code. They alleged that approximately 1,500 violations of this code had arisen since the term of their lease began. The Landlord and Tenant Branch of the District of Columbia Court of General Sessions ruled the evidence of the housing code violations inadmissible, and the appellate court affirmed.

DECISION Judgment reversed and case remanded for proceedings consistent with this opinion.

OPINION Traditionally, a lease conveyed an interest in land. Consequently, courts applied the general rules governing real property transactions to lease controversies. The rigid doctrines of real property law have inhibited the application of implied warranties to real estate transactions. Today's tenant is not interested in land, however, but in a suitable place for occupation. The value of the lease for a modern apartment dweller is that it gives him a place to live that includes adequate heat, light, ventilation, serviceable plumbing facilities, secure doors and windows, proper sanitation, and proper maintenance. A tenant's tenure in a specific place often is not sufficient to justify efforts at repairs. Since the lease specifies a particular period of time for the tenant to use the apartment, he may legitimately expect that it will be fit for habitation during this rental period. The landlord, then, should be obligated to keep the premises in a habitable condition. This court, therefore, holds that a warranty of habitability, measured by housing standards regulations, is implied in leases of units covered by those regulations. In this case, the tenants' obligation to pay rent was dependent upon the landlord's performance of its obligations, which now include the warranty to maintain the premises in a habitable condition. First National has not fulfilled its implied warranty of habitability; therefore, it cannot sue for possession due to the tenants' default.

INTERPRETATION Most states impose an implied warranty of habitability that requires leased premises to be fit for ordinary residential purposes.

Repair Under the common law, unless there is a specific provision in the lease or a statutory duty to do so, the landlord has *no* obligation to **repair** or restore the premises. The landlord does, however, have a duty to maintain, repair, and keep in safe condition those parts of the premises that remain under her control. For example, an apartment house owner who controls the building's stairways, elevators, lobbies, and other common areas is liable for keeping them maintained and repaired and is responsible for injuries that occur because of her failure to do so. With respect to apartment buildings, the courts presume that any portion of the premises that is not specifically leased to the tenants remains under the

> **Repair** unless there is a statute or a specific provision in the lease, the landlord has no duty to repair or restore the premises

landlord's control. Thus, in such cases, the landlord is liable for making external repairs, including repairs to the roof. The courts have further expanded the "common areas" rule to individual rental unit equipment that is connected to a central system, such as central heating and air conditioning, hot water, and plumbing and electrical systems. For a discussion of a landlord's duties and tort liabilities to a tenant in common areas, see the section on duties of possessors in Chapter 8.

While at common law the landlord is under no duty to repair, restore, or keep the premises in a livable condition, she may and often does assume those duties in the lease. However, her breach of such obligations under a lease does not entitle a tenant to abandon the premises and refuse to pay rent. Unless the lease specifically provides the tenant this right, the common law allows him only an action for damages.

Landlord's Liability for Injury Caused by Third Parties Chapter 7 discusses the duties and tort liabilities of a landlord to a tenant for defects in common areas and for the failure to disclose hidden defects in the rented premises of which the landlord knew or should have known. Under the common law, a landlord also was liable if he did not exercise reasonable care in repairing such defects. Today, by statute or judicial decision, many states require landlords to maintain leased premises in good repair and hold them liable for a negligent failure to do so.

Some states hold landlords liable for injuries their tenants and others suffer as a result of the foreseeable criminal conduct of third parties. Although landlords cannot insure their tenants' safety, courts have held landlords liable for failure "to take minimal precautions to protect members of the public from the reasonably foreseeable criminal acts of third persons."

CONCURRENT OWNERSHIP

Co-tenants persons who hold title concurrently

As we mentioned in Chapter 49, property may be owned by one individual or by two or more persons concurrently. Two or more persons who hold title concurrently generally are known as **co-tenants**. Each is entitled to an undivided interest in the entire property, and neither has a claim to any specific part of it. Each may have an equal undivided interest, or one may have a larger undivided share than the other.

The two major types of concurrent ownership are joint tenancy and tenancy in common. Both provide an undivided interest in the whole, the right of both tenants to possession, and the right of either to sell his interest during life and thus terminate the original relationship. Other forms of concurrent ownership of real estate are tenancy by the entireties, community property, condominiums, and cooperatives.

Tenancy in Common

Tenancy in common co-ownership whereby each tenant holds an undivided interest with no right of survivorship

Under a **tenancy in common**, the most frequently used form of concurrent ownership, each co-owner has both an undivided interest in the property and the right to possession; but none claims any specific portion of the property. Tenants in common need not have acquired their interests at the same time or by the same instrument, and their interests may differ as to duration and scope. Because there is no right of survivorship, the interests of tenants in common may be devised by will or pass by intestate succession. By statute in all states, a transfer of title to two or more persons is presumed to create a tenancy in common.

Partition is a physical division of the property that changes undivided interests into smaller, individually owned parcels. The size of the individual parcels is based upon the size of the owners' prior shares of the undivided interest.

Partition physical division of undivided property into smaller, individually owned parcels

Joint Tenancy

The most significant feature of joint tenancy is the right of *survivorship*. On the death of a joint tenant, title to the entire property passes by operation of law to the survivor or survivors. Neither the heirs of the deceased joint tenant nor his general creditors have a claim to his interest, and a joint tenant cannot transfer his interest by executing a will. Any joint tenant may sever the joint tenancy, however, by conveying or mortgaging his interest to a third party. Further, the interest of either co-tenant is subject to levy and sale on execution. To *sever* a joint tenancy is to forfeit the right of survivorship: following severance, the tenancy becomes a tenancy in common among the remaining joint tenants and the transferee.

To sustain a **joint tenancy**, the common law requires the presence of what are known as the **four unities** of time, title, interest, and possession. The unity of time means that all the tenants' interests must take effect at the same time; the unity of title means that all the tenants must acquire title by the same instrument; the unity of interest means that the tenants' interests must be identical in duration and scope; and the unity of possession means that the tenants have identical rights of possession and enjoyment. The absence of any unity will prevent the creation of a joint tenancy. The presence of the fourth unity and any two of the others, however, will result in the creation of a tenancy in common, because the only unity required of a tenancy in common is the unity of possession.

Joint tenancy co-ownership with the presence of the four unities and the right of survivorship

Four unities time, title, interest, and possession

ESTATE OF GULLEDGE District of Columbia Court of Appeals, 1996, 673 A.2d 1278

FACTS Clayton and Margie Gulledge owned a house at 532 Somerset Place, N.W. (the Somerset property) as tenants by the entirety. They had three children: Bernis Gulledge, Johnsie Walker, and Marion Watkins. When Margie Gulledge died in 1970, Clayton became the sole owner of the Somerset property. The following year, Clayton remarried, but the marriage was unsuccessful. To avoid a possible loss of the Somerset property, Bernis forwarded Clayton funds to satisfy the second wife's financial demands. In exchange, Clayton conveyed the property to Bernis and himself as joint tenants. In 1988, Clayton conveyed his interest in the Somerset property to his daughter, Marion Watkins. In 1991, Clayton died. Bernis died in 1993 and Johnsie Walker died in 1994. In these proceedings, Marion Watkins claims to be a tenant in common with the estate of Bernis Gulledge. The estate claims that when Clayton died, Watkin's interest was extinguished and Bernis became the sole owner of the Somerset property.

DECISION Judgment for Watkins.

OPINION The applicable rule in a large majority of jurisdictions is that either party to a joint tenancy may sever that tenancy by unilaterally disposing of his interest, that the consent of the other tenant is not required, and that the transfer converts the estate into a tenancy in common. This position is supported by the nature of a joint tenancy. It is established that a "[j]oint tenancy cannot exist unless there be present unity of interest, title, time and possession; that is to say, the interests must be identical, they must accrue by the same conveyance, they must commence at the same time and the estate must be held by the same undivided possession." The interests held by Marion Watkins and Bernis Gulledge were not created by the same conveyance and were not created at the same time. Therefore, the unities of title and time did not exist between these interests and no joint tenancy could have existed. When Clayton conveyed his interest to Marion, he unilaterally severed the joint tenancy held by him and Bernis and created a tenancy in common between Bernis and Marion.

INTERPRETATION Either party to a joint tenancy may sever the tenancy and thus convert the estate into a tenancy in common.

Tenancy by the Entireties

Tenancy by the entireties
co-ownership by spouses in
which neither may convey
his or her interest during life

Tenancy by the entireties, recognized in some, but not all states, is created only by a conveyance to a *husband and wife*. It is distinguished from joint tenancy by the inability of either spouse to convey separately his or her interest during life and thus destroy the right of survivorship. Likewise, the interest of either spouse cannot be attached by creditors. By the nature of the tenancy, divorce would terminate the relationship, and partition would then be available as a method of creating separate interests in the property.

Figure 52–2 compares the rights of concurrent owners in joint tenancy, tenancy in common, and tenancy by the entireties.

Community Property

Community property
rights of each spouse in
property acquired by the
other during marriage

In Arizona, California, Idaho, Louisiana, Nevada, New Mexico, Puerto Rico, Texas, Washington, and Wisconsin, under the **community property** system, one-half of any property acquired by either the husband or the wife belongs to each spouse.

In most instances, the only property that belongs separately to either spouse is any property acquired before the marriage or acquired subsequent to it by gift or inheritance. On the death of either spouse, one-half of the community property belongs outright to the survivor, and the interest of the deceased spouse in the other half may go to the heirs of the decedent or as directed by will.

Condominiums

Condominium separate
ownership of an individual
unit with tenancy in common
with respect to common
areas

Condominiums embody a form of concurrent ownership now common in the United States. All states have enacted statutes authorizing this form of ownership. The purchaser of a condominium acquires separate ownership to the unit and becomes a tenant in common with respect to its common facilities, such as the land on which the project is built, recreational facilities, hallways, parking areas, and spaces between the units. The common elements are maintained by a condominium association funded by assessments levied on each unit. The transfer of a condominium conveys both the separate ownership of the unit and the share in the common elements.

Cooperatives

Cooperative the corporate
owner of the property leases
units to its shareholders as
tenants

Cooperatives involve an indirect form of common ownership. A cooperative, usually a corporation, purchases or constructs dwelling units and then leases the units to its shareholders as tenants, who acquire the right to use and occupy their units.

NONPOSSESSORY INTERESTS

Though a nonpossessory interest in land entitles the holder to use the land or to take something from it, the interest does not give him the right to possess the land. Nonpossessory interests include easements, *profits à prendre*, and licenses.

FIGURE 52–2 Rights of Concurrent Owners

	Undivided Interest	Right to Possession	Right to Sell	Right to Mortgage	Levy by Creditors	Right to Will	Right of Survivorship
Joint Tenancy	yes	yes	yes	yes	yes	no	yes
Tenancy in Common	yes	yes	yes	yes	yes	yes	no
Tenancy by Entireties	yes	yes	no	no	no	no	yes

Definition of Easements

An **easement** is a *limited right* to use another's land in a specific manner that is created by the acts of the parties or by operation of law and that has all the attributes of an estate in the land itself. For example, a typical easement exists where Liz sells part of her land to Bill and expressly provides in the same document or in a separate one that Bill, as the adjoining landowner, shall have a right-of-way over a strip of Liz's remaining parcel of land. Bill's land is said to be the **dominant** parcel (land whose owner has rights in other land), and Liz's land, which is subject to the easement, is the **servient** parcel. Easements may, of course, exist for many different uses, as, for example, the right to run a ditch across another's land, to lay pipe under the surface, to erect power lines, or, in the case of adjacent buildings, to use a stairway or a common or "party" wall.

> **Easement** limited right to use the land of another in a specific manner

> **Dominant** land whose owner has rights in other land

> **Servient** land subject to an easement

Types of Easements

Easements fall into two classes: easements appurtenant and easements in gross. **Appurtenant easements** are by far the more common, and, as the name indicates, the rights and duties they create pertain to the land itself, not to the individuals who have created such easements. Therefore, the easement usually stays with the land when it is sold. For example, continuing with the illustration of Liz and Bill above, if Liz sells her servient parcel to Kyle, who has actual notice of the easement for the benefit of Bill's land or constructive notice through a local recording act, Kyle takes the parcel subject to the easement. Likewise, if Bill sells his dominant parcel to Daniel, the deed from Bill to Daniel does not need to refer specifically to the easement in order to give to Daniel, as the dominant parcel's new owner, the right to use the right-of-way over the servient parcel.

> **Appurtenant easements** *(ap·pur'·te·nant)* an easement interest that attaches to land and passes with it

The second type of easement is an **easement in gross**, which is personal to the particular individual who receives the right. It does not depend on the ownership of land and actually amounts to little more than an irrevocable personal right to use another's land.

> **Easement in gross** personal right to use another's land

NELSON v. JOHNSON Supreme Court of Idaho, 1984, 106 Idaho 385, 679 P.2d 662

FACTS Robert and Majorie Wake owned land that they used as both a cattle ranch and a farm. Each spring and autumn, the Wakes would drive their cattle from the ranch portion of the operation across an access road on the farmland to Butler Springs, which was also on the farmland.

In December 1956, the Wakes sold the farm to Jesse and Maud Hess but retained for themselves a right-of-way over the farm access road and the right to use Butler Springs for watering their livestock. In 1963, the Hesses sold the farm to the Johnsons, granting them uninterrupted possession of the property "excepting only that permissive use of the premises" owned by the Wakes.

The Wakes continued to use the access road and Butler Springs until 1964, when they sold their ranch and granted the new owners "their rights to the water of Butler Springs," but they said nothing about the access road. The ranch was subsequently sold several times, and all the owners used the access road and watering hole. In

1978, the Nelsons purchased the ranch. Shortly thereafter, the Johnsons notified the Nelsons that they had revoked the Nelsons' right to use the access road and Butler Springs. In 1979, the Johnsons closed the access road by locking the gates across the road. The Nelsons brought this action, claiming easements to both the access road and Butler Springs. The trial court ruled in favor of the Nelsons, and the Johnsons appealed.

DECISION Judgment of the district court affirmed.

OPINION The Johnsons allege that the Butler Springs easement was "in gross," and therefore personal to the Wakes. An easement in gross is merely a personal interest in the land of another. However, an easement appurtenant is an interest that is annexed to the possession of the dominant tenement and which passes with the land to subsequent owners. An instrument granting an easement is to be interpreted in connection with the parties' intention and the circumstances in existence at the time of the easement's creation. The

continued

trial court determined that the Butler Springs easement created in the 1956 Wake-Hess contract was appurtenant in nature, with a dominant estate in the cattle ranch and a servient estate in the farmland. The Butler Springs easement consequently has passed with the cattle ranch (dominant estate) upon each transfer of title. The evidence presented at trial fully supports this interpretation.

INTERPRETATION An appurtenant easement is an easement that stays with the land and is transferred to subsequent owners.

Creation of Easements

The most common way to create an easement is by *express grant* or reservation. For example, when Amy sells part of her land to Robert, she may, in the same deed, expressly grant him an easement over her remaining property.

Easements by *implication* arise whenever an owner of adjacent properties establishes an *apparent* and *permanent* use in the nature of an easement and then conveys one of the properties without mention of any easement. An easement may also arise by *necessity*: if Andrew conveys part of his land to Sharon, and the part conveyed to Sharon is so situated that she would have no access to it except across Andrew's remaining land, the law implies a grant by Andrew to Sharon of an easement by necessity across his remaining land.

Finally, an easement may arise by *prescription* in most states if certain required conditions are met. To obtain an easement by prescription, a person must use a portion of land owned by another in a way (1) that is adverse to the rightful owner's use, (2) that is open and generally known, and (3) that continues, uninterrupted, for a specific period that varies from state to state. The claimant acquires no easement by prescription, however, if given the owner's permission to use the land.

Creation of easements easements may be created by (1) express grant or reservation, (2) implied grant or reservation, (3) necessity, and (4) prescription (adverse use)

Profits à Prendre

Coming from the French, the phrase *profit à prendre* means the right to remove the produce from another's land. An example would be the grant by B to A, an adjoining landowner, of the right to remove coal, fish, or timber from B's land or to graze his cattle on B's land. Like an easement, a *profit à prendre* may arise by prescription, but if it comes about through an act of the parties, it must be created with all the formalities accorded the grant of an estate in real property. Unless the right is clearly designated as exclusive, the owner of the land is entitled to exercise it as well. Unlike A in the example above, even those who do not own adjacent land may hold the right to take profits. Thus, C may have a right to remove crushed gravel from B's acreage even though C lives in another part of the county.

Profit à prendre *(pro'·fad a prondur)* right to remove produce from another's land

Licenses

Permission to use another's land generally constitutes a **license** that creates no interest in the property and is usually exercised only at the will of and subject to revocation by the owner at any time. For example, if A tells B she may cut across A's land to pick hickory nuts, B has nothing but a license subject to revocation at any time. Nonetheless, should B, on the basis of that license, expend funds to exercise the right, the courts may prevent A from revoking the license simply because penalizing B would be unfair, given the circumstances. In such a case, B's interest would be, in practice, indistinguishable from an easement.

License permission to use another's land

THE LAW AND YOU Renting a Home

What Is a Residential Lease?

A lease is an agreement between a landlord and a tenant concerning the rights and duties of each. In the agreement, the landlord gives possession of an apartment, house or property to the tenant in exchange for rent, which is usually money, but can be property or services, given to the landlord by the tenant. In the residential lease, the tenant has both the use and possession of the property.

Please note that different laws may apply to mobile homes.

Is a Verbal Agreement Effective?

Yes. A verbal agreement is valid in Pennsylvania if it is a typical residential lease and is for less than a three-year term. However, it is usually better to have a lease in writing. Without a written lease, the parties to it may disagree about the terms and conditions. If a lease is for a period of more than three years, it must be in writing.

Does a Written Lease Have to Be in a Special Form?

No, but it does have to be written in "plain language." Pennsylvania law requires that all written residential leases be easy to read and understand. For example, there can be no "fine print" and simple everyday words must be used throughout the document. When the lease says that a tenant is to give up certain legal rights, the language used must clearly state what rights are being given up and what could happen to the tenant as a result.

It is a violation of the law for a landlord to require a tenant to sign a lease that does not conform to the plain language law. However, if a tenant does sign a residential lease that is not in plain language, the lease is still effective and the tenant must still abide by all the agreements in

the lease. If this happens, the tenant may have the right to bring a suit in court against the landlord for special damages or to prevent enforcement of any provision not written in plain language.

What Is a Security Deposit?

A security deposit is a sum of money given to the landlord, usually before a tenant moves in, to protect the rented property from any damages that may occur during the time of the lease or for unpaid rent.

Can a Security Deposit Be Required?

Yes. A landlord has the option of requiring a security deposit. During the first year of a lease, the deposit cannot exceed the amount of two month's rent. During the second and subsequent years, it cannot exceed one month's rent. During the third and subsequent years, the landlord must deposit all sums over $100 in a special interest-bearing account and annually pay to the tenant a portion of the interest earned on that account.

Will the Security Deposit Be Returned?

When the lease ends or the tenant returns possession of the property to the landlord, the tenant should ask the landlord in writing for the return of the security deposit, as well as give the date the tenant is moving and a forwarding address. The tenant should keep a copy of this letter. Within 30 days after the end of the lease or within 30 days from the time the property is returned to the landlord, whichever comes first, the landlord must either return the entire deposit or send the tenant an itemized list of damages and deductions from the deposit, together with the balance, if any.

If the landlord does not provide such a list or does not return the

appropriate deposit, the tenant has certain rights, including the right to file suit against the landlord for up to double the amount of the deposit. If the tenant receives a list of damages and believes the list is wrong, the tenant may also be able to sue the landlord. For more information on filing suit before a district justice, contact the Pennsylvania Bar Association for the pamphlet, "Bringing Suit Before a District Justice."

Are There Restrictions on Rent Increases?

Unless the rental unit is under a special government program or subject to governmental rent control, the amount of rent is not limited. A landlord may increase the amount of rent at the expiration of the term of the lease. While the amount of notice required is not specified by law, the landlord should give at least 30 days notice of any increase in rent, or as the lease provides.

What If the Landlord Doesn't Make Repairs?

Most written leases specify who is obligated to make ordinary repairs. If you sign a written lease, read it carefully. Quite often it will state that the tenant is responsible for ordinary repairs.

However, under Pennsylvania law, every residential lease includes the landlord's implied warranty of habitability (livability), which is part of the agreement even if it is not included in writing. This means that, if the rental property needs repairs or is unsafe, the tenant must notify the landlord and the landlord is obligated to repair the condition so that the property is habitable.

If the landlord does not make the repairs within a reasonable amount of time, there are specific rules about what the tenant may do. The tenant may be able to pursue several actions, including moving, repairing

continued

the defect and deducting the cost from rent payments, or getting a court to order the landlord to repair the defects. The tenant should consult an attorney before deciding which of these actions is appropriate, if any. The tenant should also keep records of contacts with the landlord about these problems.

Can a Tenant Break a Lease?

If there is a month-to-month lease, either the landlord or the tenant can terminate the lease at the end of a monthly period. Even if the lease does not require it, the tenant should give the landlord at least 30 days written notice of moving.

If there is a written lease, the lease itself usually states the amount of notice the tenant must give the landlord before leaving. If the tenant moves out before the lease expires or without proper notice, the tenant may be legally liable for paying the remaining rent due under the entire term of the lease.

If the tenant wishes to end a lease without giving the proper notice, the tenant should talk to the landlord to try to reach an understanding which will be agreeable to both parties. Otherwise, the tenant should discuss the matter with an attorney before breaking a lease or violating the terms of it.

How Can a Tenant Be Evicted?

If the lease term ends or a tenant breaks the lease agreement, the landlord can evict if the tenant does not move voluntarily. However, while the tenant is in possession of the property, the landlord does not have the right to change the locks, move the tenant's belongings from the leased property, or turn off the utilities to force the tenant out of the leased property. The landlord must go to court and use legal process.

In the absence of some other agreement between the parties, the landlord must give the tenant a written eviction notice. If the eviction is for failure to pay rent after demand, the notice must be at least 10 days. If the eviction is for any other reason, it must be 15 days for a lease of a year or less or 30 days for a lease of more than a year.

If the eviction is solely for nonpayment of rent, the tenant can avoid an eviction by paying the rent owed and court costs, at any time before the eviction actually takes place.

Does a Tenant Have to Pay Rent If an Eviction Notice Is Received?

Probably. In general, as long as a tenant remains in the apartment or house, rent must be paid to the landlord, even if an eviction notice has been received.

What If an Eviction Order Is Entered?

The tenant has the right to file an appeal, but must do so within 10 days of the date of the district justice judgment. If the tenant wants to remain in the home during the time of the appeal, the tenant must also pay either three month's rent or the amount of rent the district justice finds due, whichever is less, plus ongoing rent during the appeal. A tenant who is a victim of domestic violence may only have to pay ongoing rent. A tenant who wants to file an appeal should consult an attorney.

What If Back Rent Is Still Owed?

Even if the term of the lease has expired and the tenant's security deposit has been taken, the tenant remains responsible for any back rent or damages that are still owed to the landlord. The landlord can use further legal process to collect what is owed. If legal action is taken by the landlord, the tenant could lose property, including money in banks and motor vehicles.

[The material in this feature has been issued to inform and not to advise. It is based on Pennsylvania law. The statements are general, and individual facts in a given case may alter their application or involve other laws not referred to here.]

The material appearing herein has been reprinted with permission from the Pennsylvania Bar Association and the Pennsylvania Bar Trust Fund.

CHAPTER SUMMARY

Freehold Estates	**Fee Estates** right to immediate possession of real property for an indefinite time
	■ *Fee Simple* absolute ownership of property
	■ *Qualified Fee* ownership subject to its being taken away upon the happening of an event

Life Estates
- *Conventional Life Estates* ownership right in property for the life of a designated person, while remainder is the ownership estate that takes effect when the prior estate terminates
- *Established by Law* includes dower (wife's estate in the real property of her husband) and curtesy (husband's estate in the real property of his wife)

Future Interests
- *Reversion* grantor's right to property upon termination of another estate
- *Remainders* are of two kinds: vested remainders (unconditional remainder that is a fixed, present interest to be enjoyed in the future) and contingent remainders (remainder interest conditional upon the happening of an event in addition to the termination of the preceding estate)

Leasehold Estates

Lease both (1) a contract for use and possession of land and (2) a grant of an estate in land
- *Landlord* owner of land who grants a leasehold interest to another while retaining a reversionary interest in the property
- *Tenant* possessor of the leasehold interest in the land

Duration of Leases
- *Definite Term* lease that automatically expires at the end of the term
- *Periodic Tenancy* lease consisting of specific terms that continue in indefinite succession
- *Tenancy at Will* lease that is terminable at any time
- *Tenancy at Sufferance* possession of real property without a lease

Transfer of Tenant's Interest
- *Assignment* transfer of all of the tenant's interest in the leasehold
- *Sublease* transfer of less than all of the tenant's interest in the leasehold

Tenant's Obligations the tenant has an obligation to pay a specified rent at specified times or, if none is specified, to pay a reasonable amount at the end of the term
- *Destruction of the Premises* under the common law, if the premises are destroyed, the tenant is not relieved of his obligation to pay rent and cannot terminate the lease
- *Eviction* if the tenant breaches one of the covenants of her lease, the landlord may terminate the lease and evict (remove) her from the premises
- *Abandonment* if tenant abandons property and the landlord reenters or relets it, tenant's obligation to pay rent terminates

Landlord's Obligations
- *Quiet Enjoyment* the right of the tenant to have physical possession of the premises free of landlord interference
- *Fitness for Use* most courts impose for residential leases an implied warranty of habitability that the leased premises are fit for ordinary residential purposes
- *Repair* unless there is a statute or a specific provision in the lease, the landlord has no duty to repair or restore the premises

Concurrent Ownership	**Tenancy in Common** co-ownership in which each tenant holds an undivided interest with no right of survivorship
	Joint Tenancy co-ownership with the right of survivorship; requires the presence of the four unities (time, title, interest, and possession)
	Tenancy by the Entireties co-ownership by spouses in which neither may convey his or her interest during life
	Community Property spouses' rights in property acquired by the other during their marriage
	Condominium separate ownership of an individual unit with tenancy in common with respect to common areas
	Cooperative the corporate owner of the property leases units to its shareholders as tenants

Nonpossessory Interests	**Easement** limited right to use the land of another in a specified manner
	■ *Appurtenant* rights and duties created by the easement pertain to and run with the land of the owner of the easement (dominant parcel) and the land subject to the easement (servient parcel)
	■ *In Gross* rights and duties created by the easement are personal to the individual who received the right
	■ *Creation of Easements* easements may be created by (1) express grant or reservation, (2) implied grant or reservation, (3) necessity, and (4) prescription (adverse use)
	Profits à Prendre right to remove produce from the land of another
	Licenses permission to use the land of another

QUESTIONS

1. Define and discuss the following freehold interests: (a) fee simple, (b) qualified fee, (c) life estate, (d) remainder interest, (e) dower, (f) curtesy, and (g) reversionary interest.
2. Distinguish between a vested and a contingent remainder.
3. Discuss the primary rights and obligations of landlords and tenants.
4. Identify and discuss the various forms of concurrent ownership of real property.
5. Identify and discuss the various ways in which an easement may be created.

Internet Question. Find and explore information about the rights of residential tenants.

PROBLEMS

1. Kirkland conveyed a farm to Sandler to have and to hold for and during his life and on Sandler's death to Rubin. Some years thereafter, oil was discovered in the vicinity. Sandler thereupon made an oil and gas lease, and the oil company set up its machinery to begin drilling operations. Rubin then filed suit to enjoin the operations. Assuming an injunction to be the proper form of remedy, what decision?

2. Smith owned Blackacre in fee simple. In section 3 of a properly executed will, Smith devised Blackacre as follows: "I devise my farm Blackacre to my son Darwin so long as it is used as a farm." Sections 5 and 6 of the will made gifts to persons other than Darwin. The last clause of Smith's will provided: "All the remainder of my real and personal property not disposed of heretofore in this will, I devise and bequeath to Stanford University."

Smith died in 1994, survived by her son Darwin. Smith's estate has been administered. Darwin has been offered $100,000 for Blackacre if he can convey title to it in fee simple.

What interests in Blackacre were created by Smith's will?

3. Panessi leased to Barnes, for a term of ten years beginning May 1, certain premises located at 527–529 Main Street in Cleveland. The premises were improved with a three-story building, the first floor being occupied by stores and the upper stories by apartments. On May 1 of the following year, Barnes leased one of the apartments to Clinton for one year. On July 5, a fire destroyed the second and third floors of the building. The first floor was not burned but was rendered unusable. Neither the lease from Panessi to Barnes nor the lease from Barnes to Clinton contained any provision regarding loss by fire. Discuss the liability of Barnes and Clinton to continue to pay rent.

4. Ames leased an apartment to Boor for $200 a month, payable the last day of each month. The term of the written lease was from January 1, 1993, through April 30, 1994. On March 15, 1993, Boor moved out, telling Ames that he disliked all the other tenants. Ames replied, "Well, you're no prize as a tenant; I can probably get more rent from someone more agreeable." Ames and Boor then had a minor physical altercation in which neither was injured. Boor sent the apartment keys to Ames by mail. Ames wrote Boor, "It will be my pleasure to hold you for every penny you owe me. I am renting the apartment on your behalf to Clay until April 30, 1994, at $175 a month." Boor had paid his rent through February 28, 1993. Clay entered the premises on April 1, 1993.

How much rent, if any, may Ames recover from Boor?

5. Jay signed a two-year lease containing a clause that expressly prohibited subletting. After six months, Jay asked the landlord for permission to sublet the apartment for one year. The landlord refused. This angered Jay, and he immediately assigned his right under the lease to Kay. Kay was a distinguished gentleman, and Jay knew that everyone would consider him a desirable tenant. Is Jay's assignment of his lease to Kay valid?

6. In 1981, Roy Martin and his wife, Alice; their son, Hiram; and Hiram's wife, Myrna, acquired title to a 240-acre farm. The deed ran to Roy Martin and Alice Martin, the father and mother, as joint tenants with the right of survivorship, and to Hiram Martin and Myrna Martin, the son and his wife, as joint tenants with the right of survivorship. Alice Martin died in 1986, and in 1989, Roy Martin married Agnes Martin. By his will, Roy Martin bequeathed and devised his entire estate to Agnes Martin. When Roy Martin died

in 1991, Hiram and Myrna Martin assumed complete control of the farm.

State the interest in the farm, if any, of Agnes, Hiram, and Myrna Martin on the death of Roy Martin.

7. In her will, Teressa granted a life estate to Amos in certain real estate, with remainder to Brenda and Clive in joint tenancy. All the rest of Teressa's estate was left to Hillman College. While going to Teressa's funeral, the car in which Amos, Brenda, and Clive were driving was wrecked. Brenda was killed, Clive died a few minutes later, and Amos died on his way to the hospital. Who is entitled to the real estate in question?

8. Otis Olson, the owner of two adjoining city lots, A and B, built a house on each. He laid a drainpipe from lot B across lot A to the main sewer pipe under the alley beyond lot A. Olson then sold and conveyed lot A to Fred Ford. The deed, which made no mention of the drainpipe, was promptly recorded. Ford had no actual knowledge or notice of the drainpipe, although it would have been apparent to anyone inspecting the premises because it was only partially buried. Later, Olson sold and conveyed lot B to Luke Lane. This deed also made no reference to the drainpipe and was promptly recorded.

A few weeks later, Ford discovered the drainpipe across lot A and removed it. Did he have the right to do so?

9. At the time of his marriage to Ann, Robert owned several parcels of real estate in joint tenancy with his brother, Sam. During his marriage, Robert purchased a house and put the title in his name and his wife's name as joint tenants, not as tenants in common. Robert died; within a month of his death, Smith obtained a judgment against Robert's estate. What are the relative rights of Sam, Smith, and Ann?

10. In 1966, Ogle owned two adjoining lots numbered 6 and 7 fronting at the north on a city street. In that year, she laid out and built a concrete driveway along and two feet in front of what she erroneously believed to be the west boundary of lot 7. Ogle used the driveway for access to buildings situated at the southern end of both lots. Later in the same year, she conveyed lot 7 to Dale, and thereafter in the same year, she conveyed lot 6 to Pace. Neither deed made any reference to the driveway, and after the conveyance, Dale used it exclusively for access to lot 7. In 1992, a survey by Pace established that the driveway overlapped six inches on lot 6, and he brought an appropriate action to establish his lawful ownership of the strip on which the driveway approaches, to enjoin its use by Dale, and to require Dale to remove the overlap. Decision?

11. Temco, Inc. conveyed to the Wynns certain property adjoining an apartment complex being developed by Sonnett Realty Company. Although nothing to this effect was contained in the deed, the sales contract

gave the purchaser of the property use of the apartment's swimming pool. Temco's sales agent also emphasized that use of the pool would be a desirable feature in the event that the Wynns decided to sell the property.

Seven years later, the Bunns contracted to buy the property from the Wynns through the latter's agent, Sonnett Realty. Although both the Wynns and Sonnett Realty's agent told the Bunns that use of the apartment's pool went with the purchased property, neither the contract nor the deed subsequently conveyed to the Bunns so provided. When the Bunns requested pool passes from Temco and Offutt, the company that owned the apartments, their request was refused. The Bunns then brought this action. Decision?

12. In 1905, a deed for land in Pitt County, North Carolina, was executed and delivered by Joel and Louisa Tyson "unto M. H. Jackson and wife Maggie Jackson, for and during the term of their natural lives and after their death to the children of the said M. H. Jackson and Maggie Jackson that shall be born to their intermarriage as shall survive them to them and their heirs and assigns in fee simple forever." Thelma Jackson Vester, a daughter of M. H. and Maggie Jackson, died in 1957, survived by three children. M. H. Jackson, who survived his wife, Maggie Jackson, died in 1958, survived by four sons. The children of Thelma Jackson Vester brought this action against M. P. Jackson, a son of and executor of the will of M. H. Jackson. The children of Vester contended that through their deceased mother they were entitled to a one-fifth interest in the land conveyed by the deed of 1905. The executor contended that the deed conveyed a contingent remainder and that only those children who survived the parents took an interest in the land. Decision?

CHAPTER 53

Transfer and Control of Real Property

The law has always been extremely cautious about the transfer of title to real estate. Personal property may, for the most part, be passed easily and informally from owner to owner, but real property can be transferred only through compliance with a variety of formalities.

Title to land may be transferred in three principal ways: (1) by deed, (2) by will or by the law of descent on the death of the owner, and (3) by open, continuous, and adverse possession by a nonowner for a statutorily prescribed period of time. In this chapter, we will discuss the first and third methods of transfer; we will cover the second method in Chapter 54.

In addition to the legal restrictions placed on the transfer of real property, a number of other controls apply to the use of privately owned property. Some of these, including zoning and the taking of property by eminent domain, are imposed by governmental units. Others are imposed by private parties through restrictive covenants. We will consider these three controls in the second part of this chapter.

TRANSFER OF REAL PROPERTY

The transfer of real property occurs most commonly by deed. Such transfers usually involve a contract for the sale of the land, the subsequent delivery of the deed, and the payment of the agreed-upon consideration. The transfer of real estate by deed, however, does not require consideration to be valid; it may be made as a gift. In most cases, the real estate purchaser must borrow part of the purchase price, using the real property as security. An unusual and far less common method of transferring title, adverse possession, requires no contract, deed, or other formality.

CONTRACT OF SALE

As indicated in the chapters on general contracts, general contract law governs the sale of real property. In addition, the Fair Housing Act (Title VIII of the Civil Rights Act, as amended) prohibits discrimination in the real estate market on the basis of race, color, religion, gender, national origin, handicap, or familial status. The act exempts the sale or rental of a single-family house owned by a private individual who owns fewer than four houses, provided that the owner does not use a broker or discriminatory advertising. Nevertheless, these exemptions do not apply to discrimination based on race or color; in the sale or rental of property, the act prohibits all discrimination based on these factors.

Formation

Because an oral agreement for the sale of an interest in land is not enforceable under the statute of frauds, the buyer and seller not only must reduce the agreement to *writing* but must have it signed by the other party in order to be able to enforce the agreement against that party. The simplest agreement should contain (1) the names and addresses of the parties, (2) a description of the property to be conveyed, (3) the time for the conveyance (called the *closing*), (4) the type of deed to be given, and (5) the price and manner of payment. To avoid dispute and to assure adequately both parties' rights, a properly drawn contract for the sale of land will cover many other points as well.

Marketable Title

The law of conveyancing firmly establishes that a contract for the sale of land carries with it an *implied* obligation on the part of the seller to transfer marketable title. **Marketable title** means that the title is free from (1) encumbrances (such as mortgages, easements, liens, leases, and restrictive covenants); (2) defects in the chain of title appearing in the land records (such as a prior recorded conveyance of the same property by the seller); and (3) events that deprive the seller of title, such as adverse possession or eminent domain. The obligation to convey marketable title is significant: if the title search reveals any defect not *specifically* excepted in the contract, the seller has materially breached the contract. The buyer's remedies for breach include specific performance with a price reduction, rescission and restitution, or damages for loss of bargain.

Before title to the property passes, the buyer should ensure that she is receiving good title by having the title searched. A title search involves examining prior transfers of and encumbrances to the property. Such an examination does not, however, guarantee rightful ownership; consequently, most buyers purchase title insurance as well. Issued in the amount of the purchase price of the property, *title insurance* guarantees the owner against any loss due to defects in the title to the property or due to liens or encumbrances, except for those the policy identifies as existing when the policy was issued. Such policies also may be issued to protect the interests of mortgagees or tenants of property.

Implied Warranty of Habitability

Because the obligation to transfer marketable title covers only the title to the property conveyed, such an obligation does not apply to the quality of any improvements to the land. The traditional common law rule is *caveat emptor*—let the buyer beware. Under this rigid maxim, the buyer must thoroughly inspect the property before the sale is completed, since any undiscovered defect would not be the seller's responsibility. The seller is liable only for any misrepresentations or *express* warranties he may have made about the property.

A majority of states have relaxed the harshness of the common law in sales made by one who builds and then sells residential dwellings. In such a sale, the builder-seller *impliedly* warrants a newly constructed house to be free of latent defects, that is, those defects not apparent upon a reasonable inspection of the house at the time of sale. In some states, this implied warranty of habitability benefits only the original purchaser; other states have extended it to subsequent purchasers for a reasonable period of time. In addition, many jurisdictions now require *all* sellers to disclose hidden defects that materially affect the property's value if reasonable examination would not reveal such defects. (See Chapter 11 for a discussion of misrepresentation.)

GAITO v. AUMAN Supreme Court of North Carolina, 1985, 313 N.C. 243, 327 S.E.2d 870

FACTS Sam and Eleanor Gaito purchased a home from Howard Frank Auman, Jr., in the spring of 1978. Auman had completed the construction of the house in November 1973. In the interim, three different parties had lived in the house for brief periods, but Auman had retained ownership. The last tenants, the Ashleys, experienced difficulties with the home's air-conditioning system. Repairs were attempted, but no effort was made to change the capacity of the air-conditioning unit.

When the Gaitos moved into the house in June 1978, they too had problems with the air-conditioning. The system created only a ten-degree difference between the outside and inside temperatures. The Gaitos complained to Auman on a number of occasions, but extensive repairs failed to correct the cooling problem. In May 1981, the Gaitos brought an action against Auman, alleging that the purchase price of the home included central air-conditioning and that Auman had breached the implied warranty of habitability. At trial, an expert in the field of heating and air-conditioning testified that a four-ton air-conditioning system, rather than the three-and-one-half-ton system originally installed, was appropriate for the Gaitos's house. The jury returned a verdict in favor of the Gaitos in the amount of $3,655, and the court of appeals affirmed.

DECISION Judgment for the Gaitos affirmed.

OPINION The theory of implied warranty of habitability of a recently completed dwelling relaxed the rigid common law rule of *caveat emptor*. The theory was originally stated in North Carolina as follows: "[I]n every contract for the sale of a recently completed dwelling, . . . the vendor, if he be in the business of building such dwellings, shall . . . impliedly warrant to the initial vendee that . . . the dwelling, together with all its fixtures, is sufficiently free from major structural defects." Any defect must be latent or not reasonably discoverable at the time of sale or possession. Auman was in the business of building houses, and the Gaitos were the initial vendees. Auman argues, however, that the theory is inapplicable to this case in that the dwelling was not "recently completed" and that any implied warranty that may have arisen was invalidated by the previous occupancy of the house by tenants. The standard of reasonableness is proper for determining whether a house has been recently completed. Thus, this issue was a question of fact for the jury. The effect of the occupancy by tenants was another factor that was properly allowed consideration by the jury, since many kinds of major structural defects are unaffected by the presence of tenants. Auman also contends that an air-conditioning unit is not governed by an implied warranty because it is not "an absolute essential utility to a dwelling house." The warranty, however, includes "the dwelling, together with all its fixtures." A defective air-conditioning system may properly be considered a major structural defect.

INTERPRETATION The implied warranty of habitability requires the builder/seller to be responsible for latent defects in a newly constructed home.

DEEDS

A **deed** is a formal document transferring any interest in land. The party who transfers property by a deed is called the **grantor**; the transferee of the property is the **grantee**.

> **Deed** a formal document transferring any type of interest in land
>
> **Grantor** seller
>
> **Grantee** buyer

Types of Deeds
The rights a deed conveys depend on the type of deed used. Deeds are of three basic types: warranty, special warranty, and quitclaim.

Warranty Deed By a **warranty deed**, the grantor promises the grantee that the grantor has a valid title to the property. In addition, under a warranty deed, the grantor, either expressly or implicitly, obliges herself to make the grantee whole for any damage the grantee suffers should the grantor's title prove defective. A warranty deed includes certain promises or covenants, the most usual of which are *title, against encumbrances, quiet enjoyment,* and *warranty*. These various covenants constitute an assurance that the grantee will have undisturbed possession of the land and will, in turn, be able to transfer it without adverse claims of third parties. A phrase common in a warranty deed is "convey

> **Warranty deed** seller promises that she has valid title

and warrant," although in a number of states the phrase "grant, bargain, and sell" is used, together with the seller's covenant (appearing later in the deed) that she will "warrant and defend the title."

Special warranty deed seller promises that he has not impaired title

Special Warranty Deed Whereas a warranty deed contains a general warranty of title, a **special warranty deed** warrants only that the title has not been impaired, encumbered, or made defective because of any act or omission *of the grantor*. The grantor merely warrants the title so far as it concerns his acts or omissions. He does *not* warrant title as to the acts or omissions of others.

Quitclaim deed seller transfers whatever interest she has in the property

Quitclaim Deed By a **quitclaim deed**, the grantor, in effect, says no more than "I make no promise as to what interest I do have in this land, but whatever it is I convey it to you." A quitclaim deed usually provides that the grantor "conveys and quitclaims" or more simply "quitclaims all interest" in the property. Quitclaim deeds are used most frequently in transfers requiring persons who appear to have an interest in land to release their interest.

Formal Requirements

Requirements the deed must (1) be written, (2) contain certain words of conveyance and a description of the property, (3) end with the signature of the grantor, a seal, and an acknowledgment before a notary public, and (4) be delivered

As we noted previously, any transfer of an interest in land that is of more than a limited duration falls within the statute of frauds and must therefore be in writing. Almost every deed, whatever the type, contains substantially similar wording.

Often, the deed will first describe the land. The description must be sufficiently clear to permit identification of the property conveyed. After describing the property, the deed usually will proceed to describe the quantity of estate conveyed to the grantee. Deeds generally end with the grantor's signature, a seal, and an acknowledgment before a notary public or other official authorized to verify the authenticity of documents.

Delivery of Deeds

Delivery intent that the deed take effect, as evidenced by acts or statements of the grantor

A deed does not transfer title to land until it is delivered. **Delivery**, or an *intent* that the deed is to take effect, is evidenced by the acts or statements of the grantor. Physical transfer of the deed is usually the best evidence of this intent, but it is not necessary. Frequently, in a transfer known as an **escrow**, a grantor will turn a deed over to a third party (the escrow agent) to hold until the grantee performs certain conditions. When the grantee so performs, the escrow agent must give her the deed.

Escrow holding by a third party of a document or funds until certain conditions are performed

Recordation

Recordation required to protect the buyer's interest against third parties; consists of delivery of a duly executed and acknowledged deed to the appropriate recorder's office

In almost all states, recording a deed is not necessary to pass title from grantor to grantee. Unless the grantee has the deed recorded, however, a subsequent good faith purchaser for value of the property will acquire title superior to that of the grantee. **Recordation** consists of delivering a duly executed and acknowledged deed to the recorder's office in the county where the property is located. There, a copy of the instrument is inserted in the current deed book and indexed.

In some states, called *notice* states, unrecorded instruments are invalid against any subsequent purchaser without notice. In *notice-race* states, an unrecorded deed is invalid against any subsequent purchaser without notice of who recorded first. Finally, in a few states, called *race* states, an unrecorded deed is invalid against any deed recorded before it.

SECURED TRANSACTIONS

As we discussed in Chapter 39, a **secured transaction** essentially involves two elements: (1) a debt or obligation to pay money, and (2) the creditor's interest in specific property that secures performance of the obligation. A security interest in property cannot exist apart from the debt it secures: discharging the debt in any manner terminates the interest. Transactions involving the use of real estate as security for a debt are subject to real estate law, which consists of statutes and rules developed through common law interpretations of mortgages and trust deeds. In these cases, the real estate itself is used to secure the obligation, which is evidenced by a note and by either a mortgage or deed of trust. The debtor is referred to as the **mortgagor**; the creditor is the **mortgagee**. The Uniform Commercial Code does *not* apply to real estate mortgages or deeds of trust.

Form of Mortgages

A **mortgage** is a security interest in land. The instrument that embodies a mortgage must meet all the requirements for such a document: it must be in writing, it must contain an adequate description of the property, and it must be executed and delivered. Nearly identical to a mortgage, a **deed of trust** contains one major difference: under a deed of trust, the property is conveyed not to the creditor as security but to a third person, who acts as trustee for the benefit of the creditor. The deed of trust creates rights almost the same as those created by a mortgage. In some states, it is customary to use a deed of trust in lieu of the ordinary form of mortgage.

As with all interests in realty, the mortgage or deed of trust should be promptly recorded to protect the mortgagee's rights against third persons who acquire an interest in the mortgaged property without knowledge of the mortgage.

Rights and Duties

The rights and duties of the parties to a mortgage may depend on whether it is considered to create a lien or to transfer legal title to the mortgagee. Most states have adopted the *lien* theory. The mortgagor retains title and, even in the absence of any stipulation in the mortgage, is entitled to possession of the premises to the exclusion of the mortgagee, even if the mortgagor defaults. Only through foreclosure (sale) or through the court appointment of a receiver can the right of possession be taken from the mortgagor. Other states have adopted the common law *title* theory, which gives the mortgagee the right of ownership and possession. In most cases, as a practical matter, the mortgagor retains possession simply because the mortgagee does not care about possession unless the mortgagor defaults.

Even though the mortgagor generally is entitled to possession and to many of the advantages of unrestricted ownership, he has a responsibility to deal with the property in a manner that will not impair the security. In most instances, *waste* (impairment of the security) results from the mortgagor's failure to prevent the actual or threatened actions of third parties against the land. For example, the debtor's failure to pay taxes or to discharge a prior lien may seriously impair the mortgagee's security. In such cases, the courts usually permit the mortgagee to pay the obligation and add it to his claim against the mortgagor.

Secured transaction a secured transaction involves (1) a debt or obligation to pay money, (2) an interest of the creditor in specific property that secures performance, and (3) the debtor's right to redeem the property (remove the security interest) by paying the debt

Mortgagor debtor who uses real estate to secure an obligation

Mortgagee creditor of a secured transaction involving real estate

Mortgage interest in land created by a written document that provides security for payment of a debt

Deed of trust interest in real property that is conveyed to a third person as trustee for the creditor

Redemption debtor's right to remove the mortgage by paying the debt

The mortgagor may relieve his property from a mortgage lien by paying the debt that the mortgage secures. Characteristic of a mortgage, this right of **redemption** can be defeated only by operation of law. The right to redeem carries with it the obligation to pay the debt, and payment in full, with interest, is prerequisite to redemption. See Figure 53–1 for the fundamental rights of the mortgagor and mortgagee.

Transfer of the Interests Under the Mortgage

The interests of the original mortgagor and mortgagee can be transferred, and the rights and obligations of their assignees will depend primarily on (1) the agreement of the parties to the assignment and (2) the legal rules protecting the interest of one who is party to the mortgage but not to the transfer.

Assumes the mortgage purchaser of mortgaged property becomes personally liable to pay the debt

Subject to the mortgage purchaser is not personally obligated to pay the debt, but the property remains subject to the mortgage

If the mortgagor conveys the land, the purchaser is *not* personally liable for the mortgage debt unless she expressly assumes the mortgage. If she **assumes the mortgage**, she is personally obligated to pay the debt the mortgagor owes to the mortgagee. Furthermore, the mortgagee can also hold the mortgagor on his promise to pay. In contrast, a transfer of mortgaged property **"subject to" the mortgage** does *not* personally obligate the transferee to pay the mortgage debt. In such a case, the transferee's risk of loss is limited to the property.

A mortgagee has the right to assign the mortgage to another person without the mortgagor's consent. An assignee of a mortgage is well advised to obtain the assignment in a writing duly executed by the mortgagee and to record it promptly with the proper public official. This will protect her rights against persons who subsequently acquire an interest in the mortgaged property without knowledge of the assignment.

Foreclosure

Foreclosure sale of the mortgaged property upon default to satisfy the debt

The right to foreclose usually arises upon default by the mortgagor. **Foreclosure** is an action through which the mortgage holder takes the property from the mortgagor, ends the mortgagor's rights in the property, and sells the property to pay the mortgage debt. If the proceeds are not sufficient to satisfy the debt in full, the debtor-mortgagor remains liable for paying the balance. Generally, the mortgagee will obtain a *deficiency judgment* for any unsatisfied balance of the debt and may proceed to enforce the payment of this amount out of the mortgagor's other assets. The mortgagor's default by nonperformance of other promises in the mortgage also may give the mortgagee the right to foreclose. For example, a mortgage may provide that the mortgagor's failure to pay taxes

FIGURE 53–1 Fundamental Rights of Mortgagor and Mortgagee

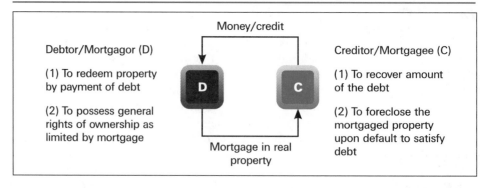

is a default that permits foreclosure. Mortgages also commonly provide that default in the payment of an installment makes the entire unpaid balance of the debt immediately due and payable, permitting foreclosure for the entire amount.

ADVERSE POSSESSION

It is possible, although very rare, that title to land may be transferred *involuntarily*, without any deed or other formality, through adverse possession. In most states, a person who openly and continuously occupies the land of another for a statutorily prescribed period, typically twenty years, will gain title to the land by **adverse possession**. The **possession** must be actual. Courts have held that living on land, farming it, building on it, or maintaining structures on it is sufficient to constitute possession. However, the possession must be adverse. In other words, any act of dominion by the true owner, such as her entry on the land or assertion of ownership, will stop the period from running. Once broken, the statutory period would have to begin again, from the point at which the owner interrupted it.

By statute, some jurisdictions have established shorter periods of adverse possession where possession exists in conjunction with some other claim, such as the payment of taxes for seven years and an apparent claim of title, even if it is not valid.

Adverse possession acquisition of title to land by open, continuous, and adverse occupancy for a statutorily prescribed period

Possession must be actual and without intervening dominion by true owner

PUBLIC AND PRIVATE CONTROLS

In exercising its police power for the benefit of the community, the state can and does place controls on the use of privately owned land. Furthermore, the state does not compensate the owner for loss or damage he sustains because of such legitimate controls. The enforcement of zoning laws, which is a proper exercise of the police power, is not a taking of property but a regulation of its use. The taking of private property for a public use or purpose under the state's power of eminent domain is not, however, an exercise of police power, and the owners of the property so taken are entitled to be paid its fair and reasonable value. In addition, by means of restrictive covenants, which we will also consider in this section, the use of privately owned property may be privately controlled.

ZONING

Zoning is the principal method of public control over *land use*. The validity of zoning is rooted in the police power of the state, the inherent power of government to provide for the public health, safety, morals, and welfare. Police power can be used only to regulate private property, never to "take" it. It is firmly established that regulation having no reasonable relation to public health, safety, morals, or welfare is unconstitutional as a denial of due process of law.

Zoning public control over private land use

Enabling Acts and Zoning Ordinances
The power to zone generally is delegated to local city and village authorities by statutes known as enabling statutes. A typical enabling statute grants

Enabling acts the power to zone is generally delegated to local authorities by statutes

municipalities the following powers: (1) to regulate and limit the height and bulk of buildings to be erected; (2) to establish, regulate, and limit the building or setback lines on or along any street, trafficway, drive, or parkway; (3) to regulate and limit the intensity of the use of lot areas and to regulate and determine the area of open spaces within and around buildings; (4) to classify, regulate, and restrict the location of trades and industries and the location of buildings designated for specified industrial, business, residential, and other uses; (5) to divide the entire municipality into districts of such number, shape, area, and class (or classes) as may be deemed best suited to carry out the purposes of the statute; and (6) to set standards to which buildings or structures must conform.

Under these powers, the local authorities may enact zoning ordinances, consisting of a map and its accompanying descriptive text. The map divides the municipality into districts designated principally as industrial, commercial, or residential, with possible subclassifications. A well-drafted zoning ordinance will carefully define the uses permitted in each area. A special use (also called a conditional use or special exception) is a use authorized by the zoning ordinance but only upon specific approval by the zoning authorities on a case-by-case basis. Special uses include churches, schools, hospitals, homes for the disabled, and cemeteries.

Variance

Variance a use differing from that provided in the zoning ordinance and granted in order to avoid undue hardship

Enabling statutes permit zoning authorities to grant variances when application of a zoning ordinance to specific property would cause its owner "particular hardship" unique or peculiar to the property. A **variance** permits a deviation from the zoning ordinance. Special circumstances applicable to particular property might include its unusual shape, topography, size, location, or surroundings. A variance is not available, however, if the hardship is caused by conditions general to the neighborhood or by the actions of the property owner. It must affirmatively appear that the property as presently zoned cannot yield a reasonable return on the owner's investment.

Nonconforming Uses

Nonconforming use preexisting use not in accordance with the zoning ordinance

A zoning ordinance may not immediately terminate a lawful use that existed before the ordinance was enacted. Rather, this **nonconforming use** must be permitted to continue for at least a reasonable time. Most ordinances provide that a nonconforming use may be terminated (1) when the use is discontinued, (2) when a nonconforming structure is destroyed or substantially damaged, or (3) when a nonconforming structure has been permitted to exist for the period of its useful life, as fixed by municipal authorities.

Judicial Review of Zoning

Judicial review zoning ordinances may be reviewed to determine if they are invalid or a confiscation of property

Although the zoning process traditionally is considered as legislative, it is subject to judicial review on several grounds, including the following: (1) that the resulting zoning ordinance is invalid, (2) that the ordinance has been applied unreasonably, and (3) that the ordinance amounts to a confiscation, or taking, of property. For example, a zoning ordinance may be invalid as a whole either because it bears no reasonable relation to public health, safety, morals, or welfare or because it involves the exercise of powers that the enabling act has not granted to the municipality.

CITY OF RENTON v. PLAYTIME THEATERS Supreme Court of the United States, 1986, 475 U.S. 41, 106 S.Ct. 925, 89 L.Ed.2d 29

FACTS The respondents, Playtime Theaters and Sea-First Properties, purchased two theaters in Renton, Washington, with the intention of exhibiting adult films. About the same time, the respondents filed suit in district court seeking injunctive relief and a declaratory judgment that the First and Fourteenth Amendments were violated by a city ordinance that prohibits adult motion picture theaters from locating within 1,000 feet of any residential zone, single- or multiple-family dwelling, church, park, or school. The district court found in favor of the city, holding that the ordinance did not violate the Constitution. The Court of Appeals reversed, holding that the ordinance did constitute a substantial restriction on the First Amendment.

DECISION Judgment of the Court of Appeals reversed in favor of the city.

OPINION Such an ordinance is a valid governmental response to the serious problems created by adult theaters and satisfies the dictates of the First Amendment. Since the ordinance does not ban adult theaters altogether, it is properly analyzed as a "form of time, place, and manner regulation." Such content-neutral regulations are acceptable so long as they are designed to serve a substantial governmental interest and do not unreasonably limit alternative avenues of communication. The ordinance is designed to serve a substantial governmental interest while allowing for reasonable alternative avenues of communication. A city's interest in attempting to preserve the quality of urban life, as in the case at bar, must be accorded high respect.

INTERPRETATION An ordinance that is designed to serve a substantial government interest and does not unreasonably limit alternative methods of communication will not be held invalid.

ETHICAL DILEMMA Where Should Cities House the Disadvantaged?

FACTS Susan Kate is a member of the city council in Wissahicken City. The Clinton Living Center, Inc. has just applied for a special use permit to allow the center to lease a building to use as a group house for the emotionally ill. The home will provide supervised group living quarters for individuals who have suffered from a wide range of emotional problems, including depression, anxiety, substance abuse, and sexual disorders. A small percentage of the proposed occupants will be criminal offenders embarking on the rehabilitative phase of their sentencing, with the ultimate goal of reentering the community. Many of the members will attend school and other job training programs under supervision during the day.

The Wissahicken zoning ordinance requires that a special permit be obtained annually for hospitals for the insane, the mentally retarded, alcoholics, or drug addicts and for penal or correctional institutions. The building the Center wishes to lease is in an R-3 zone that expressly permits apartment houses, multiple dwellings, hospitals, or nursing homes, but excludes penal institutions and homes for the insane, the mentally retarded, alcoholics, or drug addicts. In addition, the building is not far from an upper middle-class neighborhood consisting of single-family homes. The home would be across the street from a junior high school.

Public hearings have been held, and there is widespread community opposition to the proposed lease. Susan Kate, a new and politically ambitious member of the city council, must cast the deciding vote as to whether the special permit should be issued.

Social, Policy, and Ethical Considerations

1. What are the goals of zoning classifications?
2. Is there any justification for requiring a special permit in the

circumstances? What are the community's concerns? Are these concerns justified?

3. What is the social policy behind placing rehabilitative group homes in the heart of a thriving community rather than in an isolated neighborhood?

4. Should a permit be refused for the purpose of preserving property values? Consider the concerns of a sixty-year-old couple who are close to retirement, who have modest cash savings, and who have always planned to sell their house in their mid-sixties and move to an apartment. Consider also the concerns of a young, newly married couple in search of affordable housing in a stable, established neighborhood.

5. Would your answers change if the special permit request were for a meeting home for homosexuals or for a group home for the profoundly retarded?

Subdivision Master Plans

Most states have legislation enabling local authorities to require municipality approval of every land subdivision plat. These enabling statutes provide penalties for failure to secure such approval where required by local ordinance. Some statutes make it a criminal offense to sell lots by reference to unrecorded plats and provide that such plats may not be recorded unless approved by the local planning board. Other statutes provide that building permits will not be issued unless the plat is approved and recorded.

EMINENT DOMAIN

Eminent domain power to take (buy) private property for public use

The power to take private property for public use, known as the power of **eminent domain**, is recognized as one of the inherent powers of government both in the U.S. Constitution and in state constitutions. Nevertheless, this power is carefully circumscribed and controlled. The Fifth Amendment to the federal Constitution provides, "[N]or shall private property be taken for public use without just compensation," and the constitutions of the states contain similar or identical provisions. Consequently, constitutional provisions directly prohibit the taking of private property without just compensation and implicitly prohibit the taking of private property for other than public use. Moreover, both federal and state constitutions entitle to due process of law the individual from whom property is to be taken.

LUCAS v. SOUTH CAROLINA COASTAL COUNCIL Supreme Court of the United States, 1992, 505 U.S. 1003, 112 S.Ct. 2886, 120 L.Ed.2d 789

FACTS In 1972, South Carolina enacted a Coastal Zone Management Act requiring any person using land in a "critical area" to obtain a permit for any uses other than those to which the critical area was devoted when the act went into effect on September 28, 1977. In 1986, Lucas paid $975,000 for two residential lots on the Isle of Palms in Charleston County, South Carolina, on which he intended to develop a residential subdivision known as "Beachwood East." Because no portion of those lots was included in a "critical area" at that time, Lucas was not required to obtain a permit. In 1988, however, South Carolina enacted the Beachfront Management Act, which established a "baseline" for the landward-most points of erosion and in effect barred the erection of any permanent habitable structures on his two parcels. Lucas filed suit in state court, claiming that the new statute violated his Fifth and Fourteenth Amendment rights by taking property without compensation. He did not challenge South Carolina's police power; rather, he argued that he was entitled to just compensation. The trial court agreed. Stating that the new act had permanently deprived Lucas of construction rights and of any reasonable economic use of the lots, the court awarded him $1,232,387.50. The Supreme Court of South Carolina reversed, holding that the new act was a valid use of

state police power to protect a legitimate state interest. It stated further that when a state regulation is designed to protect against public harm, no compensation is required under the Fourteenth Amendment.

DECISION Judgment of the Supreme Court of South Carolina reversed and case remanded.

OPINION The U.S. Supreme Court has held that while property may be regulated, regulation that goes too far will be recognized as a taking. Although there is no set formula for making this determination, two discrete categories of regulatory action are compensable without case-specific inquiry into the public interest. First, compensation is required when regulations compel the property owner to suffer a physical "invasion" of his property—no matter how minute the intrusion and no matter how strong the public purpose. Second, compensation is required where regulation denies all economically beneficial or productive use of land.

The second category is pertinent here. Where the state seeks to sustain regulation that deprives land of all economically beneficial use, the state may resist providing compensation only if the nature of the owner's use interests were not originally part of his title. This means that when an owner takes title to his land, he must expect that the state may restrict the uses of his

continued

property from time to time, by legitimate police power actions. Any limitation that prohibits all economically beneficial use of land, however, cannot be newly legislated but must be based on the legal principles, with regard to property and nuisance, that the state already places upon land ownership.

Hence, consideration of the "total taking" here will entail, under state nuisance laws, analysis of several factors, including (1) the degree of harm to public lands and resources, or to adjacent private property, posed by the claimant's proposed activities, (2) the social value of the claimant's activities and their suitability to the locality, and (3) the relative ease with which the alleged harm can be avoided. The fact that similarly situated owners have long engaged in a particular use ordinarily imports a lack of any common law prohibition. So also does the fact that other landowners, similarly situated, are permitted to continue the use denied to the claimant. A state may not transform private property into public property without compensation. Instead, as it would be required to do if it sought to restrain Lucas in a common law action for public nuisance, South Carolina must identify background principles of nuisance and property law that prohibit the uses he now intends. Only then can South Carolina prevail.

INTERPRETATION The prohibition against a state taking private property without paying the owner just compensation applies to regulatory takings that deny all economically beneficial or productive use of the land.

Public Use

As noted, there is an implicit constitutional prohibition against taking private property for other than public use. Most states interpret **public use** to mean "public advantage." Thus, the power of eminent domain may be delegated to railroad and public utility companies. Because it enables such companies to offer continued and improved service to the public, the reasonable exercise of such power is upheld as a public advantage. As society grows more complex, other public purposes become legitimate grounds for exercising the power of eminent domain. One such use is in the area of urban renewal. Most states have legislation permitting the establishment of housing authorities with the power to condemn slum, blighted, and vacant areas and to finance, construct, and maintain housing projects. Some states have recently gone further by allowing private companies to exercise the power of eminent domain, provided the use is primarily for the public benefit, including the alleviation of unemployment or economic decay within the community.

Public use public advantage

Just Compensation

When the power of eminent domain is exercised, the owners of the property taken must receive **just compensation**. The measure of compensation is the fair market value of the property as of the time of taking. The compensation goes to holders of vested interests in the condemned property.

For an overview of eminent domain see Figure 53–2.

Just compensation the owner of the property taken by eminent domain must be paid the fair market value of the property

PRIVATE RESTRICTIONS ON LAND USE

Owners of real property may impose private restrictions, called **restrictive covenants**, on the use of land. Historically, two types of private restrictions developed—real covenants and equitable servitudes. The two had different, although overlapping, requirements. Today, equitable servitudes have nearly replaced real covenants. Accordingly, this section will cover only equitable servitudes, which we will identify by the more general term restrictive covenant.

Restrictive covenant private restriction on property contained in a conveyance

FIGURE 53–2 Eminent Domain

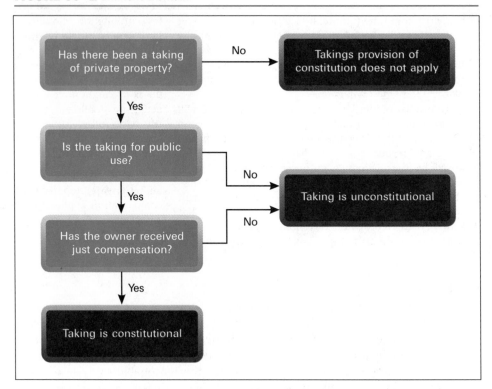

Requirements for Running Covenants

Running covenants
covenants that bind not only the original parties but also subsequent owners of the property

If certain conditions are satisfied, a restrictive covenant will bind not only the original parties to it but also remote parties who subsequently acquire the property. A restrictive covenant that binds remote parties is said to "run with the land." To run with the land, the covenant must involve promises that are enforceable under the law of contracts. Accordingly, a majority of courts hold that restrictive covenants must be in writing. The parties who agree to the restrictive covenant must intend that the covenant bind their successors. Moreover, the covenant must "touch and concern" the land, affecting its use, utility, or value. Finally, a restrictive covenant will bind only those successors who have had actual or constructive notice of the covenant.

Restrictive Covenants in Subdivisions

Covenants in subdivision
bind purchasers of lots in the subdivision as if the restrictions had been inserted in their own deeds

Restrictive covenants are widely used in subdivisions. The owners of lots are subject to restrictive covenants that, if actually brought to the attention of subsequent purchasers or recorded by original deed or by means of a recorded plat or separate agreement, bind purchasers of lots in the subdivision as though the restrictions had actually been inserted in their own deeds. If the entire subdivision has been subjected to a general building plan designed to benefit all of the lots, any lot owner in the subdivision has the right to enforce the restriction against a purchaser whose title descends from a common grantor. If a restriction is clearly intended to benefit an entire tract, the covenant will be enforced against a subsequent purchaser of one of the lots in the tract if (1) the restriction was apparently intended to benefit the purchaser of any lot in the tract and (2) the restriction appears somewhere in the chain of title to which the lot is subject.

THE LAW AND YOU Buying and Selling Real Estate

Nearly everyone, at some time in life, faces the problems of buying and selling real estate. The purchase of a home is probably the largest single investment a person will ever undertake and, therefore, careful consideration should be given to the technical difficulties involved in the transfer of real estate before any action is taken.

Contracts

Once you've found the house you'd like to buy and have agreed on the price, you will probably be asked to sign a paper and pay a deposit. This paper may be called a binder, receipt, purchase offer or agreement and is usually prepared by the seller's agent (that is, the seller's real estate broker or attorney).

Any one of these papers may constitute a binding contract requiring you to purchase the house. Before signing it, you should consider seeking legal advice. Remember that once a contract has been signed, your rights and obligations are fixed concerning the transaction and your attorney may not have the opportunity to structure the contract to meet your objectives.

Whether you are seller or buyer, you should understand the contract terms and how they affect you. The other parties to the contract may not be under any obligation to tell you what the contract means and you may not understand the legal meaning of much of the terminology.

So, if you are going to have an attorney represent you in the transaction, the time to consult one is before you sign any papers.

The contract of sale should state the parties, the purchase price and how it is to be paid, an adequate description of the property being sold, the kind of deed to be delivered, the quality of the seller's title to the property, a description of personal property included in the sale, the date you are to take possession, and other clauses relating to the property and the parties' respective responsibilities to each other.

The contract should also permit the buyer to cancel the contract if financing can't be obtained and provide for the return of the down payment if the sale falls through. Or, perhaps the seller may want to retain possession of the property for some time in order to find new accommodations. If so, appropriate clauses can be included in the contract defining such rights.

These are only a few matters usually covered in the contract. However, they illustrate the variety of terms and conditions to be considered when you enter into such a transaction.

Plain Language

All contracts and mortgage documents for the purchase and sale of real estate costing $50,000 or less must be written in non-technical language and in a clear and coherent manner. This requirement applies only to real estate which is, or will be, personally used by the buyer or seller.

Title

The "title" to real estate is the right of the owner to its peaceful possession and use, free from the claims of others. Often, however, the exercise of that right is limited by the existence of other rights which are called easements. To obtain electricity, sewers, telephone, etc., an owner gives the municipality or public utility the right to run its lines or pipes across his or her property to the house. Other often encountered easements provide for drainage of surface water, or access rights of way such as for a jointly-used driveway. These easements must be recognized by the owner in the use of the property and considered by the buyer who is purchasing the property.

There are other ways in which the use of the owner's property may be limited. One is by restrictions in the deed; another is by local zoning law. Also, almost all land is subject to real property taxes, which if not paid, may result in the loss of title. Other debts owed on the property (for example, special assessments or levies) can also cause problems later on.

When you buy a home, you should be certain that you have the right to occupy it without interference and that you later will be able to sell or mortgage it without problems.

Title Searches

After the contract has been signed, you should satisfy yourself that the seller can convey a "marketable" title to the property to you as agreed upon in the contract of sale.

In different areas of the state, varying methods are used to make sure that the title received from the seller is marketable.

In some areas, your lawyer will make his or her own examination of the records and issue a certificate indicating the findings. In other areas, your lawyer may supply you with a written title opinion based on an abstract of title (which is simply a title history) prepared by a commercial abstractor. In still other areas, your attorney may take out a title insurance policy. Or, a combination of any of these methods may be used.

A word about title insurance—while it may give you protection against financial loss and the possible expense of defending your title in court, it does not lessen the importance of your lawyer's advice. Your lawyer can advise you whether and how to obtain title insurance and also on the terms, exceptions, and conditions of a title insurance policy.

Form of Deed

In residential transactions there are two generally used Forms of Deed.

continued

The first is called a "Warranty Deed," which assures the buyer that the title is good against anyone who may claim a superior title. The second commonly used Form of Deed is the "Bargain and Sale Deed With Covenant Against Grantor's Acts." This deed assures the buyer that the seller has done nothing to affect the title to the property through his or her own acts. In both instances, if the title is insured by a title insurance company, the buyer will look to the title insurer for protection against claims even though the buyer may make claim against the seller.

Representation

Remember one important point—the seller, broker, and bank in the transaction may have an attorney representing each of their interests. An attorney representing any of these parties (even though you may be charged with a fee, as in the case of a bank), is not your attorney. It is your own responsibility, as the buyer, to seek the professional advice of an attorney to protect yourself and to be sure that you get precisely what you are legally entitled to receive.

Closing

The "closing" of the purchase of your home is the transaction in which you receive all the documents required to convey the title of your home.

At the closing these documents are reviewed to be sure that the conditions and promises of the purchase contract are fulfilled. Also at this time, the balance of the purchase price is paid to the seller.

Arrangements are made at the closing for the time when you will occupy the home. Normally, when the full purchase price is paid, the keys to the house are delivered to the buyer, who then has the right to move in immediately. However, your purchase agreement may also specify that you move in at a later date.

The important thing to remember is that buying a home is a major investment. It usually involves making payments over a period of years. In the long run, it's likely to be more economical to have competent professional advice—your attorney's advice—in making the purchase than to risk the trouble and expense that could result from not having that advice in the first place.

[The material in this feature is intended to inform and not to advise. No one should attempt to apply or interpret any law without the aid of a trained expert. This is particularly true of real property law.]

Subdivisions may involve many types of restrictive covenants. The more common ones limit the use of property to residential purposes, restrict the area of the lot on which a structure can be built, or provide for a special type of architecture. Frequently, a subdivider will specify a minimum size for each house in an attempt to maintain structural unity in a neighborhood.

Restrictive covenants are construed strictly against the party asserting their applicability.

Termination of Restrictive Covenants

A restrictive covenant may end by the terms of the original agreement. For example, the developer of a subdivision may provide that the restrictive covenant will terminate after thirty-five years unless a specified majority of the property owners reaffirm the covenant. In addition, a court will not enforce a restrictive covenant if changed circumstances make enforcement inequitable and oppressive. Evidence of *changed conditions* may be found either within the tract covered by the original covenant or within the area adjacent to or surrounding the tract.

Validity of Restrictive Covenants

Although restrictions on land use have never been popular in the law, the courts will enforce a restriction that apparently will operate to the general benefit of the owners of all the land the restriction will affect. The usual method of enforcing such agreements is by injunction to restrain a violation.

The law for many years, however, has held that under the Fourteenth Amendment to the Constitution, a state or municipality cannot impose racial restrictions by statute or ordinance. In 1947, in holding that state courts, as an arm of state government, cannot enforce private racial restrictive covenants, the Supreme Court effectively invalidated such covenants.

CORNER v. MILLS Court of Appeals of Indiana, 1995, 650 N.E.2d 712

FACTS Christiana Acres is a subdivision consisting of thirty-two lots in Elkhart, Indiana. The tract was divided in 1937 by then owners Perry and Florence Shupert. Between 1939 and 1941, four lots were sold without restrictions. In 1942, one of the lots was sold with several restrictions, including: a residential use restriction; a sideline and setback provision; a minimum lot size to build restriction; a prohibition of noxious or offensive activities; a racial restriction (prohibiting occupancy by nonwhites); a restriction against temporary residential structures; and a minimum building size and cost restriction. Between 1942 and 1946, two of the lots were sold; one with the above restrictions and one without. In 1946, the tract was recorded without any restrictions by all of the owners. At the time, all of the owners were using their lots for residential purposes. Subsequently, thirteen lots were sold. These lots all had restrictions, although they did not all have identical restrictions. All but one had a residential use restriction.

The plaintiffs own lots in the subdivision that are located near a commercialized thoroughfare. They believed that their property would be more valuable if used for commercial purposes and filed a complaint seeking declaratory relief to have the restrictive covenants on their property lifted. The defendants, who are also residents of the subdivision, filed a counterclaim seeking enforcement of the covenants. The trial court found the racial covenants unenforceable but upheld the residential use restrictions on Christiana Acres.

DECISION Judgment affirmed.

OPINION Restrictive covenants are express contracts between grantor and grantee. As in other contracts, illegal covenants can be removed if to do so would not affect the intent or symmetry of the remaining covenants. Removing the racial covenants only destroys a small portion of the prevailing and apparent intent to keep Christiana Acres residential. Therefore, contrary to the plaintiffs' contention, the racial covenants, which are illegal, can be removed without disturbing the residential covenants.

The plaintiffs also argue that the residential covenants are not enforceable because the lack of uniformity in restrictions in the subdivision shows there was no general plan for residential development. In determining if there was a general plan, the focus is on whether the facts of the case, including the language of the deeds and the grantors' actions, reveal an intent by them to create such a plan or scheme. Every current owner can trace their title back to those owning the lots in 1946, when the subdivision plat was first recorded. Since all the owners in 1946 joined in the recording and all maintained their property for residential use, it is reasonable to infer that they intended to combine their efforts to keep Christiana Acres residential.

Finally, the plaintiffs argue that the commercial development adjacent to Christiana Acres makes preserving the residential nature of the subdivision unfeasible. However, it is only where the use of property and the surrounding area has so radically changed from what was originally envisioned, making the covenants no longer sustainable, that they will be lifted as unenforceable. Since 1946, all of the lots have remained residential and there is no evidence to show that it is no longer practical to maintain the subdivision as a residential neighborhood. The plaintiffs' unilateral speculation that their properties are worth more if developed commercially is insufficient by itself to nullify the otherwise valid covenants for residential use.

INTERPRETATION Illegal covenants can be removed from an agreement, provided it will not affect the intent or symmetry of the remaining covenants.

CHAPTER SUMMARY

Transfer

Contract of Sale

Formation a contract to transfer any interest in land must be in writing to be enforceable

Marketable Title the seller must transfer marketable title, which is a title free from any defects or encumbrances

Quality of Improvements
- *Common Law Rule* under *caveat emptor* ("let the buyer beware") the seller is not liable for any undiscovered defects
- *Implied Warranty of Habitability* in a number of states, the builder-seller of a dwelling impliedly warrants that a newly constructed house is free from latent defects

Deeds

Definition a formal document transferring any type of interest in land

Types
- *Warranty Deed* the grantor (seller) promises the grantee (buyer) that she has valid title to the property without defect
- *Special Warranty Deed* the seller promises that he has not impaired the title
- *Quitclaim Deed* the seller transfers whatever interest she has in the property

Requirements the deed must (1) be written, (2) contain certain words of conveyance and a description of the property, (3) end with the signature of the grantor, a seal, and an acknowledgment before a notary public, and (4) be delivered

Delivery intent that the deed take effect, as evidenced by acts or statements of the grantor

Recordation required to protect the buyer's interest against third parties; consists of delivery of a duly executed and acknowledged deed to the appropriate recorder's office

Secured Transactions

Elements a secured transaction involves (1) a debt or obligation to pay money, (2) an interest of the creditor in specific property that secures performance, and (3) the debtor's right to redeem the property (remove the security interest) by paying the debt

Mortgage interest in land created by a written document that provides security to the mortgagee (secured party) for payment of the mortgagor's debt

Deed of Trust an interest in real property that is conveyed to a third person as trustee for the benefit of the creditor

Transfer
- *Assumes the Mortgage* the purchaser of mortgaged property becomes personally liable to pay the debt
- *Subject to the Mortgage* purchaser is not personally liable to pay the debt, but the property remains subject to the mortgage

Foreclosure upon default, sale of the mortgaged property to satisfy the debt

Adverse Possession	**Definition** acquisition of title to land by open, continuous, and adverse occupancy for a statutorily prescribed period **Possession** must be actual and without intervening dominion by true owner

Public and Private Controls

Zoning	**Definition** principal method of public control over private land use, involves regulation of land but may not constitute a taking of the property **Authority** the power to zone is generally delegated to local authorities by statutes known as *enabling acts* **Variance** a use differing from that provided in the zoning ordinance and granted in order to avoid undue hardship **Nonconforming Use** a use not in accordance with, but existing prior to, a zoning ordinance; permitted to continue for at least a reasonable time **Judicial Review** zoning ordinances may be reviewed to determine if they are invalid or a confiscation of property

Eminent Domain	**Definition** the power of a government to take (buy) private land for public use **Public Use** public advantage **Just Compensation** The owner of the property taken by eminent domain must be paid the fair market value of the property

Restrictive Covenants	**Definition** private restrictions on property contained in a conveyance **Running Covenants** covenants that bind not only the original parties but also subsequent owners of the property **Covenants in Subdivision** bind purchasers of lots in the subdivision as if the restrictions had been inserted in their own deeds

QUESTIONS

1. Distinguish among warranty, special warranty, and quitclaim deeds.
2. Distinguish between the obligations of a purchaser who assumes a mortgage and one who buys the property subject to the mortgage.
3. Describe the fundamental requirements of a valid deed.
4. Define and give an example of (a) a variance and (b) a nonconforming use.
5. Describe the nature and types of restrictive covenants.

Internet Question. Find and compare the rates among mortgage providers on (a) 30-year mortgages, (b) 15-year mortgages, and (c) adjustable rate mortgages.

PROBLEMS

1. A was the father of B, C, and D and the owner of Redacre, Blackacre, and Greenacre.

   A made and executed a warranty deed conveying Redacre to B. The deed provided that "this deed shall only become effective on the death of the grantor." A retained possession of the deed and died, leaving the deed in his safe deposit box.

   A made and executed a warranty deed conveying Blackacre to C. This deed also provided that "this deed shall only become effective on the death of the grantor." A delivered the deed to C. After A died, C recorded the deed.

   A made and executed a warranty deed conveying Greenacre to D. A delivered the deed to X with specific instructions to deliver the deed to D on A's death. X duly delivered the deed to D when A died.

   (a) What is the interest of B in Redacre, if any?

   (b) What is the interest of C in Blackacre, if any?

   (c) What is the interest of D in Greenacre, if any?

2. Arkin, the owner of Redacre, executed a real estate mortgage to the Shawnee Bank and Trust Company for $10,000. After the mortgage was executed and recorded, Arkin constructed a dwelling on the premises and planted a corn crop. After Arkin defaulted in the payment of the mortgage debt, the bank proceeded to foreclose the mortgage. At the time of the foreclosure sale, the corn crop was mature and unharvested. Arkin contends (a) that the value of the dwelling should be credited to him and (b) that he is entitled to the corn crop. Decision?

3. Robert and Stanley held legal title of record to adjacent tracts of land, each consisting of eighty acres. Stanley fenced his eighty acres in 1970, placing his east fence fifteen feet onto Robert's property. Thereafter, he was in possession of this fifteen-foot strip of land and kept it fenced and cultivated continuously until he sold his tract of land to Nathan on March 1, 1975. Nathan took possession under deed from Stanley, and continued possession and cultivation of the fifteen-foot strip until May 27, 1994, when Robert, having on several occasions strenuously objected to Nathan's possession, brought suit against Nathan for trespass. What decision?

4. Marcia executed a mortgage of Blackacre to secure her indebtedness to Ajax Savings and Loan Association in the amount of $25,000. Later, Marcia sold Blackacre to Morton. The deed contained the following provision: "This deed is subject to the mortgage executed by the Grantor herein to Ajax Savings and Loan Association."

   The sale price of Blackacre to Morton was $50,000. Morton paid $25,000 in cash, deducting the $25,000 mortgage debt from the purchase price. On default in the payment of the mortgage debt, Ajax brings an action against Marcia and Morton to recover a judgment for the amount of the mortgage debt and to foreclose the mortgage. Decision?

5. On January 1, 1983, Davis and Hershey owned Blackacre as tenants in common. On July 1, 1983, Davis made a written contract to sell Blackacre to Dibbert for $25,000. Pursuant to this contract, Dibbert paid Davis $25,000 on August 1, 1993, and Davis executed and delivered to Dibbert a warranty deed to Blackacre. On May 1, 1994, Hershey quitclaimed his interest in Blackacre to Davis. Dibbert brings an action against Davis for breach of warranty of title. What judgment?

6. John Doe, for valuable consideration, agreed to convey to Richard Roe eighty acres of land. He delivered a deed, the material portions of which read:

   "I, John Doe, grant and convey to Richard Roe eighty acres of land [land description]: To have and to hold unto Richard Roe, his heirs, and assigns forever.

   "I, John Doe, covenant to warrant and defend the premises hereby conveyed against all persons claiming the same or any part thereof by or through me."

   Thereafter, Roe conveyed "all my right, title, and interest" in the eighty acres to Paul Poe. It develops that Doe had no title to the land when he conveyed it to Roe. Subsequently, Doe inherited an undivided one-half interest in the property.

   What rights, if any, does Poe have against Doe and Roe?

7. Barker operated a retail bakery, Davidson a drugstore, Farrell a food store, Gibson a gift shop, and Harper a hardware store in adjoining locations along one side of a single suburban village block. As the population grew, the business section developed at the other end of the village, and the establishments of Barker, Davidson, Farrell, Gibson, and Harper were surrounded for at least a mile in each direction solely by residences. A zoning ordinance with the usual provisions was adopted by the village, and the area including the five stores was declared to be a "residential district for single-family dwellings." Thereafter, Barker tore down the frame building that housed the bakery and began to construct a modern brick bakery. Davidson found her business increasing to such an extent that she began to build an addition on the drugstore to extend it to the rear alley. Farrell's building was destroyed by fire, and he started to reconstruct it to restore it to its former condition. Gibson changed the gift shop into a sporting goods store and after six months of operation decided to go back into the gift shop business. Harper sold his hardware store to Hempstead.

   The village building commission brings an action under the zoning ordinance to enjoin the construction work of Barker, Davidson, and Farrell and to enjoin the carrying on of any business by Gibson and Hempstead. Assume the ordinance is valid. What result?

8. Alda and Mattingly are residents of Unit I of Chimney Hills Subdivision. The lots owned by Alda and Mattingly are subject to the following restrictive covenant: "Lots shall be for single-family residence purposes only." Alda intends to convert her carport into a beauty shop, and Mattingly brings suit against Alda to enjoin her from doing so. Alda argues that the covenant restricts only the type of building that can be constructed, not the incidental use to which residential structures are put. Decision?

9. The city of Boston sought to condemn land in fee simple for use in constructing an entrance to an underground terminal for a subway. The owners of the land contend that no more than surface and subsurface easements are necessary for the terminal entrance and seek to retain air rights above thirty-six feet. The city argues that any building using this airspace would require structural supports that would interfere with the city's plan for the terminal. The city concedes that the properties around the condemned property could be assembled and structures could be designed to span over the condemned property, in which case the air rights would be quite valuable. Decision?

10. For seven years, Desford Potts had owned a six-acre tract of land within the corporate limits of the city of Franklin. The tract contained a livestock barn in which Potts stored lumber and other building materials. Bricks were also stored in stacks four or five feet high outside and behind the barn. Franklin passed a zoning ordinance by virtue of which Potts's lot was classified as residential property. Soon afterward, Potts moved some saw logs onto his back lot, and the city complained that Potts's use of his property for storage of building materials was a "nonconforming use." Potts then brought an action to enjoin interference by the city of Franklin. Decision?

11. In May 1963, Fred Parramore executed four deeds, each conveying a life estate in his land to him and his wife and a remainder interest in one-fourth of his land to each of his four children: Alney, Eudell, Bernice, and Iris. Although Fred executed and acknowledged the four deeds as part of his plan to distribute his estate at his death, he did not deliver them to his children at this time. Instead, he placed the deeds with his will in a safe deposit box and instructed the children to pick up their deeds at his death. Fred later conveyed Alney's deed to Alney, thereby vesting Alney's interest in that parcel, but Eudell, Bernice, and Iris's deeds were never handed over to them during Fred's lifetime. Fred, however, acted as if the land was beyond his control, and on one occasion told a prospective buyer that the land had already been deeded away. When Fred died in November 1974, Alney brought this action, claiming that the deeds to Eudell, Bernice, and Iris were ineffective because they had never been handed over during Fred's lifetime. Accordingly, Alney

argued the remaining land should pass in equal shares to each of the four children under the residuary clause of Fred's will. Decision?

12. The Gerwitz family resides on a piece of land known as Lot #24 of the Belleville tract, which they acquired by deed in 1957. Shortly thereafter, the Gerwitzes began to use the adjacent vacant Lot #25. At various times they planted grass seed, flowers, and shrubs on the land and used it for picnics and cookouts. In 1977, Gelsomin acquired Lot #25 and constructed a foundation on it so that he could place a house there. The Gerwitzes then brought this action to stop him, claiming title to Lot #25 by adverse possession. Decision?

13. Leo owned a one-story, one-family dwelling in a single-family residential zoning district in Detroit. He attempted to sell the house with its adjoining lot for $38,500. Houses in the neighborhood generally sold for $20,000 to $25,000. Immediately to the west of Leo's property was a gasoline service station. In addition, Leo's property was located on a corner frequented with heavy traffic. After he received no offers from residence-use buyers during the period of over a year that the property was listed and offered for sale, Leo applied to the board of zoning appeals for a variance to permit the use of the property as a dental and medical clinic and to use the side yard for off-street parking. The variance would be subject to certain conditions, including the preservation of the building's exterior as that of a one-family dwelling. Puritan-Greenfield Improvement Association, a nonprofit corporation, filed a complaint against Leo's variance request. Decision?

14. The Glendale Church purchased a twenty-one-acre parcel of land in a canyon along the banks of Mill Creek in Angeles National Forest. The church used the twelve flat acres next to the stream to operate a campground for handicapped children. This area had a number of improved buildings located on it. In July 1977, a forest fire destroyed all ground cover upstream from the church's campground, and a subsequent flood destroyed all the buildings. In response, the county of Los Angeles enacted an interim ordinance that temporarily prohibited the church from constructing new buildings. At trial, the question presented was whether the church was as entitled to compensation for a temporary taking of its property as it would have been in a formal eminent domain proceeding. Decision?

15. Robert V. Gross owned certain land on which he proposed to construct an eighty-three-unit apartment house. The land, however, was subject to a restriction imposed by a 1947 deed to a predecessor in title that provided that no part of the premises could be used for business purposes other than raising, growing, and selling live bait, fishing tackle, and sporting goods. Gross sought a decree stating that the restriction did not prohibit the construction and operation of an apartment house. Decision?

CHAPTER 54

Trusts and Wills

In previous chapters, we have seen that real and personal property may be transferred in a number of ways, including by sale and by gift. Another important way in which a person may convey property or allow others to use or benefit from it is through trusts and wills. Trusts may take effect during the transferor's lifetime, or, when used in a will, they may become effective upon his death. Wills enable individuals to control the transfer of their property at their death. Upon a person's death, his or her property must pass to someone, and individuals are well advised to decide how their property should be distributed. Except for the limitations of dower and curtesy, the law permits individuals to make such distributions by sale, gift, trust, and will. If, however, an individual dies without a will—that is, *intestate*—state law prescribes who shall be entitled to the property that the individual owned at death. In this chapter, we will examine both trusts and wills, as well as the manner in which property descends when a person dies intestate.

TRUSTS

Trust transfer of property to one party for the benefit of another

A **trust** is a *fiduciary relationship* in which one or more persons hold legal title to property while its use, enjoyment, and benefit (equitable title) belong to another. Allowed to serve any purpose that is not against the law or public policy, a trust may be created by agreement of the parties, by a grant in a will, or by a court decree. However fashioned, the relationship is known as a trust. The party creating the trust is the **creator** or **settlor**, the party holding the legal title to the property is the **trustee** of the trust, and the person who receives the benefit of the trust is the **beneficiary** (see Figure 54–1).

Settlor creator of the trust

Trustee holder of legal title to property for the benefit of another

TYPES OF TRUSTS

Beneficiary equitable owner of trust property

Although there are many varieties, all trusts fall into one of two major groups: express or implied. The implied trusts, which are imposed upon property by court order, are categorized as either "constructive" or "resulting" trusts.

Express Trusts

Express trust a trust established by voluntary action; usually in writing, although it may be oral

The **express trust** is, as the name indicates, a trust established by voluntary action and is represented either by a written document or, under some conditions, by an oral statement or conduct of the settlor. In a majority of jurisdictions, an express trust of real property must be in writing to meet the requirements of the statute of frauds.

FIGURE 54–1 Trusts

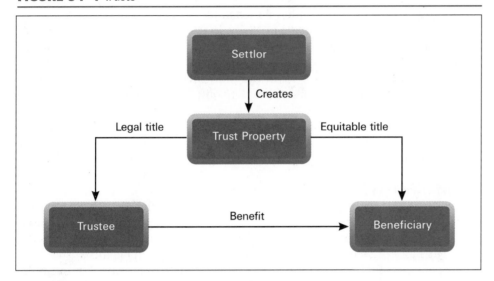

No particular words are necessary to create a trust, provided that the settlor's intent to establish a trust is unmistakable. Determining whether a settlor really intended to create a trust is not always easy. Sometimes, in connection with a gift, a settlor will use words of request or recommendation that imply or express hope that the gift should or will be used for a particular purpose. Thus, instead of leaving property "to X for the benefit and use of Y," a settlor may leave property to X "in full confidence and with hope that he will care for Y." Such a **precatory** (wishful) expression may be so definite as to impose a trust upon the property for Y's benefit. Whether the expression will create a trust or will constitute nothing more than a gratuitous wish depends on whether the court believes from all the facts that the settlor genuinely intended a trust.

Precatory expressing a wish

Testamentary Trust Trusts employed in wills are known as **testamentary trusts** because they become effective after the settlor's death.

Testamentary trust trust established by a will

Inter Vivos Trust A trust established during the settlor's lifetime is referred to as an *inter vivos*, or "between-the-living," **trust**.

Inter vivos **trust** trust established during the settlor's lifetime

Charitable Trusts Almost any trust that has for its purpose the improvement of the whole or a class of humankind is a **charitable trust**, unless it is so vague that it cannot be enforced. Gifts for public museums, for park maintenance, and for the dissemination of a particular political doctrine or religious belief have been upheld as charitable.

Charitable trust trust designed to benefit humankind

Spendthrift Trusts A settlor who believes that a beneficiary cannot be trusted to preserve even the limited rights granted her as beneficiary may provide in the trust instrument that the beneficiary cannot, by assignment or otherwise, impair her rights to receive principal or income and that creditors of the beneficiary cannot attach the fund or the income. Such a trust is called a **spendthrift trust**. Spendthrift provisions are valid in most states. However, once the beneficiary actually receives income from the trust, creditors may seize it or the beneficiary may use it as she pleases.

Spendthrift trust trust designed to remove the trust estate from the beneficiary's control

Totten trust a tentative trust consisting of a joint bank account opened by the settlor

Totten Trusts A **totten trust** or savings account trust involves a joint bank account opened by the trust settlor. For example, Sally deposits a sum of money into a savings account in the name of "Sally, in trust for Justin." Sally may make additional deposits into the account and may withdraw money from it whenever she pleases. Because the settlor may revoke a totten trust by withdrawing the funds or by changing the form of the account, such a trust is tentative. Usually the transfer of ownership becomes complete only on the depositor's death.

Implied Trusts In some cases, the courts, in the absence of any expressed intent to create a trust, will impose a trust on property because the parties' acts appear to warrant such a construction. An **implied trust** owes its existence to the law.

Implied trust a trust created by operation of law

Constructive trust trust arising by operation of law to prevent unjust enrichment

Constructive Trusts A **constructive trust** results when a court imposes a trust on property to rectify fraud or to prevent unjust enrichment. A court will establish a constructive trust where a confidential relationship has been abused or where actual fraud or duress constitutes an equitable ground for creating the trust. The mere existence of a confidential relationship prohibits the trustee from seeking any personal benefit during the course of the relationship. For example, a director of a corporation who takes advantage of a "corporate opportunity" or who makes an undisclosed profit in a transaction with the corporation will be treated as a trustee for the corporation with respect to the property or profits he has acquired. Likewise, a trustee under an express trust who permits a lease held by the trust to expire and then acquires a new lease of the property in his individual capacity will be required to hold the new lease in a confidential trust for the beneficiary.

IN RE ESTATE OF WELCH Court of Appeals of Iowa, 1995, 534 N.W.2d 109

FACTS George Welch, a wealthy man, died on April 25, 1991, and was survived by his second wife, Dorothy Welch, and his daughter by his first marriage, Patricia Fisher. At the time George and Dorothy were married, George was in very poor health and he relied on Dorothy to care for him. During the eight months George and Dorothy were married, George became isolated from his family and his health deteriorated. Prior to his death, George transferred the bulk of his assets to Dorothy. Dorothy assisted in the transfer of George's assets and often completed checks and other papers for George's signature. George also made a new will that named Dorothy as his sole beneficiary. Patricia was the sole beneficiary of his prior will. Through the transfers of assets and the new will, Dorothy received $570,000, about 60 percent of George's estate. Patricia sought to set aside the will and the transfers based on undue influence. The will contest was submitted to the jury, which found undue influence and set aside the will. However, the trial court, which considered the transfers of assets, did not find undue influence and refused to create a constructive trust over the assets. Patricia appeals the trial court's ruling.

DECISION Judgment reversed and remanded.

OPINION A constructive trust is a remedial device by which the holder of legal title is held to be a trustee for the benefit of another who in good conscience is entitled to the beneficial interest. It is an equitable doctrine applied for purposes of restitution, to prevent unjust enrichment by fraud or other unconscionable conduct. One form of unconscionable conduct that may justify a constructive trust is undue influence.

The facts of this case indicate that Dorothy exercised undue influence over George in the months prior to his death. There are four elements to sustain a finding of undue influence: (1) the grantor's susceptibility to undue influence; (2) opportunity to exercise such influence and effect the wrongful purpose; (3) disposition to influence unduly for the purpose of procuring an improper favor; and (4) a result that is clearly the effect of undue influence. George's susceptibility to undue influence is clear from his poor health. He was an alcoholic and a crippling heart attack in 1988 left him with only a few years to live. Also, the death of his first wife during the same year left him lonely and desperate for companionship. In addition, Dorothy had

continued

the opportunity to exercise undue influence and take advantage of George's susceptibility. Within a few days of his first wife's death, Dorothy told George she had always loved him and if he did not marry her, she would commit suicide. During the last months of George's life, Dorothy positioned herself as a dominant influence over him. At the same time, George became particularly susceptible to being influenced due to his advancing age, impending death, deteriorating physical condition, and unstable emotional health. Furthermore, Dorothy isolated George from his family and friends as well as complete medical care, indicating a disposition to influence unduly. Finally, the manner in which George and Dorothy conducted their business, as well as Dorothy's actions after George died, reveal a pattern of unfair persuasion or influence

from which Dorothy benefited. George was isolated and vulnerable and the transfers of his assets were rushed transactions conducted at odd times. The facts clearly indicate that George was susceptible to undue influence, Dorothy had the opportunity to exercise undue influence, Dorothy had the disposition to wrongfully influence George, and Dorothy benefited from the undue influence. The various financial arrangements between George and Dorothy were not normal transactions between a husband and wife, rather they were the result of undue influence.

INTERPRETATION A court may impose a constructive trust to prevent the unjust enrichment of a person who has abused a confidential relationship with another.

Resulting Trusts A **resulting trust** serves to effect the inferred or presumed *intent* of parties who have inadequately expressed their actual wishes. Such a trust depends not on contract or agreement but on presumed intent, as evidenced by the parties' acts. Since a resulting trust is created by implication and operation of law, it need not be evidenced in writing. The most common example of a resulting trust is where Joel pays the purchase price for property and takes title in Ellen's name. Here, the courts presume that the parties intended Ellen to hold the property for Joel's benefit, and Ellen will be treated as a trustee.

> **Resulting trust** trust arising to fulfill the parties' presumed intent

CREATION OF TRUSTS

Each trust has (1) a creator or settlor, (2) a "corpus" or trust property, (3) a trustee, and (4) a beneficiary. As we mentioned before, no particular words are necessary to create a trust, provided that the settlor's intent to establish a trust is unmistakable. Consideration is not essential to an enforceable trust. In this respect, a trust is more like a conveyance than a contract.

Settlor
Any person legally capable of making a contract may create a trust. But if a settlor's conveyance would be voidable or void because of infancy, incompetency, or some other reason, the settlor's declaration of trust is also voidable or void.

Subject Matter
One major requirement of a trust is that the trust corpus or *res* must consist of property that is definite and specific. A trust cannot be effective immediately for property not yet in existence or yet to be acquired.

Trustee
Anyone legally capable of holding title to and dealing with property may be a trustee. The lack of a trustee, however, will not destroy a trust. The court will appoint an individual or institution to act as trustee if the settlor neglects to appoint one, if the named trustee does not qualify, or if the named trustee declines to serve.

Duties the three primary duties of a trustee are to (1) carry out the purposes of the trust, (2) act prudently, and (3) act with utmost loyalty

Duties of the Trustee A trustee has three primary **duties:** (1) to carry out the purposes of the trust, (2) to administer the trust prudently and carefully, and (3) to exercise a high degree of loyalty toward the beneficiary.

Ordinarily, no special skills are required of a trustee, who is required simply to act with the same degree of care that a *prudent person* would use to carry out his or her personal affairs. The trustee has a duty to make the trust property productive and thus to invest it in income-producing assets. Given the myriad circumstances of any particular case, what constitutes the care of a "prudent person" is, of course, not easy to generalize.

The duty of loyalty arises from the fiduciary character of the relationship between the trustee and the beneficiary. In all his dealings with the trust property, the beneficiary, and third parties, the trustee must act exclusively in the beneficiary's interest.

STURGIS v. STINSON Supreme Court of Virginia, 1991, 241 Va. 531, 404 S.E.2d 56

FACTS Dr. Williams J. Sturgis, Jr. died testate in 1986, leaving an estate valued at $1,140,462. The estate consisted of stocks and bonds, an automobile, and two pieces of real estate—the Bush Hill Farm, valued at $708,500, and another parcel valued at $126,000. His will provided that his widow, Anne Sturgis, was to receive all the income from his estate for her lifetime. Upon her death, the residue of the estate was to pass to their children, Susan Sturgis Stinson and Christopher S. Sturgis (the remaindermen). Dr. Sturgis's will named Robert C. Oliver as executor. The first paragraph of the will declared that Mrs. Sturgis was "to receive all of the income of my estate, of every nature and wheresoever situate," during her lifetime. The second paragraph provided that "if at anytime, . . . in the opinion of my executor, . . . the income of my estate together with such other income available to my wife is insufficient to meet any unusual expense . . . or to provide for her comfortable maintenance and welfare, then such executor may pay to my wife . . . such amounts from the principal or corpus of my estate as such executor deems necessary." The sixth paragraph granted the executor the power to convert and reinvest corpus assets.

In 1989, Mrs. Sturgis complained that the income derived from the estate was insufficient, based upon the value of the estate assets, and asked that the Bush Hill Farm be sold and the proceeds reinvested so as to produce greater income. The remaindermen opposed the sale of the property, maintaining that the trust assets could not be sold without their consent. The trial court decreed that the will created a trust and held that (1) Oliver, as executor, had the obligation to deliver all the net income of the trust to Mrs. Sturgis and to invade the trust corpus when he determined the income from it was insufficient to meet her needs as income beneficiary and (2) that he had the authority to convert assets of the estate to other forms.

At the time of trial, the Bush Hill Farm constituted 75 percent of the corpus of the trust and had a fair market value of $1.5 million. The maximum annual income from this property was $1,265.99. Mrs. Sturgis asserted that this return on the property was so small a percentage of its market value that it classified the property as an unproductive asset and that the executor therefore was obligated to sell the property and reinvest the sale proceeds. In response, the executor and the remaindermen contended that the general law of trusts should not apply to the Bush Hill Farm because the testator, Dr. Sturgis, intended that the farm not be sold unless such sale were necessary to meet the needs of Mrs. Sturgis.

DECISION Judgment of the trial court reversed and remanded.

OPINION Under general trust principles, where a trust is created for successive beneficiaries, the trustee has a duty to deal with them impartially. Under the Restatement of Trusts, the trustee is under a duty to the beneficiary to use reasonable care and skill to make the trust property productive. Unless the terms of the trust provide otherwise, if property held in trust to pay the income to a beneficiary for a period and thereafter to pay the principal to another produces no income or an income substantially less than the current rate of return on trust investments, and is likely to continue to be unproductive or underproductive, the trustee is under a duty to the beneficiary entitled to the income to sell such property within a reasonable time.

Oliver and the remaindermen assert that the terms of the will provide for the disposition and management of the farm and that Dr. Sturgis intended that the farm not be sold unless such sale were necessary to meet the needs of the income beneficiary. Basically, they argue that the general law of trusts should not apply because

continued

the testator provided otherwise. However, the will places no condition or limitation on the disposition of the farm or any other assets. Furthermore, nothing in the will or the record suggests that the executor was required to treat the Bush Hill Farm differently from the other assets.

INTERPRETATION A trustee is under a duty to manage trust assets with prudence and care and to act exclusively in the beneficiary's interest.

Powers of the Trustee The **powers** of a trustee are determined by (1) the authority granted him by the settlor in the instrument creating the trust and (2) the rules of law in the jurisdiction in which the trust is established. State laws affecting the powers of trustees have their greatest impact on the investments a trustee may make with trust funds. Most states prescribe a prudent investor rule. Some, however, still follow the historical test, which prescribes a list of types of securities qualified for trust investment. In some jurisdictions, this list is permissive; in others, it is mandatory. If the list is permissive, the trustee may invest in securities of types not listed, though he carries the burden of showing that he made a prudent choice. The trust instrument itself may give the trustee wide discretion as to investments, in which case, the trustee need not adhere to the list deemed advisable under the statute.

Powers generally established by the trust instrument and state law

Allocation of Principal and Income Trusts often settle a life estate in the trust corpus on one beneficiary and a remainder interest on another beneficiary. For example, on his death, Bill leaves his property to a trustee who is instructed to pay the income from the property to Bill's widow during her life and to distribute the property to his children when she dies. In an instance such as this, the trustee must distribute the principal to one party (the remainderman) and the income to another (the life tenant or income beneficiary). The trustee must also allocate receipts and charge expenses between the income beneficiary and the remainderman. If the trust agreement does not specify how the funds should be allocated, the trustee is provided statutory guidance, embodied in most states in the *Uniform Principal and Income Act*. A trustee who fails to comply with the trust agreement or the statute is personally liable for any loss.

The general rule in allocating benefits and burdens between income beneficiaries and remaindermen is that *ordinary* or current receipts and expenses are chargeable to the income beneficiary, whereas *extraordinary* receipts and expense are allocated to the remainderman. (Figure 54–2 illustrates these four types of allocations.) Ordinary income is money paid for the use of trust property and any gain or profit from such use, while either property received as a substitute for or a change in the form of the original trust property is trust principal.

Beneficiary

There are very few restrictions on who (or what) may be a beneficiary. Charitable uses are a common purpose of trusts, and if the settlor's object does not outrage public policy or morals, the courts will uphold almost any purpose that happens to strike a settlor's fancy.

A person named as a trust beneficiary may accept or reject the trust. In the absence of restrictive provisions in the trust instrument, such as a spendthrift clause, a beneficiary's interest may be reached by his creditors, or the beneficiary may sell or dispose of his interest. Upon death, if he held more than a life estate

FIGURE 54–2 Allocation of Principal and Income

	Receipts	Expenses
Ordinary—Income Beneficiary	Rents Royalties Cash dividends (regular and extraordinary) Interest	Interest payments Insurance Ordinary taxes Ordinary repairs Depreciation
Extraordinary—Remainderman	Stock dividends Stock splits Proceeds from sale or exchange of corpus Settlement of claims for injury to corpus	Extraordinary repairs Long-term improvements Principal amortization Costs incurred in the sale or purchase of corpus

in the trust, the beneficiary's interest, unless disposed of by his will, passes to his heirs or personal representatives.

TERMINATION OF A TRUST

Termination the general rule is that the trust is irrevocable unless a power of revocation is reserved in the trust instrument

Unless the settlor reserves a power of revocation, the general rule is that a trust, once validly created, is *irrevocable*. If so reserved, the trust may be terminated at the settlor's discretion.

Normally, the instrument creating a trust establishes the date on which the trust will terminate. The instrument may specify a period of years for which the trust is to last, or the settlor may provide that the trust shall continue during the life of a named individual. The death of the trustee or beneficiary does not terminate the trust if neither of their lives is the measure of the trust's duration.

Though a court will usually decree a trust terminated if the beneficiary acquires legal title to the trust assets, courts will not order the termination of a trust simply because all of the beneficiaries petition the court to do so. The purposes the settlor set forth in the trust instrument, not the beneficiaries' wishes, will govern the court's actions.

If the same beneficiary holds both the equitable and legal title, the *merger doctrine* applies and the beneficiary holds the property outright. In order for a trust to exist, the trustee and beneficiary must be different persons.

DECENDENTS' ESTATES

Testament will

Intestate dying without a will

The assets (the estate) of a person who dies leaving a valid will are to be distributed according to the directions contained in the will. A will is also called a **testament**; the maker of a will is called a testator; and gifts made in a will are called devises or bequests. If a person dies without leaving a will, her property will pass to her heirs and next of kin in the proportions provided in the applicable state statute. This is known as **intestate** (dying-without-a-will) succession. If a person dies without a will and leaves no heirs or next of kin, her property *escheats* (reverts) to the state. Nonetheless, not all of the decedent's property will pass through the probate estate (the distribution of a decedent's estate to her successors). Certain property will pass through arrangements unaffected by distribution. For instance, the decedent's life insurance policy or pension plan will pass to the beneficiary of the policy or plan, property the decedent jointly owned with a right of survivorship will pass to the survivor, and property subject to a trust will be governed by the trust instrument.

WILLS

A **will** is a written instrument, executed according to statutorily dictated formalities, whereby a person makes a disposition of his property, which is to take effect after his death. One major characteristic of a will sets it apart from other transactions such as deeds and contracts: a will is revocable at any time during life. There is no such thing as an irrevocable will. A will takes effect only on the death of the testator.

> **Will** a properly executed written instrument whereby a person makes a disposition of his property

Mental Capacity

In order to make a valid will, the testator must have both the "power" and the "capacity" to do so. In addition, the requisite testamentary intent must also be present.

Testamentary Capacity and Power The state grants the *power* to make a will to persons of a class whose members are believed generally able to handle their affairs without regard to personal limitations. Thus, in most states, children under a certain age cannot make valid wills.

> **Testamentary capacity** for a will to be valid the testator must be sufficiently competent to intend the document to be her will

The *capacity* to make a will refers to the measures by which the courts determine whether a particular person belonging to the class generally granted the power to make wills is, in fact, mentally fit enough to do so. A person who is capable of understanding the nature and extent of her property, appreciating the natural objects of her bounty, and formulating an orderly plan of disposition has mental capacity sufficient to make a will.

Conduct Invalidating a Will Any document appearing to be a will that reflects an intent other than the testator's is not a valid will. This is the basis for the rule that a will that transmits property as a result of *duress, undue influence,* or *fraud* is no will at all.

> **Conduct invalidating a will** a will that is the product of duress, undue influence, or fraud is invalid and of no effect

For there to be undue influence, there must be improper pressure directed specifically to the act of making the will. The charge of undue influence most frequently arises when a testator leaves his property to one who is not a blood relative, such as a friend who took care of the testator in his last illness or during his last years. If the evidence demonstrates that the beneficiary under the will was in close contact with the testator and that the will ignores the natural objects of the testator's bounty, a suggestion of undue influence exists. (But see *In Re Estate of Hobelsberger.*) The charge of fraud can also be used to invalidate a will.

Formal Requirements of a Will

By statute in all jurisdictions, a will must comply with certain formalities to be valid. Such formalities are necessary not only to indicate that the testator understood what she was doing but also to help prevent fraud.

> **Formal requirements** a will must be (1) in writing, (2) signed, and (3) attested to by witnesses

Writing A basic requirement for a valid will is that it be in writing. The writing may be informal, as long as it substantially meets the basic statutory formalities.

Pencil, ink, and photocopy are equally valid media, and valid wills have been made on scratch paper and on an envelope.

It is also valid to incorporate into a will by reference another document that in itself is not a will because it was improperly executed. To incorporate a memorandum into a will by reference, the following four conditions must exist: (1) the memorandum must be in writing; (2) it must be in existence when the will is executed; (3) it must be adequately described in the will; and (4) it must be described in the will as being in existence.

Signature The testator must sign her will; the signature verifies that the will has been executed. Most statutes require the signature to be at the end of the will. Even in jurisdictions that do not so specify, an ending signature will preclude the charge that the portions of the will that follow the signature were written after its execution and are therefore invalid.

IN RE ESTATE OF HOLBELSBERGER Supreme Court of South Dakota, 1970, 181 N.W.2d 455

FACTS John Hobelsberger lived alone on his farm near Kranzburg, South Dakota. A grandniece, Phyllis Raml, and her husband, Ralph, lived on and operated a farm about two miles away. Hobelsberger and the Ramls had a friendly and cordial relationship. The Ramls visited him rather frequently and largely cared for him during his later years. Hobelsberger was hospitalized on October 23, 1966, and his condition was diagnosed as intermittent cerebral insufficiency. During his hospitalization, he requested that the Ramls send an attorney to see him about the preparation of a will. Thomas Green, an attorney, interviewed the testator on or about November 10 and prepared a will in compliance with his instructions.

Hobelsberger was transferred to a nursing home on November 19. On November 22, Green and a secretary went to the nursing home and witnessed his signing of the will. Hobelsberger was then eighty years old. He subscribed the will with a mark because he was having trouble with his hands. Hobelsberger died on July 19, 1967, survived by twenty-seven nieces and nephews and seven grandnieces and grandnephews. The will, after providing for the payment of debts and funeral expenses, left Hobelsberger's entire estate to Phyllis Raml. Nine of the nieces and nephews contested the will, claiming lack of testamentary capacity, undue influence by the Ramls, and improper execution. The county court admitted the will to probate, the circuit court affirmed, and the contestants appealed.

DECISION Decree holding that the will is valid is affirmed.

OPINION Clearly, Hobelsberger was aged and infirm when he executed the will. However, one may be physically weak and aged and still possess a sound mind. The testimony concerning Hobelsberger's state of mind during the period when he executed the will was conflicting. The Ramls and the attesting witnesses, however, all testified to his mental competence. This position was supported by the attending physician in the hospital, who saw the testator on a daily basis until November 19, and by the nurse's records for the period of hospitalization. The trial judge's finding that Hobelsberger was of sound mind and had testamentary capacity to execute the will was thus not clearly erroneous and will not be set aside.

The contestants claimed that the Ramls exerted undue influence upon Hobelsberger. They urged that the distribution of the estate made by the will was unnatural. However, the will simply preferred a grandniece who had given the testator needed help over the years. The contestants also pointed out that the Ramls had the motive and opportunity to exert undue influence. This fact, though, does not prove that they did so. Moreover, no presumption of undue influence results from the fact that the Ramls obtained the benefits they received under the will by acts of kindness toward the testator. This presumption could only have arisen had the Ramls actively participated in the preparation of the will. All the Ramls did was to inform an attorney of Hobelsberger's desire to discuss the matter.

Finally, the contestants argued that, since the testator knew how to write, he was not authorized to execute the will by signing with a mark. However, the evidence indicates that Hobelsberger could not write at the time of execution because he was having trouble with his hands. Thus, he was able to avail himself of the privilege of subscribing with a mark.

INTERPRETATION A valid will requires the testator to have mental capacity and freedom from the undue influence of others.

Attestation With the exception of a few isolated types of wills (noted later in this chapter) that are valid in a limited number of jurisdictions, a written will must be attested, or certified, by witnesses. The number and qualifications of witnesses and the manner of attestation generally are determined by statute. Usually, two or three witnesses are required.

Witnesses serve to acknowledge that the testator did execute the will and that she had the required intent and capacity. It is important that the testator sign first in the presence of all the witnesses; each witness should then sign in the testator's presence and in the presence of the other witnesses.

The most common restriction on a person's ability to act as a witness is that a witness must not have any interest under the will. At least two types of statute express this requirement. One type disqualifies a witness who is also a beneficiary under the will. The other voids the bequest or devise to the interested witness, thus making him a disinterested, and thereby qualified, witness.

Revocation of a Will

By definition, a will is revocable by the testator. Under certain circumstances, a will may be revoked by operation of law. Nevertheless, certain formalities are still necessary to effect a **revocation**. Most jurisdictions specify by statute the methods by which a will may be revoked.

Revocation a will is revocable by the testator and under certain circumstances may be revoked by operation of law

Destruction or Alteration Tearing, burning, or otherwise destroying a will is a strong sign that the testator intended to revoke it, and, unless such destruction is proven to be inadvertent, it is an effective way of revoking a will. In some states, partial revocation may be accomplished by erasing or obliterating part of the will. But substituted or additional bequests inserted between the written or printed lines of a will are not effective without reexecution and reattestation.

BARKSDALE v. PENDERGRASS Supreme Court of Alabama, 1975, 294 Ala. 526, 319 So.2d 267

FACTS Mamie Henry, a widow, died on October 18, 1972. She had no children, but was survived by several nieces and nephews. At first no will was found, and Joe Barksdale, a nephew, was appointed administrator of Mrs. Henry's estate. Later, Rita Pendergrass produced a copy of a will allegedly made by Mrs. Henry. The will left all of Mrs. Henry's property to Mrs. Pendergrass and appointed her as executrix. When Mrs. Pendergrass sought to have the will admitted to probate, Joe Barksdale and Olen Barksdale filed a contest on the grounds that the purported will was never duly executed, or, if executed, was destroyed by Mrs. Henry prior to her death. The jury found in favor of Rita Pendergrass, and judgment was entered ordering the admission of the will to probate.

DECISION Judgment affirmed.

OPINION In order to have an allegedly lost or destroyed will admitted to probate, the one asserting its effectiveness must first establish that it is a validly executed will and, second, rebut the presumption arising from the loss or destruction of the will that it was revoked by its maker. Since Mrs. Pendergrass fulfilled both of these requirements here, she is entitled to submit Mrs. Henry's will to probate. First, Mrs. Pendergrass established that the document was a validly executed will. It was signed by Mrs. Henry and attested by two witnesses in Mrs. Henry's presence with her express or implied knowledge or consent. Second, Mrs. Pendergrass also succeeded in rebutting the presumption that Mrs. Henry had revoked her will by showing that Mrs. Henry wanted Mrs. Pendergrass and not her nieces and nephews to receive her property at her death.

INTERPRETATION If a lost will is found after the death of its maker, the one who asserts that the will is effective must prove that the will was not revoked by the maker.

Subsequent Will The execution of a second will does not in itself constitute a revocation of an earlier will. The first will is revoked only to the extent that the second will is inconsistent with the first. The most certain manner of revocation is through the execution of a later will containing a declaration that all former wills are revoked. In some, but not all, jurisdictions, a testator may revoke a will by a written declaration to this effect in a subsequent document, such as a letter, even if that document does not meet the formal requirements of a will.

Codicils A codicil is an addition to or a revision of a will, generally by a separate instrument, that expressly refers to the will and that, in effect, incorporates the will by reference. Codicils must by executed with all the formal requirements of a will.

Operation of Law A *marriage* generally revokes a will executed before the marriage. *Divorce*, on the other hand, generally does *not* revoke a provision in the will of one party for the benefit of the other.

The *birth* of a child after a will's execution may revoke the will, at least as far as that child is concerned, if the testator apparently has omitted a provision for the child. In some jurisdictions, the subsequent birth of a child will not revoke the will, if the child's omission from it is not apparently intentional; however, the share to which the child is entitled is equal to the share he would have received if the testator had died without a will.

Renunciation by the Surviving Spouse Statutes generally provide a surviving spouse the right to renounce a will and describe the method by which the spouse may do so. Such statutory provisions enable the spouse to decide which method of taking—under the will or under intestate succession—would be most advantageous.

Special Types of Wills

There are many special types of wills, including nuncupative wills, holographic wills, and soldiers' and sailors' wills.

Nuncupative Wills A nuncupative will is an unwritten oral declaration made before witnesses. In the few jurisdictions that authorize them, such declarations usually may be made only by a testator in his last illness. Under most statutes permitting nuncupative wills, only limited amounts of personal property may be passed by such wills.

Holographic Wills In some jurisdictions, a will entirely in the handwriting of the testator is a valid testamentary document even if the will is *not* witnessed. Such an instrument, referred to as a holographic will, must comply strictly with the statutory requirements for such wills.

Soldiers' and Sailors' Wills For soldiers on active duty and sailors at sea, most statutes relax the formal requirements for a will and permit a testamentary disposition to be valid regardless of the informality of the document. In most jurisdictions, however, such a will cannot pass title to real estate.

Living Wills Almost all states have adopted statutes that permit an individual to execute a living will. A living will is a document by which an individual states that she does not wish to receive extraordinary medical treatment in order to preserve her life. Through such a will, which must comply with applicable statutory requirements, the individual rejects the use of life-prolonging procedures that artificially delay the dying process and asks to be allowed to die naturally should she contract an incurable illness or suffer an incurable injury. See Ethical Dilemma.

INTESTATE SUCCESSION

Property not effectively disposed of before death or by will passes in accordance with the law of intestate succession. The rules set forth in statutes for determining, in cases involving intestacy, to whom the decedent's property shall be distributed not only assure an orderly transfer of title to property but also purport to effect what probably would be the decedent's wishes. However, even if its requirements run contrary to the clear intention of the decedent, the intestacy statute will still govern the distribution.

Intestate *(in·tes´·tate)* person who dies without a valid will

---

FERGUSON v. CROOM Court of Appeals of North Carolina, 1985, 326 S.E.2d 373, 73 N.C. App. 316

FACTS On June 21, 1983, George W. Croom died testate. In his will, Croom left various bequests of real and personal property to his children and a grandchild. Also in his will, Croom stated, "I leave nothing whatsoever to my daughter Kathryn Elizabeth Turner and my son Ernest Edward Croom." At his death, Croom left three optional share certificates in Carolina Savings & Loan Association issued to George Croom or Kimberly Croom, his minor daughter. Each of these certificates purported to create a joint account with a right of survivorship. Two of them were signed by George Croom only, and the third agreement was not signed at all. None of these certificates were specifically devised by Croom's will, and the will contained no residuary clause. Ferguson, as administrator of George's will, brought suit seeking a determination as to who was entitled to these certificates. Kimberly Croom contended that the share certificates should pass to her by right of survivorship. Kathryn and Ernest argued that regardless of George's intent to leave them nothing, they were entitled to a portion of the certificates under the laws of intestate

succession. The trial court entered judgment for Kimberly Croom.

DECISION Judgment reversed and case remanded for entry of judgment consistent with this opinion.

OPINION The optional share certificates did not satisfy the statutory requirements necessary to pass by joint survivorship. Thus, they become part of the Croom estate. Since there was no residuary clause, the certificates must be distributed by the laws of intestate succession. North Carolina statutes direct that such property must pass by intestate succession without regard to the testator's intent expressed in his will. Under the Intestate Succession Act, each of the testator's children is entitled to take an equal share of the property not disposed of by his will. Therefore, despite George's contrary intent, Kathryn and Ernest are entitled to their equal share of the certificates.

INTERPRETATION Property not validly disposed of before death or by will passes in accordance with the law of intestate succession.

The rules of descent vary widely from state to state, but as a general rule and except for the specific statutory rights of the widow, the intestate property passes in equal shares to each child of the decedent living at the time of his death, with the share of any child who dies before the decedent to be divided equally among that child's children. For example, if A dies intestate, leaving a widow and children, his widow generally will receive one-third of his real estate and personal

Course of descent each state prescribes rules for the passage of property not governed by a valid will; as a general rule the property passes in equal shares to each child after the widow's statutory or dower rights have been settled

ETHICAL DILEMMA When Should Life Support Cease?

FACTS Marge Hilton, an inhalation therapist at Lankard Hospital, was recently assigned to a unit that has been treating Leslie Andrews. Andrews, a single, twenty-eight-year-old woman, was in a car accident two weeks ago and remains in a coma. All of her nutrition and hydration must be administered through a gastrostomy tube. Andrews, who was a dental assistant, has no known relatives, no medical insurance, and no significant assets.

Her medical condition offers no hope for recovery. Andrews does not have a living will, and the only evidence concerning whether she would wish to have life-sustaining efforts continued is a casual statement, related to Lankard's administration by two of her friends, that she "would not want to live like that." She had said this after the three attended a movie in which a young female character had been comatose for many years.

When Hilton was performing inhalation therapy for Leslie, she observed Andrews groan. She brought this to the attention of two physicians. The doctors explained that this did not indicate Andrews was showing signs of recovery or was regaining consciousness. The doctors did state that the patient may be experiencing discomfort, but reassured Hilton that properly administered medication should take care of any pain.

Social, Policy, and Ethical Considerations

1. Under what circumstances should life-sustaining mechanisms be removed? Who should make the decision?
2. How would your answer change if Leslie were discovered to be six months pregnant?
3. If attending physicians must make the decision, should they be subject to civil or criminal liability arising out of their actions?

Per stirpes *(per stir´·peez)* a class or group of distributees take the share to which their deceased ancestor would have been entitled, taking thus by their right of representing such ancestor and not as so many individuals

Per capita *(per cap´·a·ta)* an equal share is given to each of several persons, all of whom stand in equal degree to the decedent, without reference to the right of representation

property, and the remainder will pass to his children in the manner stated above. If his wife does not survive A, his entire estate passes to their children. If A dies and leaves two surviving children, B and C, and two grandchildren, D_1 and D_2, the children of a predeceased child D, the estate will go one-third to B, one-third to C, and one-sixth each to D_1 and D_2, the grandchildren, who divide equally their parent's one-third share. This result is described legally by the statement that *lineal* descendants of predeceased children take property **per stirpes**, or by representation of their parent. If A had executed a will, he may have provided that all his lineal descendants, regardless of generation, would share equally. In that case, A's estate would be divided into four equal parts, and his descendants would be said to take the property **per capita** (see Figure 54–3).

If only the widow and relatives other than children survive the decedent, a larger share usually is allotted the widow. She may receive all the decedent's personal property and one-half his real estate or, in some states, his entire estate.

At common law, property could not lineally ascend; parents of an intestate decedent did not share in his estate. Today, in many states, if a decedent has no lineal descendants or a surviving spouse, the statute provides that parents are the next to share.

Most statutes make some provision for brothers and sisters in the event that no spouse, parents, or children survive the decedent. Brothers and sisters, together with nieces, nephews, aunts, and uncles, are termed *collateral* heirs. Beyond these limits, most statutes provide that, if there are no survivors in the named classes, the property shall be distributed equally among the next of kin in equal degree.

The common law did not consider a *stepchild* as an heir or next of kin, that is, as one to whom property would descend by operation of law; and this rule prevails today. Legally *adopted* children are, however, recognized as lawful heirs of their adoptive parents.

FIGURE 54–3 *Per Stirpes* and *Per Capita*

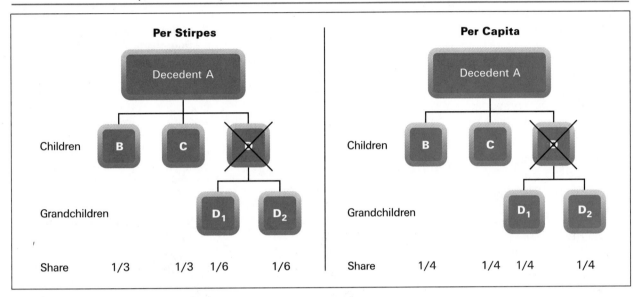

These generalities should be accepted as such; few fields of the law of property are so strictly a matter of statute, and the rights of heirs cannot reasonably be predicted without a knowledge of the exact terms of the applicable statute.

ADMINISTRATION OF ESTATES

The rules and procedures controlling the management of a decedent's estate are statutory and therefore vary somewhat from state to state. In all jurisdictions, the estate is managed and finally disbursed under the supervision of a court. The procedure of managing the distribution of decedents' estates is referred to as **probate**, and the court that supervises the procedure is often designated the probate court.

The first legal step after death is usually to determine whether the deceased left a will. If a will exists, the testator has likely named her **executor** in it. If there is no will or if there is a will that fails to name an executor, the court will, on petition, appoint an **administrator**. The closest adult relative who is a resident of the state is entitled to this appointment.

Once approved or appointed by the court, the *executor* or *administrator* holds title to all the personal property of the deceased and is accountable to her creditors and beneficiaries. The estate is his responsibility.

If there is a will, the witnesses must prove it before the court by testifying to the signing of the will by all signatories and by confirming the mental condition of the testator at the time she executed the will. If the witnesses are dead, proof of their handwriting is necessary. If satisfied that the will is proved, the court will enter a formal decree admitting the will to probate.

Soon after the admission of the will to probate, the decedent's personal representative—the executor or administrator—must file an inventory of the estate. The personal representative will then begin his duties of collecting the assets, paying the debts, and disbursing the remainder. The executor or administrator occupies a *fiduciary* position not unlike that of a trustee, and his responsibility for investing proceeds and otherwise managing the estate is just as demanding.

Probate the distribution of a decedent's estate

Executor or Administrator a person who is responsible for collecting the assets, paying the debts, and disbursing the remainder according to the will or intestate statute

Executor the person named in the will and appointed by the court to administer the will

Administrator a person appointed by the court to administer the estate when there is no will or when the person named in the will fails to qualify

THE LAW AND YOU Wills

1. What Is a Will?

A will is a signed writing in which a person (often referred to as the "testator") directs what is to be done with his or her property after death. Each state has its own very specific laws as to what is necessary for a will to be valid in that state.

2. Who May Make a Will?

Any mentally competent person who is at least 18 years old may make a will. However, later proof of any fraud, duress, or undue influence by another person on the testator may cause the will to be invalid.

3. Who Should Have a Will, and Why?

Every mentally competent adult should have a will. Here are a few of the reasons:

- You can direct how you want your property divided at your death.
- You can name the person you want to handle your estate (called the "executor" or "personal representative").
- You can reduce the expenses of administering your estate.
- You can save taxes.
- You can nominate a guardian for your minor children.
- You may provide for a trust for the support and education of your children without the necessity of costly court proceedings.

4. Must a Will Be Witnessed? Must It Be Notarized?

In Virginia, the signing of a will must generally be witnessed by two competent persons, who also must sign the will in front of the testator. (An exception to the witness requirement is made if the testator writes out the entire will in his or her own handwriting, and signs and dates it.)

Although the law does not require a will to be notarized, it is a highly recommended practice, followed by most lawyers. If the testator's and witnesses' signatures have been notarized, the will is presumed to be properly executed and is accepted by the court without testimony from the witnesses.

5. How Long Is a Will Valid?

Your will is valid until you revoke it, generally either by physical destruction (tearing or burning it up, for example) or by signing a superseding will or written revocation. However, if you get divorced after signing a will, the law may consider the will partially revoked. Also, if you are married, your spouse may have rights in your estate regardless of what is provided in your will.

6. May a Will Be Changed?

Your will does not take effect until you die; therefore, it can be changed at any time during your life as long as you are mentally competent. Traditionally, wills were changed by an amending instrument called a "codicil," but with the development of modern word processing technology, it is usually better and just as easy to sign an entirely new will when you wish to make a change.

7. What Happens If You Don't Have a Will?

If you don't have a will, a state statute directs who will receive your property, regardless of your wishes. In Virginia, if you are married, your estate generally passes entirely to your surviving spouse; however, if you have children who are not also the children of your spouse, your children divide two-thirds of your estate, and your spouse takes the other one-third.

8. Is Joint Ownership a Substitute for a Will?

In most cases, joint ownership is not an acceptable substitute for a will. Contrary to popular belief, joint ownership of assets between husband and wife often results in excessive estate taxes. Joint ownership between parent and child may foster disputes between family members and cause unexpected and unnecessary gift taxes.

9. Is a Living Trust a Substitute for a Will?

A funded revocable ("living") trust can be a valuable and important part of the estate plan for many people, but it does not eliminate the need for a will. If you have a living trust, you will still need a will to dispose of those assets that have not or cannot be placed in the trust.

As useful as they are, living trusts are not appropriate for everyone. Only your lawyer can tell you if you should consider one, and only your lawyer should prepare it.

10. Who Should Draft Your Will?

A person who drafts a will must be familiar with the law in order to avoid the many pitfalls and to comply with the formalities necessary to assure the will's validity. Only a practicing lawyer is professionally qualified to give you advice regarding your will, to prepare your will, and to supervise its signing.

[The material in this feature was prepared as a public service and is intended for general information purposes only. The frequent changes in state law could affect this material, and such law also varies from state to state.]

Reprinted with permission from the Trusts and Estates Section of the VIRGINIA STATE BAR.

The administration of every estate involves probate expenses, as well as fees to be paid to the executor or administrator and to the attorney who handles the estate. In addition, taxes are imposed at death by both the federal and state governments. The federal government imposes an *estate tax* on the transfer of property at death, whereas most state governments impose an *inheritance tax* on the privilege of an heir or beneficiary to receive the property. These taxes are separate from the basic income tax that the estate must pay on income received during estate administration.

CHAPTER SUMMARY

Trusts	**Definition** a fiduciary relationship in which legal title to property is held by one or more parties (the trustee) for the use, enjoyment, and benefit of another (the beneficiary)
	Express Trust a trust established by voluntary action; usually in writing, although it may be oral
	■ *Charitable Trust* a trust that has as its purpose the benefit of humankind
	■ *Spendthrift Trust* a trust designed to remove the trust estate from the beneficiary's control and from liability for his individual debts
	■ *Totten Trust* a tentative trust consisting of a joint bank account opened by the settlor (creator of the trust)
	Implied Trust a trust created by operation of law
	■ *Constructive Trust* an implied trust imposed to rectify fraud or to prevent unjust enrichment
	■ *Resulting Trust* an implied trust imposed to fulfill the presumed intent of the settlor
	Trustee anyone legally capable of holding title to and dealing with property may be a trustee
	■ *Duties* the three primary duties of a trustee are to (1) carry out the purposes of the trust, (2) act prudently, and (3) act with utmost loyalty
	■ *Powers* generally established by the trust instrument and state law
	■ *Allocation of Principal and Income* see Figure 54–2
	Termination the general rule is that the trust is irrevocable unless a power of revocation is reserved in the trust instrument

Wills	**Definition** a will (or testament) is a written instrument, executed with the formalities required by statute, whereby a person makes a disposition of his property to take effect after his death
	Mental Capacity
	■ *Testamentary Capacity* for a will to be valid the testator must be sufficiently competent to intend the document to be her will
	■ *Conduct Invalidating a Will* a will that is the product of duress, undue influence, or fraud is invalid and of no effect
	Formal Requirements a will must be (1) in writing, (2) signed, and (3) attested to by witnesses
	Revocation a will is revocable by the testator and under certain circumstances may be revoked by operation of law

- **Destruction or Alteration** revokes a will
- **Subsequent Will** revokes prior wills to the extent they are inconsistent
- **Codicil** an addition to or revision of a will executed with all the formalities of a will
- **Marriage** generally revokes a will executed before the marriage
- **Birth of a Child** may revoke a will at least as far as that child is concerned
- **Renunciation by Surviving Spouse** surviving spouse may elect to take under laws of descent

Special Types of Wills generally binding only in specific situations and may have limitations upon their use

Intestate Succession	**Interstate** person who dies without a valid will **Course of Descent** each state prescribes rules for the passage of property not governed by a valid will; as a general rule the property passes in equal shares to each child after the widow's statutory or dower rights have been settled

Administration of Estates	**Probate** the court's supervision of the management and distribution of the estate **Executor or Administrator** a person who is responsible for collecting the assets, paying the debts, and disbursing the remainder according to the will or interstate statute ■ **Executor** the person named in the will and appointed by the court to administer the will ■ **Administrator** a person appointed by the court to administer the estate when there is no will or when the person named in the will fails to qualify

QUESTIONS

1. Define the following types of trusts: (a) express, (b) charitable, (c) spendthrift, (d) totten, (e) implied, (f) constructive, and (g) resulting.
2. Describe the powers and duties of a trustee.
3. Discuss the formal requirements of making a valid will and the various ways in which a will may be revoked.
4. Define the following types of wills: (a) nuncupative, (b) holographic, and (c) soldiers' and sailors'.
5. Discuss intestate succession.

Internet Question. Find the last will and testament of three celebrities.

PROBLEMS

1. State whether or not a trust is created in each of the following situations:
   (a) A declares herself trustee of "the bulk of my securities" in trust for B.
   (b) A, the owner of Blackacre, purports to convey to B in trust for C "a small part" of Blackacre.
   (c) A orders B, a stockbroker, to buy 2,000 shares of American Steel or any part thereof at $20 per share. After the broker has bought 500 shares but before A knows whether any shares have been bought for him, A declares himself trustee for C of such shares of American Steel as B has bought.

(d) A owns ten bonds. He declares himself trustee for B of such five of the bonds as B may select at any time within a month.

(e) A deposits $1,000 in a savings bank. He declares himself trustee of the deposit in trust to pay B $500 out of the deposit, reserving the power to withdraw from the deposit any amounts not in excess of $500.

2. Testator gives property to Timothy in trust for Barney's benefit, providing that Barney cannot anticipate the income by assignment or pledge. Barney borrows money from Linda, assigning his future income under the trust for a stated period. Can Linda obtain any judicial relief to prevent Barney from collecting this income?

3. Collins was trustee for Indolent under the will of Indolent's father. Indolent, a middle-aged doctor, gave little concern to the management of the trust fund, contenting himself with receiving the income paid to him by the trustee. Among the assets of the trust were 100 shares of ABC Corporation and 100 shares of XYZ Corporation. About two years before the termination of the trust, Collins purchased the ABC stock from the trust at a fair price and after a full explanation to Indolent. At the same time but without saying anything to Indolent, he purchased the XYZ stock at a price higher than its current market value. At the termination of the trust, both stocks had advanced in market value well beyond the prices paid by Collins, and Indolent demanded that Collins either account for this advance in the value of both stocks or replace the stocks. What are Indolent's rights?

4. On September 1, 1982, Joe Brown gave $35,000 to his wife, Mary, with which to buy real property. They orally agreed that title to the real property should be taken in the name of Mary Brown but that she should hold the property in trust for Joe Brown. There were two witnesses to the oral agreement, both of whom are still living. Mary purchased the property on September 2, and a deed to it with Mary Brown as the grantee was delivered.

Mary died on October 5, 1993, without a will. The real property is now worth $100,000. Joe Brown is claiming the property as the beneficiary of a trust. Mary's children are claiming that the property belongs to Mary's estate and have pleaded the statute of limitations and the statute of frauds as defenses to Joe's claim. There is no evidence to prove whether Mary would or would not have conveyed the property to Joe during her lifetime if she had been requested to do so.

What are Joe's ownership rights to this particular real property?

5. On March 10, 1993, John Carver executed his will, which was witnessed by William Hobson and Sam Witt. By his will, Carver devised his farm, Stonecrest, to his nephew, Roy White. The residue of his estate was given to his sister, Florence Carver.

A codicil to his will executed April 15, 1993, provided that $5,000 be given to Carver's niece, Mary Jordan, and $5,000 to Wanda White, Roy White's wife. The codicil was witnessed by Roy White and Harold Brown. John Carver died September 1, 1993, and the will and codicil were admitted to probate.

How should Carver's estate be distributed?

6. Edwin Fuller, a bachelor, prepared his will in his office. The will, which contained no residuary clause, provided that one-third of his estate would go to his nephew, Tom Fuller, one-third to the city of Emanon to be used for park improvements, and one-third to his brother, Kurt.

He signed the will in his office and then went to the office of his nephew, Tom Fuller, who signed the will as a witness at Edwin's request. No other persons were available in Tom's office, so Edwin then went to the bank, where Frank Cash, the cashier, also signed as a witness at Edwin's request. In each instance, Edwin stated that he had signed the document but did not state that it was his will.

Edwin returned to his office and placed the will in his safe. Subsequently, Edwin died, survived by Kurt, his only heir-at-law. How should the estate be distributed?

7. Arnold executed a one-page will in which he devised his farm to Burton. Later, after a quarrel with Burton, Arnold wrote the words "I hereby cancel and revoke this will /s/Arnold" in the margin of the will but did not destroy the will. Arnold then executed a deed to the farm, naming Connie as grantee, and placed the deed and will in his safe. Shortly afterward, Arnold married Donna, with whom he had one child, Ernest. Arnold died some time later, and the deed and will were found in his safe. Burton, Connie, and Ernest claim the farm, and Donna claims dower. Discuss the validity of each claim.

8. John Walker, a widower, made a will containing the following provisions:

"I give and bequeath my piano to my daughter Nancy. I give and bequeath to my daughter Jennifer the sum of $1,000. I give and bequeath to my son John the sum of $1,000 to be paid out of my account at the Tenth National Bank in the city of Erehwon. All the rest and residue of my estate I give to Nancy, Jennifer, and John, share and share alike."

After the will was executed, Walker sold his piano for $2,300 and deposited the proceeds in the Citizens Bank of Erehwon. He withdrew the money he had on deposit in the Tenth National Bank and purchased a new automobile.

When Walker died, he had no debts. The account in the Citizens Bank of Erehwon had a balance of $2,300, which constituted his entire net estate after all administration expenses were paid. How should Walker's estate be distributed?

9. The validly executed will of John Dane contained the following provision: "I give and devise to my daughter, Mary, Redacre for and during her natural life and, at her death, the remainder to go to Wilmore College." The will also provided that the residue of his estate should go to Wilmore College. Thereafter, Dane sold Redacre and then added a validly executed codicil to his will, "Due to the fact that I have sold Redacre, which I previously gave to my daughter, Mary, I now give and devise Blackacre to Mary in place and instead of Redacre."

Another clause of the codicil provided: "I give my one-half interest in the oil business that I own in common with William Steele to my son, Henry." Subsequently, Dane acquired all of the interest in the oil business from his partner, Steele, and, at the time of his death, Dane owned the entire oil business. The will and codicil have been admitted to probate.

   (a) What interest, if any, does Mary acquire in Blackacre?

   (b) What interest, if any, does Henry acquire in the oil business?

10. Leonard Wolfe was killed in an automobile accident while driving his 1969 Buick Electra. The car was rendered a total loss, and Wolfe's insurance carrier paid his estate $3,550 for damage to the vehicle. Under the terms of Wolfe's will, any car owned at his death was to be given to his brother, David. Wolfe's daughter, Carol, however, brought an action, claiming that the gift of the car to David was adeemed by its total destruction and that she, as the residuary legatee under the will, was entitled to the insurance proceeds. Decision?

11. In April 1961, Grace Peterson, a spinster then aged seventy-four, asked Chester Gustafson, a Minneapolis attorney, to draw a will for her. Gustafson, who had also probated Peterson's sister's estate, drew this first will and six subsequent wills and codicils free of charge because he claimed that she had no money to pay for his services. Over the five-year period during which Gustafson redrew Peterson's will, an increasing amount of property was devised to Gustafson's chil-

dren, until, finally, the seventh will so devised Peterson's entire estate. Peterson, however, hardly knew the children except from several chance encounters ten years before. She died on February 1, 1966, without ever having changed the seventh will, and Gustafson, who was named as executor, now seeks to have the will admitted to probate. Decision?

12. By his last will and testament, Henry Nussbaum made a residual bequest and devise of his estate to his niece, Jane Blair, as trustee, in trust for the education of his grandchildren. If the trust could not be fulfilled, the residue was to revert to the plaintiff, Dorothy Witmer. After Nussbaum died in 1960, the plaintiff contended that the trustee had breached her fiduciary duty by failing to invest the trust corpus. A considerable portion of the trust funds were held in a checking account from 1962 to 1971. The trustee claimed that the will failed to specify when and what investments were to be made and, hence, such matters were left to her good-faith discretion. She also explained the large checking account balances by the fact that college for the grandchild, Janice, "was talked about through high school." Decision?

13. Rodney Sharp was a fifty-six-year-old dairy farmer whose education did not go beyond the eighth grade. Upon the death of his wife of thirty-two years, Sharp developed a very close relationship with Jean Kosmalski, a schoolteacher sixteen years his junior. Sharp eventually proposed to Kosmalski, but when she refused, he continued to make gifts to her in hopes of changing her mind. He also gave her access to his bank account, from which she withdrew substantial amounts of money; made a will naming her as sole beneficiary; and executed a deed naming her as a joint owner of his farm. Then, in September 1971, Sharp transferred his remaining joint interest in the farm to Kosmalski. In February 1973, Kosmalski ordered Sharp to move out of his home and to vacate the farm. She then took possession of both, leaving Sharp with assets of $300. Sharp brought this action to impose a constructive trust on the property transferred to Kosmalski. The trial court dismissed the plaintiff's complaint, and the decision was affirmed by the appellate court. Decision?

The Constitution of the United States of America

We the People of the United States, in Order to form a more perfect Union, establish Justice, insure domestic Tranquility, provide for the common defense, promote the general Welfare, and secure the Blessings of Liberty to ourselves and our Posterity, do ordain and establish this Constitution for the United States of America.

ARTICLE I

Section 1

All legislative Powers herein granted shall be vested in a Congress of the United States, which shall consist of a Senate and House of Representatives.

Section 2

The House of Representatives shall be composed of Members chosen every second Year by the People of the several States, and the Electors in each State shall have the Qualifications requisite for Electors of the most numerous Branch of the State Legislature.

No Person shall be a Representative who shall not have attained to the Age of twenty five Years, and been seven Years a Citizen of the United States, and who shall not, when elected, be an Inhabitant of that State in which he shall be chosen.

Representatives and direct Taxes shall be apportioned among the several States which may be included within this Union, according to their respective Numbers, which shall be determined by adding to the whole Number of free Persons, including those bound to Service for a Term of Years, and excluding Indians not taxed, three fifths of all other Persons. The actual Enumeration shall be made within three Years after the first Meeting of the Congress of the United States, and within every subsequent Term of ten Years, in such Manner as they shall by Law direct. The number of Representatives shall not exceed one for every thirty Thousand, but each State shall have at Least one Representative; and until such enumeration shall be made, the State of New Hampshire shall be entitled to chuse three, Massachusetts eight, Rhode Island and Providence Plantations one, Connecticut five, New-York six, New Jersey four, Pennsylvania eight, Delaware one, Maryland six, Virginia ten, North Carolina five, South Carolina five, and Georgia three.

When vacancies happen in the Representation from any State, the Executive Authority thereof shall issue Writs of Election to fill such vacancies.

The House of Representatives shall chuse their Speaker and other Officers; and shall have the sole Power of Impeachment.

Section 3

The Senate of the United States shall be composed of two Senators from each State, chosen by the Legislature thereof, for six Years; and each Senator shall have one Vote.

Immediately after they shall be assembled in Consequence of the first Election, they shall be divided as equally as may be into three Classes. The Seats of the Senators of the first Class shall be vacated at the Expiration of the second Year, of the second Class at the Expiration of the fourth Year, and of the third Class at the Expiration of the sixth Year, so that one third may be chosen every second Year; and if Vacancies happen by Resignation or otherwise, during the Recess of the Legislature of any State, the Executive thereof may make temporary Appointments until the next Meeting of the Legislature, which shall then fill such Vacancies.

No Person shall be a Senator who shall not have attained to the Age of thirty Years, and been nine Years a Citizen of the United States, and who shall not, when elected, be an Inhabitant of that State for which he shall be chosen.

The Vice President of the United States shall be President of the Senate, but shall have no Vote, unless they be equally divided.

The Senate shall chuse their other Officers, and also a President pro tempore, in the Absence of the Vice President, or when he shall exercise the Office of President of the United States.

The Senate shall have the sole power to try all Impeachments. When sitting for that Purpose, they shall be an Oath or Affirmation. When the President of the United States is tried, the Chief Justice shall preside: And no Person shall be convicted without the Concurrence of two thirds of the Members present.

Judgment in Cases of Impeachment shall not extend further than to removal from Office, and disqualification to hold and enjoy any Office of honor, Trust or Profit under the United States: but the Party convicted shall nevertheless be liable and subject to Indictment, Trial, Judgment and Punishment, according to Law.

Section 4

The Times, Places and Manner of holding Elections for Senators and Representatives, shall be prescribed in each State by the Legislature thereof: but the Congress may at any time by Law make or alter such Regulations, except as to the Places of chusing Senators.

The Congress shall assemble at least once in every Year, and such Meeting shall be on the first Monday in December, unless they shall by Law appoint a different Day.

Section 5

Each House shall be the Judge of the Elections, Returns and Qualifications of its own Members, and a Majority of each shall constitute a Quorum to do Business; but a smaller Number may adjourn from day to day, and may be authorized to compel the Attendance of absent Members, in such Manner, and under such Penalties as each House may provide.

Each House may determine the Rules of its Proceedings, punish its Members for disorderly Behaviour, and, with the Concurrence of two thirds, expel a Member.

Each House shall keep a Journal of its Proceedings, and from time to time publish the same, excepting such Parts as may in their Judgment require Secrecy; and the Yeas and Nays of the Members of either House on any question shall, at the Desire of one fifth of those Present, be entered on the Journal.

Neither House, during the Session of Congress, shall, without the Consent of the other, adjourn for more than three days, nor to any other Place than that in which the two Houses shall be sitting.

Section 6

The Senators and Representatives shall receive a Compensation for their Services, to be ascertained by Law, and paid out of the Treasury of the United States. They shall in all Cases, except Treason, Felony and Breach of the Peace, be privileged from Arrest and Breach of the Peace, be privileged from Arrest during their Attendance at the Session of their respective Houses, and in going to and returning from the same; and for any Speech or Debate in either House, they shall not be questioned in any other Place.

No Senator or Representative shall, during the Time for which he was elected, be appointed to any civil Office under the Authority of the United States, which shall have been created, or the Emoluments whereof shall have been encreased during such time; and no Person holding any Office under the United States, shall be a Member of either House during his Continuance in Office.

Section 7

All Bills for raising Revenue shall originate in the House of Representatives; but the Senate may propose or concur with Amendments as on other Bills.

Every Bill which shall have passed the House of Representatives and the Senate, shall, before it become a Law, be presented to the President of the United States; If he approve he shall sign it, but if not he shall return it, with his Objections to that House in which it shall have originated, who shall enter the Objections at large on their Journal, and proceed to reconsider it. If after such Reconsideration two thirds of that House

shall agree to pass the Bill, it shall be sent, together with the Objections, to the other House, by which it shall likewise be reconsidered, and if approved by two thirds of that House, it shall become a Law. But in all such Cases the Votes of both Houses shall be determined by Yeas and Nays, and the Names of the Persons voting for and against the Bill shall be entered on the Journal of each House respectively. If any Bill shall not be returned by the President within ten Days (Sundays excepted) after it shall have been presented to him, the Same shall be a Law, in like Manner as if he had signed it, unless the Congress by their Adjournment prevent its Return, in which Case it shall not be a Law.

Every Order, Resolution, or Vote to which the Concurrence of the Senate and House of Representatives may be necessary (except on a question of Adjournment) shall be presented to the President of the United States; and before the Same shall take Effect, shall be approved by him, or being disapproved by him, shall be repassed by two thirds of the Senate and House of Representatives, according to the Rules and Limitations prescribed in the Case of a Bill.

Section 8

The Congress shall have Power to lay and collect Taxes, Duties, Imposts and Excises, to pay the Debts and provide for the common Defense and general Welfare of the United States; but all Duties, Imposts and Excises shall be uniform throughout the United States;

To borrow Money on the credit of the United States;

To regulate Commerce with foreign Nations, and among the several States, and with the Indian Tribes;

To establish an uniform Rule of Naturalization, and uniform Laws on the subject of Bankruptcies throughout the United States;

To coin Money, regulate the Value thereof, and of foreign Coin, and fix the Standard of Weights and Measures;

To provide for the Punishment of counterfeiting the Securities and current Coin of the United States;

To establish Post Offices and post Roads;

To promote the Progress of Science and useful Arts, by securing for limited Times to Authors and Inventors the exclusive Right to their respective Writings and Discoveries;

To constitute Tribunals inferior to the supreme Court;

To define and punish Piracies and Felonies committed on the high Seas, and Offenses against the Law of Nations;

To declare War, grant Letters of Marque and Reprisal, and make Rules concerning Captures on Land and Water;

To raise and support Armies, but no Appropriation of Money to that Use shall be for a longer Term than two Years;

To provide and maintain a Navy;

To make Rules for the Government and Regulation of the land and naval Forces;

To provide for calling forth the Militia to execute the Laws of the Union, suppress Insurrections and repel Invasions;

To provide for organizing, arming, and disciplining, the Militia, and for governing such Part of them as may be employed in the Service of the United States, reserving to the States respectively, the Appointment of the Officers, and the Authority of training the Militia according to the discipline described by Congress;

To exercise exclusive Legislation in all Cases whatsoever, over such District (not exceeding ten Miles square) as may, by

Cession of particular States, and the Acceptance of Congress, become the Seat of the Government of the United States, and to exercise like Authority over all Places purchased by the Consent of the Legislature of the State in which the Same shall be, for the Erection of Forts, Magazines, Arsenals, dock-Yards, and other needful Buildings;—And

To make all Laws which shall be necessary and proper for carrying into Execution the foregoing Powers, and all other Powers vested by this Constitution in the Government of the United States, or in any Department or Officer thereof.

Section 9

The Migration or Importation of such Persons as any of the States now existing shall think proper to admit, shall not be prohibited by the Congress prior to the Year one thousand eight hundred and eight, but a Tax of Duty may be imposed on such Importation, not exceeding ten dollars for each Person.

The Privilege of the Writ of Habeas Corpus shall not be suspended, unless when in Cases of Rebellion or Invasion the public Safety may require it.

No Bill of Attainder or ex post facto Law shall be passed.

No Capitation, or other direct, Tax shall be laid, unless in Proportion to the Census or Enumeration herein before directed to be taken.

No Tax or Duty shall be laid on Articles exported from any State.

No Preference shall be given by any Regulation of Commerce or Revenue to the Ports of one State over those of another; nor shall Vessels bound to, or from, one State, be obliged to enter, clear, or pay Duties in another.

No Money shall be drawn from the Treasury, but in Consequence of Appropriations made by Laws; and a regular Statement and Account of the Receipts and Expenditures of all public Money shall be published from time to time.

No Title of Nobility shall be granted by the United States: And no Person holding any Office of Profit or Trust under them, shall, without the Consent of the Congress, accept of any present, Emolument, Office, or Title, of any kind whatever, from any King, Prince, or foreign State.

Section 10

No State shall enter into any Treaty, Alliance, or Confederation; grant Letters of Marque and Reprisal; coin Money; emit Bills of Credit; make any Thing but gold and silver Coin a Tender in Payment of Debts; pass any Bill of Attainder, ex post facto Law, or Law impairing the Obligation of Contracts, or grant any Title of Nobility.

No State shall, without the Consent of the Congress, lay any Imposts or Duties on Imports or Exports, except what may be absolutely necessary for executing its inspection Laws: and the net Produce of all Duties and Imposts, laid by any State on Imports or Exports, shall be for the Use of the Treasury of the United States; and all such Laws shall be subject to the Revision and Controul of the Congress.

No State shall, without the Consent of Congress, lay any Duty of Tonnage, keep Troops, or Ships of War in time of Peace, enter into any Agreement or Compact with another State, or with a foreign Power, or engage in War, unless actually invaded, or in such imminent Danger as will not admit of delay.

ARTICLE II

Section 1

The executive Power shall be vested in a President of the United States of America. He shall hold his Office during the Term of four Years, and, together with the Vice President, chosen for the same Term, be elected, as follows:

Each State shall appoint, in such Manner as the Legislature thereof may direct, a Number of Electors, equal to the whole Number of Senators and Representatives to which the State may be entitled in the Congress: but no Senator or Representative, or Person holding an Office of Trust or Profit under the United States, shall be appointed an Elector.

The Electors shall meet in their respective States, and vote by Ballot for two Persons, of whom one at least shall not be an Inhabitant of the same State with themselves. And they shall make a list of all the Persons voted for, and of the Number of Votes for each; which List they shall sign and certify, and transmit sealed to the Seat of the Government of the United States, directed to the President of the Senate. The President of the Senate shall, in the presence of the Senate and House of Representatives, open all the Certificates, and the Votes shall be counted. The Person having the greatest Number of Votes shall be the President, if such Number be a Majority of the whole Number of Electors appointed; and if there be more than one who have such Majority, and have an equal Number of Votes, then the House of Representatives shall immediately chuse by Ballot one of them for President; and if no Person have a Majority, then from the five highest on the List the said House shall in like Manner chuse the President. But in chusing the President, the Votes shall be taken by States, the Representation from each State having one Vote; A quorum for this Purpose shall consist of a Member or Members from two thirds of the States, and a Majority of all the States shall be necessary to a Choice. In every Case, after the Choice of the President, the Person having the Greatest Number of Votes of the Electors shall be the Vice President. But if there should remain two or more who have equal Votes, the Senate shall chuse from them by Ballot the Vice President.

The Congress may determine the Time of Chusing the Electors, and the Day on which they shall give their Votes; which Day shall be the same throughout the United States.

No Person except a natural born Citizen, or a Citizen of the United States, at the time of the Adoption of this Constitution, shall be eligible to the Office of President; neither shall any Person be eligible to that Office who shall not have attained to the Age of thirty five Years, and been fourteen Years a Resident within the United States.

In Case of the Removal of the President from Office, or of his Death, Resignation, or Inability to discharge the Powers and Duties of the said Office, the Same shall devolve on the Vice President, and the Congress may by Law provide for the Case of Removal, Death, Resignation or Inability, both of the President and Vice President, declaring what Officer shall then act as President, and such Officer shall act accordingly, until the Disability be removed, or a President shall be elected.

The President shall, at stated Times, receive for his Services, a Compensation, which shall neither be encreased nor diminished during the Period for which he shall have been elected, and he shall not receive within that Period any other Emolument from the United States, or any of them.

Before he enter on the Execution of his Office, he shall take the following Oath or Affirmation:—"I do solemnly swear (or affirm) that I will faithfully execute the Office of President of the United States, and will to the best of my Ability, preserve, protect and defend the Constitution of the United States."

Section 2

The President shall be Commander in Chief of the Army and Navy of the United States, and of the Militia of the several States, when called into the actual Service of the United States; he may require the Opinion, in writing, of the principal Officer in each of the executive Departments, upon any Subject relating to the Duties of their respective Offices, and he shall have Power to grant Reprieves and Pardons for Offences against the United States, except in Cases of Impeachment.

He shall have Power, by and with the Advice and Consent of the Senate, to make Treaties, providing two thirds of the Senators present concur; and he shall nominate, and by and with the Advice and Consent of the Senate, shall appoint Ambassadors, other public Ministers and Consuls, Judges of the supreme Court, and all other Officers of the United States, whose Appointments are not herein otherwise provided for, and which shall be established by Law: but the Congress may by Law vest the Appointment of such inferior Officers, as they think proper, in the President alone, in the Courts of Law, or in the Heads of Departments.

The President shall have Power to fill up all Vacancies that may happen during the Recess of the Senate, by granting Commissions which shall expire at the End of their next Session.

Section 3

He shall from time to time give to the Congress Information of the State of the Union, and recommend to their Consideration such Measures as he shall judge necessary and expedient; he may, on extraordinary Occasions, convene both Houses, or either of them, and in Case of Disagreement between them, with Respect to the Time of Adjournment, he may adjourn them to such Time as he shall think proper, he shall receive Ambassadors and other public Ministers; he shall take Care that the Laws be faithfully executed, and shall Commission all the Offices of the United States.

Section 4

The President, Vice President and all civil Officers of the United States, shall be removed from Office on Impeachment for, and Conviction of, Treason, Bribery, or other Crimes and Misdemeanors.

ARTICLE III

Section 1

The judicial Power of the United States, shall be vested in one supreme Court, and in such inferior Courts as the Congress may from time to time ordain and establish. The Judges, both of the supreme and inferior Courts, shall hold their Offices during good Behaviour, and shall, at Times, receive for their Services, a Compensation, which shall not be diminished during their Continuance in Office.

Section 2

The judicial Power shall extend to all Cases, in Law and Equity, arising under this Constitution, the Laws of the United States, and Treaties made, or which shall be made, under their Authority;—to all Cases affecting Ambassadors, other public Ministers and Consuls;—to all Cases of admiralty and maritime Jurisdiction;—to Controversies to which the United States shall be a Party;—to controversies between two or more States;—between a State and Citizens of another State;—between Citizens of different States;—between Citizens of the same State claiming Lands under Grants of different States; and between a State, or the Citizens thereof, and foreign States, Citizens or Subjects.

In all Cases affecting Ambassadors, other public Ministers and Consuls, and those in which a State shall be Party, the supreme Court shall have original Jurisdiction. In all the other Cases before mentioned, the supreme Court shall have appellate Jurisdiction, both as to Law and Fact, with such Exceptions, and under such Regulations as the Congress shall make.

The Trial of all Crimes, except in Cases of Impeachment, shall be by Jury; and such Trial shall be held in the State where the said Crimes shall have been committed; but when not committed within any State, the Trial shall be at such Place or Places as the Congress may by Law have directed.

Section 3

Treason against the United States, shall consist only in levying War against them, or in adhering to their Enemies, giving them Aid and Comfort. No Person shall be convicted of Treason unless on the Testimony of two Witnesses to the same overt Act, or on Confession in open Court.

The Congress shall have Power to declare the Punishment of Treason, but no Attainder of Treason shall work Corruption of Blood, or Forfeiture except during the Life of the Person attainted.

ARTICLE IV

Section 1

Full Faith and Credit shall be given in each State to the public Acts, Records, and judicial Proceedings of every other State. And the Congress may by general Laws prescribe the Manner in which such Arts, Records and Proceedings shall be proved, and the Effect thereof.

Section 2

The Citizens of each State shall be entitled to all Privileges and Immunities of Citizens in the several States.

A Person charged in any State with Treason, Felony, or other Crime, who shall flee from Justice, and be found in another State, shall on Demand of the executive Authority of the State from which he fled, be delivered up, to be removed to the State having Jurisdiction of the Crime.

No Person held to Service or Labour in one State, under the Laws thereof, escaping into another, shall, in Consequence of any Law or Regulation therein, be discharged from such Service or Labour, but shall be delivered up on Claim of the Party to whom such Service or Labour may be due.

Section 3

New States may be admitted by the Congress into this Union; but no new State shall be formed or erected within the Jurisdiction of any other State; nor any State be formed by the Junction of two or more States, or Parts of States, without the Consent of the Legislatures of the States concerned as well as the Congress.

The Congress shall have Power to dispose of and make all needful Rules and Regulations respecting the Territory or other Property belonging to the United States; and nothing in this Constitution shall be so construed as to Prejudice any Claims of the United States, or of any particular State.

Section 4

The United States shall guarantee to every State in this Union a Republican Form of Government, and shall protect each of them against Invasion; and on Application of the Legislature, or of the Executive (when the Legislature cannot be convened) against domestic Violence.

ARTICLE V

The Congress, whenever two thirds of both Houses shall deem it necessary, shall propose Amendments to this Constitution, or, on the Application of the Legislatures of two thirds of the several States, shall call a Convention for proposing Amendments, which, in either Case, shall be valid to all Intents and Purposes, as Part of this Constitution, when ratified by the Legislatures of three fourths of the several States, or by Conventions in three fourths thereof, as the one or the other Mode of Ratification may be proposed by the Congress; Provided that no Amendment which may be made prior to the Year One thousand eight hundred and eight shall in any Manner affect the first and fourth Clauses in the Ninth Section of the first Article; and that no State, without its Consent, shall be deprived of its equal Suffrage in the Senate.

ARTICLE VI

All Debts contracted and Engagements entered into, before the Adoption of this Constitution, shall be as valid against the United States under this Constitution, as under the Confederation.

This Constitution, and the Laws of the United States which shall be made in Pursuance thereof; and all Treaties made, or which shall be made, under the Authority of the United States, shall be the supreme Law of the Land; and the Judges in every State shall be bound thereby, any Thing in the Constitution or Laws of any State to the Contrary notwithstanding.

The Senators and Representatives before mentioned, and the Members of the several State Legislatures, and all executive and judicial Officers, both of the United States and of the Several States, shall be bound by Oath or Affirmation, to support this Constitution; but no religious Test shall ever be required as a Qualification to any Office or public Trust under the United States.

ARTICLE VII

The Ratification of the Conventions of nine States, shall be sufficient for the Establishment of this Constitution between the States so ratifying the Same.

Amendment I [1791]

Congress shall make no law respecting an establishment of religion, or prohibiting the free exercise thereof; or abridging the freedom of speech, or the press; or the right of the people peaceably to assemble, and to petition the Government for a redress of grievances.

Amendment II [1791]

A well regulated Militia, being necessary to the security for a free State, the right of the people to keep and bear Arms, shall not be infringed.

Amendment III [1791]

No Soldier shall, in time of peace be quartered in any house, without the consent of the Owner, nor in time of war, but in a manner to be prescribed by law.

Amendment IV [1791]

The right of the people to be secure in their persons, houses, papers, and effects, against unreasonable searches and seizures, shall not be violated, and no Warrants shall issue, but upon probable cause, supported by Oath or Affirmation, and particularly describing the place to be searched, and the persons or things to be seized.

Amendment V [1791]

No person shall be held to answer for a capital, or otherwise infamous crime, unless on a presentment or indictment of a Grand Jury, except in cases arising in the land or naval forces, or in the Militia, when in actual service in time of War or public danger; nor shall any person be subject for the same offense to be twice put in jeopardy of life or limb; nor shall be compelled in any criminal case to be a witness against himself, nor be deprived of life, liberty, or property, without due process of law; nor shall private property be taken for public use, without just compensation.

Amendment VI [1791]

In all criminal prosecutions, the accused shall enjoy the right to a speedy and public trial, by an impartial jury of the State and district wherein the crime shall have been committed, which district shall have been previously ascertained by law, and to be informed of the nature and cause of the accusation; to be confronted with the Witnesses against him; to have compulsory process for obtaining witnesses in his favor, and to have the Assistance of counsel for his defense.

Amendment VII [1791]

In suits at common law, where the value in controversy shall exceed twenty dollars, the right of trial by jury shall be preserved, and no fact tried by a jury, shall be otherwise re-examined in any Court of the United States, than according to the rules of the common law.

Amendment VIII [1791]

Excessive bail shall not be required, no excessive fines imposed, nor cruel and unusual punishments inflicted.

Amendment IX [1791]

The enumeration in the Constitution, of certain rights, shall not be construed to deny or disparage others retained by the people.

Amendment X [1791]

The powers not delegated to the United States by the Constitution, nor prohibited by it to the States, are reserved to the States respectively, or to the people.

Amendment XI [1798]

The judicial power of the United States shall not be construed to extend to any suit in law or equity, commenced or prosecuted against one of the United States by Citizens of another State, or by Citizens or Subjects of any Foreign State.

Amendment XII [1804]

The Electors shall meet in their respective states and vote by ballot for President and Vice-President, one of whom, at least, shall not be an inhabitant of the same state with themselves; they shall name in their ballots the person voted for as President, and in distinct ballots the person voted for as Vice-President, and they shall make distinct lists of all persons voted for as President, and of all persons voted for as Vice-President, and of the number of votes for each, which lists they shall sign and certify, and transmit sealed to the seat of the government of the United States, directed to the President of the Senate;—The President of the Senate shall, in the presence of the Senate and House of Representatives, open all the certificates and the votes shall then be counted;—The person having the greatest number of votes for President, shall be the President, if such a number be a majority of the whole number of Electors appointed; and if no person have such majority, then from the persons having the highest numbers not exceeding three on the list of those voted for as President, the House of Representatives shall choose immediately, by ballot, the President. But in choosing the President, the votes shall be taken by states, the representation from each state having one vote; a quorum for this purpose shall consist of a member or members from two-thirds of the states, and a majority of all the states shall be necessary to a choice. And if the House of Representatives shall not choose a President whenever the right of choice shall devolve upon them, before the fourth day of March next following, then the Vice-President shall act as President, as in the case of the death or other constitutional disability of the President. The person having the greatest number of votes as Vice-President, shall be the Vice-president, if such number be a majority of the whole number of Electors appointed, and if no person have a majority, then from the two highest numbers on the list, the Senate shall choose the Vice-President; a quorum for the purpose shall consist of two-thirds of the whole number of Senators, and a majority of the whole number shall be necessary to a choice. But no person constitutionally ineligible to the office of President shall be eligible to that of the Vice-President of the United States.

Amendment XIII [1865]

Section 1

Neither slavery nor involuntary servitude, except as a punishment for crime whereof the party shall have been duly convicted, shall exist within the United States, or any place subject to their jurisdiction.

Section 2

Congress shall have power to enforce this article by appropriate legislation.

Amendment XIV [1868]

Section 1

All persons born or naturalized in the United States, and subject to the jurisdiction thereof, are citizens of the United States and of the State wherein they reside. No State shall make or enforce any law which shall abridge the privileges or immunities of citizens of the United States; nor shall any State deprive any person of life, liberty, or property, without due process of law; nor deny to any person within its jurisdiction the equal protection of the laws.

Section 2

Representatives shall be appointed among the several States according to their respective numbers, counting the whole number of persons in each State, excluding Indians not taxed. But when the right to vote at any election for the choice of electors for President and Vice President of the United States, Representatives in Congress, the Executive and Judicial officers of a State, or the members of the Legislature thereof, is denied to any of the male inhabitants of such State, being twenty-one years of age, and citizens of the United States, or in any way abridged, except for participation in rebellion, or other crime, the basis of representation therein shall be reduced in the proportion which the number of such male citizens shall bear the whole number of male citizens twenty-one years of age in such State.

Section 3

No person shall be a Senator or Representative in Congress, or elector of President and Vice President, or hold any office, civil or military, under the United States, or under any State, who, having previously taken an oath, as a member of Congress, or as an officer of the United States, or as a member of any State legislature, or as an executive or judicial officer of any State, to support the Constitution of the United States, shall have engaged in insurrection or rebellion against the same, or given aid or comfort to the enemies thereof. But Congress may by a vote of two-thirds of each House, remove such disability.

Section 4

The validity of the public debt of the United States, authorized by law, including debts incurred for payment of pensions and bounties for services in suppressing insurrection or rebellion, shall not be questioned. But neither the United States nor any State shall assume or pay any debt or obligation incurred in aid of insurrection of rebellion against the United States, or any claim for the loss or emancipation of any slave; but all such debts, obligations and claims shall be held illegal and void.

Section 5

The Congress shall have power to enforce, by appropriate legislation, the provisions of this article.

Amendment XV [1870]

Section 1

The right of citizens of the United States to vote shall not be denied or abridged by the United States or by any State on account of race, color, or previous condition of servitude.

Section 2

The Congress shall have power to enforce this article by appropriate legislation.

Amendment XVI [1913]

The Congress shall have power to lay and collect taxes on incomes, from whatever source derived, without apportionment among the several States, and without regard to any census or enumeration.

Amendment XVII [1913]

The Senate of the United States shall be composed of two Senators from each State, elected by the people thereof, for six years; and each Senator shall have one vote. The electors in each State shall have the qualifications requisite for electors of the most numerous branch of the State legislatures.

When vacancies happen in the representation of any State in the Senate, the executive authority of each State shall issue writs of election to fill such vacancies; *Provided*, That the legislature of any State may empower the executive thereof to make temporary appointments until the people fill the vacancies by election as the legislature may direct.

This amendment shall not be construed as to affect the election or term of any Senator chosen before it becomes valid as part of the Constitution.

Amendment XVIII [1919]

Section 1

After one year from the ratification of this article the manufacture, sale, or transportation of intoxicating liquors within, the importation thereof into, or the exportation thereof from the United States and all territory subject to the jurisdiction thereof for beverage purposes is hereby prohibited.

Section 2

The Congress and the several States shall have concurrent power to enforce this article by appropriate legislation.

Section 3

This article shall be inoperative unless it shall have been ratified as an amendment to the Constitution by the legislatures of the several States, as provided in the Constitution, within seven years from the date of the submission hereof to the States by the Congress.

Amendment XIX [1920]

The right of citizens of the United States to vote shall not be denied or abridged by the United States or by any State on account of sex.

Congress shall have power to enforce this article by appropriate legislation.

Amendment XX [1933]

Section 1

The terms of the President and Vice President shall end at noon on the 20th day of January, and the terms of Senators and Representatives at noon on the 3d day of January, of the years in which such terms would have ended if this article had not been ratified; and the terms of their successors shall then begin.

Section 2

The Congress shall assemble at least once in every year, and such meeting shall begin at noon on the 3d day of January, unless they shall by law appoint a different day.

Section 3

If, at the time fixed for the beginning of the term of the President, the President elect shall have died, the Vice President elect shall become President. If a President shall not have been chosen before the time fixed for the beginning of his term, or if the President elect shall have failed to qualify, then the Vice President elect shall act as President until a President shall have qualified; and the Congress may by law provide for the case wherein neither a President elect nor a Vice President elect shall have qualified, declaring who shall then act as President, or the manner in which one who is to act shall be selected, and such person shall act accordingly until a President or Vice President shall have qualified.

Section 4

The Congress may by law provide for the case of the death of any of the persons from whom the House of Representatives may choose a President whenever the right of choice shall have devolved upon them, and for the case of the death of any of the persons from whom the Senate may choose a Vice President whenever the right of choice shall have devolved upon them.

Section 5

Sections 1 and 2 shall take effect on the 15th day of October following the ratification of this article.

Section 6

This article shall be inoperative unless it shall have been ratified as an amendment to the Constitution by the legislatures of three-fourths of the several States within seven years from the date of its submission.

Amendment XXI [1933]

Section 1

The eighteenth article of amendment to the Constitution of the United States is hereby repealed.

Section 2

The transportation or importation into any State, Territory, or possession of the United States for delivery or use therein of intoxicating liquors, in violation of the laws thereof, is hereby prohibited.

Section 3

This article shall be inoperative unless it shall have been ratified as an amendment to the Constitution by conventions in the several States, as provided in the Constitution, within seven years from the date of the submission hereof to the States by the Congress.

Amendment XXII [1951]

Section 1

No person shall be elected to the office of the President more than twice, and no person who has held the office of President, or acted as President, for more than two years of a term to which some other person was elected President shall be elected to the office of the President more than once. But this Article shall not apply to any person holding the office of President when this Article was proposed by the Congress, and shall not prevent any person who may be holding the office of President, or acting as President, during the term within which this Article becomes operative from holding the office of President, or acting as President during the remainder of such term.

Section 2

This article shall be inoperative unless it shall have been ratified as an amendment to the Constitution by the legislatures of three-fourths of the several States within seven years from the date of its submission to the States by the Congress.

Amendment XXIII [1961]

Section 1

The District constituting the seat of Government of the United States shall appoint in such manner as the Congress may direct:

A number of electors of President and Vice President equal to the whole number of Senators and Representatives in Congress to which the District would be entitled if it were a State, but in no event more than the least populous State; they shall be in addition to those appointed by the States, but they shall be considered, for the purposes of the election of President and Vice President, to be electors appointed by a State; and they shall meet in the District and perform such duties as provided by the twelfth article of amendment.

Section 2

The Congress shall have power to enforce this article by appropriate legislation.

Amendment XXIV [1964]

Section 1

The right of citizens of the United States to vote in any primary or other election for President or Vice President, for electors for President or Vice President or for Senator or Representative in Congress, shall not be denied or abridged by the United States or any State by reason of failure to pay any poll tax or other tax.

Section 2

The Congress shall have power to enforce this article by appropriate legislation.

Amendment XXV [1967]

Section 1

In case of the removal of the President from office or of his death or resignation, the Vice President shall become President.

Section 2

Whenever there is a vacancy in the office of the Vice President, the President shall nominate a Vice President who shall take office upon confirmation by a majority vote of both Houses of Congress.

Section 3

Whenever the President transmits to the President pro tempore of the Senate and the Speaker of the House of Representatives his written declaration that he is unable to discharge the powers and duties of his office, and until he transmits to them a written declaration to the contrary, such powers and duties shall be discharged by the Vice President as Acting President.

Section 4

Whenever the Vice President and a majority of either the principal officers of the executive departments or of such other body as Congress may by law provide, transmit to the President pro tempore of the Senate and the Speaker of the House of Representatives their written declaration that the President is unable to discharge the powers and duties of his office, the Vice President shall immediately assume the powers and duties of the office as Acting President.

Thereafter, when the President transmits to the President pro tempore of the Senate and the Speaker of the House of Representatives his written declaration that no inability exists, he shall resume the powers and duties of his office unless the Vice President and a majority of either the principal officers of the executive department or of such other body as Congress may by law provide, transmit within four days to the President pro tempore of the Senate and the Speaker of the House of Representatives their written declaration that the President is unable to discharge the powers and duties of his office. Thereupon Congress shall decide the issue, assembling within forty-eight hours for that purpose if not in session. If the Congress, within twenty-one days after receipt of the latter written declaration, or, if Congress is not in session, within twenty-one days after Congress is required to assemble, determines by two-thirds vote of both Houses that the President shall continue to discharge the same as Acting President; otherwise, the President shall resume the powers and duties of his office.

Amendment XXVI [1971]

Section 1

The right of citizens of the United States, who are eighteen years of age or older, to vote shall not be denied or abridged by the United States or by any State on account of age.

Section 2

The Congress shall have power to enforce this article by appropriate legislation.

Uniform Commercial Code*
(Selected Provisions)

ARTICLE 1: GENERAL PROVISIONS

Part 1—Short Title, Construction, Application and Subject Matter of the Act

§ 1–101. Short Title

This Act shall be known and may be cited as Uniform Commercial Code.

§ 1–102. Purposes; Rules of Construction; Variation by Agreement

(1) This Act shall be liberally construed and applied to promote its underlying purposes and policies.

(2) Underlying purposes and policies of this Act are
(a) to simplify, clarify and modernize the law governing commercial transactions;
(b) to permit the continued expansion of commercial practices through custom, usage and agreement of the parties;
(c) to make uniform the law among the various jurisdictions.

(3) The effect of provisions of this Act may be varied by agreement, except as otherwise provided in this Act and except that the obligations of good faith, diligence, reasonableness and care prescribed by this Act may not be disclaimed by agreement but the parties may by agreement determine the standards by which the performance of such obligations is to be measured if such standards are not manifestly unreasonable.

(4) The presence in certain provisions of this Act of the words "unless otherwise agreed" or words of similar import does not imply that the effect of other provisions may not be varied by agreement under subsection (3).

(5) In this Act unless the context otherwise requires
(a) words in the singular number include the plural, and in the plural include the singular;
(b) words of the masculine gender include the feminine and the neuter, and when the sense so indicates words of the neuter gender may refer to any gender.

*Copyright ©1989 by The American Law Institute and the National Conference of Commissioners on Uniform State Laws. Reproduced with permission.

§ 1–103. Supplementary General Principles of Law Applicable

Unless displaced by the particular provisions of this Act, the principles of law and equity, including the law merchant and the law relative to capacity to contract, principal and agent, estoppel, fraud, misrepresentation, duress, coercion, mistake, bankruptcy, or other validating or invalidating cause shall supplement its provisions.

§ 1–106. Remedies to Be Liberally Administered

(1) The remedies provided by this Act shall be liberally administered to the end that the aggrieved party may be put in as good a position as if the other party had fully performed but neither consequential or special nor penal damages may be had except as specifically provided in this Act or by other rule of law.

(2) Any right or obligation declared by this Act is enforceable by action unless the provision declaring it specifies a different and limited effect.

§ 1–107. Waiver or Renunciation of Claim or Right After Breach

Any claim or right arising out of an alleged breach can be discharged in whole or in part without consideration by a written waiver or renunciation signed and delivered by the aggrieved party.

Part 2—General Definitions and Principles of Interpretation

§ 1–201. General Definitions

Subject to additional definitions contained in the subsequent Articles of this Act which are applicable to specific Articles or Parts thereof, and unless the context otherwise requires, in this Act:

(1) "Action" in the sense of a judicial proceeding includes recoupment, counterclaim, set-off, suit in equity and any other proceedings in which rights are determined.

(2) "Aggrieved party" means a party entitled to resort to a remedy.

(3) "Agreement" means the bargain of the parties in fact as found in their language or by implication from other circumstances including course of dealing or usage of trade or course of

performance as provided in this Act (Sections 1–205 and 2–208). Whether an agreement has legal consequences is determined by the provisions of this Act, if applicable; otherwise by the law of contracts (Section 1–103). (Compare "Contract".)

(4) "Bank" means any person engaged in the business of banking.

(5) "Bearer" means the person in possession of an instrument, document of title, or certificated security payable to bearer or indorsed in blank.

(6) "Bill of lading" means a document evidencing the receipt of goods for shipment issued by a person engaged in the business of transporting or forwarding goods, and includes an airbill. "Airbill" means a document serving for air transportation as a bill of lading does for marine or rail transportation, and includes an air consignment note or air waybill.

(7) "Branch" includes a separately incorporated foreign branch of a bank.

(8) "Burden of establishing" a fact means the burden of persuading the triers of fact that the existence of the fact is more probable than its non-existence.

(9) "Buyer in ordinary course of business" means a person who in good faith and without knowledge that the sale to him is in violation of the ownership rights or security interest of a third party in the goods buys in ordinary course from a person in the business of selling goods of that kind but does not include a pawnbroker. All persons who sell minerals or the like (including oil and gas) at wellhead or minehead shall be deemed to be persons in the business of selling goods of that kind. "Buying" may be for cash or by exchange of other property or on secured or unsecured credit and includes receiving goods or documents of title under a pre-existing contract for sale but does not include a transfer in bulk or as security for or in total or partial satisfaction of a money debt.

(10) "Conspicuous": A term or clause is conspicuous when it is so written that a reasonable person against whom it is to operate ought to have noticed it. A printed heading in capitals (as: NON-NEGOTIABLE BILL OF LADING) is conspicuous. Language in the body of a form is "conspicuous" if it is in larger or other contrasting type or color. But in a telegram any stated term is "conspicuous". Whether a term or clause is "conspicuous" or not is for decision by the court.

(11) "Contract" means the total legal obligation which results from the parties' agreement as affected by this Act and any other applicable rules of law. (Compare "Agreement".)

(12) "Creditor" includes a general creditor, a secured creditor, a lien creditor and any representative of creditors, including an assignee for the benefit of creditors, a trustee in bankruptcy, a receiver in equity and an executor or administrator of an insolvent debtor's or assignor's estate.

(13) "Defendant" includes a person in the position of defendant in a cross-action or counterclaim.

(14) "Delivery" with respect to instruments, documents of title, chattel paper, or certificated securities means voluntary transfer of possession.

(15) "Document of title" includes bill of lading, dock warrant, dock receipt, warehouse receipt or order for the delivery of goods, and also any other document which in the regular course of business or financing is treated as adequately evidencing that the person in possession of it is entitled to receive, hold and dispose of the document and the goods it covers. To be a document of title a document must purport to be issued by or addressed to a bailee and purport to cover goods in the bailee's possession which are either identified or are fungible portions of an identified mass.

(16) "Fault" means wrongful act, omission or breach.

(17) "Fungible" with respect to goods or securities means goods or securities of which any unit is, by nature or usage of trade, the equivalent of any other like unit. Goods which are not fungible shall be deemed fungible for the purposes of this Act to the extent that under a particular agreement or document unlike units are treated as equivalents.

(18) "Genuine" means free of forgery or counterfeiting.

(19) "Good faith" means honesty in fact in the conduct or transaction concerned.

(20) "Holder" means a person who is in possession of a document of title or an instrument or a certificated investment security drawn, issued, or indorsed to him or his order or to bearer or in blank.

(21) To "honor" is to pay or to accept and pay, or where a credit so engages to purchase or discount a draft complying with the terms of the credit.

(22) "Insolvency proceedings" includes any assignment for the benefit of creditors or other proceedings intended to liquidate or rehabilitate the estate of the person involved.

(23) A person is "insolvent" who either has ceased to pay his debts in the ordinary course of business or cannot pay his debts as they become due or is insolvent within the meaning of the federal bankruptcy law.

(24) "Money" means a medium of exchange authorized or adopted by a domestic or foreign government as a part of its currency.

(25) A person has "notice" of a fact when

    (a) he has actual knowledge of it; or

    (b) he has received a notice or notification of it; or

    (c) from all the facts and circumstances known to him at the time in question he has reason to know that it exists.

A person "knows" or has "knowledge" of a fact when he has actual knowledge of it. "Discover" or "learn" or a word or phrase of similar import refers to knowledge rather than to reason to know. The time and circumstances under which a notice or notification may cease to be effective are not determined by this Act.

(26) A person "notifies" or "gives" a notice or notification to another by taking such steps as may be reasonably required to inform the other in ordinary course whether or not such other actually comes to know of it. A person "receives" a notice or notification when

    (a) it comes to his attention; or

    (b) it is duly delivered at the place of business through which the contract was made or at any other place held out by him as the place for receipt of such communications.

(27) Notice, knowledge or a notice or notification received by an organization is effective for a particular transaction from the time when it is brought to the attention of the individual conducting that transaction, and in any event from the time when it would have been brought to his attention if the organization had exercised due diligence. An organization exercises due diligence if it maintains reasonable routines for communicating significant information to the person conducting the transaction and there is reasonable compliance with the routines. Due diligence does not require an individual acting for the organization to communicate information unless such communication is part

of his regular duties or unless he has reason to know of the transaction and that the transaction would be materially affected by the information.

(28) "Organization" includes a corporation, government or governmental subdivision or agency, business trust, estate, trust, partnership or association, two or more persons having a joint or common interest, or any other legal or commercial entity.

(29) "Party", as distinct from "third party", means a person who has engaged in a transaction or made an agreement within this Act.

(30) "Person" includes an individual or an organization (See Section 1–102).

(31) "Presumption" or "presumed" means that the trier of fact must find the existence of the fact presumed unless and until evidence is introduced which would support a finding of its non-existence.

(32) "Purchase" includes taking by sale, discount, negotiation, mortgage, pledge, lien, or re-issue, gift or any other voluntary transaction creating an interest in property.

(33) "Purchaser" means a person who takes by purchase.

(34) "Remedy" means any remedial right to which an aggrieved party is entitled with or without resort to a tribunal.

(35) "Representative" includes an agent, an officer of a corporation or association, and a trustee, executor or administrator of an estate, or any other person empowered to act for another.

(36) "Rights" includes remedies.

(37) "Security interest" means an interest in personal property or fixtures which secures payment or performance of an obligation. The retention or reservation of title by a seller of goods notwithstanding shipment or delivery to the buyer (Section 2–401) is limited in effect to a reservation of a "security interest". The term also includes any interest of a buyer of accounts or chattel paper which is subject to Article 9. The special property interest of a buyer of goods on identification of such goods to a contract for sale under Section 2–401 is not a "security interest", but a buyer may also acquire a "security interest" by complying with Article 9. Unless a lease or consignment is intended as security, reservation of title thereunder is not a "security interest" but a consignment is in any event subject to the provisions on consignment sales (Section 2–326). Whether a lease is intended as security is to be determined by the facts of each case; however, (a) the inclusion of an option to purchase does not of itself make the lease one intended for security, and (b) an agreement that upon compliance with the terms of the lease the leasee shall become or has the option to become the owner of the property for no additional consideration or for a nominal consideration does make the lease one intended for security.

(38) "Send" in connection with any writing or notice means to deposit in the mail or delivery for transmission by any other usual means of communication with postage or cost of transmission provided for and properly addressed and in the case of an instrument to an address specified thereon or otherwise agreed, or if there be none to any address reasonable under the circumstances. The receipt of any writing or notice within the time at which it would have arrived if properly sent has the effect of a proper sending.

(39) "Signed" includes any symbol executed or adopted by a party with present intention to authenticate a writing.

(40) "Surety" includes guarantor.

(41) "Telegram" includes a message transmitted by radio, teletype, cable, any mechanical method of transmission, or the like.

(42) "Term" means that portion of an agreement which relates to a particular matter.

(43) "Unauthorized" signature or indorsement means one made without actual, implied or apparent authority and includes a forgery.

(44) "Value". Except as otherwise provided with respect to negotiable instruments and bank collections (Sections 3–303, 4–208 and 4–209) a person gives "value" for rights if he acquires them

(a) in return for a binding commitment to extend credit or for the extension of immediately available credit whether or not drawn upon or whether or not a chargeback is provided for in the event of difficulties in collection; or

(b) as security for or in total or partial satisfaction of a pre-existing claim; or

(c) by accepting delivery pursuant to a pre-existing contract for purchase; or

(d) generally, in return for any consideration sufficient to support a simple contract.

(45) "Warehouse receipt" means a receipt issued by a person engaged in the business of storing goods for hire.

(46) "Written" or "writing" includes printing, typewriting or any other intentional reduction to tangible form. Amended in 1962, 1972 and 1977.

§ 1–203. Obligation of Good Faith

Every contract or duty within this Act imposes an obligation of good faith in its performance or enforcement.

§ 1–204. Time; Reasonable Time; "Seasonably"

(1) Whenever this Act requires any action to be taken within a reasonable time, any time which is not manifestly unreasonable may be fixed by agreement.

(2) What is a reasonable time for taking any action depends on the nature, purpose and circumstances of such action.

(3) An action is taken "seasonably" when it is taken at or within the time agreed or if no time is agreed at or within a reasonable time.

§ 1–205. Course of Dealing and Usage of Trade

(1) A course of dealing is a sequence of previous conduct between the parties to a particular transaction which is fairly to be regarded as establishing a common basis of understanding for interpreting their expressions and other conduct.

(2) A usage of trade is any practice or method of dealing having such regularity of observance in a place, vocation or trade as to justify an expectation that it will be observed with respect to the transaction in question. The existence and scope of such a usage are to be proved as facts. If it is established that such a usage is embodied in a written trade code or similar writing the interpretation of the writing is for the court.

(3) A course of dealing between parties and any usage of trade in the vocation or trade in which they are engaged or of which they are or should be aware give particular meaning to and supplement or qualify terms of an agreement.

(4) The express terms of an agreement and an applicable course of dealing or usage of trade shall be construed wherever reasonable as consistent with each other, but when such construction is

unreasonable express terms control both course of dealing and usage of trade and course of dealing controls usage of trade.

(5) An applicable usage of trade in the place where any part of performance is to occur shall be used in interpreting the agreement as to that part of the performance.

(6) Evidence of a relevant usage of trade offered by one party is not admissible unless and until he has given the other party such notice as the court finds sufficient to prevent unfair surprise to the latter.

§ 1–206. Statute of Frauds for Kinds of Personal Property Not Otherwise Covered

(1) Except in the cases described in subsection (2) of this section a contract for the sale of personal property is not enforceable by way of action or defense beyond five thousand dollars in amount or value of remedy unless there is some writing which indicates that a contract for sale has been made between the parties at a defined or stated price, reasonably identifies the subject matter, and is signed by the party against whom enforcement is sought or by his authorized agent.

(2) Subsection (1) of this section does not apply to contracts for the sale of goods (Section 2–201) nor of securities (Section 8–319) nor to security agreements (Section 9–203).

ARTICLE 2: SALES

Part 1—Short Title, Construction and Subject Matter

§ 2–101. Short Title

This Article shall be known and may be cited as Uniform Commercial Code—Sales.

§ 2–102. Scope; Certain Security and Other Transactions Excluded From This Article

Unless the context otherwise requires, this Article applies to transactions in goods; it does not apply to any transaction which although in the form of an unconditional contract to sell or present sale is intended to operate only as a security transaction nor does this Article impair or repeal any statute regulating sales to consumers, farmers or other specified classes of buyers.

§ 2–103. Definitions and Index of Definitions

(1) In this Article unless the context otherwise requires
  (a) "Buyer" means a person who buys or contracts to buy goods.
  (b) "Good faith" in the case of a merchant means honesty in fact and the observance of reasonable commercial standards of fair dealing in the trade.
  (c) "Receipt" of goods means taking physical possession of them.
  (d) "Seller" means a person who sells or contracts to sell goods.

(2) Other definitions applying to this Article or to specified Parts thereof, and the sections in which they appear are:
  "Acceptance". Section 2–606.
  "Banker's credit". Section 2–325.
  "Between merchants". Section 2–104.
  "Cancellation". Section 2–106(4).
  "Commercial unit". Section 2–105.
  "Confirmed credit". Section 2–325.
  "Conforming to contract". Section 2–106.
  "Contract for sale". Section 2–106.
  "Cover". Section 2–712.
  "Entrusting". Section 2–403.
  "Financing agency". Section 2–104.
  "Future goods". Section 2–105.
  "Goods". Section 2–105.
  "Identification". Section 2–501.
  "Installment contract". Section 2–612.
  "Letter of Credit". Section 2–325.
  "Lot". Section 2–105.
  "Merchant". Section 2–104.
  "Overseas". Section 2–323.
  "Person in position of seller". Section 2–707.
  "Present sale". Section 2–106.
  "Sale". Section 2–106.
  "Sale on approval". Section 2–326.
  "Sale or return". Section 2–326.
  "Termination". Section 2–106.

(3) The following definitions in other Articles apply to this Article:
  "Check". Section 3–104.
  "Consignee". Section 7—102.
  "Consignor". Section 7—102.
  "Consumer goods". Section 9—109.
  "Dishonor". Section 3–507.
  "Draft". Section 3–104.

(4) In addition Article 1 contains general definitions and principles of construction and interpretation applicable throughout this Article.

§ 2–104. Definitions: "Merchant"; "Between Merchants"; "Financing Agency"

(1) "Merchant" means a person who deals in goods of the kind or otherwise by his occupation holds himself out as having knowledge or skill peculiar to the practices or goods involved in the transaction or to whom such knowledge or skill may be attributed by his employment of an agent or broker or other intermediary who by his occupation holds himself out as having such knowledge or skill.

(2) "Financing agency" means a bank, finance company or other person who in the ordinary course of business makes advances against goods or documents of title or who by arrangement with either the seller or the buyer intervenes in ordinary course to make or collect payment due or claimed under the contract for sale, as by purchasing or paying the seller's draft or making advances against it or by merely taking it for collection whether or not documents of title accompany the draft. "Financing agency" includes also a bank or other person who similarly intervenes between persons who are in the position of seller and buyer in respect to the goods (Section 2–707).

(3) "Between merchants" means in any transaction with respect to which both parties are chargeable with the knowledge or skill of merchants.

§ 2–105. Definitions: Transferability; "Goods"; "Future" Goods; "Lot"; "Commercial Unit"

(1) "Goods" means all things (including specially manufactured goods) which are movable at the time of identification to the contract for sale other than the money in which the price is to be paid, investment securities (Article 8) and things in action. "Goods" also includes the unborn young of animals and growing crops and other identified things attached to realty as described in the section on goods to be severed from realty (Section 2–107).

(2) Goods must be both existing and identified before any interest in them can pass. Goods which are not both existing and identified are "future" goods. A purported present sale of future goods or of any interest therein operates as a contract to sell.

(3) There may be a sale of a part interest in existing identified goods.

(4) An undivided share in an identified bulk of fungible goods is sufficiently identified to be sold although the quantity of the bulk is not determined. Any agreed proportion of such a bulk or any quantity thereof agreed upon by number, weight or other measure may to the extent of the seller's interest in the bulk be sold to the buyer who then becomes an owner in common.

(5) "Lot" means a parcel or a single article which is the subject matter of a separate sale or delivery, whether or not it is sufficient to perform the contract.

(6) "Commercial unit" means such a unit of goods as by commercial usage is a single whole for purposes of sale and division of which materially impairs its character or value on the market or in use. A commercial unit may be a single article (as a machine) or a set of articles (as a suite of furniture or an assortment of sizes) or a quantity (as a bale, gross, or carload) or any other unit treated in use or in the relevant market as a single whole.

§ 2–106. Definitions: "Contract"; "Agreement"; "Contract for Sale"; "Sale"; "Present Sale"; "Conforming" to Contract; "Termination"; "Cancellation"

(1) In this Article unless the context otherwise requires "contract" and "agreement" are limited to those relating to the present or future sale of goods. "Contract for sale" includes both a present sale of goods and a contract to sell goods at a future time. A "sale" consists in the passing of title from the seller to the buyer for a price (Section 2–401). A "present sale" means a sale which is accomplished by the making of the contract.

(2) Goods or conduct including any part of a performance are "conforming" or conform to the contract when they are in accordance with the obligations under the contract.

(3) "Termination" occurs when either party pursuant to a power created by agreement or law puts an end to the contract otherwise than for its breach. On "termination" all obligations which are still executory on both sides are discharged but any right based on prior breach or performance survives.

(4) "Cancellation" occurs when either party puts an end to the contract for breach by the other and its effect is the same as that of "termination" except that the cancelling party also retains any remedy for breach of the whole contract or any unperformed balance.

§ 2–107. Goods to Be Severed from Realty: Recording

(1) A contract for the sale of minerals or the like (including oil and gas) or a structure or its materials to be removed from realty is a contract for the sale of goods within this Article if they are to be severed by the seller but until severance a purported present sale thereof which is not effective as a transfer of an interest in land is effective only as a contract to sell.

(2) A contract for the sale apart from the land of growing crops or other things attached to realty and capable of severance without material harm thereto but not described in subsection (1) or of timber to be cut is a contract for the sale of goods within this Article whether the subject matter is to be severed by the buyer or by the seller even though it forms part of the realty at the time of contracting, and the parties can by identification effect a present sale before severance.

(3) The provisions of this section are subject to any third party rights provided by the law relating to realty records, and the contract for sale may be executed and recorded as a document transferring an interest in land and shall then constitute notice to third parties of the buyer's rights under the contract for sale.

Part 2—Form, Formation and Readjustment of Contract

§ 2–201. Formal Requirements; Statute of Frauds

(1) Except as otherwise provided in this section a contract for the sale of goods for the price of $500 or more is not enforceable by way of action or defense unless there is some writing sufficient to indicate that a contract for sale has been made between the parties and signed by the party against whom enforcement is sought or by his authorized agent or broker. A writing is not insufficient because it omits or incorrectly states a term agreed upon but the contract is not enforceable under this paragraph beyond the quantity of goods shown in such writing.

(2) Between merchants if within a reasonable time a writing in confirmation of the contract and sufficient against the sender is received and the party receiving it has reason to know its contents, it satisfies the requirements of subsection (1) against such party unless written notice of objection to its contents is given within ten days after it is received.

(3) A contract which does not satisfy the requirements of subsection (1) but which is valid in other respects is enforceable

  (a) if the goods are to be specially manufactured for the buyer and are not suitable for sale to others in the ordinary course of the seller's business and the seller, before notice of repudiation is received and under circumstances which reasonably indicate that the goods are for the buyer, has made either a substantial beginning of their manufacture or commitments for their procurement; or

  (b) if the party against whom enforcement is sought admits in his pleading, testimony or otherwise in court that a contract for sale was made, but the contract is not enforceable under this provision beyond the quantity of goods admitted; or

  (c) with respect to goods for which payment has been made and accepted or which have been received and accepted (Section 2–606).

§ 2–202. Final Written Expression: Parol or Extrinsic Evidence

Terms with respect to which the confirmatory memoranda of the parties agree or which are otherwise set forth in a writing intended by the parties as a final expression of their agreement with respect to such terms as are included therein may not be contradicted by evidence of any prior agreement or of a contemporaneous oral agreement but may be explained or supplemented

(a) by course of dealing or usage of trade (Section 1–205) or by course of performance (Section 2–208); and

(b) by evidence of consistent additional terms unless the court finds the writing to have been intended also as a complete and exclusive statement of the terms of the agreement.

§ 2–203. Seals Inoperative

The affixing of a seal to a writing evidencing a contract for sale or an offer to buy or sell goods does not constitute the writing a sealed instrument and the law with respect to sealed instruments does not apply to such a contract or offer.

§ 2–204. Formation in General

(1) A contract for sale of goods may be made in any manner sufficient to show agreement, including conduct by both parties which recognizes the existence of such a contract.

(2) An agreement sufficient to constitute a contract for sale may be found even though the moment of its making is undetermined.

(3) Even though one or more terms are left open a contract for sale does not fail for indefiniteness if the parties have intended to make a contract and there is a reasonably certain basis for giving an appropriate remedy.

§ 2–205. Firm Offers

An offer by a merchant to buy or sell goods in a signed writing which by its terms gives assurance that it will be held open is not revocable, for lack of consideration, during the time stated or if no time is stated for reasonable time, but in no event may such period of irrevocability exceed three months; but any such term of assurance on a form supplied by the offeree must be separately signed by the offeror.

§ 2–206. Offer and Acceptance in Formation of Contract

(1) Unless other unambiguously indicated by the language or circumstances

(a) an offer to make a contract shall be construed as inviting acceptance in any manner and by any medium reasonable in the circumstances;

(b) an order or other offer to buy goods for prompt or current shipment shall be construed as inviting acceptance either by a prompt promise to ship or by the prompt or current shipment of conforming or nonconforming goods, but such a shipment of non-conforming goods does not constitute an acceptance if the seller seasonably notifies the buyer that the shipment is offered only as an accommodation to the buyer.

(2) Where the beginning of a requested performance is a reasonable mode of acceptance an offeror who is not notified of acceptance within a reasonable time may treat the offer as having lapsed before acceptance.

§ 2–207. Additional Terms in Acceptance or Confirmation

(1) A definite and seasonable expression of acceptance or a written confirmation which is sent within a reasonable time operates as an acceptance even though it states terms additional to or different from those offered or agreed upon, unless acceptance is expressly made conditional on assent to the additional or different terms.

(2) The additional terms are to be construed as proposals for addition to the contract. Between merchants such terms become part of the contract unless:

(a) the offer expressly limits acceptance to the terms of the offer;

(b) they materially alter it; or

(c) notification of objection to them has already been given or is given within a reasonable time after notice of them is received.

(3) Conduct by both parties which recognizes the existence of a contract is sufficient to establish a contract for sale although the writings of the parties do not otherwise establish a contract. In such case the terms of the particular contract consist of those terms on which the writings of the parties agree, together with any supplementary terms incorporated under any other provisions of this Act.

§ 2–208. Course of Performance or Practical Construction

(1) Where the contract for sale involves repeated occasions for performance by either party with knowledge of the nature of the performance and opportunity for objection to it by the other, any course of performance accepted or acquiesced in without objection shall be relevant to determine the meaning of the agreement.

(2) The express terms of the agreement and any such course of performance, as well as any course of dealing and usage of trade, shall be construed whenever reasonable as consistent with each other; but when such construction is unreasonable, express terms shall control course of performance and course of performance shall control both course of dealing and usage of trade (Section 1–205).

(3) Subject to the provisions of the next section on modification and waiver, such course of performance shall be relevant to show a waiver or modification of any term inconsistent with such course of performance.

§ 2–209. Modification, Rescission and Waiver

(1) An agreement modifying a contract within this Article needs no consideration to be binding.

(2) A signed agreement which excludes modification or rescission except by a signed writing cannot be otherwise modified or rescinded, but except as between merchants such a requirement on a form supplied by the merchant must be separately signed by the other party.

(3) The requirements of the statute of frauds section of this Article (Section 2–201) must be satisfied if the contract as modified is within its provisions.

(4)   Although an attempt at modification or rescission does not satisfy the requirements of subsection (2) or (3) it can operate as a waiver.

(5)   A party who has made a waiver affecting an executory portion of the contract may retract the waiver by reasonable notification received by the other party that strict performance will be required of any term waived, unless the retraction would be unjust in view of a material change of position in reliance on the waiver.

§ 2–210. Delegation of Performance; Assignment of Rights

(1)   A party may perform his duty through a delegate unless otherwise agreed or unless the other party has a substantial interest in having his original promisor perform or control the acts required by the contract. No delegation of performance relieves the party delegating of any duty to perform or any liability for breach.

(2)   Unless otherwise agreed all rights of either seller or buyer can be assigned except where the assignment would materially change the duty of the other party, or increase materially the burden or risk imposed on him by his contract, or impair materially his chance of obtaining return performance. A right to damages for breach of the whole contract or a right arising out of the assignor's due performance of his entire obligation can be assigned despite agreement otherwise.

(3)   Unless the circumstances indicate the contrary a prohibition of assignment of "the contract" is to be construed as barring only the delegation to the assignee of the assignor's performance.

(4)   An assignment of "the contract" or of "all my rights under the contract" or an assignment in similar general terms is an assignment of rights and unless the language or the circumstances (as in an assignment for security) indicate the contrary, it is a delegation of performance of the duties of the assignor and its acceptance by the assignee constitutes a promise by him to perform those duties. This promise is enforceable by either the assignor or the other party to the original contract.

(5)   The other party may treat any assignment which delegates performance as creating reasonable grounds for insecurity and may without prejudice to his rights against the assignor demand assurances from the assignee (Section 2–609).

Part 3—General Obligation and Construction of Contract

§ 2–301. General Obligations of Parties

The obligation of the seller is to transfer and deliver and that of the buyer is to accept and pay in accordance with the contract.

§ 2–302. Unconscionable Contract or Clause

(1)   If the court as a matter of law finds the contract or any clause of the contract to have been unconscionable at the time it was made the court may refuse to enforce the contract, or it may enforce the remainder of the contract without the unconscionable clause, or it may so limit the application of any unconscionable clause as to avoid any unconscionable result.

(2)   When it is claimed or appears to the court that the contract or any clause thereof may be unconscionable the parties shall be afforded a reasonable opportunity to present evidence as to its commercial setting, purpose and effect to aid the court in making the determination.

§ 2–303. Allocation or Division of Risks

Where this Article allocates a risk or a burden as between the parties "unless otherwise agreed", the agreement may not only shift the allocation, but may also divide the risk or burden.

§ 2–304. Price Payable in Money, Goods, Realty, or Otherwise

(1)   The price can be made payable in money or otherwise. If it is payable in whole or in part in goods each party is a seller of the goods which he is to transfer.

(2)   Even though all or part of the price is payable in an interest in realty the transfer of the goods and the seller's obligations with reference to them are subject to this Article, but not the transfer of the interest in realty or the transferor's obligations in connection therewith.

§ 2–305. Open Price Term

(1)   The parties if they so intend can conclude a contract for sale even though the price is not settled. In such a case the price is a reasonable price at the time for delivery if

(a) nothing is said as to price; or

(b) the price is left to be agreed by the parties and they fail to agree; or

(c) the price is to be fixed in terms of some agreed market or other standard as set or recorded by a third person or agency and it is not so set or recorded.

(2)   A price to be fixed by the seller or by the buyer means a price for him to fix in good faith.

(3)   When a price left to be fixed otherwise than by agreement of the parties fails to be fixed through fault of one party the other may at his option treat the contract as cancelled or himself fix a reasonable price.

(4)   Where, however, the parties intend not to be bound unless the price be fixed or agreed and it is not fixed or agreed there is no contract. In such a case the buyer must return any goods already received or if unable so to do must pay their reasonable value at the time of delivery and the seller must return any portion of the price paid on account.

§ 2–306. Output, Requirements and Exclusive Dealings

(1)   A term which measures the quantity by the output of the seller or the requirements of the buyer means such actual output or requirements as may occur in good faith, except that no quantity unreasonably disproportionate to any stated estimate or in the absence of a stated estimate to any normal or otherwise comparable prior output or requirements may be tendered or demanded.

(2)   A lawful agreement by either the seller or the buyer for exclusive dealing in the kind of goods concerned imposes unless otherwise agreed an obligation by the seller to use best efforts to supply the goods and by the buyer to use best efforts to promote their sale.

§ 2–307. Delivery in Single Lot or Several Lots

Unless otherwise agreed all goods called for by a contract for sale must be tendered in a single delivery and payment is due only on such tender but where the circumstances give either party the right to make or demand delivery in lots the price if it can be apportioned may be demanded for each lot.

§ 2–308. Absence of Specified Place for Delivery

Unless otherwise agreed

(a) the place for delivery of goods is the seller's place of business or if he has none his residence; but

(b) in a contract for sale of identified goods which to the knowledge of the parties at the time of contracting are in some other place, that place is the place for their delivery; and

(c) documents of title may be delivered through customary banking channels.

§ 2–309. Absence of Specific Time Provisions; Notice of Termination

(1) The time for shipment or delivery or any other action under a contract if not provided in this Article or agreed upon shall be a reasonable time.

(2) Where the contract provides for successive performances but is indefinite in duration it is valid for a reasonable time but unless otherwise agreed may be terminated at any time by either party.

(3) Termination of a contract by one party except on the happening of an agreed event requires that reasonable notification be received by the other party and an agreement dispensing with notification is invalid if its operation would be unconscionable.

§ 2–310. Open Time for Payment or Running of Credit; Authority to Ship Under Reservation

Unless otherwise agreed

(a) payment is due at the time and place at which the buyer is to receive the goods even though the place of shipment is the place of delivery; and

(b) if the seller is authorized to send the goods he may ship them under reservation, and may tender the documents of title, but the buyer may inspect the goods after their arrival before payment is due unless such inspection is inconsistent with the terms of the contract (Section 2–513); and

(c) if delivery is authorized and made by way of documents of title otherwise than by subsection (b) then payment is due at the time and place at which the buyer is to receive the documents regardless of where the goods are to be received; and

(d) where the seller is required or authorized to ship the goods on credit the credit period runs from the time of shipment but post-dating the invoice or delaying its dispatch will correspondingly delay the starting of the credit period.

§ 2–311. Options and Cooperation Respecting Performance

(1) An agreement for sale which is otherwise sufficiently definite (subsection (3) of Section 2–204) to be a contract is not made invalid by the fact that it leaves particulars of performance to be specified by one of the parties. Any such specification must be made in good faith and within limits set by commercial reasonableness.

(2) Unless otherwise agreed specifications relating to assortment of the goods are at the buyer's option and except as otherwise provided in subsections (1)(c) and (3) of Section 2–319 specifications or arrangements relating to shipment are at the seller's option.

(3) Where such specification would materially affect the other party's performance but is not seasonably made or where one party's cooperation is necessary to the agreed performance of the other but is not seasonably forthcoming, the other party in addition to all other remedies

(a) is excused for any resulting delay in his own performance; and

(b) may also either proceed to perform in any reasonable manner or after the time for a material part of his own performance treat the failure to specify or to cooperate as a breach by failure to deliver or accept the goods.

§ 2–312. Warranty of Title and Against Infringement; Buyer's Obligation Against Infringement

(1) Subject to subsection (2) there is in a contract for sale a warranty by the seller that

(a) the title conveyed shall be good, and its transfer rightful; and

(b) the goods shall be delivered free from any security interest or other lien or encumbrance of which the buyer at the time of contracting has no knowledge.

(2) A warranty under subsection (1) will be excluded or modified only by specific language or by circumstances which give the buyer reason to know that the person selling does not claim title in himself or that he is purporting to sell only such right or title as he or a third person may have.

(3) Unless otherwise agreed a seller who is a merchant regularly dealing in goods of the kind warrants that the goods shall be delivered free of the rightful claim of any third person by way of infringement or the like but a buyer who furnishes specifications to the seller must hold the seller harmless against any such claim which arises out of compliance with the specifications.

§ 2–313. Express Warranties by Affirmation, Promise, Description, Sample

(1) Express warranties by the seller are created as follows:

(a) Any affirmation of fact or promise made by the seller to the buyer which relates to the goods and becomes part of the basis of the bargain creates an express warranty that the goods shall conform to the affirmation or promise.

(b) Any description of the goods which is made part of the basis of the bargain creates an express warranty that the goods shall conform to the description.

(c) Any sample or model which is made part of the basis of the bargain creates an express warranty that the whole of the goods shall conform to the sample or model.

(2) It is not necessary to the creation of an express warranty that the seller use formal words such as "warrant" or "guarantee" or that he have a specific intention to make a warranty, but an affirmation merely of the value of the goods or a statement purporting to be merely the seller's opinion or commendation of the goods does not create a warranty.

§ 2–314. Implied Warranty: Merchantability; Usage of Trade

(1)　Unless excluded or modified (Section 2–316), a warranty that the goods shall be merchantable is implied in a contract for their sale if the seller is a merchant with respect to goods of that kind. Under this section the serving for value of food or drink to be consumed either on the premises or elsewhere is a sale.

(2)　Goods to be merchantable must be at least such as

(a) pass without objection in the trade under the contract description; and

(b) in the case of fungible goods, are of fair average quality within the description; and

(c) are fit for the ordinary purpose for which such goods are used; and

(d) run, within the variations permitted by the agreement, of even kind, quality and quantity within each unit and among all units involved; and

(e) are adequately contained, packaged, and labeled as the agreement may require; and

(f) conform to the promises or affirmations of fact made on the container or label if any.

(3)　Unless excluded or modified (Section 2–316) other implied warranties may arise from course of dealing or usage of trade.

§ 2–315. Implied Warranty: Fitness for Particular Purpose

Where the seller at the time of contracting has reason to know any particular purpose for which the goods are required and that the buyer is relying on the seller's skill or judgment to select or furnish suitable goods, there is unless excluded or modified under the next section an implied warranty that the goods shall be fit for such purpose.

§ 2–316. Exclusion or Modification of Warranties

(1)　Words or conduct relevant to the creation of an express warranty and words or conduct tending to negate or limit warranty shall be construed wherever reasonable as consistent with each other, but subject to the provisions of this Article on parol or extrinsic evidence (Section 2–202) negation or limitation is inoperative to the extent that such construction is unreasonable.

(2)　Subject to subsection (3), to exclude or modify the implied warranty of merchantability or any part of it the language must mention merchantability and in case of a writing must be conspicuous, and to exclude or modify any implied warranty of fitness the exclusion must be by a writing and conspicuous. Language to exclude all implied warranties of fitness is sufficient if it states, for example, that "There are no warranties which extend beyond the description on the face hereof."

(3)　Notwithstanding subsection (2)

(a) unless the circumstances indicate otherwise, all implied warranties are excluded by expressions like "as is", "with all faults" or other language which in common understanding calls the buyer's attention to the exclusion of warranties and makes plain that there is no implied warranty; and

(b) when the buyer before entering into the contract has examined the goods or the sample or model as fully as he desired or has refused to examine the goods there is no implied warranty with regard to defects which an examination ought in the circumstances to have revealed to him; and

(c) an implied warranty can also be excluded or modified by course of dealing or course of performance or usage of trade.

(4)　Remedies for breach of warranty can be limited in accordance with the provisions of this Article on liquidation or limitation of damages and on contractual modification of remedy (Sections 2–718 and 2–719).

§ 2–317. Cumulation and Conflict of Warranties Express or Implied

Warranties whether express or implied shall be construed as consistent with each other and as cumulative, but if such construction is unreasonable the intention of the parties shall determine which warranty is dominant. In ascertaining that intention the following rules apply:

(a)　Exact or technical specifications displace an inconsistent sample or model or general language of description.

(b)　A sample from an existing bulk displaces inconsistent general language of description.

(c)　Express warranties displace inconsistent implied warranties other than an implied warranty of fitness for a particular purpose.

§ 2–318. Third Party Beneficiaries of Warranties Express or Implied

Note: If this Act is introduced in the Congress of the United States this section should be omitted. (States to select one alternative.)

Alternative A　A seller's warranty whether express or implied extends to any natural person who is in the family or household of his buyer or who is a guest in his home if it is reasonable to expect that such person may use, consume or be affected by the goods and who is injured in person by breach of the warranty. The seller may not exclude or limit the operation of this section.

Alternative B　A seller's warranty whether express or implied extends to any natural person who may reasonably be expected to use, consume or be affected by the goods and who is injured in person by breach of the warranty. A seller may not exclude or limit the operation of this section.

Alternative C　A seller's warranty whether express or implied extends to any person who may reasonably be expected to use, consume or be affected by the goods and who is injured by breach of the warranty. A seller may not exclude or limit the operation of this section with respect to injury to the person of an individual to whom the warranty extends. As amended 1966.

§ 2–319. F.O.B. and F.A.S. Terms

(1)　Unless otherwise agreed the term F.O.B. (which means "free on board") at a named place, even though used only in connection with the stated price, is a delivery term under which

(a) when the term is F.O.B. the place of shipment, the seller must at that place ship the goods in the manner provided in this Article (Section 2–504) and bear the expense and risk of putting them into the possession of the carrier; or

(b) when the term is F.O.B. the place of destination, the seller must at his own expense and risk transport the goods to that place and there tender delivery of them in the manner provided in this Article (Section 2–503);

(c) when under either (a) or (b) the term is also F.O.B. vessel, car or other vehicle, the seller must in addition at his own expense and risk load the goods on board. If the term is F.O.B. vessel the buyer must name the vessel and in an appropriate case the seller must comply with the provisions of this Article on the form of bill of lading (Section 2–323).

(2) Unless otherwise agreed the term F.A.S. vessel (which means "free alongside") at a named port, even though used only in connection with the stated price, is a delivery term under which the seller must

(a) at his own expense and risk deliver the goods alongside the vessel in the manner usual in that port or on a dock designated and provided by the buyer; and

(b) obtain and tender a receipt for the goods in exchange for which the carrier is under a duty to issue a bill of lading.

(3) Unless otherwise agreed in any case falling within subsection (1)(a) or (c) or subsection (2) the buyer must seasonably give any needed instructions for making delivery, including when the term is F.A.S. or F.O.B. the loading berth of the vessel and in an appropriate case its name and sailing date. The seller may treat the failure of needed instructions as a failure of cooperation under this Article (Section 2–311). He may also at his option move the goods in any reasonable manner preparatory to delivery or shipment.

(4) Under the term F.O.B. vessel or F.A.S. unless otherwise agreed the buyer must make payment against tender of the required documents and the seller may not tender nor the buyer demand delivery of the goods in substitution for the documents.

§ 2–320. C.I.F. and C. & F. Terms

(1) The term C.I.F. means that the price includes in a lump sum the cost of the goods and the insurance and freight to the named destination. The term C. & F. or C.F. means that the price so includes cost and freight to the named destination.

(2) Unless otherwise agreed and even though used only in connection with the stated price and destination, the term C.I.F. destination or its equivalent requires the seller at his own expense and risk to

(a) put the goods into the possession of a carrier at the port for shipment and obtain a negotiable bill or bills of lading covering the entire transportation to the named destination; and

(b) load the goods and obtain a receipt from the carrier (which may be contained in the bill of lading) showing that the freight has been paid or provided for; and

(c) obtain a policy or certificate of insurance, including any war risk insurance, of a kind and on terms then current at the port of shipment in the usual amount, in the currency of the contract, shown to cover the same goods covered by the bill of lading and providing for payment of loss to the order of the buyer or for the account of whom it may concern; but the seller may add to the price the amount of premium for any such war risk insurance; and

(d) prepare an invoice of the goods and procure any other documents required to effect shipment or to comply with the contract; and

(e) forward and tender with commercial promptness all the documents in due form and with any indorsement necessary to perfect the buyer's rights.

(3) Unless otherwise agreed the term C. & F. or its equivalent has the same effect and imposes upon the seller the same obligations and risks as a C.I.F. term except the obligation as to insurance.

(4) Under the term C.I.F. or C. & F. unless otherwise agreed the buyer must make payment against tender of the required documents and the seller may not tender nor the buyer demand delivery of the goods in substitution for the documents.

§ 2–321. C.I.F. or C. & F.: "Net Landed Weights"; "Payment on Arrival"; Warranty of Condition on Arrival

Under a contract containing a term C.I.F. or C. & F.

(1) Where the price is based on or is to be adjusted according to "net landed weights", "delivered weights", "out turn" quantity or quality or the like, unless otherwise agreed the seller must reasonably estimate the price. The payment due on tender of the documents called for by the contract is the amount so estimated, but after final adjustment of the price a settlement must be made with commercial promptness.

(2) An agreement described in subsection (1) or any warranty of quality or condition of the goods on arrival places upon the seller the risk of ordinary deterioration, shrinkage and the like in transportation but has no effect on the place or time of identification to the contract for sale or delivery or on the passing of the risk of loss.

(3) Unless otherwise agreed where the contract provides for payment on or after arrival of the goods the seller must before payment allow such preliminary inspection as is feasible; but if the goods are lost delivery of the documents and payment are due when the goods should have arrived.

§ 2–322. Delivery "Ex-Ship"

(1) Unless otherwise agreed a term for delivery of goods "ex-ship" (which means from the carrying vessel) or in equivalent language is not restricted to a particular ship and requires delivery from a ship which has reached a place at the named port of destination where goods of the kind are usually discharged.

(2) Under such a term unless otherwise agreed

(a) the seller must discharge all liens arising out of the carriage and furnish the buyer with a direction which puts the carrier under a duty to deliver the goods; and

(b) the risk of loss does not pass to the buyer until the goods leave the ship's tackle or are otherwise properly unloaded.

§ 2–323. Form of Bill of Lading Required in Overseas Shipment; "Overseas"

(1) Where the contract contemplates overseas shipment and contains a term C.I.F. or C. & F. or F.O.B. vessel, the seller unless otherwise agreed must obtain a negotiable bill of lading stating that the goods have been loaded on board or, in the case of a term C.I.F. or C. & F., received for shipment.

(2) Where in a case within subsection (1) a bill of lading has been issued in a set of parts, unless otherwise agreed if the documents are not to be sent from abroad the buyer may demand tender of the full set; otherwise only one part of the

bill of lading need be tendered. Even if the agreement expressly requires a full set

    (a) due tender of a single part is acceptable within the provisions of this Article on cure of improper delivery (subsection (1) of Section 2–508); and

    (b) even though the full set is demanded, if the documents are sent from abroad the person tendering an incomplete set may nevertheless require payment upon furnishing an indemnity which the buyer in good faith deems adequate.

(3) A shipment by water or by air or a contract contemplating such shipment is "overseas" insofar as by usage of trade or agreement it is subject to the commercial, financing or shipping practices characteristic of international deep water commerce.

§ 2–324. "No Arrival, No Sale" Term

Under a term "no arrival, no sale" or terms of like meaning, unless otherwise agreed,

(a) the seller must properly ship conforming goods and if they arrive by any means he must tender them on arrival but he assumes no obligation that the goods will arrive unless he has caused the non-arrival; and

(b) where without fault of the seller the goods are in part lost or have so deteriorated as no longer to conform to the contract or arrive after the contract time, the buyer may proceed as if there had been casualty to identified goods (Section 2–613).

§ 2–326. Sale on Approval and Sale or Return; Consignment Sales and Rights of Creditors

(1) Unless otherwise agreed, if delivered goods may be returned by the buyer even though they conform to the contract, the transaction is

    (a) a "sale on approval" if the goods are delivered primarily for use, and

    (b) a "sale or return" if the goods are delivered primarily for resale.

(2) Except as provided in subsection (3), goods held on approval are not subject to the claims of the buyer's creditors until acceptance; goods held on sale or return are subject to such claims while in the buyer's possession.

(3) Where goods are delivered to a person for sale and such person maintains a place of business at which he deals in goods of the kind involved, under a name other than the name of the person making delivery, then with respect to claims of creditors of the person conducting the business the goods are deemed to be on sale or return. The provisions of this subsection are applicable even though an agreement purports to reserve title to the person making delivery until payment or resale or uses such words as "on consignment" or "on memorandum". However, this subsection is not applicable if the person making delivery

    (a) complies with an applicable law providing for a consignor's interest or the like to be evidenced by a sign, or

    (b) establishes that the person conducting the business is generally known by his creditors to be substantially engaged in selling the goods of others, or

    (c) complies with the filing provisions of the Article on Secured Transactions (Article 9).

(4) Any "or return" term of a contract for sale is to be treated as a separate contract for sale within the statute of frauds section of this Article (Section 2–201) and as contradicting the sale

aspect of the contract within the provisions of this Article on parol or extrinsic evidence (Section 2–202).

§ 2–327. Special Incidents of Sale on Approval and Sale or Return

(1) Under a sale on approval unless otherwise agreed

    (a) although the goods are identified to the contract the risk of loss and the title do not pass to the buyer until acceptance; and

    (b) use of the goods consistent with the purpose of trial is not acceptance but failure seasonably to notify the seller of election to return the goods is acceptance, and if the goods conform to the contract acceptance of any part is acceptance of the whole; and

    (c) after due notification of election to return, the return is at the seller's risk and expense but a merchant buyer must follow any reasonable instructions.

(2) Under a sale or return unless otherwise agreed

    (a) the option to return extends to the whole or any commercial unit of the goods while in substantially their original condition, but must be exercised seasonably; and

    (b) the return is at the buyer's risk and expense.

§ 2–328. Sale by Auction

(1) In a sale by auction if goods are put up in lots each lot is the subject of a separate sale.

(2) A sale by auction is complete when the auctioneer so announces by the fall of the hammer or in other customary manner. Where a bid is made while the hammer is falling in acceptance of a prior bid the auctioneer may in his discretion reopen the bidding or declare the goods sold under the bid on which the hammer was falling.

(3) Such a sale is with reserve unless the goods are in explicit terms put up without reserve. In an auction with reserve the auctioneer may withdraw the goods at any time until he announces completion of the sale. In an auction without reserve, after the auctioneer calls for bids on an article or lot, that article or lot cannot be withdrawn unless no bid is made within a reasonable time. In either case a bidder may retract his bid until the auctioneer's announcement of completion of the sale, but a bidder's retraction does not revive any previous bid.

(4) If the auctioneer knowingly receives a bid on the seller's behalf or the seller makes or procures such a bid, and notice has not been given that liberty for such bidding is reserved, the buyer may at his option avoid the sale or take the goods at the price of the last good faith bid prior to the completion of the sale. This subsection shall not apply to any bid at a forced sale.

Part 4—Title, Creditors and Good Faith Purchasers

§ 2–401. Passing of Title; Reservation for Security; Limited Application of This Section

Each provision of this Article with regard to the rights, obligations and remedies of the seller, the buyer, purchasers or other third parties applies irrespective of title to the goods except where the provision refers to such title. Insofar as situations are not covered by the other provisions of this Article and matters concerning title became material the following rules apply:

(1) Title to goods cannot pass under a contract for sale prior to their identification to the contract (Section 2–501), and unless otherwise explicitly agreed the buyer acquires by their identification a special property as limited by this Act. Any retention or reservation by the seller of the title (property) in goods shipped or delivered to the buyer is limited in effect to a reservation of a security interest. Subject to these provisions and to the provisions of the Article on Secured Transactions (Article 9), title to goods passes from the seller to the buyer in any manner and on any conditions explicitly agreed on by the parties.

(2) Unless otherwise explicitly agreed title passes to the buyer at the time and place at which the seller completes his performance with reference to the physical delivery of the goods, despite any reservation of a security interest and even though a document of title is to be delivered at a different time or place; and in particular and despite any reservation of a security interest by the bill of lading

    (a) if the contract requires or authorizes the seller to send the goods to the buyer but does not require him to deliver them at destination, title passes to the buyer at the time and place of shipment; but

    (b) if the contract requires delivery at destination, title passes on tender there.

(3) Unless otherwise explicitly agreed where delivery is to be made without moving the goods,

    (a) if the seller is to deliver a document of title, title passes at the time when and the place where he delivers such documents; or

    (b) if the goods are at the time of contracting already identified and no documents are to be delivered, title passes at the time and place of contracting.

(4) A rejection or other refusal by the buyer to receive or retain the goods, whether or not justified, or a justified revocation of acceptance revests title to the goods in the seller. Such revesting occurs by operation of law and is not a "sale."

§ 2–403. Power to Transfer; Good Faith Purchase of Goods; "Entrusting"

(1) A purchaser of goods acquires all title which his transferor had or had power to transfer except that a purchaser of a limited interest acquires rights only to the extent of the interest purchased. A person with voidable title has power to transfer a good title to a good faith purchaser for value. When goods have been delivered under a transaction of purchase the purchaser has such power even though

    (a) the transferor was deceived as to the identity of the purchaser, or

    (b) the delivery was in exchange for a check which is later dishonored, or

    (c) it was agreed that the transaction was to be a "cash sale", or

    (d) the delivery was procured through fraud punishable as larcenous under the criminal law.

(2) Any entrusting of possession of goods to a merchant who deals in goods of that kind gives him power to transfer all rights of the entruster to a buyer in ordinary course of business.

(3) "Entrusting" includes any delivery and any acquiescence in retention of possession regardless of any condition expressed between the parties to the delivery or acquiescence and regardless of whether the procurement of the entrusting

or the possessor's disposition of the goods have been such as to be larcenous under the criminal law.

(4) The rights of other purchasers of goods and of lien creditors are governed by the Articles on Secured Transactions (Article 9), Bulk Transfers (Article 6) and Documents of Title (Article 7).

Part 5—Performance

§ 2–501. Insurable Interest in Goods; Manner of Identification of Goods

(1) The buyer obtains a special property and an insurable interest in goods by identification of existing goods as goods to which the contract refers even though the goods so identified are nonconforming and he has an option to return or reject them. Such identification can be made at any time and in any manner explicitly agreed to by the parties. In the absence of explicit agreement identification occurs

    (a) when the contract is made if it is for the sale of goods already existing and identified;

    (b) if the contract is for the sale of future goods other than those described in paragraph (c), when goods are shipped, marked or otherwise designated by the seller as goods to which the contract refers;

    (c) when the crops are planted or otherwise become growing crops or the young are conceived if the contract is for the sale of unborn young to be born within twelve months after contracting or for the sale of crops to be harvested within twelve months or the next normal harvest season after contracting whichever is longer.

(2) The seller retains an insurable interest in goods so long as title to or any security interest in the goods remains in him and where the identification is by the seller alone he may until default or insolvency or notification to the buyer that the identification is final substitute other goods for those identified.

(3) Nothing in this section impairs any insurable interest recognized under any other statute or rule of law.

§ 2–502. Buyer's Right to Goods on Seller's Insolvency

(1) Subject to subsection (2) and even though the goods have not been shipped a buyer who has paid a part or all of the price of goods in which he has a special property under the provisions of the immediately preceding section may on making and keeping good a tender of any unpaid portion of their price recover them from the seller if the seller becomes insolvent within ten days after receipt of the first installment on their price.

(2) If the identification creating his special property has been made by the buyer he acquires the right to recover the goods only if they conform to the contract for sale.

§ 2–503. Manner of Seller's Tender of Delivery

(1) Tender of delivery requires that the seller put and hold conforming goods at the buyer's disposition and give the buyer any notification reasonably necessary to enable him to take delivery. The manner, time and place for tender are determined by the agreement and this Article, and in particular

    (a) tender must be at a reasonable hour, and if it is of goods they must be kept available for the period reasonably necessary to enable the buyer to take possession; but

(b) unless otherwise agreed the buyer must furnish facilities reasonably suited to the receipt of the goods.

(2) Where the case is within the next section respecting shipment tender requires that the seller comply with its provisions.

(3) Where the seller is required to deliver at a particular destination tender requires that he comply with subsection (1) and also in any appropriate case tender documents as described in subsections (4) and (5) of this section.

(4) Where goods are in the possession of a bailee and are to be delivered without being moved

(a) tender requires that the seller either tender a negotiable document of title covering such goods or procure acknowledgment by the bailee of the buyer's right to possession of the goods; but

(b) tender to the buyer of a non-negotiable document of title or of a written direction to the bailee to deliver is sufficient tender unless the buyer seasonably objects, and receipt by the bailee of notification of the buyer's rights fixes those rights as against the bailee and all third persons; but risk of loss of the goods and of any failure by the bailee to honor the non-negotiable document of title or to obey the direction remains on the seller until the buyer has had a reasonable time to present the document or direction, and a refusal by the bailee to honor the document or to obey the direction defeats the tender.

(5) Where the contract requires the seller to deliver documents

(a) he must tender all such documents in correct form, except as provided in this Article with respect to bills of lading in a set (subsection (2) of Section 2–323); and

(b) tender through customary banking channels is sufficient and dishonor of a draft accompanying the documents constitutes non-acceptance or rejection.

§ 2–504. Shipment by Seller

Where the seller is required or authorized to send the goods to the buyer and the contract does not require him to deliver them at a particular destination, then unless otherwise agreed he must

(a) put the goods in the possession of such a carrier and make such a contract for their transportation as may be reasonable having regard to the nature of the goods and other circumstances of the case; and

(b) obtain and promptly deliver or tender in due form any document necessary to enable the buyer to obtain possession of the goods or otherwise required by the agreement or by usage of trade; and

(c) promptly notify the buyer of the shipment.

Failure to notify the buyer under paragraph (c) or to make a proper contract under paragraph (a) is a ground for rejection only if material delay or loss ensues.

§ 2–507. Effect of Seller's Tender; Delivery on Condition

(1) Tender of delivery is a condition to the buyer's duty to accept the goods and, unless otherwise agreed, to his duty to pay for them. Tender entitles the seller to acceptance of the goods and to payment according to the contract.

(2) Where payment is due and demanded on the delivery to the buyer of goods or documents of title, his right as against the seller to retain or dispose of them is conditional upon his making the payment due.

§ 2–508. Cure by Seller of Improper Tender or Delivery; Replacement

(1) Where any tender or delivery by the seller is rejected because non-conforming and the time for performance has not yet expired, the seller may seasonably notify the buyer of his intention to cure and may then within the contract time make a conforming delivery.

(2) Where the buyer rejects a non-conforming tender which the seller had reasonable grounds to believe would be acceptable with or without money allowance the seller may if he seasonably notifies the buyer have a further reasonable time to substitute a conforming tender.

§ 2–509. Risk of Loss in the Absence of Breach

(1) Where the contract requires or authorizes the seller to ship the goods by carrier

(a) if it does not require him to deliver them at a particular destination, the risk of loss passes to the buyer when the goods are duly delivered to the carrier even though the shipment is under reservation (Section 2–505); but

(b) if it does require him to deliver them at a particular destination and the goods are there duly tendered while in the possession of the carrier, the risk of loss passes to the buyer when the goods are there duly so tendered as to enable the buyer to take delivery.

(2) Where the goods are held by a bailee to be delivered without being moved, the risk of loss passes to the buyer

(a) on his receipt of a negotiable document of title covering the goods; or

(b) on acknowledgment by the bailee of the buyer's right to possession of the goods; or

(c) after his receipt of a non-negotiable document of title or other written direction to deliver, as provided in subsection (4)(b) of Section 2–503.

(3) In any case not within subsection (1) or (2), the risk of loss passes to the buyer on his receipt of the goods if the seller is a merchant; otherwise, the risk passes to the buyer on tender of delivery.

(4) The provisions of this section are subject to contrary agreement of the parties and to the provisions of this Article on sale on approval (Section 2–327) and on effect of breach on risk of loss (Section 2–510).

§ 2–510. Effect of Breach on Risk of Loss

(1) Where a tender or delivery of goods so fails to conform to the contract as to give a right of rejection the risk of their loss remains on the seller until cure or acceptance.

(2) Where the buyer rightfully revokes acceptance he may to the extent of any deficiency in his effective insurance coverage treat the risk of loss as having rested on the seller from the beginning.

(3) Where the buyer as to conforming goods already identified to the contract for sale repudiates or is otherwise in breach before risk of their loss has passed to him, the seller may to the extent of any deficiency in his effective insurance coverage treat the risk of loss as resting on the buyer for a commercially reasonable time.

§ 2–511. Tender of Payment by Buyer; Payment by Check

(1)   Unless otherwise agreed tender of payment is a condition to the seller's duty to tender and complete any delivery.

(2)   Tender of payment is sufficient when made by any means or in any manner current in the ordinary course of business unless the seller demands payment in legal tender and gives any extension of time reasonably necessary to procure it.

(3)   Subject to the provisions of this Act on the effect of an instrument on an obligation (Section 3–802), payment by check is conditional and is defeated as between the parties by dishonor of the check on due presentment.

§ 2–512. Payment by Buyer Before Inspection

(1)   Where the contract requires payment before inspection non-conformity of the goods does not excuse the buyer from so making payment unless

  (a) the non-conformity appears without inspection; or
  (b) despite tender of the required documents the circumstances would justify injunction against honor under the provisions of this Act (Section 5–114).

(2)   Payment pursuant to subsection (1) does not constitute an acceptance of goods or impair the buyer's right to inspect or any of his remedies.

§ 2–513. Buyer's Right to Inspection of Goods

(1)   Unless otherwise agreed and subject to subsection (3), where goods are tendered or delivered or identified to the contract for sale, the buyer has a right before payment or acceptance to inspect them at any reasonable place and time and in any reasonable manner. When the seller is required or authorized to send the goods to the buyer, the inspection may be after their arrival.

(2)   Expenses of inspection must be borne by the buyer but may be recovered from the seller if the goods do not conform and are rejected.

(3)   Unless otherwise agreed and subject to the provisions of this Article on C.I.F. contracts (subsection (3) of Section 2–321), the buyer is not entitled to inspect the goods before payment of the price when the contract provides

  (a) for delivery "C.O.D." or on other like terms; or
  (b) for payment against documents of title, except where such payment is due only after the goods are to become available for inspection.

(4)   A place or method of inspection fixed by the parties is presumed to be exclusive but unless otherwise expressly agreed it does not postpone identification or shift the place for delivery or for passing the risk of loss. If compliance becomes impossible, inspection shall be as provided in this section unless the place or method fixed was clearly intended as an indispensable condition failure of which avoids the contract.

Part 6—Breach, Repudiation and Excuse

§ 2–601. Buyer's Rights on Improper Delivery

Subject to the provisions of this Article on breach in installment contracts (Section 2–612) and unless otherwise agreed under the sections on contractual limitations of remedy (Sections 2–718 and 2–719), if the goods or the tender of delivery fail in any respect to conform to the contract, the buyer may

  (a) reject the whole; or
  (b) accept the whole; or
  (c) accept any commercial unit or units and reject the rest.

§ 2–602. Manner and Effect of Rightful Rejection

(1)   Rejection of goods must be within a reasonable time after their delivery or tender. It is ineffective unless the buyer seasonably notifies the seller.

(2)   Subject to the provisions of the two following sections on rejected goods (Sections 2–603 and 2–604),

  (a) after rejection any exercise of ownership by the buyer with respect to any commercial unit is wrongful as against the seller; and
  (b) if the buyer has before rejection taken physical possession of goods in which he does not have a security interest under the provisions of this Article (subsection (3) of Section 2–711), he is under a duty after rejection to hold them with reasonable care at the seller's disposition for a time sufficient to permit the seller to remove them; but
  (c) the buyer has no further obligations with regard to goods rightfully rejected.

(3)   The seller's rights with respect to goods wrongfully rejected are governed by the provisions of this Article on seller's remedies in general (Section 2–703).

§ 2–603. Merchant Buyer's Duties as to Rightfully Rejected Goods

(1)   Subject to any security interest in the buyer (subsection (3) of Section 2–711), when the seller has no agent or place of business at the market of rejection a merchant buyer is under a duty after rejection of goods in his possession or control to follow any reasonable instructions received from the seller with respect to the goods and in the absence of such instructions to make reasonable efforts to sell them for the seller's account if they are perishable or threaten to decline in value speedily. Instructions are not reasonable if on demand indemnity for expenses is not forthcoming.

(2)   When the buyer sells goods under subsection (1), he is entitled to reimbursement from the seller or out of the proceeds for reasonable expenses of caring for and selling them, and if the expenses include no selling commission then to such commission as is usual in the trade or if there is none to a reasonable sum not exceeding ten per cent on the gross proceeds.

(3)   In complying with this section the buyer is held only to good faith and good faith conduct hereunder is neither acceptance nor conversion nor the basis of an action for damages.

§ 2–604. Buyer's Options as to Salvage of Rightfully Rejected Goods

Subject to the provisions of the immediately preceding section on perishables if the seller gives no instructions within a reasonable time after notification of rejection the buyer may store the rejected goods for the seller's account or reship them to him or resell them for the seller's account with reimbursement as provided in the preceding section. Such action is not acceptance or conversion.

§ 2–605. Waiver of Buyer's Objections by Failure to Particularize

(1) The buyer's failure to state in connection with rejection a particular defect which is ascertainable by reasonable inspection precludes him from relying on the unstated defect to justify rejection or to establish breach

(a) where the seller could have cured it if stated seasonably; or

(b) between merchants when the seller has after rejection made a request in writing for a full and final written statement of all defects on which the buyer proposes to rely.

(2) Payment against documents made without reservation of rights precludes recovery of the payment for defects apparent on the face of the documents.

§ 2–606. What Constitutes Acceptance of Goods

(1) Acceptance of goods occurs when the buyer

(a) after a reasonable opportunity to inspect the goods signifies to the seller that the goods are conforming or that he will take or retain them in spite of their nonconformity; or

(b) fails to make an effective rejection (subsection (1) of Section 2–602), but such acceptance does not occur until the buyer has had a reasonable opportunity to inspect them; or

(c) does any act inconsistent with the seller's ownership; but if such act is wrongful as against the seller it is an acceptance only if ratified by him.

(2) Acceptance of a part of any commercial unit is acceptance of that entire unit.

§ 2–607. Effect of Acceptance; Notice of Breach; Burden of Establishing Breach After Acceptance; Notice of Claim or Litigation to Person Answerable Over

(1) The buyer must pay at the contract rate for any goods accepted.

(2) Acceptance of goods by the buyer precludes rejection of the goods accepted and if made with knowledge of a non-conformity cannot be revoked because of it unless the acceptance was on the reasonable assumption that the non-conformity would be seasonably cured but acceptance does not of itself impair any other remedy provided by this Article for non-conformity.

(3) Where a tender has been accepted

(a) the buyer must within a reasonable time after he discovers or should have discovered any breach notify the seller of breach or be barred from any remedy; and

(b) if the claim is one for infringement or the like (subsection (3) of Section 2–312) and the buyer is sued as a result of such a breach he must so notify the seller within a reasonable time after he receives notice of the litigation or be barred from any remedy over for liability established by the litigation.

(4) The burden is on the buyer to establish any breach with respect to the goods accepted.

(5) Where the buyer is sued for breach of a warranty or other obligation for which his seller is answerable over

(a) he may give his seller written notice of the litigation. If the notice states that the seller may come in and defend and that if the seller does not do so he will be bound in any action against him by his buyer by any determination of fact common to the two litigations, then unless the seller after seasonable receipt of the notice does come in and defend he is so bound.

(b) if the claim is one for infringement or the like (subsection (3) of Section 2–312) the original seller may demand in writing that his buyer turn over to him control of the litigation including settlement or else be barred from any remedy over and if he also agrees to bear all expense and to satisfy any adverse judgment, then unless the buyer after seasonable receipt of the demand does turn over control the buyer is so barred.

(6) The provisions of subsections (3), (4) and (5) apply to any obligation of a buyer to hold the seller harmless against infringement or the like (subsection (3) of Section 2–312).

§ 2–608. Revocation of Acceptance in Whole or in Part

(1) The buyer may revoke his acceptance of a lot or commercial unit whose non-conformity substantially impairs its value to him if he has accepted it

(a) on the reasonable assumption that its non-conformity would be cured and it has not been seasonably cured; or

(b) without discovery of such non-conformity if his acceptance was reasonably induced either by the difficulty of discovery before acceptance or by the seller's assurances.

(2) Revocation of acceptance must occur within a reasonable time after the buyer discovers or should have discovered the ground for it and before any substantial change in condition of the goods which is not caused by their own defects. It is not effective until the buyer notifies the seller of it.

(3) A buyer who so revokes has the same rights and duties with regard to the goods involved as if he had rejected them.

§ 2–609. Right to Adequate Assurance of Performance

(1) A contract for sale imposes an obligation on each party that the other's expectation of receiving due performance will not be impaired. When reasonable grounds for insecurity arise with respect to the performance of either party the other may in writing demand adequate assurance of due performance and until he receives such assurance may if commercially reasonable suspend any performance for which he has not already received the agreed return.

(2) Between merchants the reasonableness of grounds for insecurity and the adequacy of any assurance offered shall be determined according to commercial standards.

(3) Acceptance of any improper delivery or payment does not prejudice the aggrieved party's right to demand adequate assurance of future performance.

(4) After receipt of a justified demand failure to provide within a reasonable time not exceeding thirty days such assurance of due performance as is adequate under the circumstances of the particular case is a repudiation of the contract.

§ 2–610. Anticipatory Repudiation

When either party repudiates the contract with respect to a performance not yet due the loss of which will substantially impair the value of the contract to the other, the aggrieved party may

(a) for a commercially reasonable time await performance by the repudiating party; or

(b) resort to any remedy for breach (Section 2–703 or Section 2–711), even though he has notified the repudiating party that he would await the latter's performance and has urged retraction; and

(c) in either case suspend his own performance or proceed in accordance with the provisions of this Article on the seller's right to identify goods to the contract notwithstanding breach or to salvage unfinished goods (Section 2–704).

§ 2–611. Retraction of Anticipatory Repudiation

(1) Until the repudiating party's next performance is due he can retract his repudiation unless the aggrieved party has since the repudiation cancelled or materially changed his position or otherwise indicated that he considers the repudiation final.

(2) Retraction may be by any method which clearly indicates to the aggrieved party that the repudiating party intends to perform, but must include any assurance justifiably demanded under the provisions of this Article (Section 2–609).

(3) Retraction reinstates the repudiating party's rights under the contract with due excuse and allowance to the aggrieved party for any delay occasioned by the repudiation.

§ 2–612. "Installment Contract"; Breach

(1) An "installment contract" is one which requires or authorizes the delivery of goods in separate lots to be separately accepted, even though the contract contains a clause "each delivery is a separate contract" or its equivalent.

(2) The buyer may reject any installment which is non-conforming if the non-conformity substantially impairs the value of that installment and cannot be cured or if the non-conformity is a defect in the required documents; but if the non-conformity does not fall within subsection (3) and the seller gives adequate assurance of its cure the buyer must accept that installment.

(3) Whenever non-conformity or default with respect to one or more installments substantially impairs the value of the whole contract there is a breach of the whole. But the aggrieved party reinstates the contract if he accepts a non-conforming installment without seasonably notifying of cancellation or if he brings an action with respect only to past installments or demands performance as to future installments.

§ 2–613. Casualty to Identified Goods

Where the contract requires for its performance goods identified when the contract is made, and the goods suffer casualty without fault of either party before the risk of loss passes to the buyer, or in a proper case under a "no arrival, no sale" term (Section 2–324) then

(a) if the loss is total the contract is avoided; and

(b) if the loss is partial or the goods have so deteriorated as no longer to conform to the contract the buyer may nevertheless demand inspection and at his option either treat the contract as avoided or accept the goods with due allowance from the contract price for the deterioration or the deficiency in quantity but without further right against the seller.

§ 2–614. Substituted Performance

(1) Where without fault of either party the agreed berthing, loading, or unloading facilities fail or an agreed type of carrier becomes unavailable or the agreed manner of delivery otherwise becomes commercially impracticable but a commercially reasonable substitute is available, such substitute performance must be tendered and accepted.

(2) If the agreed means or manner of payment fails because of domestic or foreign governmental regulation, the seller may withhold or stop delivery unless the buyer provides a means or manner of payment which is commercially a substantial equivalent. If delivery has already been taken, payment by the means or in the manner provided by the regulation discharges the buyer's obligation unless the regulation is discriminatory, oppressive or predatory.

§ 2–615. Excuse by Failure of Presupposed Conditions

Except so far as a seller may have assumed a greater obligation and subject to the preceding section on substituted performance:

(a) Delay in delivery or non-delivery in whole or in part by a seller who complies with paragraphs (b) and (c) is not a breach of his duty under a contract for sale if performance as agreed has been made impracticable by the occurrence of a contingency the non-occurrence of which was a basic assumption on which the contract was made or by compliance in good faith with any applicable foreign or domestic governmental regulation or order whether or not it later proves to be invalid.

(b) Where the causes mentioned in paragraph (a) affect only a part of the seller's capacity to perform, he must allocate production and deliveries among his customers but may at his option include regular customers not then under contract as well as his own requirements for further manufacture. He may so allocate in any manner which is fair and reasonable.

(c) The seller must notify the buyer seasonably that there will be delay or non-delivery and, when allocation is required under paragraph (b), of the estimated quota thus made available for the buyer.

§ 2–702. Seller's Remedies on Discovery of Buyer's Insolvency

(1) Where the seller discovers the buyer to be insolvent he may refuse delivery except for cash including payment for all goods theretofore delivered under the contract, and stop delivery under this Article (Section 2–705).

(2) Where the seller discovers that the buyer has received goods on credit while insolvent he may reclaim the goods upon demand made within ten days after the receipt, but if misrepresentation of solvency has been made to the particular seller in writing within three months before delivery the ten day limitation does not apply. Except as provided in this subsection the seller may not base a right to reclaim goods on the buyer's fraudulent or innocent misrepresentation of solvency or of intent to pay.

(3) The seller's right to reclaim under subsection (2) is subject to the rights of a buyer in ordinary course or other good faith purchaser under this Article (Section 2–403). Successful reclamation of goods excludes all other remedies with respect to them.

§ 2–703. Seller's Remedies in General

Where the buyer wrongfully rejects or revokes acceptance of goods or fails to make a payment due on or before delivery or repudiates with respect to a part or the whole, then with respect to any goods directly affected and, if the breach is of the whole contract (Section 2–612), then also with respect to the whole undelivered balance, the aggrieved seller may

(a) withhold delivery of such goods;

(b) stop delivery by any bailee as hereafter provided (Section 2–705);

(c) proceed under the next section respecting goods still unidentified to the contract;

(d) resell and recover damages as hereafter provided (Section 2–706);

(e) recover damages for non-acceptance (Section 2–708) or in a proper case the price (Section 2–709);

(f) cancel.

§ 2–704. Seller's Right to Identify Goods to the Contract Notwithstanding Breach or to Salvage Unfinished Goods

(1) An aggrieved seller under the preceding section may

    (a) identify to the contract conforming goods not already identified if at the time he learned of the breach they are in his possession or control;

    (b) treat as the subject of resale goods which have demonstrably been intended for the particular contract even though those goods are unfinished.

(2) Where the goods are unfinished an aggrieved seller may in the exercise of reasonable commercial judgment for the purposes of avoiding loss and of effective realization either complete the manufacture and wholly identify the goods to the contract or cease manufacture and resell for scrap or salvage value or proceed in any other reasonable manner.

§ 2–705. Seller's Stoppage of Delivery in Transit or Otherwise

(1) The seller may stop delivery of goods in the possession of a carrier or other bailee when he discovers the buyer to be insolvent (Section 2–702) and may stop delivery of carload, truckload, planeload or larger shipments of express or freight when the buyer repudiates or fails to make a payment due before delivery or if for any other reason the seller has a right to withhold or reclaim the goods.

(2) As against such buyer the seller may stop delivery until

    (a) receipt of the goods by the buyer; or

    (b) acknowledgment to the buyer by any bailee of the goods except a carrier that the bailee holds the goods for the buyer; or

    (c) such acknowledgment to the buyer by a carrier by reshipment or as warehouseman; or

    (d) negotiation to the buyer of any negotiable document of title covering the goods.

(3) (a) To stop delivery the seller must so notify as to enable the bailee by reasonable diligence to prevent delivery of the goods.

    (b) After such notification the bailee must hold and deliver the goods according to the directions of the seller but the seller is liable to the bailee for any ensuing charges or damages.

    (c) If a negotiable document of title has been issued for goods the bailee is not obliged to obey a notification to stop until surrender of the document.

    (d) A carrier who has issued a non-negotiable bill of lading is not obliged to obey a notification to stop received from a person other than the consignor.

§ 2–706. Seller's Resale Including Contract for Resale

(1) Under the conditions stated in Section 2–703 on seller's remedies, the seller may resell the goods concerned or the undelivered balance thereof. Where the resale is made in good faith and in a commercially reasonable manner the seller may recover the difference between the resale price and the contract price together with any incidental damages allowed under the provisions of this Article (Section 2–710), but less expenses saved in consequence of the buyer's breach.

(2) Except as otherwise provided in subsection (3) or unless otherwise agreed resale may be at public or private sale including sale by way of one or more contracts to sell or of identification to an existing contract of the seller. Sale may be as a unit or in parcels and at any time and place and on any terms but every aspect of the sale including the method, manner, time, place and terms must be commercially reasonable. The resale must be reasonably identified as referring to the broken contract, but it is not necessary that the goods be in existence or that any or all of them have been identified to the contract before the breach.

(3) Where the resale is at private sale the seller must give the buyer reasonable notification of his intention to resell.

(4) Where the resale is at public sale

    (a) only identified goods can be sold except where there is a recognized market for a public sale of futures in goods of the kind; and

    (b) it must be made at a usual place or market for public sale if one is reasonably available and except in the case of goods which are perishable or threaten to decline in value speedily the seller must give the buyer reasonable notice of the time and place of the resale; and

    (c) if the goods are not to be within the view of those attending the sale the notification of sale must state the place where the goods are located and provide for their reasonable inspection by prospective bidders; and

    (d) the seller may buy.

(5) A purchaser who buys in good faith at a resale takes the goods free of any rights of the original buyer even though the seller fails to comply with one or more of the requirements of this section.

(6) The seller is not accountable to the buyer for any profit made on any resale. A person in the position of a seller (Section 2–707) or a buyer who has rightfully rejected or justifiably revoked acceptance must account for any excess over the amount of his security interest, as hereinafter defined (subsection (3) of Section 2–711).

§ 2–707. "Person in the Position of a Seller"

(1) A "person in the position of a seller" includes as against a principal an agent who has paid or become responsible for the price of goods on behalf of his principal or anyone who otherwise holds a security interest or other right in goods similar to that of a seller.

(2) A person in the position of a seller may as provided in this Article withhold or stop delivery (Section 2–705) and resell (Section 2–706) and recover incidental damages (Section 2–710).

§ 2–708. Seller's Damages for Non-Acceptance or Repudiation

(1) Subject to subsection (2) and to the provisions of this Article with respect to proof of market price (Section 2–723), the measure of damages for non-acceptance or repudiation by the buyer is the difference between the market price at the time and place for tender and the unpaid contract price together with any incidental damages provided in this Article (Section 2–710), but less expenses saved in consequence of the buyer's breach.

(2) If the measure of damages provided in subsection (1) is inadequate to put the seller in as good a position as performance would have done then the measure of damages is the profit (including reasonable overhead) which the seller would have made from full performance by the buyer, together with any incidental damages provided in this Article (Section 2–710), due allowance for costs reasonably incurred and due credit for payments or proceeds of resale.

§ 2–709. Action for the Price

(1) When the buyer fails to pay the price as it becomes due the seller may recover, together with any incidental damages under the next section, the price

(a) of goods accepted or of conforming goods lost or damaged within a commercially reasonable time after risk of their loss has passed to the buyer; and

(b) of goods identified to the contract if the seller is unable after reasonable effort to resell them at a reasonable price or the circumstances reasonably indicate that such effort will be unavailing.

(2) Where the seller sues for the price he must hold for the buyer any goods which have been identified to the contract and are still in his control except that if resale becomes possible he may resell them at any time prior to the collection of the judgment. The net proceeds of any such resale must be credited to the buyer and payment of the judgment entitles him to any goods not resold.

(3) After the buyer has wrongfully rejected or revoked acceptance of the goods or has failed to make a payment due or has repudiated (Section 2–610), a seller who is held not entitled to the price under this section shall nevertheless be awarded damages for non-acceptance under the preceding section.

§ 2–710. Seller's Incidental Damages

Incidental damages to an aggrieved seller include any commercially reasonable charges, expenses or commissions incurred in stopping delivery, in the transportation, care and custody of goods after the buyer's breach, in connection with return or resale of the goods or otherwise resulting from the breach.

§ 2–711. Buyer's Remedies in General; Buyer's Security Interest in Rejected Goods

(1) Where the seller fails to make delivery or repudiates or the buyer rightfully rejects or justifiably revokes acceptance then with respect to any goods involved, and with respect to the whole if the breach goes to the whole contract (Section 2–612), the buyer may cancel and whether or not he has done so may in addition to recovering so much of the price as has been paid

(a) "cover" and have damages under the next section as to all the goods affected whether or not they have been identified to the contract; or

(b) recover damages for non-delivery as provided in this Article (Section 2–713).

(2) Where the seller fails to deliver or repudiates the buyer may also

(a) if the goods have been identified recover them as provided in this Article (Section 2–502); or

(b) in a proper case obtain specific performance or replevy the goods as provided in this Article (Section 2–716).

(3) On rightful rejection or justifiable revocation of acceptance a buyer has a security interest in goods in his possession or control for any payments made on their price and any expenses reasonably incurred in their inspection, receipt, transportation, care and custody and may hold such goods and resell them in like manner as an aggrieved seller (Section 2–706).

§ 2–712. "Cover"; Buyer's Procurement of Substitute Goods

(1) After a breach within the preceding section the buyer may "cover" by making in good faith and without unreasonable delay any reasonable purchase of or contract to purchase goods in substitution for those due from the seller.

(2) The buyer may recover from the seller as damages the difference between the cost of cover and the contract price together with any incidental or consequential damages as hereinafter defined (Section 2–715), but less expenses saved in consequence of the seller's breach.

(3) Failure of the buyer to effect cover within this section does not bar him from any other remedy.

§ 2–713. Buyer's Damages for Non-Delivery or Repudiation

(1) Subject to provisions of this Article with respect to the proof of market price (Section 2–723), the measure of damages for non-delivery or repudiation by the seller is the difference between the market price at the time when the buyer learned of the breach and the contract price together with any incidental and consequential damages provided in this Article (Section 2–715), but less expenses saved in consequence of the seller's breach.

(2) Market price is to be determined as of the place for tender or, in cases of rejection after arrival or revocation of acceptance, as of the place of arrival.

§ 2–714. Buyer's Damages for Breach in Regard to Accepted Goods

(1) Where the buyer has accepted goods and given notification (subsection (3) of Section 2–607) he may recover as damages for any non-conformity of tender the loss resulting in the ordinary course of events from the seller's breach as determined in any manner which is reasonable.

(2) The measure of damages for breach of warranty is the difference at the time and place of acceptance between the value of the goods accepted and the value they would have had if they had been as warranted, unless special circumstances show proximate damages of a different amount.

(3) In a proper case any incidental and consequential damages under the next section may be recovered.

§ 2–715. Buyer's Incidental and Consequential Damages

(1) Incidental damages resulting from the seller's breach include expenses reasonably incurred in inspection, receipt, transportation and care and custody of goods rightfully rejected, any commercially reasonable charges, expenses or commissions in connection with effecting cover and any other reasonable expense incident to the delay or other breach.

(2) Consequential damages resulting from the seller's breach include

(a) any loss resulting from general or particular requirements and needs of which the seller at the time of contracting had reason to know and which could not reasonably be prevented by cover or otherwise; and

(b) injury to person or property proximately resulting from any breach of warranty.

§ 2–716. Buyer's Right to Specific Performance or Replevin

(1) Specific performance may be decreed where the goods are unique or in other proper circumstances.

(2) The decree for specific performance may include such terms and conditions as to payment of the price, damages, or other relief as the court may deem just.

(3) The buyer has a right of replevin for goods identified to the contract if after reasonable effort he is unable to effect cover for such goods or the circumstances reasonably indicate that such effort will be unavailing or if the goods have been shipped under reservation and satisfaction of the security interest in them has been made or tendered.

§ 2–717. Deduction of Damages From the Price

The buyer on notifying the seller of his intention to do so may deduct all or any part of the damages resulting from any breach of the contract from any part of the price still due under the same contract.

§ 2–718. Liquidation or Limitation of Damages; Deposits

(1) Damages for breach by either party may be liquidated in the agreement but only at an amount which is reasonable in the light of the anticipated or actual harm caused by the breach, the difficulties of proof of loss, and the inconvenience or nonfeasibility of otherwise obtaining an adequate remedy. A term fixing unreasonably large liquidated damages is void as a penalty.

(2) Where the seller justifiably withholds delivery of goods because of the buyer's breach, the buyer is entitled to restitution of any amount by which the sum of his payments exceeds

(a) the amount to which the seller is entitled by virtue of terms liquidating the seller's damages in accordance with subsection (1), or

(b) in the absence of such terms, twenty per cent of the value of the total performance for which the buyer is obligated under the contract or $500, whichever is smaller.

(3) The buyer's right to restitution under subsection (2) is subject to offset to the extent that the seller establishes

(a) a right to recover damages under the provisions of this Article other than subsection (1), and

(b) the amount or value of any benefits received by the buyer directly or indirectly by reason of the contract.

(4) Where a seller has received payment in goods their reasonable value or the proceeds of their resale shall be treated as payments for the purposes of subsection (2); but if the seller has notice of the buyer's breach before reselling goods received in part performance, his resale is subject to the conditions laid down in this Article on resale by an aggrieved seller (Section 2–706).

§ 2–719. Contractual Modification or Limitation of Remedy

(1) Subject to the provisions of subsections (2) and (3) of this section and of the preceding section on liquidation and limitation of damages,

(a) the agreement may provide for remedies in addition to or in substitution for those provided in this Article and may limit or alter the measure of damages recoverable under this Article, as by limiting the buyer's remedies to return of the goods and repayment of the price or to repair and replacement of non-conforming goods or parts; and

(b) resort to a remedy as provided is optional unless the remedy is expressly agreed to be exclusive, in which case it is the sole remedy.

(2) Where circumstances cause an exclusive or limited remedy to fail of its essential purpose, remedy may be had as provided in this Act.

(3) Consequential damages may be limited or excluded unless the limitation or exclusion is unconscionable. Limitation of consequential damages for injury to the person in the case of consumer goods is prima facie unconscionable but limitation of damages where the loss is commercial is not.

§ 2–721. Remedies for Fraud

Remedies for material misrepresentation or fraud include all remedies available under this Article for non-fraudulent breach. Neither rescission or a claim for rescission of the contract for sale nor rejection or return of the goods shall bar or be deemed inconsistent with a claim for damages or other remedy.

§ 2–725. Statute of Limitations in Contracts for Sale

(1) An action for breach of any contract for sale must be commenced within four years after the cause of action has accrued. By the original agreement the parties may reduce the period of limitation to not less than one year but may not extend it.

(2) A cause of action occurs when the breach occurs, regardless of the aggrieved party's lack of knowledge of the breach. A breach of warranty occurs when tender of delivery is made, except that where a warranty explicitly extends to future performance of the goods and discovery of the breach must await the time of such performance the cause of action accrues when the breach is or should have been discovered.

(3) Where an action commenced within the time limited by subsection (1) is so terminated as to leave available a remedy by another action for the same breach such other action may be commenced after the expiration of the time limited and within six months after the termination of the first action unless the termination resulted from voluntary discontinuance or from dismissal for failure or neglect to prosecute.

(4) This section does not alter the law on tolling of the statute of limitations nor does it apply to causes of action which have accrued before this Act becomes effective.

[REVISED] ARTICLE 3: NEGOTIABLE INSTRUMENTS

Part 1—General Provisions and Definitions

§ 3–101. Short Title

This Article may be cited as Uniform Commercial Code—Negotiable Instruments.

§ 3–102. Subject Matter

(a) This Article applies to negotiable instruments. It does not apply to money or to payment orders governed by Article 4A. A negotiable instrument that is also a certificated security under Section 8–102(1)(a) is subject to Article 8 and to this Article.

(b) In the event of conflict between the provisions of this Article and those of Article 4, Article 8, or Article 9, the provisions of Article 4, Article 8 and Article 9 prevail over those of this Article.

(c) Regulations of the Board of Governors of the Federal Reserve System and operating circulars of the Federal Reserve Banks supersede any inconsistent provision of this Article to the extent of the inconsistency.

§ 3–103. Definitions

(a) In this Article:

(1) "Acceptor" means a drawee that has accepted a draft.

(2) "Drawee" means a person ordered in a draft to make payment.

(3) "Drawer" means a person that signs a draft as a person ordering payment.

(4) "Good faith" means honesty in fact and the observance of reasonable commercial standards of fair dealing.

(5) "Maker" means a person that signs a note as promisor of payment.

(6) "Order" means a written instruction to pay money signed by the person giving the instruction. The instruction may be addressed to any person, including the person giving the instruction, or to one or more persons jointly or in the alternative but not in succession. An authorization to pay is not an order unless the person authorized to pay is also instructed to pay.

(7) "Ordinary care" in the case of a person engaged in business means observance of reasonable commercial standards, prevailing in the area in which that person is located, with respect to the business in which that person is engaged. In the case of a bank that takes an instrument for processing for collection or payment by automated means, reasonable commercial standards do not require the bank to examine the instrument if the failure to examine does not violate the bank's prescribed procedures and the bank's procedures do not vary unreasonably from general banking usage not disapproved by this Article or Article 4.

(8) "Party" means party to an instrument.

(9) "Promise" means a written undertaking to pay money signed by the person undertaking to pay. An acknowledgment of an obligation by the obligor is not a promise unless the obligor also undertakes to pay the obligation.

(10) "Prove" with respect to a fact means to meet the burden of establishing the fact (Section 1–201(8)).

(11) "Remitter" means a person that purchases an instrument from its issuer if the instrument is payable to an identified person other than the purchaser.

(b) Other definitions applying to this Article and the sections in which they appear are:

"Acceptance" Section 3–409.
"Accommodated party" Section 3–419.
"Accommodation indorsement" Section 3–205.
"Accommodation party" Section 3–419.
"Alteration" Section 3–407.
"Blank indorsement" Section 3–205.
"Cashier's check" Section 3–104.
"Certificate of deposit" Section 3–104.
"Certified check" Section 3–409.
"Check" Section 3–104.
"Consideration" Section 3–303.
"Draft" Section 3–104.
"Fiduciary" Section 3–307.
"Guarantor" Section 3–417.
"Holder in due course" Section 3–302.
"Incomplete instrument" Section 3–115.
"Indorsement" Section 3–204.
"Indorser" Section 3–204.
"Instrument" Section 3–104.
"Issue" Section 3–105.
"Issuer" Section 3–105.
"Negotiable instrument" Section 3–104.
"Negotiation" Section 3–201.
"Note" Section 3–104.
"Payable at a definite time" Section 3–108.
"Payable on demand" Section 3–108.
"Payable to bearer" Section 3–109.
"Payable to order" Section 3–110.
"Payment" Section 3–603.
"Person entitled to enforce" Section 3–301.
"Presentment" Section 3–501.
"Reacquisition" Section 3–207.
"Represented person" Section 3–307.
"Special indorsement" Section 3–205.
"Teller's check" Section 3–104.
"Traveler's check" Section 3–104.
"Value" Section 3–303.

(c) The following definitions in other Articles apply to this Article:

"Bank" Section 4–105.
"Banking day" Section 4–104.
"Clearing house" Section 4–104.
"Collecting bank" Section 4–105.
"Customer" Section 4–104.
"Depositary bank" Section 4–105.
"Documentary draft" Section 4–104.
"Intermediary bank" Section 4–105.
"Item" Section 4–104.
"Midnight deadline" Section 4–104.
"Payor bank" Section 4–105.
"Suspends payments" Section 4–104.

(d) In addition, Article 1 contains general definitions and principles of construction and interpretation applicable throughout this Article.

§ 3–104. Negotiable Instrument

(a) "Negotiable instrument" means an unconditional promise or order to pay a fixed amount of money, with or without interest or other charges described in the promise or order, if it:

(1) is payable to bearer or to order at the time it is issued or first comes into possession of a holder;

(2) is payable on demand or at a definite time; and

(3) does not state any other undertaking or instruction by the person promising or ordering payment to do any act in addition to the payment of money except that the promise or order may contain (i) an undertaking or power to give, maintain, or protect collateral to secure payment, (ii) an authorization or power to the holder to confess judgment or realize on or dispose of collateral, or (iii) a waiver of the benefit of any law intended for the advantage or protection of any obligor.

(b) "Instrument" means negotiable instrument.

(c) An order that meets all of the requirements of subsection (a) except subparagraph (1) and otherwise falls within the definition of "check" in subsection (f) is a negotiable instrument and a check.

(d) Notwithstanding subsection (a), a promise or order other than a check is not an instrument if, at the time it is issued or first comes into possession of a holder, it contains a conspicuous statement, however expressed, indicating that the writing is not an instrument governed by this Article.

(e) An instrument is a "note" if it is a promise, and is a "draft" if it is an order. If an instrument falls within the definition of both "note" and "draft," the person entitled to enforce the instrument may treat it as either.

(f) "Check" means (i) a draft, other than a documentary draft, payable on demand and drawn on a bank or (ii) a cashier's check or teller's check. An instrument may be a check even though it is described on its face by another term such as "money order."

(g) "Cashier's check" means a draft with respect to which the drawer and drawee are the same bank or branches of the same bank.

(h) "Teller's check" means a draft drawn by a bank (i) on another bank, or (ii) payable at or through a bank.

(i) "Traveler's check" means an instrument that (i) is payable on demand, (ii) is drawn on or payable at or through a bank, (iii) is designated by the term "traveler's check" or by a substantially similar term, and (iv) requires, as a condition to payment, a countersignature by a person whose specimen signature appears on the instrument.

(j) "Certificate of deposit" means an instrument containing an acknowledgment by a bank that a sum of money has been received by the bank, and a promise by the bank to repay the sum of money. A certificate of deposit is a note of the bank.

§ 3–105. Issue of Instrument

(a) "Issue" means the first delivery of an instrument by the maker or drawer, whether to a holder or nonholder, for the purpose of giving rights on the instrument to any person.

(b) An unissued instrument, or an unissued incomplete instrument (Section 3–115) that is completed, is binding on the maker or drawer, but nonissuance is a defense. An instrument that is conditionally issued or is issued for a special purpose is binding on the maker or drawer, but failure of the condition or special purpose to be fulfilled is a defense.

(c) "Issuer" applies to issued and unissued instruments and means any person that signs an instrument as maker or drawer.

§ 3–106. Unconditional Promise or Order

(a) Except as provided in subsections (b) and (c), for the purposes of Section 3–104(a), a promise or order is unconditional unless it states (i) an express condition to payment or (ii) that the promise or order is subject to or governed by another writing, or that rights or obligations with respect to the promise or order are stated in another writing; however, a mere reference to another writing does not make the promise or order conditional.

(b) A promise or order is not made conditional (i) by a reference to another writing for a statement of rights with respect to collateral, prepayment, or acceleration, or (ii) because payment is limited to resort to a particular fund or source.

(c) If a promise or order requires, as a condition to payment, a countersignature by a person whose specimen signature appears on the promise or order, the condition does not make the promise or order conditional for the purposes of Section 3–104(a). If the person whose specimen signature appears on an instrument fails to countersign the instrument, the failure to countersign is a defense to the obligation of the issuer, but the failure does not prevent a transferee of the instrument from becoming a holder of the instrument.

(d) If a promise or order at the time it is issued or first comes into possession of a holder contains a statement, required by applicable statutory or administrative law, to the effect that the rights of a holder or transferee are subject to claims or defenses that the issuer could assert against the original payee, the promise or order is not thereby made conditional for the purposes of Section 3–104(a), but there cannot be a holder in due course of the promise or order.

§ 3–107. Instrument Payable in Foreign Money

Unless the instrument otherwise provides, an instrument that states the amount payable in foreign money may be paid in the foreign money or in an equivalent amount in dollars calculated by using the current bank-offered spot rate at the place of payment for the purchase of dollars on the day on which the instrument is paid.

§ 3–108. Payable on Demand or at a Definite Time

(a) A promise or order is "payable on demand" if (i) it states that it is payable on demand or at sight, or otherwise indicates that it is payable at the will of the holder, or (ii) it does not state any time of payment.

(b) A promise or order is "payable at a definite time" if it is payable on elapse of a definite period of time after sight or acceptance or at a fixed date or dates or at a time or times readily ascertainable at the time the promise or order is issued, subject to rights of (i) prepayment, (ii) acceleration, or (iii) extension at the option of the holder or (iv) extension to a further definite time at the option of the maker or acceptor or automatically upon or after a specified act or event.

(c) If an instrument, payable at a fixed date, is also payable upon demand made before the fixed date, the instrument is payable on demand until the fixed date and, if demand for payment is not made before that date, becomes payable at a definite time on the fixed date.

§ 3–109. Payable to Bearer or to Order

(a) A promise or order is payable to bearer if it:

(1) states that it is payable to bearer or to the order of bearer or otherwise indicates that the person in possession of the promise or order is entitled to payment,

(2) does not state a payee, or

(3) states that it is payable to or to the order of cash or otherwise indicates that it is not payable to an identified person.

(b) A promise or order that is not payable to bearer is payable to order if it is payable (i) to the order of an identified person or (ii) to an identified person or order. A promise or order that is payable to order is payable to the identified person.

(c) An instrument payable to bearer may become payable to an identified person if it is specially indorsed as stated in Section 3–205(a). An instrument payable to an identified person may become payable to bearer if it is indorsed in blank as stated in Section 3–205(b).

§ 3–110. Identification of Person to Whom Instrument Is Payable

(a) A person to whom an instrument is payable is determined by the intent of the person, whether or not authorized, signing as, or in the name or behalf of, the maker or drawer. The instrument is payable to the person intended by the signer even if that person is identified in the instrument by a name or other identification that is not that of the intended person. If more than one person signs in the name or behalf of the maker or drawer and all the signers do not intend the same person as payee, the instrument is payable to any person intended by one or more of the signers.

(b) If the signature of the maker or drawer of an instrument is made by automated means such as a check-writing machine, the payee of the instrument is determined by the intent of the person who supplied the name or identification of the payee, whether or not authorized to do so.

(c) A person to whom an instrument is payable may be identified in any way including by name, identifying number, office, or account number. For the purpose of determining the holder of an instrument, the following rules apply:

(1) If an instrument is payable to an account and the account is identified only by number, the instrument is payable to the person to whom the account is payable. If an instrument is payable to an account identified by number and by the name of a person, the instrument is payable to the named person, whether or not that person is the owner of the account identified by number.

(2) If an instrument is payable to:

(i) a trust, estate, or a person described as trustee or representative of a trust or estate, the instrument is payable to the trustee, the representative, or a successor of either, whether or not the beneficiary or estate is also named;

(ii) a person described as agent or similar representative of a named or identified person, the instrument is payable either to the represented person, the representative, or a successor of the representative;

(iii) a fund or organization that is not a legal entity, the instrument is payable to a representative of the members of the fund or organization; or

(iv) an office or to a person described as holding an office, the instrument is payable to the named person, the incumbent of the office, or a successor to the incumbent.

(d) If an instrument is payable to two or more persons alternatively, it is payable to any of them and may be negotiated, discharged, or enforced by any of them in possession of the instrument. If an instrument is payable to two or more persons not alternatively, it is payable to all of them and may be negotiated, discharged, or enforced only by all of them. If an instrument payable to two or more persons is ambiguous as to whether it is payable to the persons alternatively, the instrument is payable to the persons alternatively.

§ 3–111. Place of Payment

Except as otherwise provided for items in Article 4, an instrument is payable at the place of payment stated in the instrument. If no place of payment is stated, an instrument is payable at the address of the drawee or maker stated in the instrument. If no address is stated, the place of payment is the place of business of the drawee or maker. If a drawee or maker has more than one place of business, the place of payment is any place of business of the drawee or maker chosen by the person entitled to enforce the instrument. If the drawee or maker has no place of business, the place of payment is the residence of the drawee or maker.

§ 3–112. Interest

(a) Unless otherwise provided in the instrument, (i) an instrument is not payable with interest, and (ii) interest on an interest-bearing instrument is payable from the date of the instrument.

(b) Interest may be stated in an instrument as a fixed or variable amount of money or it may be expressed as a fixed or variable rate or rates. The amount or rate of interest may be stated or described in the instrument in any manner and may require reference to information not contained in the instrument. If an instrument provides for interest but the amount of interest payable cannot be ascertained from the description, interest is payable at the judgment rate in effect at the place of payment of the instrument and at the time interest first accrues.

§ 3–113. Date of Instrument

(a) An instrument may be antedated or postdated. The date stated determines the time of payment if the instrument is payable at a fixed period after date. Except as provided in Section 4–401(3), an instrument payable on demand is not payable before the date of the instrument.

(b) If an instrument is undated, its date is the date of its issue or, in the case of an unissued instrument, the date it first comes into possession of a holder.

§ 3–114. Contradictory Terms of Instrument

If an instrument contains contradictory terms, typewritten terms prevail over printed terms, handwritten terms prevail over both, and words prevail over numbers.

§ 3–115. Incomplete Instrument

(a) "Incomplete instrument" means a signed writing, whether or not issued by the signer, the contents of which show at the time of signing that it is incomplete but that the signer intended it to be completed by the addition of words or numbers.

(b)   Subject to subsection (c), if an incomplete instrument is an instrument under Section 3–104, it may be enforced (i) according to its terms if it is not completed, or (ii) according to its terms as augmented by completion. If an incomplete instrument is not an instrument under Section 3–104 but, after completion, the requirements of Section 3–104 are met, the instrument may be enforced according to its terms as augmented by completion.

(c)   If words or numbers are added to an incomplete instrument without authority of the signer, there is an alteration of the incomplete instrument governed by Section 3–407.

(d)   The burden of establishing that words or numbers were added to an incomplete instrument without authority of the signer is on the person asserting the lack of authority.

§ 3–116. Joint and Several Liability; Contribution

(a)   Except as otherwise provided in the instrument, two or more persons who have the same liability on an instrument as makers, drawers, acceptors, indorsers who are indorsing joint payees, or anomalous indorsers, are jointly and severally liable in the capacity in which they sign.

(b)   Except as provided in Section 3–417(e) or by agreement of the affected parties, a party with joint and several liability that pays the instrument is entitled to receive from any party with the same joint and several liability contribution in accordance with applicable law.

(c)   Discharge of one party with joint and several liability by a person entitled to enforce the instrument does not affect the right under subsection (b) of a party with the same joint and several liability to receive contribution from the party discharged.

§ 3–117. Other Agreements Affecting an Instrument

Subject to applicable law regarding exclusion of proof of contemporaneous or prior agreements, the obligation of a party to an instrument to pay the instrument may be modified, supplemented, or nullified by a separate agreement of the obligor and a person entitled to enforce the instrument if the instrument is issued or the obligation is incurred in reliance on the agreement or as part of the same transaction giving rise to the agreement. To the extent an obligation is modified, supplemented, or nullified by an agreement under this section, the agreement is a defense to the obligation.

§ 3–118. Statute of Limitations

(a)   Except as provided in subsection (e), an action to enforce the obligation of a party to pay a note payable at a definite time must be commenced within six years after the payment date or dates stated in the note or, if a payment date is accelerated, within six years after the accelerated payment date.

(b)   Except as provided in subsection (d) or (e), if demand for payment is made to the maker of a note payable on demand, an action to enforce the obligation of a party to pay the note must be commenced within six years after the demand. If no demand for payment is made to the maker, an action to enforce the note is barred if neither principal nor interest on the note has been paid for a continuous period of 10 years.

(c)   Except as provided in subsection (d), an action to enforce the obligation of a party to an unaccepted draft to pay the draft must be commenced within six years after dishonor of the draft or 10 years after the date of the draft, whichever period expires first.

(d)   An action to enforce the obligation of the acceptor of a certified check or the issuer of a teller's check, cashier's check, or traveler's check must be commenced within six years after demand for payment is made to the acceptor or issuer, as the case may be.

(e)   An action to enforce the obligation of a party to a certificate of deposit to pay the instrument must be commenced within six years after demand for payment is made to the maker, but if the instrument states a maturity date and the maker is not required to pay before that date, the six-year period begins when a demand for payment is in effect and the maturity date has passed.

(f)   This subsection applies to an action to enforce the obligation of a party to pay an accepted draft, other than a certified check. If the obligation of the acceptor is payable at a definite time, the action must be commenced within six years after the payment date or dates stated in the draft or acceptance. If the obligation of the acceptor is payable on demand, the action must be commenced within six years after the date of the acceptance.

(g)   Unless governed by other law regarding claims for indemnity or contribution, an action (i) for conversion of an instrument, for money had and received, or like action based on conversion, (ii) for breach of warranty, or (iii) to enforce an obligation, duty, or right arising under this Article and not governed by this section must be commenced within three years after the cause of action accrues.

§ 3–119. Notice of Right to Defend Action

In an action for breach of an obligation for which a third person is answerable over pursuant to this Article or Article 4, the defendant may give the third person written notice of the litigation, and the person notified may then give similar notice to any other person who is answerable over. If the notice states (i) that the person notified may come in and defend and (ii) that failure to do so will bind the person notified in an action later brought by the person giving the notice as to any determination of fact common to the two litigations, the person notified is so bound unless after seasonable receipt of the notice the person notified does come in and defend.

Part 2—Negotiation, Transfer and Indorsement

§ 3–201. Negotiation

(a)   "Negotiation" means a transfer of possession, whether voluntary or involuntary, of an instrument to a person who thereby becomes its holder if possession is obtained from a person other than the issuer of the instrument.

(b)   Except for a negotiation by a remitter, if an instrument is payable to an identified person, negotiation requires transfer of possession of the instrument and its indorsement by the holder. If an instrument is payable to bearer, it may be negotiated by transfer of possession alone.

§ 3–202. Negotiation Subject to Rescission

(a) Negotiation is effective even if obtained (i) from an infant, a corporation exceeding its powers, or a person without capacity, or (ii) by fraud, duress, or mistake, or in breach of duty or as part of an illegal transaction.

(b) To the extent permitted by law, negotiation may be rescinded or may be subject to other remedies, but those remedies may not be asserted against a subsequent holder in due course or a person paying the instrument in good faith and without knowledge of facts that are a basis for rescission or other remedy.

§ 3–203. Rights Acquired by Transfer

(a) An instrument is transferred when it is delivered by a person other than its issuer for the purpose of giving to the person receiving delivery the right to enforce the instrument.

(b) Transfer of an instrument, regardless of whether the transfer is a negotiation, vests in the transferee any right of the transferor to enforce the instrument, including any right as a holder in due course, but the transferee cannot acquire rights of a holder in due course by a transfer, directly or indirectly, from a holder in due course if the purchaser engaged in fraud or illegality affecting the instrument.

(c) Unless otherwise agreed, if an instrument is transferred for value and the transferee does not become a holder because of lack of indorsement by the transferor, the transferee has a specifically enforceable right to the unqualified indorsement of the transferor, but negotiation of the instrument does not occur until the indorsement is made.

(d) If a transferor purports to transfer less than the entire instrument, negotiation of the instrument does not occur. The transferee obtains no rights under this Article and has only the rights of a partial assignee.

§ 3–204. Indorsement

(a) "Indorsement" means a signature, other than that of a maker, drawer, or acceptor, that alone or accompanied by other words, is made on an instrument for the purpose of (i) negotiating the instrument, (ii) restricting payment of the instrument, or (iii) incurring indorser's liability on the instrument, but regardless of the intent of the signer, a signature and its accompanying words is an indorsement unless the accompanying words, the terms of the instrument, the place of the signature, or other circumstances unambiguously indicate that the signature was made for a purpose other than indorsement. For the purpose of determining whether a signature is made on an instrument, a paper affixed to the instrument is a part of the instrument.

(b) "Indorser" means a person who makes an indorsement.

(c) For the purpose of determining whether the transferee of an instrument is a holder, an indorsement that transfers a security interest in the instrument is effective as an unqualified indorsement of the instrument.

(d) If an instrument is payable to a holder under a name that is not the name of the holder, indorsement may be made by the holder in the name stated in the instrument or in the holder's name or both, but signature in both names may be required by a person paying or taking the instrument for value or collection.

§ 3–205. Special Indorsement; Blank Indorsement; Anomalous Indorsement

(a) If an indorsement is made by the holder of an instrument, whether payable to an identified person or payable to bearer, and the indorsement identifies a person to whom it makes the instrument payable, it is a "special indorsement." When specially indorsed, an instrument becomes payable to the identified person and may be negotiated only by the indorsement of that person. The principles stated in Section 3–110 apply to special indorsements.

(b) If an indorsement is made by the holder of an instrument and it is not a special indorsement, it is a "blank indorsement." When indorsed in blank, an instrument becomes payable to bearer and may be negotiated by transfer of possession alone until specially indorsed.

(c) The holder may convert a blank indorsement that consists only of a signature into a special indorsement by writing, above the signature of the indorser, words identifying the person to whom the instrument is made payable.

(d) "Anomalous indorsement" means an indorsement made by a person that is not the holder of the instrument. An anomalous indorsement does not affect the manner in which the instrument may be negotiated.

§ 3–206. Restrictive Indorsement

(a) An indorsement limiting payment to a particular person or otherwise prohibiting further transfer or negotiation of the instrument is not effective to prevent further transfer or negotiation of the instrument.

(b) An indorsement stating a condition to the right of the indorsee to receive payment does not affect the right of the indorsee to enforce the instrument. A person paying the instrument or taking it for value or collection may disregard the condition, and the rights and liabilities of that person are not affected by whether the condition has been fulfilled.

(c) The following rules apply to an instrument bearing an indorsement (i) described in Section 4–201(2), or (ii) in blank or to a particular bank using the words "for deposit," "for collection," or other words indicating a purpose of having the instrument collected for the indorser or for a particular account:

   (1) A person, other than a bank, that purchases the instrument when so indorsed converts the instrument unless the proceeds of the instrument are received by the indorser or are applied consistently with the indorsement.

   (2) A depositary bank that purchases the instrument or takes it for collection when so indorsed converts the instrument unless the proceeds of the instrument are received by the indorser or applied consistently with the indorsement.

   (3) A payor bank that is also the depositary bank or that takes the instrument for immediate payment over the counter from a person other than a collecting bank converts the instrument unless the proceeds of the instrument are received by the indorser or applied consistently with the indorsement.

   (4) Except as otherwise provided in paragraph (3), a payor bank or intermediary bank may disregard the indorsement and is not liable if the proceeds of the instrument are not received by the indorser or applied consistently with the indorsement.

(d) Except for an indorsement covered by subsection (c), the following rules apply to an instrument bearing an indorsement using words to the effect that payment is to be made to the indorsee as agent, trustee, or other fiduciary for the benefit of the indorser or another person:

(1) Unless there is notice of breach of fiduciary duty as provided in Section 3–307, a person that purchases the instrument from the indorsee or takes the instrument from the indorsee for collection or payment may pay the proceeds of payment or the value given for the instrument to the indorsee without regard to whether the indorsee violates a fiduciary duty to the indorser.

(2) A later transferee of the instrument or person that pays the instrument is neither given notice nor otherwise affected by the restriction in the indorsement unless the transferee or payor knows that the fiduciary dealt with the instrument or its proceeds in breach of fiduciary duty.

(e) Purchase of an instrument bearing an indorsement to which this section applies does not prevent the purchaser from becoming a holder in due course of the instrument unless the purchaser is a converter under subsection (c).

(f) In an action to enforce the obligation of a party to pay the instrument, the obligor has a defense if payment would violate an indorsement to which this section applies and the payment is not permitted by this section.

§ 3–207. Reacquisition

Reacquisition of an instrument occurs if it is transferred, by negotiation or otherwise, to a former holder. A former holder that reacquires the instrument may cancel indorsements made after the reacquirer first became a holder of the instrument. If the cancellation causes the instrument to be payable to the reacquirer or to bearer, the reacquirer may negotiate the instrument. An indorser whose indorsement is canceled is discharged, and the discharge is effective against any later holder.

Part 3—Enforcement of Instruments

§ 3–301. Person Entitled to Enforce Instrument

"Person entitled to enforce" an instrument means (i) the holder of the instrument, (ii) a nonholder in possession of the instrument who has the rights of a holder, or (iii) a person not in possession of the instrument who is entitled to enforce the instrument pursuant to Section 3–309. A person may be a person entitled to enforce the instrument even though the person is not the owner of the instrument or is in wrongful possession of the instrument.

§ 3–302. Holder in Due Course

(a) Subject to subsection (c) and Section 3–106(d), "holder in due course" means the holder of an instrument if:

(1) the instrument when issued or negotiated to the holder does not bear such apparent evidence of forgery or alteration or is not otherwise so irregular or incomplete as to call into question its authenticity, and

(2) the holder took the instrument (i) for value, (ii) in good faith, (iii) without notice that the instrument is overdue or has been dishonored or that there is an uncured default with respect to payment of another instrument issued as

part of the same series, (iv) without notice that the instrument contains an unauthorized signature or has been altered, (v) without notice of any claim to the instrument stated in Section 3–306, and (vi) without notice that any party to the instrument has any defense or claim in recoupment stated in Section 3–305(a).

(b) Notice of discharge of a party to the instrument, other than discharge in an insolvency proceeding, is not notice of a defense under subsection (a), but discharge is effective against a person who became a holder in due course with notice of the discharge. Public filing or recording of a document does not of itself constitute notice of a defense, claim in recoupment, or claim to the instrument.

(c) Except to the extent a transferor or predecessor in interest has rights as a holder in due course, a person does not acquire rights of a holder in due course of an instrument taken (i) by legal process or by purchase at an execution, bankruptcy, or creditor's sale or similar proceeding, (ii) by purchase as part of a bulk transaction not in ordinary course of business of the transferor, or (iii) as the successor in interest to an estate or other organization.

(d) If, under Section 3–303(a)(1), the promise of performance that is the consideration for an instrument has been partially performed, the holder may assert rights as a holder in due course of the instrument only to the fraction of the amount payable under the instrument equal to the value of the partial performance divided by the value of the promised performance.

(e) If (i) the person entitled to enforce an instrument has only a security interest in the instrument and (ii) the person obliged to pay the instrument has a defense, claim in recoupment or claim to the instrument that may be asserted against the person who granted the security interest, the person entitled to enforce the instrument may assert rights as a holder in due course only to an amount payable under the instrument which, at the time of enforcement of the instrument, does not exceed the amount of the unpaid obligation secured.

(f) To be effective, notice must be received at such time and in such manner as to give a reasonable opportunity to act on it.

(g) This section is subject to any law limiting status as a holder in due course in particular classes of transactions.

§ 3–303. Value and Consideration

(a) An instrument is issued or transferred for value if:

(1) the instrument is issued or transferred for a promise of performance, to the extent the promise has been performed;

(2) the transferee acquires a security interest or other lien in the instrument other than a lien obtained by judicial proceedings;

(3) the instrument is issued or transferred as payment of, or as security for, an existing obligation of any person, whether or not the obligation is due;

(4) the instrument is issued or transferred in exchange for a negotiable instrument; or

(5) the instrument is issued or transferred in exchange for the incurring of an irrevocable obligation to a third party by the person taking the instrument.

(b) "Consideration" means any consideration sufficient to support a simple contract. The drawer or maker of an instrument has a defense if the instrument is issued without consideration. If an instrument is issued for a promise of performance, the drawer or maker has a defense to the extent performance of the promise is due and the promise has not been performed. If an instrument is issued for value as stated in subsection (a), the instrument is also issued for consideration.

§ 3–304. Overdue Instrument

(a) An instrument payable on demand becomes overdue at the earliest of the following times:

(1) on the day after the day demand for payment is duly made;

(2) if the instrument is a check, 90 days after its date; or

(3) if the instrument is not a check, when the instrument has been outstanding for a period of time after its date which is unreasonably long under the circumstances of the particular case in light of the nature of the instrument and trade usage.

(b) With respect to an instrument payable at a definite time the following rules apply: (1) If the principal is payable in installments and a due date has not been accelerated, the instrument becomes overdue upon default under the instrument for nonpayment of an installment, and the instrument remains overdue until the default is cured. (2) If the principal is not payable in installments and the due date has not been accelerated, the instrument becomes overdue on the day after the due date. (3) If a due date with respect to principal has been accelerated, the instrument becomes overdue on the day after the accelerated due date.

(c) Unless the due date of principal has been accelerated, an instrument does not become overdue if there is default in payment of interest but no default in payment of principal.

§ 3–305. Defenses and Claims in Recoupment

(a) Except as stated in subsection (b), the right to enforce the obligation of a party to pay the instrument is subject to the following:

(1) A defense of the obligor based on (i) infancy of the obligor to the extent it is a defense to a simple contract, (ii) duress, lack of legal capacity, or illegality of the transaction that nullifies the obligation of the obligor, (iii) fraud that induced the obligor to sign the instrument with neither knowledge nor reasonable opportunity to learn of its character or its essential terms, or (iv) discharge of the obligor in insolvency proceedings.

(2) A defense of the obligor stated in another section of this Article or a defense of the obligor that would be available if the person entitled to enforce the instrument were enforcing a right to payment under a simple contract.

(3) A claim in recoupment of the obligor against the original payee of the instrument if the claim arose from the transaction that gave rise to the instrument. The claim of the obligor may be asserted against a transferee of the instrument only to reduce the amount owing on the instrument at the time the action is brought.

(b) The right of a holder in due course to enforce the obligation of a party to pay the instrument is subject to defenses of the obligor stated in subsection (a)(1), but is not subject to defenses of the obligor stated in subsection (a)(2) or claims in recoupment stated in subsection (a)(3) against a person other than the holder.

(c) Except as stated in subsection (d), in an action to enforce the obligation of a party to pay the instrument, the obligor may not assert against the person entitled to enforce the instrument a defense, claim in recoupment, or claim to the instrument (Section 3–306) of another person, but the other person's claim to the instrument may be asserted by the obligor if the other person is joined in the action and personally asserts the claim against the person entitled to enforce the instrument. An obligor is not obliged to pay the instrument if the person seeking enforcement of the instrument does not have rights of a holder in due course and the obligor proves that the instrument is a lost or stolen instrument.

(d) In an action to enforce the obligation of an accommodation party to pay an instrument, the accommodation party may assert against the person entitled to enforce the instrument any defense or claim in recoupment under subsection (a) that the accommodated party could assert against the person entitled to enforce the instrument, except the defenses of discharge in insolvency proceedings, infancy, or lack of legal capacity.

§ 3–306. Claims to an Instrument

A person taking an instrument, other than a person having rights of a holder in due course, is subject to a claim of a property or possessory right in the instrument or its proceeds, including a claim to rescind a negotiation and to recover the instrument or its proceeds. A person having rights of a holder in due course takes free of the claim to the instrument.

§ 3–307. Notice of Breach of Fiduciary Duty

(a) This section applies if (i) an instrument is taken from a fiduciary for payment or collection or for value, (ii) the taker has knowledge of the fiduciary status of the fiduciary, and (iii) the represented person makes a claim to the instrument or its proceeds on the basis that the transaction of the fiduciary is a breach of fiduciary duty. Notice of breach of fiduciary duty by the fiduciary is notice of the claim of the represented person. "Fiduciary" means an agent, trustee, partner, corporation officer or director, or other representative owing a fiduciary duty with respect to the instrument. "Represented person" means the principal, beneficiary, partnership, corporation, or other person to whom the duty is owed.

(b) If the instrument is payable to the fiduciary, as such, or to the represented person, the taker has notice of the breach of fiduciary duty if the instrument is (i) taken in payment of or as security for a debt known by the taker to be the personal debt of the fiduciary, (ii) taken in a transaction known by the taker to be for the personal benefit of the fiduciary, or (iii) deposited to an account other than an account of the fiduciary, as such, or an account of the represented person.

(c) If the instrument is made or drawn by the fiduciary, as such, payable to the fiduciary personally, the taker does not have notice of the breach of fiduciary duty unless the taker knows of the breach of fiduciary duty.

(d) If the instrument is made or drawn by or on behalf of the represented person to the taker as payee, the taker has notice of the breach of fiduciary duty if the instrument is (i) taken in payment of or as security for a debt known by the taker to be the personal debt of the fiduciary, (ii) taken in a transaction known by the taker to be for the personal benefit of the fiduciary, or (iii) deposited to an account other than an account of the fiduciary, as such, or an account of the represented person.

§ 3–308. Proof of Signatures and Status as Holder in Due Course

(a) In an action with respect to an instrument, the authenticity of, and authority to make, each signature on the instrument is admitted unless specifically denied in the pleadings. If the validity of a signature is denied in the pleadings, the burden of establishing validity is on the person claiming validity, but the signature is presumed to be authentic and authorized unless the action is to enforce the liability of the purported signer and the signer is dead or incompetent at the time of trial of the issue of validity of the signature. If an action to enforce the instrument is brought against a person as the undisclosed principal of a person who signed the instrument as a party to the instrument, the plaintiff has the burden of establishing that the defendant is liable on the instrument as a represented person pursuant to Section 3–402(a).

(b) If the validity of signatures is admitted or proved and there is compliance with subsection (a), a plaintiff producing the instrument is entitled to payment if the plaintiff proves entitlement to enforce the instrument under Section 3–301, unless the defendant proves a defense or claim in recoupment. If a defense or claim in recoupment is proved, the right to payment of the plaintiff is subject to the defense or claim except to the extent the plaintiff proves that the plaintiff has rights of a holder in due course which are not subject to the defense or claim.

§ 3–309. Enforcement of Lost, Destroyed, or Stolen Instrument

(a) A person not in possession of an instrument is entitled to enforce the instrument if (i) that person was in rightful possession of the instrument and entitled to enforce it when loss of possession occurred, (ii) the loss of possession was not the result of a voluntary transfer by that person or a lawful seizure, and (iii) that person cannot reasonably obtain possession of the instrument because the instrument was destroyed, its whereabouts cannot be determined, or it is in the wrongful possession of an unknown person or a person that cannot be found or is not amenable to service of process.

(b) A person seeking enforcement of an instrument pursuant to subsection (a) must prove the terms of the instrument and the person's right to enforce the instrument. If that proof is made, Section 3–308 applies to the case as though the person seeking enforcement had produced the instrument. The court may not enter judgment in favor of the person seeking enforcement unless it finds that the person required to pay the instrument is adequately protected against loss that might occur by reason of a claim by another person to enforce the instrument. Adequate protection may be provided by any reasonable means.

§ 3–310. Effect of Instrument on Obligation for Which Taken

(a) Unless otherwise agreed, if a certified check, cashier's check, or teller's check is taken for an obligation, the obligation is discharged to the same extent discharge would result if an amount of money equal to the amount of the instrument were

taken in payment of the obligation. Discharge of the obligation does not affect any liability that the obligor may have as an indorser of the instrument.

(b) Unless otherwise agreed and except as provided in subsection (a), if a note or an uncertified check is taken for an obligation, the obligation is suspended to the same extent the obligation would be discharged if an amount of money equal to the amount of the instrument were taken.

    (1) In the case of an uncertified check, suspension of the obligation continues until dishonor of the check or until it is paid or certified. Payment or certification of the check results in discharge of the obligation to the extent of the amount of the check.

    (2) In the case of a note, suspension of the obligation continues until dishonor of the note or until it is paid. Payment of the note results in discharge of the obligation to the extent of the payment.

    (3) If the check or note is dishonored and the obligee of the obligation for which the instrument was taken has possession of the instrument, the obligee may enforce either the instrument or the obligation. In the case of an instrument of a third person which is negotiated to the obligee by the obligor, discharge of the obligor on the instrument also discharges the obligation.

    (4) If the person entitled to enforce the instrument taken for an obligation is a person other than the obligee, the obligee may not enforce the obligation to the extent the obligation is suspended. If the obligee is the person entitled to enforce the instrument but no longer has possession of it because it was lost, stolen, or destroyed, the obligation may not be enforced to the extent of the amount payable on the instrument, and to that extent the obligee's rights against the obligor are limited to enforcement of the instrument.

(c) If an instrument other than one described in subsection (a) or (b) is taken for an obligation, the effect is (i) that stated in subsection (a) if the instrument is one on which a bank is liable as maker or acceptor, or (ii) that stated in subsection (b) in any other case.

§ 3–311. Accord and Satisfaction by Use of Instrument

(a) This section applies if a person against whom a claim is asserted proves that (i) that person in good faith tendered an instrument to the claimant as full satisfaction of the claim, (ii) the amount of the claim was unliquidated or subject to a bona fide dispute, and (iii) the claimant obtained payment of the instrument.

(b) Unless subsection (c) applies, the claim is discharged if the person against whom the claim is asserted proves that the instrument or an accompanying written communication contained a conspicuous statement to the effect that the instrument was tendered as full satisfaction of the claim.

(c) Subject to subsection (d), a claim is not discharged under subsection (b) if the claimant is an organization and proves that within a reasonable time before the tender, the claimant sent a conspicuous statement to the person against whom the claim is asserted that communications concerning disputed debts, including an instrument tendered as full satisfaction of a debt, are to be sent to a designated person, office or place, and the instrument or accompanying communication was not received by that designated person, office, or place.

(d) Notwithstanding subsection (c), a claim is discharged under subsection (b) if the person against whom the claim is asserted proves that within a reasonable time before collection of the instrument was initiated, an agent of the claimant having direct responsibility with respect to the disputed obligation knew that the instrument was tendered in full satisfaction of the claim, or received the instrument and any accompanying written communication.

Part 4—Liability of Parties

§ 3–401. Signature

(a) A person is not liable on an instrument unless (i) the person signed the instrument, or (ii) the person is represented by an agent or representative who signed the instrument and the signature is binding on the represented person under Section 3–402.

(b) A signature may be made (i) manually or by means of a device or machine, and (ii) by the use of any name, including any trade or assumed name, or by any word, mark, or symbol executed or adopted by a person with present intention to authenticate a writing.

§ 3–402. Signature by Representative

(a) If a person acting, or purporting to act, as a representative signs an instrument by signing either the name of the represented person or the name of the signer, the represented person is bound by the signature to the same extent the represented person would be bound if the signature were on a simple contract. If the represented person is bound, the signature of the representative is the "authorized signature of the represented person" and the represented person is liable on the instrument, whether or not identified in the instrument.

(b) If a representative signs the name of the representative to an instrument and that signature is an authorized signature of the represented person, the following rules apply:

> **(1)** If the form of the signature shows unambiguously that the signature is made on behalf of the represented person who is identified in the instrument, the representative is not liable on the instrument.

> **(2)** Subject to subsection (c), if (i) the form of the signature does not show unambiguously that the signature is made in a representative capacity or (ii) the represented person is not identified in the instrument, the representative is liable on the instrument to a holder in due course that took the instrument without notice that the representative was not intended to be liable on the instrument. With respect to any other person, the representative is liable on the instrument unless the representative proves that the original parties to the instrument did not intend the representative to be liable on the instrument.

(c) If a representative signs the name of the representative as drawer of a check without indication of the representative status and the check is payable from an account of the represented person who is identified on the check, the signer is not liable on the check if the signature is an authorized signature of the represented person.

§ 3–403. Unauthorized Signature

(a) Except as otherwise provided in this Article, an unauthorized signature is ineffective except as the signature of the unauthorized signer in favor of a person who in good faith pays the instrument or takes it for value. An unauthorized signature may be ratified for all purposes of this Article.

(b) If the signature of more than one person is required to constitute the authorized signature of an organization, the signature of the organization is unauthorized if one of the required signatures is missing.

(c) The civil or criminal liability of a person who makes an unauthorized signature is not affected by any provision of this Article that makes the unauthorized signature effective for the purposes of this Article.

§ 3–404. Impostors; Fictitious Payees

(a) If an impostor by use of the mails or otherwise induces the maker or drawer of an instrument to issue the instrument to the impostor, or to a person acting in concert with the impostor, by impersonating the payee of the instrument or a person authorized to act for the payee, an indorsement of the instrument by any person in the name of the payee is effective as the indorsement of the payee in favor of any person that in good faith pays the instrument or takes it for value or for collection.

(b) If (i) a person whose intent determines to whom an instrument is payable (Section 3–110(a) or (b)) does not intend the person identified as payee to have any interest in the instrument, or (ii) the person identified as payee of the instrument is a fictitious person, the following rules apply until the instrument is negotiated by special indorsement:

> **(1)** Any person in possession of the instrument is its holder.

> **(2)** An indorsement by any person in the name of the payee stated in the instrument is effective as the indorsement of the payee in favor of any person that in good faith pays the instrument or takes it for value or for collection.

(c) Under subsection (a) or (b) an indorsement is made in the name of a payee if (i) it is made in a name substantially similar to that of the payee or (ii) the instrument, whether or not indorsed, is deposited in a depositary bank to an account in a name substantially similar to that of the payee.

(d) With respect to an instrument to which subsection (a) or (b) applies, if a person paying the instrument or taking it for value or for collection fails to exercise ordinary care in paying or taking the instrument and that failure substantially contributes to loss resulting from payment of the instrument, the person bearing the loss may recover from the person failing to exercise ordinary care to the extent the failure to exercise ordinary care contributed to the loss.

§ 3–405. Employer Responsibility for Fraudulent Indorsement by Employee

(a) This section applies to fraudulent indorsements of instruments with respect to which an employer has entrusted an employee with responsibility as part of the employee's duties. The following definitions apply to this section:

> **(1)** "Employee" includes, in addition to an employee of an employer, an independent contractor and employee of an independent contractor retained by the employer.

(2) "Fraudulent indorsement" means (i) in the case of an instrument payable to the employer, a forged indorsement purporting to be that of the employer, or (ii) in the case of an instrument with respect to which the employer is drawer or maker, a forged indorsement purporting to be that of the person identified as payee.

(3) "Responsibility" with respect to instruments means authority (i) to sign or indorse instruments on behalf of the employer, (ii) to process instruments received by the employer for bookkeeping purposes, for deposit to an account, or for other disposition, (iii) to prepare or process instruments for issue in the name of the employer, (iv) to supply information determining the names or addresses of payees of instruments to be issued in the name of the employer, (v) to control the disposition of instruments to be issued in the name of the employer, or (vi) to otherwise act with respect to instruments in a responsible capacity. "Responsibility" does not include the assignment of duties that merely allow an employee to have access to instruments or blank or incomplete instrument forms that are being stored or transported or are part of incoming or outgoing mail, or similar access.

(b) For the purpose of determining the rights and liabilities of a person who, in good faith, pays an instrument or takes it for value or for collection, if an employee entrusted with responsibility with respect to the instrument or a person acting in concert with the employee makes a fraudulent indorsement to the instrument, the indorsement is effective as the indorsement of the person to whom the instrument is payable if it is made in the name of that person. If the person paying the instrument or taking it for value or for collection fails to exercise ordinary care in paying or taking the instrument and that failure substantially contributes to loss resulting from the fraud, the person bearing the loss may recover from the person failing to exercise ordinary care to the extent the failure to exercise ordinary care contributed to the loss.

(c) Under subsection (b) an indorsement is made in the name of the person to whom an instrument is payable if (i) it is made in a name substantially similar to the name of that person or (ii) the instrument, whether or not indorsed, is deposited in a depositary bank to an account in a name substantially similar to the name of that person.

§ 3–406. Negligence Contributing to Forged Signature or Alteration of Instrument

(a) A person whose failure to exercise ordinary care substantially contributes to an alteration of an instrument or to the making of a forged signature on an instrument is precluded from asserting the alteration or the forgery against a person that, in good faith, pays the instrument or takes it for value.

(b) If the person asserting the preclusion fails to exercise ordinary care in paying or taking the instrument and that failure substantially contributes to loss, the loss is allocated between the person precluded and the person asserting the preclusion according to the extent to which the failure of each to exercise ordinary care contributed to the loss.

(c) Under subsection (a) the burden of proving failure to exercise ordinary care is on the person asserting the preclusion. Under subsection (b) the burden of proving failure to exercise ordinary care is on the person precluded.

§ 3–407. Alteration

(a) "Alteration" means (i) an unauthorized change in an instrument that purports to modify in any respect the obligation of a party to the instrument, or (ii) an unauthorized addition of words or numbers or other change to an incomplete instrument relating to the obligation of any party to the instrument.

(b) Except as provided in subsection (c), an alteration fraudulently made by the holder discharges any party to whose obligation the alteration applies unless that party assents or is precluded from asserting the alteration. No other alteration discharges any party, and the instrument may be enforced according to its original terms.

(c) If an instrument that has been fraudulently altered is acquired by a person having rights of a holder in due course, it may be enforced by that person according to its original terms. If an incomplete instrument is completed and is then acquired by a person having rights of a holder in due course, it may be enforced by that person as completed, whether or not the completion is a fraudulent alteration.

§ 3–408. Drawee Not Liable on Unaccepted Draft

A check or other draft does not of itself operate as an assignment of funds in the hands of the drawee available for its payment, and the drawee is not liable on the instrument until the drawee accepts it.

§ 3–409. Acceptance of Draft; Certified Check

(a) "Acceptance" means the drawee's signed agreement to pay a draft as presented. It must be written on the draft and may consist of the drawee's signature alone. Acceptance may be made at any time and becomes effective when notification pursuant to instructions is given or the accepted draft is delivered for the purpose of giving rights on the acceptance to any person.

(b) A draft may be accepted although it has not been signed by the drawer, is otherwise incomplete, is overdue, or has been dishonored.

(c) If a draft is payable at a fixed period after sight and the acceptor fails to date the acceptance, the holder may complete the acceptance by supplying a date in good faith.

(d) "Certified check" means a check accepted by the bank on which it is drawn. Acceptance may be made as stated in subsection (a) or by a writing on the check which indicates that the check is certified. The drawee of a check has no obligation to certify the check, and refusal to certify is not dishonor of the check.

§ 3–410. Acceptance Varying Draft

(a) If the terms of a drawee's acceptance vary from the terms of the draft as presented, the holder may refuse the acceptance and treat the draft as dishonored. In that case, the drawee may cancel the acceptance.

(b) The terms of a draft are not varied by an acceptance to pay at a particular bank or place in the United States, unless the acceptance states that the draft is to be paid only at that bank or place.

(c) If the holder assents to an acceptance varying the terms of a draft, the obligation of each drawer and indorser that does not expressly assent to the acceptance is discharged.

§ 3–411. Refusal to Pay Cashier's Checks, Teller's Checks, and Certified Checks

(a) In this section, "obligated bank" means the acceptor of a certified check or the issuer of a cashier's check or teller's check bought from the issuer.

(b) If the obligated bank wrongfully (i) refuses to pay a cashier's check or certified check, (ii) stops payment of a teller's check, or (iii) refuses to pay a dishonored teller's check, the person asserting the right to enforce the check is entitled to compensation for expenses and loss of interest resulting from the nonpayment and may recover consequential damages if the obligated bank refused to pay after receiving notice of particular circumstances giving rise to the damages.

(c) Expenses or consequential damages under subsection (b) are not recoverable if the refusal of the obligated bank to pay occurs because (i) the bank suspends payments, (ii) the obligated bank is asserting a claim or defense of the bank that it has reasonable grounds to believe is available against the person entitled to enforce the instrument, (iii) the obligated bank has a reasonable doubt whether the person demanding payment is the person entitled to enforce the instrument, or (iv) payment is prohibited by law.

§ 3–412. Obligation of Maker

A maker of a note is obliged to pay the note (i) according to its terms at the time it was issued or, if not issued, at the time it first came into possession of a holder, or (ii) if the maker signed an incomplete instrument, according to its terms when completed as stated in Sections 3–115 and 3–407. The obligation is owed to a person entitled to enforce the note or to an indorser that paid the note pursuant to Section 3–415.

§ 3–413. Obligation of Acceptor

(a) An acceptor of a draft is obliged to pay the draft (i) according to its terms at the time it was accepted, even though the acceptance states that the draft is payable "as originally drawn" or equivalent terms, (ii) if the acceptance varies the terms of the draft, according to the terms of the draft as varied, or (iii) if the acceptance is of a draft that is an incomplete instrument, according to its terms when completed as stated in Sections 3–115 and 3–407. The obligation is owed to a person entitled to enforce the draft or to the drawer or an indorser that paid the draft pursuant to Section 3–414 or 3–415.

(b) If the certification of a check or other acceptance of a draft states the amount certified or accepted, the obligation of the acceptor is that amount. If (i) the certification or acceptance does not state an amount, (ii) the instrument is subsequently altered by raising its amount, and (iii) the instrument is then negotiated to a holder in due course, the obligation of the acceptor is the amount of the instrument at the time it was negotiated to the holder in due course.

§ 3–414. Obligation of Drawer

(a) If an unaccepted draft is dishonored, the drawer is obliged to pay the draft (i) according to its terms at the time it was issued or, if not issued, at the time it first came into possession of a holder, or (ii) if the drawer signed an incomplete instrument, according to its terms when completed as stated in Sections 3–115 and 3–407. The obligation is owed to a person entitled to enforce the draft or to an indorser that paid the draft pursuant to Section 3–415.

(b) If a draft is accepted by a bank and the acceptor dishonors the draft, the drawer has no obligation to pay the draft because of the dishonor, regardless of when or by whom acceptance was obtained.

(c) If a draft is accepted and the acceptor is not a bank, the obligation of the drawer to pay the draft if the draft is dishonored by the acceptor is the same as the obligation of an indorser stated in Section 3–415(a) and (c).

(d) Words in a draft indicating that the draft is drawn without recourse are effective to disclaim all liability of the drawer to pay the draft if the draft is not a check or a teller's check, but they are not effective to disclaim the obligation stated in subsection (a) if the draft is a check or a teller's check.

(e) If (i) a check is not presented for payment or given to a depositary bank for collection within 30 days after its date, (ii) the drawee suspends payments after expiration of the 30-day period without paying the check, and (iii) because of the suspension of payments the drawer is deprived of funds maintained with the drawee to cover payment of the check, the drawer to the extent deprived of funds may discharge its obligation to pay the check by assigning to the person entitled to enforce the check the rights of the drawer against the drawee with respect to the funds.

§ 3–415. Obligation of Indorser

(a) Subject to subsections (b), (c) and (d) and to Section 3–419(d), if an instrument is dishonored, an indorser is obliged to pay the amount due on the instrument (i) according to the terms of the instrument at the time it was indorsed, or (ii) if the indorser indorsed an incomplete instrument, according to its terms when completed as stated in Sections 3–115 and 3–407. The obligation of the indorser is owed to a person entitled to enforce the instrument or to a subsequent indorser that paid the instrument pursuant to this section.

(b) If an indorsement states that it is made "without recourse" or otherwise disclaims liability of the indorser, the indorser is not liable under subsection (a) to pay the instrument.

(c) If notice of dishonor of an instrument is required by Section 3–503 and notice of dishonor complying with that section is not given to an indorser, the liability of the indorser under subsection (a) is discharged.

(d) If a draft is accepted by a bank after an indorsement was made and the acceptor dishonors the draft, the indorser is not liable under subsection (a) to pay the instrument.

(e) If an indorser of a check is liable under subsection (a) and the check is not presented for payment, or given to a depositary bank for collection, within 30 days after the day the indorsement was made, the liability of the indorser under subsection (a) is discharged.

§ 3–416. Transfer Warranties

(a) A person that transfers an instrument for consideration warrants to the transferee and, if the transfer is by indorsement, to any subsequent transferee that:

    (1) the warrantor is a person entitled to enforce the instrument,

    (2) all signatures on the instrument are authentic and authorized,

(3) the instrument has not been altered,

(4) the instrument is not subject to a defense or claim in recoupment stated in Section 3–305(a) of any party that can be asserted against the warrantor, and

(5) the warrantor has no knowledge of any insolvency proceeding commenced with respect to the maker or acceptor or, in the case of an unaccepted draft, the drawer.

(b)   A person to whom the warranties under subsection (a) are made and who took the instrument in good faith may recover from the warrantor as damages for breach of warranty an amount equal to the loss suffered as a result of the breach, but not more than the amount of the instrument plus expenses and loss of interest incurred as a result of the breach.

(c)   The warranties stated in subsection (a) cannot be disclaimed with respect to checks. Unless notice of a claim for breach of warranty is given to the warrantor within 30 days after the claimant has reason to know of the breach and the identity of the warrantor, the warrantor is discharged to the extent of any loss caused by the delay in giving notice of the claim.

(d)   A cause of action for breach of warranty under this section accrues when the claimant has reason to know of the breach.

§ 3–417. Presentment Warranties

(a)   If an unaccepted draft is presented to the drawee for payment or acceptance and the drawee pays or accepts the draft, (i) the person obtaining payment or acceptance, at the time of presentment, and (ii) a previous transferor of the draft, at the time of transfer, warrant to the drawee making payment or accepting the draft in good faith that:

(1) the warrantor is or was, at the time the warrantor transferred the draft, a person entitled to enforce the draft or authorized to obtain payment or acceptance of the draft on behalf of a person entitled to enforce the draft;

(2) the draft has not been altered; and

(3) the warrantor has no knowledge that the signature of the purported drawer of the draft is unauthorized.

(b)   A drawee making payment may recover from any warrantor damages for breach of warranty equal to the amount paid by the drawee less the amount the drawee received or is entitled to receive from the drawer because of payment of the draft. In addition the drawee is entitled to compensation for expenses and loss of interest resulting from the breach. The right of the drawee to recover damages under this subsection is not affected by any failure of the drawee to exercise ordinary care in making payment. If the drawee accepts the draft (i) breach of warranty is a defense to the obligation of the acceptor, and (ii) if the acceptor makes payment with respect to the draft, the acceptor is entitled to recover from any warrantor for breach of warranty the amounts stated in the first two sentences of this subsection.

(c)   If a drawee asserts a claim for breach of warranty under subsection (a) based on an unauthorized indorsement of the draft or an alteration of the draft, the warrantor may defend by proving that the indorsement is effective under Section 3–404 or 3–405 or the drawer is precluded under Section 3–406 or 4–406 from asserting against the drawee the unauthorized indorsement or alteration.

(d)   This subsection applies if (i) a dishonored draft is presented for payment to the drawer or an indorser or (ii) any other instrument is presented for payment to a party obliged to pay the instrument, and payment is received. The person obtaining payment and a prior transferor of the instrument warrant to the person making payment in good faith that the warrantor is or was, at the time the warrantor transferred the instrument, a person entitled to enforce the instrument or authorized to obtain payment on behalf of a person entitled to enforce the instrument. The person making payment may recover from any warrantor for breach of warranty an amount equal to the amount paid plus expenses and loss of interest resulting from the breach.

(e)   The warranties stated in subsections (a) and (d) cannot be disclaimed with respect to checks. Unless notice of a claim for breach of warranty is given to the warrantor within 30 days after the claimant has reason to know of the breach and the identity of the warrantor, the warrantor is discharged to the extent of any loss caused by the delay in giving notice of the claim.

(f)   A cause of action for breach of warranty under this section accrues when the claimant has reason to know of the breach.

§ 3–418. Payment or Acceptance by Mistake

(a)   Except as provided in subsection (c), if the drawee of a draft pays or accepts the draft and the drawee acted on the mistaken belief that (i) payment of the draft had not been stopped under Section 4–403, (ii) the signature of the purported drawer of the draft was authorized, or (iii) the balance in the drawer's account with the drawee represented available funds, the drawee may recover the amount paid from the person to whom or for whose benefit payment was made or, in the case of acceptance, may revoke the acceptance. Rights of the drawee under this subsection are not affected by failure of the drawee to exercise ordinary care in paying or accepting the draft.

(b)   Except as provided in subsection (c), if an instrument has been paid or accepted by mistake and the case is not covered by subsection (a), the person paying or accepting may recover the amount paid or revoke acceptance to the extent allowed by the law governing mistake and restitution.

(c)   The remedies provided by subsection (a) or (b) may not be asserted against a person who took the instrument in good faith and for value. This subsection does not limit remedies provided by Section 3–417 for breach of warranty.

§ 3–419. Instruments Signed for Accommodation

(a)   If an instrument is issued for value given for the benefit of a party to the instrument ("accommodated party") and another party to the instrument ("accommodation party") signs the instrument for the purpose of incurring liability on the instrument without being a direct beneficiary of the value given for the instrument, the instrument is signed by the accommodation party "for accommodation."

(b)   An accommodation party may sign the instrument as maker, drawer, acceptor, or indorser and, subject to subsection (d), is obliged to pay the instrument in the capacity in which the accommodation party signs. The obligation of an accommodation party may be enforced notwithstanding any statute of frauds and regardless of whether the accommodation party receives consideration for the accommodation.

(c)   A person signing an instrument is presumed to be an accommodation party and there is notice that the instrument is signed for accommodation if the signature is an anomalous indorsement or is accompanied by words indicating that the signer is acting as surety or guarantor with respect to the obligation of another party to the instrument. Except as provided in Section 3–606, the obligation of an accommodation party to pay the instrument is not affected by the fact that the person enforcing the obligation had notice when the instrument was taken by that person that the accommodation party signed the instrument for accommodation.

(d) If the signature of a party to an instrument is accompanied by words indicating unambiguously that the party is guaranteeing collection rather than payment of the obligation of another party to the instrument, the signer is obliged to pay the amount due on the instrument to a person entitled to enforce the instrument only if (i) execution of judgment against the other party has been returned unsatisfied, (ii) the other party is insolvent or in an insolvency proceeding, (iii) the other party cannot be served with process, or (iv) it is otherwise apparent that payment cannot be obtained from the party whose obligation is guaranteed.

(e) An accommodation party that pays the instrument is entitled to reimbursement from the accommodated party and is entitled to enforce the instrument against the accommodated party. An accommodated party that pays the instrument has no right of recourse against, and is not entitled to contribution from, an accommodation party.

§ 3–420. Conversion of Instrument

(a) The law applicable to conversion of personal property applies to instruments. An instrument is also converted if the instrument lacks an indorsement necessary for negotiation and it is purchased or taken for collection or the drawee takes the instrument and makes payment to a person not entitled to receive payment. An action for conversion of an instrument may not be brought by (i) the maker, drawer, or acceptor of the instrument or (ii) a payee or indorsee who did not receive delivery of the instrument either directly or through delivery to an agent or a co-payee.

(b) In an action under subsection (a), the measure of liability is presumed to be the amount payable on the instrument, but recovery may not exceed the amount of the plaintiff's interest in the instrument.

(c) A representative, other than a depositary bank, that has in good faith dealt with an instrument or its proceeds on behalf of one who was not the person entitled to enforce the instrument is not liable in conversion to that person beyond the amount of any proceeds that it has not paid out.

Part 5—Dishonor

§ 3–501. Presentment

(a) "Presentment" means a demand (i) to pay an instrument made to the maker, drawee, or acceptor or, in the case of a note or accepted draft payable at a bank, to the bank, or (ii) to accept a draft made to the drawee, by a person entitled to enforce the instrument.

(b) Subject to Article 4, agreement of the parties, clearing house rules and the like,

     (1) presentment may be made at the place of payment of the instrument and must be made at the place of payment if the instrument is payable at a bank in the United States; may be made by any commercially reasonable means, including an oral, written, or electronic communication; is effective when the demand for payment or acceptance is received by the person to whom presentment is made; is effective if made to any one of two or more makers, acceptors, drawees or other payors; and

     (2) without dishonoring the instrument, the party to whom presentment is made may (i) treat presentment as occurring on the next business day after the day of presentment if the party to whom presentment is made has established a cut-off hour not earlier than 2 P.M. for the receipt and processing of instruments presented for payment or acceptance and presentment is made after the cut-off hour, (ii) require exhibition of the instrument, (iii) require reasonable identification of the person making presentment and evidence of authority to make it if made on behalf of another person, (iv) require a signed receipt on the instrument for any payment made or surrender of the instrument if full payment is made, (v) return the instrument for lack of a necessary indorsement, or (vi) refuse payment or acceptance for failure of the presentment to comply with the terms of the instrument, an agreement of the parties, or other law or applicable rule.

§ 3–502. Dishonor

(a) Dishonor of a note is governed by the following rules:

     (1) If the note is payable on demand, the note is dishonored if presentment is duly made and the note is not paid on the day of presentment.

     (2) If the note is not payable on demand and is payable at or through a bank or the terms of the note require presentment, the note is dishonored if presentment is duly made and the note is not paid on the day it becomes payable or the day of presentment, whichever is later.

     (3) If the note is not payable on demand and subparagraph (2) does not apply, the note is dishonored if it is not paid on the day it becomes payable.

(b) Dishonor of an unaccepted draft other than a documentary draft is governed by the following rules:

     (1) If a check is presented for payment otherwise than for immediate payment over the counter, the check is dishonored if the payor bank makes timely return of the check or sends timely notice of dishonor or nonpayment under Section 4–301 or 4–302, or becomes accountable for the amount of the check under Section 4–302.

     (2) If the draft is payable on demand and subparagraph (1) does not apply, the draft is dishonored if presentment for payment is duly made and the draft is not paid on the day of presentment.

     (3) If the draft is payable on a date stated in the draft, the draft is dishonored if (i) presentment for payment is duly made and payment is not made on the day the draft becomes payable or the day of presentment, whichever is later, or (ii) presentment for acceptance is duly made before the day the draft becomes payable and the draft is not accepted on the day of presentment.

     (4) If the draft is payable on elapse of a period of time after sight or acceptance, the draft is dishonored if presentment for acceptance is duly made and the draft is not accepted on the day of presentment.

(c) Dishonor of an unaccepted documentary draft occurs according to the rules stated in subparagraphs (2), (3), and (4) of subsection (b) except that payment or acceptance may be delayed without dishonor until no later than the close of the third business day of the drawee following the day on which payment or acceptance is required by those subparagraphs.

(d) Dishonor of an accepted draft is governed by the following rules:

    (1) If the draft is payable on demand, the draft is dishonored if presentment for payment is duly made and the draft is not paid on the day of presentment.

    (2) If the draft is not payable on demand, the draft is dishonored if presentment for payment is duly made and payment is not made on the day it becomes payable or the day of presentment, whichever is later.

(e) In any case in which presentment is otherwise required for dishonor under this section and presentment is excused under Section 3–504, dishonor occurs without presentment if the instrument is not duly accepted or paid.

(f) If a draft is dishonored because timely acceptance of the draft was not made and the person entitled to demand acceptance consents to a late acceptance, from the time of acceptance the draft is treated as never having been dishonored.

§ 3–503. Notice of Dishonor

(a) The obligation of an indorser stated in Section 3–415(a) and the obligation of a drawer stated in Section 3–414(c) may not be enforced unless (i) the indorser or drawer is given notice of dishonor of the instrument complying with this section or (ii) notice of dishonor is excused under Section 3–504(c).

(b) Notice of dishonor may be given by any person; may be given by any commercially reasonable means including an oral, written, or electronic communication; is sufficient if it reasonably identifies the instrument and indicates that the instrument has been dishonored or has not been paid or accepted. Return of an instrument given to a bank for collection is a sufficient notice of dishonor.

(c) Subject to Section 3–504(d), with respect to an instrument taken for collection by a collecting bank, notice of dishonor must be given (i) by the bank before midnight of the next banking day following the banking day on which the bank receives notice of dishonor of the instrument, and (ii) by any other person within 30 days following the day on which the person receives notice of dishonor. With respect to any other instrument, notice of dishonor must be given within 30 days following the day on which dishonor occurs.

§ 3–504. Excused Presentment and Notice of Dishonor

(a) Presentment for payment or acceptance of an instrument is excused if (i) the person entitled to present the instrument cannot with reasonable diligence make presentment, (ii) the maker or acceptor has repudiated an obligation to pay the instrument or is dead or in insolvency proceedings, (iii) by the terms of the instrument presentment is not necessary to enforce the obligation of indorsers or the drawer, or (iv) the drawer or indorser whose obligation is being enforced waived presentment or otherwise had no reason to expect or right to require that the instrument be paid or accepted.

(b) Presentment for payment or acceptance of a draft is also excused if the drawer instructed the drawee not to pay or accept the draft or the drawee was not obligated to the drawer to pay the draft.

(c) Notice of dishonor is excused if (i) by the terms of the instrument notice of dishonor is not necessary to enforce the obligation of a party to pay the instrument, or (ii) the party whose obligation is being enforced waived notice of dishonor. A waiver of presentment is also a waiver of notice of dishonor.

(d) Delay in giving notice of dishonor is excused if the delay was caused by circumstances beyond the control of the person giving the notice and the person giving the notice exercised reasonable diligence after the cause of the delay ceased to operate.

§ 3–505. Evidence of Dishonor

(a) The following are admissible as evidence and create a presumption of dishonor and of any notice of dishonor stated:

    (1) a document regular in form as provided in subsection (b) which purports to be a protest;

    (2) a purported stamp or writing of the drawee, payor bank, or presenting bank on or accompanying the instrument stating that acceptance or payment has been refused unless reasons for the refusal are stated and the reasons are not consistent with dishonor;

    (3) a book or record of the drawee, payor bank, or collecting bank, kept in the usual course of business which shows dishonor, even if there is no evidence of who made the entry.

(b) A protest is a certificate of dishonor made by a United States consul or vice consul, or a notary public or other person authorized to administer oaths by the law of the place where dishonor occurs. It may be made upon information satisfactory to that person. The protest must identify the instrument and certify either that presentment has been made or, if not made, the reason why it was not made, and that the instrument has been dishonored by nonacceptance or nonpayment. The protest may also certify that notice of dishonor has been given to some or all parties.

Part 6—Discharge and Payment

§ 3–601. Discharge and Effect of Discharge

(a) The obligation of a party to pay the instrument is discharged as stated in this Article or by an act or agreement with the party which would discharge an obligation to pay money under a simple contract.

(b) Discharge of the obligation of a party is not effective against a person acquiring rights of a holder in due course of the instrument without notice of the discharge.

§ 3–602. Payment

(a) Subject to subsection (b), an instrument is paid to the extent payment is made (i) by or on behalf of a party obliged to pay the instrument, and (ii) to a person entitled to enforce the instrument. To the extent of the payment, the obligation of the party obliged to pay the instrument is discharged even though payment is made with knowledge of a claim to the instrument under Section 3–306 by another person.

(b) The obligation of a party to pay the instrument is not discharged under subsection (a) if:

(1) a claim to the instrument under Section 3–306 is enforceable against the party receiving payment and (i) payment is made with knowledge by the payor that payment is prohibited by injunction or similar process of a court of competent jurisdiction, or (ii) in the case of an instrument other than a cashier's check, teller's check, or certified check, the party making payment accepted, from the person having a claim to the instrument, indemnity against loss resulting from refusal to pay the person entitled to enforce the instrument, or

(2) the person making payment knows that the instrument is a stolen instrument and pays a person that it knows is in wrongful possession of the instrument.

§ 3–603. Tender of Payment

(a) If tender of payment of an obligation of a party to an instrument is made to a person entitled to enforce the obligation, the effect of tender is governed by principles of law applicable to tender of payment of an obligation under a simple contract.

(b) If tender of payment of an obligation to pay the instrument is made to a person entitled to enforce the instrument and the tender is refused, there is discharge, to the extent of the amount of the tender, of the obligation of an indorser or accommodation party having a right of recourse against the obligor making the tender.

(c) If tender of payment of an amount due on an instrument is made by or on behalf of the obligor to the person entitled to enforce the instrument, the obligation of the obligor to pay interest after the due date on the amount tendered is discharged. If presentment is required with respect to an instrument and the obligor is able and ready to pay on the due date at every place of payment stated in the instrument, the obligor is deemed to have made tender of payment on the due date to the person entitled to enforce the instrument.

§ 3–604. Discharge by Cancellation or Renunciation

(a) A person entitled to enforce an instrument may, with or without consideration, discharge the obligation of a party to pay the instrument (i) by an intentional voluntary act such as surrender of the instrument to the party, destruction, mutilation, or cancellation of the instrument, cancellation or striking out of the party's signature, or the addition of words to the instrument indicating discharge, or (ii) by agreeing not to sue or otherwise renouncing rights against the party by a signed writing.

(b) Cancellation or striking out of an indorsement pursuant to subsection (a) does not affect the status and rights of a party derived from the indorsement.

§ 3–605. Discharge of Indorsers and Accommodation Parties

(a) For the purposes of this section, the term "indorser" includes a drawer having the obligation stated in Section 3–414(c).

(b) Discharge of the obligation of a party to the instrument under Section 3–605 does not discharge the obligation of an indorser or accommodation party having a right of recourse against the discharged party.

(c) If a person entitled to enforce an instrument agrees, with or without consideration, to a material modification of the obligation of a party to the instrument, including an extension of the due date, there is discharge of the obligation of an indorser or accommodation party having a right of recourse against the person whose obligation is modified to the extent the modification causes loss to the indorser or accommodation party with respect to the right of recourse. The indorser or accommodation party is deemed to have suffered loss as a result of the modification equal to the amount of the right of recourse unless the person enforcing the instrument proves that no loss was caused by the modification or that the loss caused by the modification was less than the amount of the right of recourse.

(d) If the obligation of a party to an instrument is secured by an interest in collateral and impairment of the value of the interest is caused by a person entitled to enforce the instrument, there is discharge of the obligation of an indorser or accommodation party having a right of recourse against the obligor to the extent of the impairment. The value of an interest in collateral is impaired to the extent (i) the value of the interest is reduced to an amount less than the amount of the right of recourse of the party asserting discharge, or (ii) the reduction in value of the interest causes an increase in the amount by which the amount of the right of recourse exceeds the value of the interest. The burden of proving impairment is on the party asserting discharge.

(e) If the obligation of a party to an instrument is secured by an interest in collateral not provided by an accommodation party and the value of the interest is impaired by a person entitled to enforce the instrument, the obligation of any party who is jointly and severally liable with respect to the secured obligation is discharged to the extent the impairment causes the party asserting discharge to pay more than that party would have been obliged to pay, taking into account rights of contribution, if impairment had not occurred. If the party asserting discharge is an accommodation party not entitled to discharge under subsection (d), the party is deemed to have a right to contribution based on joint and several liability rather than a right to reimbursement. The burden of proving impairment is on the party asserting discharge.

(f) Under subsection (d) or (e) causation of impairment includes (i) failure to obtain or maintain perfection or recordation of the interest in collateral, (ii) release of collateral without substitution of collateral of equal value, (iii) failure to perform a duty to preserve the value of collateral owed, under Article 9 or other law, to a debtor or surety or other person secondarily liable, or (iv) failure to comply with applicable law in disposing of collateral.

(g) An accommodation party is not discharged under subsection (c) or (d) unless the person agreeing to the modification or causing the impairment knows of the accommodation or has notice under Section 3–419(c) that the instrument was signed for accommodation. There is no discharge of any party under subsection (c), (d), or (e) if (i) the party asserting discharge consents to the event or conduct that is the basis of the discharge, or (ii) the instrument or a separate agreement of the party provides for waiver of discharge under this section either specifically or by general language indicating that parties to the instrument waive defenses based on suretyship or impairment of collateral.

ARTICLE 4: BANK DEPOSITS AND COLLECTIONS

Part 1

§ 4–101. Short Title.

This Article may be cited as Uniform Commercial Code—Bank Deposits and Collections.

§ 4–102. Applicability.

(a) To the extent that items within this Article are also within Articles 3 and 8, they are subject to those Articles. If there is conflict, this Article governs Article 3, but Article 8 governs this Article.

(b) The liability of a bank for action or non-action with respect to an item handled by it for purposes of presentment, payment, or collection is governed by the law of the place where the bank is located. In the case of action or non-action by or at a branch or separate office of a bank, its liability is governed by the law of the place where the branch or separate office is located.

§ 4–103. Variation by Agreement; Measure of Damages; Action Constituting Ordinary Care.

(a) The effect of the provisions of this Article may be varied by agreement, but the parties to the agreement cannot disclaim a bank's responsibility for its lack of good faith or failure to exercise ordinary care or limit the measure of damages for the lack or failure. However, the parties may determine by agreement the standards by which the bank's responsibility is to be measured if those standards are not manifestly unreasonable.

(b) Federal Reserve regulations and operating circulars, clearing-house rules, and the like have the effect of agreements under subsection (a), whether or not specifically assented to by all parties interested in items handled.

(c) Action or non-action approved by this Article or pursuant to Federal Reserve regulations or operating circulars is the exercise of ordinary care and, in the absence of special instructions, action or non-action consistent with clearing-house rules and the like or with a general banking usage not disapproved by this Article, is prima facie the exercise of ordinary care.

(d) The specification or approval of certain procedures by this Article is not disapproval of other procedures that may be reasonable under the circumstances.

(e) The measure of damages for failure to exercise ordinary care in handling an item is the amount of the item reduced by an amount that could not have been realized by the exercise of ordinary care. If there is also bad faith it includes any other damages the party suffered as a proximate consequence.

§ 4–104. Definitions and Index of Definitions.

(a) In this Article, unless the context otherwise requires:

(1) "Account" means any deposit or credit account with a bank, including a demand, time, savings, passbook, share draft, or like account, other than an account evidenced by a certificate of deposit;

(2) "Afternoon" means the period of a day between noon and midnight;

(3) "Banking day" means the part of a day on which a bank is open to the public for carrying on substantially all of its banking functions;

(4) "Clearing house" means an association of banks or other payors regularly clearing items;

(5) "Customer" means a person having an account with a bank or for whom a bank has agreed to collect items, including a bank that maintains an account at another bank;

(6) "Documentary draft" means a draft to be presented for acceptance or payment if specified documents, certificated securities (Section 8–102) or instructions for uncertificated securities (Section 8–102), or other certificates, statements, or the like are to be received by the drawee or other payor before acceptance or payment of the draft;

(7) "Draft" means a draft as defined in Section 3–104 or an item, other than an instrument, that is an order;

(8) "Drawee" means a person ordered in a draft to make payment;

(9) "Item" means an instrument or a promise or order to pay money handled by a bank for collection or payment. The term does not include a payment order governed by Article 4A or a credit or debit card slip;

(10) "Midnight deadline" with respect to a bank is midnight on its next banking day following the banking day on which it receives the relevant item or notice or from which the time for taking action commences to run, whichever is later;

(11) "Settle" means to pay in cash, by clearing-house settlement, in a charge or credit or by remittance, or otherwise as agreed. A settlement may be either provisional or final;

(12) "Suspends payments" with respect to a bank means that it has been closed by order of the supervisory authorities, that a public officer has been appointed to take it over, or that it ceases or refuses to make payments in the ordinary course of business.

(b) Other definitions applying to this Article and the sections in which they appear are:

"Agreement for electronic presentment" Section 4–110.
"Bank" Section 4–105.
"Collecting bank" Section 4–105.
"Depository bank" Section 4–105.
"Intermediary bank" Section 4–105.
"Payor bank" Section 4–105.
"Presenting bank" Section 4–105.
"Presentment notice" Section 4–110.

(c) The following definitions in other Articles apply to this Article:

"Acceptance" Section 3–409.
"Alteration" Section 3–407.
"Cashier's check" Section 3–104.
"Certificate of deposit" Section 3–104.
"Certified check'" Section 3–109.
"Check" Section 3–104.
"Good faith" Section 3–103.
"Holder in due course" Section 3–302.
"Instrument" Section 3–104.
"Notice of dishonor" Section 3–503.
"Order" Section 3–103.
"Ordinary care" Section 3–103.

"Person entitled to enforce" Section 3–301.

"Presentment" Section 3–501

"Promise" Section 3–103

"Prove" Section 3–103

"Teller's check" Section 3–104

"Unauthorized signature" Section 3–403

(d) In addition, Article 1 contains general definitions and principles of construction and interpretation applicable throughout this Article.

As amended in 1990 and 1994.

§ 4–105. "Bank"; "Depositary Bank"; "Payor Bank"; "Intermediary Bank"; "Collecting Bank"; "Presenting Bank".

In this Article:

(1) "Bank" means a person engaged in the business of banking, including a savings bank, savings and loan association, credit union, or trust company;

(2) "Depositary bank" means the first bank to take an item even though it is also the payor bank, unless the item is presented for immediate payment over the counter;

(3) "Payor bank" means a bank that is the drawee of a draft;

(4) "Intermediary bank" means a bank to which an item is transferred in course of collection except the depositary or payor bank;

(5) "Collecting bank" means a bank handling an item for collection except the payor bank;

(6) "Presenting bank" means a bank presenting an item except a payor bank.

§ 4–106. Payable Through or Payable at Bank: Collection Bank.

(a) If an item states that it is "payable through" a bank identified in the item, (i) the item designates the bank as a collecting bank and does not by itself authorize the bank to pay the item, and (ii) the item may be presented for payment only by or through the bank.

ALTERNATIVE A

(b) If an item states that it is "payable at" a bank identified in the item, the item is equivalent to a draft drawn on the bank.

ALTERNATIVE B

(b) If an item states that it is "payable at" a bank identified in the item, (i) the item designates the bank as a collecting bank and does not by itself authorize the bank to pay the item, and (ii) the item may be presented for payment only by or through the bank.

(c) If a draft names a nonbank drawee and it is unclear whether a bank named in the draft is a co-drawee or a collecting bank, the bank is a collecting bank.

§ 4–107. Separate Office of Bank.

A branch or separate office of a bank is a separate bank for the purpose of computing the time within which and determining the place at or to which action may be taken or notices or orders shall be given under this Article and under Article 3.

§ 4–108. Time of Receipt of Items.

(a) For the purpose of allowing time to process items, prove balances, and make the necessary entries on its books to determine its position for the day, a bank may fix an afternoon hour of 2 P.M. or later as a cutoff hour for the handling of money and items and the making of entries on its books.

(b) An item or deposit of money received on any day after a cutoff hour so fixed or after the close of the banking day may be treated as being received at the opening of the next banking day.

§ 4–109. Delays.

(a) Unless otherwise instructed, a collecting bank in a good faith effort to secure payment of a specific item drawn on a payor other than a bank, and with or without the approval of any person involved, may waive, modify, or extend time limits imposed or permitted by this [Act] for a period not exceeding two additional banking days without discharge of drawers or indorsers or liability to its transferor or a prior party.

(b) Delay by a collecting bank or payor bank beyond time limits prescribed or permitted by this [Act] or by instructions is excused if (i) the delay is caused by interruption of communication or computer facilities, suspension of payments by another bank, war, emergency conditions, failure of equipment, or other circumstances beyond the control of the bank, and (ii) the bank exercises such diligence as the circumstances require.

§ 4–110. Electronic Presentment.

(a) "Agreement for electronic presentment" means an agreement, clearing-house rule, or Federal Reserve regulation or operating circular, providing that presentment of an item may be made by transmission of an image of an item or information describing the item ("presentment notice") rather than delivery of the item itself. The agreement may provide for procedures governing retention, presentment, payment, dishonor, and other matters concerning items subject to the agreement.

(b) Presentment of an item pursuant to an agreement for presentment is made when the presentment notice is received.

(c) If presentment is made by presentment notice, a reference to "item" or "check" in this Article means the presentment notice unless the context otherwise indicates.

§ 4–111. Statute of Limitations.

An action to enforce an obligation, duty, or right arising under this Article must be commenced within three years after the [cause of action] accrues.

Part 2—Collection of Items: Depositary and Collecting Banks

§ 4–201. Status of Collecting Bank as Agent and Provisional Status of Credits; Applicability of Article; Item Indorsed "Pay Any Bank".

(a) Unless a contrary intent clearly appears and before the time that a settlement given by a collecting bank for an item is or becomes final, the bank, with respect to an item, is an agent or sub-agent of the owner of the item and any settlement given for the item is provisional. This provision applies regardless of the form of indorsement or lack of indorsement and even though credit given for the item is subject to immediate withdrawal as of right or is in fact withdrawn; but the continuance of ownership of an item by its owner and any rights of the owner to proceeds of the item are subject to rights of a collecting bank, such as those resulting from outstanding advances on the item and rights of recoupment or setoff. If an item is handled by banks for purposes of presentment, payment, collection, or return, the relevant provisions of this Article apply even though action of the parties clearly establishes that a particular bank has purchased the item and is the owner of it.

(b) After an item has been indorsed with the words "pay any bank" or the like, only a bank may acquire the rights of a holder until the item has been:

(1) returned to the customer initiating collection; or

(2) specially indorsed by a bank to a person who is not a bank.

§4–202. Responsibility for Collection or Return; When Action Timely.

(a) A collecting bank must exercise ordinary care in:

(1) presenting an item or sending it for presentment;

(2) sending notice of dishonor or nonpayment or returning an item other than a documentary draft to the bank's transferor after learning that the item has not been paid or accepted, as the case may be;

(3) settling for an item when the bank receives final settlement; and

(4) notifying its transferor of any loss or delay in transit within a reasonable time after discovery thereof.

(b) A collecting bank exercises ordinary care under subsection (a) by taking proper action before its midnight deadline following receipt of an item, notice, or settlement. Taking proper action within a reasonably longer time may constitute the exercise of ordinary care, but the bank has the burden of establishing timeliness.

(c) Subject to subsection (a)(1), a bank is not liable for the insolvency, neglect, misconduct, mistake, or default of another bank or person or for loss or destruction of an item in the possession of others or in transit.

§ 4–203. Effect of Instructions.

Subject to Article 3 concerning conversion of instruments (Section 3–420) and restrictive endorsements (Section 3–206), only a collecting bank's transferor can give instructions that affect the bank or constitute notice to it, and a collecting bank is not liable to prior parties for any action taken pursuant to the instructions or in accordance with any agreement with its transferor.

§ 4–204. Methods of Sending and Presenting, Sending Directly to Payor Bank.

(a) A collecting bank shall send items by a reasonably prompt method, taking into consideration relevant instructions, the nature of the item, the number of those items on hand, the cost of collection involved, and the method generally used by it or others to present those items.

(b) A collecting bank may send:

(1) an item directly to the payor bank;

(2) an item to a nonbank payor if authorized by its transferor; and

(3) an item other than documentary drafts to a nonbank payor, if authorized by Federal Reserve regulation or operating circular, clearing-house rule, or the like.

(c) Presentment may be made by a presenting bank at a place where the payor bank or other payor has requested that presentment be made.

§ 4–205. Depositary Bank Holder of Unindorsed Item.

If a customer delivers an item to a depositary bank for collection:

(1) the depositary bank becomes a holder of the item at the time it receives the item for collection if the customer at the time of delivery was a holder of the item, whether or not the customer indorses the item, and, if the bank satisfies the other requirements of Section 3–302, it is a holder in due course; and

(2) the depositary bank warrants to collecting banks, the payor bank or other payor, and the drawer that the amount of the item was paid to the customer or deposited to the customer's account.

§ 4–206. Transfer Between Banks.

Any agreed method that identifies the transferor bank is sufficient for the item's further transfer to another bank.

§ 4–207. Transfer Warranties.

(a) A customer or collecting bank that transfers an item and receives a settlement or other consideration warrants to the transferee and to any subsequent collecting bank that:

(1) the warrantor is a person entitled to enforce the item;

(2) all signatures on the item are authentic and authorized;

(3) the item has not been altered;

(4) the item is not subject to a defense or claim in recoupment (Section 3–305(a)) of any party that can be asserted against the warrantor; and

(5) the warrantor has no knowledge of any insolvency proceeding commenced with respect to the maker or acceptor or, in the case of an unaccepted draft, the drawer.

(b) If an item is dishonored, a customer or collecting bank transferring the item and receiving settlement or other consideration is obliged to pay the amount due on the item (i) according to the terms of the item at the time it was transferred, or (ii) if the transfer was of an incomplete item, according to its terms when completed as stated in Sections 3–115 and 3–407. The obligation of a transferor is owed to the transferee and to any subsequent collecting bank that takes the item in good faith. A transferor cannot disclaim its obligation under this subsection by an indorsement stating that it is made "without recourse" or otherwise disclaiming liability.

(c) A person to whom the warranties under subsection (a) are made and who took the item in good faith may recover from the warrantor as damages for breach of warranty an amount equal to the loss suffered as a result of the breach, but not more than the amount of the item plus expenses and loss of interest incurred as a result of the breach.

(d) The warranties stated in subsection (a) cannot be disclaimed with respect to checks. Unless notice of a claim for breach of warranty is given to the warrantor within 30 days after the claimant has reason to know of the breach and the identity of the warrantor, the warrantor is discharged to the extent of any loss caused by the delay in giving notice of the claim.

(e) A cause of action for breach of warranty under this section accrues when the claimant has reason to know of the breach.

§ 4–208. Presentment Warranties.

(a) If an unaccepted draft is presented to the drawee for payment or acceptance and the drawee pays or accepts the draft, (i) the person obtaining payment or acceptance, at the time of presentment, and (ii) a previous transferor of the draft, at the time of transfer, warrant to the drawee that pays or accepts the draft in good faith that:

> (1) the warrantor is, or was, at the time the warrantor transferred the draft, a person entitled to enforce the draft or authorized to obtain payment or acceptance of the draft on behalf of a person entitled to enforce the draft;
>
> (2) the draft has not been altered; and
>
> (3) the warrantor has no knowledge that the signature of the purported drawer of the draft is unauthorized.

(b) A drawee making payment may recover from a warrantor damages for breach of warranty equal to the amount paid by the drawee less the amount the drawee received or is entitled to receive from the drawer because of the payment. In addition, the drawee is entitled to compensation for expenses and loss of interest resulting from the breach. The right of the drawee to recover damages under this subsection is not affected by any failure of the drawee to exercise ordinary care in making payment. If the drawee accepts the draft (i) breach of warranty is a defense to the obligation of the acceptor, and (ii) if the acceptor makes payment with respect to the draft, the acceptor is entitled to recover from a warrantor for breach of warranty the amounts stated in this subsection.

(c) If a drawee asserts a claim for breach of warranty under subsection (a) based on an unauthorized indorsement of the draft or an alteration of the draft, the warrantor may defend by proving that the indorsement is effective under Section 3–404 or 3–405 or the drawer is precluded under Section 3–406 or 4–406 from asserting against the drawee the unauthorized indorsement or alteration.

(d) If (i) a dishonored draft is presented for payment to the drawer or an indorser or (ii) any other item is presented for payment to a party obliged to pay the item, and the item is paid, the person obtaining payment and a prior transferor the item warrant to the person making payment in good faith that the warrantor is, or was, at the time the warrantor transferred the item, a person entitled to enforce the item or authorized to obtain payment on behalf of a person entitled to enforce the item. The person making payment may recover from any warrantor for breach of warranty an amount equal to the amount paid plus expenses and loss of interest resulting from the breach.

(e) The warranties stated in subsections (a) and (d) cannot be disclaimed with respect to checks. Unless notice of a claim for breach of warranty is given to the warrantor within 30 days after the claimant has reason to know of the breach and the identity of the warrantor, the warrantor is discharged to the extent of any loss caused by the delay in giving notice of the claim.

(f) A cause of action for breach of warranty under this section accrues when the claimant has reason to know of the breach.

§ 4–209. Encoding and Retention Warranties.

(a) A person who encodes information on or with an item after issue warrants to any subsequent collecting bank and to the payor bank or other payor that the information is correctly encoded. If the customer of a depositary bank encodes, that bank also makes the warranty.

(b) A person who undertakes to retain an item pursuant to an agreement for electronic presentment warrants to any subsequent collecting bank and to the payor bank or other payor that retention and presentment of the item comply with the agreement. If a customer of a depositary bank undertakes to retain an item, that bank also makes this warranty.

(c) A person to whom warranties are made under this section and who took the item in good faith may recover from the warrantor as damages for breach of warranty an amount equal to the loss suffered as a result of the breach, plus expenses and loss of interest incurred as a result of the breach.

§ 4–210. Security Interest of Collecting Bank in Items, Accompanying Documents and Proceeds.

(a) A collecting bank has a security interest in an item and any accompanying documents or the proceeds of either:

> (1) in case of an item deposited in an account, to the extent to which credit given for the item has been withdrawn or applied;
>
> (2) in case of an item for which it has given credit available for withdrawal as of right, to the extent of the credit given, whether or not the credit is drawn upon or there is a right of charge-back; or
>
> (3) if it makes an advance on or against the item.

(b) If credit given for several items received at one time or pursuant to a single agreement is withdrawn or applied in part, the security interest remains upon all the items, any accompanying documents or the proceeds of either. For the purpose of this section, credits first given are first withdrawn.

(c) Receipt by a collecting bank of a final settlement for an item is a realization on its security interest in the item, accompanying documents, and proceeds. So long as the bank does not receive final settlement for the item or give up possession of the item or accompanying documents for purposes other than collection, the security interest continues to that extent and is subject to Article 9, but:

> (1) no security agreement is necessary to make the security interest enforceable (Section 9–203 (1)(a));
>
> (2) no filing is required to perfect the security interest; and
>
> (3) the security interest has priority over conflicting perfected security interests in the item, accompanying documents, or proceeds.

§ 4–211. When Bank Gives Value for Purposes of Holder in Due Course.

For purposes of determining its status as a holder in due course, a bank has given value to the extent it has a security interest in an item, if the bank otherwise complies with the requirements of Section 3–302 on what constitutes a holder in due course.

§ 4–212. Presentment by Notice of Item Not Payable by, Through, or at Bank; Liability of Drawer or Indorser.

(a) Unless otherwise instructed, a collecting bank may present an item not payable by, through, or at a bank by sending to the party to accept or pay a written notice that the bank holds the item for acceptance or payment. The notice must be sent in time to be received on or before the day when presentment is due and the bank must meet any requirements of the party to accept or pay under Section 3–501 by the close of the bank's next banking day after it knows of the requirement.

(b) If presentment is made by notice and payment, acceptance, or request for compliance with a requirement under Section 3–501 is not received by the close of business on the day after maturity or, in the case of demand items, by the close of business on the third banking day after notice was sent, the presenting bank may treat the item as dishonored and charge any drawer or indorser by sending it notice of the facts.

§ 4–213. Medium and Time of Settlement by Bank.

(a) With respect to settlement by a bank, the medium and time of settlement may be prescribed by Federal Reserve regulations or circulars, clearing-house rules, and the like, or agreement. In the absence of such prescription:

(1) the medium of settlement is cash or credit to an account in a Federal Reserve bank of or specified by the person to receive settlement; and

(2) the time of settlement, is:

(i) with respect to tender of settlement by cash, a cashier's check, or teller's check, when the cash or check is sent or delivered;

(ii) with respect to tender of settlement by credit in an account in a Federal Reserve Bank, when the credit is made;

(iii) with respect to tender of settlement by a credit or debit to an account in a bank, when the credit or debit is made or, in the case of tender of settlement by authority to charge an account, when the authority is sent or delivered; or

(iv) with respect to tender of settlement by a funds transfer, when payment is made pursuant to Section 4A–406(a) to the person receiving settlement.

(b) If the tender of settlement is not by a medium authorized by subsection (a) or the time of settlement is not fixed by subsection (a), no settlement occurs until the tender of settlement is accepted by the person receiving settlement.

(c) If settlement for an item is made by cashier's check or teller's check and the person receiving settlement, before its midnight deadline:

(1) presents or forwards the check for collection, settlement is final when the check is finally paid; or

(2) fails to present or forward the check for collection, settlement is final at the midnight deadline of the person receiving settlement.

(d) If settlement for an item is made by giving authority to charge the account of the bank giving settlement in the bank receiving settlement, settlement is final when the charge is made by the bank receiving settlement if there are funds available in the account for the amount of the item.

§ 4–214. Right of Charge-Back or Refund: Liability of Collecting Bank: Return of Item.

(a) If a collecting bank has made provisional settlement with its customer for an item and fails by reason of dishonor, suspension of payments by a bank, or otherwise to receive settlement for the item which is or becomes final, the bank may revoke the settlement given by it, charge back the amount of any credit given for the item to its customer's account, or obtain refund from its customer, whether or not it is able to return the item, if by its midnight deadline or within a longer reasonable time after it learns the facts it returns the item or sends notification of the facts. If

the return or notice is delayed beyond the bank's midnight deadline or a longer reasonable time after it learns the facts, the bank may revoke the settlement, charge back the credit, or obtain refund from its customer, but it is liable for any loss resulting from the delay. These rights to revoke, charge back, and obtain refund terminate if and when a settlement for the item received by the bank is or becomes final.

(b) A collecting bank returns an item when it is sent or delivered to the bank's customer or transferor or pursuant to its instructions.

(c) A depositary bank that is also the payor may charge back the amount of an item to its customer's account or obtain refund in accordance with the section governing return of an item received by a payor bank for credit on its books (Section 4–301).

(d) The right to charge back is not affected by:

(1) previous use of a credit given for the item; or

(2) failure by any bank to exercise ordinary care with respect to the item, but a bank so failing remains liable.

(e) A failure to charge back or claim refund does not affect other rights of the bank against the customer or any other party.

(f) If credit is given in dollars as the equivalent of the value of an item payable in foreign money, the dollar amount of any charge-back or refund must be calculated on the basis of the bank-offered spot rate for the foreign money prevailing on the day when the person entitled to the charge-back or refund learns that it will not receive payment in ordinary course.

As amended in 1990.

§ 4–215. Final Payment of Item by Payor Bank; When Provisional Debits and Credits Become Final; When Certain Credits Become Available for Withdrawal.

(a) An item is finally paid by a payor bank when the bank has first done any of the following:

(1) paid the item in cash;

(2) settled for the item without having a right to revoke the settlement under statute, clearing-house rule, or agreement; or

(3) made a provisional settlement for the item and failed to revoke the settlement in the time and manner permitted by statute, clearing-house rule, or agreement.

(b) If provisional settlement for an item does not become final, the item is not finally paid.

(c) If provisional settlement for an item between the presenting and payor banks is made through a clearing house or by debits or credits in an account between them, then to the extent that provisional debits or credits for the item are entered in accounts between the presenting and payor banks or between the presenting and successive prior collecting banks seriatim, they become final upon final payment of the item by the payor bank.

(d) If a collecting bank receives a settlement for an item, which is or becomes final, the bank is accountable to its customer for the amount of the item and any provisional credit given for the item in an account with its customer becomes final.

(e) Subject to (i) applicable law stating a time for availability of funds and (ii) any right of the bank to apply the credit to an obligation of the customer, credit given by a bank for an item in a customer's account becomes available for withdrawal as of right:

(1) if the bank has received a provisional settlement for the item, when the settlement becomes final and the bank has had a reasonable time to receive return of the item and the item has not been received within that time:

(2) if the bank is both the depositary bank and the payor bank, and the item is finally paid, at opening of the bank's second banking day following receipt of the item.

(f) Subject to applicable law stating a time for availability of funds and any right of a bank to apply a deposit to an obligation of the depositor, a deposit of money becomes available for withdrawal as of right at the opening of the bank's next banking day after receipt of the deposit.

§ 4–216. Insolvency and Preference.

(a) If an item is in or comes into the possession of a payor or collecting bank that suspends payment and the item has not been finally paid, the item must be returned by the receiver, trustee, or agent in charge of the closed bank to the presenting bank or the closed bank's customer.

(b) If a payor bank finally pays an item and suspends payments without making a settlement for the item with its customer or the presenting bank which settlement is or becomes final, the owner of the item has a preferred claim against the payor bank.

(c) If a payor bank gives or a collecting bank gives or receives a provisional settlement for an item and thereafter suspends payments, the suspension does not prevent or interfere with the settlement's becoming final if the finality occurs automatically upon the lapse of certain time or the happening of certain events.

(d) If a collecting bank receives from subsequent parties subsequent parties settlement for an item, which settlement is or becomes final and the bank suspends payments without making a settlement for the item with its customer which settlement is or becomes final, the owner of the item has a preferred claim against the collecting bank.

Part 3—Collection of Items: Payor Banks

§ 4–301. Deferred Posting; Recovery of Payment by Return of Items; Time of Dishonor; Return of Items by Payor Bank.

(a) If a payor bank settles for a demand item other than a documentary draft presented otherwise than for immediate payment over the counter before midnight of the banking day of receipt, the payor bank may revoke the settlement and recover the settlement if, before it has made final payment and before its midnight deadline, it

    (1) returns the item; or

    (2) sends written notice of dishonor or nonpayment if the item is unavailable for return.

(b) If a demand item is received by a payor bank for credit on its books, it may return the item or send notice of dishonor and may revoke any credit given or recover the amount thereof withdrawn by its customer, if it acts within the time limit and in the manner specified in subsection (a).

(c) Unless previous notice of dishonor has been sent, an item is dishonored at the time when for purposes of dishonor it is returned or notice sent in accordance with this section.

(d) An item is returned:

    (1) as to an item presented through a clearing house, when it is delivered to the presenting or last collecting bank or to the clearing house or is sent or delivered in accordance with clearing-house rules; or

    (2) in all other cases, when it is sent or delivered to the bank's customer or transferor or pursuant to instructions.

§ 4–302. Payor Bank's Responsibility for Late Return of Item.

(a) If an item is presented to and received by a payor bank, the bank is accountable for the amount of:

    (1) a demand item, other than a documentary draft, whether properly payable or not, if the bank, in any case in which it is not also the depositary bank, retains the item beyond midnight of the banking day of receipt without settling for it or, whether or not it is also the depositary bank, does not pay or return the item or send notice of dishonor until after its midnight deadline; or

    (2) any other properly payable item unless, within the time allowed for acceptance or payment of that item, the bank either accepts or pays the item or returns it and accompanying documents.

(b) The liability of a payor bank to pay an item pursuant to subsection (a) is subject to defenses based on breach of a presentment warranty (Section 4–208) or proof that the person seeking enforcement of the liability presented or transferred the item for the purpose of defrauding the payor bank.

§ 4–303. When Items Subject to Notice, Stop-Payment Order, Legal Process, or Setoff; Order in Which Items May Be Charged or Certified.

(a) Any knowledge, notice, or stop-payment order received by, legal process served upon, or setoff exercised by a payor bank comes too late to terminate, suspend, or modify the bank's right or duty to pay an item or to charge its customer's account for the item if the knowledge, notice, stop-payment order, or legal process is received or served and a reasonable time for the bank to act thereon expires or the setoff is exercised after the earliest of the following:

    (1) the bank accepts or certifies the item;

    (2) the bank pays the item in cash;

    (3) the bank settles for the item without having a right to revoke the settlement under statute, clearing-house rule, or agreement;

    (4) the bank becomes accountable for the amount of the item under Section 4–302 dealing with the payor bank's responsibility for late return of items; or

    (5) with respect to checks, a cutoff hour no earlier than one hour after the opening of the next banking day after the banking day on which the bank received the check and no later than the close of that next banking day or, if no cutoff hour is fixed, the close of the next banking day after the banking day on which the bank received the check.

(b) Subject to subsection (a), items may be accepted, paid, certified, or charged to the indicated account of its customer in any order.

Part 4—Relationship Between Payor Bank and Its Customer

§ 4–401. When Bank May Charge Customer's Account.

(a) A bank may charge against the account of a customer an item that is properly payable from the account even though the charge creates an overdraft. An item is properly payable if it is authorized by the customer and is in accordance with any agreement between the customer and bank.

(b) A customer is not liable for the amount of an overdraft if the customer neither signed the item nor benefited from the proceeds of the item.

(c) A bank may charge against the account of a customer a check that is otherwise properly payable from the account, even though payment was made before the date of the check, unless the customer has given notice to the bank of the postdating describing the check with reasonable certainty. The notice is effective for the period stated in Section 4–403(b) for stop-payment orders, and must be received at such time and in such manner as to afford the bank a reasonable opportunity to act on it before the bank takes any action with respect to the check described in Section 4–303. If a bank charges against the account of a customer a check before the date stated in the notice of postdating, the bank is liable for damages for the loss resulting from its act. The loss may include damages for dishonor of subsequent items under Section 4–402.

(d) A bank that in good faith makes payment to a holder may charge the indicated account of its customer according to:

> **(1)** the original terms of the altered item; or
>
> **(2)** the terms of the completed item, even though the bank knows the item has been completed unless the bank has notice that the completion was improper.

§ 4–402. Bank's Liability to Customer for Wrongful Dishonor; Time of Determining Insufficiency of Account

(a) Except as otherwise provided in this Article, a payor bank wrongfully dishonors an item if it dishonors an item that is properly payable, but a bank may dishonor an item that would create an overdraft unless it has agreed to pay the overdraft.

(b) A payor bank is liable to its customer for damages proximately caused by the wrongful dishonor of an item. Liability is limited to actual damages proved and may include damages for an arrest or prosecution of the customer or other consequential damages. Whether any consequential damages are proximately caused by the wrongful dishonor is a question of fact to be determined in each case.

(c) A payor bank's determination of the customer's account balance on which a decision to dishonor for insufficiency of available funds is based may be made at any time between the time the item is received by the payor bank and the time that the payor bank returns the item or gives notice in lieu of return, and no more than one determination need be made. If, at the election of the payor bank, a subsequent balance determination is made for the purpose of reevaluating the bank's decision to dishonor the item, the account balance at that time is determinative of whether a dishonor for insufficiency of available funds is wrongful.

> As amended in 1990.
>
> *See Appendix IX for material relating to changes made in text in 1990.*

§ 4–403. Customer's Right to Stop Payment; Burden of Proof of Loss.

(a) A customer or any person authorized to draw on the account if there is more than one person may stop payment of any item drawn on the customer's account or close the account by an order to the bank describing the item or account with reasonable certainty received at a time and in a manner that affords the bank a reasonable opportunity to act on it before any action by the bank with respect to the item described in Section 4–303. If the signature of more than one person is required to draw on an account, any of these persons may stop payment or close the account.

(b) A stop-payment order is effective for six months, but it lapses after 14 calendar days if the original order was oral and was not confirmed in writing within that period. A stop-payment order may be renewed for additional six month periods by a writing given to the bank within a period during which the stop-payment order is effective.

(c) The burden of establishing the fact and amount of loss resulting from the payment of an item contrary to a stop-payment order or order to close an account is on the customer. The loss from payment of an item contrary to a stop-payment order may include damages for dishonor of subsequent items under Section 4–402.

§ 4–404. Bank Not Obliged to Pay Check More Than Six Months Old.

A bank is under no obligation to a customer having a checking account to pay a check, other than a certified check, which is presented more than six months after its date, but it may charge its customer's account for a payment made thereafter in good faith.

§ 4–405. Death or Incompetence of Customer.

(a) A payor or collecting bank's authority to accept, pay, or collect an item or to account for proceeds of its collection, if otherwise effective, is not rendered ineffective by incompetence of a customer of either bank existing at the time the item is issued or its collection is undertaken if the bank does not know of an adjudication of incompetence. Neither death nor incompetence of a customer revokes the authority to accept, pay, collect, or account until the bank knows of the fact of death or of an adjudication of incompetence and has a reasonable opportunity to act on it.

(b) Even with knowledge, a bank may for 10 days after the date of death pay or certify checks drawn on or before that date unless ordered to stop payment by a person claiming an interest in the account.

§ 4–406. Customer's Duty to Discover and Report Unauthorized Signature or Alteration.

(a) A bank that sends or makes available to a customer a statement of account showing payment of items for the account shall either return or make available to the customer the items paid or provide information in the statement of account sufficient to allow the customer reasonably to identify the items paid. The statement of account provides sufficient information if the item is described by item number, amount, and date of payment.

(b) If the items are not returned to the customer, the person retaining the items shall either retain the items or, if the items are destroyed, maintain the capacity to furnish legible copies of the items until the expiration of seven years after receipt of the items. A customer may request an item from the bank that paid the item, and that bank must provide in a reasonable time either the item or, if the item has been destroyed or is not otherwise obtainable, a legible copy of the item.

(c) If a bank sends or makes available a statement of account or items pursuant to subsection (a), the customer must exercise reasonable promptness in examining the statement or the items to determine whether any payment was not authorized because of an alteration of an item or because a purported signature by or on behalf of the customer was not authorized. If, based on the statement or items provided, the customer should reasonably have discovered the unauthorized payment, the customer must promptly notify the bank of the relevant facts.

(d) If the bank proves that the customer failed, with respect to an item, to comply with the duties imposed on the customer by subsection (c), the customer is precluded from asserting against the bank:

(1) the customer's unauthorized signature or any alteration on the item, if the bank also proves that it suffered a loss by reason of the failure; and

(2) the customer's unauthorized signature or alteration by the same wrong-doer on any other item paid in good faith by the bank if the payment was made before the bank received notice from the customer of the unauthorized signature or alteration and after the customer had been afforded a reasonable period of time, not exceeding 30 days, in which to examine the item or statement of account and notify the bank.

(e) If subsection (d) applies and the customer proves that the bank failed to exercise ordinary care in paying the item and that the failure substantially contributed to loss, the loss is allocated between the customer precluded and the bank asserting the preclusion according to the extent to which the failure of the customer to comply with subsection (c) and the failure of the bank to exercise ordinary care contributed to the loss. If the customer proves that the bank did not pay the item in good faith, the preclusion under subsection (d) does not apply.

(f) Without regard to care or lack of care of either the customer or the bank, a customer who does not within one year after the statement or items are made available to the customer (subsection (a)) discover and report the customer's unauthorized signature on or any alteration on the item is precluded from asserting against the bank the unauthorized signature or alteration. If there is a preclusion under this subsection, the payor bank may not recover for breach or warranty under Section 4–208 with respect to the unauthorized signature or alteration to which the preclusion applies.

§ 4–407. Payor Bank's Right to Subrogation on Improper Payment.

If a payor bank has paid an item over the order of the drawer or maker to stop payment, or after an account has been closed, or otherwise under circumstances giving a basis for objection by the drawer or maker, to prevent unjust enrichment and only to the extent necessary to prevent loss to the bank by reason of its payment of the item, the payor bank is subrogated to the rights

(1) of any holder in due course on the item against the drawer or maker;

(2) of the payee or any other holder of the item against the drawer or maker either on the item or under the transaction out of which the item arose; and

(3) of the drawer or maker against the payee or any other holder of the item with respect to the transaction out of which the item arose.

Part 5—Collection of Documentary Drafts

§ 4–501. Handling of Documentary Drafts; Duty to Send for Presentment and to Notify Customer of Dishonor.

A bank that takes a documentary draft for collection shall present or send the draft and accompanying documents for presentment and, upon learning that the draft has not been paid or accepted in due course, shall seasonably notify its customer of the fact even though it may have discounted or bought the draft or extended credit available for withdrawal as of right.

§ 4–502. Presentment of "On Arrival" Drafts.

If a draft or the relevant instructions require presentment "on arrival", "when goods arrive" or the like, the collecting bank need not present until in its judgment a reasonable time for arrival of the goods has expired. Refusal to pay or accept because the goods have not arrived is not dishonor; the bank must notify its transferor of the refusal but need not present the draft again until it is instructed to do so or learns of the arrival of the goods.

§ 4–503. Responsibility of Presenting Bank for Documents and Goods; Report of Reasons for Dishonor; Referee in Case of Need.

Unless otherwise instructed and except as provided in Article 5, a bank presenting a documentary draft:

(1) must deliver the documents to the drawee on acceptance of the draft if it is payable more than three days after presentment; otherwise, only on payment; and

(2) upon dishonor, either in the case of presentment for acceptance or presentment for payment, may seek and follow instructions from any referee in case of need designated in the draft or, if the presenting bank does not choose to utilize the referee's services, it must use diligence and good faith to ascertain the reason for dishonor, must notify its transferor of the dishonor and of the results of its effort to ascertain the reasons therefor, and must request instructions.

However the presenting bank is under no obligation with respect to goods represented by the documents except to follow any reasonable instructions seasonably received; it has a right to reimbursement for any expense incurred in following instructions and to prepayment of or indemnity for those expenses.

§ 4–504. Privilege of Presenting Bank to Deal With Goods; Security Interest for Expenses.

(a) A presenting bank that, following the dishonor of a documentary draft, has seasonably requested instructions but does not receive them within a reasonable time may store, sell, or otherwise deal with the goods in any reasonable manner.

(b) For its reasonable expenses incurred by action under subsection (a) the presenting bank has a lien upon the goods or their proceeds, which may be foreclosed in the same manner as an unpaid seller's lien.

ARTICLE 9: SECURED TRANSACTIONS; SALES OF ACCOUNTS AND CHATTEL PAPER

Note: The adoption of this Article should be accompanied by the repeal of existing statutes dealing with conditional sales, trust receipts, factor's liens where the factor is given a non-possessory lien, chattel mortgages, crop mortgages, mortgages on railroad equipment, assignment of accounts and generally statutes regulating security interests in personal property.

Where the state has a retail installment selling act or small loan act, that legislation should be carefully examined to determine what changes in those acts are needed to conform them to this Article. This Article primarily sets out rules defining rights of a secured party against persons dealing with the debtor; it does not prescribe regulations and controls which may be necessary to curb abuses arising in the small loan business or in the financing of consumer purchases on credit. Accordingly there is no intention to repeal existing regulatory acts in those fields by enactment or re-enactment of Article 9. See Section 9–203(4) and the Note thereto.

Part 1—Short Title, Applicability and Definitions

§ 9–101. Short Title

This Article shall be known and may be cited as Uniform Commercial Code—Secured Transactions.

§ 9–102. Policy and Subject Matter of Article

(1) Except as otherwise provided in Section 9–104 on excluded transactions, this Article applies

   (a) to any transaction (regardless of its form) which is intended to create a security interest in personal property or fixtures including goods, documents, instruments, general intangibles, chattel paper or accounts; and also

   (b) to any sale of accounts or chattel paper.

(2) This Article applies to security interests created by contract including pledge, assignment, chattel mortgage, chattel trust, trust deed, factor's lien, equipment trust, conditional sale, trust receipt, other lien or title retention contract and lease or consignment intended as security. This Article does not apply to statutory liens except as provided in Section 9–310.

(3) The application of this Article to a security interest in a secured obligation is not affected by the fact that the obligation is itself secured by a transaction or interest to which this Article does not apply.

   Amended in 1972.

§ 9–103. Perfection of Security Interest in Multiple State Transactions

(1) Documents, instruments and ordinary goods.

   (a) This subsection applies to documents and instruments and to goods other than those covered by a certificate of title described in subsection (2), mobile goods described in subsection (3), and minerals described in subsection (5).

   (b) Except as otherwise provided in this subsection, perfection and the effect of perfection or non-perfection of a security interest in collateral are governed by the law of the jurisdiction where the collateral is when the last event occurs on which is based the assertion that the security interest is perfected or unperfected.

   (c) If the parties to a transaction creating a purchase money security interest in goods in one jurisdiction understand at the time that the security interest attaches that the goods will be kept in another jurisdiction, then the law of the other jurisdiction governs the perfection and the effect of perfection or non-perfection of the security interest from the time it attaches until thirty days after the debtor receives possession of the goods and thereafter if the goods are taken to the other jurisdiction before the end of the thirty-day period.

   (d) When collateral is brought into and kept in this state while subject to a security interest perfected under the law of the jurisdiction from which the collateral was removed, the security interest remains perfected, but if action is required by Part 3 of this Article to perfect the security interest,

      (i) if the action is not taken before the expiration of the period of perfection in the other jurisdiction or the end of four months after the collateral is brought into this state, whichever period first expires, the security interest be comes unperfected at the end of that period and is thereafter deemed to have been unperfected as against a person who became a purchaser after removal;

      (ii) if the action is taken before the expiration of the period specified in subparagraph (i), the security interest continues perfected thereafter;

      (iii) for the purpose of priority over a buyer of consumer goods (subsection (2) of Section 9–307), the period of the effectiveness of a filing in the jurisdiction from which the collateral is removed is governed by the rules with respect to perfection in subparagraphs (i) and (ii).

(2) Certificate of title.

   (a) This subsection applies to goods covered by a certificate of title issued under a statute of this state or of another jurisdiction under the law of which indication of a security interest on the certificate is required as a condition of perfection.

   (b) Except as otherwise provided in this subsection, perfection and the effect of perfection or non-perfection of the security interest are governed by the law (including the conflict of laws rules) of the jurisdiction issuing the certificate until four months after the goods are removed from that jurisdiction and thereafter until the goods are registered in another jurisdiction, but in any event not beyond surrender of the certificate. After the expiration of that period, the goods are not covered by the certificate of title within the meaning of this section.

   (c) Except with respect to the rights of a buyer described in the next paragraph, a security interest, perfected in another jurisdiction otherwise than by notation on a certificate of title, in goods brought into this state and thereafter covered by a certificate of title issued by this state is subject to the rules stated in paragraph (d) of subsection (1).

   (d) If goods are brought into this state while a security interest therein is perfected in any manner under the law of the jurisdiction from which the goods are removed and a certificate of title is issued by this state and the certificate does not show that the goods are subject to the security interest or that they may be subject to security interests not shown on the certificate, the security interest is subordinate to the rights of a buyer of the goods who is not in the business of selling goods of that kind to the extent that he gives value and receives delivery of the goods after issuance of the certificate and without knowledge of the security interest.

(3) Accounts, general intangibles and mobile goods.

(a) This subsection applies to accounts (other than an account described in subsection (5) on minerals) and general intangibles (other than uncertificated securities) and to goods which are mobile and which are of a type normally used in more than one jurisdiction, such as motor vehicles, trailers, rolling stock, airplanes, shipping containers, road building and construction machinery and commercial harvesting machinery and the like, if the goods are equipment or are inventory leased or held for lease by the debtor to others, and are not covered by a certificate of title described in subsection (2).

(b) The law (including the conflict of laws rules) of the jurisdiction in which the debtor is located governs the perfection and the effect of perfection or non-perfection of the security interest.

(c) If, however, the debtor is located in a jurisdiction which is not a part of the United States, and which does not provide for perfection of the security interest by filing or recording in that jurisdiction, the law of the jurisdiction in the United States in which the debtor has its major executive office in the United States governs the perfection and the effect of perfection or non-perfection of the security interest through filing. In the alternative, if the debtor is located in a jurisdiction which is not a part of the United States or Canada and the collateral is accounts or general intangibles for money due or to become due, the security interest may be perfected by notification to the account debtor. As used in this paragraph, "United States" includes its territories and possessions and the Commonwealth of Puerto Rico.

(d) A debtor shall be deemed located at his place of business if he has one, at his chief executive office if he has more than one place of business, otherwise at his residence. If, however, the debtor is a foreign air carrier under the Federal Aviation Act of 1958, as amended, it shall be deemed located at the designated office of the agent upon whom service of process may be made on behalf of the foreign air carrier.

(e) A security interest perfected under the law of the jurisdiction of the location of the debtor is perfected until the expiration of four months after a change of the debtor's location to another jurisdiction, or until perfection would have ceased by the law of the first jurisdiction, whichever period first expires. Unless perfected in the new jurisdiction before the end of that period, it becomes unperfected thereafter and is deemed to have been unperfected as against a person who became a purchaser after the change.

(4) Chattel paper.

The rules stated for goods in subsection (1) apply to a possessory security interest in chattel paper. The rules stated for accounts in subsection (3) apply to a non-possessory security interest in chattel paper, but the security interest may not be perfected by notification to the account debtor.

(5) Minerals.

Perfection and the effect of perfection or non-perfection of a security interest which is created by a debtor who has an interest in minerals or the like (including oil and gas) before extraction and which attaches thereto as extracted, or which attaches to an account resulting from the sale thereof at the wellhead or minehead are governed by the law (including the conflict of laws rules) of the jurisdiction wherein the wellhead or minehead is located.

(6) Uncertificated securities.

The law (including the conflict of laws rules) of the jurisdiction of organization of the issuer governs the perfection and the effect of perfection or non-perfection of a security interest in uncertificated securities.

Amended in 1972 and 1977.

§ 9–104. Transactions Excluded From Article

This Article does not apply

(a) to a security interest subject to any statute of the United States, to the extent that such statute governs the rights of parties to and third parties affected by transactions in particular types of property; or

(b) to a landlord's lien; or

(c) to a lien given by statute or other rule of law for services or materials except as provided in Section 9–310 on priority of such liens; or

(d) to a transfer of a claim for wages, salary or other compensation of an employee; or

(e) to a transfer by a government or governmental subdivision or agency; or

(f) to a sale of accounts or chattel paper as part of a sale of the business out of which they arose, or an assignment of accounts or chattel paper which is for the purpose of collection only, or a transfer of a right to payment under a contract to an assignee who is also to do the performance under the contract or a transfer of a single account to an assignee in whole or partial satisfaction of a preexisting indebtedness; or

(g) to a transfer of an interest in or claim in or under any policy of insurance, except as provided with respect to proceeds (Section 9–306) and priorities in proceeds (Section 9–312); or

(h) to a right represented by a judgment (other than a judgment taken on a right to payment which was collateral); or

(i) to any right of set-off; or

(j) except to the extent that provision is made for fixtures in Section 9–313, to the creation or transfer of an interest in or lien on real estate, including a lease or rents thereunder; or

(k) to a transfer in whole or in part of any claim arising out of tort; or

(l) to a transfer of an interest in any deposit account (subsection (1) of Section 9–105), except as provided with respect to proceeds (Section 9–306) and priorities in proceeds (Section 9–312).

Amended in 1972.

§ 9–105. Definitions and Index of Definitions

(1) In this Article unless the context otherwise requires:

(a) "Account debtor" means the person who is obligated on an account, chattel paper or general intangible;

(b) "Chattel paper" means a writing or writings which evidence both a monetary obligation and a security interest in or a lease of specific goods, but a charter or other contract involving the use or hire of a vessel is not chattel paper. When a transaction is evidenced both by such a security agreement or a lease and by an instrument or a series of instruments, the group of writings taken together constitutes chattel paper;

(c) "Collateral" means the property subject to a security interest, and includes accounts and chattel paper which have been sold;

(d) "Debtor" means the person who owes payment or other performance of the obligation secured, whether or not he owns or has rights in the collateral, and includes the seller of accounts or chattel paper. Where the debtor and the owner of the collateral are not the same person, the term "debtor" means the owner of the collateral in any provision of the Article dealing with the collateral, the obligor in any provision dealing with the obligation, and may include both where the context so requires;

(e) "Deposit account" means a demand, time, savings, passbook or like account maintained with a bank, savings and loan association, credit union or like organization, other than an account evidenced by a certificate of deposit;

(f) "Document" means document of title as defined in the general definitions of Article 1 (Section 1–201), and a receipt of the kind described in subsection (2) of Section 7–201;

(g) "Encumbrance" includes real estate mortgages and other liens on real estate and all other rights in real estate that are not ownership interests;

(h) "Goods" includes all things which are movable at the time the security interest attaches or which are fixtures (Section 9–313), but does not include money, documents, instruments, accounts, chattel paper, general intangibles, or minerals or the like (including oil and gas) before extraction. "Goods" also includes standing timber which is to be cut and removed under a conveyance or contract for sale, the unborn young of animals, and growing crops;

(i) "Instrument" means a negotiable instrument (defined in Section 3–104), or a certificated security (defined in Section 8–102) or any other writing which evidences a right to the payment of money and is not itself a security agreement or lease and is of a type which is in ordinary course of business transferred by delivery with any necessary indorsement or assignment;

(j) "Mortgage" means a consensual interest created by a real estate mortgage, a trust deed on real estate, or the like;

(k) An advance is made "pursuant to commitment" if the secured party has bound himself to make it, whether or not a subsequent event of default or other event not within his control has relieved or may relieve him from his obligation;

(l) "Security agreement" means an agreement which creates or provides for a security interest;

(m) "Secured party" means a lender, seller or other person in whose favor there is a security interest, including a person to whom accounts or chattel paper have been sold. When the holders of obligations issued under an indenture of trust, equipment trust agreement or the like are represented by a trustee or other person, the representative is the secured party;

(n) "Transmitting utility" means any person primarily engaged in the railroad, street railway or trolley bus business, the electric or electronics communications transmission business, the transmission of goods by pipeline, or the transmission or the production and transmission of electricity, steam, gas or water, or the provision of sewer service.

(2) Other definitions applying to this Article and the sections in which they appear are:

"Account". Section 9–106.
"Attach". Section 9–203.
"Construction mortgage". Section 9–313(1).
"Consumer goods". Section 9–109(1).
"Equipment". Section 9–109(2).
"Farm products". Section 9–109(3).
"Fixture". Section 9–313(1).
"Fixture filing". Section 9–313(1).
"General intangibles". Section 9–106.
"Inventory". Section 9–109(4).
"Lien creditor". Section 9–301(3).
"Proceeds". Section 9–306(1).
"Purchase money security interest". Section 9–107.
"United States". Section 9–103.

(3) The following definitions in other Articles apply to this Article:

"Check". Section 3–104.
"Contract for sale". Section 2–106.
"Holder in due course". Section 3–302.
"Note". Section 3–104.
"Sale". Section 2–106.

(4) In addition Article 1 contains general definitions and principles of construction and interpretation applicable throughout this Article.

Amended in 1966, 1972 and 1977.

§ 9–106. Definitions: "Account"; "General Intangibles"

"Account" means any right to payment for goods sold or leased or for services rendered which is not evidenced by an instrument or chattel paper, whether or not it has been earned by performance. "General intangibles" means any personal property (including things in action) other than goods, accounts, chattel paper, documents, instruments, and money. All rights to payment earned or unearned under a charter or other contract involving the use or hire of a vessel and all rights incident to the charter or contract are accounts.

Amended in 1966, 1972.

§ 9–107. Definitions: "Purchase Money Security Interest"

A security interest is a "purchase money security interest" to the extent that it is

(a) taken or retained by the seller of the collateral to secure all or part of its price; or

(b) taken by a person who by making advances or incurring an obligation gives value to enable the debtor to acquire rights in or the use of collateral if such value is in fact so used.

§ 9–108. When After-Acquired Collateral Not Security for Antecedent Debt

Where a secured party makes an advance, incurs an obligation, releases a perfected security interest, or otherwise gives new value which is to be secured in whole or in part by after-acquired property his security interest in the after-acquired collateral shall be deemed to be taken for new value and not as security for an antecedent debt if the debtor acquires his rights in such collateral either in the ordinary course of his business or under a contract of purchase made pursuant to the security agreement within a reasonable time after new value is given.

§ 9–109. Classification of Goods; "Consumer Goods"; "Equipment"; "Farm Products"; "Inventory"

Goods are

(1) "consumer goods" if they are used or bought for use primarily for personal, family or household purposes;

(2) "equipment" if they are used or bought for use primarily in business (including farming or a profession) or by a debtor who is a non-profit organization or a governmental subdivision or agency or if the goods are not included in the definitions of inventory, farm products or consumer goods;

(3) "farm products" if they are crops or livestock or supplies used or produced in farming operations or if they are products of crops or livestock in their unmanufactured states (such as ginned cotton, wool-clip, maple syrup, milk and eggs), and if they are in the possession of a debtor engaged in raising, fattening, grazing or other farming operations. If goods are farm products they are neither equipment nor inventory;

(4) "inventory" if they are held by a person who holds them for sale or lease or to be furnished under contracts of service or if he has so furnished them, or if they are raw materials, work in process or materials used or consumed in a business. Inventory of a person is not to be classified as his equipment.

§ 9–110. Sufficiency of Description

For purposes of this Article any description of personal property or real estate is sufficient whether or not it is specific if it reasonably identifies what is described.

§ 9–113. Security Interests Arising Under Article on Sales

A security interest arising solely under the Article on Sales (Article 2) is subject to the provisions of this Article except that to the extent that and so long as the debtor does not have or does not lawfully obtain possession of the goods

(a) no security agreement is necessary to make the security interest enforceable; and

(b) no filing is required to perfect the security interest; and

(c) the rights of the secured party on default by the debtor are governed by the Article on Sales (Article 2).

Part 2—Validity of Security Agreement and Rights of Parties Thereto

§ 9–201. General Validity of Security Agreement

Except as otherwise provided by this Act a security agreement is effective according to its terms between the parties, against purchasers of the collateral and against creditors. Nothing in this Article validates any charge or practice illegal under any statute or regulation thereunder governing usury, small loans, retail installment sales, or the like, or extends the application of any such statute or regulation to any transaction not otherwise subject thereto.

§ 9–202. Title to Collateral Immaterial

Each provision of this Article with regard to rights, obligations and remedies applies whether title to collateral is in the secured party or in the debtor.

§ 9–203. Attachment and Enforceability of Security Interest; Proceeds; Formal Requisites

(1) Subject to the provisions of Section 4–208 on the security interest of a collecting bank, Section 8–321 on security interests in securities and Section 9–113 on a security interest arising under the Article on Sales, a security interest is not enforceable against the debtor or third parties with respect to the collateral and does not attach unless:

> **(a)** the collateral is in the possession of the secured party pursuant to agreement, or the debtor has signed a security agreement which contains a description of the collateral and in addition, when the security interest covers crops growing or to be grown or timber to be cut, a description of the land concerned;
>
> **(b)** value has been given; and
>
> **(c)** the debtor has rights in the collateral.

(2) A security interest attaches when it becomes enforceable against the debtor with respect to the collateral. Attachment occurs as soon as all of the events specified in subsection (1) have taken place unless explicit agreement postpones the time of attaching.

(3) Unless otherwise agreed a security agreement gives the secured party the rights to proceeds provided by Section 9–306.

(4) A transaction, although subject to this Article, is also subject to . . .*, and in the case of conflict between the provisions of this Article and any such statute, the provisions of such statute control. Failure to comply with any applicable statute has only the effect which is specified therein.

Amended in 1972 and 1977.

Note: *At * in subsection (4) insert reference to any local statute regulating small loans, retail installment sales and the like.*

The foregoing subsection (4) is designed to make it clear that certain transactions, although subject to this Article, must also comply with other applicable legislation.

This Article is designed to regulate all the "security" aspects of transactions within its scope. There is, however, much regulatory legislation, particularly in the consumer field, which supplements this Article and should not be repealed by its enactment. Examples are small loan acts, retail installment selling acts and the like. Such acts may provide for licensing and rate regulation and may prescribe particular forms of contract. Such provisions should remain in force despite the enactment of this Article. On the other hand if a retail installment selling act contains provisions on filing, rights on default, etc., such provisions should be repealed as inconsistent with this Article except that inconsistent provisions as to deficiencies, penalties, etc., in the Uniform Consumer Credit Code and other recent related legislation should remain because those statutes were drafted after the substantial enactment of the Article and with the intention of modifying certain provisions of this Article as to consumer credit.

§ 9–204. After-Acquired Property; Future Advances

(1) Except as provided in subsection (2), a security agreement may provide that any or all obligations covered by the security agreement are to be secured by after-acquired collateral.

(2) No security interest attaches under an after-acquired property clause to consumer goods other than accessions (Section 9–314) when given as additional security unless the debtor acquires rights in them within ten days after the secured party gives value.

(3) Obligations covered by a security agreement may include future advances or other value whether or not the advances or value are given pursuant to commitment (subsection (1) of Section 9–105).

Amended in 1972.

§ 9–205. Use or Disposition of Collateral Without Accounting Permissible

A security interest is not invalid or fraudulent against creditors by reason of liberty in the debtor to use, commingle or dispose of all or part of the collateral (including returned or repossessed goods) or to collect or compromise accounts or chattel paper, or to accept the return of goods or make repossessions, or to use, commingle or dispose of proceeds, or by reason of the failure of the secured party to require the debtor to account for proceeds or replace collateral. This section does not relax the requirements of possession where perfection of a security interest depends upon possession of the collateral by the secured party or by a bailee.

Amended in 1972.

§ 9–206. Agreement Not to Assert Defenses Against Assignee; Modification of Sales Warranties Where Security Agreement Exists

(1) Subject to any statute or decision which establishes a different rule for buyers or lessees of consumer goods, an agreement by a buyer or lessee that he will not assert against an assignee any claim or defense which he may have against the seller or lessor is enforceable by an assignee who takes his assignment for value, in good faith and without notice of a claim or defense, except as to defenses of a type which may be asserted against a holder in due course of a negotiable instrument under the Article on Commercial Paper (Article 3). A buyer who as part of one transaction signs both a negotiable instrument and a security agreement makes such an agreement.

(2) When a seller retains a purchase money security interest in goods the Article on Sales (Article 2) governs the sale and any disclaimer, limitation or modification of the seller's warranties.

Amended in 1962.

§ 9–207. Rights and Duties When Collateral is in Secured Party's Possession

(1) A secured party must use reasonable care in the custody and preservation of collateral in his possession. In the case of an instrument or chattel paper reasonable care includes taking necessary steps to preserve rights against prior parties unless otherwise agreed.

(2) Unless otherwise agreed, when collateral is in the secured party's possession

    (a) reasonable expenses (including the cost of any insurance and payment of taxes or other charges) incurred in the custody, preservation, use or operation of the collateral are chargeable to the debtor and are secured by the collateral;

    (b) the risk of accidental loss or damage is on the debtor to the extent of any deficiency in any effective insurance coverage;

    (c) the secured party may hold as additional security any increase or profits (except money) received from the collateral, but money so received, unless remitted to the debtor, shall be applied in reduction of the secured obligation;

    (d) the secured party must keep the collateral identifiable but fungible collateral may be commingled;

    (e) the secured party may repledge the collateral upon terms which do not impair the debtor's right to redeem it.

(3) A secured party is liable for any loss caused by his failure to meet any obligation imposed by the preceding subsections but does not lose his security interest.

(4) A secured party may use or operate the collateral for the purpose of preserving the collateral or its value or pursuant to the order of a court of appropriate jurisdiction or, except in the case of consumer goods, in the manner and to the extent provided in the security agreement.

Part 3—Rights of Third Parties; Perfected and Unperfected Security Interests; Rules of Priority

§ 9–301. Persons Who Take Priority Over Unperfected Security Interests; Rights of "Lien Creditor"

(1) Except as otherwise provided in subsection (2), an unperfected security interest is subordinate to the rights of

    (a) persons entitled to priority under Section 9–312;

    (b) a person who becomes a lien creditor before the security interest is perfected;

    (c) in the case of goods, instruments, documents, and chattel paper, a person who is not a secured party and who is a transferee in bulk or other buyer not in ordinary course of business or is a buyer of farm products in ordinary course of business, to the extent that he gives value and receives delivery of the collateral without knowledge of the security interest and before it is perfected;

    (d) in the case of accounts and general intangibles, a person who is not a secured party and who is a transferee to the extent that he gives value without knowledge of the security interest and before it is perfected.

(2) If the secured party files with respect to a purchase money security interest before or within ten days after the debtor receives possession of the collateral, he takes priority over the rights of a transferee in bulk or of a lien creditor which arise between the time the security interest attaches and the time of filing.

(3) A "lien creditor" means a creditor who has acquired a lien on the property involved by attachment, levy or the like and includes an assignee for benefit of creditors from the time of assignment, and a trustee in bankruptcy from the date of the filing of the petition or a receiver in equity from the time of appointment.

(4) A person who becomes a lien creditor while a security interest is perfected takes subject to the security interest only to the extent that it secures advances made before he becomes a lien creditor or within 45 days thereafter or made without knowledge of the lien or pursuant to a commitment entered into without knowledge of the lien.

Amended in 1972.

§ 9–302. When Filing Is Required to Perfect Security Interest; Security Interests to Which Filing Provisions of This Article Do Not Apply

(1) A financing statement must be filed to perfect all security interests except the following:

(a) a security interest in collateral in possession of the secured party under Section 9–305;

(b) a security interest temporarily perfected in instruments or documents without delivery under Section 9–304 or in proceeds for a 10 day period under Section 9–306;

(c) a security interest created by an assignment of a beneficial interest in a trust or a decedent's estate;

(d) a purchase money security interest in consumer goods; but filing is required for a motor vehicle required to be registered; and fixture filing is required for priority over conflicting interests in fixtures to the extent provided in Section 9–313;

(e) an assignment of accounts which does not alone or in conjunction with other assignments to the same assignee transfer a significant part of the outstanding accounts of the assignor;

(f) a security interest of a collecting bank (Section 4–208) or in securities (Section 8–321) or arising under the Article on Sales (see Section 9–113) or covered in subsection (3) of this section;

(g) an assignment for the benefit of all the creditors of the transferor, and subsequent transfers by the assignee thereunder.

(2) If a secured party assigns a perfected security interest, no filing under this Article is required in order to continue the perfected status of the security interest against creditors of and transferees from the original debtor.

(3) The filing of a financing statement otherwise required by this Article is not necessary or effective to perfect a security interest in property subject to

(a) a statute or treaty of the United States which provides for a national or international registration or a national or international certificate of title or which specifies a place of filing different from that specified in this Article for filing of the security interest; or

(b) the following statutes of this state; [list any certificate of title statute covering automobiles, trailers, mobile homes, boats, farm tractors, or the like, and any central filing statute]; but during any period in which collateral is inventory held for sale by a person who is in the business of selling goods of that kind, the filing provisions of this Article (Part 4) apply to a security interest in that collateral created by him as debtor; or

(c) a certificate of title statute of another jurisdiction under the law of which indication of a security interest on the certificate is required as a condition of perfection (subsection (2) of Section 9–103).

(4) Compliance with a statute or treaty described in subsection (3) is equivalent to the filing of a financing statement under this Article, and a security interest in property subject to the statute or treaty can be perfected only by compliance therewith except as provided in Section 9–103 on multiple state transactions. Duration and renewal of perfection of a security interest perfected by compliance with the statute or treaty are governed by the provisions of the statute or treaty; in other respects the security interest is subject to this Article.

Amended in 1972 and 1977.

§ 9–303. When Security Interest Is Perfected; Continuity of Perfection

(1) A security interest is perfected when it has attached and when all of the applicable steps required for perfection have been taken. Such steps are specified in Sections 9–302, 9–304, 9–305 and 9–306. If such steps are taken before the security interest attaches, it is perfected at the time when it attaches.

(2) If a security interest is originally perfected in any way permitted under this Article and is subsequently perfected in some other way under this Article, without an intermediate period when it was unperfected, the security interest shall be deemed to be perfected continuously for the purposes of this Article.

§ 9–304. Perfection of Security Interest in Instruments, Documents, and Goods Covered by Documents; Perfection by Permissive Filing; Temporary Perfection Without Filing or Transfer of Possession

(1) A security interest in chattel paper or negotiable documents may be perfected by filing. A security interest in money or instruments (other than certificated securities or instruments which constitute part of chattel paper) can be perfected only by the secured party's taking possession, except as provided in subsections (4) and (5) of this section and subsections (2) and (3) of Section 9–306 on proceeds.

(2) During the period that goods are in the possession of the issuer of a negotiable document therefor, a security interest in the goods is perfected by perfecting a security interest in the document, and any security interest in the goods otherwise perfected during such period is subject thereto.

(3) A security interest in goods in the possession of a bailee other than one who has issued a negotiable document therefor is perfected by issuance of a document in the name of the secured party or by the bailee's receipt of notification of the secured party's interest or by filing as to the goods.

(4) A security interest in instruments (other than certificated securities) or negotiable documents is perfected without filing or the taking of possession for a period of 21 days from the time it attaches to the extent that it arises for new value given under a written security agreement.

(5) A security interest remains perfected for a period of 21 days without filing where a secured party having a perfected security interest in an instrument (other than a certificated security), a negotiable document or goods in possession of a bailee other than one who has issued a negotiable document therefor

(a) makes available to the debtor the goods or documents representing the goods for the purpose of ultimate sale or exchange or for the purpose of loading, unloading, storing, shipping, transshipping, manufacturing, processing or otherwise dealing with them in a manner preliminary to their sale or exchange, but priority between conflicting security interests in the goods is subject to subsection (3) of Section 9–312; or

(b) delivers the instrument to the debtor for the purpose of ultimate sale or exchange or of presentation, collection, renewal or registration of transfer.

(6) After the 21 day period in subsections (4) and (5) perfection depends upon compliance with applicable provisions of this Article.

Amended in 1972 and 1977.

§ 9–305. When Possession by Secured Party Perfects Security Interest Without Filing

A security interest in letters of credit and advices of credit (sub-section (2)(a) of Section 5–116), goods, instruments (other than certificated securities), money, negotiable documents, or chattel paper may be perfected by the secured party's taking possession of the collateral. If such collateral other than goods covered by a negotiable document is held by a bailee, the secured party is deemed to have possession from the time the bailee receives notification of the secured party's interest. A security interest is perfected by possession from the time possession is taken with-out a relation back and continues only so long as possession is retained, unless otherwise specified in this Article. The security interest may be otherwise perfected as provided in this Article before or after the period of possession by the secured party.

Amended in 1972 and 1977.

§ 9–306. "Proceeds"; Secured Party's Rights on Disposition of Collateral

(1) "Proceeds" includes whatever is received upon the sale, exchange, collection or other disposition of collateral or pro-ceeds. Insurance payable by reason of loss or damage to the col-lateral is proceeds, except to the extent that it is payable to a person other than a party to the security agreement. Money, checks, deposit accounts, and the like are "cash proceeds". All other proceeds are "non-cash proceeds".

(2) Except where this Article otherwise provides, a security interest continues in collateral notwithstanding sale, exchange or other disposition thereof unless the disposition was autho-rized by the secured party in the security agreement or other-wise, and also continues in any identifiable proceeds including collections received by the debtor.

(3) The security interest in proceeds is a continuously per-fected security interest if the interest in the original collateral was perfected but it ceases to be a perfected security interest and becomes unperfected ten days after receipt of the proceeds by the debtor unless

(a) a filed financing statement covers the original collateral and the proceeds are collateral in which a security interest may be perfected by filing in the office or offices where the financing statement has been filed and, if the proceeds are acquired with cash proceeds, the description of collateral in the financing statement indicates the types of property constituting the proceeds; or

(b) a filed financing statement covers the original collateral and the proceeds are identifiable cash proceeds; or

(c) the security interest in the proceeds is perfected before the expiration of the ten day period.

Except as provided in this section, a security interest in pro-ceeds can be perfected only by the methods or under the cir-cumstances permitted in this Article for original collateral of the same type.

(4) In the event of insolvency proceedings instituted by or against a debtor, a secured party with a perfected security inter-est in proceeds has a perfected security interest only in the fol-lowing proceeds:

(a) in identifiable non-cash proceeds and in separate deposit accounts containing only proceeds;

(b) in identifiable cash proceeds in the form of money which is neither commingled with other money nor deposited in a deposit account prior to the insolvency pro-ceedings;

(c) in identifiable cash proceeds in the form of checks and the like which are not deposited in a deposit account prior to the insolvency proceedings; and

(d) in all cash and deposit accounts of the debtor in which proceeds have been commingled with other funds, but the perfected security interest under this paragraph (d) is

(i) subject to any right to set-off; and

(ii) limited to an amount not greater than the amount of any cash proceeds received by the debtor within ten days fore the institution of the insolvency proceedings less the sum of (I) the payments to the secured party on account of cash proceeds received by the debtor during such period and (II) the cash proceeds received by the debtor during such period to which the secured party is entitled under paragraphs (a) through (c) of this subsection (4).

(5) If a sale of goods results in an account or chattel paper which is transferred by the seller to a secured party, and if the goods are returned to or are repossessed by the seller or the secured party, the following rules determine priorities:

(a) If the goods were collateral at the time of sale, for an indebtedness of the seller which is still unpaid, the orig-inal security interest attaches again to the goods and con-tinues as a perfected security interest if it was perfected at the time when the goods were sold. If the security interest was originally perfected by a filing which is still effective, nothing further is required to continue the per-fected status; in any other case, the secured party must take possession of the returned or repossessed goods or must file.

(b) An unpaid transferee of the chattel paper has a security interest in the goods against the transferor. Such security interest is prior to a security interest asserted under para-graph (a) to the extent that the transferee of the chattel paper was entitled to priority under Section 9–308.

(c) An unpaid transferee of the account has a security interest in the goods against the transferor. Such security interest is subordinate to a security interest asserted under paragraph (a).

(d) A security interest of an unpaid transferee asserted under paragraph (b) or (c) must be perfected for protection against creditors of the transferor and purchasers of the returned or repossessed goods.

Amended in 1972.

§ 9–307. Protection of Buyers of Goods

(1) A buyer in ordinary course of business (subsection (9) of Section 1–201) other than a person buying farm products from a person engaged in farming operations takes free of a security interest created by his seller even though the security interest is perfected and even though the buyer knows of its existence.

(2) In the case of consumer goods, a buyer takes free of a security interest even though perfected if he buys without knowledge of the security interest, for value and for his own personal, family or household purposes unless prior to the purchase the secured party has filed a financing statement cov-ering such goods.

(3) A buyer other than a buyer in ordinary course of business (subsection (1) of this section) takes free of a security interest to the extent that it secures future advances made after the secured party acquires knowledge of the purchase, or more than 45 days after the purchase, whichever first occurs, unless made pursuant to a commitment entered into without knowledge of the purchase and before the expiration of the 45 day period.

Amended in 1972.

§ 9–308. Purchase of Chattel Paper and Instruments

A purchaser of chattel paper or an instrument who gives new value and takes possession of it in the ordinary course of his business has priority over a security interest in the chattel paper or instrument.

(a) which is perfected under Section 9–304 (permissive filing and temporary perfection) or under Section 9–306 (perfection as to proceeds) if he acts without knowledge that the specific paper or instrument is subject to a security interest; or

(b) which is claimed merely as proceeds of inventory subject to a security interest (Section 9–306) even though he knows that the specific paper or instrument is subject to the security interest.

Amended in 1972.

§ 9–309. Protection of Purchasers of Instruments, Documents and Securities

Nothing in this Article limits the rights of a holder in due course of a negotiable instrument (Section 3–302) or a holder to whom a negotiable document of title has been duly negotiated (Section 7–501) or a bona fide purchaser of a security (Section 8–302) and the holders or purchasers take priority over an earlier security interest even though perfected. Filing under this Article does not constitute notice of the security interest to such holders or purchasers.

Amended in 1977.

§ 9–310. Priority of Certain Liens Arising by Operation of Law

When a person in the ordinary course of his business furnishes services or materials with respect to goods subject to a security interest, a lien upon goods in the possession of such person given by statute or rule of law for such materials or services takes priority over a perfected security interest unless the lien is statutory and the statute expressly provides otherwise.

§ 9–312. Priorities Among Conflicting Security Interests in the Same Collateral

(1) The rules of priority stated in other sections of this Part and in the following sections shall govern when applicable: Section 4–208 with respect to the security interests of collecting banks in items being collected, accompanying documents and proceeds; Section 9–103 on security interests related to other jurisdictions; Section 9–114 on consignments.

(2) A perfected security interest in crops for new value given to enable the debtor to produce the crops during the production season and given not more than three months before the crops become growing crops by planting or otherwise takes priority over an earlier perfected security interest to the extent that such earlier interest secures obligations due more than six months before the crops become growing crops by planting or otherwise, even though the person giving new value had knowledge of the earlier security interest.

(3) A perfected purchase money security interest in inventory has priority over a conflicting security interest in the same inventory and also has priority in identifiable cash proceeds received on or before the delivery of the inventory to a buyer if

    (a) the purchase money security interest is perfected at the time the debtor receives possession of the inventory; and

    (b) the purchase money secured party gives notification in writing to the holder of the conflicting security interest if the holder had filed a financing statement covering the same types of inventory (i) before the date of the filing made by the purchase money secured party, or (ii) before the beginning of the 21 day period where the purchase money security interest is temporarily perfected without filing or possession (subsection (5) of Section 9–304); and

    (c) the holder of the conflicting security interest receives the notification within five years before the debtor receives possession of the inventory; and

    (d) the notification states that the person giving the notice has or expects to acquire a purchase money security interest in inventory of the debtor, describing such inventory by item or type.

(4) A purchase money security interest in collateral other than inventory has priority over a conflicting security interest in the same collateral or its proceeds if the purchase money security interest is perfected at the time the debtor receives possession of the collateral or within ten days thereafter.

(5) In all cases not governed by other rules stated in this section (including cases of purchase money security interests which do not qualify for the special priorities set forth in subsections (3) and (4) of this section), priority between conflicting security interests in the same collateral shall be determined according to the following rules:

    (a) Conflicting security interests rank according to priority in time of filing or perfection. Priority dates from the time a filing is first made covering the collateral or the time the security interest is first perfected, whichever is earlier, provided that there is no period thereafter when there is neither filing nor perfection.

    (b) So long as conflicting security interests are unperfected, the first to attach has priority.

(6) For the purposes of subsection (5) a date of filing or perfection as to collateral is also a date of filing or perfection as to proceeds.

(7) If future advances are made while a security interest is perfected by filing, the taking of possession, or under Section 8–321 on securities, the security interest has the same priority for the purposes of subsection (5) with respect to the future advances as it does with respect to the first advance. If a commitment is made before or while the security interest is so perfected, the security interest has the same priority with respect to advances made pursuant thereto. In other cases a perfected security interest has priority from the date the advance is made.

Amended in 1972 and 1977.

§ 9–313. Priority of Security Interests in Fixtures

(1) In this section and in the provisions of Part 4 of this Article referring to fixture filing, unless the context otherwise requires

(a) goods are "fixtures" when they become so related to particular real estate that an interest in them arises under real estate law

(b) a "fixture filing" is the filing in the office where a mortgage on the real estate would be filed or recorded of a financing statement covering goods which are or are to become fixtures and conforming to the requirements of subsection (5) of Section 9–402

(c) a mortgage is a "construction mortgage" to the extent that it secures an obligation incurred for the construction of an improvement on land including the acquisition cost of the land, if the recorded writing so indicates.

(2) A security interest under this Article may be created in goods which are fixtures or may continue in goods which become fixtures, but no security interest exists under this Article in ordinary building materials incorporated into an improvement on land.

(3) This Article does not prevent creation of an encumbrance upon fixtures pursuant to real estate law.

(4) A perfected security interest in fixtures has priority over the conflicting interest of an encumbrancer or owner of the real estate where

(a) the security interest is a purchase money security interest, the interest of the encumbrancer or owner arises before the goods become fixtures, the security interest is perfected by a fixture filing before the goods become fixtures or within ten days thereafter, and the debtor has an interest of record in the real estate or is in possession of the real estate; or

(b) the security interest is perfected by a fixture filing before the interest of the encumbrancer or owner is of record, the security interest has priority over any conflicting interest of a predecessor in title of the encumbrancer or owner, and the debtor has an interest of record in the real estate or is in possession of the real estate; or

(c) the fixtures are readily removable factory or office machines or readily removable replacements of domestic appliances which are consumer goods, and before the goods become fixtures the security interest is perfected by any method permitted by this Article; or

(d) the conflicting interest is a lien on the real estate obtained by legal or equitable proceedings after the security interest was perfected by any method permitted by this Article.

(5) A security interest in fixtures, whether or not perfected, has priority over the conflicting interest of an encumbrancer or owner of the real estate where

(a) the encumbrancer or owner has consented in writing to the security interest or has disclaimed an interest in the goods as fixtures; or

(b) the debtor has a right to remove the goods as against the encumbrancer or owner. If the debtor's right terminates, the priority of the security interest continues for a reasonable time.

(6) Notwithstanding paragraph (a) of subsection (4) but otherwise subject to subsections (4) and (5), a security interest in fixtures is subordinate to a construction mortgage recorded before the goods become fixtures if the goods become fixtures before the completion of the construction. To the extent that it is given to refinance a construction mortgage, a mortgage has this priority to the same extent as the construction mortgage.

(7) In cases not within the preceding subsections, a security interest in fixtures is subordinate to the conflicting interest of an encumbrancer or owner of the related real estate who is not the debtor.

(8) When the secured party has priority over all owners and encumbrancers of the real estate, he may, on default, subject to the provisions of Part 5, remove his collateral from the real estate but he must reimburse any encumbrancer or owner of the real estate who is not the debtor and who has not otherwise agreed for the cost of repair of any physical injury, but not for any diminution in value of the real estate caused by the absence of the goods removed or by any necessity of replacing them. A person entitled to reimbursement may refuse permission to remove until the secured party gives adequate security for the performance of this obligation.

Amended in 1972.

§ 9–314. Accessions

(1) A security interest in goods which attaches before they are installed in or affixed to other goods takes priority as to the goods installed or affixed (called in this section "accessions") over the claims of all persons to the whole except as stated in subsection (3) and subject to Section 9–315(1).

(2) A security interest which attaches to goods after they become part of a whole is valid against all persons subsequently acquiring interests in the whole except as stated in subsection (3) but is invalid against any person with an interest in the whole at the time the security interest attaches to the goods who has not in writing consented to the security interest or disclaimed an interest in the goods as part of the whole.

(3) The security interests described in subsections (1) and (2) do not take priority over

(a) a subsequent purchaser for value of any interest in the whole; or

(b) a creditor with a lien on the whole subsequently obtained by judicial proceedings; or

(c) a creditor with a prior perfected security interest in the whole to the extent that he makes subsequent advances if the subsequent purchase is made, the lien by judicial proceedings obtained or the subsequent advance under the prior perfected security interest is made or contracted for without knowledge of the security interest and before it is perfected. A purchaser of the whole at a foreclosure sale other than the holder of a perfected security interest purchasing at his own foreclosure sale is a subsequent purchaser within this section.

(4) When under subsections (1) or (2) and (3) a secured party has an interest in accessions which has priority over the claims of all persons who have interests in the whole, he may on default subject to the provisions of Part 5 remove his collateral from the whole but he must reimburse any encumbrancer or owner of the whole who is not the debtor and who has not otherwise agreed for the cost of repair of any physical injury but not for any diminution in value of the whole caused by the absence of the goods removed or by any necessity for replacing them. A person entitled to reimbursement may refuse permission to

remove until the secured party gives adequate security for the performance of this obligation.

§ 9–315. Priority When Goods Are Commingled or Processed

(1) If a security interest in goods was perfected and subsequently the goods or a part thereof have become part of a product or mass, the security interest continues in the product or mass if

(a) the goods are so manufactured, processed, assembled or commingled that their identity is lost in the product or mass; or

(b) a financing statement covering the original goods also covers the product into which the goods have been manufactured, processed or assembled.

In a case to which paragraph (b) applies, no separate security interest in that part of the original goods which has been manufactured, processed or assembled into the product may be claimed under Section 9–314.

(2) When under subsection (1) more than one security interest attaches to the product or mass, they rank equally according to the ratio that the cost of the goods to which each interest originally attached bears to the cost of the total product or mass.

§ 9–316. Priority Subject to Subordination

Nothing in this Article prevents subordination by agreement by any person entitled to priority.

§ 9–318. Defenses Against Assignee; Modification of Contract After Notification of Assignment; Term Prohibiting Assignment Ineffective; Identification and Proof of Assignment

(1) Unless an account debtor has made an enforceable agreement not to assert defenses or claims arising out of a sale as provided in Section 9–206 the rights of an assignee are subject to

(a) all the terms of the contract between the account debtor and assignor and any defense or claim arising therefrom; and

(b) any other defense or claim of the account debtor against the assignor which accrues before the account debtor receives notification of the assignment.

(2) So far as the right to payment or a part thereof under an assigned contract has not been fully earned by performance, and notwithstanding notification of the assignment, any modification of or substitution for the contract made in good faith and in accordance with reasonable commercial standards is effective against an assignee unless the account debtor has otherwise agreed but the assignee acquires corresponding rights under the modified or substituted contract. The assignment may provide that such modification or substitution is a breach by the assignor.

(3) The account debtor is authorized to pay the assignor until the account debtor receives notification that the amount due or to become due has been assigned and that payment is to be made to the assignee. A notification which does not reasonably identify the rights assigned is ineffective. If requested by the account debtor, the assignee must seasonably furnish reasonable proof that the assignment has been made and unless he does so the account debtor may pay the assignor.

(4) A term in any contract between an account debtor and an assignor is ineffective if it prohibits assignment of an account or

prohibits creation of a security interest in a general intangible for money due or to become due or requires the account debtor's consent to such assignment or security interest.

Amended in 1972.

Part 4—Filing

§ 9–401. Place of Filing; Erroneous Filing; Removal of Collateral

First Alternative Subsection (1)

(1) The proper place to file in order to perfect a security interest is as follows:

(a) when the collateral is timber to be cut or is minerals or the like (including oil and gas) or accounts subject to subsection (5) of Section 9–103, or when the financing statement is filed as a fixture filing (Section 9–313) and the collateral is goods which are or are to become fixtures, then in the office where a mortgage on the real estate would be filed or recorded;

(b) in all other cases, in the office of the [Secretary of State].

Second Alternative Subsection (1)

(1) The proper place to file in order to perfect a security interest is as follows:

(a) when the collateral is equipment used in farming operations, or farm products, or accounts or general intangibles arising from or relating to the sale of farm products by a farmer, or consumer goods, then in the office of the _____ in the county of the debtor's residence or if the debtor is not a resident of this state then in the office of the _____ in the county where the goods are kept, and in addition when the collateral is crops growing or to be grown in the office of the _____ in the county where the land is located;

(b) when the collateral is timber to be cut or is minerals or the like (including oil and gas) or accounts subject to subsection (5) of Section 9–103, or when the financing statement is filed as a fixture filing (Section 9–313) and the collateral is goods which are or are to become fixtures, then in the office where a mortgage on the real estate would be filed or recorded;

(c) in all other cases, in the office of the [Secretary of State].

Third Alternative Subsection (1)

(1) The proper place to file in order to perfect a security interest is as follows:

(a) when the collateral is equipment used in farming operations, or farm products, or accounts or general intangibles arising from or relating to the sale of farm products by a farmer, or consumer goods, then in the office of the _____ in the county of the debtor's residence or if the debtor is not a resident of this state then in the office of the _____ in the county where the goods are kept, and in addition when the collateral is crops growing or to be grown in the office of the _____ in the county where the land is located;

(b) when the collateral is timber to be cut or is minerals or the like (including oil and gas) or accounts subject to subsection (5) of Section 9–103, or when the financing statement is filed as a fixture filing (Section 9–313) and the collateral is goods which are or are to become fixtures, then in the office where a mortgage on the real estate would be filed or recorded;

(c) in all other cases, in the office of the [Secretary of State] and in addition, if the debtor has a place of business in only one county of this state, also in the office of _____ of such county, or, if the debtor has no place of business in this state, but resides in the state, also in the office of _____ of the county in which he resides.

Note: *One of the three alternatives should be selected as subsection (1).*

(2) A filing which is made in good faith in an improper place or not in all of the places required by this section is nevertheless effective with regard to any collateral as to which the filing complied with the requirements of this Article and is also effective with regard to collateral covered by the financing statement against any person who has knowledge of the contents of such financing statement.

(3) A filing which is made in the proper place in this state continues effective even though the debtor's residence or place of business or the location of the collateral or its use, whichever controlled the original filing, is thereafter changed.

Alternative Subsection (3)

[(3) A filing which is made in the proper county continues effective for four months after a change to another county of the debtor's residence or place of business or the location of the collateral, whichever controlled the original filing. It becomes ineffective thereafter unless a copy of the financing statement signed by the secured party is filed in the new county within said period. The security interest may also be perfected in the new county after the expiration of the four-month period; in such case perfection dates from the time of perfection in the new county. A change in the use of the collateral does not impair the effectiveness of the original filing.]

(4) The rules stated in Section 9–103 determine whether filing is necessary in this state.

(5) Notwithstanding the preceding subsections, and subject to subsection (3) of Section 9–302, the proper place to file in order to perfect a security interest in collateral, including fixtures, of a transmitting utility is the office of the [Secretary of State]. This filing constitutes a fixture filing (Section 9–313) as to the collateral described therein which is or is to become fixtures.

(6) For the purposes of this section, the residence of an organization is its place of business if it has one or its chief executive office if it has more than one place of business.

Amended in 1962 and 1972.

Note: *Subsection (6) should be used only if the state chooses the Second or Third Alternative Subsection (1).*

§ 9–402. Formal Requisites of Financing Statement; Amendments; Mortgage as Financing Statement

(1) A financing statement is sufficient if it gives the names of the debtor and the secured party, is signed by the debtor, gives an address of the secured party from which information concerning the security interest may be obtained, gives a mailing address of the debtor and contains a statement indicating the types, or describing the items, of collateral. A financing statement may be filed before a security agreement is made or a security interest otherwise attaches. When the financing statement covers crops growing or to be grown, the statement must also contain a description of the real estate concerned. When the financing

statement covers timber to be cut or covers minerals or the like (including oil and gas) or accounts subject to subsection (5) of Section 9–103, or when the financing statement is filed as a fixture filing (Section 9–313) and the collateral is goods which are or are to become fixtures, the statement must also comply with subsection (5). A copy of the security agreement is sufficient as a financing statement if it contains the above information and is signed by the debtor. A carbon, photographic or other reproduction of a security agreement or a financing statement is sufficient as a financing statement if the security agreement so provides or if the original has been filed in this state.

(2) A financing statement which otherwise complies with subsection (1) is sufficient when it is signed by the secured party instead of the debtor if it is filed to perfect a security interest in

(a) collateral already subject to a security interest in another jurisdiction when it is brought into this state, or when the debtor's location is changed to this state. Such a financing statement must state that the collateral was brought into this state or that the debtor's location was changed to this state under such circumstances; or

(b) proceeds under Section 9–306 if the security interest in the original collateral was perfected. Such a financing statement must describe the original collateral; or

(c) collateral as to which the filing has lapsed; or

(d) collateral acquired after a change of name, identity or corporate structure of the debtor (subsection (7)).

(3) A form substantially as follows is sufficient to comply with subsection (1):

Name of debtor (or assignor) _____

Address _____

Name of secured party (or assignee) _____

Address _____

1. This financing statement covers the following types (or items) of property:

(Describe) _____

2. (If collateral is crops) The above described crops are growing or are to be grown on:

(Describe Real Estate) _____

3. (If applicable) The above goods are to become fixtures on*

*Where appropriate substitute either "The above timber is standing on _____" or "The above minerals or the like (including oil and gas) or accounts will be financed at the wellhead or minehead of the well or mine located on"

(Describe Real Estate) _____ and this financing statement is to be filed [for record] in the real estate records. (If the debtor does not have an interest of record) The name of a record owner is _____

4. (If products of collateral are claimed) Products of the collateral are also covered.

(use . . . .
whichever   Signature of Debtor (or Assignor)
    is   . . . .
applicable)   Signature of Secured Party (or Assignee)

(4) A financing statement may be amended by filing a writing signed by both the debtor and the secured party. An amendment does not extend the period of effectiveness of a financing

statement. If any amendment adds collateral, it is effective as to the added collateral only from the filing date of the amendment. In this Article, unless the context otherwise requires, the term "financing statement" means the original financing statement and any amendments.

(5) A financing statement covering timber to be cut or covering minerals or the like (including oil and gas) or accounts subject to subsection (5) of Section 9–103, or a financing statement filed as a fixture filing (Section 9–313) where the debtor is not a transmitting utility, must show that it covers this type of collateral, must recite that it is to be filed [for record] in the real estate records, and the financing statement must contain a description of the real estate [sufficient if it were contained in a mortgage of the real estate to give constructive notice of the mortgage under the law of this state]. If the debtor does not have an interest of record in the real estate, the financing statement must show the name of a record owner.

(6) A mortgage is effective as a financing statement filed as a fixture filing from the date of its recording if

    (a) the goods are described in the mortgage by item or type; and

    (b) the goods are or are to become fixtures related to the real estate described in the mortgage; and

    (c) the mortgage complies with the requirements for a financing statement in this section other than a recital that it is to be filed in the real estate records; and

    (d) the mortgage is duly recorded.

No fee with reference to the financing statement is required other than the regular recording and satisfaction fees with respect to the mortgage.

(7) A financing statement sufficiently shows the name of the debtor if it gives the individual, partnership or corporate name of the debtor, whether or not it adds other trade names or names of partners. Where the debtor so changes his name or in the case of an organization its name, identity or corporate structure that a filed financing statement becomes seriously misleading, the filing is not effective to perfect a security interest in collateral acquired by the debtor more than four months after the change, unless a new appropriate financing statement is filed before the expiration of that time. A filed financing statement remains effective with respect to collateral transferred by the debtor even though the secured party knows of or consents to the transfer.

(8) A financing statement substantially complying with the requirements of this section is effective even though it contains minor errors which are not seriously misleading.

    Amended in 1972.

    Note: *Language in brackets is optional.*

    Note: *Where the state has any special recording system for real estate other than the usual grantor-grantee index (as, for instance, a tract system or a title registration or Torrens system) local adaptations of subsection (5) and Section 9–403(7) may be necessary. See Mass. Gen.Laws Chapter 106, Section 9–409.*

§ 9–403. What Constitutes Filing; Duration of Filing; Effect of Lapsed Filing; Duties of Filing Officer

(1) Presentation for filing of a financing statement and tender of the filing fee or acceptance of the statement by the filing officer constitutes filing under this Article.

(2) Except as provided in subsection (6) a filed financing statement is effective for a period of five years from the date of filing. The effectiveness of a filed financing statement lapses on the expiration of the five year period unless a continuation statement is filed prior to the lapse. If a security interest perfected by filing exists at the time insolvency proceedings are commenced by or against the debtor, the security interest remains perfected until termination of the insolvency proceedings and thereafter for a period of sixty days or until expiration of the five year period, whichever occurs later. Upon lapse the security interest becomes unperfected, unless it is perfected without filing. If the security interest becomes unperfected upon lapse, it is deemed to have been unperfected as against a person who became a purchaser or lien creditor before lapse.

(3) A continuation statement may be filed by the secured party within six months prior to the expiration of the five year period specified in subsection (2). Any such continuation statement must be signed by the secured party, identify the original statement by file number and state that the original statement is still effective. A continuation statement signed by a person other than the secured party of record must be accompanied by a separate written statement of assignment signed by the secured party of record and complying with subsection (2) of Section 9–405, including payment of the required fee. Upon timely filing of the continuation statement, the effectiveness of the original statement is continued for five years after the last date to which the filing was effective whereupon it lapses in the same manner as provided in subsection (2) unless another continuation statement is filed prior to such lapse. Succeeding continuation statements may be filed in the same manner to continue the effectiveness of the original statement. Unless a statute on disposition of public records provides otherwise, the filing officer may remove a lapsed statement from the files and destroy it immediately if he has retained a microfilm or other photographic record, or in other cases after one year after the lapse. The filing officer shall so arrange matters by physical annexation of financing statements to continuation statements or other related filings, or by other means, that if he physically destroys the financing statements of a period more than five years past, those which have been continued by a continuation statement or which are still effective under subsection (6) shall be retained.

(4) Except as provided in subsection (7) a filing officer shall mark each statement with a file number and with the date and hour of filing and shall hold the statement or a microfilm or other photographic copy thereof for public inspection. In addition the filing officer shall index the statement according to the name of the debtor and shall note in the index the file number and the address of the debtor given in the statement.

(5) The uniform fee for filing and indexing and for stamping a copy furnished by the secured party to show the date and place of filing for an original financing statement or for a continuation statement shall be $_____ if the statement is in the standard form prescribed by the [Secretary of State] and otherwise shall be $_____, plus in each case, if the financing statement is subject to subsection (5) of Section 9–402, $_____. The uniform fee for each name more than one required to be indexed shall be $_____. The secured party may at his option show a trade name for any person and an extra uniform indexing fee of $_____ shall be paid with respect thereto.

(6) If the debtor is a transmitting utility (subsection (5) of Section 9–401) and a filed financing statement so states, it is effective until a termination statement is filed. A real estate mortgage which is effective as a fixture filing under subsection (6) of Section 9–402 remains effective as a fixture filing until the mortgage is released or satisfied of record or its effectiveness otherwise terminates as to the real estate.

(7) When a financing statement covers timber to be cut or covers minerals or the like (including oil and gas) or accounts subject to subsection (5) of Section 9–103, or is filed as a fixture filing, [it shall be filed for record and] the filing officer shall index it under the names of the debtor and any owner of record shown on the financing statement in the same fashion as if they were the mortgagors in a mortgage of the real estate described, and, to the extent that the law of this state provides for indexing of mortgages under the name of the mortgagee, under the name of the secured party as if he were the mortgagee thereunder, or where indexing is by description in the same fashion as if the financing statement were a mortgage of the real estate described.

Amended in 1972.

Note: *In states in which writings will not appear in the real estate records and indices unless actually recorded the bracketed language in subsection (7) should be used.*

§ 9–404. Termination Statement

(1) If a financing statement covering consumer goods is filed on or after _____, then within one month or within ten days following written demand by the debtor after there is no outstanding secured obligation and no commitment to make advances, incur obligations or otherwise give value, the secured party must file with each filing officer with whom the financing statement was filed, a termination statement to the effect that he no longer claims a security interest under the financing statement, which shall be identified by file number. In other cases whenever there is no outstanding secured obligation and no commitment to make advances, incur obligations or otherwise give value, the secured party must on written demand by the debtor send the debtor, for each filing officer with whom the financing statement was filed, a termination statement to the effect that he no longer claims a security interest under the financing statement, which shall be identified by file number. A termination statement signed by a person other than the secured party of record must be accompanied by a separate written statement of assignment signed by the secured party of record complying with subsection (2) of Section 9–405, including payment of the required fee. If the affected secured party fails to file such a termination statement as required by this subsection, or to send such a termination statement within ten days after proper demand therefor, he shall be liable to the debtor for one hundred dollars, and in addition for any loss caused to the debtor by such failure.

(2) On presentation to the filing officer of such a termination statement he must note it in the index. If he has received the termination statement in duplicate, he shall return one copy of the termination statement to the secured party stamped to show the time of receipt thereof. If the filing officer has a microfilm or other photographic record of the financing statement, and of any related continuation statement, statement of assignment and statement of release, he may remove the originals from the files at any time after receipt of the termination statement, or if he has no such record, he may remove them from the files at any time after one year after receipt of the termination statement.

(3) If the termination statement is in the standard form prescribed by the [Secretary of State], the uniform fee for filing and indexing the termination statement shall be $_____, and otherwise shall be $_____, plus in each case an additional fee of $_____ for each name more than one against which the termination statement is required to be indexed.

Amended in 1972.

Note: *The date to be inserted should be the effective date of the revised Article 9.*

Part 5—Default

§ 9–501. Default; Procedure When Security Agreement Covers Both Real and Personal Property

(1) When a debtor is in default under a security agreement, a secured party has the rights and remedies provided in this Part and except as limited by subsection (3) those provided in the security agreement. He may reduce his claim to judgment, foreclose or otherwise enforce the security interest by any available judicial procedure. If the collateral is documents the secured party may proceed either as to the documents or as to the goods covered thereby. A secured party in possession has the rights, remedies and duties provided in Section 9–207. The rights and remedies referred to in this subsection are cumulative.

(2) After default, the debtor has the rights and remedies provided in this Part, those provided in the security agreement and those provided in Section 9–207.

(3) To the extent that they give rights to the debtor and impose duties on the secured party, the rules stated in the subsections referred to below may not be waived or varied except as provided with respect to compulsory disposition of collateral (subsection (3) of Section 9–504 and Section 9–505) and with respect to redemption of collateral (Section 9–506) but the parties may by agreement determine the standards by which the fulfillment of these rights and duties is to be measured if such standards are not manifestly unreasonable:

   (a) subsection (2) of Section 9–502 and subsection (2) of Section 9–504 insofar as they require accounting for surplus proceeds of collateral;

   (b) subsection (3) of Section 9–504 and subsection (1) of Section 9–505 which deal with disposition of collateral;

   (c) subsection (2) of Section 9–505 which deals with acceptance of collateral as discharge of obligation;

   (d) Section 9–506 which deals with redemption of collateral; and

   (e) subsection (1) of Section 9–507 which deals with the secured party's liability for failure to comply with this Part.

(4) If the security agreement covers both real and personal property, the secured party may proceed under this Part as to the personal property or he may proceed as to both the real and the personal property in accordance with his rights and remedies in respect of the real property in which case the provisions of this Part do not apply.

(5) When a secured party has reduced his claim to judgment the lien of any levy which may be made upon his collateral by virtue of any execution based upon the judgment shall relate back to the date of the perfection of the security interest in such collateral. A judicial sale, pursuant to such execution, is a foreclosure of the security interest by judicial procedure within the meaning of this section, and the secured party may purchase at

the sale and thereafter hold the collateral free of any other requirements of this Article.

Amended in 1972.

§ 9–502. Collection Rights of Secured Party

(1) When so agreed and in any event on default the secured party is entitled to notify an account debtor or the obligor on an instrument to make payment to him whether or not the assignor was theretofore making collections on the collateral, and also to take control of any proceeds to which he is entitled under Section 9–306.

(2) A secured party who by agreement is entitled to charge back uncollected collateral or otherwise to full or limited recourse against the debtor and who undertakes to collect from the account debtors or obligors must proceed in a commercially reasonable manner and may deduct his reasonable expenses of realization from the collections. If the security agreement secures an indebtedness, the secured party must account to the debtor for any surplus, and unless otherwise agreed, the debtor is liable for any deficiency. But, if the underlying transaction was a sale of accounts or chattel paper, the debtor is entitled to any surplus or is liable for any deficiency only if the security agreement so provides.

Amended in 1972.

§ 9–503. Secured Party's Right to Take Possession After Default

Unless otherwise agreed a secured party has on default the right to take possession of the collateral. In taking possession a secured party may proceed without judicial process if this can be done without breach of the peace or may proceed by action. If the security agreement so provides the secured party may require the debtor to assemble the collateral and make it available to the secured party at a place to be designated by the secured party which is reasonably convenient to both parties. Without removal a secured party may render equipment unusable, and may dispose of collateral on the debtor's premises under Section 9–504.

§ 9–504. Secured Party's Right to Dispose of Collateral After Default; Effect of Disposition

(1) A secured party after default may sell, lease or otherwise dispose of any or all of the collateral in its then condition or following any commercially reasonable preparation or processing. Any sale of goods is subject to the Article on Sales (Article 2). The proceeds of disposition shall be applied in the order following to

(a) the reasonable expenses of retaking, holding, preparing for sale or lease, selling, leasing and the like and, to the extent provided for in the agreement and not prohibited by law, the reasonable attorneys' fees and legal expenses incurred by the secured party;

(b) the satisfaction of indebtedness secured by the security interest under which the disposition is made;

(c) the satisfaction of indebtedness secured by any subordinate security interest in the collateral if written notification of demand therefor is received before distribution of the proceeds is completed. If requested by the secured party, the holder of a subordinate security interest must seasonably furnish reasonable proof of his interest, and unless he

does so, the secured party need not comply with his demand.

(2) If the security interest secures an indebtedness, the secured party must account to the debtor for any surplus, and, unless otherwise agreed, the debtor is liable for any deficiency. But if the underlying transaction was a sale of accounts or chattel paper, the debtor is entitled to any surplus or is liable for any deficiency only if the security agreement so provides.

(3) Disposition of the collateral may be by public or private proceedings and may be made by way of one or more contracts. Sale or other disposition may be as a unit or in parcels and at any time and place and on any terms but every aspect of the disposition including the method, manner, time, place and terms must be commercially reasonable. Unless collateral is perishable or threatens to decline speedily in value or is of a type customarily sold on a recognized market, reasonable notification of the time and place of any public sale or reasonable notification of the time after which any private sale or other intended disposition is to be made shall be sent by the secured party to the debtor, if he has not signed after default a statement renouncing or modifying his right to notification of sale. In the case of consumer goods no other notification need be sent. In other cases notification shall be sent to any other secured party from whom the secured party has received (before sending his notification to the debtor or before the debtor's renunciation of his rights) written notice of a claim of an interest in the collateral. The secured party may buy at any public sale and if the collateral is of a type customarily sold in a recognized market or is of a type which is the subject of widely distributed standard price quotations he may buy at private sale.

(4) When collateral is disposed of by a secured party after default, the disposition transfers to a purchaser for value all of the debtor's rights therein, discharges the security interest under which it is made and any security interest or lien subordinate thereto. The purchaser takes free of all such rights and interests even though the secured party fails to comply with the requirements of this Part or of any judicial proceedings

(a) in the case of a public sale, if the purchaser has no knowledge of any defects in the sale and if he does not buy in collusion with the secured party, other bidders or the person conducting the sale; or

(b) in any other case, if the purchaser acts in good faith.

(5) A person who is liable to a secured party under a guaranty, indorsement, repurchase agreement or the like and who receives a transfer of collateral from the secured party or is subrogated to his rights has thereafter the rights and duties of the secured party. Such a transfer of collateral is not a sale or disposition of the collateral under this Article.

Amended in 1972.

§ 9–505. Compulsory Disposition of Collateral; Acceptance of the Collateral as Discharge of Obligation

(1) If the debtor has paid sixty per cent of the cash price in the case of a purchase money security interest in consumer goods or sixty per cent of the loan in the case of another security interest in consumer goods, and has not signed after default a statement renouncing or modifying his rights under this Part a secured party who has taken possession of collateral must dispose of it under Section 9–504 and if he fails to do so within ninety days after he takes possession the debtor at his

option may recover in conversion or under Section 9–507(1) on secured party's liability.

(2) In any other case involving consumer goods or any other collateral a secured party in possession may, after default, propose to retain the collateral in satisfaction of the obligation. Written notice of such proposal shall be sent to the debtor if he has not signed after default a statement renouncing or modifying his rights under this subsection. In the case of consumer goods no other notice need be given. In other cases notice shall be sent to any other secured party from whom the secured party has received (before sending his notice to the debtor or before the debtor's renunciation of his rights) written notice of a claim of an interest in the collateral. If the secured party receives objection in writing from a person entitled to receive notification within twenty-one days after the notice was sent, the secured party must dispose of the collateral under Section 9–504. In the absence of such written objection the secured party may retain the collateral in satisfaction of the debtor's obligation.

Amended in 1972.

§ 9–506. Debtor's Right to Redeem Collateral

At any time before the secured party has disposed of collateral or entered into a contract for its disposition under Section 9–504 or before the obligation has been discharged under Section 9–505(2) the debtor or any other secured party may unless otherwise agreed in writing after default redeem the collateral by tendering fulfillment of all obligations secured by the collateral as well as the expenses reasonably incurred by the secured party in retaking, holding and preparing the collateral for disposition, in arranging for the sale, and to the extent provided in the agreement and not prohibited by law, his reasonable attorneys' fees and legal expenses.

§ 9–507. Secured Party's Liability for Failure to Comply With This Part

(1) If it is established that the secured party is not proceeding in accordance with the provisions of this Part disposition may be ordered or restrained on appropriate terms and conditions. If the disposition has occurred the debtor or any person entitled to notification or whose security interest has been made known to the secured party prior to the disposition has a right to recover from the secured party any loss caused by a failure to comply with the provisions of this Part. If the collateral is consumer goods, the debtor has a right to recover in any event an amount not less than the credit service charge plus 10 per cent of the principal amount of the debt or the time price differential plus 10 per cent of the cash price.

(2) The fact that a better price could have been obtained by a sale at a different time or in a different method from that selected by the secured party is not of itself sufficient to establish that the sale was not made in a commercially reasonable manner. If the secured party either sells the collateral in the usual manner in any recognized market therefor or if he sells at the price current in such market at the time of his sale or if he has otherwise sold in conformity with reasonable commercial practices among dealers in the type of property sold he has sold in a commercially reasonable manner. The principles stated in the two preceding sentences with respect to sales also apply as may be appropriate to other types of disposition. A disposition which has been approved in any judicial proceeding or by any bona fide creditors' committee or representative of creditors shall conclusively be deemed to be commercially reasonable, but this sentence does not indicate that any such approval must be obtained in any case nor does it indicate that any disposition not so approved is not commercially reasonable.

Uniform Partnership Act

Part I. Preliminary Provisions

§ 1. Name of Act

This act may be cited as Uniform Partnership Act.

§ 2. Definition of Terms

In this act, "Court" includes every court and judge having jurisdiction in the case.

"Business" includes every trade, occupation, or profession.

"Person" includes individuals, partnerships, corporations, and other associations.

"Bankrupt" includes bankrupt under the Federal Bankruptcy Act or insolvent under any state insolvent act.

"Conveyance" includes every assignment, lease, mortgage, or encumbrance.

"Real property" includes land and any interest or estate in land.

§ 3. Interpretation of Knowledge and Notice

(1) A person has "knowledge" of a fact within the meaning of this act not only when he has actual knowledge thereof, but also when he has knowledge of such other facts as in the circumstances shows bad faith.

(2) A person has "notice" of a fact within the meaning of this act when the person who claims the benefit of the notice

    (a) States the fact to such person, or

    (b) Delivers through the mail, or by other means of communication, a written statement of the fact to such person or to a proper person at his place of business or residence.

§ 4. Rules of Construction

(1) The rule that statutes in derogation of the common law are to be strictly construed shall have no application to this act.

(2) The law of estoppel shall apply under this act.

(3) The law of agency shall apply under this act.

(4) This act shall be so interpreted and construed as to effect its general purpose to make uniform the law of those states which enact it.

(5) This act shall not be construed so as to impair the obligations of any contract existing when the act goes into effect, nor to affect any action or proceedings begun or right accrued before this act takes effect.

§ 5. Rules for Cases Not Provided for in This Act

In any case not provided for in this act the rules of law and equity, including the law merchant, shall govern.

Part II. Nature of Partnership

§ 6. Partnership Defined

(1) A partnership is an association of two or more persons to carry on as co-owners a business for profit.

(2) But any association formed under any other statute of this state, or any statute adopted by authority, other than the authority of this state, is not a partnership under this act, unless such association would have been a partnership in this state prior to the adoption of this act; but this act shall apply to limited partnerships except in so far as the statutes relating to such partnerships are inconsistent herewith.

§ 7. Rules for Determining the Existence of a Partnership

In determining whether a partnership exists, these rules shall apply:

(1) Except as provided by Section 16 persons who are not partners as to each other are not partners as to third persons.

(2) Joint tenancy, tenancy in common, tenancy by the entireties, joint property, common property, or part ownership does not of itself establish a partnership, whether such co-owners do or do not share any profits made by the use of the property.

(3) The sharing of gross returns does not of itself establish a partnership, whether or not the persons sharing them have a joint or common right or interest in any property from which the returns are derived.

(4) The receipt by a person of a share of the profits of a business is prima facie evidence that he is a partner in the business, but no such inference shall be drawn if such profits were received in payment:

    (a) As a debt by installments or otherwise,

    (b) As wages of an employee or rent to a landlord,

    (c) As an annuity to a widow or representative of a deceased partner,

(d) As interest on a loan, though the amount of payment vary with the profits of the business.

(e) As the consideration for the sale of a good will of a business or other property by installments or otherwise.

§ 8. Partnership Property

(1) All property originally brought into the partnership stock or subsequently acquired by purchase or otherwise, on account of the partnership, is partnership property.

(2) Unless the contrary intention appears, property acquired with partnership funds is partnership property.

(3) Any estate in real property may be acquired in the partnership name. Title so acquired can be conveyed only in the partnership name.

(4) A conveyance to a partnership in the partnership name, though without words of inheritance, passes the entire estate of the grantor unless a contrary intent appears.

Part III. Relations of Partners to Persons Dealing with the Partnership

§ 9. Partner Agent of Partnership as to Partnership Business

(1) Every partner is an agent of the partnership for the purpose of its business, and the act of every partner, including the execution in the partnership name of any instrument, for apparently carrying on in the usual way the business of the partnership of which he is a member binds the partnership, unless the partner so acting has in fact no authority to act for the partnership in the particular matter, and the person with whom he is dealing has knowledge of the fact that he has no such authority.

(2) An act of a partner which is not apparently for the carrying on of the business of the partnership in the usual way does not bind the partnership unless authorized by the other partners.

(3) Unless authorized by the other partners or unless they have abandoned the business, one or more but less than all the partners have no authority to:

    (a) Assign the partnership property in trust for creditors or on the assignee's promise to pay the debts of the partnership,

    (b) Dispose of the good will of the business,

    (c) Do any other act which would make it impossible to carry on the ordinary business of a partnership,

    (d) Confess a judgment,

    (e) Submit a partnership claim or liability to arbitration or reference.

(4) No act of a partner in contravention of a restriction on authority shall bind the partnership to persons having knowledge of the restriction.

§ 10. Conveyance of Real Property of the Partnership

(1) Where title to real property is in the partnership name, any partner may convey title to such property by a conveyance executed in the partnership name; but the partnership may recover such property unless the partner's act binds the partnership under the provisions of paragraph (1) of section 9 or unless such property has been conveyed by the grantee or a person claiming through such grantee to a holder for value without knowledge that the partner, in making the conveyance, has exceeded his authority.

(2) Where title to real property is in the name of the partnership, a conveyance executed by a partner, in his own name, passes the equitable interest of the partnership, provided the act is one within the authority of the partner under the provisions of paragraph (1) of section 9.

(3) Where title to real property is in the name of one or more but not all the partners, and the record does not disclose the right of the partnership, the partners in whose name the title stands may convey title to such property, but the partnership may recover such property if the partners' act does not bind the partnership under the provisions of paragraph (1) of section 9, unless the purchaser or his assignee, is a holder for value, without knowledge.

(4) Where the title to real property is in the name of one or more or all the partners, or in a third person in trust for the partnership, a conveyance executed by a partner in the partnership name, or in his own name, passes the equitable interest of the partnership, provided the act is one within the authority of the partner under the provisions of paragraph (1) of section 9.

(5) Where the title to real property is in the names of all the partners a conveyance executed by all the partners passes all their rights in such property.

§ 11. Partnership Bound by Admission of Partner

An admission or representation made by any partner concerning partnership affairs within the scope of his authority as conferred by this act is evidence against the partnership.

§ 12. Partnership Charged With Knowledge of or Notice to Partner

Notice to any partner of any matter relating to partnership affairs, and the knowledge of the partner acting in the particular matter, acquired while a partner or then present to his mind, and the knowledge of any other partner who reasonably could and should have communicated it to the acting partner, operate as notice to or knowledge of the partnership, except in the case of a fraud on the partnership committed by or with the consent of that partner.

§ 13. Partnership Bound by Partner's Wrongful Act

Where, by any wrongful act or omission of any partner acting in the ordinary course of the business of the partnership or with the authority of his co-partners, loss or injury is caused to any person, not being a partner in the partnership, or any penalty is incurred, the partnership is liable therefor to the same extent as the partner so acting or omitting to act.

§ 14. Partnership Bound by Partner's Breach of Trust

The partnership is bound to make good the loss:

    (a) Where one partner acting within the scope of his apparent authority receives money or property of a third person and misapplies it; and

    (b) Where the partnership in the course of its business receives money or property of a third person and the money or property so received is misapplied by any partner while it is in the custody of the partnership.

§ 15. Nature of Partner's Liability

All partners are liable

(a) Jointly and severally for everything chargeable to the partnership under sections 13 and 14.

(b) Jointly for all other debts and obligations of the partnership; but any partner may enter into a separate obligation to perform a partnership contract.

§ 16. Partner by Estoppel

(1) When a person, by words spoken or written or by conduct, represents himself, or consents to another representing him to any one, as a partner in an existing partnership or with one or more persons not actual partners, he is liable to any such person to whom such representation has been made, who has, on the faith of such representation, given credit to the actual or apparent partnership, and if he has made such representation or consented to its being made in a public manner he is liable to such person, whether the representation has or has not been made or communicated to such person so giving credit by or with the knowledge of the apparent partner making the representation or consenting to its being made.

(a) When a partnership liability results, he is liable as though he were an actual member of the partnership.

(b) When no partnership liability results, he is liable jointly with the other persons, if any, so consenting to the contract or representation as to incur liability, otherwise separately.

(2) When a person has been thus represented to be a partner in an existing partnership, or with one or more persons not actual partners, he is an agent of the persons consenting to such representation to bind them to the same extent and in the same manner as though he were a partner in fact, with respect to persons who rely upon the representation. Where all the members of the existing partnership consent to the representation, a partnership act or obligation results; but in all other cases it is the joint act or obligation of the person acting and the persons consenting to the representation.

§ 17. Liability of Incoming Partner

A person admitted as a partner into an existing partnership is liable for all the obligations of the partnership arising before his admission as though he had been a partner when such obligations were incurred, except that this liability shall be satisfied only out of partnership property.

Part IV. Relations of Partners to One Another

§ 18. Rules Determining Rights and Duties of Partners

The rights and duties of the partners in relation to the partnership shall be determined, subject to any agreement between them, by the following rules:

(a) Each partner shall be repaid his contributions, whether by way of capital or advances to the partnership property and share equally in the profits and surplus remaining after all liabilities, including those to partners, are satisfied; and must contribute towards the losses, whether of capital or otherwise, sustained by the partnership according to his share in the profits.

(b) The partnership must indemnify every partner in respect of payments made and personal liabilities reasonably incurred by him in the ordinary and proper conduct of its business, or for the preservation of its business or property.

(c) A partner, who in aid of the partnership makes any payment or advance beyond the amount of capital which he agreed to contribute, shall be paid interest from the date of the payment or advance.

(d) A partner shall receive interest on the capital contributed by him only from the date when repayment should be made.

(e) All partners have equal rights in the management and conduct of the partnership business.

(f) No partner is entitled to remuneration for acting in the partnership business, except that a surviving partner is entitled to reasonable compensation for his services in winding up the partnership affairs.

(g) No person can become a member of a partnership without the consent of all the partners.

(h) Any difference arising as to ordinary matters connected with the partnership business may be decided by a majority of the partners; but no act in contravention of any agreement between the partners may be done rightfully without the consent of all the partners.

§ 19. Partnership Books

The partnership books shall be kept, subject to any agreement between the partners, at the principal place of business of the partnership, and every partner shall at all times have access to and may inspect and copy any of them.

§ 20. Duty of Partners to Render Information

Partners shall render on demand true and full information of all things affecting the partnership to any partner or the legal representative of any deceased partner or partner under legal disability.

§ 21. Partner Accountable as a Fiduciary

(1) Every partner must account to the partnership for any benefit, and hold as trustee for it any profits derived by him without the consent of the other partners from any transaction connected with the formation, conduct, or liquidation of the partnership or from any use by him of its property.

(2) This section applies also to the representatives of a deceased partner engaged in the liquidation of the affairs of the partnership as the personal representatives of the last surviving partner.

§ 22. Right to an Account

Any partner shall have the right to a formal account as to partnership affairs:

(a) If he is wrongfully excluded from the partnership business or possession of its property by his co-partners,

(b) If the right exists under the terms of any agreement,

(c) As provided by section 21,

(d) Whenever other circumstances render it just and reasonable.

§ 23. Continuation of Partnership Beyond Fixed Term

(1) When a partnership for a fixed term or particular undertaking is continued after the termination of such term or particular undertaking without any express agreement, the rights and

duties of the partners remain the same as they were at such termination, so far as is consistent with a partnership at will.

(2) A continuation of the business by the partners or such of them as habitually acted therein during the term, without any settlement or liquidation of the partnership affairs, is prima facie evidence of a continuation of the partnership.

Part V. Property Rights of a Partner

§ 24. Extent of Property Rights of a Partner

The property rights of a partner are (1) his rights in specific partnership property, (2) his interest in the partnership, and (3) his right to participate in the management.

§ 25. Nature of a Partner's Right in Specific Partnership Property

(1) A partner is co-owner with his partners of specific partnership property holding as a tenant in partnership.

(2) The incidents of this tenancy are such that:

(a) A partner, subject to the provisions of this act and to any agreement between the partners, has an equal right with his partners to possess specific partnership property for partnership purposes; but he has no right to possess such property for any other purpose without the consent of his partners.

(b) A partner's right in specific partnership property is not assignable except in connection with the assignment of rights of all the partners in the same property.

(c) A partner's right in specific partnership property is not subject to attachment or execution, except on a claim against the partnership. When partnership property is attached for a partnership debt the partners, or any of them, or the representatives of a deceased partner, cannot claim any right under the homestead or exemption laws.

(d) On the death of a partner his right in specific partnership property vests in the surviving partner or partners, except where the deceased was the last surviving partner, when his right in such property vests in his legal representative. Such surviving partner or partners, or the legal representative of the last surviving partner, has no right to possess the partnership property for any but a partnership purpose.

(e) A partner's right in specific partnership property is not subject to dower, curtesy, or allowances to widows, heirs, or next of kin.

§ 26. Nature of Partner's Interest in the Partnership

A partner's interest in the partnership is his share of the profits and surplus, and the same is personal property.

§ 27. Assignment of Partner's Interest

(1) A conveyance by a partner of his interest in the partnership does not of itself dissolve the partnership, nor, as against the other partners in the absence of agreement, entitle the assignee, during the continuance of the partnership to interfere in the management or administration of the partnership business or affairs, or to require any information or account of partnership transactions, or to inspect the partnership books; but it merely entitles the assignee to receive in accordance with his contract the profits to which the assigning partner would otherwise be entitled.

(2) In case of a dissolution of the partnership, the assignee is entitled to receive his assignor's interest and may require an account from the date only of the last account agreed to by all the partners.

§ 28. Partner's Interest Subject to Charging Order

(1) On due application to a competent court by any judgment creditor of a partner, the court which entered the judgment, order, or decree, or any other court, may charge the interest of the debtor partner with payment of the unsatisfied amount of such judgment debt with interest thereon; and may then or later appoint a receiver of his share of the profits, and of any other money due or to fall due to him in respect of the partnership, and make all other orders, directions, accounts and inquiries which the debtor partner might have made, or which the circumstances of the case may require.

(2) The interest charged may be redeemed at any time before foreclosure, or in case of a sale being directed by the court may be purchased without thereby causing a dissolution:

(a) With separate property, by any one or more of the partners, or

(b) With partnership property, by any one or more of the partners with the consent of all the partners whose interests are not so charged or sold.

(3) Nothing in this act shall be held to deprive a partner of his right, if any, under the exemption laws, as regards his interest in the partnership.

Part VI. Dissolution and Winding Up

§ 29. Dissolution Defined

The dissolution of a partnership is the change in the relation of the partners caused by any partner ceasing to be associated in the carrying on as distinguished from the winding up of the business.

§ 30. Partnership Not Terminated by Dissolution

On dissolution the partnership is not terminated, but continues until the winding up of partnership affairs is completed.

§ 31. Causes of Dissolution

Dissolution is caused:

(1) Without violation of the agreement between the partners,

(a) By the termination of the definite term or particular undertaking specified in the agreement,

(b) By the express will of any partner when no definite term or particular undertaking is specified,

(c) By the express will of all the partners who have not assigned their interests or suffered them to be charged for their separate debts, either before or after the termination of any specified term or particular undertaking,

(d) By the expulsion of any partner from the business bona fide in accordance with such a power conferred by the agreement between the partners;

(2) In contravention of the agreement between the partners, where the circumstances do not permit a dissolution under any other provision of this section, by the express will of any partner at any time;

(3) By any event which makes it unlawful for the business of the partnership to be carried on or for the members to carry it on in partnership;
(4) By the death of any partner;
(5) By the bankruptcy of any partner or the partnership;
(6) By decree of court under section 32.

§ 32. Dissolution by Decree of Court

(1) On application by or for a partner the court shall decree a dissolution whenever:

(a) A partner has been declared a lunatic in any judicial proceeding or is shown to be of unsound mind,

(b) A partner becomes in any other way incapable of performing his part of the partnership contract,

(c) A partner has been guilty of such conduct as tends to affect prejudicially the carrying on of the business,

(d) A partner wilfully or persistently commits a breach of the partnership agreement, or otherwise so conducts himself in matters relating to the partnership business that it is not reasonably practicable to carry on the business in partnership with him,

(e) The business of the partnership can only be carried on at a loss,

(f) Other circumstances render a dissolution equitable.

(2) On the application of the purchaser of a partner's interest under sections 27 or 28:

(a) After the termination of the specified term or particular undertaking,

(b) At any time if the partnership was a partnership at will when the interest was assigned or when the charging order was issued.

§ 33. General Effect of Dissolution on Authority of Partner

Except so far as may be necessary to wind up partnership affairs or to complete transactions begun but not then finished, dissolution terminates all authority of any partner to act for the partnership,

(1) With respect to the partners,

(a) When the dissolution is not by the act, bankruptcy or death of a partner; or

(b) When the dissolution is by such act, bankruptcy or death of a partner, in cases where section 34 so requires.

(2) With respect to persons not partners, as declared in section 35.

§ 34. Right of Partner to Contribution From Copartners After Dissolution

Where the dissolution is caused by the act, death or bankruptcy of a partner, each partner is liable to his copartners for his share of any liability created by any partner acting for the partnership as if the partnership had not been dissolved unless

(a) The dissolution being by act of any partner, the partner acting for the partnership had knowledge of the dissolution, or

(b) The dissolution being by the death or bankruptcy of a partner, the partner acting for the partnership had knowledge or notice of the death or bankruptcy.

§ 35. Power of Partner to Bind Partnership to Third Persons After Dissolution

(1) After dissolution a partner can bind the partnership except as provided in Paragraph (3)

(a) By any act appropriate for winding up partnership affairs or completing transactions unfinished at dissolution;

(b) By any transaction which would bind the partnership if dissolution had not taken place, provided the other party to the transaction.

(I) Had extended credit to the partnership prior to dissolution and had no knowledge or notice of the dissolution; or

(II) Though he had not so extended credit, had nevertheless known of the partnership prior to dissolution, and, having no knowledge or notice of dissolution, the fact of dissolution had not been advertised in a newspaper of general circulation in the place (or in each place if more than one) at which the partnership business was regularly carried on.

(2) The liability of a partner under paragraph (1b) shall be satisfied out of partnership assets alone when such partner had been prior to dissolution

(a) Unknown as a partner to the person with whom the contract is made; and

(b) So far unknown and inactive in partnership affairs that the business reputation of the partnership could not be said to have been in any degree due to his connection with it.

(3) The partnership is in no case bound by any act of a partner after dissolution

(a) Where the partnership is dissolved because it is unlawful to carry on the business, unless the act is appropriate for winding up partnership affairs; or

(b) Where the partner has become bankrupt; or

(c) Where the partner has no authority to wind up partnership affairs; except by a transaction with one who

(I) Had extended credit to the partnership prior to dissolution and had no knowledge or notice of his want of authority; or

(II) Had not extended credit to the partnership prior to dissolution, and, having no knowledge or notice of his want of authority, the fact of his want of authority has not been advertised in the manner provided for advertising the fact of dissolution in paragraph (1bII).

(4) Nothing in this section shall affect the liability under section 16 of any person who after dissolution represents himself or consents to another representing him as a partner in a partnership engaged in carrying on business.

§ 36. Effect of Dissolution on Partner's Existing Liability

(1) The dissolution of the partnership does not of itself discharge the existing liability of any partner.

(2) A partner is discharged from any existing liability upon dissolution of the partnership by an agreement to that effect between himself, the partnership creditor and the person or partnership continuing the business; and such agreement may be inferred from the course of dealing between the creditor having knowledge of the dissolution and the person or partnership continuing the business.

(3) Where a person agrees to assume the existing obligations of a dissolved partnership, the partners whose obligations have

been assumed shall be discharged from any liability to any creditor of the partnership who, knowing of the agreement, consents to a material alteration in the nature or time of payment of such obligations.

(4) The individual property of a deceased partner shall be liable for all obligations of the partnership incurred while he was a partner but subject to the prior payment of his separate debts.

§ 37. Right to Wind Up

Unless otherwise agreed the partners who have not wrongfully dissolved the partnership or the legal representative of the last surviving partner, not bankrupt, has the right to wind up the partnership affairs; provided, however, that any partner, his legal representative or his assignee, upon cause shown, may obtain winding up by the court.

§ 38. Rights of Partners to Application of Partnership Property

(1) When dissolution is caused in any way, except in contravention of the partnership agreement, each partner as against his co-partners and all persons claiming through them in respect of their interests in the partnership, unless otherwise agreed, may have the partnership property applied to discharge its liabilities, and the surplus applied to pay in cash the net amount owing to the respective partners. But if dissolution is caused by expulsion of a partner, bona fide under the partnership agreement and if the expelled partner is discharged from all partnership liabilities, either by payment or agreement under section 36(2), he shall receive in cash only the net amount due him from the partnership.

(2) When dissolution is caused in contravention of the partnership agreement the rights of the partners shall be as follows:

(a) Each partner who has not caused dissolution wrongfully shall have,

(I) All the rights specified in paragraph (1) of this section, and

(II) The right, as against each partner who has caused the dissolution wrongfully, to damages for breach of the agreement.

(b) The partners who have not caused the dissolution wrongfully, if they all desire to continue the business in the same name, either by themselves or jointly with others, may do so, during the agreed term for the partnership and for that purpose may possess the partnership property, provided they secure the payment by bond approved by the court, or pay to any partner who has caused the dissolution wrongfully, the value of his interest in the partnership at the dissolution, less any damages recoverable under clause (2aII) of the section, and in like manner indemnify him against all present or future partnership liabilities.

(c) A partner who has caused the dissolution wrongfully shall have:

(I) If the business is not continued under the provisions of paragraph (2b) all the rights of a partner under paragraph (1), subject to clause (2aII), of this section,

(II) If the business is continued under paragraph (2b) of this section the right as against his co-partners and all claiming through them in respect of their interests in the partnership, to have the value of his interest in

the partnership, less any damages caused to his co-partners by the dissolution, ascertained and paid to him in cash, or the payment secured by bond approved by the court, and to be released from all existing liabilities of the partnership; but in ascertaining the value of the partner's interest the value of the good will of the business shall not be considered.

§ 39. Rights Where Partnership Is Dissolved for Fraud or Misrepresentation

Where a partnership contract is rescinded on the ground of the fraud or misrepresentation of one of the parties thereto, the party entitled to rescind is, without prejudice to any other right, entitled,

(a) To a lien on, or right of retention of, the surplus of the partnership property after satisfying the partnership liabilities to third persons for any sum of money paid by him for the purchase of an interest in the partnership and for any capital or advances contributed by him; and

(b) To stand, after all liabilities to third persons have been satisfied, in the place of the creditors of the partnership for any payments made by him in respect of the partnership liabilities; and

(c) To be indemnified by the person guilty of the fraud or making the representation against all debts and liabilities of the partnership.

§ 40. Rules for Distribution

In settling accounts between the partners after dissolution, the following rules shall be observed, subject to any agreement to the contrary:

(a) The assets of the partnership are:

(I) The partnership property,

(II) The contributions of the partners necessary for the payment of all the liabilities specified in clause (b) of this paragraph.

(b) The liabilities of the partnership shall rank in order of payment, as follows:

(I) Those owing to creditors other than partners,

(II) Those owing to partners other than for capital and profits,

(III) Those owing to partners in respect of capital,

(IV) Those owing to partners in respect of profits.

(c) The assets shall be applied in the order of their declaration in clause (a) of this paragraph to the satisfaction of the liabilities.

(d) The partners shall contribute, as provided by section 18(a) the amount necessary to satisfy the liabilities; but if any, but not all, of the partners are insolvent, or, not being subject to process, refuse to contribute, the other parties shall contribute their share of the liabilities, and, in the relative proportions in which they share the profits, the additional amount necessary to pay the liabilities.

(e) An assignee for the benefit of creditors or any person appointed by the court shall have the right to enforce the contributions specified in clause (d) of this paragraph.

(f) Any partner or his legal representative shall have the right to enforce the contributions specified in clause (d) of this paragraph, to the extent of the amount which he has paid in excess of his share of the liability.

(g) The individual property of a deceased partner shall be liable for the contributions specified in clause (d) of this paragraph.

(h) When partnership property and the individual properties of the partners are in possession of a court for distribution, partnership creditors shall have priority on partnership property and separate creditors on individual property, saving the rights of lien or secured creditors as heretofore.

(i) Where a partner has become bankrupt or his estate is insolvent the claims against his separate property shall rank in the following order:

(I) Those owing to separate creditors,

(II) Those owing to partnership creditors,

(III) Those owing to partners by way of contribution.

§ 41. Liability of Persons Continuing the Business in Certain Cases

(1) When any new partner is admitted into an existing partnership, or when any partner retires and assigns (or the representative of the deceased partner assigns) his rights in partnership property to two or more of the partners, or to one or more of the partners and one or more third persons, if the business is continued without liquidation of the partnership affairs, creditors of the first or dissolved partnership are also creditors of the person or partnership so continuing the business.

(2) When all but one partner retire and assign (or the representative of a deceased partner assigns) their rights in partnership property to the remaining partner, who continues the business without liquidation of partnership affairs, either alone or with others, creditors of the dissolved partnership are also creditors of the person or partnership so continuing the business.

(3) When any partner retires or dies and the business of the dissolved partnership is continued as set forth in paragraphs (1) and (2) of this section, with the consent of the retired partners or the representative of the deceased partner, but without any assignment of his right in partnership property, rights of creditors of the dissolved partnership and of the creditors of the person or partnership continuing the business shall be as if such assignment had been made.

(4) When all the partners or their representatives assign their rights in partnership property to one or more third persons who promise to pay the debts and who continue the business of the dissolved partnership, creditors of the dissolved partnership are also creditors of the person or partnership continuing the business.

(5) When any partner wrongfully causes a dissolution and the remaining partners continue the business under the provisions of section 38(2b), either alone or with others, and without liquidation of the partnership affairs, creditors of the dissolved partnership are also creditors of the person or partnership continuing the business.

(6) When a partner is expelled and the remaining partners continue the business either alone or with others, without liquidation of the partnership affairs, creditors of the dissolved partnership are also creditors of the person or partnership continuing the business.

(7) The liability of a third person becoming a partner in the partnership continuing the business, under this section, to the creditors of the dissolved partnership shall be satisfied out of partnership property only.

(8) When the business of a partnership after dissolution is continued under any conditions set forth in this section the creditors of the dissolved partnership, as against the separate creditors of the retiring or deceased partner or the representative of the deceased partner, have a prior right to any claim of the retired partner or the representative of the deceased partner against the person or partnership continuing the business, on account of the retired or deceased partner's interest in the dissolved partnership or on account of any consideration promised for such interest or for his right in partnership property.

(9) Nothing in this section shall be held to modify any right of creditors to set aside any assignment on the ground of fraud.

(10) The use by the person or partnership continuing the business of the partnership name, or the name of a deceased partner as part thereof, shall not of itself make the individual property of the deceased partner liable for any debts contracted by such person or partnership.

§ 42. Rights of Retiring or Estate of Deceased Partner When the Business Is Continued

When any partner retires or dies, and the business is continued under any of the conditions set forth in section 41(1, 2, 3, 5, 6), or section 38(2b), without any settlement of accounts as between him or his estate and the person or partnership continuing the business, unless otherwise agreed, he or his legal representative as against such persons or partnership may have the value of his interest at the date of dissolution ascertained, and shall receive as an ordinary creditor an amount equal to the value of his interest in the dissolved partnership with interest, or, at his option or at the option of his legal representative, in lieu of interest, the profits attributable to the use of his right in the property of the dissolved partnership; provided that the creditors of the dissolved partnership as against the separate creditors, or the representative of the retired or deceased partner, shall have priority on any claim arising under this section, as provided by section 41(8) of this act.

§ 43. Accrual of Actions

The right to an account of his interest shall accrue to any partner, or his legal representative, as against the winding up partners or the surviving partners or the person or partnership continuing the business, at the date of dissolution, in the absence of any agreement to the contrary.

Part VII. Miscellaneous Provisions

§ 44. When Act Takes Effect

This act shall take effect on the _____ day of _____ one thousand nine hundred and _____.

§ 45. Legislation Repealed

All acts or parts of acts inconsistent with this act are hereby repealed.

Revised Model Business Corporation Act (Selected Provisions)

§ 1.40 Act Definitions

In this Act:

(1) "Articles of incorporation" include amended and restated articles of incorporation and articles of merger.

(2) "Authorized shares" means the shares of all classes a domestic or foreign corporation is authorized to issue.

(3) "Conspicuous" means so written that a reasonable person against whom the writing is to operate should have noticed it. For example, printing in italics or boldface or contrasting color, or typing in capitals or underlined, is conspicuous.

(4) "Corporation" or "domestic corporation" means a corporation for profit, which is not a foreign corporation, incorporated under or subject to the provisions of this Act.

(5) "Deliver" includes mail.

(6) "Distribution" means a direct or indirect transfer of money or other property (except its own shares) or incurrence of indebtedness by a corporation to or for the benefit of its shareholders in respect of any of its shares. A distribution may be in the form of a declaration or payment of a dividend; a purchase, redemption, or other acquisition of shares; a distribution of indebtedness; or otherwise.

(7) "Effective date of notice" is defined in section 1.41.

(8) "Employee" includes an officer but not a director. A director may accept duties that make him also an employee.

(9) "Entity" includes corporation and foreign corporation; not-for-profit corporation; profit and not-for-profit unincorporated association; business trust, estate, partnership, trust, and two or more persons having a joint or common economic interest; and state, United States, and foreign government.

(10) "Foreign corporation" means a corporation for profit incorporated under a law other than the law of this state.

(11) "Governmental subdivision" includes authority, county, district, and municipality.

(12) "Includes" denotes a partial definition.

(13) "Individual" includes the estate of an incompetent or deceased individual.

(14) "Means" denotes an exhaustive definition.

(15) "Notice" is defined in section 1.41.

(16) "Person" includes individual and entity.

(17) "Principal office" means the office (in or out of this state) so designated in the annual report where the principal executive offices of a domestic or foreign corporation are located.

(18) "Proceeding" includes civil suit and criminal, administrative, and investigatory action.

(19) "Record date" means the date established under chapter 6 or 7 on which a corporation determines the identity of its shareholders for purposes of this Act.

(20) "Secretary" means the corporate officer to whom the board of directors has delegated responsibility under section 8.40(c) for custody of the minutes of the meetings of the board of directors and of the shareholders and for authenticating records of the corporation.

(21) "Share" means the unit into which the proprietary interests in a corporation are divided.

(22) "Shareholder" means the person in whose name shares are registered in the records of a corporation or the beneficial owner of shares to the extent of the rights granted by a nominee certificate on file with a corporation.

(23) "State," when referring to a part of the United States, includes a state and commonwealth (and their agencies and governmental subdivisions) and a territory, and insular possession (and their agencies and governmental subdivisions) of the United States.

(24) "Subscriber" means a person who subscribes for shares in a corporation, whether before or after incorporation.

(25) "United States" includes district, authority, bureau, commission, department, and any other agency of the United States.

(26) "Voting group" means all shares of one or more classes or series that under the articles of incorporation or this Act are entitled to vote and be counted together collectively on a matter at a meeting of shareholders. All shares entitled by the articles of incorporation or this Act to vote generally on the matter are for that purpose a single voting group.

§ 2.01 Incorporators

One or more persons may act as the incorporator or incorporators of a corporation by delivering articles of incorporation to the secretary of state for filing.

§ 2.02 Articles of Incorporation

(a) The articles of incorporation must set forth:

(1) a corporate name for the corporation that satisfies the requirements of section 4.01;

(2) the number of shares the corporation is authorized to issue;

(3) the street address of the corporation's initial registered office and the name of its initial registered agent at that office; and

(4) the name and address of each incorporator.

(b) The articles of incorporation may set forth:

(1) the names and addresses of the individuals who are to serve as the initial directors;

(2) provisions not inconsistent with law regarding:

(i) the purpose or purposes for which the corporation is organized;

(ii) managing the business and regulating the affairs of the corporation;

(iii) defining, limiting, and regulating the powers of the corporation, its board of directors, and shareholders;

(iv) a par value for authorized shares or classes of shares;

(v) the imposition of personal liability on shareholders for the debts of the corporation to a specified extent and upon specified conditions; and

(3) any provision that under this Act is required or permitted to be set forth in the bylaws.

(4) a provision eliminating or limiting the liability of a director to the corporation or its shareholders for money damages for any action taken, or any failure to take any action, as a director, except liability for (A) the amount of a financial benefit received by a director to which he is not entitled; (B) an intentional infliction of harm on the corporation or the shareholders; (C) a violation of section 8.33; or (D) an intentional violation of criminal law.

(c) The articles of incorporation need not set forth any of the corporate powers enumerated in this Act.

§ 2.03 Incorporation

(a) Unless a delayed effective date is specified, the corporate existence begins when the articles of incorporation are filed.

(b) The secretary of state's filing of the articles of incorporation is conclusive proof that the incorporators satisfied all conditions precedent to incorporation except in a proceeding by the state to cancel or revoke the incorporation or involuntarily dissolve the corporation.

§ 2.04 Liability for Preincorporation Transactions

All persons purporting to act as or on behalf of a corporation, knowing there was no incorporation under this Act, are jointly and severally liable for all liabilities created while so acting.

§ 2.05 Organization of Corporation

(a) After incorporation:

(1) if initial directors are named in the articles of incorporation, the initial directors shall hold an organizational meeting, at the call of a majority of the directors, to complete the organization of the corporation by appointing officers, adopting bylaws, and carrying on any other business brought before the meeting;

(2) if initial directors are not named in the articles, the incorporator or incorporators shall hold an organizational meeting at the call of a majority of the incorporators:

(i) to elect directors and complete the organization of the corporation; or

(ii) to elect a board of directors who shall complete the organization of the corporation.

(b) Action required or permitted by this Act to be taken by incorporators at an organizational meeting may be taken without a meeting if the action taken is evidenced by one or more written consents describing the action taken and signed by each incorporator.

(c) An organizational meeting may be held in or out of this state.

§ 2.06 Bylaws

(a) The incorporators or board of directors of a corporation shall adopt initial bylaws for the corporation.

(b) The bylaws of a corporation may contain any provision for managing the business and regulating the affairs of the corporation that is not inconsistent with law or the articles of incorporation.

§ 3.01 Purposes

(a) Every corporation incorporated under this Act has the purpose of engaging in any lawful business unless a more limited purpose is set forth in the articles of incorporation.

(b) A corporation engaging in a business that is subject to regulation under another statute of this state may incorporate under this Act only if permitted by, and subject to all limitations of, the other statute.

§ 3.02 General Powers

Unless its articles of incorporation provide otherwise, every corporation has perpetual duration and succession in its corporate name and has the same powers as an individual to do all things necessary or convenient to carry out its business and affairs, including without limitation power:

(1) to sue and be sued, complain and defend in its corporate name;

(2) to have a corporate seal, which may be altered at will, and to use it, or a facsimile of it, by impressing or affixing it or in any other manner reproducing it;

(3) to make and amend bylaws, not inconsistent with its articles of incorporation or with the laws of this state, for managing the business and regulating the affairs of the corporation;

(4) to purchase, receive, lease, or otherwise acquire, and own, hold, improve, use, and otherwise deal with, real or personal property, or any legal or equitable interest in property, wherever located;

(5) to sell, convey, mortgage, pledge, lease, exchange, and otherwise dispose of all or any part of its property;

(6) to purchase, receive, subscribe for, or otherwise acquire; own, hold, vote, use, sell, mortgage, lend, pledge, or otherwise dispose of; and deal in and with shares or other interests in, or obligations of, any other entity;

(7) to make contracts and guarantees, incur liabilities, borrow money, issue its notes, bonds, and other obligations, (which may be convertible into or include the option to purchase other securities of the corporation), and secure any of its obligations by mortgage or pledge of any of its property, franchises, or income;

(8) to lend money, invest and reinvest its funds, and receive and hold real and personal property as security for repayment;

(9) to be a promoter, partner, member, associate, or manager of any partnership, joint venture, trust, or other entity;

(10) to conduct its business, locate offices, and exercise the powers granted by this Act within or without this state;

(11) to elect directors and appoint officers, employees, and agents of the corporation, define their duties, fix their compensation, and lend them money and credit;

(12) to pay pensions and establish pension plans, pension trusts, profit sharing plans, share bonus plans, share option plans, and benefit or incentive plans for any or all of its current or former directors, officers, employees, and agents;

(13) to make donations for the public welfare or for charitable, scientific, or educational purposes;

(14) to transact any lawful business that will aid governmental policy;

(15) to make payments or donations, or do any other act, not inconsistent with law, that furthers the business and affairs of the corporation.

§ 3.04 Ultra Vires

(a) Except as provided in subsection (b), the validity of corporate action may not be challenged on the ground that the corporation lacks or lacked power to act.

(b) A corporation's power to act may be challenged:

(1) in a proceeding by a shareholder against the corporation to enjoin the act;

(2) in a proceeding by the corporation, directly, derivatively, or through a receiver, trustee, or other legal representative, against an incumbent or former director, officer, employee, or agent of the corporation; or

(3) in a proceeding by the Attorney General under section 14.30.

(c) In a shareholder's proceeding under subsection (b)(1) to enjoin an unauthorized corporate act, the court may enjoin or set aside the act, if equitable and if all affected persons are parties to the proceeding, and may award damages for loss (other than anticipated profits) suffered by the corporation or another party because of enjoining the unauthorized act.

§ 4.01 Corporate Name

(a) A corporate name:

(1) must contain the word "corporation," "incorporated," "company," or "limited," or the abbreviation "corp.," "inc.," "co.," or "ltd.", or words or abbreviations of like import in another language; and

(2) may not contain language stating or implying that the corporation is organized for a purpose other than that permitted by section 3.01 and its articles of incorporation.

(b) Except as authorized by subsections (c) and (d), a corporate name must be distinguishable upon the records of the secretary of state from:

(1) the corporate name of a corporation incorporated or authorized to transact business in this state;

(2) a corporate name reserved or registered under section 4.02 or 4.03;

(3) the fictitious name adopted by a foreign corporation authorized to transact business in this state because its real name is unavailable; and

(4) the corporate name of a not-for-profit corporation incorporated or authorized to transact business in this state.

(c) A corporation may apply to the secretary of state for authorization to use a name that is not distinguishable upon his records from one or more of the names described in subsection (b). The secretary of state shall authorize use of the name applied for if:

(1) the other corporation consents to the use in writing and submits an undertaking in form satisfactory to the secretary of state to change its name to a name that is distinguishable upon the records of the secretary of state from the name of the applying corporation; or

(2) the applicant delivers to the secretary of state a certified copy of the final judgment of a court of competent jurisdiction establishing the applicant's right to use the name applied for in this state.

(d) A corporation may use the name (including the fictitious name) of another domestic or foreign corporation that is used in this state if the other corporation is incorporated or authorized to transact business in this state and the proposed user corporation:

(1) has merged with the other corporation;

(2) has been formed by reorganization of the other corporation; or

(3) has acquired all or substantially all of the assets, including the corporate name, of the other corporation.

(e) This Act does not control the use of fictitious names.

§ 5.01 Registered Office and Registered Agent

Each corporation must continuously maintain in this state:

(1) a registered office that may be the same as any of its places of business; and

(2) a registered agent, who may be:

(i) an individual who resides in this state and whose business office is identical with the registered office;

(ii) a domestic corporation or not-for-profit domestic corporation whose business office is identical with the registered office; or

(iii) a foreign corporation or not-for-profit foreign corporation authorized to transact business in this state whose business office is identical with the registered office.

§ 6.01 Authorized Shares

(a) The articles of incorporation must prescribe the classes of shares and the number of shares of each class that the corporation is authorized to issue. If more than one class of shares is authorized, the articles of incorporation must prescribe a distinguishing designation for each class, and prior to the issuance of shares of a class the preferences, limitations, and relative rights of that class must be described in the articles of incorporation. All shares of a class must have preferences, limitations, and relative rights identical with those of other shares of the same class except to the extent otherwise permitted by section 6.02.

(b) The articles of incorporation must authorize (1) one or more classes of shares that together have unlimited voting rights, and (2) one or more classes of shares (which may be the same class or classes as those with voting rights) that together are entitled to receive the net assets of the corporation upon dissolution.

(c) The articles of incorporation may authorize one or more classes of shares that:

(1) have special, conditional, or limited voting rights, or no right to vote, except to the extent prohibited by this Act;

(2) are redeemable or convertible as specified in the articles of incorporation (i) at the option of the corporation, the shareholder, or another person or upon the occurrence of a designated event; (ii) for cash, indebtedness, securities, or other property; (iii) in a designated amount or in an amount determined in accordance with a designated formula or by reference to extrinsic data or events;

(3) entitle the holders to distributions calculated in any manner, including dividends that may be cumulative, noncumulative, or partially cumulative;

(4) have preference over any other class of shares with respect to distributions, including dividends and distributions upon the dissolution of the corporation.

(d) The description of the designations, preferences, limitations, and relative rights of share classes in subsection (c) is not exhaustive.

§ 6.02 Terms of Class or Series Determined by Board of Directors

(a) If the articles of incorporation so provide, the board of directors may determine, in whole or part, the preferences, limitations, and relative rights (within the limits set forth in section 6.01) of (1) any class of shares before the issuance of any shares of that class or (2) one or more series within a class before the issuance of any shares of that series.

(b) Each series of a class must be given a distinguishing designation.

(c) All shares of a series must have preferences, limitations, and relative rights identical with those of other shares of the same series and, except to the extent otherwise provided in the description of the series, of those of other series of the same class.

(d) Before issuing any shares of a class or series created under this section, the corporation must deliver to the secretary of state for filing articles of amendment, which are effective without shareholder action, that set forth:

(1) the name of the corporation;

(2) the text of the amendment determining the terms of the class or series of shares;

(3) the date it was adopted; and

(4) a statement that the amendment was duly adopted by the board of directors.

§ 6.03 Issued and Outstanding Shares

(a) A corporation may issue the number of shares of each class or series authorized by the articles of incorporation. Shares that are issued are outstanding shares until they are reacquired, redeemed, converted, or cancelled.

(b) The reacquisition, redemption, or conversion of outstanding shares is subject to the limitations of subsection (c) of this section and to section 6.40.

(c) At all times that shares of the corporation are outstanding, one or more shares that together have unlimited voting rights and one or more shares that together are entitled to receive the net assets of the corporation upon dissolution must be outstanding.

§ 6.20 Subscription for Shares Before Incorporation

(a) A subscription for shares entered into before incorporation is irrevocable for six months unless the subscription agreement provides a longer or shorter period or all the subscribers agree to revocation.

(b) The board of directors may determine the payment terms of subscriptions for shares that were entered into before incorporation, unless the subscription agreement specifies them. A call for payment by the board of directors must be uniform so far as practicable as to all shares of the same class or series, unless the subscription agreement specifies otherwise.

(c) Shares issued pursuant to subscriptions entered into before incorporation are fully paid and nonassessable when the corporation receives the consideration specified in the subscription agreement.

(d) If a subscriber defaults in payment of money or property under a subscription agreement entered into before incorporation, the corporation may collect the amount owed as any other debt. Alternatively, unless the subscription agreement provides otherwise, the corporation may rescind the agreement and may sell the shares if the debt remains unpaid more than 20 days after the corporation sends written demand for payment to the subscriber.

(e) A subscription agreement entered into after incorporation is a contract between the subscriber and the corporation subject to section 6.21.

§ 6.21 Issuance of Shares

(a) The powers granted in this section to the board of directors may be reserved to the shareholders by the articles of incorporation.

(b) The board of directors may authorize shares to be issued for consideration consisting of any tangible or intangible property or benefit to the corporation, including cash, promissory notes, services performed, contracts for services to be performed, or other securities of the corporation.

(c) Before the corporation issues shares, the board of directors must determine that the consideration received or to be received for shares to be issued is adequate. That determination by the board of directors is conclusive insofar as the adequacy of consideration for the issuance of shares relates to whether the shares are validly issued, fully paid, and nonassessable.

(d) When the corporation receives the consideration for which the board of directors authorized the issuance of shares, the shares issued therefor are fully paid and nonassessable.

(e) The corporation may place in escrow shares issued for a contract for future services or benefits or a promissory note, or make other arrangements to restrict the transfer of the shares, and may credit distributions in respect of the shares against their purchase price, until the services are performed, the note is paid, or the benefits received. If the services are not performed, the note is not paid, or the benefits are not received, the shares escrowed or restricted and the distributions credited may be cancelled in whole or part.

§ 6.22 Liability of Shareholders

(a) A purchaser from a corporation of its own shares is not liable to the corporation or its creditors with respect to the shares except to pay the consideration for which the shares were authorized to be issued (section 6.21) or specified in the subscription agreement (section 6.20).

(b) Unless otherwise provided in the articles of incorporation, a shareholder of a corporation is not personally liable for the acts or debts of the corporation except that he may become personally liable by reason of his own acts or conduct.

§ 6.23 Share Dividends

(a) Unless the articles of incorporation provide otherwise, shares may be issued pro rata and without consideration to the corporation's shareholders or to the shareholders of one or more classes or series. An issuance of shares under this subsection is a share dividend.

(b) Shares of one class or series may not be issued as a share dividend in respect of shares of another class or series unless (1) the articles of incorporation so authorize, (2) a majority of the votes entitled to be cast by the class or series to be issued approve the issue, or (3) there are no outstanding shares of the class or series to be issued.

(c) If the board of directors does not fix the record date for determining shareholders entitled to a share dividend, it is the date the board of directors authorizes the share dividend.

§ 6.24 Share Options

A corporation may issue rights, options, or warrants for the purchase of shares of the corporation. The board of directors shall determine the terms upon which the rights, options, or warrants are issued, their form and content, and the consideration for which the shares are to be issued.

§ 6.27 Restriction on Transfer of Shares and Other Securities

(a) The articles of incorporation, bylaws, an agreement among shareholders, or an agreement between shareholders and the corporation may impose restrictions on the transfer or registration of transfer of shares of the corporation. A restriction does not affect shares issued before the restriction was adopted unless the holders of the shares are parties to the restriction agreement or voted in favor of the restriction.

(b) A restriction on the transfer or registration of transfer of shares is valid and enforceable against the holder or a transferee of the holder if the restriction is authorized by this section and its existence is noted conspicuously on the front or back of the certificate or is contained in the information statement required by section 6.26(b). Unless so noted, a restriction is not enforceable against a person without knowledge of the restriction.

(c) A restriction on the transfer or registration of transfer of shares is authorized:

(1) to maintain the corporation's status when it is dependent on the number or identity of its shareholders;

(2) to preserve exemptions under federal or state securities law;

(3) for any other reasonable purpose.

(d) A restriction on the transfer or registration of transfer of shares may:

(1) obligate the shareholder first to offer the corporation or other persons (separately, consecutively, or simultaneously) an opportunity to acquire the restricted shares;

(2) obligate the corporation or other persons (separately, consecutively, or simultaneously) to acquire the restricted shares;

(3) require the corporation, the holders of any class of its shares, or another person to approve the transfer of the restricted shares, if the requirement is not manifestly unreasonable;

(4) prohibit the transfer of the restricted shares to designated persons or classes of persons, if the prohibition is not manifestly unreasonable.

(e) For purposes of this section, "shares" includes a security convertible into or carrying a right to subscribe for or acquire shares.

§ 6.30 Shareholders' Preemptive Rights

(a) The shareholders of a corporation do not have a preemptive right to acquire the corporation's unissued shares except to the extent the articles of incorporation so provide.

(b) A statement included in the articles of incorporation that "the corporation elects to have preemptive rights" (or words of similar import) means that the following principles apply except to the extent the articles of incorporation expressly provide otherwise:

(1) The shareholders of the corporation have a preemptive right, granted on uniform terms and conditions prescribed by the board of directors to provide a fair and reasonable opportunity to exercise the right, to acquire proportional amounts of the corporation's unissued shares upon the decision of the board of directors to issue them.

(2) A shareholder may waive his preemptive right. A waiver evidenced by a writing is irrevocable even though it is not supported by consideration.

(3) There is no preemptive right with respect to:

(i) shares issued as compensation to directors, officers, agents, or employees of the corporation, its subsidiaries or affiliates;

(ii) shares issued to satisfy conversion or option rights created to provide compensation to directors, officers, agents, or employees of the corporation, its subsidiaries or affiliates;

(iii) shares authorized in articles of incorporation that are issued within six months from the effective date of incorporation;

(iv) shares sold otherwise than for money.

(4) Holders of shares of any class without general voting rights but with preferential rights to distributions or assets have no preemptive rights with respect to shares of any class.

(5) Holders of shares of any class with general voting rights but without preferential rights to distributions or assets have no preemptive rights with respect to shares of any class with preferential rights to distributions or assets unless the shares with preferential rights are convertible into or carry a right to subscribe for or acquire shares without preferential rights.

(6) Shares subject to preemptive rights that are not acquired by shareholders may be issued to any person for

a period of one year after being offered to shareholders at a consideration set by the board of directors that is not lower than the consideration set for the exercise of pre-emptive rights. An offer at a lower consideration or after the expiration of one year is subject to the shareholders' preemptive rights.

(c) For purposes of this section, "shares" includes a security convertible into or carrying a right to subscribe for or acquire shares.

§ 6.31 Corporation's Acquisition of Its Own Shares

(a) A corporation may acquire its own shares and shares so acquired constitute authorized but unissued shares.

(b) If the articles of incorporation prohibit the reissue of acquired shares, the number of authorized shares is reduced by the number of shares acquired, effective upon amendment of the articles of incorporation.

(c) Articles of amendment may be adopted by the board of directors without shareholder action, shall be delivered to the secretary of state for filing, and shall set forth:

(1) the name of the corporation;

(2) the reduction in the number of authorized shares, itemized by class and series; and

(3) the total number of authorized shares, itemized by class and series, remaining after reduction of the shares.

§ 6.40 Distributions to Shareholders

(a) A board of directors may authorize and the corporation may make distributions to its shareholders subject to restriction by the articles of incorporation and the limitation in subsection (c).

(b) If the board of directors does not fix the record date for determining shareholders entitled to a distribution (other than one involving a purchase, redemption, or other acquisition of the corporation's shares), it is the date the board of directors authorizes the distribution.

(c) No distribution may be made if, after giving it effect:

(1) the corporation would not be able to pay its debts as they become due in the usual course of business; or

(2) the corporation's total assets would be less than the sum of its total liabilities plus (unless the articles of incorporation permit otherwise) the amount that would be needed, if the corporation were to be dissolved at the time of the distribution, to satisfy the preferential rights upon dissolution of shareholders whose preferential rights are superior to those receiving the distribution.

(d) The board of directors may base a determination that a distribution is not prohibited under subsection (c) either on financial statements prepared on the basis of accounting practices and principles that are reasonable in the circumstances or on a fair valuation or other method that is reasonable in the circumstances.

(e) Except as provided in subsection (g), the effect of a distribution under subsection (c) is measured:

(1) in the case of distribution by purchase, redemption, or other acquisition of the corporation's shares, as of the earlier of (i) the date money or other property is transferred or debt incurred by the corporation or (ii) the date the shareholder ceases to be a shareholder with respect to the acquired shares;

(2) in the case of any other distribution of indebtedness, as of the date the indebtedness is distributed; and

(3) in all other cases, as of (i) the date the distribution is authorized if the payment occurs within 120 days after the date of authorization or (ii) the date the payment is made if it occurs more than 120 days after the date of authorization.

(f) A corporation's indebtedness to a shareholder incurred by reason of a distribution made in accordance with this section is at parity with the corporation's indebtedness to its general, unsecured creditors except to the extent subordinated by agreement.

(g) Indebtedness of a corporation, including indebtedness issued as a distribution, is not considered a liability for purposes of determinations under subsection (c) if its terms provide that payment of principal and interest are made only if and to the extent that payment of a distribution to shareholders could then be made under this section. If the indebtedness is issued as a distribution, each payment of principal or interest is treated as a distribution, the effect of which is measured on the date the payment is actually made.

§ 7.01 Annual Meeting

(a) A corporation shall hold annually at a time stated in or fixed in accordance with the bylaws a meeting of shareholders.

(b) Annual shareholders' meetings may be held in or out of this state at the place stated in or fixed in accordance with the bylaws. If no place is stated in or fixed in accordance with the bylaws, annual meetings shall be held at the corporation's principal office.

(c) The failure to hold an annual meeting at the time stated in or fixed in accordance with a corporation's bylaws does not affect the validity of any corporate action.

§ 7.02 Special Meeting

(a) A corporation shall hold a special meeting of shareholders:

(1) on call of its board of directors or the person or persons authorized to do so by the articles of incorporation or bylaws; or

(2) if the holders of at least 10 percent of all the votes entitled to be cast on any issue proposed to be considered at the proposed special meeting sign, date, and deliver to the corporation's secretary one or more written demands for the meeting describing the purpose or purposes for which it is to be held.

(b) If not otherwise fixed under sections 7.03 or 7.07, the record date for determining shareholders entitled to demand a special meeting is the date the first shareholder signs the demand.

(c) Special shareholders' meetings may be held in or out of this state at the place stated in or fixed in accordance with the bylaws. If no place is stated or fixed in accordance with the bylaws, special meetings shall be held at the corporation's principal office.

(d) Only business within the purpose or purposes described in the meeting notice required by section 7.05(c) may be conducted at a special shareholders' meeting.

§ 7.04 Action Without Meeting

(a) Action required or permitted by this Act to be taken at a shareholders' meeting may be taken without a meeting if the action is taken by all the shareholders entitled to vote on the action. The action must be evidenced by one or more written consents describing the action taken, signed by all the shareholders entitled to vote on the action, and delivered to the corporation for inclusion in the minutes or filing with the corporate records.

(b) If not otherwise determined under sections 7.03 or 7.07, the record date for determining shareholders entitled to take action without a meeting is the date the first shareholder signs the consent under subsection (a).

(c) A consent signed under this section has the effect of a meeting vote and may be described as such in any document.

(d) If this Act requires that notice of proposed action be given to nonvoting shareholders and the action is to be taken by unanimous consent of the voting shareholders, the corporation must give its nonvoting shareholders written notice of the proposed action at least 10 days before the action is taken. The notice must contain or be accompanied by the same material that, under this Act, would have been required to be sent to nonvoting shareholders in a notice of meeting at which the proposed action would have been submitted to the shareholders for action.

§ 7.05 Notice of Meeting

(a) A corporation shall notify shareholders of the date, time, and place of each annual and special shareholders' meeting no fewer than 10 nor more than 60 days before the meeting date. Unless this Act or the articles of incorporation require otherwise, the corporation is required to give notice only to shareholders entitled to vote at the meeting.

(b) Unless this Act or the articles of incorporation require otherwise, notice of an annual meeting need not include a description of the purpose or purposes for which the meeting is called.

(c) Notice of a special meeting must include a description of the purpose or purposes for which the meeting is called.

(d) If not otherwise fixed under sections 7.03 or 7.07, the record date for determining shareholders entitled to notice of and to vote at an annual or special shareholders' meeting is the close of business on the day before the first notice is delivered to shareholders.

(e) Unless the bylaws require otherwise, if an annual or special shareholders' meeting is adjourned to a different date, time, or place, notice need not be given of the new date, time, or place if the new date, time, or place is announced at the meeting before adjournment. If a new record date for the adjourned meeting is or must be fixed under section 7.07, however, notice of the adjourned meeting must be given under this section to persons who are shareholders as of the new record date.

§ 7.06 Waiver of Notice

(a) A shareholder may waive any notice required by this Act, the articles of incorporation, or bylaws before or after the date and time stated in the notice. The waiver must be in writing, be signed by the shareholder entitled to the notice, and be delivered to the corporation for inclusion in the minutes or filing with the corporate records.

(b) A shareholder's attendance at a meeting:

(1) waives objection to lack of notice or defective notice of the meeting, unless the shareholder at the beginning of the meeting objects to holding the meeting or transacting business at the meeting;

(2) waives objection to consideration of a particular matter at the meeting that is not within the purpose or purposes described in the meeting notice, unless the shareholder objects to considering the matter when it is presented.

§ 7.21 Voting Entitlement of Shares

(a) Except as provided in subsections (b) and (c) or unless the articles of incorporation provide otherwise, each outstanding share, regardless of class, is entitled to one vote on each matter voted on at a shareholders' meeting. Only shares are entitled to vote.

(b) Absent special circumstances, the shares of a corporation are not entitled to vote if they are owned, directly or indirectly, by a second corporation, domestic or foreign, and the first corporation owns, directly or indirectly, a majority of the shares entitled to vote for directors of the second corporation.

(c) Subsection (b) does not limit the power of a corporation to vote any shares, including its own shares, held by it in a fiduciary capacity.

(d) Redeemable shares are not entitled to vote after notice of redemption is mailed to the holders and a sum sufficient to redeem the shares has been deposited with a bank, trust company, or other financial institution under an irrevocable obligation to pay the holders the redemption price on surrender of the shares.

§ 7.22 Proxies

(a) A shareholder may vote his shares in person or by proxy.

(b) A shareholder may appoint a proxy to vote or otherwise act for him by signing an appointment form, either personally or by his attorney-in-fact.

(c) An appointment of a proxy is effective when received by the secretary or other officer or agent authorized to tabulate votes. An appointment is valid for 11 months unless a longer period is expressly provided in the appointment form.

(d) An appointment of a proxy is revocable by the shareholder unless the appointment form conspicuously states that it is irrevocable and the appointment is coupled with an interest. Appointments coupled with an interest include the appointment of:

(1) a pledgee;

(2) a person who purchased or agreed to purchase the shares;

(3) a creditor of the corporation who extended it credit under terms requiring the appointment;

(4) an employee of the corporation whose employment contract requires the appointment; or

(5) a party to a voting agreement created under section 7.31.

(e) The death or incapacity of the shareholder appointing a proxy does not affect the right of the corporation to accept the proxy's authority unless notice of the death or incapacity is received by the secretary or other officer or agent authorized to tabulate votes before the proxy exercises his authority under the appointment.

(f) An appointment made irrevocable under subsection (d) is revoked when the interest with which it is coupled is extinguished.

(g) A transferee for value of shares subject to an irrevocable appointment may revoke the appointment if he did not know of its existence when he acquired the shares and the existence of the irrevocable appointment was not noted conspicuously on the certificate representing the shares or on the information statement for shares without certificates.

(h) Subject to section 7.24 and to any express limitation on the proxy's authority appearing on the face of the appointment form, a corporation is entitled to accept the proxy's vote or other action as that of the shareholder making the appointment.

§ 7.25 Quorum and Voting Requirements for Voting Groups

(a) Shares entitled to vote as a separate voting group may take action on a matter at a meeting only if a quorum of those shares exists with respect to that matter. Unless the articles of incorporation or this Act provide otherwise, a majority of the votes entitled to be cast on the matter by the voting group constitutes a quorum of that voting group for action on that matter.

(b) Once a share is represented for any purpose at a meeting, it is deemed present for quorum purposes for the remainder of the meeting and for any adjournment of that meeting unless a new record date is or must be set for that adjourned meeting.

(c) If a quorum exists, action on a matter (other than the election of directors) by a voting group is approved if the votes cast within the voting group favoring the action exceed the votes cast opposing the action, unless the articles of incorporation or this Act require a greater number of affirmative votes.

(d) An amendment of articles of incorporation adding, changing, or deleting a quorum or voting requirement for a voting group greater than specified in subsection (b) or (c) is governed by section 7.27.

(e) The election of directors is governed by section 7.28.

§ 7.27 Greater Quorum or Voting Requirements

(a) The articles of incorporation may provide for a greater quorum or voting requirement for shareholders (or voting groups of shareholders) than is provided for by this Act.

(b) An amendment to the articles of incorporation that adds, changes, or deletes a greater quorum or voting requirement must meet the same quorum requirement and be adopted by the same vote and voting groups required to take action under the quorum and voting requirements then in effect or proposed to be adopted, whichever is greater.

§ 7.28 Voting for Directors; Cumulative Voting

(a) Unless otherwise provided in the articles of incorporation, directors are elected by a plurality of the votes cast by the shares entitled to vote in the election at a meeting at which a quorum is present.

(b) Shareholders do not have a right to cumulate their votes for directors unless the articles of incorporation so provide.

(c) A statement included in the articles of incorporation that "[all] [a designated voting group of] shareholders are entitled to cumulate their votes for directors" (or words of similar import) means that the shareholders designated are entitled to multiply the number of votes they are entitled to cast by the number of directors for whom they are entitled to vote and cast the product for a single candidate or distribute the product among two or more candidates.

(d) Shares otherwise entitled to vote cumulatively may not be voted cumulatively at a particular meeting unless:

(1) the meeting notice or proxy statement accompanying the notice states conspicuously that cumulative voting is authorized; or

(2) a shareholder who has the right to cumulate his votes gives notice to the corporation not less than 48 hours before the time set for the meeting of his intent to cumulate his votes during the meeting, and if one shareholder gives this notice all other shareholders in the same voting group participating in the election are entitled to cumulate their votes without giving further notice.

§ 7.30 Voting Trusts

(a) One or more shareholders may create a voting trust, conferring on a trustee the right to vote or otherwise act for them, by signing an agreement setting out the provisions of the trust (which may include anything consistent with its purpose) and transferring their shares to the trustee. When a voting trust agreement is signed, the trustee shall prepare a list of the names and addresses of all owners of beneficial interests in the trust, together with the number and class of shares each transferred to the trust, and deliver copies of the list and agreement to the corporation's principal office.

(b) A voting trust becomes effective on the date the first shares subject to the trust are registered in the trustee's name. A voting trust is valid for not more than 10 years after its effective date unless extended under subsection (c).

(c) All or some of the parties to a voting trust may extend it for additional terms of not more than 10 years each by signing an extension agreement and obtaining the voting trustee's written consent to the extension. An extension is valid for 10 years from the date the first shareholder signs the extension agreement. The voting trustee must deliver copies of the extension agreement and list of beneficial owners to the corporation's principal office. An extension agreement binds only those parties signing it.

§ 7.31 Voting Agreements

(a) Two or more shareholders may provide for the manner in which they will vote their shares by signing an agreement for that purpose. A voting agreement created under this section is not subject to the provisions of section 7.30.

(b) A voting agreement created under this section is specifically enforceable.

§ 8.01 Requirement for and Duties of Board of Directors

(a) Except as provided in subsection (c), each corporation must have a board of directors.

(b) All corporate powers shall be exercised by or under the authority of, and the business and affairs of the corporation managed under the direction of, its board of directors, subject to any limitation set forth in the articles of incorporation.

(c) A corporation having 50 or fewer shareholders may dispense with or limit the authority of a board of directors by describing in its articles of incorporation who will perform some or all of the duties of a board of directors.

§ 8.03 Number and Election of Directors

(a) A board of directors must consist of one or more individuals, with the number specified in or fixed in accordance with the articles of incorporation or bylaws.

(b) If a board of directors has power to fix or change the number of directors, the board may increase or decrease by 30 percent or less the number of directors last approved by the shareholders, but only the shareholders may increase or decrease by more than 30 percent the number of directors last approved by the shareholders.

(c) The articles of incorporation or bylaws may establish a variable range for the size of the board of directors by fixing a minimum and maximum number of directors. If a variable range is established, the number of directors may be fixed or changed from time to time, within the minimum and maximum, by the shareholders or the board of directors. After shares are issued, only the shareholders may change the range for the size of the board or change from a fixed to a variable-range size board or vice versa.

(d) Directors are elected at the first annual shareholders' meeting and at each annual meeting thereafter unless their terms are staggered under section 8.06.

§ 8.04 Election of Directors by Certain Classes of Shareholders

If the articles of incorporation authorize dividing the shares into classes, the articles may also authorize the election of all or a specified number of directors by the holders of one or more authorized classes of shares. Each class (or classes) of shares entitled to elect one or more directors is a separate voting group for purposes of the election of directors.

§ 8.08 Removal of Directors by Shareholders

(a) The shareholders may remove one or more directors with or without cause unless the articles of incorporation provide that directors may be removed only for cause.

(b) If a director is elected by a voting group of shareholders, only the shareholders of that voting group may participate in the vote to remove him.

(c) If cumulative voting is authorized, a director may not be removed if the number of votes sufficient to elect him under cumulative voting is voted against his removal. If cumulative voting is not authorized, a director may be removed only if the number of votes cast to remove him exceeds the number of votes cast not to remove him.

(d) A director may be removed by the shareholders only at a meeting called for the purpose of removing him and the meeting notice must state that the purpose, or one of the purposes, of the meeting is removal of the director.

§ 8.11 Compensation of Directors

Unless the articles of incorporation or bylaws provide otherwise, the board of directors may fix the compensation of directors.

§ 8.20 Meetings

(a) The board of directors may hold regular or special meetings in or out of this state.

(b) Unless the articles of incorporation or bylaws provide otherwise, the board of directors may permit any or all directors to participate in a regular or special meeting by, or conduct the meeting through the use of, any means of communication by which all directors participating may simultaneously hear each other during the meeting. A director participating in a meeting by this means is deemed to be present in person at the meeting.

§ 8.21 Action Without Meeting

(a) Unless the articles of incorporation or bylaws provide otherwise, action required or permitted by this Act to be taken at a board of directors' meeting may be taken without a meeting if the action is taken by all members of the board. The action must be evidenced by one or more written consents describing the action taken, signed by each director, and included in the minutes or filed with the corporate records reflecting the action taken.

(b) Action taken under this section is effective when the last director signs the consent, unless the consent specifies a different effective date.

(c) A consent signed under this section has the effect of a meeting vote and may be described as such in any document.

§ 8.24 Quorum and Voting

(a) Unless the articles of incorporation or bylaws require a greater number, a quorum of a board of directors consists of:

    (1) a majority of the fixed number of directors if the corporation has a fixed board size; or

    (2) a majority of the number of directors prescribed, or if no number is prescribed the number in office immediately before the meeting begins, if the corporation has a variable-range size board.

(b) The articles of incorporation or bylaws may authorize a quorum of a board of directors to consist of no fewer than one-third of the fixed or prescribed number of directors determined under subsection (a).

(c) If a quorum is present when a vote is taken, the affirmative vote of a majority of directors present is the act of the board of directors unless the articles of incorporation or bylaws require the vote of a greater number of directors.

(d) A director who is present at a meeting of the board of directors or a committee of the board of directors when corporate action is taken is deemed to have assented to the action taken unless: (1) he objects at the beginning of the meeting (or promptly upon his arrival) to holding it or transacting business at the meeting; (2) his dissent or abstention from the action taken is entered in the minutes of the meeting; or (3) he delivers written notice of his dissent or abstention to the presiding officer of the meeting before its adjournment or to the corporation immediately after adjournment of the meeting. The right of dissent or abstention is not available to a director who votes in favor of the action taken.

§ 8.30 General Standards for Directors

(a) A director shall discharge his duties as a director, including his duties as a member of a committee:

    (1) in good faith;

    (2) with the care an ordinarily prudent person in a like position would exercise under similar circumstances; and

    (3) in a manner he reasonably believes to be in the best interests of the corporation.

(b) In discharging his duties a director is entitled to rely on information, opinions, reports, or statements, including financial statements and other financial data, if prepared or presented by:

(1) one or more officers or employees of the corporation whom the director reasonably believes to be reliable and competent in the matters presented;

(2) legal counsel, public accountants, or other persons as to matters the director reasonably believes are within the person's professional or expert competence; or

(3) a committee of the board of directors of which he is not a member if the director reasonably believes the committee merits confidence.

(c)   A director is not acting in good faith if he has knowledge concerning the matter in question that makes reliance otherwise permitted by subsection (b) unwarranted.

(d)   A director is not liable for any action taken as a director, or any failure to take any action, if he performed the duties of his office in compliance with this section.

§ 8.33 Liability for Unlawful Distributions

(a)   A director who votes for or assents to a distribution made in violation of section 6.40 or the articles of incorporation is personally liable to the corporation for the amount of the distribution that exceeds what could have been distributed without violating section 6.40 or the articles of incorporation if it is established that he did not perform his duties in compliance with section 8.30. In any proceeding commenced under this section, a director has all of the defenses ordinarily available to a director.

(b)   A director held liable under subsection (a) for an unlawful distribution is entitled to contribution:

(1) from every other director who could be held liable under subsection (a) for the unlawful distribution; and

(2) from each shareholder for the amount the shareholder accepted knowing the distribution was made in violation of section 6.40 or the articles of incorporation.

(c)   A proceeding under this section is barred unless it is commenced within two years after the date on which the effect of the distribution was measured under section 6.40(e) or (g).

§ 8.40 Required Officers

(a)   A corporation has the officers described in its bylaws or appointed by the board of directors in accordance with the bylaws.

(b)   A duly appointed officer may appoint one or more officers or assistant officers if authorized by the bylaws or the board of directors.

(c)   The bylaws or the board of directors shall delegate to one of the officers responsibility for preparing minutes of the directors' and shareholders' meetings and for authenticating records of the corporation.

(d)   The same individual may simultaneously hold more than one office in a corporation.

§ 8.41 Duties of Officers

Each officer has the authority and shall perform the duties set forth in the bylaws or, to the extent consistent with the bylaws, the duties prescribed by the board of directors or by direction of an officer authorized by the board of directors to prescribe the duties of other officers.

§ 8.42 Standards of Conduct for Officers

(a)   An officer with discretionary authority shall discharge his duties under that authority:

(1) in good faith;

(2) with the care an ordinarily prudent person in a like position would exercise under similar circumstances; and

(3) in a manner he reasonably believes to be in the best interests of the corporation.

(b)   In discharging his duties an officer is entitled to rely on information, opinions, reports, or statements, including financial statements and other financial data, if prepared or presented by:

(1) one or more officers or employees of the corporation whom the officer reasonably believes to be reliable and competent in the matters presented; or

(2) legal counsel, public accountants, or other persons as to matters the officer reasonably believes are within the person's professional or expert competence.

(c)   An officer is not acting in good faith if he has knowledge concerning the matter in question that makes reliance otherwise permitted by subsection (b) unwarranted.

(d)   An officer is not liable for any action taken as an officer, or any failure to take any action, if he performed the duties of his office in compliance with this section.

§ 8.61 Judicial Action

(a)   A transaction effected or proposed to be effected by a corporation (or by a subsidiary of the corporation or any other entity in which the corporation has a controlling interest) that is not a director's conflicting interest transaction may not be enjoined, set aside, or give rise to an award of damages or other sanctions, in a proceeding by a shareholder or by or in the right of the corporation, because a director of the corporation, or any person with whom or which he has a personal, economic, or other association, has an interest in the transaction.

(b)   A director's conflicting interest transaction may not be enjoined, set aside, or give rise to an award of damages or other sanctions, in a proceeding by a shareholder or by or in the right of the corporation, because the director, or any person with whom or which he has a personal, economic, or other association, has an interest in the transaction, if:

(1) directors' action respecting the transaction was at any time taken in compliance with section 8.62;

(2) shareholders' action respecting the transaction was at any time taken in compliance with section 8.63;

(3) the transaction, judged according to the circumstances at the time of commitment, is established to have been fair to the corporation.

§ 8.62 Directors' Action

(a)   Directors' action respecting a transaction is effective for purposes of section 8.61(b)(1) if the transaction received the affirmative vote of a majority (but no fewer than two) of those qualified directors on the board of directors or on a duly empowered committee of the board who voted on the transaction after either required disclosure to them (to the extent the information was not known by them) or compliance with subsection (b); provided that action by a committee is so effective only if (1) all its members are qualified directors, and (2) its members are either all the qualified directors on the board or are appointed by the affirmative vote of a majority of the qualified directors on the board.

(b)   If a director has a conflicting interest respecting a transaction, but neither he nor a related person of the director specified in section 8.60(3)(i) is a party to the transaction, and if the director has a duty under law or professional canon, or a duty of confidentiality to another person, respecting information relating to the transaction such that the director may not make the disclosure described in section 8.60(4)(ii), then disclosure is sufficient for purposes of subsection (a) if the director (1) discloses to the directors voting on the transaction the existence and nature of his conflicting interest and informs them of the character and limitations imposed by that duty before their vote on the transaction, and (2) plays no part, directly or indirectly, in their deliberations or vote.

(c) A majority (but no fewer than two) of all the qualified directors on the board of directors, or on the committee, constitutes a quorum for purposes of action that complies with this section. Directors' action that otherwise complies with this section is not affected by the presence or vote of a director who is not a qualified director.

(d) For purposes of this section, "qualified director" means, with respect to a director's conflicting interest transaction, any director who does not have either (1) a conflicting interest respecting the transaction, or (2) a familial, financial, professional, or employment relationship with a second director who does have a conflicting interest respecting the transaction, which relationship would, in the circumstances, reasonably be expected to exert an influence on the first director's judgment when voting on the transaction.

§ 8.63 Shareholders' Action

(a) Shareholders' action respecting a transaction is effective for purposes of section 8.61(b)(2) if a majority of the votes entitled to be cast by the holders of all qualified shares were cast in favor of the transaction after (1) notice to shareholders describing the director's conflicting interest transaction, (2) provision of the information referred to in subsection (d), and (3) required disclosure to the shareholders who voted on the transaction (to the extent the information was not known by them).

(b) For purposes of this section, "qualified shares" means any shares entitled to vote with respect to the director's conflicting interest transaction except shares that, to the knowledge, before the vote, of the secretary (or other officer or agent of the corporation authorized to tabulate votes), are beneficially owned (or the voting of which is controlled) by a director who has a conflicting interest respecting the transaction or by a related person of the director, or both.

(c) A majority of the votes entitled to be cast by the holders of all qualified shares constitutes a quorum for purposes of action that complies with this section. Subject to the provisions of subsections (d) and (e), shareholders' action that otherwise complies with this section is not affected by the presence of holders, or the voting, of shares that are not qualified shares.

(d) For purposes of compliance with subsection (a), a director who has a conflicting interest respecting the transaction shall, before the shareholders' vote, inform the secretary (or other office or agent of the corporation authorized to tabulate votes) of the number, and the identity of persons holding or controlling the vote, of all shares that the director knows are beneficially owned (or the voting of which is controlled) by the director or by a related person of the director, or both.

(e) If a shareholders' vote does not comply with subsection (a) solely because of a failure of a director to comply with sub-

section (d), and if the director establishes that his failure did not determine and was not intended by him to influence the outcome of the vote, the court may, with or without further proceedings respecting section 8.61(b)(3), take such action respecting the transaction and the director, and give such effect, if any, to the shareholders' vote, as it considers appropriate in the circumstances.

§ 10.01 Authority to Amend

(a) A corporation may amend its articles of incorporation at any time to add or change a provision that is required or permitted in the articles of incorporation or to delete a provision not required in the articles of incorporation. Whether a provision is required or permitted in the articles of incorporation is determined as of the effective date of the amendment.

(b) A shareholder of the corporation does not have a vested property right resulting from any provision in the articles of incorporation, including provisions relating to management, control, capital structure, dividend entitlement, or purpose or duration of the corporation.

§ 10.03 Amendment by Board of Directors and Shareholders

(a) A corporation's board of directors may propose one or more amendments to the articles of incorporation for submission to the shareholders.

(b) For the amendment to be adopted:

    (1) the board of directors must recommend the amendment to the shareholders unless the board of directors determines that because of conflict of interest or other special circumstances it should make no recommendation and communicates the basis for its determination to the shareholders with the amendment; and

    (2) the shareholders entitled to vote on the amendment must approve the amendment as provided in subsection (e).

(c) The board of directors may condition its submission of the proposed amendment on any basis.

(d) The corporation shall notify each shareholder, whether or not entitled to vote, of the proposed shareholders' meeting in accordance with section 7.05. The notice of meeting must also state that the purpose, or one of the purposes, of the meeting is to consider the proposed amendment and contain or be accompanied by a copy or summary of the amendment.

(e) Unless this Act, the articles of incorporation, or the board of directors (acting pursuant to subsection (c)) require a greater vote or a vote by voting groups, the amendment to be adopted must be approved by:

    (1) a majority of the votes entitled to be cast on the amendment by any voting group with respect to which the amendment would create dissenters' rights; and

    (2) the votes required by sections 7.25 and 7.26 by every other voting group entitled to vote on the amendment.

§ 10.20 Amendment by Board of Directors or Shareholders

(a) A corporation's board of directors may amend or repeal the corporation's bylaws unless:

    (1) the articles of incorporation or this Act reserve this power exclusively to the shareholders in whole or part; or

(2) the shareholders in amending or repealing a particular bylaw provide expressly that the board of directors may not amend or repeal that bylaw.

(b)   A corporation's shareholders may amend or repeal the corporation's bylaws even though the bylaws may also be amended or repealed by its board of directors.

§ 11.01 Merger

(a)   One or more corporations may merge into another corporation if the board of directors of each corporation adopts and its shareholders (if required by section 11.03) approve a plan of merger.

(b)   The plan of merger must set forth:

(1) the name of each corporation planning to merge and the name of the surviving corporation into which each other corporation plans to merge;

(2) the terms and conditions of the merger; and

(3) the manner and basis of converting the shares of each corporation into shares, obligations, or other securities of the surviving or any other corporation or into cash or other property in whole or part.

(c)   The plan of merger may set forth:

(1) amendments to the articles of incorporation of the surviving corporation; and

(2) other provisions relating to the merger.

§ 11.02 Share Exchange

(a)   A corporation may acquire all of the outstanding shares of one or more classes or series of another corporation if the board of directors of each corporation adopts and its shareholders (if required by section 11.03) approve the exchange.

(b)   The plan of exchange must set forth:

(1) the name of the corporation whose shares will be acquired and the name of the acquiring corporation;

(2) the terms and conditions of the exchange;

(3) the manner and basis of exchanging the shares to be acquired for shares, obligations, or other securities of the acquiring or any other corporation or for cash or other property in whole or part.

(c)   The plan of exchange may set forth other provisions relating to the exchange.

(d)   This section does not limit the power of a corporation to acquire all or part of the shares of one or more classes or series of another corporation through a voluntary exchange or otherwise.

§ 11.04 Merger of Subsidiary

(a)   A parent corporation owning at least 90 percent of the outstanding shares of each class of a subsidiary corporation may merge the subsidiary into itself without approval of the shareholders of the parent or subsidiary.

§ 12.01 Sale of Assets in Regular Course of Business and Mortgage of Assets

(a)   A corporation may, on the terms and conditions and for the consideration determined by the board of directors:

(1) sell, lease, exchange, or otherwise dispose of all, or substantially all, of its property in the usual and regular course of business,

(2) mortgage, pledge, dedicate to the repayment of indebtedness (whether with or without recourse), or otherwise encumber any or all of its property whether or not in the usual and regular course of business, or

(3) transfer any or all of its property to a corporation all the shares of which are owned by the corporation.

(b)   Unless the articles of incorporation require it, approval by the shareholders of a transaction described in subsection (a) is not required.

§ 12.02 Sale of Assets Other Than in Regular Course of Business

(a)   A corporation may sell, lease, exchange, or otherwise dispose of all, or substantially all, of its property (with or without the good will), otherwise than in the usual and regular course of business, on the terms and conditions and for the consideration determined by the corporation's board of directors, if the board of directors proposes and its shareholders approve the proposed transaction.

(b)   For a transaction to be authorized:

(1) the board of directors must recommend the proposed transaction to the shareholders unless the board of directors determines that because of conflict of interest or other special circumstances it should make no recommendation and communicates the basis for its determination to the shareholders with the submission of the proposed transaction; and

(2) the shareholders entitled to vote must approve the transaction.

§ 13.02 Right to Dissent

(a)   A shareholder is entitled to dissent from, and obtain payment of the fair value of his shares in the event of, any of the following corporate actions:

(1) consummation of a plan of merger to which the corporation is a party (i) if shareholder approval is required for the merger by section 11.03 or the articles of incorporation and the shareholder is entitled to vote on the merger or (ii) if the corporation is a subsidiary that is merged with its parent under section 11.04;

(2) consummation of a plan of share exchange to which the corporation is a party as the corporation whose shares will be acquired, if the shareholder is entitled to vote on the plan;

(3) consummation of a sale or exchange of all, or substantially all, of the property of the corporation other than in the usual and regular course of business, if the shareholder is entitled to vote on the sale or exchange, including a sale in dissolution, but not including a sale pursuant to court order or a sale for cash pursuant to a plan by which all or substantially all of the net proceeds of the sale will be distributed to the shareholders within one year after the date of sale;

(4) an amendment of the articles of incorporation that materially and adversely affects rights in respect of a dissenter's shares because it:

(i) alters or abolishes a preferential right of the shares;

(ii) creates, alters, or abolishes a right in respect of redemption, including a provision respecting a sinking fund for the redemption or repurchase, of the shares;

(iii) alters or abolishes a preemptive right of the holder of the shares to acquire shares or other securities;

(iv) excludes or limits the right of the shares to vote on any matter, or to cumulate votes, other than a limitation by dilution through issuance of shares or other securities with similar voting rights; or

(v) reduces the number of shares owned by the shareholder to a fraction of a share if the fractional share so created is to be acquired for cash under section 6.04; or

(5) any corporate action taken pursuant to a shareholder vote to the extent the articles of incorporation, bylaws, or a resolution of the board of directors provides that voting or nonvoting shareholders are entitled to dissent and obtain payment for their shares.

(b) A shareholder entitled to dissent and obtain payment for his shares under this chapter may not challenge the corporate action creating his entitlement unless the action is unlawful or fraudulent with respect to the shareholder or the corporation.

§ 14.30 Grounds for Judicial Dissolution

The [name or describe court or courts] may dissolve a corporation:

(1) in a proceeding by the attorney general if it is established that:

(i) the corporation obtained its articles of incorporation through fraud; or

(ii) the corporation has continued to exceed or abuse the authority conferred upon it by law;

(2) in a proceeding by a shareholder if it is established that:

(i) the directors are deadlocked in the management of the corporate affairs, the shareholders are unable to break the deadlock, and irreparable injury to the corporation is threatened or being suffered, or the business and affairs of the corporation can no longer be conducted to the advantage of the shareholders generally, because of the deadlock;

(ii) the directors or those in control of the corporation have acted, are acting, or will act in a manner that is illegal, oppressive, or fraudulent;

(iii) the shareholders are deadlocked in voting power and have failed, for a period that includes at least two consecutive annual meeting dates, to elect successors to directors whose terms have expired; or

(iv) the corporate assets are being misapplied or wasted;

(3) in a proceeding by a creditor if it is established that:

(i) the creditor's claim has been reduced to judgment, the execution on the judgment returned unsatisfied, and the corporation is insolvent; or

(ii) the corporation has admitted in writing that the creditor's claim is due and owing and the corporation is insolvent; or

(4) in a proceeding by the corporation to have its voluntary dissolution continued under court supervision.

§ 16.01 Corporate Records

(a) A corporation shall keep as permanent records minutes of all meetings of its shareholders and board of directors, a record of all actions taken by the shareholders or board of directors without a meeting, and a record of all actions taken by a committee of the board of directors in place of the board of directors on behalf of the corporation.

(b) A corporation shall maintain appropriate accounting records.

(c) A corporation or its agent shall maintain a record of its shareholders, in a form that permits preparation of a list of the names and addresses of all shareholders, in alphabetical order by class of shares showing the number and class of shares held by each.

(d) A corporation shall maintain its records in written form or in another form capable of conversion into written form within a reasonable time.

(e) A corporation shall keep a copy of the following records at its principal office:

(1) its articles or restated articles of incorporation and all amendments to them currently in effect;

(2) its bylaws or restated bylaws and all amendments to them currently in effect;

(3) resolutions adopted by its board of directors creating one or more classes or series of shares, and fixing their relative rights, preferences, and limitations, if shares issued pursuant to those resolutions are outstanding;

(4) the minutes of all shareholders' meetings, and records of all action taken by shareholders without a meeting, for the past three years;

(5) all written communications to shareholders generally within the past three years, including the financial statements furnished for the past three years under section 16.20;

(6) a list of the names and business addresses of its current directors and officers; and

(7) its most recent annual report delivered to the secretary of state under section 16.22.

§ 16.02 Inspection of Records by Shareholders

(a) Subject to section 16.03(c), a shareholder of a corporation is entitled to inspect and copy, during regular business hours at the corporation's principal office, any of the records of the corporation described in section 16.01(e) if he gives the corporation written notice of his demand at least five business days before the date on which he wishes to inspect and copy.

(b) A shareholder of a corporation is entitled to inspect and copy, during regular business hours at a reasonable location specified by the corporation, any of the following records of the corporation if the shareholder meets the requirements of subsection (c) and gives the corporation written notice of his demand at least five business days before the date on which he wishes to inspect and copy:

(1) excerpts from minutes of any meeting of the board of directors, records of any action of a committee of the board of directors while acting in place of the board of directors on behalf of the corporation, minutes of any meeting of the shareholders, and records of action taken by the shareholders or board of directors without a meeting, to the extent not subject to inspection under section 16.02(a);

(2) accounting records of the corporation; and

(3) the record of shareholders.

(c) A shareholder may inspect and copy the records identified in subsection (b) only if:

(1) his demand is made in good faith and for a proper purpose;

(2) he describes with reasonable particularity his purpose and the records he desires to inspect; and

(3) the records are directly connected with his purpose.

(d) The right of inspection granted by this section may not be abolished or limited by a corporation's articles of incorporation or bylaws.

(e) This section does not affect:

(1) the right of a shareholder to inspect records under section 7.20 or, if the shareholder is in litigation with the corporation, to the same extent as any other litigant;

(2) the power of a court, independently of this Act, to compel the production of corporate records for examination.

abatement Reduction or elimination of gifts by category upon the reduction in value of the estate.

absolute surety Surety liable to a creditor immediately upon the default of the principal debtor.

acceptance *Commercial paper* Acceptance is the drawee's signed engagement to honor the draft as presented. It becomes operative when completed by delivery or notification. UCC § 3–410.

    Contracts Compliance by offeree with terms and conditions of offer.

    Sale of goods UCC § 2–606 provides three ways a buyer can accept goods: (1) by signifying to the seller that the goods are conforming or that he will accept them in spite of their nonconformity, (2) by failing to make an effective rejection, and (3) by doing an act inconsistent with the seller's ownership.

acceptor Drawee who has accepted an instrument.

accession An addition to one's property by increase of the original property or by production from such property. E.g., A innocently converts the wheat of B into bread. UCC § 9–315 changes the common law where a perfected security interest is involved.

accident and health insurance Provides protection from losses due to accident or sickness.

accommodation An arrangement made as a favor to another, usually involving a loan of money or commercial paper. While a party's intent may be to aid a maker of a note by lending his credit, if he seeks to accomplish thereby legitimate objects of his own and not simply to aid the maker, the act is not for accommodation.

accommodation indorser Signer not in the chain of title.

accommodation party A person who signs commercial paper in any capacity for the purpose of lending his name to another party to an instrument. UCC § 3–415.

accord and satisfaction A method of discharging a claim whereby the parties agree to accept something in settlement, the "accord" being the agreement and the "satisfaction" its execution or performance. It is a

new contract that is substituted for an old contract, which is thereby discharged, or for an obligation or cause of action and that must have all of the elements of a valid contract.

account Any account with a bank, including a checking, time, interest or savings account. UCC § 4–194. Also, any right to payment, for goods or services, that is not evidenced by an instrument or chattel paper. E.g., account receivable.

accounting Equitable proceeding for a complete settlement of all partnership affairs.

act of state doctrine Rule that a court should not question the validity of actions taken by a foreign government in its own country.

actual authority Power conferred upon agent by actual consent given by principal.

actual express authority Actual authority derived from written or spoken words of principal.

actual implied authority Actual authority inferred from words or conduct manifested to agent by principal.

actual notice Knowledge actually and expressly communicated.

actus reas Wrongful or overt act.

ademption The removal or extinction of a devise by act of the testator.

adequacy of consideration Not required where parties have freely agreed to the exchange.

adhesion contract Standard "form" contract, usually between a large retailer and a consumer, in which the weaker party has no realistic choice or opportunity to bargain.

adjudication The giving or pronouncing of a judgment in a case; also, the judgment given.

administrative agency Governmental entity (other than courts and legislatures) having authority to affect the rights of private parties.

administrative law Law dealing with the establishment, duties, and powers of agencies in the executive branch of government.

*Authors' note: Many of the definitions are abridged and adapted from *Black's Law Dictionary*. 5th Edition.

administrative process Entire set of activities engaged in by administrative agencies while carrying out their rulemaking, enforcement, and adjudicative functions.

administrator A person appointed by the court to manage the assets and liabilities of an intestate (a person dying without a will). A person named in the will of a testator (a person dying with a will) is called the executor. Female designations are administratrix and executrix.

adversary system System in which opposing parties initiate and present their case.

adverse possession A method of acquiring title to real property by possession for a statutory period under certain conditions. The periods of time may differ, depending on whether the adverse possessor has color of title.

affidavit A written statement of facts, made voluntarily, confirmed by oath or affirmation of the party making it, and taken before an authorized officer.

affiliate Person who controls, is controlled by, or is under common control with the issuer.

affirm Uphold the lower court's judgment.

affirmative action Active recruitment of minority applicants.

affirmative defense A response that attacks the plaintiff's legal right to bring an action as opposed to attacking the truth of the claim. E.g., accord and satisfaction; assumption of risk; contributory negligence; duress; estoppel.

affirmative disclosure Requirement that an advertiser include certain information in its advertisement so that the ad is not deceptive.

after-acquired property Property the debtor may acquire at some time after the security interest attaches.

agency Relation in which one person acts for or represents another by the latter's authority.
  Actual agency Exists where the agent is really employed by the principal.
  Agency by estoppel One created by operation of law and established by proof of such acts of the principal as reasonably lead to the conclusion of its existence.
  Implied agency One created by acts of the parties and deduced from proof of other facts.

agent Person authorized to act on another's behalf.

allegation A statement of a party setting out what he expects to prove.

allonge Piece of paper firmly affixed to the instrument.

annuity contract Agreement to pay periodic sums to insured upon reaching a designated age.

annul To annul a judgment or judicial proceeding is to deprive it of all force and operation.

answer The answer is the formal written statement made by a defendant setting forth the ground of his defense.

antecedent debt Preexisting obligation.

anticipatory breach of contract (or **anticipatory repudiation**) The unjustified assertion by a party that he will not perform an obligation that he is contractually obligated to perform at a future time. See UCC §§ 610 & 611.

apparent authority Such principal power that a reasonable person would assume an agent has in light of the principal's conduct.

appeal Resort to a superior (appellate) court to review the decision of an inferior (trial) court or administrative agency.

appeal by right Mandatory review by a higher court.

appellant A party who takes an appeal from one court to another. He may be either the plaintiff or defendant in the original court proceeding.

appellee The party in a cause against whom an appeal is taken; that is, the party who has an interest adverse to setting aside or reversing the judgment. Sometimes also called the "respondent."

appropriation Unauthorized use of another person's name or likeness for one's own benefit.

appurtenances Things appurtenant pass as incident to the principal thing. Sometimes an easement consisting of a right of way over one piece of land will pass with another piece of land as being appurtenant to it.

APR Annual percentage rate.

arbitration The reference of a dispute to an impartial (third) person chosen by the parties, who agree in advance to abide by the arbitrator's award issued after a hearing at which both parties have an opportunity to be heard.

arraignment Accused is informed of the crime against him and enters a plea.

articles of incorporation (or **certificate of incorporation**) The instrument under which a corporation is formed. The contents are prescribed in the particular state's general incorporation statute.

articles of partnership A written agreement by which parties enter into a partnership, to be governed by the terms set forth therein.

as is Disclaimer of implied warranties.

assault Unlawful attempted battery; intentional infliction of apprehension of immediate bodily harm or offensive contact.

assignee Party to whom contract rights are assigned.

assignment A transfer of the rights to real or personal property, usually intangible property such as rights in a lease, mortgage, sale agreement, or partnership.

assignment of rights Voluntary transfer to a third party of the rights arising from a contract.

assignor Party making an assignment.

assumes Delegatee agrees to perform the contractual obligation of the delegator.

assumes the mortgage Purchaser of mortgaged property becomes personally liable to pay the debt.

assumption of risk Plaintiff's express or implied consent to encounter a known danger.

attachment The process of seizing property, by virtue of a writ, summons, or other judicial order, and bringing the same into the custody of the court for the purpose of securing satisfaction of the judgment ultimately to be entered in the action. While formerly the main objective was to coerce the defendant debtor to appear in court, today the writ of attachment is used primarily to seize the debtor's property in the event a judgment is rendered.
    Distinguished from execution See **execution**.
Also, the process by which a security interest becomes enforceable. Attachment may occur upon the taking of possession or upon the signing of a security agreement by the person who is pledging the property as collateral.

authority Power of an agent to change the legal status of his principal.

authorized means Any reasonable means of communication.

automatic perfection Perfection upon attachment.

award The decision of an arbitrator.

bad checks Issuing a check with funds insufficient to cover it.

bailee The party to whom personal property is delivered under a contract of bailment.
    Extraordinary bailee Absolutely liable for the safety of the bailed property without regard to the cause of loss.
    Ordinary bailee Must exercise due care.

bailment A delivery of personal property in trust for the execution of a special object in relation to such goods, beneficial either to the bailor or bailee or both, and upon a contract to either redeliver the goods to the bailor or otherwise dispose of the same in conformity with the purpose of the trust.

bailor The party who delivers goods to another in the contract of bailment.

bankrupt The state or condition of one who is unable to pay his debts as they are, or become, due.

Bankruptcy Code The Act was substantially revised in 1978, effective October 1, 1979. Straight bankruptcy is in the nature of a liquidation proceeding and involves the collection and distribution to creditors of all the bankrupt's nonexempt property by the trustee in the manner provided by the Act. The debtor rehabilitation provisions of the Act (Chapters 11 and 13) differ from straight bankruptcy in that the debtor looks to rehabilitation and reorganization, rather than liquidation, and the creditors look to future earnings of the bankrupt, rather than to property held by the bankrupt, to satisfy their claims.

bargain Negotiated exchange.

bargained exchange Mutually agreed-upon exchange.

basis of the bargain Part of the buyer's assumption underlying the sale.

battery Unlawful touching of another; intentional infliction of harmful or offensive bodily contact.

bearer Person in possession of an instrument.

bearer paper Payable to holder of the instrument.

beneficiary One who benefits from act of another. See also **third-party beneficiary**.
    Incidental A person who may derive benefit from performance on contract, though he is neither the promisee nor the one to whom performance is to be rendered. Since the incidental beneficiary is not a donee or creditor beneficiary (see **third-party beneficiary**), he has no right to enforce the contract.
    Intended beneficiary Third party intended by the two contracted parties to receive a benefit from their contract.
    Trust As it relates to trust beneficiaries, includes a person who has any present or future interest, vested or contingent, and also includes the owner of an interest by assignment or other transfer and, as it relates to a charitable trust, includes any person entitled to enforce the trust.

beyond a reasonable doubt Proof that is entirely convincing and satisfying to a moral certainty; criminal law standard.

bilateral contract Contract in which both parties exchange promises.

bill of lading Document evidencing receipt of goods for shipment issued by person engaged in business of transporting or forwarding goods; includes airbill. UCC § 1–201(6).
    Through bill of lading A bill of lading which specifies at least one connecting carrier.

bill of sale A written agreement, formerly limited to one under seal, by which one person assigns or transfers his right to or interest in goods and personal chattels to another.

binder A written memorandum of the important terms of a contract of insurance which gives temporary protection to an insured pending investigation of risk by the insurance company or until a formal policy is issued.

blue law Prohibition of certain types of commercial activity on Sunday.

blue sky laws A popular name for state statutes providing for the regulation and supervision of securities offerings and sales, to protect citizen-investors from investing in fraudulent companies.

bona fide Latin. In good faith.

bond A certificate or evidence of a debt on which the issuing company or governmental body promises to pay the bondholders a specified amount of interest for a specified length of time and to repay the loan on the expiration date. In every case, a bond represents debt—its holder is a creditor of the corporation, not a part owner, as the shareholder is.

boycott Agreement among parties not to deal with a third party.

breach Wrongful failure to perform the terms of a contract.

Material breach Nonperformance which significantly impairs the aggrieved party's rights under the contract.

bribery Offering property to a public official to influence the official's decision.

bulk transfer Transfer not in the ordinary course of the transferor's business of a major part of his inventory.

burglary Breaking and entering the home of another at night with intent to commit a felony.

business judgment rule Protects directors from liability for honest mistakes of judgment.

business trust A trust (managed by a trustee for the benefit of a beneficiary) established to conduct a business for a profit.

but for rule Person's negligent conduct is a cause of an event if the event would not have occurred in the absence of that conduct.

buyer in ordinary course of business Person who buys in ordinary course, in good faith, and without knowledge that the sale to him is in violation of anyone's ownership rights or of a security interest.

bylaws Regulations, ordinances, rules, or laws adopted by an association or corporation for its government.

callable bond Bond that is subject to redemption (reacquisition) by the corporation.

cancellation One party's putting an end to a contract because of a breach by other party.

capital Accumulated goods, possessions, and assets, used for the production of profits and wealth. Owners' equity in a business. Also used to refer to the total assets of a business or to capital assets.

capital surplus Surplus other than earned surplus.

carrier Transporter of goods.

casualty insurance Covers property loss due to causes other than fire or the elements.

cause of action The ground on which an action may be sustained.

caveat emptor Latin. Let the buyer beware. This maxim is more applicable to judicial sales, auctions, and the like than to sales of consumer goods, where strict liability, warranty, and other laws protect.

certificate of deposit A written acknowledgment by a bank or banker of a deposit with promise to pay to depositor, to his order, or to some other person or to his order. UCC § 3–104(2)(c).

certificate of title Official representation of ownership.

certification Acceptance of a check by a drawee bank.

certification of incorporation See **articles of incorporation**.

certification mark Distinctive symbol, word, or design used with goods or services to certify specific characteristics.

certiorari Latin. To be informed of. A writ of common law origin issued by a superior to an inferior court requiring the latter to produce a certified record of a particular case tried therein. It is most commonly used to refer to the Supreme Court of the United States, which uses the writ of certiorari as a discretionary device to choose the cases it wishes to hear.

chancery Equity; equitable jurisdiction; a court of equity; the system of jurisprudence administered in courts of equity.

charging order Judicial lien against a partner's interest in the partnership.

charter An instrument emanating from the sovereign power, in the nature of a grant. A charter differs from a constitution in that the former is granted by the sovereign, while the latter is established by the people themselves.

Corporate law An act of a legislature creating a corporation or creating and defining the franchise of a corporation. Also a corporation's constitution or organic law; that is to say, the articles of incorporation taken in connection with the law under which the corporation was organized.

chattel mortgage A pre-Uniform Commercial Code security device whereby the mortgagee took a security interest in personal property of the mortgagor. Such security device has generally been superseded by other types of security agreements under UCC Article 9 (Secured Transactions).

chattel paper Writings that evidence both a debt and a security interest.

check A draft drawn upon a bank and payable on demand, signed by the maker or drawer, containing an unconditional promise to pay a sum certain in money to the order of the payee. UCC § 3–104(2)(b).

Cashier's check A bank's own check drawn on itself and signed by the cashier or other authorized official. It is a direct obligation of the bank.

C. & F. Cost and freight; a shipping contract.

C.I.F. Cost, insurance, and freight; a shipping contract.

civil law Laws concerned with civil or private rights and remedies, as contrasted with criminal laws.

The system of jurisprudence administered in the Roman empire, particularly as set forth in the compilation of Justinian and his successors, as distinguished from the common law of England and the canon law. The civil law (Civil Code) is followed by Louisiana.

claim A right to payment.

clearinghouse An association of banks for the purpose of settling accounts on a daily basis.

close corporation See **corporation**.

closed-ended credit Credit extended to debtor for a specific period of time.

closed shop Employer can only hire union members.

C.O.D. Collect on delivery; generally a shipping contract.

code A compilation of all permanent laws in force consolidated and classified according to subject matter. Many states have published official codes of all laws in force, including the common law and statutes as judicially interpreted, which have been compiled by code commissions and enacted by the legislatures.

codicil A supplement or an addition to a will; it may explain, modify, add to, subtract from, qualify, alter, restrain, or revoke provisions in an existing will. It must be executed with the same formalities as a will.

cognovit judgment Written authority by debtor for entry of judgment against him in the event he defaults in payment. Such provision in a debt instrument on default confers judgment against the debtor.

collateral Secondarily liable; liable only if the party with primary liability does not perform.

collateral (security) Personal property subject to security interest.

Banking Some form of security in addition to the personal obligation of the borrower.

collateral promise Undertaking to be secondarily liable, that is, liable if the principal debtor does not perform.

collecting bank Any bank, except the payor bank, handling the item for collection. UCC § 4–105(d).

collective mark Distinctive symbol used to indicate membership in an organization.

collision insurance Protects the owner of an automobile against damage due to contact with other vehicles or objects.

commerce power Exclusive power granted by the U.S. Constitution to the federal government to regulate commerce with foreign countries and among the states.

commercial bailment Bailment in which parties derive a mutual benefit.

commercial impracticability Performance can only be accomplished with unforeseen and unjust hardship.

commercial law A phrase used to designate the whole body of substantive jurisprudence (*e.g.,* Uniform Commercial Code; Truth in Lending Act) applicable to the rights, intercourse, and relations of persons engaged in commerce, trade, or mercantile pursuits. See **Uniform Commercial Code**.

commercial paper Bills of exchange (*i.e.,* drafts), promissory notes, bank checks, and other negotiable instruments for the payment of money, which, by their form and on their face, purport to be such instruments. UCC Article 3 is the general law governing commercial paper.

commercial reasonableness Judgment of reasonable persons familiar with the business transaction.

commercial speech Expression related to the economic interests of the speaker and its audience.

common carrier Carrier open to the general public.

common law Body of law originating in England and derived from judicial decisions. As distinguished from statutory law created by the enactment of legislatures, the common law comprises the judgments and decrees of the courts recognizing, affirming, and enforcing usages and customs of immemorial antiquity.

community property Rights of a spouse in property acquired by the other during marriage.

comparable worth Equal pay for jobs of equal value to the employer.

comparative negligence Under comparative negligence statutes or doctrines, negligence is measured in terms of percentage, and any damages allowed shall be diminished in proportion to amount of negligence attributable to the person for whose injury, damage, or death recovery is sought.

complainant One who applies to the courts for legal redress by filing a complaint (*i.e.,* plaintiff).

complaint The pleading which sets forth a claim for relief. Such complaint (whether it be the original claim, counterclaim, cross-claim, or third-party claim) shall contain (1) a short, plain statement of the grounds upon which the court's jurisdiction depends, unless the court already has jurisdiction and the claim needs no new grounds of jurisdiction to support it, (2) a short, plain statement of the claim showing that the pleader is entitled to relief, and (3) a demand for judgment for the relief to which he deems himself entitled. Fed.R. Civil P. 8(a). The complaint, together with the summons, is required to be served on the defendant. Rule 4.

composition Agreement between debtor and two or more of her creditors that each will take a portion of his claim as full payment.

compulsory arbitration Arbitration required by statute for specific types of disputes.

computer crime Crime committed against or through the use of a computer or computer/services.

concealment Fraudulent failure to disclose a material fact.

conciliation Nonbinding process in which a third party acts as an intermediary between disputing parties.

concurrent jurisdiction Authority of more than one court to hear the same case.

condition An uncertain event which affects the duty of performance.
    Concurrent conditions The parties are to perform simultaneously.
    Express condition Performance is contingent on the happening or nonhappening of a stated event.

condition precedent An event which must occur or not occur before performance is due; event or events (presentment, dishonor, notice of dishonor) which must occur to hold a secondary party liable to commercial paper.

condition subsequent An event which terminates a duty of performance.

conditional acceptance An acceptance of an offer contingent upon the acceptance of an additional or different term.

conditional contract Obligations are contingent upon a stated event.

conditional guarantor of collection Surety liable to creditor only after creditor exhausts his legal remedies against the principal debtor.

confession of judgment Written agreement by debtor authorizing creditor to obtain a court judgment in the event debtor defaults. See also **cognovit judgment**.

confiscation Governmental taking of foreign-owned property without payment.

conflict of laws That branch of jurisprudence, arising from the diversity of the laws of different nations, states, or jurisdictions, that reconciles the inconsistencies, or decides which law is to govern in a particular case.

confusion Results when goods belonging to two or more owners become so intermixed that the property of any of them no longer can be identified except as part of a mass of like goods.

consanguinity Kinship; blood relationship; the connection or relation of persons descended from the same stock or common ancestor.

consensual arbitration Arbitration voluntarily entered into by the parties.

consent Voluntary and knowing willingness that an act should be done.

conservator Appointed by court to manage affairs of incompetent or to liquidate business.

consideration The cause, motive, price, or impelling influence which induces a contracting party to enter into a contract. Some right, interest, profit, or benefit accruing to one party or some forbearance, detriment, loss, or responsibility given, suffered, or undertaken by the other.

consignee One to whom a consignment is made. Person named in bill of lading to whom or to whose order the bill promises delivery. UCC § 7–102(b).

consignment Ordinarily implies an agency; denotes that property is committed to the consignee for care or sale.

consignor One who sends or makes a consignment; a shipper of goods. The person named in a bill of lading as the person from whom the goods have been received for shipment. UCC § 7–102(c).

consolidation In *corporate law*, the combination of two or more corporations into a newly created corporation. Thus, A Corporation and B Corporation consolidate to form C Corporation.

constitution Fundamental law of a government establishing its powers and limitations.

constructive That which is established by the mind of the law in its act of *construing* facts, conduct, circumstances, or instruments. That which has not in its essential nature the character assigned to it, but acquires such character in consequence of the way in which it is regarded by a rule or policy of law; hence, inferred, implied, or made out by legal interpretation;

the word "legal" being sometimes used here in lieu of "constructive."

constructive assent An assent or consent imputed to a party from a construction or interpretation of his conduct; as distinguished from one which he actually expresses.

constructive conditions Conditions in contracts which are neither expressed nor implied but rather are imposed by law to meet the ends of justice.

constructive delivery Term comprehending all those acts which, although not truly conferring a real possession of the vendee, have been held by construction of law to be equivalent to acts of real delivery.

constructive eviction Failure by the landlord in any obligation under the lease that causes a substantial and lasting injury to the tenant's enjoyment of the premises.

constructive notice Knowledge imputed by law.

constructive trust Arising by operation of law to prevent unjust enrichment. See also **trustee**.

consumer goods Goods bought or used for personal, family, or household purposes.

consumer product Tangible personal property normally used for family, household, or personal purposes.

contingent remainder Remainder interest, conditional upon the happening of an event in addition to the termination of the preceding estate.

contract An agreement between two or more persons which creates an obligation to do or not to do a particular thing. Its essentials are competent parties, subject matter, a legal consideration, mutuality of agreement, and mutuality of obligation.

Destination contract Seller is required to tender delivery of the goods at a particular destination; seller bears the expense and risk of loss.

Executed contract Fully performed by all of the parties.

Executory contract Contract partially or entirely unperformed by one or more of the parties.

Express contract Agreement of parties that is expressed in words either in writing or orally.

Formal contract Agreement which is legally binding because of its particular form or mode or expression.

Implied-in-fact contract Contract where agreement of the parties is inferred from their conduct.

Informal contract All oral or written contracts other than formal contracts.

Installment contract Goods are delivered in separate lots.

Integrated contract Complete and total agreement.

Output contract A contract in which one party agrees to sell his entire output and the other agrees to buy it; it is not illusory, though it may be indefinite.

Quasi contract Obligation not based upon contract that is imposed to avoid injustice.

Requirements contract A contract in which one party agrees to purchase his total requirements from the other party; hence, such a contract is binding, not illusory.

Substituted contract An agreement between the parties to rescind their old contract and replace it with a new contract.

Unconscionable contract One which no sensible person not under delusion, duress, or in distress would make, and such as no honest and fair person would accept. A contract the terms of which are excessively unreasonable, overreaching, and one-sided.

Unenforceable contract Contract for the breach of which the law does not provide a remedy.

Unilateral and bilateral A unilateral contract is one in which one party makes an express engagement or undertakes a performance, without receiving in return any express engagement or promise of performance from the other. Bilateral (or reciprocal) contracts are those by which the parties expressly enter into mutual engagements.

contract clause Prohibition against the states' retroactively modifying public and private contracts.

contractual liability Obligation on a negotiable instrument, based upon signing the instrument.

contribution Payment from cosureties of their proportionate share.

contributory negligence An act or omission amounting to a want of ordinary care on the part of the complaining party, which, concurring with defendant's negligence, is proximate cause of injury.

The defense of contributory negligence is an absolute bar to any recovery in some states; because of this, it has been replaced by the doctrine of comparative negligence in many other states.

conversion Unauthorized and wrongful exercise of dominion and control over another's personal property, to exclusion of or inconsistent with rights of the owner.

convertible bond Bond that may be exchanged for other securities of the corporation.

copyright Exclusive right granted by federal government to authors of original works including literary, musical, dramatic, pictorial, graphic, sculptural, and film works.

corporation A legal entity ordinarily consisting of an association of numerous individuals. Such entity is regarded as having a personality and existence distinct from that of its several members and is vested with the capacity of continuous succession, irrespective of changes in its membership, either in perpetuity or for a limited term of years.

Closely held or close corporation Corporation that is owned by few shareholders and whose shares are not actively traded.

Corporation de facto One existing under color of law and in pursuance of an effort made in good faith to organize a corporation under the statute. Such a corporation is not subject to collateral attack.

Corporation de jure That which exists by reason of full compliance with requirements of an existing law permitting organization of such corporation.

Domestic corporation Corporation created under the laws of a given state.

Foreign corporation Corporation created under the laws of any other state, government, or country.

Publicly held corporation Corporation whose shares are owned by a large number of people and are widely traded.

Subchapter S corporation A small business corporation which, under certain conditions, may elect to have its undistributed taxable income taxed to its shareholders. I.R.C. § 1371 *et seq.* Of major significance is the fact that Subchapter S status usually avoids the corporate income tax, and corporate losses can be claimed by the shareholders.

Subsidiary and parent Subsidiary corporation is one in which another corporation (called parent corporation) owns at least a majority of the shares and over which it thus has control.

corrective advertising Disclosure in an advertisement that previous ads were deceptive.

costs A pecuniary allowance, made to the successful party (and recoverable from the losing party), for his expenses in prosecuting or defending an action or a distinct proceeding within an action. Generally, "costs" do not include attorneys' fees unless such fees are by a statute denominated costs or are by statute allowed to be recovered as costs in the case.

cosureties Two or more sureties bound for the same debt of a principal debtor.

co-tenants Persons who hold title concurrently.

counterclaim A claim presented by a defendant in opposition to or deduction from the claim of the plaintiff.

counteroffer A statement by the offeree which has the legal effect of rejecting the offer and of proposing a new offer to the offeror. However, the provisions of UCC § 2–207(2) modify this principle by providing that the "additional terms are to be construed as proposals for addition to the contract."

course of dealing A sequence of previous acts and conduct between the parties to a particular transaction which is fairly to be regarded as establishing a common basis of understanding for interpreting their expressions and other conduct. UCC § 1–205(1).

course of performance Conduct between the parties concerning performance of the particular contract.

court above—court below In appellate practice, the "court above" is the one to which a cause is removed for review, whether by appeal, writ of error, or certiorari, while the "court below" is the one from which the case is being removed.

covenant Used primarily with respect to promises in conveyances or other instruments dealing with real estate.

Covenants against encumbrances A stipulation against all rights to or interests in the land which may subsist in third persons to the diminution of the value of the estate granted.

Covenant appurtenant A covenant which is connected with land of the grantor, not in gross. A covenant running with the land and binding heirs, executors, and assigns of the immediate parties.

Covenant for further assurance An undertaking, in the form of a covenant, on the part of the vendor of real estate to do such further acts for the purpose of perfecting the purchaser's title as the latter may reasonably require.

Covenant for possession A covenant by which the grantee or lessee is granted possession.

Covenant for quiet enjoyment An assurance against the consequences of a defective title, and against any disturbances thereupon.

Covenants for title Covenants usually inserted in a conveyance of land, on the part of the grantor, and binding him for the completeness, security, and continuance of the title transferred to the grantee. They comprise covenants for seisin, for right to convey, against encumbrances, or quiet enjoyment, sometimes for further assurance, and almost always of warranty.

Covenant in gross Such as do not run with the land.

Covenant of right to convey An assurance by the covenantor that the grantor has sufficient capacity and title to convey the *estate* which he by his deed undertakes to convey.

Covenant of seisin An assurance to the purchaser that the grantor has the very estate in quantity and quality which he purports to convey.

Covenant of warranty An assurance by the grantor of an estate that the grantee shall enjoy the same without interruption by virtue of paramount title.

Covenant running with land A covenant which goes with the land, as being annexed to the estate, and which cannot be separated from the land or transferred without it. A covenant is said to run with the land when not only the original parties or their representatives, but each successive owner of the land, will be entitled to its benefit, or be liable (as the case may be) to its obligation. Such a covenant is said to be one which "touches and concerns" the land itself, so that its benefit or obligation passes with the ownership. Essentials are that the grantor and grantee must have intended that the covenant run with the land, the covenant must affect or concern the land with which it runs, and there must be privity of estate between the party claiming the benefit and the party who rests under the burden.

covenant not to compete Agreement to refrain from entering into a competing trade, profession, or business.

cover Buyer's purchase of goods in substitution for those not delivered by breaching seller.

credit beneficiary See **third-party beneficiary.**

creditor Any entity having a claim against the debtor.

crime An act or omission in violation of a public law and punishable by the government.

criminal duress Coercion by threat of serious bodily injury.

criminal intent Desired or virtually certain consequences of one's conduct.

criminal law The law that involves offenses against the entire community.

cure The right of a seller under the UCC to correct a nonconforming delivery of goods to buyer within the contract period. § 2–508.

curtesy Husband's estate in the real property of his wife.

cy-pres As near (as possible). Rule for the construction of instruments in equity, by which the intention of the party is carried out *as near as may be*, when it would be impossible or illegal to give it literal effect.

damage Loss, injury, or deterioration caused by the negligence, design, or accident of one person, with respect to another's person or property. The word is to be distinguished from its plural, "damages," which means a compensation in money for a loss or damage.

damages Money sought as a remedy for breach of contract or for tortious acts.

Actual damages Real, substantial, and just damages, or the amount awarded to a complainant in compensation for his actual and real loss or injury, as opposed, on the one hand, to "nominal" damages and, on the other, to "exemplary" or "punitive" damages. Synonymous with "compensatory damages" and "general damages."

Benefit-of-the-bargain damages Difference between the value received and the value of the fraudulent party's performance as represented.

Compensatory damages Compensatory damages are such as will compensate the injured party for the injury sustained, and nothing more; such as will simply make good or replace the loss caused by the wrong or injury.

Consequential damages Such damage, loss, or injury as does not flow directly and immediately from the act of the party, but only from some of the consequences or results of such act. Consequential damages resulting from a seller's breach of contract include any loss resulting from general or particular requirements and needs of which the seller at the time of contracting had reason to know and which could not reasonably be prevented by cover or otherwise, and injury to person or property proximately resulting from any breach of warranty. UCC § 2–715(2).

Exemplary or punitive damages Damages other than compensatory damages which may be awarded against a person to punish him for outrageous conduct.

Expectancy damages Calculable by subtracting the injured party's actual dollar position as a result of the breach from that party's projected dollar position had performance occurred.

Foreseeable damages Loss of which the party in breach had reason to know when the contract was made.

Incidental damages Under UCC § 2–710, such damages include any commercially reasonable charges, expenses, or commissions incurred in stopping delivery, in the transportation, care, and custody of goods after the buyer's breach, in connection with the return or resale of the goods, or otherwise resulting from the breach. Also, such damages, resulting from a seller's breach of contract, include expenses reasonably incurred in inspection, receipt, transportation, and care and custody of goods rightfully rejected, any commercially reasonable charges, expenses, or commissions in connection with effecting cover, and any other reasonable expense incident to the delay or other breach. UCC § 2–715(1).

Irreparable damages In the law pertaining to injunctions, damages for which no certain pecuniary standard exists for measurement.

Liquidated damages and penalties Damages for breach by either party may be liquidated in the agreement but only at an amount which is reasonable in the light of the anticipated or actual harm caused by the breach, the difficulties of proof of loss, and the inconvenience or nonfeasibility of otherwise obtaining an adequate remedy. A term fixing unreasonably large liquidated damages is void as a penalty. UCC § 2–718(1).

Mitigation of damages A plaintiff may not recover damages for the effects of an injury which she reasonably could have avoided or substantially ameliorated. This limitation on recovery is generally denominated as "mitigation of damages" or "avoidance of consequences."

Nominal damages A small sum awarded where a contract has been breached but the loss is negligible or unproven.

Out-of-pocket damages Difference between the value received and the value given.

Reliance damages Contract damages placing the injured party in as good a position as he would have been in had the contract not been made.

Treble damages Three times actual loss.

de facto In fact, in deed, actually. This phrase is used to characterize an officer, a government, a past action, or a state of affairs which must be accepted for all practical purposes but which is illegal or illegitimate. See also **corporation**, *corporation de facto*.

de jure Descriptive of a condition in which there has been total compliance with all requirements of law. In this sense it is the contrary of *de facto*. See also **corporation**, *corporation de jure*.

de novo Anew; afresh; a second time.

debenture Unsecured bond.

debt security Any form of corporate security reflected as debt on the books of the corporation in contrast to equity securities such as stock; *e.g.*, bonds, notes, and debentures are debt securities.

debtor Person who owes payment or performance of an obligation.

deceit A fraudulent and cheating misrepresentation, artifice, or device used to deceive and trick one who is ignorant of the true facts, to the prejudice and damage of the party imposed upon. See also **fraud; misrepresentation**.

decree Decision of a court of equity.

deed A conveyance of realty; a writing, signed by a grantor, whereby title to realty is transferred from one party to another.

deed of trust Interest in real property which is conveyed to a third person as trustee for the creditor.

defamation Injury of a person's reputation by publication of false statements.

default judgment Judgment against a defendant who fails to respond to a complaint.

defendant The party against whom legal action is sought.

definite term Lease that automatically expires at end of the term.

delectus personae Partner's right to choose who may become a member of the partnership.

delegatee Third party to whom the delegator's duty is delegated.

delegation of duties Transferring to another all or part of one's duties arising under a contract.

delegator Party delegating his duty to a third party.

delivery The physical or constructive transfer of an instrument or of goods from one person to another. See also **constructive delivery**.

demand Request for payment made by the holder of the instrument.

demand paper Payable on request.

demurrer An allegation of a defendant that even if the facts as stated in the pleading to which objection is taken be true, their legal consequences are not such as to require the demurring party to answer them or to proceed further with the cause.

The Federal Rules of Civil Procedure do not provide for the use of a demurrer, but provide an equivalent to a general demurrer in the motion to dismiss for failure to state a claim on which relief may be granted. Fed.R. Civil P. 12(b).

deposition The testimony of a witness taken upon interrogatories, not in court, but intended to be used in court. See also **discovery**.

depository bank The first bank to which an item is transferred for collection even though it may also be the payor bank. UCC § 4–105(a).

descent Succession to the ownership of an estate by inheritance or by any act of law, as distinguished from "purchase."

Descents are of two sorts, *lineal* and *collateral*. Lineal descent is descent in a direct or right line, as from father or grandfather to son or grandson. Collateral descent is descent in a collateral or oblique line, that is, up to the common ancestor and then down from him, as from brother to brother, or between cousins.

design defect Plans or specifications inadequate to ensure the product's safety.

devise A testamentary disposition of land or realty; a gift of real property by the last will and testament of the donor. When used as a noun, means a testamentary disposition of real or personal property; when used as a verb, means to dispose of real or personal property by will.

dictum Generally used as an abbreviated form of *obiter dictum*, "a remark by the way"; that is, an observation or remark made by a judge which does not embody the resolution or determination of the court and which is made without argument or full consideration of the point.

directed verdict In a case in which the party with the burden of proof has failed to present a prima facie case for jury consideration, the trial judge may order the entry of a verdict without allowing the jury to consider it because, as a matter of law, there can be only one such verdict. Fed.R. Civil P. 50(a).

disaffirmance Avoidance of a contract.

discharge Termination of certain allowed claims against a debtor.

disclaimer Negation of warranty.

discount A discount by a bank means a drawback or deduction made upon its advances or loans of money, upon negotiable paper or other evidences of debt payable at a future day, which are transferred to the bank.

discovery The pretrial devices that can be used by one party to obtain facts and information about the case from the other party in order to assist the party's preparation for trial. Under the Federal Rules of Civil Procedure, tools of discovery include depositions upon oral and written questions, written interrogatories, production of documents or things, permission to enter upon land or other property, physical and mental examinations, and requests for admission. Rules 26–37.

dishonor To refuse to accept or pay a draft or to pay a promissory note when duly presented. UCC § 3–507(1); § 4–210. See also **protest**.

disparagement Publication of false statements resulting in harm to another's monetary interests.

disputed debt Obligation whose existence or amount is contested.

dissenting shareholder One who opposes a fundamental change and has the right to receive the fair value of her shares.

dissolution The dissolution of a partnership is the change in the relation of the partners caused by any partner's ceasing to be associated with the carrying on, as distinguished from the winding up, of the business. See also **winding up**.

distribution Transfer of partnership property from the partnership to a partner; transfer of property from a corporation to any of its shareholders.

dividend The payment designated by the board of directors of a corporation to be distributed pro rata among a class or classes of the shares outstanding.

document Document of title.

document of title Instrument evidencing ownership of the document and the goods it covers.

domicile That place where a person has his true, fixed, and permanent home and principal establishment, and to which whenever he is absent he has the intention of returning.

dominant Land whose owner has rights in other land.

donee Recipient of a gift.

donee beneficiary See **third-party beneficiary**.

donor Maker of a gift.

dormant partner One who is both a silent and a secret partner.

dower A species of life-estate which a woman is, by law, entitled to claim on the death of her husband, in the lands and tenements of which he was seised in fee during the marriage, and which her issue, if any, might by possibility have inherited.

Dower has been abolished in the majority of the states and materially altered in most of the others.

draft A written order by the first party, called the drawer, instructing a second party, called the drawee (such as a bank), to pay a third party, called the payee. An order to pay a sum certain in money, signed by a drawer, payable on demand or at a definite time, and to order or bearer. UCC § 3–104.

drawee A person to whom a bill of exchange or draft is directed, and who is requested to pay the amount of money therein mentioned. The drawee of a check is the bank on which it is drawn.

When a drawee accepts, he engages that he will pay the instrument according to its tenor at the time of his engagement or as completed. UCC § 3–413(1).

drawer The person who draws a bill or draft. The drawer of a check is the person who signs it.

The drawer engages that upon dishonor of the draft and any necessary notice of dishonor or protest, he will pay the amount of the draft to the holder or to any indorser who takes it up. The drawer may disclaim this liability by drawing without recourse. UCC § 3–413(2).

due negotiation Transfer of a negotiable document in the regular course of business to a holder, who takes in good faith, without notice of any defense or claim, and for value.

duress Unlawful constraint exercised upon a person, whereby he is forced to do some act against his will.

Physical duress Coercion involving physical force or the threat of physical force.

duty Legal obligation requiring a person to perform or refrain from performing an act.

earned surplus Undistributed net profits, income, gains, and losses.

earnest The payment of a part of the price of goods sold, or the delivery of part of such goods, for the purpose of binding the contract.

easement A right in the owner of one parcel of land, by reason of such ownership, to use the land of another for a special purpose not inconsistent with a general property right in the owner. This right is distinguishable from a "license," which merely confers a personal privilege to do some act on the land.

Affirmative easement One where the servient estate must permit something to be done thereon, as to pass over it, or to discharge water on it.

Appurtenant easement An incorporeal right which is attached to a superior right and inheres in land to which it is attached and is in the nature of a covenant running with the land.

Easement by necessity Such arises by operation of law when land conveyed is completely shut off from access to any road by land retained by the grantor or by land of the grantor and that of a stranger.

Easement by prescription A mode of acquiring title to property by immemorial or long-continued enjoyment; refers to personal usage restricted to claimant and his ancestors or grantors.

Easement in gross An easement in gross is not appurtenant to any estate in land or does not belong to any person by virtue of ownership of an estate in other land but is a mere personal interest in or a right to use the land of another; it is purely personal and usually ends with death of grantee.

Easement of access Right of ingress and egress to and from the premises of a lot owner to a street appurtenant to the land of the lot owner.

ejectment An action to determine whether the title to certain land is in the plaintiff or is in the defendant.

electronic funds transfer A transaction with a financial institution by means of computer, telephone, or other electronic instrument.

emancipation The act by which an infant is liberated from the control of a parent or guardian and made his own master.

embezzlement The taking, in violation of a trust, of the property of one's employer.

emergency Sudden, unexpected event calling for immediate action.

eminent domain Right of the people or government to take private property for public use upon giving fair consideration.

employment discrimination Hiring, firing, compensating, promoting, or training of employees based on race, color, sex, religion, or national origin.

employment relationship One in which employer has right to control the physical conduct of employee.

endowment contract Agreement to pay insured a lump sum upon reaching a specified age or in event of death.

entirety Used to designate that which the law considers as a single whole incapable of being divided into parts.

entrapment Induced by a government official into committing a crime.

entrusting Transfer of possession of goods to a merchant who deals in goods of that kind and who may in turn transfer valid title to a buyer in the ordinary course of business.

equal pay Equivalent pay for the same work.

equal protection Requirement that similarly situated persons be treated similarly by government action.

equipment Goods used primarily in business.

equitable Just, fair, and right. Existing in equity; available or sustainable only in equity, or only upon the rules and principles of equity.

equity Justice administered according to fairness, as contrasted with the strictly formulated rules of common law. It is based on a system of rules and principles which originated in England as an alternative to the harsh rules of common law and which were based on what was fair in a particular situation.

equity of redemption The right of the mortgagor of an estate to redeem the same after it has been forfeited, at law, by a breach of the condition of the mortgage, upon paying the amount of debt, interest, and costs.

equity securities Stock or similar security, in contrast to debt securities such as bonds, notes, and debentures.

error A mistake of law, or a false or irregular application of it, such as vitiates legal proceedings and warrants reversal of the judgment.

Harmless error In appellate practice, an error committed in the progress of the trial below which was not prejudicial to the rights of the party assigning it and for which, therefore, the appellate court will not reverse the judgment.

Reversible error In appellate practice, such an error as warrants the appellate court's reversal of the judgment before it.

escrow A system of document transfer in which a deed, bond, or funds is or are delivered to a third person to hold until all conditions in a contract are fulfilled; *e.g.,* delivery of deed to escrow agent under installment land sale contract until full payment for land is made.

estate The degree, quantity, nature, and extent of interest which a person has in real and personal property. An estate in lands, tenements, and hereditaments signifies such interest as the tenant has therein.

Also, the total property of whatever kind that is owned by a decedent prior to the distribution of that property in accordance with the terms of a will or, when there is no will, by the laws of inheritance in the state of domicile of the decedent.

Future estate An estate limited to commence in possession at a future day, either without the intervention of a precedent estate or on the determination by lapse of time, or otherwise, of a precedent estate created at the same time. Examples include reversions and remainders.

estoppel A bar or impediment raised by the law which precludes a person from alleging or from denying a certain fact or state of facts, in consequence of his or her previous allegation, denial, conduct, or admission, or in consequence of a final adjudication of the matter in a court of law. See also **waiver**.

eviction Dispossession by process of law; the act of depriving a person of the possession of lands which he has held, pursuant to the judgment of a court.

evidence Any species of proof or probative matter legally presented at the trial of an issue by the act of the parties and through the medium of witnesses, records, documents, concrete objects, etc., for the purpose of inducing belief in the minds of the court or jury as to the parties' contention.

exception A formal objection to the action of the court, during the trial of a cause, in refusing a request or overruling an objection; implying that the party excepting does not acquiesce in the decision of the court but will seek to procure its reversal, and that he means to save the benefit of his request or objection in some future proceeding.

exclusionary rule Prohibition of illegally obtained evidence.

exclusive dealing Sole right to sell goods in a defined market.

exclusive jurisdiction Such jurisdiction that permits only one court (state or federal) to hear a case.

exculpatory clause Excusing oneself from fault or liability.

execution *Execution of contract* includes performance of all acts necessary to render it complete as an instrument; implies that nothing more need be done to make the contract complete and effective.

Execution upon a money judgment is the legal process of enforcing the judgment, usually by seizing and selling property of the debtor.

executive order Legislation issued by the president or a governor.

executor A person appointed by a testator to carry out the directions and requests in his will and to dispose of the property according to his testamentary provisions after his decease. The female designation is executrix. A person appointed by the court in an intestacy situation is called the administrator(rix).

executory That which is yet to be executed or performed; that which remains to be carried into operation or effect; incomplete; depending upon a future performance or event. The opposite of executed.

executory contract See **contracts**.

executory promise Unperformed obligation.

exemplary damages See **damages**.

exoneration Relieved of liability.

express Manifested by direct and appropriate language, as distinguished from that which is inferred from conduct. The word is usually contrasted with "implied."

express warranty Explicitly made contractual promise regarding property or contract rights transferred; in a sale of goods, an affirmation of fact or a promise about the goods or a description, including a sample, of goods which becomes part of the basis of the bargain.

expropriation Governmental taking of foreign-owned property for a public purpose and with payment.

ex-ship Risk of loss passes to buyer when the goods leaving the ship. See UCC § 2–322. See also **F.A.S.**

extortion Making threats to obtain property.

fact An event that took place or a thing that exists.

false imprisonment Intentional interference with a person's freedom of movement by unlawful confinement.

false light Offensive publicity placing another in a false light.

false pretenses Intentional misrepresentation of fact in order to cheat another.

farm products Crops, livestock, or stock used or produced in farming.

F.A.S. Free alongside. Term used in sales price quotations indicating that the price includes all costs of transportation and delivery of the goods alongside the ship. See UCC § 2–319(2).

federal preemption First right of the federal government to regulate matters within its powers to the possible exclusion of state regulation.

federal question Any case arising under the Constitution, statutes, or treaties of the United States.

fee simple

Absolute A fee simple absolute is an estate that is unlimited as to duration, disposition, and descendibility. It is the largest estate and most extensive interest that can be enjoyed in land.

Conditional Type of transfer in which grantor conveys fee simple on condition that something be done or not done.

Defeasible Type of fee grant which may be defeated on the happening of an event. An estate which may last forever, but which may end upon the happening of a specified event, is a "fee simple defeasible".

Determinable Created by conveyance which contains words effective to create a fee simple and, in addition, a provision for automatic expiration of the estate on occurrence of stated event.

fee tail An estate of inheritance, descending only to a certain class or classes of heirs; *e.g.,* an estate is conveyed or devised "to A. and the heirs of his body," or "to A. and the heirs male of his body," or "to A., and the heirs female of his body."

fellow servant rule Common law defense relieving employer from liability to an employee for injuries caused by negligence of fellow employee.

felony Serious crime.

fiduciary A person or institution who manages money or property for another and who must exercise in such management activity a standard of care imposed by law or contract; *e.g.,* executor of estate; receiver in bankruptcy; trustee.

fiduciary duty Duty of utmost loyalty and good faith, such as that owed by a fiduciary such as an agent to her principal.

field warehouse Secured party takes possession of the goods but the debtor has access to the goods.

final credit Payment of the instrument by the payor bank.

financing statement Under the Uniform Commercial Code, a financing statement is used under Article 9 to reflect a public record that there is a security interest or claim to the goods in question to secure a debt. The financing statement is filed by the security holder with the secretary of state or with a similar public body; thus filed, it becomes public record. See also **secured transaction**.

fire (property) insurance Provides protection against loss due to fire or other related perils.

firm offer Irrevocable offer to sell or buy goods by a merchant in a signed writing which gives assurance that it will not be rescinded for up to three months.

fitness for a particular purpose Goods are fit for a stated purpose, provided that the seller selects the product knowing the buyer's intended use and that the buyer is relying on the seller's judgment.

fixture An article in the nature of personal property which has been so annexed to realty that it is regarded as a part of the land. Examples include a furnace affixed to a house or other building, counters permanently affixed to the floor of a store, and a sprinkler system installed in a building. UCC § 9–313(1)(a).

   Trade fixtures Such chattels as merchants usually possess and annex to the premises occupied by them to enable them to store, handle, and display their goods, which generally are removable without material injury to the premises.

F.O.B. Free on board at some location (for example, F.O.B shipping point; F.O.B destination); the invoice price includes delivery at seller's expense to that location.

Title to goods usually passes from seller to buyer at the F.O.B location. UCC § 2–319(1).

foreclosure Procedure by which mortgaged property is sold on default of mortgagor in satisfaction of mortgage debt.

forgery Intentional falsification of a document with intent to defraud.

four unities Time, title, interest, and possession.

franchise A privilege granted or sold, such as to use a name or to sell products or services. The right given by a manufacturer or supplier to a retailer to use his products and name on terms and conditions mutually agreed upon.

fraud Elements include false representation; of a present or past fact; made by defendant; action in reliance thereon by plaintiff; and damage resulting to plaintiff from such misrepresentation.

fraud in the execution Misrepresentation that deceives the other party as to the nature of a document evidencing the contract.

fraud in the inducement Misrepresentation regarding the subject matter of a contract that induces the other party to enter into the contract.

fraudulent misrepresentation False statement made with knowledge of its falsity and intent to mislead.

freehold An estate for life or in fee. It must possess two qualities: (1) immobility, that is, the property must be either land or some interest issuing out of or annexed to land; and (2) indeterminate duration.

friendly fire Fire contained where it is intended to be.

frustration of purpose doctrine Excuses a promisor in certain situations when the objectives of contract have been utterly defeated by circumstances arising after formation of the agreement, and performance is excused under this rule even though there is no impediment to actual performance.

full warranty One under which warrantor will repair the product and, if unsuccessful, will replace it or refund its cost.

fungibles With respect to goods or securities, those of which any unit is, by nature or usage of trade, the equivalent of any other like unit. UCC § 1–201(17); *e.g.,* a bushel of wheat or other grain.

future estate See **estate**.

garnishment A statutory proceeding whereby a person's property, money, or credits in the possession or control of another are applied to payment of the former's debt to a third person.

general intangible Catchall category for collateral not otherwise covered.

general partner Member of either a general or limited partnership with unlimited liability for its debts, full management powers, and a right to share in the profits.

gift A voluntary transfer of property to another made gratuitously and without consideration. Essential requisites of "gift" are capacity of donor, intention of donor to make gift, completed delivery to or for donee, and acceptance of gift by donee.

gift causa mortis A gift in view of death is one which is made in contemplation, fear, or peril of death and with the intent that it shall take effect only in case of the death of the giver.

good faith Honesty in fact in conduct or in a transaction.

good faith purchaser Buyer who acts honestly, gives value, and takes the goods without notice or knowledge of any defect in the title of his transferor.

goods A term of variable content and meaning. It may include every species of personal property, or it may be given a very restricted meaning. Sometimes the meaning of "goods" is extended to include all tangible items, as in the phrase "goods and services."

All things (including specially manufactured goods) which are movable at the time of identification to a contract for sale other than the money in which the price is to be paid, investment securities, and things in action. UCC § 2–105(1).

grantee Transferee of property.

grantor A transferor of property. The creator of a trust is usually designated as the grantor of the trust.

gratuitous promise Promise made without consideration.

group insurance Covers a number of individuals.

guaranty A promise to answer for the payment of some debt, or the performance of some duty, in case of the failure of another person who, in the first instance, is liable for such payment or performance.

The terms *guaranty* and *suretyship* are sometimes used interchangeably; but they should not be confounded. The distinction between contract of suretyship and contract of guaranty is whether or not the undertaking is a joint undertaking with the principal or a separate and distinct contract; if it is the former, it is one of "suretyship," and if the latter, it is one of "guaranty." See also **surety**.

guardianship The relationship under which a person (the guardian) is appointed by a court to preserve and control the property of another (the ward).

heir A person who succeeds, by the rules of law, to an estate in lands, tenements, or hereditaments, upon the death of his ancestor, by descent and right of relationship.

holder Person who is in possession of a document of title or an instrument or an investment security drawn, issued, or indorsed to him or to his order, or to bearer, or in blank. UCC § 1–201(20).

holder in due course A holder who takes an instrument for value, in good faith, and without notice that it is overdue or has been dishonored or of any defense against or claim to it on the part of any person.

holograph A will or deed written entirely by the testator or grantor with his own hand and not witnessed (attested). State laws vary with respect to the validity of the holographic will.

homicide Unlawful taking of another's life.

horizontal privity Who may bring a cause of action.

horizontal restraints Agreements among competitors.

hostile fire Any fire outside its intended or usual place.

identified goods Designated goods as a part of a particular contract.

illegal per se Conclusively presumed unreasonable and therefore illegal.

illusory promise Promise imposing no obligation on the promisor.

implied-in-fact condition Contingencies understood but not expressed by the parties.

implied-in-law condition Contingency that arises from operation of law.

implied warranty Obligation imposed by law upon the transferor of property or contract rights; implicit in the sale arising out of certain circumstances.

implied warranty of habitability Leased premises are fit for ordinary residential purposes.

impossibility Performance that cannot be done.

in personam Against the person. Action seeking judgment against a person involving his personal rights and based on jurisdiction of his person, as distinguished from a judgment against property (*i.e.,* in rem).

in personam jurisdiction Jurisdiction based on claims against a person, in contrast to jurisdiction over his property.

in re In the affair; in the matter of; concerning; regarding. This is the usual method of entitling a judicial proceeding in which there are no adversary parties, but merely some *res* concerning which judicial action is to be taken, such as a bankrupt's estate, an estate in the probate court, a proposed public highway, etc.

in rem A technical term used to designate proceedings or actions instituted *against the thing*, in contradistinction to personal actions, which are said to be *in personam*.

Quasi in rem A term applied to proceedings which are not strictly and purely *in rem*, but are brought against the defendant personally, though the real object is to deal with particular property or subject property to the discharge of claims asserted; for example, foreign attachment, or proceedings to foreclose a mortgage, remove a cloud from title, or effect a partition.

in rem jurisdiction Jurisdiction based on claims against property.

incidental beneficiary Third party whom the two parties to a contract have no intention of benefiting by their contract.

income bond Bond that conditions payment of interest on corporate earnings.

incontestability clause The prohibition of an insurer to avoid an insurance policy after a specified period of time.

indemnification Duty owed by principal to agent to pay agent for losses incurred while acting as directed by principal.

indemnify To reimburse one for a loss already incurred.

indenture A written agreement under which bonds and debentures are issued, setting forth maturity date, interest rate, and other terms.

independent contractor Person who contracts with another to do a particular job and who is not subject to the control of the other.

indicia Signs; indications. Circumstances which point to the existence of a given fact as probable, but not certain.

indictment Grand jury charge that the defendant should stand trial.

indispensable paper Chattel paper, instruments, and documents.

indorsee The person to whom a negotiable instrument, promissory note, bill of lading, etc., is assigned by indorsement.

indorsement The act of a payee, drawee, accommodation indorser, or holder of a bill, note, check, or other negotiable instrument, in writing his name upon the back of the same, with or without further or qualifying words, whereby the property in the same is assigned and transferred to another. UCC § 3–202 *et seq.*

Blank indorsement No indorsee is specified.

Qualified indorsement Without recourse, limiting one's liability on the instrument.

Restrictive indorsement Limits the rights of the indorser in some manner.

Special indorsement Designates an indorsee to be paid.

infliction of emotional distress Extreme and outrageous conduct intentionally or recklessly causing severe emotional distress.

information Formal accusation of a crime brought by a prosecutor.

infringement Unauthorized use.

injunction An equitable remedy forbidding the party defendant from doing some act which he is threatening or attempting to commit, or restraining him in the continuance thereof, such act being unjust and inequitable, injurious to the plaintiff, and not such as can be adequately redressed by an action at law.

innkeeper Hotel or motel operator.

inquisitorial system System in which the judiciary initiates, conducts, and decides cases.

insider Relative or general partner of debtor, partnership in which debtor is a partner, or corporation in which debtor is an officer, director, or controlling person.

insiders Directors, officers, employees, and agents of the issuer as well as those the issuer has entrusted with information solely for corporate purposes.

insolvency Under the UCC, a person is insolvent who either has ceased to pay his debts in the ordinary course of business or cannot pay his debts as they fall due or is insolvent within the meaning of the Federal Bankruptcy Law. UCC § 1–201(23).

Insolvency (bankruptcy) Total liabilities exceed total value of assets.

Insolvency (equity) Inability to pay debts in ordinary course of business or as they become due.

inspection Examination of goods to determine whether they conform to a contract.

instrument Negotiable instruments, stocks, bonds, and other investment securities.

insurable interest Exists where insured derives pecuniary benefit or advantage by preservation and continued existence of property or would sustain pecuniary loss from its destruction.

insurance A contract whereby, for a stipulated consideration, one party undertakes to compensate the other for loss on a specified subject by specified perils. The party agreeing to make the compensation is usually called the "insurer" or "underwriter"; the other, the "insured" or "assured"; the written contract, a "policy"; the events insured against, "risks" or "perils"; and the subject, right, or interest to be protected, the "insurable interest." Insurance is a contract whereby one undertakes to indemnify another against loss, damage, or liability arising from an unknown or contingent event.

Co-insurance A form of insurance in which a person insures property for less than its full or stated value and agrees to share the risk of loss.

Life insurance Payment of a specific sum of money to a designated beneficiary upon the death of the insured.

Ordinary life Life insurance with a savings component that runs for the life of the insured.

Term life Life insurance issued for a limited number of years that does not have a savings component.

intangible property Protected interests that are not physical.

intangibles Accounts and general intangibles.

intent Desire to cause the consequences of an act or knowledge that the consequences are substantially certain to result from the act.

inter alia Among other things.

inter se or **inter sese** Latin. Among or between themselves; used to distinguish rights or duties between two or more parties from their rights or duties to others.

interest in land Any right, privilege, power, or immunity in real property.

interest in partnership Partner's share in the partnership's profits and surplus.

interference with contractual relations Intentionally causing one of the parties to a contract not to perform the contract.

intermediary bank Any bank, except the depositary or payor bank, to which an item is transferred in the course of collection. UCC § 4–105(c).

intermediate test Requirement that legislation have a substantial relationship to an important governmental objective.

international law Deals with the conduct and relations of nation-states and international organizations.

interpretation Construction or meaning of a contract.

interpretative rules Statements issued by an administrative agency indicating its construction of its governing statute.

intestate A person is said to die intestate when he dies without making a will. The word is also often used to signify the person himself. *Compare* **testator**.

intrusion Unreasonable and highly offensive interference with the seclusion of another.

inventory Goods held for sale or lease or consumed in a business.

invitee A person is an "invitee" on land of another if (1) he enters by invitation, express or implied, (2) his entry is connected with the owner's business or with an activity the owner conducts or permits to be conducted on his land, and (3) there is mutual benefit or a benefit to the owner.

joint liability Liability where creditor must sue all of the partners as a group.

joint and several liability Liability where creditor may sue partners jointly as a group or separately as individuals.

joint stock company A general partnership with some corporate attributes.

joint tenancy See **tenancy**.

joint venture An association of two or more persons to carry on a single business transaction for profit.

judgment The official and authentic decision of a court of justice upon the respective rights and claims of the parties to an action or suit therein litigated and submitted to its determination.

judgment in personam A judgment against a particular person, as distinguished from a judgment against a thing or a right or *status*.

judgment in rem An adjudication pronounced upon the status of some particular thing or subject matter, by a tribunal having competent authority.

judgment n. o. v. Judgment non obstante veredicto in its broadest sense is a judgment rendered in favor of one party notwithstanding the finding of a verdict in favor of the other party.

judgment notwithstanding the verdict A final binding determination on the merits made by the judge after and contrary to the jury's verdict.

judgment on the pleadings Final binding determination on the merits made by the judge after the pleadings.

judicial lien Interest in property that is obtained by court action to secure payment of a debt.

judicial review Power of the courts to determine the constitutionality of legislative and executive acts.

jurisdiction The right and power of a court to adjudicate concerning the subject matter in a given case.

jurisdiction over the parties Power of a court to bind the parties to a suit.

jury A body of persons selected and summoned by law and sworn to try the facts of a case and to find according to the law and the evidence. In general, the province of the jury is to find the facts in a case, while the judge passes upon pure questions of law. As a matter of fact, however, the jury must often pass upon mixed questions of law and fact in determining the case, and in all such cases the instructions of the judge as to the law become very important.

justifiable reliance Reasonably influenced by a misrepresentation.

labor dispute Any controversy concerning terms or conditions of employment or union representation.

laches Based upon maxim that equity aids the vigilant and not those who slumber on their rights. It is defined as neglect to assert a right or claim which, taken together with a lapse of time and other circumstances causing prejudice to the adverse party, operates as a bar in a court of equity.

landlord The owner of an estate in land, or a rental property, who has leased it to another person, called the "tenant." Also called "lessor."

larceny Trespassory taking and carrying away of the goods of another with the intent to permanently deprive.

last clear chance Final opportunity to avoid an injury.

lease Any agreement which gives rise to relationship of landlord and tenant (real property) or lessor and lessee (real or personal property).

The person who conveys is termed the "lessor," and the person to whom conveyed, the "lessee"; and when the lessor conveys land or tenements to a lessee, he is said to lease, demise, or let them.

Sublease, or underlease One executed by the lessee of an estate to a third person, conveying the same estate for a shorter term than that for which the lessee holds it.

leasehold An estate in realty held under a lease. The four principal types of leasehold estates are the estate for years, periodic tenancy, tenancy at will, and tenancy at sufferance.

leasehold estate Right to possess real property.

legacy "Legacy" is a gift or bequest by will of personal property, whereas a "devise" is a testamentary disposition of real estate.

Demonstrative legacy A bequest of a certain sum of money, with a direction that it shall be paid out of a particular fund. It differs from a specific legacy in this respect: that, if the fund out of which it is payable fails for any cause, it is nevertheless entitled to come on the estate as a general legacy. And it differs from a general legacy in this: that it does not abate in that class, but in the class of specific legacies.

General legacy A pecuniary legacy, payable out of the general assets of a testator.

Residuary legacy A bequest of all the testator's personal estate not otherwise effectually disposed of by his will.

Specific legacy One which operates on property particularly designated. A legacy or gift by will of a particular specified thing, as of a horse, a piece of furniture, a term of years, and the like.

legal aggregate A group of individuals not having a legal existence separate from its members.

legal benefit Obtaining something to which one had no legal right.

legal detriment Doing an act one is not legally obligated to do or not doing an act one has a legal right to do.

legal entity An organization having a legal existence separate from that of its members.

legal sufficiency Benefit to promisor or detriment to promisee.

legislative rules Substantive rules issued by an administrative agency under the authority delegated to it by the legislature.

letter of credit An engagement by a bank or other person made at the request of a customer that the issuer will honor drafts or other demands for payment upon compliance with the conditions specified in the credit.

letters of administration Formal document issued by probate court appointing one an administrator of an estate.

letters testamentary The formal instrument of authority and appointment given to an executor by the proper court, empowering him to enter upon the discharge of his office as executor. It corresponds to letters of administration granted to an administrator.

levy To assess; raise; execute; exact; tax; collect; gather; take up; seize. Thus, to levy (assess, exact, raise, or collect) a tax; to levy an execution, *i.e.*, to levy or collect a sum of money on an execution.

liability insurance Covers liability to others by reason of damage resulting from injuries to another's person or property.

liability without fault Crime to do a specific act or cause a certain result without regard to the care exercised.

libel Defamation communicated by writing, television, radio, or the like.

liberty Ability of individuals to engage in freedom of action and choice regarding their personal lives.

license License with respect to real property is a privilege to go on premises for a certain purpose, but does not operate to confer on or vest in the licensee any title, interest, or estate in such property.

licensee Person privileged to enter or remain on land by virtue of the consent of the lawful possessor.

lien A qualified right of property which a creditor has in or over specific property of his debtor, as security for the debt or charge or for performance of some act.

lien creditor A creditor who has acquired a lien on the property by attachment.

life estate An estate whose duration is limited to the life of the party holding it or of some other person. Upon the death of the life tenant, the property will go to the holder of the remainder interest or to the grantor by reversion.

limited liability Liability limited to amount invested in a business enterprise.

limited partner Member of a limited partnership with liability for its debts only to the extent of her capital contribution.

limited partnership See **partnership**.

limited partnership association A partnership which closely resembles a corporation.

liquidated Ascertained; determined; fixed; settled; made clear or manifest. Cleared away; paid; discharged.

liquidated damages See **damages**.

liquidated debt Obligation that is certain in amount.

liquidation The settling of financial affairs of a business or individual, usually by liquidating (turning to cash) all assets for distribution to creditors, heirs, etc. To be distinguished from dissolution.

loss of value Value of promised performance minus value of actual performance.

lost property Property with which the owner has involuntarily parted and which she does not know where to find or recover, not including property which she has intentionally concealed or deposited in a secret place for safekeeping. Distinguishable from mislaid property, which has been deliberately placed somewhere and forgotten.

main purpose rule Where object of promisor/surety is to provide an economic benefit for herself, the promise is considered outside of the statute of frauds.

maker One who makes or executes; as the maker of a promissory note. One who signs a check; in this context, synonymous with drawer. See **draft**.

mala in se Morally wrong.

mala prohibita Wrong by law.

mandamus Latin, we command. A legal writ compelling the defendant to do an official duty.

manslaughter Unlawful taking of another's life without malice.

> *Involuntary manslaughter* Taking the life of another by criminal negligence or during the course of a misdemeanor.
>
> *Voluntary manslaughter* Intentional killing of another under extenuating circumstances.

manufacturing defect Not produced according to specifications.

mark Trade symbol.

market allocations Division of market by customers, geographic location, or products.

marketable title Free from any defects, encumbrances, or reasonable objections to one's ownership.

marshaling of assets Segregating the assets and liabilities of a partnership from the assets and liabilities of the individual partners.

master See **principal**.

material Matters to which a reasonable investor would attach importance in deciding whether to purchase a security.

material alteration Any change that changes the contract of any party to an instrument.

maturity The date at which an obligation, such as the principal of a bond or a note, becomes due.

maxim A general legal principle.

mechanic's lien A claim created by state statutes for the purpose of securing priority of payment of the price or value of work performed and materials furnished in erecting or repairing a building or other structure; as such, attaches to the land as well as buildings and improvements erected thereon.

mediation Nonbinding process in which a third party acts as an intermediary between the disputing parties and proposes solutions for them to consider.

mens rea Criminal intent.

mentally incompetent Unable to understand the nature and effect of one's acts.

mercantile law An expression substantially equivalent to commercial law. It designates the system of rules, customs, and usages generally recognized and adopted by merchants and traders that, either in its simplicity or as modified by common law or statutes, constitutes the law for the regulation of their transactions and the solution of their controversies. The Uniform Commercial Code is the general body of law governing commercial or mercantile transactions.

merchant A person who deals in goods of the kind involved in a transaction or who otherwise by his occupation holds himself out as having knowledge or skill peculiar to the practices or goods involved in the transaction or to whom such knowledge or skill may be attributed by his employment of an agent or broker or other intermediary who by his occupation holds himself out as having such knowledge or skill. UCC § 2–104(1).

merchantability Merchant seller guarantees that the goods are fit for their ordinary purpose.

merger The fusion or absorption of one thing or right into another. In corporate law, the absorption of one company by another, the latter retaining its own name and identity and acquiring the assets, liabilities, franchises, and powers of the former, which ceases to exist as separate business entity. It differs from a consolidation, wherein all the corporations terminate their separate existences and become parties to a new one.

> *Conglomerate merger* An acquisition, which is not horizontal or vertical, by one company of another.
>
> *Horizontal merger* Merger between business competitors, such as manufacturers of the same type of products or distributors selling competing products in the same market area.
>
> *Short-form merger* Merger of a 90 percent subsidiary into its parent.

Vertical merger Union with corporate customer or supplier.

midnight deadline Midnight of the next banking day after receiving an item.

mining partnership A specific type of partnership for the purpose of extracting raw minerals.

minor Under the age of legal majority (usually eighteen).

mirror image rule An acceptance cannot deviate from the terms of the offer.

misdemeanor Less serious crime.

mislaid property Property which an owner has put deliberately in a certain place that she is unable to remember, as distinguished from lost property, which the owner has left unwittingly in a location she has forgotten. See also **lost property**.

misrepresentation Any manifestation by words or other conduct by one person to another that, under the circumstances, amounts to an assertion not in accordance with the facts. A "misrepresentation" that justifies the rescission of a contract is a false statement of a substantive fact, or any conduct which leads to a belief of a substantive fact material to proper understanding of the matter in hand. See also **deceit; fraud**.

Fraudulent misrepresentation False statement made with knowledge of its falsity and intent to mislead.

Innocent misrepresentation Misrepresentation made without knowledge of its falsity but with due care.

Negligent misrepresentation Misrepresentation made without due care in ascertaining its falsity.

M'Naughten Rule Right/wrong test for criminal insanity.

modify Change the lower court's judgment.

money Medium of exchange issued by a government body.

monopoly Ability to control price or exclude others from the marketplace.

mortgage A mortgage is an interest in land created by a written instrument providing security for the performance of a duty or the payment of a debt.

mortgagor Debtor who uses real estate to secure an obligation.

multinational enterprise Business that engages in transactions involving the movement of goods, information, money, people, or services across national borders.

multiple product order Order requiring an advertiser to cease and desist from deceptive statements on all products it sells.

murder Unlawful and premeditated taking of another's life.

mutual mistake Where the common but erroneous belief of both parties forms the basis of a contract.

necessaries Items needed to maintain a person's station in life.

negligence The omission to do something which a reasonable person, guided by those ordinary considerations which ordinarily regulate human affairs, would do, or the doing of something which a reasonable and prudent person would not do.

Culpable negligence Greater than ordinary negligence but less than gross negligence.

negligence *per se* Conclusive on the issue of negligence (duty of care and breach).

negotiable Legally capable of being transferred by indorsement or delivery. Usually said of checks and notes and sometimes of stocks and bearer bonds.

negotiable instrument Signed document (such as a check or promissory note) containing an unconditional promise to pay a "sum certain" of money at a definite time to order or bearer.

negotiation Transferee becomes a holder.

net assets Total assets minus total debts.

no arrival, no sale A destination contract, but if goods do not arrive, seller is excused from liability unless such is due to the seller's fault.

no-fault insurance Compensates victims of automobile accidents regardless of fault.

nonconforming use Preexisting use not in accordance with a zoning ordinance.

nonprofit corporation One whose profits must be used exclusively for the charitable, educational, or scientific purpose for which it was formed.

nonsuit Action in form of a judgment taken against a plaintiff who has failed to appear to prosecute his action or failed to prove his case.

note See **promissory note**.

novation A novation substitutes a new party and discharges one of the original parties to a contract by agreement of all three parties. A new contract is created with the same terms as the original one; only the parties have changed.

nuisance Nuisance is that activity which arises from the unreasonable, unwarranted, or unlawful use by a person of his own property, working obstruction or injury to the right of another or to the public, and producing such material annoyance, inconvenience, and discomfort that law will presume resulting damage.

obiter dictum See **dictum**.

objective fault Gross deviation from reasonable conduct.

objective manifestation What a reasonable person under the circumstances would believe.

objective satisfaction Approval based upon whether a reasonable person would be satisfied.

objective standard What a reasonable person under the circumstances would reasonably believe or do.

obligee Party to whom a duty of performance is owed (by delegator and delegatee).

obligor Party owing a duty (to the assignor).

offer A manifestation of willingness to enter into a bargain, so made as to justify another person in understanding that his assent to that bargain is invited and will conclude it. Restatement, Second, Contracts, § 24

offeree Recipient of the offer.

offeror Person making the offer.

open-ended credit Credit arrangement under which debtor has rights to enter into a series of credit transactions.

opinion Belief in the existence of a fact or a judgment as to value.

option Contract providing that an offer will stay open for a specified period of time.

order A final disposition made by an agency.

order paper Payable to a named person or to anyone designated by that person.

order to pay Direction or command to pay.

original promise Promise to become primarily liable.

output contract See **contracts**.

palpable unilateral mistake Erroneous belief by one party that is recognized by the other.

parent corporation Corporation which controls another corporation.

parol evidence Literally oral evidence, but now includes prior to and contemporaneous, oral, and written evidence.

parol evidence rule Under this rule, when parties put their agreement in writing, all previous oral agreements merge in the writing and the contract as written cannot be modified or changed by parol evidence, in the absence of a plea of mistake or fraud in the preparation of the writing. But the rule does not forbid a resort to parol evidence not inconsistent with the matters stated in the writing. Also, as regards sales of goods, such written agreement may be explained or supplemented by course of dealing, usage of trade, or course of conduct, and by evidence of consistent additional terms, unless the court finds the writing to have been intended also as a complete and exclusive statement of the terms of the agreement. UCC § 2–202.

part performance In order to establish part performance taking an oral contract for the sale of realty out of the statute of frauds, the acts relied upon as part performance must be of such a character that they reasonably can be naturally accounted for in no other way than that they were performed in pursuance of the contract, and they must be in conformity with its provisions. See UCC § 2–201(3).

partial assignment Transfer of a portion of contractual rights to one or more assignees.

partition The dividing of lands held by joint tenants, copartners, or tenants in common into distinct portions, so that the parties may hold those lands in severalty.

partnership An association of two or more persons to carry on, as co-owners, a business for profit.

Partnerships are treated as a conduit and are, therefore, not subject to taxation. The various items of partnership income (gains and losses, etc.) flow through to the individual partners and are reported on their personal income tax returns.

Limited partnership Type of partnership comprised of one or more general partners who manage business and who are personally liable for partnership debts, and one or more limited partners who contribute capital and share in profits but who take no part in running business and incur no liability with respect to partnership obligations beyond contribution.

Partnership at will One with no definite term or specific undertaking.

partnership capital Total money and property contributed by partners for permanent use by the partnership.

partnership property Sum of all of the partnership's assets.

past consideration An act done before the contract is made.

patent Exclusive right to an invention.

payee The person in whose favor a bill of exchange, promissory note, or check is made or drawn.

payer, or **payor** One who pays or who is to make a payment, particularly the person who is to make payment of a check, bill, or note. Correlative to "payee."

payor bank A bank by which an item is payable as drawn or accepted. UCC § 4–105(b). Correlative to "Drawee bank."

per capita This term, derived from the civil law and much used in the law of descent and distribution, denotes that method of dividing an intestate estate by which an equal share is given to each of a number of persons, all of whom stand in equal degree to the decedent, without reference to their stocks or the right of representation. The opposite of *per stirpes*.

per stirpes This term, derived from the civil law and much used in the law of descent and distribution, denotes that method of dividing an intestate estate where a class or group of distributees takes the share to which its deceased would have been entitled, taking thus by its right of representing such ancestor and not as so many individuals. The opposite of *per capita*.

perfect tender rule Seller's tender of delivery must conform exactly to the contract.

perfection of security interest Acts required of a secured party in the way of giving at least constructive notice so as to make his security interest effective at least against lien creditors of the debtor. See UCC §§ 9–302 through 9–306. In most cases, the secured party may obtain perfection either by filing with the secretary of state or by taking possession of the collateral.

performance Fulfillment of one's contractual obligations. See also **part performance; specific performance**.

periodic tenancy Lease with a definite term that is to be continued.

personal defenses Contractual defenses which are good against holders but not holders in due course.

personal property Any property other than an interest in land.

petty crime Misdemeanor punishable by imprisonment of six months or less.

plaintiff The party who initiates a civil suit.

pleadings The formal allegations by the parties of their respective claims and defenses.

> *Rules or codes of civil procedure* Unlike the rigid technical system of common law pleading, pleadings under federal and state rules or codes of civil procedure have a far more limited function, with determination and narrowing of facts and issues being left to discovery devices and pretrial conferences. In addition, the rules and codes permit liberal amendment and supplementation of pleadings.

> Under rules of civil procedure, the pleadings consist of a complaint, an answer, a reply to a counterclaim, an answer to a cross-claim, a third-party complaint, and a third-party answer.

pledge A bailment of goods to a creditor as security for some debt or engagement.

> Much of the law of pledges has been replaced by the provisions for secured transactions in Article 9 of the UCC.

possibility of reverter The interest which remains in a grantor or testator after the conveyance or devise of a fee simple determinable and which permits the grantor to be revested automatically of his estate on breach of the condition.

possibility test Under the statute of frauds, asks whether performance could possibly be completed within one year.

power of appointment A power of authority conferred by one person by deed or will upon another (called the "donee") to appoint, that is, to select and nominate, the person or persons who is or are to receive and enjoy an estate or an income therefrom or from a fund, after the testator's death, or the donee's death, or after the termination of an existing right or interest.

power of attorney An instrument authorizing a person to act as the agent or attorney of the person granting it.

power of termination The interest left in the grantor or testator after the conveyance or devise of a fee simple on condition subsequent or conditional fee.

precatory Expressing a wish.

precedent An adjudged case or decision of a court, considered as furnishing an example or authority for an identical or similar case afterwards arising or a similar question of law. See also **stare decisis**.

preemptive right The privilege of a stockholder to maintain a proportionate share of ownership by purchasing a proportionate share of any new stock issues.

preference The act of an insolvent debtor who, in distributing his property or in assigning it for the benefit of his creditors, pays or secures to one or more creditors the full amount of their claims or a larger amount than they would be entitled to receive on a *pro rata* distribution. The treatment of such preferential payments in bankruptcy is governed by the Bankruptcy Act, § 547.

preliminary hearing Determines whether there is probable cause.

premium The price for insurance protection for a specified period of exposure.

preponderance of the evidence Greater weight of the evidence; standard used in civil cases.

prescription Acquisition of a personal right to use a way, water, light, and air by reason of continuous usage. See also **easement**.

presenter's warranty Warranty given to any payor or acceptor of an instrument.

presentment The production of a negotiable instrument to the drawee for his acceptance, or to the drawer or acceptor for payment; or of a promissory note to the party liable, for payment of the same. UCC § 3–504(1).

presumption A presumption is a rule of law, statutory or judicial, by which a finding of a basic fact gives rise to the existence of presumed fact, until presumption is rebutted. A presumption imposes on the party against whom it is directed the burden of going forward with evidence to rebut or meet the presumption, but does not shift to such party the burden of proof in the sense of the risk of nonpersuasion, which remains throughout the trial upon the party on whom it was originally cast.

price discrimination Price differential.

price fixing Any agreement for the purpose and effect of raising, depressing, fixing, pegging, or stabilizing prices.

prima facie *Latin.* At first sight; on the first appearance; on the face of it; so far as can be judged from the first disclosure; presumably; a fact presumed to be true unless disproved by some evidence to the contrary.

primary liability Absolute obligation to pay a negotiable instrument.

principal *Law of agency* The term "principal" describes one who has permitted or directed another (*i.e.,* an agent or a servant) to act for his benefit and subject to his direction and control. Principal includes in its meaning the term "master" or employer, a species of principal who, in addition to other control, has a right to control the physical conduct of the species of agents known as servants or employees, as to whom special rules are applicable with reference to harm caused by their physical acts.

    Disclosed principal One whose existence and identity are known.

    Partially disclosed principal One whose existence is known but whose identity is not known.

    Undisclosed principal One whose existence and identity are not known.

principal debtor Person whose debt is being supported by a surety.

priority Precedence in order of right.

private carrier Carrier which limits its service and is not open to the general public.

private corporation One organized to conduct either a privately owned business enterprise for profit or a nonprofit corporation.

private law The law involving relationships among individuals and legal entities.

privilege Immunity from tort liability.

privity Contractual relationship.

privity of contract That connection or relationship which exists between two or more contracting parties. The absence of privity as a defense in actions for damages in contract and tort actions is generally no longer viable with the enactment of warranty statutes (*e.g.,* UCC § 2–318), acceptance by states of the doctrine of strict liability, and court decisions which have extended the right to sue to third-party beneficiaries and even innocent bystanders.

probable cause Reasonable belief of the offense charged.

probate Court procedure by which a will is proved to be valid or invalid, though in current usage this term has been expanded to include generally all matters and proceedings pertaining to administration of estates, guardianships, etc.

procedural due process Requirement that governmental action depriving a person of life, liberty, or property be done through a fair procedure.

procedural law Rules for enforcing substantive law.

procedural rules Rules issued by an administrative agency establishing its organization, method of operation, and rules of conduct for practice before it.

procedural unconscionability Unfair or irregular bargaining.

proceeds Consideration for the sale, exchange, or other disposition of collateral.

process *Judicial process* In a wide sense, this term may include all the acts of a court from the beginning to the end of its proceedings in a given cause; more specifically, it means the writ, summons, mandate, or other process which is used to inform the defendant of the institution of proceedings against him and to compel his appearance, in either civil or criminal cases.

    Legal process This term is sometimes used as equivalent to "lawful process." Thus, it is said that legal process means process not merely fair on its face but valid in fact. But properly it means a summons, writ, warrant, mandate, or other process issuing from a court.

profit corporation One founded for the purpose of operating a business for profit.

profit à prendre Right to make some use of the soil of another, such as a right to mine metals; carries with it the right of entry and the right to remove.

promise to pay Undertaking to pay an existing obligation.

promisee Person to whom a promise is made.

promisor Person making a promise.

promissory estoppel Arises where there is a promise which promisor should reasonably expect to induce action or forbearance on part of promisee and which does induce such action or forbearance, and where injustice can be avoided only by enforcement of the promise.

promissory note An unconditional written promise to pay a specified sum of money on demand or at a specified date. Such a note is negotiable if signed by the maker and containing an unconditional promise to pay a sum certain in money either on demand or at a definite time and payable to order or bearer. UCC § 3–104.

promoters In the law relating to corporations, those persons who first associate themselves for the purpose of organizing a company, issuing its prospectus, procuring subscriptions to the stock, securing a charter, etc.

property Interest that is legally protected.

    Abandoned property Intentionally disposed of by the owner.

Lost property Unintentionally left by the owner.

Mislaid property Intentionally placed by the owner but unintentionally left.

prosecute To bring a criminal proceeding.

protest A formal declaration made by a person interested or concerned in some act about to be done, or already performed, whereby he expresses his dissent or disapproval or affirms the act against his will. The object of such a declaration usually is to preserve some right which would be lost to the protester if his assent could be implied, or to exonerate him from some responsibility which would attach to him unless he expressly negatived his assent.

Notice of protest A notice given by the holder of a bill or note to the drawer or indorser that the bill has been protested for refusal of payment or acceptance. UCC § 3–509.

provisional credit Tentative credit for the deposit of an instrument until final credit is given.

proximate cause Where the act or omission played a substantial part in bringing about or actually causing the injury or damage and where the injury or damage was either a direct result or a reasonably probable consequence of the act or omission.

proxy (Contracted from "procuracy.") Written authorization given by one person to another so that the second person can act for the first, such as that given by a shareholder to someone else to represent him and vote his shares at a shareholders' meeting.

public corporation One created to administer a unit of local civil government or one created by the United States to conduct public business.

public disclosure of private facts Offensive publicity given to private information about another person.

public law The law dealing with the relationship between government and individuals.

puffery Sales talk that is considered general bragging or overstatement.

punitive damages Damages awarded in excess of normal compensation to punish a defendant for a serious civil wrong.

purchase money security interest Security interest retained by a seller of goods in goods purchased with the loaned money.

qualified fee Ownership subject to its being taken away upon the happening of an event.

quantum meruit Expression "quantum meruit" means "as much as he deserves"; describes the extent of liability on a contract implied by law. Elements essential to recovery under quantum meruit are (1) valuable services rendered or materials furnished (2) for the person sought to be charged, (3) which services and materials such person accepted, used, and enjoyed, (4) under such circumstances as reasonably notified her that plaintiff, in performing such services, was expected to be paid by the person sought to be charged.

quasi Latin. As if; almost as it were; analogous to. Negatives the idea of identity but points out that the conceptions are sufficiently similar to be classed as equals of one another.

quasi contract Legal fiction invented by common law courts to permit recovery by contractual remedy in cases where, in fact, there is no contract, but where circumstances are such that justice warrants a recovery as though a promise had been made.

quasi in rem See **in rem**.

quasi in rem jurisdiction Jurisdiction over property not based on claims against it.

quiet enjoyment Right of a tenant not to have his physical possession of premises interfered with by the landlord.

quitclaim deed A deed of conveyance operating by way of release; that is, intended to pass any title, interest, or claim which the grantor may have in the premises but neither professing that such title is valid nor containing any warranty or covenants for title.

quorum When a committee, board of directors, meeting of shareholders, legislature, or other body of persons cannot act unless at least a certain number of them are present.

rape Unlawful, nonconsensual sexual intercourse.

ratification In a broad sense, the confirmation of a previous act done either by the party himself or by another; as, for example, confirmation of a voidable act.

In the law of principal and agent, the adoption and confirmation by one person, with knowledge of all material facts, of an act or contract performed or entered into in his behalf by another who at the time assumed without authority to act as his agent.

rational relationship test Requirement that legislation bear a rational relationship to a legitimate governmental interest.

real defenses Defenses that are valid against all holders, including holders in due course.

real property Land, and generally whatever is erected or growing upon or affixed to land. Also, rights issuing out of, annexed to, and exercisable within or about land. See also **fixture**.

reasonable man standard Duty of care required to avoid being negligent; one who is careful, diligent, and prudent.

receiver A fiduciary of the court, whose appointment is incident to other proceedings wherein certain ultimate relief is prayed. He is a trustee or ministerial officer representing the court, all parties in interest in the litigation, and the property or funds entrusted to him.

recognizance Formal acknowledgment of indebtedness made in court.

redemption The realization of a right to have the title of property restored free and clear of a mortgage, performance of the mortgage obligation being essential for such purpose.

Repurchase by corporation of its own shares.

reformation Equitable remedy used to reframe written contracts to reflect accurately real agreement between contracting parties when, either through mutual mistake or unilateral mistake coupled with actual or equitable fraud by the other party, the writing does not embody the contract as actually made.

regulatory license Requirement to protect the public interest.

reimbursement Duty owed by principal to pay back authorized payments agent has made on principal's behalf. Duty owed by a principal debtor to repay surety who pays principal debtor's obligation.

rejection The refusal to accept an offer; manifestation of an unwillingness to accept the goods (sales).

release The relinquishment, concession, or giving up of a right, claim, or privilege, by the person in whom it exists or to whom it accrues, to the person against whom it might have been demanded or enforced.

remainder An estate limited to take effect and be enjoyed after another estate is determined.

remand To send back. The sending by the appellate court of a cause back to the same court out of which it came, for the purpose of having some further action taken on it there.

remedy The means by which the violation of a right is prevented, redressed, or compensated. Though a remedy may be by the act of the party injured, by operation of law, or by agreement between the injurer and the injured, we are chiefly concerned with one kind of remedy, the judicial remedy, which is by action or suit.

rent Consideration paid for use or occupation of property. In a broader sense, it is the compensation or fee paid, usually periodically, for the use of any property, land, buildings, equipment, etc.

replevin An action whereby the owner or person entitled to repossession of goods or chattels may recover those goods or chattels from one who has wrongfully distrained or taken such goods or chattels or who wrongfully detains them.

reply Plaintiff's pleading in response to the defendant's answer.

repudiation Repudiation of a contract means refusal to perform duty or obligation owed to other party.

requirements contract See **contracts**.

res ipsa loquitur "The thing speaks for itself"; permits the jury to infer both negligent conduct and causation.

rescission An equitable action in which a party seeks to be relieved of his obligations under a contract on the grounds of mutual mistake, fraud, impossibility, etc.

residuary Pertaining to the residue; constituting the residue; giving or bequeathing the residue; receiving or entitled to the residue. See also **legacy**, *residuary legacy*.

respondeat superior Latin. Let the master answer. This maxim means that a master or employer is liable in certain cases for the wrongful acts of his servant or employee, and a principal for those of his agent.

respondent In equity practice, the party who makes an answer to a bill or other proceeding. In appellate practice, the party who contends against an appeal; *i.e.,* the appellee. The party who appeals is called the "appellant."

restitution An equitable remedy under which a person who has rendered services to another seeks to be reimbursed for the costs of his acts (but not his profits) even though there was never a contract between the parties.

restraint on alienation A provision in an instrument of conveyance which prohibits the grantee from selling or transferring the property which is the subject of the conveyance. Many such restraints are unenforceable as against public policy and the law's policy of free alienability of land.

restraint of trade Agreement that eliminates or tends to eliminate competition.

restrictive covenant Private restriction on property contained in a conveyance.

revenue license Measure to raise money.

reverse An appellate court uses the term "reversed" to indicate that it annuls or avoids the judgment, or vacates the decree, of the trial court.

reverse discrimination Employment decisions taking into account race or gender in order to remedy past discrimination.

reversion The term reversion has two meanings. First, it designates the estate left in the grantor during the continuance of a particular estate; second, it denotes the residue left in grantor or his heirs after termination of a particular estate. It differs from a remainder in that it arises by an act of law, whereas a remainder arises by an act of the parties. A reversion, moreover, is the remnant left in the grantor, while a remainder is the remnant of the whole estate disposed of after a preceding part of the same has been given away.

revocation The recall of some power, authority, or thing granted, or a destroying or making void of some deed that had existence until the act of revocation made it void.

revocation of acceptance Rescission of one's acceptance of goods based upon a nonconformity of the goods which substantially impairs their value.

right Legal capacity to require another person to perform or refrain from performing an act.

right of entry The right to take or resume possession of land by entering on it in a peaceable manner.

right of redemption The right (granted by statute only) to free property from the encumbrance of a foreclosure or other judicial sale, or to recover the title passing thereby, by paying what is due, with interest, costs, etc. Not to be confounded with the "equity of redemption," which exists independently of statute but must be exercised before sale. See also **equity of redemption**.

right to work law State statute that prohibits union shop contracts.

rights in collateral Personal property the debtor owns, possesses, or is in the process of acquiring.

risk of loss Allocation of loss between seller and buyer where the goods have been damaged, destroyed, or lost.

robbery Larceny from a person by force or threat of force.

rule Agency statement of general or particular applicability designed to implement, interpret, or process law or policy.

rule against perpetuities Principle that no interest in property is good unless it must vest, if at all, not later than twenty-one years, plus period of gestation, after some life or lives in being at time of creation of interest.

rule of reason Balancing the anticompetitive effects of a restraint against its procompetitive effects.

sale Transfer of title to goods from seller to buyer for a price.

sale on approval Transfer of possession without title to buyer for trial period.

sale or return Sale where buyer has option to return goods to seller.

sanction Means of enforcing legal judgments.

satisfaction The discharge of an obligation by paying a party what is due to him (as on a mortgage, lien, or contract) or what has been awarded to him by the judgment of a court or otherwise. Thus, a judgment is satisfied by the payment of the amount due to the party who has recovered such judgment, or by his levying the amount. See also **accord and satisfaction**.

scienter Latin. Knowingly.

seal Symbol that authenticates a document.

secondary liability Obligation to pay is subject to the conditions of presentment, dishonor, notice of dishonor, and sometimes protest.

secret partner Partner whose membership in the partnership is not disclosed.

Section 402A Strict liability in tort.

secured bond A bond having a lien on specific property.

secured claim Claim with a lien on property of the debtor.

secured party Creditor who possesses a security interest in collateral.

secured transaction A transaction founded on a security agreement. Such agreement creates or provides for a security interest. UCC § 9–105(h).

securities Stocks, bonds, notes, convertible debentures, warrants, or other documents that represent a share in a company or a debt owed by a company.
  Certificated security Security represented by a certificate.
  Exempt security Security not subject to registration requirements of 1933 Act.
  Exempt transaction Issuance of securities not subject to the registration requirements of 1933 Act.
  Restricted securities Securities issued under an exempt transaction.
  Uncertificated security Security not represented by a certificate.

security agreement Agreement that grants a security interest.

security interest Right in personal property securing payment or performance of an obligation.

seisin Possession with an intent on the part of him who holds it to claim a freehold interest.

self-defense Force to protect oneself against attack.

separation of powers Allocation of powers among the legislative, executive, and judicial branches of government.

service mark Distinctive symbol, word, or design that is used to identify the services of a provider.

servient Land subject to an easement.

setoff A counterclaim demand which defendant holds against plaintiff, arising out of a transaction extrinsic to plaintiff's cause of action.

settlor Creator of a trust.

severance The destruction of any one of the unities of a joint tenancy. It is so called because the estate is no longer a joint tenancy, but is severed.

Term may also refer to the cutting of crops, such as corn, wheat, etc., or to the separation of anything from realty.

share A proportionate ownership interest in a corporation.

Shelley's case, rule in Where a person takes an estate of freehold, legally or equitably, under a deed, will, or other writing, and in the same instrument there is a limitation by way of remainder of any interest of the same legal or equitable quality to his heirs, or heirs of his body, as a class of persons to take in succession from generation to generation, the limitation to the heirs entitles the ancestor to the whole estate.

The rule was adopted as a part of the common law of this country, though it has long since been abolished by most states.

shelter rule Transferee gets rights of transferor.

shipment contract Seller is authorized or required only to bear the expense of placing goods with the common carrier and bears the risk of loss only up to such point.

short-swing profits Profits made by insider through sale or other disposition of corporate stock within six months after purchase.

sight draft An instrument payable on presentment.

signature Any symbol executed with intent to validate a writing.

silent partner Partner who takes no part in the partnership business.

slander Oral defamation.

small claims courts Inferior civil courts with jurisdiction limited by dollar amount.

social security Measures by which the government provides economic assistance to disabled or retired employees and their dependents.

sole proprietorship A form of business in which one person owns all the assets of the business, in contrast to a partnership or a corporation.

sovereign immunity Foreign country's freedom from a host country's laws.

special warranty deed Seller promises that he has not impaired title.

specific performance The doctrine of specific performance is that where damages would compensate inadequately for the breach of an agreement, the contractor or vendor will be compelled to perform specifically what he has agreed to do; *e.g.,* ordered to execute a specific conveyance of land.

With respect to the sale of goods, specific performance may be decreed where the goods are unique or in other proper circumstances. The decree for specific performance may include such terms and conditions as

to payment of the price, damages, or other relief as the court may deem just. UCC §§ 2–711(2)(b), 2–716.

standardized business form A preprinted contract.

stare decisis Doctrine that once a court has laid down a principle of law as applicable to a certain state of facts, it will adhere to that principle and apply it to all future cases having substantially the same facts, regardless of whether the parties and property are the same or not.

state action Actions by governments, as opposed to actions taken by private individuals.

state-of-the-art Made in accordance with the level of technology at the time the product is made.

stated capital Consideration, other than that allocated to capital surplus, received for issued stock.

statute of frauds A celebrated English statute, passed in 1677, which has been adopted, in a more or less modified form, in nearly all of the United States. Its chief characteristic is the provision that no action shall be brought on certain contracts unless there be a note or memorandum thereof in writing, signed by the party to be charged or by his authorized agent.

statute of limitation A statute prescribing limitations to the right of action on certain described causes of action; that is, declaring that no suit shall be maintained on such causes of action unless brought within a specified period after the right accrued.

statutory lien Interest in property, arising solely by statute, to secure payment of a debt.

stock "Stock" is distinguished from "bonds" and, ordinarily, from "debentures" in that it gives a right of ownership in part of the assets of a corporation and a right to interest in any surplus after the payment of debt. "Stock" in a corporation is an equity, representing an ownership interest. It is to be distinguished from obligations such as notes or bonds, which are not equities and represent no ownership interest.

Capital stock See **capital**.

Common stock Securities which represent an ownership interest in a corporation. If the company has also issued preferred stock, both common and preferred have ownership rights. Claims of both common and preferred stockholders are junior to claims of bondholders or other creditors of the company. Common stockholders assume the greater risk, but generally exercise the greater control and may gain the greater reward in the form of dividends and capital appreciation.

Convertible stock Stock which may be changed or converted into common stock.

Cumulative preferred Stock having a provision that if one or more dividends are omitted, the omitted dividends must be paid before dividends may be paid on the company's common stock.

Preferred stock is a separate portion or class of the stock of a corporation that is accorded, by the charter or by-laws, a preference or priority in respect to dividends, over the remainder of the stock of the corporation, which in that case is called *common stock*.

Stock warrant A certificate entitling the owner to buy a specified amount of stock at a specified time(s) for a specified price. Differs from a stock option only in that options are granted to employees and warrants are sold to the public.

Treasury stock Shares reacquired by a corporation.

stock option Contractual right to purchase stock from a corporation.

stop payment Order for a drawee not to pay an instrument.

strict liability A concept applied by the courts in product liability cases in which a seller is liable for any and all defective or hazardous products which unduly threaten a consumer's personal safety. This concept applies to all members involved in the manufacture and sale of any facet of the product.

strict scrutiny test Requirement that legislation be necessary to promote a compelling governmental interest.

subagent Person appointed by agent to perform agent's duties.

subject matter jurisdiction Authority of a court to decide a particular kind of case.

subject to the mortgage Purchaser is not personally obligated to pay the debt, but the property remains subject to the mortgage.

subjective fault Desired or virtually certain consequences of one's conduct.

subjective satisfaction Approval based upon a party's honestly held opinion.

sublease Transfer of less than all of a tenant's interest in a leasehold.

subpoena A subpoena is a command to appear at a certain time and place to give testimony upon a certain matter. A subpoena duces tecum requires production of books, papers, and other things.

subrogation The substitution of one thing for another, or of one person into the place of another with respect to rights, claims, or securities.

Subrogation denotes the putting of a third person who has paid a debt in the place of the creditor to whom he has paid it, so that he may exercise against the debtor all the rights which the creditor, if unpaid, might have exercised.

subscribe Literally, to write underneath, as one's name. To sign at the end of a document. Also, to agree in writing to furnish money or its equivalent, or to agree to purchase some initial stock in a corporation.

subscriber Person who agrees to purchase initial stock in a corporation.

subsidiary corporation Corporation controlled by another corporation.

substantial performance Equitable doctrine protects against forfeiture for technical inadvertence, trivial variations, or omissions in performance.

substantive due process Requirement that governmental action be compatible with individual liberties.

substantive law The basic law of rights and duties (contract law, criminal law, tort law, law of wills, etc.), as opposed to procedural law (law of pleading, law of evidence, law of jurisdiction, etc.).

substantive unconscionability Oppressive or grossly unfair contractual terms.

sue To begin a lawsuit in a court.

suit "Suit" is a generic term of comprehensive signification that applies to any proceeding in a court of justice in which the plaintiff pursues, in such court, the remedy which the law affords him for the redress of an injury or the recovery of a right.

Derivative suit Suit brought by a shareholder on behalf of a corporation to enforce a right belonging to the corporation.

Direct suit Suit brought by a shareholder against a corporation based upon his ownership of shares.

summary judgment Rule of Civil Procedure 56 permits any party to a civil action to move for a summary judgment on a claim, counterclaim, or cross-claim when he believes that there is no genuine issue of material fact and that he is entitled to prevail as a matter of law.

summons Writ or process directed to the sheriff or other proper officer, requiring him to notify the person named that an action has been commenced against him in the court from which the process has issued and that he is required to appear, on a day named, and answer the complaint in such action.

superseding cause Intervening event that occurs after the defendant's negligent conduct and relieves him of liability.

supreme law Law that takes precedence over all conflicting laws.

surety One who undertakes to pay money or to do any other act in event that his principal debtor fails therein.

suretyship A guarantee of debts of another.

surplus Excess of net assets over stated capital.

tangible property Physical objects.

tariff Duty or tax imposed on goods moving into or out of a country.

tenancy Possession or occupancy of land or premises under lease.

Joint tenancy Joint tenants have one and the same interest, accruing by one and the same conveyance, commencing at one and the same time, and held by one and the same undivided possession. The primary incident of joint tenancy is survivorship, by which the entire tenancy on the decease of any joint tenant remains to the survivors, and at length to the last survivor.

Tenancy at sufferance Only naked possession which continues after tenant's right of possession has terminated.

Tenancy at will Possession of premises by permission of owner or landlord, but without a fixed term.

Tenancy by the entirety A tenancy which is created between a husband and wife and by which together they hold title to the whole with right of survivorship so that, upon death of either, the other takes the whole to the exclusion of the deceased's heirs. It is essentially a "joint tenancy," modified by the common law theory that husband and wife are one person.

Tenancy for a period A tenancy for years or for some fixed period.

Tenancy in common A form of ownership whereby each tenant (*i.e.*, owner) holds an undivided interest in property. Unlike the interest of a joint tenant or a tenant by the entirety, the interest of a tenant in common does not terminate upon his or her prior death (*i.e.*, there is no right of survivorship).

tenancy in partnership Type of joint ownership that determines partners' rights in specific partnership property.

tenant Possessor of a leasehold interest.

tender An offer of money; the act by which one produces and offers to a person holding a claim or demand against him the amount of money which he considers and admits to be due, in satisfaction of such claim or demand, without any stipulation or condition.

Also, there may be a tender of performance of a duty other than the payment of money.

tender of delivery Seller makes available to buyer goods conforming to the contract and so notifies the buyer.

tender offer General invitation to all shareholders to purchase their shares at a specified price.

testament Will.

testator One who makes or has made a testament or will; one who dies leaving a will.

third-party beneficiary One for whose benefit a promise is made in a contract but who is not a party to the contract.

Creditor beneficiary Where performance of a promise in a contract will benefit a person other than the promisee, that person is a creditor beneficiary if

no purpose to make a gift appears from the terms of the promise, in view of the accompanying circumstances, and performance of the promise will satisfy an actual, supposed, or asserted duty of the promisee to the beneficiary.

Donee beneficiary The person who takes the benefit of the contract even though there is no privity between him and the contracting parties. A third-party beneficiary who is not a creditor beneficiary. See also **beneficiary**.

time paper Payable at definite time.

time-price doctrine Permits sellers to have different prices for cash sales and credit sales.

title The means whereby the owner of lands or of personalty has the just possession of his property.

title insurance Provides protection against defect in title to real property.

tort A private or civil wrong or injury, other than breach of contract, for which a court will provide a remedy in the form of an action for damages.

Three elements of every tort action are the existence of a legal duty from defendant to plaintiff, breach of that duty, and damage as proximate result.

tortfeasor One who commits a tort.

trade acceptance A draft drawn by a seller which is presented for signature (acceptance) to the buyer at the time goods are purchased and which then becomes the equivalent of a note receivable of the seller and the note payable of the buyer.

trade name Name used in trade or business to identify a particular business or manufacturer.

trade secrets Private business information.

trademark Distinctive insignia, word, or design of a good that is used to identify the manufacturer.

transferor's warranty Warranty given by any person who transfers an instrument and receives consideration.

treaty An agreement between or among independent nations.

treble damages Three times actual loss.

trespass At common law, trespass was a form of action brought to recover damages for any injury to one's person or property or relationship with another.

Trespass to chattels or personal property An unlawful and serious interference with the possessory rights of another to personal property.

Trespass to land At common law, every unauthorized and direct breach of the boundaries of another's land was an actionable trespass. The present prevailing position of the courts finds liability for trespass only in the case of intentional intrusion, or negligence, or some "abnormally dangerous activity" on the part of the defendant. *Compare* **nuisance**.

trespasser Person who enters or remains on the land of another without permission or privilege to do so.

trust Any arrangement whereby property is transferred with the intention that it be administered by a trustee for another's benefit.

A trust, as the term is used in the Restatement, when not qualified by the word "charitable," "resulting," or "constructive," is a fiduciary relationship with respect to property, subjecting the person by whom the title to the property is held to equitable duties to deal with the property for the benefit of another person, which arises through a manifestation of an intention to create such benefit. Restatement, Second, Trusts § 2.

Charitable trust To benefit humankind.

Constructive trust Wherever the circumstances of a transaction are such that the person who takes the legal estate in property cannot also enjoy the beneficial interest without necessarily violating some established principle of equity, the court will immediately raise a *constructive trust* and fasten it upon the conscience of the legal owner, so as to convert him into a trustee for the parties who in equity are entitled to the beneficial enjoyment.

Inter vivos trust Established during the settlor's lifetime.

Resulting trust One that arises by implication of law, where the legal estate in property is disposed of, conveyed, or transferred, but the intent appears or is inferred from the terms of the disposition, or from the accompanying facts and circumstances, that the beneficial interest is not to go or be enjoyed with the legal title.

Spendthrift trust Removal of the trust estate from the beneficiary's control.

Testamentary trust Established by a will.

Totten trust A tentative trust which is a joint bank account opened by the settlor.

Voting trust A trust which holds the voting rights to stock in a corporation. It is a useful device when a majority of the shareholders in a corporation cannot agree on corporate policy.

trustee In a strict sense, a "trustee" is one who holds the legal title to property for the benefit of another, while, in a broad sense, the term is sometimes applied to anyone standing in a fiduciary or confidential relation to another, such as agent, attorney, bailee, etc.

trustee in bankruptcy Representative of the estate in bankruptcy who is responsible for collecting, liquidating, and distributing the debtor's assets.

tying arrangement Conditioning a sale of a desired product (tying product) on the buyer's purchasing a second product (tied product).

ultra vires Acts beyond the scope of the powers of a corporation, as defined by its charter or by the laws of its state of incorporation. By the doctrine of ultra vires, a contract made by a corporation beyond the scope of its corporate powers is unlawful.

unconscionable Unfair or unduly harsh.

unconscionable contract See **contracts**.

underwriter Any person, banker, or syndicate that guarantees to furnish a definite sum of money by a definite date to a business or government in return for an issue of bonds or stock. In insurance, the one assuming a risk in return for the payment of a premium.

undisputed debt Obligation whose existence and amount are not contested.

undue influence Term refers to conduct by which a person, through his power over the mind of a testator, makes the latter's desires conform to his own, thereby overmastering the volition of the testator.

unemployment compensation Compensation awarded to workers who have lost their jobs and cannot find other employment.

unenforceable Contract under which neither party can recover.

unfair employer practice Conduct in which an employer is prohibited from engaging.

unfair labor practice Conduct in which an employer or union is prohibited from engaging.

unfair union practice Conduct in which a union is prohibited from engaging.

Uniform Commercial Code One of the Uniform Laws, drafted by the National Conference of Commissioners on Uniform State Laws, governing commercial transactions (sales of goods, commercial paper, bank deposits and collections, letters of credit, bulk transfers, warehouse receipts, bills of lading, investment securities, and secured transactions).

unilateral mistake Erroneous belief on the part of only one of the parties to a contract.

union shop Employer can hire nonunion members, but such employees must then join the union.

universal life Ordinary life divided into two components, a renewable term insurance policy and an investment portfolio.

unliquidated debt Obligation that is uncertain or contested in amount.

unqualified indorsement (see **indorsement**) One that imposes liability upon the indorser.

unreasonably dangerous Danger beyond that which the ordinary consumer contemplates.

unrestrictive indorsement (see **indorsement**) One that does not attempt to restrict the rights of the indorsee.

usage of trade Any practice or method of dealing having such regularity of observance in a place, vocation, or trade as to justify an expectation that it will be observed with respect to the transaction in question.

usury Collectively, the laws of a jurisdiction regulating the charging of interest rates. A usurious loan is one whose interest rates are determined to be in excess of those permitted by the usury laws.

value The performance of legal consideration, the forgiveness of an antecedent debt, the giving of a negotiable instrument, or the giving of an irrevocable commitment to a third party. UCC § 1–201(44).

variance A use differing from that provided in a zoning ordinance in order to avoid undue hardship.

vendee A purchaser or buyer; one to whom anything is sold. See also **vendor**.

vendor The person who transfers property by sale, particularly real estate; "seller" being more commonly used for one who sells personalty. See also **vendee**.

venue "Jurisdiction" of the court means the inherent power to decide a case, whereas "venue" designates the particular county or city in which a court with jurisdiction may hear and determine the case.

verdict The formal and unanimous decision or finding of a jury, impaneled and sworn for the trial of a cause, upon the matters or questions duly submitted to it upon the trial.

vertical privity Who is liable to the plaintiff.

vertical restraints Agreements among parties at different levels of the distribution chain.

vested Fixed; accrued; settled; absolute. To be "vested," a right must be more than a mere expectation based on an anticipation of the continuance of an existing law; it must have become a title, legal or equitable, to the present or future enforcement of a demand, or a legal exemption from the demand of another.

vested remainder Unconditional remainder that is a fixed present interest to be enjoyed in the future.

vicarious liability Indirect legal responsibility; for example, the liability of an employer for the acts of an employee or that of a principal for the torts and contracts of an agent.

void Null; ineffectual; nugatory; having no legal force or binding effect; unable, in law, to support the purpose for which it was intended.

This difference separates the words "void" and "voidable": *void* in the strict sense means that an instrument or transaction is nugatory and ineffectual, so that nothing can cure it; *voidable* exists when an imperfection or defect can be cured by the act or confirmation of the person who could take advantage of it.

Frequently, the word "void" is used and construed as having the more liberal meaning of "voidable."

voidable Capable of being made void. See also **void**.

voir dire Preliminary examination of potential jurors.

voluntary Resulting from free choice. The word, especially in statutes, often implies knowledge of essential facts.

voting trust Transfer of corporate shares' voting rights to a trustee.

wager (gambling) Agreement that one party will win or lose depending upon the outcome of an event in which the only interest is the gain or loss.

waiver Terms "estoppel" and "waiver" are not synonymous; "waiver" means the voluntary, intentional relinquishment of a known right, and "estoppel" rests upon principle that, where anyone has done an act or made a statement that would be a fraud on his part to controvert or impair, because the other party has acted upon it in belief that what was done or said was true, conscience and honest dealing require that he not be permitted to repudiate his act or gainsay his statement. See also **estoppel**.

ward An infant or insane person placed by authority of law under the care of a guardian.

warehouse receipt Receipt issued by a person storing goods.

warehouser Storer of goods for compensation.

warrant, *v.* In contracts, to engage or promise that a certain fact or state of facts, in relation to the subject matter, is, or shall be, as it is represented to be.

In conveyancing, to assure the title to property sold, by an express covenant to that effect in the deed of conveyance.

warranty A warranty is a statement or representation made by a seller of goods, contemporaneously with and as a part of a contract of sale, though collateral to express the object of the sale, having reference to the character, quality, or title of goods, and by which the seller promises or undertakes to ensure that certain facts are or shall be as he then represents them.

The general statutory law governing warranties on sales of goods is provided in UCC § 2–312 *et seq.* The three main types of warranties are (1) express warranty; (2) implied warranty of fitness; (3) implied warranty of merchantability.

warranty deed Deed in which grantor warrants good clear title. The usual covenants of title are warranties of seisin, quiet enjoyment, right to convey, freedom from encumbrances, and defense of title as to all claims.

Special warranty deed Seller warrants that he has not impaired title.

warranty liability Applies to persons who transfer an instrument or receive payment or acceptance.

warranty of title Obligation to convey the right to ownership without any lien.

waste Any act or omission that does permanent injury to the realty or unreasonably changes its value.

white-collar crime Corporate crime.

will A written instrument executed with the formalities required by statutes, whereby a person makes a disposition of his property to take effect after his death.

winding up To settle the accounts and liquidate the assets of a partnership or corporation, for the purpose of making distribution and terminating the concern.

without reserve Auctioneer may not withdraw the goods from the auction.

workers' compensation Compensation awarded to an employee who is injured, when the injury arose out of and in the course of his employment.

writ of certiorari Discretionary review by a higher court. See also **certiorari**.

writ of execution Order served by sheriff upon debtor demanding payment of a court judgment against debtor.

zoning Public control over land use.

INDEX